Discovering Computers & Microsoft® Office 2007

A Fundamental Combined Approach

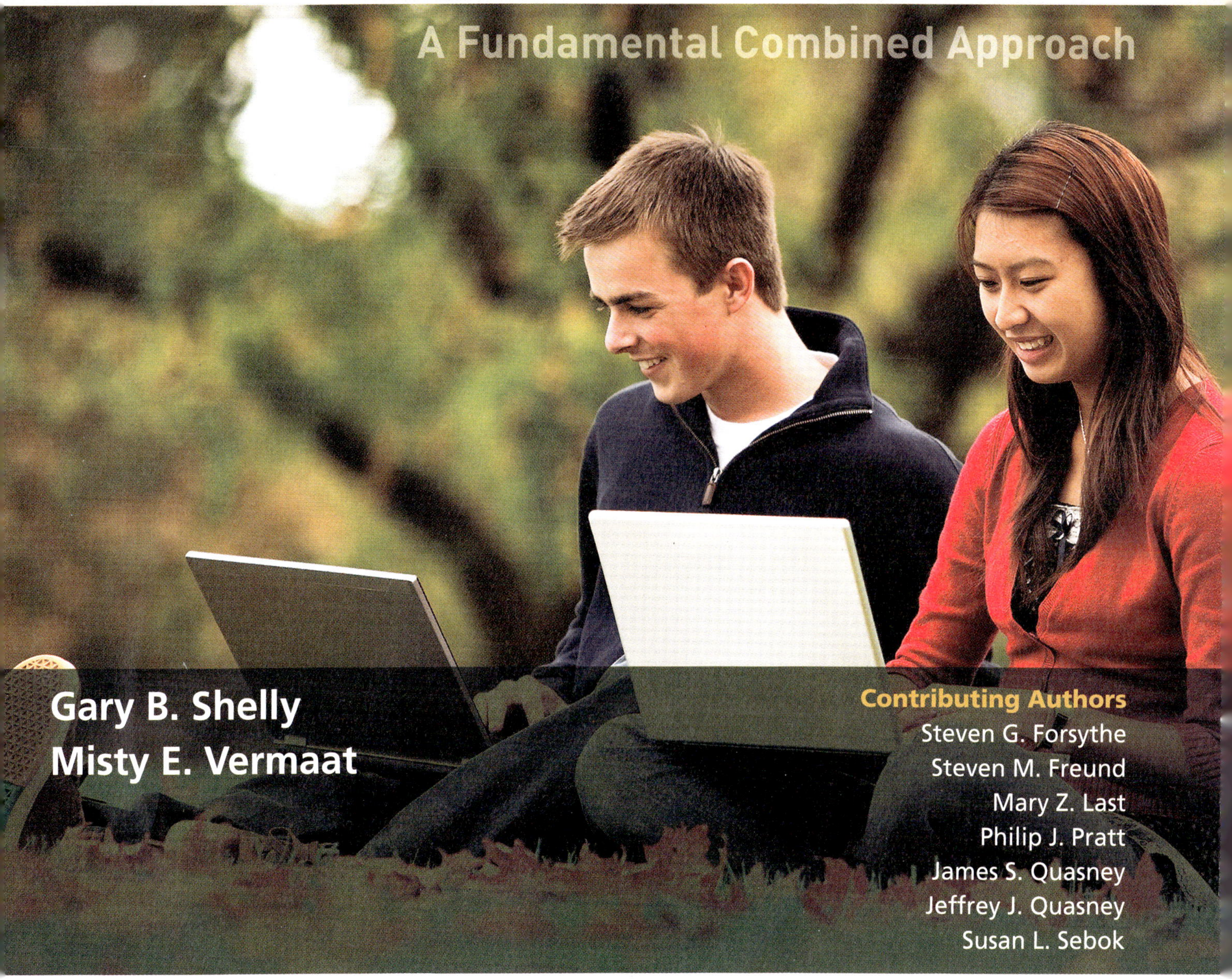

Gary B. Shelly
Misty E. Vermaat

Contributing Authors
Steven G. Forsythe
Steven M. Freund
Mary Z. Last
Philip J. Pratt
James S. Quasney
Jeffrey J. Quasney
Susan L. Sebok

Australia • Canada • Denmark • Japan • Mexico • New Zealand • Philippines • Puerto Rico • Singapore • South Africa • Spain • United Kingdom • United States

Discovering Computers & Microsoft Office 2007: A Fundamental Combined Approach
Gary B. Shelly
Misty E. Vermaat

Vice President, Publisher: Nicole Pinard
Executive Editor: Kathleen McMahon
Product Manager: Crystal Parenteau
Associate Product Manager: Jon Farnham
Editorial Assistant: Lauren Brody
Director of Marketing: Cheryl Costantini
Marketing Manager: Tristen Kendall
Marketing Coordinator: Stacey Leasca
Print Buyer: Julio Esperas
Director of Production: Patty Stephan
Content Project Manager: Matthew Hutchinson
Development Editor: Lyn Markowicz
Proofreader: Kim Kosmatka
Indexer: Rich Carlson
Art Director: Marissa Falco
Cover Designer: Lisa Kuhn, Curio Press, LLC
Cover Photo: Tom Kates Photography
Compositor: Pre-Press PMG

© 2011 Course Technology, Cengage Learning

ALL RIGHTS RESERVED. No part of this work covered by the copyright herein may be reproduced, transmitted, stored or used in any form or by any means graphic, electronic, or mechanical, including but not limited to photocopying, recording, scanning, digitizing, taping, Web distribution, information networks, or information storage and retrieval systems, except as permitted under Section 107 or 108 of the 1976 United States Copyright Act, without the prior written permission of the publisher.

> For product information and technology assistance, contact us at
> **Cengage Learning Customer & Sales Support, 1-800-354-9706**
>
> For permission to use material from this text or product, submit all requests online at **cengage.com/permissions**
> Further permissions questions can be emailed to
> **permissionrequest@cengage.com**

Library of Congress Control Number: 2010920332

ISBN-13: 978-0-538-47934-9

ISBN-10: 0-538-47934-5

Course Technology
20 Channel Center Street
Boston, MA 02210
USA

Cengage Learning is a leading provider of customized learning solutions with office locations around the globe, including Singapore, the United Kingdom, Australia, Mexico, Brazil and Japan. Locate your local office at:
international.cengage.com/region

Cengage Learning products are represented in Canada by Nelson Education, Ltd.

For your course and learning solutions, visit **www.cengage.com**

To learn more about Course Technology, visit **www.cengage.com/coursetechnology**

Purchase any of our products at your local college store or at our preferred online store **www.CengageBrain.com**

Microsoft and the Office logo are either registered trademarks or trademarks of Microsoft Corporation in the United States and/or other countries. Course Technology, a part of Cengage Learning, is an independent entity from the Microsoft Corporation, and not affiliated with Microsoft in any manner.

We dedicate this book to the memory of James S. Quasney (1940 – 2009), who for 18 years co-authored numerous books with Tom Cashman and Gary Shelly and provided extraordinary leadership to the Shelly Cashman Series editorial team. As series editor, Jim skillfully coordinated, organized, and managed the many aspects of our editorial development processes and provided unending direction, guidance, inspiration, support, and advice to the Shelly Cashman Series authors and support team members. He was a trusted, dependable, loyal, well-respected leader, mentor, and friend. We are forever grateful to Jim for his faithful devotion to our team and eternal contributions to our series.

The Shelly Cashman Series Team

Printed in the United States of America
1 2 3 4 5 6 7 16 15 14 13 12 11

Discovering Computers & Microsoft® Office 2007
A Fundamental Combined Approach

Table of Contents at a Glance

Discovering Computers—Selected Chapters from Fundamentals, 2011 Edition

Chapter 1
Introduction to Computers 1

Special Feature 1
Living Digitally 37

Chapter 2
The Internet and World Wide Web 43

Special Feature 2
Making Use of the Web 79

Chapter 3
Application Software 95

Special Feature 3
Digital Video Technology 129

Chapter 4
Operating Systems and Utility Programs 135

Special Feature 4
Digital Communications 167

Chapter 5
Computer Security and Safety, Ethics, and Privacy 181

Special Feature 5
Buyer's Guide 2011: How to Purchase
Computers and Mobile Devices 217

Quiz Yourself Answers 229

Microsoft Office 2007

Microsoft Windows Vista 2007
Introduction to Windows Vista .... WIN 1

Microsoft Windows Internet Explorer 8
Introduction to Internet Explorer .... IE 1

Microsoft Office Word 2007
Chapter 1
Creating and Editing a Word Document .... WD 1

Chapter 2
Creating a Research Paper .... WD 73

Microsoft Office PowerPoint 2007
Chapter 1
Creating and Editing a Presentation .... PPT 1

Chapter 2
Creating a Presentation with Illustrations and Shapes ... PPT 81

Microsoft Office Excel 2007
Chapter 1
Creating a Worksheet and an Embedded Chart .... EX 1

Chapter 2
Formulas, Functions, Formatting, and Web Queries .... EX 81

Microsoft Office Access 2007
Chapter 1
Creating and Using a Database .... AC 1

Chapter 2
Querying a Database .... AC 73

Microsoft Office Integration 2007
Integrating Office 2007 Programs
and the World Wide Web .... INT 1

Discovering Computers & Microsoft® Office 2007
A Fundamental Combined Approach

Table of Contents

CHAPTER 1
Introduction to Computers 1
A WORLD OF COMPUTERS 2
WHAT IS A COMPUTER? 3
    Data and Information 4
    Information Processing Cycle 4
THE COMPONENTS OF A COMPUTER 4
    Input Devices 4
    Output Devices 5
    System Unit 6
    Storage Devices 6
    Communications Devices 6
ADVANTAGES AND DISADVANTAGES OF USING COMPUTERS ... 7
    Advantages of Using Computers 7
    Disadvantages of Using Computers 7
NETWORKS AND THE INTERNET 8
COMPUTER SOFTWARE 11
    System Software 11
    Application Software 12
    Installing and Running Programs 12
    Software Development 13
CATEGORIES OF COMPUTERS 14
PERSONAL COMPUTERS 15
    Desktop Computers 16
MOBILE COMPUTERS AND MOBILE DEVICES 16
    Notebook Computers 16
    Mobile Devices 16
GAME CONSOLES 18
SERVERS 19
MAINFRAMES 19
SUPERCOMPUTERS 19
EMBEDDED COMPUTERS 19
EXAMPLES OF COMPUTER USAGE 20
    Home User 20
    Small Office/Home Office User 22
    Mobile User 22
    Power User 23
    Enterprise User 23
COMPUTER APPLICATIONS IN SOCIETY 24
    Education 24
    Finance 25
    Government 25
    Health Care 25
    Science 26
    Publishing 27
    Travel 27
    Manufacturing 27
CHAPTER SUMMARY 28
COMPANIES ON THE CUTTING EDGE 29
    Apple 29
    Amazon 29
TECHNOLOGY TRAILBLAZERS 29
    Bill Gates 29
    Tom Anderson 29
CHAPTER REVIEW 30
KEY TERMS 31
CHECKPOINT 32
PROBLEM SOLVING 33
LEARN HOW TO 34
LEARN IT ONLINE 35
WEB RESEARCH 36

Special Feature 1
Living Digitally 37

CHAPTER 2
The Internet and World Wide Web 43
THE INTERNET 44
    Connecting to the Internet 45
    Access Providers 46
    How Data and Information Travel the Internet ... 47
    Internet Addresses 48
THE WORLD WIDE WEB 49
    Browsing the Web 49
    Web Addresses 51
    Navigating Web Pages 52
    Searching the Web 53
    Types of Web Sites 55
    Evaluating a Web Site 58
    Multimedia on the Web 58
    Web Publishing 62
    E-Commerce 62
OTHER INTERNET SERVICES 63
    E-Mail 63
    Mailing Lists 66
    Instant Messaging 66
    Chat Rooms 67
    VoIP 68
    FTP 68
    Newsgroups and Message Boards 68
NETIQUETTE 69
CHAPTER SUMMARY 70
COMPANIES ON THE CUTTING EDGE 71
    Google 71
    eBay 71
TECHNOLOGY TRAILBLAZERS 71
    Tim Berners-Lee 71
    Mark Zuckerberg 71
CHAPTER REVIEW 72
KEY TERMS 73
CHECKPOINT 74
PROBLEM SOLVING 75
LEARN HOW TO 76
LEARN IT ONLINE 77
WEB RESEARCH 78

Special Feature 2
Making Use of the Web 79

CHAPTER 3
Application Software 95
- APPLICATION SOFTWARE 96
  - The Role of System Software 97
  - Working with Application Software 98
- BUSINESS SOFTWARE 100
  - Word Processing Software 101
  - Developing a Document 102
  - Spreadsheet Software 103
  - Database Software 104
  - Presentation Software 105
  - Note Taking Software 106
  - Business Software Suite 106
  - Project Management Software 106
  - Personal Information Manager Software 106
  - Business Software for Phones 106
  - Accounting Software 107
  - Document Management Software 107
  - Enterprise Computing Software 107
- GRAPHICS AND MULTIMEDIA SOFTWARE 108
  - Computer-Aided Design 109
  - Desktop Publishing Software
    (for the Professional) 109
  - Paint/Image Editing Software
    (for the Professional) 109
  - Video and Audio Editing Software
    (for the Professional) 110
  - Multimedia Authoring Software 110
  - Web Page Authoring Software 110
- SOFTWARE FOR HOME, PERSONAL, AND
  EDUCATIONAL USE 111
  - Personal Finance Software 112
  - Legal Software 113
  - Tax Preparation Software 113
  - Desktop Publishing Software (for Personal Use) ... 113
  - Paint/Image Editing Software (for Personal Use) .. 114
  - Clip Art/Image Gallery 114
  - Video and Audio Editing Software (for Personal Use) 114
  - Home Design/Landscaping Software 115
  - Travel and Mapping Software 115
  - Reference and Educational Software 115
  - Entertainment Software 116
- WEB APPLICATIONS 116
- APPLICATION SOFTWARE FOR COMMUNICATIONS 118
- LEARNING TOOLS FOR APPLICATION SOFTWARE 119
  - Web-Based Training 119
- CHAPTER SUMMARY 120
- COMPANIES ON THE CUTTING EDGE 121
  - Adobe Systems 121
  - Microsoft 121
- TECHNOLOGY TRAILBLAZERS 121
  - Dan Bricklin 121
  - Masayoshi Son 121
- CHAPTER REVIEW 122
- KEY TERMS 123
- CHECKPOINT 124
- PROBLEM SOLVING 125
- LEARN HOW TO 126
- LEARN IT ONLINE 127
- WEB RESEARCH 128

Special Feature 3
Digital Video Technology 129

CHAPTER 4
Operating Systems and Utility Programs 135
- SYSTEM SOFTWARE 136
- OPERATING SYSTEMS 137
- OPERATING SYSTEM FUNCTIONS 138
  - Starting and Shutting Down a Computer 138
  - Providing a User Interface 138
  - Managing Programs 139
  - Managing Memory 141
  - Coordinating Tasks 141
  - Configuring Devices 142
  - Establishing an Internet Connection 142
  - Monitoring Performance 143
  - Providing File Management and Other Utilities ... 143
  - Updating Software Automatically 143
  - Controlling a Network 143
  - Administering Security 144
- TYPES OF OPERATING SYSTEMS 145
- STAND-ALONE OPERATING SYSTEMS 146
  - Windows 7 146
  - Mac OS X 147
  - UNIX 147
  - Linux 148
- SERVER OPERATING SYSTEMS 148
- EMBEDDED OPERATING SYSTEMS 149
- UTILITY PROGRAMS 150
  - File Manager 151
  - Search Utility 151
  - Uninstaller 151
  - Image Viewer 151
  - Disk Cleanup 152
  - Disk Defragmenter 152
  - Backup and Restore Utilities 152
  - Screen Saver 153
  - Personal Firewall 153
  - Antivirus Programs 154
  - Spyware and Adware Removers 155
  - Internet Filters 155
  - File Compression 156
  - Media Player 156
  - Disc Burning 157
  - Personal Computer Maintenance 157
- CHAPTER SUMMARY 158
- COMPANIES ON THE CUTTING EDGE 159
  - VeriSign 159
  - Research in Motion (RIM) 159
- TECHNOLOGY TRAILBLAZERS 159
  - Steve Wozniak 159
  - Linus Torvalds 159
- CHAPTER REVIEW 160
- KEY TERMS 161
- CHECKPOINT 162
- PROBLEM SOLVING 163
- LEARN HOW TO 164
- LEARN IT ONLINE 165
- WEB RESEARCH 166

Special Feature 4
Digital Communications 167

CHAPTER 5
Computer Security and Safety, Ethics, and Privacy 181
COMPUTER SECURITY RISKS 182
INTERNET AND NETWORK ATTACKS 184
    Computer Viruses, Worms, Trojan Horses, and Rootkits 184
    Safeguards against Computer Viruses and Other Malware 185
    Botnets 187
    Denial of Service Attacks 187
    Back Doors 188
    Spoofing 188
    Safeguards against Botnets, DoS Attacks, Back Doors, and Spoofing 188
    Firewalls 188
    Intrusion Detection Software 189
UNAUTHORIZED ACCESS AND USE 189
    Safeguards against Unauthorized Access and Use 189
    Identifying and Authenticating Users 189
    Digital Forensics 192
HARDWARE THEFT AND VANDALISM 193
    Safeguards against Hardware Theft and Vandalism 193
SOFTWARE THEFT 193
    Safeguards against Software Theft 193
INFORMATION THEFT 195
    Safeguards against Information Theft 195
    Encryption 195
SYSTEM FAILURE 196
    Safeguards against System Failure 196
BACKING UP — THE ULTIMATE SAFEGUARD 196
WIRELESS SECURITY 197
HEALTH CONCERNS OF COMPUTER USE 198
    Computers and Health Risks 198
    Ergonomics and Workplace Design 199
    Computer Addiction 199
ETHICS AND SOCIETY 199
    Information Accuracy 200
    Intellectual Property Rights 201
    Green Computing 201
INFORMATION PRIVACY 202
    Electronic Profiles 203
    Cookies 203
    Spyware and Adware 204
    Spam 204
    Phishing 205
    Social Engineering 205
    Privacy Laws 206
    Employee Monitoring 207
    Content Filtering 207
CHAPTER SUMMARY 208
COMPANIES ON THE CUTTING EDGE 209
    McAfee 209
    Symantec 209
TECHNOLOGY TRAILBLAZERS 209
    Richard Stallman 209
    Gene Spafford 209
CHAPTER REVIEW 210
KEY TERMS 211
CHECKPOINT 212
PROBLEM SOLVING 213
LEARN HOW TO 214
LEARN IT ONLINE 215
WEB RESEARCH 216

Special Feature 5
Buyer's Guide 2011: How to Purchase Computers and Mobile Devices 217

Quiz Yourself Answers 229

Microsoft Windows Vista 2007
Introduction to Windows Vista WIN1
OBJECTIVES ..... WIN 1
WHAT IS AN OPERATING SYSTEM? ..... WIN 2
    Overview ..... WIN 2
    What Is a User Interface? ..... WIN 3
WINDOWS VISTA ..... WIN 4
WINDOWS VISTA OPERATING SYSTEM EDITIONS ..... WIN 5
    Windows Vista Basic Interface and Windows Aero ..... WIN 6
    Starting Windows Vista ..... WIN 7
    Logging On the Computer ..... WIN 8
    To Log On the Computer ..... WIN 8
THE WINDOWS VISTA DESKTOP ..... WIN 9
    To Close the Welcome Center Window ..... WIN 10
    To Add a Gadget to the Windows Sidebar ..... WIN 10
    To Remove a Gadget from the Windows Sidebar ..... WIN 12
    To Display the Start Menu ..... WIN 13
    To Scroll Using Scroll Arrows, the Scroll Bar, and the Scroll Box ..... WIN 15
    To Add an Icon to the Desktop ..... WIN 16
    To Open a Window Using a Desktop Icon ..... WIN 18
    Folder Windows ..... WIN 18
    To Minimize and Redisplay a Window ..... WIN 19
    To Maximize and Restore a Window ..... WIN 20
    To Close a Window ..... WIN 21
    To Open a Window Using the Start Menu ..... WIN 21
    To Move a Window by Dragging ..... WIN 22
    To Expand the Folders List ..... WIN 23
    To Size a Window by Dragging ..... WIN 23
    To Collapse the Folders List ..... WIN 24
    To Close a Window ..... WIN 24
    To Delete a Desktop Icon by Right-Dragging ..... WIN 25
    Summary of Mouse and Windows Operations ..... WIN 26
THE KEYBOARD AND KEYBOARD SHORTCUTS ..... WIN 26
STARTING A PROGRAM ..... WIN 27
    What Is Internet Explorer? ..... WIN 27
    To Start a Program Using the Start Menu ..... WIN 27
WEB ADDRESS ..... WIN 28
BROWSING THE WORLD WIDE WEB ..... WIN 29
    To Browse the Web by Entering a Web Address ..... WIN 30
    To Open a Link in a New Tab ..... WIN 31
    To Switch between Tabs ..... WIN 33
    To Close a Tab ..... WIN 33
WORKING WITH FOLDERS ..... WIN 34
    To Work with Folders ..... WIN 34
    Using a Hierarchical Format to Organize Files and Folders ..... WIN 36
    Removable Media and Network Drives ..... WIN 37
    To Plug a USB Flash Drive into a USB Port ..... WIN 38
    Naming a Folder ..... WIN 38
    To Create a Folder on a Removable Drive ..... WIN 39

Downloading a Hierarchy of Folders
into the Freshman Folder . . . . WIN 40
To Download a Hierarchy of Folders
into the Freshman Folder . . . . WIN 40
To Expand a Drive. . . . . WIN 42
To Collapse a Folder . . . . WIN 43
To Display the Contents of a Folder . . . . WIN 44
**CREATING A DOCUMENT AND FOLDER
USING WORDPAD** . . . . WIN 44
To Start WordPad Using the Start
Search Box . . . . WIN 45
To Type Text . . . . WIN 47
To Save a WordPad Document
in a New Folder . . . . WIN 47
To Verify the Contents of a Folder . . . . WIN 52
FILE MANAGEMENT . . . . WIN 52
To Copy a File by Right-Dragging . . . . WIN 52
To Display the Contents of a Folder . . . . WIN 54
To Rename a File . . . . WIN 55
To Delete a File by Right-Clicking . . . . WIN 56
To Close Expanded Folders . . . . WIN 57
To Close the Computer Window . . . . WIN 58
USING HELP AND SUPPORT . . . . WIN 58
To Open the Windows Help and Support
Window . . . . WIN 58
To Browse for Help Topics in
Windows Basics . . . . WIN 60
To Search for Help Topics Using the Table
of Contents. . . . . WIN 62
To Close the Windows Help and Support
Window . . . . WIN 63
**LOGGING OFF AND TURNING OFF
THE COMPUTER** . . . . WIN 64
To Log Off the Computer . . . . WIN 64
To Turn Off the Computer . . . . WIN 66
CHAPTER SUMMARY . . . . WIN 66
LEARN IT ONLINE . . . . WIN 67
IN THE LAB . . . . WIN 68

Microsoft Windows Internet Explorer 8
Introduction to Internet Explorer . . . . IE 1
OBJECTIVES. . . . . IE 1
INTRODUCTION . . . . IE 2
Overview. . . . . IE 2
THE INTERNET . . . . IE 3
THE WORLD WIDE WEB. . . . . IE 5
Security Concerns on the Internet. . . . . IE 6
Web Address. . . . . IE 7
Hypertext Markup Language . . . . IE 9
Home Pages . . . . IE 10
Web Browsers. . . . . IE 10
WHAT IS INTERNET EXPLORER 8? . . . . IE 10
Starting Internet Explorer . . . . IE 11
To Start Internet Explorer . . . . IE 11
The Internet Explorer Window . . . . IE 12
Command Bar. . . . . IE 14
BROWSING THE WORLD WIDE WEB. . . . . IE 15
To Browse the Web by Entering a
Web Address . . . . IE 16
Stopping the Transfer of a Page . . . . IE 20
Refreshing a Web Page . . . . IE 20
To Refresh a Web Page . . . . IE 21
Finding a Previously Displayed Web Page . . . . IE 21

Finding a Recently Displayed Web Page
Using the Navigation Buttons. . . . . IE 22
To Use the Navigation Buttons to Find Recently
Displayed Web Pages. IE 23
To Display a Web Page Using the Recent Pages List . . . IE 25
Using the History List to Display Web Pages . . . . . . IE 26
To Display a Web Page Using the History List . . . . . IE 27
KEEPING TRACK OF FAVORITE WEB PAGES . . . . IE 30
To Add a Web Page to the Favorites Center . . . . . . IE 30
To Display the Home Page Using
the Home Button . . . . IE 32
To Display a Web Page Using the
Favorites Center . . . . IE 33
To Remove a Web Page from
the Favorites Center. . . . . IE 34
**SAVING INFORMATION OBTAINED WITH INTERNET
EXPLORER** . . . . IE 35
To Save a Web Page . . . . IE 36
To Save a Picture on a Web Page . . . . IE 37
Copying and Pasting Using the Clipboard . . . . IE 39
To Start WordPad . . . . IE 39
To Display the Yellowstone National
Park Web Page. . . . . IE 41
To Copy and Paste Text from a Web Page
into a WordPad Document . . . . IE 42
To Copy and Paste a Picture from a Web
Page into a WordPad Document . . . . IE 44
To Save the WordPad Document and
Quit WordPad . . . . IE 46
**PRINTING A WEB PAGE IN INTERNET
EXPLORER** . . . . IE 47
To Print a Web Page. . . . . IE 48
INTERNET EXPLORER HELP . . . . IE 49
To Access Internet Explorer Help. . . . . IE 49
QUITTING INTERNET EXPLORER . . . . IE 52
To Quit Internet Explorer. . . . . IE 52
CHAPTER SUMMARY . . . . IE 53
LEARN IT ONLINE . . . . IE 54
APPLY YOUR KNOWLEDGE . . . . IE 54
EXTEND YOUR KNOWLEDGE. . . . . IE 58
IN THE LAB . . . . IE 59
CASES AND PLACES . . . . IE 70

Microsoft Office Word 2007
CHAPTER 1
Creating and Editing a Word Document. . . . . WD 1
OBJECTIVES. . . . . WD 1
WHAT IS MICROSOFT OFFICE WORD 2007? . . . . WD 2
PROJECT — DOCUMENT WITH A PICTURE . . . . WD 2
Overview. . . . . WD 4
STARTING WORD . . . . WD 4
To Start Word . . . . WD 5
THE WORD WINDOW. . . . . WD 6
Document Window . . . . WD 6
Ribbon. . . . . WD 7
Mini Toolbar and Shortcut Menus. . . . . WD 9
Quick Access Toolbar . . . . WD 10
Office Button . . . . WD 11
Key Tips . . . . WD 12
ENTERING TEXT . . . . WD 12
To Type Text . . . . WD 13
To Display Formatting Marks. . . . . WD 14
Wordwrap. . . . . WD 14

To Wordwrap Text as You Type	WD 15
To Insert a Blank Line	WD 15
Spelling and Grammar Check	WD 16
To Check Spelling and Grammar as You Type	WD 16
To Enter More Text	WD 18
SAVING THE PROJECT	**WD 18**
To Save a Document	WD 19
FORMATTING PARAGRAPHS AND CHARACTERS IN A DOCUMENT	**WD 22**
Fonts, Font Sizes, Styles, and Themes	WD 23
To Apply Styles	WD 24
To Center a Paragraph	WD 26
Formatting Single Versus Multiple Paragraphs and Characters	WD 26
To Select a Line	WD 27
To Change the Font Size of Selected Text	WD 28
To Change the Font of Selected Text	WD 29
To Select Multiple Paragraphs	WD 30
To Change the Font Size of Selected Text	WD 31
To Format a Line	WD 31
To Bullet a List of Paragraphs	WD 32
To Undo and Redo an Action	WD 32
To Select a Group of Words	WD 33
To Bold Text	WD 34
To Underline a Word	WD 35
To Italicize Text	WD 36
Document Formats	WD 36
To Change the Style Set	WD 37
To Change Theme Colors	WD 39
To Change Theme Fonts	WD 39
INSERTING AND FORMATTING A PICTURE IN A WORD DOCUMENT	**WD 40**
To Insert a Picture	WD 41
Scrolling	WD 43
To Apply a Picture Style	WD 44
To Change a Picture Border Color	WD 45
To Zoom the Document	WD 45
To Resize a Graphic	WD 46
ENHANCING THE PAGE	**WD 48**
To Add a Page Border	WD 48
To Change Spacing Above and Below Paragraphs	WD 50
To Zoom the Document	WD 50
CHANGING DOCUMENT PROPERTIES AND SAVING AGAIN	**WD 50**
To Change Document Properties	WD 51
To Save an Existing Document with the Same File Name	WD 53
PRINTING A DOCUMENT	**WD 53**
To Print a Document	WD 54
QUITTING WORD	**WD 55**
To Quit Word with One Document Open	WD 55
STARTING WORD AND OPENING A DOCUMENT	**WD 55**
To Start Word	WD 55
To Open a Document from Word	WD 56
CORRECTING ERRORS	**WD 57**
Types of Changes Made to Documents	WD 57
To Insert Text in an Existing Document	WD 58
Deleting Text from an Existing Document	WD 59
To Select a Word and Delete It	WD 59
Closing the Entire Document	WD 59
WORD HELP	**WD 60**
To Search for Word Help	WD 60
To Quit Word	WD 62
CHAPTER SUMMARY	**WD 62**
LEARN IT ONLINE	**WD 63**
APPLY YOUR KNOWLEDGE	**WD 63**
EXTEND YOUR KNOWLEDGE	**WD 65**
MAKE IT RIGHT	**WD 66**
IN THE LAB	**WD 67**
CASES AND PLACES	**WD 71**

CHAPTER 2
Creating a Research Paper — WD 73

OBJECTIVES	**WD 73**
INTRODUCTION	**WD 74**
PROJECT — RESEARCH PAPER	**WD 74**
Overview	WD 74
MLA Documentation Style	WD 76
CHANGING DOCUMENT SETTINGS	**WD 77**
To Start Word	WD 77
To Display Formatting Marks	WD 77
Adjusting Line and Paragraph Spacing	WD 78
To Double-Space Text	WD 78
To Remove Space after a Paragraph	WD 79
Headers and Footers	WD 79
To Switch to the Header	WD 80
To Right-Align a Paragraph	WD 81
To Enter Text	WD 81
To Insert a Page Number	WD 82
To Close the Header	WD 83
TYPING THE RESEARCH PAPER TEXT	**WD 83**
To Enter Name and Course Information	WD 84
To Click and Type	WD 85
Shortcut Keys	WD 86
To Format Text Using Shortcut Keys	WD 86
To Save a Document	WD 87
To Display the Rulers	WD 87
To First-Line Indent Paragraphs	WD 88
To Create a Quick Style	WD 90
To AutoCorrect as You Type	WD 91
To Use the AutoCorrect Options Button	WD 92
To Create an AutoCorrect Entry	WD 93
The AutoCorrect Dialog Box	WD 94
To Enter More Text	WD 94
Citations	WD 94
To Change the Bibliography Style	WD 95
To Insert a Citation and Create Its Source	WD 96
To Edit a Citation	WD 98
To Enter More Text	WD 99
Footnotes	WD 99
To Insert a Footnote Reference Mark	WD 100
To Enter Footnote Text	WD 100
To Insert a Citation Placeholder	WD 101
Footnote Text Style	WD 102
To Modify a Style Using a Shortcut Menu	WD 102
To Edit a Source	WD 104
To Edit a Citation	WD 105
Working with Footnotes and Endnotes	WD 106
To Enter More Text	WD 106
To Count Words	WD 107
Automatic Page Breaks	WD 107
To Enter More Text and Insert a Citation Placeholder	WD 108

To Edit a Source	WD 109
To Edit a Citation	WD 110
To Enter More Text	WD 111
To Save an Existing Document with the Same File Name	WD 111
CREATING AN ALPHABETICAL WORKS CITED PAGE	**WD 111**
To Page Break Manually	WD 112
To Center the Title of the Works Cited Page	WD 112
To Create the Bibliographical List	WD 113
To Modify a Style Using the Styles Task Pane	WD 114
To Create a Hanging Indent	WD 116
To Modify a Source and Update the Bibliographical List	WD 117
PROOFING AND REVISING THE RESEARCH PAPER	**WD 118**
To Use the Select Browse Object Menu	WD 118
Moving Text	WD 119
To Select a Sentence	WD 120
Selecting Text	WD 120
To Move Selected Text	WD 121
To Display the Paste Options Menu	WD 122
To Find and Replace Text	WD 123
Find and Replace Dialog Box	WD 124
To Find and Insert a Synonym	WD 124
To Check Spelling and Grammar at Once	WD 125
The Main and Custom Dictionaries	WD 127
To Use the Research Task Pane to Look Up Information	WD 128
Research Task Pane Options	WD 129
To Change Document Properties	WD 130
To Save an Existing Document with the Same File Name	WD 130
To Print Document Properties and then the Document	WD 130
To Quit Word	WD 132
CHAPTER SUMMARY	**WD 132**
LEARN IT ONLINE	**WD 133**
APPLY YOUR KNOWLEDGE	**WD 133**
EXTEND YOUR KNOWLEDGE	**WD 135**
MAKE IT RIGHT	**WD 136**
IN THE LAB	**WD 138**
CASES AND PLACES	**WD 143**

Microsoft Office PowerPoint 2007

CHAPTER 1
Creating and Editing a Presentation . . . . PPT 1

OBJECTIVES	**PPT 1**
WHAT IS MICROSOFT OFFICE POWERPOINT 2007?	**PPT 2**
PROJECT — PRESENTATION WITH BULLETED LISTS	**PPT 3**
Overview	PPT 4
STARTING POWERPOINT	**PPT 5**
To Start PowerPoint	PPT 5
THE POWERPOINT WINDOW	**PPT 6**
PowerPoint Window	PPT 6
PowerPoint Views	PPT 8
Ribbon	PPT 8
Mini Toolbar and Shortcut Menus	PPT 11
Quick Access Toolbar	PPT 13
Office Button	PPT 14
Key Tips	PPT 15
CHOOSING A DOCUMENT THEME	**PPT 16**
To Choose a Document Theme	PPT 16
CREATING A TITLE SLIDE	**PPT 18**
To Enter the Presentation Title	PPT 18
Correcting a Mistake When Typing	PPT 19
Paragraphs	PPT 19
To Enter the Presentation Subtitle Paragraph	PPT 20
FORMATTING CHARACTERS IN A PRESENTATION	**PPT 21**
Fonts and Font Styles	PPT 21
To Select a Paragraph	PPT 21
To Italicize Text	PPT 22
To Select Multiple Paragraphs	PPT 22
To Change the Text Color	PPT 23
To Select a Group of Words	PPT 24
To Increase Font Size	PPT 24
To Bold Text	PPT 25
To Decrease the Title Slide Title Text Font Size	PPT 25
SAVING THE PROJECT	**PPT 26**
To Save a Presentation	PPT 27
ADDING A NEW SLIDE TO A PRESENTATION	**PPT 29**
To Add a New Text Slide with a Bulleted List	PPT 29
CREATING A TEXT SLIDE WITH A SINGLE-LEVEL BULLETED LIST	**PPT 31**
To Enter a Slide Title	PPT 31
To Select a Text Placeholder	PPT 31
To Type a Single-Level Bulleted List	PPT 32
CREATING A TEXT SLIDE WITH A MULTI-LEVEL BULLETED LIST	**PPT 33**
To Add a New Slide and Enter a Slide Title	PPT 33
To Type a Multi-Level Bulleted List	PPT 34
To Type the Remaining Text for Slide 3	PPT 36
To Create Slide 4	PPT 37
To Create a Third-Level Paragraph	PPT 37
To Type the Remaining Text for Slide 4	PPT 39
ENDING A SLIDE SHOW WITH A CLOSING SLIDE	**PPT 40**
To Duplicate a Slide	PPT 40
To Arrange a Slide	PPT 41
To Delete All Text in a Placeholder	PPT 42
CHANGING DOCUMENT PROPERTIES AND SAVING AGAIN	**PPT 43**
To Change Document Properties	PPT 44
To Save an Existing Presentation with the Same File Name	PPT 45
MOVING TO ANOTHER SLIDE IN NORMAL VIEW	**PPT 46**
To Use the Scroll Box on the Slide Pane to Move to Another Slide	PPT 47
VIEWING THE PRESENTATION IN SLIDE SHOW VIEW	**PPT 48**
To Start Slide Show View	PPT 49
To Move Manually through Slides in a Slide Show	PPT 50
To Display the Pop-Up Menu and Go to a Specific Slide	PPT 51
To Use the Pop-Up Menu to End a Slide Show	PPT 52
QUITTING POWERPOINT	**PPT 52**
To Quit PowerPoint with One Document Open	PPT 53
STARTING POWERPOINT AND OPENING A PRESENTATION	**PPT 53**
To Start PowerPoint	PPT 53
To Open a Presentation from PowerPoint	PPT 54

CHECKING A PRESENTATION FOR	
SPELLING ERRORS	PPT 55
To Check Spelling	PPT 56
CORRECTING ERRORS	PPT 58
Types of Corrections Made to Presentations	PPT 58
Deleting Text	PPT 58
Replacing Text in an Existing Slide	PPT 59
DISPLAYING A PRESENTATION IN GRAYSCALE	PPT 59
To Display a Presentation in Grayscale	PPT 59
PRINTING A PRESENTATION	PPT 61
To Print a Presentation	PPT 61
Making a Transparency	PPT 62
POWERPOINT HELP	PPT 63
To Search for PowerPoint Help	PPT 63
To Quit PowerPoint	PPT 65
CHAPTER SUMMARY	PPT 65
LEARN IT ONLINE	PPT 66
APPLY YOUR KNOWLEDGE	PPT 66
EXTEND YOUR KNOWLEDGE	PPT 67
MAKE IT RIGHT	PPT 68
IN THE LAB	PPT 69
CASES AND PLACES	PPT 78

CHAPTER 2
Creating a Presentation with Illustrations and Shapes....... **PPT 81**

OBJECTIVES	PPT 81
INTRODUCTION	PPT 82
PROJECT — PRESENTATION WITH ILLUSTRATIONS AND A SHAPE	PPT 82
Overview	PPT 82
STARTING POWERPOINT	PPT 84
To Start PowerPoint	PPT 85
CREATING SLIDES FROM A BLANK PRESENTATION	PPT 85
To Create a Title Slide	PPT 85
To Create the First Text Slide with a Single-Level Bulleted List	PPT 86
To Create the Second Text Slide with a Single-Level Bulleted List	PPT 87
To Create the Third Text Slide with a Single-Level Bulleted List	PPT 88
To Choose a Background Style	PPT 89
To Save a Presentation	PPT 90
CHANGING VIEWS TO REVIEW A PRESENTATION	PPT 90
To Change the View to Slide Sorter View	PPT 91
To Change the View to Normal View	PPT 91
CHANGING LAYOUTS	PPT 92
To Change the Slide Layout to Two Content	PPT 92
To Change the Slide Layout to Two Content	PPT 93
To Change the Slide Layout to Picture with Caption	PPT 94
INSERTING CLIP ART AND PHOTOGRAPHS INTO SLIDES	PPT 95
The Clip Art Task Pane	PPT 95
To Insert a Clip from the Clip Organizer into a Content Placeholder	PPT 96
Photographs and the Clip Organizer	PPT 97
To Insert a Photograph from the Clip Organizer into a Slide	PPT 98
To Insert a Photograph from a File into a Slide	PPT 99

RESIZING CLIP ART AND PHOTOGRAPHS	PPT 101
To Resize Clip Art	PPT 101
To Resize a Photograph	PPT 103
To Delete a Placeholder	PPT 104
To Move Clips	PPT 105
To Save an Existing Presentation with the Same File Name	PPT 106
FORMATTING TITLE AND CONTENT TEXT	PPT 106
To Format Title Text Using Quick Styles	PPT 106
To Format Remaining Title Text Using Quick Styles	PPT 107
To Change the Heading Font	PPT 109
To Shadow Text	PPT 110
To Change Font Color	PPT 110
Format Painter	PPT 111
To Format Slide 3 Text Using the Format Painter	PPT 112
To Format Remaining Title Text	PPT 113
To Size Slide 4 Text	PPT 114
ADDING AND FORMATTING A SHAPE	PPT 115
To Increase Title Slide Font Size	PPT 115
To Add a Shape	PPT 116
To Resize a Shape	PPT 117
To Add Text to a Shape	PPT 119
To Format Shape Text and Add a Shape Quick Style	PPT 119
To Delete a Placeholder	PPT 121
ADDING A TRANSITION	PPT 122
To Add a Transition between Slides	PPT 122
To Change Document Properties	PPT 124
To Save an Existing Presentation with the Same File Name	PPT 125
To Run an Animated Slide Show	PPT 125
PRINTING A PRESENTATION AS AN OUTLINE AND HANDOUTS	PPT 126
To Preview and Print an Outline	PPT 126
To Preview and Print Handouts	PPT 129
Saving and Quitting PowerPoint	PPT 130
To Quit PowerPoint	PPT 131
CHAPTER SUMMARY	PPT 131
LEARN IT ONLINE	PPT 132
APPLY YOUR KNOWLEDGE	PPT 132
EXTEND YOUR KNOWLEDGE	PPT 134
MAKE IT RIGHT	PPT 135
IN THE LAB	PPT 136
CASES AND PLACES	PPT 142

Microsoft Office Excel 2007

Chapter 1
Creating a Worksheet and an Embedded Chart .... **EX 1**

OBJECTIVES	EX 1
WHAT IS MICROSOFT OFFICE EXCEL 2007?	EX 2
PROJECT — WORKSHEET WITH AN EMBEDDED CHART	EX 2
Overview	EX 4
STARTING EXCEL	EX 6
To Start Excel	EX 6
THE EXCEL WORKBOOK	EX 7
The Worksheet	EX 7
WORKSHEET WINDOW	EX 9
Status Bar	EX 9
Ribbon	EX 9

Formula Bar	EX 12
Mini Toolbar and Shortcut Menus	EX 12
Quick Access Toolbar	EX 13
Office Button	EX 14
Key Tips	EX 15
SELECTING A CELL	**EX 15**
ENTERING TEXT	**EX 15**
To Enter the Worksheet Titles	EX 17
Entering Text in a Cell	EX 18
Correcting a Mistake while Typing	EX 19
AutoCorrect	EX 19
To Enter Column Titles	EX 19
To Enter Row Titles	EX 21
ENTERING NUMBERS	**EX 22**
To Enter Numbers	EX 23
CALCULATING A SUM	**EX 24**
To Sum a Column of Numbers	EX 25
USING THE FILL HANDLE TO COPY A CELL TO ADJACENT CELLS	**EX 26**
To Copy a Cell to Adjacent Cells in a Row	EX 27
To Determine Multiple Totals at the Same Time	EX 28
SAVING THE PROJECT	**EX 29**
To Save a Workbook	EX 30
FORMATTING THE WORKSHEET	**EX 33**
Font Type, Style, Size, and Color	EX 34
To Change a Cell Style	EX 35
To Change the Font Type	EX 36
To Bold a Cell	EX 38
To Increase the Font Size of a Cell Entry	EX 38
To Change the Font Color of a Cell Entry	EX 39
To Center Cell Entries across Columns by Merging Cells	EX 40
To Format Column Titles and the Total Row	EX 42
To Format Numbers in the Worksheet	EX 44
To Adjust the Column Width	EX 46
USING THE NAME BOX TO SELECT A CELL	**EX 47**
To Use the Name Box to Select a Cell	EX 47
Other Ways to Select Cells	EX 48
ADDING A 3-D CLUSTERED COLUMN CHART TO THE WORKSHEET	**EX 49**
To Add a 3-D Clustered Column Chart to the Worksheet	EX 50
CHANGING DOCUMENT PROPERTIES AND SAVING AGAIN	**EX 54**
To Change Document Properties	EX 55
To Save an Existing Workbook with the Same File Name	EX 56
PRINTING A WORKSHEET	**EX 57**
To Print a Worksheet	EX 58
QUITTING EXCEL	**EX 59**
To Quit Excel with One Workbook Open	EX 59
STARTING EXCEL AND OPENING A WORKBOOK	**EX 60**
To Start Excel	EX 60
To Open a Workbook from Excel	EX 60
AUTOCALCULATE	**EX 62**
To Use the AutoCalculate Area to Determine a Maximum	EX 62
CORRECTING ERRORS	**EX 63**
Correcting Errors while You Are Typing Data into a Cell	EX 63
Correcting Errors after Entering Data into a Cell	EX 63
Undoing the Last Cell Entry	EX 65
Clearing a Cell or Range of Cells	EX 66
Clearing the Entire Worksheet	EX 66
EXCEL HELP	**EX 67**
To Search for Excel Help	EX 67
To Quit Excel	EX 69
CHAPTER SUMMARY	**EX 69**
LEARN IT ONLINE	**EX 70**
APPLY YOUR KNOWLEDGE	**EX 70**
EXTEND YOUR KNOWLEDGE	**EX 72**
MAKE IT RIGHT	**EX 73**
IN THE LAB	**EX 74**
CASES AND PLACES	**EX 79**

Chapter 2
Formulas, Functions, Formatting, and Web Queries — EX 81

OBJECTIVES	**EX 81**
INTRODUCTION	**EX 82**
PROJECT — WORKSHEET WITH FORMULAS, FUNCTIONS, AND WEB QUERIES	**EX 82**
Overview	EX 84
To Start Excel	EX 86
ENTERING THE TITLES AND NUMBERS INTO THE WORKSHEET	**EX 87**
To Enter the Worksheet Title and Subtitle	EX 87
To Enter the Column Titles	EX 87
To Enter the Portfolio Summary Data	EX 88
To Enter the Row Titles	EX 88
To Change Workbook Properties and Save the Workbook	EX 90
ENTERING FORMULAS	**EX 90**
To Enter a Formula Using the Keyboard	EX 91
Arithmetic Operations	EX 92
Order of Operations	EX 92
To Enter Formulas Using Point Mode	EX 93
To Copy Formulas Using the Fill Handle	EX 95
Smart Tags and Option Buttons	EX 96
To Determine Totals Using the Sum Button	EX 97
To Determine the Total Percent Gain/Loss	EX 98
USING THE AVERAGE, MAX, AND MIN FUNCTIONS	**EX 98**
To Determine the Average of a Range of Numbers Using the Keyboard and Mouse	EX 99
To Determine the Highest Number in a Range of Numbers Using the Insert Function Box	EX 101
To Determine the Lowest Number in a Range of Numbers Using the Sum Menu	EX 102
To Copy a Range of Cells across Columns to an Adjacent Range Using the Fill Handle	EX 104
To Save a Workbook Using the Same File Name	EX 106
VERIFYING FORMULAS USING RANGE FINDER	**EX 106**
To Verify a Formula Using Range Finder	EX 106
FORMATTING THE WORKSHEET	**EX 107**
To Change the Workbook Theme	EX 109
To Format the Worksheet Titles	EX 110
To Change the Background Color and Apply a Box Border to the Worksheet Title and Subtitle	EX 110
To Apply a Cell Style to the Column Headings and Format the Total Rows	EX 112

To Center Data in Cells and Format Dates	EX 113
Formatting Numbers Using the Ribbon	EX 114
To Apply an Accounting Style Format and Comma Style Format Using the Ribbon	EX 115
To Apply a Currency Style Format with a Floating Dollar Sign Using the Format Cells Dialog Box	EX 116
To Apply a Percent Style Format and Use the Increase Decimal Button	EX 118
Conditional Formatting	EX 118
To Apply Conditional Formatting	EX 119
Conditional Formatting Operators	EX 121
Changing the Widths of Columns and Heights of Rows	EX 122
To Change the Widths of Columns	EX 122
To Change the Heights of Rows	EX 125
CHECKING SPELLING	**EX 127**
To Check Spelling on the Worksheet	EX 127
Additional Spell Checker Considerations	EX 129
PREPARING TO PRINT THE WORKSHEET	**EX 129**
To Change the Worksheet's Margins, Header, and Orientation in Page Layout View	EX 130
PREVIEWING AND PRINTING THE WORKSHEET	**EX 132**
To Preview and Print a Worksheet	EX 132
To Print a Section of the Worksheet	EX 134
DISPLAYING AND PRINTING THE FORMULAS VERSION OF THE WORKSHEET	**EX 135**
To Display the Formulas in the Worksheet and Fit the Printout on One Page	EX 136
To Change the Print Scaling Option Back to 100%	EX 137
IMPORTING EXTERNAL DATA FROM A WEB SOURCE USING A WEB QUERY	**EX 137**
To Import Data from a Web Source Using a Web Query	EX 138
CHANGING THE WORKSHEET NAMES	**EX 140**
To Change the Worksheet Names	EX 141
E-MAILING A WORKBOOK FROM WITHIN EXCEL	**EX 142**
To E-Mail a Workbook from within Excel	EX 142
To Save the Workbook and Quit Excel	EX 143
CHAPTER SUMMARY	**EX 143**
LEARN IT ONLINE	**EX 144**
APPLY YOUR KNOWLEDGE	**EX 145**
EXTEND YOUR KNOWLEDGE	**EX 147**
MAKE IT RIGHT	**EX 148**
IN THE LAB	**EX 149**
CASES AND PLACES	**EX 156**

Microsoft Office Access 2007

Chapter 1
Creating and Using a Database .... AC 1

OBJECTIVES	AC 1
WHAT IS MICROSOFT OFFICE ACCESS 2007?	AC 2
PROJECT — DATABASE CREATION	AC 3
Overview	AC 4
DESIGNING A DATABASE	AC 6
Database Requirements	AC 6
Naming Tables and Fields	AC 8
Identifying the Tables	AC 8
Determining the Primary Keys	AC 8
Determining Additional Fields	AC 8
Determining and Implementing Relationships Between the Tables	AC 9
Determining Data Types for the Fields	AC 9
Identifying and Removing Redundancy	AC 10
STARTING ACCESS	**AC 12**
To Start Access	AC 12
CREATING A DATABASE	**AC 13**
To Create a Database	AC 14
THE ACCESS WINDOW	**AC 17**
Navigation Pane and Access Work Area	AC 18
Ribbon	AC 19
Mini Toolbar and Shortcut Menus	AC 21
Quick Access Toolbar	AC 22
Office Button	AC 22
Key Tips	AC 23
CREATING A TABLE	**AC 23**
To Define the Fields in a Table	AC 24
Making Changes to the Structure	AC 26
To Save a Table	AC 27
To Change the Primary Key	AC 28
To Add Records to a Table	AC 30
Making Changes to the Data	AC 34
AutoCorrect	AC 34
To Close a Table	AC 35
QUITTING ACCESS	**AC 35**
To Quit Access	AC 36
STARTING ACCESS AND OPENING A DATABASE	**AC 36**
To Start Access	AC 36
To Open a Database from Access	AC 37
To Add Additional Records to a Table	AC 38
PREVIEWING AND PRINTING THE CONTENTS OF A TABLE	**AC 40**
To Preview and Print the Contents of a Table	AC 41
CREATING ADDITIONAL TABLES	**AC 44**
To Create an Additional Table	AC 44
To Modify the Primary Key and Field Properties	AC 46
To Add Records to an Additional Table	AC 49
CREATING A REPORT	**AC 50**
To Create a Report	AC 51
To Print a Report	AC 56
To Create Additional Reports	AC 56
USING A FORM TO VIEW DATA	**AC 57**
To Create a Split Form	AC 57
To Use a Split Form	AC 58
CHANGING DATABASE PROPERTIES	**AC 60**
To Change Database Properties	AC 60
ACCESS HELP	**AC 61**
To Search for Access Help	AC 62
To Quit Access	AC 63
CHAPTER SUMMARY	**AC 63**
LEARN IT ONLINE	**AC 64**
APPLY YOUR KNOWLEDGE	**AC 64**
EXTEND YOUR KNOWLEDGE	**AC 65**
MAKE IT RIGHT	**AC 66**
IN THE LAB	**AC 67**
CASES AND PLACES	**AC 71**

CHAPTER 2
Querying a Database .... AC 73

OBJECTIVES	AC 73
INTRODUCTION	AC 74
PROJECT — QUERYING A DATABASE	AC 74
Overview	AC 76

STARTING ACCESS	AC 77
To Start Access	AC 77
To Open a Database	AC 77
CREATING QUERIES	AC 78
To Use the Simple Query Wizard to Create a Query	AC 78
Using Queries	AC 80
To Use a Criterion in a Query	AC 81
To Print the Results of a Query	AC 83
To Create a Query in Design View	AC 83
To Add Fields to the Design Grid	AC 85
ENTERING CRITERIA	AC 85
To Use Text Data in a Criterion	AC 86
To Use a Wildcard	AC 87
To Use Criteria for a Field Not Included in the Results	AC 88
Creating a Parameter Query	AC 89
To Create a Parameter Query	AC 90
To Save a Query	AC 91
To Use a Saved Query	AC 92
To Use a Number in a Criterion	AC 93
To Use a Comparison Operator in a Criterion	AC 94
Using Compound Criteria	AC 95
To Use a Compound Criterion Involving AND	AC 95
To Use a Compound Criterion Involving OR	AC 96
SORTING	AC 97
To Clear the Design Grid	AC 98
To Sort Data in a Query	AC 98
To Omit Duplicates	AC 100
To Sort on Multiple Keys	AC 101
To Create a Top-Values Query	AC 102
JOINING TABLES	AC 103
To Join Tables	AC 105
To Save the Query	AC 107
To Change Join Properties	AC 108
To Create a Report Involving a Join	AC 109
To Print a Report	AC 111
To Restrict the Records in a Join	AC 112
CALCULATIONS	AC 113
To Use a Calculated Field in a Query	AC 113
To Change a Caption	AC 116
Calculating Statistics	AC 117
To Calculate Statistics	AC 118
To Use Criteria in Calculating Statistics	AC 120
To Use Grouping	AC 121
CROSSTAB QUERIES	AC 122
To Create a Crosstab Query	AC 123
To Customize the Navigation Pane	AC 126
To Quit Access	AC 127
CHAPTER SUMMARY	AC 127
LEARN IT ONLINE	AC 128
APPLY YOUR KNOWLEDGE	AC 128
EXTEND YOUR KNOWLEDGE	AC 129
MAKE IT RIGHT	AC 130
IN THE LAB	AC 131
CASES AND PLACES	AC 135

Microsoft Office Integration 2007
CHAPTER 1
Integrating Office 2007 Programs and the World Wide Web . . . . INT 1

OBJECTIVES	INT 1
INTRODUCTION	INT 2
PROJECT — INTEGRATING OFFICE 2007 PROGRAMS AND THE WORLD WIDE WEB	INT 2
Overview	INT 3
ADDING HYPERLINKS TO A WORD DOCUMENT	INT 6
To Start Word, Open an Existing Document, and Save the Document with Another File Name	INT 6
To Insert a Table into a Word Document	INT 8
To Remove the Table Border, View Gridlines, and AutoFit the Table Contents	INT 9
To Insert Text for Hyperlinks	INT 11
To Create a Hyperlink to PowerPoint Web Pages	INT 11
To Insert the Remaining Hyperlinks	INT 12
EMBEDDING AN EXCEL CHART INTO A WORD DOCUMENT	INT 13
To Start Excel and Open an Existing Workbook	INT 13
To Embed an Excel Chart into a Word Document	INT 14
Copy Methods	INT 16
To Change the Size of an Embedded Object	INT 17
To Quit Excel	INT 19
VIEWING THE WORD DOCUMENT IN YOUR BROWSER AND SAVING IT AS A WEB PAGE	INT 19
To Add a Button to the Quick Access Toolbar	INT 19
To Preview the Web Page	INT 22
To Save a Document with a New File Name	INT 22
To Reset the Quick Access Toolbar and Quit Word	INT 23
CREATING A POWERPOINT PRESENTATION WEB PAGE	INT 23
To Start PowerPoint and Open an Existing Presentation	INT 23
To Add Text for a Hyperlink into a PowerPoint Presentation	INT 24
To Insert a Hyperlink into a PowerPoint Presentation	INT 25
To Add a Button to the Quick Access Toolbar and View the Web Page in Your Browser	INT 26
Using Hyperlinks in PowerPoint	INT 27
To Save the PowerPoint Presentation as a Web Page	INT 27
To Remove a Button from the Quick Access Toolbar, Quit PowerPoint, and Close Your Browser	INT 28
CREATING A WEB PAGE FROM AN ACCESS REPORT	INT 28
To Start Access and Open an Existing Database	INT 28
To Create a Report Using the Report Wizard	INT 29
To Add a Hyperlink to a Report and Change the Text Background Color	INT 32
To Save the Report and View It in Your Browser	INT 36
To Close Your Browser and Quit Access	INT 37
TESTING THE WEB SITE	INT 38
To Test the Web Site	INT 38
To Verify the Hyperlinks	INT 39
To Quit the E-Mail Program and Close Your Browser	INT 39
CHAPTER SUMMARY	INT 40
LEARN IT ONLINE	INT 40

IN THE LAB	INT 41
CASES AND PLACES	INT 46

Appendix A
Project Planning Guidelines . . . . APP 1
USING PROJECT PLANNING GUIDELINES . . . . APP 1
    Determine the Project's Purpose. . . . . APP 1
    Analyze Your Audience . . . . APP 1
    Gather Possible Content . . . . APP 2
    Determine What Content to Present
        to Your Audience. . . . . APP 2
SUMMARY . . . . APP 2

Appendix B
Microsoft Office 2007 Help . . . . APP 3
USING MICROSOFT OFFICE HELP . . . . APP 3
    To Open the Word Help Window . . . . APP 4
THE WORD HELP WINDOW. . . . . APP 5
    Search Features . . . . APP 5
    Toolbar Buttons . . . . APP 6
SEARCHING WORD HELP . . . . APP 7
    To Obtain Help Using the
        'Type words to search for' Text Box . . . . APP 7
    To Obtain Help Using the Help Links . . . . APP 9
    To Obtain Help Using the Help Table
        of Contents. . . . . APP 10
OBTAINING HELP WHILE WORKING IN WORD. . . . . APP 11
USE HELP . . . . APP 12

Appendix C
Customizing Microsoft Office 2007. . . . . APP 13
CHANGING SCREEN RESOLUTION. APP 13
    To Change the Screen Resolution . . . . APP 13
    Screen Resolution and the Appearance
        of the Ribbon in Office 2007 Programs . . . . APP 16
CUSTOMIZING THE WORD WINDOW . . . . APP 17
    To Minimize the Ribbon in Word . . . . APP 17
    Customizing and Resetting
        the Quick Access Toolbar. . . . . APP 18
    To Change the Location
        of the Quick Access Toolbar . . . . APP 18
    To Add Commands to the Quick Access
        Toolbar Using the Customize Quick
        Access Toolbar Menu. . . . . APP 19
    To Add Commands to the Quick Access
        Toolbar Using the Shortcut Menu. . . . . APP 20
    To Add Commands to the Quick Access
        Toolbar Using Word Options. . . . . APP 21
    To Remove a Command from the Quick
        Access Toolbar . . . . APP 24
    To Reset the Quick Access Toolbar . . . . APP 25
CHANGING THE WORD COLOR SCHEME . . . . APP 26
    To Change the Word Color Scheme . . . . APP 26

INDEX	IND 1
CREDITS	IND 29
QUICK REFERENCE SUMMARY	QR 1

Preface

The Shelly Cashman Series® offers the finest textbooks in computer education. This book is intended to provide instructors and students with a singular textbook that meets the needs of the combined computer concepts and Microsoft Office 2007 application course.

    The early chapters of *Discovering Computers & Microsoft Office 2007: A Fundamental Combined Approach* present introductory computer subjects in an educationally sound, highly visual, and easy-to-follow pedagogy. The computer concepts chapters are followed by an introduction to Microsoft Office 2007 with the Shelly Cashman's step-by-step, screen-by-screen, project-oriented approach. This combination of concepts and applications coverage designed by the renowned Shelly Cashman Series author team provides the ultimate solution for the introductory computing course.

Objectives of This Textbook

Discovering Computers & Microsoft Office 2007: A Fundamental Combined Approach is intended for a full-semester, introductory course that includes an introduction to both computer concepts and Microsoft Office 2007. No experience with a computer is assumed, and no mathematics beyond the high school freshman level is required. The objectives of this book are:

- To provide a concise introduction to computers
- To present the most up-to-date technology in an ever-changing discipline

- To teach the fundamentals of computers and computer nomenclature, particularly with respect to personal computers, software, and the Web
- To present the material in a visually appealing and exciting manner that motivates students to learn
- To present strategies for purchasing a desktop computer, notebook computer, smart phone, portable media player, and digital camera
- To offer an introduction to the following Microsoft products: Windows Vista, Internet Explorer 8, Word 2007, PowerPoint 2007, Excel 2007, and Access 2007
- To expose students to practical examples of the computer as a useful tool
- To acquaint students with the proper procedures to use a computer; interact with the Web; and create documents, presentations, worksheets, and databases suitable for coursework, professional purposes, and personal use
- To help students discover the underlying functionality of Microsoft Office 2007 so that they can become more productive
- To develop an exercise-oriented approach that allows learning by doing
- To offer alternative learning techniques and reinforcement via the Web
- To offer distance-education providers a textbook with a meaningful and exercise-rich Online Companion

The Shelly Cashman Approach

To date, more than six million students have learned about computers using a *Discovering Computers* textbook. Our series of Microsoft Office 4.3, Microsoft Office 95, Microsoft Office 97, Microsoft Office 2000, Microsoft Office XP, Microsoft Office 2003 textbooks, and Microsoft Office 2007 have been the most widely used books in education. Features of this book include:

- **A Proven Pedagogy** Careful explanations of computer concepts and applications, educationally-sound elements, and reinforcement highlight this proven method of presentation.
- **A Visually Appealing Book that Maintains Student Interest** The latest technology, pictures, drawings, and text are combined artfully to produce a visually appealing and easy-to-understand book. Many of the figures include a step-by-step presentation, which simplifies the more complex computer concepts and application techniques.
- **Extensive End-of-Chapter Student Assignments** A notable strength of this book is the extensive student assignments and activities at the end of each chapter. Well-structured student assignments can make the difference between students merely participating in a class and students retaining the information they learn.

DISTINGUISHING FEATURES OF DISCOVERING COMPUTERS—SELECTED CHAPTERS FROM FUNDAMENTALS, 2011 EDITION

- **Innovative Computing** Innovative Computing boxes engage students with examples of how particular technologies are used in creative ways, and Computer Usage @ Work boxes describe how computers are utilized in five different professional industries.
- **At the Movies videos** CNET At the Movies videos highlight current technology events of interest to students, involving them in the constant evolution of the computing world.

- **Learn It Online** The Learn It Online end-of-chapter exercises, which include online videos, practice tests, interactive labs, learning games, and Web-based activities, offer a wealth of online reinforcement.
- **Problem Solving** The Problem Solving and Collaboration end-of-chapter exercises tackle everyday computer problems and put the information presented in each chapter to practical use.

DISTINGUISHING FEATURES OF MICROSOFT OFFICE 2007

- **Project Orientation** Each chapter in the book presents a project with a practical problem and complete solution using an easy-to-understand approach.
- **Step-by-Step, Screen-by-Screen Instructions** Each of the tasks required to complete a project is clearly identified throughout the chapter. Now, the step-by-step instructions provide a context beyond point-and-click. Each step explains why students are performing a task, or the result of performing a certain action. Found on the screens accompanying each step, call-outs give students the information they need to know when they need to know it. Now, we have used color to distinguish the content in the call-outs. The Explanatory call-outs (in black) summarize what is happening on the screen, and the Navigational call-outs (in red) show students where to click.
- **Learn It Online** Every chapter features a Learn It Online section that is comprised of six exercises. These exercises include True/False, Multiple Choice, and Short Answer; Flash Cards; Practice Test; Who Wants To Be a Computer Genius?; Wheel of Terms; and Crossword Puzzle Challenge.
- **Make It Right** This exercise requires students to analyze a document, identify errors and issues, and correct those errors and issues using skills learned in the chapter.
- **In the Lab** Three in-depth assignments per chapter require students to utilize the chapter concepts and techniques to solve problems on a computer.
- **Video Companion** The DVD located at the front of this book offers around 200 engaging videos that correlate to the Microsoft Office Table of Contents and mirror the step-by-step pedagogy found in the application chapters.

Online Companion

The Discovering Computers & Microsoft Office 2007 Online Companion content is integrated into each page of the text, giving students easy access to current information on important topics, reinforcement activities, and alternative learning techniques. Integrating the Online Companion into the classroom keeps today's students engaged and involved in the learning experience. For each computer concepts chapter in the text, students can access a variety of interactive Quizzes and Learning Games, Exercises, Web Links, Videos, and other features that specifically reinforce and build on the concepts presented in the chapter. For each Microsoft Office chapter, students can practice the skills they have learned with the Learn It Online exercises, including chapter reinforcement, practice tests, flash cards, learning games, and more. This online content encourages students to take learning into their own hands and explore related content on their own to learn even more about subjects in which they are especially interested. With all of these resources, the Discovering Computers & Microsoft Office 2007 Online Companion enables students to get more comfortable using technology and applications and helps prepare students to use the Internet as a tool to enrich their lives.

Instructor Resources

The Instructor Resources include both teaching and testing aids.

INSTRUCTOR'S MANUAL Includes lecture notes summarizing the chapter sections, figures and boxed elements found in every chapter, teacher tips, classroom activities, lab activities, and quick quizzes in Microsoft Word files.

LECTURE SUCCESS SYSTEM Includes intermediate files that correspond to certain figures in the book, which allow you to step through the creation of a project in a chapter during a lecture without entering large amounts of data.

SYLLABUS Contains easily customizable sample syllabi that cover policies, assignments, exams, and other course information.

FIGURE FILES Illustrations for every figure in the textbook are available in electronic form. Figures are provided both with and without callouts.

POWERPOINT PRESENTATIONS A one-click-per-slide presentation system provides PowerPoint slides for every subject in each chapter. Several computer-related video clips are available for optional presentation. Presentations are based on chapter objectives.

SOLUTIONS TO EXERCISES Includes solutions for all end-of-chapter exercises. Also includes Tip Sheets, which are suggested starting points for the Problem Solving exercises in the concepts chapters, and chapter reinforcement solutions for the Microsoft Office 2007 chapters.

RUBRICS AND ANNOTATED SOLUTION FILES Grading rubrics provide a customizable framework for assigning point values to the laboratory exercises. Annotated solution files correspond to the grading rubrics to make it easy for you to compare students' results with the correct solutions whether you receive their homework as hard copy or via e-mail.

TEST BANK AND TEST ENGINE Test Banks include 112 questions for every chapter, featuring objective-based and critical-thinking question types, and include page number references and figure references, when appropriate. Also included is the test engine, ExamView, the ultimate tool for your objective-based testing needs.

PRINTED TEST BANK A Rich Text Format (.rtf) version of the test bank you can print.

LAB TESTS/TEST OUT Parallel to the Microsoft Office 2007 In the Lab assignments, and can be used for testing students in the laboratory on the chapter material or for testing students out of the course.

DATA FILES FOR STUDENTS Includes all the files that are required by students to complete the exercises.

ADDITIONAL ACTIVITIES FOR STUDENTS Consists of Chapter Reinforcement Exercises for the Microsoft Office 2007 chapters, which are true/false, multiple-choice, and short answer questions that help students gain confidence in the material learned.

Content for Online Learning

Course Technology has partnered with the leading distance learning solution providers and class-management platforms today. To access this material, instructors will visit our password-protected instructor resources available at www.cengage.com/coursetechnology. Instructor resources include the following: additional case projects, sample syllabi, PowerPoint presentations per chapter, and more. For additional information or for an instructor user name and password, please contact your sales representative. For students to access this material, they must have purchased a WebTutor PIN-code specific to this title and your campus platform. The resources for students may include (based on instructor preferences), but are not limited to: topic review, review questions, and practice tests.

SAM: SKILLS ASSESSMENT MANAGER

SAM 2007 is designed to help bring students from the classroom to the real world. It allows students to train on and test important computer skills in an active, hands-on environment.

SAM's easy-to-use system includes powerful interactive exams, training, and projects on the most commonly used Microsoft Office applications. SAM simulates the Microsoft Office 2007 application environment, allowing students to demonstrate their knowledge and think through the skills by performing real-world tasks such as bolding word text or setting up slide transitions. Add in live-in-the-application projects, and students are on their way to truly learning and applying skills to business-centric documents.

Designed to be used with the Shelly Cashman Series, SAM includes handy page references so that students can print helpful study guides that match the Shelly Cashman textbooks used in class. For instructors, SAM also includes robust scheduling and reporting features.

COURSENOTES

Course Technology's CourseNotes are six-panel quick reference cards that reinforce the most important and widely used features of a software application in a visual and user-friendly format. CourseNotes serve as a great reference tool during and after the student completes the course. CourseNotes are available for software applications such as Microsoft Office 2007, Word 2007, Excel 2007, Access 2007, PowerPoint 2007, and Windows 7. Topic-based CourseNotes are available for Best Practices in Social Networking, Hot Topics in Technology, and Web 2.0. Visit www.cengage.com/ct/coursenotes to learn more!

A GUIDED TOUR

Add excitement and interactivity to your classroom with "*A Guided Tour*" product line. Play one of the brief mini-movies to spice up your lecture and spark classroom discussion. Or, assign a movie for homework and ask students to complete the correlated assignment that accompanies each topic. "*A Guided Tour*" product line takes the prep work out of providing your students with information about new technologies and applications and helps keep students engaged with content relevant to their lives; all in under an hour!

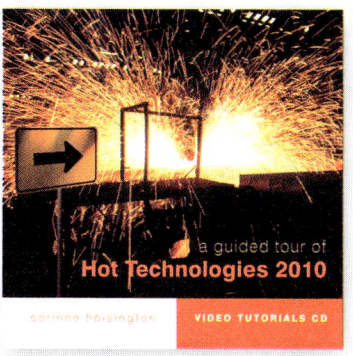
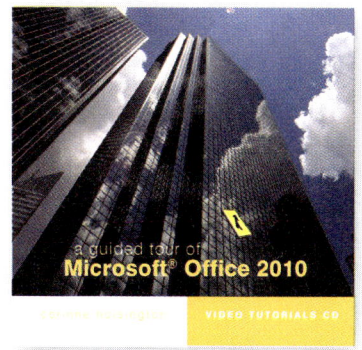
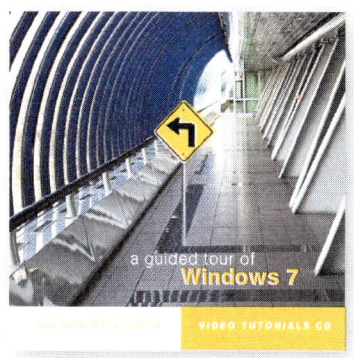

About Our Covers

The Shelly Cashman Series is continually updating our approach and content to reflect the way today's students learn and experience new technology. This focus on student success is reflected on our covers, which feature real students from Bentley University using the Shelly Cashman Series in their courses, and reflect the varied ages and backgrounds of the students learning with our books. When you use the Shelly Cashman Series, you can be assured that you are learning computer skills using the most effective courseware available.

Textbook Walk-Through
Discovering Computers—Selected Chapters from Fundamentals, 2011 Edition

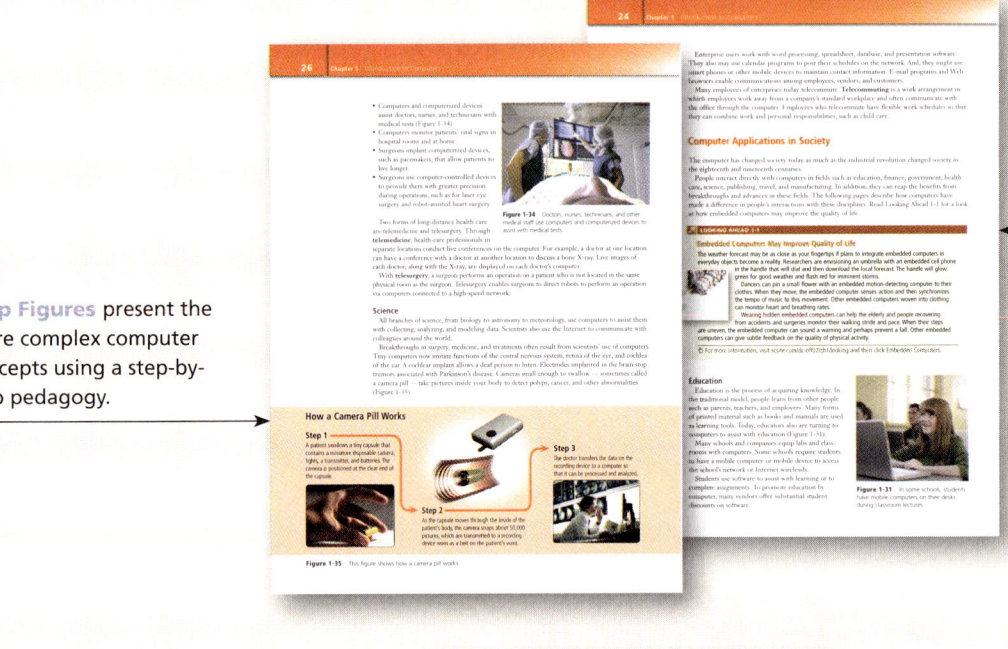

Looking Ahead boxes offer a glimpse of the latest advances in computer technology that will be available, usually within five years.

Step Figures present the more complex computer concepts using a step-by-step pedagogy.

Web Links provide current information and a different perspective about key terms and concepts by visiting the Web Links found in the margins throughout the book.

Innovative Computing boxes present different and innovative ways of using various technologies and help students learn how computing is applied creatively to solve problems.

Quiz Yourself boxes help ensure retention by reinforcing sections of the chapter material, rather than waiting for the end of chapter to test. Use the Quiz Yourself boxes for a quick check of the answers, and access additional Quiz Yourself quizzes via the Online Companion.

Ethics & Issues boxes raise controversial, computer-related topics of the day, challenging readers to consider closely general concerns of computers in society.

Companies on the Cutting Edge and Technology Trailblazers at the end of every chapter present the key computer-related companies and the more famous leaders of the computer industry.

Learn It Online exercises, which include At the Movies online CNET videos, practice test, interactive labs, learning games, and Web-based activities, offer a wealth of online reinforcement.

Computer Usage @ Work boxes explain how computers are used in five different professional industries, including transportation, entertainment, construction, education, and national and local security.

Learn How To end-of-chapter activities allow students to apply the concepts in the chapter to everyday life with hands-on activities. Learn how the Learn How To activities fit into your life with relevant scenarios, visual demonstrations, and practice questions via the Online Companion.

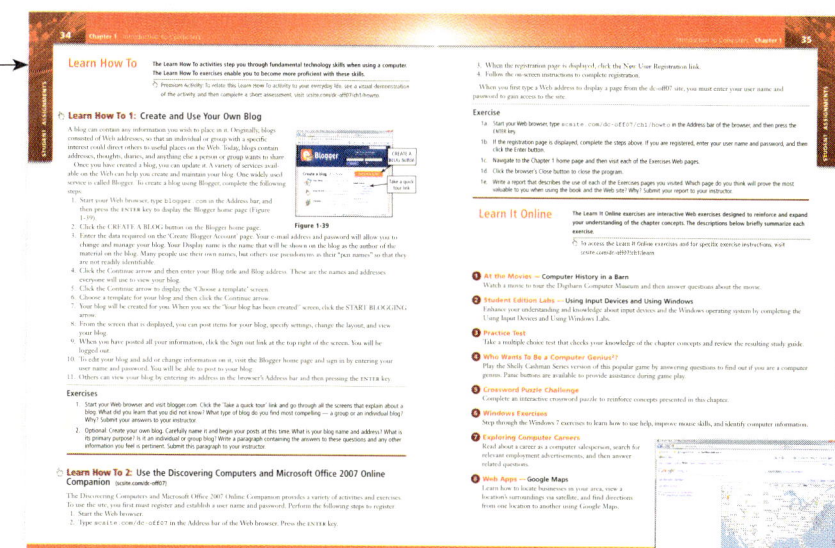

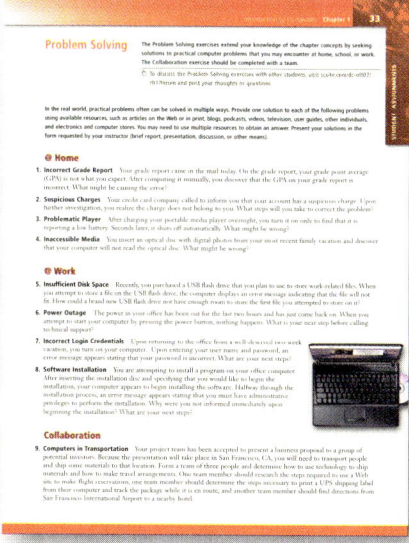

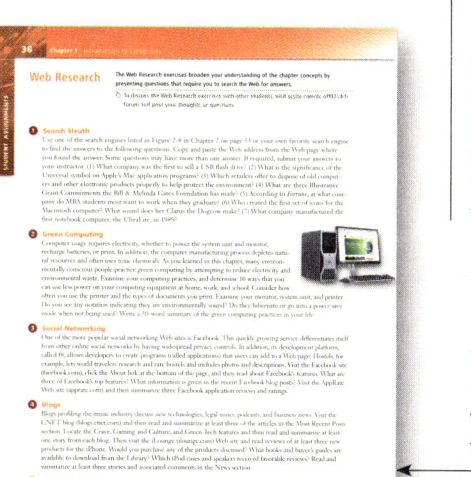

Problem Solving and Collaboration exercises tackle everyday computer problems and put the information presented in each chapter to practical use. Students work as a team to solve the Collaboration exercise.

Web Research exercises require follow-up research on the Web and suggest writing a short article or presenting the findings of the research to the class.

Textbook Walk-Through
Microsoft Office 2007

Plan Ahead boxes prepare students to create successful projects by encouraging them to think strategically about what they are trying to accomplish before they begin working.

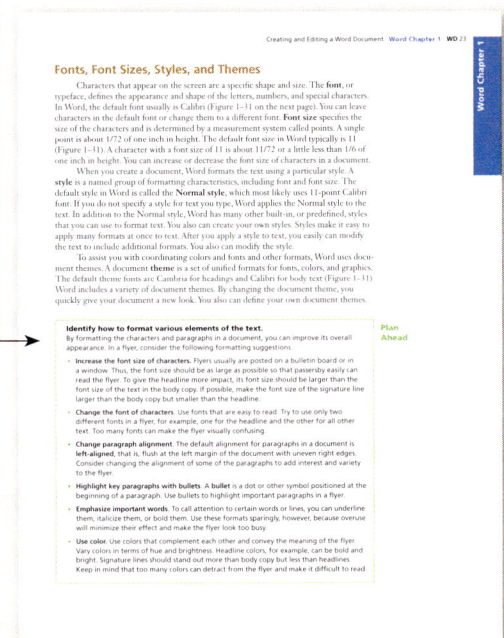

Step-by-step instructions now provide a context beyond the point-and-click. Each step provides information on why students are performing each task or what will occur as a result.

Explanatory callouts in black summarize what is happening on screen.

Navigational callouts in red show students where to click.

Q&A boxes offer questions students may have when working through the steps and provide additional information about what they are doing right where they need it.

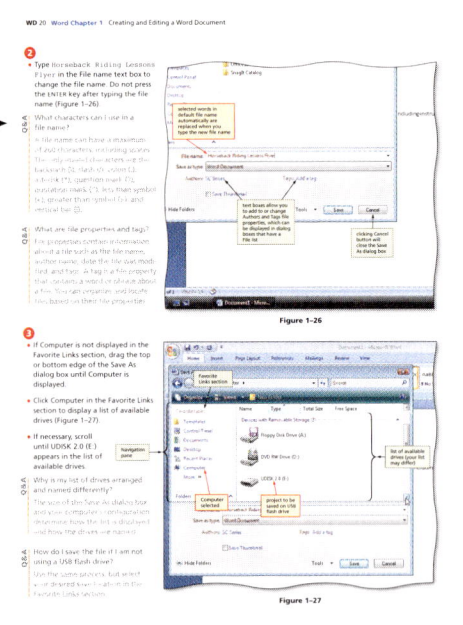

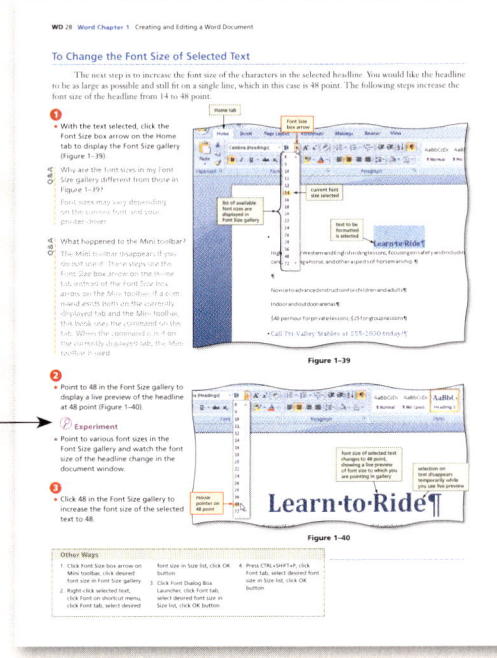

Experiment steps within our step-by-step instructions encourage students to explore, experiment, and take advantage of the features of the Office 2007 user interface. These steps are not necessary to complete the projects but are designed to increase confidence with the software and build problem solving skills.

Some steps ask students to personalize their assignments to help them better keep track of files and discourage academic dishonesty.

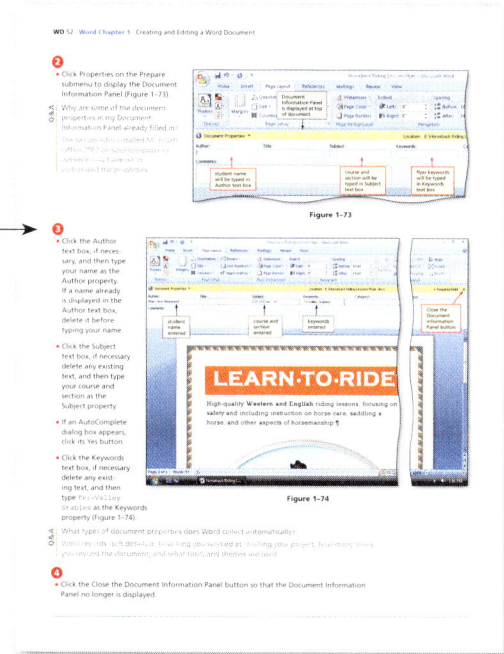

Extend Your Knowledge projects at the end of each chapter allow students to extend and expand on the skills learned within the chapter. Students use critical thinking to experiment with new skills to complete each project.

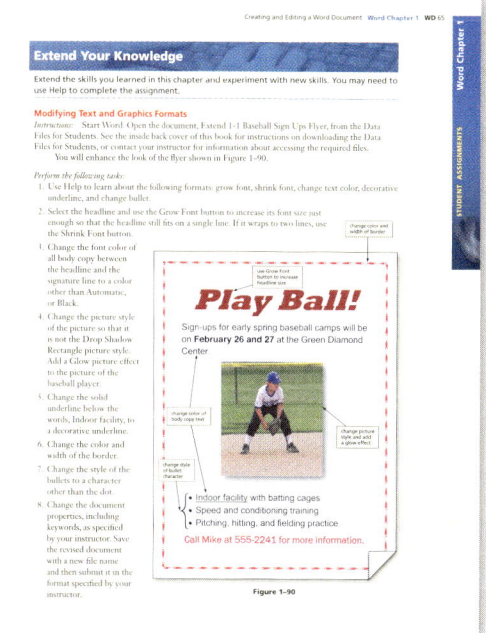

Make It Right projects call on students to analyze a file, discover errors in it, and fix them using the skills they learned in the chapter.

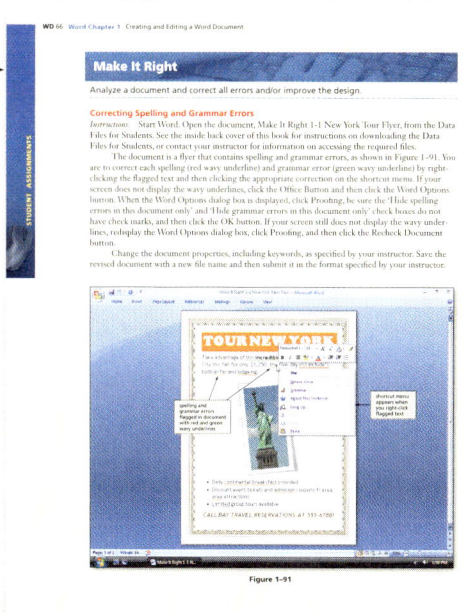

Found within the Cases & Places exercises, the **Make It Personal** activities call on students to create an open-ended project that relates to their personal lives.

Discovering Computers—Selected Chapters from Fundamentals, 2011 Edition

Chapter One

Introduction to Computers

Objectives

After completing this chapter, you will be able to:

1. Explain why computer literacy is vital to success in today's world
2. Describe the five components of a computer: input devices, output devices, system unit, storage devices, and communications devices
3. Discuss the advantages and disadvantages that users experience when working with computers
4. Discuss the uses of the Internet and World Wide Web
5. Distinguish between system software and application software
6. Differentiate among types, sizes, and functions of computers in each of these categories: personal computers (desktop), mobile computers and mobile devices, game consoles, servers, mainframes, supercomputers, and embedded computers
7. Explain how home users, small office/home office users, mobile users, power users, and enterprise users each interact with computers
8. Discuss how society uses computers in education, finance, government, health care, science, publishing, travel, and manufacturing

A World of Computers

Computers are everywhere: at work, at school, and at home (Figure 1-1). Mobile devices, such as many cell phones, often are classified as computers. Computers are a primary means of local and global communication for billions of people. Employees correspond with clients, students with classmates and teachers, and family with friends and other family members.

Through computers, society has instant access to information from around the globe. Local and national news, weather reports, sports scores, airline schedules, telephone directories, maps and directions, job listings, credit reports, and countless forms of educational material always are accessible. From the computer, you can make a telephone call, meet new friends, share photos and videos, share opinions, shop, book flights, file taxes, take a course, receive alerts, and automate your home.

In the workplace, employees use computers to create correspondence such as e-mail messages, memos, and letters; manage calendars; calculate payroll; track inventory; and generate invoices. At school, teachers use computers to assist with classroom instruction. Students use computers to complete assignments and research. Instead of attending class on campus, some students take entire classes directly from their computer.

Figure 1-1   People use all types and sizes of computers in their daily activities.

People also spend hours of leisure time using a computer. They play games, listen to music or radio broadcasts, watch or compose videos and movies, read books and magazines, share stories, research genealogy, retouch photos, and plan vacations.

Many people believe that computer literacy is vital to success. **Computer literacy**, also known as **digital literacy**, involves having a current knowledge and understanding of computers and their uses. Because the requirements that determine computer literacy change as technology changes, you must keep up with these changes to remain computer literate.

This book presents the knowledge you need to be computer literate today. As you read this first chapter, keep in mind it is an overview. Many of the terms and concepts introduced in this chapter will be discussed in more depth later in the book.

What Is a Computer?

A **computer** is an electronic device, operating under the control of instructions stored in its own memory, that can accept data, process the data according to specified rules, produce results, and store the results for future use.

Data and Information

Computers process data into information. **Data** is a collection of unprocessed items, which can include text, numbers, images, audio, and video. **Information** conveys meaning and is useful to people.

As shown in Figure 1-2, for example, computers process several data items to print information in the form of a cash register receipt.

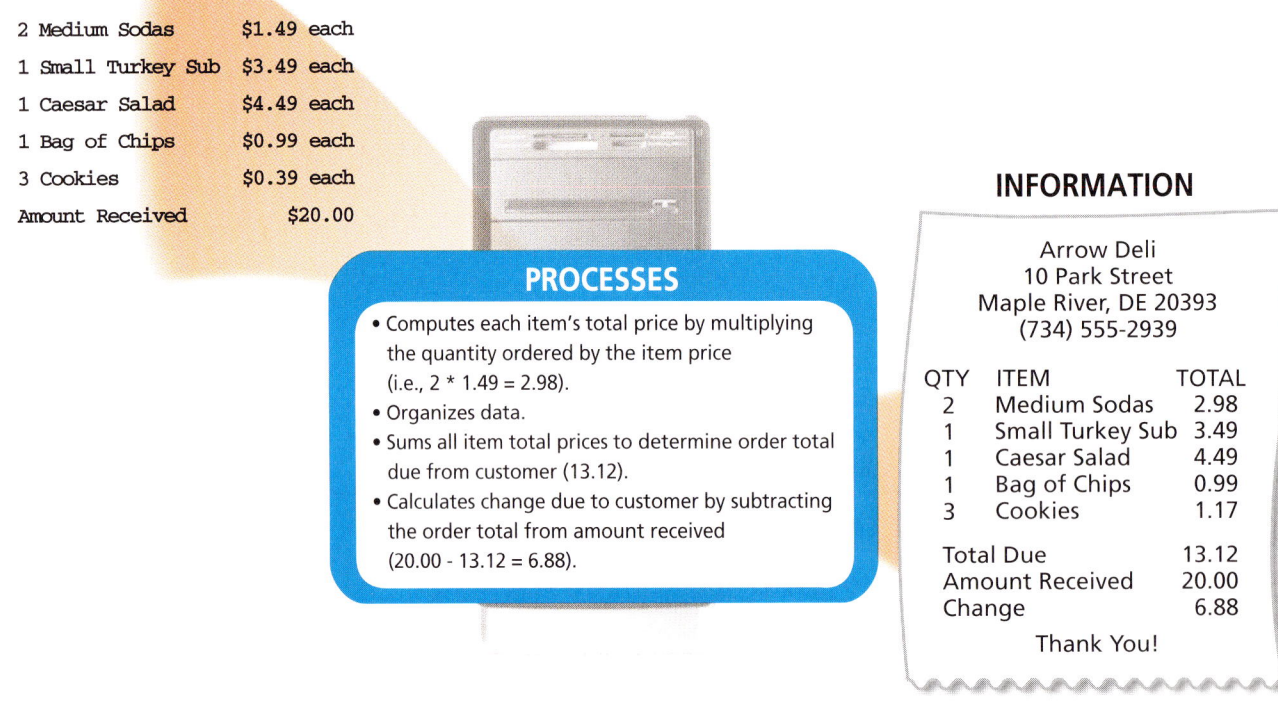

Figure 1-2 A computer processes data into information. In this simplified example, the item ordered, item price, quantity ordered, and amount received all represent data. The computer processes the data to produce the cash register receipt (information).

Information Processing Cycle

Computers process data (input) into information (output). Computers carry out processes using instructions, which are the steps that tell the computer how to perform a particular task. A collection of related instructions organized for a common purpose is referred to as software. A computer often holds data, information, and instructions in storage for future use. Some people refer to the series of input, process, output, and storage activities as the **information processing cycle**. Recently, communications also has become an essential element of the information processing cycle.

The Components of a Computer

A computer contains many electric, electronic, and mechanical components known as **hardware**. These components include input devices, output devices, a system unit, storage devices, and communications devices. Figure 1-3 shows some common computer hardware components.

Input Devices

An **input device** is any hardware component that allows you to enter data and instructions into a computer. Five widely used input devices are the keyboard, mouse, microphone, scanner, and Web cam (Figure 1-3).

A computer keyboard contains keys you press to enter data into the computer. A mouse is a small handheld device. With the mouse, you control movement of a small symbol on the screen, called the pointer, and you make selections from the screen.

A microphone allows a user to speak into the computer. A scanner converts printed material (such as text and pictures) into a form the computer can use.

A Web cam is a digital video camera that allows users to create movies or take pictures and store them on the computer instead of on tape or film.

Output Devices

An **output device** is any hardware component that conveys information to one or more people. Three commonly used output devices are a printer, a monitor, and speakers (Figure 1-3).

A printer produces text and graphics on a physical medium such as paper. A monitor displays text, graphics, and videos on a screen. Speakers allow you to hear music, voice, and other audio (sounds).

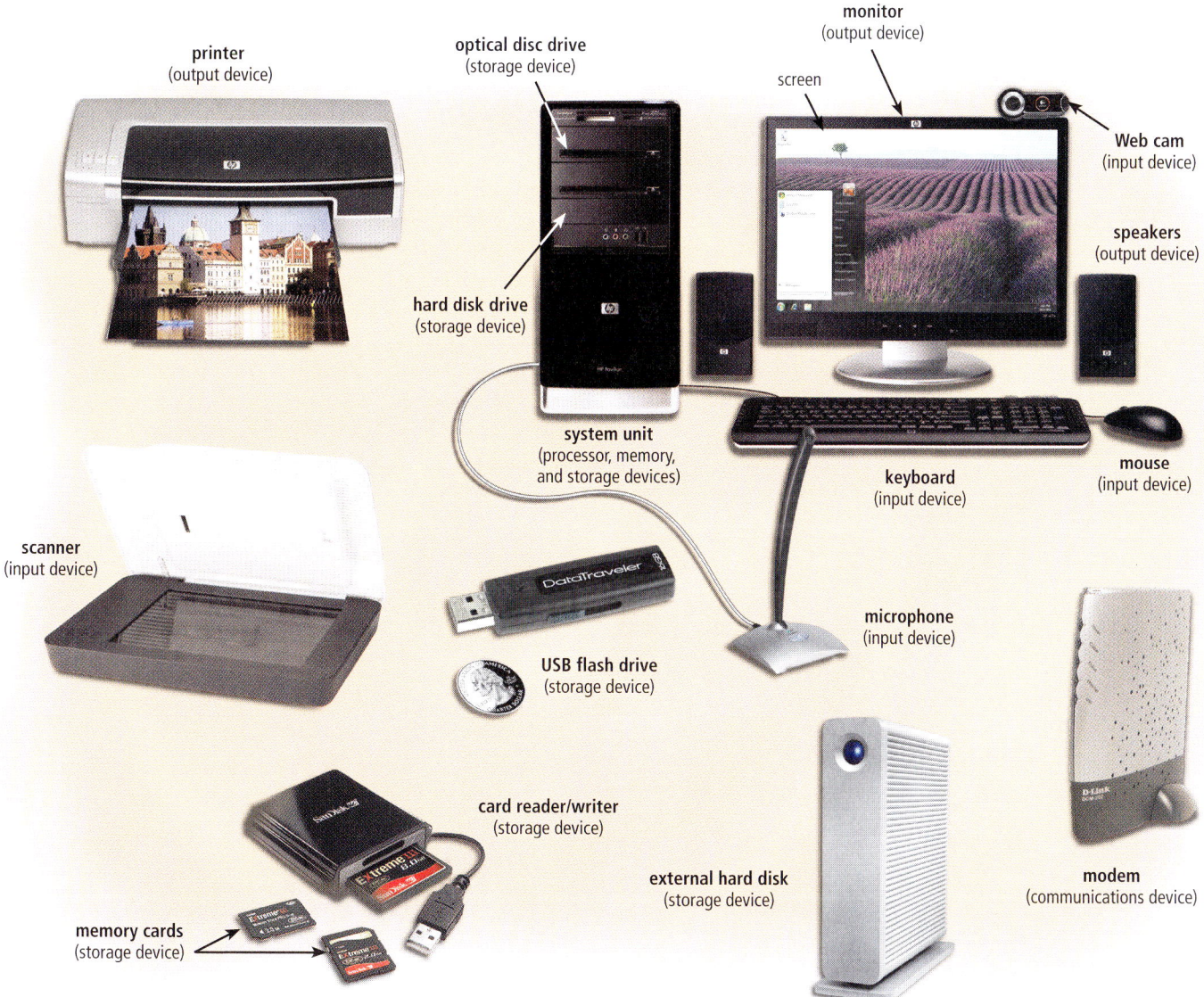

Figure 1-3 Common computer hardware components include the keyboard, mouse, microphone, scanner, Web cam, printer, monitor, speakers, system unit, hard disk drive, external hard disk, optical disc drive(s), USB flash drive, card reader/writer, memory cards, and modem.

System Unit

The **system unit** is a case that contains electronic components of the computer that are used to process data (Figure 1-3 on the previous page). The circuitry of the system unit usually is part of or is connected to a circuit board called the motherboard.

Two main components on the motherboard are the processor and memory. The **processor**, also called the **CPU** (**central processing unit**), is the electronic component that interprets and carries out the basic instructions that operate the computer. **Memory** consists of electronic components that store instructions waiting to be executed and data needed by those instructions. Most memory keeps data and instructions temporarily, which means its contents are erased when the computer is shut off.

Storage Devices

Storage holds data, instructions, and information for future use. For example, computers can store hundreds or millions of customer names and addresses. Storage holds these items permanently.

A computer keeps data, instructions, and information on **storage media**. Examples of storage media are USB flash drives, hard disks, optical discs, and memory cards. A **storage device** records (writes) and/or retrieves (reads) items to and from storage media. Storage devices often function as a source of input because they transfer items from storage to memory.

A USB flash drive is a portable storage device that is small and lightweight enough to be transported on a keychain or in a pocket (Figure 1-3). The average USB flash drive can hold about 4 billion characters.

A hard disk provides much greater storage capacity than a USB flash drive. The average hard disk can hold more than 320 billion characters. Hard disks are enclosed in an airtight, sealed case. Although some are portable, most are housed inside the system unit (Figure 1-4). Portable hard disks are either external or removable. An external hard disk is a separate, freestanding unit, whereas you insert and remove a removable hard disk from the computer or a device connected to the computer.

An optical disc is a flat, round, portable metal disc with a plastic coating. CDs, DVDs, and Blu-ray Discs are three types of optical discs. A CD can hold from 650 million to 1 billion characters. Some DVDs can store two full-length movies or 17 billion characters (Figure 1-5). Blu-ray Discs can store about 46 hours of standard video, or 100 billion characters.

Some mobile devices, such as digital cameras, use memory cards as the storage media. You can use a card reader/writer (Figure 1-3) to transfer stored items, such as digital photos, from the memory card to a computer or printer.

Figure 1-4 Most hard disks are housed inside the system unit.

Figure 1-5 A DVD in a DVD drive.

Communications Devices

A **communications device** is a hardware component that enables a computer to send (transmit) and receive data, instructions, and information to and from one or more computers or mobile devices. A widely used communications device is a modem (Figure 1-3).

Communications occur over cables, telephone lines, cellular radio networks, satellites, and other transmission media. Some transmission media, such as satellites and cellular radio networks, are wireless, which means they have no physical lines or wires.

Advantages and Disadvantages of Using Computers

Society has reaped many benefits from using computers. A **user** is anyone who communicates with a computer or utilizes the information it generates. Both business and home users can make well-informed decisions because they have instant access to information from anywhere in the world. Students, another type of user, have more tools to assist them in the learning process.

Advantages of Using Computers

The benefits from using computers are possible because computers have the advantages of speed, reliability, consistency, storage, and communications.
- **Speed:** When data, instructions, and information flow along electronic circuits in a computer, they travel at incredibly fast speeds. Many computers process billions or trillions of operations in a single second.
- **Reliability:** The electronic components in modern computers are dependable and reliable because they rarely break or fail.
- **Consistency:** Given the same input and processes, a computer will produce the same results — consistently. Computers generate error-free results, provided the input is correct and the instructions work.
- **Storage:** Computers store enormous amounts of data and make this data available for processing anytime it is needed.
- **Communications:** Most computers today can communicate with other computers, often wirelessly. Computers allow users to communicate with one another.

Disadvantages of Using Computers

Some disadvantages of computers relate to the violation of privacy, public safety, the impact on the labor force, health risks, and the impact on the environment.
- **Violation of Privacy:** In many instances, where personal and confidential records stored on computers were not protected properly, individuals have found their privacy violated and identities stolen.
- **Public Safety:** Adults, teens, and children around the world are using computers to share publicly their photos, videos, journals, music, and other personal information. Some of these unsuspecting, innocent computer users have fallen victim to crimes committed by dangerous strangers.
- **Impact on Labor Force:** Although computers have improved productivity and created an entire industry with hundreds of thousands of new jobs, the skills of millions of employees have been replaced by computers. Thus, it is crucial that workers keep their education up-to-date. A separate impact on the labor force is that some companies are outsourcing jobs to foreign countries instead of keeping their homeland labor force employed.
- **Health Risks:** Prolonged or improper computer use can lead to health injuries or disorders. Computer users can protect themselves from health risks through proper workplace design, good posture while at the computer, and appropriately spaced work breaks. Two behavioral health risks are computer addiction and technology overload. Computer addiction occurs when someone becomes obsessed with using a computer. Individuals suffering from technology overload feel distressed when deprived of computers and mobile devices.
- **Impact on Environment:** Computer manufacturing processes and computer waste are depleting natural resources and polluting the environment. **Green computing** involves reducing the electricity consumed and environmental waste generated when using a computer. Strategies that support green computing include recycling, regulating manufacturing processes, extending the life of computers, and immediately donating or properly disposing of replaced computers.

Green Computing

For more information, visit scsite.com/dc-off0//ch1/ weblink and then click Green Computing.

✓ QUIZ YOURSELF 1-1

Instructions: Find the true statement below. Then, rewrite the remaining false statements so that they are true.

1. A computer is a motorized device that processes output into input.
2. A storage device records (reads) and/or retrieves (writes) items to and from storage media.
3. An output device is any hardware component that allows you to enter data and instructions into a computer.
4. Computer literacy involves having a current knowledge and understanding of computers and their uses.
5. Three commonly used input devices are a printer, a monitor, and speakers.

 **Quiz Yourself Online:** To further check your knowledge of pages 2 through 7, visit scsite.com/dc-off07/ch1/quiz and then click Objectives 1 – 3.

Networks and the Internet

A **network** is a collection of computers and devices connected together, often wirelessly, via communications devices and transmission media. When a computer connects to a network, it is **online**. Networks allow computers to share **resources**, such as hardware, software, data, and information. Sharing resources saves time and money.

The **Internet** is a worldwide collection of networks that connects millions of businesses, government agencies, educational institutions, and individuals (Figure 1-6). More than one billion people around the world use the Internet daily for a variety of reasons, including the following: to communicate with and meet other people; to conduct research and access a wealth of information and news; to shop for goods and services; to bank and invest; to participate in online training; to engage in entertaining activities, such as planning vacations, playing online games, listening to music, watching or editing videos, and books and magazines; to share information, photos, and videos; to download music and videos; and to access and interact with Web applications. Figure 1-7 shows examples in each of these areas.

🖑 **The Internet**
For more information, visit scsite.com/dc-off07/ch1/weblink and then click The Internet.

Figure 1-6 The Internet is the largest computer network, connecting millions of computers and devices around the world.

Introduction to Computers Chapter 1 9

Figure 1-7 Home and business users access the Internet for a variety of reasons.

People connect to the Internet to exchange information with others around the world. E-mail allows you to send and receive messages to and from other users (read Ethics & Issues 1-1 for a related discussion). With instant messaging, you can have a live conversation with another connected user. In a chat room, you can communicate with multiple users at the same time — much like a group discussion. You also can use the Internet to make a telephone call.

Businesses, called access providers, offer access to the Internet free or for a fee. By subscribing to an access provider, you can use your computer and a modem to connect to the many services of the Internet.

The **Web**, short for World Wide Web, is one of the more popular services on the Internet. The Web contains billions of documents called Web pages. A **Web page** can contain text, graphics, animation, audio, and video. The nine screens shown in Figure 1-7 on the previous page are examples of Web pages.

Web pages often have built-in connections, or links, to other documents, graphics, other Web pages, or Web sites. A **Web site** is a collection of related Web pages. Some Web sites allow users to access music and videos that can be downloaded, or transferred to storage media in a computer or portable media player. Once downloaded, you can listen to the music through speakers, headphones, or earbuds, or view the videos on a display device.

Anyone can create a Web page and then make it available, or publish it, on the Internet for others to see. Millions of people worldwide join online communities, each called a **social networking Web site** or **online social network**, that encourage members to share their interests, ideas, stories, photos, music, and videos with other registered users. Hundreds of thousands of people today also use blogs to publish their thoughts on the Web. A **blog** is an informal Web site consisting of time-stamped articles in a diary or journal format, usually listed in reverse chronological order. As others read the articles in a blog, they reply with their own thoughts (to learn more about creating and using blogs, complete the Learn How To 1 activity on page 34). Podcasts are a popular way people verbally share information on the Web. A **microblog**, such as Twitter, allows users to publish short messages, usually between 100 and 200 characters, for others to read. A **podcast** is recorded audio stored on a Web site that can be downloaded to a computer or a portable media player such as an iPod.

A **Web application** is a Web site that allows users to access and interact with software from any computer or device that is connected to the Internet. Examples of software available as Web applications include those that allow you to send and receive e-mail messages, prepare your taxes, organize digital photos, create documents, and play games.

Web sites such as social networking Web sites, blogs, and Web applications are categorized as Web 2.0 sites. The term **Web 2.0** refers to Web sites that provide a means for users to share personal information (such as social networking Web sites), allow users to modify the Web site contents (such as some blogs), and/or have software built into the site for users to access (such as Web applications).

ETHICS & ISSUES 1-1

What Should Be Done about Identity Theft?

Using e-mail and other techniques on the Internet, scam artists are employing a technique known as phishing to try to steal your personal information, such as credit card numbers, banking information, and passwords. For example, an e-mail message may appear to be a request from your bank to verify your Social Security number and online banking password. Instead, the information you submit ends up in the hands of the scammer, who then uses the information for a variety of unethical and illegal acts. Sadly, the result often is identity theft. You can help to deter identity theft in several ways: 1) shred your financial documents before discarding them, 2) do not click links in unsolicited e-mail messages, and 3) enroll in a credit monitoring service. Consumer advocates often blame credit card companies and credit bureaus for lax security standards. Meanwhile, the companies blame consumers for being too gullible and forthcoming with private information. Both sides blame the government for poor privacy laws and light punishments for identity thieves. But while the arguments go on, law enforcement agencies bear the brunt of the problem by spending hundreds of millions of dollars responding to complaints and finding and processing the criminals.

Who should be responsible for protecting the public from online identity theft? Why? Should laws be changed to stop it, or should consumers change behavior? What is an appropriate punishment for identity thieves? Given the international nature of the Internet, how should foreign identity thieves be handled? Why?

FAQ 1-1

What U.S. Web sites are visited most frequently?

A recent survey found that Google's Web site is visited most frequently, with Microsoft and Yahoo! not far behind. The chart to the right shows the five most frequently visited Web sites, as well as the approximate number of unique visitors per month.

👆 For more information, visit scsite.com/dc-off07/ch1/faq and then click Top Web Sites.

An **FAQ** (frequently asked question) helps you find answers to commonly asked questions.

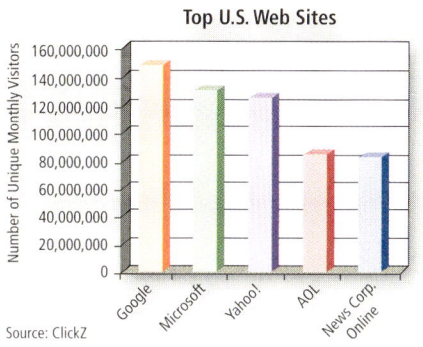

Computer Software

Software, also called a **program**, is a series of related instructions, organized for a common purpose, that tells the computer what task(s) to perform and how to perform them. You interact with a program through its user interface. Software today often has a graphical user interface. With a **graphical user interface** (**GUI** pronounced gooey), you interact with the software using text, graphics, and visual images such as icons. An icon is a miniature image that represents a program, an instruction, or some other object. You can use the mouse to select icons that perform operations such as starting a program.

The two categories of software are system software and application software. Figure 1-8 shows an example of each of these categories of software, which are explained in the following sections.

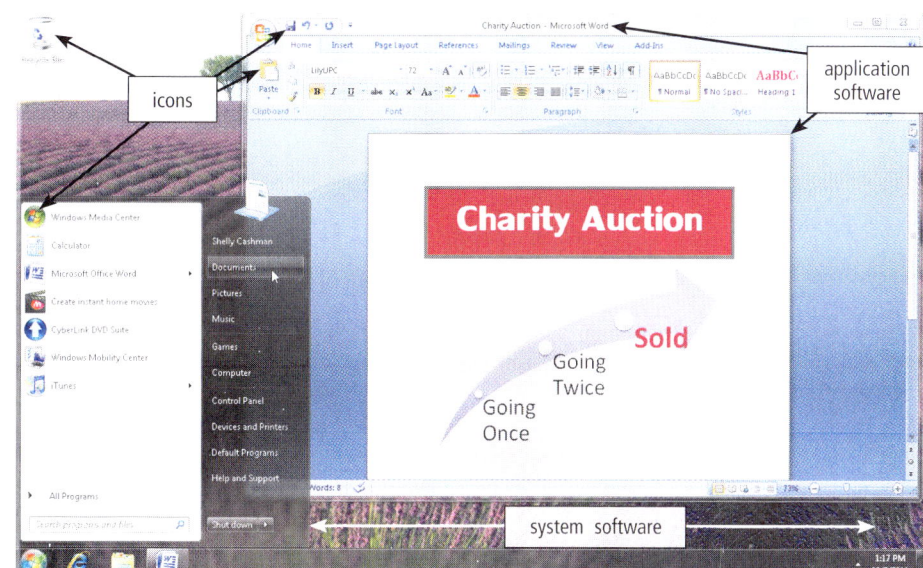

Figure 1-8 Today's system software and application software usually have a graphical user interface.

System Software

System software consists of the programs that control or maintain the operations of the computer and its devices. System software serves as the interface between the user, the application software, and the computer's hardware. Two types of system software are the operating system and utility programs.

Operating System An **operating system** is a set of programs that coordinates all the activities among computer hardware devices. It provides a means for users to communicate with the computer and other software. Many of today's computers use Microsoft's Windows, the latest version of which is shown in Figure 1-8, or Mac OS, Apple's operating system.

When a user starts a computer, portions of the operating system are copied into memory from the computer's hard disk. These parts of the operating system remain in memory while the computer is on.

 **Windows**

For more information, visit scsite.com/dc-off07/ch1/ weblink and then click Windows.

Utility Program A **utility program** allows a user to perform maintenance-type tasks usually related to managing a computer, its devices, or its programs. For example, you can use a utility program to transfer digital photos to an optical disc. Most operating systems include several utility programs for managing disk drives, printers, and other devices and media. You also can buy utility programs that allow you to perform additional computer management functions.

Application Software

Application software consists of programs designed to make users more productive and/or assist them with personal tasks. A widely used type of application software related to communications is a Web browser, which allows users with an Internet connection to access and view Web pages or access programs. Other popular application software includes word processing software, spreadsheet software, database software, and presentation software.

Many other types of application software exist that enable users to perform a variety of tasks. These include personal information management, note taking, project management, accounting, document management, computer-aided design, desktop publishing, paint/image editing, audio and video editing, multimedia authoring, Web page authoring, personal finance, legal, tax preparation, home design/landscaping, travel and mapping, education, reference, and entertainment (e.g., games or simulations).

Software is available at stores that sell computer products (Figure 1-9) and also online at many Web sites.

Figure 1-9 Stores that sell computer products have shelves stocked with software for sale.

Installing and Running Programs

When purchasing software from a retailer, you typically receive a box that includes an optical disc(s) that contains the program. If you acquire software from a Web site on the Internet, you may be able to download the program; that is, the program transfers from the Web site to the hard disk in your computer.

The instructions in software are placed on storage media, either locally or online. To use software that is stored locally, such as on a hard disk or optical disc, you usually need to install the software. Web applications that are stored online, by contrast, usually do not need to be installed.

Installing is the process of setting up software to work with the computer, printer, and other hardware. When you buy a computer, it usually has some software preinstalled on its hard disk. This enables you to use the computer the first time you turn it on. To begin installing additional software from an optical disc, insert the program disc in an optical disc drive. To install downloaded software, the Web site typically provides instructions for how to install the program on your hard disk.

Once installed, you can run the program. When you instruct the computer to **run** an installed program, the computer loads it, which means the program is copied from storage to memory. Once in memory, the computer can carry out, or **execute**, the instructions in the program so that you can use the program. Figure 1-10 illustrates the steps that occur when a user installs and runs a program.

Installing and Running a Computer Program

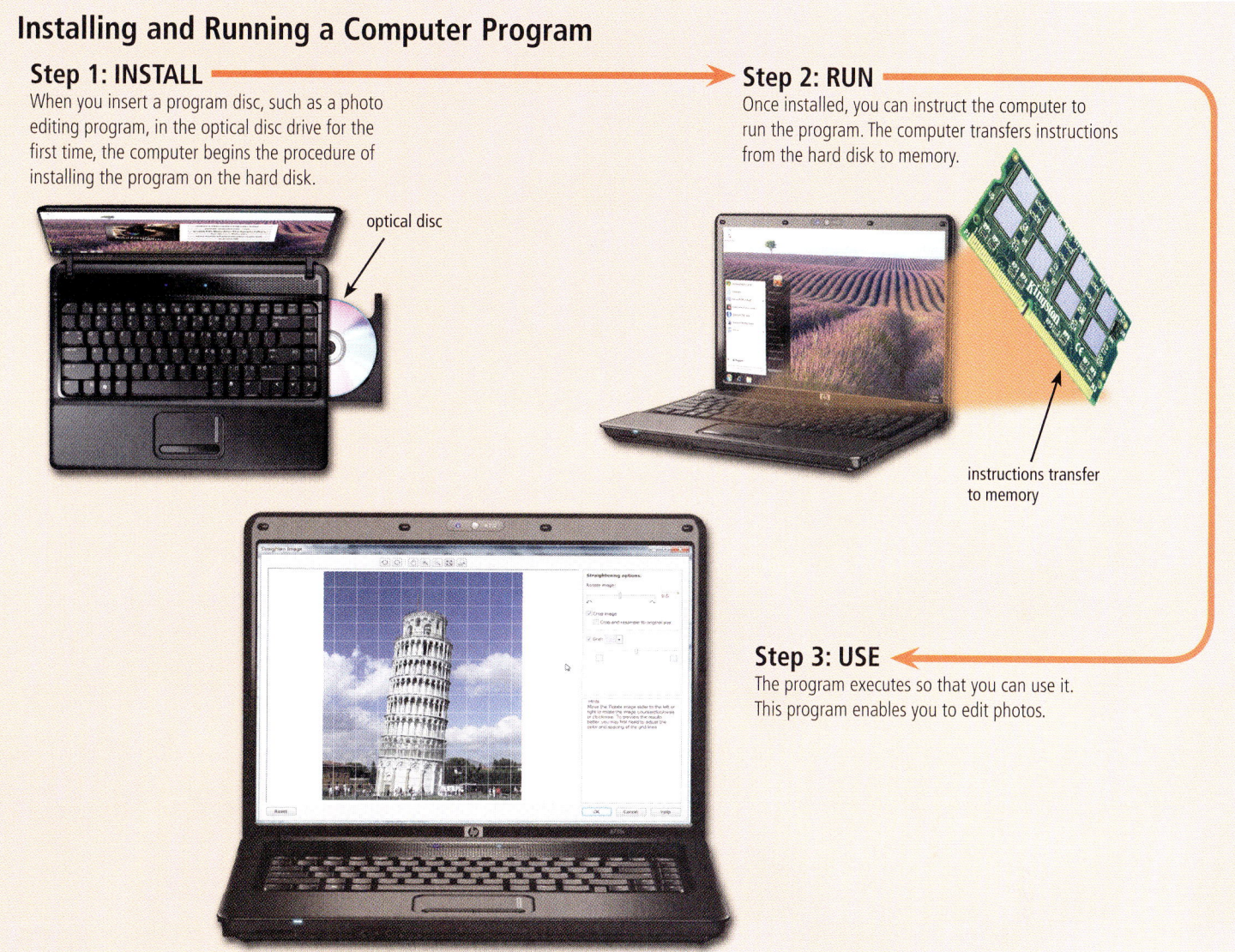

Figure 1-10 This figure shows how to install and run a computer program.

Software Development

A **programmer**, sometimes called a **developer**, is someone who develops software or writes the instructions that direct the computer to process data into information. Complex programs can require thousands to millions of instructions.

Programmers use a programming language or program development tool to create computer programs. Popular programming languages include C++, Visual C#, Visual Basic, JavaScript, and Java. Figure 1-11 shows a simple Visual Basic program.

```
Public Class frmPayrollInformation

    Private Sub btnCalculatePay_Click(ByVal sender As System.Object, ByVal e As System.
    EventArgs) Handles btnCalculatePay.Click
        'This procedure executes when the user clicks the
        'Calculate Pay button. It calculates regular
        'and overtime pay and displays it in the window.

        ' Declare variables
        Dim strHoursWorked As String
        Dim strHourlyRate As String
        Dim decHoursWorked As Decimal
        Dim decHourlyRate As Decimal
        Dim decRegularPay As Decimal
        Dim decOvertimeHours As Decimal
        Dim decOvertimePay As Decimal
        Dim decTotalPay As Decimal

        ' Calculate and display payroll information
        strHoursWorked = Me.txtHoursWorked.Text
        strHourlyRate = Me.txtHourlyRate.Text
        decHoursWorked = Convert.ToDecimal(strHoursWorked)
        decHourlyRate = Convert.ToDecimal(strHourlyRate)

        If decHoursWorked > 40 Then
            decRegularPay = 40 * decHourlyRate
            Me.txtRegularPay.Text = decRegularPay.ToString("C")
            decOvertimeHours = decHoursWorked - 40
            decOvertimePay = (1.5 * decOvertimeHours) * decHourlyRate
            Me.txtOvertimePay.Text = decOvertimePay.ToString("C")
            decTotalPay = decRegularPay + decOvertimePay
            Me.txtTotalPay.Text = decTotalPay.ToString("C")
        Else
            decRegularPay = decHoursWorked * decHourlyRate
            Me.txtRegularPay.Text = decRegularPay.ToString("C")
            Me.txtOvertimePay.Text = "$0.00"
            Me.txtTotalPay.Text = decRegularPay.ToString("C")
        End If
    End Sub
End Class
```

Figure 1-11 Some of the instructions in a program.

✓ QUIZ YOURSELF 1-2

Instructions: Find the true statement below. Then, rewrite the remaining false statements so that they are true.

1. A resource is a collection of computers and devices connected together via communications devices and transmission media.
2. Installing is the process of setting up software to work with the computer, printer, and other hardware.
3. Popular system software includes Web browsers, word processing software, spreadsheet software, database software, and presentation software.
4. The Internet is one of the more popular services on the Web.
5. Two types of application software are the operating system and utility programs.

👆 **Quiz Yourself Online:** To further check your knowledge of pages 8 through 13, visit scsite.com/dc-off07/ch1/quiz and then click Objectives 4 – 5.

Categories of Computers

Industry experts typically classify computers in seven categories: personal computers (desktop), mobile computers and mobile devices, game consoles, servers, mainframes, supercomputers, and embedded computers. A computer's size, speed, processing power, and price determine the category it best fits. Due to rapidly changing technology, however, the distinction among categories is not always clear-cut. This trend of computers and devices with technologies that overlap, called **convergence**, leads to computer manufacturers continually releasing newer models that include similar functionality and features. For example, newer cell phones often include media player, camera, and Web browsing capabilities. As devices converge, users need fewer devices for the functionality that they require. When consumers replace outdated computers and devices, they should dispose of them properly (read Ethics & Issues 1-2 for a related discussion).

Figure 1-12 summarizes the seven categories of computers. The following pages discuss computers and devices that fall in each category.

ETHICS & ISSUES 1-2

Should Recycling of Electronics Be Made Easier?

Experts estimate that about one billion computers have been discarded to date. The discarded items often are known as e-waste. As technology advances and prices fall, many people think of computers, cell phones, and portable media players as disposable items. These items often contain several toxic elements, including lead, mercury, and barium. Computers and mobile devices thrown into landfills or burned in incinerators can pollute the ground and the air. A vast amount of e-waste ends up polluting third world countries. One solution is to recycle old electronic equipment, but the recycling effort has made little progress especially when compared to recycling programs for paper, glass, and plastic.

Some lawmakers prefer an aggressive approach, such as setting up a recycling program that would be paid for by adding a $10 fee to the purchase price of computers and computer equipment, or forcing computer manufacturers to be responsible for collecting and recycling their products. California already requires a recycling fee for any products sold that include certain electronic equipment. Manufacturers have taken steps, such as offering to recycle old computers and using energy efficient and environmentally friendly manufacturing techniques, but some claim that consumers should bear the responsibility of disposing of their old computer parts. While some companies have set up recycling programs, many claim that forcing them to bear the cost of recycling programs puts the company at a competitive disadvantage when compared to foreign companies that may not be forced to maintain a recycling program.

Why is electronics recycling not as popular as other types of recycling? How can companies make it easier to recycle electronics while being compensated fairly for the cost of recycling? Should the government, manufacturers, or users be responsible for recycling of obsolete equipment? Why? Should the government mandate a recycling program for electronics? Why or why not?

Categories of Computers

Category	Physical Size	Number of Simultaneously Connected Users	General Price Range
Personal computers (desktop)	Fits on a desk	Usually one (can be more if networked)	Several hundred to several thousand dollars
Mobile computers and mobile devices	Fits on your lap or in your hand	Usually one	Less than a hundred dollars to several thousand dollars
Game consoles	Small box or handheld device	One to several	Several hundred dollars or less
Servers	Small cabinet	Two to thousands	Several hundred to a million dollars
Mainframes	Partial room to a full room of equipment	Hundreds to thousands	$300,000 to several million dollars
Supercomputers	Full room of equipment	Hundreds to thousands	$500,000 to several billion dollars
Embedded computers	Miniature	Usually one	Embedded in the price of the product

Figure 1-12 This table summarizes some of the differences among the categories of computers. These should be considered general guidelines only because of rapid changes in technology.

Personal Computers

A **personal computer** is a computer that can perform all of its input, processing, output, and storage activities by itself. A personal computer contains a processor, memory, and one or more input, output, and storage devices. Personal computers also often contain a communications device.

Two popular architectures of personal computers are the PC (Figure 1-13) and the Apple (Figure 1-14). The term, PC-compatible, refers to any personal computer based on the original IBM personal computer design. Companies such as Dell and Toshiba sell PC-compatible computers. PC and PC-compatible computers usually use a Windows operating system. Apple computers usually use a Macintosh operating system (Mac OS).

Two types of personal computers are desktop computers and notebook computers.

FAQ 1-2

Are PCs or Apple computers more popular?

While PCs still are more popular than Apple computers, Apple computer sales have been rising consistently during the past few years. In fact, Apple computer sales now account for more than 20 percent of all computer sales in the United States, with that number estimated to grow for the foreseeable future.

For more information, visit scsite.com/dc-off07/ch1/faq and then click Personal Computer Sales.

Figure 1-13 PC and PC-compatible computers usually use a Windows operating system.

Figure 1-14 Apple computers, such as the iMac, usually use a Macintosh operating system.

Desktop Computers

A **desktop computer** is designed so that the system unit, input devices, output devices, and any other devices fit entirely on or under a desk or table. In some models, the monitor sits on top of the system unit, which is placed on the desk. The more popular style of system unit is the tall and narrow tower, which can sit on the floor vertically.

Mobile Computers and Mobile Devices

A **mobile computer** is a personal computer you can carry from place to place. Similarly, a **mobile device** is a computing device small enough to hold in your hand. The most popular type of mobile computer is the notebook computer.

Notebook Computers

A **notebook computer**, also called a **laptop computer**, is a portable, personal computer often designed to fit on your lap. Notebook computers are thin and lightweight, yet can be as powerful as the average desktop computer. A **netbook**, which is a type of notebook computer, is smaller, lighter, and often not as powerful as a traditional notebook computer. Most netbooks cost less than traditional notebook computers, usually only a few hundred dollars. Some notebook computers have touch screens, allowing you to interact with the device by touching the screen, usually with the tip of a finger.

On a typical notebook computer, the keyboard is on top of the system unit, and the display attaches to the system unit with hinges (Figure 1-15). These computers weigh on average from 2.5 to more than 10 pounds (depending on configuration), which allows users easily to transport the computers from place to place. Most notebook computers can operate on batteries or a power supply or both.

Tablet PCs Resembling a letter-sized slate, the **Tablet PC** is a special type of notebook computer that allows you to write or draw on the screen using a digital pen (Figure 1-16). For users who prefer typing instead of handwriting, you can attach a keyboard to Tablet PCs that do not include one already. Most Tablet PCs have touch screens. Tablet PCs are useful especially for taking notes in locations where the standard notebook computer is not practical.

Mobile Devices

Mobile devices, which are small enough to carry in a pocket, usually store programs and data permanently on memory inside the system unit or on small storage media such as memory cards. You often can connect a mobile device to a personal computer to exchange information. Some mobile devices are **Internet-enabled**, meaning they can connect to the Internet wirelessly. Because of their reduced size, the screens on handheld computers are small.

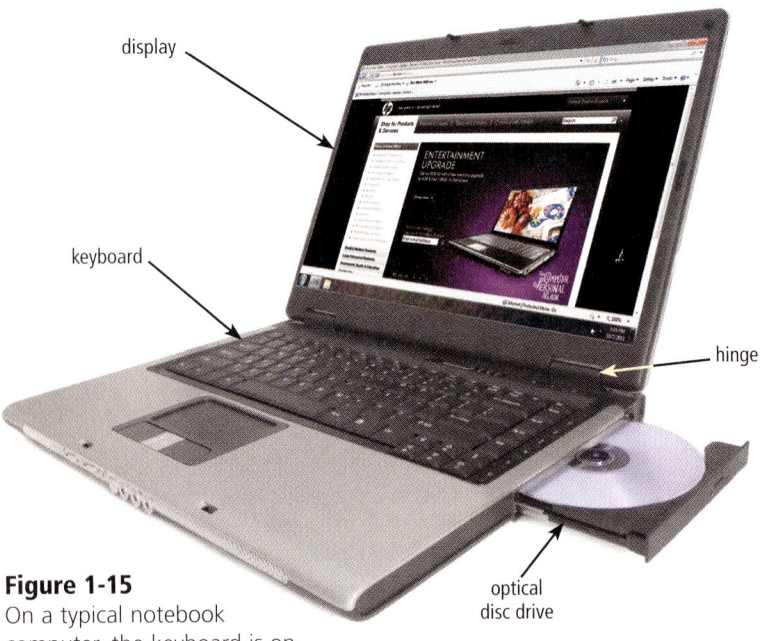

Figure 1-15
On a typical notebook computer, the keyboard is on top of the system unit, and the display attaches to the system unit with hinges.

Figure 1-16
A Tablet PC combines the features of a traditional notebook computer with the simplicity of pencil and paper.

Five popular types of mobile devices are smart phones, PDAs, handheld computers, portable media players, and digital cameras.

Smart Phones Offering the convenience of one-handed operation, a **smart phone** (Figure 1-17) is an Internet-enabled phone that usually also provides personal information management functions such as a calendar, an appointment book, an address book, a calculator, and a notepad. In addition to basic phone capabilities, a smart phone allows you to send and receive e-mail messages and access the Web — usually for an additional fee. Many models also function as a portable media player and include built-in digital cameras so that you can share photos or videos. Many smart phones also offer a variety of application software such as word processing, spreadsheet, and games.

Figure 1-17 Some smart phones have touch screens; others have mini keyboards.

Many smart phones have keypads that contain both numbers and letters so that you can use the same keypad to dial phone numbers and enter messages. Others have a built-in mini keyboard. Some have touch screens. Instead of calling someone's smart phone or cell phone, users often send messages to others by pressing buttons on their phone's keypad, keys on the mini keyboard, or images on an on-screen keyboard. Types of messages users send with smart phones include text messages, instant messages, picture messages, and video messages.

- A **text message** is a short note, typically fewer than 300 characters, sent to or from a smart phone or other mobile device.
- An **instant message** is a real-time Internet communication, where you exchange messages with other connected users.
- A **picture message** is a photo or other image, sometimes along with sound and text, sent to or from a smart phone or other mobile device. A phone that can send picture messages often is called a **camera phone**.
- A **video message** is a short video clip, usually about 30 seconds, sent to or from a smart phone or other mobile device. A phone that can send video messages often is called a **video phone**.

PDAs A **PDA** (personal digital assistant) provides personal information management functions such as a calendar, an appointment book, an address book, a calculator, and a notepad (Figure 1-18). Most PDAs also offer a variety of other application software such as word processing, spreadsheet, personal finance, and games.

A common input device for a PDA is a stylus. Many PDAs are Internet-enabled so that users can check e-mail and access the Web. Some also provide camera and phone capabilities and can function as a portable media player.

stylus

Figure 1-18 A PDA.

Handheld Computers A **handheld computer**, sometimes referred to as an **Ultra-Mobile PC** (**UMPC**), is a computer small enough to fit in one hand. Industry-specific handheld computers serve mobile employees, such as parcel delivery people, whose jobs require them to move from place to place.

Portable Media Players A **portable media player** is a mobile device on which you can store, organize, and play digital media (Figure 1-19). For example, you can listen to music; watch videos, movies, and television shows; and view photos on the device's screen. With most, you download the digital media from a computer to the portable media player or to media that you insert in the device.

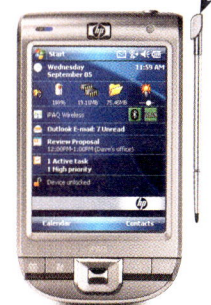

Figure 1-19 The iPod, shown here, is a popular portable media player.

earbuds

Portable media players usually include a set of earbuds, which are small speakers that rest inside each ear canal. Some portable media players have a touch screen; others have a touch-sensitive pad that you operate with a thumb or finger, to navigate through digital media, adjust volume, and customize settings.

Digital Cameras A **digital camera** is a device that allows users to take pictures and store the photographed images digitally, instead of on traditional film (Figure 1-20). Although digital cameras usually have some amount of internal storage to hold images, most users store images on small storage media such as memory cards. Digital cameras typically allow users to review, and sometimes modify, images while they are in the camera.

Often users prefer to download images from the digital camera to the computer. Or, you can remove the storage media such as a memory card from the digital camera and insert it in a card reader in or attached to the computer.

Figure 1-20 With a digital camera, users can view photographed images immediately through a small screen on the camera to see if the picture is worth keeping.

🖑 **Digital Cameras**
For more information, visit scsite.com/dc-off07/ch1/ weblink and then click Digital Cameras.

❗ INNOVATIVE COMPUTING 1-1

Wii a Welcome Medical Skill Builder

A patient awaiting laparoscopic procedures may be less tense knowing that the surgeons have honed their dexterity and coordination using a Nintendo Wii. Preliminary studies have found that doctors can improve their fine motor control by playing video games that emphasize subtle hand movements used in minimally invasive surgeries. Researchers are developing Wii surgery simulators that will allow doctors to practice their skills at home or in break rooms at hospitals.

The Wii game system is finding a medical home in other nontraditional places. Physical therapists urge arthritic patients to use Wiihabilitation to build endurance and increase their range of motion. Therapeutic recreation with the Wii's sports games may help patients recovering from strokes, fractures, and combat injuries.

Researchers in a testing lab in California are experimenting with using the Wii's motion-activated controls in non-gaming applications, such as allowing doctors to explain X-ray images to patients.

🖑 For more information, visit scsite.com/ dc-off07/ch1/innovative and then click Medical Wii.

Game Consoles

A **game console** is a mobile computing device designed for single-player or multiplayer video games (Figure 1-21). Standard game consoles use a handheld controller(s) as an input device(s); a television screen as an output device; and hard disks, optical discs, and/or memory cards for storage. The compact size and light weight of game consoles make them easy to use at home, in the car, in a hotel, or any location that has an electrical outlet. Three popular models are Microsoft's Xbox 360, Nintendo's Wii (pronounced wee), and Sony's PlayStation 3. Read Innovative Computing 1-1 for a look at how Nintendo Wii applications are being used in the medical field.

A handheld game console is small enough to fit in one hand. With the handheld game console, the controls, screen, and speakers are built into the device. Some models use cartridges to store games; others use a memory card or a miniature optical disc. Many handheld game consoles can communicate wirelessly with other similar consoles for multi-player gaming. Two popular models are Nintendo DS Lite and Sony's PlayStation Portable (PSP).

In addition to gaming, many game console models allow users to listen to music, watch movies, keep fit, and connect to the Internet.

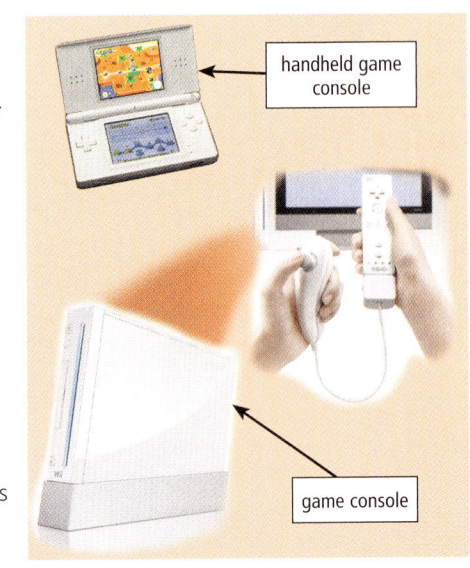

Figure 1-21 Game consoles provide hours of video game entertainment.

Servers

A **server** controls access to the hardware, software, and other resources on a network and provides a centralized storage area for programs, data, and information (Figure 1-22). Servers support from two to several thousand connected computers at the same time.

People use personal computers or terminals to access data, information, and programs on a server. A terminal is a device with a monitor, keyboard, and memory.

Figure 1-22 A server controls access to resources on a network.

Mainframes

A **mainframe** is a large, expensive, powerful computer that can handle hundreds or thousands of connected users simultaneously (Figure 1-23). Mainframes store huge amounts of data, instructions, and information. Most major corporations use mainframes for business activities. With mainframes, enterprises are able to bill millions of customers, prepare payroll for thousands of employees, and manage thousands of items in inventory. One study reported that mainframes process more than 83 percent of transactions around the world.

Servers and other mainframes can access data and information from a mainframe. People also can access programs on the mainframe using terminals or personal computers.

Figure 1-23 Mainframe computers can handle thousands of connected computers and process millions of instructions per second.

Supercomputers

A **supercomputer** is the fastest, most powerful computer — and the most expensive (Figure 1-24). The fastest supercomputers are capable of processing more than one quadrillion instructions in a single second.

Applications requiring complex, sophisticated mathematical calculations use supercomputers. Large-scale simulations and applications in medicine, aerospace, automotive design, online banking, weather forecasting, nuclear energy research, and petroleum exploration use a supercomputer.

Figure 1-24 This supercomputer, IBM's Roadrunner, can process more than one quadrillion instructions in a single second.

Embedded Computers

An **embedded computer** is a special-purpose computer that functions as a component in a larger product. A variety of everyday products contain embedded computers:
- Consumer electronics
- Home automation devices
- Automobiles
- Process controllers and robotics
- Computer devices and office machines

Because embedded computers are components in larger products, they usually are small and have limited hardware. Embedded computers perform various functions, depending on the requirements of the product in which they reside. Embedded computers in printers, for example, monitor the amount of paper in the tray, check the ink or toner level, signal if a paper jam has occurred, and so on. Figure 1-25 shows some of the many embedded computers in cars.

Adaptive cruise control systems detect if cars in front of you are too close and, if necessary, adjust the vehicle's throttle, may apply brakes, and/or sound an alarm.

Advanced airbag systems have crash-severity sensors that determine the appropriate level to inflate the airbag, reducing the chance of airbag injury in low-speed accidents.

Tire pressure monitoring systems send warning signals if tire pressure is insufficient.

Cars equipped with wireless communications capabilities, called telematics, include such features as navigation systems, remote diagnosis and alerts, and Internet access.

Drive-by-wire systems sense pressure on the gas pedal and communicate electronically to the engine how much and how fast to accelerate.

Figure 1-25 Some of the embedded computers designed to improve your safety, security, and performance in today's automobiles.

Examples of Computer Usage

Every day, people around the world rely on different types of computers for a variety of applications. To illustrate the range of uses for computers, this section takes you on a visual and narrative tour of five categories of users: a home user, a small office/home office (SOHO) user, a mobile user, a power user, and an enterprise user.

Home User

In an increasing number of homes, the computer is a basic necessity. Each family member, or **home user**, spends time on the computer for different reasons. These include personal financial management, Web access, communications, and entertainment (Figure 1-26).

On the Internet, home users access a huge amount of information, conduct research, take college classes, pay bills, manage investments, shop, listen to the radio, watch movies, read books, file taxes, book airline reservations, make telephone calls, and play games. They also communicate with others around the world through e-mail, blogs, instant messages, and chat rooms. Home users share ideas, interests, photos, music, and videos on social networking Web sites.

With a digital camera, home users take photos and then send the electronic images to others. Many home users have a portable media player, so that they can listen to downloaded music and/or podcasts at a later time through earbuds attached to the player. They also usually have one or more game consoles to play video games.

Today's homes typically have one or more desktop computers. Some home users network multiple desktop computers throughout the house, often wirelessly. These small networks allow family members to share an Internet connection and a printer.

Home users have a variety of software. They type letters, homework assignments, and other documents with word processing software. Personal finance software helps the home user with personal finances, investments, and family budgets. Other software assists with preparing taxes, keeping a household inventory, setting up maintenance schedules, and protecting computers against threats and unauthorized intrusions.

Reference software, such as encyclopedias, medical dictionaries, or a road atlas, provides valuable information for everyone in the family. With entertainment software, the home user can play games, compose music, research genealogy, or create greeting cards. Educational software helps adults learn to speak a foreign language and youngsters to read, write, count, and spell.

❓ FAQ 1-3

How many households do not use the Internet or related technologies?

A recent survey estimates that 18 percent of U.S. households have no Internet access. Furthermore, about 20 percent of U.S. heads of households have never sent an e-mail message. The chart to the right illustrates the lack of experience with computer and Internet technology.

👆 For more information, visit scsite.com/dc-off07/ch1/faq and then click Experience with Technology.

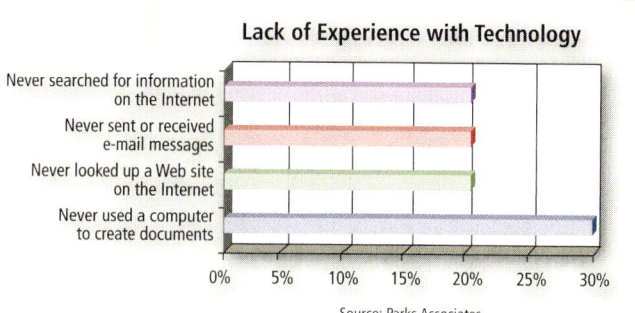

Lack of Experience with Technology
Source: Parks Associates

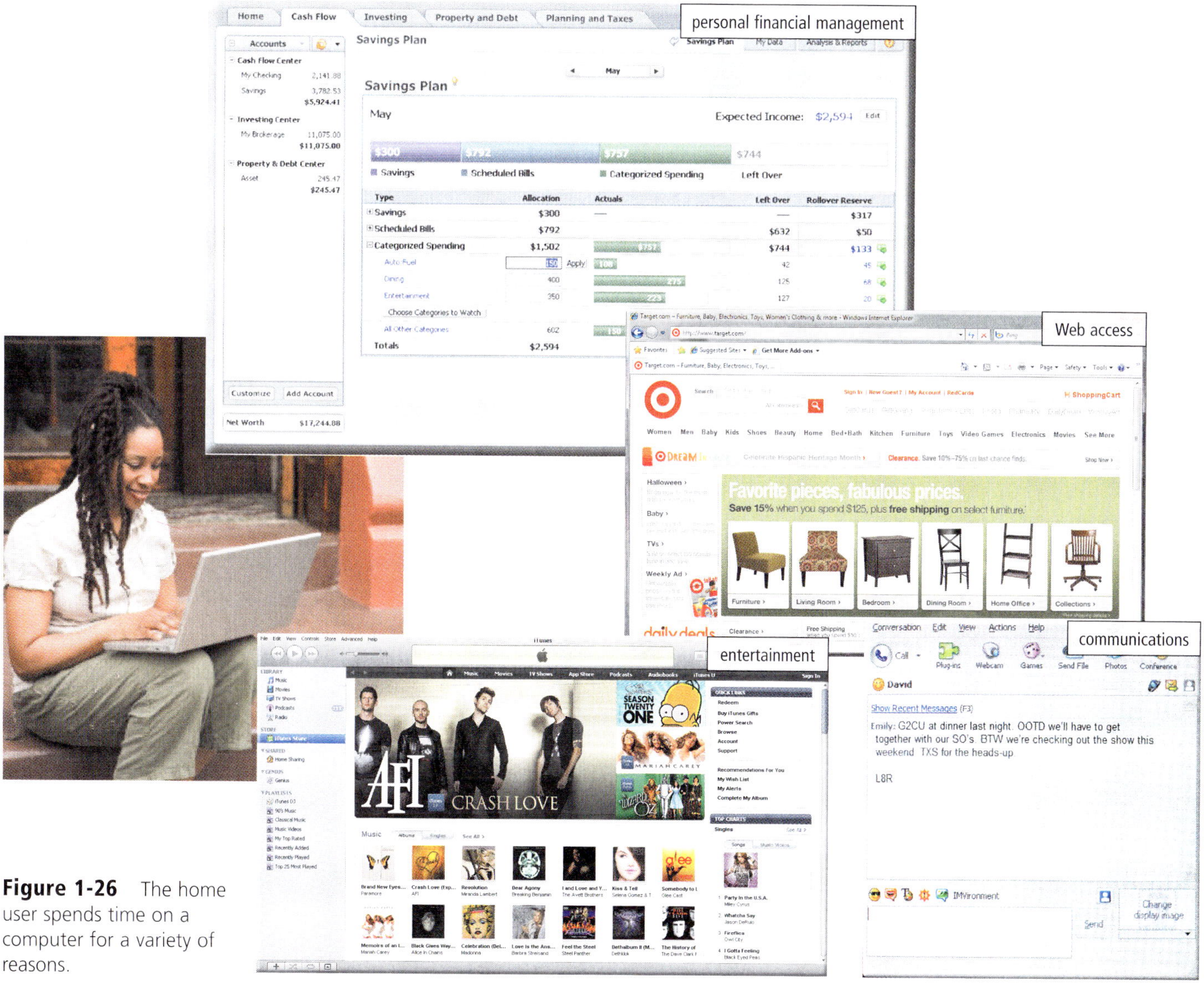

Figure 1-26 The home user spends time on a computer for a variety of reasons.

(personal financial management, Web access, entertainment, communications)

Small Office/Home Office User

Computers assist small business and home office users in managing their resources effectively. A **small office/home office** (**SOHO**) includes any company with fewer than 50 employees, as well as the self-employed who work from home. Small offices include local law practices, accounting firms, travel agencies, and florists. SOHO users typically use a desktop computer. Many also use smart phones.

SOHO users access the Internet — often wirelessly — to look up information such as addresses, directions, postal codes, flights (Figure 1-27a), and package shipping rates or to send and receive e-mail messages, or make telephone calls. Many have entered the e-commerce arena and conduct business on the Web. Their Web sites advertise products and services and may provide a means for taking orders.

To save money on hardware and software, small offices often network their computers. For example, the small office connects one printer to a network for all employees to share.

SOHO users often work with basic business software such as word processing and spreadsheet programs that assist with document preparation and finances (Figure 1-27b). They are likely to use other industry-specific types of software. An auto parts store, for example, will have software that allows for looking up parts, taking orders and payments, and updating inventory.

Mobile User

Today, businesses and schools are expanding to serve people across the country and around the world. Thus, increasingly more employees and students are **mobile users**, who work on a mobile computer or device while away from a main office, home office, or school (Figure 1-28). Some examples of mobile users are sales representatives, real estate agents, insurance agents, meter readers, package delivery people, journalists, and students.

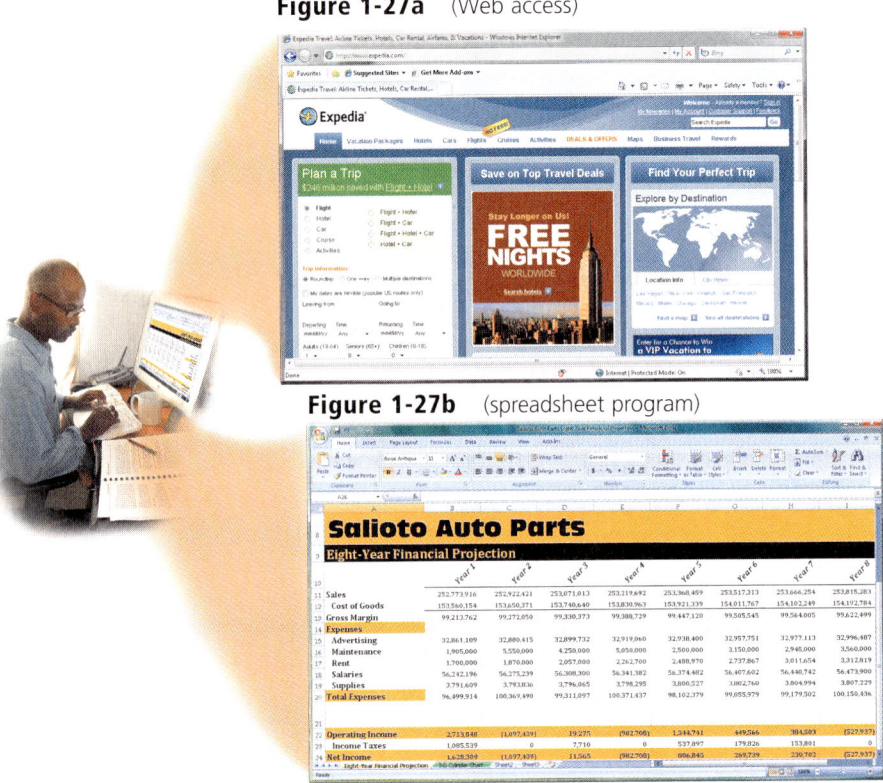

Figure 1-27a (Web access)

Figure 1-27b (spreadsheet program)

Figure 1-27 People with a home office and employees in small offices typically use a personal computer for some or all of their duties.

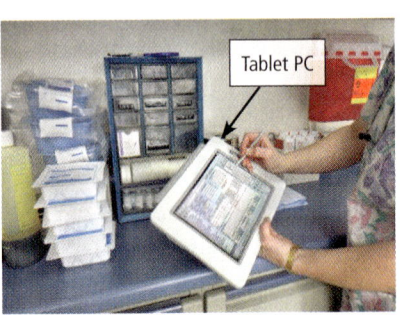

Figure 1-28 Mobile users have a variety of computers and devices so that they can work, do homework, send messages, connect to the Internet, or play games while away from a wired connection.

Mobile users often have a mobile computer and/or mobile device. With these computers and devices, the mobile user can connect to other computers on a network or the Internet, often wirelessly accessing services such as e-mail and the Web. Mobile users can transfer information between their mobile devices and another computer. For entertainment, the mobile user plays video games on a handheld game console and listens to music or watches movies on a portable media player.

The mobile user works with basic business software such as word processing and spreadsheet software. With presentation software, the mobile user can create and deliver presentations to a large audience by connecting a mobile computer or device to a video projector that displays the presentation on a full screen.

Power User

Another category of user, called a **power user**, requires the capabilities of a powerful desktop computer, called a workstation. Examples of power users include engineers, scientists, architects, desktop publishers, and graphic artists (Figure 1-29). Power users typically work with multimedia, combining text, graphics, audio, and video into one application. These users need computers with extremely fast processors because of the nature of their work.

The power user's workstation contains industry-specific software. For example, engineers and architects use software to draft and design floor plans, mechanical assemblies, or vehicles. A desktop publisher uses software to prepare marketing literature. A graphic artist uses software to create sophisticated drawings. This software usually is expensive because of its specialized design.

Power users exist in all types of businesses. Some also work at home. Their computers typically have network connections and Internet access.

Figure 1-29 This graphic artist uses a powerful computer to develop computer games.

Enterprise User

An enterprise has hundreds or thousands of employees or customers that work in or do business with offices across a region, the country, or the world. Each employee or customer who uses a computer in the enterprise is an **enterprise user** (Figure 1-30).

Many large companies use the words, **enterprise computing**, to refer to the huge network of computers that meets their diverse computing needs. The network facilitates communications among employees at all locations. Users access the network through desktop computers, mobile computers, and mobile devices.

Enterprises use computers and the computer network to process high volumes of transactions in a single day. Although they may differ in size and in the products or services offered, all generally use computers for basic business activities. For example, they bill millions of customers or prepare payroll for thousands of employees. Some enterprises use blogs to open communications among employees and/or customers.

Enterprises typically have e-commerce Web sites, allowing customers and vendors to conduct business online. The Web site showcases products, services, and other company information. Customers, vendors, and other interested parties can access this information on the Web.

The marketing department in an enterprise uses desktop publishing software to prepare marketing literature. The accounting department uses software for accounts receivable, accounts payable, billing, general ledger, and payroll activities.

Figure 1-30 An enterprise can have hundreds or thousands of users in offices across a region, the country, or the world.

Enterprise Computing
For more information, visit scsite.com/dc-off07/ch1/ weblink and then click Enterprise Computing.

Enterprise users work with word processing, spreadsheet, database, and presentation software. They also may use calendar programs to post their schedules on the network. And, they might use smart phones or other mobile devices to maintain contact information. E-mail programs and Web browsers enable communications among employees, vendors, and customers.

Many employees of enterprises today telecommute. **Telecommuting** is a work arrangement in which employees work away from a company's standard workplace and often communicate with the office through the computer. Employees who telecommute have flexible work schedules so that they can combine work and personal responsibilities, such as child care.

Computer Applications in Society

The computer has changed society today as much as the industrial revolution changed society in the eighteenth and nineteenth centuries.

People interact directly with computers in fields such as education, finance, government, health care, science, publishing, travel, and manufacturing. In addition, they can reap the benefits from breakthroughs and advances in these fields. The following pages describe how computers have made a difference in people's interactions with these disciplines. Read Looking Ahead 1-1 for a look at how embedded computers may improve the quality of life.

↗ LOOKING AHEAD 1-1

Embedded Computers May Improve Quality of Life

The weather forecast may be as close as your fingertips if plans to integrate embedded computers in everyday objects become a reality. Researchers are envisioning an umbrella with an embedded cell phone in the handle that will dial and then download the local forecast. The handle will glow green for good weather and flash red for imminent storms.

Dancers can pin a small flower with an embedded motion-detecting computer to their clothes. When they move, the embedded computer senses action and then synchronizes the tempo of music to this movement. Other embedded computers woven into clothing can monitor heart and breathing rates.

Wearing hidden embedded computers can help the elderly and people recovering from accidents and surgeries monitor their walking stride and pace. When their steps are uneven, the embedded computer can sound a warning and perhaps prevent a fall. Other embedded computers can give subtle feedback on the quality of physical activity.

For more information, visit scsite.com/dc-off07/ch1/looking and then click Embedded Computers.

Education

Education is the process of acquiring knowledge. In the traditional model, people learn from other people such as parents, teachers, and employers. Many forms of printed material such as books and manuals are used as learning tools. Today, educators also are turning to computers to assist with education (Figure 1-31).

Many schools and companies equip labs and classrooms with computers. Some schools require students to have a mobile computer or mobile device to access the school's network or Internet wirelessly.

Students use software to assist with learning or to complete assignments. To promote education by computer, many vendors offer substantial student discounts on software.

Figure 1-31 In some schools, students have mobile computers on their desks during classroom lectures.

Sometimes, the delivery of education occurs at one place while the learning occurs at other locations. For example, students can take a class on the Web. More than 70 percent of colleges offer distance learning classes. A few even offer entire degrees online.

Finance

Many people and companies use computers to help manage their finances. Some use finance software to balance checkbooks, pay bills, track personal income and expenses, manage investments, and evaluate financial plans. This software usually includes a variety of online services. For example, computer users can track investments and do online banking. With **online banking**, users access account balances, pay bills, and copy monthly transactions from the bank's computer right into their computers (Figure 1-32).

Investors often use **online investing** to buy and sell stocks and bonds — without using a broker. With online investing, the transaction fee for each trade usually is much less than when trading through a broker.

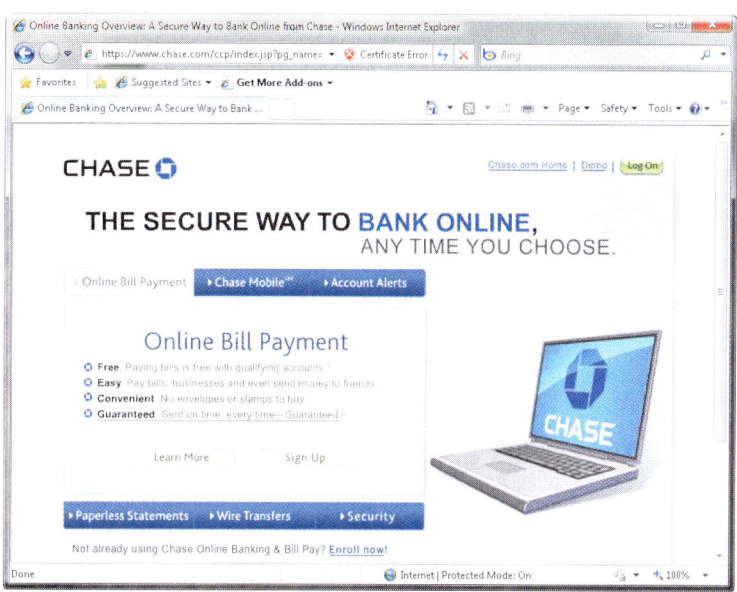

Figure 1-32 An online banking Web site.

Government

A government provides society with direction by making and administering policies. To provide citizens with up-to-date information, most government offices have Web sites. People access government Web sites to file taxes, apply for permits and licenses, pay parking tickets, buy stamps, report crimes, apply for financial aid, and renew vehicle registrations and driver's licenses.

Employees of government agencies use computers as part of their daily routine. Military and other agency officials use the U.S. Department of Homeland Security's network of information about domestic security threats to help protect our nation. Law enforcement officers have online access to the FBI's National Crime Information Center (NCIC) through in-vehicle computers, fingerprint readers, and mobile devices (Figure 1-33). The NCIC contains more than 52 million missing persons and criminal records, including names, fingerprints, parole/probation records, mug shots, and other information.

Figure 1-33 Law enforcement officials have in-vehicle computers and mobile devices to access emergency, missing person, and criminal records in computer networks in local, state, and federal agencies.

Health Care

Nearly every area of health care uses computers. Whether you are visiting a family doctor for a regular checkup, having lab work or an outpatient test, or being rushed in for emergency surgery, the medical staff around you will be using computers for various purposes:

- Doctors use the Web and medical software to assist with researching and diagnosing health conditions.
- Doctors use e-mail to correspond with patients.
- Pharmacists use computers to file insurance claims.
- Robots deliver medication to nurse stations in hospitals.
- Hospitals and doctors use computers and mobile devices to maintain and access patient records.

- Computers and computerized devices assist doctors, nurses, and technicians with medical tests (Figure 1-34).
- Computers monitor patients' vital signs in hospital rooms and at home.
- Surgeons implant computerized devices, such as pacemakers, that allow patients to live longer.
- Surgeons use computer-controlled devices to provide them with greater precision during operations, such as for laser eye surgery and robot-assisted heart surgery.

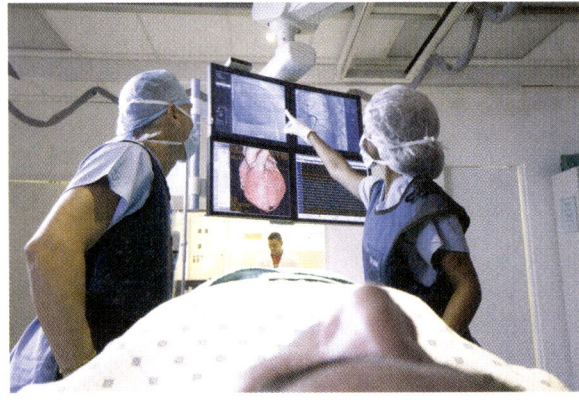

Figure 1-34 Doctors, nurses, technicians, and other medical staff use computers and computerized devices to assist with medical tests.

Two forms of long-distance health care are telemedicine and telesurgery. Through **telemedicine**, health-care professionals in separate locations conduct live conferences on the computer. For example, a doctor at one location can have a conference with a doctor at another location to discuss a bone X-ray. Live images of each doctor, along with the X-ray, are displayed on each doctor's computer.

With **telesurgery**, a surgeon performs an operation on a patient who is not located in the same physical room as the surgeon. Telesurgery enables surgeons to direct robots to perform an operation via computers connected to a high-speed network.

Science

All branches of science, from biology to astronomy to meteorology, use computers to assist them with collecting, analyzing, and modeling data. Scientists also use the Internet to communicate with colleagues around the world.

Breakthroughs in surgery, medicine, and treatments often result from scientists' use of computers. Tiny computers now imitate functions of the central nervous system, retina of the eye, and cochlea of the ear. A cochlear implant allows a deaf person to listen. Electrodes implanted in the brain stop tremors associated with Parkinson's disease. Cameras small enough to swallow — sometimes called a camera pill — take pictures inside your body to detect polyps, cancer, and other abnormalities (Figure 1-35).

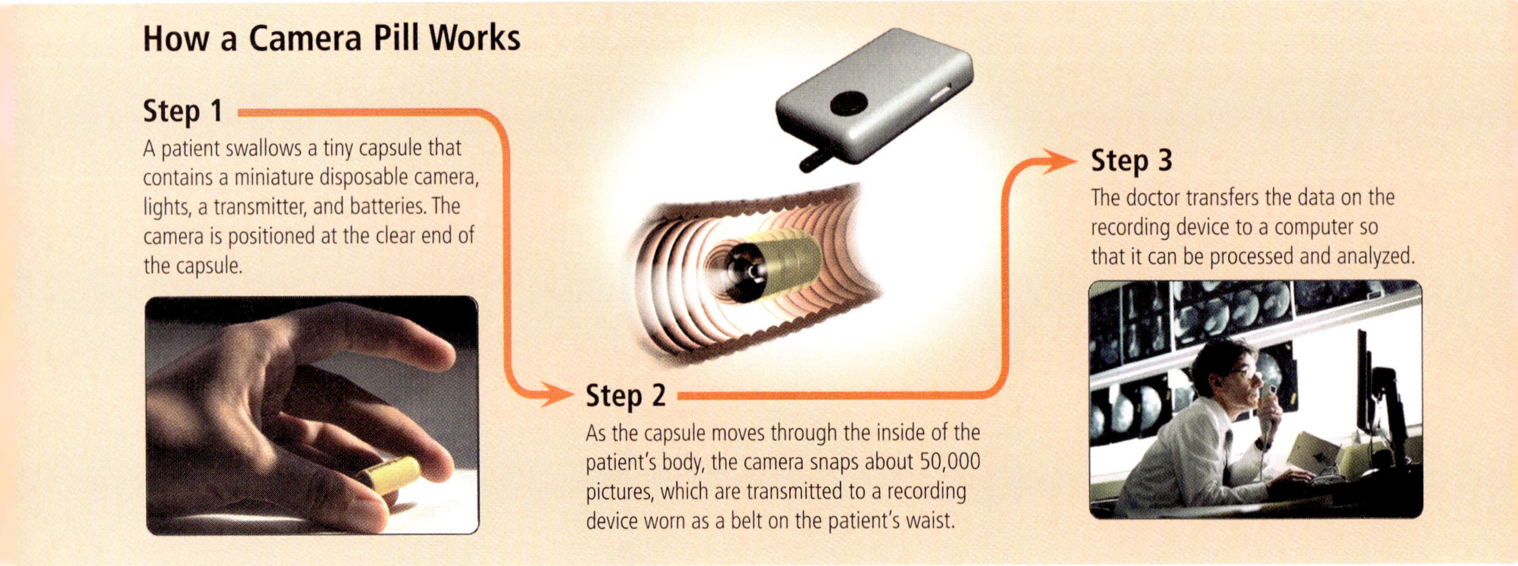

How a Camera Pill Works

Step 1
A patient swallows a tiny capsule that contains a miniature disposable camera, lights, a transmitter, and batteries. The camera is positioned at the clear end of the capsule.

Step 2
As the capsule moves through the inside of the patient's body, the camera snaps about 50,000 pictures, which are transmitted to a recording device worn as a belt on the patient's waist.

Step 3
The doctor transfers the data on the recording device to a computer so that it can be processed and analyzed.

Figure 1-35 This figure shows how a camera pill works.

Publishing

Publishing is the process of making works available to the public. These works include books, magazines, newspapers, music, film, and video. Special software assists graphic designers in developing pages that include text, graphics, and photos; artists in composing and enhancing songs; filmmakers in creating and editing film; and journalists and mobile users in capturing and modifying video clips.

Many publishers make their works available online (Figure 1-36). Some Web sites allow you to copy the work, such as a book or music, to your desktop computer, mobile computer, smart phone, or other mobile device.

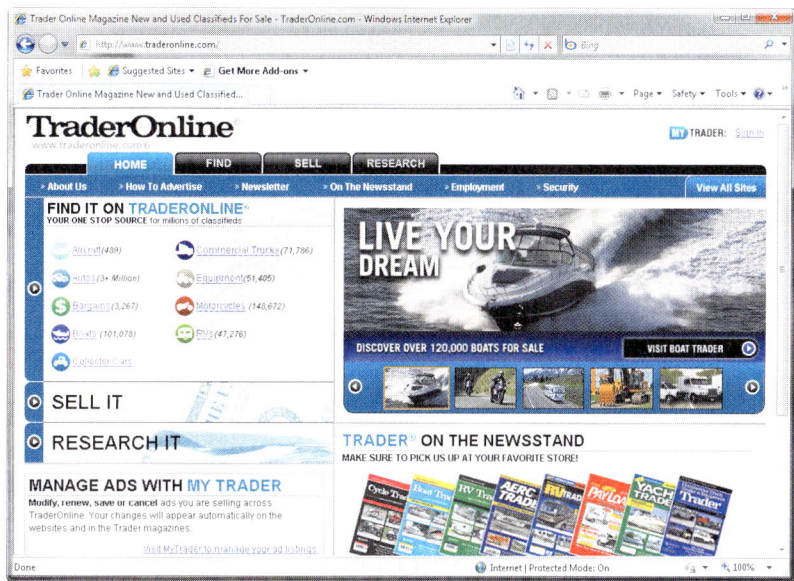

Figure 1-36 Many magazine and newspaper publishers make the content of their publications available online.

Travel

Many vehicles manufactured today include some type of onboard navigation system. Some mobile users prefer to carry specialized handheld navigation devices (Figure 1-37).

In preparing for a trip, you may need to reserve a car, hotel, or flight. Many Web sites offer these services to the public. For example, you can order airline tickets on the Web. If you plan to drive somewhere and are unsure of the road to take to your destination, you can print directions and a map from the Web.

Figure 1-37 This handheld navigation device gives users turn-by-turn voice-prompted directions to a destination.

Manufacturing

Computer-aided manufacturing (**CAM**) refers to the use of computers to assist with manufacturing processes such as fabrication and assembly. Often, robots carry out processes in a CAM environment. CAM is used by a variety of industries, including oil drilling, power generation, food production, and automobile manufacturing. Automobile plants, for example, have an entire line of industrial robots that assemble a car (Figure 1-38).

Figure 1-38 Automotive factories use industrial robots to weld car bodies.

QUIZ YOURSELF 1-3

Instructions: Find the true statement below. Then, rewrite the remaining false statements so that they are true.

1. A desktop computer is a portable, personal computer designed to fit on your lap.
2. A personal computer contains a processor, memory, and one or more input, output, and storage devices.
3. Each enterprise user spends time on the computer for different reasons that include personal financial management, Web access, communications, and entertainment.
4. A home user requires the capabilities of a workstation or other powerful computer.
5. Mainframes are the fastest, most powerful computers — and the most expensive.
6. With embedded computers, users access account balances, pay bills, and copy monthly transactions from the bank's computer right into their personal computers.

Quiz Yourself Online: To further check your knowledge of pages 14 through 27, visit scsite.com/dc-off07/ch1/quiz and then click Objectives 6 – 8.

Chapter Summary

Chapter 1 introduced you to basic computer concepts. You learned about the components of a computer. Next, the chapter discussed networks, the Internet, and computer software. The many different categories of computers, computer users, and computer applications in society also were presented.

This chapter is an overview. Many of the terms and concepts introduced will be discussed further in later chapters. For information about digital products in our lives, read the Living Digitally feature that follows this chapter.

Computer Usage @ Work

Transportation

What is transportation like without computers? Delivery drivers use clipboards to hold their records. Human navigators use paper maps to track routes for pilots. Ship captains rely solely on experience to navigate through shallow waters. Today, the transportation industry relies heavily on computer usage.

As presented in this chapter, many vehicles include onboard navigation systems to help you navigate from one location to another. These systems also usually provide other services such as dispatching roadside assistance, unlocking the driver's side door if you lock the keys in your vehicle, and tracking the vehicle if it is stolen.

The shipping and travel industries identify items during transport using bar codes, which are identification codes that consist of lines and spaces of different lengths. When you ship a package, the shipping company, such as UPS or FedEx, places a bar code on the package to indicate its destination to a computer. Because a package might travel to its destination by way of several trucks, trains, and airplanes, computers automatically route the package as efficiently as possible.

When you travel by airplane, baggage handling systems ensure that your luggage reaches its destination on time. When you check in your baggage at the airport, a bar code identifies the airplane on which the bags should be placed. If you change planes, automated baggage handling systems route your bags to connecting flights with very little, if any, human intervention. When the bags reach their destination, they are routed automatically to the baggage carousel in the airport's terminal building.

Pilots of high-technology commercial, military, and space aircraft today work in a glass cockpit, which features computerized instrumentation, navigation, communication, weather reports, and an autopilot. The electronic flight information shown on high-resolution displays is designed to reduce pilot workload, decrease fatigue, and enable pilots to concentrate on flying safely.

Boats and ships also are equipped with computers that include detailed electronic maps, help the captain navigate, as well as calculate the water depth and provide a layout of the underwater surface so that the captain can avoid obstructions.

As you travel the roadways, airways, and waterways, bear in mind that computers often are responsible for helping you to reach your destination as quickly and safely as possible.

For more information, visit scsite.com/dc-off07/ch1/work and then click Transportation.

Companies on the Cutting Edge

APPLE Innovative Industry Products

Apple recently sold more than one million of its latest iPhone models in three days, establishing the company's appeal to both consumer and corporate cell phone users. Apple is noted for introducing innovative products, starting with the Apple II, which was the first mass-marketed personal computer, in 1977 and the Macintosh, which featured a graphical user interface, in 1984.

Steve Jobs and Steve Wozniak founded Apple in 1976 when they marketed the Apple I, a circuit board they had developed in Jobs's garage. Under Jobs's direction as CEO, Apple developed the OS X operating system; iLife for working with photos, music, videos, and Web sites; and iWork, a collection of business programs. Apple also is leading the digital media revolution with its iPod portable media players and iTunes online store, which is the most popular Web site selling music. In 2009, more than one million people downloaded the latest version of their Safari Web browser in just three days.

AMAZON Retailer Focused on Consumers

Online shoppers can find practically any product they desire on Amazon.com. Billing itself as the "Earth's most customer-centric company," it offers books, movies, electronics, clothing, toys, and many other items.

Jeff Bezos founded Amazon in 1995 knowing that book lovers would gravitate toward a Web site offering the convenience of browsing through millions of book titles in one sitting. He fulfilled orders for customers in every U.S. state and 45 additional countries during the first 30 days of business, all shipped from his Seattle-area garage.

The company has grown to permit third parties to sell products on its Web site. Its Kindle portable reader wirelessly downloads more than 300,000 books along with blogs, magazines, and newspapers to a high-resolution electronic paper display. In 2009, it acquired Zappos.com, Inc., a leading online apparel and footwear retailer.

For more information, visit scsite.com/dc-off07/ch1/companies.

Technology Trailblazers

BILL GATES Microsoft Founder

When Bill Gates stepped down from his day-to-day activities at Microsoft in 2008, his action marked the end of an era that shaped the computer world. He remains the company's chairman and advisor, but he now devotes much of his time directing the Bill & Melinda Gates Foundation, a philanthropic organization working to help people worldwide lead healthy, productive lives.

Gates learned to program computers when he was 13 years old. Early in his career, he developed the BASIC programming language for the MITS Altair, one of the first microcomputers. He founded Microsoft in 1975 with Paul Allen, and five years later they licensed the first operating system, called PC-DOS, to IBM for $80,000. This decision to license, rather than sell, the software is considered one of the wisest business decisions Gates ever made. Today, Microsoft's Windows and Office products dominate the software market.

TOM ANDERSON MySpace Cofounder and President

Having more than 240 million friends is all in a day's work for Tom Anderson, the current president and one of the founders of MySpace, the world's largest online social network. Every MySpace account includes Anderson as a default first friend who is invited to view each personal network.

When Anderson's own rock group failed, he needed a place to post his songs. He started MySpace in 2003 with his friend, Chris DeWolfe, as a free tool to help musicians promote their songs and allow music lovers to create their own Web pages devoted to sharing their favorite music with like-minded admirers. Two years later they sold the business to Rupert Murdoch's News Corporation for $580 million. Anderson graduated from the University of California – Los Angeles in 2001 with a master's degree in film and from the University of California – Berkeley in 1998 with a bachelor's degree in English and rhetoric.

For more information, visit scsite.com/dc-off07/ch1/trailblazers.

Chapter Review

The Chapter Review reinforces the main concepts presented in this chapter.

☞ To obtain help from other students about any concept in this chapter, visit scsite.com/dc-off07/ch1/forum and post your thoughts or questions.

1. **Why Is Computer Literacy Vital to Success in Today's World?** **Computer literacy**, also called digital literacy, involves having current knowledge and understanding of computers and their uses. As computers become an increasingly important part of daily living, many people believe that computer literacy is vital to success. Because the requirements that determine computer literacy change as technology changes, you must keep up with these changes to remain computer literate.

2. **List and Describe the Five Components of a Computer.** A **computer** is an electronic device, operating under the control of instructions stored in its own memory, that can accept data, process the data according to specified rules, produce results, and store the results for future use. The electric, electronic, and mechanical components of a computer, or **hardware**, include input devices, output devices, a system unit, storage devices, and communications devices. An **input device** allows you to enter data or instructions into a computer. An **output device** conveys information to one or more people. The **system unit** is a case that contains the electronic components of a computer that are used to process data. A **storage device** records and/or retrieves items to and from **storage media**. A **communications device** enables a computer to send and receive data, instructions, and information to and from one or more computers.

3. **What Are the Advantages and Disadvantages That Users Experience When Working with Computers?** A **user** is anyone who communicates with a computer or utilizes the information it generates. Advantages of using a computer include speed, reliability, consistency, storage, and communications. The disadvantages include violation of privacy, public safety, impact on the labor force, health risks, and impact on the environment.

☞ Visit scsite.com/dc-off07/ch1/quiz and then click Objectives 1 – 3.

4. **How Are the Internet and World Wide Web Used?** The Internet is a worldwide collection of networks that connects millions of businesses, government agencies, educational institutions, and individuals. People use the Internet to communicate with and meet other people; conduct research and access information and news; shop for goods and services; bank and invest; participate in online training; engage in entertaining activities; download music and videos; share information, photos, and videos; and to access and interact with Web applications. The **Web**, short for World Wide Web, contains billions of documents called Web pages.

5. **What Are the Differences between System Software and Application Software?** **Software**, also called a **program**, is a series of related instructions, organized for a common purpose, that tells the computer what tasks to perform and how to perform them. The two categories of software are system software and application software. **System software** consists of the programs that control or maintain the operations of a computer and its devices. Two types of system software are the **operating system**, which coordinates activities among computer hardware devices, and **utility programs**, which perform maintenance-type tasks usually related to managing a computer, its devices, or its programs. **Application software** consists of programs designed to make users more productive and/or assist them with personal tasks. Popular application software includes a Web browser, word processing software, spreadsheet software, database software, and presentation software.

☞ Visit scsite.com/dc-off07/ch1/quiz and then click Objectives 4 – 5.

6. **What Are the Differences among the Types, Sizes, and Functions in the Following Categories: Personal Computers (Desktop), Mobile Computers and Mobile Devices, Game Consoles, Servers, Mainframes, Supercomputers, and Embedded Computers?** A **personal computer** is a computer that can perform all of its input, processing, output, and storage activities by itself. A **mobile computer** is a personal computer that you can carry from place to place, and a **mobile device** is a computing device small enough to hold in your hand. A game console is a mobile computing device designed for single-player or multiplayer video games. A **server** controls access to the hardware, software, and other resources on a network and provides a centralized storage area for programs, data, and information. A **mainframe** is a large, expensive, powerful computer that can handle hundreds or thousands of connected users simultaneously and can store huge amounts of data, instructions, and information. A **supercomputer** is the fastest, most powerful, and most expensive computer and is used for applications requiring complex, sophisticated mathematical calculations. An **embedded computer** is a special-purpose computer that functions as a component in a larger product.

7. **How Do the Various Types of Computer Users Interact with Computers?** Computer users can be separated into five categories: home user, small office/home office user, mobile user, power user, and enterprise user. A **home user** is a family member who uses a computer for a variety of reasons, such as personal financial management, Web access, communications, and entertainment. A **small office/home office** (**SOHO**) includes any company with fewer than 50 employees or a self-employed individual who works from home and uses basic business software and sometimes industry-specific software. **Mobile users** are employees and students who work on a computer while away from a main office, home office, or school. A **power user** can exist in all types of businesses and uses powerful computers to work with industry-specific software. An **enterprise user** works in or interacts with a company with many employees and uses a computer and computer network that processes high volumes of transactions in a single day.

8. **How Does Society Use Computers in Education, Finance, Government, Health Care, Science, Publishing, Travel, and Manufacturing?** In education, students use computers and software to assist with learning or take distance learning classes. In finance, people use computers for **online banking** to access information and **online investing** to buy and sell stocks and bonds. Government offices have Web sites to provide citizens with up-to-date information, and government employees use computers as part of their daily routines. In health care, computers are used to maintain patient records, assist doctors with medical tests and research, file insurance claims, provide greater precision during operations, and as implants. All branches of science use computers to assist with collecting, analyzing, and modeling data and to communicate with scientists around the world. Publishers use computers to assist in developing pages and make their works available online. Many vehicles use some type of online navigation system to help people travel more quickly and safely. Manufacturers use **computer-aided manufacturing** (**CAM**) to assist with manufacturing processes.

👆 Visit scsite.com/dc-off07/ch1/quiz and then click Objectives 6 – 8.

Key Terms

You should know the Key Terms. The list below helps focus your study.

👆 To see an example of and a definition for each term, and to access current and additional information from the Web, visit scsite.com/dc-off07/ch1/terms.

application software (12)
blog (10)
camera phone (17)
communications device (6)
computer (3)
computer literacy (3)
computer-aided manufacturing (CAM) (27)
convergence (14)
CPU (central processing unit) (6)
data (4)
desktop computer (16)
developer (13)
digital camera (18)
digital literacy (3)
embedded computer (19)
enterprise computing (23)
enterprise user (23)
execute (12)
FAQ (11)
game console (18)

graphical user interface (GUI) (11)
green computing (7)
handheld computer (17)
hardware (4)
home user (20)
information (4)
information processing cycle (4)
input device (4)
installing (12)
instant message (17)
Internet (8)
Internet-enabled (16)
laptop computer (16)
mainframe (19)
memory (6)
microblog (10)
mobile computer (16)
mobile device (16)
mobile users (22)
netbook (16)
network (8)
notebook computer (16)

online (8)
online banking (25)
online investing (25)
online social network (10)
operating system (11)
output device (5)
PDA (17)
personal computer (15)
picture message (17)
podcast (10)
portable media player (17)
power user (23)
processor (6)
program (11)
programmer (13)
resources (8)
run (12)
server (19)
small office/home office (SOHO) (22)
smart phone (17)
social networking Web site (10)

software (11)
storage device (6)
storage media (6)
supercomputer (19)
system software (11)
system unit (6)
Tablet PC (16)
telecommuting (24)
telemedicine (26)
telesurgery (26)
text message (17)
Ultra-Mobile PC (UMPC) (17)
user (7)
utility program (12)
video message (17)
video phone (17)
Web (10)
Web 2.0 (10)
Web application (10)
Web page (10)
Web site (10)

Checkpoint

The Checkpoint exercises test your knowledge of the chapter concepts. The page number containing the answer appears in parentheses after each exercise.

👆 To complete the Checkpoint exercises interactively, visit scsite.com/dc-off07/ch1/check.

Multiple Choice Select the best answer.

1. Computer literacy, also known as digital literacy, involves having a current knowledge and understanding of _____. (3)
   a. computer programming
   b. computers and their uses
   c. computer repair
   d. all of the above

2. _____ is/are a collection of unprocessed items, which can include text, numbers, images, audio, and video. (4)
   a. Data   b. Instructions
   c. Programs   d. Information

3. Millions of people worldwide join online communities, each called _____, that encourage members to share their interests, ideas, stories, photos, music, and videos with other registered users. (10)
   a. a podcast
   b. enterprise computing
   c. a social networking Web site or online social network
   d. a blog

4. _____ consists of the programs that control or maintain the operations of the computer and its devices. (11)
   a. A graphical user interface (GUI)
   b. A communications device
   c. System software
   d. Application software

5. Two types of _____ are desktop computers and notebook computers. (15)
   a. servers
   b. supercomputers
   c. mainframe computers
   d. personal computers

6. Five popular types of _____ are smart phones, PDAs, handheld computers, portable media players, and digital cameras. (17)
   a. mobile devices
   b. notebook computers
   c. desktop computers
   d. tower computers

7. A(n) _____ message is a real-time Internet communication, where you exchange messages with other connected users. (17)
   a. text   b. instant
   c. picture   d. video

8. Many large companies use the word(s), _____, to refer to the huge network of computers that meets their diverse computing needs. (23)
   a. information technology
   b. telecommuting
   c. enterprise computing
   d. multimedia

Matching Match the terms with their definitions.

_____ 1. information processing cycle (4)
_____ 2. processor (6)
_____ 3. storage device (6)
_____ 4. portable media player (17)
_____ 5. digital camera (18)

a. records (writes) and/or retrieves (reads) items to and from storage media
b. mobile device on which you can store, organize, and play digital media
c. fastest, most powerful computer — and the most expensive
d. electronic component that interprets and carries out the basic instructions for a computer
e. series of input, process, output, and storage activities
f. device that allows users to take pictures and store the photographed images digitally, instead of on traditional film

Short Answer Write a brief answer to each of the following questions.

1. What does it mean to be computer literate? _____ What is a computer? _____
2. Describe two health risks posed by computers. _____ How might computers have a negative effect on the environment? _____
3. What are five common storage devices? _____ How are they different? _____
4. What is a Web application? _____ What are some features of a Web 2.0 site? _____
5. How is hardware different from software? _____ What are two types of system software and how are they used? _____
6. How do computers benefit individuals' health care? _____ How does telesurgery differ from telemedicine? _____

Introduction to Computers   Chapter 1   **33**

Problem Solving

The Problem Solving exercises extend your knowledge of the chapter concepts by seeking solutions to practical computer problems that you may encounter at home, school, or work. The Collaboration exercise should be completed with a team.

👆 To discuss the Problem Solving exercises with other students, visit scsite.com/dc-off07/ch1/forum and post your thoughts or questions.

In the real world, practical problems often can be solved in multiple ways. Provide one solution to each of the following problems using available resources, such as articles on the Web or in print, blogs, podcasts, videos, television, user guides, other individuals, and electronics and computer stores. You may need to use multiple resources to obtain an answer. Present your solutions in the form requested by your instructor (brief report, presentation, discussion, or other means).

@ Home

1. **Incorrect Grade Report**   Your grade report came in the mail today. On the grade report, your grade point average (GPA) is not what you expect. After computing it manually, you discover that the GPA on your grade report is incorrect. What might be causing the error?

2. **Suspicious Charges**   Your credit card company called to inform you that your account has a suspicious charge. Upon further investigation, you realize the charge does not belong to you. What steps will you take to correct the problem?

3. **Problematic Player**   After charging your portable media player overnight, you turn it on only to find that it is reporting a low battery. Seconds later, it shuts off automatically. What might be wrong?

4. **Inaccessible Media**   You insert an optical disc with digital photos from your most recent family vacation and discover that your computer will not read the optical disc. What might be wrong?

@ Work

5. **Insufficient Disk Space**   Recently, you purchased a USB flash drive that you plan to use to store work-related files. When you attempt to store a file on the USB flash drive, the computer displays an error message indicating that the file will not fit. How could a brand new USB flash drive not have enough room to store the first file you attempted to store on it?

6. **Power Outage**   The power in your office has been out for the last two hours and has just come back on. When you attempt to start your computer by pressing the power button, nothing happens. What is your next step before calling technical support?

7. **Incorrect Login Credentials**   Upon returning to the office from a well-deserved two-week vacation, you turn on your computer. Upon entering your user name and password, an error message appears stating that your password is incorrect. What are your next steps?

8. **Software Installation**   You are attempting to install a program on your office computer. After inserting the installation disc and specifying that you would like to begin the installation, your computer appears to begin installing the software. Halfway through the installation process, an error message appears stating that you must have administrative privileges to perform the installation. Why were you not informed immediately upon beginning the installation? What are your next steps?

Collaboration

9. **Computers in Transportation**   Your project team has been accepted to present a business proposal to a group of potential investors. Because the presentation will take place in San Francisco, CA, you will need to transport people and ship some materials to that location. Form a team of three people and determine how to use technology to ship materials and how to make travel arrangements. One team member should research the steps required to use a Web site to make flight reservations, one team member should determine the steps necessary to print a UPS shipping label from their computer and track the package while it is en route, and another team member should find directions from San Francisco International Airport to a nearby hotel.

Learn How To

The Learn How To activities step you through fundamental technology skills when using a computer. The Learn How To exercises enable you to become more proficient with these skills.

> **Premium Activity:** To relate this Learn How To activity to your everyday life, see a visual demonstration of the activity, and then complete a short assessment, visit scsite.com/dc-off07/ch1/howto.

Learn How To 1: Create and Use Your Own Blog

A blog can contain any information you wish to place in it. Originally, blogs consisted of Web addresses, so that an individual or group with a specific interest could direct others to useful places on the Web. Today, blogs contain addresses, thoughts, diaries, and anything else a person or group wants to share.

Once you have created a blog, you can update it. A variety of services available on the Web can help you create and maintain your blog. One widely used service is called Blogger. To create a blog using Blogger, complete the following steps:

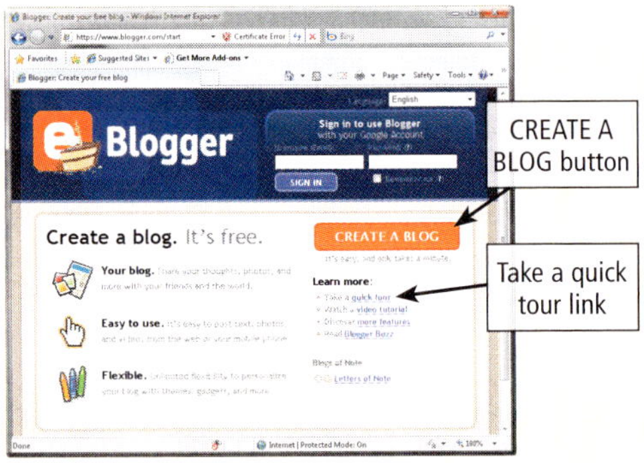

1. Start your Web browser, type `blogger.com` in the Address bar, and then press the ENTER key to display the Blogger home page (Figure 1-39).
2. Click the CREATE A BLOG button on the Blogger home page.
3. Enter the data required on the 'Create Blogger Account' page. Your e-mail address and password will allow you to change and manage your blog. Your Display name is the name that will be shown on the blog as the author of the material on the blog. Many people use their own names, but others use pseudonyms as their "pen names" so that they are not readily identifiable.
4. Click the Continue arrow and then enter your Blog title and Blog address. These are the names and addresses everyone will use to view your blog.
5. Click the Continue arrow to display the 'Choose a template' screen.
6. Choose a template for your blog and then click the Continue arrow.
7. Your blog will be created for you. When you see the 'Your blog has been created!' screen, click the START BLOGGING arrow.
8. From the screen that is displayed, you can post items for your blog, specify settings, change the layout, and view your blog.
9. When you have posted all your information, click the Sign out link at the top right of the screen. You will be logged out.
10. To edit your blog and add or change information on it, visit the Blogger home page and sign in by entering your user name and password. You will be able to post to your blog.
11. Others can view your blog by entering its address in the browser's Address bar and then pressing the ENTER key.

Figure 1-39

Exercises

1. Start your Web browser and visit blogger.com. Click the 'Take a quick tour' link and go through all the screens that explain about a blog. What did you learn that you did not know? What type of blog do you find most compelling — a group or an individual blog? Why? Submit your answers to your instructor.
2. Optional: Create your own blog. Carefully name it and begin your posts at this time. What is your blog name and address? What is its primary purpose? Is it an individual or group blog? Write a paragraph containing the answers to these questions and any other information you feel is pertinent. Submit this paragraph to your instructor.

Learn How To 2: Use the Discovering Computers and Microsoft Office 2007 Online Companion (scsite.com/dc-off07)

The Discovering Computers and Microsoft Office 2007 Online Companion provides a variety of activities and exercises. To use the site, you first must register and establish a user name and password. Perform the following steps to register:

1. Start the Web browser.
2. Type `scsite.com/dc-off07` in the Address bar of the Web browser. Press the ENTER key.

3. When the registration page is displayed, click the New User Registration link.
4. Follow the on-screen instructions to complete registration.

When you first type a Web address to display a page from the dc-off07 site, you must enter your user name and password to gain access to the site.

Exercise

1a. Start your Web browser, type `scsite.com/dc-off07/ch1/howto` in the Address bar of the browser, and then press the ENTER key.

1b. If the registration page is displayed, complete the steps above. If you are registered, enter your user name and password, and then click the Enter button.

1c. Navigate to the Chapter 1 home page and then visit each of the Exercises Web pages.

1d. Click the browser's Close button to close the program.

1e. Write a report that describes the use of each of the Exercises pages you visited. Which page do you think will prove the most valuable to you when using the book and the Web site? Why? Submit your report to your instructor.

Learn It Online

The Learn It Online exercises are interactive Web exercises designed to reinforce and expand your understanding of the chapter concepts. The descriptions below briefly summarize each exercise.

👆 To access the Learn It Online exercises and for specific exercise instructions, visit scsite.com/dc-off07/ch1/learn.

❶ At the Movies — Computer History in a Barn
Watch a movie to tour the Digibarn Computer Museum and then answer questions about the movie.

❷ Student Edition Labs — Using Input Devices and Using Windows
Enhance your understanding and knowledge about input devices and the Windows operating system by completing the Using Input Devices and Using Windows Labs.

❸ Practice Test
Take a multiple choice test that checks your knowledge of the chapter concepts and review the resulting study guide.

❹ Who Wants To Be a Computer Genius^2?
Play the Shelly Cashman Series version of this popular game by answering questions to find out if you are a computer genius. Panic buttons are available to provide assistance during game play.

❺ Crossword Puzzle Challenge
Complete an interactive crossword puzzle to reinforce concepts presented in this chapter.

❻ Windows Exercises
Step through the Windows 7 exercises to learn how to use help, improve mouse skills, and identify computer information.

❼ Exploring Computer Careers
Read about a career as a computer salesperson, search for relevant employment advertisements, and then answer related questions.

❽ Web Apps — Google Maps
Learn how to locate businesses in your area, view a location's surroundings via satellite, and find directions from one location to another using Google Maps.

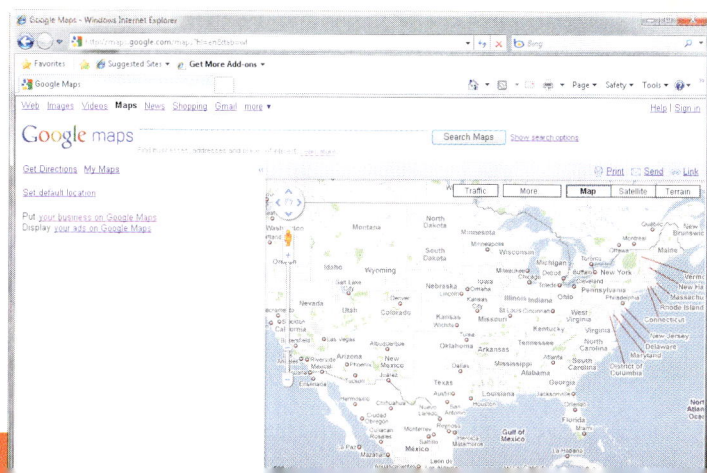

Web Research

The Web Research exercises broaden your understanding of the chapter concepts by presenting questions that require you to search the Web for answers.

👆 To discuss the Web Research exercises with other students, visit scsite.com/dc-off07/ch1/forum and post your thoughts or questions.

❶ Search Sleuth
Use one of the search engines listed in Figure 2-8 in Chapter 2 on page 53 or your own favorite search engine to find the answers to the following questions. Copy and paste the Web address from the Web page where you found the answer. Some questions may have more than one answer. If required, submit your answers to your instructor. (1) What company was the first to sell a USB flash drive? (2) What is the significance of the Universal symbol on Apple's Mac application programs? (3) Which retailers offer to dispose of old computers and other electronic products properly to help protect the environment? (4) What are three Illustrative Grant Commitments the Bill & Melinda Gates Foundation has made? (5) According to *Fortune*, at what company do MBA students most want to work when they graduate? (6) Who created the first set of icons for the Macintosh computer? What sound does her Clarus the Dogcow make? (7) What company manufactured the first notebook computer, the UltraLite, in 1989?

❷ Green Computing
Computer usage requires electricity, whether to power the system unit and monitor, recharge batteries, or print. In addition, the computer manufacturing process depletes natural resources and often uses toxic chemicals. As you learned in this chapter, many environmentally conscious people practice green computing by attempting to reduce electricity and environmental waste. Examine your computing practices, and determine 10 ways that you can use less power on your computing equipment at home, work, and school. Consider how often you use the printer and the types of documents you print. Examine your monitor, system unit, and printer. Do you see any notation indicating they are environmentally sound? Do they hibernate or go into a power save mode when not being used? Write a 50-word summary of the green computing practices in your life.

❸ Social Networking
One of the more popular social networking Web sites is Facebook. This quickly growing service differentiates itself from other online social networks by having widespread privacy controls. In addition, its development platform, called f8, allows developers to create programs (called applications) that users can add to a Web page. Hostels, for example, lets world travelers research and rate hostels and includes photos and descriptions. Visit the Facebook site (facebook.com), click the About link at the bottom of the page, and then read about Facebook's features. What are three of Facebook's top features? What information is given in the recent Facebook blog posts? Visit the AppRate Web site (apprate.com) and then summarize three Facebook application reviews and ratings.

❹ Blogs
Blogs profiling the music industry discuss new technologies, legal issues, podcasts, and business news. Visit the CNET blog (blogs.cnet.com) and then read and summarize at least three of the articles in the Most Recent Posts section. Locate the Crave, Gaming and Culture, and Green Tech features and then read and summarize at least one story from each blog. Then visit the iLounge (ilounge.com) Web site and read reviews of at least three new products for the iPhone. Would you purchase any of the products discussed? What books and buyer's guides are available to download from the Library? Which iPod cases and speakers received favorable reviews? Read and summarize at least three stories and associated comments in the News section.

❺ Ethics in Action
The Internet has increased the ease with which students can plagiarize material for research paper assignments. Teachers are using online services, such as Turnitin and PlagiarismDetect.com, to help detect plagiarized papers and to help students understand how to cite sources correctly. Visit the Turnitin Web site (turnitin.com) and then write a summary of how this service is used. How does this service attempt to prevent plagiarism through the Turnitin Write Cycle? How prevalent is plagiarism on your campus? What is your school's official policy on disciplining students who submit plagiarized papers? Does your school have an honor code? If required, submit your summary to your instructor.

Special Feature

Living Digitally

OUR DIGITAL LIVES are filled with a variety of products. We listen on portable media players to audio files we create or download. We record and view video content that matches our viewing interests. We play recorded files wherever and whenever we desire. We play games solo or with multiple friends across the globe. Our home networks link security, energy monitoring, and leisure activities throughout the house. Wherever we go in our lives, technology is a pervasive part of our daily existence.

Microsoft Xbox 360

PSPgo

3-D video display

Sony PlayStation 3

avatar

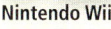
Slingbox

Rock Band

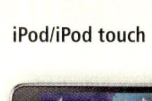
Nintendo Wii

flat-screen TV

head-mounted display

iPod/iPod touch

TiVo

Digital products in our lives often include features that overlap in various entertainment and home automation categories.

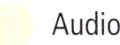 Audio

 Video

 Recording

Gaming

Digital Home

Nintendo DSi

video camera

speakers

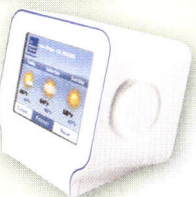
chumby

smart phone

GarageBand

Nero optical disc burning software

combination drive

Dolby logo

digital frames

Netflix

multi-room audio system

docking station

home automation dashboard

38 Special Feature

Audio

THE MUSIC INDUSTRY is a major part of our everyday lives, and digital music sales generate more than $10 billion each year. Audio files can be played on iPods and other portable media players and mobile devices. Musicians of all skill levels can create their own music with Rock Band and Guitar Hero handheld instruments.

Figure 1 Apple has sold hundreds of millions of iPods. The iPod accessory market has grown to a billion-dollar industry, with inventors developing earbuds, cases, and docking stations.

Figure 3 Rock the night away playing legendary songs from The Beatles, Aerosmith, Metallica, and other musical groups. Online multiplayer modes and downloadable songs expand the concert experience.

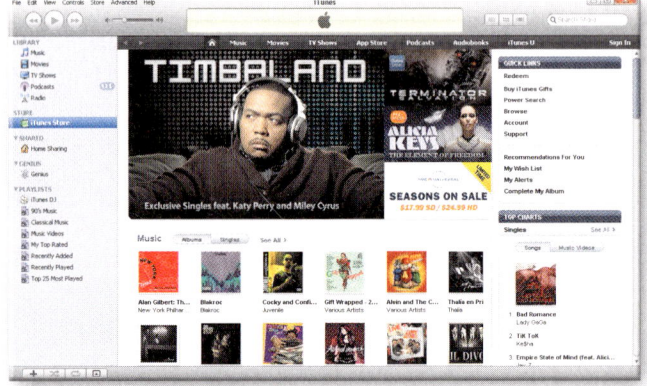

Figure 2 Music downloading services allow you to purchase individual tracks or entire albums and then download the music to a computer or portable media player. More than 500 downloading services are available; Apple iTunes and Amazon MP3 are the sales leaders.

Figure 4 Ray Dolby founded Dolby Laboratories in 1965. His company has become the world leader in defining high-quality products, including audio and surround sound in theaters, home entertainment systems, and broadcasting.

Living Digitally

Video

WHETHER IN A COMFY CHAIR or on the go, watching television and movies has changed dramatically. Viewers download content and then watch the programs when and where they desire on devices ranging from large flat-screen display devices to compact smart phones. Glasses and 3-D displays add a new dimension to the viewing experience.

Figure 5 A multitude of video streaming devices is infiltrating the marketplace as companies expand their services to add subscribers and bring movies and television programs to homes via a broadband Internet connection. Apple TV takes control of your home theater system by streaming HD movies, television programs, iTunes music, podcasts, and photos to display devices.

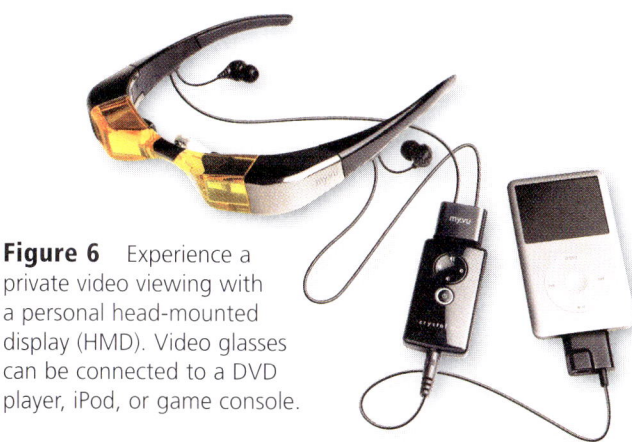

Figure 6 Experience a private video viewing with a personal head-mounted display (HMD). Video glasses can be connected to a DVD player, iPod, or game console.

Figure 7 View your favorite television programs anywhere in the world as long as you have a broadband connection and a Slingbox. This device streams video and audio from your home to any Internet-connected device.

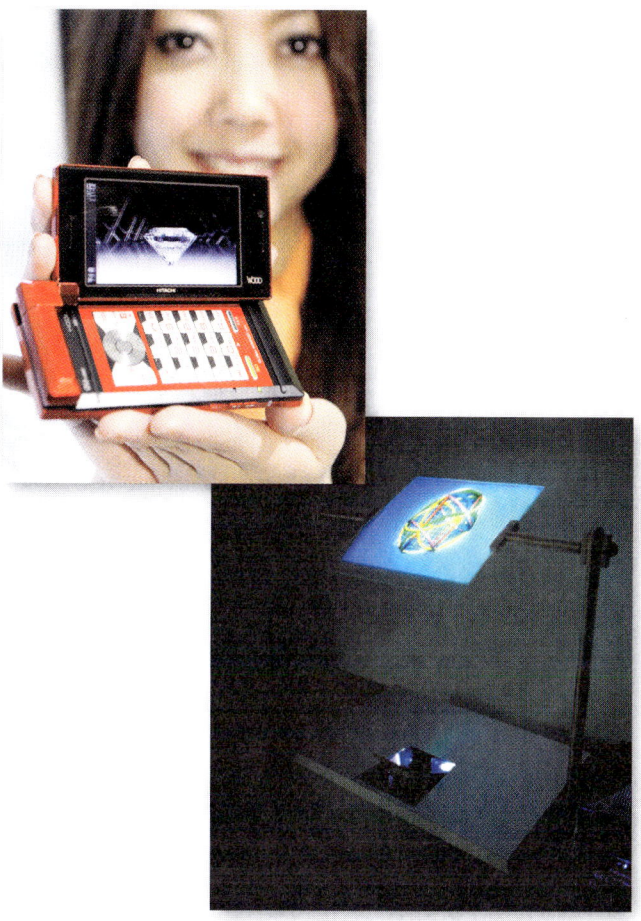

Figure 8 True 3-D video images can be seen on cell phones and video displays without special glasses or goggles. Applications include medical imaging, CAD drawings, mapping, and entertainment.

Figure 9 High-definition (HD) digital video recorders (DVRs), such as the TiVo, let you locate and record current and off-air digital broadcasts, pause and rewind live television programs, and create your own instant replays with slow motion.

Recording

WHETHER YOU ARE WORKING OUT at the gym or driving to Grandma's house for dinner, you might want to download or record your favorite audio, video, and photos to transport them from one location to another or upload them to share with friends and family. You also can record movies or television programs when you are not at home and then play them at your convenience on a home entertainment system or portable media player.

Figure 10 Use optical disc burning software to create optical discs quickly and easily with multiformat burners and rewritable drives to store your movies, photos, music, and digital data.

Figure 12 Record, edit, and mix songs created with your virtual and real bands using Apple's GarageBand software, which is part of the iLife software suite. Then, upload your music to iWeb.

Figure 11 Capture video using your video camera and then, with the press of a button, upload recorded clips to social networking Web sites. Each minute, more than 20 hours of video are uploaded to YouTube.

Figure 13 Capture video of friends and family, upload the clips to your computer, and use video editing software to rearrange the sequence of events, add music and titles, and record narration.

Living Digitally **41**

Gaming   REVENUE GENERATED BY THE VIDEO GAMING INDUSTRY quickly is approaching $100 billion. The areas experiencing the fastest growth are online and mobile gaming as new game consoles and advanced networking become mainstream.

Figure 14   The three gaming consoles — Nintendo Wii, Sony PlayStation 3, and Microsoft Xbox 360 — offer a variety of game titles.

Figure 16   In a computer role-playing game (CRPG), players interact with one another and generally attempt to accomplish a quest. Massively multiplayer online games (MMOGs) unite millions of gamers worldwide.

Figure 17   Handheld game consoles have large, high-resolution screens and incredible sound to play audio and video files and can display photos. Bluetooth and Wi-Fi technology allows networked gaming and synchronizing with other handheld units or personal computers.

Figure 15   Gaming reaches all generations. The Wii game console's interactive quality appeals to players of all ages. The iPod touch's accelerometer, which detects movement and changes the display accordingly, and 3-D graphics immerse players in the action.

Figure 18   Outdoor treasure hunters use their GPS receivers and navigational skills to create and locate hidden caches throughout the world.

42 Special Feature

Digital Home

THE AVERAGE HOUSEHOLD has 21 consumer electronics devices, and many of them are linked via home networks and broadband connections that simplify our lives and provide entertainment in innovative ways. Digital music and video are recorded and streamed to multiple devices. Meanwhile, automation systems monitor security, energy usage, and room temperatures to provide optimal conditions.

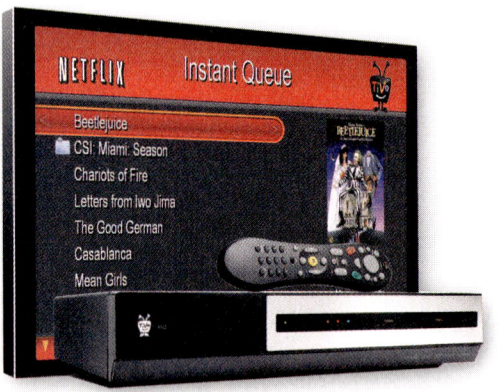

Figure 19 Set-top boxes stream movies from the Web to your televisions, computers, and mobile devices. On average, Netflix ships approximately two million DVDs each day.

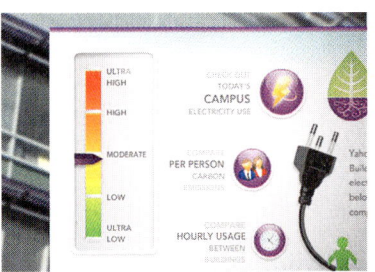

Figure 21 LED screens provide information about home electricity, gas, and water use, and they compare the rates with previous consumption.

Figure 22 Digital picture frames, some as large as 40 inches wide, are among the more popular consumer electronic devices; more than 3 million are sold each year. They provide a convenient method of displaying the billions of digital photos taken each day and may play songs and Web broadcasts.

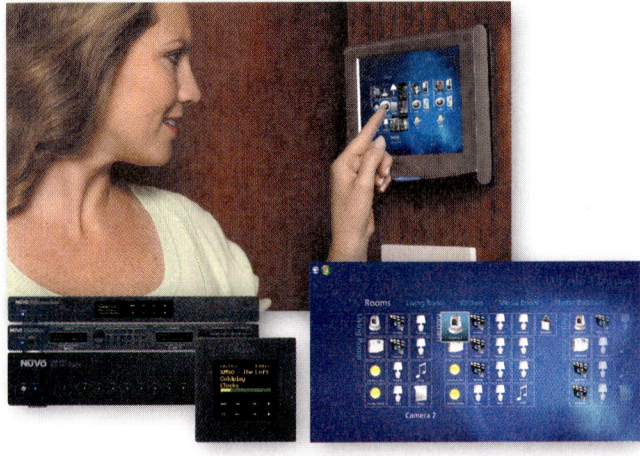

Figure 20 Program an entire home to fit your lifestyle and needs. A home automation system can set room temperatures, open and close window shades, water the grass, watch for intruders, and play music to wake you or relax you to sleep.

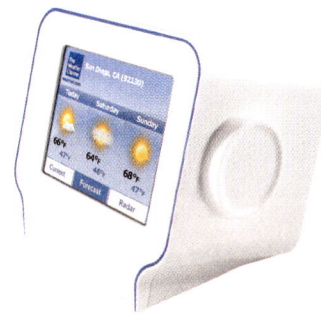

Figure 23 The wireless chumby connects to the Internet and streams news, entertainment, sports scores, video clips, interactive games, photos, and hundreds of favorite widgets.

Computer technology impacts virtually every facet of our lives. From the largest media rooms to the smallest portable media players, we can watch our favorite television programs and movies any place at any time. We can browse the Web, play games with partners on the other side of the world, listen to music we created with handheld instruments, and have fun wherever life takes us. No matter where we are, our digital lives are filled with information and entertainment.

Chapter Two

The Internet and World Wide Web

Objectives

After completing this chapter, you will be able to:

1. Identify and briefly describe various broadband Internet connections
2. Describe the types of Internet access providers: Internet service providers, online service providers, and wireless Internet service providers
3. Explain the purpose of a Web browser and identify the components of a Web address
4. Describe how to use a search engine to search for information on the Web
5. Describe the types of Web sites: portal, news, informational, business/marketing, blog, wiki, online social network, educational, entertainment, advocacy, Web application, content aggregator, and personal
6. Recognize how Web pages use graphics, animation, audio, video, virtual reality, and plug-ins
7. Identify the steps required for Web publishing
8. Explain how e-mail, mailing lists, instant messaging, chat rooms, VoIP, FTP, and newsgroups and message boards work
9. Identify the rules of netiquette

The Internet

One of the major reasons business, home, and other users purchase computers is for Internet access. The **Internet**, also called the **Net**, is a worldwide collection of networks that links millions of businesses, government agencies, educational institutions, and individuals. The Internet is a widely used research tool, providing society with access to global information and instant communications.

Today, more than one billion home and business users around the world access a variety of services on the Internet, some of which are shown in Figure 2-1. The World Wide Web, or simply the Web, and e-mail are two of the more widely used Internet services. Other services include chat rooms, instant messaging, and VoIP (Voice over Internet Protocol).

The Internet has its roots in a networking project started by an agency of the U.S. Department of Defense. The goal was to build a network that (1) allowed scientists at different locations to share information and work together on military and scientific projects and (2) could function even if part of the network were disabled or destroyed by a disaster such as a nuclear attack. That network, called ARPANET, became functional in September 1969, linking scientific and academic researchers across the United States.

The original ARPANET consisted of four main computers, one each located at the University of California at Los Angeles, the University of California at Santa Barbara, the Stanford Research Institute, and the University of Utah. Each of these computers served as a host on the network. A host or server is any computer that provides services and connections to other computers on a network. By 1984, ARPANET had more than 1,000 individual computers linked as hosts. Today, more than 550 million hosts connect to this network, which is known now as the Internet.

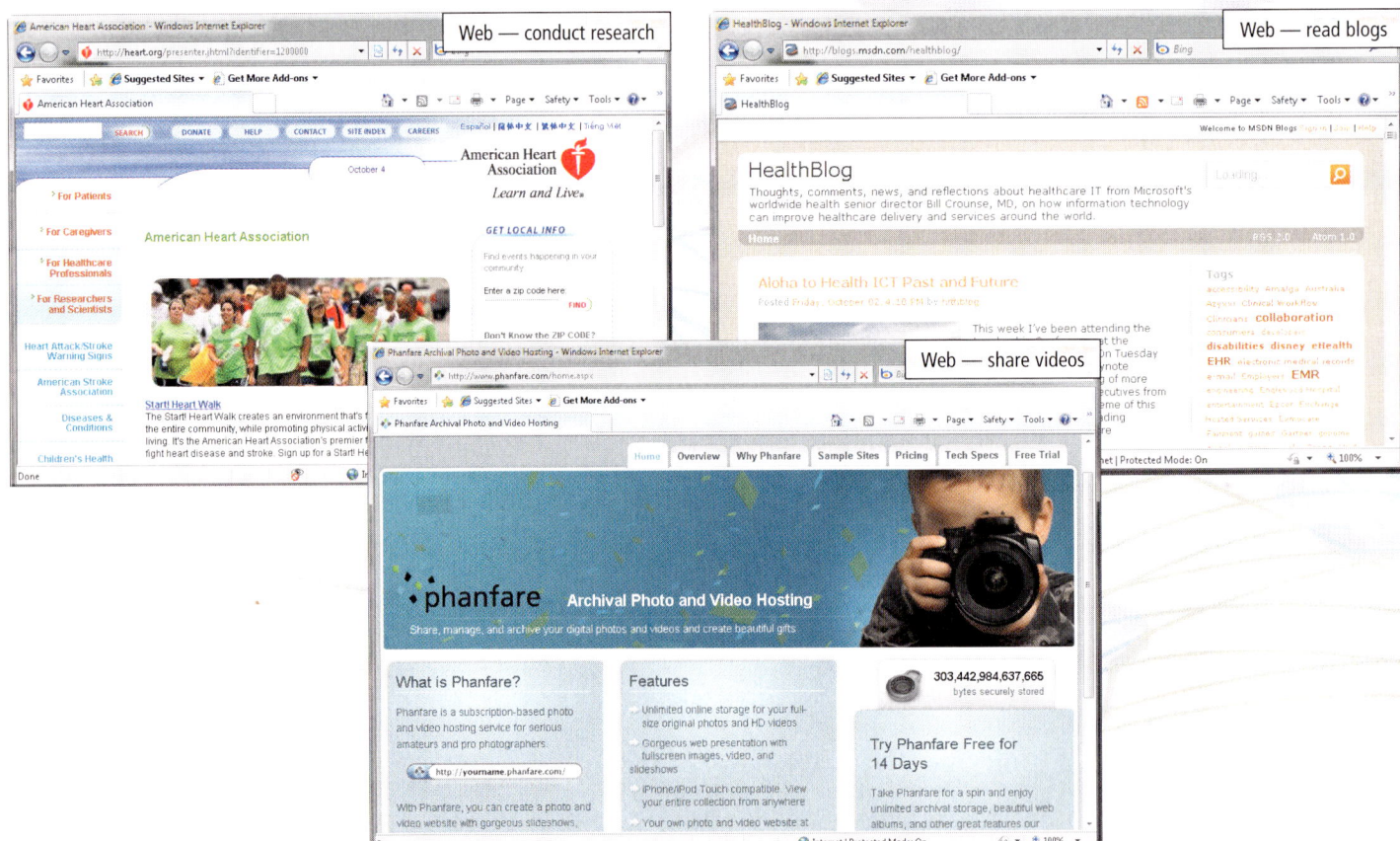

Figure 2-1 People around the world use a variety of Internet services in daily activities. Internet services allow home and business users to access the Web for activities such as conducting research, reading blogs, or sharing videos; to send e-mail messages; or to converse with others using chat rooms, instant messaging, or VoIP.

The Internet consists of many local, regional, national, and international networks. Both public and private organizations own networks on the Internet. These networks, along with telephone companies, cable and satellite companies, and the government, all contribute toward the internal structure of the Internet.

Each organization on the Internet is responsible only for maintaining its own network. No single person, company, institution, or government agency controls or owns the Internet. The World Wide Web Consortium (W3C), however, oversees research and sets standards and guidelines for many areas of the Internet. More than 350 organizations from around the world are members of the W3C.

Connecting to the Internet

Many home and small business users connect to the Internet via high-speed **broadband** Internet service. With broadband Internet service, your computer or mobile device usually is connected to the Internet the entire time it is powered on. Examples of broadband Internet service include the following:

- **Cable Internet service** provides high-speed Internet access through the cable television network via a cable modem.
- **DSL** (digital subscriber line) provides high-speed Internet connections using regular telephone lines.
- **Fiber to the Premises (FTTP)** uses fiber-optic cable to provide high-speed Internet access to home and business users.
- **Fixed wireless** provides high-speed Internet connections using a dish-shaped antenna on your house or business to communicate with a tower location via radio signals.
- A **Wi-Fi** (wireless fidelity) network uses radio signals to provide high-speed Internet connections to wireless computers and devices.

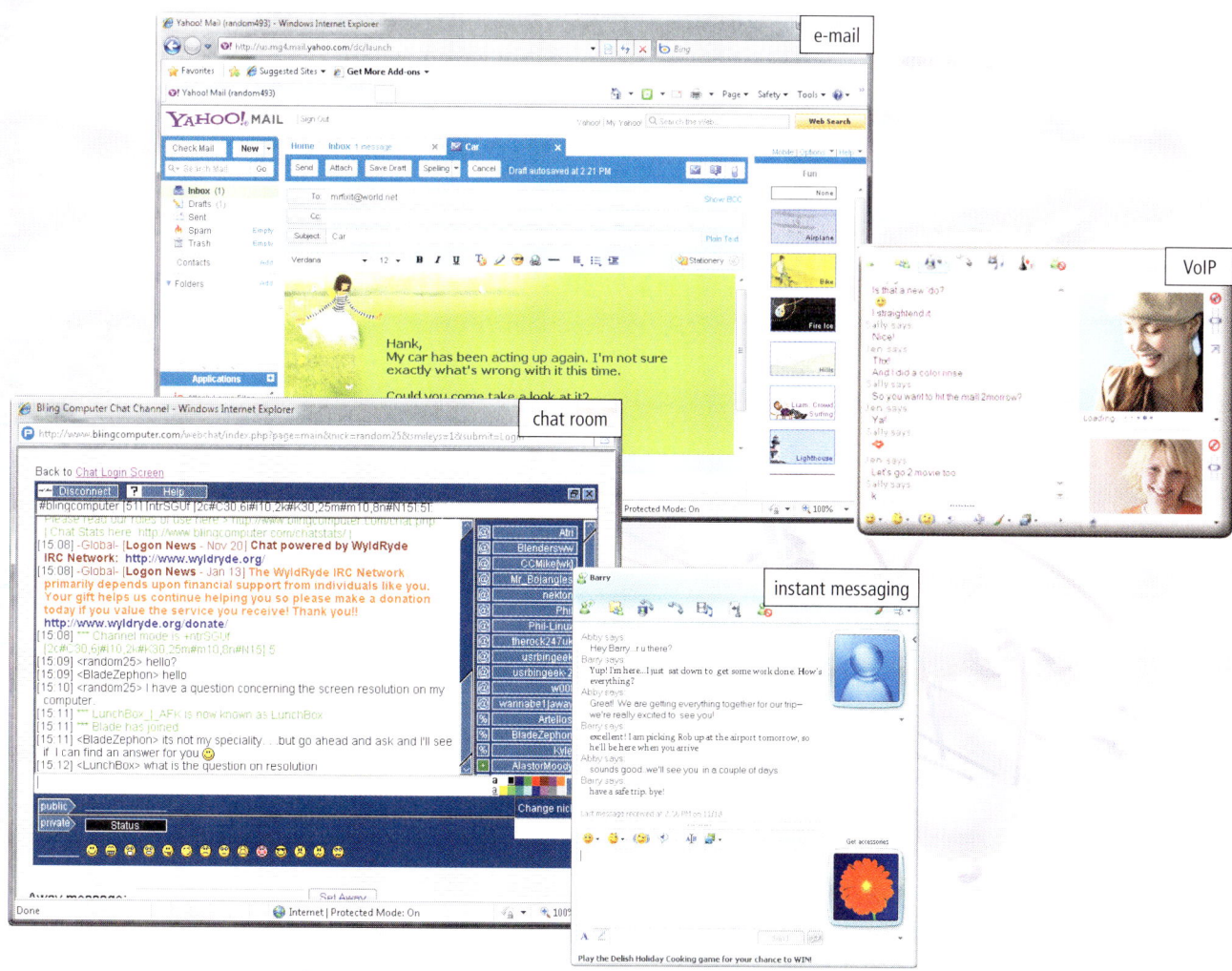

- A **cellular radio network** offers high-speed Internet connections to devices with built-in compatible technology or computers with wireless modems.
- **Satellite Internet service** provides high-speed Internet connections via satellite to a satellite dish that communicates with a satellite modem.

Employees and students typically connect their computers to the Internet through a business or school network. The business or school network connects to a high-speed broadband Internet service.

Mobile users access the Internet using a variety of services. Most hotels and airports provide wired or wireless Internet connections. Wireless Internet services such as Wi-Fi networks, allow mobile users to connect easily to the Internet with notebook computers, smart phones, and other mobile devices while away from a telephone, cable, or other wired connection. Many public locations, such as airports, hotels, schools, and coffee shops, are **hot spots** that provide Wi-Fi Internet connections to users with mobile computers or devices.

Many home users set up a Wi-Fi network, which sends signals to a communications device that is connected to a high-speed Internet service such as cable or DSL. Instead of using broadband Internet service, however, some home users connect to the Internet via dial-up access, which is a slower-speed technology. **Dial-up access** takes place when the modem in your computer connects to the Internet via a standard telephone line that transmits data and information using an analog (continuous wave pattern) signal. Users may opt for dial-up access because of its lower price or because broadband access is not available in their area.

❓ FAQ 2-1

How popular is broadband?
According to a study performed by Pew Internet & American Life Project, 63 percent of American adults have broadband Internet connections at home. Adoption of broadband connections increases during good economic times, while some may hesitate to make the switch during an economic downturn. It is believed that once the price of a broadband connection decreases, and broadband is available in more rural areas, its popularity will increase further.

👆 For more information, visit scsite.com/dc-off07/ch2/faq and then click Broadband.

Access Providers

An **access provider** is a business that provides individuals and organizations access to the Internet free or for a fee. For example, some Wi-Fi networks provide free access while others charge a per use fee. Other access providers often charge a fixed amount for an Internet connection, usually about $5 to $24 per month for dial-up access and $13 to $120 for higher-speed access. Many Internet access providers offer services such as news, weather, financial data, games, travel guides, e-mail, photo communities, and online storage to hold digital photos and other files. (A file is a named unit of storage.)

Access providers are categorized as ISPs, online service providers, and wireless Internet service providers. An **ISP (Internet service provider)** is a regional or national access provider. A regional ISP usually provides Internet access to a specific geographic area. A national ISP is a business that provides Internet access in cities and towns nationwide. National ISPs usually offer more services and have a larger technical support staff than regional ISPs. Examples of national ISPs are AT&T and EarthLink.

In addition to providing Internet access, an **online service provider (OSP)** also has many members-only features such as instant messaging or their own customized version of a Web browser. The two more popular OSPs are AOL (America Online) and MSN (Microsoft Network). AOL also provides free access to its services to any user with a high-speed Internet connection.

A **wireless Internet service provider**, sometimes called a wireless data provider, is a company that provides wireless Internet access to computers and mobile devices, such as smart phones and portable media players with built-in wireless capability (such as Wi-Fi) or to computers using wireless modems or wireless access devices. Wireless modems usually are in the form of a USB flash drive or a card that inserts in a slot in a computer or mobile device. Examples of wireless Internet service providers include AT&T, Boingo Wireless, Sprint Broadband Direct, T-Mobile, and Verizon Wireless.

Wireless Modems
For more information, visit scsite.com/dc-off07/ch2/ weblink and then click Wireless Modems.

How Data and Information Travel the Internet

Computers connected to the Internet work together to transfer data and information around the world using various wired and wireless transmission media. Several main transmission media carry the heaviest amount of traffic on the Internet. These major carriers of network traffic are known collectively as the **Internet backbone.**

In the United States, the transmission media that make up the Internet backbone exchange data and information at several different major cities across the country. That is, they transfer data and information from one network to another until reaching the final destination (Figure 2-2).

FAQ 2-2

What types of Web sites do mobile Internet users visit?

More than 87 million individuals subscribe to a wireless Internet service provider. Mobile Internet users most frequently visit weather, entertainment, and e-mail Web sites. The chart to the right illustrates various types of Web sites and their associated increase in traffic resulting from mobile Internet users.

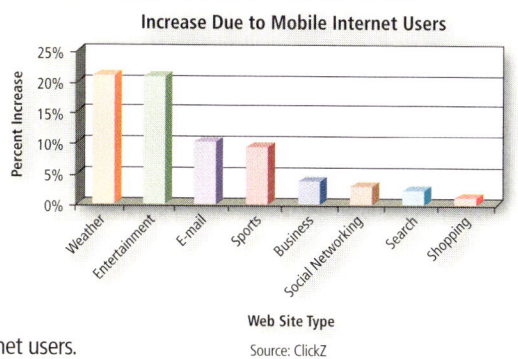

Increase Due to Mobile Internet Users
Percent Increase
25%
20%
15%
10%
5%
0%
Weather
Entertainment
E-mail
Sports
Business
Social Networking
Search
Shopping
Web Site Type
Source: ClickZ

For more information, visit scsite.com/dc-off07/ch2/faq and then click Mobile Internet.

How a Home User's Data and Information Might Travel the Internet Using a Cable Modem Connection

Step 1
You initiate an action to request data or information from the Internet. For example, you request to display a Web page on your computer screen.
Step 2
A cable modem transfers the computer's digital signals to the cable television line in your house.
Step 3
Your request (digital signals) travels through cable television lines to a central cable system, which is shared by up to 500 homes in a neighborhood.
Step 4
The central cable system sends your request over high-speed fiber-optic lines to the cable operator, who often also is the ISP.
Step 5
The ISP routes your request through the Internet backbone to the destination server (in this example, the server that contains the requested Web site).
Step 6
The server retrieves the requested Web page and sends it back through the Internet backbone to your computer.
Last Chance Buys
While supplies last!
SPECIALBUYS
eValues

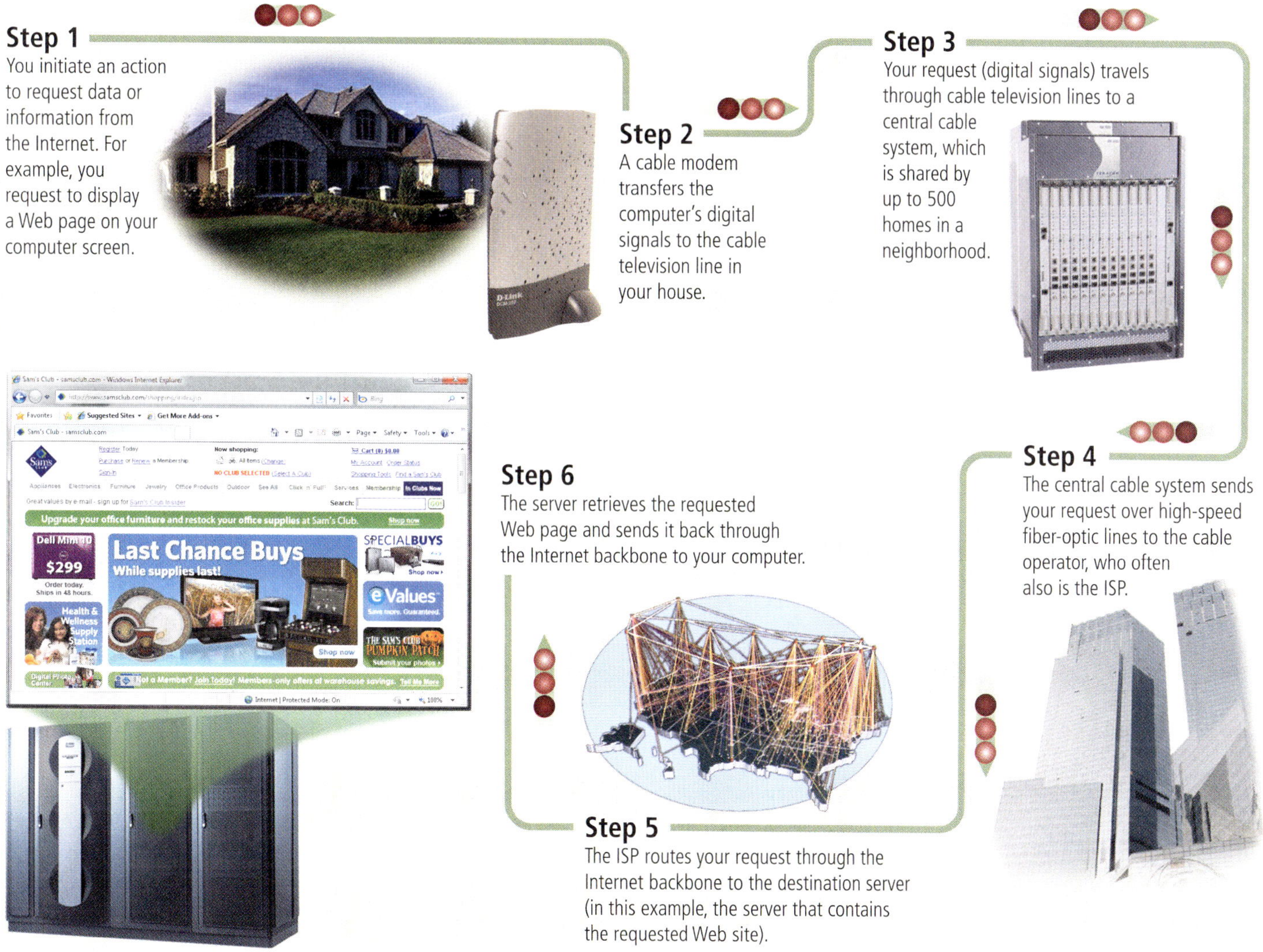

Figure 2-2 This figure shows how a home user's data and information might travel the Internet using a cable modem connection.

Internet Addresses

The Internet relies on an addressing system much like the postal service to send data and information to a computer at a specific destination. An **IP address**, short for Internet Protocol address, is a number that uniquely identifies each computer or device connected to the Internet. The IP address usually consists of four groups of numbers, each separated by a period. In general, the first portion of each IP address identifies the network and the last portion identifies the specific computer.

These all-numeric IP addresses are difficult to remember and use. Thus, the Internet supports the use of a text name that represents one or more IP addresses. A **domain name** is the text version of an IP address. Figure 2-3 shows an IP address and its associated domain name. As with an IP address, the components of a domain name are separated by periods.

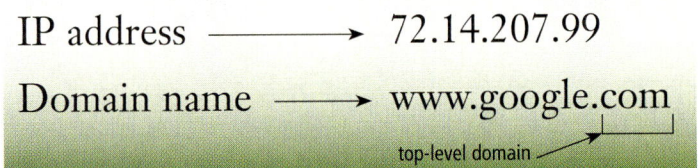

Figure 2-3 The IP address and domain name for the Google Web site.

The text in the domain name up to the first period identifies the type of Internet server. In Figure 2-3, for example, the www indicates a Web server. The Internet server portion of a domain name often is not required.

Every domain name contains a **top-level domain** (**TLD**), which is the last section of the domain name. A generic TLD (gTLD), such as the com in Figure 2-3, identifies the type of organization associated with the domain. Figure 2-4 lists some gTLDs. For international Web sites outside the United States, the domain name also includes a country code TLD (ccTLD), which is a two-letter country code, such as au for Australia or fr for France.

When you specify a domain name, a server translates the domain name to its associated IP address so that data and information can be routed to the correct computer. This server is an Internet server that usually is associated with an Internet access provider.

Examples of Generic Top-Level Domains

Generic TLD	Intended Purpose	Generic TLD	Intended Purpose
aero	Aviation community members	mil	Military organizations
biz	Businesses of all sizes	mobi	Delivery and management of mobile Internet services
cat	Catalan cultural community	museum	Accredited museums
com	Commercial organizations, businesses, and companies	name	Individuals or families
coop	Business cooperatives such as credit unions and rural electric co-ops	net	Network providers or commercial companies
		org	Nonprofit organizations
edu	Educational institutions	pro	Certified professionals such as doctors, lawyers, and accountants
gov	Government agencies		
info	Business organizations or individuals providing general information	tel	Internet communications
		travel	Travel industry
jobs	Employment or human resource businesses		

Figure 2-4 In addition to the generic TLDs listed in this table, proposals for newer TLDs continually are evaluated.

QUIZ YOURSELF 2-1

Instructions: Find the true statement below. Then, rewrite the remaining false statements so that they are true.

1. An access provider is a business that provides individuals and organizations access to the Internet free or for a fee.
2. A wireless Internet service provider is a number that uniquely identifies each computer or device connected to the Internet.
3. An IP address, such as www.google.com, is the text version of a domain name.
4. Satellite Internet service provides high-speed Internet access through the cable television network via a cable modem.

Quiz Yourself Online: To further check your knowledge of pages 44 through 48, visit scsite.com/dc-off07/ch2/quiz and then click Objectives 1 – 2.

The World Wide Web

The **World Wide Web** (**WWW**), or **Web**, a widely used service on the Internet, consists of a worldwide collection of electronic documents. Each electronic document on the Web, called a **Web page**, can contain text, graphics, animation, audio, and video. Additionally, Web pages usually have built-in connections to other documents. A **Web site** is a collection of related Web pages and associated items, such as documents and pictures, stored on a Web server. A **Web server** is a computer that delivers requested Web pages to your computer. Some industry experts use the term **Web 2.0** to refer to Web sites that provide a means for users to share personal information (such as social networking Web sites), allow users to modify Web site content (such as wikis, which are discussed later in this chapter), and have application software built into the site for visitors to use (such as e-mail and word processing programs). Read Looking Ahead 2-1 for a look at Web 3.0.

Browsing the Web

A **Web browser**, or **browser**, is application software that allows users to access and view Web pages or access Web 2.0 programs. To browse the Web, you need a computer or mobile device that is connected to the Internet and that has a Web browser. The more widely used Web browsers for personal computers are Internet Explorer, Firefox, Opera, Safari, and Google Chrome.

LOOKING AHEAD 2-1

Web 3.0 to Reinvent the Virtual World

When Tim Berners-Lee developed the World Wide Web 20 years ago, he envisioned a service that allowed users to exchange information seamlessly. The Web has evolved through versions 1.0 and 2.0, and work is underway to develop Web 3.0, also known as the Semantic Web.

This next generation of the Web is predicted to perform practically any imaginable task, according to some researchers. For example, your computer will be able to scan a Web page much as you do to look for specific useful information. If you need the location of the nearest eye doctor and the time when your brother's flight from Chicago actually will land, Web 3.0 will provide those facts and then search your calendar to see if you can fit the doctor's appointment in your schedule in time to pick up your brother at the airport. In essence, the Web will become one huge searchable database, and automated agents of every type will retrieve the data we need to live productive lives.

For more information, visit scsite.com/dc-off07/ch2/looking and then click Web 3.0.

FAQ 2-3

Which Web browser currently has the highest market share?

Windows Internet Explorer (IE) currently is the most popular browser, with approximately 68 percent of the market share. The chart to the right illustrates the market share of the more popular Web browsers.

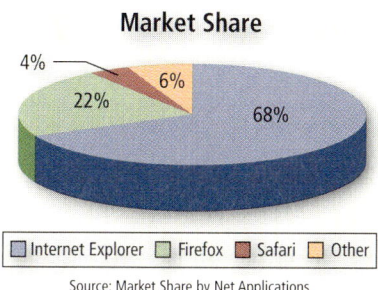

Market Share

4%, 6%, 22%, 68%

■ Internet Explorer ■ Firefox ■ Safari ■ Other

Source: Market Share by Net Applications

For more information, visit scsite.com/dc-off07/ch2/faq and then click Browser Market Share.

With an Internet connection established, you start a Web browser. The browser retrieves and displays a starting Web page, sometimes called the browser's home page. Figure 2-5 shows how a Web browser displays a home page.

Another use of the term, **home page**, refers to the first page that a Web site displays. Similar to a book cover or a table of contents for a Web site, the home page provides information about the Web site's purpose and content. Often it provides connections to other documents, Web pages, or Web sites, which can be downloaded to a computer or mobile device. **Downloading** is the process of a computer or device receiving information, such as a Web page, from a server on the Internet.

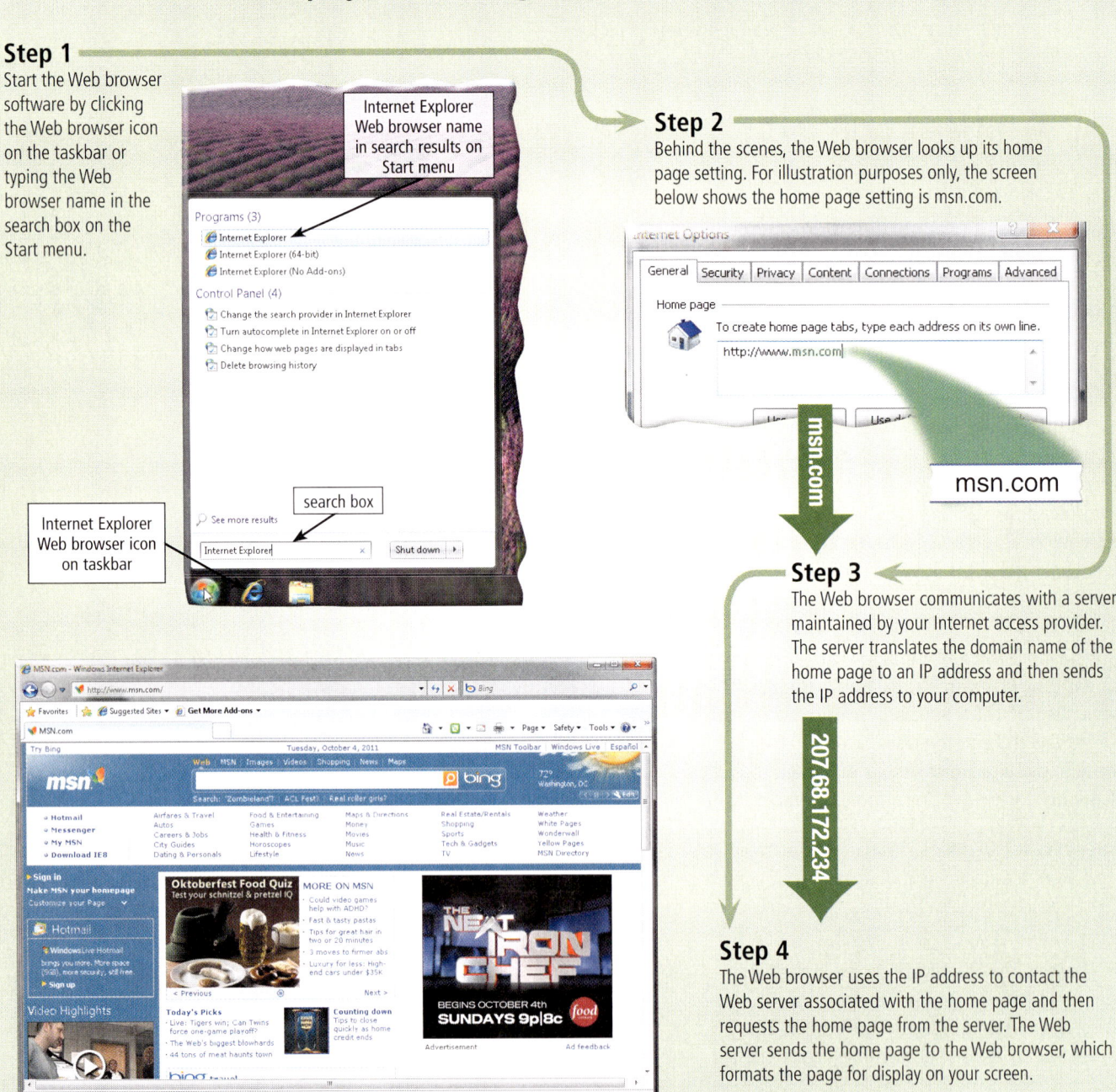

Figure 2-5 This figure shows how a Web browser displays a home page.

Web Addresses

A Web page has a unique address, which is called a **URL** (Uniform Resource Locator) or **Web address**. For example, the home page for the United States National Park Service Web site has a Web address of http://www.nps.gov. A Web browser retrieves a Web page using its Web address.

If you know the Web address of a Web page, you can type it in the Address bar at the top of the browser window. If you type http://www.nps.gov/grsm/planyourvisit/wildlifeviewing.htm as the Web address in the Address bar and then press the ENTER key, the browser downloads and displays the Web page shown in Figure 2-6.

A Web address consists of a protocol, domain name, and sometimes the path to a specific Web page or location on a Web page. Many Web page addresses begin with http://. The http, which stands for Hypertext Transfer Protocol, is a set of rules that defines how pages transfer on the Internet. To help minimize errors, many browsers and Web sites do not require you enter the http:// and www portions of the Web address.

When you enter the Web address, http://www.nps.gov/grsm/planyourvisit/wildlifeviewing.htm in the Web browser, it sends a request to the Web server that contains the nps.com Web site. The server then retrieves the Web page that is named wildlifeviewing.htm in the grsm/planyourvisit path and delivers it to your browser, which then displays the Web page on the screen.

To save time, many users create bookmarks for their frequently visited Web pages. A **bookmark**, or **favorite**, is a saved Web address that you access by clicking the bookmark name in a list. That is, instead of entering a Web address to display a Web page, you can click a previously saved bookmark.

For information about useful Web sites and their associated Web addresses, read the Making Use of the Web feature that follows this chapter.

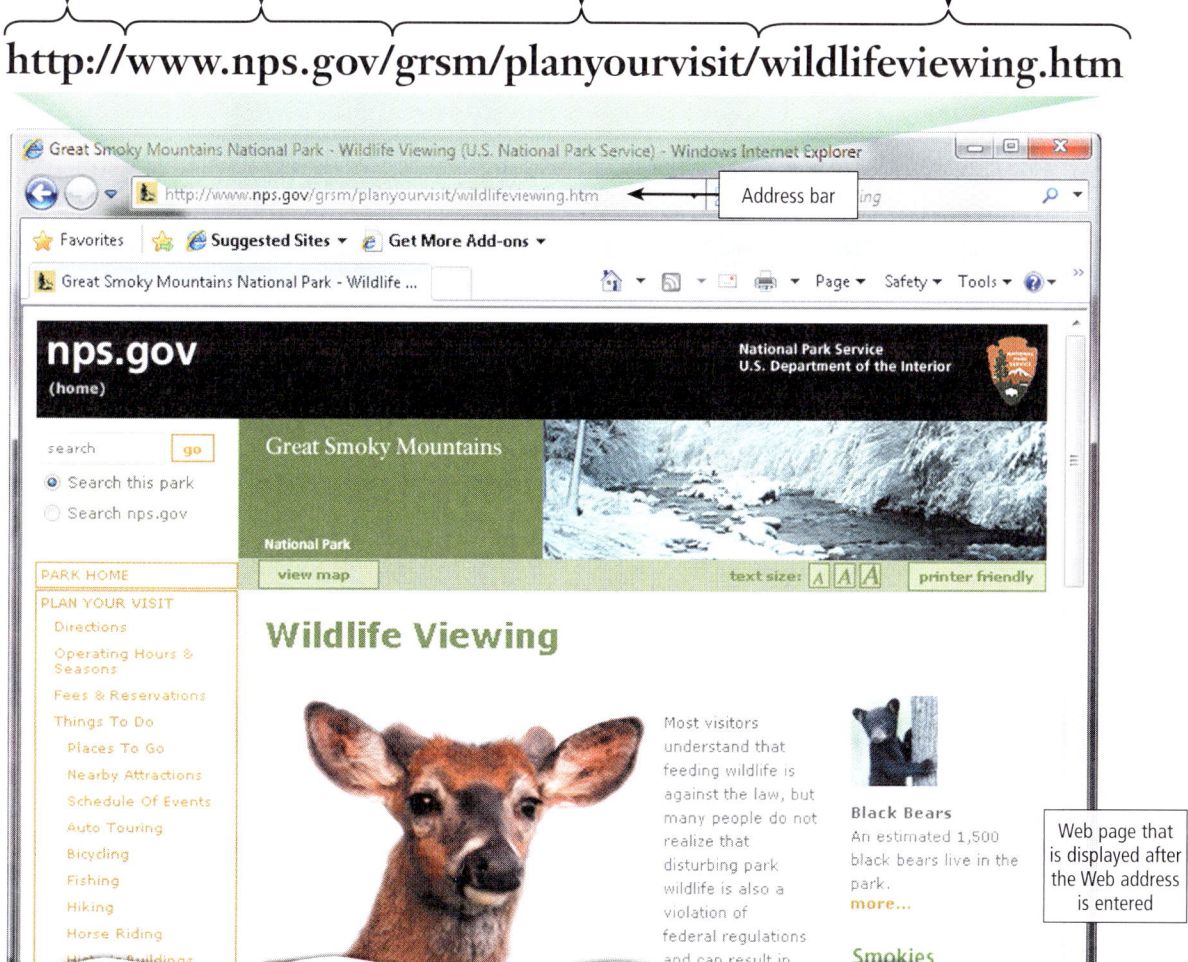

Figure 2-6 After entering http://www.nps.gov/grsm/planyourvisit/wildlifeviewing.htm as the Web address in the Address bar, this Web page at the United States National Park Service Web site is displayed.

Navigating Web Pages

Most Web pages contain links. A **link**, short for **hyperlink**, is a built-in connection to another related Web page or part of a Web page. Links allow you to obtain information in a nonlinear way. That is, instead of accessing topics in a specified order, you move directly to a topic of interest.

Branching from one related topic to another in a nonlinear fashion is what makes links so powerful. Some people use the phrase, **surfing the Web**, to refer to the activity of using links to explore the Web.

A link can be text or an image. Text links may be underlined and/or displayed in a color different from other text on the Web page. Pointing to, or positioning the pointer on, a link on the screen typically changes the shape of the pointer to a small hand with a pointing index finger. Pointing to a link also sometimes causes the link to change in appearance or play a sound. The Web page shown in Figure 2-7 contains a variety of link types, with the pointer on one of the links.

Each link on a Web page corresponds to a Web address or document. To activate a link, you **click** it, that is, point to the link and then press the left mouse button. Clicking a link causes the Web page or document associated with the link to be displayed on the screen. The linked object might be on the same Web page, a different Web page at the same Web site, or a separate Web page at a different Web site in another city or country.

Most current Web browsers support **tabbed browsing**, where the top of the browser displays a tab (similar to a file folder tab) for each Web page you open. To move from one open Web page to another, you click the tab in the Web browser.

Because some Web sites attempt to track your browsing habits or gather personal information, some current Web browsers include a feature that allows you to disable and/or more tightly control the dissemination of your browsing habits and personal information. Read Ethics & Issues 2-1 for a related discussion.

Tabbed Browsing
For more information, visit scsite.com/dc-off07/ch2/ weblink and then click Tabbed Browsing.

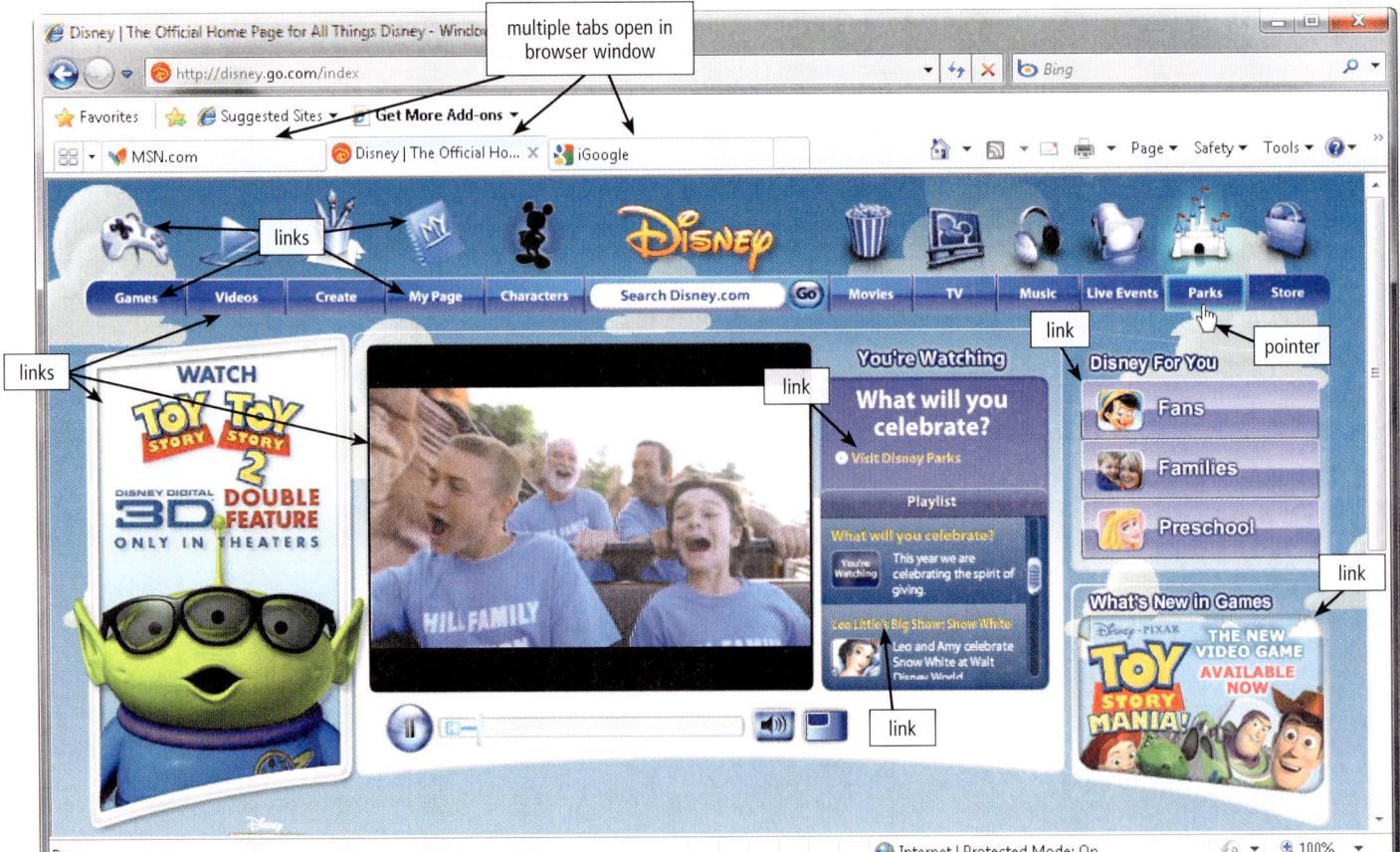

Figure 2-7 This browser window has several open tabs. The current tab shows a Web page that has various types of links.

ETHICS & ISSUES 2-1

Should the Government Allow You to Sign Up for a Do-Not-Track List?

When you visit a Web site that includes an advertisement, someone probably is recording the fact that you visited that Web site and viewed the advertisement with your browser. Over time, companies that specialize in tracking who views which online advertisements can amass an enormous amount of information about your online Web surfing habits. Through tracking the Web sites a user visits, the products they buy, and the articles they read, a company may attempt to profile the visitor's beliefs, associations, and habits. Although a user may think he or she is anonymous while navigating the Web, the company can attempt through various means to link the user's true identity with the user's online profile. The company can sell online profiles, with or without the user's true identity, to other advertisers or organizations. Some privacy groups have called for the government to allow consumers to sign up for a do-not-track list modeled after the popular do-not-call list.

Should organizations be allowed to track your Web surfing habits? Why or why not? Should organizations be allowed to associate your real identity with your online identity and profit from the information? Should the government force companies to give you the option of not being tracked? Why or why not? What are the benefits and dangers of online tracking?

Searching the Web

The Web is a worldwide resource of information. A primary reason that people use the Web is to search for specific information, including text, pictures, music, and video. The first step in successful searching is to identify the main idea or concept in the topic about which you are seeking information. Determine any synonyms, alternate spellings, or variant word forms for the topic. Then, use a search tool to locate the information.

Two types of search tools are search engines and subject directories. A **search engine** is a program that finds Web sites, Web pages, images, videos, news, maps, and other information related to a specific topic. A **subject directory** classifies Web pages in an organized set of categories or groups, such as sports or shopping, and related subcategories.

Some Web sites offer the functionality of both a search engine and a subject directory. Google and Yahoo!, for example, are widely used search engines that also provide a subject directory. To use Google or Yahoo!, you enter the Web address (google.com or yahoo.com) in the Address bar in a browser window. The table in Figure 2-8 lists the Web addresses of several popular general-purpose search engines and subject directories.

Widely Used Search Tools

Search Tool	Web Address	Search Engine	Subject Directory
A9	a9.com	X	
AlltheWeb	alltheweb.com	X	
AltaVista	altavista.com	X	
AOL Search	search.aol.com	X	
Ask	ask.com	X	
Bing	bing.com	X	
Cuil (pronounced cool)	cuil.com	X	
Dogpile	dogpile.com	X	
Excite	excite.com	X	X
Gigablast	gigablast.com	X	X
Google	google.com	X	X
Lycos	lycos.com	X	
MSN	msn.com	X	X
Open Directory Project	dmoz.org	X	X
WebCrawler	webcrawler.com	X	
Yahoo!	yahoo.com	X	X

Figure 2-8
Popular search engines and subject directories.

Search Engines A search engine is helpful in locating information for which you do not know an exact Web address or are not seeking a particular Web site. Some search engines look through Web pages for all types of information. Others can restrict their searches to a specific type of information, such as images, videos, audio, news, maps, people or businesses, and blogs.

Search engines require that you enter a word or phrase, called **search text**, that describes the item you want to find. Your search text can be broad, such as spring break destinations, or more specific, such as Walt Disney World. Figure 2-9 shows one way to use the Google search engine to search for the phrase, Aspen Colorado ski resorts. The results shown in Step 3 include nearly 150,000 links to Web pages, called hits, that reference Aspen Colorado ski resorts. Each hit in the list has a link that, when clicked, displays an associated Web site or Web page. Most search engines sequence the hits based on how close the words in the search text are to one another in the titles and descriptions of the hits. Thus, the first few links probably contain more relevant information.

How to Use a Search Engine

Step 1
Type the search engine's Web address (in this case, google.com) in the Address bar in the Web browser.

Step 2
Press the ENTER key. When the Google home page is displayed, type `Aspen Colorado ski resorts` as the search text and then point to the Google Search button.

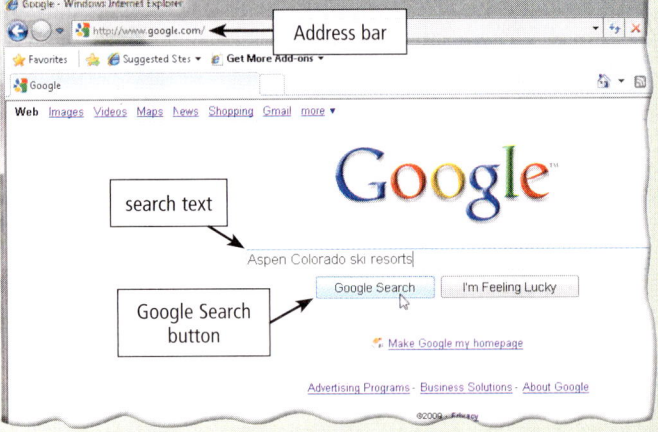

Step 4
Click the Aspen Snowmass link to display a Web page with a description and links to skiing in Aspen.

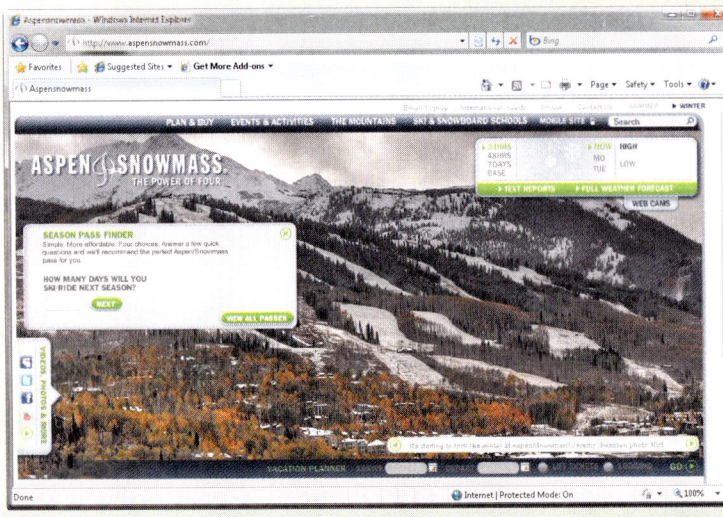

Step 3
Click the Google Search button. When the results of the search are displayed, scroll through the links and read the descriptions. Point to the Aspen Snowmass link.

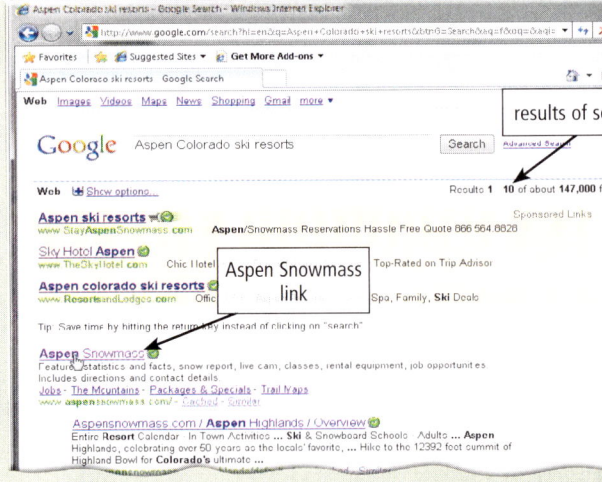

Figure 2-9 This figure shows how to use a search engine.

Some Web browsers contain an Instant Search box that, when filled in, uses a predefined or default search engine to perform searches. Using the Instant Search box eliminates the steps of displaying the search engine's Web page prior to entering the search text.

If you enter a phrase with spaces between the words in the search text, most search engines display results (hits) that include all of the words. The following list identifies techniques you can use to improve your searches. To learn more about searching for information, complete the Learn How To 2 activity on pages 76 and 77.

- Use specific nouns.
- Put the most important terms first in the search text.
- Use the asterisk (*) to substitute characters in words. For example, retriev* displays hits containing retrieves, retrieval, retriever, and any other variation.
- Use quotation marks to create phrases so that the search engine finds an exact sequence of words.
- List all possible spellings, for example, email, e-mail.
- Before using a search engine, read its Help information.
- If the search is unsuccessful with one search engine, try another.

Subject Directories A subject directory provides categorized lists of links arranged by subject (Figure 2-10). Using this search tool, you locate a particular topic by clicking links through different levels, moving from the general to the specific.

Types of Web Sites

Thirteen types of Web sites are portal, news, informational, business/marketing, blog, wiki, online social network, educational, entertainment, advocacy, Web application, content aggregator, and personal. Many Web sites fall into more than one of these categories.

Portal A **portal** is a Web site that offers a variety of Internet services from a single, convenient location (Figure 2-11a). Most portals offer these free services: search engine; news; sports and weather; Web publishing; reference tools such as yellow pages, stock quotes, and maps; shopping; and e-mail communications services. Popular portals include AltaVista, AOL, Excite, GO.com, iGoogle, Lycos, MSN, and Yahoo!.

News A news Web site contains newsworthy material including stories and articles relating to current events, life, money, sports, and the weather (Figure 2-11b). Newspapers and television and radio stations are some of the media that maintain news Web sites.

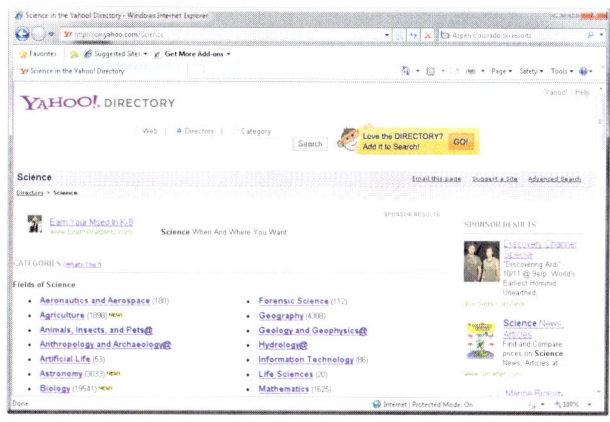

Figure 2-10 A subject directory provides categorized lists of links.

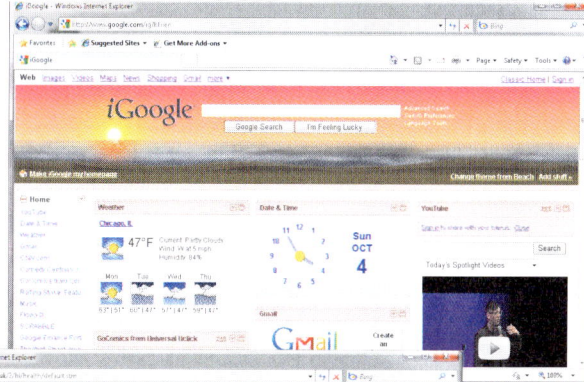

Figure 2-11a (portal)

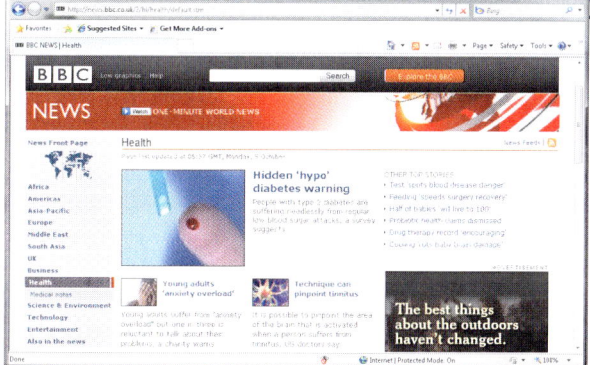

Figure 2-11b (news)

Figure 2-11 Types of Web sites. *(continued on next page)*

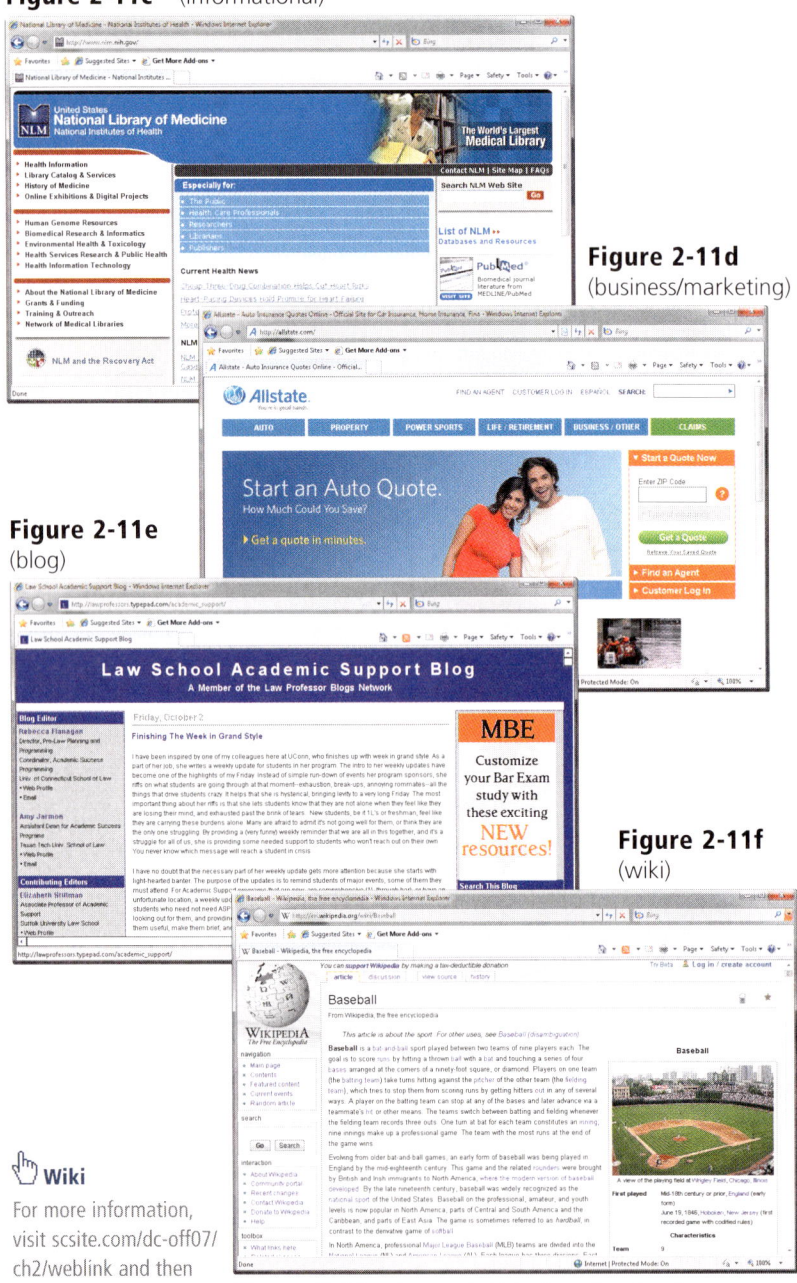

Figure 2-11c (informational)

Figure 2-11d (business/marketing)

Figure 2-11e (blog)

Figure 2-11f (wiki)

Figure 2-11 Types of Web sites. *(continued)*

👆 **Wiki**
For more information, visit scsite.com/dc-off07/ch2/weblink and then click Wiki.

Informational An informational Web site contains factual information (Figure 2-11c). Many United States government agencies have informational Web sites providing information such as census data, tax codes, and the congressional budget. Other organizations provide information such as public transportation schedules and published research findings.

Business/Marketing A business/marketing Web site contains content that promotes or sells products or services (Figure 2-11d). Nearly every enterprise has a business/marketing Web site. Many companies also allow you to purchase their products or services online.

Blog A **blog**, short for Weblog, is an informal Web site consisting of time-stamped articles, or posts, in a diary or journal format, usually listed in reverse chronological order (Figure 2-11e). A blog that contains video clips is called a **video blog** or **vlog**. A **microblog** allows users to publish short messages, usually between 100 and 200 characters, for others to read. Twitter is a popular microblog. The term **blogosphere** refers to the worldwide collection of blogs, and the **vlogosphere** refers to all vlogs worldwide. Blogs reflect the interests, opinions, and personalities of the author and sometimes site visitors. Blogs have become an important means of worldwide communications.

Wiki A **wiki** is a collaborative Web site that allows users to create, add to, modify, or delete the Web site content via their Web browser. Most wikis are open to modification by the general public. Wikis usually collect recent edits on a Web page so that someone can review them for accuracy. The difference between a wiki and a blog is that users cannot modify original posts made by the blogger. A popular wiki is Wikipedia, a free Web encyclopedia (Figure 2-11f). Read Ethics & Issues 2-2 for a related discussion.

ETHICS & ISSUES 2-2

Should You Trust a Wiki for Academic Research?

As wikis have grown in number, size, and popularity, some educators and librarians have shunned the sites as valid sources of research. While many wikis are tightly controlled with a limited number of contributors and expert editors, these usually focus on narrowly-defined, specialized topics. Most large wikis, such as Wikipedia, often involve thousands of editors, many of whom remain anonymous. Recently, television station reporters purposefully vandalized entries on Wikipedia for John Lennon and Elvis Presley in an attempt either to discredit Wikipedia or to test how quickly corrections are made. Editors quickly corrected the information. In other situations, rival political factions falsified or embellished wiki entries in an attempt to give their candidate an advantage. Some wiki supporters argue that most wikis provide adequate controls to correct false or misleading content quickly and to punish those who submit it. One popular wiki now requires an experienced editor to verify changes made to certain types of articles. Some propose that wikis should be used as a starting point for researching a fact, but that the fact should be verified using traditional sources.

Should wikis be allowed as valid sources for academic research? Why or why not? Would you submit a paper to your instructor that cites a wiki as a source? An encyclopedia? Why or why not? What policies could wikis enforce that could garner more confidence from the public? If a wiki provided verification of the credentials of the author, would you trust the wiki more? Why or why not?

Online Social Networks An **online social network**, also called a **social networking Web site**, is a Web site that encourages members in its online community to share their interests, ideas, stories, photos, music, and videos with other registered users (Figure 2-11g). Popular social networking Web sites include MySpace and Facebook, with Facebook alone boasting more than 300 million active users. A **media sharing Web site** is a specific type of online social network that enables members to share media such as photos, music, and videos. Flickr, Fotki, and Webshots are popular photo sharing communities; PixelFish and YouTube are popular video sharing communities.

Educational An educational Web site offers exciting, challenging avenues for formal and informal teaching and learning (Figure 2-11h). For a more structured learning experience, companies provide online training to employees; and colleges offer online classes and degrees. Instructors often use the Web to enhance classroom teaching by publishing course materials, grades, and other pertinent class information.

Entertainment An entertainment Web site offers an interactive and engaging environment (Figure 2-11i). Popular entertainment Web sites offer music, videos, sports, games, ongoing Web episodes, sweepstakes, chat rooms, and more.

Advocacy An advocacy Web site contains content that describes a cause, opinion, or idea (Figure 2-11j). These Web sites usually present views of a particular group or association.

Web Application A **Web application**, or **Web app**, is a Web site that allows users to access and interact with software through a Web browser on any computer or device that is connected to the Internet. Some Web applications provide free access to their software (Figure 2-11k). Others offer part of their software free and charge for access to more comprehensive features or when a particular action is requested. Examples of Web applications include Google Docs (word processing, spreadsheets, presentations), TurboTax Online (tax preparation), and Windows Live Hotmail (e-mail).

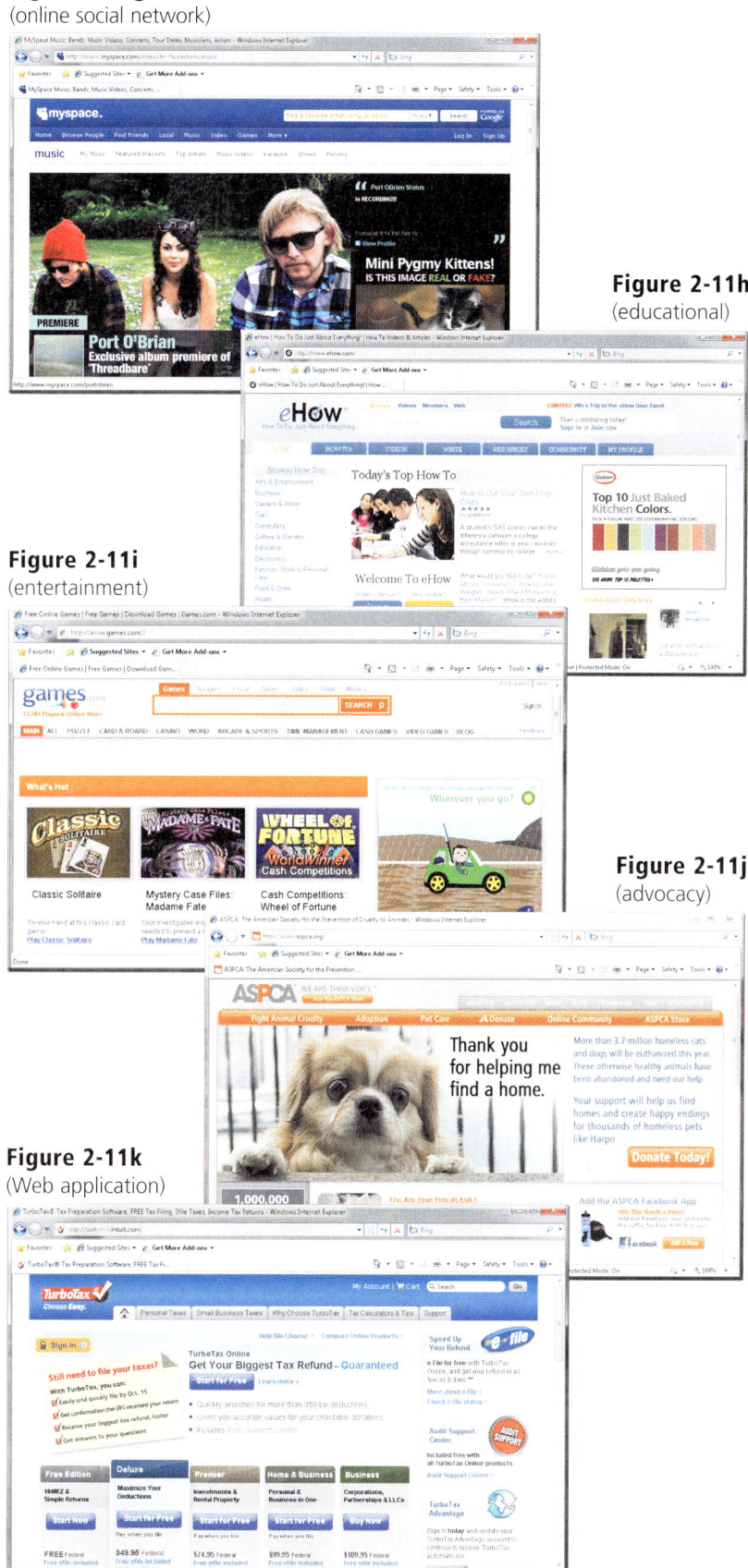

Figure 2-11g (online social network)

Figure 2-11h (educational)

Figure 2-11i (entertainment)

Figure 2-11j (advocacy)

Figure 2-11k (Web application)

Figure 2-11 Types of Web sites. (*continued on next page*)

Figure 2-11l (content aggregator)

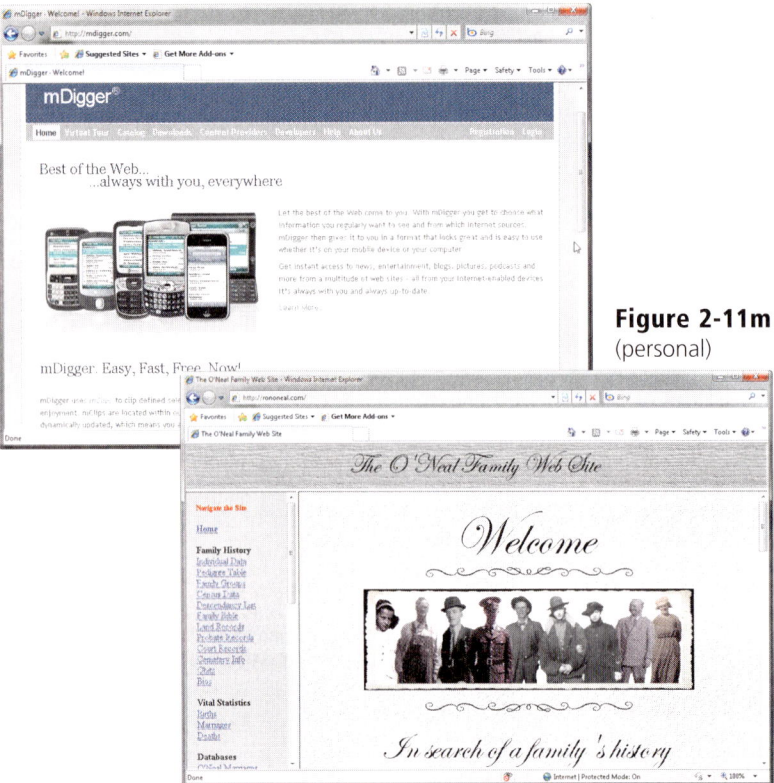

Figure 2-11m (personal)

Figure 2-11 Types of Web sites. *(continued)*

Criteria for Evaluating a Web Site's Content	
Evaluation Criteria	**Reliable Web Sites**
Affiliation	A reputable institution should support the Web site without bias in the information.
Audience	The Web site should be written at an appropriate level.
Authority	The Web site should list the author and the appropriate credentials.
Content	The Web site should be well organized and the links should work.
Currency	The information on the Web page should be current.
Design	The pages at the Web site should download quickly, be visually pleasing, and easy to navigate.
Objectivity	The Web site should contain little advertising and be free of preconceptions.

Figure 2-12 Criteria for evaluating a Web site's content.

Content Aggregator A **content aggregator** is a business that gathers and organizes Web content and then distributes, or feeds, the content to subscribers for free or a fee (Figure 2-11l). Examples of distributed content include news, music, video, and pictures. Subscribers select content in which they are interested. Whenever this content changes, it is downloaded automatically (pushed) to the subscriber's computer or mobile device. **RSS 2.0**, which stands for Really Simple Syndication, is a specification that content aggregators use to distribute content to subscribers.

Personal A private individual or family not usually associated with any organization may maintain a personal Web site (Figure 2-11m). People publish personal Web pages for a variety of reasons. Some are job hunting. Others simply want to share life experiences with the world.

Evaluating a Web Site

Do not assume that information presented on the Web is correct or accurate. Any person, company, or organization can publish a Web page on the Internet. No one oversees the content of these Web pages. Figure 2-12 lists guidelines for assessing the value of a Web site or Web page before relying on its content.

Multimedia on the Web

Most Web pages include more than just formatted text and links. The more exciting Web pages use multimedia. **Multimedia** refers to any application that combines text with graphics, animation, audio, video, and/or virtual reality. Multimedia Web pages often require specific hardware and software and take more time to download because they contain large graphics files or video or audio clips. The sections that follow discuss how the Web uses graphics, animation, audio, video, and virtual reality.

Graphics A **graphic**, or graphical image, is a digital representation of nontext information such as a drawing, chart, or photo. Many Web pages use colorful graphical designs and images to convey messages (Figure 2-13). Read Innovative Computing 2-1 to find out how astronomers share graphics of the universe.

Figure 2-13 This Web page uses colorful graphical designs and images to convey its messages.

INNOVATIVE COMPUTING 2-1

View the Wonders of Space through the WorldWide Telescope

The phrase, reach for the stars, takes on a new meaning when using Microsoft's WorldWide Telescope. Users can access the Telescope from a Web browser or download free software. They then can view a variety of multimedia, including high-resolution graphics from telescopes located on Earth and in space, with Web 2.0 services to allow people to explore the final frontier from their computers.

Users can pan and zoom around the night sky by looking through a specific telescope, such as the Hubble Space Telescope, and view the universe in the past, present, or future. In addition, they can browse graphics of a specific planet, the Milky Way Galaxy, black holes, and other celestial bodies in our solar system, galaxy, and beyond. They also can select different wavelengths, such as X-ray or visible light, to search for objects. Astronomers and educators also have created narrated tours of the sky to help interpret the images.

For more information, visit scsite.com/dc-off07/ch2/innovative and then click WorldWide Telescope.

Of the graphics formats that exist on the Web, the two more common are JPEG and GIF formats. JPEG (pronounced JAY-peg) is a format that compresses graphics to reduce their file size, which means the file takes up less storage space. The goal with JPEG graphics is to reach a balance between image quality and file size. Digital photos often use the JPEG format. GIF (pronounced jiff) graphics also use compression techniques to reduce file sizes. The GIF format works best for images that have only a few distinct colors, such as company logos.

Some Web sites use thumbnails on their pages because graphics can be time-consuming to display. A **thumbnail** is a small version of a larger graphic. You usually can click a thumbnail to display a larger image.

Animation Many Web pages use **animation**, which is the appearance of motion created by displaying a series of still images in sequence. Animation can make Web pages more visually interesting or draw attention to important information or links.

Audio On the Web, you can listen to audio clips and live audio. **Audio** includes music, speech, or any other sound. Simple applications on the Web consist of individual audio files available for download to a computer or device. Once downloaded, you can play (listen to) the contents of these files. Audio files are compressed to reduce their file sizes. For example, the **MP3** format reduces an audio file to about one-tenth its original size, while preserving much of the original quality of the sound.

Some music publishers have Web sites that allow users to download sample tracks free to persuade them to buy all the songs contained on the CD. Others allow a user to purchase and download an entire CD (Figure 2-14). It is legal to download copyrighted music only if the song's copyright holder has granted permission for users to download and play the song.

To listen to an audio file on your computer, you need special software called a **player**. Most current operating systems contain a player, for example, Windows Media Player. Some audio files, however, might require you to download a player. Players available for download include iTunes and RealPlayer.

Some applications on the Web use streaming audio. **Streaming** is the process of transferring data in a continuous and even flow. Streaming allows users to access and use a file while it is transmitting. For example, streaming audio enables you to listen to music as it downloads to your computer.

Podcasting is another popular method of distributing audio. A **podcast** is recorded audio, usually an MP3 file, stored on a Web site that can be downloaded to a computer or a portable media player such as an iPod. Examples of podcasts include music, radio shows, news stories, classroom lectures, political messages, and television commentaries. Podcasters register their podcasts with content aggregators. Subscribers select podcast feeds they want to be downloaded automatically whenever they connect. Most smart phone users who subscribe to a wireless Internet service provider can listen to streaming audio and podcasts.

Figure 2-14 This figure shows how to purchase and download music using iTunes.

Video On the Web, you can view video clips or watch live video. **Video** consists of images displayed in motion. Most video also has accompanying audio. You can use the Internet to watch live and prerecorded coverage of your favorite television programs or enjoy a live performance of your favorite vocalist. You can upload, share, or view video clips at a video sharing Web site such as YouTube. Educators, politicians, and businesses are using video blogs and video podcasts to engage students, voters, and consumers.

Video files often are compressed because they are quite large in size. These clips also are quite short in length, usually less than 10 minutes, because they can take a long time to download. The Moving Pictures Experts Group (MPEG) defines a popular video compression standard, a widely used one called MPEG-4 or **MP4**. Another popular video format is Adobe Flash. As with streaming audio, streaming video allows you to view longer or live video images as they download to your computer.

> **FAQ 2-4**
>
> **How are social networking Web sites and Internet video affecting Internet traffic?**
>
> A report from Cisco Systems states that Internet traffic will double every two years until 2012. The volume of Internet traffic is increasing mostly because of Internet videos and social networking. In addition, the increased use of video conferencing by business users accounts for the increase in traffic.
>
> For more information, visit scsite.com/dc-off07/ch2/faq and then click Internet Traffic.

Virtual Reality Virtual reality (**VR**) is the use of computers to simulate a real or imagined environment that appears as a three-dimensional (3-D) space. VR involves the display of 3-D images that users explore and manipulate interactively. A VR Web site, for example, might show a house for sale. Potential buyers walk through rooms in the VR house by moving an input device forward, backward, or to the side.

Plug-ins Most Web browsers have the capability of displaying basic multimedia elements on a Web page. Sometimes, a browser might need an additional program, called a plug-in. A **plug-in**, or **add-on**, is a program that extends the capability of a browser. You can download many plug-ins at no cost from various Web sites (Figure 2-15).

Popular Plug-Ins

Plug-In Application		Description	Web Address
Acrobat Reader	Get ADOBE READER	View, navigate, and print Portable Document Format (PDF) files — documents formatted to look just as they look in print	adobe.com
Flash Player	Get ADOBE FLASH PLAYER	View dazzling graphics and animation, hear outstanding sound and music, display Web pages across an entire screen	adobe.com
Java	Get it Now	Enable Web browser to run programs written in Java, which add interactivity to Web pages	java.com
QuickTime	Get QuickTime Free Download	View animation, music, audio, video, and VR panoramas and objects directly on a Web page	apple.com
RealPlayer	real RealPlayer DOWNLOAD	Listen to live and on-demand near-CD-quality audio and newscast-quality video, stream audio and video content for faster viewing, play MP3 files, create music CDs	real.com
Shockwave Player	Get ADOBE SHOCKWAVE PLAYER	Experience dynamic interactive multimedia, 3-D graphics, and streaming audio	adobe.com
Silverlight	Install Microsoft Silverlight	Experience high-definition video, high-resolution interactive multimedia, and streaming audio and video	microsoft.com
Windows Media Player	Windows Media Player	Listen to live and on-demand audio, play or edit WMA and MP3 files, burn CDs, and watch DVD movies	microsoft.com

Figure 2-15 Most plug-ins can be downloaded free from the Web.

Web Publishing

Before the World Wide Web, the means to share opinions and ideas with others easily and inexpensively was limited to the media, classroom, work, or social environments. Today, businesses and individuals convey information to millions of people by creating their own Web pages.

Web publishing is the development and maintenance of Web pages. To develop a Web page, you do not have to be a computer programmer. For the small business or home user, Web publishing is fairly easy as long as you have the proper tools.

The five major steps to Web publishing are as follows:
1. Plan a Web site: Think about issues that could affect the design of the Web site.
2. Analyze and design a Web site: Design the layout of elements of the Web site such as links, text, graphics, animation, audio, video, and virtual reality.
3. Create a Web site: Use a word processing program to create basic Web pages or Web page authoring software to create more sophisticated Web sites.
4. Deploy a Web site: Transfer the Web pages from your computer to a Web server.
5. Maintain a Web site: Ensure the Web site contents remain current and all links work properly.

E-Commerce

E-commerce, short for electronic commerce, is a business transaction that occurs over an electronic network such as the Internet. Anyone with access to a computer or mobile device, an Internet connection, and a means to pay for purchased goods or services can participate in e-commerce.

Three types of e-commerce are business-to-consumer, consumer-to-consumer, and business-to-business. Business-to-consumer (B2C) e-commerce consists of the sale of goods and services to the general public. For example, Apple has a B2C Web site. Instead of visiting a retail store to purchase an iPod, for example, customers can order one directly from Apple's Web site.

E-retail, short for electronic retail, occurs when businesses use the Web to sell products (Figure 2-16). A customer (consumer) visits an online business through an **electronic storefront**, which contains product

> **Web Page Authoring Software**
> For more information, visit scsite.com/dc-off07/ch2/weblink and then click Web Page Authoring Software.

An Example of E-Retail

Step 1 The customer displays the e-retailer's electronic storefront.

Step 2 The customer collects purchases in an electronic shopping cart.

Step 3 The customer enters payment information on a secure Web site. The e-retailer sends financial information to a bank.

Step 4 The bank performs security checks and sends authorization back to the e-retailer.

Step 5 The e-retailer's Web server sends confirmation to the customer, processes the order, and then sends it to the fulfillment center.

Step 6 The fulfillment center packages the order, prepares it for shipment, and then sends a report to the server where records are updated.

Step 7 While the order travels to the customer, shipping information is posted on the Web.

Step 8 The order is delivered to the customer, who may be required to sign a handheld computer or document to acknowledge receipt.

Figure 2-16 This figure shows an example of e-retail.

descriptions, images, and a shopping cart. The **shopping cart** allows the customer to collect purchases. When ready to complete the sale, the customer enters personal data and the method of payment, which should be through a secure Internet connection.

Consumer-to-consumer (C2C) e-commerce occurs when one consumer sells directly to another, such as in an online auction. With an **online auction**, users bid on an item being sold by someone else. The highest bidder at the end of the bidding period purchases the item. eBay is one of the more popular online auction Web sites.

As an alternative to entering credit card, bank account, or other financial information online, some shopping and auction Web sites allow consumers to use an online payment service such as PayPal or Google Checkout. To use an online payment service, you create an account that is linked to your credit card or funds at a financial institution. When you make a purchase, you use your online payment service account, which transfers money for you without revealing your financial information.

Most e-commerce, though, actually takes place between businesses, which is called business-to-business (B2B) e-commerce. Many businesses provide goods and services to other businesses, such as online advertising, recruiting, credit, sales, market research, technical support, and training.

Google Checkout
For more information, visit scsite.com/dc-off07/ch2/weblink and then click Google Checkout.

✔ QUIZ YOURSELF 2-2

Instructions: Find the true statement below. Then, rewrite the remaining false statements so that they are true.

1. A blog is a Web site that uses a regularly updated journal format to reflect the interests, opinions, and personalities of the author and sometimes site visitors.
2. A Web browser classifies Web pages in an organized set of categories and related subcategories.
3. Business-to-consumer e-commerce occurs when one consumer sells directly to another, such as in an online auction.
4. The more widely used search engines for personal computers are Internet Explorer, Firefox, Opera, Safari, and Google Chrome.
5. To develop a Web page, you have to be a computer programmer.

Quiz Yourself Online: To further check your knowledge of pages 49 through 63, visit scsite.com/dc-off07/ch2/quiz and then click Objectives 3 – 7.

Other Internet Services

The Web is only one of the many services on the Internet. The Web and other Internet services have changed the way we communicate. We use computers and mobile devices to send e-mail messages to the president, have a discussion with experts about the stock market, chat with someone in another country about genealogy, and talk about homework assignments with classmates via instant messages. Many times, these communications take place completely in writing — without the parties ever meeting each other.

The following pages discuss these Internet services: e-mail, mailing lists, instant messaging, chat rooms, VoIP (Voice over IP), FTP (File Transfer Protocol), and newsgroups and message boards.

E-Mail

E-mail (short for electronic mail) is the transmission of messages and files via a computer network. Today, e-mail is a primary communications method for both personal and business use.

You use an **e-mail program** to create, send, receive, forward, store, print, and delete e-mail messages. Outlook and Windows Live Mail are two popular desktop e-mail programs.

64 Chapter 2 The Internet and World Wide Web

The steps in Figure 2-17 illustrate how to send an e-mail message using Outlook; Gmail and Windows Live Hotmail are two popular free e-mail Web applications. The message can be simple text or can include an attachment such as a word processing document, a graphic, an audio clip, or a video clip. To learn more about how to attach a file to an e-mail message, complete the Learn How To 1 activity on page 76.

Just as you address a letter when using the postal system, you address an e-mail message with the e-mail address of your intended recipient. Likewise, when someone sends you a message, he or she must have your e-mail address. An **e-mail address** is a combination of a user name and a domain name that

How to Send an E-Mail Message Using Outlook

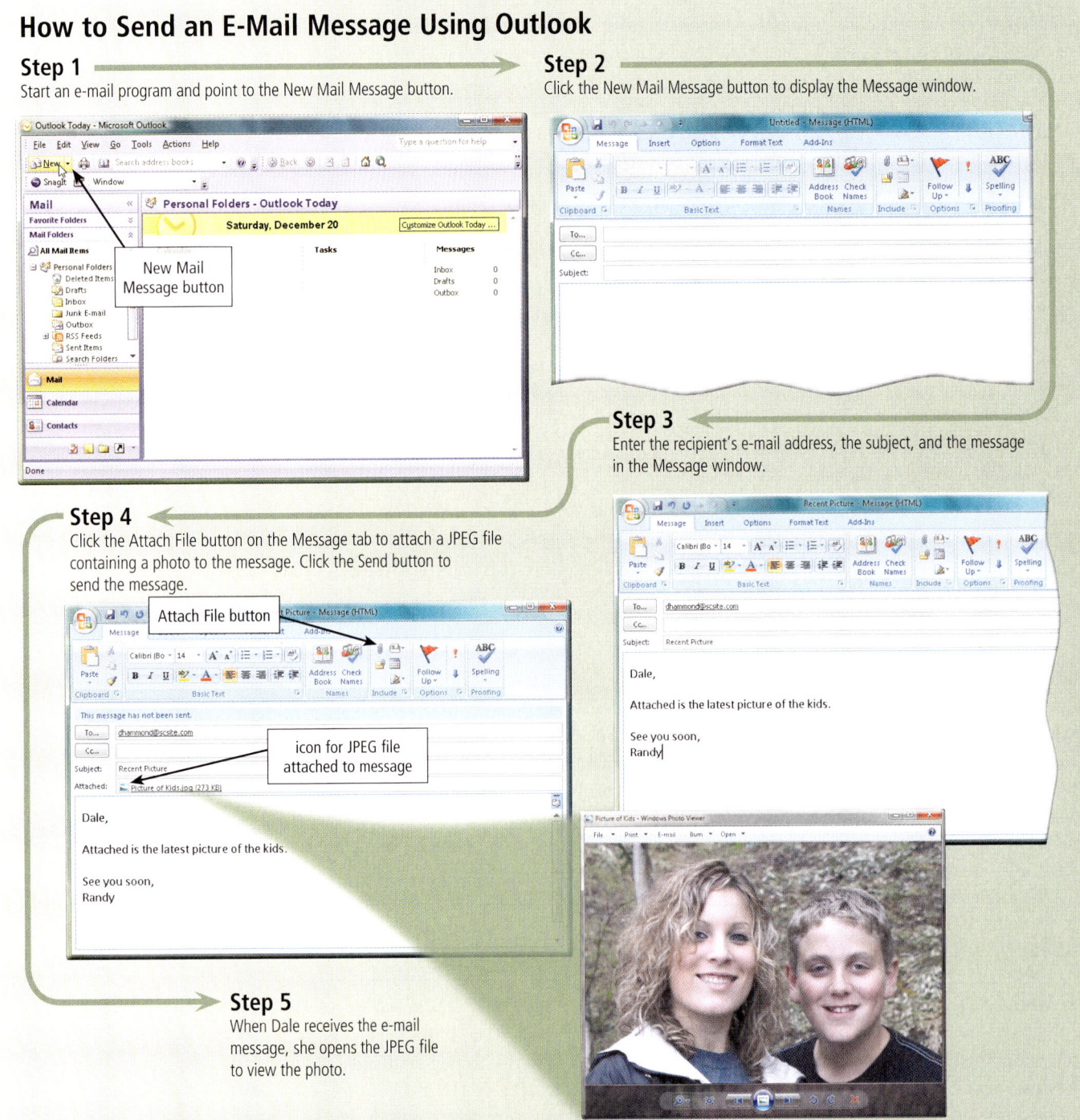

Figure 2-17 This figure shows how to send an e-mail message using Outlook.

identifies a user so that he or she can receive Internet e-mail. A **user name** is a unique combination of characters, such as letters of the alphabet and/or numbers, that identifies a specific user.

In an Internet e-mail address, an @ (pronounced at) symbol separates the user name from the domain name. Your service provider supplies the domain name. A possible e-mail address for Kiley Barnhill would be kbarnhill@scsite.com, which would be read as follows: K Barnhill at s c site dot com. Most e-mail programs allow you to create an **address book**, or contacts folder, which contains a list of names and e-mail addresses.

When you send an e-mail message, an outgoing mail server that is operated by your Internet access provider determines how to route the message through the Internet and then sends the message. As you receive e-mail messages, an incoming mail server — also operated by your Internet access provider — holds the messages in your mailbox until you use your e-mail program to retrieve them. Most e-mail programs have a mail notification alert that informs you via a message and/or sound when you receive new mail. Figure 2-18 illustrates how an e-mail message may travel from a sender to a receiver using a desktop e-mail program.

E-Mail
For more information, visit scsite.com/dc-off07/ch2/weblink and then click E-Mail.

FAQ 2-5

Can my computer get a virus through e-mail?
Yes. A virus is a computer program that can damage files and the operating system. One way that virus authors attempt to spread a virus is by sending virus-infected e-mail attachments. If you receive an e-mail attachment, you should use an antivirus program to verify that it is virus free.

For more information, read the section about viruses and antivirus programs in Chapter 4, and visit scsite.com/dc-off07/ch2/faq and then click Viruses.

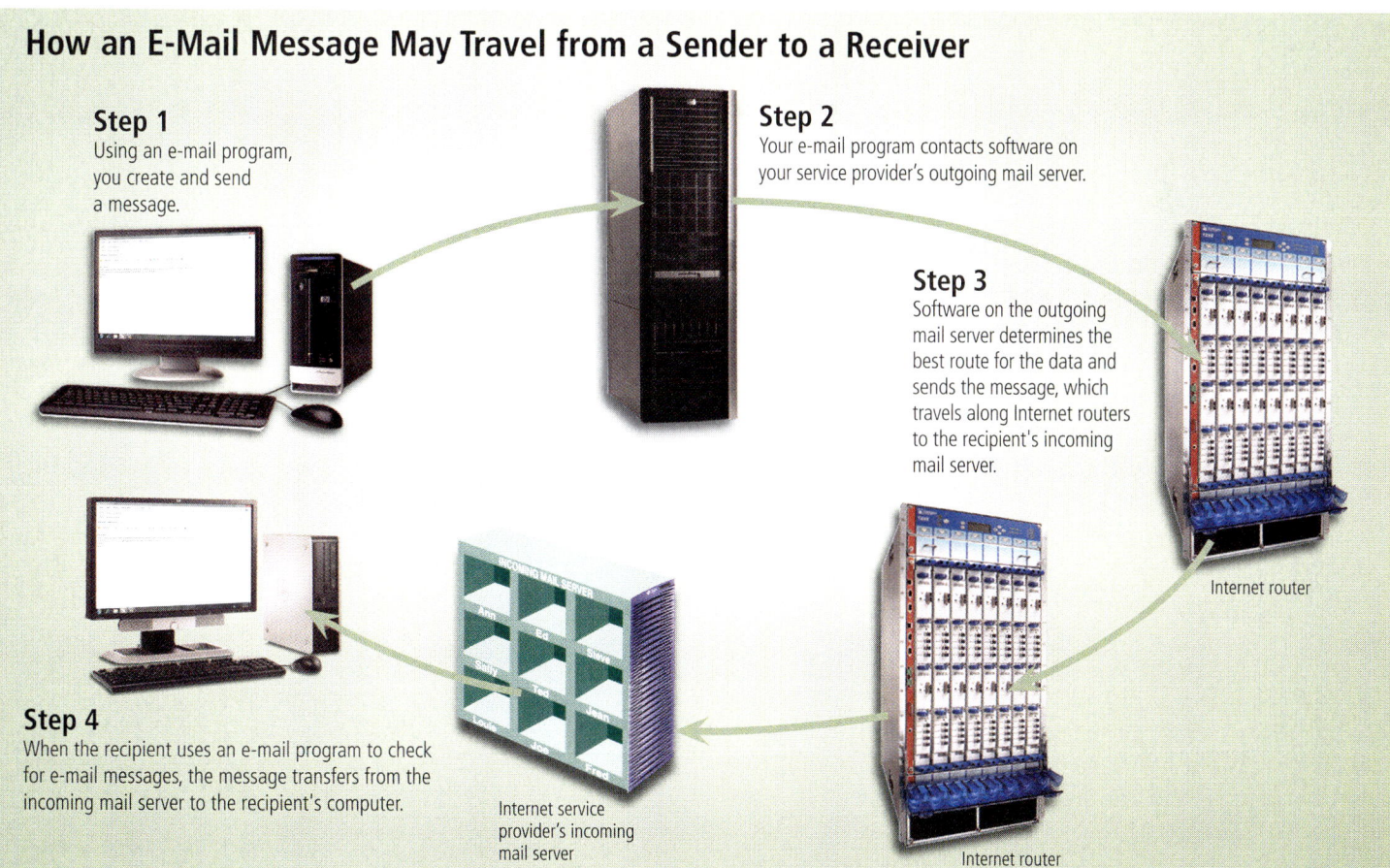

Figure 2-18 This figure shows how an e-mail message may travel from a sender to a receiver.

Mailing Lists

A **mailing list**, also called an e-mail list or distribution list, is a group of e-mail names and addresses given a single name. When a message is sent to a mailing list, every person on the list receives a copy of the message in his or her mailbox. For example, your credit card company may add you to its mailing list in order to send you special offers. To add your e-mail name and address to a mailing list, you **subscribe** to it. To remove your name, you **unsubscribe** from the mailing list.

Thousands of mailing lists exist about a variety of topics in areas of entertainment, business, computers, society, culture, health, recreation, and education.

Instant Messaging

Instant messaging (**IM**) is a real-time Internet communications service that notifies you when one or more people are online and then allows you to exchange messages or files or join a private chat room with them (Figure 2-19). **Real time** means that you and the people with whom you are conversing are online at the same time. Some IM services support voice and video conversations. For IM to work, both parties must be online at the same time. Also, the receiver of a message must be willing to accept messages.

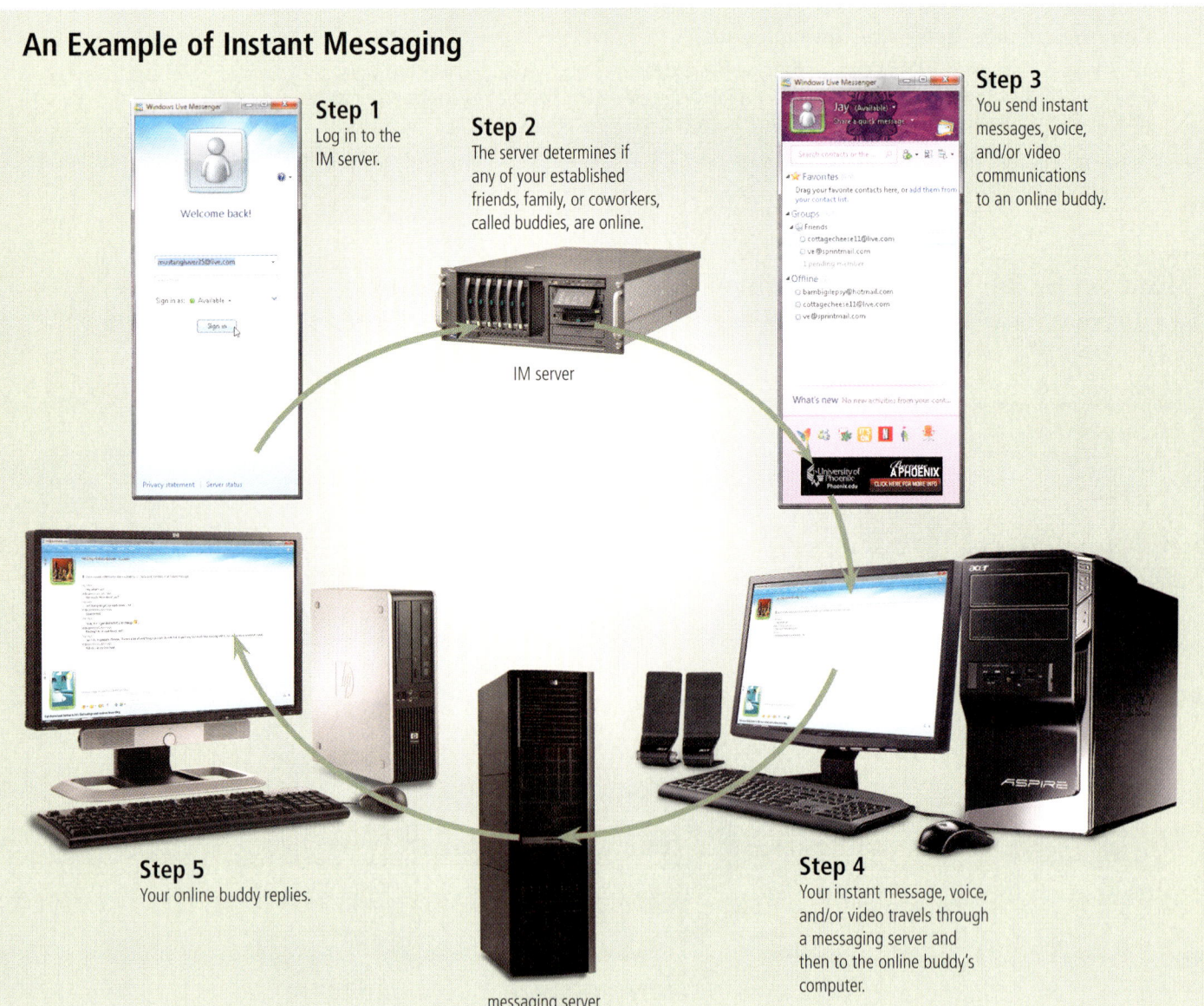

Figure 2-19 This figure shows an example of instant messaging.

To use IM, you may have to install instant messenger software on the computer or device, such as a smart phone, you plan to use. Some operating systems, such as Windows, include an instant messenger. Few IM programs follow IM standards. To ensure successful communications, all individuals on the contact list need to use the same or a compatible instant messenger.

Chat Rooms

A **chat** is a real-time typed conversation that takes place on a computer. A **chat room** is a location on an Internet server that permits users to chat with each other. Anyone in the chat room can participate in the conversation, which usually is specific to a particular topic.

As you type on your keyboard, a line of characters and symbols is displayed on the computer screen. Others connected to the same chat room server also see what you type (Figure 2-20). Some chat rooms support voice chats and video chats, in which people hear or see each other as they chat.

To start a chat session, you connect to a chat server through a program called a chat client. Today's browsers usually include a chat client. If yours does not, you can download a chat client from the Web. Once you have installed a chat client, you can create or join a conversation on the chat server to which you are connected.

Chat Rooms
For more information, visit scsite.com/dc-off07/ch2/ weblink and then click Chat Rooms.

Figure 2-20 As you type, the words and symbols you enter are displayed on the computer screens of other people in the same chat room. To save time many chat and IM users type abbreviations and acronyms for phrases, such as 'r u there?', which stands for 'Are You There?'.

VoIP

VoIP (Voice over IP, or Internet Protocol), also called Internet telephony, enables users to speak to other users over the Internet (instead of the public switched telephone network).

To place an Internet telephone call, you need a high-speed Internet connection (e.g., via cable or DSL modem); Internet telephone service; a microphone or telephone, depending on the Internet telephone service; and Internet telephone software or VoIP router, or a telephone adapter, depending on the Internet telephone service (Figure 2-21). VoIP services also are available on some mobile devices that have wireless Internet service. Calls to other parties with the same Internet telephone service often are free, while calls that connect to the telephone network typically cost about $15 to $35 per month.

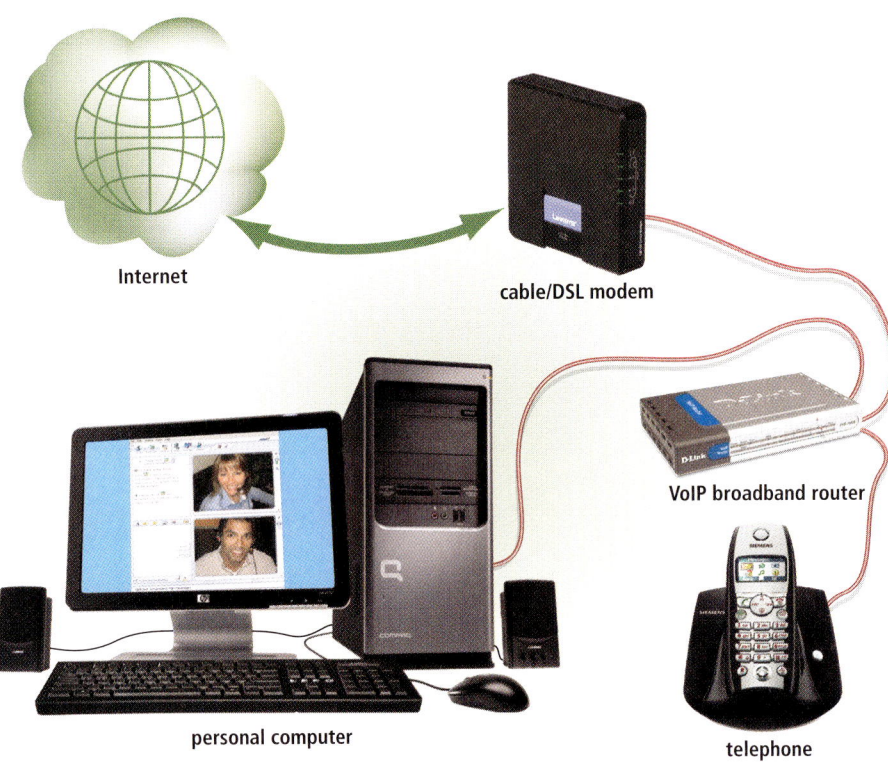

Figure 2-21 One type of equipment configuration for a user making a call via VoIP.

FTP

FTP (File Transfer Protocol) is an Internet standard that permits the process of file uploading and downloading with other computers on the Internet. Uploading is the opposite of downloading; that is, **uploading** is the process of transferring documents, graphics, and other objects from your computer to a server on the Internet.

Many operating systems include FTP capabilities. An FTP site is a collection of files including text, graphics, audio clips, video clips, and program files that reside on an FTP server. Many FTP sites have anonymous FTP, whereby anyone can transfer some, if not all, available files. Some FTP sites restrict file transfers to those who have authorized accounts (user names and passwords) on the FTP server.

Newsgroups and Message Boards

A **newsgroup** is an online area in which users have written discussions about a particular subject (Figure 2-22). To participate in a discussion, a user sends a message to the newsgroup, and other users in the newsgroup read and reply to the message.

Some newsgroups require you to enter a user name and password to participate in the discussion. For example, a newsgroup for students taking a college course may require a user name

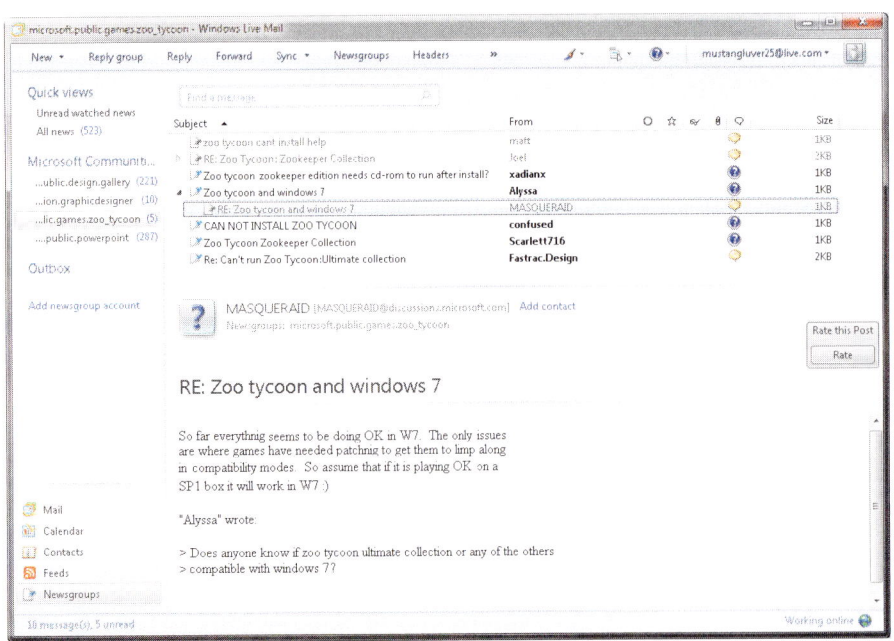

Figure 2-22 Users in a newsgroup read and reply to other users' messages.

and password to access the newsgroup. This ensures that only students in the course participate in the discussion. To participate in a newsgroup, typically you use a program called a newsreader.

A popular Web-based type of discussion group that does not require a newsreader is a **message board**. Many Web sites use message boards instead of newsgroups because they are easier to use.

Netiquette

Netiquette, which is short for Internet etiquette, is the code of acceptable behaviors users should follow while on the Internet; that is, it is the conduct expected of individuals while online. Netiquette includes rules for all aspects of the Internet, including the World Wide Web, e-mail, instant messaging, chat rooms, FTP, and newsgroups and message boards. Figure 2-23 outlines some of the rules of netiquette. Read Ethics & Issues 2-3 for a related discussion.

NETIQUETTE — Golden Rule: Treat others as you would like them to treat you.

1. In e-mail, chat rooms, and newsgroups:
   - Keep messages brief. Use proper grammar, spelling, and punctuation.
   - Be careful when using sarcasm and humor, as it might be misinterpreted.
   - Be polite. Avoid offensive language.
   - Read the message before you send it.
   - Use meaningful subject lines.
   - Avoid sending or posting flames, which are abusive or insulting messages. Do not participate in flame wars, which are exchanges of flames.
   - Avoid sending spam, which is the Internet's version of junk mail. Spam is an unsolicited e-mail message or newsgroup posting sent to many recipients or newsgroups at once.
   - Do not use all capital letters, which is the equivalent of SHOUTING!
   - Use **emoticons** to express emotion. Popular emoticons include
     :) Smile   :| Indifference   :o Surprised
     :(Frown   :\ Undecided
   - Use abbreviations and acronyms for phrases:
     btw   by the way
     imho   in my humble opinion
     fyi   for your information
     ttfn   ta ta for now
     fwiw   for what it's worth
     tyvm   thank you very much
   - Clearly identify a spoiler, which is a message that reveals a solution to a game or ending to a movie or program.
2. Read the FAQ (frequently asked questions), if one exists. Many newsgroups and Web pages have an FAQ.
3. Do not assume material is accurate or up-to-date. Be forgiving of other's mistakes.
4. Never read someone's private e-mail.

Figure 2-23 Some of the rules of netiquette.

ETHICS & ISSUES 2-3

Would Banning Anonymous Comments Reduce Cyberbullying?

Recently, several high-profile cases highlighted the issue of cyberbullying. Cyberbullying is the harassment of computer users, often teens and preteens, through various forms of Internet communications. The behavior typically occurs via e-mail, instant messaging, and chat rooms, and can result in a traumatic experience for the recipient. The bullying may be in the form of threats, spreading of rumors, or humiliation. Usually, the perpetrators of cyberbullying remain anonymous. Many people believe that the anonymous nature of the Internet directly leads to this unscrupulous behavior. Some government officials and advocacy groups have asked for laws that would ban anonymous comments in chat rooms and require that Internet access providers verify and record the true identity of all users. Others have proposed that it be illegal to sign up for an e-mail account or instant messaging account with a fake screen name. Opponents of such plans claim that anonymity and privacy are too important to give up. They state, for example, that the right to be critical of the government in an anonymous forum is a basic right. The rights of everyone should not be infringed upon due to bad behavior of a small group of people.

Would banning anonymous comments reduce cyberbullying? Why or why not? What are the positive and negative aspects of the freedom to remain anonymous on the Internet? What other measures can be taken to reduce cyberbullying? What role can parents play in reducing cyberbullying?

QUIZ YOURSELF 2-3

Instructions: Find the true statement below. Then, rewrite the remaining false statements so that they are true.

1. A chat room is a location on an Internet server that permits users to chat with each other.
2. An e-mail address is a combination of a user name and an e-mail program that identifies a user so that he or she can receive Internet e-mail.
3. FTP uses the Internet (instead of the public switched telephone network) to connect a calling party to one or more called parties.
4. Netiquette is the code of unacceptable behaviors while on the Internet.
5. VoIP enables users to subscribe to other users over the Internet.

👆 **Quiz Yourself Online:** To further check your knowledge of pages 63 through 69, visit scsite.com/dc-off07/ch2/quiz and then click Objectives 8 – 9.

Chapter Summary

This chapter presented the history and structure of the Internet. It discussed the World Wide Web at length, including topics such as browsing, navigating, searching, Web publishing, and e-commerce. It also introduced other services available on the Internet, such as e-mail, mailing lists, instant messaging, chat rooms, VoIP, FTP, and newsgroups and message boards. Finally, the chapter listed rules of netiquette.

Computer Usage @ Work

Entertainment

Do you wonder how music on the radio sounds so perfectly in tune, how animated motion pictures are created, or how one controls lighting during a concert? Not only does the entertainment industry rely on computers to advertise and sell their services on the Internet, computers also assist in other aspects, including audio and video composition, lighting control, computerized animation, and computer gaming.

As mentioned in this chapter, entertainment Web sites provide music and movies you can purchase and download to your computer or mobile device; live news broadcasts, performances, and sporting events; games you can play with other online users; and much more.

As early as 1951, computers were used to record and play music. Today, computers play a much larger role in the music industry. For example, if you are listening to a song on the radio and notice that not one note is out of tune, it is possible that software was used to change individual notes without altering the rest of the song.

Many years ago, creating cartoons or animated motion pictures was an extremely time-consuming task because artists were responsible for sketching thousands of drawings by hand. Currently, artists use computers to create these drawings in a fraction of the time, which significantly can reduce the time and cost of development.

Computers also are used in the game industry. While some game developers create games from scratch, others might use game engines that simplify the development process. For example, LucasArts created the GrimE game engine, which is designed to create adventure games.

During a concert, lighting technicians use computer programs to turn lights off and on, change color, or change location at specified intervals. In fact, once a performance begins, the technicians often merely are standing by, monitoring the computer as it performs most of the work. A significant amount of time and effort, however, is required to program the computer to perform its required tasks during a live show.

The next time you listen to a song, watch a movie, play a game, or attend a concert, think about the role computers play in contributing to your entertainment.

👆 For more information, visit scsite.com/dc-off07/ch2/work and then click Entertainment.

Companies on the Cutting Edge

GOOGLE Popular Search Engine and Services

Google founders Sergey Brin and Larry Page have done very little advertising, but their Web site has become a household word, largely on favorable word-of-mouth reviews. They launched the Web site in 1998 in a friend's garage with the goal of providing the best possible experience for their loyal users who are looking for information presented clearly and quickly.

Google regularly scans more than one trillion Web pages in search of unique phrases and terms. Its thousands of connected computers deliver organized search results for the hundreds of millions of queries users input daily. In 2009, the company updated its Google Earth product to allow users to explore the Moon, and also updated its popular advertising product, AdWords. Among its other services are Google Docs and YouTube.

eBAY World's Largest Online Marketplace

Millions of products are traded daily on eBay auctions, whether it is across town or across the globe. The more than 88 million registered worldwide shoppers generate at least $1.8 billion in annual revenue through purchases on the main Web site, eBay, along with items on Shopping.com, tickets on StubHub, classifieds on Kijiji, and other e-commerce venues.

The shoppers likely pay for their merchandise using PayPal, another eBay service. This merchant service allows buyers to transfer money from savings accounts or use their credit card without having to expose the account number to the seller. Other eBay companies are Rent.com, which offers listings for apartments and houses, and Shopping.com, which allows consumers to find and compare products. In 2009, eBay introduced a program to more easily identify its top-rated sellers. It also invited buyers and sellers to become members of the eBay Green Team, which encourages and promotes environmentally friendly business practices.

For more information, visit scsite.com/dc-off07/ch2/companies.

Technology Trailblazers

TIM BERNERS-LEE Creator of the World Wide Web

Being the creator of the World Wide Web is an impressive item on any resume, and it certainly helped Tim Berners-Lee become the 3Com Founders Professor of Engineering at the Massachusetts Institute of Technology in 2008. As a professor in the electrical engineering and computer science departments, he researches social and technical collaboration on the Internet.

Berners-Lee's interest in sharing information via Web servers, browsers, and Web addresses developed in 1989 while working at CERN, the European Organization for Nuclear Research, in Geneva, Switzerland. He continued to improve his design of a program that tracked random associations for several years and then became the director of the World Wide Web Consortium (W3C), a forum to develop Web standards, in 1994.

Queen Elizabeth bestowed the Order of Merit – the highest civilian honor – upon the British-born Berners-Lee in 2007.

MARK ZUCKERBERG Facebook Founder and CEO

As one of the youngest self-made billionaires in history, Mark Zuckerberg could have his choice of the finest things in life. Instead, he lives very modestly and walks to Facebook's Palo Alto headquarters.

Both Microsoft and AOL had recruited Zuckerberg during his senior year in high school in New Hampshire. He declined their job offers and decided to attend Harvard. In college, he and some friends developed several projects, laying the foundation that led to Facebook's eventual start. Harvard administrators claimed these Web sites violated students' privacy. He, however, had instant success launching Facebook from his dorm room, and the Web site's popularity quickly spread to other Ivy League and Boston-area colleges and then worldwide. He left his studies at Harvard University in 2004 and moved to California.

Today, Zuckerberg says he spends the majority of his time running the $15 billion company on very little sleep.

For more information, visit scsite.com/dc-off07/ch2/trailblazers.

Chapter Review

The Chapter Review reinforces the main concepts presented in this chapter.

👆 To obtain help from other students about any concept in this chapter, visit scsite.com/dc-off07/ch2/forum and post your thoughts and questions.

1. **What Are the Various Broadband Internet Connections?** The **Internet** is a worldwide collection of networks that links millions of businesses, government agencies, educational institutions, and individuals. Many home and small business users connect to the Internet via high-speed **broadband** Internet service. **Cable Internet service** provides high-speed Internet access through the cable television network via a cable modem. **DSL** (digital subscriber line) provides high-speed Internet connections using regular telephone lines. **Fiber to the Premises** (**FTTP**) uses fiber-optic cable to provide high-speed Internet access. **Fixed wireless** high-speed Internet connections use a dish-shaped antenna to communicate via radio signals. A **Wi-Fi** network uses radio signals to provide Internet connections to wireless computers and devices. A **cellular radio network** offers high-speed Internet connections to devices with built-in compatible technology or computers with wireless modems. **Satellite Internet service** communicates with a satellite dish to provide high-speed Internet connections. Some home and small businesses connect to the Internet with **dial-up access**, which uses a modem in the computer and a standard telephone line.

2. **What Are the Types of Internet Access Providers?** An **access provider** is a business that provides access to the Internet free or for a fee. An **ISP** (**Internet service provider**) is a regional or national access provider. An **online service provider** (**OSP**) provides Internet access in addition to members-only features, such as instant messaging or customized Web browsers. A **wireless Internet service provider** provides wireless Internet access to computers and mobile devices with built-in wireless capability (such as Wi-Fi) or to computers using wireless modems or wireless access devices.

👆 Visit scsite.com/dc-off07/ch2/quiz and then click Objectives 1 – 2.

3. **What Is the Purpose of a Web Browser, and What Are the Components of a Web Address?** A **Web browser**, or **browser**, is application software that allows users to access and view Web pages or access Web 2.0 programs. A **Web address** is the unique address for each **Web page** and consists of a protocol, a domain name, and sometimes the path to a specific Web page or location on a Web page.

4. **How Do You Use a Search Engine to Search for Information on the Web?** A **search engine** is a program that finds Web sites, Web pages, images, videos, news, maps, and other information related to a specific topic. A search engine is helpful in locating information for which you do not know an exact Web address or are not seeking a particular Web site. Search engines require **search text** that describes the item you want to find. After performing the search, the search engine returns a list of hits, each one a **link** to an associated Web page.

5. **What Are the Types of Web Sites?** A **portal** is a Web site that offers a variety of Internet services from a single location. A news Web site contains newsworthy material. An informational Web site contains factual information. A business/marketing Web site promotes or sells products or services. A **blog** is an informal Web site consisting of time-stamped articles, or posts, in a diary or journal format, usually listed in reverse chronological order. A **wiki** is a collaborative Web site that allows users to create, add to, modify, or delete the Web site content via their Web browser. An **online social network**, or **social networking Web site**, encourages members to share their interests, ideas, stories, photos, music, and videos with other registered users. An educational Web site offers avenues for teaching and learning. An entertainment Web site offers an interactive and engaging environment. An advocacy Web site describes a cause, opinion, or idea. A **Web application**, or **Web app**, is a Web site that allows users to access and interact with software through a Web browser on any computer connected to the Internet. A **content aggregator** is a business that gathers and organizes Web content and then distributes, or feeds, the content to subscribers for free or a fee. A personal Web site is maintained by a private individual or family.

6. **How Do Web Pages Use Graphics, Animation, Audio, Video, Virtual Reality, and Plug-Ins?** More exciting Web sites use **multimedia**, which refers to any application that combines text with graphics, animation, video, and/or virtual reality. A **graphic**, or graphical image, is a digital representation of nontext information such as a drawing, chart, or photo. **Animation** is the appearance of motion created by displaying a series of still images in sequence. **Audio** includes music, speech, or any other sound. **Video** consists of full-motion images that are played back at various speeds. **Virtual reality** (**VR**) is the use of computers to simulate a real or imagined environment as a 3-D space. A **plug-in** is a program that extends the capability of a browser.

7. **What Are the Steps Required for Web Publishing?** **Web publishing** is the development and maintenance of Web pages. The five major steps to Web publishing are: (1) plan a Web site, (2) analyze and design a Web site, (3) create a Web site, (4) deploy a Web site, and (5) maintain a Web site.

   Visit scsite.com/dc-off07/ch2/quiz and then click Objectives 3 – 7.

8. **How Do E-Mail, Mailing Lists, Instant Messaging, Chat Rooms, VoIP, FTP, and Newsgroups and Message Boards Work?** E-mail (short for electronic mail) is the transmission of messages and files via a computer network. A **mailing list** is a group of e-mail names and addresses given a single name, so that everyone on the list receives a message sent to the list. **Instant messaging (IM)** is a **real-time** Internet communications service that notifies you when one or more people are online. A **chat room** is a location on an Internet server that permits users to **chat**, or conduct real-time typed conversations. **VoIP** (Voice over IP, or Internet Protocol) enables users to speak to other users over the Internet instead of the public switched telephone network. **FTP** (File Transfer Protocol) is an Internet standard that permits file **uploading** and **downloading** with other computers on the Internet. A **newsgroup** is an online area in which users have written discussions about a particular subject. A **message board** is a popular Web-based type of discussion group that is easier to use than a newsgroup.

9. **What Are the Rules of Netiquette?** **Netiquette**, which is short for Internet etiquette, is the code of acceptable behaviors users should follow while on the Internet. Keep messages short. Be polite. Use **emoticons**. Read the FAQ if one exists. Do not assume material is accurate or up-to-date, and never read someone's private e-mail.

   Visit scsite.com/dc-off07/ch2/quiz and then click Objectives 8 – 9.

Key Terms

You should know the Key Terms. The list below helps focus your study.

To see an example of and a definition for each term, and to access current and additional information from the Web, visit scsite.com/dc-off07/ch2/terms.

access provider (46)
add-on (61)
address book (65)
animation (59)
audio (60)
blog (56)
blogosphere (56)
bookmark (51)
broadband (45)
browser (49)
cable Internet service (45)
cellular radio network (46)
chat (67)
chat room (67)
click (52)
content aggregator (58)
dial-up access (46)
domain name (48)
downloading (50)
DSL (45)
e-commerce (62)
electronic storefront (62)
e-mail address (64)
e-mail program (63)
emoticons (69)

favorite (51)
Fiber to the Premises (FTTP) (45)
fixed wireless (45)
FTP (68)
graphic (58)
home page (50)
hot spots (46)
hyperlink (52)
instant messaging (IM) (66)
Internet (44)
Internet backbone (47)
IP address (48)
ISP (Internet service provider) (46)
link (52)
mailing list (66)
media sharing Web site (57)
message board (69)
microblog (56)
MP3 (60)
MP4 (61)
multimedia (58)
Net (44)
netiquette (69)

newsgroup (68)
online auction (63)
online service provider (OSP) (46)
online social network (57)
player (60)
plug-in (61)
podcast (60)
portal (55)
real time (66)
RSS 2.0 (58)
satellite Internet service (46)
search engine (53)
search text (54)
shopping cart (63)
social networking Web site (57)
streaming (60)
subject directory (53)
subscribe (66)
surfing the Web (52)
tabbed browsing (52)
thumbnail (59)
top-level domain (TLD) (48)
unsubscribe (66)

uploading (68)
URL (51)
user name (65)
video (61)
video blog (56)
virtual reality (VR) (61)
vlog (56)
vlogosphere (56)
VoIP (68)
Web (49)
Web 2.0 (49)
Web address (51)
Web app (57)
Web application (57)
Web browser (49)
Web page (49)
Web publishing (62)
Web server (49)
Web site (49)
Wi-Fi (45)
wiki (56)
wireless Internet service provider (46)
World Wide Web (WWW) (49)

Checkpoint

The Checkpoint exercises test your knowledge of the chapter concepts. The page number containing the answer appears in parentheses after each exercise.

☝ To complete the Checkpoint exercises interactively, visit scsite.com/dc-off07/ch2/check.

Multiple Choice   Select the best answer.

1. _____ offers high-speed Internet connections to devices with built-in compatible technology or computers with wireless modems. (46)
   a. Cable Internet service
   b. A digital subscriber line
   c. A cellular radio network
   d. Fiber to the Premises (FTTP)

2. Instead of using broadband Internet service some home users connect to the Internet via _____, which is a slower-speed technology. (46)
   a. satellite Internet service
   b. cable Internet service
   c. DSL
   d. dial-up access

3. _____ is the process of a computer or device receiving information, such as a Web page, from a server on the Internet. (50)
   a. Uploading
   b. Social networking
   c. Downloading
   d. Blogging

4. A _____ is a Web site that allows users to post short text updates, usually between 100 and 200 characters. (56)
   a. podcast
   b. wiki
   c. microblog
   d. portal

5. A _____ is a specific type of online social network that enables members to share photos, music, and videos. (57)
   a. blog
   b. wiki
   c. podcast
   d. media sharing Web site

6. A(n) _____ is a small version of a larger graphic. (59)
   a. thumbnail
   b. wiki
   c. MP3
   d. portal

7. In _____ e-commerce, one consumer sells directly to another. (63)
   a. consumer-to-business
   b. business-to-business
   c. consumer-to-consumer
   d. business-to-consumer

8. The _____ standard permits uploading and downloading of files on the Internet. (68)
   a. FTP
   b. newsgroup
   c. message board
   d. mailing list

Matching   Match the terms with their definitions.

_____ 1. home page (50)
_____ 2. search engine (53)
_____ 3. MP3 (60)
_____ 4. e-mail address (64)
_____ 5. emoticons (69)

a. used to express emotions in e-mail, chat rooms, and newsgroups
b. the first page that a Web site displays
c. combination of a user name and a domain name that identifies an Internet user
d. program that finds Web sites, Web pages, images, videos, news, maps, and other information related to a specific topic
e. built-in connection to a related Web page or part of a Web page
f. format that reduces an audio file to about one-tenth its original size

Short Answer   Write a brief answer to each of the following questions.

1. Describe three different types of broadband Internet services. _____ What is the difference between a regional ISP and a national ISP? _____
2. How is a Web page different from a Web site? _____ How can you use a Web address to display a Web page? _____
3. What are the differences between blogs, wikis, and podcasts? _____ When might you use each? _____
4. What is a Web application? _____ What are some features and examples of Web applications? _____
5. What is one specification used by content aggregators to distribute content? _____ How might you evaluate the accuracy of a Web site? _____

Problem Solving

The Problem Solving exercises extend your knowledge of the chapter concepts by seeking solutions to practical computer problems that you may encounter at home, school, or work. The Collaboration exercise should be completed with a team.

☞ To discuss the Problem Solving exercises with other students, visit scsite.com/dc-off07/ch2/forum and post your thoughts or questions.

In the real world, practical problems often can be solved in multiple ways. Provide one solution to each of the following problems using available resources, such as articles on the Web or in print, blogs, podcasts, videos, television, user guides, other individuals, and electronics and computer stores. You may need to use multiple resources to obtain an answer. Present your solutions in the form requested by your instructor (brief report, presentation, discussion, or other means).

@ Home

1. **Slow Internet Connection**   You just installed VoIP telephone service in your house. Each time you are on the telephone, however, you notice that your Internet connection slows down significantly. What could be causing this?

2. **No Wireless Connection**   When you return home to visit your parents and turn on your new notebook computer, it does not connect automatically to their wireless network. What is your next step?

3. **Incorrect Search Engine**   A class project requires that you conduct research on the Web. After typing the Web address for Google's home page and pressing the ENTER key, your Web browser redirects you to a different search engine. What could be wrong?

4. **New Browser Windows**   While browsing the Web, each time you click a link, the link's destination opens in a new browser window. You prefer to have each link open in a new tab so that your taskbar does not become cluttered. How will you resolve this?

@ Work

5. **Access Denied**   During your lunch hour, you decide to search the Web for possible vacation destinations. After visiting several airline and hotel Web sites, you attempt to visit the Web site for a Caribbean resort. Much to your surprise, the Web browser informs you that the Web site has been blocked. Why might this happen?

6. **Sporadic E-Mail Message Delivery**   The e-mail program on your computer has been delivering new messages only every hour, on the hour. Historically, new e-mail messages would arrive and be displayed immediately upon being sent by the sender. Furthermore, your coworkers claim that they sometimes do not receive your e-mail messages until hours after they are sent. What might be the problem?

7. **E-Mail Message Formatting**   A friend sent an e-mail message containing a photo to your e-mail account at work. Upon receiving the e-mail message, the photo does not display. You also notice that e-mail messages never display any formatting, such as different fonts, font sizes, and font colors. What might be causing this?

8. **Automatic Response**   When you return from vacation, a colleague informs you that when she sent e-mail messages to your e-mail address, she would not always receive your automatic response stating that you were out of the office. Why might your e-mail program not respond automatically to every e-mail message received?

Collaboration

9. **Computers in Entertainment**   The drama department at a local high school is considering developing a movie and has asked for your help. The drama teacher would like to incorporate technology wherever possible, in hopes that it would decrease the costs of the movie's production. Form a team of three people to help determine what technology can be used to assist in the movie's production. One team member should research the type of technology that can be used during the filming process. Another team member should research the types of hardware and software available for editing footage, and the third team member should research the hardware and software requirements for creating the media to distribute the finished product.

Learn How To

The Learn How To activities step you through fundamental technology skills when using a computer. The Learn How To exercises enable you to become more proficient with these skills.

👆 **Premium Activity:** To relate this Learn How To activity to your everyday life, see a visual demonstration of the activity, and then complete a short assessment, visit scsite.com/dc-off07/ch2/howto.

Learn How To 1: Attach a File to an E-Mail Message

When you send an e-mail message, it sometimes is necessary to attach a file to supplement the body of the e-mail message. Most e-mail programs allow you to attach a file to your e-mail messages easily, but many do not allow you to attach files exceeding a specified size limit (which varies by your e-mail service). You can attach a file to an e-mail message by completing the following steps:

1. Start your e-mail program and compose a new e-mail message to your recipient. Make sure that you have a descriptive subject and that you explain in the e-mail message that you are attaching a file.
2. To attach a file, locate and click the Attach File button or link. If you are unable to locate this button, you may find an icon with a picture of a paperclip or a menu command to attach a file. Some e-mail programs also may have a text box in the new message window with an adjacent Browse button. In this case, click the Browse button.
3. Locate and click the file you wish to attach and then click the Open (or Insert or Select) button (Figure 2-24).
4. Verify that your e-mail message contains the attachment and then click the Send button.

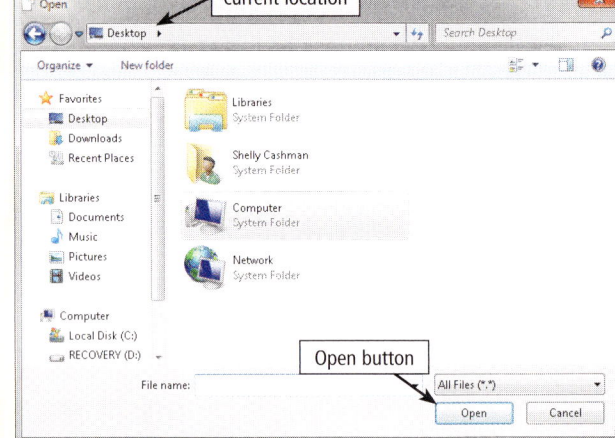

Figure 2-24

When the recipient opens the e-mail message, he or she also will be able to open the attachment.

Exercises

1. Start your e-mail program. Compose a new e-mail message to your instructor, and attach a file containing your current course schedule. Verify that your message has been received and then close your e-mail program.
2. Locate three free e-mail Web applications. How many file attachments do these e-mail programs allow you to attach to one e-mail message? Is a maximum file size specified for an e-mail attachment? Can you pay to upgrade your e-mail account so that these restrictions are lifted? Submit these answers to your instructor.

Learn How To 2: Search the Web for Driving Directions, Addresses, and Telephone Numbers

In addition to searching the Web for information using search engines such as Google and Yahoo!, some Web sites are designed specifically to search for other information such as driving directions, addresses, and telephone numbers.

Search for Driving Directions

1. Start your Web browser, type `mapquest.com` in the Address bar, press the ENTER key to display the MapQuest home page, and then click the Directions tab.
2. Type the starting address (or intersection), city, state, and ZIP code (if you know it) in the appropriate text boxes in the Starting Location area of the Directions page.
3. Type the ending address (or intersection), city, state, and ZIP code (if you know it) in the appropriate text boxes in the Ending Location area of the Directions page.
4. Click the Get Directions button to display the driving directions.

Search for the Address and Telephone Number of a Business

1. If necessary, start your Web browser. Type `yellowpages.com` in the Address bar, and then press the ENTER key to display the Yellow Pages Local Directory home page.

2. Type the name of the business in the Find text box, and type the city, state, and ZIP (if you know it) in the Location text box.
3. Click the FIND button to display the search results.
4. Close your Web browser.

Exercises

1. If necessary, start Internet Explorer by clicking the Start button, and then click Internet Explorer on the Start menu. Type `mapquest.com` in the Address bar, and then press the ENTER key. Search for driving directions between your address and the address of a friend or family member. How many miles are between the two addresses? How long would it take you to drive from your address to the other address? Write a paragraph explaining whether you would or would not use MapQuest to retrieve driving directions. Submit this paragraph to your instructor.

2. Use the Web to search for another Web site that provides driving directions. Use the Web site to search for directions between the same two locations from Exercise 1. Are the driving directions the same as the ones that MapQuest provided? If not, why might they be different? Which Web site did you use? Do you prefer this Web site to MapQuest? Why or why not? Write a paragraph with your answers and submit it to your instructor.

3. Think about a company for which you would like to work. In your Web browser, display the Yellow Pages Web page (yellowpages.com) and then search for the address and telephone number of this company. If Yellow Pages does not display the desired information, what other Web sites might you be able to use to search for the address and telephone number for a company?

Learn It Online

The Learn It Online exercises are interactive Web exercises designed to reinforce and expand your understanding of the chapter concepts. The descriptions below briefly summarize each exercise.

To access the Learn It Online exercise instructions, visit scsite.com/dc-off07/ch2/learn.

1 At the Movies — Tell Your Stories via Vlog
Watch a movie to learn about how to post your thoughts to a vlog and then answer questions about the movie.

2 Student Edition Labs — Connecting to the Internet, Getting the Most out of the Internet, and E-mail
Enhance your understanding and knowledge about the Internet and e-mail by completing the Connecting to the Internet, Getting the Most out of the Internet, and E-mail Labs.

3 Practice Test
Take a multiple choice test that checks your knowledge of the chapter concepts and review the resulting study guide.

4 Who Wants To Be a Computer Genius^2?
Play the Shelly Cashman Series version of this popular game by answering questions to find out if you are a computer genius. Panic buttons are available to provide assistance during game play.

5 Crossword Puzzle Challenge
Complete an interactive crossword puzzle to reinforce concepts presented in this chapter.

6 Windows Exercises
Step through the Windows 7 exercises to learn about Internet properties, dial-up networking connections, and using Help to understand the Internet.

7 Exploring Computer Careers
Read about a career as a Web developer, search for related employment advertisements, and then answer related questions.

8 Web Apps — Windows Live Hotmail
Learn how to sign up for a free e-mail account, add a contact to your address book, and send an e-mail message.

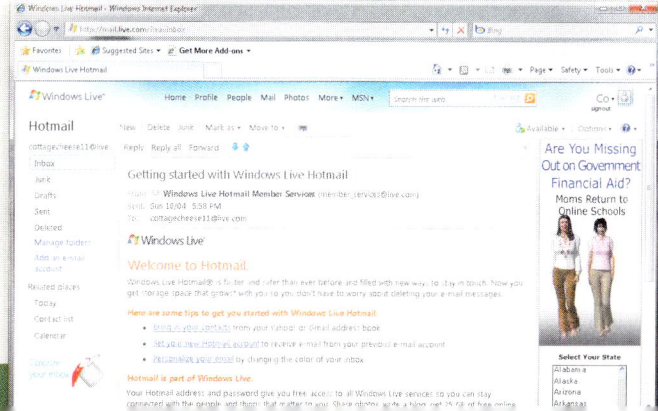

Web Research

The Web Research exercises broaden your understanding of the chapter concepts by presenting questions that require you to search the Web for answers.

☞ To discuss any of the Web Research exercises with other students, visit scsite.com/dc-off07/ch2/forum and post your thoughts or questions.

① Search Sleuth

Use one of the search engines listed in Figure 2-8 in Chapter 2 on page 53 or your own favorite search engine to find the answers to the following questions. Copy and paste the Web address from the Web page where you found the answer. Some questions may have more than one answer. If required, submit your answers to your instructor. (1) What were the title, date of publication, and purpose of the Internet Engineering Task Force's RFC 1 document? (2) What is the mission of the World Wide Web Consortium (W3C)? (3) What topic does the film *Adina's Deck* address? (4) What are the current figures on the Reporters Without Borders' Press Freedom Barometer? (5) What was eBay's original name, and what was the first item offered for auction? (6) Why did ConnectU sue Facebook in 2008 and 2004? (7) What is the cost to use Google's 411 service?

② Green Computing

EcoSearch is a search engine dedicated to supporting the Earth's natural resources. Visit this Web site (ecosearch.org), use your word processing program to answer the following questions, and then, if required, submit your answers to your instructor. (1) From what company do the search results come? (2) Click the Learn More link on the page. What charities does EcoSearch support? (3) How can you get involved to help EcoSearch? (4) Click the EcoSearch Home link at the bottom of the page to return to the EcoSearch home page. In the text box, type `ecosearch donate profits` and then click the Search button. Click several of the resulting links and review the information. Write a 50-word summary of the information, including what percent of EcoSearch proceeds is donated to charities and how much money EcoSearch expects to donate each year.

③ Social Networking

MySpace is considered one of the pioneering Web sites that helped popularize the online social networking phenomenon. Calling itself "a place for friends," it allows the millions of registered members to create profiles for free and then invite friends to join their networks. The growth of this Web site has helped it emerge as one of the more popular search engines. Visit the MySpace site (myspace.com), type the name of your favorite musical artist or group in the search text box, and then click the Search button. How many search results were found? Visit some of these profiles. Which music videos, playlists, and ringtones are featured? How do you create and edit your own playlists and add a song to your profile? Then click the Safety Tips link at the bottom of the page and read the guidelines for posting information and reporting inappropriate content. Summarize the music profiles you viewed and the guidelines. If required, submit your summary to your instructor.

④ Blogs

Many of the best blogs in the blogosphere have received awards for their content and design. For example, loyal blogging fans nominate and vote for their favorite blogs by visiting the Blogger's Choice Awards Web site (bloggerschoiceawards.com). Visit this Web site, click the Best Blog Design, Best Blog About Blogging, and Best Education Blog links, and view some of the blogs receiving the largest number of votes. Then visit other award sites, including the Interactive Media Awards (interactivemediaawards.com), Bloggies (bloggies.com), and the Best of Blogs (thebestofblogs.com). Which blogs, if any, received multiple awards on the different Web sites? Who casts the votes? What criteria are used to judge these blogs?

⑤ Ethics in Action

Some Internet access providers have admitted they monitored their users' Web surfing activities without giving notice of this eavesdropping practice. Embarq and Charter Communications secretly tested advertising technology to gather data about specific Web searches and then display advertisements relating to these searches. Privacy experts claim these Internet access providers' practices violate federal privacy laws, including the wiretapping statute. Locate news articles discussing the Internet access providers' Web eavesdropping. Then locate Web sites that oppose this practice. Summarize the views of the advertisers and the privacy proponents. If required, submit your summary to your instructor.

Special Feature

Making Use of the Web

INFORMATION LITERACY IS DEFINED as having the practical skills needed to evaluate information critically from print and electronic resources and to use this information accurately in daily life. Locating Web sites may be profitable for your educational and professional careers, as the resources may help you research class assignments and make your life more fulfilling and manageable.

Because the Web does not have an organizational structure to assist you in locating reliable material, you may need additional resources to guide you in searching. To help you find useful Web sites, this Special Feature describes specific information about a variety of Web pages, and it includes tables of Web addresses so that you can get started. The material is organized in several areas of interest.

Web Exercises at the end of each area will reinforce the material and help you discover Web sites that may add a treasure trove of knowledge to your life.

Areas of Interest

Fun and Entertainment	Shopping and Auctions
Research	Weather, Sports, and News
Blogs	Learning
Online Social Networks and Media Sharing	Science
Travel	Health
Environment	Careers
Finance	Literature and Arts
Government	

Fun and Entertainment

That's Entertainment

Rock 'n' Roll on the Web

Consumers place great significance on buying entertainment products for fun and recreation. Nearly 10 percent of the United States's economy is spent on attending concerts and buying optical discs, reading materials, sporting goods, and toys.

Many Web sites supplement our cravings for fun and entertainment. For example, you can see and hear the musicians inducted into the Rock and Roll Hall of Fame and Museum. If you need an update on your favorite reality-based television program or a preview of an upcoming movie, E! Online and Entertainment Weekly provide the latest features about actors and actresses. The Internet Movie Database contains reviews of more than one million titles (Figure 1).

Watch the surfers riding the waves and romp with pandas at the San Diego Zoo. Web cams can display live video on Web pages, taking armchair travelers across the world for views of natural attractions, monuments, and cities. Many Web sites featuring Web cams are listed in the table in Figure 2.

Fun and Entertainment Web Sites

Entertainment	Web Address
allmusic	allmusic.com
E! Online	eonline.com
Entertainment Weekly's EW	ew.com/ew
Games.com	games.com
Internet Movie Database	imdb.com
Old Time Radio (OTR) — Radio Days: A Radio History	otr.com
Rock and Roll Hall of Fame and Museum	rockhall.com
World Radio Network	wrn.org
Yahoo! Entertainment	entertainment.yahoo.com

Web Cams	Web Address
Camvista	camvista.com
Discovery Kids — Live Cams	kids.discovery.com/cams/cams.html
EarthCam — Webcam Network	earthcam.com
ESRL/GMD Mauna Loa Live Camera	esrl.noaa.gov/gmd/obop/mlo/livecamera.html
Gatorland	gatorland.com/gatorcam.php
Geocaching — The Official Global GPS Cache Hunt Site	geocaching.com
Panda Cam San Diego Zoo	sandiegozoo.org/zoo/ex_panda_station.html
WebCam Central	camcentral.com
Wild Birds Unlimited Bird FeederCam	wbu.com/feedercam_home.html

👆 For more information about fun and entertainment Web sites, visit scsite.com/dc-off07/ch2/web.

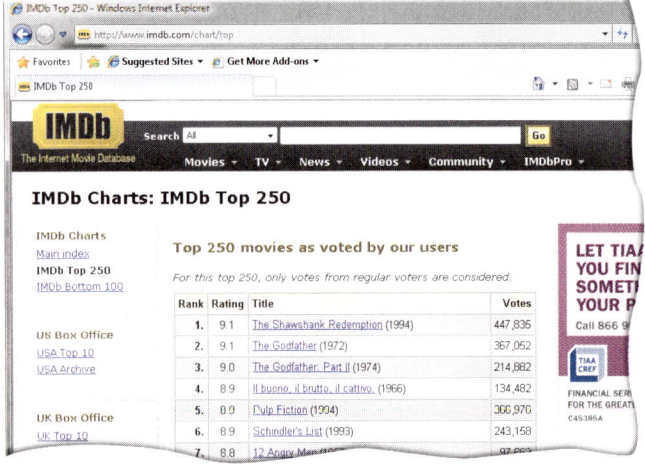

Figure 1 Visitors exploring the Internet Movie Database will find the latest news about their favorite television programs and movies.

Figure 2 When you visit Web sites offering fun and entertainment resources, you can be both amused and informed.

Fun and Entertainment Web Exercises

1 **Visit the Geocaching site listed in Figure 2.** Find the geocaches within five miles of your home or school and then print a map showing their locations. Then, visit the Discovery Kids — Live Cams Web site and view one of the animal cams in the Live Cams. What do you observe? Visit another Web site listed in Figure 2 and describe the view. What are the benefits of having Web cams at these locations throughout the world?

2 **What are your favorite movies?** Use the Internet Movie Database Web site listed in Figure 2 to search for information about two films, and write a brief description of the biographies of the major stars and director for each movie. Then, visit one of the entertainment Web sites and describe three of the featured stories. At the Rock and Roll Hall of Fame and Museum Web site, view the information about The Beatles and one of your favorite musicians. Write a paragraph describing the information available about these rock stars.

Research
Search and Ye Shall Find

Information on the Web

A recent Web Usability survey conducted by the Nielsen Norman Group found that 88 percent of people who connect to the Internet use a search engine as their first online action. Search engines require users to type words and phrases that characterize the information being sought. Bing (Figure 3), Google, and AltaVista are some of the more popular search engines. The key to effective searching on the Web is composing search queries that narrow the search results and place the more relevant Web sites at the top of the results list.

Keep up with the latest computer and related product developments by viewing online dictionaries and encyclopedias that add to their collections on a regular basis. Shopping for a new computer can be a daunting experience, but many online guides can help you select the components that best fit your needs and budget. If you are not confident in your ability to solve a problem alone, turn to online technical support. Hardware and software reviews, price comparisons, shareware, technical questions and answers, and breaking technology news are found on comprehensive portals. Figure 4 lists popular research Web sites.

Research Web Sites

Research	Web Address
A9.com	a9.com
AccessMyLibrary	accessmylibrary.com
AltaVista	altavista.com
Answers.com	answers.com
Ask	ask.com
Bing	bing.com
ChaCha	chacha.com
CNET	cnet.com
eHow	ehow.com
Google	google.com
HotBot	hotbot.com
Librarians' Internet Index	lii.org
PC911	pcnineoneone.com
Switchboard	switchboard.com
Webopedia	webopedia.com
ZDNet	zdnet.com

For more information about research Web sites, visit scsite.com/dc-off07/ch2/web.

Figure 3 The Bing Web site provides a search engine for images, videos, shopping, news, maps, and travel.

Figure 4 Web users can find information by using research Web sites.

Research Web Exercises

1. Visit two of the research Web sites listed in Figure 4 to find three Web sites that review the latest digital cameras from Kodak and Canon. Make a table listing the research Web sites, the located Web site names, and the cameras' model numbers, suggested retail price, and features.

2. Visit the Webopedia Web site. Search this site for five terms of your choice. Create a table with two columns: one for the term and one for the Web definition. Then, create a second table listing five recently added or updated words and their definitions on this Web site. Next, visit the CNET Web site to choose the components you would buy if you were building a customized desktop computer and notebook computer. Create a table for both computers, listing the computer manufacturer, processor model name or number and manufacturer, clock speed, RAM, cache, number of expansion slots, and number of bays.

Blogs
Express Yourself

Blogosphere Growing Swiftly

Internet users are feeling the need to publish their views, and they are finding Weblogs, or blogs for short, the ideal vehicle. The blogosphere began as an easy way for individuals to express their opinions on the Web. Today, this communications vehicle has become a powerful tool, for individuals, groups, and corporations are using blogs to promote their ideas and advertise their products. It is not necessary to have a background in Web design to be able to post to a blog.

Bloggers generally update their Web sites frequently to reflect their views. Their posts range from a paragraph to an entire essay and often contain links to other Web sites. The more popular blogs discuss politics, lifestyles, and technology.

Individuals easily may set up a blog free or for a fee, using Web sites such as Blogger, Bloglines (Figure 5), and TypePad. In addition, online social networks may have a built-in blogging feature. Be cautious of the information you post on your blog, especially if it is accessible to everyone online.

Corporate blogs, such as The GM FastLane Blog, discuss all aspects of the company's products, whereas all-encompassing blogs, such as the MetaFilter Community Weblog and others in Figure 6, are designed to keep general readers entertained and informed.

Blogs are affecting the manner in which people communicate, and some experts predict they will one day become our primary method of sharing information.

Blogs Web Sites

Blog	Web Address
A List Apart	alistapart.com
Blog.com	blog.com
Blog Flux	topsites.blogflux.com
Blogger	blogger.com
Bloglines	bloglines.com
Blogstream	blogstream.com
Davenetics*Remote Control Revolutionary	davenetics.com
Geek News Central	geeknewscentral.com
GM FastLane Blog	fastlane.gmblogs.com
kottke.org	kottke.org
MetaFilter Community Weblog	metafilter.com
Rocketboom	rocketboom.com
TreeHugger	treehuggertv.com
Twitter	twitter.com
TypePad	typepad.com

For more information about blogs Web sites, visit scsite.com/dc-off07/ch2/web.

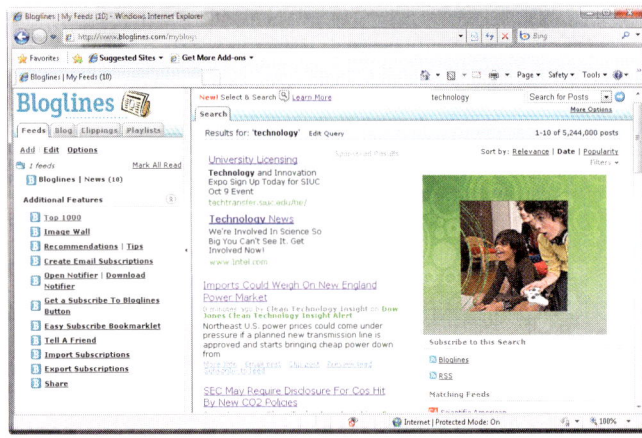

Figure 5 Bloglines keeps readers abreast of the latest technology, entertainment, and political news in the blogosphere.

Figure 6 These blogs offer information about technology, news, politics, and entertainment.

Blogs Web Exercises

1 Visit three of the blog Web sites listed in Figure 6. Make a table listing the blog name, its purpose, the author, its audience, and advertisers, if any, who sponsor the blog. Then, write a paragraph that describes the information you found on each of these blogs.

2 Many Internet users read the technology blogs to keep abreast of the latest developments. Visit the Geek News Central and Bloglines blogs listed in Figure 6 and write a paragraph describing the top story in each blog. Read the posted comments, if any. Then, write another paragraph describing two other stories found on these blogs that cover material you have discussed in this course. Write a third paragraph discussing which one is more interesting to you. Would you add reading blogs to your list of Internet activities? Why or why not?

Online Social Networks and Media Sharing
Check Out My New Photos

Online Social Networks and Media Sharing Web Sites Gain Popularity

Do you ever wonder what your friends are doing? What about your friends' friends? The popularity of online social networks has increased dramatically in recent years. Online social networks, such as those listed in Figure 7, allow you to create a personalized profile that others are able to view online. These profiles may include information about you such as your hometown, your age, your hobbies, and pictures. You also may create links to your friends' pages, post messages for individual friends, or bulletins for all of your friends to see. Online social networks are great places to keep in touch with your friends and to network with professionals for business purposes.

If you would like to post pictures and videos and do not require the full functionality of an online social network, you might consider a media sharing Web site, which is a type of online social network. Media sharing Web sites such as YouTube and Phanfare (Figure 8) allow you to post media, including photos and videos, for others to view, print, and/or download. Media sharing Web sites, which may be free or charge a fee, provide a quick, efficient way to share photos of your last vacation or videos of your family reunion.

Online Social Networks and Media Sharing	
Online Social Networks	**Web Address**
Club Penguin	clubpenguin.com
Facebook	facebook.com
LinkedIn	linkedin.com
MySpace — a place for friends	myspace.com
orkut	orkut.com
Windows Live Spaces	spaces.live.com
Media Sharing	**Web Address**
flickr	flickr.com
Phanfare	phanfare.com
Photobucket	photobucket.com
Picasa	picasa.com
Shutterfly	shutterfly.com
Yahoo! Video	video.yahoo.com
YouTube	youtube.com

For more information about online social networks and media sharing Web sites, visit scsite.com/dc-off07/ch2/web.

Figure 7 Online social networks and media sharing Web sites are popular ways to keep in touch with friends, meet new people, and share media.

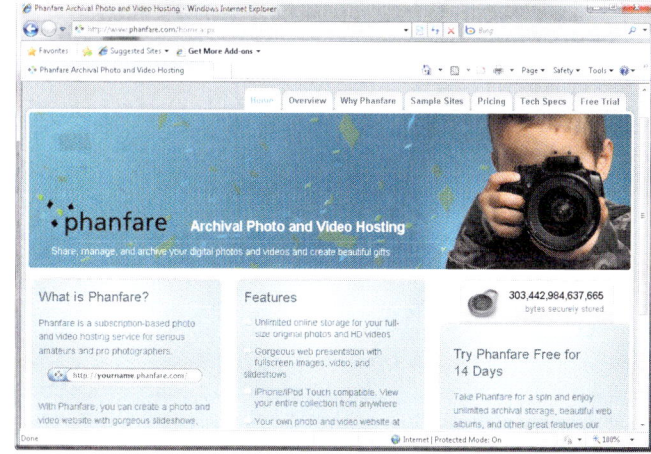

Figure 8 The Phanfare Web site allows users to share their photo and video files with people throughout the world.

Online Social Networks and Media Sharing Web Exercises

1. **Many individuals now use online social networks.** Visit two online social networks listed in Figure 7. (If you are attempting to access an online social network from your classroom and are unable to do so, your school may have restricted use of social networking Web sites.) Compare and contrast these two sites by performing the following actions and recording your findings. First, create a profile on each of these sites. If you find a Web site that charges a fee to sign up, choose another Web site. How easy is the sign-up process? Does either Web site ask for any personal information you are uncomfortable sharing? If so, what information? Once you sign up, make a list of five of your closest friends, and search for their profiles on each of these two sites. Which site contains more of your friends? Browse each site and make a list of its features. In your opinion, which site is better? Explain why.

2. **Media sharing Web sites make it easy to share photos and videos with friends, family, and colleagues.** Before choosing a media sharing Web site to use, do some research. Visit two media sharing Web sites in Figure 7. Is there a fee to post media to these Web sites? If so, how much? Are these Web sites supported by advertisements? Locate the instructions for posting media to these Web sites. Are the instructions straightforward? Do these Web sites impose a limit on the number and/or size of media files you can post? Summarize your responses to these questions in two or three paragraphs.

Travel
Get Packing!

Explore the World without Leaving Home

When you are ready to arrange your next travel adventure or just want to explore destination possibilities, the Internet provides ample resources to set your plans in motion.

To discover exactly where your destination is on this planet, cartography Web sites, including MapQuest and Yahoo! Maps, allow you to pinpoint your destination. View your exact destination using satellite imagery with Google Maps and Bing Maps (Figure 9).

Some excellent starting places are general travel Web sites such as Expedia Travel, Cheap Tickets, Orbitz, and Travelocity. Many airline Web sites allow you to reserve hotel rooms, activities, and rental cars while booking a flight. These all-encompassing Web sites, including those in Figure 10, have tools to help you find the lowest prices and details about flights, car rentals, cruises, and hotels. Comprehensive online guidebooks can provide useful details about maximizing your vacation time while saving money.

Travel Web Sites	
General Travel	**Web Address**
CheapTickets	cheaptickets.com
Expedia Travel	expedia.com
Kayak	kayak.com
Orbitz	orbitz.com
SideStep	sidestep.com
Travelocity	travelocity.com
Cartography	**Web Address**
Bing Maps	bing.com/maps
Google Maps	maps.google.com
MapQuest	mapquest.com
Maps.com	maps.com
Yahoo! Maps	maps.yahoo.com
Travel and City Guides	**Web Address**
Frommer's Travel Guides	frommers.com
GoPlanit	goplanit.com
U.S.-Parks US National Parks Travel Guide	www.us-parks.com
Virtual Tourist	virtualtourist.com

👉 For more information about travel Web sites, visit scsite.com/dc-off07/ch2/web.

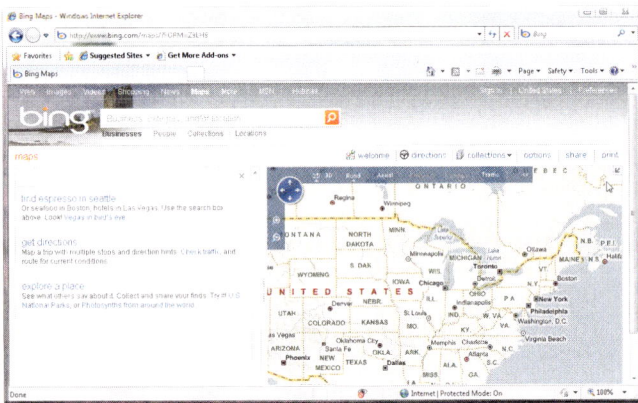

Figure 9 Bing Maps provides location information and satellite imagery for many regions on this planet.

Figure 10 These travel resources Web sites offer travel information to exciting destinations throughout the world.

Travel Web Exercises

1 Visit one of the cartography Web sites listed in Figure 10 and obtain the directions from your campus to one of these destinations: the Washington Monument in Washington, D.C.; the Statue of Liberty on Ellis Island in New York; Disneyland in Anaheim, California; or the Grand Old Opry in Nashville, Tennessee. How many miles is it to your destination? What is the estimated driving time? Use the Google Maps Web site to obtain an overhead image of this destination. Then, visit one of the general travel Web sites listed in the table and plan a flight from the nearest major airport to one of the four destinations for the week after finals and a return trip one week later. Which airline, flight numbers, and departure and arrival times did you select?

2 Visit one of the travel and city guides Web sites listed in Figure 10, and choose a destination for a getaway this coming weekend. Write a one-page paper giving details about this location, such as popular hotels and lodging, expected weather, population, local colleges and universities, parks spd recreation, ancient and modern history, and tours. Include a map or satellite photo of this place. Why did you select this destination? How would you travel there and back? What is the breakdown of expected costs for this weekend, including travel expenditures, meals, lodging, and tickets to events and activities? Which Web addresses did you use to complete this exercise?

Environment
The Future of the Planet

Making a Difference for Earth

From the rain forests of Africa to the marine life in the Pacific Ocean, the fragile ecosystem is under extreme stress. Many environmental groups have developed informative Web sites, including those listed in Figure 11, in attempts to educate worldwide populations and to increase resource conservation. The Environmental Defense Fund Web site (Figure 12) contains information for people who would like to help safeguard the environment.

On an international scale, the Environmental Sites on the Internet Web page developed by the Royal Institute of Technology in Stockholm, Sweden, has been rated as one of the better ecological Web sites. Its comprehensive listing of environmental concerns range from aquatic ecology to wetlands.

The U.S. federal government has a number of Web sites devoted to specific environmental concerns. For example, the U.S. Environmental Protection Agency (EPA) provides pollution data, including ozone levels and air pollutants, for specific areas. Its AirData Web site displays air pollution emissions and monitoring data from the entire United States and is the world's most extensive collection of air pollution data.

Environment Web Sites

Name	Web Address
Central African Regional Program for the Environment (CARPE)	carpe.umd.edu
Earthjustice	earthjustice.org
EarthTrends: Environmental Information	earthtrends.wri.org
Environmental Defense Fund	edf.org
Environmental Sites on the Internet	www.ima.kth.se/im/envsite/envsite.htm
EPA AirData — Access to Air Pollution Data	epa.gov/air/data
Global Warming	globalwarming.org
Green Computing Impact Organization	gcio.org
GreenNet	gn.apc.org
New American Dream	newdream.org
University of Wisconsin — Milwaukee Environmental Health and Safety Resources	uwm.edu/Dept/EHSRM/EHSLINKS
USGS Branch of Quality Systems	bqs.usgs.gov/acidrain

For more information about environment Web sites, visit scsite.com/dc-off07/ch2/web.

Figure 11 Environment Web sites provide vast resources for ecological data and action groups.

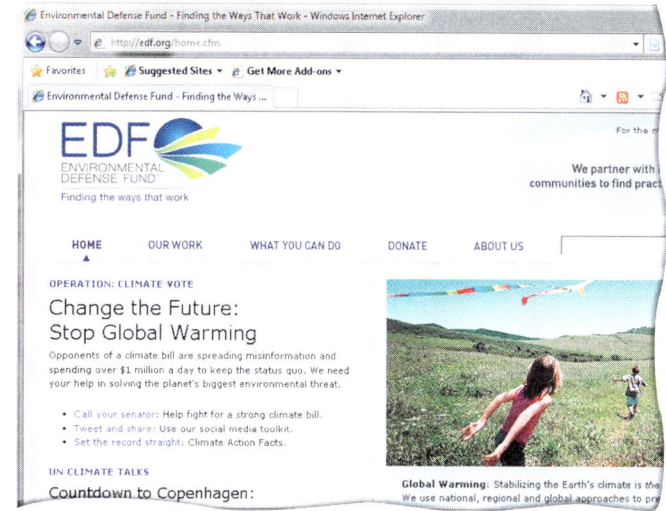

Figure 12 A visit to the Environmental Defense Fund Web site provides practical advice about protecting the environment.

Environment Web Exercises

1 **The New American Dream Web site encourages consumers to reduce the amount of junk mail sent to their homes.** Using the table in Figure 11, visit the Web site to learn how many trees are leveled each year to provide paper for these mailings and how many garbage trucks are needed to haul this waste. Read the letters used to eliminate names from bulk mail lists. To whom would you mail these letters? How long does it take to stop these unsolicited letters?

2 **Visit the EPA AirData Web site.** What is the highest ozone level recorded in your state this past year? Where are the nearest air pollution monitoring Web sites, and what are their levels? Where are the nearest sources of air pollution? Read two reports about two different topics, such as acid rain and air quality, and summarize their findings. Include information about who sponsored the research, who conducted the studies, when the data was collected, and the impact of this pollution on the atmosphere, water, forests, and human health. Whom would you contact for further information regarding the data and studies?

Finance
Money Matters

Cashing In on Financial Advice

You can manage your money with advice from financial Web sites that offer online banking, tax help, personal finance, and small business and commercial services.

If you do not have a personal banker or a financial planner, consider a Web adviser to guide your investment decisions. The MSN Money Web site (Figure 13) provides financial news and investment information.

If you are ready to ride the ups and downs of the Dow and the NASDAQ, an abundance of Web sites listed in Figure 14, including Reuters and Morningstar, can help you select companies that fit your interests and financial needs.

Claiming to be the fastest, easiest tax publication on the planet, the Internal Revenue Service Web site contains procedures for filing tax appeals and contains IRS forms, publications, and legal regulations.

Finance Web Sites	
Advice and Education	**Web Address**
Bankrate	bankrate.com
ING Direct	ingdirect.com
LendingTree	lendingtree.com
Loan.com	loan.com
The Motley Fool	fool.com
MSN Money	moneycentral.msn.com
Wells Fargo	wellsfargo.com
Yahoo! Finance	finance.yahoo.com
Stock Market	**Web Address**
E*TRADE	us.etrade.com
Financial Engines	financialengines.com
Merrill Lynch	ml.com
Morningstar	morningstar.com
Reuters	reuters.com/investing
Valic	valic.com
Vanguard	vanguard.com
Taxes	**Web Address**
H&R Block	hrblock.com
Internal Revenue Service	www.irs.gov
Jackson Hewitt	jacksonhewitt.com
Liberty Tax Service	libertytax.com

For more information about finance Web sites, visit scsite.com/dc-off07/ch2/web.

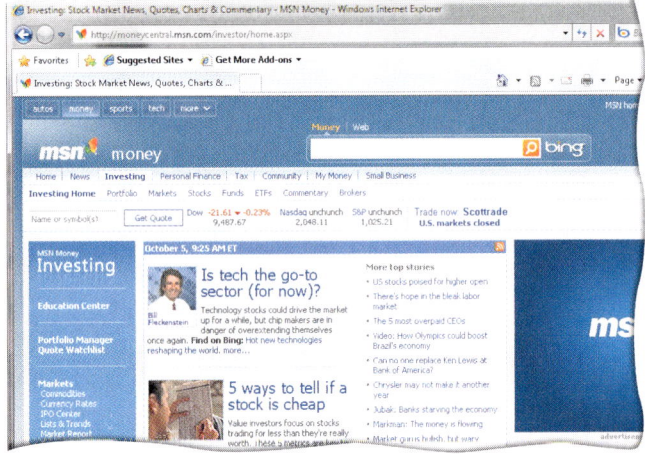

Figure 13 The MSN Money Web site contains features and information related to college and family finances.

Figure 14 Financial resources Web sites offer general information, stock market analyses, and tax advice, as well as guidance and money-saving tips.

Finance Web Exercises

1. **Visit three advice and education Web sites listed in Figure 14** and read their top business world reports. Write a paragraph about each, summarizing these stories. Which stocks or mutual funds do these Web sites predict as being sound investments today? What are the current market indexes for the DJIA (Dow Jones Industrial Average), S&P 500, and NASDAQ, and how do these figures compare with the previous day's numbers?

2. **Using two of the stock market Web sites listed in Figure 14,** search for information about Microsoft, Apple, and one other software vendor. Write a paragraph about each of these stocks describing the revenues, net incomes, total assets for the previous year, current stock price per share, highest and lowest prices of each stock during the past year, and other relevant investment information.

Government
Stamp of Approval

Making a Federal Case for Useful Information

When it is time to buy stamps to mail your correspondence, you no longer need to wait in long lines at your local post office. The U.S. Postal Service has authorized several organizations to sell stamps online.

You can recognize U.S. Government Web sites on the Internet by their gov top-level domain. For example, the Library of Congress Web site is loc.gov (Figure 15). Government and military Web sites offer a wide range of information. The Time Service Department Web site will provide you with the correct time. If you are looking for a federal document, FedWorld lists thousands of documents distributed by the government on its Web site. For access to the names of your congressional representatives, visit the extensive HG.org Web site. Figure 16 shows some of the more popular U.S. Government Web sites.

Government Resources Web Sites

Postage	Web Address
Endicia	endicia.com
Pitney Bowes	pb.com
Stamps.com	stamps.com

Government	Web Address
FedWorld	www.fedworld.gov
HG.org — Worldwide Legal Directories	hg.org
Library of Congress	loc.gov
National Agricultural Library	nal.usda.gov
Smithsonian Institution	smithsonian.org
THOMAS (Library of Congress)	thomas.loc.gov
Time Service Department	tycho.usno.navy.mil
U.S. Department of Education	ed.gov
United States Department of the Treasury	treas.gov
U.S. Government Printing Office	www.access.gpo.gov
United States National Library of Medicine	nlm.nih.gov
United States Patent and Trademark Office	uspto.gov
USAJOBS	usajobs.opm.gov
The White House	whitehouse.gov

For more information about government Web sites, visit scsite.com/dc-off07/ch2/web.

Figure 16 These Web sites offer information about buying U.S.-approved postage online and researching federal agencies.

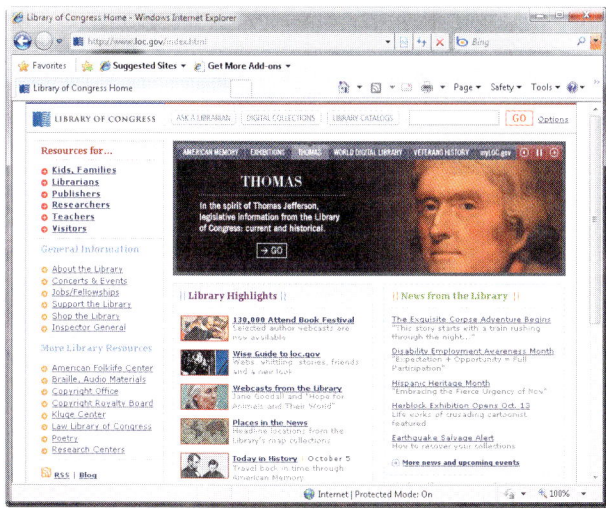

Figure 15 The Library of Congress Web site has resources about American history, world culture, and digital preservation.

Government Web Exercises

1 View the three postage Web sites listed in Figure 16. Compare and contrast the available services on each one. Consider postage cost, necessary equipment, shipping services, security techniques, and tracking capability. Explain why you would or would not like to use this service.

2 Visit the HG.org Web site listed in Figure 16. What are the names, addresses, and phone numbers of your two state senators and your local congressional representative? On what committees do they serve? Who is the chief justice of the Supreme Court, and what has been this justice's opinion on two recently decided cases? Who are the members of the president's cabinet? Then, visit two other Web sites listed in Figure 16. Write a paragraph about each Web site describing its content and features.

Shopping and Auctions
Bargains Galore

Let Your Mouse Do Your Shopping

From groceries to clothing to computers, you can buy just about everything you need with just a few clicks of your mouse. More than one-half of Internet users will make at least one online purchase this year. Books, computer software and hardware, and music are the hottest commodities.

The two categories of Internet shopping Web sites are those with physical counterparts, such as Walmart and Fry's Electronics (Figure 17), and those with only a Web presence, such as Amazon and Buy. Popular Web shopping sites are listed in Figure 18.

Another method of shopping for the items you need, and maybe some you really do not need, is to visit auction Web sites, including those listed in Figure 18. Categories include antiques and collectibles, automotive, computers, electronics, music, sports, sports cards and memorabilia, and toys. Online auction Web sites can offer unusual items, including *Star Wars* memorabilia or a round of golf with Tiger Woods. eBay is one of thousands of Internet auction Web sites and is the world's largest personal online trading community. In addition, craigslist is a free online equivalent of classified advertisements.

Shopping and Auctions Web Sites

Auctions	Web Address
craigslist	craigslist.org
eBay	ebay.com
Sotheby's	sothebys.com
uBid	ubid.com
U.S. Treasury — Seized Property Auctions	ustreas.gov/auctions

Books and Music	Web Address
Amazon	amazon.com
Barnes & Noble	bn.com
BookFinder	bookfinder.com

Computers and Electronics	Web Address
BestBuy	bestbuy.com
Buy	buy.com
Fry's Electronics	frys.com

Miscellaneous	Web Address
drugstore	drugstore.com
Google Product Search	google.com/products
SmashBuys	smashbuys.com
Walmart	walmart.com

For more information about shopping and auctions Web sites, visit scsite.com/dc-off07/ch2/web.

Figure 17 Fry's is a popular electronic retailer that sells a variety of products.

Figure 18 Making online purchases can help ease the burden of driving to and fighting the crowds in local malls.

Shopping and Auctions Web Exercises

1. **Visit two of the computers and electronics and two of the miscellaneous Web sites listed in Figure 18.** Write a paragraph describing the features these Web sites offer compared with the same offerings from stores. In another paragraph, describe any disadvantages of shopping at these Web sites instead of actually visiting a store. Then, describe their policies for returning unwanted merchandise and for handling complaints.

2. **Using one of the auction Web sites listed in Figure 18, search for two objects pertaining to your hobbies.** For example, if you are a sports fan, you can search for a complete set of Upper Deck cards. If you are a car buff, search for your dream car. Describe these two items. How many people have bid on these items? Who are the sellers? What are the opening and current bids?

Weather, Sports, and News
What's News?

Weather, Sports, and News Web Sites Score Big Hits

Rain or sun? Hot or cold? Weather is the leading online news item, with at least 10,000 Web sites devoted to this field. Millions of people view The Weather Channel Web site (Figure 19) each month.

Baseball may be the national pastime, but sports aficionados yearn for everything from auto racing to cricket. The Internet has millions of pages of multimedia sports news, entertainment, and merchandise.

The Internet has emerged as a major source for news, with more than one-third of Americans going online at least once a week and 15 percent going online daily for reports of major news events. Many of these viewers are using RSS (Really Simple Syndication) technology to be notified when new stories about their favorite topics are available on the Internet. Popular weather, sports, and news Web sites are listed in Figure 20.

Weather, Sports, and News Web Sites

Weather	Web Address
AccuWeather	accuweather.com
Infoplease Weather	infoplease.com/weather.html
Intellicast	www.intellicast.com
National Weather Service	www.crh.noaa.gov
The Weather Channel	weather.com

Sports	Web Address
CBS Sports	cbssports.com
ESPN	espn.com
NASCAR	nascar.com
International Olympic Committee	www.olympic.org
Sporting News Radio	radio.sportingnews.com
Yahoo! Sports	sports.yahoo.com

News	Web Address
FactCheck	factcheck.org
Geek.com	geek.com
Google News	news.google.com
MSNBC	msnbc.com
Onlinenewspapers	onlinenewspapers.com
privacy.org	privacy.org
SiliconValley	siliconvalley.com
starting page	startingpage.com/html/news.html
USA TODAY	usatoday.com
Washington Post	washingtonpost.com

For more information about weather, sports, and news Web sites, visit scsite.com/dc-off07/ch2/web.

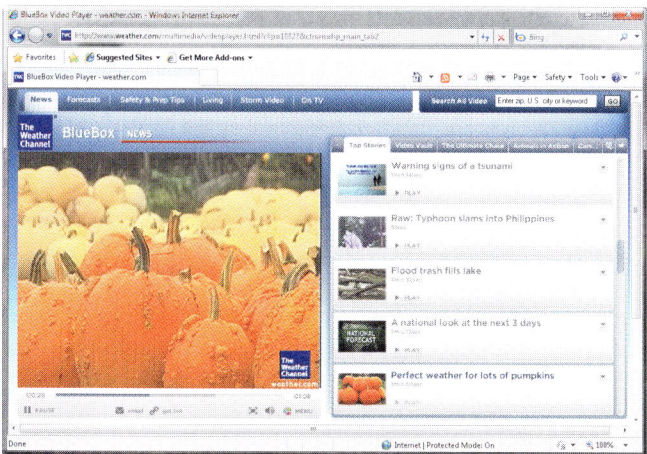

Figure 19 Local, national, and international weather conditions and details about breaking weather stories are available on The Weather Channel Web site.

Figure 20 Keep informed about the latest weather, sports, and news events with these Web sites.

Weather, Sports, and News Web Exercises

1 Visit two of the sports Web sites in Figure 20 and write a paragraph describing the content these Web sites provide concerning your favorite sport. Visit Google News and then search for stories about this sports team or athlete. Then, create a customized news page with stories about your sports interests. Include RSS feeds to get regularly updated summaries on this subject.

2 Visit the Onlinenewspapers and starting page Web sites listed in Figure 20 and select two newspapers from each site. Write a paragraph describing the top national news story featured in each of these four Web pages. Then, write another paragraph describing the top international news story displayed at each Web site. In the third paragraph, discuss which of the four Web sites is the most interesting in terms of story selection, photos, and Web page design.

Special Feature

Learning
Yearn to Learn

Discover New Worlds Online

While you may believe your education ends when you finally graduate from college, learning is a lifelong process. You can increase your technological knowledge by visiting several Web sites (Figure 21) with tutorials about building your own Web sites, the latest news about the Internet, and resources for visually impaired users.

Learning Web Sites	
Learning How To's	**Web Address**
Bartleby: Great Books Online	bartleby.com
AT&T Knowledge Network Explorer	www.kn.pacbell.com/wired
BBC Learning	bbc.co.uk/learning
CBT Nuggets	cbtnuggets.com
HowStuffWorks	howstuffworks.com
Internet Public Library	ipl.org
Learn the Net	learnthenet.com
ScienceMaster	sciencemaster.com
Search Engine Watch	searchenginewatch.com
Wiredguide	wiredguide.com
Cooking	**Web Address**
Betty Crocker	bettycrocker.com
Chef2Chef	chef2chef.net
Food Network	foodnetwork.com

For more information about learning Web sites, visit scsite.com/dc-off07/ch2/web.

Figure 21 The information gleaned from these Web sites can help you learn about many aspects of our existence.

The HowStuffWorks Web site has won numerous awards for its clear, comprehensive articles that demystify aspects of our everyday life. It includes ratings and reviews of products written by *Consumer Guide* editors.

A consortium of colleges maintains the Internet Public Library, which includes subject collections, reference materials, and a reading room filled with magazines and books. Volunteer librarians will answer your personal questions asked in its Ask an IPL Librarian form.

Enhancing your culinary skills can be a rewarding endeavor. No matter if you are a gourmet chef or a weekend cook, you will be cooking in style with the help of online resources, including those listed in Figure 21.

Have you ever wondered how to make a key lime pie? How about learning how to cook some easy, low-calorie dishes? Are you seeking advice from expert chefs? The Food Network Web site (Figure 22) is filled with information related to cooking, grilling, and healthy eating.

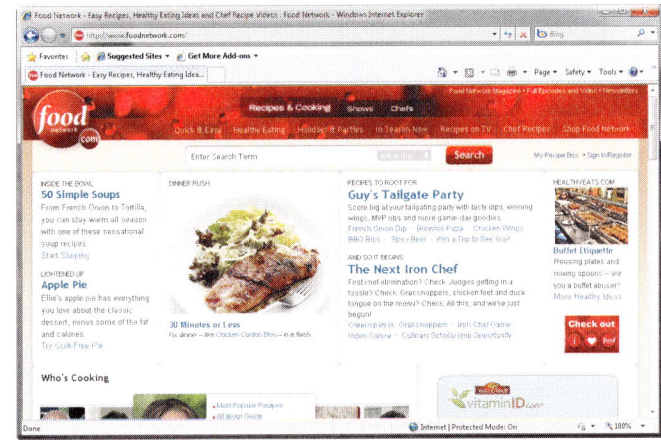

Figure 22 The Food Network Web site provides access to healthy recipes, grilling tips, and cookware.

Learning Web Exercises

1. **Using one of the Learning How To's Web sites listed in Figure 21,** search for information about installing memory in a computer. Write a paragraph about your findings. Then, review the material in the HowStuffWorks Web site listed in Figure 21, and write a paragraph describing articles on this Web site that are pertinent to your major.

2. **Visit one of the cooking Web sites listed in Figure 21** and find two recipes or cooking tips that you can use when preparing your next meal. Write a paragraph about each one, summarizing your discoveries. Which Web sites allow you to create your own online recipe book? What are the advantages and disadvantages of accessing these Web sites on the new appliances and gadgets that might someday be in your kitchen?

Science
$E = mc^2$

Rocket Science on the Web

For some people, space exploration is a hobby. Building and launching model rockets allow these at-home scientists to participate in exploring the great frontier of space. For others, space exploration is their life. Numerous Web sites, including those in Figure 23, provide in-depth information about the universe.

NASA's Web site contains information about rockets, space exploration, the International Space Station, space transportation, and communications. Other science resources explore space-related questions about astronomy, physics, the earth sciences, microgravity, and robotics.

Rockets and space are not the only areas to explore in the world of science. Where can you find the latest pictures taken with the Hubble Space Telescope? Do you know how climate change is affecting the human body? You can find the answers to these questions and many others through the New Scientist Web site (newscientist.com) shown in Figure 24.

The National Science Foundation's Web site features overviews of current topics and an extensive Multimedia Gallery with audio and video files, photos, and paintings.

Science.gov is an outstanding resource for scientific databases and thousands of authoritative science Web sites. The U.S. government science information provided offers 200 million pages of research, with search results ranked by relevance and sorted by topic and year.

Science Web Sites

Periodicals	Web Address
Archaeology Magazine	archaeology.org
Astronomy Magazine	astronomy.com
New Scientist	newscientist.com
OceanLink	oceanlink.island.net
Science Magazine	sciencemag.org
Scientific American	sciam.com

Resources	Web Address
National Science Foundation (NSF)	nsf.gov
Science.gov: USA.gov for Science	science.gov
Thomson Reuters	scientific.thomson.com/free/

Science Community	Web Address
American Scientist	amsci.org
Federation of American Scientists	fas.org
NASA	www.nasa.gov
Sigma Xi, The Scientific Research Society	sigmaxi.org

For more information about science Web sites, visit scsite.com/dc-off07/ch2/web.

Figure 23 Resources available on the Internet offer a wide range of subjects for enthusiasts who want to delve into familiar and unknown territories in the world of science.

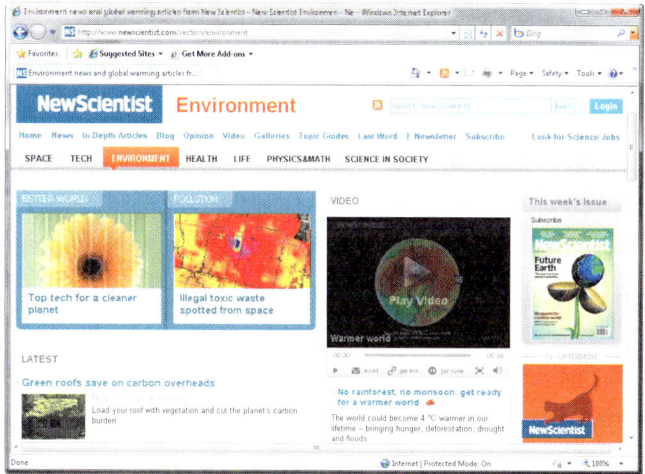

Figure 24 The New Scientist Web site covers news about space exploration, the environment, and technology.

Science Web Exercises

1. **Visit the National Science Foundation Web site listed in the table in Figure 23.** What are the topics of the latest science news and special reports? Which speeches and lectures are featured? What are the titles of image, video, and audio files in the Multimedia Gallery?

2. **Visit the NASA Web site listed in the table in Figure 23.** Click the Missions link and then click the Mission Calendar link. When are the next two launches scheduled? What are the purposes of these missions? Click the Careers @ NASA topic and then write a paragraph describing the internships, cooperative programs, and summer employment opportunities. Then, view two of the science community Web sites listed in Figure 23 and write a paragraph about each of these Web sites describing the information each contains.

Health
No Pain, All Gain

Store Personal Health Records Online

More than 75 million consumers use the Internet yearly to search for health information, so using the Web to store personal medical data is a natural extension of the Internet's capabilities. Internet health services and portals are available to store your personal health history, including prescriptions, lab test results, doctor visits, allergies, and immunizations.

Google Health allows users to create a health profile, import medical records, and locate medical services and doctors. Web sites such as healthfinder.gov (Figure 25) provide free wellness information to consumers. Wise consumers, however, verify the online information they read with their personal physician.

In minutes, you can register with a health Web site by choosing a user name and password. Then, you create a record to enter your medical history. You also can store data for your emergency contacts, primary care physicians, specialists, blood type, cholesterol levels, blood pressure, and insurance plan. No matter where you are in the world, you and medical personnel can obtain records via the Internet or fax machine. Some popular online health databases are shown in Figure 26.

Health Web Sites

Medical History	Web Address
Google Health	google.com/health
Lifestar	mylifestarphr.com
Medem	medem.com
PersonalMD	personalmd.com
Practice Solutions	practicesolutions.ca
Records for Living, Inc — Personal Health and Living Management	recordsforliving.com
WebMD	webmd.com

General Health	Web Address
Consumer and Patient Health Information Section (CAPHIS)	caphis.mlanet.org/consumer
Centers for Disease Control and Prevention	cdc.gov
familydoctor	familydoctor.org
healthfinder	healthfinder.gov
KidsHealth	kidshealth.org
LIVESTRONG.COM	livestrong.com
MedlinePlus	medlineplus.gov
PE Central: Health and Nutrition Web Sites	pecentral.org/websites/healthsites.html
Physical Activity Guidelines	health.gov/paguidelines

👆 For more information about health Web sites, visit scsite.com/dc-off07/ch2/web.

Figure 25 The healthfinder.gov Web site provides advice and tools to prevent illnesses and check drug interactions.

Figure 26 These health Web sites allow you to organize your medical information and store it in an online database and also obtain information about a variety of medical conditions and treatments.

Health Web Exercises

1 **Access one of the health Web sites listed in Figure 26.** Register yourself or a family member and then enter the full health history. Create an emergency medical card if the Web site provides the card option. Submit this record and emergency card to your instructor. If you feel uncomfortable disclosing medical information for yourself or a family member, you may enter fictitious information.

2 **Visit three of the health Web sites listed in Figure 26.** Describe the features of each. Which of the three is the most user-friendly? Why? Describe the privacy policies of these three Web sites. Submit your analysis of these Web sites to your instructor.

Careers
In Search of the Perfect Job

Web Helps Career Hunt

While your teachers give you valuable training to prepare you for a career, they rarely teach you how to begin that career. You can broaden your horizons by searching the Internet for career information and job openings.

First, examine some of the job search Web sites. These resources list thousands of openings in hundreds of fields, companies, and locations. For example, the USAJOBS Web site, shown in Figure 27, allows you to find information for Federal jobs. This information may include the training and education required, salary data, working conditions, job descriptions, and more. In addition, many companies advertise careers on their Web sites.

When a company contacts you for an interview, learn as much about it and the industry as possible before the interview. Many of the Web sites listed in Figure 28 include detailed company profiles and links to their corporate Web sites.

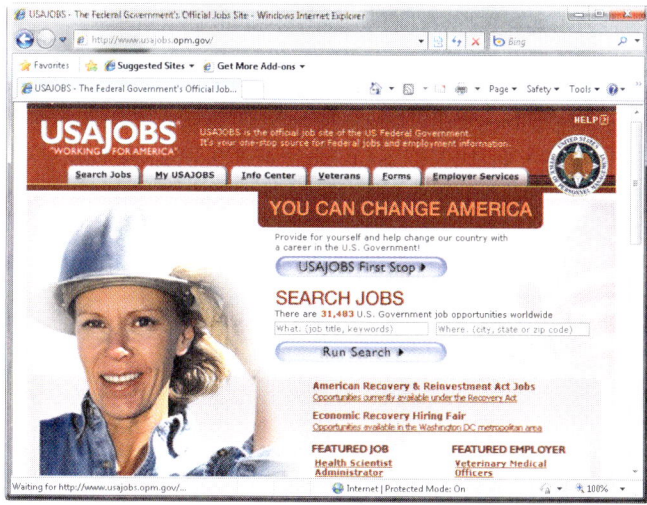

Figure 27 The USAJOBS Web site is the official location for federal jobs and information for job seekers.

Career Web Sites

Job Search	Web Address
BestJobsUSA	bestjobsusa.com
CareerBuilder	careerbuilder.com
Careerjet	careerjet.com
CareerNET	careernet.com
CAREERXCHANGE	careerxchange.com
CollegeGrad.com	collegegrad.com
EmploymentGuide.com	employmentguide.com
Job.com	job.com
Job Bank USA	jobbankusa.com
JobWeb	jobweb.com
Monster	monster.com
USAJOBS	www.usajobs.gov
VolunteerMatch	volunteermatch.org
Yahoo! HotJobs	hotjobs.yahoo.com
Company/Industry Information	**Web Address**
Careers.org	careers.org
Forbes	forbes.com/leadership/careers
Fortune	fortune.com
Hoover's	hoovers.com
Occupational Outlook Handbook	stats.bls.gov/oco

For more information about career Web sites, visit scsite.com/dc-off07/ch2/web.

Figure 28 Career Web sites provide a variety of job openings and information about major companies worldwide.

Careers Web Exercises

1. **Use two of the job search Web sites listed in Figure 28** to find three companies with job openings in your field. Make a table listing the Web site name, position available, description, salary, location, desired education, and desired experience.

2. **It is a good idea to acquire information before graduation about the industry in which you would like to work.** Are you interested in the automotive manufacturing industry, the restaurant service industry, or the financial industry? Use two of the company/industry information Web sites listed in Figure 28 to research a particular career related to your major. Write a paragraph naming the Web sites and the specific information you found, such as the nature of the work, recommended training and qualifications, employment outlook, and earnings. Then, use two other Web sites to profile three companies with positions available in this field. Write a paragraph about each of these companies, describing the headquarters' location, sales and earnings for the previous year, total number of employees, working conditions, benefits, and competitors.

Special Feature

Literature and Arts
Find Some Culture

Get Ready to Read, Paint, and Dance

Brush up your knowledge of Shakespeare, grab a canvas, and put on your dancing shoes. Literature and arts Web sites, including those in Figure 29, are about to sweep you off your cyberfeet.

Literature and Arts Web Sites	
Literature	**Web Address**
Bartleby	bartleby.com
Bibliomania	bibliomania.com
The Complete Review	www.complete-review.com
eNotes	enotes.com
Fantastic Fiction	fantasticfiction.co.uk
Literary History	literaryhistory.com
Nobel Prize in Literature	nobelprize.org/nobel_prizes/literature/laureates/1909/press.html
Project Gutenberg	gutenberg.org
Project MUSE	muse.jhu.edu
Arts	**Web Address**
absolutearts	absolutearts.com
The Children's Museum of Indianapolis	childrensmuseum.org
ARTINFO Gallery Guide	artinfo.com/galleryguide/
The Getty	getty.edu
Louvre Museum	louvre.fr
Montreal Museum of Fine Arts	mmfa.qc.ca
The Museum of Online Museums	coudal.com/moom
National Gallery of Art	nga.gov
Virtual Library museums pages (VLmp)	icom.museum/vlmp

👉 For more information about literature and arts Web sites, visit scsite.com/dc-off07/ch2/web.

Figure 29 Discover culture throughout the world by visiting these literature and arts Web sites.

The full text of hundreds of books is available online from the Bibliomania and Project Gutenberg Web sites. The Complete Review provides summaries, reviews, and Web links about a variety of books and their authors. The Bartleby Web site features biographies, definitions, quotations, dictionaries, and indexes.

When you are ready to absorb more culture, you can turn to various art Web sites. Many museums have images of their collections online. Among them are the Getty Museum in Los Angeles, the Montreal Museum of Fine Arts, and the Louvre Museum in Paris (Figure 30).

The absolutearts Web site focuses on contemporary art and includes video interviews with artists, art history research, and artists' blogs.

The Museum of Online Museums Web site provides links to museum and gallery Web sites, such as the Museum of Modern Art, The Bauhaus Archive, and The Art Institute of Chicago.

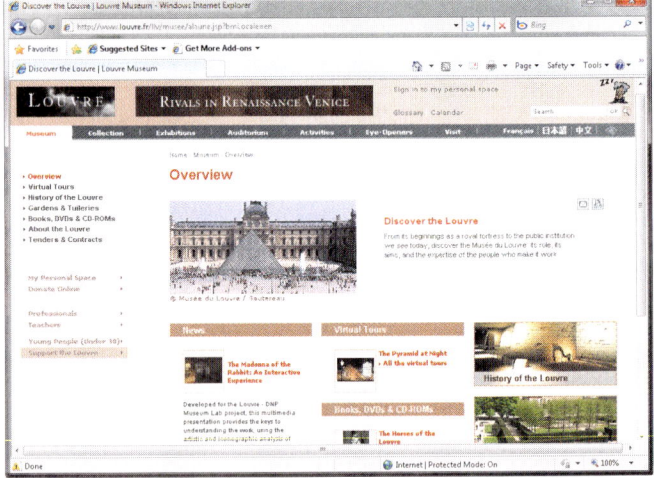

Figure 30 Permanent and temporary exhibitions, educational activities, and a bookstore are featured on the Louvre Museum Web site.

Literature and Arts Web Exercises

1 **Visit the Literary History Web site listed in Figure 29** and view one author in the Twentieth Century Literature, Nineteenth Century Literature, British Poets, and African American Literature sections. Read two literary criticism articles about each of the four authors and write a paragraph describing which of these authors is the most interesting to you. What are the advantages and disadvantages of reading literary criticism electronically?

2 **Using the arts Web sites listed in Figure 29,** search for three temporary exhibitions in galleries throughout the world. Describe the venues, the artists, and the works. Which permanent collections are found in these museums? Some people shop for gifts in the museums' stores. View and describe three items for sale.

Chapter Three

Application Software

Objectives

After completing this chapter, you will be able to:

1. Identify the four categories of application software
2. Describe characteristics of a user interface
3. Identify the key features of widely used business programs: word processing, spreadsheet, database, presentation, note taking, personal information manager, business software for phones, business software suite, project management, accounting, document management, and enterprise computing
4. Identify the key features of widely used graphics and multimedia programs: computer-aided design, professional desktop publishing, professional paint/image editing, professional photo editing, professional video and audio editing, multimedia authoring, and Web page authoring
5. Identify the key features of widely used home, personal, and educational programs: personal finance, legal, tax preparation, personal desktop publishing, personal paint/image editing, personal photo editing and photo management, clip art/image gallery, personal video and audio editing, travel and mapping, reference and educational, and entertainment
6. Discuss Web applications
7. Identify the types of application software used in communications
8. Describe the learning aids available for application software

Application Software

With the proper software, a computer is a valuable tool. Software allows users to create letters, reports, and other documents; develop multimedia presentations; design Web pages and diagrams; draw images; enhance audio and video clips; prepare taxes; play games; compose e-mail messages and instant messages; and much more. To accomplish these and many other tasks, users work with application software. **Application software** consists of programs designed to make users more productive and/or assist them with personal tasks. Application software has a variety of uses:

1. To make business activities more efficient
2. To assist with graphics and multimedia projects
3. To support home, personal, and educational tasks
4. To facilitate communications

The table in Figure 3-1 categorizes popular types of application software by their general use. Although many types of communications software exist, the ones listed in Figure 3-1 are application software oriented.

Application software is available in a variety of forms: packaged, custom, Web application, open source, shareware, freeware, and public domain.

- **Packaged software** is mass-produced, copyrighted retail software that meets the needs of a wide variety of users, not just a single user or company. Packaged software is available in retail stores or on the Web. Figure 3-1 shows some images of packaged software.
- **Custom software** performs functions specific to a business or industry. Sometimes a company cannot find packaged software that meets its unique requirements. In this case, the company may use programmers to develop tailor-made custom software.
- A **Web application** is a Web site that allows users to access and interact with software from any computer or device that is connected to the Internet. Types of Web applications include e-mail, word processing, and game programs.

Four Categories of Application Software

Business
- Word Processing
- Spreadsheet
- Database
- Presentation
- Note Taking
- Personal Information Manager (PIM)
- Business Software for Phones
- Business Software Suite
- Project Management
- Accounting
- Document Management
- Enterprise Computing

Graphics and Multimedia
- Computer-Aided Design (CAD)
- Desktop Publishing (for the Professional)
- Paint/Image Editing (for the Professional)
- Photo Editing (for the Professional)
- Video and Audio Editing (for the Professional)
- Multimedia Authoring
- Web Page Authoring

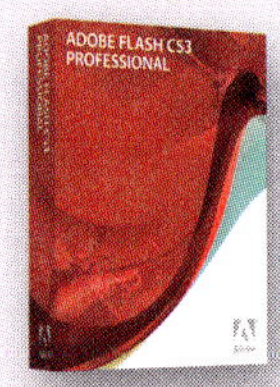

Home/Personal/Educational
- Software Suite (for Personal Use)
- Personal Finance
- Legal
- Tax Preparation
- Desktop Publishing (for Personal Use)
- Paint/Image Editing (for Personal Use)
- Photo Editing and Photo Management (for Personal Use)
- Clip Art/Image Gallery
- Video and Audio Editing (for Personal Use)
- Home Design/Landscaping
- Travel and Mapping
- Reference and Educational
- Entertainment

Communications

- Web Browser
- RSS Aggregator
- E-Mail
- Blogging
- Instant Messaging
- Newsgroup/Message Board
- Chat Room
- FTP
- Text, Picture, Video Messaging
- VoIP
- Video Conferencing

Figure 3-1 The four major categories of popular application software are outlined in this table. Communications software often is bundled with other application or system software.

- **Open source software** is software provided for use, modification, and redistribution. This software has no restrictions from the copyright holder regarding modification of the software's internal instructions and its redistribution. Open source software usually can be downloaded from the Internet, often at no cost.
- **Shareware** is copyrighted software that is distributed at no cost for a trial period. To use a shareware program beyond that period, you send payment to the program developer.
- **Freeware** is copyrighted software provided at no cost to a user by an individual or a company that retains all rights to the software.
- **Public-domain software** has been donated for public use and has no copyright restrictions. Anyone can copy or distribute public-domain software to others at no cost.

Thousands of shareware, freeware, and public-domain programs are available on the Internet for users to download. Examples include communications, graphics, and game programs.

The Role of System Software

System software serves as the interface between the user, the application software, and the computer's hardware (Figure 3-2). To use application software, such as a word processing program, your computer must be running system software — specifically, an operating system. Three popular personal computer operating systems are Windows, Mac OS, and Linux.

Each time you start a computer, the operating system is loaded (copied) from the computer's hard disk into memory. Once the operating system is loaded, it coordinates all the activities of the computer. This includes starting application software and transferring data among input and output devices and memory. While the computer is running, the operating system remains in memory.

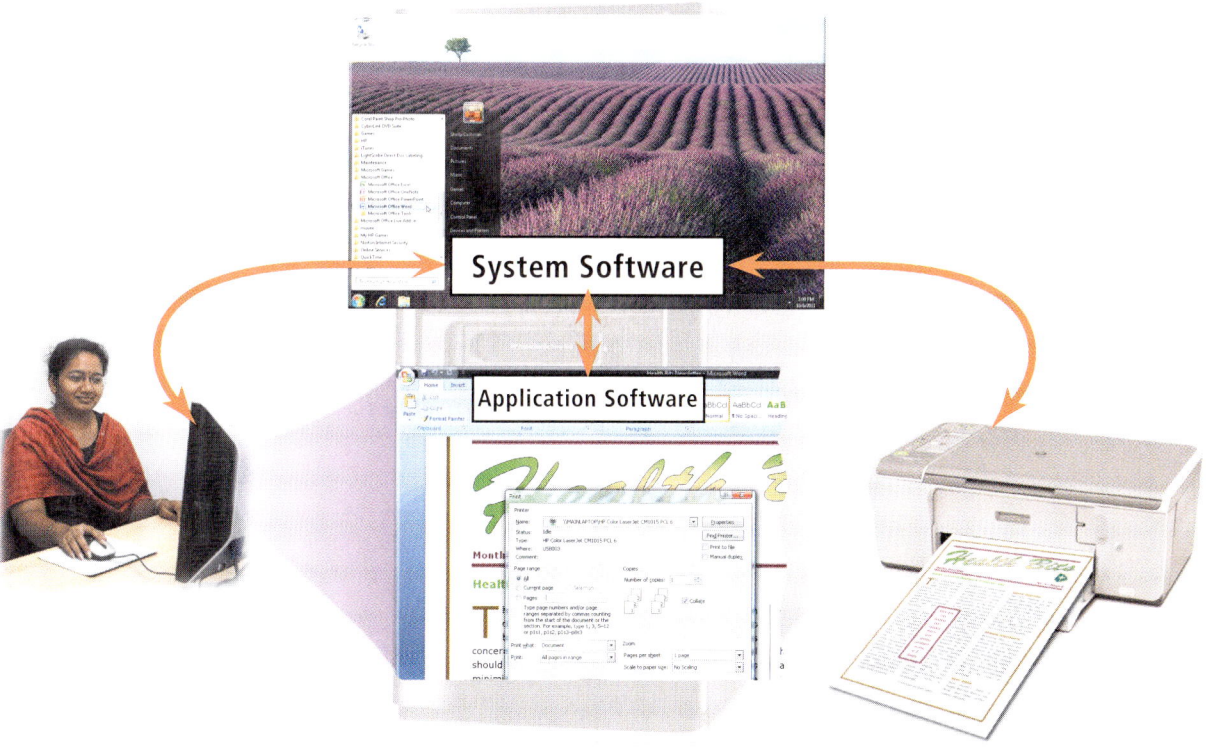

Figure 3-2 A user does not communicate directly with the computer hardware. Instead, system software is the interface between the user, the application software, and the hardware. For example, when a user instructs the application software to print a document, the application software sends the print instruction to the system software, which in turn sends the print instruction to the hardware.

Antivirus Programs
For more information, visit scsite.com/dc-off07/ch3/ weblink and then click Antivirus Programs.

Utility Programs A utility program is a type of system software that assists users with controlling or maintaining the operation of a computer, its devices, or its software. Utility programs typically offer features that provide an environment conducive to successful use of application software. For example, utility programs protect a computer against malicious software and unauthorized intrusions, manage files and disks, compress files, play media files, and burn optical discs. (To learn more about how to compress files, complete the Learn How To 2 activity on pages 126 and 127.)

One of the more important utility programs protects a computer against malicious software, or **malware**, which is a program that acts without a user's knowledge and deliberately alters the computer's operations. A computer virus is a type of malicious software. Chapter 4 discusses system software and utility programs in more depth.

FAQ 3-1

How many viruses exist on the Internet?

More than one million viruses exist on the Internet. This statistic stresses the importance of protecting your computer from various threats on the Internet, as well as practicing safe Web browsing habits. Not only is it possible to get a computer virus from downloading and opening an infected file or by opening an infected e-mail message, you also can fall victim to a computer virus simply by visiting a malicious Web site.

For more information, visit scsite.com/dc-off07/ch3/faq and then click Computer Viruses.

Working with Application Software

To use application software, you must instruct the operating system to start the program. The steps in Figure 3-3 illustrate one way to start and interact with the Paint program, which is included with the Windows operating system. The following paragraphs explain the steps in Figure 3-3.

Personal computer operating systems often use the concept of a desktop to make the computer easier to use. The **desktop** is an on-screen work area that has a graphical user interface. Step 1 of Figure 3-3 shows icons, a button, a pointer, and a menu on the Windows desktop. An **icon** is a small image displayed on the screen that represents a program, a document, or some other object. A **button** is a graphical element that you activate to cause a specific action to occur. One way to activate a button is to click it. To **click** a button on the screen requires moving the pointer to the button and then pressing and releasing a button on the mouse (usually the left mouse button). The **pointer** is a small symbol displayed on the screen that moves as you interact with the mouse or other pointing device. Common pointer shapes are an I-beam (I), a block arrow, and a pointing hand.

The Windows desktop contains a Start button on the lower-left corner of the taskbar. When you click the Start button, the Start menu is displayed on the desktop. A **menu** contains a list of commands from which you make selections. A **command** is an instruction that causes a program to perform a specific action.

As illustrated in Steps 1 and 2 of Figure 3-3, when you click the Start button and then click the All Programs command on the Start menu, the All Programs list is displayed on the Start menu. Clicking the Accessories folder in the All Programs list displays the Accessories list.

To start a program, you can click its program name on a menu or in a list. This action instructs the operating system to start the program, which means the program's instructions load from a storage medium (such as a hard disk) into memory. For example, when you click Paint in the Accessories list, Windows loads the Paint program instructions from the computer's hard disk into memory.

Once loaded into memory, the program appears in a window on the desktop (Step 3 of Figure 3-3). A **window** is a rectangular area of the screen that displays data and information. The top of a window has a **title bar**, which is a horizontal space that contains the window's name.

With the program loaded, you can create a new file or open an existing one. A **file** is a named collection of stored data, instructions, or information. A file can contain text, images, audio, and video. To distinguish among various files, each file has a file name. The title bar of the document window usually displays a document's file name. Step 4 of Figure 3-3 shows the contents of the file, Baby Buffalo, displaying in the Paint window.

In some cases, when you instruct a program to perform an activity such as print, the program displays a dialog box. A dialog box is a window that provides information, presents available options, or requests a response. Dialog boxes, such as the one shown in Step 5 of Figure 3-3, often contain option buttons, text boxes, check boxes, and command buttons.

One Way to Start and Interact with a Program from Windows

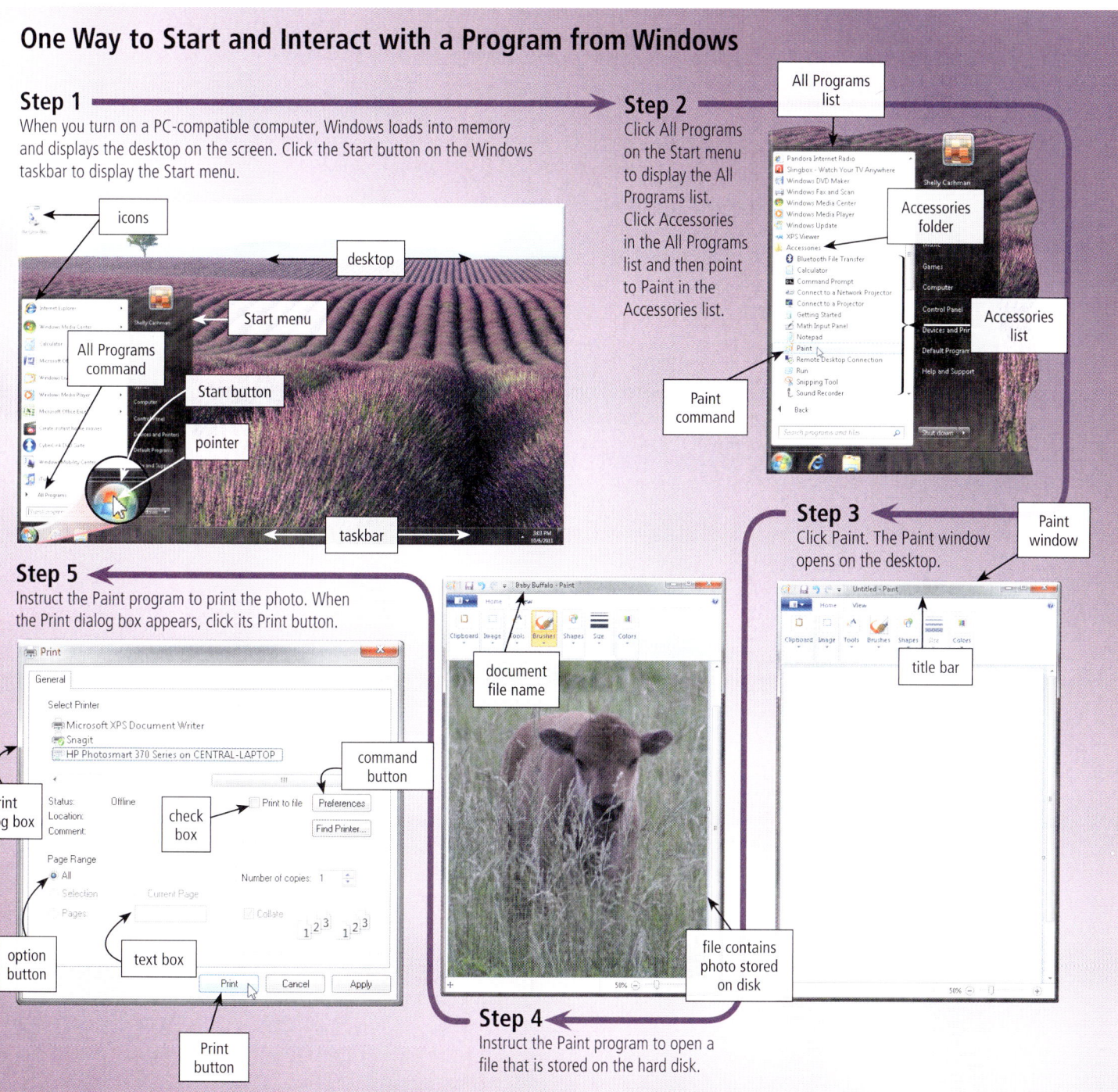

Figure 3-3 This figure shows one way to start and interact with a program from Windows.

QUIZ YOURSELF 3-1

Instructions: Find the true statement below. Then, rewrite the remaining false statements so that they are true.

1. Application software is used to make business activities more efficient; assist with graphics and multimedia projects; support home, personal, and educational tasks; and facilitate communications.
2. Public-domain software is mass-produced, copyrighted retail software that meets the needs of a wide variety of users, not just a single user or company.
3. To use system software, your computer must be running application software.
4. When a program is started, its instructions load from memory into a storage medium.

👆 **Quiz Yourself Online:** To further check your knowledge of pages 96 through 99, visit scsite.com/dc-off07/ch3/quiz and then click Objectives 1 – 2.

Business Software

Business software is application software that assists people in becoming more effective and efficient while performing their daily business activities. Business software includes programs such as word processing, spreadsheet, database, presentation, note taking, personal information manager, business software for phones, business software suites, project management, accounting, document management, and enterprise computing software. Figure 3-4 lists popular programs for each of these categories.

Popular Business Programs

Application Software	Manufacturer	Program Name	Application Software	Manufacturer	Program Name
Word Processing	Microsoft	Word	Business Software Suite (for the Professional)	Microsoft	Office
	Apple	Pages			Office for Mac
	Corel	WordPerfect		Apple	iWork
Spreadsheet	Microsoft	Excel		Google	Google Docs
	Apple	Numbers		Sun	OpenOffice.org
	Corel	Quattro Pro			StarOffice
Database	Microsoft	Access		Corel	WordPerfect Office
	Corel	Paradox		IBM	Lotus SmartSuite
	Oracle	Oracle Database	Project Management	CS Odessa	ConceptDraw PROJECT
	Sun	MySQL		Microsoft	Project
Presentation	Microsoft	PowerPoint		Oracle	Primavera SureTrak Project Manager
	Apple	Keynote			
	Corel	Presentations	Accounting	Intuit	QuickBooks
Note Taking	Microsoft	OneNote		Microsoft	Accounting
	Agilix	GoBinder		Sage Software	Peachtree
	Corel	Grafigo	Document Management	Adobe	Acrobat
	SnapFiles	KeyNote		Enfocus	PitStop
Personal Information Manager (PIM)	Microsoft	Outlook		Nuance	PDF Converter
	Google	Calendar	Enterprise Computing	Oracle	PeopleSoft Enterprise Human Capital Management
	IBM	Lotus Organizer			
	Palm	Desktop			
	Mozilla	Thunderbird		Sage Software	Sage MAS 500
Business Software for Phones	CNetX	Pocket SlideShow		MSC Software	MSC.SimManager
	DataViz	Documents To Go		Oracle	Oracle Manufacturing
	Microsoft	Word Mobile Excel Mobile PowerPoint Mobile Outlook Mobile		SAP	mySAP Customer Relationship Management
				NetSuite	NetERP
	Mobile Systems	MobiSystems Office Suite		Syntellect	Syntellect Interaction Management Suite
	Ultrasoft	Money			

Figure 3-4 Popular business software.

Word Processing Software

Word processing software, sometimes called a word processor, allows users to create and manipulate documents containing mostly text and sometimes graphics (Figure 3-5). Millions of people use word processing software every day to develop documents such as letters, memos, reports, mailing labels, newsletters, and Web pages.

A major advantage of using word processing software is that users easily can change what they have written. Word processing software also has many features to make documents look professional and visually appealing. For example, you can change the shape, size, and color of characters; apply special effects such as three-dimensional shadows; and organize text in newspaper-style columns.

Most word processing software allows users to incorporate graphical images, such as digital photos and clip art, in documents. **Clip art** is a collection of drawings, photos, and other images. In Figure 3-5, a user inserted an image of a baseball player in the document. With word processing software, you easily can modify the appearance of an image after inserting it in the document.

You can use word processing software to define the size of the paper on which to print and specify the margins. A feature, called wordwrap, allows users to type words in a paragraph continually without pressing the ENTER key at the end of each line. As you type more lines of text than can be displayed on the screen, the top portion of the document moves upward, or scrolls, off the screen. Read Ethics & Issues 3-1 for a related discussion.

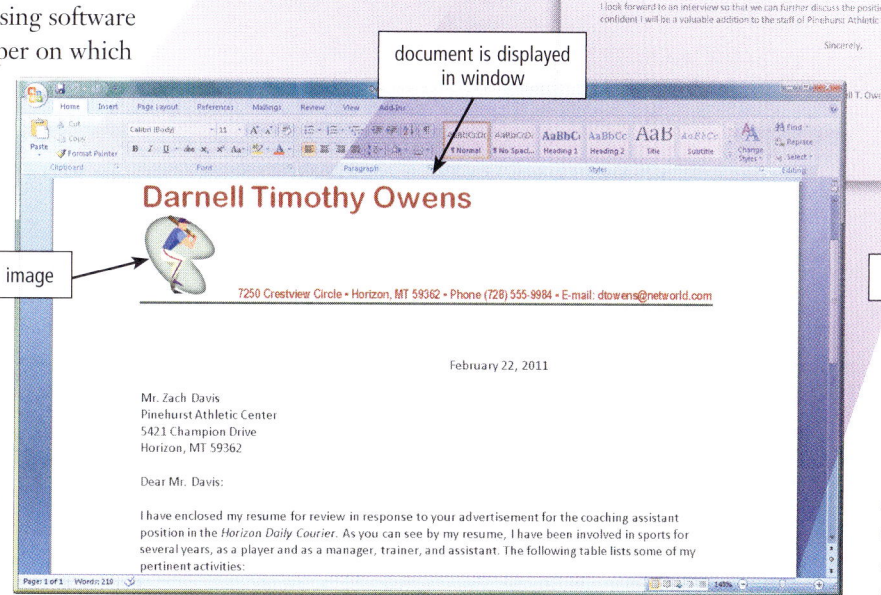

Figure 3-5 Word processing software enables users to create professional and visually appealing documents.

ETHICS & ISSUES 3-1

Are Word Processing Programs Making Students Lazy?

Today, word processing programs fix spelling and grammar mistakes, automatically format documents with templates, help correctly reference works cited in a document, and seem to do everything short of generating an idea for a document. Some educators believe that the proliferation of word processing automation is cheating students of the fundamental ability to perform these tasks on their own. Research shows that as word processing programs became more popular over the past years, the quality of written work done without the aid of this software has dropped dramatically. Opponents of using word processing software for assignments point out the quality of e-mail and instant messages is markedly worse than works written with the aid of modern word processing programs.

Proponents of the use of word processing programs for educational use point out that automation is the way writing should be done now and in the future. The higher quality of works produced using the software is well worth not sacrificing time toward teaching students less modern tactics. Students are more productive and able to focus on the topics at hand, rather than worry about spelling errors.

Are word processing programs making students lazy? Why or why not? Should educators have the ability to turn off time-saving features, such as the AutoCorrect and grammar checker features, in their student's word processing programs? Why? Do students need the ability manually to check spelling and grammar, format a document, and reference cited works in a document, in the same way that students still learn multiplication and long division? Why or why not?

Word Processing Software
For more information, visit scsite.com/dc-off07/ch3/ weblink and then click Word Processing Software.

Word processing software typically includes a spelling checker, which reviews the spelling of individual words, sections of a document, or the entire document. The spelling checker compares the words in the document with an electronic dictionary that is part of the word processing software. Some word processing programs also check for contextual spelling errors, such as a misuse of homophones (words pronounced the same but have different spellings or meanings, such as one and won).

Developing a Document

With application software, such as a word processing program, users create, edit, format, save, and print documents. When you **create** a document, you enter text or numbers, insert images, and perform other tasks using an input device such as a keyboard, mouse, or digital pen. If you are using Microsoft Word to design a flyer, for example, you are creating a document.

To **edit** a document means to make changes to its existing content. Common editing tasks include inserting, deleting, cutting, copying, and pasting. Inserting text involves adding text to a document. Deleting text means that you are removing text or other content. Cutting is the process of removing a portion of the document and storing it in a temporary storage location, sometimes called a clipboard. Pasting is the process of transferring an item from a clipboard to a specific location in a document.

When users **format** a document, they change its appearance. Formatting is important because the overall look of a document significantly can affect its ability to communicate clearly. Examples of formatting tasks are changing the font, font size, and font style.

A **font** is a name assigned to a specific design of characters. Cambria and Calibri are examples of fonts. **Font size** indicates the size of the characters in a particular font. Font size is gauged by a measurement system called points. A single point is about 1/72 of an inch in height. The text you are reading in this book is about 10 point. Thus, each character is about 5/36 (10/72) of an inch in height. A **font style** adds emphasis to a font. Bold, italic, underline, and color are examples of font styles. Figure 3-6 illustrates fonts, font sizes, and font styles.

During the process of creating, editing, and formatting a document, the computer holds it in memory. To keep the document for future use requires that you save it. When you **save** a document, the computer transfers the document from memory to a storage medium such as a USB flash drive or hard disk. Once saved, a document is stored permanently as a file on the storage medium. To learn more about how to save a file, complete the Learn How To 1 activity on page 126.

When you **print** a document, the computer places the contents of the document on paper or some other medium. Instead of printing a document and physically distributing it, some users e-mail the document to others on a network such as the Internet.

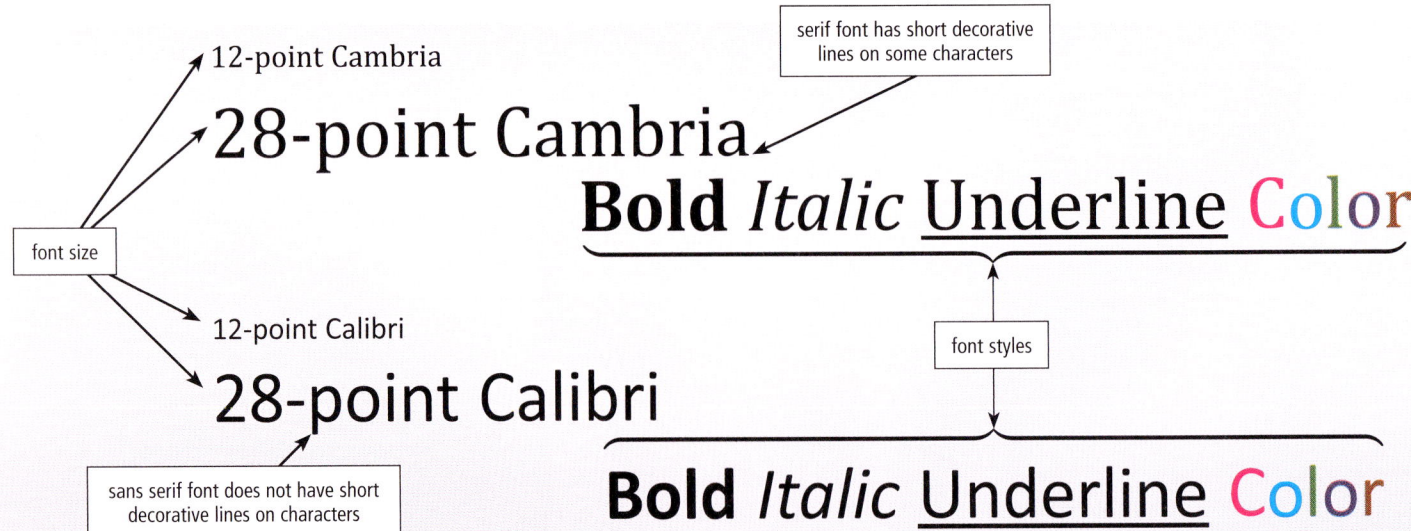

Figure 3-6 The Cambria and Calibri fonts are shown in two font sizes and a variety of font styles.

Spreadsheet Software

Spreadsheet software allows users to organize data in rows and columns and perform calculations on the data. These rows and columns collectively are called a **worksheet** (Figure 3-7). Most spreadsheet software has basic features to help users create, edit, and format worksheets. The following sections describe the features of most spreadsheet programs.

Spreadsheet Organization A spreadsheet file is similar to a notebook that can contain more than 1,000 related individual worksheets. Data is organized vertically in columns and horizontally in rows on each worksheet (Figure 3-7). Each worksheet usually can have more than 16,000 columns and 1 million rows. One or more letters identify each column, and a number identifies each row. Only a small fraction of these columns and rows are visible on the screen at one time. Scrolling through the worksheet displays different parts of it on the screen.

A cell is the intersection of a column and row. The spreadsheet software identifies cells by the column and row in which they are located. For example, the intersection of column B and row 4 is referred to as cell B4. As shown in Figure 3-7, cell B4 contains the number, $3,383,909.82, which represents the sales for January.

Cells may contain three types of data: labels, values, and formulas. The text, or label, entered in a cell identifies the worksheet data and helps organize the worksheet. Using descriptive labels, such as Gross Margin and Total Expenses, helps make a worksheet more meaningful.

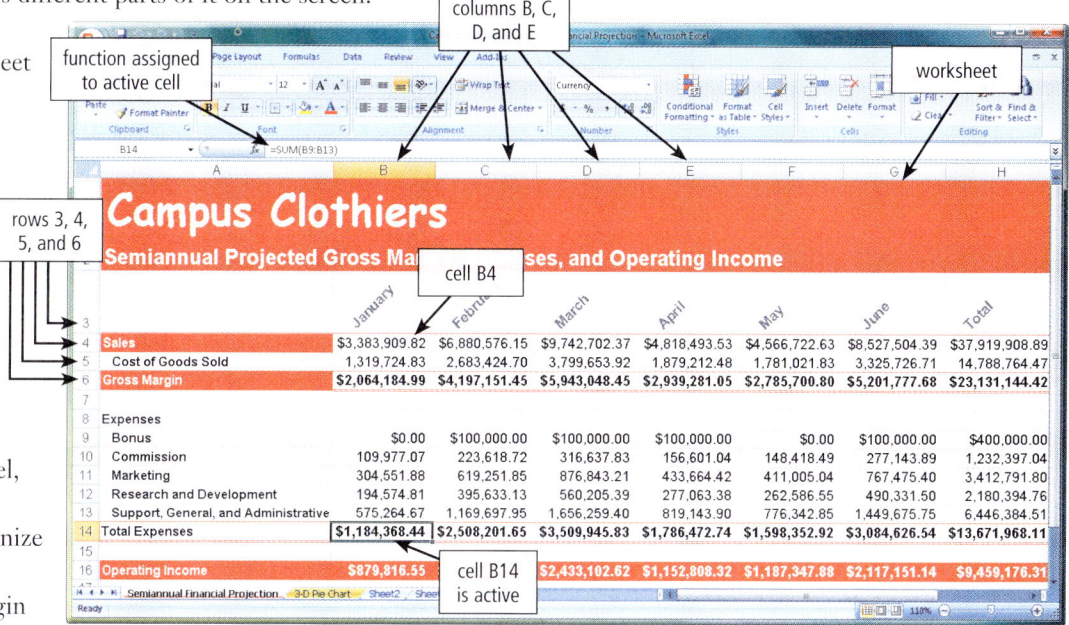

Figure 3-7 With spreadsheet software, you create worksheets that contain data arranged in rows and columns, and you can perform calculations on the data in the worksheets.

Calculations Many of the worksheet cells shown in Figure 3-7 contain a number, called a value, that can be used in a calculation. Other cells, however, contain formulas that generate values. A formula performs calculations on the data in the worksheet and displays the resulting value in a cell, usually the cell containing the formula. When creating a worksheet, you can enter your own formulas. In Figure 3-7, for example, cell B14 could contain the formula B9+B10+B11+B12+B13, which would add together (sum) the contents of cells B9, B10, B11, B12, and B13. That is, this formula calculates the total expenses for January.

A function is a predefined formula that performs common calculations such as adding the values in a group of cells or generating a value such as the time or date. For example, the function =SUM(B9:B13) instructs the spreadsheet program to add all of the numbers in cells B9 through B13.

Recalculation One of the more powerful features of spreadsheet software is its capability of recalculating the rest of the worksheet when data in a worksheet changes. Spreadsheet software's capability of recalculating data also makes it a valuable budgeting, forecasting, and decision making tool.

Spreadsheet Software
For more information, visit scsite.com/dc-off07/ch3/ weblink and then click Spreadsheet Software.

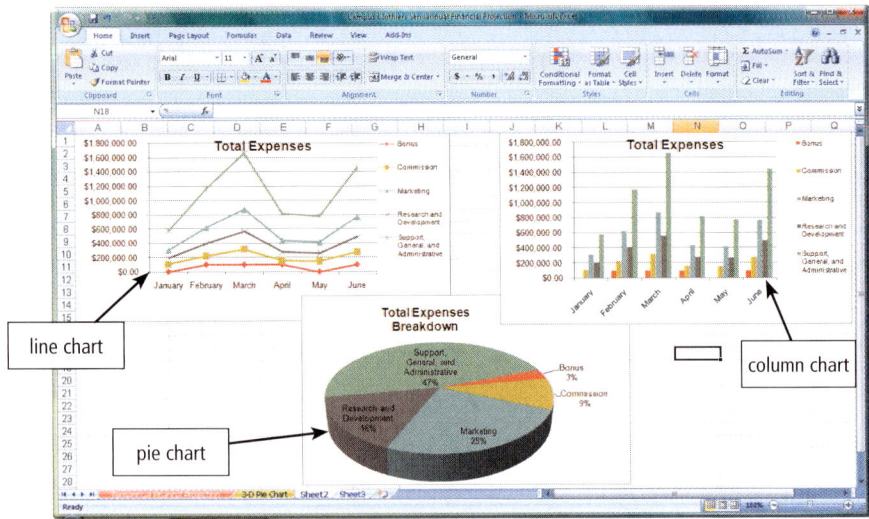

Figure 3-8 Three basic types of charts provided with spreadsheet software are line charts, column charts, and pie charts. The charts shown here were created using the data in the worksheet in Figure 3-7.

Charting Another standard feature of spreadsheet software is charting, which depicts the data in graphical form. A visual representation of data through charts often makes it easier for users to see at a glance the relationship among the numbers. Three popular chart types are line charts, column charts, and pie charts. Figure 3-8 shows examples of these charts that were plotted using the five types of expenses for each of the months shown in the worksheet in Figure 3-7 on the previous page. A line chart shows a trend during a period of time, as indicated by a rising or falling line. A column chart, also called a bar chart, displays bars of various lengths to show the relationship of data. The bars can be horizontal, vertical, or stacked on top of one another. A pie chart, which has the shape of a round pie cut into slices, shows the relationship of parts to a whole.

Database Software

A **database** is a collection of data organized in a manner that allows access, retrieval, and use of that data. In a manual database, you might record data on paper and store it in a filing cabinet. With a computerized database, such as the one shown in Figure 3-9, the computer stores the data in an electronic format on a storage medium such as a hard disk.

Database software is application software that allows users to create, access, and manage a database. Using database software, you can add, change, and delete data in a database; sort and retrieve data from the database; and create forms and reports using the data in the database.

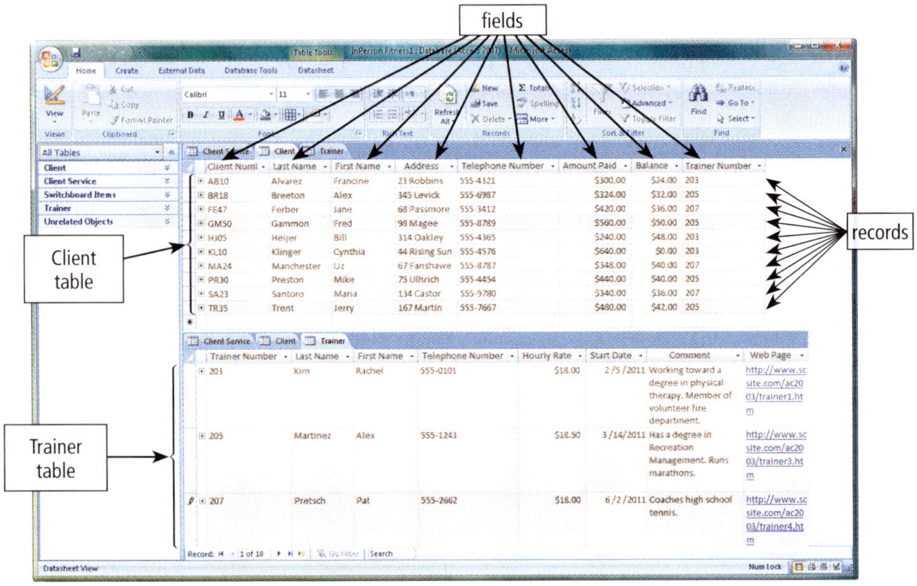

With most personal computer database programs, a database consists of a collection of tables, organized in rows and columns. Each row, called a record, contains data about a given person, product, object, or event. Each column, called a field, contains a specific category of data within a record.

The Fitness database shown in Figure 3-9 consists of two tables: a Client table and a Trainer table. The Client table contains ten records (rows), each storing data about one client. The client data is grouped into eight fields (columns): Client Number, Last Name, First Name, Address, Telephone Number, Amount Paid, Balance, and Trainer Number. The Balance field, for instance, contains the balance due

Figure 3-9 This database contains two tables: one for the clients and one for the trainers. The Client table has ten records and eight fields; the Trainer table has three records and eight fields.

from the client. The Client and Trainer tables relate to one another through a common field, Trainer Number.

Users run queries to retrieve data. A query is a request for specific data from the database. For example, a query might request a list of clients whose balance is greater than $45. Database software can take the results of a query and present it in a window on the screen or send it to the printer.

Presentation Software

Presentation software is application software that allows users to create visual aids for presentations to communicate ideas, messages, and other information to a group. The presentations can be viewed as slides, sometimes called a slide show, that are displayed on a large monitor or on a projection screen (Figure 3-10).

Presentation software typically provides a variety of predefined presentation formats that define complementary colors for backgrounds, text, and graphical accents on the slides. This software also provides a variety of layouts for each individual slide such as a title slide, a two-column slide, and a slide with clip art, a chart, a table, or a diagram. In addition, you can enhance any text, charts, and graphical images on a slide with 3-D, animation, and other special effects such as shading, shadows, and textures.

When building a presentation, users can set the slide timing so that the presentation automatically displays the next slide after a preset delay. Presentation software allows you to apply special effects to the transition between slides. One slide, for example, might fade away as the next slide appears.

Presentation software typically includes a clip gallery that provides images, photos, video clips, and audio clips to enhance multimedia presentations. Some audio and video editing programs work with presentation software, providing users with an easy means to record and insert video, music, and audio commentary in a presentation.

You can view or print a finished presentation in a variety of formats, including an outline of text from each slide and audience handouts that show completed slides.

Presentation software incorporates features such as checking spelling, formatting, research, and creating Web pages from existing slide shows.

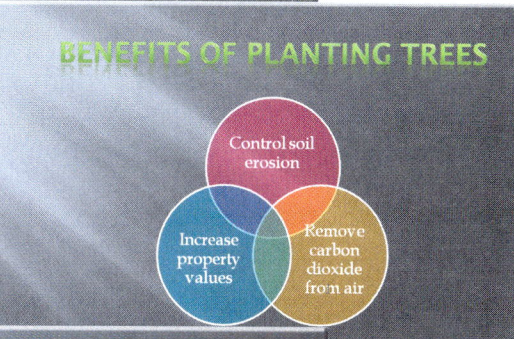

Figure 3-10
This presentation created with presentation software consists of five slides.

Note Taking Software

Note taking software is application software that enables users to enter typed text, handwritten comments, drawings, or sketches anywhere on a page and then save the page as part of a notebook (Figure 3-11). Users also can include audio recordings as part of their notes. Users find note taking software convenient during meetings, class lectures, conferences, in libraries, and other settings that previously required a pencil and tablet of paper for recording thoughts and discussions.

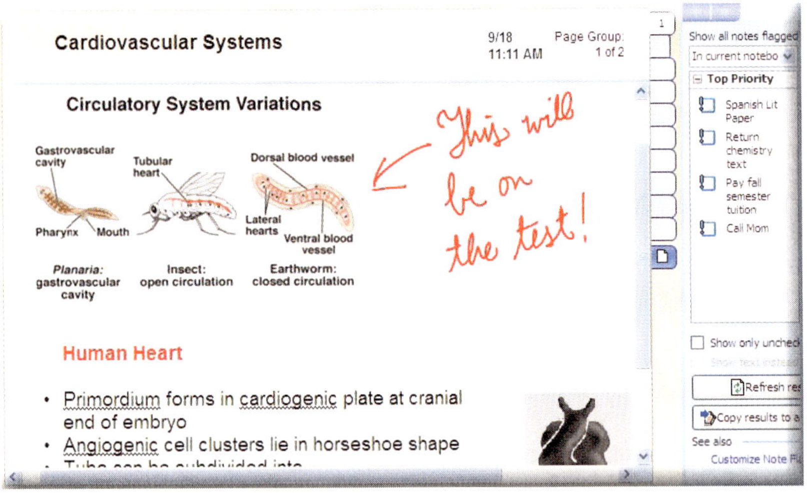

Business Software Suite

A **software suite** is a collection of individual programs available together as a unit. Business software suites typically include, at a minimum, the following programs: word processing, spreadsheet, presentation, and e-mail. Popular software suites are Microsoft Office, Apple iWork, Corel WordPerfect Office, and Google Docs.

Software suites offer two major advantages: lower cost and ease of use. When you purchase a collection of programs as a software suite, the suite usually costs significantly less than purchasing them individually. Software suites provide ease of use because the programs in the suite normally use a similar interface and share features such as clip art and spelling checker.

Figure 3-11 With note taking software, mobile users can handwrite notes, draw sketches, and type text.

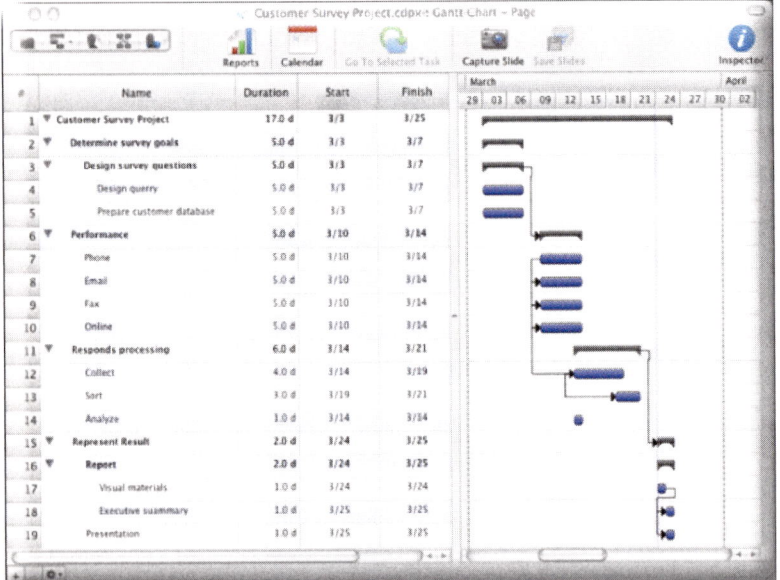

Figure 3-12 With project management software, you plan and schedule a project.

Project Management Software

Project management software allows a user to plan, schedule, track, and analyze the events, resources, and costs of a project. Project management software helps users manage project variables, allowing them to complete a project on time and within budget. A customer service manager might use project management software to schedule the process of administering customer surveys, evaluating responses, and presenting recommendations (Figure 3-12).

Personal Information Manager Software

A **personal information manager** (**PIM**) is application software that includes an appointment calendar, address book, notepad, and other features to help users organize personal information.

Mobile devices such as smart phones and PDAs include, among many other features, PIM functionality. You can synchronize, or coordinate, information so that both the mobile device and your personal computer and/or organization's server have the latest version of any updated information.

Business Software for Phones

In addition to PIM software, a huge variety of business and other software is available for phones. Some software is preloaded on the phone, while other programs can be downloaded or accessed on memory cards. Business software for phones enables users to create documents and worksheets, manage databases and lists, create slide shows, take notes, manage budgets and finances, view and edit photos, read electronic books, plan travel routes, compose and read e-mail messages, send instant messages, send text and picture messages, view maps and directions, read the latest news articles, and browse the Web. Many of the programs discussed in this chapter have scaled-down versions that work with smart phones and other mobile devices.

Accounting Software

Accounting software helps companies record and report their financial transactions (Figure 3-13). With accounting software, business users perform accounting activities related to the general ledger, accounts receivable, accounts payable, purchasing, invoicing, and payroll functions. Accounting software also enables business users to write and print checks, track checking account activity, and update and reconcile balances on demand.

Most accounting software supports online credit checks, invoicing, bill payment, direct deposit, and payroll services. Some accounting software offers more complex features such as job costing and estimating, time tracking, multiple company reporting, foreign currency reporting, and forecasting the amount of raw materials needed for products. The cost of accounting software for small businesses ranges from less than one hundred to several thousand dollars. Accounting software for large businesses can cost several hundred thousand dollars.

Document Management Software

Document management software provides a means for sharing, distributing, and searching through documents by converting them into a format that can be viewed by any user. The converted document, which mirrors the original document's appearance, can be viewed and printed without the software that created the original document.

A popular file format that document management software uses to save converted documents is **PDF** (Portable Document Format), developed by Adobe Systems. To view and print a PDF file, you need Acrobat Reader software (Figure 3-14), which can be downloaded free from Adobe's Web site.

Enterprise Computing Software

A large organization, commonly referred to as an enterprise, requires special computing solutions because of its size and large geographical distribution. A typical enterprise consists of a wide variety of departments, centers, and divisions — collectively known as functional units. Nearly every enterprise has the following functional units: human resources, accounting and finance, engineering or product development, manufacturing, marketing, sales, distribution, customer service, and information technology. Each of these functional units has specialized software requirements.

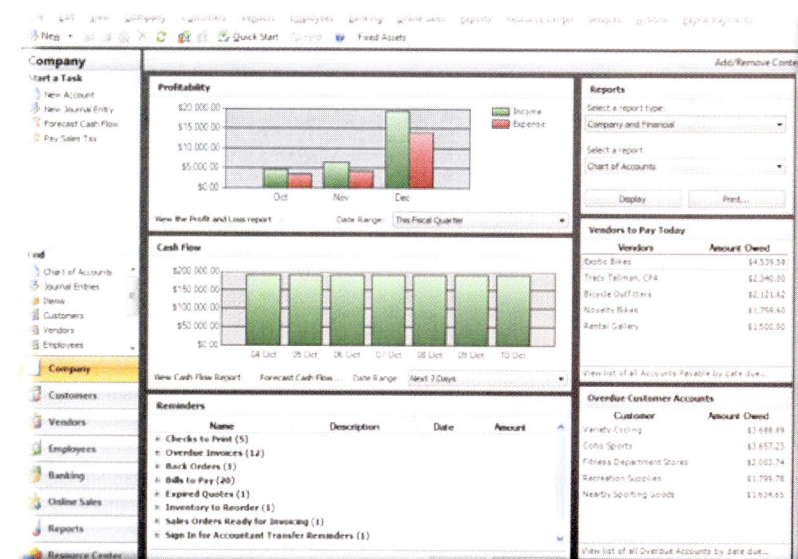

Figure 3-13 Accounting software helps companies record and report their financial transactions.

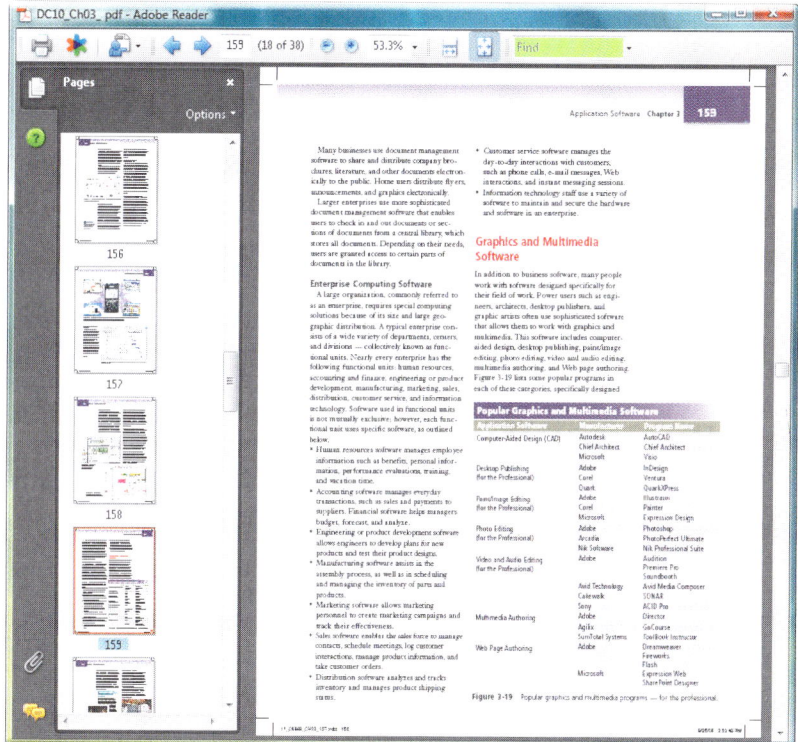

Figure 3-14 With Adobe Reader, you can view any PDF file.

Graphics and Multimedia Software

In addition to business software, many people work with software designed specifically for their field of work. Power users such as engineers, architects, desktop publishers, and graphic artists often use sophisticated software that allows them to work with graphics and multimedia. This software includes computer-aided design, desktop publishing, paint/image editing, photo editing, video and audio editing, multimedia authoring, and Web page authoring. Figure 3-15 lists the more popular programs for each of these categories, specifically designed for professional or more technically astute users.

Many graphics and multimedia programs incorporate user-friendly interfaces, or scaled-down versions, making it possible for the home and small business users to create documents using these programs. The following sections discuss the features and functions of graphics and multimedia software. Read Innovative Computing 3-1 to find out how fireworks shows can be produced using multimedia software.

Graphics Software
For more information, visit scsite.com/dc-off07/ch3/ weblink and then click Graphics Software.

Popular Graphics and Multimedia Software

Application Software	Manufacturer	Program Name	Application Software	Manufacturer	Program Name
Computer-Aided Design (CAD)	Autodesk	AutoCAD	Video and Audio Editing (for the Professional)	Adobe	Audition Premiere Pro Soundbooth
	Chief Architect	Chief Architect		Avid Technology	Avid Media Composer
	Microsoft	Visio		Cakewalk	SONAR
Desktop Publishing (for the Professional)	Adobe	InDesign		Sony	ACID Pro
	Corel	Ventura	Multimedia Authoring	Adobe	Director
	Quark	QuarkXPress		Agilix	GoCourse
Paint/Image Editing (for the Professional)	Adobe	Illustrator		SumTotal Systems	ToolBook Instructor
	Corel	Painter	Web Page Authoring	Adobe	Dreamweaver Fireworks Flash
	Microsoft	Expression Design			
Photo Editing (for the Professional)	Adobe	Photoshop		Microsoft	Expression Web SharePoint Designer
	Arcadia	PhotoPerfect Ultimate			
	Nik Software	Nik Professional Suite			

Figure 3-15 Popular graphics and multimedia programs — for the professional.

❗ INNOVATIVE COMPUTING 3-1

Fireworks Software Creates a Real Blast

The "oohs" and "aahs" you hear at a fireworks show may be in response to the music and pyrotechnics synchronized with special multimedia software. Major fireworks productions on Independence Day and at

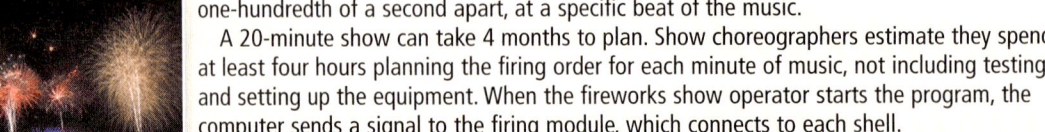

theme parks are choreographed with programs designed to fire each shell, sometimes only one-hundredth of a second apart, at a specific beat of the music.

A 20-minute show can take 4 months to plan. Show choreographers estimate they spend at least four hours planning the firing order for each minute of music, not including testing and setting up the equipment. When the fireworks show operator starts the program, the computer sends a signal to the firing module, which connects to each shell.

The multimedia software can cost from $2,000 to $8,000, while the firing hardware that the computer synchronizes wirelessly or with wires can cost between $30,000 and $50,000.

For more information, visit scsite.com/dc-off07/ch3/innovative and then click Fireworks.

Computer-Aided Design

Computer-aided design (CAD) software is a sophisticated type of application software that assists a professional user in creating engineering, architectural, and scientific designs. For example, engineers create design plans for vehicles and security systems. Architects design building structures and floor plans (Figure 3-16). Scientists design drawings of molecular structures.

Figure 3-16 Architects use CAD software to design building structures.

Desktop Publishing Software (for the Professional)

Desktop publishing (DTP) software enables professional designers to create sophisticated documents that contain text, graphics, and many colors (Figure 3-17). Professional DTP software is ideal for the production of high-quality color documents such as textbooks, corporate newsletters, marketing literature, product catalogs, and annual reports. Designers and graphic artists can print finished publications on a color printer, take them to a professional printer, or post them on the Web in a format that can be viewed by those without DTP software.

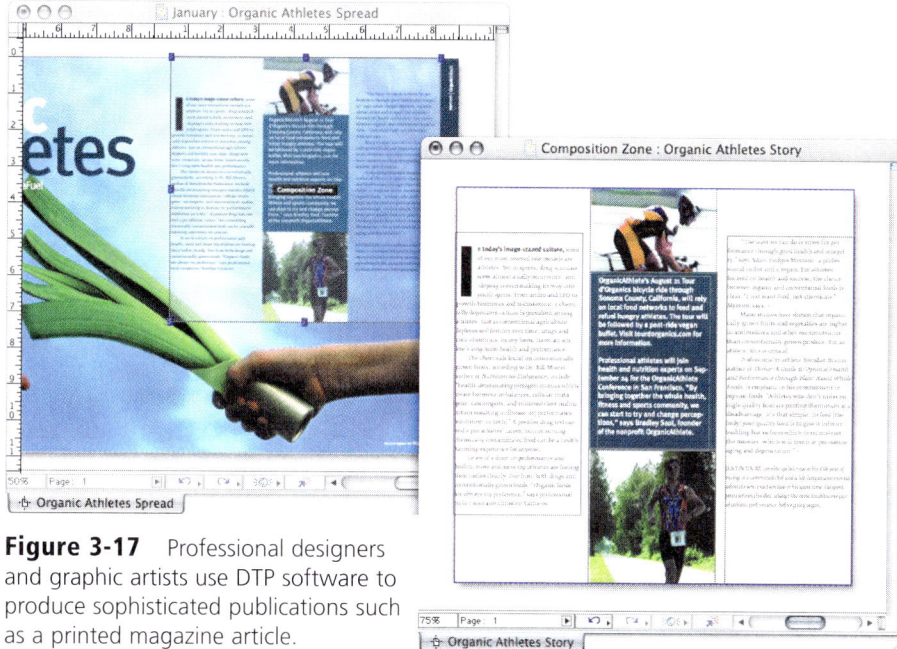

Figure 3-17 Professional designers and graphic artists use DTP software to produce sophisticated publications such as a printed magazine article.

Paint/Image Editing Software (for the Professional)

Graphic artists, multimedia professionals, technical illustrators, and desktop publishers use paint software and image editing software to create and modify graphical images such as those used in DTP documents and Web pages. **Paint software**, also called illustration software, allows users to draw pictures (Figure 3-18), shapes, and other graphical images with various on-screen tools such as a pen, brush, eyedropper, and paint bucket. **Image editing software** provides the capabilities of paint software and also includes the capability to enhance and modify existing pictures and images. Modifications can include adjusting or enhancing image colors, adding special effects such as shadows and glows, creating animations, and image stitching, which is the process of combining multiple images into a larger image.

Professional photo editing software is a type of image editing software that allows photographers, videographers, engineers, scientists, and other high-volume digital photo users to edit and customize digital photos. With professional photo editing software, users can retouch photos, crop images, remove red-eye, change image shapes, color-correct images, straighten images, remove or rearrange objects in a photo, and apply filters.

Figure 3-18 This graphic artist uses paint software to draw characters in a computer game.

Video and Audio Editing Software (for the Professional)

Video editing software allows professionals to modify a segment of a video, called a clip. For example, users can reduce the length of a video clip, reorder a series of clips, or add special effects such as words that move horizontally across the screen. Video editing software typically includes audio editing capabilities. **Audio editing software** lets users modify audio clips, produce studio-quality soundtracks, and add audio to video clips (Figure 3-19). Most television shows and movies are created or enhanced using video and audio editing software.

Figure 3-19 With audio editing software, users modify audio clips.

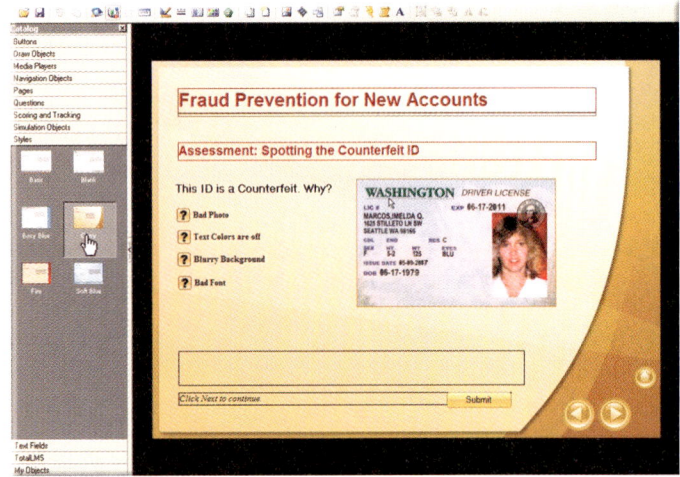

Figure 3-20 Multimedia authoring software allows you to create dynamic presentations that include text, graphics, video, sound, and animation.

Multimedia Authoring Software

Multimedia authoring software allows users to combine text, graphics, audio, video, and animation in an interactive application (Figure 3-20). With this software, users control the placement of text and images and the duration of sounds, video, and animation. Once created, multimedia presentations often take the form of interactive computer-based presentations or Web-based presentations designed to facilitate learning, demonstrate product functionality, and elicit direct-user participation. Training centers, educational institutions, and online magazine publishers all use multimedia authoring software to develop interactive applications. These applications may be available on an optical disc, over a local area network, or via the Internet.

Web Page Authoring Software

Web page authoring software helps users of all skill levels create Web pages that include graphical images, video, audio, animation, and special effects with interactive content. In addition, many Web page authoring programs allow users to organize, manage, and maintain Web sites.

Application software, such as Word and Excel, often includes Web page authoring features. This allows home and small business users to create basic Web pages using application software they already own. For more sophisticated Web pages, users work with Web page authoring software.

✓ QUIZ YOURSELF 3-2

Instructions: Find the true statement below. Then, rewrite the remaining false statements so that they are true.

1. Enterprise computing software provides the capabilities of paint software and also includes the capability to modify existing images.
2. Millions of people use spreadsheet software every day to develop documents such as letters, memos, reports, mailing labels, newsletters, and Web pages.
3. Professional accounting software is ideal for the production of high-quality color documents such as textbooks, corporate newsletters, marketing literature, product catalogs, and annual reports.
4. Database software is application software that allows users to create visual aids for presentations to communicate ideas, messages, and other information to a group.
5. Popular CAD programs include Microsoft Office, Apple iWork, Corel WordPerfect Office, and Google Docs.
6. Web page authoring software helps users of all skill levels create Web pages.

☞ **Quiz Yourself Online:** To further check your knowledge of pages 100 through 110, visit scsite.com/dc-off07/ch3/quiz and then click Objectives 3 – 4.

Software for Home, Personal, and Educational Use

A large amount of application software is designed specifically for home, personal, and educational use. Most of the programs in this category are relatively inexpensive, often priced less than $100. Figure 3-21 lists popular programs for many of these categories. The following pages discuss the features and functions of this application software.

Popular Programs for Home/Personal/Educational Use

Application Software	Manufacturer	Program Name	Application Software	Manufacturer	Program Name
Personal Finance	IGG Software	iBank	Clip Art/Image Gallery	Broderbund	ClickArt
	Intuit	Quicken		Nova Development	Art Explosion
Legal	Broderbund	Home and Business Lawyer		CoolArchive	CoolArchive
		WillWriter	Video and Audio Editing (for Personal Use)	Corel	VideoStudio
	Cosmi	Perfect Attorney		Microsoft	Windows Live Movie Maker
	Nolo	Quicken Legal Business Quicken WillMaker		Pinnacle Systems	Studio
				Roxio	Buzz
Tax Preparation	2nd Story Software	TaxACT	Home Design/ Landscaping	Broderbund	Instant Architect
	H&R Block	TaxCut		Chief Architect	Better Homes and Gardens Home Designer
	Intuit	TurboTax			
Desktop Publishing (for Personal Use)	Broderbund	The Print Shop PrintMaster		IMSI/Design	TurboFLOORPLAN
			Travel and Mapping	DeLorme	Street Atlas
	Microsoft	Publisher		Microsoft	Streets & Trips
Paint/Image Editing (for Personal Use)	Corel	CorelDRAW Painter Essentials		Google	Earth Maps
	The GIMP Team	The Gimp	Reference	Fogware Publishing	Merriam-Webster Collegiate Dictionary & Thesaurus
Photo Editing and Photo Management (for Personal Use)	Adobe	Photoshop Elements Photoshop Express			
	Corel	Paint Shop Pro Photo Ulead PhotoImpact MediaOne Plus		Microsoft	MSN Encarta
	Yahoo!	Flickr			
	Google	Picasa			
	Microsoft	Windows Live Photo Gallery			
	Roxio	PhotoShow			

Figure 3-21 Many popular programs are available for home, personal, and educational use.

Personal Finance Software

Personal finance software is a simplified accounting program that helps home users and small office/home office users balance their checkbooks, pay bills, track personal income and expenses (Figure 3-22), track investments, and evaluate financial plans.

Most personal finance software includes financial planning features, such as analyzing home and personal loans, preparing income taxes, and managing retirement savings. Other features include managing home inventory and setting up budgets. Most of these programs also offer a variety of online services, such as online banking, which require access to the Internet.

? FAQ 3-2

How many people bank online?
The number of people banking online is approximately 50 million, with that number expected to continue growing. The chart to the right depicts the more popular online banking activities.

For more information, visit scsite.com/dc-off07/ch3/faq and then click Online Banking.

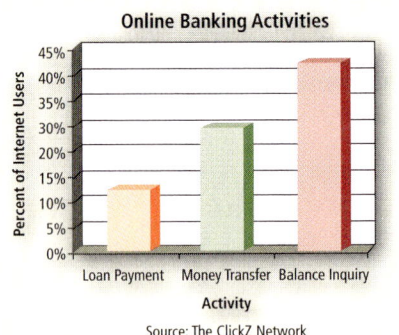

Figure 3-22 Personal finance software assists home users with tracking personal accounts, such as the savings account shown here.

Legal Software

Legal software assists in the preparation of legal documents and provides legal information to individuals, families, and small businesses (Figure 3-23). Legal software provides standard contracts and documents associated with buying, selling, and renting property; estate planning; marriage and divorce; and preparing a will or living trust. By answering a series of questions or completing a form, the legal software tailors the legal document to specific needs.

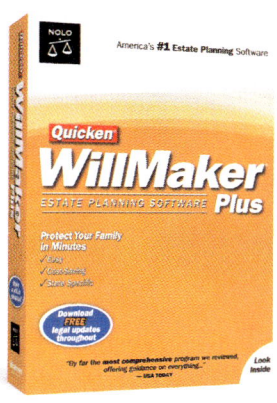

Figure 3-23 Legal software provides legal information and assists in record keeping and the preparation of legal documents.

Tax Preparation Software

Tax preparation software, which is available both as packaged software and Web applications, can guide individuals, families, or small businesses through the process of filing federal taxes (Figure 3-24). These programs forecast tax liability and offer money-saving tax tips, designed to lower your tax bill. After you answer a series of questions and complete basic forms, the software creates and analyzes your tax forms to search for missed potential errors and deduction opportunities.

Once the forms are complete, you can print any necessary paperwork, and then they are ready for filing. Some tax preparation programs also allow you to file your tax forms electronically.

Figure 3-24 Tax preparation software guides individuals, families, or small businesses through the process of filing federal taxes.

Desktop Publishing Software (for Personal Use)

Personal DTP software helps home and small business users create newsletters, brochures, flyers (Figure 3-25), advertisements, postcards, greeting cards, letterhead, business cards, banners, calendars, logos, and Web pages. Although many word processing programs include DTP features, users often prefer to create DTP documents using DTP software because of its enhanced features. For example, personal DTP programs provide hundreds of thousands of graphical images. You also can import (bring in) your own digital photos into the documents. These programs typically guide you through the development of a document by asking a series of questions. Then, you can print a finished publication on a color printer or post it on the Web.

Many personal DTP programs also include paint/image editing software and photo editing and photo management software.

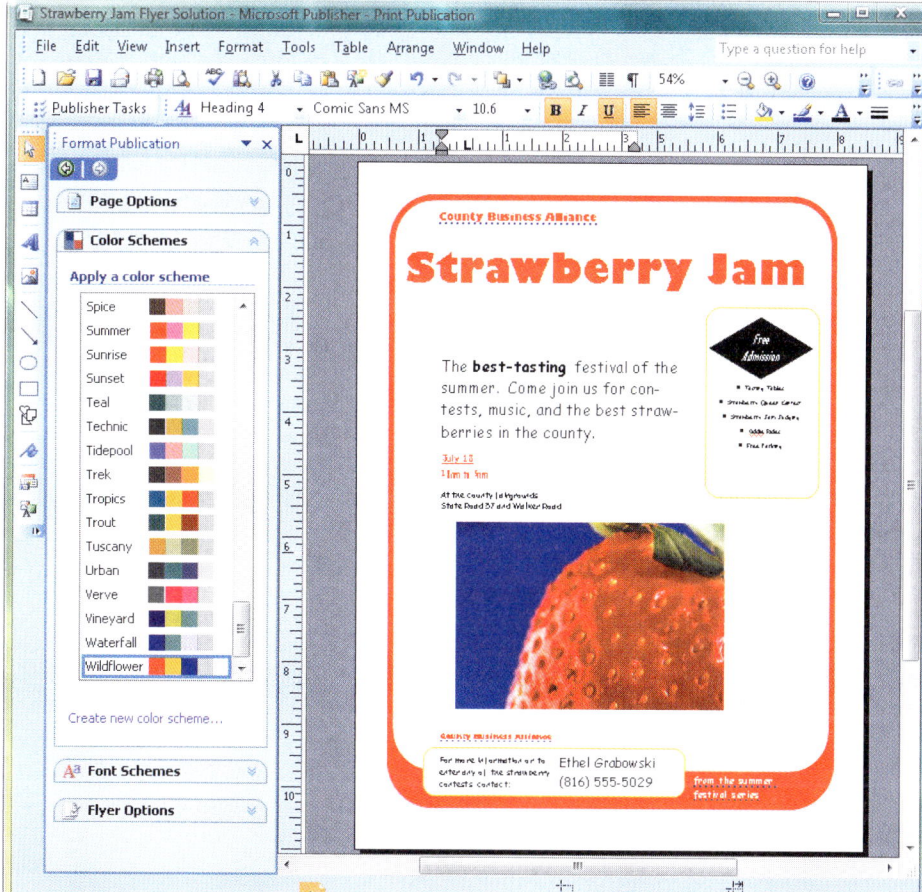

Figure 3-25 With desktop publishing software, home and small business users can create flyers.

Paint/Image Editing Software (for Personal Use)

Personal paint/image editing software provides an easy-to-use interface; includes various simplified tools that allow you to draw pictures, shapes, and other images; and provides the capability of modifying existing graphics and photos. These products also include many templates to assist you in adding images to documents such as greeting cards, banners, calendars, signs, labels, business cards, and letterhead.

Personal photo editing software, a popular type of image editing software available both as packaged software and as Web applications, allows users to edit digital photos by removing red-eye, erasing blemishes, restoring aged photos, adding special effects, enhancing image quality, or creating electronic photo albums. When you purchase a digital camera, it usually includes photo editing software (Figure 3-26). Some digital cameras even have basic photo editing software built in so that you can edit the image directly on the camera. You can print edited photos on labels, calendars, business cards, and banners, or you can post them on the Web.

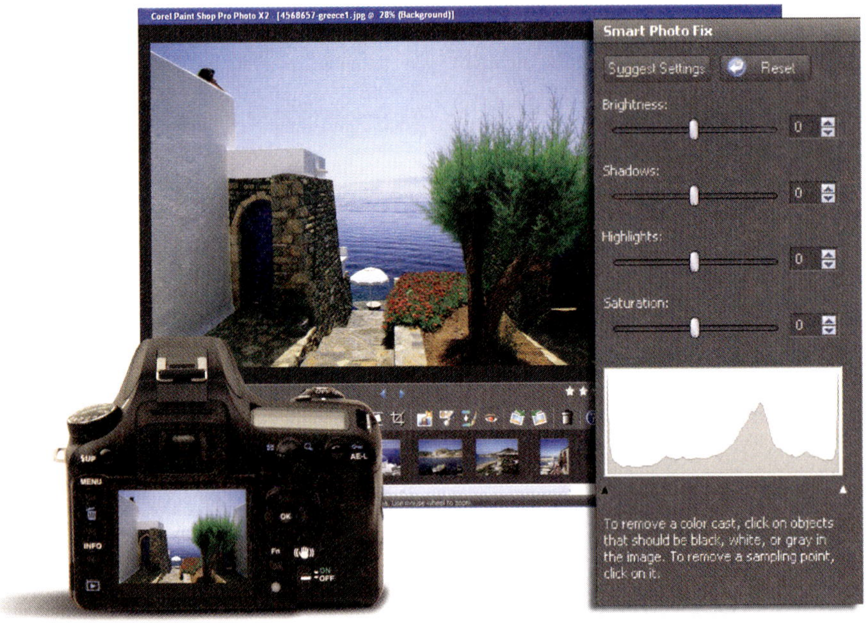

Figure 3-26 As shown here, home users adjust color on their digital photos with personal photo editing software.

With **photo management software**, you can view, organize, sort, catalog, print, and share digital photos. Some photo editing software includes photo management functionality.

Clip Art/Image Gallery

Application software often includes a **clip art/image gallery**, which is a collection of clip art and photos. Some programs have links to additional clips available on the Web or are available as Web applications. You also can purchase clip art/image gallery software that contains thousands of images (Figure 3-27).

In addition to clip art, many clip art/image galleries provide fonts, animations, sounds, video clips, and audio clips. You can use the images, fonts, and other items from the clip art/image gallery in all types of documents, including word processing, desktop publishing, spreadsheet, and presentations.

Figure 3-27 Clip art/image gallery software contains thousands of images.

Video and Audio Editing Software (for Personal Use)

Many home users work with easy-to-use video and audio editing software, which is much simpler to use than its professional counterpart, for small-scale movie making projects (Figure 3-28). With these programs, home users can edit home movies, add music or other sounds to the video, and share their movies on the Web. Some operating systems include video editing and audio editing software.

Figure 3-28 With personal video and audio editing software, home users can edit their home movies.

Home Design/Landscaping Software

Homeowners or potential homeowners can use **home design/landscaping software** to assist them with the design, remodeling, or improvement of a home, deck, or landscape (Figure 3-29). This software includes hundreds of predrawn plans that you can customize to meet your needs. These programs show changes to home designs and landscapes, allowing homeowners to preview proposed modifications.

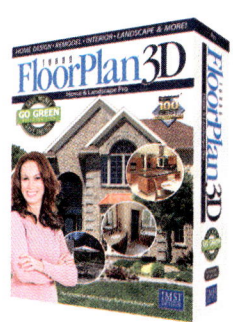

Figure 3-29 Home design/landscaping software can help you design or remodel a home, deck, or landscape.

Travel and Mapping Software

Travel and mapping software enables users to view maps, determine route directions, and locate points of interest (Figure 3-30). Using travel and mapping software, which is available both as packaged software and as Web applications, you can display maps by searching for an address, postal code, telephone number, or point of interest (such as airports, lodging, and historical sites). Most programs also allow you to download construction reports and calculate mileage, time, and expenses. Read Looking Ahead 3-1 for a look at the next generation of navigation software.

↗ LOOKING AHEAD 3-1

Sensors Help Drivers Find Their Way

Navigating through town may become less burdensome with products under development at Microsoft. Current devices are touted as being small enough to fit in a pocket, but this size can be a hindrance for people with large hands. When they attempt to place their fingers on the touch screen to press the commands, their fingers cover information they are trying to see.

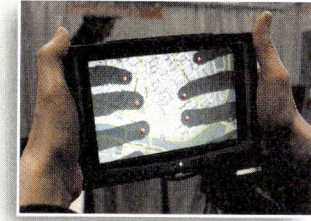

Microsoft's prototype LucidTouch solves this problem by allowing users to place their hands underneath the device, in-between it and a camera attached to the back. The camera captures an image of their hands, and the device overlays a semitransparent shadow of their fingers on the screen.

Microsoft also is developing sensors for a cell phone that collect data as a driver passes through town. These accelerometers sense speed, braking, and even when the driver hits a pothole, and the cell phone's microphone can detect the car's horn. Another potential use of Microsoft's sensors in cell phones is to monitor the behavior and health status of the elderly so that they can lead independent lives.

👆 For more information, visit scsite.com/dc-off07/ch3/looking and then click Mapping.

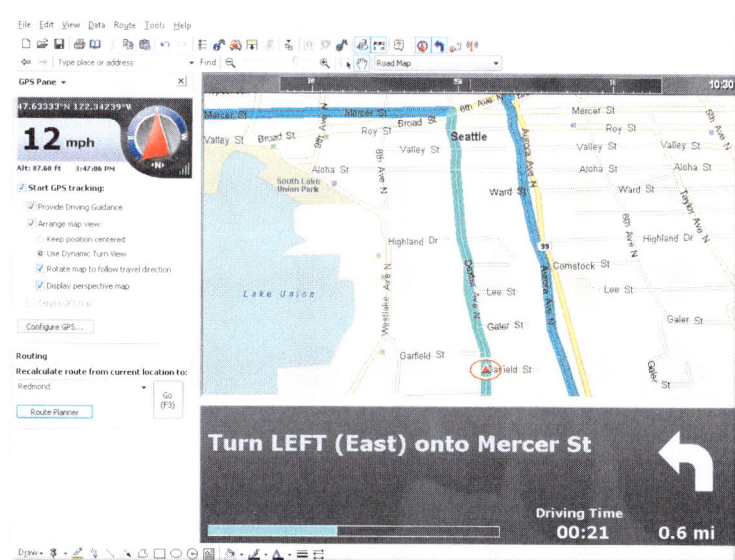

Figure 3-30 This software provides turn-by-turn directions, along with estimated travel times.

Reference and Educational Software

Reference software provides valuable and thorough information for all individuals. Popular reference software includes encyclopedias, dictionaries, and health/medical guides.

Educational software teaches a particular skill. Educational software exists for just about any subject, from learning how to type (Figure 3-31) to learning how to cook to preparing for college entrance exams. Educational software often includes games and other content to make the learning experience more fun. Many educational programs use a computer-based training approach. **Computer-based training (CBT)** is a type of education in which students learn by using and completing exercises with instructional software. CBT typically consists of self-directed, self-paced instruction about a topic.

Figure 3-31 Educational software can teach a skill.

Entertainment Software

Entertainment software for personal computers includes interactive games, videos, and other programs designed to support a hobby or provide amusement and enjoyment. For example, you might use entertainment software to play games individually (Figure 3-32) or with others online, make a family tree, or fly an aircraft. Many games are available as Web applications, allowing you to play individually or with other online players.

? FAQ 3-3

How popular is entertainment software?
The popularity of entertainment software has increased greatly during the past few years. More than 65 percent of American households play computer or video games. Further, more than 36 percent play games on a mobile device such as a smart phone or PDA.

👆 For more information, visit scsite.com/dc-off07/ch3/faq and then click Entertainment Software.

👆 Game Software
For more information, visit scsite.com/dc-off07/ch3/weblink and then click Game Software.

Figure 3-32 Entertainment software can provide hours of recreation on personal computers, game consoles, and mobile devices.

Web Applications

As previously mentioned, a Web application, or **Web app**, is a Web site that allows users to access and interact with software from any computer or device that is connected to the Internet. Users often interact with Web applications directly at the Web site, referred to as the host, through their Web browser. Some Web sites, however, require you download the software to your local computer or device. Web application hosts often store users' data and information on their servers. Some Web applications provide users with an option of storing data locally on their own personal computer or mobile device. Many of the previously discussed types of application software are available as Web applications (Figure 3-33). Read Ethics & Issues 3-2 for a related discussion.

Popular Web Applications

Program Name	Type of Application Software	Program Name	Type of Application Software
Britannica.com	Reference	MSN Encarta	Reference
Dictionary.com	Reference	Photoshop Express	Photo Editing
Flickr	Photo Editing and Photo Management	Picnik	Photo Editing
		TaxACT Online	Tax Preparation
Gmail	E-Mail	TurboTax Online	Tax Preparation
Google Docs	Productivity Suite	Windows Live Calendar	Personal Information Manager
Google Earth	Travel and Mapping	Windows Live Hotmail	E-Mail
Google Maps	Travel and Mapping	YouSendIt	File Transfer and E-Mail

Figure 3-33 Some popular Web applications. For practice using Web applications, complete the last Learn It Online exercise in each chapter.

Many Web application hosts provide free access to their software, such as Google Docs shown in Figure 3-34. Others, such as Google Earth, offer part of their Web application free and charge for access to a more comprehensive program. Some Web applications allow you to use the Web application free and pay a fee when a certain action occurs. For example, you can prepare your tax return free, but if you elect to print it or file it electronically, you pay a minimal fee.

Experts often use the term Web 2.0 to describe Web applications. Recall that Web 2.0 refers to Web sites that provide users with a means to share personal information, allow users to modify Web site content, and/or have application software built into the site for visitors to use.

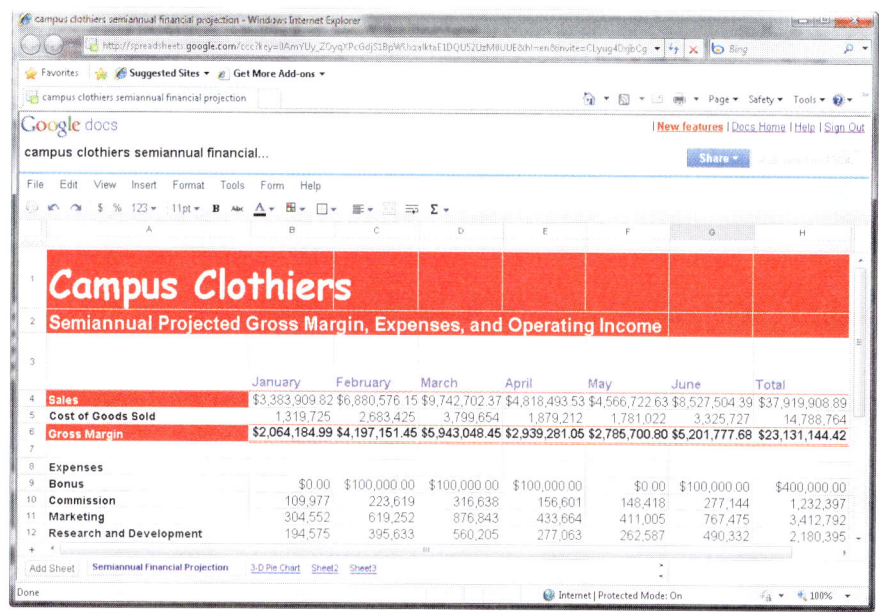

Figure 3-34 The spreadsheet shown here in Google Docs is the same Microsoft Excel spreadsheet that is shown in Figure 3-7 on page 103. Differences between the two figures are due to different features in the two programs.

ETHICS & ISSUES 3-2

Should Online Mapping Services Make You Feel More Secure or More Vulnerable?

Most Internet users find that online maps, such as Google Maps and Bing Maps, provide tremendous convenience and reliability. Instead of searching the house or car for maps or making phone calls for directions, a quick Web search results in a readable map with exact directions. Sometimes, even photos of the route and location are available. Some parents and advocacy groups, however, claim that the services allow predators to locate potential victims quickly. Google Maps, for example, provides photos for neighborhoods of entire cities. The opponents of the services believe that predators may find potential victims in the photos, or find likely locations where a crime may be easier to commit. Opponents of this point of view state that mapping services allow known predators and high-crime areas to be more readily identified. The services, therefore, increase personal security because the location of known predators can be pinpointed before they find victims. The services also provide much more positive value than any potential problems that they create, and, therefore, should thrive.

Do online mapping services make you feel more secure or more vulnerable? Why? Should parents and neighborhood associations have the legal right to have photos and personal information removed from mapping services? Why or why not? Would you feel comfortable if a service such as Google Maps showed a photo of you walking your normal route from home to work or school? Why?

Application Software for Communications

One of the main reasons people use computers is to communicate and share information with others. Some communications software is considered system software because it works with hardware and transmission media. Other communications software performs specific tasks for users, and thus, is considered application software. Chapter 2 presented a variety of application software for communications, which is summarized in the table in Figure 3-35.

> **? FAQ 3-4**
>
> **Does text messaging improve typing skills?**
>
> Although some individuals are able to send text messages from their phones quickly, the differences in layout between a phone keypad and a standard computer keyboard might not allow for their typing skills to improve at the same rate. Some individuals are able to send text messages more quickly than they can type. In fact, a 20-year-old college student won $50,000 in a text messaging competition when he typed more than 125 characters in 50 seconds with no mistakes.
>
> 👆 For more information, visit scsite.com/dc-off07/ch3/faq and then click Text Messaging.

Application Software for Communications

Web Browser
- Allows users to access and view Web pages on the Internet
- Requires a Web browser program
  - Integrated in some operating systems
  - Available for download on the Web free or for a fee

E-Mail
- Messages and files sent via a network such as the Internet
- Requires an e-mail program
  - Integrated in many software suites and operating systems
  - Available free at portals on the Web
  - Included with paid Internet access service
  - Can be purchased separately from retailers

Instant Messaging
- Real-time exchange of messages, files, audio, and/or video with another online user
- Requires instant messenger software
  - Integrated in some operating systems
  - Available for download on the Web, usually at no cost
  - Included with some paid Internet access services

Chat Room
- Real-time, online typed conversation
- Requires chat client software
  - Integrated in some operating systems, e-mail programs, and Web browsers
  - Available for download on the Web, usually at no cost
  - Included with some paid Internet access services
  - Built into some Web sites

Text, Picture, Video Messaging
- Short text, picture, or video messages sent and received, mainly on mobile devices
- Requires text, picture, video messenger software
  - Integrated in most mobile devices
  - Available for download on the Web, usually at no cost, for personal computers

RSS Aggregator
- Keeps track of changes made to Web sites by checking RSS feeds
- Requires RSS aggregator program
  - Integrated in some e-mail programs and Web browsers
  - Available for download on the Web, usually at no cost

Blogging
- Time-stamped articles, or posts, in a diary or journal format, usually listed in reverse chronological order
- Blogger needs blog software, or blogware, to create/maintain blog
  - Some Web sites do not require installation of blog software

Newsgroup/Message Board
- Online area where users have written discussions
- Newsgroup may require a newsreader program
  - Integrated in some operating systems, e-mail programs, and Web browsers

FTP
- Method of uploading and downloading files with other computers on the Internet
- May require an FTP program
  - Integrated in some operating systems
  - Available for download on the Web for a small fee

VoIP (Internet Telephony)
- Allows users to speak to other users over the Internet
- Requires Internet connection, Internet telephone service, microphone or telephone, and Internet telephone software or telephone adapter

Video Conferencing
- Meeting between geographically separated people who use a network such as the Internet to transmit video/audio
- Requires video conferencing software, a microphone, speakers, and sometimes a video camera attached to your computer

Figure 3-35 A summary of application software for home and business communications.

Learning Tools for Application Software

Learning how to use application software effectively involves time and practice. To assist in the learning process, many programs provide online Help (Figure 3-36) and Web-based Help.

Online Help is the electronic equivalent of a user manual. When working with a program, you can use online Help to ask a question or access the Help topics in subject or alphabetical order. Most online Help also links to Web sites that offer Web-based help, which provides updates and more comprehensive resources to respond to technical issues about software.

Many books are available to help you learn to use the features of personal computer programs. These books typically are available in bookstores and software stores.

Web-Based Training

Web-based training (**WBT**) is a type of computer-based training (CBT) that uses Internet technology and consists of application software on the Web. Similar to CBT, WBT typically consists of self-directed, self-paced instruction about a topic. WBT is popular in business, industry, and schools for teaching new skills or enhancing existing skills of employees, teachers, or students.

Many Web sites offer WBT to the general public. Such training covers a wide range of topics, from how to change a flat tire to creating documents in Word. Many of these Web sites are free. Others require registration and payment to take the complete Web-based course.

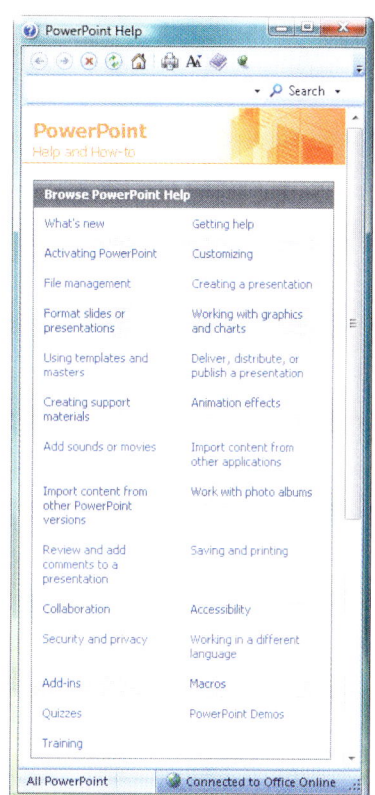

Figure 3-36 Many programs include online Help.

WBT often is combined with other materials for distance learning and e-learning. **Distance learning** is the delivery of education at one location while the learning takes place at other locations. **E-learning**, short for electronic learning, is the delivery of education via some electronic method such as the Internet, networks, or optical discs. To enhance communications, e-learning systems also may include video conferencing, e-mail, blogs, wikis, newsgroups, chat rooms, and groupware (Figure 3-37).

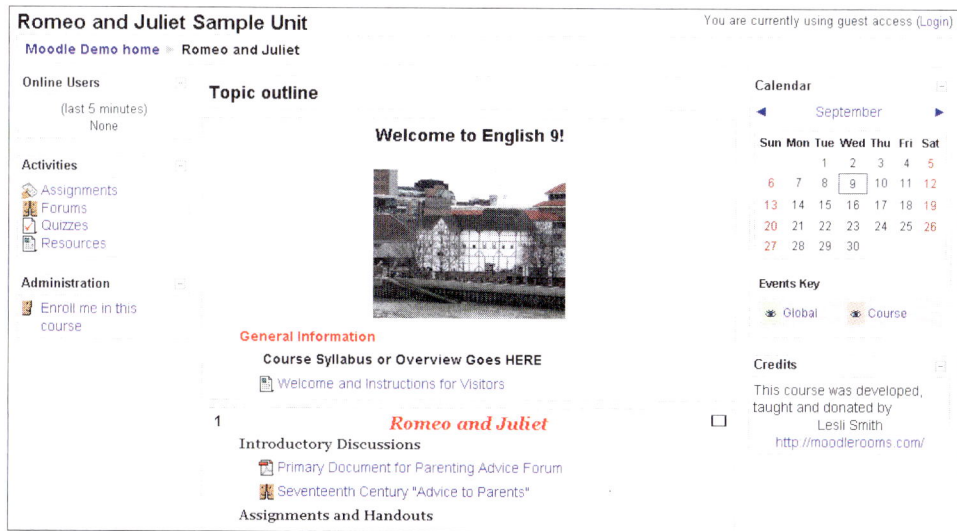

Figure 3-37 E-learning systems enable instructors to post course materials for their students.

QUIZ YOURSELF 3-3

Instructions: Find the true statement below. Then, rewrite the remaining false statements so that they are true.

1. All Web application hosts provide free access to their software.
2. Computer-based training is a type of Web-based training that uses Internet technology and consists of application software on the Web.
3. E-mail and Web browsers are examples of communications software that are considered application software.
4. Legal software is a simplified accounting program that helps home users and small office/home office users balance their checkbooks, pay bills, track investments, and evaluate financial plans.
5. Personal DTP software is a popular type of image editing software that allows users to edit digital photos.

Quiz Yourself Online: To further check your knowledge of pages 111 through 119, visit scsite.com/dc-off07/ch3/quiz and then click Objectives 5 – 8.

Chapter Summary

This chapter illustrated how to start and interact with application software. It presented an overview of a variety of business software, graphics and multimedia software, and home/personal/educational software. Finally, Web applications, application software for communications, and learning tools for application software were presented.

Computer Usage @ Work

Construction

Walking the streets, you stop to admire a new skyscraper with the most striking architectural features you ever have seen. You think to yourself that those responsible for designing the building are nothing less than brilliant. While a great deal of work goes into the design and construction of a building, computers and technology also play an important role in the process. In fact, the role of computers not only saves time and provides for more accurate results, it also allows us to preview how a building will look before construction even begins.

As mentioned in the chapter, computer-aided design (CAD) software is a sophisticated type of application software that assists a professional user in creating engineering, architectural, and scientific plans. During the preliminary design process, architects and design firms use CAD software to design the appearance and layout of a new building and can provide clients with a three-dimensional walkthrough of a building so that they can determine whether the proposed design will meet their needs. Later, the program can be used to include the placement of support beams, walls, roof shape, and so on, and also conform to building code.

CAD software allows engineers in various fields, such as mechanical and electrical, to design separate layers in a structure. The CAD software then can superimpose the designs to check for interactions and conflicts, such as if a structural beam in one layer covers a drain in another layer. The CAD software makes it easy to modify and correct the structure before it is built, which can save time and money during the construction process. This software also eliminates most, if not all, of the manual drafting required.

Engineers use computers to determine the type of foundation required to support the building and its occupants; the heating, ventilating, and air conditioning (HVAC); and the electrical requirements, as well as how the building may withstand external threats such as hurricanes and tornadoes.

During construction, contractors and builders are able to use computer software to estimate accurately the amount of materials and time required to complete the job. Without computers, determining materials and time required is a cumbersome and time-consuming task.

The next time you notice a building under construction, stop to think about how computer technology has increased the efficiency of the design and construction process.

For more information, visit scsite.com/dc-off07/ch3/work and then click Construction.

Companies on the Cutting Edge

ADOBE SYSTEMS Design Software Leader

Practically all creative professionals involved with art and photography have a copy of Adobe Photoshop on their computer, and the leading computer manufacturers ship their products with a copy of Adobe Reader installed. The worldwide presence of Adobe Systems software attests to the company's success in developing programs that help people communicate effectively.

Charles Geschke and John Warnock founded the company in 1982 and named it after a creek that ran behind Warnock's house in California. Creative Suite contains the fundamental tools that help photographers, designers, and publishers develop and maintain their documents and Web sites, and it includes Dreamweaver, Flash, Fireworks, Contribute, InDesign, Illustrator, and Photoshop.

In 2009, Adobe was voted one of the 100 Best Companies to Work For.

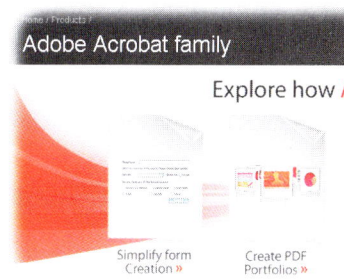

MICROSOFT Computer Technology Innovator

Internet users view Microsoft's Web site more than 2.4 million times each day, attesting to the company's presence as the largest software company in the world. Its Office and Internet Explorer programs dominate the computer industry, and it also has assets in the MSNBC cable television network, the Encarta multimedia encyclopedia, SharePoint, and gaming software, including Flight Simulator and Zoo Tycoon. Microsoft also manufactures hardware, such as the Xbox, Zune, mouse devices, keyboards, fingerprint readers, Web cams, and game controllers.

When Microsoft was incorporated in 1975, the company had three programmers, one product, and revenues of $16,000. The company now employs more than 92,000 people and has annual revenues in excess of $58 billion. In 2009, Microsoft released Windows 7, the latest version of its flagship operating system.

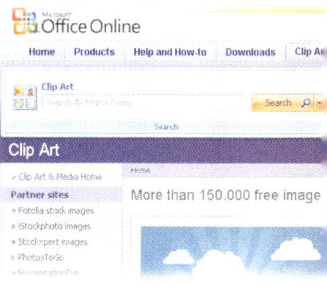

✋ For more information, visit scsite.com/dc-off07/ch3/companies.

Technology Trailblazers

DAN BRICKLIN VisiCalc Developer

Dan Bricklin introduced wikiCalc in 2007 as a free software tool for Web pages that have data in lists and tables. This program is an offshoot of a prototype program he had developed 30 years earlier, named VisiCalc, that performed a series of calculations automatically when numbers were entered.

Bricklin and a friend founded a company, Software Arts, to develop VisiCalc, short for Visible Calculator. They programmed the software using Apple Basic on an Apple II computer. This small program was the first type of application software that provided a reason for businesses to buy Apple computers. It included many features found in today's spreadsheet software.

Bricklin founded a small consulting company, Software Garden, to develop and market software such as wikiCalc. The company also distributes resources to help programmers learn about licensing their products and about open source software.

MASAYOSHI SON Softbank President and CEO

In the 1970s, Masayoshi Son was convinced that the microchip was going to change people's lives. As an economics major at the University of California, Berkeley, each day he attempted to develop one original use for computer technology. One of these ideas made him a millionaire: a multilingual pocket translating device that he sold to Sharp Corporation.

At age 23, Son founded Softbank, which is one of Japan's largest telecommunications and media corporations. He now is one of the richest men in the world with a net worth of $3.7 billion.

In 2008, Softbank partnered with Apple to develop a version of the iPhone for the Japanese market. In addition, Son's company collaborated with Tiffany & Co. to manufacture 10 cell phones, each worth more than $910,000, with 400 diamonds weighing more than 20 karats total.

✋ For more information, visit scsite.com/dc-off07/ch3/trailblazers.

Chapter Review

The Chapter Review reinforces the main concepts presented in this chapter.

👆 To obtain help from other students about any concept in this chapter, visit scsite.com/dc-off07/ch3/forum and post your thoughts and questions.

1. **What Are the Four Categories of Application Software?** **Application software** consists of programs designed to make users more productive and/or assist them with personal tasks. The major categories of application software are business software; graphics and multimedia software; home, personal, and educational software; and communications software.

2. **What Is the User Interface of Application Software?** Personal computer operating systems often use the concept of a **desktop**, which is an on-screen work area that has a graphical user interface. One way to start a program in Windows is to move the **pointer** to the Start **button** on the taskbar and **click** the Start button by pressing and releasing a button on the mouse. Then, click the program name on the menu or in a list. Once loaded in memory, the program is displayed in a **window** on the desktop.

   👆 Visit scsite.com/dc-off07/ch3/quiz and then click Objectives 1 – 2.

3. **What Are the Key Features of Widely Used Business Programs?** **Business software** assists people in becoming more effective and efficient while performing daily business activities. Business software includes the following programs. **Word processing software** allows users to **create** a document by entering text or numbers and inserting graphical images, **edit** the document by making changes to its existing content, and **format** the document by changing its appearance. **Spreadsheet software** allows users to organize data in rows and columns, perform calculations, recalculate when data changes, and chart the data in graphical form. **Database software** allows users to create a **database**, which is a collection of data organized in a manner that allows access, retrieval, and use of that data. **Presentation software** allows users to create slides that are displayed on a monitor or on a projection screen. **Note taking software** enables users to enter typed text, handwritten comments, drawings, and sketches. A **personal information manager (PIM)** includes an appointment calendar, address book, notepad, and other features to help users organize personal information. In addition to PIM software, a huge variety of business and other software is available for phones. A **software suite** is a collection of individual programs available together as a unit. **Project management software** allows users to plan, schedule, track, and analyze the events, resources, and costs of a project. **Accounting software** helps companies record and report their financial transactions. **Document management software** provides a means for sharing, distributing, and searching through documents by converting them into a format that can be viewed by any user.

4. **What Are the Key Features of Widely Used Graphics and Multimedia Programs?** Graphics and multimedia software includes the following. **Computer-aided design (CAD) software** assists a professional user in creating engineering, architectural, and scientific designs. **Desktop publishing (DTP) software** enables professional designers to create sophisticated documents that contain text, graphics, and colors. **Paint software** allows users to draw pictures, shapes, and other graphical images with various on-screen tools. **Image editing software** provides the capabilities of paint software and also includes the capability to modify existing images. **Professional photo editing software** is a type of image editing software that allows photographers, videographers, engineers, scientists, and other high-volume digital photo users to edit and customize digital photos. **Video editing software** allows professionals to modify a segment of a video, called a clip. **Audio editing software** lets users modify audio clips, produce studio-quality soundtracks, and add audio to video clips. **Multimedia authoring software** allows users to combine text, graphics, audio, video, and animation into an interactive application. **Web page authoring software** helps users create Web pages and organize and maintain Web sites.

   👆 Visit scsite.com/dc-off07/ch3/quiz and then click Objectives 3 – 4.

5. **What Are the Key Features of Widely Used Home, Personal, and Educational Programs?** Software for home, personal, and educational use includes the following. **Personal finance software** is a simplified accounting program that helps users balance their checkbooks, pay bills, track personal income and expenses, track investments, and evaluate financial plans. **Legal software** assists in the preparation of legal documents and provides legal information. **Tax preparation software** can guide users through the process of filing federal taxes. **Personal DTP software** helps home and small business users create newsletters, brochures, flyers, advertisements, postcards, greeting cards, letterhead, business cards, banners, calendars, logos, and Web pages. **Personal paint/image editing software** provides an easy-to-use interface and includes various simplified tools that allow you to draw pictures, shapes, and other images and to modify existing graphics and photos. Application software

often includes a **clip art/image gallery**, which is a collection of clip art and photos. **Home design/landscaping software** assists users with the design, remodeling, or improvement of a home, deck, or landscape. **Travel and mapping software** allows users to view maps, determine routes, and locate points of interest. **Reference software** provides valuable and thorough information for all individuals. **Educational software** teaches a particular skill. **Entertainment software** includes interactive games, video, and other programs.

6. **What Are Web Applications?** A **Web application**, or **Web app**, is a Web site that allows users to access and interact with software from any computer or device that is connected to the Internet. Users often interact with Web applications directly at the Web site, referred to as the host, through their Web browser. Some Web sites require you to download the software to your computer or device.

7. **What Are the Types of Application Software Used in Communications?** Application software for communications includes Web browsers to access and view Web pages; e-mail programs to transmit messages via a network; instant messaging software for real-time exchange of messages or files; chat room software to have real-time, online typed conversations; text, picture, and video messaging software; RSS aggregator program to keep track of changes made to Web sites; blog software, or blogware, to create and maintain a blog; newsgroup/message board programs that allow online written discussions; FTP programs to upload and download files on the Internet; VoIP (Internet telephony), which allows users to speak to other users over the Internet; and video conferencing software for meetings on a network.

8. **What Learning Aids Are Available for Application Software?** To assist in the learning process, many programs provide **online Help**, which is the electronic equivalent of a user manual. Most online Help also links to Web-based Help, which provides updates and more comprehensive resources to respond to technical issues about software. Popular in business, industry, and schools, **Web-based training** (**WBT**) uses Internet technology and consists of application software on the Web.

Visit scsite.com/dc-off07/ch3/quiz and then click Objectives 5 – 8.

Key Terms

You should know the Key Terms. The list below helps focus your study.

To see an example of and a definition for each term, and to access current and additional information from the Web, visit scsite.com/dc-off07/ch3/terms.

accounting software (107)
application software (96)
audio editing software (110)
business software (100)
button (98)
click (98)
clip art (101)
clip art/image gallery (114)
command (98)
computer-aided design (CAD) software (109)
computer-based training (CBT) (115)
create (102)
custom software (96)
database (104)
database software (104)
desktop (98)
desktop publishing (DTP) software (109)
distance learning (119)
document management software (107)

edit (102)
educational software (115)
e-learning (119)
entertainment software (116)
file (98)
font (102)
font size (102)
font style (102)
format (102)
freeware (97)
home design/landscaping software (115)
icon (98)
image editing software (109)
legal software (113)
malware (98)
menu (98)
multimedia authoring software (110)
note taking software (106)
online Help (119)
open source software (97)
packaged software (96)

paint software (109)
PDF (107)
personal DTP software (113)
personal finance software (112)
personal information manager (PIM) (106)
personal paint/image editing software (114)
personal photo editing software (114)
photo management software (114)
pointer (98)
presentation software (105)
print (102)
professional photo editing software (109)
project management software (106)
public-domain software (97)
reference software (115)
save (102)

shareware (97)
software suite (106)
spreadsheet software (103)
system software (97)
tax preparation software (113)
title bar (98)
travel and mapping software (115)
video editing software (110)
Web app (116)
Web application (96)
Web page authoring software (110)
Web-based training (WBT) (119)
window (98)
word processing software (101)
worksheet (103)

Checkpoint

The Checkpoint exercises test your knowledge of the chapter concepts. The page number containing the answer appears in parentheses after each exercise.

👆 To complete the Checkpoint exercises interactively, visit scsite.com/dc-off07/ch3/check.

Multiple Choice Select the best answer.

1. _____ is mass-produced, copyrighted retail software that meets the needs of a wide variety of users, not just a single user or company. (96)
   a. Custom software
   b. Open source software
   c. A Web application
   d. Packaged software

2. A feature, called _____, allows users of word processing software to type words continually without pressing the ENTER key at the end of each line. (101)
   a. AutoFormat
   b. clipboard
   c. AutoCorrect
   d. wordwrap

3. When using spreadsheet software, a function _____. (103)
   a. depicts data in graphical form
   b. changes certain values to reveal the effects of the changes
   c. is a predefined formula that performs common calculations
   d. contains the formatting necessary for a specific worksheet type

4. _____ combines application software such as word processing, spreadsheet, presentation graphics, and e-mail. (106)
   a. Shareware
   b. A software suite
   c. Packaged software
   d. Custom software

5. _____ software provides a means for sharing, distributing, and searching through documents by converting them into a format that can be viewed by any user. (107)
   a. Portable Document Format (PDF)
   b. Document management
   c. Database
   d. Word processing

6. With _____, you can view, organize, sort, catalog, print, and share digital photos. (114)
   a. spreadsheet software
   b. photo management software
   c. clip art
   d. desktop publishing software

7. A(n) _____ is an online area where users have written discussions. (118)
   a. FTP program
   b. text message
   c. newsgroup/message board
   d. Web browser

8. _____ is the electronic equivalent of a user manual. (119)
   a. Distance learning
   b. Online Help
   c. Web-based training
   d. E-learning

Matching Match the terms with their definitions.

_____ 1. command (98)
_____ 2. format (102)
_____ 3. note taking software (106)
_____ 4. personal finance software (112)
_____ 5. Web app (116)

a. delivers applications to meet a specific business need
b. simplified accounting program that helps home users and small office/home office users balance their checkbooks, pay bills, track personal income and expenses, set up budgets, manage home inventory, track investments, and evaluate financial plans
c. an instruction that causes a program to perform a specific action
d. Web site that allows users to access and interact with software from any computer or device that is connected to the Internet
e. enables users to enter typed text, handwritten comments, drawings, or sketches anywhere on a page
f. change the appearance of a document

Short Answer Write brief answer to each of the following questions.

1. Describe some types of utility programs. _____ What is malware? _____
2. What are the features of presentation software? _____ What types of media might a person use to enhance a presentation? _____
3. How is video editing software used? _____ How is multimedia authoring software used? _____
4. How is travel and mapping software used? _____ What are some examples of educational software? _____
5. Describe how many Web sites utilize Web-based training. _____ What are some ways that e-learning enhances communications? _____

Problem Solving

The Problem Solving exercises extend your knowledge of the chapter concepts by seeking solutions to practical computer problems that you may encounter at home, school, or work. The Collaboration exercise should be completed with a team.

☞ To discuss the Problem Solving exercises with other students, visit scsite.com/dc-off07/ch3/forum and post your thoughts or questions.

In the real world, practical problems often can be solved in multiple ways. Provide one solution to each of the following problems using available resources, such as articles on the Web or in print, blogs, podcasts, videos, television, user guides, other individuals, and electronics and computer stores. You may need to use multiple resources to obtain an answer. Present your solutions in the form requested by your instructor (brief report, presentation, discussion, or other means).

@ Home

1. **Program Not Responding**   While working with a document, Microsoft Word suddenly fails to recognize when you click the mouse or type on the keyboard. The title bar also indicates that the program is not responding. What could be wrong?

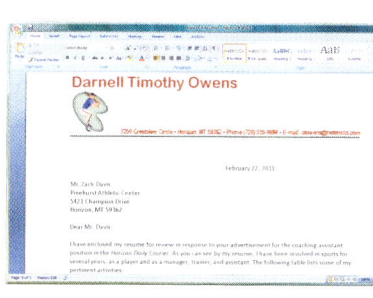

2. **Unwanted Page**   A local charity in which you are active has asked you to design a one-page brochure. Each time you print the brochure, it prints the first page correctly, but a blank second page also comes out. What steps will you take to eliminate the blank second page?

3. **Audio Not Playing**   You are attempting for the first time to transfer video from your video recorder directly to your computer. When you save the file on your computer and play it back, the video quality is acceptable, but there is no audio. What is the first step you will take to troubleshoot this problem?

4. **Unusual File Size**   You are using photo editing software to remove red eye from a photo. After successfully removing the red eye, you save the file and notice that the size of the file nearly has doubled. What might be causing this?

@ Work

5. **Missing Font**   A coworker has sent you a document that was created in Microsoft Word. She asks you to format the heading of the document with a specific font; however, the font name does not appear in your list of fonts. What steps will you take to retrieve the font?

6. **Insufficient Permission**   When reviewing a document in your company's document management system, you attempt to correct a typographical error for the next person who views the file. The document management system prohibits this action and informs you that you do not have the proper permission. What will you do to resolve this problem?

7. **Trial Version Expired**   New job responsibilities require that you use Adobe Photoshop to create a new company logo. Your boss has been unable to purchase the latest version of the software for you, and recommends that you download and install the trial version until she is able to purchase the software. The trial period now has expired and you are unable to use the program. How might you be able to continue using the software?

8. **Web-Based Training Difficulties**   You have signed up for Web-based training that is designed to teach you how to use your company's new accounting system. During your training, you notice that the Web-based training Web site is not keeping track of your progress. Consequently, you have to start from the beginning each time you log in. What might be causing this?

Collaboration

9. **Computers in Construction**   As a student in a drafting class, your instructor has challenged you to design your dream home by using application software wherever possible. Form a team of three people that will determine how to accomplish this objective. One team member should compare and contrast two programs that can be used to create a two-dimensional floor plan, another team member should compare and contrast two computer-aided design programs that can create a more detailed design of the house, and the third team member should compare and contrast two programs that can assist with other aspects of the design process such as landscaping and interior design.

Learn How To

The Learn How To activities step you through fundamental technology skills when using a computer. The Learn How To exercises enable you to become more proficient with these skills.

> Premium Activity: To relate this Learn How To activity to your everyday life, see a visual demonstration of the activity, and then complete a short assessment, visit scsite.com/dc-off07/ch3/howto.

Learn How To 1: Save a File in Application Software

When you use application software, most of the time you either will be creating a new file or modifying an existing file. For example, if you are using a word processor, when you create a new document, the document is a file.

When you create or modify a file, it is contained in RAM. If you turn off your computer or lose electrical power, the file will not be retained. In order to retain the file, you must save it on disk or other permanent storage, such as a USB flash drive.

As you create the file, you should save the file often. To save a new file, you must complete several tasks:

1. Initiate an action indicating you want to save the file, such as selecting Save on the File menu.
2. Designate where the file should be stored. This includes identifying both the device (such as drive C) and the folder or library.
3. Specify the name of the file, using the file name rules as specified by the application or operating system.
4. Click the Save button to save the file.

Tasks 2 through 4 normally can be completed using a dialog box such as the one shown in Figure 3-38.

If you use application software to create or modify a file and attempt to close the program prior to saving the new or modified file, the program may display a dialog box that asks if you want to save the file. If you click the Yes button, a modified file will be saved using the same file name in the same location from which it was retrieved. Saving a new file requires that you complete tasks 2 through 4.

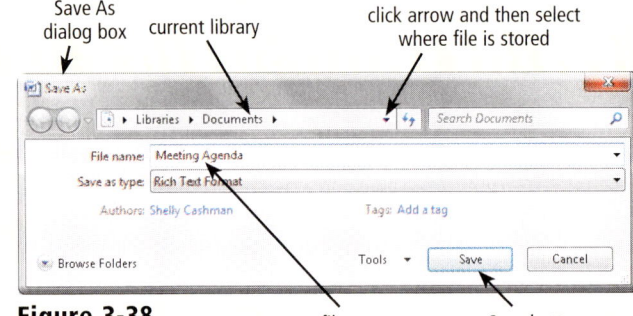

Figure 3-38

Exercise

1a. Start the WordPad program from the Accessories list in the All Programs list. Type `Saving a file is the best insurance against losing work.`

1b. Click the Save button on the Quick Access Toolbar. What dialog box is displayed? Where will the file be saved? What is the default file name? If you wanted to save the file on the desktop, what would you do? Click the Cancel button in the dialog box. Submit your answers to your instructor.

1c. Click the Close button in the upper-right corner of the WordPad window. What happened? Click the Yes button in the WordPad dialog box. What happened? Connect a USB flash drive to one of the computer's USB ports. Select the USB flash drive as the location for saving the file. Save the file with the name, Chapter 3 Learn How To 1. What happened when you clicked the Save button? Submit your answers to your instructor.

Learn How To 2: Zip/Compress a File

When you zip or compress one or more files in Windows, it attempts to shrink the file size(s) by reducing the amount of unneeded space. Compressing a file is particularly useful when you attach files to an e-mail message and wish to keep the file size as small as possible. It also is useful when you compress multiple files simultaneously, because Windows compresses the multiple files into a single file. You can compress a file or folder by completing the following steps:

1. Locate the file(s) or folder(s) you want to compress. If the files or folders you wish to compress are located in multiple locations, it might be helpful to first move them so that they are in a single location.
2. Select the file(s) or folder(s) you would like to compress. If you are selecting multiple files or folders, click the first one and then hold down the CTRL key while you select the remaining files and/or folders. Once you are finished making your selections, release the CTRL key.

Application Software Chapter 3 127

3. Right-click the selection to display a shortcut menu, point to Send to on the shortcut menu to display the Send to submenu (Figure 3-39), and then click Compressed (zipped) folder to create the compressed folder.
4. If necessary, type a new name for the compressed folder and then press the ENTER key.

Exercise

1. To better organize your hard disk, you decide to compress files you rarely use, but would like to keep as a backup. Click the Start button to display the Start menu, click Pictures to display the Pictures library, and then double-click the Sample Pictures folder to display sample pictures included with Windows 7. Select three pictures and compress them into one compressed folder. Use your first initial and last name as the name of the new compressed folder and then e-mail the folder to your instructor.

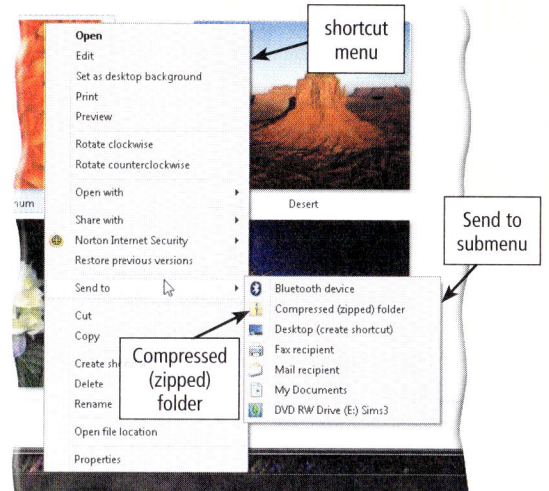

Figure 3-39

Learn It Online

The Learn It Online exercises are interactive Web exercises designed to reinforce and expand your understanding of the chapter concepts. The descriptions below briefly summarize each exercise.

☞ To access the Learn It Online exercises and for specific exercise instructions, visit scsite.com/dc-off07/ch3/learn.

❶ At the Movies — MediaCell Video Converter
Watch a movie to learn how to use the MediaCell Video Converter and then answer questions about the movie.

❷ Student Edition Labs — Word Processing, Spreadsheets, Databases, and Presentation Software
Enhance your understanding and knowledge about business application software by completing the Word Processing, Spreadsheets, Databases, and Presentation Software Labs.

❸ Practice Test
Take a multiple choice test that checks your knowledge of the chapter concepts and review the resulting study guide.

❹ Who Wants To Be a Computer Genius^2?
Play the Shelly Cashman Series version of this popular game by answering questions to find out if you are a computer genius. Panic buttons are available to provide assistance during game play.

❺ Crossword Puzzle Challenge
Complete an interactive crossword puzzle to reinforce concepts presented in this chapter.

❻ Windows Exercises
Step through the Windows 7 exercises to learn about working with application programs, creating a word processing document, using WordPad Help, and business software products.

❼ Exploring Computer Careers
Read about a career as a help desk specialist, search for related employment advertisements, and then answer related questions.

❽ Web Apps — Britannica.com
Learn how to browse world history and search for various encyclopedia articles using Britannica.com.

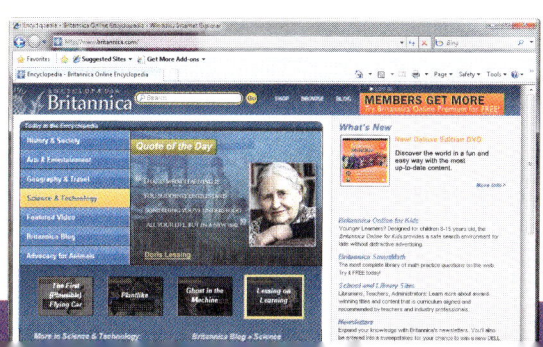

Web Research

The Web Research exercises broaden your understanding of chapter concepts by presenting questions that require you to search the Web for answers.

👆 To discuss any of the Web Research exercises in this chapter with other students, visit scsite.com/dc-off07/ch3/forum and post your thoughts or questions.

1 Search Sleuth

Use one of the search engines listed in Figure 2-8 in Chapter 2 on page 53 or your own favorite search engine to find the answers to the following questions. Copy and paste the Web address from the Web page where you found the answer. Some questions may have more than one answer. If required, submit your answers to your instructor. (1) What company did Bruce Artwick form in 1977, and what game did it license to Microsoft in 1982? (2) In what year did the United States Department of Revenue first provide tax forms and booklets in Adobe PDF format on its Web site? (3) What is the latest security incident listed on the United States Computer Emergency Readiness Team (US-CERT) Web site? (4) What is the name of the sans serif font the German Bauhaus movement developed in 1928? (5) What United States president's speech did Peter Norvig turn into a lighthearted PowerPoint presentation?

2 Green Computing

A typical desktop computer and 17-inch monitor that always are turned on release 750 pounds of carbon dioxide in one year, which is the same amount of carbon dioxide released by a car driven 820 miles. Power management software helps conserve a computer's electricity consumption while maintaining acceptable performance. The programs determine when a computer is inactive and, in turn, power down the computer. Use one of the search engines listed in Figure 2-8 in Chapter 2 on page 53 or your own favorite search engine to find information about power management software. What average return-on-investment do they promise? What features do they have, such as generating reports and exempting critical programs from powering down? What is their cost? Powering down the computer stresses critical components, such as the CPU and memory, so does this practice actually result in more waste because these parts must be replaced? Write a report summarizing your findings, and include a table of links to Web sites that you viewed.

3 Social Networking

Career-minded professionals have turned to LinkedIn as a resource for online networking. The more than 45 million registered users, who represent each of the FORTUNE 500 companies, create public profiles that recruiters scour in search of new talent. Users can link to work contacts who, in turn, give access to their work contacts. Visit the LinkedIn Web site (linkedin.com), click the What is LinkedIn? link at the top of the page, and then read the information about reconnecting with current and former colleagues and classmates, job hunting, and obtaining advice from experts. Click the LinkedIn Jobs link at the bottom of the page, type a keyword describing the type of job you would like to have, and then browse the listings. What tips for finding jobs does LinkedIn provide? Summarize the listings and job information you read.

4 Blogs

Vehicle buyers know that the Internet provides a wealth of information that helps direct them toward the best vehicle for their needs. Those consumers who research blogs can obtain price, safety, performance, and maintenance facts and then employ savvy negotiation techniques that help them make the purchase confidently. Visit several automotive blogs, including those from Popular Mechanics (popularmechanics.com/blogs/automotive_news), Autoblog (autoblog.com), Autoblog Green (autobloggreen.com), Autopia (blog.wired.com/cars), and Ask Patty — Car Advice for Women (caradvice.askpatty.com). What new hybrid, luxury, and high-performance vehicles are profiled? Which are promoted as being environmentally friendly? Write a report summarizing the vehicle information you read.

5 Ethics in Action

A hacker is someone who tries to access a computer or network illegally. Although hacking activity sometimes is a harmless prank, at times it causes extensive damage. Some hackers say their activities allow them to test their skills. Others say their activities are a form of civil disobedience that forces companies to make their products more secure. View online sites such as The Ethical Hacker Network (ethicalhacker.net) that provide information about when hackers provide some benefit to the Internet society. Write a report summarizing your findings and include a table of links to Web sites that provide additional details.

Special Feature

Digital Video Technology

Everywhere you look, people are capturing moments they want to remember. They shoot movies of their vacations, birthday parties, activities, accomplishments, sporting events, weddings, and more. Because of the popularity of digital video cameras and mobile devices with built-in digital cameras, increasingly more people desire to capture their memories digitally, instead of on film. As shown in Figure 1, people have the ability to modify and share the digital videos they create. When you use special hardware and/or software, you can copy, manipulate, and distribute digital videos using your personal computer and the Internet. Amateurs can achieve professional quality results by using more sophisticated hardware and software. This feature describes how to select a video camera, record a video, transfer and manage videos, edit a video, and distribute a video.

Digital recordings deliver significant benefits over film-based movie making. With digital video cameras, recordings reside on storage media such as a hard disk, optical disc, or memory card. Unlike film, storage media can be reused, which reduces costs, saves time, and provides immediate results. Digital technology allows greater control over the creative process, both while recording video and in the editing process. You can check results immediately after capturing a video to determine whether it meets your expectations. If you are dissatisfied with a video, you can erase it and recapture it, again and again. Today, many mobile devices, such as smart phones and PDAs, allow you to capture video.

As shown in Figure 1, digital video cameras, and mobile devices function as input devices when they transmit video to a personal computer. You can transmit video by connecting the video camera or mobile device to your personal computer using a USB or FireWire port, or by placing the storage media used on the camera or mobile device in the computer. Some cameras and devices also can transmit wirelessly to a computer or to the media sharing Web sites.

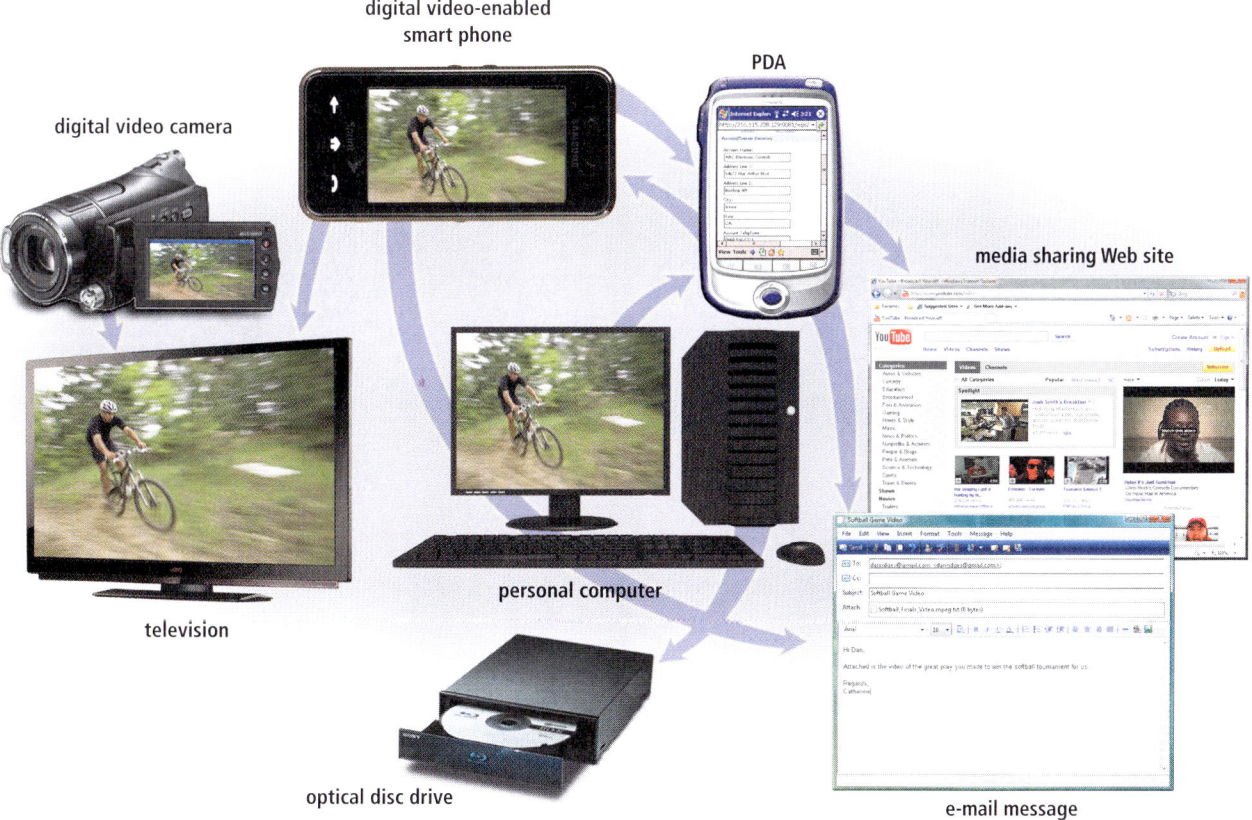

Figure 1 A variety of input, output, and storage devices are used by home users to process and edit digital video.

When you transmit video that was captured with a digital video camera or mobile device to a computer, you can edit the video using video editing software. If desired, you often can preview the video during the editing process on a television. Finally, you save the finished result to the desired media, such as an optical disc or, perhaps, e-mail the edited video or post it to a media sharing Web site. In this example, an optical disc drive also can be used to input video from an optical disc. Also in the example shown in Figure 1 on the previous page, a mobile device that includes a video camera sends a video directly to a media sharing Web site.

Digital video technology allows you to input, edit, manage, publish, and share your videos using a personal computer. With digital video technology, you can transform home videos into Hollywood-style movies by enhancing the videos with scrolling titles and transitions, cutting out or adding scenes, and adding background music and voice-over narration. The following sections outline the steps involved in the process of using digital video technology.

1 Select a Video Camera

Video cameras record in either analog or digital format. **Analog formats** include 8mm, Hi8, VHS-C, and Super VHS-C. **Digital formats** include Mini-DV, MICROMV, Digital8, DVD, Blu-ray, and HDV (high-definition video format). Some digital video cameras record on an internal hard disk. Others may allow you to record directly on an optical disc drive. Digital video cameras fall into three general categories: high-end consumer, consumer, and webcasting and monitoring (Figure 2). Consumer digital video cameras are by far the most popular type among consumers. High-end consumer models may support the Blu-ray or HDV standards. A video recorded in high-definition can be played back on a high-definition display. Many mobile devices allow you to record video that you later can transmit to your computer or e-mail from the device. Some devices allow you to upload video directly to video sharing Web sites. Digital video cameras provide more features than analog video cameras, such as a higher level of zoom, better sound, or greater control over color and lighting.

2 Record a Video

Most video cameras provide you with a choice of recording programs, which sometimes are called automatic settings. Each recording program includes a different combination of camera settings, so that you can adjust the exposure and other functions to match the recording environment. Usually, several different programs are available, such as point-and-shoot, point-and-shoot with manual adjustment, sports, portrait, spotlit scenes, and low light. You also have the ability to select special digital effects, such as fade, wipe, and black and white. If you are shooting outside on a windy day, then you can enable the windscreen to prevent wind noise. If you are shooting home videos or video meant for a Web site, then the point-and-shoot recording program is sufficient.

3 Transfer and Manage Videos

After recording the video, the next step is to transfer the video to your personal computer or to the Internet. Most video cameras connect directly to a USB or FireWire port on a personal computer (Figure 3). Transferring video with a

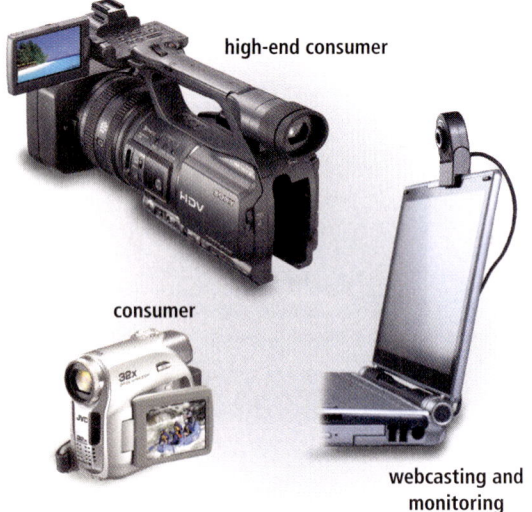

Figure 2 The high-end consumer digital video camera can produce professional-grade results. The consumer digital video camera produces amateur-grade results. The webcasting and monitoring digital video camera is appropriate for webcasting and security monitoring.

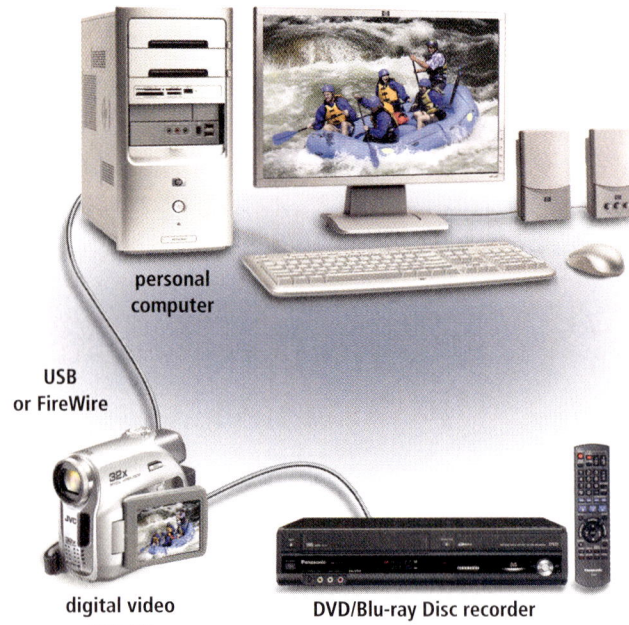

Figure 3 A digital video camera is connected to the personal computer or DVD/Blu-ray Disc recorder via a USB or FireWire port. No additional hardware is needed.

digital camera or mobile device is easy, because the video already is in a digital format that the computer can recognize. Many mobile devices include a special cable used to connect the device to a personal computer or allow you to transfer the videos to a media sharing Web site or your own Web site.

Some people own analog format video tapes that require additional hardware to convert the analog signals to a digital format before the video can be manipulated on a personal computer. The additional hardware includes a special video capture card using a standard RCA video cable or an S-video cable (Figure 4). **S-video** cables provide sharper images and greater overall quality. A personal computer also can record video to an optical disc, or it can be connected to an external DVD/Blu-ray Disc recorder to record videos. Video conversion services often specialize in converting older analog video to a variety of digital formats.

When transferring video, plan to use approximately 15 to 30 GB of hard disk storage per hour of digital video. High-definition formats may require much more storage per hour. A typical video project requires about four times the amount of raw footage as the final product. At the high end, therefore, a video that lasts an hour may require up to 120 GB of storage for the raw footage, editing process, and final video. This storage requirement can vary depending on the software you use to copy the video from the video camera to the hard disk and the format you select to save the video. For example, Microsoft's Windows Live Movie Maker can save 15 hours of standard video in 10 GB when creating video for playback on a computer, but saves only 1 hour of video in 10 GB when creating video for playback on a DVD. A high-definition video file may require more than 10 GB per hour.

The video transfer requires application software on the personal computer (Figure 5). The Windows Live Movie Maker software, available as a free download from Microsoft's Web site, allows you to transfer the video from

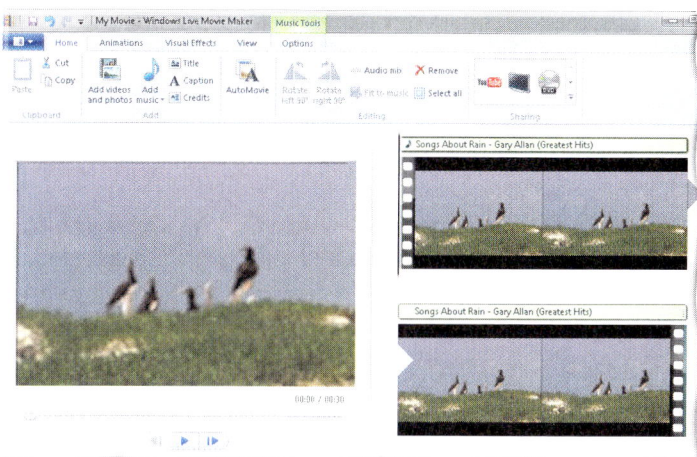

Figure 5 Some video editing software allows you to transfer a video from any video source to a hard disk.

a video camera. Depending on the length of video and the type of connection used, the video may take a long time to transfer. Make certain that no other programs are running on your personal computer while transferring the video.

The frame rate of a video refers to the number of frames per second (fps) that are captured in the video. The most widely used frame rate is 30 fps. A smaller frame rate results in a smaller file size for the video, but playback of the video will not be as smooth as one recorded with a higher frame rate.

When transferring video, the software may allow you to choose a file format and a codec to store the video. A video **file format** holds the video information in a manner specified by a vendor, such as Apple or Microsoft. Six of the more popular file formats are listed in Figure 6. The 3GP format is widely used on mobile devices.

File formats support codecs to encode the audio and video into the file formats. A **codec** specifies how the audio and video is compressed and stored within the file. A particular file format may be able to store audio and video in a number of

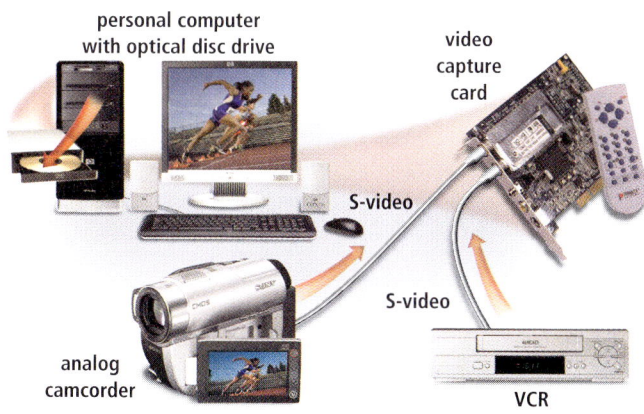

Figure 4 An analog camcorder or VCR is connected to the personal computer via an S-video port on a video capture card.

Popular Video File Formats	
File Format	**File Extensions**
Apple QuickTime	.MOV or .QT
DivX	.DIVX
Microsoft Windows Media Video	.WMV or .ASF
MPEG-4 Part 4	.MP4
Real RealMedia	.RM or .RAM
3GP	.3GP or .3G2

Figure 6 Apple, DivX, Microsoft, and Real offer the more popular video file formats.

different codecs. Figure 7 shows some options available for specifying a file format and video quality settings in a video capture program. The file format and codec you choose often is based on what you plan to do with the movie. For example, if you plan to upload your video to the YouTube video sharing Web site, the best choices are DivX and MPEG-4 file formats. Many users find that they are unable to play their own or others' videos, and the problem often is that the proper codec is not installed on the user's personal computer. Video conversion software often allows the user to convert a video in a less popular format to a better supported format. Many of these programs are available as freeware.

After transferring the video to a personal computer or the Internet, and before manipulating the video, you should store the video files in appropriate folders, named correctly, and backed up. Most video transfer application software helps manage these tasks.

4 Edit a Video

Once the video is stored on your hard disk or the Internet, the next step is to edit, or manipulate, the video. If you used a video capture card to transfer analog video to the computer (Figure 4 on the previous page), the files may require extra initial processing. Some Web sites allow you to perform minor editing and other tasks on the Web site. When you use a video capture card, some of the video frames may be lost in the transfer process. Some video editing programs allow you to fix this problem with **frame rate correction** tools.

The first step in the editing process is to split the video into smaller pieces, or scenes, that you can manipulate more easily. This process is called splitting. Most video software automatically splits the video into scenes, thus sparing you the task. After splitting, you should delete unwanted scenes or portions of scenes. This process is called pruning.

After creating the scenes you want to use in the final production, you edit each individual scene. You can crop, or change the size of, scenes. That is, you may want to delete the top or a side of a scene that is irrelevant. You also can resize the scene. For example, you may be creating a video that will be displayed on a media sharing Web site. Making a smaller video, such as 320 × 200 pixels, instead of 640 × 480 pixels, results in a smaller file that transmits faster over the Internet. Some media sharing Web sites recommend smaller video resolutions, such as 320 × 200 pixels, and some will perform the conversion for you automatically.

Figure 7 Video editing software allows you to specify a combination of file format and video quality settings when saving a video.

If a video has been recorded over a long period, using different cameras or under different lighting conditions, the video may need color correction. Color correction tools analyze your video and match brightness, colors, and other attributes of video clips to ensure a smooth look to the video (Figure 8).

You can add logos, special effects, or titles to scenes. You can place a company logo or personal logo in a video to identify yourself or the company producing the video. Logos often are added on the lower-right corner of a video and remain for the duration of the video. Special effects include warping, changing from color to black and white, morphing, or zoom motion. Morphing is a special effect in which one video image is transformed into another image over the course of several frames of video, creating the illusion of metamorphosis. You usually add titles at the beginning and ending of a video to give the video context. A training video may have titles throughout the video to label a particular scene, or each scene may begin with a title.

The next step in editing a video is to add audio effects, including voice-over narration and background music. Many video editing programs allow you to add additional tracks, or layers, of sound to a video in addition to the sound that was recorded on the video camera or mobile device. You also can add special audio effects.

The final step in editing a video is to combine the scenes into a complete video (Figure 9). This process involves ordering scenes and adding transition effects between scenes. Video editing software allows you to combine scenes and separate each scene with a transition. Transitions include fading, wiping, blurry, bursts, ruptures, erosions, and more.

Figure 8 Color correction tools in video editing software allow a great deal of control over the mood of your video creation.

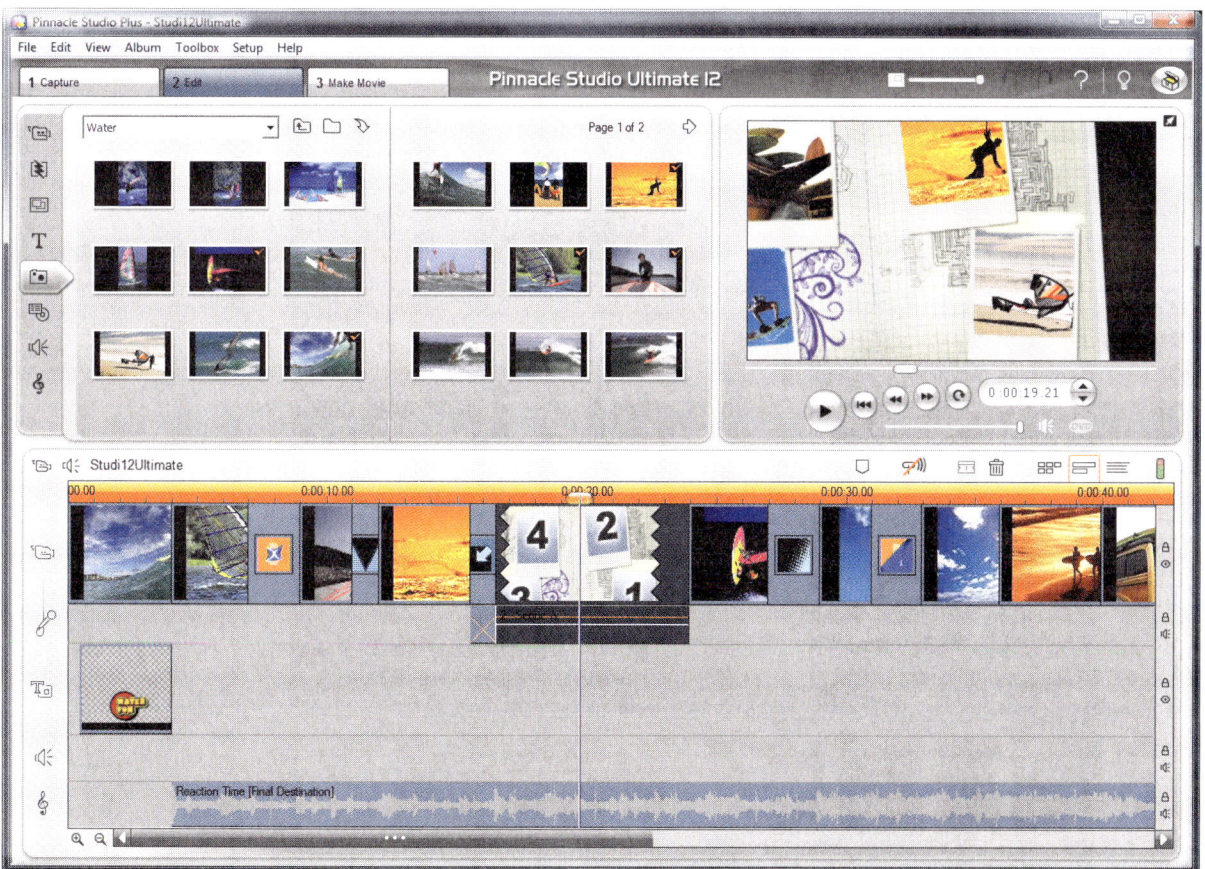

Figure 9 Scenes are combined into a sequence on the bottom of the screen.

5 Distribute the Video

After editing the video, the final step is to distribute it or save it on an appropriate medium. You can save video in a variety of formats. Video recorded on a mobile device often requires conversion to a more widely accepted format.

Video also can be stored in digital formats in any of several optical disc formats or on a media sharing Web site. **Optical disc creation software**, which often is packaged with video editing software, allows you to create, or master, optical discs. You can add interactivity to your optical disc creations. For example, you can allow viewers to jump to certain scenes using a menu.

You also can save your video creation in electronic format for distribution over the Web, via e-mail, or to a mobile device. Some cameras include a button that allows users to upload directly to a media sharing Web site. Popular media sharing Web sites, such as YouTube (Figure 10), have recommendations for the best file format and codecs to use for video that you upload to them (Figure 11). Your video editing software must support the file format and codec you want to use. For example, Apple's iMovie software typically saves files in the QuickTime file format.

Professionals use hardware and software that allow them to create a film version of digital video that can be played in movie theaters. This technology is becoming increasingly popular. The cost of professional video editing software ranges from thousands to hundreds of thousands of dollars. Video editing software for the home user is available for a few hundred dollars or less. Some Hollywood directors believe that eventually all movies will be recorded and edited digitally.

After creating your final video for distribution or for your personal video collection, you should back up the final video file. You can save your scenes for inclusion in other video creations or create new masters using different effects, transitions, and ordering of scenes.

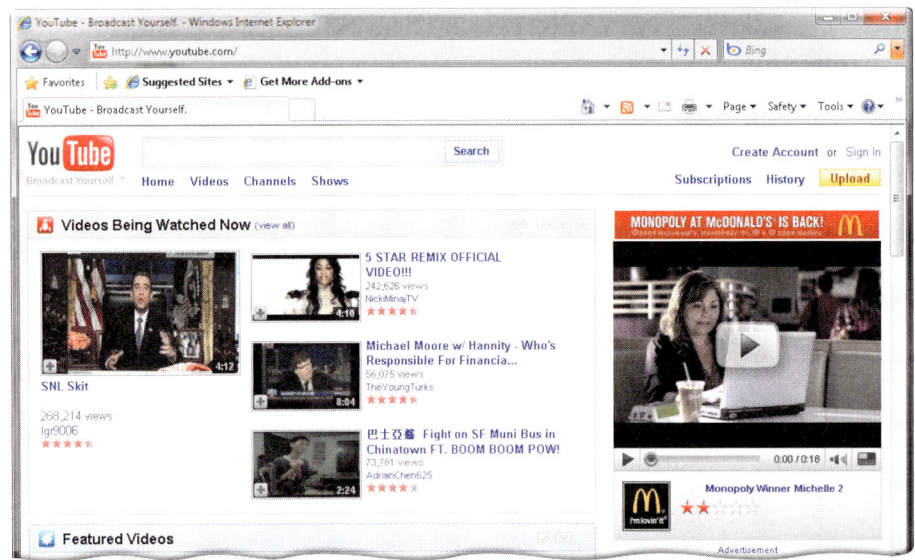

Figure 10 Media sharing Web sites allow you to share your videos with acquaintances or the entire world.

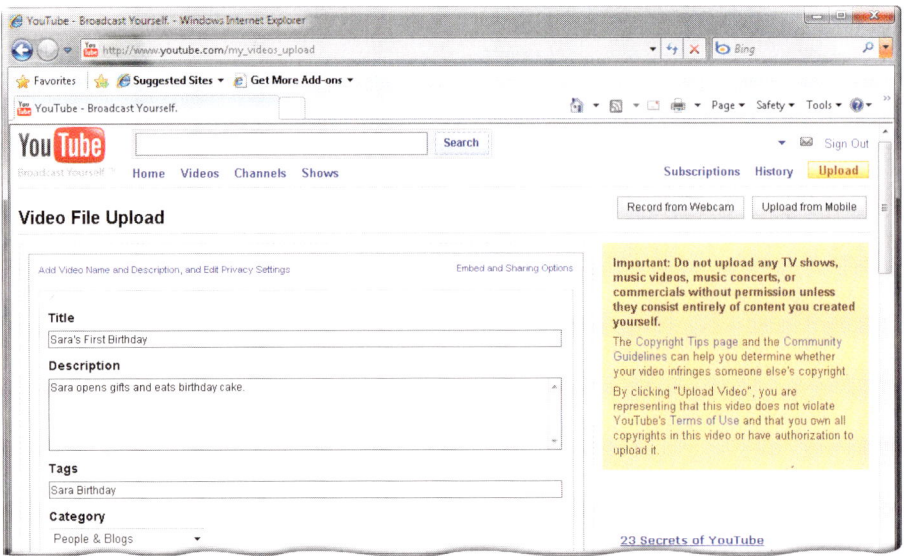

Figure 11 Media sharing Web sites, such as YouTube, provide tools that simplify the process of uploading videos to the site.

Chapter Four

Operating Systems and Utility Programs

Objectives

After completing this chapter, you will be able to:

1. Define system software and identify the two types of system software
2. Describe each of these functions of an operating system: starting and shutting down a computer, providing a user interface, managing memory, coordinating tasks, configuring devices, establishing an Internet connection, monitoring performance, providing file management and other utilities, updating automatically, controlling a network, and administering security
3. Summarize the features of several stand-alone operating systems: Windows, Mac OS, UNIX, and Linux
4. Identify various server operating systems
5. Briefly describe several embedded operating systems: Windows Embedded CE, Windows Mobile, Palm OS, iPhone OS, BlackBerry, Google Android, Embedded Linux, and Symbian OS
6. Explain the purpose of several utility programs: file manager, search utility, image viewer, uninstaller, disk cleanup, disk defragmenter, backup and restore utilities, screen saver, personal firewall, antivirus programs, spyware and adware removers, Internet filters, file compression, media player, disc burning, and personal computer maintenance

System Software

When you purchase a personal computer, it usually has system software installed on its hard disk. **System software** consists of the programs that control or maintain the operations of the computer and its devices. System software serves as the interface between the user, the application software, and the computer's hardware.

Two types of system software are operating systems and utility programs. This chapter discusses the operating system and its functions, as well as several types of utility programs for personal computers.

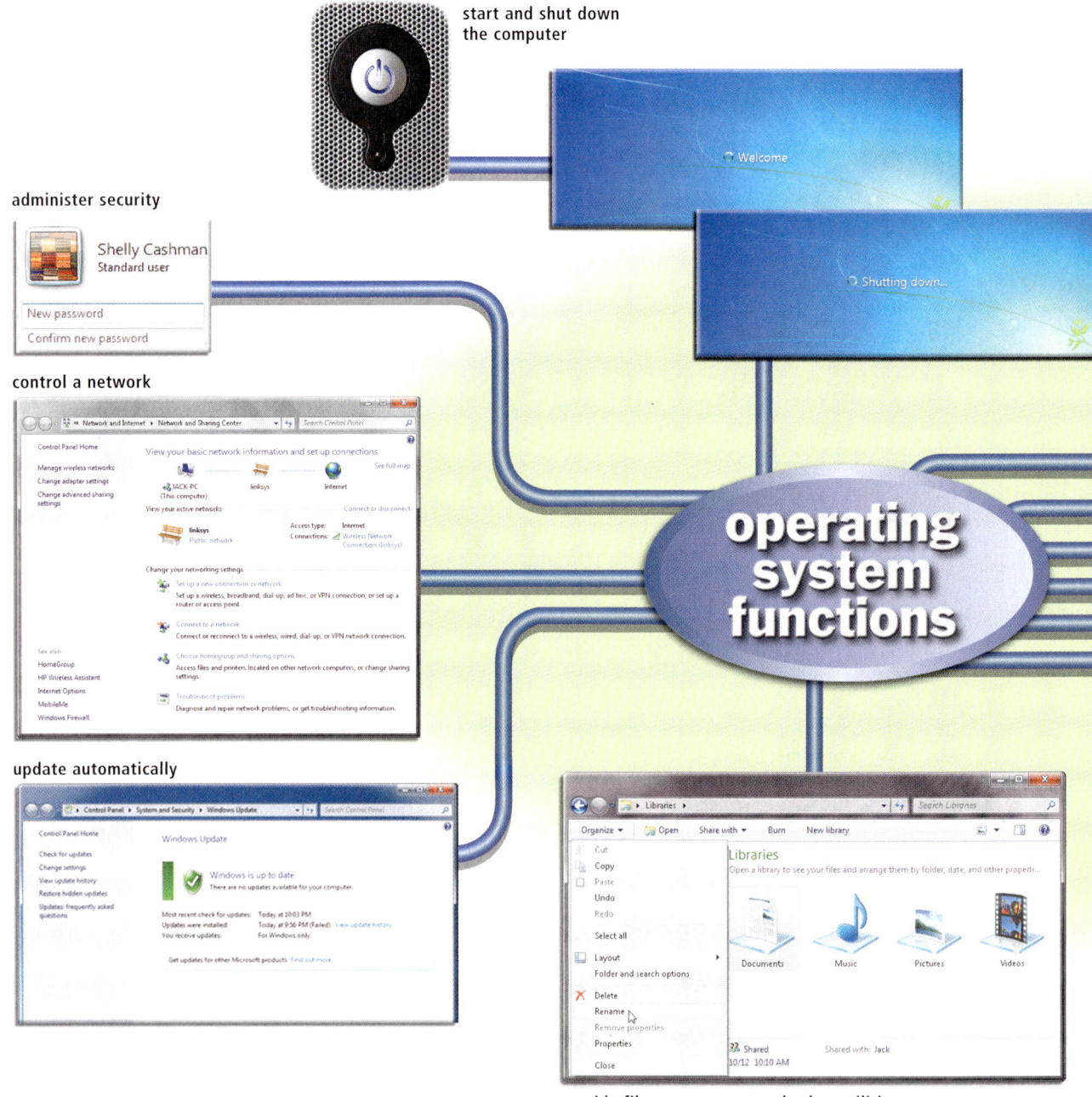

Figure 4-1 Most operating systems perform similar functions, which are illustrated with the latest version of Windows in this figure.

Operating Systems

An **operating system** (**OS**) is a set of programs containing instructions that work together to coordinate all the activities among computer hardware resources. Most operating systems perform similar functions that include starting and shutting down a computer, providing a user interface, managing programs, managing memory, coordinating tasks, configuring devices, establishing an Internet connection, monitoring performance, providing file management and other utilities, and automatically updating itself and certain utility programs. Some operating systems also allow users to control a network and administer security (Figure 4-1).

Although an operating system can run from an optical disc and/or flash memory mobile media, in most cases, the operating system is installed and resides on the computer's hard disk. On handheld computers and many mobile devices, the operating system may reside on a ROM chip.

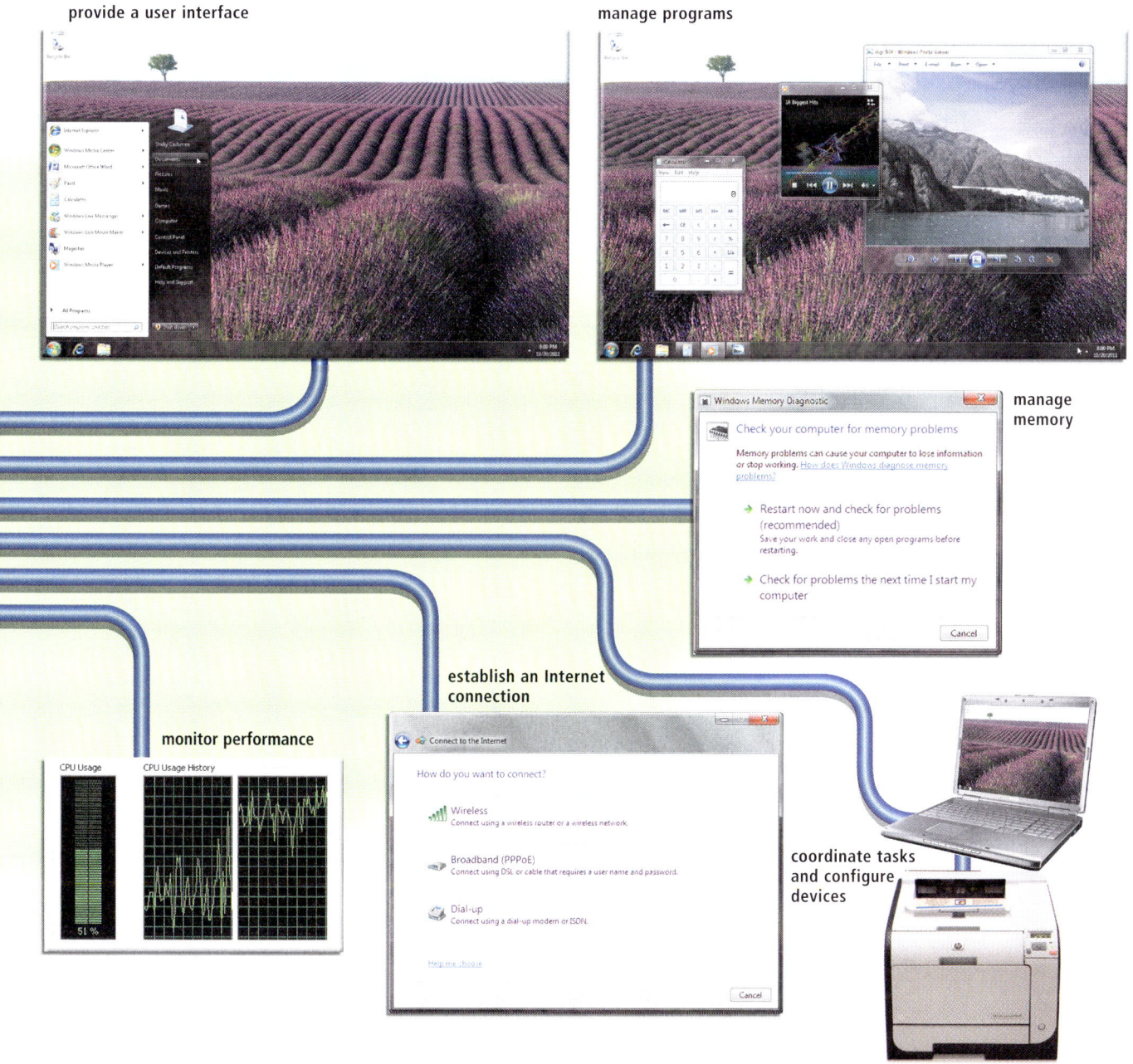

Different sizes of computers typically use different operating systems because operating systems generally are written to run on a specific type of computer. For example, a mainframe computer does not use the same operating system as a personal computer. Even the same types of computers, such as desktop computers, may not use the same operating system. Some, however, can run multiple operating systems. When purchasing application software, you must ensure that it works with the operating system installed on your computer or mobile device.

The operating system that a computer uses sometimes is called the platform. With purchased application software, the package or specifications identify the required platform (operating system). A cross-platform program is one that runs the same on multiple operating systems.

Operating System Functions

Many different operating systems exist; however, most operating systems provide similar functions. The following sections discuss functions common to most operating systems. The operating system handles many of these functions automatically, without requiring any instruction from a user.

Starting and Shutting Down a Computer

Booting is the process of starting or restarting a computer. When turning on a computer that has been powered off completely, you are performing a **cold boot**. A **warm boot**, by contrast, is the process of using the operating system to restart a computer. With Windows, for example, you can perform a warm boot by clicking a menu command (Figure 4-2).

When you install new software or update existing software, often an on-screen prompt instructs you to restart the computer. In this case, a warm boot is appropriate.

Each time you boot a computer, the kernel and other frequently used operating system instructions are loaded, or copied, from storage into the computer's memory (RAM). The kernel is the core of an operating system that manages memory and devices, maintains the computer's clock, starts programs, and assigns the computer's resources, such as devices, programs, data, and information. The kernel is memory resident, which means it remains in memory while the computer is running. Other parts of the operating system are nonresident, that is, these instructions remain on a storage medium until they are needed.

When you boot a computer, a series of messages may appear on the screen. The actual information displayed varies depending on the make and type of the computer and the equipment installed. The boot process, however, is similar for large and small computers.

Although some users leave their computers running continually and never turn them off, others choose to shut them down. Shut down options including powering off the computer, placing the computer in sleep mode, and hibernating the computer. Both sleep mode and hibernate are designed to save time when you resume working on the computer. **Sleep mode** saves any open documents and programs to RAM, turns off all unneeded functions, and then places the computer in a low-power state. **Hibernate**, by contrast, saves any open documents and programs to a hard disk before removing power from the computer.

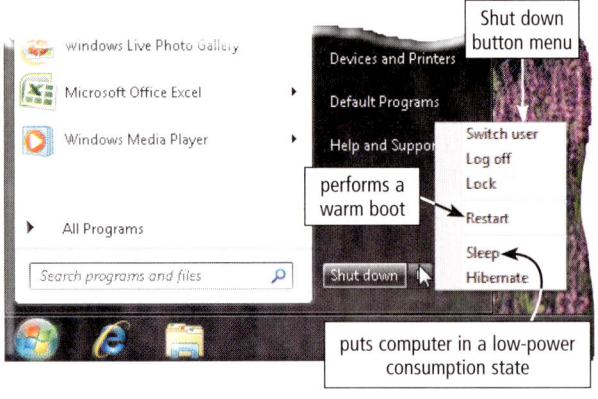

Figure 4-2 To reboot a running computer, click the Shut down button arrow and then click Restart.

Providing a User Interface

You interact with software through its user interface. That is, a **user interface** controls how you enter data and instructions and how information is displayed on the screen. Two types of user interfaces are graphical and command-line (Figure 4-3). Operating systems sometimes use a combination of these interfaces to define how a user interacts with a computer.

Graphical User Interface Most users today work with a graphical user interface. With a **graphical user interface** (**GUI**), you interact with menus and visual images such as buttons and other graphical objects to issue commands (Figure 4-3a). Many current GUI operating systems incorporate features similar to those of a Web browser.

Windows 7 offers two different GUIs, depending on your hardware configuration. Computers with less than 1 GB of RAM work with the Windows 7 Basic interface. Computers with more than 1 GB of RAM that have the required hardware may be able to work with the Windows 7 Aero interface, also known as **Windows Aero**, shown in Figure 4-3a, which provides an enhanced visual look, additional navigation options, and animation.

Command-Line Interface To configure devices, manage system resources, and troubleshoot network connections, network administrators and other advanced users work with a command-line interface. In a **command-line interface**, a user types commands or presses special keys on the keyboard to enter data and instructions (Figure 4-3b). Some people consider command-line interfaces difficult to use because they require exact spelling, grammar, and punctuation.

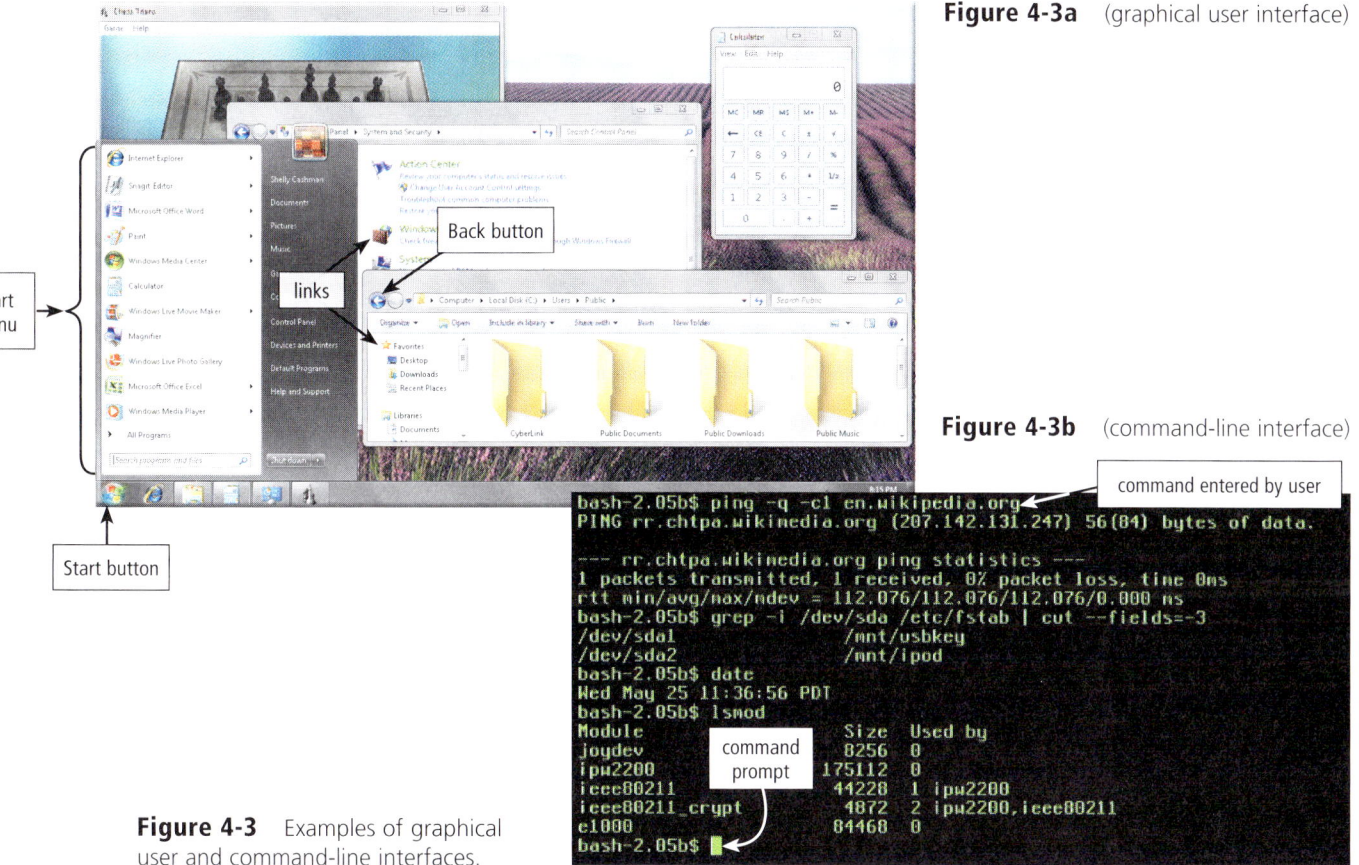

Figure 4-3a (graphical user interface)

Figure 4-3b (command-line interface)

Figure 4-3 Examples of graphical user and command-line interfaces.

Managing Programs

Some operating systems support a single user and only one running program at a time. Others support thousands of users running multiple programs. How an operating system handles programs directly affects your productivity.

A single user/single tasking operating system allows only one user to run one program at a time. Smart phones and other mobile devices often use a single user/single tasking operating system.

A single user/multitasking operating system allows a single user to work on two or more programs that reside in memory at the same time. Users today typically run multiple programs concurrently. It is common to have an e-mail program and Web browser open at all times, while working with application programs such as word processing or graphics.

When a computer is running multiple programs concurrently, one program is in the foreground and the others are in the background. The one in the foreground is the active program, that is, the one you currently are using. The other programs running but not in use are in the background. In Figure 4-4, the Windows Live Movie Maker program is in the foreground, and three other programs are running in the background (Windows Media Player, Microsoft PowerPoint, and Chess Titans).

The foreground program typically is displayed on the desktop but the background programs often are hidden partially or completely behind the foreground program. You easily can switch between foreground and background programs. To make a program active (in the foreground) in Windows, click its program button on the taskbar. This causes the operating system to place all other programs in the background.

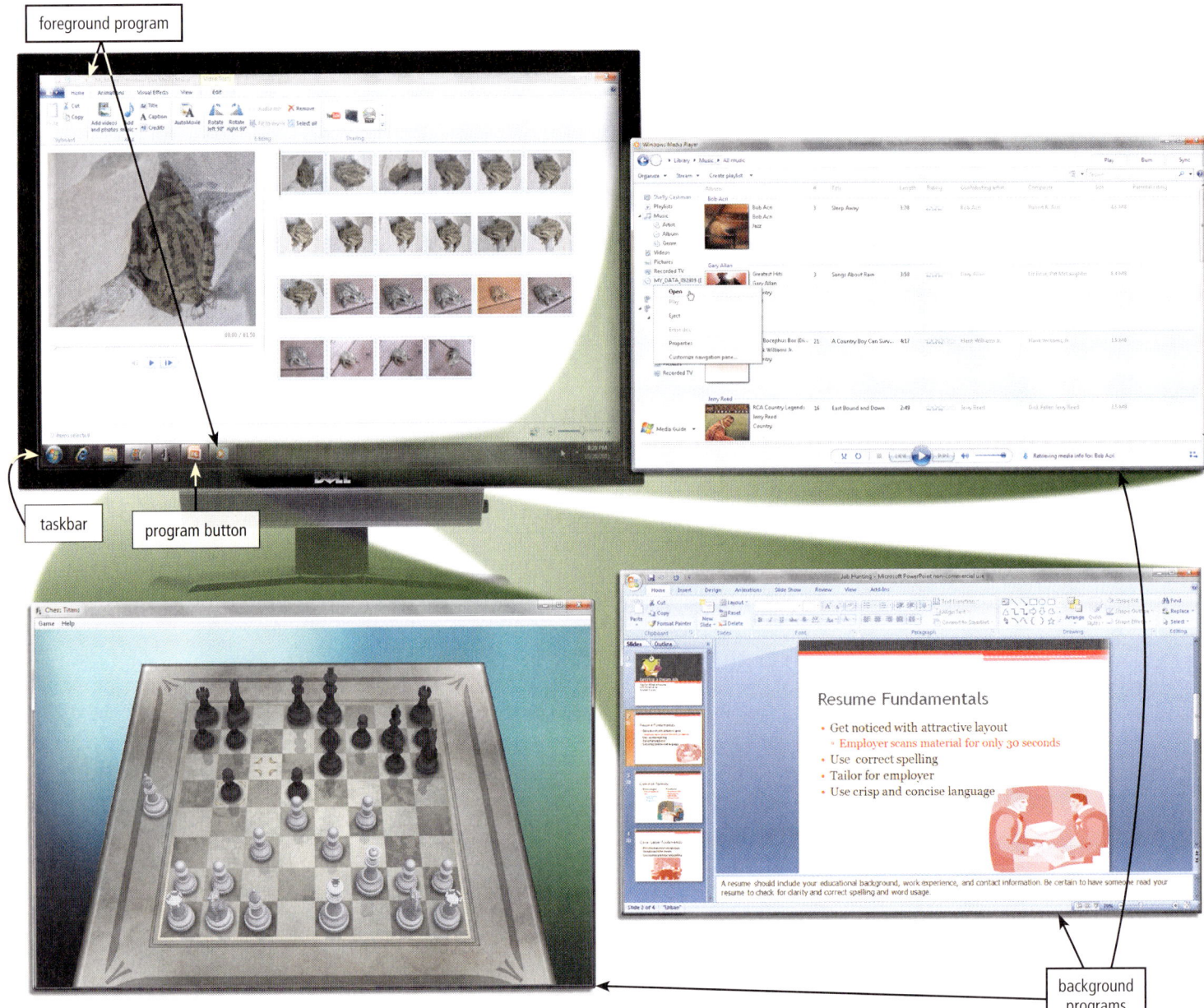

Figure 4-4 The foreground program, Windows Live Movie Maker, is displayed on the desktop. The other programs (Windows Media Player, Microsoft PowerPoint, and Chess Titans) are in the background.

A **multiuser** operating system enables two or more users to run programs simultaneously. Networks, servers, mainframes, and supercomputers allow hundreds to thousands of users to connect at the same time, and thus are multiuser.

A **multiprocessing** operating system supports two or more processors running programs at the same time. Multiprocessing involves the coordinated processing of programs by more than one processor. Multiprocessing increases a computer's processing speed.

Managing Memory

The purpose of **memory management** is to optimize the use of random access memory (RAM). RAM consists of one or more chips on the motherboard that hold items such as data and instructions while the processor interprets and executes them. The operating system allocates, or assigns, data and instructions to an area of memory while they are being processed. Then, it carefully monitors the contents of memory. Finally, the operating system releases these items from being monitored in memory when the processor no longer requires them.

Virtual memory is a concept in which the operating system allocates a portion of a storage medium, usually the hard disk, to function as additional RAM. As you interact with a program, part of it may be in physical RAM, while the rest of the program is on the hard disk as virtual memory. Because virtual memory is slower than RAM, users may notice the computer slowing down while it uses virtual memory.

The operating system uses an area of the hard disk for virtual memory, in which it swaps (exchanges) data, information, and instructions between memory and storage. The technique of swapping items between memory and storage is called paging. When an operating system spends much of its time paging, instead of executing application software, it is said to be thrashing. If application software, such as a Web browser, has stopped responding and the hard disk's LED blinks repeatedly, the operating system probably is thrashing.

Instead of using a hard disk as virtual memory, Windows users can increase the size of memory through **Windows ReadyBoost**, which can allocate available storage space on removable flash memory devices as additional memory cache. Users notice better performance with Windows ReadyBoost versus hard disk virtual memory because the operating system accesses a flash memory device, such as a USB flash drive or SD memory card, more quickly than it accesses a hard disk.

Coordinating Tasks

The operating system determines the order in which tasks are processed. A task, or job, is an operation the processor manages. Tasks include receiving data from an input device, processing instructions, sending information to an output device, and transferring items from storage to memory and from memory to storage.

A multiuser operating system does not always process tasks on a first-come, first-served basis. Sometimes, one user may have a higher priority than other users. In this case, the operating system adjusts the schedule of tasks.

Sometimes, a device already may be busy processing one task when it receives a second task. This occurs because the processor operates at a much faster rate of speed than peripheral devices. For example, if the processor sends five documents to a printer, the printer can print only one document at a time and store as many documents as its memory can handle.

While waiting for devices to become idle, the operating system places items in buffers. A **buffer** is a segment of memory or storage in which items are placed while waiting to be transferred from an input device or to an output device.

The operating system commonly uses buffers with printed documents. This process, called **spooling**, sends documents to be printed to a buffer instead of sending them immediately to the printer. If a printer does not have its own internal memory or if its memory is full, the operating system's buffer holds the information waiting to print while the printer prints from the buffer at its own rate of speed. By spooling documents to a buffer, the processor can continue interpreting and executing instructions while the printer prints. This allows users to work on the computer for other

Spooling
For more information, visit scsite.com/dc-off07/ch4/ weblink and then click Spooling.

tasks while a printer is printing. Multiple print jobs line up in a **queue** (pronounced Q) in the buffer. A program, called a print spooler, intercepts documents to be printed from the operating system and places them in the queue (Figure 4-5).

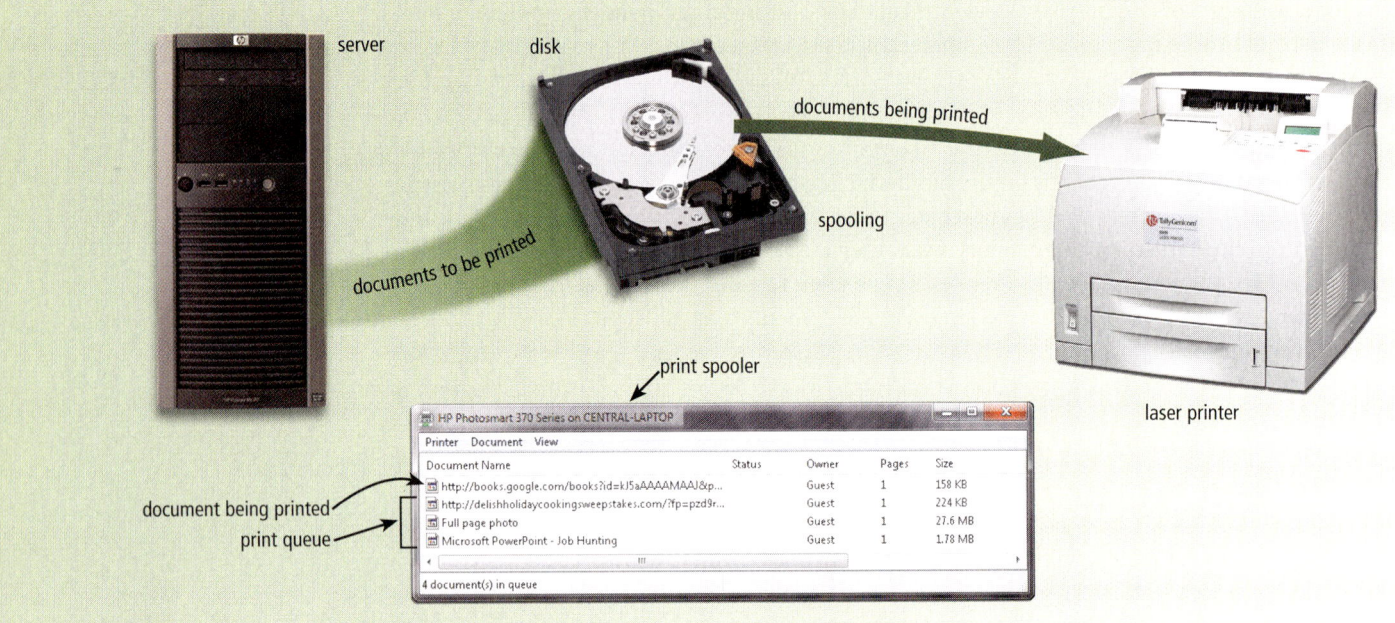

Figure 4-5 Spooling increases both processor and printer efficiency by placing documents to be printed in a buffer on disk before they are printed. This figure illustrates three documents in the queue with one document printing.

Configuring Devices

A **driver** is a small program that tells the operating system how to communicate with a specific device. Each device on a computer, such as the mouse, keyboard, monitor, printer, and scanner, has its own specialized set of commands and thus requires its own specific driver. When you boot a computer, the operating system loads each device's driver.

If you attach a new device to a computer, such as a printer or scanner, its driver must be installed before you can use the device. Today, most devices and operating systems support Plug and Play. **Plug and Play** means the operating system automatically configures new devices as you install them. With Plug and Play, a user can plug in a device, turn on the computer, and then use the device without having to configure the system manually.

 **Plug and Play**
For more information, visit scsite.com/dc-off07/ch4/ weblink and then click Plug and Play.

Establishing an Internet Connection

Operating systems typically provide a means to establish Internet connections. For example, Windows includes a Set Up a Connection or Network wizard that guides users through the process of setting up a connection between a computer and an Internet access provider (Figure 4-6).

Some operating systems also include a Web browser and an e-mail program, enabling you to begin using the Web and communicate with others as soon as you set up the Internet connection. Some also include utilities to protect computers from unauthorized intrusions and unwanted software such as viruses and spyware.

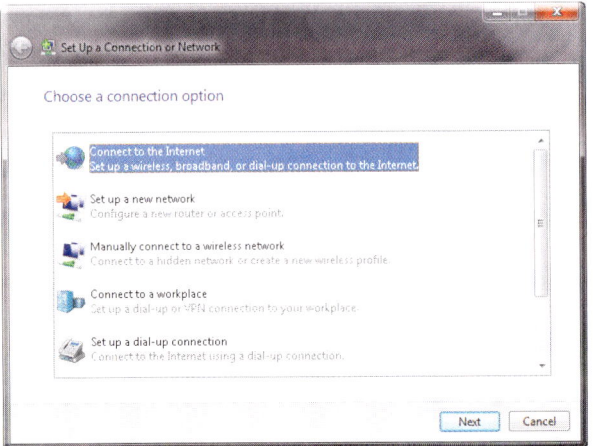

Figure 4-6 To connect to a network using Windows, click the Start button, click Control Panel, click Network and Internet, click Network and Sharing Center, and then click 'Set up a new connection or network' to open the window shown here.

Monitoring Performance

Operating systems typically contain a performance monitor. A **performance monitor** is a program that assesses and reports information about various computer resources and devices (shown in Figure 4-1 on pages 136 and 137).

The information in performance reports helps users and administrators identify a problem with resources so that they can try to resolve any problems. If a computer is running extremely slow, for example, the performance monitor may determine that the computer's memory is being used to its maximum. Thus, you might consider installing additional memory in the computer. Read Looking Ahead 4-1 for a look at a future type of health-based performance monitor.

↗ LOOKING AHEAD 4-1

Contact Lenses Monitor Glaucoma

The future looks good for contact lenses that will help study and treat glaucoma. Biomedical engineers at the University of California – Davis are developing lenses that measure eye pressure and then flow if the readings are abnormal.

Glaucoma occurs when the fluid pressure inside the eye increases. This intraocular pressure can result in total blindness if the optic nerve, which sends messages from the eyes to the brain, is damaged. Doctors can measure the amount of pressure and then perform surgery to correct the blockage in the back of the eye that prevents the fluid from draining. As an alternative to the pressure measurement, the new contact lenses can perform the fluidic resistance evaluation for the drainage network of the eye, which prevents dangerously high levels in the early glaucomatous eyes.

Lasers, too, are expected to become part of a doctor's means of detecting glaucoma. A high-resolution laser can measure 28 million areas of the optic nerve, and then software can create a 3-D view of the eye and assess signs of the disease.

🖑 For more information, visit scsite.com/dc-off07/ch4/looking and then click Contact Lenses.

Providing File Management and Other Utilities

Operating systems often provide users with the capability of managing files, searching for files, viewing images, securing a computer from unauthorized access, uninstalling programs, cleaning up disks, defragmenting disks, diagnosing problems, backing up files and disks, and setting up screen savers. A later section in the chapter discusses these and other utilities in depth.

Updating Software Automatically

Many popular programs, including most operating systems, include an **automatic update** feature that automatically provides updates to the program. With an operating system, these updates can include fixes to program bugs (errors), enhancements to security, modifications to device drivers, access to new or expanded components such as desktop themes or games, and even updates to application software on the computer such as a Web browser or an e-mail program.

Many software makers provide free downloadable updates, sometimes called a **service pack**, to users who have registered and/or activated their software. With operating systems, the automatic update feature automatically alerts users when an update is available; further, it can be configured to download and install the update automatically. Users without an Internet connection usually can order the updates on an optical disc for a minimal shipping fee. To learn about keeping Windows up-to-date, complete the Learn How To 2 exercise on pages 164 and 165.

Controlling a Network

Some operating systems are designed to work with a server on a network. A **server operating system** is an operating system that organizes and coordinates how multiple users access and share resources on a network. Resources include hardware, software, data, and information. For example, a server operating system allows multiple users to share a printer, Internet access, files, and programs.

Some operating systems have network features built into them. In other cases, the server operating system is a set of programs separate from the operating system on the client computers that access the network. When not connected to the network, the client computers use their own operating system. When connected to the network, the server operating system may assume some of the operating system functions.

The network administrator, the person overseeing network operations, uses the server operating system to add and remove users, computers, and other devices to and from the network. The network administrator also uses the server operating system to install software and administer network security.

Administering Security

Computer and network administrators typically have an **administrator account** that enables them to access all files and programs on the computer or network, install programs, and specify settings that affect all users on a computer or network. Settings include creating user accounts and establishing permissions. These permissions define who can access certain resources and when they can access those resources.

For each user, the network administrator establishes a user account, which enables a user to access, or **log on** to, a computer or a network (Figure 4-7). Each user account typically consists of a user name and password. A **user name**, or **user ID**, is a unique combination of characters, such as letters of the alphabet or numbers, that identifies one specific user. Many users select a combination of their first and last names as their user name. A user named Henry Baker might choose H Baker as his user name.

A **password** is a private combination of characters associated with the user name that allows access to certain computer resources. Some operating systems allow the computer or network administrator to assign passwords to files and commands, restricting access to only authorized users.

To prevent unauthorized users from accessing computer resources, keep your password confidential. While users type a password, most computers hide the actual password characters by displaying some other characters, such as asterisks (*) or dots. After entering a user name and password, the operating system compares the user's entry with a list of authorized user names and passwords. If the entry matches the user name and password kept on file, the operating system grants the user access. If the entry does not match, the operating system denies access to the user.

The operating system records successful and unsuccessful logon attempts in a file. This allows the computer or network administrator to review who is using or attempting to use the computer. The administrators also use these files to monitor computer usage.

To protect sensitive data and information as it travels over a network, the operating system may encrypt it. Encryption is the process of encoding data and information into an unreadable form. Administrators can specify that data be encrypted as it travels over a network to prevent unauthorized users from reading the data. When an authorized user attempts to read the data, it automatically is decrypted, or converted back into a readable form.

Figure 4-7 Most multiuser operating systems allow each user to log on, which is the process of entering a user name and a password into the computer.

❓ FAQ 4-1

What are the guidelines for selecting a good password?

Choose a password that is easy to remember, and that no one could guess. Do not use any part of your first or last name, your spouse's or child's name, telephone number, street address, license plate number, Social Security number, birthday, and so on. Be sure your password is at least eight characters long, mixed with uppercase and lowercase letters, numbers, and special characters. You also should avoid using single-word passwords that are found in the dictionary. Security experts also recommend using a passphrase, which is similar to a password, but comprised of several words separated by spaces.

👆 For more information, visit scsite.com/dc-off07/ch4/faq and then click Passwords.

QUIZ YOURSELF 4-1

Instructions: Find the true statement below. Then, rewrite the remaining false statements so that they are true.

1. A buffer is a small program that tells the operating system how to communicate with a specific device.
2. A warm boot is the process of using the operating system to restart a computer.
3. A password is a public combination of characters associated with the user name that allows access to certain computer resources.
4. The program you currently are using is in the background, and the other programs running but not in use are in the foreground.
5. Two types of system software are operating systems and application programs.

👆 **Quiz Yourself Online:** To further check your knowledge of pages 136 through 144, visit scsite.com/dc-off07/ch4/quiz and then click Objectives 1 – 2.

Types of Operating Systems

When you purchase a new computer or mobile device, it typically has an operating system preinstalled. As new versions of the operating system are released, users upgrade their existing computers and mobile devices to incorporate features of the new version. Purchasing an operating system upgrade usually costs less than purchasing the entire operating system.

New versions of an operating system usually are backward compatible. That is, they recognize and work with application software written for an earlier version of the operating system (or platform). By contrast, the application software may or may not be upward compatible, meaning it may or may not run on new versions of the operating system.

The three basic categories of operating systems that exist today are stand-alone, server, and embedded. The table in Figure 4-8 lists names of operating systems in each category. The following pages discuss a variety of operating systems.

Categories of Operating Systems

Category	Operating System Name
Stand-alone	• DOS • Early Windows versions (Windows 3.x, Windows 95, Windows NT Workstation, Windows 98, Windows 2000 Professional, Windows Millennium Edition, Windows XP, Windows Vista) • Windows 7 • Mac OS X • UNIX • Linux
Server	• Early Windows Server versions (Windows NT Server, Windows 2000 Server, Windows Server 2003) • Windows Server 2008 • UNIX • Linux • Solaris • NetWare
Embedded	• Windows Embedded CE • Windows Mobile • Palm OS • iPhone OS • BlackBerry • Google Android • Embedded Linux • Symbian OS

Figure 4-8 Examples of stand-alone, server, and embedded operating systems. Some stand-alone operating systems include the capability of configuring small home or office networks.

FAQ 4-2

Which operating systems have the most market share?

The Windows operating system family currently dominates the operating system market with more than 93 percent market share. The Mac operating system is in second place with nearly 5 percent market share. The chart to the right illustrates the market share for various operating systems.

Operating System Market Share

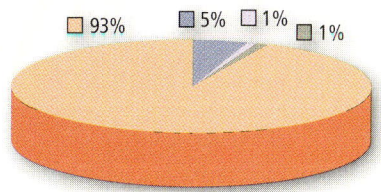
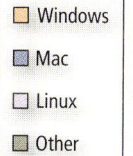

Source: Market Share by Net Applications

👆 For more information, visit scsite.com/dc-off07/ch4/faq and then click Operating System Market Share.

Stand-Alone Operating Systems

A **stand-alone operating system** is a complete operating system that works on a desktop computer, notebook computer, or mobile computing device. Some stand-alone operating systems are called client operating systems because they also work in conjunction with a server operating system. Client operating systems can operate with or without a network. Other stand-alone operating systems include networking capabilities, allowing the home and small business user to set up a small network. Examples of currently used stand-alone operating systems are Windows 7, Mac OS X, UNIX, and Linux.

Windows 7

In the mid-1980s, Microsoft developed its first version of Windows, which provided a graphical user interface (GUI). Since then, Microsoft continually has updated its Windows operating system, incorporating innovative features and functions with each new version. **Windows 7** is Microsoft's fastest, most efficient operating system to date, offering quicker program start up, built-in diagnostics, automatic recovery, improved security, enhanced searching and organizing capabilities, and an easy-to-use interface (Figure 4-9).

Most users choose one of these Windows 7 editions: Windows 7 Starter, Windows 7 Home Premium, Windows 7 Ultimate, or Windows 7 Professional.

- Windows 7 Starter, designed for netbooks and other small notebook computers, uses the Windows 7 Basic interface and allows users easily to search for files, connect to printers and devices, browse the Internet, join home networks, and connect to wireless networks. This edition of Windows typically is preinstalled on new computers and not available for purchase in retail stores.
- Windows 7 Home Premium, which includes all the capabilities of Windows 7 Starter, also includes Windows Aero with its Aero Flip 3D feature and provides tools to create and edit high-definition movies, record and watch television shows, connect to a game console, and read from and write on Blu-ray Discs.
- Windows 7 Ultimate, which includes all features of Windows 7 Home Premium, provides additional features designed to keep your files secure and support for 35 languages.
- With Windows 7 Professional, users in all sizes of businesses are provided a secure operating environment that uses Windows Aero where they easily can search for files, protect their computers from unauthorized intruders and unwanted programs, use improved backup technologies, securely connect to Wi-Fi networks, quickly view messages on a powered-off, specially equipped notebook computer, easily share documents and collaborate with other users, and watch and record live television.

Windows 7 adapts to the hardware configuration on which it is installed. Thus, two users with the same edition of Windows 7 may experience different functionality and interfaces.

Windows 7
For more information, visit scsite.com/dc-off07/ch4/ weblink and then click Windows 7.

Figure 4-9 Windows 7 has a new interface, easier navigation and searching techniques, and improved security.

Mac OS X

Since it was released with Macintosh computers in 1984, Apple's **Macintosh operating system** has set the standard for operating system ease of use and has been the model for most of the new GUIs developed for non-Macintosh systems. The latest version, **Mac OS X**, is a multitasking operating system available only for computers manufactured by Apple (Figure 4-10).

Mac OS X
For more information, visit scsite.com/dc-off07/ch4/ weblink and then click Mac OS X.

Figure 4-10 Mac OS X is the operating system used with Apple Macintosh computers.

UNIX

UNIX (pronounced YOU-nix) is a multitasking operating system. Several versions of this operating system exist, each slightly different. Although some versions of UNIX have a command-line interface, most versions of UNIX offer a graphical user interface (Figure 4-11). Today, a version of UNIX is available for most computers of all sizes. Power users often work with UNIX because of its flexibility and power.

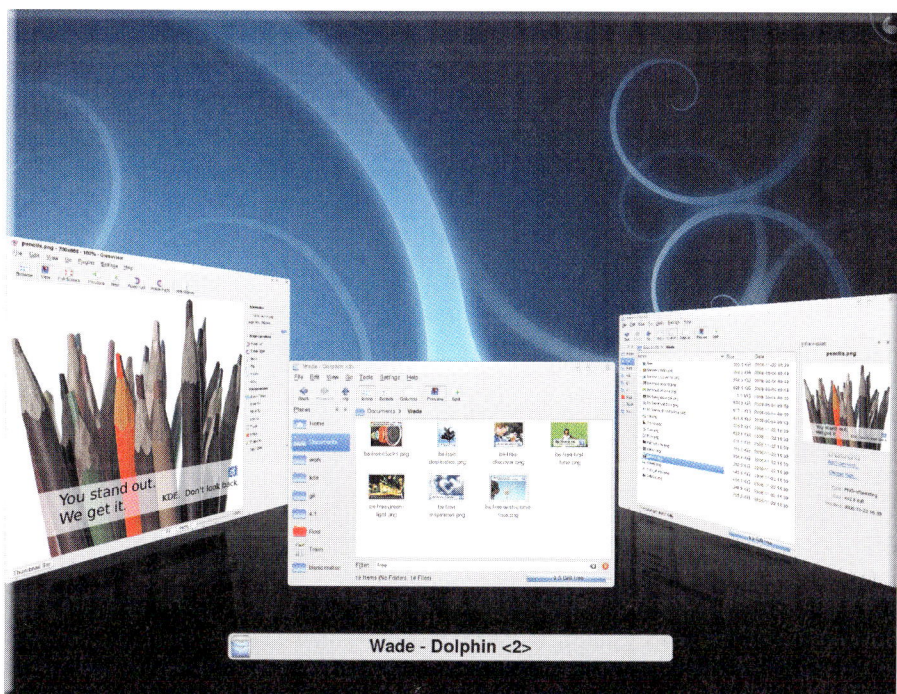

Figure 4-11 Many versions of UNIX have a graphical user interface.

Linux

Linux is one of the faster growing operating systems. **Linux** (pronounced LINN-uks), introduced in 1991, is a popular, multitasking UNIX-type operating system. In addition to the basic operating system, Linux also includes many free programming languages and utility programs. Linux is not proprietary software like the operating systems discussed thus far. Instead, Linux is open source software, which means its code is available to the public for use, modification, and redistribution. Read Ethics & Issues 4-1 for a related discussion.

Linux is available in a variety of forms, known as distributions. Some distributions of Linux are command-line. Others are GUI (Figure 4-12). Users obtain Linux in a variety of ways. Some people download it free from the Web. Others purchase it from vendors, who bundle their own software with the operating system. Linux optical discs are included in many Linux books and also are available for purchase from vendors. For purchasers of new personal computers, some retailers such as Dell will preinstall Linux on the hard disk on request. If you want to preview the Linux operating system, you can obtain a Live CD or Live USB.

Linux
For more information, visit scsite.com/dc-off07/ch4/ weblink and then click Linux.

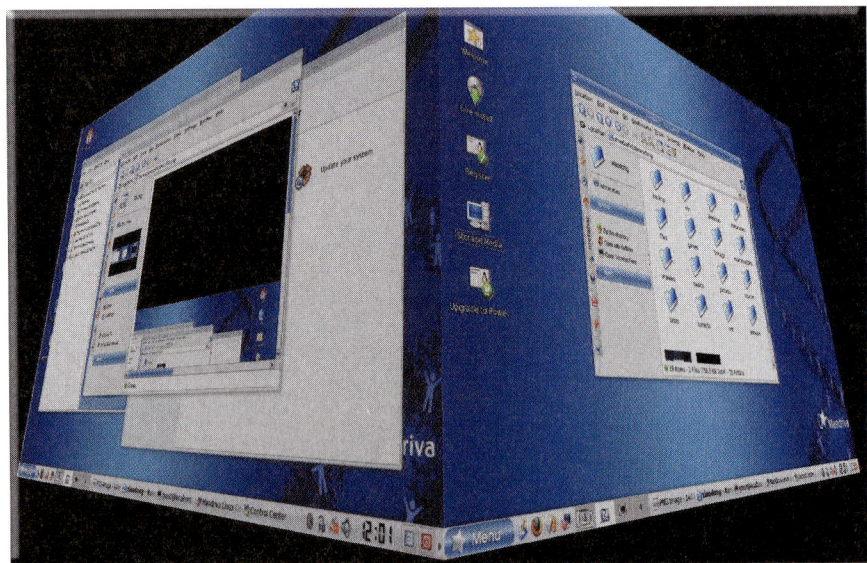

Figure 4-12 This distribution of Linux has a graphical user interface.

ETHICS & ISSUES 4-1

Closed Source vs. Open Source Operating Systems

One of the features that make Linux different from other operating systems is that Linux is open source and its source code, along with any changes, remains public. Often, when closed source operating system developers refuse to share some or all of the operating system code, third-party software developers become hindered when developing application software for the operating system. Supporters of open source maintain that source code should be open to the public so that it can be scrutinized, corrected, and enhanced. In light of concerns about security and fears of possible virus problems, however, some people are not sure open source software is a good idea. Besides, they argue, companies and programmers should be able to control, and profit from, the operating systems they create. On the other hand, open source software can be scrutinized for errors by a much larger group of people and changes can be made immediately, resulting in better software.

Are open source operating systems a good idea? Why or why not? How can the concerns about open source software be addressed? What are the advantages and disadvantages of open versus closed source operating systems? Does the open source model lead to better software?

Server Operating Systems

As discussed earlier in this chapter, a server operating system is an operating system that is designed specifically to support a network. A server operating system typically resides on a server. The client computers on the network rely on the server(s) for resources.

Many of the stand-alone operating systems discussed in the previous section function as clients and work in conjunction with a server operating system. Some of these stand-alone operating systems do include networking capability; however, server operating systems are designed specifically to support all sizes of networks, including medium- to large-sized businesses and Web servers.

Following are examples of server operating systems:
- Windows Server 2008 is an upgrade to Windows Server 2003.
- UNIX and Linux often are called multipurpose operating systems because they are both stand-alone and server operating systems.
- Solaris, a version of UNIX developed by Sun Microsystems, is a server operating system designed specifically for e-commerce applications.
- Novell's NetWare is a server operating system designed for client/server networks.

Embedded Operating Systems

The operating system on most mobile devices and many consumer electronics, called an **embedded operating system**, resides on a ROM chip. Popular embedded operating systems include Windows Embedded CE, Windows Mobile, Palm OS, iPhone OS, BlackBerry, Google Android, embedded Linux, and Symbian OS.

- Windows Embedded CE is a scaled-down Windows operating system designed for use on communications, entertainment, and computing devices with limited functionality. Examples of devices that use Windows Embedded CE include VoIP telephones, digital cameras, point-of-sale terminals, automated teller machines, digital photo frames, fuel pumps, handheld navigation devices, portable media players, ticket machines, and computerized sewing machines.
- Windows Mobile, an operating system based on Windows Embedded CE, works on specific types of smart phones and PDAs. With the Windows Mobile operating system and a compatible device, users have access to the basic PIM (personal information manager) functions such as contact lists, schedules, tasks, calendars, and notes. These devices also can check e-mail, browse the Web, listen to music, take pictures or record video, watch a video, send and receive text messages and instant messages, record a voice message, manage finances, view a map, read an e-book, or play a game.
- Palm OS, a competing operating system to Windows Mobile, runs on smart phones and PDAs. With Palm OS and a compatible device, users manage schedules and contacts, phone messages, notes, tasks and address lists, and appointments. Many Palm OS devices allow users to connect wirelessly to the Internet; browse the Web; send and receive e-mail messages, text messages, and instant messages; listen to music; record voice messages; and view digital photos.
- iPhone OS is an operating system for the iPhone and iPod touch. With finger motions, users can manage contacts and notes, send and receive e-mail and text messages, take pictures, record videos, record voice messages, view a compass, connect to the Internet wirelessly and browse the Web, check stocks, access maps and obtain directions, listen to music, watch movies and videos, and display photos. iPhone OS devices also provide Wi-Fi access to the iTunes Music Store.
- The BlackBerry operating system runs on handheld devices supplied by RIM (Research In Motion), shown in Figure 4-13. BlackBerry devices provide PIM, phone, and wireless capabilities such as sending e-mail messages, text messages, and instant messages; connecting to the Internet and browsing the Web; and accessing Bluetooth devices. Some also allow you to take pictures, play music, and access maps and directions.
- Google Android is an operating system designed by Google for mobile devices. Used on more than 20 different types of mobile devices, Google Android allows programmers to design programs specifically for devices supporting this operating system. Google Android contains features such as access to e-mail accounts, an alarm clock, video capture, access to Google Apps, Wi-Fi access, and easy Web browsing.
- Embedded Linux is a scaled-down Linux operating system designed for smart phones, PDAs, portable media players, Internet telephones, and many other types of devices and computers requiring an embedded operating system. Devices with embedded Linux offer calendar and address book and other PIM functions, touch screens, and handwriting recognition.
- Symbian OS is an open source multitasking operating system designed for smart phones. Users enter data by pressing keys on the keypad or keyboard, touching the screen, and writing on the screen with a stylus.

Figure 4-13 A smart phone that uses the BlackBerry operating system.

✓ QUIZ YOURSELF 4-2

Instructions: Find the true statement below. Then, rewrite the remaining false statements so that they are true.

1. Pocket PCs use Palm OS as their operating system.
2. Examples of embedded operating systems include Windows Server 2008, UNIX, Linux, Solaris, and NetWare.
3. Windows 7 Starter uses Windows Aero.
4. Mac OS X is a multitasking operating system available only for computers manufactured by Apple.
5. Aero Flip 3D is a UNIX-type operating system that is open source software.

Quiz Yourself Online: To further check your knowledge of pages 145 through 149, visit scsite.com/dc-off07/ch4/quiz and then click Objectives 3 – 5.

Utility Programs

A **utility program**, also called a **utility**, is a type of system software that allows a user to perform maintenance-type tasks, usually related to managing a computer, its devices, or its programs. Most operating systems include several built-in utility programs (Figure 4-14). Users often buy stand-alone utilities, however, because they offer improvements over those included with the operating system.

Functions provided by utility programs include the following: managing files, searching for files, uninstalling programs, viewing images, cleaning up disks, defragmenting disks, backing up files and disks, setting up screen savers, securing a computer from unauthorized access, protecting against viruses, removing spyware and adware, filtering Internet content, compressing files, playing media files, burning optical discs, and maintaining a personal computer. The following sections briefly discuss each of these utilities. Read Innovative Computing 4-1 to find out about utility programs that can help you recover deleted files.

Figure 4-14 To display the utilities available in the Windows System Tools list, click the Start button, click All Programs, click Accessories, and then click System Tools.

❗ INNOVATIVE COMPUTING 4-1

Utility Programs Locate Deleted Files

If you delete a file mistakenly from a USB flash drive, removable flash memory device, or hard disk, you easily can recover that erased file with utility programs. A few of the more popular utility programs have names that explain their purpose: Recuva, Recover My Files, FreeUndelete, FileMakerRecovery, R-Studio, and Recovery Toolbox. Most can be downloaded from the Web, often free of charge.

Data recovery experts offer advice on actions to take immediately when you realize you have erased files, even if you have emptied the Recycle Bin. Although the file name does not appear in the list of files on that storage medium, the file actually remains intact on the storage medium. The computer marks the space on the disk as free so that another file can overwrite the contents of the deleted file. As long as you do not save any file, no matter how small, the utility program generally can locate the marked space and then retrieve the contents of the file.

👆 For more information, visit scsite.com/dc-off07/ch4/innovative and then click Recovering Deleted Files.

File Manager

A **file manager** is a utility that performs functions related to file management. Some of the file management functions that a file manager performs are displaying a list of files on a storage medium (Figure 4-15); organizing files in folders; and copying, renaming, deleting, moving, and sorting files. A **folder** is a specific named location on a storage medium that contains related documents. Operating systems typically include a file manager.

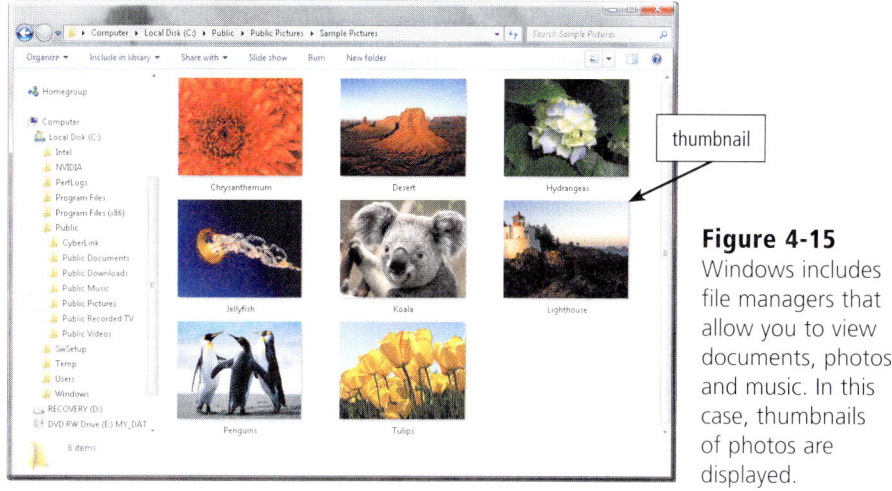

Figure 4-15 Windows includes file managers that allow you to view documents, photos, and music. In this case, thumbnails of photos are displayed.

Search Utility

A **search utility** is a program that attempts to locate a file on your computer based on criteria you specify (Figure 4-16). The criteria could be a word or words contained in a file, date the file was created or modified, size of the file, location of the file, file name, author/artist, and other similar properties. Search utilities can look through documents, photos, music, and other files. Operating systems typically include a built-in search utility.

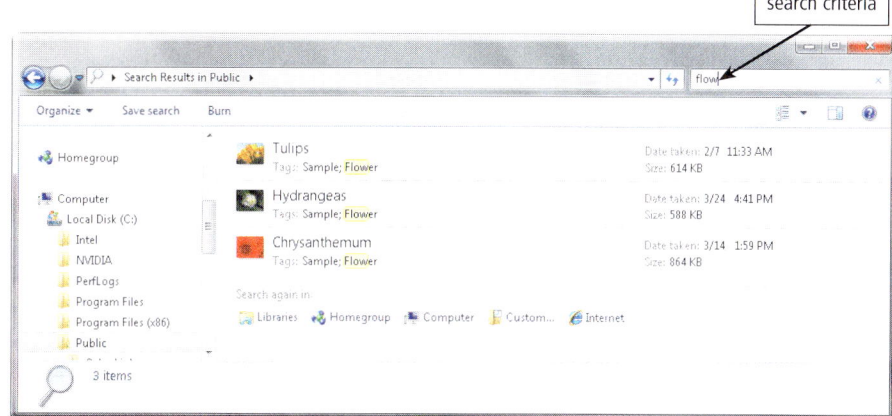

Figure 4-16 This search displays files whose name or contents contain the text, flow.

Uninstaller

An **uninstaller** is a utility that removes a program, as well as any associated entries in the system files. When you install a program, the operating system records the information it uses to run the software in the system files. The uninstaller deletes files and folders from the hard disk, as well as removes program entries from the system files.

Image Viewer

An **image viewer** is a utility that allows users to display, copy, and print the contents of a graphics file. With an image viewer, users can see images without having to open them in a paint or image editing program. Most operating systems include an image viewer. Windows image viewer is called Windows Photo Viewer (Figure 4-17).

Figure 4-17 Windows Photo Viewer allows users to see the contents of a photo file.

Disk Cleanup

A **disk cleanup** utility searches for and removes unnecessary files. Unnecessary files may include downloaded program files, temporary Internet files, deleted files, and unused program files. Operating systems, such as Windows, include a disk scanner utility.

Disk Defragmenter

A **disk defragmenter** is a utility that reorganizes the files and unused space on a computer's hard disk so that the operating system accesses data more quickly and programs run faster. When an operating system stores data on a disk, it places the data in the first available sector on the disk. It attempts to place data in sectors that are contiguous (next to each other), but this is not always possible. When the contents of a file are scattered across two or more noncontiguous sectors, the file is fragmented.

Fragmentation slows down disk access and thus the performance of the entire computer. **Defragmenting** the disk, or reorganizing it so that the files are stored in contiguous sectors, solves this problem (Figure 4-18). Operating systems usually include a disk defragmenter. Windows Disk Defragmenter is available in the System Tools list.

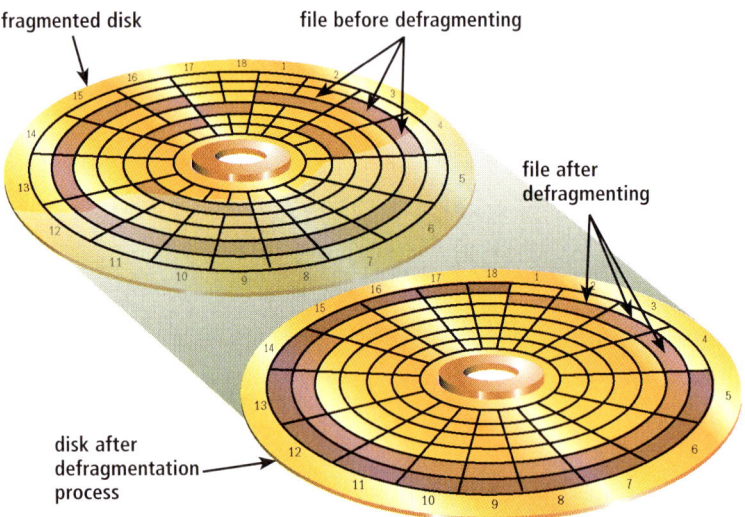

Figure 4-18 A fragmented disk has many files stored in noncontiguous sectors. Defragmenting reorganizes the files so that they are located in contiguous sectors, which speeds access time.

Backup and Restore Utilities

A **backup utility** allows users to copy, or back up, selected files or an entire hard disk to another storage medium such as another hard disk, optical disc, USB flash drive, or tape. During the backup process, the backup utility monitors progress and alerts you if it needs additional media, such as another disc. Many backup programs compress, or shrink the size of, files during the backup process. By compressing the files, the backup program requires less storage space for the backup files than for the original files.

Because they are compressed, you usually cannot use backup files in their backed up form. In the event you need to use a backup file, a **restore utility** reverses the process and returns backed up files to their original form. Backup utilities work with a restore utility.

You should back up files and disks regularly in the event your originals are lost, damaged, or destroyed. Operating systems include backup and restore utilities. Instead of backing up to a local disk storage device, some users opt to use cloud storage to back up their files. Cloud storage is a service on the Web that provides storage to computer users, usually for free or for a minimal monthly fee.

Screen Saver

A **screen saver** is a utility that causes a display device's screen to show a moving image or blank screen if no keyboard or mouse activity occurs for a specified time. When you press a key on the keyboard or move the mouse, the screen saver disappears and the screen returns to the previous state.

Screen savers originally were developed to prevent a problem called ghosting, in which images could be etched permanently on a monitor's screen. Although ghosting is not as severe of a problem with today's displays, manufacturers continue to recommend that users install screen savers for this reason. Screen savers also are popular for security, business, and entertainment purposes. To secure a computer, users configure their screen saver to require a password to deactivate. In addition to those included with the operating system, many screen savers are available for a minimal fee in stores and on the Web.

Personal Firewall

A **personal firewall** is a utility that detects and protects a personal computer from unauthorized intrusions. Personal firewalls constantly monitor all transmissions to and from a computer.

When connected to the Internet, your computer is vulnerable to attacks from a hacker. A hacker is someone who tries to access a computer or network illegally. Users with broadband Internet connections, such as through DSL and cable Internet service, are even more susceptible than those with dial-up access because the Internet connection always is on.

Operating systems often include a personal firewall. Windows automatically enables its built-in personal firewall, called Windows Firewall, upon installation of the operating system. If your operating system does not include a personal firewall or you want additional protection, you can purchase a stand-alone personal firewall utility (Figure 4-19) or a hardware firewall, which is a device such as a router that has a built-in firewall.

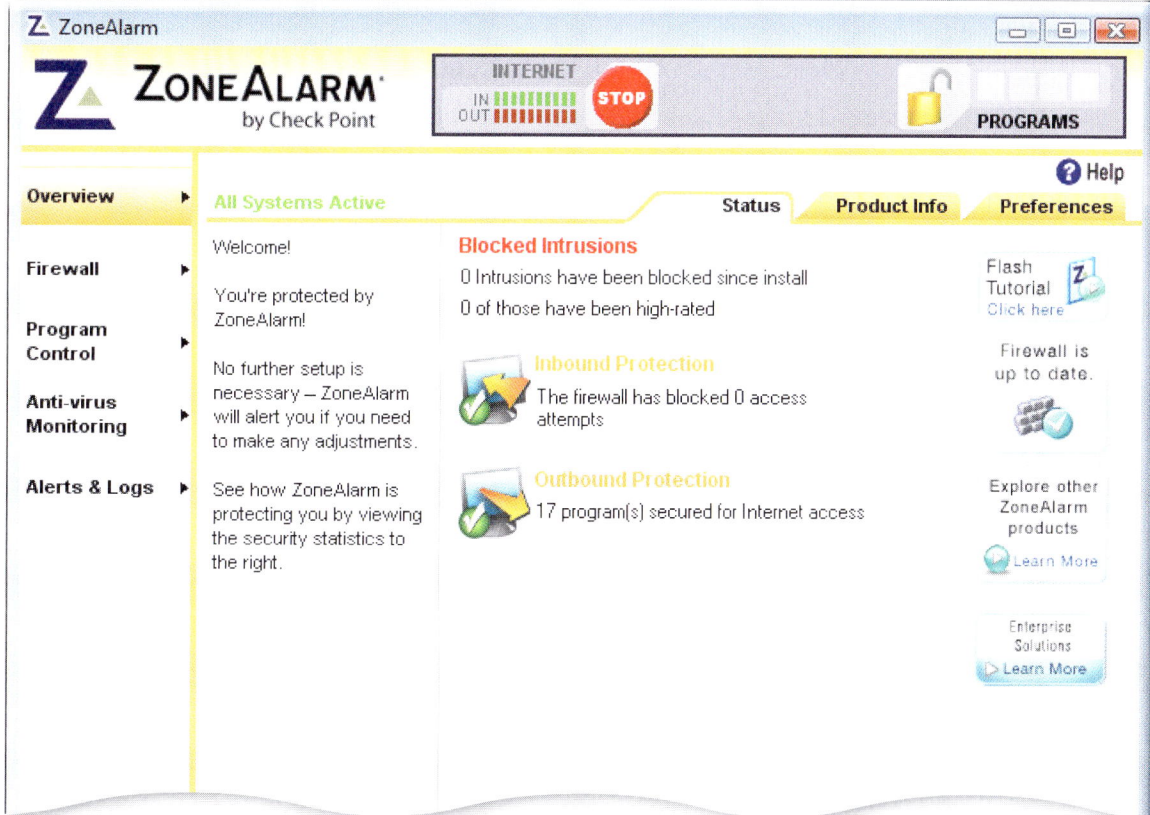

Figure 4-19 A stand-alone personal firewall utility.

Antivirus Programs

The term, computer **virus**, describes a potentially damaging computer program that affects, or infects, a computer negatively by altering the way the computer works without the user's knowledge or permission. Once the virus is in a computer, it can spread throughout and may damage your files and operating system.

Computer viruses do not generate by chance. The programmer of a virus, known as a virus author, intentionally writes a virus program. Some virus authors find writing viruses a challenge. Others write them to cause destruction. Writing a virus program usually requires significant programming skills.

Some viruses are harmless pranks that simply freeze a computer temporarily or display sounds or messages. The Music Bug virus, for example, instructs the computer to play a few chords of music. Other viruses destroy or corrupt data stored on the hard disk of the infected computer. If you notice any unusual changes in your computer's performance, it may be infected with a virus (Figure 4-20).

A **worm** copies itself repeatedly, for example, in memory or over a network, using up system resources and possibly shutting the system down. A **Trojan horse** hides within or looks like a legitimate program such as a screen saver. A certain condition or action usually triggers the Trojan horse. Unlike a virus or worm, a Trojan horse does not replicate itself to other computers. Currently, more than one million known threats to your computer exist.

To protect a computer from virus attacks, users should install an antivirus program and update it frequently. An **antivirus program** protects a computer against viruses by identifying and removing any computer viruses found in memory, on storage media, or on incoming files (Figure 4-21). Most antivirus programs also protect against worms and Trojan horses. When you purchase a new computer, it often includes antivirus software.

Three more popular antivirus programs are McAfee VirusScan, Norton AntiVirus, and Windows Live OneCare, most of which also contains spyware removers, Internet filters, and other utilities. As an alternative to purchasing these products on disc, both McAfee and Norton offer Web-based antivirus programs.

? FAQ 4-3

What steps should I take to prevent virus infections on my computer?

Set up the antivirus program to scan on a regular basis. Never open an e-mail attachment unless you are expecting the attachment and it is from a trusted source. Set macro security in programs such as word processing and spreadsheet so that you can enable or disable macros. Write-protect your recovery disk. Back up files regularly.

For more information, visit scsite.com/dc-off07/ch4/faq and then click Virus Infections.

Signs of Virus Infection

- An unusual message or image is displayed on the computer screen
- An unusual sound or music plays randomly
- The available memory is less than what should be available
- A program or file suddenly is missing
- An unknown program or file mysteriously appears
- The size of a file changes without explanation
- A file becomes corrupted
- A program or file does not work properly
- System properties change
- The computer operates much slower than usual

Figure 4-20 Viruses attack computers in a variety of ways. This list indicates some of the more common signs of virus infection.

Operating Systems and Utility Programs   Chapter 4   155

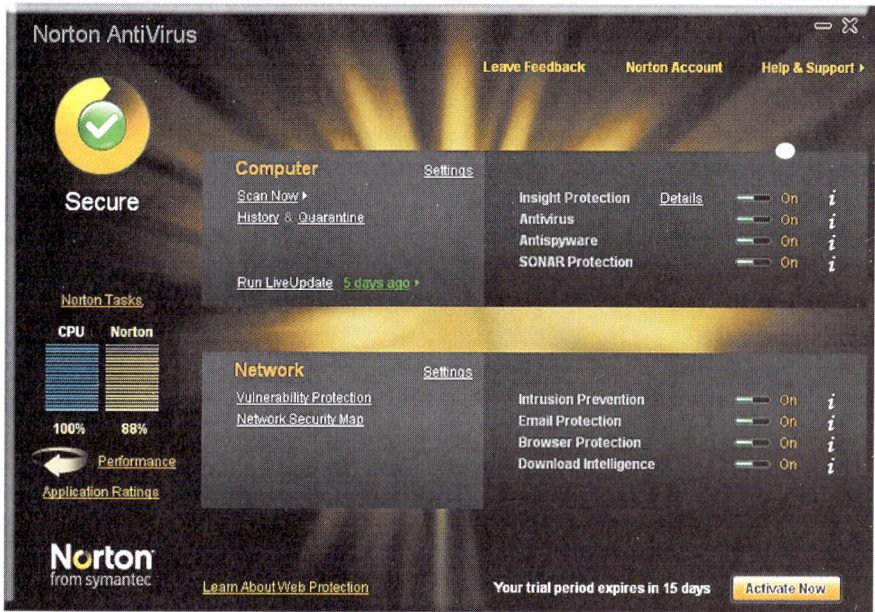

Figure 4-21 An antivirus program scans memory, disks, and incoming e-mail messages and attachments for viruses and attempts to remove any viruses it finds.

Spyware and Adware Removers

Spyware is a program placed on a computer without the user's knowledge that secretly collects information about the user, often related to Web browsing habits. The spyware program communicates information it collects to some outside source while you are online. Adware is a program that displays an online advertisement in a banner or pop-up window on Web pages, e-mail, or other Internet services. Sometimes, spyware is hidden in adware.

A **spyware remover** is a program that detects and deletes spyware, and similar programs. An **adware remover** is a program that detects and deletes adware. Most spyware and adware removers cost less than $50; some are available on the Web at no cost. Some operating systems include spyware and adware removers.

Internet Filters

Filters are programs that remove or block certain items from being displayed. Four widely used Internet filters are anti-spam programs, Web filters, phishing filters, and pop-up blockers.

Anti-Spam Programs **Spam** is an unsolicited e-mail message or newsgroup posting sent to many recipients or newsgroups at once. Spam is Internet junk mail. An **anti-spam program** is a filtering program that attempts to remove spam before it reaches your inbox. Internet access providers often filter spam as a service for their subscribers.

? FAQ 4-4

Where does spam originate?
Research indicates that spam originates from various countries throughout the world. Symantec Corporation found that in a 30-day period, the United States was responsible for more spam than any other country. The chart to the right illustrates the countries responsible for the most spam worldwide.

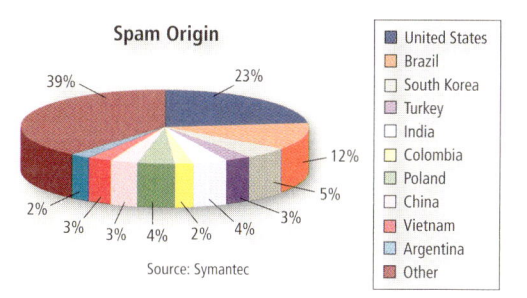

For more information, visit scsite.com/dc-off07/ch4/faq and then click Spam.

Web Filters **Web filtering software** is a program that restricts access to certain material on the Web. Some restrict access to specific Web sites; others filter sites that use certain words or phrases. Many businesses use Web filtering software to limit employee's Web access. Some schools, libraries, and parents use this software to restrict access to minors. Windows 7 contains parental controls, which allow parents to record and control the types of content their children can access on the Internet.

Phishing Filters **Phishing** is a scam in which a perpetrator attempts to obtain your personal and/or financial information. A **phishing filter** is a program that warns or blocks you from potentially fraudulent or suspicious Web sites. Some Web browsers include phishing filters.

Pop-Up Blockers A pop-up ad is an Internet advertisement that suddenly appears in a new window in the foreground of a Web page displayed in your browser. A **pop-up blocker** is a filtering program that stops pop-up ads from displaying on Web pages. Many Web browsers include a pop-up blocker. You also can download pop-up blockers from the Web at no cost.

File Compression

A **file compression utility** shrinks the size of a file(s). A compressed file takes up less storage space than the original file. Compressing files frees up room on the storage media and improves system performance. Attaching a compressed file to an e-mail message, for example, reduces the time needed for file transmission. Uploading and downloading compressed files to and from the Internet reduces the file transmission time.

WinZip
For more information, visit scsite.com/dc-off07/ch4/weblink and then click WinZip.

Compressed files sometimes are called **zipped files**. When you receive or download a compressed file, you must uncompress it. To **uncompress**, or unzip, a file, you restore it to its original form. Some operating systems such as Windows include file compression and uncompression capabilities. Two popular stand-alone file compression utilities are PKZIP and WinZip.

Media Player

A **media player** is a program that allows you to view images and animation, listen to audio, and watch video files on your computer (Figure 4-22). Media players may also include the capability to organize media files, convert them to different formats, connect to and purchase media from an online media store, download podcasts and vodcasts, burn audio CDs, and transfer media to portable media players. Windows includes Windows Media Player. Three other popular media players are iTunes, RealPlayer, and Rhapsody. Read Ethics & Issues 4-2 for a related discussion.

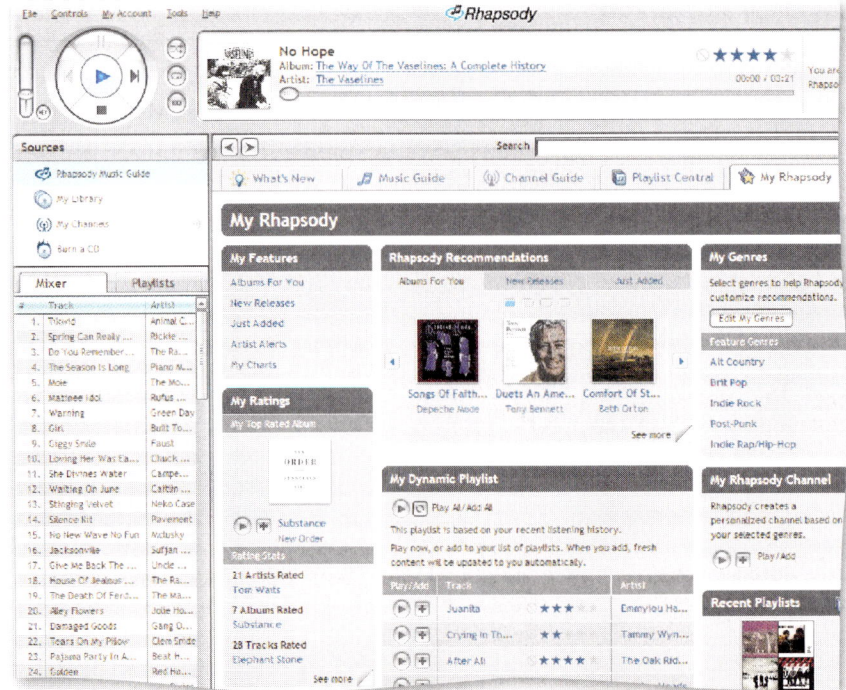

Figure 4-22
A popular media player.

ETHICS & ISSUES 4-2

Should the Government Tax Media Downloads?

When you purchase a DVD or Blu-ray Disc that contains a season or two of your favorite television show, chances are that you also pay a state and/or local sales tax. If you purchase and download the same material online in a digital format, however, chances are that you do not pay a sales tax. Some government taxing bodies seek to change that discrepancy. Two main reasons for the pressure to tax include: state and local governments feeling the pinch of lost revenue to legally downloaded digital content because consumers purchase less taxable, physical media; and pressure from the media industry to recoup lost sales due to illegally downloaded digital content. Some governments go as far as funneling collected taxes directly to the multimedia industry as compensation for illegally downloaded content that occurs in a region. Critics of the new taxes claim that government should not tax the greenest form of media purchases. Digitally downloaded content eliminates packaging, optical discs, trips to the store, and use of delivery vehicles. Critics also claim that governments single out multimedia content due to pressure from the multimedia industry. For example, some governments tax the purchase of newspapers, magazines and books, but often the same content is sold online and is not taxed. Typically, government taxing bodies tax goods, but not food and services.

Should the government tax media downloads, such as music, video, e-books, newspaper articles, and magazine articles? Why or why not? Should digital content delivery be considered a service rather than a good by taxing bodies? Why?

Disc Burning

Disc burning software writes text, graphics, audio, and video files on a recordable or rewritable CD, DVD, or Blu-ray Disc. This software enables the home user easily to back up contents of their hard disk on an optical disc and make duplicates of uncopyrighted music or movies. Disc burning software usually also includes photo editing, audio editing, and video editing capabilities (Figure 4-23). To learn about burning files to a disc, complete the Learn How To 1 exercise on page 164.

When you buy a recordable or rewritable disc, it typically includes burning software. You also can buy disc burning software for a cost of less than $100.

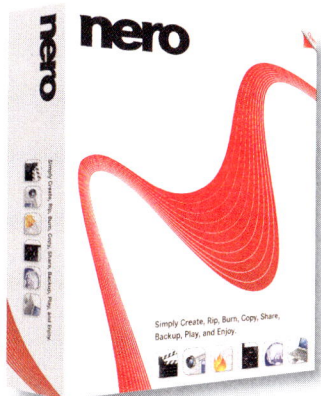

Figure 4-23 You can copy text, graphics, audio, and video files to discs using the digital media suite shown here, provided you have the correct type of drive and media.

Personal Computer Maintenance

Operating systems typically include a diagnostic utility that diagnoses computer problems but does not repair them. A **personal computer maintenance utility** identifies and fixes operating system problems, detects and repairs disk problems, and includes the capability of improving a computer's performance. Additionally, some personal computer maintenance utilities continuously monitor a computer while you use it to identify and repair problems before they occur. Norton SystemWorks is a popular personal computer maintenance utility designed for Windows operating systems (Figure 4-24).

Figure 4-24 A popular maintenance program for Windows users.

✓ QUIZ YOURSELF 4-3

Instructions: Find the true statement below. Then, rewrite the remaining false statements so that they are true.

1. A pop-up blocker shrinks the size of a file(s).
2. An anti-spam program protects a computer against viruses.
3. A personal firewall is a utility that detects and protects a personal computer from unauthorized intrusions.
4. You should uninstall files and disks regularly in the event your originals are lost, damaged, or destroyed.
5. Web filtering software writes text, graphics, audio, and video files to a recordable or rewritable disc.

🖑 **Quiz Yourself Online:** To further check your knowledge of pages 150 through 157, visit scsite.com/dc-off07/ch4/quiz and then click Objective 6.

Chapter Summary

This chapter defined an operating system and then discussed the functions common to most operating systems. The chapter introduced a variety of stand-alone operating systems, server operating systems, and embedded operating systems. Finally, the chapter described several utility programs. For a consolidated look at various forms of digital communications, read the special feature that follows this chapter.

Computer Usage @ Work

Education

Teachers and students have been using computers in education for many years. Teachers have been taking advantage of advances in computer technology to help provide a better educational experience for their students.

Many grade schools throughout the United States, as well as other countries, enable parents to track their child's performance online. In the past, parents would rely solely on their child bringing home graded assignments and tests to know how he or she was doing. In some cases, parents would be surprised when they saw their child's grades on report cards every two to three months. Teachers now have the opportunity to engage parents in their child's education not only by giving them an up-to-the-minute snapshot of grades, but also by posting lesson plans online so that parents know what their child is learning.

Computers and technology also benefit students in the classroom. Schools now have one or more computers in almost every classroom, enabling students to access the Internet to do research that they otherwise would have had to visit the library to perform. Schools also are able to offer additional technology courses such as Web page design, digital media, and computer programming.

At the college level, many instructors today rely heavily on e-learning systems to provide students with Web-based access to course materials and assessments, discussion forums, chat rooms, and e-mail. Once used mainly in online classes, e-learning systems provide instructors with an easy way to allow students access to the class at any time of the day.

Most instructors go beyond e-learning systems and use additional technologies to enhance their classes. For example, digital media instructors might require students to upload their assignments to a photo sharing community, and an English instructor might save paper by requiring students to upload research papers to Google Docs and share them with the instructor.

Computer use in education not only enhances the teaching experience for instructors and learning experience for students, it also provides students with technological knowledge that will benefit them for the rest of their lives.

🖑 For more information, visit scsite.com/dc-off07/ch4/work and then click Education.

Companies on the Cutting Edge

VERISIGN Internet Infrastructure Services

Technology users desire immediate access to information and services. Their ability to communicate and conduct commerce securely is aided in large part by VeriSign. More than 30 billion times a day, people interact on the Internet, and their purchases, text messages, downloads, and other transactions are enabled and protected by VeriSign's infrastructure services.

The company's encryption and identity services help protect businesses and consumers by authenticating communications and detecting online fraud. Its domain name services department registers all .com, .net, .cc, and .tv domain names. The VeriSign Secured Seal, which has been issued to more than 90,000 domains in 145 countries, ensures companies and consumers that the Web site is secure.

The California-based company was founded in 1995 and has more than 2,800 employees worldwide. VeriSign has invested $500 million in Project Titan, which will increase its infrastructure and security system to allow 4 trillion queries per day.

RESEARCH IN MOTION (RIM) Wireless Mobile Communications Devices Manufacturer

By 2012, 800 million people worldwide are expected to access social networking Web sites on smart phones, up from 82 million in 2007. Research in Motion (RIM) helped fuel this networking frenzy by partnering with MySpace in 2008 to help connect networkers on the go. They can access MySpace Mobile on a BlackBerry smart phone, which is RIM's key product.

The Canadian company was founded in 1984 by Mike Lazaridis, who serves as its president and co-CEO. Lazaridis's vision for wireless technology developed in high school when he was a member of the local amateur radio and television club. He developed RIM's first major product, the Inter@active Pager, which was integrated in the first BlackBerry product in 1998. The BlackBerry gained attention for having the capability to combine a wireless mailbox with a corporate mailbox so that users could assess e-mail continuously.

In 2009, Research in Motion launched BlackBerry App World, an application store that allows BlackBerry users to download personal and business programs.

For more information, visit scsite.com/dc-off07/ch4/companies.

Technology Trailblazers

STEVE WOZNIAK Apple Cofounder

Mixing fun with work comes naturally for Steve Wozniak. As Apple's cofounder, he says his computer designing career began and still continues to be a hobby filled with creativity, humor, games, and education. In his opinion, Apple's success evolved because he designed computers that had minimal parts and maximum performance.

Wozniak designed the original Apple computer in 1975 with Apple's current CEO, Steve Jobs, and wrote most of the software. Ten years later he cofounded Pixar, the award winning animation studio. He left Apple in 1985 to spend time with his family, work on community projects, and teach, but he still serves as an advisor to the corporation.

Wozinak was inducted into the Consumer Electronics Hall of Fame and the National Inventors Hall of Fame. One of his current passions is applying artificial intelligence to the area of robotics. He also is a member of the Silicon Valley Aftershocks, a polo team that plays using Segway electric transportation devices.

LINUS TORVALDS Linux Creator

Inductees to the Computer History Museum in Mountain View, CA, are noted for their contribution to computer technology. Linus Torvalds joined the Museum's Hall of Fellows in 2008 for his creation of the open source operating system, Linux.

When he developed an operating system in 1991, he announced his project in an Internet newsgroup. He made the source code available and asked readers for suggestions to enhance the product. Computer users responded by reviewing the system and offering enhancements. Three years later he released a greatly enhanced version he called Linux.

Torvalds developed this innovative operating system when he was a 21-year-old computer science student in Finland. Today, he leads the development of Linux as a fellow at OSDL (Open Source Development Labs), a not-for-profit consortium of companies dedicated to developing and promoting the operating system. Torvalds says his daily involvement with Linux involves coordinating and merging the lines of code submitted by users so that the software runs smoothly.

For more information, visit scsite.com/dc-off07/ch4/trailblazers.

Chapter Review

The Chapter Review reinforces the main concepts presented in this chapter.

👆 To obtain help from other students about any concept in this chapter, visit scsite.com/dc-off07/ch4/forum and post your thoughts and questions.

1. **What Is System Software, and What Are the Two Types of System Software?** **System software** consists of the programs that control or maintain the operations of a computer and its devices. Two types of system software are operating systems and utility programs. System software serves as the interface between the user, the application software, and the computer's hardware. An **operating system** (**OS**) is a set of programs that contains instructions that work together to coordinate all the activities among computer hardware resources. Different sizes of computers typically use different operating systems because operating systems generally are written to run on a specific type of computer. A **utility program,** or **utility,** performs maintenance-type tasks, usually related to managing a computer, its devices, or its programs.

2. **What Are the Functions of an Operating System?** The operating system starts and shuts down a computer, provides a user interface, manages programs, manages memory, coordinates tasks, configures devices, establishes an Internet connection, monitors performance, provides file management and other utilities, updates automatically, controls a network, and administers security. The **user interface** controls how data and instructions are entered and how information is displayed. Two types of user interfaces are a **graphical user interface** (**GUI**) and a **command-line interface**. Managing programs refers to how many users, and how many programs, an operating system can support at one time. An operating system can be single user/single tasking, single user/multitasking, **multiuser,** or **multiprocessing**. **Memory management** optimizes the use of random access memory (RAM). **Virtual memory** is a concept in which the operating system allocates a portion of a storage medium, usually the hard disk, to function as additional RAM. Coordinating tasks determines the order in which tasks are processed. Configuring devices involves loading each device's driver when a user boots the computer. A **driver** is a small program that tells the operating system how to communicate with a specific device. Establishing an Internet connection sets up a connection between a computer and an Internet access provider. A **performance monitor** is a program that assesses and reports information about computer resources and devices. Operating systems often provide the capability of managing and searching for files, viewing images, securing a computer from unauthorized access, uninstalling programs, and other tasks. Most operating systems include an **automatic update** feature that provides updates to the program. A **server operating system** is an operating system that organizes and coordinates how multiple users access and share network resources. Network administrators typically have an **administrator account** that enables them to access files, install programs, and specify network settings.

👆 Visit scsite.com/dc-off07/ch4/quiz and then click Objectives 1 – 2.

3. **What Are Features of Windows 7, Mac OS X, UNIX, and Linux Operating Systems?** **Windows 7** is Microsoft's fastest, most efficient operating system to date, offering quicker program start up, built-in diagnostics, automatic recovery, improved security, enhanced searching and organizing capabilities, and an easy-to-use interface. Most users choose between Windows 7 Starter, Windows 7 Home Premium, Windows 7 Ultimate, or Windows 7 Professional editions. **Mac OS X** is a multitasking GUI operating system available only for Apple computers. **UNIX** is a multitasking operating system that is flexible and powerful. **Linux** is a popular, multitasking UNIX-type operating system that is open source software, which means its code is available to the public for use, modification, and redistribution.

4. **What Are the Various Server Operating Systems?** Server operating systems are designed to support all sizes of networks, including medium- to large-sized businesses and Web servers. An example of a server operating system is Windows Server 2008. UNIX and Linux often are called multipurpose operating systems because they are both stand-alone and server operating systems. Solaris is a server operating system designed specifically for e-commerce applications. Novell's NetWare is a server operating system designed for client/server networks.

5. **What Are Several Embedded Operating Systems?** Most mobile devices and many consumer electronics have an **embedded operating system** that resides on a ROM chip. Popular embedded operating systems include the following. Windows Embedded CE is a scaled-down Windows operating system designed for use on communications, entertainment, and computing devices with limited functionality, such as VoIP telephones, digital cameras, point-of-sale terminals, automated teller machines, digital photo frames, handheld navigation devices, and portable media players. Windows Mobile, an operating system based on Windows Embedded CE, works on smart phones and PDAs. Palm OS is an operating system

used on smart phones and PDAs. iPhone OS is an operating system for iPhone and iPod touch. The BlackBerry operating system runs on handheld devices supplied by RIM. Google Android is an operating system developed by Google for mobile devices. Embedded Linux is a scaled-down Linux operating system for smart phones, PDAs, portable media players, and other devices. Symbian OS is an open source multitasking operating system designed for smart phones.

Visit scsite.com/dc-off07/ch4/quiz and then click Objectives 3 – 5.

6. **What Is the Purpose of Several Utility Programs?** Most operating systems include several built-in utility programs. A **file manager** performs functions related to file management. A **search utility** attempts to locate a file on your computer based on criteria you specify. An **image viewer** displays, copies, and prints the contents of a graphics file. An **uninstaller** removes a program and any associated entries in the system files. A **disk cleanup** utility searches for and removes unnecessary files. A **disk defragmenter** reorganizes the files and unused space on a computer's hard disk. A **backup utility** is used to copy, or back up, selected files or an entire hard disk to another storage medium. A **restore utility** reverses the backup process and returns backed up files to their original form. A **screen saver** displays a moving image or blank screen if no keyboard or mouse activity occurs for a specified time. A **personal firewall** detects and protects a personal computer from unauthorized intrusions. An **antivirus program** protects computers against a **virus**, or potentially damaging computer program, by identifying and removing any computer viruses. A **spyware remover** detects and deletes spyware and similar programs. An **adware remover** detects and deletes adware. An **anti-spam program** attempts to remove **spam** before it reaches your inbox. **Web filtering software** restricts access to certain material on the Web. A **phishing filter** warns or blocks you from potentially fraudulent or suspicious Web sites. A **pop-up blocker** stops pop-up ads from displaying on Web pages. A **file compression utility** shrinks the size of a file. A **media player** allows you to view images and animation, listen to audio, and watch video files on a computer. **Disc burning software** writes on a recordable or rewritable CD, DVD, or Blu-ray Disc. A **personal computer maintenance utility** identifies and fixes operating system or disk problems and improves a computer's performance.

Visit scsite.com/dc-off07/ch4/quiz and then click Objective 6.

Key Terms

You should know each key term. The list below helps focus your study.

To see an example of and a definition for each term, and to access current and additional information from the Web, visit scsite.com/dc-off07/ch4/terms.

administrator account (144)
adware remover (155)
anti-spam program (155)
antivirus program (154)
automatic update (143)
backup utility (152)
booting (138)
buffer (141)
cold boot (138)
command-line interface (139)
defragmenting (152)
disc burning software (157)
disk cleanup (152)
disk defragmenter (152)
driver (142)
embedded operating system (149)
file compression utility (156)
file manager (151)

folder (151)
graphical user interface (GUI) (139)
hibernate (138)
image viewer (151)
Linux (148)
log on (144)
Mac OS X (147)
Macintosh operating system (147)
media player (156)
memory management (141)
multiprocessing (141)
multiuser (141)
operating system (OS) (137)
password (144)
performance monitor (143)
personal computer maintenance utility (157)

personal firewall (153)
phishing (156)
phishing filter (156)
Plug and Play (142)
pop-up blocker (156)
queue (142)
restore utility (152)
screen saver (153)
search utility (151)
server operating system (143)
service pack (143)
sleep mode (138)
spam (155)
spooling (141)
spyware remover (155)
stand-alone operating system (146)
system software (136)
Trojan horse (154)

uncompress (156)
uninstaller (151)
UNIX (147)
user ID (144)
user interface (138)
user name (144)
utility (150)
utility program (150)
virtual memory (141)
virus (154)
warm boot (138)
Web filtering software (156)
Windows 7 (146)
Windows Aero (139)
Windows ReadyBoost (141)
worm (154)
zipped files (156)

Checkpoint

The Checkpoint exercises test your knowledge of the chapter concepts. The page number containing the answer appears in parentheses after each exercise.

👆 To complete the Checkpoint exercises interactively, visit scsite.com/dc-off07/ch4/check.

Multiple Choice Select the best answer.

1. In the Windows 7 operating system, _____ provides an enhanced visual look, additional navigation options, and animation. (139)
    a. Windows Aero
    b. Plug and Play
    c. Mac OS X
    d. Windows 7 Starter

2. Windows users can increase the size of memory through _____, which can allocate available storage space on removable flash memory devices as additional memory cache. (141)
    a. Windows Aero
    b. Plug and Play
    c. Windows ReadyBoost
    d. a disk defragmenter

3. A _____ is a small program that tells the operating system how to communicate with a specific device. (142)
    a. buffer
    b. driver
    c. performance monitor
    d. device

4. Computer and network administrators typically have a(n) _____ that enables them to access all files and programs on the computer or network, install programs, and specify settings that affect all users on a computer or network. (144)
    a. file manager
    b. personal computer maintenance utility
    c. administrator account
    d. graphical user interface

5. The operating system on most mobile devices and many consumer electronics, called a(n) _____, resides on a ROM chip. (149)
    a. network operating system
    b. embedded operating system
    c. stand-alone operating system
    d. stand-alone utility program

6. A _____ is a specific named location on a storage medium that contains related documents. (151)
    a. file
    b. buffer
    c. utility
    d. folder

7. A(n) _____ is a program that warns or blocks you from potentially fraudulent or suspicious Web sites. (156)
    a. phishing filter
    b. adware remover
    c. Web filter
    d. Trojan horse

8. A(n) _____ is a program that allows you to view images and animation, listen to audio, and watch video files on your computer. (156)
    a. file manager
    b. media player
    c. service pack
    d. image viewer

Matching Match the terms with their definitions.

_____ 1. sleep mode (138)
_____ 2. hibernate (138)
_____ 3. virus (154)
_____ 4. worm (154)
_____ 5. spam (155)

a. a potentially damaging computer program that affects, or infects, a computer negatively by altering the way the computer works without the user's knowledge or permission
b. copies itself repeatedly using up system resources and possibly shutting the system down
c. saves any open documents and programs to a hard disk before removing power from the computer
d. hides within or looks like a legitimate program such as a screen saver
e. saves any open documents and programs to RAM, turns off all unneeded functions, and then places the computer in a low-power state
f. an unsolicited e-mail message or newsgroup posting sent to many recipients or newsgroups at once

Short Answer Write a brief answer to each of the following questions.

1. How is a cold boot different from a warm boot? _____ How is a memory-resident part of an operating system different from a nonresident part of an operating system? _____
2. What is the purpose of an automatic update feature? _____ Why and when might a user receive a service pack? _____
3. How does a file become fragmented? _____ How does a disk defragmenter work? _____
4. What are the differences between Windows 7 Starter and Windows 7 Home Premium? _____ What is the difference between Windows 7 Ultimate and Windows 7 Professional? _____
5. What is a backup utility, and what happens during a backup? _____ What is the purpose of a restore utility? _____

Problem Solving

The Problem Solving exercises extend your knowledge of the chapter concepts by seeking solutions to practical computer problems that you may encounter at home, school, or work. The Collaboration exercise should be completed with a team.

👆 To discuss the Problem Solving exercises with other students, visit scsite.com/dc-off07/ch4/forum and post your thoughts or questions.

In the real world, practical problems often can be solved in multiple ways. Provide one solution to each of the following problems using available resources, such as articles on the Web or in print, blogs, podcasts, videos, television, user guides, other individuals, and electronics and computer stores. You may need to use multiple resources to obtain an answer. Present your solutions in the form requested by your instructor (brief report, presentation, discussion, or other means).

@ Home

1. **Computer Cannot Boot**   You recently purchased a computer from your friend. When you turn on the computer, a message displays that says, "Operating system not found." What steps will you take before calling technical support?

2. **Incorrect Display Settings**   You have been using the same display settings since purchasing your computer several months ago. You recently turn on your computer and notice that the screen resolution, desktop background, and color scheme has changed, even though you have not changed the display settings. What might have caused Windows to change your display settings? What are your next steps?

3. **Maximum CPU Usage**   Because your computer is performing slowly, you start the Windows Task Manager to investigate. You see that the CPU usage is near 100%. You are not aware of any other programs currently running. What might be causing this?

4. **Unwanted Programs**   The new computer that you ordered online arrived today. You anxiously unpack it, connect all the components, and then turn it on. After answering a series of questions to set up the computer, you notice it includes programs that you do not want. How will you remove these unwanted programs?

@ Work

5. **Password Required**   After turning on your computer, it prompts you to type a password to continue the boot process; however, you forgot the password. What are your next steps to allow the computer to continue the boot process, start Windows, and access the files on the hard disk?

6. **Automatic Updates**   Two or three times per month, your coworker receives a notification on his computer that the computer recently has been updated. You ask your coworker about these messages, and he says that Microsoft periodically installs updates automatically to protect the computer from various threats, as well as to improve performance. You never have seen this message appear on your computer. Does this mean that your computer does not update automatically? How can you configure your computer to update automatically?

7. **Antivirus Schedule**   You recently changed your work schedule so that you work until 6:00 p.m. instead of 5:00 p.m. At 5:00 p.m. each day, you notice that the antivirus program on your computer automatically begins scanning all files on your hard disk. This process slows your computer, and the program usually still is scanning when you leave the office. How can you change the configuration so that the antivirus program does not start until after you leave?

8. **Minimum Battery Power**   When you use your notebook computer and it is not plugged in, the battery lasts for only one hour, but the documentation states that the computer can last for two hours on battery power. What are some ways that you can increase the battery life?

Collaboration

9. **Computers in Education**   A private elementary school in your neighborhood has received a grant to create a computer lab with Internet access so that students can learn about computers and related technologies. Your neighbor, who also is a teacher at the school, asks for advice regarding how they should spend the grant money. Form a team of three people to determine the best configuration for the lab. One team member should research whether a PC or Mac is more beneficial. Another team member should research the application software that should be installed on these computers, and the other team member should determine what, if any, peripheral devices should be attached to the computers in the lab. Compile your findings and submit them to your instructor.

Learn How To

The Learn How To activities step you through fundamental technology skills when using a computer. The Learn How To exercises enable you to become more proficient with these skills.

👆 Premium Activity: To relate this Learn How To activity to your everyday life, see a visual demonstration of the activity, and then complete a short assessment, visit scsite.com/dc-off07/ch4/howto.

👆 Learn How To 1: Burn Files to an Optical Disc

Many people use USB flash drives to transport files from one location to another. If they wish to share files with someone else, however, they might choose to distribute these files on an optical disc. To learn how to burn files to an optical disc using Windows 7, complete the following steps:
1. Insert a blank optical disc into the optical disc drive.
2. When the AutoPlay dialog box is displayed, click the Burn files to disc using Windows Explorer link.
3. If necessary, change the Disc title, click the 'Like a USB flash drive' option button, and then click the Next button in the Burn a Disc dialog box to prepare the blank disc.
4. Drag the files you wish to burn to the empty window that opens.
5. Click the 'Burn to disk' button.
6. Click the Next button to burn the files to the disc. When the disc has finished burning, remove the disc from the optical disc drive.

Exercise
1. Locate photos on your computer that you are willing to share with others. If you are unable to locate any photos or are using someone else's computer, download at least three photos from the Internet. Insert a blank optical disc into your optical disc drive and then burn the photos to the disc. Once you have finished burning the disc, eject it, write your name on it, and then submit it to your instructor.

👆 Learn How To 2: Keep Windows Up-to-Date

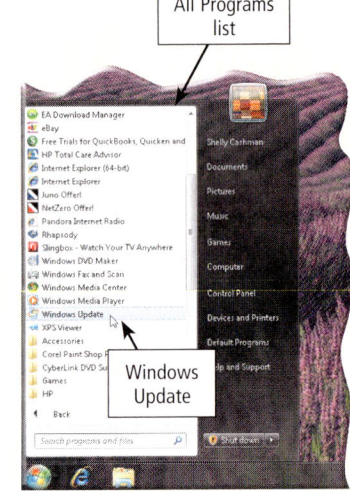

Figure 4-25

Keeping Windows up-to-date is a critical part of keeping your computer in working order. The updates made available by Microsoft for no charge over the Internet can help to keep errors from occurring on your computer and attempt to ensure that all security safeguards are in place. To update Windows, complete the next steps:
1. Click the Start button on the Windows taskbar, click All Programs, and then click Windows Update in the All Programs list (Figure 4-25) to open the Windows Update window.
2. Click the link indicating that updates are available.
3. If necessary, select those updates you wish to install and then click the OK button. Be aware that some updates might take 20 minutes or more to download and install, based primarily on your Internet access speed.
4. Often, after installation of updates, you must restart your computer to allow those updates to take effect. Be sure to save any open files before restarting your computer.

You also can schedule automatic updates for your computer. To do so, complete the following steps:
1. Click the Start button on the Windows taskbar and then click Control Panel on the Start menu.
2. In the Control Panel window, click System and Security to open the System and Security window.
3. In the System and Security window, click 'Turn automatic updating on or off' to open the Change settings window (Figure 4-26).
4. Select the option you want to use for Windows updates. Microsoft, together with all security and operating system experts, strongly recommends you select 'Install updates automatically' so that updates will be installed on your computer automatically. Notice that if you select 'Install updates automatically', you also should select a time when your computer will be on and be connected to the Internet. A secondary choice is to download the suggested updates and then choose when you want to install them, and a third choice allows you to check for updates and then choose when you want to download and install them.
5. When you have made your selection, click the OK button in the Change settings window.

Updating Windows on your computer is vital to maintain security and operational integrity.

Exercises

1. Open the Windows Update window. Make a list of the important updates to Windows on the computer you are using. Add to the list the optional updates that are available. If you are using your own computer, install the updates of your choice on your computer. Submit the list of updates to your instructor.

2. **Optional: If you are not using your own computer, do not complete this exercise.** Open the Control Panel, click System and Security, and then click 'Turn automatic updating on or off'. Select the level of automatic updates you want to use. Write a report justifying your choice of automatic updates and then submit the report to your instructor.

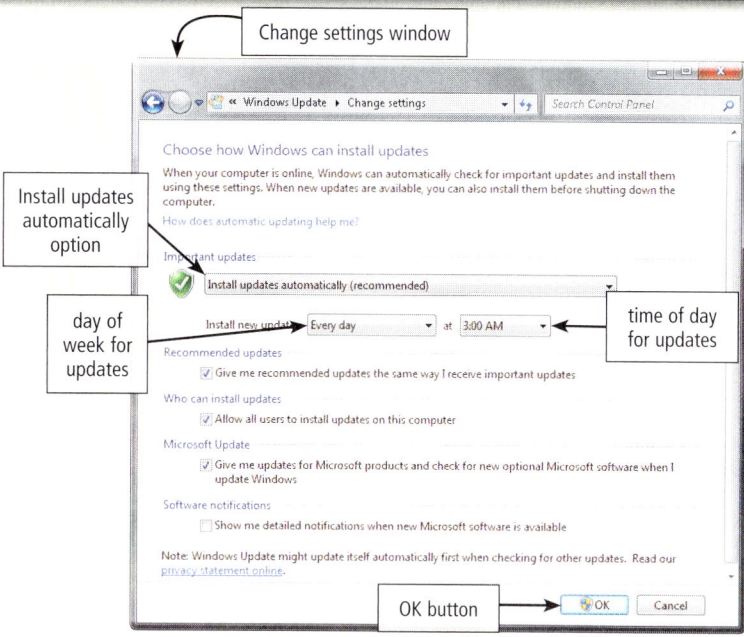

Figure 4-26

Learn It Online

The Learn It Online exercises are interactive Web exercises designed to reinforce and expand your understanding of the chapter concepts. The descriptions below briefly summarize each exercise.

👆 To access the Learn It Online exercises and for specific exercise instructions, visit scsite.com/dc-off07/ch4/learn.

❶ At the Movies — Free Online Antivirus
Watch a movie to learn why it is important to run antivirus software on your computer and how to scan your computer for malware online for no cost and then answer questions about the movie.

❷ Student Edition Labs — Installing and Uninstalling Software and Keeping Your Computer Virus Free
Enhance your understanding and knowledge about installing and uninstalling software and keeping your computer virus free by completing the Installing and Uninstalling Software and Keeping Your Computer Virus Free Labs.

❸ Practice Test
Take a multiple choice test that checks your knowledge of the chapter concepts and review the resulting study guide.

❹ Who Wants To Be a Computer Genius^2?
Play the Shelly Cashman Series version of this popular game by answering questions to find out if you are a computer genius. Panic buttons are available to provide assistance during game play.

❺ Crossword Puzzle Challenge
Complete an interactive crossword puzzle to reinforce concepts presented in this chapter.

❻ Windows Exercises
Step through the Windows 7 exercises to learn about Windows, using a screen saver, changing desktop colors, customizing the desktop for multiple users, and backing up a computer.

❼ Exploring Computer Careers
Read about a career as a systems programmer, search for related employment advertisements, and then answer related questions.

❽ Web Apps — Photoshop Express
Learn how to use Photoshop Express to upload new photos as well as photos stored on other photo sharing communities, edit photos, create new pictures, and share them with others.

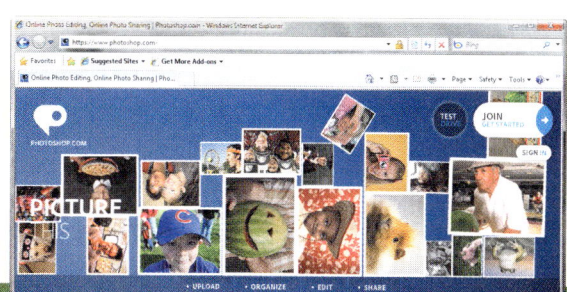

Web Research

The Web Research exercises broaden your understanding of chapter concepts by presenting questions that require you to search the Web for answers.

👆 To discuss any of the Web Research exercises in this chapter with other students, visit scsite.com/dc-off07/ch4/forum and post your thoughts or questions.

1 Search Sleuth

Use one of the search engines listed in Figure 2-8 in Chapter 2 on page 53 or your own favorite search engine to find the answers to the following questions. Copy and paste the Web address from the Web page where you found the answer. Some questions may have more than one answer. If required, submit your answers to your instructor. (1) Who are the "goons" who attend DEFCON? What color shirts do they wear? (2) Which product does IBM propose in its "Reincarnating PCs with Portable SoulPads" paper? (3) Which bird is the mascot for Linux? What is the mascot's name? (4) Why do some computer experts consider the term, spool, a backronym? (5) Who invented the Control-Alt-Delete (CTRL+ALT+DEL) key combination used to reboot a computer? (6) Which virus did the Farooq Alvi brothers invent? (7) Why would a programmer use the EICAR test file? (8) Why are UNIX programmers concerned about the "Year 2038 problem"?

2 Green Computing

Operating systems can help monitor computer energy use and suggest methods of reducing electricity through efficient power management. Experts claim monitoring systems can save each computer user at least $60 per year in electricity costs. Suggestions include not using a screen saver, turning down a monitor's brightness level, maximizing the standby and sleep settings, and using a power saver or high performance power setting that balances processing power with notebook computer battery life. View online Web sites that provide information about power management. Which methods are effective in reducing power consumption, especially for notebook computers? Which sleep state setting gives significant power savings? Which power management settings are recommended for balanced, power saver, and high performance? Write a report summarizing your findings, and include a table of links to Web sites that provide additional details.

3 Social Networking

Social networking Web site advertisers in the United States spent $108 million in 2009, an increase of 119 percent in one year. General Motors and Proctor & Gamble are two of the larger marketers exploring the placement of advertising on social networking Web sites. Millions of registered online social networking users have posted demographic information about themselves, including age, gender, and geographical location. This data helps marketing managers deliver specific advertisements to each user in an attempt to raise revenue to support their Web sites. Adknowledge (adknowledge.com) is one of the primary companies that gathers and studies data regarding online users and then sells targeted ads on social networking, e-mail, and gaming Web sites. Visit the Adknowledge Web site, view the information about targeting social network consumers, and then read articles in the About Us and Press Room sections. How are advertisers using virtual currency? How do traffic networks help advertisers create marketing campaigns? View the posts in the Adverblog Web site (adverblog.com) to read about interactive marketing trends. Summarize the information you read and viewed.

4 Blogs

Search engines help locate Web pages about certain topics based on the search text specified. A number of the search engine Web sites feature blogs describing popular search topics. For example, Ask.com's blog (blog.ask.com) lists its Blogroll, which gives recommended research and search engine Web sites. The Yahoo! Search blog (ysearchblog.com) includes news about consumer search trends (Yahoo! Buzz) and innovations in Web search technology. Google Blog Search (blogsearch.google.com) has search engines to help users find blogs about particular topics, including politics, technology, sports, and business. Visit these sites and read the posts. What topics are discussed? Compose search queries about issues and products discussed in this chapter, such as personal firewalls or antivirus programs, and read a few of the blogs describing these topics. Summarize the information you read and viewed.

5 Ethics in Action

Several automobile insurers, including Progressive Casualty Insurance Company, are promising drivers insurance premium discounts if they install a data recorder in their cars to track their driving and then exercise good driving behavior. Progressive customers voluntarily using the MyRate wireless device hope to decrease their insurance bills by a maximum of 25 percent. Privacy experts predict more insurance companies will offer this monitoring system and that it eventually will become mandatory. These critics fear that negative data will be used against poor drivers and possibly be subpoenaed in litigation. View online sites that provide information about vehicle monitoring devices. Write a report summarizing your findings, and include a table of links to Web sites that provide additional details.

Special Feature

Digital Communications

DIGITAL COMMUNICATIONS, which factor largely in many people's personal and business lives, include any transmission of information from one computer or mobile device to another (Figure 1). This feature covers many forms of digital communications: e-mail; text messaging, instant messaging, and picture/video messaging; digital voice communications; blogs and wikis; online social networks, chat rooms, and Web conferences; and content sharing.

With the Internet, cell phone networks, and other wireless networks increasing in size and speed, digital communications have become more and more prevalent. The most common devices used to communicate digitally are desktop computers, notebook computers, smart phones, and other mobile devices.

Successful use of digital communications involves selecting both the proper communications device and the proper mode of communication for a given situation. Each computer or mobile device and communications method has advantages and disadvantages that you should consider.

The following pages describe how people use different types of digital communications in their personal and business lives to enhance collaboration and increase productivity. The final section of the feature includes an example of how you might use digital communications.

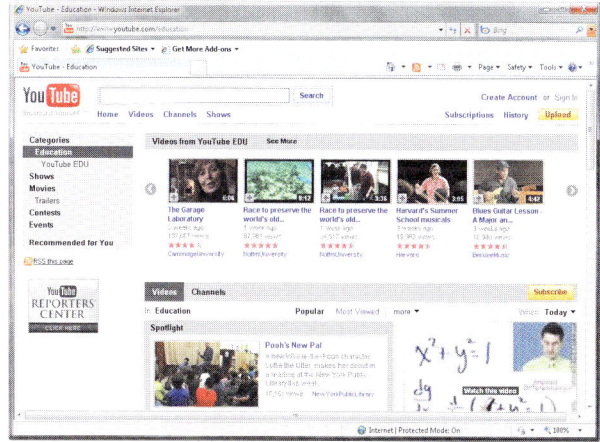

Figure 1 People use a variety of methods in their personal and business lives to engage in digital communications.

E-Mail

E-mail is the transmission of messages and files via a computer network. E-mail quickly has become one of the more widely used forms of digital communications. Although e-mail is primarily a text-based form of digital communications, it also can be used to share photos, videos, and other types of files by attaching files to e-mail messages.

E-Mail: The Personal Perspective

With a computer or mobile device connected to the Internet, you can use e-mail to keep in contact with friends, family, stores, companies, schools, and government agencies. Some people maintain several different e-mail addresses for use in different situations. Figure 2 lists some advantages, disadvantages, and good practices of personal e-mail use. Some e-mail programs are application programs that run on your computer, while others are Web applications (shown in Figure 3).

Personal E-Mail Use

Advantages
- One of the most preferred methods of online communications.
- Available on nearly any computer or mobile device with Internet access.
- Send files, called attachments, via e-mail messages to others.
- Fast, reliable, and proven technology.
- Allows messages to be sent anywhere free of charge or inexpensively.
- Allows communications with more than one person at a time.
- Provides an electronic forum for communications in which the originator has time to consider a thought before it is sent or spoken, unlike face-to-face meetings or telephone conversations.

Disadvantages
- Number of messages received can become overwhelming and unmanageable.
- Spam can overwhelm your e-mail inbox.
- Message tone can be misunderstood.
- Many computer viruses and other malicious programs are transmitted via e-mail messages.

Good practices
- Keep messages as short as possible.
- Check with the recipient before sending attachments, especially large attachments.
- Respond to messages promptly.
- Use a reputable Internet access provider that uses a spam filter, which is a program that detects and removes spam, and use an e-mail program that includes a spam filter.
- Never respond to unsolicited advertisements or spam.
- Informal language and shortcuts are acceptable when communicating with friends and family (e.g., suitable to use HRU? as a shortcut for How are you?).
- Always include a Subject line.
- Always reread your message and edit it before sending it.
- When replying to questions or comments included with a previous message, include the original message.

Figure 2 Personal e-mail remains one of the more popular reasons to use the Internet.

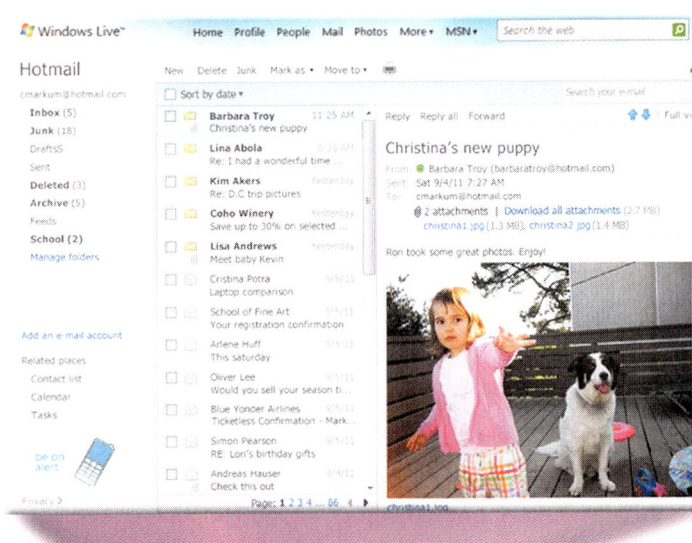

Figure 3 Many home users have e-mail Web applications.

E-Mail: The Business Perspective

Most businesses use e-mail for internal communications among employees and external communications with customers and business partners. E-mail gradually has replaced typed and copied memos, letters, and faxes while increasing the reliability, cost effectiveness, and speed of the communications. Figure 4 indicates some advantages, disadvantages, and good practices of e-mail use in business. Many of the notes listed in Figure 2 also apply to e-mail communications in business. Figure 5 shows an example of the inbox of a business e-mail program user and an example of an appropriate business e-mail message.

E-Mail Use in Business

Advantages
- Easily archive, or store long-term, all e-mail messages sent from or received by the business.
- Generally can guarantee delivery of any e-mail message that is sent within the business.
- A replacement for memos, letters, faxes, and other internal and external business communications when permitted by company policy.
- Communicate with someone who is not available at the time you need to communicate.

Disadvantages
- Volume of e-mail messages often becomes overwhelming.
- Often leads to overcommunication, which can result in important information being lost because it is ignored.
- Sometimes leads to avoidance of personal contact, such as a meeting or telephone call.

Good practices
- Because most companies archive, or save, all e-mail messages, use e-mail when you want a permanent record of a communication.
- Understand your company's e-mail policies. Many companies prohibit sending personal e-mail messages from a business computer.
- Never include any language that would be considered inappropriate in a business environment.
- Check your e-mail inbox regularly.
- Follow your company's or department's guidelines for formatting messages and including contact information and any appropriate disclaimers.
- In most cases, it is appropriate to send larger attachments in business e-mail messages as compared to those permissible in personal messages.
- Avoid sending messages to many people simultaneously or replying to large groups of people. For example, it is almost always inappropriate to send a message to the entire company.
- Avoid using e-mail messages when the content involves sensitive issues, such as a negotiation, legal matter, or employee review.
- When you need to know that the recipient has read your e-mail message, use the return receipt feature of your e-mail program to receive automatic notification as soon as the message is read.

Figure 4 Most businesses provide written policies and guidelines regarding use of e-mail programs.

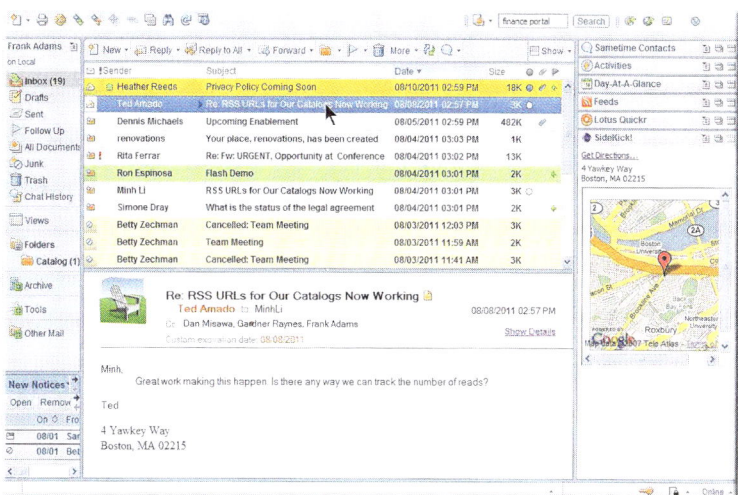

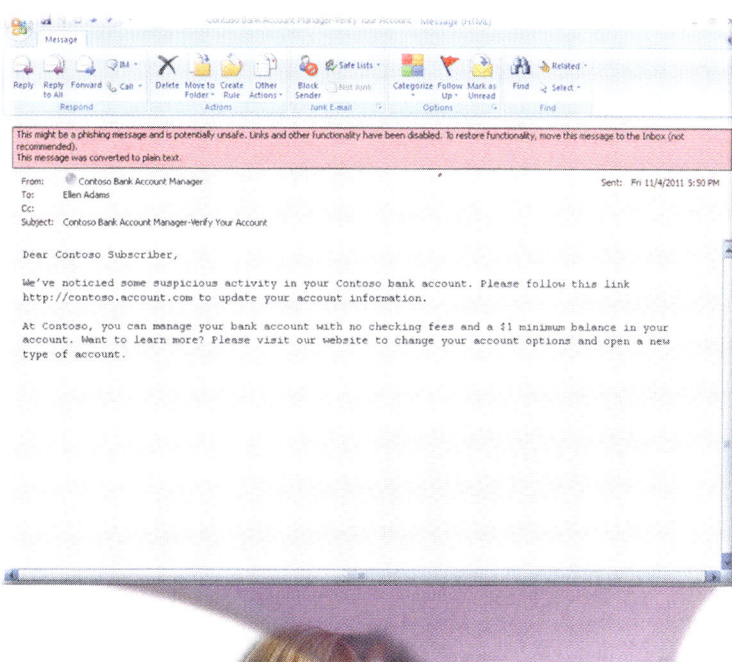

Figure 5 Businesses often use more sophisticated e-mail programs than do home users.

Text Messaging, Instant Messaging, and Picture/Video Messaging

Text messaging, instant messaging, and picture/video messaging allow you to exchange short messages and small multimedia files with other online users. Text messaging is a wireless messaging service that allows users to send and receive short notes on a smart phone or other mobile device. Instant messaging is a real-time Internet communications service that notifies a user when one or more people are online and allows the user to exchange messages or files or join a private chat room with those people. Picture messaging is a wireless messaging service that allows users to send and receive photos and sound files, as well as short text messages, to and from a mobile device, or computer. Video messaging is a wireless messaging service that allows users to send and receive short video clips, usually up to 30 seconds, in addition to all picture messaging services.

Text Messaging, Instant Messaging, and Picture/Video Messaging: The Personal Perspective

Text messaging, instant messaging, and picture/video messaging typically are used on smart phones. Instant messaging often is used on desktop and notebook computers. Virtually instantaneous communication is possible with the various forms of messaging. Figure 6 indicates some advantages, disadvantages, and good practices of using instant messaging, text messaging, and picture/video messaging in your personal life. Figure 7 shows some examples of people using messaging.

Personal Text Messaging, Instant Messaging, and Picture/Video Messaging Use

Advantages
- Virtually instantaneous form of digital communications.
- Fast, reliable, and popular method of digital communications.
- Useful when you prefer an immediate response from the recipient.
- Allows you to carry on several conversations at any time.

Disadvantages
- Can be addictive in nature.
- Receiving a constant stream of messages can be distracting.
- May be very expensive on mobile devices.
- Text messaging: Overuse may result in repetitive stress injuries (RSIs).

Good practices
- Know the person with whom you are exchanging messages.
- Keep in mind that any text, picture, or video you send can be sent to others by the recipient.
- When messaging with a new contact, do not share personal information quickly.
- Always reread your text messages and preview your pictures and videos before you send them.
- Respect the status of others when they indicate they are busy.
- Instant messaging: If the program allows you to indicate your status to others, such as "Busy" or "Do not disturb," use these indicators to let others know when you are unavailable.
- Picture/video messaging: When sending picture/video messages, make sure the content is appropriate.

Figure 6 People use various types of messaging for different reasons. (Where noted, some bullet points apply only to particular technologies.)

Figure 7 Many people interact with messaging software both at home and while away from home or work.

Text Messaging, Instant Messaging, and Picture/Video Messaging: The Business Perspective

Businesses typically use more secure, feature-rich messaging programs that allow all messages to be archived. Archiving of messages often is required by law and allows old messages to be available for future reference. Messaging allows colleagues to collaborate, or work together, online. Figure 8 indicates some advantages, disadvantages, and good practices of text messaging, instant messaging, and picture/video messaging use in business. Many of the notes listed in Figure 6 also apply to the various forms of messaging in business. Figure 9 shows an example of business-level instant messaging software and video messaging at job sites.

Text Messaging, Instant Messaging, and Picture/Video Messaging Use in Business

Advantages
- When used properly, greatly increases collaboration and communications because users have instantaneous access to each other.
- All messages can be archived for retrieval at a later date or for meeting legal requirements.
- Immediate contact with customers when allowed by company policy and agreed to by the customer.
- Collaboration with geographically separated colleagues.
- Instant messaging: Some programs allow conferences of several people at one time, eliminating the need for scheduling meeting rooms or conference calls.
- Picture/video messaging: Provides instant views of remote locations, such as work sites or company assets.

Disadvantages
- Despite policies, business conversations often lead to personal conversations.
- Often leads to over-reliance on simply messaging a colleague for an answer to a question rather than determining the answer on your own.
- Can lead to a significant decline in important face-to-face contact with coworkers, customers, and business partners.
- Instant messaging: Because all messages can be archived, it can lead to difficult situations when inappropriate content is shared.

Good practices
- When beginning a messaging conversation, make your point quickly and keep messages concise.
- Separate your personal messaging habits from your business messaging habits, avoiding use of emoticons and shortcuts, such as "brb" as a shortcut for "Be right back."
- Use proper spelling, grammar, and punctuation, and avoid colloquialisms.
- Be aware of cultural differences that might arise during casual conversations.
- Acknowledge the end of a messaging conversation.
- Follow your company's policies regarding the type of information that can be conveyed in a message and with whom you may engage in messaging.
- Always try to meet or telephone a person to introduce yourself before sending a first message to him or her.
- Review all messages you send to colleagues to make sure that the contents are appropriate for the workplace.

Figure 8 Businesses use a variety of messaging methods to allow employees to collaborate in a timely and secure manner. (Where noted, some bullet points apply only to particular technologies.)

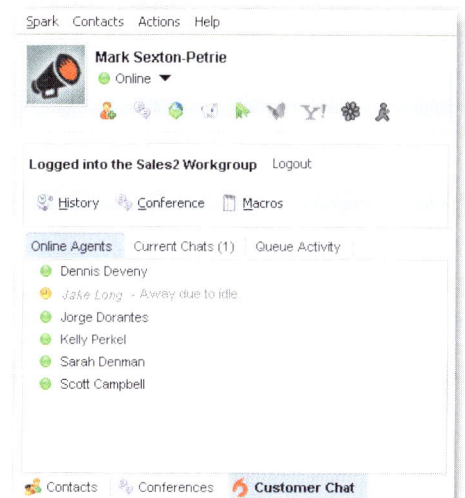

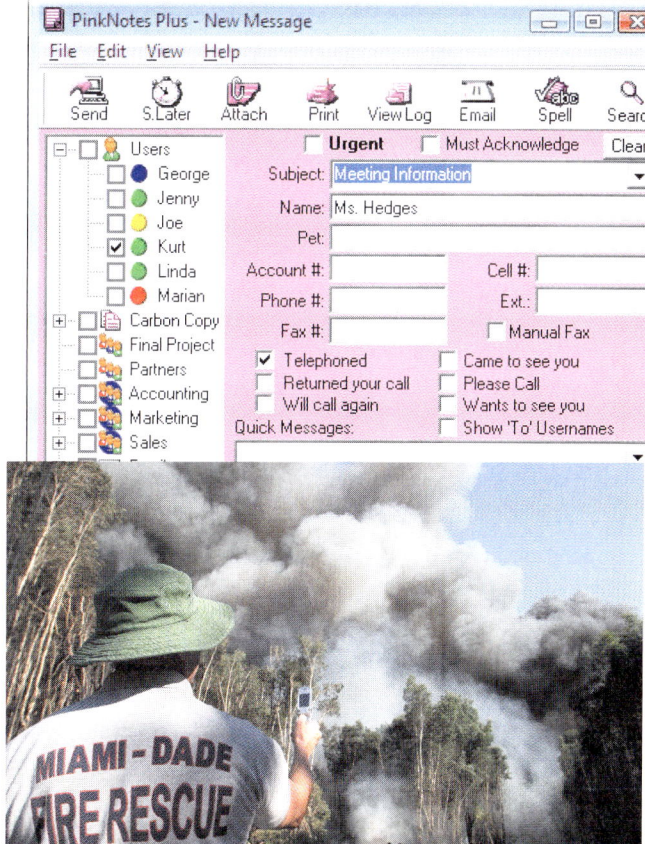

Figure 9 Business users employ instant messaging and video messaging to communicate ideas and multimedia information quickly.

Digital Voice Communications

Digital voice communications includes the use of cell phones, smart phones, and VoIP (Voice over IP). VoIP is a technology that allows users to speak to other users via the Internet. VoIP can be used as a replacement for the traditional telephone at work or in the home.

Digital Voice Communications: The Personal Perspective

With more than 200 million in use in the United States, cell phones are a primary source of digital voice communications. Cell phones can act as a suitable replacement for the traditional, wired, public switched telephone network. Smart phones offer features such as e-mail, text messaging, picture/video messaging, and playing or streaming multimedia.

Figure 10 indicates some advantages, disadvantages, and good practices of digital voice communications in your personal life. Figure 11 shows some examples of digital voice communications, including visual voice mail, which is a service that automatically translates voice mail into text messages or allows you to download voice messages to your smart phone and listen to them at your convenience.

Personal Digital Voice Communications Use

Advantages
- Increase productivity through greater and more timely communications.
- Both cell phones and VoIP offer more choice in providers than the public switched telephone network.
- Cell phones: Widespread coverage of cell phone networks provides voice communications nearly everywhere in the United States.
- Cell phones: Have been instrumental in saving lives in emergency situations.
- VoIP: Often offers free features, such as voice mail, unlimited in-country long distance calling, three-way calling, and call forwarding.
- VoIP: Typically is less expensive for both local and long distance calls than the public switched telephone network.

Disadvantages
- Cell phones: In some situations, such as while driving a car, can contribute to accidents.
- VoIP: Not as strictly regulated as the public switched telephone network, meaning that the quality of service may be lower.
- With many VoIP providers and some cell phone providers, connecting to a local service, such as 911 for emergencies, may be difficult or cumbersome.

Good practices
- Cell phones: Use a headset if you must use a cell phone while driving. Be aware of laws in your area that prohibit or limit cell phone use while driving.
- Cell phones: When using in public, be mindful of and courteous to those around you.
- Cell phones: Be aware of rules or policies at some locations, such as schools, medical facilities, or religious facilities.
- Cell phones: In public locations, use an alternative ring method, such as a vibration setting, to avoid interrupting others.

Figure 10 Cell phones and other forms of digital voice communications have become an essential means of communications throughout the world. (Where noted, some bullet points apply only to particular technologies.)

Figure 11 People use cell phones, VoIP, and visual voice mail in their everyday lives for contact with friends and family.

Digital Voice Communications: The Business Perspective

Businesses embrace digital voice communications because of increased collaboration and productivity, cost savings, and mobility. Figure 12 lists many of the advantages, disadvantages, and good practices of digital voice communications use in business. Many of the notes listed in Figure 10 also apply to the various forms of digital voice communications in business. Figure 13 shows an example of a simple VoIP system.

Digital Voice Communications Use in Business

Advantages
- Increased communications and collaboration can result in increased productivity and cost savings.
- Cell phones: Ability to contact a person almost anywhere at any time.
- VoIP: With some systems, employees can listen to and manage their voice messages on their personal computer.
- VoIP: A computer is not necessary to use a VoIP system.
- VoIP: Allows large companies to consolidate communications between geographically diverse locations.
- VoIP: Implement as an alternative to the public switched telephone network because VoIP allows businesses to use their existing network more efficiently and provides more features than the public switched telephone network.

Disadvantages
- With many VoIP providers and some cell phone providers, connecting to a local service, such as 911 for emergencies, may be difficult or cumbersome.
- The quality of calls may change at times due to excessive network usage.
- Cell phones: Misuse often leads to rude behavior or disruption of meetings.
- Cell phones: Using a cell phone provided by an employer for personal calls may have undesirable tax consequences.
- VoIP: Large companies may find it expensive and difficult to manage.
- VoIP: Unlike a public switched telephone network, many VoIP systems and equipment will not function during a power outage.

Good practices
- Cell phones: Follow company policy regarding the use for business communications. Limit personal calls on your cell phone during business hours.
- Cell phones: Disable the ringer when in meetings or during important discussions.
- Cell phones: Resist the need to answer every call at all times, such as when you are on breaks or when you are not at work.
- Cell phones: Avoid speaking loudly on the phone when walking through others' work areas.
- VoIP: When possible, use a VoIP telephone rather than a cell phone because it generally is less expensive for the company on a per-call basis.

Figure 12 Digital voice communications are used when a more personal form of communications than e-mail or messaging is required in real time. (Where noted, some bullet points apply only to particular technologies.)

Figure 13 VoIP allows businesses to connect their telephone system to their internal network and the Internet for voice telephone calls.

Blogs and Wikis

A **blog** is an informal Web site consisting of time-stamped articles, or posts, in a diary or journal format, usually listed in reverse chronological order. A **wiki** is a collaborative Web site that allows users to create, add to, modify, or delete the Web site content via their Web browser.

Blogs and Wikis: The Personal Perspective

Blog topics often include family life, social life, a personal project, or events during a vacation. You might read and contribute to a wiki regarding classical guitar techniques if your hobbies included playing classical guitar. While blogs can be modified only by the author, a wiki can be authored and edited by any user. Another difference between blogs and wikis is that blog entries typically are not included in search results from search engines, such as Google, while wiki entries are recognized by search engine queries. Figure 14 indicates some advantages, disadvantages, and good practices of using blogs and wikis in your personal life. Figure 15 shows examples of blog and wiki entries.

Personal Blog and Wiki Use

Advantages
- Some blogs and wikis provide secure access so that only a select group of qualified or desired individuals are allowed to read and write entries.
- Blogs: Easy, accessible, and often free method of keeping a group of people informed about events.
- Blogs: Easy way to keep up with an acquaintance or expand your knowledge about political or social points of view.
- Blogs: Often can be read or written using Internet-enabled mobile devices.
- Wikis: Provide free access to concise, almost encyclopedic, information about nearly any topic.

Disadvantages
- Vulnerable to fraudulent or biased entries placed by businesses or special interest groups in an effort to sway public opinion.
- Blogs: Often are biased towards a particular point of view.
- Blogs: Some blogging Web sites are often sources of malicious programs.
- Wikis: Publicly accessible wikis sometimes are vulnerable to vandalism or subject to errors.

Good practices
- Blogs: When writing a blog, be aware that the contents of your blog may be accessible publicly and associated with your identity for a long time.
- Blogs: When reading blogs, be aware of the source of the information and evaluate the credibility of the source.
- Wikis: When performing research using a wiki, check any provided sources and, if possible, check the editorial history of the entries.
- Wikis: If you locate an error, notify the author or editor of the wiki page, or, if possible, edit the page yourself to make the correction.
- Wikis: When possible, contribute your own knowledge to wikis that interest you, being sure to follow the guidelines of the wiki.

Figure 14 While blogs and wikis provide a great deal of information sharing, users and contributors alike should be aware of the risks involved. (Where noted, some bullet points apply only to particular technologies.)

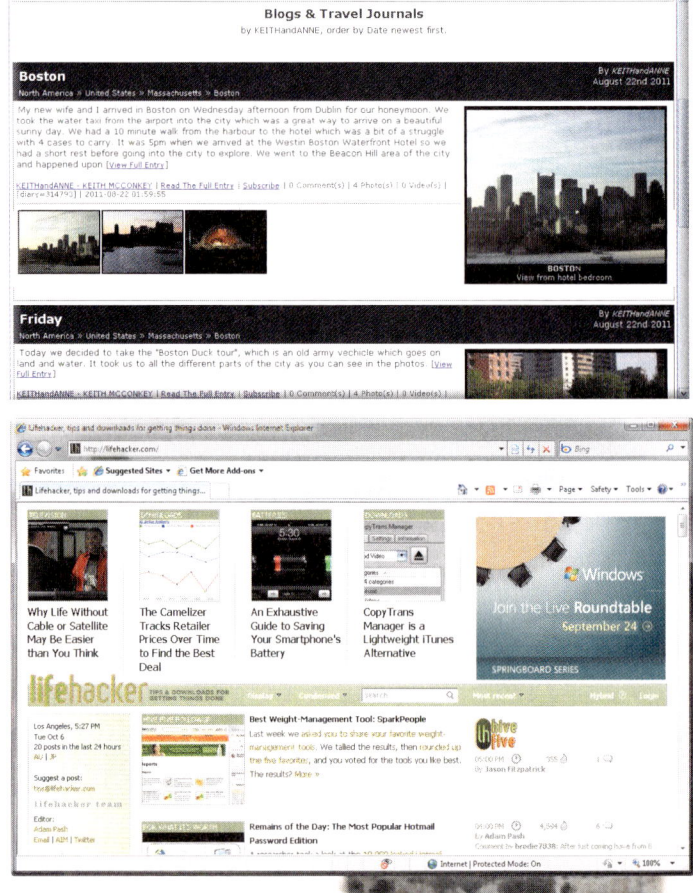

Figure 15 Blogs and wikis allow people to share their knowledge, experience, viewpoints, and personal events on the Internet. People use mobile blogging while away from home or while in interesting locations.

Blogs and Wikis: The Business Perspective

Many businesses use blogs and wikis to share knowledge within the company. One large company claims to maintain more than 300,000 blogs and wikis internally. A key reason that blogs and wikis are so popular in business is that they can be written, read, and searched easily. As the company's resident expert regarding a particular topic, an employee may blog to keep others informed about topics relating to that expertise. A business-oriented wiki may contain a wealth of historical knowledge for a particular department in the company. Figure 16 indicates some advantages, disadvantages, and good practices of using blogs and wikis in business. Many of the notes listed in Figure 14 also apply to using blogs and wikis in business. Figure 17 shows examples of typical business-oriented blog and wiki entries.

Blog and Wiki Use in Business

Advantages
- Provide easy access to gained knowledge and experience.
- Easily can be searched by employees.
- Some may be made available to customers, business partners, or the general public.
- Blogs: Publicly accessible blogs often are used as an effective means to promote products or services.

Disadvantages
- Mistakes, inaccuracies, and inconsistencies in entries can lead to lost productivity and increased costs.
- Internal company blogs and wikis often contain proprietary company information that easily can be leaked to competitors or the press.
- Blogs: When contributing to a blog, some employees become engrossed with capturing every detail of their job.
- Wikis: Information often may become old, or stale, if it is not updated regularly.

Good practices
- Search your company's blogs and wikis for information before telephoning, instant messaging, or e-mailing a colleague with a question.
- If you do not find an answer to a question on your company's blogs or wikis, then contribute to a blog or wiki once you find the answer.
- When contributing to a blog or wiki entry, read your company's policies regarding content, formatting, and style. Some companies employ full-time bloggers and writers who can help you contribute a valuable entry.
- When contributing to a blog or wiki entry, stay on topic and create links within your entry to other related or relevant Web pages, including other blog and wiki entries.
- Blogs: When engaging in personal blogging, do not discredit your employer or potential future employers; many people have lost their jobs as a result of engaging in such behavior.
- Blogs: When engaging in personal blogging, be careful not to divulge proprietary company information.

Figure 16 Business blog and wiki use typically is governed by more guidelines and rules than those for personal blogs and wikis. (Where noted, some bullet points apply only to particular technologies.)

Figure 17 Increasingly more businesses use blogs and wikis to allow employees to share information with each other, customers, and business partners.

Online Social Networks, Chat Rooms, and Web Conferences

An **online social network** is a Web site that encourages members in its online community to share their interest, ideas, stories, photos, music, and videos with other registered users. A **chat room** is a location on the Internet that permits users to chat with one another. A **Web conference** allows two or more people to engage in an online meeting and often allows the attendees to access programs and digital content, such as documents, audio, and video, during the meeting.

Online Social Networks, Chat Rooms, and Web Conferences: The Personal Perspective

The popularity of online social networks such as Facebook continues to skyrocket. Most online social networks allow you to maintain a personal Web site that you can share with other registered users who, after being invited, may view or contribute content to your site. Those invited to your online social network often are known as friends. While chat rooms have decreased in popularity over the years, people often use them for targeted discussions about specific topics. Web conferences often are used by consumers to obtain technical support or assistance from companies and government agencies or in educational settings to engage in online learning. Figure 18 indicates some advantages, disadvantages, and good practices of using online social networks, chat rooms, and Web conferences in your personal life. Figure 19 shows an example of an online social network and a virtual chat room discussion.

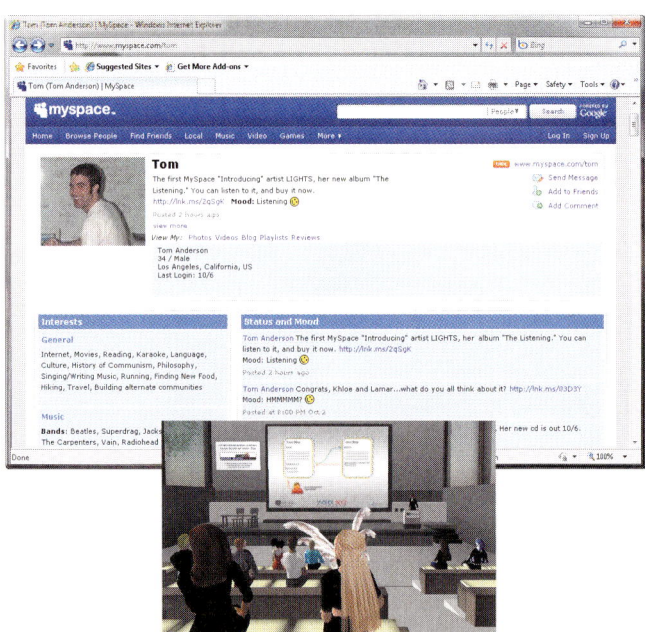

Figure 19 Online social networks and virtual chat rooms allow groups of people with similar interests or lifestyles to enjoy real-time communications.

Personal Use of Online Social Networks, Chat Rooms, and Web Conferences

Advantages
- Online social networks/chat rooms: Easily find friends throughout the world with similar interests or traits.
- Online social networks/chat rooms: Can expand your knowledge about political or social points of view.
- Web conferences: Use Web conferencing when offered by a company for technical support issues because the tenor of the interaction is more personal than a telephone call.
- Web conferences: Often effectively provides the necessary communications to avoid a visit to a store location or a visit from a repair technician.

Disadvantages
- Online social networks/chat rooms: Some people are susceptible to overusing these forms of communications in lieu of real, in-person contacts and relationships. Overuse of these forms of communications may lead to addiction.
- Online social networks/chat rooms: People often hide their real identity to lure others into revealing too much personal information.
- Online social networks/chat rooms: Several high-profile incidents occurred in which people engaged in illegal activity using online social networks and chat rooms.

Good practices
- Online social networks: When submitting information, be aware that the information may be accessible publicly and associated with your identity for a long time.
- Online social networks: While many online social networks encourage the practice, do not try to gather too many friends in your social network. Some experts believe that a functional social network is limited to a maximum of 150 people.
- Chat rooms/Web conferences: Be as polite and courteous as you would be to someone in person.

Figure 18 People use online social networks, chat rooms, and Web conferences as a means of extending their social lives beyond their physical surroundings. (Where noted, some bullet points apply only to particular technologies.)

Online Social Networks, Chat Rooms, and Web Conferences: The Business Perspective

Online social networks, chat rooms, and Web conferences allow business users to interact and collaborate as teams. While online social networks have not been as popular as other forms of digital communications in business, their use is showing promise for many companies and groups who use it for business purposes. One company claims to have signed up more than five million business users for its business-oriented online social network. Chat rooms and Web conferences often serve as forums for online meetings. Figure 20 indicates some advantages, disadvantages, and good practices of using online social networks, chat rooms, and Web conferences in business. Many of the notes listed in Figure 6 on page 170 and Figure 18 also apply to these forms of digital communication in business. Figure 21 shows an example of a business-oriented online social network, chat room, and Web conference.

Online Social Network, Chat Room, and Web Conference Use in Business

Advantages
- Online social networks: Encourage people to collaborate with others with whom they typically would not collaborate.
- Online social networks/chat rooms: Often can be accessed using Internet-enabled mobile devices, providing instant collaboration almost anywhere.
- Online social networks/chat rooms: Provide forums for meeting potential customers, employers, and employees.
- Web conferences: Programs often allow application program sharing, which means that all participants can view the contents of one or more participant's computer screen.
- Online social networks/chat rooms: Some are located internally within a company and allow only employees access to the sites.
- Online social networks/chat rooms: Some are subscription-based and allow people to interact freely with others in related fields or industries.

Disadvantages
- Employees often over-rely on these means of online digital communications and do not interact with others in more personal ways.
- Online social networks: Can be cumbersome and expensive to maintain.

Good practices
- When engaging in online social networks, chat rooms, and Web conferences outside of your company, be careful not to divulge proprietary company information.
- Always maintain a professional demeanor. Often, those who use this technology in their personal lives are quick to behave more casually than is appropriate in a business setting.
- Divulge only that information about yourself that is relevant to the reasons you are participating in an online social network or chat room.

Figure 20 Businesses have embraced online social networks, chat rooms, and Web conferences to drive collaboration among geographically separated teams, employees, and other business contacts. (Where noted, some bullet points apply only to particular technologies.)

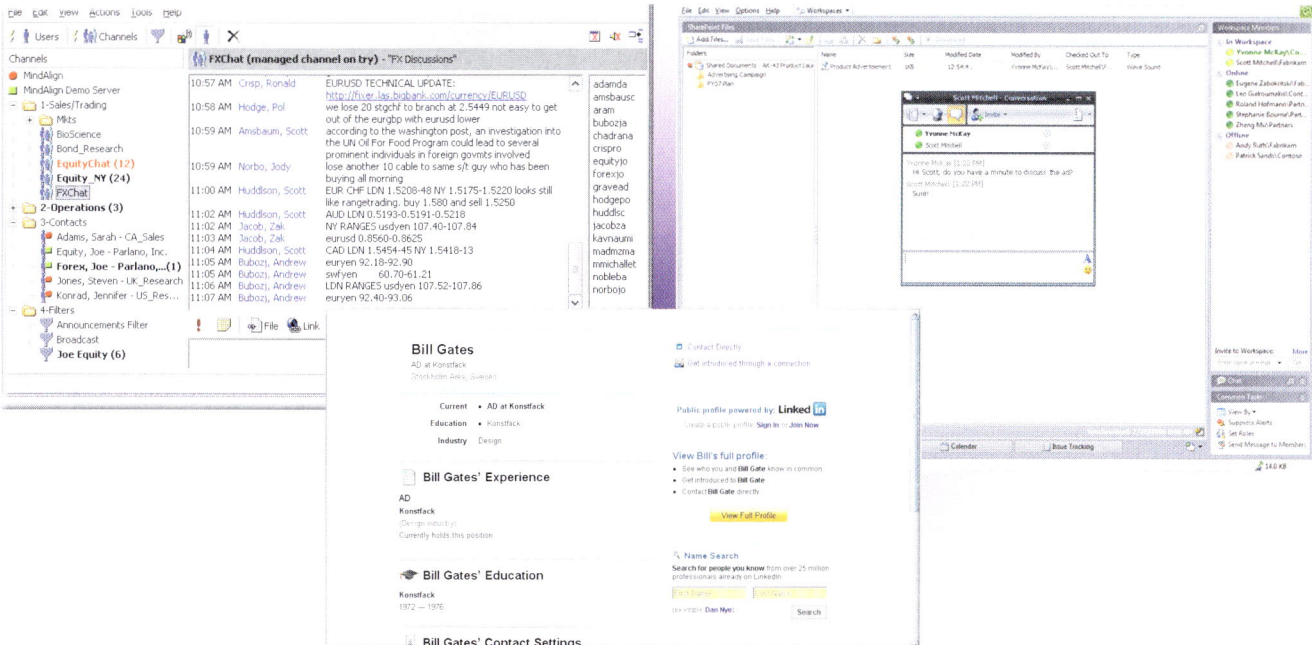

Figure 21 Businesses use online social networks, chat rooms, and Web conferences to allow employees and teams to communicate more effectively.

Content Sharing

Content sharing provides a means by which rich content, such as audio, video, photos, and documents, can be communicated digitally.

Content Sharing: The Personal Perspective

The prolific spread of digital cameras and digital video cameras combined with ever-increasing speeds of home and mobile Internet connections has resulted in the explosive growth of media sharing Web sites, such as YouTube and Flickr. In addition to sharing media, people are sharing documents, spreadsheets, and other content on Web sites. Figure 22 indicates some advantages, disadvantages, and good practices of content sharing in your personal life. Figure 23 shows some examples of a video sharing Web site, a photo sharing group Web site, and a personal photo sharing Web site.

Personal Content Sharing Use

Advantages
- Ability to view broadcasts of events that may not be available through traditional broadcasts in your area.
- Media sharing Web sites provide almost limitless information and entertainment at little or no cost.
- Some services allow you to edit your content or the content of others directly on the site using a Web application.
- View or listen to live broadcasts of sporting events.
- View or listen to news stories.
- Much like online social networks, media sharing Web sites can provide a sense of community to a group of geographically separated individuals.

Disadvantages
- You may find it difficult to locate media and content that interests you.
- When sharing video and photos on a media sharing Web site, you may be giving up some of your rights to the media.
- Many people have been embarrassed by content posted by others to media sharing Web sites.

Good practices
- Before placing your content on a media sharing Web site, make a good effort to edit the content for brevity and clarity. For example, make certain that audio is clear in a video, and use photo editing software to remove red-eye.
- Take advantage of the fact that most media and content sharing Web sites allow you to limit who can access your media and content.
- Before you allow somebody to record video of you or take your picture, remember that the video or photo may end up on a media sharing Web site.
- Before placing your multimedia content on a media sharing Web site, check the terms of the service agreement and make certain you agree to give up certain legal rights to your multimedia content.
- Do not post pictures or videos that are protected by a copyright.

Figure 22 While most people act as consumers of content shared on the Internet, some share their own content.

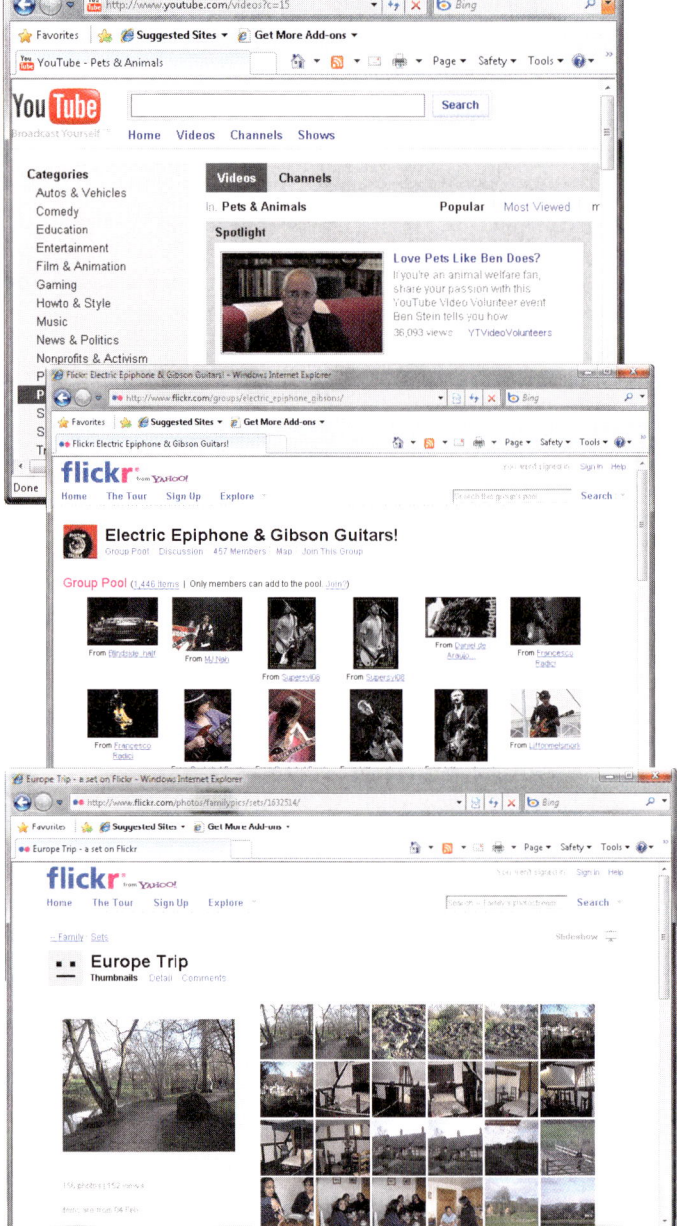

Figure 23 People share and view content on the Internet in a number of ways.

Content Sharing: The Business Perspective

Media sharing Web sites allow business to interact creatively with employees, customers, and prospective customers. Video conferencing is the oldest form of real-time multimedia content sharing in business. Figure 24 outlines some advantages, disadvantages, and good practices of content sharing in business. Many of the notes listed in Figure 22 also apply to content sharing in business. Figure 25 shows examples of content shared in an educational setting and a document management system, which allows for secure storage and management of a company's documents.

Content Sharing Use in Business

Advantages
- Multimedia sharing sites allow companies to archive video conferences, advertisements, employee photos, and other multimedia content.
- Executives and managers create podcasts or vodcasts to spread their vision or message. Vodcasts are podcasts that contain video and usually audio.
- Video conferences allow geographically separate people to transmit audio and video and engage in a meeting remotely.
- Most business-based content sharing software provides for enhanced collaboration by making the content accessible and searchable.
- Multimedia content, such as videos and photos, can be stored in a document management system to archive information about important projects or events.

Disadvantages
- Production and distribution of multimedia content often is more expensive than traditional methods.
- Security on business content sharing systems often frustrates employees who are denied access to information without special approval.

Good practices
- Unless you have permission, do not share company-owned photos and videos on publicly available media sharing Web sites, such as YouTube or Flickr.
- When viewing or sharing photos and videos in the workplace, be certain that the content is appropriate for the workplace. Some businesses have a media department that manages all of the company's multimedia content.

Figure 24 Businesses provide secure content sharing repositories and real-time multimedia.

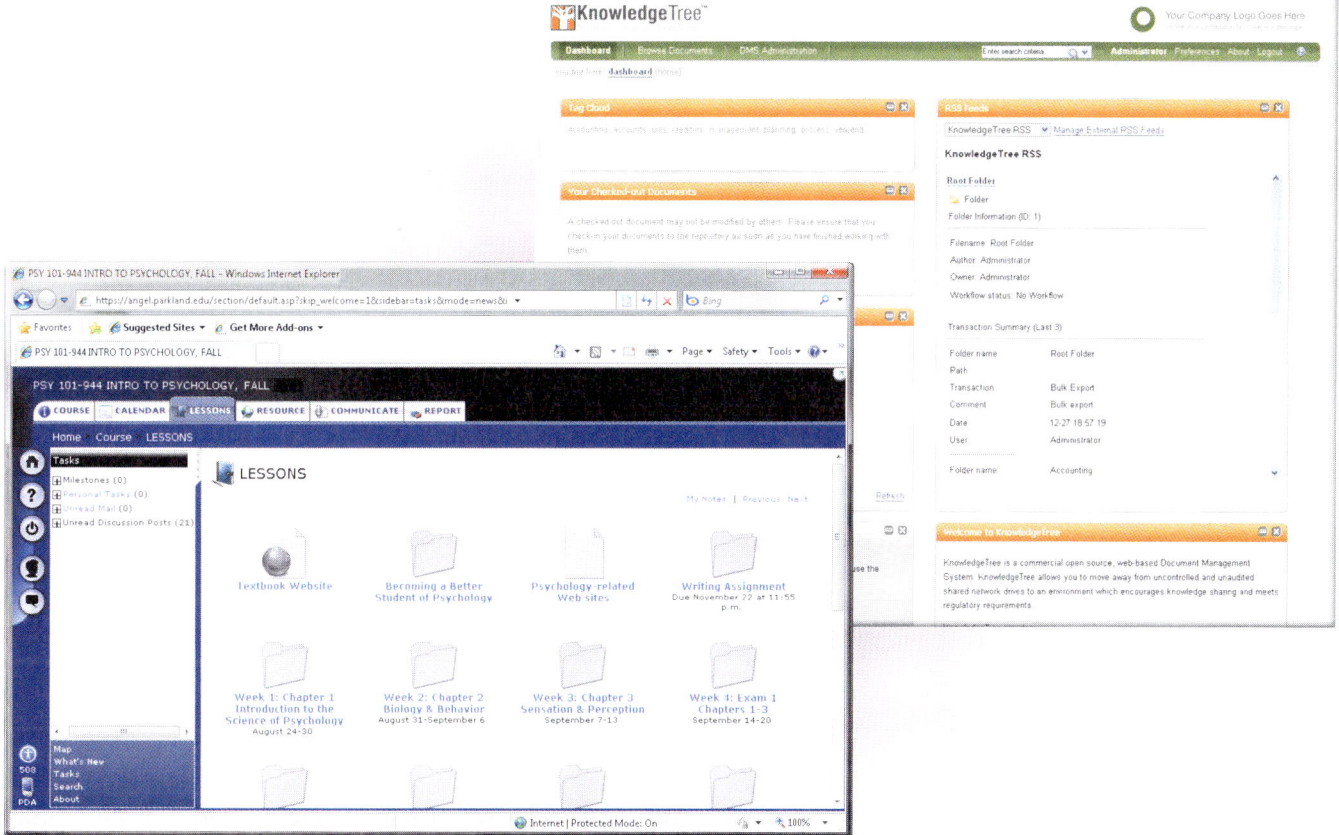

Figure 25 Businesses and other institutions share a variety of digital content in order to facilitate collaboration.

Special Feature

Digital Communications in Your Life

Many people use various forms of digital communications in both their personal and business lives. Imagine you are working in your chosen field and making decisions every day regarding how to communicate best with family, friends, and business contacts. The following scenario presents several situations and decisions regarding digital communications made during a single day.

8:15 a.m.

SITUATION: Before leaving for work, you remember that you are expecting an e-mail confirmation from your travel agent regarding plans for a trip to a friend's birthday party.

RESOLUTION: E-mail is a good tool when instant communication is not necessary. Personal business, such as travel arrangements, is negotiated or confirmed easily via e-mail messages, resulting in a permanent record of the communication.

You receive the e-mail message on your personal computer from your travel agent with the news that your trip is booked.

8:47 a.m.

SITUATION: While riding the bus to work, you use your smart phone to access wirelessly the newest song from your favorite band. The phone number of an incoming call appears on the smart phone's display, and you recognize it as your boss's phone number. Should you take the call?

RESOLUTION: Many people feel uncomfortable answering business calls while on personal time or in a public place. The decision whether to allow work life to interfere with personal life varies with each individual. You know that your boss calls your cell phone only for important reasons. You answer the call and your boss explains that she would like you to join a video conference with an important customer. After hanging up the phone, you resume listening to your song.

9:11 a.m.

SITUATION: After arriving at work, your first task is to check e-mail messages. You have more than 30 new e-mail messages since you last checked your e-mail inbox at 5:00 p.m. yesterday.

RESOLUTION: Business e-mail programs usually include several methods for organizing and managing your e-mail inbox. As you view your inbox, a few items have red exclamation marks next to them, indicating that the sender marked them as urgent. Your e-mail program also allows you to mark e-mail messages in your inbox with colored flags. You quickly flag the urgent items with a red flag, meaning that you will handle these immediately after you flag the remaining messages. You flag messages from customers with a yellow flag. By skimming the subject, you place blue, green, and black flags next to some messages. You use the colors to code messages based on the priority of the messages.

Good practices often suggest you respond by phone to urgent messages or messages from important customers. You put on your headset, and, using your VoIP phone, you begin the process of calling some of the people whose messages you marked with red and yellow flags. When you are finished talking on the phone, you respond to several of the other messages. By 9:45 a.m. your inbox is empty.

10:00 a.m.

SITUATION: By the time you arrive at your office's video conferencing room, five other coworkers already have gathered. After sitting down, you see a large monitor and a camera in front of you. A group of people in another conference room in London appears on the monitor. Your boss whispers that your shirt is a bit bright for the video conference. During the meeting, the cell phone in your pocket buzzes a number of times. Should you take the call?

RESOLUTION: At first, most people find video conferences to be uncomfortable experiences. In comparison to a typical meeting, some people tend to fidget more, tap their fingers, or speak more nervously in a video conference. People tend to recognize those actions when they view others on a monitor in a video conference, so experts suggest keeping these types of actions to a minimum.

You ignore the cell phone calls during the meeting. You plan to check your visual voice mail on your cell phone later.

9:15 p.m.

SITUATION: As you end the day at home, you log on to the online social network that you joined earlier in the year. When you add a friend to your list of contacts, you notice that she currently is logged on. You start your instant messaging program and begin instant messaging with your friend. Your friend reminds you that you still have a home page on another online social network from your days in school.

RESOLUTION: You log on to the old online social network that you used when you were in school. You decide to delete the site. People often forget that once they put content on an online social network, in a blog, or on a wiki that it may remain there forever unless they delete or edit it. Periodically, consider checking how others might perceive you based on content you have placed on the Internet.

Chapter Five

Computer Security and Safety, Ethics, and Privacy

Objectives

After completing this chapter, you will be able to:

1. Describe various types of Internet and network attacks (computer viruses, worms, Trojan horses, rootkits, botnets, denial of service attacks, back doors, and spoofing), and identify ways to safeguard against these attacks, including firewalls and intrusion detection software

2. Discuss techniques to prevent unauthorized computer access and use

3. Identify safeguards against hardware theft and vandalism

4. Explain the ways to protect against software theft and information theft

5. Discuss the types of devices available that protect computers from system failure

6. Identify risks and safeguards associated with wireless communications

7. Discuss ways to prevent health-related disorders and injuries due to computer use

8. Discuss issues surrounding information privacy, including electronic profiles, cookies, spyware and adware, spam, phishing, privacy laws, social engineering, employee monitoring, and content filtering

Computer Security Risks

Today, people rely on computers to create, store, and manage critical information. Thus, it is crucial that users take measures to protect their computers and data from loss, damage, and misuse.

A **computer security risk** is any event or action that could cause a loss of or damage to computer hardware, software, data, information, or processing capability. While some breaches to computer security are accidental, many are intentional. Some intruders do no damage; they merely access data, information, or programs on the computer. Other intruders indicate some evidence of their presence either by leaving a message or by deliberately altering or damaging data.

An intentional breach of computer security often involves a deliberate act that is against the law. Any illegal act involving a computer generally is referred to as a **computer crime**. The term **cybercrime** refers to online or Internet-based illegal acts. Today, cybercrime is one of the FBI's top three priorities.

Perpetrators of cybercrime and other intrusions fall into seven basic categories: hacker, cracker, script kiddie, corporate spy, unethical employee, cyberextortionist, and cyberterrorist.

- The term **hacker**, although originally a complimentary word for a computer enthusiast, now has a derogatory meaning and refers to someone who accesses a computer or network illegally. Some hackers claim the intent of their security breaches is to improve security.
- A **cracker** also is someone who accesses a computer or network illegally but has the intent of destroying data, stealing information, or other malicious action. Both hackers and crackers have advanced computer and network skills.
- A **script kiddie** has the same intent as a cracker but does not have the technical skills and knowledge. Script kiddies often use prewritten hacking and cracking programs to break into computers.
- Some corporate spies have excellent computer and networking skills and are hired to break into a specific computer and steal its proprietary data and information. Unscrupulous companies hire corporate spies, a practice known as corporate espionage, to gain a competitive advantage.
- Unethical employees break into their employers' computers for a variety of reasons. Some simply want to exploit a security weakness. Others seek financial gains from selling confidential information. Disgruntled employees may want revenge.
- A **cyberextortionist** is someone who uses e-mail as a vehicle for extortion. These perpetrators send an organization a threatening e-mail message indicating they will expose confidential information, exploit a security flaw, or launch an attack that will compromise the organization's network — if they are not paid a sum of money.

- A **cyberterrorist** is someone who uses the Internet or network to destroy or damage computers for political reasons. The cyberterrorist might target the nation's air traffic control system, electricity-generating companies, or a telecommunications infrastructure. Cyberterrorism usually requires a team of highly skilled individuals, millions of dollars, and several years of planning.

Business and home users must protect, or safeguard, their computers from breaches of security and other computer security risks. Some organizations hire individuals previously convicted of computer crimes to help identify security risks and implement safeguards because these individuals know how criminals attempt to breach security.

The more common computer security risks include Internet and network attacks, unauthorized access and use, hardware theft, software theft, information theft, and system failure (Figure 5-1). The following pages describe these computer security risks and also discuss safeguards users might take to minimize or prevent their consequences.

Figure 5-1 Computers and computer users are exposed to several types of security risks.

Internet and Network Attacks

Information transmitted over networks has a higher degree of security risk than information kept on an organization's premises. In an organization, network administrators usually take measures to protect a network from security risks. On the Internet, where no central administrator is present, the security risk is greater.

Internet and network attacks that jeopardize security include computer viruses, worms, Trojan horses, and rootkits; botnets; denial of service attacks; back doors; and spoofing. The following sections address these computer security risks and suggest measures organizations and individuals can take to protect their computers while on the Internet or connected to a network.

Computer Viruses, Worms, Trojan Horses, and Rootkits

Every unprotected computer is susceptible to the first type of computer security risk — a computer virus, worm, Trojan horse, and/or rootkit.

- A computer **virus** is a potentially damaging computer program that affects, or infects, a computer negatively by altering the way the computer works without the user's knowledge or permission. Once the virus infects the computer, it can spread throughout and may damage files and system software, including the operating system.
- A **worm** is a program that copies itself repeatedly, for example in memory or on a network, using up resources and possibly shutting down the computer or network.
- A **Trojan horse** (named after the Greek myth) is a program that hides within or looks like a legitimate program. A certain condition or action usually triggers the Trojan horse. Unlike a virus or worm, a Trojan horse does not replicate itself to other computers.
- A **rootkit** is a program that hides in a computer and allows someone from a remote location to take full control of the computer. Once the rootkit is installed, the rootkit author can execute programs, change settings, monitor activity, and access files on the remote computer.

Computer viruses, worms, Trojan horses, and rootkits are classified as **malware** (short for malicious software), which are programs that act without a user's knowledge and deliberately alter the computer's operations. Unscrupulous programmers write malware and then test it to ensure it can deliver its payload. The **payload** is the destructive event or prank the program is intended to deliver. A computer infected by a virus, worm, Trojan horse, or rootkit often has one or more of the following symptoms:

- Operating system runs much slower than usual
- Available memory is less than expected
- Files become corrupted
- Screen displays unusual message or image
- Unknown programs or files mysteriously appear
- Music or unusual sound plays randomly
- Existing programs and files disappear
- Programs or files do not work properly
- System properties change
- Operating system does not start up
- Operating system shuts down unexpectedly

Currently, more than 300,000 Web sites can infect your computer with known viruses, worms, Trojan horses, rootkits, and other malware. These malicious programs deliver their payload on a computer in a variety of ways: when a user (1) opens an infected file, (2) runs an infected program, (3) boots the computer with infected removable media inserted in a drive or plugged in a port, (4) connects an unprotected computer to a network, or (5) when a certain condition or event occurs, such as the computer's clock changing to a specific date. A common way computers become infected with viruses and other malware is through users opening infected e-mail attachments (Figure 5-2).

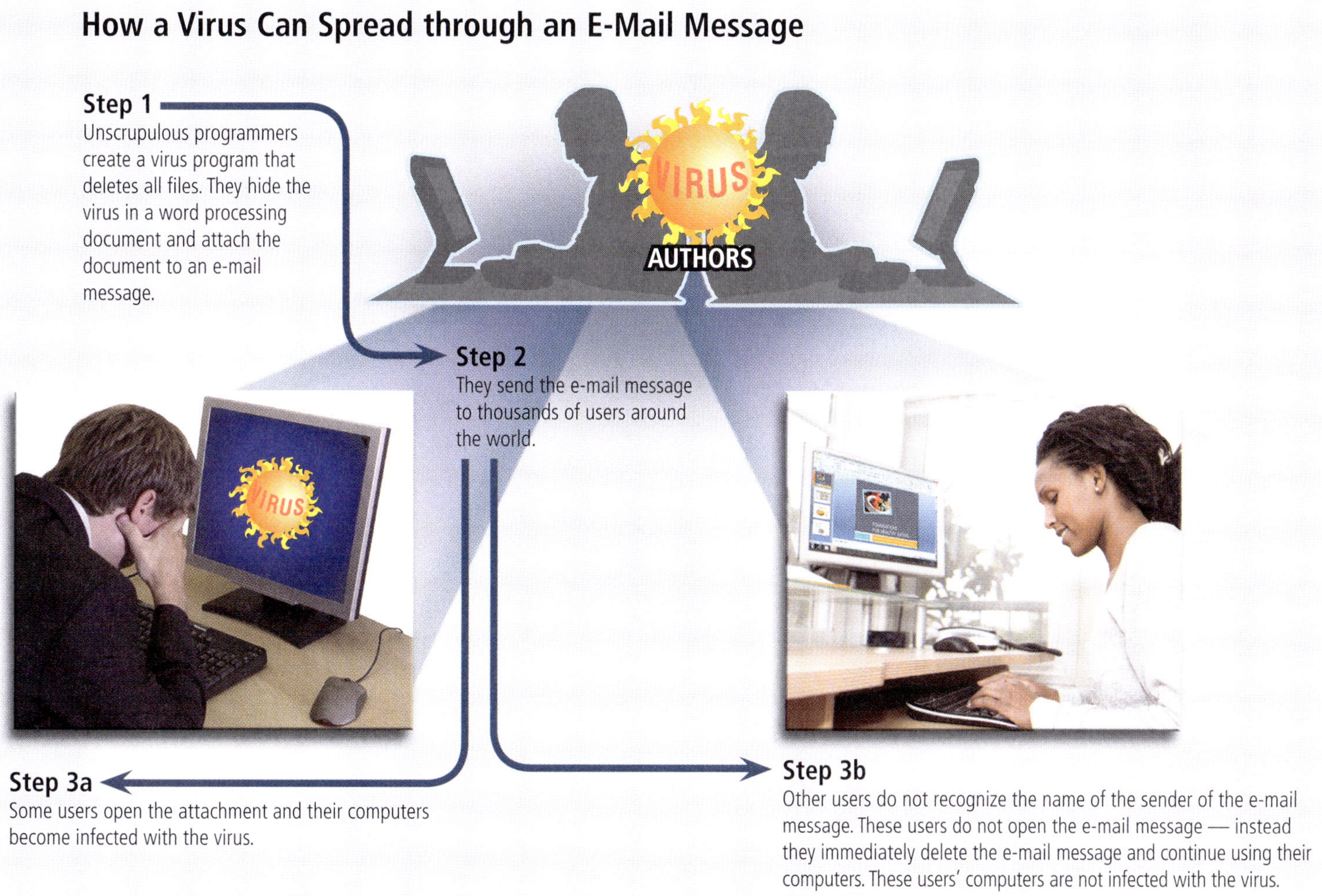

How a Virus Can Spread through an E-Mail Message

Step 1
Unscrupulous programmers create a virus program that deletes all files. They hide the virus in a word processing document and attach the document to an e-mail message.

Step 2
They send the e-mail message to thousands of users around the world.

Step 3a
Some users open the attachment and their computers become infected with the virus.

Step 3b
Other users do not recognize the name of the sender of the e-mail message. These users do not open the e-mail message — instead they immediately delete the e-mail message and continue using their computers. These users' computers are not infected with the virus.

Figure 5-2 This figure shows how a virus can spread through an e-mail message.

FAQ 5-1

Can multimedia files be infected with a virus?
Yes. The increase in popularity of media sharing Web sites provides a great opportunity to distribute malicious programs. During one year, approximately 500,000 people downloaded what they thought was a media file from the Internet. In fact, the file was a Trojan horse that infected many computers with spyware. For this reason, it is important to scan all media files for malware before playing them.

For more information, visit scsite.com/dc-off07/ch5/faq and then click Infected Media Files.

Safeguards against Computer Viruses and Other Malware

Users can take several precautions to protect their home and work computers and mobile devices from these malicious infections. The following paragraphs discuss these precautionary measures.

Do not start a computer with removable media, such as optical discs and USB flash drives, in the drives or ports — unless you are certain the media are uninfected or from a trusted source. A **trusted source** is an organization or person you believe will not send a virus infected file knowingly. Never open an e-mail attachment unless you are expecting the attachment *and* it is from a trusted source. If the e-mail message is from an unknown source, delete the e-mail message immediately — without opening or executing any attachments. If the e-mail message is from a trusted source, but you were not expecting an attachment, carefully check the spelling of the e-mail address and contents of the message for errors because perpetrators often make typographical errors. If the message is error-free, verify with the source that they intended to send you an attachment — before opening it.

Some viruses are hidden in macros, which are instructions saved in software such as a word processing or spreadsheet program. In programs that allow users to write macros, you should set the macro security level so that the application software warns users that a document they are attempting to open contains a macro. From this warning, a user chooses to disable or enable the macro. If the document is from a trusted source, the user can enable the macro. Otherwise, it should be disabled.

Users should install an antivirus program and update it frequently. An **antivirus program** protects a computer against viruses by identifying and removing any computer viruses found in memory, on storage media, or on incoming files. Most antivirus programs also protect against other malware. When you purchase a new computer, it often includes antivirus software. Many e-mail servers also have antivirus programs installed to check incoming and outgoing e-mail messages for malware.

An antivirus program scans for programs that attempt to modify the boot program, the operating system, and other programs that normally are read from but not modified. In addition, many antivirus programs automatically scan files downloaded from the Web, e-mail attachments, opened files, and all removable media inserted in the computer.

One technique that antivirus programs use to identify a virus is to look for virus signatures. A **virus signature**, also called a **virus definition**, is a known specific pattern of virus code. Computer users should update their antivirus program's signature files regularly (Figure 5-3). This extremely important activity allows the antivirus program to protect against viruses written since the antivirus program was released and/or its last update. Most antivirus programs contain an automatic update feature that regularly prompts users to download the virus signature, usually at least once a week. The vendor usually provides this service to registered users at no cost for a specified time.

If an antivirus program identifies an infected file, it attempts to remove the malware. If the antivirus program cannot remove the infection, it often quarantines the infected file. A **quarantine** is a separate area of a hard disk that holds the infected file until the infection can be removed. This step ensures other files will not become infected. Quarantined files remain on your computer until you delete them or restore them.

Some users also install a personal firewall program to protect a computer and its data from unauthorized intrusions. A section later in this chapter discusses firewalls.

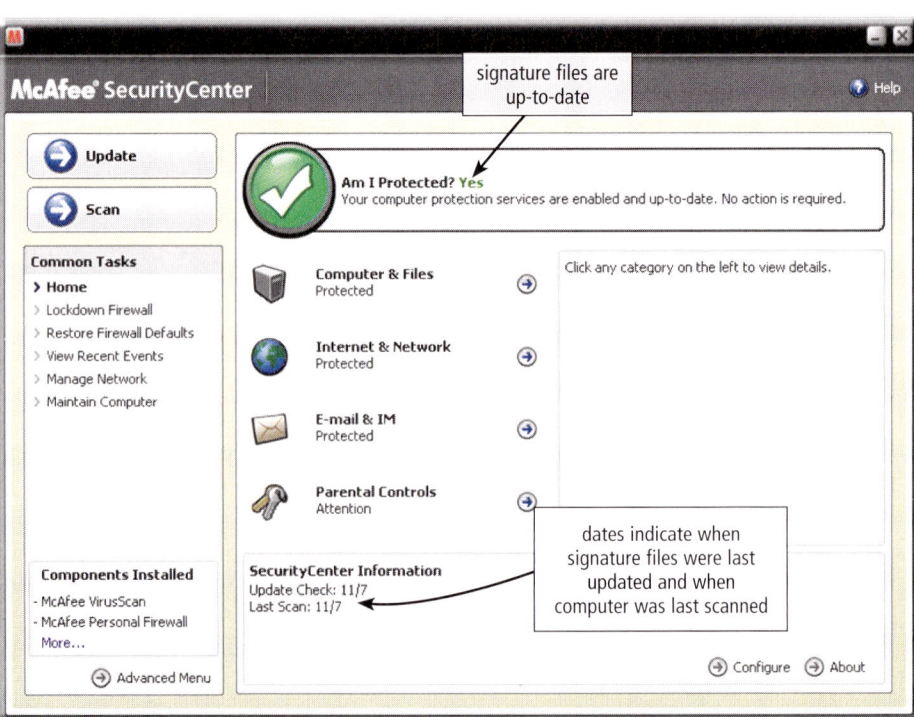

Figure 5-3
This antivirus program, which protects a computer from a variety of malware, regularly checks for the latest virus signatures and other important updates.

Finally, stay informed about new virus alerts and virus hoaxes. A **virus hoax** is an e-mail message that warns users of a nonexistent virus or other malware. Often, these virus hoaxes are in the form of a chain letter that requests the user to send a copy of the e-mail message to as many people as possible. The content of the hoax message, for example, may inform users that an important operating system file on their computer is a virus and encourage them to delete the file, which could make their computer unusable. Instead of forwarding the message, visit a Web site that publishes a list of virus alerts and virus hoaxes.

The list in Figure 5-4 summarizes important tips for protecting your computer from viruses and other malware.

Tips for Preventing Viruses and Other Malware

1. Never start a computer with removable media inserted in the drives or plugged in the ports, unless the media are uninfected.
2. Never open an e-mail attachment unless you are expecting it *and* it is from a trusted source.
3. Set the macro security in programs so that you can enable or disable macros. Enable macros only if the document is from a trusted source and you are expecting it.
4. Install an antivirus program on all of your computers. Update the software and the virus signature files regularly.
5. Scan all downloaded programs for viruses and other malware.
6. If the antivirus program flags an e-mail attachment as infected, delete or quarantine the attachment immediately.
7. Before using any removable media, scan the media for malware. Follow this procedure even for shrink-wrapped software from major developers. Some commercial software has been infected and distributed to unsuspecting users.
8. Install a personal firewall program.
9. Stay informed about new virus alerts and virus hoaxes.

Figure 5-4 With the growing number of new viruses and other malware, it is crucial that users take steps to protect their computers.

Botnets

A **botnet** is a group of compromised computers connected to a network such as the Internet that are used as part of a network that attacks other networks, usually for nefarious purposes. A compromised computer, known as a **zombie**, is one whose owner is unaware the computer is being controlled remotely by an outsider. Cybercriminals use botnets to send spam via e-mail, spread viruses and other malware, or commit a denial of service attack.

 FAQ 5-2

How can I tell if my computer is a zombie or in a botnet?

The number of zombie computers is increasing at a rapid rate. Your computer may be a zombie or part of a botnet if you notice unusually high disk activity, a slower than normal Internet connection, or devices connected to your computer becoming increasingly unresponsive. The chances of your computer becoming a zombie or part of a botnet greatly increase if you do not have an effective firewall.

For more information, visit scsite.com/dc-off07/ch5/faq and then click Zombies and Botnets.

Denial of Service Attacks

A **denial of service attack**, or **DoS attack**, is an assault whose purpose is to disrupt computer access to an Internet service such as the Web or e-mail. Perpetrators carry out a DoS attack in a variety of ways. For example, they may use an unsuspecting computer to send an influx of confusing data messages or useless traffic to a computer network. The victim computer network slows down considerably and eventually becomes unresponsive or unavailable, blocking legitimate visitors from accessing the network.

Perpetrators have a variety of motives for carrying out a DoS attack. Those who disagree with the beliefs or actions of a particular organization claim political anger motivates their attacks. Some perpetrators use the attack as a vehicle for extortion. Others simply want the recognition, even though it is negative.

 DoS Attacks

For more information, visit scsite.com/dc-off07/ch5/ weblink and then click DoS Attacks.

Back Doors

A **back door** is a program or set of instructions in a program that allow users to bypass security controls when accessing a program, computer, or network. Once perpetrators gain access to unsecure computers, they often install a back door or modify an existing program to include a back door, which allows them to continue to access the computer remotely without the user's knowledge.

Spoofing

Spoofing is a technique intruders use to make their network or Internet transmission appear legitimate to a victim computer or network. E-mail spoofing occurs when the sender's address or other components of the e-mail header are altered so that it appears the e-mail originated from a different sender. E-mail spoofing commonly is used for virus hoaxes, spam, and phishing scams. IP spoofing occurs when an intruder computer fools a network into believing its IP address is associated with a trusted source. Perpetrators of IP spoofing trick their victims into interacting with a phony Web site.

Safeguards against Botnets, DoS Attacks, Back Doors, and Spoofing

To defend against botnets, DoS attacks, improper use of back doors, and spoofing, users can implement firewall solutions and install intrusion detection software. The following sections discuss these safeguards.

Firewalls

A **firewall** is hardware and/or software that protects a network's resources from intrusion by users on another network such as the Internet (Figure 5-5). All networked and online computer users should implement a firewall solution.

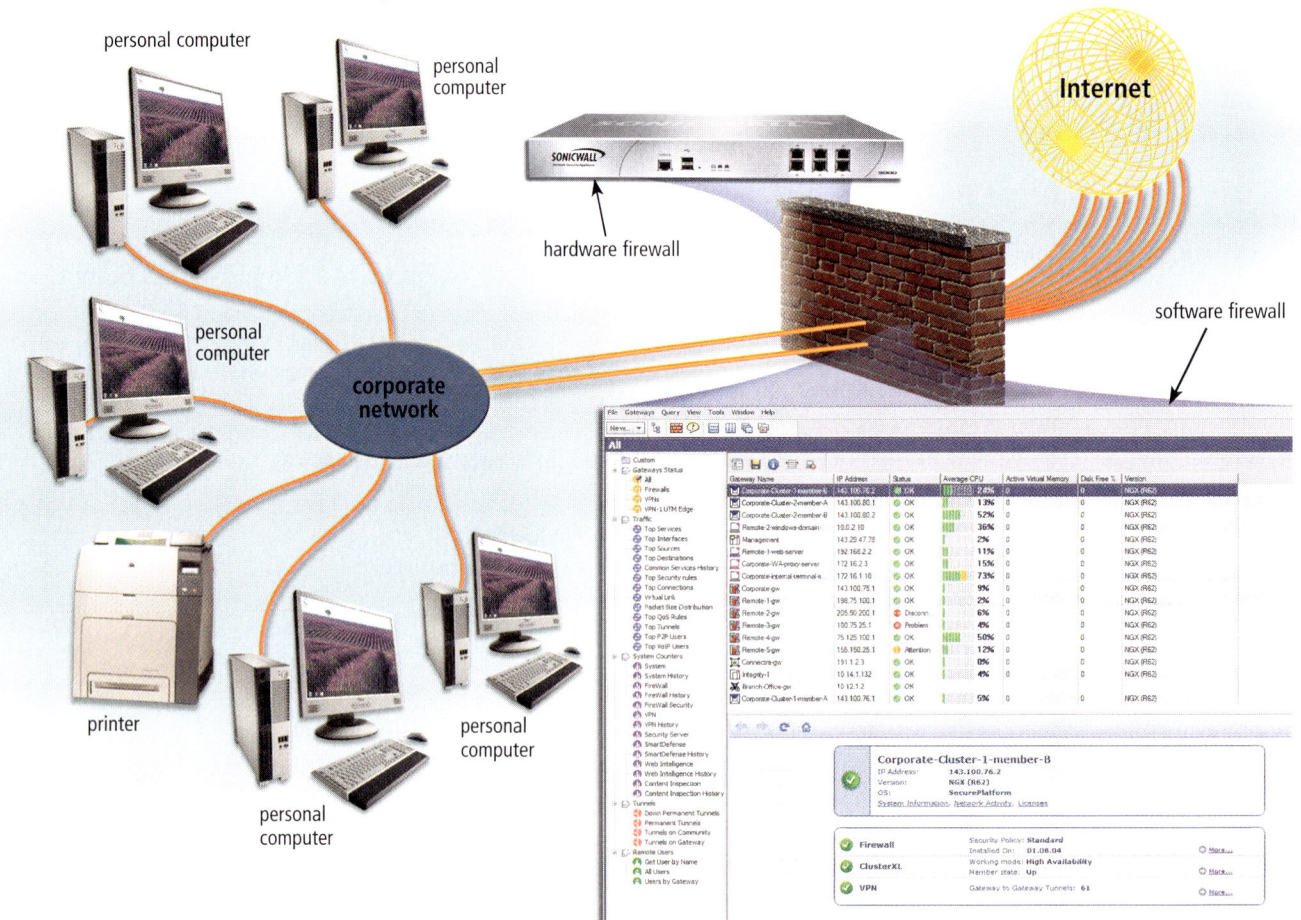

Figure 5-5 A firewall is hardware and/or software that protects a network's resources from intrusion by users on another network such as the Internet.

Organizations use firewalls to protect network resources from outsiders and to restrict employees' access to sensitive data such as payroll or personnel records. They can implement a firewall solution themselves or outsource their needs to a company specializing in providing firewall protection. Large organizations often route all their communications through a proxy server, which is a component of the firewall. A proxy server is a server outside the organization's network that controls which communications pass into the organization's network.

Home and small office/home office users often protect their computers with a personal firewall utility. A **personal firewall** is a utility program that detects and protects a personal computer and its data from unauthorized intrusions. Some operating systems, such as Windows, include personal firewalls.

Some small office/home office users purchase a hardware firewall, such as a router or other device that has a built-in firewall, in addition to or instead of personal firewall software. Hardware firewalls stop intrusions before they attempt to affect your computer maliciously.

Intrusion Detection Software

To provide extra protection against hackers and other intruders, large organizations sometimes use intrusion detection software to identify possible security breaches. **Intrusion detection software** automatically analyzes all network traffic, assesses system vulnerabilities, identifies any unauthorized access (intrusions), and notifies network administrators of suspicious behavior patterns or system breaches.

To utilize intrusion detection software requires the expertise of a network administrator because the programs are complex and difficult to use and interpret. These programs also are quite expensive.

Unauthorized Access and Use

Another type of computer security risk is unauthorized access and use. **Unauthorized access** is the use of a computer or network without permission. **Unauthorized use** is the use of a computer or its data for unapproved or possibly illegal activities. Unauthorized use includes a variety of activities: an employee using an organization's computer to send personal e-mail messages, an employee using the organization's word processing software to track his or her child's soccer league scores, or someone gaining access to a bank computer and performing an unauthorized transfer.

Safeguards against Unauthorized Access and Use

Organizations take several measures to help prevent unauthorized access and use. At a minimum, they should have a written acceptable use policy (AUP) that outlines the computer activities for which the computer and network may and may not be used. An organization's AUP should specify the acceptable use of computers by employees for personal reasons. Some organizations prohibit such use entirely. Others allow personal use on the employee's own time such as a lunch hour.

Other measures that safeguard against unauthorized access and use include firewalls and intrusion detection software, which were discussed in the previous section, and identifying and authenticating users.

Identifying and Authenticating Users

Many organizations use access controls to minimize the chance that a perpetrator intentionally may access or an employee accidentally may access confidential information on a computer. An **access control** is a security measure that defines who can access a computer, when they can access it, and what actions they can take while accessing the computer. In addition, the computer should maintain an **audit trail** that records in a file both successful and unsuccessful access attempts. An unsuccessful access attempt could result from a user mistyping his or her password, or it could result from a hacker trying thousands of passwords.

Organizations should investigate unsuccessful access attempts immediately to ensure they are not intentional breaches of security. They also should review successful access for irregularities, such as use of the computer after normal working hours or from remote computers.

Firewalls
For more information, visit scsite.com/dc-off07/ch5/ weblink and then click Firewalls.

Many systems implement access controls using a two-phase process called identification and authentication. Identification verifies that an individual is a valid user. Authentication verifies that the individual is the person he or she claims to be. Three methods of identification and authentication include user names and passwords, possessed objects, and biometric devices. The technique(s) an organization uses should correspond to the degree of risk associated with the unauthorized access.

User Names and Passwords A **user name**, or user ID (identification), is a unique combination of characters, such as letters of the alphabet or numbers, that identifies one specific user. A **password** is a private combination of characters associated with the user name that allows access to certain computer resources.

Most multiuser (networked) operating systems require that users correctly enter a user name and a password before they can access the data, information, and programs stored on a computer or network (Figure 5-6).

Multiuser systems typically require that users select their own passwords. Users typically choose an easy-to-remember word or series of characters for passwords. If your password is too obvious, however, such as your initials or birthday, others can guess it easily. Easy passwords make it simple for hackers and other intruders to break into a system. Hackers use computer automated tools to assist them with guessing passwords. Thus, you should select a password carefully. Longer passwords provide greater security than shorter ones. Each character added to a password significantly increases the number of possible combinations and the length of time it might take for someone or for a hacker's computer to guess the password (Figure 5-7).

In addition to a user name and password, some systems ask users to enter one of several pieces of personal information. Such items can include a spouse's first name, a birth date, a place of birth, or a mother's maiden name. As with a password, if the user's response does not match the information on file, the system denies access.

Some Web sites use a CAPTCHA to further protect a user's password. A **CAPTCHA**, which stands for Completely Automated Public Turing test to tell Computers and Humans Apart, is a program that verifies user input is not computer generated. A CAPTCHA displays a series of distorted characters and requires the user to enter the characters correctly to continue using the Web site. For visually impaired users, the CAPTCHA text can be read aloud. Because unscrupulous individuals attempt to circumvent or decode CAPTCHAs, developers continually are seeking ways to make them more secure or develop alternative authentication techniques.

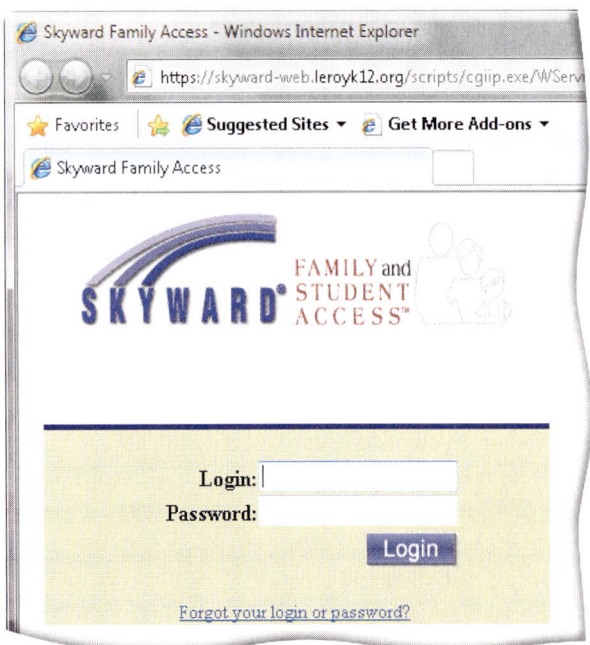

Figure 5-6 Many Web sites that maintain personal and confidential data require a user to enter a user name and password.

Password Protection

Number of Characters	Possible Combinations	AVERAGE TIME TO DISCOVER	
		Human	Computer
1	36	3 minutes	.000018 second
2	1,300	2 hours	.00065 second
3	47,000	3 days	.02 second
4	1,700,000	3 months	1 second
5	60,000,000	10 years	30 seconds
10	3,700,000,000,000,000	580 million years	59 years

- Possible characters include the letters A–Z and numbers 0–9
- Human discovery assumes 1 try every 10 seconds
- Computer discovery assumes 1 million tries per second
- Average time assumes the password would be discovered in approximately half the time it would take to try all possible combinations

Figure 5-7 This table shows the effect of increasing the length of a password that consists of letters and numbers. The longer the password, the more effort required to discover it. Long passwords, however, are more difficult for users to remember.

Possessed Objects A **possessed object** is any item that you must carry to gain access to a computer or computer facility. Examples of possessed objects are badges, cards, smart cards, and keys. The card you use in an automated teller machine (ATM) is a possessed object that allows access to your bank account.

Possessed objects often are used in combination with personal identification numbers. A **personal identification number** (**PIN**) is a numeric password, either assigned by a company or selected by a user. PINs provide an additional level of security. An ATM card typically requires a four-digit PIN. PINs are passwords. Select them carefully and protect them as you do any other password.

Biometric Devices A **biometric device** authenticates a person's identity by translating a personal characteristic, such as a fingerprint, into a digital code that is compared with a digital code stored in the computer verifying a physical or behavioral characteristic. If the digital code in the computer does not match the personal characteristic code, the computer denies access to the individual.

Biometric devices grant access to programs, computers, or rooms using computer analysis of some biometric identifier. Examples of biometric devices and systems include fingerprint readers (Figure 5-8), hand geometry systems, face recognition systems, voice verification systems, signature verification systems, iris recognition systems, and retinal scanners. Many grocery stores, retail stores, and gas stations now use **biometric payment**, where the customer's fingerprint is read by a fingerprint reader that is linked to a specific payment method such as a checking account or credit card.

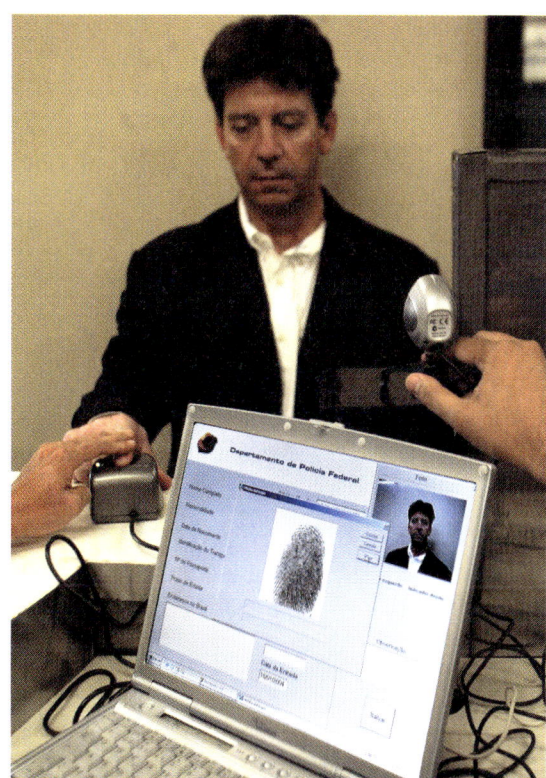

Figure 5-8
A fingerprint reader verifies this traveler's identity.

? FAQ 5-3

How many people are victims of identity theft each year?

Studies reveal that identity theft is the fastest growing crime in the United States. In fact, identity theft costs banks, victims, and the government millions of dollars each year, with that amount continually increasing. The chart to the right illustrates the reported number of identity theft cases grouped by age.

👆 For more information, visit scsite.com/dc-off07/ch5/faq and then click Identity Theft.

Identity Theft — Complaints by Victim Age
- 60 and over: 9%
- Under 18: 5%
- 18–29: 29%
- 30–39: 24%
- 40–49: 20%
- 50–59: 13%

Source: FTC.gov

Digital Forensics

Digital forensics, also called computer forensics, network forensics, or cyberforensics, is the discovery, collection, and analysis of evidence found on computers and networks. Digital forensics involves the examination of computer media, programs, data and log files on computers, servers, and networks. Many areas use digital forensics, including law enforcement, criminal prosecutors, military intelligence, insurance agencies, and information security departments in the private sector.

A digital forensics examiner must have knowledge of the law, technical experience with many types of hardware and software products, superior communication skills, familiarity with corporate structures and policies, a willingness to learn and update skills, and a knack for problem solving. For a look at the next generation of forensics, read Looking Ahead 5-1.

↗ LOOKING AHEAD 5-1

Brain Waves, Behavior Tracked to Prevent and Solve Crimes

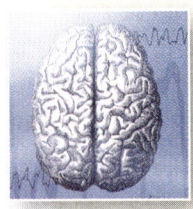

The brain may one day become part of a crime scene investigation. When a person has committed a criminal or fraudulent act, his brain generates unique waves involuntarily when confronted with pictures, sounds, and words related to the crime scene. Computers can capture and analyze this brain fingerprint of distinctive brain waves to determine if a person has stored critical details of a particular felony or misdemeanor situation.

Similarly, behavior detection systems study a person's body language, facial expressions, speech, and emotions to isolate specific patterns that criminals commonly exhibit. The surveillance systems can recognize microexpressions, which are the split-second emotions lasting one-fifteenth of a second, on a person's face.

The U.S. Department of Homeland Security is testing its Future Attribute Screening Technologies (FAST) program, which uses cameras, infrared heat sensors, and lasers to measure pulse and breathing rates. The trial technology is being tested for use at airports and sporting and music events.

👆 For more information, visit scsite.com/dc-off07/ch5/looking and then click Brain Fingerprinting.

✓ QUIZ YOURSELF 5-1

Instructions: Find the true statement below. Then, rewrite the remaining false statements so that they are true.

1. A back door attack is an assault whose purpose is to disrupt computer access to an Internet service such as the Web or e-mail.
2. All networked and online computer users should implement a firewall solution.
3. Computer viruses, worms, Trojan horses, and rootkits are malware that acts with a user's knowledge.
4. Shorter passwords provide greater security than longer ones.
5. Updating an antivirus program's quarantine protects a computer against viruses written since the antivirus program was released.

👆 **Quiz Yourself Online:** To further check your knowledge of pages 182 through 192, visit scsite.com/dc-off07/ch5/quiz and then click Objectives 1 – 2.

Hardware Theft and Vandalism

Hardware theft and vandalism are other types of computer security risks. **Hardware theft** is the act of stealing computer equipment. **Hardware vandalism** is the act of defacing or destroying computer equipment. Hardware vandalism takes many forms, from someone cutting a computer cable to individuals breaking into a business or school computer lab and aimlessly smashing computers.

Companies, schools, and other organizations that house many computers are at risk of hardware theft and vandalism, especially those that have smaller system units that easily can fit in a backpack or briefcase. Mobile users also are susceptible to hardware theft. It is estimated that more than 600,000 notebook computers are stolen each year. The size and weight of these computers, especially netbooks, make them easy to steal.

Safeguards against Hardware Theft and Vandalism

To help reduce the chances of theft, companies and schools use a variety of security measures. Physical access controls, such as locked doors and windows, usually are adequate to protect the equipment. Many businesses, schools, and some homeowners install alarm systems for additional security. School computer labs and other areas with a large number of semifrequent users often attach additional physical security devices such as cables that lock the equipment to a desk (Figure 5-9), cabinet, or floor. Small locking devices also exist that require a key to access a hard disk or optical disc drive.

Some businesses use a **real time location system** (**RTLS**) to track and identify the location of high-risk or high-value items. One implementation of RTLS places RFID tags in items to be tracked.

Mobile computer users must take special care to protect their equipment. Some users attach a physical device such as a cable to lock a mobile computer temporarily to a stationary object. Other mobile users install a mini-security system in the notebook computer. Some of these security systems shut down the computer and sound an alarm if the computer moves outside a specified distance. Others can be configured to photograph the thieves when they use the computer. Notebook computer security systems and tracking software also can track the location of a stolen notebook computer.

Some notebook computers use passwords, possessed objects, and biometrics as methods of security. When you start these computers, you must enter a password, slide a card in a card reader, or press your finger on a fingerprint reader before the hard disk unlocks. This type of security does not prevent theft, but it renders the computer useless if it is stolen.

RTLS
For more information, visit scsite.com/dc-off07/ch5/ weblink and then click RTLS.

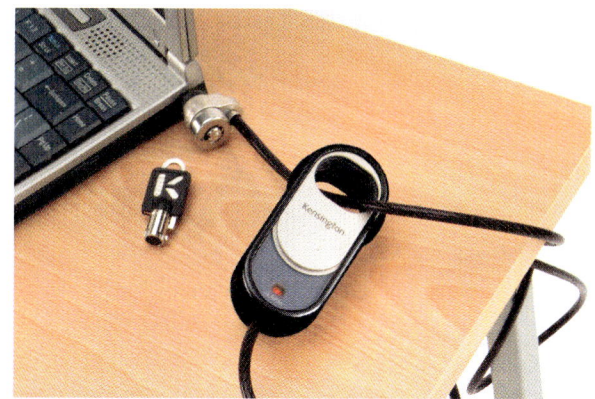

Figure 5-9 Using cables to lock computers can help prevent the theft of computer equipment.

Software Theft

Another type of computer security risk is software theft. **Software theft** occurs when someone steals software media, intentionally erases programs, illegally copies a program, or illegally registers and/or activates a program. One form of software theft involves someone physically stealing the media that contain the software or the hardware that contains the media, as described in the previous section. Another form of software theft occurs when software is stolen from software manufacturers. This type of theft, called piracy, is by far the most common form of software theft. Software **piracy** is the unauthorized and illegal duplication of copyrighted software. A related form of software theft involves users illegally obtaining registration numbers and/or activation codes.

Safeguards against Software Theft

To protect software media from being stolen, owners should keep original software boxes and media in a secure location. All computer users should back up their files and disks regularly, in the event of theft.

To protect themselves from software piracy, software manufacturers issue users license agreements. A **license agreement** is the right to use the software. That is, you do not own the software. The license agreement provides specific conditions for use of the software, which a user must accept before using the software (Figure 5-10). These terms usually are displayed when you install the software.

The most common type of license included with software purchased by individual users is a single-user license agreement, also called an end-user license agreement (EULA). A single-user license agreement typically includes many of the following conditions that specify a user's responsibility upon acceptance of the agreement.

Users are permitted to:
- Install the software on only one computer. (Some license agreements allow users to install the software on one desktop computer and one notebook computer.)
- Make one copy of the software as a backup.
- Give or sell the software to another individual, but only if the software is removed from the user's computer first.

Users are not permitted to:
- Install the software on a network, such as a school computer lab.
- Give copies to friends and colleagues, while continuing to use the software.
- Export the software.
- Rent or lease the software.

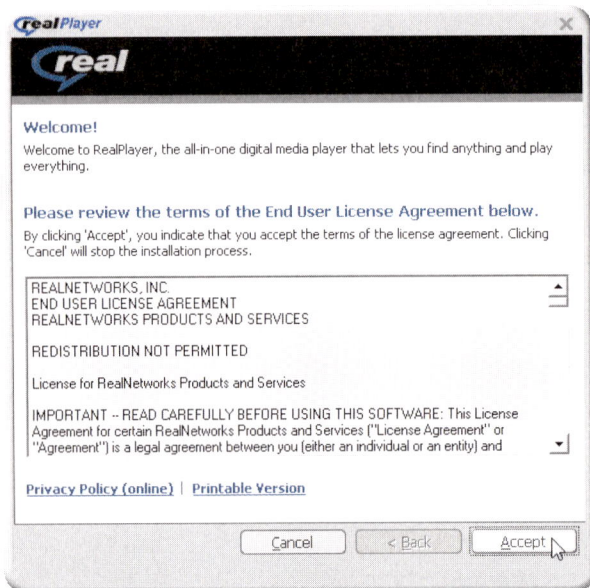

Figure 5-10 A user must accept the terms in the license agreement before using the software.

Unless otherwise specified by a license agreement, you do not have the right to copy, loan, borrow, rent, or in any way distribute software. Doing so is a violation of copyright law. It also is a federal crime. Despite this, some experts estimate for every authorized copy of software in use, at least one unauthorized copy exists. Read Ethics & Issues 5-1 for a related discussion.

In an attempt to prevent software piracy, Microsoft and other manufacturers have incorporated an activation process into many of its consumer products. During the **product activation**, which is conducted either online or by telephone, users provide the software product's 25-character identification number to receive an installation identification number unique to the computer on which the software is installed.

If you are not completely familiar with your school or employer's policies governing installation of software, check with the information technology department or your school's technology coordinator.

ETHICS & ISSUES 5-1

Should Online Auctions Be Liable for Pirated Software Sales?

Currently, software companies patrol online auction sites looking for pirated copies of their software that might be for sale. When they find such activity, the software company takes legal action against the seller of the pirated software. With the explosion of online auctions, however, the companies are fighting an uphill battle given the amount of time it takes to discover the sales, find the perpetrators, and then individually bring each perpetrator to justice. Many software companies have joined forces to demand that auction sites, such as eBay, legally be held liable for pirated software sold on their Web sites, and they have offered more than 20 suggestions as to how auction sites could better police their Web sites for pirated software. Online auction Web sites claim that the law clearly states they are not responsible for such sales, but that the software companies legally are responsible for controlling pirated sales. For its part, eBay claims already to enforce more than 13,000 rules to check for suspicious activity on its Web site, and offers trademark holders a special program in which they can enroll and have additional rules enforced.

Should online auctions be liable for pirated software sales on their Web sites? Why or why not? Should new or clearer laws be written to force online auctions to check whether software for sale on their Web sites is pirated? Why? Would you purchase software at an online auction being sold at a substantial discount to prices offered elsewhere? Why or why not?

Information Theft

Information theft is yet another type of computer security risk. **Information theft** occurs when someone steals personal or confidential information. An unethical company executive may steal or buy stolen information to learn about a competitor. A corrupt individual may steal credit card numbers to make fraudulent purchases.

Safeguards against Information Theft

Most companies attempt to prevent information theft by implementing the user identification and authentication controls discussed earlier in this chapter. These controls are best suited for protecting information on computers located on an organization's premises. Information transmitted over networks offers a higher degree of risk because unscrupulous users can intercept it during transmission. To protect information on the Internet and networks, companies and individuals use a variety of encryption techniques.

Encryption

Encryption is the process of converting readable data into unreadable characters to prevent unauthorized access. You treat encrypted data just like any other data. That is, you can store it or send it in an e-mail message. To read the data, the recipient must **decrypt**, or decipher, it into a readable form.

In the encryption process, the unencrypted, readable data is called plaintext. The encrypted (scrambled) data is called ciphertext. An **encryption algorithm** is a set of steps that can convert readable plaintext into unreadable ciphertext. Figure 5-11 shows examples of some simple encryption algorithms. Encryption programs typically use more than one encryption algorithm, along with an encryption key. An **encryption key** is a programmed formula that the originator of the data uses to encrypt the plaintext and the recipient of the data uses to decrypt the ciphertext.

Simple Encryption Algorithms

Name	Algorithm	Plaintext	Ciphertext	Explanation
Transposition	Switch the order of characters	SOFTWARE	OSTFAWER	Adjacent characters swapped
Substitution	Replace characters with other characters	INFORMATION	WLDIMXQUWIL	Each letter replaced with another
Expansion	Insert characters between existing characters	USER	UYSYEYRY	Letter Y inserted after each character
Compaction	Remove characters and store elsewhere	ACTIVATION	ACIVTIN	Every third letter removed (T, A, O)

Figure 5-11 This table shows four simple encryption algorithms. Most encryption keys use a combination of algorithms.

Some operating systems and e-mail programs allow you to encrypt the contents of files and messages that are stored on your computer. You also can purchase an encryption program, such as Pretty Good Privacy (PGP).

A **digital signature** is an encrypted code that a person, Web site, or organization attaches to an electronic message to verify the identity of the message sender. Digital signatures often are used to ensure that an impostor is not participating in an Internet transaction. That is, digital signatures help to prevent e-mail forgery. A digital signature also can verify that the content of a message has not changed.

Many Web browsers and Web sites use encryption. A Web site that uses encryption techniques to secure its data is known as a **secure site** (Figure 5-12). Secure sites often use digital certificates. A **digital certificate** is a notice that guarantees a user or a Web site is legitimate. A **certificate authority** (CA)

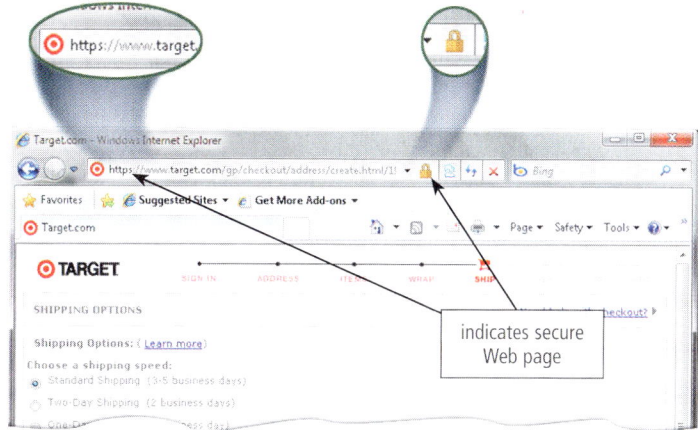

Figure 5-12 Web addresses of secure sites often begin with https instead of http. Browsers also often display a lock symbol in the window.

Digital Certificates
For more information, visit scsite.com/dc-off07/ch5/ weblink and then click Digital Certificates.

is an authorized person or a company that issues and verifies digital certificates. Users apply for a digital certificate from a CA. The digital certificate typically contains information such as the user's name, the issuing CA's name and signature, and the serial number of the certificate. The information in a digital certificate is encrypted.

System Failure

System failure is yet another type of computer security risk. A **system failure** is the prolonged malfunction of a computer. System failure can cause loss of hardware, software, data, or information. A variety of causes can lead to system failure. These include aging hardware; natural disasters such as fires, floods, or hurricanes; random events such as electrical power problems; and even errors in computer programs.

One of the more common causes of system failure is an electrical power variation. Electrical power variations can cause loss of data and loss of equipment. If the computer equipment is networked, a single power disturbance can damage multiple systems.

Safeguards against System Failure

To protect against electrical power variations, use a surge protector. A **surge protector** uses special electrical components to provide a stable current flow to the computer and other electronic equipment (Figure 5-13). Sometimes resembling a power strip, the computer and other devices plug in the surge protector, which plugs in the power source.

No surge protectors are 100 percent effective. Typically, the amount of protection offered by a surge protector is proportional to its cost. That is, the more expensive, the more protection the protector offers.

If your computer connects to a network or the Internet, also be sure to have protection for your modem, telephone lines, DSL lines, Internet cable lines, and network lines. Many surge protectors include plug-ins for telephone lines and other cables.

Surge Protectors
For more information, visit scsite.com/dc-off07/ch5/ weblink and then click Surge Protectors.

Figure 5-13 Circuits inside a surge protector safeguard against electrical power variations.

For additional electrical protection, some users connect an uninterruptible power supply to the computer. An **uninterruptible power supply** (**UPS**) is a device that contains surge protection circuits and one or more batteries that can provide power during a loss of power (Figure 5-14). A UPS connects between your computer and a power source.

As another measure of protection, some companies use duplicate components or computers as a safeguard against system failure.

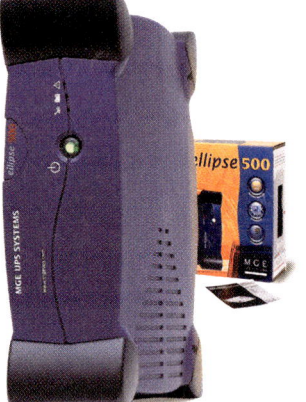

Figure 5-14 If power fails, an uninterruptible power supply (UPS) uses batteries to provide electricity for a limited amount of time.

Backing Up — The Ultimate Safeguard

To protect against data loss caused by a system failure or hardware/software/information theft, computer users should back up files regularly. A **backup** is a duplicate of a file, program, or disk that can be used if the original is lost, damaged, or destroyed. Thus, to **back up** a file means to make a copy of it. In the case of a system failure or the discovery of corrupted files, you **restore** the files by copying the backed up files to their original location on the computer.

You can use just about any media to store backups. A good choice for a home user might be optical discs or external hard disks. Keep backup copies in a fireproof and heatproof safe or vault, or offsite. Offsite means in a location separate from the computer site. A growing trend is to use cloud storage as an offsite location. Recall that cloud storage is an Internet service that provides storage to computer users. To learn more about how to back up files using an Internet service, complete the Learn How To 1 activity on pages 214 and 215.

Most backup programs for the home user provide for a full backup and a selective backup. A full backup copies all of the files in the computer. With a selective backup, users choose which folders and files to include in a backup.

Some users implement a three-generation backup policy to preserve three copies of important files. The grandparent is the oldest copy of the file. The parent is the second oldest copy of the file. The child is the most recent copy of the file. Others use RAID to duplicate the contents of a disk. Instead of multiple backup copies, some users choose continuous backup, where data is backed up whenever a change is made.

Most operating systems include a backup program. Backup devices, such as external disk drives, also include backup programs. Numerous stand-alone backup utilities exist. Many of these can be downloaded from the Web at no cost.

Wireless Security

Wireless technology has made dramatic changes in the way computer users communicate worldwide. Billions of home and business users have notebook computers, smart phones, and other mobile devices to access the Internet, send e-mail and instant messages, chat online, or share network connections — all without wires. Home users set up wireless home networks. Mobile users access wireless networks in hot spots at airports, hotels, shopping malls, bookstores, restaurants, and coffee shops. Schools have wireless networks so that students can access the school network using their mobile computers and devices as they move from building to building.

Although wireless access provides many conveniences to users, it also poses additional security risks. One study showed that about 80 percent of wireless networks have no security protection. Some perpetrators connect to other's wireless networks to gain free Internet access; others may try to access an organization's confidential data.

To access the network, the individual must be in range of the wireless network. Some intruders intercept and monitor communications as they transmit through the air. Others connect to a network through an unsecured wireless access point (WAP). In one technique, called **war driving**, individuals attempt to detect wireless networks via their notebook computer or mobile device while driving a vehicle through areas they suspect have a wireless network.

In addition to using firewalls, some safeguards that improve the security of wireless networks include reconfiguring the wireless access point and ensuring equipment uses one or more wireless security standards such as Wi-Fi Protected Access and 802.11i.
- A wireless access point (WAP) should be configured so that it does not broadcast a network name. The WAP also can be programmed so that only certain devices can access it.
- **Wi-Fi Protected Access** (WPA) is a security standard that improves on older security standards by authenticating network users and providing more advanced encryption techniques.
- An **802.11i** network, sometimes called WPA2, the most recent network security standard, conforms to the government's security standards and uses more sophisticated encryption techniques than WPA.

By implementing these security measures, you can help to prevent unauthorized access to wireless networks.

✔ QUIZ YOURSELF 5-2

Instructions: Find the true statement below. Then, rewrite the remaining false statements so that they are true.
1. An end-user license agreement (EULA) permits users to give copies to friends and colleagues, while continuing to use the software.
2. Encryption is a process of converting ciphertext into plaintext to prevent unauthorized access.
3. Mobile users are not susceptible to hardware theft.
4. Two wireless security standards are Wi-Fi Protected Access and 802.11i.
5. To protect against data loss caused by a system failure, computer users should restore files regularly.

👆 **Quiz Yourself Online:** To further check your knowledge of pages 193 through 197, visit scsite.com/dc-off07/ch5/quiz and then click Objectives 3 – 6.

Health Concerns of Computer Use

Users are a key component in any information system. Thus, protecting users is just as important as protecting hardware, software, and data.

The widespread use of computers has led to some important user health concerns. The following sections discuss health risks and preventions, along with measures users can take to keep the environment healthy.

Computers and Health Risks

A **repetitive strain injury** (**RSI**) is an injury or disorder of the muscles, nerves, tendons, ligaments, and joints. Computer-related RSIs include tendonitis and carpal tunnel syndrome. RSIs are the largest job-related injury and illness problem in the United States today.

Tendonitis is inflammation of a tendon due to some repeated motion or stress on that tendon. Carpal tunnel syndrome (CTS) is inflammation of the nerve that connects the forearm to the palm of the wrist. Repeated or forceful bending of the wrist can cause CTS or tendonitis of the wrist. Symptoms of tendonitis of the wrist include extreme pain that extends from the forearm to the hand, along with tingling in the fingers. Symptoms of CTS include burning pain when the nerve is compressed, along with numbness and tingling in the thumb and first two fingers.

Long-term computer work can lead to tendonitis or CTS. Factors that cause these disorders include prolonged typing, prolonged mouse usage, or continual shifting between the mouse and the keyboard. If untreated, these disorders can lead to permanent physical damage.

You can take many precautions to prevent these types of injuries. Take frequent breaks during the computer session to exercise your hands and arms (Figure 5-15). To prevent injury due to typing, place a wrist rest between the keyboard and the edge of your desk. To prevent injury while using a mouse, place the mouse at least six inches from the edge of the desk. In this position, your wrist is flat on the desk. Finally, minimize the number of times you switch between the mouse and the keyboard, and avoid using the heel of your hand as a pivot point while typing or using the mouse.

Hand Exercises
- Spread fingers apart for several seconds while keeping wrists straight.
- Gently push back fingers and then thumb.
- Dangle arms loosely at sides and then shake arms and hands.

Figure 5-15 To reduce the chance of developing tendonitis or carpal tunnel syndrome, take frequent breaks during computer sessions to exercise your hands and arms.

Another type of health-related condition due to computer usage is **computer vision syndrome** (**CVS**). You may have CVS if you have sore, tired, burning, itching, or dry eyes; blurred or double vision; distance blurred vision after prolonged staring at a display device; headache or sore neck; difficulty shifting focus between a display device and documents; difficulty focusing on the screen image; color fringes or after-images when you look away from the display device; and increased sensitivity to light. Eyestrain associated with CVS is not thought to have serious or long-term consequences. Figure 5-16 outlines some techniques you can follow to ease eyestrain.

People who spend their workday using the computer sometimes complain of lower back pain, muscle fatigue, and emotional fatigue. Lower back pain sometimes is caused from poor posture. Always sit

Techniques to Ease Eyestrain
- Every 10 to 15 minutes, take an eye break.
  - Look into the distance and focus on an object for 20 to 30 seconds.
  - Roll your eyes in a complete circle.
  - Close your eyes and rest them for at least one minute.
- Blink your eyes every five seconds.
- Place your display device about an arm's length away from your eyes with the top of the screen at eye level or below.
- Use large fonts.
- If you wear glasses, ask your doctor about computer glasses.
- Adjust the lighting.

Figure 5-16 Following these tips may help reduce eyestrain while working on a computer.

properly in the chair while you work. To alleviate back pain, muscle fatigue, and emotional fatigue, take a 15- to 30-minute break every 2 hours — stand up, walk around, stretch, and relax. Another way to help prevent these injuries is to be sure your workplace is designed ergonomically.

Ergonomics and Workplace Design

Ergonomics is an applied science devoted to incorporating comfort, efficiency, and safety into the design of items in the workplace. Ergonomic studies have shown that using the correct type and configuration of chair, keyboard, display device, and work surface helps users work comfortably and efficiently and helps protect their health. For the computer work space, experts recommend an area of at least two feet by four feet. Figure 5-17 illustrates additional guidelines for setting up the work area.

Figure 5-17 A well-designed work area should be flexible to allow adjustments to the height and build of different individuals. Good lighting and air quality also are important considerations.

Computer Addiction

Computers can provide entertainment and enjoyment. Some computer users, however, become obsessed with the computer and the Internet. **Computer addiction** occurs when the computer consumes someone's entire social life. Computer addiction is a growing health problem but can be treated through therapy and support groups. Symptoms of a user with computer addiction include the following:

- Craves computer time
- Overjoyed when at the computer
- Neglects family and friends
- Irritable when not at the computer
- Unable to stop computer activity
- Problems at work or school

Ethics and Society

As with any powerful technology, computers can be used for both good and bad intentions. The standards that determine whether an action is good or bad are known as ethics.

Computer ethics are the moral guidelines that govern the use of computers and information systems. Six frequently discussed areas of computer ethics are unauthorized use of computers and networks, software theft (piracy), information accuracy, intellectual property rights, green computing, and information privacy.

Previous sections in this chapter discussed unauthorized use of computers and networks, and software theft (piracy). The following sections discuss issues related to information accuracy, intellectual property rights, green computing, and information privacy. The questionnaire in Figure 5-18 raises issues in each of these areas.

Your Thoughts?

	Ethical	Unethical
1. An organization requires employees to wear badges that track their whereabouts while at work.	☐	☐
2. A supervisor reads an employee's e-mail.	☐	☐
3. An employee uses his computer at work to send e-mail messages to a friend.	☐	☐
4. An employee sends an e-mail message to several coworkers and blind copies his supervisor.	☐	☐
5. An employee forwards an e-mail message to a third party without permission from the sender.	☐	☐
6. An employee uses her computer at work to complete a homework assignment for school.	☐	☐
7. The vice president of your Student Government Association (SGA) downloads a photo from the Web and uses it in a flyer recruiting SGA members.	☐	☐
8. A student copies text from the Web and uses it in a research paper for his English Composition class.	☐	☐
9. An employee sends political campaign material to individuals on her employer's mailing list.	☐	☐
10. As an employee in the registration office, you have access to student grades. You look up grades for your friends, so that they do not have to wait for delivery of grade reports from the postal service.	☐	☐
11. An employee makes a copy of software and installs it on her home computer. No one uses her home computer while she is at work, and she uses her home computer only to finish projects from work.	☐	☐
12. An employee who has been laid off installs a computer virus on his employer's computer.	☐	☐
13. A person designing a Web page finds one on the Web similar to his requirements, copies it, modifies it, and publishes it as his own Web page.	☐	☐
14. A student researches using only the Web to write a report.	☐	☐
15. In a society in which all transactions occur online (a cashless society), the government tracks every transaction you make and automatically deducts taxes from your bank account.	☐	☐
16. Someone copies a well-known novel to the Web and encourages others to read it.	☐	☐
17. A person accesses an organization's network and reports to the organization any vulnerabilities discovered.	☐	☐
18. Your friend uses a neighbor's wireless network to connect to the Internet and check e-mail.	☐	☐
19. A company uses recycled paper to print a 50-page employee benefits manual that is distributed to 425 employees.	☐	☐
20. Your friend donates her old computers and mobile devices to local schools when she purchases newer models.	☐	☐

Figure 5-18 Indicate whether you think the situation described is ethical or unethical. Discuss your answers with your instructor and other students.

Information Accuracy

Information accuracy today is a concern because many users access information maintained by other people or companies, such as on the Internet. Do not assume that because the information is on the Web that it is correct. Users should evaluate the value of a Web page before relying on its content. Be aware that the organization providing access to the information may not be the creator of the information.

In addition to concerns about the accuracy of computer input, some individuals and organizations raise questions about the ethics of using computers to alter output, primarily graphical output such as retouched photos. Using graphics equipment and software, users easily can digitize photos and then add, change, or remove images (Figure 5-19).

One group that completely opposes any manipulation of an image is the National Press Photographers Association. It believes that allowing even the slightest alteration could lead to misrepresentative photos. Others believe that digital photo retouching is acceptable as long as the significant content or meaning of the photo does not change. Digital retouching is an area in which legal precedents so far have not been established.

Figure 5-19 A digitally altered photo shows sports legend Michael Jordan (born in 1963) meeting the famous scientist Albert Einstein (who died in 1955).

Intellectual Property Rights

Intellectual property (IP) refers to unique and original works such as ideas, inventions, art, writings, processes, company and product names, and logos. **Intellectual property rights** are the rights to which creators are entitled for their work. Certain issues arise surrounding IP today because many of these works are available digitally.

A **copyright** gives authors and artists exclusive rights to duplicate, publish, and sell their materials. A copyright protects any tangible form of expression.

A common infringement of copyright is piracy. People pirate (illegally copy) software, movies, and music. Many areas are not clear-cut with respect to the law, because copyright law gives the public fair use to copyrighted material. The issues surround the phrase, fair use, which allows use for educational and critical purposes.

This vague definition is subject to widespread interpretation and raises many questions:
- Should individuals be able to download contents of your Web site, modify it, and then put it on the Web again as their own?
- Should a faculty member have the right to print material from the Web and distribute it to all members of the class for teaching purposes only?
- Should someone be able to scan photos or pages from a book, publish them to the Web, and allow others to download them?
- Should students be able to post term papers they have written on the Web, making it tempting for other students to download and submit them as their own work?

These issues with copyright law led to the development of **digital rights management** (DRM), a strategy designed to prevent illegal distribution of movies, music, and other digital content.

 **Digital Rights Management**
For more information, visit scsite.com/dc-off07/ch5/ weblink and then click Digital Rights Management.

Green Computing

Green computing involves reducing the electricity and environmental waste while using a computer. People use, and often waste, resources such as electricity and paper while using a computer.

The United States government developed the **ENERGY STAR program** to help reduce the amount of electricity used by computers and related devices. This program encourages manufacturers to create energy-efficient devices that require little power when they are not in use. Computers and devices that meet the ENERGY STAR guidelines display an ENERGY STAR label.

Green Computing Suggestions

1. Use computers and devices that comply with the ENERGY STAR program.
2. Do not leave the computer running overnight.
3. Turn off the monitor, printer, and other devices when not in use.
4. Use LCD monitors instead of CRT monitors.
5. Use paperless methods to communicate.
6. Recycle paper.
7. Buy recycled paper.
8. Recycle toner cartridges.
9. Recycle old computers, printers, and other devices.
10. Telecommute (saves gas).
11. Use video conferencing and VoIP for meetings.

Figure 5-20 A list of suggestions to make computing healthy for the environment.

Users should not store obsolete computers and devices in their basement, storage room, attic, warehouse, or any other location. Computers, monitors, and other equipment contain toxic materials and potentially dangerous elements including lead, mercury, and flame retardants. In a landfill, these materials release into the environment. Recycling and refurbishing old equipment are much safer alternatives for the environment.

Experts estimate that more than 700 million personal computers are obsolete. Because of the huge volumes of electronic waste, the U.S. federal government has proposed a bill that would require computer recycling across the country. Many state and local governments have methods in place to make it easy for consumers to recycle this type of equipment.

To reduce the environmental impact of computing further, users simply can alter a few habits. Figure 5-20 lists the ways you can contribute to green computing. To learn more about green computing, complete the Green Computing exercise on the Web Research pages in this book.

Information Privacy

Information privacy refers to the right of individuals and companies to deny or restrict the collection and use of information about them. In the past, information privacy was easier to maintain because information was kept in separate locations. Each retail store had its own credit files. Each government agency maintained separate records. Doctors had their own patient files.

Today, huge databases store this data online. Much of the data is personal and confidential and should be accessible only to authorized users. Many individuals and organizations, however, question whether this data really is private.

Figure 5-21 lists measures you can take to make your personal data private. The following pages address techniques companies and employers use to collect your personal data. Read Innovative Computing 5-1 to find out how merchants watch shoppers' behaviors.

INNOVATIVE COMPUTING 5-1

Customers' Behavior, Conversations Monitored

Deciding whether to display peanut butter next to jelly on a supermarket shelf is made easier with consumer-monitoring technology. Leading stores, including Best Buy, Walmart, Walgreens, Office Depot, and Abercrombie & Fitch, have installed video cameras and recorders, heat sensors, and sometimes microphones to track customers' movement throughout the store and their buying patterns.

One system, called Smartlane, counts the number of people, known as "hot blobs," entering and exiting the store and records how quickly clerks are completing transactions at cash registers. It alerts management when many hot blobs are waiting in checkout lanes or have entered the store in a short period of time so that additional clerks can be made available to reduce checkout waiting times.

Another system, BehaviorIQ, collects data on where customers walk throughout the store, when and for how long they stop to browse, and what they take from shelves and racks. Some stores claim information gleaned from these monitoring systems has increased sales 300 percent.

Privacy experts warn that consumers might object to being recorded and analyzed. The monitoring companies, however, dispel these concerns by explaining that the data actually resembles audio recordings made when calling customer-service hotlines and when being observed for loss prevention purposes.

👆 For more information, visit scsite.com/dc-off07/ch5/innovative and then click Shopping Behavior.

How to Safeguard Personal Information

1. Fill in only necessary information on rebate, warranty, and registration forms.
2. Do not preprint your telephone number or Social Security number on personal checks.
3. Have an unlisted or unpublished telephone number.
4. If Caller ID is available in your area, find out how to block your number from displaying on the receiver's system.
5. Do not write your telephone number on charge or credit receipts.
6. Ask merchants not to write credit card numbers, telephone numbers, Social Security numbers, and driver's license numbers on the back of your personal checks.
7. Purchase goods with cash, rather than credit or checks.
8. Avoid shopping club and buyer cards.
9. If merchants ask personal questions, find out why they want to know before releasing the information.
10. Inform merchants that you do not want them to distribute your personal information.
11. Request, in writing, to be removed from mailing lists.
12. Obtain your credit report once a year from each of the three major credit reporting agencies (Equifax, Experian, and TransUnion) and correct any errors.
13. Request a free copy of your medical records once a year from the Medical Information Bureau.
14. Limit the amount of information you provide to Web sites. Fill in only required information.
15. Install a cookie manager to filter cookies.
16. Clear your history file when you are finished browsing.
17. Set up a free e-mail account. Use this e-mail address for merchant forms.
18. Turn off file and printer sharing on your Internet connection.
19. Install a personal firewall.
20. Sign-up for e-mail filtering through your Internet access provider or use an anti-spam program such as Brightmail.
21. Do not reply to spam for any reason.
22. Surf the Web anonymously with a program such as Freedom WebSecure or through an anonymous Web site such as Anonymizer.com.

Figure 5-21 Techniques to keep personal data private.

Electronic Profiles

When you fill out a form such as a magazine subscription, product warranty registration card, or contest entry form, the merchant that receives the form usually enters it into a database. Likewise, every time you click an advertisement on the Web or register software online, your information and preferences enter a database. Merchants then sell the contents of their databases to national marketing firms and Internet advertising firms. By combining this data with information from public sources such as driver's licenses and vehicle registrations, these firms create an electronic profile of individuals.

Critics contend that the information in an electronic profile reveals more about an individual than anyone has a right to know. They also claim that companies should inform people if they plan to provide personal information to others. Many companies today allow people to specify whether they want their personal information distributed.

Cookies

E-commerce and other Web applications often rely on cookies to identify users. A **cookie** is a small text file that a Web server stores on your computer. Cookie files typically contain data about you, such as your user name or viewing preferences.

Many commercial Web sites send a cookie to your browser, and then your computer's hard disk stores the cookie. The next time you visit the Web site, your browser retrieves the cookie from your hard disk and sends the data in the cookie to the Web site.

Web sites use cookies for a variety of purposes:

- Most Web sites that allow for personalization use cookies to track user preferences. On such sites, users may be asked to fill in a form requesting personal information, such as their name, postal code, or site preferences. A news Web site, for example, might allow users to customize their viewing preferences to display certain stock quotes or local weather forecasts. The Web site stores their preferences in a cookie on the users' hard disks.

- Some Web sites use cookies to store users' passwords, so that they do not need to enter it every time they log in to the Web site.
- Online shopping sites generally use a session cookie to keep track of items in a user's shopping cart. This way, users can start an order during one Web session and finish it on another day in another session. Session cookies usually expire after a certain time, such as a week or a month.
- Some Web sites use cookies to track how often users visit a site and the Web pages they visit while at the site.
- Web sites may use cookies to target advertisements. These sites store a user's interests and browsing habits in the cookie.

Cookies
For more information, visit scsite.com/dc-off07/ch5/weblink and then click Cookies.

You can set a browser to accept cookies automatically, prompt you if you want to accept a cookie, or disable cookie use altogether. Keep in mind if you disable cookie use, you will not be able to use many of the e-commerce Web sites. Figure 5-22 illustrates how Web sites work with cookies.

Figure 5-22 This figure shows how cookies work.

Spyware and Adware

Spyware is a program placed on a computer without the user's knowledge that secretly collects information about the user. Some vendors or employers use spyware to collect information about program usage or employees. Internet advertising firms often collect information about users' Web browsing habits by hiding spyware in adware. **Adware** is a program that displays an online advertisement in a banner or pop-up window on Web pages, e-mail messages, or other Internet services. To remove spyware and adware, you can obtain a spyware and adware remover that can detect and delete spyware and adware. Some operating systems and Web browsers include spyware removers.

Spam

Spam is an unsolicited e-mail message or newsgroup posting sent to multiple recipients or newsgroups at once. Spam is Internet junk mail (Figure 5-23). The content of spam ranges from selling a product or service, to promoting a business opportunity, to advertising offensive material. One study indicates more than 92 percent of e-mail is spam.

Users can reduce the amount of spam they receive with a number of techniques. Some e-mail programs have built-in settings that allow users to delete spam automatically. Users also can sign up for e-mail filtering from their Internet access provider. **E-mail filtering** is a service that blocks e-mail messages from designated sources. An alternative to e-mail filtering is to purchase an **anti-spam program** that attempts to remove spam before it reaches your inbox. The disadvantage of e-mail filters and anti-spam programs is that sometimes they remove valid e-mail messages. Thus, users should review the contents of the spam messages periodically to ensure they do not contain valid messages.

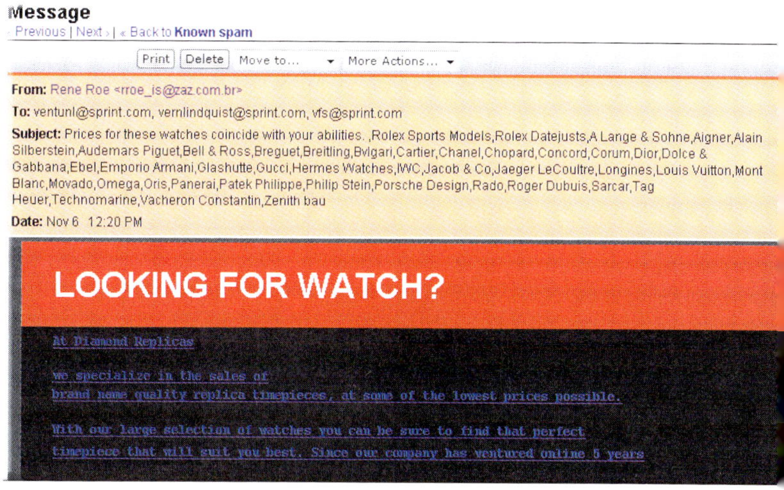

Phishing

Phishing is a scam in which a perpetrator sends an official looking e-mail message that attempts to obtain your personal and financial information (Figure 5-24). Some phishing e-mail messages ask you to reply with your information; others direct you to a phony Web site, or a pop-up window that looks like a Web site, that collects the information.

If you receive an e-mail that looks legitimate and requests you update credit card numbers, Social Security numbers, bank account numbers, passwords, or other private information, the FTC recommends you visit the Web site directly to determine if the request is valid. Never click a link in an e-mail message; instead retype the Web address in your browser.

A **phishing filter** is a program that warns or blocks you from potentially fraudulent or suspicious Web sites. Some Web browsers include phishing filters.

Pharming is a scam, similar to phishing, where a perpetrator attempts to obtain your personal and financial information, except they do so via spoofing. That is, when you type a Web address in the Web browser, you are redirected to a phony Web site that looks legitimate. The phony Web site requests you enter confidential information.

Clickjacking is yet another similar scam. With **clickjacking**, an object that can be clicked on a Web site, such as a button, image, or link, contains a malicious program. When users click the disguised object, for example, they may be redirected to a phony Web site that requests personal information, or a virus may download to their computer.

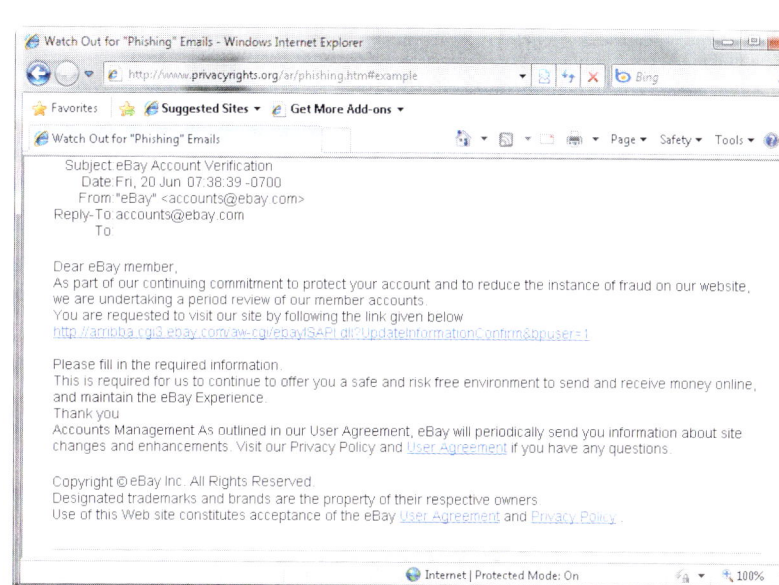

Figure 5-23 An example of spam.

Figure 5-24 An example of a phishing e-mail message.

Social Engineering

As related to the use of computers, **social engineering** is defined as gaining unauthorized access or obtaining confidential information by taking advantage of the trusting human nature of some victims and the naivety of others. Some social engineers trick their victims into revealing confidential information such as user names and passwords on the telephone, in person, or on the Internet. Techniques they use include pretending to be an administrator or other authoritative figure, feigning an emergency situation, or impersonating an acquaintance. Social engineers also obtain information from users who do not destroy or conceal information properly. These perpetrators sift through company dumpsters, watch or film people dialing telephone numbers or using ATMs, and snoop around computers looking for openly displayed confidential information.

Privacy Laws

The concern about privacy has led to the enactment of federal and state laws regarding the storage and disclosure of personal data (Figure 5-25).

Common points in some of these laws include the following:
1. Information collected and stored about individuals should be limited to what is necessary to carry out the function of the business or government agency collecting the data.

Date	Law	Purpose
2006	Telephone Records and Privacy Protection Act	Makes it illegal to use fraudulent means to obtain someone's telephone records.
2003	CAN-SPAM Act	Gives law enforcement the right to impose penalties on people using the Internet to distribute spam.
2002	Sarbanes-Oxley Act	Requires corporate officers, auditors, and attorneys of publicly-traded companies follow strict financial reporting guidelines.
2001	Children's Internet Protection Act (CIPA)	Protects minors from inappropriate content when accessing the Internet in schools and libraries.
2001	Provide Appropriate Tools Required to Intercept and Obstruct Terrorism (PATRIOT) Act	Gives law enforcement the right to monitor people's activities, including Web and e-mail habits.
1999	Gramm-Leach-Bliley Act (GLBA) or Financial Modernization Act	Protects consumers from disclosure of their personal financial information and requires institutions to alert customers of information disclosure policies.
1998	Children's Online Privacy Protection Act (COPPA)	Requires Web sites protect personal information of children under 13 years of age.
1998	Digital Millennium Copyright Act (DMCA)	Makes it illegal to circumvent antipiracy schemes in commercial software; outlaws sale of devices that copy software illegally.
1997	No Electronic Theft (NET) Act	Closes a narrow loophole in the law that allowed people to give away copyrighted material (such as software) on the Internet without legal repercussions.
1996	Health Insurance Portability and Accountability Act (HIPAA)	Protects individuals against the wrongful disclosure of their health information.
1996	National Information Infrastructure Protection Act	Penalizes theft of information across state lines, threats against networks, and computer system trespassing.
1994	Computer Abuse Amendments Act	Amends 1984 act to outlaw transmission of harmful computer code such as viruses.
1992	Cable Act	Extends the privacy of the Cable Communications Policy Act of 1984 to include cellular and other wireless services.
1991	Telephone Consumer Protection Act	Restricts activities of telemarketers.
1988	Computer Matching and Privacy Protection Act	Regulates the use of government data to determine the eligibility of individuals for federal benefits.
1988	Video Privacy Protection Act	Forbids retailers from releasing or selling video-rental records without customer consent or a court order.
1986	Electronic Communications Privacy Act (ECPA)	Provides the same right of privacy protection for the postal delivery service and telephone companies to the new forms of electronic communications, such as voice mail, e-mail, and cell phones.
1984	Cable Communications Policy Act	Regulates disclosure of cable television subscriber records.
1984	Computer Fraud and Abuse Act	Outlaws unauthorized access of federal government computers.
1978	Right to Financial Privacy Act	Strictly outlines procedures federal agencies must follow when looking at customer records in banks.
1974	Privacy Act	Forbids federal agencies from allowing information to be used for a reason other than that for which it was collected.
1974	Family Educational Rights and Privacy Act	Gives students and parents access to school records and limits disclosure of records to unauthorized parties.
1970	Fair Credit Reporting Act	Prohibits credit reporting agencies from releasing credit information to unauthorized people and allows consumers to review their own credit records.

Figure 5-25 Summary of the major U.S. government laws concerning privacy.

2. Once collected, provisions should be made to restrict access to the data to those employees within the organization who need access to it to perform their job duties.
3. Personal information should be released outside the organization collecting the data only when the person has agreed to its disclosure.
4. When information is collected about an individual, the individual should know that the data is being collected and have the opportunity to determine the accuracy of the data.

Employee Monitoring

Employee monitoring involves the use of computers to observe, record, and review an employee's use of a computer, including communications such as e-mail messages, keyboard activity (used to measure productivity), and Web sites visited. Many programs exist that easily allow employers to monitor employees. Further, it is legal for employers to use these programs.

A frequently debated issue is whether an employer has the right to read employee e-mail messages. Actual policies vary widely. Some companies declare that they will review e-mail messages regularly, and others state that e-mail is private. In some states, if an organization does not have a formal e-mail policy, it can read e-mail messages without employee notification. Several lawsuits have been filed against employers because many believe that such internal communications should be private. Read Ethics & Issues 5-2 for a related discussion.

Another controversial issue relates to the use of cameras to monitor employees, customers, and the public. Many people feel that this use of video cameras is a violation of privacy.

ETHICS & ISSUES 5-2

Should Text Messages Sent by Employees Be Private?

When an employee sends or receives an e-mail message using his or her employer's e-mail server, the company most likely retains a backup of the message, which can be used as evidence against the employee if the employee is suspected of engaging in unscrupulous activity. When an employee sends a text message using a company-issued smart phone for such activity, however, the smart phone provider may store a record of the message. Even if an employer requires an employee to disclose all text message communications with customers, vendors, and competitors, the employee is not required legally to divulge those communications. If the employer accuses an employee of possibly violating only company policy, rather than a law, then the smart phone provider is not allowed to disclose the communications. While recent court rulings only confuse the issue further, the courts seem to side with employee privacy regarding the content of sent text messages. Employers argue, however, that because they provide the devices and service to the employee, they should have a right to view the content of the messages.

Should text messages sent by employees be private? Why or why not? How can employers create and enforce policies regarding the content of text messages sent on employer-issued smart phones? Should employers demand that smart phone providers offer the option to send all employee text message communications to the company on a monthly basis? Why or why not?

Content Filtering

One of the more controversial issues that surround the Internet is its widespread availability of objectionable material, such as racist literature, violence, and obscene pictures. Some believe that such materials should be banned. Others believe that the materials should be filtered, that is, restricted. **Content filtering** is the process of restricting access to certain material on the Web. Content filtering opponents argue that banning any materials violates constitutional guarantees of free speech and personal rights.

Many businesses use content filtering to limit employees' Web access. These businesses argue that employees are unproductive when visiting inappropriate or objectionable Web sites. Some schools, libraries, and parents use content filtering to restrict access to minors.

Web filtering software is a program that restricts access to specified Web sites. Some also filter sites that use specific words. Others allow you to filter e-mail messages, chat rooms, and programs. Many Internet security programs include a firewall, antivirus program, and filtering capabilities combined (Figure 5-26).

Figure 5-26 Many Internet security programs include content filtering capabilities, where users can block specified Web sites and applications.

QUIZ YOURSELF 5-3

Instructions: Find the true statement below. Then, rewrite the remaining false statements so that they are true.

1. Factors that cause CVS include prolonged typing, prolonged mouse usage, or continual shifting between the mouse and the keyboard.
2. Phishing is the discovery, collection, and analysis of evidence found on computers and networks.
3. Spam is Internet junk mail.
4. You can assume that information on the Web is correct.

Quiz Yourself Online: To further check your knowledge of pages 198 through 207, visit scsite.com/dc-off07/ch5/fquiz and then click Objectives 7 – 8.

Chapter Summary

This chapter identified some potential computer risks and the safeguards that organizations and individuals can implement to minimize these risks. Wireless security risks and safeguards also were discussed.

The chapter presented computer-related health issues and their preventions. The chapter ended with a discussion about ethical issues surrounding information accuracy, intellectual property rights, green computing, and information privacy.

For detailed personal computer and mobile device purchasing guidelines, read the Buyer's Guide feature that follows this chapter.

Computer Usage @ Work

National and Local Security

Since 2001, the federal government, local governments, businesses, and individuals have been implementing aggressive new security measures because of the increase in terrorist activity. A security threat can exist anywhere, and it is nearly impossible for humans alone to protect the country. As a result, computers now assist governments, law enforcement officials, business owners, and other individuals with monitoring and maintaining security.

Advancements in computer vision enable computers to monitor indoor and outdoor areas that might be subject to a high amount of criminal activity. For example, some cities are installing cameras in problematic areas. A computer program analyzes the output from the camera and can determine whether two or more people in close proximity to one another might be engaged in a physical confrontation. If the computer detects suspicious behavior, it automatically notifies local law enforcement.

Computers also use facial recognition to identify individuals who do not belong in a particular area. For example, one theme park in Florida often takes a picture of individuals they escort out of and ban from the park. As visitors walk from their cars to the park, surveillance cameras positioned in strategic locations scan visitors' faces and compare them to the database containing images of those who are banned from the park. If the computer finds a match, it alerts a security officer who then can investigate the situation. Thousands of people visit theme parks each day, and computers make it easier to perform the otherwise impossible task of identifying those who might be trespassing.

The federal government, particularly the Department of Homeland Security, uses a computerized No Fly List to track individuals who are not authorized to travel on commercial flights within the United States. When an individual makes a reservation, a computer compares his or her name to the names on the No Fly List. If the computer finds a match, the individual must prove that he or she is not the person on the list before being allowed to board an aircraft.

Whether you are walking outside, visiting an attraction, or traveling, the chances are good that computers are, in some way, ensuring your safety.

For more information, visit scsite.com/dc-off07/ch5/work and then click National and Local Security.

Companies on the Cutting Edge

MCAFEE Intrusion Prevention Products Developer

The McAfee Initiative to Fight Cybercrime is a global effort to thwart security threats and criminal activity. The world's largest dedicated security technology company has partnered with experts in law enforcement, education, government, and society to investigate, prosecute, and attempt to prevent security breaches.

McAfee products protect more than 60 million consumers, small- and medium-sized businesses, governmental agencies, and large corporations from malware, spam, and unauthorized access. In addition, more than 100 million mobile devices are protected with McAfee software. The corporation takes its name from its founder, John McAfee, who started the company in 1987 from his Santa Clara, California, home.

In 2009, McAfee launched a new online backup service with unlimited capacity that allows consumers to back up and encrypt their important files such as documents, photos, music, and e-mail messages.

SYMANTEC Computer Security Solutions Leader

Symantec's programmers analyzed every line of code, rewrote programs, and developed a new security model to create its latest versions of Norton AntiVirus and Norton Internet Security. The results are programs that use less hard disk space, decrease starting and scanning time, and average less than 7 MB of memory. The more than 100 performance improvements offer advanced protection for millions of computer users worldwide.

The California-based company is one of the ten largest software corporations in the world. It was founded in 1982 and has offices in more than 40 countries. Its primary manufacturing facility is located in Dublin, Ireland.

In 2009, Symantec released the latest version of its Norton Internet Security software. A rating service tested the level of protection provided by 10 different security products and gave Norton Internet Security the only perfect score.

For more information, scsite.com/dc-off07/ch5/companies.

Technology Trailblazers

RICHARD STALLMAN Software Freedom Advocate

The relationship between software and freedom is key to Richard Stallman's philosophy. Since his days as a physics student at Harvard University, he has advocated free software and campaigned against software patents and copyright laws. His pioneering work developed the concept of copyleft, which gives each person who has purchased a software product the ability to copy, adapt, and distribute the program as long as the new software also has the same lack of restrictions.

Stallman began the GNU/Linux Project in 1983 as an effort to develop and use the copyleft concept. Linux is an outgrowth of this project, which continues to be a forum for software development, ethical practices, and political campaigning. He also started the Free Software Foundation (FSF) in 1985 to promote writing free software for the GNU Project. The Free Software Directory catalogs more than 5,300 packages that run on the Linux and GNU operating systems.

GENE SPAFFORD Computer Security Expert

The Morris Worm, also called the MBDF virus, is considered the first computer worm distributed on the Internet, and Gene Spafford gained fame for deconstructing and analyzing this 1988 attack. His work led to the conviction of a Cornell University student, Robert Morris. Today, Spafford, who also is known as Spaf, is recognized as one of the world's foremost experts in the computer security, intelligence, cybercrime, and software engineering fields.

For 30 years, he has advised major corporations, including Microsoft, Intel, and Unisys, the U.S. Air Force, the Federal Bureau of Investigation, and two U.S. presidents. He is noted for several firsts in the computer security field. For example, he defined the terms, software forensics and firewall, wrote the first English-language book on the topics of viruses and malware, and founded the world's first multidisciplinary academic security awareness group: the Center for Education and Research in Information Assurance and Security (CERIAS).

For more information, scsite.com/dc-off07/ch5/trailblazers.

Chapter Review

The Chapter Review reinforces the main concepts presented in this chapter.

👆 To obtain help from other students about any concept in this chapter, scsite.com/dc-off07/ch5/forum and post your thoughts and questions.

1. **What Are Various Internet and Network Attacks, and How Can Users Safeguard against These Attacks?** A computer **virus** is a potentially damaging program that infects a computer and negatively affects the way the computer works. A **worm** is a program that copies itself repeatedly, using up resources and possibly shutting down the computer or network. A **Trojan horse** is a program that hides within or looks like a legitimate program. A **rootkit** is a program that hides in a computer and allows someone from a remote location to take full control of the computer. Users can take precautions to guard against this **malware**. Do not start a computer with removable media in the drives or ports unless the media are uninfected. Never open an e-mail attachment unless it is from a **trusted source**. Disable macros in documents that are not from a trusted source. Install an **antivirus program** and a personal firewall program. Stay informed about any new virus alert or **virus hoax**. To defend against a **botnet**, a **denial of service attack**, improper use of a **back door**, and **spoofing**, users can install a **firewall** and install **intrusion detection software**.

2. **What Are Techniques to Prevent Unauthorized Access and Use?** **Unauthorized access** is the use of a computer or network without permission. **Unauthorized use** is the use of a computer or its data for unapproved or illegal activities. A written acceptable use policy (AUP) outlines the activities for which the computer and network may and may not be used. Other measures include firewalls and intrusion detection software. An **access control** defines who can access a computer, when they can access it, and what actions they can take. An **audit trail** records in a file both successful and unsuccessful access attempts. Access controls include a **user name** and **password**, a **possessed object**, and a **biometric device**.

   👆 Visit scsite.com/dc-off07/ch5/quiz and then click Objectives 1 – 2.

3. **What Are Safeguards against Hardware Theft and Vandalism?** **Hardware theft** is the act of stealing computer equipment. **Hardware vandalism** is the act of defacing or destroying computer equipment. Physical devices and practical security measures, passwords, possessed objects, and biometrics can reduce the risk of theft or render a computer useless if it is stolen.

4. **How Do Software Manufacturers Protect against Software Theft and Information Theft?** **Software theft** occurs when someone steals software, intentionally erases programs, illegally copies programs, or illegally registers/activates a program. Software **piracy** is the unauthorized and illegal duplication of copyrighted software. To protect themselves from software piracy, manufacturers issue a **license agreement** that provides specific conditions for use of the software. During **product activation**, users provide the product's identification number to receive an installation identification number unique to their computer. Companies attempt to prevent **information theft** through user identification and authentication controls, **encryption**, a **digital signature**, a **digital certificate**, or a **certificate authority**.

5. **What Types of Devices Are Available to Protect Computers from System Failure?** A **system failure** is the prolonged malfunction of a computer. A common cause of system failure is an electrical power variation. A **surge protector** uses special electrical components to provide a stable current flow to the computer. An **uninterruptible power supply** (**UPS**) contains surge protection circuits and one or more batteries that can provide power during a power loss.

6. **What Risks and Safeguards Are Associated with Wireless Communications?** Wireless access poses additional security risks. Intruders connect to other wireless networks to gain free Internet access or to access an organization's confidential data. Some individuals intercept and monitor communications as they are transmitted. Others connect to a network through an unsecured wireless access point (WAP). Some safeguards include firewalls, reconfiguring the WAP, and ensuring equipment uses a wireless security standard, such as **Wi-Fi Protected Access** and **802.11i**.

   👆 Visit scsite.com/dc-off07/ch5/quiz and then click Objectives 3 – 6.

7. **How Can Health-Related Disorders and Injuries Due to Computer Use Be Prevented?** A **repetitive strain injury** (**RSI**) is an injury or disorder of the muscles, nerves, tendons, ligaments, and joints. Computer-related RSIs include tendonitis and carpal tunnel syndrome (CTS). Another health-related condition is eyestrain associated with **computer vision**

syndrome (CVS). To prevent health-related disorders, take frequent breaks, use precautionary exercises and techniques, and incorporate ergonomics when planning the workplace. **Computer addiction** occurs when the computer consumes someone's entire social life.

8. **What Are Issues Surrounding Information Privacy?** **Information privacy** is the right of individuals and companies to restrict the collection and use of information about them. An electronic profile combines data about an individual's Web use with data from public sources. A **cookie** is a file that a Web server stores on a computer to collect data about the user. **Spyware** is a program placed on a computer that secretly collects information about the user. **Adware** is a program that displays an online advertisement in a banner or pop-up window. **Spam** is an unsolicited e-mail message or newsgroup posting sent to many recipients. **Phishing** is a scam in which a perpetrator sends an official looking e-mail message that attempts to obtain a user's personal and financial information. The concern about privacy has led to the enactment of many federal and state laws regarding the storage and disclosure of data. As related to the use of computers, **social engineering** is defined as gaining unauthorized access or obtaining confidential information by taking advantage of the trusting human nature of some victims and the naivety of others. **Employee monitoring** uses computers to observe, record, and review an employee's computer use. **Content filtering** restricts access to certain material on the Web.

Visit scsite.com/dc-off07/ch5/quiz and then click Objectives 7 – 8.

Key Terms

You should know each key term. The list below helps focus your study.

To see an example of and a definition for each term, and to access current and additional information from the Web, scsite.com/dc-off07/ch5/terms.

802.11i (197)
access control (189)
adware (204)
anti-spam program (205)
antivirus program (186)
audit trail (189)
back door (188)
back up (196)
backup (196)
biometric device (191)
biometric payment (191)
botnet (187)
CAPTCHA (190)
certificate authority (195)
clickjacking (205)
computer addiction (199)
computer crime (182)
computer ethics (199)
computer security risk (182)
computer vision syndrome (198)
content filtering (207)
cookie (203)
copyright (201)
cracker (182)
cybercrime (182)

cyberextortionist (182)
cyberterrorist (183)
decrypt (195)
denial of service attack (187)
digital certificate (195)
digital forensics (192)
digital rights management (201)
digital signature (195)
DoS attack (187)
e-mail filtering (205)
employee monitoring (207)
encryption (195)
encryption algorithm (195)
encryption key (195)
ENERGY STAR program (201)
firewall (188)
green computing (201)
hacker (182)
hardware theft (193)
hardware vandalism (193)
information privacy (202)
information theft (195)
intellectual property rights (201)

intrusion detection software (189)
license agreement (194)
malware (184)
password (190)
payload (184)
personal firewall (189)
personal identification number (PIN) (191)
pharming (205)
phishing (205)
phishing filter (205)
piracy (193)
possessed object (191)
product activation (194)
quarantine (186)
real time location system (RTLS) (193)
repetitive strain injury (RSI) (198)
restore (196)
rootkit (184)
script kiddie (182)
secure site (195)
social engineering (205)
software theft (193)

spam (204)
spoofing (188)
spyware (204)
surge protector (196)
system failure (196)
Trojan horse (184)
trusted source (185)
unauthorized access (189)
unauthorized use (189)
uninterruptible power supply (UPS) (196)
user name (190)
virus (184)
virus definition (186)
virus hoax (187)
virus signature (186)
war driving (197)
Web filtering software (207)
Wi-Fi Protected Access (197)
worm (184)
zombie (187)

Checkpoint

The Checkpoint exercises test your knowledge of the chapter concepts. The page number containing the answer appears in parentheses after each exercise.

☝ To complete the Checkpoint exercises interactively, visit scsite.com/dc-off07/ch5/check.

Multiple Choice Select the best answer.

1. A _____ is a program that hides in a computer and allows someone from a remote location to take full control of the computer. (184)
   a. worm
   b. rootkit
   c. payload
   d. cookie

2. Malware is a term that can be used to describe _____. (184)
   a. viruses
   b. rootkits
   c. Trojan horses
   d. all of the above

3. The _____ is the destructive event or prank that malware is intended to deliver. (184)
   a. hash
   b. payload
   c. cookie
   d. spam

4. A _____ is an assault whose purpose is to disrupt computer access to an Internet service such as the Web or e-mail. (187)
   a. zombie
   b. denial of service attack
   c. Trojan horse
   d. virus hoax

5. _____ involves the examination of computer media, programs, data and log files on computers, servers, and networks. (192)
   a. Encryption key
   b. E-mail filtering
   c. Digital forensics
   d. Trusted source

6. Physical access controls, such as locked doors and windows, usually are adequate to protect against _____. (193)
   a. software piracy
   b. unauthorized access
   c. hardware theft
   d. all of the above

7. A(n) _____ is a programmed formula that the originator of the data uses to encrypt the plaintext and the recipient of the data uses to decrypt the ciphertext. (195)
   a. botnet
   b. certificate authority
   c. encryption algorithm
   d. encryption key

8. As related to the use of computers, _____ is defined as gaining unauthorized access or obtaining confidential information by taking advantage of the trusting human nature of some victims and the naivety of others. (205)
   a. phishing
   b. a virus hoax
   c. social engineering
   d. pharming

Matching Match the terms with their definitions.

_____ 1. virus (184)
_____ 2. trusted source (185)
_____ 3. spoofing (188)
_____ 4. encryption algorithm (195)
_____ 5. surge protector (196)

a. organization or person you believe will not send a virus infected file knowingly
b. set of steps that can convert readable plaintext into unreadable ciphertext
c. potentially damaging computer program that affects, or infects, a computer negatively by altering the way the computer works without the user's knowledge or permission
d. technique intruders use to make their network or Internet transmission appear legitimate to a victim computer or network
e. uses special electrical components to provide a stable current flow to the computer and other electronic equipment
f. service that blocks e-mail messages from designated sources

Short Answer Write a brief answer to each of the following questions.

1. How do antivirus programs detect and identify a virus? _____ What is a virus hoax? _____
2. Describe the ENERGY STAR program. _____ How should users handle obsolete computers? _____
3. What is information privacy? _____ List five ways to safeguard your personal information. _____
4. What are two methods for avoiding phishing attacks? _____ How does clickjacking work? _____
5. What is content filtering, and who uses it? _____ Why is content filtering controversial? _____

Problem Solving

The Problem Solving exercises extend your knowledge of the chapter concepts by seeking solutions to practical computer problems that you may encounter at home, school, or work. The Collaboration exercise should be completed with a team.

👆 To discuss the Problem Solving exercises with other students, visit scsite.com/dc-off07/ch5/forum and post your thoughts or questions.

In the real world, practical problems often can be solved in multiple ways. Provide one solution to each of the following problems using available resources, such as articles on the Web or in print, blogs, podcasts, videos, television, user guides, other individuals, and electronics and computer stores. You may need to use multiple resources to obtain an answer. Present your solutions in the form requested by your instructor (brief report, presentation, discussion, or other means).

@ Home

1. **Infected File Detected**   A message appears on your computer screen stating that your antivirus program detected an infected file on your computer and is unable to move it to quarantine. What are your next steps?

2. **Product Key in Use**   While installing the latest version of Microsoft Office, the installation program prompts you to enter the product key. Once you finish entering the product key, you receive an error message stating that the product key already is in use. What might be causing this?

3. **Questionable Fair Use**   A media company's attorney has sent you a letter stating that you are violating their rights by including a short movie clip from one of their movies in one of your videos posted on YouTube. You believe that you are within fair use guidelines by including the movie clip but also feel that you should respond to the attorney's letter. What are your next steps?

4. **Verifying Photo Validity**   You are writing a research paper for your history class and have found a photo on the Web that you would like to use. You are cautious about using photos on the Web because of copyright issues and photos that have been altered digitally. How might you verify the validity of a photo on the Web?

@ Work

5. **Password Management**   You must remember multiple user names and passwords to access various computer resources within your company. Each time your company introduces a new system, you must remember a new user name and password, some of which you are unable to customize. What steps will you take to manage your passwords?

6. **Problem Reinstalling Software**   After recovering from a computer crash, you attempt to reinstall a program that was previously installed. When you insert the installation media, begin the installation, and type the product key, you receive an indication that you are unable to continue installing the software because you have installed it the maximum number of allowable times. What are your next steps?

7. **Missing Security Cable Key**   To protect your notebook computer from theft, you use a security cable to secure it to the desk in your cubicle. Your boss assigns you some work to take home and suggests that you take home your notebook computer. You discover, however, that you are unable to locate the key that releases the security cable from the computer. What are your next steps?

8. **Monitored Computer Activities**   You receive an e-mail message from the IT department stating that it randomly will monitor employee computers throughout the workday to ensure that they are being used for legitimate purposes. Shortly thereafter, you begin to notice that your computer slows significantly at random times once or twice per week. You suspect the performance decrease is a result of the computer monitoring. How will you address this?

Collaboration

9. **Computers in National and Local Security**   National and local security agencies often use computers to protect citizens. For example, computers are used to maintain a list of individuals not cleared to board a commercial aircraft. Form a team of three people to create a list of the various ways computers help to keep us safe. One team member should research how local agencies, such as police departments, use computers to ensure security. Another team member should research ways national security agencies use computers to protect us from threats, and the last team member should research ways that private businesses use computers to guarantee security. Compile these findings into a report and submit it to your instructor.

Learn How To

The Learn How To activities step you through fundamental technology skills when using a computer. The Learn How To exercises enable you to become more proficient with these skills.

👆 **Premium Activity:** To relate this Learn How To activity to your everyday life, see a visual demonstration of the activity, and then complete a short assessment, visit scsite.com/dc-off07/ch5/howto.

Learn How To 1: Back Up Files on an Offsite Internet Server

Note: The service described in this exercise allows 15 days of free access. After that time, you may be billed automatically for service unless you cancel your service in the given time frame.

Backing up files stored on your computer on another disk or computer located in a different geographical location is the ultimate safeguard for data on your computer. A good way to back up data is to use one of the services available on the Web. A leading service is found at IBackup.com. To subscribe to the IBackup service, complete the following steps:

1. Start a Web browser, type the Web address `IBackup.com` in the Address bar and then press the ENTER key.
2. When the IBackup Web page is displayed, click Signup on the top horizontal toolbar.
3. Enter your e-mail address in the E-mail Address text box and then click the Continue with Registration button to display a form (Figure 5-27).
4. Fill in the form. Select the plan you want in the Select a Storage Plan list. If you want to try the service for a short period of time before subscribing, select 5 GB 15 day Free Trial Plan.
5. To continue to the next pages, you must enter credit card information. If you select the 15-day trial, your credit card will not be charged at this time, and an automatic billing at the end of 15 days will occur. After entering the required information, click the Continue button at the bottom of the page.
6. A message is displayed that confirms that you have signed up with IBackup and also provides a link for you to download the IBackup for Windows program.
7. Click the DOWNLOAD button to download the IBackup for Windows program and then follow the instructions to install the program on your computer.

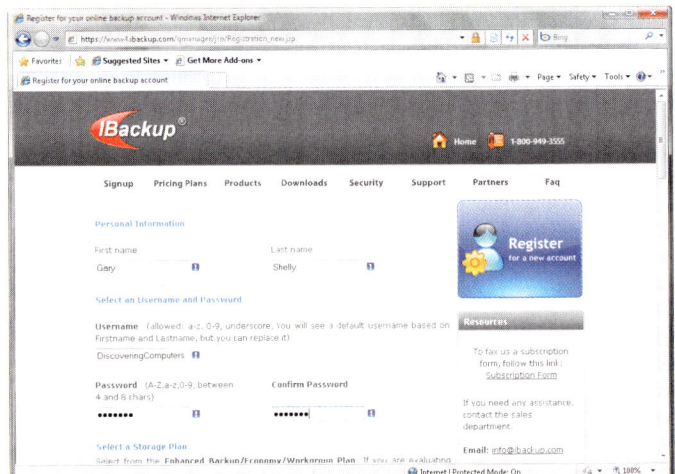

Figure 5-27

After establishing an account, you can use it for the time for which you subscribed. Complete the following steps to use the service:

1. Start the IBackup for Windows program.
2. Enter your user name and password and then click the Connect button to open a window containing your files, as well as the contents of your My IBackup folder (Figure 5-28).
3. To upload a file, locate the file in the left pane of the IBackup window and drag it to the right pane. The Backup Progress dialog box will be displayed while the file is uploading. The file will be placed in the My IBackup folder.

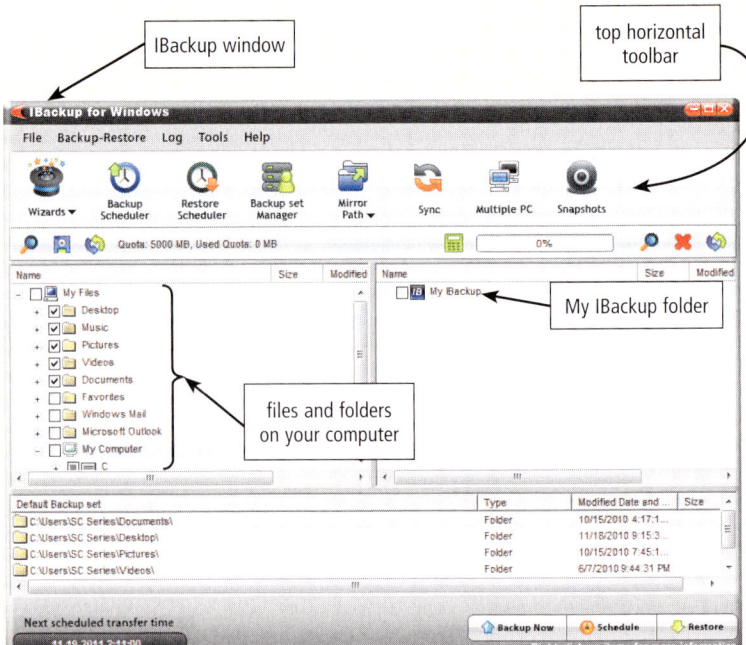

Figure 5-28

4. For further activities you can accomplish in this program for backing up your files, click the buttons on the top horizontal toolbar and experiment.

Exercises

1. Visit the IBackup Web site. Click View Demo and then follow the screen prompts to view all the services offered by IBackup. Which service is most appropriate for your home computer? Which service is most useful for the server that is used in the computer lab at your school? If you had critical data you needed to back up, would you use a service like this? Why or why not? Submit your answers to your instructor.

2. **Optional: Perform this exercise only for your own computer. Do not perform this exercise on a school computer.** Establish an account on IBackup.com. Upload two or more files from your computer. Download the files you uploaded back to your computer. Is this an efficient way to back up your files? Do you think the IBackup service would be useful for businesses? Submit your answers to your instructor.

Learn It Online

The Learn It Online exercises are interactive Web exercises designed to reinforce and expand your understanding of the chapter concepts. The descriptions below briefly summarize each exercise.

👉 To access the Learn It Online exercises and for specific exercise instructions, visit scsite.com/dc-off07/ch5/learn.

❶ At the Movies — Attack of the Mobile Viruses
Watch a movie to learn about the recent wave of viruses plaguing mobile device users and then answer questions about the movie.

❷ Student Edition Labs — Protecting Your Privacy Online and Computer Ethics
Enhance your understanding and knowledge about online privacy and computer ethics by completing the Protecting Your Privacy Online and Computer Ethics Labs.

❸ Practice Test
Take a multiple choice test that checks your knowledge of the chapter concepts and review the resulting study guide.

❹ Who Wants To Be a Computer Genius^2?
Play the Shelly Cashman Series version of this popular game by answering questions to find out if you are a computer genius. Panic buttons are available to provide assistance during game play.

❺ Crossword Puzzle Challenge
Complete an interactive crossword puzzle to reinforce concepts presented in this chapter.

❻ Windows Exercises
Step through the Windows 7 exercises to learn about playing audio compact discs, understanding multimedia properties, dragging and dropping Windows objects, and checking for system updates.

❼ Exploring Computer Careers
Read about a career as a digital forensics examiner, search for related employment advertisements, and then answer related questions.

❽ Web Apps — Dictionary.com
Learn how to use Dictionary.com to search for a dictionary entry, translate a word to other languages, and search for Web pages containing your search term.

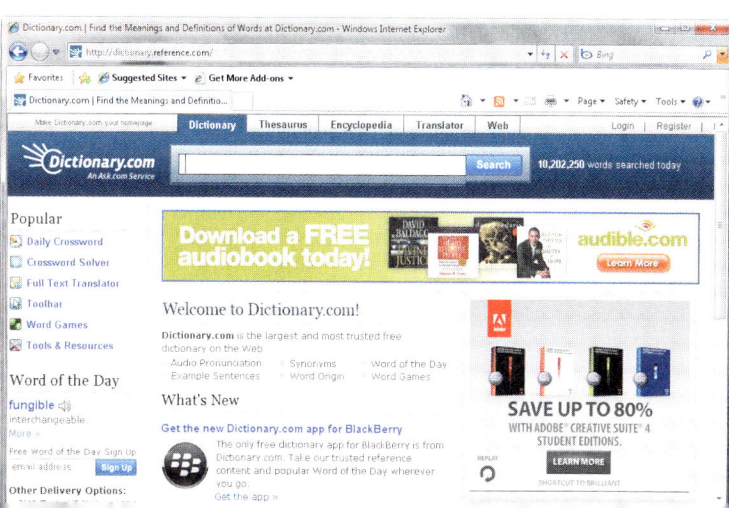

Web Research

The Web Research exercises broaden your understanding of chapter concepts by presenting questions that require you to search the Web for answers.

👆 To discuss any of the Web Research exercises in this chapter with other students, visit scsite.com/dc-off07/ch5/forum and post your thoughts or questions.

1 Search Sleuth

Use one of the search engines listed in Figure 2-8 in Chapter 2 on page 53 or your own favorite search engine to find the answers to the following questions. Copy and paste the Web address from the Web page where you found the answer. Some questions may have more than one answer. If required, submit your answers to your instructor. (1) Which five words are among the most commonly used passwords? (2) What do e-mail messages with the subject lines "Sending You All My Love," "Laughing Kitty," and "You've Received a Postcard from a Family Member" have in common? (3) T'ai chi, yoga, and the Alexander technique might offer some relief to computer users suffering from which injury? (4) For which purpose is a gas discharge arrestor used? (5) How many computers in the business world have antivirus software that has been disabled or never was installed properly?

2 Green Computing

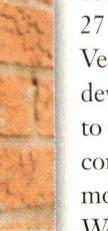

The more than 1 billion computers in the world each emit an average of 1,000 pounds of carbon dioxide each year. Many home computer users can help reduce their carbon footprint with the help of devices that monitor energy consumption. Computers are not the only home devices that draw a lot of current; the average home has 27 products that always are turned on, including the television, appliances, and heating and cooling systems. Verdiem's free download, Edison, helps consumers manage their computer power usage. Smart metering devices made by Control4, Colorado vNet, and ZigBee track power usage and give automated tips on how to reduce energy costs. View online Web sites that provide information about reducing home electricity consumption. How do the monitoring devices work? How much do they cost? How do they calculate the money and energy saved per year? Write a report summarizing your findings, and include a table of links to Web sites that provide additional details.

3 Social Networking

People with unique and special talents often desire to share their passions and pastimes with others. Online social networks provide them an opportunity to share their hobbies and creations. In fact, 69 percent of online social networking members say they have a connection with special-interest Web sites. For example, members of the Sports MatchMaker (sportsmatchmaker.com) community can find people who want to play any sport or participate in any hobby at a specific date and time. ShowOffDemo (showoffdemo.com) members spotlight their talents on a virtual stage, and the Instructables community (instructables.com) collaborates to provide instructions for arts, crafts, food, electronics, and games. Visit these Web sites and view the members' products. Which items are popular? Which are unusual? Which photos provide details on documenting the steps necessary to complete a project? How do members share project ideas and requests for information? Summarize the information you read and viewed.

4 Blogs

More than 80,000 blogs are created daily according to Umbria Communications, a service that tracks new Internet media. Many information technology (IT) professionals maintain these blogs to tout companies' products and express personal observations. IT bloggers include Robert Scoble on video (scobleizer.com); Jeff Jaffe, Novell's chief technical officer (novell.com/ctoblog); Ed Brill on IBM (edbrill.com); and Tom Kyte on Oracle (tkyte.blogspot.com). Visit these blogs and read some of the posts. What new products are mentioned? What are the bloggers' backgrounds? What controversial topics are discussed? What personal views do the bloggers express?

5 Ethics in Action

Radio frequency identification (RFID) tags are expected to help merchants in many ways. By placing these tags on such items as prescriptions, computer peripherals, and clothing, retailers hope to reduce theft, track inventory, reduce labor costs, and keep their shelves stocked. Privacy experts, however, claim the tags can store information about consumers' shopping habits and whereabouts. Law enforcement officials, lawyers, marketers, and even thieves could use this detailed electronic data to track people at all times of the day. View Web sites that discuss using RFID tags in stores and the privacy issues that arise from their use. Write a report summarizing your findings, and include a table of links to Web sites that provide additional details.

Special Feature

Buyer's Guide 2011: How to Purchase Computers and Mobile Devices

AT SOME POINT, perhaps while you are taking this course, you may decide to buy a computer or mobile device (Figure 1). The decision is an important one and will require an investment of both time and money. Like many buyers, you may have little experience with technology and find yourself unsure of how to proceed. You can start by talking to your friends, coworkers, and instructors about their computers and mobile devices. What type of computers and mobile devices did they buy? Why? For what purposes do they use their computers and mobile devices?

desktop computer

notebook computer

portable media player

smart phone

digital camera

Figure 1 Computers and mobile devices.

How to Purchase a Desktop Computer

A **desktop computer** sits on or below a desk or table in a stationary location such as a home, office, or dormitory room. Desktop computers are a good option if you work mostly in one place and have plenty of space in a work area. Desktop computers generally provide more performance for your money. Today, manufacturers are placing more emphasis on style by offering bright colors, stylish displays, and theme-based displays so that the computer looks attractive if it is in an area of high visibility. Once you have decided that a desktop computer is most suited to your computing needs, the next step is to determine specific software, hardware, peripheral devices, and services to purchase, as well as where to buy the computer.

❶ Determine the specific software to use on your computer.

Before deciding to purchase software, be sure it contains the features necessary for the tasks you want to perform. Rely on the computer users in whom you have confidence to help you decide on the software to use. In addition, consider purchasing software that might help you perform tasks at home that you otherwise would perform at another location, such as at school or at work. The minimum requirements of the software you select may determine the operating system (Microsoft Windows, Mac OS, Linux) you need. If you decide to use a particular operating system that does not support software you want to use, you may be able to purchase similar software from other manufacturers.

Many Web sites and trade magazines provide reviews of software products. These Web sites frequently have articles that rate computers and software on cost, performance, and support.

Your hardware requirements depend on the minimum requirements of the software you will run on your computer. Some software requires more memory and disk space than others, as well as additional input, output, and storage devices. For example, suppose you want to run software that can copy one optical disc's contents directly to another optical disc, without first copying the data to the hard disk. To support that, you should consider a desktop computer or a high-end notebook computer, because the computer will need two optical disc drives: one that reads from an optical disc, and one that writes on an optical disc. If you plan to run software that allows your computer to function as an entertainment system, then you will need an optical disc drive, quality speakers, and an upgraded sound card.

❷ Know the system requirements of the operating system.

After determining the software you want to run on your new computer, the next step is to determine the operating system to use. If, however, you purchase a new computer, chances are it will have the latest version of your preferred operating system (Windows, Mac OS, Linux).

❸ Look for bundled software.

When you purchase a computer, it may include bundled software. Some sellers even let you choose which software you want. Remember, however, that bundled software has value only if you would have purchased the software even if it had not been included with the computer. At the very least, you probably will want word processing software and an antivirus program. If you need additional programs, such as a spreadsheet, a database, or presentation software, consider purchasing or downloading Microsoft Office, Microsoft Works, OpenOffice.org, or Sun StarOffice, which include several programs at a reduced price or at no cost.

❹ Avoid buying the least powerful computer available.

Once you know the application software you want to use, then consider the following important criteria about the computer's components: (1) processor speed, (2) size and types of memory (RAM) and storage, (3) types of input/output devices, (4) types of ports and adapter cards, and (5) types of communications devices. You also should consider if the computer is upgradeable and to what extent you are able to upgrade. For example, all manufacturers limit the amount of memory you can add. The information in Figure 2 on pages 219 and 220 can help you determine which computer components are best for you and outlines considerations for specific hardware components. For a sample Base Components worksheet that lists PC recommendations for each category of user discussed in this

Considerations for Hardware Components

Card Reader/Writer: A card reader/writer is useful for transferring data directly to and from a memory card, such as the type used in a digital camera, smart phone, or portable media player. Make sure the card reader/writer can read from and write on the memory cards that you use.

Digital Video Capture Device: A digital video capture device allows you to connect a computer to a video camera or VCR and record, edit, manage, and then write video back on an optical disc or VCR tape. To create quality video (true 30 frames per second, full-sized TV), the digital video capture device should have a USB or FireWire port.

External Hard Disk: An external hard disk can serve many purposes: it can serve as extra storage for your computer, provide a way to store and transport large files or large quantities of files, and provide a convenient way to back up data on other internal and external hard disks. External hard disks can be purchased with the same capacity as any internal disk.

Fingerprint Reader: For added security, you may want to consider purchasing a fingerprint reader. It helps prevent unauthorized access to your computer and also allows you to log onto Web sites quickly via your fingerprint, rather than entering a user name and password each time you access the site. Most use a USB connection and require software installation.

Hard Disk: It is recommended that you buy a computer with at least a 320 GB hard disk if your primary interests are browsing the Web and using e-mail and Office suite-type programs; 1 TB if you also want to edit digital photos or if you plan to edit digital video or manipulate large audio files even occasionally; and 2 TB if you will edit digital video, movies, or photos often; store audio files and music; or consider yourself to be a power user. Internal hard disk controllers are available with the RAID option for added data protection.

Joystick/Wheel: If you use the computer to play games, then you will want to purchase a joystick or a wheel. These devices, especially the more expensive ones, provide for realistic game play with force feedback, programmable buttons, and specialized levers and wheels.

Keyboard: The keyboard is one of the more important devices used to communicate with the computer. For this reason, make sure the keyboard you purchase has 101 to 105 keys, is comfortable and easy to use, and has a USB connection. A wireless keyboard should be considered, especially if you have a small desk area.

Microphone: If you plan to record audio or use speech recognition to enter text and commands, then purchase a close-talk headset with gain adjustment support.

Modem: Most computers include a modem so that you can use a telephone line to access the Internet. Some modems also have fax capabilities. Your modem should be rated at 56 Kbps.

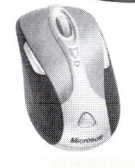

Monitor: The monitor is where you will view documents, read e-mail messages, and view pictures. A minimum of a 19" LCD flat-panel monitor is recommended, but if you plan to use the computer for graphic design or game playing, then you may want to purchase a 22" or 27" monitor. Instead of a single large, widescreen monitor, you may want to consider a side-by-side monitor setup.

Mouse: While working with a desktop computer, you use the mouse constantly. Make sure the mouse has a wheel, which acts as a third button in addition to the top two buttons on the left and right. An ergonomic design also is important because your hand is on the mouse most of the time when you are using the computer. A wireless mouse should be considered to eliminate the cord and allow you to work at short distances from the computer.

Optical Disc Drives: Most computers include a DVD±RW combination drive and/or DVD/Blu-ray Disc drive. A DVD±RW or a Blu-ray Disc drive allows you to read optical discs and to write data on (burn) an optical disc. It also will allow you to store and share video files, digital photos, and other large files with other people who have access to a DVD/Blu-ray Disc drive. A Blu-ray Disc has a capacity of at least 25 GB, and a DVD has a capacity of at least 4.7 GB, versus the 650 MB capacity of a CD.

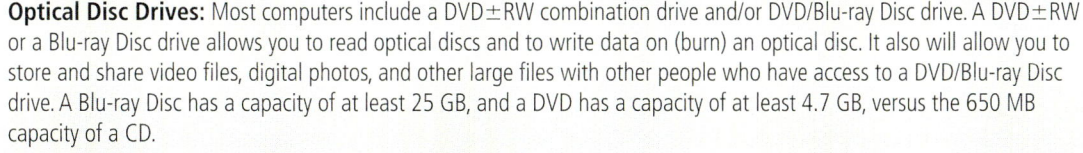

Figure 2 Hardware guidelines. *(continues)*

Considerations for Hardware Components

Ports: Depending on how you are using the computer, you may need anywhere from 4 to 10 USB ports. USB ports have become the connection of choice in the computer industry. They offer an easy way to connect peripheral devices such as printers, digital cameras, and portable media players. Many computers intended for home or professional audio/video use have built-in FireWire ports. Most personal computers include a minimum of six USB ports, two FireWire ports, and an Ethernet port.

Printer: Your two basic printer choices are ink-jet and laser. Color ink-jet printers cost on average between $50 and $300. Laser printers cost from $200 to $2,000. In general, the less expensive the printer, the lower the resolution and speed, and the more often you are required to change the ink cartridges or toner. Laser printers print faster and with a higher quality than an ink-jet, and their toner on average costs less.

Processor: For a personal computer, an Intel Core i7 processor at 2.93 GHz is more than enough processor power for most home and small office/home office users. Game home, enterprise, and power users should upgrade to faster, more powerful processors.

RAM: RAM plays a vital role in the speed of a computer. Make sure the computer you purchase has at least 2 GB of RAM. If you have extra money to invest in a computer, consider increasing the RAM. The extra money for RAM will be well spent because more RAM typically translates into more speed.

Scanner: The most popular scanner purchased with a computer today is the flatbed scanner. When evaluating a flatbed scanner, check the color depth and resolution. Do not buy anything less than a color depth of 48 bits and a resolution of 1200 x 2400 dpi. The higher the color depth, the more accurate the color. A higher resolution picks up the more subtle gradations of color.

Sound Card: Many computers include a standard sound card that supports Dolby 5.1 surround and are capable of recording and playing digital audio. Make sure they are suitable in the event you decide to use the computer as an entertainment or gaming system.

Speakers: Once you have a good sound card, quality speakers and a separate subwoofer that amplifies the bass frequencies of the speakers can turn the computer into a premium stereo system.

USB Flash Drive: If you work on different computers and need access to the same data and information, then this portable flash memory device is ideal. USB flash drive capacity varies from 1 GB to 16 GB.

USB Hub: If you plan to connect several peripheral devices to the computer at the same time, then you need to be concerned with the number of ports available on the computer. If the computer does not have enough ports, then you should purchase a USB hub. A USB hub plugs into a single USB port and provides several additional ports.

Video Card: Most standard video cards satisfy the monitor display needs of most home and small office users. If you are a game home user or a graphic designer, you will want to upgrade to a higher quality video card. The higher refresh rates will further enhance the display of games, graphics, and movies.

Web Cam: A Web cam is a small digital video camera that can capture and display live video on a Web page. You also can capture, edit, and share video and still photos. Recommended minimum specifications include 640 x 480 resolution, a video with a rate of 30 frames per second, and a USB or FireWire port. Some Web cams are built into computer monitors.

Wireless LAN Access Point: A wireless LAN access point allows you to network several computers, so that multiple users can share files and access the Internet through a single broadband connection. Each device that you connect requires a wireless card. A wireless LAN access point can offer a range of operations up to several hundred feet, so be sure the device has a high-powered antenna.

Figure 2 Hardware guidelines. *(continued)*

book, see scsite.com/dc-off07/ch5/buyers. In the worksheet, the Home User category is divided into two groups: Application Home User and Game Home User.

Computer technology changes rapidly, meaning a computer that seems powerful enough today may not serve your computing needs in several years. In fact, studies show that many users regret not buying a more powerful computer. To avoid this, plan to buy a computer that will last for at least two to three years. You can help delay obsolescence by purchasing the fastest processor, the most memory, and the largest hard disk you can afford. If you must buy a less powerful computer, be sure you can upgrade it with additional memory, components, and peripheral devices as your computer requirements grow.

5 Consider upgrades to the mouse, keyboard, monitor, printer, microphone, and speakers.

You use these peripheral devices to interact with the computer, so make sure they are up to your standards. Review the peripheral devices listed in Figure 2 and then visit both local computer dealers and large retail stores to test the computers and devices on display. Ask the salesperson which input and output devices would be best for you and whether you should upgrade beyond the standard product. Consider purchasing a wireless keyboard and wireless mouse to eliminate wires on your desktop. A few extra dollars spent on these components when you initially purchase a computer can extend its usefulness by years.

6 Determine whether to use a broadband or dial-up connection to access the Internet.

If your computer has a modem, you can access the Internet using a standard telephone line. Ordinarily, you call a local or toll-free 800 number to connect to an Internet access provider. Using a dial-up Internet connection usually is relatively inexpensive but slow.

Broadband connections provide much faster Internet connections, which are ideal if you want faster file download speeds for software, digital photos, digital video, and music. As you would expect, they can be more expensive than a dial-up connection. If you want to use a broadband connection, your computer should have an Ethernet card installed, unless you are using a wireless broadband connection such as WiMax or 3G. If you will be using a dial-up connection, your computer should have a modem installed.

7 Use a worksheet to compare computers, services, and other considerations.

You can use a separate sheet of paper to take notes about each vendor's computer and then summarize the information on a worksheet. For a sample worksheet that compares prices for a PC or a Mac, see scsite.com/dc-off07/ch5/buyers. Most

companies advertise a price for a base computer that includes components housed in the system unit (processor, RAM, sound card, video card, network card), hard disks, optical disc drives, a keyboard, mouse, monitor, printer, speakers, and modem. Be aware, however, that some advertisements list prices for computers with only some of these components. Monitors and printers, for example, often are not included in a base computer's price. Depending on how you plan to use the computer, you may want to invest in additional or more powerful components. When comparing the prices of computers, make sure you are comparing identical or similar configurations.

8 If you are buying a new computer, you have several purchasing options: buying from a school bookstore, a local computer dealer, a local large retail store, or ordering by mail via telephone or the Web.

Each purchasing option has certain advantages. Many college bookstores, for example, sign exclusive pricing agreements with computer manufacturers and, thus, can offer student discounts. Local dealers and local large retail stores, however, more easily can provide hands-on support. Mail-order companies that sell computers by telephone or online via the Web (Figure 3) often provide the lowest prices, but extend less personal service. Some major mail-order companies, however, have started to provide next-business-day, on-site services. A credit card usually is required to buy from a mail-order company.

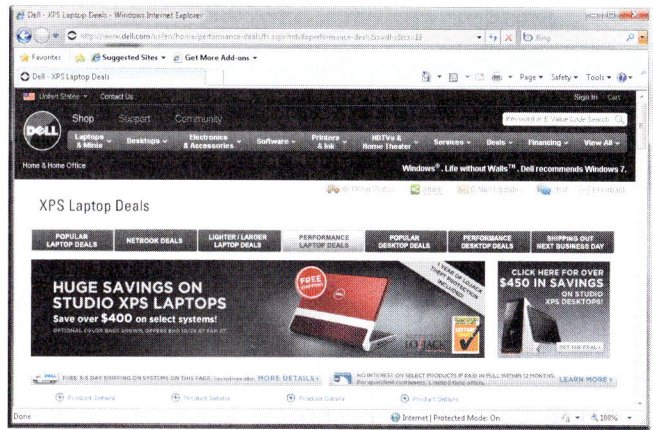

Figure 3 Mail-order companies, such as Dell, sell computers online.

9 If you are buying a used computer, stay with name brands such as Dell, Apple, HP, and Gateway.

Although brand-name equipment can cost more, most brand-name computers have longer, more comprehensive warranties, are better supported, and have more authorized centers for repair services. As with new computers, you can purchase a used computer from local computer dealers, local large retail stores, or mail order via the telephone or the Web. Classified ads and used computer sellers offer additional outlets for purchasing used computers.

10 If you have a computer and are upgrading to a new one, then consider selling or trading in the old one.

If you are a replacement buyer, your older computer still may have value. If you cannot sell the computer through the classified ads, via a Web site, or to a friend, then ask if the computer dealer will buy your old computer.

An increasing number of companies are taking trade-ins, but do not expect too much money for your old computer. Other companies offer to recycle your old computer free or for a fee.

11 Be aware of hidden costs.

Before purchasing, be sure to consider any additional costs associated with buying a computer, such as an additional telephone line, a broadband modem, an uninterruptible power supply (UPS), computer furniture, a USB flash drive, paper, and computer training classes you may want to take. Depending on where you buy the computer, the seller may be willing to include some or all of these in the computer purchase price.

12 Consider more than just price.

The lowest-cost computer may not be the best long-term buy. Consider such intangibles as the vendor's time in business, regard for quality, and reputation for support. If you need to upgrade a computer often, you may want to consider a leasing arrangement, in which you pay monthly lease fees, but can upgrade or add on to your computer as your equipment needs change. No matter what type of buyer you are, insist on a 30-day, no-questions-asked return policy on the computer.

13 Avoid restocking fees.

Some companies charge a restocking fee of 10 to 20 percent as part of their money-back return policy. In some cases, no restocking fee for hardware is applied, but it is applied for software. Ask about the existence and terms of any restocking policies before you buy.

14 Use a credit card to purchase a new computer.

Many credit cards offer purchase protection and extended warranty benefits that cover you in case of loss of or damage to purchased goods. Paying by credit card also gives you time to install and use the computer before you have to pay for it. Finally, if you are dissatisfied with the computer and are unable to reach an agreement with the seller, paying by credit card gives you certain rights regarding withholding payment until the dispute is resolved. Check your credit card terms for specific details.

15 Consider purchasing an extended warranty or service plan.

If you use your computer for business or require fast resolution to major computer problems, consider purchasing an extended warranty or a service plan through a local dealer or third-party company. Most extended warranties cover the repair and replacement of computer components beyond the standard warranty. Most service plans ensure that your technical support calls receive priority response from technicians. You also can purchase an on-site service plan that states that a technician will arrive at your home, work, or school within 24 hours. If your computer includes a warranty and service agreement for a year or less, consider extending the service for two or three years when you buy the computer.

How to Purchase a Notebook Computer

If you need computing capability when you travel or to use in lectures or meetings, you may find a notebook computer to be an appropriate choice. The guidelines mentioned in the previous section also apply to the purchase of a notebook computer. The following are additional considerations unique to notebook computers, including netbooks and Tablet PCs.

1 Determine which computer fits your mobile computing needs.

Before purchasing a notebook computer, you need to determine whether a traditional notebook computer, netbook, or Tablet PC will meet your needs. If you spend most of your time working on spreadsheets, writing and/or editing documents, e-mail, or using the Internet, then a traditional notebook computer will suffice. If your primary use will be to access the Internet while traveling and you are not concerned as much with processing power or hard disk capacity, consider a netbook. If you find yourself in need of a computer in class or that you spend more time in meetings than in your office, then the Tablet PC may be the answer. Before you invest money in a Tablet PC, however, determine which programs you plan to use on it. You should not buy a Tablet PC simply because it is an interesting type of computer.

② Purchase a notebook computer with a sufficiently large screen.

Active-matrix screens display high-quality color that is viewable from all angles. Less expensive, passive-matrix screens sometimes are difficult to see in low-light conditions and cannot be viewed from an angle.

Notebook computers typically include a 12.1-inch, 13.3-inch, 14.1-inch, 15.4-inch, or 17-inch display. Netbooks have screens as small as 7 inches. For most users, a 14.1-inch display is satisfactory. If you intend to use the notebook computer as a desktop computer replacement, however, you may opt for a 15.4-inch or 17-inch display. The WSXGA+ standard (1680 × 1050) is popular with 17-inch displays, so if you intend to watch HD movies on the computer, take this into consideration. Dell offers a notebook computer with a 20.1-inch display that looks like a briefcase when closed. Some notebook computers with these larger displays weigh more than 10 pounds, however, so if you travel a lot and portability is essential, you might want a lighter computer with a smaller display. The lightest notebook computers, which weigh less than 3 pounds, are equipped with a 12.1-inch display.

Regardless of size, the resolution of the display should be at least 1024 × 768 pixels. To compare the screen size on various notebook computers, including netbooks and Tablet PCs, visit the company Web sites. Tablet PCs use a digitizer below a standard 10.4-inch motion-sensitive LCD display to make the writing experience on the screen feel like writing on paper. To ensure you experience the maximum benefits from the Clear-Type technology, make sure the LCD display has a resolution of 800 × 600 in landscape mode and a 600 × 800 in portrait mode.

③ Experiment with different keyboards, pointing devices, and digital pens.

Notebook computer keyboards, especially netbook keyboards, are far less standardized than those for desktop computers. Some notebook computers, for example, have wide wrist rests, while others have none, and keyboard layouts on notebook computers often vary. Notebook computers also use a range of pointing devices, including touchpads, pointing sticks, trackballs, and, in the case of Tablet PCs, digital pens.

Before purchasing a notebook computer, try various types of keyboards and pointing devices to determine which is easiest for you to use. Regardless of the device you select, you also may want to purchase a standard mouse to use when you are working at a desk or other large surface. Figure 4 compares the standard point-and-click of a mouse with the gestures made with a digital pen. Other gestures with the digital pen replicate some of the commonly used keys on a keyboard.

Mouse and Digital Pen Operations	
Mouse	**Digital Pen**
Point	Point
Click	Tap
Double-click	Double-tap
Right-click	Tap and hold
Click and drag	Drag

Figure 4 Standard point-and-click of a mouse compared with the gestures made with a digital pen.

④ Make sure the notebook computer you purchase has an optical disc drive.

Most mobile computers include an optical disc drive. Although DVD/Blu-ray Disc drives are slightly more expensive, they allow you to play CDs, DVDs, and Blu-ray Discs using your notebook computer and hear the sound through earbuds. If you decide to purchase a netbook, it might not include an optical disc drive. Instead, you might need to purchase an external optical disc drive.

⑤ If necessary, upgrade the processor, memory, and disk storage at the time of purchase.

As with a desktop computer, upgrading a notebook computer's memory and disk storage usually is less expensive at the time of initial purchase. Some disk storage is custom designed for notebook computer manufacturers, meaning an upgrade might not be available in the future. If you are purchasing a lightweight notebook computer or Tablet PC, then it should include at least an Intel Core 2 Quad processor, 2 GB RAM, and 250 GB of storage. If you are purchasing a netbook, it should have an Intel Atom processor, at least 1 GB RAM, and 120 GB of storage.

⑥ The availability of built-in ports and slots and a USB hub on a notebook computer is important.

A notebook computer does not have much room to add adapter cards. If you know the purpose for which you plan to use the notebook computer, then you can determine the ports you will need. Netbooks typically have fewer ports than traditional notebook computers and Tablet PCs. Most notebook computers include common ports, such as a video port, audio port, network port, FireWire port, and multiple USB ports. If you plan to connect the notebook computer to a television, however, then you will need a PC to TV port. To optimize television viewing, you may want to consider DisplayPort, DVI, or HDMI ports. If you want to connect to networks at school or in various offices via a network cable, make sure the notebook computer you purchase has a network port. If the notebook computer does not contain a network port, you will have to purchase an external network card that slides into an expansion slot in your computer, as well as a network cable. You also may want to consider adding a card reader.

7 If you plan to use your notebook computer for note-taking at school or in meetings, consider a convertible Tablet PC.

Some computer manufacturers have developed convertible Tablet PCs that allow the screen to rotate 180 degrees on a central hinge and then fold down to cover the keyboard (Figure 5). You then can use a digital pen to enter text or drawings into the computer by writing on the screen. Some notebook computers have wide screens for better viewing and editing, and some even have a screen on top of the unit in addition to the regular screen. If you spend much of your time attending lectures or meetings, then the slate Tablet PC is ideal. With a slate Tablet PC, users can attach a removable keyboard.

Figure 5
A convertible Tablet PC.

8 If you purchase a Tablet PC, determine whether you require multi-touch technology.

Newer operating systems now support hardware with multi-touch technology. If you choose an operating system that supports this technology, the Tablet PC also must support this technology.

9 Purchase a notebook computer with an integrated Web cam.

If you will be using a notebook computer to connect to the Internet and chat with friends online, consider purchasing one with an integrated Web cam.

10 Check with your wireless carrier to see if it offers netbooks for sale.

Most wireless carriers now offer wireless data plans allowing you to connect to the Internet from almost anywhere with a cell phone signal. Some wireless carriers now are selling netbooks with built-in capability to connect wirelessly to the Internet using a wireless data plan.

11 Purchase a notebook computer with a built-in wireless network connection.

A wireless network connection (Bluetooth, Wi-Fi a/b/g/n, WiMAX, etc.) can be useful when you travel or as part of a home network. Increasingly more airports, hotels, schools, and cafés have wireless networks that allow you to connect to the Internet. Many users today are setting up wireless home networks. With a wireless home network, your notebook computer can access the Internet, as well as other computers in the house, from any location to share files and hardware, such as a printer, and browse the Web. Most home wireless networks allow connections from distances of 150 to 800 feet.

12 If you plan to use your notebook computer for long periods without access to an electrical outlet, purchase a second battery.

The trend among notebook computer users today is power and size over battery life. Many notebook computer users today are willing to give up longer battery life for a larger screen, faster processor, and more storage. In addition, some manufacturers typically sell the notebook computer with the lowest capacity battery. For this reason, be careful in choosing a notebook computer if you plan to use it without access to electrical outlets for long periods, such as an airplane flight. You also might want to purchase a second battery as a backup. If you anticipate running the notebook computer on batteries frequently, choose a computer that uses lithium-ion batteries, which last longer than nickel cadmium or nickel hydride batteries.

13 Purchase a well-padded and well-designed carrying case.

An amply padded carrying case will protect your notebook computer from the bumps it will receive while traveling. A well-designed carrying case will have room for accessories such as spare optical discs, pens, and paperwork (Figure 6). Although a netbook may be small enough to fit in a handbag, make sure that the bag has sufficient padding to protect the computer.

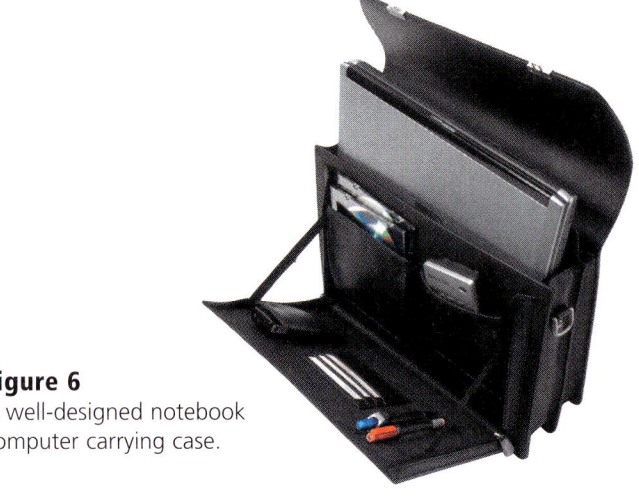

Figure 6
A well-designed notebook computer carrying case.

Buyer's Guide 2011: How to Purchase Computers and Mobile Devices

14 **If you plan to connect your notebook computer to a video projector, make sure the notebook computer is compatible with the video projector.**

You should check, for example, to be sure that your notebook computer will allow you to display an image on the computer screen and projection device at the same time. Also, ensure that the notebook computer has the ports required to connect to the video projector. You also may consider purchasing a notebook computer with a built-in Web cam for video conferencing purposes.

15 **For improved security and convenience, consider a fingerprint reader.**

More than half a million notebook computers are stolen or lost each year. If you have critical information stored on your notebook computer, consider purchasing one with a fingerprint reader (Figure 7) to protect the data if your computer is stolen or lost. Fingerprint security offers a level of protection that extends well beyond the standard password protection. If your notebook computer is stolen, the odds of recovering it improve dramatically with anti-theft tracking software. Manufacturers claim recovery rates of 90 percent or more for notebook computers using their product. For convenience, fingerprint readers also allow you to log onto several Web sites in lieu of entering user name and password information.

Figure 7 Fingerprint reader technology offers greater security than passwords.

16 **Review the docking capabilities of the Tablet PC.**

The Tablet Technology in the Windows operating system supports a grab-and-go form of docking, so that you can pick up and take a docked Tablet PC with you, just as you would pick up a notepad on your way to a meeting (Figure 8).

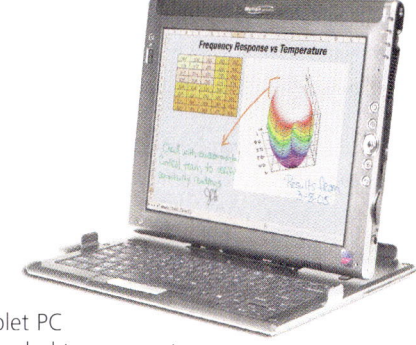

Figure 8 A Tablet PC docked to create a desktop computer with the Tablet PC as the monitor.

How to Purchase a Smart Phone

You probably will use a smart phone more often than other mobile devices. For this reason, it is important to choose a phone that is available through your preferred wireless carrier, available in your price range, and offers access to the features you will use most frequently. This section lists guidelines you should consider when purchasing a smart phone.

1 **Choose a wireless carrier and plan that satisfies your needs and budget.**

Multiple wireless carriers exist today, and each one offers a different line of smart phones. For example, the Samsung Alias is available only through Verizon Wireless. Alternatively, some smart phones, such as the BlackBerry line of smart phones, are available from multiple wireless carriers. Before deciding on a smart phone, you first should research the wireless carriers in your area, and be sure to ascertain whether the coverage is acceptable. Additionally, compare the calling plans for the various carriers and determine which one best meets your needs. Once you have determined the wireless carrier to use, you then can choose from one of their available smart phones. Once you purchase a smart phone, most carriers allow you to perform a risk-free evaluation for 30 days. If you are not satisfied with the phone or its performance, you can return the phone and pay only for the service you have used.

2 **Decide on the size, style, and weight of the smart phone that will work best for you.**

Smart phones are available in various sizes, weights, shapes, and colors. Some people prefer larger, heavier phones because they feel that they are more durable, while others prefer smaller, lightweight phones for easy portability. Some smart phones are flip phones, meaning that you have to open the phone (like a clamshell) to display the screen and keypad, some open by sliding the phone, and others do not need to be opened to use them. Figure 9 shows the various smart phone styles.

Figure 9 Various smart phone styles.

❸ **Determine whether you prefer a touch screen, keypad, or mini-keyboard.**

Modern smart phones provide various ways to enter text. During the past several years, smart phones with touch screens as their primary input device have been penetrating the market. Some smart phone users prefer touch screens because the phone does not require additional space for a keypad or mini-keyboard, but others find it more difficult to type on a touch screen. Most newer smart phones with touch screens also include handwriting recognition. Smart phones with keypads might make it easier to type for some users, but others do not like the unfamiliar feeling of keys arranged in alphabetical order. In addition, you often have to press the keys multiple times before reaching the letter you want to type. Mini-keyboards are available on some smart phones, such as the BlackBerry and Samsung Alias. Mini-keyboards provide a key for each letter, but the keys are significantly smaller than those on a standard keyboard. Most smart phone users type on mini-keyboards using their thumbs.

❹ **If you will be synchronizing your smart phone with a program on your computer, select a smart phone that is compatible with the program you wish to use.**

Programs such as Microsoft Outlook allow you to synchronize your e-mail messages, contacts, and calendar with your smart phone. If you would like this functionality, purchase a smart phone that can synchronize with Microsoft Outlook. Similarly, if your company uses a BlackBerry Enterprise server or Microsoft Exchange server, you should consider purchasing a smart phone that can synchronize, either using wires or wirelessly, with those servers.

❺ **Compare battery life.**

Any smart phone is useful only if it has the power required to run. Talking and using the Internet on your smart phone will shorten battery life more quickly than when the phone is powered on but not in use. If you have a choice, be sure to purchase a battery that will allow the phone to function all day. Pay particular attention to the talk time and standby time. If you plan to talk on the phone more than the advertised talk time, you might consider purchasing a second battery or an extended battery if your phone supports it.

❻ **Make sure your smart phone has enough memory and storage.**

If you are using the smart phone to send and receive picture, video, and e-mail messages, and to store music, purchase a memory card that not only is compatible with your computer and smart phone, but also has adequate storage space for your messages and files. If you purchase a memory card and eventually fill it, you easily can transfer the data to a larger memory card.

❼ **Check out the accessories.**

Determine which accessories you want for the smart phone. Accessories include carrying cases, screen protectors, synchronization cradles and cables, and car chargers.

How to Purchase a Portable Media Player

Portable media players are becoming the preferred device for listening to music and watching videos on the go. When choosing a portable media player, it is important to consider features and characteristics other than the physical size and amount of storage space. This section lists guidelines you should consider when purchasing a portable media player.

❶ **Choose a device with sufficient storage capacity.**

Audio and video files can consume a great deal of storage space, so be sure to purchase a portable media player that has enough capacity to store your audio and video files. You also should consider approximately how many media files you acquire each year, and make sure that your device has enough storage space to accommodate these files for years to come.

❷ **Determine which file formats your new portable media player should support and how you will add files to your library.**

Some portable media players are designed to accept new audio and video files only through a program installed on a computer. For example, it is easiest to add media files to an iPod using the iTunes program. Other portable media players connect to a computer using a cable and are displayed in Windows as a removable disk. You then can add files to the media player by dragging the files to the removable disk icon in Windows. The portable media player must support the file formats you are using. You can determine the file format by looking at the file extension on the media files you wish to transfer to your portable media player. Before purchasing a portable media player, make sure that it can support the file formats you are using.

❸ **Consider a portable media player that can play video.**

Some users prefer to watch videos on their portable media player in addition to playing music. You typically can download videos for portable media players less expensively than purchasing the movie on a DVD/Blu-ray Disc. Although the display on a portable media player is small, many still find entertainment value because they are able to watch videos and stay occupied while waiting for a bus, on an airplane, or at other locations where they otherwise might not have anything to occupy them.

4 Read reviews about the sound quality on the portable media players you are considering.

Sound quality may vary greatly among portable media players. If you are unable to try the portable media player before buying it, read reviews and make sure that those reviewing the devices find the sound quality to be acceptable. You also may consider purchasing higher-quality earbuds or headphones to enhance the sound quality.

5 Select a size and style that works best for you.

Portable media players are available in various shapes and styles. For example, Apple offers the iPod shuffle, iPod nano, iPod classic, and iPod touch (Figure 10). Each type of iPod varies in size and style, and some have capabilities (such as video) that others do not. Choose a size and style that meets your needs and fits your personality.

Figure 10 Portable media players are available in different shapes, styles, and colors.

6 Check out additional memory cards.

Most portable media players have internal storage for your media files. If you wish to increase the available storage, consider purchasing a portable media player that allows you to increase storage capacity by inserting memory cards. Similar to most computers, it is less expensive initially to purchase the largest amount of storage that you can afford, but it is helpful to be able to increase your storage at a later date.

7 Consider rechargeable batteries.

Although most portable media players include rechargeable batteries, some still use traditional alkaline batteries. Portable media players sometimes can last for only a few hours on alkaline batteries, and battery replacement can be costly. Rechargeable batteries often last longer and create less waste. If you are not near a power source, you are unable to recharge the batteries when they die. With alkaline batteries, you simply can insert new ones and continue enjoying your player.

8 Stay within your budget.

As previously mentioned, portable media players are available in a variety of shapes and sizes, and they also are available with various storage capacities. When shopping for a portable media player, be realistic when you consider how you will use the device, as well as how much storage you require. Purchasing the latest and greatest device is not always the best option, and the cost can exceed what you care to spend.

How to Purchase a Digital Camera

Both amateur and professional photographers now are mostly purchasing digital cameras to meet their photography needs. Because digital cameras with new and improved features regularly are introduced to the marketplace, consumers should know how to compare the differences among the multiple cameras that are available. This section lists guidelines you should consider when purchasing a digital camera.

1 Determine the type of digital camera that meets your needs.

Various types of digital cameras exist, including point-and-shoot cameras, field cameras, and studio cameras. Point-and-shoot cameras typically fit in your pocket and meet the needs of most general consumers. Field cameras, which often are used by photojournalists, are portable but flexible. Field cameras allow photographers to change lenses and use other attachments, and also are more customizable than point-and-shoot cameras. Studio cameras are used in photo studios and are stationary. These cameras give you the widest range of lenses and settings.

2 The digital camera with the highest resolution is not always the best.

Many consumers mistakenly believe that the digital camera with the highest resolution is the best camera for their needs. A higher resolution increases quality and clarity of your photos, as well as the size at which you can print the photos before noticing degradation in quality. If you never plan to print photos larger than 8" × 10", for example, you do not need a camera with a resolution greater than 5 megapixels. Many cameras available today advertise higher resolutions, but taking pictures at these high resolutions can use valuable storage space. Just because your camera can take a 10-megapixel photo does not mean that you always should set the resolution to 10 megapixels.

❸ Consider size and weight.

Digital cameras are available in various sizes and weights. Some people prefer smaller, lighter cameras because they are easier to transport and take up less space. Others prefer bulkier, heavier cameras because the weight helps steady them to take a clearer picture. Many digital cameras also include an image stabilization feature that reduces the possibility of a blurry picture if you move your hands slightly while taking the picture. Some also believe that heavier cameras are of better quality, although that seldom is true. When choosing a digital camera, practice taking pictures with it and select one that feels comfortable and natural.

❹ Different cameras require different memory cards.

When purchasing a digital camera, pay careful attention to the type of memory card the camera uses. Many use SD cards, some use xD Picture cards, and some use CompactFlash memory cards. Some memory cards are more expensive to replace than others, and some have a higher capacity than other cards. If you take a lot of pictures, purchase a camera that supports a memory card with a higher storage capacity so that you can avoid carrying multiple memory cards. You also might consider purchasing a camera that uses a memory card that is compatible with your other mobile devices.

❺ Photo editing features can save you time.

Some digital cameras have integrated tools that allow you to edit photos directly from the camera. For instance, you may be able to crop photos, change the brightness, or remove red eye effects. Editing photos directly on the camera after taking them can save you from editing multiple photos at once when you transfer them to a computer. The photo editing capabilities available on digital cameras are limited when compared to photo editing programs, but in many cases they can edit a photo to your satisfaction.

❻ Make sure that you can see the LCD screen easily.

LCD screens on digital cameras allow you to configure the settings, frame a shot before taking it, and preview photos after taking them. LCD screens vary by inches, so select a camera with a screen that does not require you to strain your eyes to view. This is especially important if the camera you are considering does not have a viewfinder, because you then will be required to use the display to frame your shots.

❼ Determine whether your pictures will require you to zoom.

If you plan to take pictures of people or objects that require you to zoom in, select a digital camera that has a high optical zoom. An optical zoom enlarges the subject by adjusting the camera lens, whereas a digital zoom uses algorithms built into the camera to magnify images. Optical zooms, as opposed to digital zooms, often result in a higher quality photo. While a digital zoom might be capable of magnifying objects that are 100 feet away, the photo will suffer a loss of quality.

❽ Price is important.

As with all other devices, locate a digital camera that does not exceed your budget. If you find a great camera that is available for more than you are willing to spend, consider locating a camera with a slightly lower resolution, an alternate brand, or a smaller screen. Digital cameras can last well beyond five years if properly maintained, so consider this a longer-term investment that will create memories lasting you a lifetime.

❾ Know your batteries.

Some digital cameras require replaceable alkaline or rechargeable batteries (often AA or AAA), and others have a rechargeable battery. Similar to batteries in portable media players, using disposable batteries in digital cameras can get expensive, and they may not last as long as rechargeable battery packs. Digital camera battery life is not measured in hours (as is the case with smart phones and portable media players); instead, it is measured in how many pictures can be taken on a single charge or set of batteries. Turning off the LCD screen and flash when you take pictures can help to extend battery life.

❿ Purchase accessories.

Accessories that are available for digital cameras include carrying cases, extra batteries and battery chargers, and extra memory cards (Figure 11). Carrying cases can help protect your digital camera, especially while traveling, and the extra batteries and chargers can stay inside your carrying case so that they are readily available should you need them. Screen protectors can help protect the LCD screen on your digital camera.

Figure 11 Digital camera accessories include memory cards, cases, batteries, and battery chargers.

Multiple Web sites on the Internet allow you to purchase computers and mobile devices. For a list of Web sites that sell computers and mobile devices, visit scsite.com/dc-off07/ch5/buyers.

Quiz Yourself Answers

Following are possible answers to the Quiz Yourself boxes in Chapters 1 through 5 of this book.

Quiz Yourself 1-1
1. A computer is ~~a motorized~~an electronic device that processes ~~output~~input into ~~input~~output.
2. A storage device records (~~reads~~writes) and/or retrieves (~~writes~~reads) items to and from storage media.
3. An ~~output~~input device is any hardware component that allows you to enter data and instructions in a computer.
4. True Statement
5. Three commonly used ~~input~~output devices are a printer, a monitor, and speakers.

Quiz Yourself 1-2
1. A ~~resource~~network is a collection of computers and devices connected together via communications devices and transmission media.
2. True Statement
3. Popular ~~system~~application software includes Web browsers, word processing software, spreadsheet software, database software, and presentation software.
4. The ~~Internet~~Web is one of the more popular services on the ~~Web~~Internet.
5. Two types of ~~application~~system software are the operating system and utility programs.

Quiz Yourself 1-3
1. A ~~desktop computer~~notebook computer (or laptop computer) is a portable, personal computer designed to fit on your lap.
2. True Statement
3. Each ~~enterprise~~home user spends time on the computer for different reasons that include personal financial management, Web access, communications, and entertainment.
4. A ~~home~~power user requires the capabilities of a workstation or other powerful computer.
5. ~~Mainframes~~Supercomputers are the fastest, most powerful computers — and the most expensive.
6. With ~~embedded computers~~online banking, users access account balances, pay bills, and copy monthly transactions from the bank's computer right into their personal computers.

Quiz Yourself 2-1
1. True Statement
2. ~~A wireless Internet service provider~~An IP address (or Internet Protocol address) is a number that uniquely identifies each computer or device connected to the Internet.
3. ~~An IP address~~A domain name, such as www.google.com, is the text version of ~~a domain name~~an IP address.
4. ~~Satellite~~Cable Internet service provides high-speed Internet access through the cable television network via a cable modem.

Quiz Yourself 2-2
1. True Statement
2. A ~~Web browser~~subject directory classifies Web pages in an organized set of categories and related subcategories.
3. ~~Business~~Consumer-to-consumer e-commerce occurs when one consumer sells directly to another, such as in an online auction.
4. The more widely used ~~search engines~~Web browsers for personal computers are Internet Explorer, Firefox, Opera, Safari, and Google Chrome.
5. To develop a Web page, you do not have to be a computer programmer.

Quiz Yourself 2-3

1. True Statement
2. An e-mail address is a combination of a user name and ~~an e-mail program~~a domain name that identifies a user so that he or she can receive Internet e-mail.
3. ~~FTP~~Internet telephony uses the Internet (instead of the public switched telephone network) to connect a calling party to one or more called parties.
4. Netiquette is the code of ~~un~~acceptable behaviors while on the Internet.
5. VoIP enables users to ~~subscribe~~speak to other users over the Internet.

Quiz Yourself 3-1

1. True Statement
2. ~~Public-domain~~Packaged software is mass produced, copyrighted retail software that meets the needs of a wide variety of users, not just a single user or company.
3. To use ~~system~~application software, your computer must be running ~~application~~system software.
4. When a program is started, its instructions load from ~~memory~~a storage medium into ~~a storage medium~~memory.

Quiz Yourself 3-2

1. ~~Enterprise computing~~Image editing software provides the capabilities of paint software and also includes the ability to modify existing images.
2. Millions of people use ~~spreadsheet~~word processing software every day to develop documents such as letters, memos, reports, mailing labels, newsletters, and Web pages.
3. Professional ~~accounting~~DTP (or desktop publishing) software is ideal for the production of high-quality color documents such as textbooks, corporate newsletters, marketing literature, product catalogs, and annual reports.
4. ~~Database~~Presentation software is application software that allows users to create visual aids for presentations to communicate ideas, messages, and other information to a group.
5. Popular ~~CAD programs~~software suites include Microsoft Office, Apple iWork, Corel WordPerfect Office, and Google Docs.
6. True Statement

Quiz Yourself 3-3

1. ~~All~~Some Web application hosts provide free access to their software.
2. ~~Computer~~Web-based training is a type of ~~Web~~computer-based training that uses Internet technology and consists of application software on the Web.
3. True Statement
4. ~~Legal~~Personal finance software is a simplified accounting program that helps home users and small office/home office users balance their checkbooks, pay bills, track investments, and evaluate financial plans.
5. ~~Personal DTP~~Photo editing software is a popular type of image editing software that allows users to edit digital photos.

Quiz Yourself 4-1

1. A ~~buffer~~driver is a small program that tells the operating system how to communicate with a specific device.
2. True Statement
3. A password is a ~~public~~private combination of characters associated with the user name that allows access to certain computer resources.
4. The program you currently are using is in the ~~background~~foreground, and the other programs running but not in use are in the ~~foreground~~background.
5. Two types of system software are operating systems and ~~application~~utility programs.

Quiz Yourself 4-2
1. ~~BlackBerry~~Palm OS devices use Palm OS as their operating system.
2. Examples of ~~embedded~~server operating systems include Windows Server 2008, UNIX, Linux, Solaris, and NetWare.
3. Windows 7 Starter uses Windows ~~Aero~~Vista Basic.
4. True Statement
5. ~~Aero Flip 3D~~Linux is a UNIX-type operating system that is open source software.

Quiz Yourself 4-3
1. A ~~pop-up blocker~~file compression utility shrinks the size of a file(s).
2. An ~~anti-spam~~antivirus program protects a computer against viruses.
3. True Statement
4. You should ~~uninstall~~back up files and disks regularly in the event your originals are lost, damaged, or destroyed.
5. ~~Web filtering~~CD/DVD burning software writes text, graphics, audio, and video files to a recordable or rewritable disc.

Quiz Yourself 5-1
1. A ~~back door~~denial of service attack is an assault whose purpose is to disrupt computer access to an Internet service such as the Web or e-mail.
2. True Statement
3. Computer viruses, worms, Trojan horses, and rootkits are malware that acts with~~out~~ a user's knowledge.
4. ~~Shorter~~Longer passwords provide greater security than ~~longer~~shorter ones.
5. Updating an antivirus program's ~~quarantine~~signature file protects a computer against viruses written since the antivirus program was released.

Quiz Yourself 5-2
1. An end-user license agreement (EULA) ~~permits~~does not permit users to give copies to friends and colleagues, while continuing to use the software.
2. Encryption is a process of converting ~~ciphertext~~plaintext into ~~plaintext~~ciphertext to prevent unauthorized access.
3. Mobile users are ~~not~~ susceptible to hardware theft.
4. True Statement
5. To prevent against data loss caused by a system failure, computer users should ~~restore~~back up files regularly.

Quiz Yourself 5-3
1. Factors that cause ~~CVS~~tendonitis and CTS (carpal tunnel syndrome) include prolonged typing, prolonged mouse usage, or continual shifting between the mouse and the keyboard.
2. ~~Phishing~~Digital forensics is the discovery, collection, and analysis of evidence found on computers and networks.
3. True Statement
4. You can not assume that information on the Web is correct.

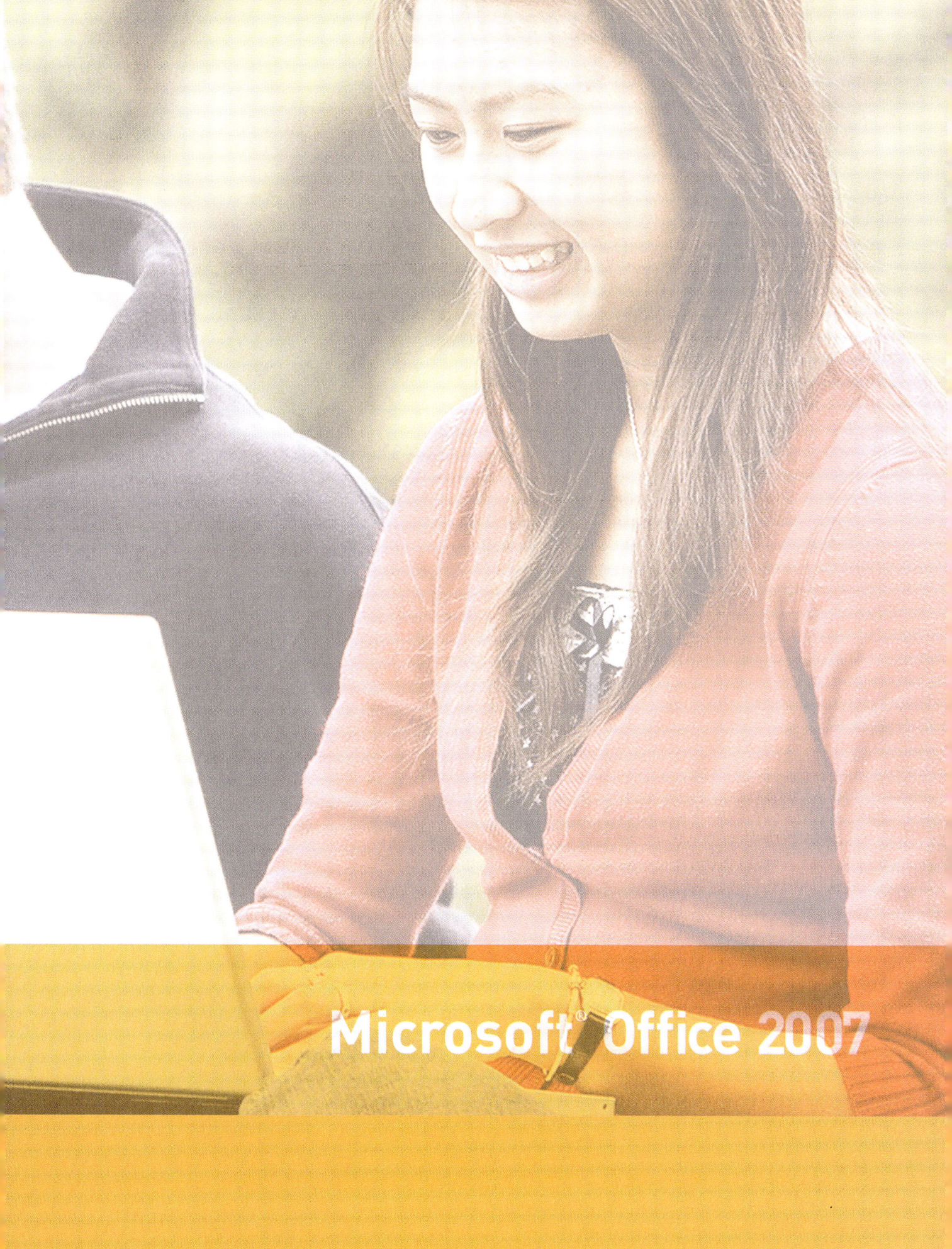

Microsoft **Windows Vista 2007**

Introduction to Windows Vista

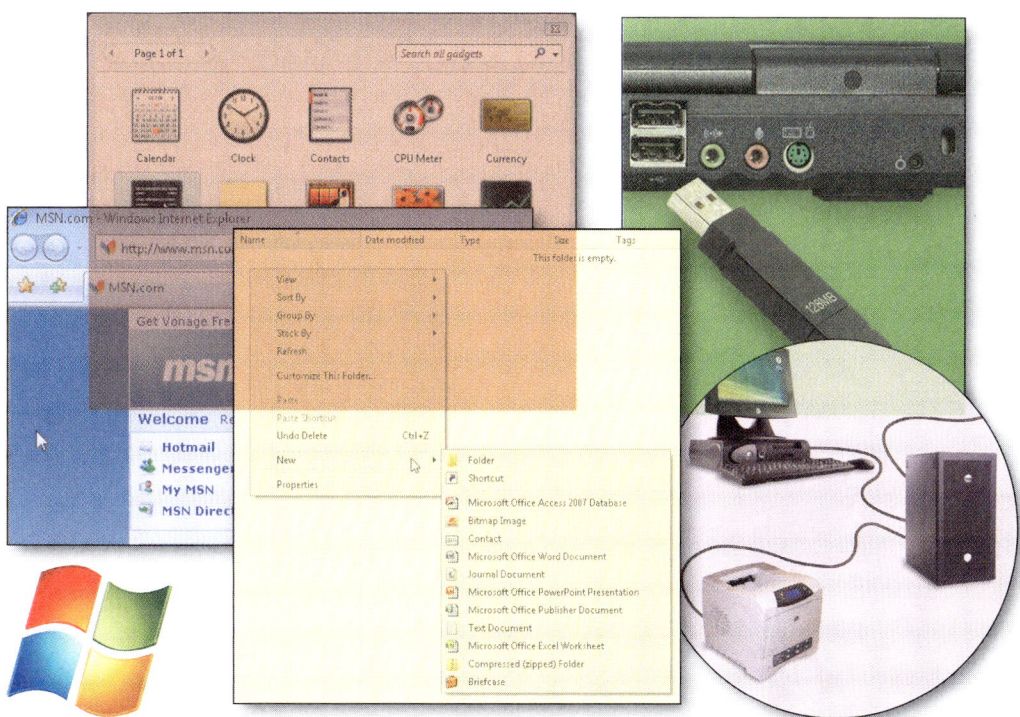

Objectives

You will have mastered the material in this chapter when you can:

- Start Windows Vista, log on the computer, and identify the objects on the desktop
- Customize the Windows Sidebar with Gadgets
- Perform basic mouse operations
- Display the Start menu and start a program
- Open, minimize, maximize, restore, move, size, scroll, and close a window
- Display drive and folder contents

- Create a folder in Folder Windows and WordPad
- Browse the Web using Windows Internet Explorer 7.0, a Web address, and tabbed browsing
- Download folders from scsite.com
- Copy, move, rename, and delete files
- Search for files using a word or phrase in the file or by name
- Use Windows Help and Support
- Log off the computer and turn it off

Microsoft Office **Windows Vista 2007**

Introduction to Windows Vista

What Is an Operating System?

An **operating system** is the set of computer instructions, called a computer program, that controls the allocation of computer hardware such as memory, hard disks, printers, and optical disc drives, and provides the capability for you to communicate with the computer. The most popular and widely used operating system is **Microsoft Windows**. **Microsoft Windows Vista** is a recent version of Microsoft Windows. Windows Vista allows you to communicate with and control the computer.

Project Planning Guidelines

> Working with an operating system requires a basic knowledge of how to start the operating system, log on and log off the computer, and identify the objects on the Windows Vista desktop. As a starting point, you must be familiar with the Start menu and its commands, and be able to start a program. You should be able to personalize the operating system to allow you to work more efficiently. You will want to know how to manipulate windows as well as create a folder, display folder contents, recognize a disk drive, and download information from the Internet. You should be able to copy, move, rename, delete, and search for files. If you encounter a problem, Windows Help and Support is available to answer any questions you may have.

Overview

As you read through this chapter, you will learn how to use the Windows Vista operating system by performing these general tasks:

- Start the Windows Vista operating system.
- Log on the computer.
- Perform basic mouse operations.
- Add and remove a gadget on the Windows Sidebar.
- Display the Start menu and start a program.
- Add and delete icons on the desktop.
- Open, minimize, maximize, restore, move, size, scroll, and close a window.
- Display drive and folder contents.
- Create folders and download folders from the Internet.
- Copy, move, rename, delete, and search for files.
- Use Help and Support.
- Log off and turn off the computer.

What Is a User Interface?

A **user interface** is the combination of hardware and software that you use to communicate with and control the computer. Through the user interface, you are able to make selections on the computer, request information from the computer, and respond to messages displayed by the computer.

Hardware and software together form the user interface. Among the hardware devices associated with a user interface are the monitor, keyboard, and mouse (Figure 1). The **monitor** displays messages and provides information. You respond by entering data in the form of a command or other response using an input device such as a **keyboard** or **mouse**.

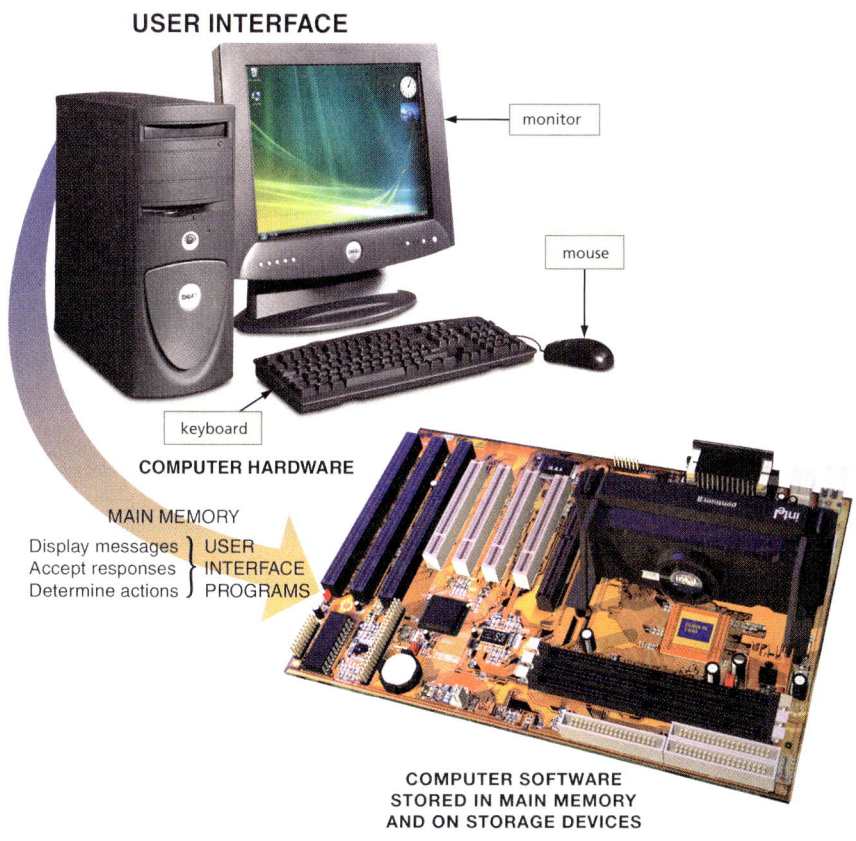

Figure 1

The computer software associated with the user interface consists of the programs that engage you in dialogue. The computer software determines the messages you receive, the manner in which you should respond, and the actions that occur based on your responses.

The goal of an effective user interface is to be **user-friendly**, which means the software can be used easily by individuals with limited training. A **graphical user interface**, or **GUI** (pronounced gooey), is a user interface that displays graphics in addition to text when it communicates with the user.

To communicate with the operating system, you can use a mouse. A mouse is a pointing device used with Windows Vista that may be attached to the computer by a cable or may be wireless.

Many common tasks, such as logging on to the computer or logging off, are performed by pointing to an item and then clicking the item. **Point** means you move the mouse across a flat surface until the mouse pointer on the monitor rests on the item of choice. As you move the mouse across a flat surface, the optical sensor on the underside of the mouse senses the movement of the mouse, and the mouse pointer moves across the computer desktop in the same direction. In Office 2007, you can point to buttons on the Ribbon in a window and observe a live preview of the effect of selecting that button.

Click means you press and release the primary mouse button, which in most cases is the left mouse button. In most cases, you must point to an item before you click it.

Windows Vista

The Windows Vista operating system simplifies the process of working with documents and programs by transferring data between documents, organizing the manner in which you interact with the computer, and using the computer to access information on the Internet or an intranet. Windows Vista is used to run **application software**, which consists of programs designed to make users more productive and/or assist them with personal tasks, such as word processing.

In business, Windows Vista is commonly used on stand-alone computers, client computers, and mobile computers. A stand-alone computer is not part of a computer network, and has access only to software that is installed on it, and hardware directly connected to it. A **client** is a computer connected to a server. A **server** is a computer that controls access to the hardware and software on a network and provides a centralized storage area for programs, data, and information. Mobile computers, often referred to as notebook computers or laptop computers, can be used either as stand-alone computers or clients. Figure 2 illustrates a simple computer network consisting of a server, three client computers, and a laser printer connected to the server.

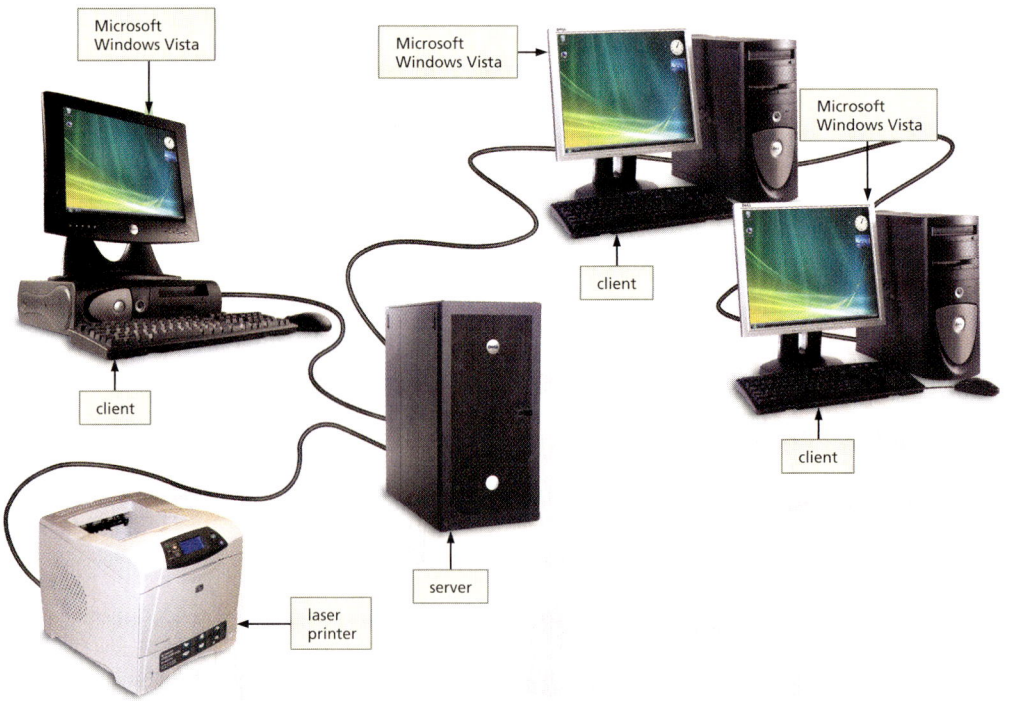

Figure 2

Windows Vista Operating System Editions

The Windows Vista operating system is available in five editions: Windows Vista Home Basic, Windows Vista Home Premium, Windows Vista Business, Windows Vista Ultimate, and Windows Vista Enterprise. Windows Vista Ultimate (called **Windows Vista** for the rest of the chapter) is an operating system that performs every function necessary for you to communicate with and use the computer. The five editions of Windows Vista are described in Table 1.

Table 1 Windows Vista Editions

Edition	Description
Windows Vista Home Basic	This edition is easy to set up and maintain, provides security and parental controls, allows access to e-mail, simplifies searching for pictures and music, and allows the creation of simple documents.
Windows Vista Home Premium Edition	This edition is designed for individuals who have a home desktop or mobile computer. The built-in Windows Media Center allows you to watch and record television, play video games, listen to music, and burn and play optical discs.
Windows Vista Business Edition	This edition is the first operating system designed specifically for the needs of small and midsized businesses. Features include keeping personal computers up-to-date and running smoothly, as well as powerful ways to find, organize, and share information on the road or in the office. Additional features include Windows Tablet PC capability, PC-to-PC synchronization, Domain Join, Group Policy support, and Encrypting File System.
Windows Vista Ultimate Edition	This edition, the most complete edition of the five, contains the most advanced capabilities and is the choice of individuals who want the power, security, and mobility needed for work and the entertainment features desired for fun. The edition includes support for Windows Tablet and Touch Technology, Windows SideShow, Windows Mobility Center, Windows DreamScene, and Windows BitLocker Secure Online Key storage.
Windows Vista Enterprise	This edition was designed to help global organizations and enterprises with complex IT infrastructures to lower IT costs, reduce risk, and stay connected. This edition is available only to Volume License customers who have personal computers covered by Microsoft Software Assurance. Windows BitLocker Drive Encryption is used to help prevent sensitive data and intellectual property from being lost or stolen.

Windows Vista Basic Interface and Windows Aero

Windows Vista offers two different GUIs, depending on your hardware configuration. Computers with up to 1 GB of RAM work with the Windows Vista Basic interface (Figure 3a). Computers with more than 1 GB of RAM can work also with the Windows Aero interface (Figure 3b), which provides an enhanced visual experience designed for Windows Vista, including additional navigation options, and animation. Windows Aero features a transparent glass design with subtle window animations and new window colors. The Windows Vista Business, Windows Vista Enterprise, Windows Vista Home Premium, and Windows Vista Ultimate editions have the ability to use Windows Aero. In this chapter, all figures were created on a computer using the Windows Vista Basic interface.

Figure 3

Starting Windows Vista

It is not an unusual occurrence for multiple people to use the same computer in a work, educational, recreational, or home setting. Windows Vista uses User Accounts to organize the resources that are made available to a person when they use the computer. A **user account** identifies to Windows Vista which resources a person can use when using the computer. Associated with a user account is a **user name**, which identifies the person to Windows Vista, and a **password**, a string of letters, numbers, and special characters, which is used to restrict access to a user account's resources to only those who know the password. In Windows Vista, you can choose a picture to associated with your user name as well.

In a work or school environment your user name and password may be set up for you automatically. Usually, you are given the option to reset the password to something that only you know. A good password is important for ensuring the security and privacy of your work. When you turn on the computer, an introductory black screen consisting of a progress bar and copyright message (© Microsoft Corporation) are displayed. After a short time, the Windows Vista logo and Welcome screen are displayed on the desktop (Figure 4).

> **Plan Ahead**
>
> **Determine a user name and password.**
> Before logging on the computer, you must have a unique user name and password.
>
> 1. Choose a user name that is unique and inoffensive. Your user name may be set automatically for you in a work or educational setting.
>
> 2. Choose a password that no one could guess. Do not use any part of your first or last name, your spouse's or child's name, telephone number, street address, license plate number, Social Security number, and so on.
>
> 3. Be sure your password is at least six characters long, mixed with letters and numbers.
>
> 4. Protect your password. Change your password frequently and do not disclose it to anyone or write it on a slip of paper kept near the computer. E-mail and telemarketing scams often ask you to disclose a password, so be wary if you did not initiate the inquiry or telephone call.

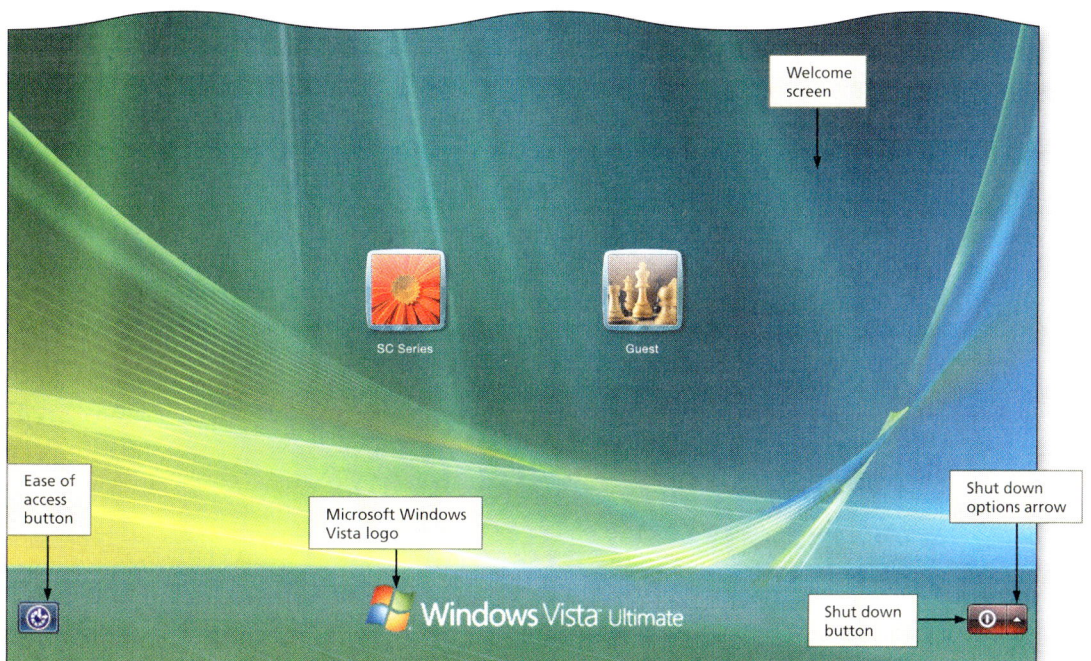

Figure 4

The **Welcome screen** shows the user names of every computer user on the computer. Clicking the user name or picture begins the process of logging on the computer. The list of user names on your computer will be different.

At the bottom of the Welcome screen is the Ease of access button, Windows Vista logo, and a Shut down button. Clicking the **Ease of access button** displays the Ease of Access Center. The Ease of Access Center provides access to tools you can use to optimize your computer to accomodate the needs of the mobility, hearing, and vision impaired. To the right of the Ease of access button is the Windows Vista logo. Located in the lower corner of the Welcome screen is the **Shut down button**. Clicking this button shuts down Windows Vista and the computer. To the right of the Shut down button is the **Shut down options arrow**, which provides access to a menu containing three commands: Restart, Sleep, and Shut Down.

The **Restart command** closes open programs, shuts down Windows Vista, and then restarts Windows Vista, and displays the Welcome screen. The **Sleep command** waits for Windows Vista to save your work and then turns off the fans and hard disk. To wake the computer from the Sleep state, press the Power button or lift the notebook computer cover, and log on the computer. The **Shut Down command** shuts down and turns off the computer.

Logging On the Computer

After starting Windows Vista, you must log on the computer. **Logging on** the computer opens your user account and makes the computer available for use.

If you are using a computer to step through the project in this chapter and you want your screen to match the figures in this book, you should change your screen's resolution to 1024 × 768. For information about how to change a computer's resolution, read Appendix C.

To Log On the Computer

The following steps log on the computer. In this chapter, the user name SC Series is used in the figures.

1
- Click your user name on the Welcome screen to display the password text box.

Q&A What is a text box?
A text box is a rectangular area in which you can enter text.

- Type your password in the password text box as shown in Figure 5.

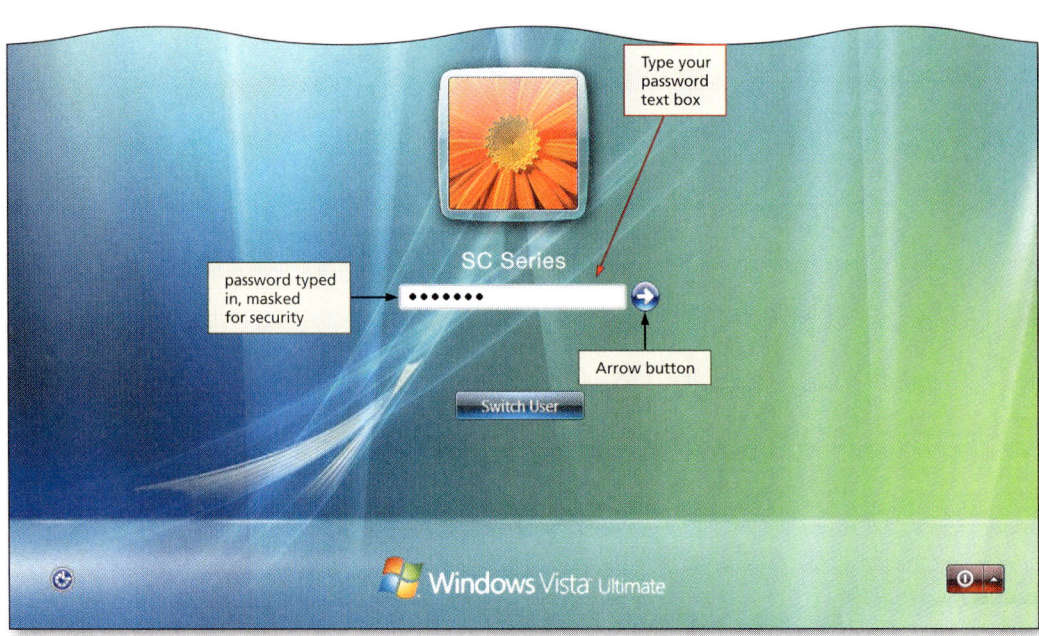

Figure 5

- Click the arrow button to log on the computer and open the Welcome Center window and Windows Sidebar on the Windows Vista desktop (Figure 6).

Q&A What is displayed on the desktop when I log on the computer?

The Recycle Bin icon, Welcome Center window, Windows Sidebar, and taskbar are displayed on the desktop.

Q&A What if the Computer displays a different desktop design?

Windows Vista offers many standard desktop backgrounds, so any background is fine. The background design shown in Figure 6 is called img24.

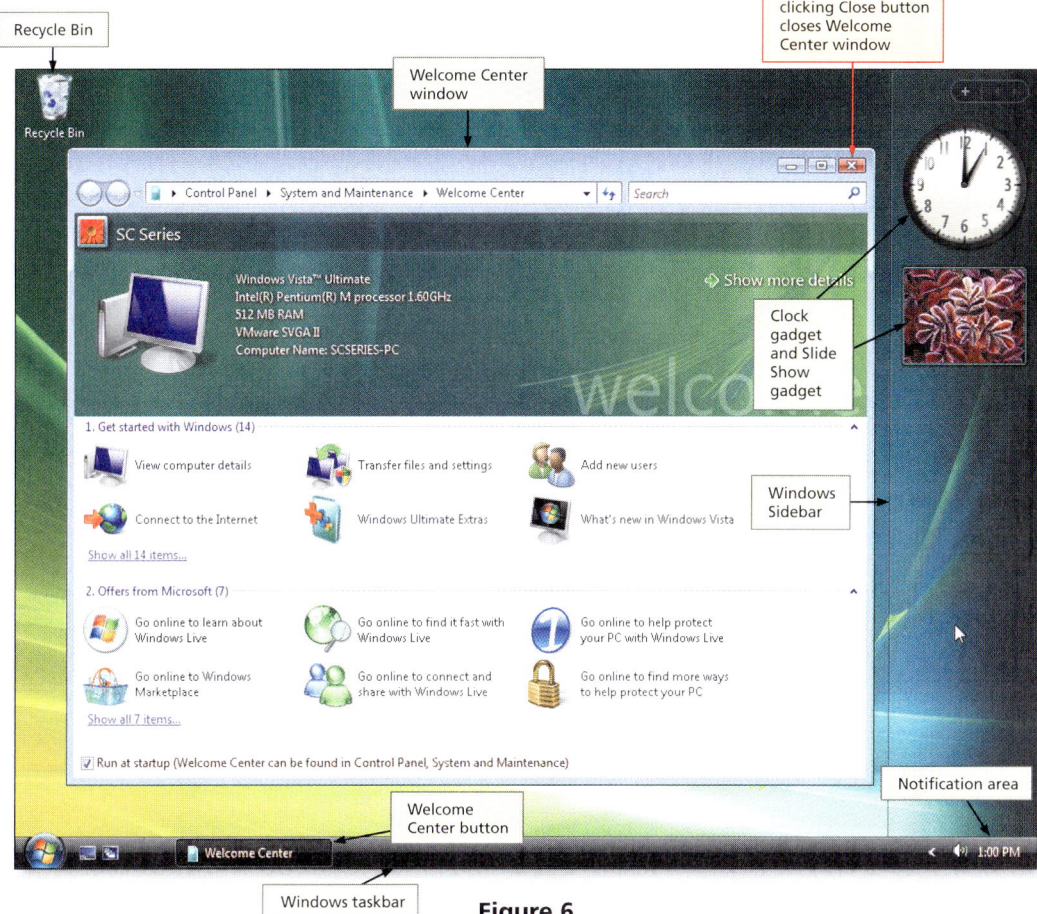

Figure 6

The Windows Vista Desktop

The Windows Vista desktop is similar to a real physical desktop. It is the main work area when you are using Windows Vista. When you start a program, it appears on the desktop. Some items are on the desktop by default. For instance, the **Recycle Bin**, the location of files that have been deleted, sits on the desktop by default. You can customize your desktop so that programs and files you use often are out on your desktop and easily accessible.

Also on the Windows Vista desktop is the Windows Sidebar. The **Windows Sidebar** is a long, vertical strip on the right edge of the desktop that holds mini-programs called gadgets (Figure 6). A **gadget** is a mini-program that provides continuously updated information, such as current weather information, news updates, traffic information, and Internet radio streams. You can customize your Sidebar to hold gadgets that you choose.

Across the bottom of the Windows Vista desktop is the Windows taskbar (Figure 6). The Windows taskbar contains the Start button, which you use to access programs, files, folders, and settings on your computer. It also shows you which programs currently are running on your computer, by displaying a button per program.

In addition, the Windows Vista desktop may contain the Welcome Center window. The **Welcome Center** window opens when the computer is used for the first time and allows you to complete a set of tasks to optimize the computer. The tasks may include adding user accounts, transferring files and settings from another computer, and connecting to the Internet.

To Close the Welcome Center Window

The Welcome Center window opens when you start Windows Vista for the first time, and subsequently unless you turn it off. If the Welcome Center window is open, you can close it prior to beginning any other operations using Windows Vista. This provides you with a clear desktop with which to work. The following step closes the Welcome Center window.

- Click the Close button in the top right corner of the Welcome Center window to close the Welcome Center window (Figure 7).

Q&A Are there other ways to access the Welcome Center if it does not open at startup?

Yes. The Welcome Center features are available in the Control Panel under System and Maintenance.

Figure 7

To Add a Gadget to the Windows Sidebar

When you start Windows Vista, some gadgets are attached to the Windows Sidebar. Many additional gadgets can be added according to personal preference. Gadgets can be found in the **Gadget Gallery**, which is a collection of gadgets. Before you can use gadgets, they must be added to the Windows Sidebar. One method to add a gadget to the Windows Sidebar is to double-click the gadget in the Gadget Gallery. **Double-click** means you quickly press and release the left mouse button twice without moving the mouse. The following steps open the Gadget Gallery and add a gadget to the Windows Sidebar.

1
- Click the Add Gadgets button to open the Gadget Gallery on the desktop (Figure 8).

Q&A Where can I find additional gadgets?

You can find more gadgets on the www.microsoft.com Web site by searching for the text, sidebar gadgets.

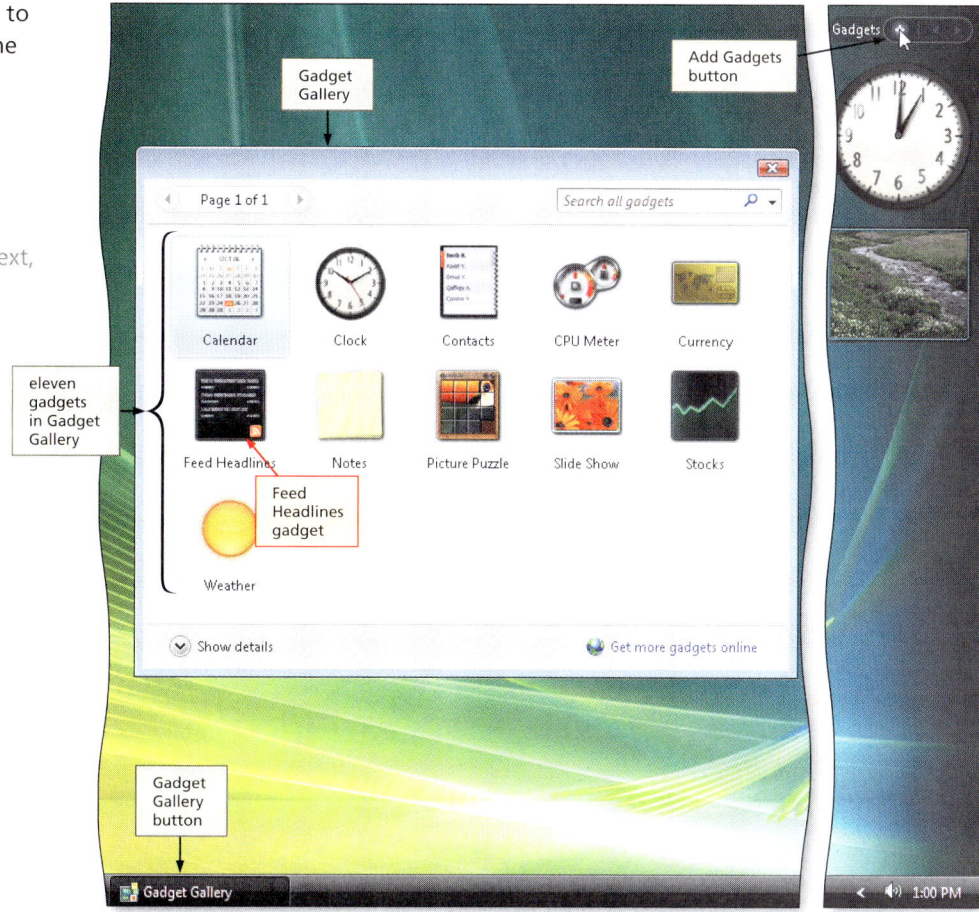

Figure 8

2
- Double-click the Feed Headlines gadget in the Gadget Gallery to add the gadget to the top of the Windows Sidebar and display frequently updated headlines (Figure 9).

3
- Click the Close button to close the Gadget Gallery.

Q&A Can I customize the Windows Sidebar?

Yes. You can select which gadgets you want to add or remove, add multiple instances of a particular gadget, and detach one or more gadgets from the Sidebar and place them on the desktop.

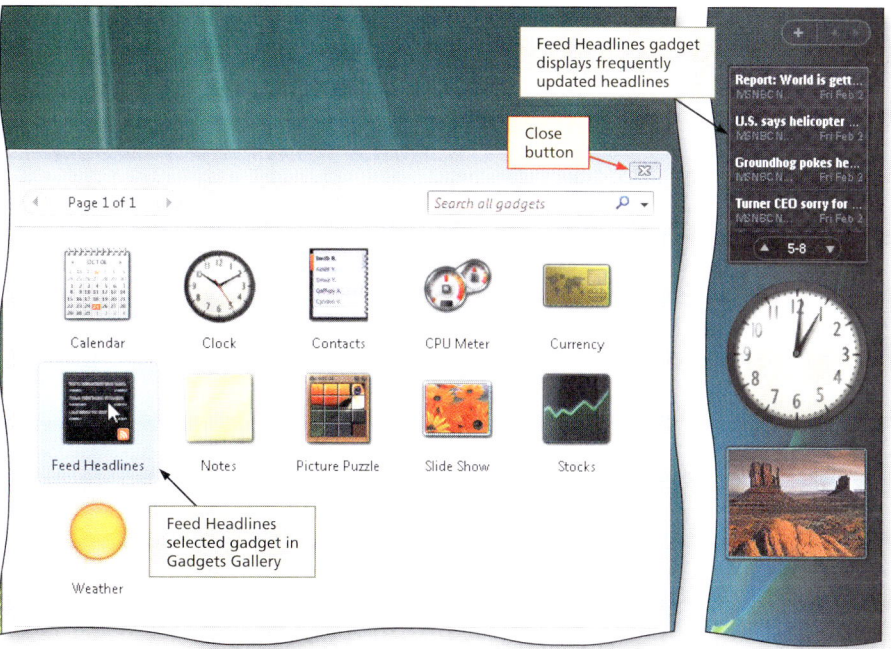

Figure 9

To Remove a Gadget from the Windows Sidebar

In addition to adding gadgets to the Windows Sidebar, you may want to customize the desktop by removing one or more gadgets from the Sidebar. The following step removes a gadget from the Windows Sidebar.

- Point to the Feed Headlines gadget to make the Close button visible (Figure 10).

- Click the Close button to remove the Feed Headlines gadget from the Windows Sidebar.

Figure 10

Other Ways
1. Right-click gadget, click Close Gadget

To Display the Start Menu

A **menu** is a list of related items, including folders, programs, and commands. Each **command** on a menu performs a specific action, such as searching for files or obtaining Help. The **Start menu** allows you to access programs and files on the computer and contains commands that allow you to connect to and browse the Internet, start an e-mail program, start programs, store and search for documents, customize the computer, and obtain Help on thousands of topics. The Start menu contains the All Programs command, Search box, and right pane. The following steps display the Start menu, the All Programs list, and then the Accessories list.

1

- Click the Start button on the Windows Vista taskbar to display the Start menu (Figure 11).

Q&A What are the various sections on the Start menu?

The left pane contains the pinned items list, frequently used programs list, All Programs command, and the Search box. The right pane contains the computer user name and illustration, list of links, Power button, Lock this computer button, and Lock menu arrow.

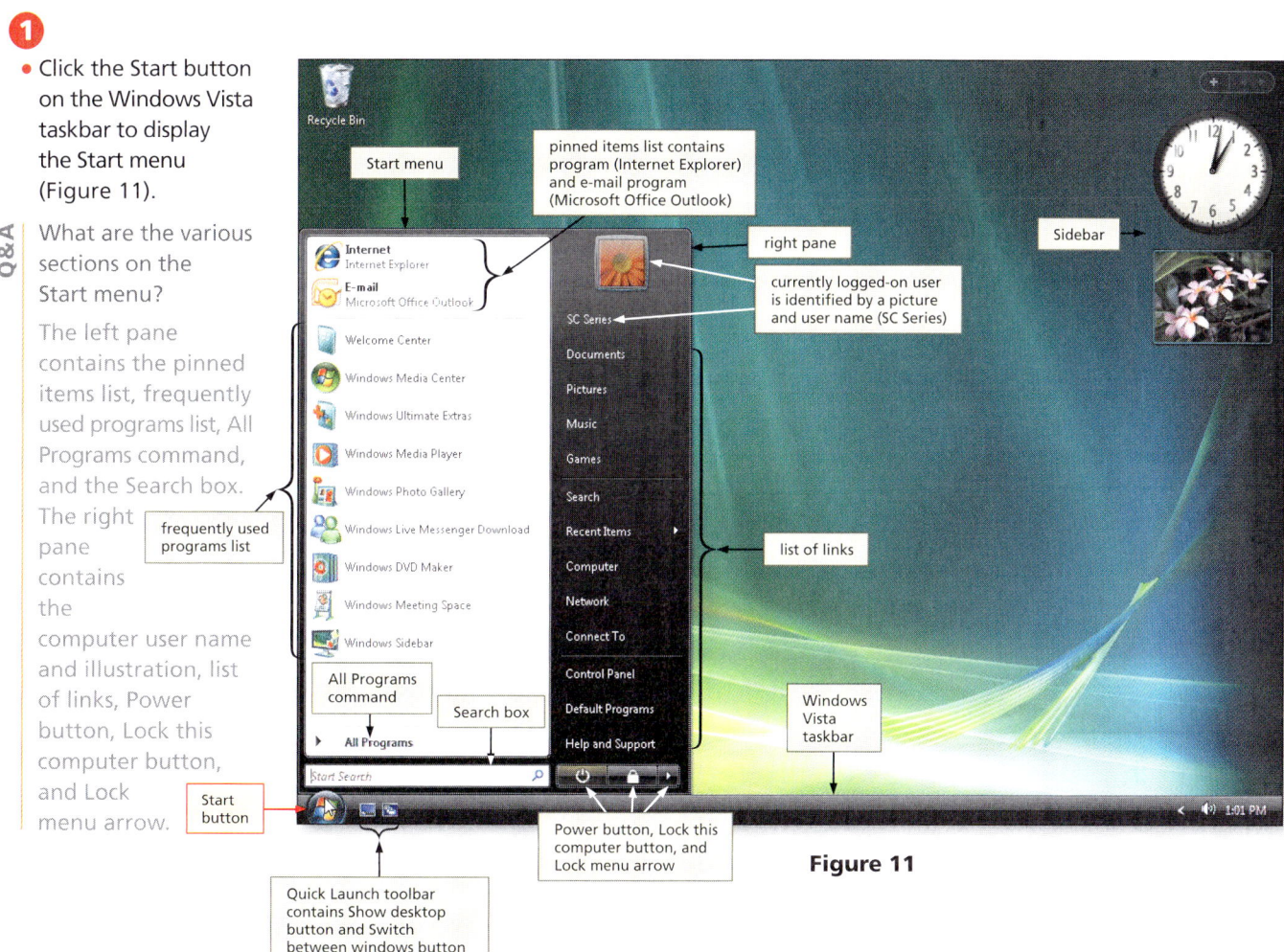

Figure 11

2

- Point to All Programs at the bottom of the left pane on the Start menu to display the All Programs list (Figure 12).

Q&A What happens when you point to All Programs on the Start menu?

The All Programs list is displayed and the Back button appears at the bottom of the All Programs list.

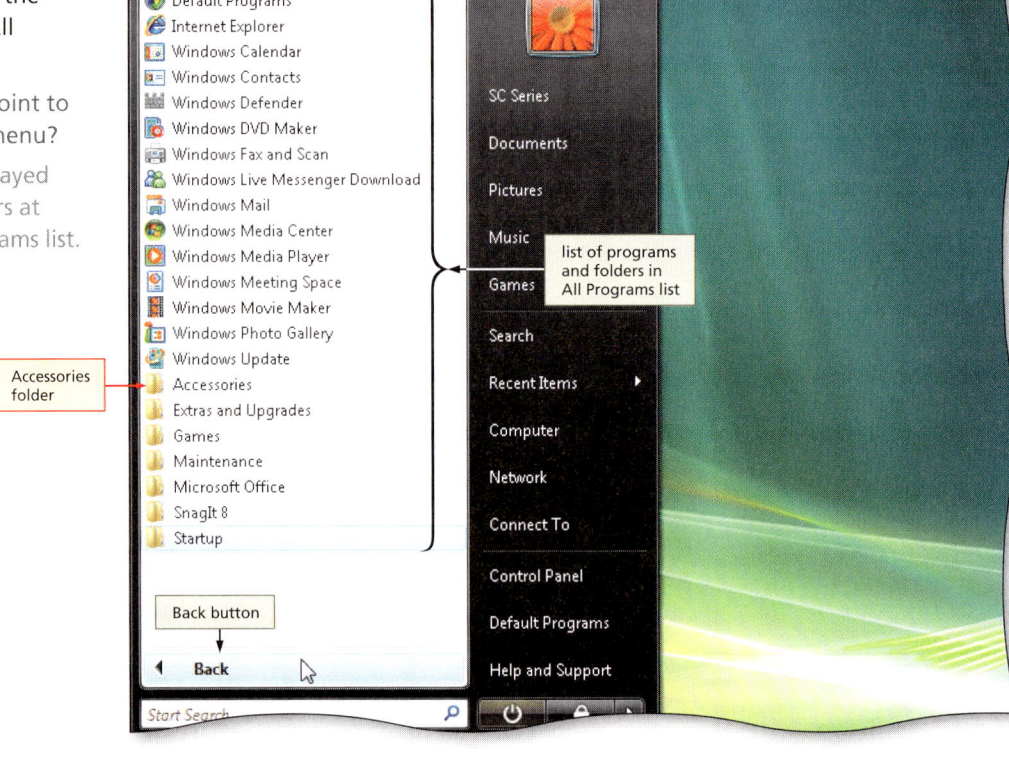

Figure 12

3

- Click Accessories to expand the list of programs and folders in the Accessories folder (Figure 13).

Q&A What are Accessories?

Accessories are programs that accomplish a variety of tasks commonly required on a computer. For example, the Accessories programs include Calculator, Notepad, Paint, and other programs.

Figure 13

To Scroll Using Scroll Arrows, the Scroll Bar, and the Scroll Box

A **scroll bar** is a bar that displays when the contents of an area may not be completely visible. A vertical scroll bar contains an **up scroll arrow**, a **down scroll arrow**, and a **scroll box** that enables you to view areas that currently are not visible. In Figure 14, a vertical scroll bar displays along the right side of the All Programs list. Scrolling can be accomplished in three ways: (1) click the scroll arrows; (2) click the scroll bar; and (3) drag the scroll box. **Drag** means you point to an item, hold down the left mouse button, move the item to the desired location, and then release the left mouse button. The following steps scroll the items in the All Programs list.

- Click the down scroll arrow on the vertical scroll bar to display additional folders at the bottom of the All Programs list (Figure 14). You may need to click more than once to show the bottom of the All Programs list.

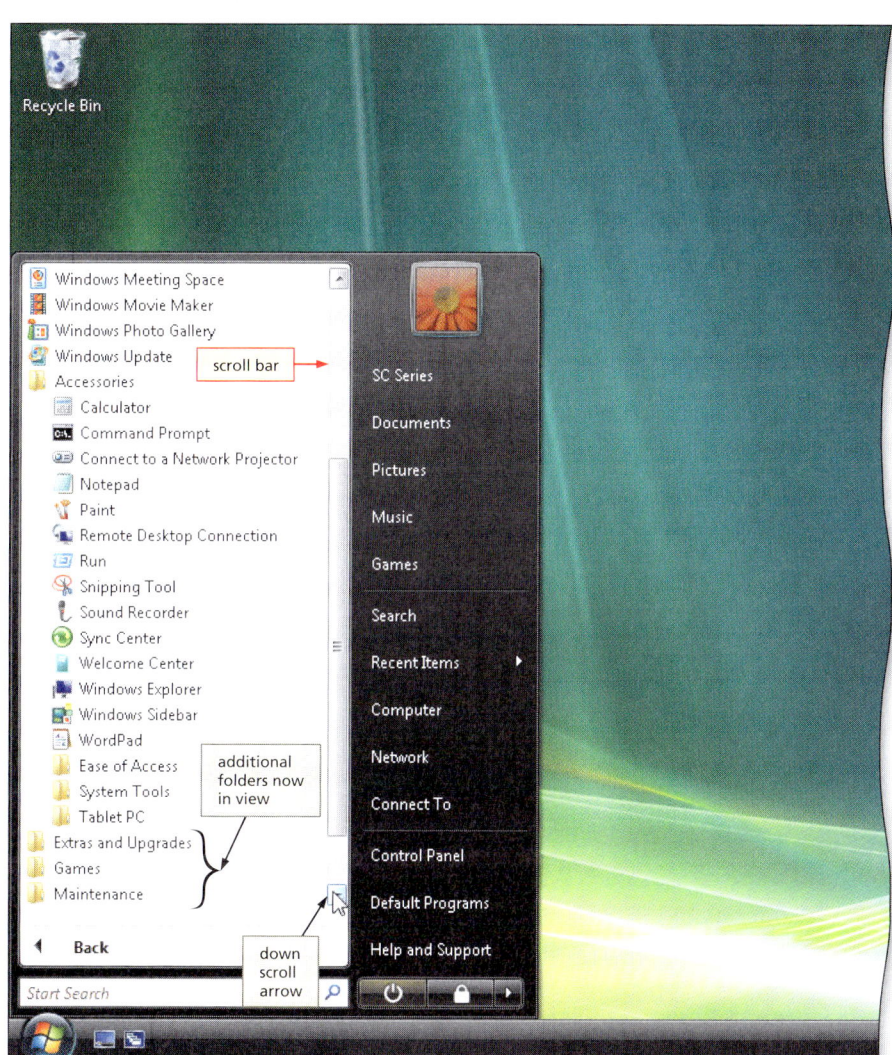

Figure 14

- Click the scroll bar above the scroll box to move the scroll box to the top of the scroll bar and display the top of the All Programs list (Figure 15).

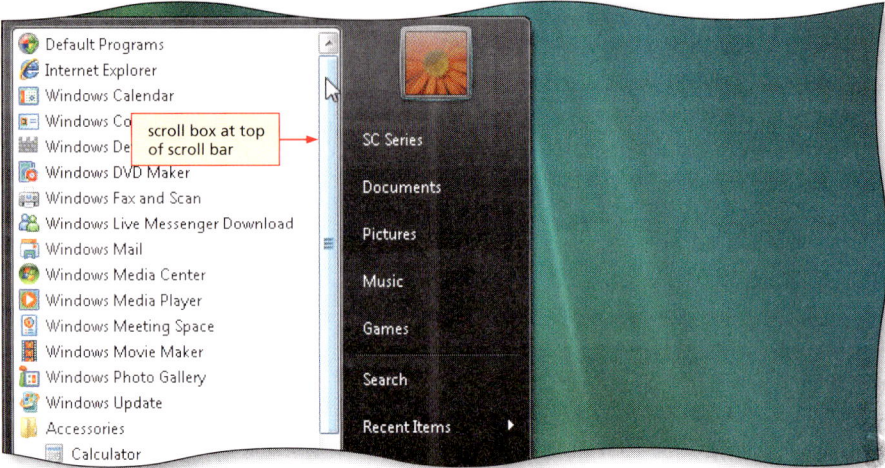

Figure 15

- Drag the scroll box down the scroll bar until the scroll box is about halfway down the scroll bar (Figure 16).

- Click an open area on the desktop to close the Start menu.

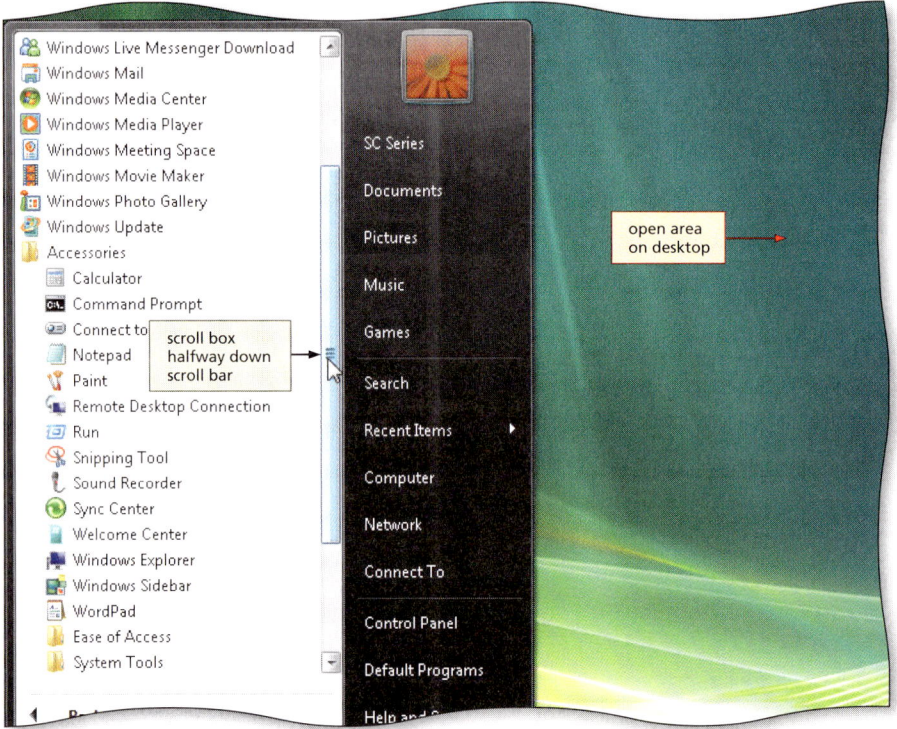

Figure 16

To Add an Icon to the Desktop

In addition to gadgets, you may want to add icons to the desktop. An **icon** is a picture that represents a file, folder, object, or program. For example, you may want to add the Computer icon to the desktop so you can view the contents of the computer folder without having to use the Start menu. The following steps add the Computer icon to the desktop.

Introduction to Windows Vista **Windows Vista Chapter** WIN 17

1

- Click the Start button to display the Start menu.

- Right-click Computer in the right pane to select the Computer link and display a shortcut menu (Figure 17).

Q&A What is a shortcut menu?

A shortcut menu appears when you right-click an object and includes commands specifically for use with the object clicked.

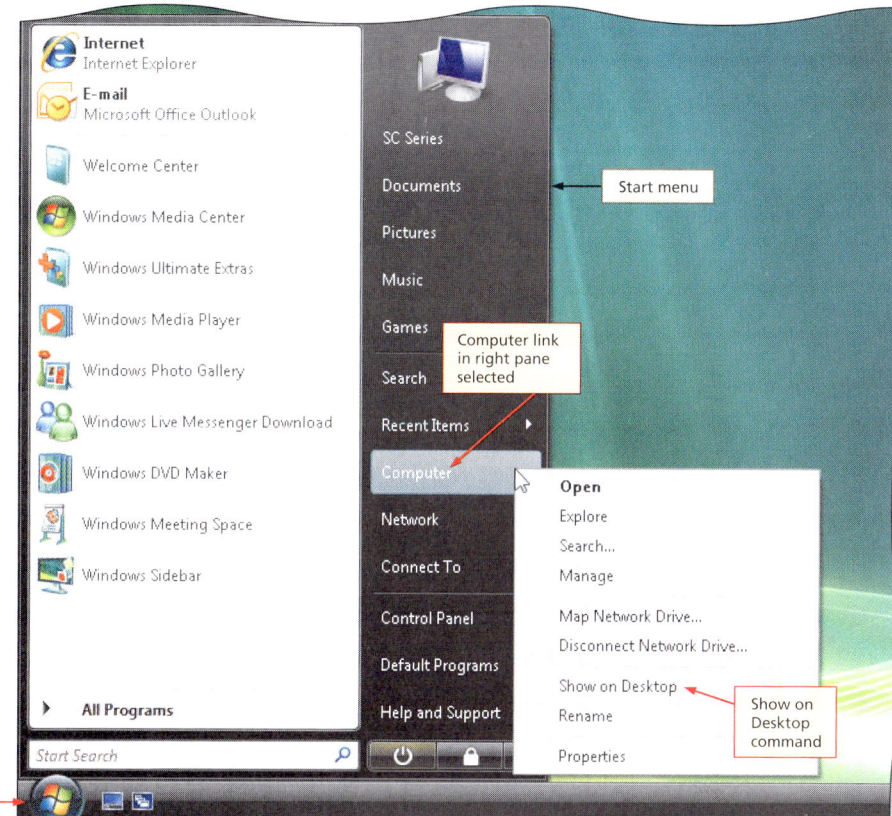

Figure 17

2

- Click Show on Desktop to close the shortcut menu and display the Computer icon on the desktop (Figure 18).

Q&A Why should I use a shortcut menu?

A shortcut menu speeds up your work and adds flexibility to your interaction with the computer by making often used items available in multiple locations.

3

- Click an open area on the desktop to close the Start menu.

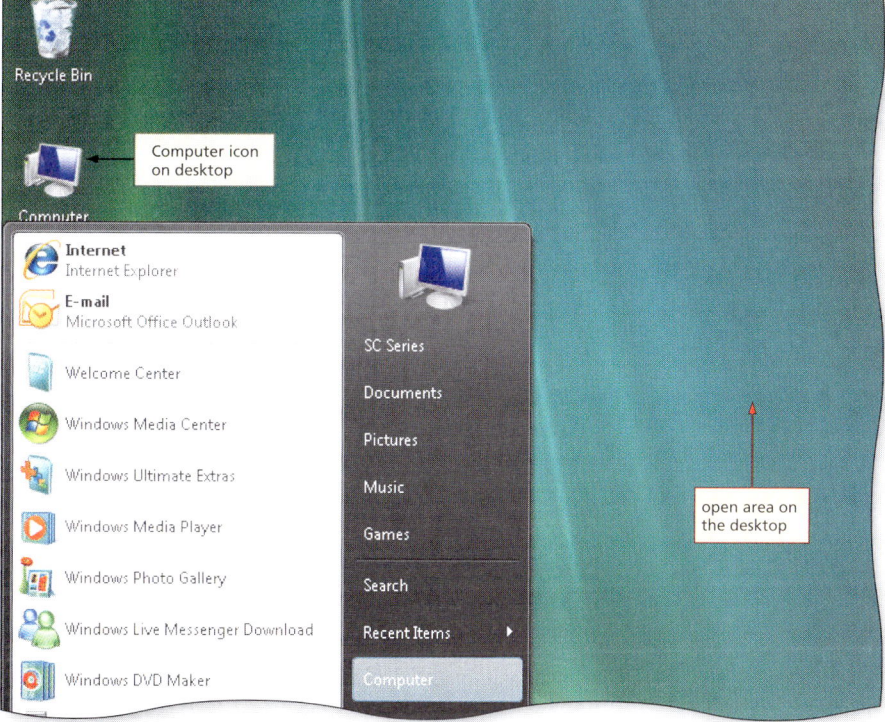

Figure 18

To Open a Window Using a Desktop Icon

When an icon, like the Computer icon, is displayed on the desktop, you can use the icon to start the program or open the window it represents. One method for opening a window with a desktop icon is to double-click the icon. The following step opens the Computer window on the desktop by double-clicking the Computer icon on the desktop.

1

- Double-click the Computer icon on the desktop to open the Computer window (Figure 19).

Q&A What does the Computer window allow me to do?

The Computer window allows you to view the contents of the computer.

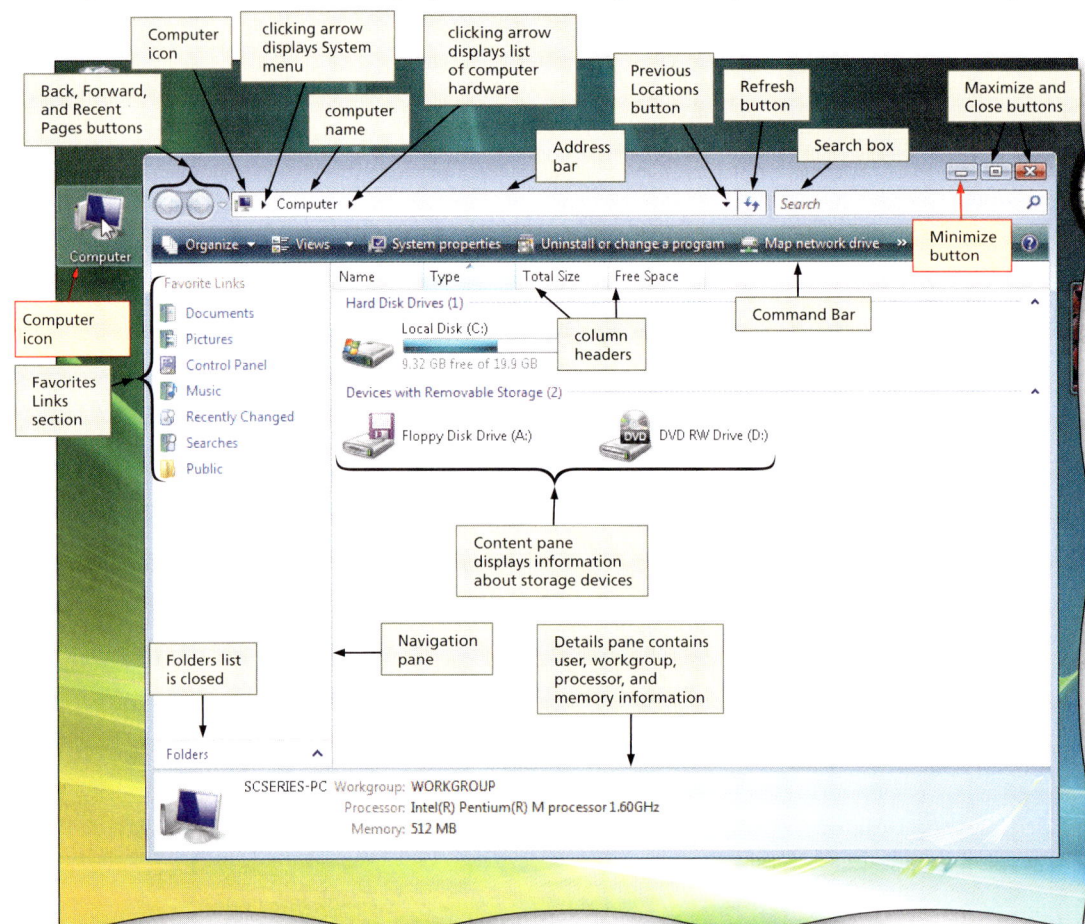

Figure 19

Other Ways
1. Right-click desktop icon, click Open on shortcut menu
2. Press WINDOWS+E

Folder Windows

Folder windows are the key tools for finding, viewing, and managing information on the computer. Folder Windows have common design elements, illustrated in Figure 19. The three buttons to the left of the **Address bar** allow you to navigate the contents of the left pane and view recent pages. On the right of the title bar are the Minimize button, Maximize button, and Close button that can be used to specify the size of the window or close the window.

The two right arrows on the Address bar allow you to visit different locations on the computer and display a list of computer hardware. The **Previous Locations button** saves the locations you have visited and displays the locations using computer path names.

The **Refresh button** at the end of the Address bar refreshes the contents of the right pane of the Computer window. The **Search box** to the right of the Address bar contains the dimmed word, Search. You can type a term in the Search box for a list of files, folders, shortcuts, and such containing that term within the location you are searching.

The **Command bar** contains five buttons used to accomplish various tasks on the computer related to organizing and managing the contents of the open window. The area below the Command bar contains the Navigation pane and four column headers (Name, Type, Total Size, and Free Space) on the right. The **Navigation pane** on the left contains the Favorite Links section and the Folders list. The **Favorite Links list** contains your documents, pictures, music files, and more.

Four **column headers** displayed in the right pane allow you to sort and group the entries below the column header.

To Minimize and Redisplay a Window

Two buttons on the title bar, the Minimize button and the Maximize button, allow you to control the way a window is displayed on the desktop. The following steps minimize and then redisplay the Computer window.

1

- Click the Minimize button on the title bar of the Computer window to minimize the Computer window (Figure 20).

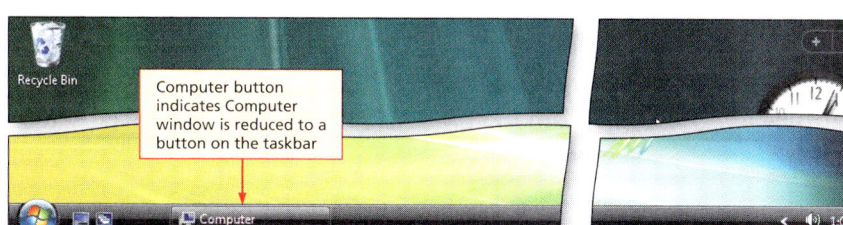

Q&A What happens to the Computer window when I click the Minimize button?

The Computer window still is available, but it no longer is the active window. It collapses to an unselected, light gray and black button on the taskbar.

Figure 20

2

- Click the Computer button on the taskbar to display the Computer window (Figure 21).

Q&A Why does the Computer button on the taskbar change?

The button changes to reflect the status of the Computer window. A selected (recessed) button indicates that the Computer window is active on the screen. An unselected button indicates that the Computer window is not active, but is open.

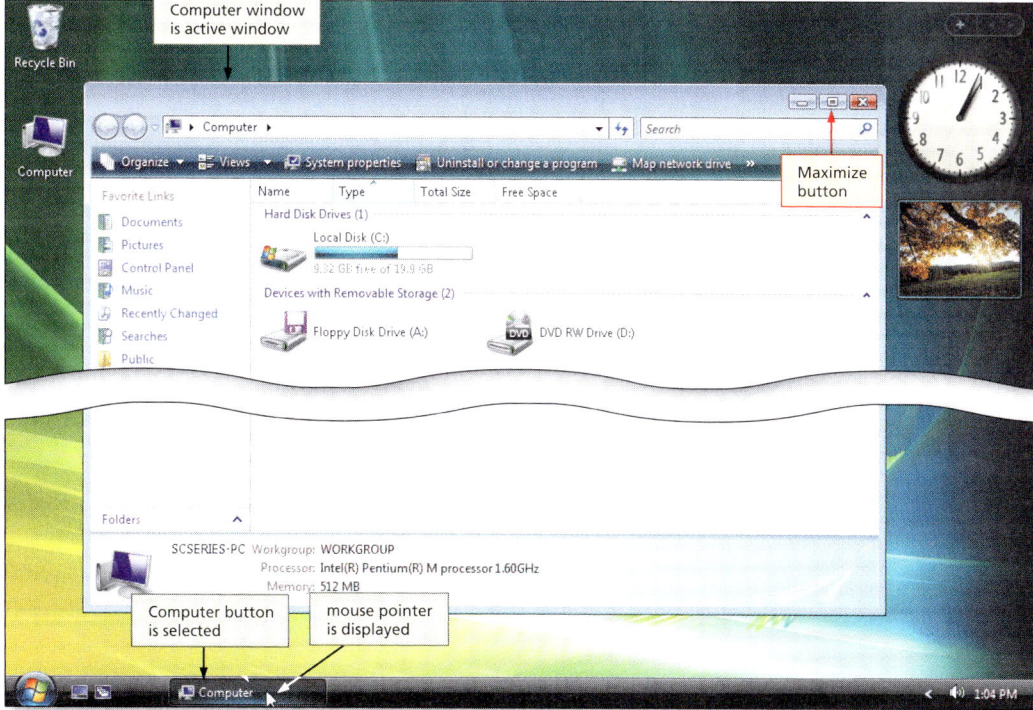

Figure 21

Other Ways
1. Right-click title bar, click Minimize, on taskbar click taskbar button 2. Press WINDOWS+M, press WINDOWS+SHIFT+M

To Maximize and Restore a Window

Sometimes information shown in a window is not completely visible. One method of displaying more contents in a window is to enlarge the window using the **Maximize button**, so that the window fills the entire screen. If a window is filling the entire screen and you want to see part of the desktop, you can use the **Restore** button to return the window to its previous state. The following steps maximize and restore the Computer window.

- Click the Maximize button on the title bar of the Computer window to maximize the Computer window (Figure 22).

Q&A When a window is maximized, can you also minimize it?

Yes. Click the Minimize button to minimize the window.

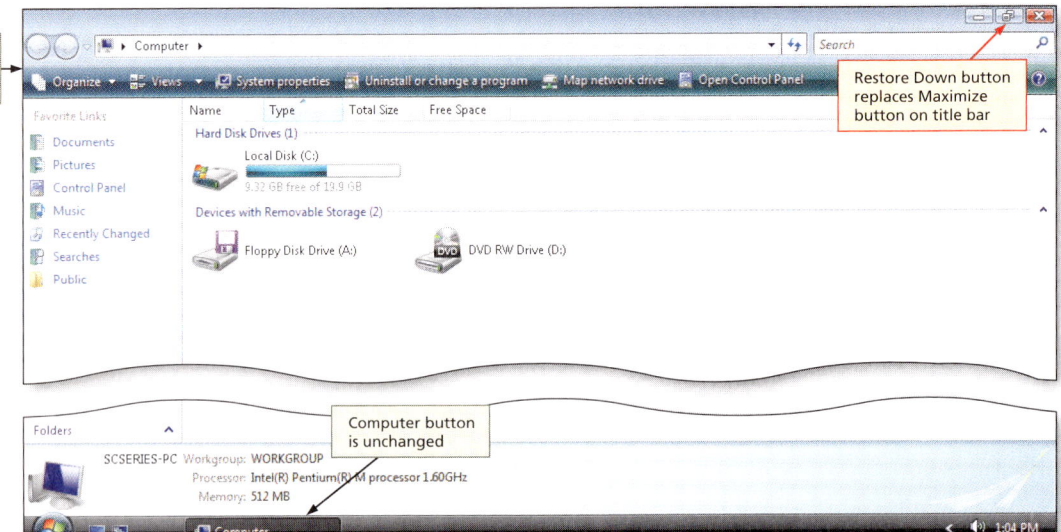

Figure 22

- Click the Restore Down button on the title bar of the Computer window to return the Computer window to its previous size (Figure 23).

Q&A What happens to the Restore Down button when I click it?

The Maximize button replaces the Restore Down button on the title bar.

Other Ways

1. Right-click title bar, click Maximize, right-click title bar, click Restore
2. Double-click title bar, double-click title bar

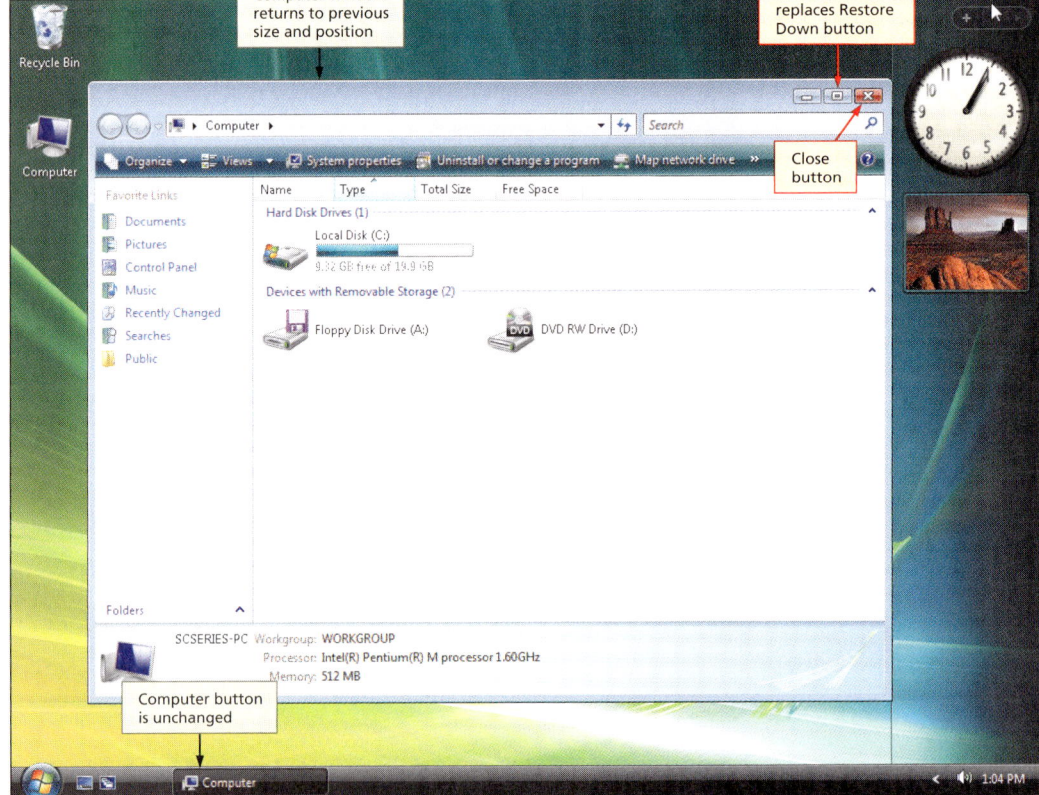

Figure 23

To Expand the Folders List

The Folders list in the Pictures window is collapsed and an up arrow appears to the right of the Folders name (see Figure 27). Clicking the up arrow or the Folders button expands the Folders list and reveals the contents of the Folders list. The following step expands the Folders list in the Pictures window.

1

- Click the Folders button to expand the Folders list in the Navigation pane of the Pictures window (Figure 28).

Q&A What is shown in the Folders list?

The Folders list displays a hierarchical structure of files, folders, and drives on the computer.

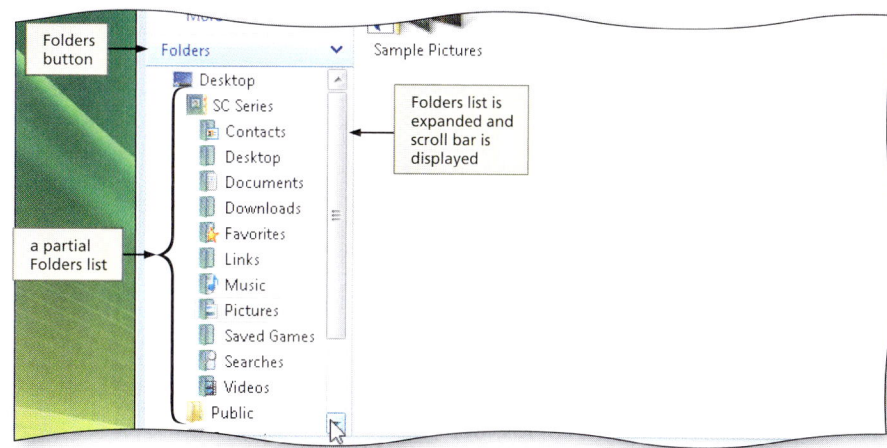

Figure 28

To Size a Window by Dragging

You can resize any open window to a more desirable size by pointing to one of the outside borders of the window and then dragging the border in or out. The following steps drag the bottom border of the Pictures window downward to enlarge the window until the contents of the Folders list is visible.

1

- Point to the bottom border of the Pictures window until the mouse pointer changes to a two-headed arrow.

- Drag the bottom border downward until the entire contents of the Folders list are visible and the scroll bar no longer appears (Figure 29).

Q&A Can I drag anything else to enlarge or shrink the window?

You can drag the left, right, and top borders and any window corner.

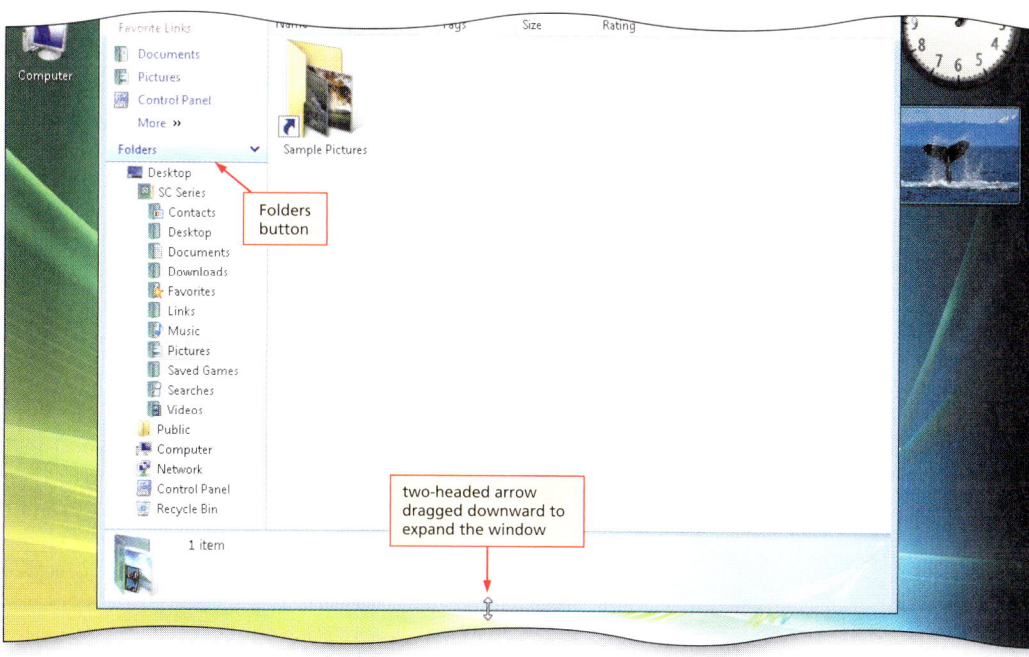

Figure 29

To Collapse the Folders List

When the Folders list is expanded, a down arrow is displayed. In the following step, you will collapse the list by clicking the Folders button.

- Click the Folders button to collapse the Folders list (Figure 30).

Q&A Is there another way to collapse the Folders list?

Yes. You can click the down arrow to collapse the Folders list.

Q&A Should I keep the Folders list expanded or collapsed?

If you need to use the contents within the Folders list, it is handy to keep the Folders list expanded. You can collapse the Folders list when the information is not needed.

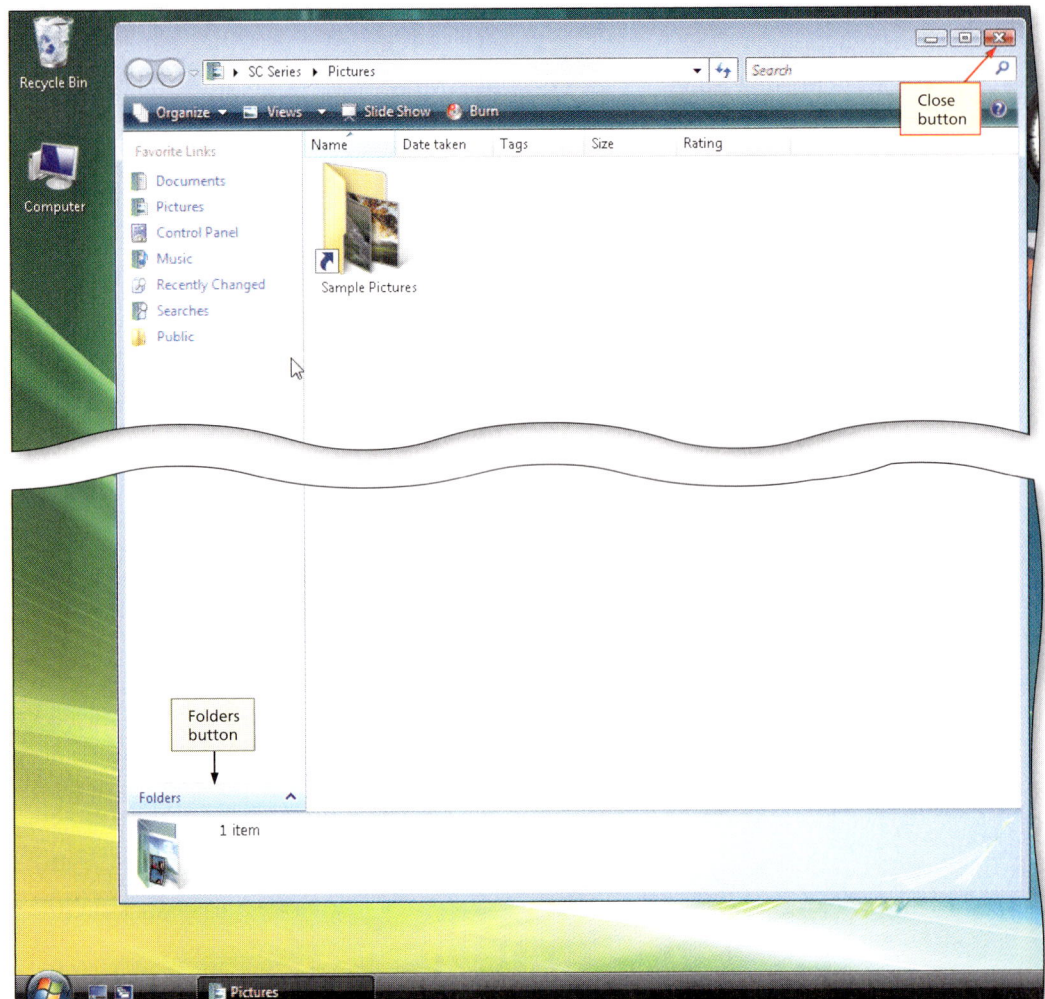

Figure 30

To Close a Window

After you have completed work in a window, normally you will close the window. The following step closes the Pictures window.

 Click the Close button on the title bar in the Pictures window to close the Pictures window.

To Delete a Desktop Icon by Right-Dragging

Sometimes, you will want to remove an icon from the desktop. One method of deleting an icon from the desktop is to right-drag the icon to the Recycle Bin icon on the desktop. **Right-drag** means you point to an item, hold down the right mouse button, move the item to the desired location, and then release the right mouse button. When you right-drag an object, a shortcut menu is displayed. The shortcut menu contains commands specifically for use with the object being dragged. The following steps delete the Computer icon by right-dragging the icon to the Recycle Bin icon. A **dialog box** is displayed whenever Windows Vista needs to supply information to you or wants you to enter information or select among several options. The Confirm Delete dialog box is used in the following steps.

1
- Point to the Computer icon on the desktop, hold down the right mouse button, drag the Computer icon over the Recycle Bin icon, and then release the right mouse button to display a shortcut menu (Figure 31).

Figure 31

2
- Click Move Here on the shortcut menu to close the shortcut menu and display the Confirm Delete dialog box (Figure 32).

Q&A Why should I right-drag instead of simply dragging?

Although you can move icons by dragging with the primary (left) mouse button and by right-dragging with the secondary (right) mouse button, it is strongly suggested you right-drag because a shortcut menu appears and, in most cases, you can specify the exact operation you want to occur. When you drag using the left mouse button, a default operation takes place and that operation may not be the operation you intended to perform.

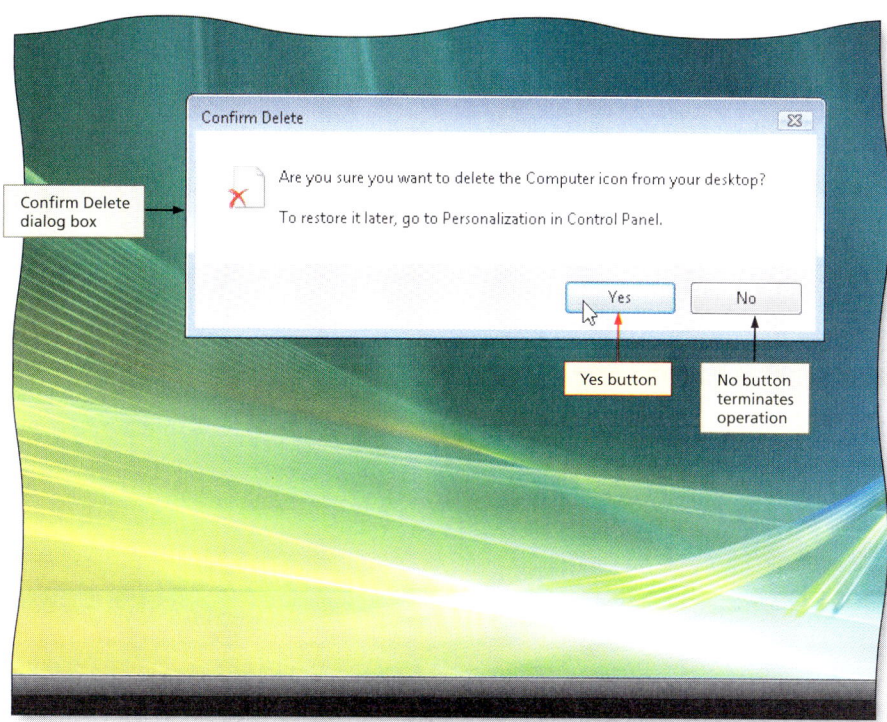

Figure 32

3
- Click the Yes button to delete the Computer icon and close the Confirm Delete dialog box.

Other Ways
1. Drag icon to Recycle Bin, click Yes button
2. Right-click icon, click Delete, click Yes button

Summary of Mouse and Windows Operations

You have seen how to use the mouse to point, click, right-click, double-click, drag, and right-drag in order to accomplish certain tasks on the desktop. The use of a mouse is an important skill when using Windows Vista. In addition, you have learned how to move around and use windows on the Windows Vista desktop.

The Keyboard and Keyboard Shortcuts

The **keyboard** is an input device on which you manually key in, or type, data. Figure 33 illustrates the rechargeable Wireless Entertainment Desktop 8000 keyboard designed for use with Microsoft Office and the Internet. Keyboards can be basic input devices, or in the case of the keyboard illustrated, can serve other purposes, such as providing USB ports for connecting hardware, and specialized buttons such as the Windows Gadget button, which allow access to certain Windows Vista features at the touch of a button.

Figure 33

Many tasks you accomplish with a mouse can also be accomplished using a keyboard. To perform tasks using the keyboard, you must understand the notation used to identify which keys to press. This notation is used throughout Windows Vista to identify a **keyboard shortcut**.

Keyboard shortcuts consist of (1) pressing a single key (such as press the F1 key); or (2) pressing and holding down one key and pressing a second key, as shown by two key names separated by a plus sign (such as press CTRL+ESC). For example, to obtain help about Windows Vista, you can press the F1 key and to display the Start menu, hold down the CTRL key and then press the ESC key (press CRTL+ESC).

Starting a Program

One of the basic tasks you can perform using Windows Vista is starting a program. A **program** is a series of related instructions that tells a computer what tasks to perform and how to perform them. As previously mentioned, application software is a program designed to make users more productive and/or assist them with personal tasks. For example, a **word processing program** is application software that allows you to create and manipulate documents containing mostly text and sometimes graphics; a **presentation program** is application software that allows you to create visual aids for presentations to communicate with a group; and a **Web browser** is application software that allows you to access and view **Web pages**, which are documents designed to be viewed using a Web browser.

The default Web browser (Internet Explorer) appears in the pinned items list on the Start menu shown in Figure 34. Because the default Web browser is selected during the installation of the Windows Vista operating system, the default Web browser on your computer may be different. In addition, you easily can select another Web browser as the default Web browser. Another frequently used Web browser is **Mozilla Firefox**.

What Is Internet Explorer?

Internet Explorer is a Web browser that allows you to search for and view Web pages, save pages you find for use in the future, maintain a list of the pages you visit, send and receive e-mail messages, and edit Web pages. The Internet Explorer program is included with the Windows Vista operating system and Microsoft Office software, or you can download it from the Internet.

To Start a Program Using the Start Menu

A common activity performed on a computer is starting a program to accomplish specific tasks. You can start a program by using the Start menu. To illustrate the use of the Start menu to start a program, the following steps start Internet Explorer using the Internet command on the Start menu.

- Display the Start menu (Figure 34).

Is Internet Explorer included in the All Programs list?

Yes. All programs stored on the computer are listed in the All Programs list. Internet Explorer also is on the pinned items list because it is used often, but you can start Internet Explorer from the All Programs list as well.

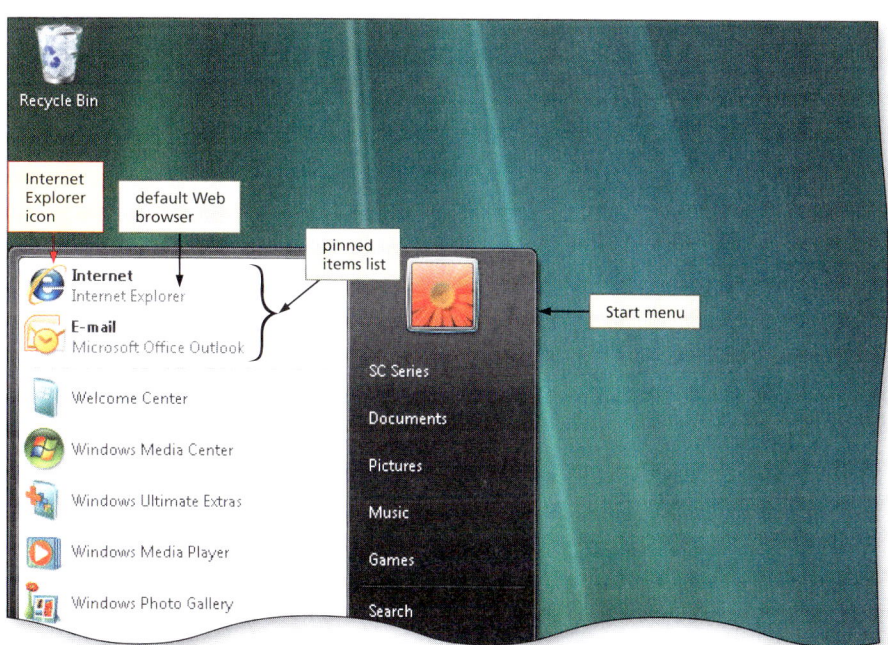

Figure 34

2
- Click the Internet Explorer icon in the pinned items list on the Start menu to start Windows Internet Explorer (Figure 35).

Q&A What is displayed in the Windows Internet Explorer window?

A title bar, Address bar, Standard toolbar, Instant Search box, scroll bar, status bar, and display area where pages from the World Wide Web are displayed.

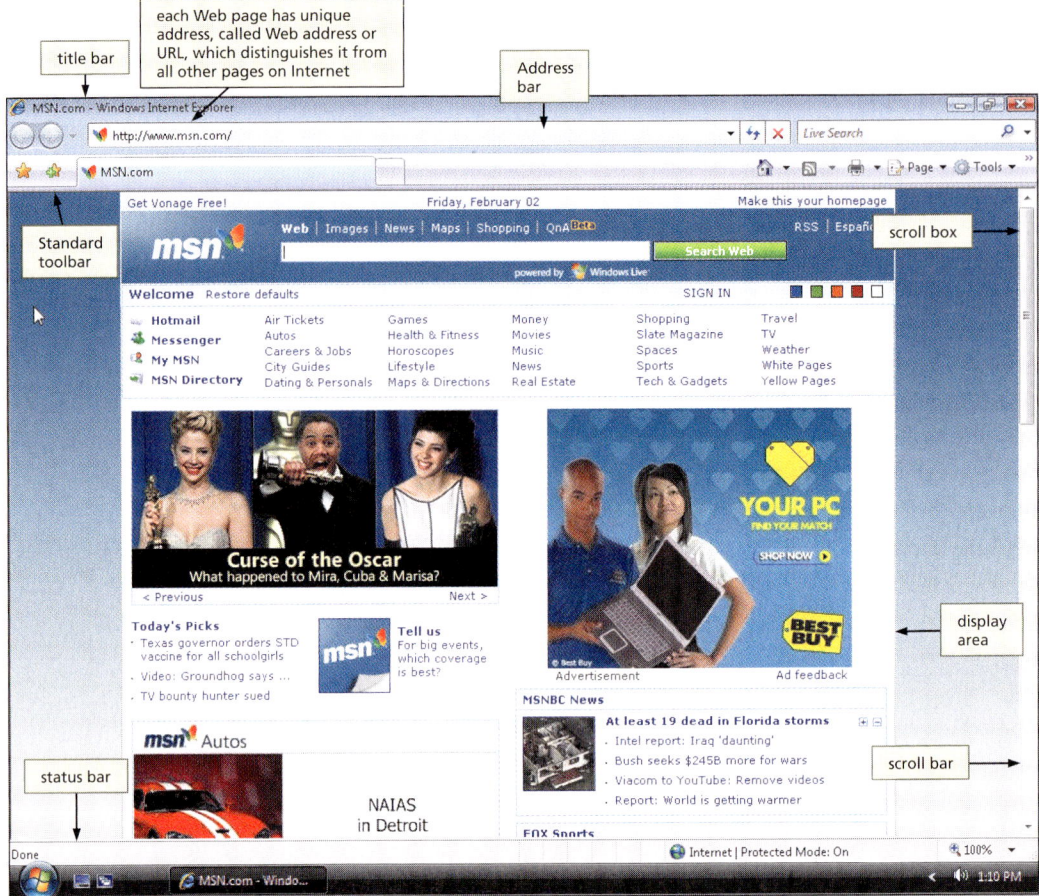

Figure 35

Other Ways
1. Click Start button, point to All Programs, click Internet Explorer

BTW

Web Sites
A collection of related Web pages on a computer is called a **Web site**. The MSN.com Web page shown in Figure 35 is the first Web page you see when you access the MSN.com Web site and is, therefore, referred to as a **home page**, or **start page**.

Web Address

A **Web address**, sometimes called a Uniform Resource Locator (URL), is the address on the World Wide Web where a Web page is located. It often is composed of three parts (Figure 36). The first part is the **protocol**. A protocol is a set of rules. Most Web pages use the Hypertext Transfer Protocol. **Hypertext Transfer Protocol** (**HTTP**) describes the rules used to transmit Web pages electronically over the Internet. You enter the protocol in lowercase as http followed by a colon and two forward slashes (http://). If you do not begin a Web address with a protocol, Internet Explorer will assume it is http, and automatically will append http:// to the front of the Web address.

The second part of a Web address is the domain name. The **domain name** is the Internet address of the computer on the Internet where the Web page is located. The domain name in the Web address in Figure 36 is www.scsite.com.

The last part of the domain name (com in Figure 36) indicates the type of organization that owns the Web site. Table 2 shows some types of organizations and their extensions. In addition to the 14 domain name extensions listed in the table, there are country specific extensions, such as .uk for the United Kingdom and .dk for Denmark.

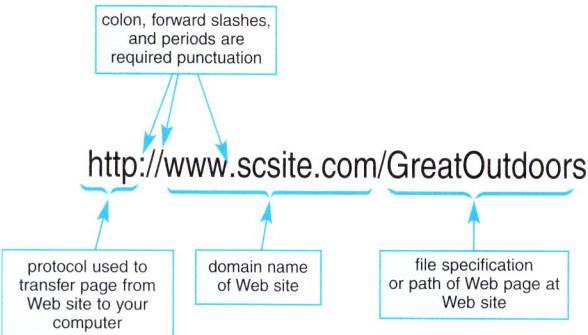

Figure 36

Table 2 Organizations and Their Domain Name Extensions			
Organization	**Extension**	**Organization**	**Extension**
Commercial	.com	aviation	.aero
Educational	.edu	businesses	.biz
Government	.gov	co-operatives	.coop
Military	.mil	general	.info
Major network support	.net	museums	.museum
Nonprofit organizations	.org	individuals	.name
International	.int	professionals	.pro

The optional third part of a Web address is the file specification of the Web page. The **file specification** includes the file name and possibly a directory or folder name. This information is called the **path**. If no file specification of a Web page is specified in the Web address, a default Web page is displayed.

Browsing the World Wide Web

One method to browse the World Wide Web is to find Web addresses that identify interesting Web sites in magazines or newspapers, on television, from friends, or even from just browsing the Web. Web addresses of well-known companies and organizations usually contain the company's name and institution's name. For example, ibm.com is the IBM Corporation Web address, and umich.edu is the Web address for the University of Michigan.

When you find a Web address of a Web page you want to visit, enter the Web address into the Address bar. The following steps show how to view a Web site provided by Course Technology and visit the Web page titled SC Site – Shelly Cashman Series Student Resources Web site, which contains student resources for use with Shelly Cashman Series textbooks. The Web address for the SC Site – Shelly Cashman Series Student Resources Web site is:

www.scsite.com

You are not required to provide the leading http:// protocol when initially typing the Web address in the Address bar. Internet Explorer will insert http:// and assume the www automatically, if you do not supply it.

To Browse the Web by Entering a Web Address

The SC Site — Shelly Cashman Series Student Resources Web site contains student resources for use with Shelly Cashman Series textbooks. The Web address for this Web page is www.scsite.com.

When you find the Web address of a Web page you want to visit, enter the Web address in the Address bar. The following steps display the Web page from the Shelly Cashman Series.

1
- Click the Address bar to select the Web address in the Address bar (Figure 37).

Q&A What happens when I click the Address bar?

Internet Explorer selects the Web address in the Address bar and the mouse pointer changes to an I-beam.

2
- Type www.scsite.com in the Address bar to display the new Web address (Figure 38).

Q&A Must I type www. in the Web address?

No. If you type scsite.com, Internet Explorer automatically will add www.

3
- Click the Go to button to display the SC Site – Shelly Cashman Series Student Resources Web site (Figure 39).

Q&A The Go to button changes after I click it. Why?

When you type the Web address, the button changes to the Go to button. After the page is displayed, the button changes to the Refresh button. When you click the Refresh button, the Web page is downloaded again from the Web server, resulting in the most up-to-date version of the page being displayed.

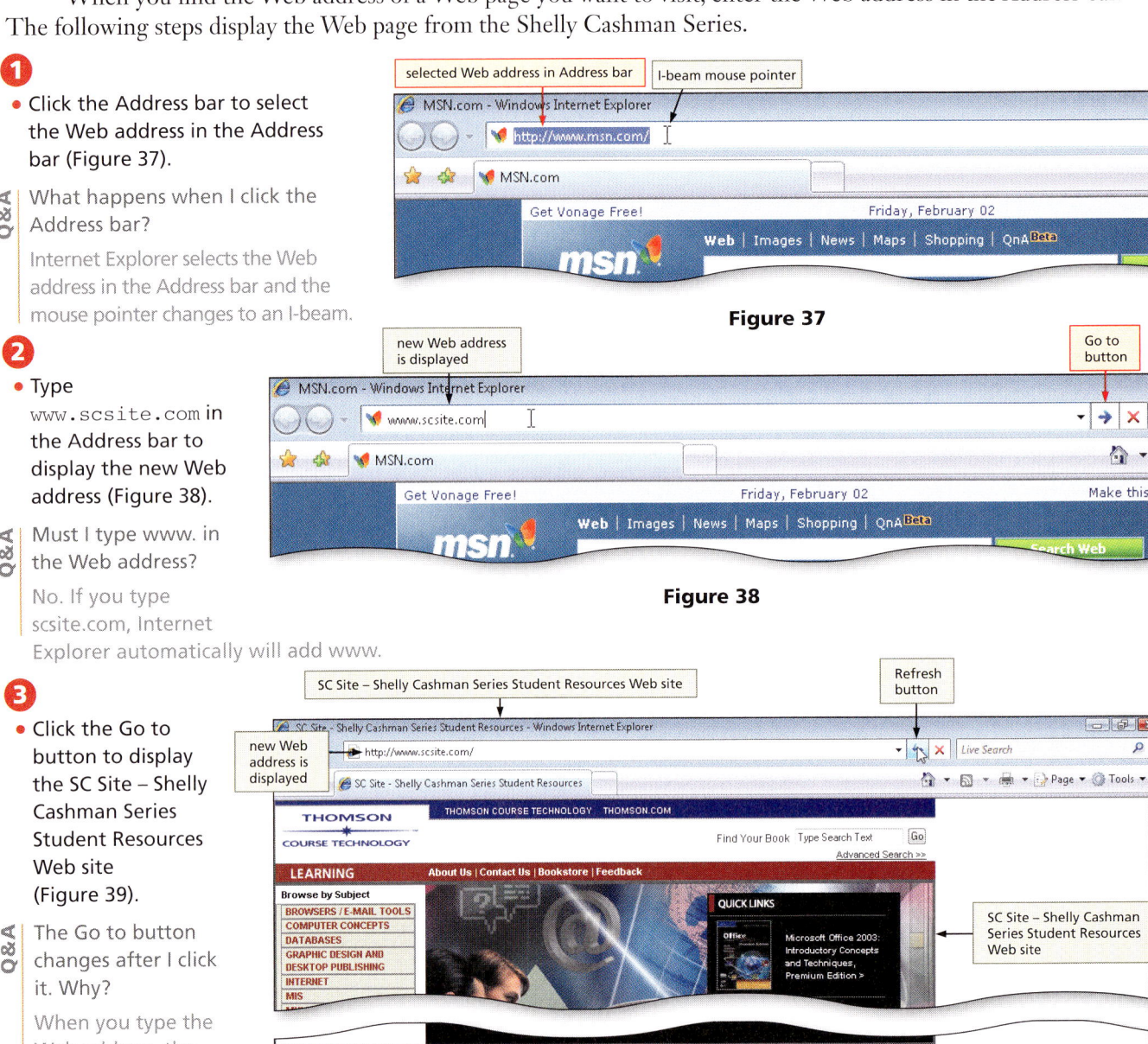

Figure 37

Figure 38

Figure 39

To Open a Link in a New Tab

You can view multiple Web pages in a single window using tabbed pages. A **tabbed page** consists of a tab in the Internet Explorer window and the associated Web page. When you start Internet Explorer only one tab is displayed, but you can open as many tabbed pages as you want. The following steps use the Instant Search box and the Course Technology – Shelly Cashman Series link to open a Web page on a new tabbed page.

1
- Click the Instant Search box and type `Shelly Cashman Series` in the Instant Search box (Figure 40).

Q&A What is an Instant Search box?

It is a text box in which you can type a term which then can be searched for by a Search engine. Internet Explorer provides an Instant Search box in the upper-right corner of the window.

Figure 40

2
- Click the Search button to the right of the Instant Search box to display the results of the Web search (Figure 41).

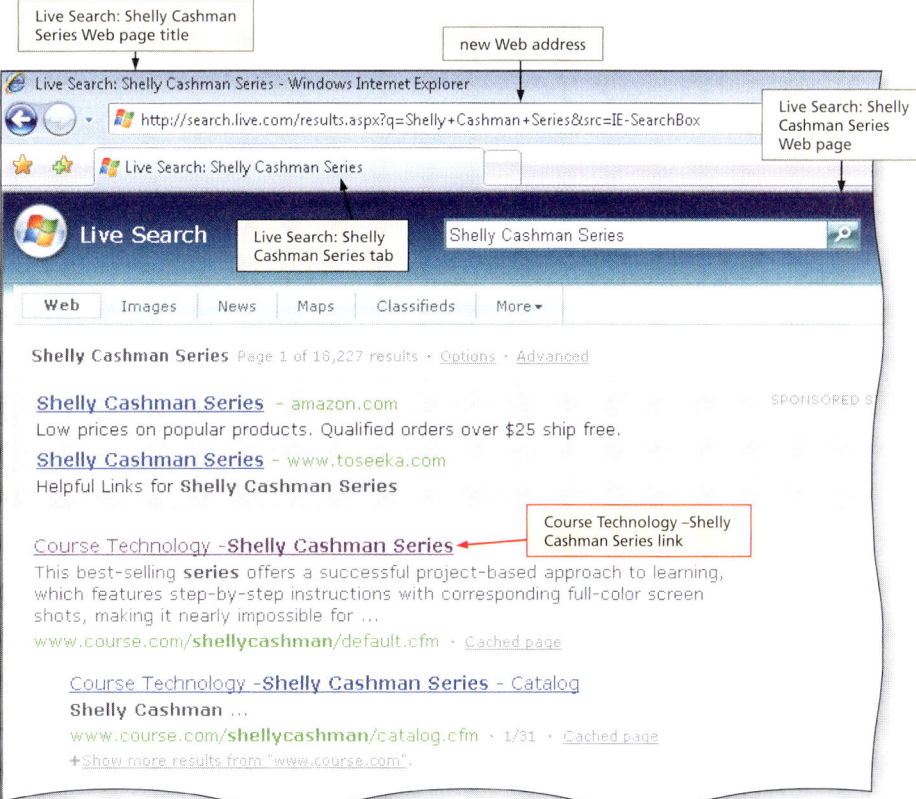

Figure 41

3

- If necessary, scroll to view the Course Technology –Shelly Cashman Series link.

- Right-click the Course Technology –Shelly Cashman Series link to display a shortcut menu (Figure 42).

Q&A What happens when I just click a link?

The Web page will be displayed on the same tabbed page as the search results and will replace the search results page.

Figure 42

4

- Click Open in New Tab on the shortcut menu to close the shortcut menu and display the Course Technology –Shelly Cashman Series tab (Figure 43).

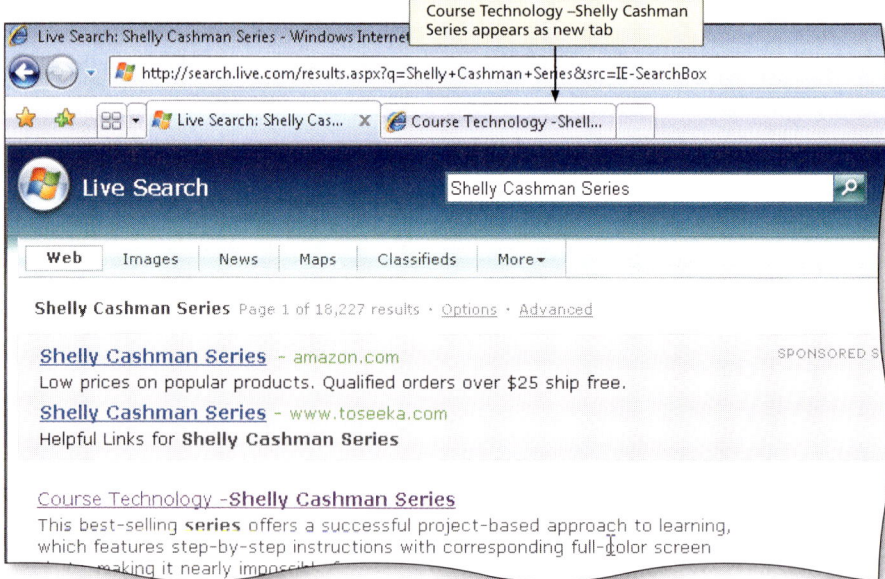

Figure 43

Other Ways

1. While holding down CTRL, click link

To Switch between Tabs

You can display the contents of any tabbed page by clicking the tab, as shown in the following step which activates the Course Technology –Shelly Cashman Series tab.

- Click the Course Technology –Shelly Cashman Series tab to activate the tab and display The Shelly Cashman Series® Web page in the display area (Figure 44).

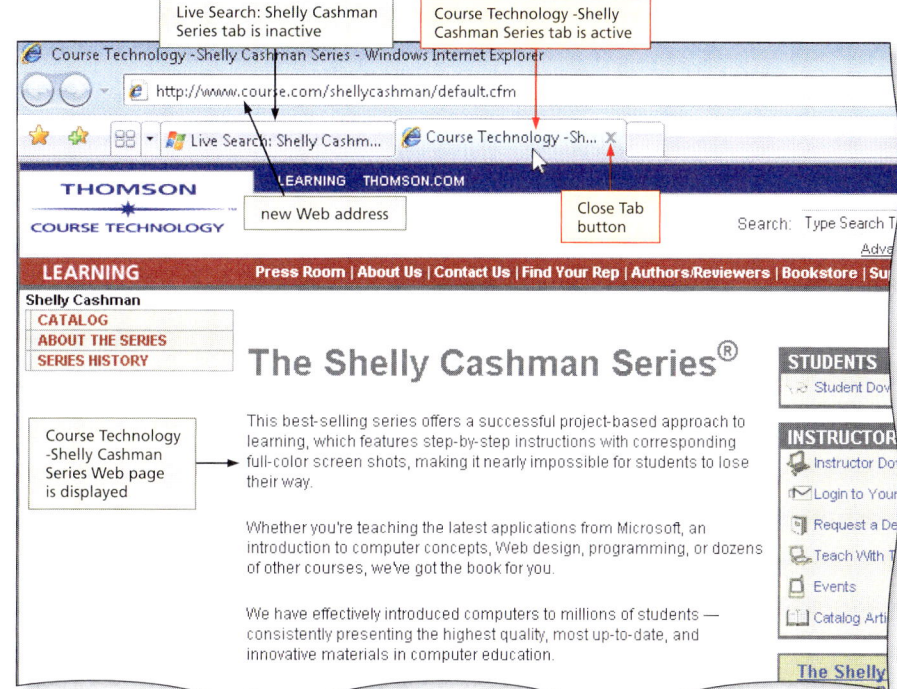

Figure 44

Other Ways	
1. Press CTRL+TAB, press CTRL+TAB	2. Press CTRL+2, press CTRL+1

To Close a Tab

You can keep as many tabbed pages open as necessary. If you no longer have a need for the tabbed page to be open, you can close the tab using the following steps.

- Click the Close Tab button in the Course Technology –Shelly Cashman Series tab to close the Course Technology –Shelly Cashman Series tab (Figure 45).

- Click the Close button on the title bar to close the Live Search: Shelly Cashman Series - Windows Internet Explorer window.

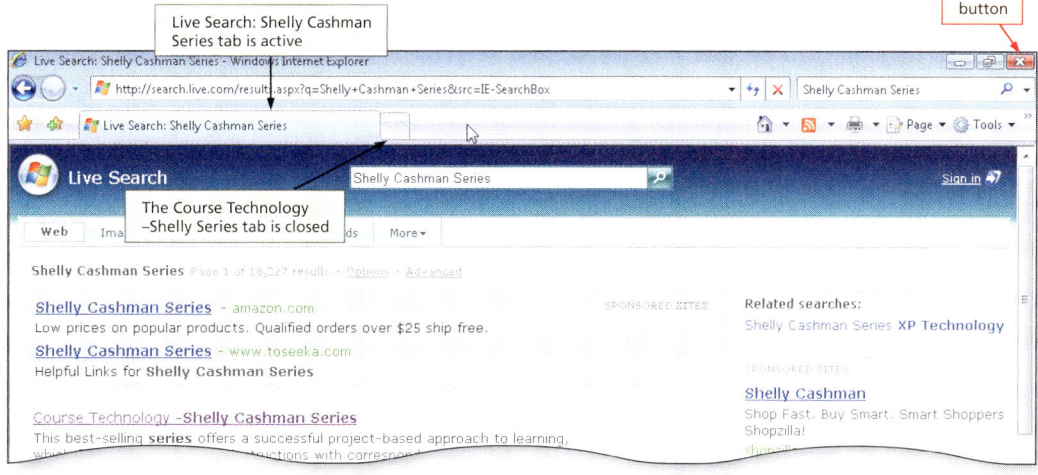

Figure 45

Working with Folders

The steps below allow you to view the contents of the computer, the hierarchy of drives and folders on the computer, and the files and folders in each folder. In this section, you will expand and collapse drives and folders, display drive and folder contents, create a new folder, copy a file between folders, and rename and then delete a file. These are common operations that you should understand how to perform.

To Work with Folders

Before working with folders, you must display the Start menu, open the Computer window, and then maximize the window, as shown in the following steps.

1
- Click the Start button to display the Start menu (Figure 46).

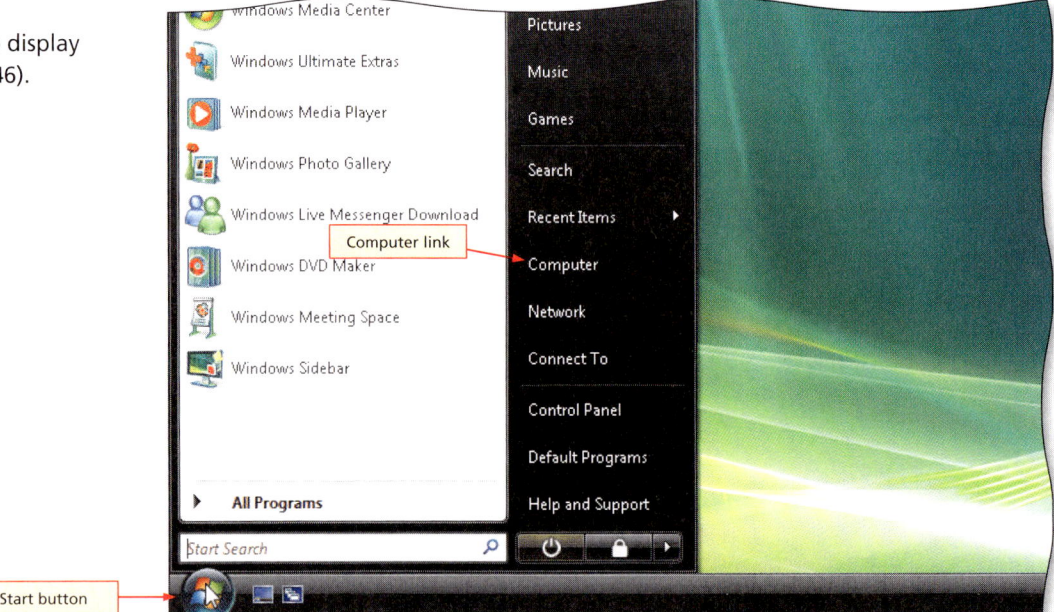

Figure 46

2
- Click Computer on the Start menu to open the Computer window (Figure 47).

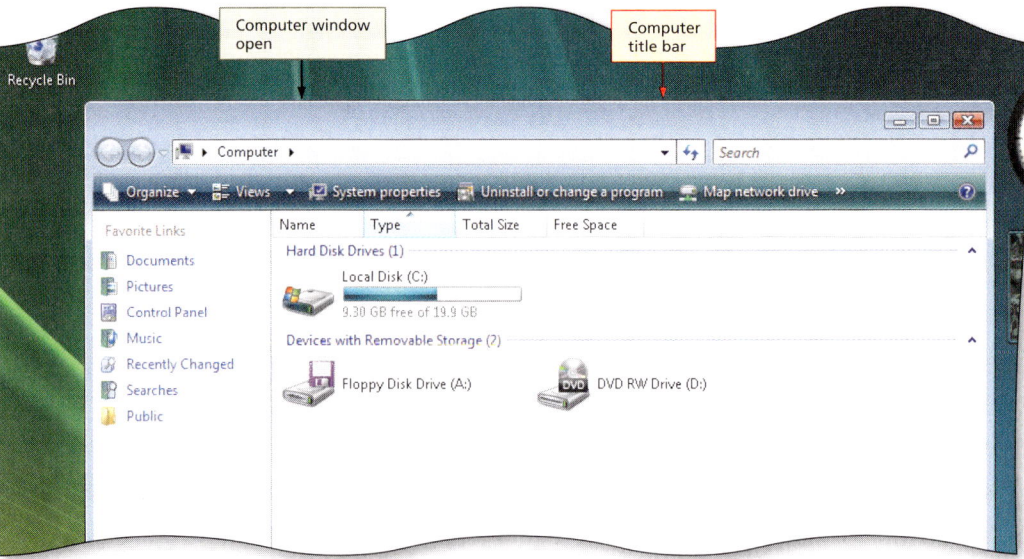

Figure 47

Introduction to Windows Vista   **Windows Vista Chapter**   **WIN** 35

3
- If necessary, double-click the Computer title bar to maximize the Computer window (Figure 48).

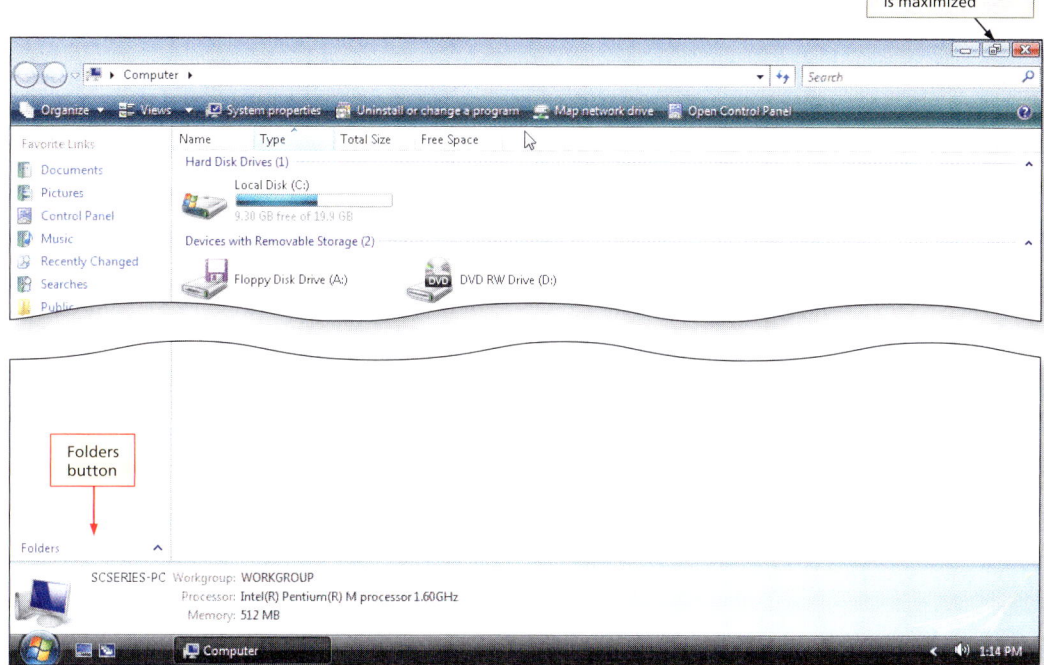

Figure 48

4
- If necessary, click the Folders button to display the Folders list (Figure 49).

Q&A Is it possible to display my folders and drives in the right pane differently than what is shown in Figure 49?

You can display files and folders in the right pane in several different views. Currently, the drives and folders in the right pane are displayed in Tiles view.

Experiment
- Click a black arrow in the Folders list and observe the changes in the window. Then, click the resulting white arrow to return the window to its previous state. Do the same for another black arrow and resulting white arrow.

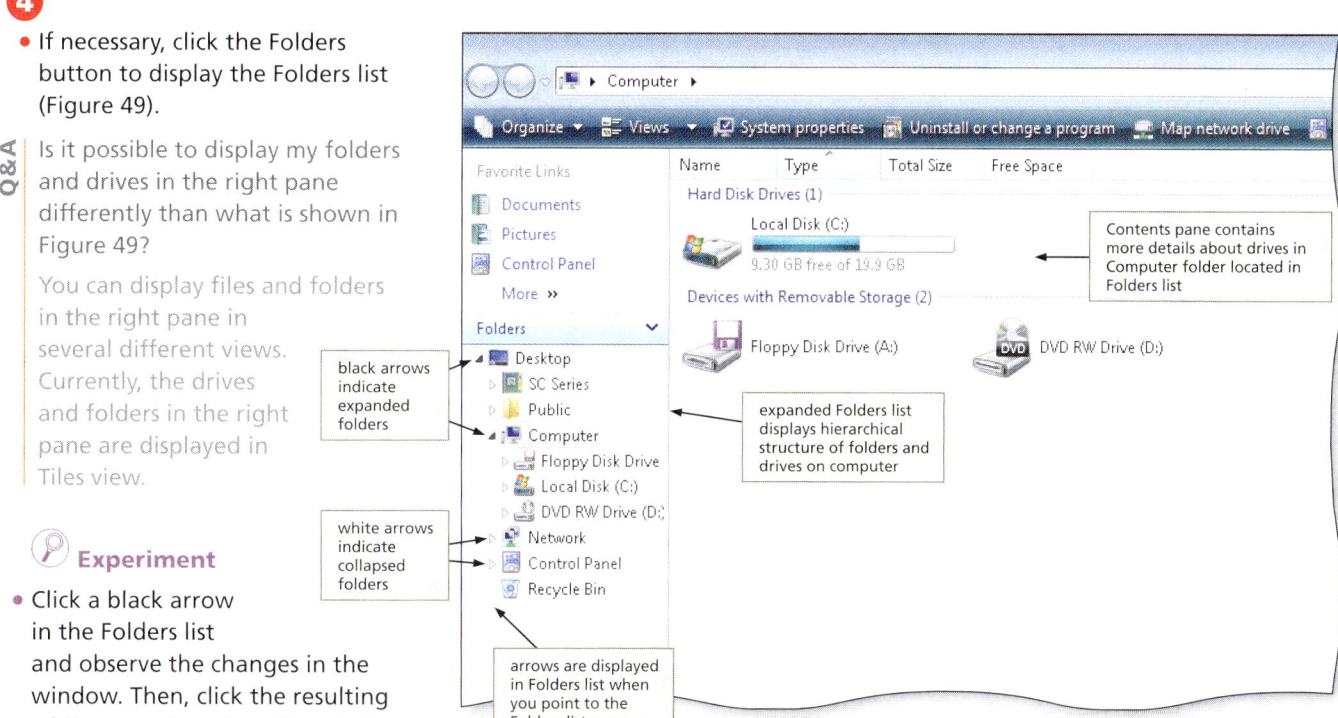

Figure 49

Other Ways
1. Click Start button, right-click Computer, click Explore on shortcut menu
2. Press WINDOWS+E

Using a Hierarchical Format to Organize Files and Folders

Besides navigating drives and folder, you also need to be able to create and organize the files and folders on the computer. A file may contain a spreadsheet assignment given by the computer teacher, a research paper assigned by the English teacher, an electronic quiz given by the Business teacher, or a study sheet designed by the Math teacher. You should organize and store these files in folders to avoid misplacing a file and to help you find a file quickly.

Assume you are a freshman taking four classes (Business, Computer, English, and Math). You want to design a series of folders for the four classes you are taking in the first semester of your freshman year. To accomplish this, you arrange the folders in a **hierarchical format**. The hierarchical structure of folders for the Freshman year is shown in Figure 50.

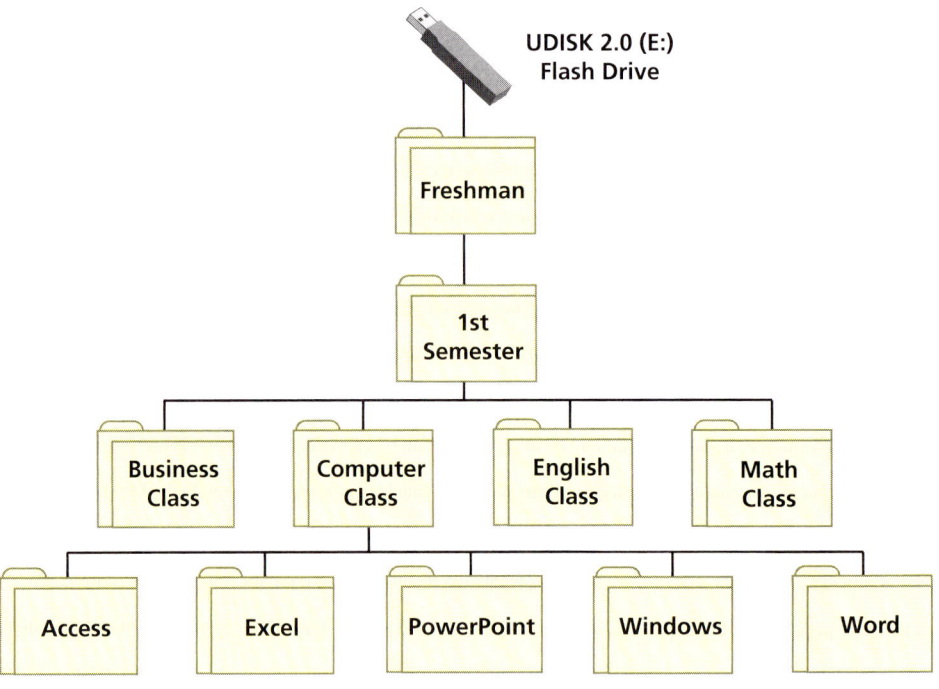

Figure 50

The hierarchy contains five levels. The first level contains the storage device, in this case a flash drive. Windows Vista identifies the storage device with a letter, and, in some cases, a name. In Figure 50, the flash drive is identified as UDISK 2.0 (E:). The second level contains the Freshman folder, the third level contains the 1st Semester folder, the fourth level contains four folders (Business Class, Computer Class, English Class, and Math Class), and the fifth level contains five folders (Access, Excel, PowerPoint, Windows, and Word).

The vertical and horizontal lines in the hierarchy chart form a pathway that allows you to navigate to a drive or folder. Each pathway is a means of navigation to a specific location on a computer or network. A **path** consists of a drive letter (preceded by a drive name when necessary) and colon, to identify the storage device, and one or more folder names. Each drive or folder in the hierarchy chart has a corresponding path. When you click a drive or folder icon in the Folders list, the corresponding path appears in the Address bar. Table 3 contains examples of paths and their corresponding drives and folders. These paths are referred to as **breadcrumb trails**, showing you where the current page or folder is in the hierarchy.

When the hierarchy in Figure 50 is created, the UDISK 2.0 (E:) drive is said "to contain" the Freshman folder, the Freshman folder is said "to contain" the 1st Semester folder, and so on. In addition, this hierarchy easily can be expanded to include folders from the Sophomore, Junior, and Senior years and any additional semesters.

Table 3 Paths and Corresponding Drives and Folders

Path	Drive and Folder
Computer ► UDISK 2.0 (E:)	Drive E (UDISK 2.0 (E:))
Computer ► UDISK 2.0 (E:) ► Freshman	Freshman folder on drive E
Computer ► UDISK 2.0 (E:) ► Freshman ► 1st Semester	1st Semester folder in Freshman folder on drive E
Computer ► UDISK 2.0 (E:) ► Freshman ► 1st Semester ► Computer Class ► Word	Word folder in Computer Class folder in 1st Semester folder in Freshman folder on drive E

Removable Media and Network Drives

Types of removable media such as USB flash drives are ideal for storing files and folders on a computer. A **USB flash drive**, sometimes called a **thumb drive**, is a flash memory storage device that plugs in a USB port on a computer. A **USB port**, short for universal serial bus port, can be found on most computers. USB flash drives, like the one shown in Figure 51, are convenient for mobile users because they are small and lightweight enough to be transported on a keychain or in a pocket.

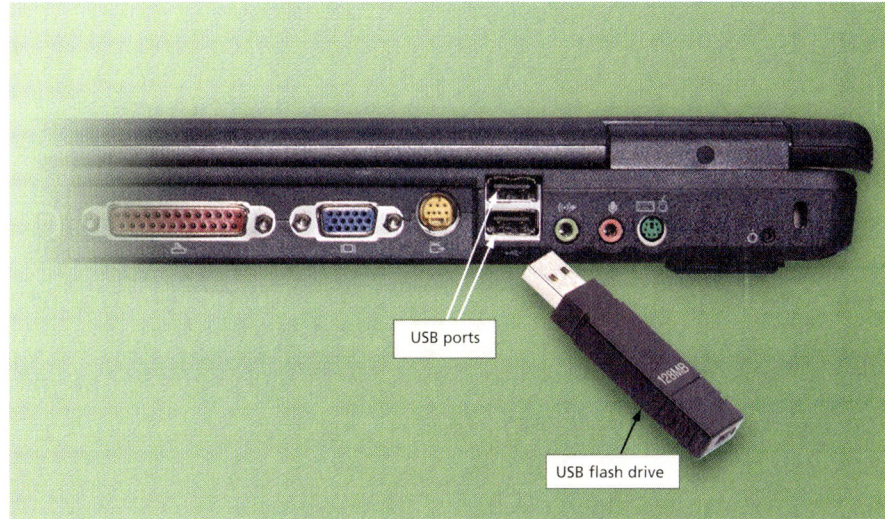

Figure 51

Instead of a USB drive, you might use files stored on a network drive. A **network** is a collection of computers and devices connected together for the purpose of sharing information between computer users. In some cases, students might be required to store their files on a network drive found on the school's computer network. A **network drive** is a storage device that is connected to the server on the computer network. A **server** controls access to the hardware, software, and other resources on the network and provides a centralized storage area for programs, data, and information. If student files reside on the network drive on the school's network, files may be accessed from a school computer, or from a personal computer with permission from the school. Ask your teacher if the school requires you to use a network drive.

To Plug a USB Flash Drive into a USB Port

Although other removable media may be used for storage, the USB flash drive is one of the more popular drives. To store files and folders on the USB flash drive, you must plug the USB flash drive into a USB port on the computer. After you do, the flash drive window is displayed on the desktop. The removable media drive name on your computer may be different. The following step plugs a USB flash drive into a USB port.

1

- Plug the USB flash drive into a USB port on the computer to open the UDISK 2.0 (E:) window (Figure 52).

Q&A What does UDISK 2.0 (E:) mean?

UDISK 2.0 is the name of a particular type of USB drive. (E:) is the drive letter assigned by Windows Vista to your removable drive. The name and drive letter of your USB drive might be different.

2

- Close the UDISK 2.0 (E:) window.

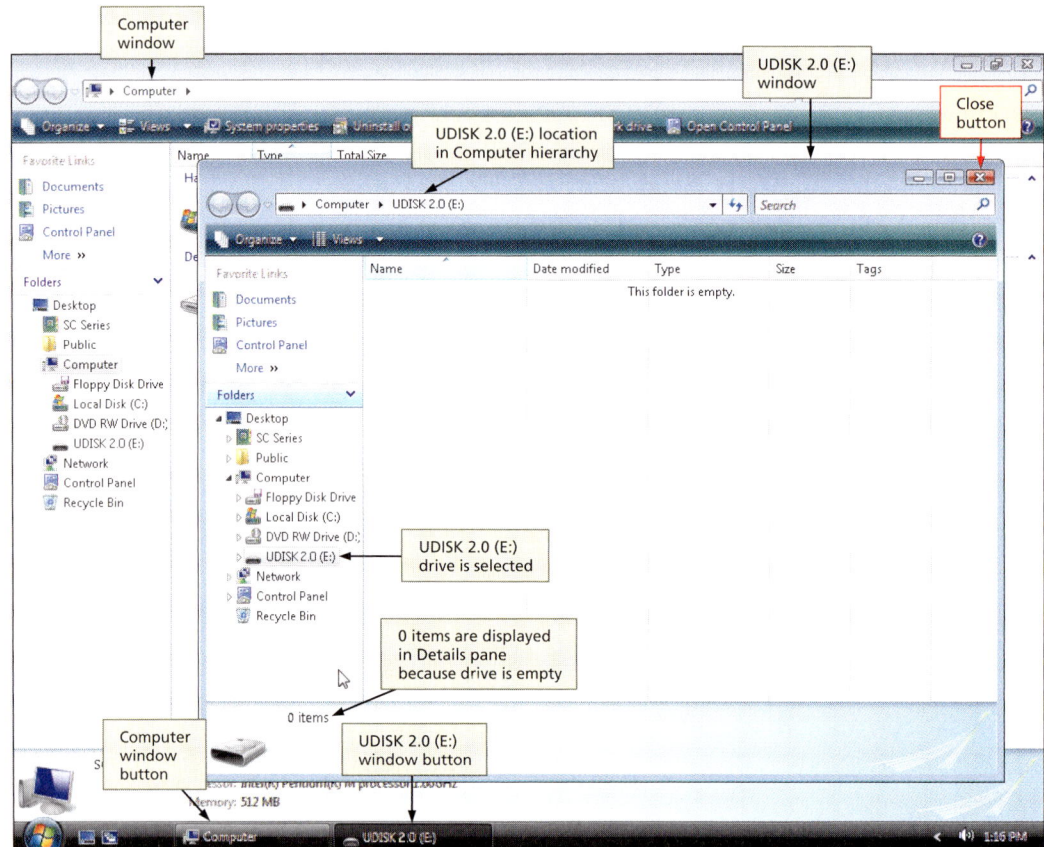

Figure 52

Naming a Folder

When you create a folder, such as the Freshman folder in Figure 50 on page WIN 36, you must name the folder. A folder name should describe the folder and its contents. A folder name can contain up to 255 characters, including spaces. Any uppercase or lowercase character is valid when creating a folder name, except a backslash (\), slash (/), colon (:), asterisk (*), question mark (?), quotation marks ("), less than symbol (<), greater than symbol (>), or vertical bar (|). Folder names cannot be CON, AUX, COM1, COM2, COM3, COM4, LPT1, LPT2, LPT3, PRN, or NUL. The same rules for naming folders also apply to naming files.

To Create a Folder on a Removable Drive

To create a folder on a removable drive, you must select the UDISK 2.0 (E:) drive and then create the folder in the right pane. The following steps create the Freshman folder on the UDISK 2.0 (E:) drive.

1
- Double-click the UDISK 2.0 (E:) icon in the Folders list to select it.
- Right-click an open area of the right pane to display a shortcut menu.
- Point to New on the shortcut menu to display the New submenu (Figure 53).

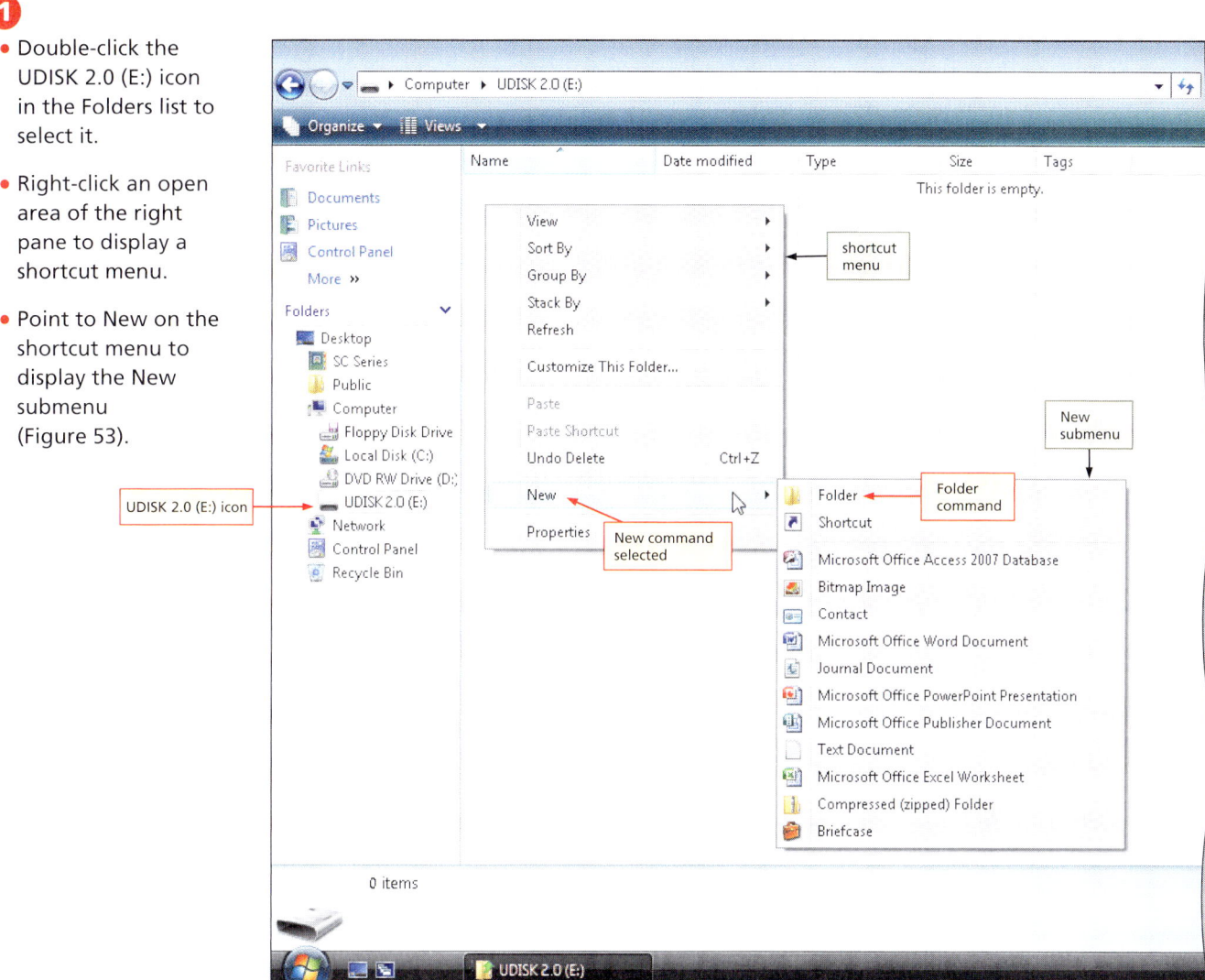

Figure 53

- Click Folder on the New submenu to display the new Folder icon.
- Type Freshman in the text box to name the folder.
- Press the ENTER key to create the Freshman folder on the UDISK 2.0 (E:) drive (Figure 54).

Q&A What happens when I press the ENTER key?

The Freshman folder is displayed in the File list, which contains the folder name, date modified, and file folder type.

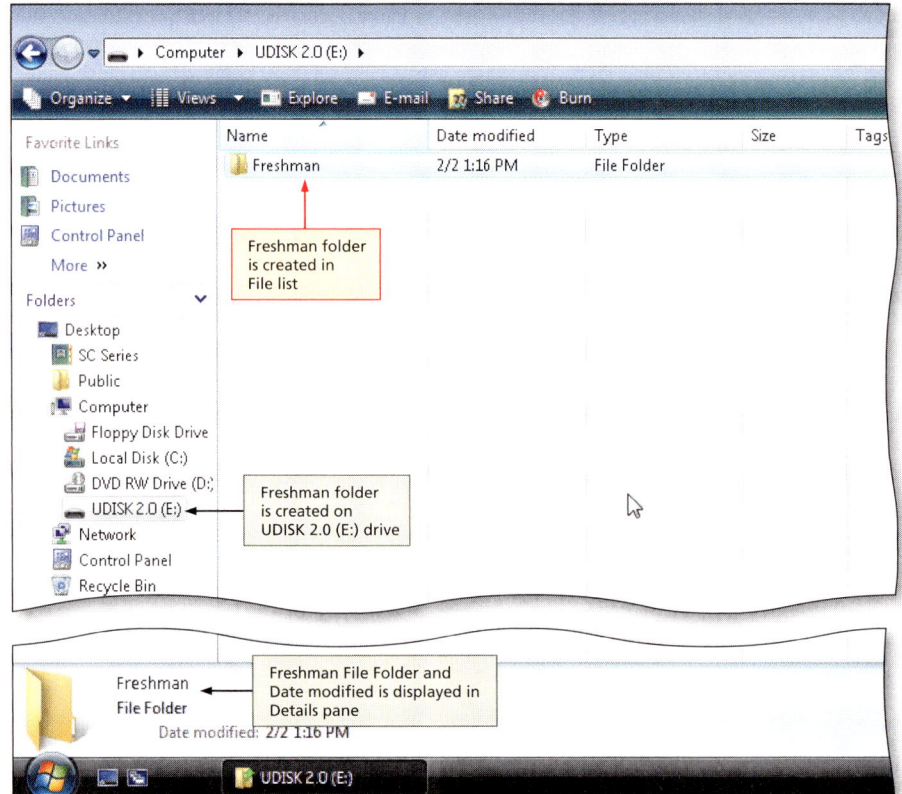

Figure 54

Downloading a Hierarchy of Folders into the Freshman Folder

After creating the Freshman folder on the UDISK 2.0 (E:) drive, the remaining folders in the hierarchical structure (see Figure 50), starting with the 1st Semester folder, should be downloaded to the Freshman folder. **Downloading** is the process of a computer receiving information, such as a set of files or folders from a Web site, from a server on the Internet. To make the task of creating the folders easier, the folders have been created and stored in a hierarchical structure on the SC Site - Shelly Cashman Series Student Resources Web site.

To Download a Hierarchy of Folders into the Freshman Folder

The following steps download the folders in the hierarchical structure into the Freshman folder.

1 Start Internet Explorer by clicking the Start button on the taskbar and then clicking Internet on the Start menu.

2 Click the Address bar, type scsite.com in the Address bar, and then click the Go button.

3. When the SC Site - Shelly Cashman Series Student Resources Web site is displayed, use the Browse by Subject navigation bar, click Office Suites, and then click Microsoft Office 2007.

4. In the center of the screen, locate your textbook and click the title (for example, Discovering Computers and Microsoft Office 2007: A Fundamental Combined Approach).

5. Scroll down to display the Data Files for Students (Windows) area and then click the Windows Vista Chapter Data Files link.

6. When the File Download – Security Warning dialog box is displayed, click the Run button.

7. When the Internet Explorer – Security Warning dialog box is displayed, click the Run button.

8. When the WinZip Self-Extractor dialog box is displayed, type the removable media drive letter of your removable media drive followed by a colon, backslash, and folder name (Freshman) (for example, E:\Freshman).

9. Click the Unzip button.

10. When Windows displays the WinZip Self-Extractor dialog box, click the OK button.

11. Click the Close button in the WinZip Self-Extractor dialog box.

12. Click the Close button in the SC Site – Shelly Cashman Series Student Resources Web site window (Figure 55).

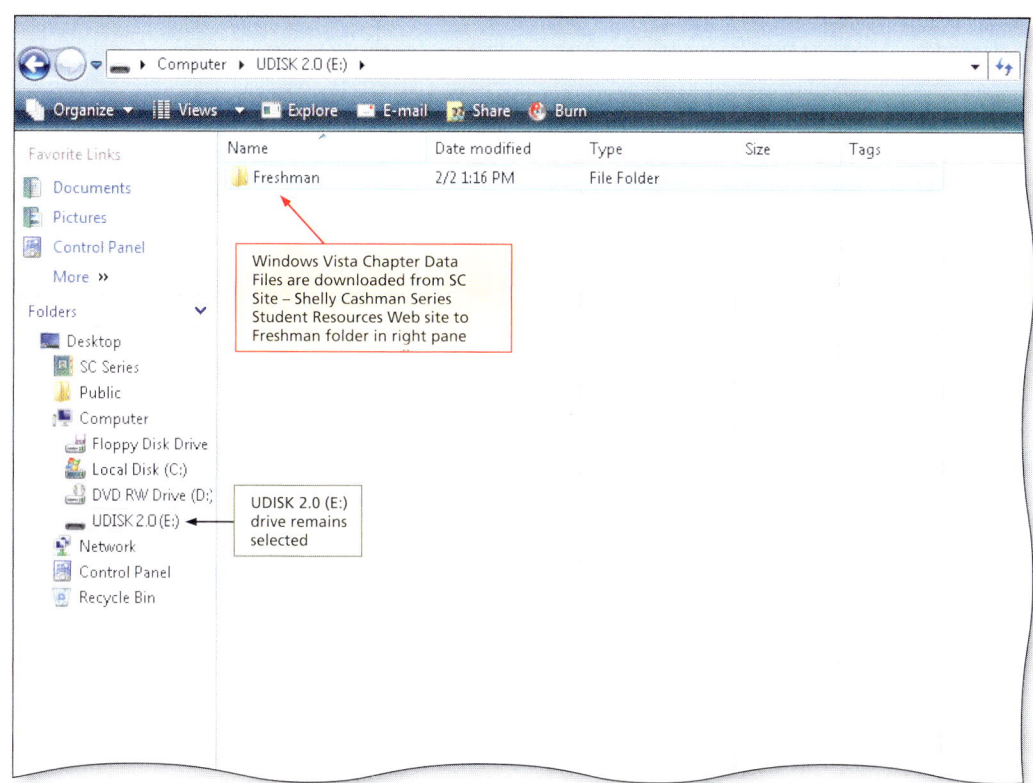

Figure 55

To Expand a Drive

Folder Windows display the hierarchy of items in the Folders list and the contents of drives and folders in the right pane. You might want to expand a drive to view its contents in the Folders list. The following step expands a drive.

- Point to any item in the Folders list to display arrows and then click the white arrow to the left of the UDISK 2.0 (E:) icon in the Folders list to display the Freshman folder.

Q&A Why are black arrows and white arrows in the Folders list?

The black arrows represent folders and drives that contain other folders that have been expanded to show their contents. The white arrows represent folders and drives that contain other folders that have not been expanded.

- Click the white arrow next to the Freshman folder and then click the white arrow next to the 1st Semester folder to display its contents (Figure 56).

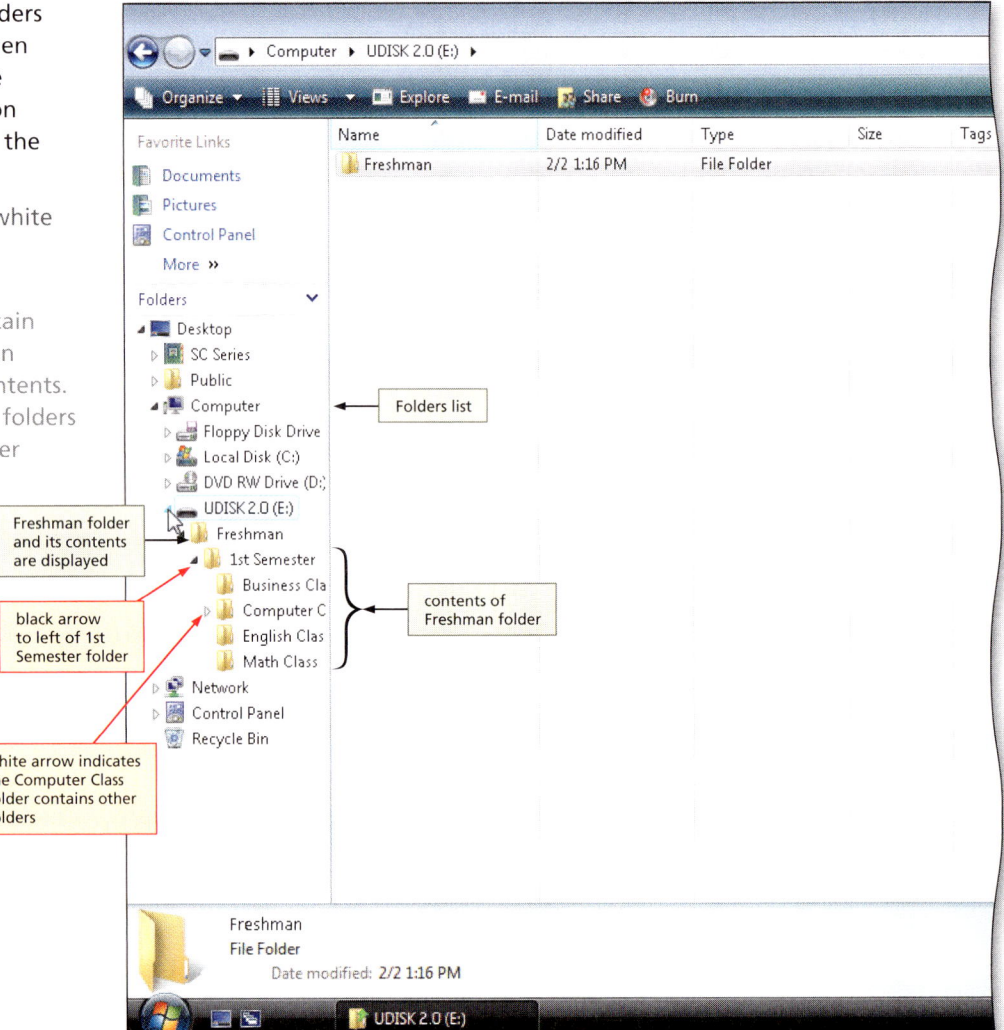

Figure 56

Other Ways

1. Double-click drive icon in Folders list
2. Select drive to expand using ARROW keys, press RIGHT ARROW on keyboard
3. Select drive to expand, press RIGHT ARROW

Introduction to Windows Vista **Windows Vista Chapter** **WIN 43**

To Collapse a Folder

When a black arrow is displayed to the left of a folder icon in the Folders list, the folder is expanded and shows all the folders it contains. The following step collapses the 1st Semester folder.

1

- Click the black arrow to the left of the 1st Semester folder icon in the Folders list to collapse the 1st Semester folder (Figure 57).

Q&A Why is the 1st Semester folder indented below the Freshman folder in the Folders list?

The folder is indented below the Freshman icon to show that the folder is contained within the Freshman folder.

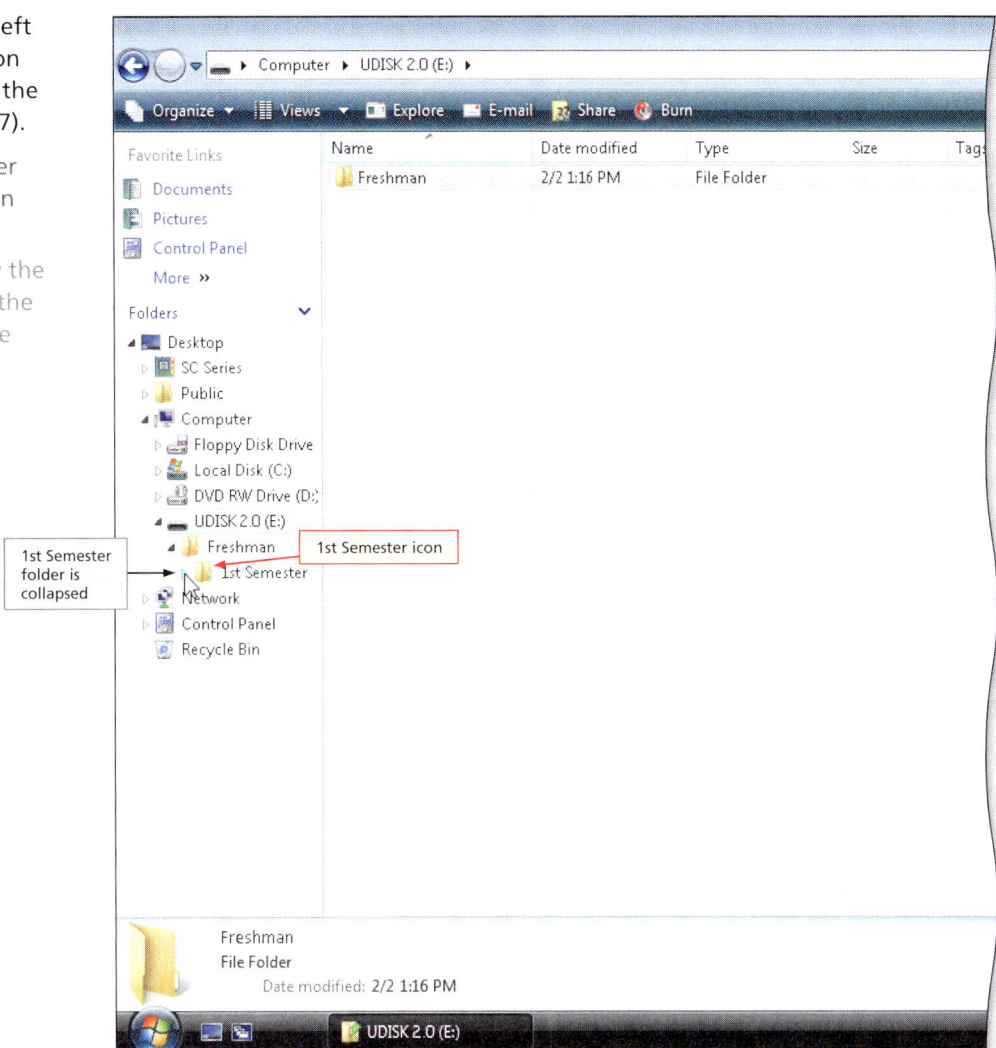

Figure 57

Other Ways

1. Double-click folder icon in Folders list
2. Select folder to collapse using ARROW keys, press LEFT ARROW on keyboard
3. Select folder to collapse, press LEFT ARROW

To Display the Contents of a Folder

Clicking a folder icon in the Folders list displays the contents of the drive or folder in the File list and displays the path in the Address bar. The following step displays the contents of the 1st Semester folder.

1

• Click the 1st Semester icon in the Folders list to display the contents of the 1st Semester folder in the File list (Figure 58).

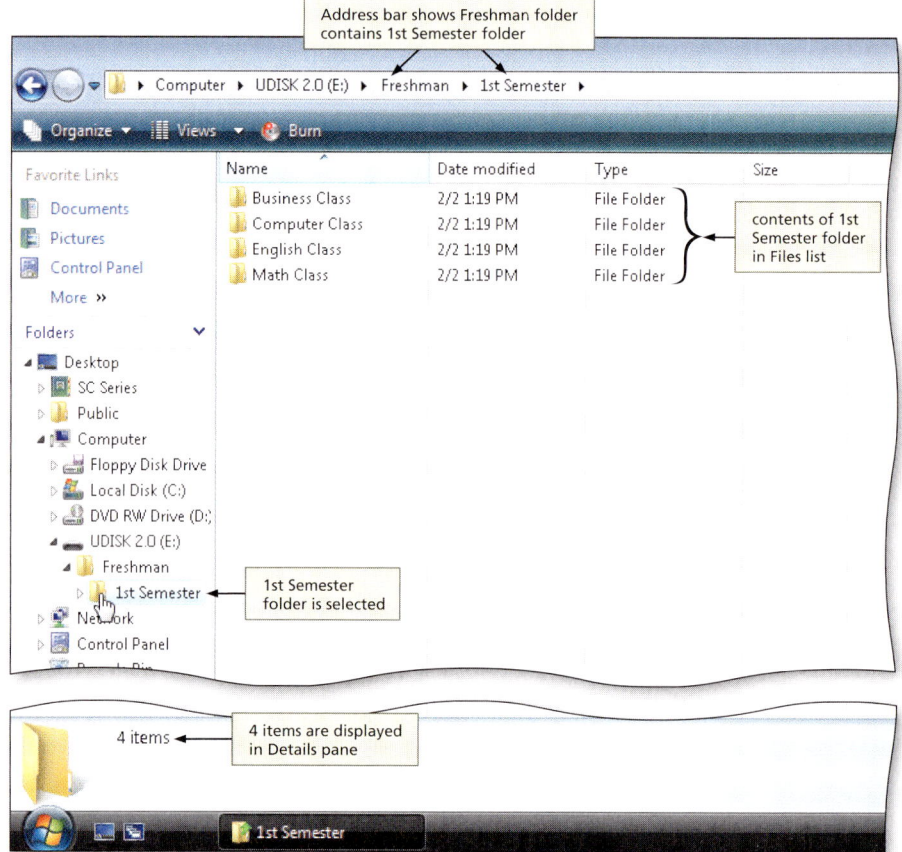

Figure 58

Other Ways

1. Right-click 1st Semester icon, click Explore on shortcut menu

Creating a Document and Folder Using WordPad

The Freshman folder was created on the UDISK 2.0 (E:) drive when you downloaded the files. You also can create a folder anytime you save a file in a Windows program. For example, you can use WordPad to create a document and then save the new document in a folder. **WordPad** is a word processing program included with Windows Vista that allows you to create a limited variety of personal and business documents.

As one of the programs in the Accessories list, one method to start WordPad is to display the Start menu, click All Programs, click Accessories, and click WordPad in the Accessories list.

An easier method to start WordPad is to use the Start Search box on the Start menu. The **Start Search** box allows you to find a specific program, file, e-mail, or Internet favorite by typing the first few letters in the Start Search box at the bottom of the Start menu.

To Start WordPad Using the Start Search Box

Assume you want to create a WordPad document that lists your homework for Friday, April 11. The first step is to start the WordPad program using the Start Search box. The following steps find and then start WordPad based on using the Start Search box at the bottom of the Start menu.

1

- Click the Start button to display the Start menu.

- Type w (the first letter in the WordPad name) in the Start Search box on the Start menu to display a list of programs, favorites, and history (Figure 59).

Q&A

What is displayed on the Start menu when I type the letter w?

A list of programs, favorites, and history that begin with the letter entered, w, are displayed. The WordPad program does not appear yet. As you type the entire program name, fewer selections remain in the list until you find your selection or no items match your search term.

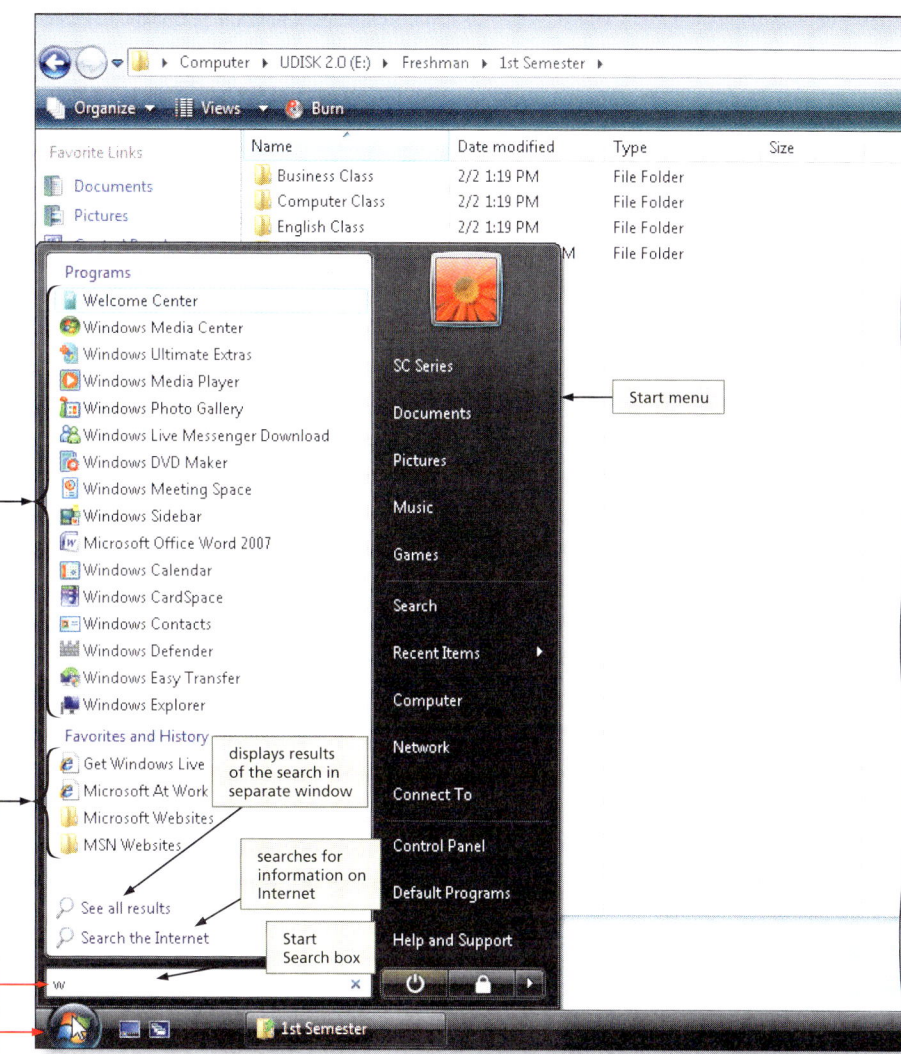

Figure 59

2

- Type the letter o (the second letter in the WordPad name) in the Start Search box on the Start menu to display a list of programs, favorites, history, and files (Figure 60).

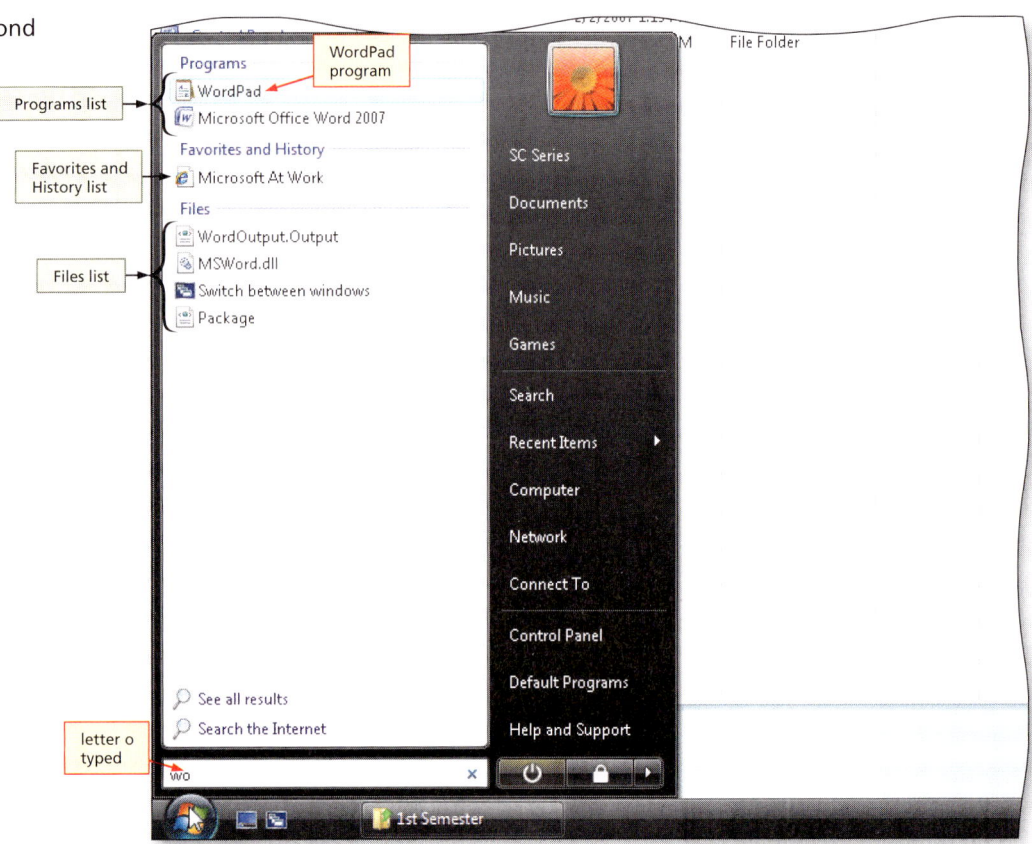

Figure 60

3

- Click WordPad in the Programs list to start the WordPad program and display a new blank document in the WordPad window (Figure 61).

- If the WordPad window is not maximized, click the Maximize button on the title bar to maximize the window.

Q&A Could I continue typing the remainder of the letters in the WordPad name?

Yes. To start the program you still need to click WordPad in the Programs list to start the WordPad program.

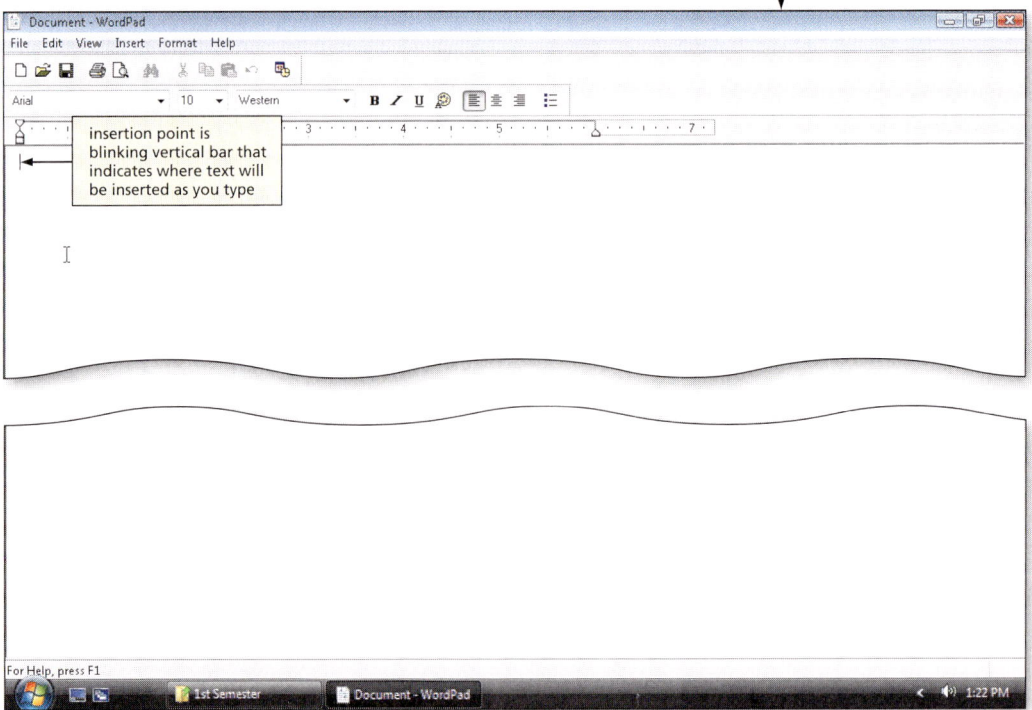

Figure 61

Introduction to Windows Vista **Windows Vista Chapter** WIN 49

4
- Click UDISK 2.0 (E:) in the Folders list to display the contents of the UDISK 2.0 (E:) folder in the File list (Figure 66).

 Why is my list of drives and folders different from the one in Figure 66?

Folders and drives can be unique for each computer.

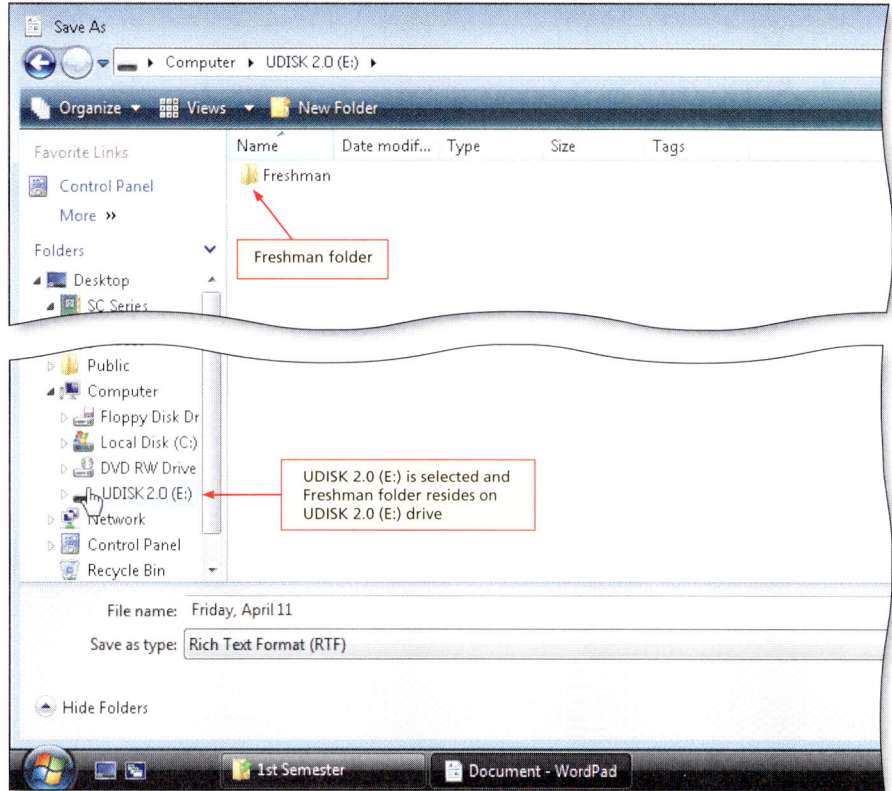

Figure 66

5
- Double-click the Freshman folder in the File list in the Save As dialog box to display the 1st Semester folder in the File list (Figure 67).

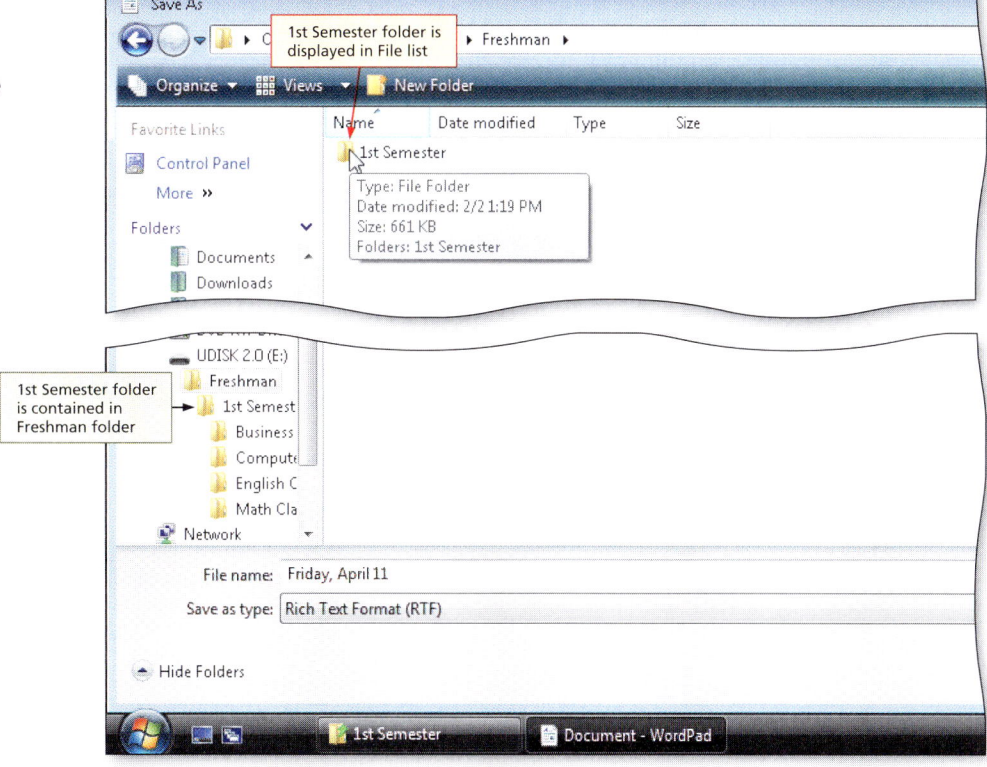

Figure 67

- Double-click the 1st Semester folder in the File list of the Save As dialog box to display the contents of the 1st Semester folder (Figure 68).

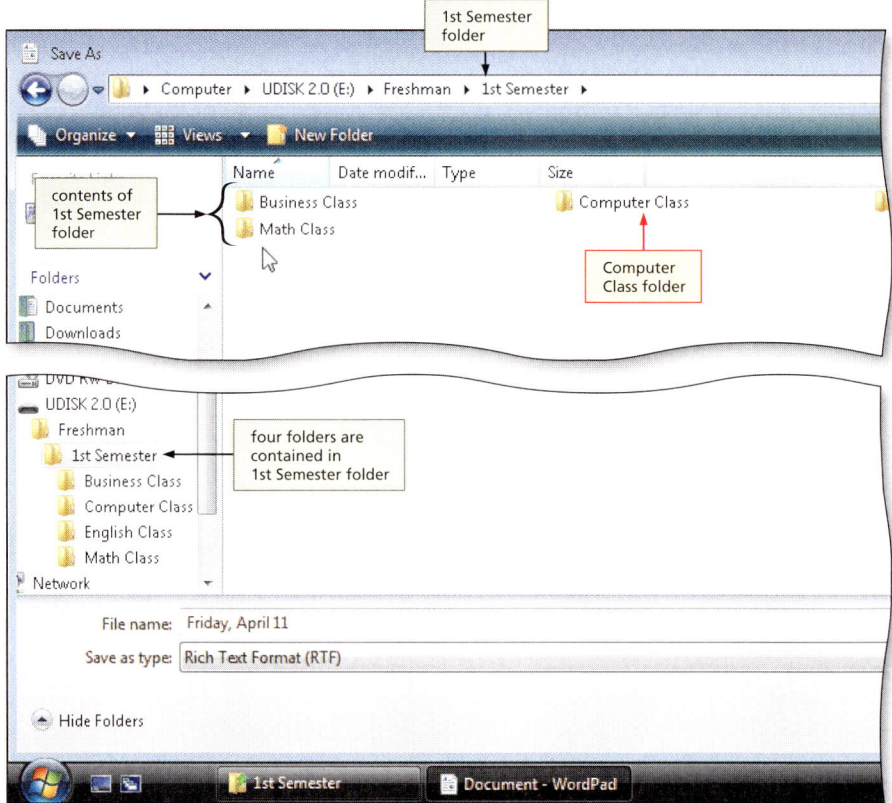

Figure 68

- Double-click the Computer Class folder in the File list in the Save As dialog box to display the contents of the Computer Class folder (Figure 69).

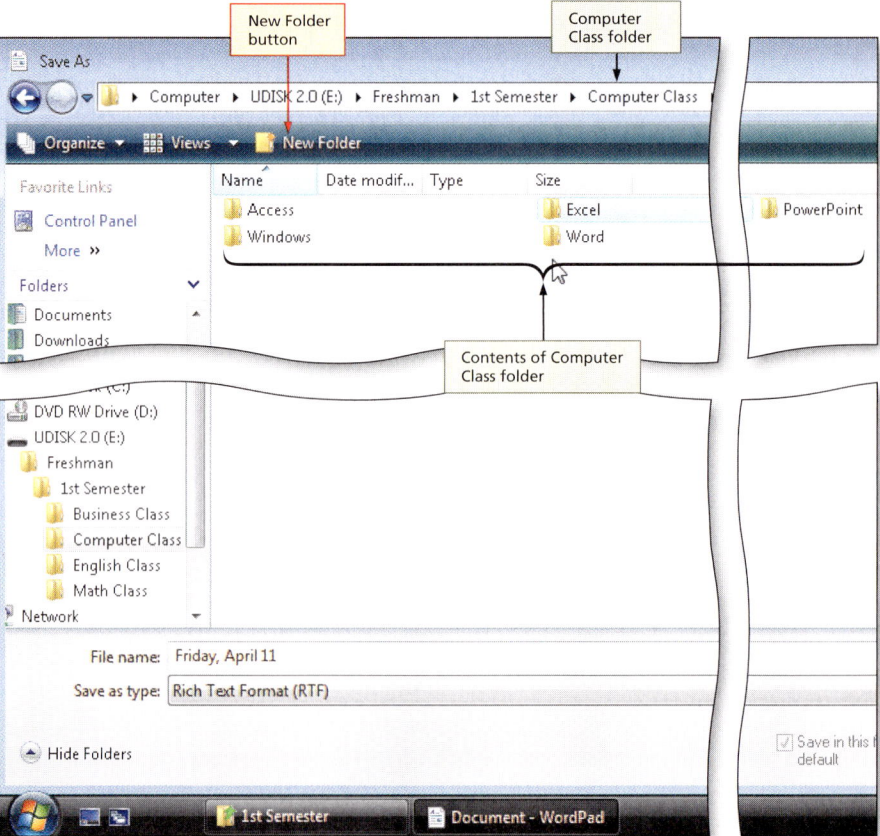

Figure 69

Introduction to Windows Vista **Windows Vista Chapter** WIN 51

8
- Click the New Folder button in the Save As dialog box to create a new folder within the Computer Class folder.
- Type Homework as the name of the folder and then press the ENTER key (Figure 70).

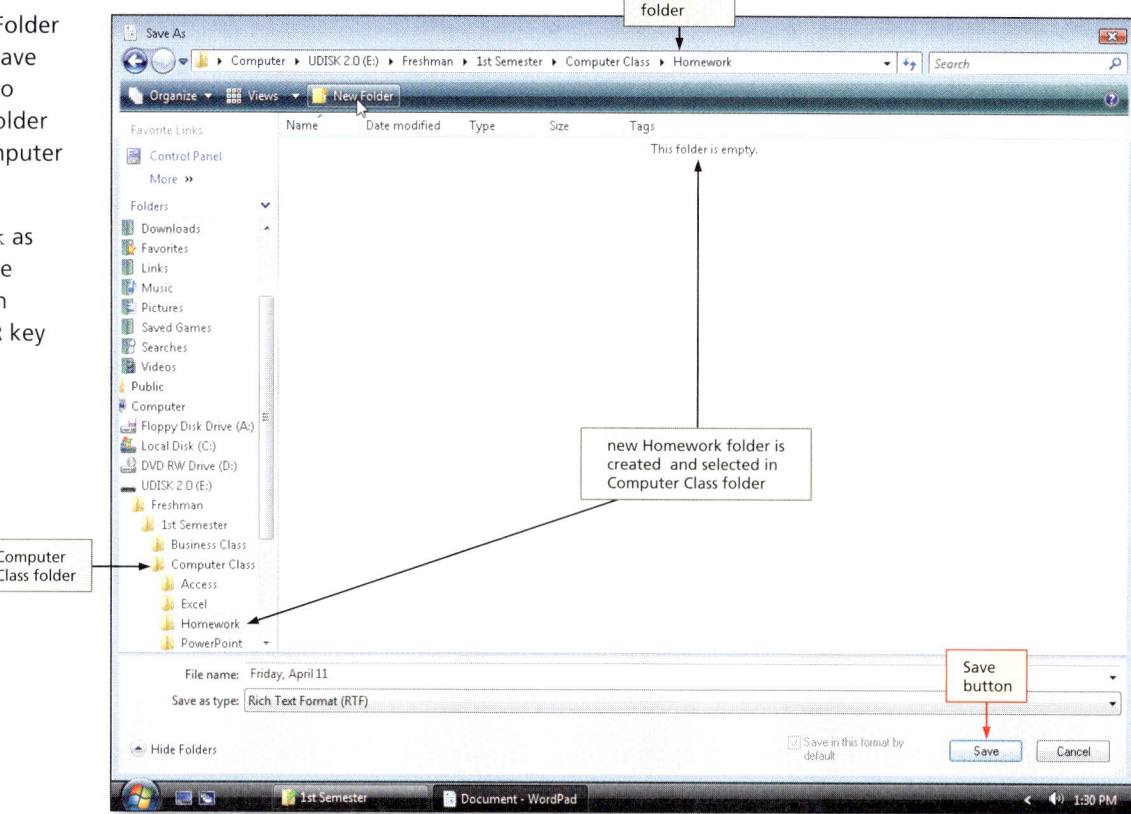

Figure 70

9
- Click the Save button in the Save As dialog box to save the Friday, April 11 document to its new location in the Homework folder (Figure 71).
- Click the Close button on the WordPad title bar to close the window.

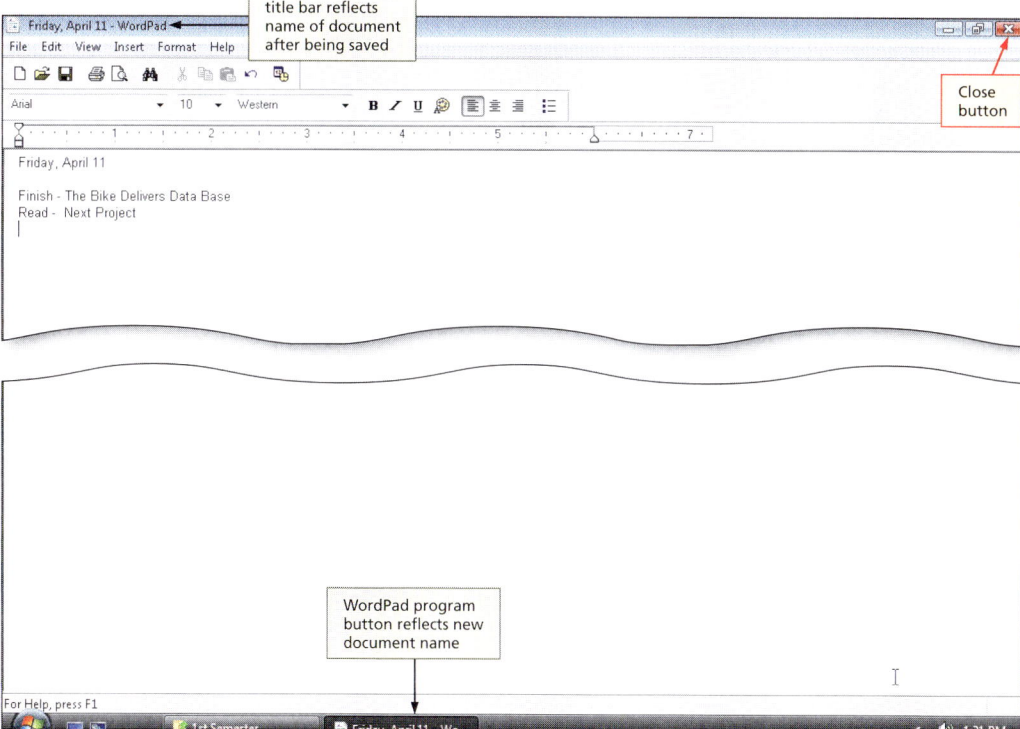

Figure 71

To Verify the Contents of a Folder

After saving the Friday, April 11 document in the Homework folder, you can verify that the document was correctly saved in the Homework folder. The following step verifies the Homework folder contains the Friday, April 11 document.

- Click the white arrow next to the 1st Semester icon in the Folders list to display the folders within the 1st Semester folder.

- Click the white arrow next to the Computer Class icon in the Folders list to display the folders within the Computer Class folder.

- Click the Homework icon in the Folders list to select the Homework folder and display the contents of the Homework folder in the right pane (Figure 72).

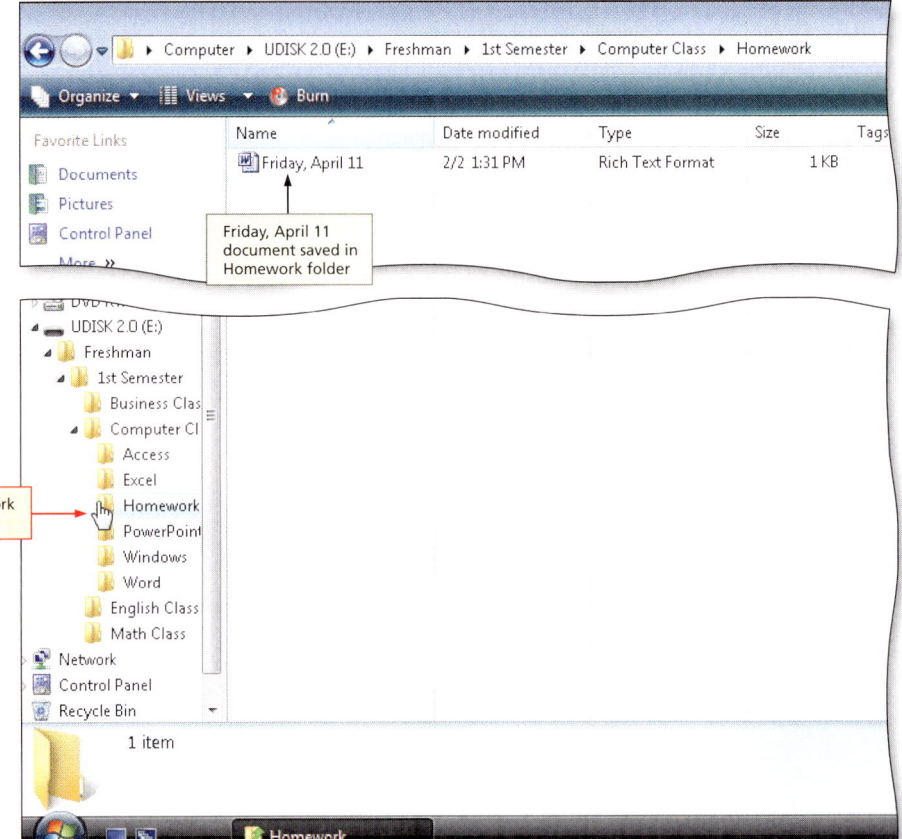

Figure 72

File Management

Being able to manage the files on the computer is one of the most important computer skills you can have. **File management** includes copying, moving, renaming, and deleting files and folders on the computer.

To Copy a File by Right-Dragging

When copying files, the drive and folder containing the files to be copied are called the **source drive** and **source folder**, respectively. The drive and folder to which the files are copied are called the **destination drive** and **destination folder**, respectively. The Access folder contains two Access database files (SciFi Scene and The Bike Delivers).

The following steps show one method of copying files — right-drag a file icon from the right pane to a folder or drive icon in the Folders list. The following steps copy the The Bike Delivers file from the Access folder (source folder) to the Homework (destination folder). The UDISK 2.0 (E:) drive is both the source drive and the destination drive.

1
- Click the Access folder in the Folders list to select the Access folder and display its contents in the right pane (Figure 73).

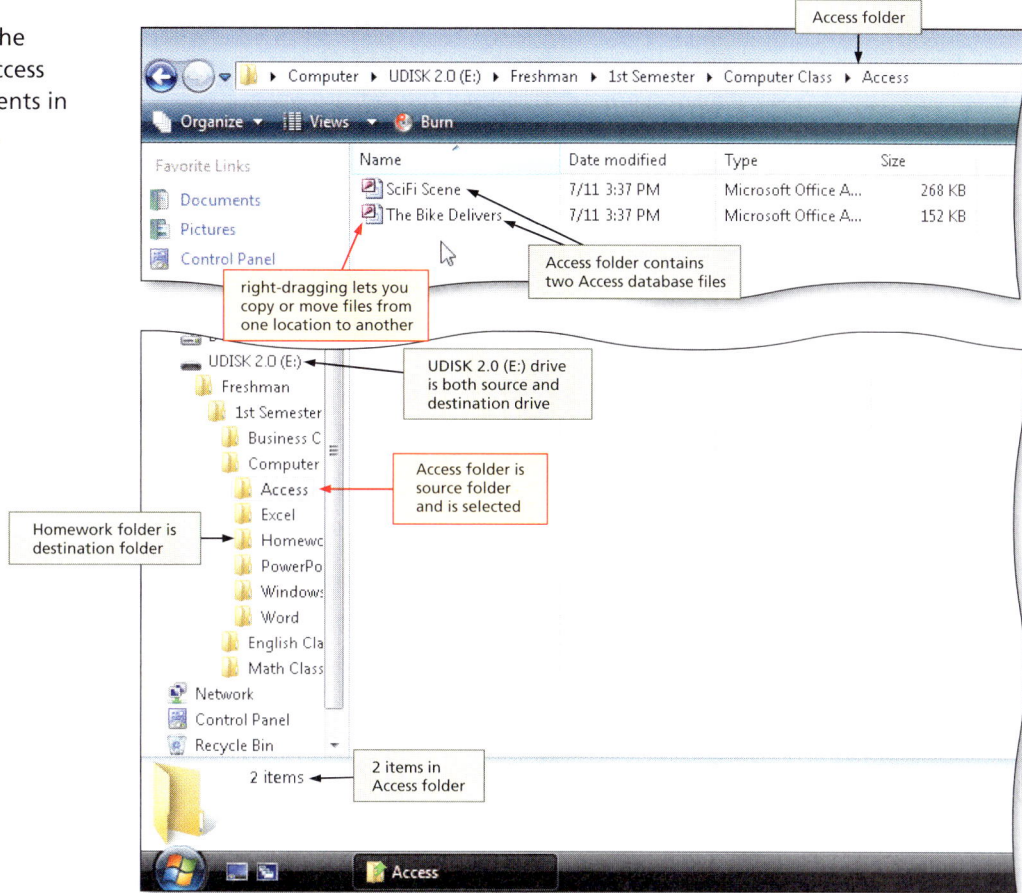

Figure 73

2
- Right-drag the The Bike Delivers icon from the right pane to the Homework folder icon in the Folders list to display the shortcut menu (Figure 74).

Q&A What should I do if I right-drag a file to the wrong folder?

Click Cancel on the shortcut menu and then right-drag the file to the correct folder.

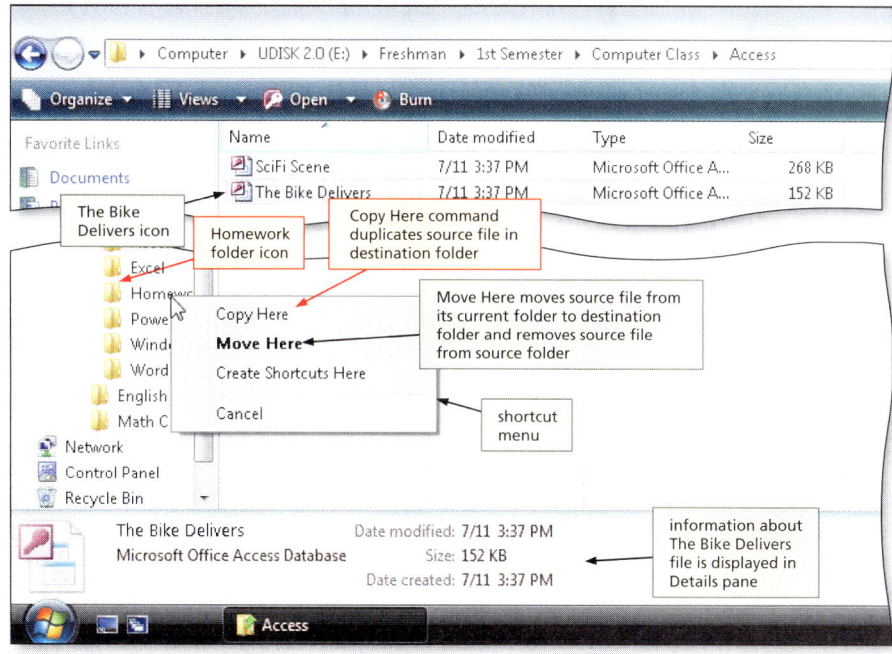

Figure 74

- Click Copy Here on the shortcut menu to copy The Bike Delivers file to the Homework folder (Figure 75).

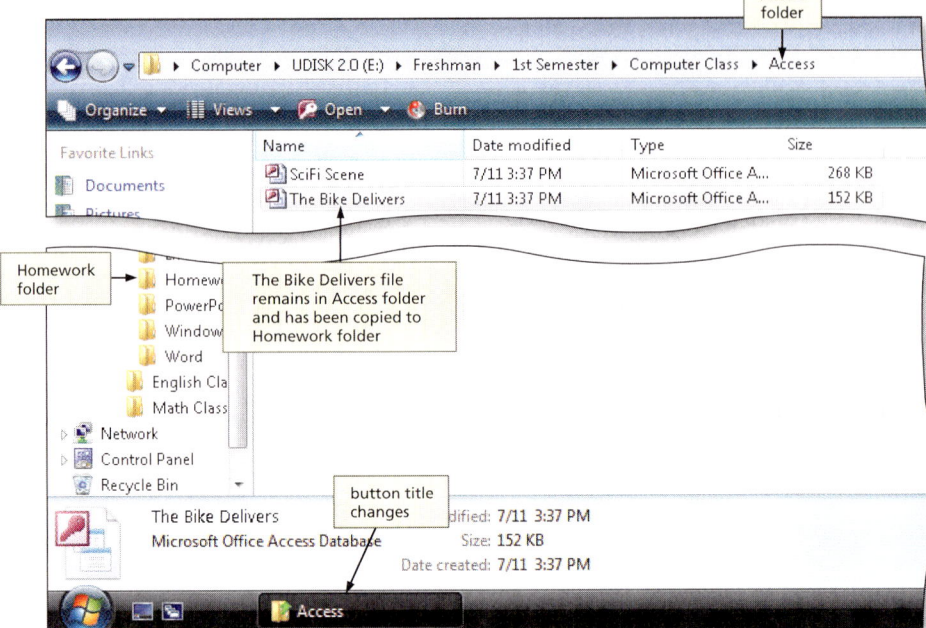

Figure 75

Other Ways

1. Right-click file to copy, click Copy on shortcut menu, right-click Homework folder, click Paste on the shortcut menu
2. Select file to copy, press CTRL+C, select Homework folder, press CTRL+V

To Display the Contents of a Folder

After copying a file, you might want to examine the folder or drive where the file was copied to ensure it was copied properly. The following step displays the contents of the Homework folder.

- Click the Homework folder in the Folders list to display the contents of the Homework folder (Figure 76).

Q&A Can I copy or move more than one file at a time?

Yes. To copy or move multiple files, select each file to be copied or moved by clicking the file icon while holding down the CTRL key. Then, right-drag the selected files to the destination folder using the same technique as right-dragging a single file.

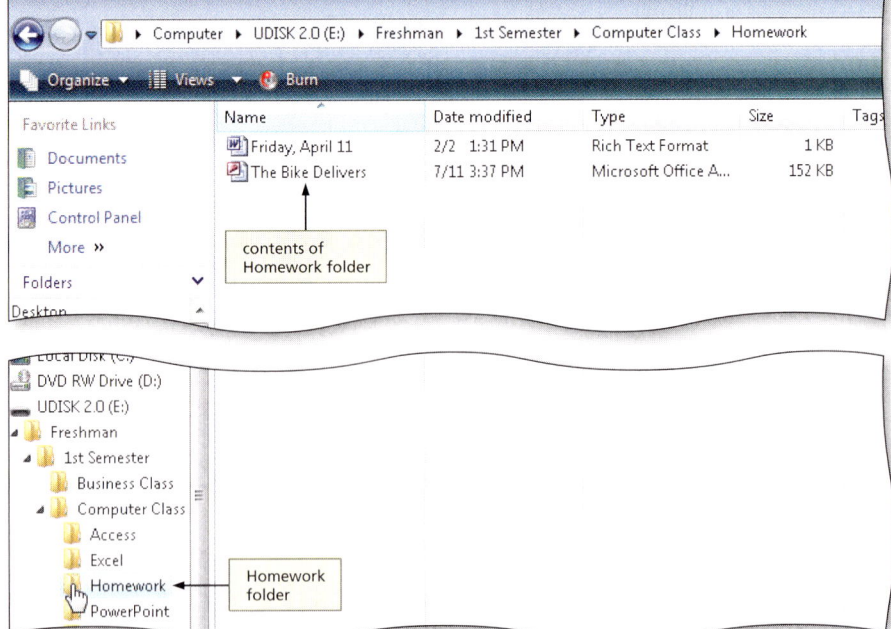

Figure 76

To Rename a File

In some circumstances, you may want to rename a file or a folder. This could occur when you want to distinguish a file in one folder or drive from a copy, or if you decide you need a better name to identify a file. The Word folder in Figure 77 contains the three Word documents (Barn and Silo, Fall Harvest, and Lake at Sunset). In this case, you decide to change the Fall Harvest name to Great Fall Harvest. The following steps change the name of the Fall Harvest file in the Word folder to Great Fall Harvest.

1
- Click the Word folder in the left pane to display the three files it contains in the right pane.
- Right-click the Fall Harvest icon in the right pane to select the Fall Harvest icon and display a shortcut menu (Figure 77).

2
- Click Rename on the shortcut menu to select the file name for renaming.
- Type `Great Fall Harvest` and then press the ENTER key (Figure 78).

Q&A Are any risks involved in renaming files that are located on the hard disk?

If you inadvertently rename a file that is associated with certain programs, the programs may not be able to find the file and, therefore, may not execute properly. Always use caution when renaming files.

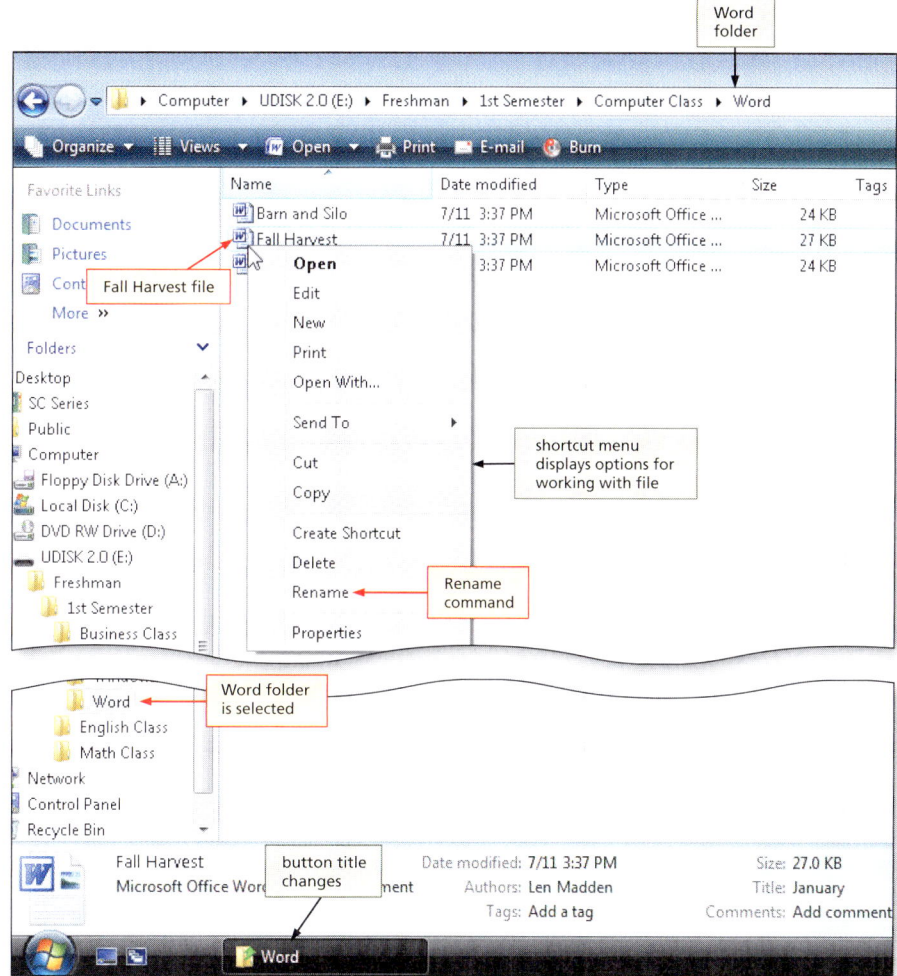

Figure 77

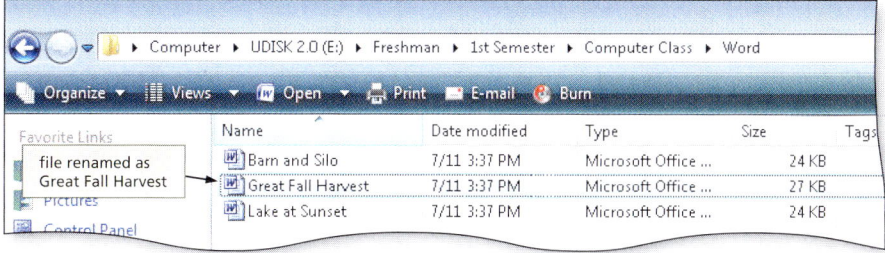

Figure 78

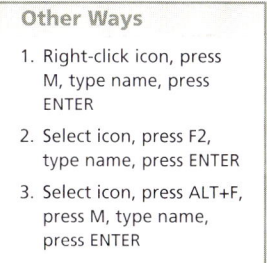

Other Ways
1. Right-click icon, press M, type name, press ENTER
2. Select icon, press F2, type name, press ENTER
3. Select icon, press ALT+F, press M, type name, press ENTER

To Delete a File by Right-Clicking

A final task you may want to perform is to delete a file. Exercise extreme caution when deleting a file or files. When you delete a file from a hard disk, the deleted file is stored in the Recycle Bin where you can recover it until you empty the Recycle Bin. If you delete a file from removable media, the file is gone permanently once you delete it. The following steps delete the Lake at Sunset file.

- Right-click the Lake at Sunset icon in the right pane to select the icon and display a shortcut menu (Figure 79).

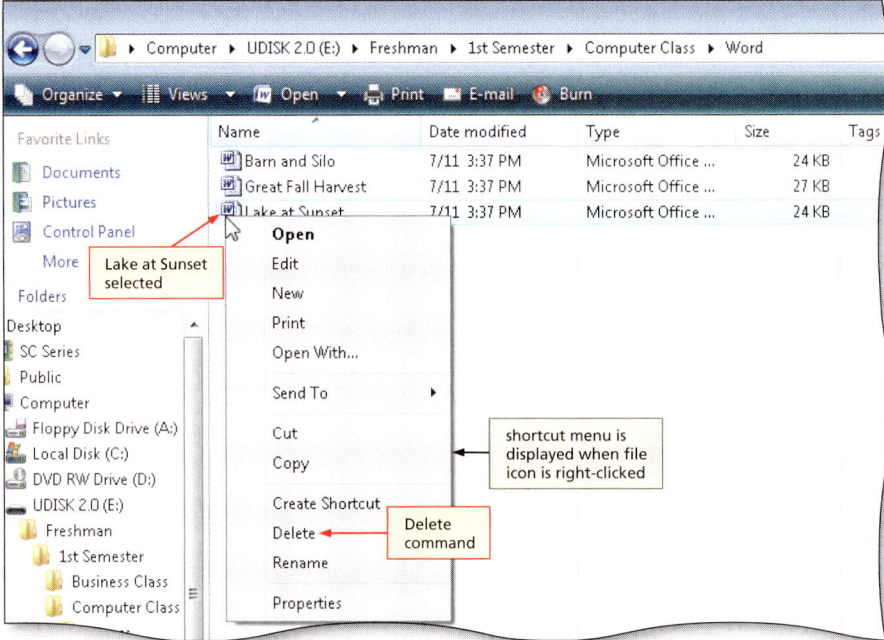

Figure 79

- Click Delete on the shortcut menu to display the Delete File dialog box (Figure 80).

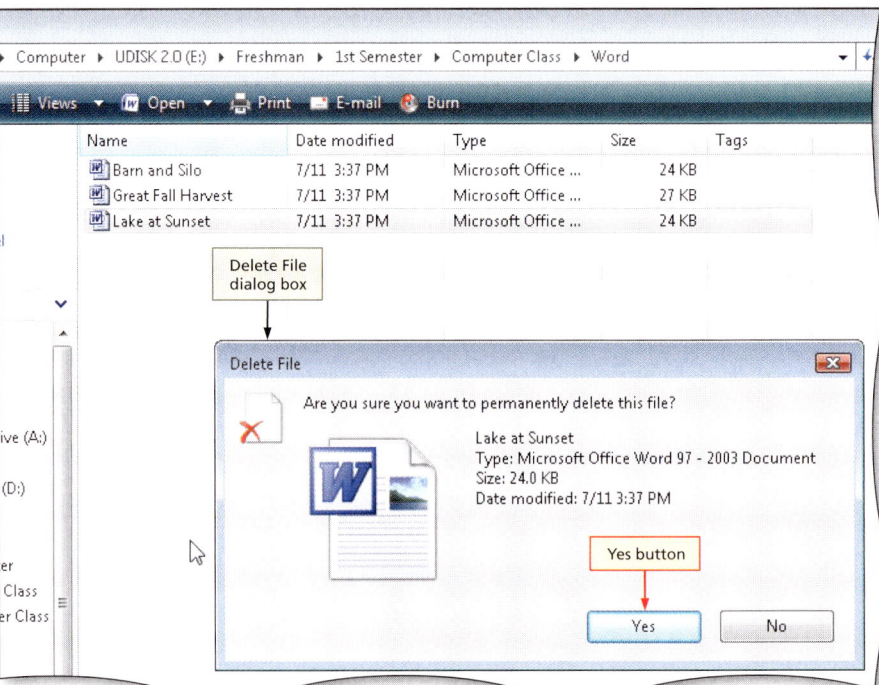

Figure 80

3

- Click the Yes button in the Delete File dialog box to delete the Lake at Sunset file (Figure 81).

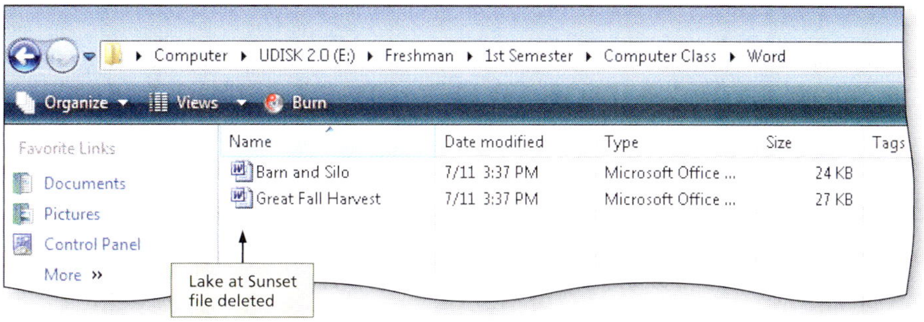

Q&A

Can I use this same technique to delete a folder?

Yes. Right-click the folder and then click Delete on the shortcut menu. When you delete a folder, all the files and folders contained in the folder you are deleting, together with any files and folders on lower hierarchical levels, are deleted as well.

Figure 81

Other Ways

1. Select icon, press ALT+F, press D, press Y

To Close Expanded Folders

Sometimes, after you have completed work with expanded folders, you will want to close the expanded folders while still leaving the Word window open. The following steps close the Computer Class folder, 1st Semester folder, Freshman folder, and UDISK 2.0 (E:) drive.

1

- Click the black arrow to the left of the Computer Class folder in the Folders list to collapse the Computer Class folder (Figure 82).

2

- Click the black arrow to the left of the 1st Semester folder to collapse the folder.

- Click the black arrow to the left of the Freshman folder to collapse the folder.

- Click the black arrow to the left of the UDISK 2.0 (E:) drive to collapse the drive.

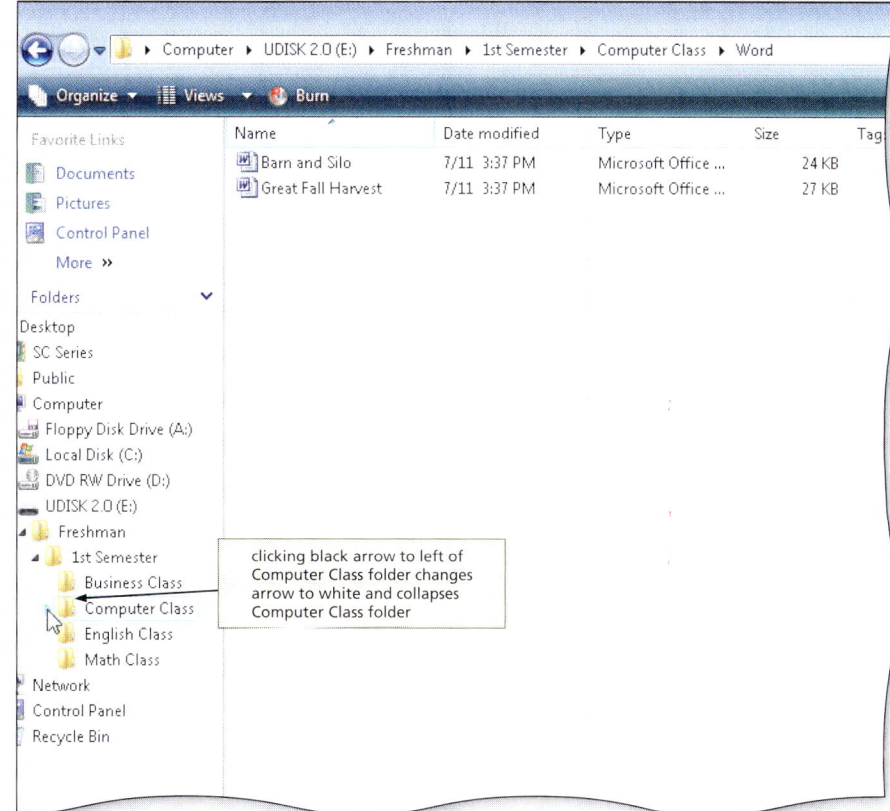

Figure 82

Other Ways

1. Click expanded folder icon, press LEFT ARROW

To Close the Computer Window

When you have finished working, you can close the Folders list and close the Computer window. The following steps close the Computer window.

1 Click the Close button on the Computer window title bar to close the Computer window.

2 Remove the USB flash drive from the USB port.

Using Help and Support

One of the more powerful Windows Vista features is Windows Help and Support. **Windows Help and Support** is available when using Windows Vista, or when using any program running under Windows Vista. It contains answers to many questions you may ask with respect to the Windows Vista operating system.

To Open the Windows Help and Support Window

Before you can access the Windows Help and Support services, you must start Help and Support. One method of starting Help and Support uses the Start menu. The following steps open the Windows Help and Support window.

- Display the Start menu (Figure 83).

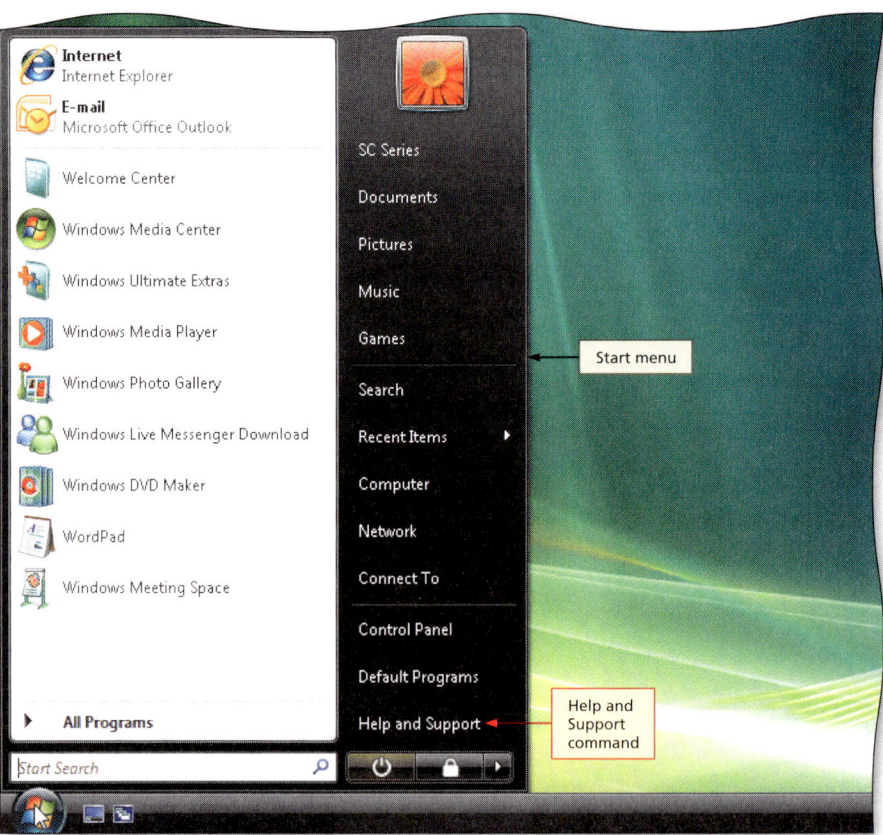

Figure 83

2

- Click Help and Support to display the Windows Help and Support window.

- If necessary, click the Maximize button on the Windows Help and Support title bar to maximize the Windows Help and Support window (Figure 84).

Q&A What does Windows Help and Support contain?

Windows Help and Support contains a title bar, navigation toolbar, Find an answer area, Ask someone area, and Information from Microsoft area.

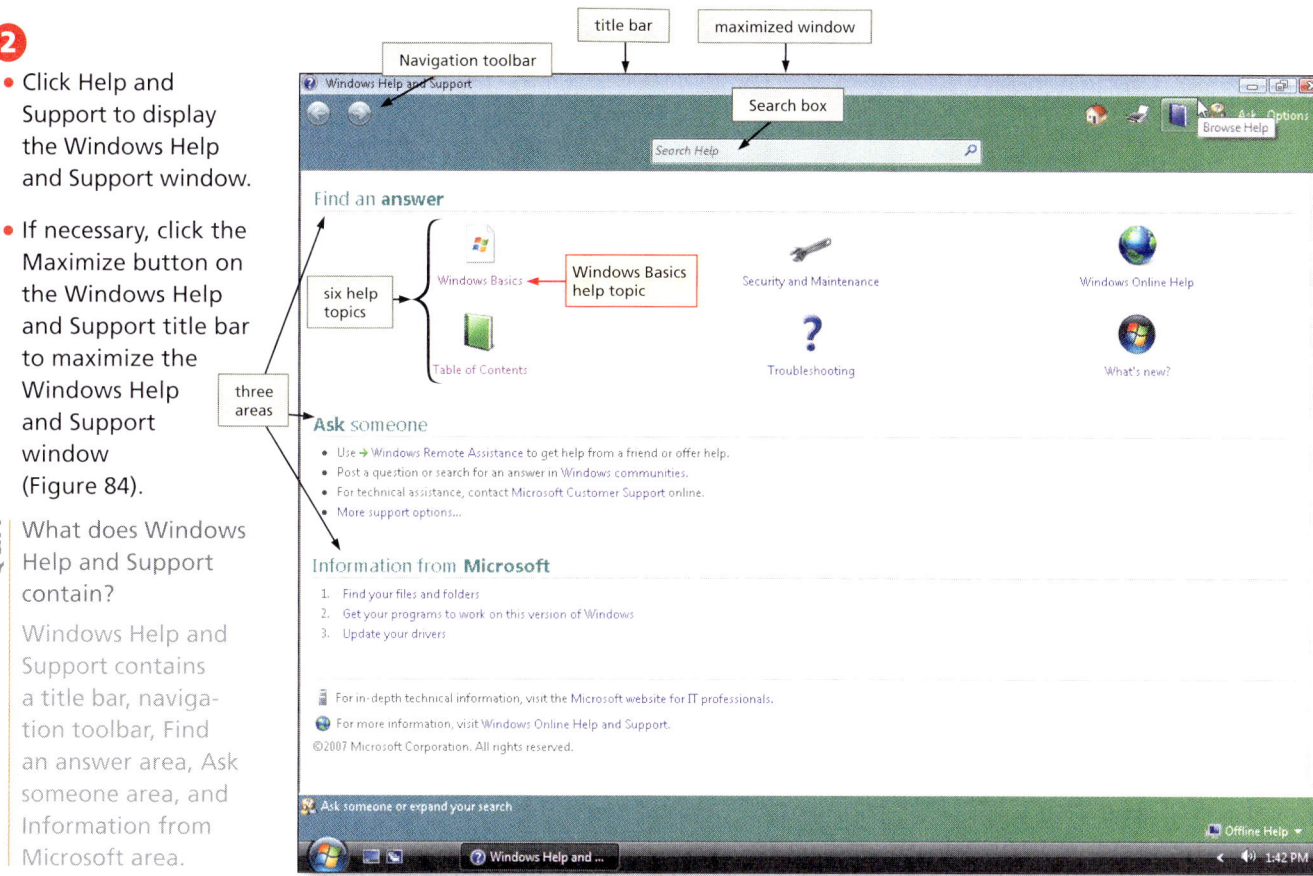

Figure 84

Other Ways
1. Press CTRL+ESC, press RIGHT ARROW, press UP ARROW, press ENTER
2. Press WINDOWS+F1

Table 4 shows the content areas in the Windows Help and Support Center.

Table 4 Windows Help and Support Center Content Areas

Area	Function
Find an answer	Area contains six Help topics: Windows Basics, Table of Contents, Security and Maintenance, Troubleshooting, Windows Online Help, and What's new? Clicking a category displays a list of subcategories and Help topics related to the category.
Ask someone	Area contains Windows Remote Assistance allowing you to get help from a friend or offer help, post a question or search for an answer in Windows communities, or get technical assistance from Microsoft Customer Support online. Clicking the 'More support options' link allows you to search the Knowledge Base, get in-depth technical information from Microsoft Website for IT professionals, and Windows Online Help and Support.
Information from Microsoft	Area contains links to 'Find your files and folders', 'Get your programs to work on this version of Windows', and 'Update your drives'.

To Browse for Help Topics in Windows Basics

After starting Windows Help and Support, the next action is to find the Help topic in which you are interested. The following steps use the 'Find an answer' area in the Windows Help and Support Center to find a Help topic that describes how to use the Windows Help and Support Center.

- Click Windows Basics in the 'Find an answer' area to display the Windows Basics: all topics heading (Figure 85).

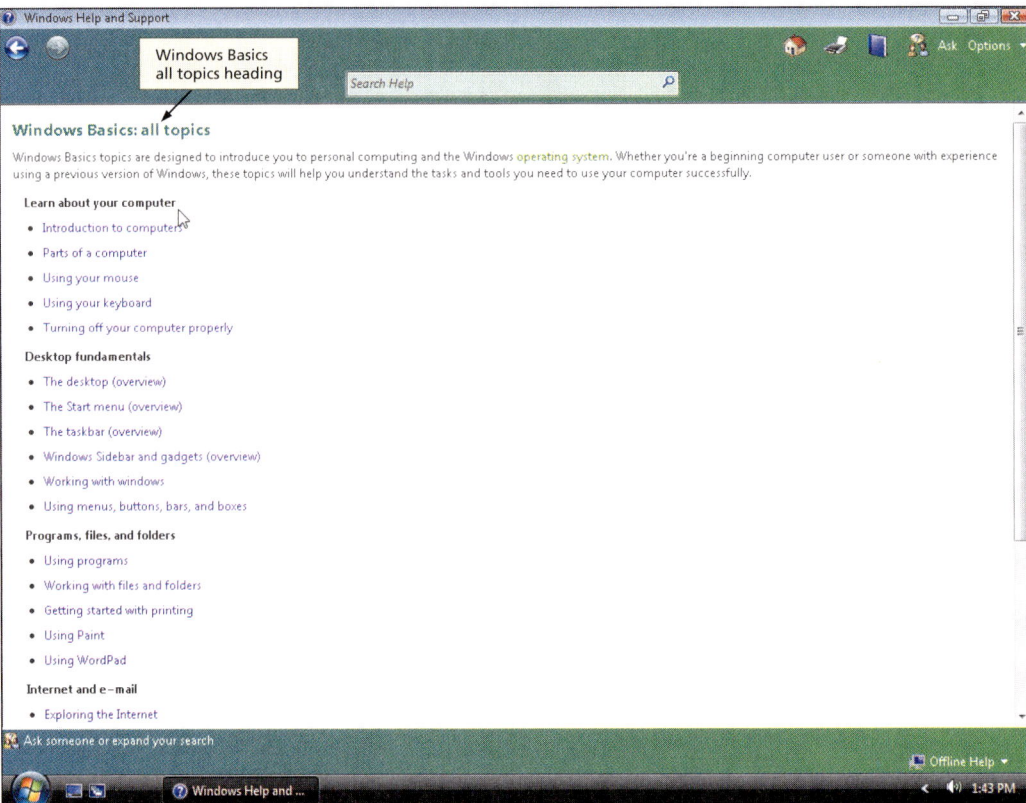

Figure 85

- Scroll down to view the Getting help topic (Figure 86).

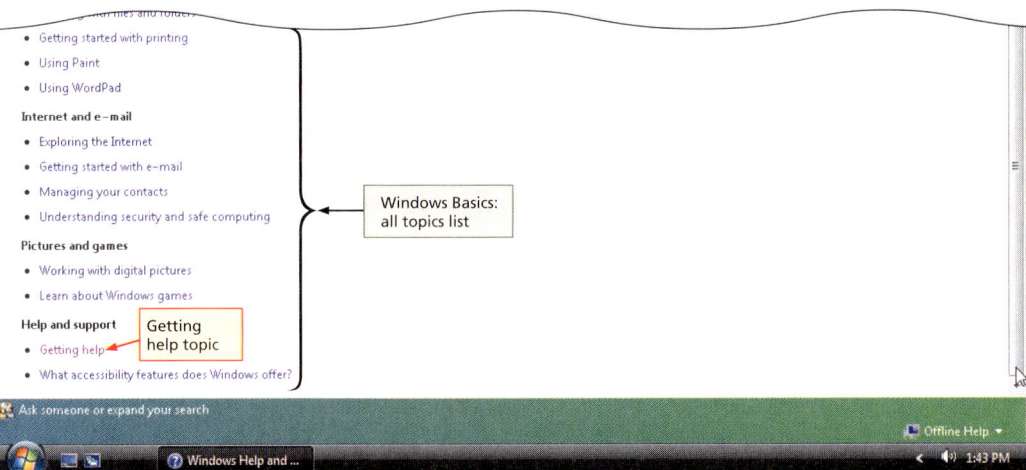

Figure 86

❸
- Click the Getting help topic (Figure 87).
- Read the information in the Getting help topic.

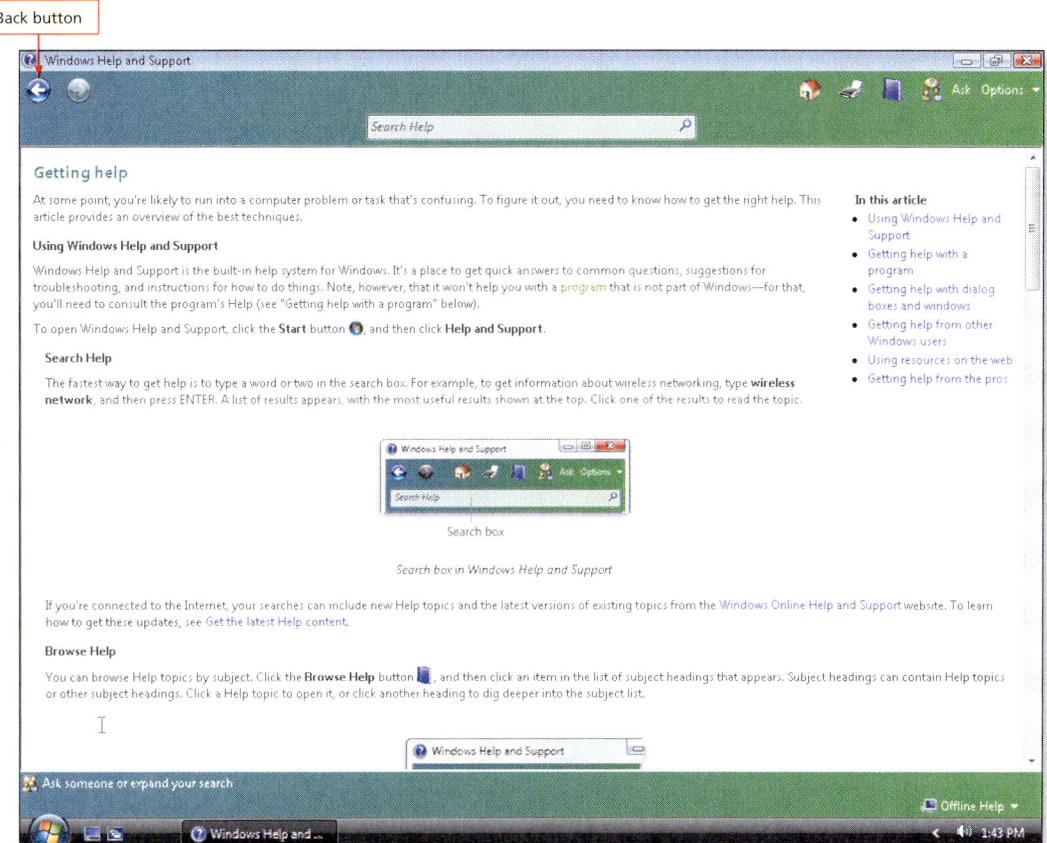

Figure 87

❹
- Click the Back button on the Navigation toolbar two times to return to the 'Find an answer' area (Figure 88).

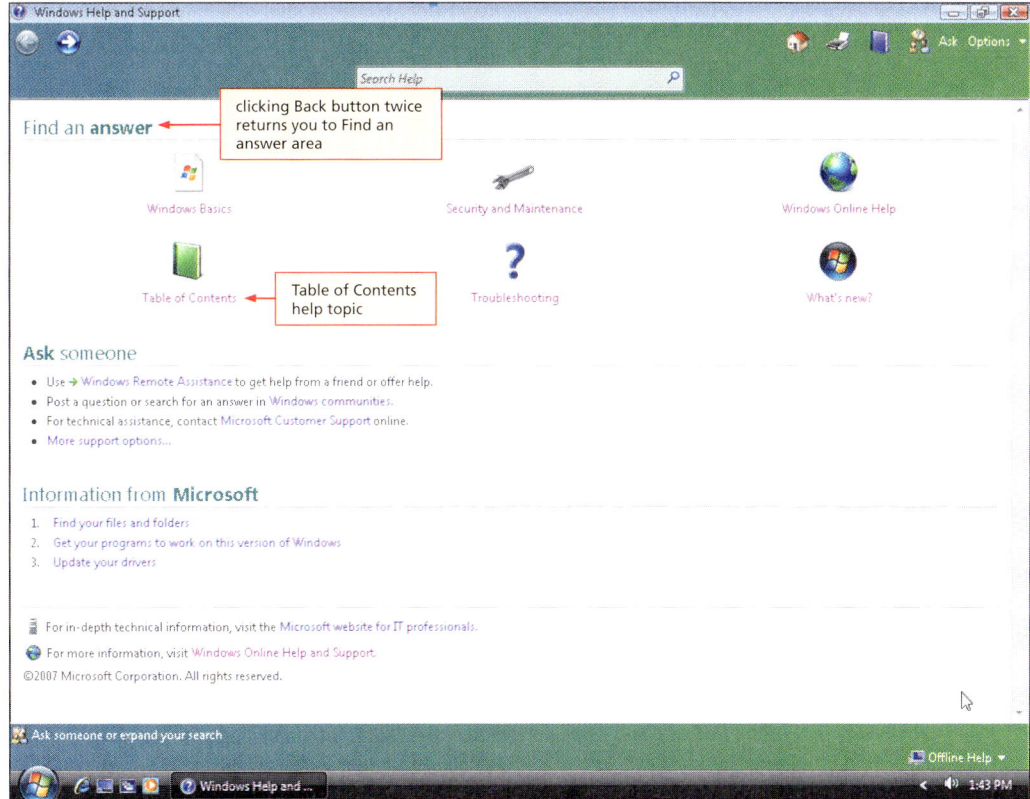

Figure 88

To Search for Help Topics Using the Table of Contents

A second method of finding answers to your questions about Windows Vista is to use the Table of Contents. The **Table of Contents** contains a list of entries, each of which references one or more Help topics. The following steps obtain help and information about what you need to set up a home network.

- Click Table of Contents in the 'Find an answer' area to display the Table of Contents (Figure 89).

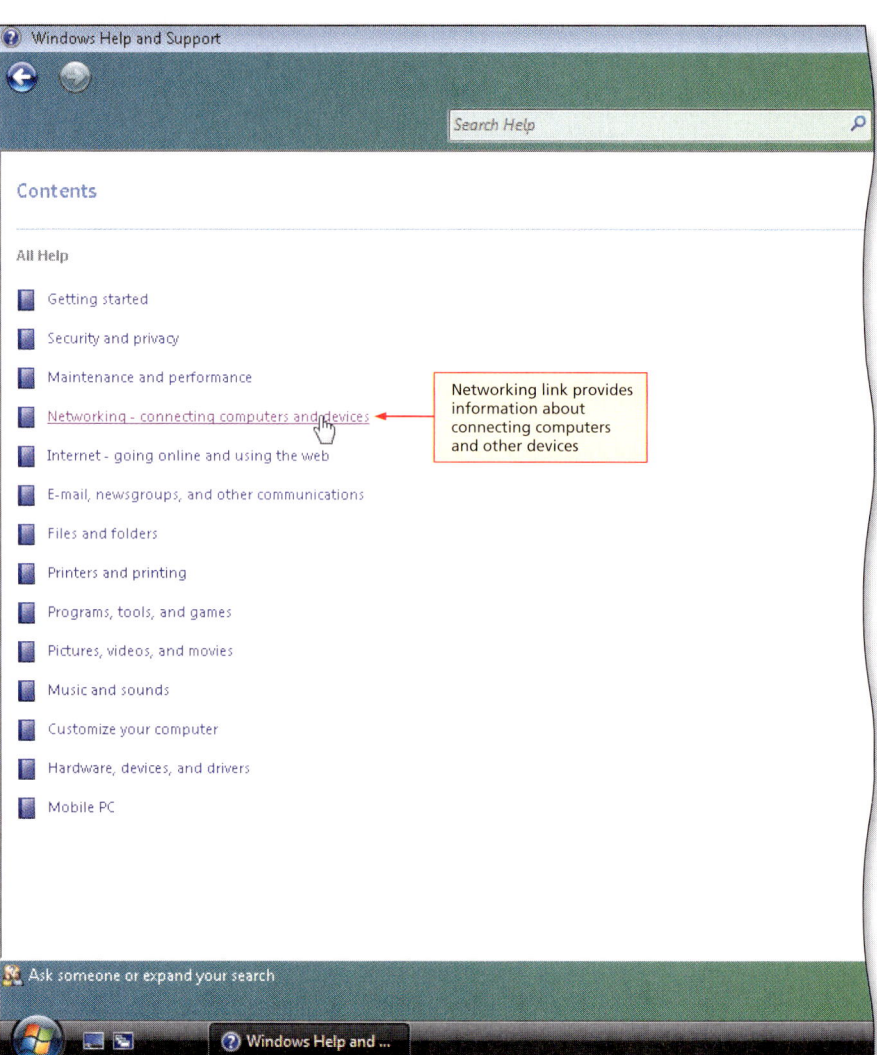

Figure 89

②
- Click the 'Networking – connecting computers and devices' link in the Contents area (Figure 90).

Q&A What happens if the topic I am interested in is not included in the table of contents?

Type the term in the Search Help text box in the Windows Help and Support window, and then press ENTER to find information about your topic.

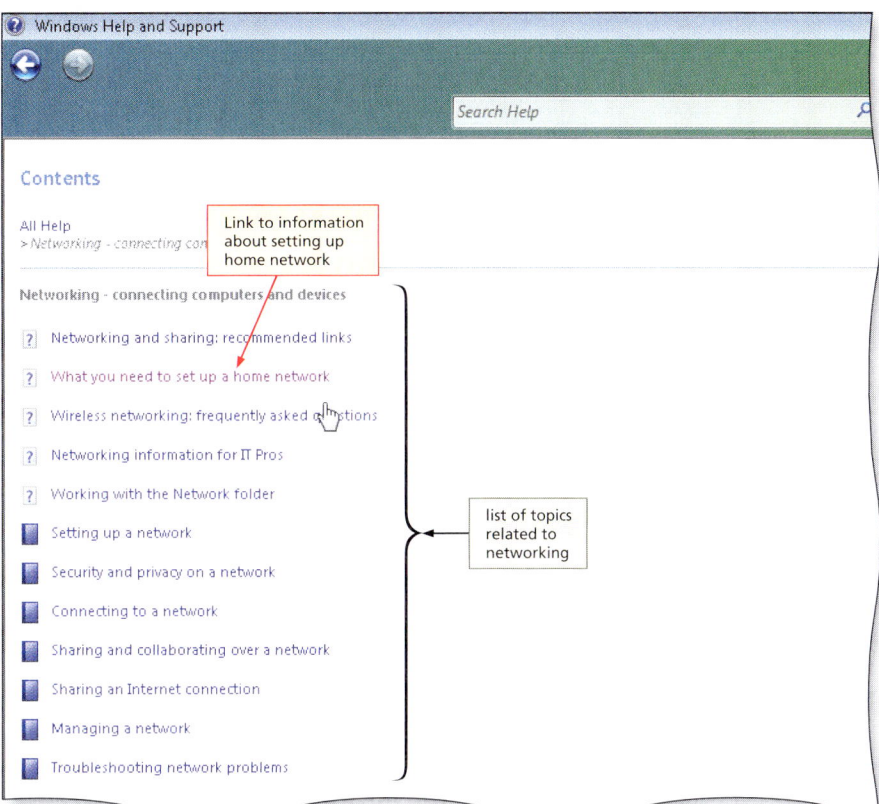

Figure 90

③
- Click the 'What you need to set up a home network' link (Figure 91).

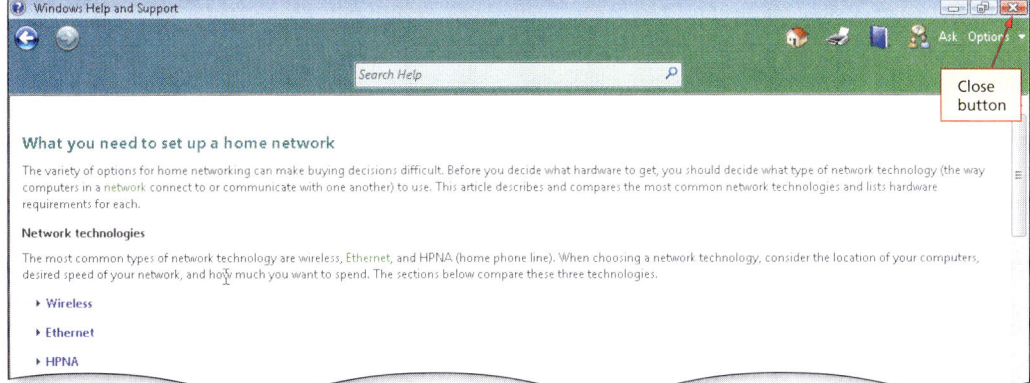

Figure 91

To Close the Windows Help and Support Window

The following step shows how to close the Windows Help and Support window.

① Click the Close button on the title bar of the Windows Help and Support window to close the Windows Help and Support window.

Logging Off and Turning Off the Computer

After completing your work with Windows Vista, you should close your user account by logging off the computer. In addition to logging off, there are several options available for ending a Windows Vista session. Table 5 illustrates the various options for ending your Windows Vista session.

Table 5 Options and Methods for Ending a Windows Vista Session	
Option	**Method**
Switch User	Click the Start button, point to the 'Lock this computer' button arrow, and then click Switch User to keep your programs running in the background (but inaccessible until you log on again), which can allow another user to log on.
Log Off	Click the Start button, point to the 'Lock this computer' button arrow, and then click Log Off to close all your programs but leave the computer running so that another user can log on.
Lock	Click the Start button and then click the Lock button to deny anyone except those you have authorized access to log on the computer.
Restart	Click the Start button, point to the 'Lock this computer' button arrow, and then click Restart to shut down and then restart the computer.
Sleep	Click the Start button, click the Sleep button, wait for Windows to save your work, and then power down to a hibernating state.
Shut Down	Click the Start button, point to the 'Lock this computer' button arrow, and then click Shut Down to quit all programs and turn off the computer.

To Log Off the Computer

Logging off the computer closes any open programs, allows you to save any unsaved documents, ends the Windows Vista session, and makes the computer available for other users. The following steps log off the computer.

- Display the Start menu (Figure 92).

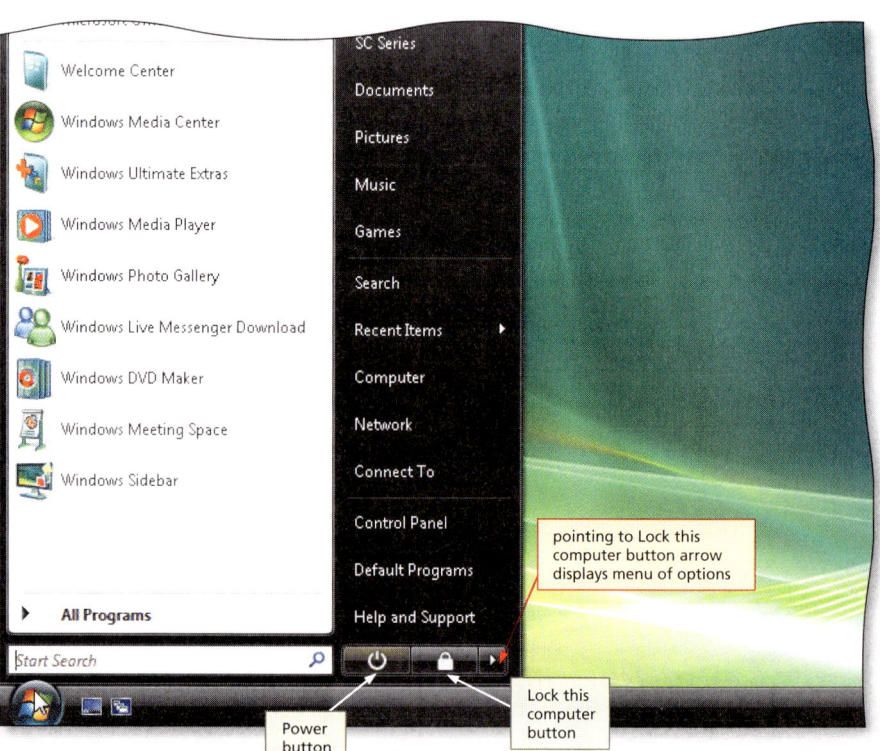

Figure 92

Introduction to Windows Vista **Windows Vista Chapter** WIN 65

2
- Point to the 'Lock this computer' button arrow to display a menu (Figure 93).

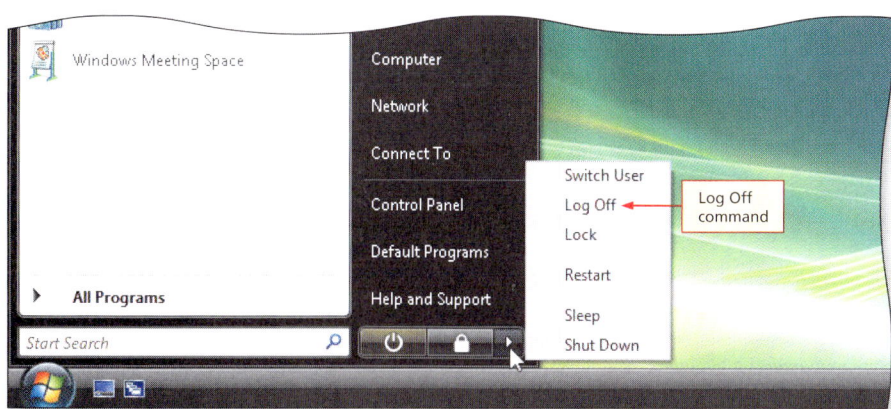

Figure 93

3
- Click Log Off on the menu and then wait for Windows Vista to prompt you to save any unsaved and log off (Figure 94).

 Q&A

Why should I log off the computer?

It is important to log off the computer so that you do not lose your work. Some users of Windows Vista have turned off their computers without following the log off procedure only to find they had lost data they thought they had stored on disk.

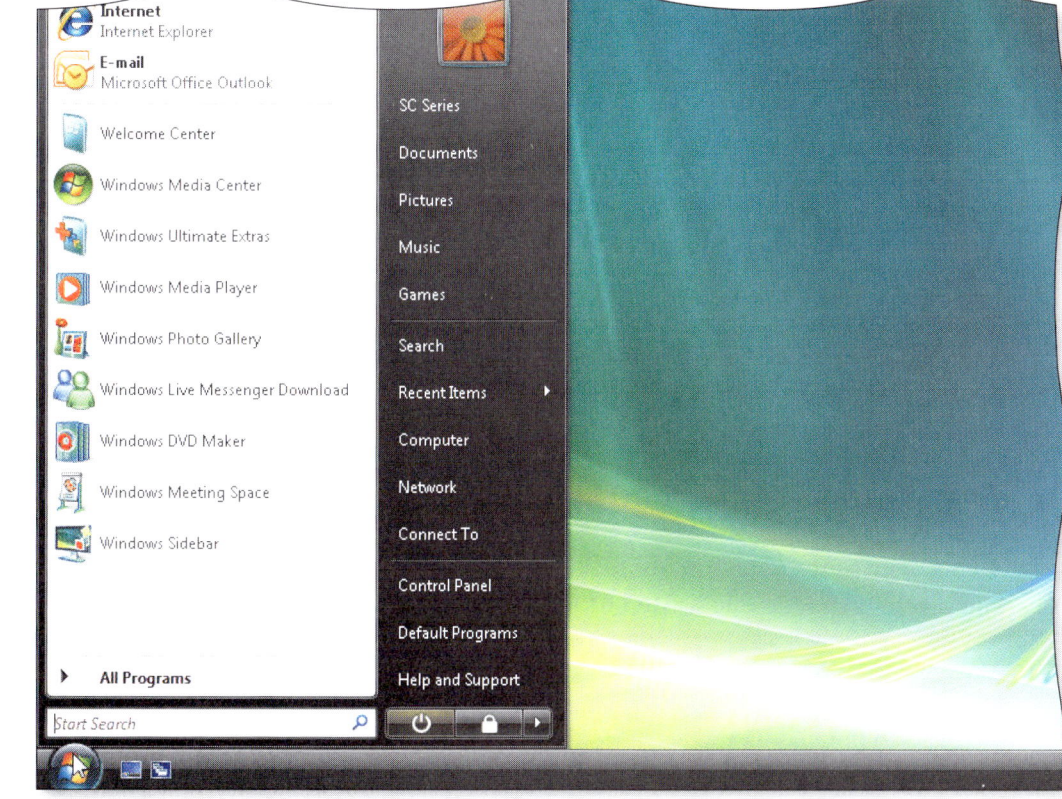

Figure 94

To Turn Off the Computer

After logging off, you also may want to shut down the computer using the Shut down button or the Shut down options arrow in the lower corner of the Welcome screen. Clicking the left button shuts down your computer, and clicking the right button displays a menu containing three commands (Restart, Sleep, and Shut Down) that can be used to restart the computer, put the computer into sleep mode, and shut down the computer. The following step turns off the computer. If you are not sure about turning off the computer, simply read the step.

- Click the Shut down button on the Welcome screen to shut down the computer.

Other Ways

1. Press ALT+F4, press the down arrow, select Shut Down, click OK button

Chapter Summary

In this chapter, you learned about the Windows Vista graphical interface. You started Windows Vista, learned the components of the desktop and the six mouse operations. You opened, closed, moved, resized, minimized, maximized, and scrolled a window. You used Folder Windows to expand and collapse drives and folders, display drive and folder contents, create a folder, copy a file between folders, and rename and then delete a file. You used Internet Explorer to browse using a Web address and tabs. You learned about the hierarchical format, removable media flash drives, and you used WordPad to type and save a document in a newly created folder. You searched for files using a word or phrase in the file or by name, you obtained Help using Windows Vista, and shut down Windows Vista.

1. Log On the Computer (WIN 8)
2. Close the Welcome Center Window (WIN 10)
3. Add a Gadget to the Windows Sidebar (WIN 10)
4. Remove a Gadget from the Windows Sidebar (WIN 12)
5. Display the Start Menu (WIN 13)
6. Scroll Using Scroll Arrows, the Scroll Bar, and the Scroll Box (WIN 15)
7. Add an Icon to the Desktop (WIN 16)
8. Open a Window Using a Desktop Icon (WIN 18)
9. Minimize and Redisplay a Window (WIN 19)
10. Maximize and Restore a Window (WIN 20)
11. Close a Window (WIN 21, WIN 24)
12. Open a Window Using the Start Menu (WIN 21)
13. Move a Window by Dragging (WIN 22)
14. Expand the Folders List (WIN 23)
15. Size a Window by Dragging (WIN 23)
16. Collapse the Folders List (WIN 24)
17. Delete a Desktop Icon by Right-Dragging (WIN 25)
18. Start a Program Using the Start Menu (WIN 27)
19. Browse the Web by Entering a Web Address (WIN 30)
20. Open a Link on a New Tab (WIN 31)
21. Switch between Tabs (WIN 33)
22. Close a Tab (WIN 33)
23. Work with Folders (WIN 34)
24. Plug a USB Flash Drive into a USB Port (WIN 38)
25. Create a Folder on a Removable Drive (WIN 39)
26. Download a Hierarchy of Folders (WIN 40)
27. Expand a Drive (WIN 42)
28. Collapse a Folder (WIN 43)
29. Display the Contents of a Folder (WIN 44)
30. Start WordPad Using the Start Search Box (WIN 45)
31. Type Text (WIN 47)
32. Save a WordPad Document in a New Folder (WIN 47)
33. Verify the Contents of a Folder (WIN 52)
34. Copy a File by Right-Dragging (WIN 52)
35. Display the Contents of a Folder (WIN 54)
36. Rename a File (WIN 55)
37. Delete a File by Right-Clicking (WIN 56)
38. Close Expanded Folders (WIN 57)
39. Open the Windows Help and Support Window (WIN 58)

40. Browse for Help Topics in Windows Basics (WIN 60)
41. Search for Help Topics Using the Table of Contents (WIN 62)
42. Close the Windows Help and Support Window (WIN 63)
43. Log Off the Computer (WIN 64)
44. Turn Off the Computer (WIN 66)

 If you have a SAM user profile, you may have access to hands-on instruction, practice, and assessment. Log in to your SAM account (http://sam2007.course.com) to launch any assigned training activities or exams that relate to the skills covered in this chapter.

Learn It Online

Test your knowledge of chapter content and key terms.

Instructions: To complete the Learn It Online exercises, start your browser, click the Address bar, and then enter the Web address `scsite.com/dc-off07/winvista2007/learn`. When the Windows Learn It Online page is displayed, click the link for the exercise you want to complete and then read the instructions.

Chapter Reinforcement TF, MC, and SA
A series of true/false, multiple choice, and short answer questions that test your knowledge of the chapter content.

Flash Cards
An interactive learning environment where you identify chapter key terms associated with displayed definitions.

Practice Test
A series of multiple choice questions that test your knowledge of chapter content and key terms.

Who Wants To Be a Computer Genius?
An interactive game that challenges your knowledge of chapter content in the style of a television quiz show.

Wheel of Terms
An interactive game that challenges your knowledge of chapter key terms in the style of the television show *Wheel of Fortune*.

Crossword Puzzle Challenge
A crossword puzzle that challenges your knowledge of key terms presented in the chapter.

In the Lab

Using the guidelines, concepts, and skills presented in this chapter, complete the following Labs.

Lab 1: Windows Vista Demos
Instructions: Use a computer to perform the following tasks.
Part 1: Windows Vista Demos
1. If necessary, start Windows Vista and then log on the computer.
2. Click the Start button and then click Help and Support on the Start menu.
3. If necessary, maximize the Windows Help and Support window.
4. Click What's new? in the 'Find an answer' area in the Windows Help and Support window.

Part 2: What's New in Windows Vista?
1. In the 'Searching and organizing' area, click the 'Demo: Working with files and folders' link, and then click the 'Watch the demo' link. As you watch the demo, answer the questions below.
   a. The Start menu provides access to several folders. What are the three folders mentioned?
   _____
   b. How do you create a new folder?
   _____
   c. If you use a folder frequently, where should you put the folder?
   _____

2. Click the Back button below the Windows Help and Support title bar to return to the What's new in Windows Vista heading.

Part 3: What's New in Security?
1. In the Security area, click the green arrow to the left of the Click to open the Security Center link. Answer the questions below.
   a. What are the four security essentials shown in the Windows Security Center?
   _____
   b. Close the Windows Security Center.
   c. In the Security area, click the Demo: Security basics link and then click the 'Read the transcript' link.
   d. What is the quickest way to check your computer's security status and fix security problems?
   _____
   e. What does a firewall do?
   _____
   f. What does it mean when all the lights in the Security Center are green?
   _____

2. Click the Back button below the Windows Help and Support title bar to return to the What's new in Windows Vista Ultimate page.

Part 4: What's New in Parental Controls?
1. Scroll down to view the Parental Controls area.
   a. In the Parental Controls area, click the What can I control with Parental Controls? link.
   b. What tasks can be accomplished with Parental Controls?
   _____

c. After setting up Parental Controls, how can a parent keep a record of a child's computer activity?
_____

2. Click the Back button below the Windows Help and Support title bar to view the topics in the Windows and Help Support window.

Part 5:   What's New in the Pictures Area?
1. Scroll down the Windows Help and Support window to view the Pictures area.
   a. In the Pictures area, click the 'Working with digital pictures' link.
   b. What are the two main ways to import pictures?
   _____
   _____

2. Click the Back button below the Windows Help and Support title bar to view the topics in the Windows Help and Support window.

Part 6:   What's New in the Ease of Access Center Area?
1. If necessary, scroll to view the Ease of Access Center features area, click the What accessibility features does Windows offer link. Answer the following question.
   a. How do you open the Ease of Access Center?
   _____
   _____

2. Click the Close button in the Windows Help and Support window.

In the Lab

Lab 2: Internet Explorer

Instructions: Use a computer to perform the following tasks.
1. Start Windows Vista and connect to the Internet.
2. Right-click the Start button on the taskbar, click Explore on the shortcut menu, and then maximize the Start Menu window.
3. If necessary, open the Folders list so the Start Menu and Programs icons are visible.
4. Click the Programs icon in the Start Menu folder.
5. Double-click the Internet Explorer shortcut icon in the Contents pane to start Internet Explorer. What is the Web address of the Web page that appears in the Address bar in the Windows Internet Explorer window? _____
6. Click the Web address in the Address bar in the Windows Internet Explorer window to select it. Type `scsite.com` and then press the ENTER key.
7. If necessary, scroll the Web page to display the Browse by Subject navigation bar containing the subject categories. Clicking a subject category displays the book titles in that category.
8. Click Operating Systems in the Browse by Subject navigation bar.
9. Click the Windows Vista link.
10. Right-click the first Windows Vista textbook cover image on the Web page, click Save Picture As on the shortcut menu, type `Windows Vista Cover` in the File name box, and then click the Save button in the Save Picture dialog box to save the image in the Pictures folder.

Continued >

In the Lab *continued*

11. Click the Close button in the Windows Internet Explorer window.
12. If necessary, scroll to the top of the Folders list to make the drive (C:) icon visible.
13. Click the black arrow to the left of the drive (C:) icon.
14. Click the Documents folder name in the Favorites Links list.
15. Click the Pictures folder name in the Folders list.
16. Right-click the Windows Vista Cover icon and then click Properties on the shortcut menu.
    a. What type of file is the Windows Vista Cover file? _____
    b. When was the file last modified? _____
    c. With what program does this file open? _____
17. Click the Cancel button in the Windows Vista Cover Properties dialog box.
18. If necessary, click the Close button in the Auto Play window.
19. Plug a USB flash drive to one of your computer's USB ports.
19. Right-drag the Windows Vista Cover icon to the USB flash drive icon in the Folders list. Click Move Here on the shortcut menu. Click the USB flash drive icon in the Folders list.
    a. Is the Windows Vista Cover file stored on the USB flash drive? _____
20. Click the Close button in the USB flash drive window.

In the Lab

Lab 3: Getting Help

Instructions: Use a computer to perform the following tasks.

Part 1: Using Windows Basics to Get Help

1. If necessary, start Windows Vista and then log on the computer.
2. Click the Start button and then click Help and Support on the Start menu.
3. If necessary, maximize the Windows Help and Support window.
4. Click Windows Basics icon in the 'Find an answer' area.
5. Click the 'Turning off your computer properly' link. Why are two different Power buttons available?

   _____
   _____

6. Click the Back button in the upper-left corner of the Windows Help and Support window.

Part 2: Using Desktop Fundamentals to Get Help

1. Look in the Desktop fundamentals area and identify the three parts of the desktop.

   _____

2. Click the 'Getting started with printing' link. List the three types of printers shown in the 'Getting started with printing' area.

   _____

3. Click the Back button in the upper-left corner of the Windows Help and Support window.

4. If necessary, scroll to view the Getting help topic below the 'Help and support' heading. Click the Getting help link. List the eight ways to get help.

_____

_____

5. Click the Back button twice in the upper-left corner of the Windows Help and Support window.

Part 3: Using Table of Contents to Get Help
1. Click the Table of Contents icon in the 'Find an answer' area.
2. Click the 'E-mail, newsgroups, and other communications' link. List six communication options.

_____

_____

3. Click Newsgroups in the Contents list.
4. Click the 'What are newsgroups?' in the Contents list.
5. What is a newsgroup?

_____

_____

6. Click the Back button four times in the upper-left corner of the Windows Help and Support window.

Part 4: Using Security and Maintenance to Get Help
1. Click the Security and Maintenance link in the 'Find an answer' area.
2. What does Windows Defender prevent?

_____

3. Why is Back up and Restore important?

_____

_____

4. Click the Back button in the upper-left corner of the Windows Help and Support window.

Part 5: Using Troubleshooting to Get Help
1. Click the Troubleshooting icon in the 'Find an answer' area.
2. Click the Connect to the Internet link under the 'Using the web' heading.
3. Click the 'What do I need to connect to the Internet?' link.
4. What do you use to connect to the Internet?

_____

5. Click the Back button three times in the upper-left corner of the Windows Help and Support.

Part 6: Using Windows Online Help to Get Help
1. Click Windows the Online Help icon in the 'Find an answer' area to open the Windows Vista: Help and How-to window.
2. Click the 'Music and sounds' icon.
3. What can you do in the 'Music and sounds' area in the Windows Help and How-to Web site?

_____

_____

4. Close the Windows Vista: Help Music window and then close the Windows Help and Support window.

In the Lab

Lab 4: Downloading the Word 2007 Chapters 1–2 Data Files

Instructions: Download the Word 2007 Chapters 1–2 Data Files into the Word folder. See the inside back cover of this book for instructions on downloading the Data Files for Students, or contact your instructor for information about accessing the required files.

Part 1: Plug the USB Flash Drive into the USB Port

1. If necessary, start Windows Vista and log on the computer.
2. Plug the USB flash drive into one of the USB ports on the computer. The UDISK 2.0 (E:) window should open on the desktop and should contain the Freshman folder.
3. If the Freshman folder is not displayed in the UDISK 2.0 (E:) window, follow the steps in this Chapter to create the hierarchy of folders shown in Figure 50 on page WIN 36.

Part 2: Download the Word 2007 Chapters 1-2 Data Files into the Word Folder

1. Start Internet Explorer by clicking the Start button on the taskbar and then clicking Internet on the Start menu.
2. Click the Address bar, type `scsite.com` in the Address bar, and then click the Go button.
3. When the SC Site — Shelly Cashman Series Student Resources Web site is displayed, use the Browse by Subject navigation bar, click Office Suites, and then click Microsoft Office 2007.
4. In the center of the screen, locate your textbook, and then click the title (for example, Discovering Computers and Microsoft Office 2007: A Fundamental Combined Approach).
5. When the page for your textbook displays, click the Word Chapters 1–2 Data Files link (you may need to scroll down the page).
6. When the File Download – Security Warning dialog box is displayed, click the Run button.
7. When the Internet Explorer – Security Warning dialog box is displayed, click the Run button.
8. When the WinZip Self-Extractor dialog box is displayed, click the Browse button.
9. Click the plus sign to the left of the removable drive, click the plus sign to the left of the Freshman folder, click the plus sign to the left of the 1st Semester folder, click the plus sign to the left of the Computer Class folder, and then click the Word folder.
10. Click the OK button in the Browse for Folder dialog box.
11. Click the Unzip button in the WinZip Self-Extractor dialog box.
12. When a smaller WinZip Self-Extractor dialog box appears, click the OK button.
13. Click the Close button in the WinZip Self-Extractor dialog box.
14. Click the Close button in the SC Site — Shelly Cashman Series Student Resources Web site window.
15. Verify the Word 2007 Chapters 1–2 Data Files folder is contained in the Word folder.
16. Close the Word window. Remove the USB flash drive from the USB port.

Microsoft Windows **Internet Explorer 8**

Introduction to Internet Explorer

Objectives

You will have mastered the material in this chapter when you can:

- Define the Internet and the World Wide Web
- Discuss security concerns on the Internet
- Explain a link, a Web address, and Hypertext Markup Language (HTML)
- Describe Internet Explorer features
- Enter a Web address
- Use the History List and the Favorites Center

- Use buttons on the toolbar
- Add and remove a favorite
- Save a picture or text from a Web page or an entire Web page
- Copy and paste text or pictures from a Web page into WordPad
- Print a WordPad document and Web page
- Use Internet Explorer Help

Introduction to Windows Internet Explorer

Introduction

The Internet is the most popular and fastest growing area in computing today. Using the Internet, you can do research, send and receive files, obtain a loan, shop for services and merchandise, search for a job, buy and sell stocks, display weather maps, obtain medical advice, watch movies, listen to high-quality music, and converse with people worldwide.

Although a complex system of hardware and software comprises the Internet, it is accessible to the general public because personal computers with user-friendly tools have reduced its complexity. The Internet, with its millions of connected computers, continues to grow with thousands of new users coming online each day. Schools, businesses, newspapers, television stations, and government agencies all can be found on the Internet. All around the world, service providers offer access to the Internet free of charge or for minimal cost.

Overview

As you read this chapter, you will learn how to browse the Web and use Internet Explorer by performing these general tasks:

- Start Internet Explorer
- Enter a Web address in the Address bar
- Browse a Web page by clicking links and using the Back and Forward buttons
- Navigate to previously viewed Web pages by using the History List and the Favorites Center
- Save a Web page
- Print a Web page

Plan Ahead

Internet Usage Guidelines

Internet usage involves navigating to, viewing, and interacting with the various resources on the Internet. Preparations you make before using the Internet will determine the effectiveness of your experience. Before using the Internet, you should follow these general guidelines:

1. **Determine whether your computer has the proper hardware and software necessary to connect to the Internet.** Connecting to the Internet requires your computer to communicate with other computers. Special hardware and software, discussed later in this chapter, are designed to facilitate this communication. If you are unsure of whether your computer is capable of connecting to the Internet, a technician from a company that provides Internet access will be able to help.

(continued)

> *(continued)*
>
> 2. **Choose an appropriate method to connect to the Internet.** The quality and speed of your Internet connection plays an important role in your overall experience. Various Internet connection options are available, and it is important to choose one that not only allows you to quickly and easily access the information that you desire, but also falls within your price range.
>
> 3. **Determine whether your computer is protected properly from threats on the Internet.** The Internet can be a breeding ground for software that can do harm to your computer. You should not connect to the Internet unless you have the proper software installed on your computer that will protect you from these various threats.
>
> 4. **Determine why you are connecting to the Internet.** Individuals connect to the Internet for many reasons. If you are connecting to the Internet to accomplish a specific task, be clear about what you want to accomplish and identify which resources might prove useful. Many individuals find it easy to become distracted from the task at hand when they are online.
>
> 5. **Determine how much time you wish to spend on the Internet.** For some individuals, the Internet can be an extremely addictive environment. In fact, many companies that provide Internet access to their employees have strict policies in place that outline what they consider to be acceptable Internet usage while on the job. The Internet has the potential to significantly lower an employee's productivity, therefore costing the employer money. Similarly, parents should be concerned that their children have a safe experience online. Parents can guide children to age-appropriate content and teach their children to keep personal information private.
>
>   Using the Internet not only can be addicting, it also can be costly. Depending upon the method you use to connect to the Internet, the amount that you are charged to connect may directly relate to the number of minutes or hours that you spend connected. Some Internet connection plans allow unlimited usage, while others may only allow you to connect for a certain number of hours before charging an additional fee.

Plan Ahead

The Internet

The **Internet** is a worldwide collection of networks (Figure 1 on the next page), each of which is composed of a collection of smaller networks. A **network** is composed of several computers connected together to share resources and data. For example, on a college campus, the network in the student computer lab can connect to the faculty computer network, which is connected to the administration network, and they all can connect to the Internet.

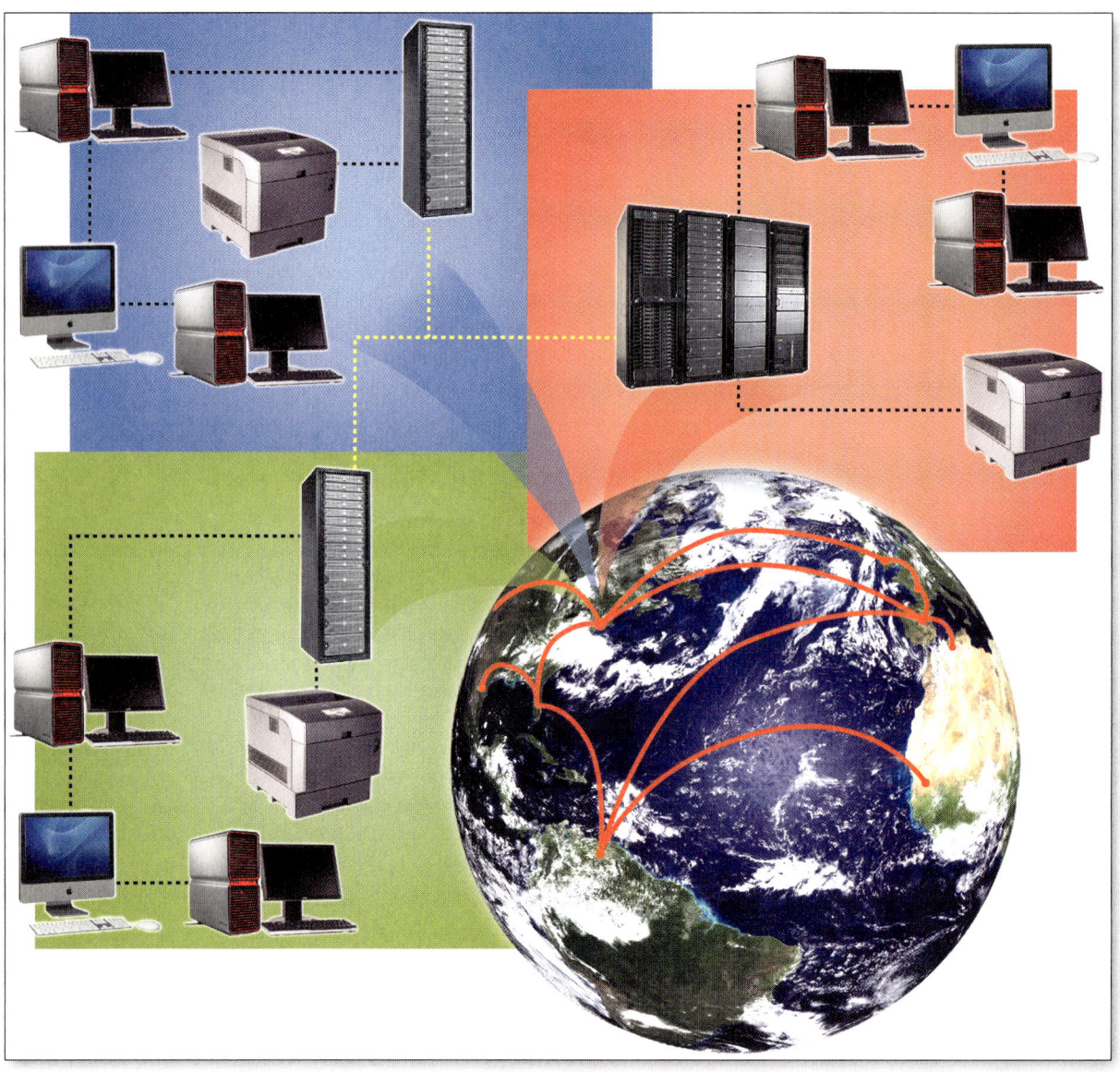

Figure 1

BTW

The Internet
The Internet started as a government experiment for the military. The military wanted the ability to connect to and communicate via different computers running different operating systems. From this experiment, a communication technique originated called Transmission Control Protocol/Internet Protocol, or TCP/IP.

Networks are connected with high-, medium-, and low-speed data lines that allow data to move from one computer to another (Figure 2). The Internet has high-speed data lines that connect major computers located around the world, which form the **Internet backbone**. Other, less powerful computers, such as those used by local ISPs (Internet service providers) often attach to the Internet backbone using medium-speed data lines. Finally, the connection between your computer at home and your local ISP, often called **the last mile**, employs low-speed data lines such as telephone lines, cable television lines, and fiber-optic cable. In some cases today, fixed wireless access is replacing wires over the last mile, which significantly improves access to the Internet.

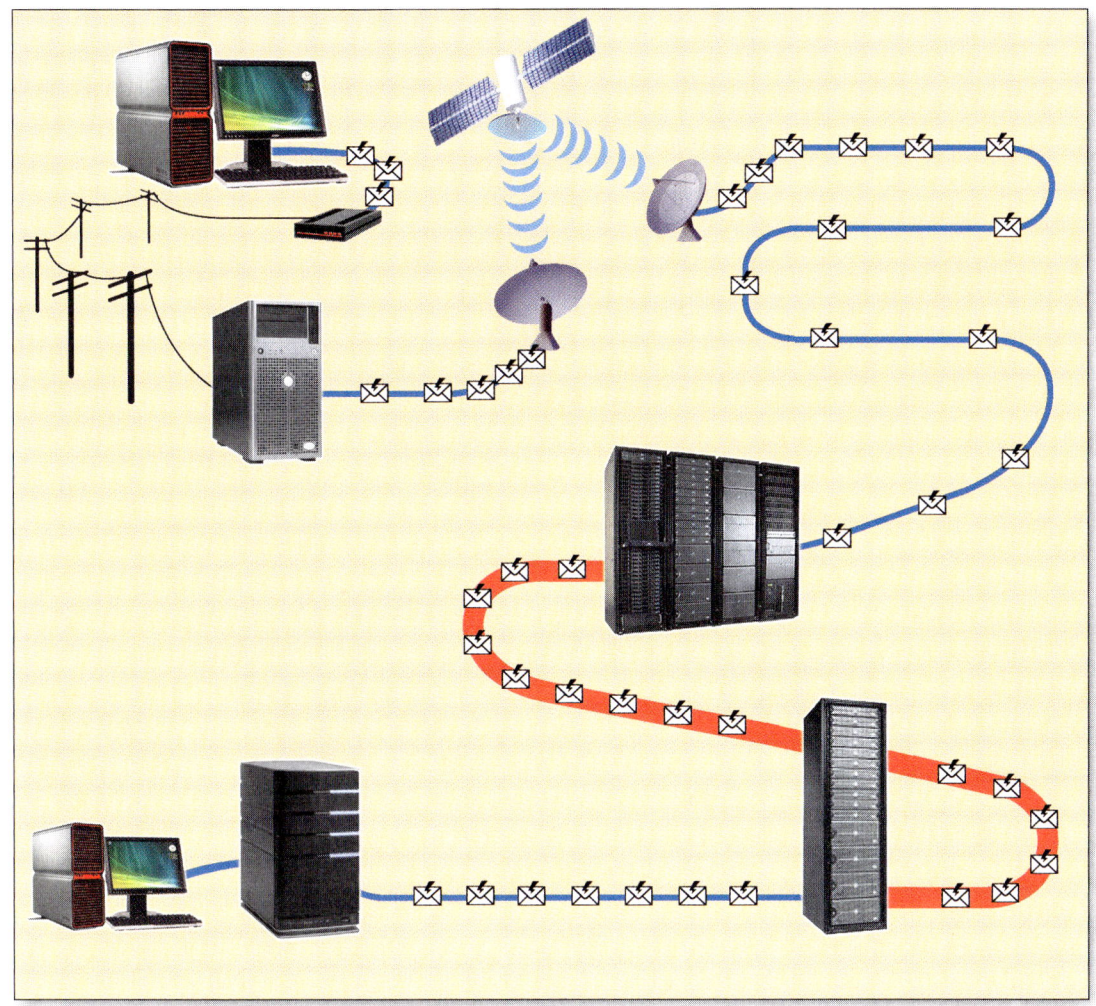

Figure 2

The World Wide Web

Modern computers have the capability of delivering information in a variety of ways, using images, sound, video, animation, virtual reality, and, of course, regular text. On the Internet, this multimedia capability is known as **hypermedia**, which is the combination of text, images, audio, video, and interactivity, delivered over the Internet.

You access hypermedia by clicking a **hyperlink**, or simply a **link**, which points to the location of the computer on which the hypermedia is stored and to the hypermedia itself. A link, which can be in the form of text or an image, can point to hypermedia on any computer connected to the Internet that is configured as a Web server. A **Web server**, which runs Web server software, provides resources such as text, images, files, and links to other computers on the Internet. Thus, clicking a link on a computer in Miami could display hypermedia located in Seattle. All of the resources and links found throughout the Internet create an interconnected network called the **World Wide Web**, which also is referred to as the **Web**, or **WWW**.

Text, images, and other hypermedia available at a Web site are stored in a file called a **Web page**, and a collection of related Web pages make up a **Web site**. When you are viewing hypermedia such as text, images, and video on the World Wide Web, you actually are viewing a Web page.

BTW

Web Sites
An organization can have more than one Web site. Separate departments may have their own Web servers, allowing faster response to requests for Web pages and local control over the Web pages stored at that Web site.

Figure 3 illustrates a Web page at the Disney.com Web site. This Web page contains numerous links. For example, the ten graphics on the top of the Web page are links. Clicking a link, such as Videos, could display a Web page located on the other side of the world.

Figure 3

Security Concerns on the Internet

Although there are many advantages to accessing and using the Internet, some disadvantages to Internet access also exist that are important to consider. When your computer connects to the Internet, other computers may be able to see your computer and possibly connect to it. Computer-savvy individuals with malicious intentions sometimes take advantage of Internet users who do not take the proper security precautions—by deleting, modifying, or even stealing their data, often without their knowledge. It also is possible for an individual or Web site to install spyware on your computer. **Spyware** is a program that tracks the actions you take on your computer, such as which Web sites you visit, what products you purchase online, and your credit card information, and sends them to a third party. Spyware can decrease your computer's performance, as well as compromise any secure information you have stored on your computer. Another type of malicious software that may be installed on your computer without your knowledge is **adware**. Adware randomly displays advertisements and other messages while you use your computer. Adware and spyware may be installed by someone who connects to an unsecure computer, or by downloading and running a program or file from the Internet. To avoid downloading harmful files

> **BTW**
>
> **Windows Defender**
> Microsoft offers Windows Defender, a program that provides spyware protection, free of charge to Windows users. To download Windows Defender, navigate to Microsoft's Web site (www.microsoft.com) and search for Windows Defender.

and programs, it is important to learn how to tell the difference between legitimate and fraudulent Web sites, files, and programs on the Internet.

In addition to adware and spyware, your computer also may be infected by a **computer virus** if you download an infected file from a Web page or open an infected e-mail attachment. Your computer also can be infected by a virus if someone exploits a security vulnerability, or bug, in a program that is installed on your computer.

Adware, spyware, and viruses are not the only problems that exist on the Internet. **Phishing scams**, or attempts by individuals to obtain confidential information from you, often via the Internet, are growing in popularity. A phishing scam works by falsifying one's identity in an attempt to convince an unsuspecting victim into disclosing information such as credit card numbers, bank account information, and social security numbers. A phisher may falsify his or her identity by sending an e-mail that appears to come from someone else, or by creating a Web site that appears to be that of a legitimate company. The worst part about a phishing scam is that the victim often does not know that someone else took advantage of him or her until it is too late. Victims of phishing scams also can be exposed to identity theft and financial loss.

To lower the risk of being victimized by a malicious Web site or a phishing scam, Internet Explorer 8 includes a **SmartScreen Filter**. The SmartScreen Filter is designed to identify malicious and fraudulent Web sites, and will inform you by displaying an appropriate message in the display area and changing the background color of the Address bar to red. While the SmartScreen Filter may not detect all malicious and fraudulent Web sites, it greatly reduces your chances of visiting a malicious Web site or becoming a victim of a phishing scam.

Because these security threats exist, it is important for everyone to practice safe browsing techniques while connected to the Internet. Before connecting your computer to the Internet, you should make sure that you have **antivirus software** installed. Antivirus software immediately will inform you if it detects a virus on your computer. Antivirus software manufacturers also release virus **definition updates** that "teach" the software how to detect newly-created viruses. In addition to installing antivirus software, you also should install a **software firewall** on your computer. A software firewall blocks unauthorized connections to and from your computer. When using your computer on the Internet, it is important to regularly scan your computer for adware and spyware. Some adware and spyware scanners are available online free or for a fee, and some are available in retail stores that sell computer software.

To combat security vulnerabilities that are present in programs installed on your computer, software manufactures may release updates, also known as **patches** or **service packs**, which correct these vulnerabilities. It is good practice to install these updates as soon as they become available. The **Automatic Update feature** in Windows, for example, can be configured to automatically download and install security updates as they become available. Finally, be selective with the Web sites you visit. Millions of Web sites exist on the Internet today, and it is easy to arrive inadvertently at a site other than the one you intended to visit. In addition, you should take extra precaution while visiting Web sites that are hosted by unknown individuals or obscure companies. Avoid downloading anything from these sites or entering any personal information. If you are unsure of whether a Web site is legitimate, it is better to be cautious and simply navigate to another site.

Web Address

Each Web page has a unique address, called a **Web address**, sometimes referred to as a Uniform Resource Locator (URL), which distinguishes it from all other pages on the Internet. The Web address in Figure 3 is http://disney.go.com/index.

BTW

Online Security
Because of the importance of protecting yourself and your computer while you are connected to the Internet, some Web sites have been developed that offer advice and guidelines for ensuring a safe online experience. For more information, visit onguardonline.gov or staysafeonline.org.

BTW

Children and the Internet
The Internet can be a great source of entertainment and education for children, but there also is the potential for children to encounter inappropriate content or behavior. While there are many ongoing efforts to make the Internet safer for children, children still should be properly supervised and educated about Internet threats. For more information, visit enough.org.

A Web address is composed of multiple parts (Figure 4). The first part is the protocol. A **protocol** is a set of rules. Most Web pages use the Hypertext Transfer Protocol. **Hypertext Transfer Protocol (HTTP)** describes the rules used to transmit Web pages electronically over the Internet. You enter the protocol in lowercase as http followed by a colon and two forward slashes (http://). If you do not begin a Web address with a protocol, Internet Explorer will assume it is http, and automatically will append http:// to the front of the Web address.

Figure 4

BTW

HTTPS
You may notice that when browsing the Web, some Web sites use the *https* protocol, instead of *http*. The https protocol is a more secure version of the http protocol. The https protocol is designed to make it difficult for others to see the data being transferred between your computer and the Web server.

The second part of a Web address is the domain name. The **domain name** is the Internet address of the computer where the Web page is located. Each computer on the Internet has a unique address, called an **Internet Protocol address**, or **IP address**. The domain name identifies where to forward a request for the Web page referenced by the Web address. The domain name in the Web address in Figure 4 is www.scsite.com. The last part of the domain name (com in Figure 4) is called an **extension** and indicates the type of organization that owns the Web site. For example, the extension .com indicates a commercial organization, usually a business or corporation. Countries throughout the world also have their own domain name extensions. For example, Germany's domain name extension is .de, and China's domain name extension is .cn. Table 1 shows some types of organizations and their extensions.

Table 1 Organizations and Their Domain Name Extensions	
Types of Organizations	**Original Domain Name Extensions**
Commercial organizations, businesses, and companies	.com
Educational institutions	.edu
Government agencies	.gov
Military organizations	.mil
Network providers	.net
Nonprofit organizations	.org
Types of Organizations	**Additional Domain Name Extensions**
Accredited museums	.museum
Aviation community members	.aero
Business cooperatives such as credit unions and rural electric co-ops	.coop
Businesses of all sizes	.biz
Businesses, organizations, or individuals providing general information	.info
Certified professionals such as doctors, lawyers, and accountants	.pro
Individuals or families	.name
Web sites offering media and other broadband content	.tv

The optional third part of a Web address is the file specification of the Web page. The **file specification** includes the file name and possibly a directory or folder name. This information is called the **path**. If no file specification of a Web page is specified in the Web address, a default Web page appears. This means you can display a Web page even though you do not know its file specification.

You can find Web addresses that identify Web sites in magazines or newspapers, on television, from friends, or even from just browsing the Web. Web addresses of well-known companies and organizations usually contain the company's name and institution's name. For example, ibm.com is the Web address for IBM (International Business Machines Corp.), and ucf.edu is the University of Central Florida.

Hypertext Markup Language

Web page authors use a special language called **Hypertext Markup Language** (**HTML**) to create Web pages. Behind all the formatted text and eye-catching graphics is plain text. Special HTML formatting codes and functions that control attributes of a page, such as font size, colors, and text alignment, surround the text and picture references. Figure 5 shows part of the hypertext markup language used to create the Web page shown in Figure 3 on page IE 6.

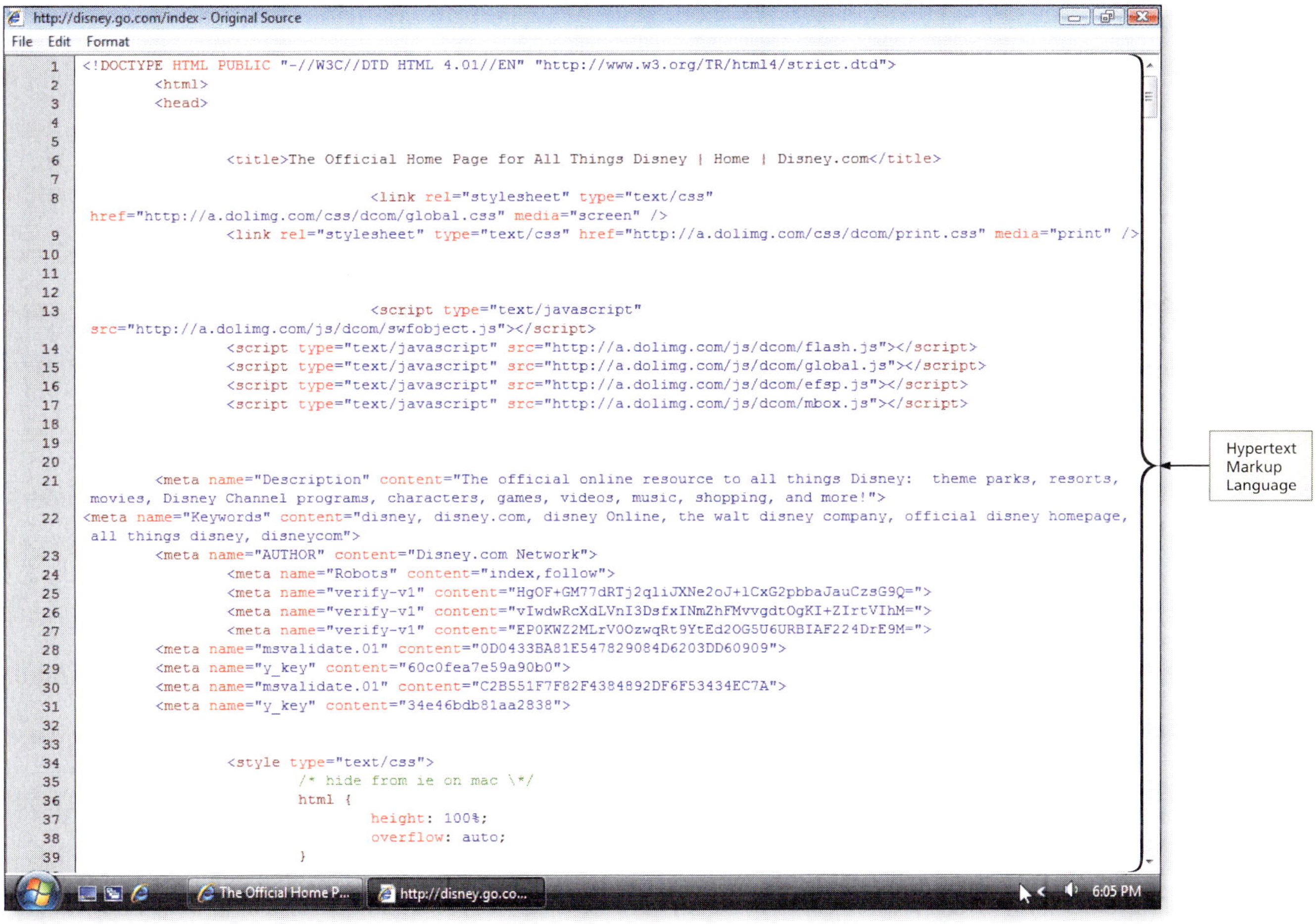

Figure 5

> **BTW**
>
> **Web Page Authoring**
> Many Web page authoring programs make it easy to create Web pages without learning HTML syntax. Editing programs include SharePoint Designer, Expression Web, Adobe Dreamweaver, CoffeeCup, WebExpress, and Cool Page.

HTML is considered a markup language. A **markup language** contains text, as well as information about the text. This information can include how the text is formatted and positioned on a page. Using HTML, you can create your own Web pages and place them on the Web for others to see. If you want to create Web pages without learning HTML, many easy-to-use Web page authoring programs are available, such as Microsoft Expression Web or Adobe Dreamweaver. New versions of HTML are released periodically to allow Web developers to take advantage of new and exciting technologies that can be delivered over the World Wide Web. As new versions of HTML are released, software on your computer must be updated to support new and updated features.

Home Pages

> **BTW**
>
> **Customize Your Home Page**
> You can change the home page by clicking Tools on the Command bar, clicking the Internet Options command, and in the General sheet clicking the Use current, Use default, or Use blank button, or typing your desired Web address in the text box.

No main menus or particular starting points exist in the World Wide Web, but most people start a visit to the Web via specially designated Web pages called home pages. A **home page** is the introductory page for a Web site. All other Web pages for that site usually are accessible from the home page via links. When you enter a domain name with no file specification, such as disneyland.com or nbc.com, the home page is the page that is displayed.

Because it is the starting point for most Web sites, Web designers try to make a good first impression. These pages often display attractive, eye-catching images, specially formatted text, and a variety of links to other pages at the Web site as well as to other related Web sites.

A home page also may refer to the first Web page, or the multiple Web pages, that appear when you start your Web browser. For example, if you normally read the news online when you connect to the Internet, you may set your browser's home page to your favorite news Web site.

Web Browsers

Graphical user interfaces (GUIs) such as Microsoft Windows simplify working with a computer by using a point-and-click method. Similarly, a browser such as Internet Explorer makes using the World Wide Web easier by removing the complexity of having to remember the syntax, or rules, of commands used to reference Web pages at Web sites. A **Web browser** takes the Web address associated with a link or the Web address entered by a user, locates the computer containing the associated Web page, and then reads the returned HTML to display a Web page.

> **BTW**
>
> **The Internet Explorer Icon**
> When you install Internet Explorer 8, the Internet Explorer icon and name are displayed in the All Programs list and also may be displayed as the first entry on the Start menu. The Internet Explorer icon also may appear on the taskbar.

What Is Internet Explorer 8?

Microsoft Windows Internet Explorer 8, also known as **Internet Explorer** or **IE,** is Web browsing software that allows you to search for and view Web pages, save links for future use, maintain a list of the pages you visit, obtain information from various sources, listen to radio stations, and watch videos. The Internet Explorer 8 program is available free of charge to Windows users on Microsoft's Web site (microsoft.com). To install Internet Explorer 8, you must be using one of the following operating systems: Windows XP, Windows Vista, Windows 7, Windows Server 2003, or Windows Server 2008. This chapter illustrates the use of the Internet Explorer 8 Web browser.

Starting Internet Explorer

If you are stepping through this chapter on a computer and want your screen to match the figures in this book, your monitor's resolution should be set to 1024 × 768. For more information about how to change the resolution on your computer, read Appendix C.

To Start Internet Explorer

The following steps, which assume Windows is running, start Internet Explorer based on a typical installation. You may need to ask your instructor how to start Internet Explorer on your computer.

- Click the Start button on the Windows taskbar to display the Start menu.

- Point to All Programs on the Start menu to display the All Programs list, and then point to Internet Explorer in the All Programs list (Figure 6).

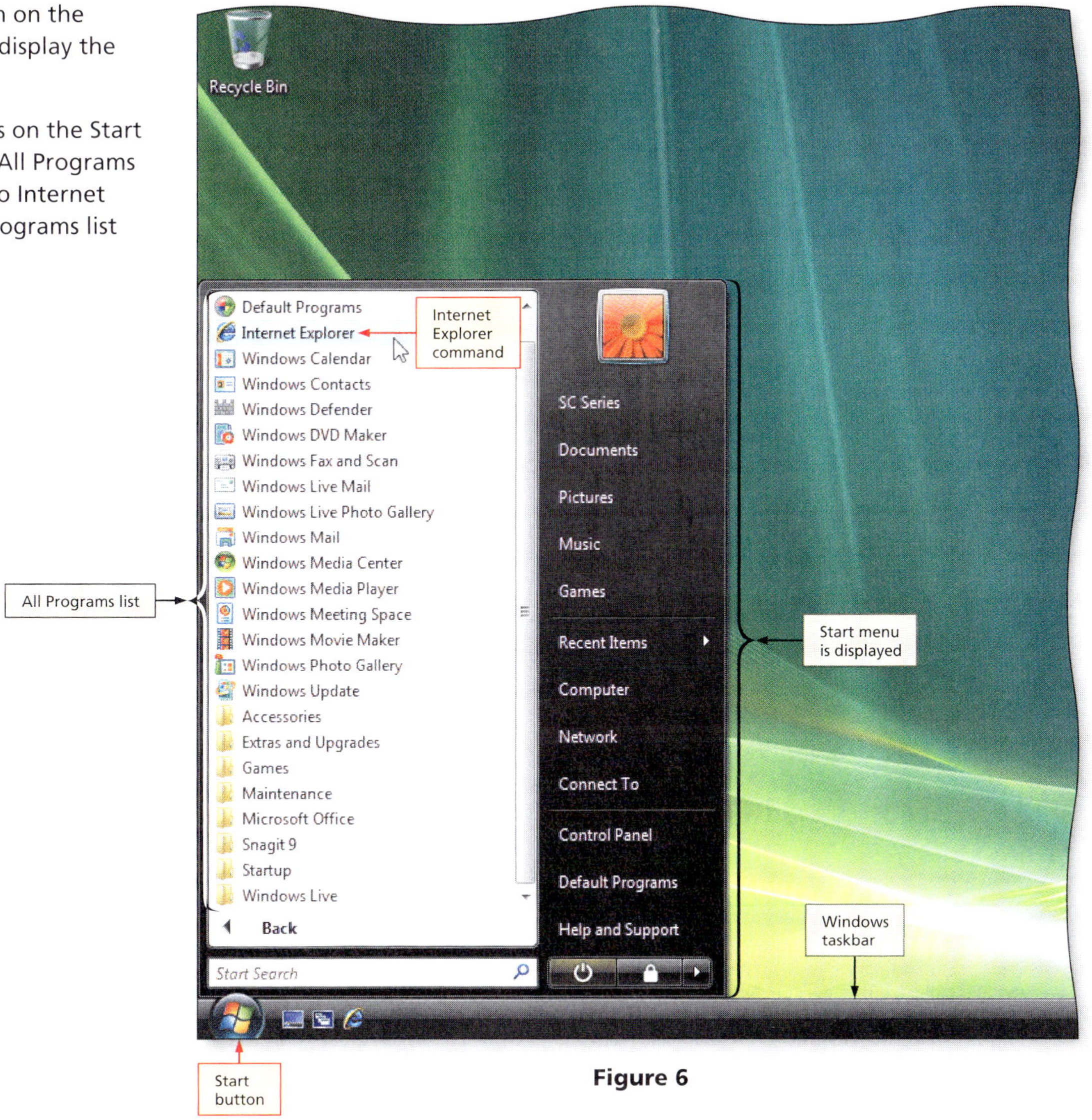

Figure 6

2

- Click Internet Explorer to start Internet Explorer and open the MSN.com - Windows Internet Explorer window (Figure 7). Depending on your computer's configuration, a different home page may display.

- If the Internet Explorer window is not maximized, double-click its title bar to maximize it.

- Press the ALT key to display the menu bar, click View to display the View menu, point to Toolbars to display the Toolbars submenu, and then click the Status Bar command to hide the status bar.

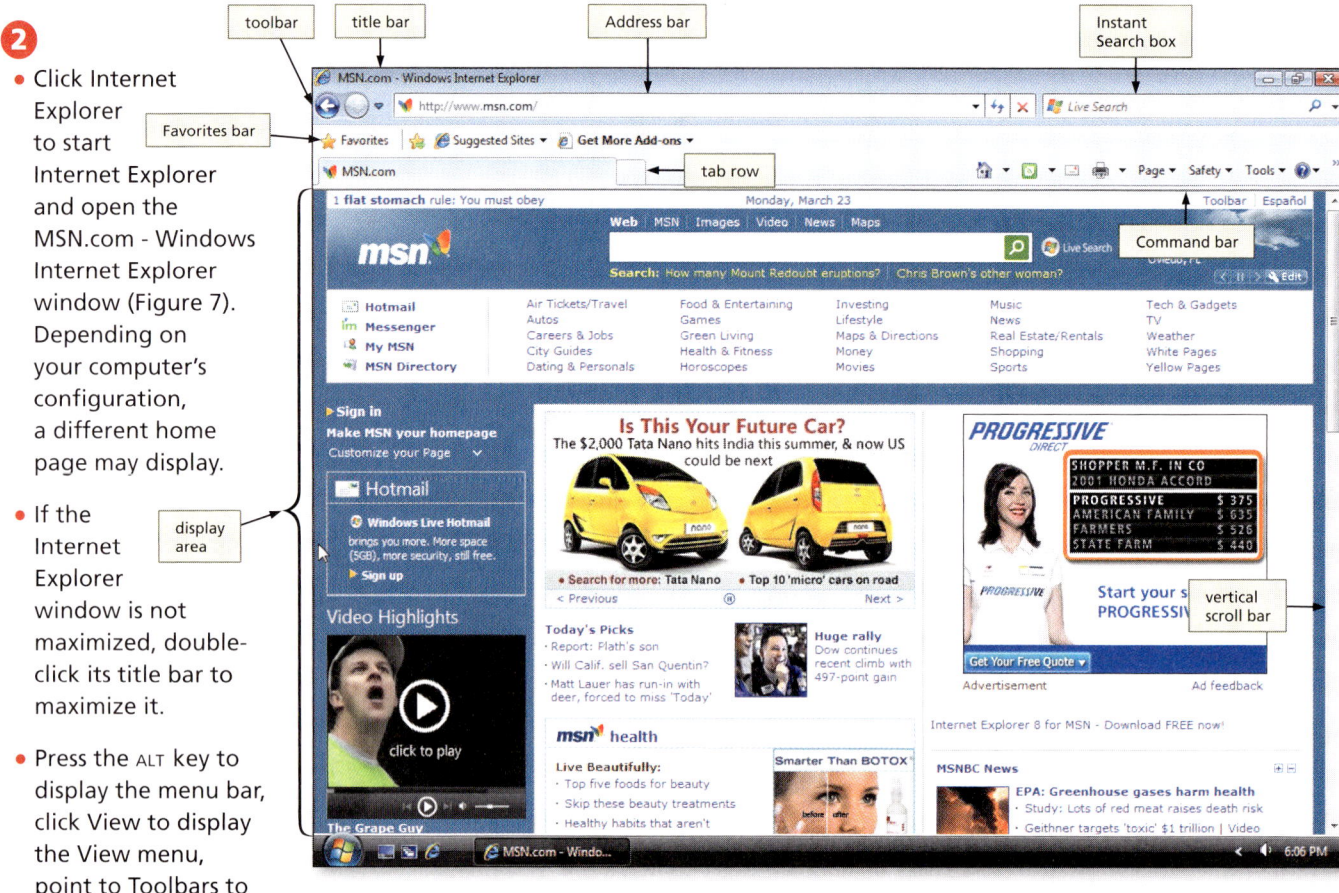

Figure 7

Other Ways

1. Click Start button on Windows taskbar, click Internet Explorer icon on Start menu
2. Double-click Internet Explorer icon on desktop
3. Press CTRL+ESC, press I, press ENTER

BTW

Full Screen Mode
If you would like Internet Explorer to display Web pages in full screen mode (without the title bar, toolbars, or other components of the window), you can either press the F11 key on the keyboard or select the Full Screen command on the View menu.

The Internet Explorer Window

The **Internet Explorer window** (Figure 7) consists of a range of features that make browsing the Internet easy. It contains a title bar, the menu bar, the Instant Search box, an Address bar, a tab row, the Command bar, Favorites bar, scroll bars, and a display area where pages from the Web appear. The menu bar, Favorites bar, Address bar, Instant Search box, Command bar, and tab row appear at the top of the screen just below the title bar. By default, the menu bar is not displayed. You can display the menu bar by right-clicking on the the Command bar and clicking the Menu Bar command, or by pressing the ALT key. The status bar appears at the bottom of the screen. Some users choose to hide the status bar so that it does not take space away from the display area.

Display Area Only a portion of most pages will be visible on the screen. You view the portion of the page displayed on the screen in the **display area** (Figure 7). To the right of the display area is a scroll bar, scroll arrows, and a scroll box, which you can use to move the text in the display area up and down and reveal other parts of the page. Occasionally a Web page may be wider than the display area can show, and a horizontal scroll bar will appear at the bottom of the display area.

Notice the links on the Internet Explorer home page shown in Figure 7. When you position the mouse pointer on one of these links, the mouse pointer changes to a pointing hand. This change in the shape of the mouse pointer identifies these elements as links. Clicking a link retrieves the Web page associated with the link and displays it in the display area.

Title Bar The title bar appears at the top of the Internet Explorer window. As shown at the top of Figure 7, the **title bar** includes the Internet Explorer menu icon on the left, the title of the active Web page, the Minimize, Restore (or Maximize), and Close buttons on the right. Clicking the **Internet Explorer menu icon** on the title bar will display the System menu, which contains commands to carry out the actions associated with the Internet Explorer window. Double-click the Internet Explorer menu icon or click the Close button to close the window and quit Internet Explorer.

Click the **Minimize button** to minimize the Internet Explorer window. When you minimize the window, it still is open but it no longer appears on the desktop and the Internet Explorer button on the taskbar becomes inactive (a lighter color). After minimizing, clicking the button with the Internet Explorer icon on the Windows taskbar displays the Internet Explorer window in the previous position it occupied on the desktop and changes the button to an active state (a darker color).

Click the **Maximize button** to maximize the Internet Explorer window so that it expands to fill the entire desktop. When the window is maximized, the Restore button replaces the Maximize button on the title bar. Click the **Restore button** to return the window to the size and position it occupied before being maximized. The Restore button changes to the Maximize button when the Internet Explorer window is in a restored state.

You also can double-click the title bar to restore and maximize the Internet Explorer window. If the window is in a restored state, you can drag the title bar to move the window around the desktop.

Menu Bar The **menu bar** is located below the title bar. Because the most common Internet Explorer commands are accessible via the Favorites bar and the Command bar, by default Internet Explorer hides the menu bar. Each **menu name** on the menu bar represents a menu of commands you can use to perform actions such as saving Web pages, copying and pasting, using the Find on this page command, sending a page as an e-mail message, setting Internet Explorer options, quitting Internet Explorer, and so on. To display a menu when the menu bar is displayed, click the menu name on the menu bar. To select a command on a menu, click the command name or press the **keyboard shortcut** shown to the right of some commands on the menu.

Navigation Buttons The **navigation buttons** (Figure 7) in Internet Explorer include the **Back button** and the **Forward button**. Clicking the Back button retrieves the previous page. To go more than one page back, click the Recent Pages list arrow, and then click a Web page title in the list. The Forward button retrieves the next page. To navigate more than one page forward, click the Recent Pages list arrow, and then click a Web page title in the list. The Forward button only is available after you have clicked the Back button one or more times to return to a previous page.

Favorites Bar The **Favorites bar** (Figure 7) contains buttons that allow you to display the Favorites Center and add a Web site to your Favorites bar. As you add to your favorites (discussed later in this chapter), more buttons may appear on this bar.

BTW

The Address Bar
To move the insertion point to the Address bar when the box is empty, or to highlight the Web address in the Address bar, press ALT+D.

Address Bar The **Address bar** (Figure 7 on page IE 12) contains the Web address for the page currently shown in the display area. The Address bar also can be used to search for information on the World Wide Web.

The Web address updates automatically as you browse from page to page. If you know the Web address of a Web page you want to visit, click the Web address in the Address bar to highlight it, type the new Web address, and then press the ENTER key to display the corresponding page. As you type a Web address in the Address bar, Internet Explorer will display a list of suggestions, including AutoComplete suggestions and previously visited Web pages, files, and feeds. In addition, you can click the **Address bar arrow** at the right end of the Address bar to display a list of previously displayed Web pages. Clicking a Web address in the Address list displays the corresponding Web page.

New to Internet Explorer 8, the Address bar now includes a security feature known as domain highlighting. **Domain highlighting** displays the top level domain in a black font, while the remainder of the Web address is displayed in a gray font (Figure 8). This helps to protect from phishing scams by allowing the user easily to identify whether the Web site currently displayed in the window is the Web site he or she intended to visit.

Figure 8

You also can access information on your computer by typing a program name in the Address bar and pressing the ENTER key to start the corresponding program, typing a folder name and pressing the ENTER key to open a folder window, typing a document name and pressing the ENTER key to start a program and display the document in the program window, or typing a keyword or phrase (search inquiry) and pressing the ENTER key to display Web pages containing the keyword or phrase.

Command Bar

The **Command bar** provides quick and easy access to most Internet Explorer functions. The buttons on the Command bar allow you to change your home page options, access your e-mail account, print the current Web page and access printing options, access Web page options, access safety options, access Internet Explorer tools, and more. You can customize the tools that appear on the Command bar by right-clicking the Command bar, pointing to Customize on the shortcut menu, and then clicking Add or Remove Commands. Depending on the size of the Command bar in your Internet Explorer window, not all commands may be displayed. If a small double caret appears to the right of the Command bar, it indicates additional Command bar options are available. The options on your Command bar may be different, depending on the software installed on your computer and your computer's configuration. Table 2 identifies the default commands on the Command bar and briefly describes the function of each command.

Table 2 Commands on the Command Bar	
Commands	Function
🏠	Displays the home page, and includes options to add, change, or remove the home page
📶 📗	When active, these buttons allow you to view the RSS feeds or Web Slices on the current Web page
✉	Starts your default e-mail program
🖨	Prints the current Web page, or displays a menu providing access to various printing options
Page ▼	Displays a menu containing selected popular commands from the menu bar's File, Edit, and View menus
Safety ▼	Displays a menu containing commands that allow you to configure safety and security options
Tools ▼	Displays commonly used commands that are also accessible on the View and Tools menus on the menu bar
❓ ▼	Displays the Help menu, which is also accessible via the menu bar

Instant Search Box The **Instant Search box** is located to the right of the Address bar and allows you to perform a search on the World Wide Web by entering your search criteria and pressing the ENTER key. By default, the Instant Search box will perform your search using Windows Live search, but other searching options are available by customizing the Instant Search box.

Tab Row The **tab row** is located adjacent to the Command bar. The tab row enables you to keep multiple Web pages open simultaneously in one browser window. After clicking the New Tab button in the tab row, you can type the Web address of the Web page in the Address bar and it will display in the new tab. The tab row also allows you to switch between tabs, reorder tabs, close single tabs, and view the Web pages you currently have open in tabs. Older versions of Web browsers, including versions of Internet Explorer prior to version 7, did not support tabbed browsing, and it was necessary to open a new browser window each time you wanted to display additional Web pages. Opening multiple browser windows consumes additional system resources, which can decrease your computer's performance. Even though you are able to open multiple Internet Explorer windows simultaneously, it is recommended that you open new Web pages in tabs. While a Web page loads in the display area, the Internet Explorer icon in the corresponding tab changes to an animated circle. When the Web page finishes loading, the Internet Explorer icon displays in the tab.

> **BTW**
> **The Command Bar**
> If the text label is not displayed on the buttons on the Command bar, right-click the Command bar, point to Customize on the shortcut menu, and then click Show All Text Labels. You also can change the size of the icons on the Command bar by using the Use Large Icons command on the shortcut menu. When a check mark appears next to the Use Large Icons command, the icons on the Command bar are displayed in their largest size. When a check mark does not appear, small icons are displayed on the Command bar.

Browsing the World Wide Web

The most common way to browse the World Wide Web is to obtain the Web address of a Web page you want to visit and then enter it into the Address bar. By visiting various Web sites, you can begin to understand the enormous appeal of the Web. The following steps show how to visit the Web page titled Great Outdoors Travel, which contains information and photographs of five popular outdoor destinations in the United States. The Web address for The Great Outdoors Web site is www.scsite.com/dc-off07/ie8/greatoutdoors.

> **BTW**
> **The Great Outdoors Travel Web Site**
> Notice that the Web address you enter for The Great Outdoors page contains a domain name (scsite.com) that belongs to the publishing company. The Great Outdoors Travel Web site has been developed exclusively for use with this chapter.

To Browse the Web by Entering a Web Address

To navigate to the home page for the Great Outdoors Travel Web site, you will need to enter the Web address in the Address bar.

- Click the Address bar to highlight the Web address (Figure 9).

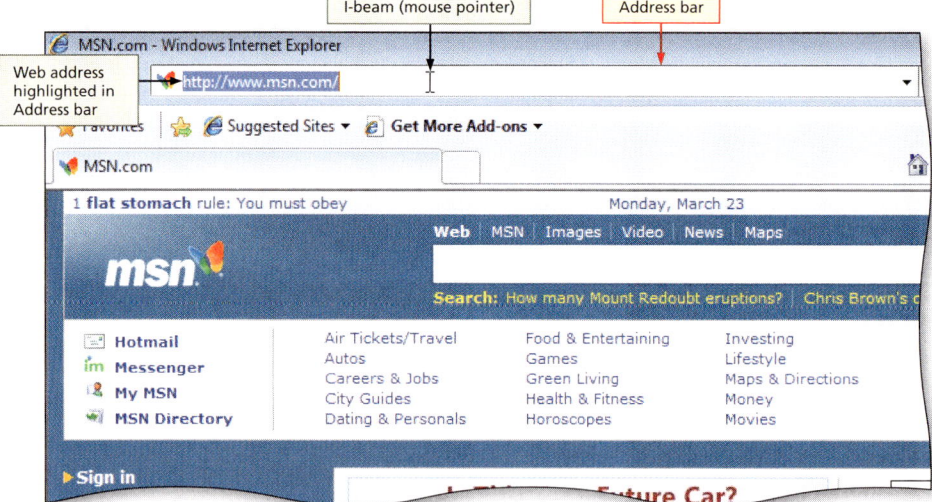

Figure 9

- Type `scsite.com/dc-off07/ie8/greatoutdoors` in the Address bar to enter the new Web address (Figure 10).

Q&A Why is it unnecessary to type http:// or www. at the beginning of each Web address?

Depending on how the Web server is configured, it may not require you to type http:// or www. at the beginning of the Web address. In the case of this Web site, you can type `scsite.com/dc-off07/ie8/greatoutdoors` or `www.scsite.com/dc-off07/ie8/greatoutdoors`.

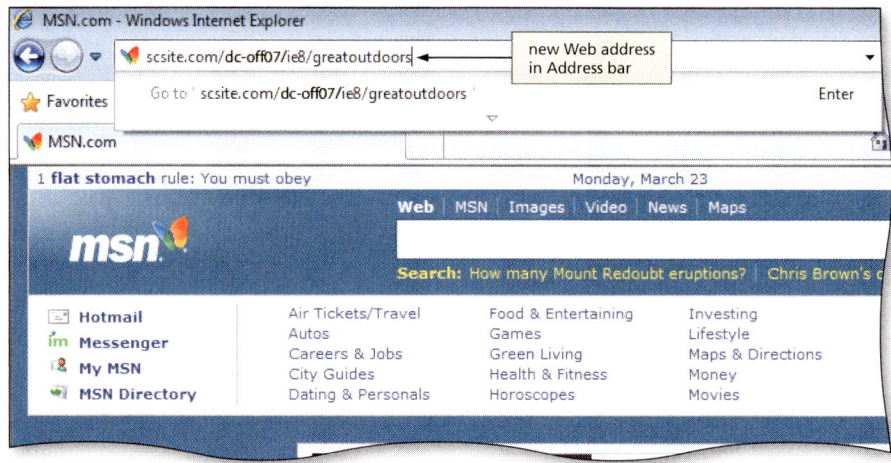

Figure 10

Q&A What happens if a Web page does not display correctly?

Internet Explorer 8 follows a more strict interpretation of HTML, and as a result some Web pages may not display as expected. If you encounter a Web page that does not display correctly, you may be able to correct the problem by displaying the Web page in Compatibility View. To display a Web page in Compatibility View, click the Compatibility View button on the Address bar.

Introduction to Internet Explorer   **Internet Explorer Chapter**   IE 17

❸
- Press the ENTER key to load the Great Outdoors Travel Web page (Figure 11).

Q&A What if I typed the wrong Web address?

If you type the wrong letter and notice the error before pressing the ENTER key, use the BACKSPACE key to erase all the characters back to and including the one that is wrong. If the error is easier to retype than correct, click the Web address in the Address bar and retype it correctly.

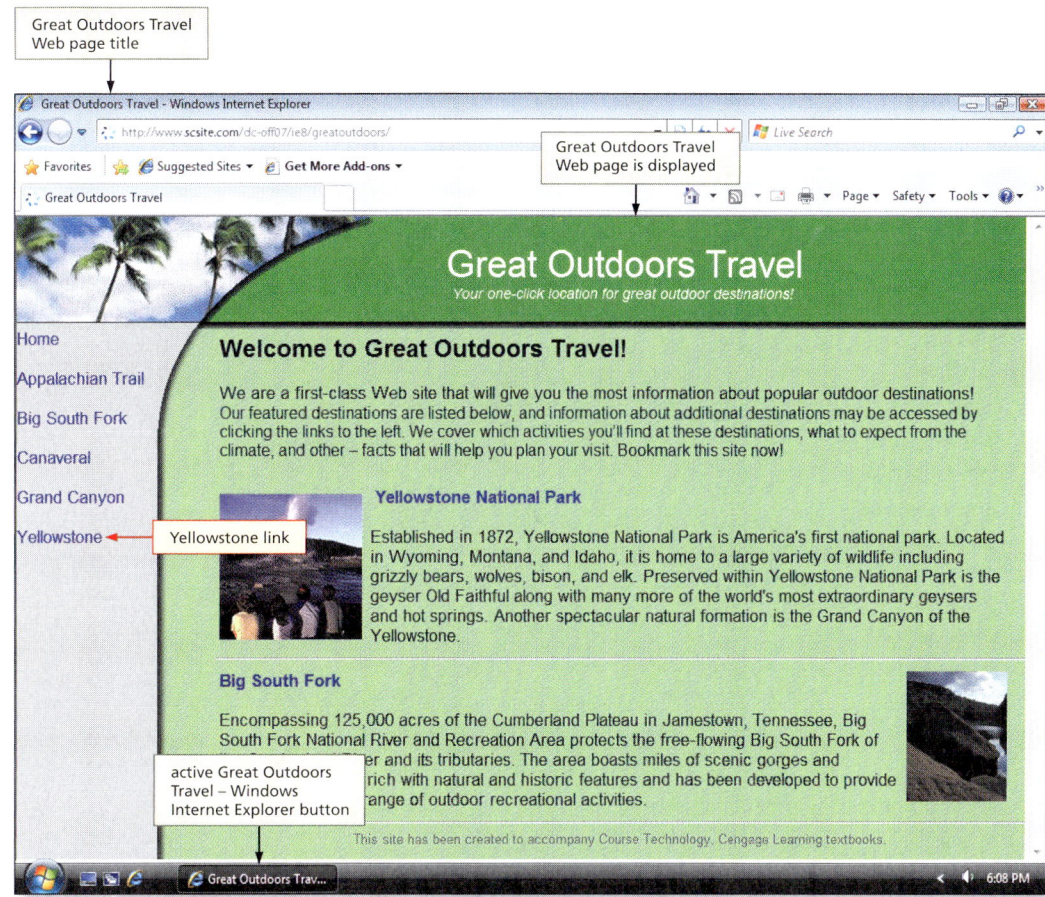

Figure 11

❹
- Click the Yellowstone link to display the Yellowstone National Park Web page (Figure 12).

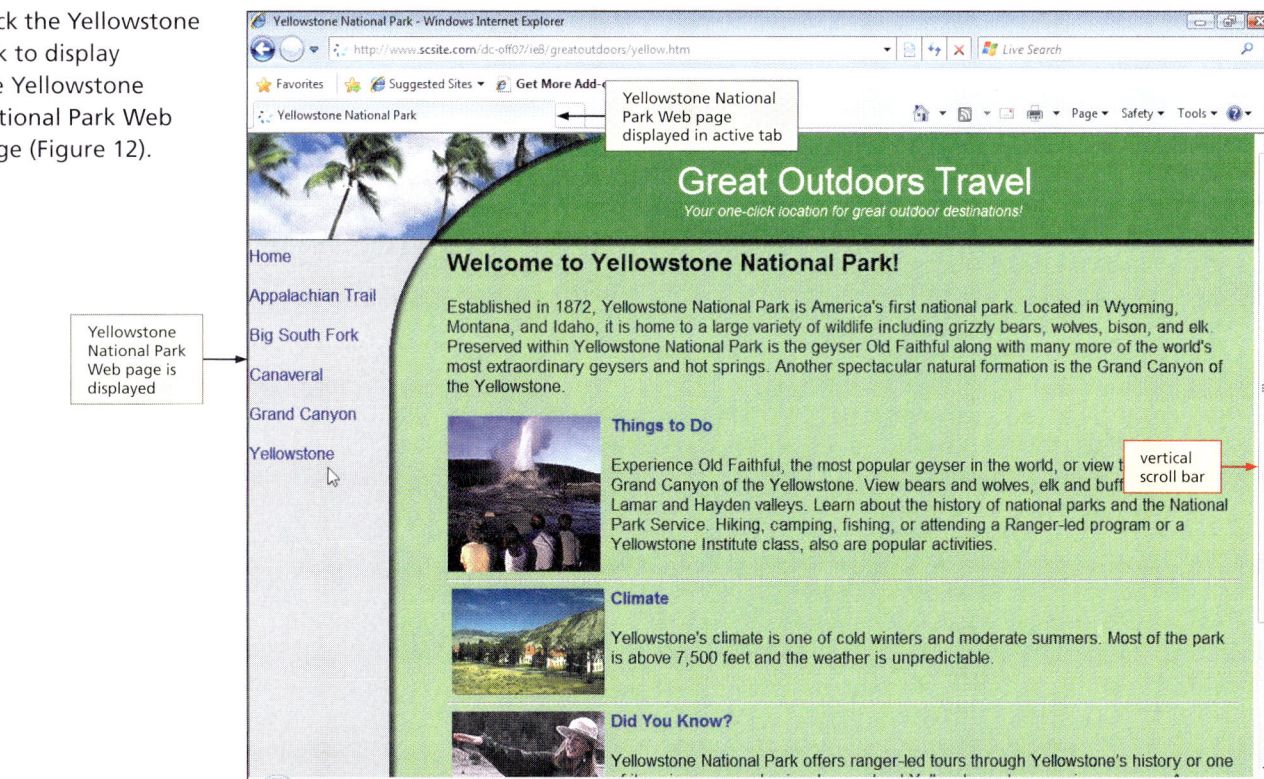

Figure 12

5
- Scroll through the display area using the vertical scroll bar to display the photo gallery link (Figure 13).

Q&A Why is the text, photo gallery, underlined?

Links to other Web pages and Web sites usually are underlined. Individuals who create Web pages typically do not underline text unless the text will act as a hyperlink.

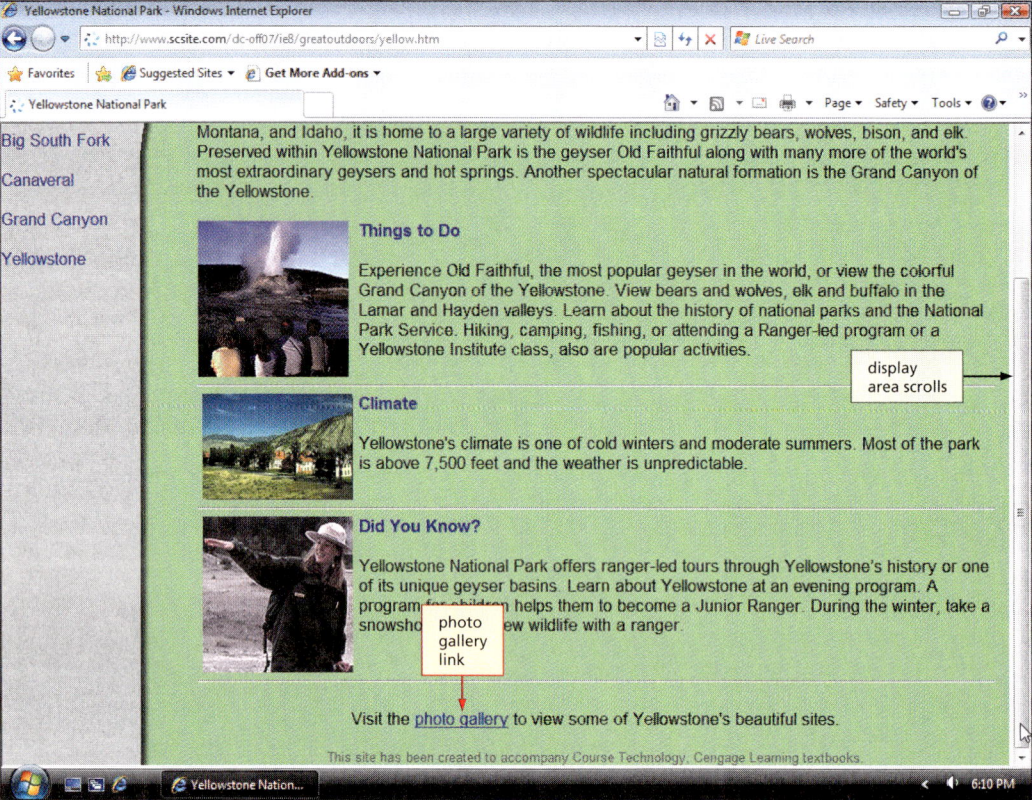

Figure 13

6
- Click the photo gallery link to display the Yellowstone National Park Photo Gallery Web page (Figure 14).

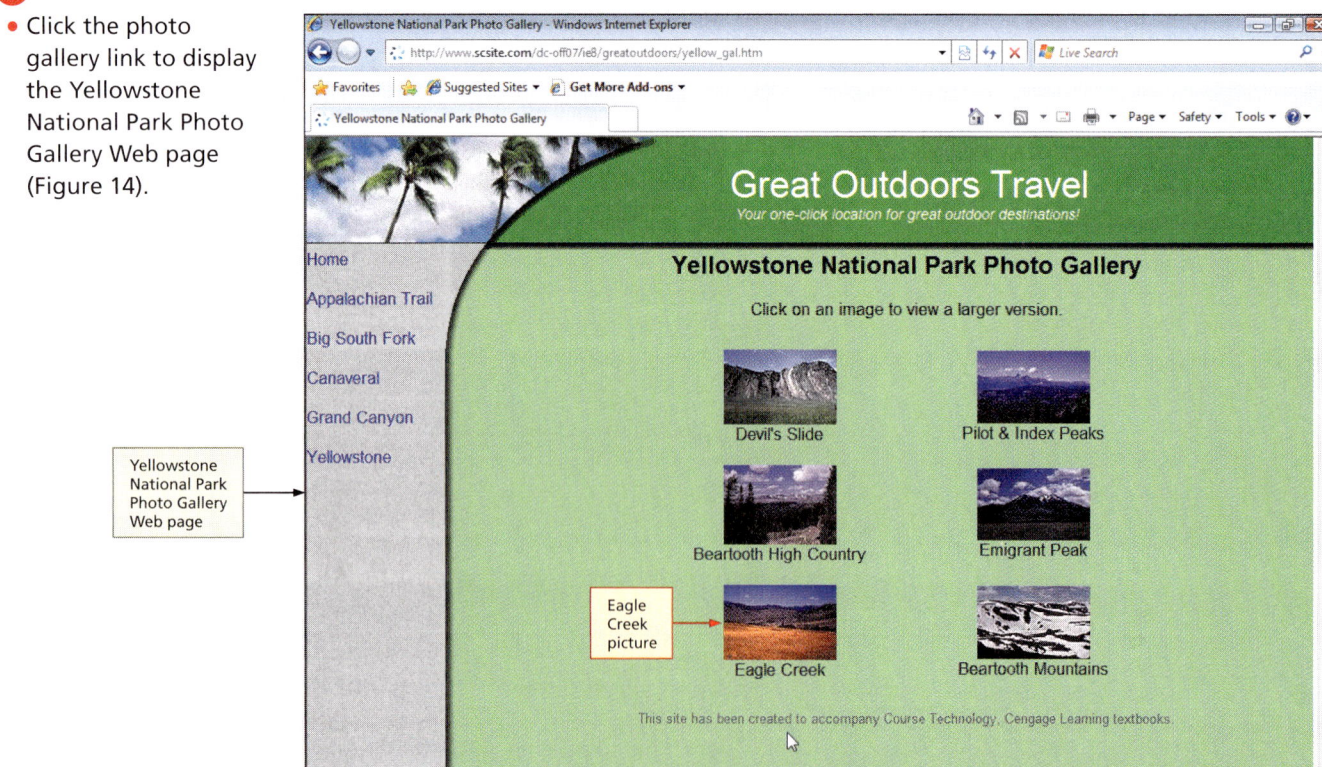

Figure 14

- If necessary, scroll through the display area to view the six pictures.

- Click the Eagle Creek picture to display the Eagle Creek Web page, which contains a larger version of the Eagle Creek picture (Figure 15).

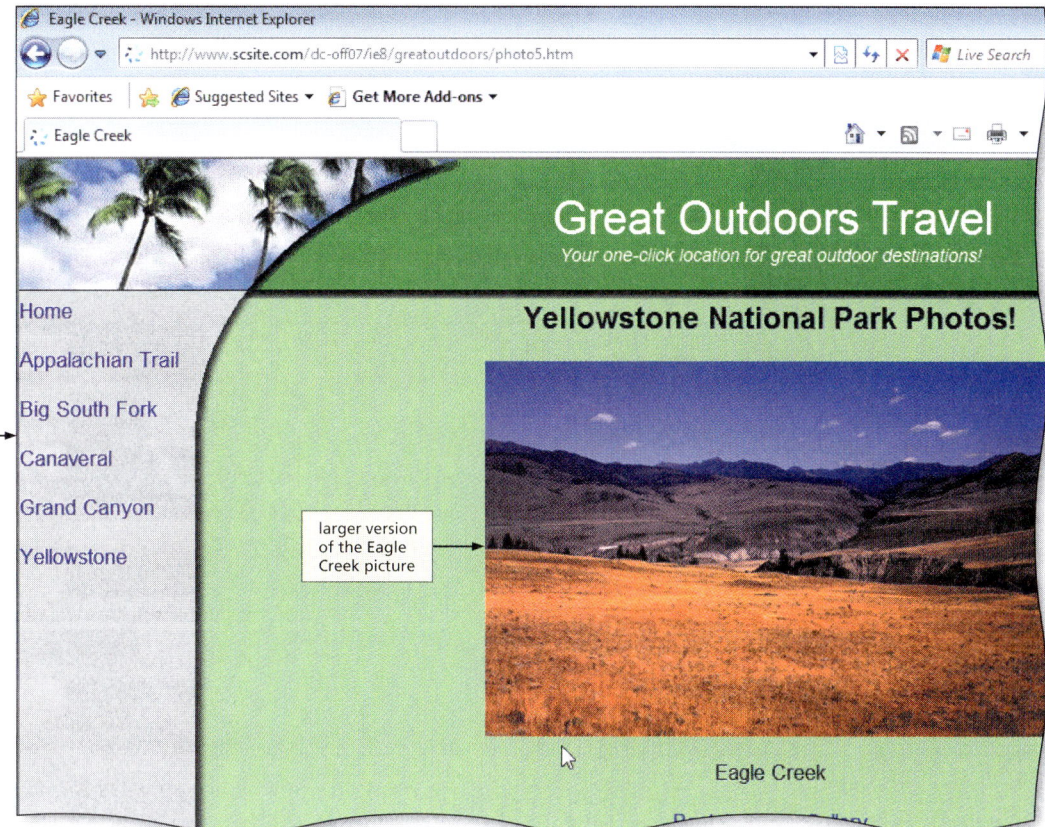

Figure 15

The preceding steps illustrate how simple it is to browse the World Wide Web. Displaying a Web page associated with a link is as easy as clicking a text or picture link.

Pointing to an image on a Web page may display **alternate text** in a small pop-up box (Figure 16 on the next page). Alternate text is text that displays in place of the image if a user configures his or her Web browser not to display images. In addition, visually impaired users typically have special software installed on their computer that reads the contents of their screen through the computer's speakers. Because this software cannot read an image, it reads the alternate text instead. Web page authors typically write alternate text that briefly describes the image it represents. Poorly written alternate text can make it difficult for visually impaired users to understand what is on the Web page.

Other Ways

1. On File menu click Open, type Web address in Open box, click OK button
2. Press CTRL+O, type Web address in Open box, click OK button
3. Press ALT+F, press O, type Web address in Open box, click OK button

Figure 16

BTW

Stopping the Transfer of a Web Page
In addition to clicking the Stop button on the toolbar to stop the transfer of a Web page, you also can click the Stop command on the View menu, press the ESC key, or press ALT+V and then press the P key.

Stopping the Transfer of a Page

If a Web page you are trying to view is taking too long to transfer or if you have clicked the wrong link, you may decide not to wait for the page to finish transferring. The Stop button on the toolbar (Figure 17) allows you to stop the transfer of a page while the transfer is in progress. You will know that the transfer still is in progress if the icon on the current tab is in motion. Stopping the transfer of a Web page will leave a partially transferred Web page in the display area. Pictures or text displaying before the Stop button is clicked remain visible in the display area and any links can be clicked to display the associated Web pages. Because high-speed Internet connections are increasingly common, Web pages load quickly and the need for the Stop button is decreasing. Individuals who connect to the Internet with a slower Internet connection, such as dial-up access, however, may have a greater need to use the Stop button.

Refreshing a Web Page

One of the great features of the Internet is how quickly content on Web pages can be updated or changed. As you display different Web pages, Internet Explorer keeps track of the pages you visit, so that you can find those pages quickly in the future. Internet Explorer stores the Web pages you visit in a folder on the hard disk. When you display a previously viewed Web page, the page is displayed quickly because Internet Explorer is able to retrieve the page from the folder on the hard disk instead of from a Web server on the Internet. For this reason, the Web page you are viewing may not be the most up-to-date version. Web pages containing stock quotes, weather, and news are updated frequently to reflect the most current information. If you are unsure of whether the content you are viewing on a Web page is current, you should refresh the Web page. You also should refresh a Web page if you think the Web page has loaded incorrectly. You can refresh the Web page by using the **Refresh button** on the toolbar (Figure 17).

To Refresh a Web Page

The following steps refresh the contents of the Web page to ensure that you are viewing the most recent version of the page.

1
- Click the Refresh button on the toolbar to cause Internet Explorer to initiate a new transfer of the Web page from the Web server to your computer (Figure 17).

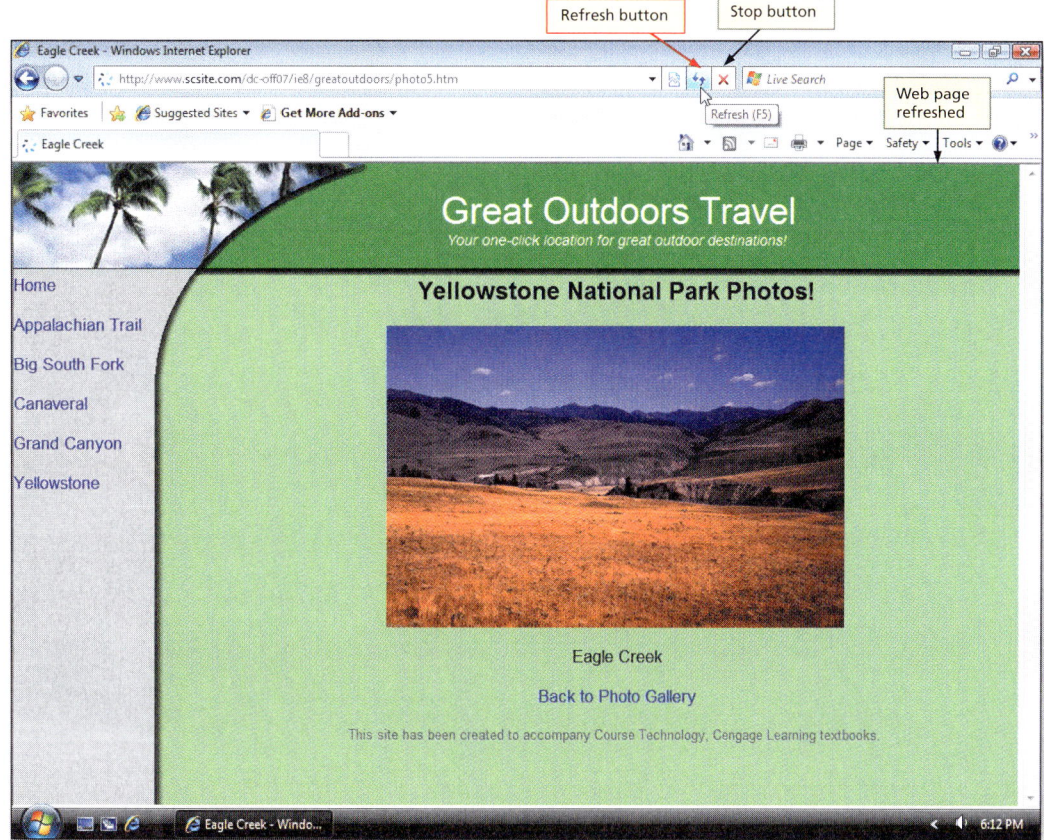

Figure 17

Other Ways
1. Click Web address in Address bar, press ENTER key
2. On View menu click Refresh
3. Press ALT+V, press R
4. Press F5

Finding a Previously Displayed Web Page

One method to find a previously displayed Web page is to use the Back button and the Recent Pages list (Figure 18a on the next page). Each time a Web page appears in the display area, the title of the Web page is added to the **Recent Pages list**. You can redisplay a previously viewed page by clicking the Recent Pages list arrow and selecting the desired Web page from the Recent Pages list (Figure 18a). The Forward button activates only after you click the Back button to return to a recent page. Each time you end an Internet session by quitting Internet Explorer, the entries on the Recent Pages list are cleared.

Another method for retrieving previously viewed pages is the **Go To list**, which contains the titles of all Web pages in the order they were displayed during the current session (Figure 18b). A check mark preceding a name in the list identifies the page currently displayed. To view the Go To list, press the ALT key to display the menu bar, click View on the menu bar, and then point to Go To on the View menu. Clicking a title in the Go To list displays the associated Web page in the display area.

A third method uses the Address bar arrow to display previously viewed Web pages. Clicking the Address bar arrow displays the **Address bar list**, which also contains a list of previously visited Web addresses (Figure 18c).

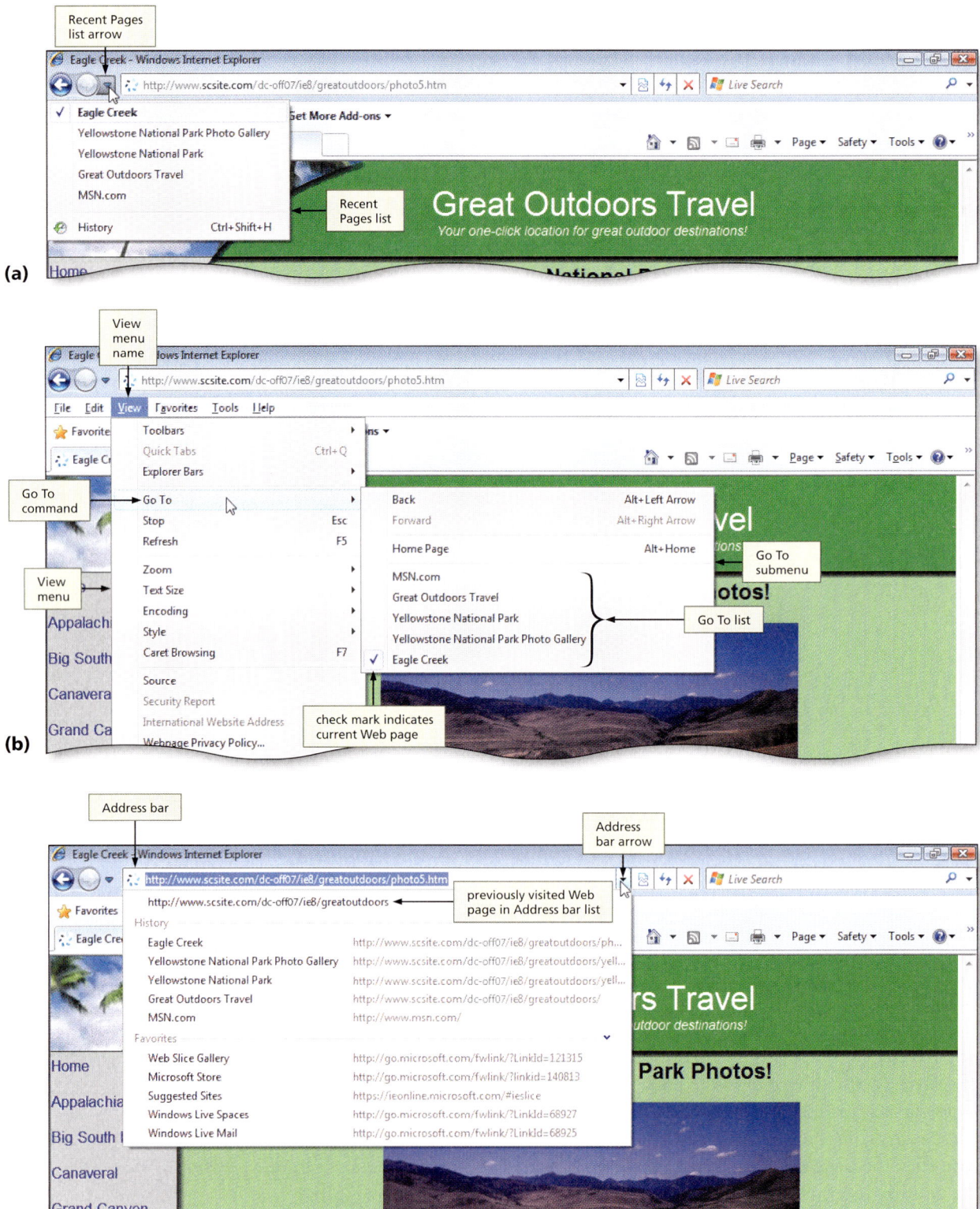

Figure 18

Finding a Recently Displayed Web Page Using the Navigation Buttons

When you visit the first Web page after starting Internet Explorer, the Back button is available for use. Pointing to the button changes the color of the button, indicating the button is active.

To Use the Navigation Buttons to Find Recently Displayed Web Pages

The Back and Forward buttons often are used when you wish to revisit a Web page you recently have visited since you last opened Internet Explorer. The following steps use the Back and Forward buttons.

1
- Click the Back button on the toolbar to display the Yellowstone National Park Photo Gallery Web page (Figure 19).

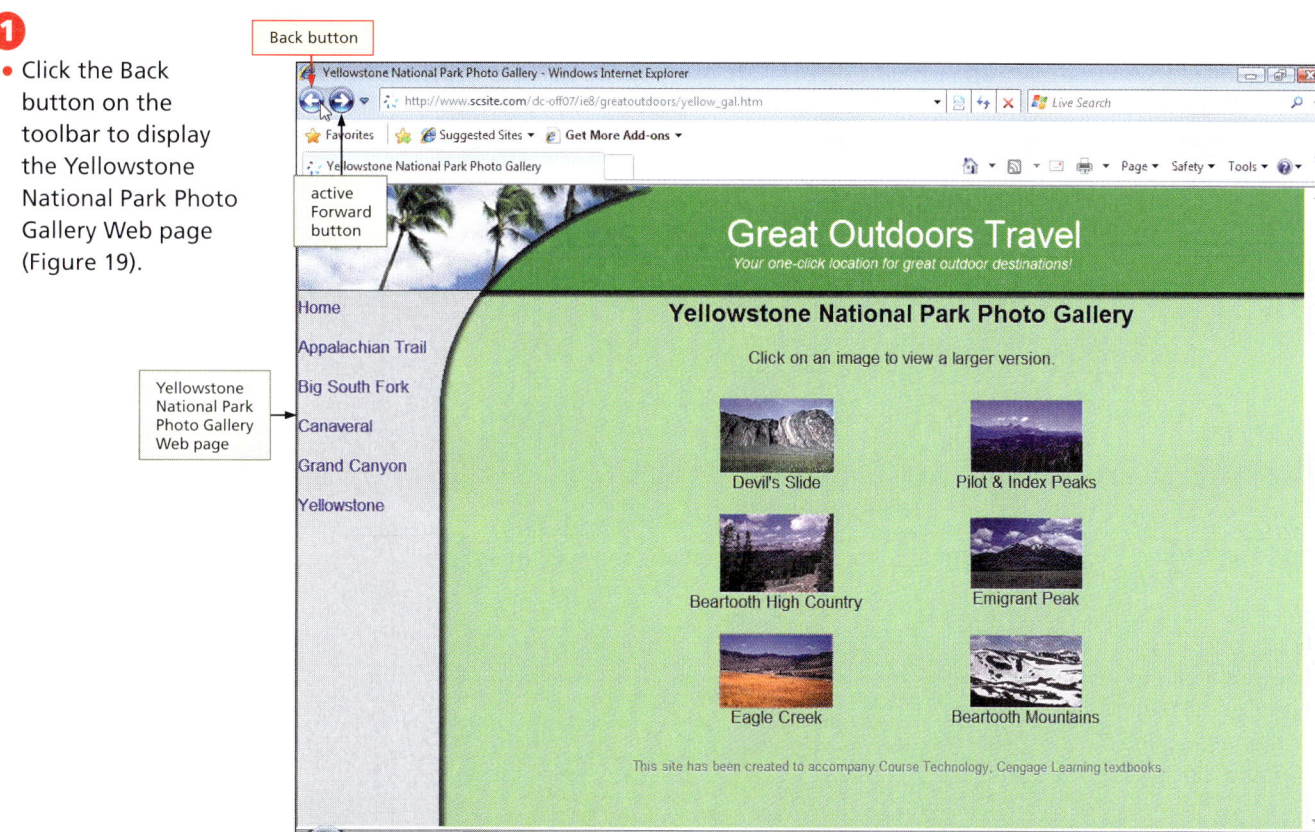

Figure 19

2
- Click the Back button again to display the Yellowstone National Park Web page (Figure 20).

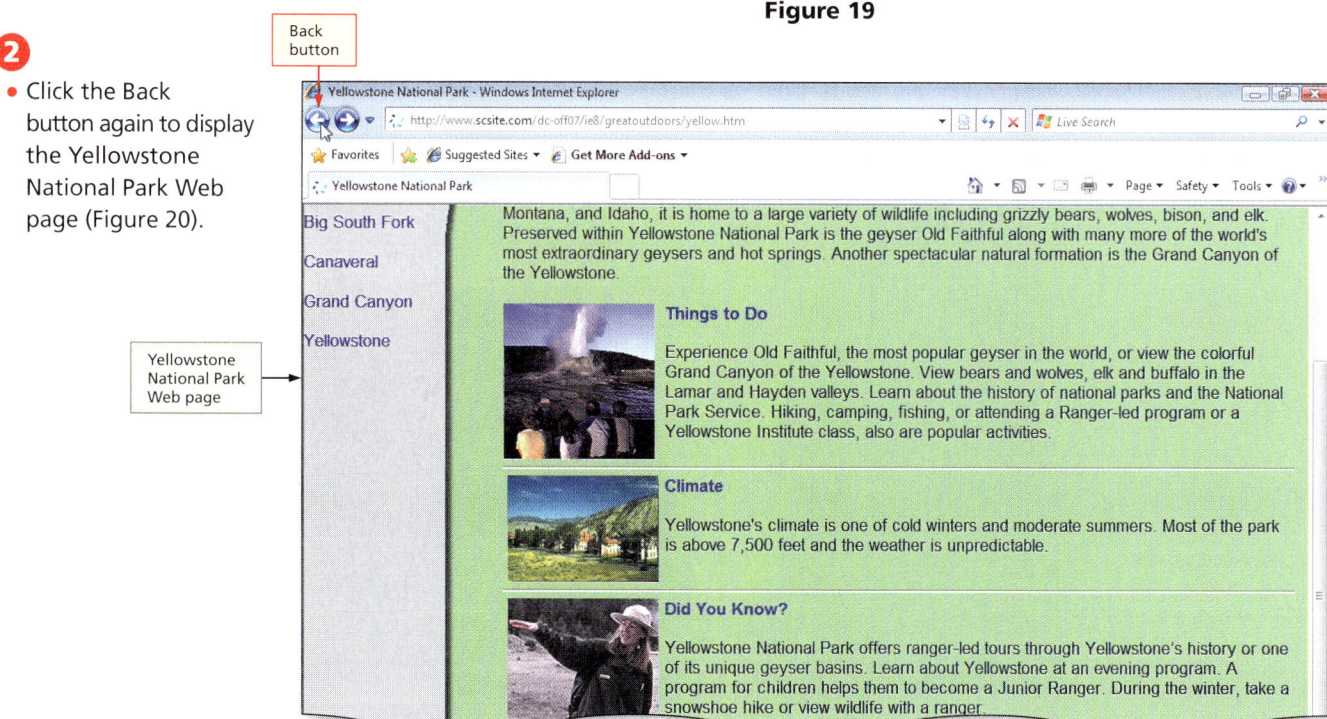

Figure 20

IE 24   Internet Explorer Chapter   Introduction to Internet Explorer

3
- Click the Forward button on the toolbar to display the Yellowstone National Park Photo Gallery Web page (Figure 21).

4
- Click the Forward button again to display the Eagle Creek Web page (Figure 22).

Other Ways
1. Click Recent Pages list arrow, click Web page title
2. On View menu, point to Go To, click Web page title on Go To submenu (or Back or Forward)
3. Back: press ALT+LEFT ARROW; forward: press ALT+RIGHT ARROW

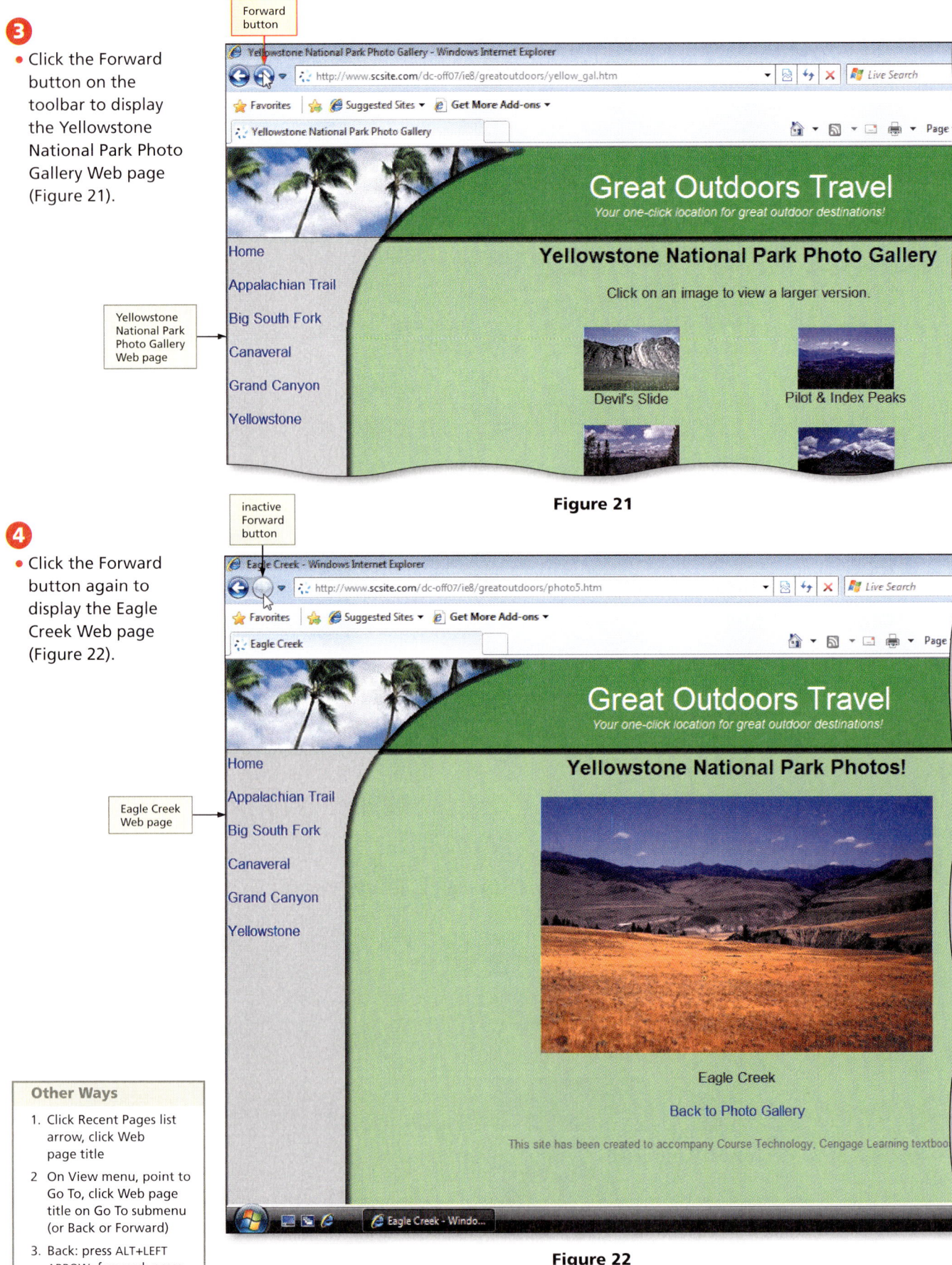

Figure 21

Figure 22

You can continue to page backward until you reach the beginning of the Recent Pages list. At that time, the Back button becomes inactive, which indicates that the list contains no additional pages to which you can move back. You can move forward, however, by clicking the Forward button.

You can see that traversing the list of pages is easy using the Back and Forward buttons. This method can be time consuming, however, if you must navigate through many pages before you reach the one you want to view.

To Display a Web Page Using the Recent Pages List

It is possible to jump to any previously visited page by clicking its title in the Recent Pages list. In this way, you can find a recently visited page without displaying an intermediate page. The following steps illustrate how to navigate quickly and easily to a recently visited page without having to click the Back button multiple times to reach the page.

1
- Click the Recent Pages list arrow on the toolbar to display the Recent Pages list (Figure 23).

Q&A Why does my Recent Pages list look different?

If Internet Explorer was running before beginning this chapter, your Recent Pages list may contain additional pages.

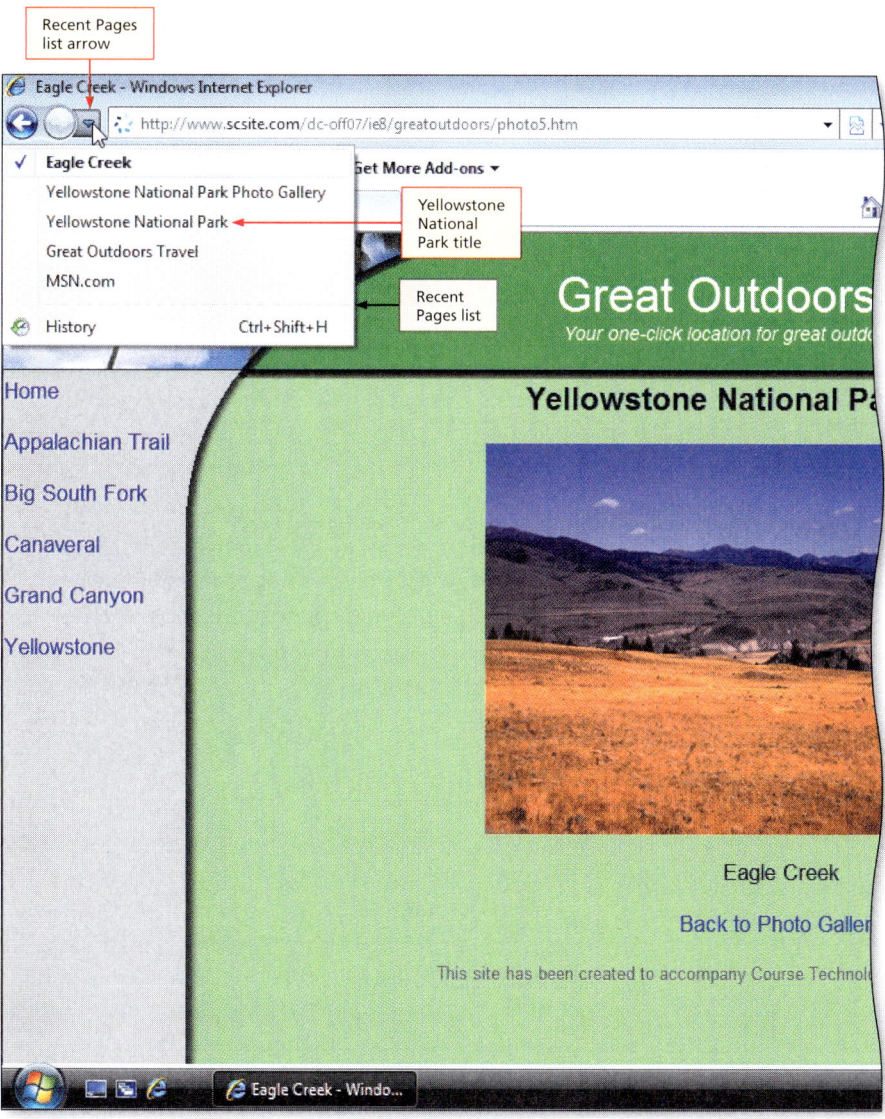

Figure 23

- Click Yellowstone National Park on the Recent Pages list to display the Yellowstone National Park Web page (Figure 24).

Q&A Why are some Web page titles displayed only partially in the Recent Pages list?

Some Web page titles are too long to display fully in the Recent Pages list. For this reason, the end of the Web page names might not display.

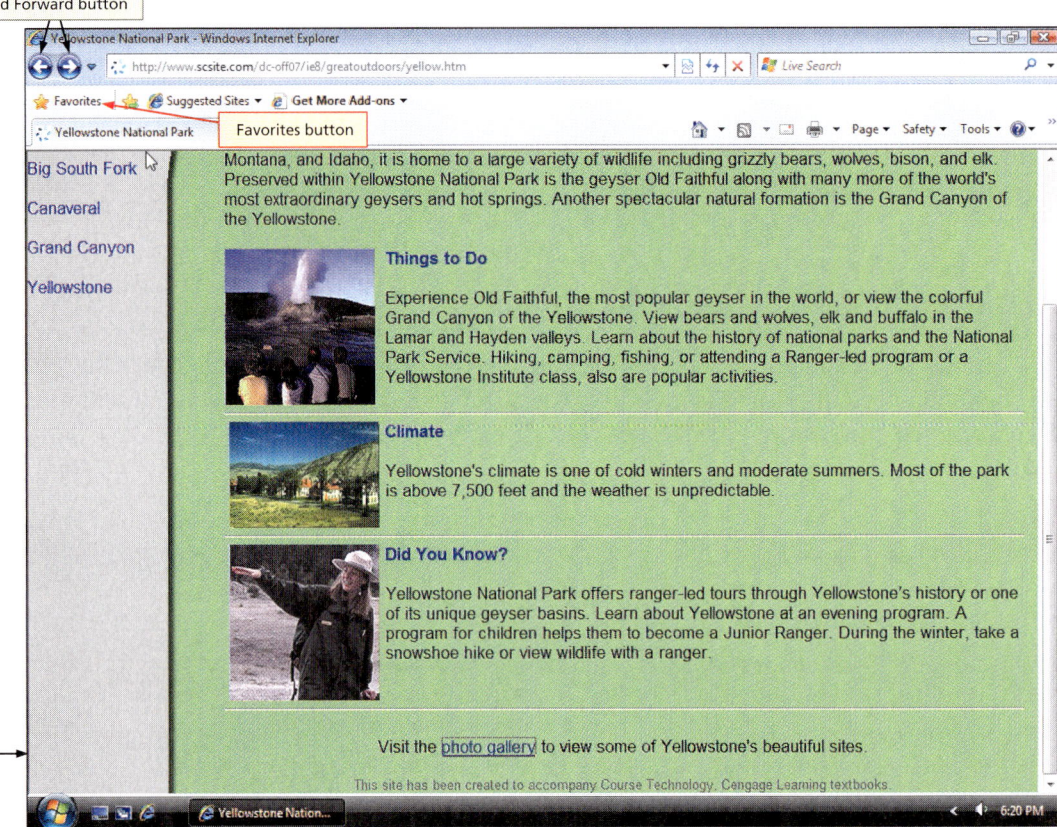

Figure 24

Other Ways
1. On View menu point to Go To, click Back on Go To submenu
2. Press ALT+LEFT ARROW

BTW

Clearing the History List
If the list of Web sites you have visited has become too large to be meaningful, you may want to clear the History List. You can clear the History List by clicking Safety on the Command bar, clicking Delete Browsing History, verifying that a check mark appears in the History check box, and then clicking the Delete button in the Delete Browsing History dialog box. Clearing the History List also clears the Address bar list.

If you have a small list of pages you have visited, or the Web page you wish to view is only one or two pages away, using the Back and Forward buttons to traverse the lists will likely be faster than displaying the Recent Pages list and selecting the correct title. If you have visited a large number of pages, however, you will need to step forward or back through many pages, and it may be easier to use the Recent Pages list to select the exact page.

Using the History List to Display Web Pages

Internet Explorer maintains another list of previously visited Web pages in the History List. The **History List** is a list of Web pages visited over a period of days or weeks (over many sessions). You can use this list to display Web pages you may have accessed during that time. Clicking the Favorites button on the Favorites bar, clicking the History tab, and then clicking Today displays the History List.

When the Explorer bar is visible, the display area contains two panes. The left pane contains the Explorer bar and the right pane contains the current Web page. The Explorer bar will remain on the screen until you close it. To find a recently visited Web page using the History List, first display the entire History List, select the order in which you want to view the history, and then click the desired Web page title. The Web page titles can be categorized by date, site, most visited, or order visited today. You also are able to search this History List for a particular Web site.

If you are browsing the World Wide Web from a public or shared computer, you might not want Internet Explorer to save any information about the Web sites you have visited. **InPrivate Browsing** is a new feature in Internet Explorer 8 that allows you to visit Web pages without the Web browser recording any information. For example, if you visit your bank's Web site using InPrivate Browsing, Internet Explorer will not save the site in your History List, nor will it save any cookies or other temporary Internet files from the Web site. To enable InPrivate Browsing, click the Safety button on the Command bar, and then click InPrivate Browsing on the Safety menu. Internet Explorer will open a new window with an InPrivate icon in the Address bar. When you wish to exit InPrivate Browsing mode, simply close the window.

To Display a Web Page Using the History List

To display a recently visited Web page without having to click the Back button multiple times, perform the following steps to display the Web page using the History List.

1

- Click the Favorites button on the Favorites bar to display the Favorites Center.

- Click the Pin the Favorites Center button to pin the Favorites Center to the Internet Explorer window (Figure 25).

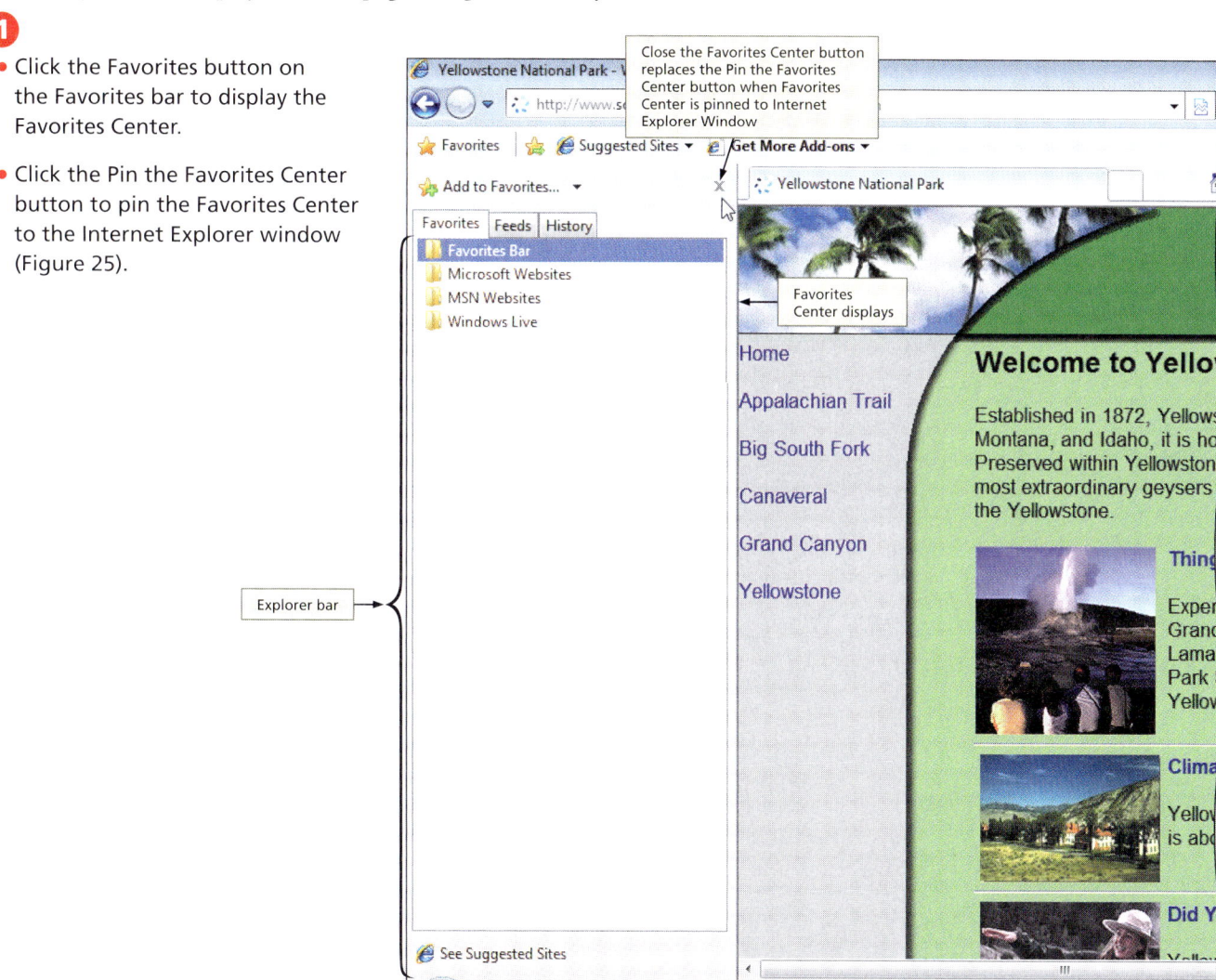

Figure 25

2
- Click the History tab on the Explorer bar to display the History List on the Explorer bar in the left pane of the Internet Explorer display area (Figure 26).

 Q&A

Why is the Explorer bar often hidden from the Internet Explorer window?

Internet Explorer reserves as much space as possible to display the Web pages in the display area. Continuously displaying the Explorer bar consumes space on the Web page, possibly resulting in visitors needing to scroll the page horizontally to view all content.

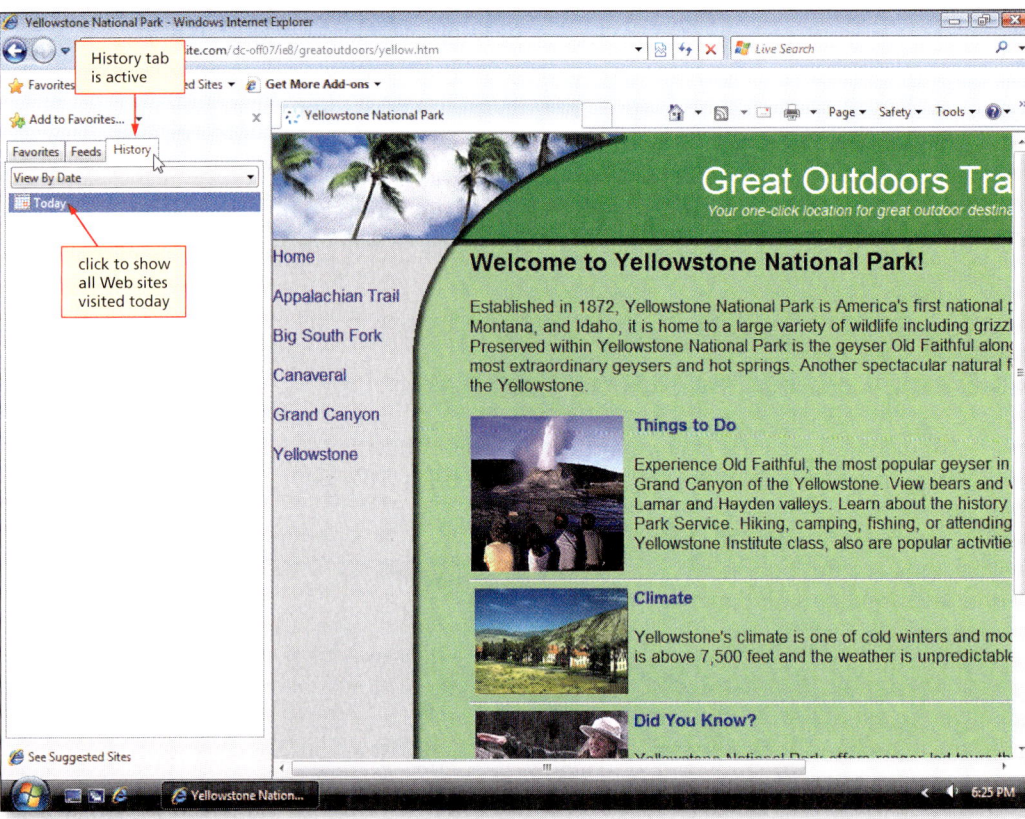

Figure 26

3
- Click Today in the History List to display a list of Web sites that have been accessed today (Figure 27). Your History List might differ.

Figure 27

- Click scsite (www.scsite.com) to display the list of Web pages that were accessed from scsite.com.
- Click Great Outdoors Travel to display the Great Outdoors Travel Web page (Figure 28).

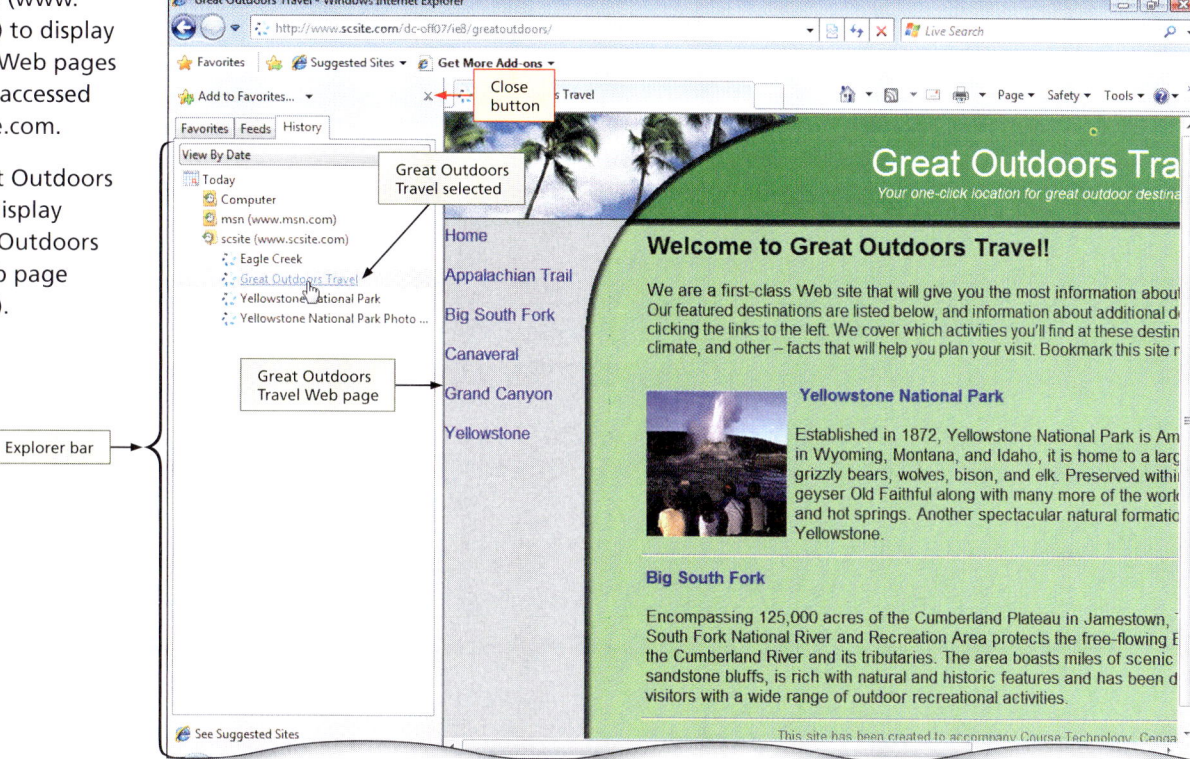

Figure 28

- Click the Close button on the Explorer bar to close the Explorer bar (Figure 29).

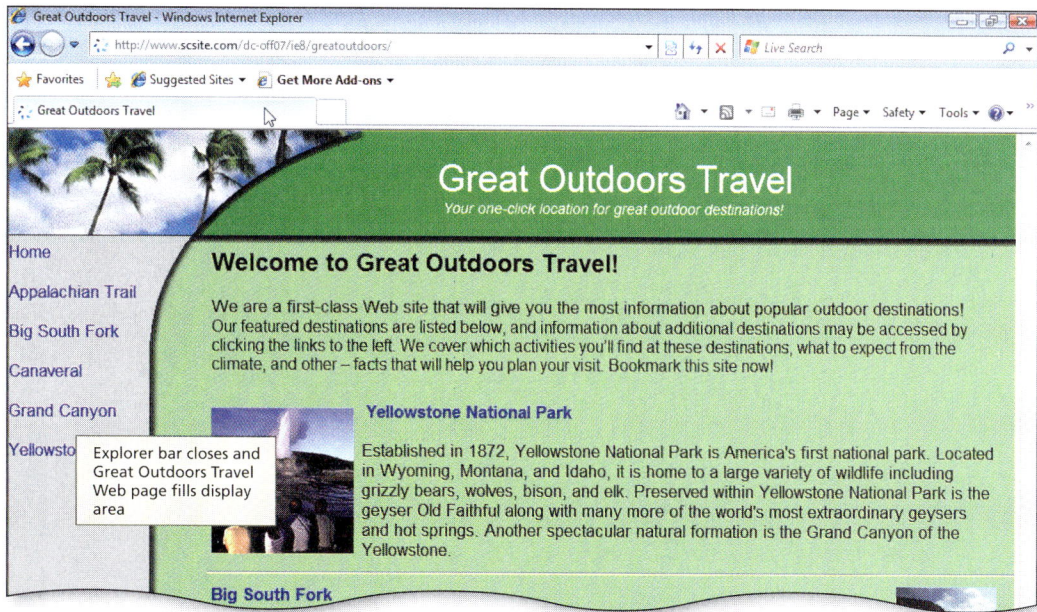

Figure 29

Other Ways

1. Click Tools on the Command bar, point to Explorer bars, click History
2. Press CTRL+SHIFT+H

BTW

Suggested Sites
The new Suggested Sites feature in Internet Explorer keeps a record of Web pages you frequently visit. It then uses this information to suggest other Web sites that might be of interest to you. To turn on Suggested Sites, click the Favorites button on the Favorites bar, and then click Turn on Suggested Sites.

The History List is useful for returning to a Web page you have visited recently. You can set the number of days Internet Explorer keeps the Web addresses in the History List by using the Internet Options command on the Tools menu. Because the History List does not keep a permanent list of Web pages you have visited, you should not use the History List to store the Web addresses of favorite or frequently visited pages.

Keeping Track of Favorite Web Pages

You can see from the previous figures that Web addresses can be long and cryptic. It is easy to make a mistake while entering complex Web addresses. Fortunately, Internet Explorer can keep track of favorite Web pages. You can store the Web addresses of favorite Web pages permanently in an area appropriately called the Favorites list.

A **favorite** consists of the title of the Web page and the Web address of that page. The title of the Web page is added to the Favorites Center. Your favorites appear in both the Favorites menu and the Favorites Center.

To Add a Web Page to the Favorites Center

The following steps add a Web page to the Favorites Center, so that you easily can access the Web page in the future.

- Click the Favorites button on the Favorites bar to display the Explorer bar.
- If necessary, click the Favorites tab to display the Favorites Center (Figure 30).

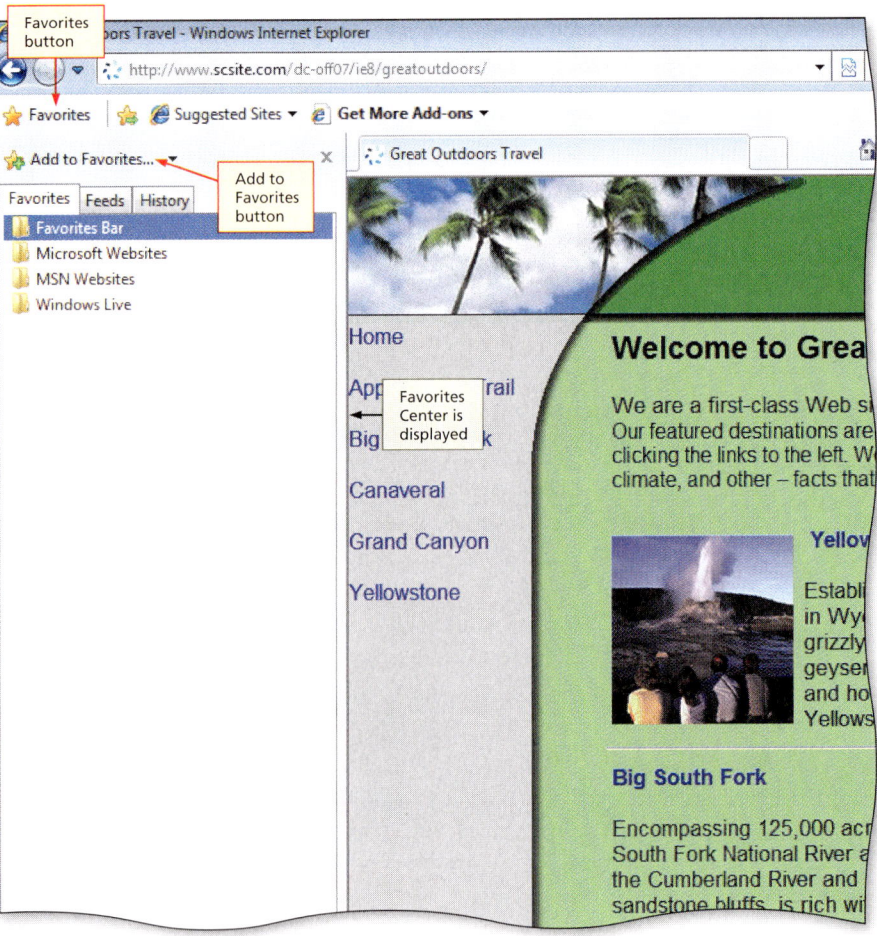

Figure 30

Introduction to Internet Explorer **Internet Explorer Chapter** IE 31

2
- Click the Add to Favorites button in the Favorites Center to display the Add a Favorite dialog box (Figure 31).

3
- Click the Add button in the Add a Favorite dialog box to add the Great Outdoors Travel Web page to the Favorites Center.

Q&A What if I want to add a Web site to my Favorites bar?

To add a Web site to your Favorites bar, simply click the Add to Favorites bar button on the Favorites bar.

Experiment
- After you add the favorite, check the Favorites menu to verify that your new favorite appears in the list. Press the ALT key to display the menu bar, click the Favorites menu, verify that the favorite appears, and then press the ESC key twice to close the Favorites menu and hide the menu bar.

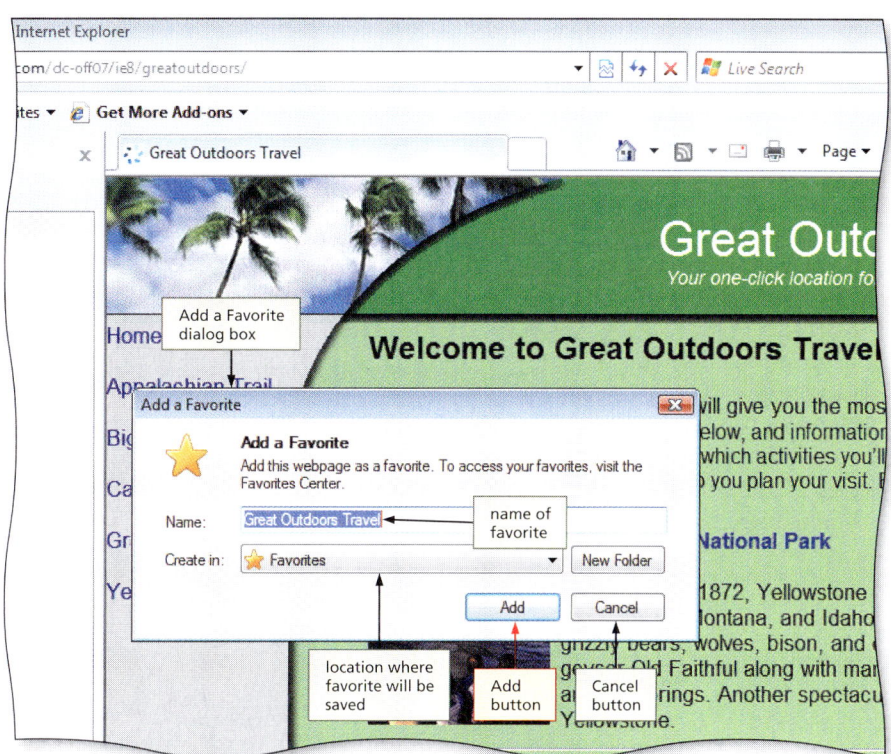

Figure 31

Other Ways
1. Press the ALT key, click Favorites on the menu bar, and then click Add to Favorites
2. Press CTRL+D
3. Press ALT+A, press A, press ENTER

In Figure 30, clicking the Add to Favorites button arrow and then clicking the Organize Favorites command displays the Organize Favorites dialog box, which allows you to move, rename, organize, and delete your favorites.

If you plan to store many favorites on your computer, you might choose to give your favorite Web sites meaningful names by renaming them and storing them in folders. In Figure 31, clicking the New Folder button adds a new folder to the Favorites list. Immediately after adding a new folder to the Favorites list, you can name the folder by typing an appropriate name and then pressing the ENTER key. After renaming the folder, you can drag an existing favorite to the folder to store the favorite in that folder. You also can change the name of a folder or favorite by clicking a folder or favorite, clicking the Rename button, typing the new name, and then pressing the ENTER key. For example, if you frequently visit many Web sites to read the news, you might choose to store the Web addresses of these sites as favorites in a News folder. A student, for example, may store school-related Web sites in an Academics folder.

BTW

Importing and Exporting Favorites
If you already have favorite Web sites set up on another computer or Web browser, or wish to transfer your favorite Web sites to another computer, you can use Internet Explorer's Import/Export Wizard to preserve your favorites. Click the Favorites button on the Favorites bar, click the Add to Favorites list arrow in the Favorites Center, and then click Import and Export to start the Import/Export Wizard. Follow the steps in the wizard to import or export your favorites.

To Display the Home Page Using the Home Button

In many cases, individuals designate the Web page they most frequently visit as their home page. The Home button on the Command bar provides a quick way to navigate to your home page. If you want to navigate back to your home page quickly and easily, perform the following step to display the home page in Internet Explorer's display area.

- Click the Home button on the toolbar to display the MSN.com home page in the Internet Explorer window (Figure 32). Your computer may display a different home page.

Figure 32

Q&A Can I have more than one home page?

Yes. If you designate more than one Web page as your home page, Internet Explorer will open each home page in a separate tab when you start Internet Explorer or when you click the Home button on the Command bar. To create multiple home pages, click Tools on the Command bar, click the Internet Options command, type the Web address for each Web page on its own line in the Home page box, and then click the OK button. You also can click the Home button list arrow, click the Add or Change Home Page command, and then click the `Add this webpage to your home page tabs´ option button to add the current page to your current home pages.

Other Ways

1. Click Home button list arrow on Command bar, click home page title
2. On View menu point to Go To, click Home Page on Go To submenu
3. Press ALT+V, press G, press H
4. Press ALT+HOME

To Display a Web Page Using the Favorites Center

The Favorites Center is used to display your list of favorite Web pages quickly, without having to navigate through several unwanted pages. Using a favorite to display a Web page is similar to using the History List to display a Web page. While you are browsing the Internet, you may want to access one of your favorites. The following steps display the Great Outdoors Travel home page by using the Favorites Center.

1

- Click the Favorites button on the Favorites bar to display the Explorer bar.

- If necessary, click the Favorites tab on the Explorer bar to display the Favorites Center (Figure 33).

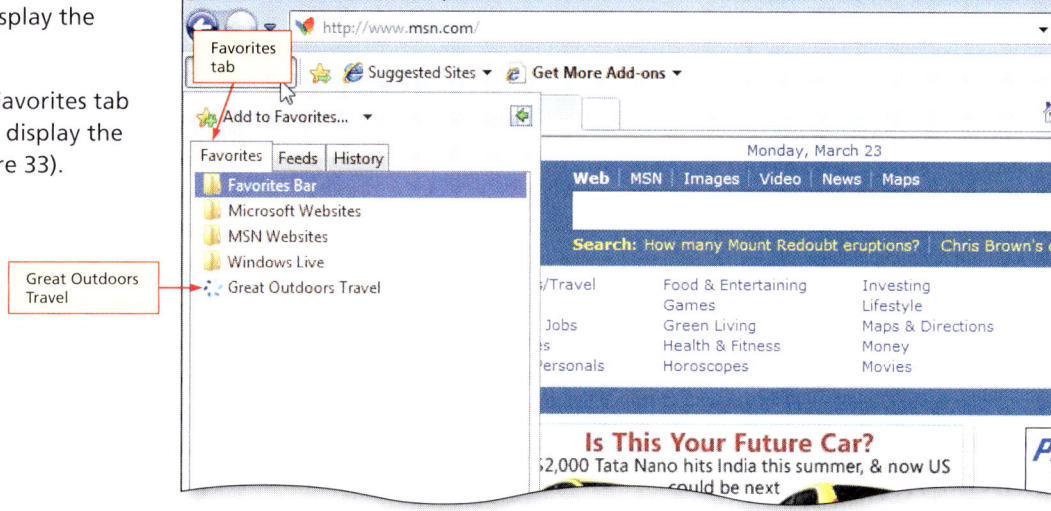

Figure 33

2

- Click the Great Outdoors Travel command on the Explorer bar to display the Great Outdoors Travel Web page in the display area (Figure 34).

Figure 34

Additional favorites are displayed in the Favorites Center shown in Figure 33. Folders included in the favorites list include the Favorites Bar folder, the Microsoft Websites folder, the MSN Websites folder, and the Windows Live folder. Other folders and favorites may display in the Favorites Center on your computer.

Other Ways

1. On Favorites menu click favorite
2. Press ALT+A, click favorite
3. Press CTRL+I, click favorite

To Remove a Web Page from the Favorites Center

You may have a variety of reasons for wanting to remove a favorite. With the Web changing every day, the Web address that worked today may not work tomorrow, or perhaps the Web site is no longer of use to you, or your favorites list is getting too big to be meaningful. Once you decide that you no longer need a favorite, the following steps delete the favorite.

- Click the Favorites button on the Favorites bar to display a list of your favorites on the Explorer bar.

- Right-click the Great Outdoors Travel entry in the Favorites Center to display a shortcut menu containing the Delete command (Figure 35).

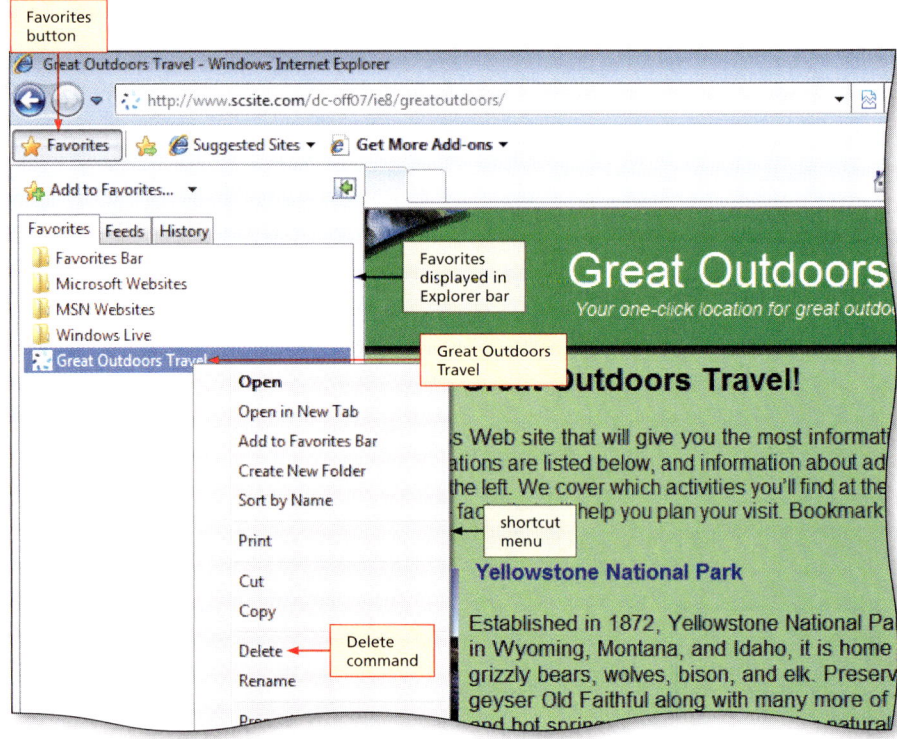

Figure 35

- Click Delete on the shortcut menu to display the Delete File dialog box (Figure 36).

Q&A

Why does the dialog box tell me that I am deleting a file?

Internet Explorer and Windows store your favorites as small text files in a folder on your computer. When you add a favorite, you are creating a file. When you delete a favorite, you are deleting a file.

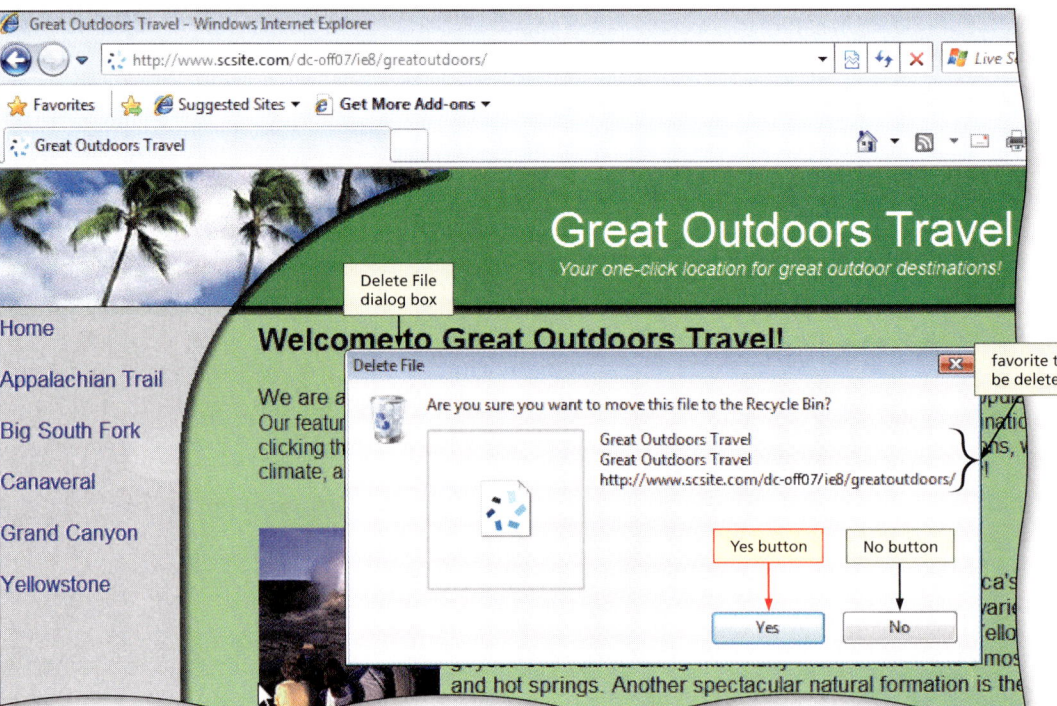

Figure 36

❸
- Click the Yes button in the Delete File dialog box to move the Great Outdoors Travel Web page to the Recycle Bin.

- Click the Favorites button to display the Explorer bar (Figure 37).

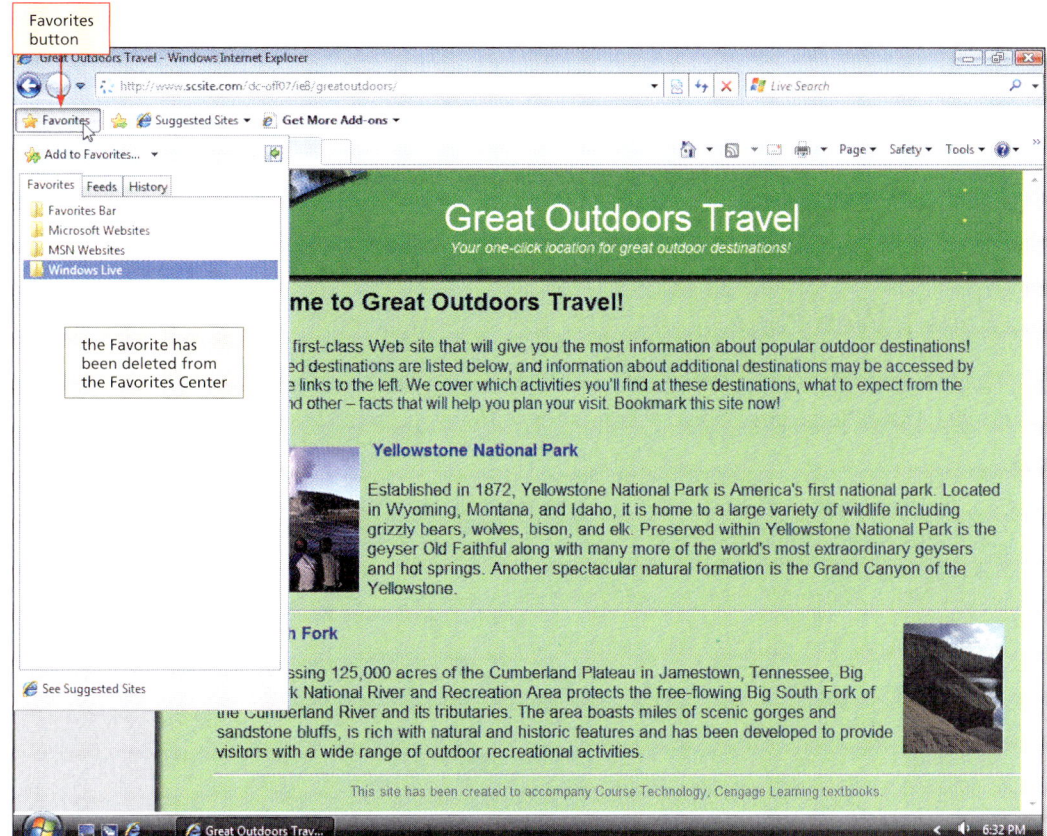

Figure 37

Other Ways
1. On Favorites menu click Organize Favorites, click favorite, click Delete button, click Yes button

The steps required to delete a folder in the favorites list are the same as those required to delete a favorite. If you delete a folder, however, Internet Explorer also will delete all favorites stored in that folder. Because favorites are stored as files on your computer, deleting a folder or favorite will move it to the Recycle Bin. The Recycle Bin stores files marked for deletion before they are permanently deleted. While a file or folder is in the Recycle Bin, it can be restored by double-clicking the Recycle Bin icon on the desktop, clicking the item you wish to restore, and then clicking the 'Restore this item' button. Because not all operating systems are configured to handle deleted items in the same manner, you should not delete a favorite or a folder unless you are sure that you no longer want it.

Saving Information Obtained with Internet Explorer

Many different types of Web pages are accessible on the World Wide Web. Because these pages can help you gather information about areas of interest, you may wish to save the information you discover for future reference. The different types of Web pages and the various uses you have for the information require different methods of saving. Internet Explorer allows you to save an entire Web page, individual pictures, or selected pieces of text. Before

BTW

Citing Web Sites
Whenever you use content from a Web site, you should cite the Web site as a source. Word Chapter 2 contains additional information about citing Internet sources.

saving a Web page or information from a Web page, you first should determine whether the information is free for you to use. If content on a Web page is protected by a copyright, or if it displays a copyright symbol, you should contact the Web page author to obtain permission before copying or using the content. Copying an image that is protected by a copyright could carry legal consequences. If you are not sure whether content is protected by a copyright, you should seek permission before duplicating it. The following pages illustrate how to save an entire Web page, how to save a single picture, and how to save text.

To Save a Web Page

One method of saving information on a Web page is to save the entire page. The following steps save the Great Outdoors Travel home page on your computer so that you can access it even when you are not connected to the Internet.

- Click the Page button on the Command bar to display the Page menu (Figure 38).

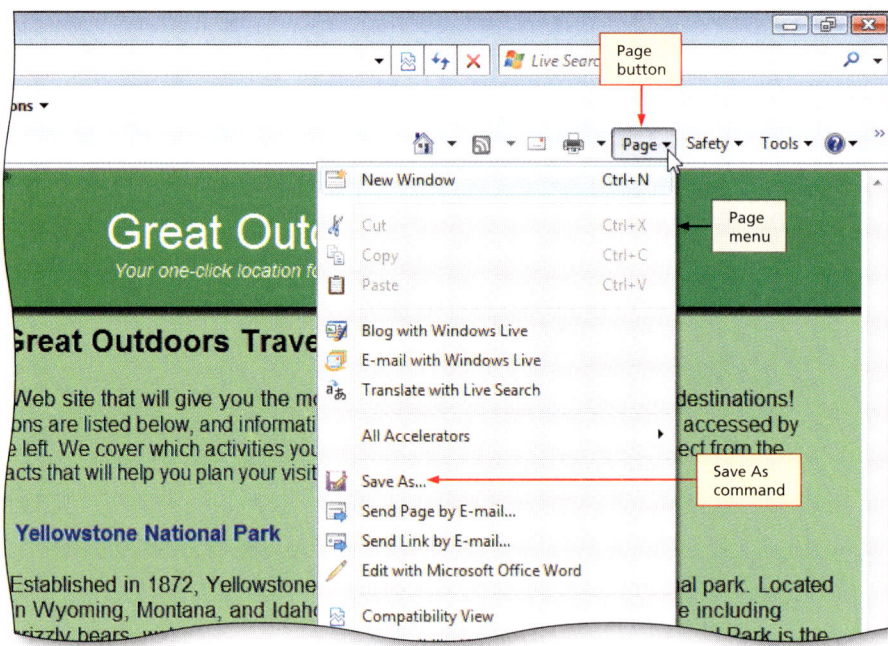

Figure 38

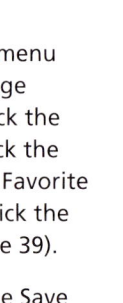
- Click Save As on the Page menu to display the Save Webpage dialog box. If necessary click the Browse Folders button, click the Documents link under the Favorite Links heading, and then click the Hide Folders button (Figure 39).

- Click the Save button in the Save Webpage dialog box to save the Web page to the Documents folder on your computer.

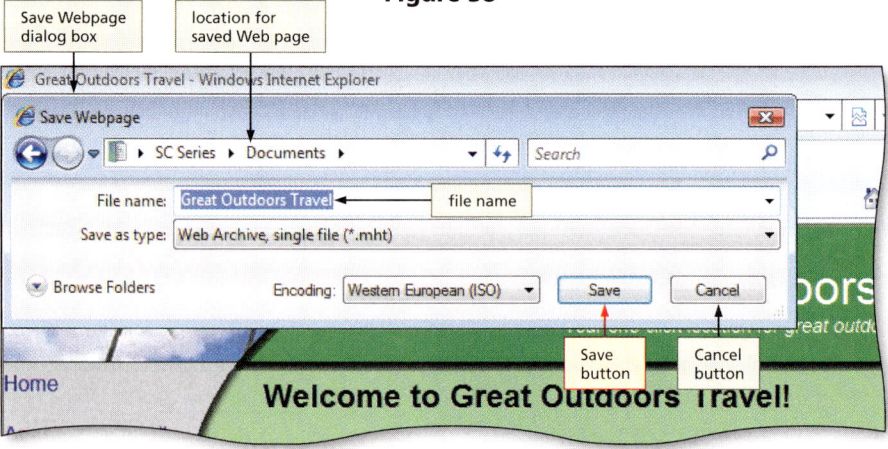

Figure 39

Other Ways
1. Press ALT+F, press A

Internet Explorer saves the instructions to display the saved Web page in the Great Outdoors Travel.mht file in the Documents folder on your computer. You can view the saved Web page in the Internet Explorer window by double-clicking the Great Outdoors Travel.mht file in your Documents folder. An .mht file is a Web archive file, capable of storing the text and images for a Web page in a single file.

To Save a Picture on a Web Page

In some cases, you may want to save only an image located on a Web page. The following steps save the Yellowstone National Park picture in the Pictures folder on your computer in the **Joint Photographic Experts Group (JPEG)** file format using the file name yellowstone.jpg. The JPEG file format is a method of encoding pictures that then can be displayed by a variety of programs.

1

- Right-click the Yellowstone National Park picture on the Great Outdoors Travel Web page to display a shortcut menu containing the Save Picture As command (Figure 40).

Q&A What else will Internet Explorer allow me to do with a picture?

The shortcut menu that is displayed after right-clicking a picture also allows you to e-mail the picture, print the picture, navigate to your Pictures folder, or set the picture as your desktop background.

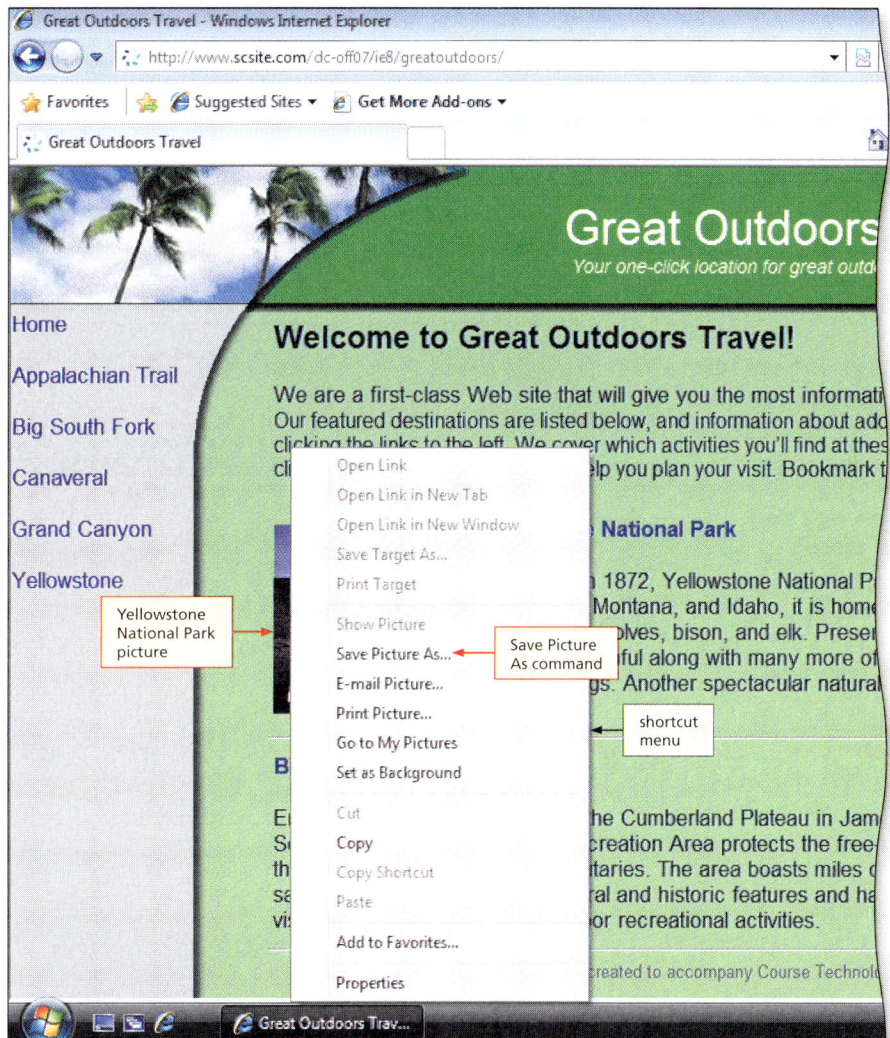

Figure 40

2
- Click Save Picture As on the shortcut menu to display the Save Picture dialog box (Figure 41).

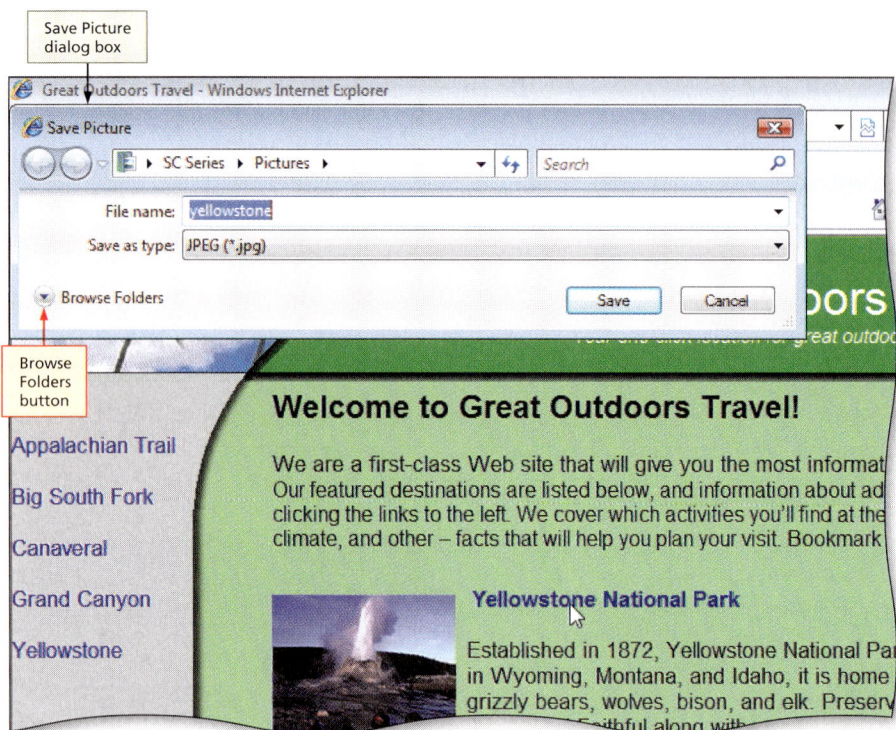

Figure 41

3
- If necessary, click the Browse Folders button to expand the Save Picture dialog box.
- If necessary, click the Pictures link in the Save Picture dialog box (Figure 42).

4
- Click the Save button in the Save Picture dialog box to save the picture in the Pictures folder on your computer and to close the Save Picture dialog box.

Q&A Should I store all my pictures in the Pictures folder?

Yes. Windows provides a Pictures folder to help you organize your pictures and make backing up the folders in the Pictures folder to another storage device for safekeeping easy. Three other folders (Documents, Music, and Videos) are available to store document, music, and video files.

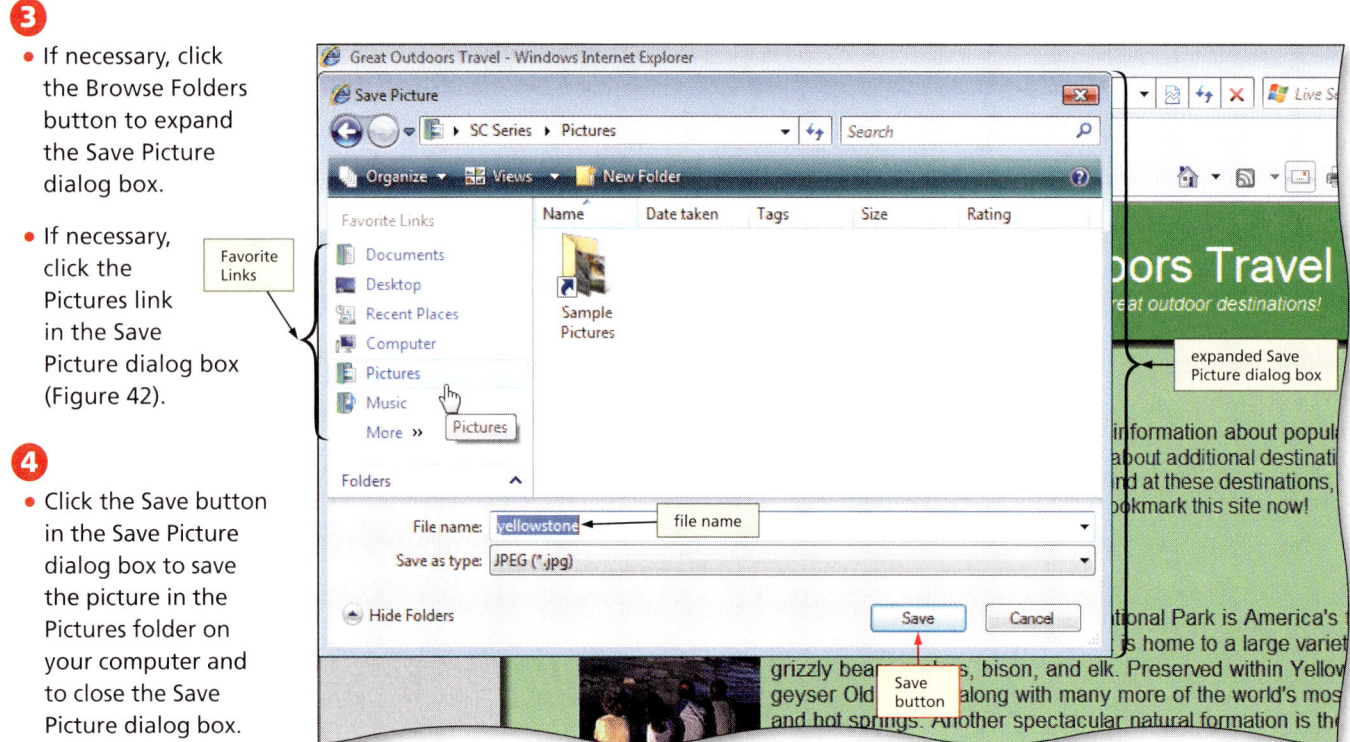

Figure 42

Copying and Pasting Using the Clipboard

A third method of saving information, called the **copy and paste method**, allows you to copy an entire Web page, or portions of a page, and insert the information into any Windows document. The **Clipboard** is a storage area in main memory that temporarily holds the information being copied. The portion of the Web page you select is **copied** from the page to the Clipboard and then **pasted** from the Clipboard into the document. Information you copy to the Clipboard remains there until you add more information or clear it.

The following pages demonstrate how to copy text and pictures from the Yellowstone National Park Web page into a WordPad document using the Clipboard. **WordPad** is a word processing program that is supplied with Microsoft Windows.

> **BTW**
>
> **Copy and Paste Web Addresses**
> You can use the copy and paste operation to insert a Web address that appears in the Address bar into a document or e-mail message. You also can copy a Web address that appears in an e-mail message into the Address bar.

To Start WordPad

Before copying information from the Web page in Internet Explorer to the Clipboard, you first should start WordPad. The following steps start WordPad.

1
- Click the Start button on the Windows taskbar to display the Start menu.
- Click All Programs on the Start menu to display the All Programs list.
- Click Accessories on the All Programs list to display the Accessories list (Figure 43).

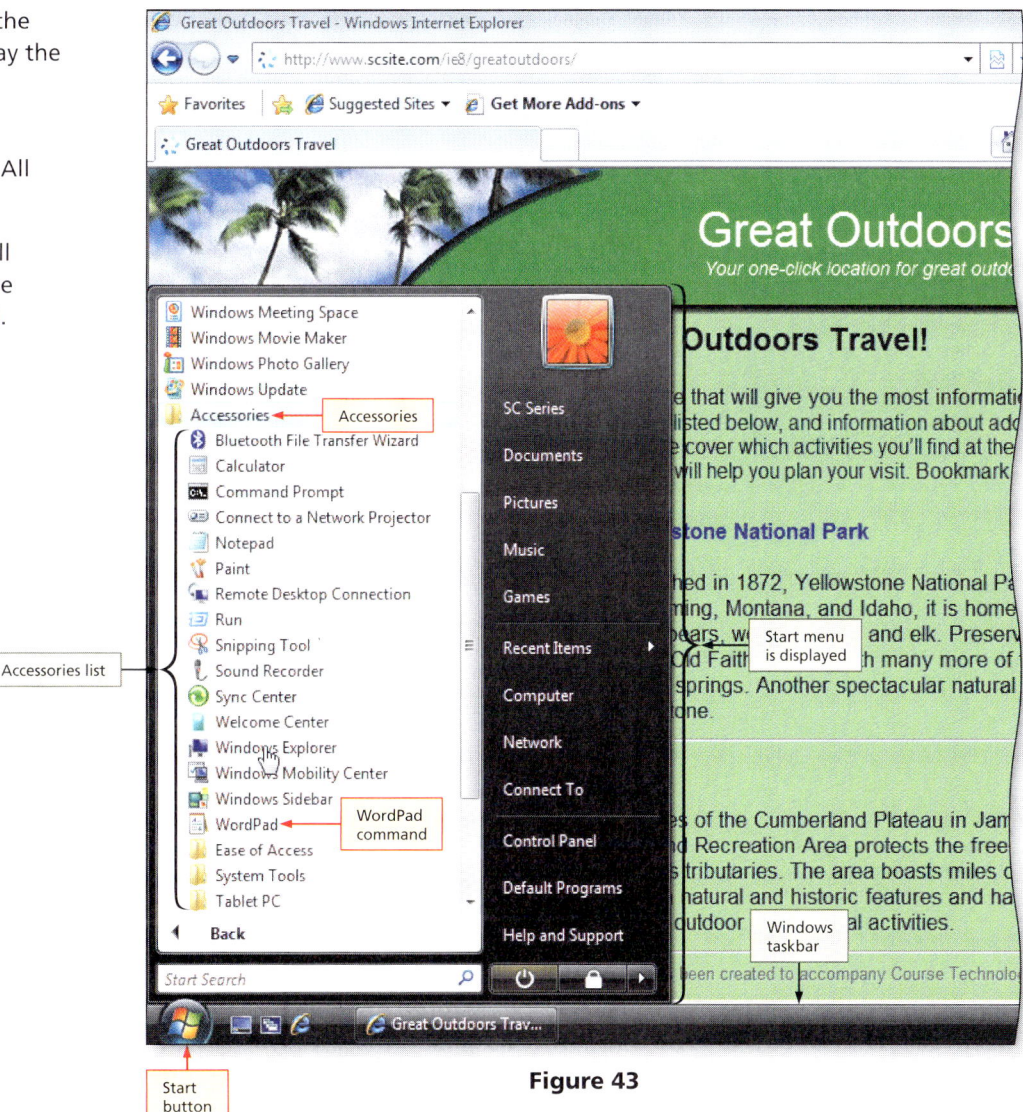

Figure 43

❷
- Click WordPad to start WordPad (Figure 44).

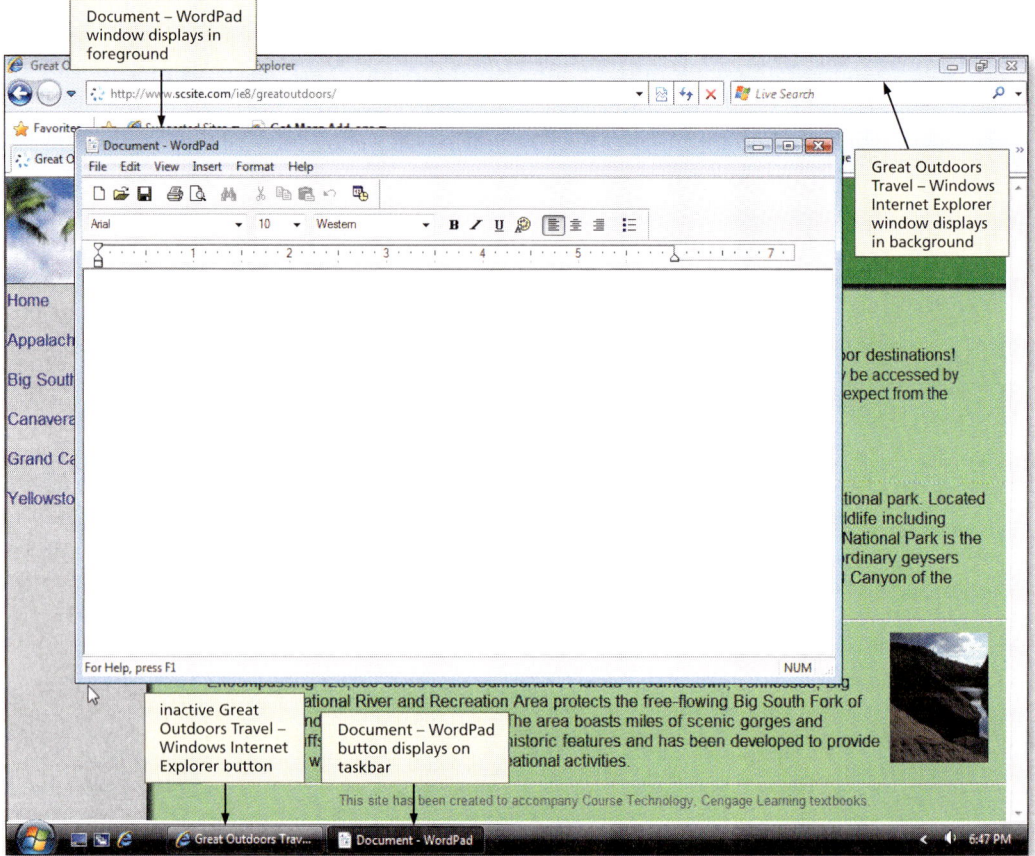

Figure 44

Other Ways
1. Click Start button, click All Programs, click Accessories, click Run, type wordpad, click OK button

The Document - WordPad window is displayed on top of the Great Outdoors Travel window. The Document - WordPad window is the active window. The **active window** means that it is the window currently being used. A dark title bar identifies the active window. The Great Outdoors Travel window is the inactive window. A light title bar identifies the **inactive window**.

To Display the Yellowstone National Park Web Page

Currently, the active Document - WordPad window displays on top of the inactive Great Outdoors Travel window. After starting WordPad and before copying text from a Web page to the Clipboard, make the Great Outdoors Travel window active and then display the Yellowstone National Park Web page. The following steps display the Yellowstone National Park Web page.

- Click the Great Outdoors Travel - Windows Internet Explorer button on the taskbar to make the Great Outdoors Travel window the active window (Figure 45).

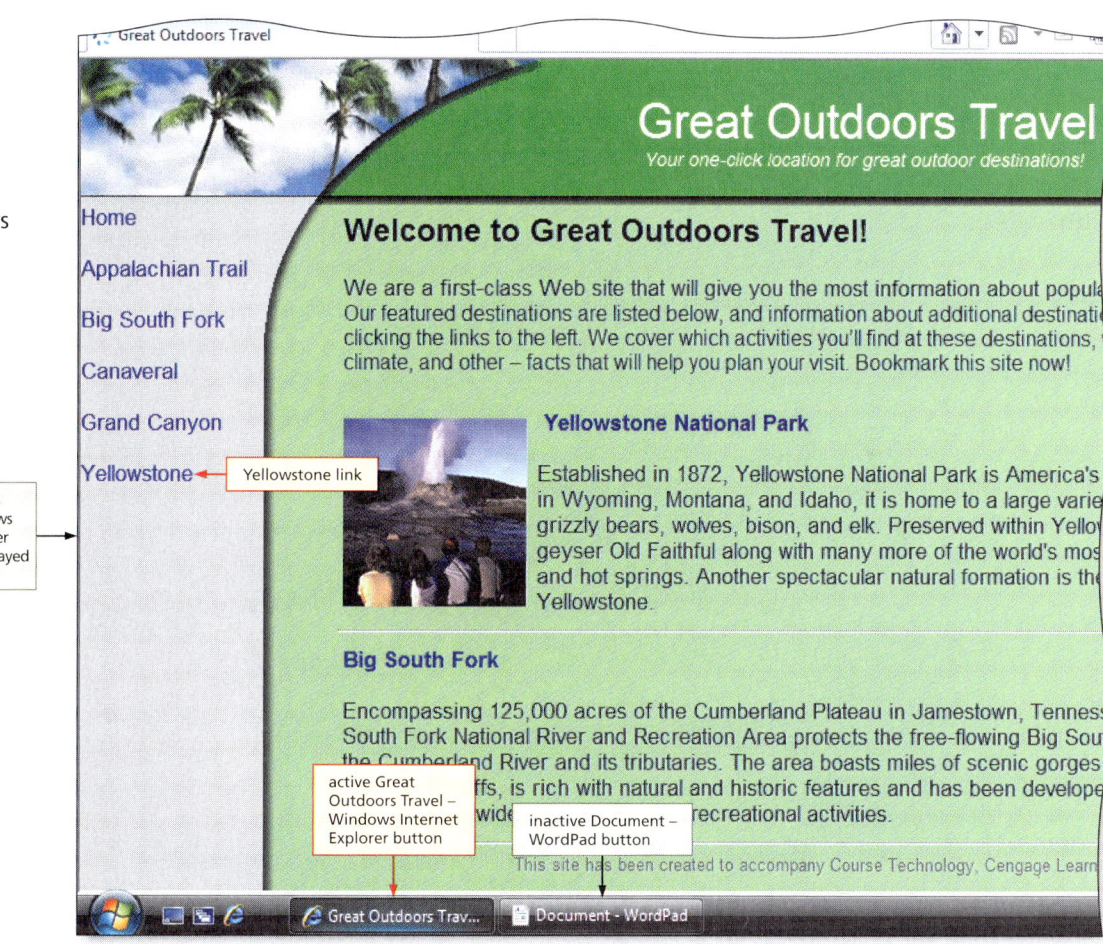

Figure 45

- Click the Yellowstone link on the Great Outdoors Travel Web page to display the Yellowstone National Park Web page (Figure 46).

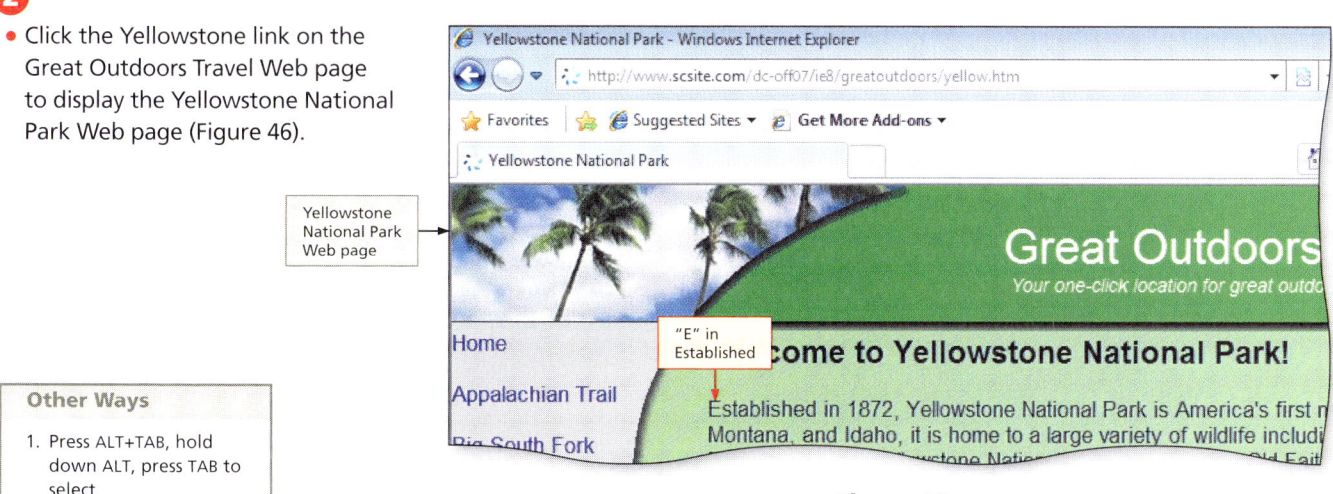

Figure 46

Other Ways

1. Press ALT+TAB, hold down ALT, press TAB to select
2. If visible, click window title bar

To Copy and Paste Text from a Web Page into a WordPad Document

With the Document - WordPad window open and the text you wish to copy contained on the Yellowstone National Park Web page, the next steps are to copy the text from the Yellowstone National Park Web page to the Clipboard, and then paste the text into the WordPad document. The following steps copy the text about Yellowstone National Park into the WordPad document.

- Position the mouse pointer (I-beam) to the left of the E in Established to prepare to select the text to be copied (Figure 47).

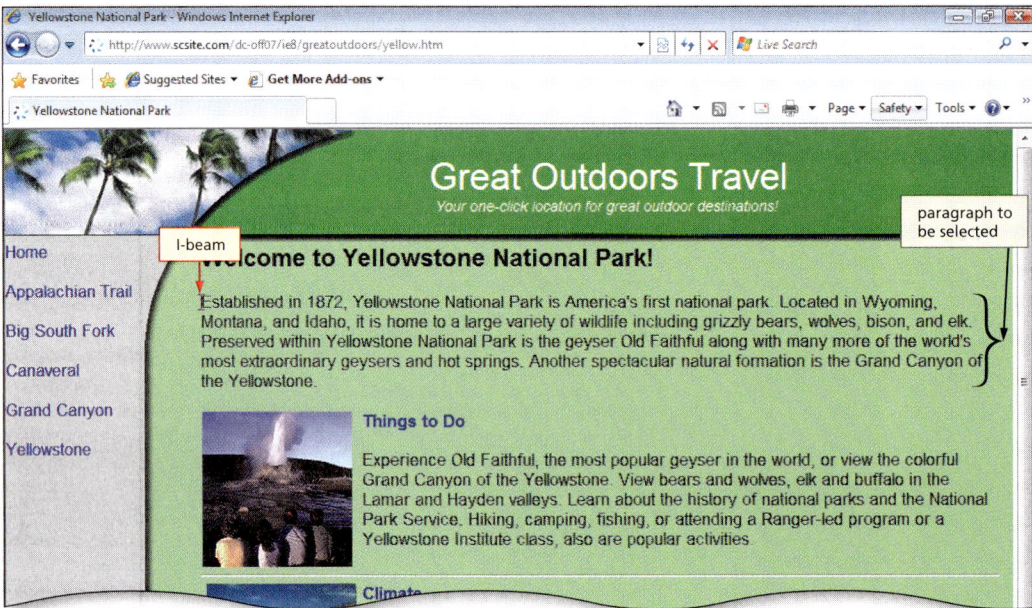

Figure 47

- Drag to select the text in the entire paragraph.
- Right-click the selected text to display a shortcut menu (Figure 48).

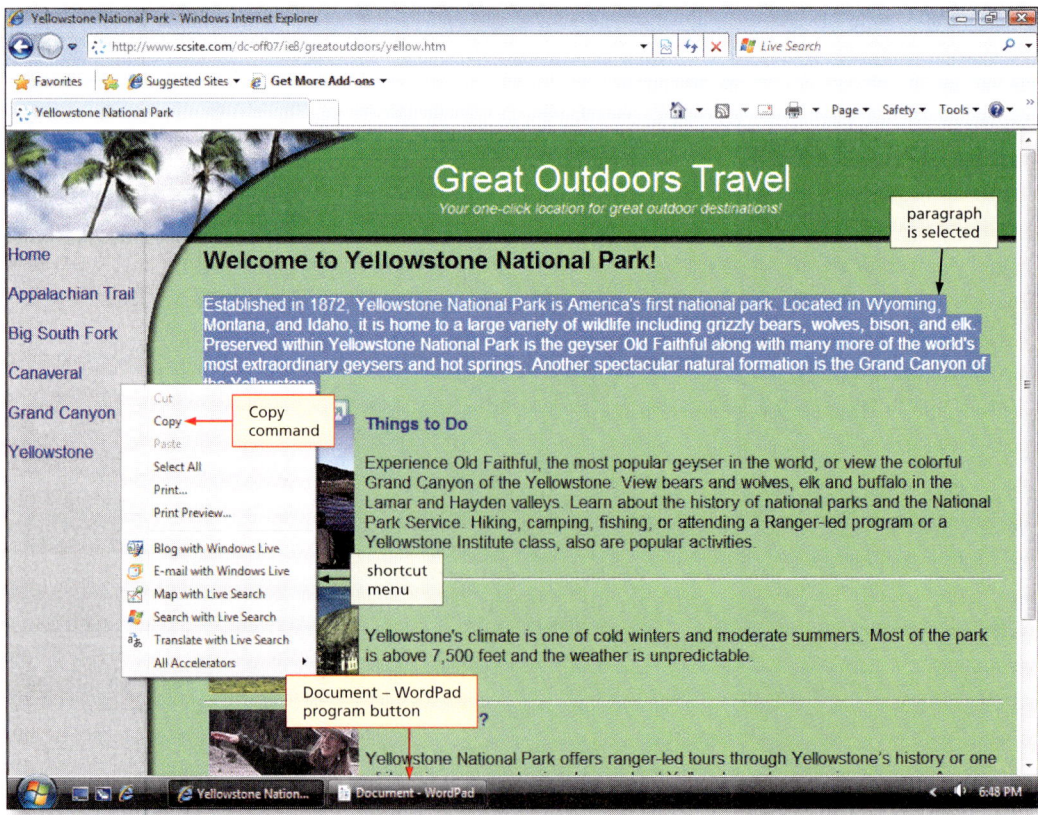

Figure 48

Introduction to Internet Explorer **Internet Explorer Chapter** IE 43

3

- Click Copy on the shortcut menu to copy the selected text to the Clipboard.

- Click the Document - WordPad button on the Windows taskbar to display the Document - WordPad window, and then right-click the empty text area in the Document - WordPad window to display a shortcut menu (Figure 49).

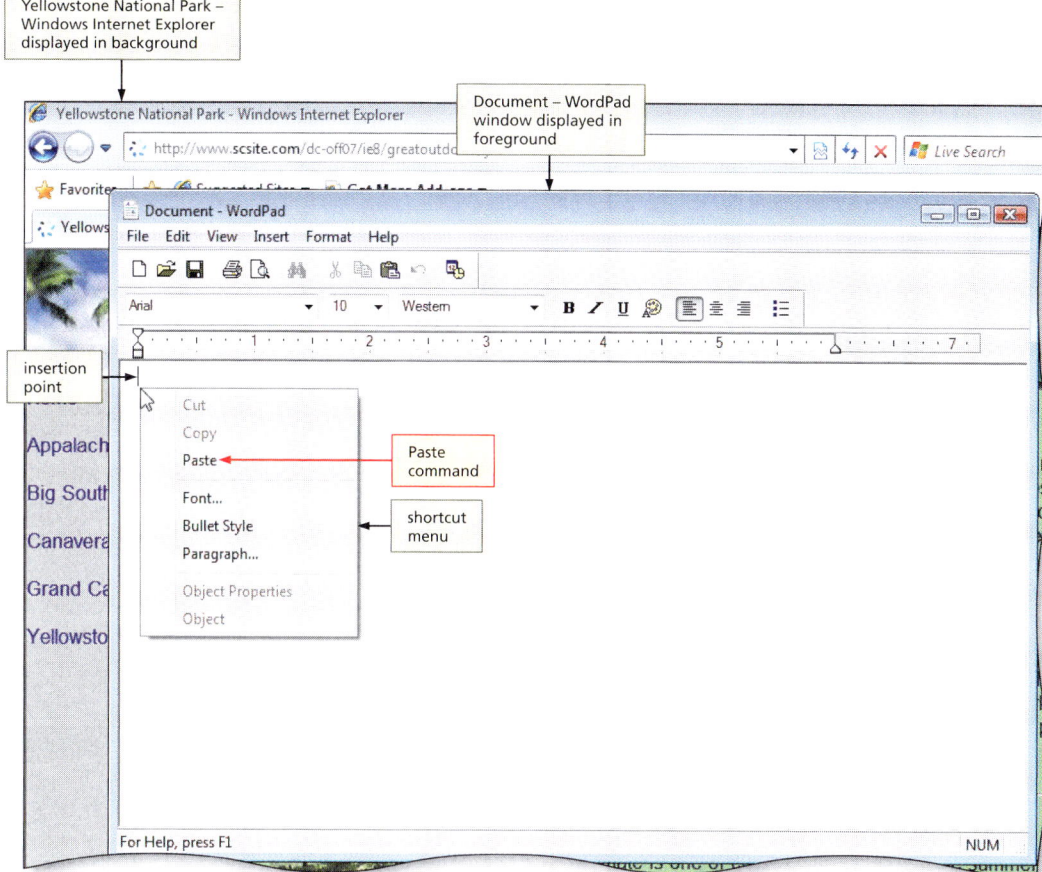

Figure 49

4

- Click Paste on the shortcut menu to paste the contents of the Clipboard in the Document - WordPad window (Figure 50).

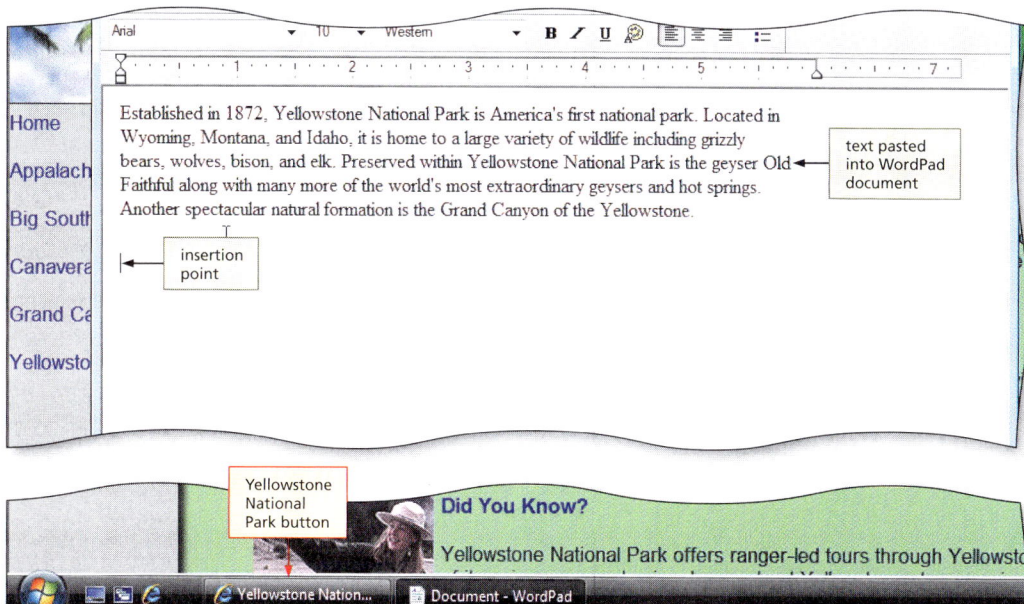

Figure 50

Other Ways
1. Select text, on Edit menu click Copy, select paste area, on Edit menu click Paste
2. Select text, on Page menu click Copy, select paste area, on Edit menu click Paste
3. Select text, press CTRL+C, select paste area, press CTRL+V
4. Select text, press ALT+E, press C, select paste area, press ALT+E, press P

To Copy and Paste a Picture from a Web Page into a WordPad Document

The steps to copy a picture from a Web page are similar to those used to copy and paste text. The following steps copy and then paste a picture from a Web page into a WordPad document.

- To activate the Yellowstone National Park Web page, click the Yellowstone National Park button on the Windows taskbar.

- Click outside the selected text to deselect the text.

- Right-click the picture to the left of the Things to Do area to display a shortcut menu (Figure 51).

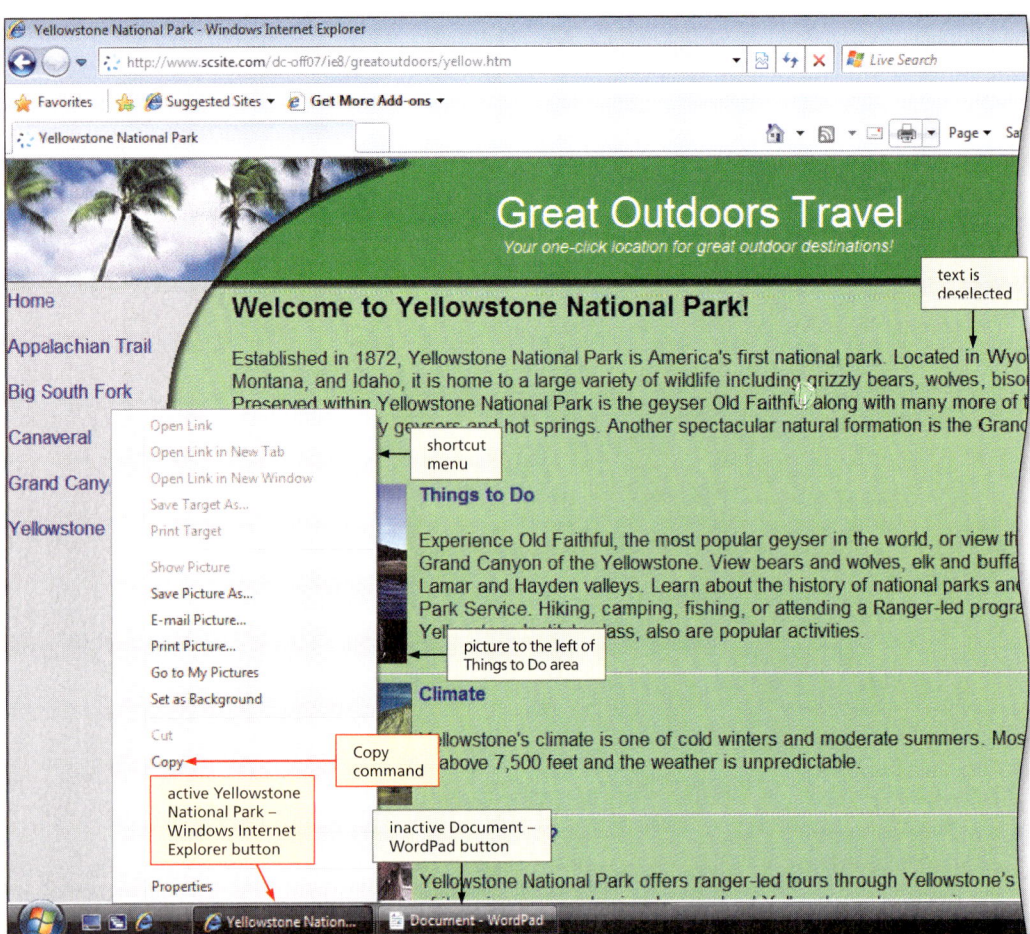

Figure 51

Introduction to Internet Explorer   **Internet Explorer Chapter**   IE 45

2
- Click Copy on the shortcut menu to copy the picture to the Clipboard.
- Activate the Document - WordPad window.
- Right-click an area below the insertion point in the Document - WordPad window to display a shortcut menu (Figure 52).

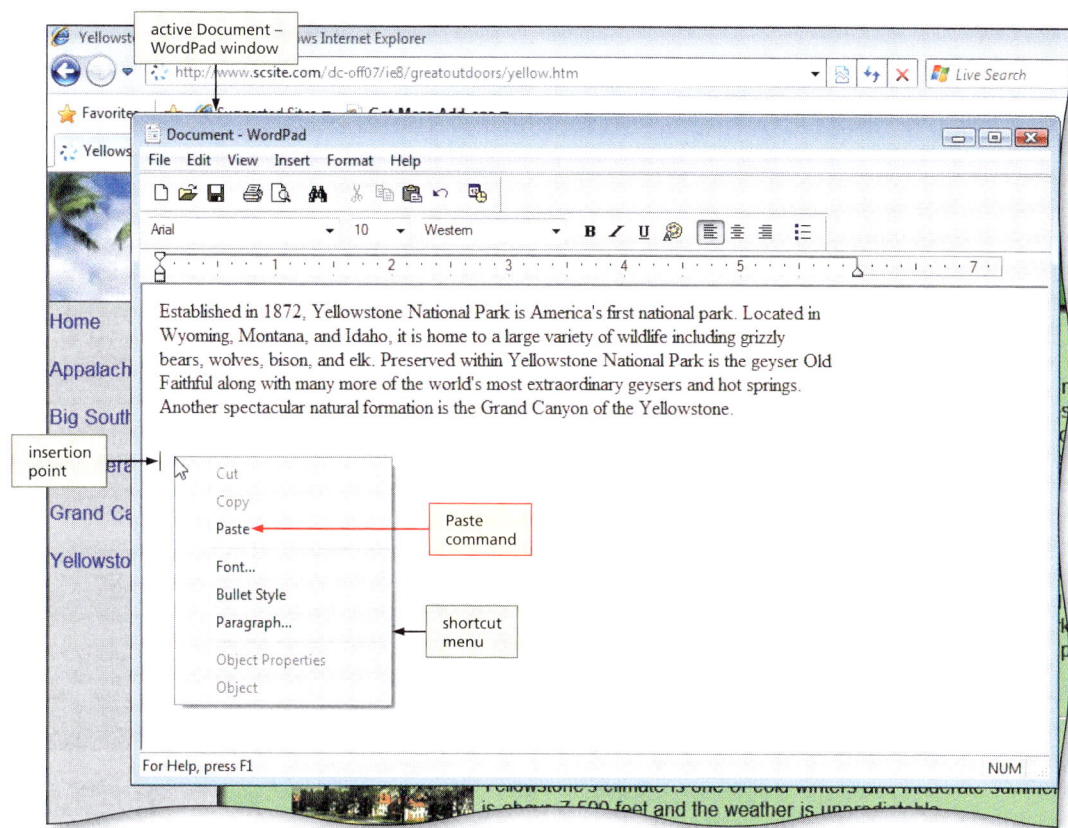

Figure 52

3
- Click Paste on the shortcut menu to paste the picture into the Document - WordPad window (Figure 53).

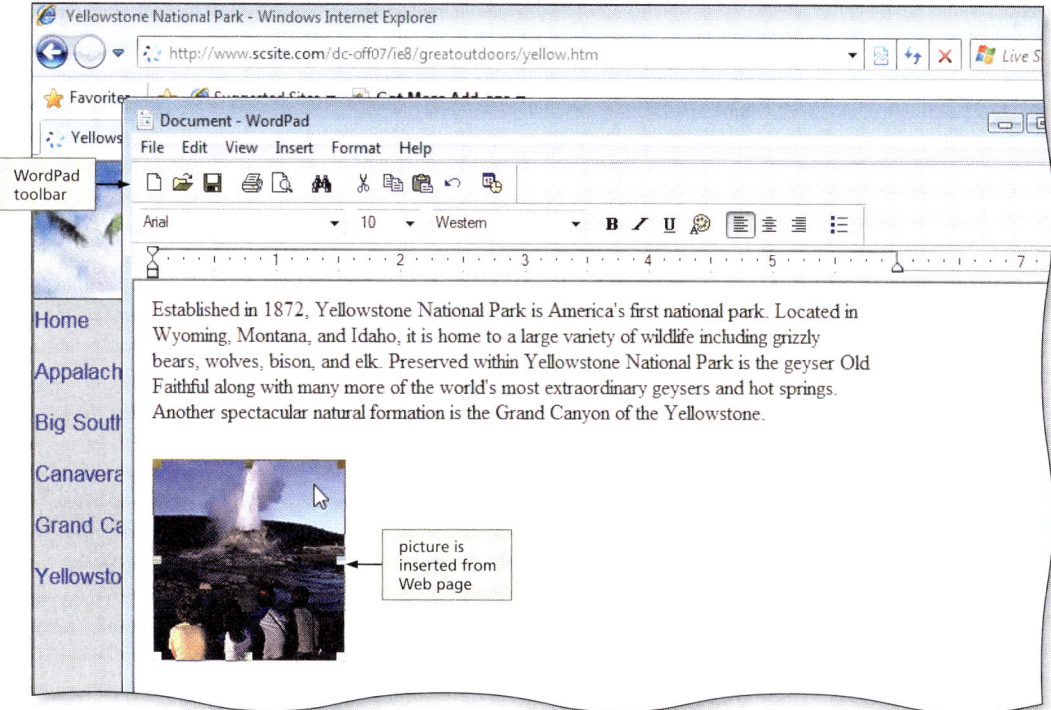

Figure 53

To Save the WordPad Document and Quit WordPad

When you are finished with the WordPad document, you can save it to your computer for later use and then quit WordPad. The following steps save the WordPad document using the Yellowstone National Park file name and then quit WordPad.

- Click the Save button on the WordPad toolbar in the Document - WordPad window to display the Save As dialog box (Figure 54).

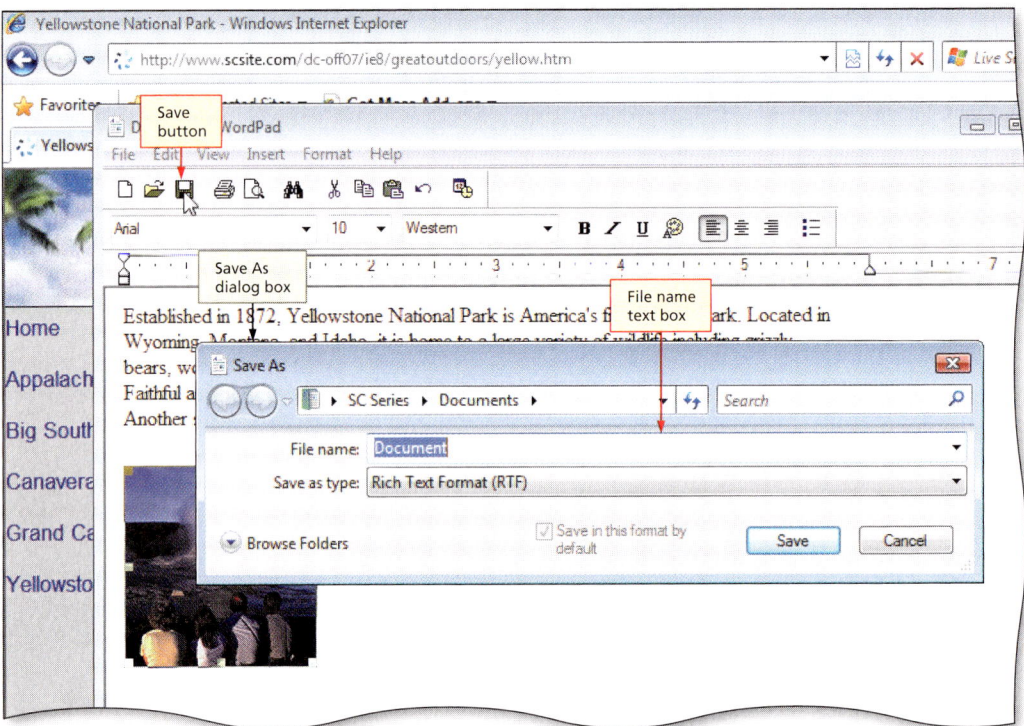

Figure 54

- Type Yellowstone National Park in the File name text box (Figure 55).

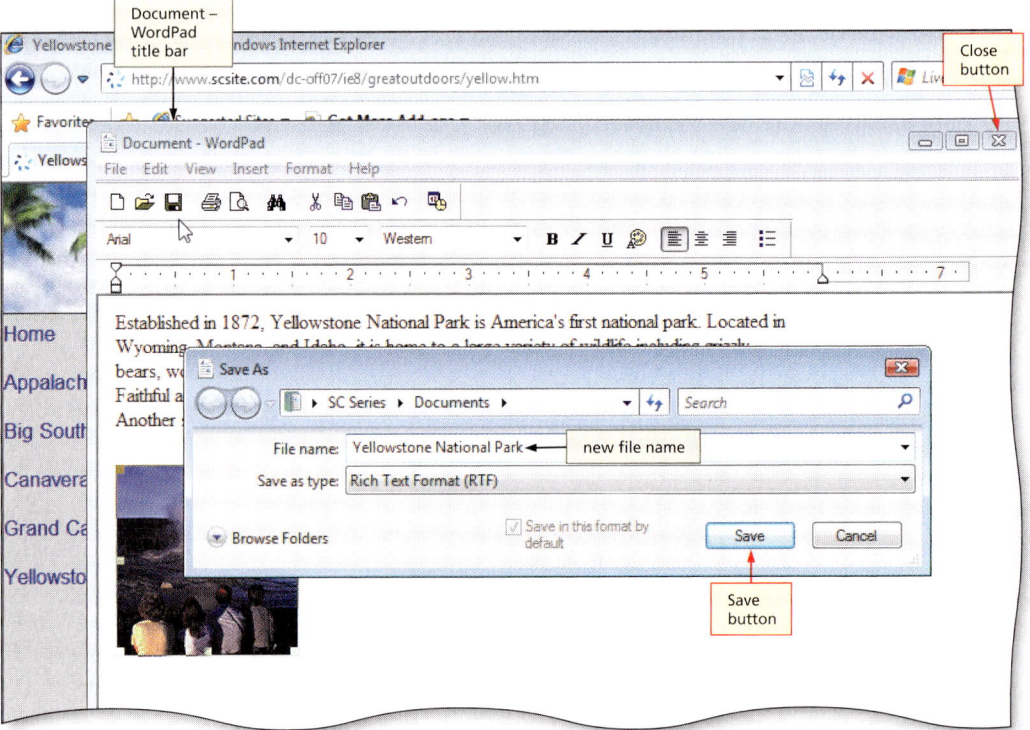

Figure 55

Introduction to Internet Explorer **Internet Explorer Chapter** IE 47

❸
- Click the Save button in the Save As dialog box to save the WordPad document.
- Click the Close button on the Yellowstone National Park - WordPad title bar to quit WordPad (Figure 56).

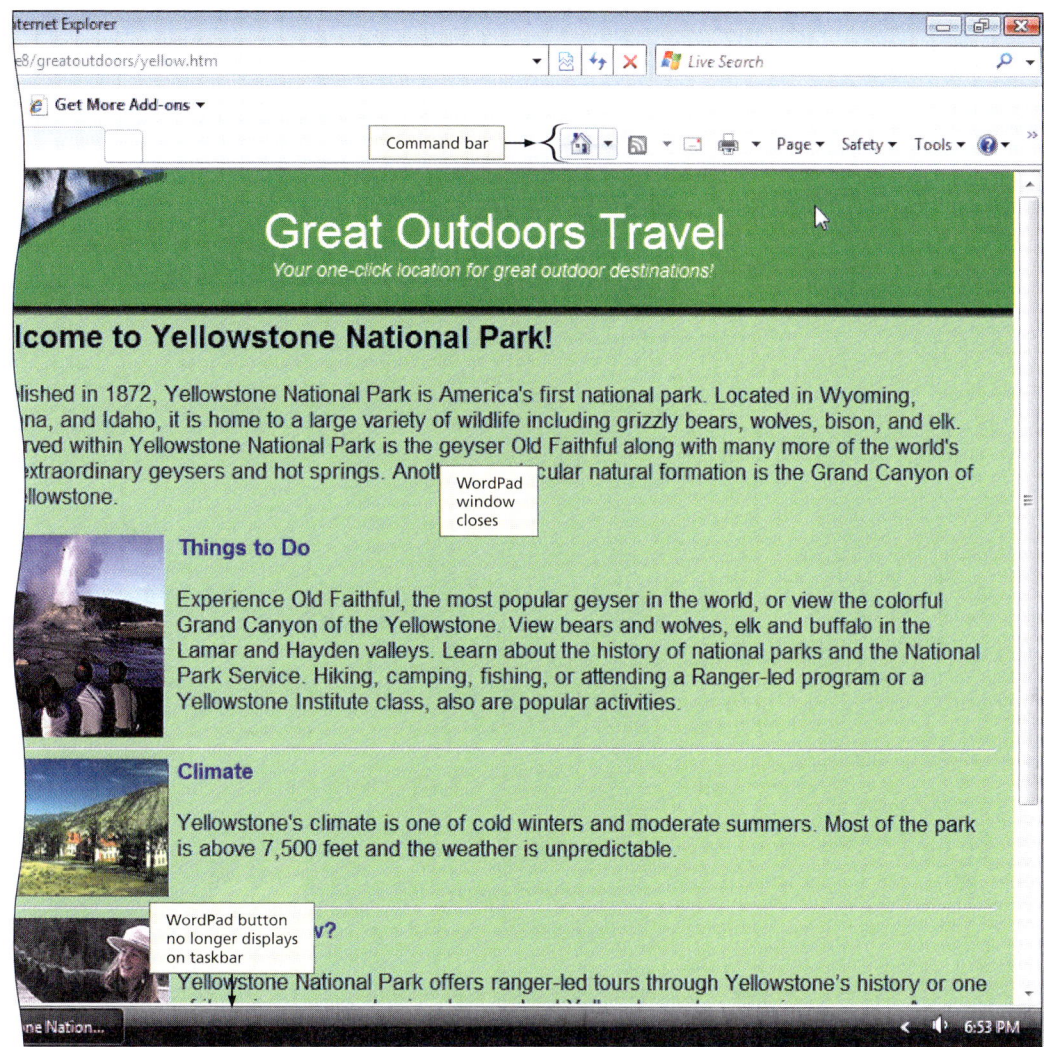

Figure 56

Other Ways
1. Press ALT+F, press A, type file name, press ENTER
2. Press CTRL+S, type file name, press ENTER

Printing a Web Page in Internet Explorer

As you browse the Web, you may want to print some of the pages you view. You may need to print driving directions, your airline ticket, or a record of your tax documents, if you submitted your taxes online. A printed version of a Web page is called a **hard copy** or **printout**.

You can suppress the title and Web address of a Web page that are displayed at the top of a printout using the Page Setup dialog box. You can display the Page Setup dialog box by clicking the Print button arrow on the Command bar and then selecting the Page Setup command. The Header and Footer buttons allow you to specify the information that is displayed in the header and footer areas of the printout.

To Print a Web Page

Internet Explorer allows you to print both the text and picture portions of a Web page. The following steps print the Yellowstone National Park Web page.

- Ready the printer according to the printer instructions.
- Point to the Print button on the Command bar (Figure 57).

Figure 57

- Click the Print button on the Command bar to begin printing the Web page.
- When the printer stops printing the document, retrieve the printout, which should look like Figure 58.

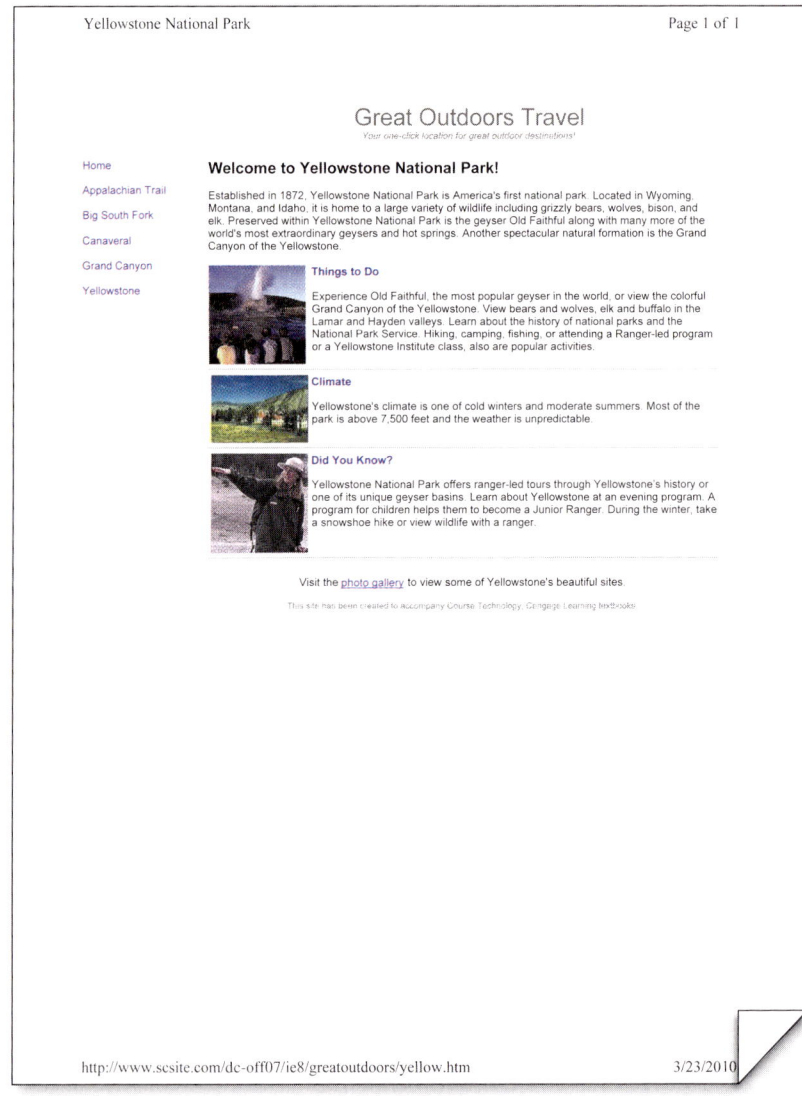

Figure 58

Other Ways

1. On File menu click Print, click Print button
2. Press CTRL+P, click Print button

Using the Print button arrow provides access to the Print Preview and Page Setup commands. The printing options available in the Print dialog box allow you to print the entire document, print selected pages of a document, print to a file, print multiple copies, change the printer properties, and cancel the print request.

Internet Explorer Help

Internet Explorer offers users many features and options. Although you will master some features and options quickly, it is not necessary for you to remember everything about all of them. Reference materials and other forms of assistance are available within **Internet Explorer Help**.

BTW

Print Options
You can choose to print a table containing a list of all links on the Web page you are printing, or you can choose to print all documents with links on the Web page. Click the Options tab in the Print dialog box and then click the `Print all linked documents´ check box or `Print table of links´ check box to print the documents or table.

To Access Internet Explorer Help

The following steps use Internet Explorer Help to find more information about favorites.

- Click the Help button arrow on the Command bar to display the Help menu (Figure 59).

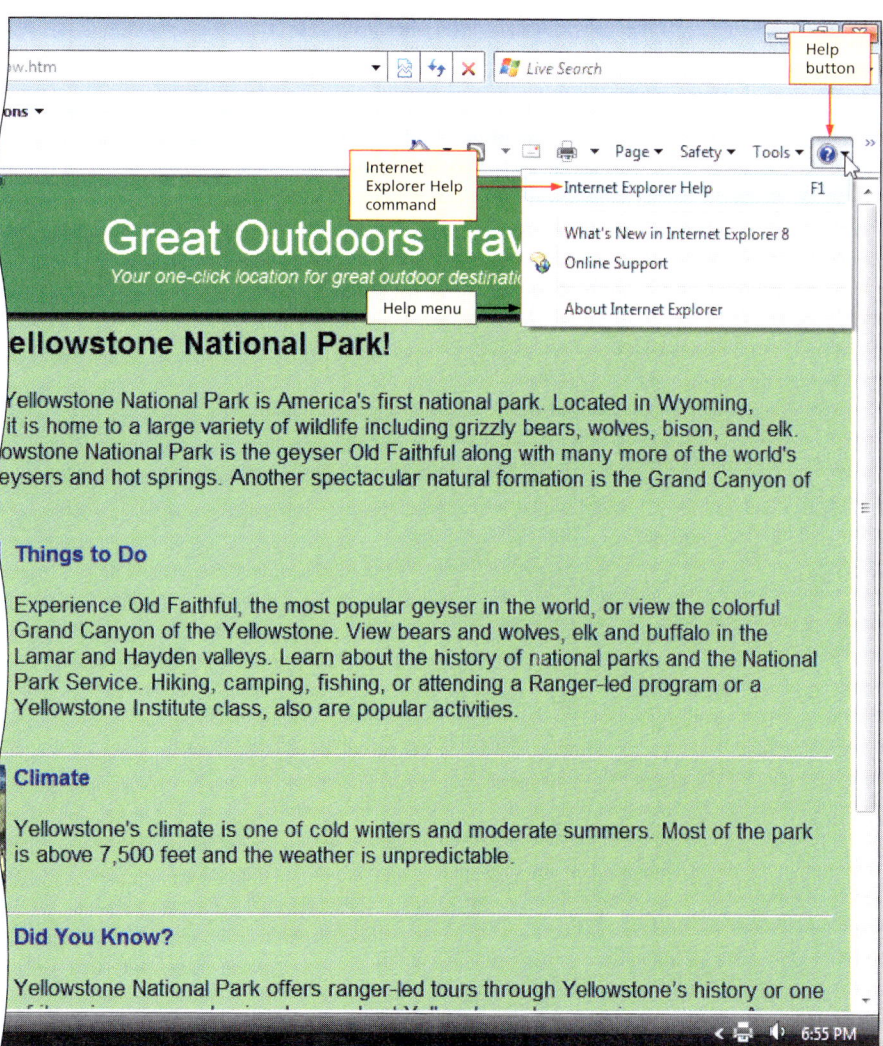

Figure 59

IE 50 Internet Explorer Chapter Introduction to Internet Explorer

2
- Click Internet Explorer Help on the Help menu to open the Windows Help and Support window (Figure 60).

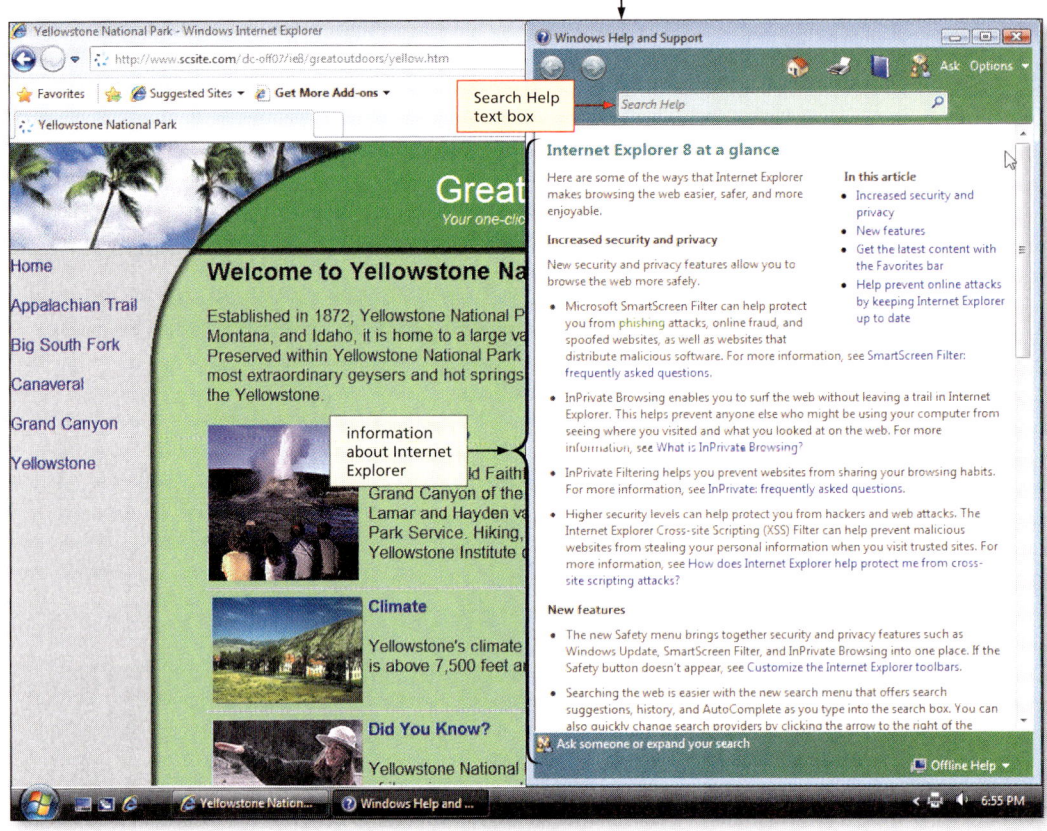

Figure 60

3
- Type favorites in the Search Help text box, and then press the ENTER key to display the search results matching your search text (Figure 61).

Q&A Why do my search results differ?

When you search for help using Windows Help and Support, your search results also include online resources that match your search criteria. Microsoft regularly updates these online resources to provide you with an effective and up-to-date Help system.

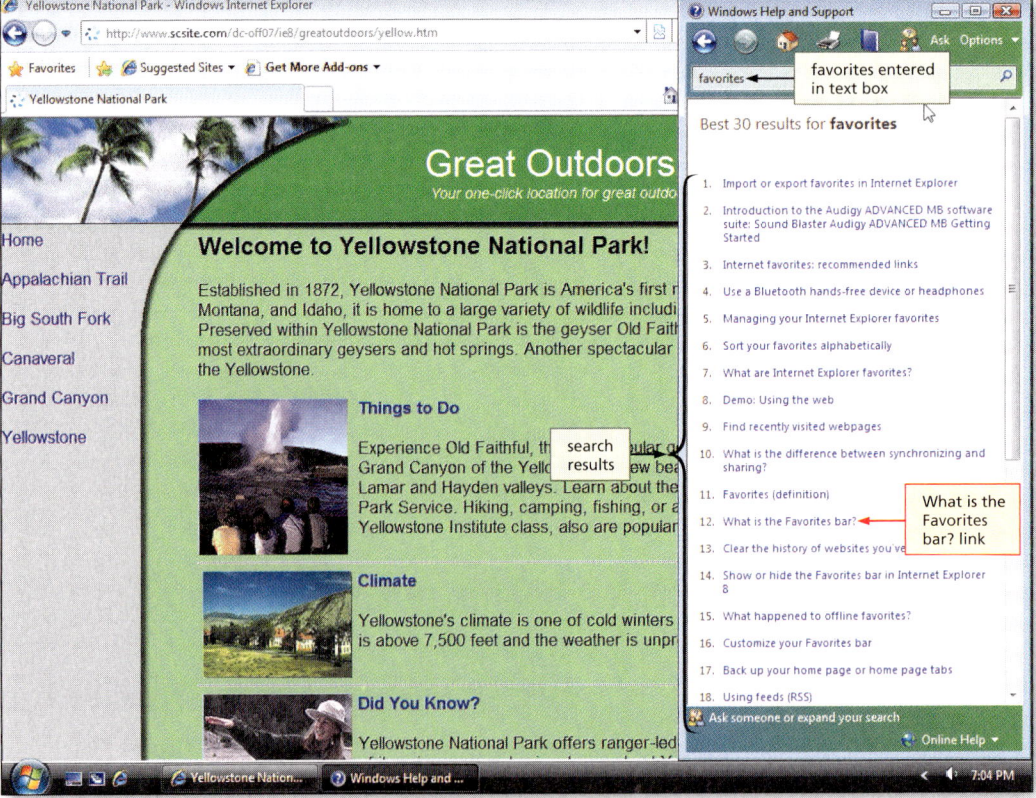

Figure 61

- Click the What is the Favorites bar? link in the list of Help topics to display information about favorites (Figure 62).

- When you are finished viewing the information, click the Close button on the right side of the title bar to close the Windows Help and Support window.

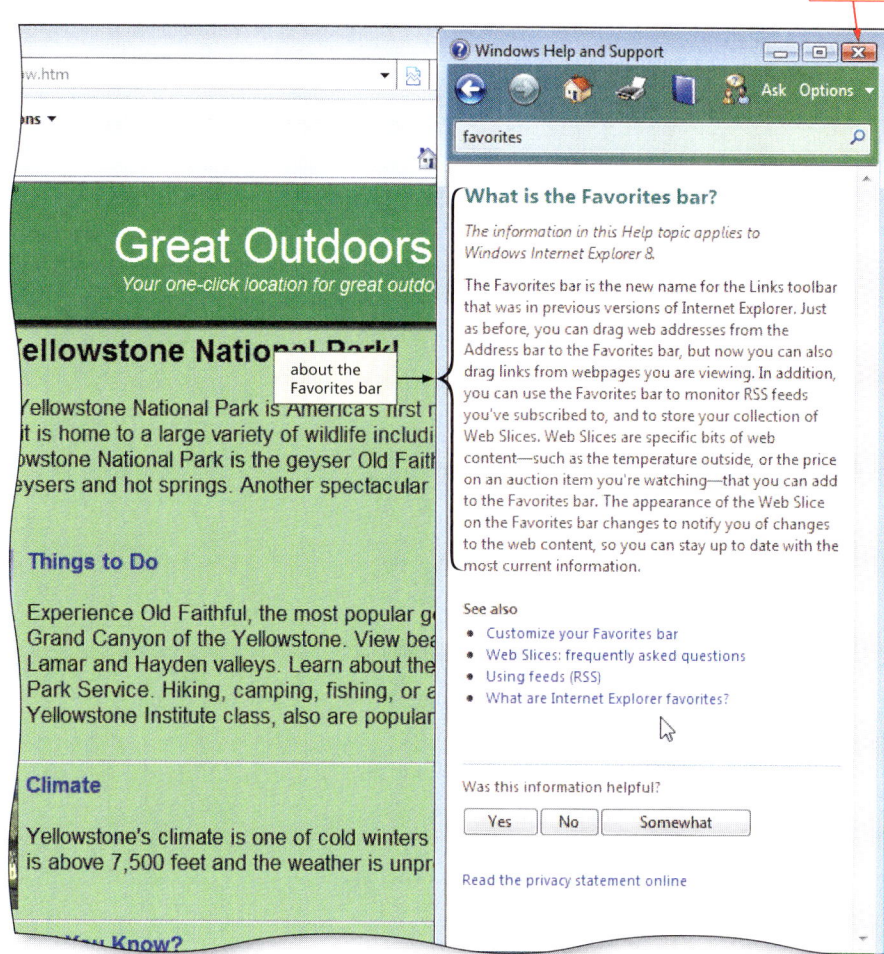

Figure 62

Other Ways

1. Press ALT+H, press I
2. Press F1

In Figure 60, buttons on the Help toolbar in the Windows Help and Support window allow you to perform activities such as going back to the most recent help topic, going forward to a help page you have visited prior to clicking the Back button, displaying the Windows Help and Support Center home page, printing the current page, requesting additional help, and changing Internet options.

The Help menu in Figure 59 on page IE 49 contains several other commands, which are summarized in Table 3.

Table 3 Commands on the Help Menu

Menu Command	Function
Internet Explorer Help	Displays the Windows Help and Support window
What's New in Internet Explorer 8	Displays a Web page highlighting new features in Internet Explorer 8
Online Support	Displays Microsoft Help and Support Web site
About Internet Explorer	Displays version, cipher strength, product ID, license information, and copyright information about Internet Explorer

Quitting Internet Explorer

After browsing the Web and learning how to navigate Web sites, add favorites, copy and paste content, and print Web pages, this chapter is complete.

To Quit Internet Explorer

The following step quits Internet Explorer.

- Click the Close button in the upper-right corner of the Internet Explorer window to close the window (Figure 63).

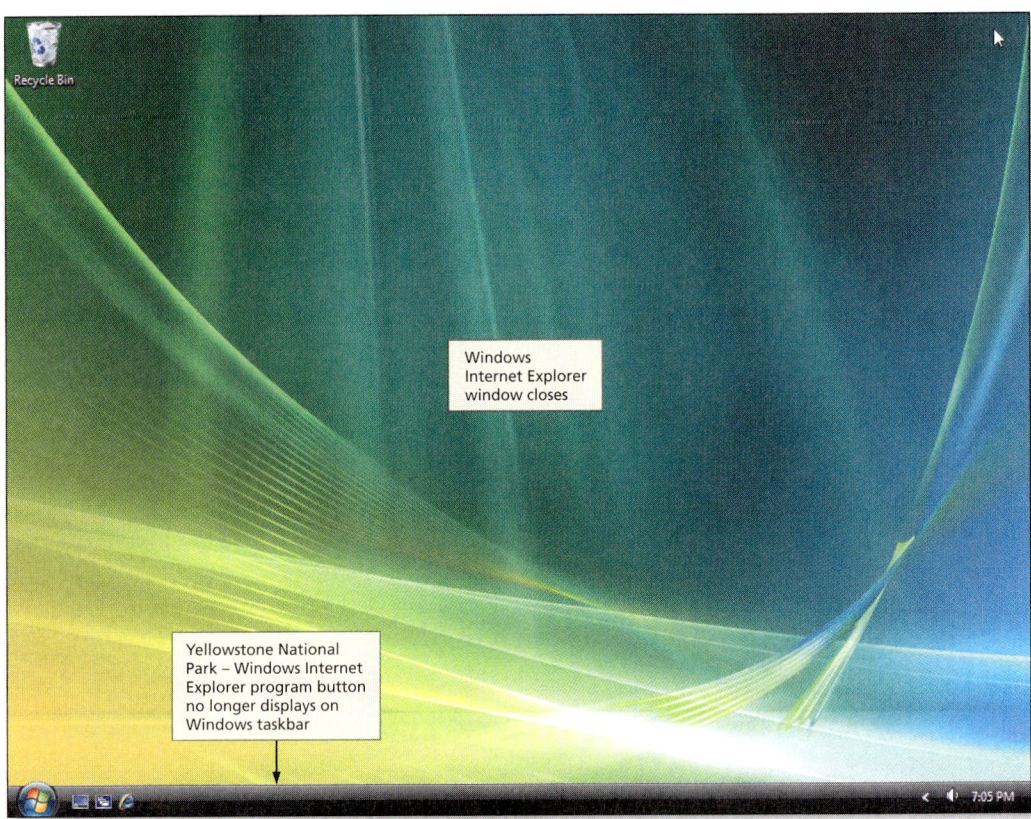

Figure 63

Other Ways

1. Double-click Internet Explorer menu icon at left end of title bar
2. On File menu click Exit
3. Press ALT+F, press X

Chapter Summary

This chapter introduced you to the Internet and World Wide Web. You learned how to start Internet Explorer; use the Address bar, Command bar, Favorites bar, History List, and the navigation buttons on the toolbar; and enter a Web address to browse the Web. You learned how to add and remove favorites; copy and paste text from a Web page into a WordPad document; print a Web page; and save text, a picture, and an entire Web page to the hard disk. In addition, you learned how to use Help to obtain help about Internet Explorer. The items listed below include all the new Internet Explorer skills you have learned in this chapter.

1. Start Internet Explorer (IE 11)
2. Browse the Web by Entering a Web Address (IE 16)
3. Refresh a Web Page (IE 21)
4. Use the Navigation Buttons to Find Recently Displayed Web Pages (IE 23)
5. Display a Web Page Using the Recent Pages List (IE 25)
6. Display a Web Page Using the History List (IE 27)
7. Add a Web Page to the Favorites Center (IE 30)
8. Display the Home Page Using the Home Button (IE 32)
9. Display a Web Page Using the Favorites Center (IE 33)
10. Remove a Web Page from the Favorites Center (IE 34)
11. Save a Web Page (IE 36)
12. Save a Picture on a Web Page (IE 37)
13. Start WordPad (IE 39)
14. Display the Yellowstone National Park Web Page (IE 41)
15. Copy and Paste Text from a Web Page into a WordPad Document (IE 42)
16. Copy and Paste a Picture from a Web Page into a WordPad Document (IE 44)
17. Save the WordPad Document and Quit WordPad (IE 46)
18. Print a Web Page (IE 48)
19. Access Internet Explorer Help (IE 49)
20. Quit Internet Explorer (IE 52)

Learn It Online

Test your knowledge of chapter content and key terms.

Instructions: To complete the Learn It Online exercises, start your browser, click the Address bar, and then enter the Web address `scsite.com/dc-off07/ie8/learn`. When the Internet Explorer 8 Learn It Online page is displayed, click the link for the exercise you want to complete and then read the instructions.

Chapter Reinforcement TF, MC, and SA
A series of true/false, multiple choice, and short-answer questions that test your knowledge of the chapter content.

Flash Cards
An interactive learning environment where you identify key terms from the chapter associated with displayed definitions.

Practice Test
A series of multiple-choice questions that test your knowledge of chapter content and key terms.

Who Wants To Be a Computer Genius?
An interactive game that challenges your knowledge of chapter content in the style of the television quiz show.

Wheel of Terms
An interactive game that challenges your knowledge of key terms from the chapter in the style of the television show *Wheel of Fortune*.

Crossword Puzzle Challenge
A crossword puzzle that challenges your knowledge of key terms presented in the chapter.

Apply Your Knowledge

Reinforce the skills and apply the concepts you learned in this chapter.

Browsing the World Wide Web Using Web Addresses and Links
Problem: You work part-time for CNN, one of the nation's leading sources of news. Your editor has asked you to search for information on several informational Web sites and print the first page of each Web site.

Instructions: Perform the following tasks.

Part 1: Using the Address Bar to Find Web Pages
1. If necessary, connect to the Internet and start Internet Explorer.

Introduction to Internet Explorer   **Internet Explorer Chapter**   IE 55

2. Click the Address bar, type www.fbi.gov in the box, and then press the ENTER key to display the Federal Bureau of Investigation's home page (Figure 64).

Figure 64

3. Click the Quick Facts link to display the Web page that contains facts about the FBI.
4. Click the Print button on the Command bar toolbar to print the Web page.
5. Use the Back button on the toolbar to display the FBI home page.
6. Click the Print button on the Command bar to print the Web page.
7. Click the Address bar, type www.nbc.com to enter the Web address, and then press the ENTER key to display the NBC home page (Figure 65 on the next page).

Continued >

Apply Your Knowledge *continued*

Figure 65

8. Click the shows link, and then click the The Office link in the NBC Web site to display the Web page about the show, *The Office*.
9. Click the Print button on the Command bar to print the Web page.
10. Click the Address bar, type `www.weather.com` in the box, and then press the ENTER key to display the weather.com home page (Figure 66).

Figure 66

11. Type your zip code in the Local Weather text box, and then click the Search button to display the Web page containing the weather report for your area.
12. Click the Print button on the Command bar to print the Web page.
13. Click the Address bar, type www.abc.com to enter the Web address, and then press the ENTER key to display the ABC home page (Figure 67).

Figure 67

14. Click the NEWS link to display the Web page containing the top news stories in a new window.
15. Click the Print button on the Command bar to print the Web page.
16. Close the Internet Explorer window displaying the news.

Part 2: Using the History List to Find a Web Page
1. Click the Home button on the Command bar to display your default home page.
2. Click the Favorites button on the Favorites bar, click the History tab to display the History List, click Today, click nbc (www.nbc.com) folder name in the History List, and then click the TV Network for Primetime, Daytime and Late Night Television Shows - NBC Official Site entry to display the NBC home page.
3. Click the Print button on the Command bar to print the Web page.
4. Click the Close button on the Explorer bar.

Part 3: Using the Back Button Arrow to Find a Web Page
1. Click the Recent Pages list arrow and then click the Home - ABC.com entry on the menu to display the ABC home page.
2. Click the Print button on the Command bar to print the Web page.

Continued >

Apply Your Knowledge *continued*

Part 4: Using the Address Bar List Arrow to Find a Web Page
1. Click the Address bar list arrow and then click http://www.weather.com in the Address list to display the weather.com home page.
2. Click the Print button on the Command bar to print the Web page.
3. Click the Close button in the Internet Explorer window.
4. Submit the printed pages to your instructor.

Extend Your Knowledge

Extend the skills you learned in this chapter and experiment with new skills. You may need to use Help to complete the assignment.

Browsing the World Wide Web Using the Instant Search Box and Links

Problem: Concerned about keeping your personal information and your computer safe when you access the Internet, you decide to visit the Web site of a leading computer security company.

Instructions: Perform the following tasks.
1. Use the Instant Search box to locate the official McAfee, Inc. Web site. What keywords did you type to locate this page?
2. Navigate to the McAfee, Inc. home page (Figure 68).

Figure 68

3. View the Web page in Print Preview. What buttons appear at the top of the Print Preview window? How many pages will it take to print this Web page?
4. Print the McAfee, Inc. home page from the Print Preview window, and then close the Print Preview window.
5. Use the links on the McAfee, Inc. home page to answer the following questions:
   a. What are five latest computer vulnerabilities?
   b. On what date was the latest vulnerability made public?
   c. How does McAfee measure the severity of threats?
   d. What must you do to protect your computer from threats? What programs does McAfee offer to help you protect your computer?
   e. What is the current Global Threat Condition?
   f. If your computer already has been infected by a threat, such as a virus or spyware, what should you do?
6. Use the History List to navigate back to the McAfee home page.
7. Browse McAfee's Web site for a page that discusses an example of current malware. Print the Web page.
8. Add the Web page to your Favorites Center.
9. Remove the Web page from your Favorites Center.
10. Organize your printed Web pages and submit them, along with the answers to the questions in this exercise, to your instructor.

In the Lab

Use Internet Explorer to navigate the World Wide Web by using the guidelines, concepts, and skills presented in this chapter. Labs are listed in order of increasing difficulty.

Lab 1: Using the History List to Locate Previously Viewed Pages

Problem: Your instructor would like you to practice browsing the Internet for Web sites and using the History List. As proof of completing this assignment, you should print the first page of each Web site you visit.

Instructions: Perform the following tasks.

Part 1: Clearing the History List
1. Click Tools on the Command bar and then click Internet Options to display the Internet Options dialog box (Figure 69 on the next page).

Continued >

In the Lab *continued*

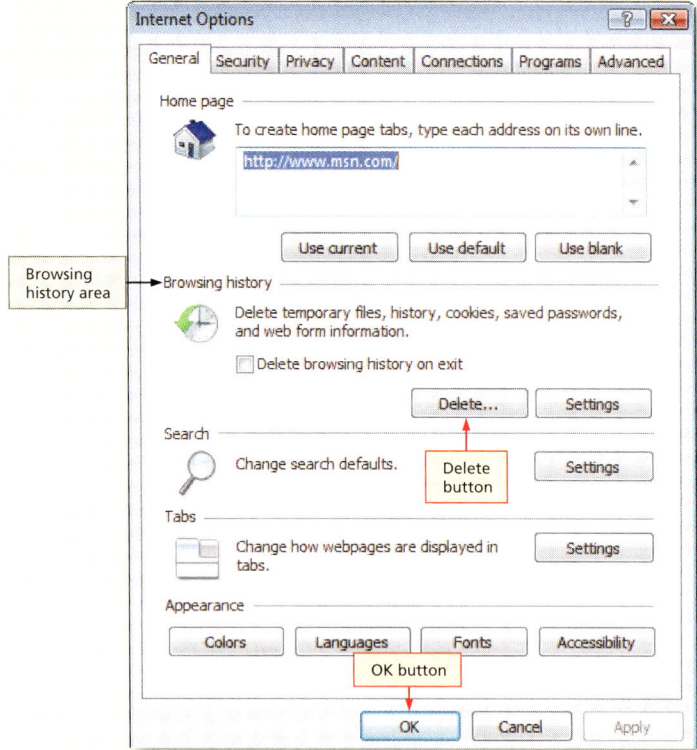

Figure 69

2. Click the Delete button in the Browsing history area, and then click the Delete button in the Delete Browsing History dialog box.
3. Click the OK button in the Internet Options dialog box.

Part 2: Browsing the World Wide Web
1. Click the Address bar, type `www.youtube.com` to enter the Web address, and then press the ENTER key to display the YouTube home page.
2. Click the Address bar, type `www.ucf.edu` to enter the Web address, and then press the ENTER key to display the University of Central Florida home page.
3. Click the Address bar, type `www.geocaching.com` to enter the Web address, and then press the ENTER key to display the Geocaching home page.
4. Click the Address bar, type `www.cbssports.com` to enter the Web address, and then press the ENTER key to display the CBSSports home page.

Part 3: Using the History List to Print a Web Page
1. Click the Favorites button on the Favorites bar, click the History tab (Figure 70), and then click Today to display the current History List.

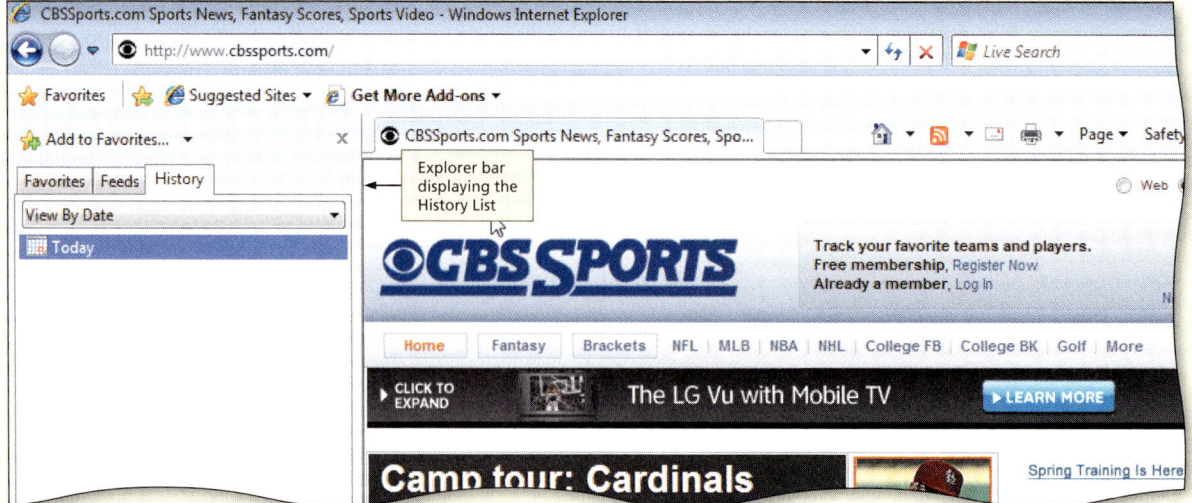

Figure 70

2. Click the ucf (www.ucf.edu) folder in the History List and then click the University of Central Florida link. Print the Web page.
3. Click the youtube (www.youtube.com) folder in the History List and then click the YouTube - Broadcast Yourself link. Print the Web page.
4. Click the cbssports (www.cbssports.com) folder in the History List and then click the CBSSports.com link. Print the Web page.
5. Delete the geocaching (www.geocaching.com) folder by right-clicking the folder, clicking Delete on the shortcut menu, and then clicking the Yes button in the WARNING dialog box.
6. If necessary, click the Close the Favorites Center button.

Part 4: Clearing the History List
1. Click Safety on the Command bar and then click Delete Browsing History to display the Delete Browsing History dialog box.
2. If necessary, click the History check box so that it contains a check mark, and then click the Delete button.
3. Click the Close button to close Internet Explorer.
4. Submit the printed Web pages to your instructor.

In the Lab

Lab 2: Adding, Viewing, Printing, and Removing Your Favorites

Problem: Your instructor would like you to practice browsing the Internet for Web sites and adding them to the Favorites Center. As proof of completing this assignment, print out the first page of each Web site you visit.

Instructions: Perform the following tasks.

Part 1: Creating a Folder in the Favorites Center
1. Click the Favorites button on the Favorites bar, click the Add to Favorites list arrow, and then click Organize Favorites to display the Organize Favorites dialog box (Figure 71 on the next page).

Continued >

In the Lab continued

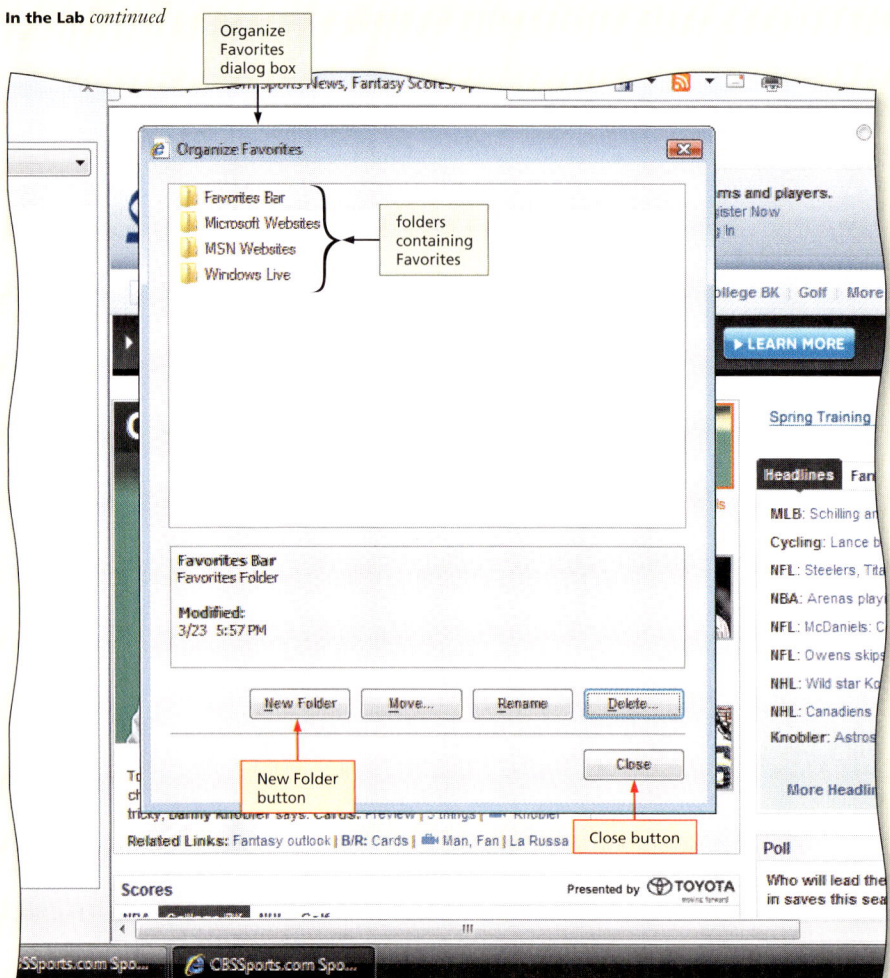

Figure 71

2. Click the New Folder button in the Organize Favorites dialog box to create a folder titled New Folder, type your first and last name as the folder name, and then press the ENTER key.
3. Click the Close button to close the Organize Favorites dialog box.

Part 2: Adding Favorites to Your Folder

1. Click the Address bar, type `www.pentagon.gov` to enter the Web address, and then press the ENTER key to display The Official Home of the Department of Defense home page.
2. Add The Official Home of the Department of Defense favorite to the folder identified by your name by clicking the Favorites button on the Favorites bar, and then clicking the Add to Favorites button (Figure 72). Click the Create in drop-down list button to display the Create in list.

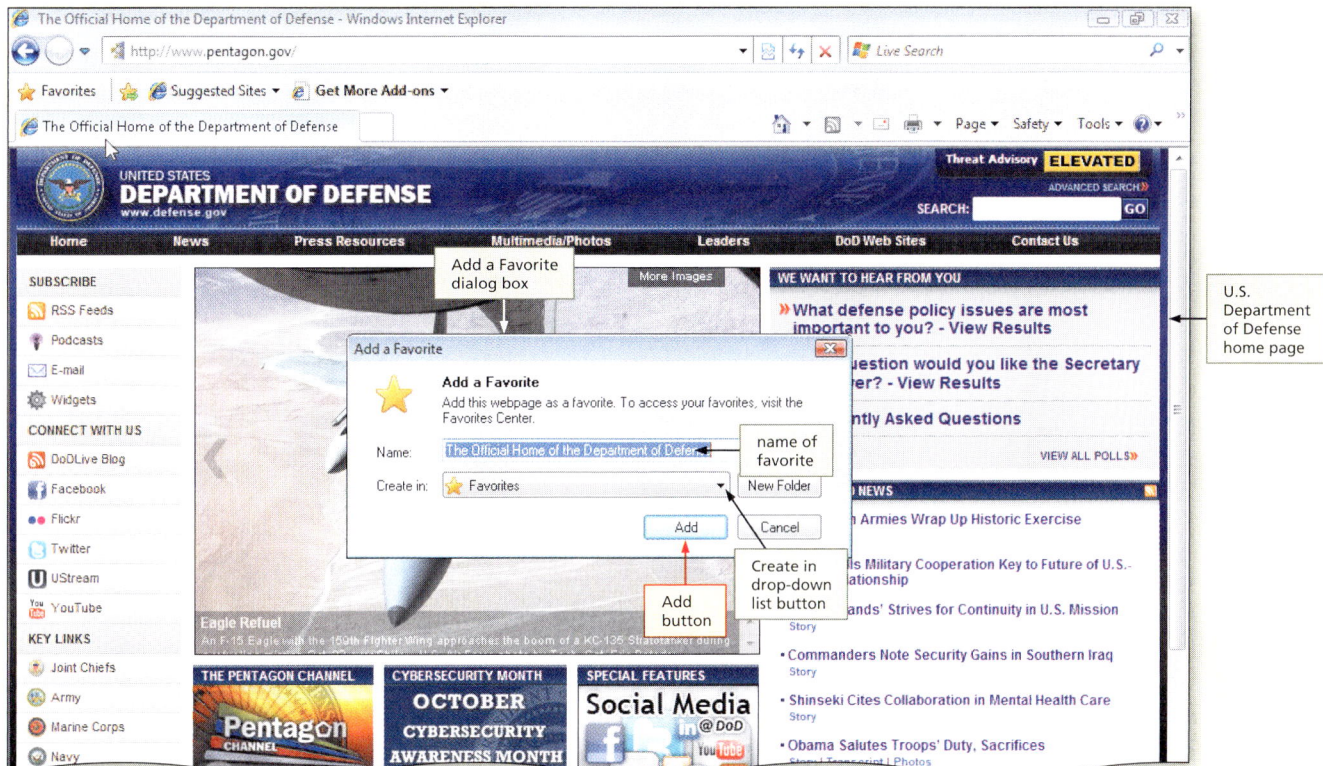

Figure 72

3. Click your folder in the Create in list and then click the Add button.
4. Click the Address bar, type www.orbitz.com to enter the Web address, and then press the ENTER key to display the Orbitz home page.
5. Add this Web page as a favorite, change the name of the favorite to Orbitz, and then create the favorite in your folder.
6. Click the Home button on the Command bar to display your default home page.

Part 3: Displaying and Printing a Favorite from Your Folder
1. Click the Favorites button on the Favorites bar to display the Favorites Center. If necessary, click the Favorites tab.
2. Click your folder in the Favorites Center and then click United States Department of Defense Official Website.
3. Print the Web page.
4. If necessary, click the Favorites button on the Favorites bar to display the Favorites Center.
5. Click Orbitz in the Favorites Center.
6. Print the Web page.

Part 4: Deleting a Folder in the Favorites Center
1. If necessary, display the Favorites Center.
2. Right-click your folder name, click the Delete command on the shortcut menu, and then click the Yes button in the Delete Folder dialog box.
3. If necessary, close the Favorites Center.
4. Verify that you have deleted your folder.
5. Close Internet Explorer.
6. Submit the printed pages to your instructor.

In the Lab

Lab 3: Printing and Saving the Current U.S. Weather Map

Problem: You are interested in finding a current United States weather map to use on a road trip starting in San Diego, California, and ending in Boston, Massachusetts. You want to print the map and save it on your hard disk.

Instructions: Perform the following tasks.

1. Type www.weather.com in the Address bar and then press the ENTER key to display the weather.com home page.
2. Click the Maps link, and then click the thumbnail image of the weather map to display an enlarged weather map for the United States. If necessary scroll down to view the weather map (Figure 73). The map that displays on your computer might differ from Figure 73.

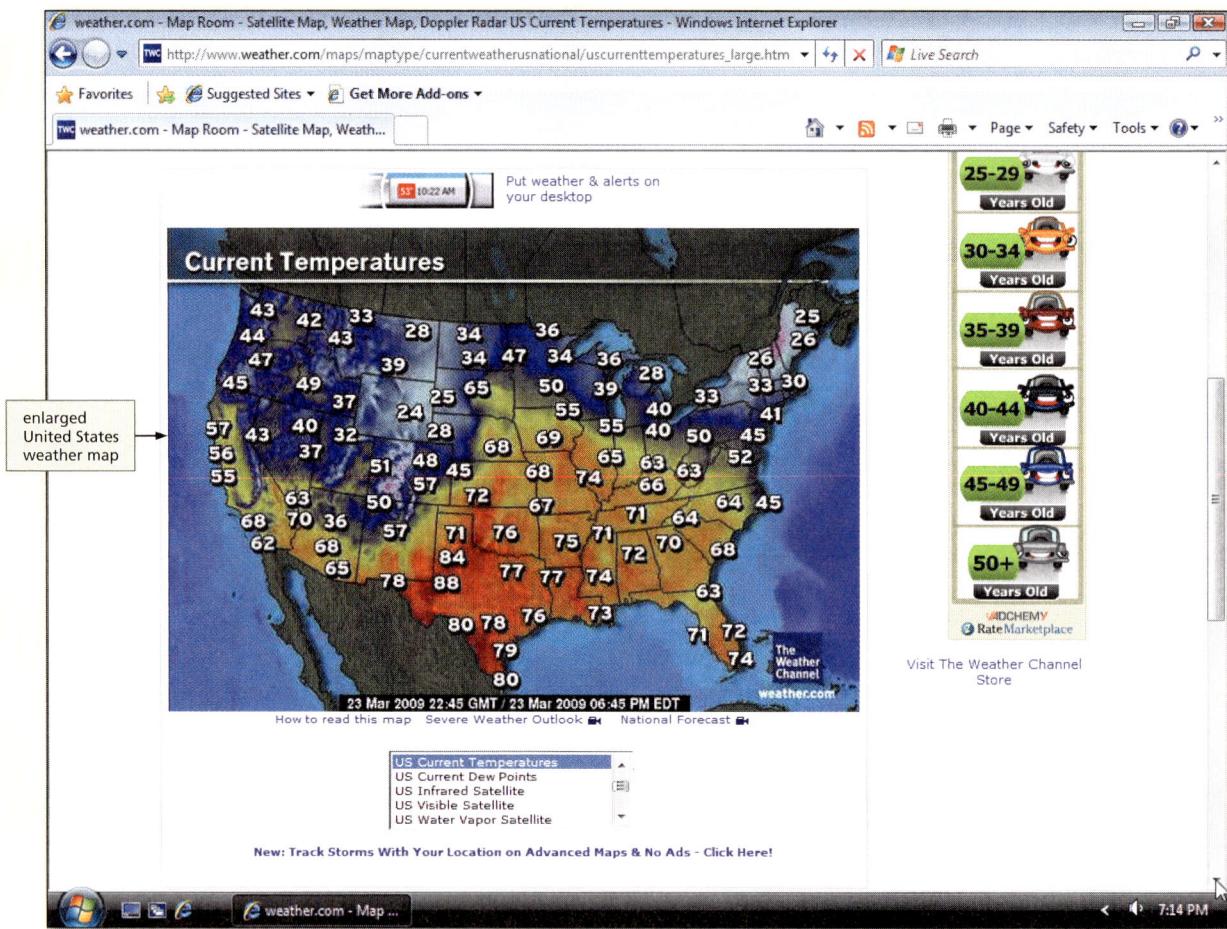

Figure 73

3. Right-click the weather map, click Print Picture on the shortcut menu, and then click the Print button in the Print dialog box to print the weather map.

4. Right-click the weather map and click Save Picture As on the shortcut menu to display the Save Picture dialog box. Click the Documents link in the left pane of the Save Picture dialog box, click the File name text box, type U.S. Weather map, and then click the Save button to save the picture on your hard disk.
5. Close Internet Explorer.
6. Submit the printed weather map to your instructor.

In the Lab

Lab 4: Collecting Biographical Information

Problem: To complete an assignment in history class, you must locate the Biography.com Web site and select an individual whose biography is on the Web site. When you find the biography of your chosen individual, copy his or her picture and the text of the biography into WordPad, and then print the WordPad document.

Instructions: Perform the following tasks.

Part 1: Retrieving a Web Page
1. Type www.biography.com in the Address bar and then press the ENTER key to display the Biography.com home page (Figure 74).

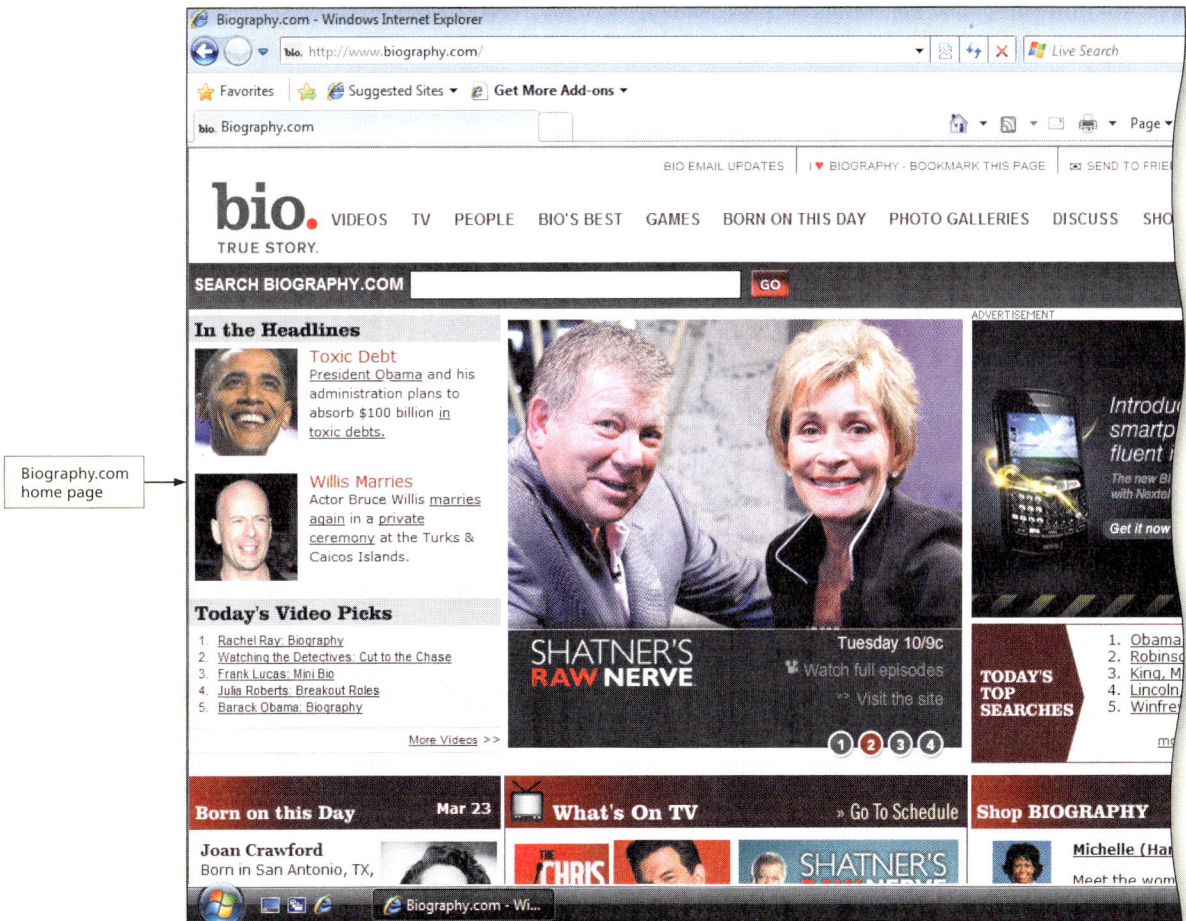

Figure 74

Continued >

In the Lab *continued*

2. Using the links on the Web site, search for the biography of an individual in whom you are interested. (Suggestions: Thomas Edison, Mia Hamm, Martin Luther King, George Lucas, Oprah Winfrey, Elvis Presley, Eleanor Roosevelt, Tiger Woods)

Part 2: Copying a Picture and Text to Microsoft WordPad
1. If a picture of the individual is available, copy the picture to the Clipboard.
2. Start Microsoft WordPad.
3. Paste the picture from the Clipboard into the WordPad document, click anywhere off the picture, and then press the ENTER key.
4. Switch back to the Internet Explorer window.
5. If necessary, click the link that contains the biography.
6. Copy the biography text to the Clipboard.
7. Switch to the WordPad window.
8. Paste the text on the Clipboard into the WordPad document.
9. Save the WordPad document on your hard disk using the file name, Biography Assignment.
10. Print the WordPad document.
11. Close WordPad and Internet Explorer.
12. Submit the WordPad document to your instructor.

In the Lab

Lab 5: Searching the Web for a Job in Computer Programming

Problem: You are job hunting for a position that uses your expertise in computer programming. Instead of using the newspaper to find a job, you decide to search for jobs on the Internet. You decide to visit three Web sites in hopes of finding the perfect job.

Instructions: Perform the following tasks.
1. Click the Address bar, type `www.computerjobs.com` to enter the Web address, and then press the ENTER key to display the ComputerJobs.com home page (Figure 75).

Figure 75

2. When the ComputerJobs.com home page displays, type computer programming in the keyword search text box and then press the ENTER key. When the first page of the computer programming listings displays, print it.

3. Type www.monster.com in the Address bar and then press the ENTER key.

4. When the Monster home page appears, type computer programming in the Enter keywords text box and then click the Search button. When the first page of the computer programming listings displays, print it.

5. Type www.careerbuilder.com in the Address bar and then press the ENTER key.

6. When the careerbuilder.com page displays, type computer programming in the Keywords text box, and then press the ENTER key. When the first page of the computer programming listings displays, print it.

7. Close Internet Explorer, and submit the printouts to your instructor.

In the Lab

Lab 6: Using Windows Help and Support to Find Information about Internet Explorer

Problem: Because you do not know much about Windows Help and Support, you decide to learn more by using it to search for the following topics: cookies, AutoComplete, certificates, content advisor, and shortcut keys.

Instructions: Use Windows Help and Support to perform the following tasks.

1. Press the F1 key to display the Windows Help and Support window, which contains general information about Internet Explorer (Figure 76).

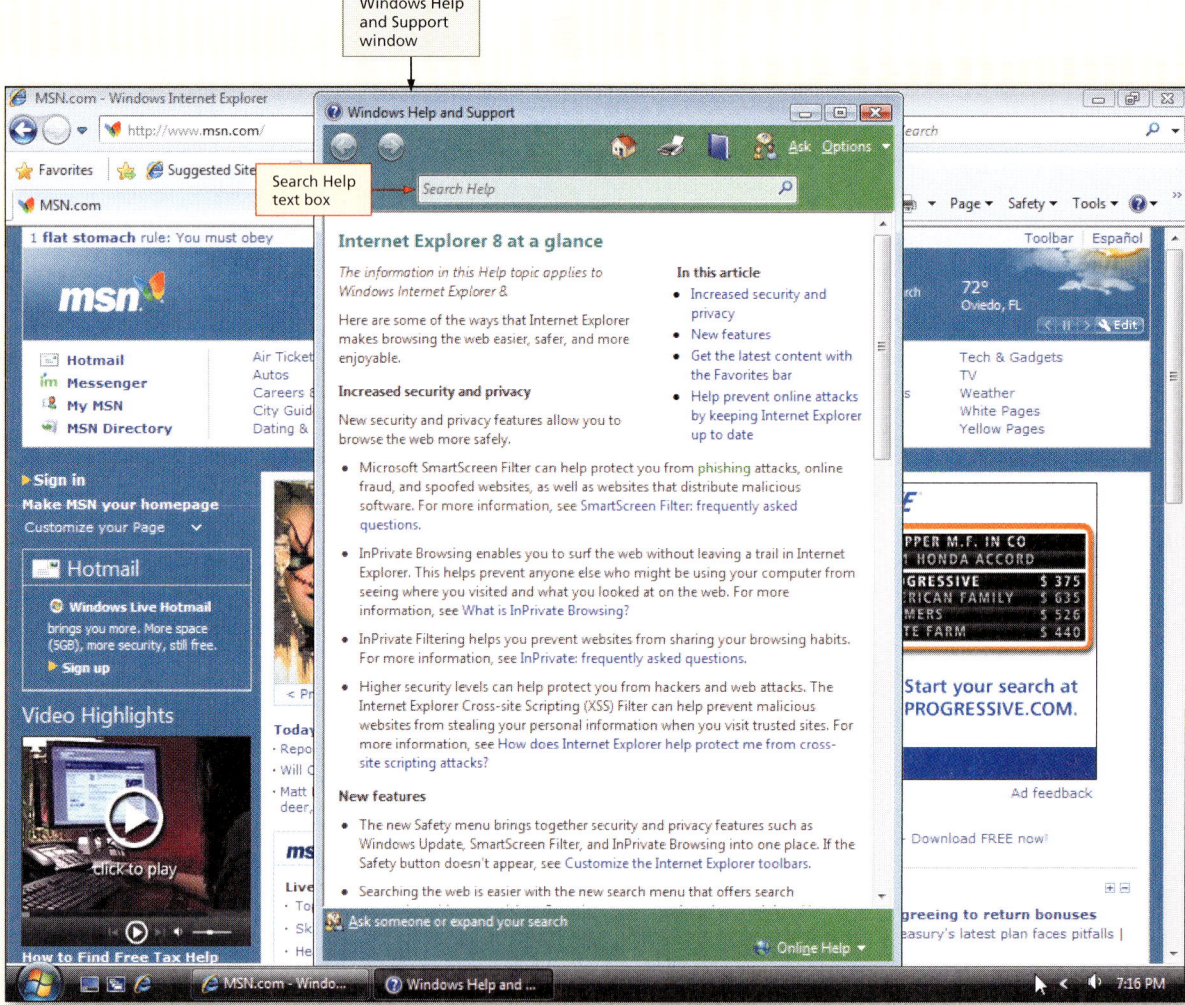

Figure 76

2. Type `cookies` in the Search Help text box, press the ENTER key, and browse the topics necessary to answer the following questions.
    a. What is a cookie?
    b. What does a cookie contain?

3. Select the text in the text box, type `autocomplete` in the box, and browse the search results to answer the following questions.
    a. What does the AutoComplete feature save?
    b. What does AutoComplete do?
4. Select the text in the text box, type `certificates` in the box, and browse the search results to answer the following questions.
    a. List two types of certificates.
    b. What is EFS?
5. Select the text in the text box, type `content advisor` in the box, and browse the search results to answer the following question.
    a. What is the purpose of Content Advisor?
6. Select the text in the text box, type `shortcut keys` in the box, and browse the search results to answer the following questions.
    a. What is the shortcut key to go to the next Web page?
    b. What is the shortcut key to refresh the current Web page?
    c. What is the shortcut key to stop downloading a Web page?
7. Close Windows Help and Support.
8. Close Internet Explorer.
9. Submit the answers to the questions to your instructor.

Cases and Places

Apply your creative thinking and problem solving skills to go online to find the information you need.

• Easier   •• More Difficult

• 1: Browsing the Web for a New Car
Your old car broke down and you are in the market for a new one. Type `autotrader.com` in the Address bar of your browser to display the AutoTrader home page. Select your favorite make, type your ZIP code, and then click the Next button to search for a new car. Select two competitors of the car you chose. Print the information on your favorite car and its two competitors.

• 2: Browsing the Web for Stock Information
Your uncle would like to invest in the stock market. He has asked you to find fundamental stock information about three companies of your choice (for example, Microsoft Corporation (MSFT), Google Inc. (GOOG), or TiVo Inc. (TIVO)). Use the Yahoo! Finance Web site (finance.yahoo.com) to obtain today's stock price, dividend rate, daily volume, 52-week range, and the P/E (price earnings ratio). To display this information, enter the stock symbol and click the Get Quotes button to display the information. Print the detailed results for each stock. In addition, when the stock information for Google displays, click the first Headline and print the page.

•• 3: Browsing the Web for Vacation Specials
You are planning a vacation to Hong Kong. You want to leave exactly one month from today and plan to stay seven days, including the travel days. Check with at least two different travel Web sites such as orbitz.com and expedia.com for travel specials to Hong Kong. Print any Web pages containing flight information and then summarize the information you find in a brief report.

•• 4: Browsing the Web for Information about Web Browsers
Although Internet Explorer may be the most widely used Web browser, it is not the only Web browser in use today. Using the Internet, computer magazines, newspapers, or other resources, prepare a brief report about three other Web browsers in use today. Describe their features, differences, and similarities.

•• 5: Shopping Online for a Computer
Make It Personal
You have decided to purchase a computer online. You plan to spend between $800 and $1,200 for a computer with a monitor and a printer. Visit three online computer stores, such as HP (hp.com), Dell (dell.com), and Gateway (gateway.com). On each site, find a computer that sells for the amount you plan to spend. For each site, print the page that provides the computer features and price. Compare the three computers. Which one is the best buy? Why?

•• 6: Comparing Newspaper Web Sites
Working Together
Have each member of your group visit a daily newspaper's Web site, such as the *Washington Post* (washingtonpost.com), *Chicago Tribune* (chicagotribune.com), *Los Angeles Times* (latimes.com), *Orlando Sentinel* (orlandosentinel.com), or a local newspaper's Web site. Print at least one page from each newspaper site. Compare the latest headline news. Navigate through each site. How are the newspaper sites similar and dissimilar? Which newspaper has the best Web site? Why? Present your findings to the class.

1 Creating and Editing a Word Document

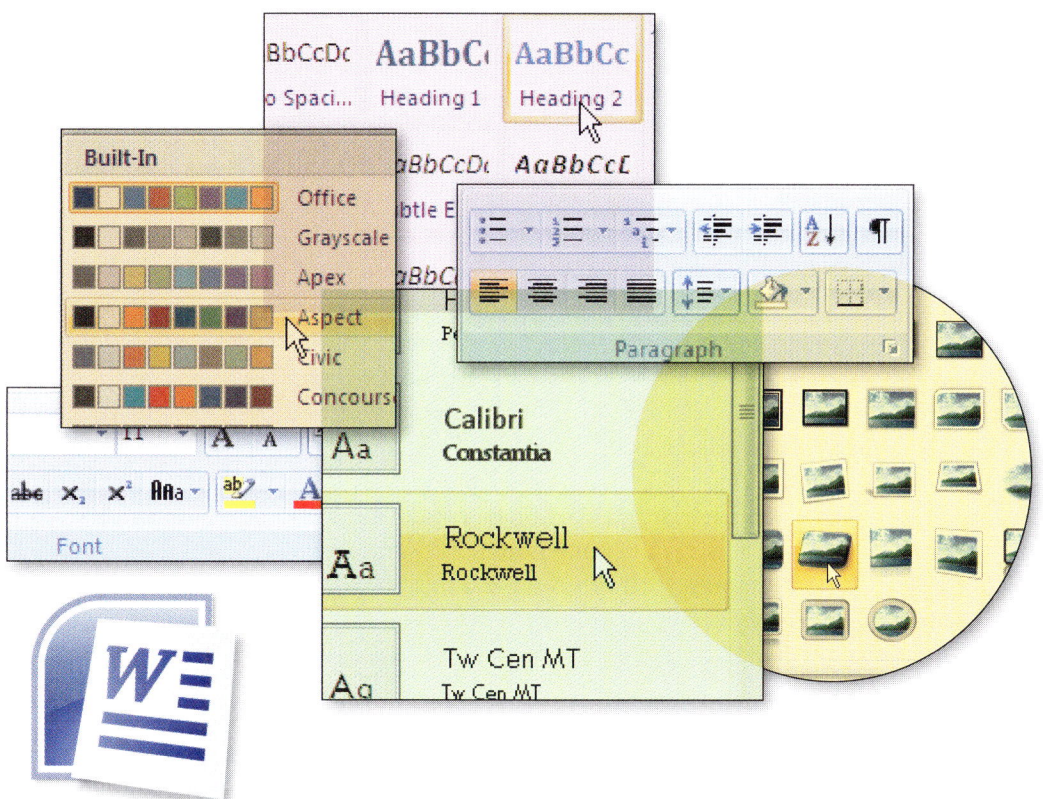

Objectives

You will have mastered the material in this chapter when you can:

- Start and quit Word
- Describe the Word window
- Enter text in a document
- Check spelling as you type
- Save a document
- Format text, paragraphs, and document elements
- Undo and redo commands or actions
- Insert a picture and format it
- Print a document
- Change document properties
- Open a document
- Correct errors in a document
- Use Word's Help

1 | Creating and Editing a Word Document

What Is Microsoft Office Word 2007?

Microsoft Office Word 2007 is a full-featured word processing program that allows you to create professional-looking documents and revise them easily. A document is a printed or electronic medium people use to communicate with others. With Word, you can develop many types of documents, including flyers, letters, memos, resumes, reports, fax cover sheets, mailing labels, and newsletters. Word also provides tools that enable you to create Web pages. From within Word, you can place these Web pages directly on a Web server.

Word has many features designed to simplify the production of documents and make documents look visually appealing. Using Word, you easily can change the shape, size, and color of text. You can include borders, shading, tables, images, pictures, charts, and Web addresses in documents.

While you are typing, Word performs many tasks automatically. For example, Word detects and corrects spelling and grammar errors in several languages. Word's thesaurus allows you to add variety and precision to your writing. Word also can format text, such as headings, lists, fractions, borders, and Web addresses, as you type.

This latest version of Word has many new features to make you more productive. For example, Word has many predefined text and graphical elements designed to assist you with preparing documents. Word also includes new charting and diagramming tools; uses themes so that you can coordinate colors, fonts, and graphics; and has a tool that enables you to convert a document to a PDF format.

To illustrate the features of Word, this book presents a series of projects that use Word to create documents similar to those you will encounter in academic and business environments.

Project Planning Guidelines

> The process of developing a document that communicates specific information requires careful analysis and planning. As a starting point, establish why the document is needed. Once the purpose is determined, analyze the intended readers of the document and their unique needs. Then, gather information about the topic and decide what to include in the document. Finally, determine the document design and style that will be most successful at delivering the message. Details of these guidelines are provided in Appendix A. In addition, each project in this book provides practical applications of these planning considerations.

Project — Document with a Picture

To advertise a sale, promote a business, publicize an event, or convey a message to the community, you may want to create a flyer and post it in a public location. Libraries, schools, religious organizations, grocery stores, and other places often provide bulletin boards or windows for flyers. These flyers announce personal items for sale or rent (car, boat, apartment); garage or block sales; services being offered (animal care, housecleaning, lessons); membership, sponsorship, or donation requests (club, religious organization, charity); and other messages. Flyers are an inexpensive means of reaching the community, yet many go unnoticed because they are designed poorly.

The project in this chapter follows general guidelines and uses Word to create the flyer shown in Figure 1–1. This colorful, eye-catching flyer advertises horseback riding lessons at Tri-Valley Stables. The picture of the horse and rider entices passersby to stop and look at the flyer. The headline on the flyer is large and colorful to draw attention into the text. The body copy below the headline briefly describes key points of the riding lessons, and the bulleted list below the picture concisely highlights important additional information. The signature line of the flyer calls attention to the stable name and telephone number. Finally, the graphical page border nicely frames and complements the contents of the flyer.

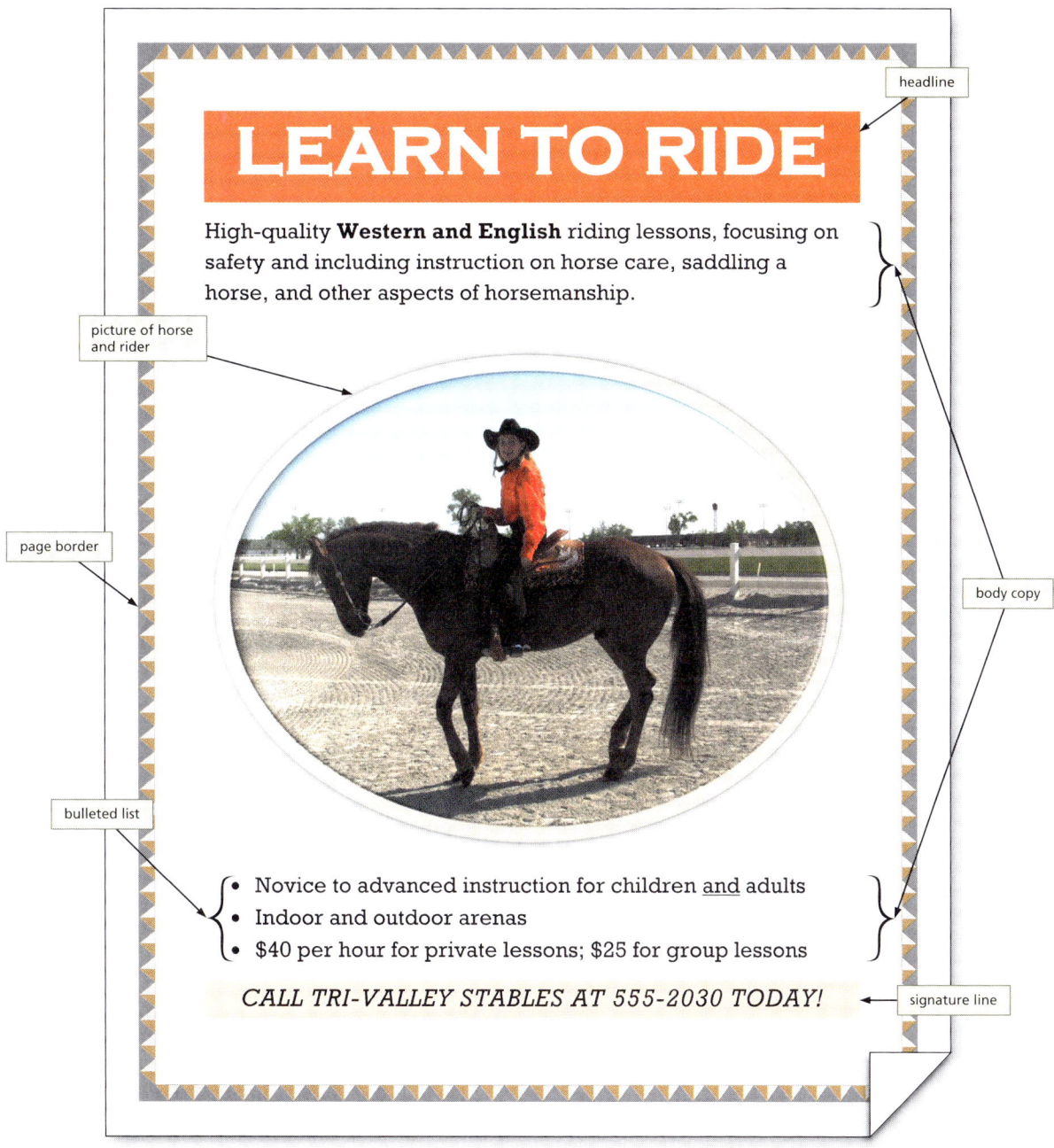

Figure 1–1

Overview

As you read this chapter, you will learn how to create the flyer shown in Figure 1–1 on the previous page by performing these general tasks:

- Enter text in the document.
- Save the document.
- Format the text in the document.
- Insert a picture in the document.
- Format the picture.
- Add a border to the page.
- Print the document.

Plan Ahead

General Project Guidelines

When creating a Word document, the actions you perform and decisions you make will affect the appearance and characteristics of the finished document. As you create a flyer, such as the project shown in Figure 1–1, you should follow these general guidelines:

1. **Choose the words for the text.** Follow the *less is more* principle. The less text, the more likely the flyer will be read. Use as few words as possible to make a point.

2. **Determine where to save the flyer.** You can store a document permanently, or **save** it, on a variety of storage media including a hard disk, USB flash drive, or optical disc. You also can indicate a specific location on the storage media for saving the document.

3. **Identify how to format various elements of the text.** The overall appearance of a document significantly affects its ability to communicate clearly. Examples of how you can modify the appearance, or **format**, of text include changing its shape, size, color, and position on the page.

4. **Find the appropriate graphical image.** An eye-catching graphical image should convey the flyer's overall message. It could show a product, service, result, or benefit, or visually convey a message that is not expressed easily with words.

5. **Establish where to position and how to format the graphical image.** The position and format of the graphical image should grab the attention of passersby and draw them into reading the flyer.

6. **Determine whether the flyer needs a page border, and if so, its style and format.** A graphical, color-coordinated page border can further draw attention to a flyer and nicely frame its contents. Be careful, however, that a page border does not make the flyer look too cluttered.

When necessary, more specific details concerning the above guidelines are presented at appropriate points in the chapter. The chapter also will identify the actions performed and decisions made regarding these guidelines during the creation of the flyer shown in Figure 1–1.

Starting Word

BTW

The Word Window
The screen in Figure 1-3 shows how the Word window looks the first time you start Word after installation on most computers. Your screen may look different depending on your screen resolution and Word settings.

If you are using a computer to step through the project in this chapter and you want your screen to match the figures in this book, you should change your screen's resolution to 1024 × 768. For information about how to change a computer's resolution, read Appendix C.

Creating and Editing a Word Document   Word Chapter 1   **WD 5**

To Start Word

The following steps, which assume Windows Vista is running, start Word based on a typical installation. You may need to ask your instructor how to start Word for your computer.

1
- Click the Start button on the Windows Vista taskbar to display the Start menu.
- Click All Programs at the bottom of the left pane on the Start menu to display the All Programs list.
- Click Microsoft Office in the All Programs list to display the Microsoft Office list (Figure 1–2).

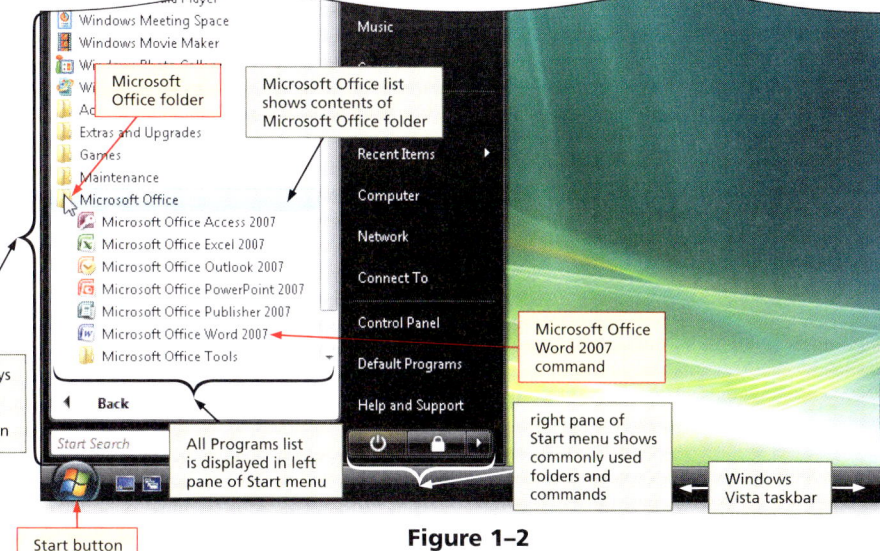

Figure 1–2

2
- Click Microsoft Office Word 2007 to start Word and display a new blank document in the Word window (Figure 1–3).

- If the Word window is not maximized, click the Maximize button next to the Close button on its title bar to maximize the window.

 What is a maximized window?

A maximized window fills the entire screen. When you maximize a window, the Maximize button changes to a Restore Down button.

3
- If the Print Layout button is not selected, click it so that your screen layout matches Figure 1–3.

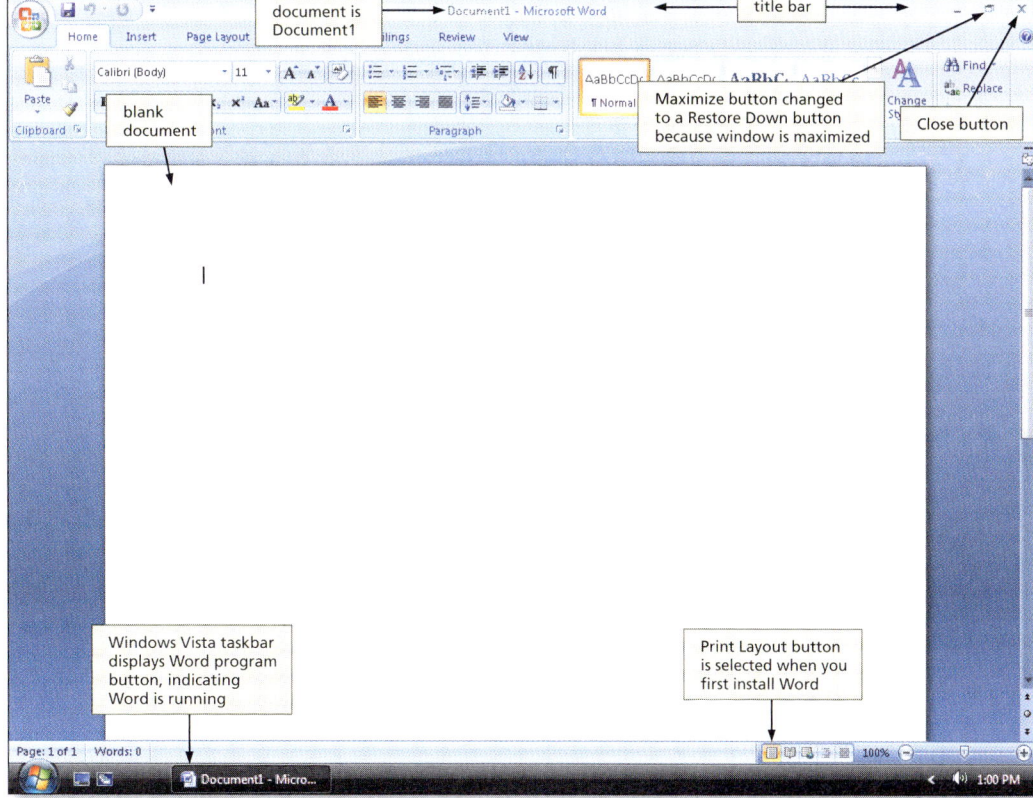

Figure 1–3

Other Ways
1. Double-click Word icon on desktop, if one is present 2. Click Microsoft Office Word 2007 on Start menu

The Word Window

The Word window consists of a variety of components to make your work more efficient and documents more professional. These include the document window, Ribbon, Mini toolbar and shortcut menus, Quick Access Toolbar, and Office Button. Some of these components are common to other Microsoft Office 2007 programs; others are unique to Word.

Document Window

You view a portion of a document on the screen through a **document window** (Figure 1–4). The default (preset) view is **Print Layout view**, which shows the document on a mock sheet of paper in the document window.

The Word document window in Figure 1–4 contains an insertion point, mouse pointer, scroll bar, and status bar. Other elements that may appear in the document window are discussed later in this chapter.

Insertion Point The **insertion point** is a blinking vertical bar that indicates where text, graphics, and other items will be inserted. As you type, the insertion point moves to the right, and when you reach the end of a line, it moves downward to the beginning of the next line.

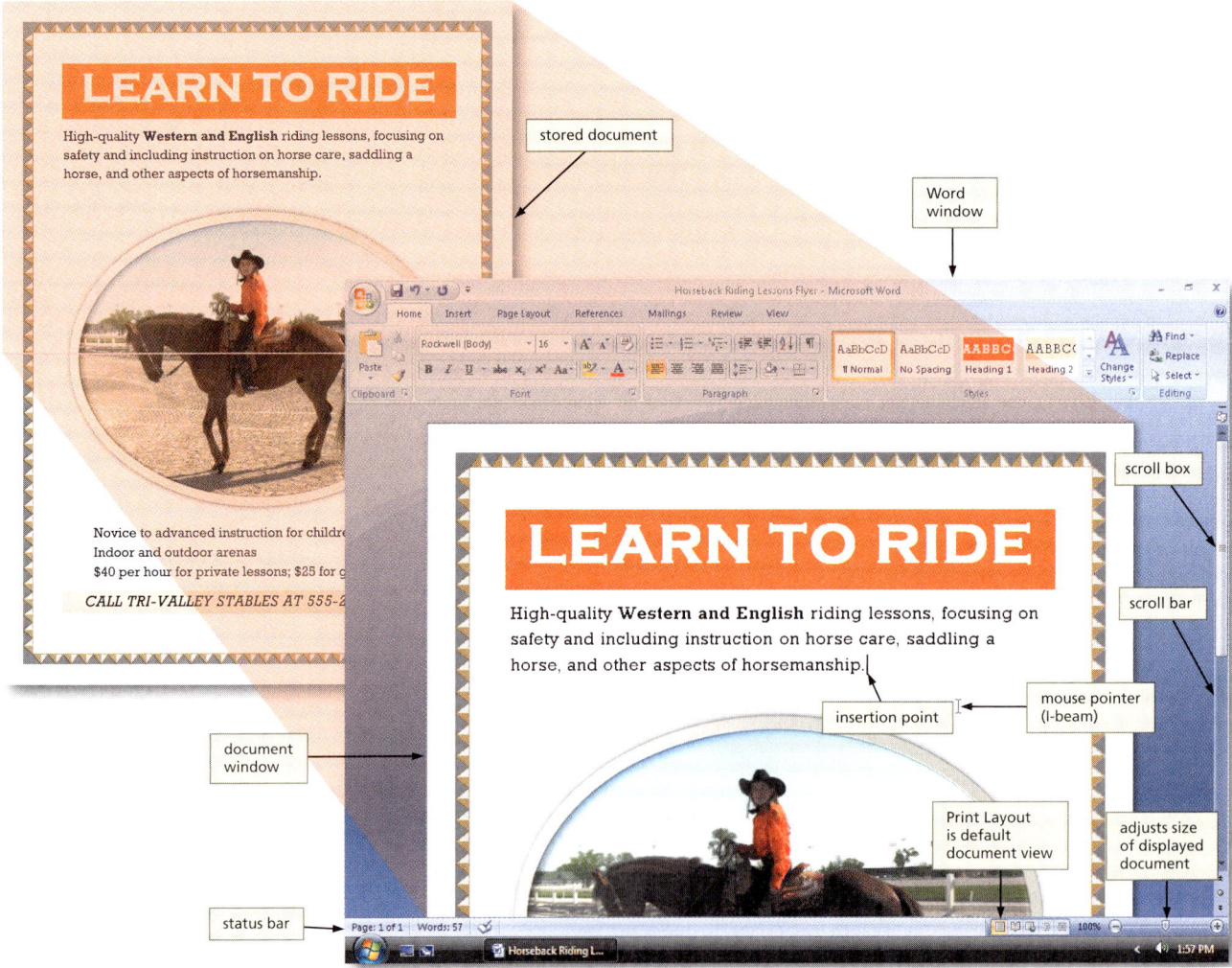

Figure 1–4

Mouse Pointer The **mouse pointer** becomes different shapes depending on the task you are performing in Word and the pointer's location on the screen. The mouse pointer in Figure 1–4 is the shape of an I-beam.

Scroll Bar You use a **scroll bar** to display different portions of a document in the document window. At the right edge of the document window is a vertical scroll bar. If a document is too wide to fit in the document window, a horizontal scroll bar also appears at the bottom of the document window. On a scroll bar, the position of the scroll box reflects the location of the portion of the document that is displayed in the document window. A **scroll arrow** is located at each end of a scroll bar. To scroll through, or display different portions of the document in the document window, you can click a scroll arrow or drag the scroll box.

Status Bar The **status bar**, located at the bottom of the document window above the Windows Vista taskbar, presents information about the document, the progress of current tasks, and the status of certain commands and keys; it also provides controls for viewing the document. As you type text or perform certain commands, various indicators and buttons may appear on the status bar.

The left edge of the status bar in Figure 1–4 shows the current page followed by the total number of pages in the document, the number of words in the document, and a button to check spelling and grammar. Toward the right edge are buttons and controls you can use to change the view of a document and adjust the size of the displayed document.

Ribbon

The Ribbon, located near the top of the Word window, is the control center in Word (Figure 1–5a). The Ribbon provides easy, central access to the tasks you perform while creating a document. The Ribbon consists of tabs, groups, and commands. Each tab surrounds a collection of groups, and each group contains related commands.

When you start Word, the Ribbon displays seven top-level tabs: Home, Insert, Page Layout, References, Mailings, Review, and View. The **Home tab**, called the primary tab, contains the more frequently used commands. To display a different tab on the Ribbon, click the top-level tab. That is, to display the Insert tab, click Insert on the Ribbon. To return to the Home tab, click Home on the Ribbon. The tab currently displayed is called the **active tab**.

To display more of the document in the document window, some users prefer to minimize the Ribbon, which hides the groups on the Ribbon and displays only the top-level tabs (Figure 1–5b). To use commands on a minimized Ribbon, click the top-level tab.

> **BTW**
>
> **Minimizing the Ribbon**
> If you want to minimize the Ribbon, right-click the Ribbon and then click Minimize the Ribbon on the shortcut menu, double-click the active tab, or press CTRL+F1. To restore a minimized Ribbon, right-click the Ribbon and then click Minimize the Ribbon on the shortcut menu, double-click any top-level tab, or press CTRL+F1. To use commands on a minimized Ribbon, click the top-level tab.

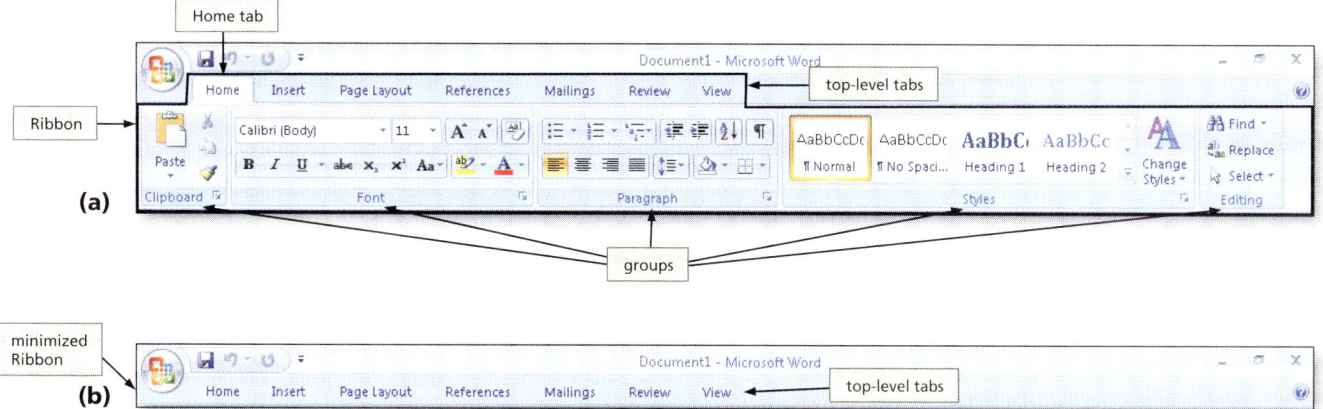

Figure 1–5

Each time you start Word, the Ribbon appears the same way it did the last time you used Word. The chapters in this book, however, begin with the Ribbon appearing as it did at the initial installation of the software. If you are stepping through this chapter on a computer and you want your Ribbon to match the figures in this book, read Appendix C.

In addition to the top-level tabs, Word displays other tabs, called **contextual tabs**, when you perform certain tasks or work with objects such as pictures or tables. If you insert a picture in the document, for example, the Picture Tools tab and its related subordinate Format tab appear (Figure 1–6). When you are finished working with the picture, the Picture Tools and Format tabs disappear from the Ribbon. Word determines when contextual tabs should appear and disappear based on tasks you perform. Some contextual tabs, such as the Table Tools tab, have more than one related subordinate tab.

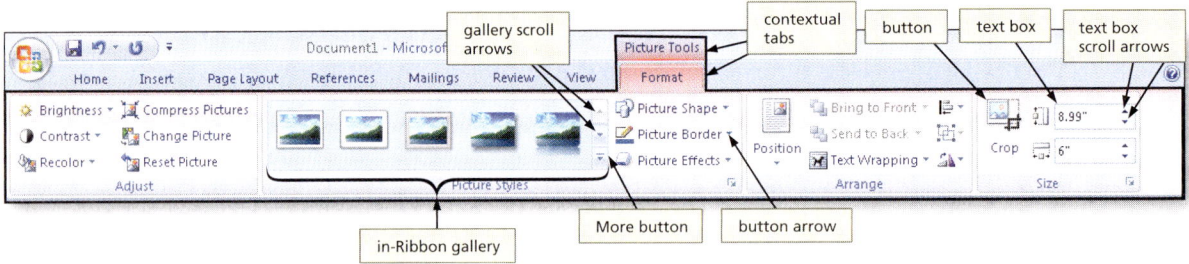

Figure 1–6

Commands on the Ribbon include buttons, boxes (text boxes, check boxes, etc.), and galleries (Figure 1–6). A **gallery** is a set of choices, often graphical, arranged in a grid or in a list. You can scroll through choices on an in-Ribbon gallery by clicking the gallery's scroll arrows. Or, you can click a gallery's More button to view more gallery options on the screen at a time. Some buttons and boxes have arrows that, when clicked, also display a gallery; others always cause a gallery to be displayed when clicked. Most galleries support **live preview**, which is a feature that allows you to point to a gallery choice and see its effect in the document — without actually selecting the choice (Figure 1–7).

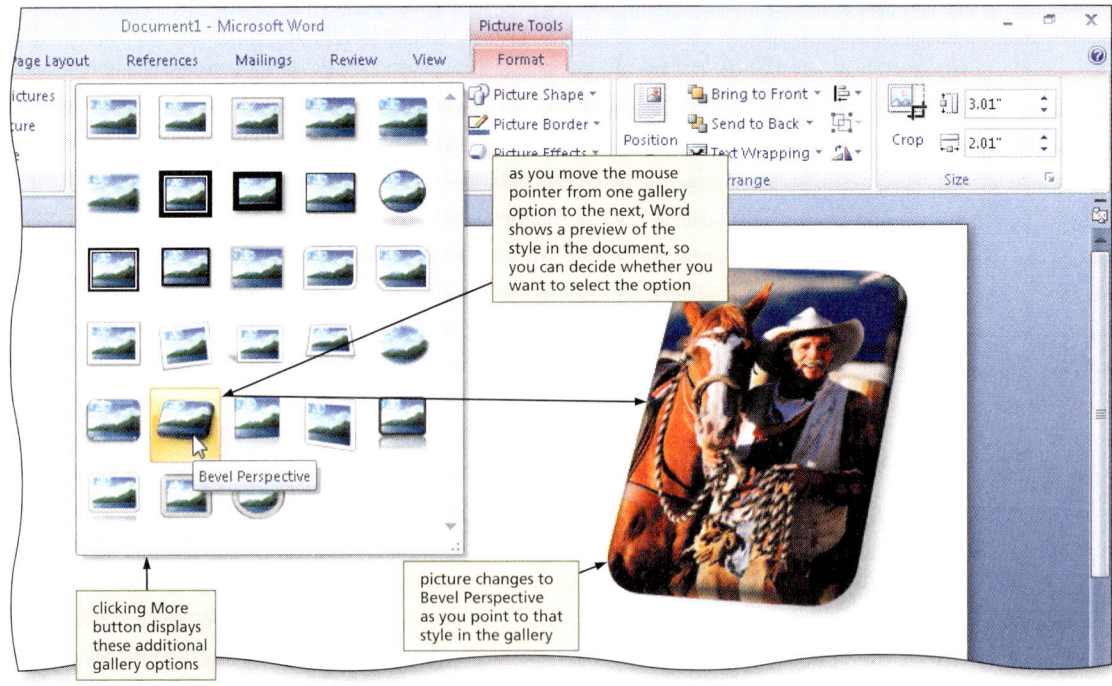

Figure 1–7

Some commands on the Ribbon display an image to help you remember their function. When you point to a command on the Ribbon, all or part of the command glows in shades of yellow and orange, and an Enhanced ScreenTip appears on the screen. An **Enhanced ScreenTip** is an on-screen note that provides the name of the command, available keyboard shortcut(s), a description of the command, and sometimes instructions for how to obtain help about the command (Figure 1–8). Enhanced ScreenTips are more detailed than a typical ScreenTip, which usually only displays the name of the command.

Figure 1–8

The lower-right corner of some groups on the Ribbon has a small arrow, called a **Dialog Box Launcher**, that when clicked, displays a dialog box or a task pane with additional options for the group (Figure 1–9). When presented with a dialog box, you make selections and must close the dialog box before returning to the document. A task pane, by contrast, is a window that can remain open and visible while you work in the document.

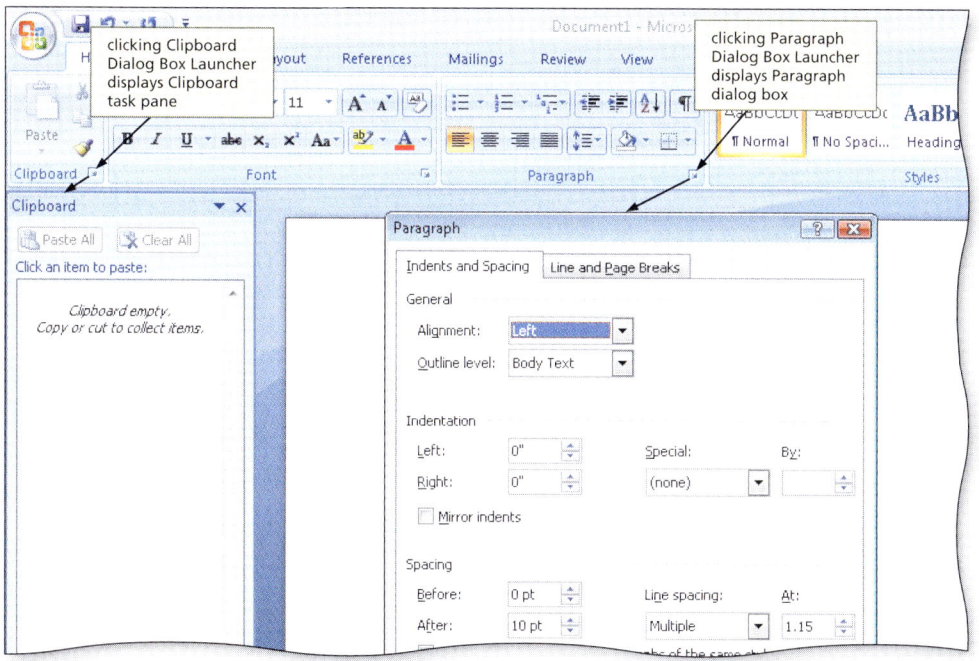

Figure 1–9

Mini Toolbar and Shortcut Menus

The **Mini toolbar**, which appears automatically based on tasks you perform, contains commands related to changing the appearance of text in a document. All commands on the Mini toolbar also exist on the Ribbon. The purpose of the Mini toolbar is to minimize mouse movement. For example, if you want to use a command that currently is not displayed on the active tab, you can use the command on the Mini toolbar — instead of switching to a different tab to use the command.

When the Mini toolbar appears, it initially is transparent (Figure 1–10a). If you do not use the transparent Mini toolbar, it disappears from the screen. To use the Mini toolbar, move the mouse pointer into the toolbar, which causes the Mini toolbar to change from a transparent to bright appearance (Figure 1–10b).

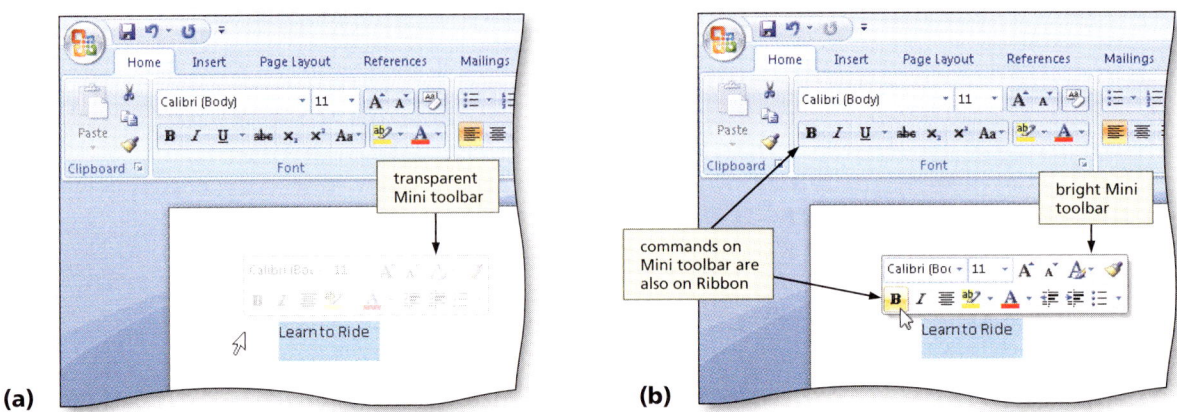

Figure 1–10

A **shortcut menu**, which appears when you right-click an object, is a list of frequently used commands that relate to the right-clicked object. When you right-click a scroll bar, for example, a shortcut menu appears with commands related to the scroll bar. If you right-click an item in the document window, Word displays both the Mini toolbar and a shortcut menu (Figure 1–11).

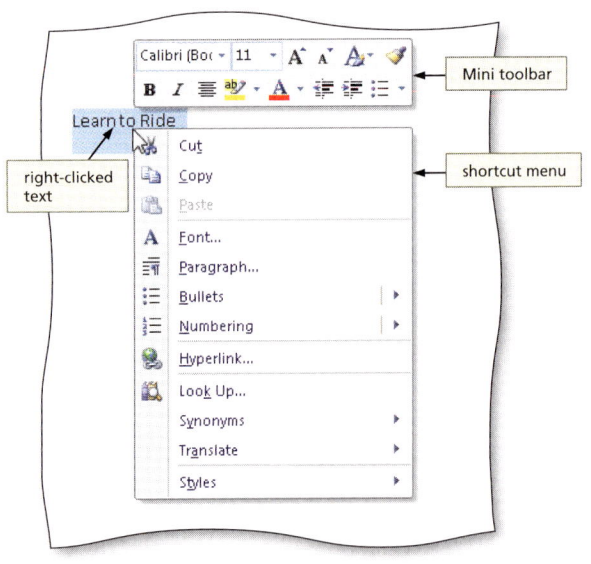

Figure 1–11

Quick Access Toolbar

The **Quick Access Toolbar**, located by default above the Ribbon, provides easy access to frequently used commands (Figure 1–12a). The commands on the Quick Access Toolbar always are available, regardless of the task you are performing. Initially, the Quick Access Toolbar contains the Save, Undo, and Redo commands. If you click the Customize Quick Access Toolbar button, Word provides a list of commands you quickly can add to and remove from the Quick Access Toolbar (Figure 1–12b).

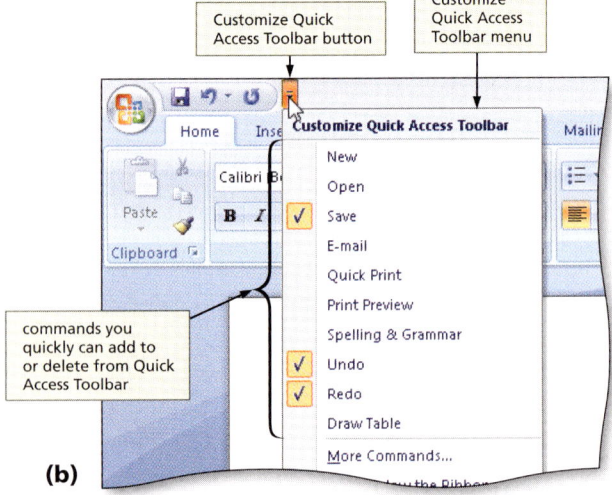

Figure 1–12

You also can add other commands to or delete commands from the Quick Access Toolbar so that it contains the commands you use most often. As you add commands to the Quick Access Toolbar, its commands may interfere with the document title on the title bar. For this reason, Word provides an option of displaying the Quick Access Toolbar below the Ribbon (Figure 1–13).

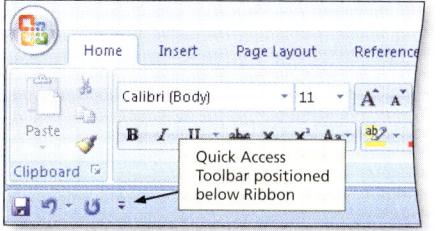

Figure 1–13

BTW

Quick Access Toolbar Commands
To add a Ribbon command to the Quick Access Toolbar, right-click the command on the Ribbon and then click Add to Quick Access Toolbar on the shortcut menu. To delete a command from the Quick Access Toolbar, right-click the command on the Quick Access Toolbar and then click Remove from Quick Access Toolbar on the shortcut menu. To display the Quick Access Toolbar below the Ribbon, right-click the Quick Access Toolbar and then click Show Quick Access Toolbar Below the Ribbon on the shortcut menu.

Each time you start Word, the Quick Access Toolbar appears the same way it did the last time you used Word. The chapters in this book, however, begin with the Quick Access Toolbar appearing as it did at the initial installation of the software. If you are stepping through this chapter on a computer and you want your Quick Access Toolbar to match the figures in this book, you should reset your Quick Access Toolbar. For more information about how to reset the Quick Access Toolbar, read Appendix C.

Office Button

While the Ribbon is a control center for creating documents, the **Office Button** is a central location for managing and sharing documents. When you click the Office Button, located in the upper-left corner of the window, Word displays the Office Button menu (Figure 1–14a). A **menu** contains a list of commands.

When you click the New, Open, Save As, and Print commands on the Office Button menu, Word displays a dialog box with additional options. The Save As, Print, Prepare, Send, and Publish commands have an arrow to their right. If you point to this arrow, Word displays a **submenu**, which is a list of additional commands associated with the selected command (Figure 1–14b). For the Prepare, Send, and Publish commands that do not display a dialog box when clicked, you can point either to the command or the arrow to display the submenu.

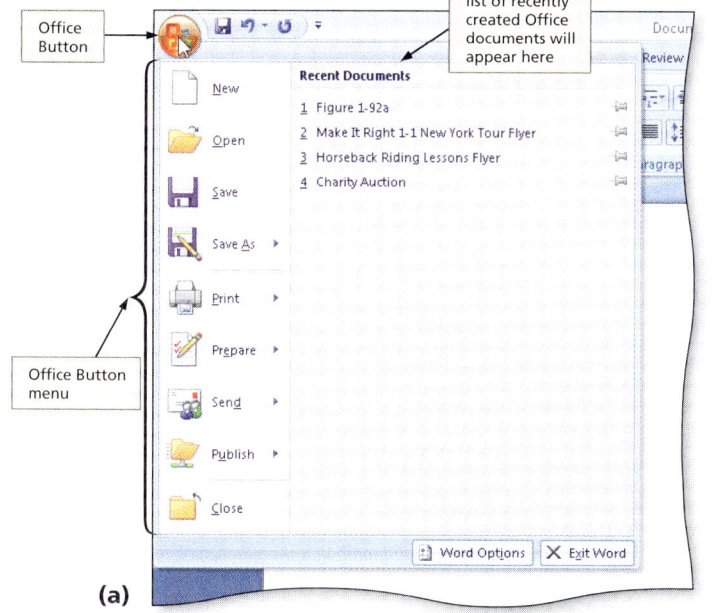

(a)

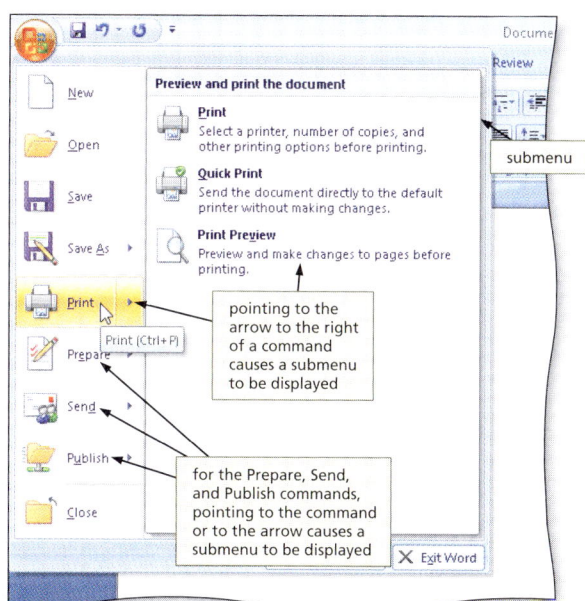

(b)

Figure 1–14

Key Tips

If you prefer using the keyboard instead of the mouse, you can press the ALT key on the keyboard to display a **Key Tip badge**, or keyboard code icon, for certain commands (Figure 1–15). To select a command using the keyboard, press its displayed code letter, or **Key Tip**. When you press a Key Tip, additional Key Tips related to the selected command may appear. For example, to select the New command on the Office Button menu, press the ALT key, then press the F key, and then press the N key.

To remove the Key Tip badges from the screen, press the ALT key or the ESC key until all Key Tip badges disappear, or click the mouse anywhere in the Word window.

Figure 1–15

Entering Text

The first step in creating a document is to enter its text by typing on the keyboard. By default, Word positions text you type at the left margin. In a later section of this chapter, you will learn how to format, or change the appearance of, the entered text.

BTW

Zooming
If text is too small for you to read on the screen, you can zoom the document by dragging the Zoom slider on the status bar or clicking the Zoom Out or Zoom In buttons on the status bar. Changing the zoom has no effect on the printed document.

Plan Ahead

Choose the words for the text.
The text in a flyer is organized into three areas: headline, body copy, and signature line.

- The headline is the first line of text on the flyer. It conveys the product or service being offered, such as a car for sale or personal lessons, or the benefit that will be gained, such as a convenience, better performance, greater security, higher earnings, or more comfort.

- The body copy consists of all text between the headline and the signature line. This text highlights the key points of the message in as few words as possible. It should be easy to read and follow. While emphasizing the positive, the body copy must be realistic, truthful, and believable.

- The signature line, which is the last line of text on the flyer, contains contact information or identifies a call to action.

To Type Text

To begin creating the flyer in this chapter, you type the headline in the document window. The following steps type this first line of text in the document.

1

- Type `Learn to Ride` as the headline (Figure 1–16).

Q&A What if I make an error while typing?

You can press the BACKSPACE key until you have deleted the text in error and then retype the text correctly.

Q&A Why did the Spelling and Grammar Check icon appear on the status bar?

When you begin typing text, the **Spelling and Grammar Check icon** appears on the status bar with an animated pencil writing on paper that indicates Word is checking for spelling and grammar errors. When you stop typing, the pencil changes to a blue check mark (no errors) or a red X (potential errors found). Word flags potential errors in the document with a red or green wavy underline. Later, this chapter shows how to fix flagged errors.

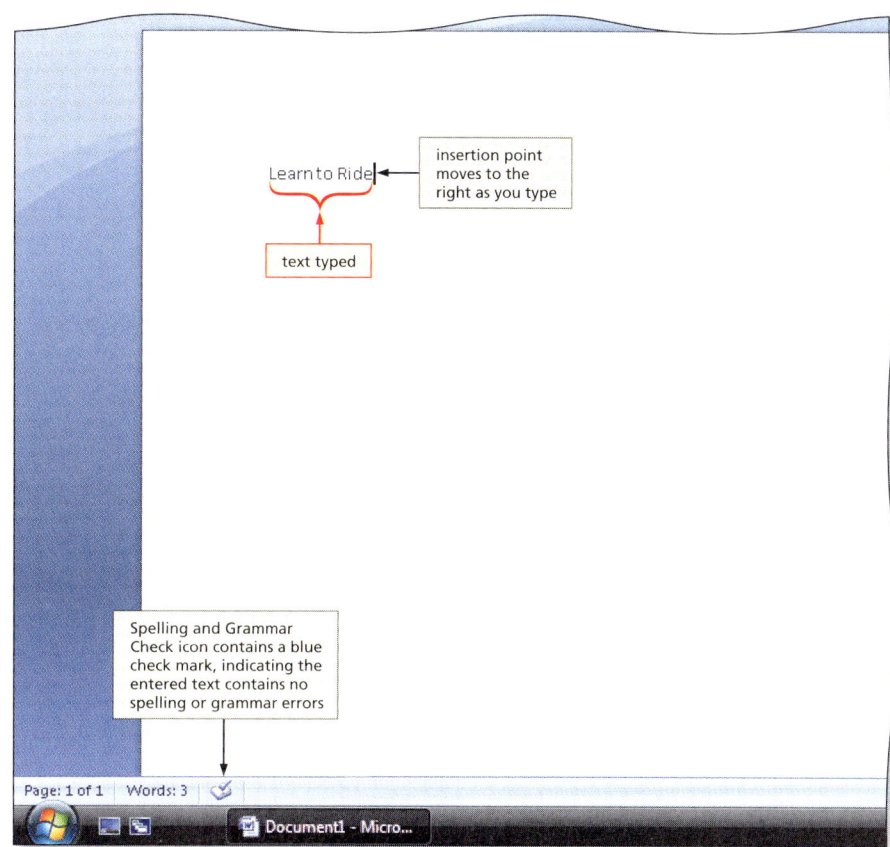

Figure 1–16

2

- Press the ENTER key to move the insertion point to the beginning of the next line (Figure 1–17).

Q&A Why did blank space appear between the headline and the insertion point?

Each time you press the ENTER key, Word creates a new paragraph and inserts blank space between the two paragraphs. Later in this chapter, you will learn how to adjust the spacing between paragraphs.

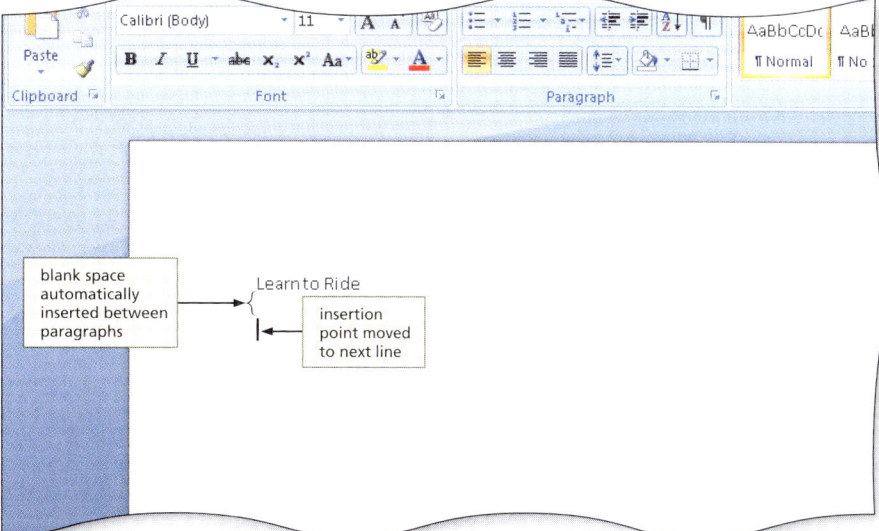

Figure 1–17

To Display Formatting Marks

To indicate where in a document you press the ENTER key or SPACEBAR, you may find it helpful to display formatting marks. A **formatting mark**, sometimes called a **nonprinting character**, is a character that Word displays on the screen but is not visible on a printed document. For example, the paragraph mark (¶) is a formatting mark that indicates where you pressed the ENTER key. A raised dot (·) shows where you pressed the SPACEBAR. Other formatting marks are discussed as they appear on the screen.

Depending on settings made during previous Word sessions, your Word screen already may display formatting marks (Figure 1–18). The following step displays formatting marks, if they do not show already on the screen.

- If necessary, click Home on the Ribbon to display the Home tab.

- If it is not selected already, click the Show/Hide ¶ button on the Home tab to display formatting marks on the screen (Figure 1–18).

Q&A What if I do not want formatting marks to show on the screen?

If you feel the formatting marks clutter the screen, you can hide them by clicking the Show/Hide ¶ button again. It is recommended that you display formatting marks so that you visually can identify when you press the ENTER key, SPACEBAR, and other keys associated with nonprinting characters; therefore, the document windows presented in this book show the formatting marks.

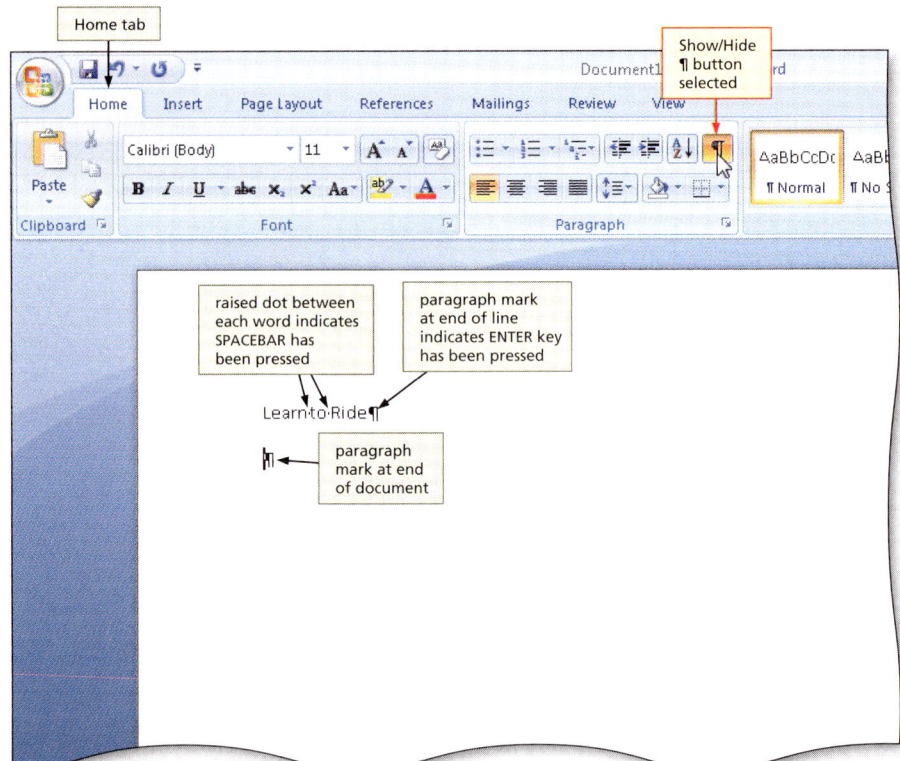

Figure 1–18

Other Ways
1. Press CTRL+SHIFT+*

BTW — Strange Formatting Marks
With some fonts, the formatting marks are not displayed on the screen properly. For example, the raised dot in each space may be displayed behind a character instead of in the space between two characters, causing the characters to look incorrect.

Wordwrap

Wordwrap allows you to type words in a paragraph continually without pressing the ENTER key at the end of each line. When the insertion point reaches the right margin, Word automatically positions the insertion point at the beginning of the next line. As you type, if a word extends beyond the right margin, Word also automatically positions that word on the next line along with the insertion point.

Word creates a new paragraph each time you press the ENTER key. Thus, as you type text in the document window, do not press the ENTER key when the insertion point reaches the right margin. Instead, press the ENTER key only in these circumstances:

1. To insert blank lines in a document
2. To begin a new paragraph
3. To terminate a short line of text and advance to the next line
4. To respond to questions or prompts in Word dialog boxes, task panes, and other on-screen objects

To Wordwrap Text as You Type

The next step in creating the flyer is to type the body copy. The following step wordwraps the text in the body copy.

- **Type** High-quality Western and English riding lessons, focusing on safety and including instruction on horse care, saddling a horse, and other aspects of horsemanship.

Q&A Why does my document wrap on different words?

Differences in wordwrap relate to the printer used by your computer. That is, the printer controls where wordwrap occurs for each line in your document. Thus, it is possible that the same document could wordwrap differently if printed on different printers.

- Press the ENTER key to position the insertion point on the next line in the document (Figure 1–19).

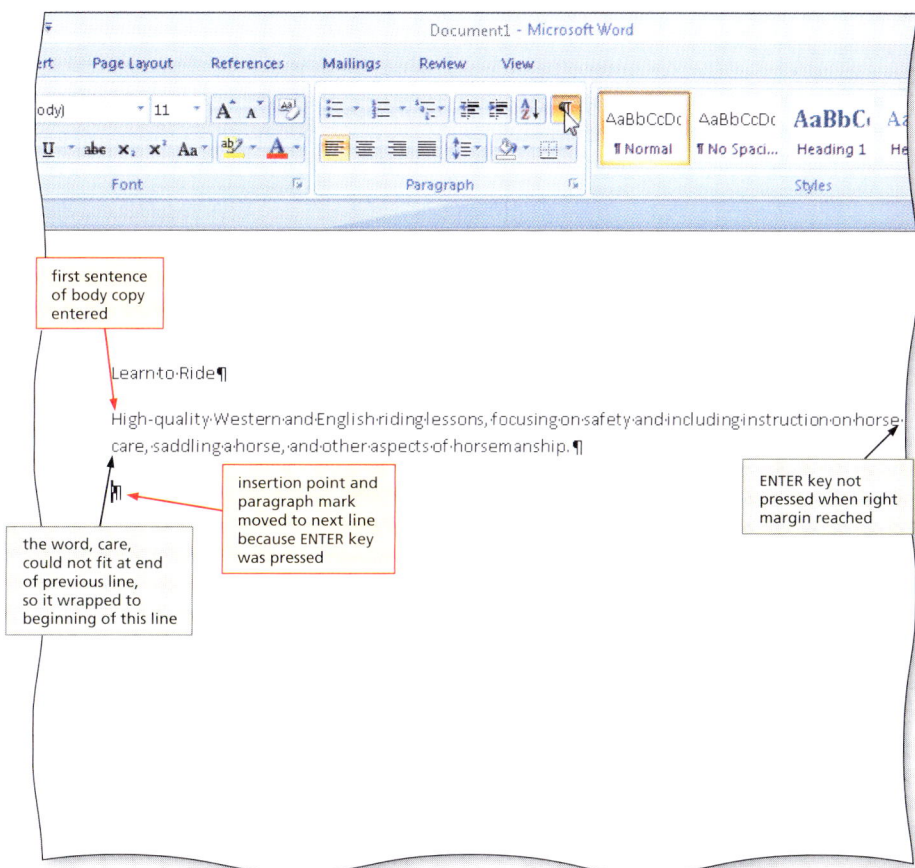

Figure 1–19

To Insert a Blank Line

In the flyer, the picture of the horse and rider should be positioned below the paragraph just entered. The picture will be inserted after all text is entered and formatted. Thus, you will leave a blank line in the document for the picture. To enter a blank line in a document, press the ENTER key without typing any text on the line. The following step inserts one blank line below the first paragraph of body copy.

- Press the ENTER key to insert a blank line in the document (Figure 1–20).

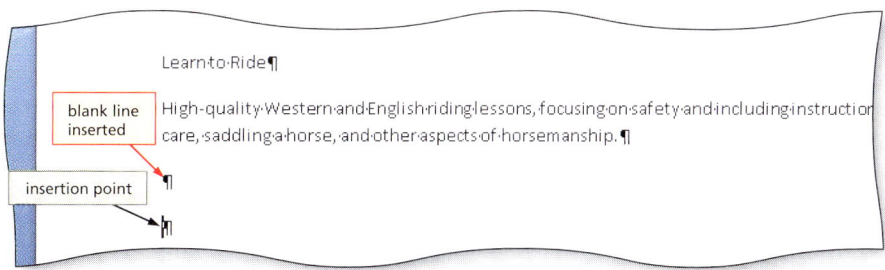

Figure 1–20

BTW

Automatic Spelling Correction

As you type, Word automatically corrects some misspelled words. For example, if you type recieve, Word automatically fixes the misspelling and displays the word, receive, when you press the SPACEBAR or type a punctuation mark. To see a complete list of automatically corrected words, click Office Button, click the Word Options button, click Proofing in the left pane of the Word Options dialog box, click the AutoCorrect Options button, and then scroll through the list of words near the bottom of the dialog box.

Spelling and Grammar Check

As you type text in a document, Word checks your typing for possible spelling and grammar errors. If all of the words you have typed are in Word's dictionary and your grammar is correct, as mentioned earlier, the Spelling and Grammar Check icon on the status bar displays a blue check mark. Otherwise, the icon shows a red X. In this case, Word flags the potential error in the document window with a red or green wavy underline. A red wavy underline means the flagged text is not in Word's dictionary (because it is a proper name or misspelled). A green wavy underline indicates the text may be incorrect grammatically. Although you can check the entire document for spelling and grammar errors at once, you also can check these flagged errors as they appear on the screen.

To display a list of corrections for flagged text, right-click the flagged text. When you right-click a flagged word, for example, a list of suggested spelling corrections appears on the screen. A flagged word, however, is not necessarily misspelled. For example, many names, abbreviations, and specialized terms are not in Word's main dictionary. In these cases, you tell Word to ignore the flagged word. As you type, Word also detects duplicate words while checking for spelling errors. For example, if your document contains the phrase, to the the store, Word places a red wavy underline below the second occurrence of the word, the.

To Check Spelling and Grammar as You Type

In the following steps, the word, instruction, has been misspelled intentionally as intrution to illustrate Word's check spelling as you type feature. If you are doing this project on a computer, your flyer may contain other misspelled words, depending on the accuracy of your typing.

1

- Type Novice to advanced intrution and then press the SPACEBAR (Figure 1–21).

Q&A

What if Word does not flag my spelling and grammar errors with wavy underlines?

To verify that the check spelling and grammar as you type features are enabled, click the Office Button and then click the Word Options button. When the Word Options dialog box is displayed, click Proofing, and then ensure the 'Check spelling as you type' and 'Mark grammar errors as you type' check boxes have check marks. Also ensure the 'Hide spelling errors in this document only' and 'Hide grammar errors in this document only' check boxes do not have check marks. Click the OK button.

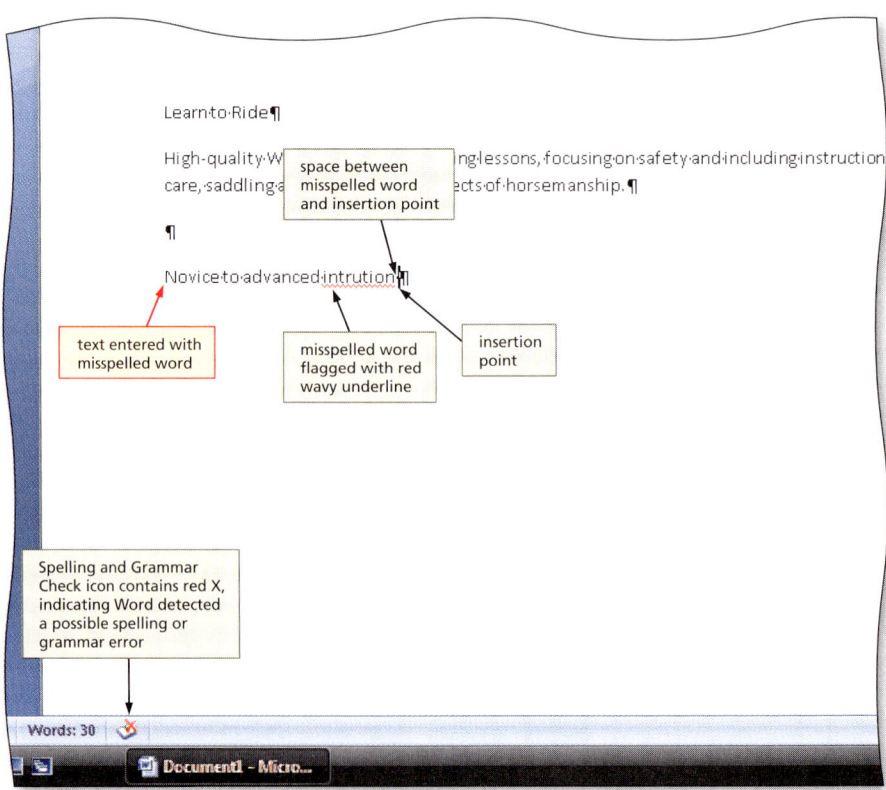

Figure 1–21

2
- Right-click the flagged word (intrution, in this case) to display a shortcut menu that includes a list of suggested spelling corrections for the flagged word (Figure 1–22).

Q&A What if, when I right-click the misspelled word, my desired correction is not in the list on the shortcut menu?

You can click outside the shortcut menu to close the menu and then retype the correct word, or you can click Spelling on the shortcut menu to display the Spelling dialog box. Chapter 2 discusses the Spelling dialog box.

Q&A What if a flagged word actually is, for example, a proper name and spelled correctly?

Right-click it and then click Ignore All on the shortcut menu to instruct Word not to flag future occurrences of the same word.

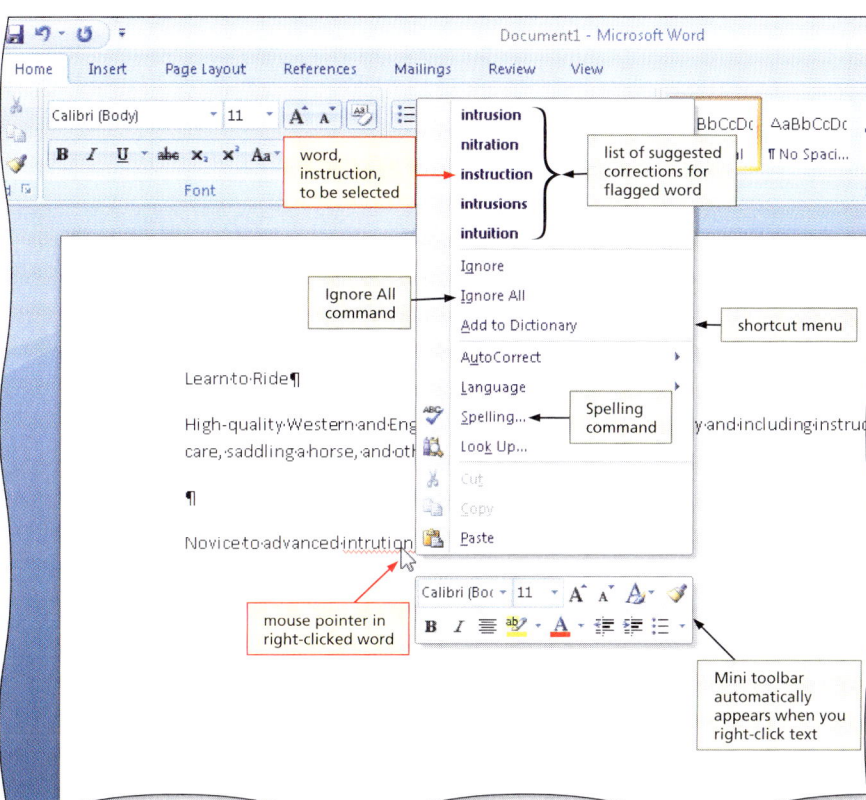

Figure 1–22

3
- Click instruction on the shortcut menu to replace the misspelled word in the document (intrution) with the word, instruction (Figure 1–23).

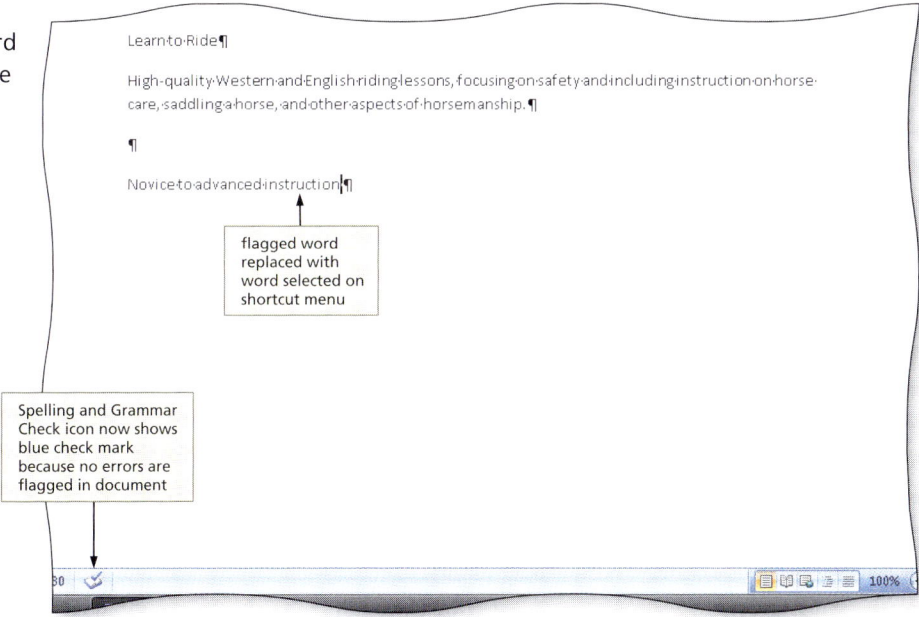

Figure 1–23

Other Ways
1. Click Spelling and Grammar Check icon on status bar, click correct word on shortcut menu

To Enter More Text

In the flyer, the text yet to be entered includes the remainder of the body copy, which will be formatted as a bulleted list, and the signature line. The following steps enter the remainder of text in the flyer.

1. Press the END key to move the insertion point to the end of the current line.

2. Type `for children and adults` and then press the ENTER key.

3. Type `Indoor and outdoor arenas` and then press the ENTER key.

4. Type `$40 per hour for private lessons; $25 for group lessons` and then press the ENTER key.

5. To complete the text in the flyer, type `Call Tri-Valley Stables at 555-2030 today!` (Figure 1–24).

> **BTW**
> **Character Widths**
> Many word processing documents use variable character fonts, where some characters are wider than others; for example, the letter w takes up more space than the letter i.

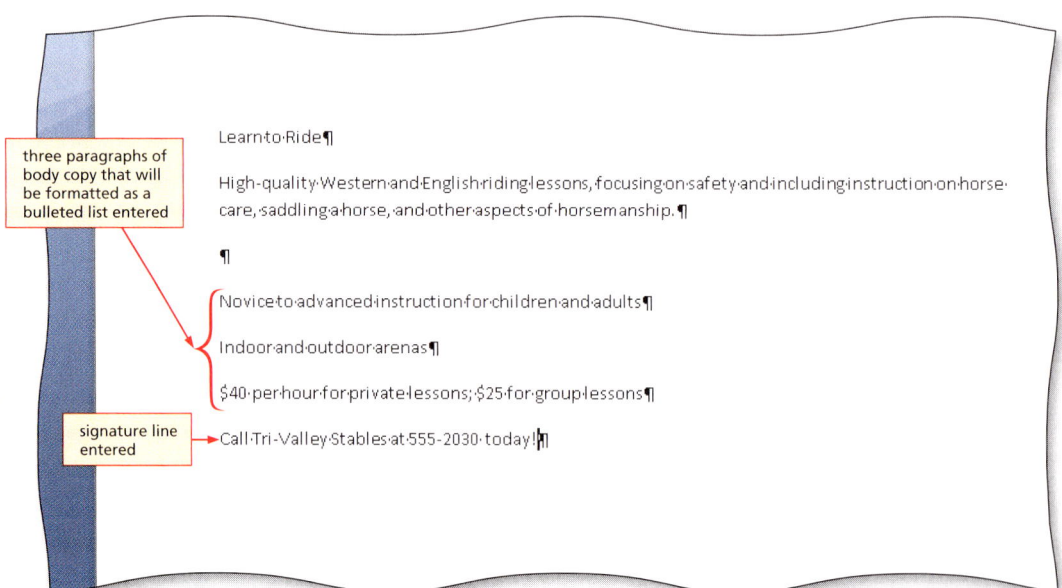

Figure 1–24

Saving the Project

While you are creating a document, the computer stores it in memory. When you save a document, the computer places it on a storage medium such as a USB flash drive, optical disc, or hard disk. A saved document is referred to as a file. A file name is the name assigned to a file when it is saved.

It is important to save a document frequently for the following reasons:

- The document in memory will be lost if the computer is turned off or you lose electrical power while Word is open.
- If you run out of time before completing your project, you may finish your document at a future time without starting over.

> **BTW**
> **File Type**
> Depending on your Windows Vista settings, the file type .docx may be displayed immediately to the right of the file name after you save the file. The file type .docx is a Word 2007 document. Previous versions of Word had a file type of .doc.

Plan Ahead

Determine where to save the document.
When saving a document, you must decide which storage medium to use.

- If you always work on the same computer and have no need to transport your projects to a different location, then your computer's hard disk will suffice as a storage location. It is a good idea, however, to save a backup copy of your projects on a separate medium in case the file becomes corrupted or the computer's hard disk fails.

- If you plan to work on your projects in various locations or on multiple computers, then you should save your projects on a portable medium, such as a USB flash drive or optical disc. The projects in this book use a USB flash drive, which saves files quickly and reliably and can be reused. Optical discs are easily portable and serve as good backups for the final versions of projects because they generally can save files only one time.

To Save a Document

You have performed many tasks while creating this project and do not want to risk losing the work completed thus far. Accordingly, you should save the document. The following steps save a document on a USB flash drive using the file name, Horseback Riding Lessons Flyer.

1
- With a USB flash drive connected to one of the computer's USB ports, click the Save button on the Quick Access Toolbar to display the Save As dialog box (Figure 1–25).

- If the Navigation pane is not displayed in the Save As dialog box, click the Browse Folders button to expand the dialog box.

- If a Folders list is displayed below the Folders button, click the Folders button to remove the Folders list.

Q&A
Do I have to save to a USB flash drive?

No. You can save to any device or folder. A **folder** is a specific location on a storage medium. You can save to the default folder or a different folder. You also can create your own folders.

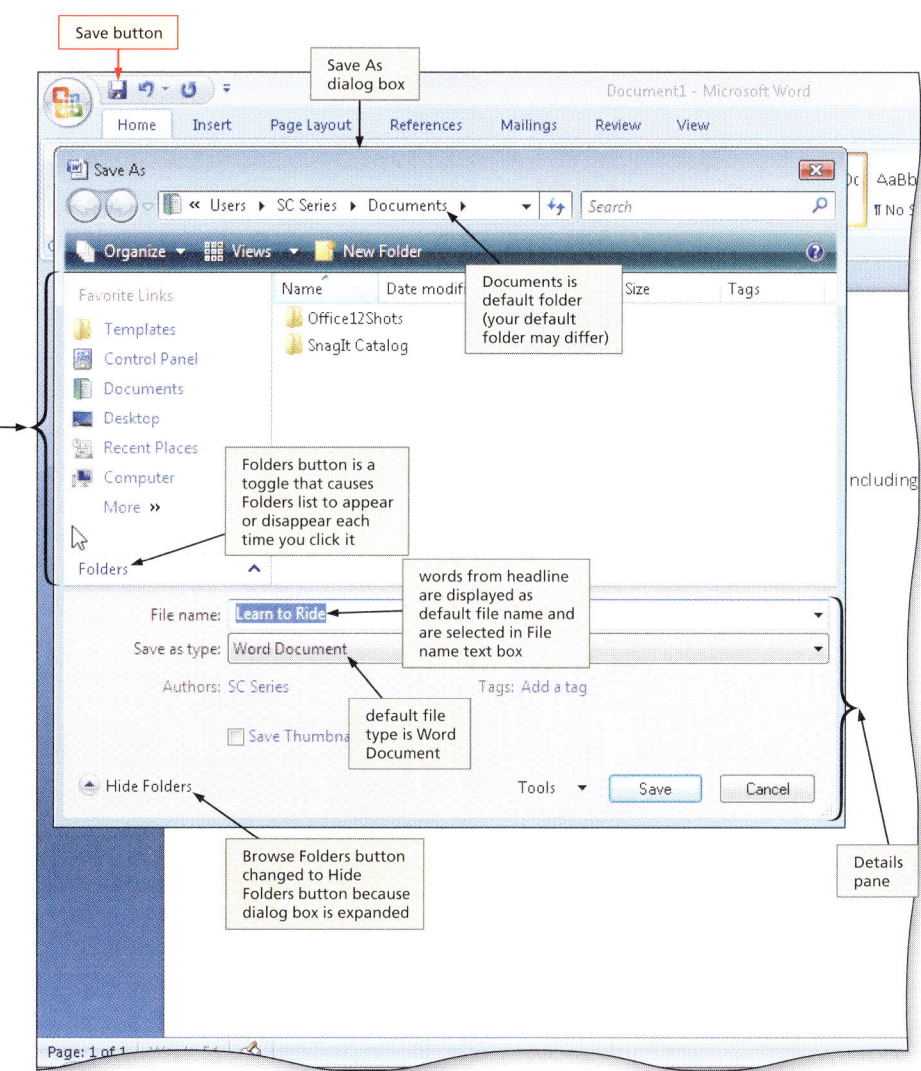

Figure 1–25

- Type `Horseback Riding Lessons Flyer` in the File name text box to change the file name. Do not press the ENTER key after typing the file name (Figure 1–26).

Q&A What characters can I use in a file name?

A file name can have a maximum of 260 characters, including spaces. The only invalid characters are the backslash (\), slash (/), colon (:), asterisk (*), question mark (?), quotation mark ("), less than symbol (<), greater than symbol (>), and vertical bar (|).

Q&A What are file properties and tags?

File properties contain information about a file such as the file name, author name, date the file was modified, and tags. A tag is a file property that contains a word or phrase about a file. You can organize and locate files based on their file properties.

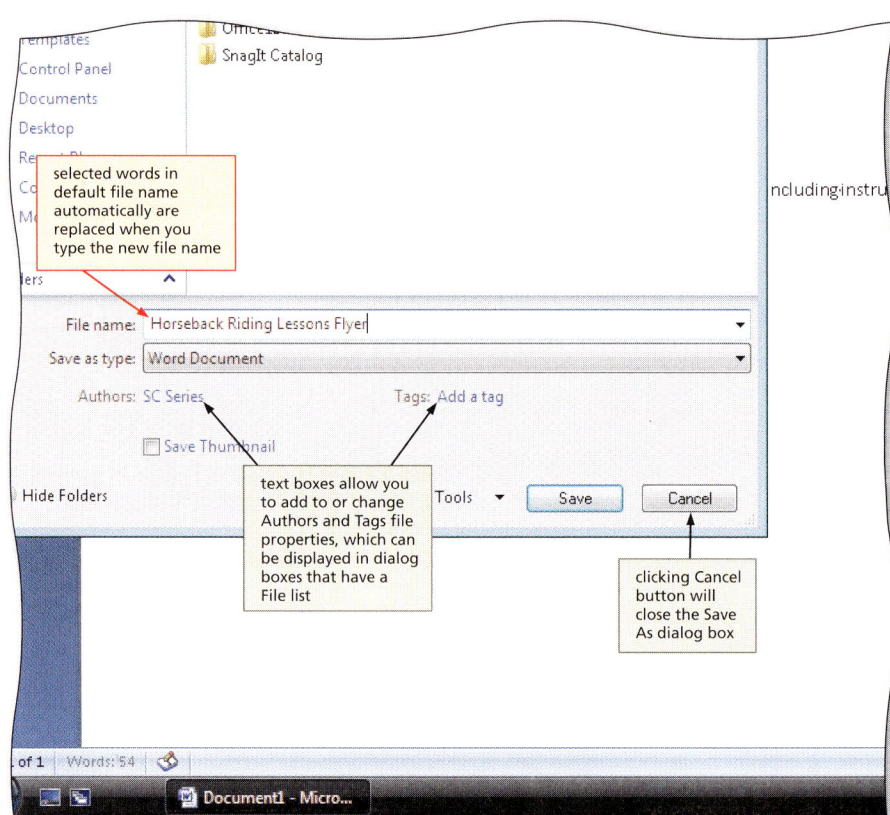

Figure 1–26

- If Computer is not displayed in the Favorite Links section, drag the top or bottom edge of the Save As dialog box until Computer is displayed.

- Click Computer in the Favorite Links section to display a list of available drives (Figure 1–27).

- If necessary, scroll until UDISK 2.0 (E:) appears in the list of available drives.

Q&A Why is my list of drives arranged and named differently?

The size of the Save As dialog box and your computer's configuration determine how the list is displayed and how the drives are named.

Q&A How do I save the file if I am not using a USB flash drive?

Use the same process, but select your desired save location in the Favorite Links section.

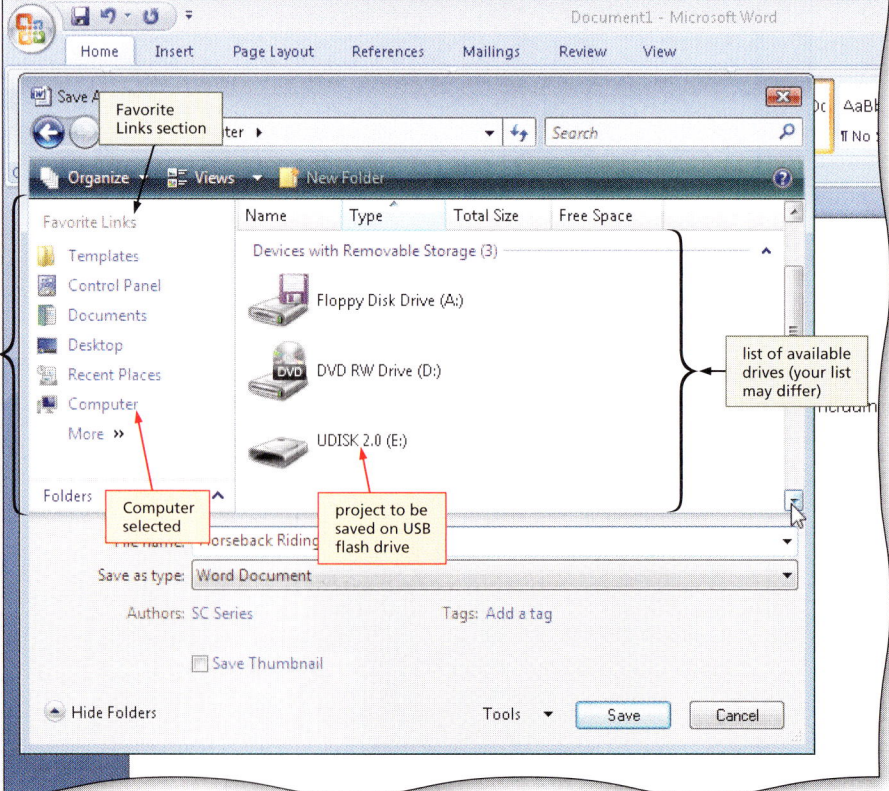

Figure 1–27

Creating and Editing a Word Document   **Word Chapter 1**   **WD** 21

4

- Double-click UDISK 2.0 (E:) in the Computer list to select the USB flash drive, Drive E in this case, as the new save location (Figure 1–28).

Q&A What if my USB flash drive has a different name or letter?

It is very likely that your USB flash drive will have a different name and drive letter and be connected to a different port. Verify the device in your Computer list is correct.

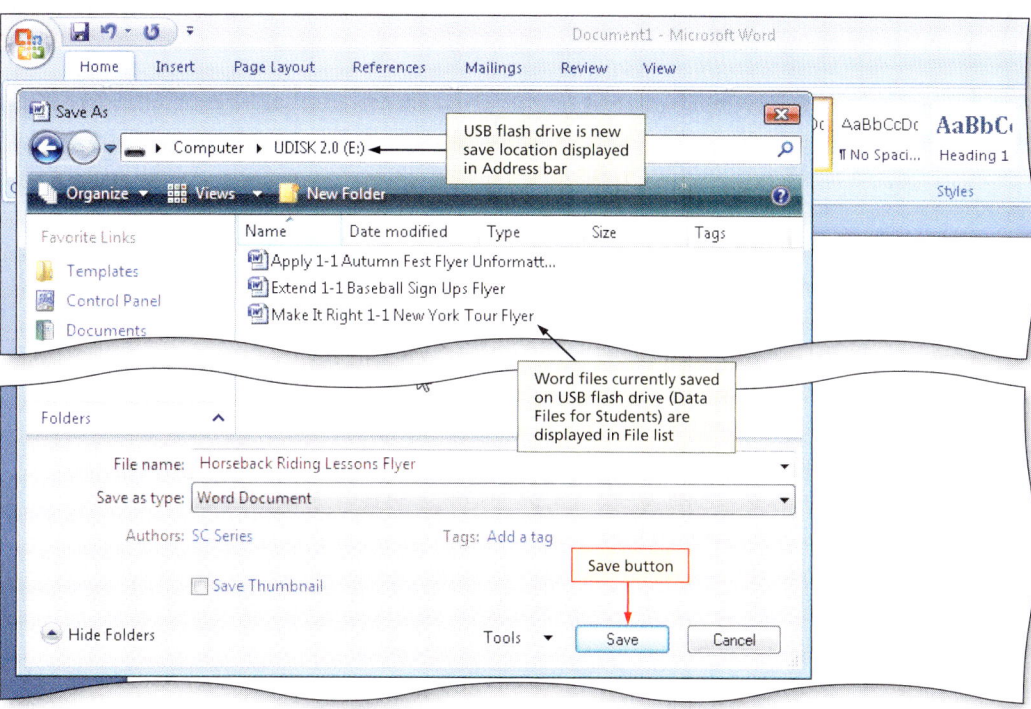

Figure 1–28

5

- Click the Save button in the Save As dialog box to save the document on the USB flash drive with the file name, Horseback Riding Lessons Flyer (Figure 1–29).

Q&A How do I know that the project is saved?

While Word is saving your file, it briefly displays a message on the status bar indicating the amount of the file saved. In addition, your USB drive may have a light that flashes during the save process.

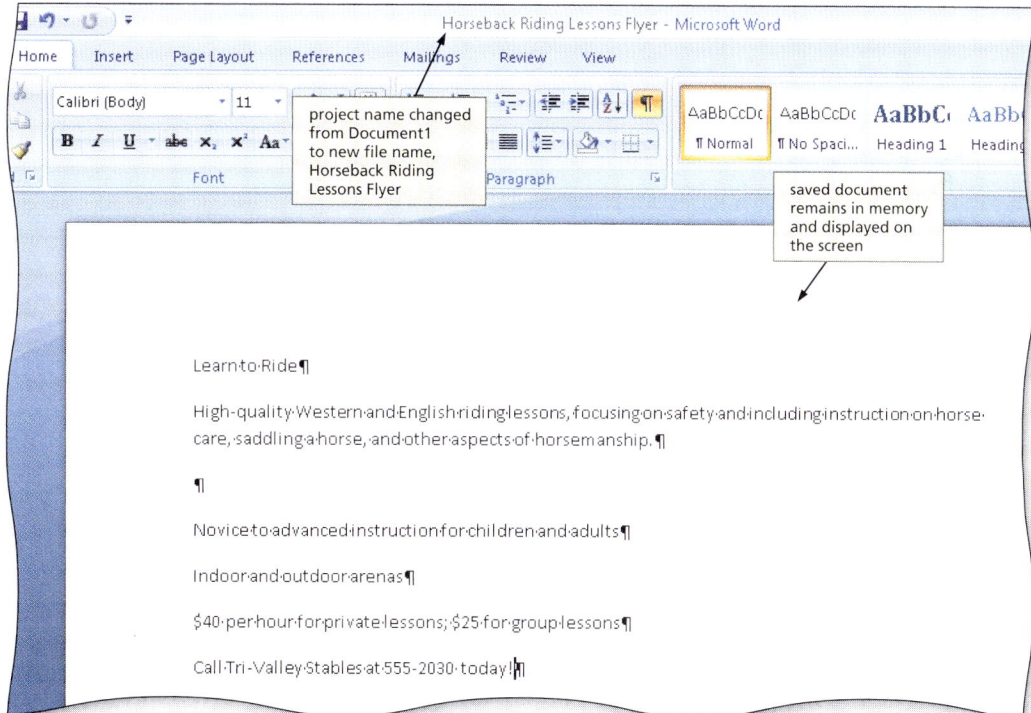

Figure 1–29

Other Ways	
1. Click Office Button, click Save, type file name, click Computer, select drive or folder, click Save button	2. Press CTRL+S or press SHIFT+F12, type file name, click Computer, select drive or folder, click Save button

Formatting Paragraphs and Characters in a Document

With the text for the flyer entered, the next step is to format its paragraphs and characters. Paragraphs encompass the text from the first character in a paragraph up to and including a paragraph mark (¶). **Paragraph formatting** is the process of changing the appearance of a paragraph. For example, you can center or indent a paragraph. Characters include letters, numbers, punctuation marks, and symbols. **Character formatting** is the process of changing the way characters appear on the screen and in print. You use character formatting to emphasize certain words and improve readability of a document. For example, you can italicize or underline characters. Often, you apply both paragraph and character formatting to the same text. For example, you may center a paragraph (paragraph formatting) and bold some of the characters in a paragraph (character formatting).

Although you can format paragraphs and characters before you type, many Word users enter text first and then format the existing text. Figure 1–30a shows the flyer in this chapter before formatting its paragraphs and characters. Figure 1–30b shows the flyer after formatting. As you can see from the two figures, a document that is formatted is easier to read and looks more professional. The following pages discuss how to format the flyer so that it looks like Figure 1–30b.

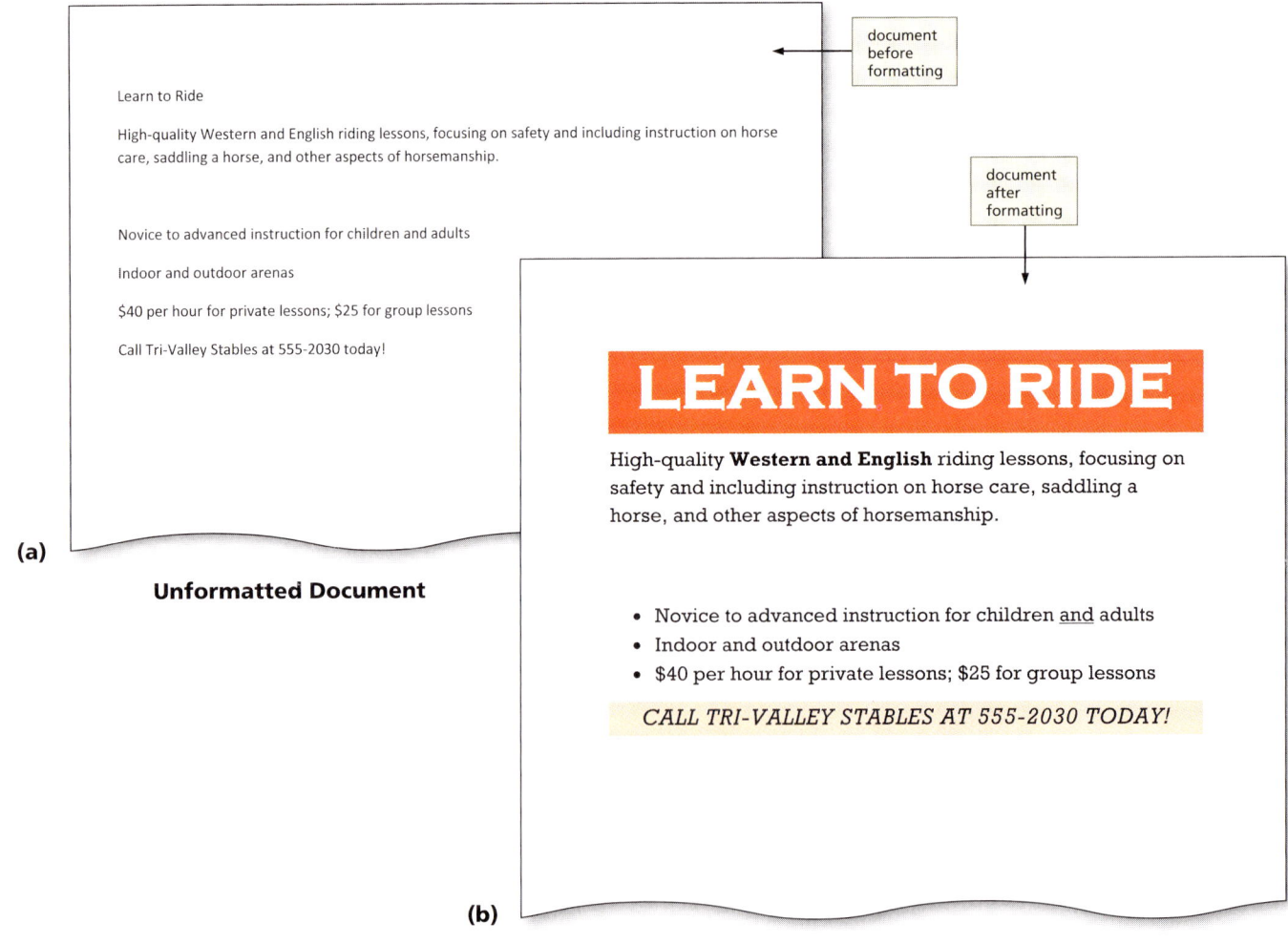

Figure 1–30

Fonts, Font Sizes, Styles, and Themes

Characters that appear on the screen are a specific shape and size. The **font**, or typeface, defines the appearance and shape of the letters, numbers, and special characters. In Word, the default font usually is Calibri (Figure 1–31 on the next page). You can leave characters in the default font or change them to a different font. **Font size** specifies the size of the characters and is determined by a measurement system called points. A single point is about 1/72 of one inch in height. The default font size in Word typically is 11 (Figure 1–31). A character with a font size of 11 is about 11/72 or a little less than 1/6 of one inch in height. You can increase or decrease the font size of characters in a document.

When you create a document, Word formats the text using a particular style. A **style** is a named group of formatting characteristics, including font and font size. The default style in Word is called the **Normal style**, which most likely uses 11-point Calibri font. If you do not specify a style for text you type, Word applies the Normal style to the text. In addition to the Normal style, Word has many other built-in, or predefined, styles that you can use to format text. You also can create your own styles. Styles make it easy to apply many formats at once to text. After you apply a style to text, you easily can modify the text to include additional formats. You also can modify the style.

To assist you with coordinating colors and fonts and other formats, Word uses document themes. A document **theme** is a set of unified formats for fonts, colors, and graphics. The default theme fonts are Cambria for headings and Calibri for body text (Figure 1–31). Word includes a variety of document themes. By changing the document theme, you quickly give your document a new look. You also can define your own document themes.

Plan Ahead

Identify how to format various elements of the text.
By formatting the characters and paragraphs in a document, you can improve its overall appearance. In a flyer, consider the following formatting suggestions.

- **Increase the font size of characters.** Flyers usually are posted on a bulletin board or in a window. Thus, the font size should be as large as possible so that passersby easily can read the flyer. To give the headline more impact, its font size should be larger than the font size of the text in the body copy. If possible, make the font size of the signature line larger than the body copy but smaller than the headline.

- **Change the font of characters**. Use fonts that are easy to read. Try to use only two different fonts in a flyer, for example, one for the headline and the other for all other text. Too many fonts can make the flyer visually confusing.

- **Change paragraph alignment**. The default alignment for paragraphs in a document is **left-aligned**, that is, flush at the left margin of the document with uneven right edges. Consider changing the alignment of some of the paragraphs to add interest and variety to the flyer.

- **Highlight key paragraphs with bullets**. A **bullet** is a dot or other symbol positioned at the beginning of a paragraph. Use bullets to highlight important paragraphs in a flyer.

- **Emphasize important words**. To call attention to certain words or lines, you can underline them, italicize them, or bold them. Use these formats sparingly, however, because overuse will minimize their effect and make the flyer look too busy.

- **Use color.** Use colors that complement each other and convey the meaning of the flyer. Vary colors in terms of hue and brightness. Headline colors, for example, can be bold and bright. Signature lines should stand out more than body copy but less than headlines. Keep in mind that too many colors can detract from the flyer and make it difficult to read.

To Apply Styles

In the flyer, you want the headline and the signature line to be emphasized more than the other text. Word provides heading styles designed to emphasize this type of text. The first step in formatting the flyer is to apply the Heading 1 style to the headline and the Heading 2 style to the signature line. The default Heading 1 style is a 14-point Cambria bold font. The default Heading 2 style is a 13-point Cambria bold font. The default theme color scheme uses shades of blue for headings.

To apply a style to a paragraph, you first position the insertion point in the paragraph and then apply the style. The following steps apply heading styles to paragraphs.

- Press CTRL+HOME (that is, press and hold down the CTRL key, press the HOME key, and then release both keys) to position the insertion point at the top of the document (Figure 1–31).

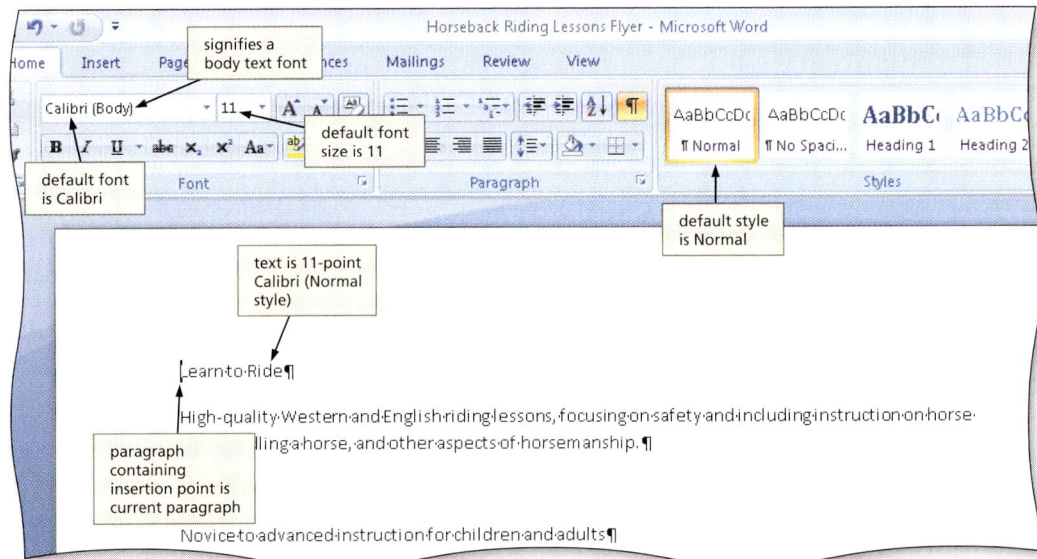

Figure 1–31

- Point to Heading 1 in the Styles gallery to display a live preview in the document of the Heading 1 style (Figure 1–32).

Q&A What happens if I move the mouse pointer?

If you move the mouse pointer away from the gallery, the text containing the insertion point returns to the Normal style.

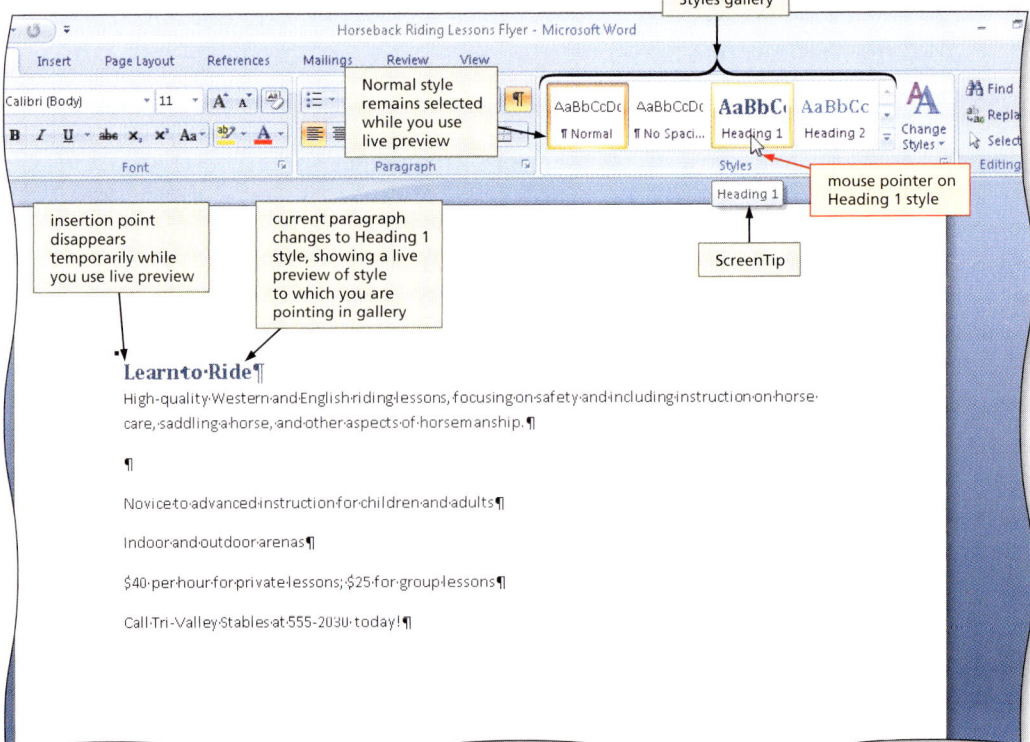

Figure 1–32

❸
- Click Heading 1 in the Styles gallery to apply the Heading 1 style to the headline (Figure 1–33).

Q&A Why did a square appear on the screen near the left edge of the headline?

The square is a nonprinting character, like the paragraph mark, that indicates text to its right has a special paragraph format applied to it.

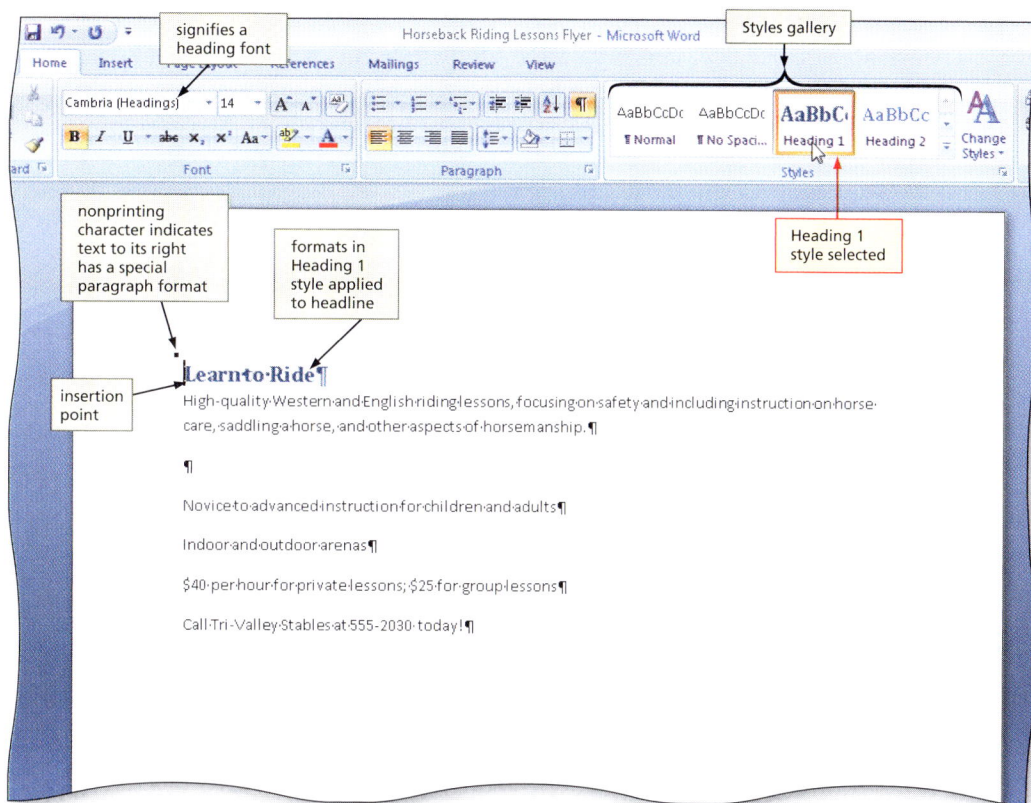

Figure 1–33

❹
- Press CTRL+END (that is, press and hold down the CTRL key, press the END key, and then release both keys) to position the insertion point at the end of the document.

- Click Heading 2 in the Styles gallery to apply the Heading 2 style to the signature line (Figure 1–34).

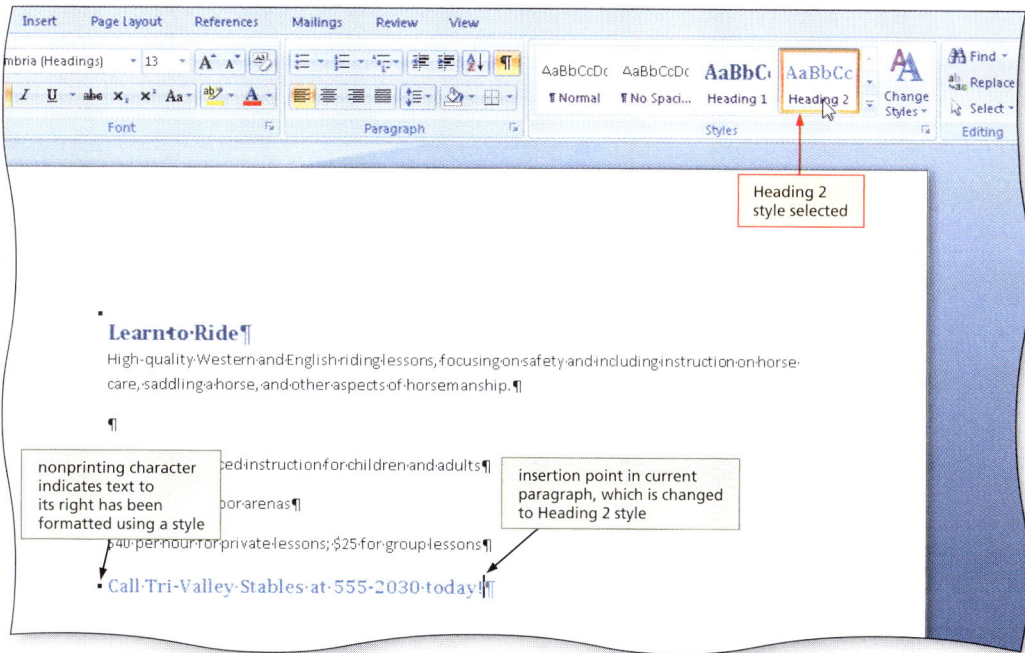

Figure 1–34

Other Ways	
1. Click Styles Dialog Box Launcher, click desired style in Styles task pane	2. Press CTRL+SHIFT+S, click Style Name box arrow in Apply Styles task pane, click desired style in list

To Center a Paragraph

The headline in the flyer currently is left-aligned (Figure 1–35). You want the headline to be **centered**, that is, positioned horizontally between the left and right margins on the page. Thus, you will center the paragraph containing the headline. Recall that Word considers a single short line of text, such as the three-word headline, a paragraph. The following steps center a paragraph.

- Click somewhere in the paragraph to be centered (in this case, the headline) to position the insertion point in the paragraph to be formatted (Figure 1–35).

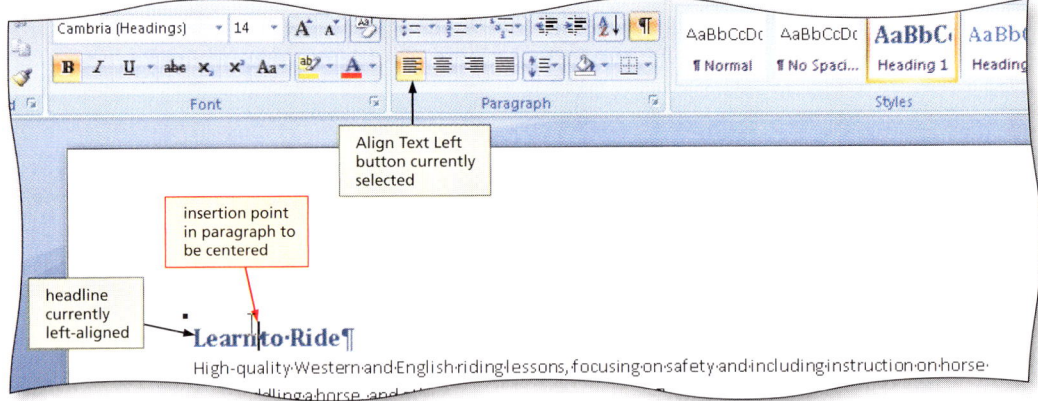

Figure 1–35

- Click the Center button on the Home tab to center the headline (Figure 1–36).

Q&A

What if I want to return the paragraph to left-aligned?

Click the Align Text Left button on the Home tab.

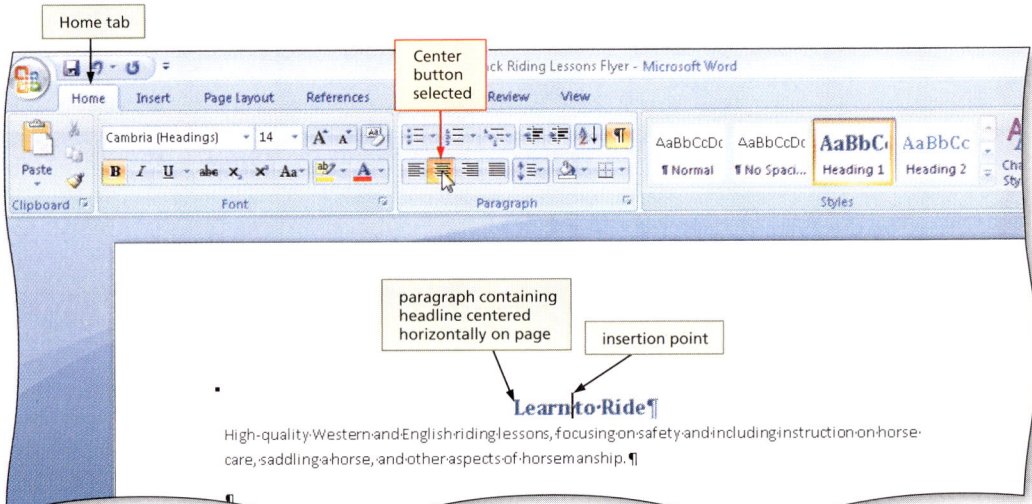

Figure 1–36

Other Ways

1. Right-click paragraph, click Center button on Mini toolbar
2. Right-click paragraph, click Paragraph on shortcut menu, click Indents and Spacing tab, click Alignment box arrow, click Centered, click OK button
3. Click Paragraph Dialog Box Launcher, click Indents and Spacing tab, click Alignment box arrow, click Centered, click OK button
4. Press CTRL+E

Formatting Single Versus Multiple Paragraphs and Characters

As shown in the previous pages, to format a single paragraph, simply move the insertion point in the paragraph and then format the paragraph. Likewise, to format a single word, position the insertion point in the word and then format the word.

To format multiple paragraphs or words, however, you first must select the paragraphs or words you want to format and then format the selection. If your screen normally displays dark letters on a light background, which is the default setting in Word, then selected text displays light letters on a dark background.

To Select a Line

The font size of characters in the Heading 1 style, 14 point, is too small for passersby to read in the headline of the flyer. To increase the font size of the characters in the headline, you must first select the line of text containing the headline. The following steps select a line.

- Move the mouse pointer to the left of the line to be selected (in this case, the headline) until the mouse pointer changes to a right-pointing block arrow (Figure 1–37).

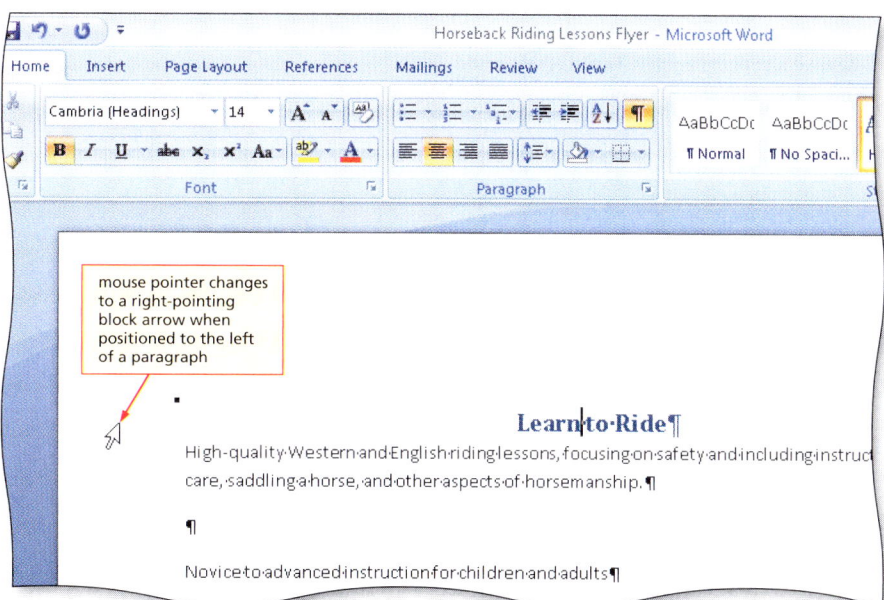

Figure 1–37

- While the mouse pointer is a right-pointing block arrow, click the mouse to select the entire line to the right of the mouse pointer (Figure 1–38).

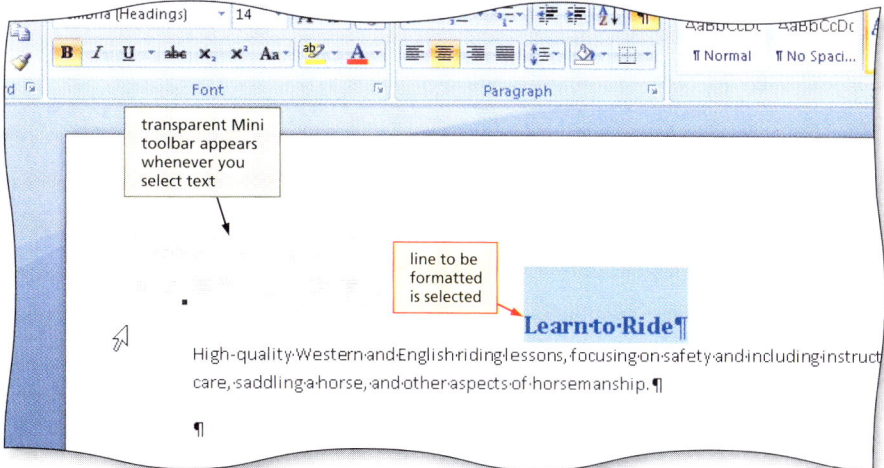

Figure 1–38

Other Ways	
1. Drag mouse through line	2. With insertion point at beginning of desired line, press SHIFT+DOWN ARROW

To Change the Font Size of Selected Text

The next step is to increase the font size of the characters in the selected headline. You would like the headline to be as large as possible and still fit on a single line, which in this case is 48 point. The following steps increase the font size of the headline from 14 to 48 point.

- With the text selected, click the Font Size box arrow on the Home tab to display the Font Size gallery (Figure 1–39).

Q&A Why are the font sizes in my Font Size gallery different from those in Figure 1–39?

Font sizes may vary depending on the current font and your printer driver.

Q&A What happened to the Mini toolbar?

The Mini toolbar disappears if you do not use it. These steps use the Font Size box arrow on the Home tab instead of the Font Size box arrow on the Mini toolbar. If a command exists both on the currently displayed tab and the Mini toolbar, this book uses the command on the tab. When the command is not on the currently displayed tab, the Mini toolbar is used.

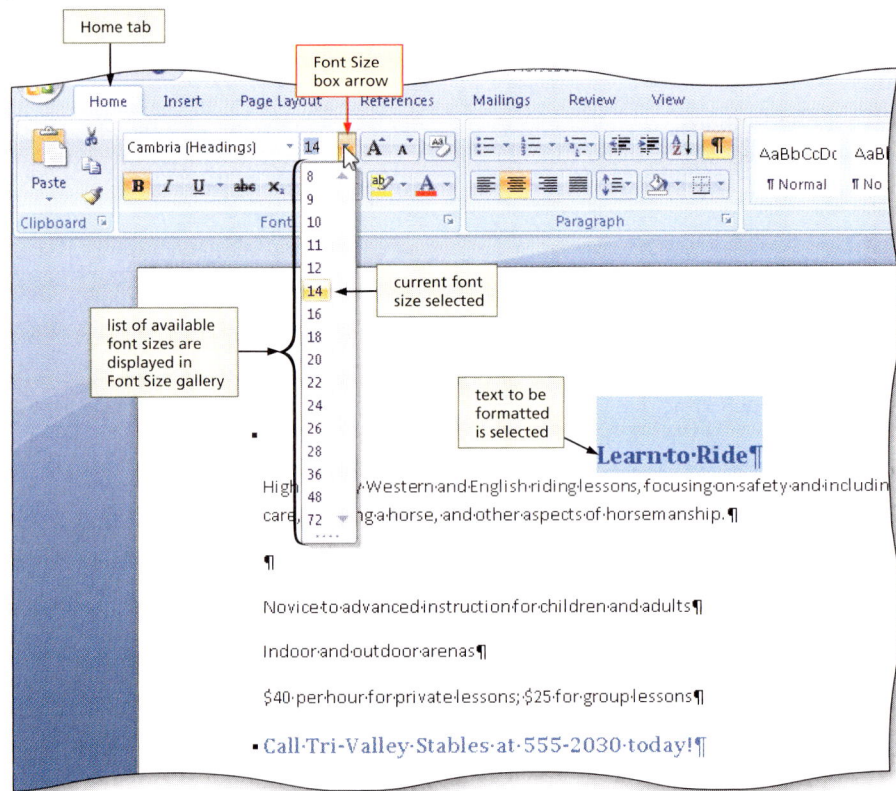

Figure 1–39

- Point to 48 in the Font Size gallery to display a live preview of the headline at 48 point (Figure 1–40).

Experiment

- Point to various font sizes in the Font Size gallery and watch the font size of the headline change in the document window.

- Click 48 in the Font Size gallery to increase the font size of the selected text to 48.

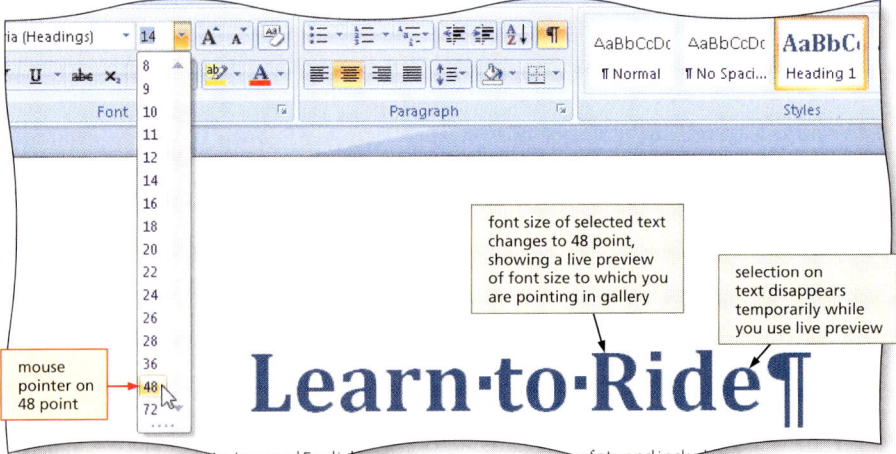

Figure 1–40

Other Ways

1. Click Font Size box arrow on Mini toolbar, click desired font size in Font Size gallery
2. Right-click selected text, click Font on shortcut menu, click Font tab, select desired font size in Size list, click OK button
3. Click Font Dialog Box Launcher, click Font tab, select desired font size in Size list, click OK button
4. Press CTRL+SHIFT+P, click Font tab, select desired font size in Size list, click OK button

To Change the Font of Selected Text

As mentioned earlier, the default Heading 1 style uses the font called Cambria. Word, however, provides many other fonts to add variety to your documents. To draw more attention to the headline, you change its font so it differs from the font of other text in the flyer. The following steps change the font from Cambria to Copperplate Gothic Bold.

- With the text selected, click the Font box arrow on the Home tab to display the Font gallery (Figure 1–41).

Q&A
Will the fonts in my Font gallery be the same as those in Figure 1–41?

Your list of available fonts may differ, depending on the type of printer you are using.

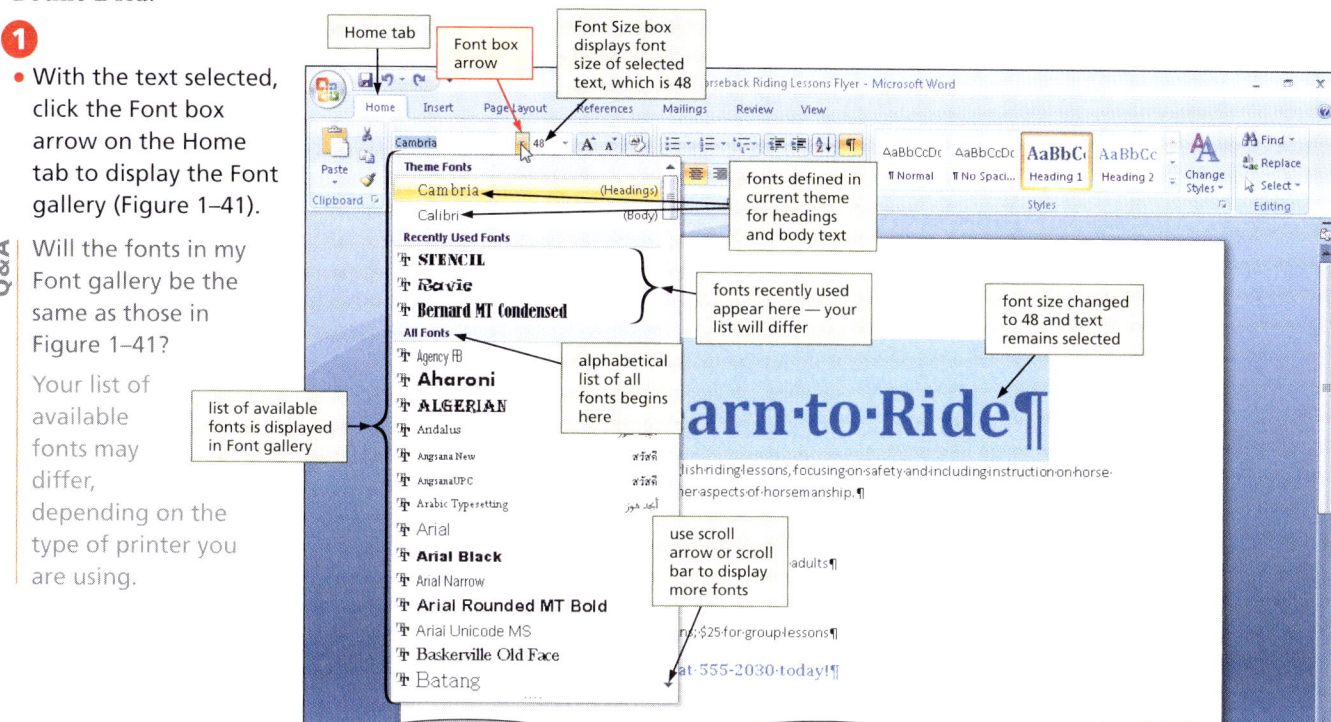

Figure 1–41

- Scroll through the Font gallery, if necessary, and then point to Copperplate Gothic Bold (or a similar font) to display a live preview of the headline in Copperplate Gothic Bold font (Figure 1–42).

Experiment

- Point to various fonts in the Font gallery and watch the font of the headline change in the document window.

- Click Copperplate Gothic Bold (or a similar font) to change the font of the selected text to Copperplate Gothic Bold.

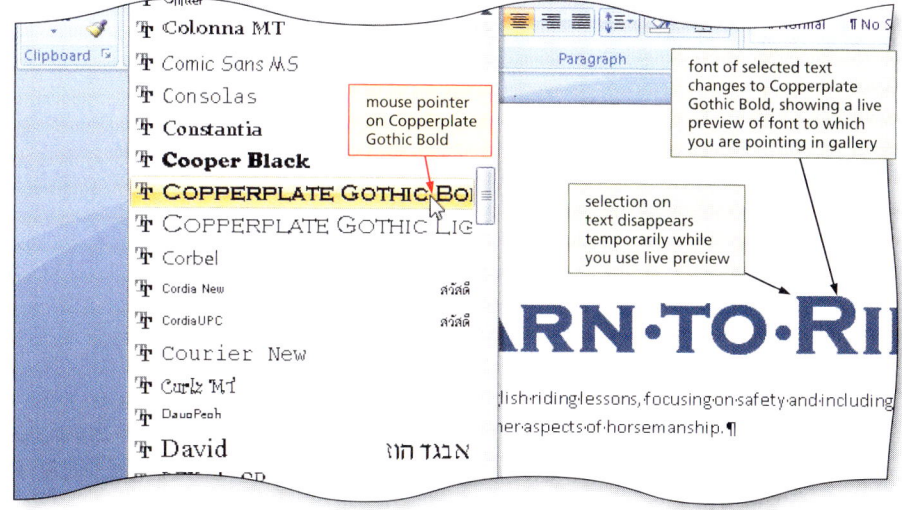

Figure 1–42

Other Ways

1. Click Font box arrow on Mini toolbar, click desired font in Font gallery
2. Right-click selected text, click Font on shortcut menu, click Font tab, select desired font in Font list, click OK button
3. Click Font Dialog Box Launcher, click Font tab, select desired font in Font list, click OK button
4. Press CTRL+SHIFT+F, click Font tab, select desired font in the Font list, click OK button

To Select Multiple Paragraphs

The next formatting step in creating the flyer is to increase the font size of the characters between the headline and the signature line so that they are easier to read from a distance. To change the font size of the characters in multiple lines, you first must select all the lines to be formatted. The following steps select multiple lines.

- Move the mouse pointer to the left of the first paragraph to be selected until the mouse pointer changes to a right-pointing block arrow (Figure 1–43).

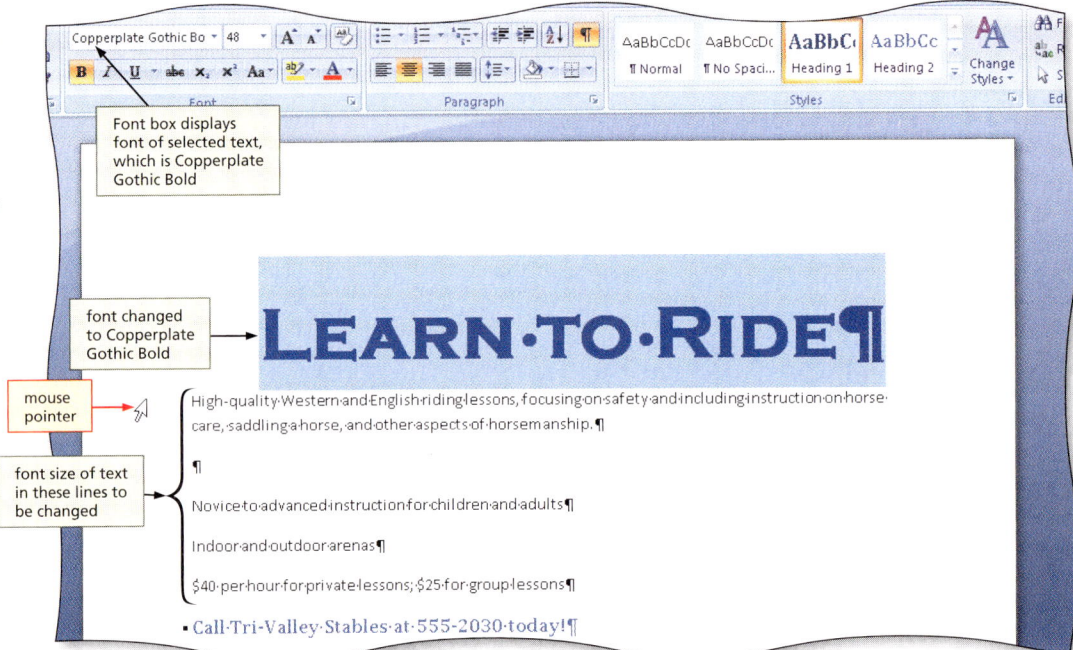

Figure 1–43

- Drag downward to select all lines that will be formatted (Figure 1–44).

Q&A How do I *drag* the mouse?

Dragging is the process of holding down the mouse button while moving the mouse and then releasing the mouse button.

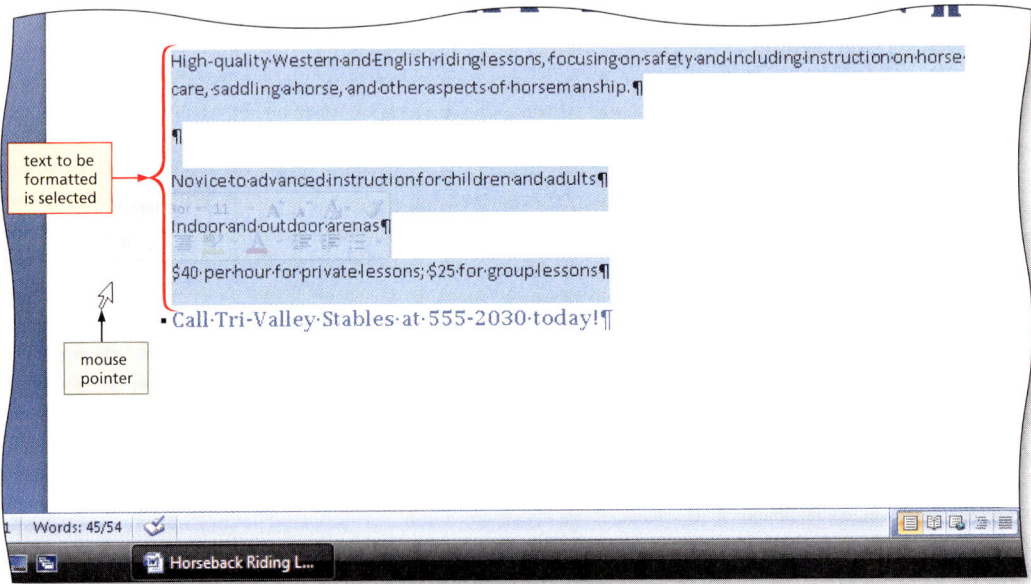

Figure 1–44

Other Ways

1. With insertion point at beginning of desired line, press SHIFT+DOWN ARROW repeatedly until all lines are selected

To Change the Font Size of Selected Text

The characters between the headline and the signature line in the flyer currently are 11 point. To make them easier to read from a distance, this flyer uses 16 point for these characters. The following steps change the font size of the selected text.

1. With the text selected, click the Font Size box arrow on the Home tab to display the Font Size gallery.

2. Click 16 in the Font Size gallery to increase the font size of the selected text to 16.

To Format a Line

In the flyer, the signature line is to be centered to match the paragraph alignment of the headline. Also, its text should have a font size larger than the rest of the body copy. The following steps center the line and increase its font size to 18.

1. Click somewhere in the paragraph to be centered (in this case, the signature line) to position the insertion point in the paragraph to be formatted.

2. Click the Center button on the Home tab to center the signature line.

3. Move the mouse pointer to the left of the line to be selected (in this case, the signature line) until the mouse pointer changes to a right-pointing block arrow and then click to select the line.

4. With the signature line selected, click the Font Size box arrow on the Home tab and then click 18 in the Font Size gallery to increase the font size of the selected text to 18 (Figure 1–45).

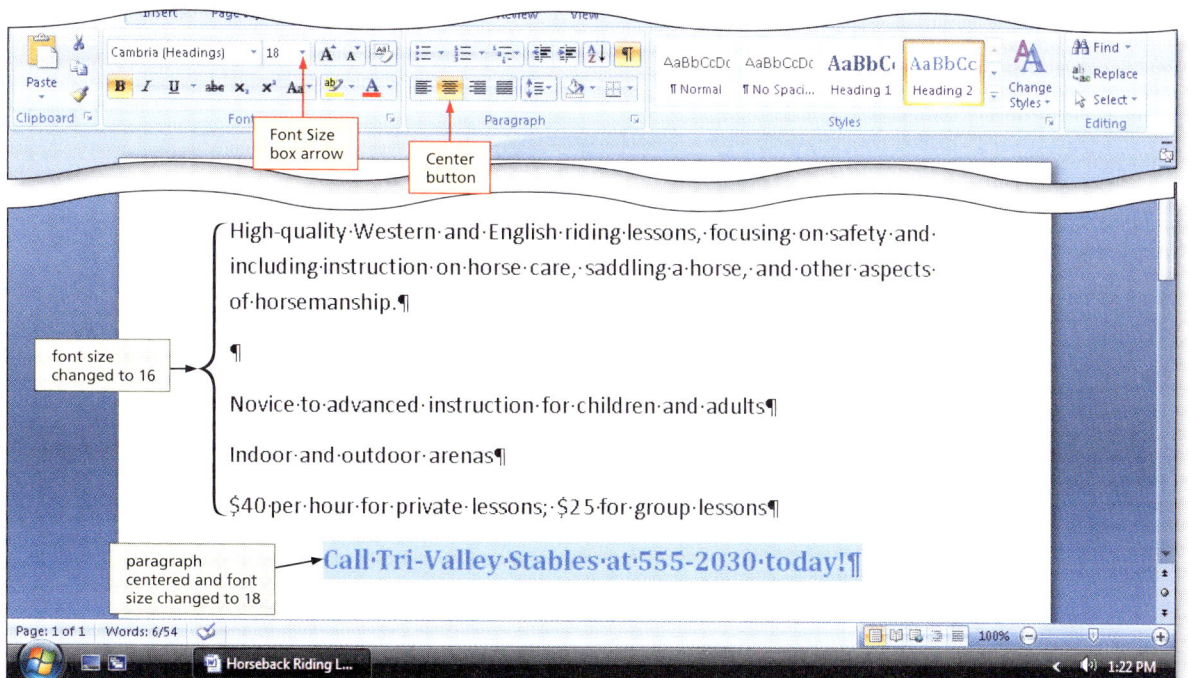

Figure 1–45

To Bullet a List of Paragraphs

The next step is to format the three important points above the signature line in the flyer as a bulleted list. A **bulleted list** is a series of paragraphs, each beginning with a bullet character. The three lines each end with a paragraph mark because you pressed the ENTER key at the end of each line. Thus, these three lines actually are three separate paragraphs.

To format a list of paragraphs with bullets, you first must select all the lines in the paragraphs. The following steps bullet a list of paragraphs.

- Move the mouse pointer to the left of the first paragraph to be selected until the mouse pointer changes to a right-pointing block arrow.

- Drag downward until all paragraphs (lines) that will be formatted with a bullet character are selected.

- Click the Bullets button on the Home tab to place a bullet character at the beginning of each selected paragraph (Figure 1–46).

Q&A How do I remove bullets from a list or paragraph?

Select the list or paragraph and click the Bullets button again.

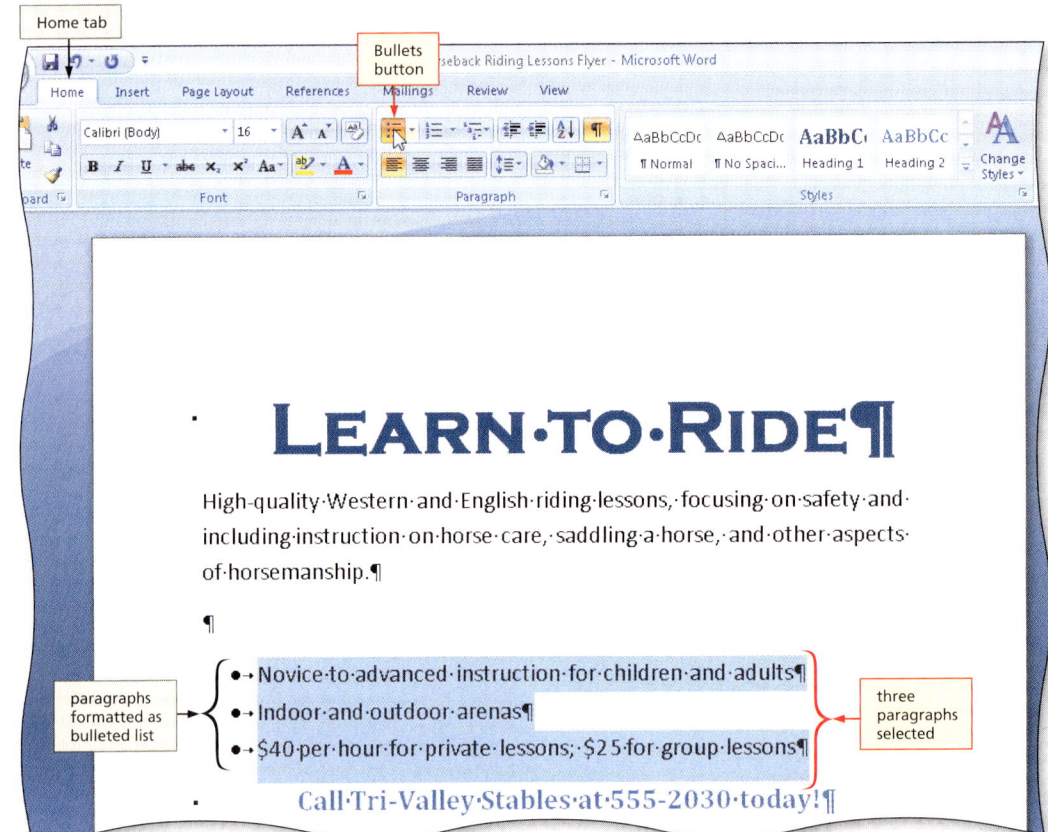

Figure 1–46

Other Ways

1. Right-click selected paragraphs, click Bullets button on Mini toolbar
2. Right-click selected paragraphs, point to Bullets on shortcut menu, click desired bullet style

To Undo and Redo an Action

Word provides a means of canceling your recent command(s) or action(s). For example, if you format text incorrectly, you can undo the format and try it again. When you point to the Undo button, Word displays the action you can undo as part of the ScreenTip.

If, after you undo an action, you decide you did not want to perform the undo, you can redo the undone action. Word does not allow you to undo or redo some actions, such as saving or printing a document. The next steps undo the bullet format just applied and then redo the bullet format.

- Click the Undo button on the Quick Access Toolbar to remove the bullets from the selected paragraphs (Figure 1–47).

- Click the Redo button on the Quick Access Toolbar to place a bullet character at the beginning of each selected paragraph again (shown in Figure 1–46).

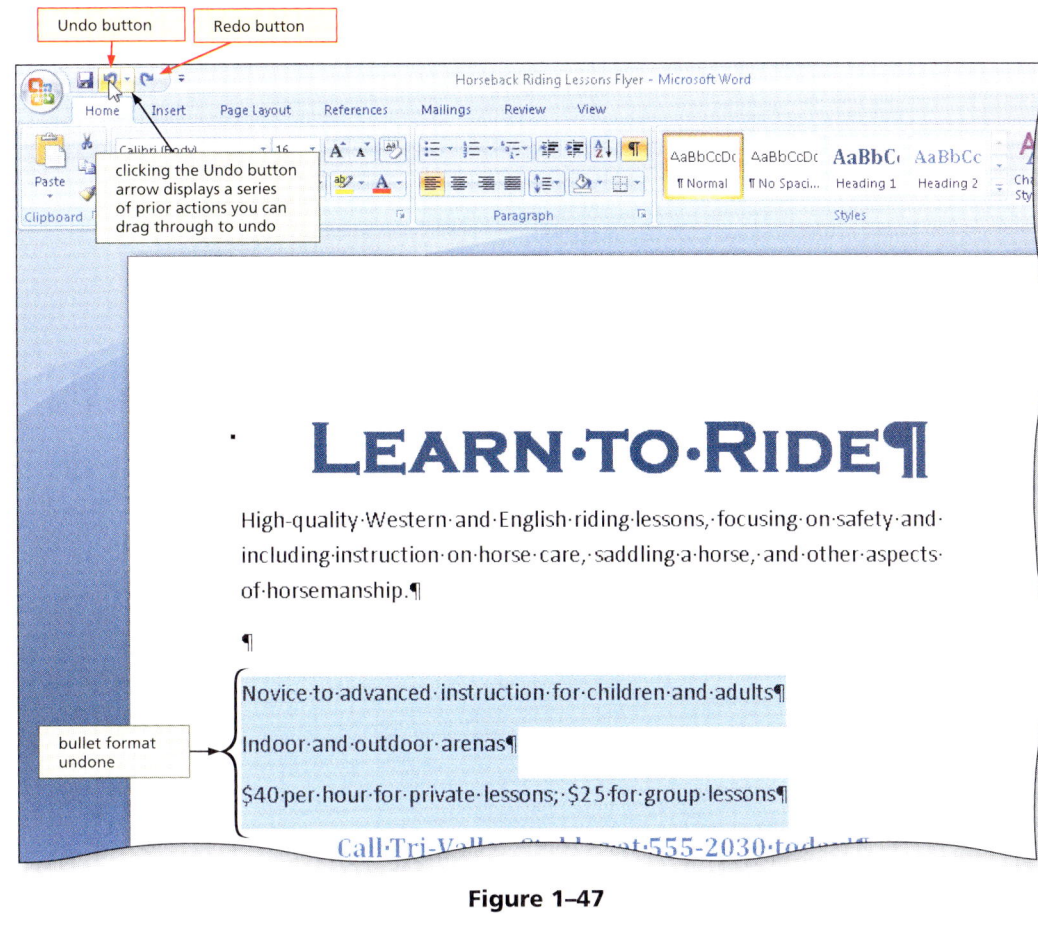

Figure 1–47

Other Ways
1. Press CTRL+Z; press CTRL+Y

To Select a Group of Words

To emphasize the types of riding lessons, Western and English, these words are bold in the flyer. To format a group of words, you first must select them. The following steps select a group of words.

- Position the mouse pointer immediately to the left of the first character of the text to be selected, in this case, the W in Western (Figure 1–48).

Q&A Why did the shape of the mouse pointer change?

The mouse pointer's shape is an I-beam when positioned in unselected text in the document window.

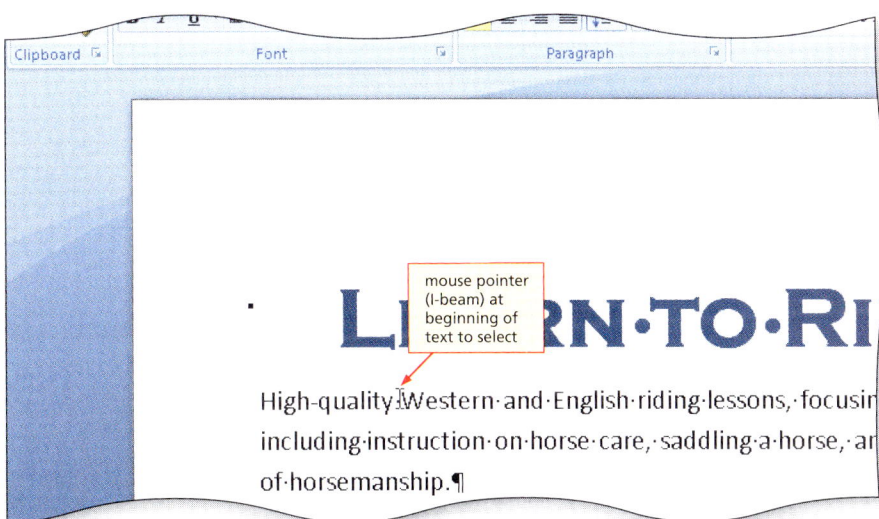

Figure 1–48

2
- Drag the mouse pointer through the last character of the text to be selected, in this case, the h in English (Figure 1–49).

Q&A Why did the mouse pointer shape change again?

When the mouse pointer is positioned in selected text, its shape is a left-pointing block arrow.

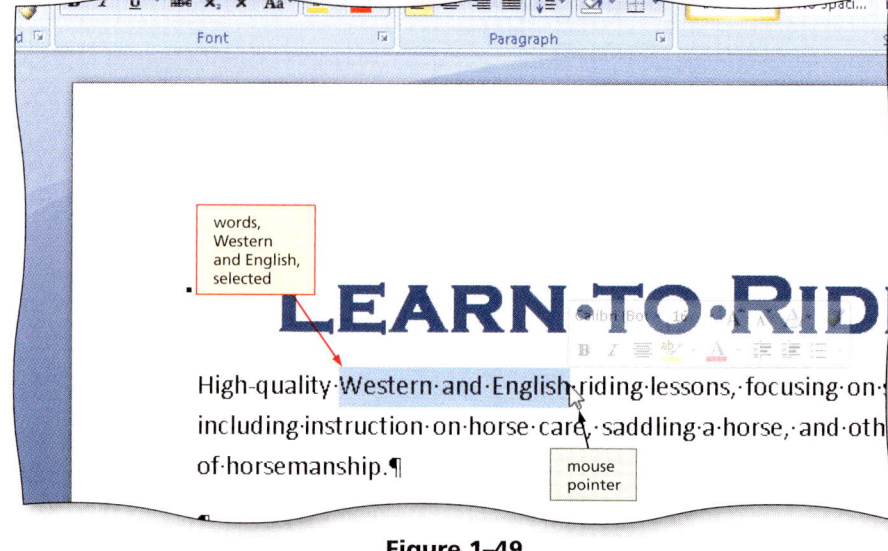

Figure 1–49

Other Ways
1. With insertion point at beginning of first word in group, press CTRL+SHIFT+RIGHT ARROW repeatedly until all words are selected

To Bold Text

Bold characters display somewhat thicker and darker than those that are not bold. The following step formats the selected words, Western and English, as bold.

- With the text selected, click the Bold button on the Home tab to format the selected text in bold (Figure 1–50).

Q&A How would I remove a bold format?

You would click the Bold button a second time, or you immediately could click the Undo button on the Quick Access Toolbar.

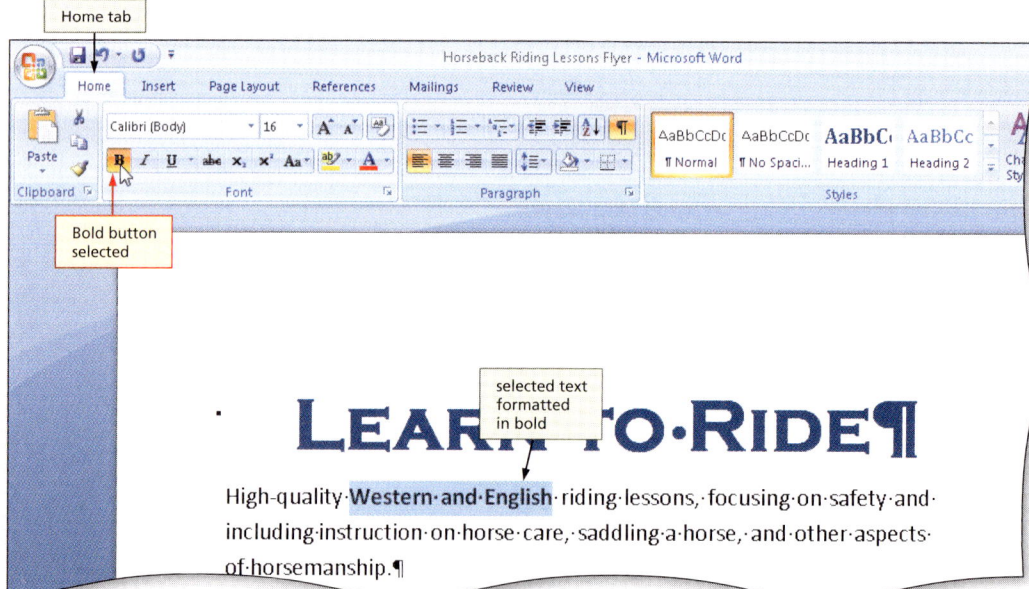

Figure 1–50

Other Ways
1. Click Bold button on Mini toolbar
2. Right-click selected text, click Font on shortcut menu, click Font tab, click Bold in Font style list, click OK button
3. Click Font Dialog Box Launcher, click Font tab, click Bold in Font style list, click OK button
4. Press CTRL+B

To Underline a Word

As with bold text, underlines are used to emphasize or draw attention to specific text. Underlined text prints with an underscore (_) below each character. In the flyer, the word, and, in the first bulleted paragraph is emphasized with an underline.

As with a single paragraph, if you want to format a single word, you do not need to select the word. Simply position the insertion point somewhere in the word and apply the desired format. The following step formats a word with an underline.

1

- Click somewhere in the word to be underlined (and, in this case).

- Click the Underline button on the Home tab to underline the word containing the insertion point (Figure 1–51).

Q&A How would I remove an underline?

You would click the Underline button a second time, or you immediately could click the Undo button on the Quick Access Toolbar.

Q&A Are other types of underlines available?

In addition to the basic solid underline shown in Figure 1–51, Word has many decorative underlines, such as double underlines, dotted underlines, and wavy underlines. You can access the decorative underlines and also change the color of an underline through the Underline gallery.

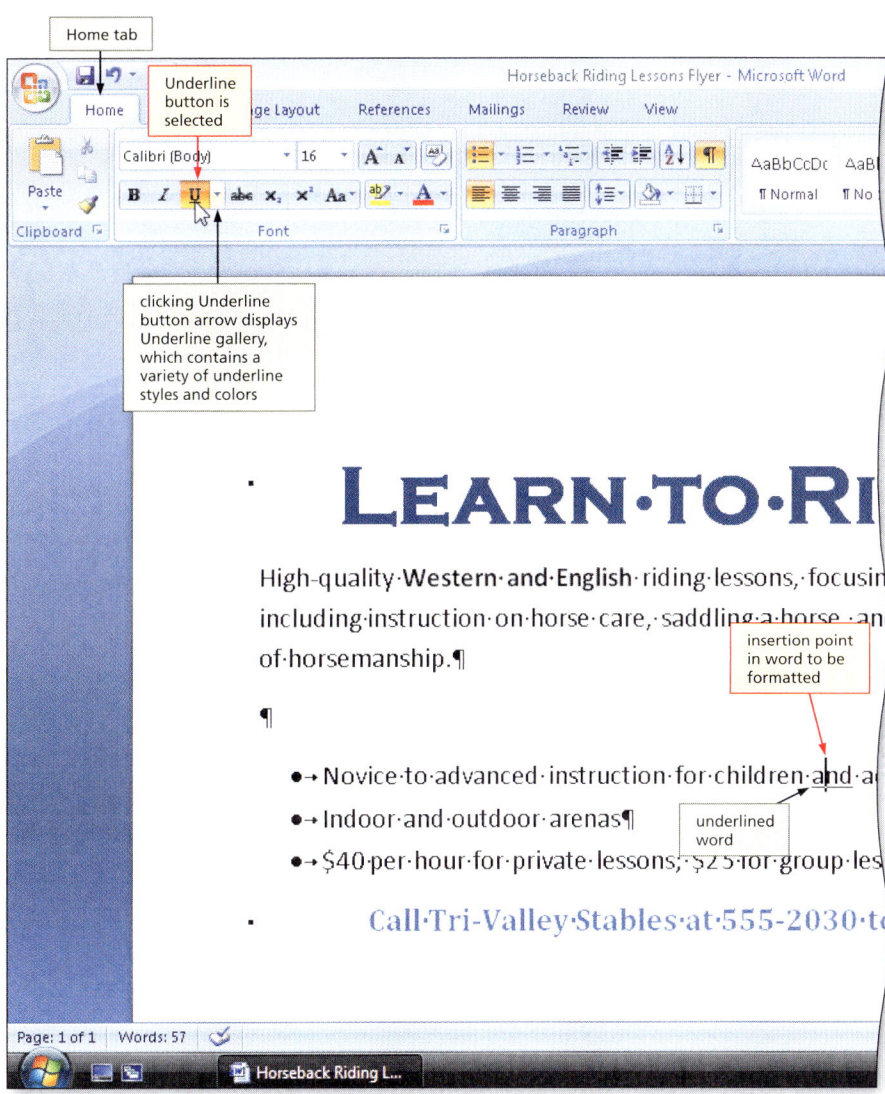

Figure 1–51

Other Ways

1. Right-click text, click Font on shortcut menu, click Font tab, click Underline style box arrow, click desired underline style, click OK button

2. Click Font Dialog Box Launcher, click Font tab, click Underline style box arrow, click desired underline style, click OK button

3. Press CTRL+U

To Italicize Text

To further emphasize the signature line, this line is italicized in the flyer. **Italicized** text has a slanted appearance. The following steps select the text and then italicize it.

- Point to the left of the line to be selected (in this case, the signature line) and click when the mouse pointer is a right-pointing block arrow.

- Click the Italic button on the Home tab to italicize the selected text.

- Click inside the selected text to remove the selection (Figure 1–52).

Q&A How would I remove an italic format?

You would click the Italic button a second time, or you immediately could click the Undo button on the Quick Access Toolbar.

Q&A How can I tell what formatting has been applied to text?

The selected buttons and boxes on the Home tab show formatting characteristics of the location of the insertion point. With the insertion point in the signature line, the Home tab shows these formats: 18-point Cambria bold italic font, centered paragraph, and Heading 2 style.

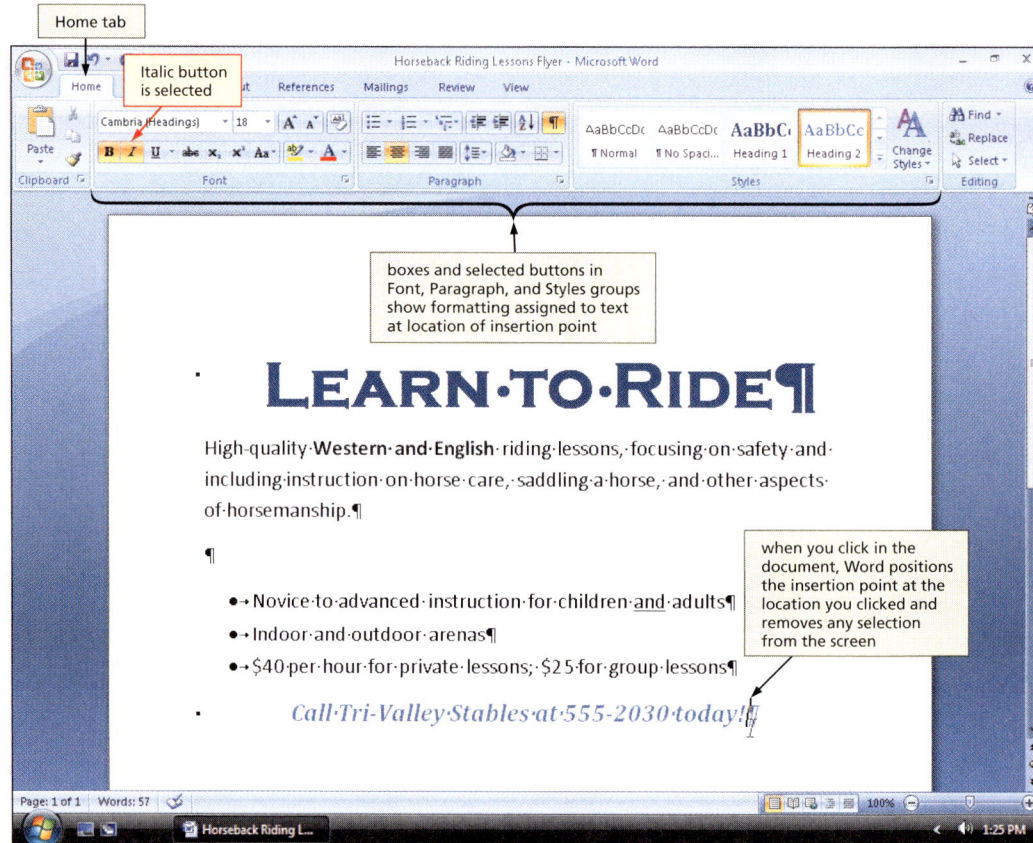

Figure 1–52

Other Ways

1. Click Italic button on Mini toolbar
2. Right-click selected text, click Font on shortcut menu, click Font tab, click Italic in Font style list, click OK button
3. Click Font Dialog Box Launcher, click Font tab, click Italic in Font style list, click OK button
4. Press CTRL+I

Document Formats

One advantage of using styles to format text is that you easily can change the formats of styles and themes in your document to give it a different or new look. Recall that a style is a named group of formatting characteristics and a theme is a set of unified formats for fonts, colors, and graphics. In Word, you can change the style set, theme colors, and theme fonts.

- The predefined styles in the Styles gallery, such as Heading 1 and Heading 2, each known as a **Quick Style**, are part of a style set. A style set consists of a group of frequently used styles formatted so they look pleasing when used together. When you change the style set, formats assigned to each Quick Style also change.

- Each **color scheme** in a theme identifies 12 complementary colors for text, background, accents, and links in a document. With more than 20 predefined color schemes, Word provides a simple way to select colors that work well together.
- Each theme has a **font set** that defines formats for two fonts: one for headings and another for body text. In Word, you can select from more than 20 predefined coordinated font sets to give the document's text a new look.

> **Plan Ahead**
>
> **Use color.**
> When choosing color, associate the meaning of color to your message:
> - Red expresses danger, power, or energy, and often is associated with sports or physical exertion.
> - Brown represents simplicity, honesty, and dependability.
> - Orange denotes success, victory, creativity, and enthusiasm.
> - Yellow suggests sunshine, happiness, hope, liveliness, and intelligence.
> - Green symbolizes growth, healthiness, harmony, blooming, and healing, and often is associated with safety or money.
> - Blue indicates integrity, trust, importance, confidence, and stability.
> - Purple represents wealth, power, comfort, extravagance, magic, mystery, and spirituality.
> - White stands for purity, goodness, cleanliness, precision, and perfection.
> - Black suggests authority, strength, elegance, power, and prestige.
> - Gray conveys neutrality and thus often is found in backgrounds and other effects.

To Change the Style Set

To symbolize perfection and precision in the flyer, the characters in the headline are white. The style set, called Modern, formats Heading 1 characters in white. It also formats the Heading 1 and Heading 2 styles in all capital letters and places a background color around the paragraphs, which further emphasize the headline and signature line in the flyer. Thus, you will change the style set from Default to Modern. The following steps change a style set.

- Click the Change Styles button on the Home tab to display the Change Styles menu (Figure 1–53).

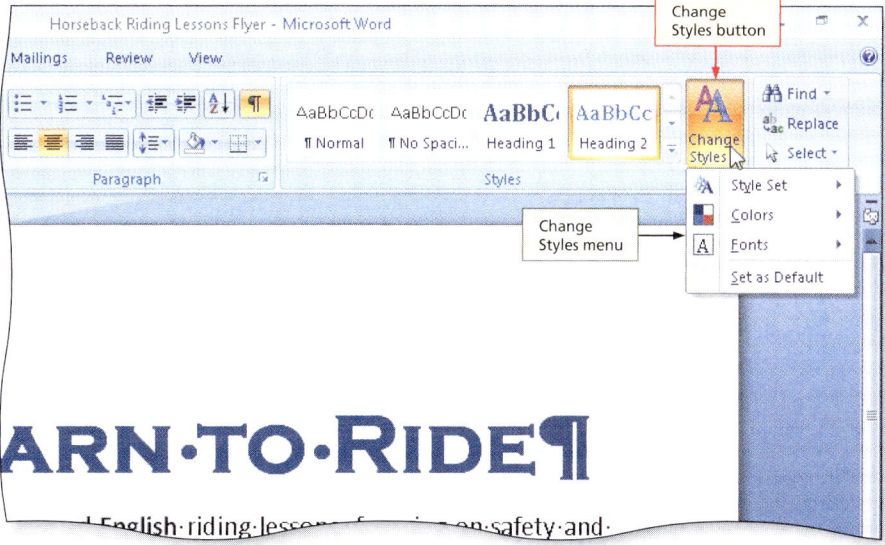

Figure 1–53

2
- Point to Style Set on the Change Styles menu to display the Style Set gallery.
- Point to Modern in the Style Set gallery to display a live preview of the formats associated with the Modern style set (Figure 1–54).

 Experiment

- Point to various style sets in the Style Set gallery and watch the formats of the styled text change in the document window.

3
- Click Modern in the Style Set gallery to change the document style set to Modern.

Q&A What if I want to return to the original style set?

You would click the Change Styles button, click Style Set on the Change Styles menu, and then click Default in the Style Set gallery, or you could click the Undo button on the Quick Access Toolbar.

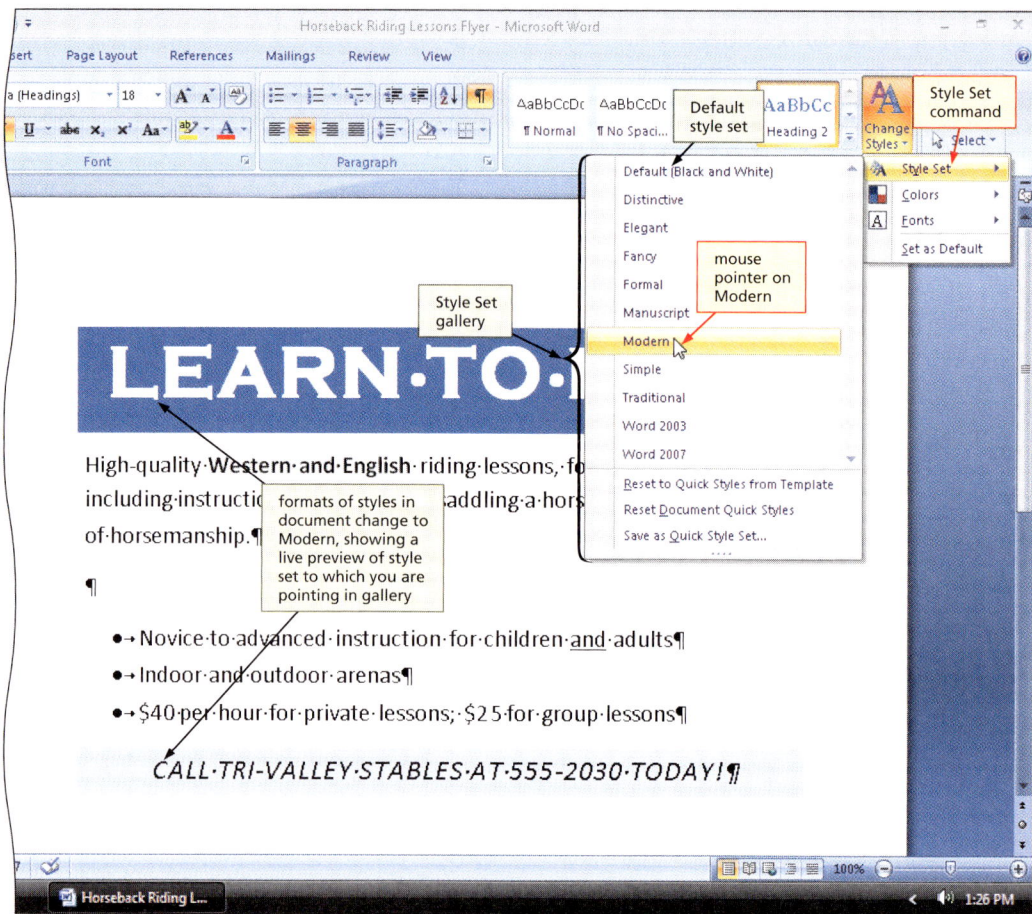

Figure 1–54

BTW

Style Formats
To see the formats assigned to a particular style in a document, click the Styles Dialog Box Launcher on the Home tab and then click the Style Inspector button in the Styles task pane. Position the insertion point in the style and then point to the Paragraph formatting or Text level formatting areas in the Style Inspector task pane to display an Enhanced ScreenTip describing formats assigned to the location of the insertion point. You also can click the Reveal Formatting button in the Style Inspector to display the Reveal Formatting task pane.

To Change Theme Colors

To suggest enthusiasm, success, and honesty, the background colors around the headline and signature line paragraphs in the flyer use shades of orange and brown. In Word, the color scheme called Aspect uses these colors. Thus, you will change the color scheme to Aspect. The following steps change theme colors.

1

- Click the Change Styles button on the Home tab to display the Change Styles menu.

- Point to Colors on the Change Styles menu to display the Colors gallery.

- Point to Aspect in the Colors gallery to display a live preview of the Aspect color scheme (Figure 1–55).

 Experiment

- Point to various color schemes in the Colors gallery and watch the paragraph background colors change in the document window.

2

- Click Aspect in the Colors gallery to change the document theme colors to Aspect.

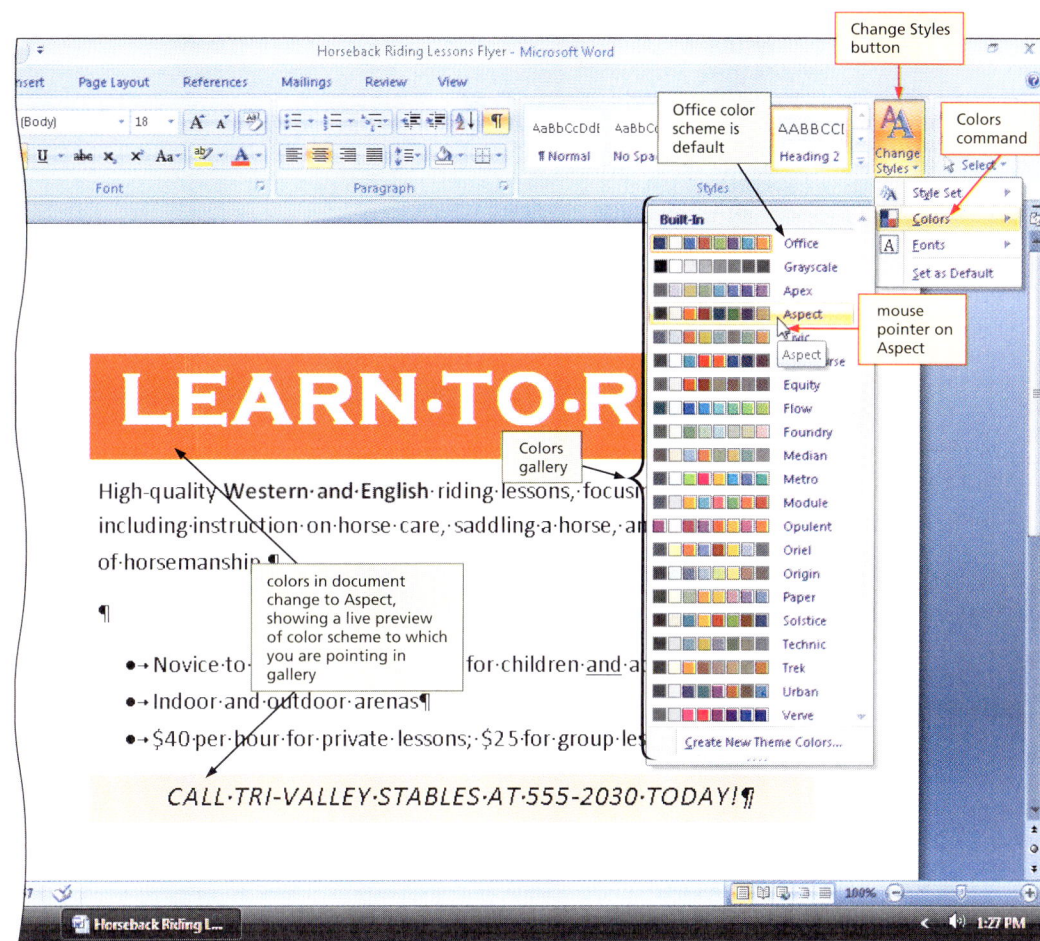

Figure 1–55

Q&A What if I want to return to the original color scheme?
You would click the Change Styles button, click Colors on the Change Styles menu, and then click Office in the Colors gallery.

Other Ways
1. Click Theme Colors button arrow on Page Layout tab, select desired color scheme

To Change Theme Fonts

Earlier in this chapter, you changed the font of the headline to Copperplate Gothic Bold. In this flyer, all text below the headline should be the Rockwell font, instead of the Calibri font, because it better matches the western tone of the flyer. Thus, the next step is to change the current font set, which is called Office, to a font set called Foundry, which uses the Rockwell font for headings and body text.

If you previously changed a font using buttons on the Ribbon or Mini toolbar, Word will not alter those when you change the font set because changes to the font set are not applied to fonts changed individually. This means the font headline in the flyer will stay as Copperplate Gothic Bold when you change the font set. The following steps change the font set to Foundry.

- Click the Change Styles button on the Home tab.
- Point to Fonts on the Change Styles menu to display the Fonts gallery.
- Scroll through the Fonts gallery until Foundry is displayed and then point to Foundry to display a live preview of the Foundry font set (Figure 1–56).

- Point to various font sets in the Fonts gallery and watch the fonts below the headline change in the document window.

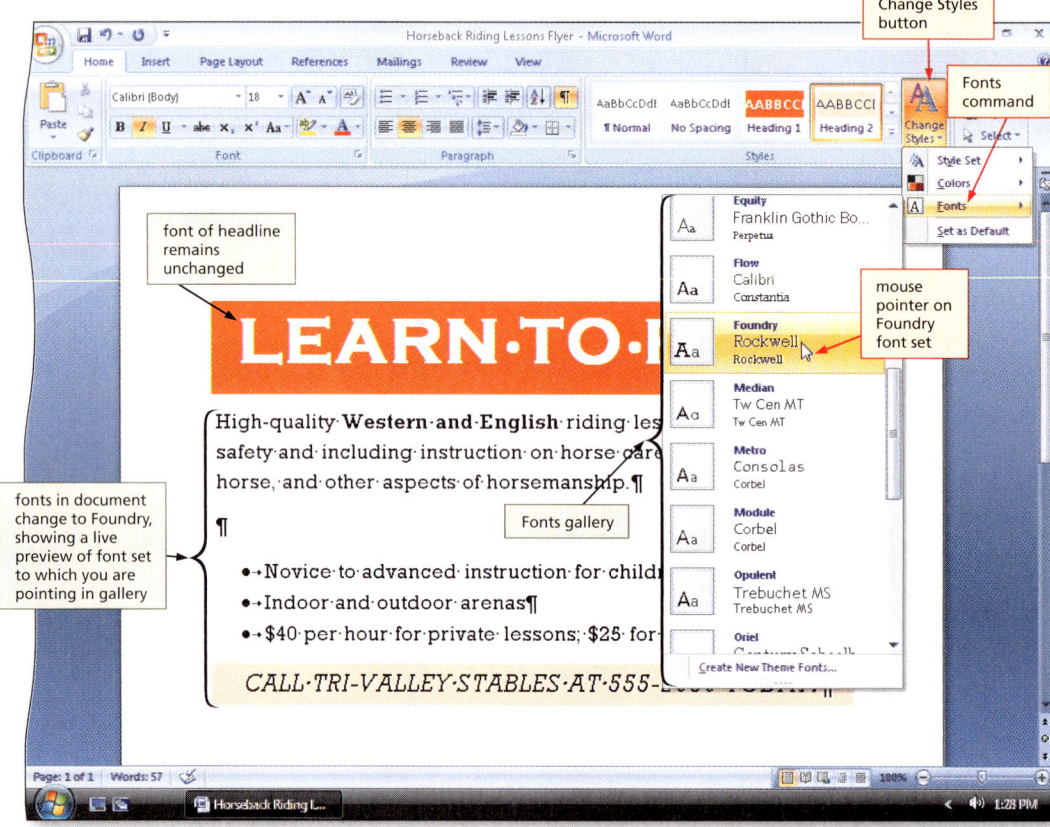

Figure 1–56

- Click Foundry in the Fonts gallery to change the document theme fonts to Foundry.

Q&A What if I want to return to the original font set?
You would click the Change Styles button, click Fonts on the Change Styles menu, and then click Office in the Fonts gallery.

Other Ways
1. Click Theme Fonts button arrow on Page Layout tab, select desired font set

Inserting and Formatting a Picture in a Word Document

With the text formatted in the flyer, the next step is to insert a picture in the flyer and format the picture. Flyers usually contain graphical images, such as a picture, to attract the attention of passersby.

> **Find the appropriate graphical image.**
> To use graphical images, also called graphics, in a Word document, the image must be stored digitally in a file. Files containing graphical images are available from a variety of sources:
>
> - Word includes a collection of predefined graphical images that you can insert in a document.
> - Microsoft has free digital images on the Web for use in a document. Other Web sites also have images available, some of which are free, while others require a fee.
> - You can take a picture with a digital camera and **download** it, which is the process of copying the digital picture from the camera to your computer.
> - With a scanner, you can convert a printed picture, drawing, or diagram to a digital file.
>
>   If you receive a picture from a source other than yourself, do not use the file until you are certain it does not contain a virus. A **virus** is a computer program that can damage files and programs on your computer. Use an antivirus program to verify that any files you use are virus free.

Plan Ahead

> **Establish where to position and how to format the graphical image.**
> The content, size, shape, position, and format of a graphic should capture the interest of passersby, enticing them to stop and read the flyer. Often, the graphic is the center of attraction and visually the largest element on a flyer. If you use colors in the graphical image, be sure they are part of the document's color scheme.

Plan Ahead

To Insert a Picture

The next step in creating the flyer is to insert the picture of the horse and rider so that it is centered on the blank line above the bulleted list. The picture, which was taken with a digital camera, is available on the Data Files for Students. See the inside back cover of this book for instructions on downloading the Data Files for Students, or contact your instructor for information about accessing the required files. The following steps insert a centered picture, which, in this example, is located on the same USB flash drive that contains the saved flyer.

1
- To position the insertion point where you want the picture to be located, press CTRL+HOME and then press the DOWN ARROW key four times.

- Click the Center button on the Home tab to center the paragraph that will contain the picture.

- Click Insert on the Ribbon to display the Insert tab (Figure 1–57).

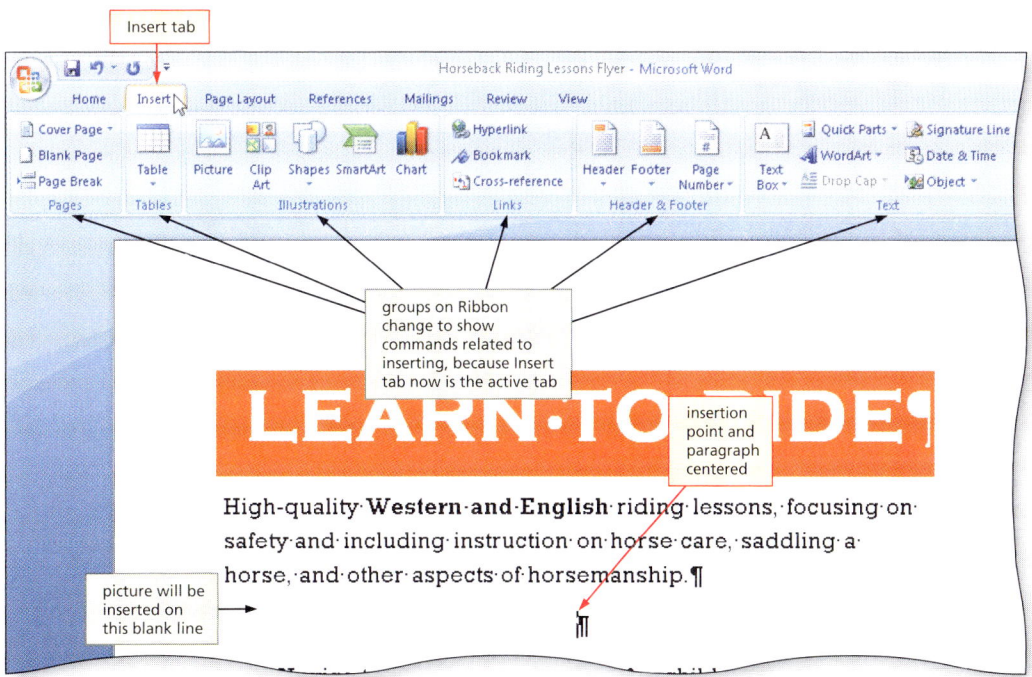

Figure 1–57

2

- With your USB flash drive connected to one of the computer's USB ports, click the Insert Picture from File button on the Insert tab to display the Insert Picture dialog box.

- If the Folders list is displayed below the Folders button, click the Folders button to remove the Folders list.

- If necessary, click Computer in the Favorite Links section and then scroll until UDISK 2.0 (E:) appears in the list of available drives.

- Double-click UDISK 2.0 (E:) to select the USB flash drive, Drive E in this case, as the device that contains the picture.

- Click Horse and Rider to select the file name (Figure 1–58).

Q&A What if the picture is not on a USB flash drive?

Use the same process, but select the device containing the picture in the Favorite Links section.

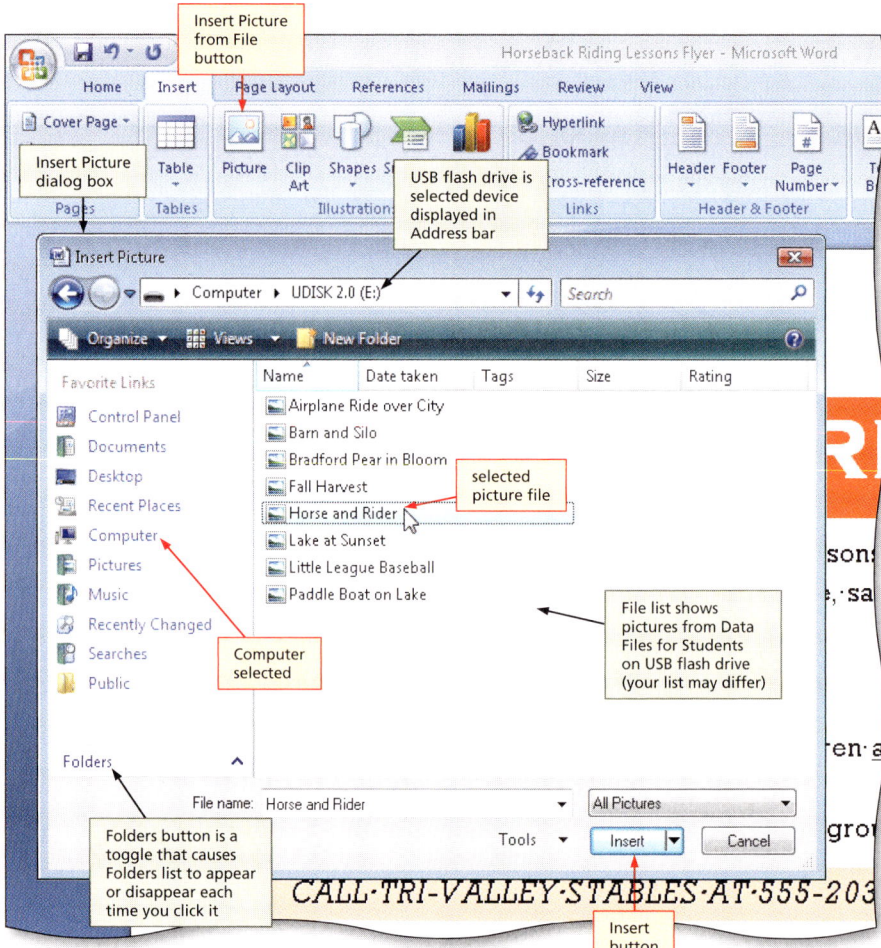

Figure 1–58

3

- Click the Insert button in the dialog box to insert the picture at the location of the insertion point in the document (Figure 1–59).

Q&A What are the symbols around the picture?

A selected graphic appears surrounded by a **selection rectangle**, which has small squares and circles, called **sizing handles**, at each corner and middle location.

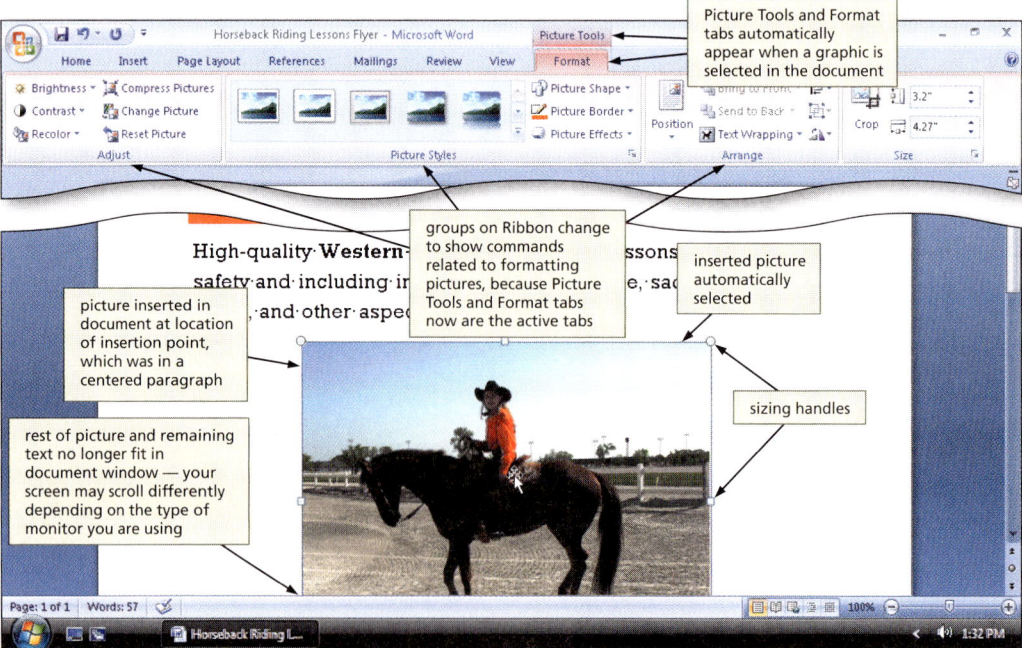

Figure 1–59

Scrolling

As mentioned at the beginning of this chapter, you view only a portion of a document on the screen through the document window. At some point when you type text or insert graphics, Word will **scroll** the top or bottom portion of the document off the screen. Although you cannot see the text and graphics once they scroll off the screen, they remain in the document.

As shown in Figure 1–59, when you insert the picture in the flyer, the text and graphics are too long to fit in the document window. Thus, to see the bottom of the flyer, you will need to scroll downward.

You may use either the mouse or the keyboard to scroll to a different location in a document. With the mouse, you can use the scroll arrows or the scroll box on the scroll bar to display a different portion of the document in the document window, and then click the mouse to move the insertion point to that location. Table 1–1 explains various techniques for using the scroll bar to scroll vertically with the mouse.

Minimize Wrist Injury
Computer users frequently switch between the keyboard and the mouse during a word processing session; such switching strains the wrist. To help prevent wrist injury, minimize switching. For instance, if your fingers already are on the keyboard, use keyboard keys to scroll. If your hand already is on the mouse, use the mouse to scroll.

Table 1–1 Using the Scroll Bar to Scroll with the Mouse

SCROLL DIRECTION	MOUSE ACTION
Up	Drag the scroll box upward.
Down	Drag the scroll box downward.
Up one screen	Click anywhere above the scroll box on the vertical scroll bar.
Down one screen	Click anywhere below the scroll box on the vertical scroll bar.
Up one line	Click the scroll arrow at the top of the vertical scroll bar.
Down one line	Click the scroll arrow at the bottom of the vertical scroll bar.

When you use the keyboard to scroll, the insertion point automatically moves when you press the appropriate keys. Table 1–2 outlines various techniques to scroll through a document using the keyboard, some of which you have seen used in this chapter.

Table 1–2 Scrolling with the Keyboard

SCROLL DIRECTION	KEY(S) TO PRESS
Left one character	LEFT ARROW
Right one character	RIGHT ARROW
Left one word	CTRL+LEFT ARROW
Right one word	CTRL+RIGHT ARROW
Up one line	UP ARROW
Down one line	DOWN ARROW
To end of line	END
To beginning of line	HOME
Up one paragraph	CTRL+UP ARROW
Down one paragraph	CTRL+DOWN ARROW
Up one screen	PAGE UP
Down one screen	PAGE DOWN
To top of document window	ALT+CTRL+PAGE UP
To bottom of document window	ALT+CTRL+PAGE DOWN
To beginning of document	CTRL+HOME
To end of document	CTRL+END

To Apply a Picture Style

Earlier in this chapter, you applied the heading styles to the headline and signature line in the flyer. Word also provides styles for pictures, allowing you easily to change the basic rectangle format to a more visually appealing style. Word provides a gallery of more than 25 picture styles, which include a variety of shapes, angles, borders, and reflections. The flyer in this chapter uses an oval picture style that has a border around its edges. The following steps apply a picture style to the picture in the flyer.

- Click the down scroll arrow on the vertical scroll bar as many times as necessary until the entire picture is displayed in the document window (Figure 1–60).

Q&A What if the Picture Tools and Format tabs no longer are displayed on my Ribbon?

Double-click the picture to display the Picture Tools and Format tabs.

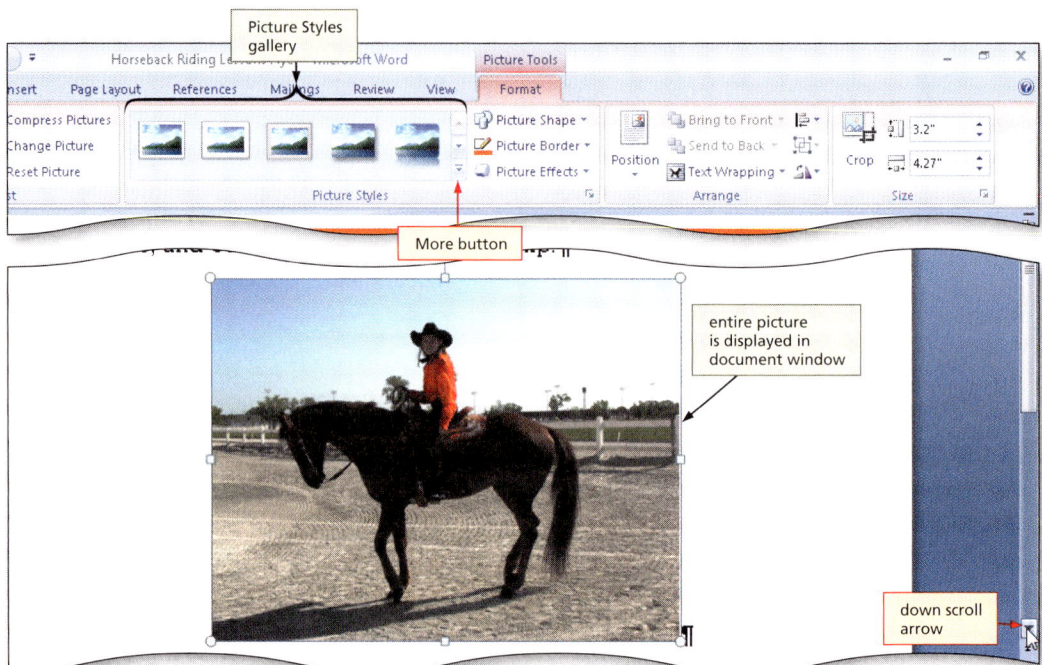

Figure 1–60

- Click the More button in the Picture Styles gallery, which shows more gallery options.
- Point to Metal Oval in the Picture Styles gallery to display a live preview of that style applied to the picture in the document (Figure 1–61).

Experiment

- Point to various picture styles in the Picture Styles gallery and watch the format of the picture change in the document window.

- Click Metal Oval in the Picture Styles gallery to apply the selected style to the picture.

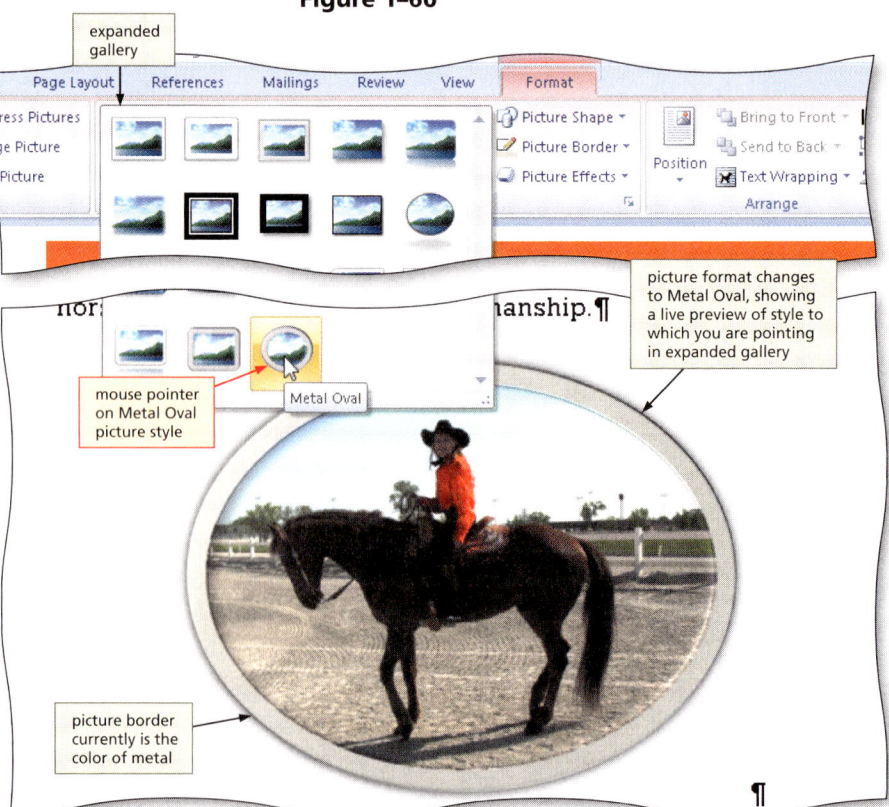

Figure 1–61

To Change a Picture Border Color

The flyer in this chapter has a tan border around the picture. Earlier in this chapter, you changed the color scheme to Aspect. To coordinate the border color with the other colors in the document, you will use a shade of tan in Aspect color scheme for the picture border. Any color galleries you display show colors defined in this current color scheme. The following steps change the picture border color.

1

- Click the Picture Border button arrow on the Format tab to display the Picture Border gallery.

Q&A What if the Picture Tools and Format tabs no longer are displayed on my Ribbon?

Double-click the picture to display the Picture Tools and Format tabs.

- Point to Tan, Background 2 (third theme color from left in the first row) in the Picture Border gallery to display a live preview of that border color on the picture (Figure 1–62).

🔍 **Experiment**

- Point to various colors in the Picture Border gallery and watch the border color on the picture change in the document window.

2

- Click Tan, Background 2 in the Picture Styles gallery to change the picture border color.

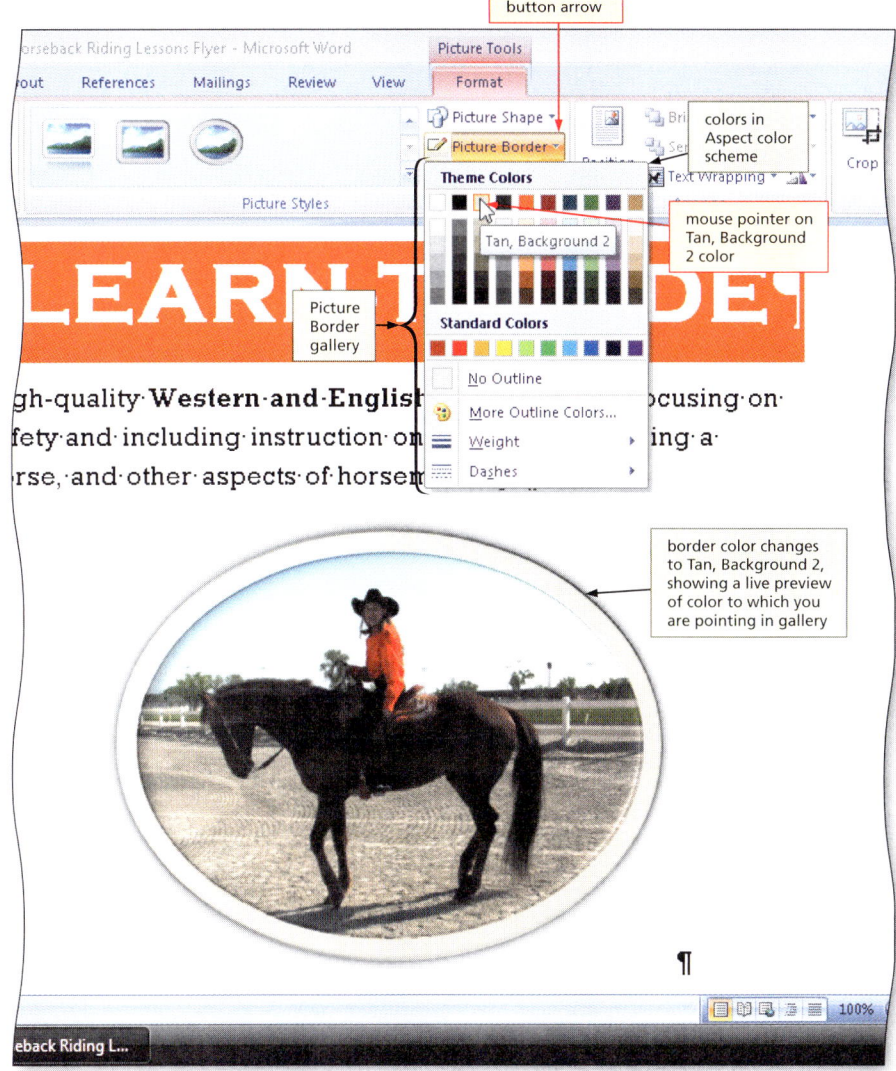

Figure 1–62

To Zoom the Document

The next step in formatting the picture is to resize it. Specifically, you will increase the size of the picture. You do not want it so large, however, that it causes the flyer text to flow to a second page. You can change the zoom so that you can see the entire document on the screen at once. Seeing the entire document at once helps you determine the appropriate size of the picture. The steps on the next page zoom the document.

Experiment

- Repeatedly click the Zoom Out and Zoom In buttons on the status bar and watch the size of the document change in the document window.

- Click the Zoom Out or Zoom In button as many times as necessary until the Zoom level button displays 50% on its face (Figure 1–63).

Q&A If I change the zoom percentage, will the document print differently?

Changing the zoom has no effect on the printed document.

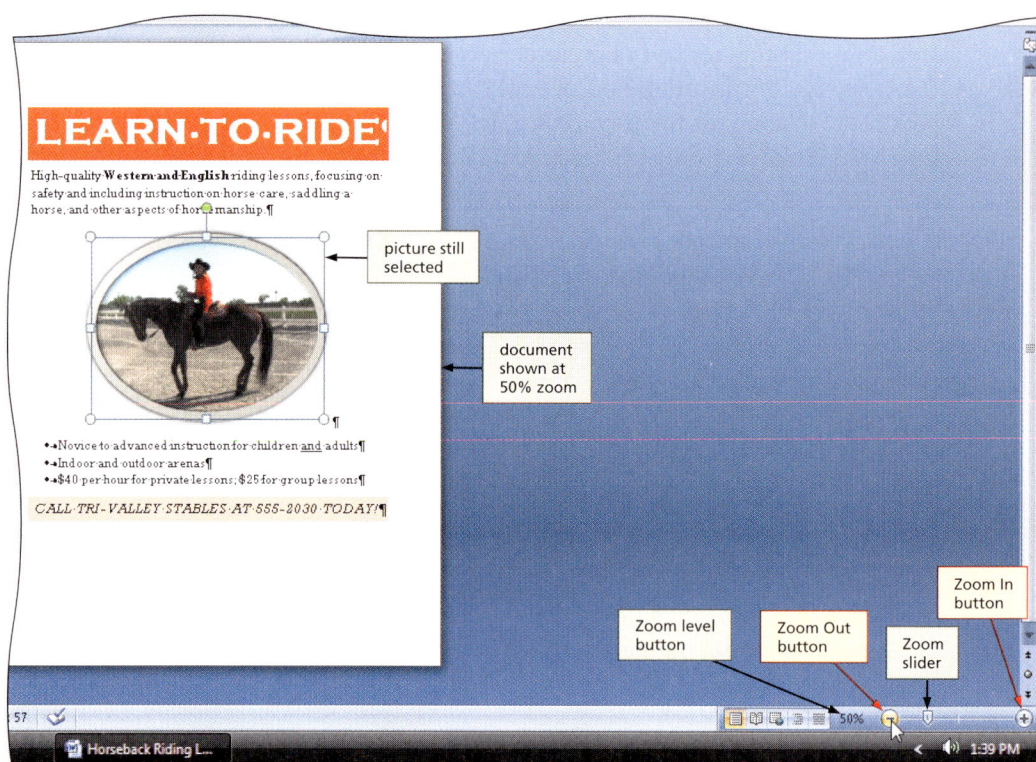

Figure 1–63

Other Ways

1. Drag Zoom slider on status bar
2. Click Zoom level button on status bar, select desired zoom percent or type, click OK button
3. Click Zoom button on View tab, select desired zoom percent or type, click OK button

To Resize a Graphic

The next step is to resize the picture. **Resizing** includes both enlarging and reducing the size of a graphic. The picture in the flyer should be as large as possible, without causing any flyer text to flow to a second page.

With the entire document displaying in the document window, you will be able to see how the resized graphic will look on the entire page. The following steps resize a selected graphic.

- With the graphic still selected, point to the upper-right corner sizing handle on the picture so that the mouse pointer shape changes to a two-headed arrow (Figure 1–64).

Q&A What if my graphic (picture) is not selected?

To select a graphic, click it.

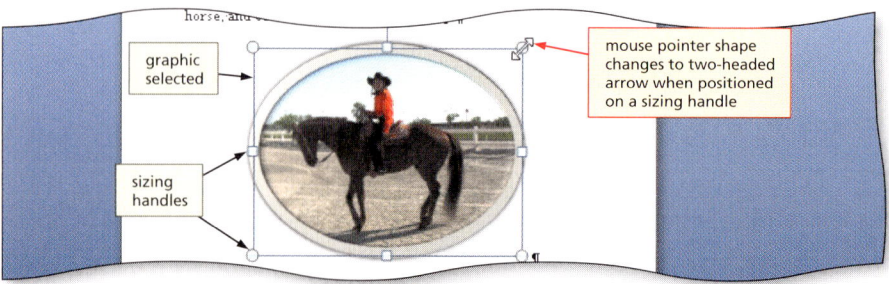

Figure 1–64

2
- Drag the sizing handle diagonally outward until the crosshair mouse pointer is positioned approximately as shown in Figure 1–65.

3
- Release the mouse button to resize the graphic.

Q&A What if the graphic is the wrong size?

Repeat Steps 1, 2, and 3.

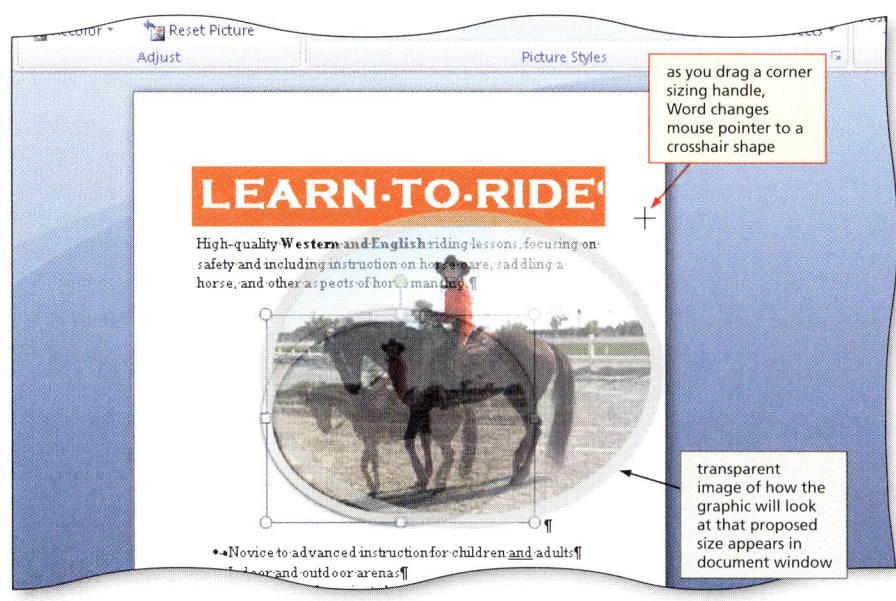

Figure 1–65

4
- Click outside the graphic to deselect it (Figure 1–66).

Q&A What happened to the Picture Tools and Format tabs?

When you click outside of a graphic or press a key to scroll through a document, Word deselects the graphic and removes the Picture Tools and Format tabs from the screen.

Q&A What if I want to return a graphic to its original size and start again?

With the graphic selected, click the Size Dialog Box Launcher on the Format tab to display the Size dialog box, click the Size tab, click the Reset button, and then click the Close button.

Figure 1–66

Other Ways

1. Enter graphic height and width in Shape Height and Shape Width text boxes in Size group on Format tab in Picture Tools tab

2. Click Size Dialog Box Launcher on Format tab in Picture Tools tab, click Size tab, enter desired height and width values in text boxes, click Close button

Enhancing the Page

With the text and graphics entered and formatted, the next step is to look at the page as a whole and determine if it looks finished in its current state. As you review the page, answer these questions:

- Does it need a page border to frame its contents, or would a page border make it look too busy?
- Is the spacing between paragraphs and graphics on the page adequate? Do any sections of text or graphics look as if they are positioned too closely to the items above or below them?

You determine that a graphical, color-coordinated border would enhance the flyer. You also notice that the flyer would look more proportionate if it had a little more space below the headline and above the graphic. The following pages make these enhancements to the flyer.

To Add a Page Border

In Word, you can add a border around the perimeter of an entire page. In this flyer, you add a graphical border that uses a shade of brown from the Aspect color scheme. The following steps add a graphical page border.

- Click Page Layout on the Ribbon to display the Page Layout tab.
- Click the Page Borders button on the Page Layout tab to display the Borders and Shading dialog box (Figure 1–67).

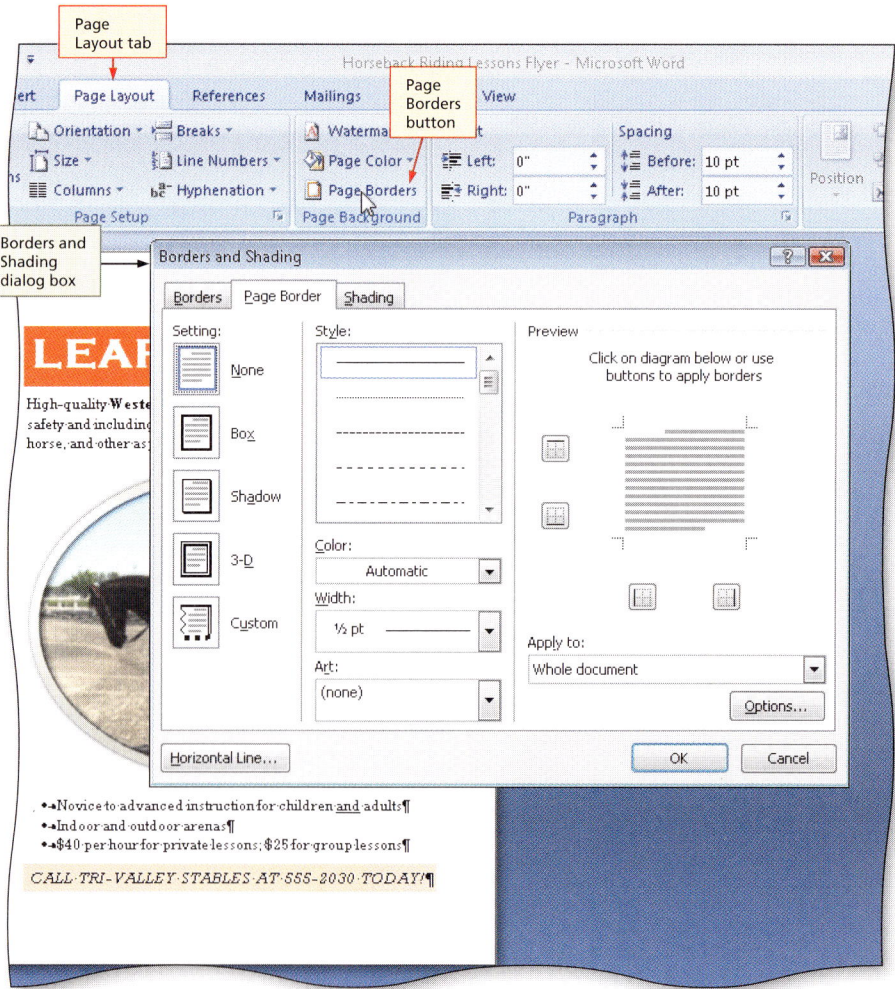

Figure 1–67

Creating and Editing a Word Document Word Chapter 1 WD 49

2
- Click the Art box arrow to display the Art gallery.
- Click the down scroll arrow in the Art gallery until the art border shown in Figure 1–68 appears.

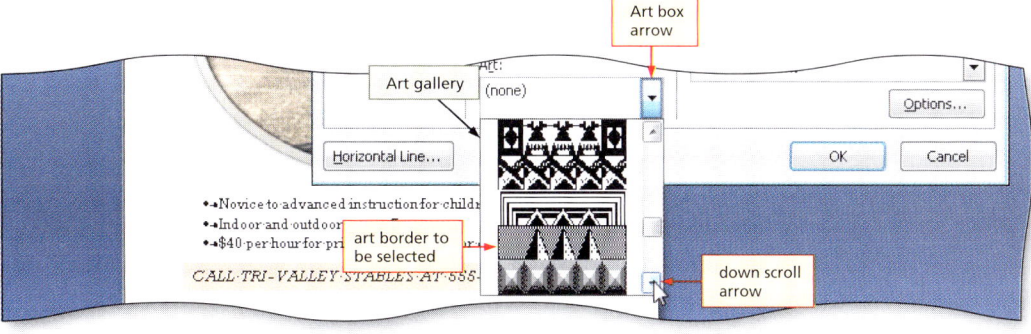

Figure 1–68

3
- Click the art border shown in Figure 1–68 to display a preview of the selection in the Preview area of the dialog box.
- Click the Color box arrow to display a Color gallery (Figure 1–69).

Q&A Do I have to use an art border?

No. You can select a solid or decorative line in the Style list.

Q&A Can I add color to every border type?

You can color all of the line styles and many of the art borders.

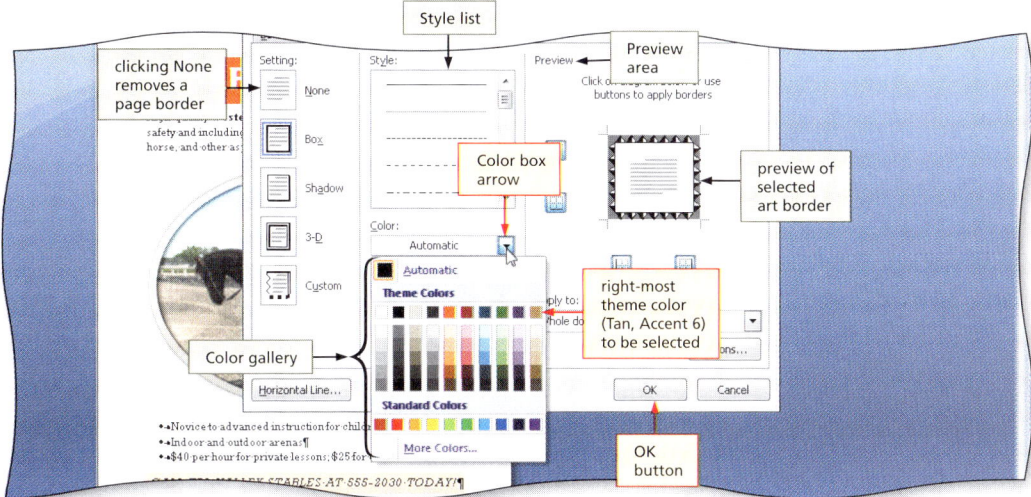

Figure 1–69

4
- Click the right-most theme color (Tan, Accent 6) in the Color gallery to display a preview of the selection in the Preview area.
- Click the OK button to add the border to the page (Figure 1–70).

Q&A What if I wanted to remove the border?

Click None in the Setting list in the Borders and Shading dialog box.

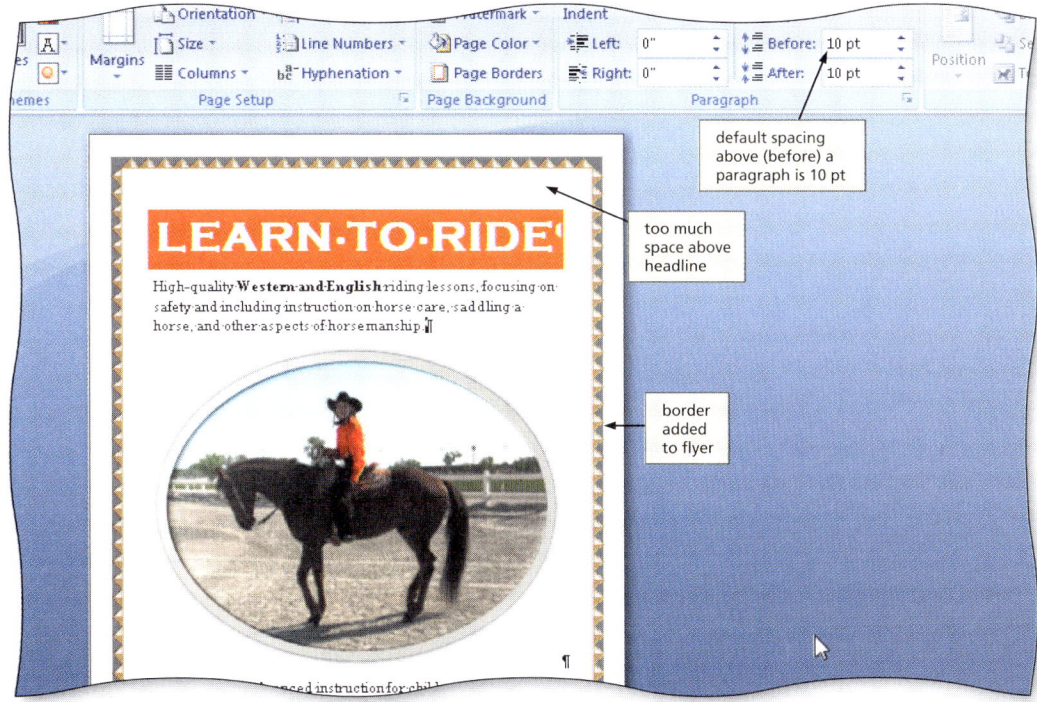

Figure 1–70

To Change Spacing Above and Below Paragraphs

The default spacing above a heading paragraph in Word is 10 points. In the flyer, you want to remove this spacing so the headline is closer to the page border. The default spacing below (after) a body text paragraph is 0 points. Below the first paragraph of body copy in the flyer, you want to increase this space. The following steps change the spacing above and below paragraphs.

- Position the insertion point in the paragraph to be adjusted, in this case, the headline.

- Click the Spacing Before box down arrow on the Page Layout tab as many times as necessary until 0 pt is displayed in the Spacing Before text box (Figure 1–71).

Q&A Why is a blank space still between the border and the headline?

The space is a result of Word's preset left, right, top, and bottom margins and other settings.

- Position the insertion point in the paragraph below the headline.

- Click the Spacing After box up arrow on the Page Layout tab as many times as necessary until 24 pt is displayed in the Spacing After text box, shown in Figure 1–72. (If the text flows to two pages, resize the picture so that it is smaller.)

Figure 1–71

BTW

Centering Page Contents Vertically
You can center page contents vertically between the top and bottom margins. To do this, click the Page Setup Dialog Box Launcher on the Page Layout tab, click the Layout tab in the dialog box, click the Vertical alignment box arrow, click Center in the list, and then click the OK button.

To Zoom the Document

You are finished enhancing the page and no longer need to view the entire page in the document window. Thus, the following step changes the zoom back to 100 percent.

1. Click the Zoom In button as many times as necessary until the Zoom level button displays 100% on its face, shown in Figure 1–72.

Changing Document Properties and Saving Again

Word helps you organize and identify your files by using **document properties**, which are the details about a file. Document properties, also known as **metadata**, can include such information as the project author, title, or subject. **Keywords** are words or phrases that further describe the document. For example, a class name or document topic can describe the file's purpose or content.

Document properties are valuable for a variety of reasons:

- Users can save time locating a particular file because they can view a document's properties without opening the document.
- By creating consistent properties for files having similar content, users can better organize their documents.
- Some organizations require Word users to add document properties so that other employees can view details about these files.

Five different types of document properties exist, but the more common ones used in this book are standard and automatically updated properties. **Standard properties** are associated with all Microsoft Office documents and include author, title, and subject. **Automatically updated properties** include file system properties, such as the date you create or change a file, and statistics, such as the file size.

BTW

Printing Document Properties
To print document properties, click the Office Button to display the Office Button menu, point to Print on the Office Button menu to display the Print submenu, click Print on the Print submenu to display the Print dialog box, click the Print what box arrow, click Document properties to instruct Word to print the document properties instead of the document, and then click the OK button.

To Change Document Properties

The **Document Information Panel** contains areas where you can view and enter document properties. You can view and change information in this panel at any time while you are creating a document. Before saving the flyer again, you want to add your name and course information as document properties. The following steps use the Document Information Panel to change document properties.

1
- Click the Office Button to display the Office Button menu.
- Point to Prepare on the Office Button menu to display the Prepare submenu (Figure 1–72).

Q&A
What other types of actions besides changing properties can you take to prepare a document for distribution?

The Prepare submenu provides commands related to sharing a document with others, such as allowing or restricting people to view and modify your document, checking to see if your document will open in earlier versions of Word, and searching for hidden personal information.

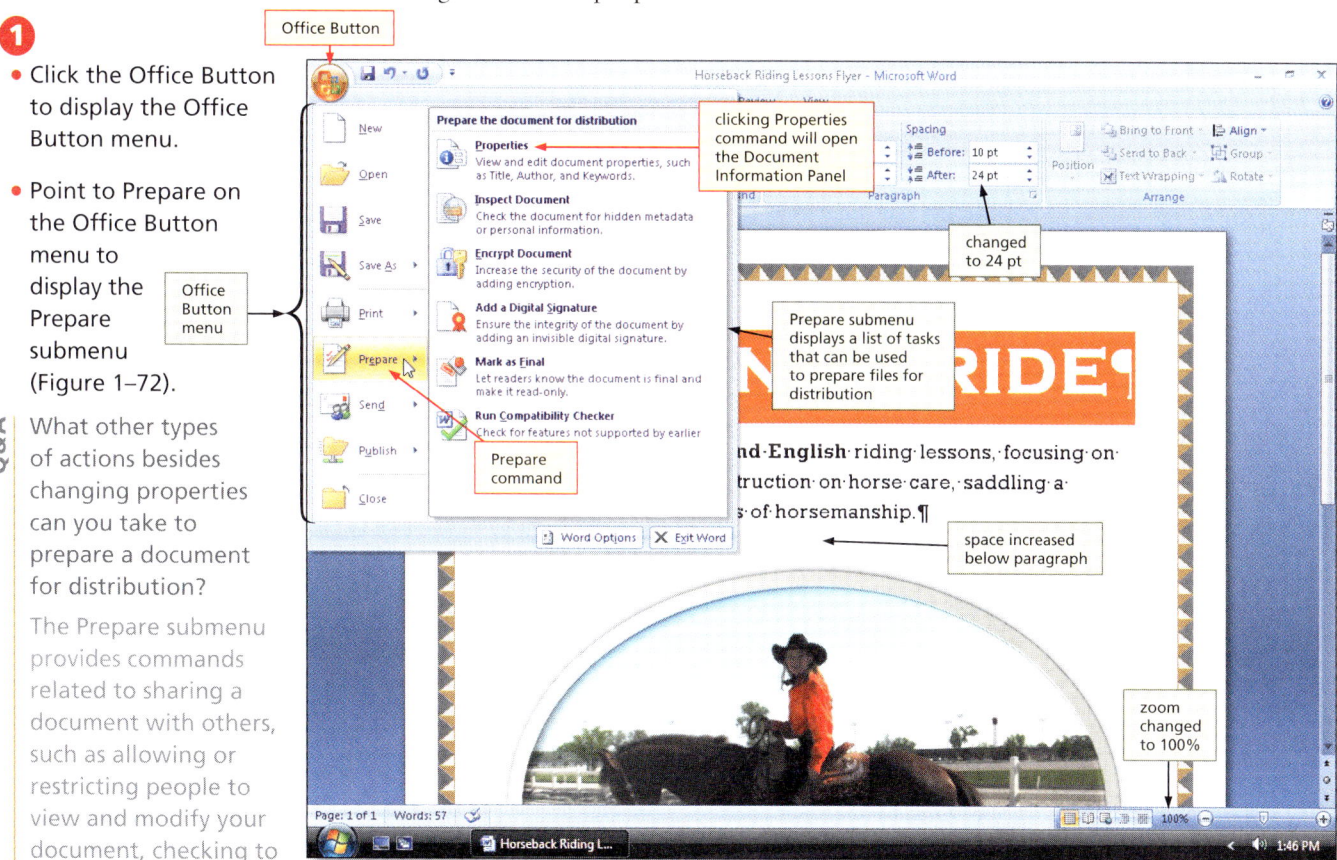

Figure 1–72

2

- Click Properties on the Prepare submenu to display the Document Information Panel (Figure 1–73).

Q&A Why are some of the document properties in my Document Information Panel already filled in?

The person who installed Microsoft Office 2007 on your computer or network may have set or customized the properties.

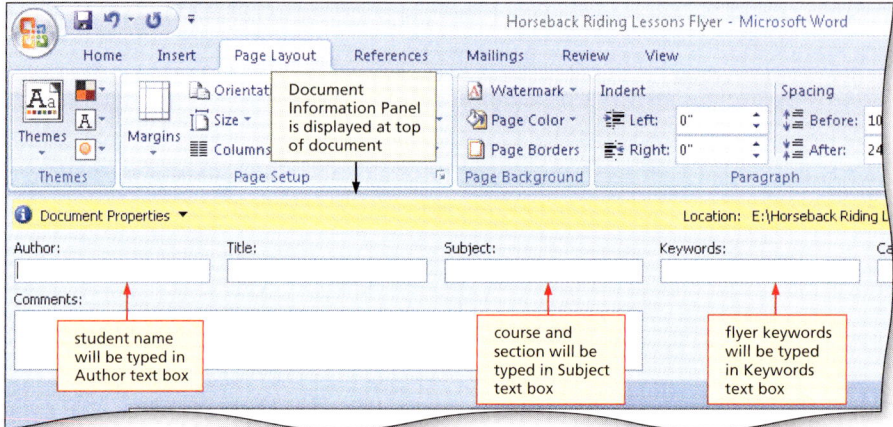

Figure 1–73

3

- Click the Author text box, if necessary, and then type your name as the Author property. If a name already is displayed in the Author text box, delete it before typing your name.

- Click the Subject text box, if necessary delete any existing text, and then type your course and section as the Subject property.

- If an AutoComplete dialog box appears, click its Yes button.

- Click the Keywords text box, if necessary delete any existing text, and then type `Tri-Valley Stables` as the Keywords property (Figure 1–74).

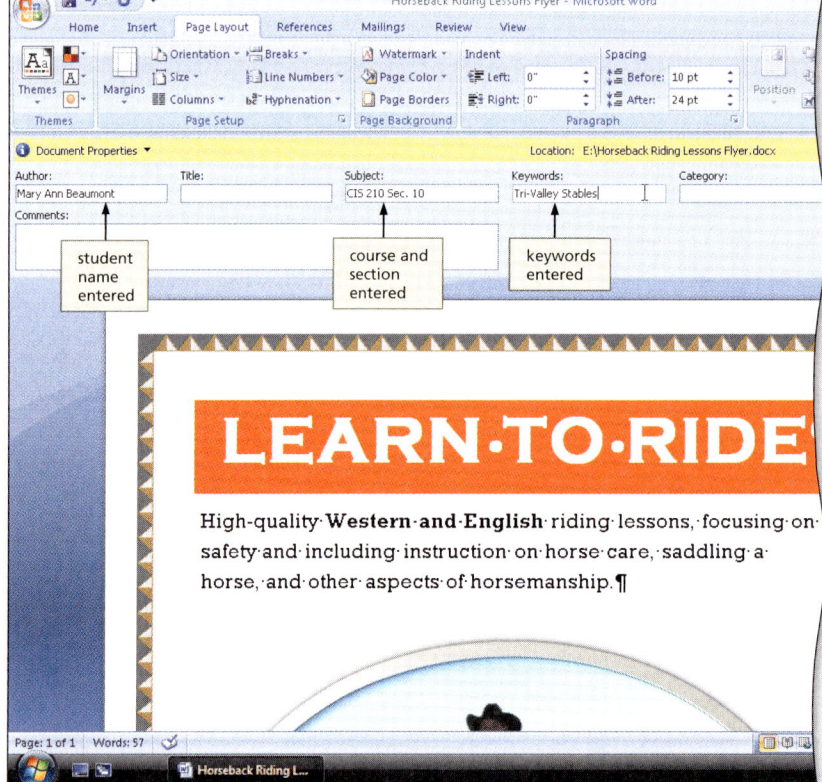

Figure 1–74

Q&A What types of document properties does Word collect automatically?

Word records such details as how long you worked at creating your project, how many times you revised the document, and what fonts and themes are used.

4

- Click the Close the Document Information Panel button so that the Document Information Panel no longer is displayed.

To Save an Existing Document with the Same File Name

Saving frequently cannot be overemphasized. You have made several modifications to the document since you saved it earlier in the chapter. When you first saved the document, you clicked the Save button on the Quick Access Toolbar, the Save As dialog box appeared, and you entered the file name, Horseback Riding Lessons Flyer. If you want to use the same file name to save the changes made to the document, you again click the Save button on the Quick Access Toolbar. The following step saves the document again.

1
- Click the Save button on the Quick Access Toolbar to overwrite the previous Horseback Riding Lessons Flyer file on the USB flash drive (Figure 1–75).

Q&A Why did the Save As dialog box not appear?

Word overwrites the document using the settings specified the first time you saved the document. To save the file with a different file name or on different media, display the Save As dialog box by clicking the Office Button and then clicking Save As on the Office Button menu. Then, fill in the Save As dialog box as described in Steps 2 through 5 on pages WD 20 and WD 21.

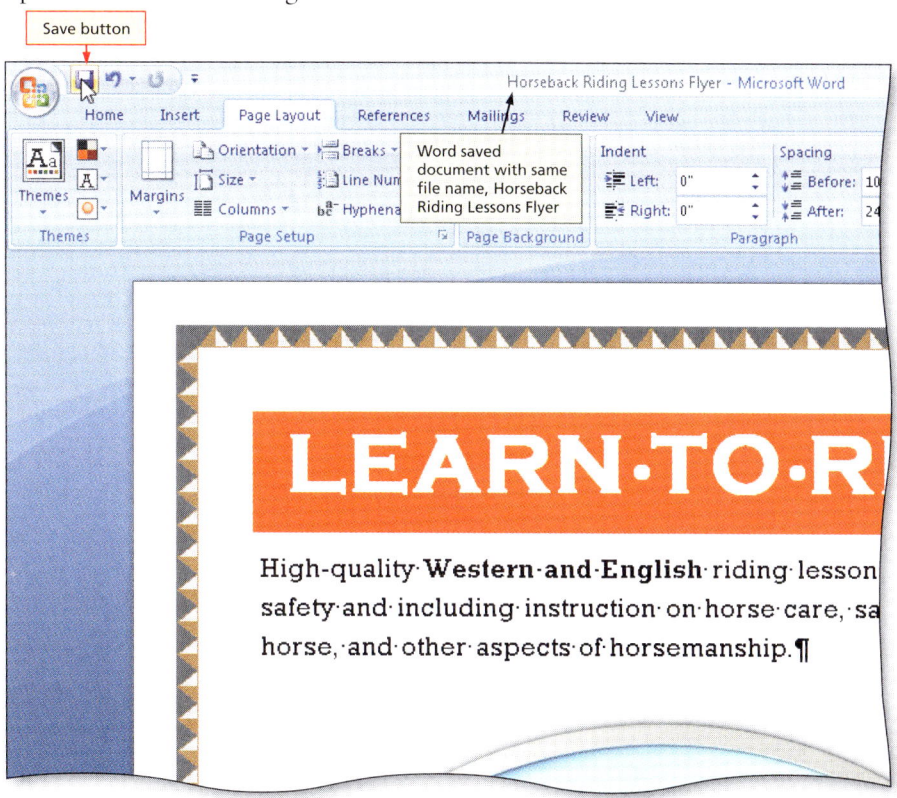

Figure 1–75

Other Ways
1. Press CTRL+S or press SHIFT+F12

Printing a Document

After you create a document, you often want to print it. A printed version of the document is called a **hard copy or printout**.

Printed copies of your document can be useful for the following reasons:

- Many people prefer proofreading a hard copy of the document rather than viewing it on the screen to check for errors and readability.
- Hard copies can serve as reference material if your storage medium is lost or becomes corrupted and you need to re-create the document.

It is a good practice to save a document before printing it, in the event you experience difficulties with the printer.

BTW

Conserving Ink and Toner
You can instruct Word to print draft quality documents to conserve ink or toner by clicking the Office Button, clicking the Word Options button, clicking Advanced in the left pane of the Word Options dialog box, scrolling to the Print area, placing a check mark in the 'Use draft quality' check box, and then clicking the OK button. To print the document with these settings, click the Office Button, point to Print, and then click Quick Print.

To Print a Document

With the completed document saved, you may want to print it. The following steps print the contents of the saved Horseback Riding Lessons Flyer project.

1
- Click the Office Button to display the Office Button menu.
- Point to Print on the Office Button menu to display the Print submenu (Figure 1–76).

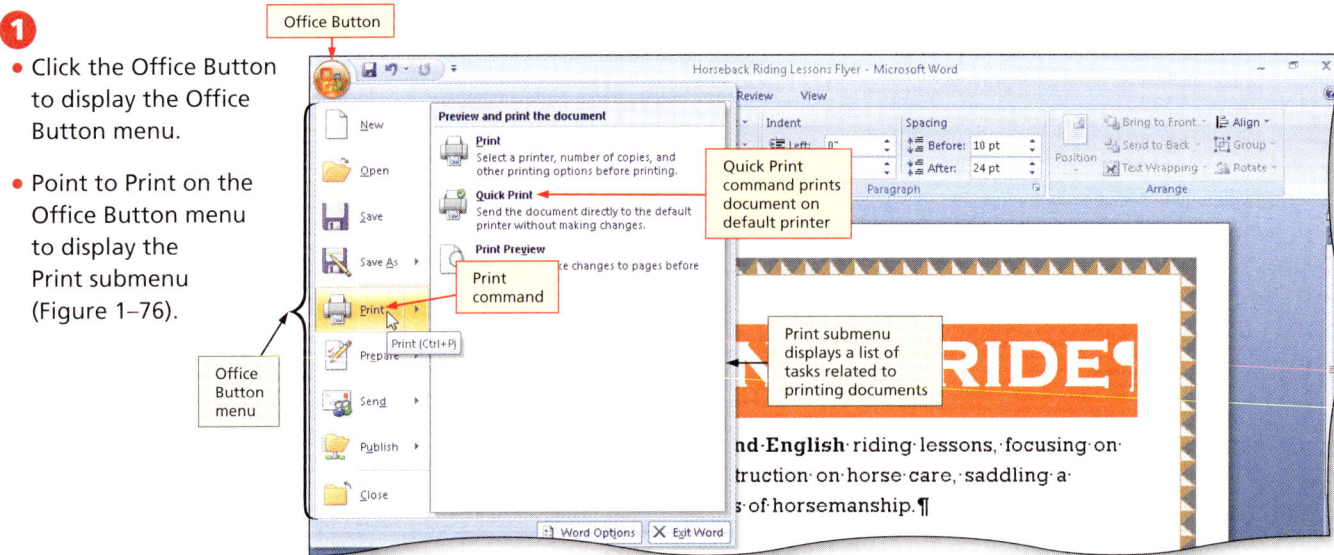

Figure 1–76

2
- Click Quick Print on the Print submenu to print the document.
- When the printer stops, retrieve the hard copy of the Horseback Riding Lessons Flyer (Figures 1–77).

Q&A How can I print multiple copies of my document other than issuing the Quick Print command twice?

Click the Office Button, point to Print on the Office Button menu, click Print on the Print submenu, increase the number in the Number of copies box, and then click the OK button.

Q&A Do I have to wait until my document is complete to print it?

No, you can follow these steps to print a document at any time while you are creating it.

BTW
Printed Borders
If one or more of your borders do not print, click the Page Borders button on the Page Layout tab, click the Options button in the dialog box, click the Measure from box arrow and click Text, change the four text boxes to 15 pt, and then click the OK button in each dialog box. Try printing the document again. If the borders still do not print, adjust the text boxes in the dialog box to a number smaller than 15 point.

Figure 1–77

Other Ways
1. Press CTRL+P, press ENTER

Quitting Word

When you quit Word, if you have made changes to a document since the last time the file was saved, Word displays a dialog box asking if you want to save the changes you made to the file before it closes that window. The dialog box contains three buttons with these resulting actions: the Yes button saves the changes and then quits Word; the No button quits Word without saving changes; and the Cancel button closes the dialog box and redisplays the document without saving the changes.

If no changes have been made to an open document since the last time the file was saved, Word will close the window without displaying a dialog box.

To Quit Word with One Document Open

You saved the document prior to printing and did not make any changes to the project. The Horseback Riding Lessons Flyer project now is complete, and you are ready to quit Word. When one Word document is open, the following steps quit Word.

1
- Point to the Close button on the right side of the Word title bar (Figure 1–78).

2
- Click the Close button to quit Word.

Q&A What if I have more than one Word document open?

You would click the Close button for each open document. When you click the last open document's Close button, Word also quits. As an alternative, you could click the Office Button and then click the Exit Word button on the Office Button menu, which closes all open Word documents and then quits Word.

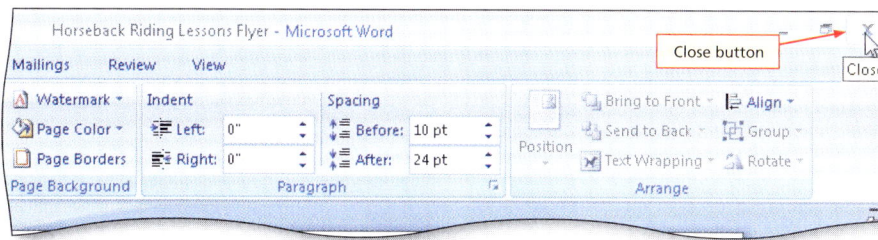

Figure 1–78

Other Ways
1. Double-click Office Button
2. With multiple documents open, click Office Button, click Exit Word on Office Button menu
3. Right-click Microsoft Word button on Windows Vista taskbar, click Close on shortcut menu
4. Press ALT+F4

Starting Word and Opening a Document

Once you have created and saved a document, you may need to retrieve it from your storage medium. For example, you might want to revise the document or reprint it. Opening a document requires that Word is running on your computer.

To Start Word

The following steps, which assume Windows Vista is running, start Word.

1 Click the Start button on the Windows Vista taskbar to display the Start menu.

2 Click All Programs at the bottom of the left pane on the Start menu to display the All Programs list and then click Microsoft Office in the All Programs list to display the Microsoft Office list.

3 Click Microsoft Office Word 2007 in the Microsoft Office list to start Word and display a new blank document in the Word window.

4 If the Word window is not maximized, click the Maximize button on its title bar to maximize the window.

To Open a Document from Word

Earlier in this chapter you saved your project on a USB flash drive using the file name, Horseback Riding Lessons Flyer. The following steps open the Horseback Riding Lessons Flyer file from the USB flash drive.

- With your USB flash drive connected to one of the computer's USB ports, click the Office Button to display the Office Button menu (Figure 1–79).

Q&A What files are shown in the Recent Documents list?

Word displays the most recently opened document file names in this list. If the name of the file you want to open appears in the Recent Documents list, you could click it to open the file.

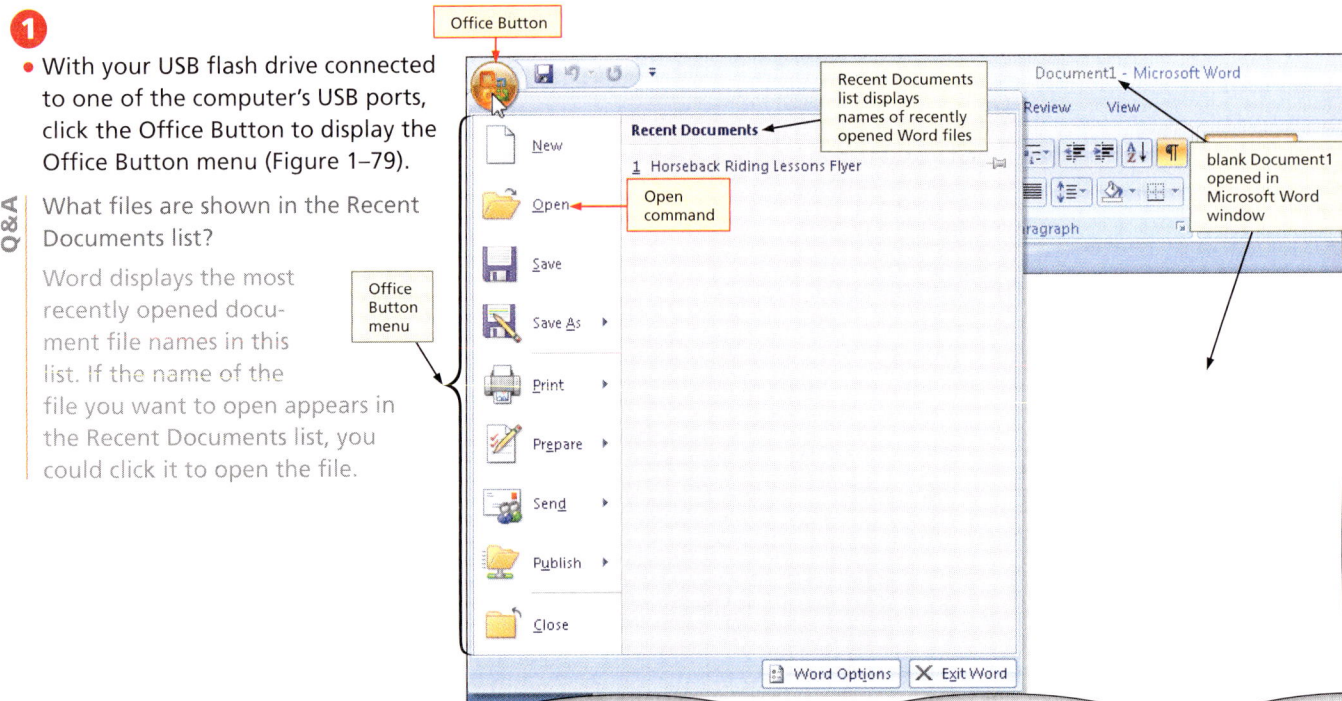

Figure 1–79

- Click Open on the Office Button menu to display the Open dialog box.

- If the Folders list is displayed below the Folders button, click the Folders button to remove the Folders list.

- If necessary, click Computer in the Favorite Links section and then scroll until UDISK 2.0 (E:) appears in the list of available drives.

- Double-click UDISK 2.0 (E:) to select the USB flash drive, Drive E in this case, as the new open location.

- Click Horseback Riding Lessons Flyer to select the file name (Figure 1–80).

Q&A How do I open the file if I am not using a USB flash drive?

Use the same process, but be certain to select your device in the Computer list.

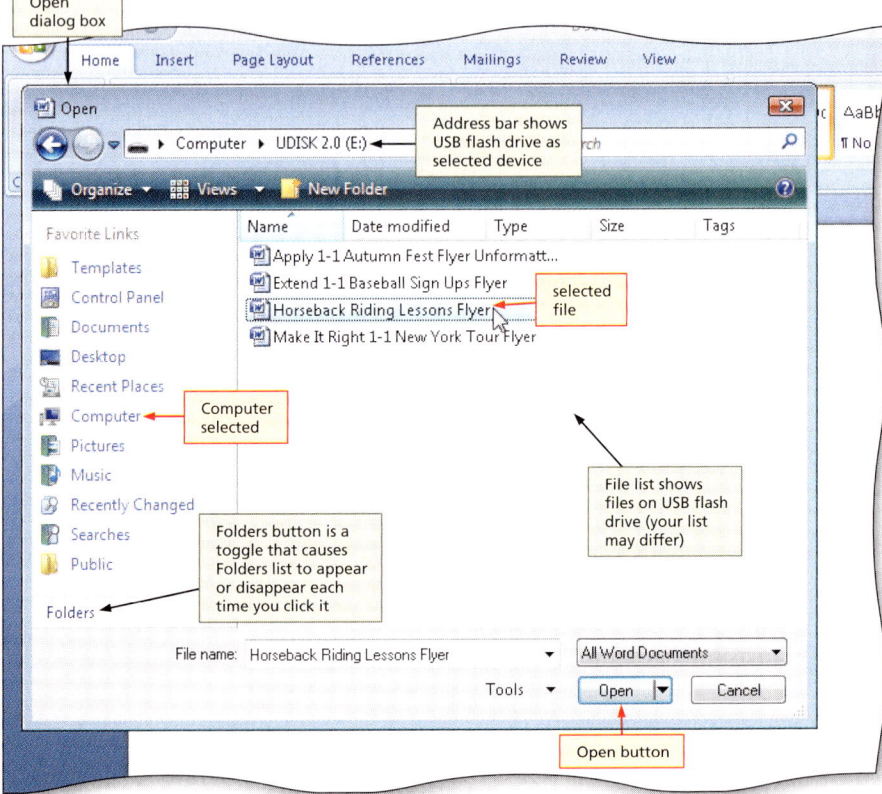

Figure 1–80

3
- Click the Open button to open the selected file and display the Horseback Riding Lessons Flyer document in the Word window (Figure 1–81).

Q&A Why is the Word icon and document name on the Windows Vista taskbar?

When you open a Word file, a Word program button is displayed on the taskbar. The button in Figure 1–81 contains an ellipsis because some of its contents do not fit in the allotted button space. If you point to a program button, its entire contents appear in a ScreenTip, which in this case would be the file name followed by the program name.

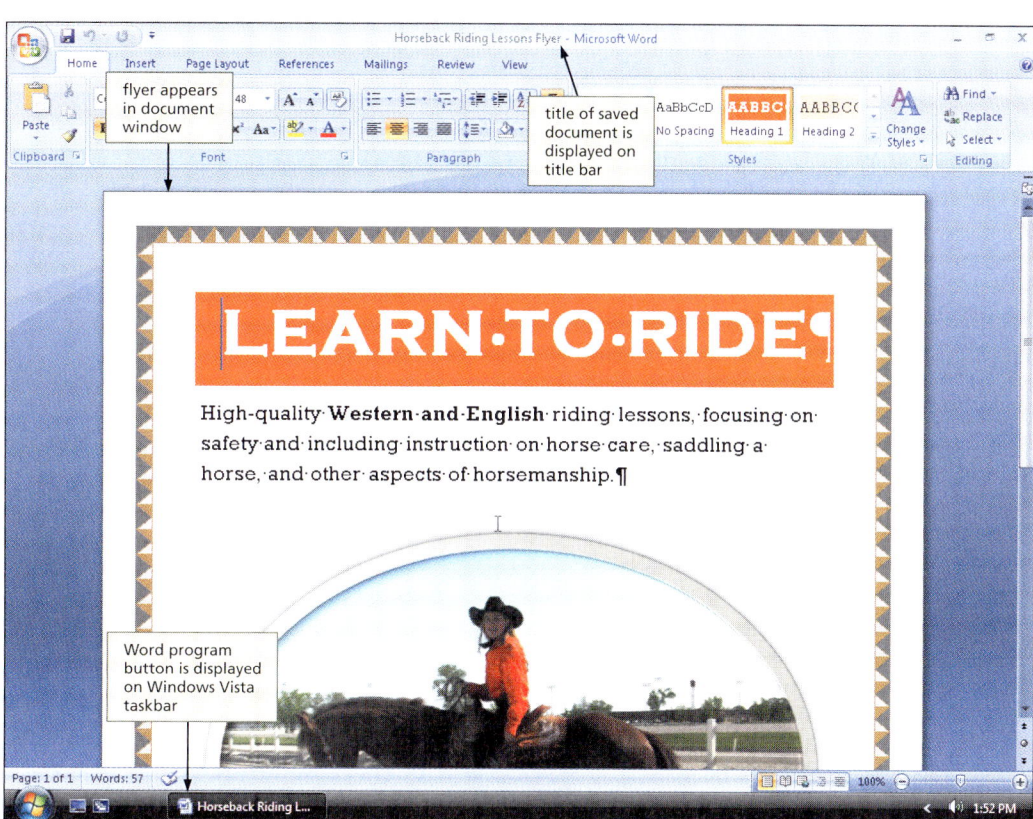

Figure 1–81

Other Ways
1. Click Office Button, click file name in Recent Documents list
2. Press CTRL+O, select file name, press ENTER

Correcting Errors

After creating a document, you often will find you must make changes to it. For example, the document may contain an error, or new circumstances may require you to add text to the document.

Types of Changes Made to Documents

The types of changes made to documents normally fall into one of the three following categories: additions, deletions, or modifications.

Additions Additional words, sentences, or paragraphs may be required in a document. Additions occur when you omit text from a document and want to insert it later. For example, additional types of riding lessons may be offered.

BTW **Print Preview**
You can preview a document before printing it by clicking the Office Button, pointing to Print, and then clicking Print Preview. When finished previewing the document, click the Close Print Preview button.

Deletions Sometimes, text in a document is incorrect or is no longer needed. For example, group lessons might not be offered. In this case, you would delete the words, $25 for group lessons, from the flyer.

Modifications If an error is made in a document or changes take place that affect the document, you might have to revise a word(s) in the text. For example, the fee per hour may change from $40 to $50 for private lessons.

To Insert Text in an Existing Document

Word inserts text to the left of the insertion point. The text to the right of the insertion point moves to the right and downward to fit the new text. The following steps insert the word, various, to the left of the word, aspects, in the flyer.

- Scroll through the document and then click to the left of the location of text to be inserted (in this case, the a in aspects) to position the insertion point where text should be inserted (Figure 1–82).

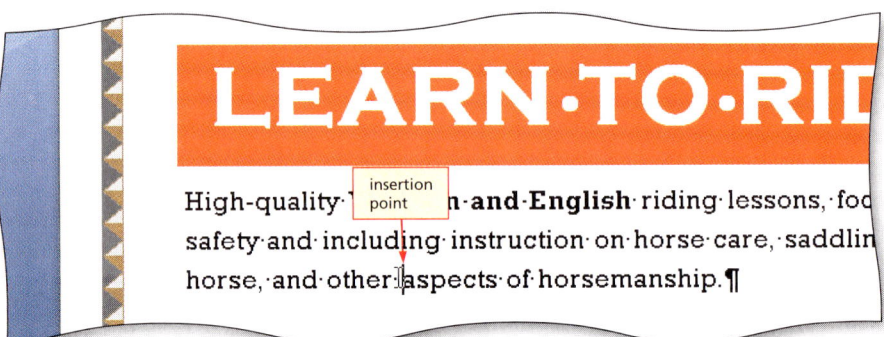

Figure 1–82

- Type various and then press the SPACEBAR to insert the word, various, to the left of the insertion point (Figure 1–83).

Why did the text move to the right as I typed?

In Word, the default typing mode is **insert mode**, which means as you type a character, Word moves all the characters to the right of the typed character one position to the right.

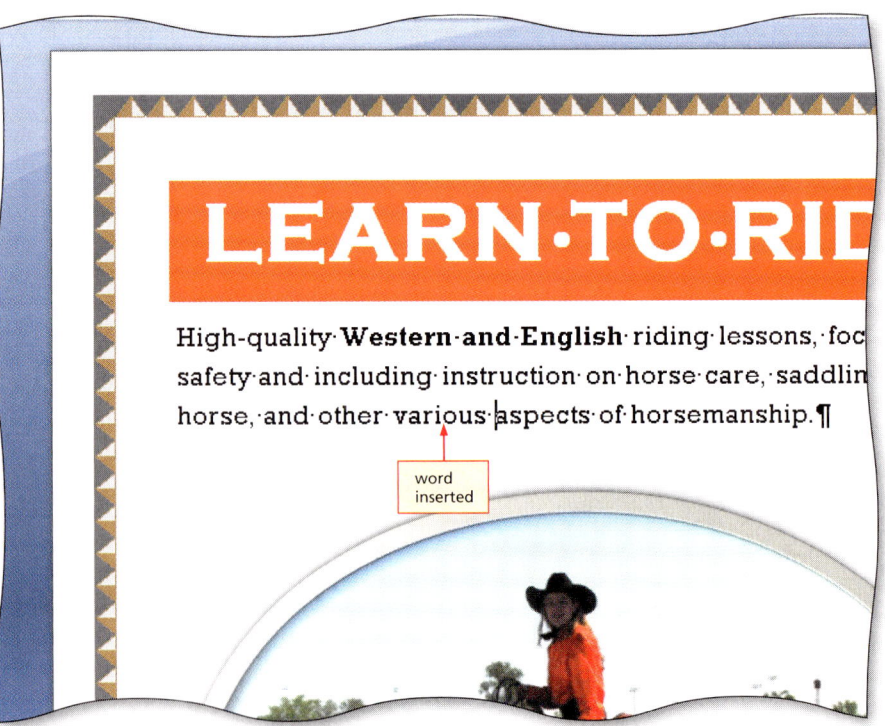

Figure 1–83

Deleting Text from an Existing Document

It is not unusual to type incorrect characters or words in a document. As discussed earlier in this chapter, you can click the Undo button on the Quick Access Toolbar to immediately undo a command or action — this includes typing. Word also provides other methods of correcting typing errors.

To delete an incorrect character in a document, simply click next to the incorrect character and then press the BACKSPACE key to erase to the left of the insertion point, or press the DELETE key to erase to the right of the insertion point.

To Select a Word and Delete It

To delete a word or phrase, you first must select the word or phrase. The following steps select the word, various, that was just added in the previous steps and then delete the selection.

- Position the mouse pointer somewhere in the word to be selected (in this case, various), as shown in Figure 1–84.

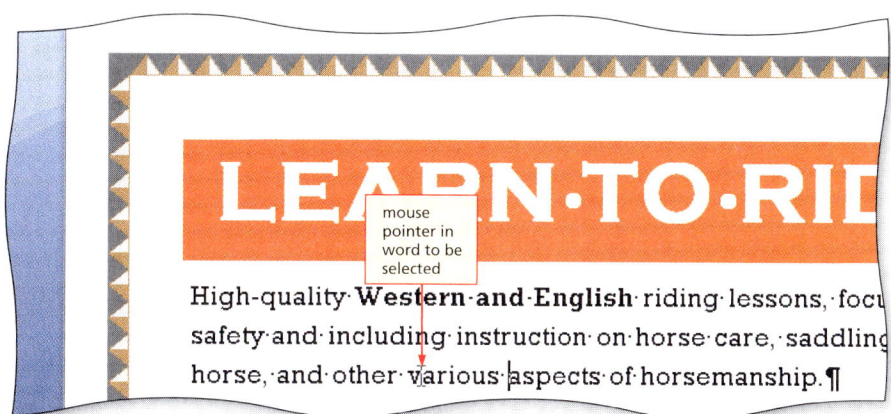

Figure 1–84

- Double-click the word to select it (Figure 1–85).

- With the text selected, press the DELETE key to delete the selected text (shown in Figure 1–82).

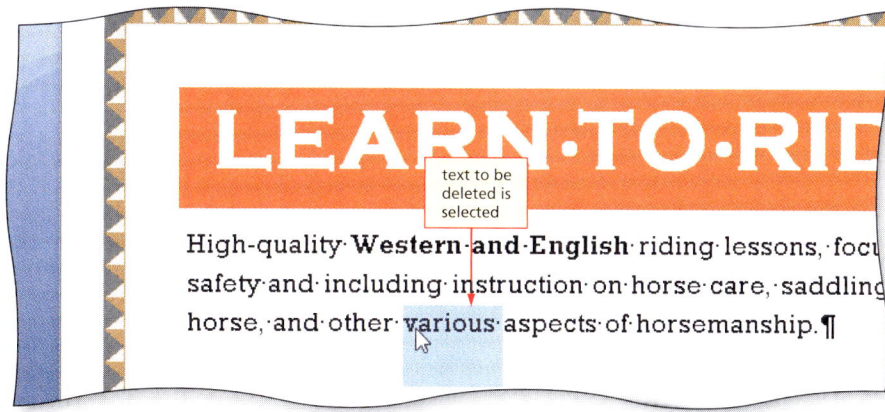

Figure 1–85

Closing the Entire Document

Sometimes, everything goes wrong. If this happens, you may want to close the document entirely and start over with a new document. You also may want to close a document when you are finished with it so you can begin your next document. If you wanted to close a document, you would use the steps on the next page.

To Close the Entire Document and Start Over

1. Click the Office Button and then click Close.
2. If Word displays a dialog box, click the No button to ignore the changes since the last time you saved the document.
3. Click the Office Button and then click New on the Office Button menu. When Word displays the New Document dialog box, click Blank document and then click the Create button.

> **BTW**
>
> **Word Help**
> The best way to become familiar with Word Help is to use it. Appendix B includes detailed information about Word Help and exercises that will help you gain confidence in using it.

Word Help

At any time while using Word, you can find answers to questions and display information about various topics through **Word Help**. Used properly, this form of assistance can increase your productivity and reduce your frustrations by minimizing the time you spend learning how to use Word.

This section introduces you to Word Help. Additional information about using Word Help is available in Appendix B.

To Search for Word Help

Using Word Help, you can search for information based on phrases such as save a document or format text, or key terms such as copy, save, or format. Word Help responds with a list of search results displayed as links to a variety of resources. The following steps, which use Word Help to search for information about selecting text, assume you are connected to the Internet.

- Click the Microsoft Office Word Help button near the upper-right corner of the Word window to open the Word Help window.

- Type select text in the 'Type words to search for' text box at the top of the Word Help window (Figure 1–86).

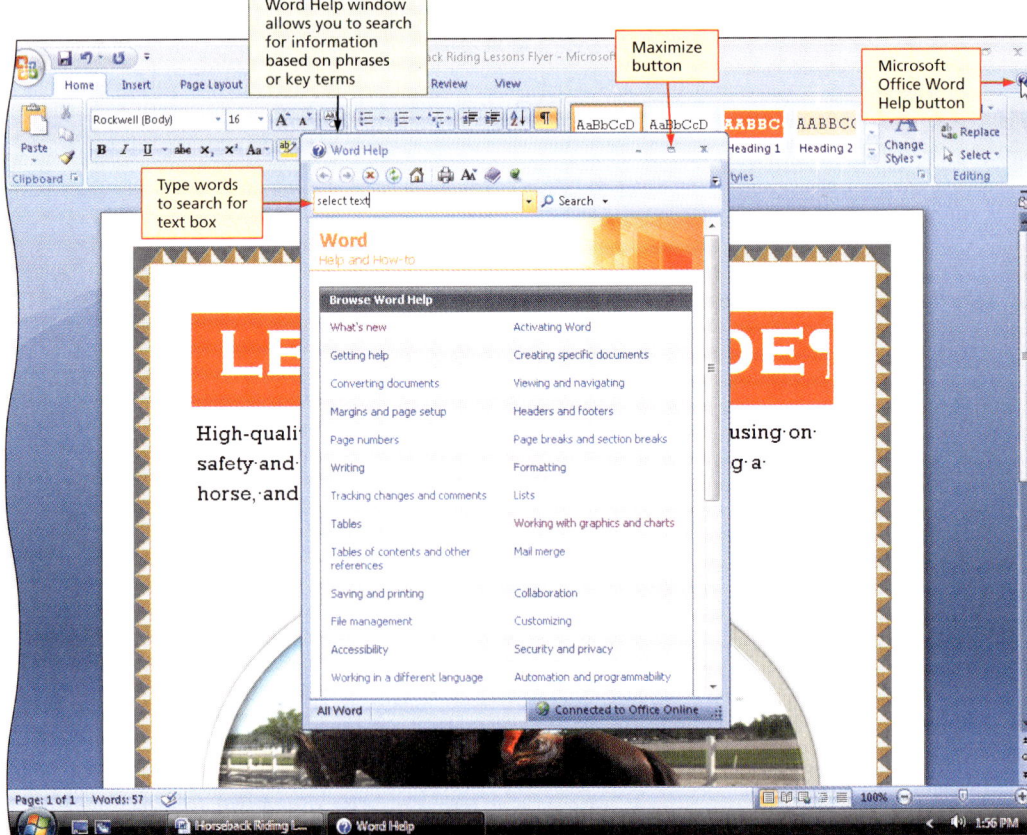

Figure 1–86

Creating and Editing a Word Document   **Word Chapter 1**   WD 61

- Press the ENTER key to display the search results.

- Click the Maximize button on the Word Help window title bar to maximize the Help window (Figure 1–87).

Q&A Where is the Word window with the Horseback Riding Lessons Flyer document?

Word is open in the background, but the Word Help window is overlaid on top of the Word window. When the Word Help window is closed, the document will reappear.

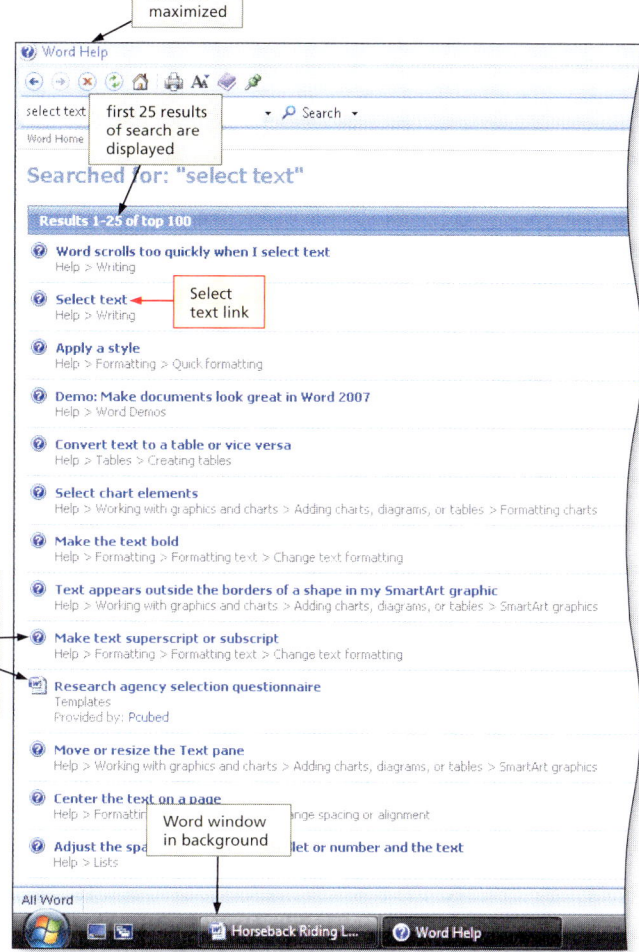

Figure 1–87

- Click the Select text link to display information about selecting text (Figure 1–88).

Q&A What is the purpose of the buttons at the top of the Word Help window?

Use the buttons in the upper-left corner of the Word Help window to navigate through Help, change the display, show the Word Help table of contents, and print the contents of the window.

- Click the Close button on the Word Help window title bar to close the Word Help window and redisplay the Word window.

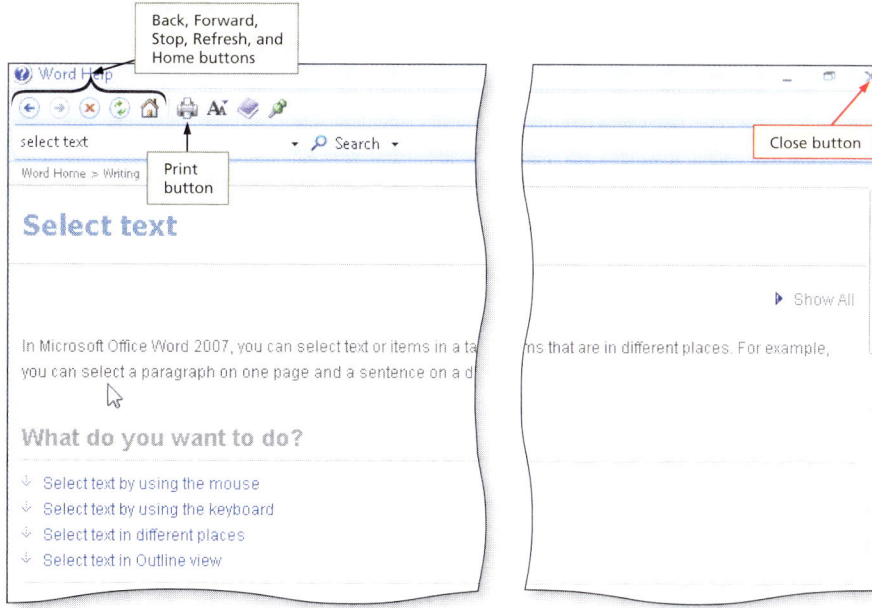

Figure 1–88

Other Ways
1. Press F1

BTW

Quick Reference
For a table that lists how to complete the tasks covered in this book using the mouse, Ribbon, shortcut menu, and keyboard, see the Quick Reference Summary at the back of this book, or visit the Word 2007 Quick Reference Web page (scsite.com/dc-off07/qr).

To Quit Word

The following steps quit Word.

1 Click the Close button on the right side of the title bar to quit Word; or if you have multiple Word documents open, click the Office Button and then click the Exit Word button on the Office Button menu to close all open documents and quit Word.

2 If necessary, click the No button in the Microsoft Office Word dialog box so that any changes you have made are not saved.

Chapter Summary

In this chapter you have learned how to enter text in a document, format text, insert a picture, format a picture, add a page border, and print a document. The items listed below include all the new Word skills you have learned in this chapter.

1. Start Word (WD 5)
2. Type Text (WD 13)
3. Display Formatting Marks (WD 14)
4. Wordwrap Text as You Type (WD 15)
5. Insert a Blank Line (WD 15)
6. Check Spelling and Grammar as You Type (WD 16)
7. Save a Document (WD 19)
8. Apply Styles (WD 24)
9. Center a Paragraph (WD 26)
10. Select a Line (WD 27)
11. Change the Font Size of Selected Text (WD 28)
12. Change the Font of Selected Text (WD 29)
13. Select Multiple Paragraphs (WD 30)
14. Bullet a List of Paragraphs (WD 32)
15. Undo and Redo an Action (WD 32)
16. Select a Group of Words (WD 33)
17. Bold Text (WD 34)
18. Underline a Word (WD 35)
19. Italicize Text (WD 36)
20. Change the Style Set (WD 37)
21. Change Theme Colors (WD 39)
22. Change Theme Fonts (WD 39)
23. Insert a Picture (WD 41)
24. Apply a Picture Style (WD 44)
25. Change a Picture Border Color (WD 45)
26. Zoom the Document (WD 45)
27. Resize a Graphic (WD 46)
28. Add a Page Border (WD 48)
29. Change Spacing Above and Below Paragraphs (WD 50)
30. Change Document Properties (WD 51)
31. Save an Existing Document with the Same File Name (WD 53)
32. Print a Document (WD 54)
33. Quit Word with One Document Open (WD 55)
34. Open a Document from Word (WD 56)
35. Insert Text in an Existing Document (WD 58)
36. Select a Word and Delete It (WD 59)
37. Close the Entire Document and Start Over (WD 60)
38. Search for Word Help (WD 60)

If you have a SAM user profile, you may have access to hands-on instruction, practice, and assessment. Log in to your SAM account (http://sam2007.course.com) to launch any assigned training activities or exams that relate to the skills covered in this chapter.

Learn It Online

Test your knowledge of chapter content and key terms.

Instructions: To complete the Learn It Online exercises, start your browser, click the Address bar, and then enter the Web address `scsite.com/dc-off07/wd2007/learn`. When the Word 2007 Learn It Online page is displayed, click the link for the exercise you want to complete and then read the instructions.

Chapter Reinforcement TF, MC, and SA
A series of true/false, multiple choice, and short answer questions that test your knowledge of the chapter content.

Flash Cards
An interactive learning environment where you identify chapter key terms associated with displayed definitions.

Practice Test
A series of multiple choice questions that test your knowledge of chapter content and key terms.

Who Wants To Be a Computer Genius?
An interactive game that challenges your knowledge of chapter content in the style of a television quiz show.

Wheel of Terms
An interactive game that challenges your knowledge of chapter key terms in the style of the television show *Wheel of Fortune*.

Crossword Puzzle Challenge
A crossword puzzle that challenges your knowledge of key terms presented in the chapter.

Apply Your Knowledge

Reinforce the skills and apply the concepts you learned in this chapter.

Modifying Text and Formatting a Document

Instructions: Start Word. Open the document, Apply 1-1 Autumn Fest Flyer Unformatted, from the Data Files for Students. See the inside back cover of this book for instructions on downloading the Data Files for Students, or contact your instructor for information about accessing the required files.

The document you open is an unformatted flyer. You are to modify text, format paragraphs and characters, and insert a picture in the flyer.

Perform the following tasks:
1. Delete the word, entire, in the sentence of body copy below the headline.
2. Insert the word, Creek, between the text, Honey Farm, in the sentence of body copy below the headline. The sentence should end: …Honey Creek Farm.
3. At the end of the signature line, change the period to an exclamation point. The sentence should end: …This Year's Fest!
4. Apply the Heading 1 style to the headline. Apply the Heading 2 style to the signature line.
5. Center the headline and the signature line.
6. Change the font and font size of the headline to 48-point Cooper Black, or a similar font.
7. Change the font size of body copy between the headline and the signature line to 22 point.
8. Change the font size of the signature line to 28 point.
9. Bullet the three lines (paragraphs) of text above the signature line.
10. Bold the text, October 4 and 5.

Continued >

Apply Your Knowledge *continued*

11. Underline the word, and, in the first bulleted paragraph.
12. Italicize the text in the signature line.
13. Change the theme colors to the Civic color scheme.
14. Change the theme fonts to the Opulent font set.
15. Change the zoom to 50 percent so the entire page is visible in the document window.
16. Change the spacing before the headline paragraph to 0 point. Change the spacing after the headline paragraph to 12 point.
17. Insert the picture of the combine centered on the blank line above the bulleted list. The picture is called Fall Harvest and is available on the Data Files for Students. Apply the Snip Diagonal Corner, White picture style to the inserted picture. Change the color of the picture border to Orange, Accent 6.
18. The entire flyer now should fit on a single page. If it flows to two pages, resize the picture or decrease spacing before and after paragraphs until the entire flyer text fits on a single page.
19. Enter the text, Honey Creek, as the keywords. Change the other document properties, as specified by your instructor.
20. Click the Office Button and then click Save As. Save the document using the file name, Apply 1-1 Autumn Fest Flyer Formatted.
21. Position the Quick Access Toolbar below the Ribbon. Save the document again by clicking the Save button. Reposition the Quick Access Toolbar above the Ribbon.
22. Submit the revised document, shown in Figure 1–89, in the format specified by your instructor.

Figure 1–89

Creating and Editing a Word Document   Word Chapter 1   WD 65

Extend Your Knowledge

Extend the skills you learned in this chapter and experiment with new skills. You may need to use Help to complete the assignment.

Modifying Text and Graphics Formats

Instructions: Start Word. Open the document, Extend 1-1 Baseball Sign Ups Flyer, from the Data Files for Students. See the inside back cover of this book for instructions on downloading the Data Files for Students, or contact your instructor for information about accessing the required files.

You will enhance the look of the flyer shown in Figure 1–90.

Perform the following tasks:

1. Use Help to learn about the following formats: grow font, shrink font, change text color, decorative underline, and change bullet.
2. Select the headline and use the Grow Font button to increase its font size just enough so that the headline still fits on a single line. If it wraps to two lines, use the Shrink Font button.
3. Change the font color of all body copy between the headline and the signature line to a color other than Automatic, or Black.
4. Change the picture style of the picture so that it is not the Drop Shadow Rectangle picture style. Add a Glow picture effect to the picture of the baseball player.
5. Change the solid underline below the words, Indoor facility, to a decorative underline.
6. Change the color and width of the border.
7. Change the style of the bullets to a character other than the dot.
8. Change the document properties, including keywords, as specified by your instructor. Save the revised document with a new file name and then submit it in the format specified by your instructor.

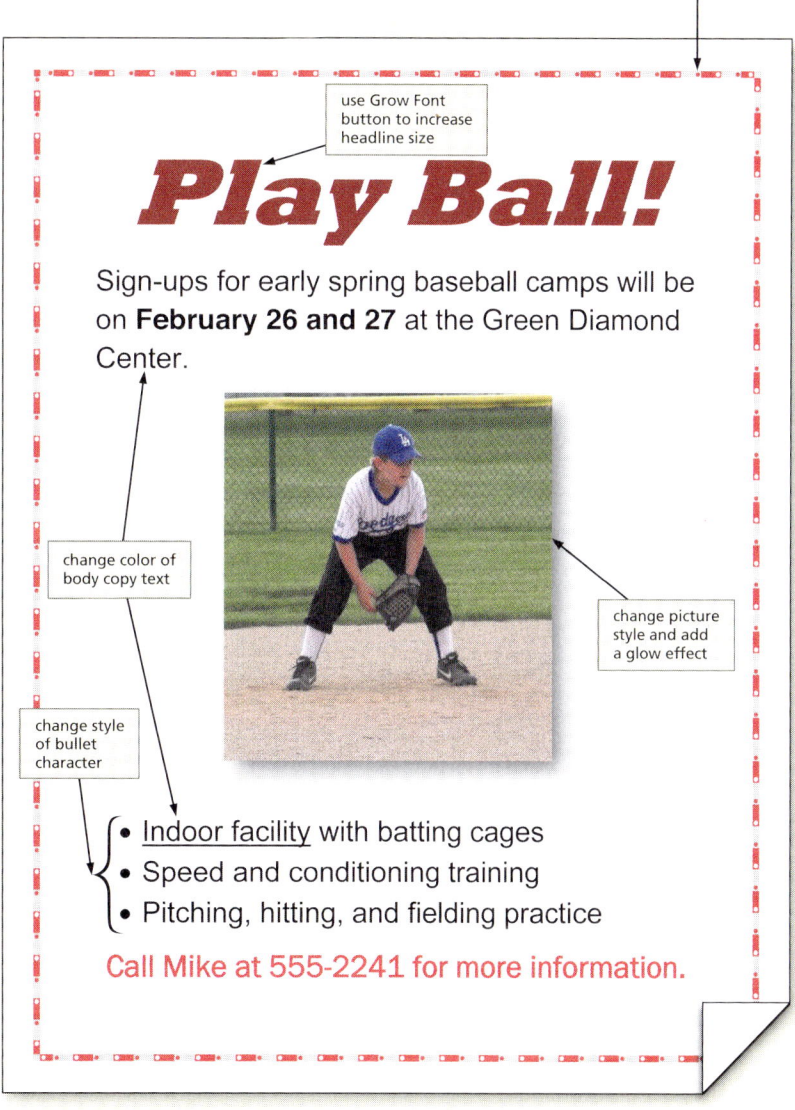

Figure 1–90

Make It Right

Analyze a document and correct all errors and/or improve the design.

Correcting Spelling and Grammar Errors

Instructions: Start Word. Open the document, Make It Right 1-1 New York Tour Flyer, from the Data Files for Students. See the inside back cover of this book for instructions on downloading the Data Files for Students, or contact your instructor for information on accessing the required files.

The document is a flyer that contains spelling and grammar errors, as shown in Figure 1–91. You are to correct each spelling (red wavy underline) and grammar error (green wavy underline) by right-clicking the flagged text and then clicking the appropriate correction on the shortcut menu. If your screen does not display the wavy underlines, click the Office Button and then click the Word Options button. When the Word Options dialog box is displayed, click Proofing, be sure the 'Hide spelling errors in this document only' and 'Hide grammar errors in this document only' check boxes do not have check marks, and then click the OK button. If your screen still does not display the wavy underlines, redisplay the Word Options dialog box, click Proofing, and then click the Recheck Document button.

Change the document properties, including keywords, as specified by your instructor. Save the revised document with a new file name and then submit it in the format specified by your instructor.

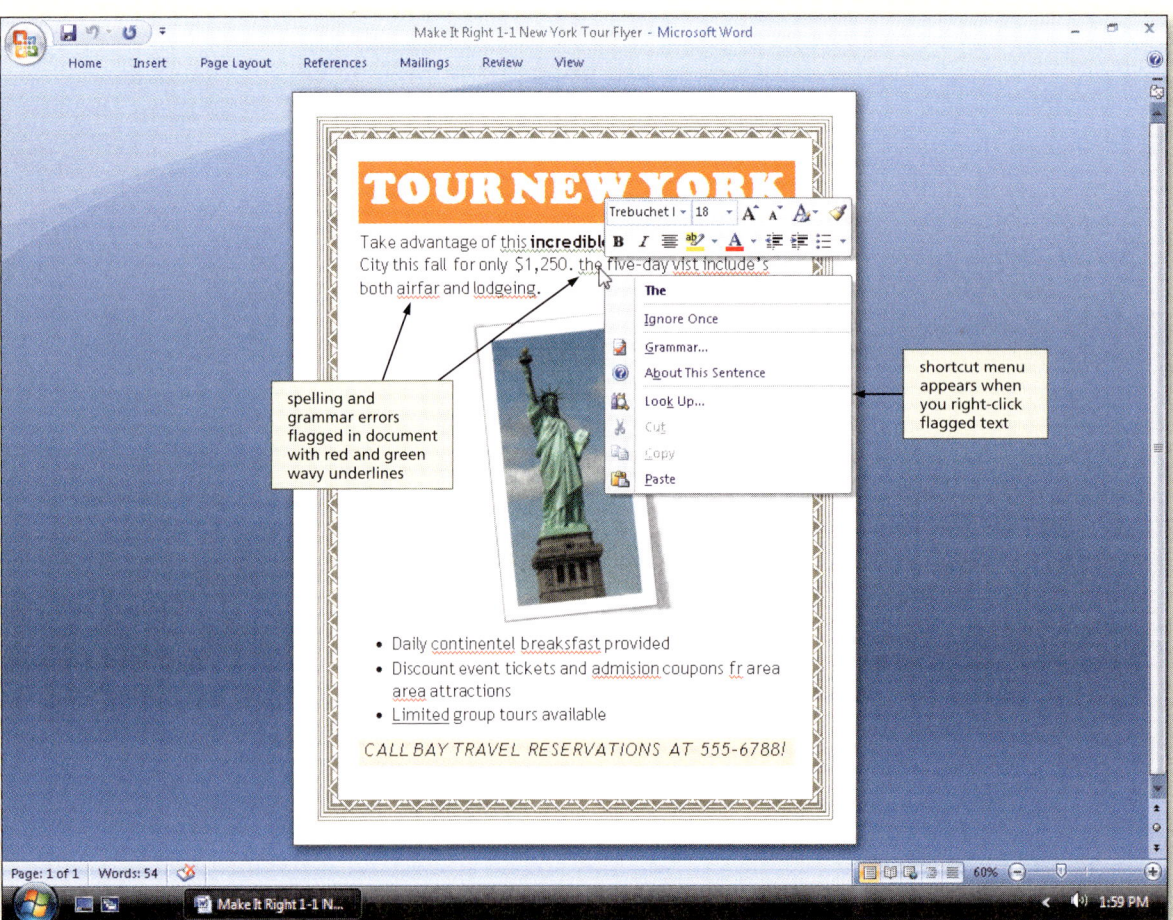

Figure 1–91

In the Lab

Design and/or create a document using the guidelines, concepts, and skills presented in this chapter. Labs are listed in order of increasing difficulty.

Lab 1: Creating a Flyer with a Picture

Problem: You work part-time at Scenic Air. Your boss has asked you to prepare a flyer that advertises aerial tours over the city of Campton. First, you prepare the unformatted flyer shown in Figure 1–92a, and then you format it so that it looks like Figure 1–92b on the next page. *Hint:* Remember, if you make a mistake while formatting the flyer, you can click the Undo button on the Quick Access Toolbar to undo your last action.

Instructions: Perform the following tasks:

1. Display formatting marks on the screen.
2. Type the flyer text, unformatted, as shown in Figure 1–92a. If Word flags any misspelled words as you type, check the spelling of these words and correct them.
3. Save the document on a USB flash drive using the file name, Lab 1-1 Airplane Rides Flyer.
4. Apply the Heading 1 style to the headline. Apply the Heading 2 style to the signature line.
5. Center the headline and the signature line.
6. Change the font and font size of the headline to 48-point Arial Rounded MT Bold, or a similar font.
7. Change the font size of body copy between the headline and the signature line to 22 point.
8. Change the font size of the signature line to 28 point.
9. Bullet the three lines (paragraphs) of text above the signature line.
10. Bold the text, change your view.
11. Italicize the word, aerial.

Airplane Rides

Gain an entirely new vision of Campton by taking an aerial tour. Visitor or local, business or pleasure, the trip will change your view of the city.

Pilots are licensed and experienced

15-, 30-, or 60-minute tours available during daylight hours

Individual and group rates

Call Scenic Air at 555-9883!

Figure 1–92a

Continued >

In the Lab *continued*

12. Underline the word, and, in the first bulleted paragraph.
13. Change the style set to Formal.
14. Change the theme fonts to the Metro font set.
15. Change the zoom to 50 percent so the entire page is visible in the document window.
16. Change the spacing before the headline to 0 point. Change the spacing after the first paragraph of body copy to 0 point. Change the spacing before the first bulleted paragraph to 12 point.
17. Insert the picture on the blank line above the bulleted list. The picture is called Airplane Ride over City and is available on the Data Files for Students. Apply the Relaxed Perspective, White picture style to the inserted picture.
18. The entire flyer should fit on a single page. If it flows to two pages, resize the picture or decrease spacing before and after paragraphs until the entire flyer text fits on a single page.
19. Change the document properties, including keywords, as specified by your instructor.
20. Save the flyer again with the same file name.
21. Submit the document, shown in Figure 1–92b, in the format specified by your instructor.

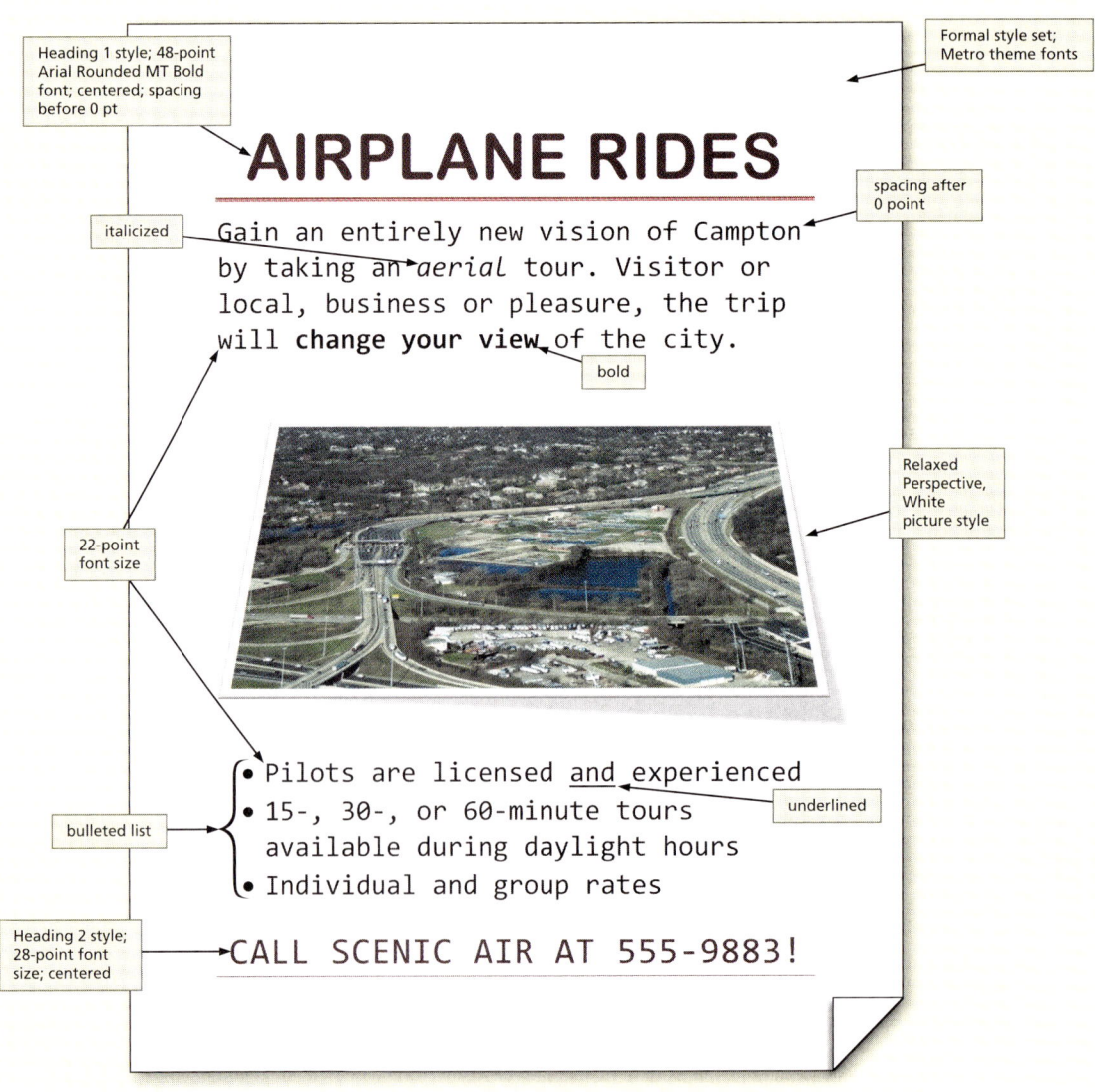

Figure 1–92b

In the Lab

Lab 2: Creating a Flyer with a Picture and a Border

Problem: Your boss at Danvers Nursery has asked you to prepare a flyer that promotes its expanded greenhouses and grounds. You prepare the flyer shown in Figure 1–93. *Hint:* Remember, if you make a mistake while formatting the flyer, you can click the Undo button on the Quick Access Toolbar to undo your last action.

Instructions: Perform the following tasks:
1. Display formatting marks on the screen.
2. Type the flyer text, unformatted. If Word flags any misspelled words as you type, check the spelling of these words and correct them.
3. Save the document on a USB flash drive using the file name, Lab 1-2 Nursery Expansion Flyer.

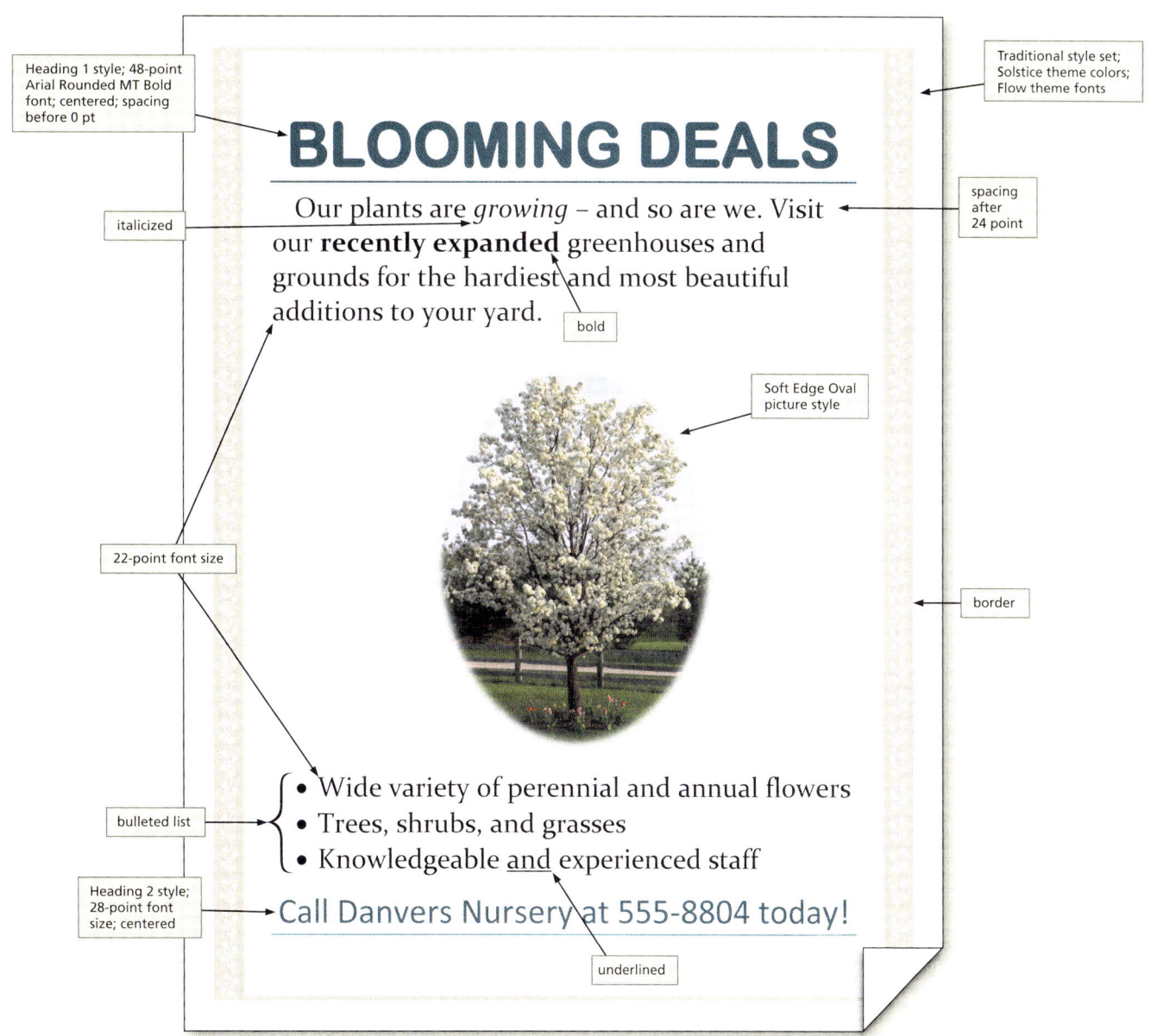

Figure 1–93

Continued >

In the Lab *continued*

4. Apply the Heading 1 style to the headline. Apply the Heading 2 style to the signature line.
5. Center the headline and the signature line.
6. Change the font and font size of the headline to 48-point Arial Rounded MT Bold, or a similar font.
7. Change the font size of body copy between the headline and the signature line to 22 point.
8. Change the font size of the signature line to 28 point.
9. Bullet the three lines (paragraphs) of text above the signature line.
10. Italicize the word, growing.
11. Bold the text, recently expanded.
12. Underline the word, and, in the third bulleted paragraph.
13. Change the style set to Traditional.
14. Change the theme colors to the Solstice color scheme.
15. Change the theme fonts to the Flow font set.
16. Change the zoom to 50 percent so the entire page is visible in the document window.
17. Change the spacing before the headline to 0 point. Change the spacing after the first paragraph of body copy to 24 point. Change the spacing before the first bulleted paragraph to 12 point.
18. Insert the picture on the blank line above the bulleted list. The picture is called Bradford Pear in Bloom and is available on the Data Files for Students. Apply the Soft Edge Oval picture style to the inserted picture.
19. The entire flyer should fit on a single page. If it flows to two pages, resize the picture or decrease spacing before and after paragraphs until the entire flyer text fits on a single page.
20. Add the graphic border, shown in Figure 1–93 on the previous page (about one-third down in the Art gallery). Change the color of the border to Tan, Background 2.
21. Change the document properties, including keywords, as specified by your instructor.
22. Save the flyer again with the same file name.
23. Submit the document, shown in Figure 1–93, in the format specified by your instructor.

In the Lab

Lab 3: Creating a Flyer with a Picture and Resized Border Art

Problem: Your neighbor has asked you to prepare a flyer that promotes her cabin rental business. You prepare the flyer shown in Figure 1–94.

Instructions: Enter the text in the flyer, checking spelling as you type, and then format it as shown in Figure 1–94. The picture to be inserted is called Paddle Boat on Lake and is available on the Data Files for Students. After adding the page border, reduce the point size of its width so that the border is not so predominant on the page. Change the document properties, including keywords, as specified by your instructor. Save the document on a USB flash drive using the file name, Lab 1-3 Cabin Rentals Flyer. Submit the document, shown in Figure 1–94, in the format specified by your instructor.

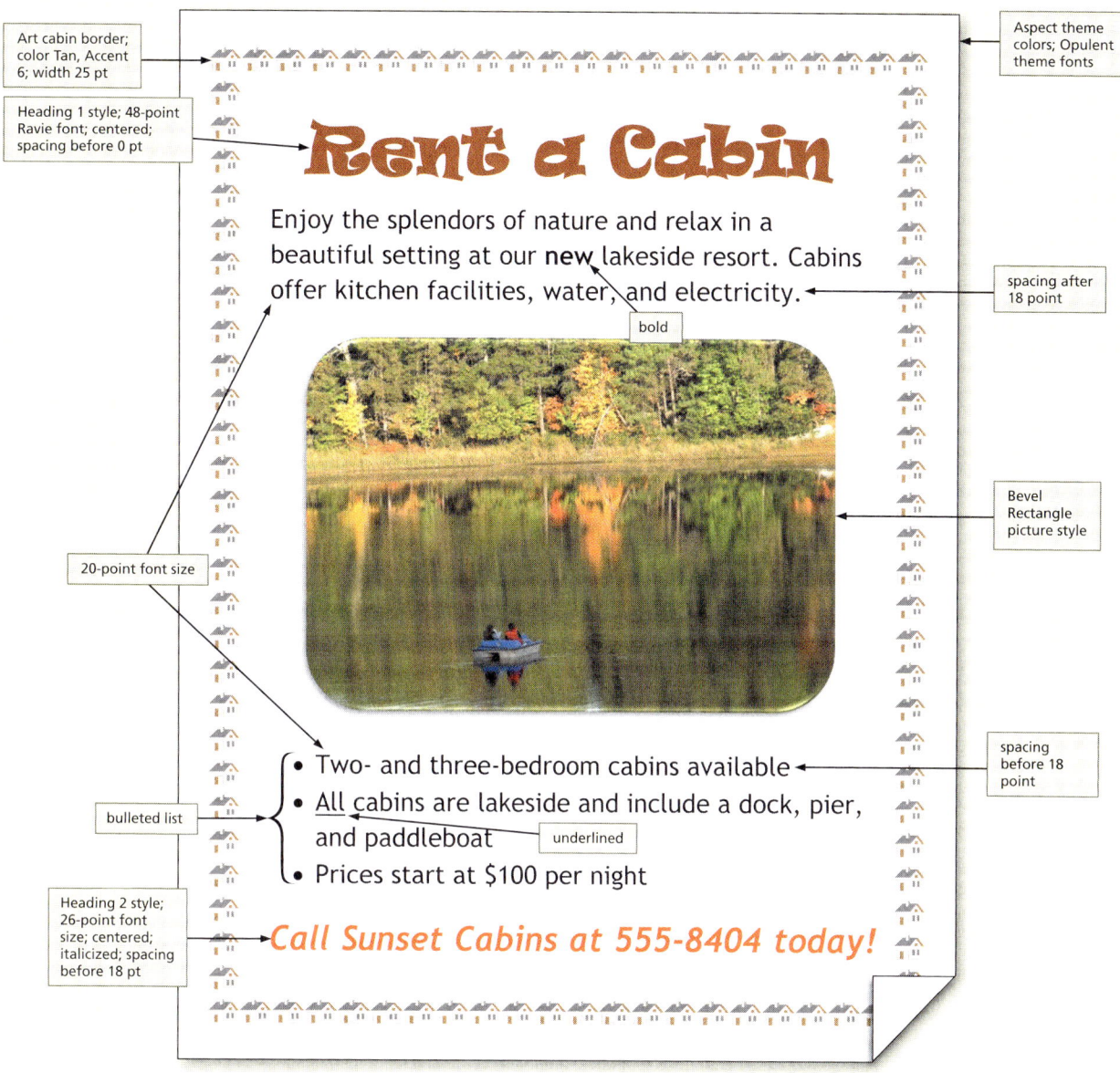

Figure 1–94

Cases and Places

Apply your creative thinking and problem solving skills to design and implement a solution.

• Easier   •• More Difficult

• **1: Design and Create a Grand Reopening Flyer**

Your friend owns the Craft Barn, a large, year-round craft fair. She recently has renovated and remodeled the facility and is planning a grand reopening. She has asked you to create a flyer advertising this fact. The flyer should contain the following headline: Craft Barn. The first paragraph of text below the headline should read: Pick up a jar of homemade jam or a handcrafted gift at the completely remodeled and renovated Craft Barn, located at 8701 County Road 300 West. Insert the photograph named, Barn and Silo, which is available on the Data Files for Students. The bullet items

Continued >

Cases and Places *continued*

under the photograph should read as follows: first bullet – Expanded and paved parking; second bullet – More than 150 booths; and third bullet – Open Monday through Saturday, 10:00 a.m. to 7:00 p.m. The last line should read: Call 555-5709 for more information! Use the concepts and techniques presented in this chapter to create and format this flyer. Be sure to check spelling and grammar.

• 2: Design and Create a Property Advertisement Flyer
As a part-time employee of Markum Realty, you have been assigned the task of preparing a flyer advertising lakefront property. The headline should read: Lakefront Lot. The first paragraph of text should read as follows: Build the house of your dreams or a weekend getaway on this beautiful lakeside property located on the north side of Lake Pleasant. Insert the photograph named, Lake at Sunset, which is available on the Data Files for Students. Below the photograph, insert the following bullet items: first bullet — City sewer and water available; second bullet – Lot size 110 × 300; third bullet – List price $65,000. The last line should read: Call Markum Realty at 555-0995 for a tour! Use the concepts and techniques presented in this chapter to create and format this flyer. Be sure to check spelling and grammar.

•• 3: Design and Create a Flyer for the Sale of a Business
After 25 years, your Uncle Mitch has decided to sell his ice cream shop and wants you to help him create a sales flyer. The shop is in a choice location at the corner of 135th and Main Street and has an established customer base. The building has an adjacent, paved parking lot, as well as an outdoor seating area. He wants to sell the store and all its contents, including the equipment, tables, booths, and chairs. The 1200-square-foot shop recently was appraised at $200,000, and your uncle is willing to sell for cash or on contract. Use the concepts and techniques presented in this chapter to create and format a sales flyer. Include a headline, descriptive body copy, a signature line, an appropriate photograph or clip art image, a bulleted list, a decorative underline, and if appropriate, a page border. Be sure to check spelling and grammar in the flyer.

•• 4: Design and Create a Flyer that Advertises You
Make It Personal
Everyone has at least one skill, talent, or special capability, which if shared with others, can lead to opportunity for growth, experience, and personal reward. Perhaps you play a musical instrument. If so, you could offer lessons. Maybe you are a skilled carpenter or other tradesman who could advertise your services. If you speak a second language, you could offer tutoring. Budding athletes might harbor a desire to pass on their knowledge by coaching a youth sports team. You may have a special knack for singing, sewing, knitting, photography, typing, housecleaning, or pet care. Carefully consider your own personal capabilities, skills, and talents and then use the concepts and techniques presented in this chapter to create a flyer advertising a service you can provide. Include a headline, descriptive body copy, a signature line, an appropriate photograph or clip art image, a bulleted list, a decorative underline, and if appropriate, a page border. Be sure to check spelling and grammar in the flyer.

•• 5: Redesign and Enhance a Poorly Designed Flyer
Working Together
Public locations, such as stores, schools, and libraries, have bulletin boards or windows for people to post flyers. Often, these bulletin boards or windows have so many flyers that some go unnoticed. Locate a posted flyer on a bulletin board or window that you think might be overlooked. Copy the text from the flyer and distribute it to each team member. Each member then independently should use this text, together with the techniques presented in this chapter, to create a flyer that would be more likely to catch the attention of passersby. Be sure to check spelling and grammar. As a group, critique each flyer and have team members redesign their flyer based on the group's recommendations. Hand in each team member's original and final flyers.

Microsoft Office **Word 2007**

2 Creating a Research Paper

Objectives

You will have mastered the material in this chapter when you can:

- Describe the MLA documentation style for research papers
- Change line and paragraph spacing in a document
- Use a header to number pages of a document
- Apply formatting using shortcut keys
- Modify paragraph indentation
- Create and modify styles
- Insert and edit citations and their sources
- Add a footnote to a document
- Insert a manual page break
- Create a bibliographical list of sources
- Move text
- Find and replace text
- Use the Research task pane to look up information

2 Creating a Research Paper

Introduction

In both academic and business environments, you will be asked to write reports. Business reports range from proposals to cost justifications to five-year plans to research findings. Academic reports focus mostly on research findings. A **research paper** is a document you can use to communicate the results of research findings. To write a research paper, you learn about a particular topic from a variety of sources (research), organize your ideas from the research results, and then present relevant facts and/or opinions that support the topic. Your final research paper combines properly credited outside information along with personal insights. Thus, no two research papers — even if about the same topic — will or should be the same.

Project — Research Paper

When preparing a research paper, you should follow a standard documentation style that defines the rules for creating the paper and crediting sources. A variety of documentation styles exists, depending on the nature of the research paper. Each style requires the same basic information; the differences in styles relate to requirements for presenting the information. For example, one documentation style uses the term bibliography for the list of sources, whereas another uses references, and yet a third prefers the title works cited. Two popular documentation styles for research papers are the **Modern Language Association of America** (**MLA**) and **American Psychological Association** (**APA**) styles. This chapter uses the MLA documentation style because it is used in a wide range of disciplines.

The project in this chapter follows research paper guidelines and uses Word to create the short research paper shown in Figure 2–1. This paper, which discusses three types of wireless communications, follows the MLA documentation style. Each page contains a page number. The first two pages present the heading (name, course, and date information), paper title, an introduction with a thesis statement, details that support the thesis, and a conclusion. This section of the paper also includes references to research sources. The third page contains a detailed, alphabetical list of the sources used in the research paper.

Overview

As you read through this chapter, you will learn how to create the research paper shown in Figure 2–1 by performing these general tasks:

- Change the document settings.
- Type the research paper.
- Save the research paper.
- Create an alphabetical list of sources.
- Proof and revise the research paper.
- Print the research paper.

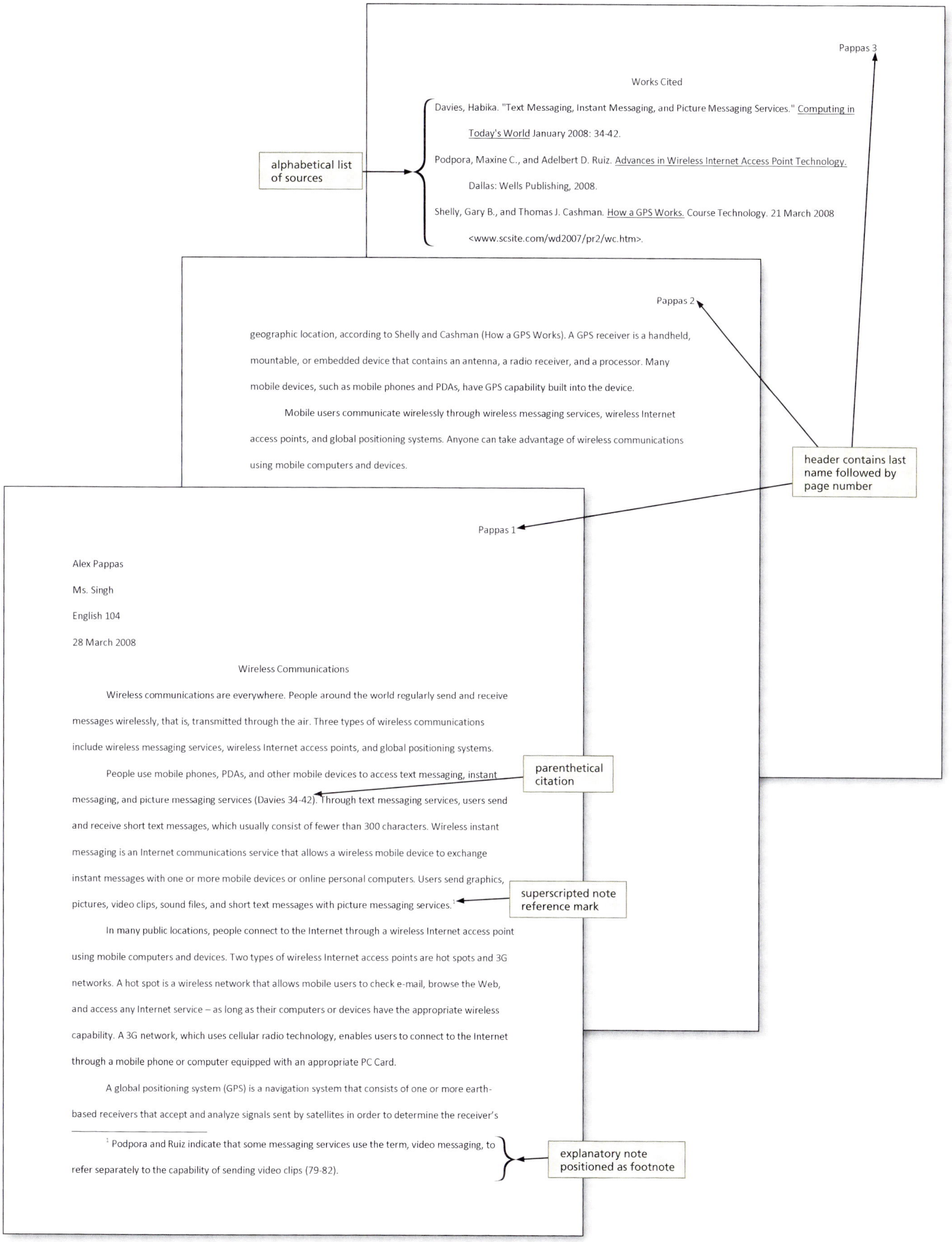

Pappas 3

Works Cited

Davies, Habika. "Text Messaging, Instant Messaging, and Picture Messaging Services." Computing in Today's World January 2008: 34-42.

Podpora, Maxine C., and Adelbert D. Ruiz. Advances in Wireless Internet Access Point Technology. Dallas: Wells Publishing, 2008.

Shelly, Gary B., and Thomas J. Cashman. How a GPS Works. Course Technology. 21 March 2008 <www.scsite.com/wd2007/pr2/wc.htm>.

alphabetical list of sources

Pappas 2

geographic location, according to Shelly and Cashman (How a GPS Works). A GPS receiver is a handheld, mountable, or embedded device that contains an antenna, a radio receiver, and a processor. Many mobile devices, such as mobile phones and PDAs, have GPS capability built into the device.

Mobile users communicate wirelessly through wireless messaging services, wireless Internet access points, and global positioning systems. Anyone can take advantage of wireless communications using mobile computers and devices.

header contains last name followed by page number

Pappas 1

Alex Pappas

Ms. Singh

English 104

28 March 2008

Wireless Communications

Wireless communications are everywhere. People around the world regularly send and receive messages wirelessly, that is, transmitted through the air. Three types of wireless communications include wireless messaging services, wireless Internet access points, and global positioning systems.

People use mobile phones, PDAs, and other mobile devices to access text messaging, instant messaging, and picture messaging services (Davies 34-42). Through text messaging services, users send and receive short text messages, which usually consist of fewer than 300 characters. Wireless instant messaging is an Internet communications service that allows a wireless mobile device to exchange instant messages with one or more mobile devices or online personal computers. Users send graphics, pictures, video clips, sound files, and short text messages with picture messaging services.[1]

parenthetical citation

superscripted note reference mark

In many public locations, people connect to the Internet through a wireless Internet access point using mobile computers and devices. Two types of wireless Internet access points are hot spots and 3G networks. A hot spot is a wireless network that allows mobile users to check e-mail, browse the Web, and access any Internet service – as long as their computers or devices have the appropriate wireless capability. A 3G network, which uses cellular radio technology, enables users to connect to the Internet through a mobile phone or computer equipped with an appropriate PC Card.

A global positioning system (GPS) is a navigation system that consists of one or more earth-based receivers that accept and analyze signals sent by satellites in order to determine the receiver's

---

[1] Podpora and Ruiz indicate that some messaging services use the term, video messaging, to refer separately to the capability of sending video clips (79-82).

explanatory note positioned as footnote

Figure 2–1

Plan Ahead

General Project Guidelines
When creating a Word document, the actions you perform and decisions you make will affect the appearance and characteristics of the finished document. As you create a research paper, such as the project shown in Figure 2–1 on the previous page, you should follow these general guidelines:

1. **Select a topic.** Spend time brainstorming ideas for a topic. Choose one you find interesting. For shorter papers, narrow down the scope of the topic; for longer papers, broaden the scope. Identify a tentative thesis statement, which is a sentence describing the paper's subject matter.

2. **Research the topic and take notes.** Gather credible, relevant information about the topic that supports the thesis statement. Sources of research include books, magazines, newspapers, and the Internet. As you record facts and ideas, list details about the source: title, author, place of publication, publisher, date of publication, etc. When taking notes, be careful not to **plagiarize**. That is, do not use someone else's work and claim it to be your own. If you copy information directly, place it in quotation marks and identify its source.

3. **Organize your ideas.** Classify your notes into related concepts. Make an outline from the categories of notes. In the outline, identify all main ideas and supporting details.

4. **Write the first draft, referencing sources.** From the outline, compose the paper. Every research paper should include an introduction containing the thesis statement, supporting details, and a conclusion. Follow the guidelines identified in the required documentation style. Reference all sources of information.

5. **Create the list of sources.** Using the formats specified in the required documentation style, completely list all sources referenced in the body of the research paper in alphabetical order.

6. **Proofread and revise the paper.** If possible, proofread the paper with a fresh set of eyes, that is, at least one to two days after completing the first draft. Proofreading involves reading the paper with the intent of identifying errors (spelling, grammar, etc.) and looking for ways to improve the paper (wording, transitions, flow, etc.). Try reading the paper out loud, which helps to identify unclear or awkward wording. Ask someone else to proofread the paper and give you suggestions for improvements.

When necessary, more specific details concerning the above guidelines are presented at appropriate points in the chapter. The chapter also will identify the actions performed and decisions made regarding these guidelines during the creation of the research paper shown in Figure 2–1.

BTW

APA Documentation Style
In the APA style, a separate title page is required instead of placing name and course information on the paper's first page. Double-space all pages of the paper with 1.5" top, bottom, left, and right margins. Indent the first word of each paragraph .5" from the left margin. In the upper-right margin of each page, including the title page, place a running head that consists of the page number double-spaced below a brief summary of the paper title.

MLA Documentation Style

The research paper in this project follows the guidelines presented by the MLA. To follow the MLA style, double-space text on all pages of the paper using one-inch top, bottom, left, and right margins. Indent the first word of each paragraph one-half inch from the left margin. At the right margin of each page, place a page number one-half inch from the top margin. On each page, precede the page number by your last name.

The MLA style does not require a title page. Instead, place your name and course information in a block at the left margin beginning one inch from the top of the page. Center the title one double-space below your name and course information.

In the text of the paper, place author references in parentheses with the page number(s) of the referenced information. The MLA style uses in-text **parenthetical citations** instead of noting each source at the bottom of the page or at the end of the paper. In the MLA style, notes are used only for optional explanatory notes.

If used, explanatory notes elaborate on points discussed in the paper. Use a superscript (raised number) to signal that an explanatory note exists, and also to sequence the notes. Position explanatory notes either at the bottom of the page as footnotes or at the end of the paper as endnotes. Indent the first line of each explanatory note one-half inch from the left margin. Place one space following the superscripted number before beginning the note text. Double-space the note text. At the end of the note text, you may list bibliographic information for further reference.

The MLA style uses the term **works cited** to refer to the bibliographic list of sources at the end of the paper. The works cited page alphabetically lists sources that are referenced directly in the paper. Place the list of sources on a separate numbered page. Center the title, Works Cited, one inch from the top margin. Double-space all lines. Begin the first line of each source at the left margin, indenting subsequent lines of the same source one-half inch from the left margin. List each source by the author's last name, or, if the author's name is not available, by the title of the source. Underline or italicize the title of each source.

Changing Document Settings

The MLA documentation style defines some global formats that apply to the entire research paper. Some of these formats are the default in Word. For example, the default left, right, top, and bottom margin settings in Word are one inch, which meets the MLA style. You will modify, however, the paragraph and line spacing and header formats as required by the MLA style.

After starting Word, the following pages adjust line and paragraph spacing and define a header for the current document.

To Start Word

If you are using a computer to step through the project in this chapter and you want your screens to match the figures in this book, you should change your computer's resolution to 1024 × 768. For information about how to change a computer's resolution, read Appendix C.

The following steps, which assume Windows Vista is running, start Word based on a typical installation. You may need to ask your instructor how to start Word for your computer.

1. Click the Start button on the Windows Vista taskbar to display the Start menu and then click All Programs at the bottom of the left pane on the Start menu to display the All Programs list.

2. Click Microsoft Office in the All Programs list to display the Microsoft Office list and then click Microsoft Office Word 2007 to start Word and display a new blank document in the Word window.

3. If the Word window is not maximized, click the Maximize button next to the Close button on its title bar to maximize the window.

4. If the Print Layout button is not selected, click it so that your screen layout matches Figure 2–2 on the next page.

5. If your zoom percent is not 100, click the Zoom Out or Zoom In button as many times as necessary until the Zoom level button displays 100% on its face.

To Display Formatting Marks

As discussed in Chapter 1, it is helpful to display formatting marks that indicate where in the document you pressed the ENTER key, SPACEBAR, and other keys. The following step displays formatting marks.

1. If necessary, click Home on the Ribbon to display the Home tab. If the Show/Hide ¶ button on the Home tab is not selected already, click it to display formatting marks on the screen.

BTW

Line Spacing
If the top of a set of characters or a graphical image is chopped off, then line spacing may be set to Exactly. To remedy the problem, change line spacing to 1.0, 1.15, 1.5, 2.0, 2.5, 3.0, or At least (in the Paragraph dialog box), all of which accommodate the largest font or image.

Adjusting Line and Paragraph Spacing

Line spacing is the amount of vertical space between lines of text in a paragraph. **Paragraph spacing** is the amount of space above and below a paragraph. By default, the Normal style places 10 points of blank space after each paragraph and inserts a vertical space equal to 1.15 lines between each line of text. It also automatically adjusts line height to accommodate various font sizes and graphics.

The MLA documentation style requires that you **double-space** the entire research paper. That is, the amount of vertical space between each line of text and above and below paragraphs should be equal to one blank line. The next sets of steps adjust line spacing and paragraph spacing according to the MLA documentation style.

To Double-Space Text

To double-space the lines in the research paper, change the line spacing to 2.0. The following steps change line spacing to double.

- Click the Line spacing button on the Home tab to display the Line spacing gallery (Figure 2–2).

Q&A What do the numbers in the Line spacing gallery represent?

The default line spacing is 1.15 lines. The options 1.0, 2.0, and 3.0 set line spacing to single, double, and triple, respectively. Similarly, the 1.5 and 2.5 options set line spacing to 1.5 and 2.5 lines. All these options adjust line spacing automatically to accommodate the largest font or graphic on a line.

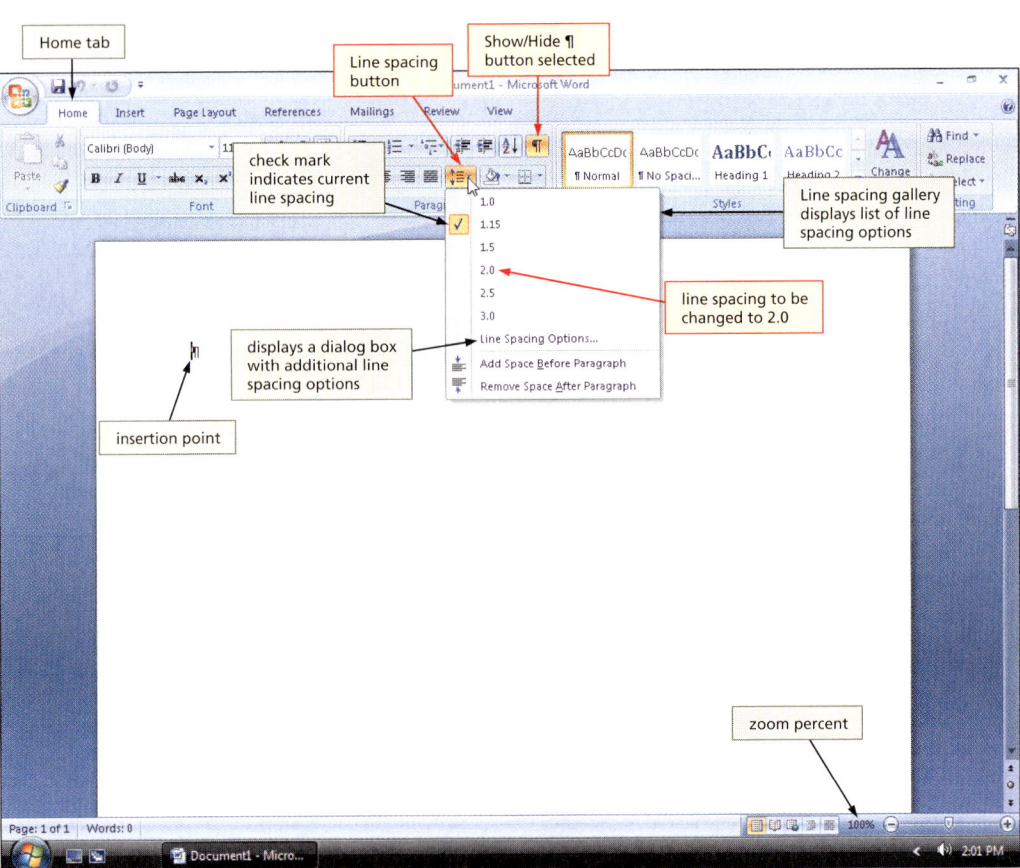

Figure 2–2

- Click 2.0 in the Line spacing gallery to change the line spacing to double at the location of the insertion point.

Q&A Can I change the line spacing of existing text?

Yes. Select the text first and then change the line spacing as described in these steps.

Other Ways

1. Right-click paragraph, click Paragraph on shortcut menu, click Indents and Spacing tab, click Line spacing box arrow, click Double, click OK button

2. Click Paragraph Dialog Box Launcher, click Indents and Spacing tab, click Line spacing box arrow, click Double, click OK button

3. Press CTRL+2

To Remove Space after a Paragraph

The research paper should not have additional blank space after each paragraph. The following steps remove space after a paragraph.

- Click the Line spacing button on the Home tab to display the Line spacing gallery (Figure 2–3).

- Click Remove Space After Paragraph in the Line spacing gallery so that no blank space appears after a paragraph.

Q&A Can I remove space after existing paragraphs?

Yes. Select the paragraphs first and then remove the space as described in these steps.

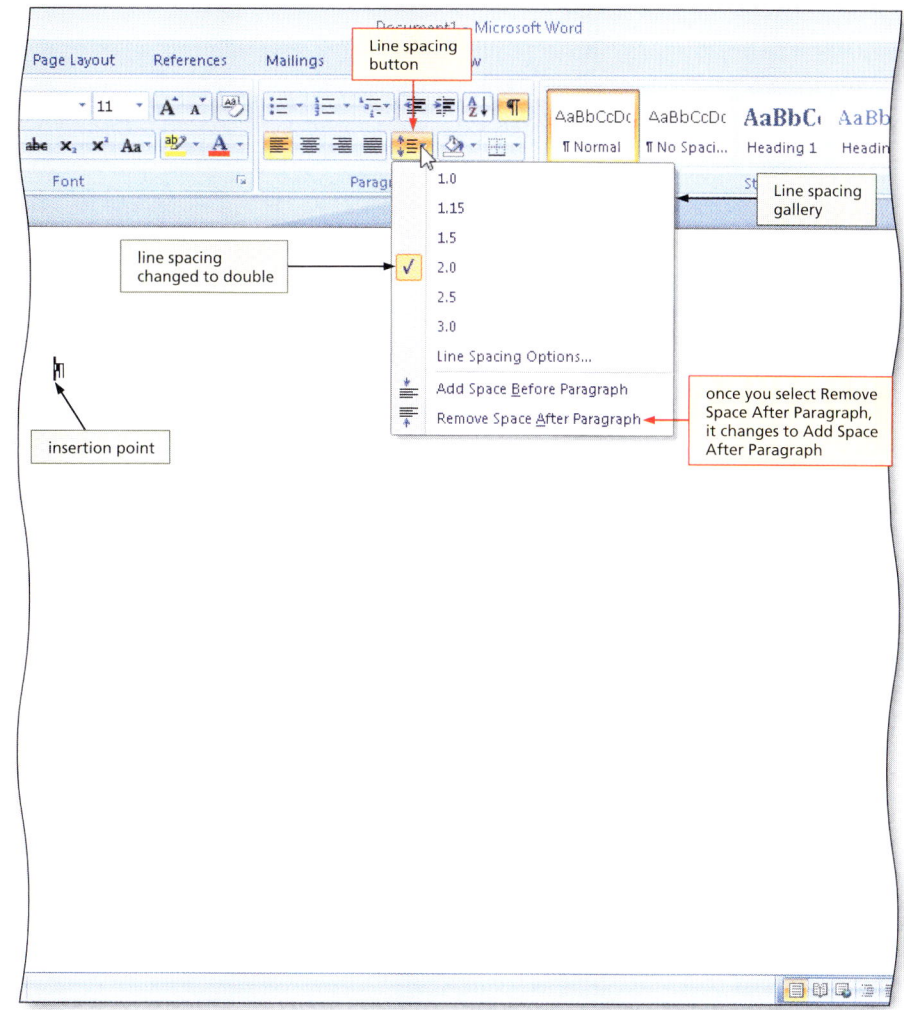

Figure 2–3

Other Ways

1. Click Spacing After box arrow on Page Layout tab until 0 pt is displayed
2. Right-click paragraph, click Paragraph on shortcut menu, click Indents and Spacing tab, click Spacing After box arrow until 0 pt is displayed, click OK button
3. Click Paragraph Dialog Box Launcher, click Indents and Spacing tab, click Spacing After box arrow until 0 pt is displayed, click OK button

Headers and Footers

A **header** is text and graphics that print at the top of each page in a document. Similarly, a **footer** is text and graphics that print at the bottom of every page. In Word, headers print in the top margin one-half inch from the top of every page, and footers print in the bottom margin one-half inch from the bottom of each page, which meets the MLA style. In addition to text and graphics, headers and footers can include document information such as the page number, current date, current time, and author's name.

In this research paper, you are to precede the page number with your last name placed one-half inch from the upper-right edge of each page. The procedures on the following pages enter your name and the page number in the header, as specified by the MLA style.

To Switch to the Header

To enter text in the header, you instruct Word to edit the header. The following steps switch from editing the document text to editing the header.

1
- Click Insert on the Ribbon to display the Insert tab.
- Click the Header button on the Insert tab to display the Header gallery (Figure 2–4).

Q&A Can I use a built-in header for this research paper?

None of the built-in headers adhere to the MLA style. Thus, you enter your own header contents, instead of using a built-in header, for this research paper.

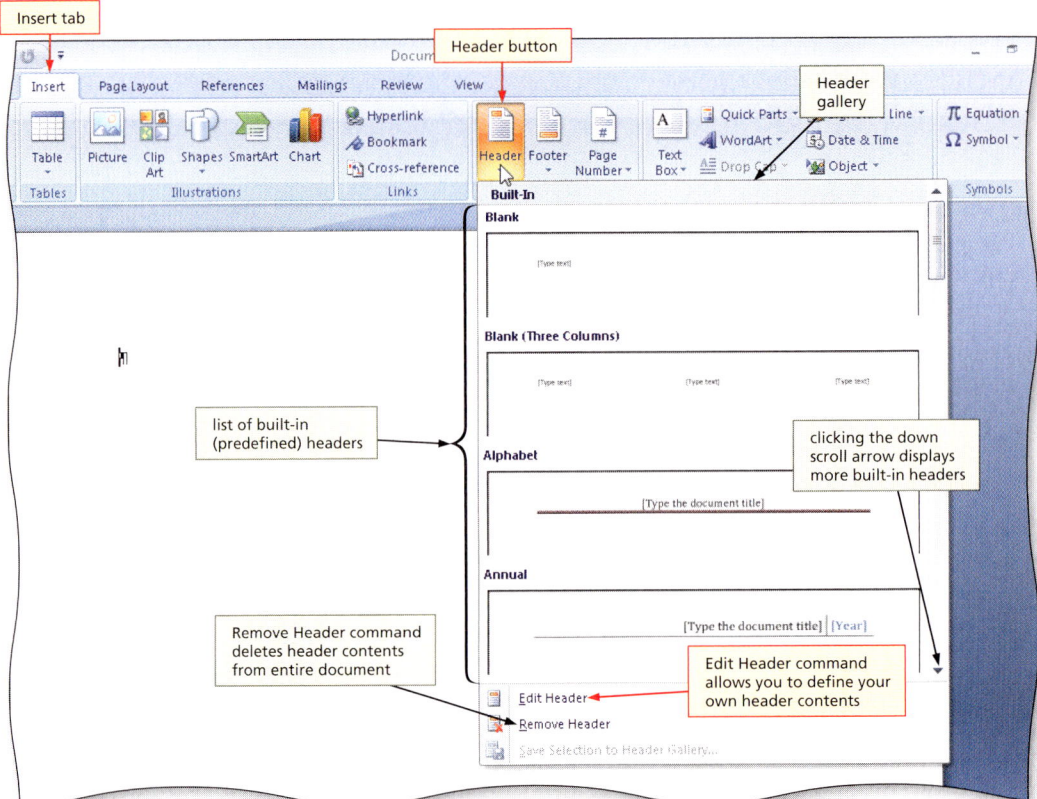

Figure 2–4

2

 Experiment
- Click the down scroll arrow in the Header gallery to see the available built-in headers.

3
- Click Edit Header in the Header gallery to switch from the document text to the header, which allows you to edit the contents of the header (Figure 2–5).

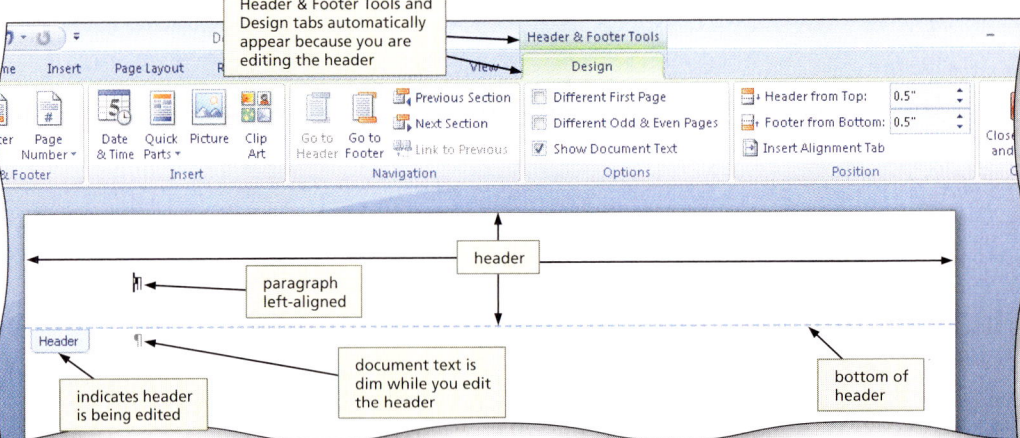

Figure 2–5

Q&A How do I remove the Header & Footer Tools and Design tabs from the Ribbon?

When you are finished editing the header, you will close it, which removes the Header & Footer Tools tabs.

Other Ways
1. Double-click dimmed header

To Right-Align a Paragraph

The paragraph in the header currently is left-aligned (Figure 2–5). Your last name and the page number should print **right-aligned**, that is, at the right margin. The following step right-aligns a paragraph.

1
- Click Home on the Ribbon to display the Home tab.
- Click the Align Text Right button on the Home tab to right-align the paragraph in the header (Figure 2–6).

Q&A What if I wanted to return the paragraph to left-aligned?

Click the Align Text Right button again, or click the Align Text Left button.

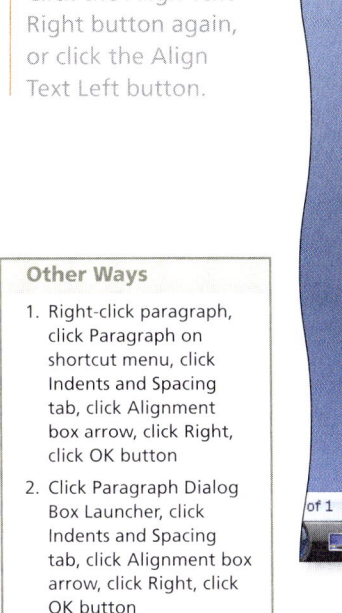

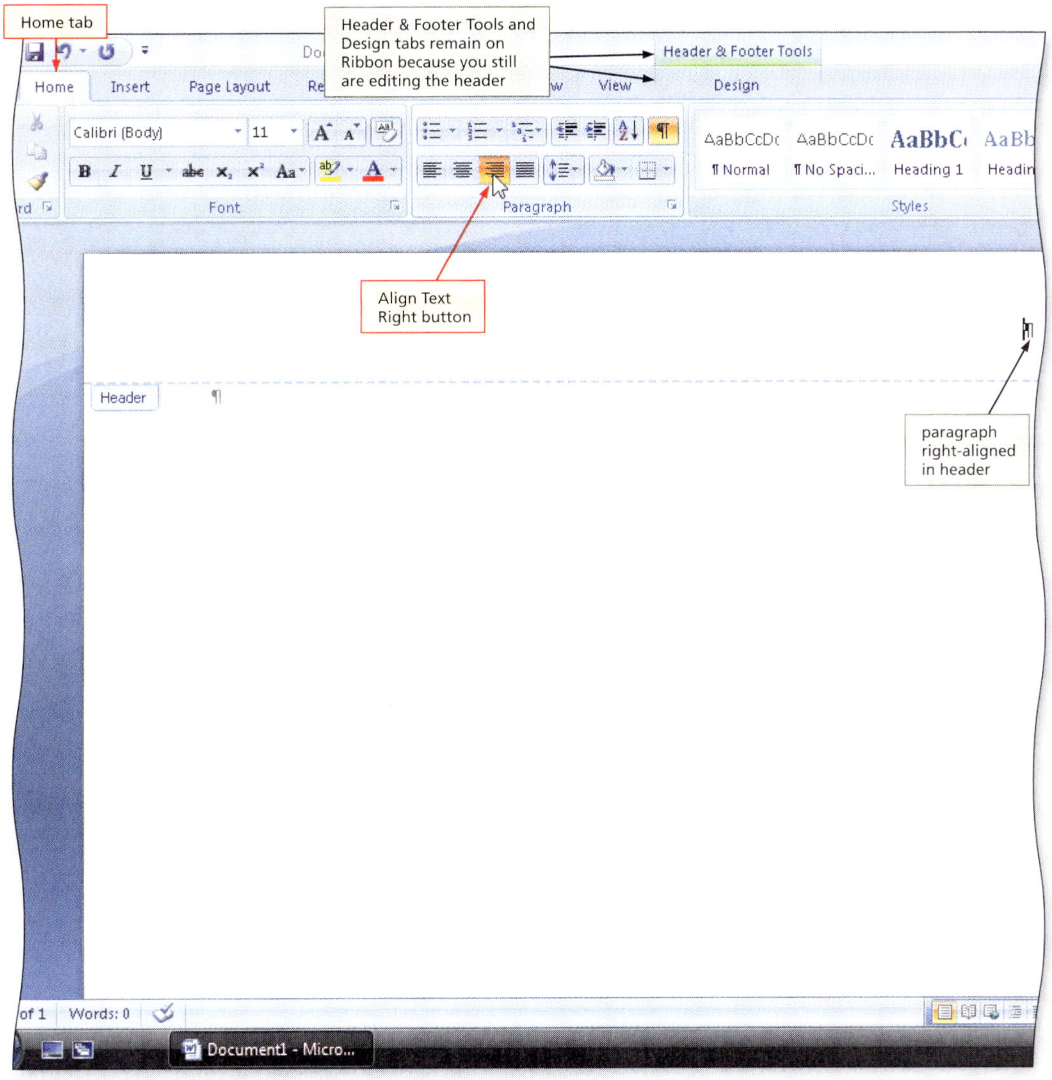

Figure 2–6

Other Ways
1. Right-click paragraph, click Paragraph on shortcut menu, click Indents and Spacing tab, click Alignment box arrow, click Right, click OK button
2. Click Paragraph Dialog Box Launcher, click Indents and Spacing tab, click Alignment box arrow, click Right, click OK button
3. Press CTRL+R

To Enter Text

The following steps enter your last name right-aligned in the header area.

1 Click Design on the Ribbon to display the Design tab.

2 Type Pappas and then press the SPACEBAR to enter the last name in the header.

BTW

Footers
If you wanted to create a footer, you would click the Footer button on the Insert tab and then select the desired built-in footer or click Edit Footer to create a customized footer.

To Insert a Page Number

The next task is to insert the current page number in the header. The following steps insert a page number at the location of the insertion point.

1
- Click the Insert Page Number button on the Design tab to display the Insert Page Number menu.
- Point to Current Position on the Insert Page Number menu to display the Current Position gallery (Figure 2–7).

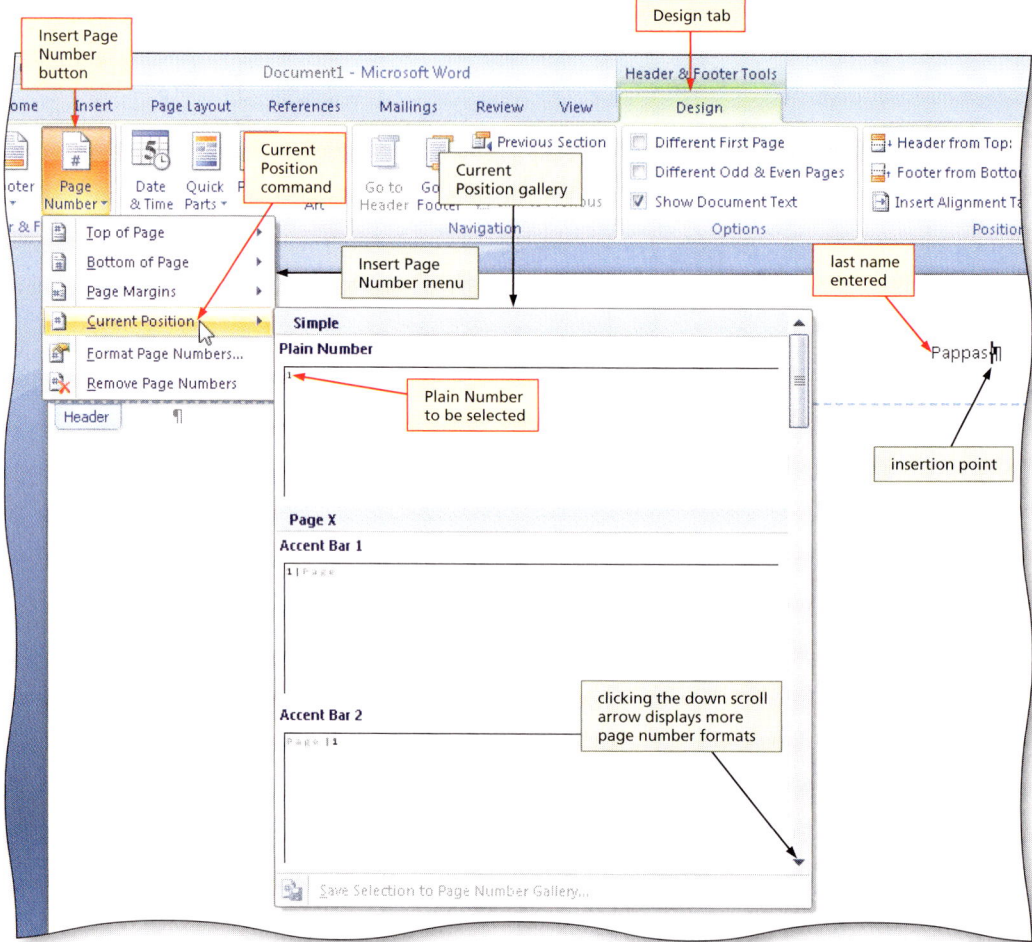

Figure 2–7

2

 Experiment
- Click the down scroll arrow in the Current Position gallery to see the available page number formats.

3
- If necessary, scroll to the top of the Current Position gallery. Click Plain Number in the Current Position gallery to insert an unformatted page number at the location of the insertion point (Figure 2–8).

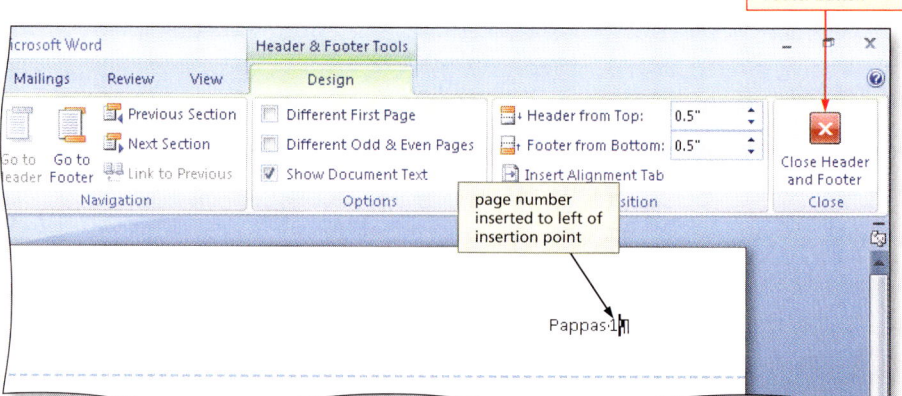

Figure 2–8

Other Ways

1. Click Insert Page Number button on Insert tab
2. Click Quick Parts button on Insert tab or on Design tab on Header & Footer Tools tab, click Field on Quick Parts menu, select Page in Field names list, click OK button

To Close the Header

You are finished entering text in the header. Thus, the next task is to switch back to the document text. The following step closes the header.

- Click the Close Header and Footer button on the Design tab (shown in Figure 2–8) to close the header and switch back to the document text (Figure 2–9).

Q&A How do I make changes to existing header text?

Switch to the header using the steps described on page WD 80, edit the header as you would edit text in the document window, and then switch back to the document text.

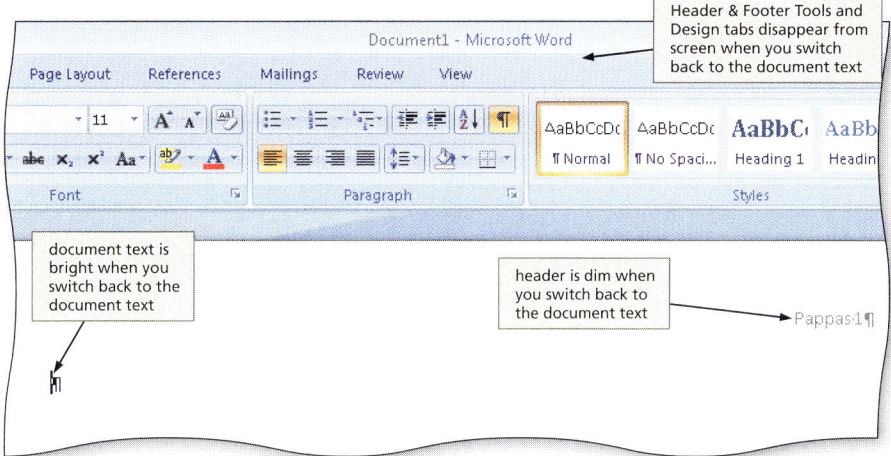

Figure 2–9

Other Ways
1. Double-click dimmed document text

Typing the Research Paper Text

The text of the research paper in this chapter encompasses the first two pages of the paper. You will type the text of the research paper and then modify it later in the chapter, so that it matches Figure 2–1 on page WD 75.

> **Plan Ahead**
>
> **Write the first draft, referencing sources.**
> As you write the first draft of your research paper, be sure it includes the proper components, uses credible sources, and does not contain any plagiarism.
>
> - **Include an introduction, body, and conclusion.** The first paragraph of the paper introduces the topic and captures the reader's attention. The body, which follows the introduction, consists of several paragraphs that support the topic. The conclusion summarizes the main points in the body and restates the topic.
>
> - **Evaluate sources for authority, currency, and accuracy.** Be especially wary of information obtained from the Web. Any person, company, or organization can publish a Web page on the Internet. Ask yourself these questions about the source:
>   - Authority: Does a reputable institution or group support the source? Is the information presented without bias? Are the author's credentials listed and verifiable?
>   - Currency: Is the information up to date? Are dates of sources listed? What is the last date revised or updated?
>   - Accuracy: Is the information free of errors? Is it verifiable? Are the sources clearly identified?
>
> - **Acknowledge all sources of information; do not plagiarize.** Not only is plagiarism unethical, but it is considered an academic crime that can have severe punishments such as failing a course or being expelled from school.
>
>   When you summarize, paraphrase (rewrite information in your own words), present facts, give statistics, quote exact words, or show a map, chart, or other graphical image, you
>
> *(continued)*

Plan Ahead

(continued)

must acknowledge the source. Information that commonly is known or accessible to the audience constitutes common knowledge and does not need to be acknowledged. If, however, you question whether certain information is common knowledge, you should document it — just to be safe.

To Enter Name and Course Information

As discussed earlier in this chapter, the MLA style does not require a separate title page for research papers. Instead, place your name and course information in a block at the top of the page, below the header, at the left margin. The following steps enter the name and course information in the research paper.

BTW

Date Formats
The MLA style prefers the day-month-year (28 March 2008) or month-day-year (March 28, 2008) format. Whichever format you select, use it consistently throughout the paper.

① Type `Alex Pappas` as the student name and then press the ENTER key.

② Type `Ms. Singh` as the instructor name and then press the ENTER key.

③ Type `English 104` as the course name and then press the ENTER key.

④ Type `28 March 2008` as the paper due date and then press the ENTER key (Figure 2–10).

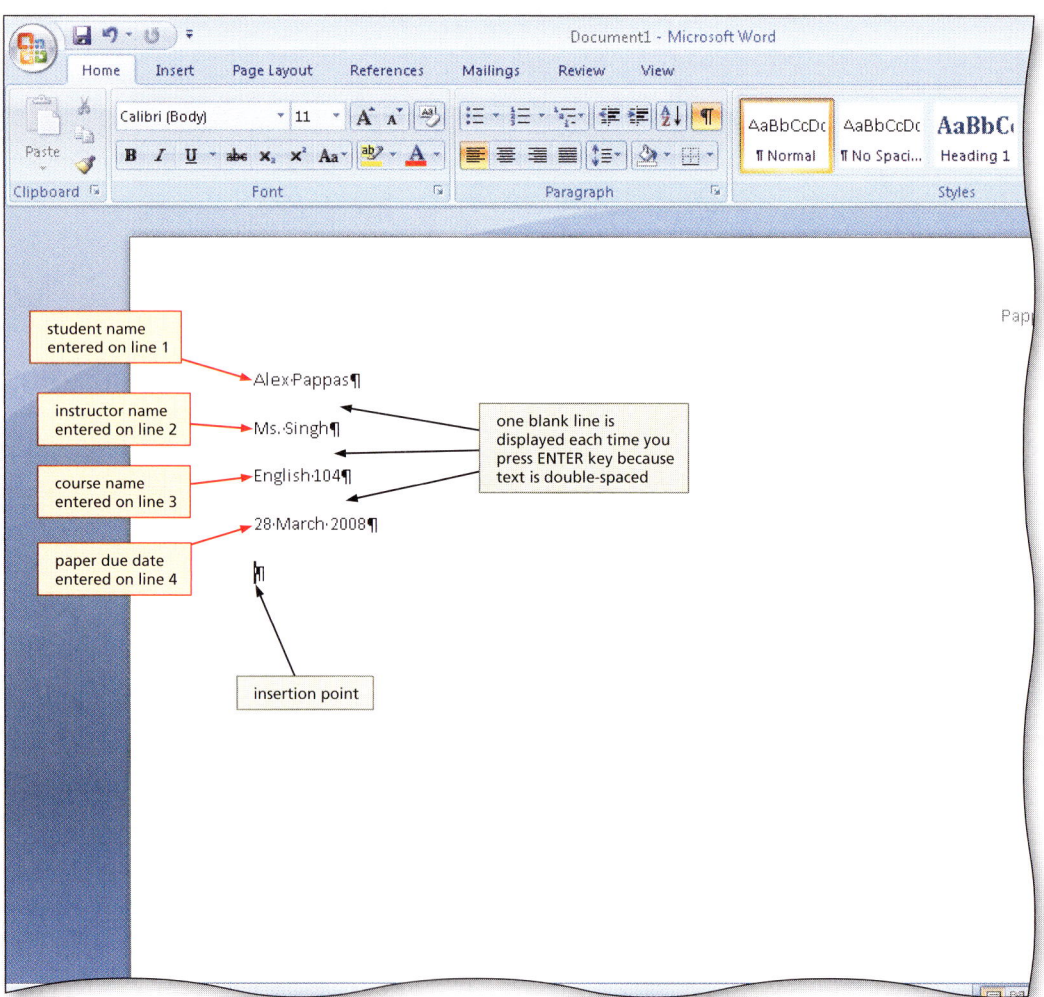

Figure 2–10

To Click and Type

The next step is to enter the title of the research paper centered between the page margins. In Chapter 1, you used the Center button on the Home tab to center text and graphics. As an alternative, you can use **Click and Type** to format and enter text, graphics, and other items. To use Click and Type, you double-click a blank area of the document window. Word automatically formats the item you enter according to the location where you just double-clicked. The following steps use Click and Type to center and then type the title of the research paper.

Experiment

- Move the mouse pointer around the document below the entered name and course information and observe the various icons that appear with the I-beam.

- Position the mouse pointer in the center of the document at the approximate location for the research paper title until a center icon appears below the I-beam (Figure 2–11).

Q&A What are the other icons that appear in the Click and Type pointer?

A left-align icon appears to the right of the I-beam when the Click and Type pointer is in certain locations on the left side of the document window. A right-align icon appears to the left of the icon when the Click and Type pointer is in certain locations on the right side of the document window.

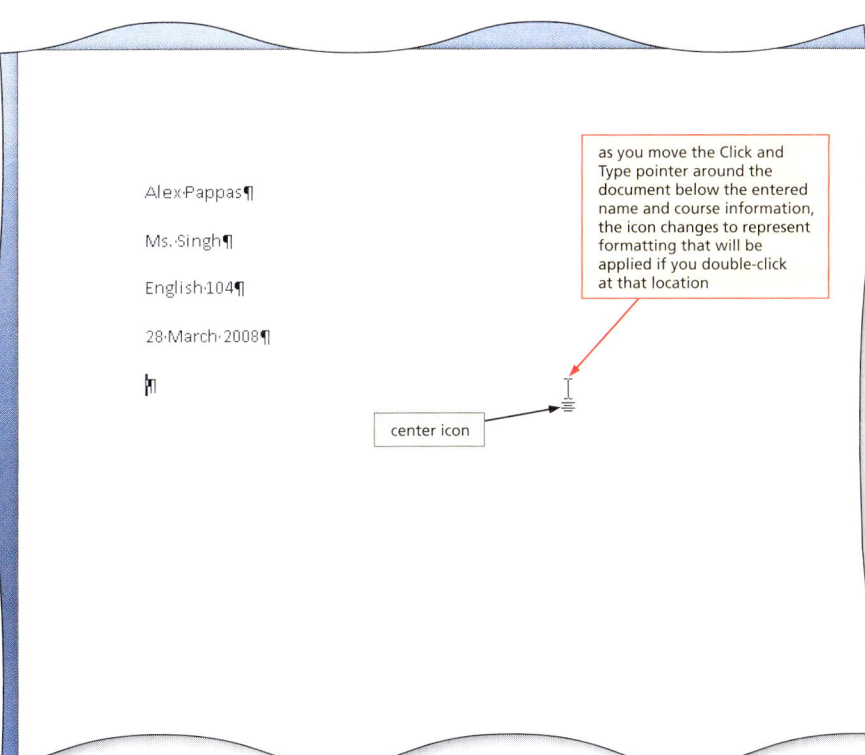

Figure 2–11

- Double-click to center the paragraph mark and insertion point between the left and right margins.

- Type `Wireless Communications` as the paper title and then press the ENTER key (Figure 2–12).

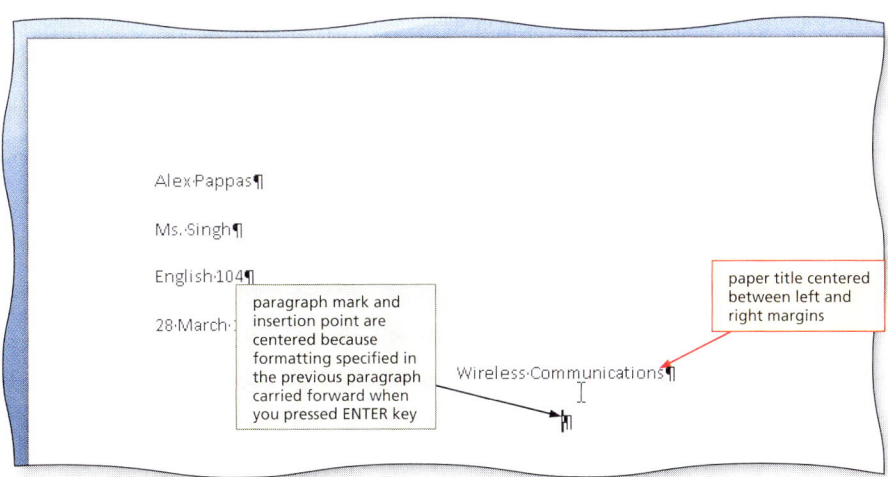

Figure 2–12

Shortcut Keys

Word has many shortcut keys for your convenience while typing. Table 2–1 lists the common shortcut keys for formatting characters. Table 2–2 lists common shortcut keys for formatting paragraphs.

Table 2–1 Shortcut Keys for Formatting Characters

Character Formatting Task	Shortcut Keys	Character Formatting Task	Shortcut Keys
All capital letters	CTRL+SHIFT+A	Italic	CTRL+I
Bold	CTRL+B	Remove character formatting (plain text)	CTRL+SPACEBAR
Case of letters	SHIFT+F3	Small uppercase letters	CTRL+SHIFT+K
Decrease font size	CTRL+SHIFT+<	Subscript	CTRL+EQUAL SIGN
Decrease font size 1 point	CTRL+[	Superscript	CTRL+SHIFT+PLUS SIGN
Double-underline	CTRL+SHIFT+D	Underline	CTRL+U
Increase font size	CTRL+SHIFT+>	Underline words, not spaces	CTRL+SHIFT+W
Increase font size 1 point	CTRL+]		

Table 2–2 Shortcut Keys for Formatting Paragraphs

Paragraph Formatting	Shortcut Keys	Paragraph Formatting	Shortcut Keys
1.5 line spacing	CTRL+5	Justify paragraph	CTRL+J
Add/remove one line above paragraph	CTRL+0 (ZERO)	Left-align paragraph	CTRL+L
Center paragraph	CTRL+E	Remove hanging indent	CTRL+SHIFT+T
Decrease paragraph indent	CTRL+SHIFT+M	Remove paragraph formatting	CTRL+Q
Double-space lines	CTRL+2	Right-align paragraph	CTRL+R
Hanging indent	CTRL+T	Single-space lines	CTRL+1
Increase paragraph indent	CTRL+M		

BTW

Shortcut Keys
To print a complete list of shortcut keys in Word, click the Microsoft Office Word Help button near the upper-right corner of the Word window, type shortcut keys in the 'Type words to search for' text box at the top of the Word Help window, press the ENTER key, click the Keyboard shortcuts for Microsoft Office Word link, click the Show All link in the upper-right corner of the Help window, click the Print button in the Help window, and then click the Print button in the Print dialog box.

To Format Text Using Shortcut Keys

The paragraphs below the paper title should be left-aligned, instead of centered. Thus, the next step is to left-align the paragraph below the paper title. When your fingers are already on the keyboard, you may prefer using **shortcut keys**, or keyboard key combinations, to format text as you type it. The following step left-aligns a paragraph using the shortcut keys CTRL+L. (Recall from Chapter 1 that a notation such as CTRL+L means to press the letter l on the keyboard while holding down the CTRL key.)

1 Press CTRL+L to left-align the current paragraph, that is, the paragraph containing the insertion point.

Q&A Why would I use a keyboard shortcut, instead of the Ribbon, to format text?
Switching between the mouse and the keyboard takes time. If your hands are already on the keyboard, use a keyboard shortcut. If your hand is on the mouse, use the Ribbon.

To Save a Document

You have performed many tasks while creating the research paper and do not want to risk losing the work completed thus far. Accordingly, you should save the document. For a detailed example of the procedure summarized below, refer to pages WD 19 through WD 21 in Chapter 1.

1 With a USB flash drive connected to one of the computer's USB ports, click the Save button on the Quick Access Toolbar to display the Save As dialog box.

2 Type `Wireless Communications Paper` in the File name text box to change the file name.

3 If Computer is not displayed in the Favorite Links section, drag the top or bottom edge of the Save As dialog box until Computer is displayed. Click Computer in the Favorite Links section and then double-click your USB flash drive in the list of available drives.

4 Click the Save button in the Save As dialog box to save the document on the USB flash drive with the file name, Wireless Communications Paper.

To Display the Rulers

According to the MLA style, the first line of each paragraph in the research paper is to be indented one-half inch from the left margin. Although you can use a dialog box to indent paragraphs, Word provides a quicker way through the **horizontal ruler**. This ruler displays at the top edge of the document window just below the Ribbon. Word also provides a **vertical ruler** that displays along the left edge of the Word window. The following steps display the rulers.

Experiment

- Repeatedly click the View Ruler button on the vertical scroll bar to see the how this button is used to both show and hide the rulers.

- If the rulers are not displayed, click the View Ruler button on the vertical scroll bar because you want to use the ruler to indent paragraphs (Figure 2–13).

Q&A Can I use the rulers for other tasks?

In addition to indenting paragraphs, you can use the rulers to set tab stops, change page margins, and adjust column widths.

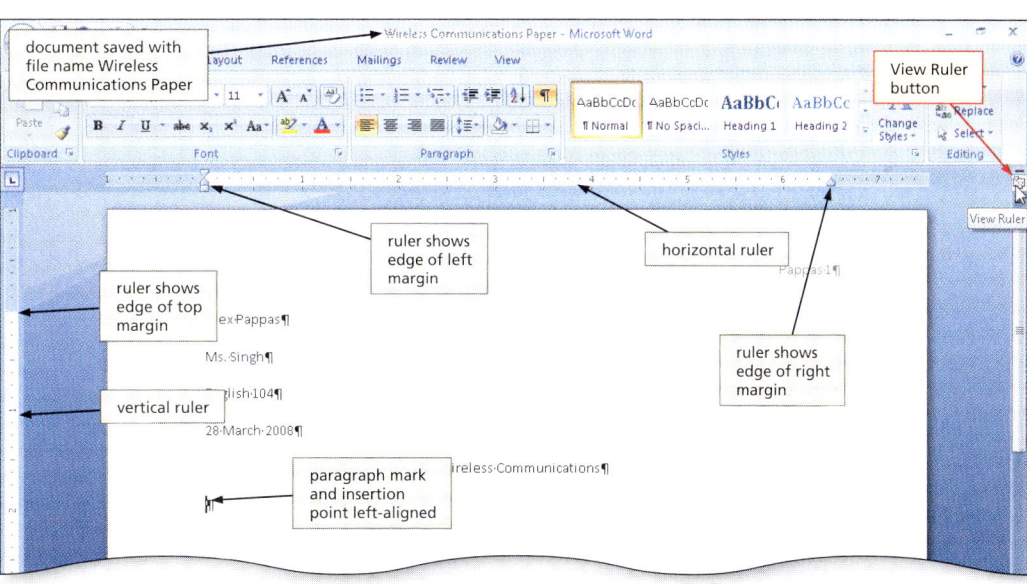

Figure 2–13

Other Ways

1. Click View Ruler check box on View tab

To First-Line Indent Paragraphs

The first line of each paragraph in the research paper is to be indented one-half inch from the left margin. You can use the horizontal ruler, usually simply called the **ruler**, to indent just the first line of a paragraph, called **first-line indent**.

The left margin on the ruler contains two triangles above a square. The **First Line Indent marker** is the top triangle at the 0" mark on the ruler (Figure 2–14). The bottom triangle is discussed later in this chapter. The small square at the 0" mark is the Left Indent marker. The **Left Indent marker** allows you to change the entire left margin, whereas the First Line Indent marker indents only the first line of the paragraph. The following steps first-line indent paragraphs in the research paper.

- With the insertion point on the paragraph mark below the research paper title, point to the First Line Indent marker on the ruler (Figure 2–14).

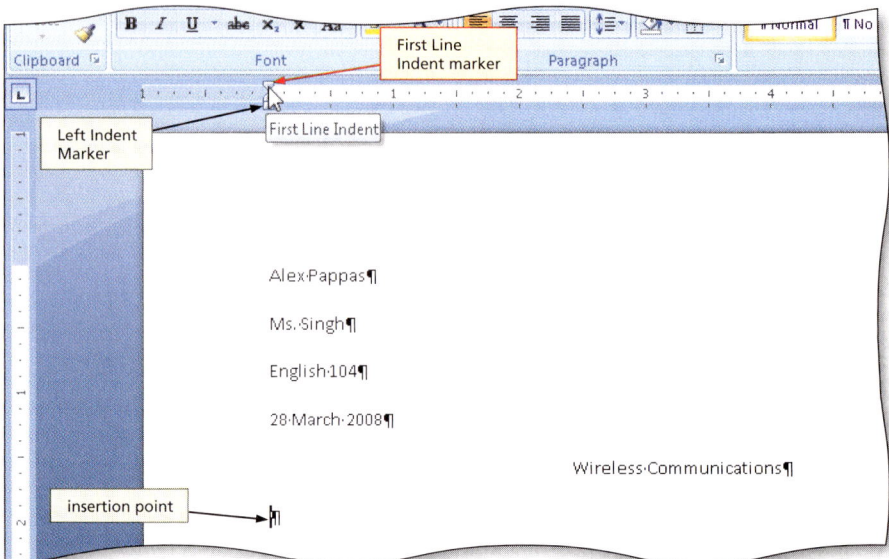

Figure 2–14

- Drag the First Line Indent marker to the .5" mark on the ruler to display a vertical dotted line in the document window, which indicates the proposed location of the first line of the paragraph (Figure 2–15).

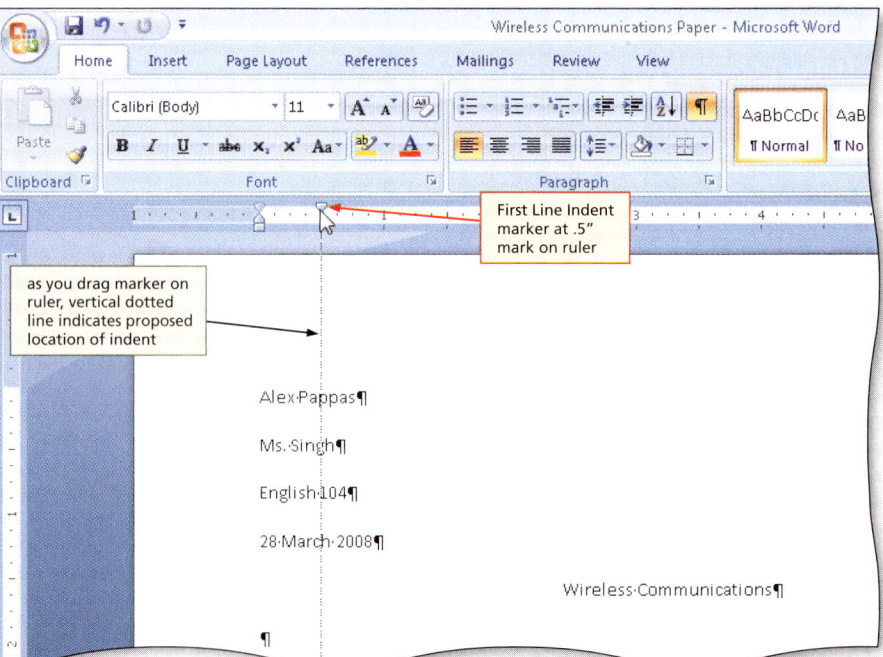

Figure 2–15

③
- Release the mouse button to place the First Line Indent marker at the .5" mark on the ruler, or one-half inch from the left margin (Figure 2–16).

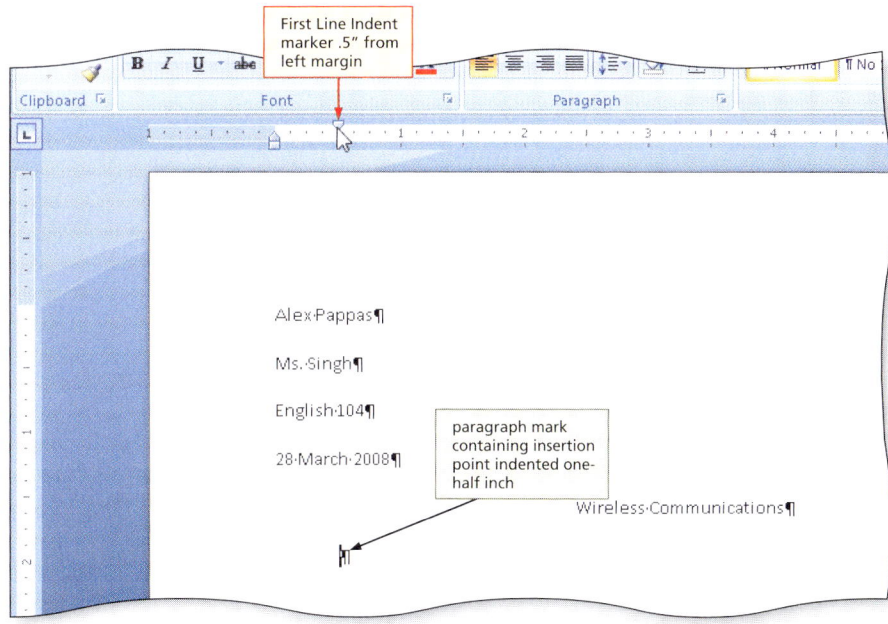

Figure 2–16

④
- Type `Wireless communications are everywhere. People around the world regularly send and receive messages wirelessly, that is, transmitted through the air.` and notice that Word automatically indented the first line of the paragraph by one-half inch (Figure 2–17).

 Will I have to set first-line indent for each paragraph in the paper?

No. Each time you press the ENTER key, paragraph formatting in the previous paragraph carries forward to the next paragraph. Thus, once you set the first-line indent, its format carries forward automatically to each subsequent paragraph you type.

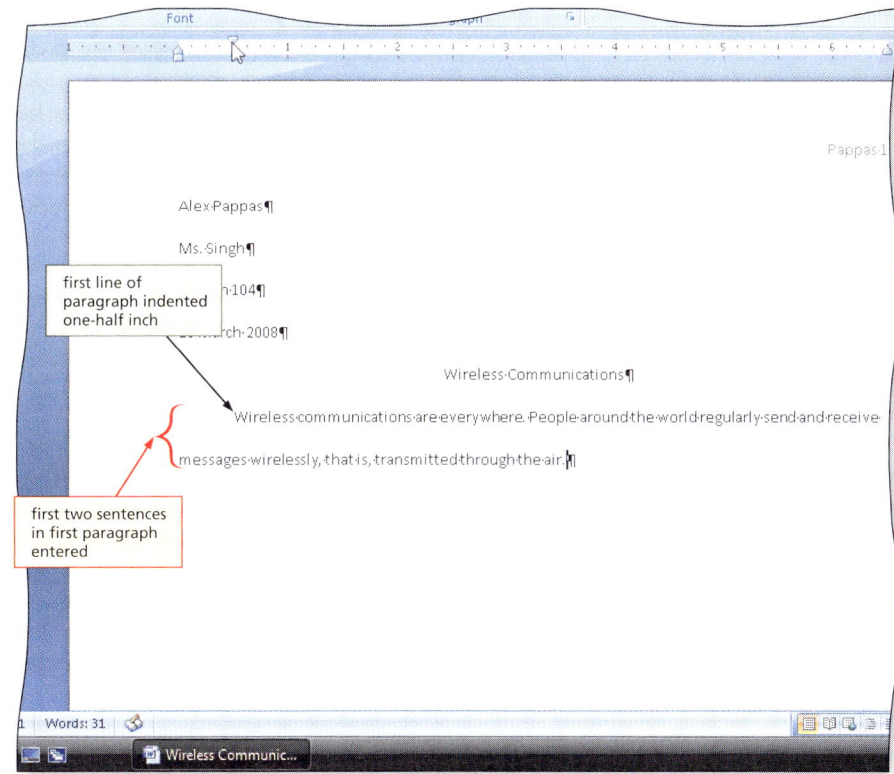

Figure 2–17

Other Ways

1. Right-click paragraph, click Paragraph on shortcut menu, click Indents and Spacing tab, click Special box arrow, click First line, click OK button
2. Click Paragraph Dialog Box Launcher, click Indents and Spacing tab, click Special box arrow, click First line, click OK button
3. Press TAB key at beginning of paragraph

To Create a Quick Style

Recall from Chapter 1 that a Quick Style is a predefined style that appears in the Styles gallery on the Ribbon. You use styles in the Styles gallery to apply defined formats to text. Later in this chapter, you will apply the formats of the research paper paragraph to the paragraphs in the footnote. To accomplish this task, you can create a Quick Style based on the formats in the current paragraph. That is, text is double-spaced with the first line of the paragraph indented and no space after the paragraph. The following steps first select the paragraph and then create a Quick Style based on the formats in the selected paragraph.

- Position the mouse pointer in the paragraph below the title and then triple-click; that is, press the mouse button three times in rapid succession, to select the paragraph.
- Right-click the selected paragraph to display a shortcut menu.
- Point to Styles on the shortcut menu to display the Styles submenu (Figure 2–18).

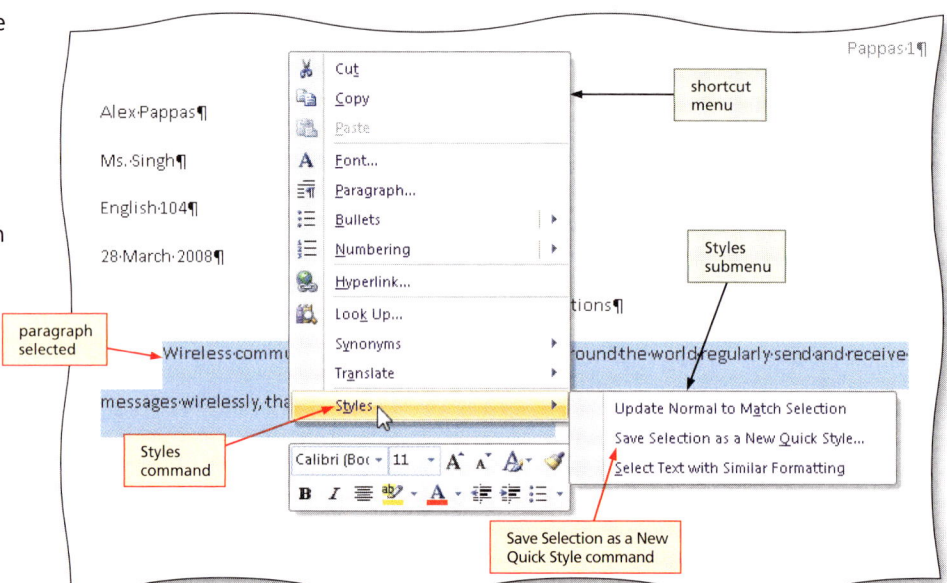

Figure 2–18

- Click Save Selection as a New Quick Style on the Styles submenu to display the Create New Style from Formatting dialog box.
- Type `Research Paper Paragraphs` in the Name text box (Figure 2–19).

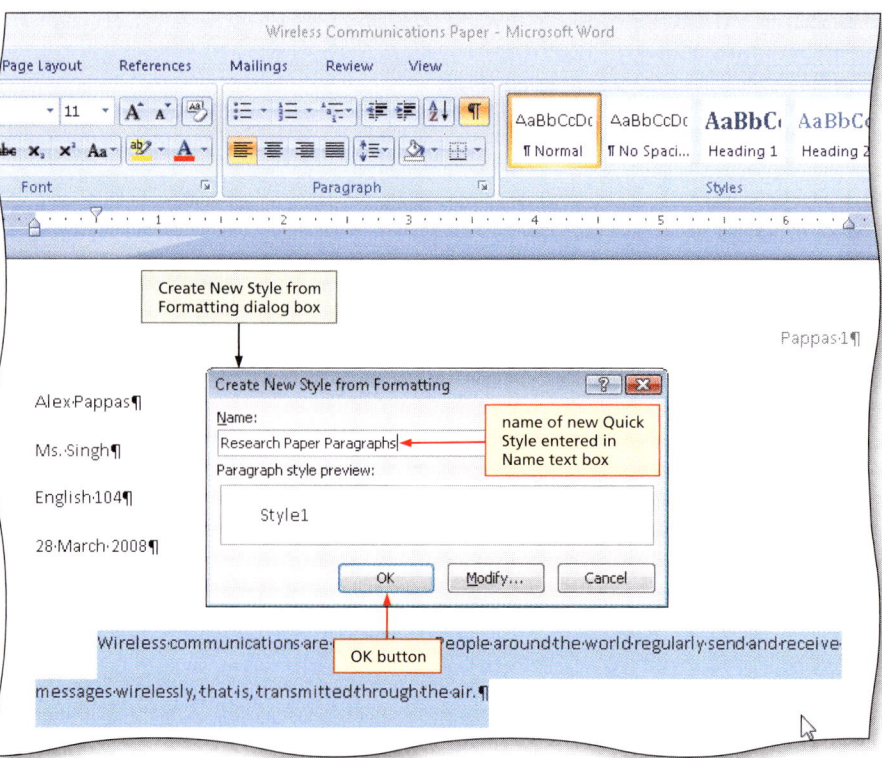

Figure 2–19

- Click the OK button to create the new Quick Style and add it to the Styles gallery (Figure 2–20).

Q&A How can I see the formats assigned to a Quick Style?

Click the Styles Dialog Box Launcher. When the Styles task pane appears, position the mouse pointer on any style to display its formats in a ScreenTip. When finished, click the Close button in the task pane.

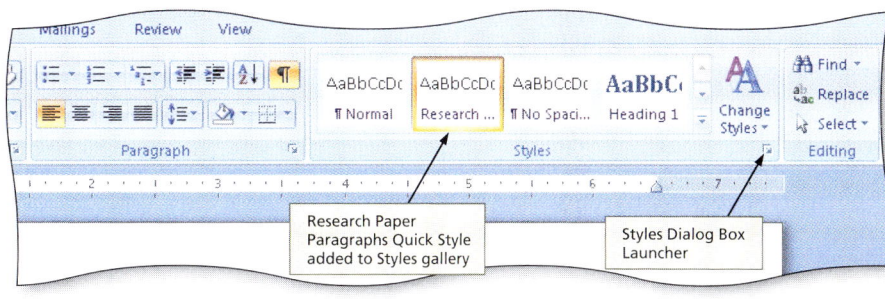

Figure 2–20

Other Ways

1. Click More button in Styles gallery on Home tab, click Save Selection as a New Quick Style, enter name of new Quick Style, click OK button

To AutoCorrect as You Type

As you type, you may make typing, spelling, capitalization, or grammar errors. For this reason, Word provides an **AutoCorrect** feature that automatically corrects these kinds of errors as you type them in the document. For example, if you type the text ahve, Word automatically changes it to the correct spelling, have, when you press the SPACEBAR or a punctuation mark key such as a period or comma.

Word has predefined many commonly misspelled words, which it automatically corrects for you. In the following steps, the word wireless is misspelled intentionally as wreless to illustrate the AutoCorrect as you type feature.

- Press CTRL+END to move the insertion point to the end of the document.

- Press the SPACEBAR.

- Type the beginning of the next sentence, misspelling the word, wireless, as follows: `Three types of wireless communications include wireless messaging services, wreless` (Figure 2–21).

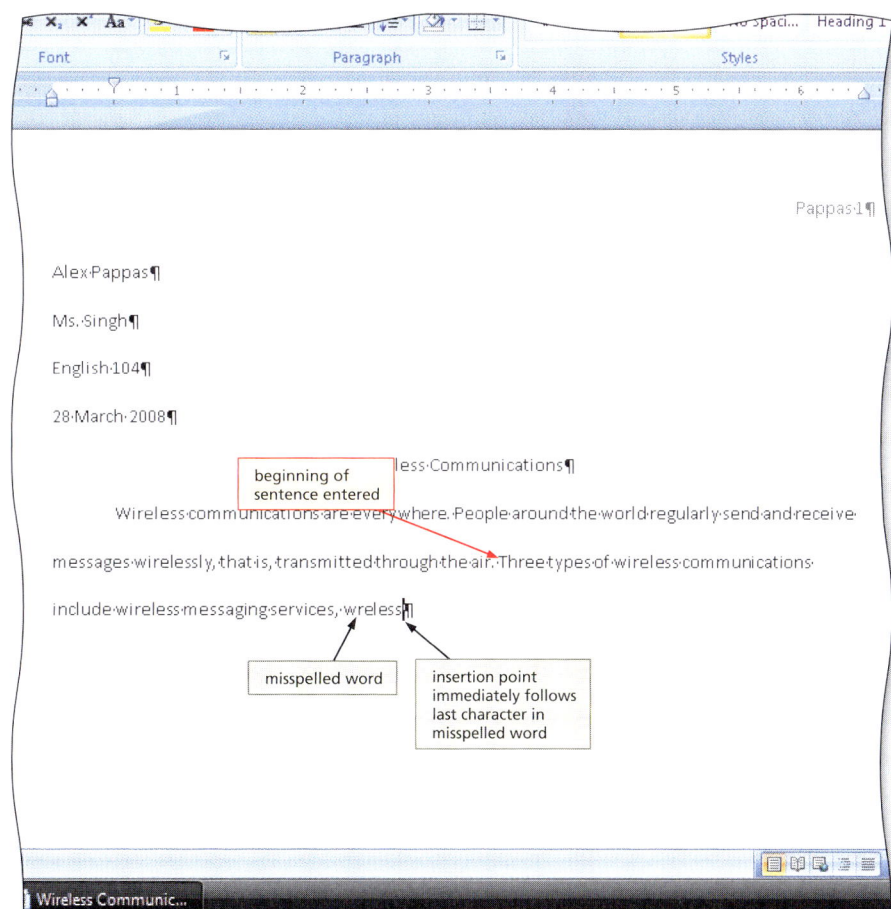

Figure 2–21

- Press the SPACEBAR and watch Word automatically correct the misspelled word.

- Type the rest of the sentence (Figure 2–22): `Internet access points, and global positioning systems.`

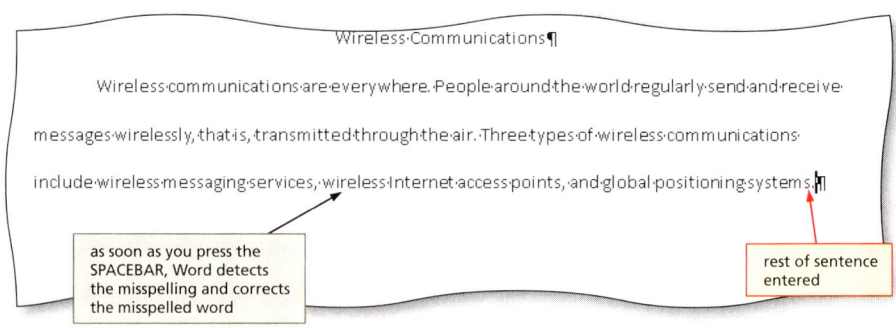

Figure 2–22

To Use the AutoCorrect Options Button

When you position the mouse pointer on text that Word automatically corrected, a small blue box appears below the text. If you point to the small blue box, Word displays the AutoCorrect Options button. When you click the **AutoCorrect Options button**, Word displays a menu that allows you to undo a correction or change how Word handles future automatic corrections of this type. The following steps illustrate the AutoCorrect Options button and menu.

- Position the mouse pointer in the text automatically corrected by Word (in this case, the word wireless) to display a small blue box below the automatically corrected word (Figure 2–23).

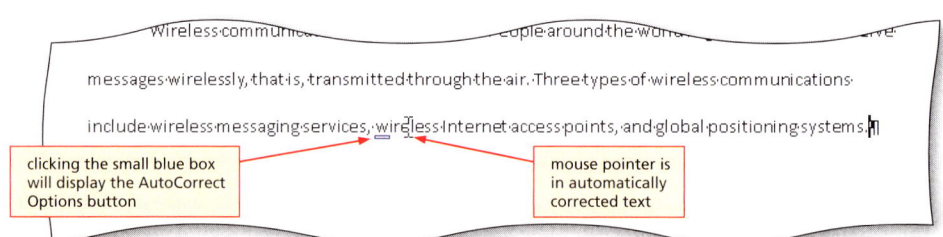

Figure 2–23

- Point to the small blue box to display the AutoCorrect Options button.

- Click the AutoCorrect Options button to display the AutoCorrect Options menu (Figure 2–24).

- Press the ESCAPE key to remove the AutoCorrect Options menu from the screen.

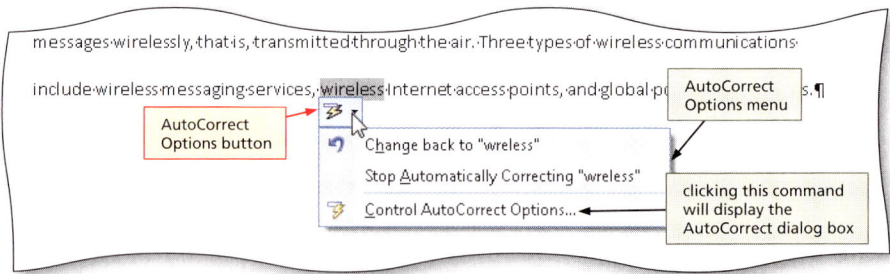

Figure 2–24

Q&A Do I need to remove the AutoCorrect Options button from the screen?

No. When you move the mouse pointer, the AutoCorrect Options button will disappear from the screen. If, for some reason, you wanted to remove the AutoCorrect Options button from the screen, you could press the ESCAPE key a second time.

To Create an AutoCorrect Entry

In addition to the predefined list of AutoCorrect spelling, capitalization, and grammar errors, you can create your own AutoCorrect entries to add to the list. For example, if you tend to type the word mobile as moble, you should create an AutoCorrect entry for it. The following steps create an AutoCorrect entry.

1
- Click the Office Button to display the Office Button menu (Figure 2–25).

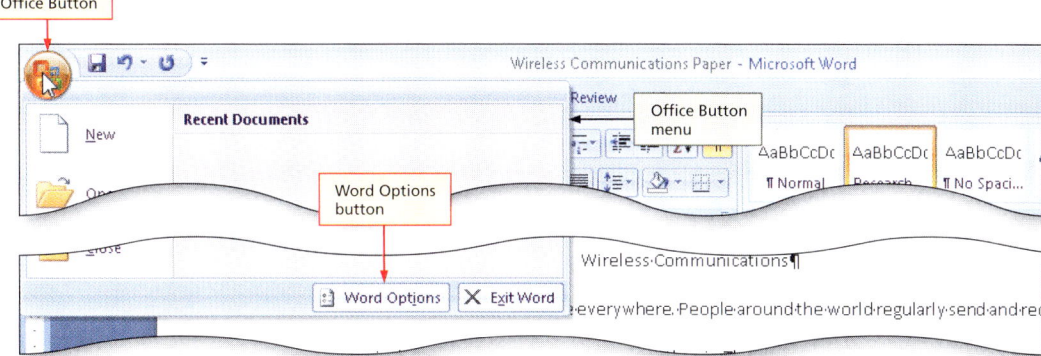

Figure 2–25

2
- Click the Word Options button on the Office Button menu to display the Word Options dialog box.

- Click Proofing in the left pane to display proofing options in the right pane.

- Click the AutoCorrect Options button in the right pane to display the AutoCorrect dialog box.

- When Word displays the AutoCorrect dialog box, type `moble` in the Replace text box.

- Press the TAB key and then type `mobile` in the With text box (Figure 2–26).

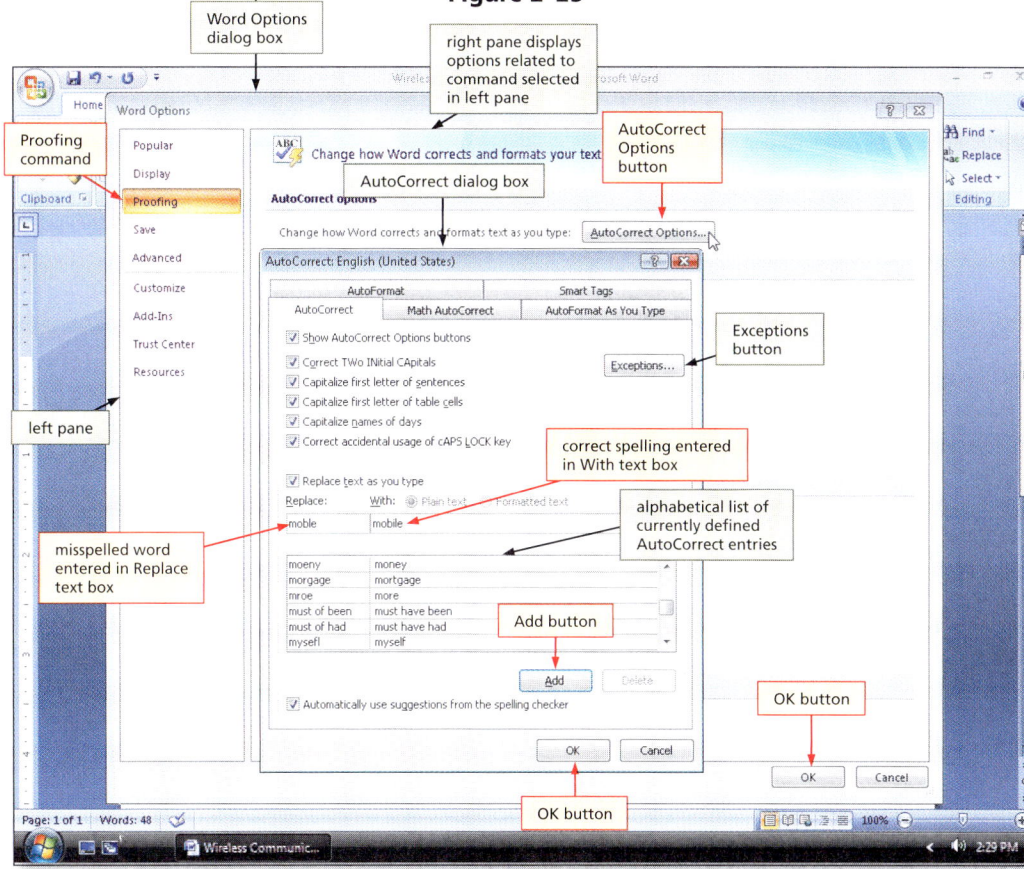

Figure 2–26

3
- Click the Add button in the AutoCorrect dialog box. (If your dialog box displays a Replace button instead, click it and then click the Yes button in the Microsoft Office Word dialog box.)

- Click the OK button to add the entry alphabetically to the list of words to correct automatically as you type.

- Click the OK button in the Word Options dialog box.

The AutoCorrect Dialog Box

In addition to creating AutoCorrect entries for words you commonly misspell or mistype, you can create entries for abbreviations, codes, and so on. For example, you could create an AutoCorrect entry for asap, indicating that Word should replace this text with the phrase, as soon as possible.

If, for some reason, you do not want Word to correct automatically as you type, you can turn off the Replace text as you type feature by clicking the Word Options button on the Office Button menu, clicking Proofing in the left pane of the Word Options dialog box, clicking the AutoCorrect Options button in the right pane of the Word Options dialog box (Figure 2–26 on the previous page), clicking the 'Replace text as you type' check box to remove the check mark, and then clicking the OK button in each open dialog box.

The AutoCorrect sheet in the AutoCorrect dialog box (Figure 2–26) contains other check boxes that correct capitalization errors if the check boxes are selected. If you type two capital letters in a row, such as TH, Word makes the second letter lowercase, Th. If you begin a sentence with a lowercase letter, Word capitalizes the first letter of the sentence. If you type the name of a day in lowercase, such as tuesday, Word capitalizes the first letter of the day, Tuesday. If you leave the CAPS LOCK key on and begin a new sentence, such as aFTER, Word corrects the typing, After, and turns off the CAPS LOCK key.

Sometimes you do not want Word to AutoCorrect a particular word or phrase. For example, you may use the code WD. in your documents. Because Word automatically capitalizes the first letter of a sentence, the character you enter following the period will be capitalized (in the previous sentence, it would capitalize the letter i in the word, in). To allow the code WD. to be entered into a document and still leave the AutoCorrect feature turned on, you should set an exception. To set an exception to an AutoCorrect rule, click the Word Options button on the Office Button menu, click Proofing in the left pane of the Word Options dialog box, click the AutoCorrect Options button in the right pane of the Word Options dialog box, click the Exceptions button (Figure 2–26), click the appropriate tab in the AutoCorrect Exceptions dialog box, type the exception entry in the text box, click the Add button, click the Close button in the AutoCorrect Exceptions dialog box, and then click the OK button in each of the remaining dialog boxes.

> **BTW**
>
> **Automatic Corrections**
> If you do not want to keep a change automatically made by Word and you immediately notice the automatic correction, you can undo the change by clicking the Undo button on the Quick Access Toolbar or pressing CTRL+Z. You also can undo a correction through the AutoCorrect Options button, which was shown on page WD 92.

To Enter More Text

The next step is to continue typing text in the research paper up to the location of the citation.

1 Press the ENTER key, so that you can begin typing the text in the second paragraph.

2 Type People use mobile phones, PDAs, and other mobile devices to access text messaging, instant messaging, and picture messaging services and then press the SPACEBAR.

Citations

Both the MLA and APA guidelines suggest the use of in-text parenthetical citations (placed at the end of a sentence), instead of footnoting each source of material in a paper. These parenthetical acknowledgments guide the reader to the end of the paper for complete information about the source.

> **Reference all sources.**
> During your research, be sure to record essential publication information about each of your sources. Following is a sample list of types of required information.
> - Book: full name of author(s), complete title of book, edition (if available), volume (if available), publication city, publication year
> - Magazine: full name of author(s), complete title of article, magazine title, date of magazine, page numbers of article
> - Web site: full name of author(s), title of Web site, date viewed, Web address

Plan Ahead

Word provides tools to assist you with inserting citations in a paper and later generating a list of sources from the citations. With a documentation style selected, Word automatically formats the citations and list of sources. The process for adding citations in Word is as follows:

1. Modify the documentation style, if necessary.
2. Insert a citation placeholder.
3. Enter the source information for the citation.

You can combine Steps 2 and 3, where you insert the citation placeholder and enter the source information at once. Or, you can insert the citation placeholder as you write and then enter the source information for the citation at a later time. While entering the research paper in this chapter, you will use both methods.

To Change the Bibliography Style

The first step in inserting a citation is to be sure the citations and sources will be formatted using the correct documentation style, called the bibliography style in Word. The following steps change the specified documentation style.

1
- Click References on the Ribbon to display the References tab.
- Click the Bibliography Style box arrow on the References tab to display a gallery of predefined documentation styles (Figure 2–27).

2
- Click MLA in the Bibliography Style gallery to change the documentation style to MLA.

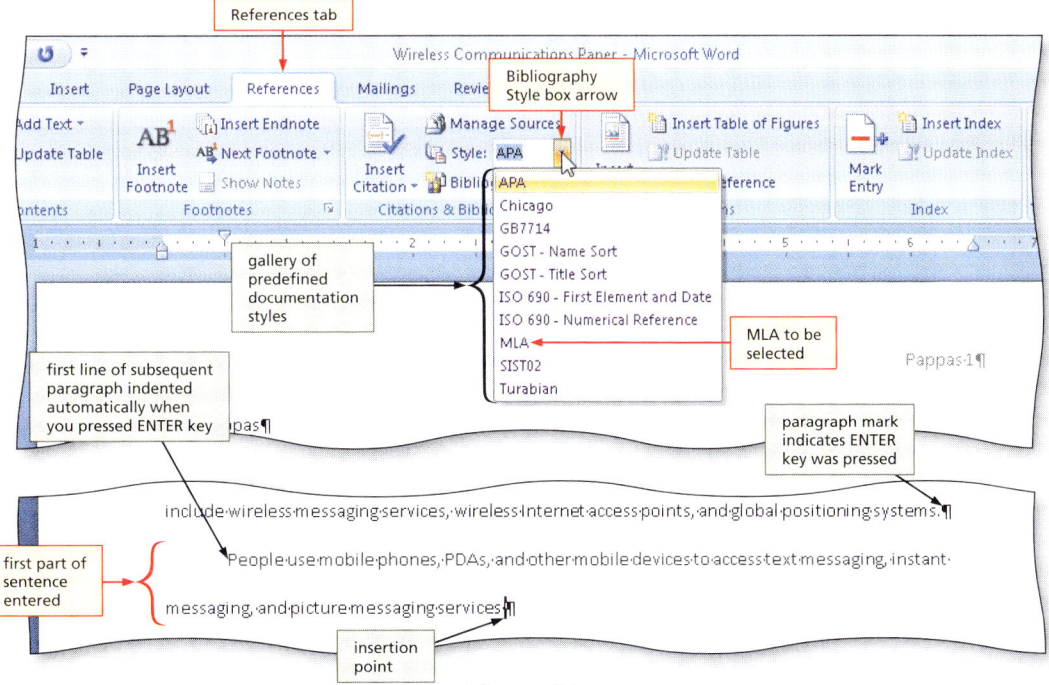

Figure 2–27

To Insert a Citation and Create Its Source

With the documentation style selected, the next task is to insert a citation placeholder and enter the source information. You can accomplish these steps at once by instructing Word to add a new source. The following steps add a new source for a magazine (periodical) article.

- Click the Insert Citation button on the References tab to display the Insert Citation menu (Figure 2–28).

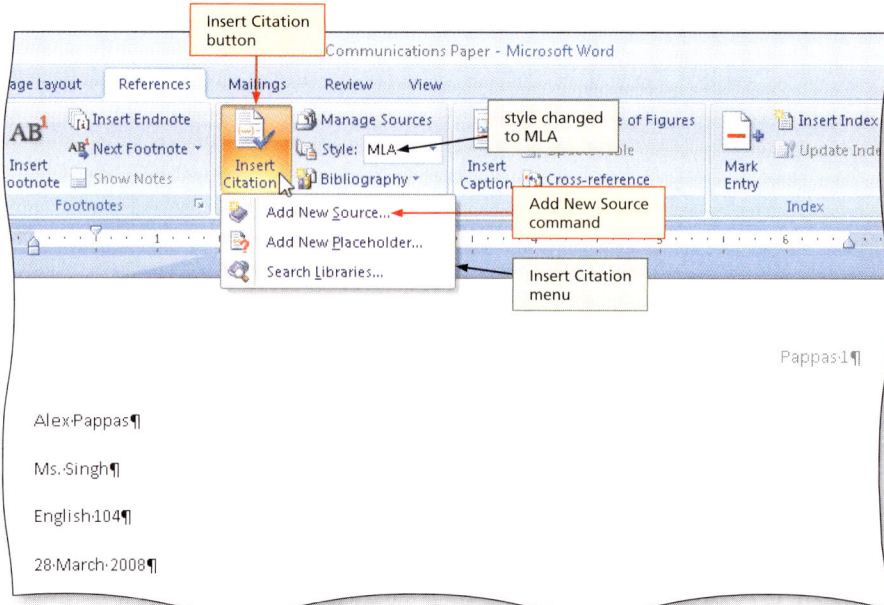

Figure 2–28

- Click Add New Source on the Insert Citation menu to display the Create Source dialog box (Figure 2–29).

Q&A What are the Bibliography Fields in the Create Source dialog box?

A **field** is a placeholder for data whose contents can change. You enter data in some fields; Word supplies data for others. In this case, you enter the contents of the fields for a particular source, for example, the author name in the Author field.

- Click the Type of Source box arrow and then click one of the source types in the list, so that you can see how the list of fields changes to reflect the source type you selected.

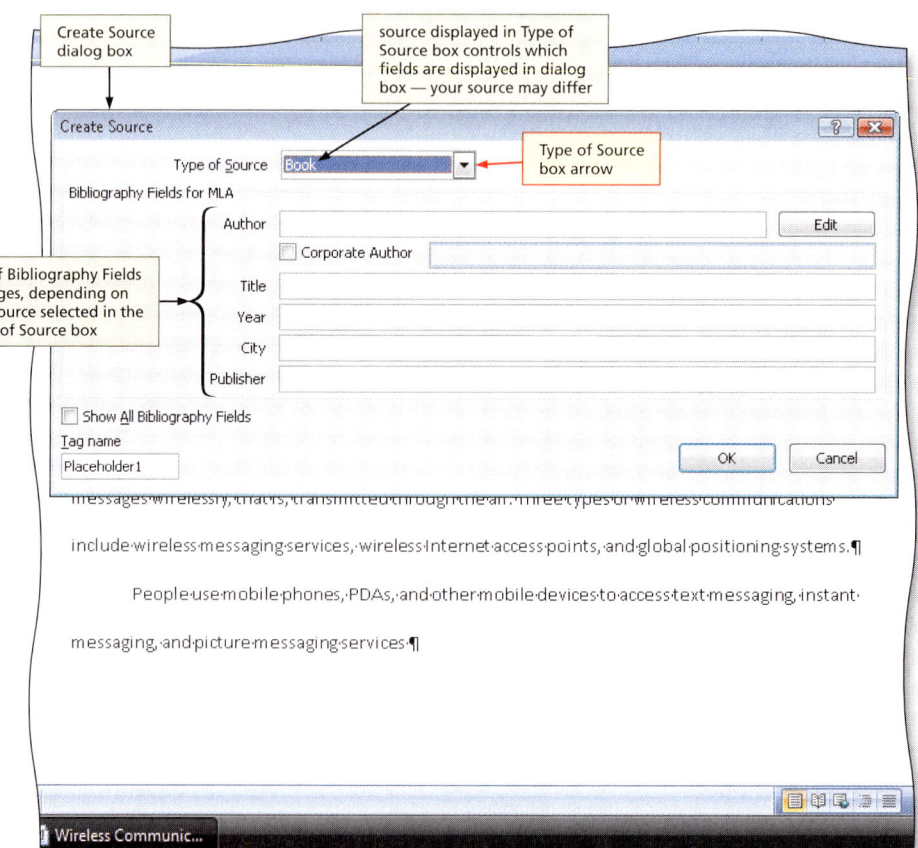

Figure 2–29

3

- If necessary, click the Type of Source box arrow and then click Article in a Periodical, so that the list shows fields required for a magazine (periodical).

- Click the Author text box. Type `Davies, Habika` as the author.

- Click the Title text box. Type `Text Messaging, Instant Messaging, and Picture Messaging` as the article title.

- Press the TAB key and then type `Computing in Today's World` as the periodical title.

- Press the TAB key and then type `2008` as the year.

- Press the TAB key and then type `January` as the month.

- Press the TAB key twice and then type `34-42` as the pages (Figure 2–30).

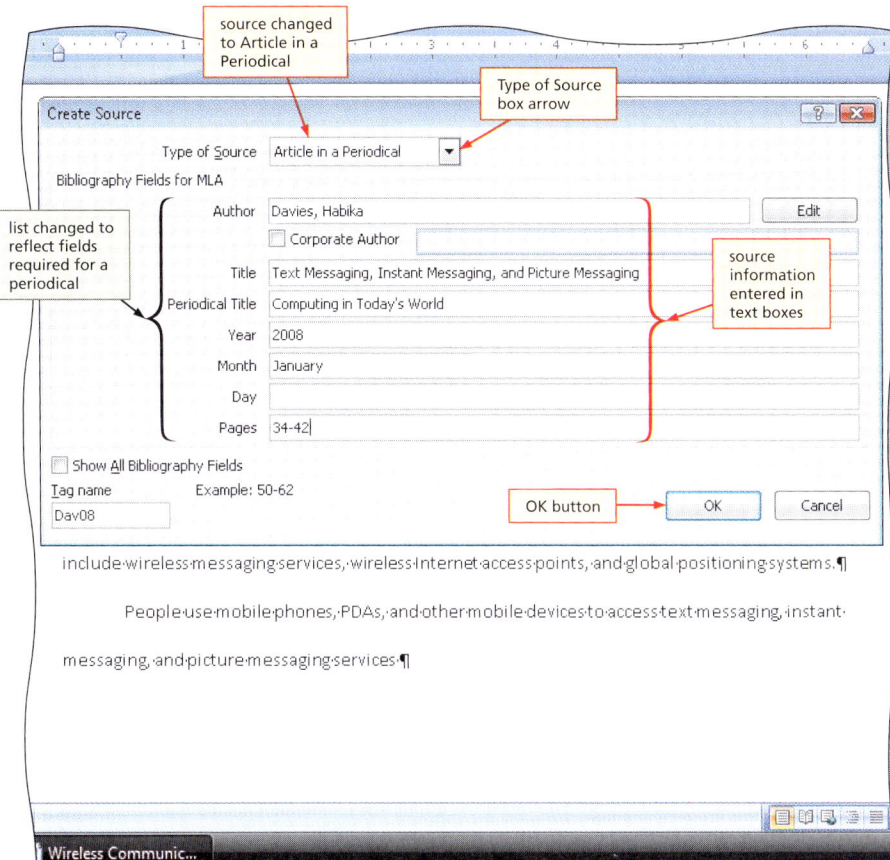

Figure 2–30

4

- Click the OK button to close the dialog box, create the source, and insert the citation in the document at the location of the insertion point (Figure 2–31).

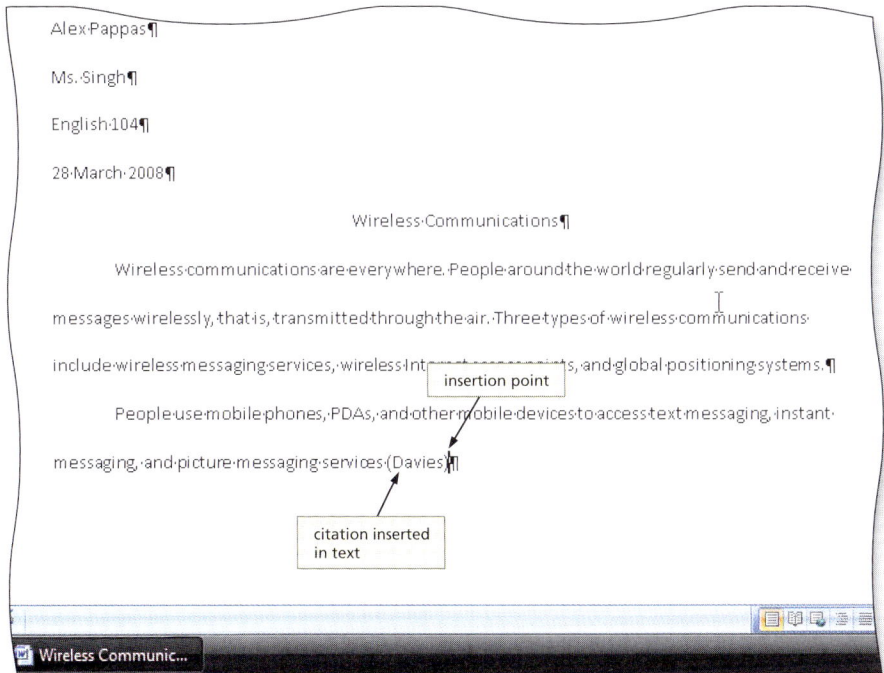

Figure 2–31

To Edit a Citation

In the MLA style, if a source has page numbers, you should include them in the citation. Thus, Word provides a means to enter the page numbers to be displayed in the citation. The following steps edit a citation, so that the page numbers appear in it.

- Click somewhere in the citation to be edited, in this case somewhere in (Davies), which selects the citation and displays the Citation Options box arrow.
- Click the Citation Options box arrow to display the Citation Options menu (Figure 2–32).

Q&A What is the purpose of the tab to the left of the selected citation?

If, for some reason, you wanted to move a citation to a different location in the document, you would select it and then drag the citation tab to the desired location.

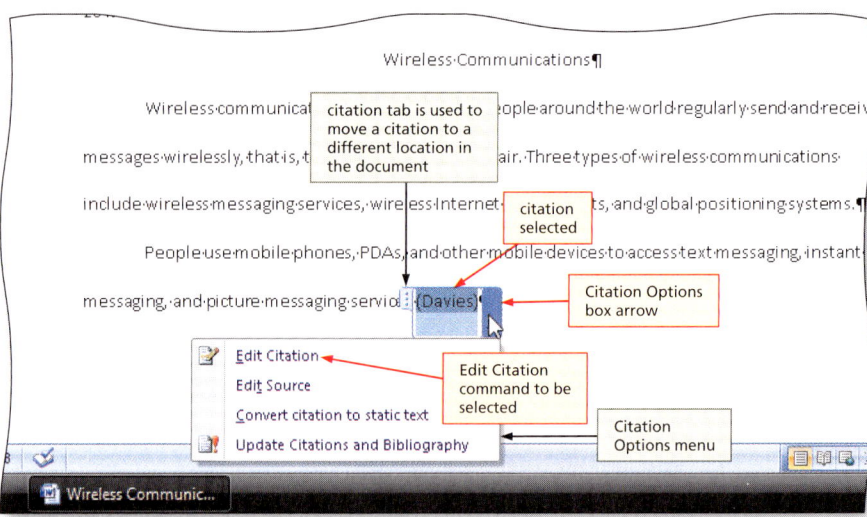

Figure 2–32

- Click Edit Citation on the Citation Options menu to display the Edit Citation dialog box.
- Type 34-42 in the Pages text box (Figure 2–33).

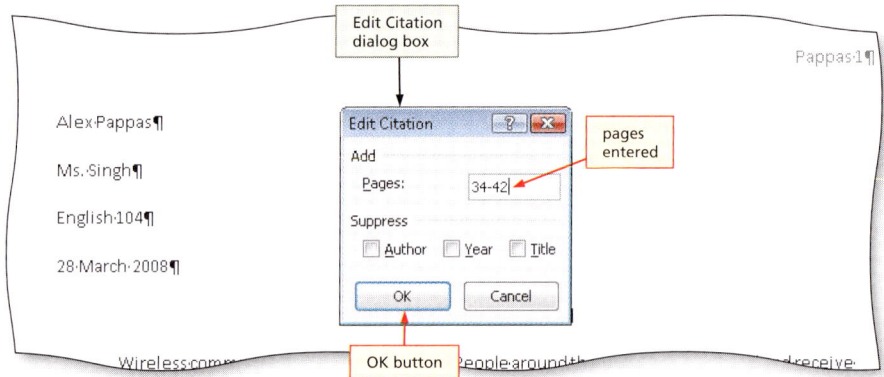

Figure 2–33

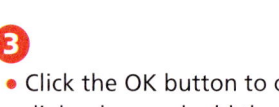

- Click the OK button to close the dialog box and add the page numbers to the citation in the document (Figure 2–34).

- Press the END key to move the insertion point to the end of the line, which also deselects the citation.
- Press the PERIOD key to end the sentence.

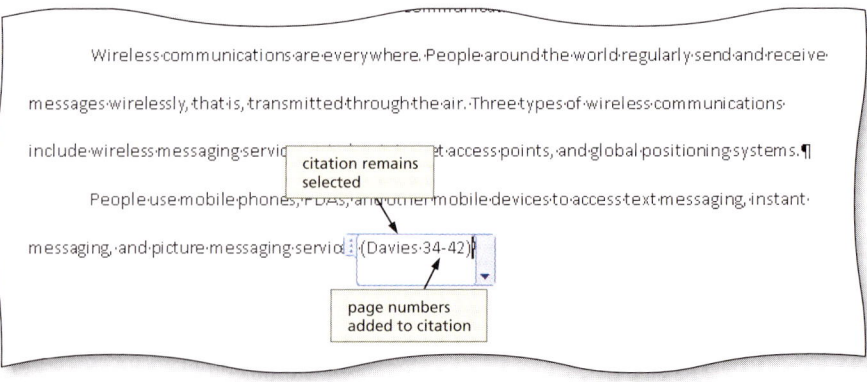

Figure 2–34

To Enter More Text

The next step is to continue typing text in the research paper up to the location of the footnote.

1 Press the SPACEBAR.

2 Type these three sentences (Figure 2–35): `Through text messaging services, users send and receive short text messages, which usually consist of fewer than 300 characters. Wireless instant messaging is an Internet communications service that allows a wireless mobile device to exchange instant messages with one or more mobile devices or online personal computers. Users send graphics, pictures, video clips, sound files, and short text messages with picture messaging services.`

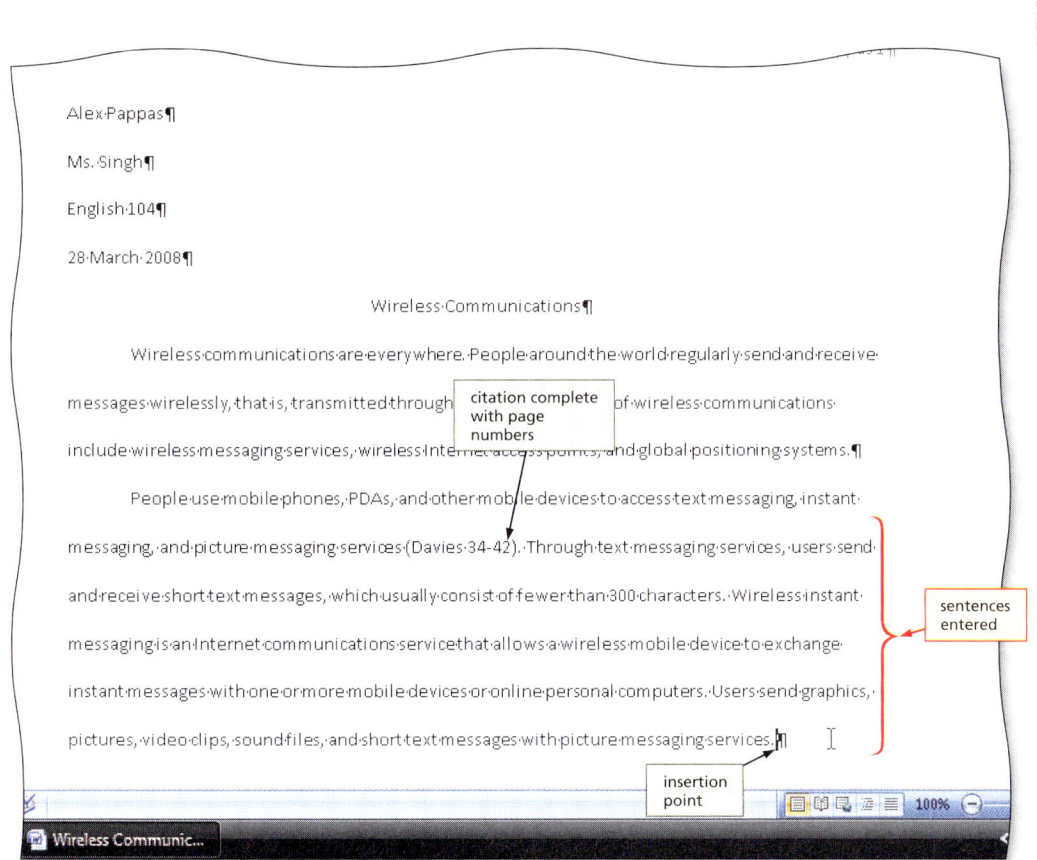

Edit a Source
To edit a source, click somewhere in the citation, click the Citation Options box arrow, and then click Edit Source on the Citation Options menu to display the Edit Source dialog box (which resembles the Create Source dialog box). Make necessary changes and then click the OK button.

Figure 2–35

Footnotes

As discussed earlier in this chapter, explanatory notes are optional in the MLA documentation style. They are used primarily to elaborate on points discussed in the body of a research paper. The MLA style specifies that a superscript (raised number) be used for a **note reference mark** to signal that an explanatory note exists either at the bottom of the page as a **footnote** or at the end of the document as an **endnote**.

In Word, **note text** can be any length and format. Word automatically numbers notes sequentially by placing a note reference mark in the body of the document and also to the left of the note text. If you insert, rearrange, or remove notes, Word renumbers any subsequent note reference marks according to their new sequence in the document.

To Insert a Footnote Reference Mark

The following step inserts a footnote reference mark in the document at the location of the insertion point and also at the location where the footnote text will be typed.

- With the insertion point positioned as shown in Figure 2–35 on the previous page, click the Insert Footnote button on the References tab to display a note reference mark (a superscripted 1) in two places: (1) in the document window at the location of the insertion point and (2) at the bottom of the page where the footnote will be positioned, just below a separator line (Figure 2–36).

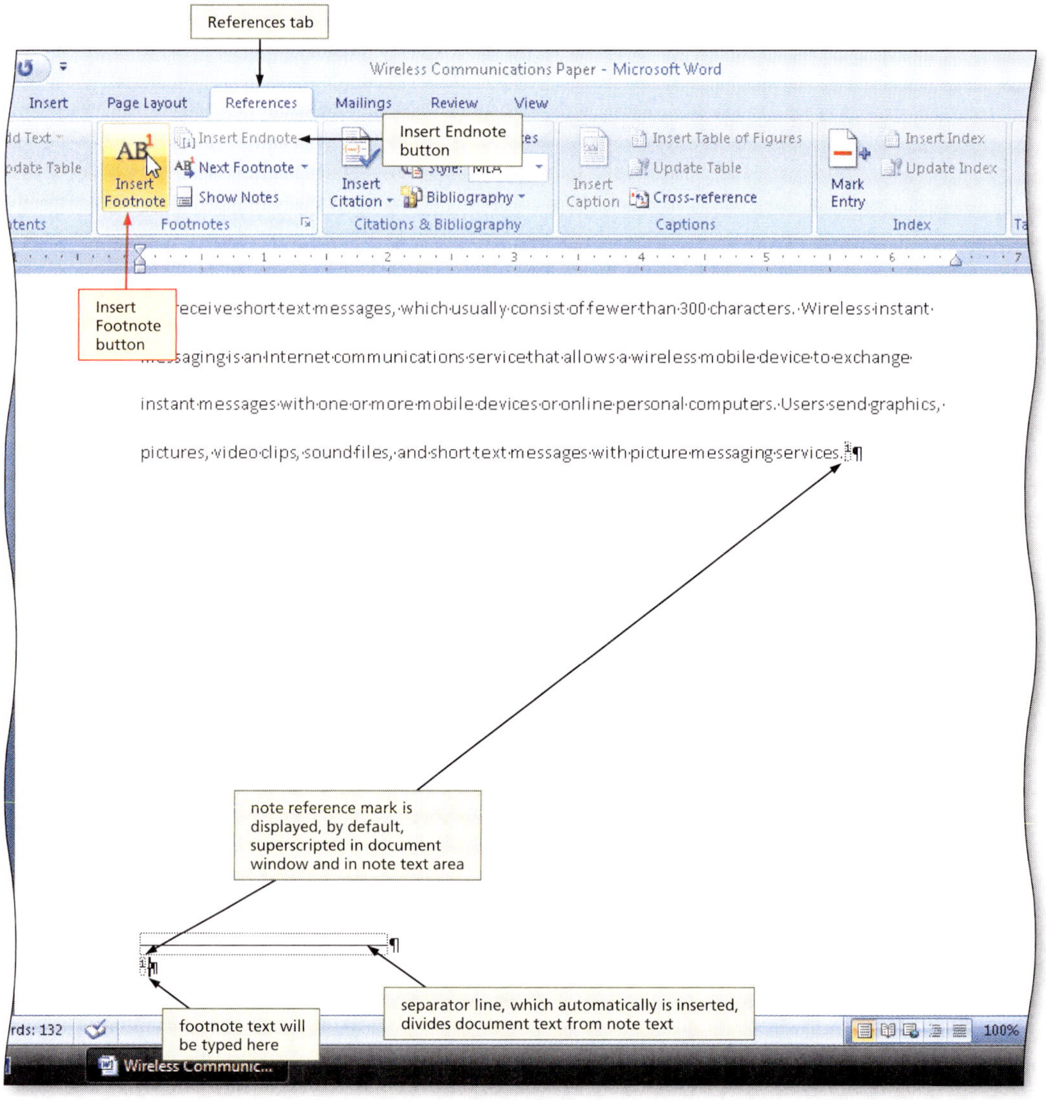

Q&A What if I wanted explanatory notes to be positioned as endnotes instead of as footnotes?

You would click the Insert Endnote button on the References tab, which places the separator line and the endnote text at the end of the document, instead of the bottom of the page containing the reference.

Figure 2–36

Other Ways

1. Press CTRL+ALT+F

To Enter Footnote Text

The next step is to type the footnote text to the right of the note reference mark below the separator line.

1. Type the footnote text up to the citation: `Podpora and Ruiz indicate that some messaging services use the term, video messaging, to refer separately to the capability of sending video clips` and then press the SPACEBAR.

To Insert a Citation Placeholder

Earlier in this chapter, you inserted a citation and its source at once. Sometimes, you may not have the source information readily available and would prefer entering it at a later time.

In the footnote, you will insert a placeholder for the citation and enter the source information later. The following steps insert a citation placeholder.

- With the insertion point positioned as shown in Figure 2–37, click the Insert Citation button on the References tab to display the Insert Citation menu (Figure 2–37).

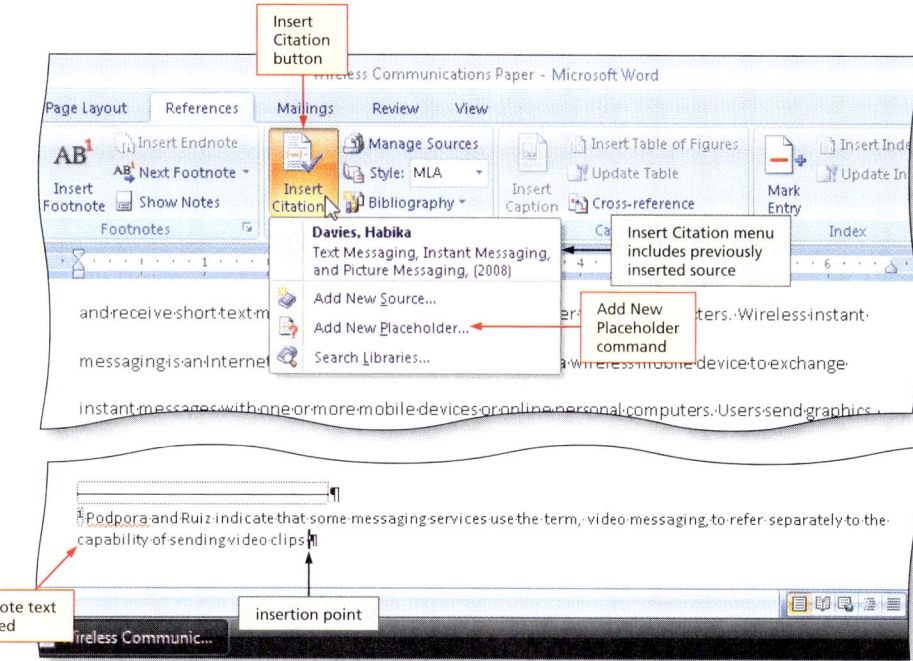

Figure 2–37

- Click Add New Placeholder on the Insert Citation menu to display the Placeholder Name dialog box.

- Type Podpora as the tag name for the source (Figure 2–38).

 What is a tag name?

A tag name is an identifier that links a citation to a source. Word automatically creates a tag name when you enter a source. When you create a citation placeholder, enter a meaningful tag name, which will appear in the citation placeholder until you edit the source.

- Click the OK button to close the dialog box and insert the tag name in the citation placeholder.

- Press the PERIOD key to end the sentence.

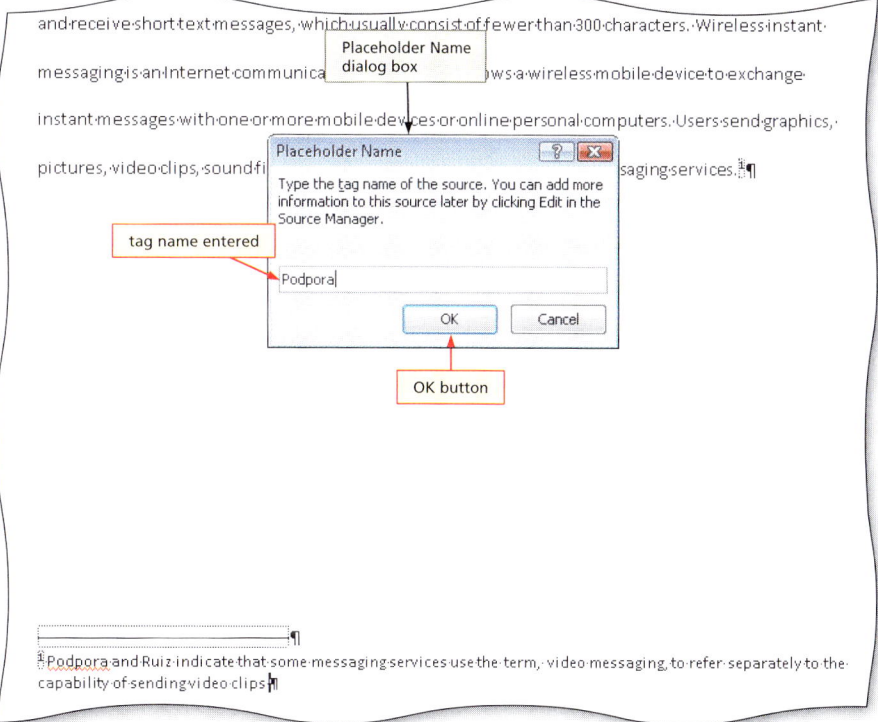

Figure 2–38

Footnote Text Style

When you insert a footnote, Word formats it using the Footnote Text style, which does not adhere to the MLA documentation style. For example, notice in Figure 2–38 on the previous page that the footnote text is single-spaced, left-aligned, and a smaller font size than the text in the research paper. According to the MLA style, notes should be formatted like all other paragraphs in the paper.

You could change the paragraph formatting of the footnote text to first-line indent and double-spacing and then change the font size from 10 to 11 point. If you use this technique, however, you will need to change the format of the footnote text for each footnote you enter into the document.

A more efficient technique is to modify the format of the Footnote Text style so that every footnote you enter in the document will use the formats defined in this style.

To Modify a Style Using a Shortcut Menu

The Footnote Text style should be based on the Research Paper Paragraphs style defined earlier in this chapter. Because the Footnote Text style specifically set paragraphs to single-spaced and the font size to 10 point, you will need to modify those formats to double-spaced paragraphs and 11-point font. The following steps modify the Footnote Text style.

- Right-click the note text in the footnote to display a shortcut menu related to footnotes (Figure 2–39).

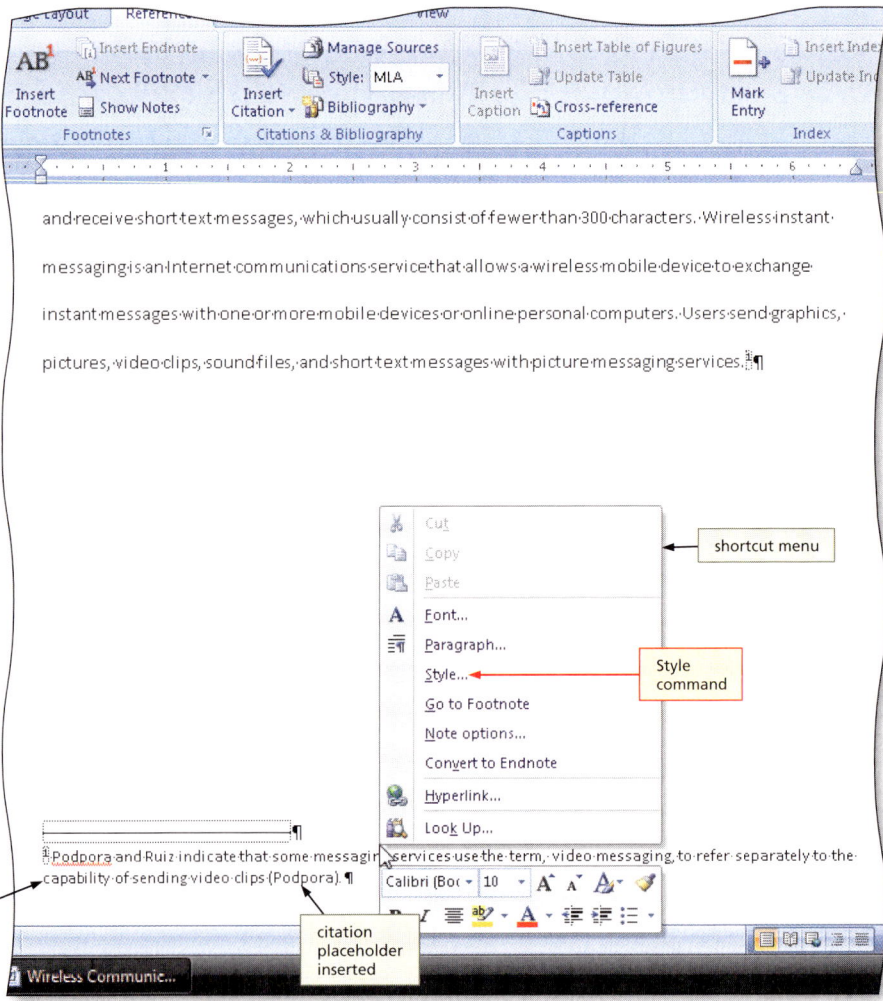

Figure 2–39

❷
- Click Style on the shortcut menu to display the Style dialog box. If necessary, click Footnote Text in the Styles list.

- Click the Modify button in the Style dialog box to display the Modify Style dialog box.

- Click the 'Style based on' box arrow and then click Research Paper Paragraphs so that the Footnote Text style is based on the Research Paper Paragraphs style.

- Click the 'Style for following paragraph' box arrow and then scroll to and click Research Paper Paragraphs so that the additional footnote paragraphs are based on the Research Paper Paragraphs style.

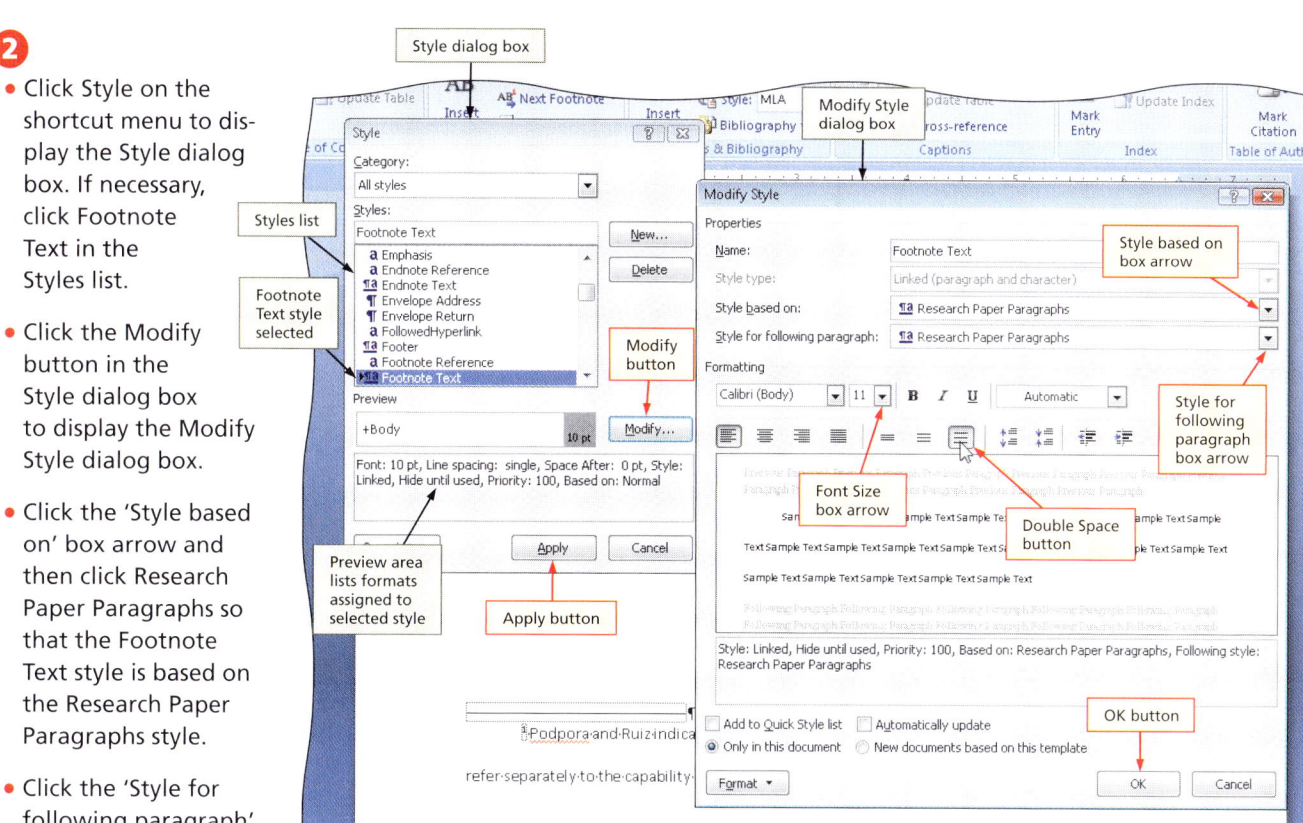

Figure 2–40

- Click the Font Size box arrow and then click 11 in the Font Size list to change the font size to 11.

- Click the Double Space button to set the line spacing to double (Figure 2–40).

❸
- Click the OK button in the Modify Style dialog box to close the dialog box.

- Click the Apply button in the Style dialog box to apply the style changes to the footnote text (Figure 2–41).

Q&A Will all footnotes use this modified style?

Yes. Any future footnotes entered in the document will use an 11-point font with the paragraphs first-line indented and double-spaced.

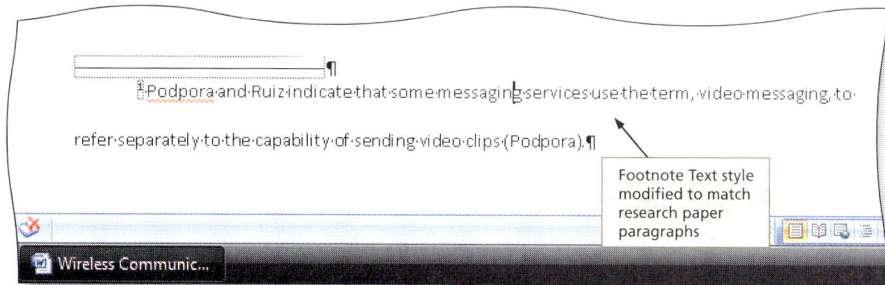

Figure 2–41

Other Ways

1. Click Styles Dialog Box Launcher, click Footnote Text in list, click Footnote Text box arrow, click Modify, change settings, click OK button

2. Click Styles Dialog Box Launcher, click Manage Styles button, scroll to Footnote Text and then select it, click Modify button, change settings, click OK button in each dialog box

To Edit a Source

When you typed the footnote text for this research paper, you inserted a citation placeholder for the source. You now have the source information and are ready to enter it. The following steps edit the source.

- Click somewhere in the citation placeholder to be edited, in this case (Podpora), to select the citation placeholder.

- Click the Citation Options box arrow to display the Citation Options menu (Figure 2–42).

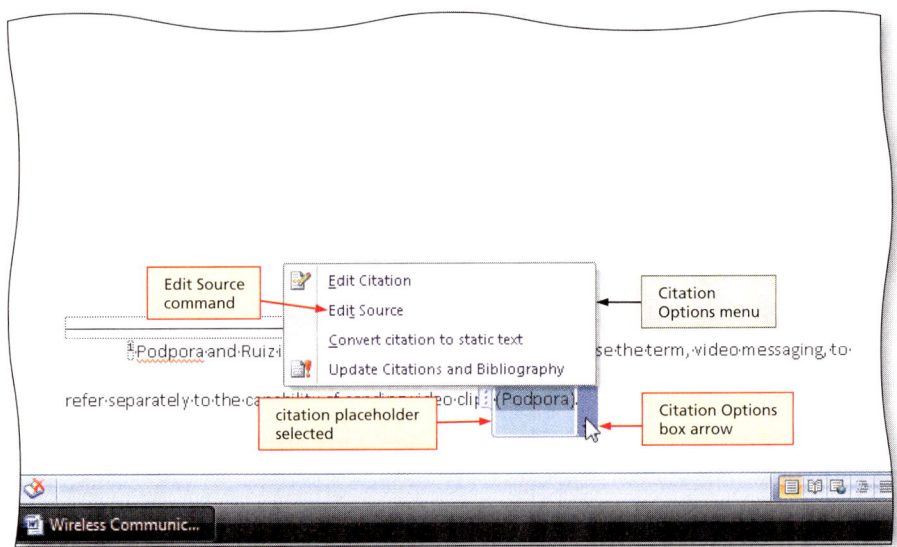

Figure 2–42

- Click Edit Source on the Citation Options menu to display the Edit Source dialog box.

- If necessary, click the Type of Source box arrow and then click Book, so that the list shows fields required for a book.

- Click the Author text box. Type `Podpora, Maxine C., and Adelbert D. Ruiz` as the author.

- Click the Title text box. Type `Advances in Wireless Internet Access Point Technology` as the book title.

- Press the TAB key and then type `2008` as the year.

- Press the TAB key and then type `Dallas` as the city.

- Press the TAB key and then type `Wells Publishing` as the publisher (Figure 2–43).

- Click the OK button to close the dialog box and create the source.

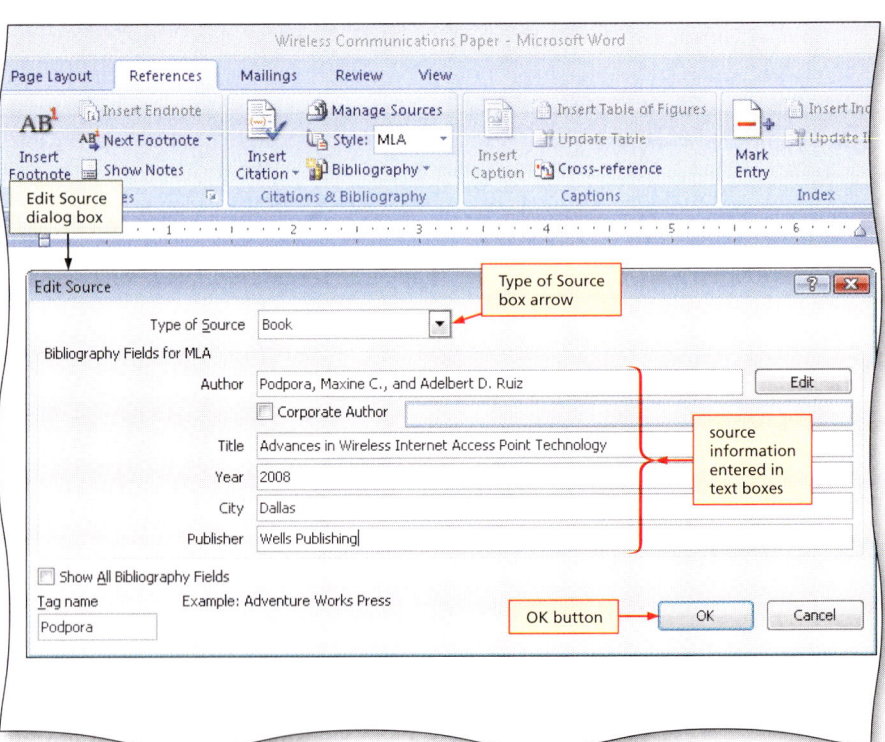

Figure 2–43

Other Ways

1. Click Manage Sources button on References tab, click placeholder source in Current List, click Edit button

To Edit a Citation

In the MLA style, if you reference the author's name in the text, you should not list it again in the parenthetical citation. Instead, just list the page number in the citation. The following steps edit the citation, suppressing the author but displaying the page numbers.

1. If necessary, click somewhere in the citation to be edited, in this case (Podpora), to select the citation and display the Citation Options box arrow.

2. Click the Citation Options box arrow to display the Citation Options menu.

3. Click Edit Citation on the Citation Options menu to display the Edit Citation dialog box.

4. Type 79-82 in the Pages text box.

5. Click the Author check box to place a check mark in it (Figure 2–44).

6. Click the OK button to close the dialog box, remove the author name from the citation in the footnote, and add page numbers to the citation.

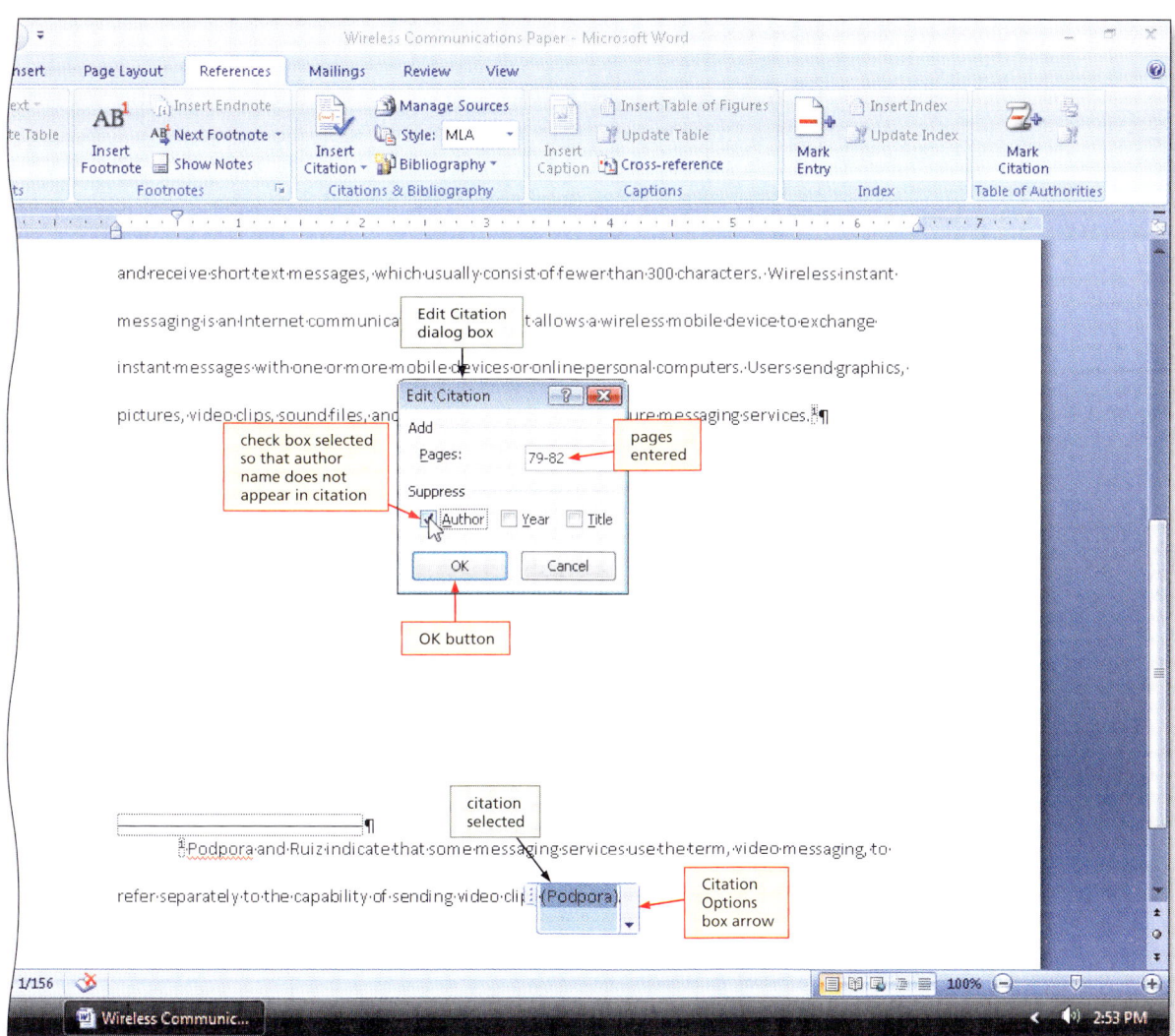

Figure 2–44

Working with Footnotes and Endnotes

You edit footnote text just as you edit any other text in the document. To delete or move a note reference mark, however, you must be in the document text (not in the footnote text).

To delete a note, select the note reference mark in the document text (not in the footnote text) by dragging through the note reference mark and then click the Cut button on the Home tab. Another way to delete a note is to click immediately to the right of the note reference mark in the document text and then press the BACKSPACE key twice, or click immediately to the left of the note reference mark in the document text and then press the DELETE key twice.

To move a note to a different location in a document, select the note reference mark in the document text (not in the footnote text), click the Cut button on the Home tab, click the location where you want to move the note, and then click the Paste button on the Home tab. When you move or delete notes, Word automatically renumbers any remaining notes in the correct sequence.

If you position the mouse pointer on the note reference mark, the note text displays above the note reference mark as a ScreenTip. To remove the ScreenTip, move the mouse pointer.

If, for some reason, you wanted to change the format of note reference marks in footnotes or endnotes (i.e., from 1, 2, 3, to A, B, C), you would click the Footnotes Dialog Box Launcher to display the Footnote and Endnote dialog box, click the Number format box arrow, click the desired number format in the list, and then click the OK button.

If, for some reason, you wanted to convert footnotes to endnotes, you would click the Footnotes Dialog Box Launcher to display the Footnote and Endnote dialog box, click the Convert button, make sure the 'Convert all footnotes to endnotes' option button is selected, click the OK button, and then click the Close button in the Footnote and Endnote dialog box.

To Enter More Text

The next step is to continue typing text in the body of the research paper.

1 Position the insertion point after the note reference mark in the document, and then press the ENTER key.

2 Type the third paragraph of the research paper (Figure 2–45): `In many public locations, people connect to the Internet through a wireless Internet access point using mobile computers and devices. Two types of wireless Internet access points are hot spots and 3-G networks. A 3-G network, which uses cellular radio technology, enables users to connect to the Internet through a mobile phone or computer equipped with an appropriate PC Card. A hot spot is a wireless network that allows mobile users to check e-mail, browse the Web, and access any Internet service - as long as their computers or devices have the proper wireless capability.`

BTW

Spacing after Punctuation
Because word processing documents use variable character fonts, it often is difficult to determine in a printed document how many times someone has pressed the SPACEBAR between sentences. The rule is to press the SPACEBAR only once after periods, colons, and other punctuation marks.

To Count Words

Often when you write papers, you are required to compose the papers with a minimum number of words. The minimum requirement for the research paper in this chapter is 325 words. You can look on the status bar and see the total number of words thus far in a document. For example, Figure 2–45 shows the research paper has 250 words, but you are not sure if that count includes the words in your footnote. The following steps display the Word Count dialog box, so that you can verify whether the footnote text is included in the count.

1
- Click the Word Count indicator on the status bar to display the Word Count dialog box.
- If necessary, place a check mark in the 'Include textboxes, footnotes and endnotes' check box (Figure 2-45).

Q&A Why do the statistics in my Word Count dialog box differ from Figure 2–45?

Depending on the accuracy of your typing, your statistics may differ.

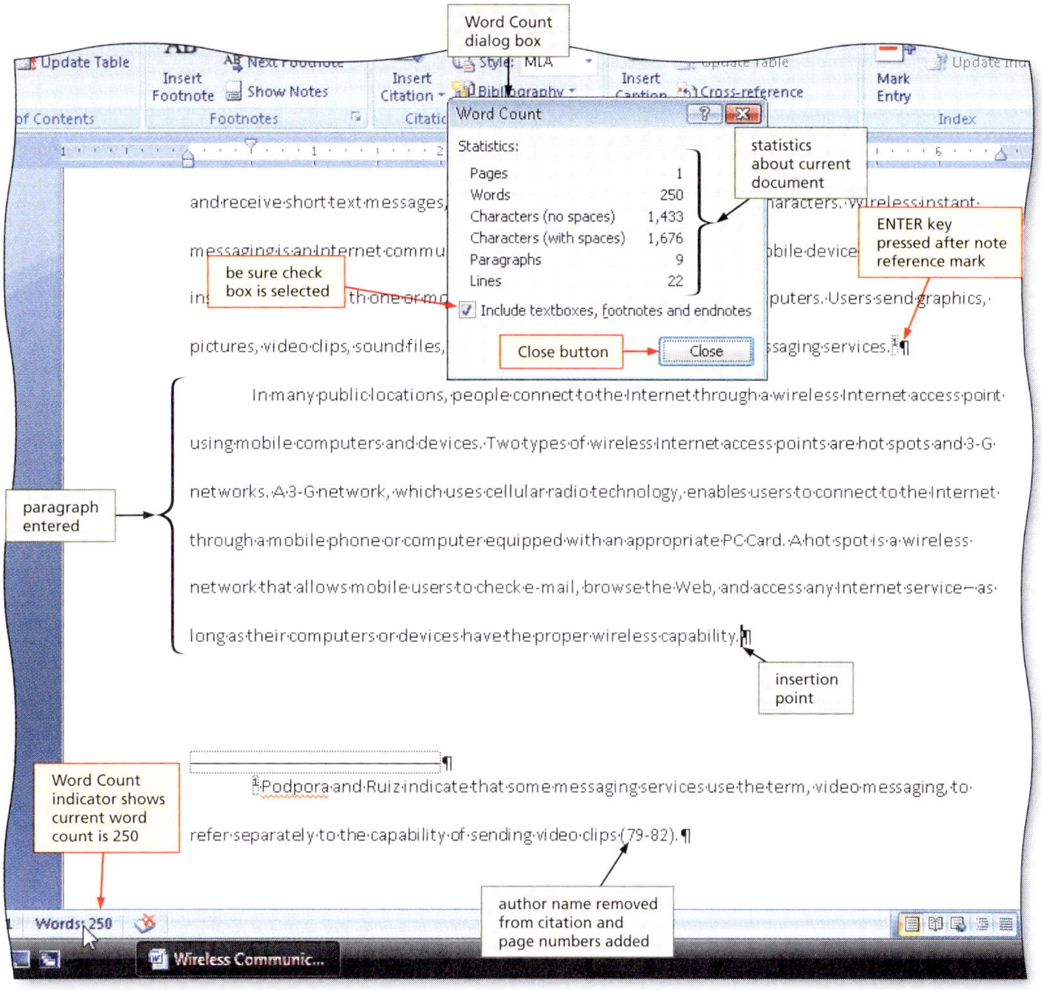

2
- Click the Close button to close the dialog box.

Q&A Can I display statistics for just a section of the document?

Yes. Select the section and then click the Word Count indicator on the status bar to display statistics about the selected text.

Figure 2–45

Other Ways
1. Click Word Count button on Review tab
2. Press CTRL+SHIFT+G

Automatic Page Breaks

As you type documents that exceed one page, Word automatically inserts page breaks, called **automatic page breaks** or **soft page breaks**, when it determines the text has filled one page according to paper size, margin settings, line spacing, and other settings. If you add text, delete text, or modify text on a page, Word recomputes the location of automatic page breaks and adjusts them accordingly.

Word performs page recomputation between the keystrokes, that is, in between the pauses in your typing. Thus, Word refers to the automatic page break task as **background repagination**. The steps on the next page illustrate Word's automatic page break feature.

To Enter More Text and Insert a Citation Placeholder

The next task is to type the fourth paragraph in the body of the research paper.

1 With the insertion point positioned at the end of the third paragraph as shown in Figure 2–45 on the previous page, press the ENTER key. Type the fourth paragraph of the research paper (Figure 2–46): `A global positioning system (GPS) is a navigation system that consists of one or more earth-based receivers that accept and analyze signals sent by satellites in order to determine the receiver's geographic location, according to Shelly and Cashman` and then press the SPACEBAR.

2 Click the Insert Citation button on the References tab to display the Insert Citation menu. Click Add New Placeholder on the Insert Citation menu to display the Placeholder Name dialog box.

3 Type `Shelly` as the tag name for the source.

4 Click the OK button to close the dialog box and insert the tag name in the citation placeholder.

5 Press the PERIOD key to end the sentence. Press the SPACEBAR. Type `A GPS receiver is a handheld, mountable, or embedded device that contains an antenna, a radio receiver, and a processor. Many mobile devices, such as mobile phones and PDAs, have GPS capability built into the device.`

6 Press the ENTER key.

BTW

Page Break Locations
As you type, your page break may occur at different locations depending on Word settings and the type of printer connected to the computer.

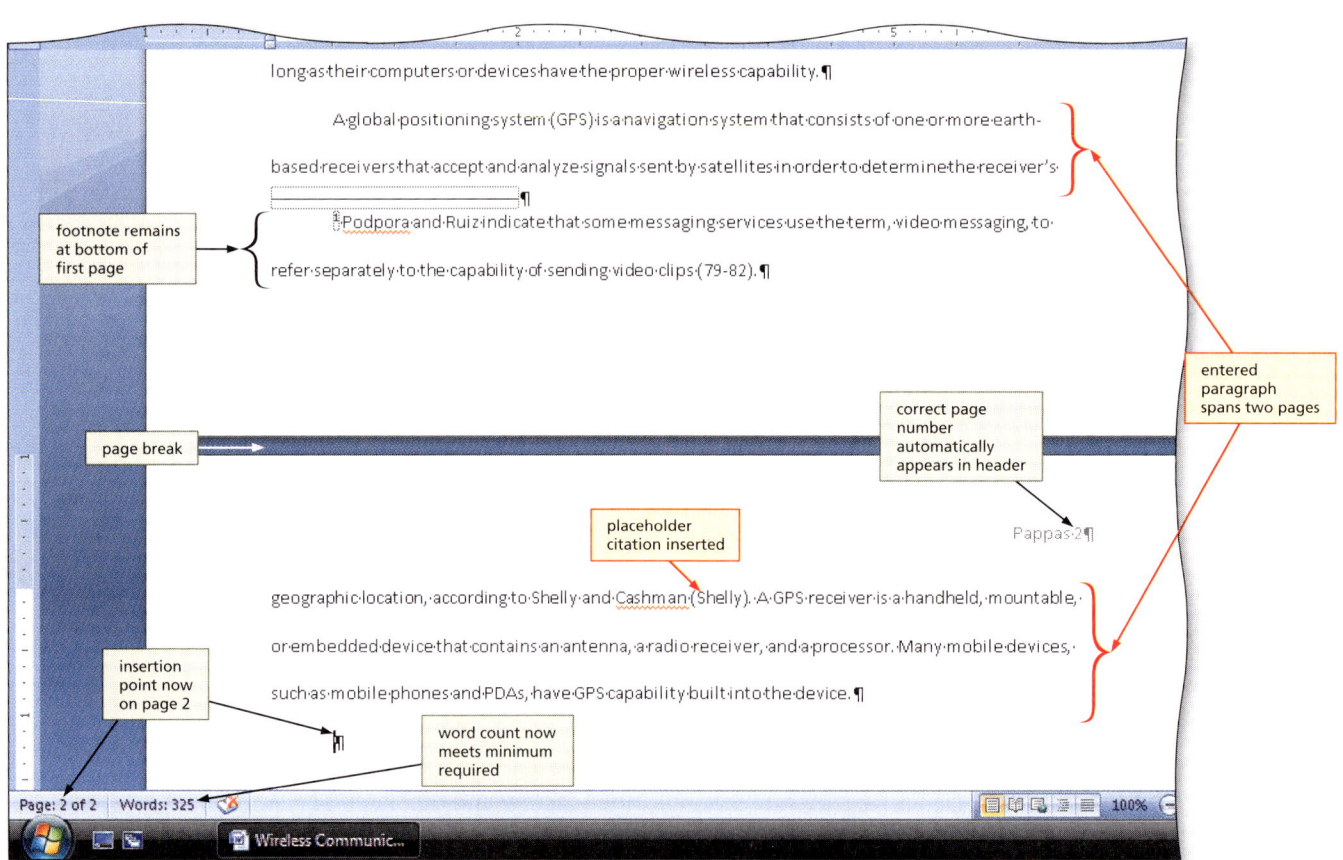

Figure 2–46

To Edit a Source

When you typed the fourth paragraph of the research paper, you inserted a citation placeholder, Shelly, for the source. You now have the source information, which is for a Web site, and are ready to enter it. The following steps edit the source for the Shelly citation placeholder.

① Click somewhere in the citation placeholder to be edited, in this case (Shelly), to select the citation placeholder.

② Click the Citation Options box arrow to display the Citation Options menu.

③ Click Edit Source on the Citation Options menu to display the Edit Source dialog box.

④ If necessary, click the Type of Source box arrow; scroll to and then click Web site, so that the list shows fields required for a Web site.

⑤ Place a check mark in the Show All Bibliography Fields check box to display more fields related to Web sites.

⑥ Click the Author text box. Type `Shelly, Gary B., and Thomas J. Cashman` as the author.

⑦ Click the Name of Web Page text box. Type `How a GPS Works` as the Web page title.

⑧ Click the Production Company text box. Type `Course Technology` as the production company.

⑨ Click the Year Accessed text box. Type `2008` as the year.

⑩ Press the TAB key and then type `March` as the month accessed.

Q&A What if some of the text boxes disappear as I enter the Web site fields?

With the Show All Bibliography Fields check box selected, all Web site fields may not be able to be displayed in the dialog box at the same time. In this case, some may scroll up.

⑪ Press the TAB key and then type `21` as the day accessed.

⑫ Press the TAB key and then type `www.scsite.com/wd2007/pr2/wc.htm` as the URL (Figure 2–47).

⑬ Click the OK button to close the dialog box and create the source.

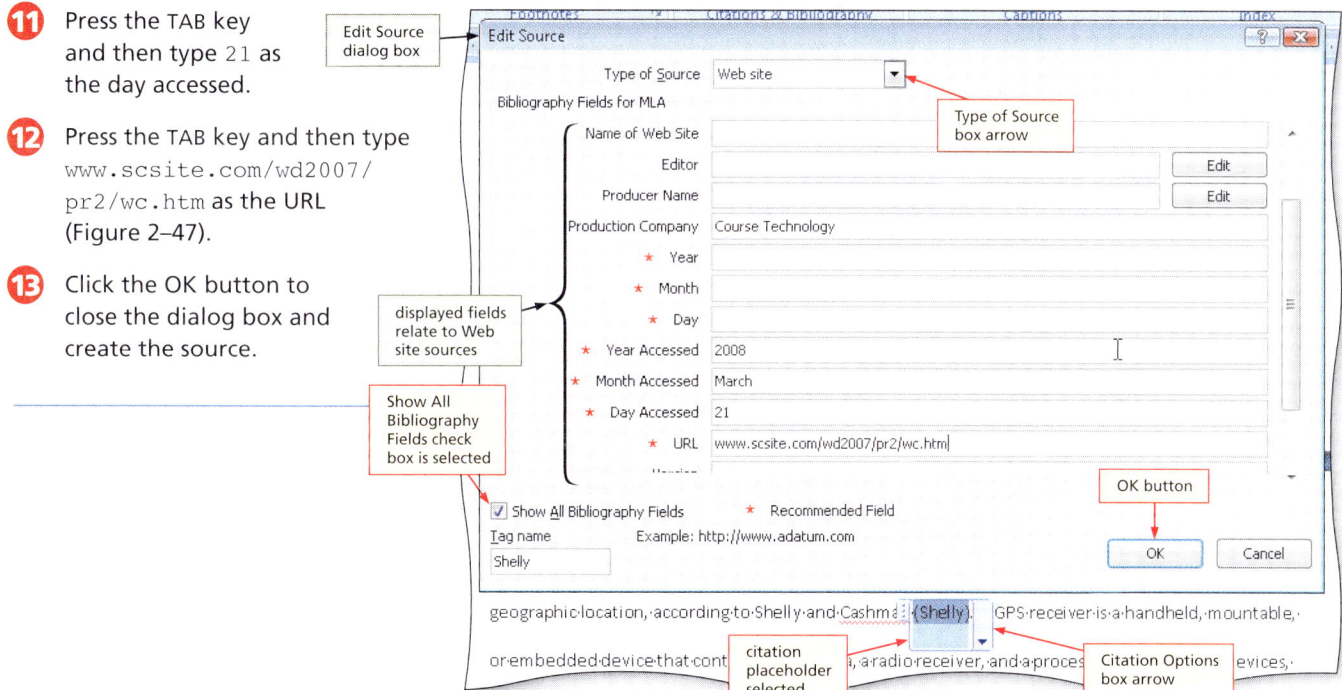

Figure 2–47

To Edit a Citation

As mentioned earlier, if you reference the author's name in the text, you should not list it again in the parenthetical citation. For Web site citations, when you suppress the author's name, the citation shows the Web site name because page numbers do not apply. The following steps edit the citation, suppressing the author and displaying the name of the Web site instead.

1 If necessary, click somewhere in the citation to be edited, in this case (Shelly), to select the citation and display the Citation Options box arrow.

2 Click the Citation Options box arrow and then click Edit Citation on the Citation Options menu to display the Edit Citation dialog box.

3 Click the Author check box to place a check mark in it (Figure 2–48).

4 Click the OK button to close the dialog box, remove the author name from the citation, and show the name of the Web site in the citation.

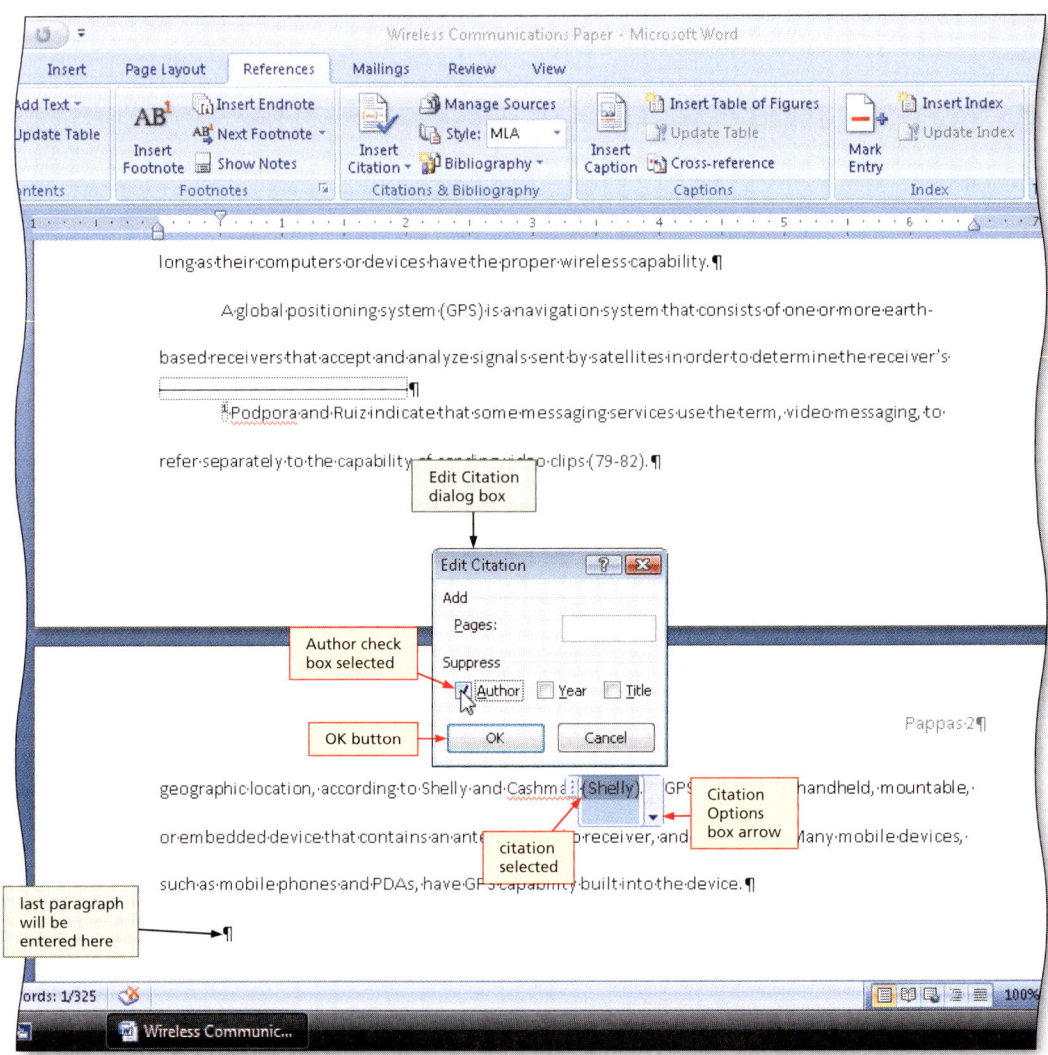

Figure 2–48

To Enter More Text

The next step is to type the last paragraph of text in the research paper.

1. Position the insertion point on the paragraph mark below the fourth paragraph in the research paper (Figure 2–48).

2. Type the last paragraph of the research paper (Figure 2–49):
   ```
   Mobile users
   communicate
   wirelessly
   through
   wireless
   messaging services, wireless Internet access points, and global
   positioning systems. Anyone can take advantage of wireless communications
   using mobile computers and devices.
   ```

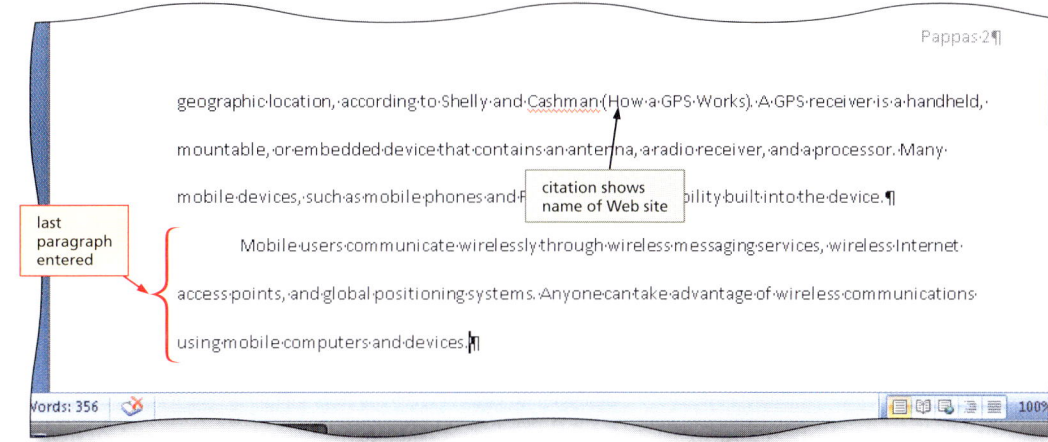

Figure 2–49

To Save an Existing Document with the Same File Name

You have made several edits to the research paper since you last saved it. Thus, you should save it again. The following step saves the document again.

1. Click the Save button on the Quick Access Toolbar to overwrite the previous Wireless Communications Paper file on the USB flash drive.

Creating an Alphabetical Works Cited Page

According to the MLA style, the **works cited page** is a list of sources that are referenced directly in a research paper. You place the list on a separate numbered page with the title, Works Cited, centered one inch from the top margin. The works are to be alphabetized by the author's last name or, if the work has no author, by the work's title. The first line of each entry begins at the left margin. Indent subsequent lines of the same entry one-half inch from the left margin.

Plan Ahead

Create the list of sources.
A **bibliography** is an alphabetical list of sources referenced in a paper. Whereas the text of the research paper contains brief references to the source (the citations), the bibliography lists all publication information about the source. Documentation styles differ significantly in their guidelines for preparing a bibliography. Each style identifies formats for various sources including books, magazines, pamphlets, newspapers, Web sites, television programs, paintings, maps, advertisements, letters, memos, and much more. You can find information about various styles and their guidelines in printed style guides and on the Web.

To Page Break Manually

The works cited are to be displayed on a separate numbered page. Thus, you must insert a manual page break following the body of the research paper so that the list of sources is displayed on a separate page. A **manual page break**, or **hard page break**, is one that you force into the document at a specific location.

Word never moves or adjusts manual page breaks; however, Word adjusts any automatic page breaks that follow a manual page break. Word inserts manual page breaks immediately above the location of the insertion point. The following step inserts a manual page break after the text of the research paper.

- With the insertion point at the end of the text of the research paper (Figure 2-49 on the previous page), press the ENTER key.

- Then, press CTRL+ENTER to insert a manual page break immediately above the insertion point and position the insertion point immediately below the manual page break (Figure 2–50).

- Scroll to position the top of the third page closer to the ruler.

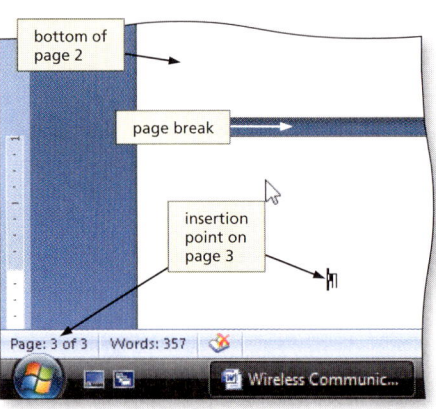
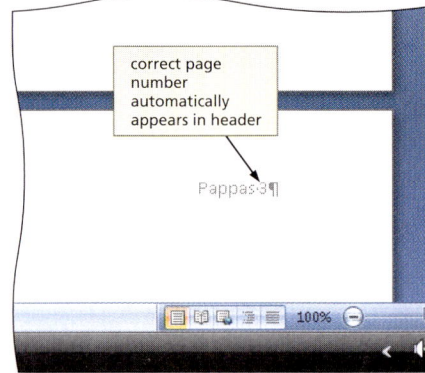

Figure 2–50

> **Other Ways**
> 1. Click Page Break button on Insert tab

To Center the Title of the Works Cited Page

The works cited title is to be centered between the margins of the paper. If you simply issue the Center command, the title will not be centered properly. Instead, it will be one-half inch to the right of the center point because earlier you set first-line indent at one-half inch. Recall that Word is indenting the first line of every paragraph one-half inch.

To properly center the title of the works cited page, you must move the First Line Indent marker back to the left margin before centering the paragraph.

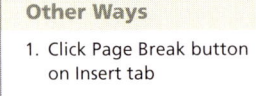

① Drag the First Line Indent marker to the 0" mark on the ruler, which is at the left margin, to remove the first-line indent setting.

② Press CTRL+E to center the paragraph mark.

③ Type Works Cited as the title.

④ Press the ENTER key.

⑤ Press CTRL+L to left-align the paragraph mark (Figure 2–51).

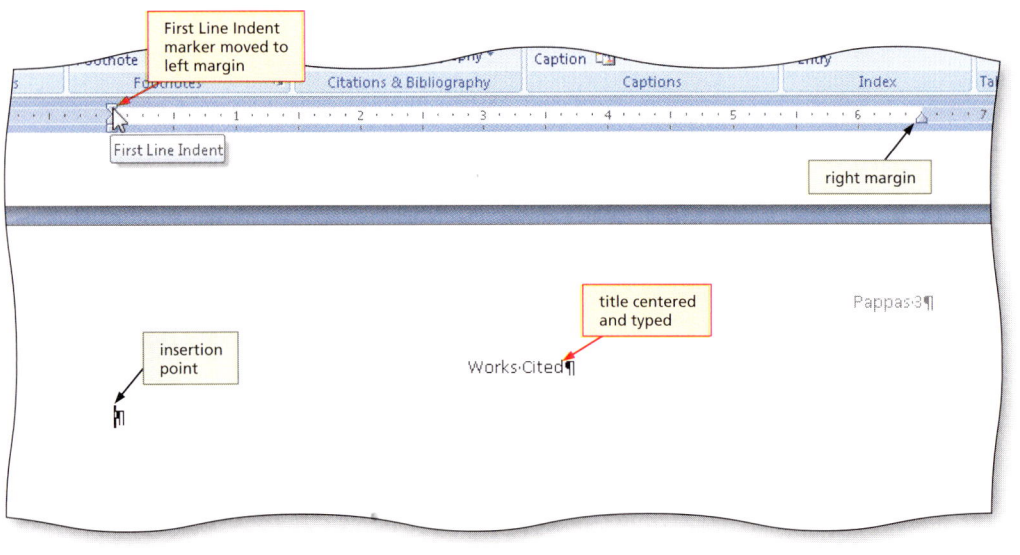

Figure 2–51

To Create the Bibliographical List

While typing the research paper, you created several citations and their sources. Word can format the list of sources and alphabetize them in a **bibliographical list**, saving you time looking up style guidelines. That is, Word will create a bibliographical list with each element of the source placed in its correct position with proper formatting and punctuation, according to the specified style. For example, in this research paper, the book source will list, in this order, the author name(s), book title, publisher city, publishing company name, and publication year with the book title underlined and the correct punctuation between each element according to the MLA style. The following steps create a MLA formatted bibliographical list from the sources previously entered.

- With the insertion point positioned as shown in Figure 2–52, click the Bibliography button on the References tab to display the Bibliography gallery (Figure 2–52).

Q&A Will I select Works Cited from the Bibliography gallery?

No. The title it inserts is not formatted according to the MLA style. Thus, you will use the Insert Bibliography command instead.

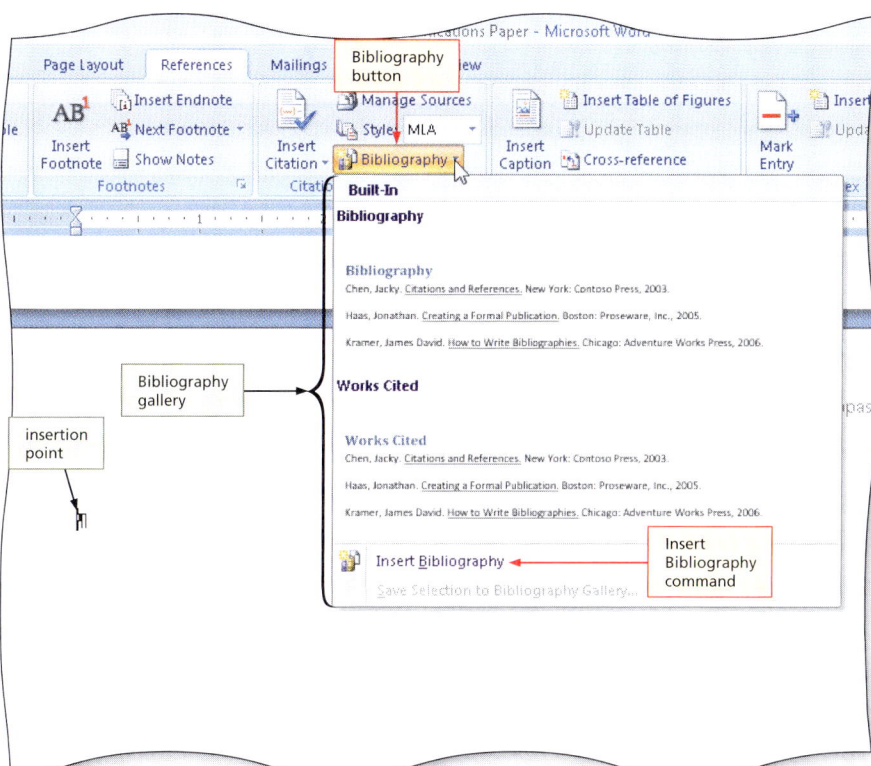

Figure 2–52

- Click Insert Bibliography in the Bibliography gallery to insert a list of sources at the location of the insertion point.

- If necessary, scroll to display the entire list of sources in the document window (Figure 2–53).

Figure 2–53

To Modify a Style Using the Styles Task Pane

Although the format within each entry in the bibliographical list meets the MLA style, the paragraph formatting does not. Currently, entries are based on the Normal style, which does not have the correct line or paragraph spacing. Thus, you will modify the style so that it is based on the No Spacing style (no blank space before or after a paragraph) and change its line spacing to double. The following steps modify the Bibliography style.

1

- Click somewhere in the list of sources to position the insertion point in a paragraph formatted with the Bibliography style.

Q&A Why did the list of sources turn gray?

The entire list of sources is a field that Word automatically updates each time you make a change to one of the sources. Word, by default, shades fields gray on the screen to help you identify them. The gray shading, however, will not appear in the printed document.

- Click Home on the Ribbon to display the Home tab.

- Click the Styles Dialog Box Launcher to display the Styles task pane.

- If necessary, scroll to Bibliography in the Styles task pane. Click Bibliography to select it, if necessary, and then click its box arrow to display the Bibliography menu (Figure 2–54).

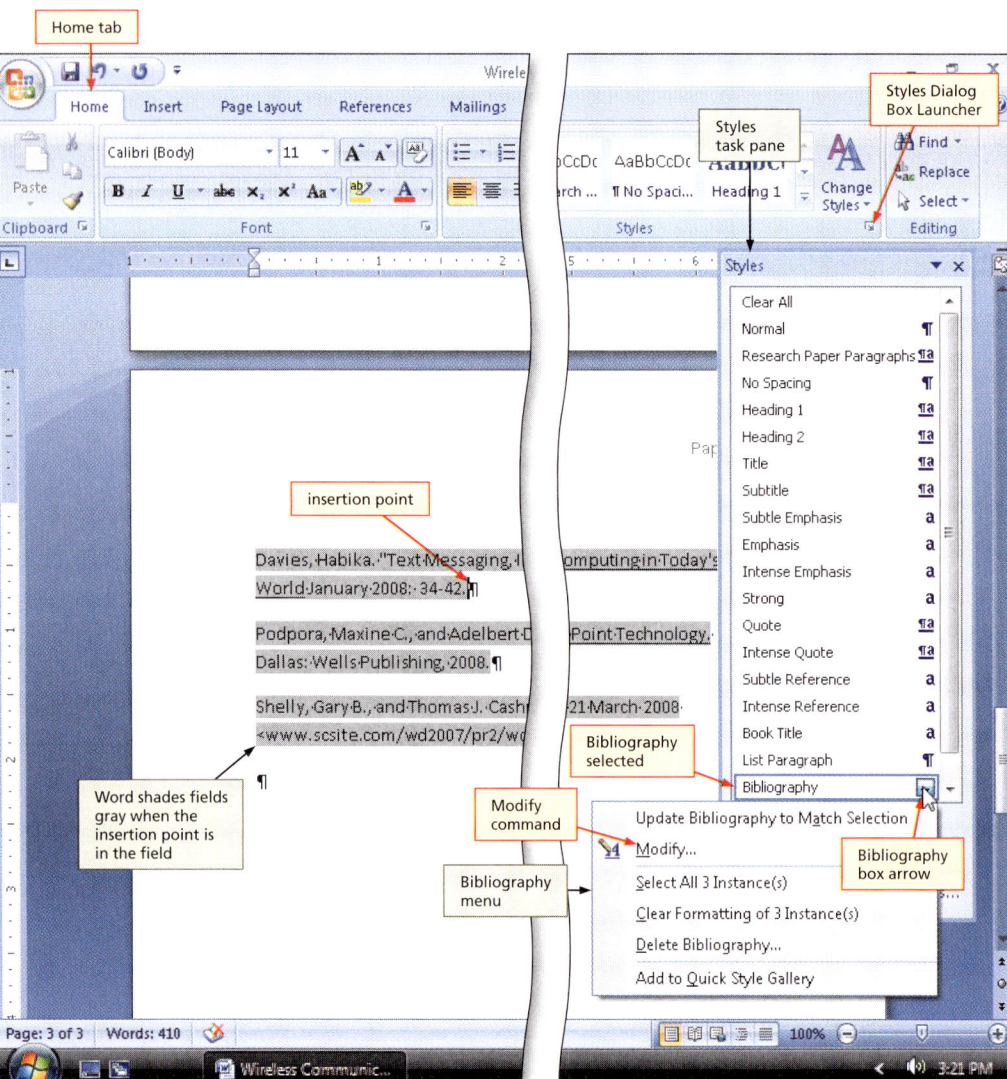

Figure 2–54

- Click Modify on the Bibliography menu to display the Modify Style dialog box.

- Click the 'Style based on' box arrow and then click No Spacing to base the Bibliography style on the No Spacing style.

- Click the 'Style for following paragraph' box arrow and then click No Spacing to base additional bibliographical paragraphs on the No Spacing style.

- Click the Double Space button to set the line spacing to double.

- Place a check mark in the Automatically update check box so that any future changes you make to the bibliographical paragraphs will update the Bibliography style automatically (Figure 2–55).

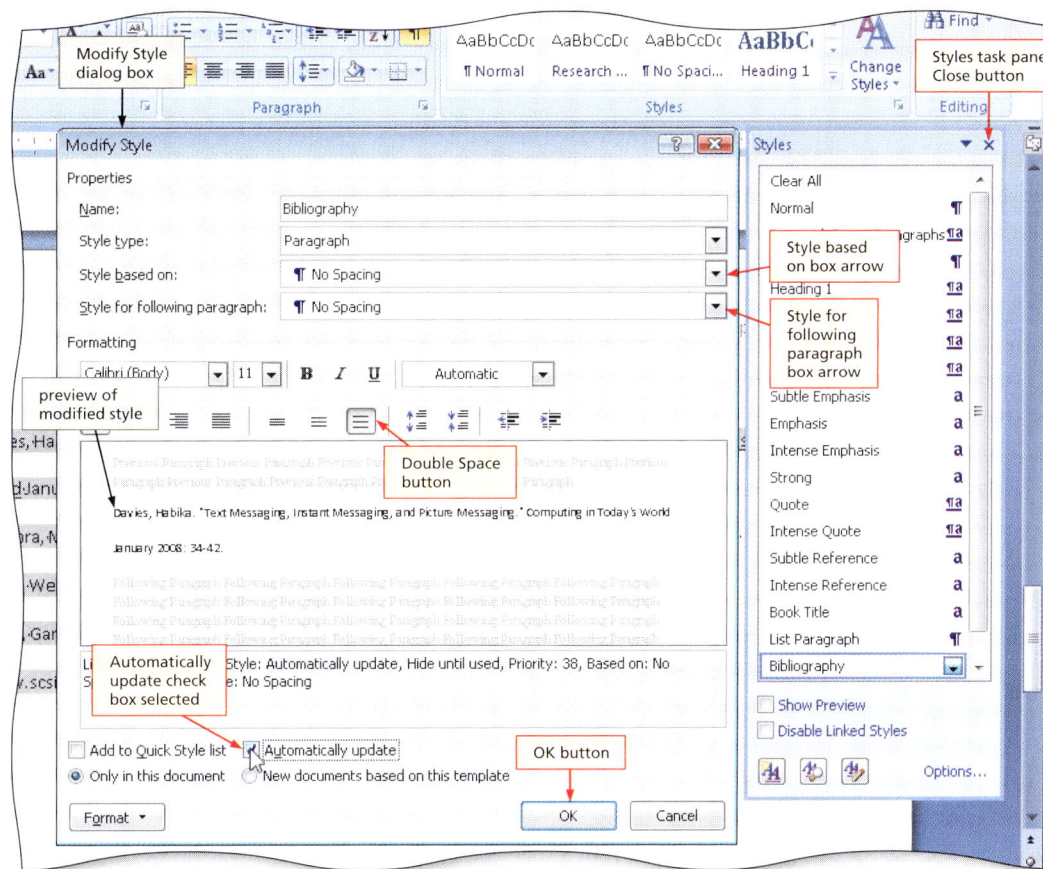

Figure 2–55

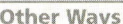

- Click the OK button in the Modify Style dialog box to close the dialog box and apply the style changes to the paragraphs in the document.

- Click the Close button on the Styles task pane title bar to close the task pane (Figure 2–56).

Other Ways

1. Click Styles Dialog Box Launcher, click Manage Styles button, scroll to style and then select it, click Modify button, change settings, click OK button in each dialog box

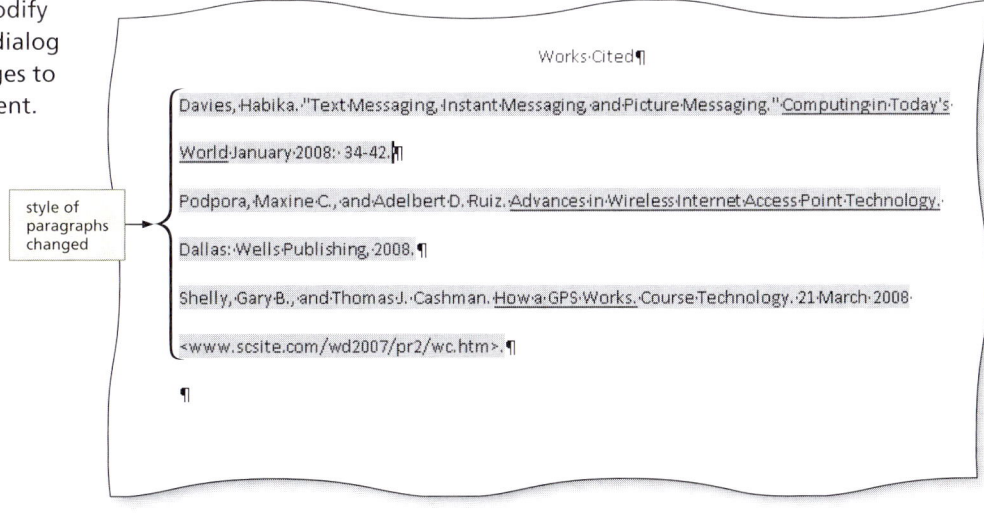

Figure 2–56

To Create a Hanging Indent

Currently, the first line of each source entry begins at the left margin. Subsequent lines in the same paragraph are to be indented one-half inch from the left margin. In essence, the first line hangs to the left of the rest of the paragraph; thus, this type of paragraph formatting is called a **hanging indent**.

One method of creating a hanging indent is to use the horizontal ruler. The **Hanging Indent marker** is the bottom triangle at the 0" mark on the ruler (Figure 2–57). The following steps create a hanging indent using the horizontal ruler.

- With the insertion point in the paragraph to format, point to the Hanging Indent marker on the ruler (Figure 2–57).

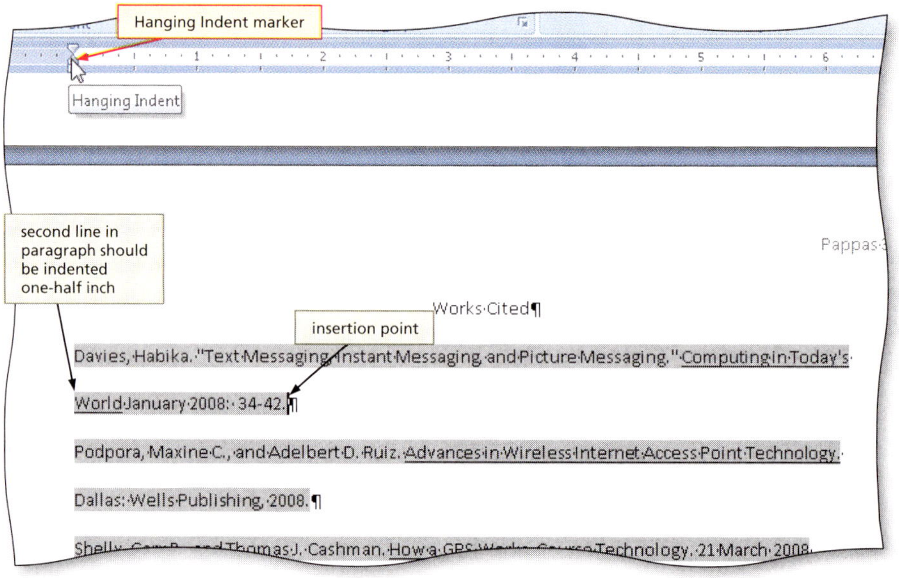

- Drag the Hanging Indent marker to the .5" mark on the ruler to set the hanging indent to one-half inch from the left margin (Figure 2–58).

Q&A

Why were all three bibliographical paragraphs formatted with a hanging indent?

When you make a change to a paragraph based on the Bibliography style, the style is updated and all paragraphs based on that style also change because you selected the Automatically update check box in the Modify Style dialog box (shown in Figure 2–55 on the previous page).

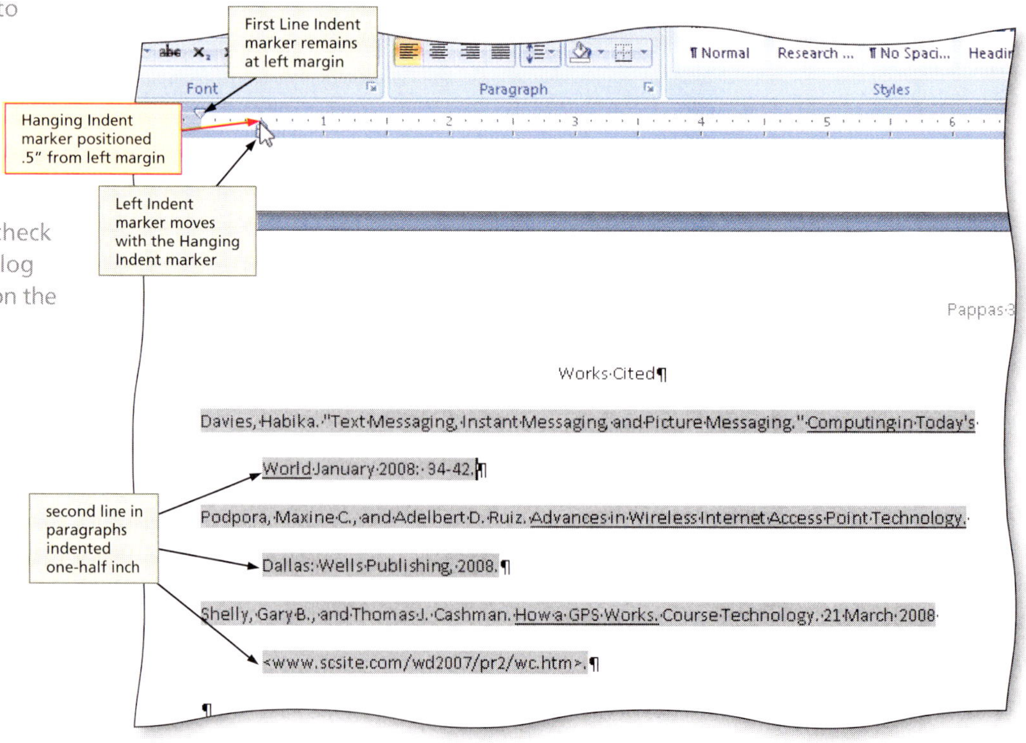

Figure 2–57

Figure 2–58

Other Ways

1. Right-click paragraph, click Paragraph on shortcut menu, click Indents and Spacing tab, click Special box arrow, click Hanging, click OK button
2. Click Paragraph Dialog Box Launcher, click Indents and Spacing tab, click Special box arrow, click Hanging, click OK button
3. Press CTRL+T

To Modify a Source and Update the Bibliographical List

If you modify the contents of any source, the list of sources automatically updates because the list is a field. The following steps modify the title of the magazine article.

1

- Click References on the Ribbon to display the References tab.

- Click the Manage Sources button on the References tab to display the Source Manager dialog box.

- Click the source you wish to edit in the Current List.

- Click the Edit button to display the Edit Source dialog box.

- In the Title text box, add the word, Services, to the end of the title (Figure 2–59).

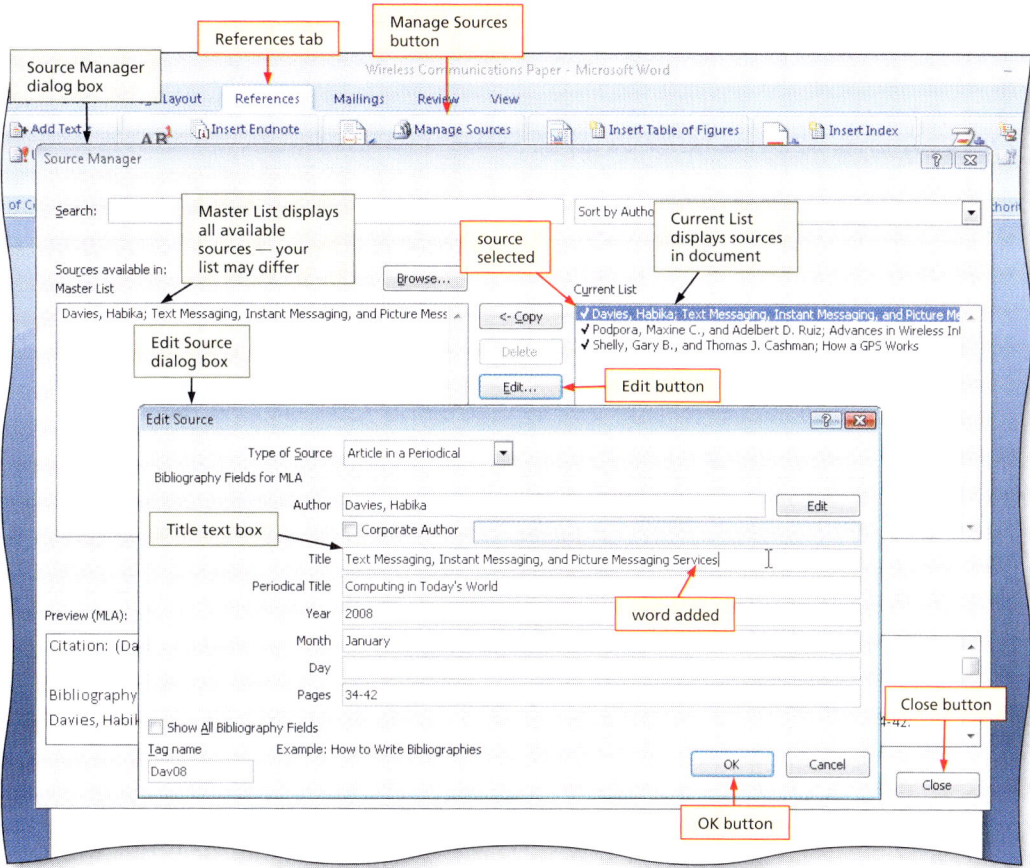

Figure 2–59

2

- Click the OK button to close the Edit Source dialog box.

- If a Microsoft Office Word dialog box appears, click its Yes button to update all occurrences of the source.

- Click the Close button in the Source Manager dialog box to update the list of sources in the document (Figure 2–60).

 What if the list of sources in the document does not update automatically?

Click in the list of sources and then press the F9 key, which is the shortcut key to update a field.

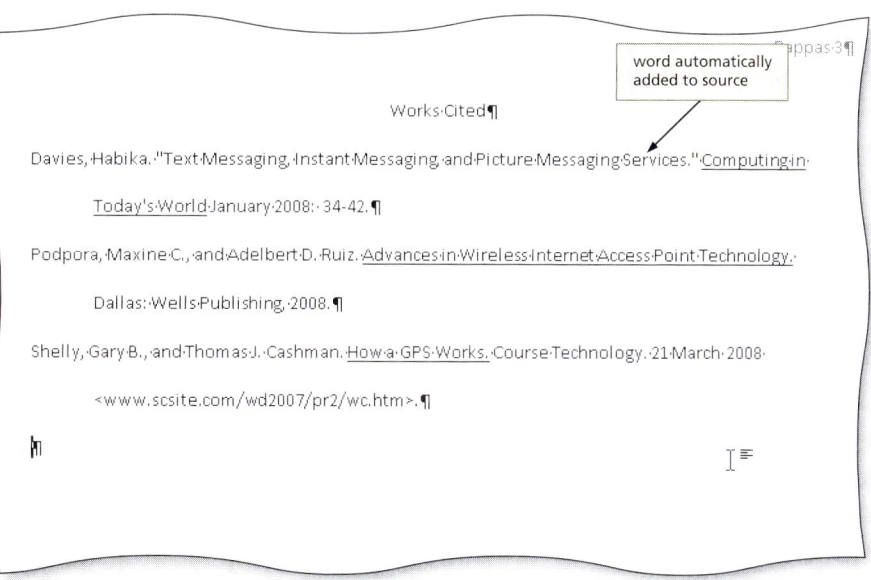

Figure 2–60

Proofing and Revising the Research Paper

As discussed in Chapter 1, once you complete a document, you might find it necessary to make changes to it. Before submitting a paper to be graded, you should proofread it. While **proofreading**, you look for grammatical errors and spelling errors. You want to be sure the transitions between sentences flow smoothly and the sentences themselves make sense.

Plan Ahead	**Proofread and revise the paper.** As you proofread the paper, look for ways to improve it. Check all grammar, spelling, and punctuation. Be sure the text is logical and transitions are smooth. Where necessary, add text, delete text, reword text, and move text to different locations. Ask yourself these questions: • Does the title suggest the topic? • Is the thesis clear? • Is the purpose of the paper clear? • Does the paper have an introduction, body, and conclusion? • Does each paragraph in the body relate to the thesis? • Is the conclusion effective? • Are all sources acknowledged?

To assist you with the proofreading effort, Word provides several tools. You can go to a specific location in a document, move text, find and replace text, insert a synonym, check spelling and grammar, and look up information. The following pages discuss these tools.

To Use the Select Browse Object Menu

Often, you would like to bring a certain page, footnote, or other object into view in the document window. To accomplish this, you could scroll through the document to find a desired page, footnote, or item. Instead of scrolling through the document, however, you can use Word to go to a specific location via the Select Browse Object menu. The following steps display the footnote in the research paper using the Select Browse Object menu.

- Click the Select Browse Object button on the vertical scroll bar to display the Select Browse Object menu and then position the mouse pointer on the Browse by Footnote icon (Figure 2–61).

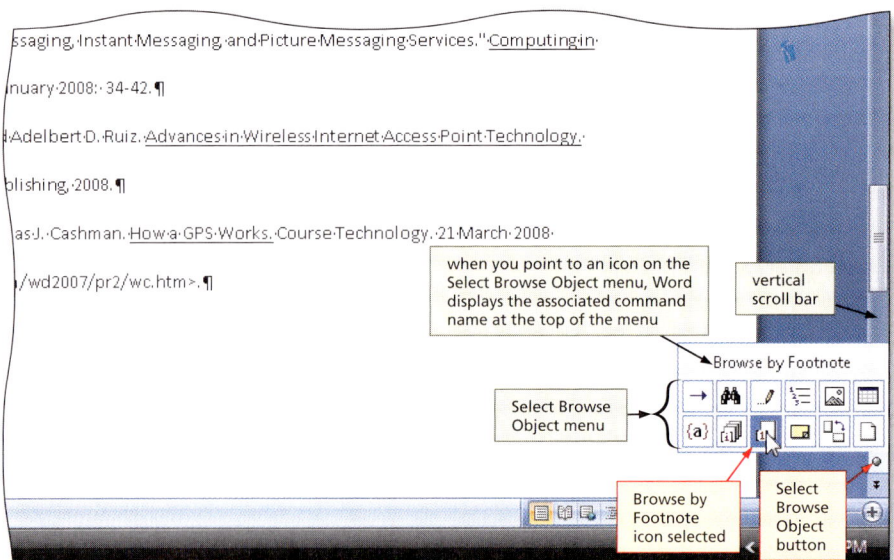

Figure 2–61

②
- Click the Browse by Footnote icon to set the browse object to footnotes.

- Position the mouse pointer on the Previous Footnote button on the vertical scroll bar (Figure 2–62).

Q&A Did the function of the button change?

Yes. By default, it is the Previous Page button. Depending on the icon you click on the Select Browse Object menu, the function of the buttons above and below the Select Browse Object button on the vertical scroll bar changes.

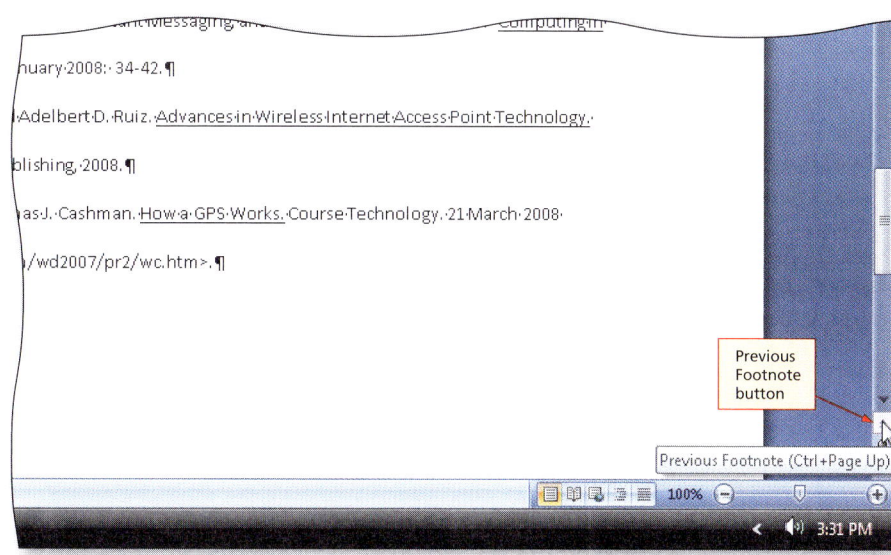

Figure 2–62

③
- Click the Previous Footnote button to display the footnote reference mark in the document window (Figure 2–63).

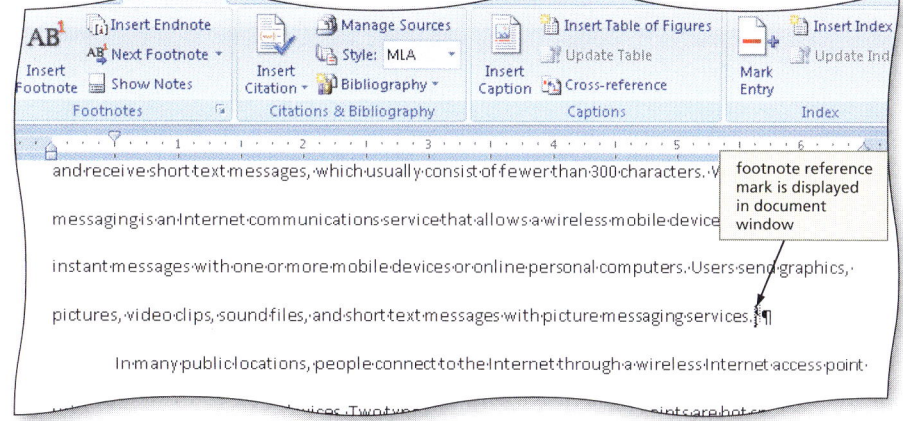

Figure 2–63

Other Ways
1. Click Page Number indicator on status bar, click desired object in Go to what list, type desired object number in Enter object number text box, click Go To button
2. Press ALT+CTRL+HOME

Moving Text

While proofreading the research paper, you realize that text in the third paragraph would flow better if the third sentence were moved to the end of the paragraph.

To move text, such as words, characters, sentences, or paragraphs, you first select the text to be moved and then use drag-and-drop editing or the cut-and-paste technique to move the selected text. With **drag-and-drop editing**, you drag the selected item to the new location and then insert, or *drop*, it there. **Cutting** involves removing the selected item from the document and then placing it on the Clipboard. The **Clipboard** is a temporary Windows storage area. **Pasting** is the process of copying an item from the Clipboard into the document at the location of the insertion point.

When moving text a long distance or between application programs, use the Clipboard task pane to cut and paste. When moving text a short distance, the drag-and-drop technique is more efficient. Thus, the steps on the following pages demonstrate drag-and-drop editing.

To Select a Sentence

To drag-and-drop a sentence in the research paper, you first must select the sentence. The following step selects a sentence.

- Position the mouse pointer in the sentence to be moved (shown in Figure 2–64).

- Press and hold down the CTRL key. While holding down the CTRL key, click the sentence to select the entire sentence.

- Release the CTRL key.

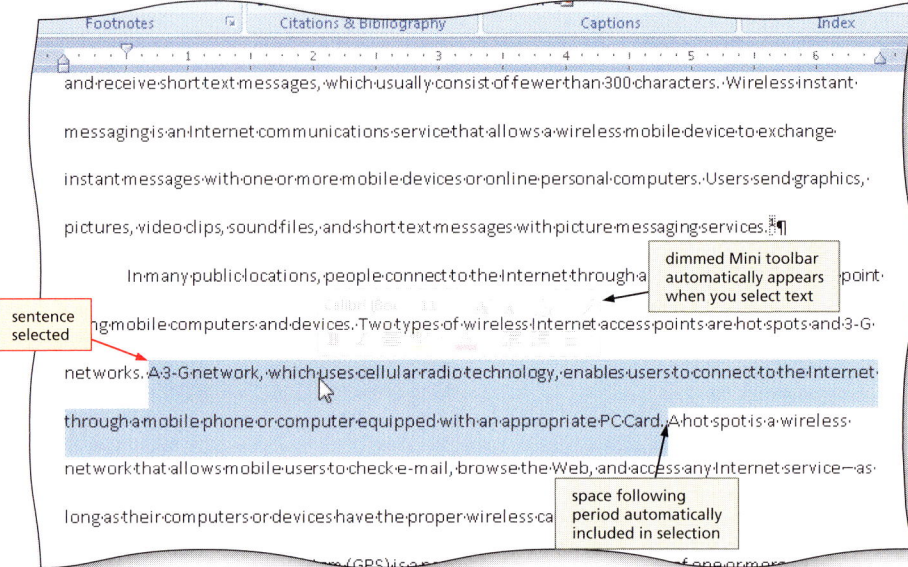

Figure 2–64

Other Ways

1. Drag through the sentence
2. With insertion point at beginning of sentence, press CTRL+SHIFT+RIGHT ARROW until sentence is selected

Selecting Text

In the previous steps and throughout Chapters 1 and 2, you have selected text. Table 2–3 summarizes the techniques used to select various items with the mouse.

BTW

Selecting Nonadjacent Items
In Word, you can select nonadjacent items, that is, items not next to each other. This is helpful when you are formatting multiple items the same way. To select nonadjacent items (text or graphics), do the following: select the first item, such as a word or paragraph, as usual. Press and hold down the CTRL key. While holding down the CTRL key, select any additional items.

Table 2–3 Techniques for Selecting Items with the Mouse	
Item To Select	**Mouse Action**
Block of text	Click at beginning of selection, scroll to end of selection, position mouse pointer at end of selection, hold down SHIFT key and then click; or drag through the text
Character(s)	Drag through character(s)
Document	Move mouse to left of text until mouse pointer changes to a right-pointing block arrow and then triple-click
Graphic	Click the graphic
Line	Move mouse to left of line until mouse pointer changes to a right-pointing block arrow and then click
Lines	Move mouse to left of first line until mouse pointer changes to a right-pointing block arrow and then drag up or down
Paragraph	Triple-click paragraph; or move mouse to left of paragraph until mouse pointer changes to a right-pointing block arrow and then double-click
Paragraphs	Move mouse to left of paragraph until mouse pointer changes to a right-pointing block arrow, double-click, and then drag up or down
Sentence	Press and hold down CTRL key and then click sentence
Word	Double-click the word
Words	Drag through words

To Move Selected Text

With the sentence to be moved selected, you can use drag-and-drop editing to move it. You should be sure that drag-and-drop editing is enabled by clicking the Word Options button on the Office Button menu, clicking Advanced in the left pane of the Word Options dialog box, verifying the 'Allow text to be dragged and dropped' check box is selected, and then clicking the OK button.

The following steps move the selected sentence so that it becomes the last sentence in the paragraph.

- With the mouse pointer in the selected text, press and hold down the mouse button (Figure 2–65).

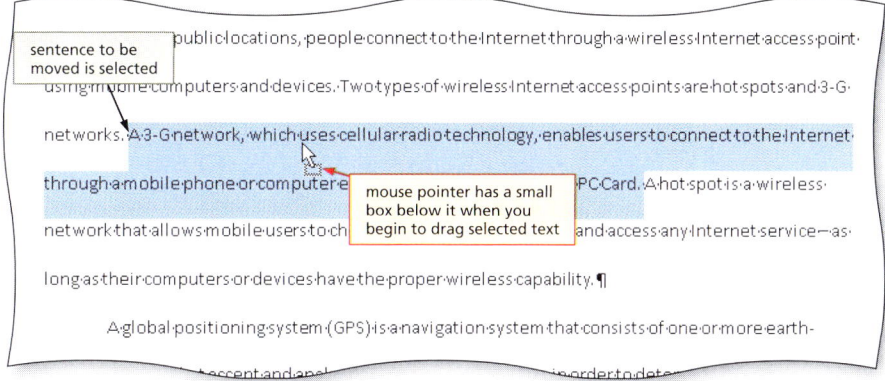

Figure 2–65

- Drag the mouse pointer to the location where the selected text is to be moved, as shown in Figure 2–66.

- Release the mouse button to move the selected text to the location of the mouse pointer.

- Click outside the selected text to remove the selection (Figure 2–67).

Q&A What if I accidentally drag text to the wrong location?

Click the Undo button on the Quick Access Toolbar and try again.

Q&A Can I use drag-and-drop editing to move any selected item?

Yes, you can select words, sentences, phrases, and graphics and then use drag-and-drop editing to move them.

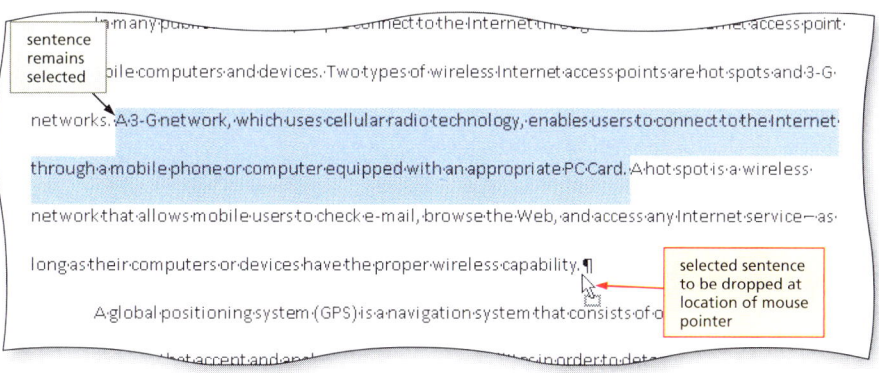

Figure 2–66

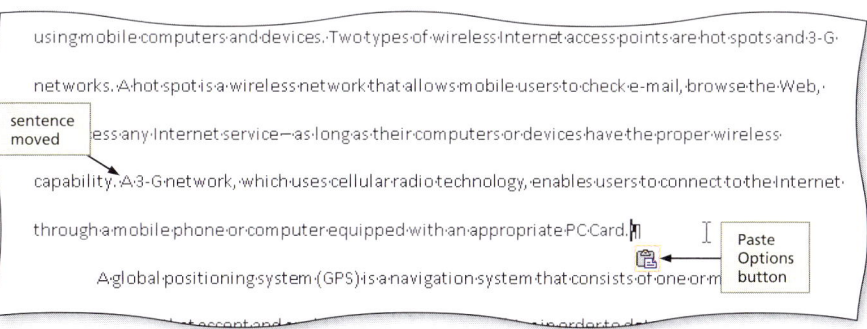

Figure 2–67

Other Ways

1. Click Cut button on Home tab, click where text is to be pasted, click Paste button on Home tab
2. Right-click selected text, click Cut on shortcut menu, right-click where text is to be pasted, click Paste on shortcut menu
3. Press CTRL+X, position insertion point where text is to be pasted, press CTRL+V

To Display the Paste Options Menu

When you drag-and-drop text, Word automatically displays a Paste Options button near the location of the drag-and-dropped text (Figure 2–67 on the previous page). If you click the **Paste Options button**, a menu appears that allows you to change the format of the item that was moved. The following steps display the Paste Options menu.

- Click the Paste Options button to display the Paste Options menu (Figure 2–68).

Q&A What is the purpose of the commands on the Paste Options menu?

In general, the first command indicates the pasted text should look the same as it did in its original location. The second command formats the pasted text to match the rest of the text where it was pasted. The third command removes all formatting from the pasted text. The last command displays the Word Options dialog box.

- Press the ESCAPE key to remove the Paste Options menu from the window.

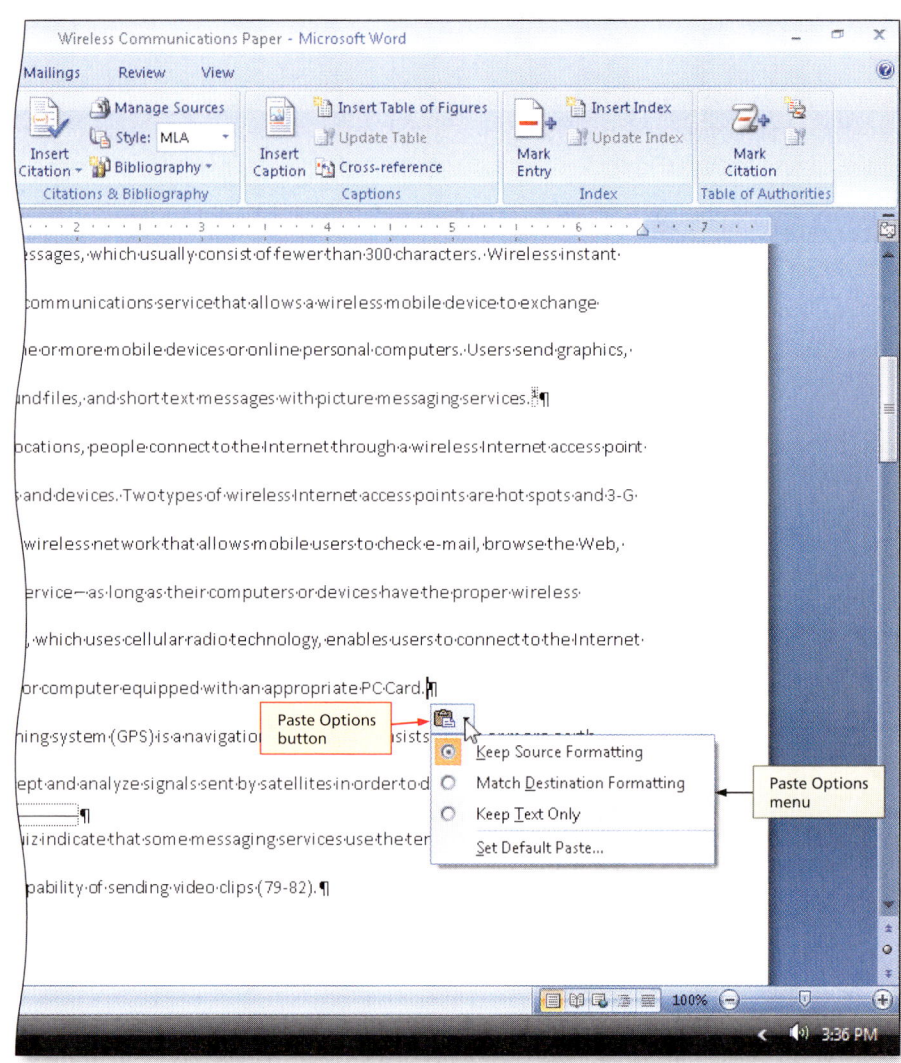

Figure 2–68

BTW

Dragging-and-Dropping
If you hold down the CTRL key while dragging a selected item, Word copies the item instead of moving it.

To Find and Replace Text

While proofreading the paper, you notice that you typed 3-G in the third paragraph (Figure 2–69). You prefer to use 3G, instead. Therefore, you need to change all occurrences of 3-G to 3G. To do this, you can use Word's find and replace feature, which automatically locates each occurrence of a word or phrase and then replaces it with specified text. The following steps use Find and Replace to replace all occurrences of 3-G with 3G.

- Click Home on the Ribbon to display the Home tab.
- Click the Replace button on the Home tab to display the Find and Replace dialog box.
- Type 3-G in the Find what text box.
- Press the TAB key. Type 3G in the Replace with text box (Figure 2–69).

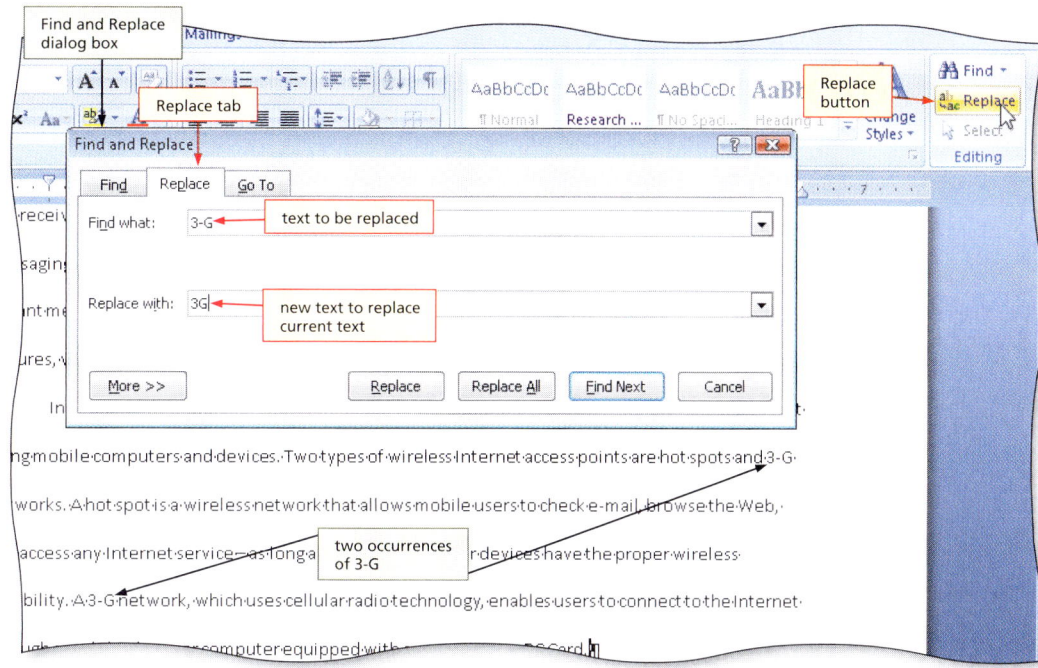

Figure 2–69

- Click the Replace All button in the Find and Replace dialog box to instruct Word to replace all occurrences of the Find what text with the Replace with text (Figure 2–70).

- Click the OK button in the Microsoft Office Word dialog box.
- Click the Close button in the Find and Replace dialog box.

Other Ways

1. Click Select Browse Object button on vertical scroll bar, click Find icon, click Replace tab
2. Click Page Number indicator on status bar, click Replace tab in dialog box
3. Press CTRL+H

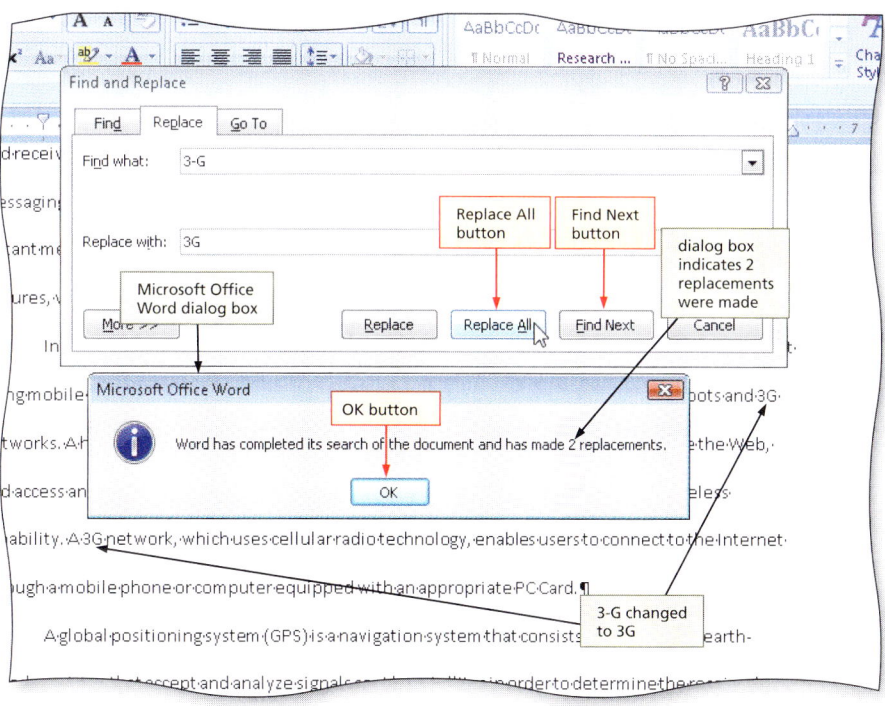

Figure 2–70

Find and Replace Dialog Box

The Replace All button in the Find and Replace dialog box replaces all occurrences of the Find what text with the Replace with text. In some cases, you may want to replace only certain occurrences of a word or phrase, not all of them. To instruct Word to confirm each change, click the Find Next button in the Find and Replace dialog box (Figure 2–70 on the previous page), instead of the Replace All button. When Word locates an occurrence of the text, it pauses and waits for you to click either the Replace button or the Find Next button. Clicking the Replace button changes the text; clicking the Find Next button instructs Word to disregard the replacement and look for the next occurrence of the Find what text.

If you accidentally replace the wrong text, you can undo a replacement by clicking the Undo button on the Standard toolbar. If you used the Replace All button, Word undoes all replacements. If you used the Replace button, Word undoes only the most recent replacement.

TO FIND TEXT

Sometimes, you may want only to find text, instead of finding and replacing text. To search for just a single occurrence of text, you would follow these steps.

1. Click the Find button on the Home tab; or click the Select Browse Object button on the vertical scroll bar and then click the Find icon on the Select Browse Object menu; or click the page indicator on the status bar and then click the Find tab; or press CTRL+F.

2. Type the text to locate in the Find what text box and then click the Find Next button. To edit the text, click the Cancel button in the Find and Replace dialog box; to find the next occurrence of the text, click the Find Next button.

> **BTW**
>
> **Finding Formatting**
> To search for formatting or a special character, click the More button in the Find dialog box. To find formatting, use the Format button in the Find dialog box. To find a special character, use the Special button.

To Find and Insert a Synonym

When writing, you may discover that you used the same word in multiple locations or that a word you used was not quite appropriate. In these instances, you will want to look up a **synonym**, or a word similar in meaning, to the duplicate or inappropriate word. A **thesaurus** is a book of synonyms. Word provides synonyms and a thesaurus for your convenience.

In this project, you would like a synonym for the word, proper, in the third paragraph of the research paper. The following steps show how to find a suitable synonym.

1

- Locate and then right-click the word for which you want to find a synonym (in this case, proper) to display a shortcut menu related to the word you right-clicked.

- Point to Synonyms on the shortcut menu to display a list of synonyms for the word you right-clicked (Figure 2–71).

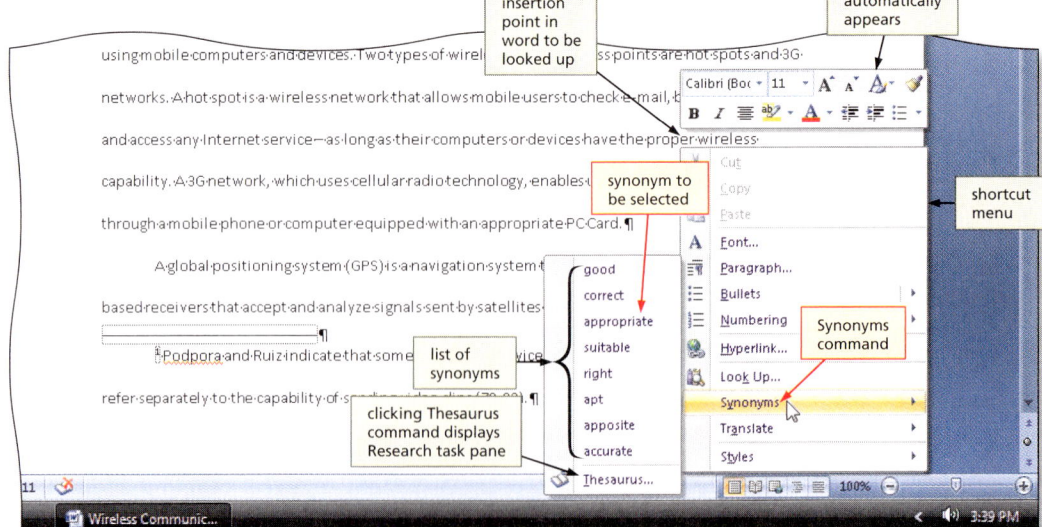

Figure 2–71

2
- Click the synonym you want (appropriate) on the Synonyms submenu to replace the word, proper, in the document with the word, appropriate (Figure 2–72).

Q&A What if the synonyms list on the shortcut menu does not display a suitable word?

You can display the thesaurus in the Research task pane by clicking Thesaurus on the Synonyms submenu. The Research task pane displays a complete thesaurus, in which you can look up synonyms for various meanings of a word. You also can look up an **antonym**, or word with an opposite meaning. The Research task pane is discussed later in this chapter.

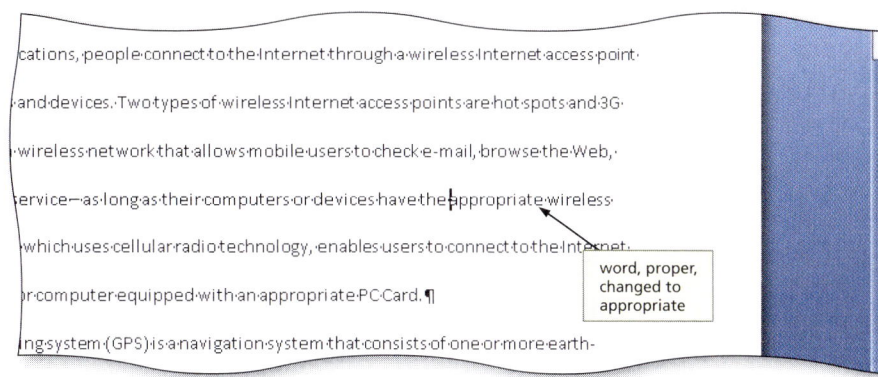

Figure 2–72

Other Ways
1. Click Thesaurus on Review tab
2. Press SHIFT+F7

To Check Spelling and Grammar at Once

As discussed in Chapter 1, Word checks spelling and grammar as you type and places a wavy underline below possible spelling or grammar errors. Chapter 1 illustrated how to check these flagged words immediately. As an alternative, you can wait and check the entire document for spelling and grammar errors at once.

Note: In the following example the word, world, has been misspelled intentionally as wrld to illustrate the use of Word's check spelling and grammar at once feature. If you are completing this project on a personal computer, your research paper may contain different misspelled words, depending on the accuracy of your typing.

1
- Press CTRL+HOME because you want the spelling and grammar check to begin from the top of the document.
- Click Review on the Ribbon to display the Review tab.
- Click the Spelling & Grammar button on the Review tab to begin the spelling and grammar check at the location of the insertion point, which in this case, is at the beginning of the document (Figure 2–73).

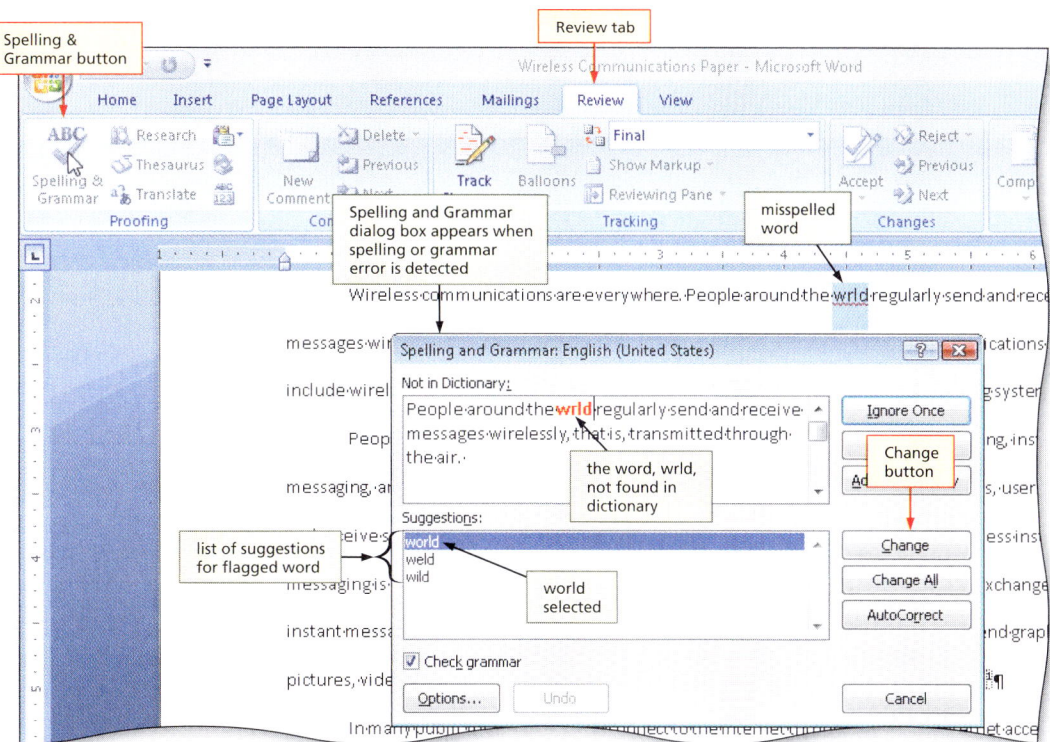

Figure 2–73

- With the word, world, selected in the Suggestions list, click the Change button in the Spelling and Grammar dialog box to change the flagged word, wrld, to the selected suggestion, world, and then continue the spelling and grammar check until the next error is identified or the end of the document is reached (Figure 2–74).

- Click the Ignore All button in the Spelling and Grammar dialog box to ignore this and future occurrences of the flagged proper noun and then continue the spelling and grammar check until the next error is identified or the end of the document is reached.

- When Word flags the proper noun, Podpora, click the Ignore All button.

- When the spelling and grammar check is finished and Word displays a dialog box, click its OK button.

Q&A Can I check spelling of just a section of a document?

Yes, select the text before starting the spelling and grammar check.

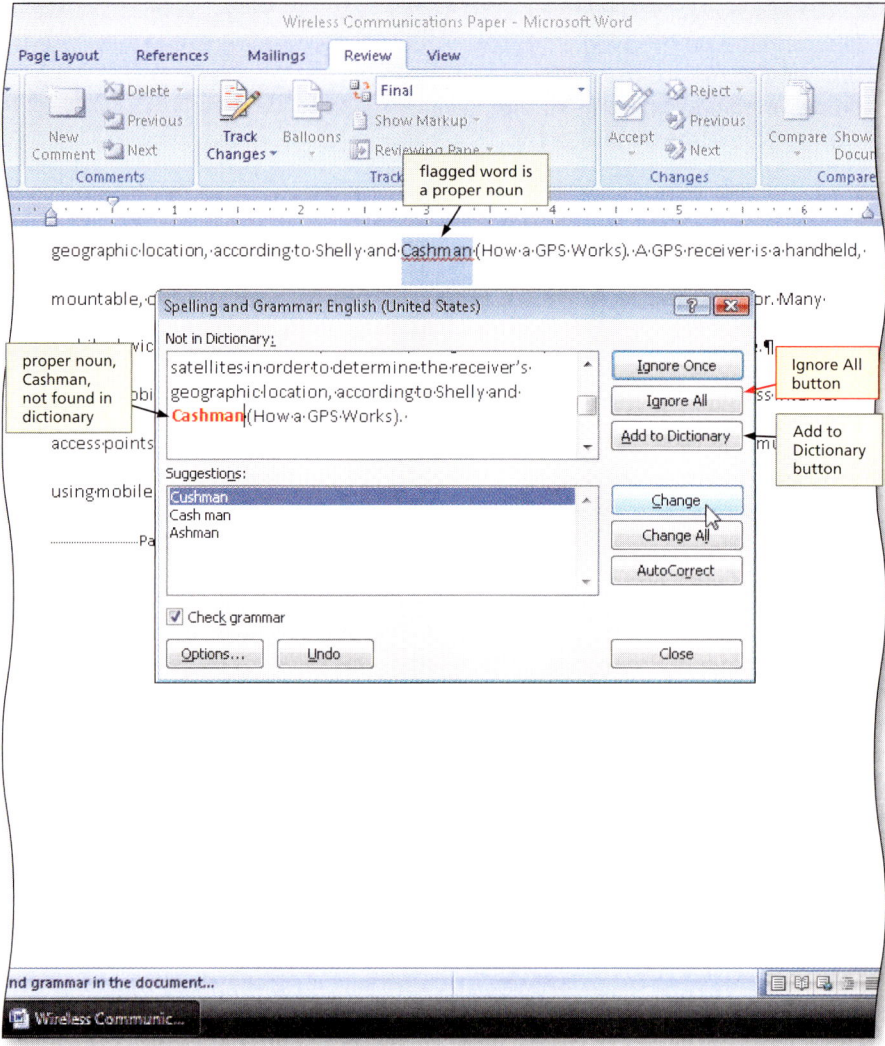

Figure 2–74

Other Ways
1. Click Spelling and Grammar Check icon on status bar, click Spelling on shortcut menu
2. Right-click flagged word, click Spelling on shortcut menu
3. Press F7

BTW

Contextual Spelling Errors
You can instruct Word to check for misuse of homophones and other types of contextual spelling errors. (Homophones are two or more words that are pronounced the same but that have different spellings or meanings, such as one and won.) With this feature, Word flags a contextual spelling error with a blue wavy underline. For example, Word would place a blue wavy underline below the words, one and knight, in this sentence: The team one the game last knight. (The correct sentence would be written as follows: The team won the game last night.) To view Word's suggested replacements for the flagged words, you could right-click each of the flagged words or start the spelling and grammar check by clicking the Spelling & Grammar button on the Review tab. On many installations of Word, the contextual spelling check is not activated by default. To activate it, click the Office Button, click Word Options on the Office Button menu, click Proofing in the left pane, place a check mark in the 'Use contextual spelling' check box, and then click the OK button.

The Main and Custom Dictionaries

As shown in the previous steps, Word may flag a proper noun as an error because the proper noun is not in its main dictionary. To prevent Word from flagging proper nouns as errors, you can add the proper nouns to the custom dictionary. To add a correctly spelled word to the custom dictionary, click the Add to Dictionary button in the Spelling and Grammar dialog box (Figure 2–74) or right-click the flagged word and then click Add to Dictionary on the shortcut menu. Once you have added a word to the custom dictionary, Word no longer will flag it as an error.

TO VIEW OR MODIFY ENTRIES IN A CUSTOM DICTIONARY

To view or modify the list of words in a custom dictionary, you would follow these steps.

1. Click the Office Button and then click the Word Options button.
2. Click Proofing in the left pane of the Word Options dialog box.
3. Click the Custom Dictionaries button.
4. When Word displays the Custom Dictionaries dialog box, place a check mark next to the dictionary name to view or modify. Click the Edit Word List button. (In this dialog box, you can add or delete entries to and from the selected custom dictionary.)
5. When finished viewing and/or modifying the list, click the OK button in the dialog box.
6. Click the OK button in the Custom Dictionaries dialog box.
7. If the 'Suggest from main dictionary only' check box is selected in the Word Options dialog box, remove the check mark. Click the OK button in the Word Options dialog box.

TO SET THE DEFAULT CUSTOM DICTIONARY

If you have multiple custom dictionaries, you can specify which one Word should use when checking spelling. To set the default custom dictionary, you would follow these steps.

1. Click the Office Button and then click the Word Options button.
2. Click Proofing in the left pane of the Word Options dialog box.
3. Click the Custom Dictionaries button.
4. When the Custom Dictionaries dialog box is displayed, place a check mark next to the desired dictionary name. Click the Change Default button.
5. Click the OK button in the Custom Dictionaries dialog box.
6. If the 'Suggest from main dictionary only' check box is selected in the Word Options dialog box, remove the check mark. Click the OK button in the Word Options dialog box.

To Use the Research Task Pane to Look Up Information

From within Word, you can search through various forms of reference information. Earlier, this chapter discussed the Research task pane with respect to looking up a synonym in a thesaurus. Other services available in the Research task pane include a dictionary and if you are connected to the Web, an encyclopedia, a search engine, and other Web sites that provide information such as stock quotes, news articles, and company profiles.

Assume you want to know more about the acronym, PDA. The following steps use the Research task pane to look up information about a word.

- Locate the word you want to look up.

- While holding down the ALT key, click the word you want to look up (in this case, PDAs) to open the Research task pane and display a dictionary entry for the ALT+CLICKED word. Release the ALT key (Figure 2–75).

- If the Research task pane does not display a dictionary entry for the ALT+CLICKED word, click the Search for box arrow and then click All Reference Books.

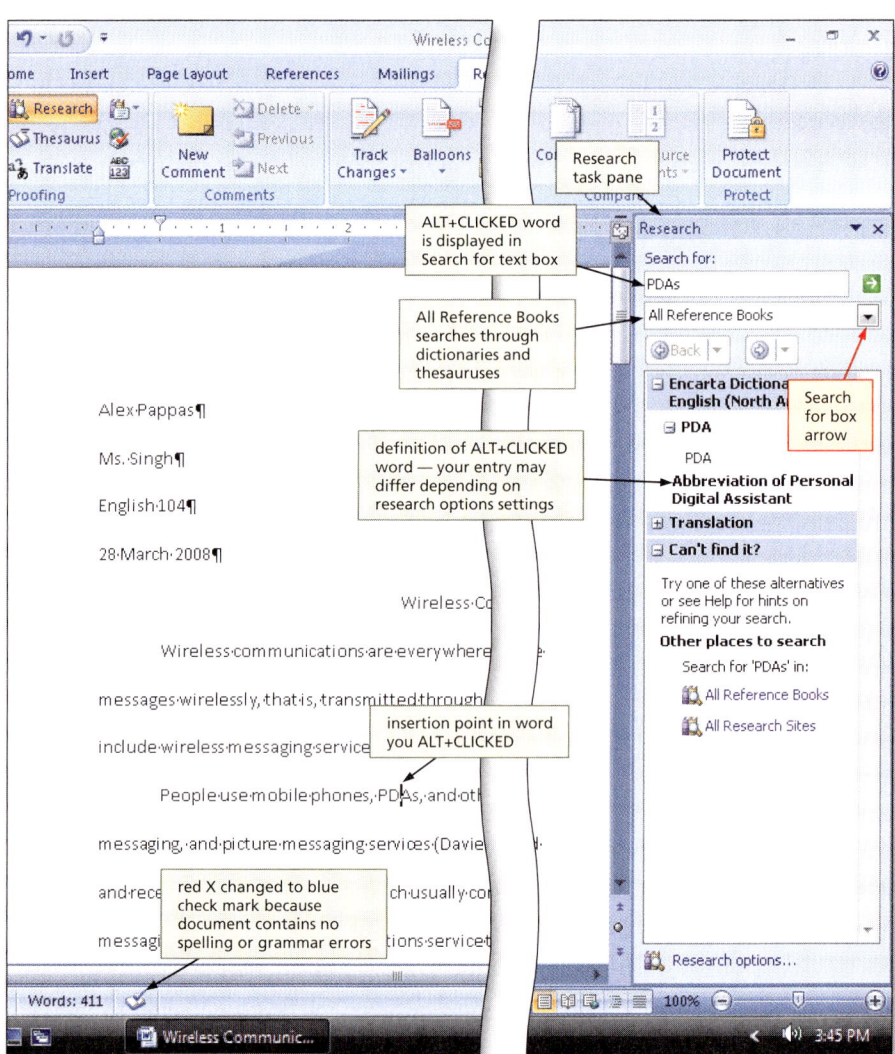

Figure 2–75

❷
- Click the Search for box arrow and then click All Research Sites in the list to display Web sites with information about the ALT+CLICKED word (Figure 2–76).

 Can I copy information from the Research task pane into my document?

Yes, you can use the Copy and Paste commands. When using Word to insert material from the Research task pane or any other online reference, however, be very careful not to plagiarize.

❸
- Click the Close button in the Research task pane.

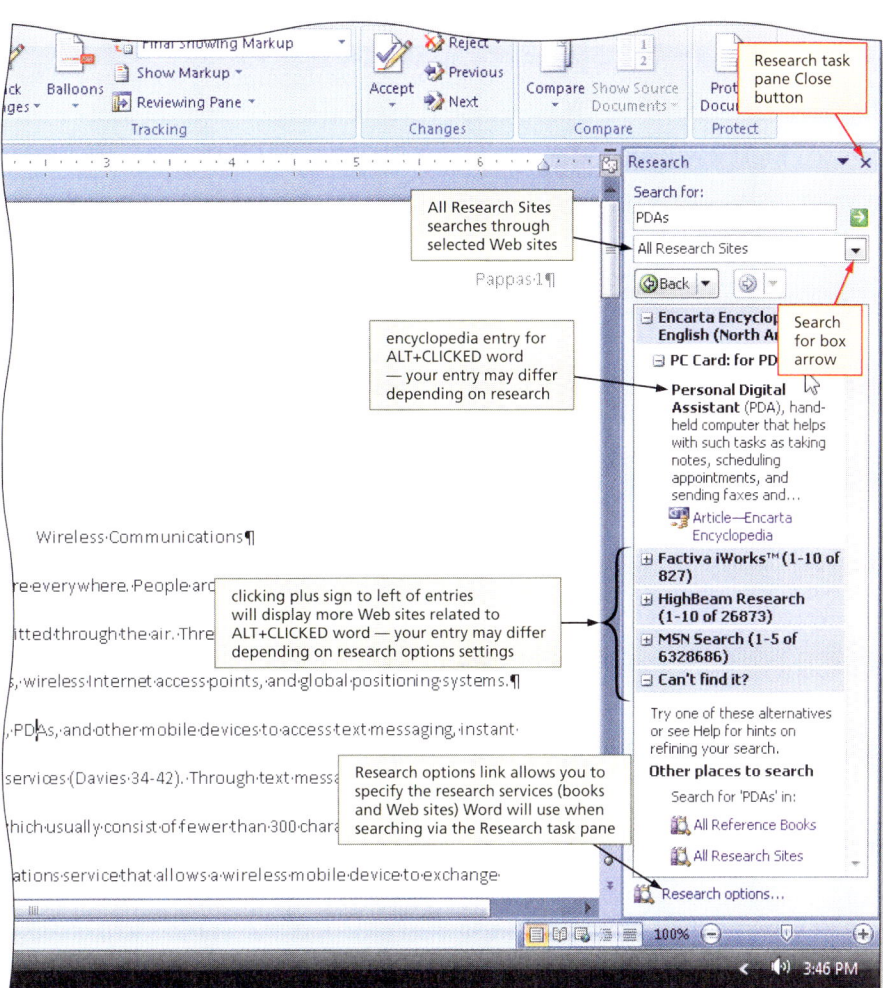

Figure 2–76

Other Ways
1. Click Research button on Review tab
2. Click Insert Citation button on References tab, click Search Libraries

Research Task Pane Options

When you install Word, it selects a series of services (reference books and Web sites) through which it searches when you use the Research task pane. You can view, modify, and update the list of services at any time.

Clicking the Research options link at the bottom of the Research task pane displays the Research Options dialog box, where you can view or modify the list of installed services. You can view information about any installed service by clicking the service in the list and then clicking the Properties button. To activate an installed service, click the check box to its left; likewise, to deactivate a service, remove the check mark. To add a particular Web site to the list, click the Add Services button, enter the Web address in the Address text box, and then click the Add button in the Add Services dialog box. To update or remove services, click the Update/Remove button, select the service in the list, click the Update (or Remove) button in the Update or Remove Services dialog box, and then click the Close button. You also can install parental controls through the Parental Control button in the Research Options dialog box, for example, if you want to restrict Web access from minor children who use Word.

To Change Document Properties

Before saving the research paper again, you want to add your name, course information, and some keywords as document properties. The following steps use the Document Information Panel to change document properties.

1. Click the Office Button to display the Office Button menu, point to Prepare on the Office Button menu, and then click Properties on the Prepare submenu to display the Document Information Panel.

2. Click the Author text box, if necessary, and then type your name as the Author property. If a name already is displayed in the Author text box, delete it before typing your name.

3. Click the Subject text box, if necessary delete any existing text, and then type your course and section as the Subject property.

4. Click the Keywords text box, if necessary delete any existing text, and then type `instant messaging, Internet access points, global positioning systems` as the Keywords property.

5. Click the Close the Document Information Panel button so that the Document Information Panel no longer is displayed.

BTW

Conserving Ink and Toner
You can instruct Word to print draft quality documents to conserve ink or toner by clicking the Office Button, clicking the Word Options button, clicking Advanced in the left pane of the Word Options dialog box, scrolling to the Print area, placing a check mark in the 'Use draft quality' check box, and then clicking the OK button. Click the Office Button, point to Print, and then click Quick Print.

To Save an Existing Document with the Same File Name

The document now is complete. You should save the research paper again. The following step saves the document again.

1. Click the Save button on the Quick Access Toolbar to overwrite the previous Wireless Communications Paper file on the USB flash drive.

To Print Document Properties and then the Document

With the document properties entered and the completed document saved, you may want to print the document properties along with the document. The following steps print the document properties, followed by the contents of the saved Wireless Communications Paper project.

- Click the Office Button to display the Office Button menu and then point to Print on the Office Button menu to display the Print submenu (Figure 2–77).

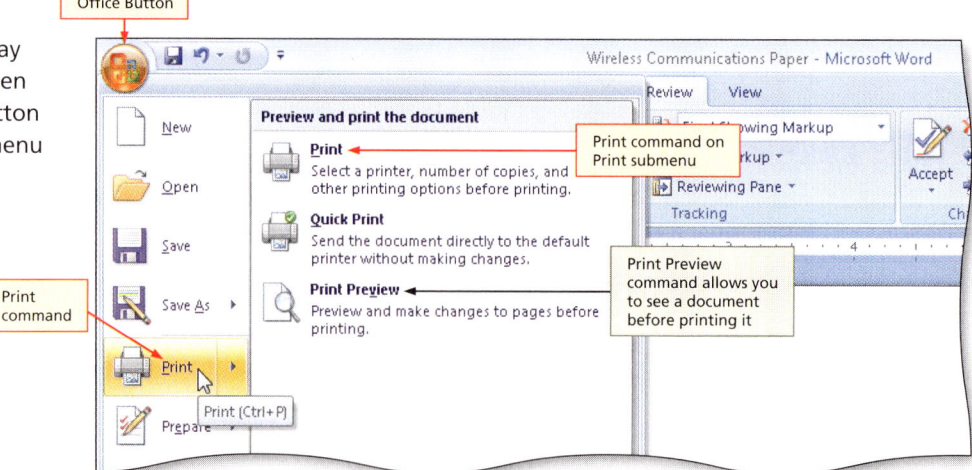

Figure 2–77

2

- Click Print on the Print submenu to display the Print dialog box.
- Click the Print what box arrow and then click Document properties to instruct Word to print the document properties instead of the document (Figure 2–78).

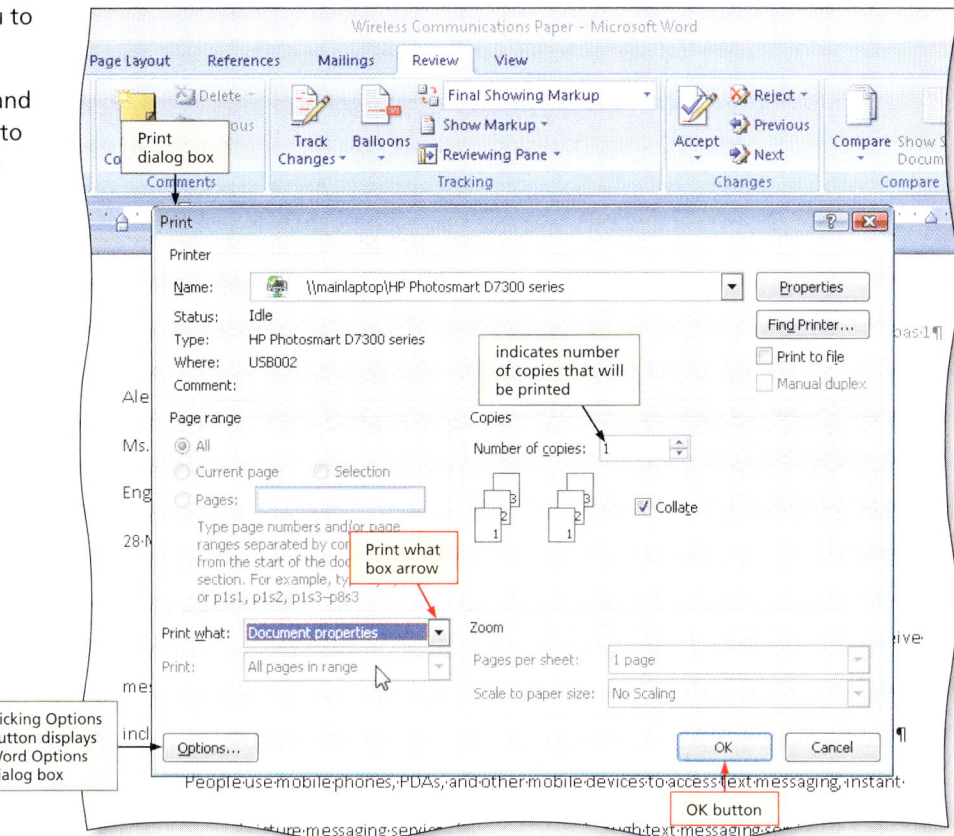

Figure 2–78

3

- Click the OK button to print the document properties (Figure 2–79).

4

- Click the Office Button again to display the Office Button menu, point to Print on the Office Button menu, and then click Quick Print on the Print submenu to print the research paper (shown in Figure 2–1 on page WD 75).

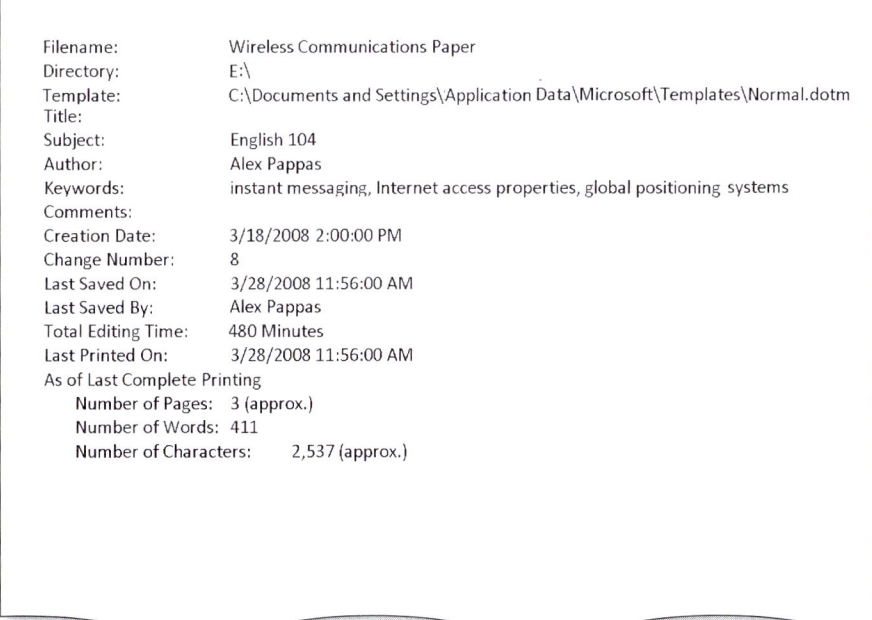

Figure 2–79

To Quit Word

This project is complete. The following steps quit Word.

1. Click the Close button on the right side of the title bar to quit Word; or if you have multiple Word documents open, click the Office Button and then click the Exit Word button on the Office Button menu to close all open documents and quit Word.

2. If necessary, click the Yes button in the Microsoft Office Word dialog box so that any changes you have made are saved.

Chapter Summary

In this chapter you have learned how to change document settings, use headers to number pages, create and modify styles, insert and edit citations and their sources, add footnotes, create a bibliographical list of sources, and use the Research task pane. The items listed below include all the new Word skills you have learned in this chapter.

1. Double-Space Text (WD 78)
2. Remove Space after a Paragraph (WD 79)
3. Switch to the Header (WD 80)
4. Right-Align a Paragraph (WD 81)
5. Insert a Page Number (WD 82)
6. Close the Header (WD 83)
7. Click and Type (WD 85)
8. Display the Rulers (WD 87)
9. First-Line Indent Paragraphs (WD 88)
10. Create a Quick Style (WD 90)
11. AutoCorrect as You Type (WD 91)
12. Use the AutoCorrect Options Button (WD 92)
13. Create an AutoCorrect Entry (WD 93)
14. Change the Bibliography Style (WD 95)
15. Insert a Citation and Create Its Source (WD 96)
16. Edit a Citation (WD 98)
17. Insert a Footnote Reference Mark (WD 100)
18. Insert a Citation Placeholder (WD 101)
19. Modify a Style Using a Shortcut Menu (WD 102)
20. Edit a Source (WD 104)
21. Count Words (WD 107)
22. Page Break Manually (WD 112)
23. Create the Bibliographical List (WD 113)
24. Modify a Style Using the Styles Task Pane (WD 114)
25. Create a Hanging Indent (WD 116)
26. Modify a Source and Update the Bibliographical List (WD 117)
27. Use the Select Browse Object Menu (WD 118)
28. Select a Sentence (WD 120)
29. Move Selected Text (WD 121)
30. Display the Paste Options Menu (WD 122)
31. Find and Replace Text (WD 123)
32. Find Text (WD 124)
33. Find and Insert a Synonym (WD 124)
34. Check Spelling and Grammar at Once (WD 125)
35. View or Modify Entries in a Custom Dictionary (WD 127)
36. Set the Default Custom Dictionary (WD 127)
37. Use the Research Task Pane to Look Up Information (WD 128)
38. Print Document Properties and then the Document (WD 130)

If you have a SAM user profile, you may have access to hands-on instruction, practice, and assessment. Log in to your SAM account (http://sam2007.course.com) to launch any assigned training activities or exams that relate to the skills covered in this chapter.

Quick Reference

For a table that lists how to complete the tasks covered in this book using the mouse, Ribbon, shortcut menu, and keyboard, see the Quick Reference Summary at the back of this book, or visit the Word 2007 Quick Reference Web page (scsite.com/dc-off07/qr).

Learn It Online

Test your knowledge of chapter content and key terms.

Instructions: To complete the Learn It Online exercises, start your browser, click the Address bar, and then enter the Web address scsite.com/dc-off07/wd2007/learn. When the Word 2007 Learn It Online page is displayed, click the link for the exercise you want to complete and then read the instructions.

Chapter Reinforcement TF, MC, and SA
A series of true/false, multiple choice, and short answer questions that test your knowledge of the chapter content.

Flash Cards
An interactive learning environment where you identify chapter key terms associated with displayed definitions.

Practice Test
A series of multiple choice questions that test your knowledge of chapter content and key terms.

Who Wants To Be a Computer Genius?
An interactive game that challenges your knowledge of chapter content in the style of a television quiz show.

Wheel of Terms
An interactive game that challenges your knowledge of chapter key terms in the style of the television show *Wheel of Fortune*.

Crossword Puzzle Challenge
A crossword puzzle that challenges your knowledge of key terms presented in the chapter.

Apply Your Knowledge

Reinforce the skills and apply the concepts you learned in this chapter.

Revising Text and Paragraphs in a Document
Instructions: Start Word. Open the document, Apply 2-1 Software Paragraphs Draft, from the Data Files for Students. See the inside back cover of this book for instructions on downloading the Data Files for Students, or contact your instructor for information about accessing the required files.

The document you open has a header and three paragraphs of text. You are to revise the document as follows: move a paragraph, move a word and change the format of the moved word, change paragraph indentation, change line spacing and paragraph spacing, replace all occurrences of a word with another word, and edit the header.

Perform the following tasks:

1. Select the last (third) paragraph. Use drag-and-drop editing to move this paragraph, so that it is the second paragraph in the document.
2. Select the underlined word, effectively, in the second sentence of the first paragraph. Use drag-and-drop editing to move the selected word, effectively, so that it follows the word, software, in the same sentence. Click the Paste Options button that displays to the right of the moved word, effectively. Remove the underline format from the moved sentence by clicking Keep Text Only on the shortcut menu.
3. Select the three paragraphs of text in the document.
4. Display the ruler, if necessary. With the paragraphs selected, use the ruler to indent the first line of the selected paragraphs one-half inch.
5. With the paragraphs still selected, change the line spacing of the selected paragraphs from single to double.

Continued >

Apply Your Knowledge continued

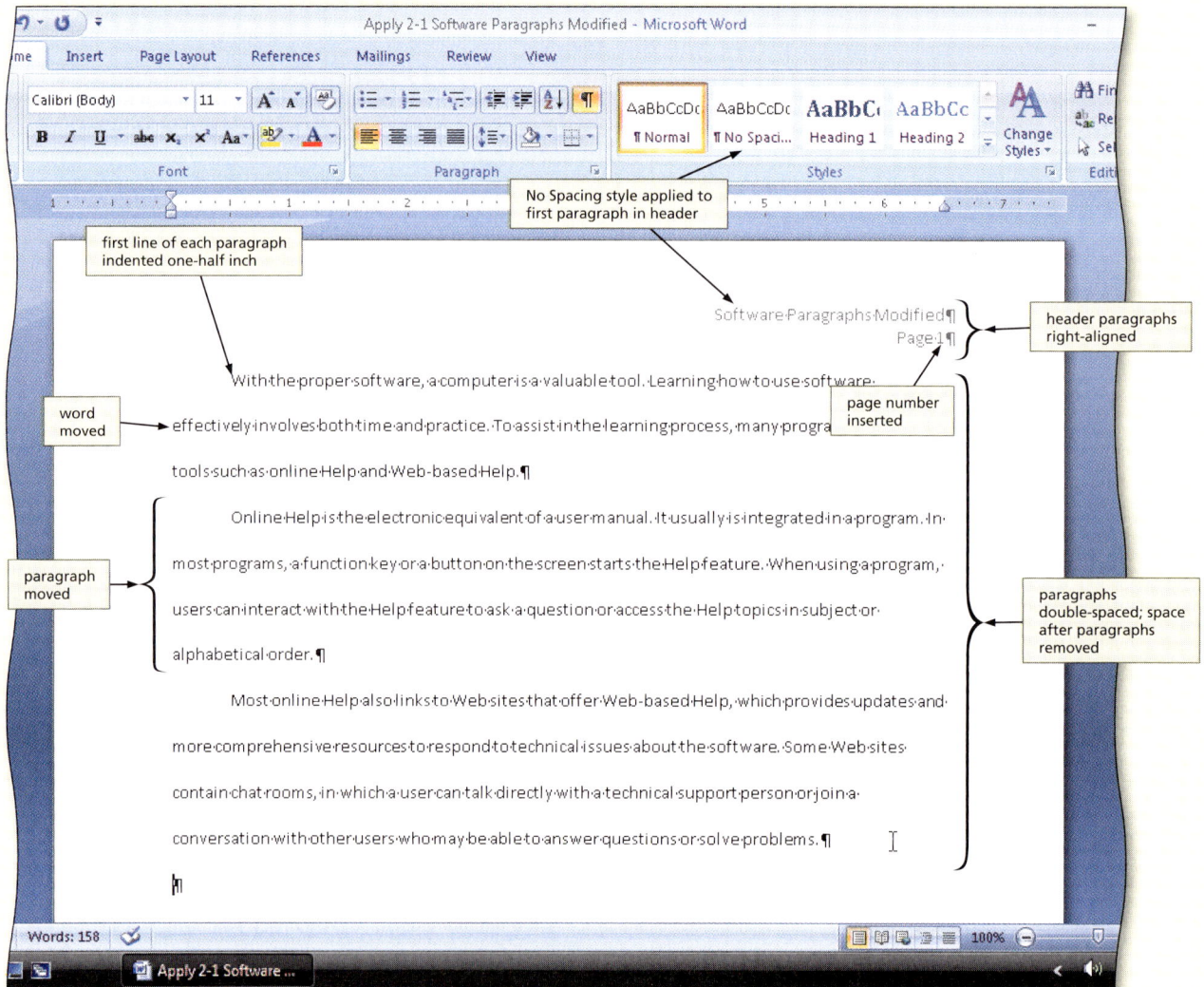

Figure 2–80

6. With the paragraphs still selected, use Line spacing box arrow to remove extra space below (after) the paragraphs. Click anywhere to remove the selection.

7. Use the Find and Replace dialog box to replace all occurrences of the word, Internet, with the word, Web. How many replacements were made?

8. Use the Find dialog box to locate the word, incorporated. Use Word's thesaurus to change the word, incorporated, to the word, integrated, in the first sentence of the second paragraph.

9. Switch to the header so that you can edit it. In the first line of the header, change the word, Draft, to the word, Modified, so that it reads: Software Paragraphs Modified. Change the first line of the header from the Normal style to the No Spacing style.

10. In the second line of the header, insert the page number (with no formatting) one space after the word, Page.

11. Change the alignment of both lines of text in the header from left-aligned to right-aligned. Switch back to the document text.

12. Change the document properties, as specified by your instructor.

13. Click the Office Button and then click Save As. Save the document using the file name, Apply 2-1 Software Paragraphs Modified.

14. Print the document properties and then print the revised document, shown in Figure 2–80.
15. Use the Research task pane to look up the definition of the word, online, in the first sentence of the second paragraph. Handwrite the COMPUTING definition of the word, online, on your printout.
16. Display the Research Options dialog box and on your printout, handwrite the currently active Reference Books, Research Sites, and Business and Financial Sites. If your instructor approves, activate one of the services.

Extend Your Knowledge

Extend the skills you learned in this chapter and experiment with new skills. You may need to use Help to complete the assignment.

Working with References and Proofing Tools

Instructions: Start Word. Open the document, Extend 2-1 Computing Options Paper Draft, from the Data Files for Students. See the inside back cover of this book for instructions on downloading the Data Files for Students, or contact your instructor for information on accessing the required files.

You will add another footnote to the paper, use the thesaurus, convert the document from MLA to APA style, convert the footnotes to endnotes, modify the Endnote Text style, change the format of the note reference marks, and translate the document to another language.

Perform the following tasks:
1. Insert a second footnote at an appropriate place in the research paper. Use the following footnote text: The Americans with Disabilities Act (ADA) requires any company with 15 or more employees to make reasonable attempts to accommodate the needs of physically challenged workers.
2. Use the Replace dialog box to find the word, imagine, in the document and then replace it with a word of your choice.
3. Save the document with a new file name and then print it. Select the entire document and then change the style of the citations and bibliography from MLA to APA. Save the APA version of the document with a new file name and then print it. Compare the two versions. Circle the differences between the two documents.
4. Convert the footnotes to endnotes.
5. Modify the Endnote Text style to 11-point Calibri font, double-spaced text with a first-line indent.
6. Change the format of the note reference marks to capital letters (A, B, etc.).
7. Save the revised document with endnotes with a new file name and then print it. On the printout with the endnotes, write the number of words, characters without spaces, characters with spaces, paragraphs, and lines in the document. Be sure to include endnote text in the statistics.
8. Translate the research paper into a language of your choice (Figure 2–81 on the next page) using the Translate button on the Review tab. Print the translated document.

Continued >

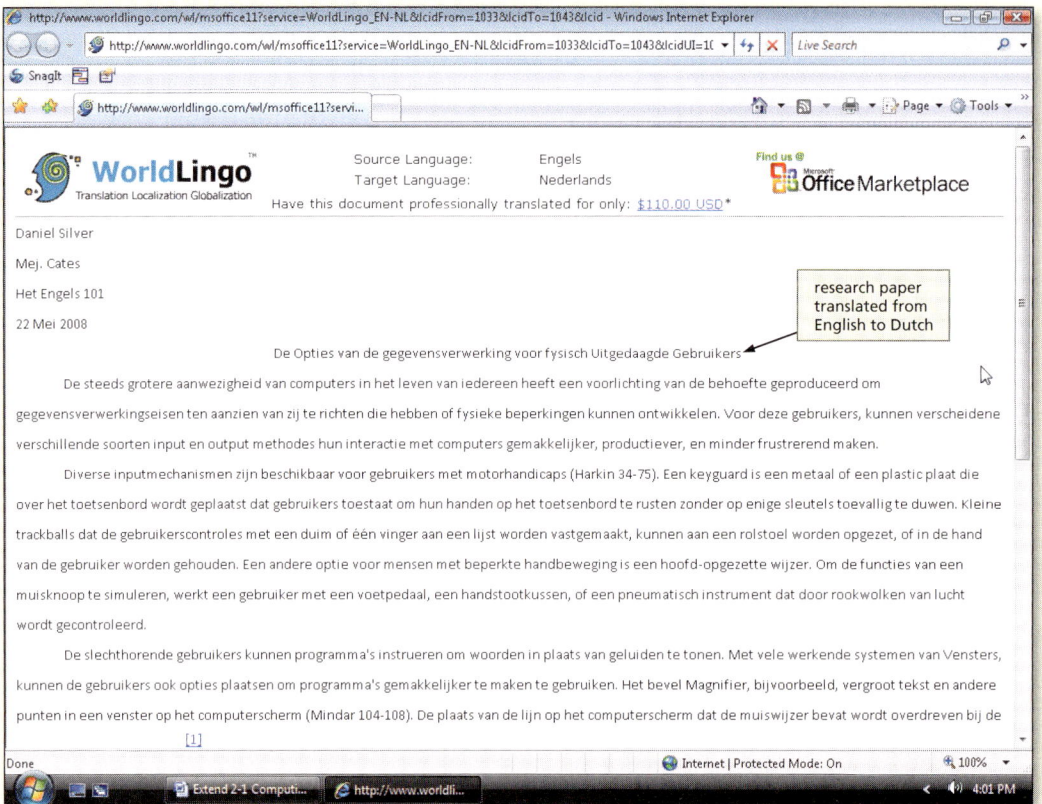

Figure 2–81

Make It Right

Analyze a document and correct all errors and/or improve the design.

Inserting Missing Elements in an MLA Style Research Paper

Instructions: Start Word. Open the document, Make It Right 2-1 Certification Paper Draft, from the Data Files for Students. See the inside back cover of this book for instructions on downloading the Data Files for Students, or contact your instructor for information on accessing the required files.

The document is a research paper that is missing several elements. You are to insert these missing elements, all formatted according to the MLA documentation style: header with a page number, heading (name, course, and date information), paper title, footnote, and source information for the first citation and the citation in the footnote.

Perform the following tasks:
1. Insert a header with a page number, heading (use your own information: name, course information, and date), and an appropriate paper title, all formatted according to the MLA style.
2. Use the Select Browse Object button to go to page 2. How many bibliographical entries currently are on the Works Cited page? You will create additional source entries in Steps 3 and 4.
3. The Otoole placeholder (tag name) is missing its source information (Figure 2–82). Use the following source information to edit the source: magazine article titled "Career Builders and Boosts," written by Sarah W. O'Toole, magazine name is *IT World and Certifications*, publication date is March 2008, article is on pages 88-93. Edit the citation so that it displays the author name and the page numbers.

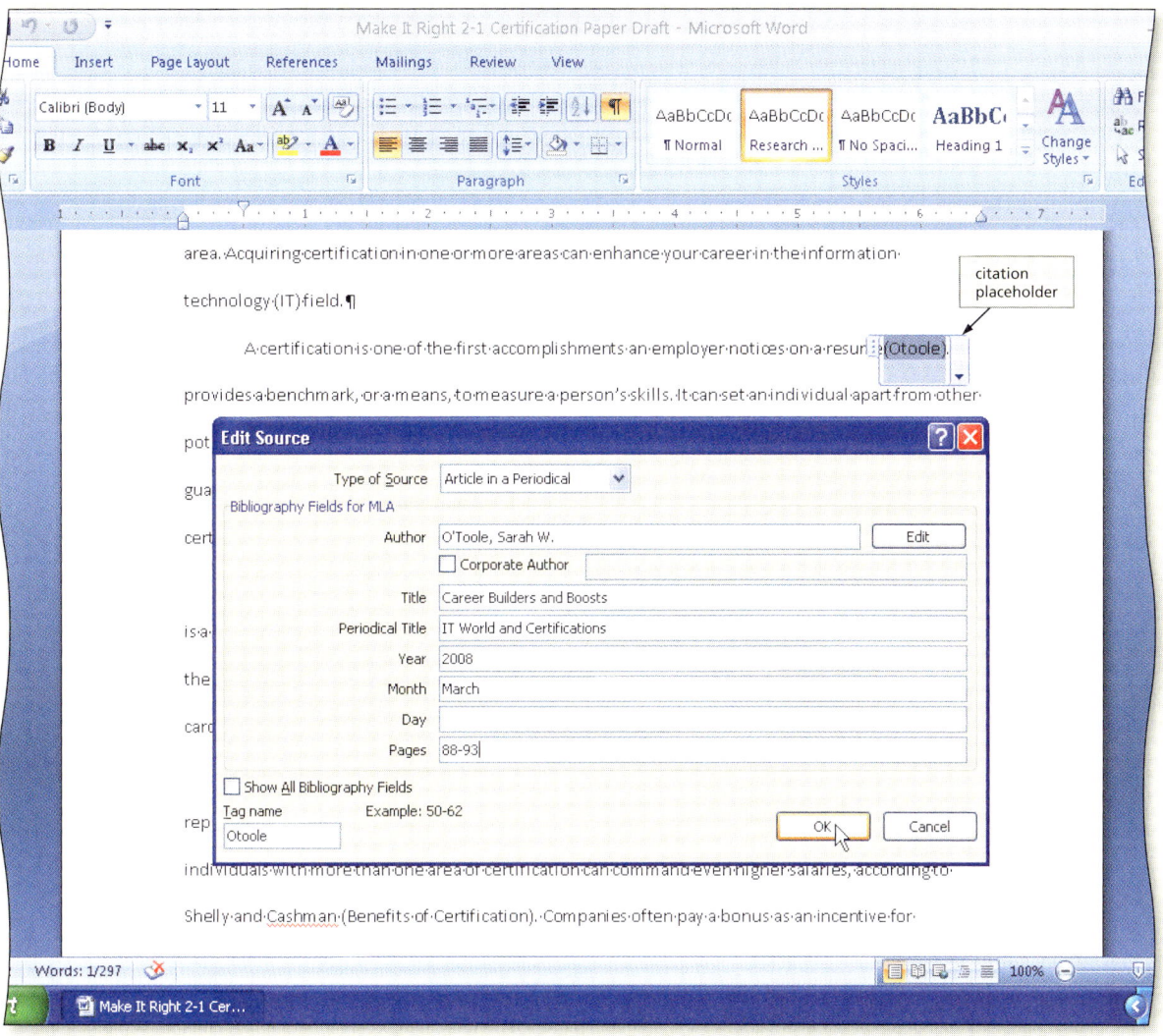

Figure 2–82

4. Insert the following footnote with the note reference at an appropriate place in the paper, formatted according to the MLA style: Debbins points out that, as an additional bonus, some certification training can be used for college credit. The citation for this footnote should be at the end of the footnote. The source information is as follows: book named *Preparing for the Future: IT Strategies*, authored by Floyd I. Debbins, published in 2008 at IT World Press in Chicago, pages 99-104. Edit the citation so that it displays only page numbers.

5. Use the Select Browse Object button to go to page 3. Be sure the bibliographical list on the Works Cited page contains all three entries. If necessary, use the F9 key to update the bibliographical list. Format the bibliographical paragraphs with a one-half inch hanging indent.

6. Modify the source of the book authored by Floyd I. Debbins, so that the publisher city is Boston instead of Chicago.

7. Use the Select Browse Object button to go to the footnote. Be sure the footnote is formatted properly.

8. Change the document properties, as specified by your instructor. Save the revised document with a new file name and then submit it in the format specified by your instructor.

In the Lab

Design and/or create a document using the guidelines, concepts, and skills presented in this chapter. Labs are listed in order of increasing difficulty.

Lab 1: Preparing a Short Research Paper

Problem: You are a college student currently enrolled in an introductory business class. Your assignment is to prepare a short research paper (300-350 words) about a computer-related job. The requirements are that the paper be presented according to the MLA documentation style and have three references. One of the three references must be from the Web. You prepare the paper shown in Figure 2–83, which discusses the computer forensics specialist.

Hankins 1

Mary Hankins

Mr. Habib

Business 102

14 March 2008

Computer Forensics Specialist

  Computer forensics, also called digital forensics, network forensics, or cyberforensics, is a rapidly growing field that involves gathering and analyzing evidence from computers and networks. Because computers and the Internet are the fastest growing technology used for criminal activity, the need for computer forensics specialists will increase in years to come.

  A computer forensics specialist examines computer media, programs, data, and log files on computers, servers, and networks. According to Shelly and Cashman (Computer Careers), many areas employ computer forensics specialists, including law enforcement, criminal prosecutors, military intelligence, insurance agencies, and information security departments in the private sector. A computer forensics specialist must have knowledge of the law, technical experience with many types of hardware and software products, superior communication skills, a willingness to learn and update skills, and a knack for problem solving.

  When a problem occurs, it is the responsibility of the computer forensics specialist to carefully take several steps to identify and retrieve possible evidence that may exist on a suspect's computer. These steps include protecting the suspect's computer, discovering all files, recovering deleted files, revealing hidden files, accessing protected or encrypted files, analyzing all the data, and providing expert consultation and/or testimony as required (Reinman 52-58).

  A computer forensics specialist must have knowledge of all aspects of the computer, from the operating system to computer architecture and hardware design. In the past, many computer forensics specialists were self-taught computer users. Today, extensive training, usually from several different

(a)

Figure 2–83

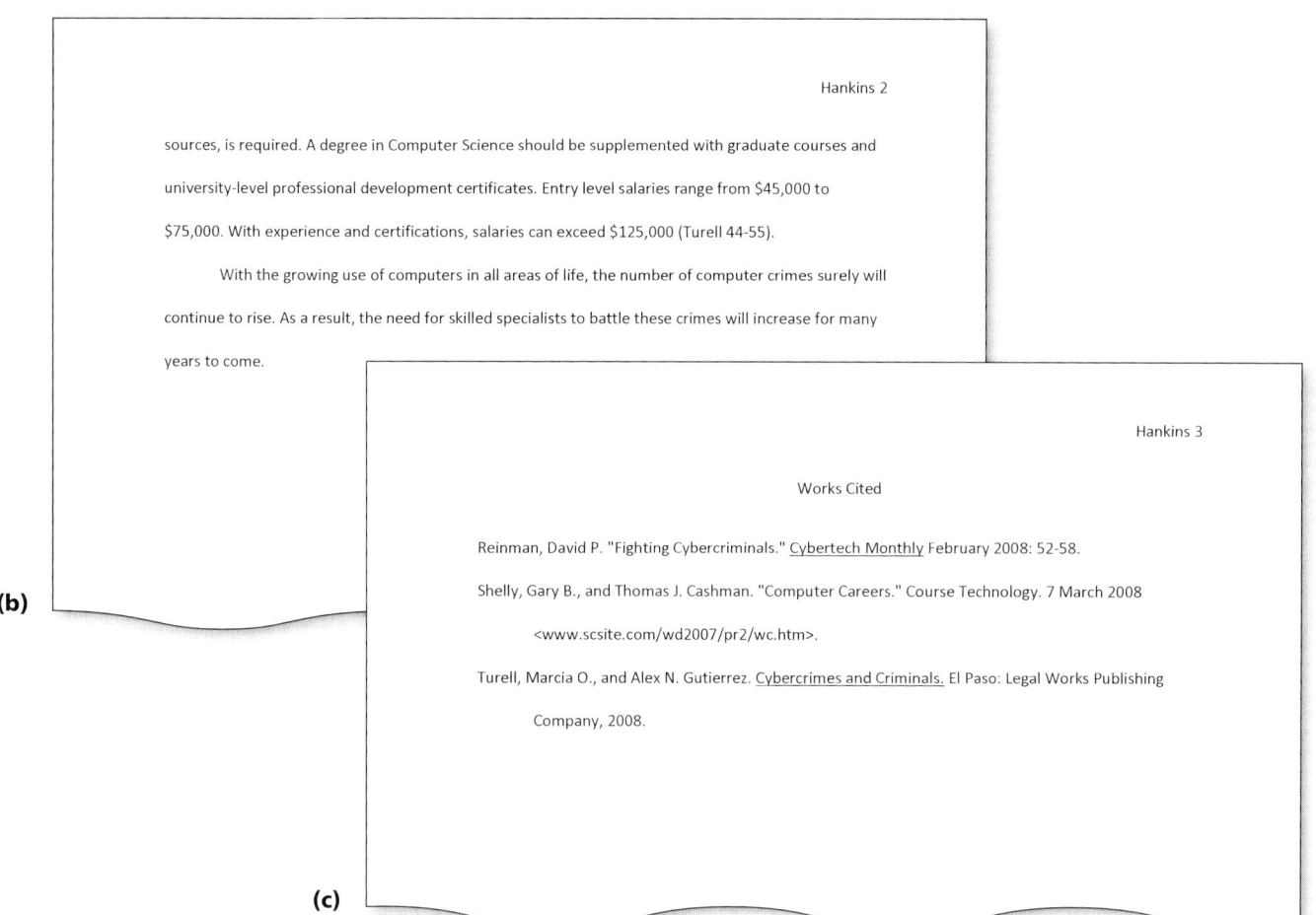

Figure 2–83 (continued)

Instructions: Perform the following tasks:
1. If necessary, display formatting marks on the screen.
2. Adjust line spacing to double.
3. Remove space below (after) paragraphs.
4. Create a header to number pages.
5. Type the name and course information at the left margin. Center and type the title.
6. Set first-line indent for paragraphs in the body of the research paper.
7. Create a Quick Style for the research paper paragraphs.
8. Type the research paper as shown in Figures 2–83a and 2–83b. Change the bibliography style to MLA. As you insert citations, enter their source information (shown in Figure 2–83c). Edit the citations so that they display according to Figures 2–83a and 2–83b.
9. At the end of the research paper text, press the ENTER key and then insert a manual page break so that the Works Cited page begins on a new page. Enter and format the works cited title (Figure 2–83c). Use Word to insert the bibliographical list (bibliography). Format the paragraphs in the list with a hanging indent.
10. Check the spelling and grammar of the paper at once.
11. Save the document on a USB flash drive using Lab 2-1 Computer Forensics Paper as the file name.
12. Print the research paper. Handwrite the number of words, paragraphs, and characters in the research paper above the title of your printed research paper.

In the Lab

Lab 2: Preparing a Research Report with a Footnote

Problem: You are a college student enrolled in an introductory English class. Your assignment is to prepare a short research paper in any area of interest to you. The requirements are that the paper be presented according to the MLA documentation style, contain at least one explanatory note positioned as a footnote, and have three references. One of the three references must be from the Internet. You prepare a paper about antivirus programs (Figure 2–84).

Yadav 1

Pahdi Yadav

Professor Milton

English 101

5 May 2008

Antivirus Programs

Today, people rely on computers to create, store, and manage critical information, many times via a home computer network. Information transmitted over networks has a higher degree of security risk than information kept in a user's home or company premises. Thus, it is crucial that they take measures to protect their computers and data from loss, damage, and misuse resulting from computer security risks. Antivirus programs are an effective way to protect a computer against viruses.

An antivirus program protects a computer against viruses by identifying and removing any computer viruses found in memory, on storage media, or on incoming files.[1] When you purchase a new computer, it often includes antivirus software. Antivirus programs work by scanning for programs that attempt to modify the boot program, the operating system, and other programs that normally are read from but not modified. In addition, many antivirus programs automatically scan files downloaded from the Web, e-mail attachments, opened files, and all types of removable media inserted in the computer (Karanos 201-205).

One technique that antivirus programs use to identify a virus is to look for virus signatures, or virus definitions, which are known specific patterns of virus code. According to Shelly and Cashman (Antivirus Programs), many vendors of antivirus programs allow registered users to update virus signature files automatically from the Web at no cost for a specified time. Updating the antivirus

_____

[1] Bulowski points out that most antivirus programs also protect against worms and Trojan horses (55-61).

(a)

Figure 2–84

(b)

> program's signature files regularly is important, because it will download any new virus definitions that have been added since the last update.
>
> Methods that guarantee a computer or network is safe from computer viruses simply do not exist. Installing, updating, and using an antivirus program, though, is an effective technique to safeguard your computer from loss.

Figure 2–84 (continued)

Instructions: Perform the following tasks:

1. Adjust line spacing to double and remove space below (after) paragraphs. Create a header to number pages. Type the name and course information at the left margin. Center and type the title. Set first-line indent for paragraphs in the body of the research paper. Create a Quick Style for the research paper paragraphs.

2. Type the research paper as shown in Figures 2–84a and 2–84b. Add the footnote as shown in Figure 2–84a. Change the Footnote Text style to the format specified in the MLA style. Change the bibliography style to MLA. As you insert citations, use the following source information:

   a. Type of Source: Periodical
      Author: Bulowski, Dana
      Title: Protection and Precaution: Keeping Your Computer Healthy
      Periodical Title: Computing Today
      Year: 2008
      Month: February
      Pages 55-61

   b. Type of Source: Book
      Author: Karanos, Hector
      Title: Internet Security
      Year: 2008
      City: Indianapolis
      Publisher: Citywide Cyber Press

   c. Type of Source: Web site
      Author: Shelly, Gary B., and Thomas J. Cashman
      Name of Web page: Antivirus Programs
      Production Company: Course Technology
      Year Accessed: 2008
      Month Accessed: February
      Day Accessed: 7
      URL: www.scsite.com/wd2007/pr2/wc.htm

3. At the end of the research paper text, press the ENTER key once and insert a manual page break so that the Works Cited page begins on a new page. Enter and format the works cited title. Use Word to insert the bibliographical list. Format the paragraphs in the list with a hanging indent.

4. Check the spelling and grammar of the paper.

5. Save the document on a USB flash drive using Lab 2-2 Antivirus Programs Paper as the file name.

6. Print the research paper. Handwrite the number of words, including the footnotes, in the research paper above the title of your printed research paper.

In the Lab

Lab 3: Composing a Research Paper from Notes

Problem: You have drafted the notes shown in Figure 2–85. Your assignment is to prepare a short research paper from these notes.

Home networks:
- Home users connect multiple computers and devices together in a home network.
- Home networking saves money and provides conveniences.
- Approximately 39 million homes have more than one computer.
- Many vendors offer home networking packages that include all the necessary hardware and software to network a home using wired or wireless techniques.

Three types of wired home networks: Ethernet, powerline cable, and phoneline (source: "Wired vs. Wireless Networks," an article on pages 24-29 in March 2008 issue of Modern Networking by Mark A. Travis).
- Traditional Ethernet networks require that each computer have built-in network capabilities or contain a network card, which connects to a central network hub or similar device with a physical cable. This may involve running cable through walls, ceilings, and floors in the house.
- The hardware and software of an Ethernet network can be difficult to configure for the average home user (source: a book called Home Networking by Frank A. Deakins, published at Current Press in New York in 2008).
- A phoneline network is an easy-to-install and inexpensive network that uses existing telephone lines in the home.
- A home powerline cable network is a network that uses the same lines that bring electricity into the house. This network requires no additional wiring.

Two types of wireless home networks: HomeRF and Wi-Fi (source: a Web site titled "Wired and Wireless Networks" by Gary B. Shelly and Thomas J. Cashman of Course Technology, viewed on April 23, 2008. Web address is www.scsite.com/wd2007/pr2/wc.htm).
- Wireless networks have the disadvantage of interference, because walls, ceilings, and other electrical devices such as cordless telephones and microwave ovens can disrupt wireless communications.
- A HomeRF (radio frequency) network uses radio waves, instead of cables, to transmit data.
- A Wi-Fi network sends signals over a wider distance than the Home RF network, which can be up to 1,500 feet in some configurations.

Figure 2–85

Instructions: Perform the following tasks:

1. Review the notes in Figure 2–85 and then rearrange and reword them. Embellish the paper as you deem necessary. Present the paper according to the MLA documentation style. Create an AutoCorrect entry that automatically corrects the spelling of the misspelled word, wird, to the correct spelling, wired. Add a footnote that refers the reader to the Web for more information. Enter citations and their sources as shown. Create the works cited page (bibliography) from the listed sources.

2. Check the spelling and grammar of the paper. Save the document on a USB flash drive using Lab 2-3 Home Networks Paper as the file name.

3. Use the Research task pane to look up a definition of a word in the paper. Copy and insert the definition into the document as a footnote. Be sure to quote the definition and cite the source.

4. Print the research paper. Handwrite the number of words, including the footnotes, in the research paper above the title of the printed research paper.

Cases and Places

Apply your creative thinking and problem solving skills to design and implement a solution.

• EASIER   •• MORE DIFFICULT

• 1: Create a Research Paper about Word Using the MLA Documentation Style

Chapter 1 of this book discussed the components of the Word window (pages WD 6 through 11). Using the material presented on those pages, write a short research paper (350–400 words) that describes the purpose and functionality of one or more of these components: document window, Ribbon, Mini toolbar and shortcut menus, Quick Access Toolbar, and Office Button. Use your textbook and Word Help as sources. Include at least two citations and one explanatory note positioned as a footnote. Add an AutoCorrect entry to correct a word you commonly mistype. Use the concepts and techniques presented in this chapter to format the paper according to the MLA documentation style. Check spelling and grammar of the finished paper.

•• 2: Create the Research Paper Presented in this Chapter Using the APA Documentation Style

As discussed in this chapter, two popular documentation styles for research papers are the Modern Language Association of America (MLA) and American Psychological Association (APA) styles. In this chapter, you created a research paper that followed guidelines of the MLA documentation style. Using the school library, this textbook, other textbooks, the Internet, magazines, or other sources, research the guidelines of the APA documentation style. Then, prepare the Wireless Communications Paper from this chapter following the guidelines of the APA documentation style. Use Figure 2–1 on page WD 75 as a starting point for the text and source information. Check spelling and grammar of the finished paper.

•• 3: Create a Research Paper that Compares Documentation Styles

This chapter discussed the requirements of the MLA documentation style. The American Psychological Association (APA) and the Chicago Manual of Style (CMS) are two other documentation styles supported by Word. Using the school library, this textbook, other textbooks, the Internet, magazines, or other sources, research the guidelines of the APA and CMS documentation styles to learn more about the differences among the MLA, APA, and CMS documentation styles. Using what you learn, write a short research paper (450-500 words) that compares the requirements and formats of the three documentation styles. Include at least two references and one explanatory note positioned as a footnote. Use the documentation style specified by your instructor to format the paper. Check spelling and grammar of the finished paper.

•• 4: Create a Research Paper about the Month You Were Born

Make It Personal

Did you ever wonder what world events took place during the month you were born (besides your birth)? For example, what happened with respect to politics, world affairs, and the economy? What made headline news? Were there any scientific breakthroughs? What was on television and at the box office? Were any famous people born? Did anyone famous die? What songs topped the charts? What was happening in the world of sports? Research the newsworthy events that took place during the month and year you were born (i.e., July 1981) by looking through newspapers, magazines, searching the Web, and/or interviewing family and friends. Write a short research paper (450-500 words) that summarizes your findings. Include at least two references and one explanatory note. Use the documentation style specified by your instructor to format the paper. Check spelling and grammar of the finished paper.

Continued >

Cases and Places *continued*

• • 5: Create a Research Paper about Spring Break Vacation Destinations

Working Together
With spring break just two months away, you and your fellow classmates are thinking about various spring break vacation destinations. Many options are available. Should you vacation close to home or travel across the country? Stay at a hotel, rent a condominium, or camp outdoors? Travel by car, train, or airplane? Book through a travel agent or the Web? Each team member is to research the attractions, accommodations, required transportation, and total cost of one spring break destination by looking through newspapers, magazines, searching the Web, and/or visiting a travel agency. Each team member is to write a minimum of 200 words summarizing his or her findings. Each team member also is to write at least one explanatory note and supply his or her source information for the citation and bibliography. Then, the team should meet as a group to compose a research paper that includes all team members' write-ups. Start by copying and pasting the text into a single document and then write an introduction and conclusion as a group. Use the documentation style specified by your instructor to format the paper. Check spelling and grammar of the finished paper. Set the default dictionary. If Word flags any of your last names as an error, add the name(s) to the custom dictionary. Hand in printouts of each team member's original write-up, as well as the final research paper.

Microsoft Office **PowerPoint 2007**

1 Creating and Editing a Presentation

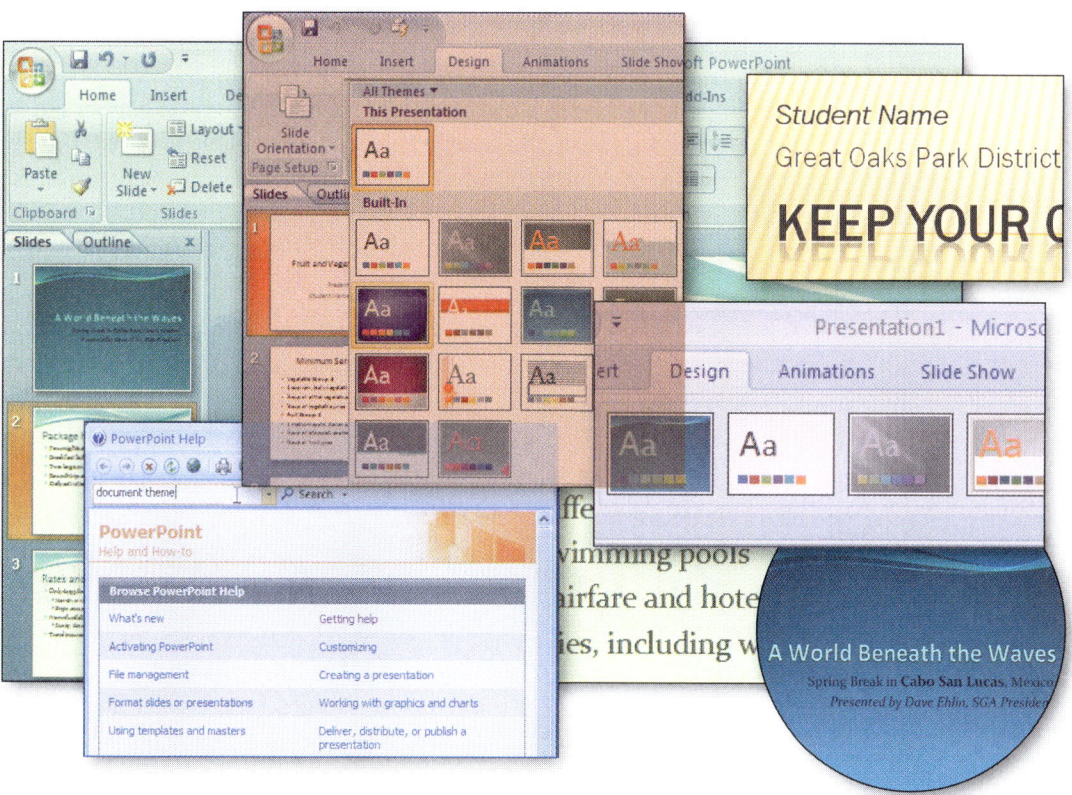

Objectives

You will have mastered the material in this chapter when you can:

- Start and quit PowerPoint
- Describe the PowerPoint window
- Select a document theme
- Create a title slide and text slides with single- and multi-level bulleted lists
- Save a presentation
- Copy elements from one slide to another
- View a presentation in Slide Show view
- Open a presentation
- Display and print a presentation in grayscale
- Check spelling
- Use PowerPoint Help

1 Creating and Editing a Presentation

What Is Microsoft Office PowerPoint 2007?

Microsoft Office PowerPoint 2007 is a complete presentation graphics program that allows you to produce professional-looking presentations (Figure 1–1). A PowerPoint **presentation** also is called a **slide show**.

PowerPoint contains several features to simplify creating a slide show. For example, the results-oriented user interface can boost productivity by making tasks and options readily accessible. Professionally designed standard layouts help you save time by formatting and creating content. You then can modify these layouts to create custom slides to fit your specific needs. To make your presentation more impressive, you can add diagrams, tables, pictures, video, sound, and animation effects. Additional PowerPoint features include the following:

- **Word processing** — Create bulleted lists, combine words and images, find and replace text, and use multiple fonts and type sizes.
- **Outlining** — Develop your presentation using an outline format. You also can import outlines from Microsoft Word or other word processing programs.
- **Charting** — Create and insert charts into your presentations and then add effects and chart elements.
- **Drawing** — Form and modify diagrams using shapes such as arcs, arrows, cubes, rectangles, stars, and triangles. Then apply Quick Styles to customize and add effects. Arrange these objects by sizing, scaling, and rotating.
- **Inserting multimedia** — Insert artwork and multimedia effects into your slide show. The Microsoft Clip Organizer contains hundreds of media files, including pictures, photos, sounds, and movies.
- **Saving to the Web** — Save presentations or parts of a presentation in HTML format so they can be viewed and manipulated using a browser. You can publish your slide show to the Internet or to an intranet.
- **E-Mailing** — Send your entire slide show as an attachment to an e-mail message.
- **Collaborating** — Share your presentation with friends and coworkers. Ask them to review the slides and then insert comments that offer suggestions to enhance the presentation.
- **Preparing delivery** — Rehearse integrating PowerPoint slides into your speech by setting timings, using presentation tools, showing only selected slides in a presentation, and packaging the presentation for an optical disc.

This latest version of PowerPoint has many new features to increase your productivity. Graphics and other shape effects allow you to add glow, shadowing, 3-D effects, and other appealing visuals. Typography effects enhance the design's impact. PowerPoint themes apply a consistent look to each graphic, font, and table color in an entire presentation. Digital signatures enable you to verify that no one has altered your presentation since you created it, and the Document Inspector removes private data, such as comments and hidden text.

PowerPoint gives you the flexibility to make presentations using a projection device attached to a personal computer or using overhead transparencies. In addition, you can take advantage of the World Wide Web and run virtual presentations on the Internet. PowerPoint also can create paper printouts of the individual slides, outlines, and speaker notes.

Project Planning Guidlines

The process of developing a presentation that communicates specific information requires careful analysis and planning. As a starting point, establish why the presentation is needed. Next, analyze the intended audience for the presentation and their unique needs. Then, gather information about the topic and decide what to include in the presentation. Finally, determine the presentation design and style that will be most successful at delivering the message. Details of these guidelines are provided in Appendix A. In addition, each project in this book provides practical applications of these planning considerations.

Project — Presentation with Bulleted Lists

In Project 1, you will follow proper design guidelines and learn to use PowerPoint to create, save, and print the slides shown in Figures 1–1a through 1–1e on this page and the next. The objective is to produce a presentation, called A World Beneath the Waves, to help the Student Government Association (SGA) President, Dave Ehlin, promote the annual spring break diving and snorkeling trip to Cabo San Lucas, Mexico. This slide show presents the highlights of this trip and promotes the included amenities, tour prices, and the inviting Pacific waters. Some of the text will have formatting and color enhancements. In addition, you will print handouts of your slides to distribute to students.

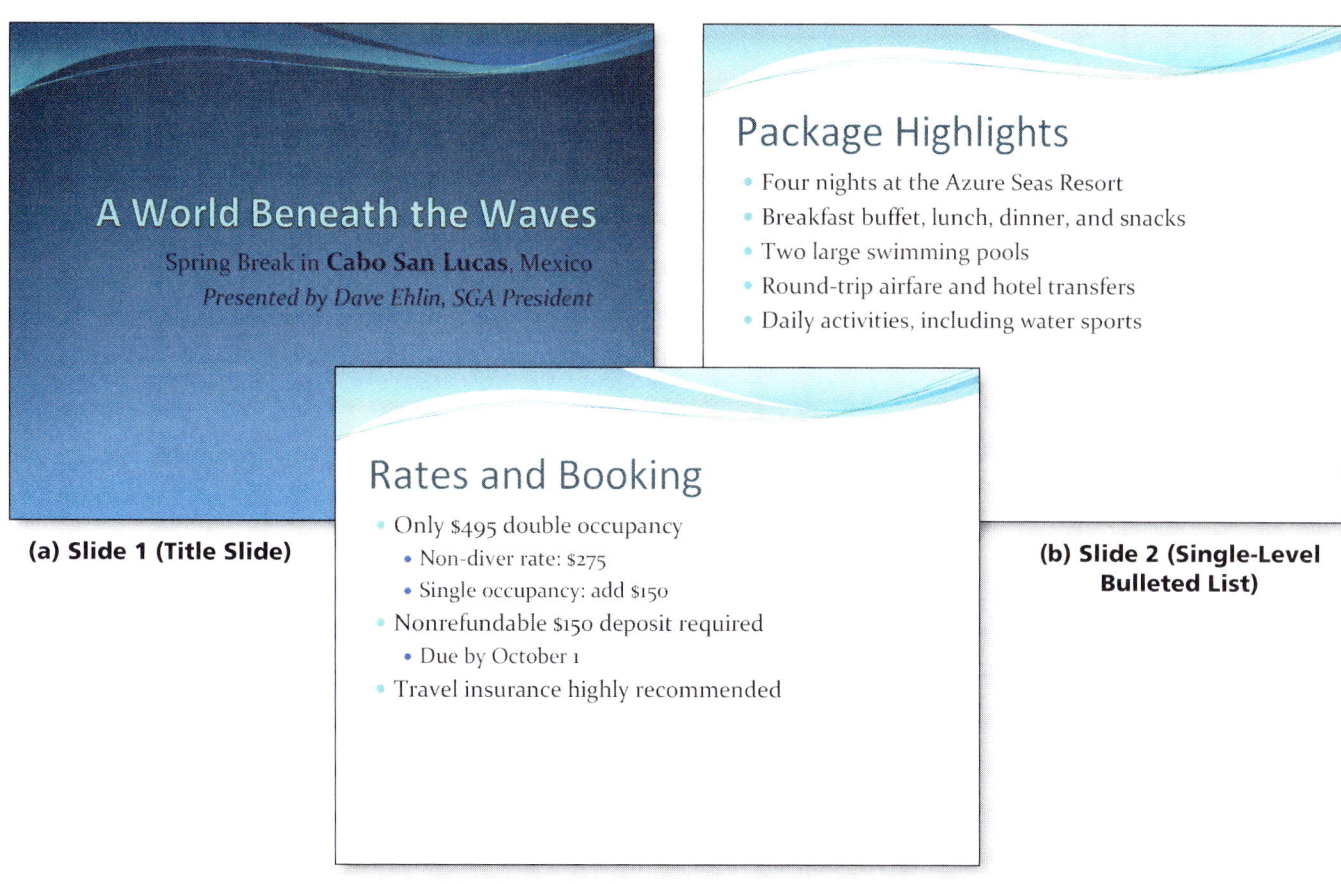

(a) Slide 1 (Title Slide)

(b) Slide 2 (Single-Level Bulleted List)

(c) Slide 3 (Multi-Level Bulleted List)

Figure 1–1

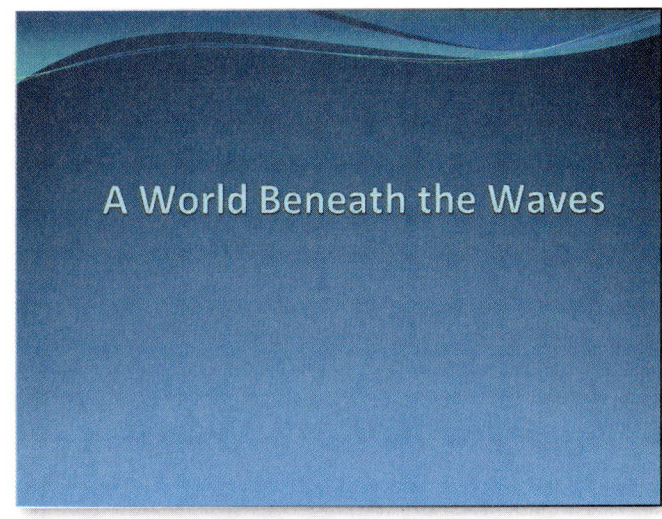

(d) Slide 4 (Multi-Level Bulleted List)   **(e) Slide 5 (Closing Slide)**

Figure 1–1 (continued)

PowerPoint allows you to produce slides to use in an academic, business, or other environment. One of the more common uses of these slides is to enhance an oral presentation. A speaker may desire to convey information, such as urging students to participate in a food drive, explaining first aid, or describing the changes in an employee benefit package. The PowerPoint slides should reinforce the speaker's message and help the audience members retain the information presented. An accompanying handout gives audience members reference notes and review material after the presentation's conclusion.

Overview

As you read this chapter, you will learn how to create the presentation shown in Figure 1–1 by performing these general tasks:

- Select an appropriate document theme.
- Enter titles and text on slides.
- Change the size, color, and style of text.
- View the presentation on your computer.
- Save the presentation so you can modify and view it at a later time.
- Print handouts of your slides.

Plan Ahead

General Project Guidelines

When creating a PowerPoint document, the actions you perform and decisions you make will affect the appearance and characteristics of the finished document. As you create a presentation such as the project shown in Figure 1–1, you should follow these general guidelines:

1. **Find the appropriate theme.** The overall appearance of a presentation significantly affects its capability to communicate information clearly. The slides' graphical appearance should support the presentation's overall message. Colors, fonts, and layouts affect how audience members perceive and react to the slide content.

2. **Choose words for each slide.** Use the less is more principle. The less text, the more likely the slides will enhance your speech. Use the fewest words possible to make a point.

(continued)

(continued)

3. **Format specific elements of the text.** Examples of how you can modify the appearance, or **format**, of text include changing its shape, size, color, and position on the slide.

4. **Determine where to save the presentation.** You can store a document permanently, or **save** it, on a variety of storage media including a hard disk, USB flash drive, or optical disc. You also can indicate a specific location on the storage media for saving the document.

When necessary, more specific details concerning the above guidelines are presented at appropriate points in the chapter. The chapter also will identify the actions performed and decisions made regarding these guidelines during the creation of the slides shown in Figure 1–1.

Plan Ahead

Decreasing Resolution
You may need to decrease your computer's resolution if you know you are going to run your presentation on another computer that uses a lower resolution, such as 800 × 600 or 640 × 480. This lower resolution, however, may affect the appearance of your slides.

Starting PowerPoint

If you are using a computer to step through the project in this chapter and you want your screen to match the figures in this book, you should change your screen's resolution to 1024 × 768. For information about how to change a computer's resolution, read Appendix C.

To Start PowerPoint

The following steps, which assume Windows Vista is running, start PowerPoint based on a typical installation. You may need to ask your instructor how to start PowerPoint for your computer.

1
- Click the Start button on the Windows Vista taskbar to display the Start menu.
- Click All Programs at the bottom of the left pane on the Start menu to display the All Programs list.
- Click Microsoft Office in the All Programs list to display the Microsoft Office (Figure 1–2).

Figure 1–2

2
- Click Microsoft Office PowerPoint 2007 to start PowerPoint and display a new blank document in the PowerPoint window (Figure 1–3).
- If the PowerPoint window is not maximized, click the Maximize button next to the Close button on its title bar to maximize the window.

Q&A

What is a maximized window?

A maximized window fills the entire screen. When you maximize a window, the Maximize button changes to a Restore Down button. When you restore a maximized window, the Restore Down button changes to a Maximize button.

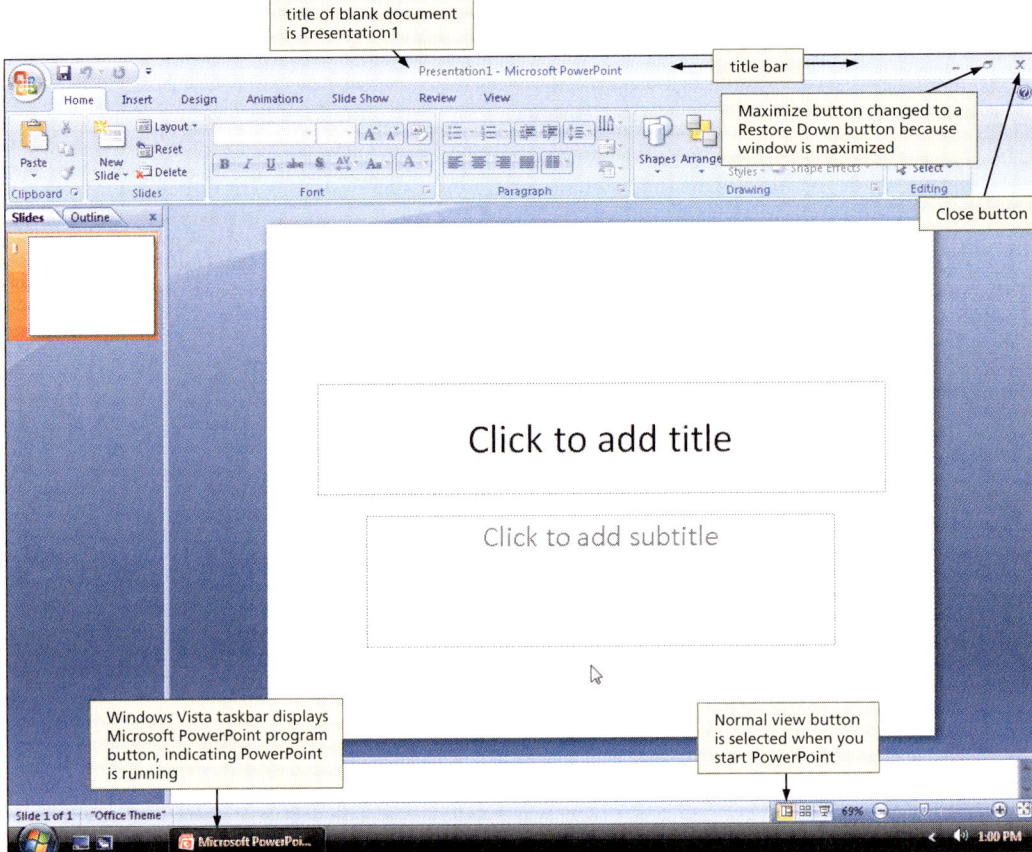

Figure 1–3

Other Ways
1. Double-click PowerPoint icon on desktop, if one is present
2. Click Microsoft Office PowerPoint 2007 on Start menu

BTW

Portrait Page Orientation
If your slide content is dominantly vertical, such as a skyscraper or a person, consider changing the slide layout to a portrait page orientation. To change the orientation, click the Slide Orientation button in the Page Setup group in the Design tab and then click the desired orientation. You can use both slide and portrait orientation in the same slide show.

The PowerPoint Window

The PowerPoint window consists of a variety of components to make your work more efficient and documents more professional. These include the document window, Ribbon, Mini toolbar and shortcut menus, Quick Access Toolbar, and Office Button. Some of these components are common to other Microsoft Office 2007 programs; others are unique to PowerPoint.

PowerPoint Window

The basic unit of a PowerPoint presentation is a **slide**. A slide may contain text and objects, such as graphics, tables, charts, and drawings. **Layouts** are used to position this content on the slide. When you open a new presentation, the default **Title Slide** layout appears (Figure 1–4). The purpose of this layout is to introduce the presentation to the audience. PowerPoint includes eight other built-in standard layouts.

The default (preset) slide layouts are set up in **landscape orientation**, where the slide width is greater than its height. In landscape orientation, the slide size is preset to 10 inches wide and 7.5 inches high when printed on a standard sheet of paper measuring 11 inches wide and 8.5 inches high.

The PowerPoint window in Figure 1–4 contains placeholders, a mouse pointer, and a status bar. Other elements that may appear in the window are discussed later.

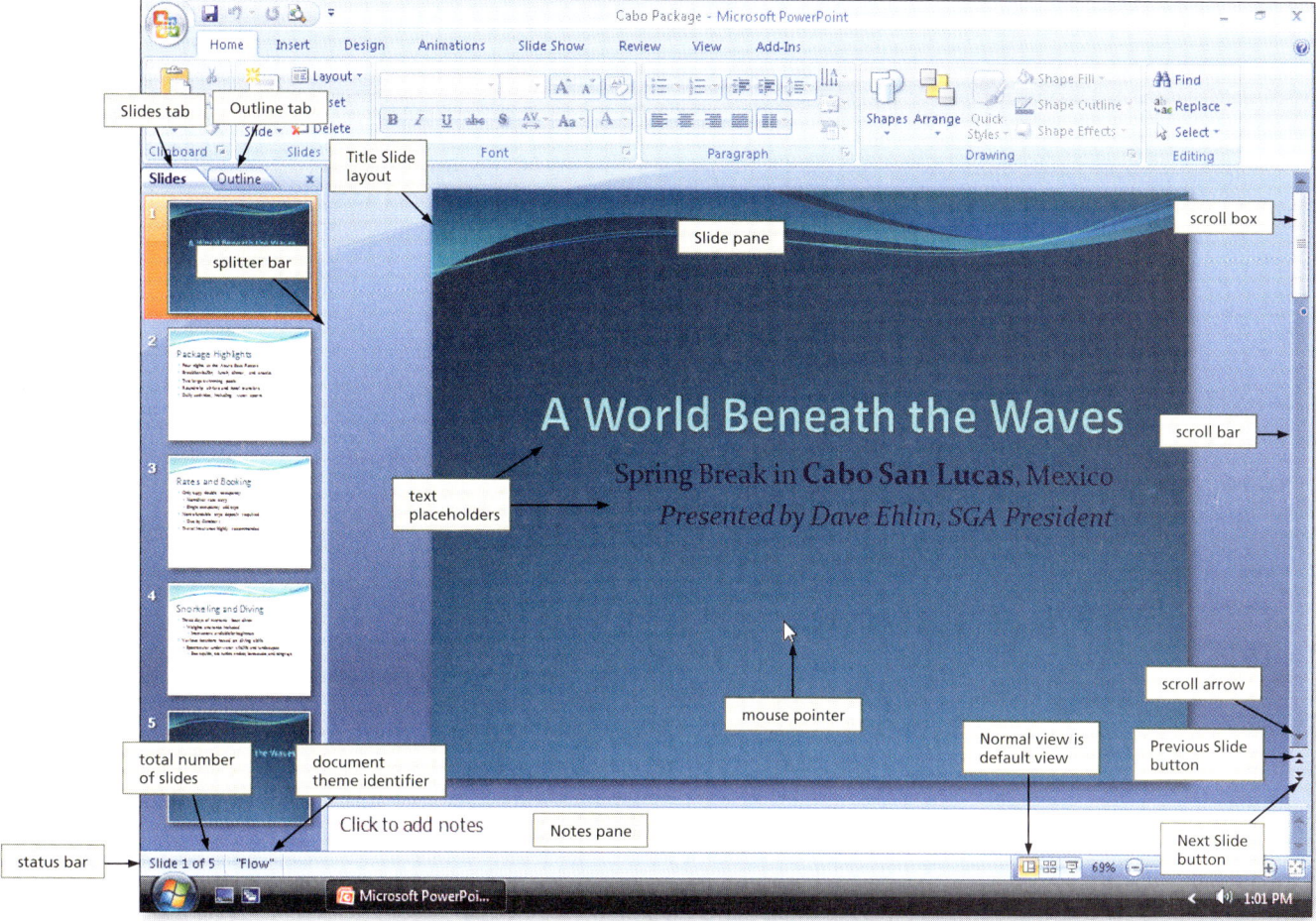

Figure 1–4

PLACEHOLDERS Placeholders are boxes with dotted or hatch-marked borders that are displayed when you create a new slide. All layouts except the Blank slide layout contain placeholders. Depending on the particular slide layout selected, title and subtitle placeholders are displayed for the slide title and subtitle; a content text placeholder is displayed for text, art, or a table, chart, picture, graphic, or movie. The title slide in Figure 1–4 has two text placeholders where you will type the main heading, or title, of a new slide and the subtitle.

MOUSE POINTER The **mouse pointer** becomes different shapes depending on the task you are performing in PowerPoint and the pointer's location on the screen. The mouse pointer in Figure 1–4 is the shape of a block arrow.

SCROLL BAR You use the **vertical scroll bar** to display different slides in the document window. When you add a second slide to a presentation, this vertical scroll bar appears on the right side of the Slide pane. On the scroll bar, the position of the **scroll box** reflects the location of the slide in the presentation that is displayed in the document window. A **scroll arrow** is located at each end of a scroll bar. To scroll through, or display different portions of the document in the document window, you can click a scroll arrow or drag the scroll box to move forward or backward through the presentation.

The Previous Slide button and the Next Slide button appear at the bottom of the vertical scroll bar. Click one of these buttons to advance through the slides backwards or forwards.

The **horizontal scroll bar** also may appear. It is located on the bottom of the Slide pane and allows you to display a portion of the slide when the entire slide does not fit on the screen.

STATUS BAR The **status bar**, located at the bottom of the document window above the Windows Vista taskbar, presents information about the document, the progress of current tasks, and the status of certain commands and keys; it also provides controls for viewing the document. As you type text or perform certain commands, various indicators may appear on the status bar.

The left edge of the status bar in Figure 1–4 shows the current slide number followed by the total number of slides in the document and a document theme identifier. A **document theme** provides consistency in design and color throughout the entire presentation by setting the color scheme, font and font size, and layout of a presentation. Toward the right edge are buttons and controls you can use to change the view of a slide and adjust the size of the displayed document.

PowerPoint Views

> **BTW**
>
> **Using the Notes Pane**
> As you create your presentation, type comments to yourself in the Notes pane. This material can be used as part of the spoken information you will share with your audience as you give your presentation. You can print these notes for yourself or to distribute to your audience.

The PowerPoint window display varies depending on the view. A **view** is the mode in which the presentation appears on the screen. PowerPoint has three main views: Normal, Slide Sorter, and Slide Show, and also Notes Page. The default view is **Normal view**, which is composed of three working areas that allow you to work on various aspects of a presentation simultaneously. The left side of the screen has a Tabs pane that consists of a **Slides tab** and an **Outline tab** that alternate between views of the presentation in a thumbnail, or miniature, view of the slides and an outline of the slide text. You can type the text of the presentation on the Outline tab and easily rearrange bulleted lists, paragraphs, and individual slides. As you type, you can view this text in the **Slide pane**, which shows a large view of the current slide on the right side of the window. You also can enter text, graphics, animations, and hyperlinks directly in the Slide pane. The **Notes pane** at the bottom of the window is an area where you can type notes and additional information. This text can consist of notes to yourself or remarks to share with your audience. If you want to work with your notes in full page format, you can display them in **Notes Page view**.

In Normal view, you can adjust the width of the Slide pane by dragging the **splitter bar** and the height of the Notes pane by dragging the pane borders. After you have created at least two slides, **scroll bars**, **scroll arrows**, and **scroll boxes** will appear on the right edge of the window.

Ribbon

The **Ribbon**, located near the top of the PowerPoint window, is the control center in PowerPoint (Figure 1–5a). The Ribbon provides easy, central access to the tasks you perform while creating a slide show. The Ribbon consists of tabs, groups, and commands. Each **tab** surrounds a collection of groups, and each group contains related commands.

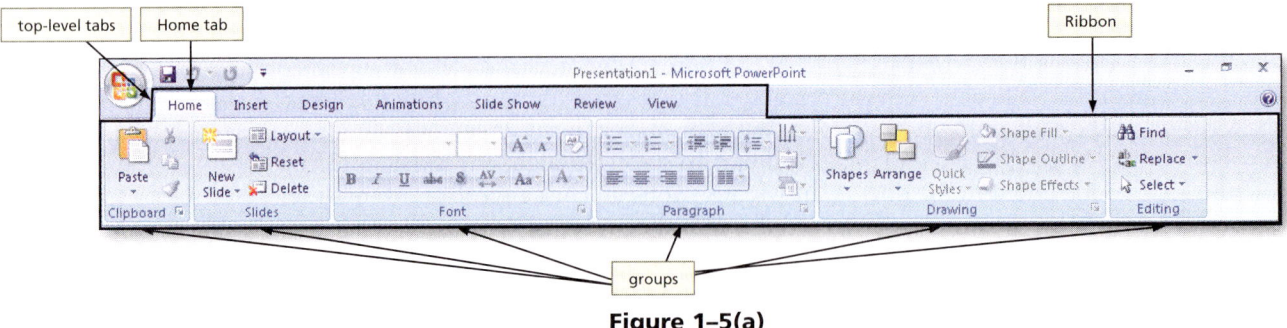

Figure 1–5(a)

When you start PowerPoint, the Ribbon displays seven top-level tabs: Home, Insert, Design, Animations, Slide Show, Review, and View. The **Home tab**, called the primary tab, contains the more frequently used commands. To display a different tab on the Ribbon, click the top-level tab. That is, to display the Insert tab, click Insert on the Ribbon. To return to the Home tab, click Home on the Ribbon. The tab currently displayed is called the **active tab**.

To display more of the document in the document window, some users prefer to minimize the Ribbon, which hides the groups on the Ribbon and displays only the top-level tabs (Figure 1–5b). To use commands on a minimized Ribbon, click the top-level tab.

Each time you start PowerPoint, the Ribbon appears the same way it did the last time you used PowerPoint. The chapters in this book, however, begin with the Ribbon appearing as it did at the initial installation of the software. If you are stepping through this chapter on a computer and you want your Ribbon to match the figures in this book, read Appendix C.

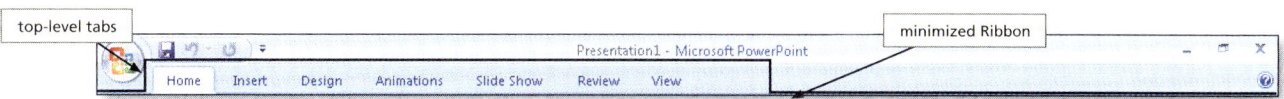

Figure 1–5(b)

In addition to the top-level tabs, PowerPoint displays other tabs, called **contextual tabs**, when you perform certain tasks or work with objects such as pictures or tables. If you insert a picture in a slide, for example, the Picture Tools tab and its related subordinate Format tab appear (Figure 1–6). When you are finished working with the picture, the Picture Tools and Format tabs disappear from the Ribbon. PowerPoint determines when contextual tabs should appear and disappear based on tasks you perform. Some contextual tabs, such as the Chart Tools tab, have more than one related subordinate tab.

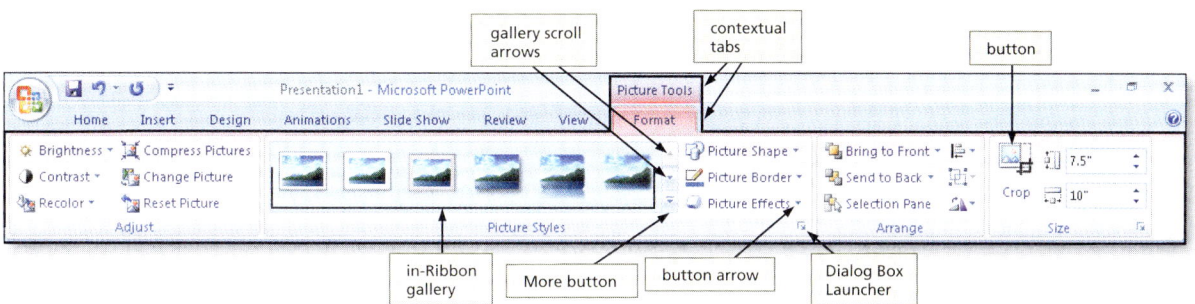

Figure 1–6

Commands on the Ribbon include buttons, boxes (text boxes, check boxes, etc.), and galleries (Figure 1–6). A **gallery** is a set of choices, often graphical, arranged in a grid or in a list. You can scroll through choices on an in-Ribbon gallery by clicking the gallery's scroll arrows. Or, you can click a gallery's More button to view more gallery options on the screen at a time. Some buttons and boxes have arrows that, when clicked, also display a gallery; others always cause a gallery to be displayed when clicked. Most galleries support **live preview**, which is a feature that allows you to point to a gallery choice and see its effect in the document - without actually selecting the choice (Figure 1–7).

BTW

Minimizing the Ribbon
If you want to minimize the Ribbon, right-click the Ribbon and then click Minimize the Ribbon on the shortcut menu, double-click the active tab, or press CTRL+F1. To restore a minimized Ribbon, right-click the Ribbon and then click Minimize the Ribbon on the shortcut menu, double-click any top-level tab, or press CTRL+F1. To use commands on a minimized Ribbon, click the top-level tab.

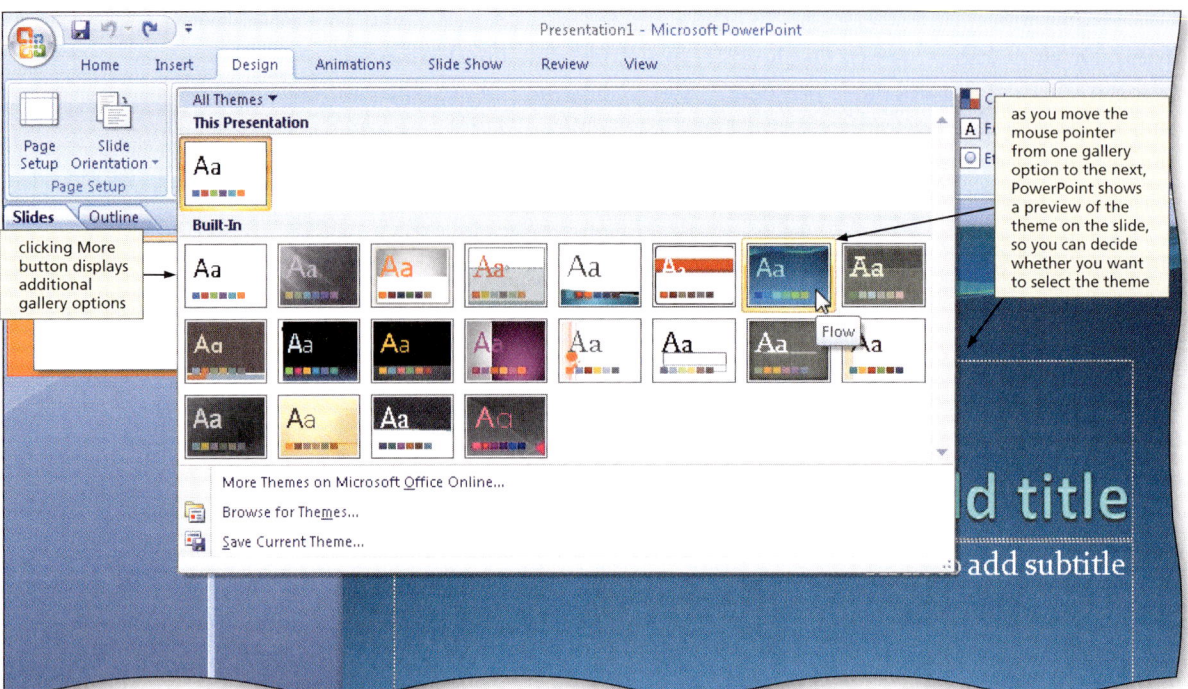

Figure 1–7

Some commands on the Ribbon display an image to help you remember their function. When you point to a command on the Ribbon, all or part of the command glows in shades of yellow and orange, and an Enhanced ScreenTip appears on the screen. An **Enhanced ScreenTip** is an on-screen note that provides the name of the command, available keyboard shortcut(s), a description of the command, and sometimes instructions for how to obtain help about the command (Figure 1–8). Enhanced ScreenTips are more detailed than a typical ScreenTip, which usually only displays the name of the command.

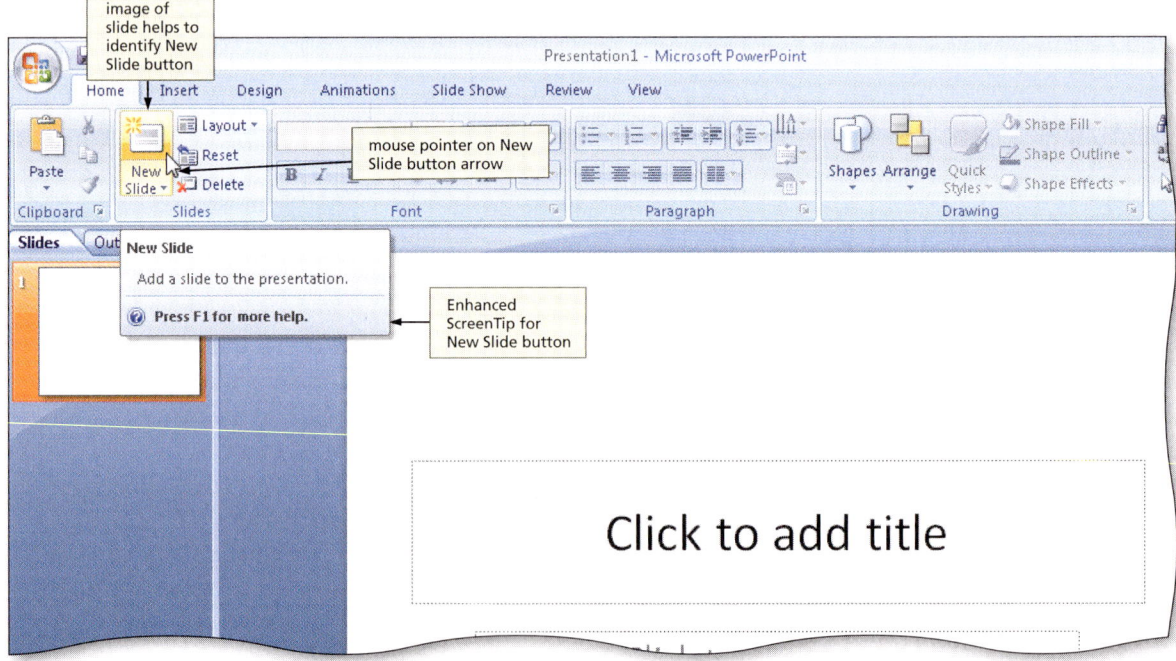

Figure 1–8

The lower-right corner of some groups on the Ribbon has a small arrow, called a **Dialog Box Launcher**, that when clicked displays a dialog box or a task pane with additional options for the group (Figure 1–9). When presented with a dialog box, you make selections and must close the dialog box before returning to the document. A **task pane**, by contrast, is a window that can remain open and visible while you work in the document.

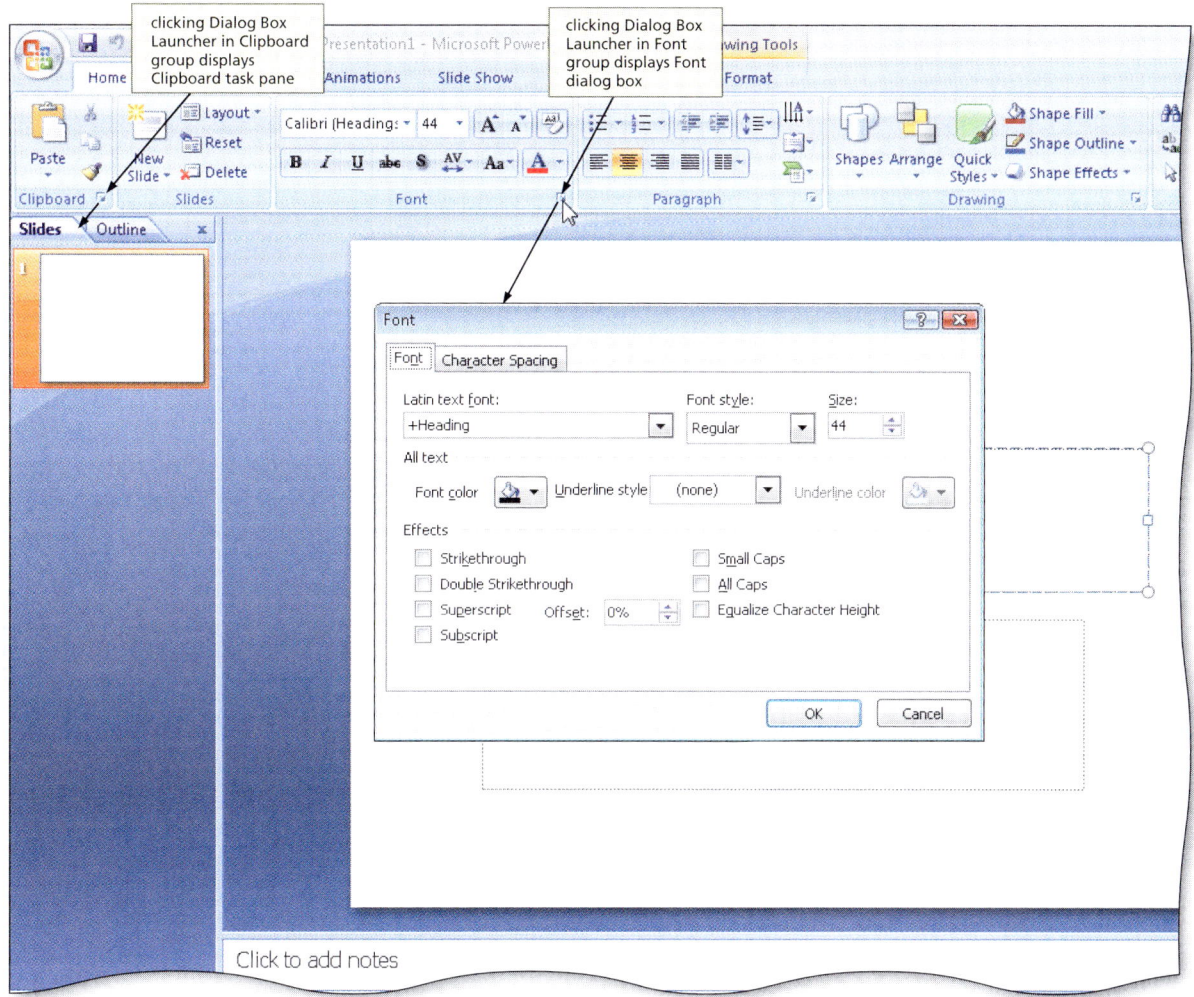

Figure 1–9

Mini Toolbar and Shortcut Menus

The **Mini toolbar**, which appears automatically based on tasks you perform, contains commands related to changing the appearance of text in a slide. All commands on the Mini toolbar also exist on the Ribbon. The purpose of the Mini toolbar is to minimize mouse movement. For example, if you want to use a command that currently is not displayed on the active tab, you can use the command on the Mini toolbar - instead of switching to a different tab to use the command.

When the Mini toolbar appears, it initially is transparent (Figure 1–10a on the next page). If you do not use the transparent Mini toolbar, it disappears from the screen. To use the Mini toolbar, move the mouse pointer into the toolbar, which causes the Mini toolbar to change from a transparent to bright appearance (Figure 1–10b on the next page).

BTW

Turning Off the Mini Toolbar
If you do not want the Mini toolbar to display, click the Office Button, click the PowerPoint Options button on the Office Button menu, and then clear the 'Show Mini Toolbar on selection' check box in the Popular panel.

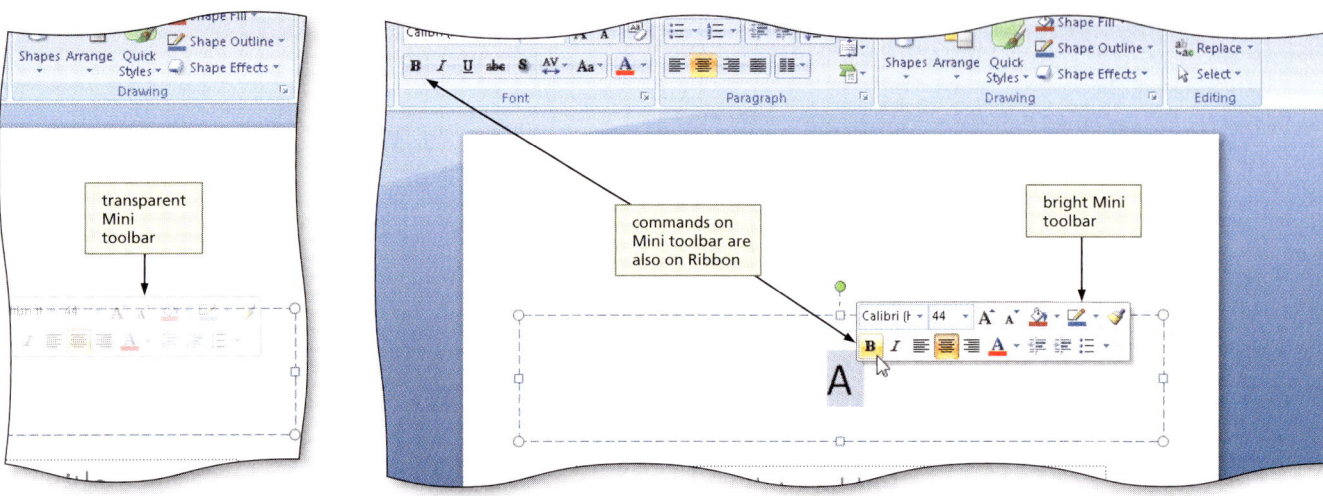

(a) Transparent Mini Toolbar **(b) Bright Mini Toolbar**

Figure 1–10

A **shortcut menu**, which appears when you right-click an object, is a list of frequently used commands that relate to the right-clicked object. When you right-click a scroll bar, for example, a shortcut menu appears with commands related to the scroll bar. If you right-click an item in the document window, PowerPoint displays both the Mini toolbar and a shortcut menu (Figure 1–11).

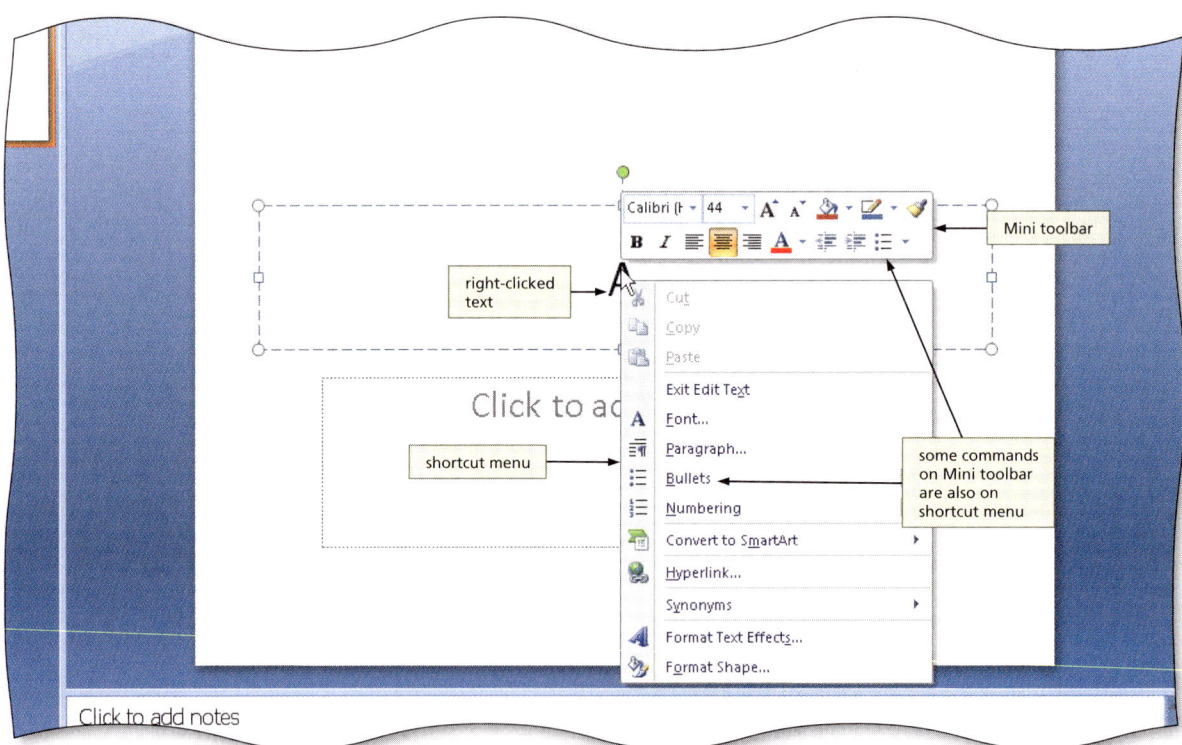

Figure 1–11

Quick Access Toolbar

The **Quick Access Toolbar**, located by default above the Ribbon, provides easy access to frequently used commands (Figure 1–12a). The commands on the Quick Access Toolbar always are available, regardless of the task you are performing. Initially, the Quick Access Toolbar contains the Save, Undo, and Redo commands. If you click the Customize Quick Access Toolbar button, PowerPoint provides a list of commands you quickly can add to and remove from the Quick Access Toolbar (Figure 1–12b).

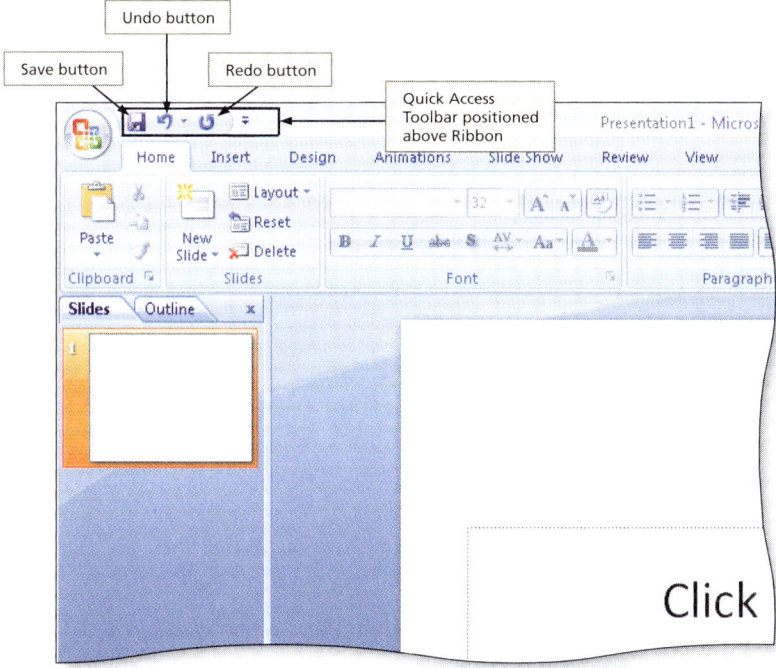

Figure 1–12(a) Quick Access Toolbar above Ribbon

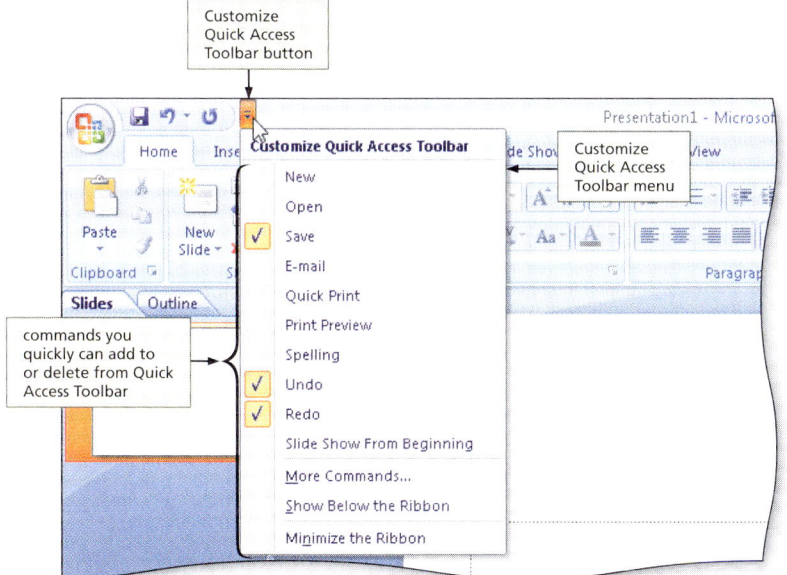

Figure 1–12(b) Customize Quick Access Toolbar

BTW

Quick Access Toolbar Commands
To add a Ribbon command to the Quick Access Toolbar, right-click the command on the Ribbon and then click Add to Quick Access Toolbar on the shortcut menu. To delete a command from the Quick Access Toolbar, right-click the command on the Quick Access Toolbar and then click Remove from Quick Access Toolbar on the shortcut menu. To display the Quick Access Toolbar below the Ribbon, right-click the Quick Access Toolbar and then click Place Quick Access Toolbar below the Ribbon on the shortcut menu.

You also can add other commands to or delete commands from the Quick Access Toolbar so that it contains the commands you use most often. As you add commands to the Quick Access Toolbar, its commands may interfere with the document title on the title bar. For this reason, PowerPoint provides an option of displaying the Quick Access Toolbar below the Ribbon (Figure 1–12c).

Figure 1–12(c) Quick Access Toolbar below Ribbon

Each time you start PowerPoint, the Quick Access Toolbar appears the same way it did the last time you used PowerPoint. The chapters in this book, however, begin with the Quick Access Toolbar appearing as it did at the initial installation of the software. If you are stepping through this chapter on a computer and you want your Quick Access Toolbar to match the figures in this book, you should reset your Quick Access Toolbar. For more information about how to reset the Quick Access Toolbar, read Appendix C.

Office Button

While the Ribbon is a control center for creating documents, the **Office Button** is a central location for managing and sharing documents. When you click the Office Button, located in the upper-left corner of the window, PowerPoint displays the Office Button menu (Figure 1–13). A **menu** contains a list of commands.

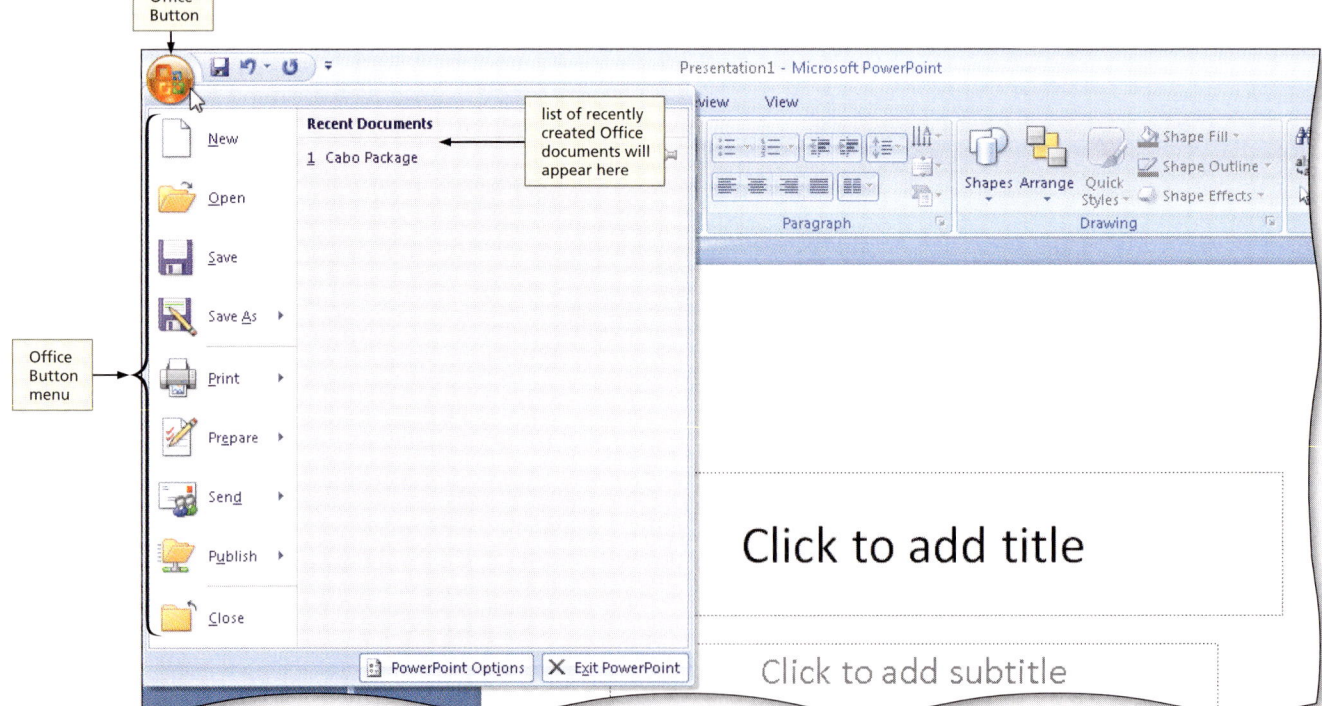

Figure 1–13

When you click the New, Open, Save As, and Print commands on the Office Button menu, PowerPoint displays a dialog box with additional options. The Save As, Print, Prepare, Send, and Publish commands have an arrow to their right. If you point to this arrow, PowerPoint displays a **submenu**, which is a list of additional commands associated with the selected command (Figure 1–14). For the Prepare, Send, and Publish commands that do not display a dialog box when clicked, you can point either to the command or the arrow to display the submenu.

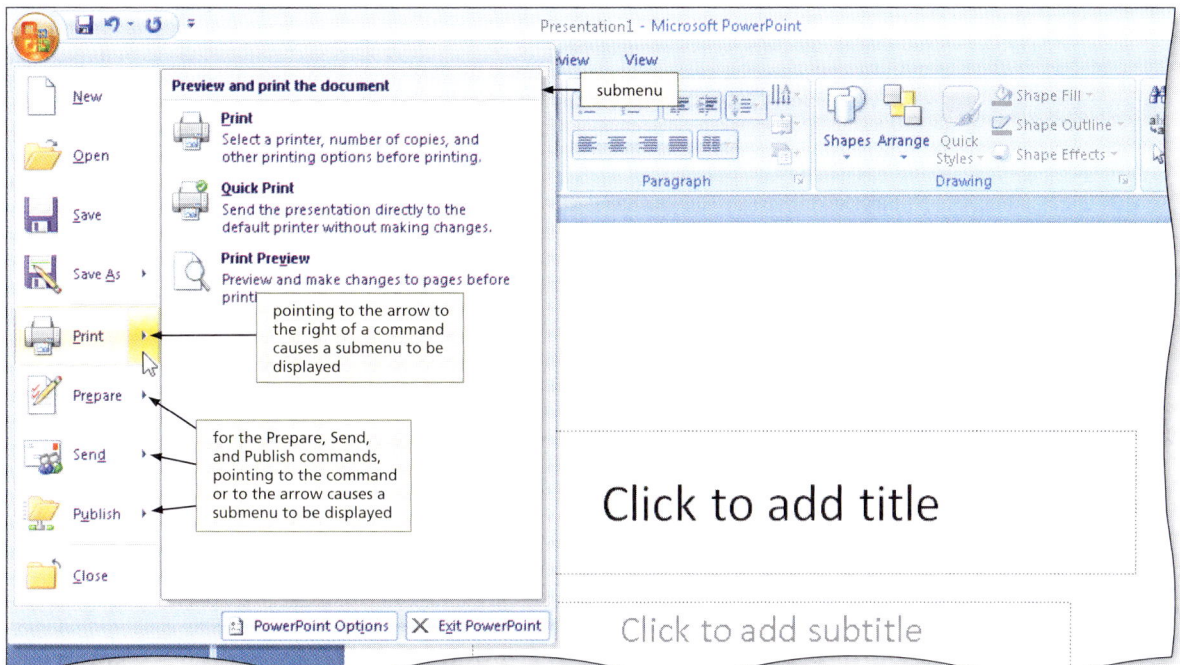

Figure 1–14

Key Tips

If you prefer using the keyboard instead of the mouse, you can press the ALT key on the keyboard to display a **Key Tip badge**, or keyboard code icon, for certain commands (Figure 1–15). To select a command using the keyboard, press its displayed code letter, or **Key Tip**. When you press a Key Tip, additional Key Tips related to the selected command may appear. For example, to select the New command on the Office Button menu, press the ALT key, then press the F key, then press the N key.

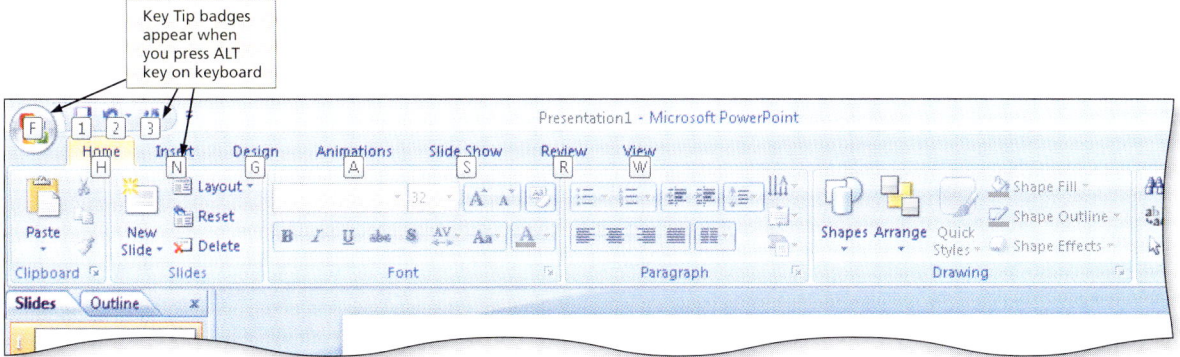

Figure 1–15

To remove the Key Tip badges from the screen, press the ALT key or the ESC key until all Key Tip badges disappear, or click the mouse anywhere in the PowerPoint window.

Choosing a Document Theme

You easily can give a presentation a professional and consistent appearance by using a document theme. This collection of formatting choices includes a set of colors (the color theme), a set of heading and content text fonts (the font theme), and a set of lines and fill effects (the effects theme). These themes allow you to choose and change the appearance of all the slides or individual slides in your presentation.

Plan Ahead

Find the appropriate theme.
In the initial steps of this project, you will select a document theme by locating a particular built-in theme in the Themes group. You could, however, apply a theme at any time while creating the presentation. Some PowerPoint slide show designers create presentations using the default Office Theme. This blank design allows them to concentrate on the words being used to convey the message and does not distract them with colors and various text attributes. Once the text is entered, the designers then select an appropriate document theme.

To Choose a Document Theme

The document theme identifier shows the theme currently used in the slide show. PowerPoint initially uses the **Office Theme** until you select a different theme. The following steps change the theme for this presentation from the Office Theme to the Flow document theme.

- Click Design on the Ribbon to display the Design tab (Figure 1–16).

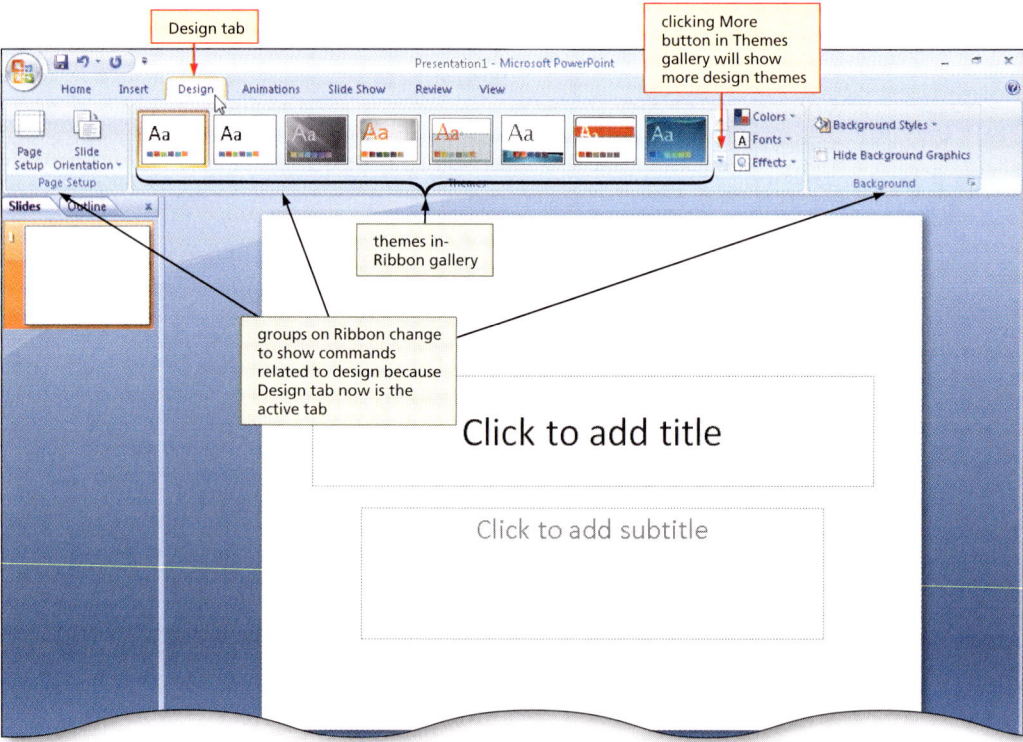

Figure 1–16

2

- Click the More button in the Themes gallery to expand the gallery, which shows more Built-In theme gallery options (Figure 1–17).

🔍 **Experiment**

- Point to various document themes in the Themes gallery and watch the colors and fonts change on the title slide.

Q&A Are the themes displayed in a specific order?

Yes. They are arranged in alphabetical order running from left to right. If you point to a theme, a ScreenTip with the design's name appears on the screen.

Q&A What if I change my mind and do not want to select a new theme?

Click anywhere outside the All Themes gallery to close the gallery.

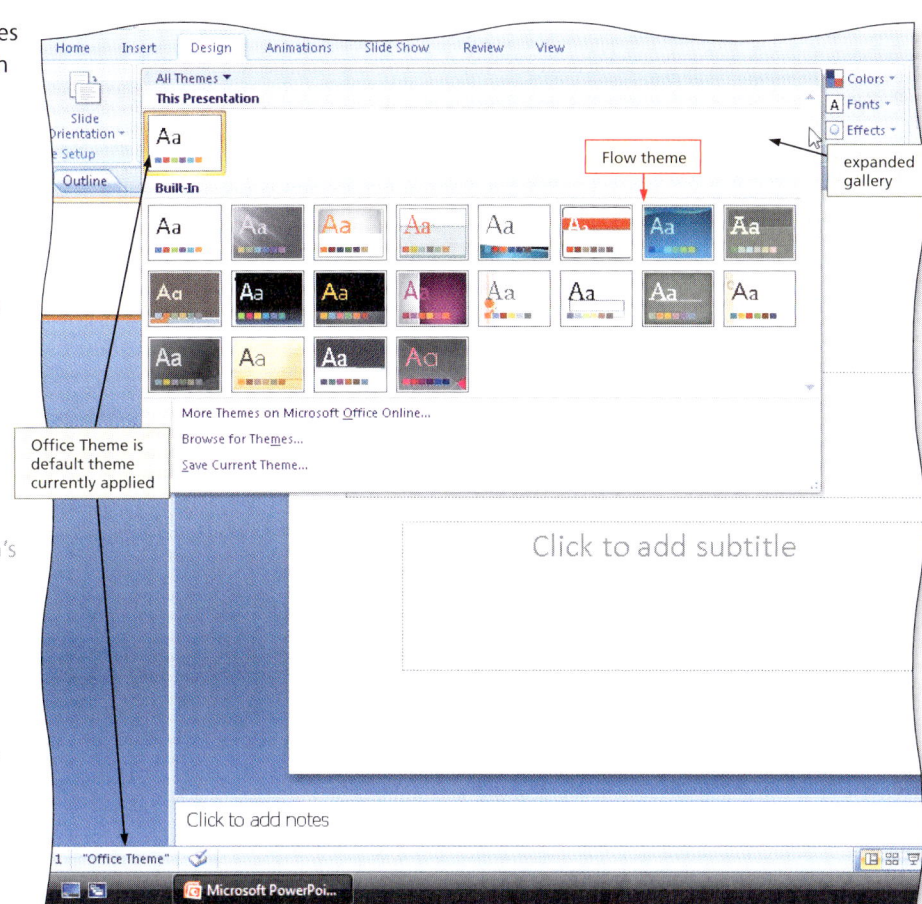

Figure 1–17

3

- Click the Flow theme to apply this theme to Slide 1 (Figure 1–18).

Q&A If I decide at some future time that this design does not fit the theme of my presentation, can I apply a different design?

Yes. You can repeat these steps at any time while creating your presentation.

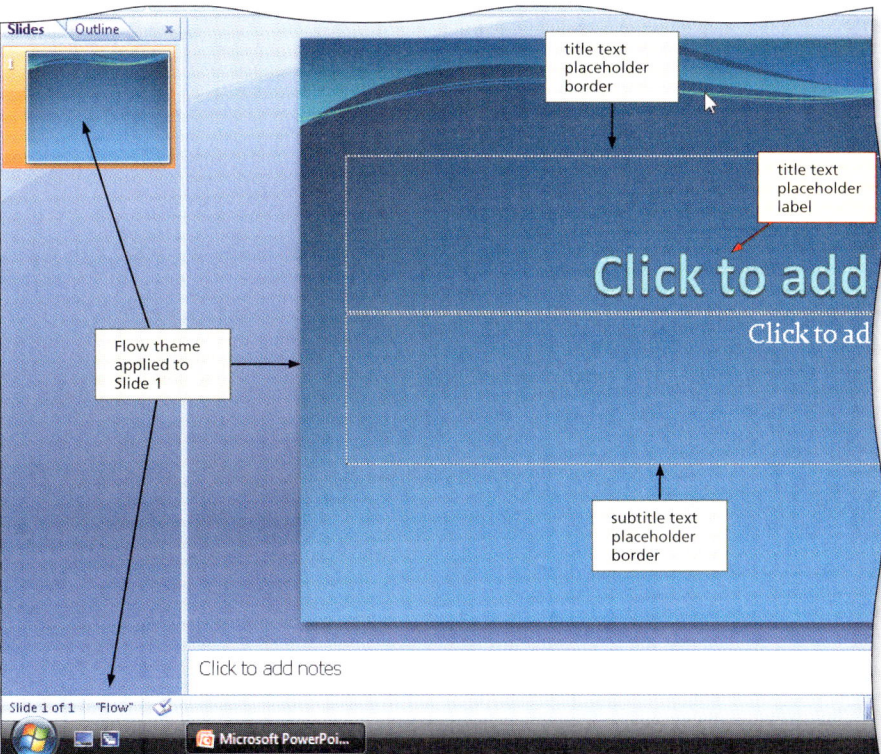

Figure 1–18

Creating a Title Slide

With the exception of a blank slide and a slide with a picture and caption, PowerPoint assumes every new slide has a title. Many of PowerPoint's layouts have both a title text placeholder and at least one content placeholder. To make creating a presentation easier, any text you type after a new slide appears becomes title text in the title text placeholder. The following steps create the title slide for this presentation.

Plan Ahead

Choose the words for the slide.
No doubt you have heard the phrase, "You get only one chance to make a first impression." The same philosophy holds true for a PowerPoint presentation. The title slide gives your audience an initial sense of what they are about to see and hear. It is, therefore, extremely important to choose the text for this slide carefully. Avoid stating the obvious in the title. Instead, create interest and curiosity using key ideas from the presentation.
Some PowerPoint users create the title slide as their last step in the design process so that it reflects the tone of the presentation. They begin by planning the final slide in the presentation so that they know where and how they want to end the slide show. All the slides in the presentation should work toward meeting this final slide.

To Enter the Presentation Title

As you begin typing text in the title text placeholder, the title text also is displayed in the Slide 1 thumbnail in the Slides tab. PowerPoint **line wraps** text that exceeds the width of the placeholder. The presentation title for Project 1 is A World Beneath the Waves. This title creates interest by introducing the concept of exploring the life under water. The following step creates the slide show's title.

- Click the label, Click to add title, located inside the title text placeholder to select the placeholder (Figure 1–19).

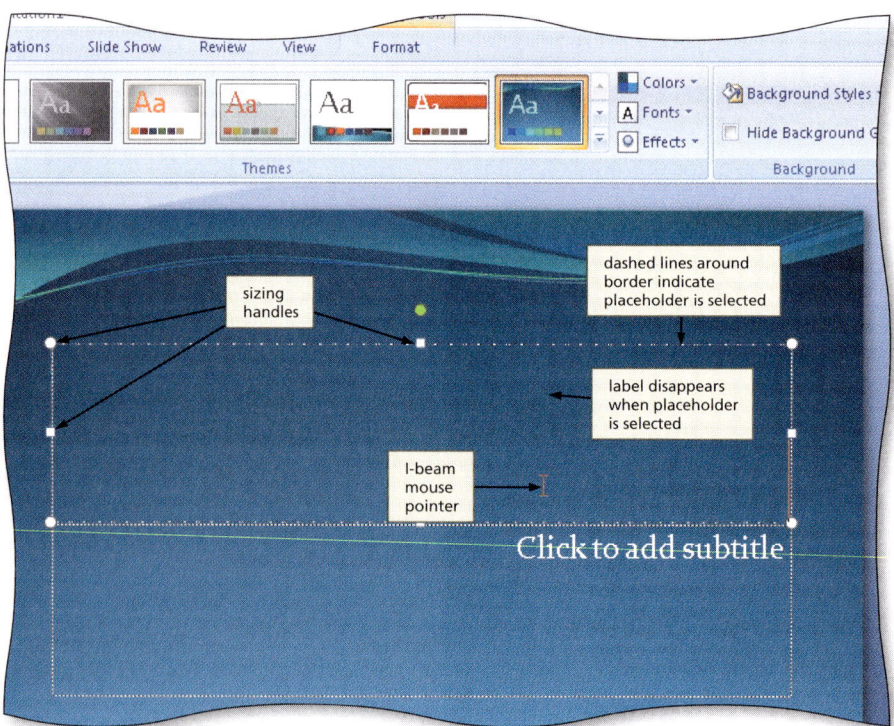

Figure 1–19

2
- Type A World Beneath the Waves in the title text placeholder. Do not press the ENTER key (Figure 1–20).

Q&A

What if a button with two lines and two arrows appears on the left side of the title text placeholder?

The **AutoFit** button displays because PowerPoint attempts to reduce the size of the letters when the title text does not fit on a single line. If you are creating a slide and need to squeeze an extra line in the text placeholder, you can click this button to resize the existing text in the placeholder so the spillover text will fit on the slide.

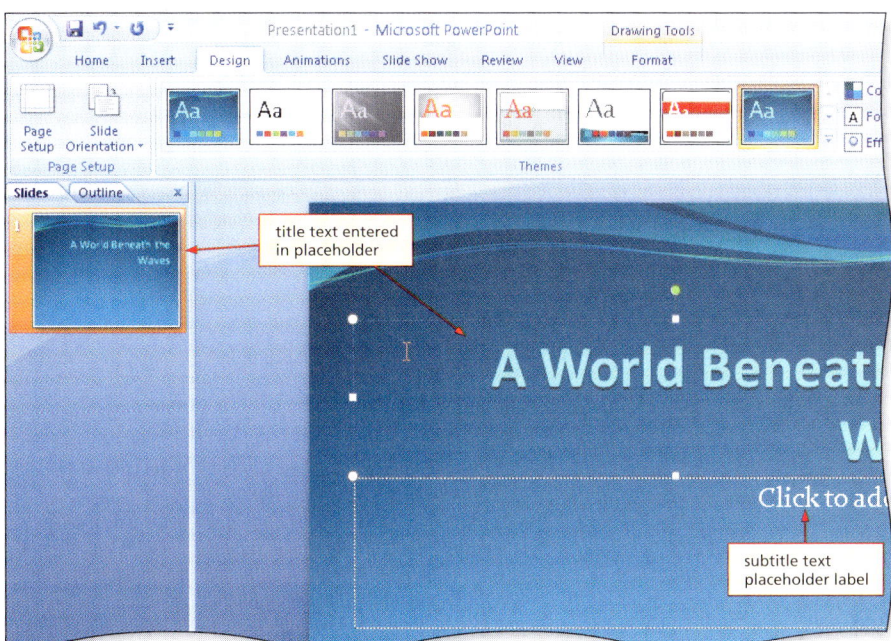

Figure 1–20

Correcting a Mistake When Typing

If you type the wrong letter, press the BACKSPACE key to erase all the characters back to and including the one that is incorrect. If you mistakenly press the ENTER key after typing the title and the insertion point is on the new line, simply press the BACKSPACE key to return the insertion point to the right of the letter s in the word Waves.

When you install PowerPoint, the default setting allows you to reverse up to the last 20 changes by clicking the Undo button on the Quick Access Toolbar. The ScreenTip that appears when you point to the Undo button changes to indicate the type of change just made. For example, if you type text in the title text placeholder and then point to the Undo button, the ScreenTip that appears is Undo Typing. For clarity, when referencing the Undo button in this project, the name displaying in the ScreenTip is referenced. You can reapply a change that you reversed with the Undo button by clicking the Redo button on the Quick Access Toolbar. Clicking the Redo button reverses the last undo action. The ScreenTip name reflects the type of reversal last performed.

Paragraphs

Subtitle text in the subtitle text placeholder supports the title text. It can appear on one or more lines in the placeholder. To create more than one subtitle line, you press the ENTER key after typing some words. PowerPoint creates a new line, which is the second paragraph in the placeholder. A **paragraph** is a segment of text with the same format that begins when you press the ENTER key and ends when you press the ENTER key again. This new paragraph is the same level as the previous paragraph. A **level** is a position within a structure, such as an outline, that indicates the magnitude of importance. PowerPoint allows for five paragraph levels.

To Enter the Presentation Subtitle Paragraph

The first subtitle paragraph links to the title by giving specific details about the vacation location, and the second paragraph gives information about the person who will be speaking to the audience. The following steps enter the presentation subtitle.

- Click the label, Click to add subtitle, located inside the subtitle text placeholder to select the placeholder (Figure 1–21).

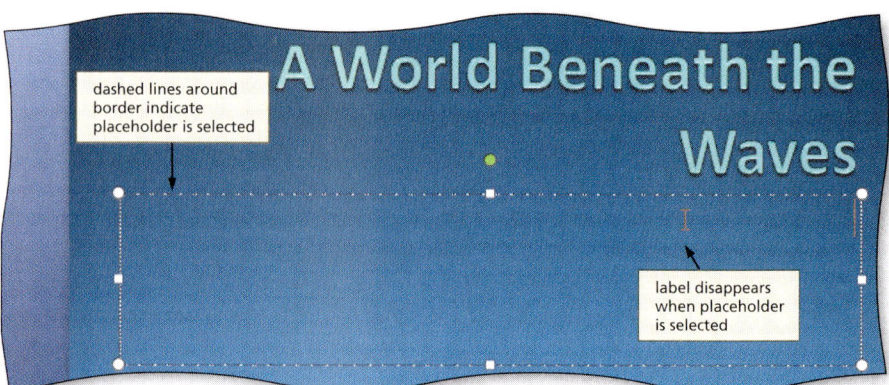

Figure 1–21

- Type `Spring Break in Cabo San Lucas, Mexico` and then press the ENTER key.
- Type `Presented by Dave Ehlin, SGA President` but do not press the ENTER key (Figure 1–22).

Q&A Why do red wavy lines appear below the words, Cabo and Ehlin?

The lines indicate possible spelling errors.

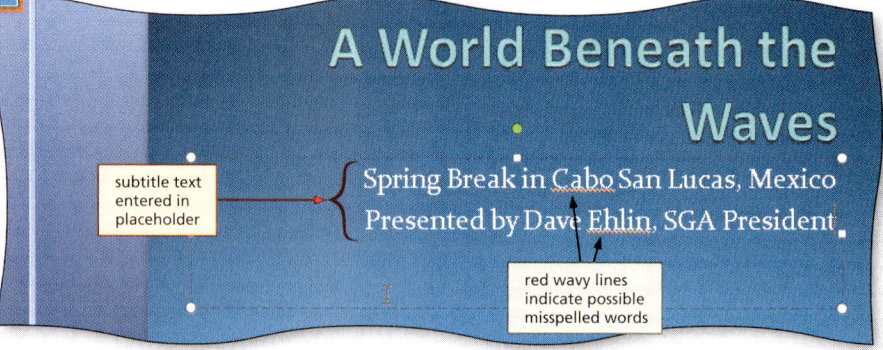

Figure 1–22

Plan Ahead

Identify how to format specific elements of the text.
Most of the time, you use the document theme's text attributes, color scheme, and layout. Occasionally, you may want to change the way a presentation looks, however, and still keep a particular document theme. PowerPoint gives you that flexibility.

Graphic designers use several rules when formatting text.

- Avoid all capital letters, if possible. Audiences have difficulty comprehending sentences typed in all capital letters, especially when the lines exceed seven words. All capital letters leaves no room for emphasis or inflection, so readers get confused about what material deserves particular attention. Some document themes, however, have a default title text style of all capital letters.

- Avoid text with a font size less than 24 point. Audience members generally will sit a maximum of 50 feet from a screen, and at this distance 24-point type is the smallest size text they can read comfortably without straining.

- Make careful color choices. Color evokes emotions, and a careless color choice may elicit the incorrect psychological response. PowerPoint provides a color palette with hundreds of colors. The built-in document themes use complementary colors that work well together. If you stray from these themes and add your own color choices, without a good reason to make the changes, your presentation is apt to become ineffective.

Formatting Characters in a Presentation

Recall that each document theme determines the color scheme, font and font size, and layout of a presentation. You can use a specific document theme and then change the characters' formats any time before, during, or after you type the text.

Fonts and Font Styles

Characters that appear on the screen are a specific shape and size. Examples of how you can modify the appearance, or **format**, of these typed characters on the screen and in print include changing the font, style, size, and color. The **font**, or typeface, defines the appearance and shape of the letters, numbers, punctuation marks, and symbols. **Style** indicates how the characters are formatted. PowerPoint's text font styles include regular, italic, bold, and bold italic. **Size** specifies the height of the characters and is gauged by a measurement system that uses points. A **point** is 1/72 of an inch in height. Thus, a character with a point size of 36 is 36/72 (or 1/2) of an inch in height. **Color** defines the hue of the characters.

This presentation uses the Flow document theme, which uses particular font styles and font sizes. The Flow document theme default title text font is named Calibri. It has a bold style with no special effects, and its size is 56 point. The Flow document theme default subtitle text font is Constantia with a font size of 26 point.

> **BTW**
>
> **Formatting Words**
> To format one word, position the insertion point anywhere in the word. Then make the formatting changes you desire. The entire word does not need to be selected for the change to occur.

To Select a Paragraph

You can use many techniques to format characters. When you want to apply the same formats to multiple words or paragraphs, it is efficient to select the desired text and then make the desired changes to all the characters simultaneously. The first formatting change you will make will apply to the second paragraph of the title slide subtitle. The following step selects this paragraph.

1

- Triple-click the paragraph, Presented by Dave Ehlin, SGA President, in the subtitle text placeholder to select the paragraph (Figure 1–23).

Q&A Can I select the paragraph using a technique other than triple-clicking?

Yes. You can move your mouse pointer to the left of the first paragraph and then drag it to the end of the line.

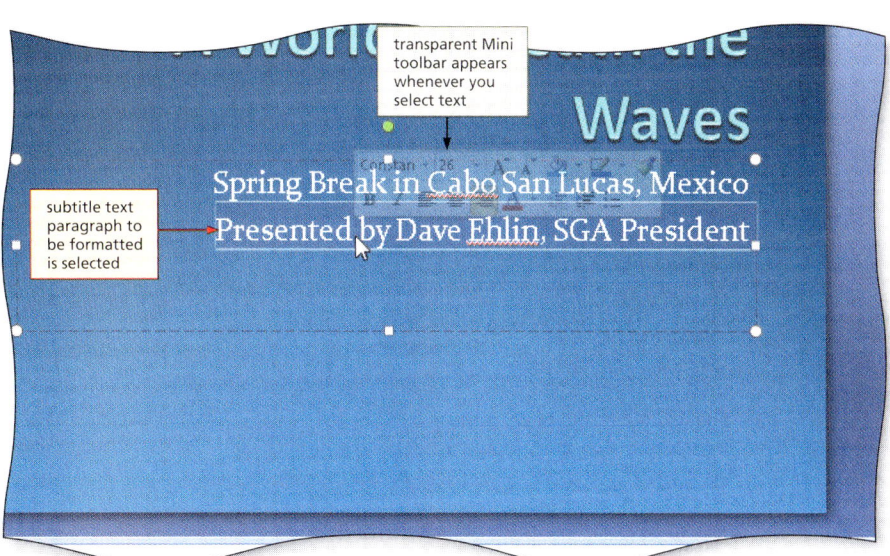

Figure 1–23

To Italicize Text

Different font styles often are used on slides to make them more appealing to the reader and to emphasize particular text. Italic type, used sparingly, draws the readers' eyes to these characters. The following step adds emphasis to the second line of the subtitle text by changing regular text to italic text.

- With the subtitle text still selected, click the Italic button on the Mini toolbar to italicize that text on the slide and on the slide thumbnail (Figure 1–24).

Q&A If I change my mind and decide not to italicize the text, how can I remove this style?

Select the italicized text and then click the Italic button. As a result, the Italic button will not be selected, and the text will not have the italic font style.

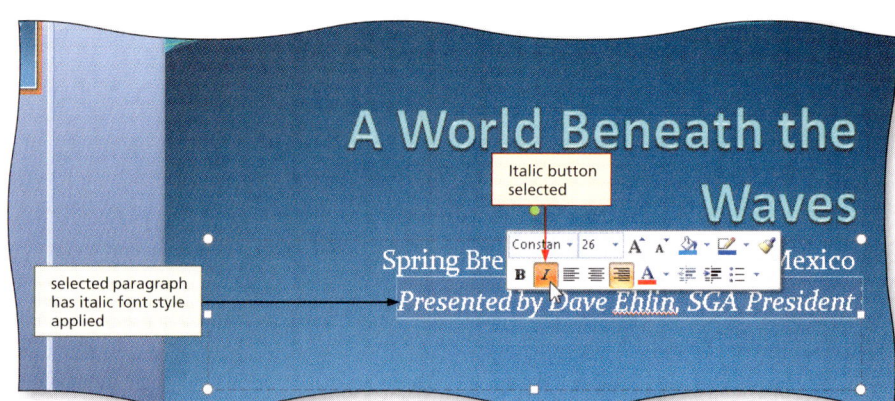

Figure 1–24

Other Ways

1. Right-click selected text, click Font on shortcut menu, click Italic in Font style list
2. Click Home tab, click Italic in Font group
3. Press CTRL+I

To Select Multiple Paragraphs

Each of the subtitle lines is a separate paragraph. As previously discussed, PowerPoint creates a new paragraph each time you press the ENTER key. To change the character formatting in both paragraphs, it is efficient to select the desired text and then make the desired changes to all the characters simultaneously.

The next formatting change you will make will apply to both title slide subtitle paragraphs. The following step selects the first paragraph so that you can format both paragraphs concurrently.

- With the second subtitle text paragraph selected, press the CTRL key and then triple-click the first subtitle text paragraph, Spring Break in Cabo San Lucas, Mexico, to select both paragraphs (Figure 1–25).

Q&A Can I use a different technique to select both subtitle text paragraphs?

Yes. Click the placeholder border so that it appears as a solid line. When the placeholder is selected in this manner, formatting changes will apply to all text in the placeholder.

Figure 1–25

> **Identify how to format specific elements of the text.**
> When selecting text colors, try to limit using red. At least 15 percent of men have difficulty distinguishing varying shades of green or red. They also often see the color purple as blue and the color brown as green. This problem is more pronounced when the colors appear in small areas, such as slide paragraphs or line chart bars.

Plan Ahead

To Change the Text Color

PowerPoint allows you to use one or more text colors in a presentation. To add more emphasis to the title slide subtitle text, you decide to change the color. The following steps add emphasis to both subtitle text paragraphs by changing the font color from white to dark blue.

1
- With both paragraphs selected, click the Font Color arrow on the Mini toolbar to display the palette of Theme Colors and Standard Colors (Figure 1–26).

Q&A If the Mini toolbar disappears from the screen, how can I display it once again?
Right-click the text, and the Mini toolbar should appear.

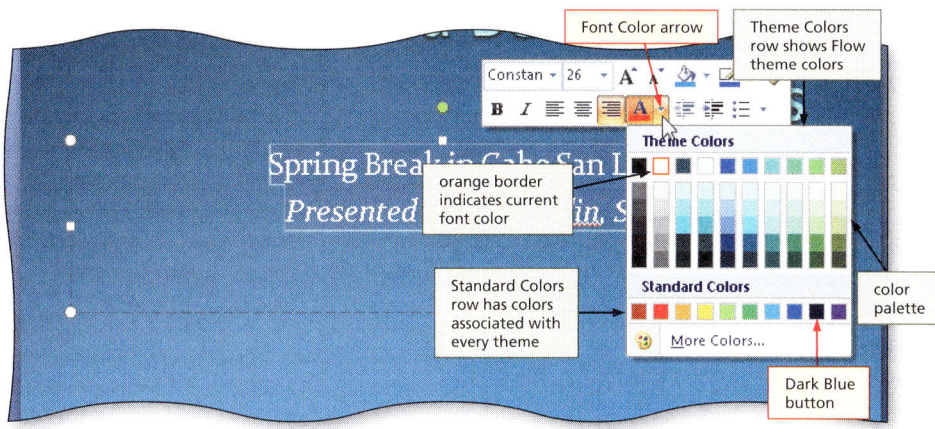

Figure 1–26

2
- Click the Dark Blue button in the Standard Colors row on the Mini toolbar (row 1, column 9) to change the font color to dark blue (Figure 1–27).

Q&A Why did I select the color, dark blue?
Dark blue is one of the 10 standard colors associated with every document theme, and it works well with the shades of blue already on the slide. An additional consideration is that dark colors print well.

Figure 1–27

3
- Click outside the selected area to deselect the two paragraphs.

Other Ways
1. Right-click selected text, click Font on shortcut menu, click Font color button, click Dark Blue in Standard Colors row
2. Click Home tab, click Font Color arrow in Font group, click Dark Blue in Standard Colors row

To Select a Group of Words

PowerPoint designers use many techniques to format characters. To apply the same formats to multiple words or paragraphs, they select the desired text and then make the desired changes to all the characters simultaneously.

To add emphasis to the vacation destination, you want to increase the font size and change the font style to bold for the words, Cabo San Lucas. You could perform these actions separately, but it is more efficient to select this group of words and then change the font attributes. The following steps select a group of words.

- Position the mouse pointer immediately to the left of the first character of the text to be selected (in this case, the C in Cabo) (Figure 1–28).

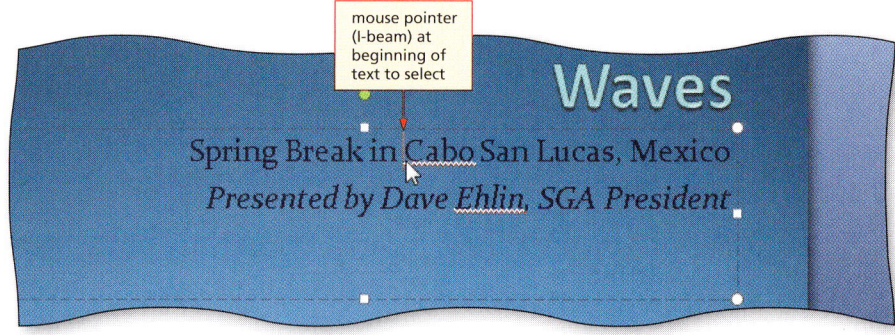

Figure 1–28

- Drag the mouse pointer through the last character of the text to be selected (in this case, the s in Lucas) (Figure 1–29).

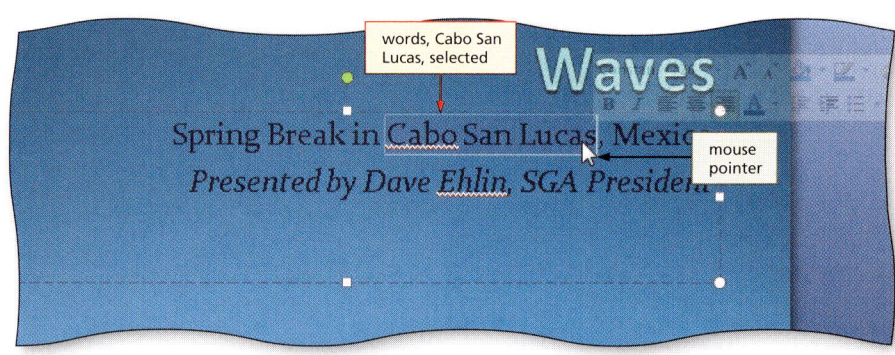

Figure 1–29

To Increase Font Size

To add emphasis, you increase the font size for Cabo San Lucas. The Increase Font Size button on the Mini toolbar increases the font size in preset increments. The following step uses this button to increase the font size.

- Click the Increase Font Size button on the Mini toolbar once to increase the font size of the selected text from 26 to 28 point (Figure 1–30).

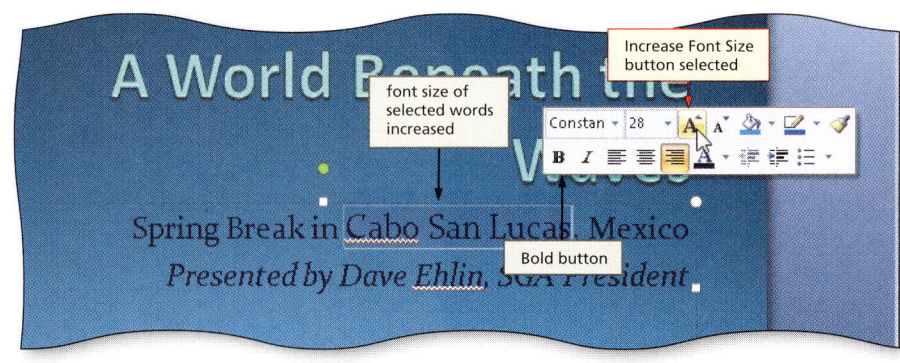

Figure 1–30

Other Ways

1. Click Home tab, click Increase Font Size button in Font group
2. Click Home tab, click Font Size box arrow, click new font size
3. Press CTRL+SHIFT+>

To Bold Text

Bold characters display somewhat thicker and darker than those that display in a regular font style. Clicking the Bold button on the Mini toolbar is an efficient method of bolding text. To add more emphasis to the vacation destination, you want to bold the words, Cabo San Lucas. The following step bolds this text.

- Click the Bold button on the Mini toolbar to bold the three selected words (Figure 1–31).

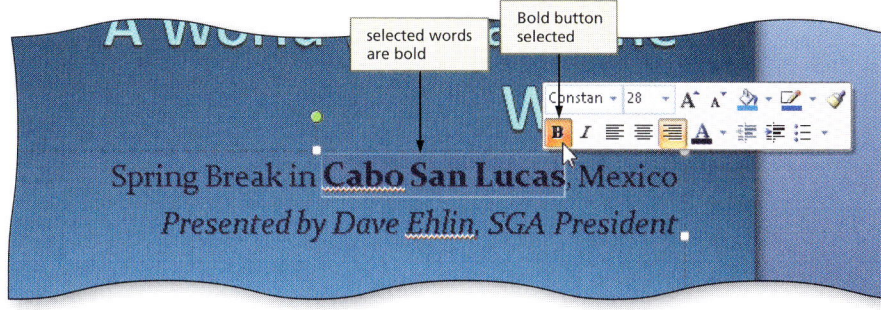

Figure 1–31

> **Other Ways**
> 1. Click Home tab, click Bold button in Font group
> 2. Press CTRL+B

Plan Ahead

Identify how to format specific elements of the text.
Avoid line wraps. Your audience's eyes want to stop at the end of a line. Thus, you must plan your words carefully or adjust the font size so that each point displays on only one line.

To Decrease the Title Slide Title Text Font Size

The last word of the title text, Waves, appears on a line by itself. For aesthetic reasons, it is advantageous to have this word appear with the rest of the title on a single line. One way to fit text on one line is to decrease the font size. The process is similar to increasing the font size. Clicking the Decrease Font Size button on the Mini toolbar decreases the size in preset increments. The following steps decrease the font size from 56 to 48 point.

- Select the title slide title text, A World Beneath the Waves (Figure 1–32).

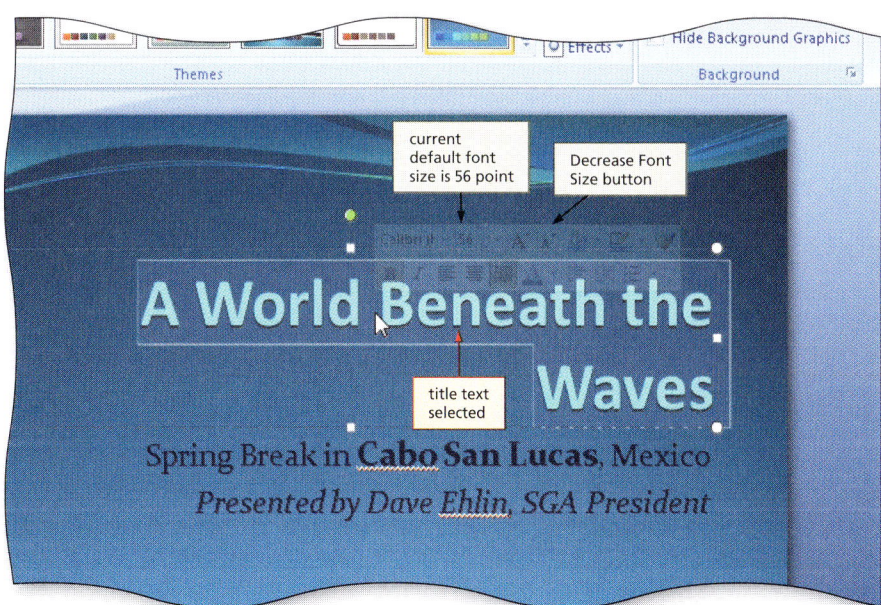

Figure 1–32

2
- Click the Decrease Font Size button on the Mini toolbar twice to decrease the font size from 56 to 48 point (Figure 1–33).

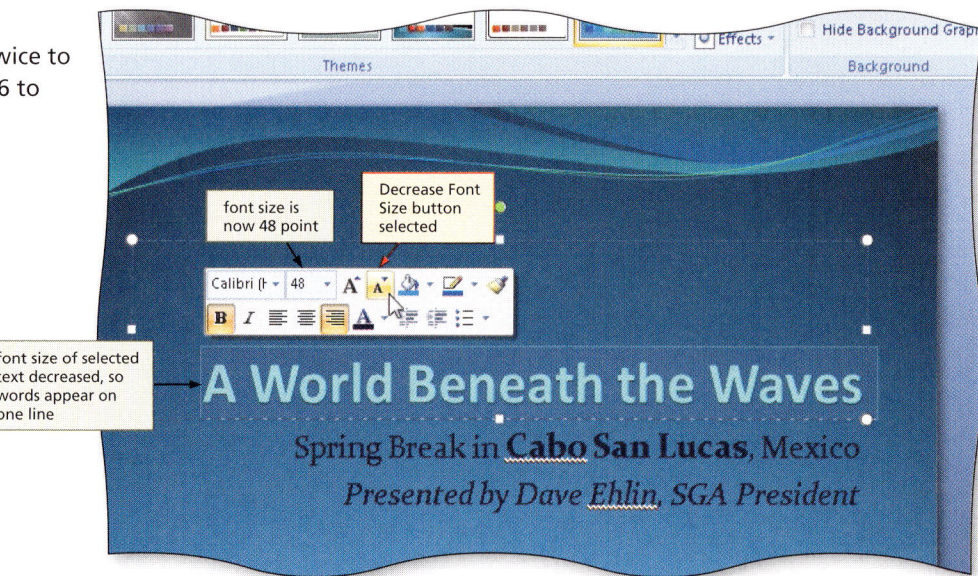

Figure 1–33

Other Ways
1. Click Home tab, click Decrease Font Size button in Font group
2. Click Home tab, click Font Size box arrow, click new font size
3. Press CTRL+SHIFT+<

Saving the Project

While you are building a presentation, the computer stores it in memory. When you save a presentation, the computer places it on a storage medium such as a USB flash drive, optical disc, or hard disk. A saved presentation is referred to as a **file**. A **file name** is the name assigned to a file when it is saved.

It is important to save the presentation frequently for the following reasons:

- The presentation in memory will be lost if the computer is turned off or you lose electrical power while PowerPoint is open.
- If you run out of time before completing your project, you may finish your presentation at a future time without starting over.

BTW

Saving in a Previous PowerPoint Format
To ensure that your presentation will open in an earlier version of PowerPoint, you must save your file in PowerPoint 97–2003 format. Files saved in this format have the .ppt extension.

Plan Ahead

Determine where to save the document.
When saving a document, you must decide which storage medium to use.

- If you always work on the same computer and have no need to transport your projects to a different location, then your computer's hard drive will suffice as a storage location. It is a good idea, however, to save a backup copy of your projects on a separate medium in case the file becomes corrupted or the computer's hard drive fails.
- If you plan to work on your projects in various locations or on multiple computers, then you should save your projects on a portable medium, such as a USB flash drive or an optical disc. The projects in this book use a USB flash drive, which saves files quickly and reliably and can be reused. Optical discs are easily portable and serve as good backups for the final versions of projects because they generally can save files only one time.

To Save a Presentation

You have performed many tasks and do not want to lose the work completed thus far. Thus, you should save the presentation. The following steps save a presentation on a USB flash drive using the file name, Cabo Package.

1
- With a USB flash drive connected to one of the computer's USB ports, click the Save button on the Quick Access Toolbar to display the Save As dialog box. (Figure 1–34).

- If the Navigation pane is not displayed in the Save As dialog box, click the Browse Folders button to expand the dialog box.

- If a Folders list is displayed below the Folders button, click the Folders button to remove the Folders list.

Q&A Do I have to save to a USB flash drive?

No. You can save to any device or folder. A **folder** is a specific location on a storage medium. You can save to the default folder or a different folder. You also can create your own folders.

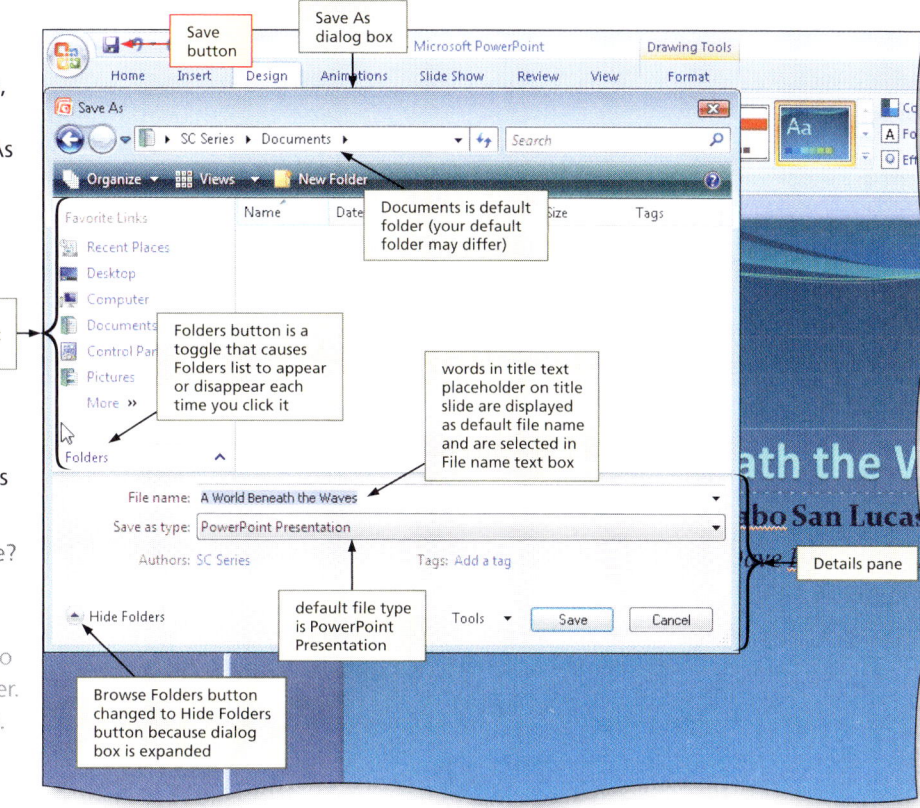

Figure 1–34

2
- Type `Cabo Package` in the File name box to change the file name. Do not press the ENTER key after typing the file name (Figure 1–35).

Q&A What characters can I use in a file name?

A file name can have a maximum of 260 characters, including spaces. The only invalid characters are the backslash (\), slash (/), colon (:), asterisk (*), question mark (?), quotation mark ("), less than symbol (<), greater than symbol (>), and vertical bar (|).

Q&A What are file properties and tags?

File properties contain information about a file such as the file name, author name, date the file was modified, and tags. A tag is a file property that contains a word or phrase about a file. You can organize and locate files based on their file properties.

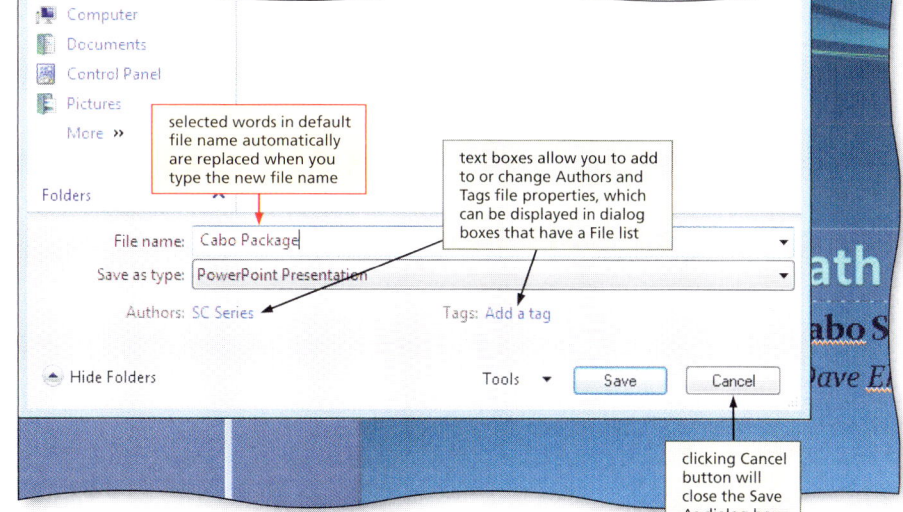

Figure 1–35

- If Computer is not displayed in the Favorite Links section, drag the top or bottom edge of the Save As dialog box until Computer is displayed.
- Click Computer in the Favorite Links section to display a list of available drives (Figure 1–36).
- If necessary, scroll until UDISK 2.0 (E:) appears in the list of available drives.

Q&A Why is my list of drives arranged and named differently?

The size of the Save As dialog box and your computer's configuration determine how the list is displayed and how the drives are named.

Q&A How do I save the file if I am not using a USB flash drive?

Use the same process, but select your desired save location in the Favorite Links section.

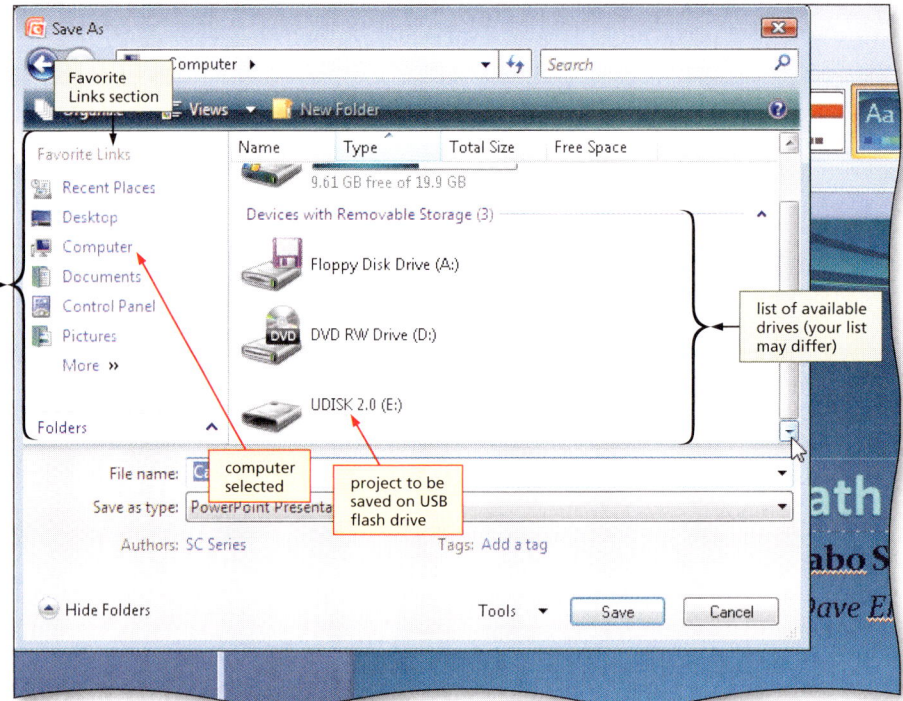

Figure 1–36

- Double-click UDISK 2.0 (E:) in the Computer list to select the USB flash drive, Drive E in this case, as the new save location (Figure 1–37).

Q&A What if my USB flash drive has a different name or letter?

It is very likely that your USB flash drive will have a different name and drive letter and be connected to a different port. Verify the device in your Computer list is correct.

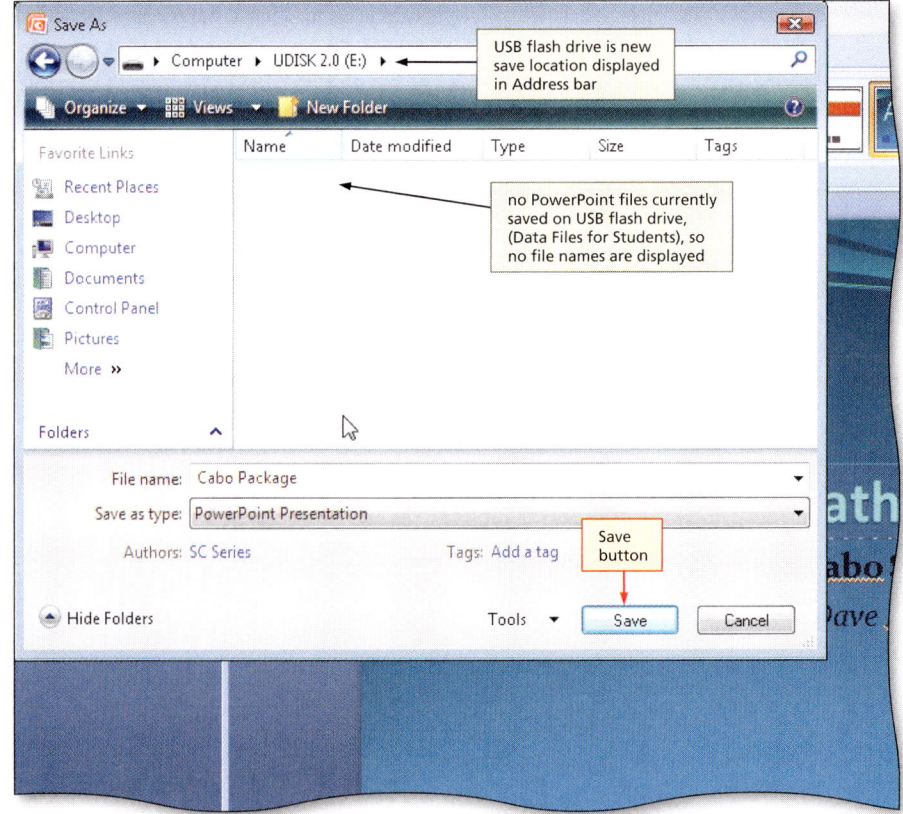

Figure 1–37

5

- Click the Save button in the Save As dialog box to save the presentation on the USB flash drive with the file name, Cabo Package (Figure 1–38).

Q&A How do I know that the project is saved?

While PowerPoint is saving your file, it briefly displays a message on the status bar indicating the amount of the file saved. In addition, your USB drive may have a light that flashes during the save process.

Q&A Why is .pptx displayed immediately to the right of the file name?

Depending on your Windows Vista settings, .pptx may be displayed after you save the file. The file type .pptx is a PowerPoint 2007 document. Previous versions of PowerPoint had a file type of .ppt.

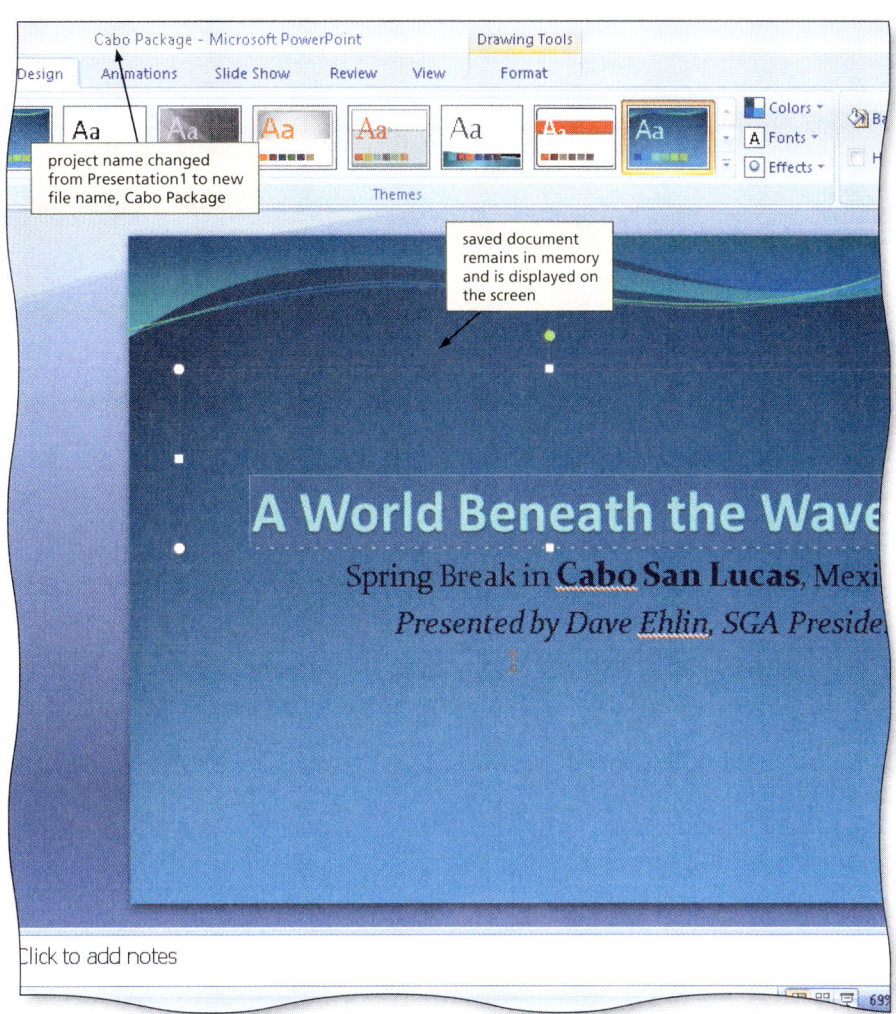

Figure 1–38

Other Ways

1. Click Office Button, click Save, type file name, click Computer, select drive or folder, click Save button
2. Press CTRL+S or press SHIFT+F12, type file name, click Computer, select drive or folder, click Save button

Adding a New Slide to a Presentation

With the title slide for the presentation created, the next step is to add the first text slide immediately after the title slide. Usually, when you create a presentation, you add slides with text, graphics, or charts. Some placeholders allow you to double-click the placeholder and then access other objects, such as media clips, charts, diagrams, and organization charts. You can change the layout for a slide at any time during the creation of a presentation.

To Add a New Text Slide with a Bulleted List

When you add a new slide, PowerPoint uses the Title and Content slide layout. This layout provides a title placeholder and a content area for text, art, charts, and other graphics. A vertical scroll bar appears in the Slide pane when you add the second slide so that you can move from slide to slide easily. A thumbnail of this slide also appears in the Slides tab. The following steps add a new slide with the Title and Content slide layout.

1
- Click Home on the Ribbon to display the Home tab (Figure 1–39).

Figure 1–39

2
- Click the New Slide button in the Slides group to insert a new slide with the Title and Content layout (Figure 1–40).

Q&A Why does the bullet character display a blue dot?

The Flow document theme determines the bullet characters. Each paragraph level has an associated bullet character.

Q&A I clicked the New Slide arrow instead of the New Slide button. What should I do?

Click the Title and Content slide thumbnail in the layout gallery.

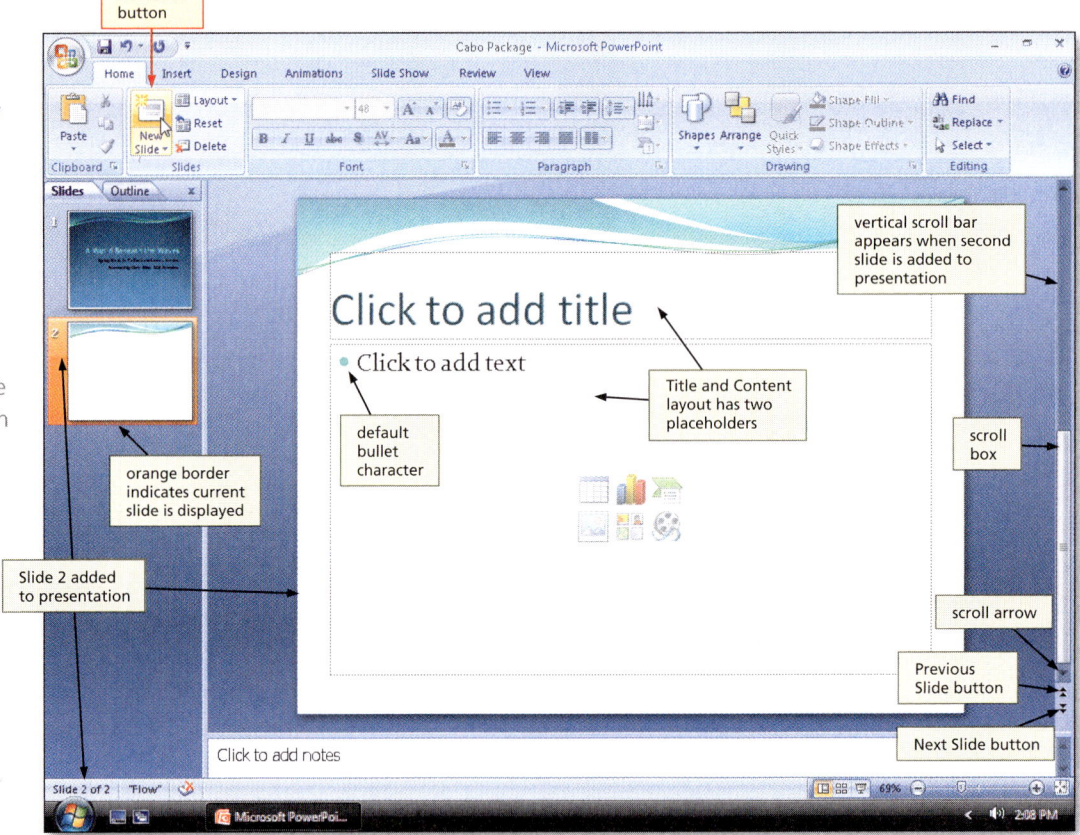

Figure 1–40

Other Ways
1. Press CTRL+M

> **Choose the words for the slide.**
> All presentations should follow the 7 × 7 rule which states that each slide should have a maximum of seven lines, and each line should have a maximum of seven words. PowerPoint designers must choose their words carefully and, in turn, help viewers read the slides easily.

Plan Ahead

Creating a Text Slide with a Single-Level Bulleted List

The information in the Slide 2 text placeholder is presented in a bulleted list. All the bullets appear at the same paragraph level, called the first level.

To Enter a Slide Title

PowerPoint assumes every new slide has a title. The title for Slide 2 is Package Highlights. The following step enters this title.

1

- Click the label, Click to add title, to select it and then type `Package Highlights` in the placeholder. Do not press the ENTER key (Figure 1–41).

Q&A What are those six icons grouped in the middle of the slide?

You can click one of the icons to insert a specific type of content: table, chart, SmartArt graphic, picture, clip art, or media clip.

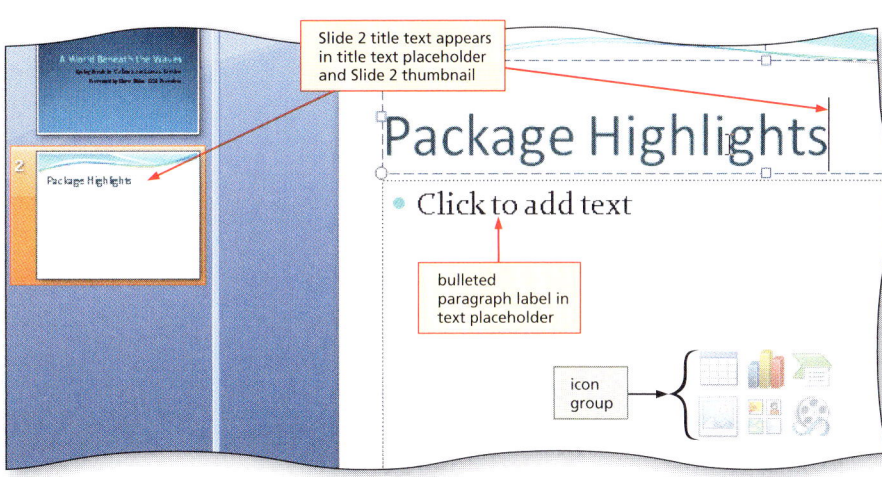

Figure 1–41

To Select a Text Placeholder

Before you can type text into the text placeholder, you first must select it. The following step selects the text placeholder on Slide 2.

1

- Click the label, Click to add text, to select the text placeholder (Figure 1–42).

Q&A Why does my mouse pointer have a different shape?

If you move the mouse pointer away from the bullet, it will change shape.

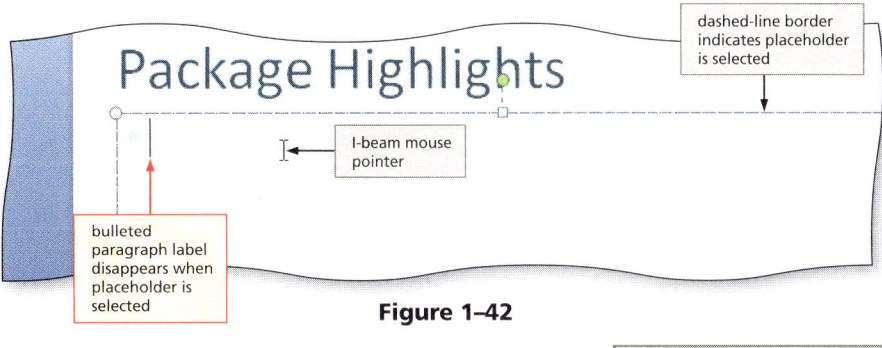

Figure 1–42

Other Ways
1. Press CTRL+ENTER

To Type a Single-Level Bulleted List

The content placeholder provides an area for the text characters. When you click inside a placeholder, you then can type or paste text. If your text exceeds the size of the placeholder, PowerPoint will attempt to make the text fit by reducing the text size and line spacing. **Line spacing** is the amount of vertical space between the lines of text.

As discussed previously, a bulleted list is a list of paragraphs, each of which is preceded by a bullet. A paragraph is a segment of text ended by pressing the ENTER key. The next step is to type the single-level bulleted list, which consists of five paragraphs (Figure 1–1b on page PPT 3). The following steps create a single-level bulleted list.

- Type `Four nights at the Azure Seas Resort` and then press the ENTER key to begin a new bulleted first-level paragraph (Figure 1–43).

Q&A Can I delete bullets on a slide?

Yes. If you do not want bullets to display on a particular paragraph, click the Bullets button in the Paragraph group on the Home tab or right-click the paragraph and then click the Bullets button on the Mini toolbar.

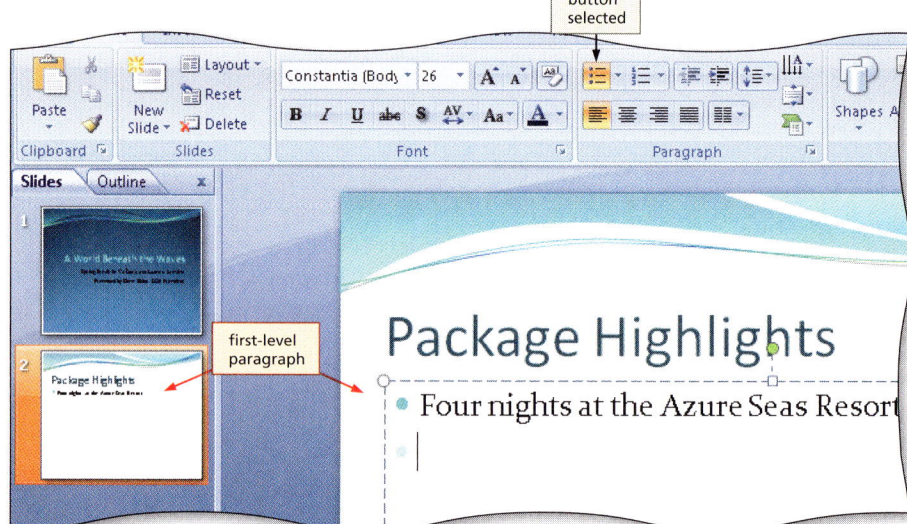

Figure 1–43

- Type `Breakfast buffet, lunch, dinner, and snacks` and then press the ENTER key.
- Type `Two large swimming pools` and then press the ENTER key.
- Type `Round-trip airfare and hotel transfers` and then press the ENTER key.
- Type `Daily activities, including water sports` but do not press the ENTER key (Figure 1–44).

Q&A I pressed the ENTER key in error, and now a new bullet appears after the last entry on this slide. How can I remove this extra bullet?

Press the BACKSPACE key.

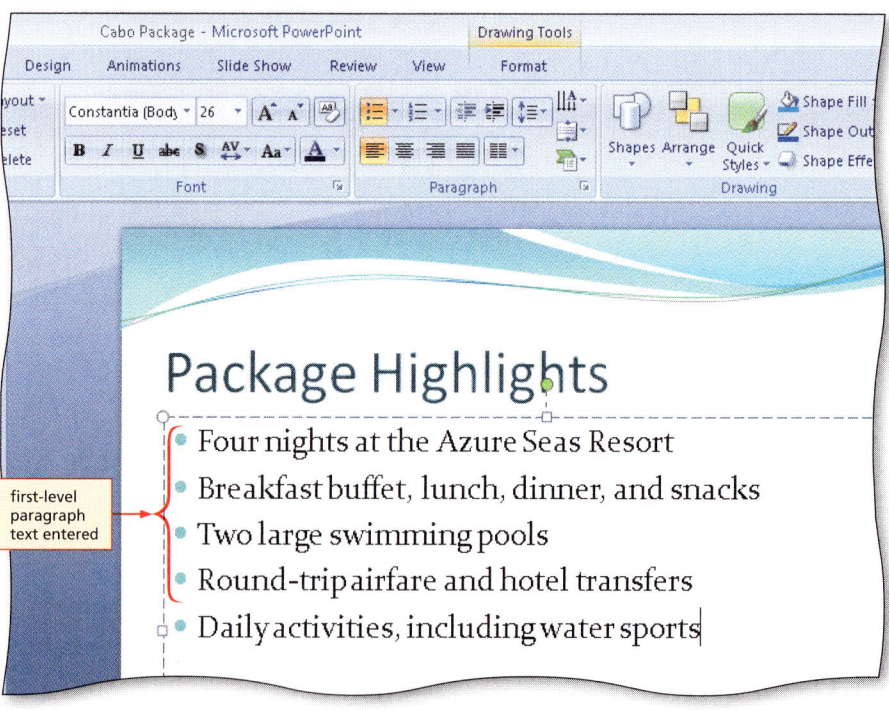

Figure 1–44

Creating a Text Slide with a Multi-Level Bulleted List

Slides 3 and 4 in Figure 1–1 on pages PPT 3–4 contain more than one level of bulleted text. A slide that consists of more than one level of bulleted text is called a **multi-level bulleted list slide**. Beginning with the second level, each paragraph indents to the right of the preceding level and is pushed down to a lower level. For example, if you increase the indent of a first-level paragraph, it becomes a second-level paragraph.

Creating a text slide with a multi-level bulleted list requires several steps. Initially, you enter a slide title in the title text placeholder. Next, you select the content text placeholder. Then, you type the text for the multi-level bulleted list, increasing and decreasing the indents as needed. The next several sections add a slide with a multi-level bulleted list.

To Add a New Slide and Enter a Slide Title

When you add a new slide to a presentation, PowerPoint keeps the same layout used on the previous slide. PowerPoint assumes every new slide has a title. The title for Slide 3 is Rates and Booking. The following steps add a new slide (Slide 3) and enter a title.

1
- Click the New Slide button in the Slides group on the Home tab to insert a new slide with the Title and Content layout (Figure 1–45).

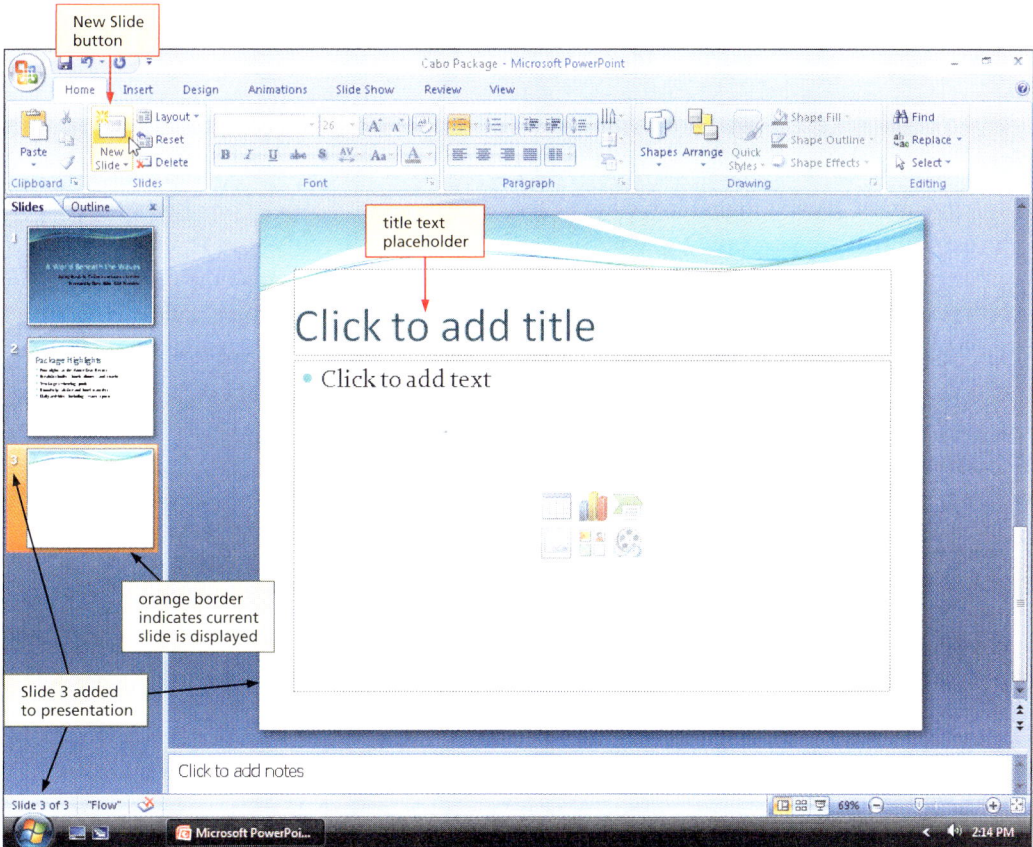

Figure 1–45

- Click the title text placeholder and then type `Rates and Booking` in this placeholder. Do not press the ENTER key (Figure 1–46).

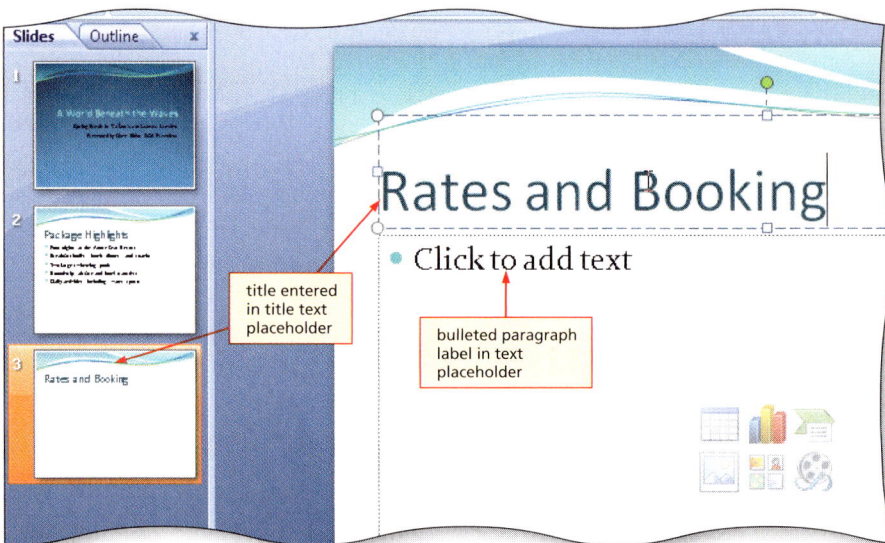

Figure 1–46

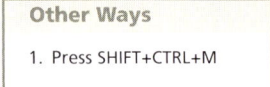

Other Ways
1. Press SHIFT+CTRL+M

To Type a Multi-Level Bulleted List

In a multi-level bulleted list, a lower-level paragraph is a subset of a higher-level paragraph. It usually contains information that supports the topic in the paragraph immediately above it.

The next step is to select the content text placeholder and then type the multi-level bulleted list, which consists of six entries (Figure 1–1c on page PPT 3). Creating a lower-level paragraph is called **demoting** text; creating a higher-level paragraph is called **promoting** text. The following steps create a list consisting of three levels.

- Click the bulleted paragraph text placeholder.
- Type `Only $495 double occupancy` and then press the ENTER key (Figure 1–47).

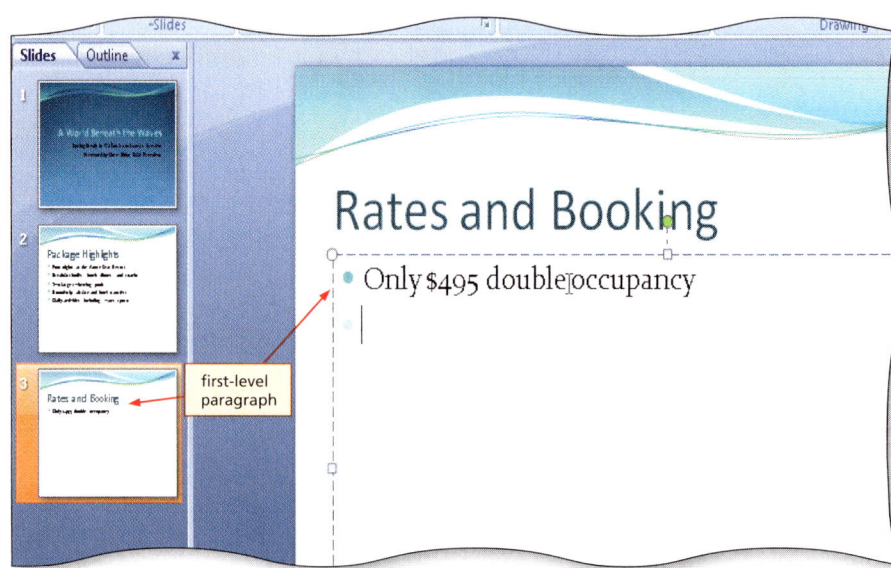

Figure 1–47

②
- Click the Increase List Level button in the Paragraph group to indent the second paragraph below the first and create a second-level paragraph (Figure 1–48).

Q&A Why does the bullet for this paragraph have a different size and color?

A different bullet is assigned to each paragraph level.

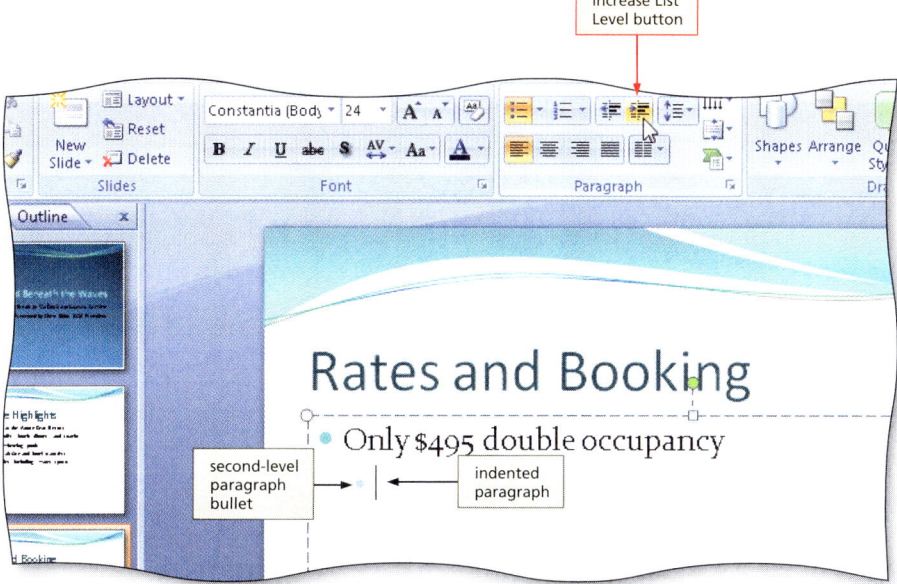

Figure 1–48

③
- Type `Non-diver rate: $275` and then press the ENTER key to add a new paragraph at the same level as the previous paragraph.
- Type `Single occupancy: add $150` and then press the ENTER key (Figure 1–49).

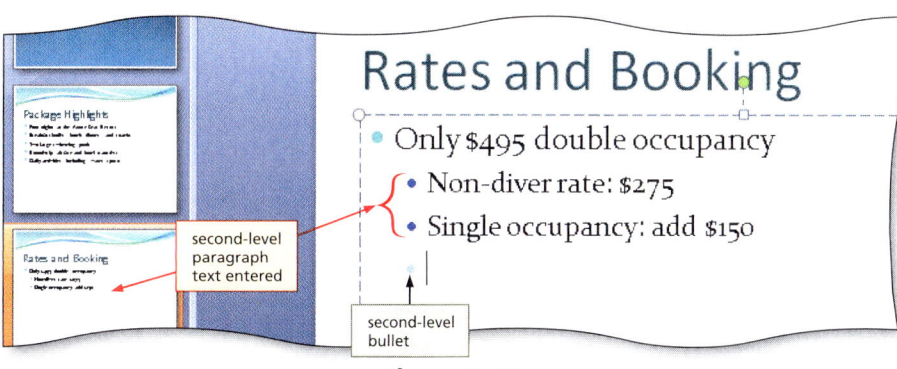

Figure 1–49

④
- Click the Decrease List Level button in the Paragraph group so that the second-level paragraph becomes a first-level paragraph (Figure 1–50).

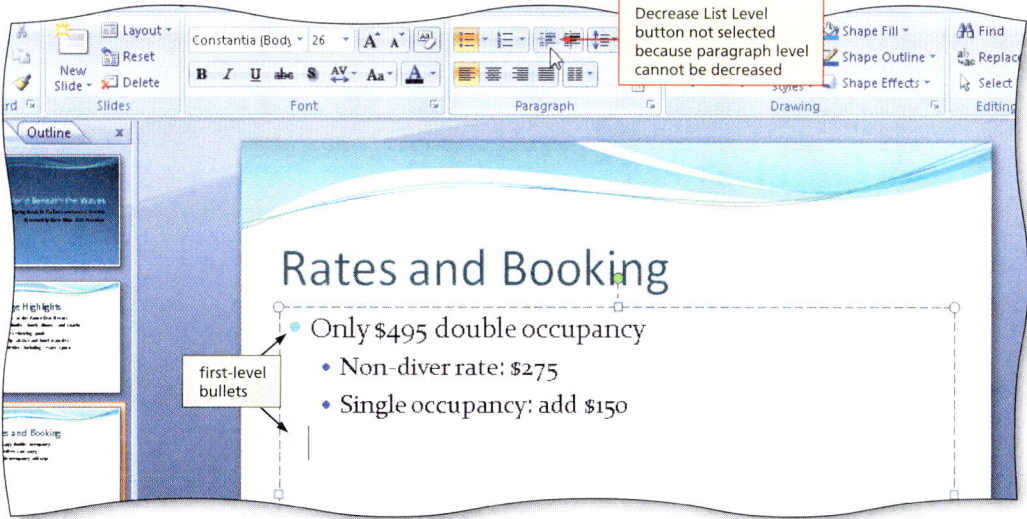

Figure 1–50

Other Ways

1. Press TAB to promote paragraph; press SHIFT+TAB to demote paragraph

To Type the Remaining Text for Slide 3

The following steps complete the text for Slide 3.

1. Type `Nonrefundable $150 deposit required` and then press the ENTER key.

2. Click the Increase List Level button in the Paragraph group to demote the paragraph.

3. Type `Due by October 1` and then press the ENTER key.

4. Click the Decrease List Level button in the Paragraph group to promote the paragraph.

5. Type `Travel insurance highly recommended` but do not press the ENTER key (Figure 1–51).

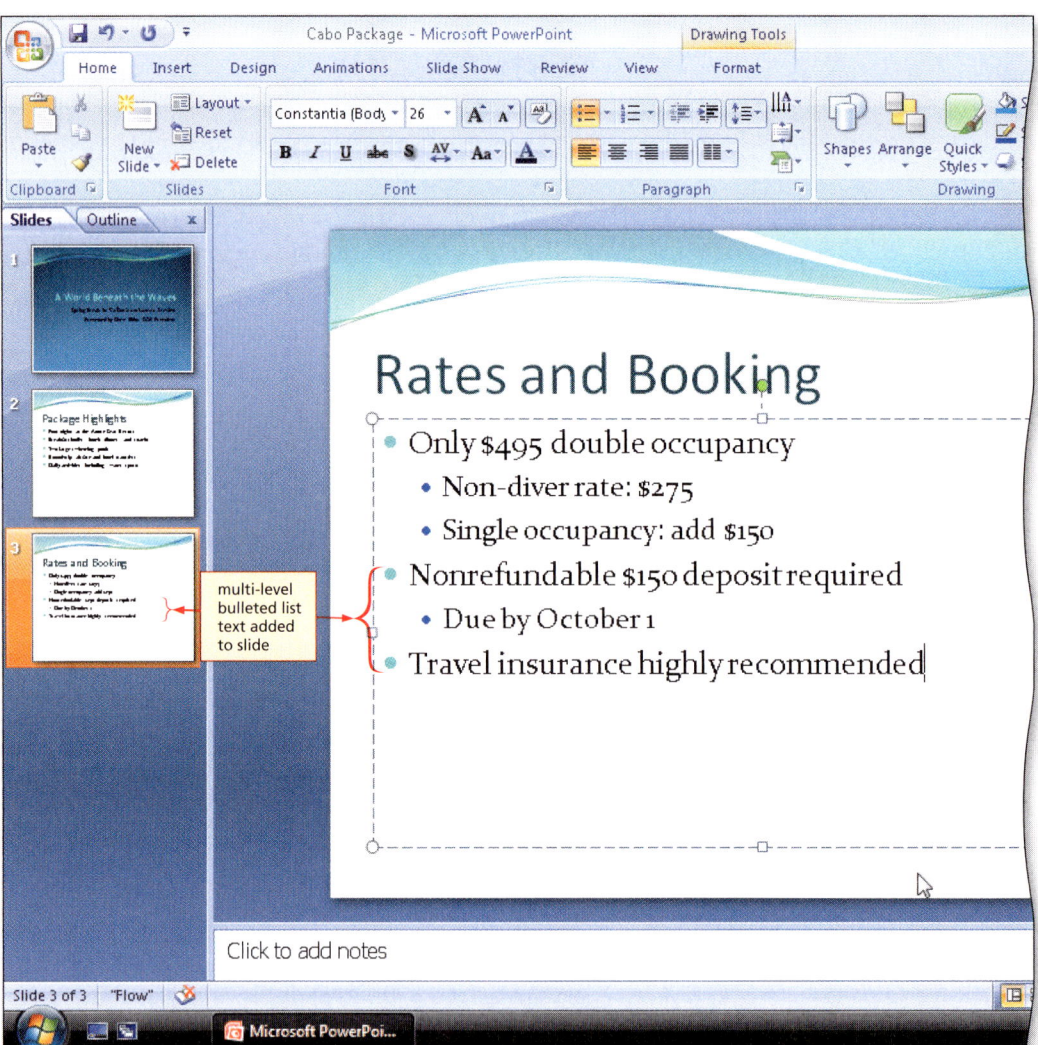

Figure 1–51

To Create Slide 4

Slide 4 is the final multi-level bulleted text slide in this presentation. It has three levels. The following steps create Slide 4.

1. Click the New Slide button in the Slides group.

2. Type Snorkeling and Diving in the title text placeholder.

3. Press CTRL+ENTER to move the insertion point to the text placeholder.

4. Type Three days of two-tank boat dives and then press the ENTER key.

5. Click the Increase List Level button. Type Weights and tanks included and then press the ENTER key (Figure 1–52).

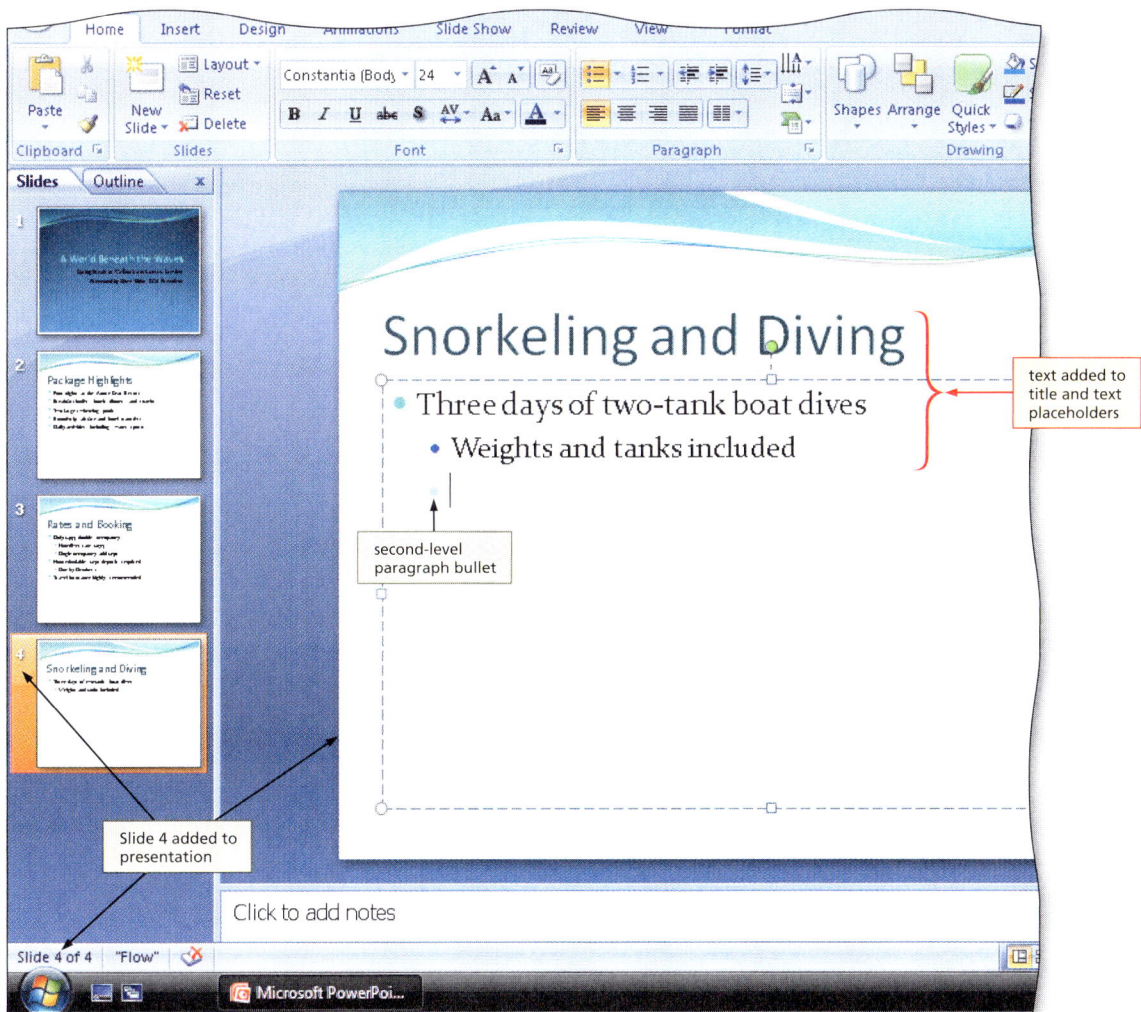

Figure 1–52

To Create a Third-Level Paragraph

Slide 4 contains detailed information about the particular dives. Each additional paragraph becomes more specific and supports the information in the paragraph above it.

The next line in Slide 4 is indented an additional level, to the third level. The following steps demote the text to a third-level paragraph.

1

- Click the Increase List Level button so that the second-level paragraph becomes a third-level paragraph (Figure 1–53).

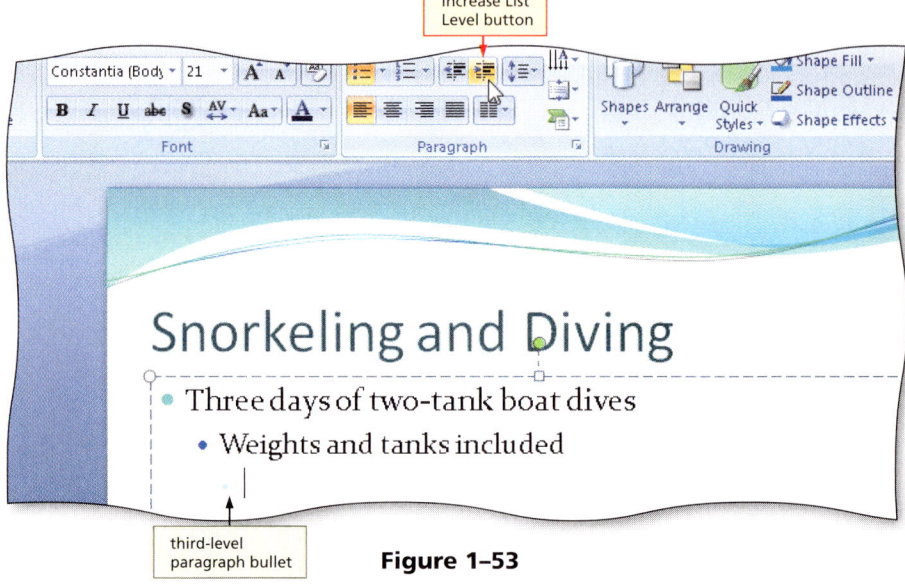

Figure 1–53

2

- Type `Instructors available for beginners` and then press the ENTER key to create a second third-level paragraph (Figure 1–54).

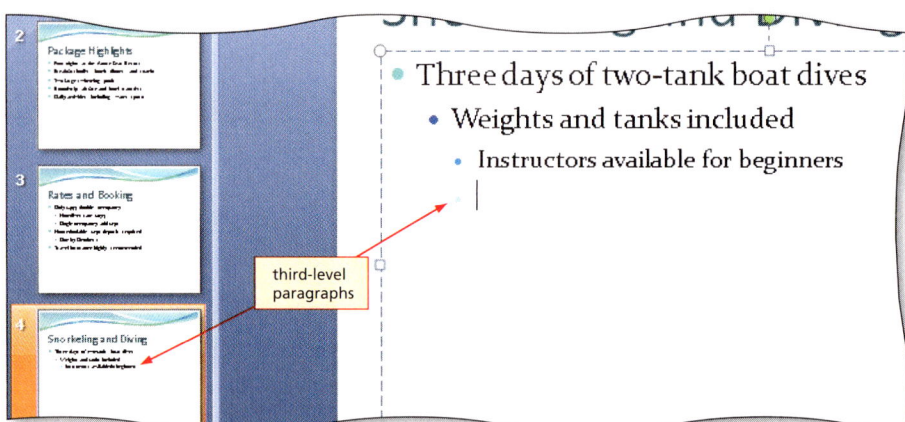

Figure 1–54

3

- Click the Decrease List Level button two times so that the insertion point appears at the first level (Figure 1–55).

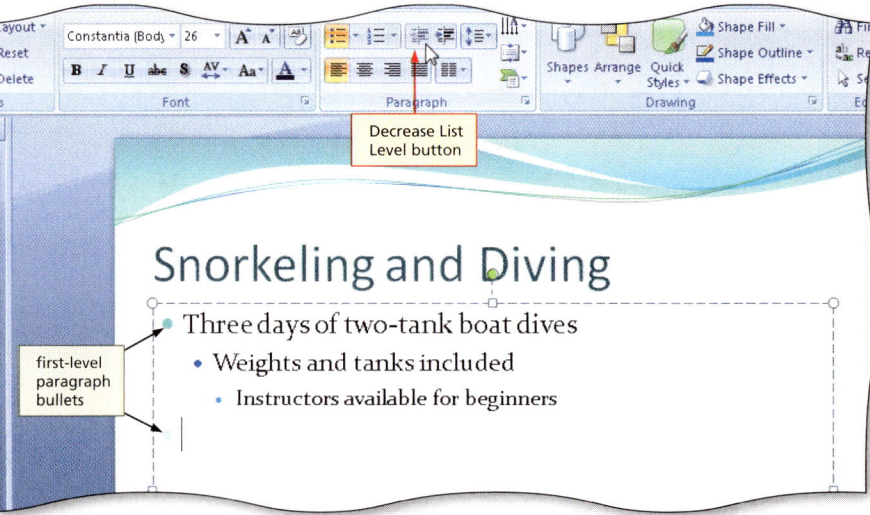

Figure 1–55

To Type the Remaining Text for Slide 4

The next three paragraphs concern what divers and snorkelers will view. The following steps type the remaining text for Slide 4.

1 Type `Various locations based on diving skills` and then press the ENTER key.

2 Press the TAB key to increase the indent to the second level.

3 Type `Spectacular underwater wildlife and landscapes` and then press the ENTER key.

4 Press the TAB key to increase the indent to the third level.

5 Type `See squids, sea turtles, snakes, barracudas, and stingrays` but do not press the ENTER key (Figure 1–56).

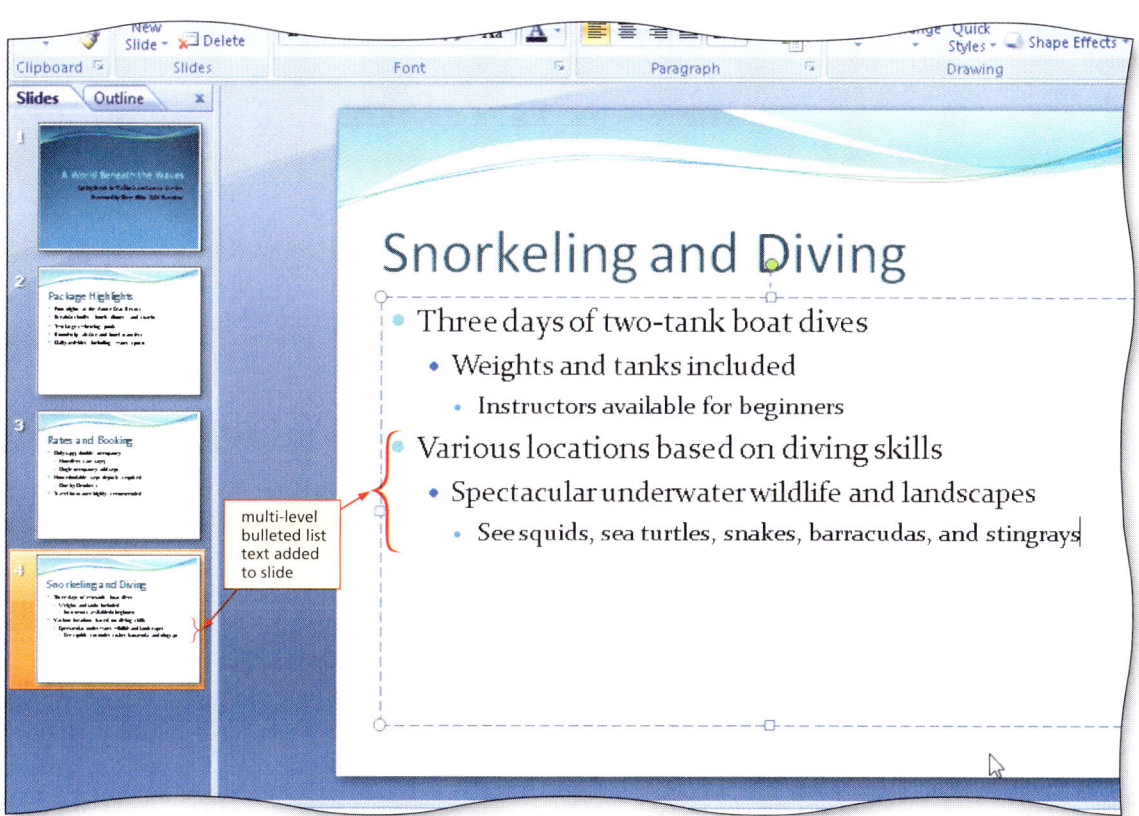

Figure 1–56

Plan Ahead

Choose the words for the slide.
After the last bulleted list slide in the slide show appears during a slide show, the default PowerPoint setting is to end the presentation with a **black slide**. This black slide appears only when the slide show is running and concludes the slide show, so your audience never sees the PowerPoint window. It is a good idea, however, to end the presentation with a final, closing slide to display at the end of the presentation. This slide ends the presentation gracefully and should be an exact copy, or a very similar copy, of your title slide. The audience will recognize that the presentation is drawing to a close when this slide appears. It can remain on the screen when the audience asks questions, approaches the speaker for further information, or exits the room.

Ending a Slide Show with a Closing Slide

All the text slides are created for the Cabo Package slide show. This presentation thus far consists of a title slide, one text slide with a single-level bulleted list, and two text slides with a multi-level bulleted list. A closing slide that resembles the title slide is the final slide to create.

To Duplicate a Slide

When two slides contain similar information and have the same format, duplicating one slide and then making minor modifications to the new slide saves time and increases consistency.

Slide 5 will have the same layout and design as Slide 1. The most expedient method of creating this slide is to copy Slide 1 and then make minor modifications to the new slide. The following steps duplicate the title slide.

1
- Click the Slide 1 thumbnail in the Slides tab to display Slide 1 (Figure 1–57).

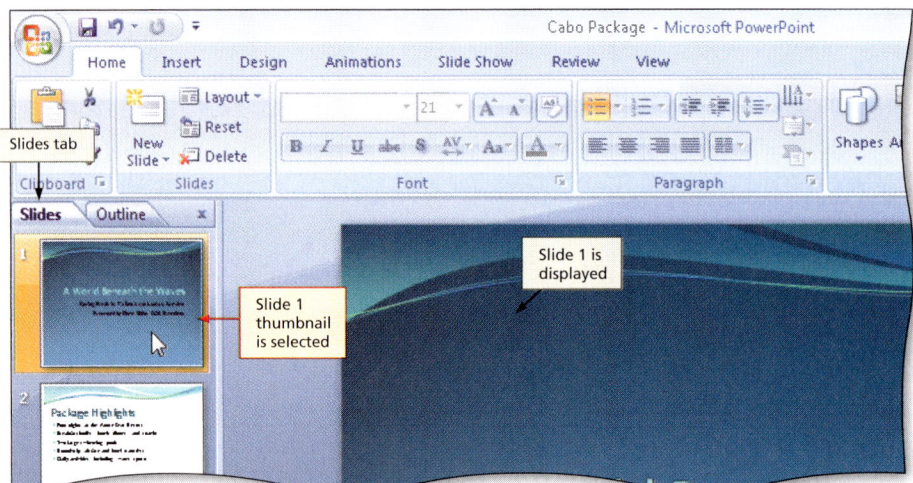

Figure 1–57

2
- Click the New Slide arrow in the Slides group on the Home tab to display the Flow layout gallery (Figure 1–58).

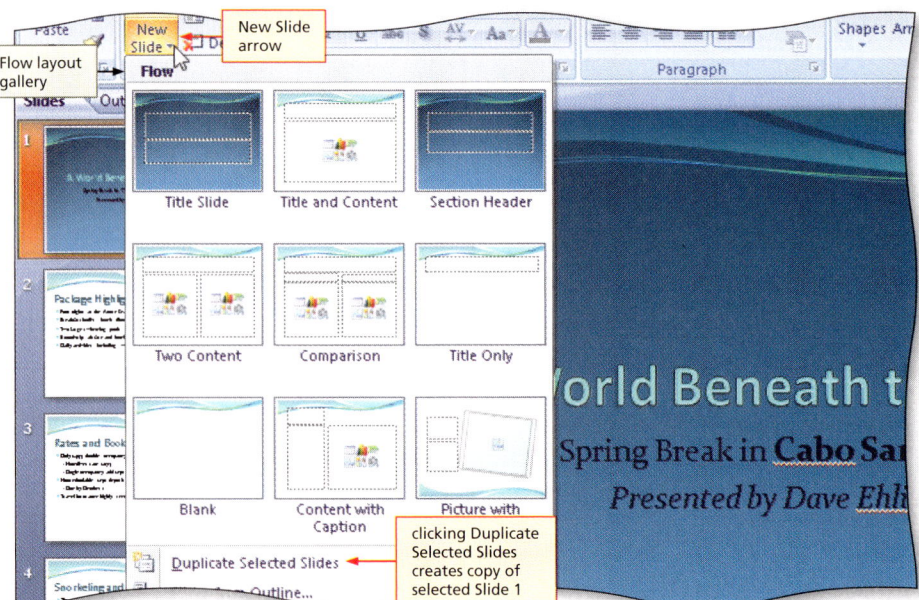

Figure 1–58

3
- Click Duplicate Selected Slides in the Flow layout gallery to create a new Slide 2, which is a duplicate of Slide 1 (Figure 1–59).

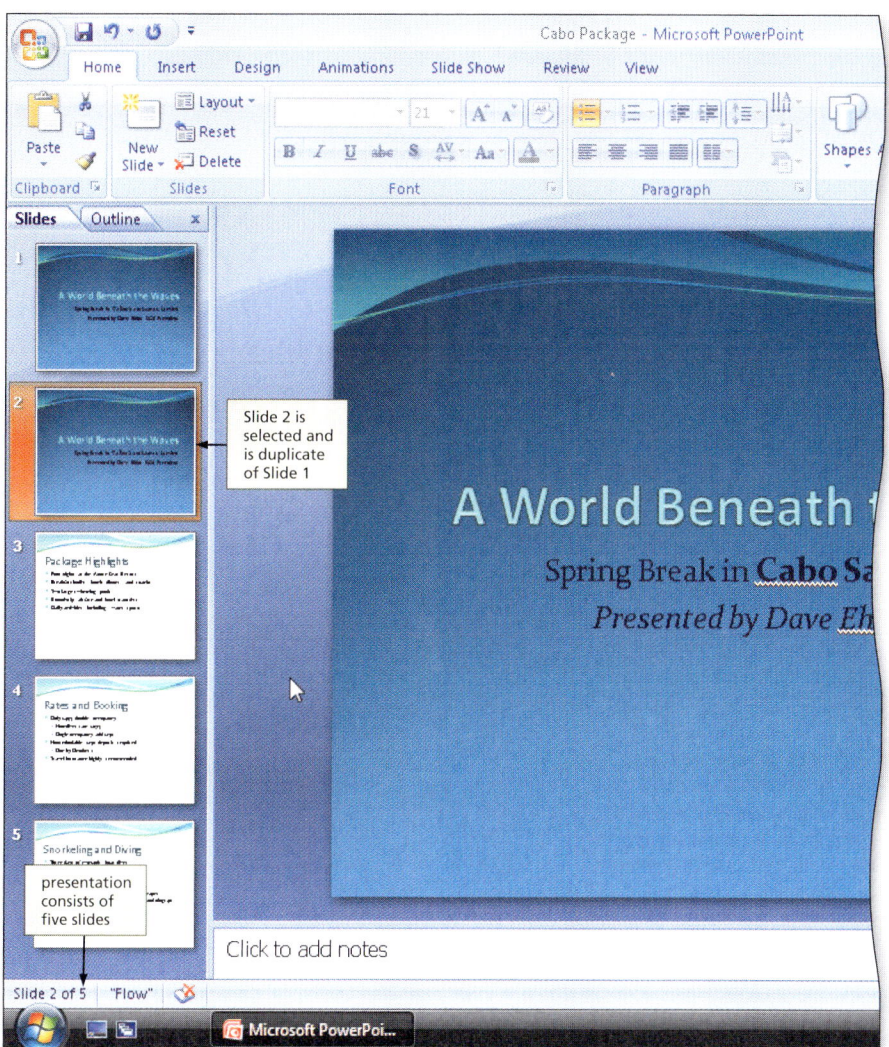

Figure 1–59

To Arrange a Slide

The new Slide 2 was inserted directly below Slide 1 because Slide 1 was the selected slide. This duplicate slide needs to display at the end of the presentation directly after the final title and content slide.

Changing slide order is an easy process and is best performed in the Tabs pane. When you click the slide thumbnail and begin to drag it to a new location, a line indicates the new location of the selected slide. When you release the mouse button, the slide drops into the desired location. Hence, this process of dragging and then dropping the thumbnail in a new location is called **drag and drop**. You can use the drag-and-drop method to move any selected item, including text and graphics. The following step moves the new Slide 2 to the end of the presentation so that it becomes a closing slide.

1
- With Slide 2 selected, drag the Slide 2 slide thumbnail in the Slides pane below the last slide thumbnail (Figure 1–60).

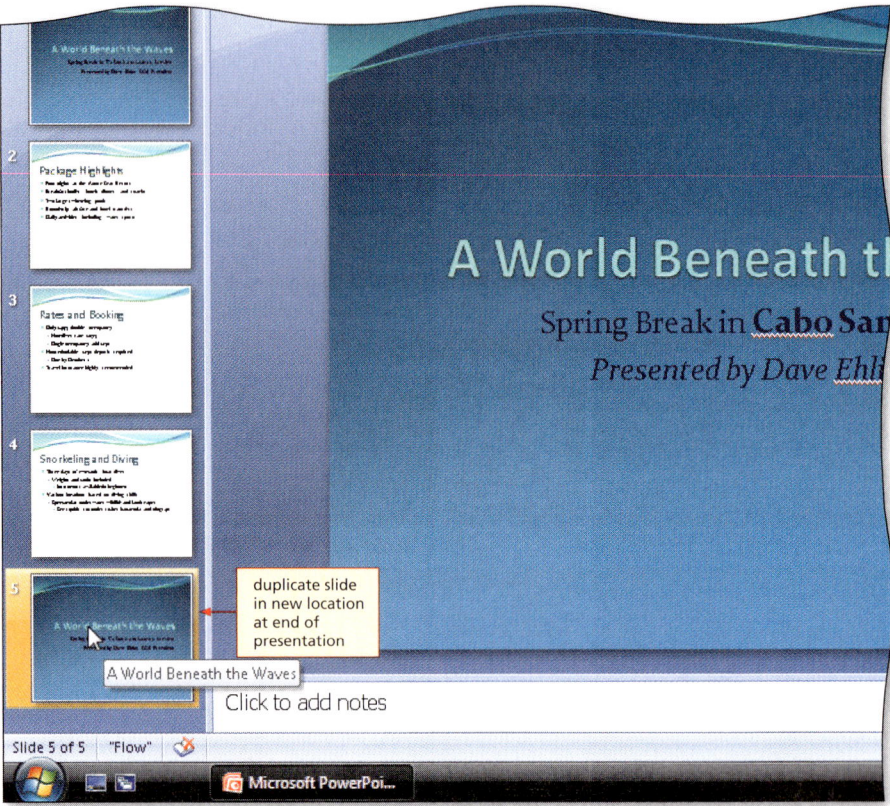

Figure 1–60

Other Ways

1. Click slide icon on Outline tab, drag icon to new location
2. In Slide Sorter view click slide thumbnail, drag thumbnail to new location

To Delete All Text in a Placeholder

To keep the ending slide clean and simple, you want only the slide show title, A World Beneath the Waves, to display on Slide 5. The following steps delete both paragraphs in the subtitle placeholder.

1
- With Slide 5 selected, click the subtitle text placeholder to select it (Figure 1–61).

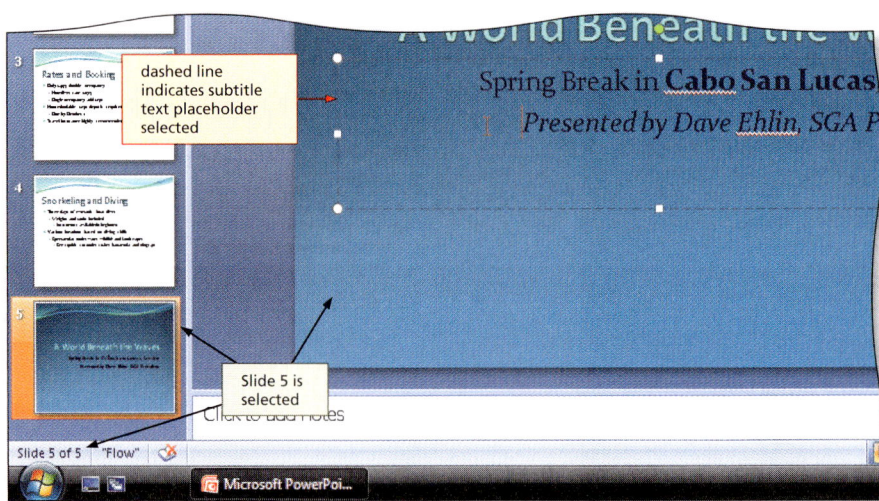

Figure 1–61

- Click the subtitle text placeholder border to change the border from a dashed line to a solid line (Figure 1–62).

Figure 1–62

- Click the Cut button in the Clipboard group on the Home tab to delete all the text in the subtitle text placeholder (Figure 1–63).

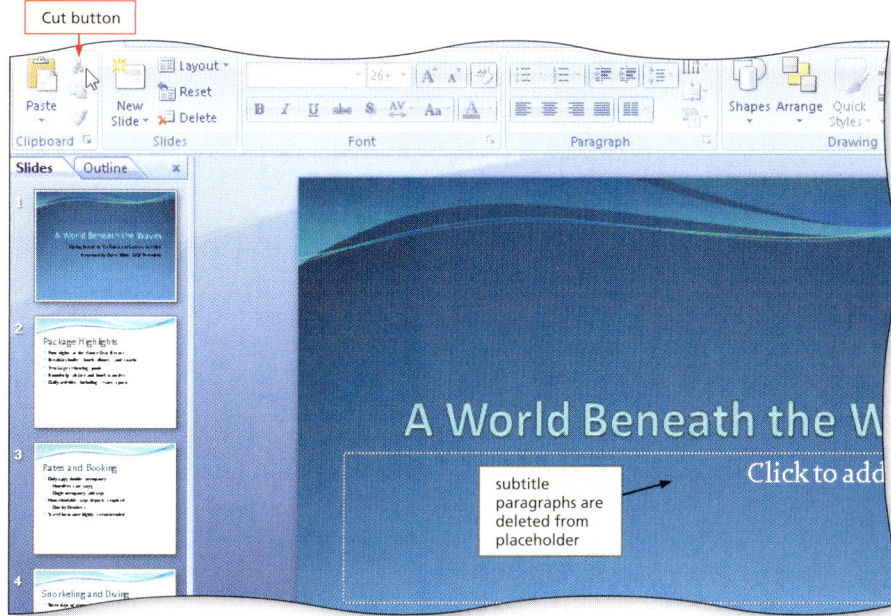

Figure 1–63

Changing Document Properties and Saving Again

PowerPoint helps you organize and identify your files by using document properties, which are the details about a file. **Document properties**, also known as **metadata**, can include such information as the project author, title, or subject. **Keywords** are words or phrases that further describe the document. For example, a class name or document topic can describe the file's purpose or content.

Document properties are valuable for a variety of reasons:

- Users can save time locating a particular file because they can view a document's properties without opening the document.
- By creating consistent properties for files having similar content, users can better organize their documents.
- Some organizations require PowerPoint users to add document properties so that other employees can view details about these files.

Five different types of document properties exist, but the more common ones used in this book are standard and automatically updated properties. **Standard properties**

Other Ways
1. Right-click selected text, click Cut on shortcut menu
2. Select text, press DELETE key
3. Select text, press CTRL+X

Converters for Earlier PowerPoint Versions
The Microsoft Web site has updates and converters if you are using earlier versions of PowerPoint. The Microsoft Office Compatibility Pack for Word, Excel and PowerPoint 2007 File Format will allow you to open, edit, and save Office 2007 documents that you receive without saving them in the earlier version's file format.

are associated with all Microsoft Office documents and include author, title, and subject. **Automatically updated properties** include file system properties, such as the date you create or change a file, and statistics, such as the file size.

To Change Document Properties

The **Document Information Panel** contains areas where you can view and enter document properties. You can view and change information in this panel at any time while you are creating a document. Before saving the presentation again, you want to add your name and class name as document properties. The following steps use the Document Information Panel to change document properties.

1
- Click the Office Button to display the Office Button menu.
- Point to Prepare on the Office Button menu to display the Prepare submenu (Figure 1–64).

Q&A What other types of actions besides changing properties can you take to set up a document for distribution?

The Prepare submenu provides commands related to sharing a document with others, such as allowing or restricting people to view and modify your document, checking to see if your presentation will run in earlier versions of PowerPoint, and searching for hidden personal information.

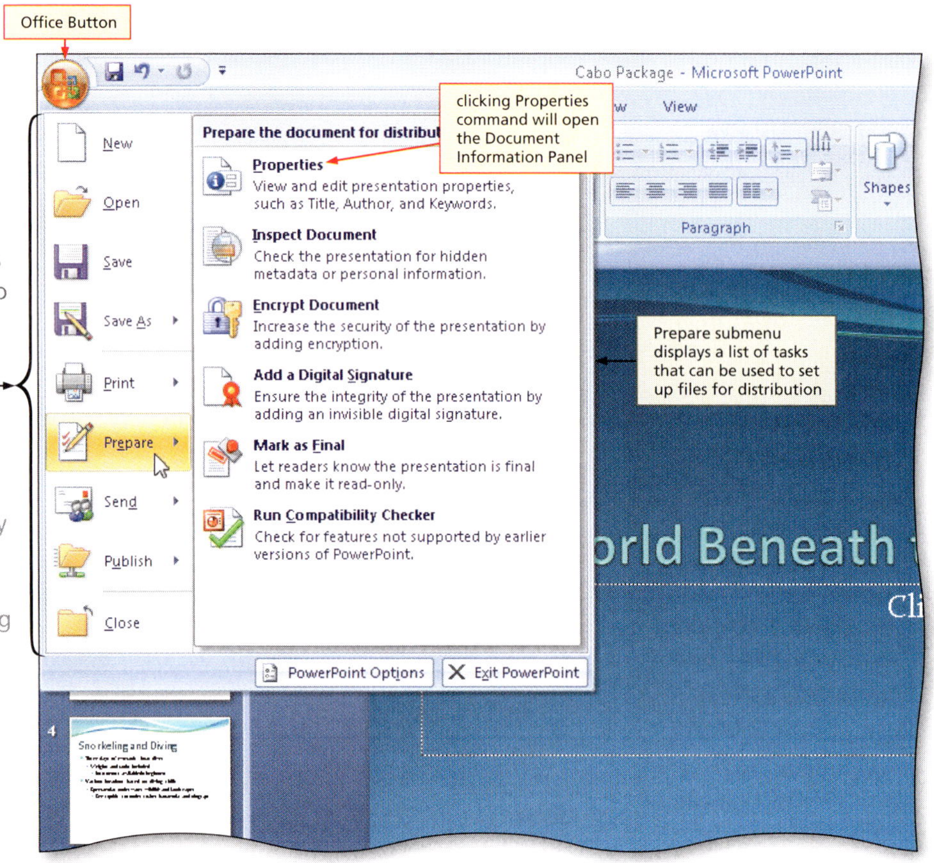

Figure 1–64

2
- Click Properties on the Prepare submenu to display the Document Information Panel (Figure 1–65).

Q&A Why are some of the document properties in my Document Information Panel already filled in?

The person who installed Microsoft Office 2007 on your computer or network may have set or customized the properties.

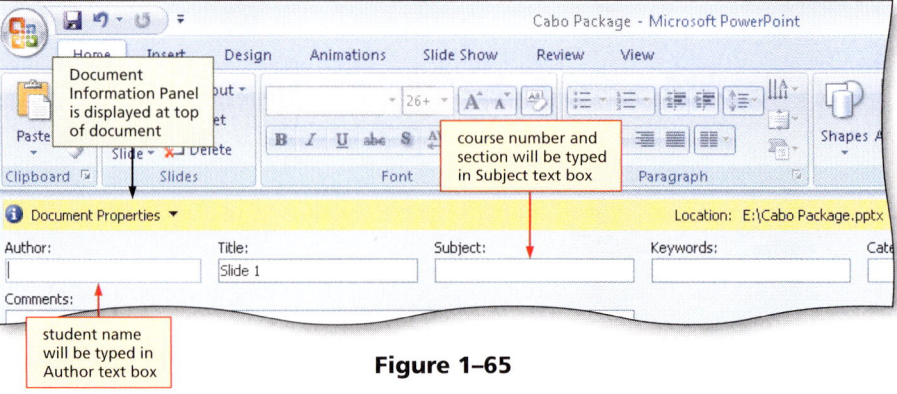

Figure 1–65

3
- Click the Author text box, if necessary, and then type your name as the Author property. If a name already is displayed in the Author text box, delete it before typing your name.

- Click the Subject text box, if necessary delete any existing text, and then type your course number and section as the Subject property (Figure 1–66).

What types of document properties does PowerPoint collect automatically?

PowerPoint records such details as how long you worked at creating your project, how many times you revised the document, and what fonts and themes are used.

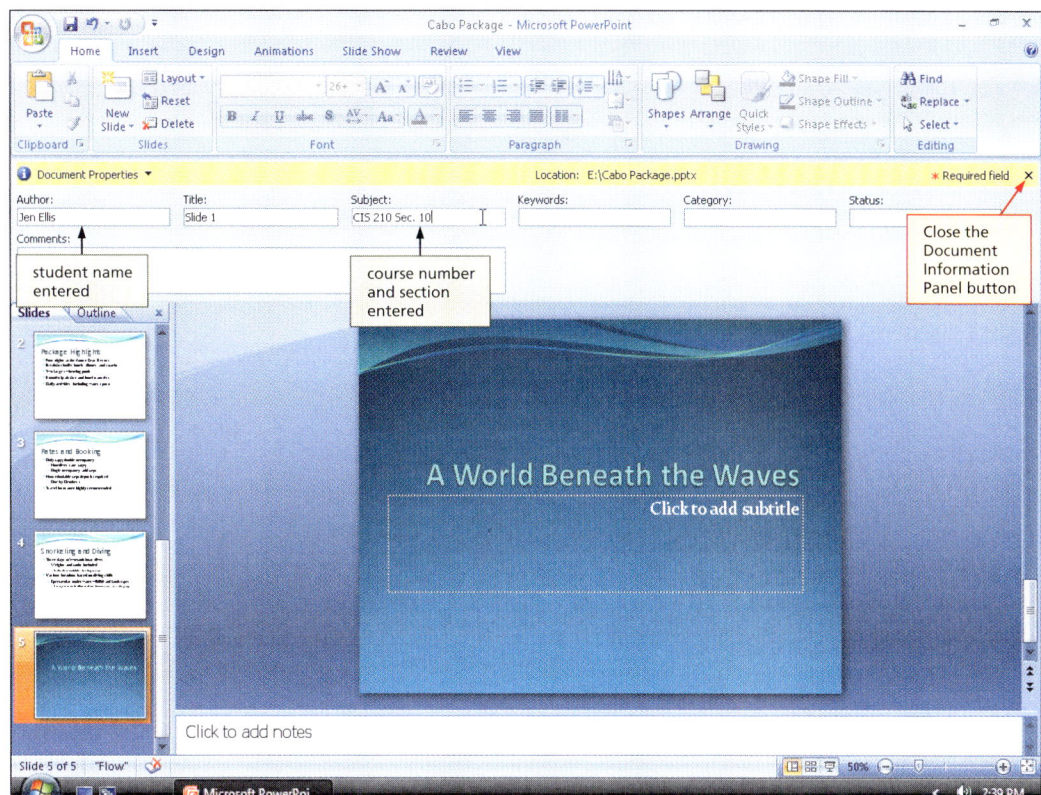

Figure 1–66

4
- Click the Close the Document Information Panel button so that the Document Information Panel no longer is displayed.

To Save an Existing Presentation with the Same File Name

Saving frequently cannot be overemphasized. You have made several modifications to the presentation since you saved it earlier in the chapter. When you first saved the document, you clicked the Save button on the Quick Access Toolbar, the Save As dialog box appeared, and you entered the file name, Cabo Package. If you want to use the same file name to save the changes made to the document, you again click the Save button on the Quick Access Toolbar. The following step saves the presentation again.

- Click the Save button on the Quick Access Toolbar to overwrite the previous Cabo Package file on the USB flash drive (Figure 1–67).

Q&A

Why did the Save As dialog box not appear?

PowerPoint overwrites the document using the settings specified the first time you saved the document. To save the file with a different file name or on different media, display the Save As dialog box by clicking the Office Button and then clicking Save As on the Office Button menu. Then, fill in the Save As dialog box as described in Steps 2 through 5 on pages PPT 27 through PPT 29.

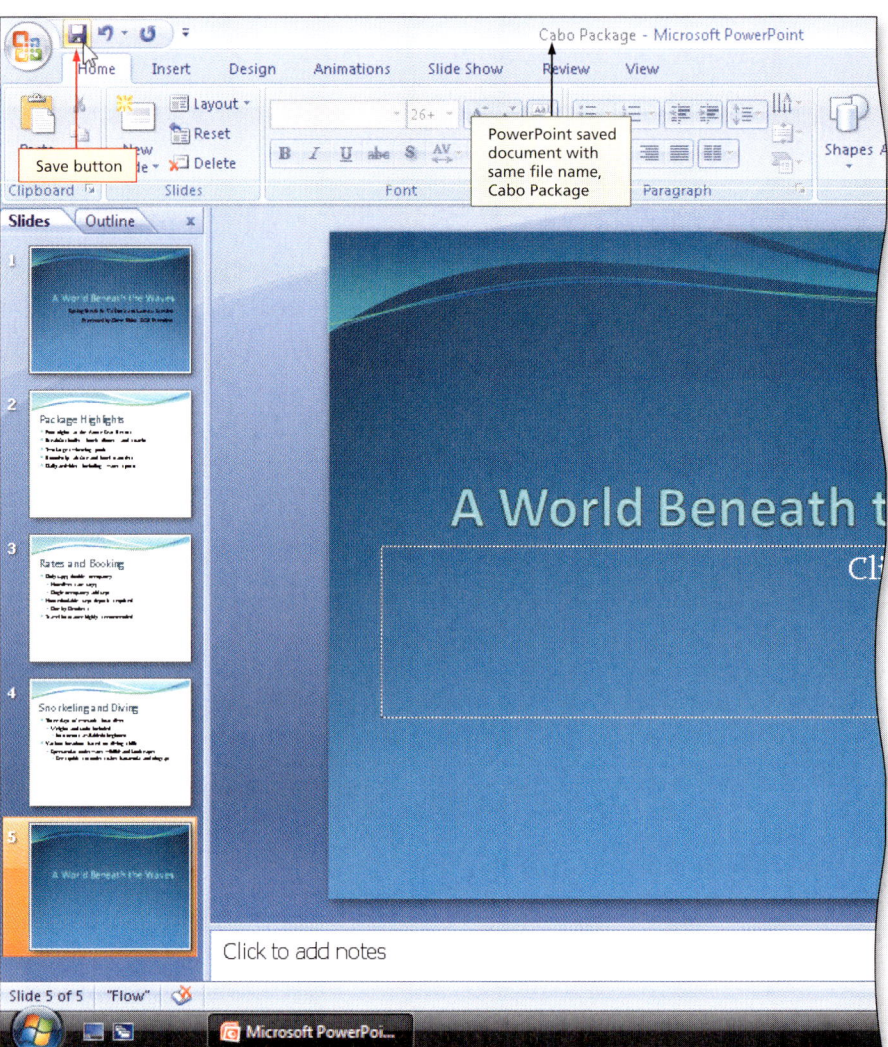

Figure 1–67

Other Ways

1. Press CTRL+S or press SHIFT+F12, press ENTER

Moving to Another Slide in Normal View

When creating or editing a presentation in Normal view, you often want to display a slide other than the current one. You can move to another slide using several methods.

- Drag the scroll box on the vertical scroll bar up or down to move through the slides in the presentation.
- Click the Next Slide or Previous Slide button on the vertical scroll bar. Clicking the Next Slide button advances to the next slide in the presentation. Clicking the Previous Slide button backs up to the slide preceding the current slide.
- On the Slides tab, click a particular slide to display that slide in the Slide pane.

To Use the Scroll Box on the Slide Pane to Move to Another Slide

Before continuing with developing this project, you want to display the title slide by dragging the scroll box on the vertical scroll bar. When you drag the scroll box, the **slide indicator** shows the number and title of the slide you are about to display. Releasing the mouse button shows the slide. The following steps move from Slide 5 to Slide 1 using the scroll box on the Slide pane.

1
- Position the mouse pointer on the scroll box.
- Press and hold down the mouse button so that Slide: 5 of 5 A World Beneath the Waves appears in the slide indicator (Figure 1–68).

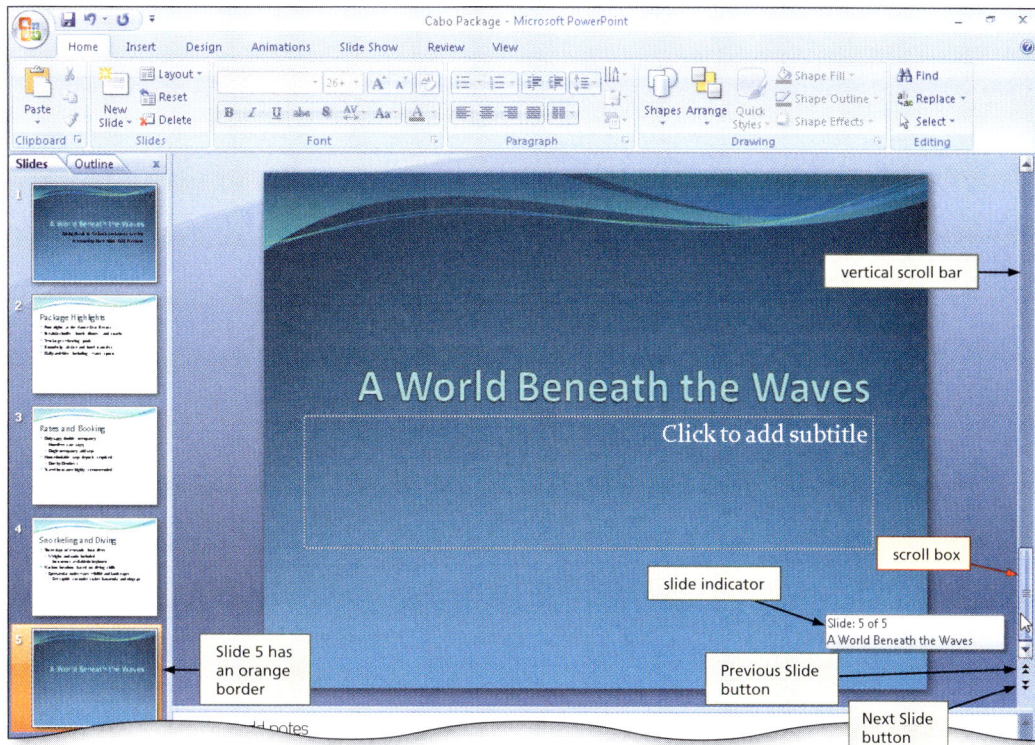

Figure 1–68

2
- Drag the scroll box up the vertical scroll bar until Slide: 1 of 5 A World Beneath the Waves appears in the slide indicator (Figure 1–69).

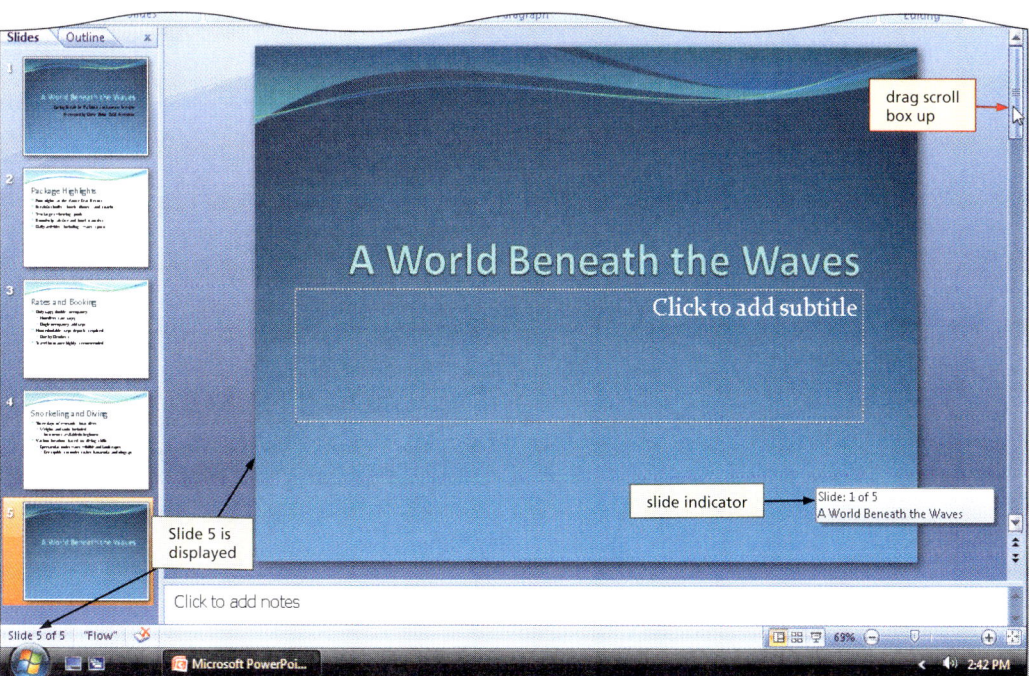

Figure 1–69

- Release the mouse button so that Slide 1 appears in the Slide pane and the Slide 1 thumbnail has an orange border in the Slides tab (Figure 1–70).

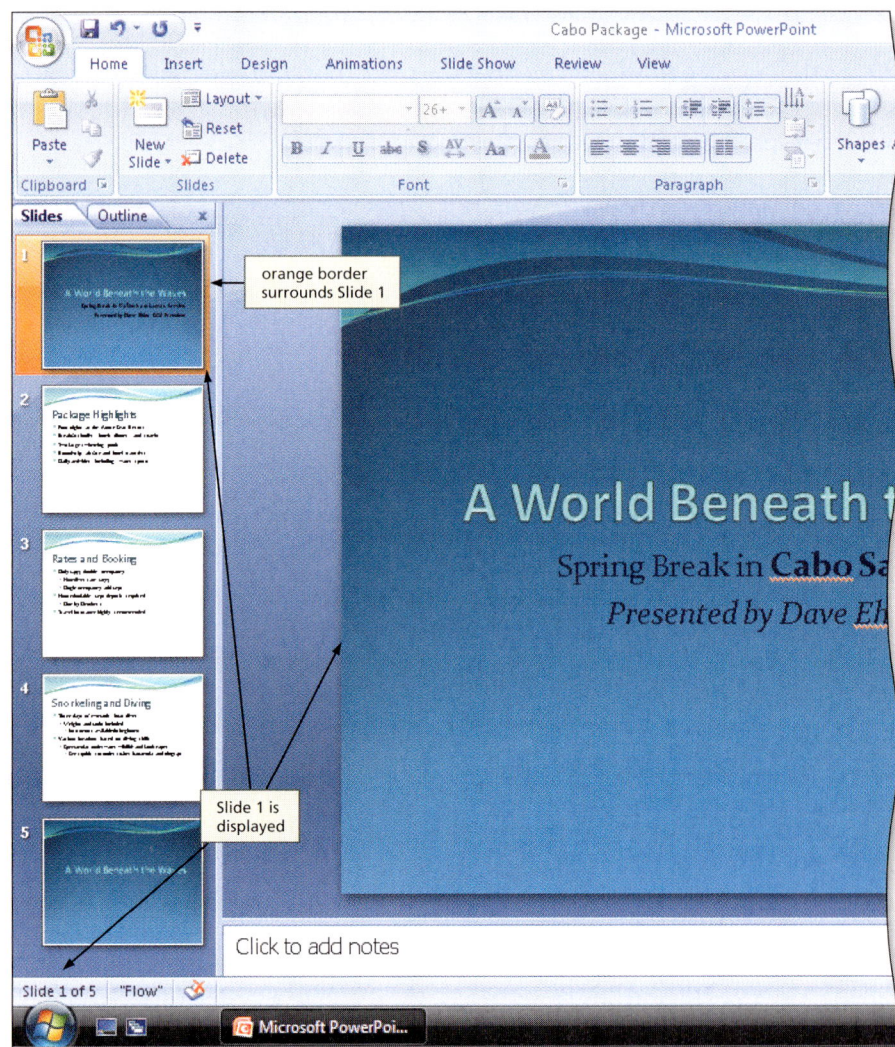

Figure 1–70

Other Ways

1. Click Next Slide button or Previous Slide button to move forward or back one slide
2. Press PAGE DOWN or PAGE UP to move forward or back one slide

Viewing the Presentation in Slide Show View

The Slide Show button, located in the lower-right corner of the PowerPoint window above the status bar, allows you to show a presentation using a computer. The computer acts like a slide projector, displaying each slide on a full screen. The full-screen slide hides the toolbars, menus, and other PowerPoint window elements.

To Start Slide Show View

When making a presentation, you use **Slide Show view**. You can start Slide Show view from Normal view or Slide Sorter view. Slide Show view begins when you click the Slide Show button in the lower-right corner of the PowerPoint window on the status bar. PowerPoint then shows the current slide on the full screen without any of the PowerPoint window objects, such as the menu bar or toolbars. The following steps start Slide Show view.

- Point to the Slide Show button in the lower-right corner of the PowerPoint window on the status bar (Figure 1–71).

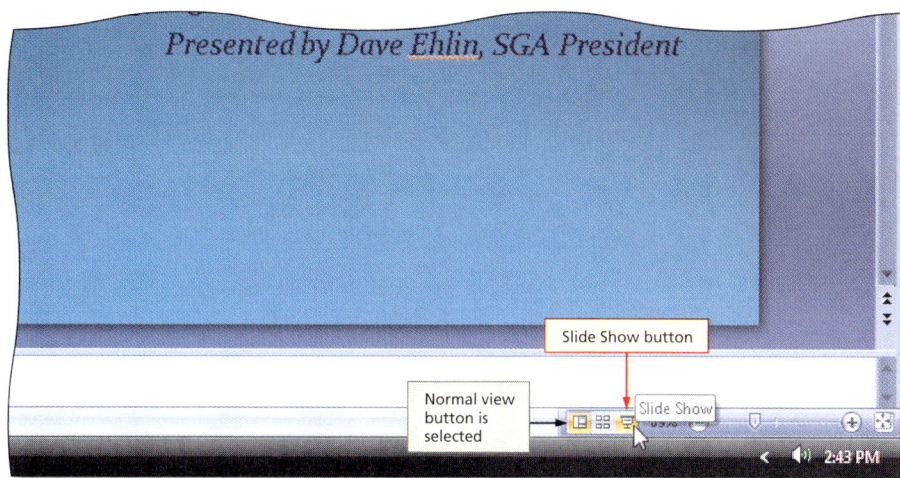

Figure 1–71

- Click the Slide Show button to display the title slide (Figure 1–72).

Where is the PowerPoint window?

When you run a slide show, the PowerPoint window is hidden. It will reappear once you end your slide show.

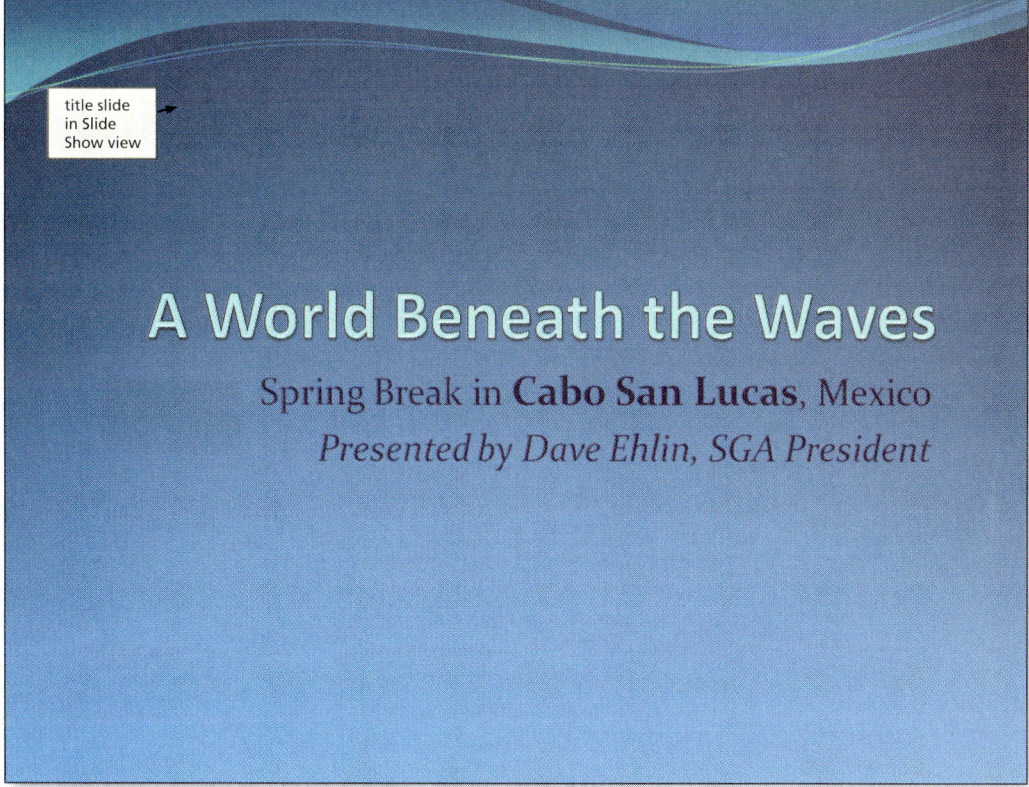

Figure 1–72

Other Ways

1. Click Slide Show tab, click From Beginning button in Start Slide Show group
2. Press F5

To Move Manually through Slides in a Slide Show

After you begin Slide Show view, you can move forward or backward through the slides. PowerPoint allows you to advance through the slides manually or automatically. During a slide show, each slide in the presentation shows on the screen, one slide at a time. Each time you click the mouse button, the next slide appears. The following steps move manually through the slides.

- Click each slide until Slide 5 (A World Beneath the Waves) is displayed (Figure 1–73).

Q&A I see a small toolbar in the lower-left corner of my slide. What is this toolbar?

The Slide Show toolbar appears when you begin running a slide show and then move the mouse pointer. The buttons on this toolbar allow you to navigate to the next slide, the previous slide, to mark up the current slide, or to change the current display.

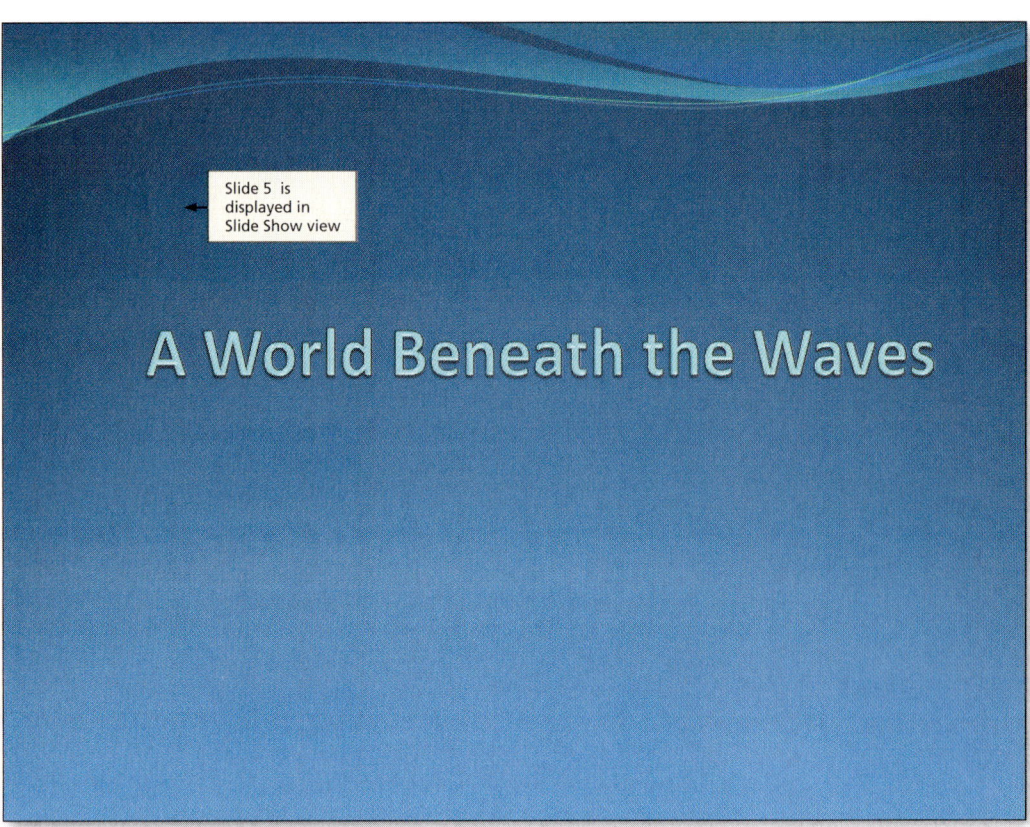

Figure 1–73

- Click Slide 5 so that the black slide appears with a message announcing the end of the slide show (Figure 1–74).

Q&A How can I end the presentation at this point?

Click the black slide to return to Normal view in the PowerPoint window or press the ESC key.

Figure 1–74

Other Ways

1. Press PAGE DOWN to advance one slide at a time, or press PAGE UP to go back one slide at a time
2. Press RIGHT ARROW or DOWN ARROW to advance one slide at a time, or press LEFT ARROW or UP ARROW to go back one slide at a time
3. If Slide Show toolbar is displayed, click Next Slide or Previous Slide button on toolbar

To Display the Pop-Up Menu and Go to a Specific Slide

Slide Show view has a shortcut menu, called a **pop-up menu**, that appears when you right-click a slide in Slide Show view. This menu contains commands to assist you during a slide show.

When the pop-up menu appears, clicking the Next command moves to the next slide. Clicking the Previous command moves to the previous slide. Pointing to the Go to Slide command and then clicking the desired slide allows you to move to any slide in the presentation. The Go to Slide submenu contains a list of the slides in the presentation. You can go to the requested slide by clicking the name of that slide. Additional pop-up menu commands allow you to change the mouse pointer to a ballpoint or felt tip pen or highlighter that draws in various colors, make the screen black or white, create speaker notes, and end the slide show. The following steps go to the title slide (Slide 1) in the Cabo Package presentation.

1
- With the black slide displaying in Slide Show view, right-click the slide to display the pop-up menu.

2
- Point to Go to Slide on the pop-up menu, and then point to 2 Package Highlights in the Go to Slide submenu (Figure 1–75).

Q&A Why does my pop-up menu appear in a different location on my screen?

The pop-up menu appears near the location of the mouse pointer at the time you right-click.

3
- Click 2 Package Highlights to display Slide 2.

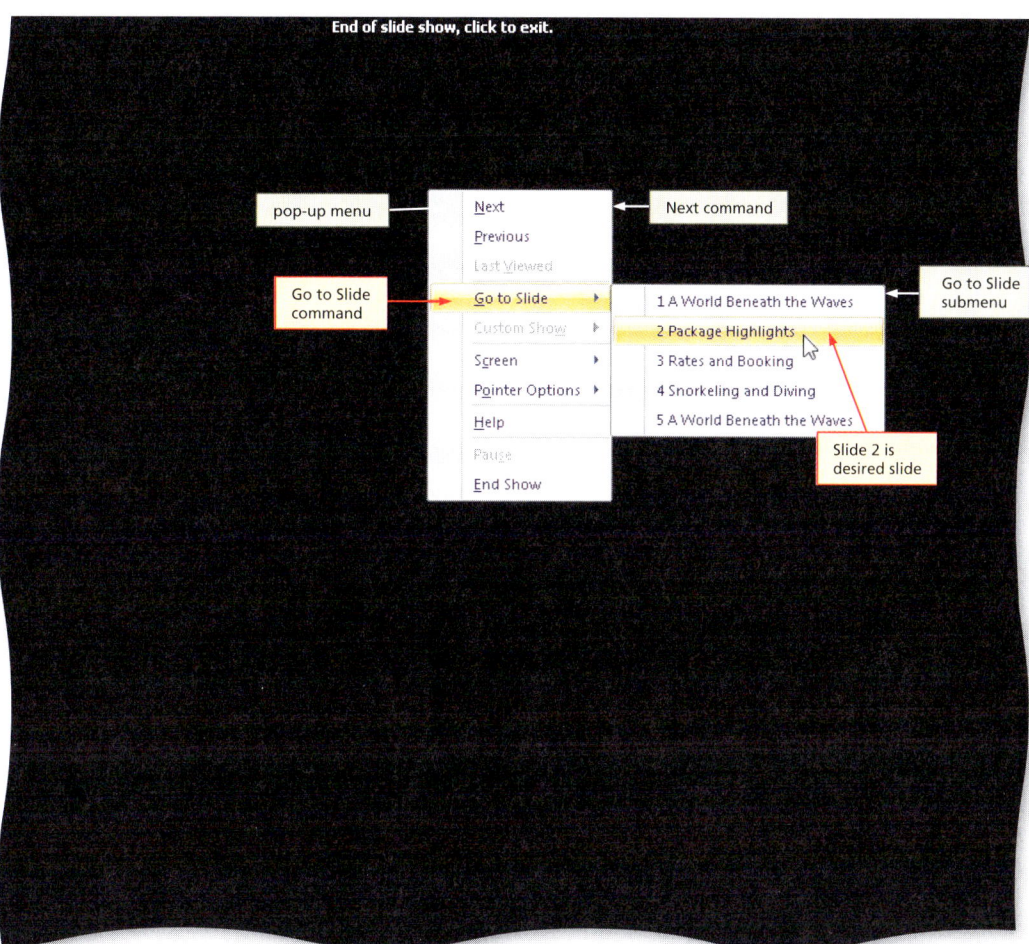

Figure 1–75

To Use the Pop-Up Menu to End a Slide Show

The End Show command on the pop-up menu ends Slide Show view and returns to the same view as when you clicked the Slide Show button. The following steps end Slide Show view and return to Normal view.

- Right-click Slide 2 and then point to End Show on the pop-up menu (Figure 1–76).

- Click End Show to return to Slide 2 in the Slide pane in Normal view.
- If the Microsoft Office PowerPoint dialog box appears, click the Yes button.

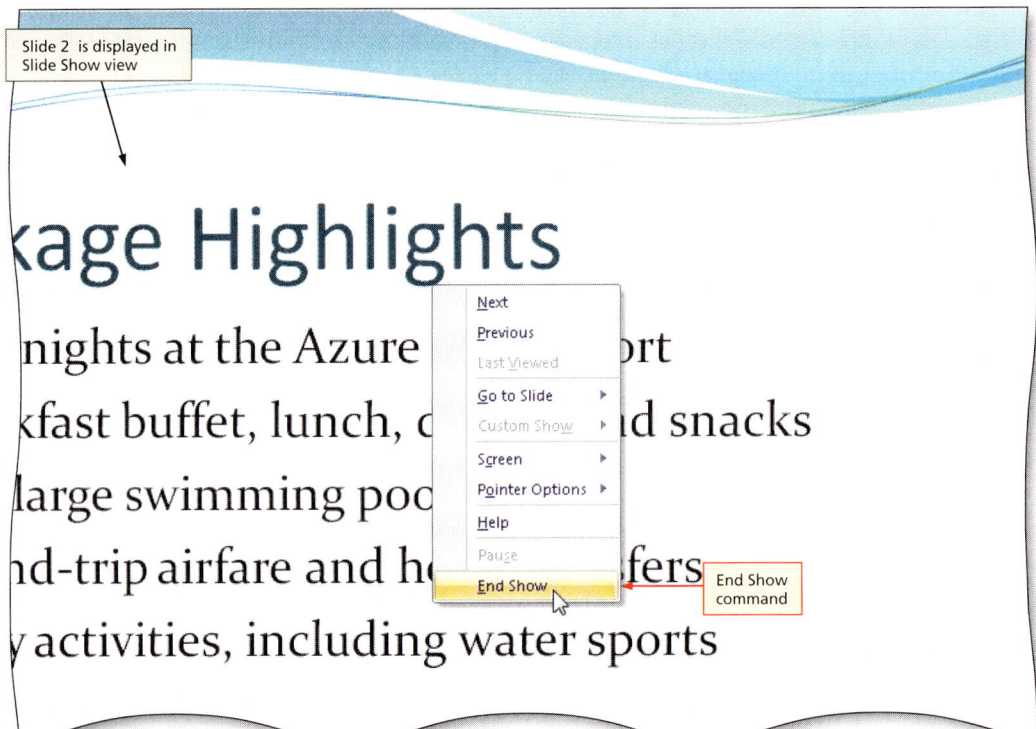

Figure 1–76

Other Ways

1. Press ESC (shows slide last viewed in Slide Show view)

Quitting PowerPoint

When you quit PowerPoint, if you have made changes to a presentation since the last time the file was saved, PowerPoint displays a dialog box asking if you want to save the changes you made to the file before it closes that window. The dialog box contains three buttons with these resulting actions:

- Yes button — Saves the changes and then quits PowerPoint
- No button — Quits PowerPoint without saving changes
- Cancel button — Closes the dialog box and redisplays the presentation without saving the changes

If no changes have been made to an open presentation since the last time the file was saved, PowerPoint will close the window without displaying a dialog box.

To Quit PowerPoint with One Document Open

You saved the presentation prior to running the slide show and did not make any changes to the project. The presentation now is complete, and you are ready to quit PowerPoint. When you have one document open, the following steps quit PowerPoint.

1

Point to the Close button on the right side of the PowerPoint title bar (Figure 1–77).

2

• Click the Close button to quit PowerPoint.

Q&A What if I have more than one PowerPoint document open?

You would click the Close button for each open document. When you click the last open document's Close button, PowerPoint also quits. As an alternative, you could click the Office Button and then click the Exit PowerPoint button on the Office Button menu, which closes all open PowerPoint documents and then quits PowerPoint.

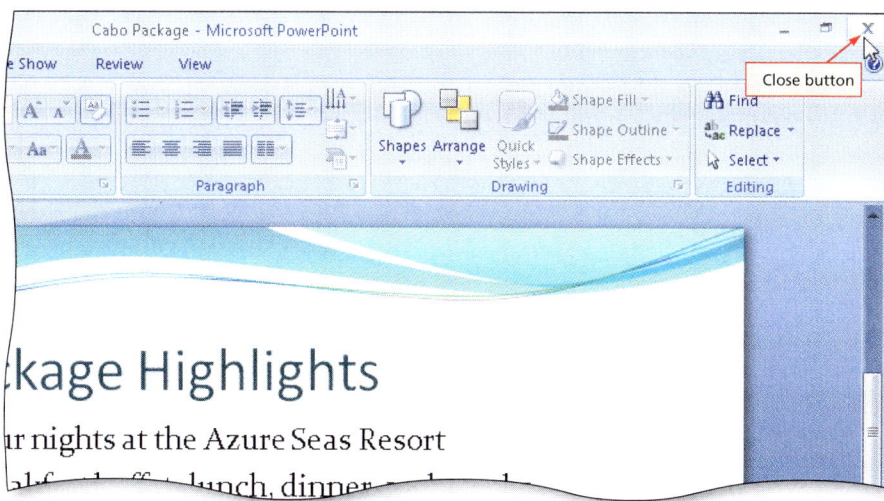

Figure 1–77

Other Ways

1. With one document open, double-click Office Button
2. Click Office Button, click Exit PowerPoint on Office Button menu
3. With one document open, right-click Microsoft PowerPoint button on Windows Vista taskbar, click Close on shortcut menu
4. With one document open, press ALT+F4

Starting PowerPoint and Opening a Presentation

Once you have created and saved a presentation, you may need to retrieve it from your storage medium. For example, you might want to revise the document or print it. Opening a presentation requires that PowerPoint is running on your computer.

To Start PowerPoint

The following steps, which assume Windows Vista is running, start PowerPoint.

1 Click the Start button on the Windows Vista taskbar to display the Start menu.

2 Click All Programs at the bottom of the left pane on the Start menu to display the All Programs list and then click Microsoft Office in the All Programs list to display the Microsoft Office list.

3 Click Microsoft Office PowerPoint 2007 on the Microsoft Office list to start PowerPoint and display a new blank presentation in the PowerPoint window.

4 If the PowerPoint window is not maximized, click the Maximize button on its title bar to maximize the window.

To Open a Presentation from PowerPoint

Earlier in this chapter you saved your project on a USB flash drive using the file name, Cabo Package. The following steps open the Cabo Package file from the USB flash drive.

- With your USB flash drive connected to one of the computer's USB ports, click the Office Button to display the Office Button menu (Figure 1–78).

Q&A What files are shown in the Recent Documents list?

PowerPoint displays the most recently opened document file names in this list. If the name of the file you want to open appears in the Recent Documents list, you could click it to open the file.

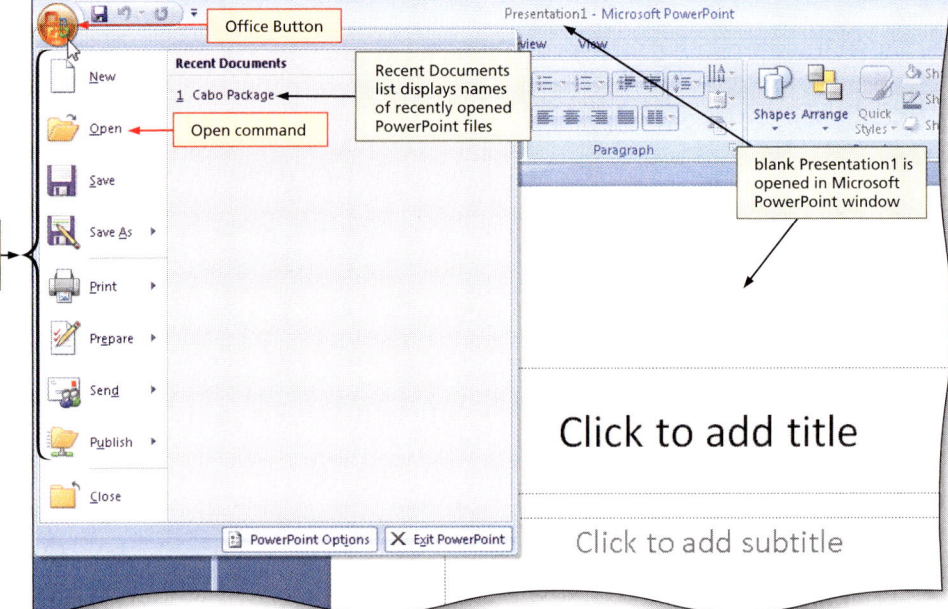

Figure 1–78

- Click Open on the Office Button menu to display the Open dialog box.

- If the Folders list is displayed below the Folders button, click the Folders button to remove the Folders list.

- If necessary, click Computer in the Favorite Links section and then scroll until UDISK 2.0 (E:) appears in the list of available drives.

- Double-click UDISK 2.0 (E:) to select the USB flash drive, Drive E in this case, as the new open location.

- Click Cabo Package to select the file name (Figure 1–79).

Q&A How do I open the file if I am not using a USB flash drive?

Use the same process, but be certain to select your device in the Computer list.

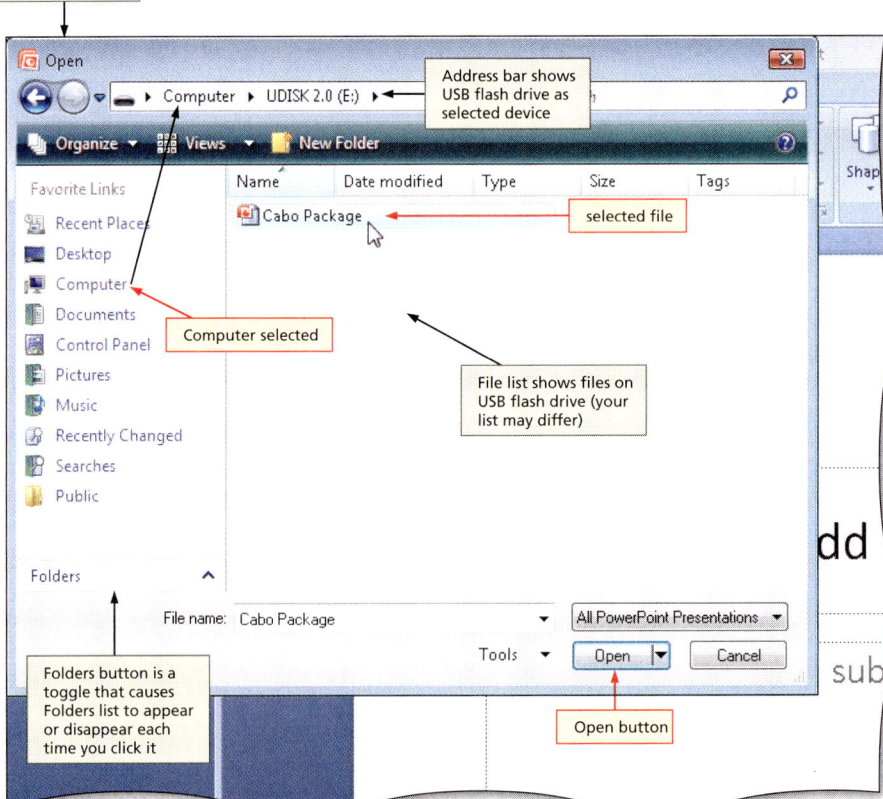

Figure 1–79

3
- Click the Open button to open the selected file and display Slide 1 in the PowerPoint window (Figure 1–80).

Q&A

Why are the PowerPoint icon and name on the Windows Vista taskbar?

When you open a PowerPoint file, a PowerPoint program button is displayed on the taskbar. The button contains an ellipsis because some of its contents do not fit in the allotted button space. If you point to a program button, its entire contents appear in a ScreenTip, which in this case would be the program name followed by the file name.

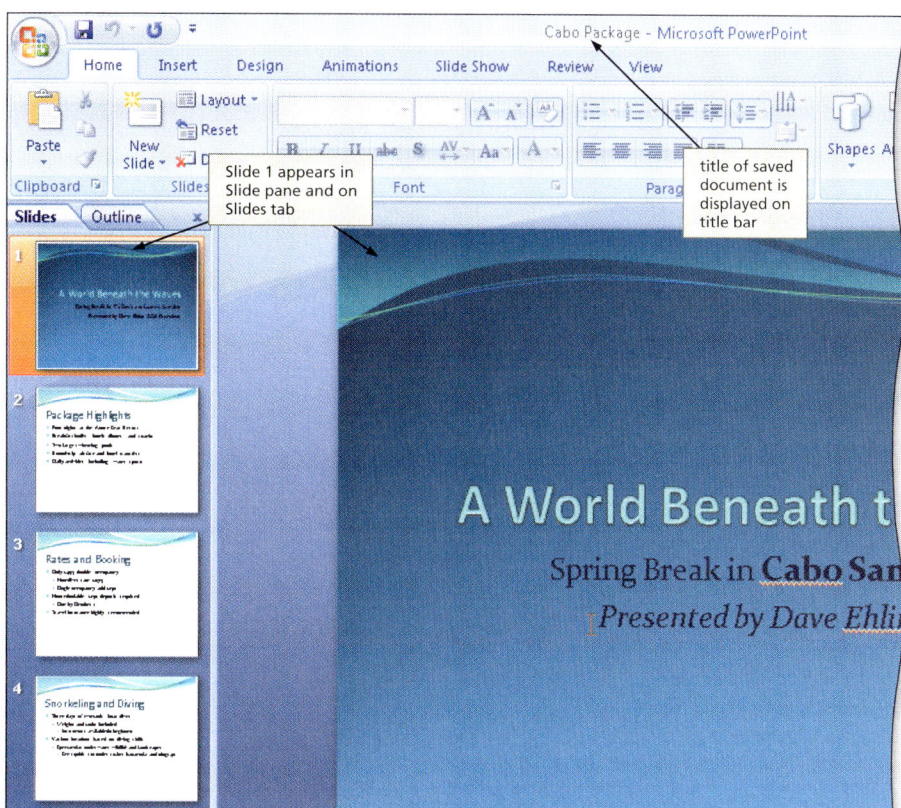

Figure 1–80

Other Ways

1. Click Office Button, double-click file name in Recent Documents list
2. Press CTRL+O, select file name, press ENTER

Checking a Presentation for Spelling Errors

After you create a presentation, you should check it visually for spelling errors and style consistency. In addition, you use PowerPoint's Spelling tool to identify possible misspellings. Do not rely on the spelling checker to catch all your mistakes. While PowerPoint's spelling checker is a valuable tool, it is not infallible. You should proofread your presentation carefully by pointing to each word and saying it aloud as you point to it. Be mindful of commonly misused words such as its and it's, through and though, and to and too.

PowerPoint checks the entire presentation for spelling mistakes using a standard dictionary contained in the Microsoft Office group. This dictionary is shared with the other Microsoft Office applications such as Word and Excel. A **custom dictionary** is available if you want to add special words such as proper names, cities, and acronyms. When checking a presentation for spelling errors, PowerPoint opens the standard dictionary and the custom dictionary file, if one exists. When a word appears in the Spelling dialog box, you can perform one of several actions.

Table 1–1 Spelling Dialog Box Buttons and Actions		
Button Name	**When To Use**	**Action**
Ignore	Word is spelled correctly but not found in dictionaries	Continues checking rest of the presentation but will flag that word again if it appears later in document.
Ignore All	Word is spelled correctly but not found in dictionaries	Ignores all occurrences of the word and continues checking rest of presentation.
Change	Word is misspelled	Click proper spelling of the word in Suggestions list. PowerPoint corrects word, continues checking rest of presentation, but will flag that word again if it appears later in document.
Change All	Word is misspelled	Click proper spelling of word in Suggestions list. PowerPoint changes all occurrences of misspelled word and continues checking rest of presentation.
Add	Add word to custom dictionary	PowerPoint opens custom dictionary, adds word, and continues checking rest of presentation.
Suggest	Correct spelling is uncertain	Lists alternative spellings. Click the correct word from the Suggestions box or type the proper spelling. Corrects the word and continues checking the rest of the presentation.
AutoCorrect	Add spelling error to AutoCorrect list	PowerPoint adds spelling error and its correction to AutoCorrect list. Any future misspelling of word is corrected automatically as you type.
Close	Stop spelling checker	PowerPoint closes spelling checker and returns to PowerPoint window.

To Check Spelling

The standard dictionary contains commonly used English words. It does not, however, contain many proper names, abbreviations, technical terms, poetic contractions, or antiquated terms. PowerPoint treats words not found in the dictionaries as misspellings. The following steps check the spelling on all slides in the Cabo Package presentation.

- Click Review on the Ribbon to display the Review tab (Figure 1–81).

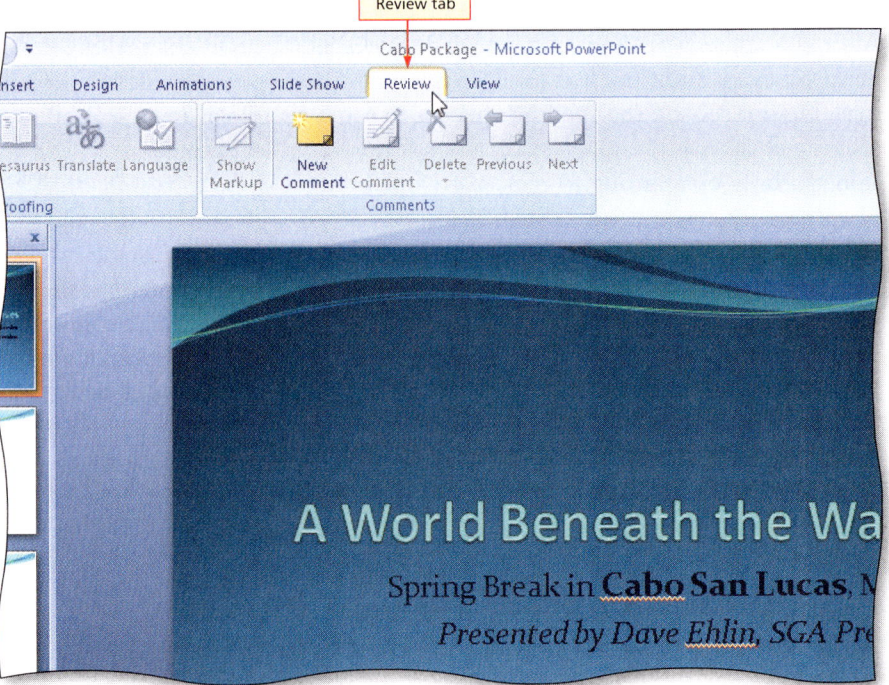

Figure 1–81

2
- Click the Spelling button in the Proofing group to start the spelling checker and display the Spelling dialog box (Figure 1–82).

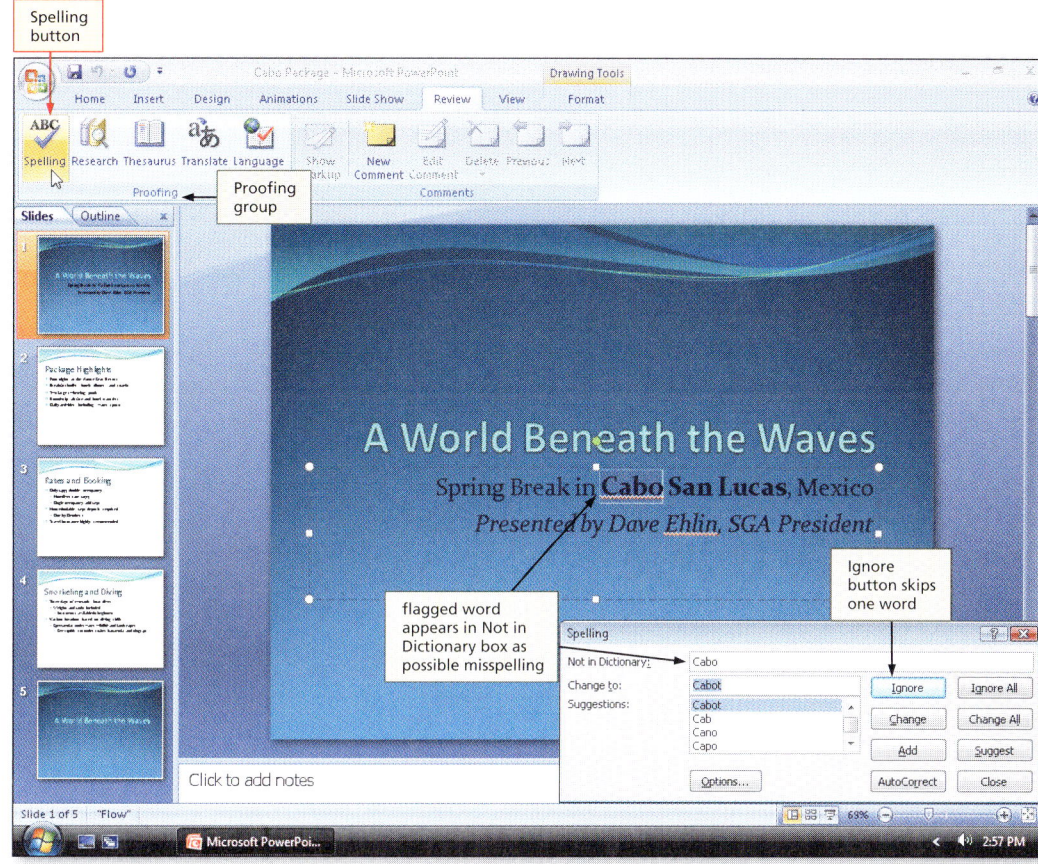

Figure 1–82

3
- Click the Ignore button to skip the word, Cabo (Figure 1–83).

Q&A Cabo is not flagged as a possible misspelled word. Why not?

Your custom dictionary contains the word, so it is recognized as a correct word.

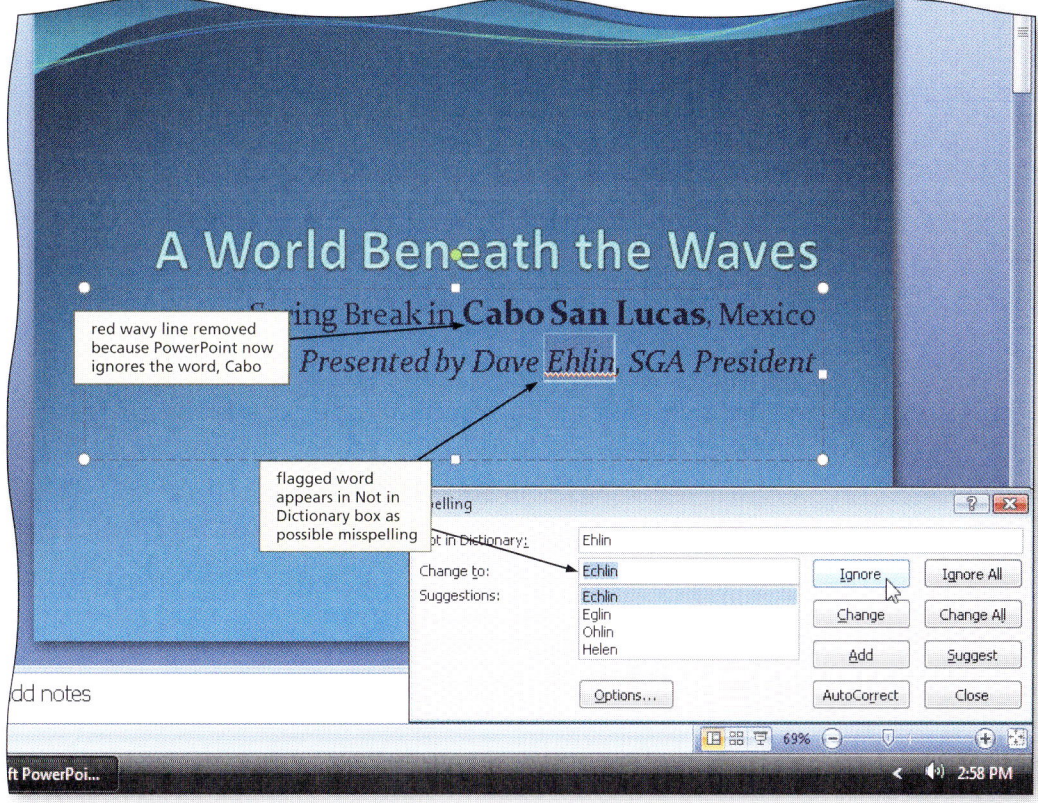

Figure 1–83

4
- Click the Ignore button to skip the word, Ehlin.

- When the Microsoft Office PowerPoint dialog box appears, click the OK button to close the spelling checker and return to the current slide, Slide 1, or to the slide where a possible misspelled word appeared.

- Click the slide to remove the box from the word, Ehlin (Figure 1–84).

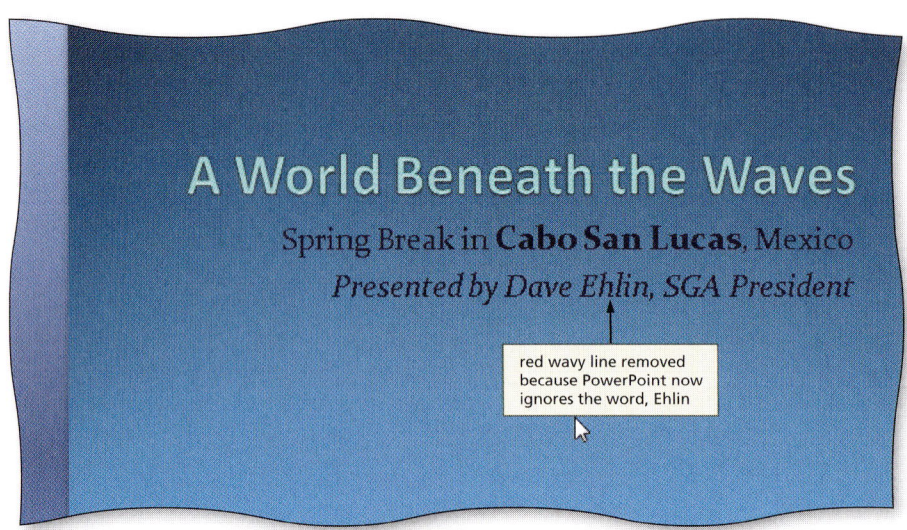

Figure 1–84

Other Ways
1. Press F7

Correcting Errors

After creating a presentation and running the spelling checker, you may find that you must make changes. Changes may be required because a slide contains an error, the scope of the presentation shifts, or the style is inconsistent. This section explains the types of errors that commonly occur when creating a presentation.

Types of Corrections Made to Presentations

You generally make three types of corrections to text in a presentation: additions, deletions, and replacements.

- Additions are necessary when you omit text from a slide and need to add it later. You may need to insert text in the form of a sentence, word, or single character. For example, you may want to add the presenter's middle name on the title slide.
- Deletions are required when text on a slide is incorrect or no longer is relevant to the presentation. For example, a slide may look cluttered. Therefore, you may want to remove one of the bulleted paragraphs to add more space.
- Replacements are needed when you want to revise the text in a presentation. For example, you may want to substitute the word, their, for the word, there.

Editing text in PowerPoint basically is the same as editing text in a word processing program. The following sections illustrate the most common changes made to text in a presentation.

Deleting Text

You can delete text using one of three methods. One is to use the BACKSPACE key to remove text just typed. The second is to position the insertion point to the left of the text you wish to delete and then press the DELETE key. The third method is to drag through the text you wish to delete and then press the DELETE key. Use the third method when deleting large sections of text.

Replacing Text in an Existing Slide

When you need to correct a word or phrase, you can replace the text by selecting the text to be replaced and then typing the new text. As soon as you press any key on the keyboard, the selected text is deleted and the new text is displayed.

PowerPoint inserts text to the left of the insertion point. The text to the right of the insertion point moves to the right (and shifts downward if necessary) to accommodate the added text.

Displaying a Presentation in Grayscale

Printing handouts of a presentation allows you to use them to make overhead transparencies. The Color/Grayscale button on the Color/Grayscale group on the View tab shows the presentation in black and white before you print. Pure Black and White alters the slides' appearance so that black lines display on a white background. Shadows and other graphical effects are hidden. Grayscale shows varying degrees of gray.

To Display a Presentation in Grayscale

The Color/Grayscale button on the Color/Grayscale group on the View tab changes from color bars to shades of black, called grayscale, and white. After you view the text objects in the presentation in grayscale, you can make any changes that will enhance printouts produced from a black and white printer or photocopier. The following steps display the presentation in grayscale.

- Click View on the Ribbon to display the View tab (Figure 1–85).

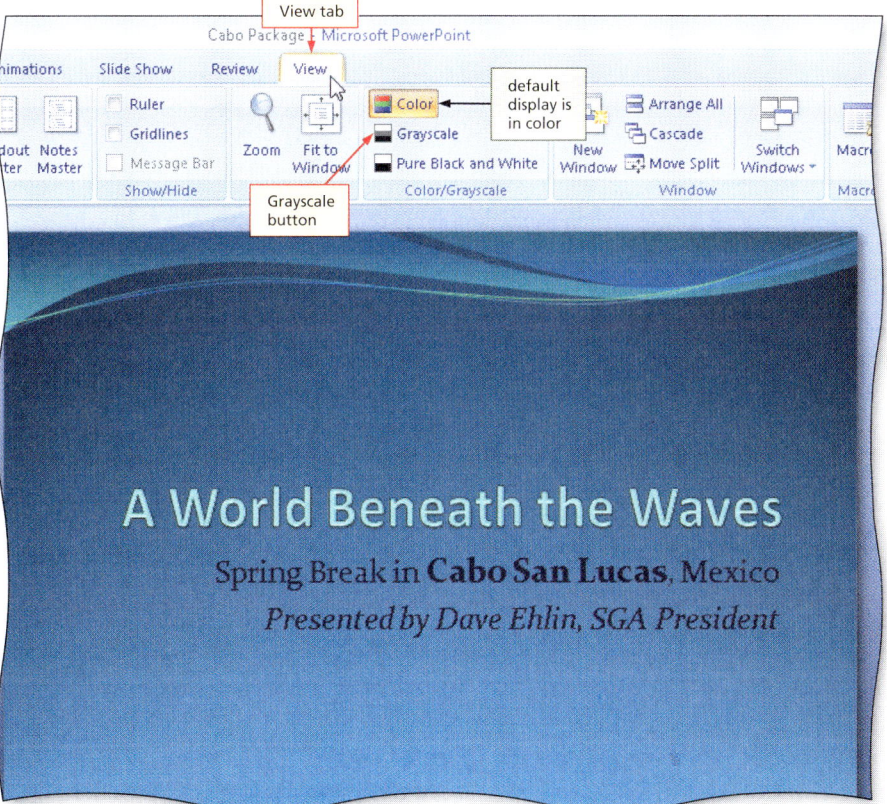

Figure 1–85

2
- Click Grayscale in the Color/Grayscale group to display Slide 1 in grayscale in the Slide pane (Figure 1–86).

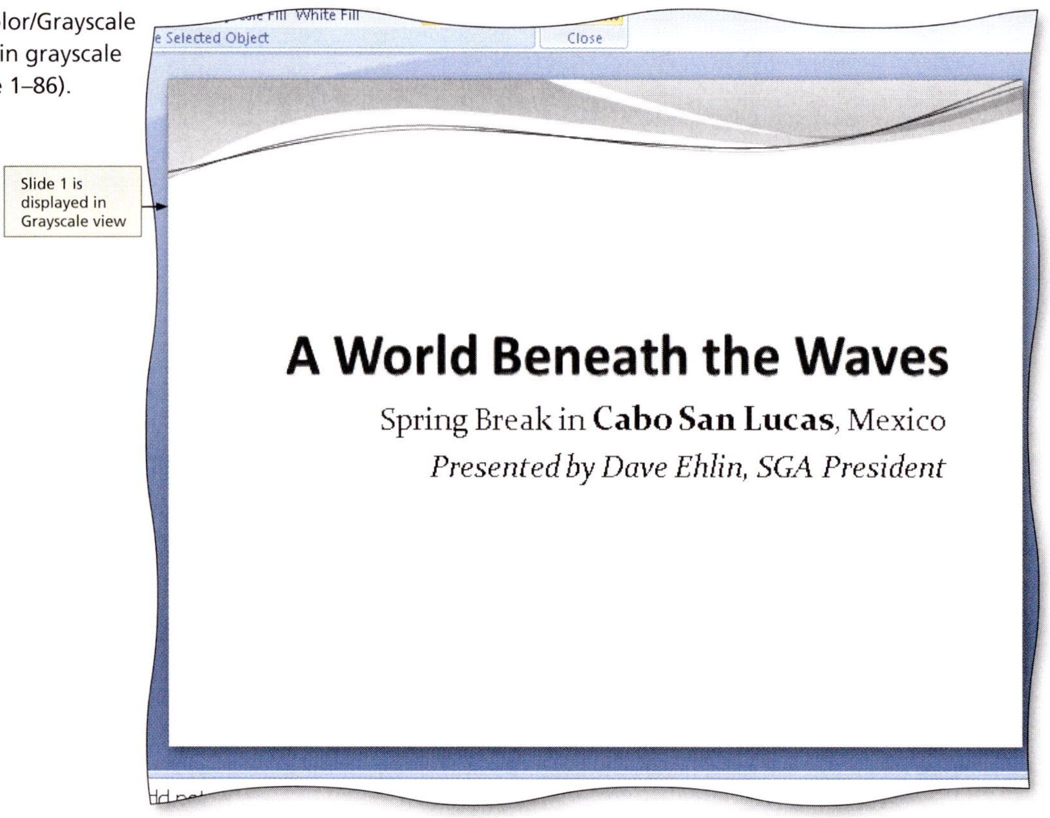

Figure 1–86

3
- Click the Next Slide button four times to view all slides in the presentation in grayscale (Figure 1–87).

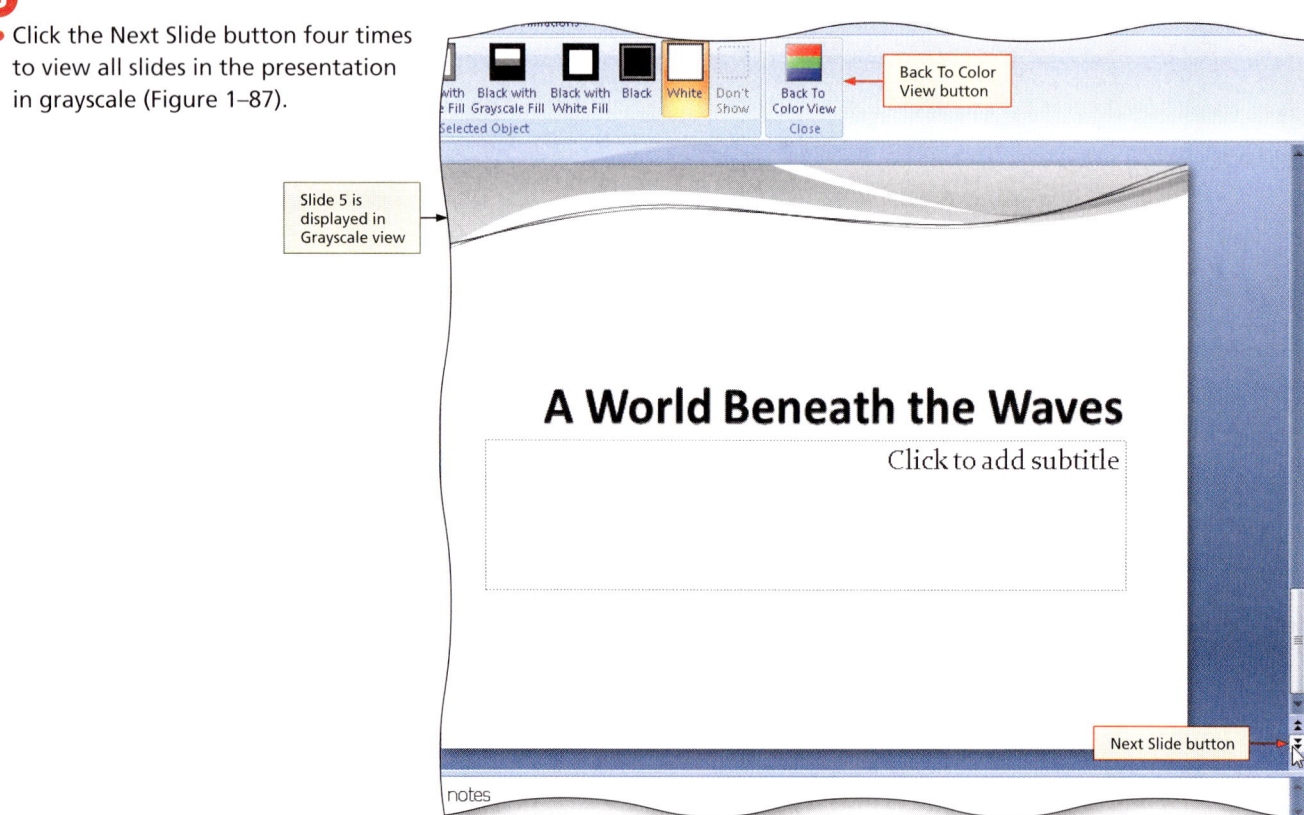

Figure 1–87

- Click the Back To Color View button in the Close group to return to the previous tab and display Slide 5 with the default Flow color scheme (Figure 1–88).

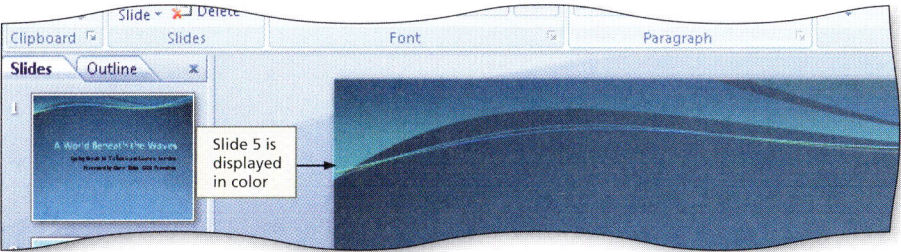

Figure 1–88

Printing a Presentation

After you create a presentation, you often want to print it. A printed version of the presentation is called a **hard copy** or **printout**.

Printed copies of your presentation can be useful for the following reasons:

- Many people prefer proofreading a hard copy of the presentation rather than viewing the slides on the screen to check for errors and readability.
- Someone without computer access or who could not attend your live presentation can view the slides' content.
- Copies can be distributed as handouts to people viewing your presentation.
- Hard copies can serve as reference material if your storage medium is lost or becomes corrupted and you need to re-create the presentation.

It is a good practice to save a presentation before printing it, in the event you experience difficulties with the printer.

To Print a Presentation

With the completed presentation saved, you may want to print it. The following steps print all five completed presentation slides in the saved Cabo Package project.

- Click the Office Button to display the Office Button menu.
- Point to Print on the Office Button menu to display the Print submenu (Figure 1–89).

Q&A Can I print my presentation in black and white to conserve ink or toner?

Yes. Click the Office Button, point to the arrow next to Print on the Office Button menu, and then click Print Preview on the Print submenu. Click the Options button on the Print Preview tab, point to Color/Grayscale on the Options button menu, and then click Pure Black and White on the Color/Grayscale submenu. Click the Print button on the Print submenu.

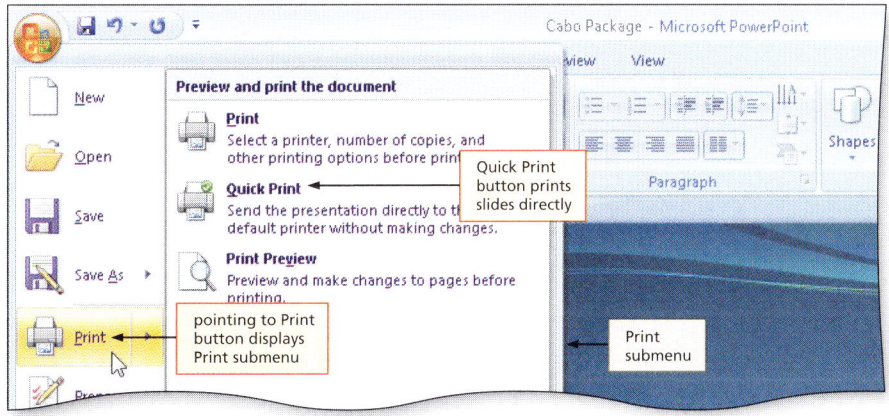

Figure 1–89

2
- Click Quick Print on the Print submenu to print the slides.
- When the printer stops, retrieve the hard copy of the five Cabo Package slides (Figures 1–90a through 1–90e).

Q&A How can I print multiple copies of my document other than clicking the Print button twice?

Click the Office Button, point to Print on the Office Button menu, click Print on the Print submenu, increase the number in the Number of copies box, and then click the OK button.

Q&A Do I have to wait until my presentation is complete to print it?

No, you can follow these steps to print your slides at any time while you are creating your presentation.

(a) Slide 1   (b) Slide 2

(c) Slide 3   (d) Slide 4

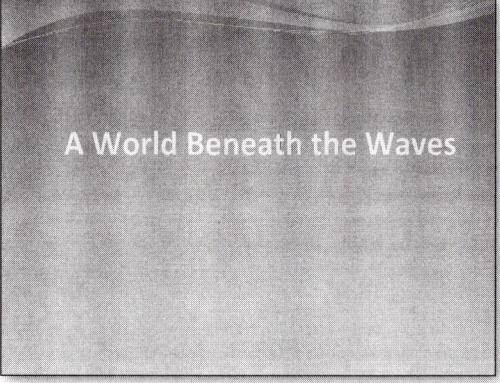

(e) Slide 5

Figure 1–90

Other Ways
1. Press CTRL+P

BTW | **Quick Reference**
For a table that lists how to complete the tasks covered in this book using the mouse, Ribbon, shortcut menu, and keyboard, see the Quick Reference Summary at the back of this book, or visit the PowerPoint 2007 Quick Reference Web page (scsite.com/dc-off07/qr).

Making a Transparency

With the handouts printed, you now can make overhead transparencies using one of several devices. One device is a printer attached to your computer, such as an inkjet printer or a laser printer. Transparencies produced on a printer may be in black and white or color, depending on the printer. Another device is a photocopier. Because each of these devices requires a special transparency film, check the user's manual for the film requirement of your specific device, or ask your instructor.

PowerPoint Help

At any time while using PowerPoint, you can find answers to questions and display information about various topics through **PowerPoint Help**. Used properly, this form of assistance can increase your productivity and reduce your frustrations by minimizing the time you spend learning how to use PowerPoint.

This section introduces you to PowerPoint Help. Additional information about using PowerPoint Help is available in Appendix B.

> **BTW**
>
> **PowerPoint Help**
> The best way to become familiar with PowerPoint Help is to use it. Appendix B includes detailed information about PowerPoint Help and exercises that will help you gain confidence in using it.

To Search for PowerPoint Help

Using PowerPoint Help, you can search for information based on phrases such as save a presentation or format a chart, or key terms such as copy, save, or format. PowerPoint Help responds with a list of search results displayed as links to a variety of resources. The following steps, which use PowerPoint Help to search for information about using document themes, assume you are connected to the Internet.

1
- Click the Microsoft Office PowerPoint Help button near the upper-right corner of the PowerPoint window to open the PowerPoint Help window.

- Type `document theme` in the 'Type words to search for' text box at the top of the PowerPoint Help window (Figure 1–91).

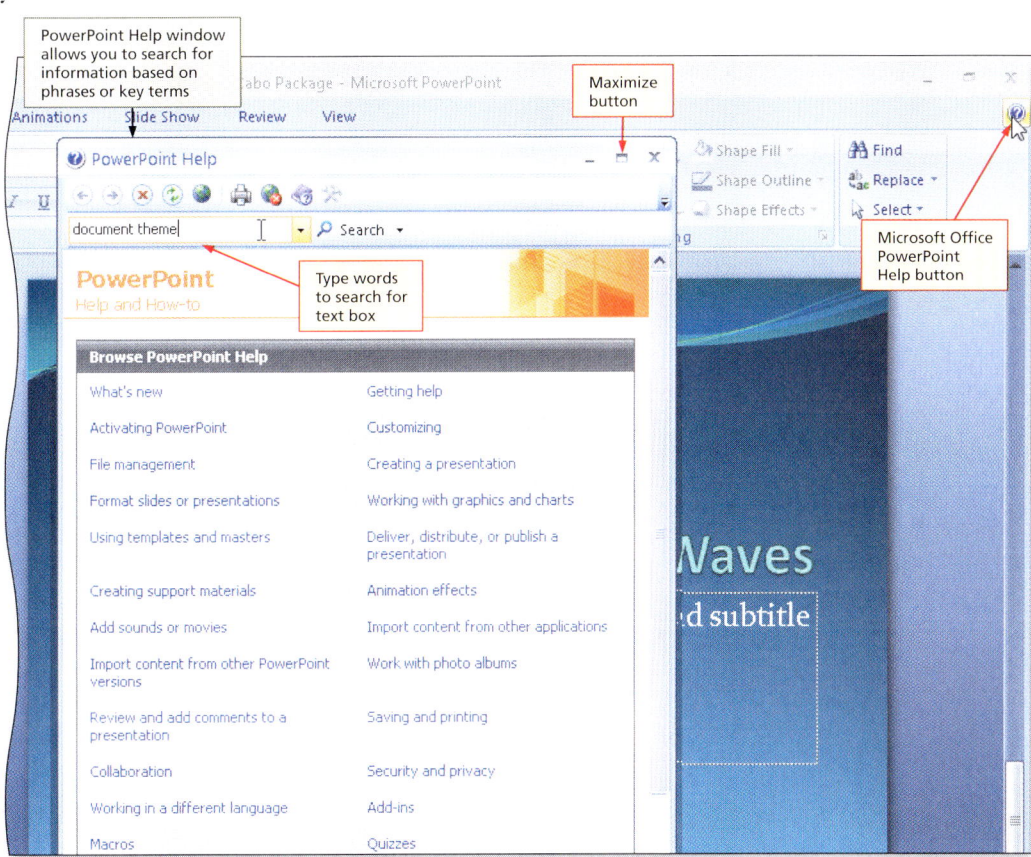

Figure 1–91

2

- Press the ENTER key to display the search results.

- Click the Maximize button on the PowerPoint Help window title bar to maximize the Help window (Figure 1–92).

Q&A Where is the PowerPoint window with Slide 1?

PowerPoint is open in the background, but the PowerPoint Help window is overlaid on top of the Microsoft PowerPoint window. When the PowerPoint Help window is closed, the slide will reappear.

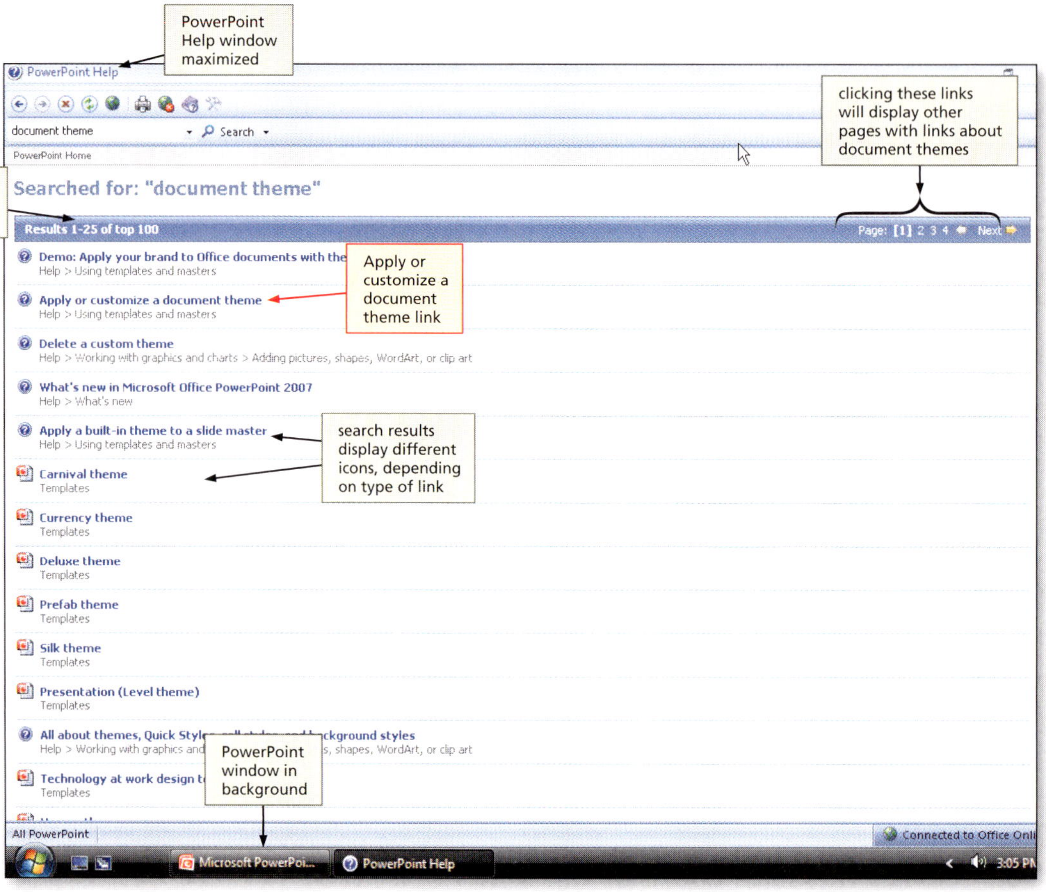

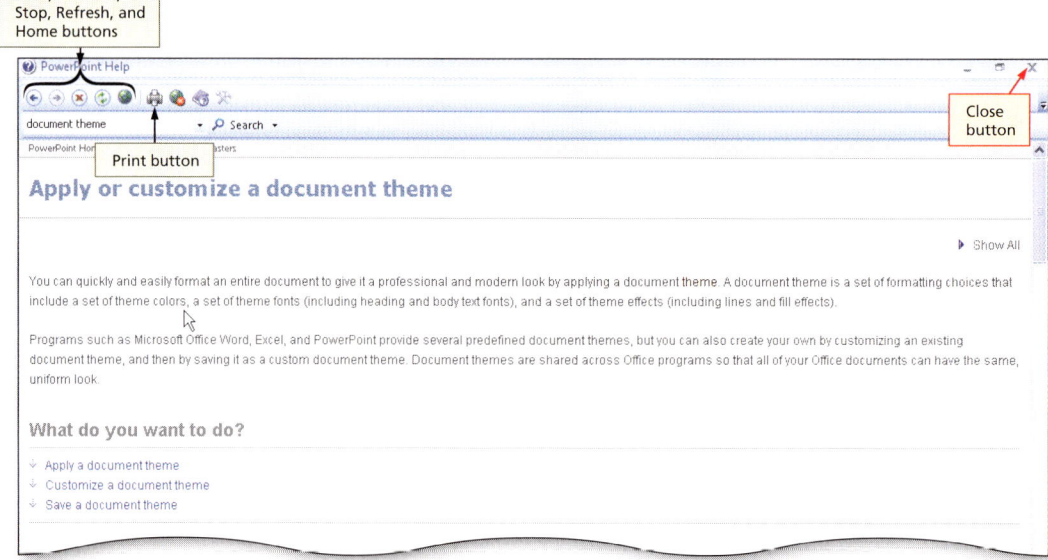

Figure 1–92

3

- Click the 'Apply or customize a document theme' link to display information regarding applying or customizing themes (Figure 1–93).

Q&A What is the purpose of the buttons at the top of the PowerPoint Help window?

Use the buttons in the upper-left corner of the PowerPoint Help window to navigate through the Help system, change the display, show the PowerPoint Help table of contents, and print the contents of the window.

Figure 1–93

4

- Click the Close button on the PowerPoint Help window title bar to close the PowerPoint Help window and display Slide 5.

Other Ways

1. Press F1

To Quit PowerPoint

The following steps quit PowerPoint.

1 Click the Close button on the right side of the title bar to quit PowerPoint; or, if you have multiple PowerPoint documents open, click the Office Button and then click the Exit PowerPoint button on the Office Button menu to close all open documents and quit PowerPoint.

2 If necessary, click the No button in the Microsoft Office PowerPoint dialog box so that any changes you have made are not saved.

Chapter Summary

In this chapter you have learned how to apply a document theme, create a title slide and text slides with bulleted lists, format text, view the presentation in Slide Show view, and print slides as handouts. The items listed below include all the new PowerPoint skills you have learned in this chapter.

1. Start PowerPoint (PPT 5)
2. Choose a Document Theme (PPT 16)
3. Enter the Presentation Title (PPT 18)
4. Enter the Presentation Subtitle Paragraph (PPT 20)
5. Select a Paragraph (PPT 21)
6. Italicize Text (PPT 22)
7. Select Multiple Paragraphs (PPT 22)
8. Change the Text Color (PPT 23)
9. Select a Group of Words (PPT 24)
10. Increase Font Size (PPT 24)
11. Bold Text (PPT 25)
12. Decrease the Title Slide Title Text Font Size (PPT 25)
13. Save a Presentation (PPT 27)
14. Add a New Text Slide with a Bulleted List (PPT 29)
15. Enter a Slide Title (PPT 31)
16. Select a Text Placeholder (PPT 31)
17. Type a Single-Level Bulleted List (PPT 32)
18. Add a New Slide and Enter a Slide Title (PPT 33)
19. Type a Multi-Level Bulleted List (PPT 34)
20. Create a Third-Level Paragraph (PPT 37)
21. Duplicate a Slide (PPT 40)
22. Arrange a Slide (PPT 41)
23. Delete All Text in a Placeholder (PPT 42)
24. Change Document Properties (PPT 44)
25. Save an Existing Presentation with the Same File Name (PPT 45)
26. Use the Scroll Box on the Slide Pane to Move to Another Slide (PPT 47)
27. Start Slide Show View (PPT 49)
28. Move Manually through Slides in a Slide Show (PPT 50)
29. Display the Pop-Up Menu and Go to a Specific Slide (PPT 51)
30. Use the Pop-Up Menu to End a Slide Show (PPT 52)
31. Quit PowerPoint with One Document Open (PPT 53)
32. Open a Presentation from PowerPoint (PPT 54)
33. Check Spelling (PPT 55)
34. Display a Presentation in Grayscale (PPT 59)
35. Print a Presentation (PPT 61)
36. Search for PowerPoint Help (PPT 63)

If you have a SAM user profile, you may have access to hands-on instruction, practice, and assessment. Log in to your SAM account (http://sam2007.course.com) to launch any assigned training activities or exams that relate to the skills covered in this chapter.

Learn It Online

Test your knowledge of chapter content and key terms.

Instructions: To complete the Learn It Online exercises, start your browser, click the Address bar, and then enter the Web address scsite.com/dc-off07/ppt2007/learn. When the Office 2007 Learn It Online page is displayed, click the link for the exercise you want to complete and then read the instructions.

Chapter Reinforcement TF, MC, and SA
A series of true/false, multiple choice, and short answer questions that test your knowledge of the chapter content.

Flash Cards
An interactive learning environment where you identify chapter key terms associated with displayed definitions.

Practice Test
A series of multiple choice questions that test your knowledge of chapter content and key terms.

Who Wants To Be a Computer Genius?
An interactive game that challenges your knowledge of chapter content in the style of a television quiz show.

Wheel of Terms
An interactive game that challenges your knowledge of chapter key terms in the style of the television show *Wheel of Fortune*.

Crossword Puzzle Challenge
A crossword puzzle that challenges your knowledge of key terms presented in the chapter.

Apply Your Knowledge

Reinforce the skills and apply the concepts you learned in this chapter.

Modifying Character Formats and Paragraph Levels

Instructions: Start PowerPoint. Open the presentation, Apply 1-1 Keep Your Cool, from the Data Files for Students. See the inside back cover of this book for instructions on downloading the Data Files for Students, or contact your instructor for more information about accessing the required files.

The two slides in the presentation stress the importance of drinking plenty of water on hot days. The document you open is an unformatted presentation. You are to modify the document theme and text, indent the paragraphs, and format the text so the slides look like Figure 1–94.

Perform the following tasks:

1. Change the document theme to Trek. Note that the Trek theme uses all capital letters for the title text. On the title slide, use your name in place of Student Name and bold and italicize your name. Increase the title text font size to 44 point.

(a) Slide 1 (Title Slide)

Figure 1–94

(b) Slide 2 (Multi-Level Bulleted List)
Figure 1–94 (continued)

2. On Slide 2, increase the indent of the second, fifth, and sixth paragraphs (Drink throughout the day; Do not substitute caffeinated beverages; Cool water is best for keeping hydrated) to second-level paragraphs. Then change paragraphs three and four (Start and end your day with water; Do not wait until you are thirsty) to third-level paragraphs.
3. Check the spelling, and then display the revised presentation in grayscale.
4. Change the document properties, as specified by your instructor. Save the presentation using the file name, Apply 1-1 Drink Water. Submit the revised document in the format specified by your instructor.

Extend Your Knowledge

Extend the skills you learned in this chapter and experiment with new skills. You may need to use Help to complete the assignment.

Changing Slide Theme and Text

Instructions: Start PowerPoint. Open the presentation, Extend 1-1 Nutrition, from the Data Files for Students. See the inside back cover of this book for instructions on downloading the Data Files for Students, or contact your instructor for more information about accessing the required files.

You will choose a theme (Figure 1–95), format slides, and create a closing slide.

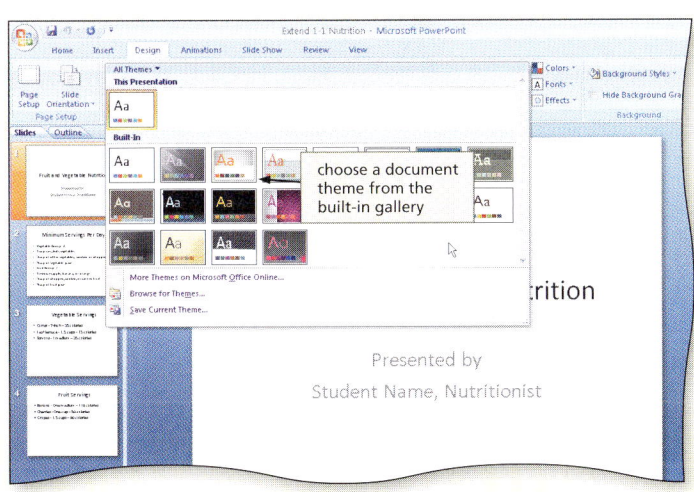

Figure 1–95

Perform the following tasks:
1. Apply an appropriate document theme.
2. On Slide 1, use your name in place of Student Name. Format the text using techniques you learned in this chapter, such as changing the font size and color and also bolding and italicizing words.

Continued >

Extend Your Knowledge *continued*

3. On Slide 2, adjust the paragraph levels so that the lines of text are arranged under vegetable and fruit categories. Edit the text so that the slide meets the 7 × 7 rule, which states that each line should have a maximum of seven words, and each slide should have a maximum of seven lines.
4. On Slides 3 and 4, create paragraphs and adjust the paragraph levels.
5. Create an appropriate closing slide using the title slide as a guide.
6. Change the document properties, as specified by your instructor. Save the presentation using the file name, Extend 1-1 Fruit and Vegetables.
7. Add the Print button to the Quick Access Toolbar and then click this button to print the slides.
8. Delete the Print button from the Quick Access Toolbar.
9. Submit the revised document in the format specified by your instructor.

Make It Right

Analyze a presentation and correct all errors and/or improve the design.

Correcting Formatting and List Levels

Instructions: Start PowerPoint. Open the presentation, Make It Right 1-1 Indulge, from the Data Files for Students. See the inside back cover of this book for instructions on downloading the Data Files for Students, or contact your instructor for more information about accessing the required files.

Correct the formatting problems and errors in the presentation while keeping in mind the guidelines presented in this chapter.

Perform the following tasks:

1. Change the document theme from Metro, shown in Figure 1–96, to Opulent.
2. On Slide 1, replace the words, Fall Semester, with your name. Format your name so that it displays prominently on the slide.
3. Move Slide 2 to the end of the presentation so that it becomes the new Slide 4.
4. Use the spell checker to correct the misspellings. Analyze the slides for other word usage errors that the spell checker did not find.

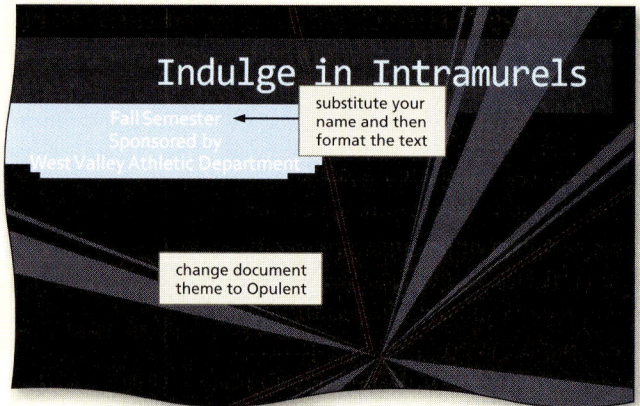

Figure 1–96

5. On Slide 2, increase the Slide 2 title (Athletic Events) font size to 40. Make the indent levels for paragraphs 2, 4, and 6 the same level.
6. On Slide 3, change the title text (Awards Ceremony) font size to 40. Make the indent levels for paragraphs 3 and 5 the same level.
7. Change the document properties, as specified by your instructor. Save the presentation using the file name, Make It Right 1-1 Intramurals.
8. Submit the revised document in the format specified by your instructor.

In the Lab

Design and/or create a presentation using the guidelines, concepts, and skills presented in this chapter. Labs 1, 2, and 3 are listed in order of increasing difficulty.

Lab 1: Creating a Presentation with Bulleted Lists

Problem: Many of the important steps you will take in your life are influenced by your credit report. Buying a car, renting an apartment, and even applying for a job often require a credit check. Your credit score can make or break your ability to obtain the goods you truly want and need. One of your assignments in your economics class is to give a speech about establishing credit. You develop the outline shown in Figure 1–97 and then prepare the PowerPoint presentation shown in Figures 1–98a through 1–98d.

Instructions: Perform the following tasks.

1. Create a new presentation using the Aspect document theme.
2. Using the typed notes illustrated in Figure 1–97, create the title slide shown in Figure 1–98a using your name in place of Marc Kantlon. Italicize your name. Decrease the font size of the title paragraph, Give Yourself Some Credit, to 40. Increase the font size of the first paragraph of the subtitle text, Understanding Your Credit Report, to 28.
3. Using the typed notes in Figure 1–97, create the three text slides with bulleted lists shown in Figures 1–98b through 1–98d.

Give Yourself Some Credit
 Understanding Your Credit Report
 Marc Kantlon
 Economics 101

Credit Report Fundamentals
  Generated by three companies
    Experian, Equifax, TransUnion
  Factors
    How much you owe to each company
    Payment history for each company
      Includes utilities, medical expenses, rent

How FICO Is Calculated
  Range - 760 (excellent) to 620 (poor)
    35% - Payment history
    30% - Amounts owed
    15% - Credit history length
    10% - New credit
    10% - Credit types

Improve Your FICO Score
  Pay bills on time
  Avoid opening many new accounts
    Open only if you intend to use
  Keep balances low
    Less than 25% of credit limit
  Review credit report yearly

Figure 1–97

Continued >

In the Lab *continued*

4. On Slide 3, change the font color of the number, 760, to green and the number, 620, to red.
5. Check the spelling and correct any errors.
6. Drag the scroll box to display Slide 1. Click the Slide Show button to start Slide Show view. Then click to display each slide.
7. Change the document properties, as specified by your instructor. Save the presentation using the file name, Lab 1-1 Credit.
8. Submit the document in the format specified by your instructor.

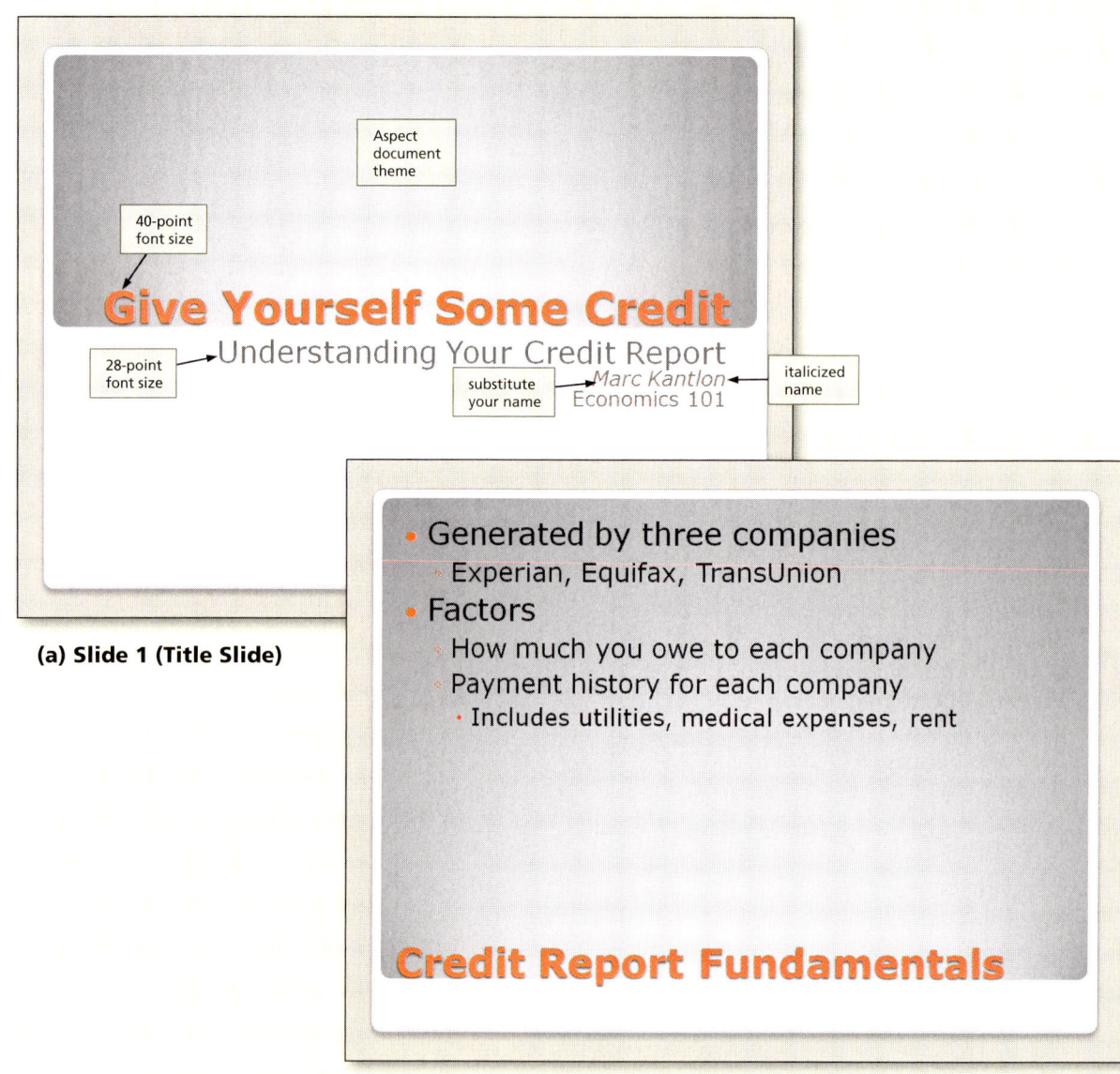

(a) Slide 1 (Title Slide)

(b) Slide 2

Figure 1–98

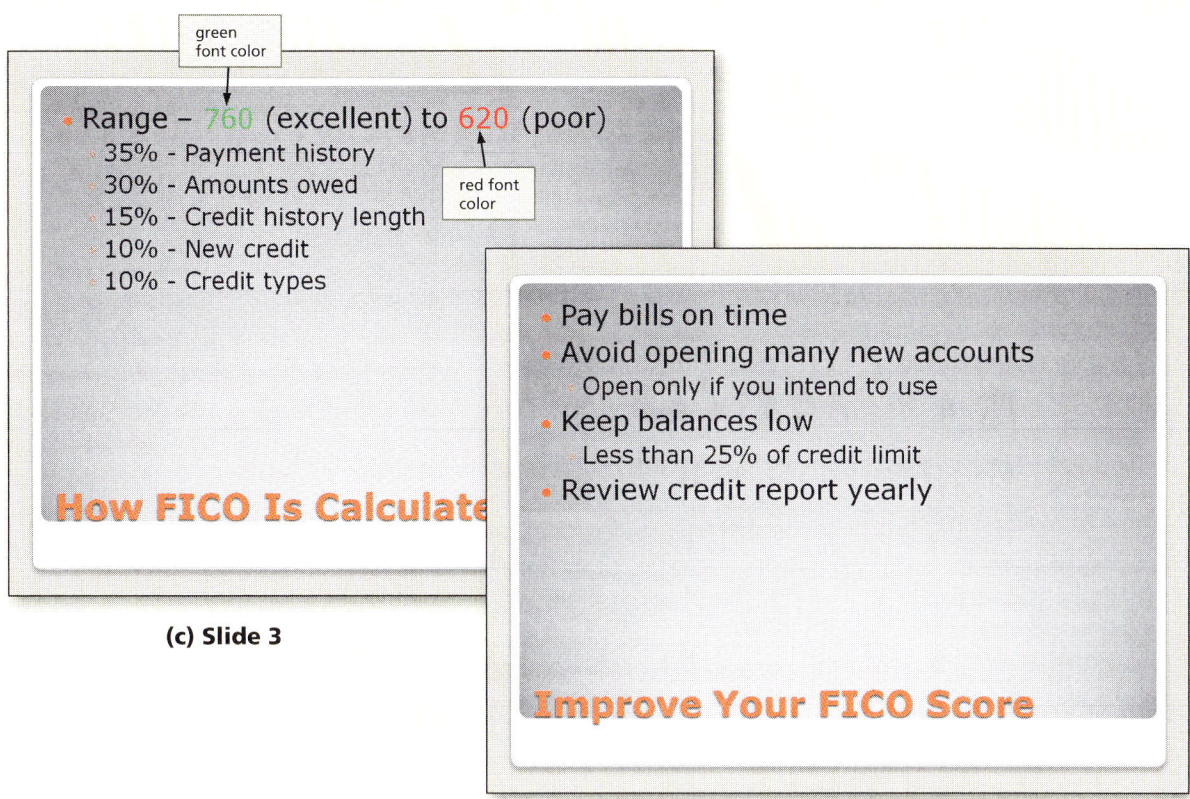

(c) Slide 3

(d) Slide 4

Figure 1–98 (continued)

In the Lab

Lab 2: Creating a Presentation with Bulleted Lists and a Closing Slide

Problem: Hybrid vehicles have received much attention in recent years. Everyone from environmentalists to movie stars are driving them, and potential buyers wait for months until the vehicles arrive in dealers' showrooms. You work part-time at Midwest State Bank, and the loan department manager, Jen Westbrook, has asked you to develop a PowerPoint presentation to accompany her upcoming speech. She hands you the outline shown in Figure 1–99 and asks you to create the presentation shown in Figures 1–100a through 1–100e.

Is a Hybrid Car Right for You?
  Jen Westbrook, Midwest State Bank Loan Department Manager

Are They a Good Value?
  Depends upon your driving habits
  Government offers tax credits
  Excellent resale value
  Efficient gas consumption

What Is Their Gas Mileage?
  Depends upon make and size
    City: Ranges from 18 to 60 mpg
    Highway: Ranges from 21 to 66 mpg
  Actual mileage affected by driving patterns

What Makes Them Work?
  Use two motors
    Gas
      Smaller, more efficient than traditional vehicle
    Electric
      Gives gas engine extra power boost
      May power car entirely

See me for your next car purchase
  Jen Westbrook, Midwest State Bank Loan Department Manager

Figure 1–99

Continued >

In the Lab *continued*

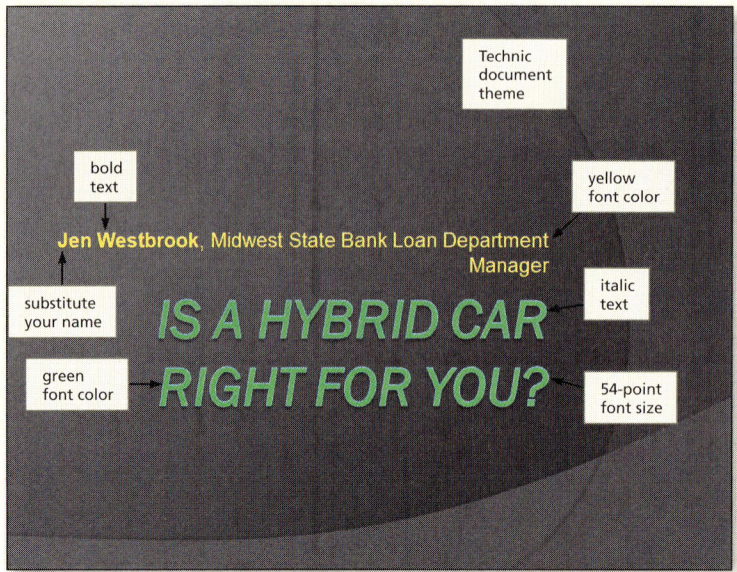

(a) Slide 1 (Title Slide)

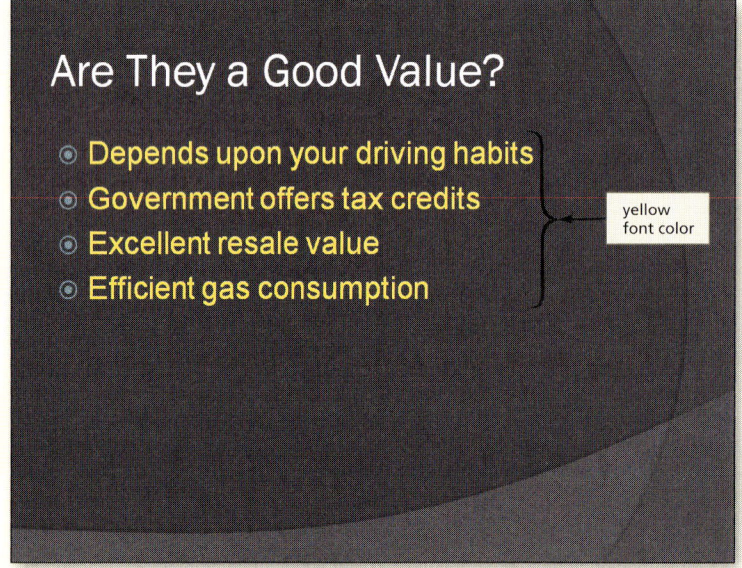

(b) Slide 2

Figure 1–100

Instructions: Perform the following tasks.

1. Create a new presentation using the Technic document theme.
2. Using the typed notes illustrated in Figure 1–99, create the title slide shown in Figure 1–100a using your name in place of Jan Westbrook. Bold your name. Italicize the title, Is a Hybrid Car Right for You?, and increase the font size to 54. Change the font color of the title text to green and the subtitle text to yellow.
3. Using the typed notes in Figure 1–99, create the three text slides with bulleted lists shown in Figures 1–100b through 1–100d. Change the color of all the bulleted list paragraph text to yellow.
4. Duplicate the title slide and then move the new closing slide to the end of the presentation. Change the Slide 5 title text, increase the font size to 66, and remove the italics.
5. Check the spelling and correct any errors.
6. Drag the scroll box to display Slide 1. Click the Slide Show button to start Slide Show view. Then click to display each slide.
7. Change the document properties, as specified by your instructor. Save the presentation using the file name, Lab 1-2 Hybrids.
8. Submit the revised document in the format specified by your instructor.

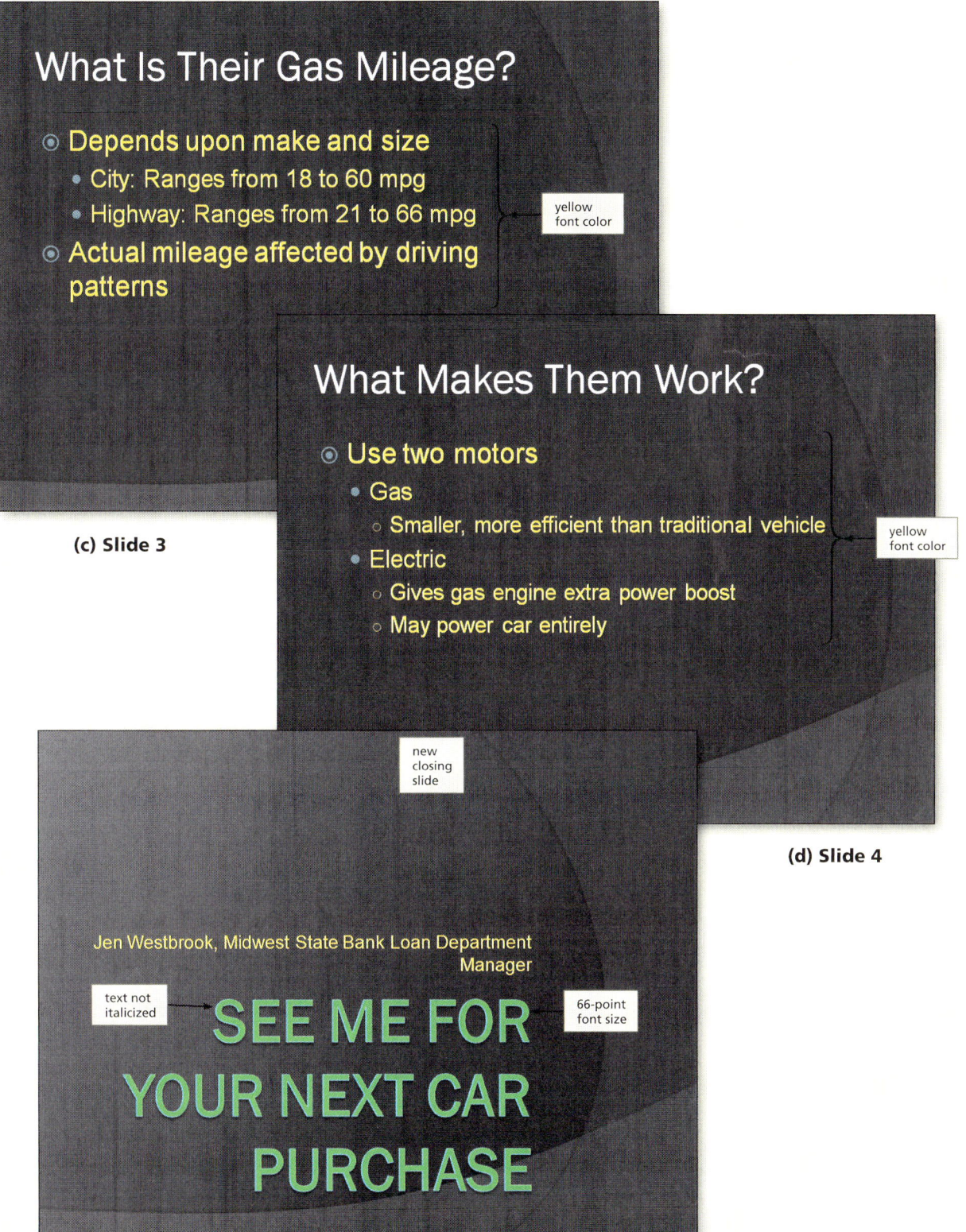

Figure 1–100 (continued)

In the Lab

Lab 3: Creating and Updating Presentations

Problem: Bobbie Willis, the public relations director for the South Haven Park District, plans activities every season for community residents and promotes the offerings using a PowerPoint presentation. The new seminars for senior citizens this spring are quilting and t'ai chi. Adults can register for gourmet cooking lessons and kickball. Teens can enroll in sailing and fencing lessons.

South Haven Park District
New Spring Seminars
Bobbie Willis, Director

Seniors' Seminars
    Quilting
        Quilts made from donated fabrics
        Sewing machines provided
    T'ai Chi
        Gentle warm-ups
        12 slow, continuous movements
        Easy cool-down exercises

Adults' Seminars
    Almost Gourmet
        Learn techniques from a professional chef
            Everyone prepares and enjoys the dinners
                Come hungry!
    Kickball
        Learn techniques and rules

Teens' Seminars
    Sailing
        Sail a 30-foot sailboat at your first class
    Fencing
        Three levels
            Level 1 – Beginning Foil
            Level 2 – Foil, Epee, and Saber
            Level 3 – Open Strip Fencing

Figure 1–101

Instructions Part 1: Using the outline in Figure 1–101, create the presentation shown in Figure 1–102. Use the Oriel document theme. On the title slide shown in Figure 1–102a, type your name in place of Bobbie Willis, increase the font size of the title paragraph, South Haven Park District, to 60 and change the text font style to italic. Increase the font size of the subtitle paragraph, New Spring Seminars, to 32, and change the font size of the subtitle paragraph with your name to 37 or to a size that displays all the text on one line. Create the three text slides with multi-level bulleted lists shown in Figures 1–102b through 1–102d.

Correct any spelling mistakes. Change the document properties, as specified by your instructor. Save the presentation using the file name, Lab 1-3 Part One Spring Seminars. Display the presentation in grayscale.

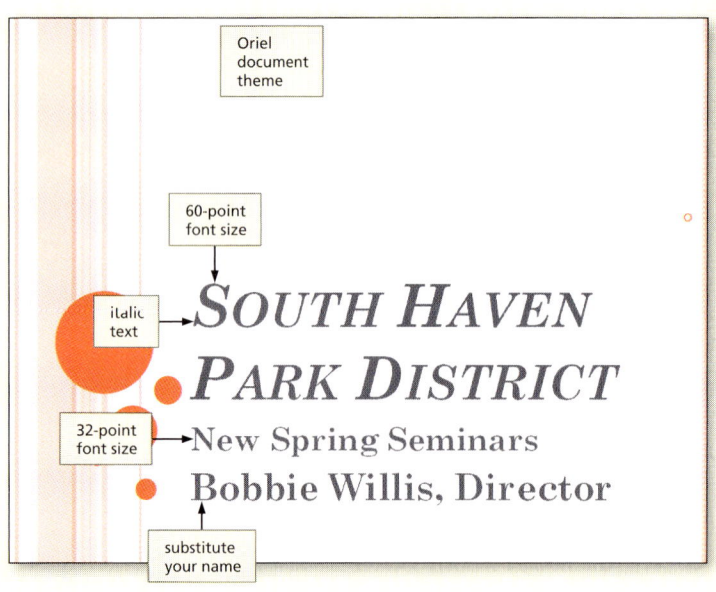

(a) Slide 1 (Title Slide)
Figure 1–102

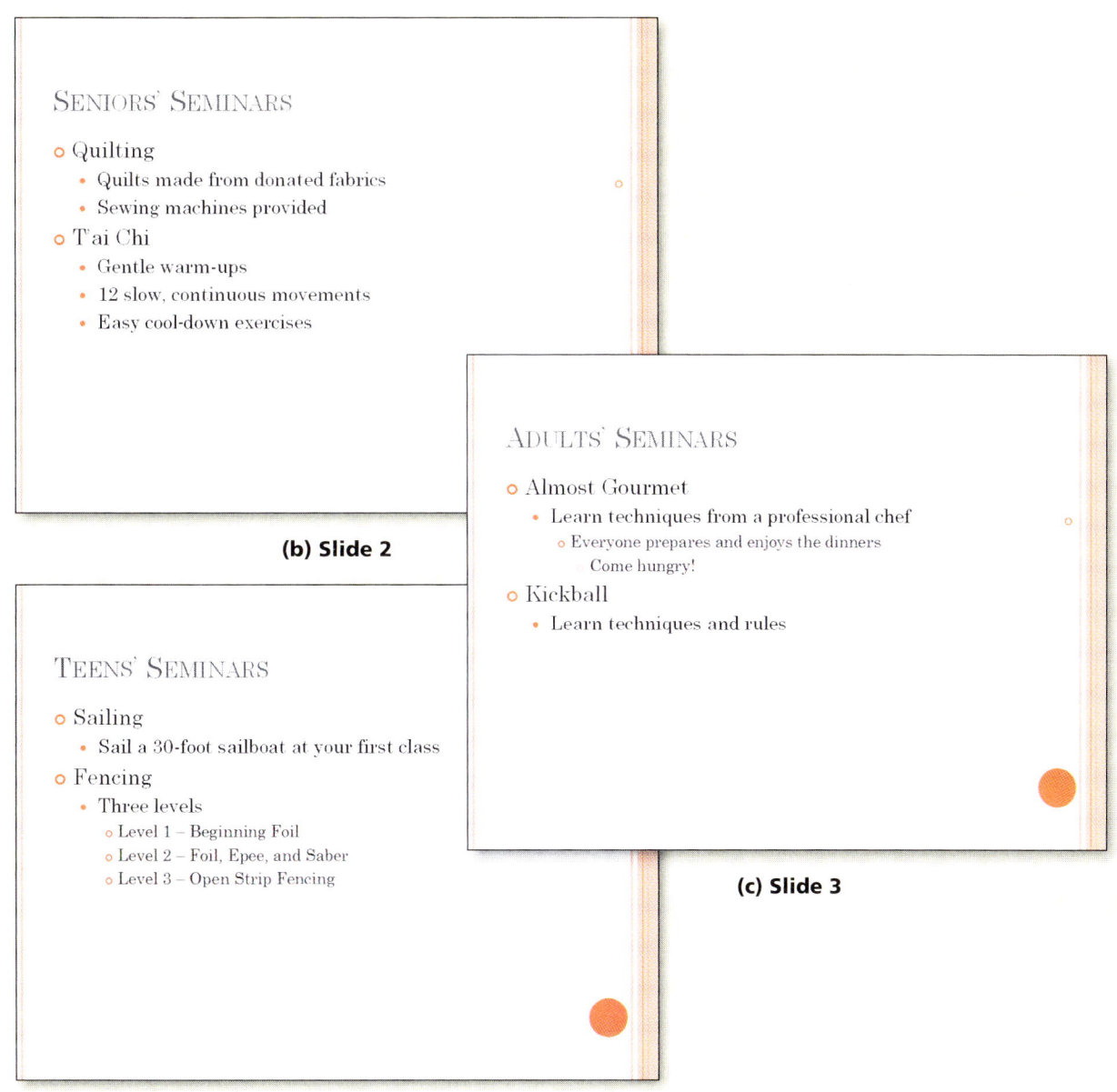

Figure 1–102 (continued)

Instructions Part 2: The South Haven Park District staff members want to update this presentation to promote the new Fall seminars. Modify the presentation created in Part 1 to create the presentation shown in Figure 1–103. To begin, save the current presentation with the new file name, Lab 1-3 Part Two Fall Seminars. Change the document theme to Civic. On the title slide, remove the italics from the title paragraph, South Haven Park District, decrease the font size to 44, and bold the text. Change the first subtitle paragraph to New Fall Seminars. Then change your title in the second subtitle paragraph to Executive Director and change the font size of the entire paragraph to 28.

On Slide 2, change the first first-level paragraph, Quilting, to Quilting for the Holidays. Change the first second-level paragraph, Quilts made from donated fabrics, to Quilts will be raffled at Annual Bazaar. Change the title of the second seminar to Intermediate T'ai Chi.

On Slide 3, change the first second-level paragraph under Almost Gourmet to Holiday feasts and parties. Then change the second-level paragraph under Kickball to Seminar concludes with single elimination tournament.

On Slide 4, change the first class from Sailing to Climbing and then change the course description second-level paragraph to Covers verbal signals, rope, knots, harnesses, belaying.

Continued >

In the Lab *continued*

Correct any spelling mistakes, and then view the slide show. Change the document properties, as specified by your instructor. Display the presentation in grayscale. Submit both Part One and Part Two documents in the format specified by your instructor.

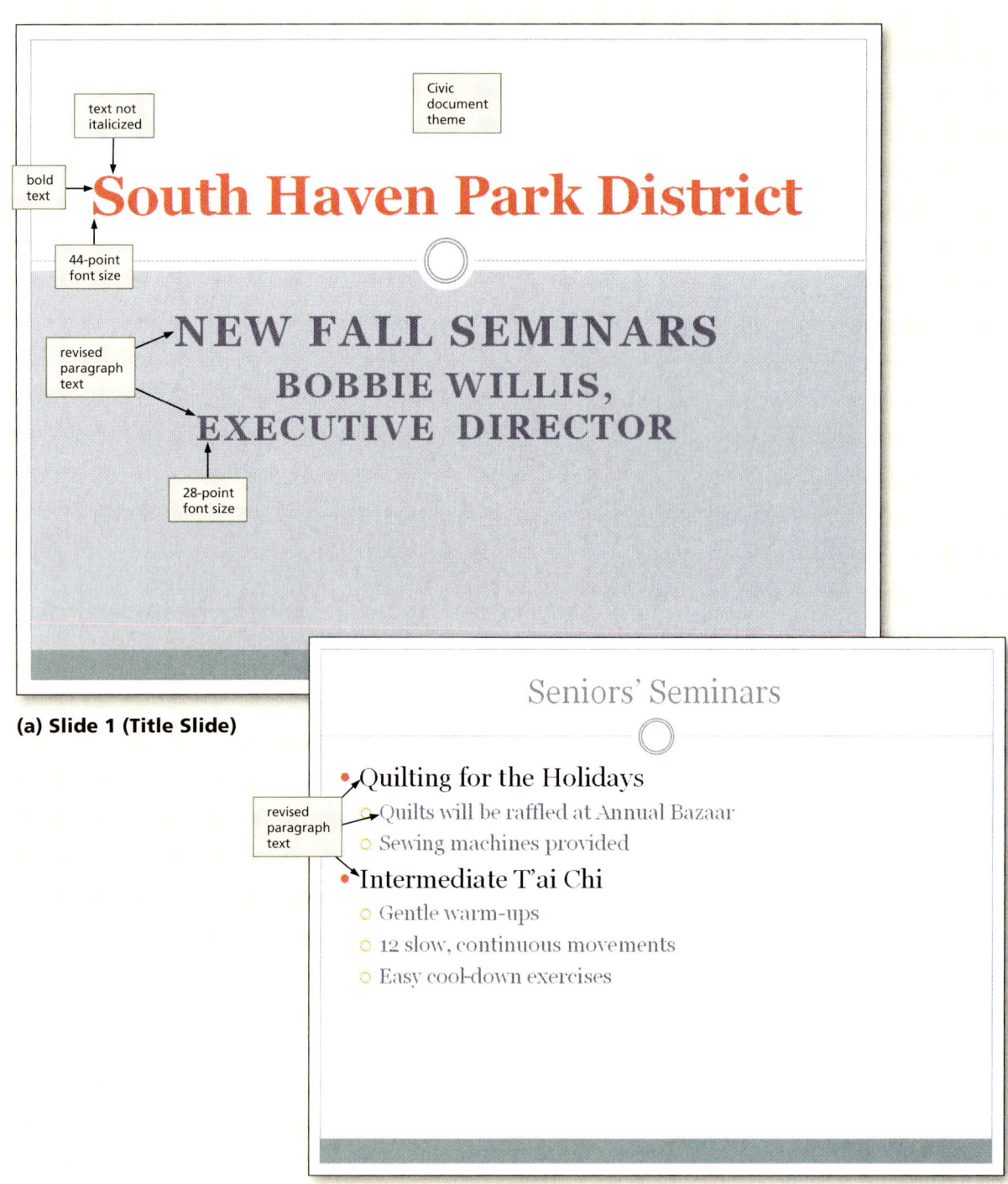

(a) Slide 1 (Title Slide)

(b) Slide 2

Figure 1–103

(c) Slide 3

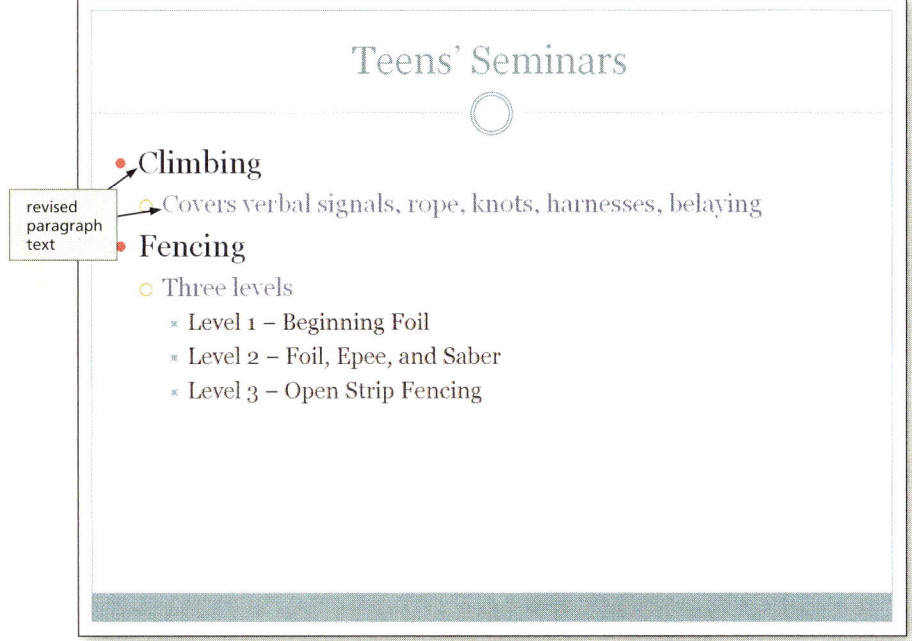

(d) Slide 4

Figure 1–103 (continued)

Cases and Places

Apply your creative thinking and problem solving skills to design and implement a solution.

• Easier   •• More Difficult

Note: Remember to use the 7 × 7 rule as you design the presentations: a maximum of seven words on a line and a maximum of seven lines on one slide.

• 1: Design and Create an Ocean and Seas Presentation

Salt water covers more than two-thirds of the Earth's surface. This water flows freely between the Earth's five oceans and seas, which all are connected. In preparation for your next snorkeling and diving adventure, you have been reading about the oceans and seas. You decide to prepare a PowerPoint presentation to accompany a speech that is required in your Earth Science class. You create the outline shown in Figure 1–104 about these waters. Use this outline along with the concepts and techniques presented in this chapter to develop and format a slide show with a title slide and three text slides with bulleted lists. Be sure to check spelling.

Water, Water, Everywhere
The Earth's Oceans and Seas
Jamel Thomas
Earth Science 203

Major Bodies of Water
　Four oceans: Pacific, Atlantic, Indian, and Arctic
　　Pacific is largest and deepest
　　　64,186,300 square miles
　　　12,925 feet average depth
　Fifth ocean delimited in 2000
　　Southern Ocean north of Antarctica

Coral Reefs
　Form in shallow, warm seas
　Made of coral polyps' skeletons
　　Grow on top of old skeletons
　Spend adult lives fixed to same spot
　Coral diseases increasing dramatically past 10 years
　　Responding to onset of bacteria, fungi, viruses

Ocean Zones
　Sunlit (down to 650 feet)
　　Sea plants and many animals
　Twilight (down to 3,300 feet)
　　Many different fish
　Sunless (down to 13,100 feet)
　　Animals feed on dead food from above

Figure 1–104

• 2: Design and Create an Industrial Revolution Presentation

The Industrial Revolution changed the way people worked and lived in many parts of the world. With its roots in Britain in the 18th century, the Industrial Revolution introduced new machines, steam power, and trains. As part of your World History homework assignments, you develop the outline shown in Figure 1–105 about the Industrial Revolution and then create an accompanying PowerPoint presentation. Use the concepts and techniques presented in this chapter to develop and format this slide show with a title slide, three text slides with bulleted lists, and a closing slide. Be sure to check spelling.

The Industrial Revolution
1700 - 1850
Sonia Banks
World History 108

British Inventors
    First machines spun and wove cloth quickly
        Wealthy businessmen built factories
            Spinning Jenny machine spun 16 threads simultaneously
    Angered people who made cloth at home
        Luddites protested by smashing machines
            Led by Ned Ludd

Steam Power
    James Watt invented first steam engine in 1782
        Hundreds of his engines used throughout Britain
    George Stephenson designed steam train, The Rocket
        Peak speed: 30 mph
        Used to transport goods in 1829

Coal Mining
    Coal needed to boil water to create steam
    Mining towns boomed
        Deep mines dug
        Men, women, and children worked long hours
            Many people killed and injured

Figure 1–105

Continued >

Cases and Places *continued*

•• 3: Design and Create a Recycling Presentation

Many communities require recycling of household waste. Residents are required to separate paper, plastics, and glass and put each material in special bins or bags. Electronic equipment also can be recycled. Your community has developed a special program for broken or obsolete computers and peripherals, office equipment and products, small home appliances, and entertainment equipment. These items include personal computers, printers, cellular telephones, toasters, televisions, DVD players, and video game consoles. Community officials will be collecting these items during the next two Fridays at your local police station and a nearby shopping center. They will not accept air conditioners, humidifiers, and hazardous wastes. Using the concepts and techniques presented in this chapter, develop a short PowerPoint presentation to show at various businesses and offices in your community. Emphasize that recycling is important because electronic products have very short useful lives. They produce waste and may contain hazardous materials, but many components can be salvaged. Include one slide with acceptable products and another with unacceptable products.

•• 4 Design and Create Your Favorite or Dream Car Presentation

Make It Personal

Ever since Henry Ford rolled the first Model T off his assembly line in 1908, people have been obsessed with cars. From the sporty Corvette to the environmentally friendly Prius, everyone has a favorite car or dream car. Use the concepts and techniques presented in this chapter to create a slide show promoting a particular vehicle. Include a title slide, at least three text slides with bulleted lists, and a closing slide. Format the text using colors, bolding, and italics where needed for emphasis. Be sure to check spelling.

•• 5: Design and Create a Financial Institutions Presentation

Working Together

Financial institutions such as banks, savings and loans, and credit unions offer a variety of products. Have each member of your team visit, telephone, or view Web sites of three local financial institutions. Gather data about:

1) Savings accounts

2) Checking accounts

3) Mortgages

4) Certificates of deposit

After coordinating the data, create a presentation with at least one slide showcasing each financial institution. As a group, critique each slide. Submit your assignment in the format specified by your instructor.

Microsoft Office **PowerPoint 2007**

2 | Creating a Presentation with Illustrations and Shapes

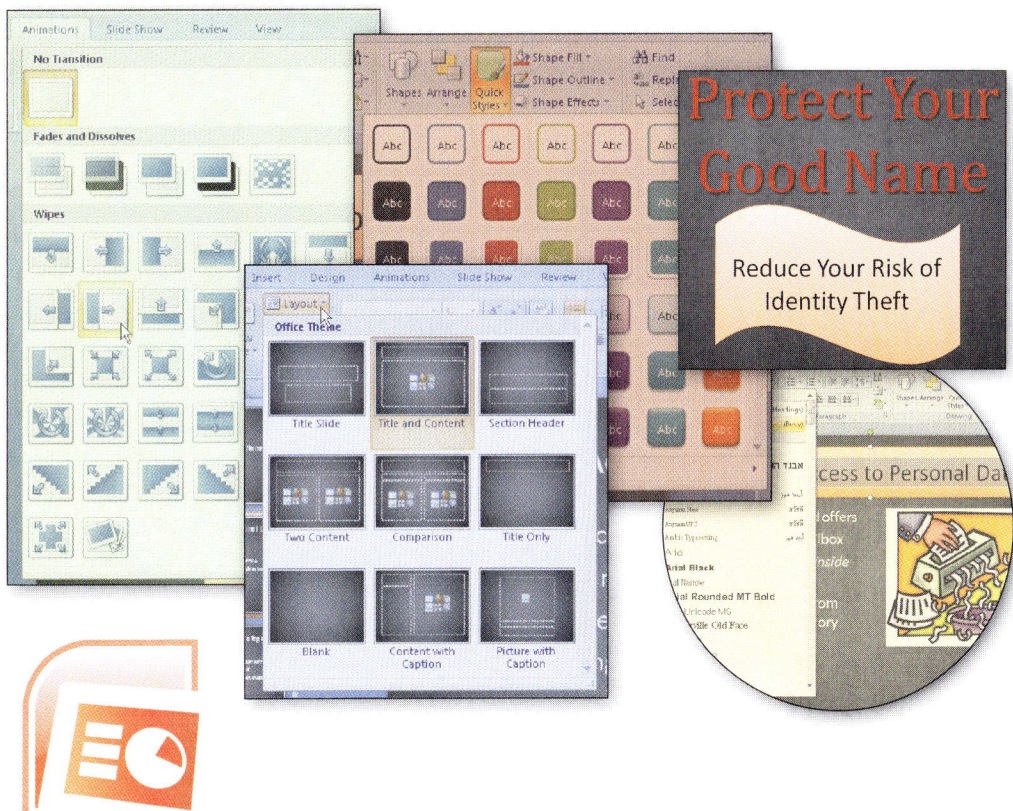

Objectives

You will have mastered the material in this chapter when you can:

- Create slides from a blank presentation
- Change views to review a presentation
- Change slide layouts
- Add a background style
- Insert, move, and size clip art
- Insert a photograph from a file
- Delete a placeholder
- Change font color
- Format text using the Format Painter
- Add and size a shape
- Apply Quick Styles to placeholders and shapes
- Select slide transitions
- Preview and print an outline and handout

2 Creating a Presentation with Illustrations and Shapes

Introduction

In our visual culture, audience members enjoy viewing effective graphics. Whether reading a document or viewing a PowerPoint presentation, people increasingly want to see photographs, artwork, graphics, and a variety of type. Researchers have known for decades that documents with visual elements are more effective than those that consist of only text because the illustrations motivate audiences to study the material. People remember at least one-third more information when the document they are seeing or reading contains visual elements. These graphics help clarify and emphasize details, so they appeal to audience members with differing backgrounds, reading levels, attention spans, and motivations.

Project — Presentation with Illustrations and a Shape

The project in this chapter follows graphical guidelines and uses PowerPoint to create the presentation shown in Figure 2–1. This slide show, which discusses identity theft, has a variety of illustrations and visual elements inserted on a gray background. Clip art and photographs add interest. Transitions help one slide flow gracefully into the next during a slide show. Slide titles have a style that blends well with the background and illustrations. The slide handouts include an outline of the slides and print all four slides on one page.

This presentation uses Quick Styles, which are collections of formatting options for objects and documents. The Quick Styles, like the document themes introduced in Chapter 1, are created by Microsoft's visual designers and give your presentation a professional look. When you rest your mouse pointer on a Quick Style thumbnail in the Quick Style gallery, you will see how the various colors, fonts, and effects are combined, and you can select the image that best fits the impression you want to present in your slide show.

Overview

As you read through this chapter, you will learn how to create the presentation shown in Figure 2–1 by performing these general tasks:

- Create a new presentation from a blank presentation.
- Review presentation in a variety of views.
- Insert and format shapes.
- Insert photographs and clips.
- Print an outline and a handout.

BTW

Delivery Skills
While illustrations and shapes help audience members retain important points in a slide show, keep in mind that a speaker's presentation skills are the most effective part of a presentation. The presenter's posture, eye contact, volume, gestures, and rate establish the tone and tempo of the presentation. A good presentation rarely overcomes poor delivery skills.

(a)

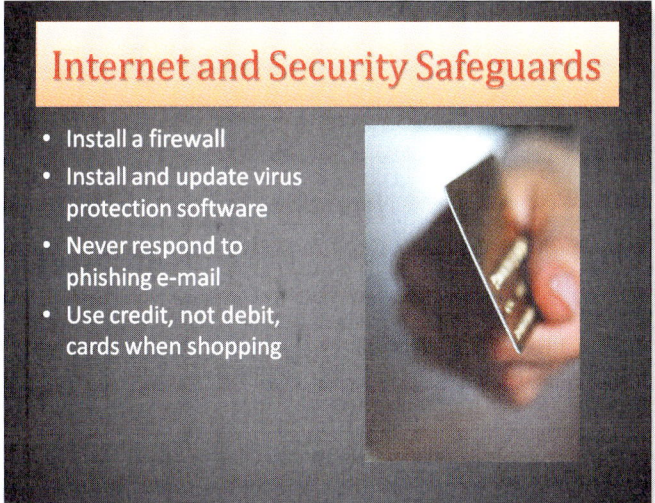

(c)

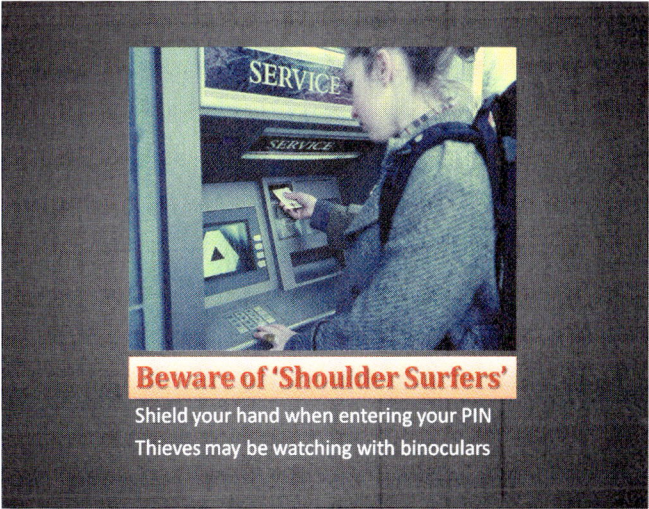

(b)

(d)

Figure 2–1

Plan Ahead

General Project Guidelines

When creating a PowerPoint presentation, the actions you perform and decisions you make will affect the appearance and characteristics of the finished document. As you create a presentation with illustrations, such as the project shown in Figure 2–1, you should follow these general guidelines:

1. **Focus on slide text content.** Give some careful thought to the words you choose to use. Some graphic designers advise starting with a blank screen so that the document theme does not distract from or influence the words.

2. **Use single quotation marks.** PowerPoint slides generally use a single quotation mark in several instances.
   - The introduction of an unfamiliar term
   - A quotation
   - Nicknames
   - Composition titles

3. **Adhere to copyright regulations.** Copyright laws apply to printed and Web-based materials. You can copy an existing photograph or artwork if it is in the public domain, if your company owns the graphic, or if you have obtained permission to use it. Be certain you have the legal right to use a desired graphic in your presentation.

4. **Use color effectively.** Your audience's eyes are drawn to color on a slide. Used appropriately, color can create interest by emphasizing material and promoting understanding. Be aware of symbolic meanings attached to colors, such as red generally representing danger, electricity, and heat.

5. **Use serif fonts for titles and sans serif fonts for body text.** Typefaces are divided into two categories: serif and sans serif. A serif letter generally has thin and thick areas, with the thin areas at the end of the lines. A sans serif letter generally is the same thickness. The letters in this box are sans serif.

6. **Choose graphics that serve a purpose.** Illustrations and art should help your audience remember and understand information. They should be uncluttered and visually appealing. Determine why you need each graphic and the kind of information it communicates.

7. **Consider graphics for multicultural audiences.** In today's intercultural society, your presentation might be viewed by people whose first language is different from yours. Some graphics have meanings specific to a culture, so be certain to learn about your intended audience and their views.

When necessary, more specific details concerning the above guidelines are presented at appropriate points in the chapter. The chapter also will identify the actions you perform and decisions made regarding these guidelines during the creation of the presentation shown in Figure 2–1.

Starting PowerPoint

Chapter 1 introduced you to starting PowerPoint, selecting a document theme, creating slides with bulleted lists, and printing a presentation. The following steps summarize starting a new presentation. To start PowerPoint, Windows Vista must be running. If you are using a computer to step through the project in this chapter and you want your screen to match the figures in this book, you should change your computer's resolution to 1024 × 768. For more information about how to change a computer's resolution, see Appendix C.

To Start PowerPoint

1. Click the Start button on the Windows Vista taskbar to display the Start menu.

2. Click All Programs at the bottom of the left pane on the Start menu to display the All Programs list and then click Microsoft Office in the All Programs list.

3. Click Microsoft Office PowerPoint 2007 to start PowerPoint and display a new blank presentation in the PowerPoint window.

4. If the PowerPoint window is not maximized, click the Maximize button next to the Close button on its title bar to maximize the window.

> **Plan Ahead**
>
> **Focus on slide text content.**
> Once you have researched your presentation topic, many methods exist to begin developing slide content.
>
> - Select a document theme and then enter text, illustration, and tables.
> - Open an existing presentation and modify the slides and theme.
> - Import an outline created in Microsoft Word.
> - Start with a blank presentation that uses the default Office Theme. Consider this practice similar to an artist who begins creating a painting with a blank, white canvas.
>
> Experiment using different methods of developing the initial content for slides. Experienced PowerPoint users sometimes find one technique works better than another to stimulate creativity or help them organize their ideas in a particular circumstance.

Creating Slides from a Blank Presentation

In Chapter 1, you selected a document theme and then typed the content for the title and text slides using single- and multi-level bulleted lists. In this chapter, you will type the slide content for the title and text slides, select a background, and then format the text.

> **BTW**
>
> **Introducing the Presentation**
> Before your audience enters the room, start the presentation and display Slide 1. This slide should be visually appealing and provide general interest in the presentation. An effective title slide gives a good first impression.

To Create a Title Slide

Recall from Chapter 1 that the title slide introduces the presentation to the audience. In addition to introducing the presentation, this project uses the title slide to capture the audience's attention by using title text and a shape, which is a movable, resizable graphical element. You will add this shape after you have typed the text for all four slides. The following step creates the slide show's title.

1. Type `Protect Your Good Name` in the title text placeholder (Figure 2–2 on the next page).

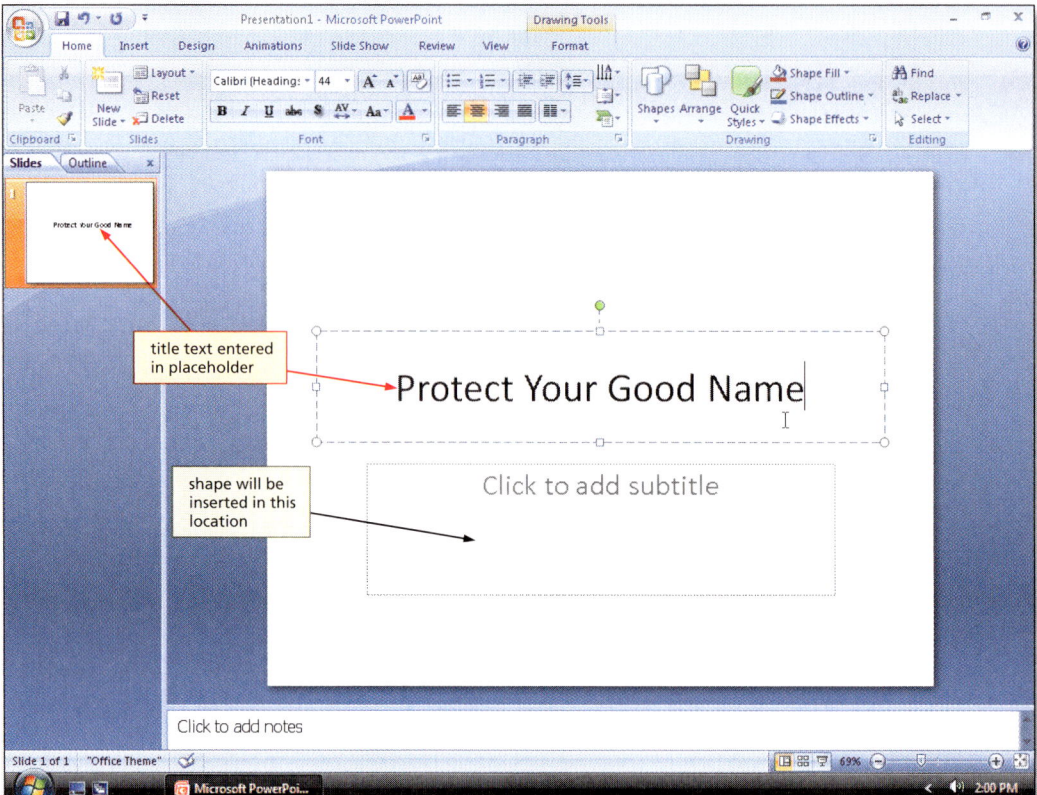

Figure 2–2

Plan Ahead

Use sans serif fonts for content text.
When a new slide is displayed during your presentation, your audience members focus on the title and then read the words in the content placeholder. Generally more words appear in the content placeholder, so designers use sans serif typefaces to decrease reading time.

To Create the First Text Slide with a Single-Level Bulleted List

The first text slide you create in Chapter 2 describes tips for helping prevent thieves from accessing personal information. The four suggestions are displayed as second-level paragraphs. The following steps add a new slide (Slide 2) and then create a text slide with a single-level bulleted list.

1. Click the New Slide button in the Slides group.

2. Type `Reduce Access to Personal Data` in the title text placeholder.

3. Press CTRL+ENTER, type `Shred credit card offers` in the content text placeholder, and then press the ENTER key.

4. Type `Use a locked mailbox` and then press the ENTER key.

Creating a Presentation with Illustrations and Shapes **PowerPoint Chapter 2** PPT 87

5. Type `Mail envelopes inside the post office` and then press the ENTER key.
6. Type `Remove listing from telephone directory` but do not press the ENTER key.
7. Italicize the word, inside, in the third bulleted paragraph (Figure 2–3).

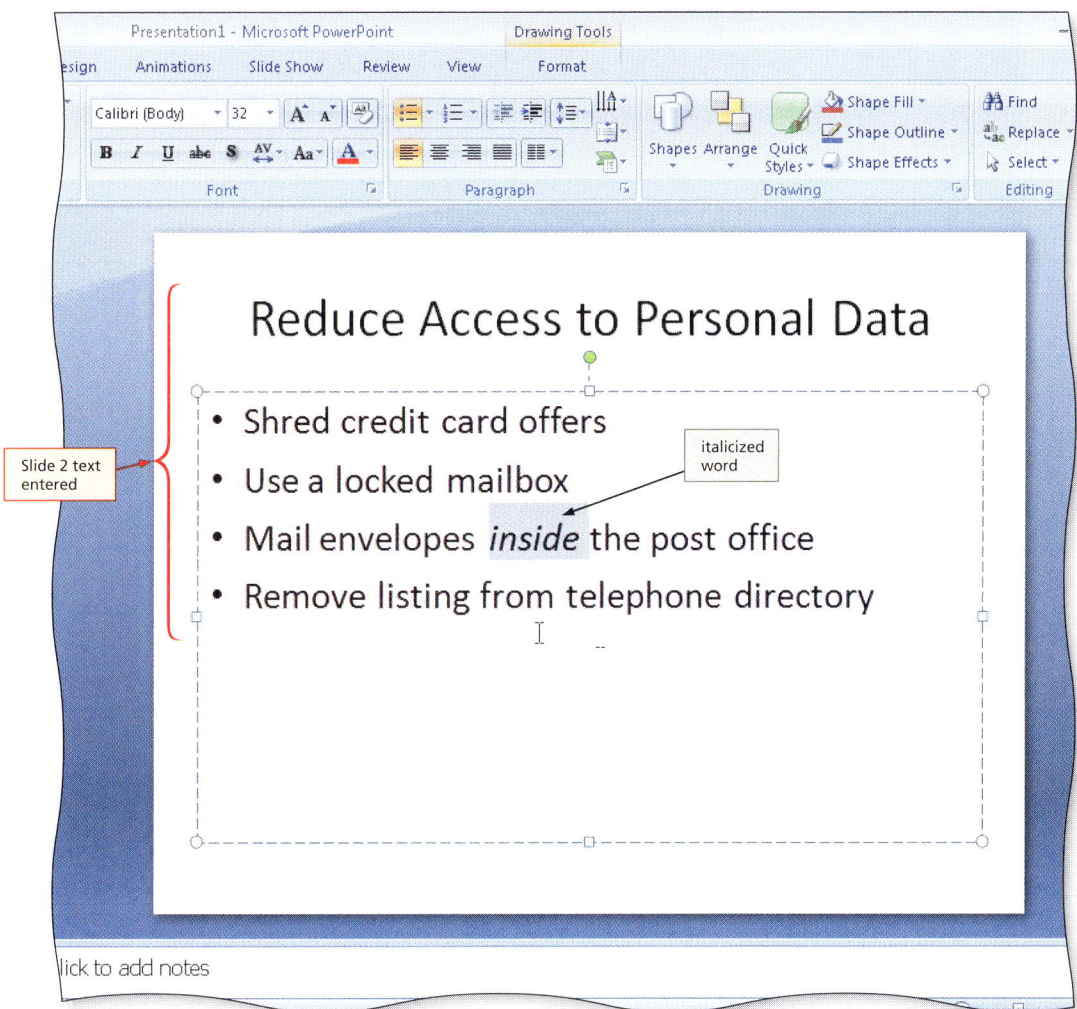

Figure 2–3

To Create the Second Text Slide with a Single-Level Bulleted List

The second text slide contains suggestions to help computer users protect their sensitive electronic files from cyber-intruders. The following steps add a new slide (Slide 3) and then create a text slide with a single-level bulleted list.

1. Click the New Slide button in the Slides group.
2. Type `Internet and Security Safeguards` in the title text placeholder.
3. Press CTRL+ENTER, type `Install a firewall` in the content text placeholder, and then press the ENTER key.
4. Type `Install and update virus protection software` and then press the ENTER key.

5 Type `Never respond to phishing e-mail` and then press the ENTER key.

6 Type `Use credit, not debit, cards when shopping` but do not press the ENTER key (Figure 2–4).

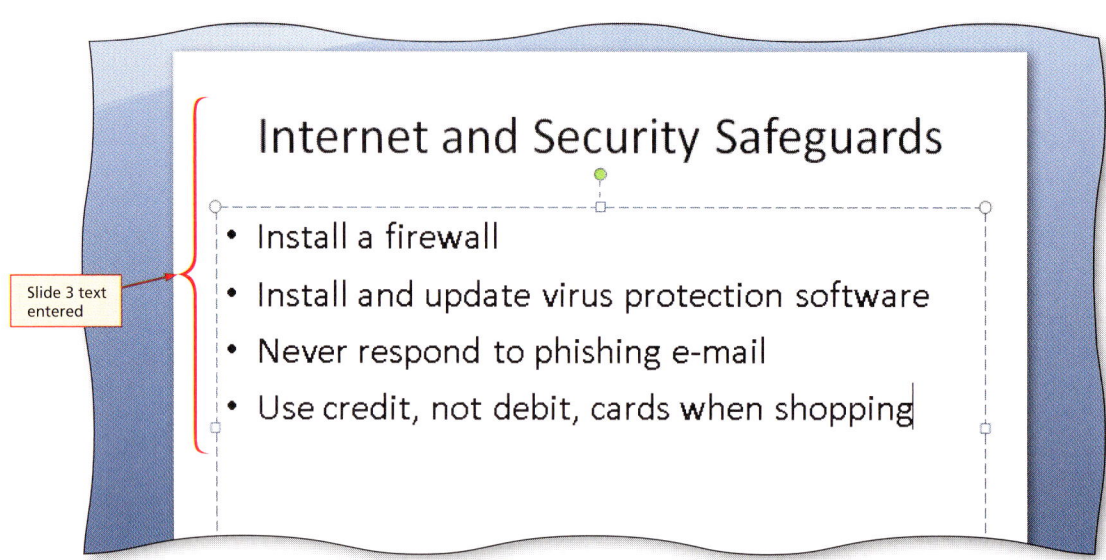

Figure 2–4

Plan Ahead

Use single quotation marks.
Type an apostrophe for the single quotation mark. PowerPoint generally will invert the first single quotation mark, making it an open-quotation mark, after you type a second single quotation mark, which then becomes a close-quotation mark.

To Create the Third Text Slide with a Single-Level Bulleted List

The final text slide in your presentation provides information to protect people using an automatic teller machine (ATM). "Shoulder surfers" position themselves near an ATM and often use binoculars and cameras to capture a user's personal identification number (PIN). The following steps add a new slide (Slide 4) and then create a text slide with two second-level bulleted paragraphs.

1 Click the New Slide button in the Slides group.

2 Type `Beware of 'Shoulder Surfers'` in the title text placeholder.

3 Press CTRL+ENTER, type `Shield your hand when entering your PIN` in the content text placeholder, and then press the ENTER key.

4 Type `Thieves may be watching with binoculars` but do not press the ENTER key (Figure 2–5).

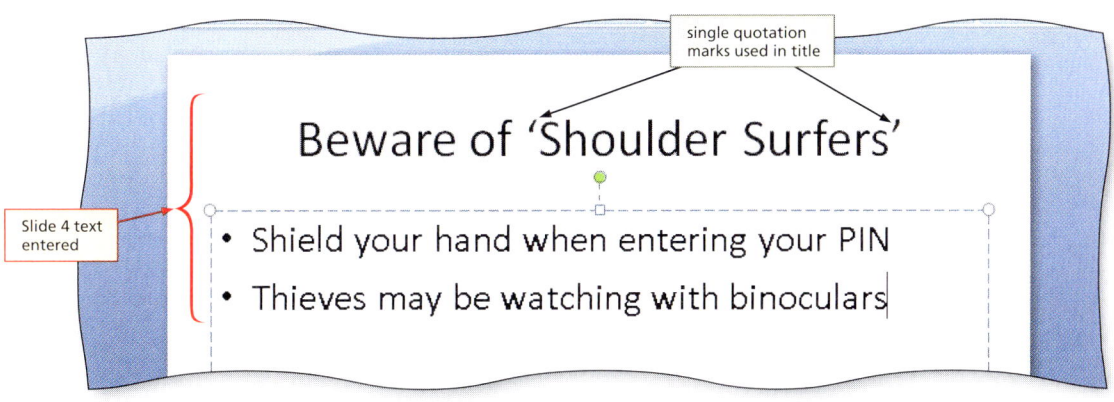

Figure 2–5

To Choose a Background Style

Now that the basic text paragraphs for the title and three text slides have been entered, you need to make design decisions. In creating Project 1, you chose a theme that determined the colors, fonts, and effects. You also can select these elements individually without choosing a theme. In Project 2, you will choose a background that fits the tone of your presentation and then choose fonts and effects. PowerPoint provides 12 white, ivory, blue, and black **background styles**. Background styles have designs that may include color, shading, patterns, and textures. **Fill effects** add pattern and texture to a background, which add depth to a slide. The following steps add a background style to all slides in the presentation.

1
- Click Design on the Ribbon to display the Design tab.
- Click the Background Styles button in the Background group to display the Background Styles gallery (Figure 2–6).

Experiment
- Point to various styles themes in the Background Styles gallery and watch the backgrounds changes on the slide.

Q&A Are the backgrounds displayed in a specific order?

Yes. They are arranged in order from white to black running from left to right. The first row has solid backgrounds; the middle row has darker fills at the bottom; the bottom row has darker fills on the sides. If you point to a background, a ScreenTip with the background's name appears on the screen.

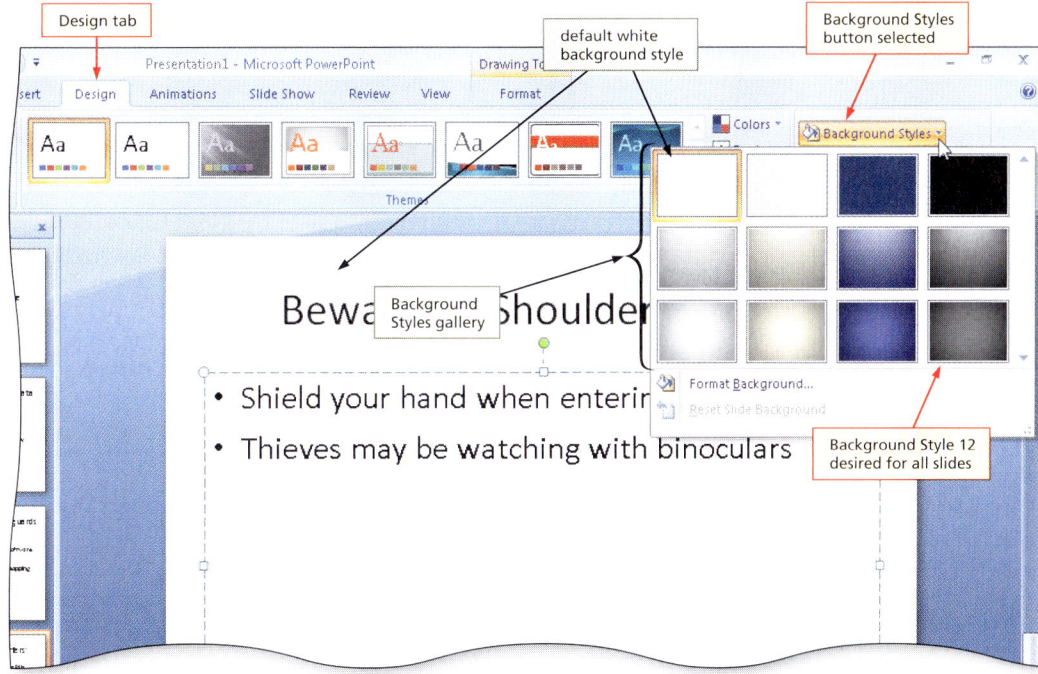

Figure 2–6

2
- Click Background Style 12 to apply this background to all the slides (Figure 2–7).

Q&A If I decide later that this background style does not fit the theme of my presentation, can I apply a different background?

Yes. You can repeat these steps at any time while creating your presentation.

Q&A What if I want to apply this background style to only one slide?

When the gallery is displaying, right-click the desired style and then click Apply to Selected Slides.

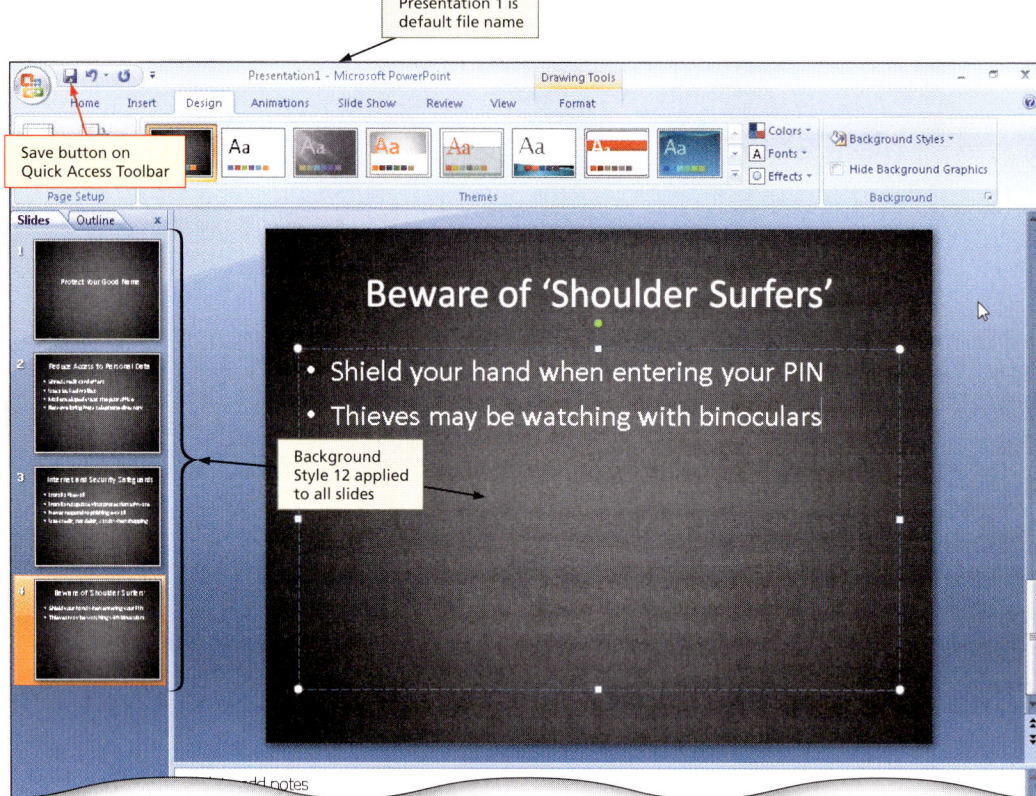

Figure 2–7

To Save a Presentation

You have performed many tasks to create the slide show and do not want to risk losing the work completed thus far. Accordingly, you should save the presentation. For a detailed example of the procedure summarized below, refer to pages PPT 27 through PPT 29 in Chapter 1.

1. With a USB flash drive connected to one of the computer's USB ports, click the Save button on the Quick Access Toolbar to display the Save As dialog box.

2. Type `Identity Theft` in the File name text box to change the file name. Do not press the ENTER key after typing the file name. If Computer is not displayed in the Favorite Links section, drag the top or bottom edge of the Save As dialog box until Computer is displayed. Click Computer in the Favorite Links section.

3. Double-click your USB flash drive in the list of available drives.

4. Click the Save button in the Save As dialog box to save the presentation on the USB flash drive with the file name, Identity Theft.

BTW

Experimenting with Normal View
As you become more comfortable using PowerPoint, experiment with using the Outline tab and with closing the Tabs pane to maximize the slide area. To close the Tabs pane, click the X to the right of the Outline tab. To redisplay the Tabs pane, click the View tab on the Ribbon and then click Normal in the Presentation Views group.

Changing Views to Review a Presentation

In Chapter 1, you displayed slides in Slide Show view to evaluate the presentation. Slide Show view, however, restricts your evaluation to one slide at a time. Recall from Chapter 1 that Slide Sorter view allows you to look at several slides at one time, which is why it is the best view to use to evaluate a presentation for content, organization, and overall appearance. After reviewing the slides, you can change the view to Normal view to continue working on the presentation.

To Change the View to Slide Sorter View

You can review the four slides in this presentation all in one window. The following step changes the view from Normal view to Slide Sorter view.

1
- Click the Slide Sorter button at the lower right of the PowerPoint window to display the presentation in Slide Sorter view (Figure 2–8).

Q&A Why is Slide 4 selected?
It is the current slide in the slide pane.

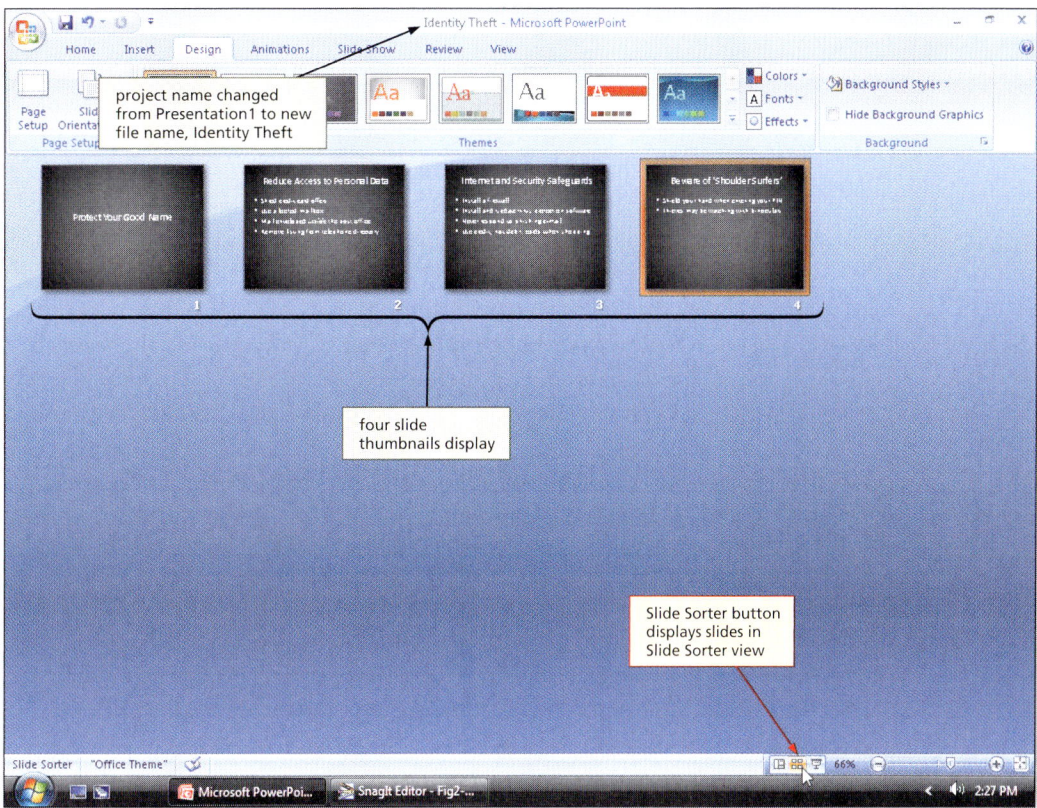

Figure 2–8

To Change the View to Normal View

You can make changes to text in Normal view and on the Outline tab. It is best, however, to change the view to Normal view when altering the slide layouts and formats so you can see the results of your changes. Switching between Slide Sorter view and Normal view helps you review your presentation, assess whether the slides have an attractive design and adequate content, and are organized for the most impact. The following steps change the view from Slide Sorter view to Normal view.

1
- Click the Normal button at the lower right of the PowerPoint window to display the presentation in Normal view (Figure 2–9).

Figure 2–9

BTW

Using the Find Command
Rather than viewing all the slides in your presentation to look for a particular word or phrase you typed, use the Find command to locate this text. Click the Home tab, click the Find button in the Editing group, type the text in the Find what text box, and then click the Find Next button.

Changing Layouts

When you developed this presentation, PowerPoint applied the Title Slide layout for Slide 1 and the Title and Content layout for the other three slides in the presentation. These layouts are the default styles. A **layout** specifies the arrangement of placeholders on a slide. These placeholders are arranged in various configurations and can contain text, such as the slide title or a bulleted list, or they can contain content, such as SmartArt graphics, pictures, charts, tables, shapes, and clip art. The placement of the text, in relationship to content, depends on the slide layout. You can specify a particular slide layout when you add a new slide to a presentation or after you have created the slide.

Using the **Layout gallery**, you can choose a slide layout. The nine layouts in this gallery have a variety of placeholders to define text and content positioning and formatting. Three layouts are for text: Title Slide, Section Header, and Title Only. Five are for text and content: Title and Content, Two Content, Comparison, Content with Caption, and Picture with Caption. The Blank layout has no placeholders. If none of these standard layouts meets your design needs, you can create a **custom layout**. A custom layout specifies the number, size, and location of placeholders, background content, and optional slide and placeholder-level properties.

When you change the layout of a slide, PowerPoint retains the text and objects and repositions them into the appropriate placeholders. Using slide layouts eliminates the need to resize objects and the font size because PowerPoint automatically sizes the objects and text to fit the placeholders.

To Change the Slide Layout to Two Content

Notice the slides have a significant amount of space and look plain. These observations indicate a need to add visual interest to the slides. The next several sections improve the presentation by changing layouts and adding clip art and photos. Before you add these graphical elements, you must change the slide layouts.

Adding clip art and a photograph to Slides 2, 3, and 4 requires two steps. First, change the slide layouts and then insert the clip or photo into the content placeholders. The following steps change the slide layout on Slide 2 from Title and Content to Two Content.

- Click the Previous Slide button on the vertical scroll bar twice to display Slide 2.
- Click Home on the Ribbon to display the Home tab.
- Click the Layout button in the Slides group on the Home tab to display the Layout gallery (Figure 2–10).

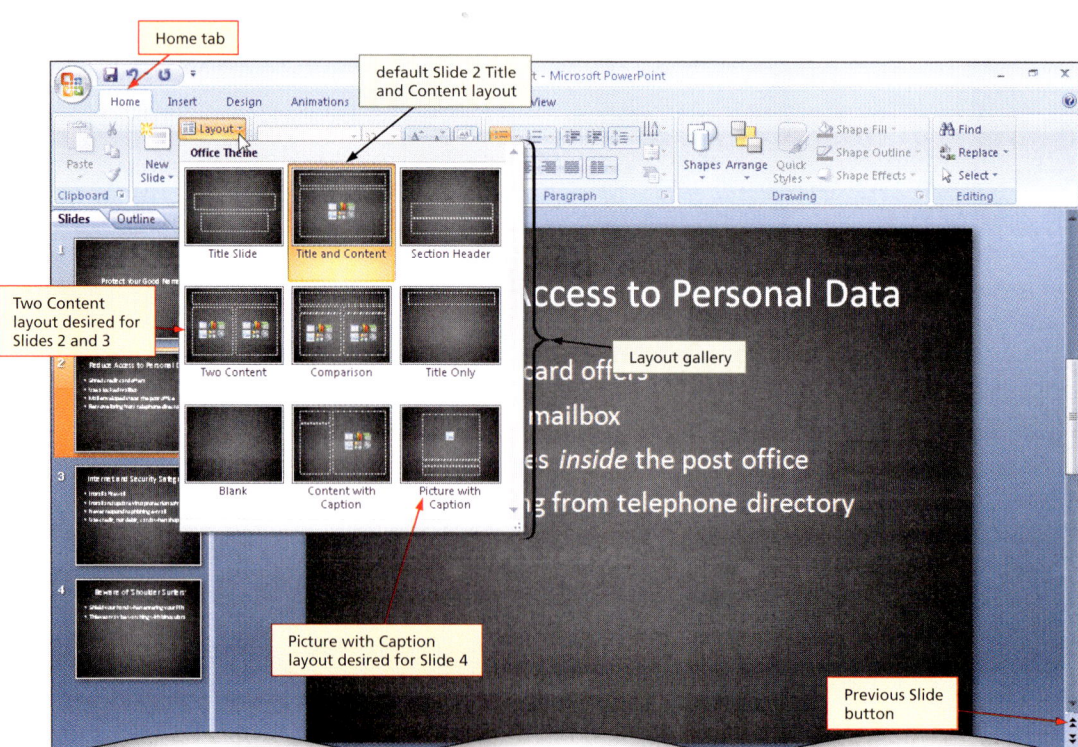

Figure 2–10

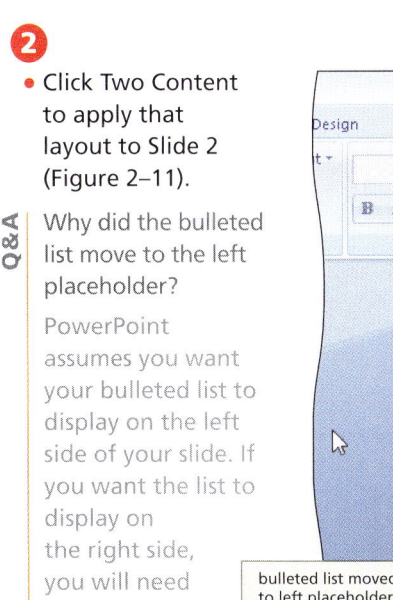

2
- Click Two Content to apply that layout to Slide 2 (Figure 2–11).

Q&A Why did the bulleted list move to the left placeholder?

PowerPoint assumes you want your bulleted list to display on the left side of your slide. If you want the list to display on the right side, you will need to move the placeholders on the slide.

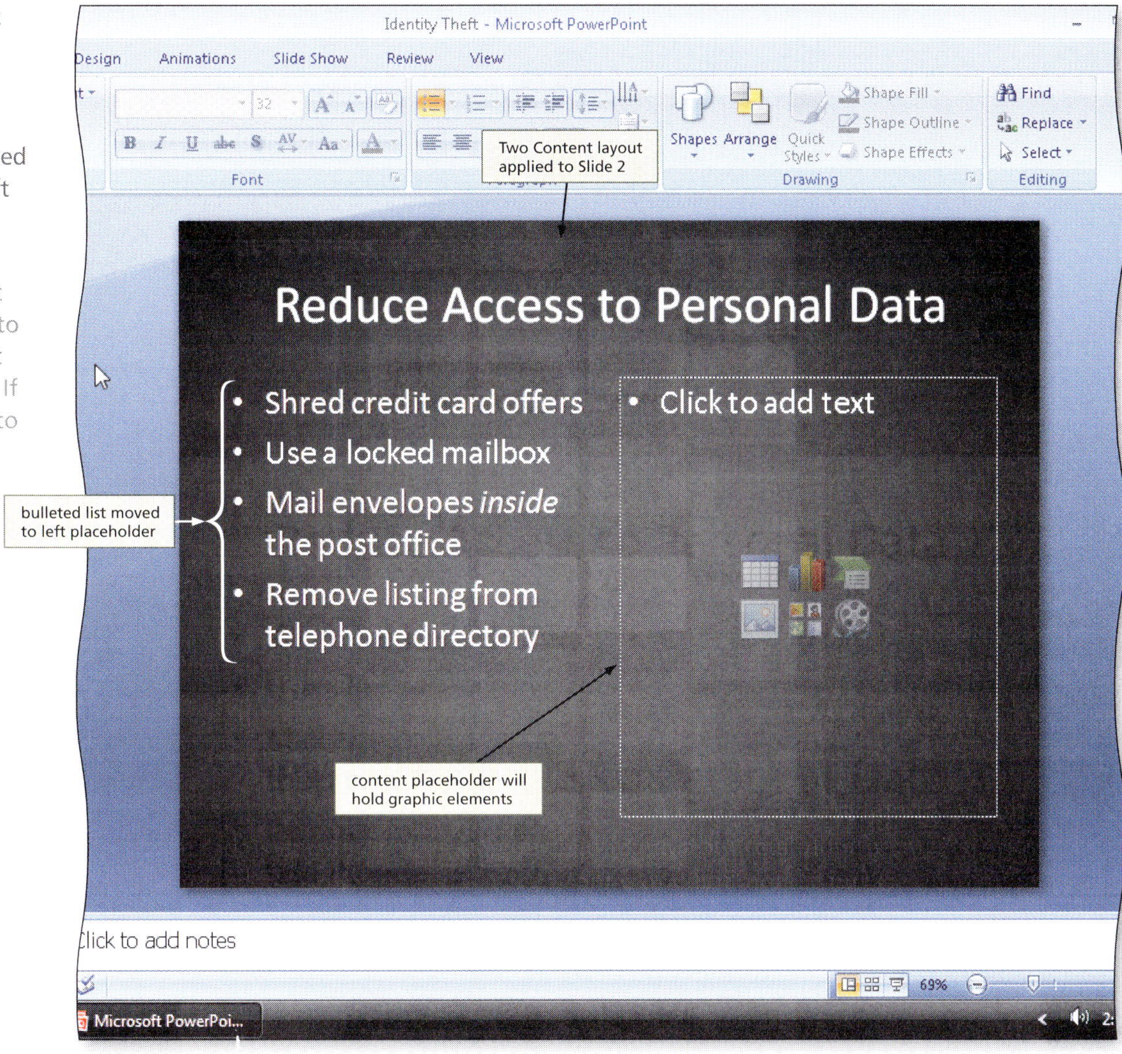

Figure 2–11

To Change the Slide Layout to Two Content

Slide 3 also will have a bulleted list and a graphic element, so the layout needs to change to accommodate this slide content. The following steps change the Slide 3 layout to Two Content.

1 Click the Next Slide button.

2 Click the Layout button in the Slides group on the Home tab to display the Layout gallery.

3 Click Two Content to apply the layout to Slide 3 (Figure 2–12).

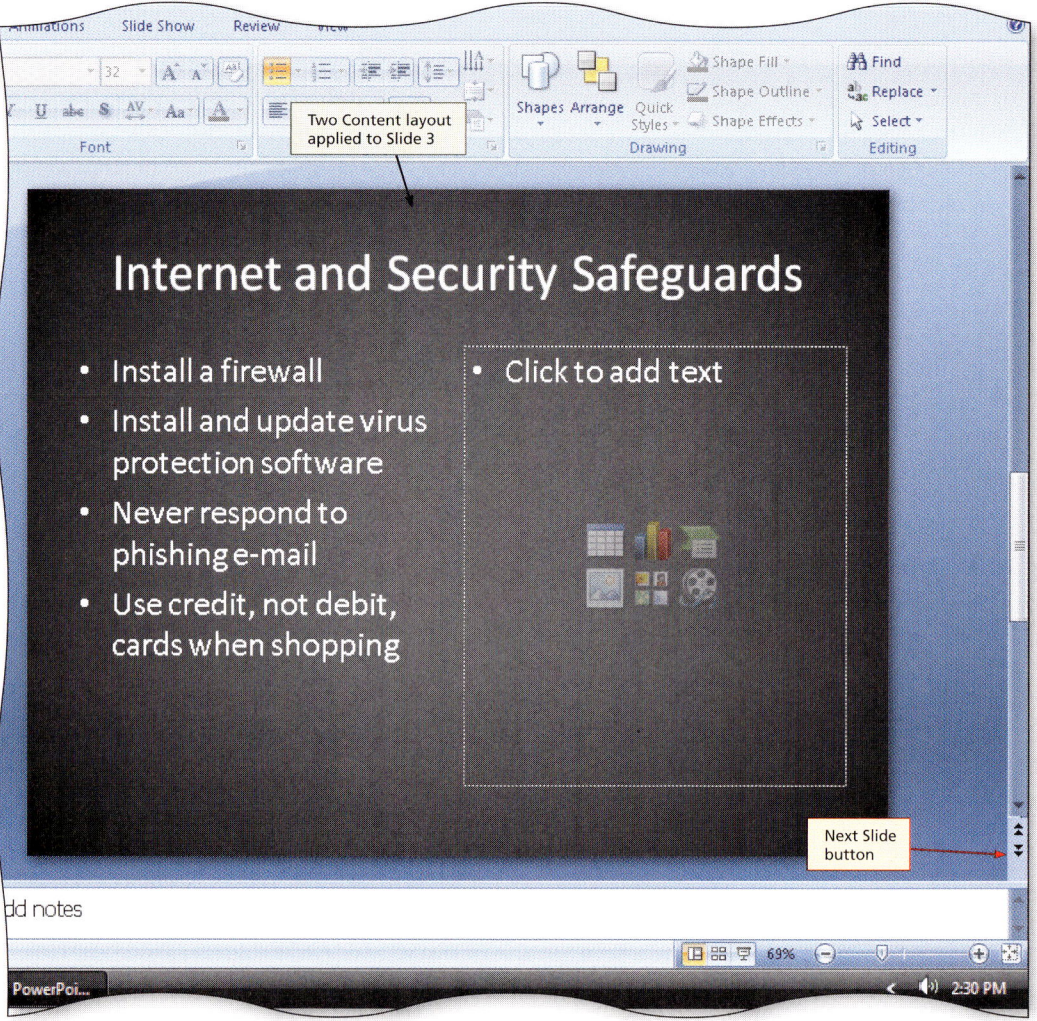

Figure 2-12

To Change the Slide Layout to Picture with Caption

The Slide 4 text discusses exercising caution while using an automatic teller machine (ATM). You have a photograph of a person using an ATM, and you want to display this graphic prominently on the slide. The Picture with Caption layout serves this purpose well, so the layout needs to change to accommodate this slide content. The following steps change the Slide 4 layout to Picture with Caption.

1 Click the Next Slide button.

2 Click the Layout button in the Slides group.

3 Click Picture with Caption to apply the layout to Slide 4 (Figure 2–13).

Q&A | Why did the font size of the title and bulleted list text decrease?
PowerPoint reduced the font size to make room for the large upper content placeholder. You can increase the font size of this text if you desire.

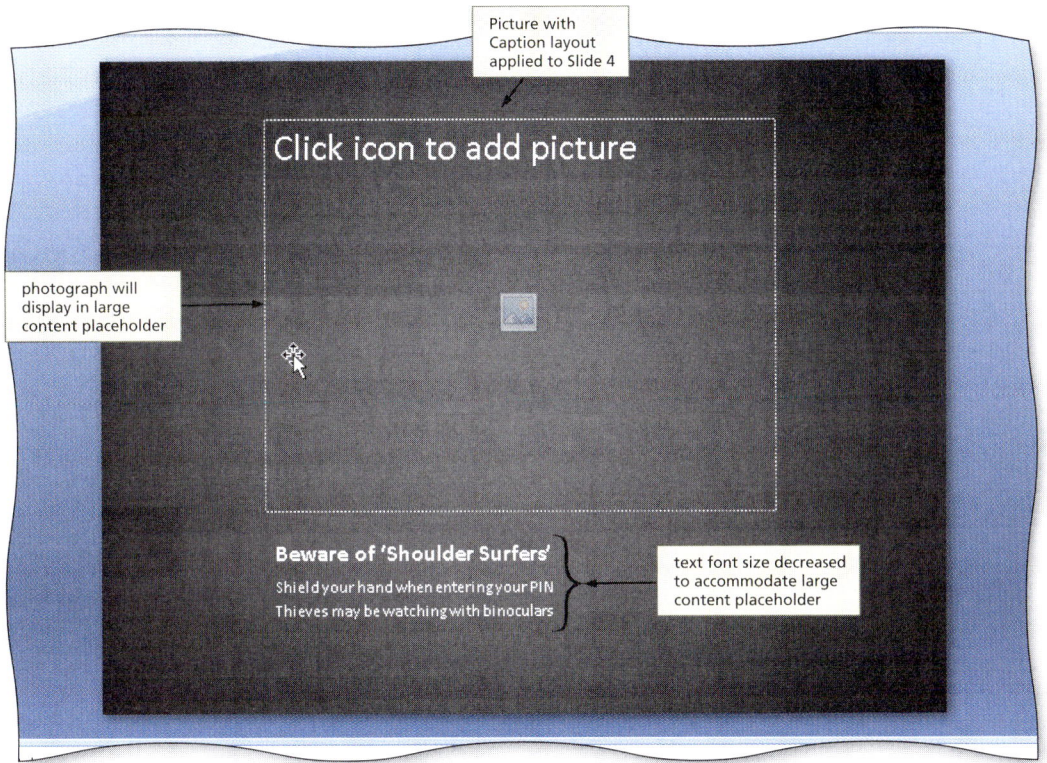

Figure 2–13

Inserting Clip Art and Photographs into Slides

A **clip** is a single media file, including art, sound, animation, and movies. Adding a clip can help increase the visual appeal of many slides and can offer a quick way to add professional-looking graphic images and sounds to a presentation without creating these files yourself. This art is contained in the **Microsoft Clip Organizer**, a collection of drawings, photographs, sounds, videos, and other media files shared with Microsoft Office applications. The **Office Collections** contains all these media files included with Microsoft Office.

You also can add your own clips to slides. You can insert these files directly from a storage medium, such as a USB flash drive. In addition, you can add them to the other files in the Clip Organizer so that you can search for and reuse these images, sounds, animations, and movies. When you create these media files, they are stored on your hard disk in **My Collections**. The Clip Organizer will find these files and create a new collection with these files. Two other locations for clips are Shared Collections and Web Collections. Files in the **Shared Collections** typically reside on a shared network file server and are accessed by multiple users. The **Web Collections** clips reside on the Microsoft Clip Art and Media Home page on the Microsoft Office Online Web site. They are available only if you have an active Internet connection.

> **BTW**
>
> **Importing Clips**
> Previous versions of PowerPoint imported clips automatically the first time a user desired to insert clips. PowerPoint 2007 requires the user to import the clips on first use by clicking the Organize clips link in the Clip Art task pane, clicking the File menu in the Favorites – Microsoft Clip Organizer dialog box, pointing to Add Clips to Organizer in the File menu, and then clicking Automatically.

The Clip Art Task Pane

You can add clips to your presentation in two ways. One way is by selecting one of the slide layouts that includes a content placeholder with a Clip Art button. A second method is by clicking the Clip Art button in the Illustrations area on the Insert tab. Clicking the Clip Art button opens the Clip Art task pane. The **Clip Art task pane** allows you to search for clips by using descriptive keywords, file names, media file formats, and clip collections. Specific file formats could be for clip art, photographs, movies, and sounds. Clips are organized in hierarchical **clip collections**, which combine topic-related clips into categories, such as Academic, Business, and Technology.

Clips have one or more keywords associated with various entities, activities, labels, and emotions. In most instances, the keywords give the name of the clip and related categories. For example, an image of a cow in the Animals category has the keywords animals, cattle, cows, dairies, farms, and Holsteins. You can enter these keywords in the Search for text box to find clips when you know one of the words associated with the image. Otherwise, you may find it necessary to scroll through several categories to find an appropriate clip.

To Insert a Clip from the Clip Organizer into a Content Placeholder

Depending on the installation of the Microsoft Clip Organizer on your computer, you may not have the clip art used in this chapter. Contact your instructor if you are missing clips used in the following steps. If you have an open connection to the Internet, clips from the Microsoft Office Online Web site will display automatically as the result of your search results.

With the Two Content layout applied to Slide 2, you insert clip art into the right content placeholder. The following steps insert clip art of a shredder into the content placeholder on Slide 2.

- Click the Previous Slide button twice to display Slide 2.
- Click the Clip Art button in the content placeholder to display the Clip Art task pane.
- Click the Search for text box in the Clip Art task pane, delete any letters that are present, and then type shredder in the Search for text box (Figure 2–14).

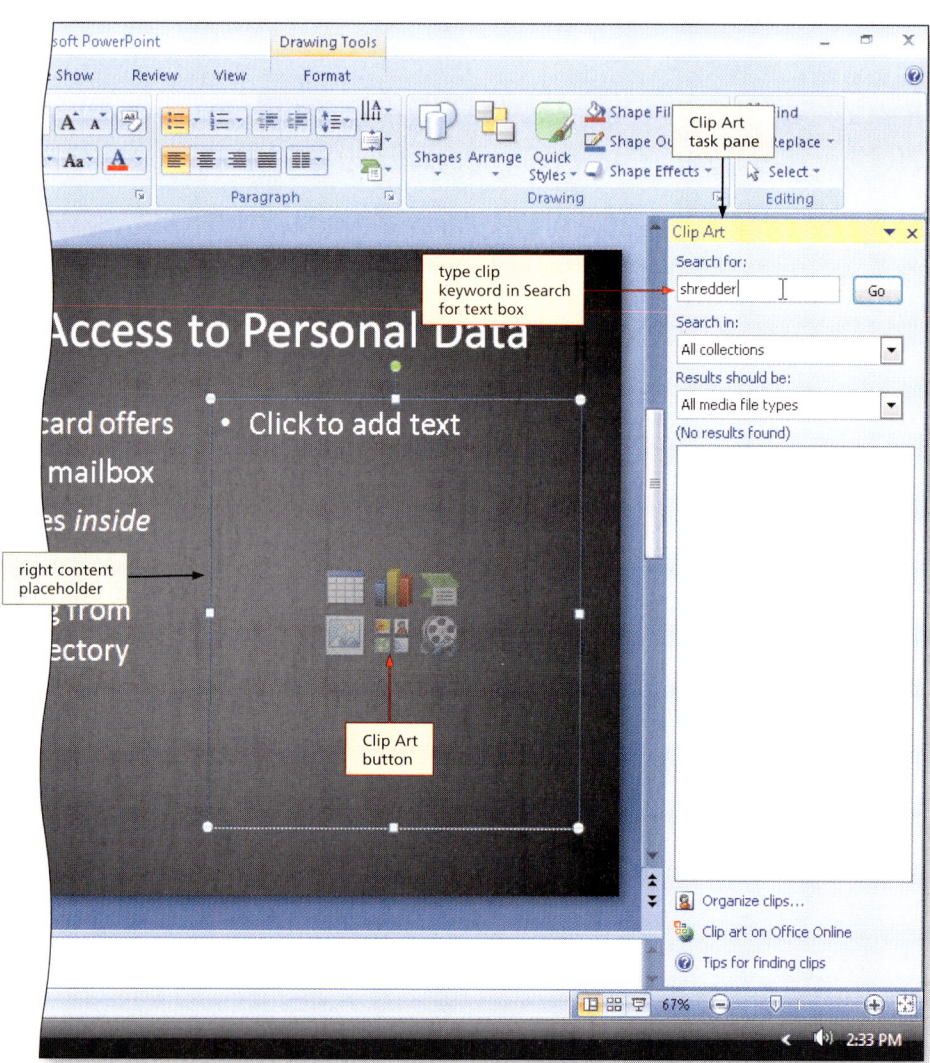

Figure 2–14

2

- Click the Go button so that the Microsoft Clip Organizer will search for and display all pictures having the keyword, shredder.

- If necessary, click the Yes button if a Microsoft Clip Organizer dialog box appears asking if you want to include additional clip art images from Microsoft Office Online.

- If necessary, scroll down the list to display the shredder clip shown in Figure 2–15

- Click the clip to insert it into the right content placeholder (Figure 2–15).

Q&A What if the shredder image displayed in Figure 2–15 is not shown in my Clip Art task pane?

Select a similar clip. Your clips may be different depending on the clips installed on your computer and if you have an open connection to the Internet.

Q&A What is the blue globe image that displays in the lower-left corner of the clips in the Clip Art task pane?

The globe indicates that the image was obtained from the Microsoft Office Online Web site.

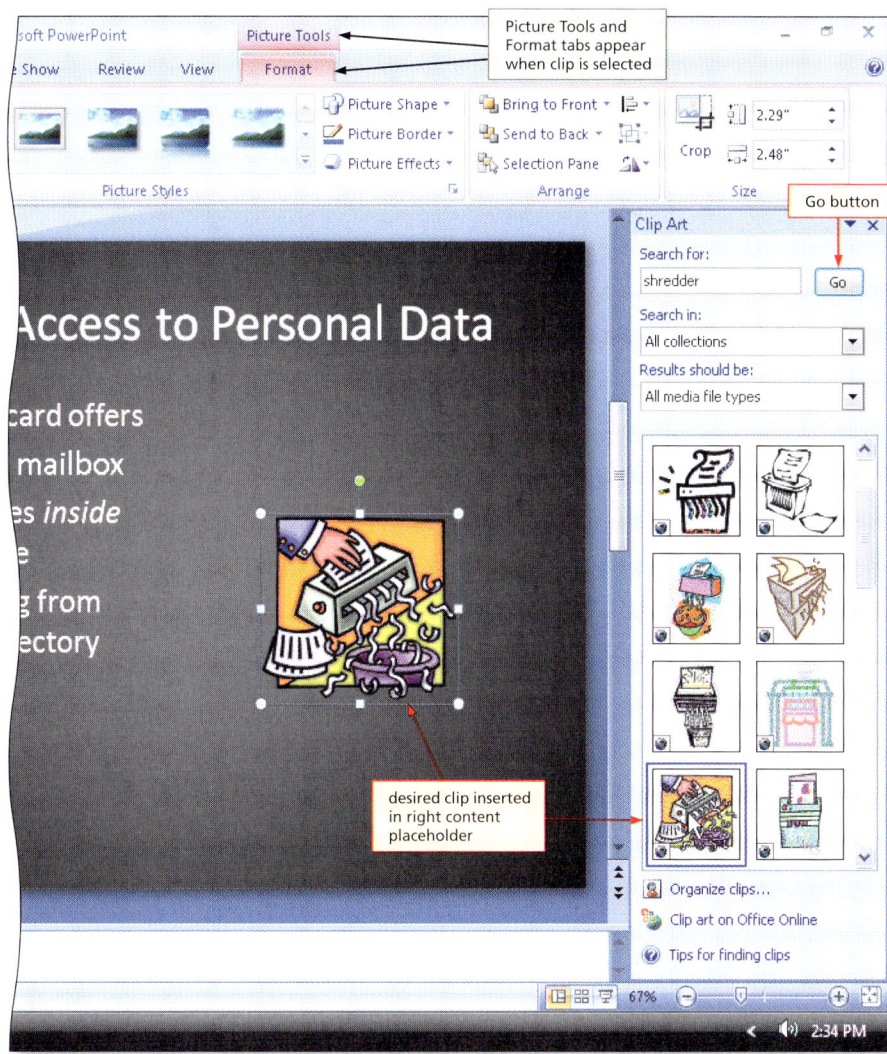

Figure 2–15

Adhere to copyright regulations.
You have permission to use the clips from the Microsoft Clip Organizer. If you want to use a clip from another source, be certain you have the legal right to insert this file in your presentation. Read the copyright notices that accompany the clip and are posted on the Web site. The owners of these images and files often ask you to give them credit for using their work, which may be satisfied by stating where you obtained the images.

Plan Ahead

Photographs and the Clip Organizer

In addition to clip art, you can insert pictures into a presentation. These may include scanned photographs, line art, and artwork from compact discs. To insert a picture into a presentation, the picture must be saved in a format that PowerPoint can recognize. Table 2–1 identifies some of the formats PowerPoint recognizes.

You can import files saved with the .emf, .gif, .jpg, .png, .bmp, .rle, .dib, and .wmf formats directly into PowerPoint presentations. All other file formats require separate filters that are shipped with the PowerPoint installation software and must be installed. You can download additional filters from the Microsoft Office Online Web site.

Table 2–1 Primary File Formats PowerPoint Recognizes

Format	File Extension
Computer Graphics Metafile	.cgm
CorelDRAW	.cdr, .cdt, .cmx, and .pat
Encapsulated PostScript	.eps
Enhanced Metafile	.emf
FlashPix	.fpx
Graphics Interchange Format	.gif
Hanako	.jsh, .jah, and .jbh
Joint Photographic Experts Group (JPEG)	.jpg
Kodak PhotoCD	.pcd
Macintosh PICT	.pct
PC Paintbrush	.pcx
Portable Network Graphics	.png
Tagged Image File Format	.tif
Windows Bitmap	.bmp, .rle, .dib
Microsoft Windows Metafile	.wmf
WordPerfect Graphics	.wpg

To Insert a Photograph from the Clip Organizer into a Slide

Next you will add a photograph to Slide 3. You will not insert this picture into a content placeholder, so it will display in the center of the slide. Later in this chapter you will resize this picture and then delete the right placeholder because it is not being used. To start the process locating this photograph, you do not need to click the Clip Art button icon in the content placeholder because the Clip Art task pane already is displayed. The following steps add a photograph to Slide 3.

1 Click the Next Slide button to display Slide 3.

2 Click the Search for text box in the Clip Art task pane and then delete the letters in the text box.

3 Type `credit card` and then click the Go button.

4 If necessary, scroll down the list to display the picture of a credit card shown in Figure 2–16 and then click the photograph to insert it into Slide 3 (Figure 2–16).

Q&A | Why is my photograph so large on the slide?
The photograph was inserted into the slide and not into a content placeholder. You will resize the picture later in this chapter.

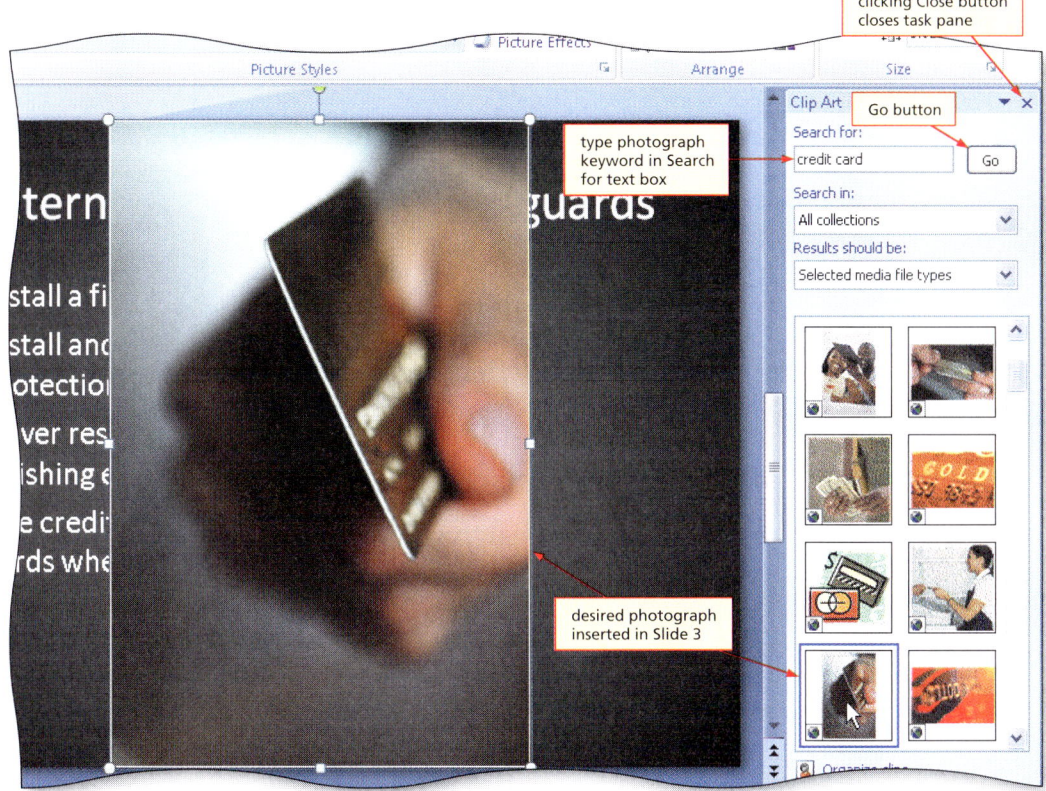

Figure 2–16

To Insert a Photograph from a File into a Slide

The final image to insert in the presentation is a photograph on Slide 4. This slide uses the Picture with Caption layout, so the picture will display in the top placeholder. The following steps add a picture from the Data Files for Students. See the inside back cover of this book for instructions on downloading the Data Files for Students, or contact your instructor for more information on accessing the required files. The following steps insert a photograph of a student using an automatic teller machine (ATM).

1
- Click the Next Slide button to display Slide 4.
- Click the Close button in the Clip Art task pane so that it no longer is displayed (Figure 2–17).

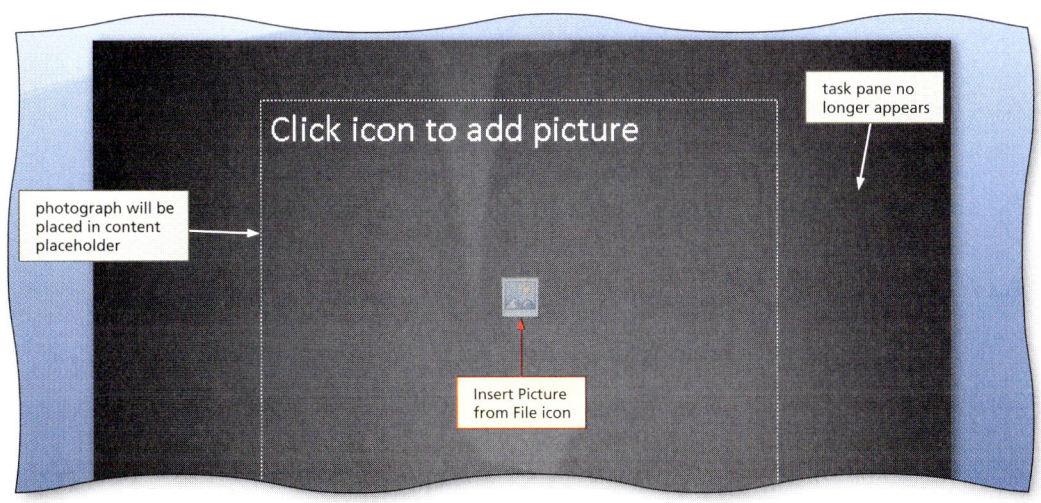

Figure 2–17

- Click the Insert Picture from File icon in the content placeholder to display the Insert Picture dialog box.

- If the Folders list is displayed below the Folders button, click the Folders button to remove the Folders list.

- With your USB flash drive connected to one of the computer's USB ports, if necessary, click Computer in the Favorite Links section and then scroll until UDISK 2.0 (E:) appears in the list of available drives.

- Double-click UDISK 2.0 (E:) to select the USB flash drive, Drive E in this case, as the device that contains the picture.

- Click ATM to select the file name (Figure 2–18).

Q&A What if the photograph is not on a USB flash drive?

Use the same process, but select the device containing the photograph in the Favorite Links section.

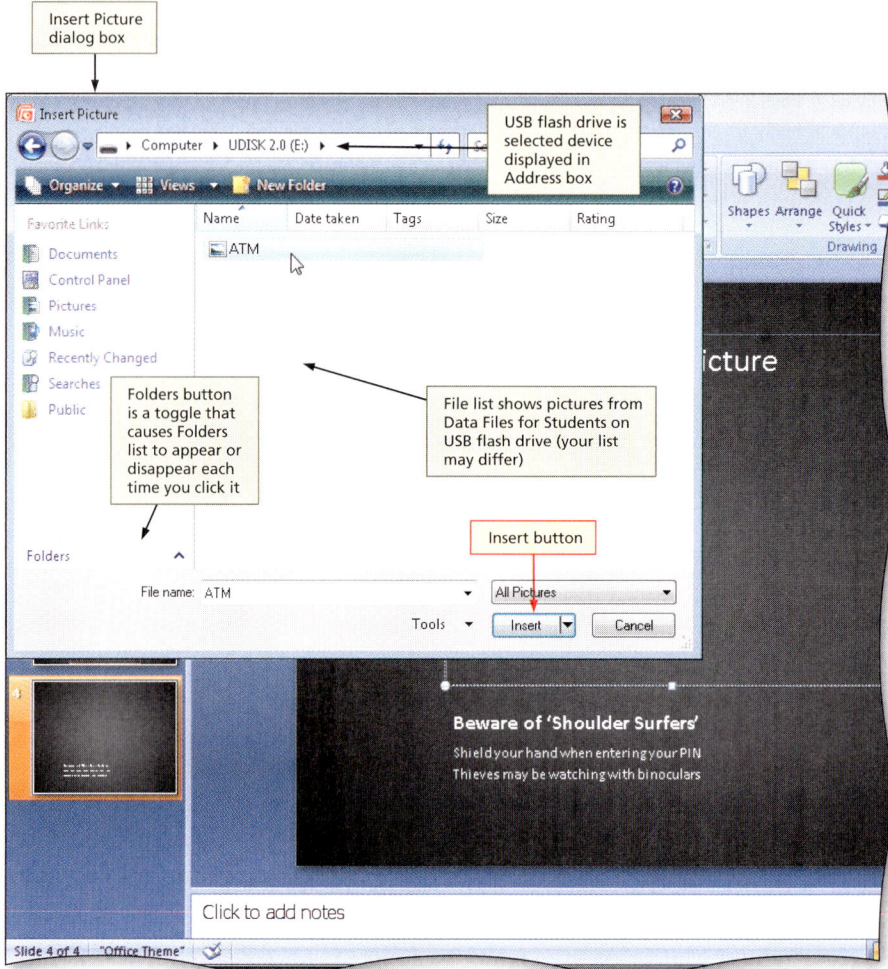

Figure 2–18

- Click the Insert button in the dialog box to insert the picture into Slide 4 (Figure 2–19).

Figure 2–19

Resizing Clip Art and Photographs

Sometimes it is necessary to change the size of clip art. **Resizing** includes both enlarging and reducing the size of a clip art graphic. You can resize clip art using a variety of techniques. One method involves changing the size of a clip by specifying exact dimensions in a dialog box. Another method involves dragging one of the graphic's sizing handles to the desired location. A selected graphic appears surrounded by a **selection rectangle**, which has small squares and circles, called **sizing handles** or move handles, at each corner and middle location.

To Resize Clip Art

On Slide 2, much space appears around the clip, so you can increase its size. The photograph on Slide 3 is too large for the slide, so you should reduce its size. To change the size, drag the corner sizing handles to view how the clip will look on the slide. Using these corner handles maintains the graphic's original proportions. Dragging the square sizing handles alters the proportions so that the graphic becomes more or less high or more or less wide. The following steps increase the size of the Slide 2 clip using a corner sizing handle.

- Click the Previous Slide button two times to display Slide 2.
- Click the shredder clip to select it and display the selection rectangle.
- Point to the upper-left corner sizing handle on the clip so that the mouse pointer shape changes to a two-headed arrow (Figure 2–20).

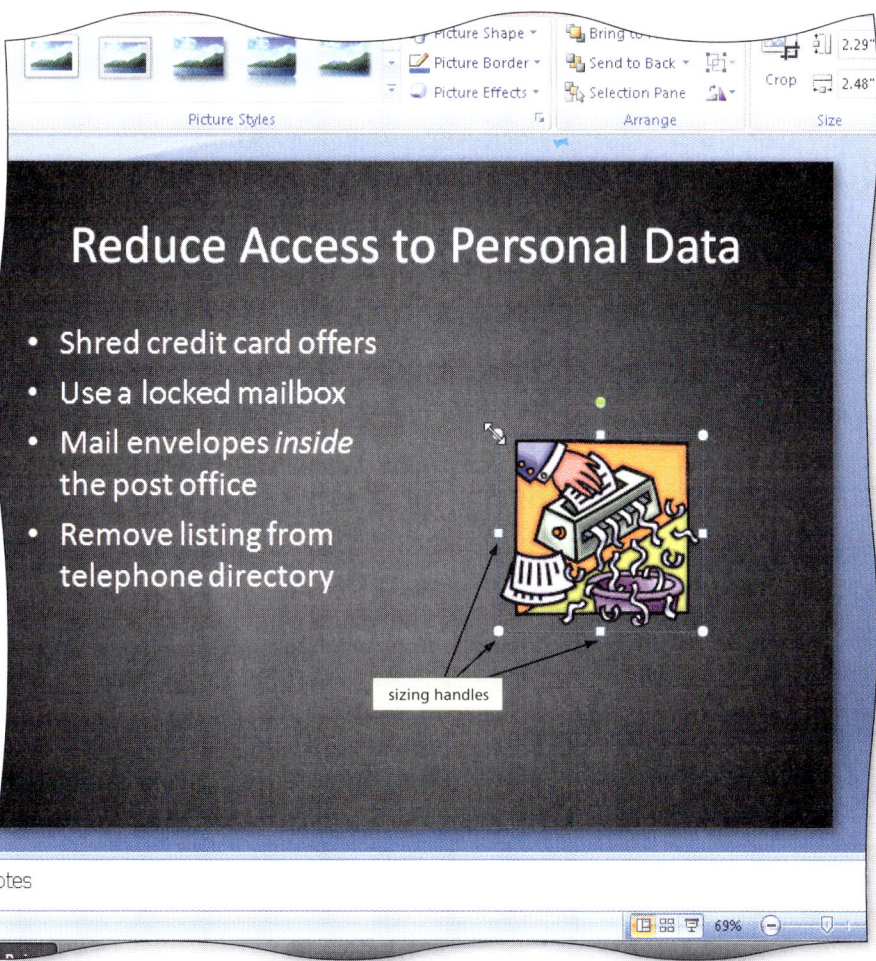

Figure 2–20

2
- Drag the sizing handle diagonally toward the center of the slide until the mouse pointer is positioned approximately as shown in Figure 2–21.

Q&A What if the clip is not the same size shown in Figure 2–21?

Repeat Steps 1 and 2.

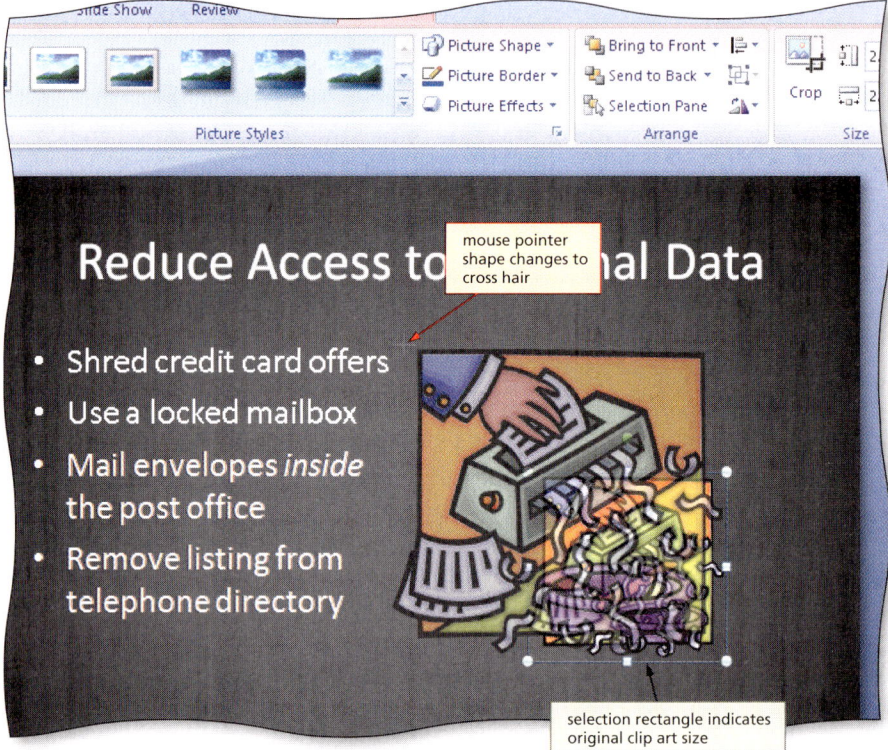

Figure 2–21

3
- Release the mouse button to resize the clip. If necessary, select the clip and then use the ARROW keys to position the clip as shown in Figure 2–21.

4
- Click outside the clip to deselect it (Figure 2–22).

Q&A What happened to the Picture Tools and Format tabs?

When you click outside the clip, PowerPoint deselects the clip and removes the Picture Tools and Format tabs from the screen.

Q&A What if I want to return the clip to its original size and start again?

With the graphic selected, click the Reset button in the Slides group on the Home tab.

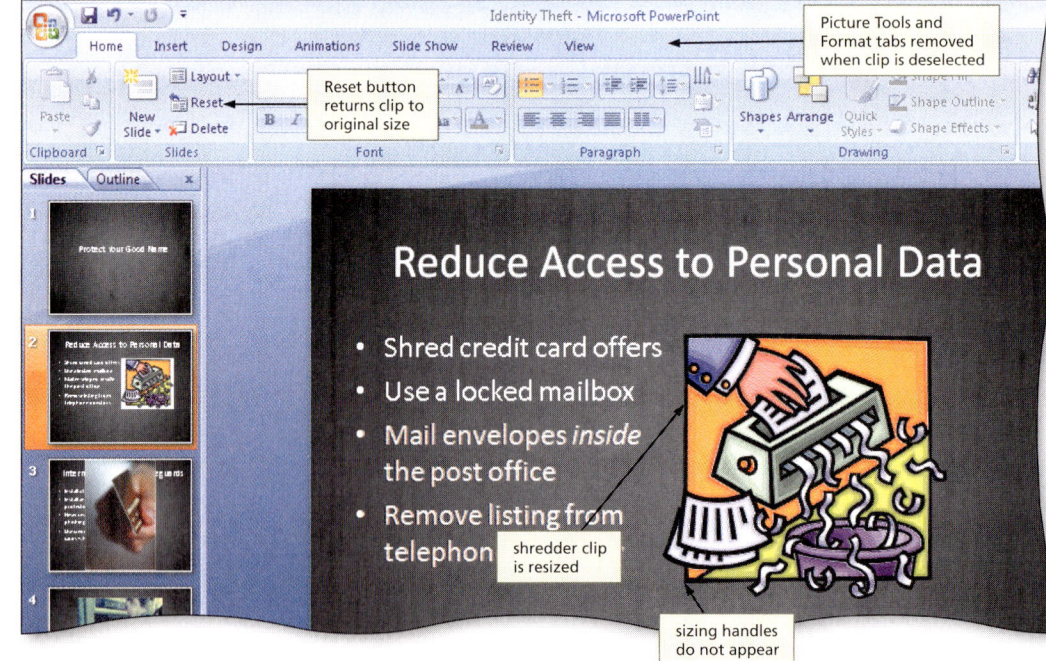

Figure 2–22

To Resize a Photograph

The credit card picture in Slide 3 fills the middle of the slide and covers some text, so you should reduce its size. The following steps resize this photograph using a sizing handle.

1. Click the Next Slide button to display Slide 3.

2. Click the credit card photograph to select it.

3. Drag the upper-left corner sizing handle on the photograph diagonally inward until the photograph is resized approximately as shown in Figure 2–23.

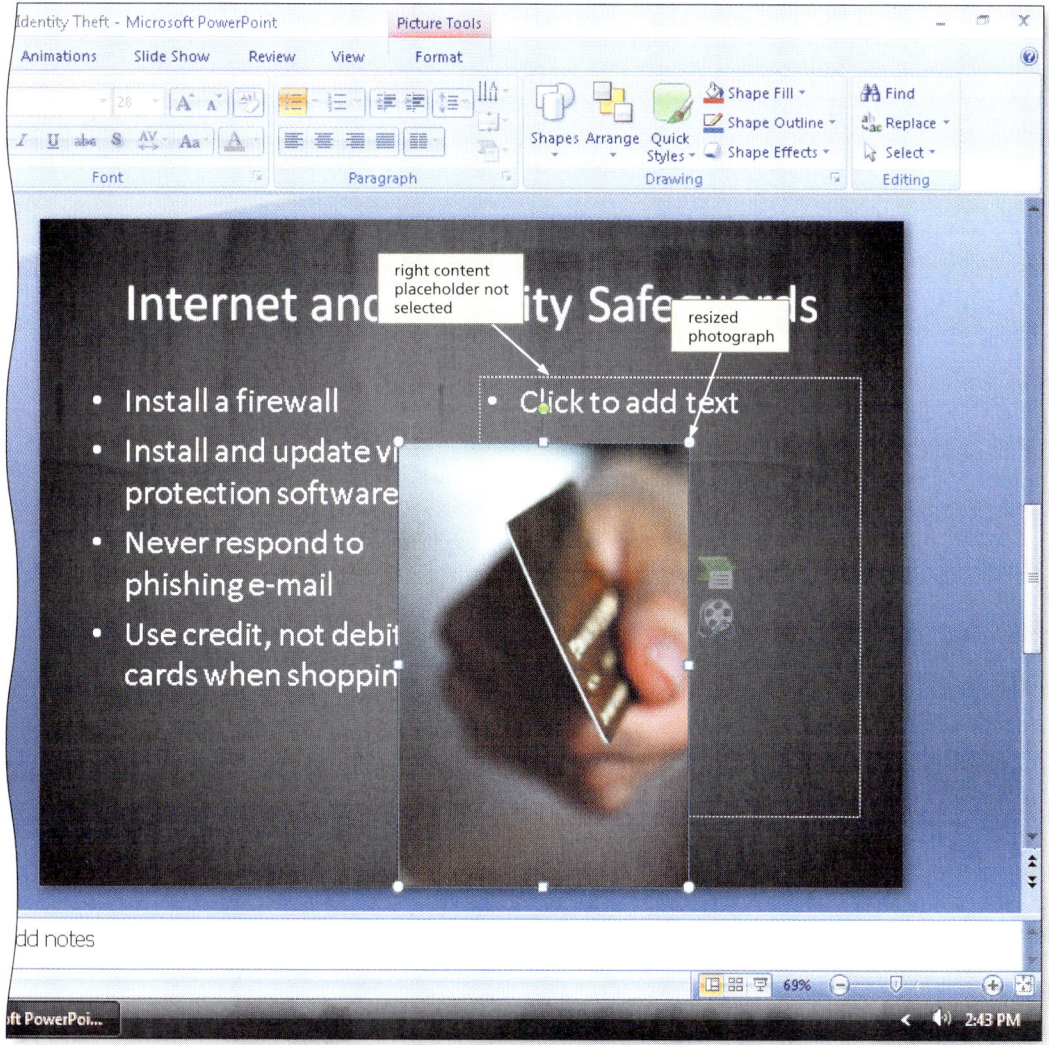

Figure 2–23

To Delete a Placeholder

The credit card photograph was inserted into the slide and not into a content placeholder. The right content placeholder, therefore, is not needed, so you can delete it from the slide. The following steps delete this placeholder.

- Click the right content placeholder to select it.
- Click the edge of the placeholder so the border is displayed as a solid line (Figure 2–24).

Figure 2–24

- Press the DELETE key to delete the placeholder from Slide 2 (Figure 2–25).

Figure 2–25

To Move Clips

After you insert clip art or a picture on a slide, you may want to reposition it. The credit card photograph on Slide 3 and the shredder clip on Slide 2 could be centered in the spaces between the bulleted text and the right edge of the slide. The following steps move these graphics.

- Click the credit card photograph on Slide 3 to select it and then press and hold down the mouse button.
- Drag the photograph diagonally upward toward the word, Safeguards (Figure 2–26).

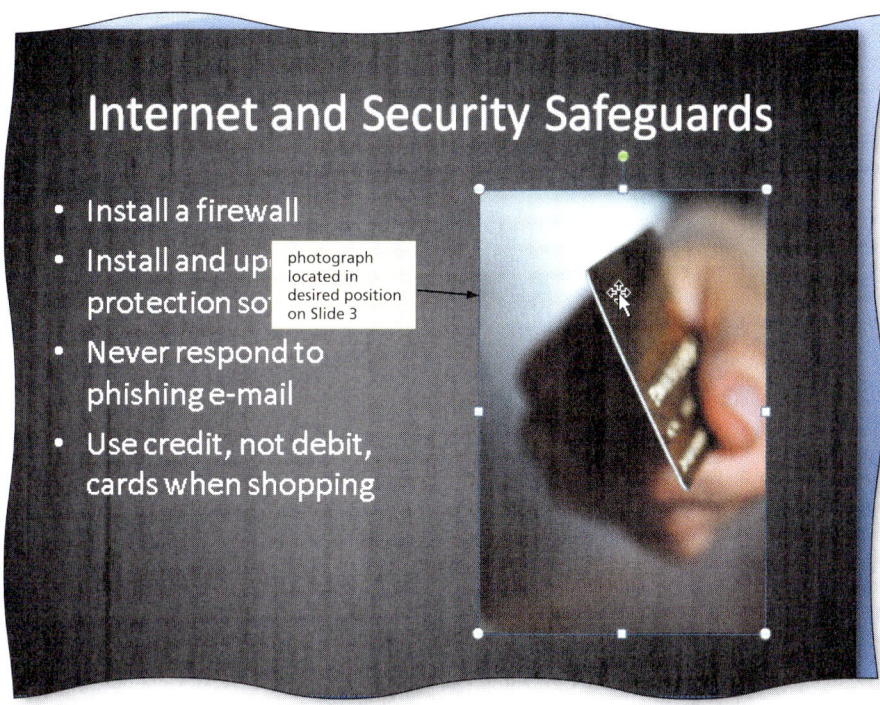

Figure 2–26

- Click the Previous Slide button to display Slide 2.
- Click the shredder clip to select it, press and hold down the mouse button, and then drag the photograph toward the right side of the slide (Figure 2–27).

Figure 2–27

BTW

Inserting Special Characters
You can insert characters not found on your keyboard, such as the Euro sign (€), the copyright sign (©), and Greek capital letters (e.g., Δ, Ε, Θ). To insert these characters, click the Insert tab on the Ribbon, and then click the Symbol button in the Text group. When the Symbol dialog box is displayed, you can use the same font you currently are using in your presentation, or you can select another font. The Webdings, Webdings 2, and Webdings 3 fonts have a variety of symbols.

To Save an Existing Presentation with the Same File Name

You have made several changes to your presentation since you last saved it. Thus, you should save it again. The following step saves the presentation again.

 Click the Save button on the Quick Access Toolbar to overwrite the previous Identity Theft file on the USB flash drive.

Formatting Title and Content Text

Choosing well-coordinated colors and styles for text and objects in a presentation is possible by using **Quick Styles**, which are defined combinations of formatting options. The styles in the Quick Styles Gallery have a wide variety of font, background, and border colors. You even can create a custom Quick Style and give it a unique name. Once you select a particular Quick Style and make any other font changes, you then can copy these changes to other text using the **Format Painter**. The Format Painter allows you to copy all formatting changes from one object to another.

To Format Title Text Using Quick Styles

The 42 Quick Styles are displayed in thumbnails in the Quick Style gallery. When you place your mouse pointer over a Quick Style thumbnail, PowerPoint changes the text and shows how the Quick Style affects the formatting. The title text in this presentation will have a light orange background, a dark orange border, and black letters. The following steps apply a Quick Style to the title text.

- Click the Slide 2 title text placeholder to select it.

- Click the Quick Styles button in the Drawing group on the Home tab to display the Quick Styles gallery. Point to the Subtle Effect – Accent 6 Quick Style (row 4, column 7) to display a live preview of the style (Figure 2–28).

- Point to various styles in the Quick Styles gallery and watch the format of the text, backgrounds, and borders change in the placeholder.

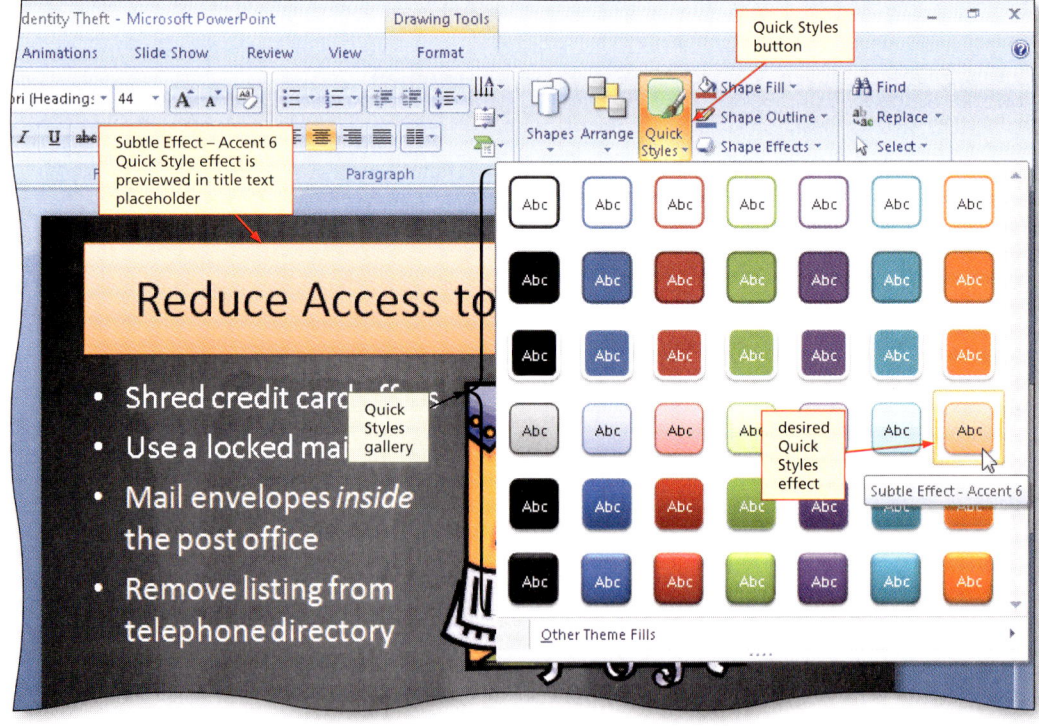

Figure 2–28

2
- Click the Subtle Effect – Accent 6 Quick Style (row 4, column 7) to apply this format to the title text placeholder (Figure 2–29).

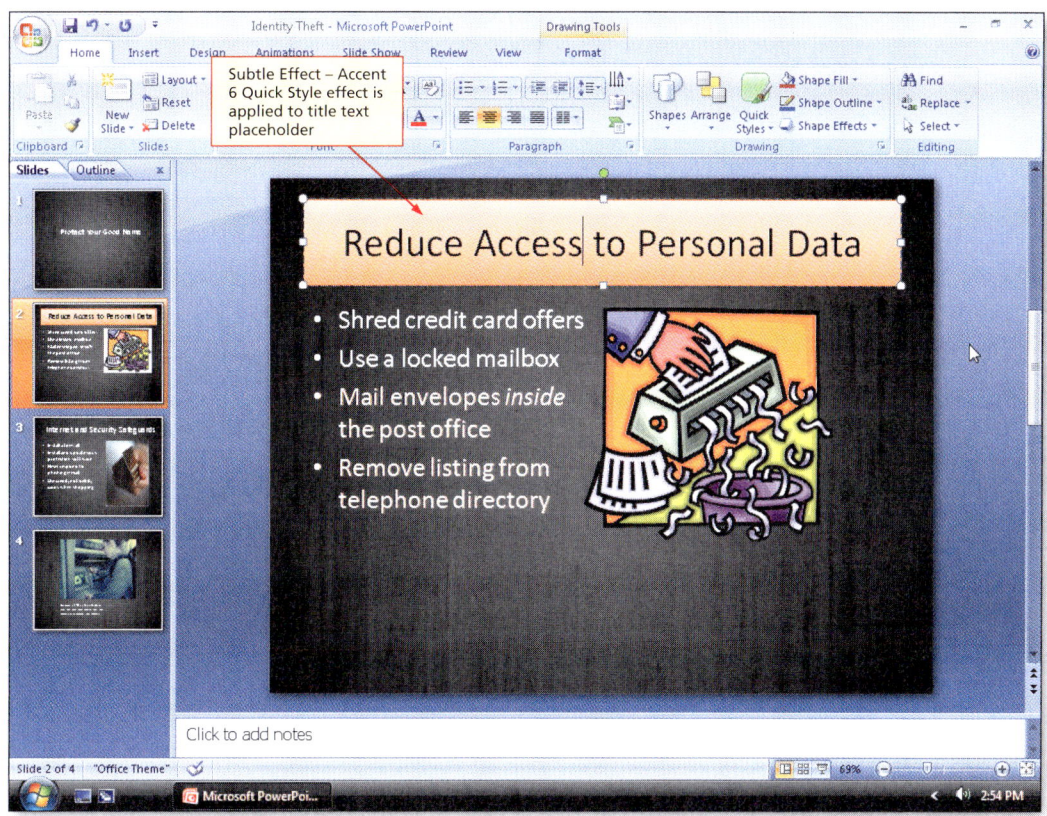

Figure 2–29

To Format Remaining Title Text Using Quick Styles

Once you have applied a Quick Style to one title text placeholder, it is a good idea to use the same style for consistency. The following steps apply the Subtle Effect – Accent 6 Quick Style to the title text placeholder on Slides 3 and 4.

1 Click the Next Slide button to display Slide 3. Click the title text placeholder and then click the Quick Styles button in the Drawing group to display the Quick Styles gallery.

② Click the Subtle Effect – Accent 6 Quick Style (row 4, column 7) to apply this format to the title text placeholder.

③ Click the Next Slide button to display Slide 4. Click the title text placeholder, click the Quick Styles button, and then click the Subtle Effect – Accent 6 Quick Style (row 4, column 7) to apply this format to the title text placeholder (Figure 2–30).

Figure 2–30

Plan Ahead

Use serif fonts for titles.
The design guidelines for title text differ from the guidelines for content body text. You would like your audience members to remember the main points of your presentation, and you can help their retention by having them read the title text more slowly than they read the words in the content text placeholder. The uneven lines in serif typefaces cause eye movement to slow down. Designers, therefore, often use serif fonts for the slide title text.

To Change the Heading Font

The default Office Theme heading and body text font is Calibri with a font size of 28 point. Calibri is a sans serif font, and designers recommend using a serif font to draw more attention to the slide title text. The following steps change the font from Calibri to Cambria.

1

- Click the Previous Slide button two times to display Slide 2. Triple-click the title text paragraph. With the text selected, click the Font box arrow in the Font group on the Home tab to display the Font gallery (Figure 2–31).

Q&A Will the fonts in my Font gallery be the same as those in Figure 2–31?

Your list of available fonts may differ, depending on the type of printer you are using.

2

- Scroll through the Font gallery, if necessary, and then point to Cambria (or a similar font) to display a live preview of the title text in Cambria font.

 Experiment

- Point to various fonts in the Font gallery and watch the font of the title text change in the document window.

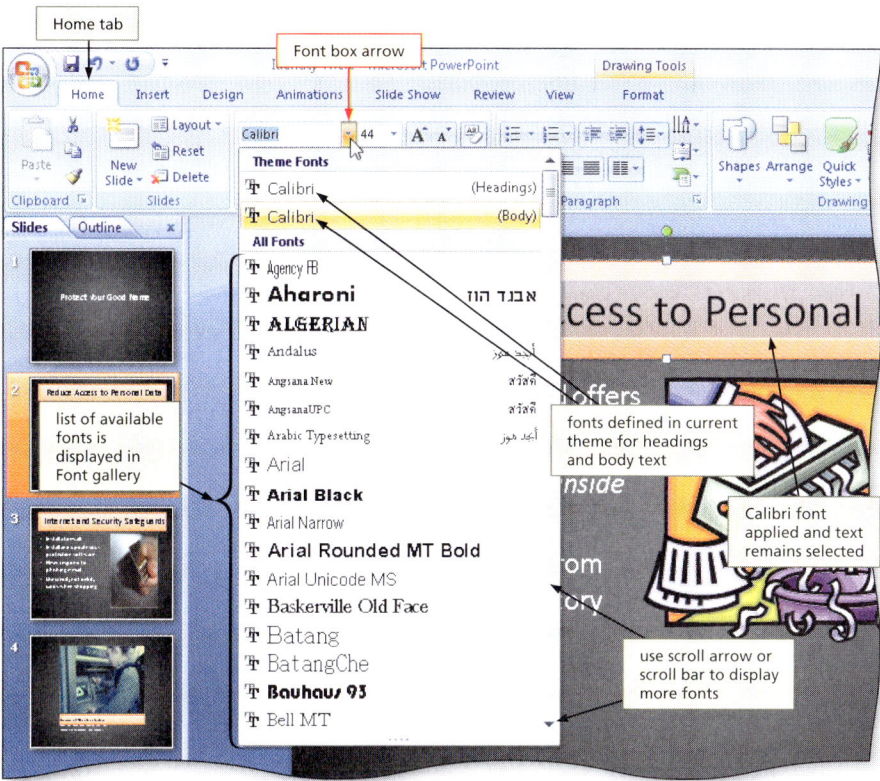

Figure 2–31

3

- Click Cambria (or a similar font) to change the font of the selected text to Cambria (Figure 2–32).

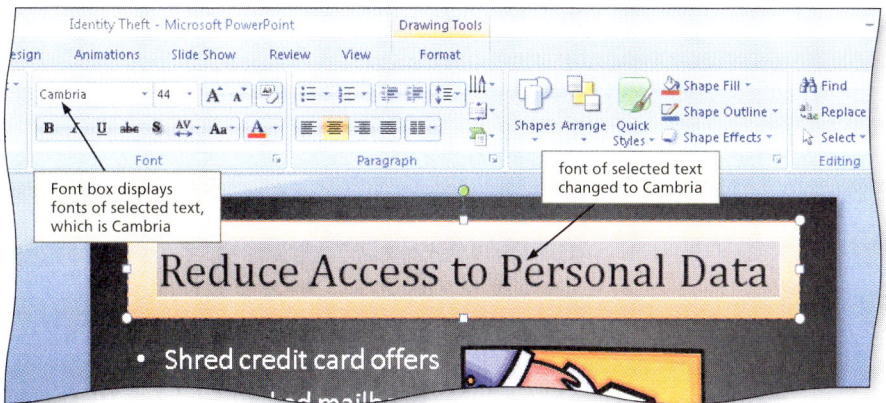

Figure 2–32

Other Ways

1. Click Font box arrow on Mini toolbar, click desired font in Font gallery
2. Right-click selected text, click Font on shortcut menu, click Font tab, select desired font in Font list or type a font in Font box, click OK button
3. Click Dialog Box Launcher in Font group, click Font tab, select desired font in Font list or type a font in Font box, click OK button
4. Press CTRL+SHIFT+F, click Font tab, select desired font in the Font list, click OK button

To Shadow Text

A **shadow** helps the letters display prominently by adding a shadow behind the text. The following step adds a shadow to the selected title text, Reduce Access to Personal Data.

- With the text selected, click the Text Shadow button in the Font group on the Home tab to add a shadow to the selected text (Figure 2–33).

Q&A How would I remove a shadow?

You would click the Shadow button a second time, or you immediately could click the Undo button on the Quick Access Toolbar.

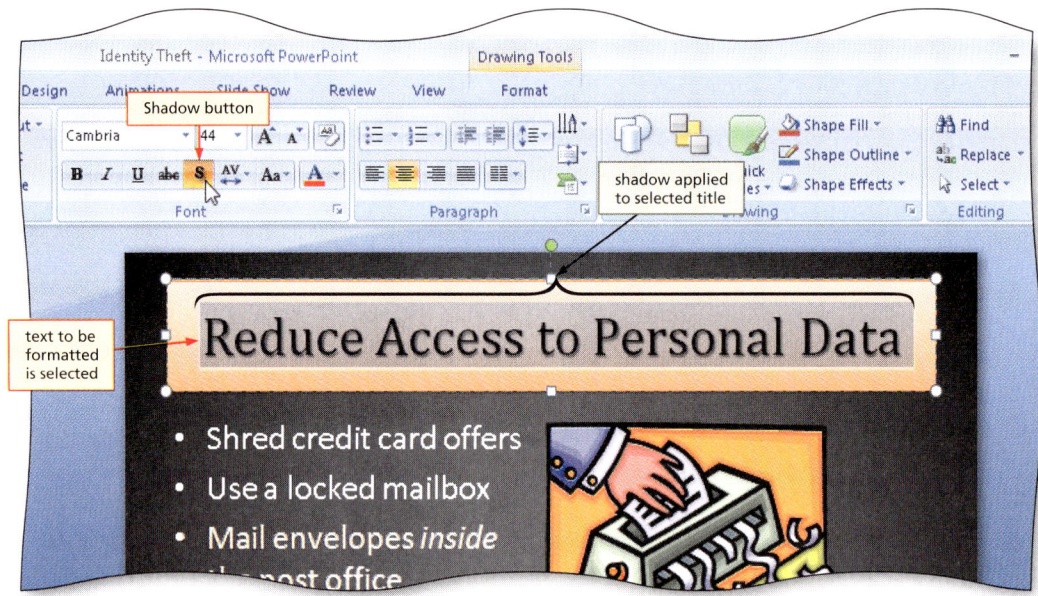

Figure 2–33

To Change Font Color

Color is used to emphasize or draw attention to specific text. The following step changes the title text font color from black to dark red.

- With the text selected, click the Font Color box arrow in the Font group on the Home tab to display the Font Color gallery (Figure 2–34).

Q&A What is the difference between the colors shown in the Theme Colors area and the Standard Colors?

The ten colors in the top row of the Theme Colors area are two text, two background, and six accent colors in the Office Theme; the five colors in each column under the top row display different transparencies. The ten standard colors are available in every document theme.

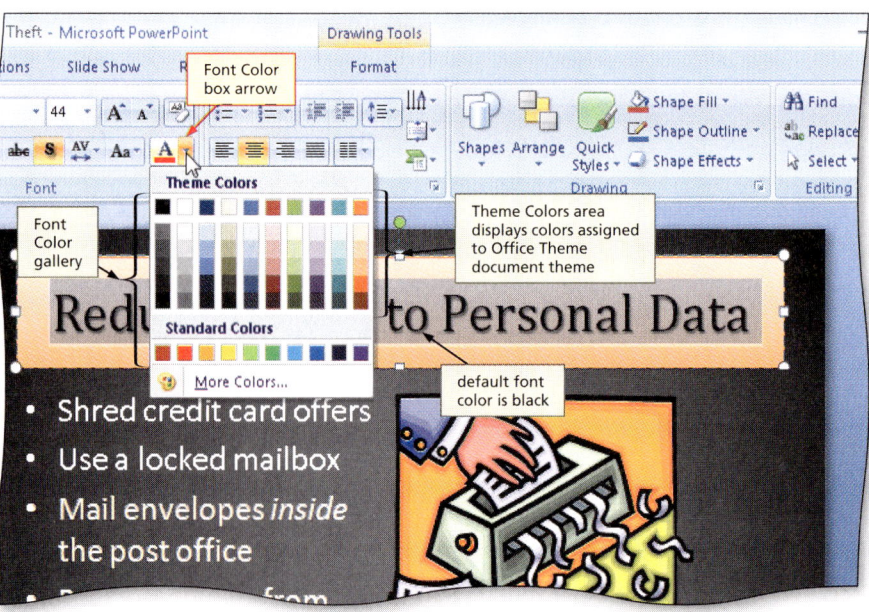

Figure 2–34

❷
- Point to the Dark Red color in the Standard Colors row to display a live preview of the title text in a Dark Red color (Figure 2–35).

  🔍 **Experiment**
- Point to various colors in the Font Color gallery and watch the title text color change in the slide.

❸
- Click Dark Red to change the title text font color.

Q&A How would I change a color?
You would click the Font Color box arrow and then select another color in the Font Color gallery.

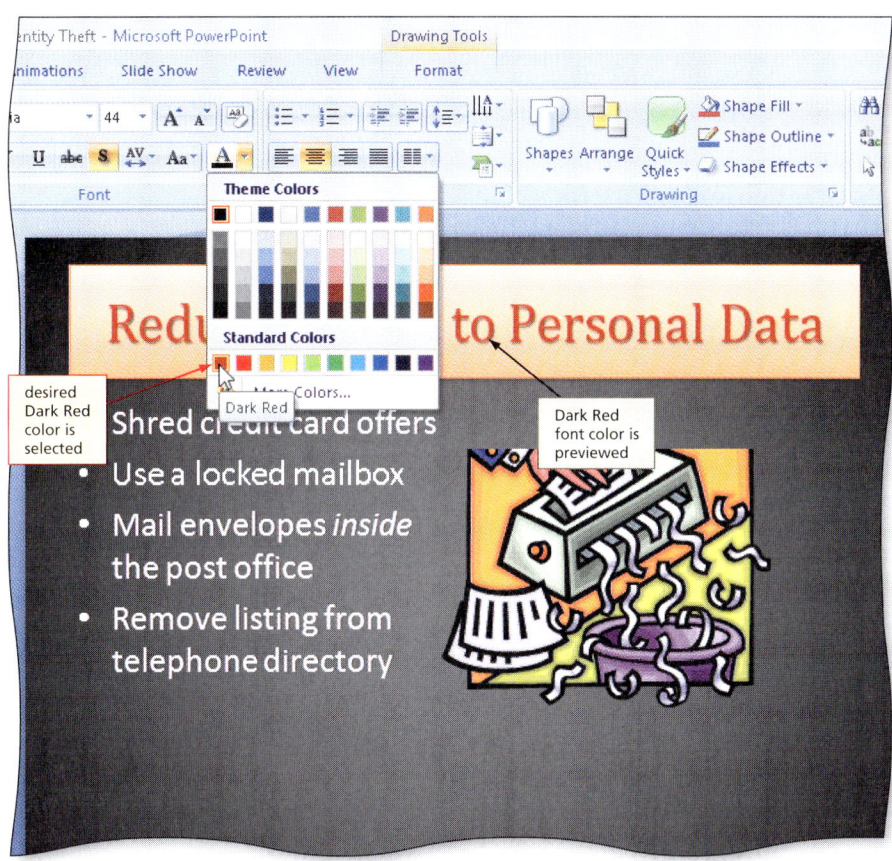

Figure 2–35

Other Ways
1. Click Font color box arrow on Mini toolbar, click desired color in Font Color gallery
2. Right-click selected text, click Font on shortcut menu, click Font tab, select desired color in Font color list, click OK button
3. Click Dialog Box Launcher in Font group, click Font tab, select desired color in Font color list, click OK button
4. Press CTRL+SHIFT+F, click Font tab, select desired color in Font color list, click OK button

Format Painter

To save time and avoid formatting errors, you can use the Format Painter to apply custom formatting to other places in your presentation quickly and easily. You can use this feature in three ways:

- To copy only character attributes, such as font and font effects, select text that has these qualities.
- To copy both paragraph attributes, such as alignment and indentation and character attributes, select the entire paragraph.
- To apply the same formatting to multiple words, phrases, or paragraphs, double-click the Format Painter button and then select each item you want to format. You then can press the ESC key or click the Format Painter button to turn off this feature.

BTW

Deleting WordArt
If you decide you no longer want the WordArt text to display on your slide, select this text, click the Format tab on the Ribbon, click the Quick Styles button, and then click Clear WordArt.

To Format Slide 3 Text Using the Format Painter

To save time and duplicated effort, you quickly can use the Format Painter to copy formatting attributes from the Slide 2 title text and apply them to Slides 3. The following steps use the Format Painter to copy formatting features.

- With the Slide 2 title text still selected, double-click the Format Painter button in the Clipboard group in the Home tab (Figure 2–36).

- Move the mouse pointer off the Ribbon.

Q&A Why did my mouse pointer change shape?

The mouse pointer changed shape by adding a paint brush to indicate that the Format Painter function is active.

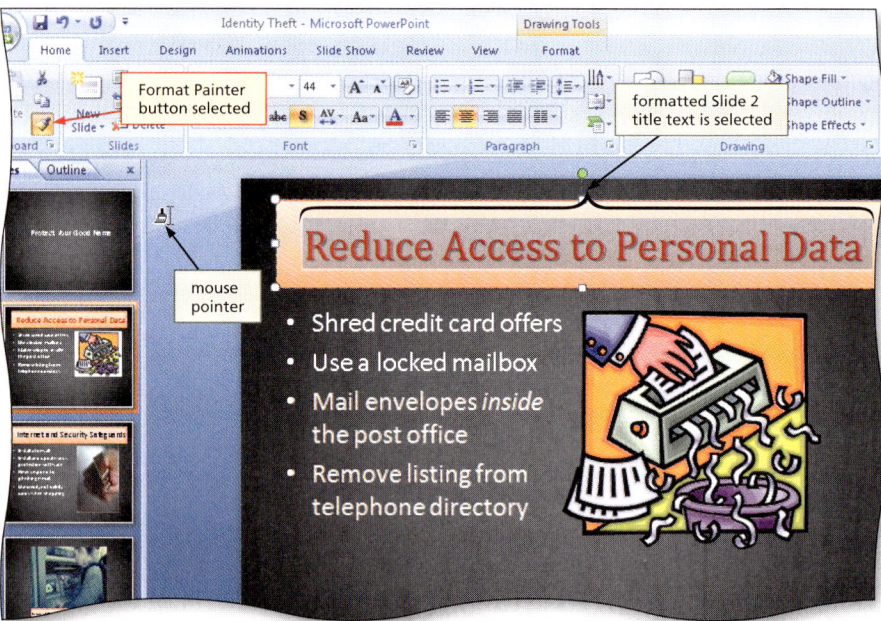

Figure 2–36

- Click the Next Slide button to display Slide 3. Triple-click the title text placeholder to apply the format to all the title text (Figure 2–37).

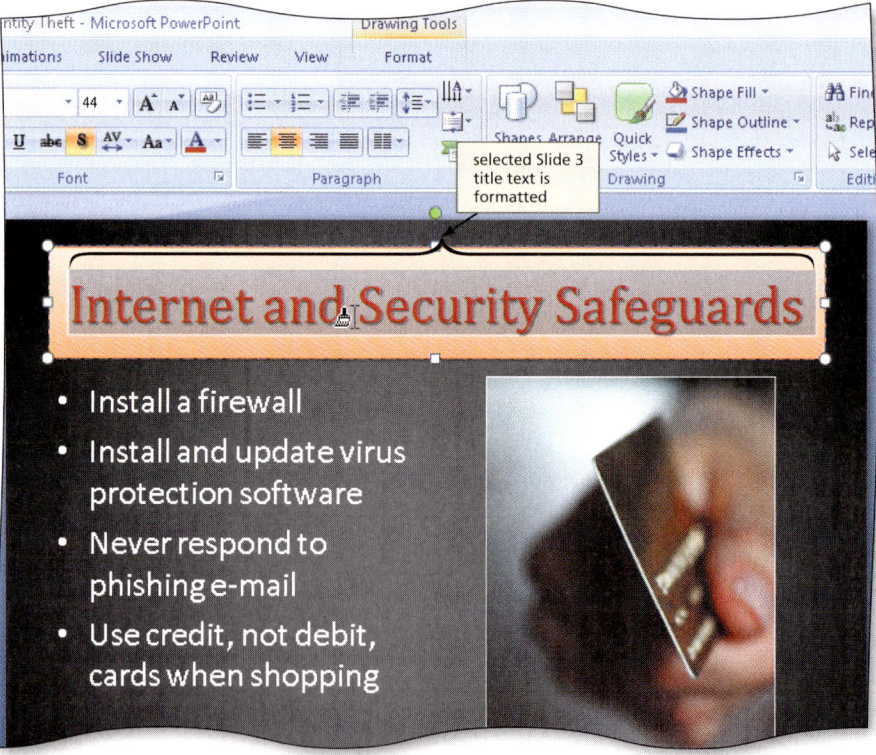

Figure 2–37

To Format Remaining Title Text

Once you have applied formatting characteristics to one text placeholder, you should maintain consistency and apply the same formats to the other title text characters. The following steps use the Format Painter to change the font and font color and apply a shadow to the Slide 4 and Slide 1 title text.

1 Click the Next Slide button to display Slide 4. Triple-click the title text placeholder to apply the format to all title text characters.

Q&A What happened to all the letters in my title?

The Format Painter applied a style that does not fit in the current placeholder. You will adjust the font size so that all the words are displayed.

2 Click the Previous Slide button three times to display Slide 1. Triple-click the title text placeholder to apply the format to all title text characters.

3 Press the ESC key to turn off the Format Painter feature (Figure 2–38).

Other Ways
1. Click Format Painter button on Mini toolbar

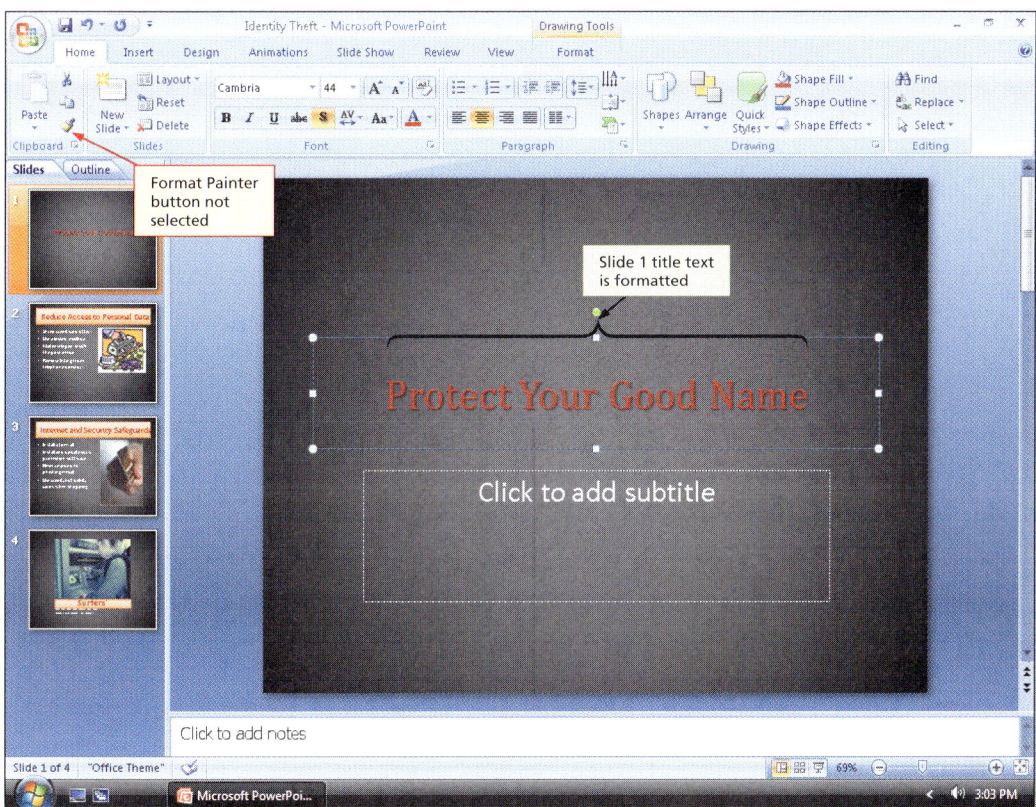

Figure 2–38

To Size Slide 4 Text

The Slide 4 title text placeholder is too small to accommodate the formatting characteristics you applied to the text. The text will fit if you reduce the font size. In addition, the body text should be enlarged for readability. The following steps adjust the size of the Slide 4 title and body text.

1. Click the Next Slide button three times to display Slide 4.

2. Select both body text paragraphs in the content text placeholder and then click the Increase Font Size button on the Mini toolbar four times to increase the font size to 24 point.

3. Triple-click the title text placeholder and then click the Decrease Font Size button on the Mini toolbar three times to reduce the font size to 32 point.

4. Click the slide anywhere outside the placeholders to deselect it (Figure 2–39).

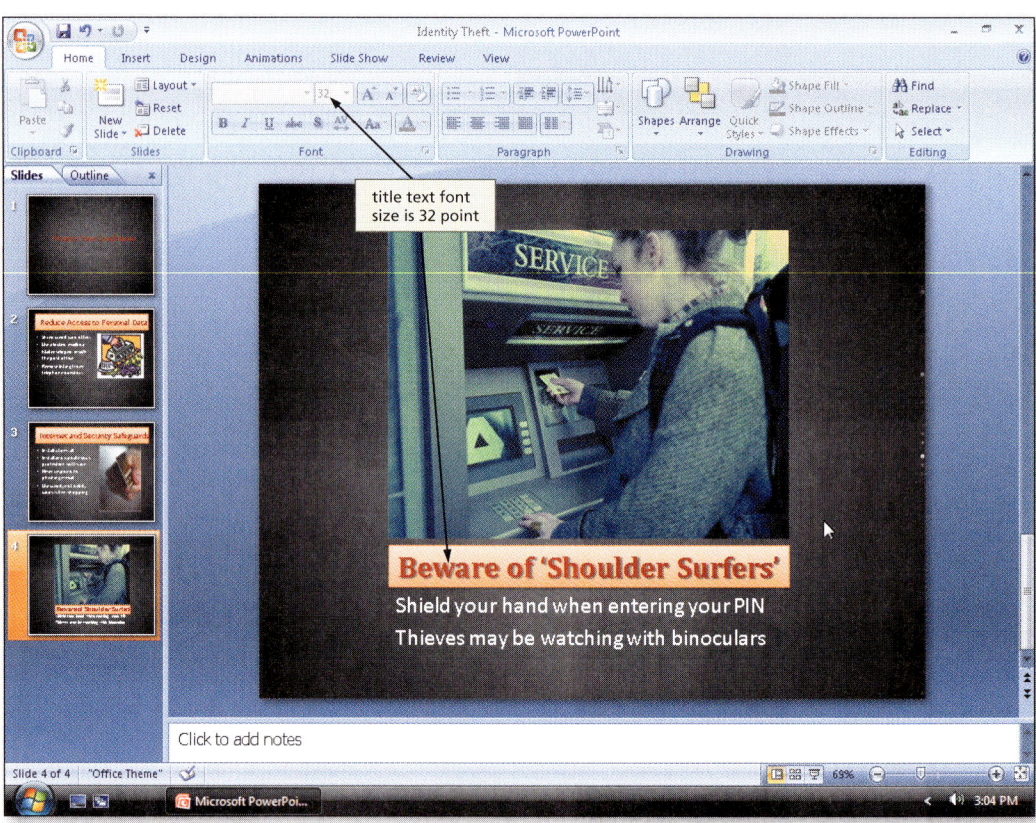

Figure 2–39

Adding and Formatting a Shape

One method of getting the audience's attention at the start of a slide show is to have graphical elements on the title slide. PowerPoint provides a wide variety of shapes that can add visual interest to a slide. Shape elements include lines, basic geometrical shapes, arrows, equation shapes, flowchart symbols, stars, banners, and callouts.

    Slide 1 in this presentation is enhanced in a variety of ways. First, the title text font size is increased to aid readability and to catch the audience's attention. Then a shape is inserted below the title text with additional formatted text. Finally, the subtitle text placeholder is deleted because it no longer is needed.

To Increase Title Slide Font Size

    The title on a slide should be large enough to stimulate the audience's interest and announce the topic of the presentation. The following steps increase the Slide 1 title text.

1. Click the Previous Slide button three times to display Slide 1.

2. Select the Slide 1 title text, Protect Your Good Name. Click the Increase Font Size button on the Mini toolbar six times until the font size is 80 point (Figure 2–40).

3. Click the slide anywhere outside the title text placeholder to deselect it.

Figure 2–40

To Add a Shape

After adding a shape to a slide, you can change its default characteristics by adding text, bullets, numbers, and Quick Styles. You also can combine multiple shapes to create a more complex graphic. The following steps add a banner shape to Slide 1.

- Click the Shapes button in the Drawing group on the Home tab to display the Shapes gallery. Point to the Wave banner shape in the Stars and Banners area (Figure 2–41).

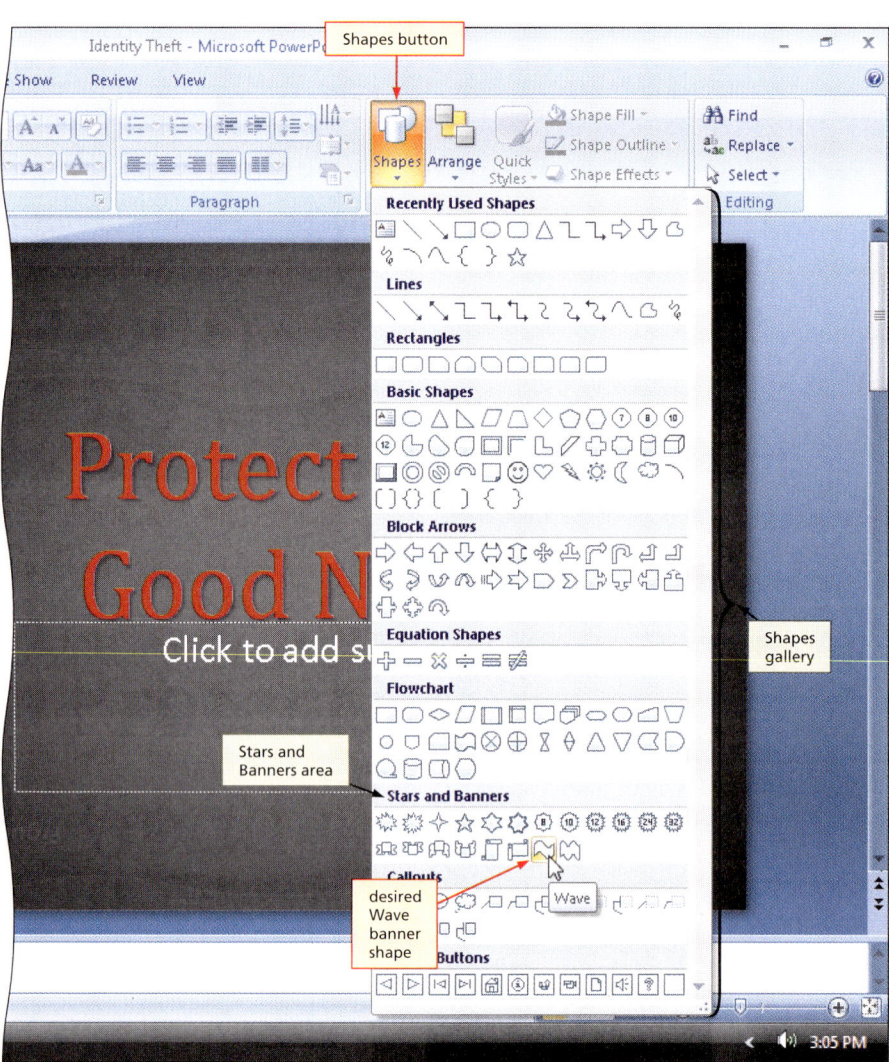

Figure 2–41

- Click the Wave shape (Figure 2–42).

Q&A Why did my pointer change shape?
The pointer changed to a plus shape to indicate the Wave shape has been added to the Clipboard.

Figure 2–42

- Click Slide 1 anywhere below the title text to insert the Wave shape (Figure 2–43).

Figure 2–43

Other Ways
1. Click More button in Insert Shapes group on Format tab in Drawing Tools tab

To Resize a Shape

The next step is to resize the Wave shape. The shape should be enlarged so that it appears prominently on the slide and can hold the subtitle text. The following steps resize the selected Wave shape.

- With the Wave shape still selected, point to the lower-right corner sizing handle on the picture so that the mouse pointer shape changes to a two-headed arrow (Figure 2–44).

Q&A What if my shape is not selected?
To select a shape, click it.

Figure 2–44

- Drag the sizing handle diagonally outward and downward until the Wave shape is the approximate size of the one shown in Figure 2–45.

Figure 2–45

- Release the mouse button to resize the shape (Figure 2–46).

Q&A What if the shape is the wrong size?
Repeat Steps 1 and 2.

Q&A What if I want to move the shape to a different location on the slide?
With the shape selected, press the ARROW keys or drag the shape to the desired location.

Other Ways

1. Enter shape height and width in Height and Width text boxes in Size group on Format tab in Drawing Tools contextual tabs
2. Click Dialog Box Launcher in Size group on Format tab in Drawing Tools contextual tabs, click Size tab, enter desired height and width values in text boxes, click Close button

Figure 2–46

To Add Text to a Shape

The banner shape is displayed on Slide 1 in the correct location. The next step is to add text stating that the presentation will cover strategies to help prevent identity theft. The following step describes how to add this information to the shape.

1

- With the Wave banner shape selected, type `Reduce Your Risk of Identity Theft` in the shape (Figure 2–47).

Figure 2–47

To Format Shape Text and Add a Shape Quick Style

Formatting text in a shape follows the same techniques as formatting text in a placeholder. You can change font, font color and size, and alignment, and you also can apply a Shape Quick Style. The following steps describe how to format the shape text by increasing the font size and adding a Shape Quick Style.

1

- Triple-click the Wave shape text to select it and then click the Increase Font Size button on the Mini toolbar five times until the font size is 36 point (Figure 2–48).

Figure 2–48

2
- Click the Shape Quick Styles button in the Drawing group on the Home tab to display the Quick Styles gallery (Figure 2–49).
- Point to the Subtle Effect – Accent 6 Shape Quick Style (row 4, column 7) to display a live preview of the style.

 Experiment
- Point to various styles in the Quick Styles gallery and watch the format of the text, backgrounds, and borders change in the Wave shape.

3
- Click the Subtle Effect – Accent 6 Shape Quick Style (row 4, column 7) to apply this format to the shape.

Figure 2–49

4
- Click outside the shape to deselect it (Figure 2–50).

Figure 2–50

To Delete a Placeholder

The subtitle placeholder no longer is necessary on Slide 1 because the shape fills the area below the title text. The following steps delete the Slide 1 subtitle placeholder.

1
- Click the subtitle text placeholder border two times to change the border to a solid line (Figure 2–51).

Figure 2–51

2
- Press the DELETE key to delete the placeholder. If necessary, select the shape and then use the ARROW keys to center the shape under the title text (Figure 2–52).

Figure 2–52

Plan Ahead	**Use simple transitions.** Transitions help segue one slide into the next seamlessly. They should not be used decoratively or be something on which an audience member focuses. For consistency, use the same transition throughout the presentation unless you have a special circumstance that warrants a different effect.

Adding a Transition

PowerPoint provides many animation effects to add interest and make a slide show presentation look professional. **Animation** includes special visual and sound effects applied to text or content. A **slide transition** is a special animation effect used to progress from one slide to the next in a slide show. You can control the speed of the transition effect and add a sound.

PowerPoint provides more than 50 different transitions in the Quick Styles group. They are arranged into five categories that describe the types of effects:

- Fades and Dissolves - Blend one slide seamlessly into the next slide
- Wipes - Gently uncover one slide to reveal the next
- Push and Cover - Appear to move one slide off the screen
- Stripes and Bars – Use blinds and checkerboard patterns
- Random – Use vertical and horizontal bars or an arbitrary pattern that changes each time you run the presentation.

To Add a Transition between Slides

In this presentation, you apply the Uncover Right transition in the Wipes category to all slides and change the transition speed to Medium. The following steps apply this transition to the presentation.

- Click the Animations tab on the Ribbon and then point to the More button in the Transition to This Slide group (Figure 2–53).

Is a transition applied now?

No. The first slide icon in the Transitions group has an orange border, which indicates no transition has been applied.

Figure 2–53

Creating a Presentation with Illustrations and Shapes **PowerPoint Chapter 2** **PPT** 123

2
- Click the More button to expand the Transitions gallery.
- Point to the Uncover Right transition (row 2, column 2) in the Wipes category in the Transitions gallery to display a live preview of this transition (Figure 2–54).

Experiment
- Point to various styles in the Transitions gallery and watch the transitions on the slide.

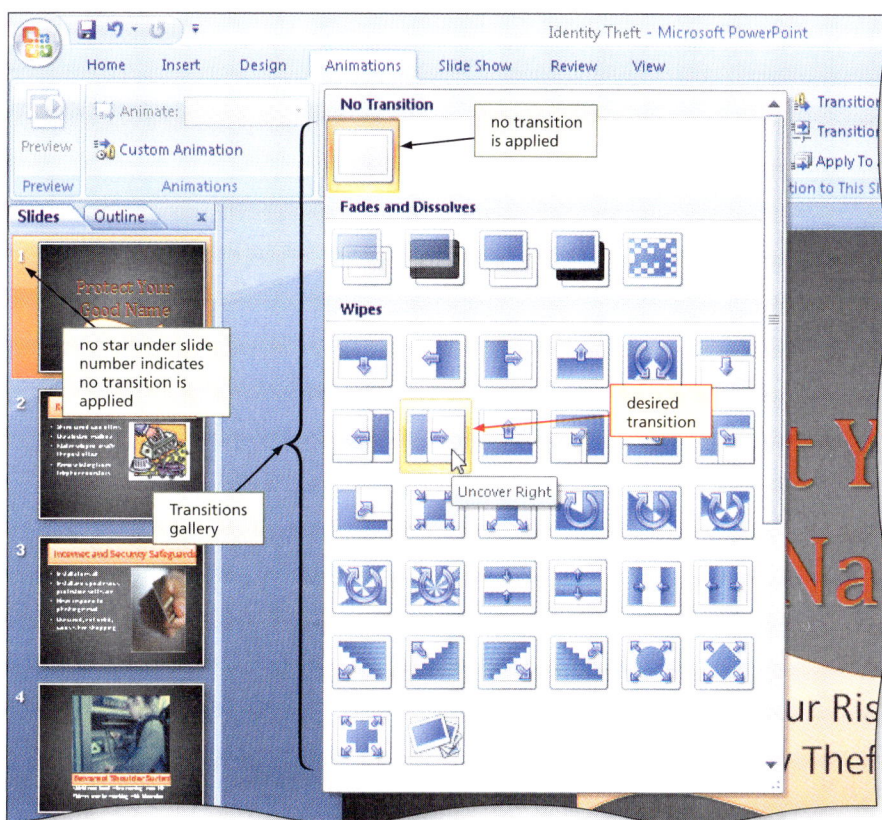

Figure 2–54

3
- Click Uncover Right in the Wipes category in the Transitions gallery to apply the Uncover Right transition to the title slide.

Q&A Why does a star appear next to Slide 1 in the Slides tab?

The star indicates that a transition animation effect is applied to that slide.

- Click the Transition Speed arrow in the Transition to This Slide group on the Animations tab to display three possible speeds: Slow, Medium, and Fast (Figure 2–55).

Figure 2–55

- Click Medium to change the transition speed for Slide 1 to Medium.

- Click the Apply to All button in the Transition to This Slide group on the Animations tab to apply the Uncover Right transition and Medium speed to all four slides in the presentation (Figure 2–56).

Q&A What if I want to apply a different transition and speed to each slide in the presentation?

Repeat Steps 2 through 4 for each slide individually.

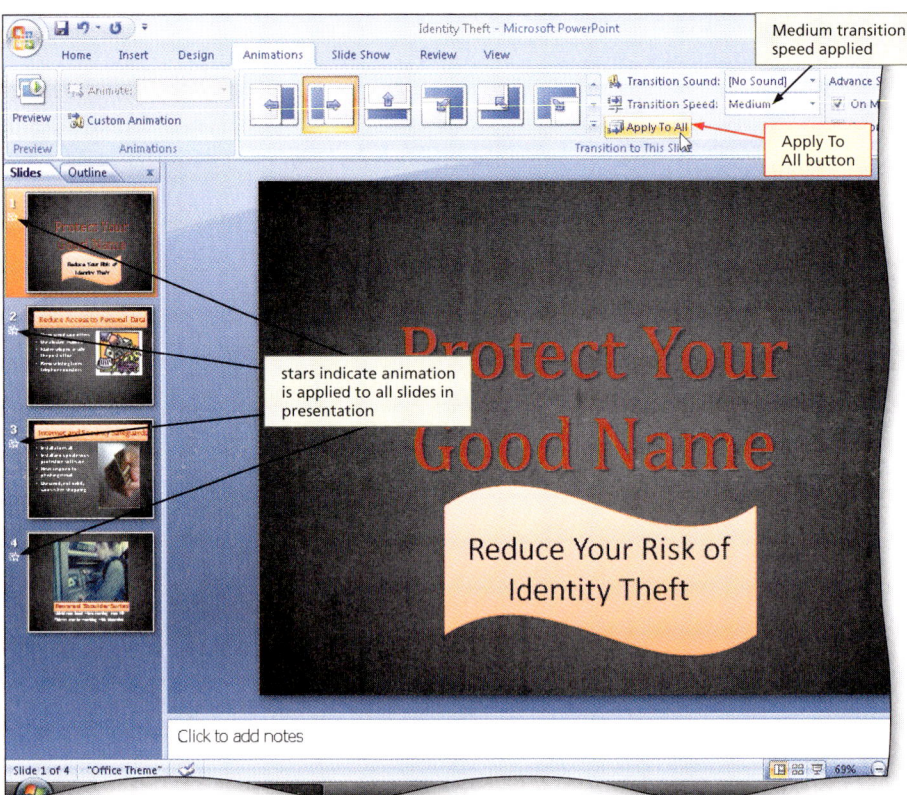

Figure 2–56

To Change Document Properties

Before saving the presentation again, you want to add your name, class name, and some keywords as document properties. The following steps use the Document Information Panel to change document properties.

1 Click the Office Button to display the Office Button menu, point to Prepare on the Office Button menu, and then click Properties on the Prepare submenu to display the Document Information Panel.

2 Click the Author text box, if necessary, and then type your name as the Author property. If a name already is displayed in the Author text box, delete it before typing your name.

3 Click the Subject text box, if necessary delete any existing text, and then type your course and section as the Subject property.

4 Click the Keywords text box, if necessary delete any existing text, and then type identity theft, Internet safeguards, PIN as the Keywords properties.

5 Click the Close the Document Information Panel button so that the Document Information Panel no longer is displayed.

To Save an Existing Presentation with the Same File Name

You have made several changes to the presentation since you last saved it. Thus, you should save it again. The following step saves the document again.

1 Click the Save button on the Quick Access Toolbar to overwrite the previous Identity Theft file on the USB flash drive.

To Run an Animated Slide Show

All changes are complete, and the presentation is saved. You now can view the Identity Theft presentation. The following step starts Slide Show view.

1 Click the Slide Show button to display the title slide (Figure 2–57).

2 Click each slide and view the transition effect and slides.

Figure 2–57

BTW

Quick Reference
For a table that lists how to complete the tasks covered in this book using the mouse, Ribbon, shortcut menu, and keyboard, see the Quick Reference Summary at the back of this book, or visit the PowerPoint 2007 Quick Reference Web page (scsite.com/dc-off07/qr).

Printing a Presentation as an Outline and Handouts

During the development of a lengthy presentation, it often is easier to review an outline in print rather than on the screen. Printing an outline also is useful for audience handouts or when your supervisor or instructor wants to review your subject matter before you develop the presentation fully. In addition, printing two or more slides on one page helps audience members see relationships between slides and also conserves paper. You can preview your print selections to see how your printout will look.

The **Print What list** in the Page Setup group or in the Print dialog box contains options for printing slides, handouts, notes, and an outline. If you want to print handouts, you can specify whether you want one, two, three, four, six, or nine slide images to display on each page. The next two sections preview and then print the presentation outline and the presentation slides as a handout.

To Preview and Print an Outline

Recall that in Chapter 1 each slide printed on a separate page when you clicked Quick Print on the Print submenu. When you want to print other materials, such as an outline, notes, or handouts, you click Print on the Print submenu and select what form of output you desire. The following steps preview and print an outline.

- Click the Office Button to display the Office Button menu.

- Point to Print on the Office Button menu to display the Print submenu (Figure 2–58).

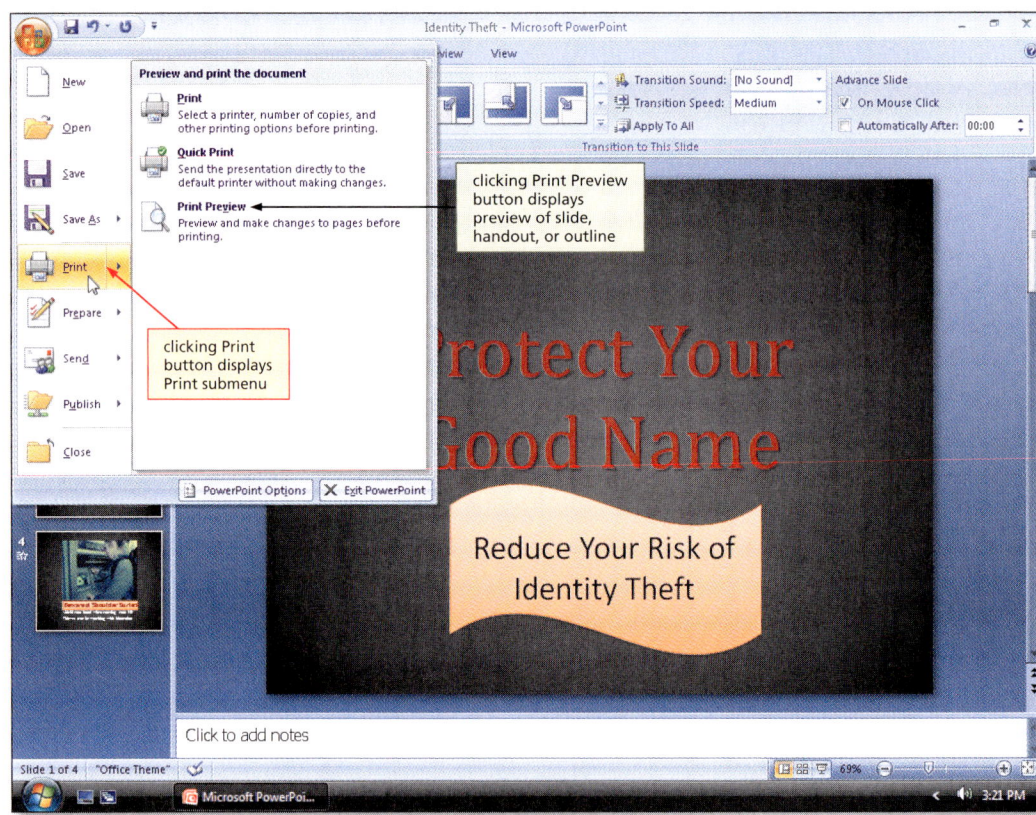

Figure 2–58

2

- Click Print Preview on the Print submenu to display a preview of a slide, handout, or outline of the presentation.

Q&A Why does the slide preview image vary among slides, handouts, and outlines?

PowerPoint retains the settings last specified for previewing and printing. If, for example, you last specified to print in Grayscale, the current document will print in Grayscale unless you change the setting.

- If an outline is not previewed, click the Print What box arrow in the Page Setup group on the Print Preview tab to display a list of output types in the Print What list (Figure 2–59).

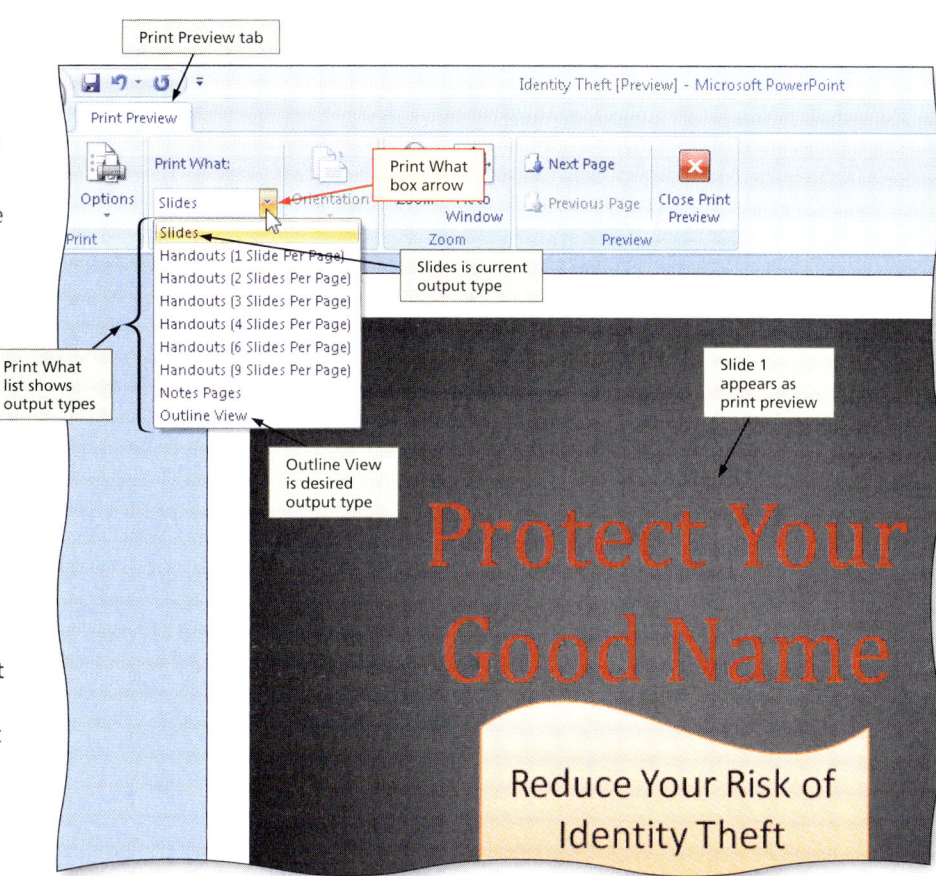

Figure 2–59

3

- Click Outline View in the Print What list if this choice is not already selected.

- Click the Zoom button in the Zoom group on the Print Preview tab to open the Zoom dialog box.

- Click 100% in the Zoom dialog box to change the zoom so that you can read the outline easily on the screen (Figure 2–60).

Q&A If I change the zoom percentage, will the document print differently?

Changing the zoom has no effect on the printed document.

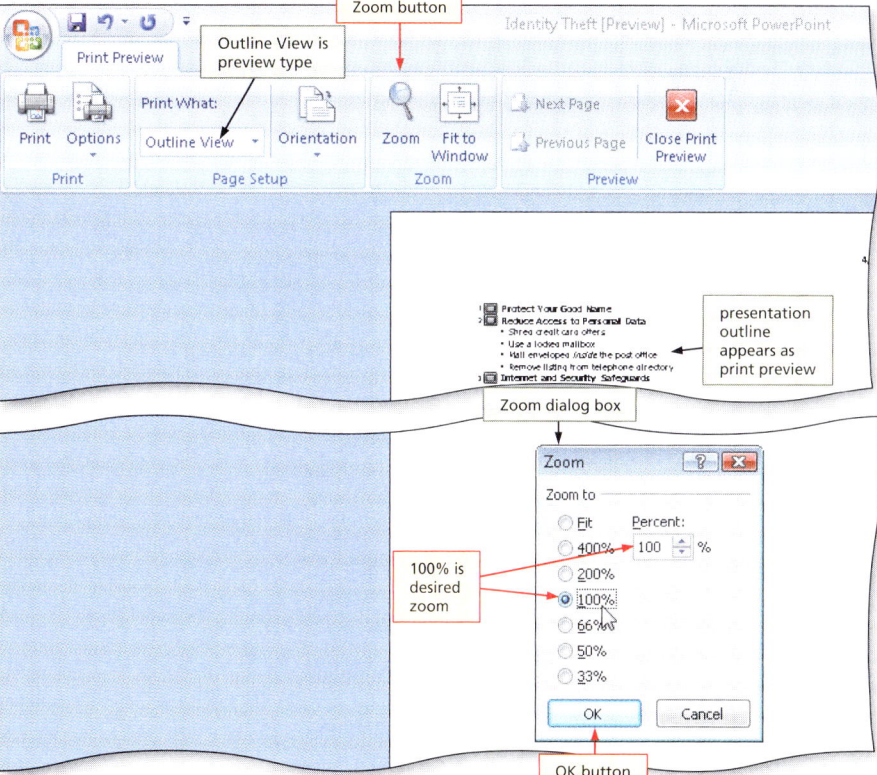

Figure 2–60

4

- Click the OK button in the Zoom dialog box to zoom the outline.

- Drag the scroll box on the vertical scroll bar up or down to move through the outline text (Figure 2–61).

Q&A If I do not want to print my outline now, can I cancel this print request?

Yes. Click the Close Print Preview button in the Print Preview window to return to Normal view.

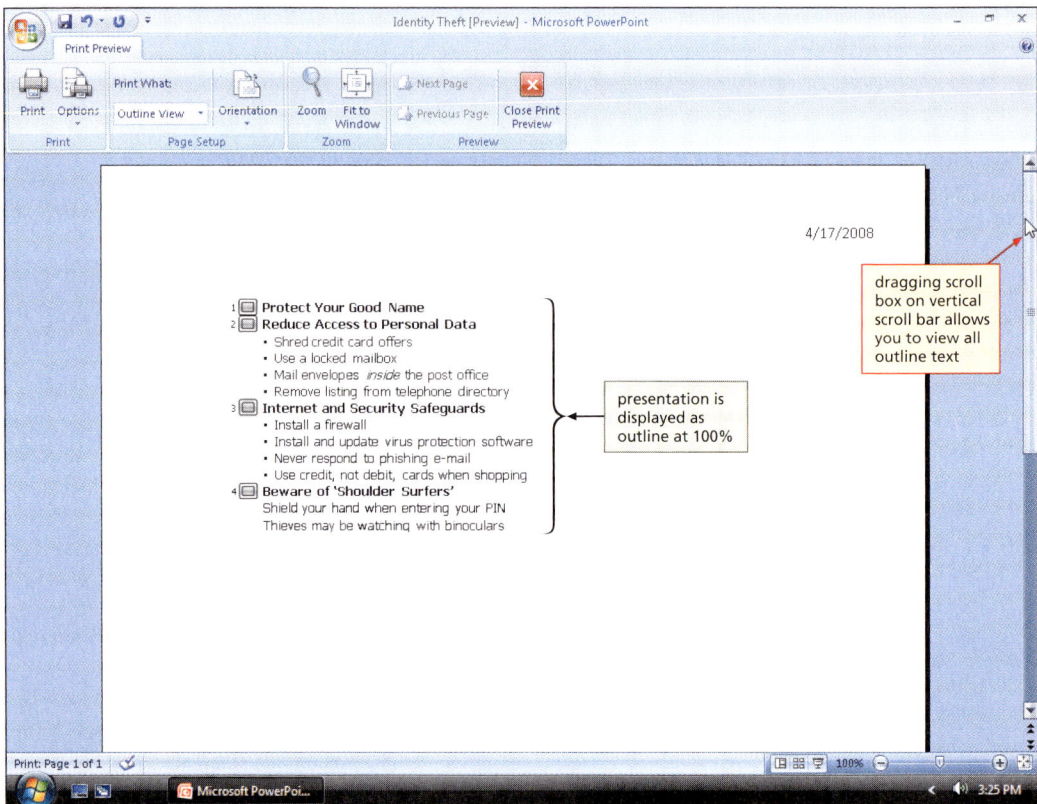

Figure 2–61

5

- Click the Print button in the Print group on the Print Preview tab to display the Print dialog box (Figure 2–62).

Q&A What if my Print dialog box displays a different printer name?

It is likely a different printer name will display. Just ensure that the printer listed is the correct device you want to use to print your outline.

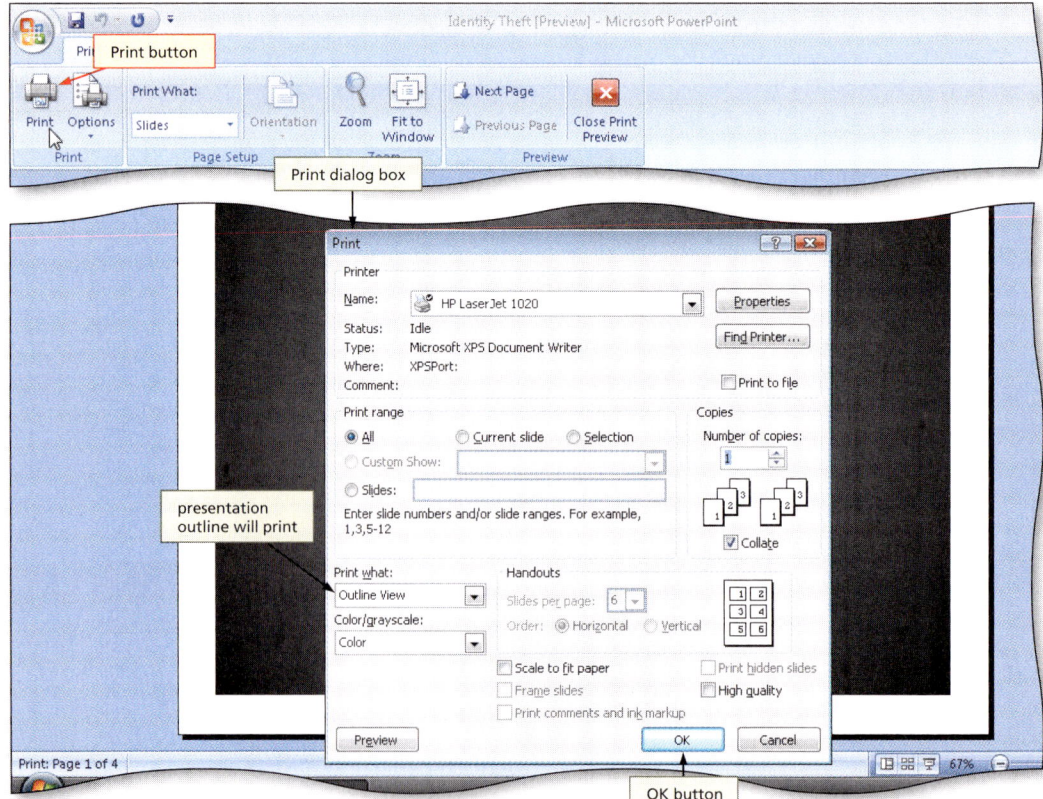

Figure 2–62

6
- Click the OK button to print the outline (Figure 2–63).

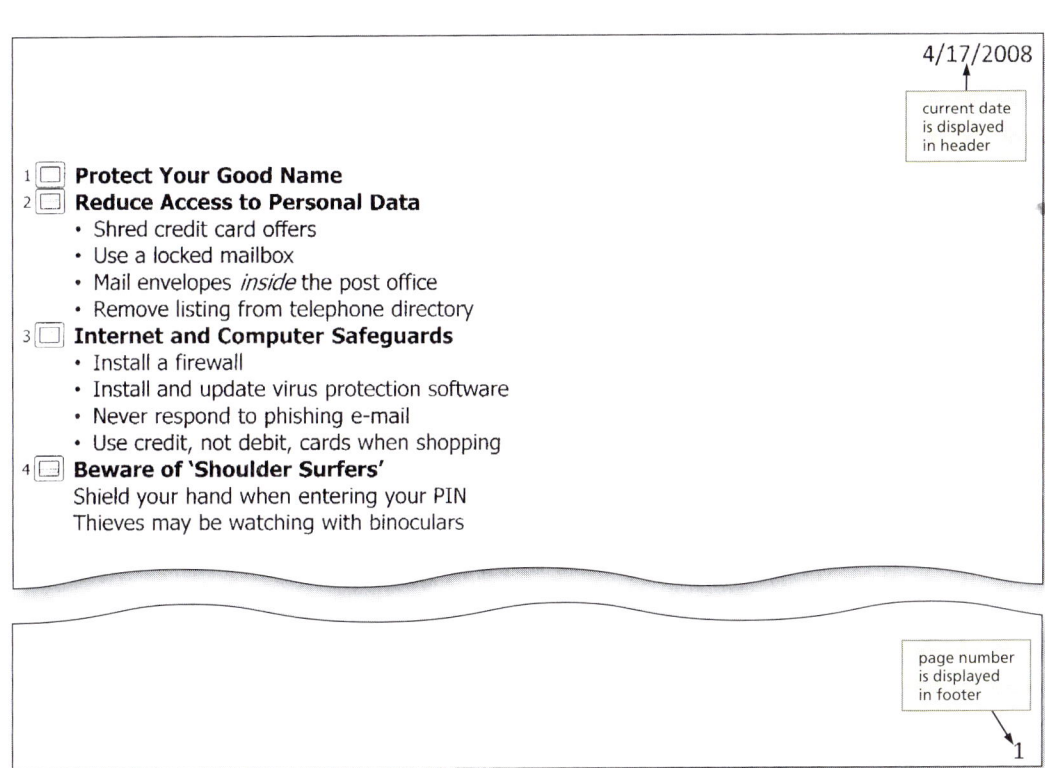

Figure 2–63

To Preview and Print Handouts

Printing handouts is useful for reviewing a presentation because you can analyze several slides displayed simultaneously on one page. Additionally, many businesses distribute handouts of the slide show before a presentation so the attendees can refer to a copy.

The default slide print order is Horizontal so that Slides 1 and 2, and 3 and 4 are adjacent to each other. You can change this order to Vertical, which shows Slides 1 and 4, and 2 and 3 adjacent to each other, by clicking Options in the Print group on the Print Preview tab and then changing the printing order.

The following steps preview and print presentation handouts.

1 Click the Print What box arrow in the Page Setup group.

2 Click Handouts (4 Slides Per Page) in the Print What list. Drag the scroll box on the vertical scroll bar up or down to move through the page.

3 Click the Print button in the Print group.

4 Click the OK button in the Print dialog box to print the handout (Figure 2–64).

5 Click the Close Print Preview button in the Preview group on the Print Preview tab to return to Normal view.

Other Ways
1. Drag Zoom slider on status bar
2. Click Zoom button on status bar, select desired zoom percent or type, click OK button

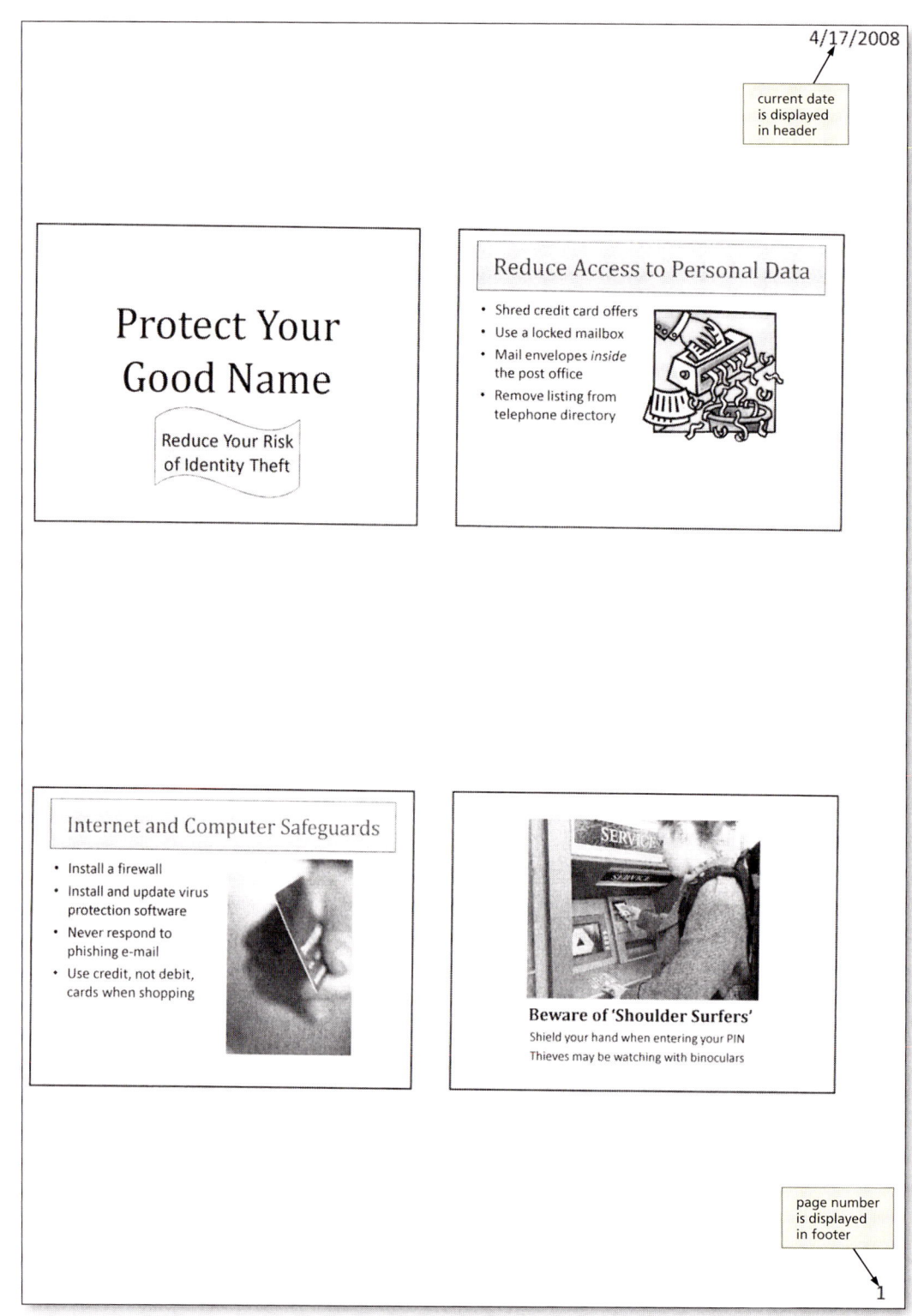

Figure 2–64

Saving and Quitting PowerPoint

If you made any changes to your presentation since your last save, you should save it again before quitting PowerPoint. The following steps save changes to the presentation and quit PowerPoint.

To Quit PowerPoint

This project is complete. The following steps quit PowerPoint.

1 Click the Office Button and then click the Exit PowerPoint button.

2 If necessary, click the Yes button in the Microsoft Office PowerPoint dialog box so that any changes you have made are saved.

Chapter Summary

In this chapter you have learned how to create slides from a blank presentation, change slide layouts, add a background style, insert clip art and pictures, size graphic elements, apply Quick Styles, select slide transitions, and preview and print an outline and handout. The items listed below include all the new PowerPoint skills you have learned in this chapter.

1. Choose a Background Style (PPT 89)
2. Change the View to Slide Sorter View (PPT 91)
3. Change the View to Normal View (PPT 91)
4. Change the Slide Layout to Two Content (PPT 92)
5. Change the Slide Layout to Picture with Caption (PPT 94)
6. Insert a Clip from the Clip Organizer into a Content Placeholder (PPT 96)
7. Insert a Photograph from the Clip Organizer into a Slide (PPT 98)
8. Insert a Photograph from a File into a Slide (PPT 99)
9. Resize Clip Art (PPT 100)
10. Resize a Photograph (PPT 103)
11. Delete a Placeholder (PPT 104)
12. Move Clips (PPT 105)
13. Format Title Text Using Quick Styles (PPT 106)
14. Format Remaining Title Text Using Quick Styles (PPT 107)
15. Change the Heading Font (PPT 109)
16. Shadow Text (PPT 110)
17. Change Font Color (PPT 110)
18. Format Text Using the Format Painter (PPT 112)
19. Format Remaining Title Text (PPT 113)
20. Add a Shape (PPT 116)
21. Resize a Shape (PPT 117)
22. Add Text to a Shape (PPT 119)
23. Format Shape Text and Add a Shape Quick Style (PPT 119)
24. Add a Transition between Slides (PPT 122)
25. Preview and Print an Outline (PPT 122)
26. Preview and Print Handouts (PPT 129)

 If you have a SAM user profile, you may have access to hands-on instruction, practice, and assessment. Log in to your SAM account (http://sam2007.course.com) to launch any assigned training activities or exams that relate to the skills covered in this chapter.

Learn It Online

Test your knowledge of chapter content and key terms.

Instructions: To complete the Learn It Online exercises, start your browser, click the Address bar, and then enter the Web address scsite.com/dc-off07/ppt2007/learn. When the Office 2007 Learn It Online page is displayed, click the link for the exercise you want to complete and then read the instructions.

Chapter Reinforcement TF, MC, and SA
A series of true/false, multiple choice, and short answer questions that test your knowledge of the chapter content.

Flash Cards
An interactive learning environment where you identify chapter key terms associated with displayed definitions.

Practice Test
A series of multiple choice questions that test your knowledge of chapter content and key terms.

Who Wants To Be a Computer Genius?
An interactive game that challenges your knowledge of chapter content in the style of a television quiz show.

Wheel of Terms
An interactive game that challenges your knowledge of chapter key terms in the style of the television show *Wheel of Fortune*.

Crossword Puzzle Challenge
A crossword puzzle that challenges your knowledge of key terms presented in the chapter.

Apply Your Knowledge

Reinforce the skills and apply the concepts you learned in this chapter.

Changing the Background and Adding Photographs and a Quick Style

Instructions: Start PowerPoint. Open the presentation, Apply 2-1 Lifestyle, from the Data Files for Students. See the inside back cover of this book for instructions on downloading the Data Files for Students, or contact your instructor for more information about accessing the required files.

The four slides in the presentation present basic guidelines for maintaining a healthy lifestyle and focus on proper weight, exercise, and food choices. The document you open is an unformatted presentation. You are to add and size photographs, change the background style, change slide layouts, apply a transition, and use the Format Painter so the slides look like Figure 2-65.

Perform the following tasks:
1. Change the background style to Style 11 (row 3, column 3). On the title slide, use your name in place of Student Name and bold and italicize your name and change the font color to orange. Increase the title text font size to 72 point, change the font to Baskerville Old Face, and change the font color to Dark Blue.
2. On Slides 2 and 4, change the layout to Two Content and then insert the photographs shown in Figure 2-65b and 2-65d from the Microsoft Clip Organizer.
3. On Slide 3, change the layout to Picture with Caption and then insert the picture shown in Figure 2-65c from the Microsoft Clip Organizer. Delete the text placeholder. Change the title text font size to 44 point, center this text, and then add the italic font style and shadow effect. Use the Format Painter to format the title text on Slides 2 and 4.
4. Apply the Subtle Effect – Accent 1 Quick Style (row 4, column 2) to the Slides 2, 3, and 4 title text placeholders. Apply the Uncover Left wipe transition (row 2, column 1) to all slides.

5. Check the spelling, and then display the revised presentation in Slide Sorter view.
6. Change the document properties, as specified by your instructor. Save the presentation using the file name, Apply 2–1 Healthy Lifestyle. Submit the revised document in the format specified by your instructor.

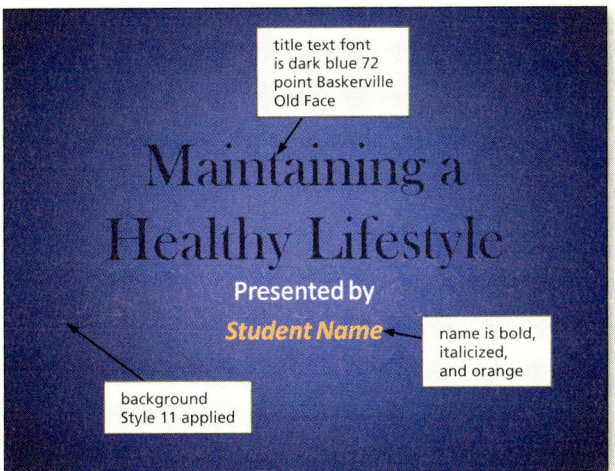
(a)

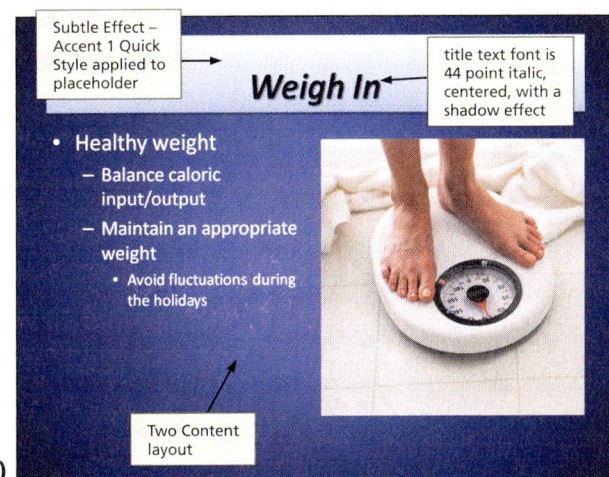
(b)

(c)

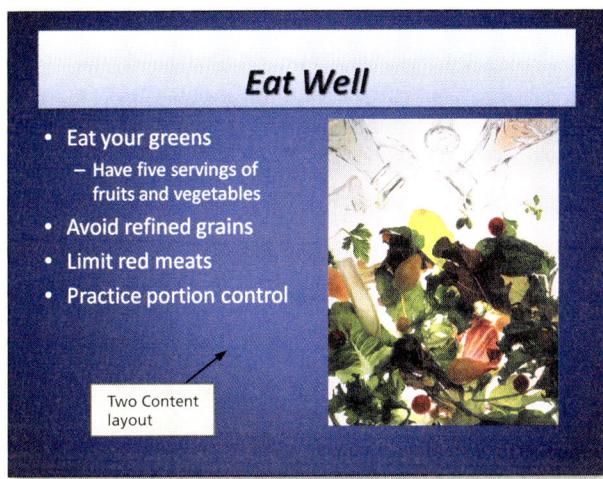
(d)

Figure 2–65

Extend Your Knowledge

Extend the skills you learned in this chapter and experiment with new skills. You may need to use Help to complete the assignment.

Changing Slide Layouts and Moving Clips

Instructions: Start PowerPoint. Open the presentation, Extend 2-1 Fats, from the Data Files for Students. See the inside back cover of this book for instructions on downloading the Data Files for Students, or contact your instructor for more information on accessing the required files.

You will choose a background, format slides, and copy clips (Figure 2–66).

Perform the following tasks:
1. Add an appropriate background style.
2. On Slide 1, use your name in place of Student Name. Format the text using techniques you learned and applied in this chapter, such as changing the font size and color and also bolding and italicizing words.
3. Slide 7 contains a variety of clips downloaded from the Microsoft Clip Organizer. Review the slides in the presentation and then move clips from Slide 7 to the appropriate slides. You do not need to use all the clips. Delete Slide 7 when you have finished moving the desired clips to the slides.
4. Change the slide layouts to accommodate the clips. Size the clips when necessary. Edit the text so that each slide meets the 7 × 7 rule, which states that each line should have a maximum of seven words, and each slide should have a maximum of seven lines.
5. Apply an appropriate transition to all slides.
6. Change the document properties, as specified by your instructor. Save the presentation using the file name, Extend 2-1 Enhanced Fats.
7. Submit the revised document in the format specified by your instructor.

Figure 2–66

Make It Right

Analyze a presentation and correct all errors and/or improve the design.

Applying Background and Quick Styles

Instructions: Start PowerPoint. Open the presentation, Make It Right 2-1 Safety, from the Data Files for Students. See the back inside cover of this book for instructions on downloading the Data Files for Students, or contact your instructor for more information on accessing the required files.

Correct the formatting problems and errors in the presentation while keeping in mind the guidelines presented in this chapter.

Perform the following tasks:

1. Change the document theme from Verve, shown in Figure 2–67, to Paper. Apply the Style 7 background style (row 2, column 3).
2. On Slide 1, replace the words, Student Name, with your name. Apply a Quick Style to your name and the title text so that they display prominently on the slide.
3. Move Slide 2 to the end of the presentation so that it becomes the new Slide 5.
4. Use the spell checker to correct the misspellings. Analyze the slides for other word usage errors that the spell checker did not find.
5. Adjust the clip art sizes so they do not overlap text and are the appropriate dimensions for the slide content.
6. Select a Quick Style to apply to the Slides 2 through 5 title text. Center the title text and apply a shadow.
7. Apply an appropriate transition to all slides. Change the speed to Slow.
8. Change the document properties, as specified by your instructor. Save the presentation using the file name, Make It Right 2-1 Home Safety.
9. Submit the revised document in the format specified by your instructor.

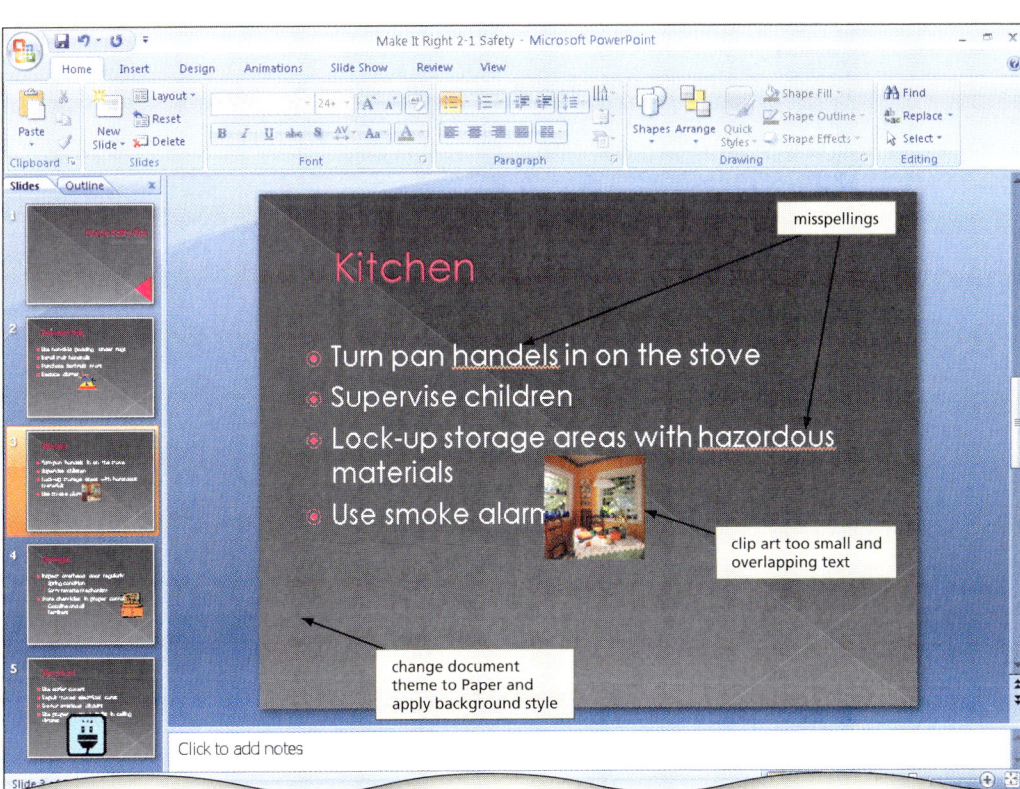

Figure 2–67

In the Lab

Design and/or create a presentation using the guidelines, concepts, and skills presented in this chapter. Labs 1, 2, and 3 are listed in order of increasing difficulty.

Lab 1: Creating a Presentation with a Clip and Shapes

Problem: The ear affects balance while it enables us to hear. This organ can be divided into three parts for analysis: outer, middle, and inner. The outer ear is composed of a flap and the auditory canal. The middle ear has three tiny bones called the auditory ossicles and the eustachian tube, which links the ear to the nose. The inner ear contains the spiral-shaped cochlea and also the semicircular canals and the vestibule, which control balance. You are studying the ear as a unit in your health class, so you decide to develop a PowerPoint slide that names these parts to help you study for a quiz. Create the slide shown in Figure 2–68 from a blank presentation.

Instructions: Perform the following tasks.

1. Apply the Style 6 background style (row 2, column 2) to the slide. Change the layout to Content with Caption. Import the ear diagram clip from the Microsoft Clip Organizer.

2. Type the slide title and caption body text shown in Figure 2–68. Use your name in place of Bill Tracy, and then italicize this text and change the font color to Blue (color 8 in the Standard Colors row). Change the color of the title text to Dark Red (color 1 in the Standard Colors row) and increase the font size to 24.

3. Use the Right Arrow, Left Arrow, Up Arrow, and Down Arrow shapes in the Block Arrow section to point to the parts of the ear shown in Figure 2–68. Add the number to each arrow. Apply the Subtle Effect – Accent 3 Quick Style (row 4, column 4) to each arrow. Change the font size of each arrow text to 24 point and bold these numbers.

4. Check the spelling and correct any errors.

5. Change the document properties, as specified by your instructor. Save the presentation using the file name, Lab 2-1 Ear.

6. Submit the revised document in the format specified by your instructor.

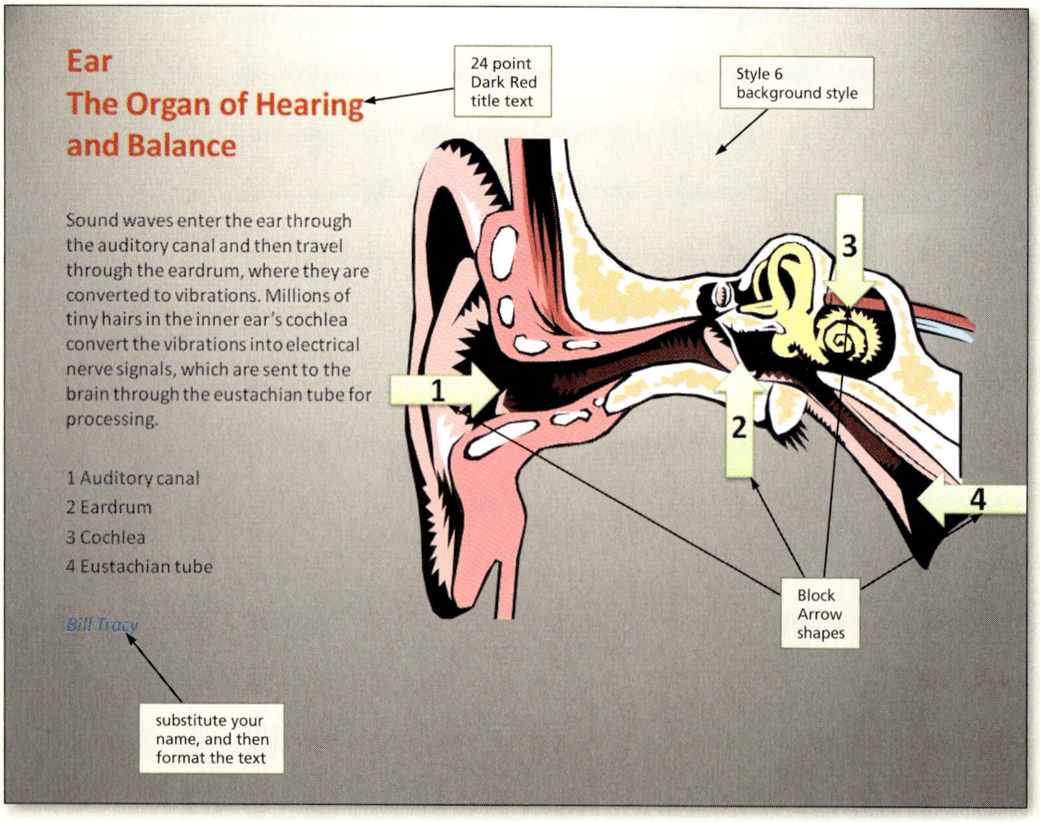

Figure 2–68

In the Lab

Lab 2: Creating a Presentation with Photographs Inserted from a File

Problem: Destructive insects damage specific species of trees throughout the world. You have learned in your Botany 202 class that the Asian Longhorn Beetle, the Emerald Ash Borer, the Gypsy Moth, and the Western Pine Beetle are among trees' biggest pests. One of your assignments in your botany class is to give a speech about common tree pests. You develop the outline shown in Figure 2–69 and then prepare the PowerPoint presentation shown in Figures 2–70a through 2–70f. You have obtained permission from the U.S. Forestry Department to copy photographs from its Web site to your slide show; these photographs are on your Data Files for Students.

Tree Pests
Creatures That Bug Our Trees
Jim DeYoung
Botany 202

Asian Longhorn Beetle
- Native to China
- Transported to United States in infested packing material

Emerald Ash Borer
- Killed 20 million trees in Michigan, Ohio, and Indiana
- Firewood quarantines to prevent new infestations

Gypsy Moth
- Spread to U.S. in 1870
- Oaks and Aspens are most common hosts
- Larva defoliate trees
- Small mammals and birds are predators

Western Pine Beetle
- Infest Ponderosa and Coulter pine trees
  - Mainly Western states
- Tree loss considered normal ecological process

Acknowledgements
- Photos and information courtesy of the USDA Forest Service
  - forestry.about.com

Figure 2–69

Continued >

In the Lab *continued*

Instructions: *Perform the following tasks.*

1. Create a new presentation using the Foundry document theme. Apply the Style 7 background style (row 2, column 3).
2. Using the typed notes illustrated in Figure 2–69, create the title slide shown in Figure 2–70a using your name in place of Jim DeYoung. Bold your name and apply a shadow.
3. Insert the Isosceles Triangle shape (row 1, column 3 in the Basic Shapes category) in the top center of Slide 1. Size the shape so that the top and bottom align with the edges of the brown area of the slide, as shown in Figure 2–70a.
4. Using the typed notes in Figure 2–69, create the five text slides with bulleted lists shown in Figures 2–70b through 2–70f. Use the Two Content slide layout for Slides 2 through 5 and the Title and Content slide layout for Slide 6.
5. Insert the appropriate pictures from your Data Files for Students on Slides 2 through 5.
6. Apply the Wedge transition (row 1, column 5 in the Wipes category) to all slides. Change the speed to Medium. Check the spelling and correct any errors.
7. Review the slides in Slide Sorter view to check for consistency, and then change the view to Normal.
8. Drag the scroll box to display Slide 1. Click the Slide Show button to start Slide Show view. Then click to display each slide.
9. Change the document properties, as specified by your instructor. Save the presentation using the file name, Lab 2-2 Tree Pests.
10. Submit the document in the format specified by your instructor.

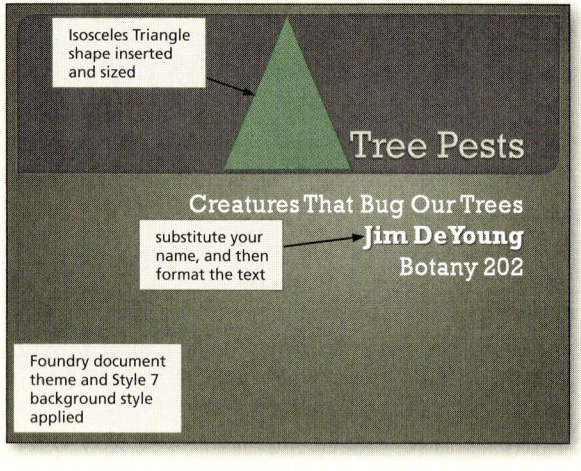
(a)

(b)

Figure 2–70

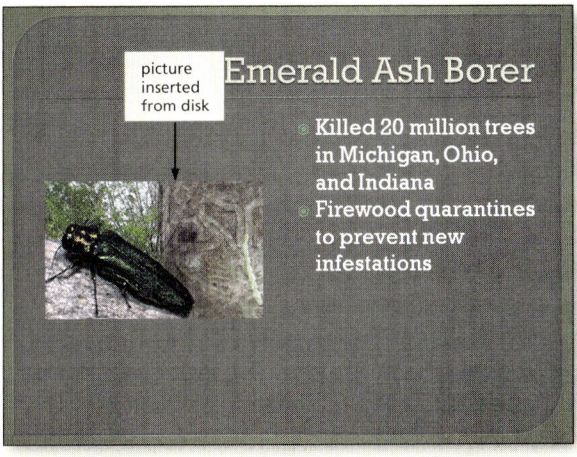
(c)

(d)

(e)

(f)

Figure 2–70

In the Lab

Lab 3: Creating a Presentation with Clips and Shapes

Problem: Snowboarding's popularity has soared in recent years; even Cameron Diaz and Space Shuttle astronauts have a passion for the sport. But with this increase in snowboarders has come a corresponding increase in injuries. The most common injuries are caused by a failure to follow common sense precautions. In order to maximize the time on the slopes, snowboarders need to prepare for the sport by wearing proper equipment, getting into condition, and snowboarding under control. Bryan Howell owns a local ski and snowboard shop in your town and has asked you to prepare a PowerPoint presentation that he can share with equipment buyers and renters. He hands you the outline shown in Figure 2–71 and asks you to create the presentation shown in Figures 2–72a through 2–72d.

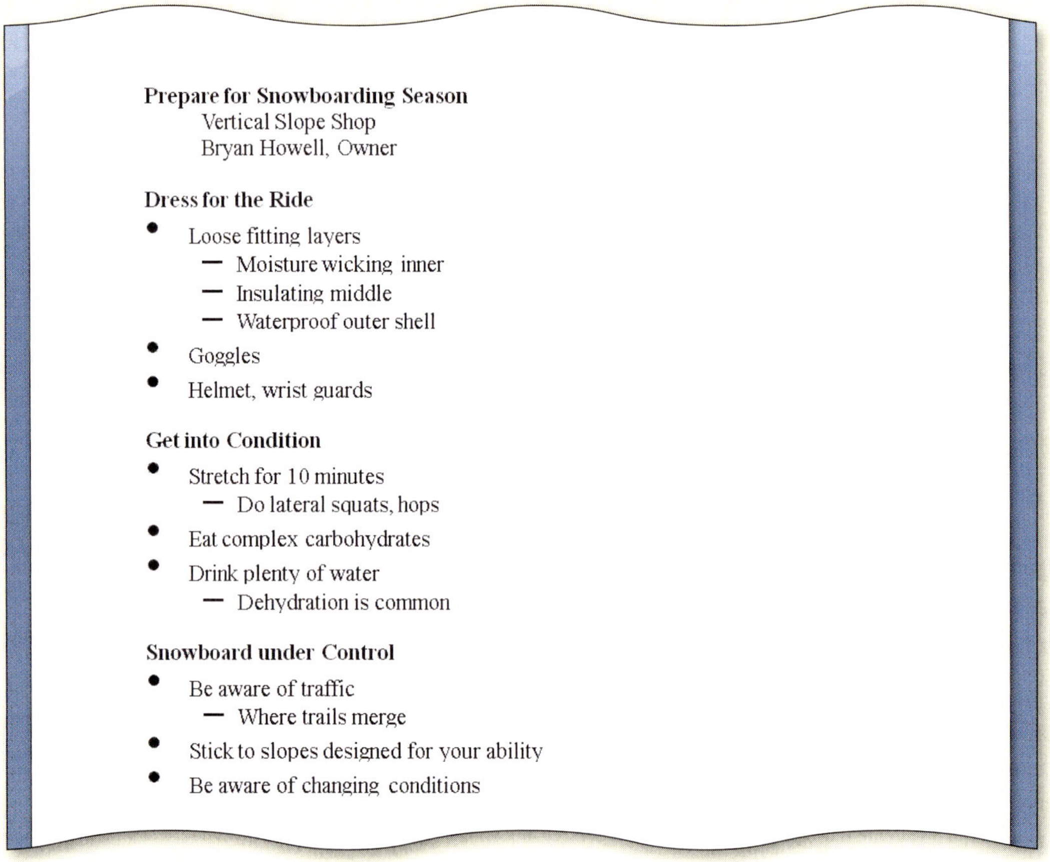

Prepare for Snowboarding Season
  Vertical Slope Shop
  Bryan Howell, Owner

Dress for the Ride
- Loose fitting layers
  - Moisture wicking inner
  - Insulating middle
  - Waterproof outer shell
- Goggles
- Helmet, wrist guards

Get into Condition
- Stretch for 10 minutes
  - Do lateral squats, hops
- Eat complex carbohydrates
- Drink plenty of water
  - Dehydration is common

Snowboard under Control
- Be aware of traffic
  - Where trails merge
- Stick to slopes designed for your ability
- Be aware of changing conditions

Figure 2–71

Instructions: Perform the following tasks.
1. Use the typed notes illustrated in Figure 2–71 to create four slides shown in Figures 2–72a through 2–72d from a blank presentation. Apply the Style 7 background style (row 2, column 3). Use your name in place of Bryan Howell on the title slide shown in Figure 2–72a. Bold your name.
2. Insert the Right Triangle shape (row 1, column 4 in the Basic Shapes category) on Slide 1. With the shape selected, click the Arrange button in the Drawing group on the Home tab, point to Rotate in the Position Objects group, and then click Flip Horizontal to turn the triangle shape. Drag the shape to the lower-right corner of the slide, increase the size to that shown in Figure 2–72a, and apply the Colored Outline - Accent 3 Quick Style (row 1, column 4).

3. Italicize the Slide 1 title text, Prepare for Snowboarding Season, align the text left, and change the font color to Black. Align the subtitle text left and change the font color to Green (color 6 in the Standard Colors row).
4. Add the photographs and clip art shown in Figures 2–72a through 2–72d from the Microsoft Clip Organizer. Adjust the clip sizes when necessary.
5. Change the Slide 2 title text font size to 54 point, change the font to Forte, and then change the color to Green. Use the Format Painter to format the title text on Slides 3 and 4 with the same features as on Slide 2.
6. Apply the Newsflash transition (row 6, column 2 in the Wipes category) to all slides. Change the speed to Medium. Check the spelling and correct any errors.
7. Click the Slide Sorter button, view the slides for consistency, and then click the Normal button.
8. Change the document properties, as specified by your instructor. Save the presentation using the file name, Lab 2-3 Snowboarding.
9. Submit the revised document in the format specified by your instructor.

(a)

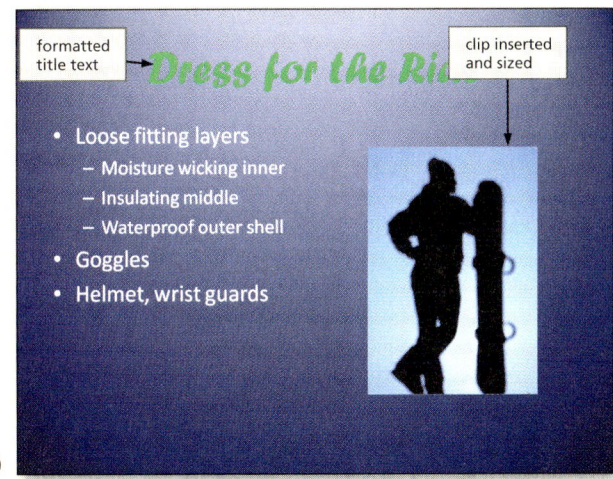
(b)

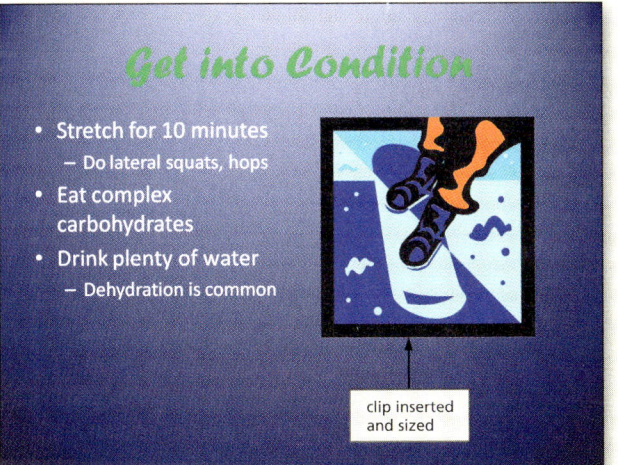
(c)

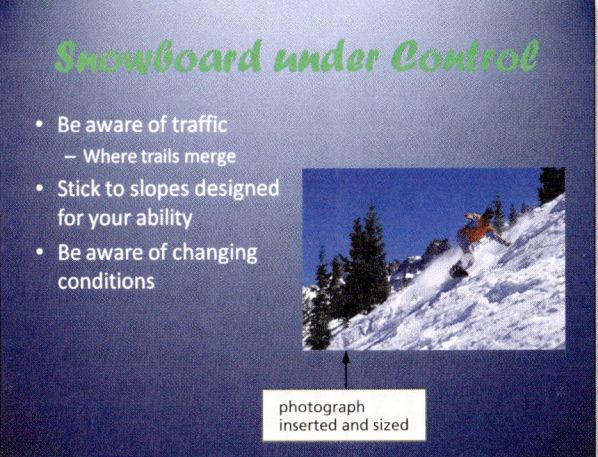
(d)

Figure 2–72

Cases and Places

Apply your creative thinking and problem solving skills to design and implement a solution.

• Easier   •• More Difficult

Note: Remember to use the 7 × 7 rule as you design the presentations: a maximum of seven words on a line and a maximum of seven lines on one slide.

• 1: Design and Create an Energy Efficiency Presentation

Global demand, industry deregulation, and regional conflicts have increased energy prices. The United States Department of Energy predicts energy use will grow 33 percent by 2030. Despite these staggering numbers, homeowners can undertake relatively simple measures to be energy efficient. Create a presentation using the outline in Figure 2–73. Apply at least three objectives found at the beginning of this chapter to develop the presentation. Add a title slide with a shape and a closing slide that cites your references. Be sure to check spelling.

Home Energy Savings Tips

Save Money While You Help the Environment

Bright Ideas
- Lighting accounts for more than 10 percent of electric bill
- Change to compact florescent lights (CFLs)
  - Use 50-75 percent less energy
  - Last up to ten times longer than conventional bulbs

Keep It Clean
- Wash only *full* loads of clothes and dishes
- Keep dryer vents clean
- Air dry dishes when possible
- Use ENERGY STAR products

Stay Out of Hot Water
- Heating water accounts for 13 percent of energy bill
- Use low-flow fixtures
- Repair leaks
- Lower thermostat
- Insulate heater

References
- www1.eere.energy.gov/consumer/tips/save_energy.html
- www.exeloncorp.com/comedcare/
- www.energystar.gov/|

Figure 2–73

• 2: Design and Create a Hypertension Presentation

According to the National Heart, Lung, and Blood Institute, nearly one-third of American adults are inflicted by the "silent killer," high blood pressure. This disease affects people of all ages and ethnicities. Use the concepts and techniques presented in this chapter to create a presentation following the outline in Figure 2–74, which includes the definition of hypertension and hypertension categories, has tips on controlling high blood pressure, and lists Web sites to view for further information. Insert photographs and clips, and apply a subtle slide transition to all slides. Be sure to check spelling.

Blood Pressure 101
Taking Control of the Silent Killer

Blood Pressure Definition
- Force of blood on vein walls
    - Pressure units: milligrams of mercury (mgHg)
- Defined by two numbers
    - Systolic: Pressure during beats
    - Diastolic: Pressure between beats
- Read as the systolic over diastolic level
    - Example: 125 over 74

Adult Blood Pressure Categories
- Normal
    - Systolic < 120
    - Diastolic < 80
- Prehypertension
    - Systolic 120 – 139
    - Diastolic 80 – 89
- Hypertension
    - Systolic > 140
    - Diastolic > 90

Detection
- No symptoms
- Person must be tested
    - Sphygmomanometer and stethoscope used

Hypertension Prevention Tips
- Eat healthy
    - Fruits, vegetables
    - Low fat diet
- Maintain weight
- Exercise regularly

References
- National Heart, Lung, and Blood Institute
    www.nhlbi.nih.gov
- American Heart Association
    www.americanheart.org/presenter.jhtml

Figure 2–74

Continued >

Cases and Places *continued*

•• 3: Design and Create a Portable Media Player Presentation

Video tape recorders were immensely popular more than three decades ago with several competing standards introduced in the market. Each technology touted different features. Today, the situation is similar with portable media players and cellular telephones that can download music from the Internet or rip files from your computer. Your supervisor at NextPhase Electronics recognizes buyers need assistance learning about these devices. She has asked you to prepare a presentation summarizing one of these players for next month's Saturday Seminar Series at the store. Research a specific portable media player and create a slide for each of the following attributes: featured model, user interface, and finding and loading songs. Select art and photographs from the Microsoft Clip Organizer, and add a title slide and summary slide to complete your presentation. Format the title slide with a shape and the text with colors and bolding where needed for emphasis.

•• 4: Design and Create a Campus Orientation Presentation

Make It Personal

Feedback from new students at your school cites difficulties navigating your campus. Incoming students mention the library, registrar, and health services as locations most often sought. To address these concerns, you volunteered as a member of the New Student Orientation Team to create a presentation and distribute a handout showing frequently accessed areas of the school. Use the concepts and techniques presented in this chapter to develop and format a slide show with a title slide and at least three text slides with bulleted lists. Create a slide for each landmark that briefly describes its location, and use clips and text to annotate it. Obtain a map of your campus and import it as a picture into your presentation. Select slide layouts that permit both the map and a bulleted list to appear on each slide. Use the arrow shapes to indicate the location of the landmark on the map. Add a background style and slide transitions. Be sure to check spelling. Print a handout with two slides on each page to distribute to new students on campus.

•• 5: Design and Create a Wellness Program Presentation

Working Together

Health care costs continue to rise at nearly double the inflation rate. Many health insurance companies are becoming proactive in containing those costs by offering reimbursement for wellness programs. Have each member of your team visit, telephone, or view Web sites of three health insurance companies. Gather information about:

1) Health screenings

2) Fitness center amenities

3) Self-Improvement classes

4) Wellness program benefits

After coordinating the data, create a presentation with a least one slide showcasing each topic. As a group, critique each slide. Submit your assignment in the format specified by your instructor.

1 Creating a Worksheet and an Embedded Chart

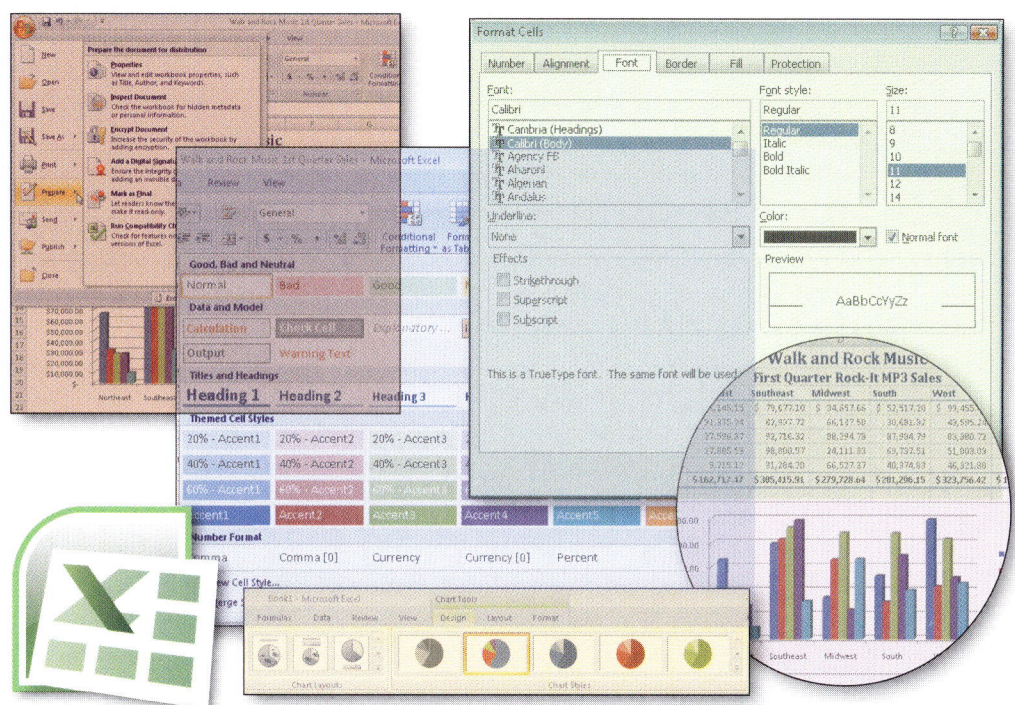

Objectives

You will have mastered the material in this chapter when you can:

- Start and quit Excel
- Describe the Excel worksheet
- Enter text and numbers
- Use the Sum button to sum a range of cells
- Copy the contents of a cell to a range of cells using the fill handle
- Save a workbook
- Format cells in a worksheet
- Create a 3-D Clustered Column chart
- Change document properties
- Save a workbook a second time using the same file name
- Print a worksheet
- Open a workbook
- Use the AutoCalculate area to determine statistics
- Correct errors on a worksheet
- Use Excel Help to answer questions

Microsoft Office **Excel 2007**

1 Creating a Worksheet and an Embedded Chart

What Is Microsoft Office Excel 2007?

Microsoft Office Excel 2007 is a powerful spreadsheet program that allows users to organize data, complete calculations, make decisions, graph data, develop professional looking reports (Figure 1–1), publish organized data to the Web, and access real-time data from Web sites. The four major parts of Excel are:

- **Workbooks and Worksheets** Workbooks are a collection of worksheets. Worksheets allow users to enter, calculate, manipulate, and analyze data such as numbers and text. The terms worksheet and spreadsheet are interchangeable.
- **Charts** Excel can draw a variety of charts.
- **Tables** Tables organize and store data within worksheets. For example, once a user enters data into a worksheet, an Excel table can sort the data, search for specific data, and select data that satisfies defined criteria.
- **Web Support** Web support allows users to save Excel worksheets or parts of a worksheet in HTML format, so a user can view and manipulate the worksheet using a browser. Excel Web support also provides access to real-time data, such as stock quotes, using Web queries.

This latest version of Excel makes it much easier than in previous versions to perform common functions by introducing a new style of user interface. It also offers the capability of creating larger worksheets, improved formatting and printing, improved charting and table functionality, industry-standard XML support that simplifies the sharing of data within and outside an organization, improved business intelligence functionality, and the capability of performing complex tasks on a server.

In this chapter, you will create a worksheet that includes a chart. The data in the worksheet and chart includes sales data for several stores that a company owns and operates.

Project Planning Guidelines

The process of developing a worksheet that communicates specific information requires careful analysis and planning. As a starting point, establish why the worksheet is needed. Once the purpose is determined, analyze the intended users of the worksheet and their unique needs. Then, gather information about the topic and decide what to include in the worksheet. Finally, determine the worksheet design and style that will be most successful at delivering the message. Details of these guidelines are provided in Appendix A. In addition, each project developed in this book provides practical applications of these planning considerations.

Project — Worksheet with an Embedded Chart

The project in this chapter follows proper design guidelines and uses Excel to create the worksheet shown in Figure 1–1. The worksheet contains sales data for Walk and Rock Music stores. The Walk and Rock Music product line includes a variety of MP3 music players, called Rock-It MP3, including players that show pictures and video, as well as a complete line of headphones and other accessories. The company sells its products at kiosks in several malls throughout the United States. By concentrating its stores near colleges and universities and keeping the newest items in stock, the Walk and Rock Music stores quickly became trendy. As sales continued to grow in the past year, senior management requested an easy-to-read worksheet that shows product sales for the first quarter by region. In addition, they asked for a chart showing first quarter sales, because the president of the company likes to have a graphical representation of sales that allows him quickly to identify stronger and weaker product types by region.

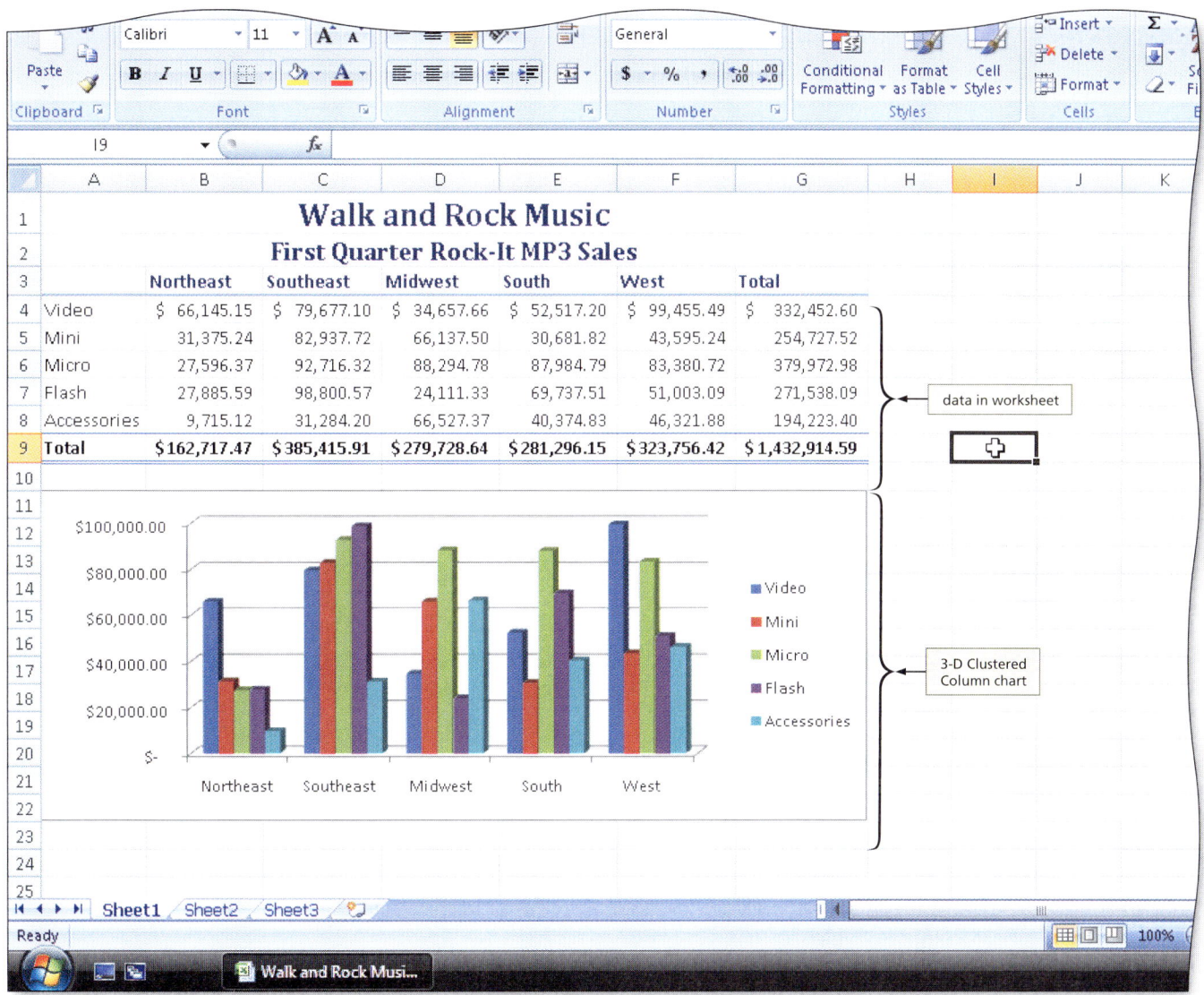

Figure 1–1

The first step in creating an effective worksheet is to make sure you understand what is required. The person or persons requesting the worksheet should supply their requirements in a requirements document. A **requirements document** includes a needs

BTW

Excel 2007 Features
With its what-if analysis tools, research capabilities, collaboration tools, streamlined user interface, smart tags, charting features, Web capabilities, hundreds of functions, and enhanced formatting capabilities, Excel 2007 is one of the easier and more powerful spreadsheet packages available.

statement, source of data, summary of calculations, and any other special requirements for the worksheet, such as charting and Web support. Figure 1–2 shows the requirements document for the new workbook to be created in this chapter.

REQUEST FOR NEW WORKBOOK	
Date Submitted:	April 15, 2008
Submitted By:	Trisha Samuels
Worksheet Title:	Walk and Rock Music First Quarter Sales
Needs:	An easy-to-read worksheet that shows Walk and Rock Music's first quarter sales for each of our sales regions in which we operate (Northeast, Southeast, Midwest, South, West). The worksheet also should include total sales for each region, total sales for each product type, and total company sales for the first quarter.
Source of Data:	The data for the worksheet is available for the end of the first quarter from the chief financial officer (CFO) of Walk and Rock Music.
Calculations:	The following calculations must be made for the worksheet: (a) total first quarter sales for each of the five regions; (b) total first quarter sales for each of the five product types; and (c) total first quarter sales for the company.
Chart Requirements:	Below the data in the worksheet, construct a 3-D Clustered Column chart that compares the total sales for each region within each type of product.

Approvals

Approval Status:	X	Approved
		Rejected
Approved By:	Stan Maderbek	
Date:	April 22, 2008	
Assigned To:	J. Quasney, Spreadsheet Specialist	

requirements document →

Figure 1–2

BTW

Worksheet Development Cycle
Spreadsheet specialists do not sit down and start entering text, formulas, and data into a blank Excel worksheet as soon as they have a spreadsheet assignment. Instead, they follow an organized plan, or methodology, that breaks the development cycle into a series of tasks. The recommended methodology for creating worksheets includes: (1) analyze requirements (supplied in a requirements document); (2) design solution; (3) validate design; (4) implement design; (5) test solution; and (6) document solution.

Overview

As you read this chapter, you will learn how to create the worksheet shown in Figure 1–1 by performing these general tasks:

- Enter text in the worksheet
- Add totals to the worksheet
- Save the workbook that contains the worksheet
- Format the text in the worksheet
- Insert a chart in the worksheet
- Save the workbook a second time using the same file name
- Print the worksheet

Plan Ahead

General Project Guidelines
While creating an Excel worksheet, you need to make several decisions that will determine the appearance and characteristics of the finished worksheet. As you create the worksheet shown in Figure 1–1, you should follow these general guidelines:

1. **Select titles and subtitles for the worksheet.** Follow the *less is more* guideline. The less text in the titles and subtitles, the more impact the titles and subtitles will have. Use the fewest words possible to specify the information presented in the worksheet to the intended audience.

(continued)

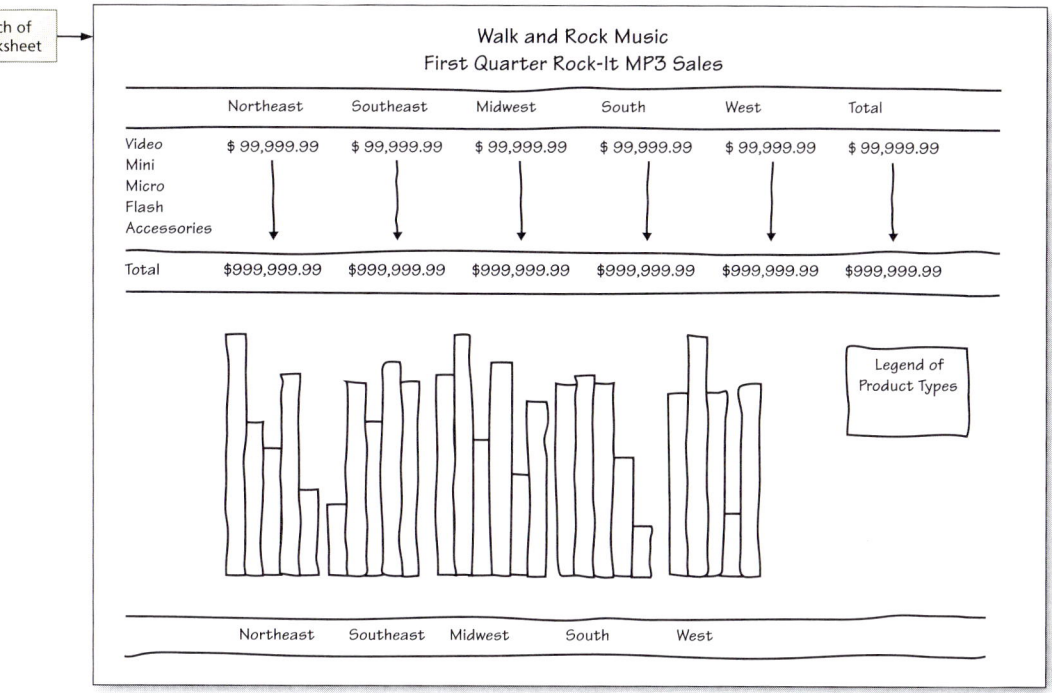

Figure 1–3

(continued)

2. **Determine the contents for rows and columns.** Rows typically contain information that is analogous to items in a list, such as the products sold by a company. Columns typically contain descriptive information about items in rows or contain information that helps to group the data in the worksheet, such as company regions.

3. **Determine the calculations that are needed.** You can decide to total data in a variety of ways, such as across rows or in columns. You also can include a grand total.

4. **Determine where to save the workbook.** You can store a workbook permanently, or **save** it, on a variety of storage media including a hard disk, USB flash drive, or optical disc. You also can indicate a specific location on the storage media for saving the workbook.

5. **Identify how to format various elements of the worksheet.** The overall appearance of a worksheet significantly affects its ability to communicate clearly. Examples of how you can modify the appearance, or **format**, of text include changing its shape, size, color, and position on the worksheet.

6. **Decide on the type of chart needed.** Excel includes the capability of creating many different types of charts, such as bar charts and pie charts. Each chart type relays a different message about the data in the worksheet. Choose a chart type that relays the message that you want to convey.

7. **Establish where to position and how to format the chart.** The position and format of the chart should command the attention of the intended audience. If possible, position the chart so that it prints with the worksheet data on a single page.

When necessary, more specific details concerning the above guidelines are presented at appropriate points in the chapter. The chapter also will identify the actions performed and decisions made regarding these guidelines during the creation of the worksheet shown in Figure 1–1 on page EX 3.

Plan Ahead

After carefully reviewing the requirements document (Figure 1–2 on page EX 4) and necessary decisions, the next step is to design a solution or draw a sketch of the worksheet based on the requirements, including titles, column and row headings, location of data values, and the 3-D Clustered Column chart, as shown in Figure 1–3 on page EX 5. The dollar signs, 9s, and commas that you see in the sketch of the worksheet indicate formatted numeric values.

With a good understanding of the requirements document, an understanding of the necessary decisions, and a sketch of the worksheet, the next step is to use Excel to create the worksheet and chart.

Starting Excel

If you are using a computer to step through the project in this chapter and you want your screen to match the figures in this book, you should change your computer's resolution to 1024 × 768. For information about how to change a computer's resolution, read Appendix C.

To Start Excel

The following steps, which assume Windows Vista is running, start Excel based on a typical installation of Microsoft Office on your computer. You may need to ask your instructor how to start Excel for your computer.

1

- Click the Start button on the Windows Vista taskbar to display the Start menu.
- Click All Programs at the bottom of left pane on the the Start menu to display the All Programs list.
- Click Microsoft Office in the All Programs list to display the Microsoft Office list (Figure 1–4).

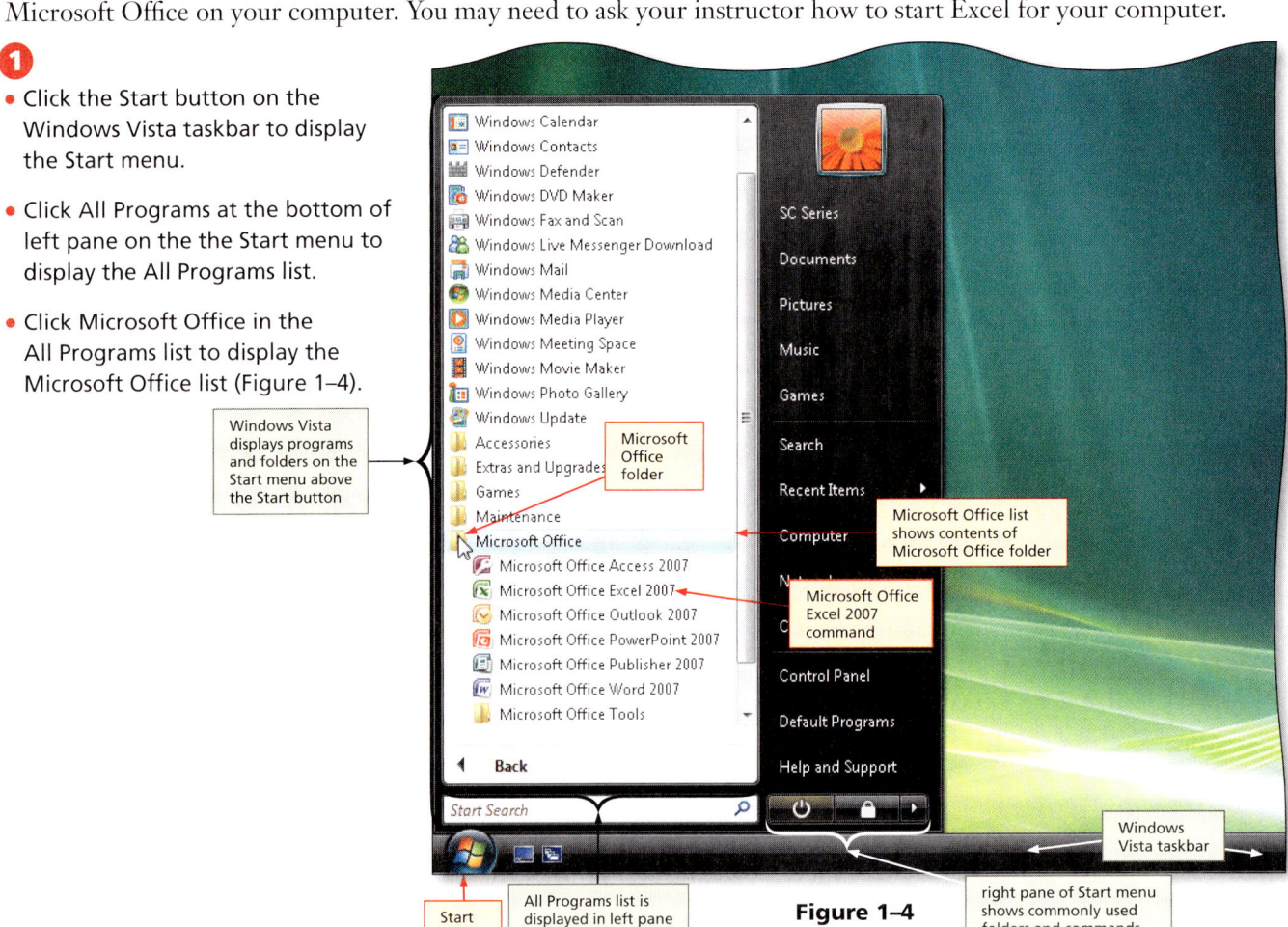

Figure 1–4

Creating a Worksheet and an Embedded Chart **Excel Chapter 1** **EX 7**

- Click Microsoft Office Excel 2007 to start Excel and display a new blank workbook titled Book1 in the Excel window (Figure 1–5).

- If the Excel window is not maximized, click the Maximize button next to the Close button on its title bar to maximize the window.

- If the worksheet window in Excel is not maximized, click the Maximize button next to the Close button on its title bar to maximize the worksheet window within Excel.

Q&A

What is a maximized window?

A maximized window fills the entire screen. When you maximize a window, the Maximize button changes to a Restore Down button. When you restore a maximized window, the window returns to its previous size and the Restore Down button changes to a Maximize button.

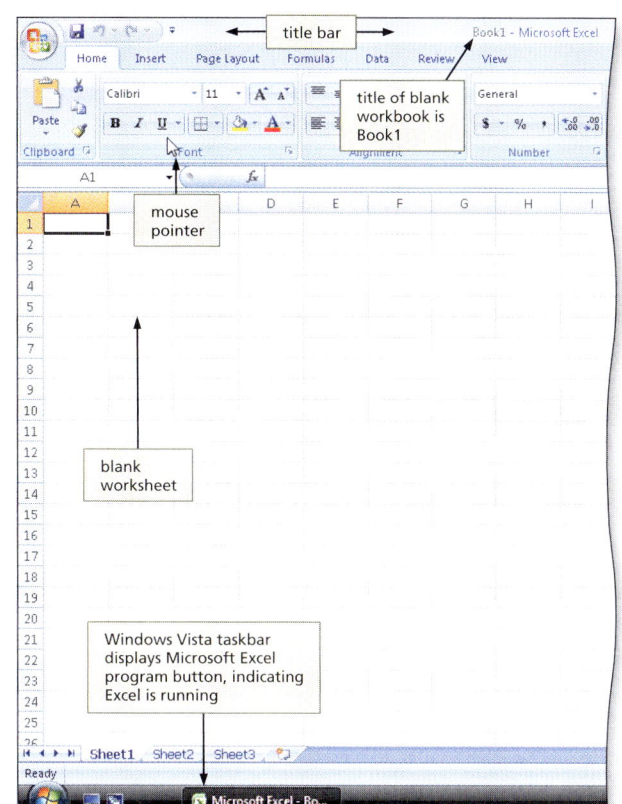

Figure 1–5

Other Ways
1. Double-click Excel 2007 icon on desktop, if one is present
2. Click Microsoft Office Excel 2007 on Start menu

The Excel Workbook

The Excel window consists of a variety of components to make your work more efficient and worksheets more professional. These include the document window, Ribbon, Mini toolbar and shortcut menus, Quick Access Toolbar, and Office Button. Some of these components are common to other Microsoft Office 2007 programs; others are unique to Excel.

When Excel starts, it creates a new blank workbook, called Book1. The **workbook** (Figure 1–6) is like a notebook. Inside the workbook are sheets, each of which is called a **worksheet**. Excel opens a new workbook with three worksheets.

If necessary, you can add additional worksheets as long as your computer has enough memory to accommodate them. Each worksheet has a sheet name that appears on a **sheet tab** at the bottom of the workbook. For example, Sheet1 is the name of the active worksheet displayed in the Book1 workbook. If you click the sheet tab labeled Sheet2, Excel displays the Sheet2 worksheet. The project in this chapter uses only the Sheet1 worksheet.

The Worksheet

The worksheet is organized into a rectangular grid containing vertical columns and horizontal rows. A column letter above the grid, also called the **column heading**, identifies each column. A row number on the left side of the grid, also called the **row heading**, identifies

BTW

Excel Help
Help with Excel is no further away than the Help button on the right side of the Ribbon. Click the Help button, type help in the 'Type words to search for' box, and then press the ENTER key. Excel responds with a list of topics you can click to learn about obtaining Help on any Excel-related topic. To find out what is new in Excel 2007, type what is new in Excel in the 'Type words to search for' box.

each row. With the screen resolution set to 1024 × 768 and the Excel window maximized, Excel displays 15 columns (A through O) and 25 rows (1 through 25) of the worksheet on the screen, as shown in Figure 1–6.

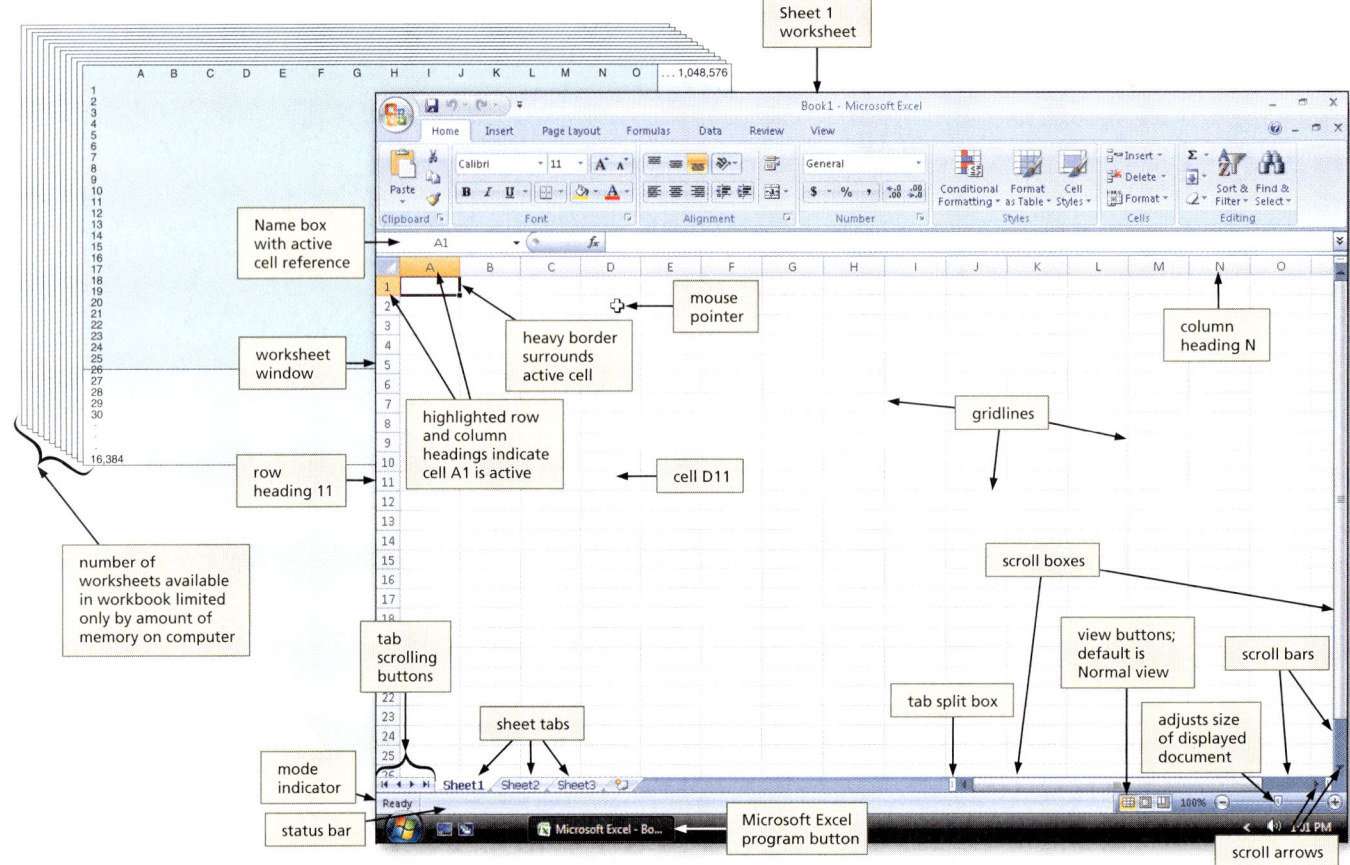

Figure 1–6

> **BTW**
>
> **Worksheet Development**
> The key to developing a useful worksheet is careful planning. Careful planning can reduce your effort significantly and result in a worksheet that is accurate, easy to read, flexible, and useful. When analyzing a problem and designing a worksheet solution, you should follow these steps: (1) define the problem, including need, source of data, calculations, charting, and Web or special requirements; (2) design the worksheet; (3) enter the data and formulas; and (4) test the worksheet.

The intersection of each column and row is a cell. A **cell** is the basic unit of a worksheet into which you enter data. Each worksheet in a workbook has 16,384 columns and 1,048,576 rows for a total of 17,179,869,180 cells. Only a small fraction of the active worksheet appears on the screen at one time.

A cell is referred to by its unique address, or **cell reference**, which is the coordinates of the intersection of a column and a row. To identify a cell, specify the column letter first, followed by the row number. For example, cell reference D11 refers to the cell located at the intersection of column D and row 11 (Figure 1–6).

One cell on the worksheet, designated the **active cell**, is the one into which you can enter data. The active cell in Figure 1–6 is A1. The active cell is identified in three ways. First, a heavy border surrounds the cell; second, the active cell reference shows immediately above column A in the Name box; and third, the column heading A and row heading 1 are highlighted so it is easy to see which cell is active (Figure 1–6).

The horizontal and vertical lines on the worksheet itself are called **gridlines**. Gridlines make it easier to see and identify each cell in the worksheet. If desired, you can turn the gridlines off so they do not show on the worksheet, but it is recommended that you leave them on for now.

The mouse pointer in Figure 1–6 has the shape of a block plus sign. The mouse pointer appears as a block plus sign whenever it is located in a cell on the worksheet. Another common shape of the mouse pointer is the block arrow. The mouse pointer turns into the block arrow whenever you move it outside the worksheet or when you drag cell contents between rows or columns. The other mouse pointer shapes are described when they appear on the screen.

Worksheet Window

You view the portion of the worksheet displayed on the screen through a **worksheet window** (Figure 1–6). The default (preset) view is **normal view**. Below and to the right of the worksheet window are **scroll bars**, **scroll arrows**, and **scroll boxes** that you can use to move the worksheet window around to view different parts of the active worksheet. To the right of the sheet tabs at the bottom of the screen is the tab split box. You can drag the **tab split box** to increase or decrease the view of the sheet tabs (Figure 1–6). When you decrease the view of the sheet tabs, you increase the length of the horizontal scroll bar, and vice versa.

Status Bar

The status bar is located immediately above the Windows Vista taskbar at the bottom of the screen (Figure 1–6). The **status bar** presents information about the worksheet, the function of the button the mouse pointer is pointing to, or the mode of Excel. **Mode indicators**, such as Enter and Ready, appear on the status bar and specify the current mode of Excel. When the mode is **Ready**, Excel is ready to accept the next command or data entry. When the mode indicator reads **Enter**, Excel is in the process of accepting data through the keyboard into the active cell.

Keyboard indicators, such as Scroll Lock, show which toggle keys are engaged. Keyboard indicators appear to the right of the mode indicator. Toward the right edge of the status bar are buttons and controls you can use to change the view of a document and adjust the size of the displayed document.

Ribbon

The **Ribbon**, located near the top of the Excel window, is the control center in Excel (Figure 1–7a). The Ribbon provides easy, central access to the tasks you perform while creating a worksheet. The Ribbon consists of tabs, groups, and commands. Each **tab** surrounds a collection of groups, and each **group** contains related commands.

> **BTW**
>
> **The Worksheet Size and Window**
> Excel's 16,384 columns and 1,048,576 rows make for a huge worksheet that – if you could imagine – takes up the entire side of a building to display in its entirety. Your computer screen, by comparison, is a small window that allows you to view only a minute area of the worksheet at one time. While you cannot see the entire worksheet, you can move the window over the worksheet to view any part of it.
>
> **BTW**
>
> **Increasing the Viewing Area**
> You can increase the size of the Excel window or viewing area to show more of the worksheet. Two ways exist to increase what you can see in the viewing area: (1) on the View tab on the Ribbon, click Full Screen; and (2) change to a higher resolution. See Appendix C for information about how to change to a higher resolution.

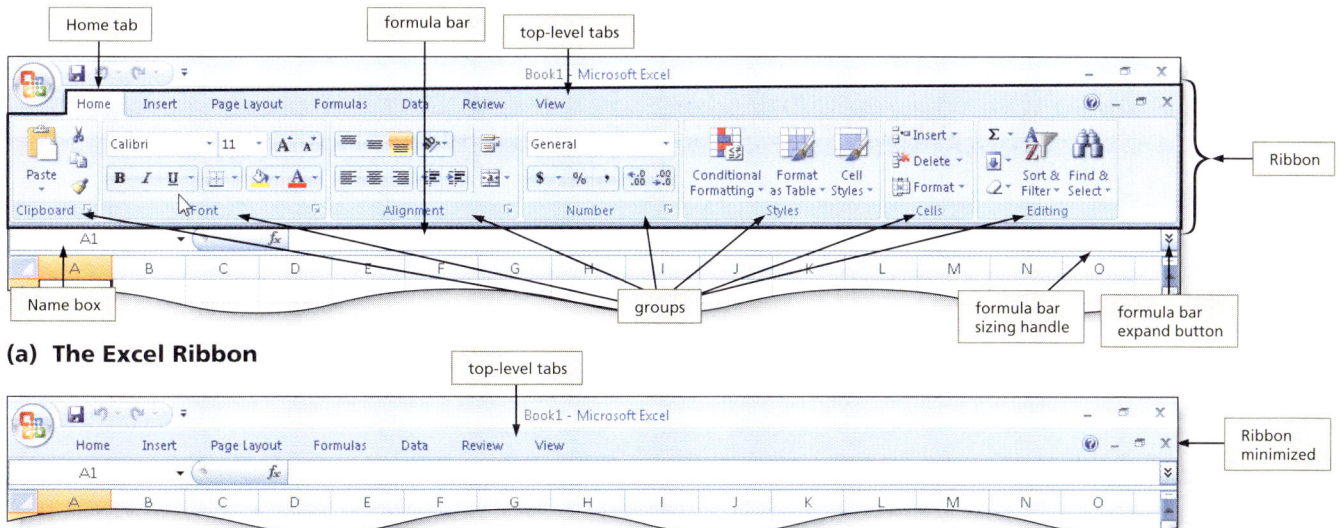

(a) The Excel Ribbon

(b) The Excel Ribbon Minimized

Figure 1–7

> **BTW**
>
> **Minimizing the Ribbon**
> If you want to minimize the Ribbon, right-click the Ribbon and then click Minimize the Ribbon on the shortcut menu, double-click the active tab, or press CTRL+F1. To restore a minimized Ribbon, right-click the Ribbon and then click Minimize the Ribbon on the shortcut menu, double-click any top-level tab, or press CTRL+F1. To use commands on a minimized Ribbon, click the top-level tab.

When you start Excel, the Ribbon displays seven top-level tabs: Home, Insert, Page Layout, Formulas, Data, Review, and View. The **Home tab**, called the primary tab, contains groups with the more frequently used commands. To display a different tab on the Ribbon, click the top-level tab. That is, to display the Insert tab, click Insert on the Ribbon. To return to the Home tab, click Home on the Ribbon. The tab currently displayed is called the **active tab**.

To display more of the document in the document window, some users prefer to minimize the Ribbon, which hides the groups on the Ribbon and displays only the top-level tabs (Figure 1–7b). To use commands on a minimized Ribbon, click the top-level tab.

Each time you start Excel, the Ribbon appears the same way it did the last time you used Excel. The chapters in this book, however, begin with the Ribbon appearing as it did at the initial installation of the software. If you are stepping through this chapter on a computer and you want your Ribbon to match the figures in this book, read Appendix C.

In addition to the top-level tabs, Excel displays other tabs, called **contextual tabs**, when you perform certain tasks or work with objects such as charts or tables. If you insert a chart in the worksheet, for example, the Chart Tools tab and its related subordinate tabs appear (Figure 1–8). When you are finished working with the chart, the Chart Tools and subordinate tabs disappear from the Ribbon. Excel determines when contextual tabs should appear and disappear, based on the tasks you perform.

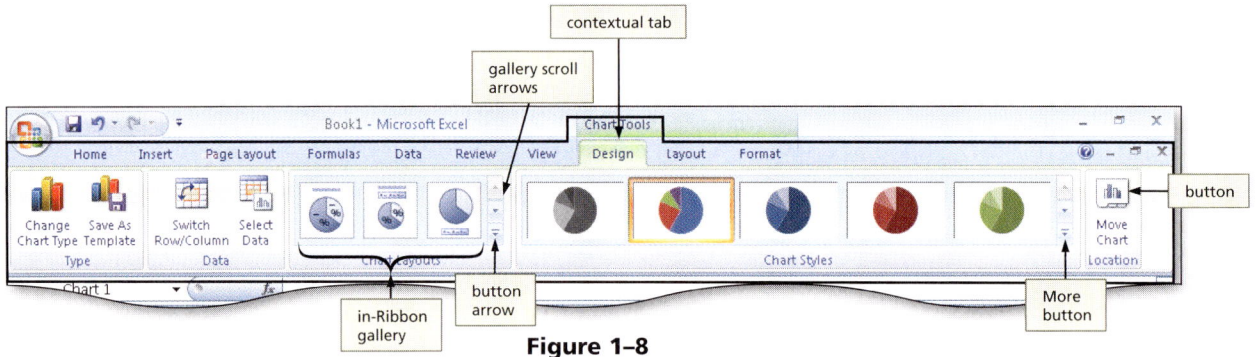

Figure 1–8

Ribbon commands include buttons, boxes (text boxes, check boxes, etc.), and galleries (Figure 1–8). A **gallery** is a set of choices, often graphical, arranged in a grid or in a list. You can scroll through choices on an in-Ribbon gallery by clicking the gallery's scroll arrows. An **in-Ribbon** gallery shows common gallery choices on the Ribbon rather than in a dropdown list. Or, you can click a gallery's More button to view more gallery options on the screen at a time. Some buttons and boxes have arrows that, when clicked, also display a gallery; others always cause a gallery to be displayed when clicked. Most galleries support **live preview**, which is a feature that allows you to point to a gallery choice and see its effect in the worksheet without actually selecting the choice (Figure 1–9).

Some commands on the Ribbon display an image to help you remember their function. When you point to a command on the Ribbon, all or part of the command glows in shades of yellow and orange, and an Enhanced ScreenTip appears on the screen. An **Enhanced ScreenTip** is an on-screen note that provides the name of the command, available keyboard shortcut(s), a description of the command, and sometimes instructions for how to obtain Help about the command (Figure 1–10). Enhanced ScreenTips are more detailed than a typical **ScreenTip**, which usually displays only the name of the command.

The lower-right corner of some groups on the Ribbon has a small arrow, called a **Dialog Box Launcher**, that when clicked displays a dialog box or a task pane (Figure 1–11). A **dialog box** contains additional commands and options for the group. When presented with a dialog box, you make selections and must close the dialog box before returning to the worksheet. A **task pane**, by contrast, is a window that contains additional commands and can stay open and visible while you work on the worksheet.

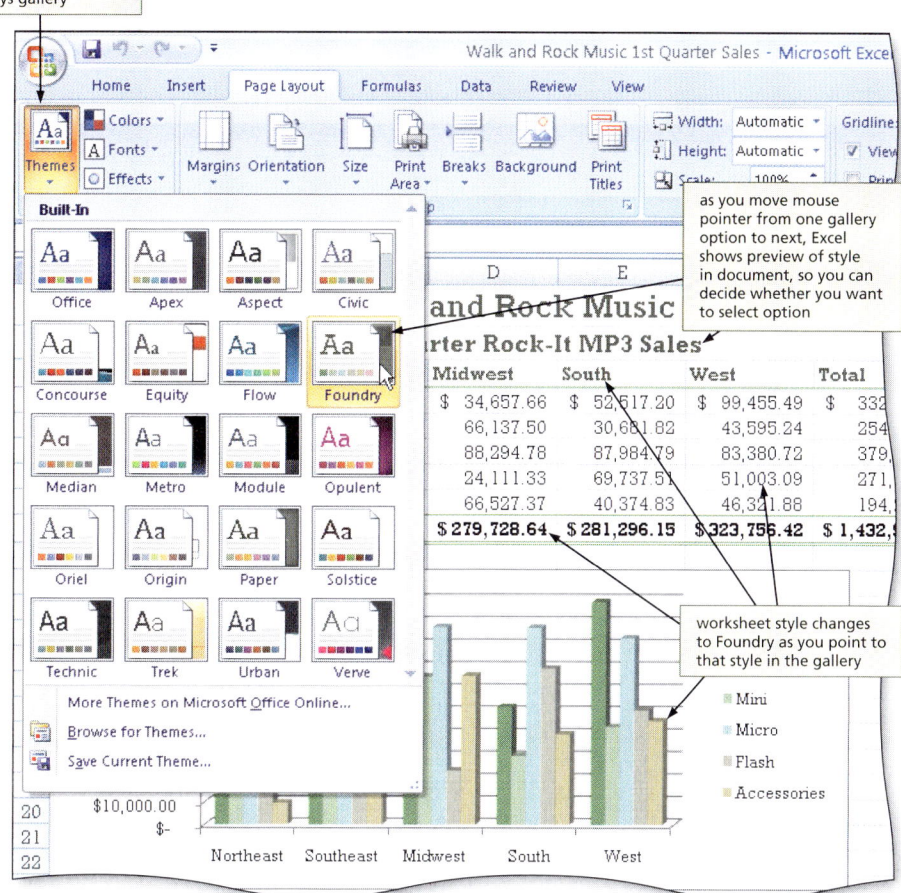

Figure 1–9

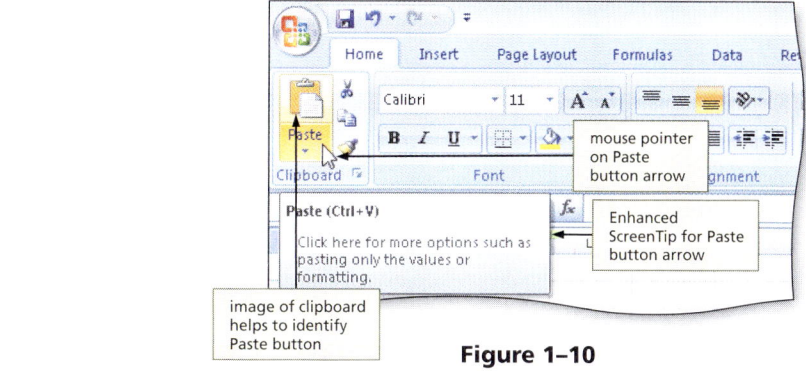

Figure 1–10

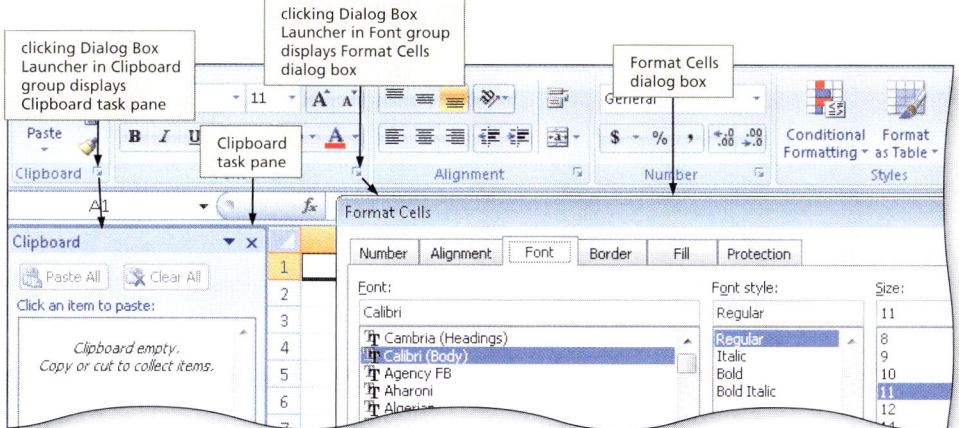

Figure 1–11

Formula Bar

The formula bar appears below the Ribbon (Figure 1–12a). As you type, Excel displays the entry in the **formula bar**. You can make the formula bar larger by dragging the sizing handle (Figure 1–7) on the formula bar or clicking the expand button to the right of the formula bar. Excel also displays the active cell reference in the **Name box** on the left side of the formula bar.

Mini Toolbar and Shortcut Menus

The **Mini toolbar**, which appears automatically based on tasks you perform (such as selecting text), contains commands related to changing the appearance of text in a worksheet. All commands on the Mini toolbar also exist on the Ribbon. The purpose of the Mini toolbar is to minimize mouse movement. For example, if you want to format text using a command that currently is not displayed on the active tab, you can use the command on the Mini toolbar — instead of switching to a different tab to use the command.

When the Mini toolbar appears, it initially is transparent (Figure 1–12a). If you do not use the transparent Mini toolbar, it disappears from the screen. To use the Mini toolbar, move the mouse pointer into the toolbar, which causes the Mini toolbar to change from a transparent to bright appearance (Figure 1–12b).

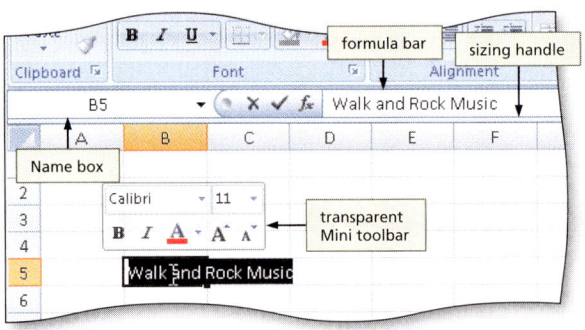

(a) Transparent Mini Toolbar

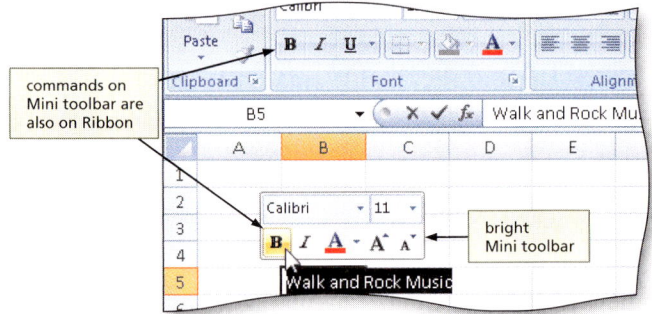

(b) Bright Mini Toolbar

Figure 1–12

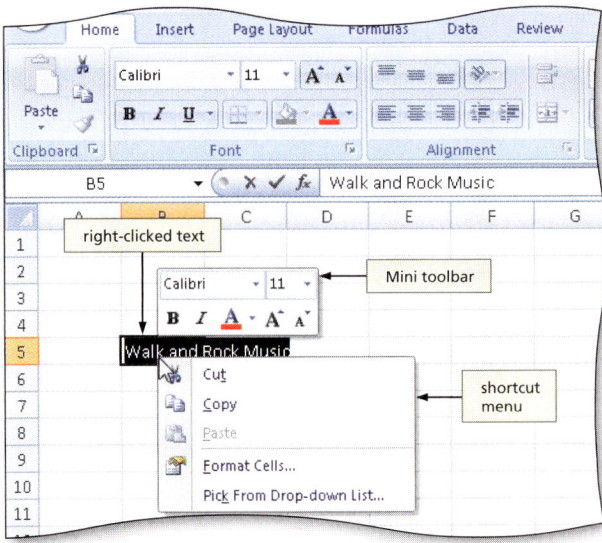

A **shortcut menu**, which appears when you right-click an object, is a list of frequently used commands that relate to the right-clicked object. If you right-click an item in the document window such as a cell, Excel displays both the Mini toolbar and a shortcut menu (Figure 1–13).

Figure 1–13

Quick Access Toolbar

The **Quick Access Toolbar**, located by default above the Ribbon, provides easy access to frequently used commands (Figure 1–14a). The commands on the Quick Access Toolbar always are available, regardless of the task you are performing. Initially, the Quick Access Toolbar contains the Save, Undo, and Redo buttons. If you click the Customize Quick Access Toolbar button, Excel provides a list of commands you quickly can add to and remove from the Quick Access Toolbar (Figure 1–14b).

You also can add other commands to or delete commands from the Quick Access Toolbar so that it contains the commands you use most often. As you add commands to the Quick Access Toolbar, its commands may interfere with the workbook title on the title bar. For this reason, Excel provides an option of displaying the Quick Access Toolbar below the Ribbon (Figure 1–14c).

> **BTW**
>
> **Quick Access Toolbar Commands**
> To add a Ribbon command as a button to the Quick Access Toolbar, right-click the command on the Ribbon and then click Add to Quick Access Toolbar on the shortcut menu. To delete a button from the Quick Access Toolbar, right-click the button on the Quick Access Toolbar and then click Remove from Quick Access Toolbar on the shortcut menu. To display the Quick Access Toolbar below the Ribbon, right-click the Quick Access Toolbar and then click Show Quick Access Toolbar Below the Ribbon on the shortcut menu.

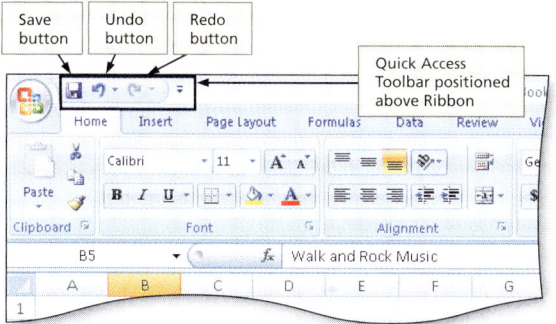

(a) Quick Access Toolbar above Ribbon

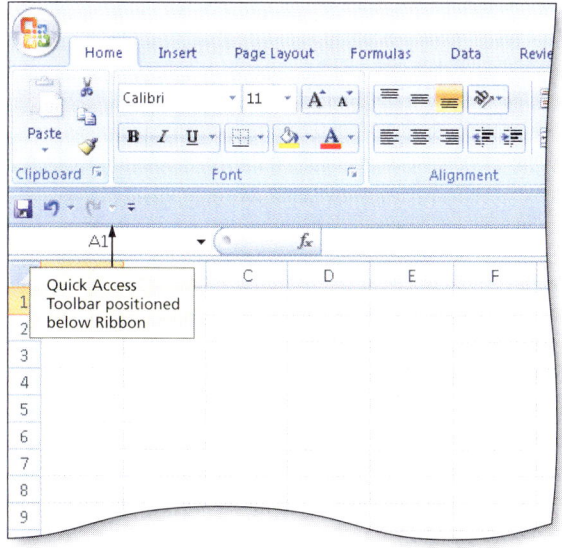

(c) Quick Access Toolbar below Ribbon

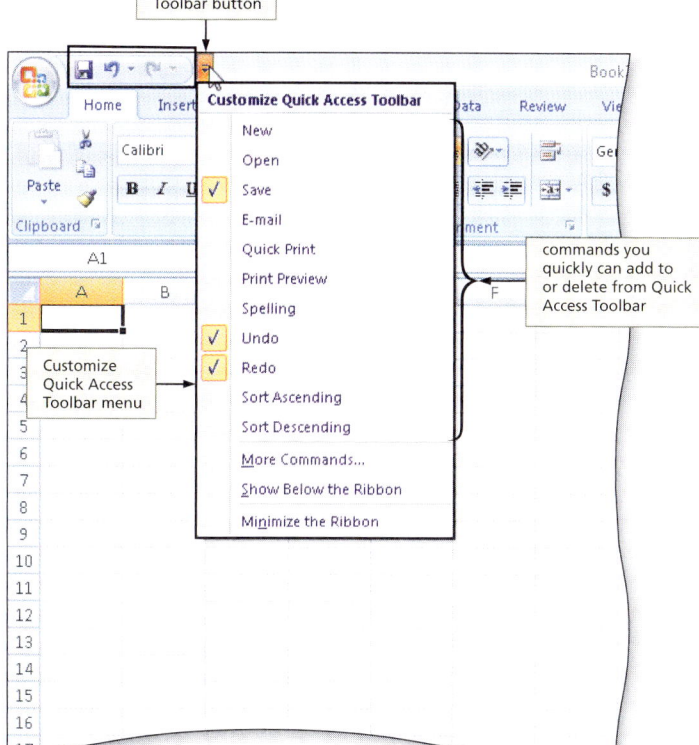

(b) Customize Quick Access Toolbar Menu

Figure 1–14

Each time you start Excel, the Quick Access Toolbar appears the same way it did the last time you used Excel. The chapters in this book, however, begin with the Quick Access Toolbar appearing as it did at the initial installation of the software. If you are stepping through this chapter on a computer and you want your Quick Access Toolbar to match the figures in this book, you should reset your Quick Access Toolbar. For more information about how to reset the Quick Access Toolbar, read Appendix C.

Office Button

While the Ribbon is a control center for creating worksheets, the **Office Button** is a central location for managing and sharing workbooks. When you click the Office Button, located in the upper-left corner of the window, Excel displays the Office Button menu (Figure 1–15). A **menu** contains a list of commands.

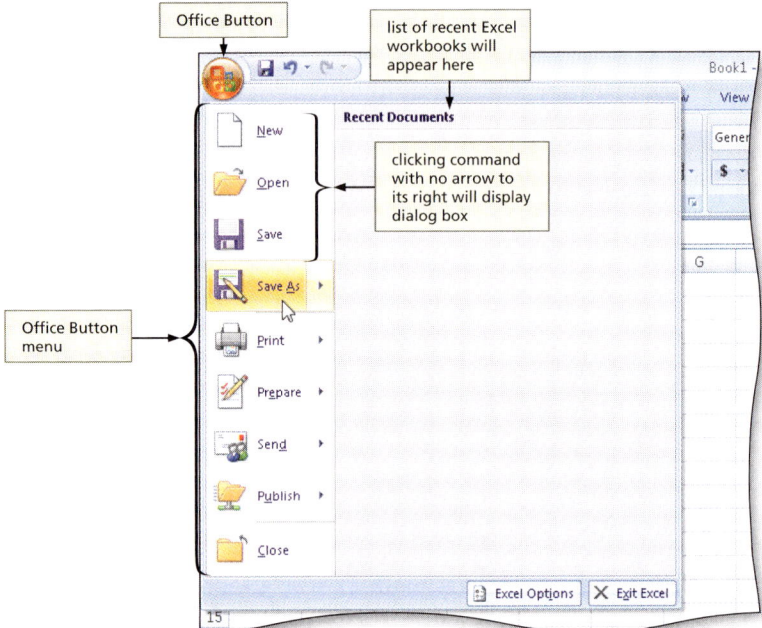

Figure 1–15

When you click the New, Open, Save As, and Print commands on the Office Button menu, Excel displays a dialog box with additional options. The Save As, Print, Prepare, Send, and Publish commands have an arrow to their right. If you point to a button that includes an arrow, Excel displays a **submenu**, which is a list of additional commands associated with the selected command (Figure 1–16). For the Prepare, Send, and Publish commands that do not display a dialog box when clicked, you can point either to the command or the arrow to display the submenu.

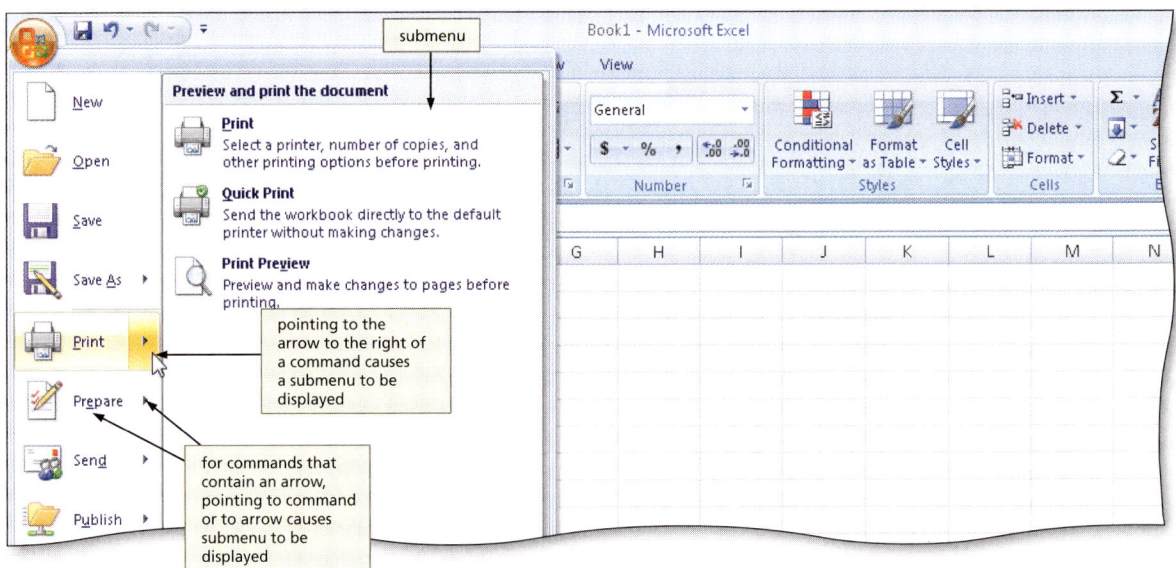

Figure 1–16

Key Tips

If you prefer using the keyboard, instead of the mouse, you can press the ALT key on the keyboard to display a **Key Tip badge**, or keyboard code icon, for certain commands (Figure 1–17). To select a command using the keyboard, press its displayed code letter, or **Key Tip**. When you press a Key Tip, additional Key Tips related to the selected command appear. For example, to select the New command on the Office Button menu, press the ALT key, then press the F key, then press the N key.

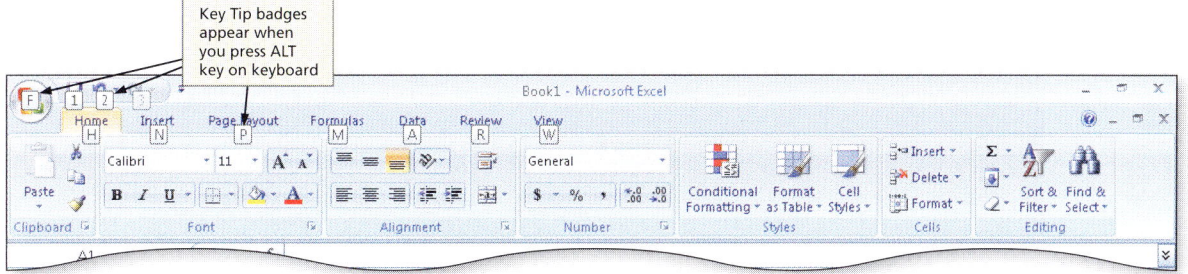

Figure 1–17

To remove the Key Tip badges from the screen, press the ALT key or the ESC key on the keyboard until all Key Tip badges disappear or click the mouse anywhere in the Excel window.

Selecting a Cell

To enter data into a cell, you first must select it. The easiest way **to select a cell** (make it active) is to use the mouse to move the block plus sign mouse pointer to the cell and then click.

An alternative method is to use the arrow keys that are located just to the right of the typewriter keys on the keyboard. An arrow key selects the cell adjacent to the active cell in the direction of the arrow on the key.

You know a cell is selected, or active, when a heavy border surrounds the cell and the active cell reference appears in the Name box on the left side of the formula bar. Excel also changes the active cell's column heading and row heading to a gold color.

> **BTW**
>
> **Selecting a Cell**
> You can select any cell by entering its cell reference, such as b4, in the Name box on the left side of the formula bar.

Entering Text

In Excel, any set of characters containing a letter, hyphen (as in a telephone number), or space is considered text. **Text** is used to place titles, such as worksheet titles, column titles, and row titles, on the worksheet.

Plan Ahead

Select titles and subtitles for the worksheet.
As previously stated, worksheet titles and subtitles should be as brief and meaningful as possible. As shown in Figure 1–18, the worksheet title, Walk and Rock Music, identifies the company for whom the worksheet is being created in Chapter 1. The worksheet subtitle, First Quarter Rock-It MP3 Sales, identifies the type of report.

Plan Ahead

Determine the contents of rows and columns.
As previously mentioned, rows typically contain information that is similar to items in a list. For the Walk and Rock Music sales data, the list of product types meets this criterion. It is more likely that in the future, the company will add more product types as opposed to more regions. Each product type, therefore, should be placed in its own row. The row titles in column A (Video, Mini, Micro, Flash, Accessories, and Total) identify the numbers in each row.

Columns typically contain descriptive information about items in rows or contain information that helps to group the data in the worksheet. In the case of the Walk and Rock Music sales data, the regions classify the sales of each product type. The regions, therefore, are placed in columns. The column titles in row 3 (Northeast, Southeast, Midwest, South, West, and Total) identify the numbers in each column.

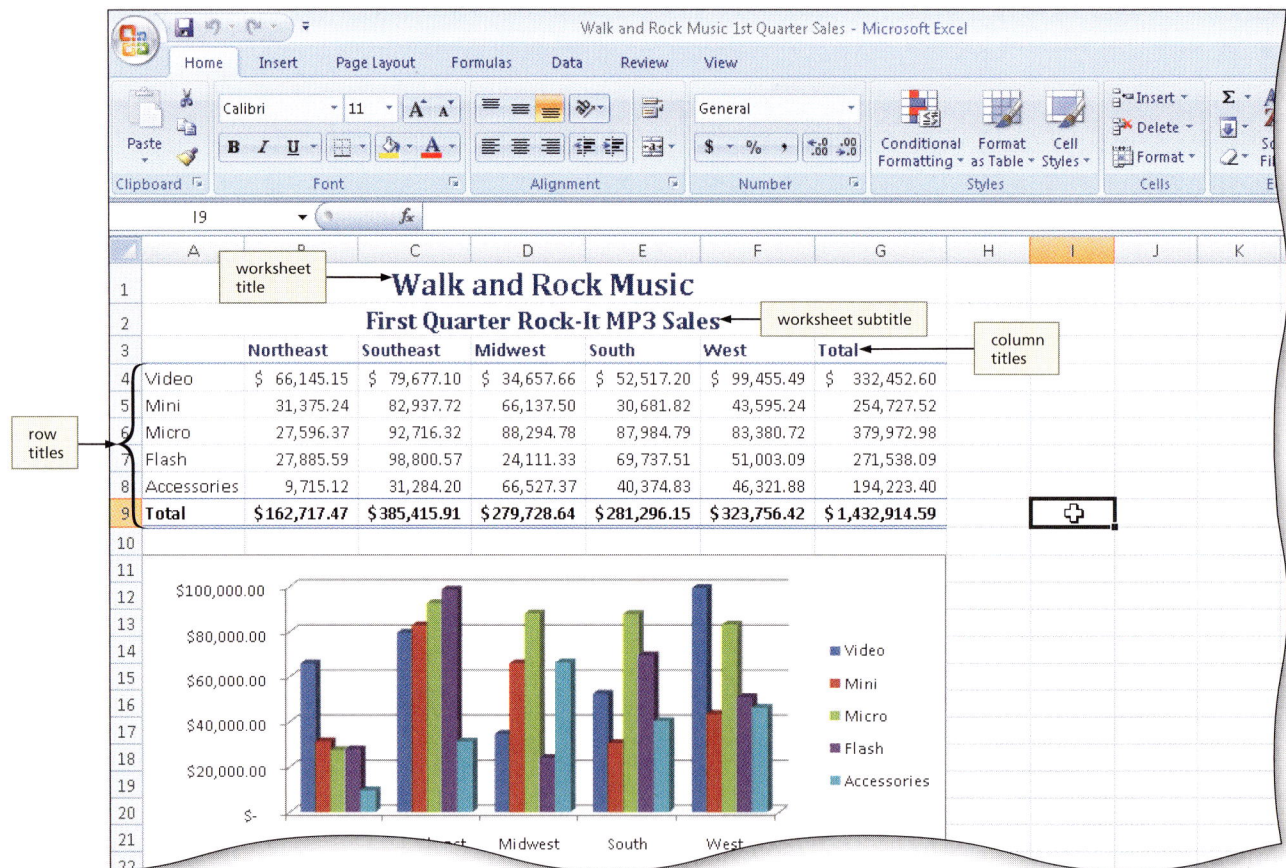

Figure 1–18

To Enter the Worksheet Titles

The following steps enter the worksheet titles in cells A1 and A2. Later in this chapter, the worksheet titles will be formatted so they appear as shown in Figure 1–18.

- Click cell A1 to make cell A1 the active cell (Figure 1–19).

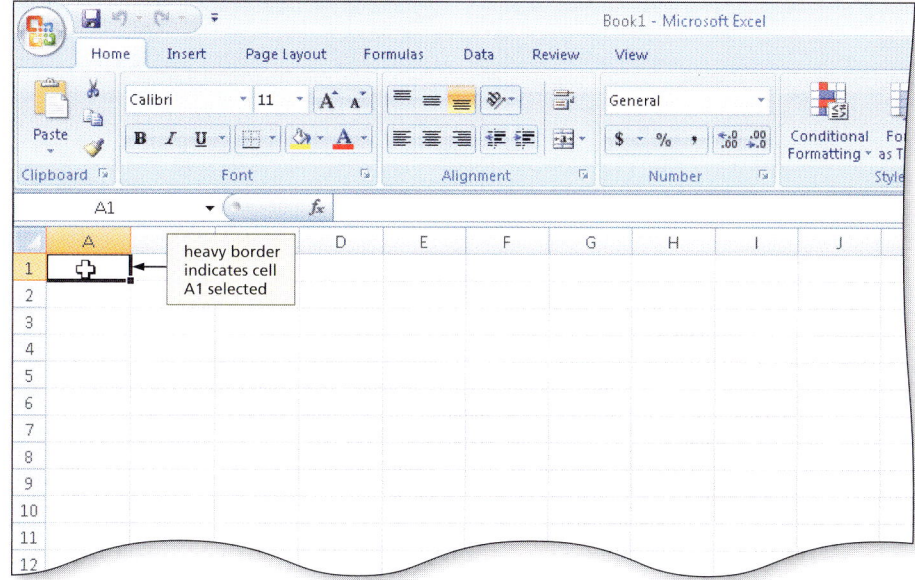

Figure 1–19

- Type 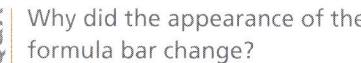 in cell A1, and then point to the Enter box in the formula bar.

Q&A Why did the appearance of the formula bar change?

Excel displays the title in the formula bar and in cell A1. When you begin typing a cell entry, Excel displays two additional boxes in the formula bar: the Cancel box and the Enter box. Clicking the **Enter box** completes an entry. Clicking the **Cancel box** cancels an entry.

Q&A What is the vertical line in cell A1?

In Figure 1–20, the text in cell A1 is followed by the insertion point. The **insertion point** is a blinking vertical line that indicates where the next typed character will appear.

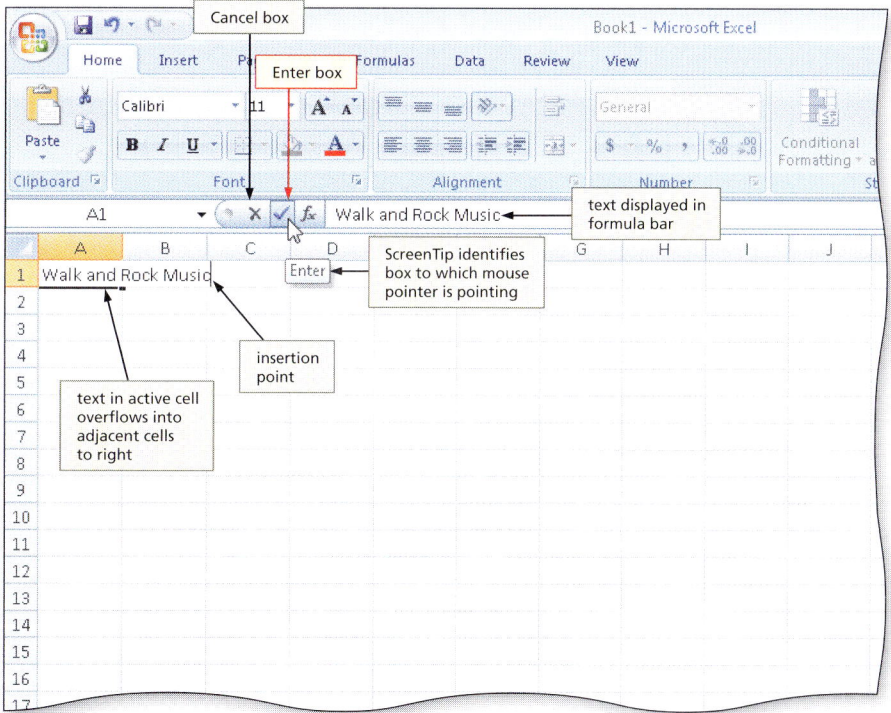

Figure 1–20

3

- Click the Enter box to complete the entry and enter the worksheet title in cell A1 (Figure 1–21).

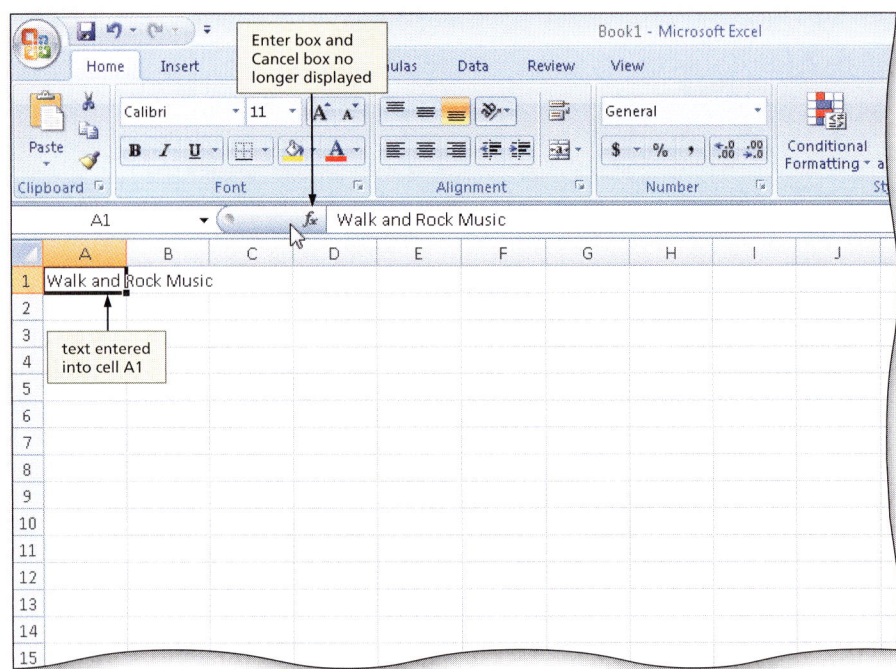

Figure 1–21

4

- Click cell A2 to select it.
- Type `First Quarter Rock-It MP3 Sales` as the cell entry.
- Click the Enter box to complete the entry and enter the worksheet subtitle in cell A2 (Figure 1–22).

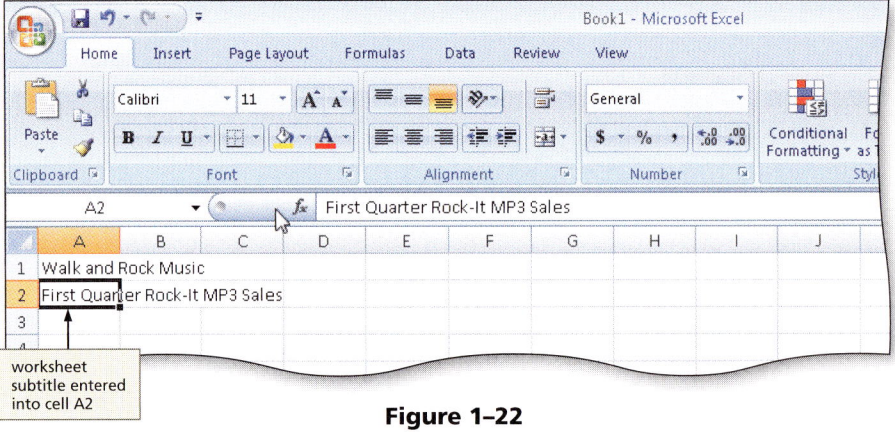

Figure 1–22

Other Ways

1. To complete entry, click any cell other than active cell
2. To complete entry, press ENTER key
3. To complete entry, press HOME, PAGE UP, PAGE DOWN, or END key
4. To complete entry, press UP, DOWN, LEFT, or RIGHT key

Entering Text in a Cell

When you complete a text entry into a cell, a series of events occurs. First, Excel positions the text left-aligned in the cell. **Left-aligned** means the cell entry is positioned at the far left in the cell. Therefore, the W in the worksheet title, Walk and Rock Music, begins in the leftmost position of cell A1.

Second, when the text is longer than the width of a column, Excel displays the overflow characters in adjacent cells to the right as long as these adjacent cells contain no data. In Figure 1–22, the width of cell A1 is approximately nine characters. The text consists of 19 characters. Therefore, Excel displays the overflow characters from cell A1 in cells B1 and C1, because cells B1 and C1 are empty. If cell B1 contained data, Excel would hide the overflow characters, so that only the first nine characters in cell A1 would appear on the worksheet. Excel stores the overflow characters in cell A1 and displays them in the formula bar whenever cell A1 is the active cell.

Third, when you complete an entry by clicking the Enter box, the cell in which the text is entered remains the active cell.

Correcting a Mistake while Typing

If you type the wrong letter and notice the error before clicking the Enter box or pressing the ENTER key, use the BACKSPACE key to delete all the characters back to and including the incorrect letter. To cancel the entire entry before entering it into the cell, click the Cancel box in the formula bar or press the ESC key. If you see an error in a cell after entering the text, select the cell and retype the entry. Later in this chapter, additional error-correction techniques are discussed.

AutoCorrect

The **AutoCorrect feature** of Excel works behind the scenes, correcting common mistakes when you complete a text entry in a cell. AutoCorrect makes three types of corrections for you:
1. Corrects two initial capital letters by changing the second letter to lowercase.
2. Capitalizes the first letter in the names of days.
3. Replaces commonly misspelled words with their correct spelling. For example, it will change the misspelled word *recieve* to *receive* when you complete the entry. AutoCorrect will correct the spelling of hundreds of commonly misspelled words automatically.

BTW

The ENTER Key
When you first install Excel, the ENTER key not only completes the entry, but it also moves the selection to an adjacent cell. You can instruct Excel not to move the selection after pressing the ENTER key by clicking the Excel Options button on the Office Button menu, clicking the Advanced option, removing the checkmark from the 'After pressing Enter, move selection' check box, and then clicking the OK button.

To Enter Column Titles

To enter the column titles in row 3, select the appropriate cell and then enter the text. The following steps enter the column titles in row 3.

1
- Click cell B3 to make cell B3 the active cell (Figure 1–23).

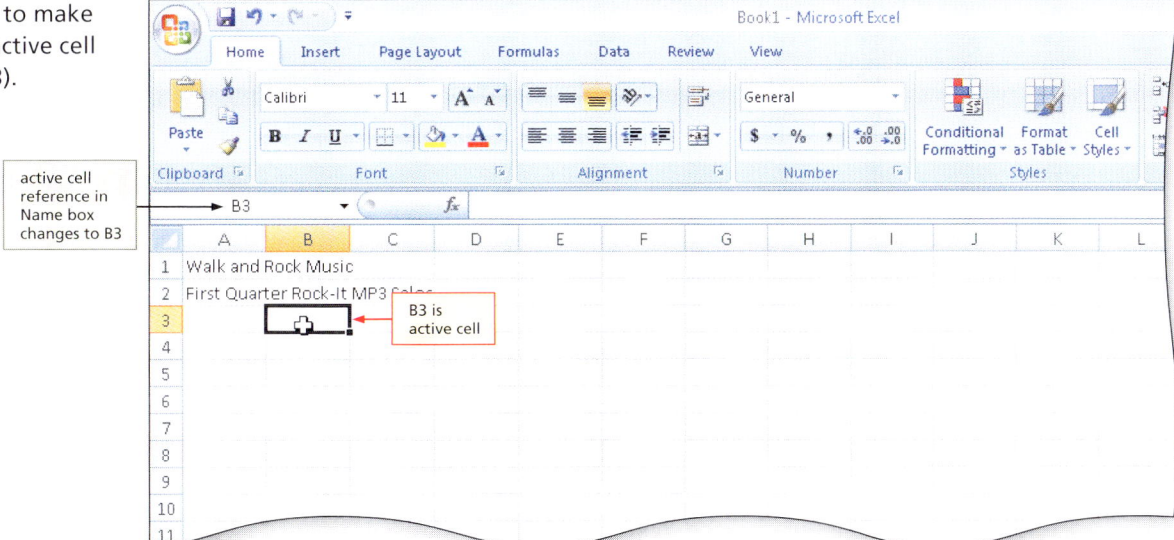

Figure 1–23

2
- Type Northeast in cell B3 (Figure 1–24).

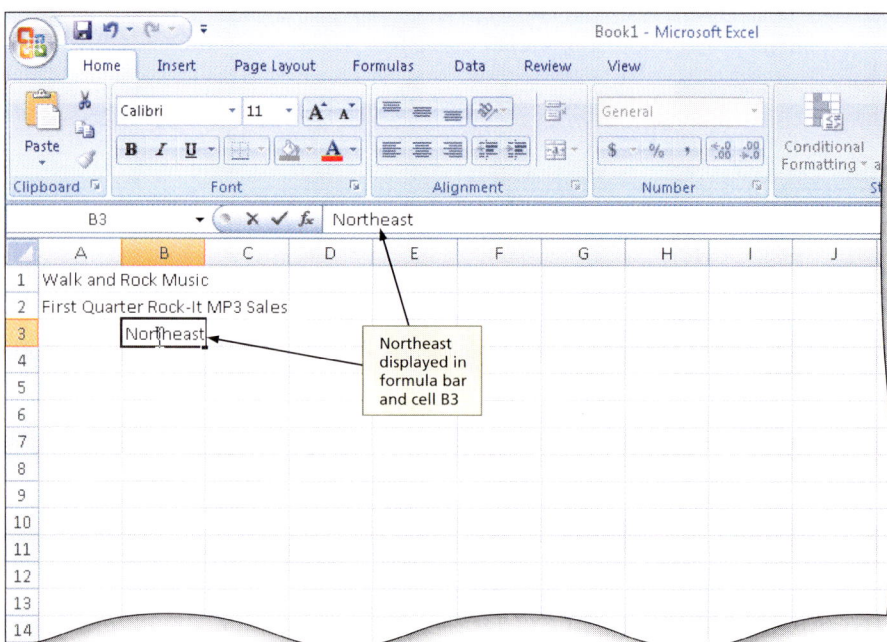

Figure 1–24

3
- Press the RIGHT ARROW key to enter the column title, Northeast, in cell B3 and make cell C3 the active cell (Figure 1–25).

Q&A Why is the RIGHT ARROW key used to complete the entry in the cell?

If the next entry is in an adjacent cell, use the arrow keys to complete the entry in a cell. When you press an arrow key to complete an entry, the adjacent cell in the direction of the arrow (up, down, left, or right) becomes the active cell. If the next entry is in a nonadjacent cell, complete an entry by clicking the next cell in which you plan to enter data. You also can click the Enter box or press the ENTER key and then click the appropriate cell for the next entry.

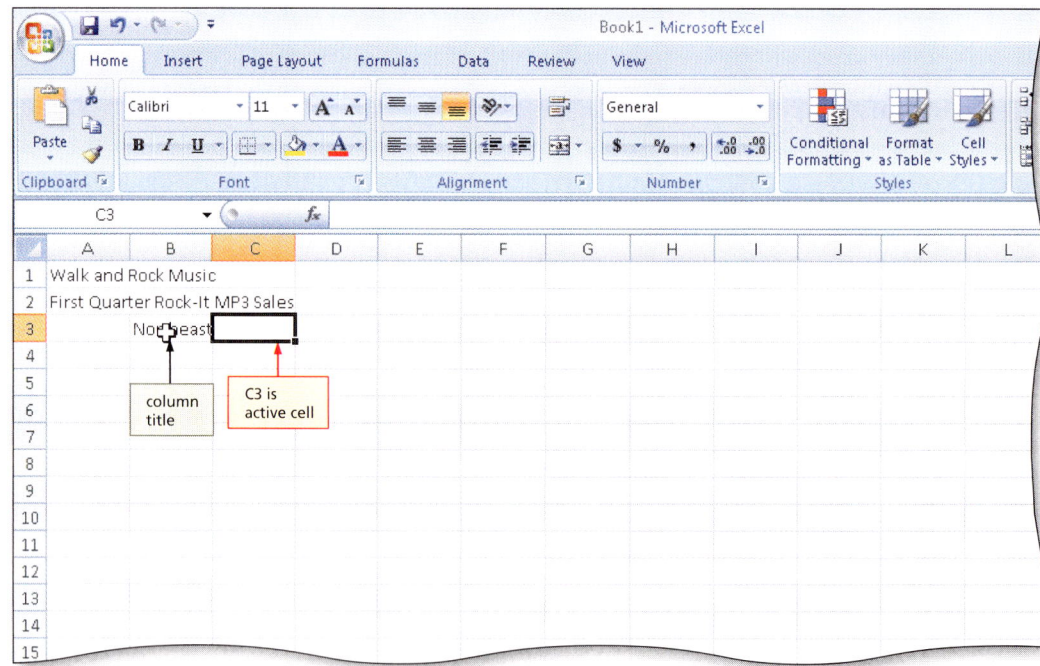

Figure 1–25

- Repeat Steps 2 and 3 to enter the remaining column titles in row 3; that is, enter `Southeast` in cell C3, `Midwest` in cell D3, `South` in cell E3, `West` in cell F3, and `Total` in cell G3 (complete the last entry in cell G3 by clicking the Enter box in the formula bar) (Figure 1–26).

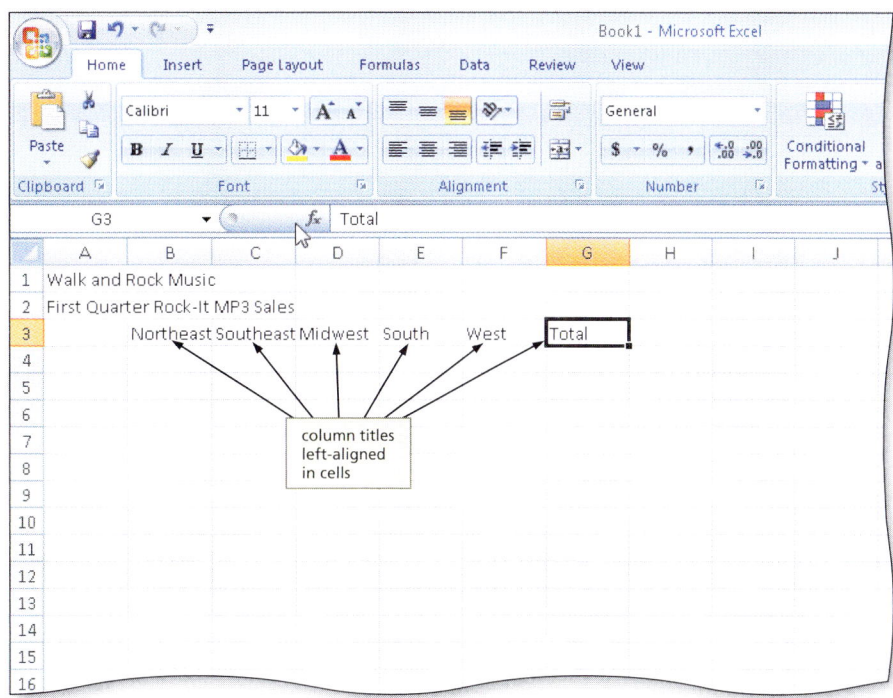

Figure 1–26

To Enter Row Titles

The next step in developing the worksheet for this project is to enter the row titles in column A. This process is similar to entering the column titles. The following steps enter the row titles in the worksheet.

- Click cell A4 to select it.
- Type `Video` and then press the DOWN ARROW key to enter the row title and make cell A5 the active cell (Figure 1–27).

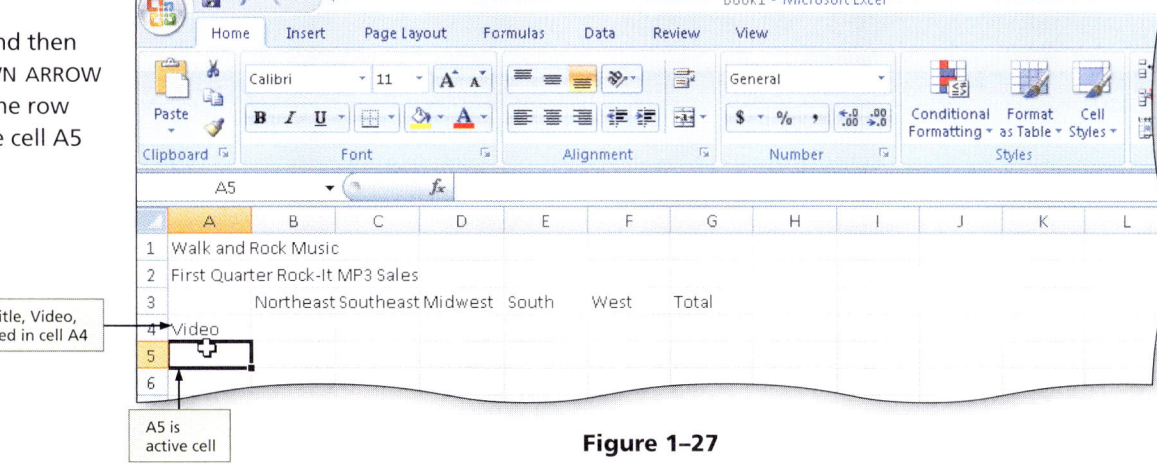

Figure 1–27

2

- Repeat Step 1 to enter the remaining row titles in column A; that is, enter `Mini` in cell A5, `Micro` in cell A6, `Flash` in cell A7, `Accessories` in cell A8, and `Total` in cell A9 (Figure 1–28).

Q&A Why is the text left-aligned in the cells?

When you enter text, Excel automatically left-aligns the text in the cell. Excel treats any combination of numbers, spaces, and nonnumeric characters as text. For example, the following entries are text:

401AX21, 921-231, 619 321, 883XTY

You can change the text alignment in a cell by realigning it. Several alignment techniques are discussed later in the chapter.

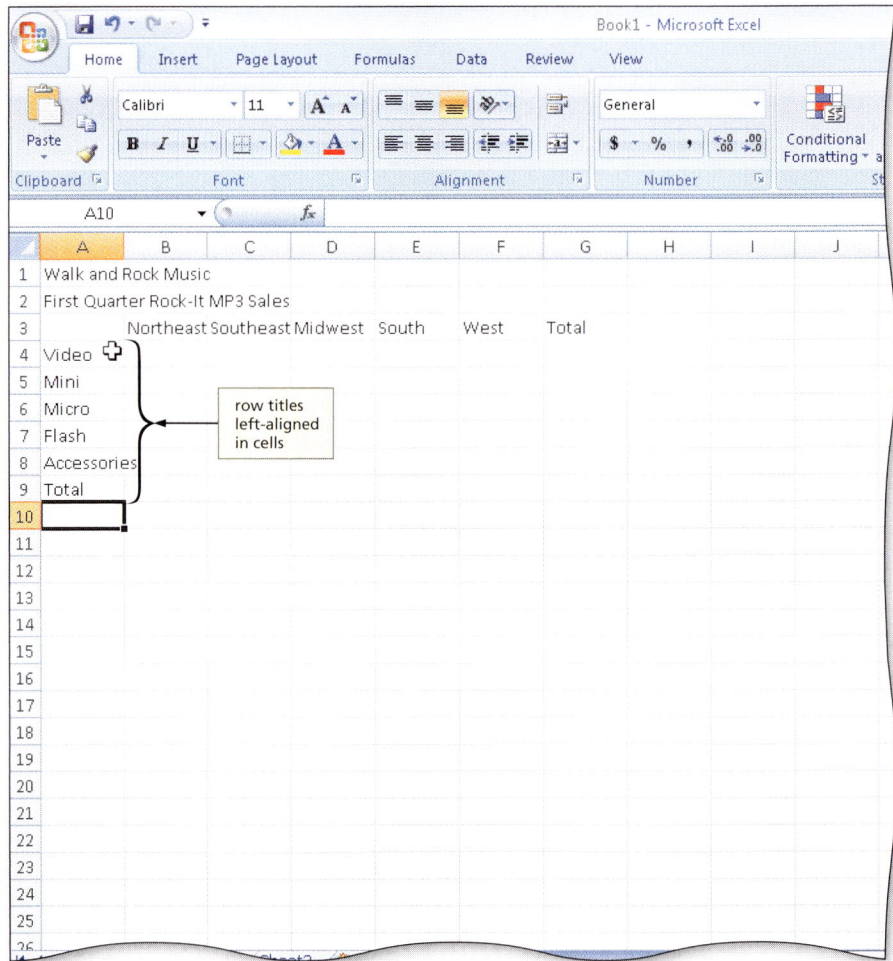

Figure 1–28

BTW

Numeric Limitations
In Excel, a number can be between approximately -1×10^{308} and 1×10^{308}, that is, between a negative 1 followed by 308 zeros and a positive 1 followed by 308 zeros. To enter a number such as 6,000,000,000,000,000, you can type 6,000,000,000,000,000, or you can type 6E15, which stands for 6×10^{15}.

Entering Numbers

In Excel, you can enter numbers into cells to represent amounts. A **number** can contain only the following characters:

0 1 2 3 4 5 6 7 8 9 + - ( ) , / . $ % E e

If a cell entry contains any other keyboard character (including spaces), Excel interprets the entry as text and treats it accordingly. The use of the special characters is explained when they are used in this book.

To Enter Numbers

The Walk and Rock Music First Quarter Rock-It MP3 Sales numbers used in Chapter 1 are summarized in Table 1–1. These numbers, which represent sales revenue for each of the product types and regions, must be entered in rows 4, 5, 6, 7, and 8.

Table 1–1 Walk and Rock Music First Quarter Rock-It MP3 Sales					
	Northeast	**Southeast**	**Midwest**	**South**	**West**
Video	66145.15	79677.10	34657.66	52517.20	99455.49
Mini	31375.24	82937.72	66137.50	30681.82	43595.24
Micro	27596.37	92716.32	88294.78	87984.79	83380.72
Flash	27885.59	98800.57	24111.33	69737.51	51003.09
Accessories	9715.12	31284.20	66527.37	40374.83	46321.88

The following steps enter the numbers in Table 1–1 one row at a time.

1

- Click cell B4.

- Type `66145.15` and then press the RIGHT ARROW key to enter the data in cell B4 and make cell C4 the active cell (Figure 1–29).

Q&A Do I need to enter dollar signs, commas, or trailing zeros for the quarterly sales numbers?

You are not required to type dollar signs, commas, or trailing zeros. When you enter a dollar value that has cents, however, you must add the decimal point and the numbers representing the cents. Later in this chapter, the numbers will be formatted to use dollar signs, commas, and trailing zeros to improve the appearance and readability of the numbers.

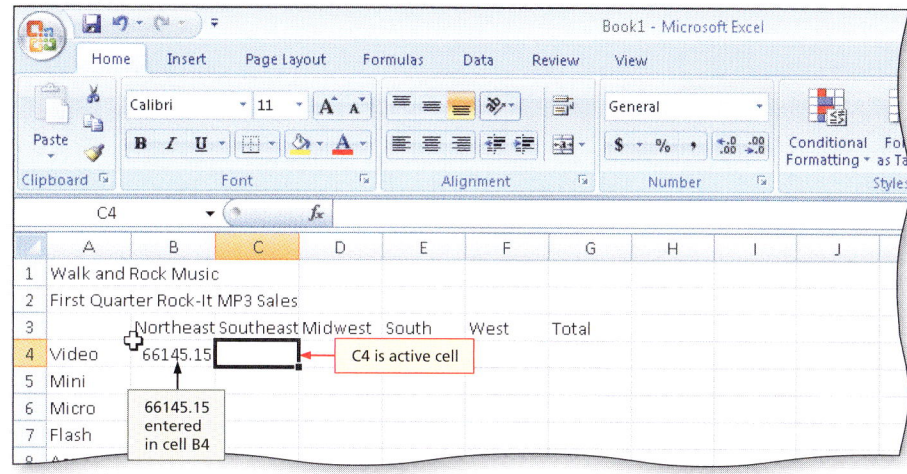

Figure 1–29

2

- Enter `79677.1` in cell C4, `34657.66` in cell D4, `52517.2` in cell E4, and `99455.49` in cell F4 (Figure 1–30).

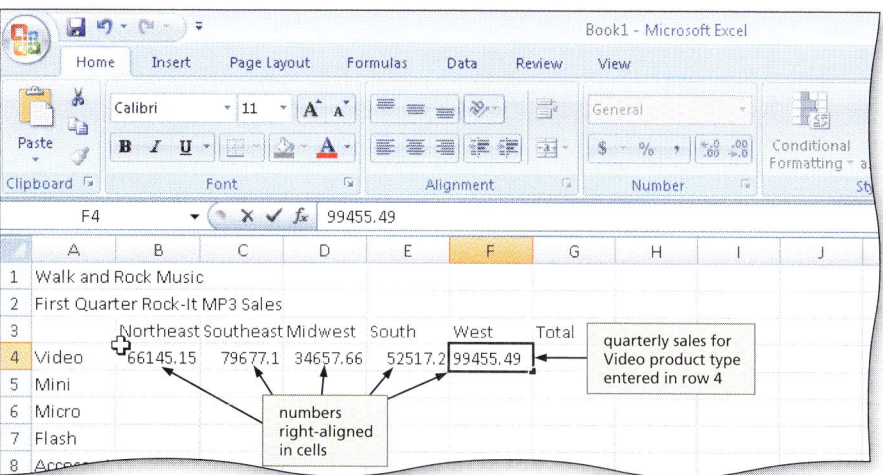

Figure 1–30

3

- Click cell B5.
- Enter the remaining first quarter sales numbers provided in Table 1–1 for each of the four remaining offerings in rows 5, 6, 7, and 8 to display the quarterly sales in the worksheet (Figure 1–31).

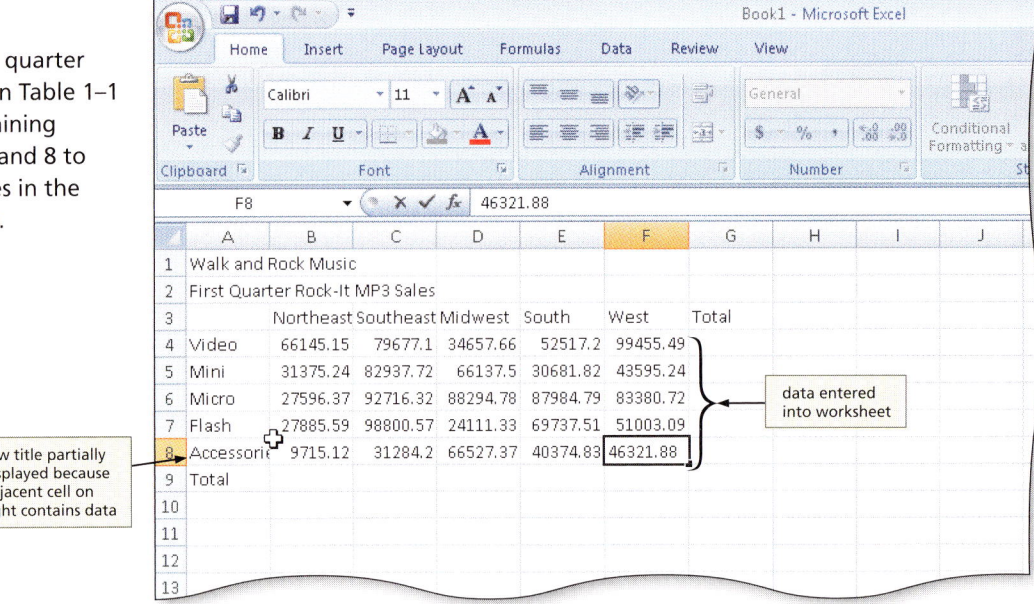

Figure 1–31

Calculating a Sum

The next step in creating the worksheet is to perform any necessary calculations, such as calculating the column and row totals.

Plan Ahead

Determine calculations that are needed.
As stated in the requirements document in Figure 1–2 on page EX 4, totals are required for each region, each product type, and the company. The first calculation is to determine the quarterly sales for the stores in the Northeast region in column B. To calculate this value in cell B9, Excel must add, or sum, the numbers in cells B4, B5, B6, B7, and B8. Excel's **SUM function**, which adds all of the numbers in a range of cells, provides a convenient means to accomplish this task.

A **range** is a series of two or more adjacent cells in a column or row or a rectangular group of cells. For example, the group of adjacent cells B4, B5, B6, B7, and B8 is called a range. Many Excel operations, such as summing numbers, take place on a range of cells.

After the total quarterly sales for the stores in the Northeast region in column B is determined, the totals for the remaining regions and totals for each product type will be determined.

BTW

Entering Numbers as Text
Sometimes, you will want Excel to treat numbers, such as Zip codes and telephone numbers, as text. To enter a number as text, start the entry with an apostrophe (').

BTW

Calculating Sums
Excel calculates sums for a variety of data types. For example, Boolean values, such as TRUE and FALSE, can be summed. Excel treats the value of TRUE as 1 and the value of FALSE as 0. Times also can be summed. For example, Excel treats the sum of 1:15 and 2:45 as 4:00.

To Sum a Column of Numbers

The following steps sum the numbers in column B.

1
- Click cell B9 to make it the active cell and then point to the Sum button on the Ribbon (Figure 1–32).

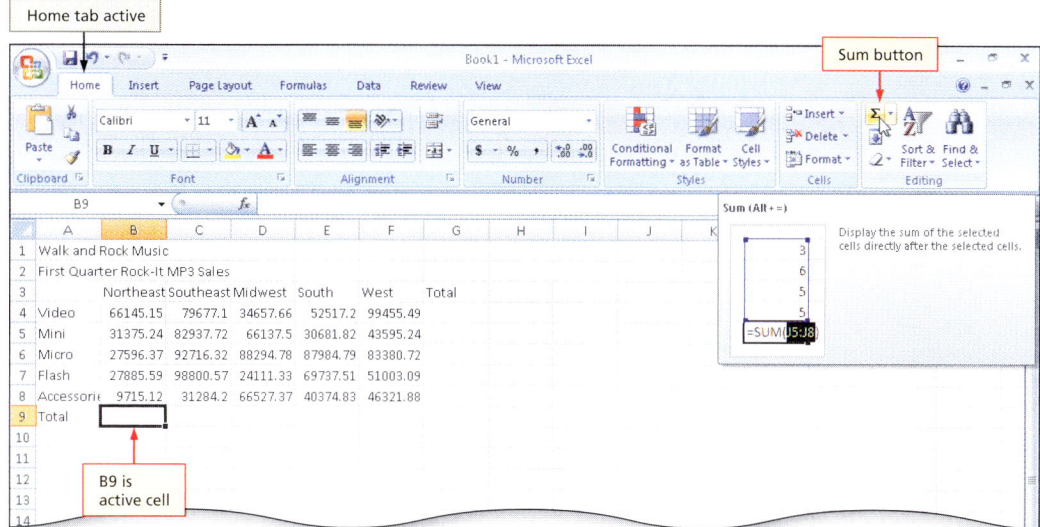

Figure 1–32

2
- Click the Sum button on the Ribbon to display =SUM(B4:B8) in the formula bar and in the active cell B9 (Figure 1–33).

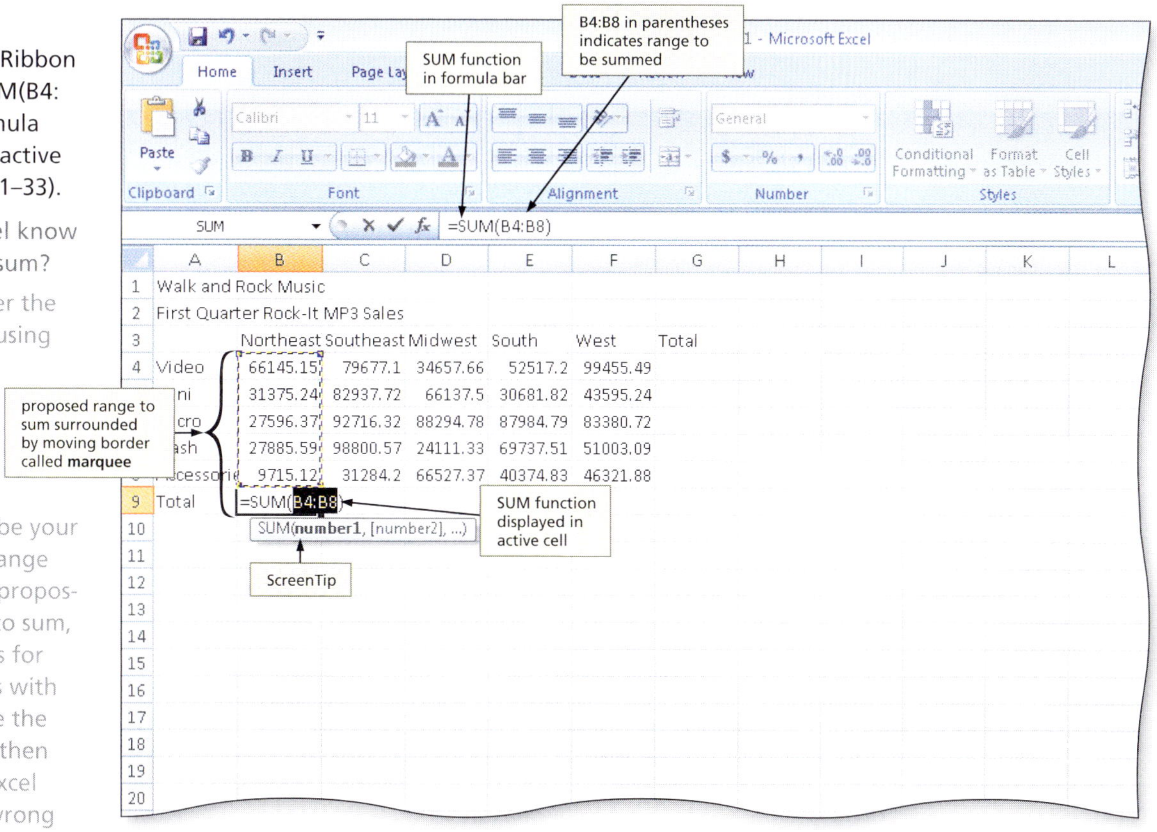

Q&A How does Excel know which cells to sum?

When you enter the SUM function using the Sum button, Excel automatically selects what it considers to be your choice of the range to sum. When proposing the range to sum, Excel first looks for a range of cells with numbers above the active cell and then to the left. If Excel proposes the wrong range, you can correct it by dragging through the correct range before pressing the ENTER key. You also can enter the correct range by typing the beginning cell reference, a colon (:), and the ending cell reference.

Figure 1–33

❸

- Click the Enter box in the formula bar to enter the sum of the first quarter sales for the five product types for the Northeast region in cell B9 (Figure 1-34).

Q&A What is the purpose of the Sum button arrow?

If you click the Sum button arrow on the right side of the Sum button (Figure 1–34), Excel displays a list of often-used functions from which you can choose. The list includes functions that allow you to determine the average, the number of items in the selected range, the minimum value, or the maximum value of a range of numbers.

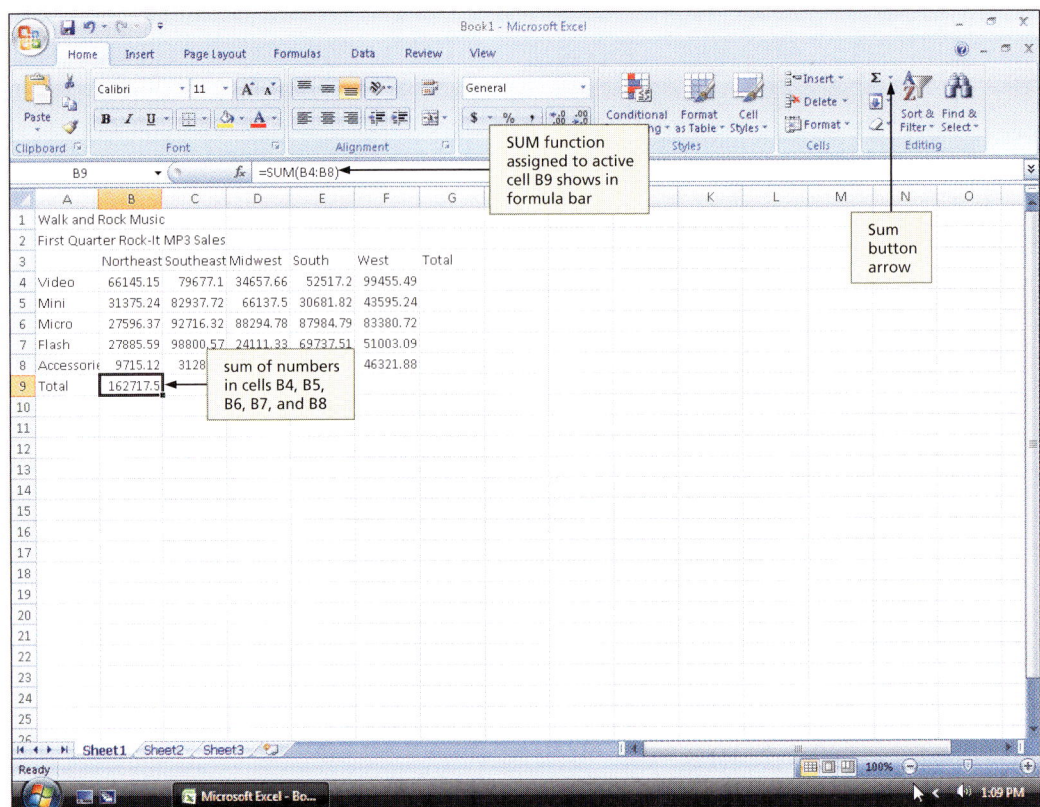

Figure 1–34

Other Ways

1. Click Insert Function button in formula bar, select SUM in Select a function list, click OK button, select range, click OK button
2. Click Sum button arrow on Ribbon, click More Functions, select SUM in Select a function list, click OK button, select range, click OK button
3. Type = s in cell, select SUM from list, select range
4. Press ALT + EQUAL SIGN (=) twice

Using the Fill Handle to Copy a Cell to Adjacent Cells

Excel also must calculate the totals for the Southeast in cell C9, the Midwest in cell D9, the South in cell E9, and for the West in cell F9. Table 1–2 illustrates the similarities between the entry in cell B9 and the entries required to sum the totals in cells C9, D9, E9, and F9.

Table 1–2 Sum Function Entries in Row 9

Cell	Sum Function Entries	Remark
B9	=SUM(B4:B8)	Sums cells B4, B5, B6, B7, and B8
C9	=SUM(C4:C8)	Sums cells C4, C5, C6, C7, and C8
D9	=SUM(D4:D8)	Sums cells D4, D5, D6, D7, and D8
E9	=SUM(E4:E8)	Sums cells E4, E5, E6, E7, and E8
F9	=SUM(F4:F8)	Sums cells F4, F5, F6, F7, and F8

To place the SUM functions in cells C9, D9, E9, and F9, you could follow the same steps shown previously in Figures 1–32 through 1–34. A second, more efficient method is to copy the SUM function from cell B9 to the range C9:F9. The cell being copied is called the **source area** or **copy area**. The range of cells receiving the copy is called the **destination area** or **paste area**.

Although the SUM function entries in Table 1–2 are similar, they are not exact copies. The range in each SUM function entry uses cell references that are one column to the right of the previous column. When you copy cell references, Excel automatically adjusts them for each new position, resulting in the SUM function entries illustrated in Table 1–2. Each adjusted cell reference is called a **relative reference**.

To Copy a Cell to Adjacent Cells in a Row

The easiest way to copy the SUM formula from cell B9 to cells C9, D9, E9, and F9 is to use the fill handle. The **fill handle** is the small black square located in the lower-right corner of the heavy border around the active cell. The following steps use the fill handle to copy cell B9 to the adjacent cells C9:F9.

- With cell B9 active, point to the fill handle (Figure 1–35).

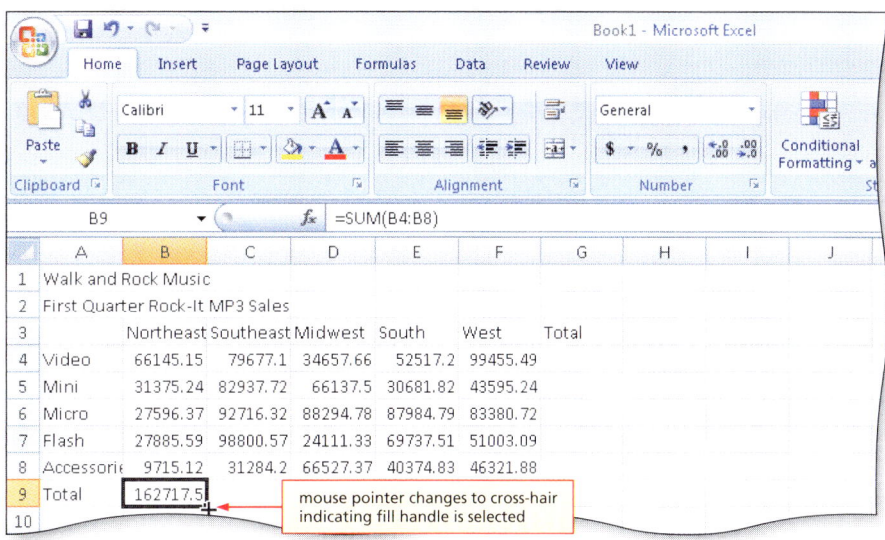

Figure 1–35

- Drag the fill handle to select the destination area, range C9:F9, to display a shaded border around the destination area, range C9:F9, and the source area, cell B9 (Figure 1–36). Do not release the mouse button.

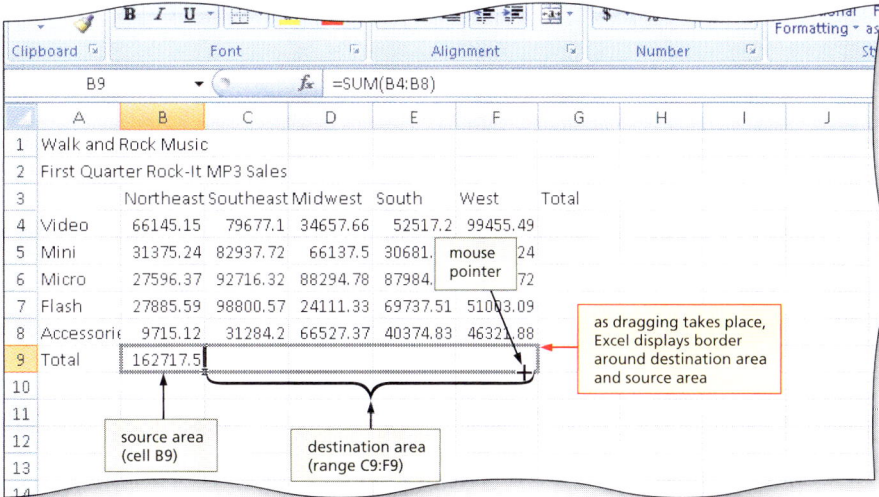

Figure 1–36

3

- Release the mouse button to copy the SUM function in cell B9 to the range C9:F9 (Figure 1–37) and calculate the sums in cells C9, D9, E9, and F9.

Q&A What is the purpose of the Auto Fill Options button?

When you copy one range to another, Excel displays an Auto Fill Options button (Figure 1–37). The Auto Fill Options button allows you to choose whether you want to copy the values from the source area to the destination area with formatting, without formatting, or copy only the format. To view the available fill options, click the Auto Fill Options button. The Auto Fill Options button disappears when you begin another activity.

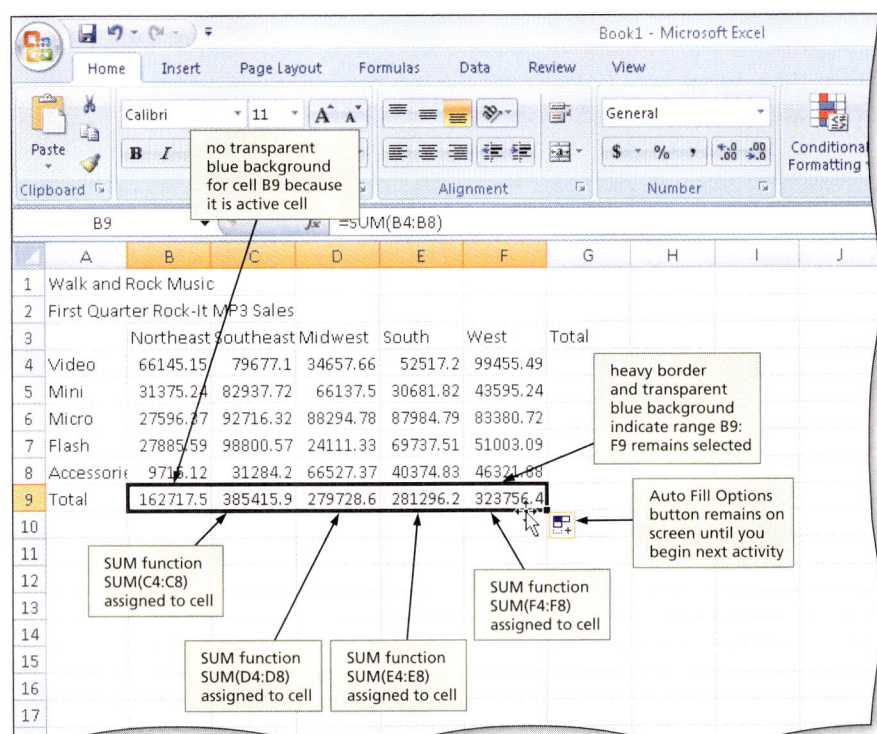

Figure 1–37

Other Ways

1. Select source area, click Copy button on Ribbon, select destination area, click Paste button on Ribbon
2. Right-click source area, click Copy on shortcut menu, right-click destination area, click Paste on shortcut menu
3. Select source area and then point to border of range; while holding down CTRL key, drag source area to destination area

To Determine Multiple Totals at the Same Time

The next step in building the worksheet is to determine the quarterly sales for each product type and total quarterly sales for the company in column G. To calculate these totals, you can use the SUM function much as it was used to total the quarterly sales by region in row 9. In this example, however, Excel will determine totals for all of the rows at the same time. The following steps illustrate this process.

1

- Click cell G4 to make it the active cell (Figure 1–38).

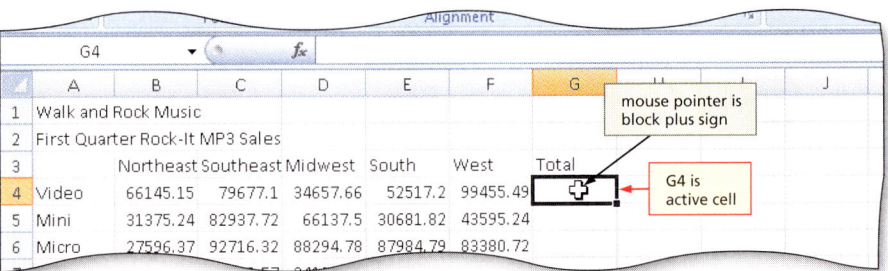

Figure 1–38

- With the mouse pointer in cell G4 and in the shape of a block plus sign, drag the mouse pointer down to cell G9 to highlight the range G4:G9 with a transparent view (Figure 1–39).

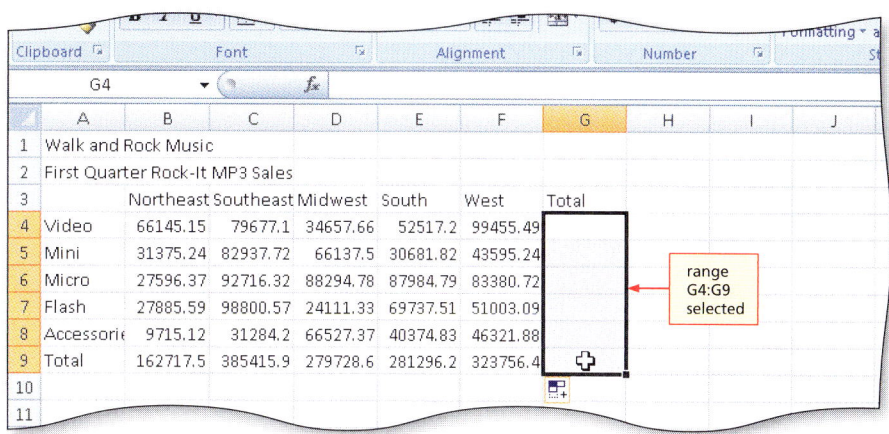

Figure 1–39

- Click the Sum button on the Ribbon to calculate and display the sums of the corresponding rows of sales in cells G4, G5, G6, G7, G8, and G9 (Figure 1–40).

- Select cell A10 to deselect the range G4:G9.

Why does Excel create totals for each row?

If each cell in a selected range is next to a row of numbers, Excel assigns the SUM function to each cell when you click the Sum button.

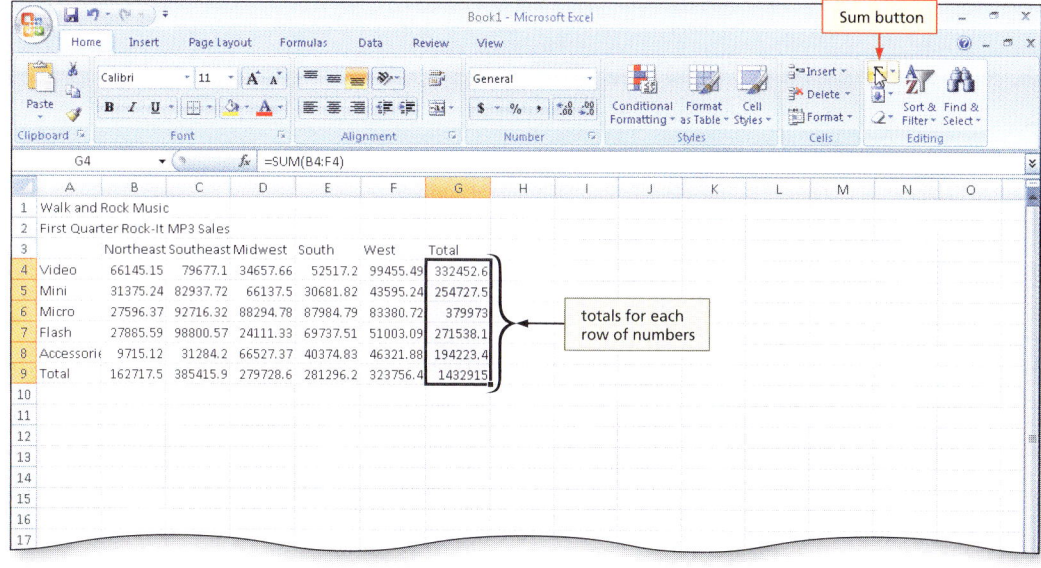

Figure 1–40

Saving the Project

While you are building a worksheet in a workbook, the computer stores it in memory. When you save a workbook, the computer places it on a storage medium such as a USB flash drive, optical disc, or hard disk. A saved workbook is referred to as a **file**. A **file name** is the name assigned to a file when it is saved. It is important to save the workbook frequently for the following reasons:

- The worksheet in memory will be lost if the computer is turned off or you lose electrical power while Excel is open.
- If you run out of time before completing your workbook, you may finish your worksheet at a future time without starting over.

BTW

Saving
Excel allows you to save a workbook in more than 30 different file formats. Choose the file format by clicking the 'Save as type' box arrow at the bottom of the Save As dialog box (Figure 1–41 on the next page). Excel Workbook is the default file format.

Plan Ahead

Determine where to save the workbook.
When saving a workbook, you must decide which storage medium to use.

- If you always work on the same computer and have no need to transport your projects to a different location, then your computer's hard drive will suffice as a storage location. It is a good idea, however, to save a backup copy of your projects on a separate medium in case the file becomes corrupted or the computer's hard drive fails.

- If you plan to work on your workbooks in various locations or on multiple computers, then you should save your workbooks on a portable medium, such as a USB flash drive or optical disc. The workbooks used in this book are saved to a USB flash drive, which saves files quickly and reliably and can be reused. Optical discs are easily portable and serve as good backups for the final versions of workbooks because they generally can save files only one time.

To Save a Workbook

You have performed many tasks while creating this project and do not want to risk losing the work completed thus far. Accordingly, you should save the workbook. The following steps save a workbook on a USB flash drive using the file name, Walk and Rock Music 1st Quarter Sales.

1

- With a USB flash drive connected to one of the computer's USB ports, click the Save button on the Quick Access Toolbar to display the Save As dialog box (Figure 1–41).

- If the Navigation pane is not displayed in the Save As dialog box, click the Browse Folders button to expand the dialog box.

- If a Folders list is displayed below the Folders button, click the Folders button to remove the Folders list.

Q&A Do I have to save to a USB flash drive?

No. You can save to any device or folder. A **folder** is a specific location on a storage medium. You can save to the default folder or a different folder. You also can create your own folders.

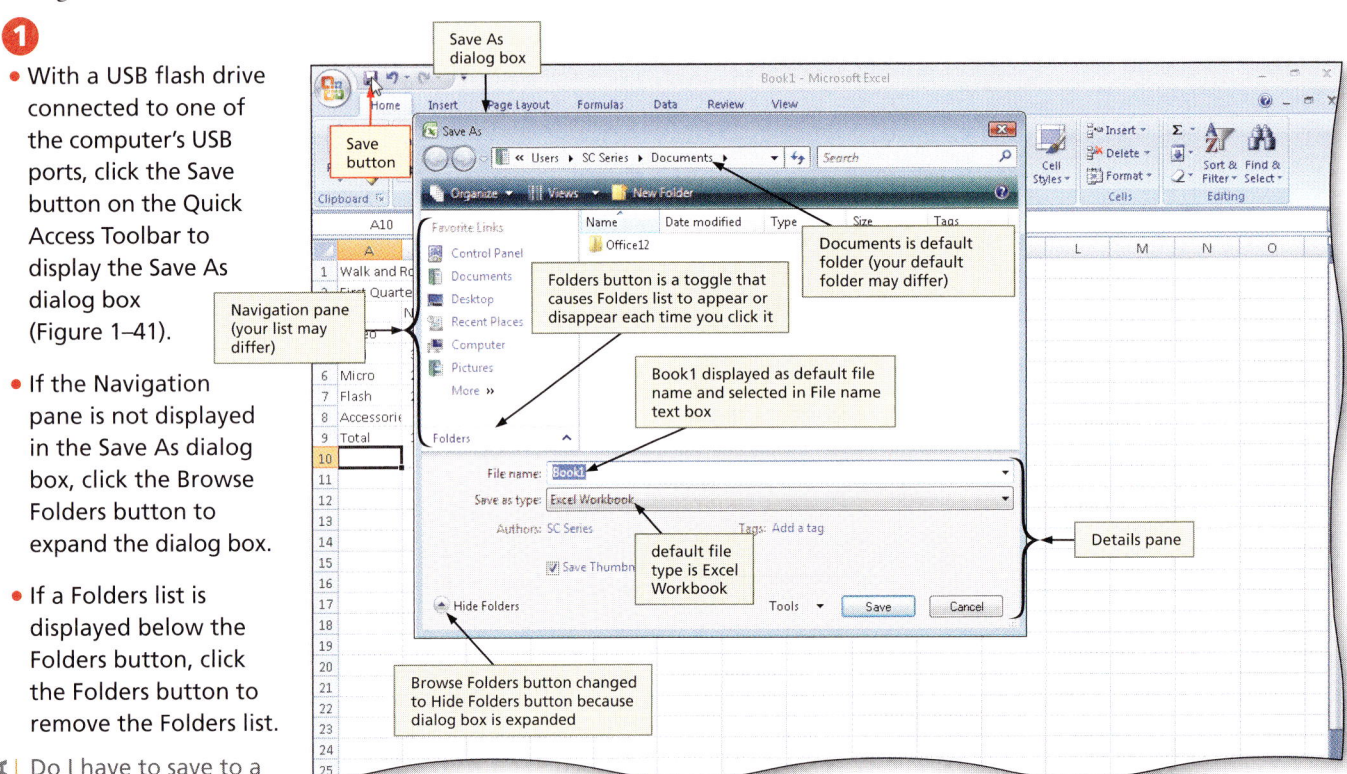

Figure 1–41

2

- Type `Walk and Rock Music 1st Quarter Sales` in the File name text box to change the file name. Do not press the ENTER key after typing the file name (Figure 1–42).

Q&A What characters can I use in a file name?

A file name can have a maximum of 255 characters, including spaces. The only invalid characters are the backslash (\), slash (/), colon (:), asterisk (*), question mark (?), quotation mark ("), less than symbol (<), greater than symbol (>), and vertical bar (|).

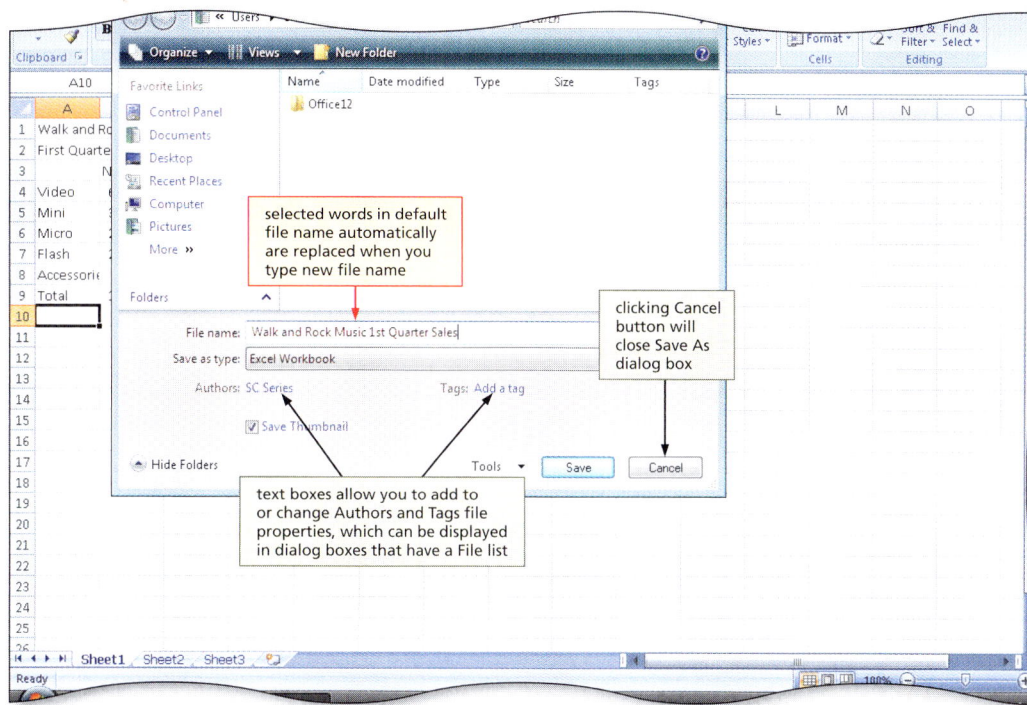

Figure 1–42

3

- If Computer is not displayed in the Favorite Links section, drag the top or bottom edge of the Save As dialog box until Computer is displayed.

- Click Computer in the Favorite Links section to display a list of available drives (Figure 1–43).

- If necessary, scroll until UDISK 2.0 (E:) appears in the list of available drives.

Q&A Why is my list of files, folders, and drives arranged and named differently from those shown in the figure?

Your computer's configuration determines how the list of files and folders is displayed and how drives are named. You can change the save location by clicking links on the **Favorite Links section**.

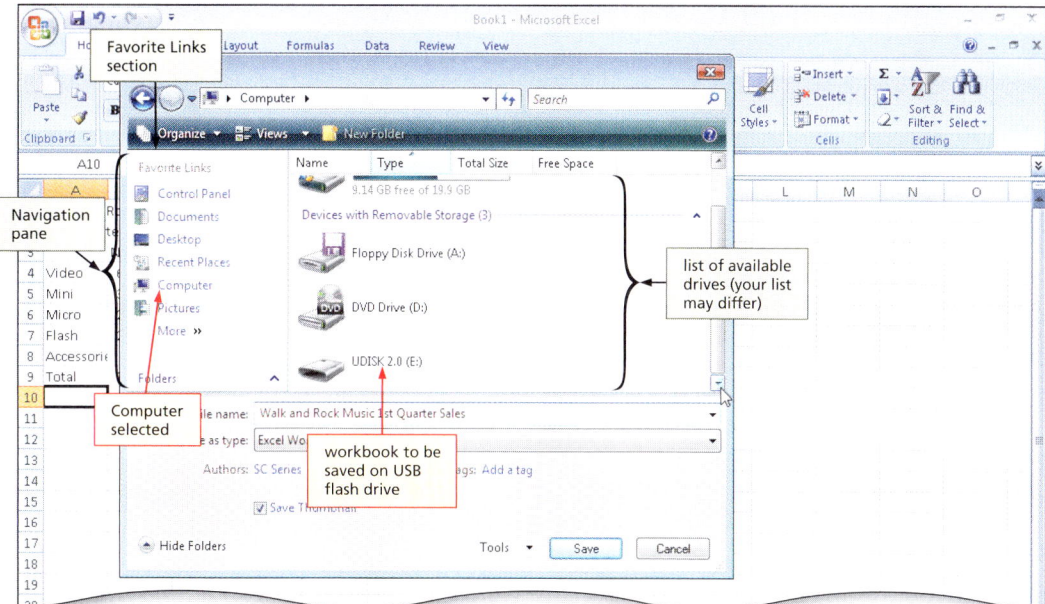

Figure 1–43

Q&A How do I save the file if I am not using a USB flash drive?

Use the same process, but be certain to select your device in the list of available drives.

4

- Double-click UDISK 2.0 (E:) in the Save in list to select the USB flash drive, Drive E in this case, as the new save location (Figure 1–44).

Q&A What if my USB flash drive has a different name or letter?

It is very likely that your USB flash drive will have a different name and drive letter and be connected to a different port.

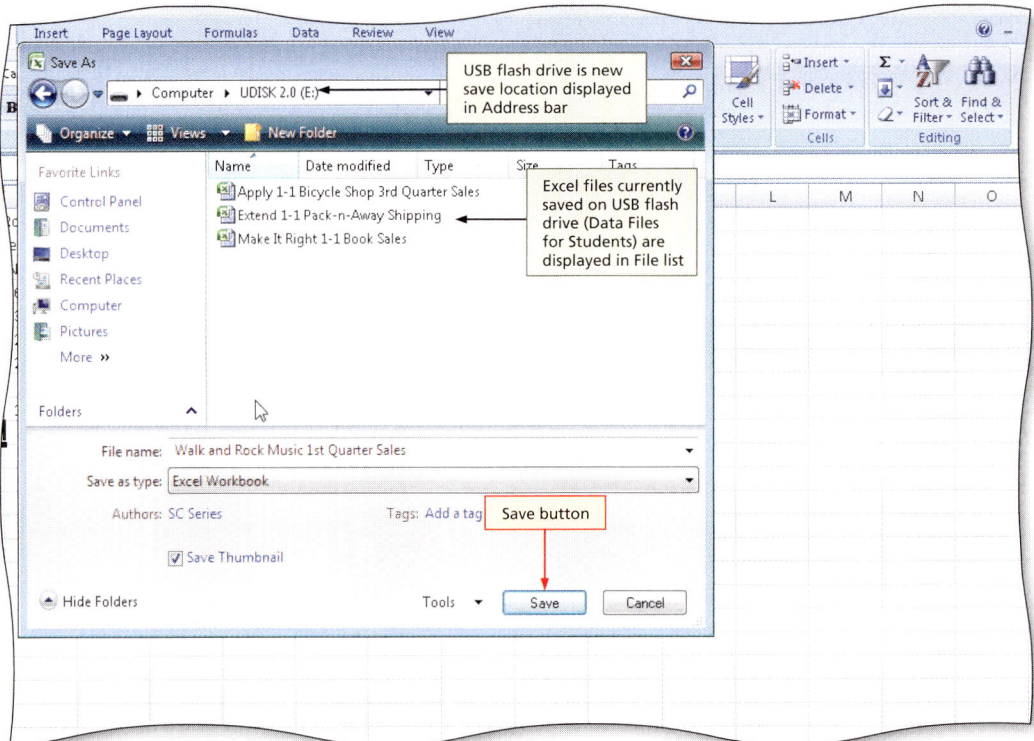

Figure 1–44

5

- Click the Save button in the Save As dialog box to save the workbook on the USB flash drive with the file name, Walk and Rock Music 1st Quarter Sales (Figure 1–45).

Q&A How do I know that Excel saved the workbook?

While Excel is saving your file, it briefly displays a message on the status bar indicating the amount of the file saved. In addition, your USB drive may have a light that flashes during the save process.

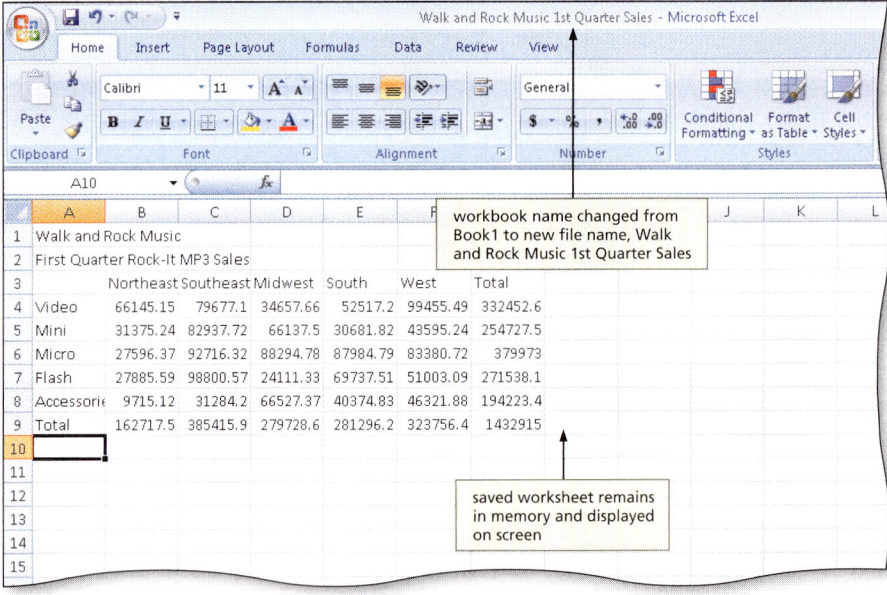

Figure 1–45

Other Ways

1. Click Office Button, click Save, type file name, select drive or folder, click Save button
2. Press CTRL+S or press SHIFT+F12, type file name, select drive or folder, click Save button

Formatting the Worksheet

The text, numeric entries, and functions for the worksheet now are complete. The next step is to format the worksheet. You **format** a worksheet to emphasize certain entries and make the worksheet easier to read and understand.

Figure 1–46a shows the worksheet before formatting. Figure 1–46b shows the worksheet after formatting. As you can see from the two figures, a worksheet that is formatted not only is easier to read but also looks more professional.

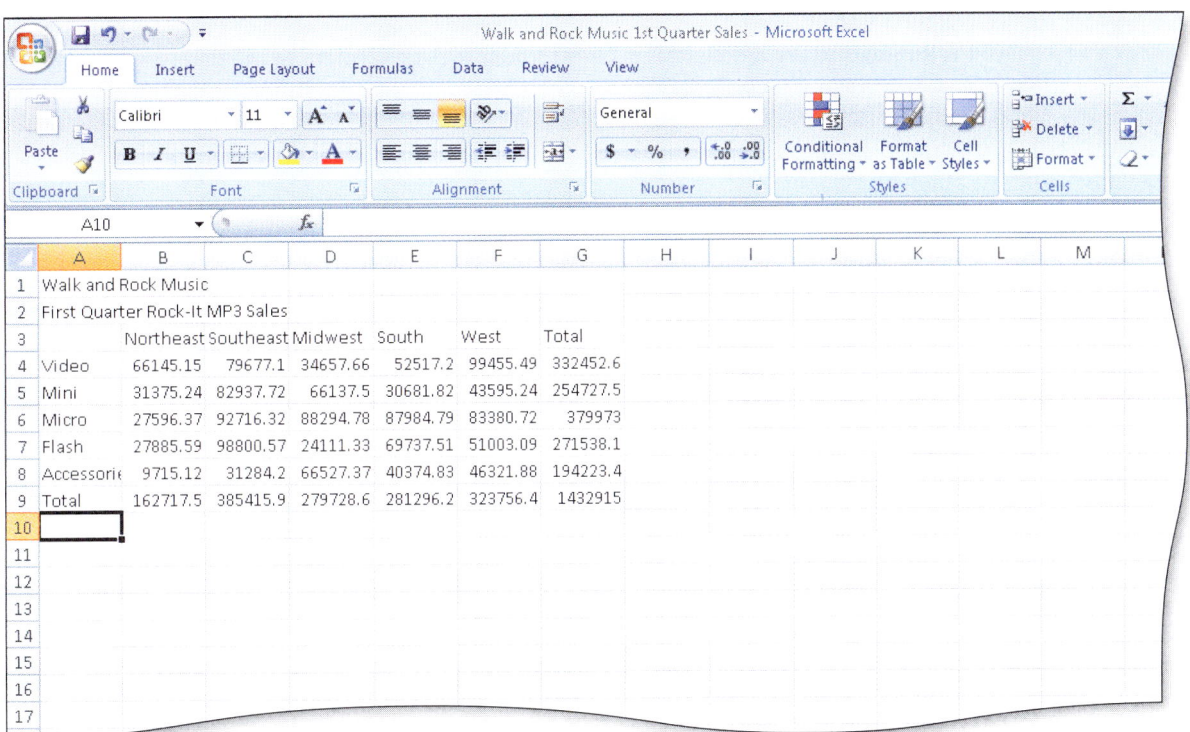

(a) Before Formatting

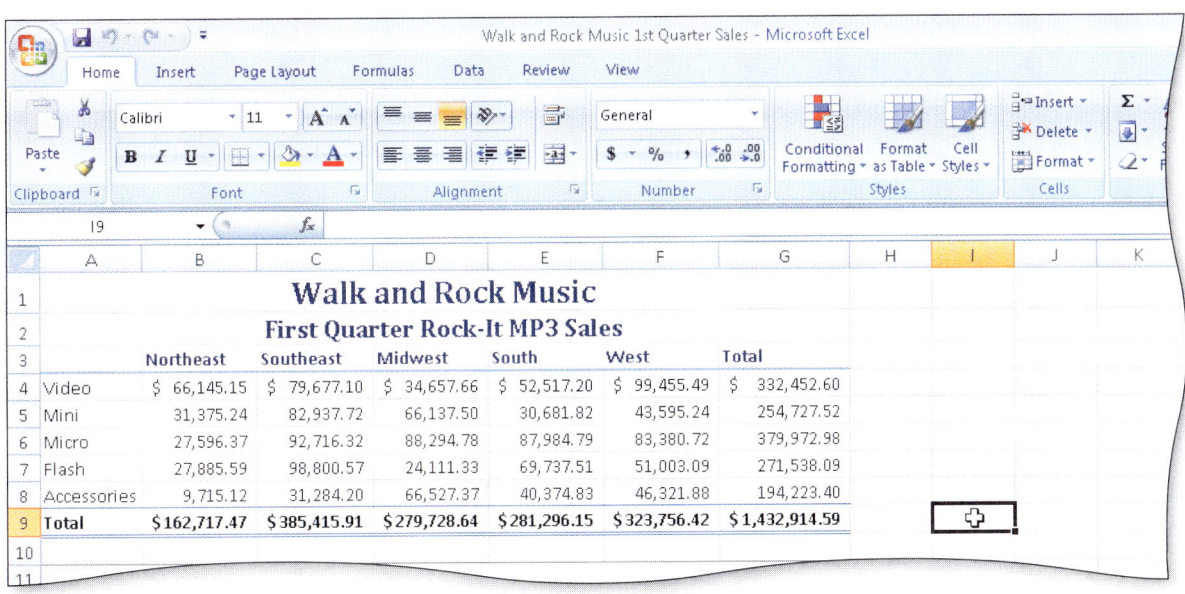

(b) After Formatting

Figure 1–46

Plan Ahead

Identify how to format various elements of the worksheet.
To change the unformatted worksheet in Figure 1–46a to the formatted worksheet in Figure 1–46b, the following tasks must be completed:

1. Change the font type, change the font style to bold, increase the font size, and change the font color of the worksheet titles in cells A1 and A2. These changes make the worksheet title prominently display to the user and inform the user of the purpose of the worksheet.

2. Center the worksheet titles in cells A1 and A2 across columns A through G.

3. Format the body of the worksheet. The body of the worksheet, range A3:G9, includes the column titles, row titles, and numbers. Formatting the body of the worksheet changes the numbers to use a dollars-and-cents format, with dollar signs in the first row (row 4) and the total row (row 9); adds underlining that emphasizes portions of the worksheet; and modifies the column widths to make the text and numbers readable.

The remainder of this section explains the process required to format the worksheet. Although the format procedures are explained in the order described above, you should be aware that you could make these format changes in any order. Modifying the column widths, however, usually is done last.

> **BTW**
> **Fonts**
> In general, use no more than two font types in a worksheet.

> **BTW**
> **Fonts and Themes**
> Excel uses default recommended fonts based on the workbook's theme. A theme is a collection of fonts and color schemes. The default theme is named Office, and the two recommended fonts for the Office theme are Calibri and Cambria. Excel, however, allows you to apply any font to a cell or range as long as the font is installed on your computer.

Font Type, Style, Size, and Color

The characters that Excel displays on the screen are a specific font type, style, size, and color. The **font type**, or font face, defines the appearance and shape of the letters, numbers, and special characters. Examples of font types include Calibri, Cambria, Times New Roman, Arial, and Courier. **Font style** indicates how the characters are emphasized. Common font styles include regular, bold, underline, or italic. The **font size** specifies the size of the characters on the screen. Font size is gauged by a measurement system called points. A single point is about 1/72 of one inch in height. Thus, a character with a **point size** of 10 is about 10/72 of one inch in height. The **font color** defines the color of the characters. Excel can display characters in a wide variety of colors, including black, red, orange, and blue.

When Excel begins, the preset font type for the entire workbook is Calibri, with a font size, font style, and font color of 11-point regular black. Excel allows you to change the font characteristics in a single cell, a range of cells, the entire worksheet, or the entire workbook.

To Change a Cell Style

Excel includes the capability of changing several characteristics of a cell, such as font type, font size, and font color, all at once by assigning a predefined cell style to a cell. The following steps assign the Title cell style to the worksheet title in cell A1.

1
- Click cell A1 to make cell A1 the active cell.
- Click the Cell Styles button on the Ribbon to display the Cell Styles gallery (Figure 1–47).

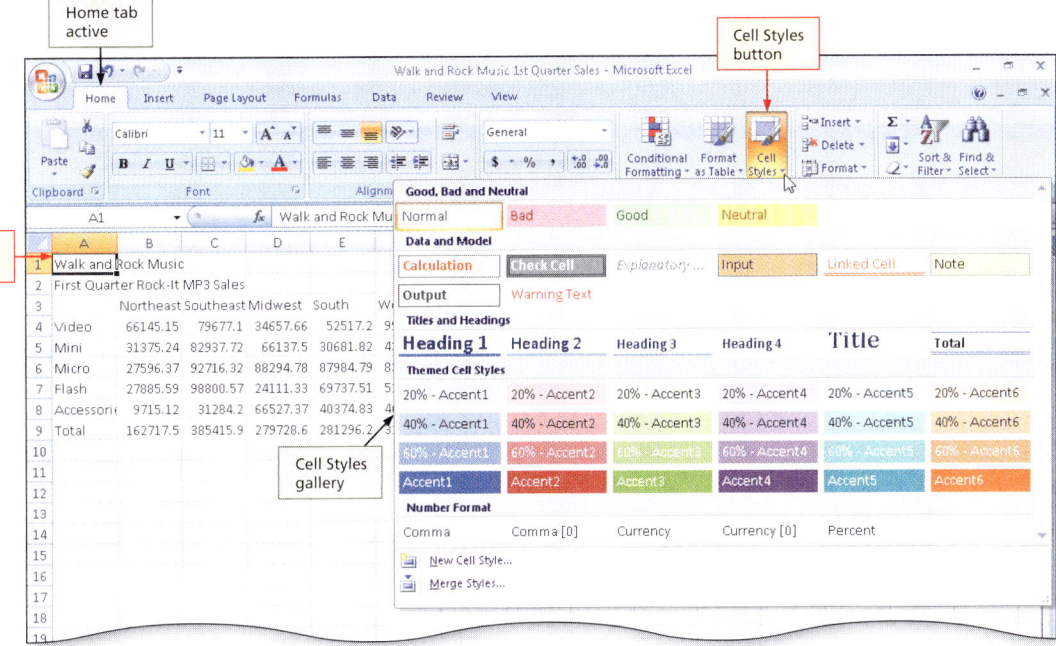

Figure 1–47

2
- Point to the Title cell style in the Titles and Headings area of the Cell Styles gallery to see a live preview of the cell style in cell A1 (Figure 1–48).

Experiment
- Point to several other cell styles in the Cell Styles gallery to see a live preview of other cell styles in cell A1.

 Why does the font type, font size, and font color change in cell A1 when I point to it?

The change in cell A1 is a result of live preview. Live preview is a feature of Excel 2007 that allows you to preview cell styles as you point to them in the Cell Styles gallery.

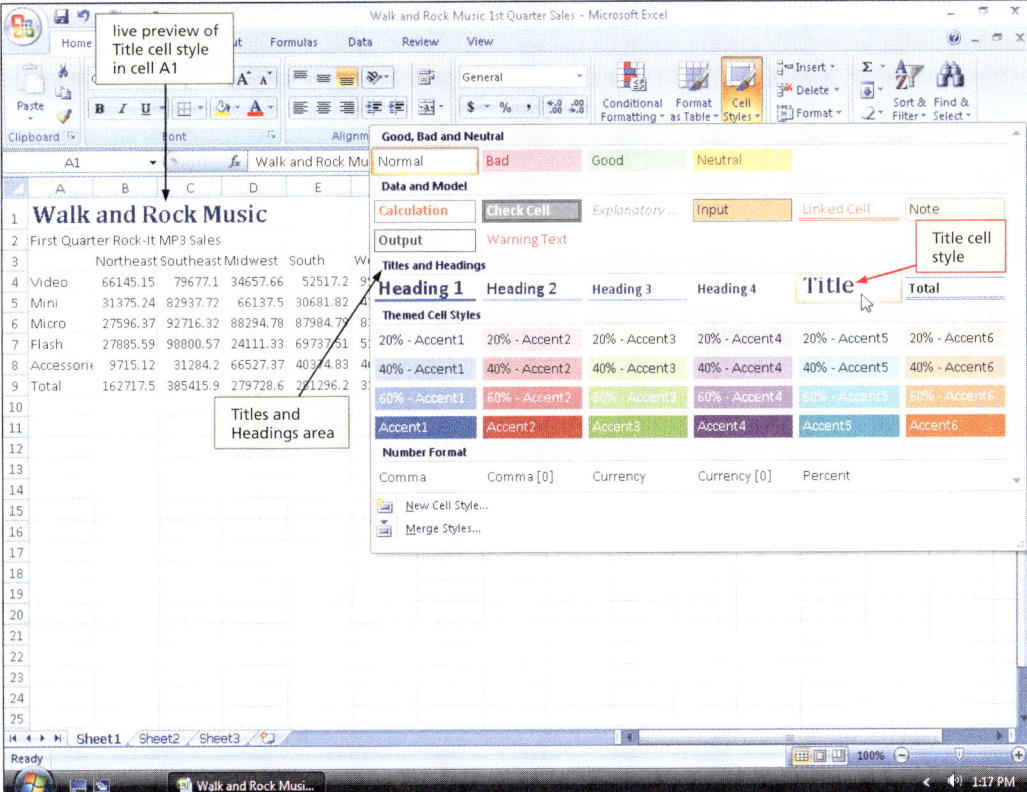

Figure 1–48

EX 36 Excel Chapter 1 Creating a Worksheet and an Embedded Chart

- Click the Title cell style to apply the cell style to cell A1 (Figure 1–49).

Q&A Why do several items in the Font group on the Ribbon change?

The changes to the Font box, Bold button, and Font Size box indicate the font changes applied to the active cell, cell A1, as a result of applying the Title cell style.

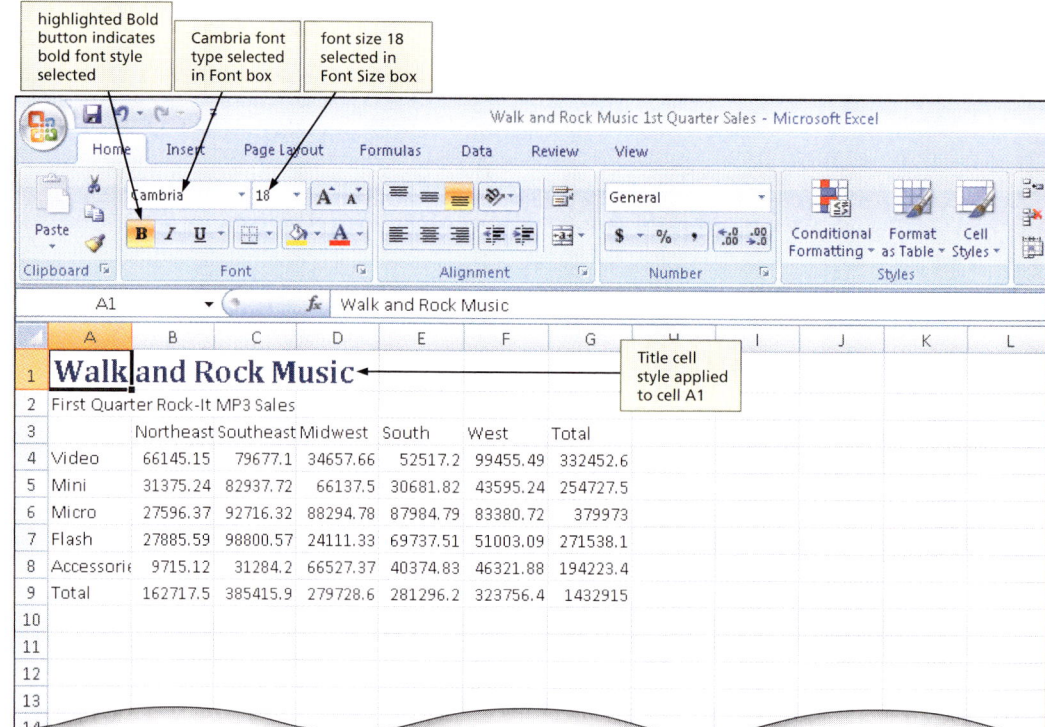

Figure 1–49

To Change the Font Type

Different font types often are used in a worksheet to make it more appealing to the reader. The following steps change the worksheet subtitle's font type from Calibri to Cambria.

- Click cell A2 to make cell A2 the active cell.

- Click the Font box arrow on the Ribbon to display the Font gallery (Figure 1–50).

Q&A Which fonts are displayed in the Font gallery?

Because many programs supply additional font types beyond what comes with the Windows Vista operating system, the number of font types available on your computer will depend on the programs installed. This book uses only font types that come with the Windows Vista operating system and Microsoft Office.

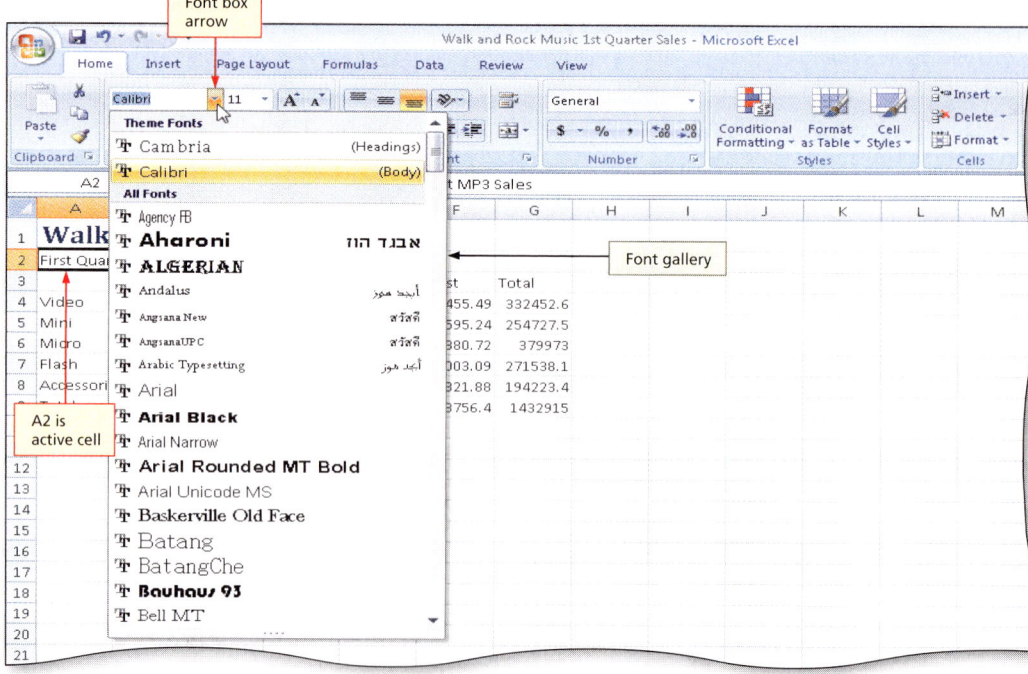

Figure 1–50

- Point to Cambria in the Theme Fonts area of the Font gallery to see a live preview of the Cambria font in cell A2 (Figure 1–51).

   **Experiment**

- Point to several other fonts in the Font gallery to see a live preview of other fonts in cell A2.

Q&A

What is the Theme Fonts area?

Excel applies the same default theme to any new workbook that you start. A **theme** is a collection of cell styles and other styles that have common characteristics, such as a color scheme and font type. The default theme for an Excel workbook is the Office theme. The Theme Fonts area of the Font gallery includes the fonts included in the default Office theme. Cambria is recommended for headings and Calibri is recommended for cells in the body of the worksheet (Figure 1–51).

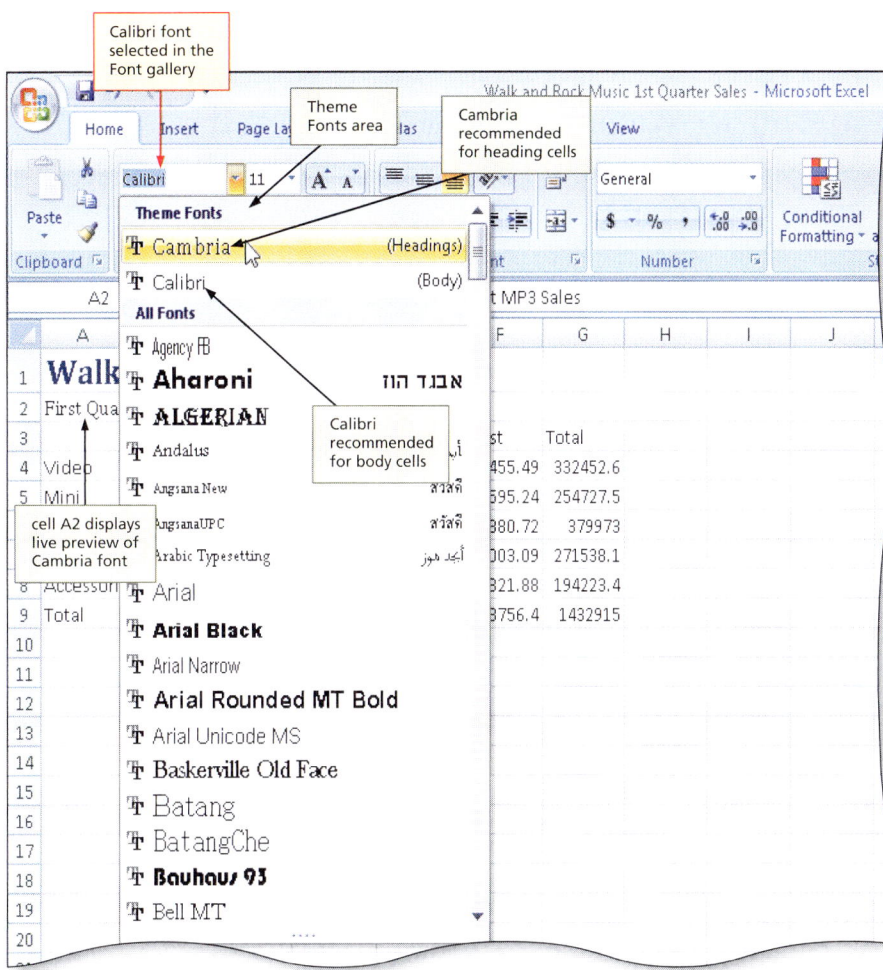

Figure 1–51

- Click Cambria in the Theme Fonts area to change the font type of the worksheet subtitle in cell A2 from Calibri to Cambria (Figure 1–52).

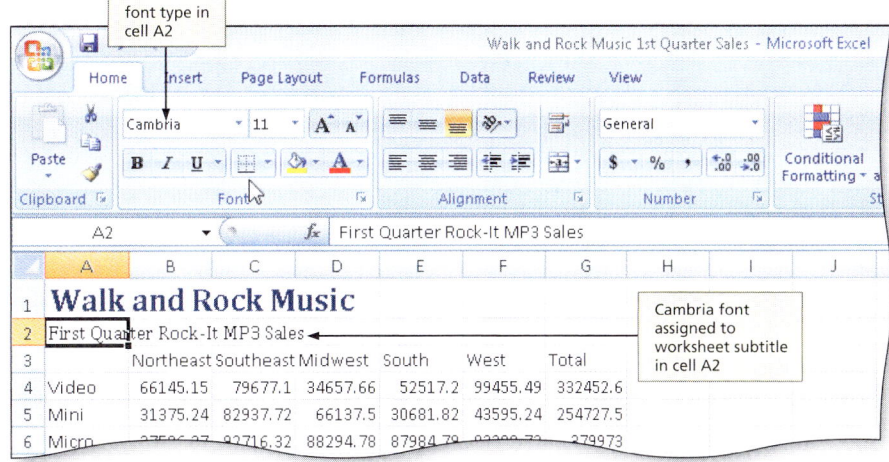

Figure 1–52

Other Ways

1. Select font type from Font list on Mini toolbar
2. Right-click cell, click Format Cells on shortcut menu, click Font tab, click desired font type, click OK button

To Bold a Cell

You **bold** an entry in a cell to emphasize it or make it stand out from the rest of the worksheet. The following step shows how to bold the worksheet subtitle in cell A2.

1

- With cell A2 active, click the Bold button on the Ribbon to change the font style of the worksheet subtitle to bold (Figure 1–53).

Q&A What if a cell already includes a bold style?

If the active cell already is bold, then Excel displays the button with a transparent orange background.

Q&A How do I remove the bold style from a cell?

Clicking the Bold button a second time removes the bold font style.

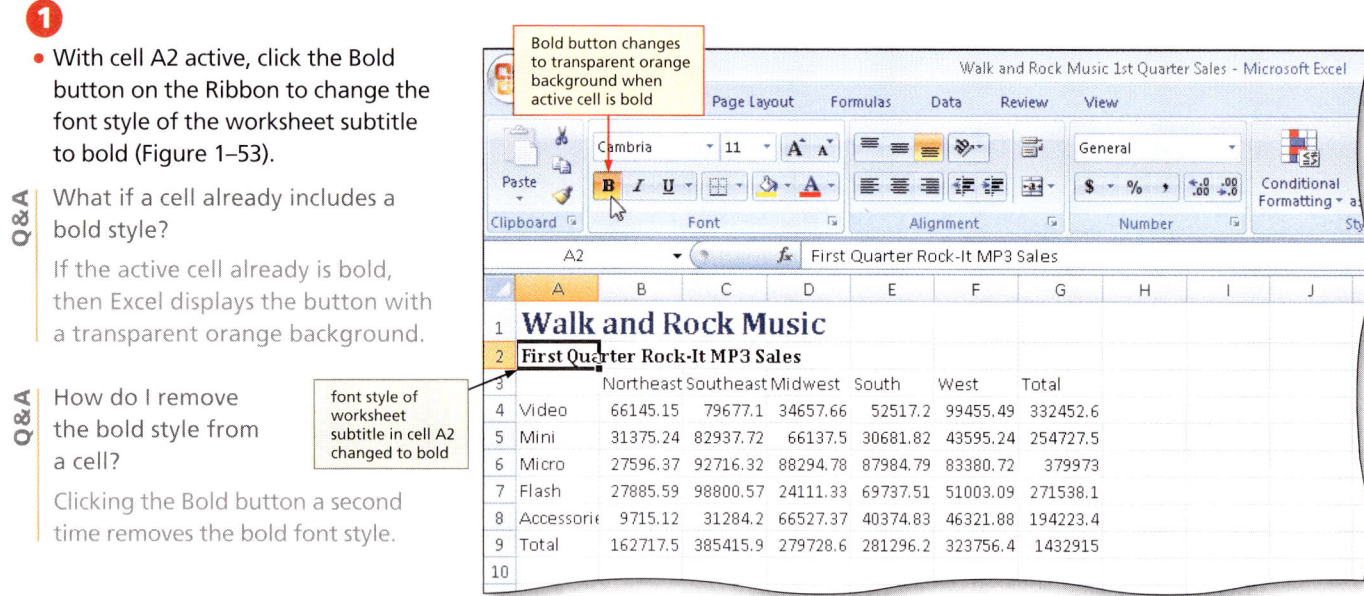

Figure 1–53

Other Ways

1. Click Bold button on Mini toolbar
2. Right-click cell, click Format Cells on shortcut menu, click Font tab, click Bold, click OK button
3. Press CTRL+B

To Increase the Font Size of a Cell Entry

Increasing the font size is the next step in formatting the worksheet subtitle. You increase the font size of a cell so the entry stands out and is easier to read. The following steps increase the font size of the worksheet subtitle in cell A2.

1

- With cell A2 selected, click the Font Size box arrow on the Ribbon to display the Font Size list.

- Point to 14 in the Font Size list to see a live preview of cell A2 with a font size of 14 (Figure 1–54).

  🔍 **Experiment**

- Point to several other font sizes in the Font Size list to see a live preview of other font sizes in cell A2.

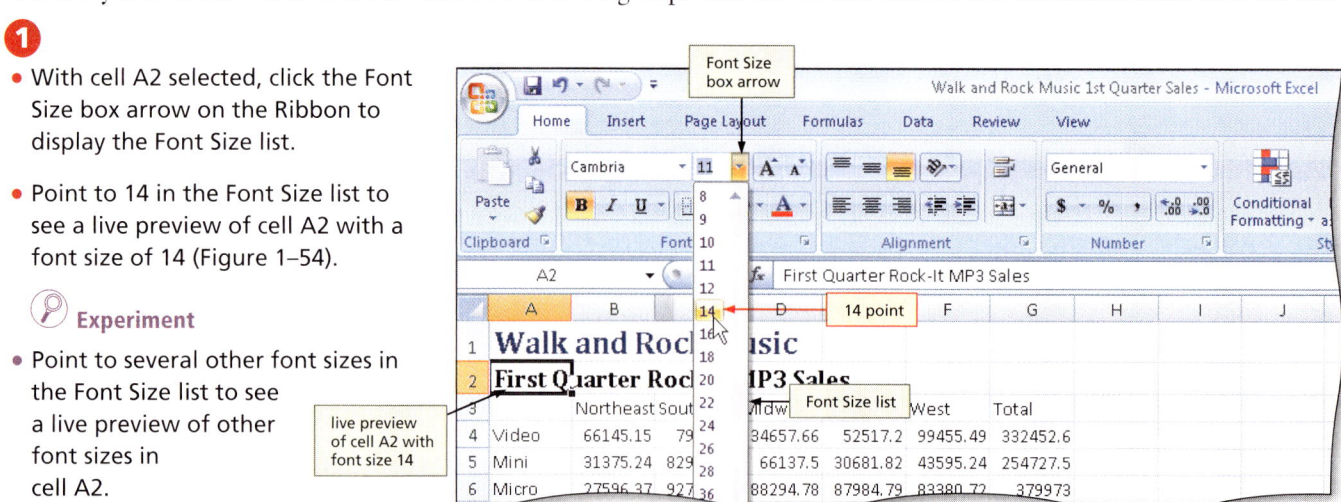

Figure 1–54

2

- Click 14 in the Font Size list to change the font in cell A2 from 11 point to 14 point (Figure 1–55).

Q&A Can I assign a font size that is not in the Font Size list?

Yes. An alternative to clicking a font size in the Font Size list is to click the Font Size box, type the font size, and then press the ENTER key. This procedure allows you to assign a font size not available in the Font Size list to a selected cell entry.

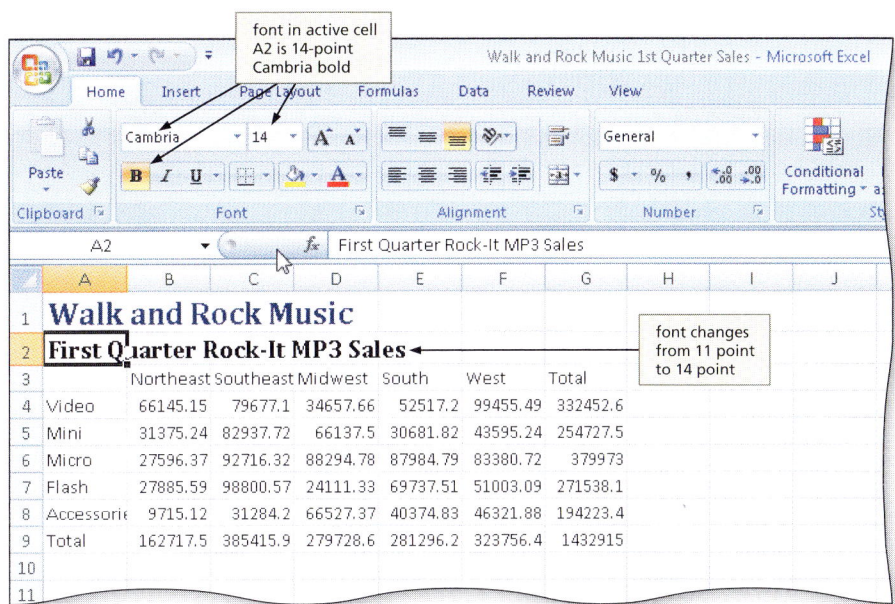

Figure 1–55

Other Ways

1. Click Increase Font Size button or Decrease Font Size button on Ribbon
2. Select font size from Font Size list on Mini toolbar
3. Right-click cell, click Format Cells on shortcut menu, click Font tab, select font size in Size box, click OK button

To Change the Font Color of a Cell Entry

The next step is to change the color of the font in cell A2 from black to dark blue. The following steps change the font color of a cell entry.

1

- With cell A2 selected, click the Font Color button arrow on the Ribbon to display the Font Color palette.

- Point to Dark Blue, Text 2 (dark blue color in column 4, row 1) in the Theme Colors area of the Font Color palette to see a live preview of the font color in cell A2 (Figure 1–56).

Experiment

- Point to several other colors in the Font Color palette to see a live preview of other font colors in cell A2.

Q&A Which colors does Excel make available on the Font Color palette?

You can choose from more than 60 different font colors on the Font Color palette (Figure 1–56). Your Font Color palette may have more or fewer colors, depending on color settings of your operating system. The Theme Colors area includes colors that are included in the current workbook's theme.

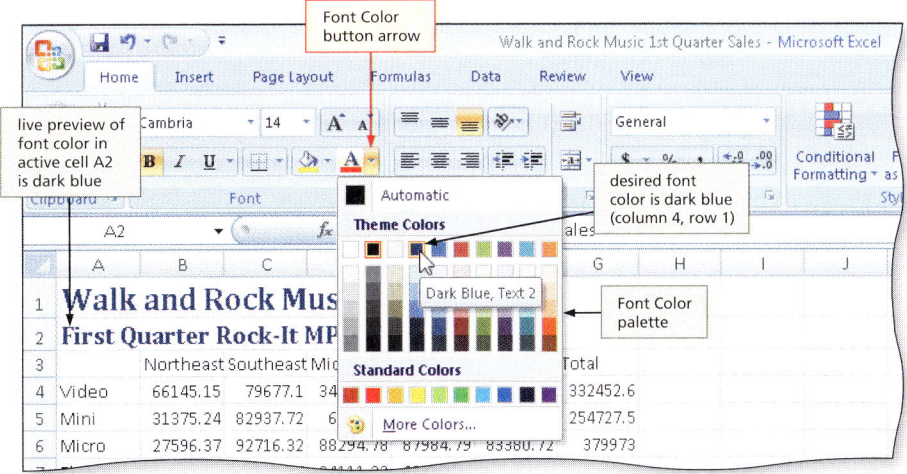

Figure 1–56

2

- Click Dark Blue, Text 2 (column 4, row 1) on the Font Color palette to change the font of the worksheet subtitle in cell A2 from black to dark blue (Figure 1–57).

Q&A

Why does the Font Color button change after I select the new font color?

When you choose a color on the Font Color palette, Excel changes the Font Color button on the Formatting toolbar to the chosen color. Thus, to change the font color of the cell entry in another cell to the same color, you need only to select the cell and then click the Font Color button.

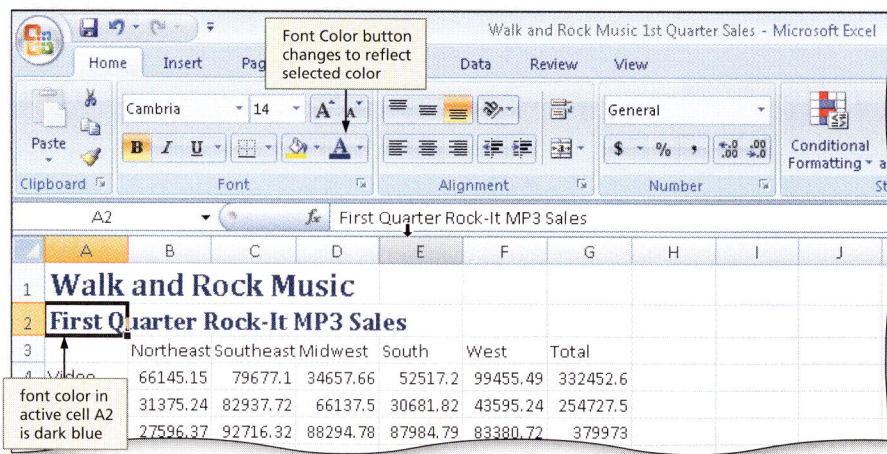

Figure 1–57

Other Ways

1. Select font color from Font Color list on Mini toolbar
2. Right-click cell, click Format Cells on shortcut menu, click Font tab, select color on Font Color palette, click OK button

To Center Cell Entries across Columns by Merging Cells

The final step in formatting the worksheet title and subtitle is to center them across columns A through G. Centering a title across the columns used in the body of the worksheet improves the worksheet's appearance. To do this, the seven cells in the range A1:G1 are combined, or merged, into a single cell that is the width of the columns in the body of the worksheet. The seven cells in the range A2:G2 also are merged in a similar manner. **Merging cells** involves creating a single cell by combining two or more selected cells. The following steps center the worksheet title and subtitle across columns by merging cells.

1

- Select cell A1 and then drag to cell G1 to highlight the range A1:G1 (Figure 1–58).

Q&A

What if a cell in the range B1:G1 contained data?

For the Merge & Center button to work properly, all the cells except the leftmost cell in the selected range must be empty.

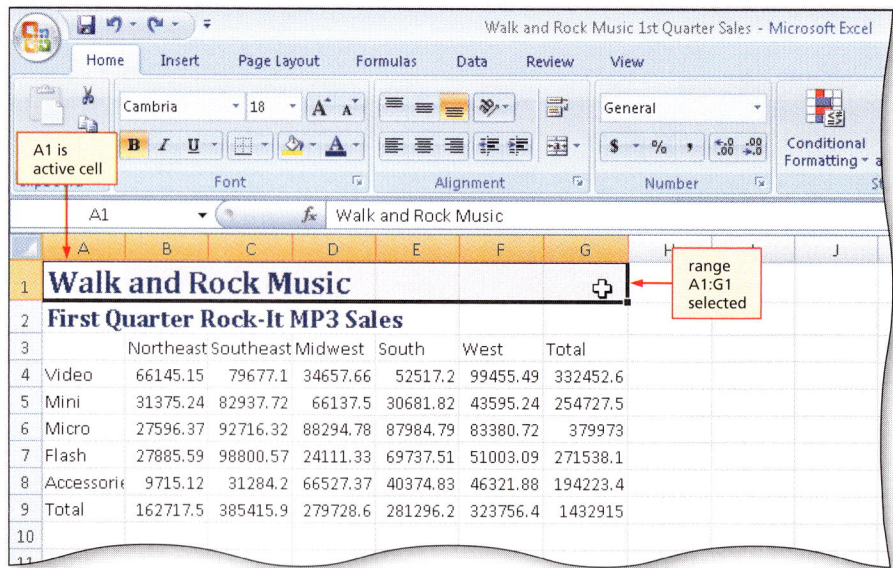

Figure 1–58

Creating a Worksheet and an Embedded Chart Excel Chapter 1 EX 41

2
- Click the Merge & Center button on the Ribbon to merge cells A1 through G1 and center the contents of cell A1 across columns A through G (Figure 1–59).

Q&A What happened to cells B1 through G1?

After the merge, cells B1 through G1 no longer exist. Cell A1 now extends across columns A through G.

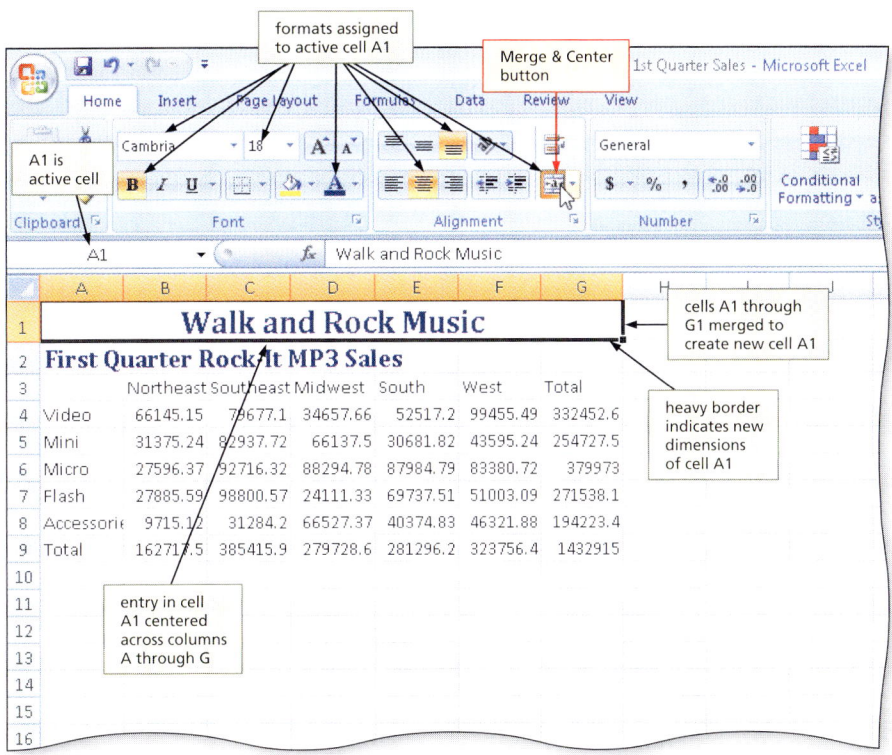

Figure 1–59

3
- Repeat Steps 1 and 2 to merge and center the worksheet subtitle across cells A2 through G2 (Figure 1–60).

Q&A Are cells B1 through G1 and B2 through G2 lost forever?

No. The opposite of merging cells is **splitting a merged cell**. After you have merged multiple cells to create one merged cell, you can unmerge, or split, the merged cell to display the original cells on the worksheet. You split a merged cell by selecting it and clicking the Merge & Center button. For example, if you click the Merge & Center button a second time in Step 2, it will split the merged cell A1 to cells A1, B1, C1, D1, E1, F1, and G1.

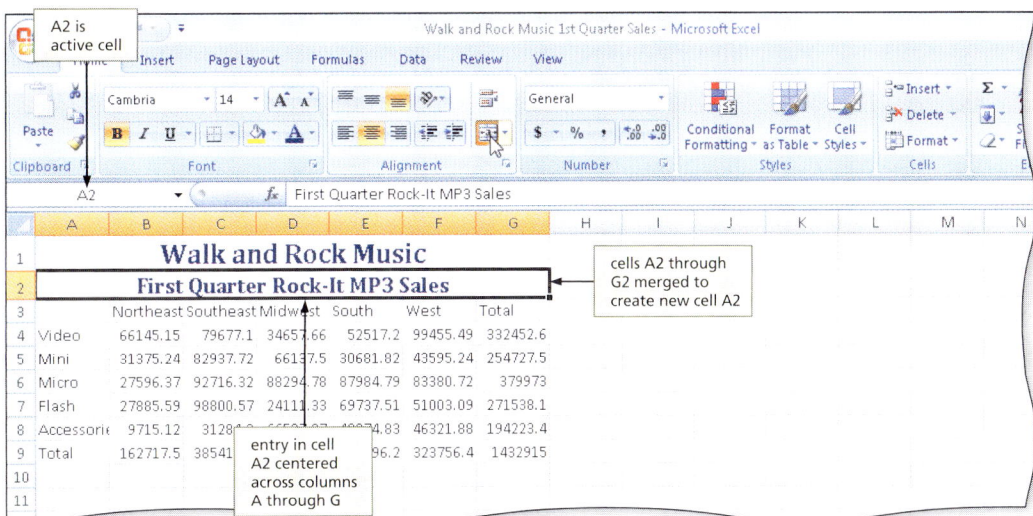

Figure 1–60

Other Ways	
1. Right-click selection, click Merge & Center button on Mini toolbar	2. Right-click selection, click Format Cells on shortcut menu, click Alignment tab, select Center Across Selection in Horizontal list, click OK button

To Format Column Titles and the Total Row

The next step to format the worksheet is to format the column titles in row 3 and the total row, row 9. Column titles and the total row should be formatted so anyone who views the worksheet can quickly distinguish the column titles and total row from the data in the body of the worksheet. The following steps format the column titles and total row using cell styles in the default worksheet theme.

- Click cell A3 and then drag the mouse pointer to cell G3 to select the range A3:G3.
- Point to the Cell Styles button on the Ribbon (Figure 1–61).

Q&A Why is cell A3 selected in the range for the column headings?

The style to be applied to the column headings includes an underline that will help to distinguish the column headings from the rest of the worksheet. Including cell A3 in the range ensures that the cell will include the underline, which is visually appealing and further helps to separate the data in the worksheet.

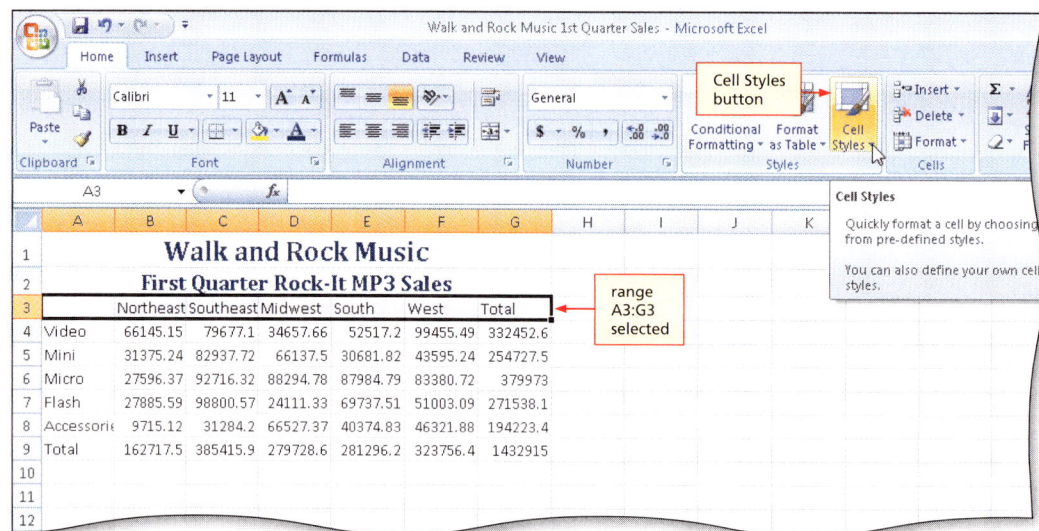

Figure 1–61

- Click the Cell Styles button to display the Cell Styles gallery.
- Point to the Heading 3 cell style in the Titles and Headings area of the Cell Styles gallery to see a live preview of the cell style in the range A3:G3 (Figure 1–62).

Experiment

- Point to other cell styles in the Titles and Headings area of the Cell Styles gallery to see a live preview of other cell styles in the range A3:G3.

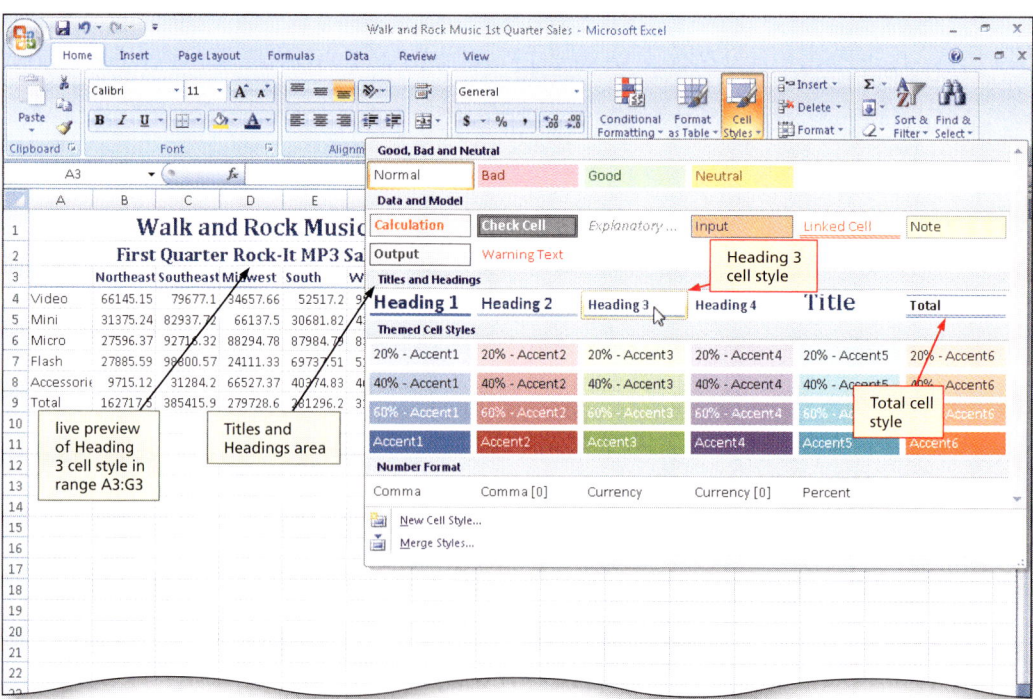

Figure 1–62

Creating a Worksheet and an Embedded Chart Excel Chapter 1 EX 43

3

- Click the Heading 3 cell style to apply the cell style to the range A3:G3.
- Click cell A9 and then drag the mouse pointer to cell G9 to select the range A9:G9.
- Point to the Cell Styles button on the Ribbon (Figure 1–63).

Q&A Why should I choose Heading 3 instead of another heading cell style?

Excel includes many types of headings, such as Heading 1 and Heading 2, because worksheets often include many levels of headings above columns. In the case of the worksheet created for this project, the Heading 3 title includes formatting that makes the column titles' font size smaller than the title and subtitle and makes the column titles stand out from the data in the body of the worksheet.

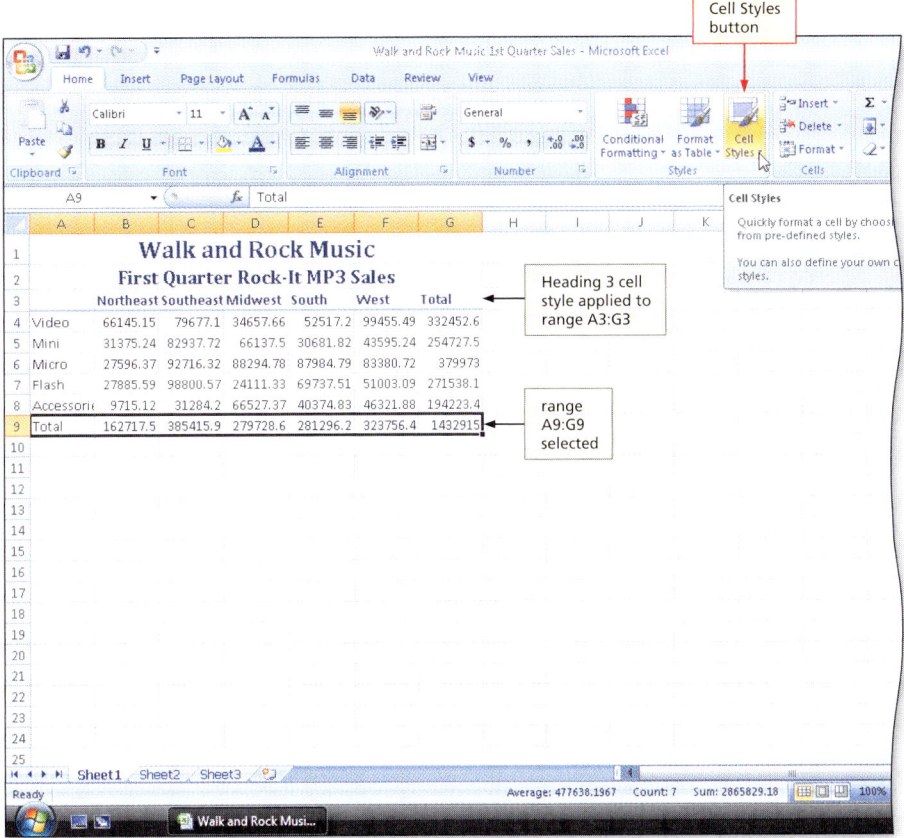

Figure 1–63

4

- Click the Cell Styles button on the Ribbon to display the Cell Styles gallery and then click the Total cell style in the Titles and Headings area to apply the Total cell style to the cells in the range A9:G9.
- Click cell A11 to select the cell (Figure 1–64).

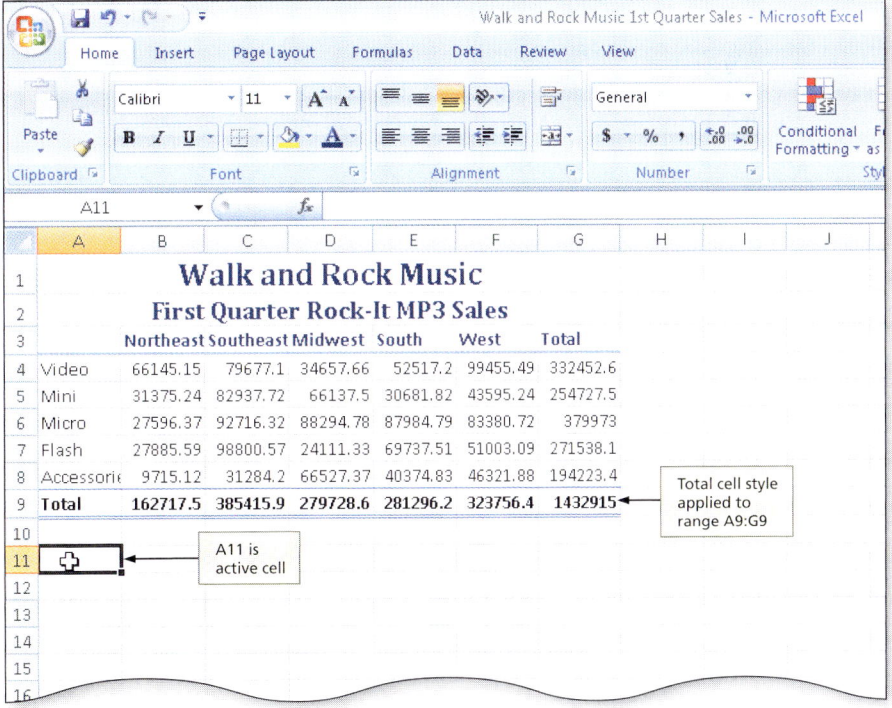

Figure 1–64

To Format Numbers in the Worksheet

As previously noted, the numbers in the worksheet should be formatted to use a dollar-and-cents format, with dollar signs in the first row (row 4) and the total row (row 9). Excel allows you to format numbers in a variety of methods, some of which are discussed in this book. The following steps use buttons on the Ribbon to format the numbers in the worksheet.

- Select cell B4 and drag the mouse pointer to cell G4 to select the range B4:G4.
- Point to the Accounting Number Format button on the Ribbon to display the Enhanced ScreenTip (Figure 1–65).

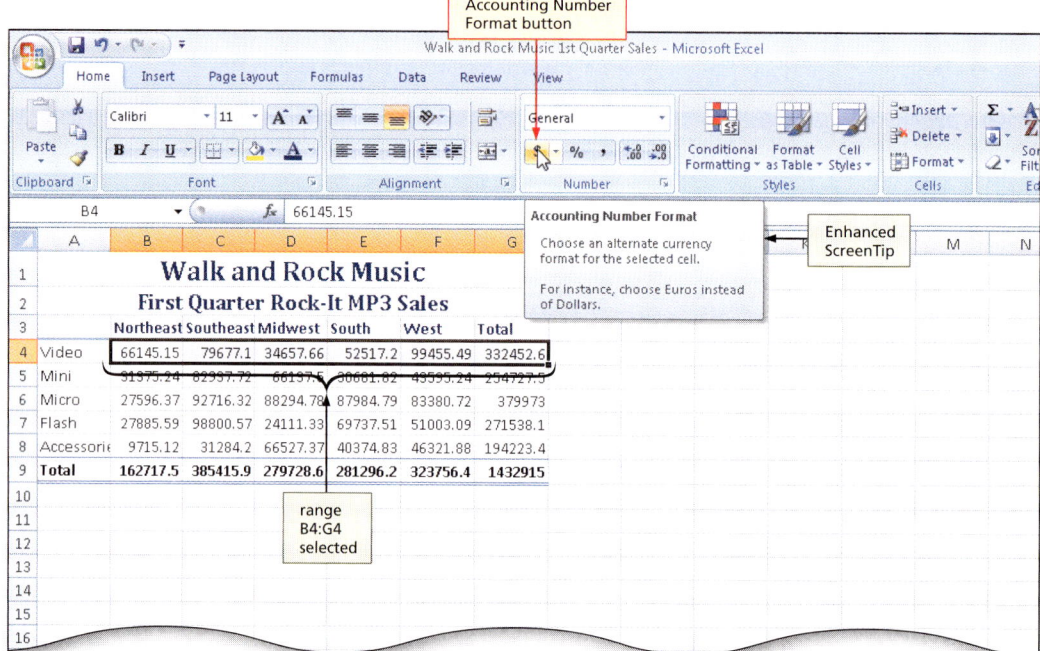

Figure 1–65

2

- Click the Accounting Number Format button on the Ribbon to apply the Accounting Number format to the cells in the range B4:G4.
- Select the range B5:G8 (Figure 1–66).

Q&A What effect does the Accounting Number format have on the selected cells?

The Accounting Number format causes the cells to display with two decimal places so that decimal places in cells below the selected cells align vertically. Cell widths are automatically adjusted to accommodate the new formatting.

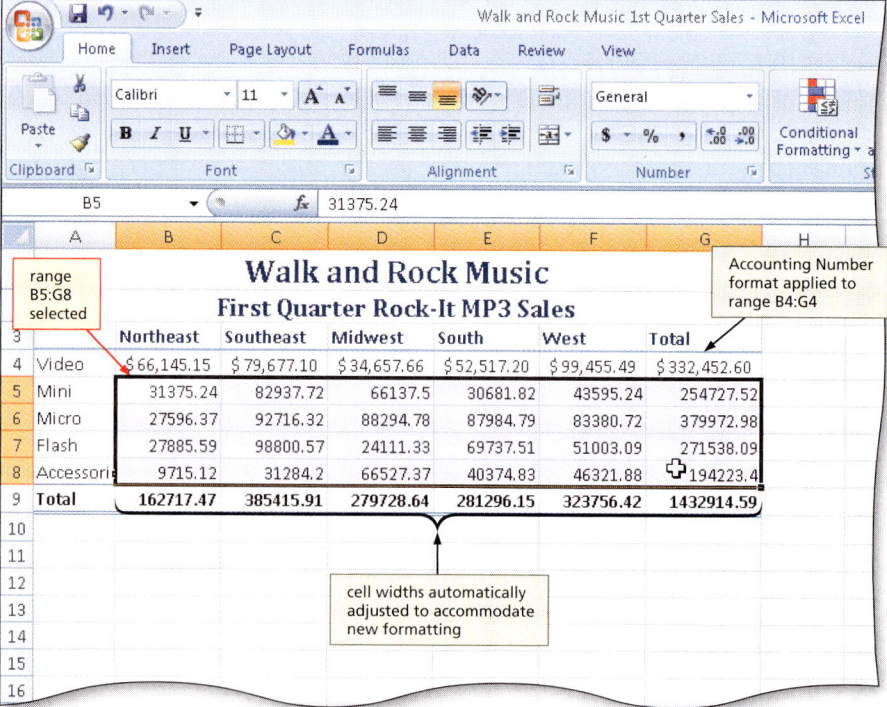

Figure 1–66

- Click the Comma Style button on the Ribbon to apply the Comma Style to the range B5:G8.

- Select the range B9:G9 (Figure 1–67).

Q&A

What effect does the Comma Style format have on the selected cells?

The Comma Style format causes the cells to display with two decimal places and commas as thousands separators.

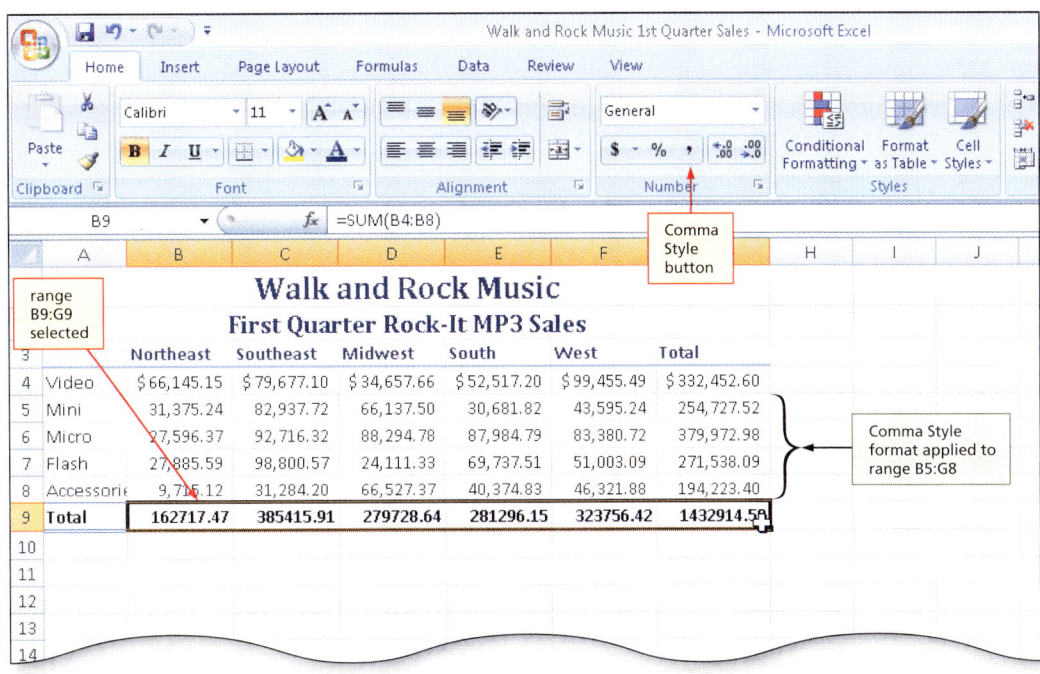

Figure 1–67

- Click the Accounting Number Format button on the Ribbon to apply the Accounting Number format to the cells in the range B9:G9.

- Select cell A11 (Figure 1-68).

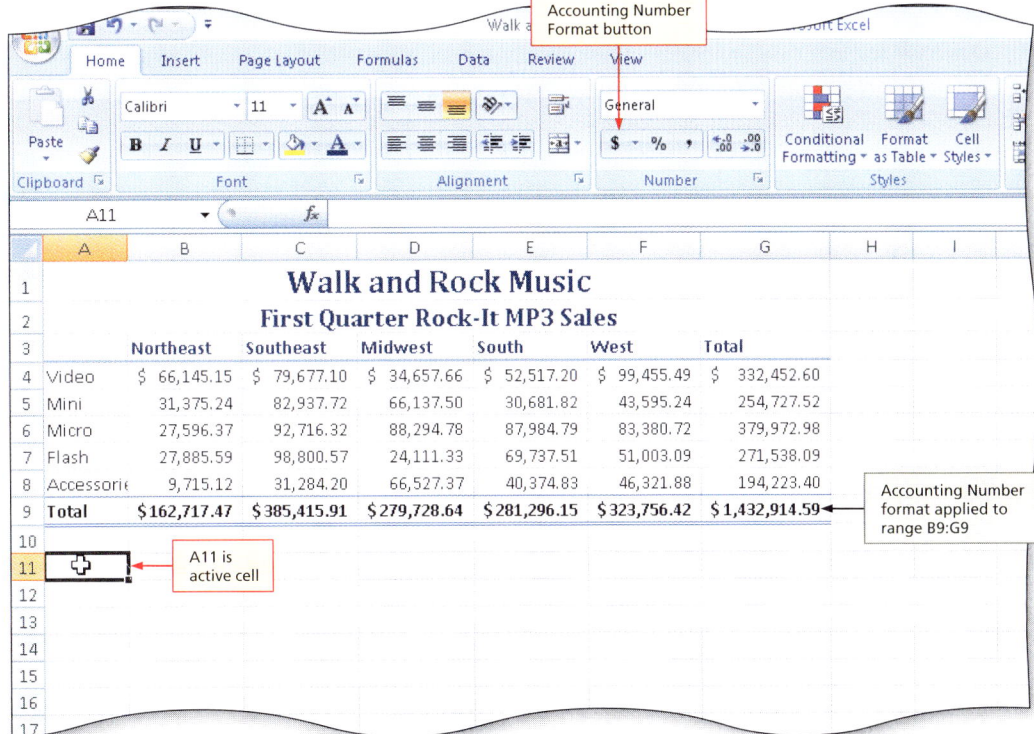

Figure 1–68

Other Ways
1. Click Accounting Number Format or Comma button on Mini toolbar 2. Right-click selection, click Format Cells on the shortcut menu, click Number tab, select Accounting in Category list or select Number and click Use 1000 Separator, click OK button

To Adjust the Column Width

The last step in formatting the worksheet is to adjust the width of column A so that the word Accessories in cell A8 is shown in its entirety in the cell. Excel includes several methods for adjusting cell widths and row heights. The following steps adjust the width of column A so that the contents of cell A8 are displayed in the cell.

1

- Point to the boundary on the right side of the column A heading above row 1 to change the mouse pointer to a split double arrow (Figure 1–69).

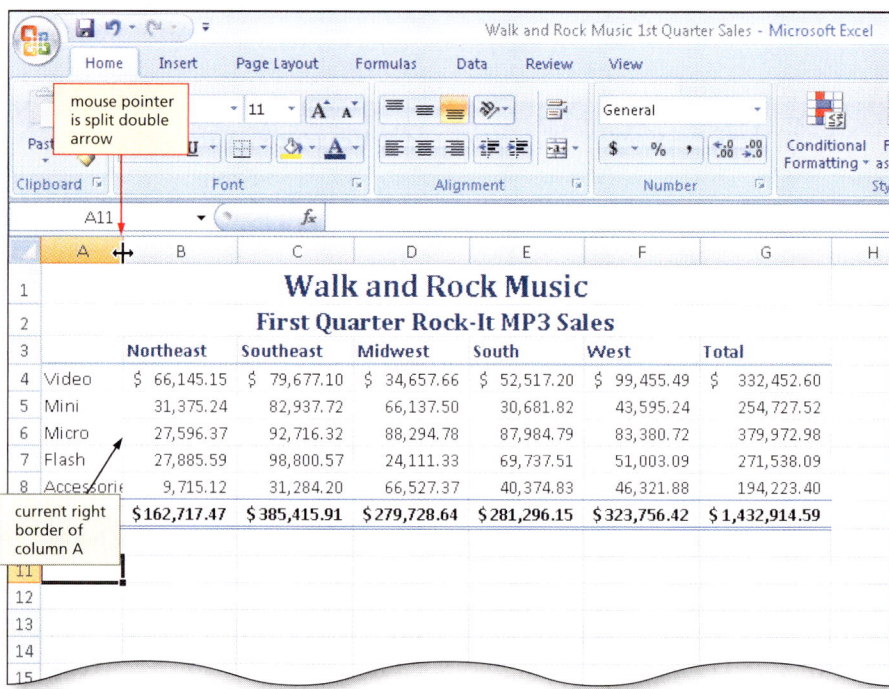

Figure 1–69

2

- Double-click on the boundary to adjust the width of column A to the width of the largest item in the column (Figure 1–70).

Q&A

What if none of the items in column A extended through the entire width of the column?

If all of the items in column A were shorter in length than the width of the column when you double-click the right side of the column A heading, then Excel still would adjust the column width to the largest item in the column. That is, Excel would reduce the width of the column to the largest item.

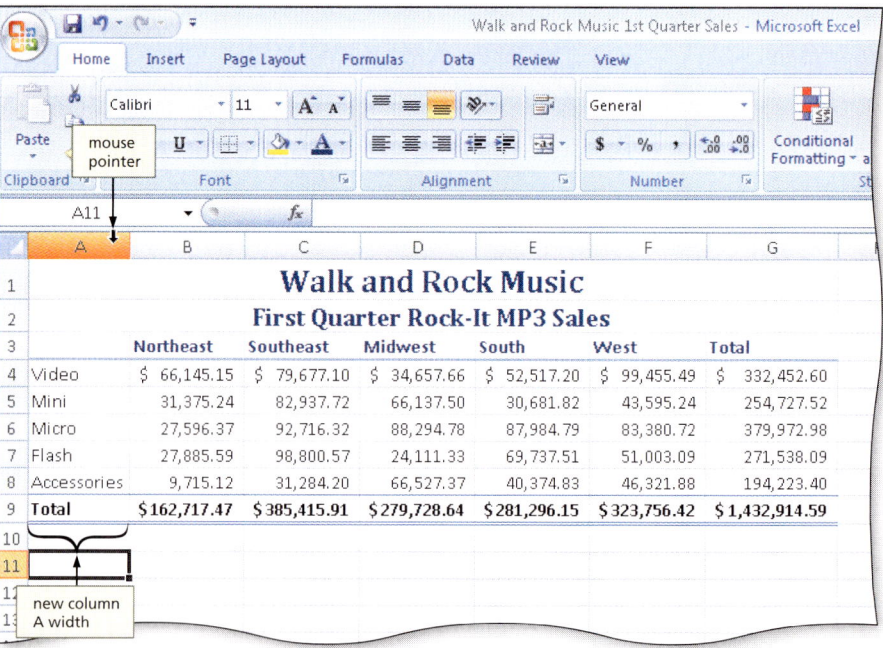

Figure 1–70

Using the Name Box to Select a Cell

The next step is to chart the quarterly sales for the five product types sold by the company. To create the chart, you must select the cell in the upper-left corner of the range to chart (cell A3). Rather than clicking cell A3 to select it, the next section describes how to use the Name box to select the cell.

To Use the Name Box to Select a Cell

As previously noted, the Name box is located on the left side of the formula bar. To select any cell, click the Name box and enter the cell reference of the cell you want to select. The following steps select cell A3.

1
- Click the Name box in the formula bar and then type a3 as the cell to select (Figure 1–71).

Q&A Why is cell A11 still selected?
Even though cell A11 is the active cell, Excel displays the typed cell reference a3 in the Name box until you press the ENTER key.

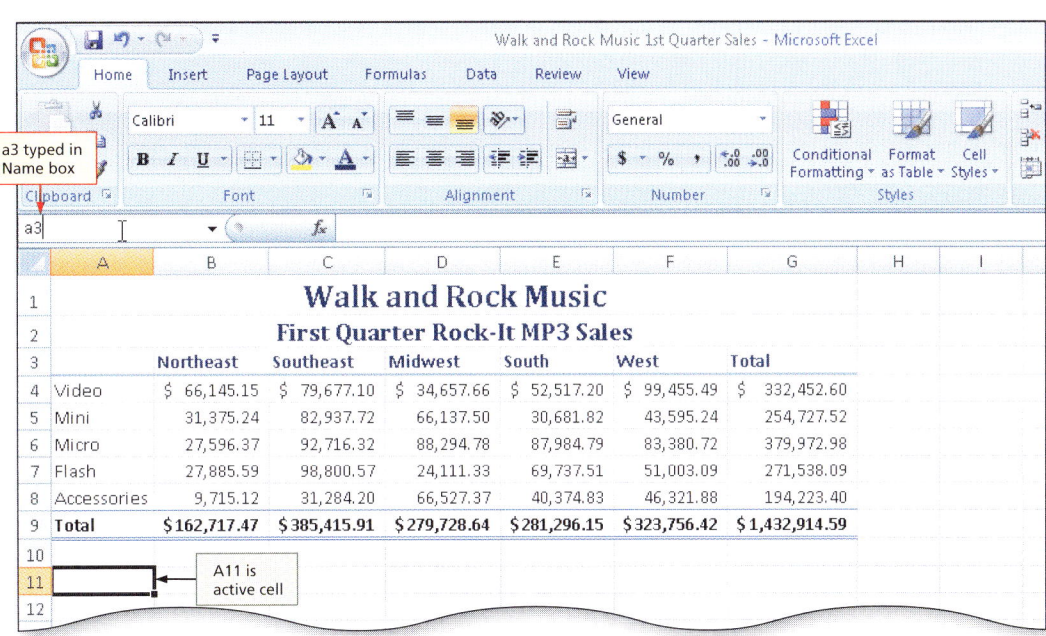

Figure 1–71

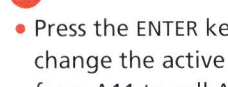
- Press the ENTER key to change the active cell from A11 to cell A3 (Figure 1–72).

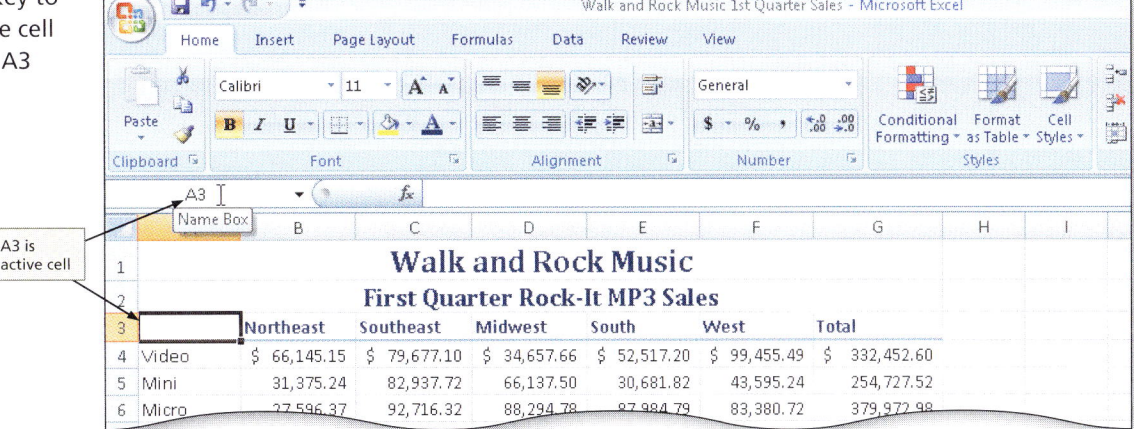

Figure 1–72

Other Ways to Select Cells

In addition to using the Name box to select any cell in a worksheet, you also can use it to assign names to a cell or range of cells. Excel supports several additional ways to select a cell, as summarized in Table 1–3.

> **BTW**
>
> **Find & Select**
> You can find and select cells based on their content. Click the Find & Select button on the Home tab on the Ribbon. Then, click the Go To Special command. Choose your desired option in the Select area of the Go To Special dialog box and then click the OK button.

Table 1–3 Selecting Cells in Excel

Key, Box, or Command	Function
ALT+PAGE DOWN	Selects the cell one worksheet window to the right and moves the worksheet window accordingly.
ALT+PAGE UP	Selects the cell one worksheet window to the left and moves the worksheet window accordingly.
ARROW	Selects the adjacent cell in the direction of the arrow on the key.
CTRL+ARROW	Selects the border cell of the worksheet in combination with the arrow keys and moves the worksheet window accordingly. For example, to select the rightmost cell in the row that contains the active cell, press CTRL+RIGHT ARROW. You also can press the END key, release it, and then press the appropriate arrow key to accomplish the same task.
CTRL+HOME	Selects cell A1 or the cell one column and one row below and to the right of frozen titles and moves the worksheet window accordingly.
Find command on Find and Select menu or SHIFT+F5	Finds and selects a cell that contains specific contents that you enter in the Find dialog box. If necessary, Excel moves the worksheet window to display the cell. You also can press CTRL+F to display the Find dialog box.
Go To command on Find and Select menu or F5	Selects the cell that corresponds to the cell reference you enter in the Go To dialog box and moves the worksheet window accordingly. You also can press CTRL+G to display the Go To dialog box.
HOME	Selects the cell at the beginning of the row that contains the active cell and moves the worksheet window accordingly.
Name box	Selects the cell in the workbook that corresponds to the cell reference you enter in the Name box.
PAGE DOWN	Selects the cell down one worksheet window from the active cell and moves the worksheet window accordingly.
PAGE UP	Selects the cell up one worksheet window from the active cell and moves the worksheet window accordingly.

Plan Ahead

Decide on the type of chart needed.
Excel includes 11 chart types from which you can choose including column, line, pie, bar, area, X Y (scatter), stock, surface, doughnut, bubble, and radar. The type of chart you choose depends on the type of data that you have, how much data you have, and the message you want to convey.

A column chart is a good way to compare values side-by-side. A Clustered Column chart can go even further in comparing values across categories. In the case of the Walk and Rock Music quarterly sales data, comparisons of product types within each region can be made side-by-side with a Clustered Column chart.

Establish where to position and how to format the chart.

- When possible, try to position charts so that both the data and chart appear on the screen on the worksheet together and so that the data and chart can be printed in the most readable manner possible. By placing the chart below the data on the Walk and Rock Music 1st Quarter Sales worksheet, both of these goals are accomplished.

- When choosing/selecting colors for a chart, consider the color scheme of the rest of the worksheet. The chart should not present colors that are in stark contrast to the rest of the worksheet. If the chart will be printed in color, minimize the amount of dark colors on the chart so that the chart both prints quickly and preserves ink.

Adding a 3-D Clustered Column Chart to the Worksheet

As outlined in the requirements document in Figure 1–2 on page EX 4, the worksheet should include a 3-D Clustered Column chart to graphically represent quarterly sales for each product type that the company sells. The 3-D Clustered Column chart shown in Figure 1–73 is called an **embedded chart** because it is drawn on the same worksheet as the data.

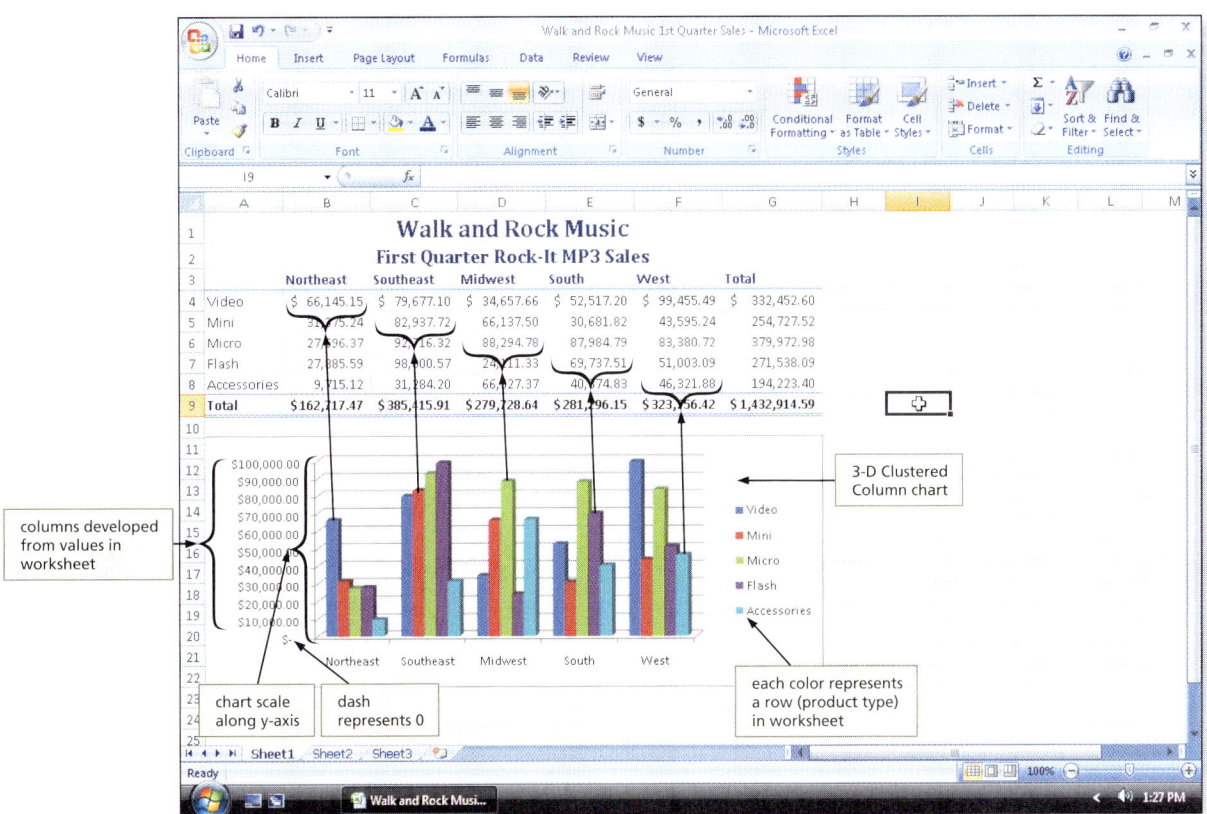

Figure 1–73

The chart uses different colored columns to represent sales for different product types. Each region uses the same color scheme for identifying product types, which allows for easy identification and comparison. For the Northeast sales region, for example, the dark blue column representing Video products shows quarterly sales of $66,145.15; for the Southeast sales region, the maroon column representing Mini products shows quarterly sales of $82,937.72; for the Midwest sales region, the pale green column representing Micro products shows quarterly sales of $88,294.78; for the South sales region, the violet column representing Flash products shows quarterly sales of $69,737.51; and for the West sales region, the light blue column representing Accessories shows quarterly sales of $46,321.88. Because the same color scheme is used in each region to represent the five product types, you easily can compare sales of product types among the sales regions. The totals from the worksheet are not represented, because the totals are not in the range specified for charting.

BTW

Cell Values and Charting
When you change a cell value on which a chart is dependent, Excel redraws the chart instantaneously, unless automatic recalculation is disabled. If automatic recalculation is disabled, then you must press the F9 key to redraw the chart. To enable or disable automatic recalculation, click the Calculations Options button on the Formulas tab on the Ribbon.

Excel derives the chart scale based on the values in the worksheet and then displays the scale along the vertical axis (also called the **y-axis** or **value axis**) of the chart. For example, no value in the range B4:F8 is less than 0 or greater than $100,000.00, so the scale ranges from 0 to $100,000.00. Excel also determines the $10,000.00 increments of the scale automatically. For the numbers along the y-axis, Excel uses a format that includes representing the 0 value with a dash (Figure 1–73 on the previous page).

To Add a 3-D Clustered Column Chart to the Worksheet

The commands to insert a chart are located on the Insert tab. With the range to chart selected, you click the Column button on the Ribbon to initiate drawing the chart. The area on the worksheet where the chart appears is called the chart location. As shown in Figure 1–73, the chart location in this worksheet is the range A11:G22, immediately below the worksheet data.

The following steps draw a 3-D Clustered Column chart that compares the quarterly sales by product type for the five sales regions.

- Click cell A3 and then drag the mouse pointer to the cell F8 to select the range A3:F8 (Figure 1–74).

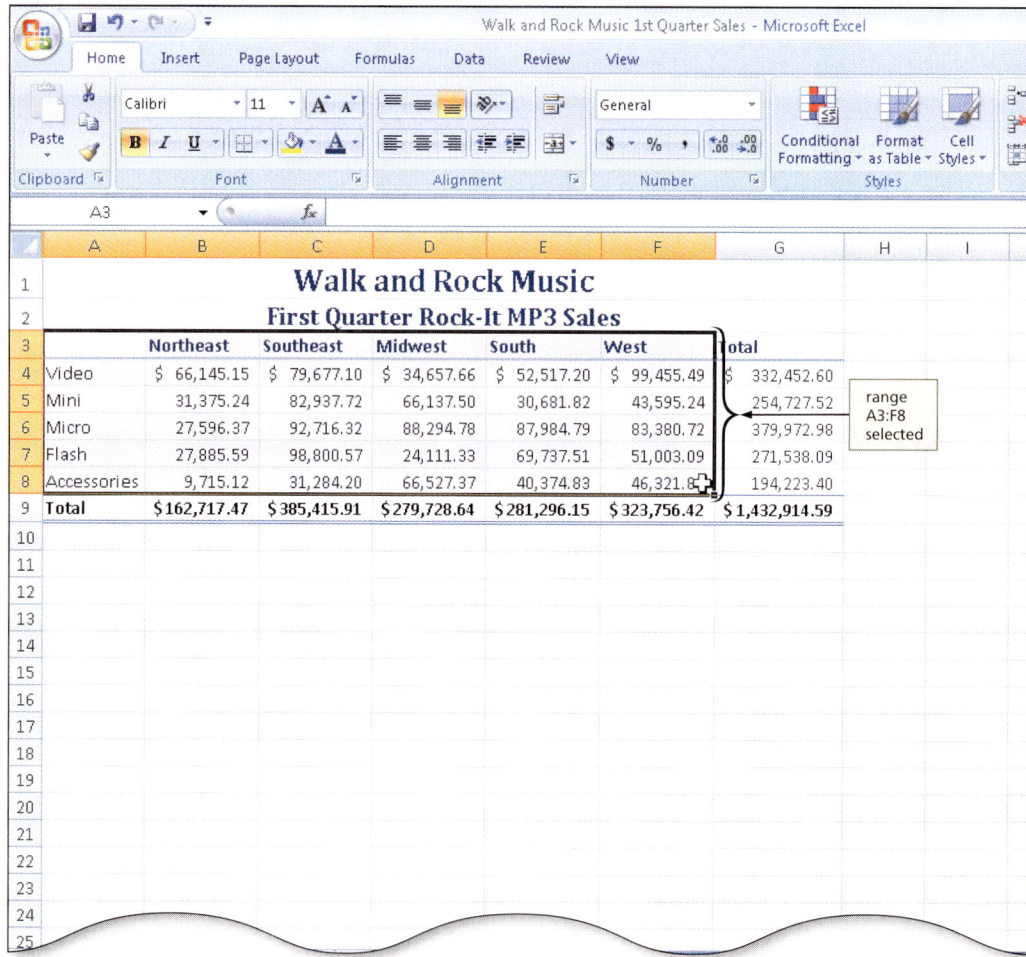

Figure 1–74

2
- Click the Insert tab to make the Insert tab the active tab (Figure 1–75).

Q&A What tasks can I perform with the Insert tab?

The Insert tab includes commands that allow you to insert various objects, such as shapes, tables, illustrations, and charts, into a worksheet. These objects will be discussed as they are used throughout this book.

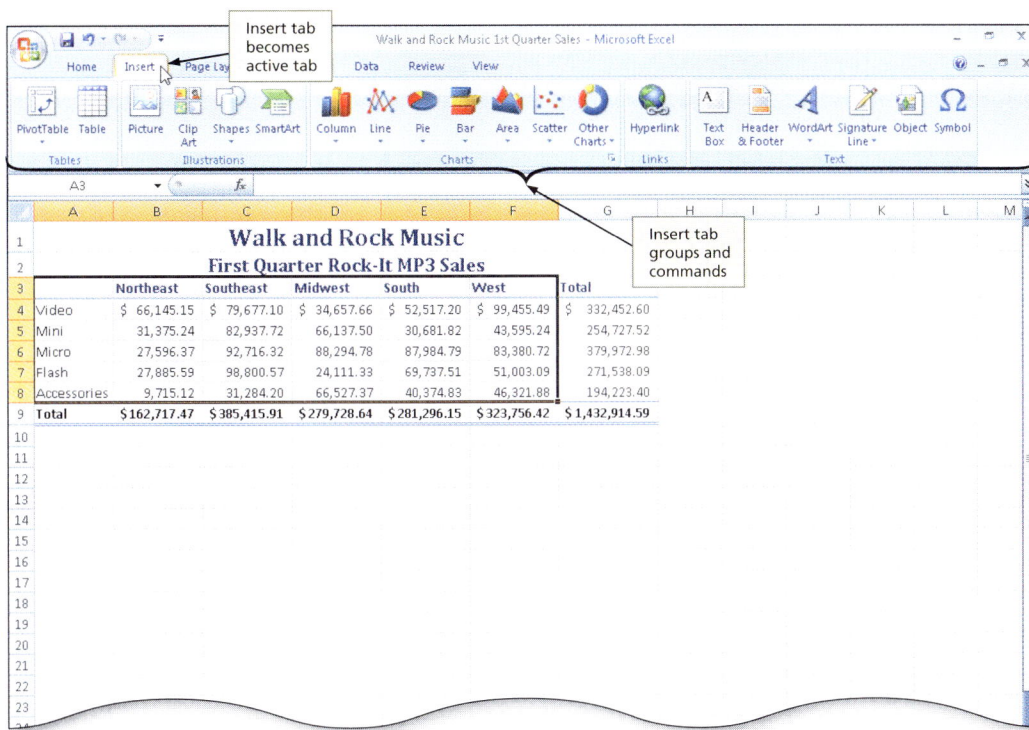

Figure 1–75

3
- Click the Column button on the Ribbon to display the Column gallery.
- Point to the 3-D Clustered Column chart type in the 3-D Column area of the Column gallery (Figure 1–76).

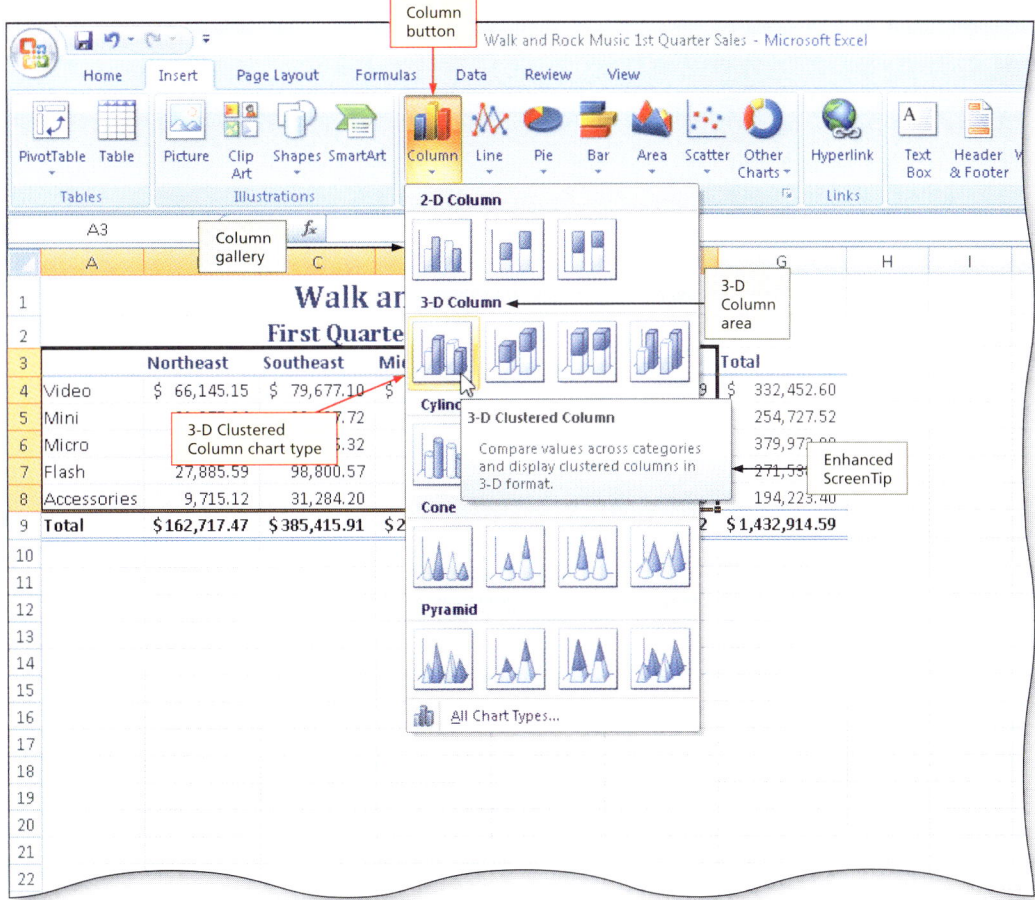

Figure 1–76

EX 52 Excel Chapter 1 Creating a Worksheet and an Embedded Chart

4

- Click the 3-D Clustered Column chart type in the 3-D Column area of the Column gallery to add a 3-D Clustered Column chart to the middle of the worksheet in a selection rectangle.

- Click the top-right edge of the selection rectangle but do not release the mouse to grab the chart and change the mouse pointer to a crosshair with four arrowheads (Figure 1–77).

Q&A Why is a new tab displayed on the Ribbon?

When you select objects such as shapes or charts, Excel displays contextual tabs that include special commands that are used to work with the type of object selected. Because a chart is selected, Excel displays the Chart Tools contextual tab. The three tabs below the Chart Tools contextual tab, Design, Layout, and Format, are tabs that include commands to work with charts.

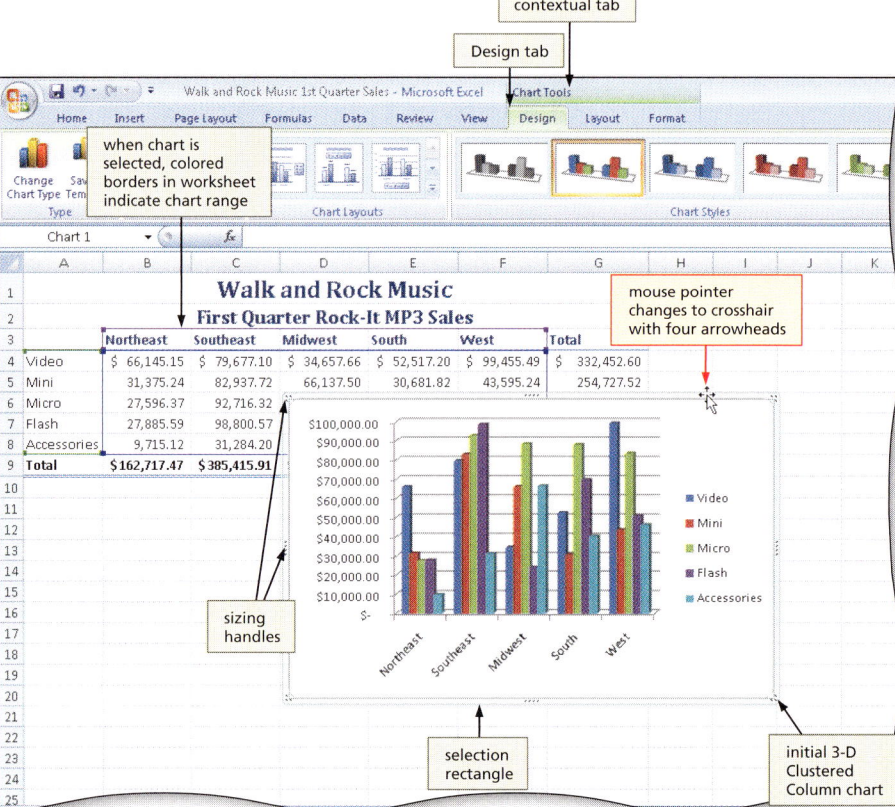

Figure 1–77

5

- Continue holding down the left mouse button while dragging the chart down and to the left to position the upper-left corner of the dotted line rectangle over the upper-left corner of cell A11. Release the mouse button to complete the move of the chart.

- Click the middle sizing handle on the right edge of the chart and do not release the mouse button (Figure 1–78).

Q&A How does Excel know how to create the chart?

Excel automatically selects the entries in the topmost row of the chart range (row 3) as the titles for the horizontal axis (also called the **x-axis** or **category axis**) and draws a column for each of the 25 cells in the range containing numbers.

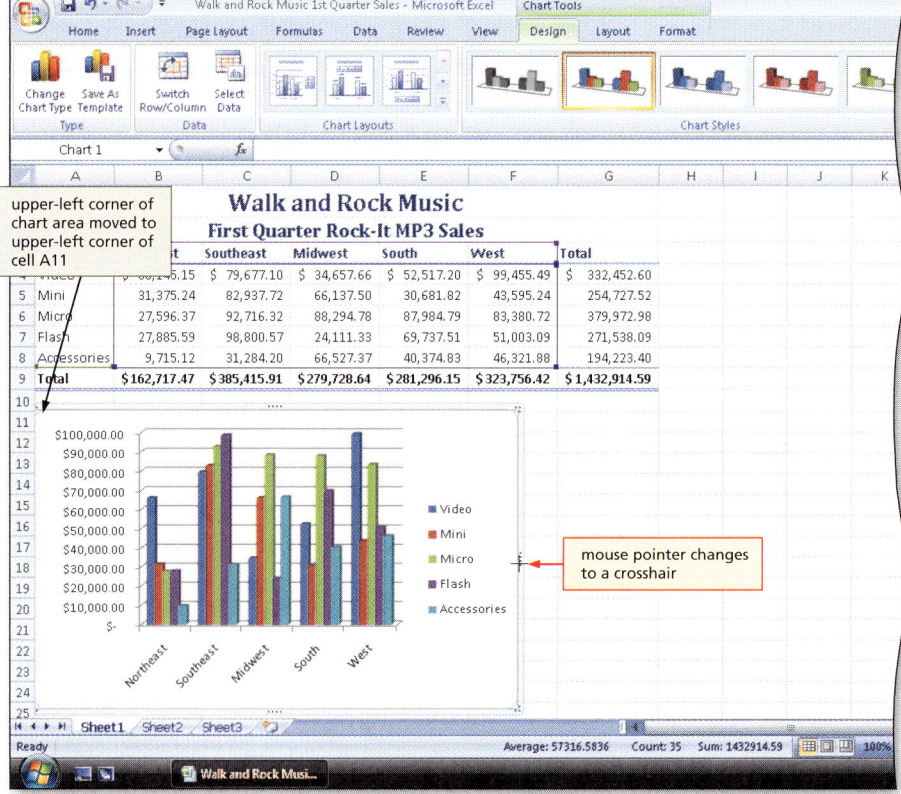

Figure 1–78

6

- While continuing to hold down the mouse button, press the ALT key and drag the right edge of the chart to the right edge of column G and then release the mouse button to resize the chart.

- Point to the middle sizing handle on the bottom edge of the selection rectangle and do not release the mouse button (Figure 1–79).

Q&A

Why should I hold the ALT key down while I resize a chart?

Holding down the ALT key while you drag a chart snaps (aligns) the edge of the chart area to the worksheet gridlines. If you do not hold down the ALT key, then you can place an edge of a chart in the middle of a column or row.

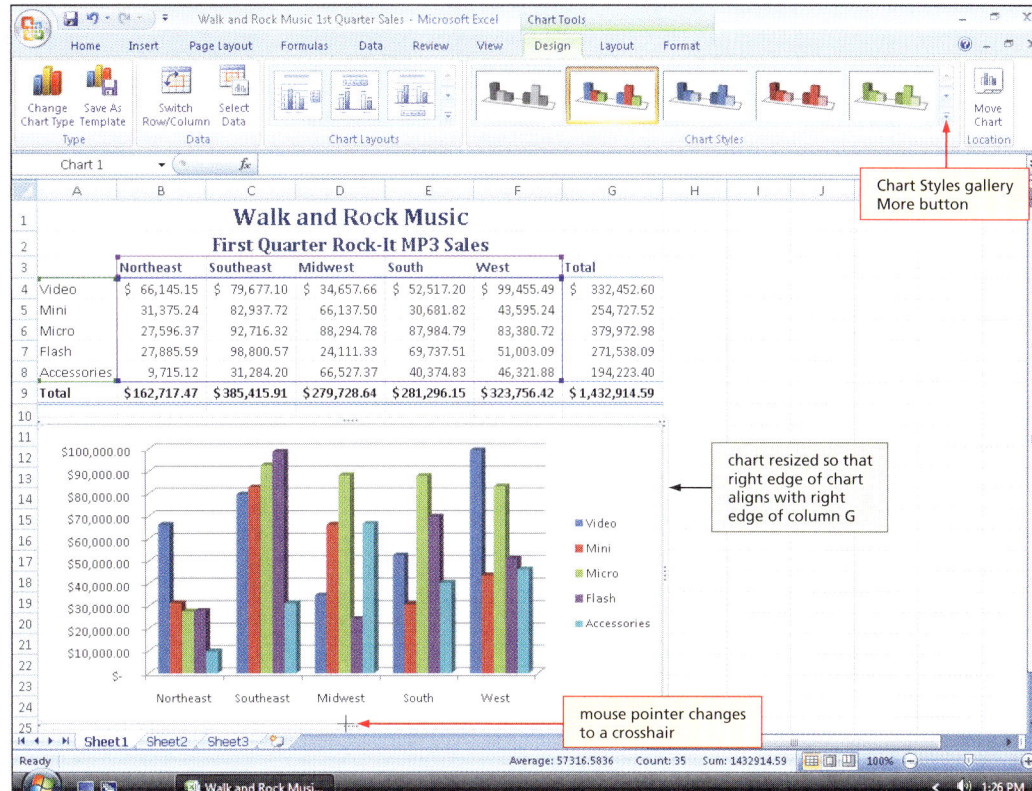

Figure 1–79

7

- While continuing to hold down the mouse button, press the ALT key and drag the bottom edge of the chart up to the bottom edge of row 22 and then release the mouse button to resize the chart.

- Click the More button in the Chart Styles gallery to expand the gallery and point to Style 2 in the gallery (column 2, row 1) (Figure 1–80).

Figure 1–80

- Click Style 2 in the Chart Styles gallery to apply the chart style Style 2 to the chart.

Experiment

- Select other chart styles in the Chart Styles gallery to apply other chart styles to the chart, but select Style 2 as your final choice.

- Click cell I9 to deselect the chart and complete the worksheet (Figure 1–81).

Q&A What is the purpose of the items on the right side of the chart?

The items to the right of the column chart in Figure 1–81 are the **legend**, which identifies the colors assigned to each bar in the chart. Excel automatically selects the entries in the leftmost column of the chart range (column A) as titles within the legend.

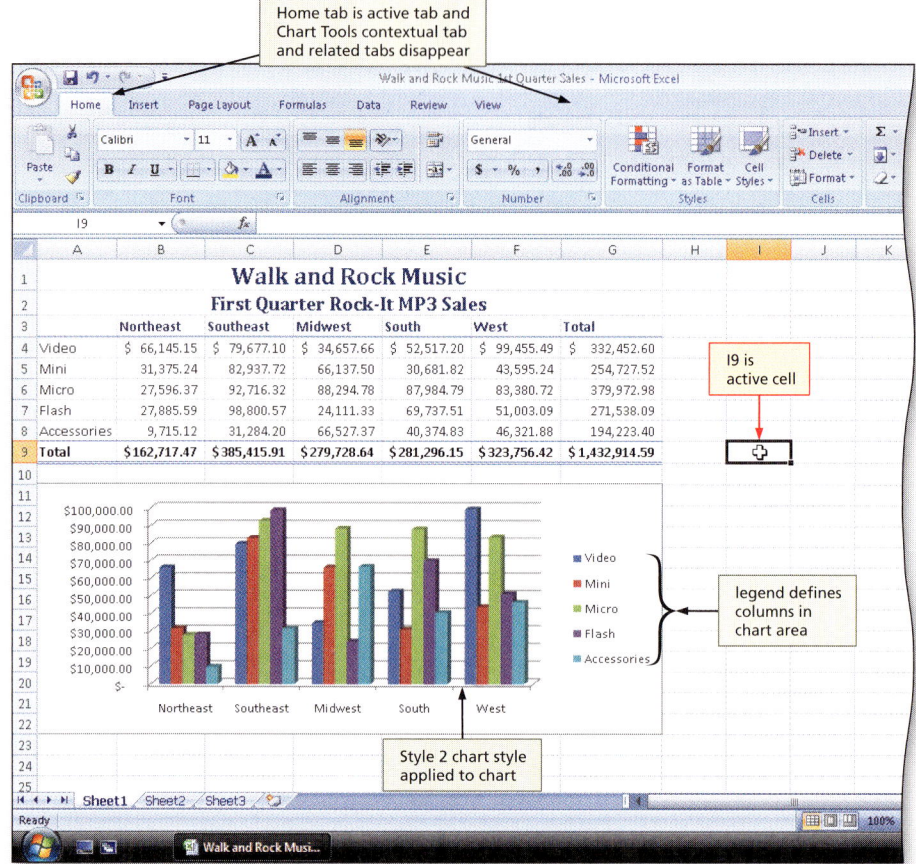

Figure 1–81

Changing Document Properties and Saving Again

BTW

Document Properties
Excel allows you to assign additional document properties by clicking the Document Properties button arrow in the Document Information Panel and then clicking Advanced Properties. You can assign custom properties, such as Department, Purpose, and Editor. Or, you can create your own document properties.

Excel helps you organize and identify your files by using **document properties**, which are the details about a file. Document properties, also known as **metadata**, can include such information as the project author, title, or subject. **Keywords** are words or phrases that further describe the document. For example, a class name or worksheet topic can describe the file's purpose or content. Document properties are valuable for a variety of reasons:

- Users can save time locating a particular file because they can view a document's properties without opening the workbook.
- By creating consistent properties for files having similar content, users can better organize their workbooks.
- Some organizations require Excel users to add document properties so that other employees can view details about these files.

Five different types of document properties exist, but the more common ones used in this book are standard and automatically updated properties. **Standard properties** are associated with all Microsoft Office documents and include author, title, and subject. **Automatically updated properties** include file system properties, such as the date you create or change a file, and statistics, such as the file size.

To Change Document Properties

The **Document Information Panel** contains areas where you can view and enter document properties. You can view and change information in this panel at any time while you are creating your workbook. Before saving the workbook again, you want to add your name and class name as document properties. The following steps use the Document Information Panel to change document properties.

1

- Click the Office Button to display the Office Button menu.

- Point to Prepare on the Office Button menu to display the Prepare submenu (Figure 1–82).

Q&A What other types of actions besides changing properties can you take to prepare a document for distribution?

The Prepare submenu provides commands related to sharing a document with others, such as allowing or restricting people to view and modify your document, checking to see if your worksheet will work in earlier versions of Excel, and searching for hidden personal information.

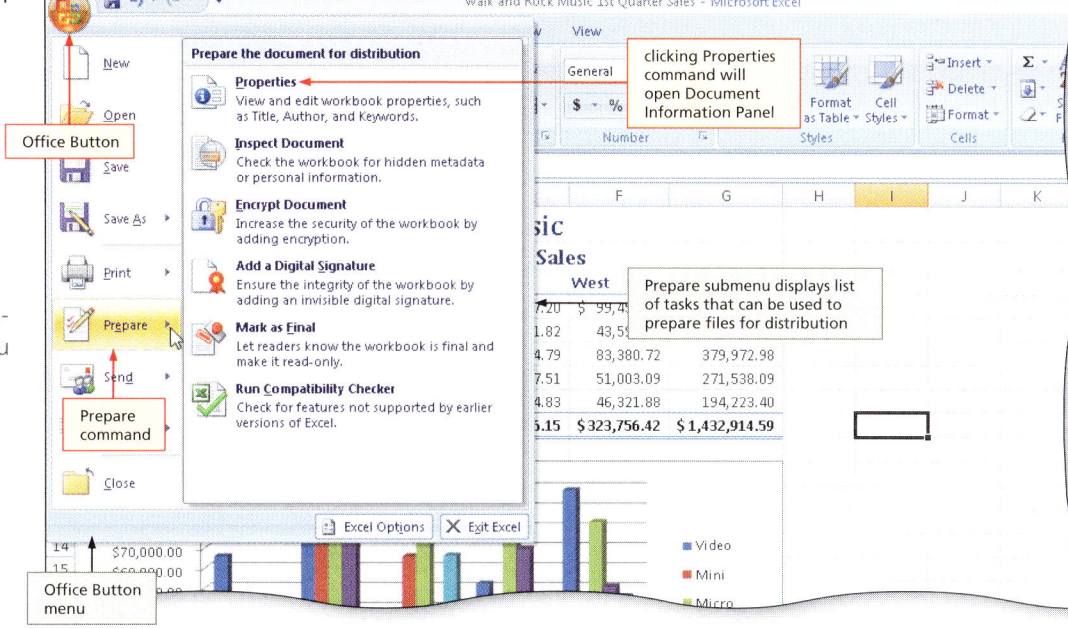

Figure 1–82

2

- Click Properties on the Prepare submenu to display the Document Information Panel (Figure 1–83).

Q&A Why are some of the document properties in my Document Information Panel already filled in?

The person who installed Microsoft Office 2007 on your computer or network may have set or customized the properties.

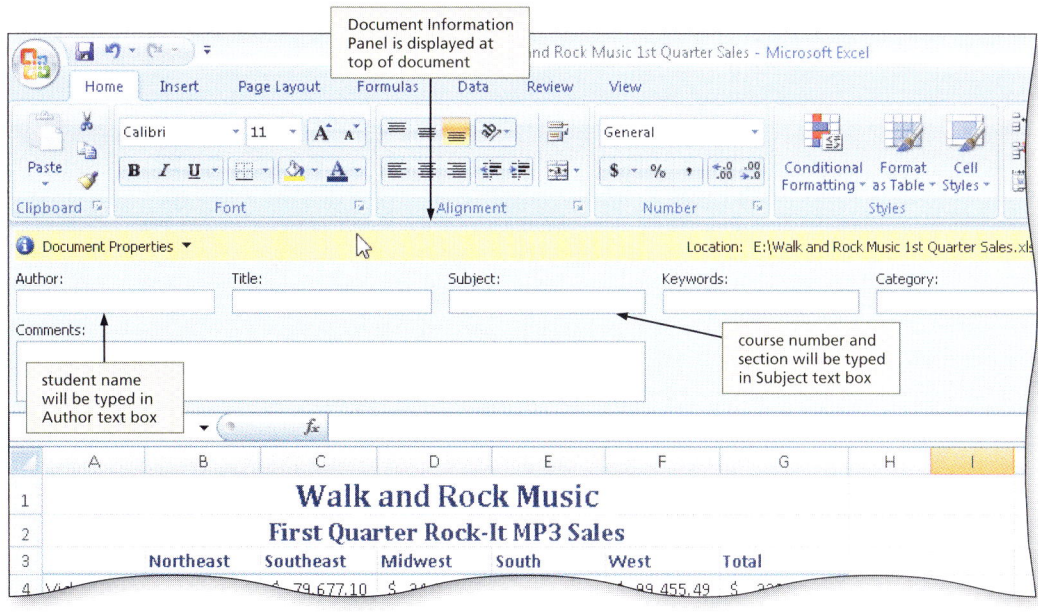

Figure 1–83

3

- Click the Author text box and then type your name as the Author property. If a name already is displayed in the Author text box, delete it before typing your name.

- Click the Subject text box, if necessary delete any existing text, and then type your course and section as the Subject property.

- Click the Keywords text box, if necessary delete any existing text, and then type `First Quarter Rock-It MP3 Sales` (Figure 1–84).

 Q&A What types of document properties does Excel collect automatically?

Excel records such details as how long you worked at creating your project, how many times you revised the document, and what fonts and themes are used.

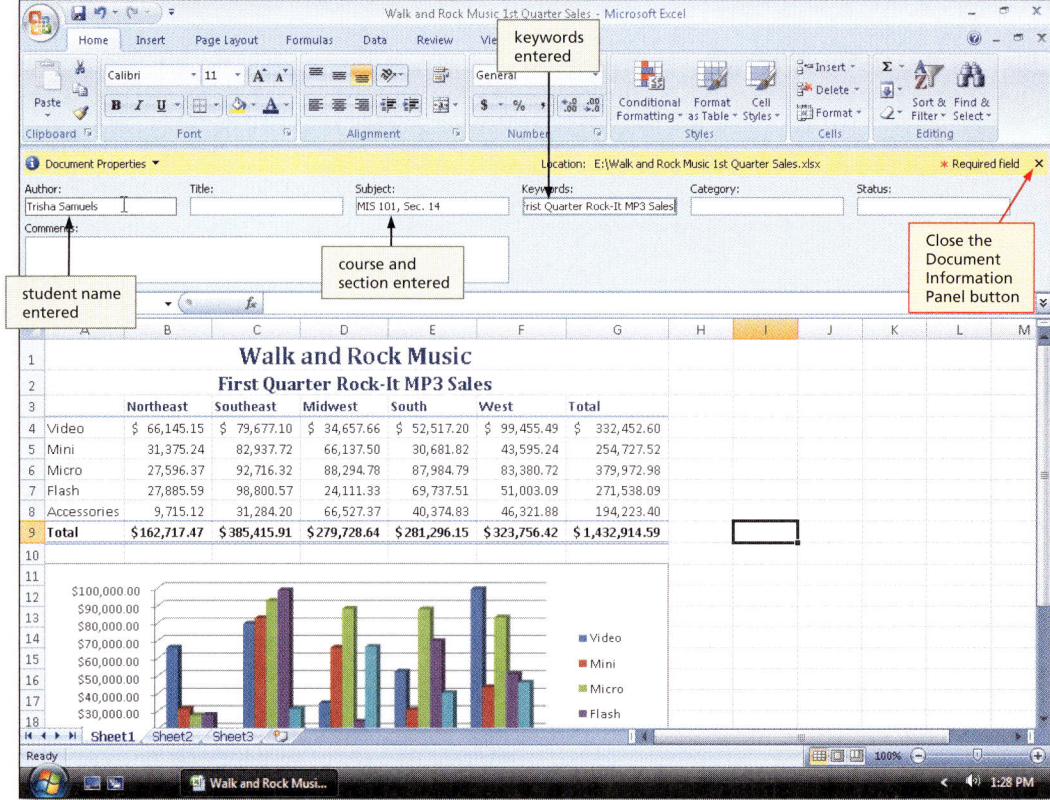

Figure 1–84

4

- Click the Close the Document Information Panel button so that the Document Information Panel no longer is displayed.

To Save an Existing Workbook with the Same File Name

Saving frequently cannot be overemphasized. Several modifications have been made to the workbook since it was saved earlier in the chapter. Earlier in this chapter, the Save button on the Quick Access Toolbar caused the Save As dialog box to appear, and the file name, Walk and Rock Music 1st Quarter Sales, was entered. Clicking the Save button on the Quick Access Toolbar causes Excel to save the changes made to the workbook since the last time it was saved. The following step saves the workbook again.

Creating a Worksheet and an Embedded Chart Excel Chapter 1 **EX 57**

1
- With your USB flash drive connected to one of the computer's USB ports, click the Save button on the Quick Access Toolbar to overwrite the previous Walk and Rock Music 1st Quarter Sales file on the USB flash drive (Figure 1–85).

Q&A

Why did the Save As dialog box not appear?

Excel overwrites the document using the settings specified the first time the document was saved. To save the file with a different file name or on different media, display the Save As dialog box by clicking the Office Button and then clicking Save As on the Office Button menu. Then, fill in the Save As dialog box as described in Steps 2 through 5 on pages EX 31 and EX 32.

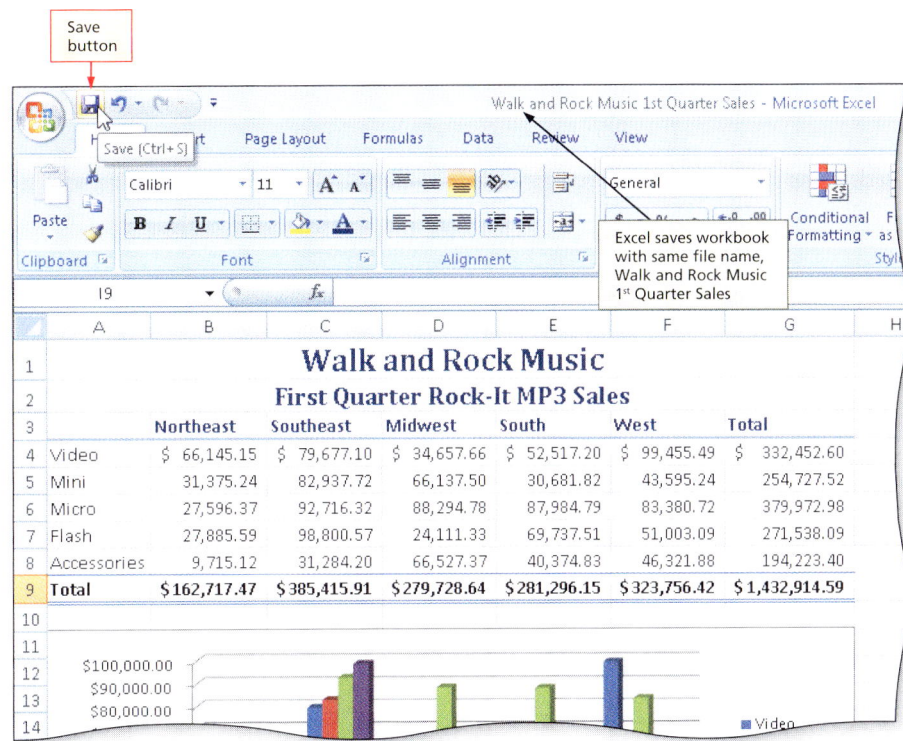

Figure 1–85

Other Ways

1. Press CTRL+S or press SHIFT+F12, press ENTER

Printing a Worksheet

After you create a worksheet, you often want to print it. A printed version of the worksheet is called a **hard copy** or **printout**. Printed copies of your worksheet can be useful for the following reasons:
- Many people prefer proofreading a hard copy of the worksheet rather than viewing the worksheet on the screen to check for errors and readability.
- Someone without computer access can view the worksheet's content.
- Copies can be distributed as handouts to people during a meeting or presentation.
- Hard copies can serve as reference material if your storage medium is lost or becomes corrupted and you need to recreate the worksheet.

It is a good practice to save a workbook before printing it, in the event you experience difficulties with the printer.

To Print a Worksheet

With the completed worksheet saved, you may want to print it. The following steps print the worksheet in the saved Walk and Rock Music 1st Quarter Sales workbook.

1
- Click the Office Button to display the Office Button menu.
- Point to Print on the Office Button menu to display the Print submenu (Figure 1–86).

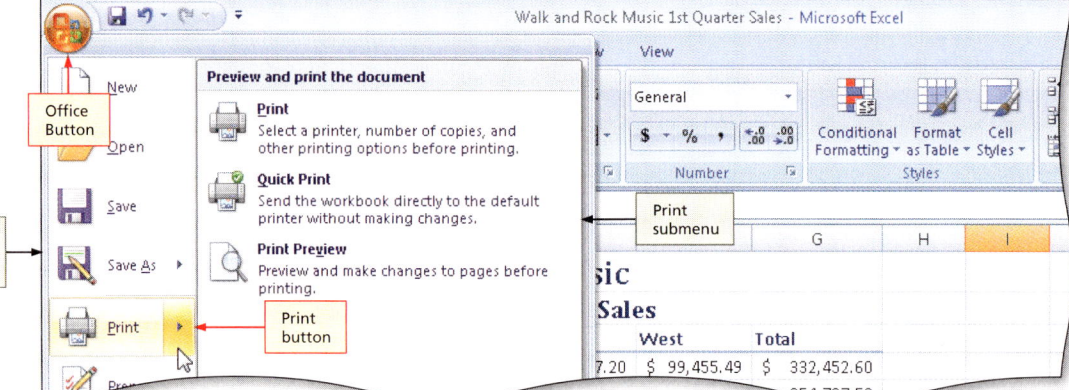

Figure 1–86

2
- Click Quick Print on the Print submenu to print the document (Figure 1–87).

 Can I print my document in black and white to conserve ink or toner?

Yes. Click the Office Button and then click the Excel Options button on the Office Button menu. When the Excel Options dialog box is displayed, click Advanced, scroll to the Print area, place a check mark in the 'Use draft quality' check box if it is displayed, and then click the OK button. Click the Office Button, point to Print, and then click Quick Print.

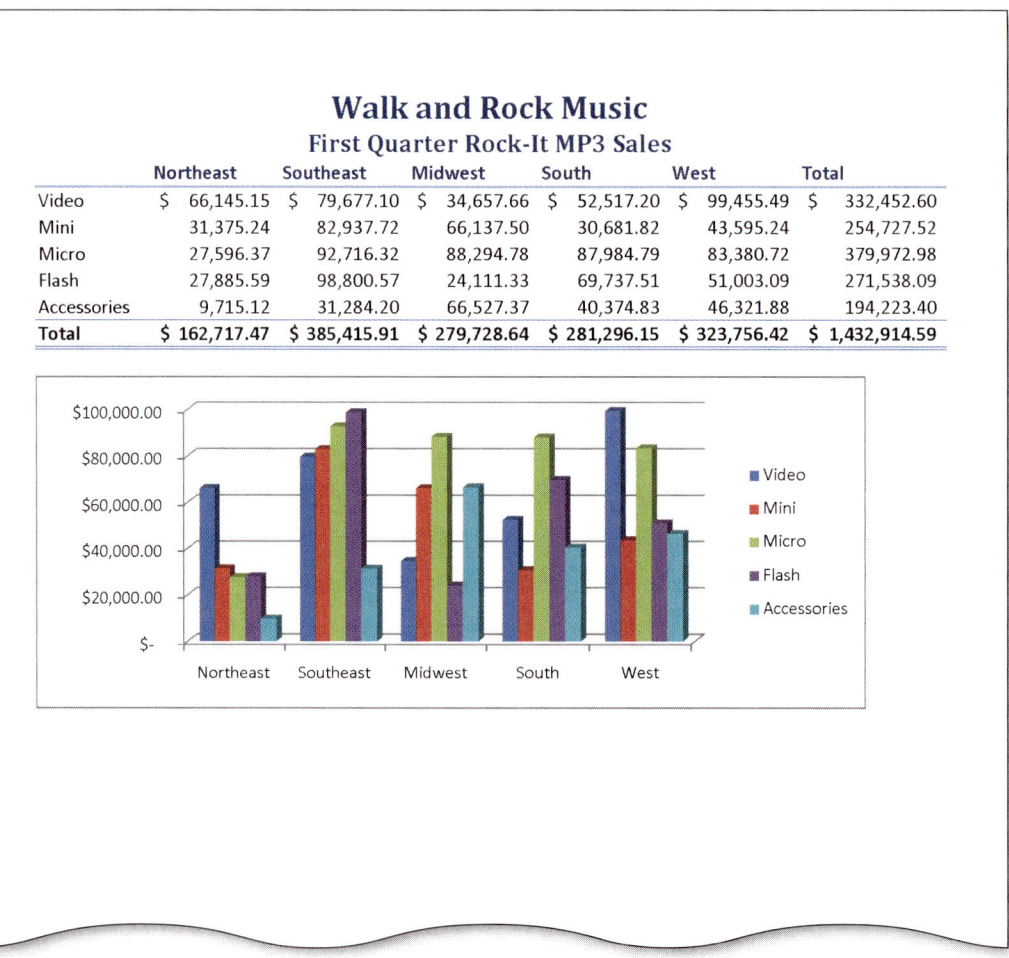

Figure 1–87

Other Ways
1. Press CTRL+P, press ENTER

Quitting Excel

When you quit Excel, if you have made changes to a workbook since the last time the file was saved, Excel displays a dialog box asking if you want to save the changes you made to the file before it closes that window. The dialog box contains three buttons with these resulting actions:

- Yes button — Saves the changes and then quits Excel
- No button — Quits Excel without saving changes
- Cancel button — Closes the dialog box and redisplays the worksheet without saving the changes

If no changes have been made to an open workbook since the last time the file was saved, Excel will close the window without displaying a dialog box.

To Quit Excel with One Workbook Open

The Walk and Rock 1st Quarter Sales worksheet is complete. The following steps quit Excel if only one workbook is open.

1
- Point to the Close button on the right side of the Excel title bar (Figure 1–88).

2
- Click the Close button to quit Excel.

Q&A

What if I have more than one Excel workbook open?

You would click the Close button on the Excel title bar for each open workbook. When you click the Close button with the last workbook open, Excel also quits. As an alternative, you could click the Office Button and then click the Exit Excel button on the Office Button menu, which closes all open workbooks and then quits Excel.

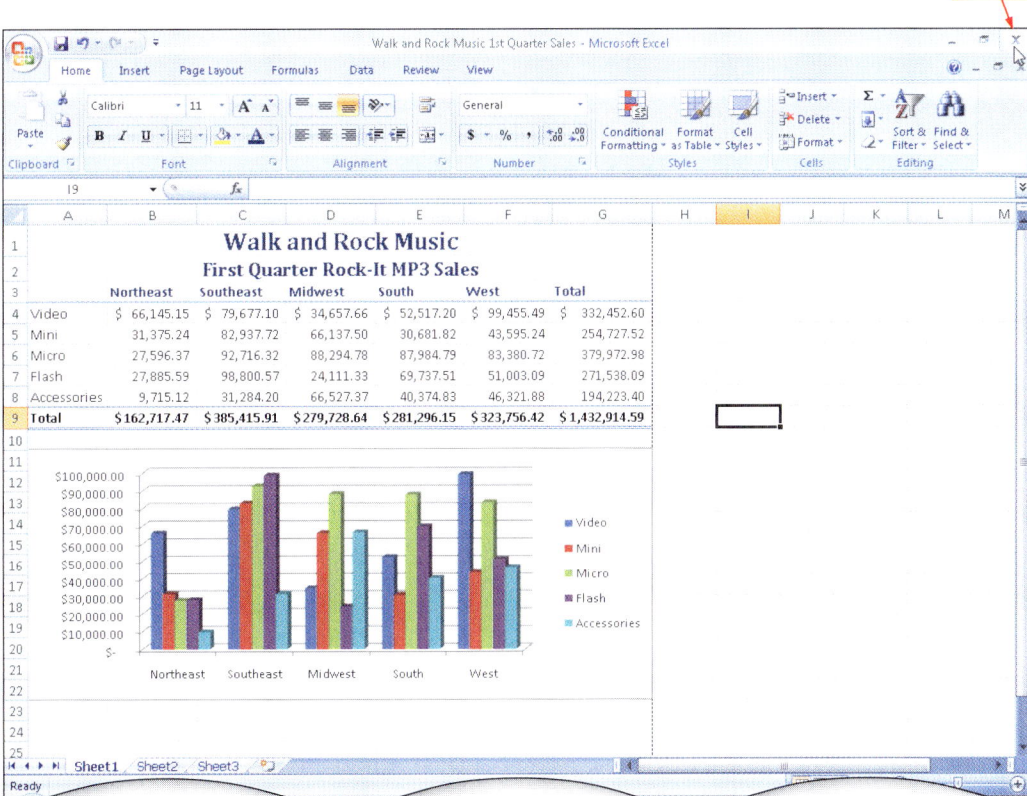

Figure 1–88

Other Ways

1. Double-click Office Button
2. With multiple workbooks open, click Office Button, click Exit Excel on Office Button menu
3. Right-click Microsoft Excel button on Windows Vista taskbar, click Close on shortcut menu
4. Press ALT+F4

BTW

Print Preview
You can preview the printout on your screen using the Print Preview command on the Print submenu (Figure 1–86 on page EX 58), make adjustments to the worksheet, and then print it only when it appears exactly as you want. Each time you preview rather than print, you save both ink and paper.

Starting Excel and Opening a Workbook

Once you have created and saved a workbook, you may need to retrieve it from your storage medium. For example, you might want to revise a worksheet or reprint it. Opening a workbook requires that Excel is running on your computer.

To Start Excel

The following steps, which assume Windows Vista is running, start Excel.

1 Click the Start button on the Windows Vista taskbar to display the Start menu.

2 Click All Programs at the bottom of the left pane on the Start menu to display the All Programs list and then click Microsoft Office in the All Programs list to display the Microsoft Office list.

3 Click Microsoft Office Excel 2007 in the Microsoft Office list to start Excel and display a new blank worksheet in the Excel window.

4 If the Excel window is not maximized, click the Maximize button on its title bar to maximize the window.

To Open a Workbook from Excel

Earlier in this chapter, the workbook was saved on a USB flash drive using the file name, Walk and Rock Music 1st Quarter Sales. The following steps open the Walk and Rock Music 1st Quarter Sales file from the USB flash drive.

1
- With your USB flash drive connected to one of the computer's USB ports, click the Office Button to display the Office Button menu (Figure 1–89).

Q&A

What files are shown in the Recent Documents list?

Excel displays the most recently opened document file names in this list. If the name of the file you want to open appears in the Recent Documents list, you could double-click it to open the file.

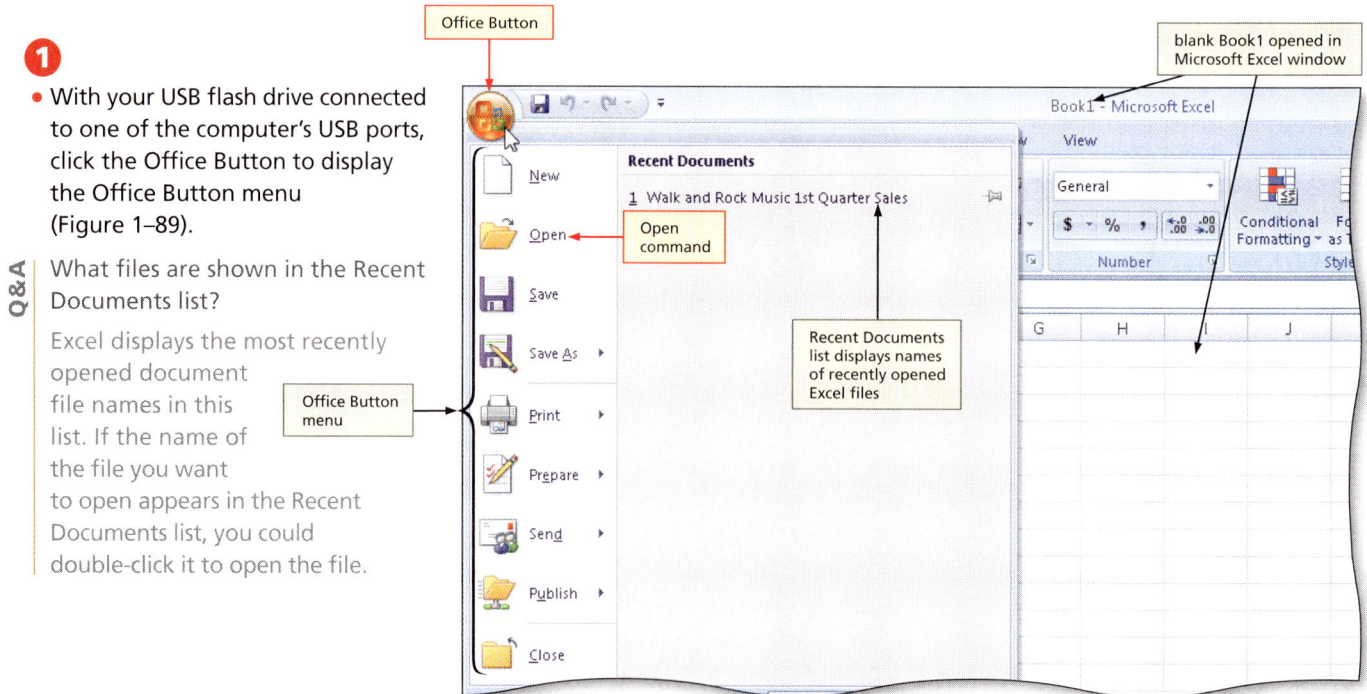

Figure 1–89

2

- Click Open on the Office Button menu to display the Open dialog box.

- If the Folders list is displayed below the Folders button, click the Folders button to remove the Folders list.

- If necessary, click Computer in the Favorite Links section and then scroll until UDISK 2.0 (E:) appears in the list of available drives.

- Double-click UDISK 2.0 (E:) to select the USB flash drive, Drive E in this case, as the new open location.

- Click Walk and Rock Music 1st Quarter Sales to select the file name (Figure 1–90).

Q&A How do I open the file if I am not using a USB flash drive?

Use the same process, but be certain to select your device in the Computer list.

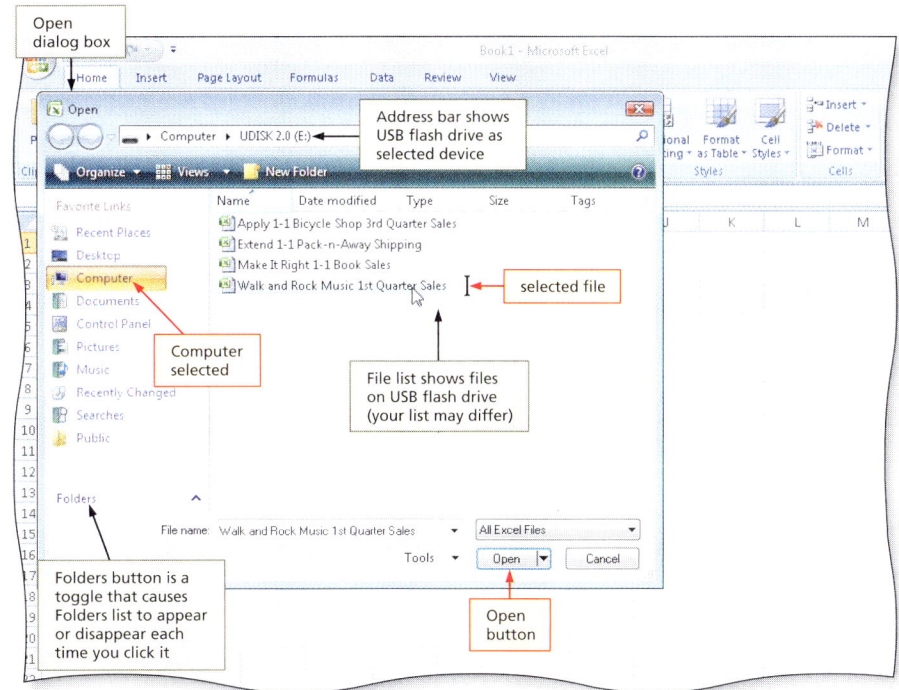

Figure 1–90

3

- Click the Open button to open the selected file and display the worksheet in the Excel window (Figure 1–91).

Q&A Why do I see the Microsoft Excel icon and name on the Windows Vista taskbar?

When you open an Excel file, the program name (Microsoft Excel) is displayed on a selected button on the Windows Vista taskbar. If you point to this button, the file name also appears in a ScreenTip.

Other Ways

1. Click Office Button, double-click file name in Recent Documents list
2. Press CTRL+O, select file name, press ENTER

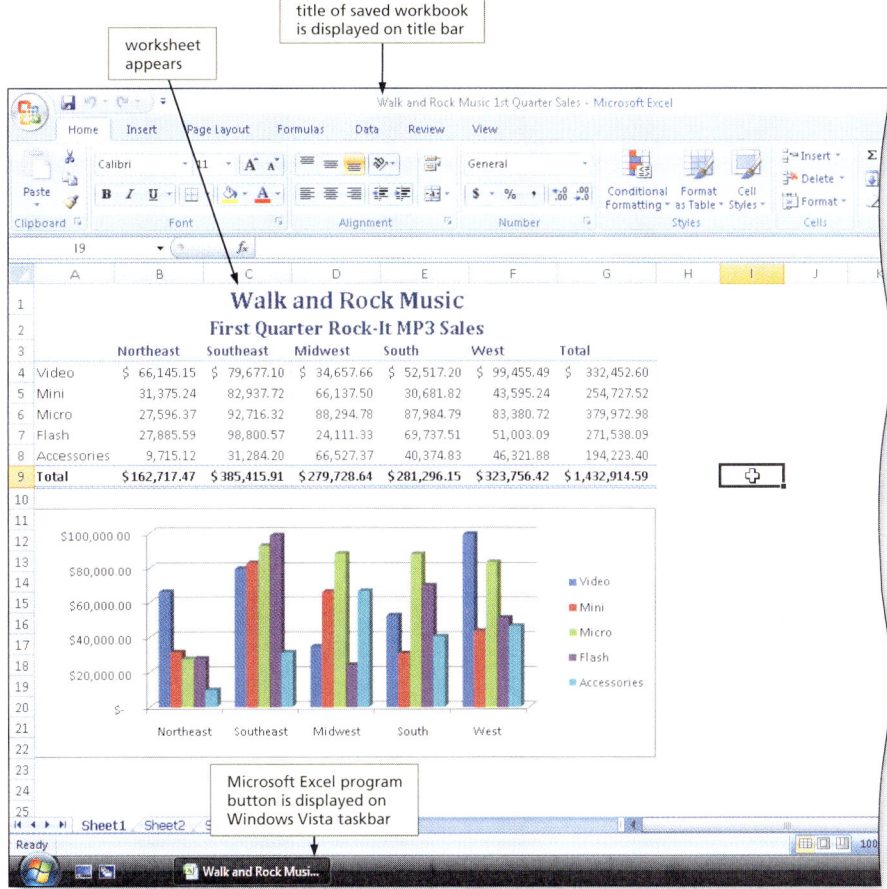

Figure 1–91

BTW

AutoCalculate
Use the AutoCalculate area on the status bar to check your work as you enter data in a worksheet. If you enter large amounts of data, you select a range of data and then check the AutoCalculate area to provide insight into statistics about the data you entered. Often, you will have an intuitive feel for whether the numbers are accurate or if you may have made a mistake while entering the data.

AutoCalculate

You easily can obtain a total, an average, or other information about the numbers in a range by using the **AutoCalculate area** on the status bar. First, select the range of cells containing the numbers you want to check. Next, right-click the AutoCalculate area to display the Status Bar Configuration shortcut menu (Figure 1–92). The check mark to the left of the active functions (Average, Count, and Sum) indicates that the sum, count, and average of the selected range are displayed in the AutoCalculate area on the status bar. The functions of the AutoCalculate commands on the Status Bar Configuration shortcut menu are described in Table 1–4.

Table 1–4 AutoCalculate Shortcut Menu Commands

Command	Function
Average	AutoCalculate area displays the average of the numbers in the selected range
Count	AutoCalculate area displays the number of nonblank cells in the selected range
Numerical Count	AutoCalculate area displays the number of cells containing numbers in the selected range
Minimum	AutoCalculate area displays the lowest value in the selected range
Maximum	AutoCalculate area displays the highest value in the selected range
Sum	AutoCalculate area displays the sum of the numbers in the selected range

To Use the AutoCalculate Area to Determine a Maximum

The following steps display the largest quarterly sales for any region for the Micro product type.

- Select the range B6:F6 and then right-click the AutoCalculate area on the status bar to display the Status Bar Configuration shortcut menu (Figure 1–92).

Q&A

What is displayed on the Status Bar Configuration shortcut menu?

This shortcut menu includes several commands that allow you to control the items displayed on the Customize Status Bar shortcut menu. The AutoCalculate area of the shortcut menu includes six commands as well as the result of the associated calculation on the right side of the menu.

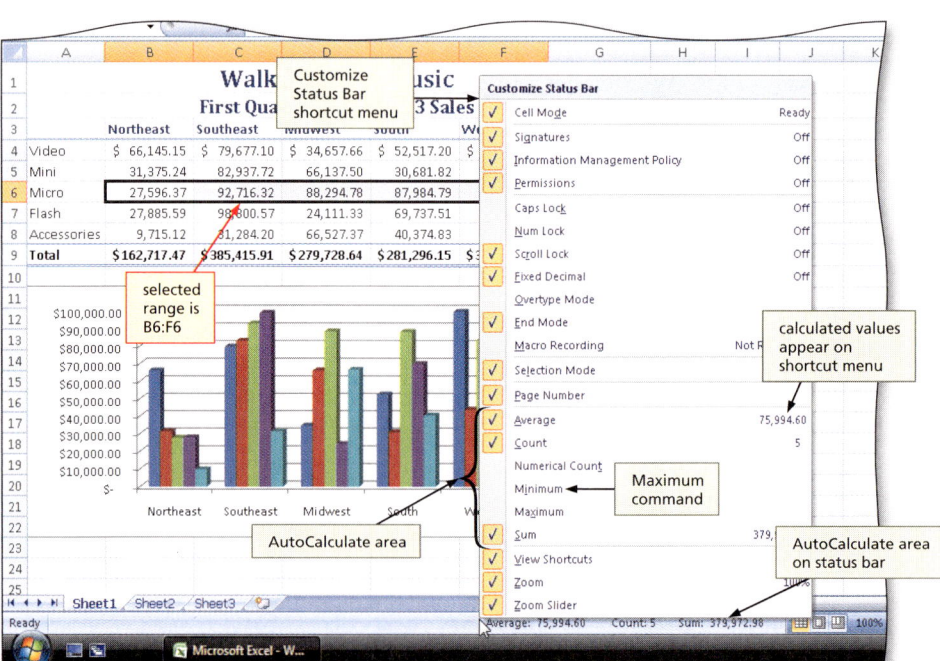

Figure 1–92

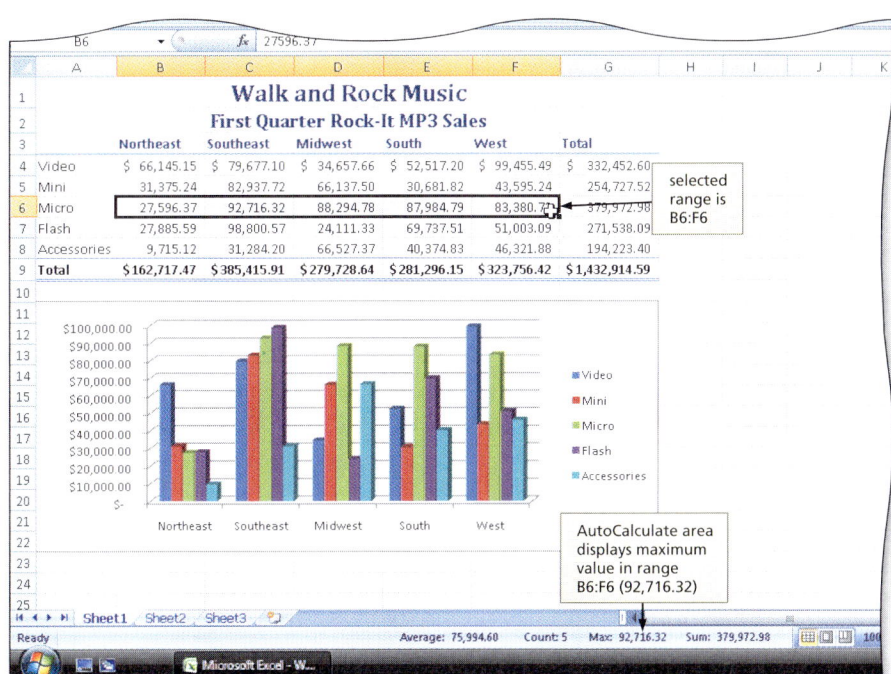

Figure 1–93

2
- Click Maximum on the shortcut menu to display the Maximum value in the range B6:F6 in the AutoCalculate area of the status bar.
- Click anywhere on the worksheet to cause the shortcut menu to disappear (Figure 1–93).

3
- Right-click the AutoCalculate area and then click Maximum on the shortcut menu to cause the Maximum value to no longer appear in the AutoCalculate area.

Correcting Errors

You can correct errors on a worksheet using one of several methods. The method you choose will depend on the extent of the error and whether you notice it while typing the data or after you have entered the incorrect data into the cell.

Correcting Errors while You Are Typing Data into a Cell

If you notice an error while you are typing data into a cell, press the BACKSPACE key to erase the incorrect characters and then type the correct characters. If the error is a major one, click the Cancel box in the formula bar or press the ESC key to erase the entire entry and then reenter the data from the beginning.

Correcting Errors after Entering Data into a Cell

If you find an error in the worksheet after entering the data, you can correct the error in one of two ways:

1. If the entry is short, select the cell, retype the entry correctly, and then click the Enter box or press the ENTER key. The new entry will replace the old entry.
2. If the entry in the cell is long and the errors are minor, using Edit mode may be a better choice than retyping the cell entry. Use the Edit mode as described below.
   a. Double-click the cell containing the error to switch Excel to Edit mode. In **Edit mode**, Excel displays the active cell entry in the formula bar and a flashing

BTW

In-Cell Editing
An alternative to double-clicking the cell to edit it is to select the cell and then press the F2 key.

insertion point in the active cell (Figure 1–94). With Excel in Edit mode, you can edit the contents directly in the cell — a procedure called **in-cell editing**.

b. Make changes using in-cell editing, as indicated below.

(1) To insert new characters between two characters, place the insertion point between the two characters and begin typing. Excel inserts the new characters at the location of the insertion point.

(2) To delete a character in the cell, move the insertion point to the left of the character you want to delete and then press the DELETE key or place the insertion point to the right of the character you want to delete and then press the BACKSPACE key. You also can use the mouse to drag through the character or adjacent characters you want to delete and then press the DELETE key or click the Cut button on the Home tab on the Ribbon.

(3) When you are finished editing an entry, click the Enter box or press the ENTER key.

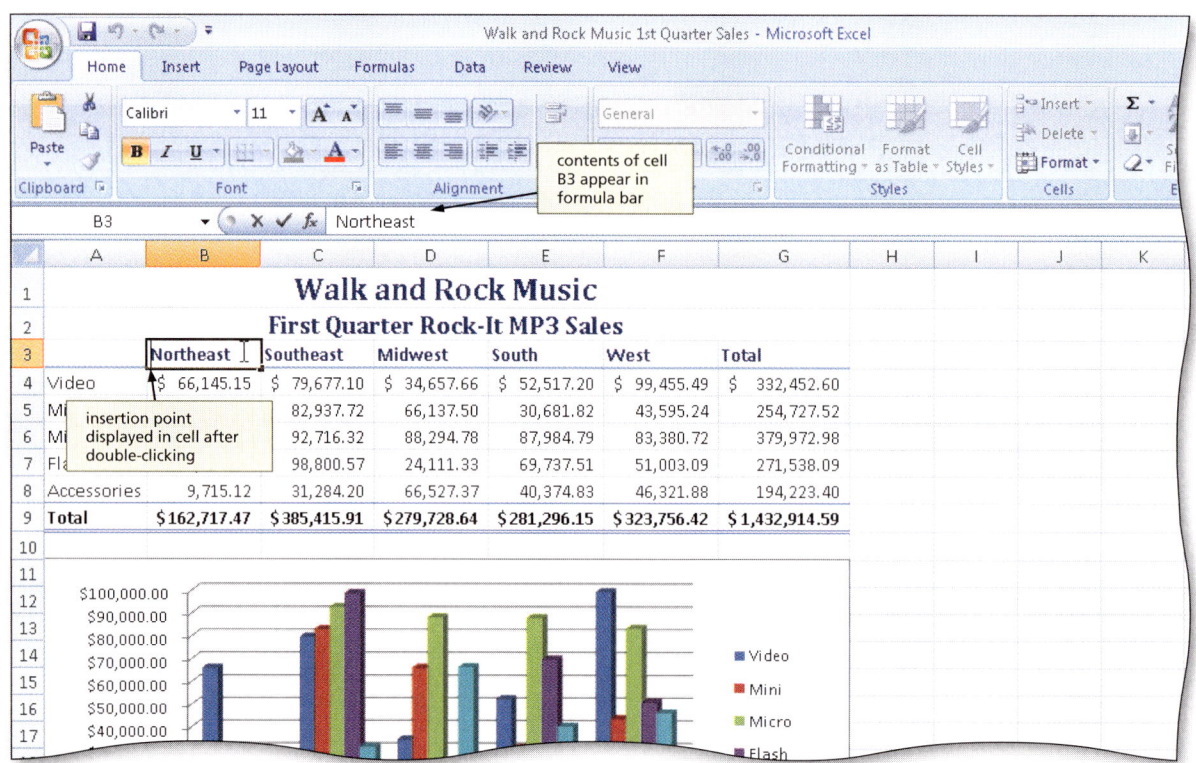

Figure 1–94

When Excel enters the Edit mode, the keyboard usually is in Insert mode. In **Insert mode**, as you type a character, Excel inserts the character and moves all characters to the right of the typed character one position to the right. You can change to Overtype mode by pressing the INSERT key. In **Overtype mode**, Excel overtypes, or replaces, the character to the right of the insertion point. The INSERT key toggles the keyboard between Insert mode and Overtype mode.

While in Edit mode, you may have reason to move the insertion point to various points in the cell, select portions of the data in the cell, or switch from inserting characters to overtyping characters. Table 1–5 summarizes the more common tasks used during in-cell editing.

BTW

Editing the Contents of a Cell
Rather than using in-cell editing, you can select the cell and then click the formula bar to edit the contents.

Table 1–5 Summary of In-Cell Editing Tasks

	Task	Mouse	Keyboard
1	Move the insertion point to the beginning of data in a cell.	Point to the left of the first character and click.	Press HOME
2	Move the insertion point to the end of data in a cell.	Point to the right of the last character and click.	Press END
3	Move the insertion point anywhere in a cell.	Point to the appropriate position and click the character.	Press RIGHT ARROW or LEFT ARROW
4	Highlight one or more adjacent characters.	Drag the mouse pointer through adjacent characters.	Press SHIFT+RIGHT ARROW or SHIFT+LEFT ARROW
5	Select all data in a cell.	Double-click the cell with the insertion point in the cell if there are no spaces in the data in the cell.	
6	Delete selected characters.	Click the Cut button on the Home tab on the Ribbon.	Press DELETE
7	Delete characters to the left of the insertion point.		Press BACKSPACE
8	Delete characters to the right of the insertion point.		Press DELETE
9	Toggle between Insert and Overtype modes.		Press INSERT

Undoing the Last Cell Entry

Excel provides the Undo command on the Quick Access Toolbar (Figure 1–95), which allows you to erase recent cell entries. Thus, if you enter incorrect data in a cell and notice it immediately, click the Undo button and Excel changes the cell entry to what it was prior to the incorrect data entry.

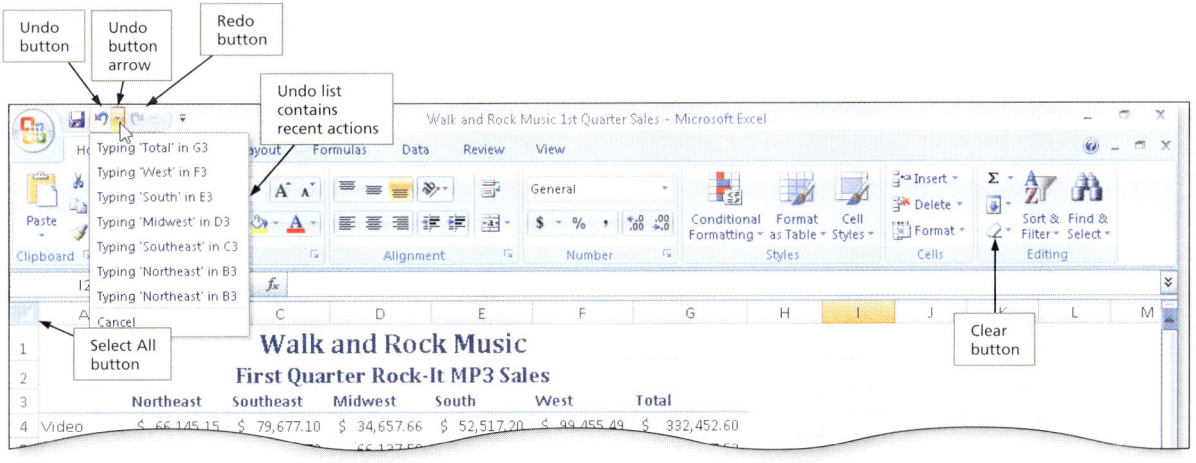

Figure 1–95

Excel remembers the last 100 actions you have completed. Thus, you can undo up to 100 previous actions by clicking the Undo button arrow to display the Undo list and then clicking the action to be undone (Figure 1–95). You can drag through several actions in the Undo list to undo all of them at once. If no actions are available for Excel to undo, then the Undo button is dimmed and inoperative.

The Redo button, next to the Undo button on the Quick Access Toolbar, allows you to repeat previous actions.

BTW

Quick Reference
For a table that lists how to complete the tasks covered in this book using the mouse, Ribbon, shortcut menu, and keyboard, see the Quick Reference Summary at the back of this book, or visit the Excel 2007 Quick Reference Web page (scsite.com/dc-off07/qr).

Clearing a Cell or Range of Cells

If you enter data into the wrong cell or range of cells, you can erase, or clear, the data using one of the first four methods listed below. The fifth method clears the formatting from the selected cells.

To Clear Cell Entries Using the Fill Handle

1. Select the cell or range of cells and then point to the fill handle so the mouse pointer changes to a crosshair.
2. Drag the fill handle back into the selected cell or range until a shadow covers the cell or cells you want to erase. Release the mouse button.

To Clear Cell Entries Using the Shortcut Menu

1. Select the cell or range of cells to be cleared.
2. Right-click the selection.
3. Click Clear Contents on the shortcut menu.

To Clear Cell Entries Using the delete Key

1. Select the cell or range of cells to be cleared.
2. Press the DELETE key.

To Clear Cell Entries and Formatting Using the Clear Button

1. Select the cell or range of cells to be cleared.
2. Click the Clear button on the Home tab (Figure 1–95 on the previous page).
3. Click Clear Contents on the menu.

To Clear Formatting Using the Cell Styles Button

1. Select the cell or range of cells from which you want to remove the formatting.
2. Click the Cell Styles button on the Home tab and point to Normal.
3. Click Normal in the Cell Styles Gallery.

The Clear button on the Home tab is the only command that clears both the cell entry and the cell formatting. As you are clearing cell entries, always remember that you should *never press the* SPACEBAR *to clear a cell*. Pressing the SPACEBAR enters a blank character. A blank character is text and is different from an empty cell, even though the cell may appear empty.

BTW

Getting Back to Normal
If you accidentally assign unwanted formats to a range of cells, you can use the Normal cell style selection in the Cell Styles gallery. Click Cell Styles on the Home tab on the Ribbon and then click Normal. Doing so changes the format to Normal style. To view the characteristics of the Normal style, right-click the style in the Cell Styles gallery and then click Modify, or press ALT+APOSTROPHE (').

Clearing the Entire Worksheet

If required worksheet edits are extremely extensive, you may want to clear the entire worksheet and start over. To clear the worksheet or delete an embedded chart, use the following steps.

To Clear the Entire Worksheet

1. Click the Select All button on the worksheet (Figure 1–95).
2. Click the Clear button on the Home tab to delete both the entries and formats.

The Select All button selects the entire worksheet. Instead of clicking the Select All button, you also can press CTRL+A. To clear an unsaved workbook, click the workbook's Close Window button or click the Close command on the Office Button menu. Click the No button if the Microsoft Excel dialog box asks if you want to save changes. To start a new, blank workbook, click the New command on the Office Button menu.

To delete an embedded chart, complete the following steps.

BTW

Excel Help
The best way to become familiar with Excel Help is to use it. Appendix B includes detailed information about Excel Help and exercises that will help you gain confidence in using it.

TO DELETE AN EMBEDDED CHART
1. Click the chart to select it.
2. Press the DELETE key.

Excel Help

At any time while using Excel, you can find answers to questions and display information about various topics through **Excel Help**. This section introduces you to Excel Help.

To Search for Excel Help

Using Excel Help, you can search for information based on phrases such as save a workbook or format a chart, or key terms such as copy, save, or format. Excel Help responds with a list of search results displayed as links to a variety of resources. The following steps, which use Excel Help to search for information about formatting a chart, assume you are connected to the Internet.

1
- Click the Microsoft Office Excel Help button near the upper-right corner of the Excel window to open the Excel Help window.

- Type `format a chart` in the Type words to search for text box at the top of the Excel Help window (Figure 1–96).

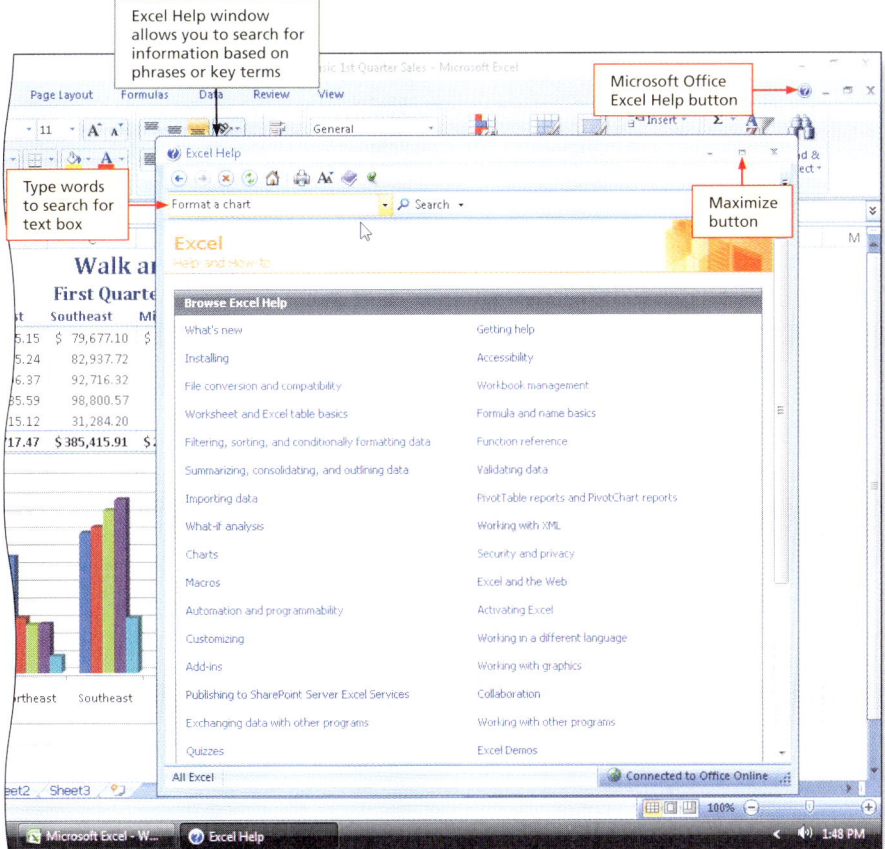

Figure 1–96

2

- Press the ENTER key to display the search results.

- Click the Maximize button on the Excel Help window title bar to maximize the Help window (Figure 1–97).

Q&A Where is the Excel window with the Walk and Rock Music 1st Quarter Sales worksheet?

Excel is open in the background, but the Excel Help window is overlaid on top of the Microsoft Excel window. When the Excel Help window is closed, the worksheet will reappear.

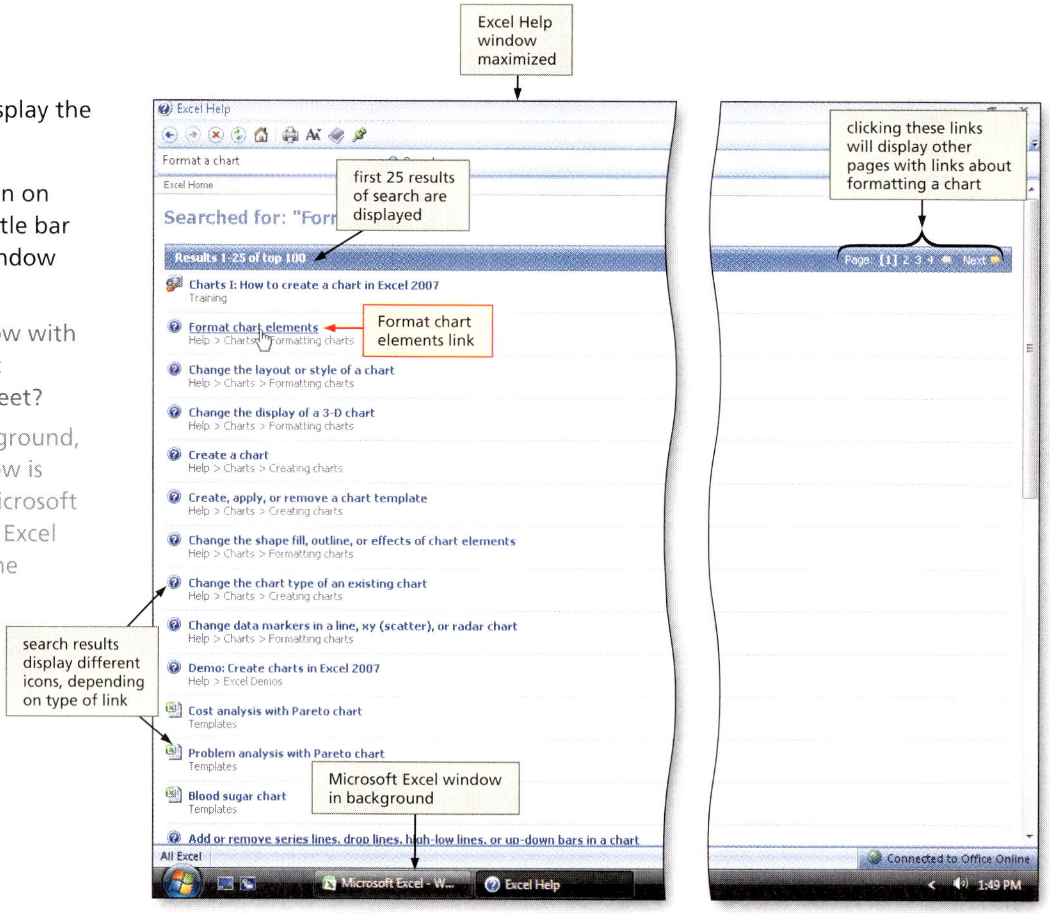

Figure 1–97

3

- Click the Format chart elements link to display information regarding formatting chart elements (Figure 1–98).

Q&A What is the purpose of the buttons at the top of the Excel Help window?

Use the buttons in the upper-left corner of the Excel Help window to navigate through the Help system, change the display, show the Excel Help table of contents, and print the contents of the window.

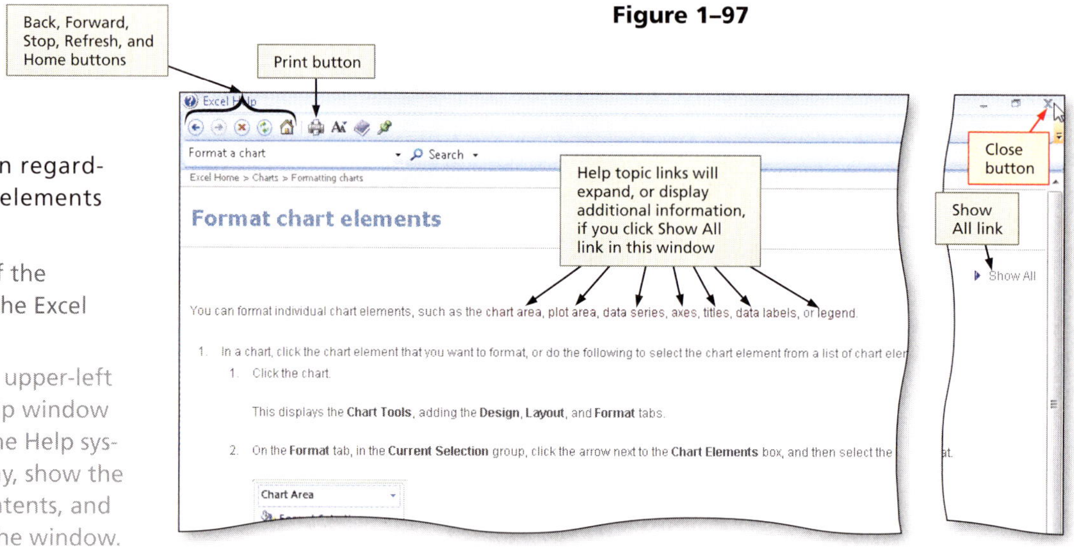

Figure 1–98

4

- Click the Close button on the Excel Help window title bar to close the Excel Help window and make Excel active.

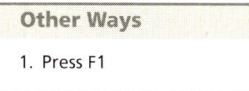

Other Ways
1. Press F1

To Quit Excel

The following steps quit Excel.

1. Click the Close button on the right side of the title bar to quit Excel; or if you have multiple Excel workbooks open, click the Office Button and then click the Exit Excel button on the Office Button menu to close all open workbooks and quit Excel.

2. If necessary, click the No button in the Microsoft Office Excel dialog box so that any changes you have made are not saved.

> **BTW**
>
> **Quitting Excel**
> Do not forget to remove your USB flash drive from the USB port after quitting Excel, especially if you are working in a laboratory environment. Nothing can be more frustrating than leaving all of your hard work behind on a USB flash drive for the next user.

Chapter Summary

In this chapter you have learned about the Excel window, how to enter text and numbers to create a worksheet, how to select a range, how to use the Sum button, save a workbook, format cells, insert a chart, print a worksheet, quit Excel, and use Excel Help. The items listed below include all the new Excel skills you have learned in this chapter.

1. Start Excel (EX 6)
2. Enter the Worksheet Titles (EX 17)
3. Enter Column Titles (EX 19)
4. Enter Row Titles (EX 21)
5. Enter Numbers (EX 23)
6. Sum a Column of Numbers (EX 25)
7. Copy a Cell to Adjacent Cells in a Row (EX 27)
8. Determine Multiple Totals at the Same Time (EX 28)
9. Save a Workbook (EX 30)
10. Change a Cell Style (EX 35)
11. Change the Font Type (EX 36)
12. Bold a Cell (EX 38)
13. Increase the Font Size of a Cell Entry (EX 38)
14. Change the Font Color of a Cell Entry (EX 39)
15. Center Cell Entries across Columns by Merging Cells (EX 40)
16. Format Column Titles and the Total Row (EX 42)
17. Format Numbers in the Worksheet (EX 44)
18. Adjust the Column Width (EX 46)
19. Use the Name Box to Select a Cell (EX 47)
20. Add a 3-D Clustered Column Chart to the Worksheet (EX 50)
21. Change Document Properties (EX 55)
22. Save an Existing Workbook with the Same File Name (EX 58)
23. Print a Worksheet (EX 58)
24. Quit Excel with One Workbook Open (EX 59)
25. Open a Workbook from Excel (EX 60)
26. Use the AutoCalculate Area to Determine a Maximum (EX 62)
27. Clear Cell Entries Using the Fill Handle (EX 66)
28. Clear Cell Entries Using the Shortcut Menu (EX 66)
29. Clear Cell Entries Using the DELETE Key (EX 66)
30. Clear Cell Entries and Formatting Using the Clear Button (EX 66)
31. Clear Formatting Using the Cell Styles Button (EX 66)
32. Clear the Entire Worksheet (EX 66)
33. Delete an Embedded Chart (EX 67)
34. Search for Excel Help (EX 67)

If you have a SAM user profile, you may have access to hands-on instruction, practice, and assessment. Log in to your SAM account (http://sam2007.course.com) to launch any assigned training activities or exams that relate to the skills covered in this chapter.

Learn It Online

Test your knowledge of chapter content and key terms.

Instructions: To complete the Learn It Online exercises, start your browser, click the Address bar, and then enter the Web address scsite.com/dc-off2007/ex2007/learn. When the Excel 2007 Learn It Online page is displayed, click the link for the exercise you want to complete and then read the instructions.

Chapter Reinforcement TF, MC, and SA
A series of true/false, multiple choice, and short answer questions that test your knowledge of the chapter content.

Flash Cards
An interactive learning environment where you identify chapter key terms associated with displayed definitions.

Practice Test
A series of multiple choice questions that test your knowledge of chapter content and key terms.

Who Wants To Be a Computer Genius?
An interactive game that challenges your knowledge of chapter content in the style of a television quiz show.

Wheel of Terms
An interactive game that challenges your knowledge of chapter key terms in the style of the television show *Wheel of Fortune*.

Crossword Puzzle Challenge
A crossword puzzle that challenges your knowledge of key terms presented in the chapter.

Apply Your Knowledge

Reinforce the skills and apply the concepts you learned in this chapter.

Changing the Values in a Worksheet

Instructions: Start Excel. Open the workbook Apply 1-1 Bicycle Shop 3rd Quarter Sales (Figure 1–99a). See the inside back cover of this book for instructions for downloading the Data Files for Students, or contact your instructor for information on accessing the files required in this book.

1. Make the changes to the worksheet described in Table 1–6 so that the worksheet appears as shown in Figure 1–99b. As you edit the values in the cells containing numeric data, watch the totals in row 8, the totals in column G, and the chart change.

2. Change the worksheet title in cell A1 to the Title cell style and then merge and center it across columns A through G. Use commands in the Font group on the Home tab on the Ribbon to change the worksheet subtitle in cell A2 to 16-point Corbel red, bold font and then center it across columns A through G. Use the Accent 1 theme color (column 5, row 1 on the Font Color palette) for the red font color.

3. Update the document properties with your name, course number, and name for the workbook. Save the workbook using the file name, Apply 1-1 Spoke-Up Bicycle Shop 3rd Quarter Sales. Submit the assignment as requested by your instructor.

Table 1–6 New Worksheet Data

Cell	Change Cell Contents To
A1	Spoke-Up Bicycle Shop
B4	11869.2
E4	9157.83
D6	5217.92
F6	6239.46
B7	3437.64

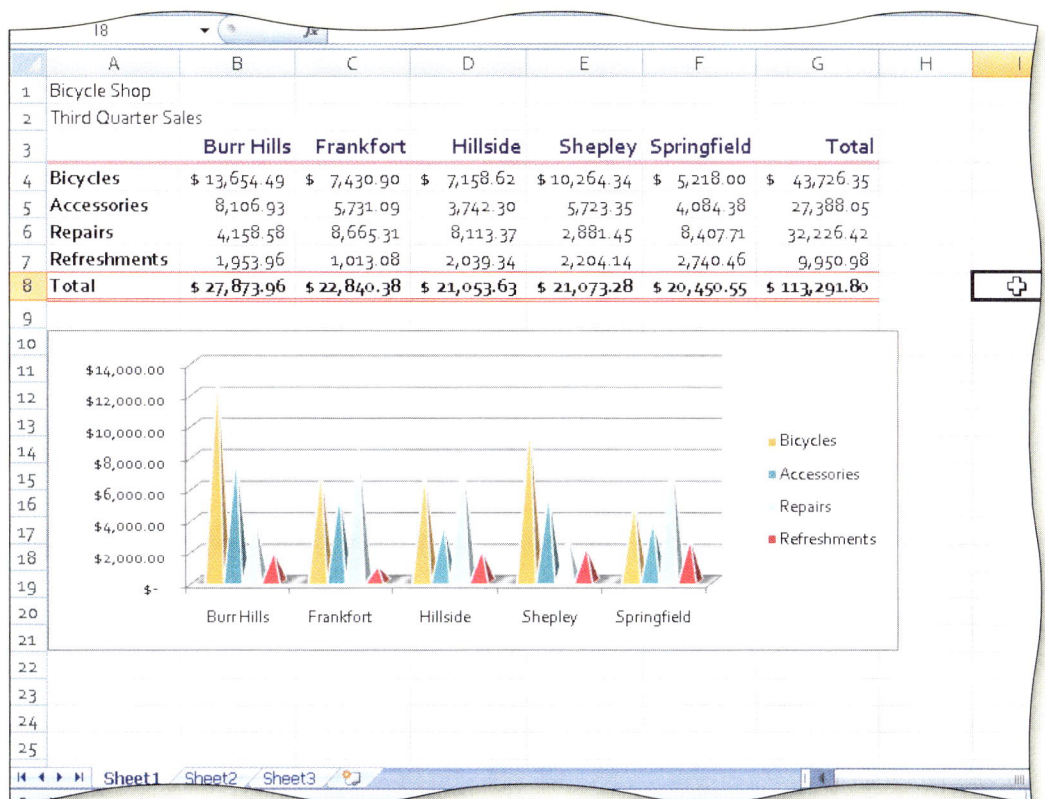

(a) Before

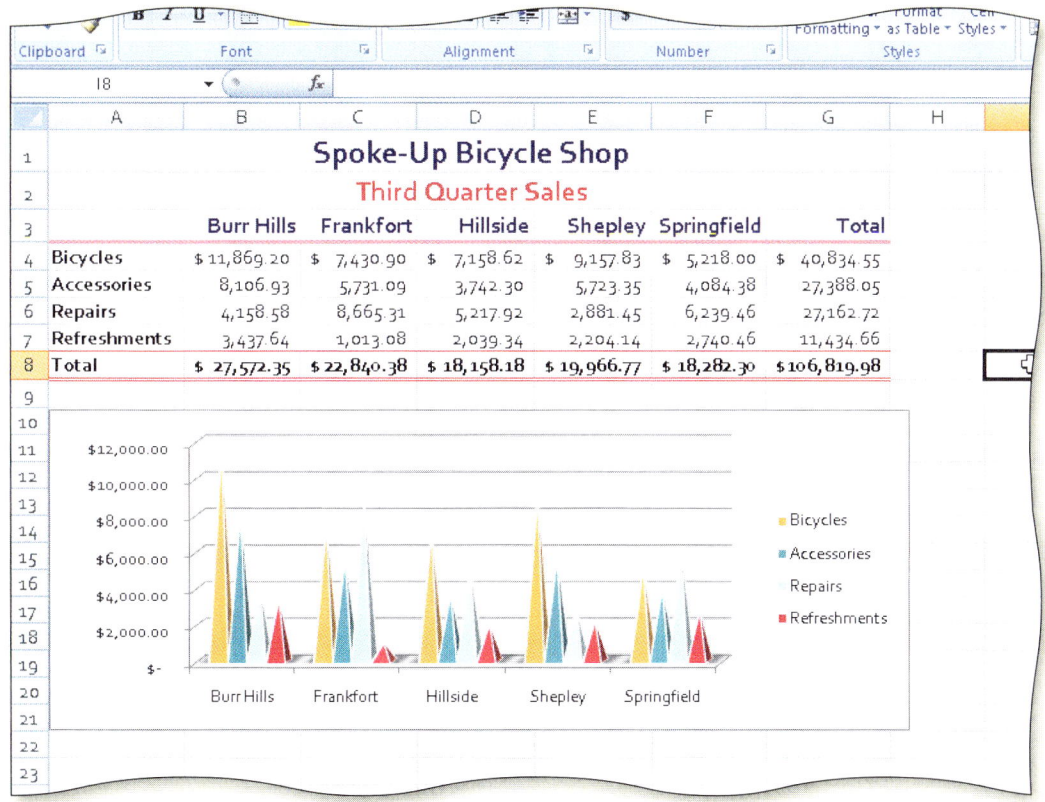

(b) After

Figure 1–99

Extend Your Knowledge

Extend the skills you learned in this chapter and experiment with new skills. You may need to use Help to complete the assignment.

Formatting Cells and Inserting Multiple Charts

Instructions: Start Excel. Open the workbook Extend 1-1 Pack-n-Away Shipping. See the inside back cover of this book for instructions for downloading the Data Files for Students, or contact your instructor for information on accessing the files required in this book. Perform the following tasks to format cells in the worksheet and to add two charts to the worksheet.

1. Use the commands in the Font group on the Home tab on the Ribbon to change the font of the title in cell A1 to 24-point Arial, red; bold and subtitle of the worksheet to 16-point Arial Narrow, blue, bold.
2. Select the range A3:E8, click the Insert tab on the Ribbon, and then click the Dialog Box Launcher in the Charts group on the Ribbon to open the Insert Chart dialog box (Figure 1–100).

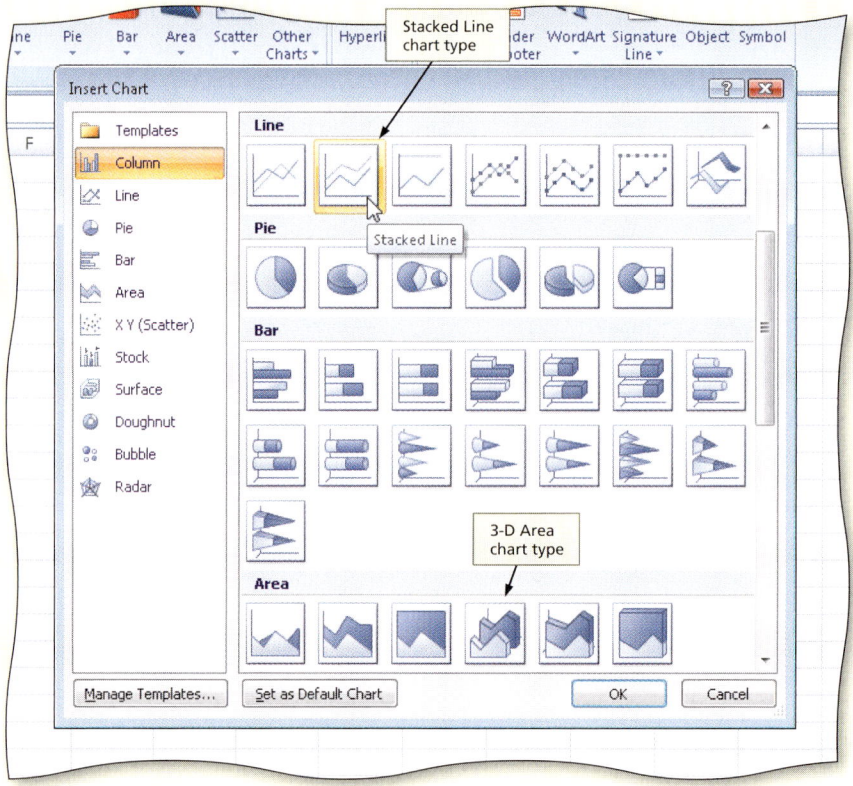

Figure 1–100

3. Insert a Stacked Line chart by clicking the Stacked Line chart in the gallery and then clicking the OK button. Move the chart either below or to the right of the data in the worksheet. Click the Design tab and apply a chart style to the chart.
4. If necessary, reselect the range A3:E8 and follow Step 3 above to insert a 3-D Area chart in the worksheet. You may need to use the scroll box on the right side of the Insert Chart dialog box to view the Area charts in the gallery. Move the chart either below or to the right of the data so that each chart does not overlap the Stacked Line chart. Choose a different chart style for this chart than the one you selected for the Stacked Line chart.

Creating a Worksheet and an Embedded Chart   Excel Chapter 1   EX 73

5. Resize each chart so that each snaps to the worksheet gridlines. Make certain that both charts are visible with the worksheet data without the need to scroll the worksheet.
6. Update the document properties with your name, course number, and name for the workbook.
7. Save the workbook using the file name, Extend 1-1 Pack-n-Away Shipping Charts. Submit the assignment as requested by your instructor.

Make It Right

Analyze a workbook and correct all errors and/or improve the design.

Correcting Formatting and Values in a Worksheet

Instructions: Start Excel. Open the workbook Make It Right 1-1 Book Sales. See the inside back cover of this book for instructions for downloading the Data Files for Students, or contact your instructor for information on accessing the files required for this book. Correct the following formatting problems and data errors (Figure 1–101) in the worksheet, while keeping in mind the guidelines presented in this chapter.

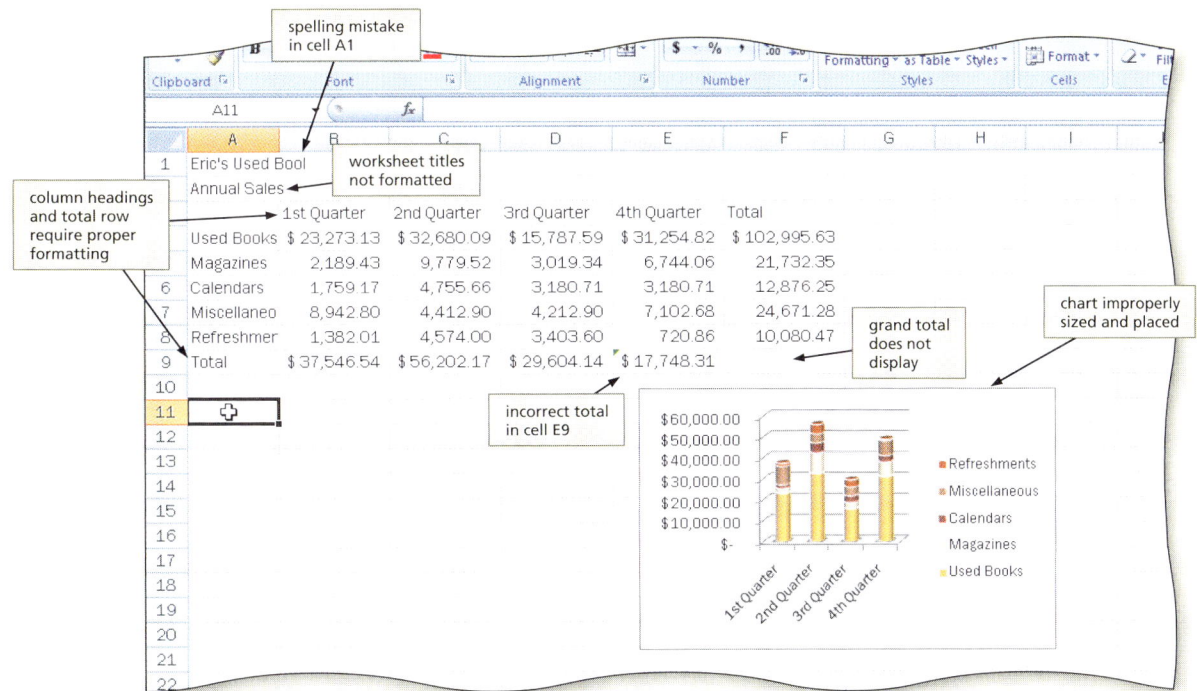

Figure 1–101

1. Merge and center the worksheet title and subtitle appropriately.
2. Format the worksheet title with a cell style appropriate for a worksheet title.
3. Format the subtitle using commands in the Font group on the Ribbon.
4. Correct the spelling mistake in cell A1 by changing Bool to Books.
5. Apply proper formatting to the column headers and total row.

Continued >

Make It Right *continued*

6. Adjust column sizes so that all data in each column is visible.
7. Use the SUM function to create the grand total for annual sales.
8. The SUM function in cell E9 does not sum all of the numbers in the column. Correct this error by editing the range for the SUM function in the cell.
9. Resize and move the chart so that it is below the worksheet data and does not extend past the right edge of the worksheet data. Be certain to snap the chart to the worksheet gridlines by holding down the ALT key as you resize the chart.
10. Update the document properties with your name, course number, and name for the workbook. Save the workbook using the file name, Make It Right 1-1 Eric's Used Books Annual Sales. Submit the assignment as requested by your instructor.

In the Lab

Design and/or create a workbook using the guidelines, concepts, and skills presented in this chapter. Labs 1, 2, and 3 are listed in order of increasing difficulty.

Lab 1: Annual Cost of Goods Worksheet

Problem: You work part-time as a spreadsheet specialist for Kona's Expresso Coffee, one of the up-and-coming coffee franchises in the United States. Your manager has asked you to develop an annual cost of goods analysis worksheet similar to the one shown in Figure 1–102.

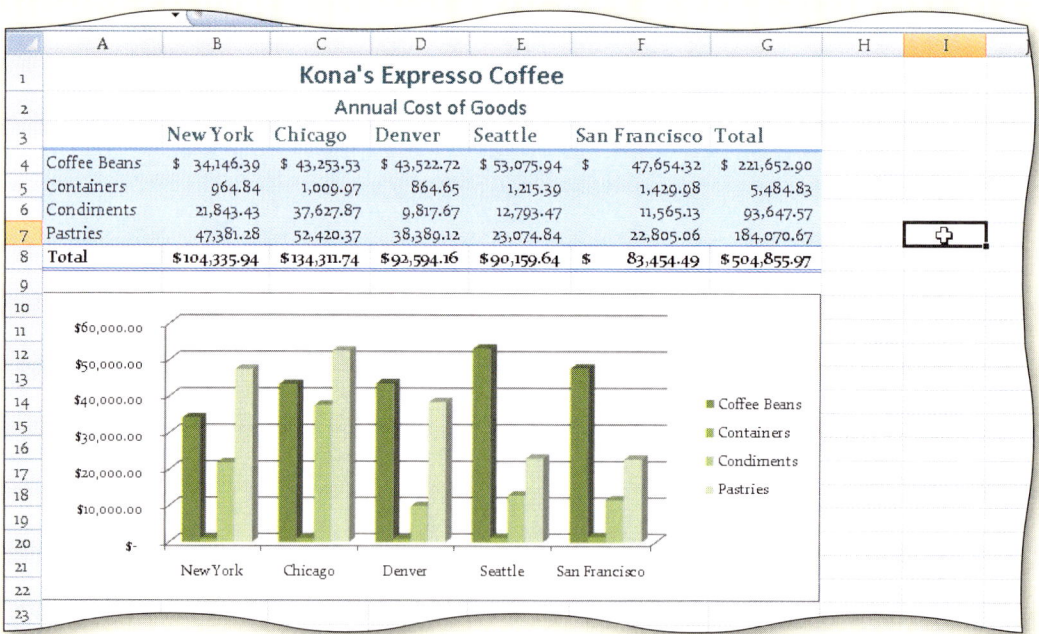

Figure 1–102

Instructions: Perform the following tasks.
1. Start Excel. Enter the worksheet title, Kona's Expresso Coffee, in cell A1 and the worksheet subtitle, Annual Cost of Goods, in cell A2. Beginning in row 3, enter the store locations, costs of goods, and supplies categories shown in Table 1–7.

Table 1–7 Kona's Expresso Coffee Annual Cost of Goods

	New York	Chicago	Denver	Seattle	San Franscisco
Coffee Beans	34146.39	43253.53	43522.72	53075.94	47654.32
Containers	964.84	1009.97	864.65	1215.39	1429.98
Condiments	21843.43	37627.87	9817.67	12793.47	11565.13
Pastries	47381.28	52420.37	38389.12	23074.84	22805.06

2. Use the SUM function to determine the totals for each store location, type of supply, and company grand total.
3. Use Cell Styles in the Styles group on the Home tab on the Ribbon to format the worksheet title with the Title cell style. Center the title across columns A through G. Do not be concerned if the edges of the worksheet title are not displayed.
4. Use buttons in the Font group on the Home tab on the Ribbon to format the worksheet subtitle to 14-point Calibri dark blue, bold font, and center it across columns A through G.
5. Use Cell Styles in the Styles group on the Home tab on the Ribbon to format the range A3:G3 with the Heading 2 cell style, the range A4:G7 with the 20% - Accent1 cell style, and the range A8:G8 with the Total cell style. Use the buttons in the Number group on the Home tab on the Ribbon to apply the Accounting Number format to the range B4:G4 and the range B8:G8. Use the buttons in the Number group on the Home tab on the Ribbon to apply the Comma Style to the range B5:G7. Adjust any column widths to the widest text entry in each column.
6. Select the range A3:F7 and then insert a 3-D Clustered Column chart. Apply the Style 8 chart style to the chart. Move and resize the chart so that it appears in the range A10:G22. If the labels along the horizontal axis (x-axis) do not appear as shown in Figure 1-102, then drag the right side of the chart so that it is displayed in the range A10:G22.
7. Update the document properties with your name, course number, and name for the workbook.
8. Save the workbook using the file name Lab 1-1 Konas Expresso Coffee Annual Cost of Goods.
9. Print the worksheet.
10. Make the following two corrections to the sales amounts: $9,648.12 for Seattle Condiments (cell E6), $12,844.79 for Chicago Pastries (cell C7). After you enter the corrections, the company totals in cell G8 should equal $462,135.04.
11. Print the revised worksheet. Close the workbook without saving the changes. Submit the assignment as requested by your instructor.

In the Lab

Lab 2: Annual Sales Analysis Worksheet

Problem: As the chief accountant for Scissors Office Supply, Inc., you have been asked by the sales manager to create a worksheet to analyze the annual sales for the company by location and customer type category (Figure 1–103). The office locations and corresponding sales by customer type for the year are shown in Table 1–8.

Continued >

In the Lab continued

Instructions: Perform the following tasks.
1. Create the worksheet shown in Figure 1–103 using the data in Table 1–8.
2. Use the SUM function to determine totals sales for the four offices, the totals for each customer type, and the company total. Add column and row headings for the totals row and totals column, as appropriate.

Table 1–8 Scissors Office Supply Annual Sales

	Boston	Miami	St. Louis	Santa Fe
Consumer	206348.81	113861.40	69854.13	242286.82
Small Business	235573.28	133511.24	199158.35	228365.51
Large Business	237317.55	234036.08	126519.10	111773.38
Government	178798.04	144548.80	135470.86	132599.75
Nonprofit	15180.63	28837.75	63924.48	21361.42

3. Format the worksheet title with the Title cell style and center it across columns A through F. Use the Font group on the Ribbon to format the worksheet subtitle to 16-point Cambria green, and bold font. Center the title across columns A through F.

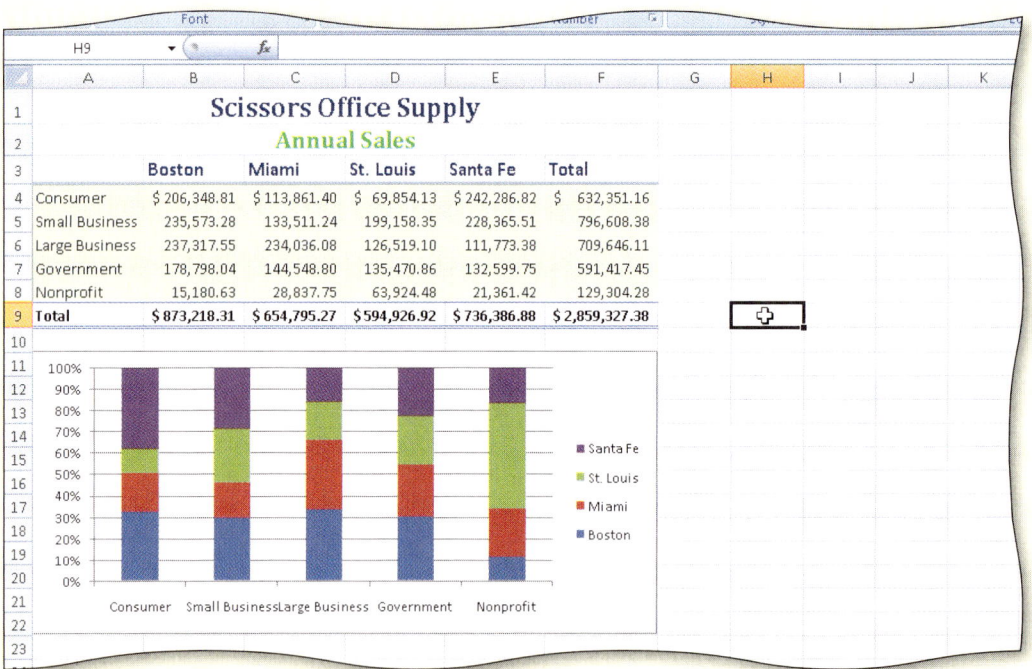

Figure 1–103

4. Format the range A3:F3 with the Heading 2 cell style, the range A4:F8 with the 20% - Accent3 cell style, and the range A9:F9 with the Total cell style. Use the Number group on the Ribbon to format cells B4:F4 and B9:F9 with the Accounting Number Format and cells B5:F8 with the Comma Style numeric format. Adjust the width of column A in order to fit contents of the column.

5. Chart the range A3:E8. Insert a 100% Stacked Column chart for the range A3:E8, as shown in Figure 1–103, by using the Column button on the Insert tab on the Ribbon. Use the chart location A11:F22.

6. Update the document properties with your name, course number, and name for the workbook.
7. Save the workbook using the file name, Lab 1-2 Scissors Office Supply Annual Sales. Print the worksheet.
8. Two corrections to the figures were sent in from the accounting department. The correct sales are $98,342.16 for Miami's annual Small Business sales (cell C5) and $48,933.75 for St. Louis's annual Nonprofit sales (cell D8). After you enter the two corrections, the company total in cell F9 should equal $2,809,167.57. Print the revised worksheet.
9. Use the Undo button to change the worksheet back to the original numbers in Table 1–8. Use the Redo button to change the worksheet back to the revised state.
10. Close Excel without saving the latest changes. Start Excel and open the workbook saved in Step 7. Double-click cell E6 and use in-cell editing to change the Santa Fe annual Large Business sales (cell E6) to $154,108.49. Write the company total in cell F9 at the top of the first printout. Click the Undo button.
11. Click cell A1 and then click the Merge & Center button to split cell A1 into cells A1, B1, C1, D1, E1, and F1. To merge the cells into one again, select the range A1:F1 and then click the Merge & Center button on the Home tab on the Ribbon.
12. Close the workbook without saving the changes. Submit the assignment as requested by your instructor.

In the Lab

Lab 3: College Cost and Financial Support Worksheet

Problem: Attending college is an expensive proposition and your resources are limited. To plan for your four-year college career, you have decided to organize your anticipated resources and costs in a worksheet. The data required to prepare your worksheet is shown in Table 1–9.

Table 1–9 College Cost and Resources

Cost	Freshman	Sophomore	Junior	Senior
Books	450.00	477.00	505.62	535.95
Room & Board	7500.00	7950.00	8427.00	8932.62
Tuition	8200.00	8692.00	9213.52	9766.33
Entertainment	1325.00	1404.50	1488.77	1578.10
Miscellaneous	950.00	1007.00	1067.42	1131.47
Clothes	725.00	768.50	814.61	863.49
Financial Support	**Freshman**	**Sophomore**	**Junior**	**Senior**
Job	3400.00	3604.00	3820.24	4049.45
Savings	4350.00	4611.00	4887.66	5180.92
Parents	4700.00	4982.00	5280.92	5597.78
Financial Aid	5500.00	5830.00	6179.80	6550.59
Other	1200.00	1272.00	1348.32	1429.22

Continued >

In the Lab *continued*

Instructions Part 1: Using the numbers in Table 1–9, create the worksheet shown in columns A through F in Figure 1–104. Format the worksheet title as Calibri 24-point bold red. Merge and center the worksheet title in cell A1 across columns A through F. Format the worksheet subtitles in cells A2 and A11 as Calibri 16-point bold green. Format the ranges A3:F3 and A12:F12 with the Heading 2 cell style, the ranges A4:F9 and A13:F17 with the 20% - Accent1 cell style, and the ranges A10:F10 and A18:F18 with the Total cell style.

Update the document properties, including the addition of at least one keyword to the properties, and save the workbook using the file name, Lab 1-3 Part 1 College Cost and Financial Support. Print the worksheet. Submit the assignment as requested by your instructor.

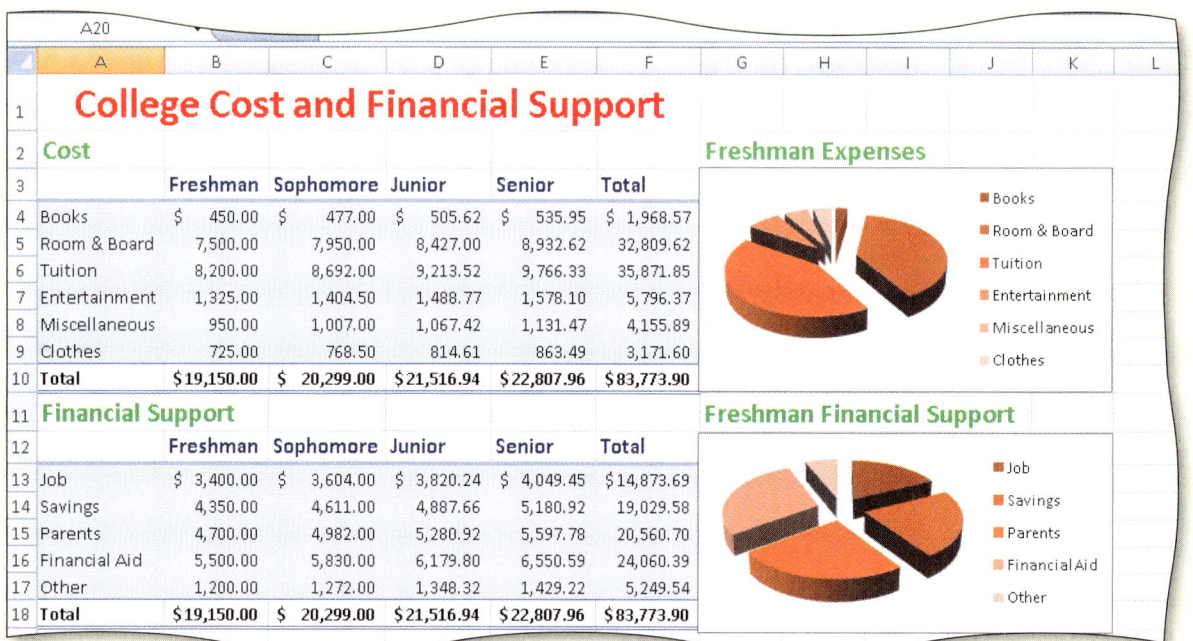

Figure 1–104

After reviewing the numbers, you realize you need to increase manually each of the Junior-year expenses in column D by $600. Change the Junior-year expenses to reflect this change. Manually change the financial aid for the Junior year in cell D16 by the amount required to cover the increase in costs. The totals in cells F10 and F18 should equal $87,373.90. Print the worksheet. Close the workbook without saving changes.

Instructions Part 2: Open the workbook Lab 1-3 Part 1 College Cost and Financial Support and then save the workbook using the file name, Lab 1-3 Part 2 College Cost and Financial Support. Insert an Exploded pie in 3-D chart in the range G3:K10 to show the contribution of each category of cost for the Freshman year. Chart the range A4:B9 and apply the Style 8 chart style to the chart. Add the Pie chart title as shown in cell G2 in Figure 1–104. Insert an Exploded pie in 3-D chart in the range G12:K18 to show the contribution of each category of financial support for the Freshman year. Chart the range A13:B17 and apply the Style 8 chart style to the chart. Add the Pie chart title shown in cell G11 in Figure 1–104. Update the identification area with the exercise part number and save the workbook. Print the worksheet. Submit the assignment as requested by your instructor.

Instructions Part 3: Open the workbook Lab 1-3 Part 2 College Cost and Financial Support. Do not save the workbook in this part. A close inspection of Table 1–9 shows that both cost and financial support figures increase 6% each year. Use Excel Help to learn how to enter the data for the last three years using a formula and the Copy and Paste buttons on the Home tab on the Ribbon. For example, the formula to enter in cell C4 is =B4*1.06. Enter formulas to replace all the numbers in the range C4:E9 and C13:E17. If necessary, reformat the tables, as described in Part 1. The worksheet should appear as shown in Figure 1–104, except that some of the totals will be off by 0.01 due to rounding errors. Save the worksheet using the file name, Lab 1-3 Part 3 College Cost and Financial Support. Print the worksheet. Press CTRL+ACCENT MARK (`) to display the formulas. Print the formulas version. Submit the assignment as requested by your instructor. Close the workbook without saving changes.

Cases and Places

Apply your creative thinking and problem solving skills to design and implement a solution.

• EASIER   •• MORE DIFFICULT

• 1: Design and Create a Workbook to Analyze Yearly Sales

You are working as a summer intern for Hit-the-Road Mobile Services. Your manager has asked you to prepare a worksheet to help her analyze historical yearly sales by type of product (Table 1–10). Use the concepts and techniques presented in this chapter to create the worksheet and an embedded 3-D Clustered Column chart.

Table 1–10 Hit-the-Road Mobile Services Sales

	2005	2006	2007	2008
Standard Mobile Phones	87598	99087	129791	188785
Camera Phones	71035	75909	96886	100512
Music Phones	65942	24923	34590	15696
Wireless PDAs	67604	58793	44483	35095
Satellite Radios	15161	27293	34763	43367
Headsets	9549	6264	2600	4048
Other Accessories	47963	108059	100025	62367

• 2: Design and Create a Worksheet and Chart to Analyze a Budget

To estimate the funds needed by your school's Environmental Club to make it through the upcoming year, you decide to create a budget for the club itemizing the expected quarterly expenses. The anticipated expenses are listed in Table 1–11. Use the concepts and techniques presented in this chapter to create the worksheet and an embedded 3-D Column chart using an appropriate chart style that compares the quarterly cost of each expense. Use the AutoCalculate area to determine the average amount spent per quarter on each expense. Manually insert the averages with appropriate titles in an empty area on the worksheet.

Table 1–11 Quarterly Environmental Club Budget

	Jan – Mar	April – June	July – Sept	Oct – Dec
Meeting Room Rent	300	300	150	450
Copies and Supplies	390	725	325	640
Travel	450	755	275	850
Refreshments	105	85	215	155
Speaker Fees	200	200	0	500
Miscellaneous	125	110	75	215

Continued >

Cases and Places *continued*

• • 3: Create a 3-D Pie Chart to Analyze Quarterly Revenue

In-the-Villa DVD Rental is a DVD movie rental store. The owner of the store is trying to decide if it is feasible to hire more employees during certain times of the year. You have been asked to develop a worksheet totaling all the revenue received last year by quarter. The revenue per quarter is: Quarter 1, $52,699.23; Quarter 2, $111,244.32; Quarter 3, $70,905.03; and Quarter 4, $87,560.10. Create a 3-D Pie chart to illustrate quarterly revenue contribution by quarter. Use the AutoCalculate area to find the average, maximum, and minimum quarterly revenue and manually enter them and their corresponding identifiers in an empty area of the worksheet.

• • 4: Design and Create a Workbook to Analyze Your Field of Interest

Make It Personal

Based on your college major, area of interest, or career, use an Internet search engine or other research material to determine the total number of people employed in your chosen field of interest in the country over the past five years. For each year, break the yearly number down into two or more categories. For example, the number for each year can be broken into management and nonmanagement employees. Create an Excel worksheet that includes this data. Place the data in appropriate rows and columns for each year and category. Create totals for each row, totals for each column, and a grand total. Format the worksheet title, column headings, and data using the concepts presented in this chapter. Create a properly formatted Clustered Cone chart for the data and place it below the data in the worksheet. Make certain that years are on the x-axis and number of employees is on the y-axis.

• • 5: Design and Create a Workbook to Analyze Your School

Working Together

Visit the registrar's office at your school and obtain data, such as age, gender, and full-time versus part-time status, for the students majoring in at least six different academic departments this semester. Have each member of your team divide the data into different categories. For example, separate the data by:

1. Age, divided into four different age groups
2. Gender, divided into male and female
3. Status, divided into full-time and part-time

After coordinating the data as a group, have each member independently use the concepts and techniques presented in this chapter to create a worksheet and appropriate chart to show the total students by characteristics by academic department. As a group, critique each worksheet and have each member modify his or her worksheet based on the group recommendations.

Microsoft Office **Excel 2007**

2 Formulas, Functions, Formatting, and Web Queries

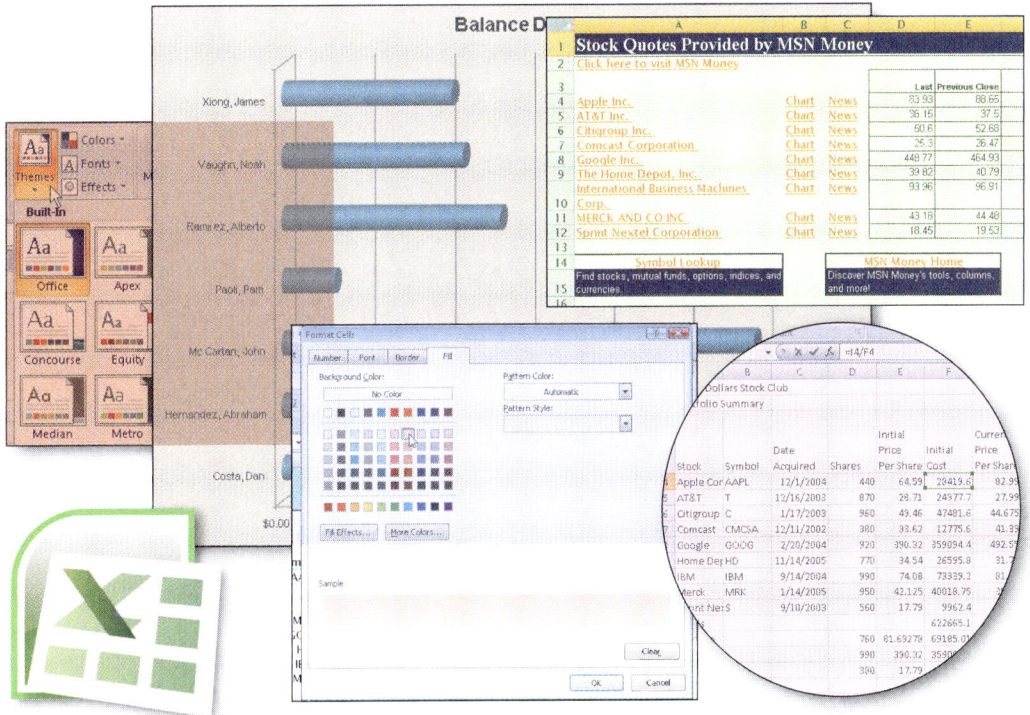

Objectives

You will have mastered the material in this chapter when you can:

- Enter formulas using the keyboard and Point mode
- Apply the AVERAGE, MAX, and MIN functions
- Verify a formula using Range Finder
- Apply a theme to a workbook
- Add conditional formatting to cells
- Change column width and row height
- Check the spelling of a worksheet

- Set margins, headers and footers in Page Layout View
- Preview and print versions of a worksheet
- Use a Web query to get real-time data from a Web site
- Rename sheets in a workbook
- E-mail the active workbook from within Excel

Microsoft Office **Excel 2007**

2 | Formulas, Functions, Formatting, and Web Queries

Introduction

In Chapter 1, you learned how to enter data, sum values, format the worksheet to make it easier to read, and draw a chart. You also learned about using Help and saving, printing, and opening a workbook. This chapter continues to highlight these topics and presents some new ones.

The new topics covered in this chapter include using formulas and functions to create a worksheet. A **function** is a prewritten formula that is built into Excel. Other new topics include smart tags and option buttons, verifying formulas, applying a theme to a worksheet, adding borders, formatting numbers and text, using conditional formatting, changing the widths of columns and heights of rows, spell checking, e-mailing from within a program, renaming worksheets, using alternative types of worksheet displays and printouts, and adding page headers and footers to a worksheet. One alternative worksheet display and printout shows the formulas in the worksheet, instead of the values. When you display the formulas in the worksheet, you see exactly what text, data, formulas, and functions you have entered into it. Finally, this chapter covers Web queries to obtain real-time data from a Web site.

Project — Worksheet with Formulas, Functions, and Web Queries

The project in the chapter follows proper design guidelines and uses Excel to create the two worksheets shown in Figure 2–1. The Silver Dollars Stock Club was started and is owned by a national academic fraternity, which pools contributions from a number of local chapters. Each local chapter contributes $150 per month; the money is then invested in the stock market for the benefit of the organization and as a tool to help members learn about investing. At the end of each month, the club's treasurer summarizes the club's financial status in a portfolio summary. This summary includes information such as the stocks owned by the club, the cost of the stocks to the club, and the gain or loss that the club has seen over time on the stock. As the complexity of the task of creating the summary increases, the treasurer wants to use Excel to create the monthly portfolio summary. The treasurer also sees an opportunity to use Excel's built-in capability to access real-time stock quotes over the Internet.

Recall that the first step in creating an effective worksheet is to make sure you understand what is required. The people who will use the worksheet usually provide requirements. The requirements document for the Silver Dollars Stock Club Portfolio Summary worksheet includes the following: needs, source of data, summary of calculations, Web requirements, and other facts about its development (Figure 2–2 on page EX 84). The real-time stock quotes (shown in Figure 2–1b) will be accessed via a Web query. The stock quotes will be returned to the active workbook on a separate worksheet. Microsoft determines the content and format of the Real-Time Stock Quotes worksheet.

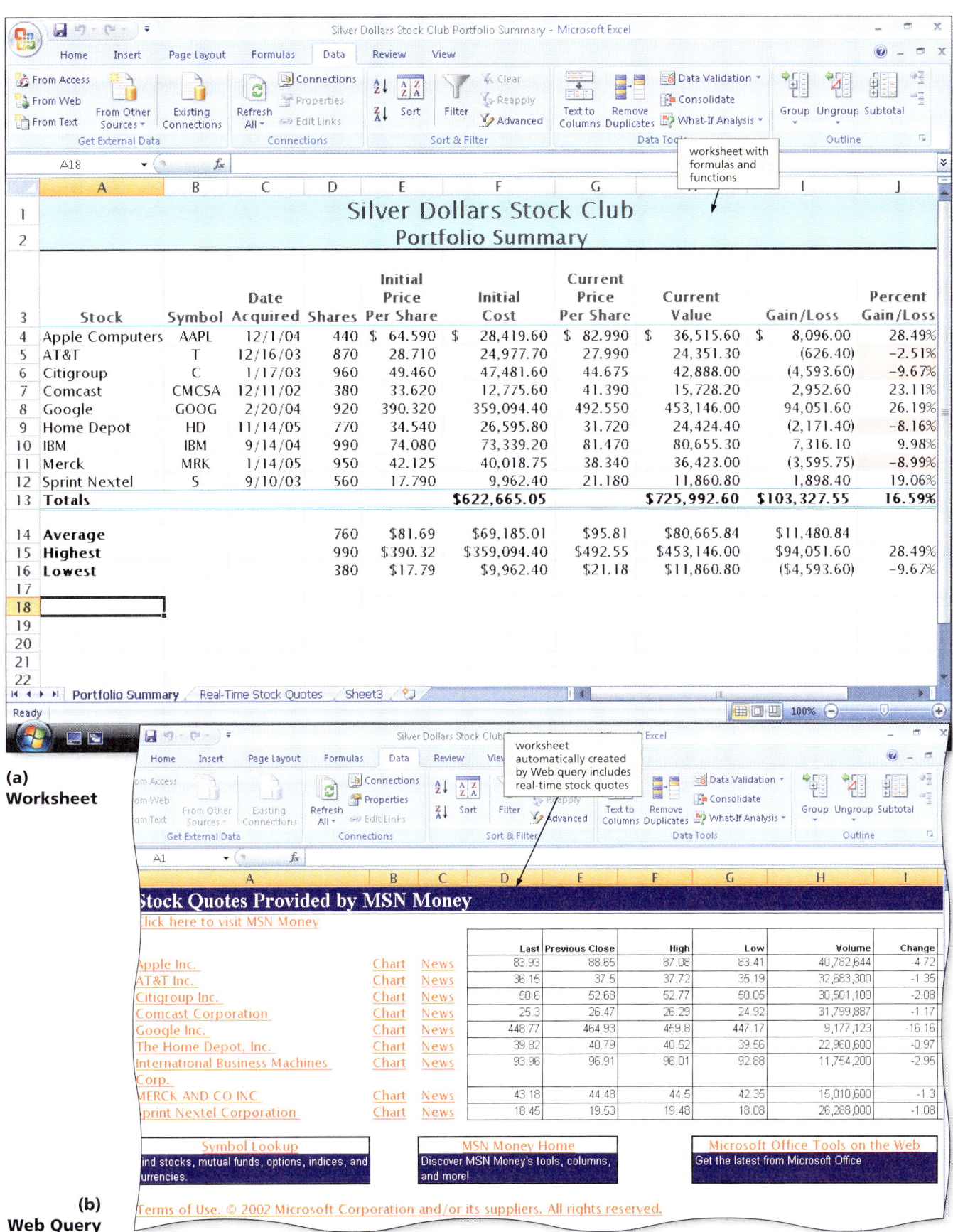

Figure 2–1

EX 83

REQUEST FOR NEW WORKSHEET

Date Submitted:	April 8, 2008
Submitted By:	Juan Castillo
Worksheet Title:	Silver Dollars Stock Club Portfolio Summary
Needs:	An easy-to-read worksheet that summarizes the club's investments (Figure 2-3). For each stock, the worksheet is to include the stock name, stock symbol, date acquired, shares, initial price per share, initial cost, current price per share, current value, gain/loss, and percent gain/loss. Also include totals and the average, highest value, and lowest value for each column of numbers. Use the import data capabilities of Excel to access real-time stock quotes using Web queries.
Source of Data:	The data supplied by Juan includes the stock names, symbols, dates acquired, number of shares, initial price per share, and current price per share. This data is shown in Table 2-1 on page EX 89.
Calculations:	The following calculations must be made for each of the stocks: 1. Initial Cost = Shares × Initial Price Per Share 2. Current Value = Shares × Current Price Per Share 3. Gain/Loss = Current Value − Initial Cost 4. Percent Gain/Loss = Gain/Loss / Initial Cost 5. Compute the totals for initial cost, current value, and gain/loss. 6. Use the AVERAGE function to determine the average for the number of shares, initial price per share, initial cost per share, current price per share, current value, and gain/loss. 7. Use the MAX and MIN functions to determine the highest and lowest values for the number of shares, initial price per share, initial cost per share, current price per share, current value, gain/loss, and percent gain/loss.
Web Requirements:	Use the Web query feature of Excel to get real-time stock quotes for the stocks owned by the Silver Dollars Stock Club.

Approvals

Approval Status:	X	Approved
		Rejected
Approved By:		Members of the Silver Dollars Stock Club
Date:		April 15, 2008
Assigned To:		J. Quasney, Spreadsheet Specialist

Figure 2–2

> **BTW**
>
> **Aesthetics versus Function**
> In designing a worksheet, functional considerations should come first, before visual aesthetics. The function, or purpose, of a worksheet is to provide a user with direct ways to accomplish tasks. Avoid the temptation to use flashy or confusing visual elements within the worksheet, unless they will help the user more easily complete a task.

Overview

As you read this chapter, you will learn how to create the worksheet shown in Figure 2–1 by performing these general tasks:

- Enter formulas and apply functions in the worksheet
- Add conditional formatting to the worksheet
- Apply a theme to the worksheet
- Work with the worksheet in Page Layout View
- Print a part of the worksheet
- Perform a Web query to get real-time data from a Web site and create a new worksheet
- E-mail the worksheet

General Project Decisions

Plan Ahead

While creating an Excel worksheet, you need to make several decisions that will determine the appearance and characteristics of the finished worksheet. As you create the worksheet required to meet the requirements shown in Figure 2–2, you should follow these general guidelines:

1. **Plan the layout of the worksheet.** As discussed in Chapter 1 and shown in Figure 2–3, rows typically contain items analogous to items in a list. In the case of the stock club's data, the individual stocks serve this purpose and each stock should be placed in a row. As the club adds more stocks, the number of rows in the worksheet will increase. Information about each stock and associated calculations should appear in columns.

2. **Determine the necessary formulas and functions needed.** Values such as initial cost and current value are calculated from known values. The formulas for these calculations should be known in advance of creating the worksheet. Values such as the average, highest, and lowest values can be calculated using Excel functions as opposed to relying on complex formulas.

3. **Identify how to format various elements of the worksheet.** As discussed in Chapter 1 and shown in Figure 2–3, the appearance of the worksheet affects its ability to communicate clearly. Numeric data should be formatted in generally accepted formats, such as using commas as thousands separators and parentheses for negative values.

4. **Establish rules for conditional formatting.** Conditional formatting allows you to format a cell based on the contents of the cell. Decide under which circumstances you would like a cell to stand out from similar cells and determine in what way the cell will stand out. In the case of the Percent Gain/Loss column on the worksheet, placing a different background color in cells that show losses is an appropriate format for the column.

5. **Specify how the printed worksheet should appear.** When it is possible that a person will want to print a worksheet, care should be taken in the development of the worksheet to ensure that the contents can be printed in a readable manner. Excel prints worksheets in landscape or portrait orientation and margins can be adjusted to fit more or less data on each page. Headers and footers add an additional level of customization to the printed page.

(continued)

Silver Dollars Stock Club
Portfolio Summary

Stock	Symbol	Date Acquired	Shares	Initial Price Per Share	Initial Cost	Current Price Per Share	Current Value	Gain/Loss	Percent Gain/Loss
XXXXXXXX	XXX	99/99/99	999	$ Z9 999	$ ZZ,ZZ9.99	$ ZZ9 999	$ ZZ,ZZ9.99	$ ZZ,ZZ9.99	Z9.99%
Total					$ ZZZ,ZZ9.99		$ ZZZ,ZZ9.99	$ ZZZ,ZZ9.99	Z9.99%
Average			999	$ Z9 999	$ ZZ,ZZ9.99	$ZZ9.999	$ ZZ,ZZ9.99	$ ZZ,ZZ9.99	Z9.99%
Highest									
Lowest									

- Xs indicate text data
- 9s indicate numeric data
- Zs indicate numeric data with 0s suppressed
- $ adjacent to Z indicates floating dollar sign
- $ not adjacent to Z indicates a fixed dollar sign

Figure 2–3

Plan Ahead

(continued)

6. **Gather information regarding the needed Web query.** You must also know what information the Web query requires in order for it to generate results that you can use in Excel.

7. **Choose names for the worksheets.** When a workbook includes multiple worksheets, each worksheet should be named. A good worksheet name is succinct, unique to the workbook, and meaningful to any user of the workbook.

In addition, using a sketch of the worksheet can help you visualize its design. The sketch for Silver Dollars Stock Club Portfolio Summary worksheet (Figure 2–3 on the previous page) includes a title, a subtitle, column and row headings, and the location of data values. It also uses specific characters to define the desired formatting for the worksheet as follows:

1. The row of Xs below the leftmost column defines the cell entries as text, such as stock names and stock symbols.

2. The rows of Zs and 9s with slashes, dollar signs, decimal points, commas, and percent signs in the remaining columns define the cell entries as numbers. The Zs indicate that the selected format should instruct Excel to suppress leading 0s. The 9s indicate that the selected format should instruct Excel to display any digits, including 0s.

3. The decimal point means that a decimal point should appear in the cell entry and indicates the number of decimal places to use.

4. The commas indicate that the selected format should instruct Excel to display a comma separator only if the number has enough digits to the left of the decimal point.

5. The slashes in the third column identify the cell entry as a date.

6. The dollar signs that are not adjacent to the Zs in the first row below the column headings and in the total row signify a fixed dollar sign. The dollar signs that are adjacent to the Zs below the total row signify a floating dollar sign, or one that appears next to the first significant digit.

7. The percent sign (%) in the far right column indicates a percent sign should appear after the number.

When necessary, more specific details concerning the above guidelines are presented at appropriate points in the chapter. The chapter also will identify the actions you perform and decisions made regarding these guidelines during the creation of the worksheet shown in Figure 2–3 on page EX 85.

With a good understanding of the requirements document, an understanding of the necessary decisions, and a sketch of the worksheet, the next step is to use Excel to create the worksheet.

To Start Excel

If you are using a computer to step through the project in this chapter and you want your screen to match the figures in this book, you should change your computer's resolution to 1024 × 768. For information about how to change a computer's resolution, read Appendix C.

The following steps, which assume Windows Vista is running, start Excel based on a typical installation of Microsoft Office on your computer. You may need to ask your instructor how to start Excel for your computer.

1. Click the Start button on the Windows Vista taskbar to display the Start menu.
2. Point to All Programs at the bottom of the left pane on the Start menu to display the All Programs list.
3. Click Microsoft Office in the All Programs list to display the Microsoft Office list.
4. Click Microsoft Office Excel to start Excel and display a blank worksheet in the Excel window.
5. If the Excel window is not maximized, click the Maximize button next to the Close button on its title bar to maximize the window.
6. If the worksheet window in Excel is not maximized, click the Maximize button next to the Close button on its title bar to maximize the worksheet window within Excel.

> **BTW**
>
> **Starting Excel**
> You can use a command-line switch to start Excel and control how it starts. First, click the Start button on the Windows Vista taskbar, and then click the Start Search box. Next, enter the complete path to Excel's program file including the switch (for example, C:\Program Files\Microsoft Office\Office12\Excel.exe/e). The switch /e starts Excel without opening a new workbook; /i starts Excel with a maximized window; /p "folder" sets the active path to folder and ignores the default folder; /r "filename" opens filename in read-only mode; and /s starts Excel in safe mode.

Entering the Titles and Numbers into the Worksheet

The first step in creating the worksheet is to enter the titles and numbers into the worksheet.

To Enter the Worksheet Title and Subtitle

The following steps enter the worksheet title and subtitle into cells A1 and A2.

1. If necessary, select cell A1. Type `Silver Dollars Stock Club` in the cell and then press the DOWN ARROW key to enter the worksheet title in cell A1.
2. Type `Portfolio Summary` in cell A2 and then press the DOWN ARROW key to enter the worksheet subtitle in cell A2 (Figure 2–4 on page EX 89).

To Enter the Column Titles

The column titles in row 3 begin in cell A3 and extend through cell J3. The column titles in Figure 2–3 include multiple lines of text. To start a new line in a cell, press ALT+ENTER after each line, except for the last line, which is completed by clicking the Enter box, pressing the ENTER key, or pressing one of the arrow keys. When you see ALT+ENTER in a step, press the ENTER key while holding down the ALT key and then release both keys.

The stock names and the row titles Totals, Average, Highest, and Lowest in the leftmost column begin in cell A4 and continue down to cell A16. This data is entered into rows 4 through 12 of the worksheet. The remainder of this section explains the steps required to enter the column titles, stock data, and row titles as shown in Figure 2–4 on page EX 89 and then save the workbook.

1. With cell A3 selected, type `Stock` and then press the RIGHT ARROW key.
2. Type `Symbol` in cell B3 and then press the RIGHT ARROW key.

BTW

Wrapping Text
If you have a long text entry, such as a paragraph, you can instruct Excel to wrap the text in a cell, rather than pressing ALT+ENTER to end a line. To wrap text, right-click in the cell, click Format Cells on the shortcut menu, click the Alignment tab, click Wrap text, and then click OK. Excel will increase the height of the cell automatically so the additional lines will fit. If you want to control where each line ends in the cell, rather than letting Excel wrap based on the cell width, however, then you must end each line with ALT+ENTER.

BTW

Two-Digit Years
When you enter a two-digit year value, Excel changes a two-digit year less than 30 to 20xx and a two-digit year of 30 and greater to 19xx. Use four-digit years to ensure that Excel interprets year values the way you intend, if necessary.

BTW

Formatting a Worksheet
With early worksheet programs, users often skipped rows to improve the appearance of the worksheet. With Excel it is not necessary to skip rows because you can increase row heights to add white space between information.

③ In cell C3, type Date and then press ALT+ENTER. Type Acquired and then press the RIGHT ARROW key.

④ In cell D3, type Shares and then press the RIGHT ARROW key.

⑤ In cell E3, type Initial and then press ALT+ENTER. Type Price and then press ALT+ENTER. Type Per Share and then press the RIGHT ARROW key.

⑥ Type Initial in cell F3 and then press ALT+ENTER. Type Cost and then press the RIGHT ARROW key.

⑦ In cell G3, type Current and then press ALT+ENTER. Type Price and then press ALT+ENTER. Type Per Share and then press the RIGHT ARROW key.

⑧ Type Current in cell H3 and then press ALT+ENTER. Type Value and then press the RIGHT ARROW key.

⑨ In cell I3, type Gain/Loss and then press the RIGHT ARROW key.

⑩ In cell J3, type Percent and then press ALT+ENTER. Type Gain/Loss.

To Enter the Portfolio Summary Data

The portfolio summary data in Table 2–1 includes a purchase date for each stock. Excel considers a date to be a number and, therefore, it displays the date right-aligned in the cell. The following steps enter the portfolio summary data shown in Table 2–1.

① Select cell A4, type Apple Computers, and then press the RIGHT ARROW key.

② Type AAPL in cell B4 and then press the RIGHT ARROW key.

③ Type 12/1/04 in cell C4 and then press the RIGHT ARROW key.

④ Type 440 in cell D4 and then press the RIGHT ARROW key.

⑤ Type 64.59 in cell E4 and then click cell G4.

⑥ Type 82.99 in cell G4 and then click cell A5.

⑦ Enter the portfolio summary data in Table 2–1 for the eight remaining stocks in rows 5 through 12 (Figure 2–4).

To Enter the Row Titles

① Select cell A13. Type Totals and then press the DOWN ARROW key. Type Average in cell A14 and then press the DOWN ARROW key.

② Type Highest in cell A15 and then press the DOWN ARROW key. Type Lowest in cell A16 and then press the ENTER key. Select cell F4 (Figure 2–4).

Table 2–1 Silver Dollars Stock Club Portfolio Summary Data

Stock	Symbol	Date Acquired	Shares	Initial Price Per Share	Current Price Per Share
Apple Computers	AAPL	12/1/04	440	64.59	82.99
AT&T	T	12/16/03	870	28.71	27.99
Citigroup	C	1/17/03	960	49.46	44.675
Comcast	CMCSA	12/11/02	380	33.62	41.39
Google	GOOG	2/20/04	920	390.32	492.55
Home Depot	HD	11/14/05	770	34.54	31.72
IBM	IBM	9/14/04	990	74.08	81.47
Merck	MRK	1/14/05	950	42.125	38.34
Sprint Nextel	S	9/10/03	560	17.79	21.18

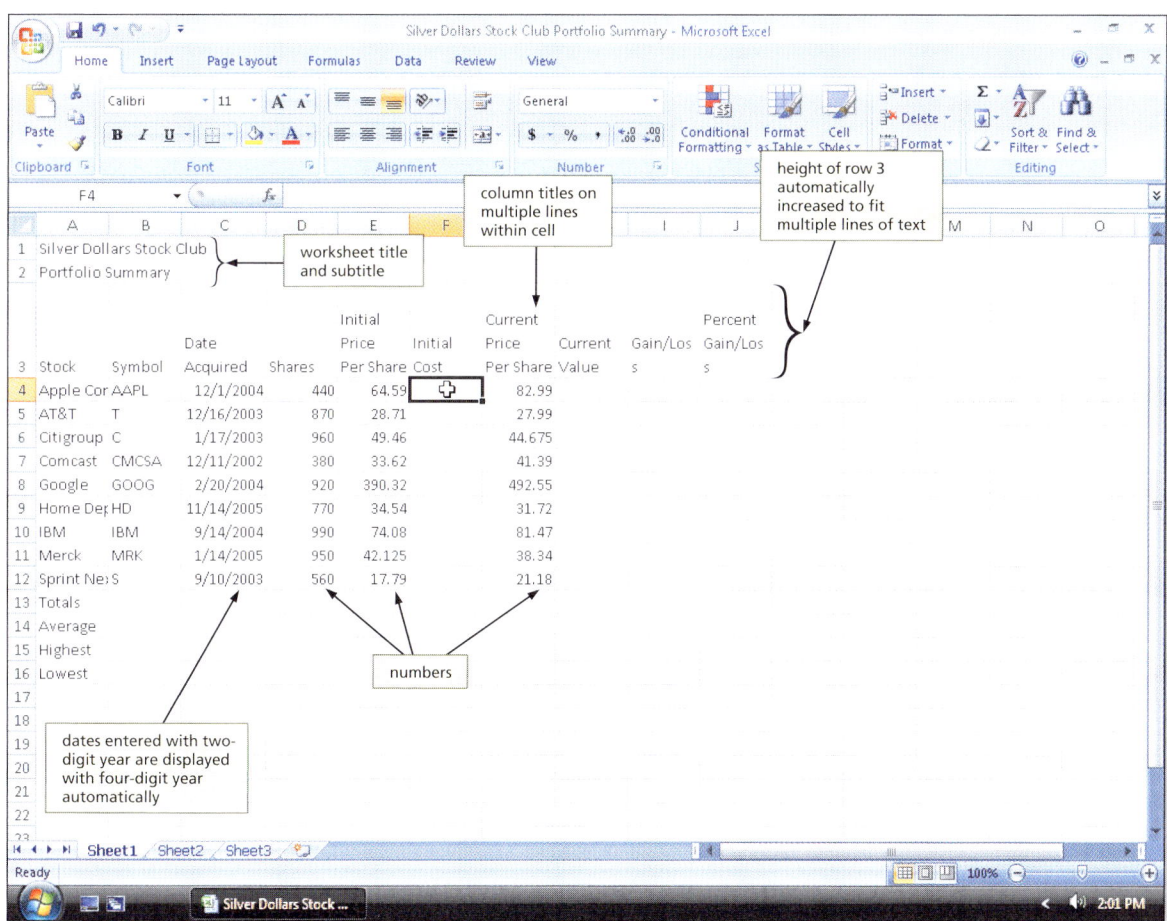

Figure 2–4

To Change Workbook Properties and Save the Workbook

With the data entered into the worksheet, the following steps save the workbook using the file name, Silver Dollars Stock Club Portfolio Summary. As you are building a workbook, it is a good idea to save it often so that you do not lose your work if the computer is turned off or if you lose electrical power. The first time you save a workbook, you should change the workbook properties.

BTW

Entering Numbers in a Range
An efficient way to enter data into a range of cells is to select a range and then enter the first number in the upper-left cell of the range. Excel responds by entering the value and moving the active cell selection down one cell. When you enter the last value in the first column, Excel moves the active cell selection to the top of the next column.

1. Click the Office Button, click Prepare on the Office Button menu, and then click Properties.
2. Update the document properties with your name and any other information required.
3. Click the Close button on the Document Properties pane.
4. With a USB flash drive connected to one of the computer's USB ports, click the Save button on the Quick Access Toolbar.
5. When Excel displays the Save As dialog box, type `Silver Dollars Stock Club Portfolio Summary` in the File name text box.
6. If the Folders list is displayed below the Folders button, click the Folders button to remove the Folders list.
7. If Computer is not displayed in the Favorite Links section, drag the top or bottom edge of the Save As dialog box until Computer is displayed.
8. Click Computer in the Favorite Links section. If necessary, scroll until UDISK 2.0 (E:) appears in the list of available drives. Double-click UDISK 2.0 (E:) (your USB flash drive may have a different name and letter). Click the Save button in the Save As dialog box to save the workbook on the USB flash drive using the file name, Silver Dollars Stock Club Portfolio Summary.

Entering Formulas

One of the reasons Excel is such a valuable tool is that you can assign a **formula** to a cell and Excel will calculate the result. Consider, for example, what would happen if you had to multiply 440 × 64.59 and then manually enter the product, 28,419.60, in cell F4. Every time the values in cells D4 or E4 changed, you would have to recalculate the product and enter the new value in cell F4. By contrast, if you enter a formula in cell F4 to multiply the values in cells D4 and E4, Excel recalculates the product whenever new values are entered into those cells and displays the result in cell F4.

Plan Ahead

Determine the necessary formulas and functions needed.
The formulas needed in the worksheet are noted in the requirements document as follows:

1. Initial Cost (column F) = Shares × Initial Price Per Share
2. Current Value (column H) = Shares × Current Price Per Share
3. Gain/Loss (column I) = Current Value − Initial Cost
4. Percent Gain/Loss (column J) = Gain/Loss / Initial Cost

The necessary functions to determine the average, highest, and lowest numbers are discussed shortly.

To Enter a Formula Using the Keyboard

The initial cost for each stock, which appears in column F, is equal to the number of shares in column D times the initial price per share in column E. Thus, the initial cost for Apple Computers in cell F4 is obtained by multiplying 440 (cell D4) by 64.59 (cell E4) or =D4*E4. The following steps enter the initial cost formula in cell F4 using the keyboard.

- With cell F4 selected, type =d4*e4 in the cell to display the formula in the formula bar and in cell F4 and to display colored borders around the cells referenced in the formula (Figure 2–5).

Q&A

What is happening on the worksheet as I enter the formula?

The **equal sign** (=) preceding d4*e4 is an important part of the formula. It alerts Excel that you are entering a formula or function and not text. Because the most common error when entering a formula is to reference the wrong cell in a formula mistakenly, Excel colors the borders of the cells referenced in the formula. The coloring helps in the reviewing process to ensure the cell references are correct. The **asterisk** (*) following d4 is the arithmetic operator that directs Excel to perform the multiplication operation.

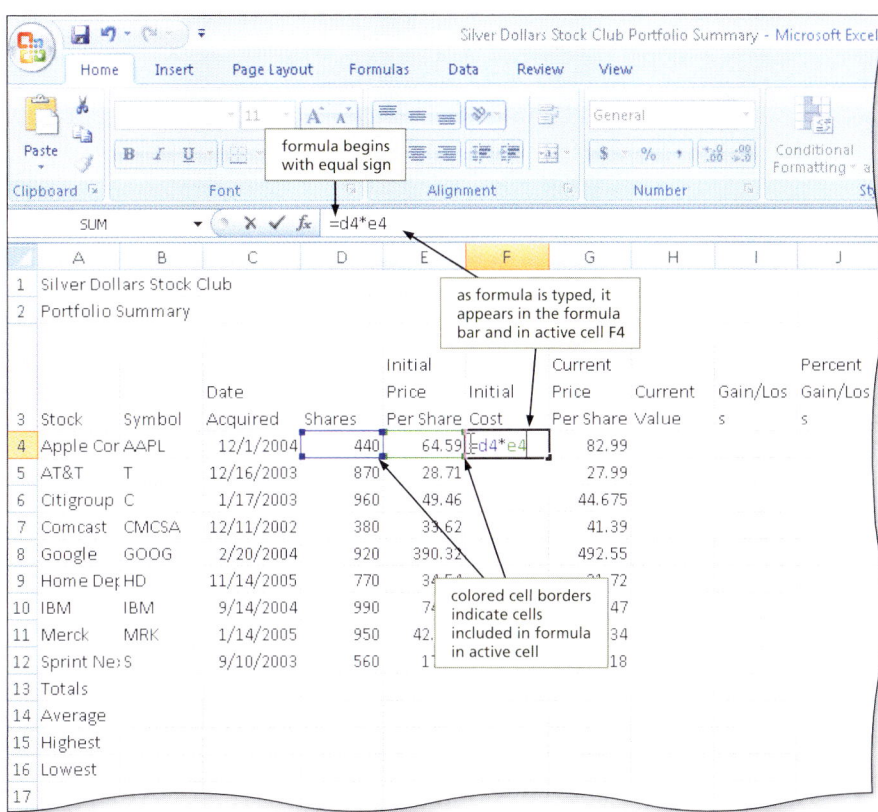

Figure 2–5

- Press the RIGHT ARROW key twice to complete the arithmetic operation indicated by the formula, display the result, 28419.6, and to select cell H4 (Figure 2–6).

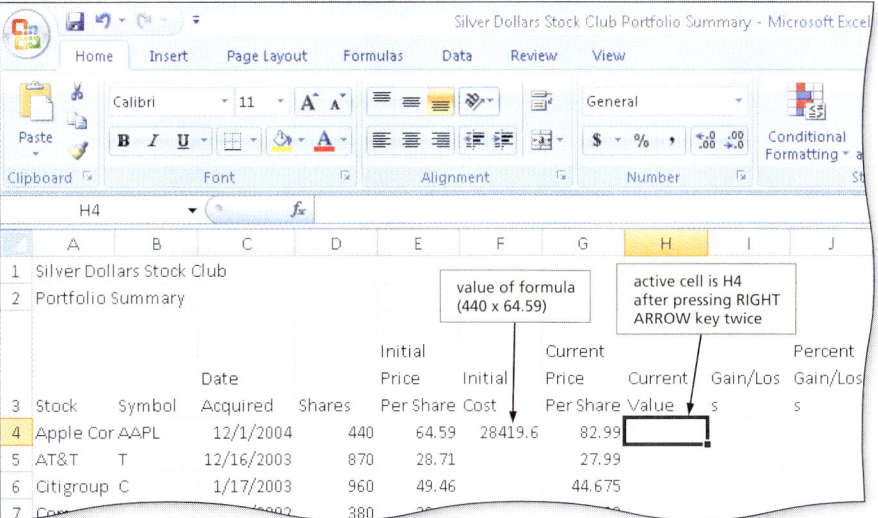

Figure 2–6

Arithmetic Operations

Table 2–2 describes multiplication and other valid Excel arithmetic operators.

Table 2–2 Summary of Arithmetic Operators

Arithmetic Operator	Meaning	Example of Usage	Meaning
–	Negation	–34	Negative 34
%	Percentage	=72%	Multiplies 72 by 0.01
^	Exponentiation	=4 ^ 6	Raises 4 to the sixth power
*	Multiplication	=22.6 * F4	Multiplies the contents of cell F4 by 22.6
/	Division	=C3 / C6	Divides the contents of cell C3 by the contents of cell C6
+	Addition	=7 + 3	Adds 7 and 3
–	Subtraction	=F12 – 22	Subtracts 22 from the contents of cell F12

BTW

Troubling Formulas
If Excel does not accept a formula, remove the equal sign from the left side and complete the entry as text. Later, after you have entered additional data or determined the error, reinsert the equal sign to change the text back to a formula and edit the formula as needed.

You can enter the cell references in formulas in uppercase or lowercase, and you can add spaces before and after arithmetic operators to make the formulas easier to read. The formula, =d4*e4, is the same as the formulas, =d4 * e4, =D4 * e4, or =D4 * E4.

Order of Operations

When more than one arithmetic operator is involved in a formula, Excel follows the same basic order of operations that you use in algebra. Moving from left to right in a formula, the **order of operations** is as follows: first negation (–), then all percentages (%), then all exponentiations (^), then all multiplications (*) and divisions (/), and finally, all additions (+) and subtractions (–).

You can use parentheses to override the order of operations. For example, if Excel follows the order of operations, 5 * 9 + 8 equals 53. If you use parentheses, however, to change the formula to 5 * (9 + 8), the result is 85, because the parentheses instruct Excel to add 9 and 8 before multiplying by 5. Table 2–3 illustrates several examples of valid Excel formulas and explains the order of operations.

Table 2–3 Examples of Excel Formulas

Formula	Meaning
=K12	Assigns the value in cell K12 to the active cell.
=10 + 4^2	Assigns the sum of 10 + 16 (or 26) to the active cell.
=3 * C20 or =C20 * 3 or =(3 * C20)	Assigns three times the contents of cell C20 to the active cell.
=50% * 12	Assigns the product of 0.50 times 12 (or 6) to the active cell.
– (H3 * Q30)	Assigns the negative value of the product of the values contained in cells H3 and Q30 to the active cell.
=12 * (N8 – O8)	Assigns the product of 12 times the difference between the values contained in cells N8 and O8 to the active cell.
=M9 / Z8 – C3 * Q19 + A3 ^ B3	Completes the following operations, from left to right: exponentiation (A3 ^ B3), then division (M9 / Z8), then multiplication (C3 * Q19), then subtraction (M9 / Z8) – (C3 * Q19), and finally addition (M9 / Z8 – C3 * Q19) + (A3 ^ B3). If cells A3 = 2, B3 = 4, C3 = 6, M9 = 3, Q19 = 4, and Z8 = 3, then Excel assigns the active cell the value 18; that is, 3 / 3 – 6 * 4 + 2 ^ 4 = -7.

To Enter Formulas Using Point Mode

The sketch of the worksheet in Figure 2–3 on page EX 85 calls for the current value, gain/loss, and percent gain/loss of each stock to appear in columns H, I, and J respectively. All three of these values are calculated using formulas in row 4:

Current Value (cell H4) = Shares × Current Price Per Share or =D4*G4

Gain/Loss (cell I4) = Current Value – Initial Cost or H4-F4

Percent Gain/Loss (cell J4) = Gain/Loss / Initial Cost or I4/F4

An alternative to entering the formulas in cells H4, I4, and J4 using the keyboard is to enter the formulas using the mouse and Point mode. **Point mode** allows you to select cells for use in a formula by using the mouse. The following steps enter formulas using Point mode.

1

- With cell H4 selected, type = (equal sign) to begin the formula and then click cell D4 to add a reference to cell D4 to the formula (Figure 2–7).

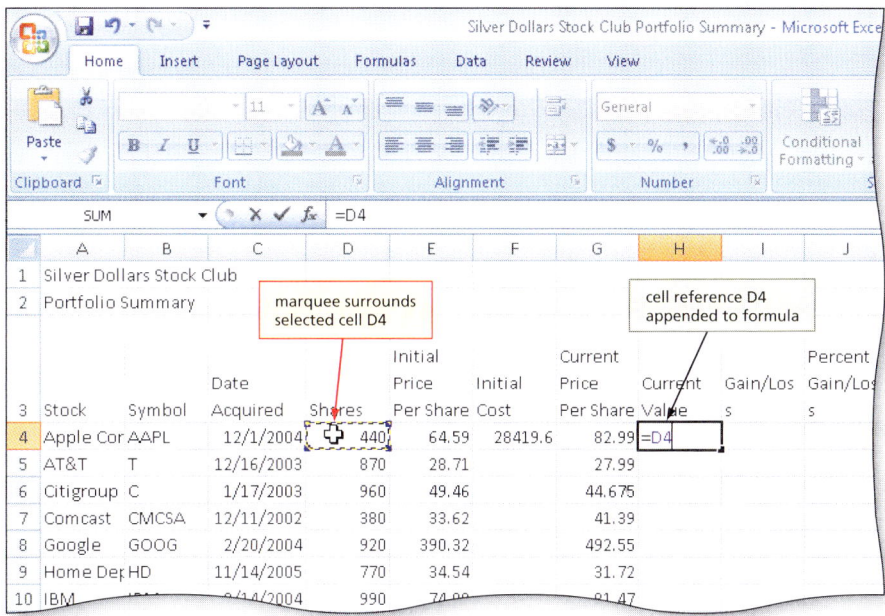

Figure 2–7

2

- Type * (asterisk) and then click cell G4 to add a multiplication operator and reference to cell G4 to the formula (Figure 2–8).

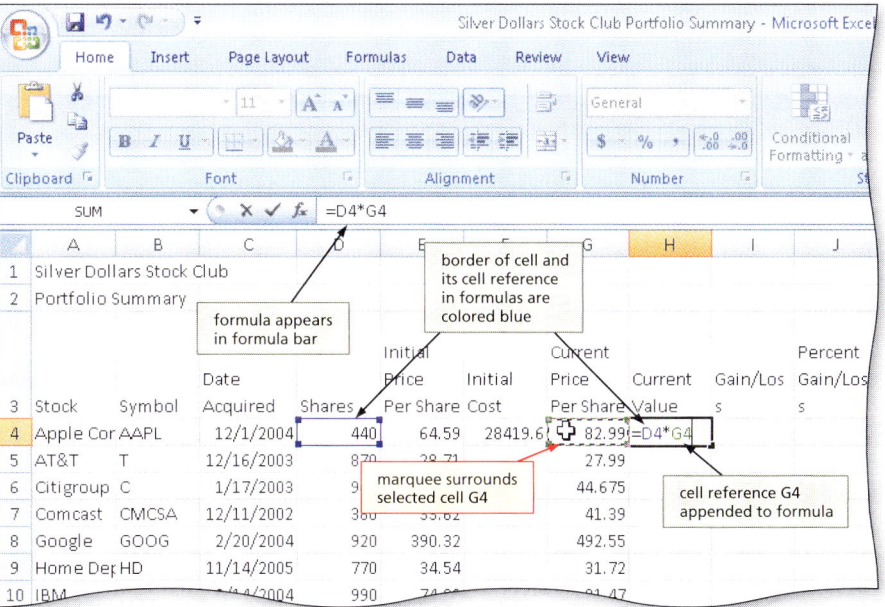

Figure 2–8

3

- Click the Enter box and then click cell I4 to select cell I4.

- Type = (equal sign) and then click cell H4 to add a reference to cell H4 to the formula.

- Type – (minus sign) and then click cell F4 to add a subtraction operator and reference to cell F4 to the formula (Figure 2–9).

Q&A When should I use Point mode to enter formulas?

Using Point mode to enter formulas often is faster and more accurate than using the keyboard to type the entire formula when the cell you want to select does not require you to scroll. In many instances, as in these steps, you may want to use both the keyboard and mouse when entering a formula in a cell. You can use the keyboard to begin the formula, for example, and then use the mouse to select a range of cells.

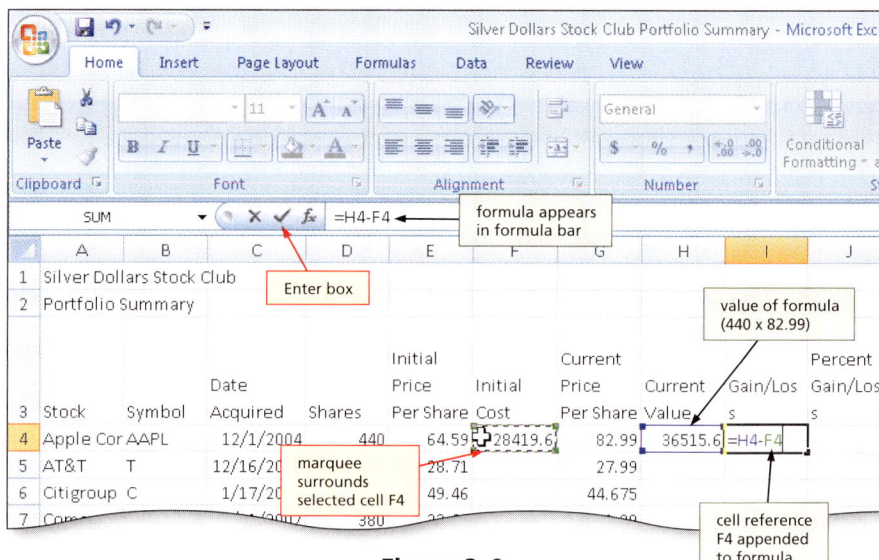

Figure 2–9

4

- Click the Enter box to enter the formula in cell I4.

- Select cell J4. Type = (equal sign) and then click cell I4 to add a reference to cell I4 to the formula.

- Type / (forward slash) and then click cell F4 to add a reference to cell F4 to the formula.

- Click the Enter box to enter the formula in cell J4 (Figure 2–10).

Q&A Why do only six decimal places show in cell J4?

The actual value assigned by Excel to cell J4 from the division operation in Step 4 is 0.284873819. While not all the decimal places appear in Figure 2–10, Excel maintains all of them for computational purposes. Thus, if referencing cell J4 in a formula, the value used for computational purposes is 0.284873819, not 0.284874. Excel displays the value in cell J4 as 0.284874 because the cell formatting is set to display only six digits after the decimal point. If you change the cell formatting of column J to display nine digits after the decimal point, then Excel displays the true value 0.284873819.

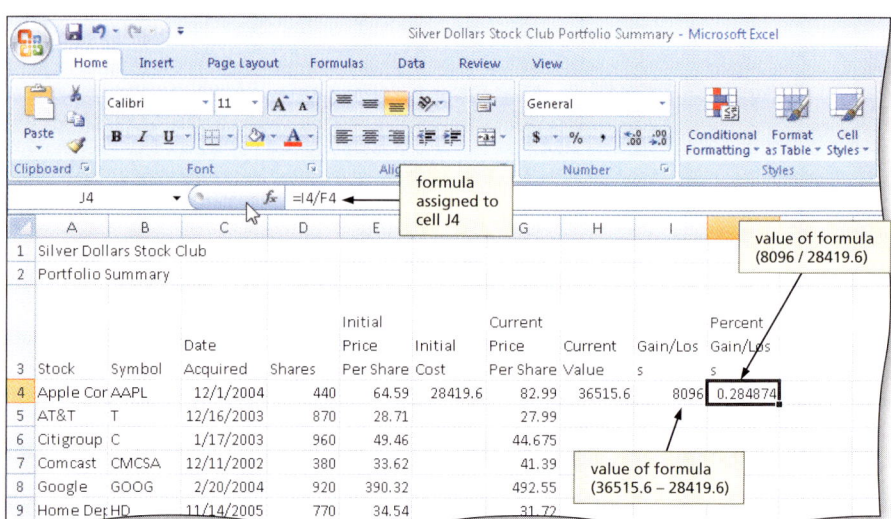

Figure 2–10

To Copy Formulas Using the Fill Handle

The four formulas for Apple Computers in cells F4, H4, I4, and J4 now are complete. You could enter the same four formulas one at a time for the eight remaining stocks. A much easier method of entering the formulas, however, is to select the formulas in row 4 and then use the fill handle to copy them through row 12. Recall from Chapter 1 that the fill handle is a small rectangle in the lower-right corner of the active cell or active range. The following steps copy the formulas using the fill handle.

1

- Select cell F4 and then point to the fill handle.
- Drag the fill handle down through cell F12 and continue to hold the mouse button to select the destination range (Figure 2–11).

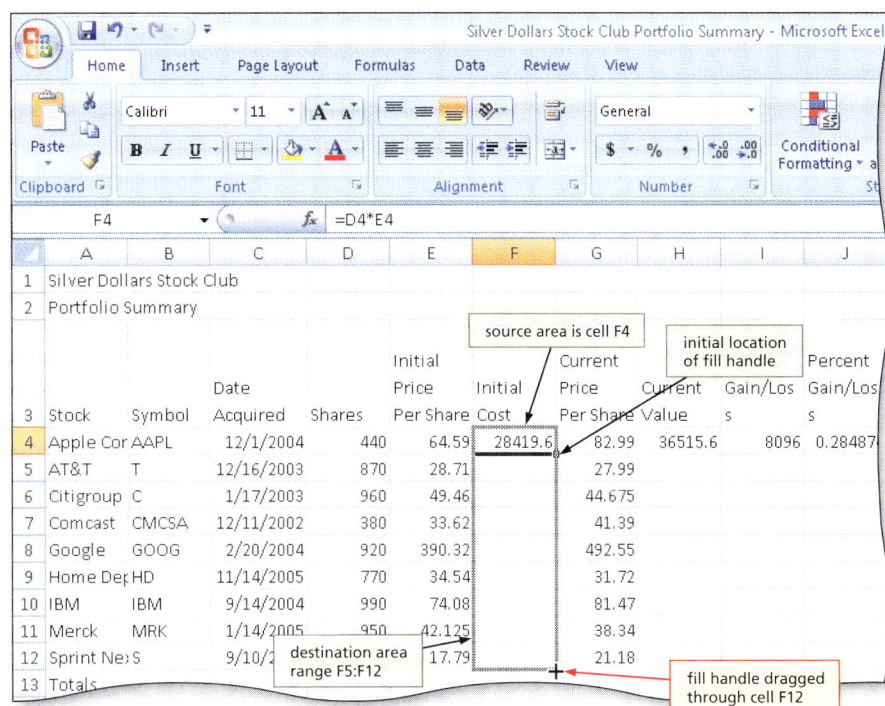

Figure 2–11

2

- Release the mouse button to copy the formula in cell F4 to the cells in the range F5:F12.
- Select the range H4:J4 and then point to the fill handle (Figure 2–12).

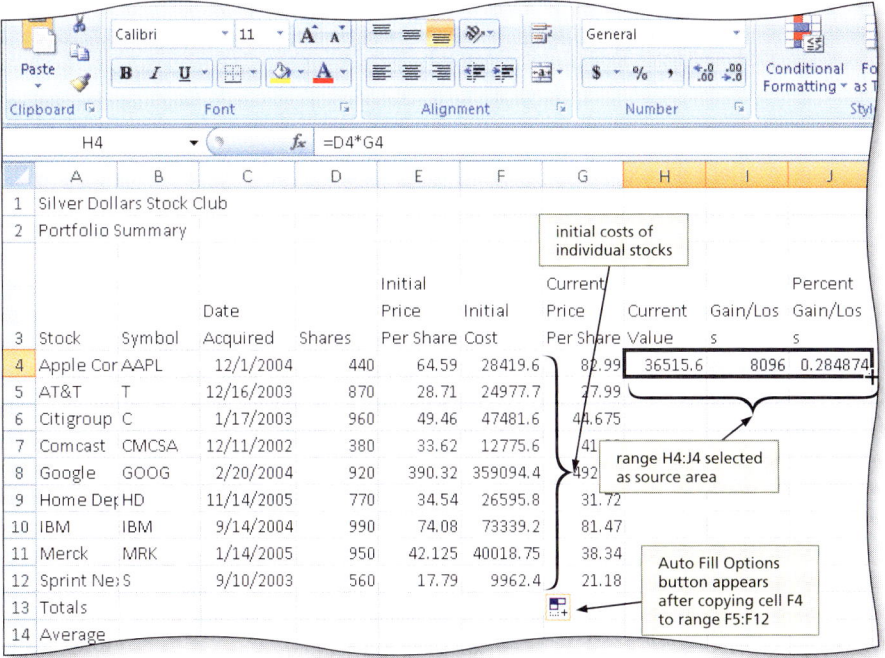

Figure 2–12

3

- Drag the fill handle down through the range H5:J12 to copy the three formulas =D4*G4 in cell H4, =H4-F4 in cell I4, and =I4/F4 in cell J4 to the range H5:J12 (Figure 2–13).

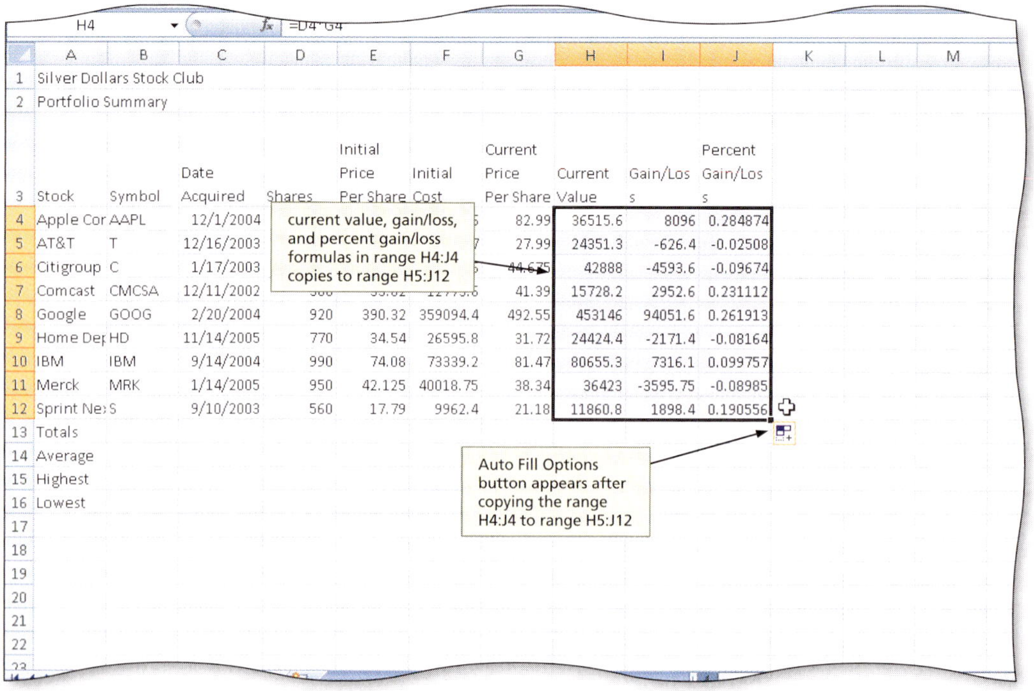

Q&A

How does Excel adjust the cell references in the formulas in the destination area?

Recall that when you copy a formula, Excel adjusts the cell references so the new formulas contain references corresponding to the new location and performs calculations using the appropriate values. Thus, if you copy downward, Excel adjusts the row portion of cell references. If you copy across, then Excel adjusts the column portion of cell references. These cell references are called **relative cell references**.

Figure 2–13

Other Ways

1. Select source area, click Copy button on Ribbon, select destination area, click Paste button on Ribbon
2. Select source area, right-click copy area, click Copy on shortcut menu, select destination area, right-click paste area, click Paste on shortcut menu

BTW

Automatic Recalculation
Every time you enter a value into a cell in the worksheet, Excel automatically recalculates all formulas. You can change to manual recalculation by clicking the Calculation Options button on the Formulas tab on the Ribbon and then clicking Manual. In manual calculation mode, press the F9 key to instruct Excel to recalculate all formulas.

Smart Tags and Option Buttons

Excel can identify certain actions to take on specific data in workbooks using **smart tags**. Data labeled with smart tags includes dates, financial symbols, people's names, and more. To use smart tags, you must turn on smart tags using the AutoCorrect Options in the Excel Options dialog box. To change AutoCorrect options, click the Office Button, click the Excel Options button on the Office Button menu, point to Proofing, and then click AutoCorrect Options. Once smart tags are turned on, Excel places a small purple triangle, called a **smart tag indicator**, in a cell to indicate that a smart tag is available. When you move the insertion point over the smart tag indicator, the Smart Tag Actions button appears. Clicking the Smart Tag Actions button arrow produces a list of actions you can perform on the data in that specific cell.

In addition to smart tags, Excel also displays Options buttons in a workbook while you are working on it to indicate that you can complete an operation using automatic features such as AutoCorrect, Auto Fill, error checking, and others. For example, the Auto Fill Options button shown in Figure 2–13 appears after a fill operation, such as dragging the fill handle. When an error occurs in a formula in a cell, Excel displays the Trace Error button next to the cell and identifies the cell with the error by placing a green triangle in the upper left of the cell.

Table 2–4 summarizes the smart tag and Options buttons available in Excel. When one of these buttons appears on your worksheet, click the button arrow to produce the list of options for modifying the operation or to obtain additional information.

Table 2-4 Smart Tag and Options Buttons in Excel		
Button	Name	Menu Function
	Auto Fill Options	Gives options for how to fill cells following a fill operation, such as dragging the fill handle.
	AutoCorrect Options	Undoes an automatic correction, stops future automatic corrections of this type, or causes Excel to display the AutoCorrect Options dialog box.
	Insert Options	Lists formatting options following an insertion of cells, rows, or columns.
	Paste Options	Specifies how moved or pasted items should appear (for example, with original formatting, without formatting, or with different formatting).
	Smart Tag Actions	Lists information options for a cell containing data recognized by Excel, such as a stock symbol.
	Trace Error	Lists error checking options following the assignment of an invalid formula to a cell.

To Determine Totals Using the Sum Button

The next step is to determine the totals in row 13 for the initial cost in column F, current value in column H, and gain/loss in column I. To determine the total initial cost in column F, the values in the range F4 through F12 must be summed. To do so, enter the function =sum(f4:f12) in cell F13 or select cell F13 and then click the Sum button on the Ribbon and then press the ENTER key. Recall that a function is a prewritten formula that is built into Excel. Similar SUM functions or the Sum button can be used in cells H13 and I13 to determine total current value and total gain/loss, respectively.

1 Select cell F13. Click the Sum button on the Ribbon and then click the Enter button.

2 Select the range H13:I13. Click the Sum button on the Ribbon to display the totals in row 13 as shown in Figure 2-14.

Selecting a Range
You can select a range using the keyboard. Press the F8 key and then use the arrow keys to select the desired range. After you are finished, make sure to press the F8 key to turn off the selection or you will continue to select ranges.

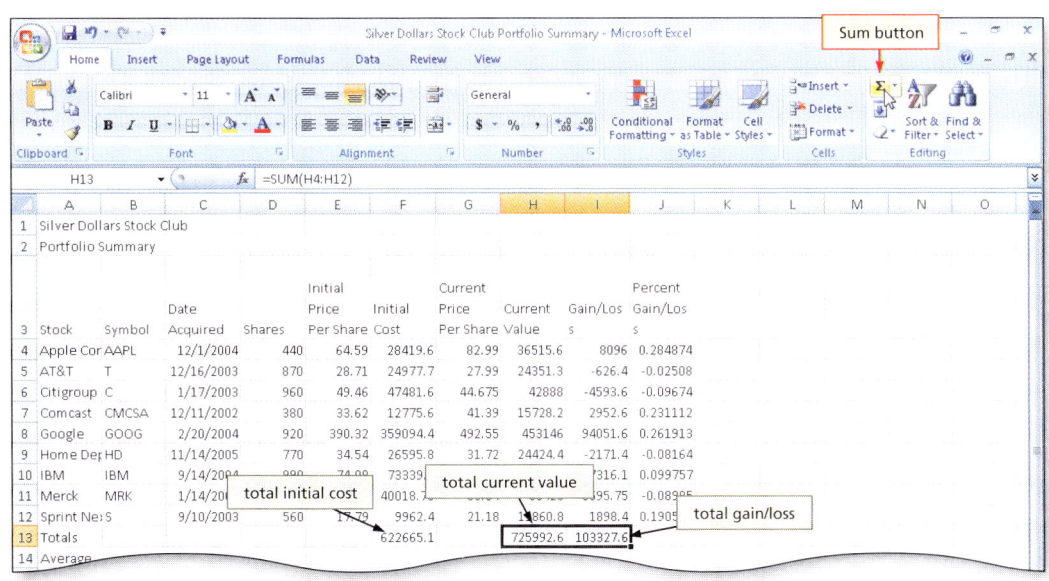

Figure 2-14

To Determine the Total Percent Gain/Loss

With the totals in row 13 determined, the next step is to copy the percent gain/loss formula in cell J12 to cell J13 as performed in the following steps.

1 Select cell J12 and then point to the fill handle.

2 Drag the fill handle down through cell J13 to copy the formula in cell J12 to cell J13 (Figure 2–15).

Q&A Why was the formula I13/F13 not copied to cell J13 earlier?

The formula, I13/F13, was not copied to cell J13 when cell J4 was copied to the range J5:J12 because both cells involved in the computation (I13 and F13) were blank, or zero, at the time. A **blank cell** in Excel has a numerical value of zero, which would have resulted in an error message in cell J13. Once the totals were determined, both cells I13 and F13 (especially F13, because it is the divisor) had nonzero numerical values.

	Stock	Symbol	Date Acquired	Shares	Initial Price Per Share	Initial Cost	Current Price Per Share	Current Value	Gain/Loss	Percent Gain/Loss
3	Stock	Symbol	Date Acquired	Shares	Per Share	Cost	Per Share	Value	s	s
4	Apple Cor	AAPL	12/1/2004	440	64.59	28419.6	82.99	36515.6	8096	0.284874
5	AT&T	T	12/16/2003	870	28.71	24977.7	27.99	24351.3	-626.4	-0.02508
6	Citigroup	C	1/17/2003	960	49.46	47481.6	44.675	42888	-4593.6	-0.09674
7	Comcast	CMCSA	12/11/2002	380	33.62	12775.6	41.39	15728.2	2952.6	0.231112
8	Google	GOOG	2/20/2004	920	390.32	359094.4	492.55	453146	94051.6	0.261913
9	Home Dep	HD	11/14/2005	770	34.54	26595.8	31.72	24424.4	-2171.4	-0.08164
10	IBM	IBM	9/14/2004	990	74.08	73339.2	81.47	80655.3	7316.1	0.099757
11	Merck	MRK	1/14/2005	950	42.125	40018.75	38.34	36423	-3595.75	-0.08985
12	Sprint Nex	S	9/10/2003	560	17.79	9962.4	21.18	11860.8	1898.4	0.190556
13	Totals					622665.1		725992.6	103327.6	0.165944
14	Average									
15	Highest									
16	Lowest									

formula is =I12/F12

formula is =I13/F13

Auto Fill Options button appears after copying cell J12 to cell J13

Figure 2–15

BTW

Entering Functions
You can drag the Function Arguments dialog box (Figure 2–20 on page EX 101) out of the way in order to select a range. You also can click the Collapse Dialog button to the right of the Number 1 box to hide the Function Arguments dialog box. After selecting the range, click the Collapse Dialog button a second time.

BTW

Statistical Functions
Excel usually considers a blank cell to be equal to 0. The statistical functions, however, ignore blank cells. Excel thus calculates the average of 3 cells with values of 7, blank, and 5 to be 6 or (7 + 5) / 2 and not 4 or (7 + 0 + 5) / 3.

Using the AVERAGE, MAX, and MIN Functions

The next step in creating the Silver Dollars Stock Club Portfolio Summary worksheet is to compute the average, highest value, and lowest value for the number of shares listed in the range D4:D12 using the AVERAGE, MAX, and MIN functions in the range D14:D16. Once the values are determined for column D, the entries can be copied across to the other columns.

Excel includes prewritten formulas called functions to help you compute these statistics. A **function** takes a value or values, performs an operation, and returns a result to the cell. The values that you use with a function are called **arguments**. All functions begin with an equal sign and include the arguments in parentheses after the function name. For example, in the function =AVERAGE(D4:D12), the function name is AVERAGE, and the argument is the range D4:D12.

With Excel, you can enter functions using one of five methods: (1) the keyboard or mouse; (2) the Insert Function box in the formula bar; (3) the Sum menu; (4) the AutoSum command on the Formulas tab on the Ribbon; and (5) the Name box area in the formula bar (Figure 2–16). The method you choose will depend on your typing skills and whether you can recall the function name and required arguments.

In the following pages, each of the first three methods will be used. The keyboard and mouse method will be used to determine the average number of shares (cell D14). The Insert Function button in the formula bar method will be used to determine the highest number of shares (cell D15). The Sum menu method will be used to determine the lowest number of shares (cell D16).

To Determine the Average of a Range of Numbers Using the Keyboard and Mouse

The **AVERAGE function** sums the numbers in the specified range and then divides the sum by the number of nonzero cells in the range. The following steps use the AVERAGE function to determine the average of the numbers in the range D4:D12.

1

- Select cell D14.
- Type =av in the cell to display the Formula AutoComplete list.
- Point to the AVERAGE function name (Figure 2–16).

Q&A

What is happening as I type?

As you type the equal sign followed by the characters in the name of a function, Excel displays the Formula AutoComplete list. This list contains those functions that alphabetically match the letters you have typed. Because you typed =av, Excel displays all the functions that begin with the letters av.

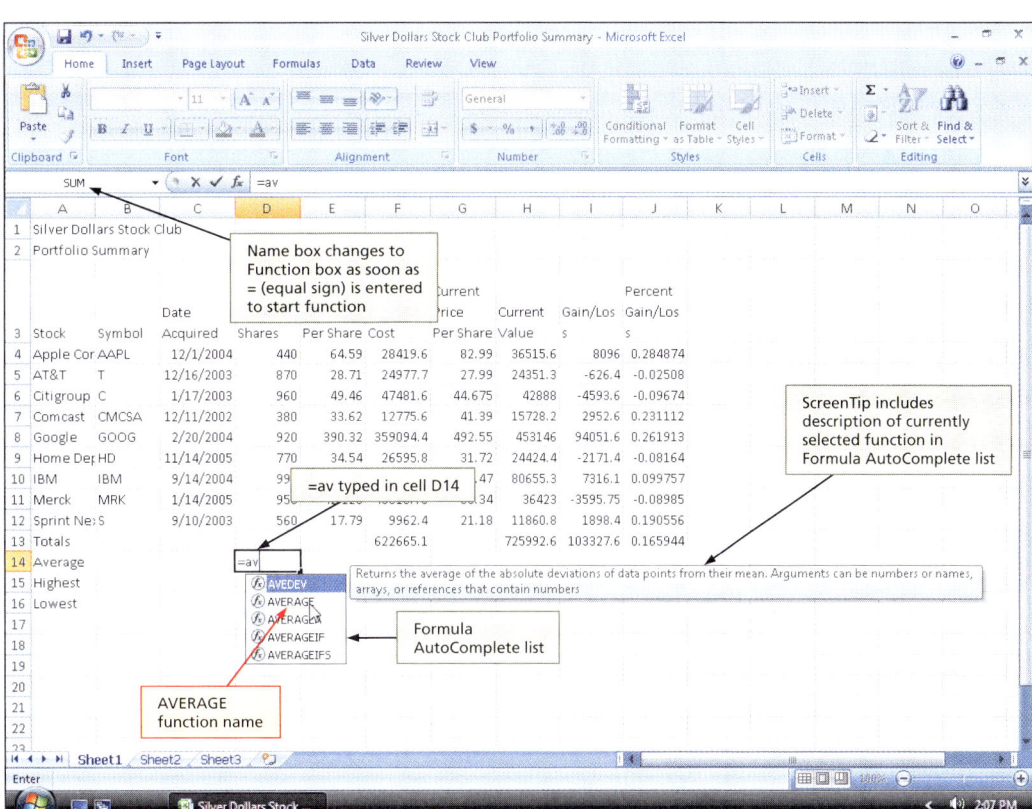

Figure 2–16

2

- Double-click AVERAGE in the Formula AutoComplete list to select the AVERAGE function.
- Select the range D4:D12 to insert the range as the argument to the AVERAGE function (Figure 2–17).

Q&A As I drag, why does the function in cell D14 change?

When you click cell D4, Excel appends cell D4 to the left parenthesis in the formula bar and surrounds cell D4 with a marquee. When you begin dragging, Excel appends to the argument a colon (:) and the cell reference of the cell where the mouse pointer is located.

3

- Click the Enter box to compute the average of the nine numbers in the range D4:D12 and display the result in cell D14 (Figure 2–18).

Q&A Can I use the arrow keys to complete the entry instead?

No. When you use Point mode you cannot use the arrow keys to complete the entry. While in Point mode, the arrow keys change the selected cell reference in the range you are selecting.

Q&A What is the purpose of the parentheses in the function?

The AVERAGE function requires that the argument (in this case, the range D4:D12) be included within parentheses following the function name. Excel automatically appends the right parenthesis to complete the AVERAGE function when you click the Enter box or press the ENTER key.

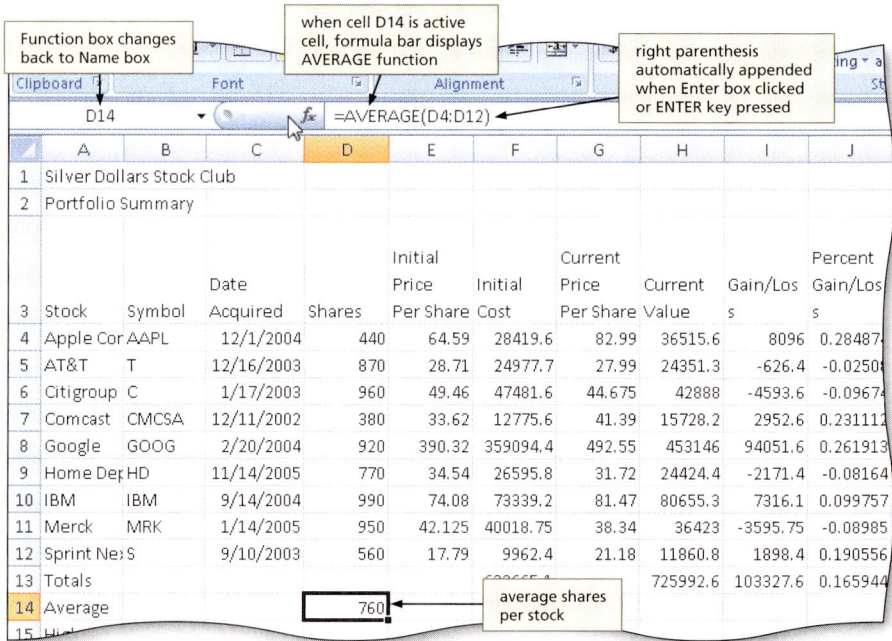

Figure 2–17

Figure 2–18

Other Ways

1. Click Insert Function box in formula bar, click AVERAGE function
2. Click Sum button arrow on Ribbon, click Average function
3. Click Formulas tab on Ribbon, click AutoSum button arrow, click Average function

To Determine the Highest Number in a Range of Numbers Using the Insert Function Box

The next step is to select cell D15 and determine the highest (maximum) number in the range D4:D12. Excel has a function called the **MAX function** that displays the highest value in a range. Although you could enter the MAX function using the keyboard and Point mode as described in the previous steps, an alternative method to entering the function is to use the Insert Function box in the formula bar, as performed in the following steps.

- Select cell D15.

- Click the Insert Function box in the formula bar to display the Insert Function dialog box.

- When Excel displays the Insert Function dialog box, click MAX in the 'Select a function' list (Figure 2–19).

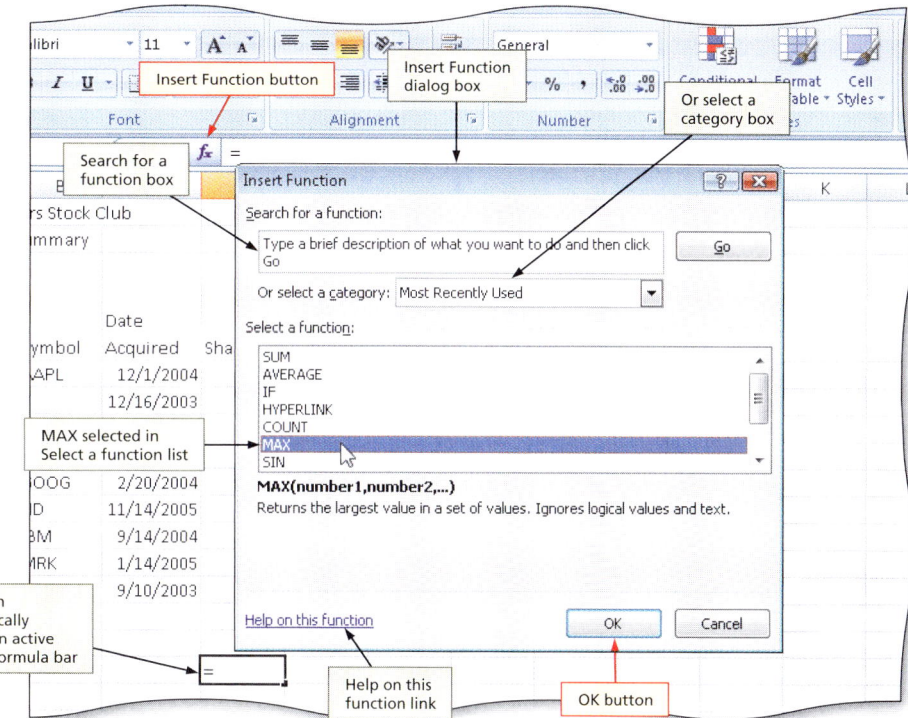

Figure 2–19

- Click the OK button.

- When Excel displays the Function Arguments dialog box, type `d4:d12` in the Number1 box (Figure 2–20).

Q&A

Why did numbers appear in the Function Arguments dialog box?

As shown in Figure 2–20, Excel displays the value the MAX function will return to cell D15 in the Function Arguments dialog box. It also lists the first few numbers in the selected range, next to the Number1 box.

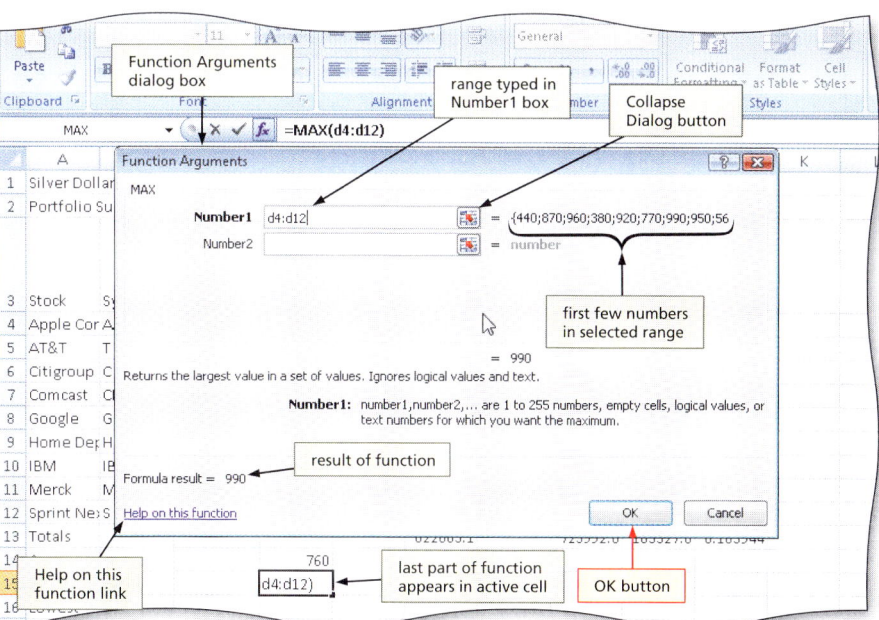

Figure 2–20

- Click the OK button to display the highest value in the range D4:D12 in cell D15 (Figure 2–21).

Q&A Why should I not just enter the highest value that I see in the range D4:D12 in cell D15?

In this example, rather than entering the MAX function, you easily could scan the range D4:D12, determine that the highest number of shares is 990, and manually enter the number 990 as a constant in cell D15. Excel would display the number the same as in Figure 2–21. Because it contains a constant, however, Excel will continue to display 990 in cell D15, even if the values in the range D4:D12 change. If you use the MAX function, Excel will recalculate the highest value in the range D4:D9 each time a new value is entered into the worksheet.

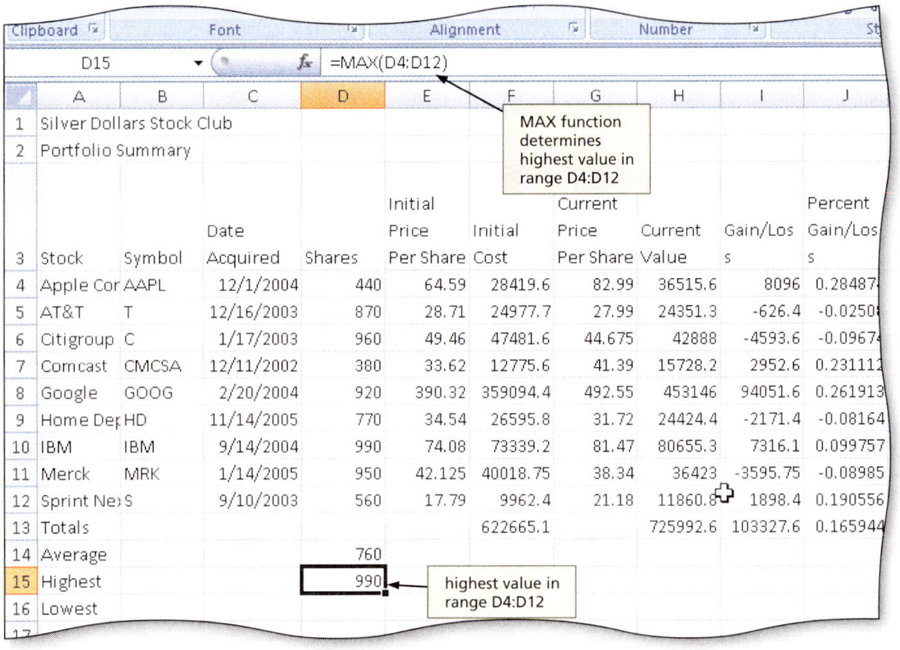

Figure 2–21

Other Ways

1. Click Sum button arrow on Ribbon, click Max function
2. Click Formulas tab on Ribbon, click AutoSum button arrow, click Max function
3. Type =MAX in cell

To Determine the Lowest Number in a Range of Numbers Using the Sum Menu

The next step is to enter the **MIN function** in cell D16 to determine the lowest (minimum) number in the range D4:D12. Although you can enter the MIN function using either of the methods used to enter the AVERAGE and MAX functions, the following steps perform an alternative using the Sum button on the Ribbon.

- Select cell D16.
- Click the Sum button arrow on the Ribbon to display the Sum button menu (Figure 2–22).

Q&A Why should I use the Sum button menu?

Using the Sum button menu allows you to enter one of five often-used functions easily into a cell, without having to memorize its name or the required arguments.

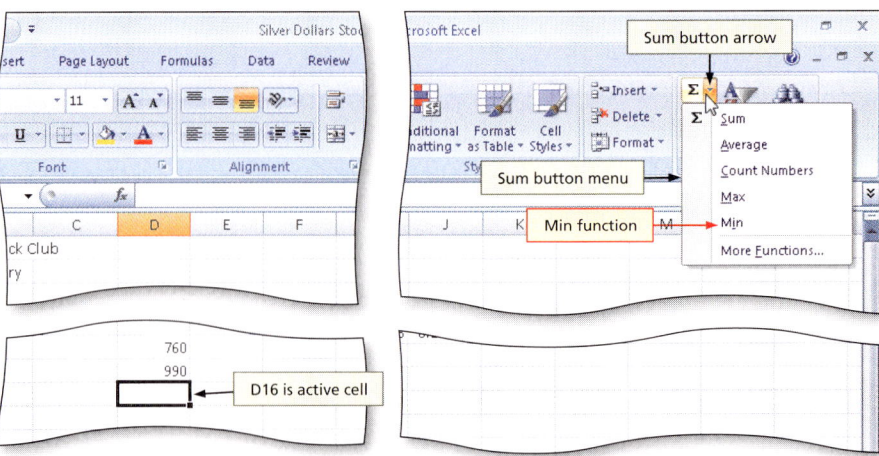

Figure 2–22

2

- Click Min to display the function =MIN(D14:D15) in the formula bar and in cell D16 (Figure 2–23).

Q&A Why does Excel select the range D14:D15?

The range D14:D15 automatically selected by Excel is not correct. Excel attempts to guess which cells you want to include in the function by looking for adjacent ranges to the selected cell that contain numeric data.

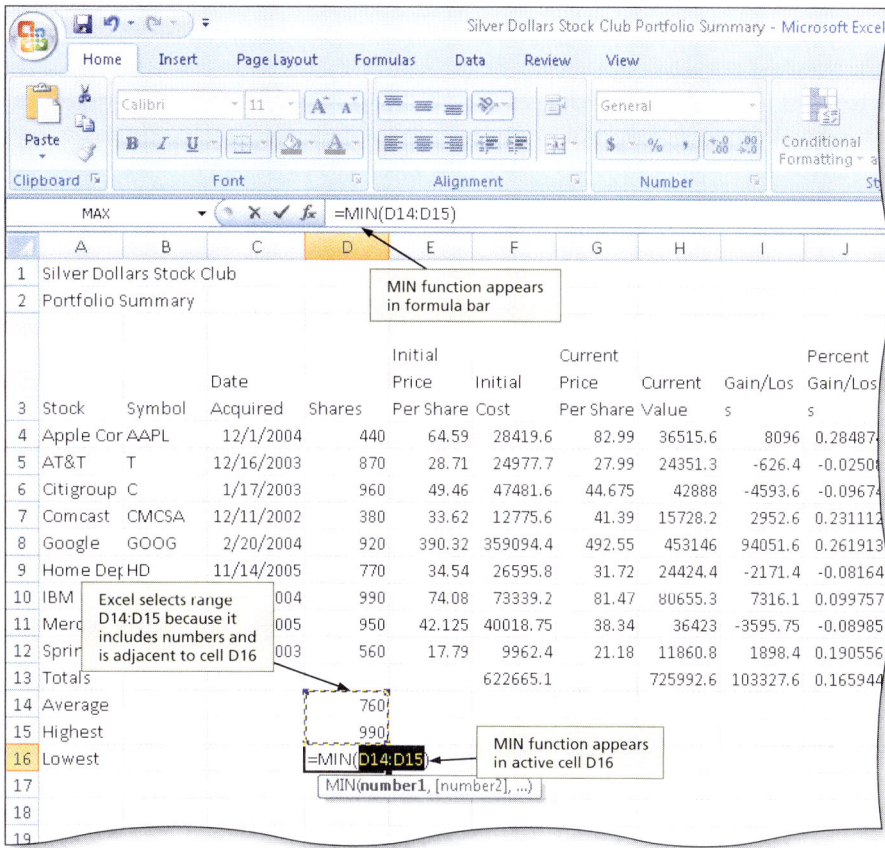

Figure 2–23

3

- Click cell D4 and then drag through cell D12 to display the function in the formula bar and in cell D14 with the new range (Figure 2–24).

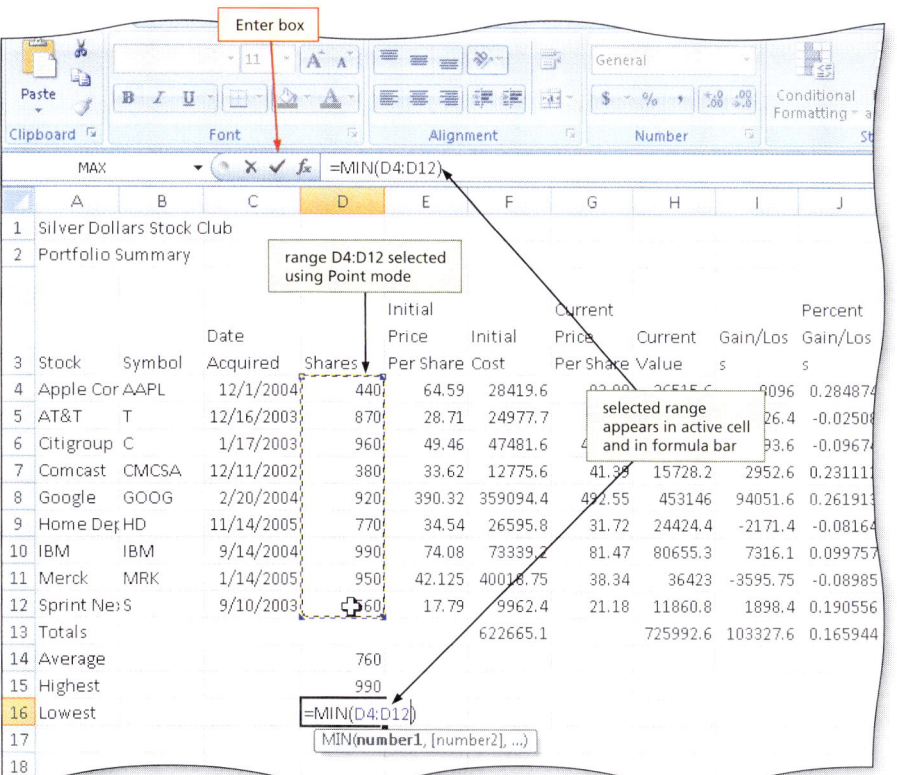

Figure 2–24

4

- Click the Enter box to determine the lowest value in D4:D12 and display the result in the formula bar and in cell D14 (Figure 2–25).

 How can I use other functions?

Excel has more than 400 additional functions that perform just about every type of calculation you can imagine. These functions are categorized in the Insert Function dialog box shown in Figure 2–19 on page EX 101. To view the categories, click the 'Or select a category' box arrow. To obtain a description of a selected function, select its name in the Insert Function dialog box. Excel displays the description of the function below the 'Select a function' list in the dialog box.

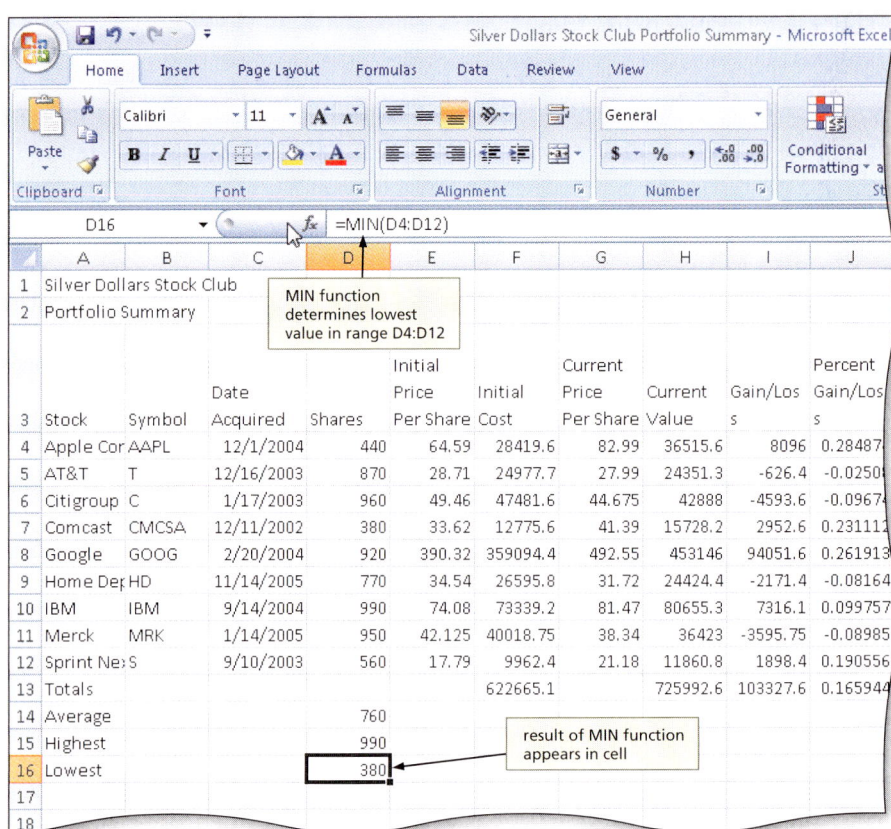

Figure 2–25

Other Ways

1. Click Insert Function box in formula bar, click MIN function
2. Click Formulas tab on Ribbon, click AutoSum button arrow, click Min function
3. Type =MIN in cell

To Copy a Range of Cells across Columns to an Adjacent Range Using the Fill Handle

The next step is to copy the AVERAGE, MAX, and MIN functions in the range D14:D16 to the adjacent range E14:J16. The following steps use the fill handle to copy the functions.

1

- Select the range D14:D16.
- Drag the fill handle in the lower-right corner of the selected range through cell J16 and continue to hold down the mouse button (Figure 2–26).

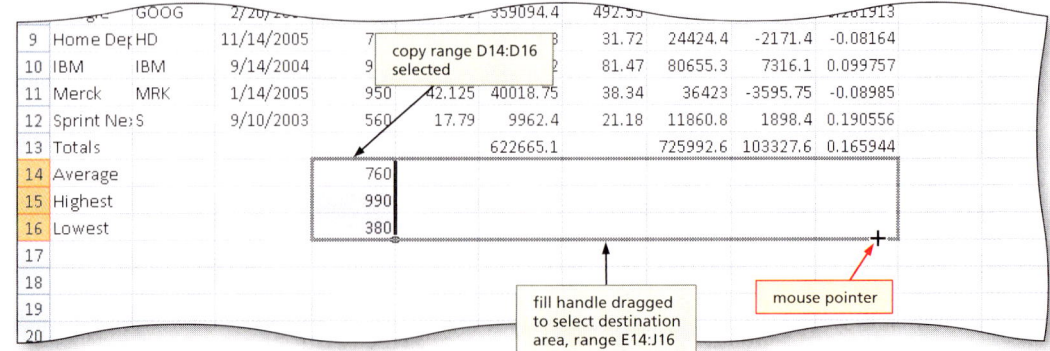

Figure 2–26

2

- Release the mouse button to copy the three functions to the range E14:J16 (Figure 2–27).

 How can I be sure that the function arguments are proper for the cells in range E14:J16?

Remember that Excel adjusts the cell references in the copied functions so each function refers to the range of numbers above it in the same column. Review the numbers in rows 14 through 16 in Figure 2–27. You should see that the functions in each column return the appropriate values, based on the numbers in rows 4 through 12 of that column.

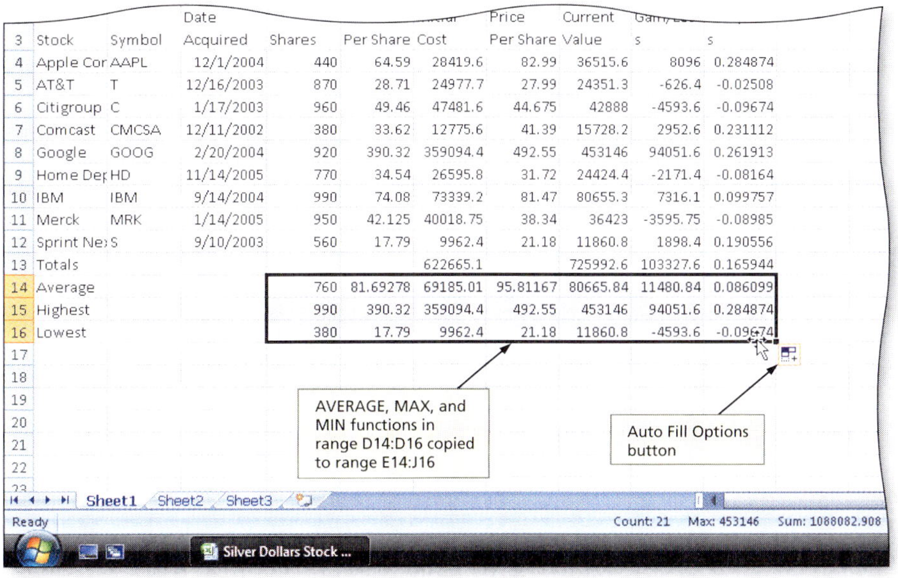

Figure 2–27

3

- Select cell J14 and press the DELETE key to delete the average of the percent gain/loss (Figure 2–28).

 Why is the formula in cell J14 deleted?

The average of the percent gain/loss in cell J14 is deleted because an average of percentages of this type is mathematically invalid.

Other Ways

1. Select source area and point to border of range, while holding down CTRL key, drag source area to destination area
2. Select source area, on Ribbon click Copy button, select destination area, on Ribbon click Paste button
3. Right-click source area, click Copy on shortcut menu, right-click destination area, click Paste on shortcut menu
4. Select source area, press CTRL+C, select destination area, press CTRL+V

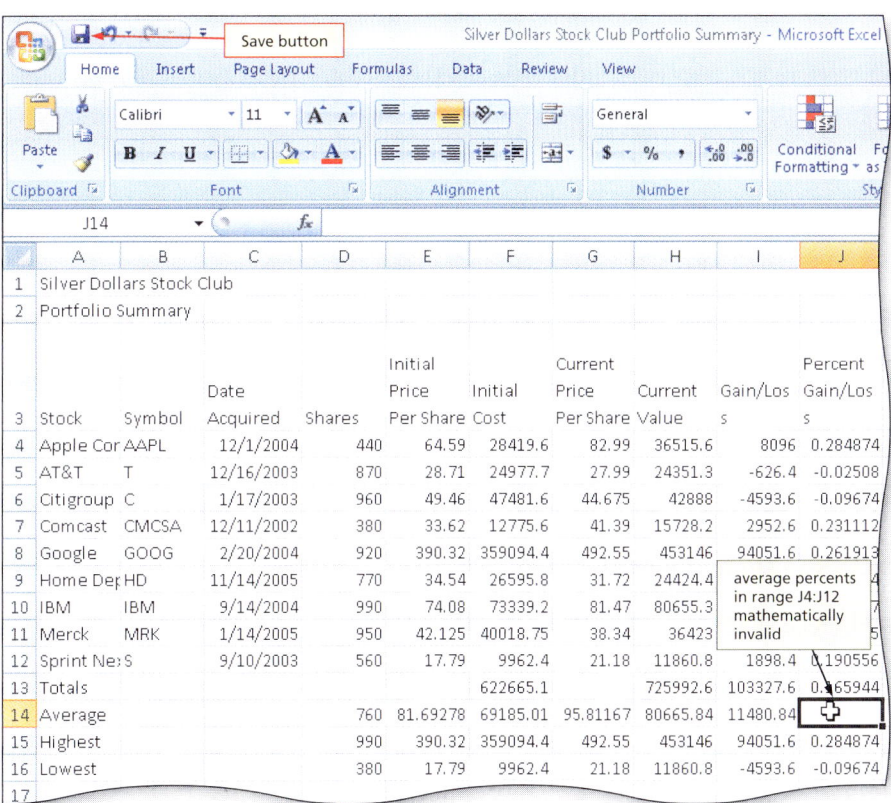

Figure 2–28

To Save a Workbook Using the Same File Name

Earlier in this project, an intermediate version of the workbook was saved using the file name, Silver Dollars Stock Club Portfolio Summary. The following step saves the workbook a second time using the same file name.

1 Click the Save button on the Quick Access Toolbar to save the workbook on the USB flash drive using the file name, Silver Dollars Stock Club Portfolio Summary.

Q&A

Why did Excel not display the Save As dialog box?

When you save a workbook a second time using the same file name, Excel will not display the Save As dialog box as it does the first time you save the workbook. Excel automatically stores the latest version of the workbook using the same file name, Silver Dollars Stock Club Portfolio Summary. You also can click Save on the Office Button menu or press SHIFT+F12 or CTRL+S to save a workbook again.

Verifying Formulas Using Range Finder

One of the more common mistakes made with Excel is to include a wrong cell reference in a formula. An easy way to verify that a formula references the cells you want it to reference is to use Excel's Range Finder. Use the **Range Finder** to check which cells are referenced in the formula assigned to the active cell. Range Finder allows you to make immediate changes to the cells referenced in a formula.

To use Range Finder to verify that a formula contains the intended cell references, double-click the cell with the formula you want to check. Excel responds by highlighting the cells referenced in the formula so you can check that the cell references are correct.

To Verify a Formula Using Range Finder

The following steps use Range Finder to check the formula in cell J4.

1
- Double-click cell J4 to activate Range Finder (Figure 2–29).

2
- Press the ESC key to quit Range Finder and then select cell A18.

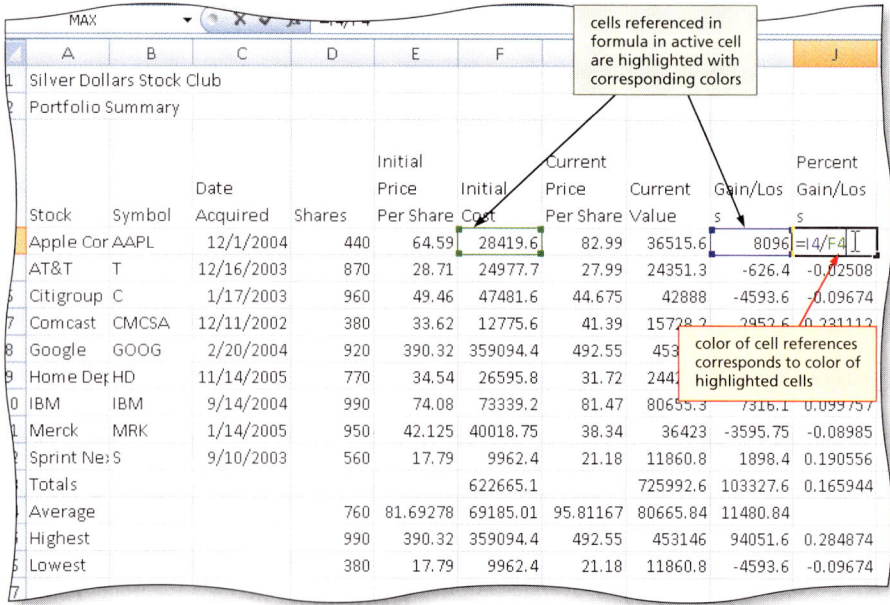

Figure 2–29

Formatting the Worksheet

Although the worksheet contains the appropriate data, formulas, and functions, the text and numbers need to be formatted to improve their appearance and readability.

In Chapter 1, cell styles were used to format much of the worksheet. This section describes how to change the unformatted worksheet in Figure 2–30a to the formatted worksheet in Figure 2–30b using a theme and other commands on the Ribbon. A **theme** is a predefined set of colors, fonts, chart styles, cell styles, and fill effects that can be applied to an entire workbook. Every new workbook that you create is assigned a default theme named Office. The colors and fonts that are used in the worksheet shown in Figure 2–30b are those that are associated with the Concourse theme.

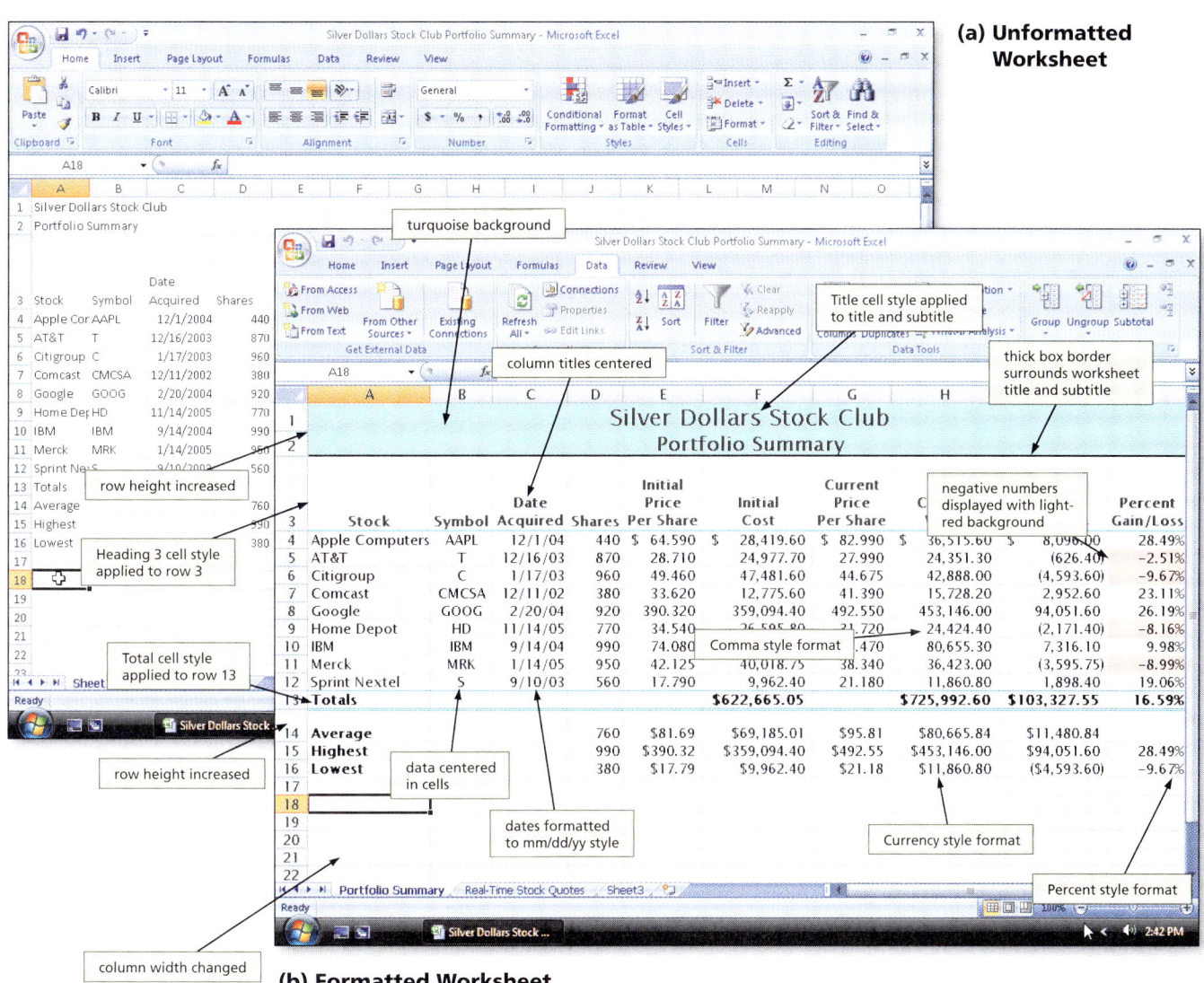

Figure 2–30

Plan Ahead

Identify how to format various elements of the worksheet.
The following outlines the formatting suggested in the sketch of the worksheet in Figure 2–3 on page EX 85:

1. Workbook theme - Concourse
2. Worksheet title and subtitle
    a. Alignment — center across columns A through J
    b. Cell style —Title
    c. Font size — title 18; subtitle 16
    d. Background color (range A1:J2) — Turquoise Accent 1, Lighter 60%
    e. Border — thick box border around range A1:J2
3. Column titles
    a. Cell style — Heading 3
    b. Alignment — center
4. Data
    a. Alignment — center data in column B
    b. Dates in column C — mm/dd/yy format
    c. Numbers in top row (range E4:I4) — Accounting style
    d. Numbers below top row (range E5:I12) — Comma style and decimal places
5. Total line
    a. Cell style — Total
    b. Numbers — Accounting style
6. Average, Highest, and Lowest rows
    a. Font style of row titles in range A14:A16 — bold
    b. Numbers — Currency style with floating dollar sign in the range E14:I16
7. Percentages in column J
    a. Numbers — Percentage style with two decimal places; if a cell in range J4:J12 is less than zero, then cell appears with background color of light red
8. Column widths
    a. Column A — 14.11 characters
    b. Columns B and C — best fit
    c. Column D — 6.00 characters
    d. Column E, G, and J — 9.00 characters
    e. Columns F, H, and I — 12.67 characters
9. Row heights
    a. Row 3 — 60.00 points
    b. Row 14 — 26.25 points
    c. Remaining rows — default

BTW

Colors
Knowing how people perceive colors helps you emphasize parts of your worksheet. Warmer colors (red and orange) tend to reach toward the reader. Cooler colors (blue, green, and violet) tend to pull away from the reader. Bright colors jump out of a dark background and are easiest to see. White or yellow text on a dark blue, green, purple, or black background is ideal.

To Change the Workbook Theme

The Concourse theme includes fonts and colors that provide the worksheet a professional and subtly colored appearance. The following steps change the workbook theme to the Concourse theme.

1

- Click the Page Layout tab on the Ribbon.

- Click the Themes button on the Ribbon to display the Theme gallery (Figure 2–31).

Experiment

- Point to several themes in the Theme gallery to see a live preview of the themes.

Q&A Why should I change the theme of a workbook?

A company or department may standardize on a specific theme so that all of their documents have a similar appearance. Similarly, an individual may want to have a theme that sets their work apart from others. Other Office programs, such as Word and PowerPoint, include the same themes included with Excel, meaning that all of your Microsoft Office documents can share a common theme.

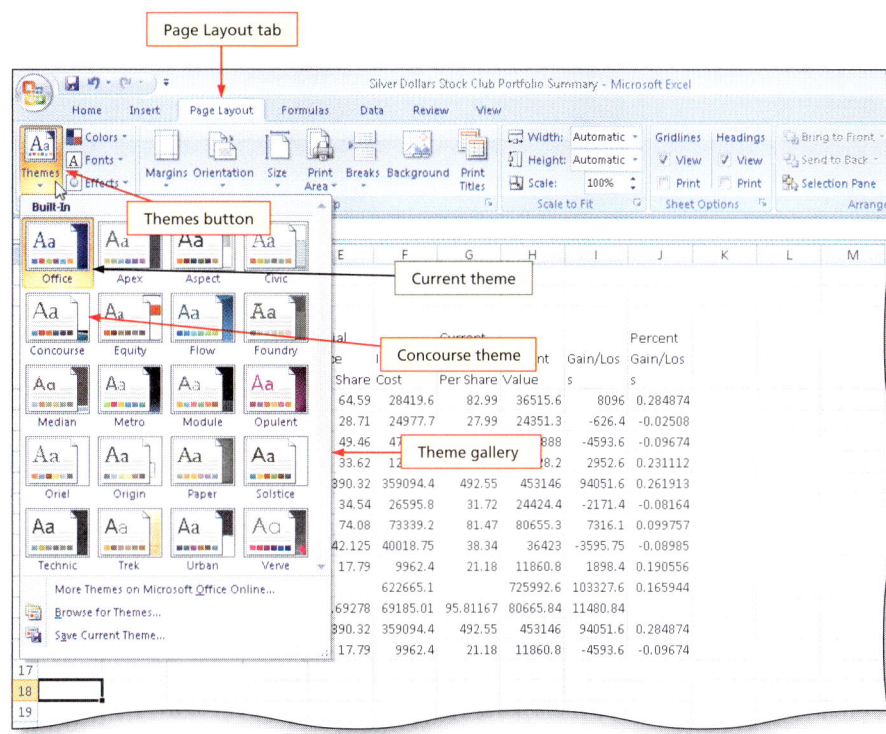

Figure 2–31

2

- Click Concourse in the Theme gallery to change the workbook theme to Concourse (Figure 2–32).

Q&A Why did the cells in the worksheet change?

The cells in the worksheet originally were formatted with the default font for the default Office theme. The default font for the Concourse theme is different than that of the default font for the Office theme and therefore changed on the worksheet when you changed the theme. If you had modified the font for any of the cells, those cells would not receive the default font for the Concourse theme.

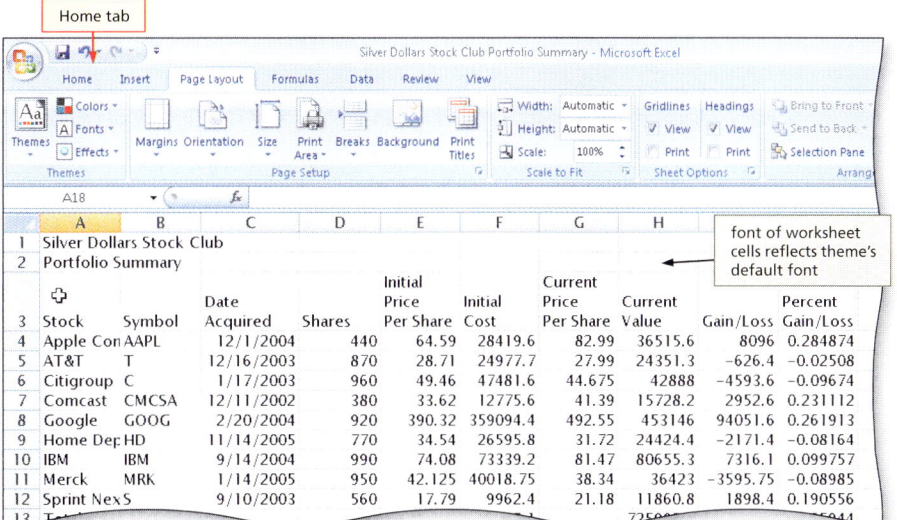

Figure 2–32

BTW

Background Colors
The most popular background color is blue. Research shows that the color blue is used most often because this color connotes serenity, reflection, and proficiency.

To Format the Worksheet Titles

The following steps merge and center the worksheet titles, apply the Title cells style to the worksheet titles, and decrease the font of the worksheet subtitle.

1. Click the Home tab on the Ribbon.

2. Select the range A1:J1 and then click the Merge & Center button on the Ribbon.

3. Select the range A2:J2 and then click the Merge & Center button on the Ribbon.

4. Select the range A1:A2, click the Cell Styles button on the Ribbon, and then click the Title cell style in the Cell Styles gallery.

5. Select cell A2 and then click the Decrease Font Size button on the Ribbon (Figure 2–33).

Q&A What is the effect of clicking the Decrease Font Size button?

When you click the Decrease Font Size button Excel assigns the next lowest font size in the Font Size gallery to the selected range. The Increase Font Size button works in a similar manner, but causes Excel to assign the next highest font size in the Font Size gallery to the selected range.

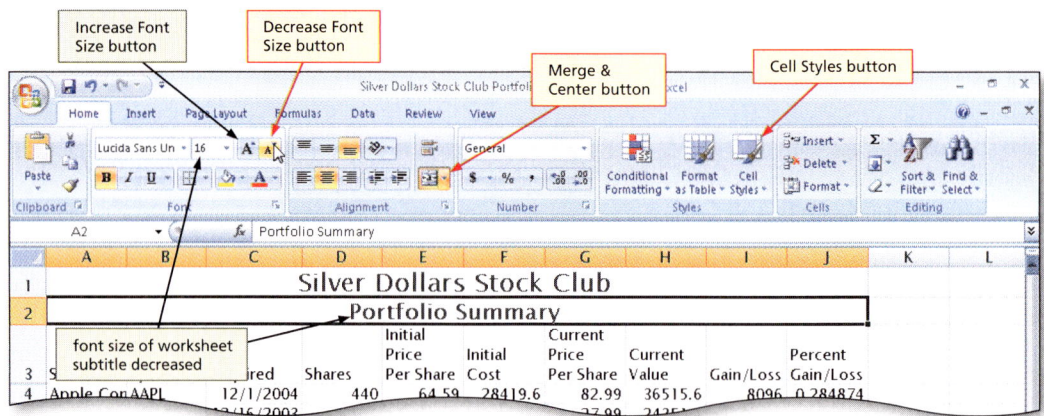

Figure 2–33

To Change the Background Color and Apply a Box Border to the Worksheet Title and Subtitle

The final formats assigned to the worksheet title and subtitle are the turquoise background color and thick box border (Figure 2–30b on page EX 107). The following steps complete the formatting of the worksheet titles.

1.
- Select the range A1:A2 and then click the Fill Color button arrow on the Ribbon to display the Fill Color palette (Figure 2–34).

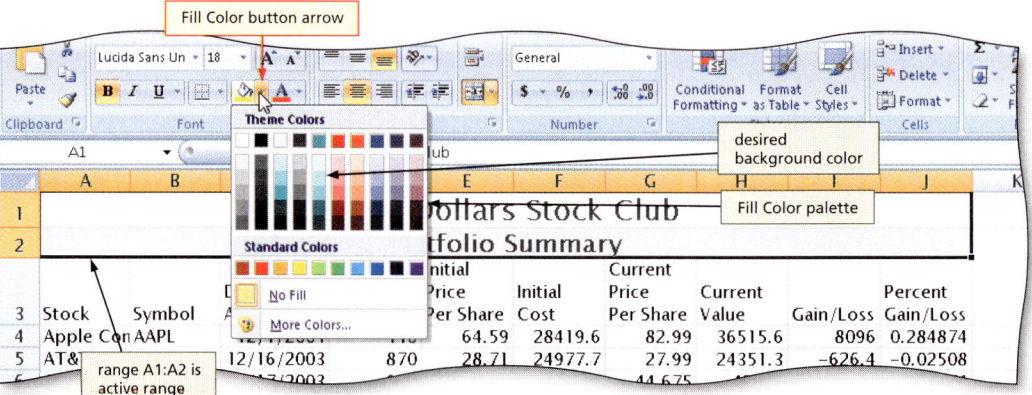

Figure 2–34

2

- Click Turquoise Accent 1, lighter 60% (column 5, row 3) on the Fill Color palette to change the background color of cells A1 and A2 from white to turquoise (Figure 2–35).

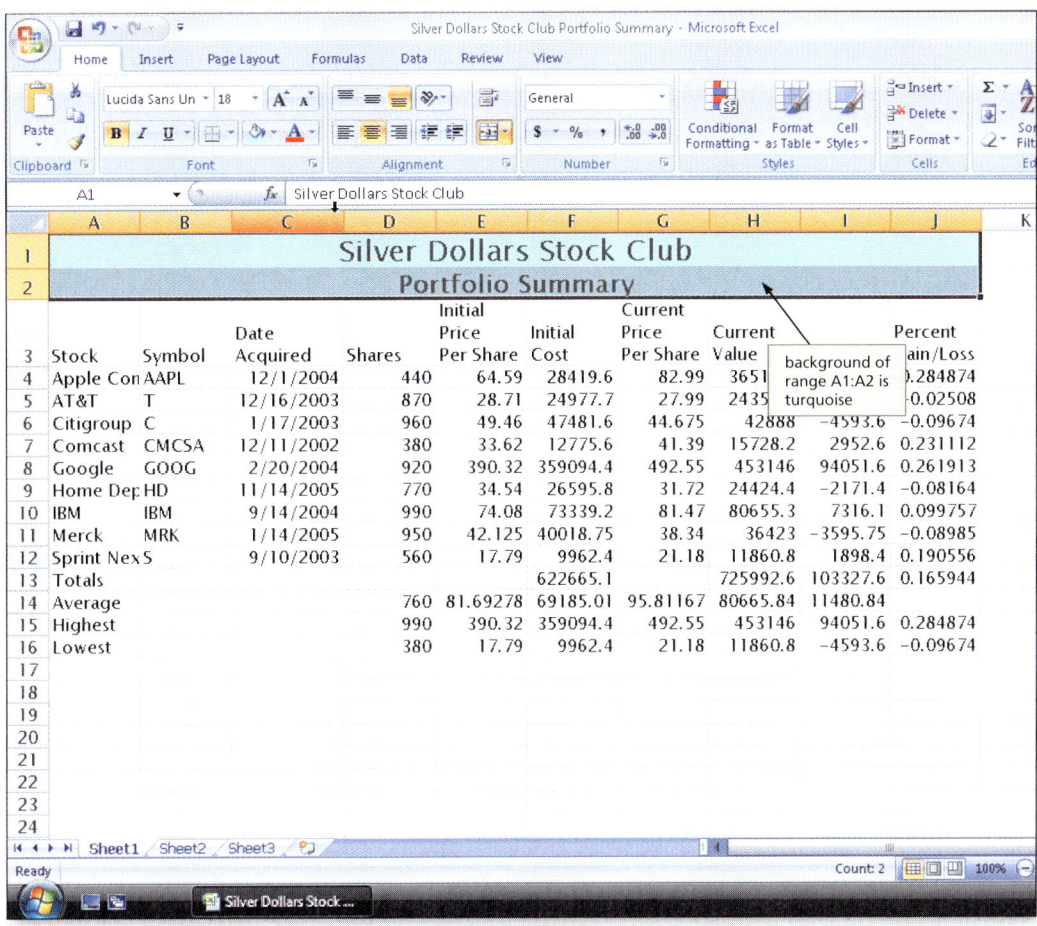

Figure 2–35

3

- Click the Borders button arrow on the Ribbon to display the Borders gallery (Figure 2–36).

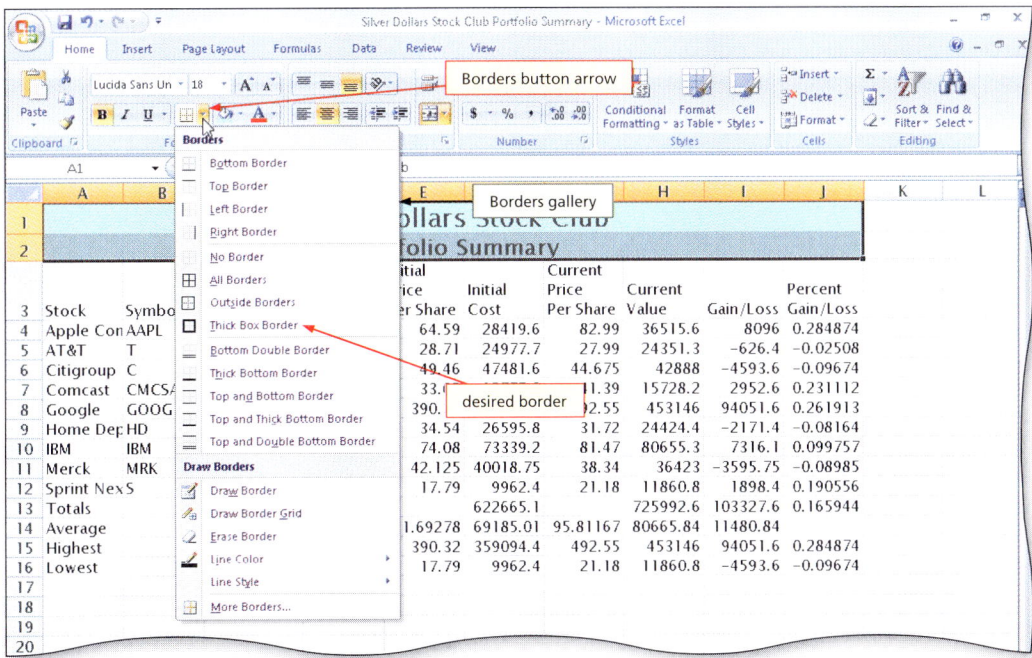

Figure 2–36

- Click the Thick Box Border command on the Borders gallery to display a thick box border around the range A1:A2.
- Click cell A18 to deselect the range A1:A2 (Figure 2–37).

Other Ways

1. On Ribbon click Format Cells Dialog Box Launcher, click appropriate tab, click desired format, click OK button
2. Right-click range, click Format Cells on shortcut menu, click appropriate tab, click desired format, click OK button
3. Press CTRL+1, click appropriate tab, click desired format, click OK button

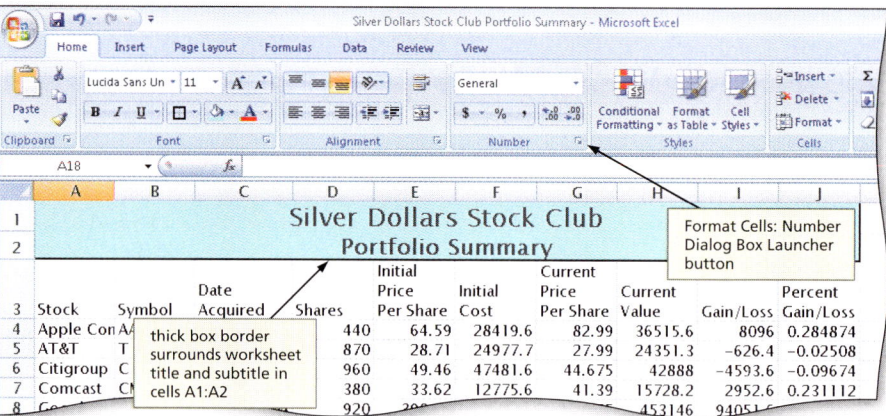

Figure 2–37

To Apply a Cell Style to the Column Headings and Format the Total Rows

As shown in Figure 2–30b on page EX 107, the column titles (row 3) have the Heading 3 cell style and the total row (row 13) has the Total cell style. The summary information headings in the range A14:A16 should be bold. The following steps assign these styles to row 3 and row 13 and the range A14:A16.

1. Select the range A3:J3.
2. Apply the Heading 3 cell style to the range A3:J3.
3. Apply the Total cell style to the range A13:J13.
4. Select the range A14:A16 and then click the Bold button on the Ribbon (Figure 2–38).

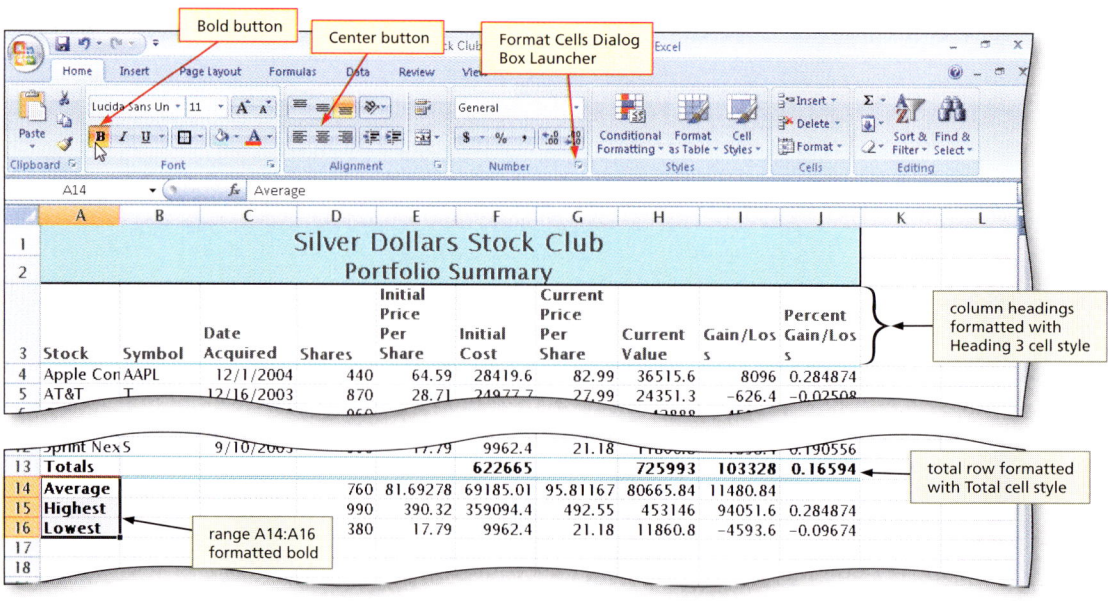

Figure 2–38

To Center Data in Cells and Format Dates

With the column titles and total rows formatted, the next step is to center the stock symbols in column B and format the dates in column C. If a cell entry is short, such as the stock symbols in column B, centering the entries within their respective columns improves the appearance of the worksheet. The following steps center the data in the range B4:B12 and format the dates in the range C4:C12.

1

- Select the range B4:B12 and then click the Center button on the Ribbon to center the data in the range B4:B12.

2

- Select the range C4:C12.

- Click the Format Cells: Number Dialog Box Launcher on the Ribbon to display the Format Cells dialog box.

- When Excel displays the Format Cells dialog box, if necessary click the Number tab, click Date in the Category list, and then click 3/14/01 in the Type list to choose the format for the range C4:C12 (Figure 2–39).

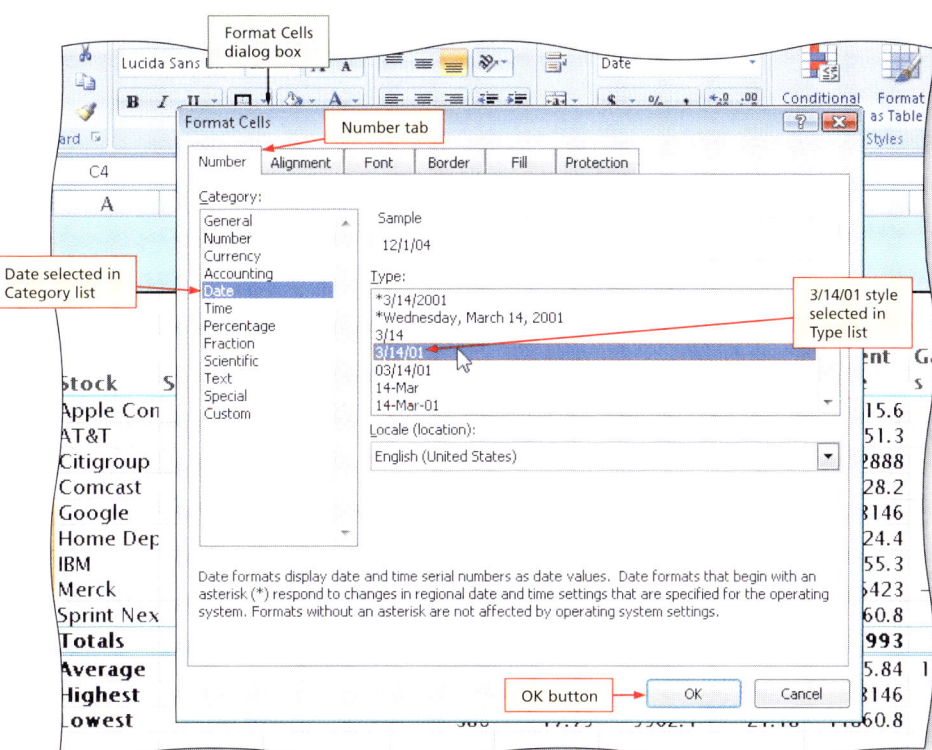

Figure 2–39

3

- Click the OK button to format the dates in column C using the date format style, mm/dd/yy.

- Select cell E4 to deselect the range C4:C13 (Figure 2–40).

Q&A Can I format an entire column at once?

Yes. Rather than selecting the range B4:B12 in Step 1, you could have clicked the column B heading immediately above cell B1, and then clicked the Center button on the Ribbon. In this case, all cells in column B down to the last cell in the worksheet would have been formatted to use center alignment. This same procedure could have been used to format the dates in column C.

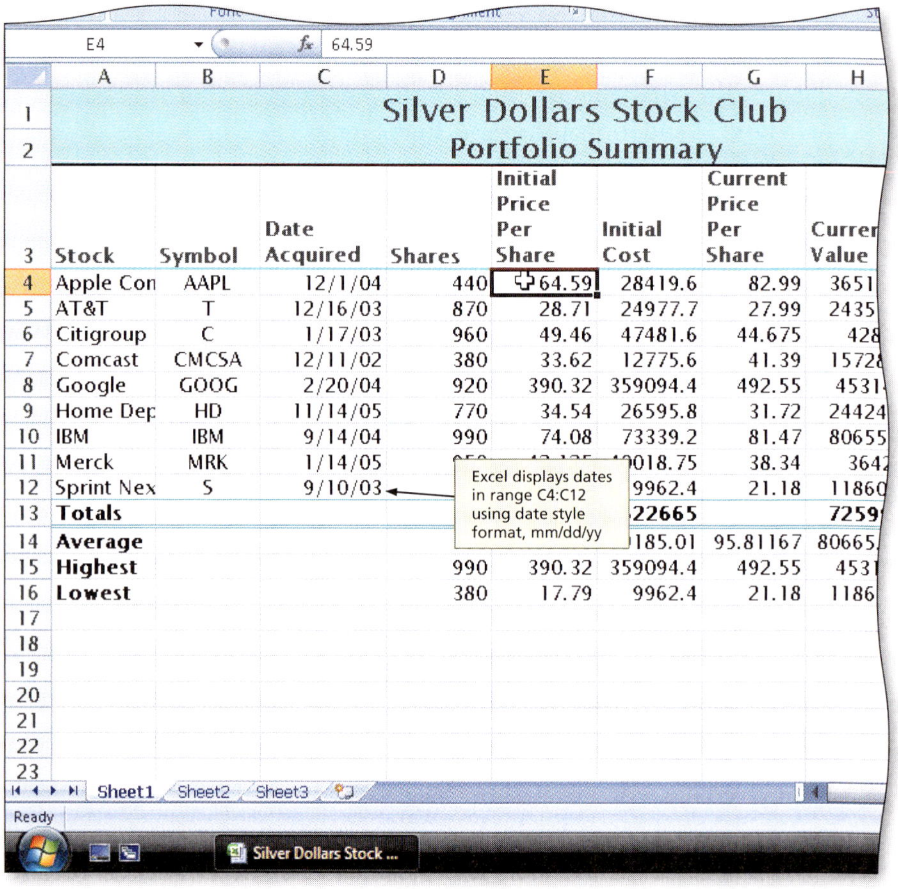

Figure 2–40

Other Ways

1. Right-click range, click Format Cells on shortcut menu, click appropriate tab, click desired format, click OK button
2. Press CTRL+1, click appropriate tab, click desired format, click OK button

BTW

Rotating and Shrinking Entries in Cells
In addition to aligning entries horizontally and vertically, you also can rotate and shrink entries to fit in a cell. To rotate or shrink entries to fit in a cell, click Format Cells on the shortcut menu, click the Alignment tab in the Format Cells dialog box, and then select the type of control you want.

Formatting Numbers Using the Ribbon

As shown in Figure 2–30b on page EX 107, the worksheet is formatted to resemble an accounting report. For example, in columns E through I, the numbers in the first row (row 4), the totals row (row 13), and the rows below the totals (rows 14 through 16) have dollar signs, while the remaining numbers (rows 5 through 12) in columns E through I do not.

To append a dollar sign to a number, you should use the Accounting number format. Excel displays numbers using the **Accounting number format** with a dollar sign to the left of the number, inserts a comma every three positions to the left of the decimal point, and displays numbers to the nearest cent (hundredths place). Clicking the Accounting Number Format button on the Ribbon assigns the desired Accounting number format. When you use the Accounting Number Format button to assign the Accounting number format, Excel displays a **fixed dollar sign** to the far left in the cell, often with spaces between it and the first digit. To assign a **floating dollar sign** that appears immediately to the left of the first digit with no spaces, use the Currency style in the Format Cells dialog box.

The Comma style format is used to instruct Excel to display numbers with commas and no dollar signs. The **Comma style format**, which can be assigned to a range of cells by clicking the Comma Style button on the Ribbon, inserts a comma every three positions to the left of the decimal point and causes numbers to be displayed to the nearest hundredths.

To Apply an Accounting Style Format and Comma Style Format Using the Ribbon

The following steps assign formats using the Accounting Number Format button and the Comma Style button on the Ribbon.

- Select the range E4:I4.
- While holding down the CTRL key, select the ranges F13:I13.
- Click the Accounting Number Format button on the Ribbon (Figure 2–41) to apply the Accounting style format with fixed dollar signs to the nonadjacent ranges E4:I4 and F13:I13 (Figure 2–41).

Q&A

What is the effect of applying the Accounting style format?

The Accounting Number Format button assigns a fixed dollar sign to the numbers in the ranges E4:I4 and F13:I13. In each cell in these ranges, Excel displays the dollar sign to the far left with spaces between it and the first digit in the cell.

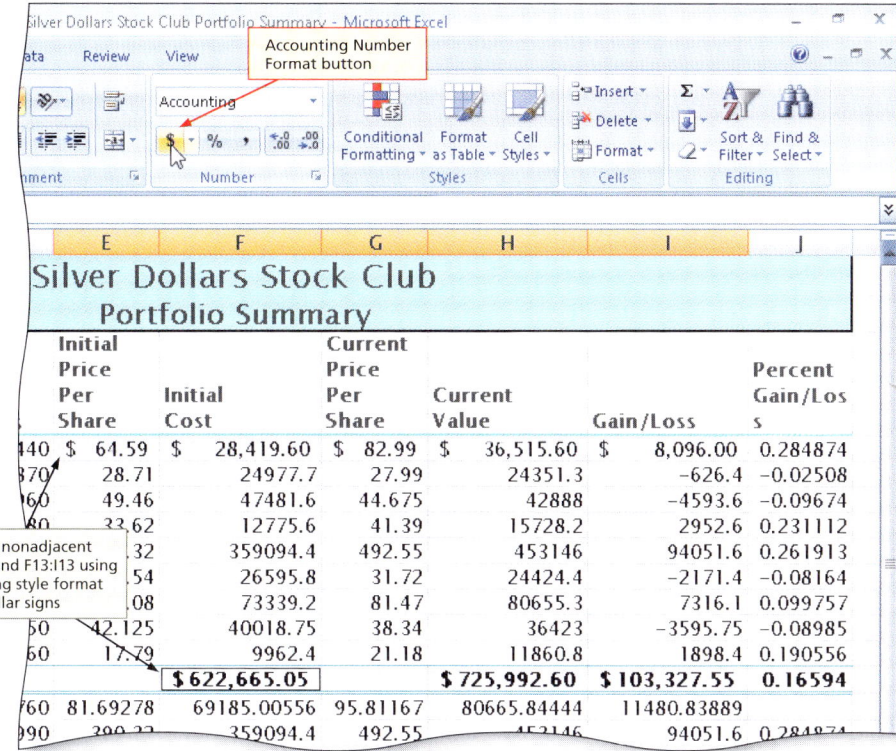

Figure 2–41

- Select the range E5:I12.
- Click the Comma Style button on the Ribbon to assign the Comma style format to the range E5:I12 (Figure 2–42).

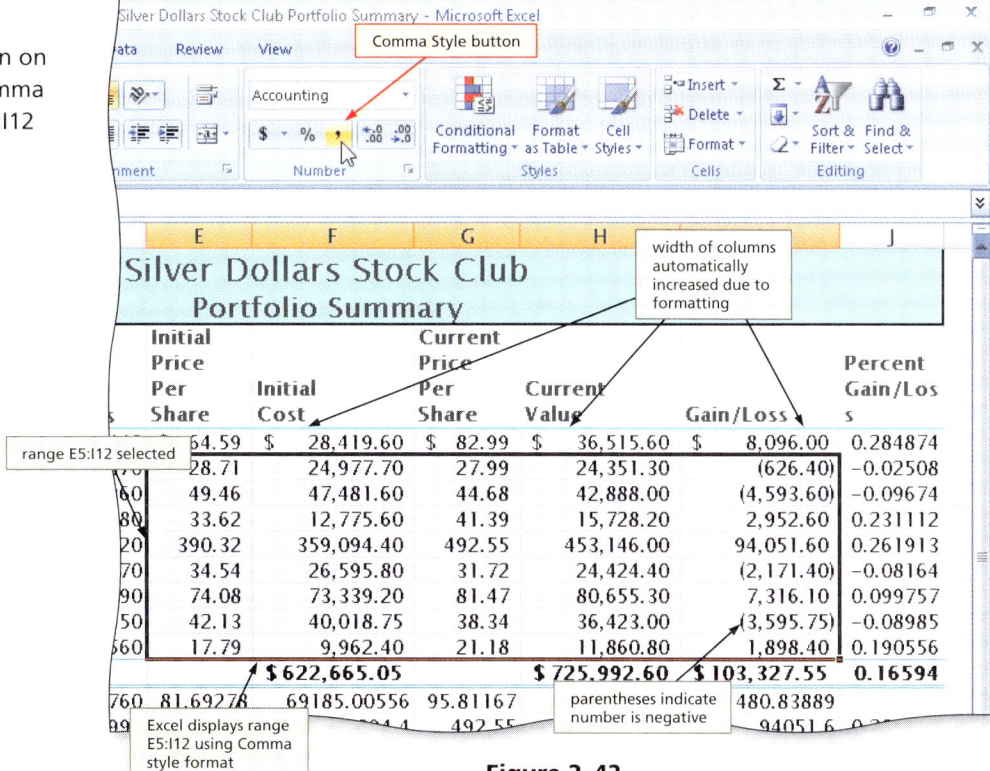

Figure 2–42

EX 116 Excel Chapter 2 Formulas, Functions, Formatting, and Web Queries

3

- Click cell E4.

- While holding down the CTRL key, select cell G4.

- Click the Increase Decimal button on the Ribbon to increase the number of decimal places displayed in cell E4 and G4.

- Select the range E5:E12. While holding down the CTRL key, select the range G5:G12.

- Click the Increase Decimal button on the Ribbon to increase the number of decimal places displayed in selected ranges (Figure 2–43).

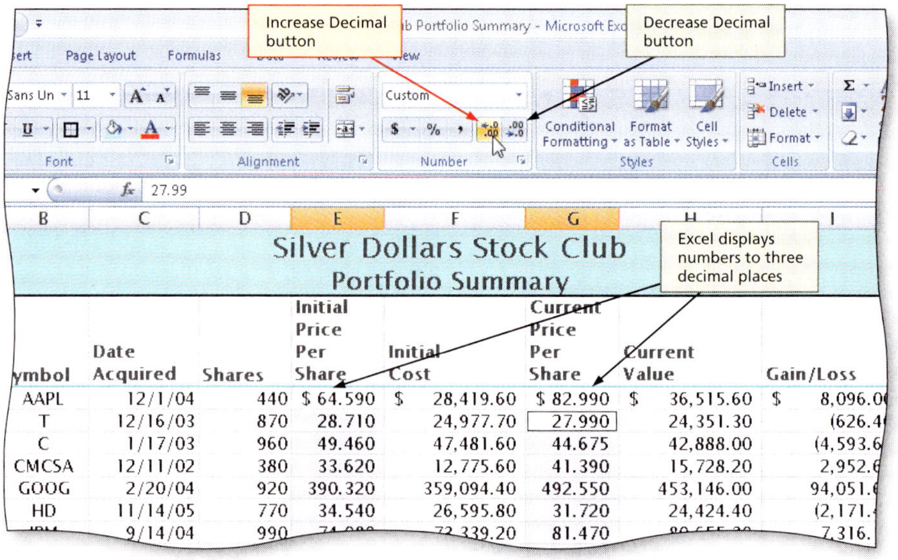

Q&A What is the effect of clicking the Increase Decimal button?

The Increase Decimal button instructs Excel to display additional decimal places in a cell. Each time you click the Increase Decimal button, Excel adds a decimal place to the selected cell.

Figure 2–43

To Apply a Currency Style Format with a Floating Dollar Sign Using the Format Cells Dialog Box

The following steps use the Format Cells dialog box to apply the Currency style format with a floating dollar sign to the numbers in the ranges E14:I16.

1

- Select the range E14:I16 and then point to the Format Cells: Number Dialog Box Launcher on the Ribbon (Figure 2–44).

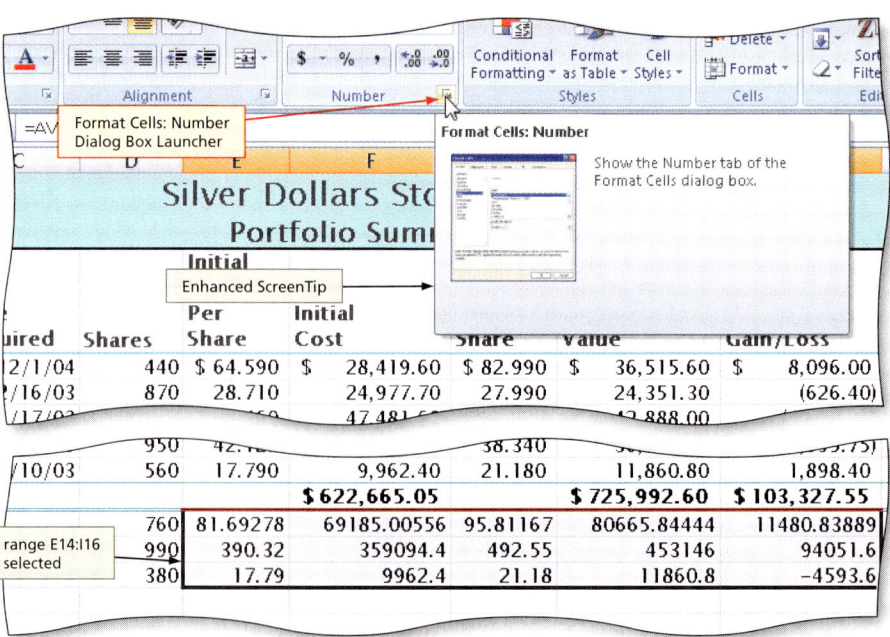

Figure 2–44

2
- Click the Format Cells: Number Dialog Box Launcher.
- If necessary, click the Number tab in the Format Cells dialog box.
- Click Currency in the Category list and then click the third style ($1,234.10) in the Negative numbers list (Figure 2–45).

Q&A How do I select the proper format?

You can choose from 12 categories of formats. Once you select a category, you can select the number of decimal places, whether or not a dollar sign should be displayed, and how negative numbers should appear. Selecting the appropriate negative numbers format is important, because doing so adds a space to the right of the number in order to align the numbers in the worksheet on the decimal points. Some of the available negative number formats do not align the numbers in the worksheet on the decimal points.

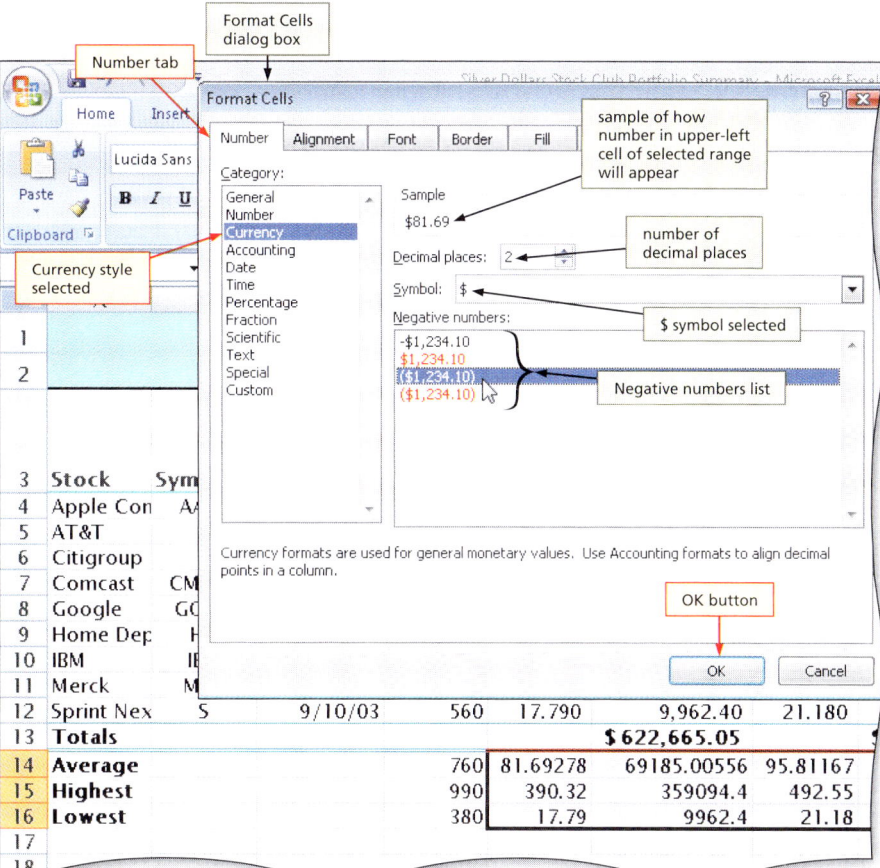

Figure 2–45

3
- Click the OK button to assign the Currency style format with a floating dollar sign to the range E14:I16 (Figure 2–46).

Q&A Should I click the Accounting Number Style button on the Ribbon or use the Format Cells dialog box?

Recall that a floating dollar sign always appears immediately to the left of the first digit, and the fixed dollar sign always appears on the left side of the cell. Cell E4, for example, has a fixed dollar sign, while cell E14 has a floating dollar sign. The Currency style was assigned to cell E14 using the Format Cells dialog box and the result is a floating dollar sign.

Figure 2–46

Other Ways

1. Press CTRL+1, click Number tab, click Currency in Category list, select format, click OK button
2. Press CTRL+SHIFT+ DOLLAR SIGN ($)

To Apply a Percent Style Format and Use the Increase Decimal Button

The next step is to format the percent gain/loss in column J. Currently, Excel displays the numbers in column J as a decimal fraction (for example, 0.284874 in cell J4). The following steps format the range J4:J16 to the Percent style format with two decimal places.

- Select the range J4:J16.
- Click the Percent Style button on the Ribbon to display the numbers in column J as a rounded whole percent.

Q&A

What is the result of clicking the Percent Style button?

The Percent Style button instructs Excel to display a value as a percentage, determined by multiplying the cell entry by 100, rounding the result to the nearest percent, and adding a percent sign. For example, when cell J4 is formatted using the Percent Style and Increase Decimal buttons, Excel displays the actual value 0.284874 as 28.49%.

- Click the Increase Decimal button on the Ribbon two times to display the numbers in column J with the Percent style format and two decimal places (Figure 2–47).

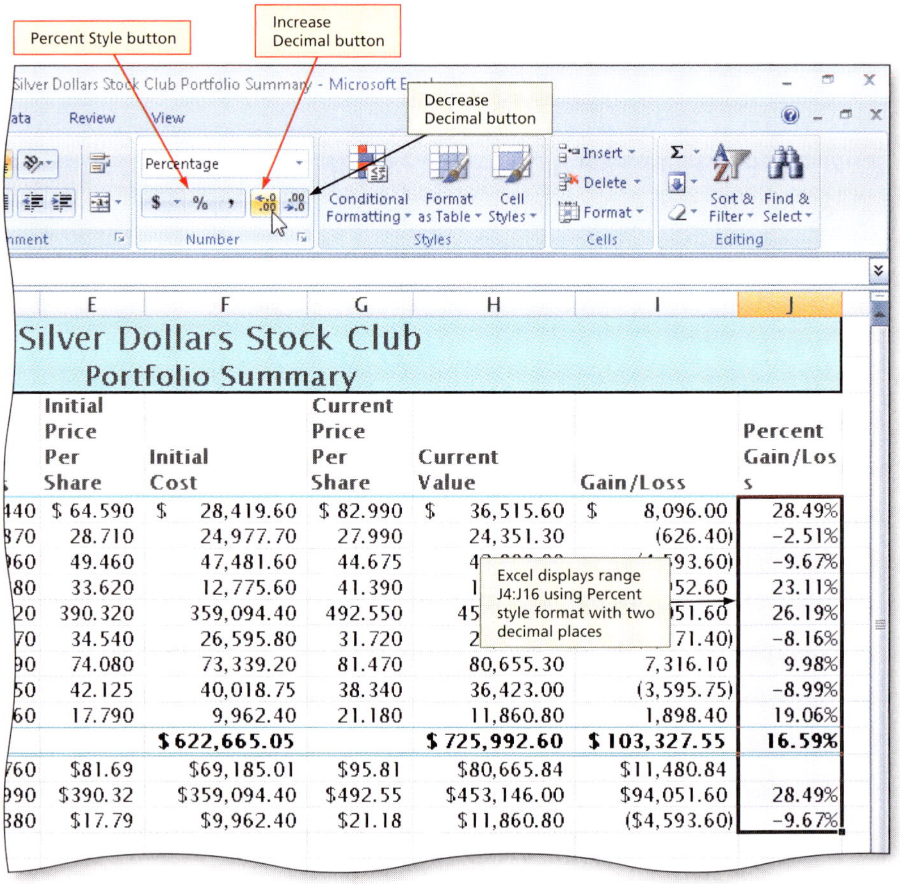

Figure 2–47

Other Ways

1. Right-click range, click Format Cells on shortcut menu, click Number tab, click Percentage in Category list, select format, click OK button
2. Press CTRL+1, click Number tab, click Percentage in Category list, select format, click OK button
3. Press CTRL+SHIFT+ PERCENT SIGN (%)

Conditional Formatting

The next step is to emphasize the negative percentages in column J by formatting them to appear with a tinted background. The Conditional Formatting button on the Ribbon will be used to complete this task.

Excel lets you apply formatting that appears only when the value in a cell meets conditions that you specify. This type of formatting is called **conditional formatting**. You can apply conditional formatting to a cell, a range of cells, the entire worksheet, or the entire workbook. Usually, you apply conditional formatting to a range of cells that contains values you want to highlight, if conditions warrant. For example, you can instruct Excel to change the color of the background of a cell if the value in the cell meets a condition, such as being less than 0 as shown in Figure 2–48.

A **condition**, which is made up of two values and a relational operator, is true or false for each cell in the range. If the condition is true, then Excel applies the formatting. If the condition is false, then Excel suppresses the formatting. What makes conditional formatting so powerful is that the cell's appearance can change as you enter new values in the worksheet.

To Apply Conditional Formatting

The following steps assign conditional formatting to the range J4:J12, so that any cell value less than zero will cause Excel to display the number in the cell with a light red background.

- Select the range J4:J12.
- Click the Conditional Formatting button on the Ribbon to display the Conditional Formatting gallery (Figure 2–48).

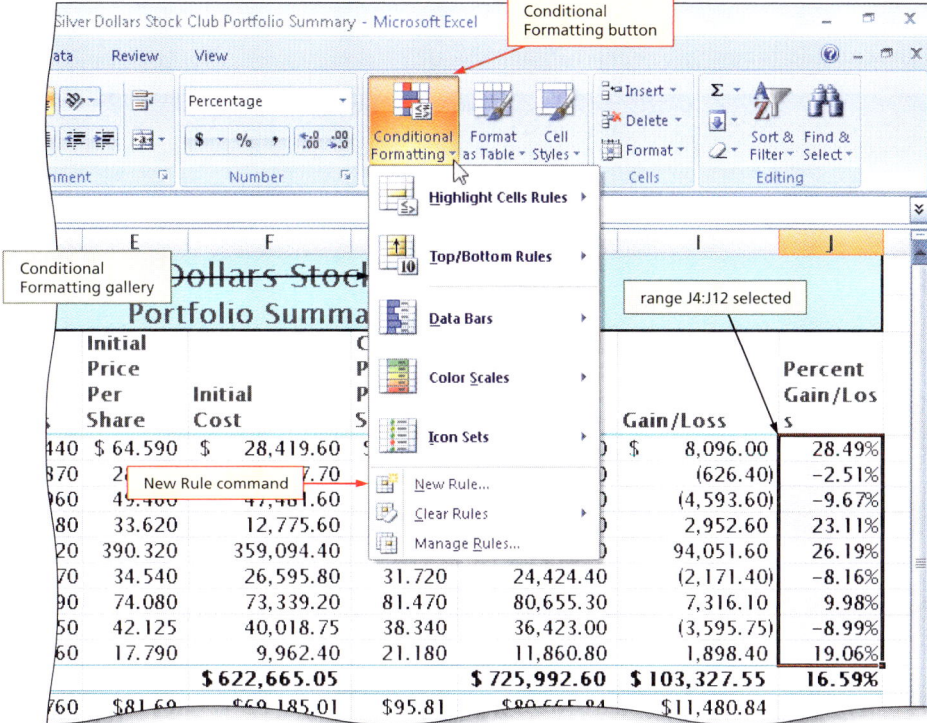

Figure 2–48

- Click New Rule in the Conditional Formatting gallery to display the New Formatting Rule dialog box.
- Click 'Format only cells that contain' in the Select a Rule Type area.
- In the Edit the Rule Description area, click the box arrow in the relational operator box (second text box) and then select less than.
- Type 0 (zero) in the rightmost box in the Edit the Rule Description area (Figure 2–49).

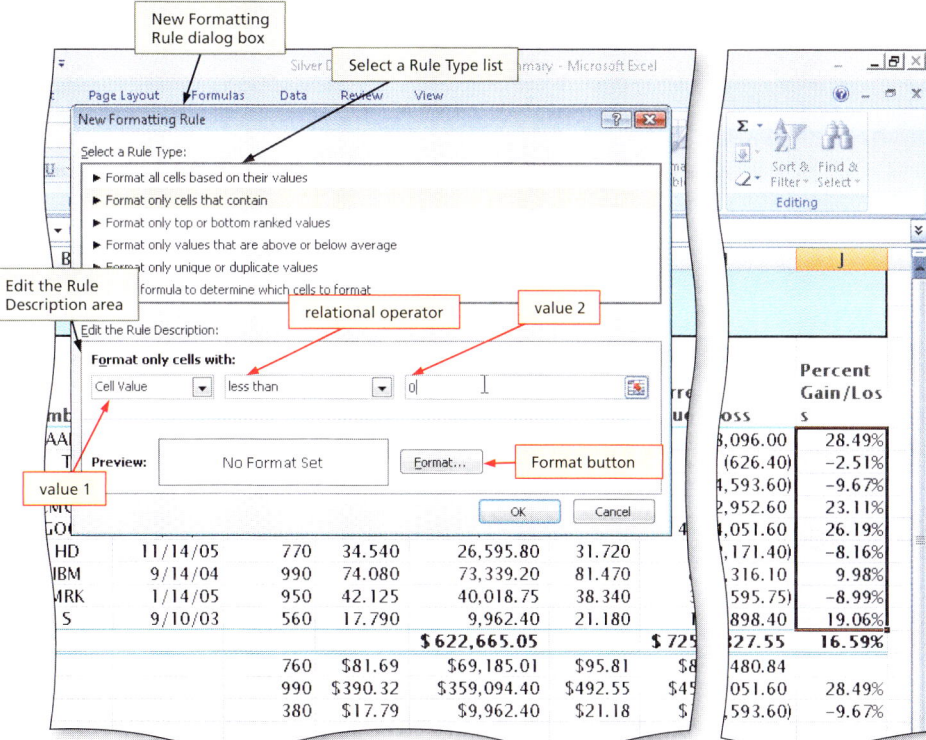

Figure 2–49

3
- Click the Format button.
- When Excel displays the Format Cells dialog box, click the Fill tab and then click the light red color in column 6, row 2 (Figure 2–50).

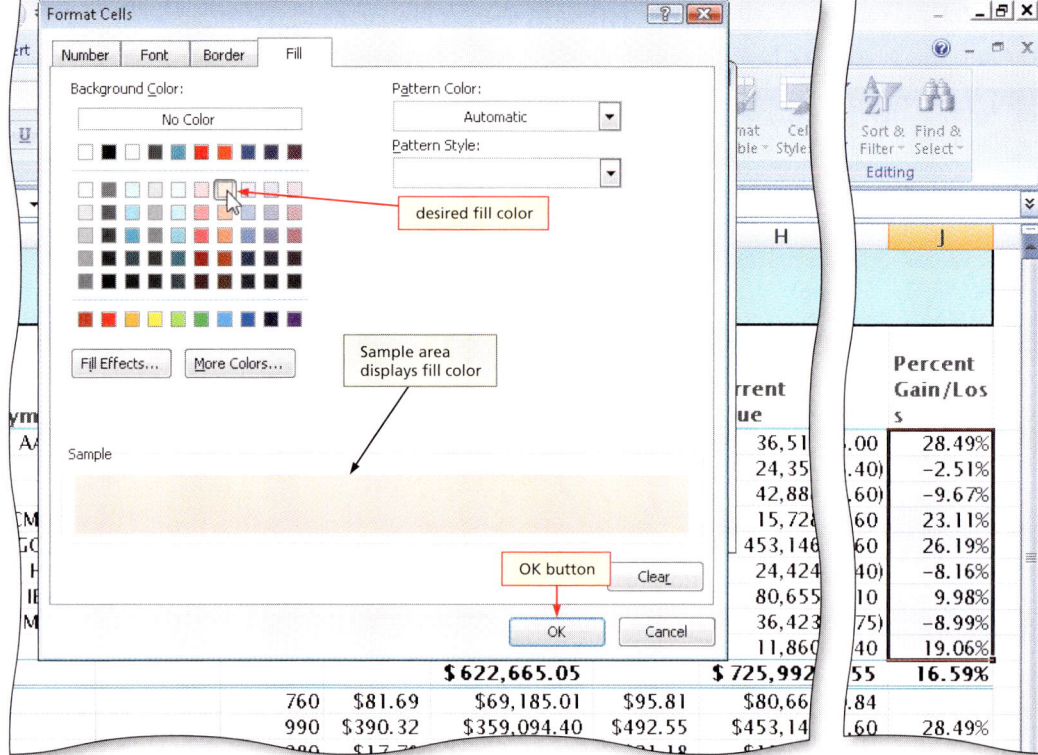

Figure 2–50

4
- Click the OK button to close the Format Cells dialog box and display the New Formatting Rule dialog box with the desired color displayed in the Preview box (Figure 2–51).

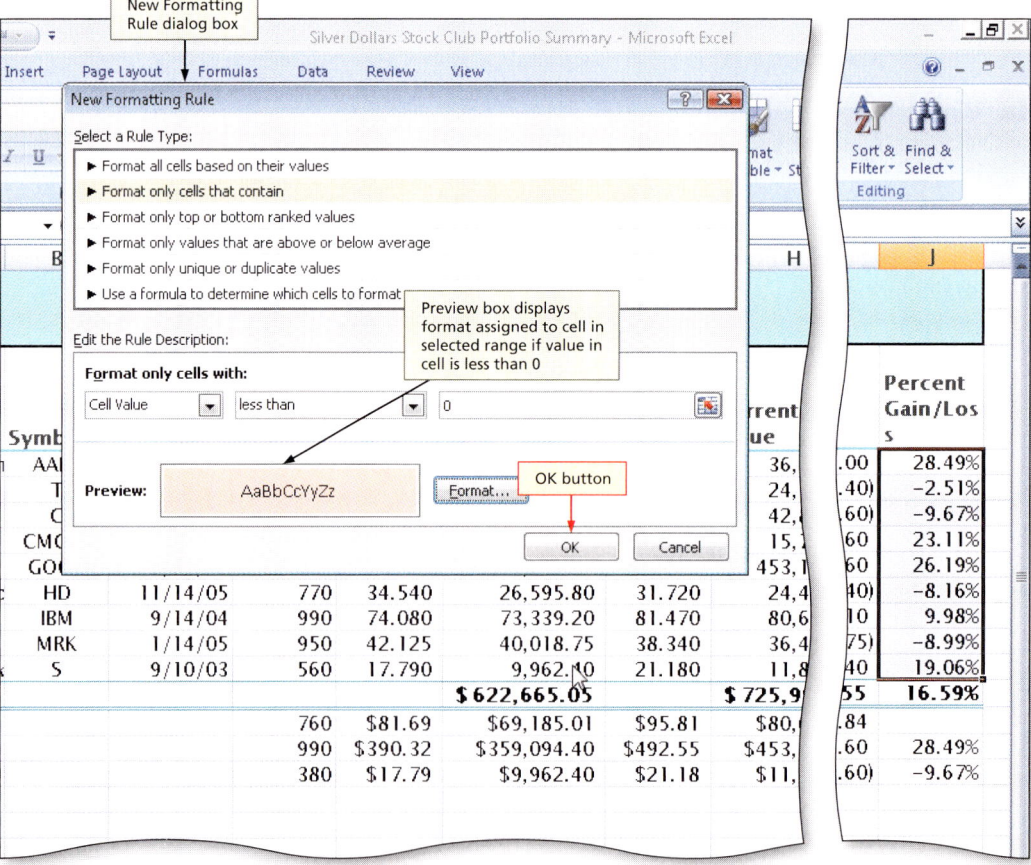

Figure 2–51

5
- Click the OK button to assign the conditional format to the range J4:J12.
- Click cell A18 to deselect the range J4:J12 (Figure 2–52).

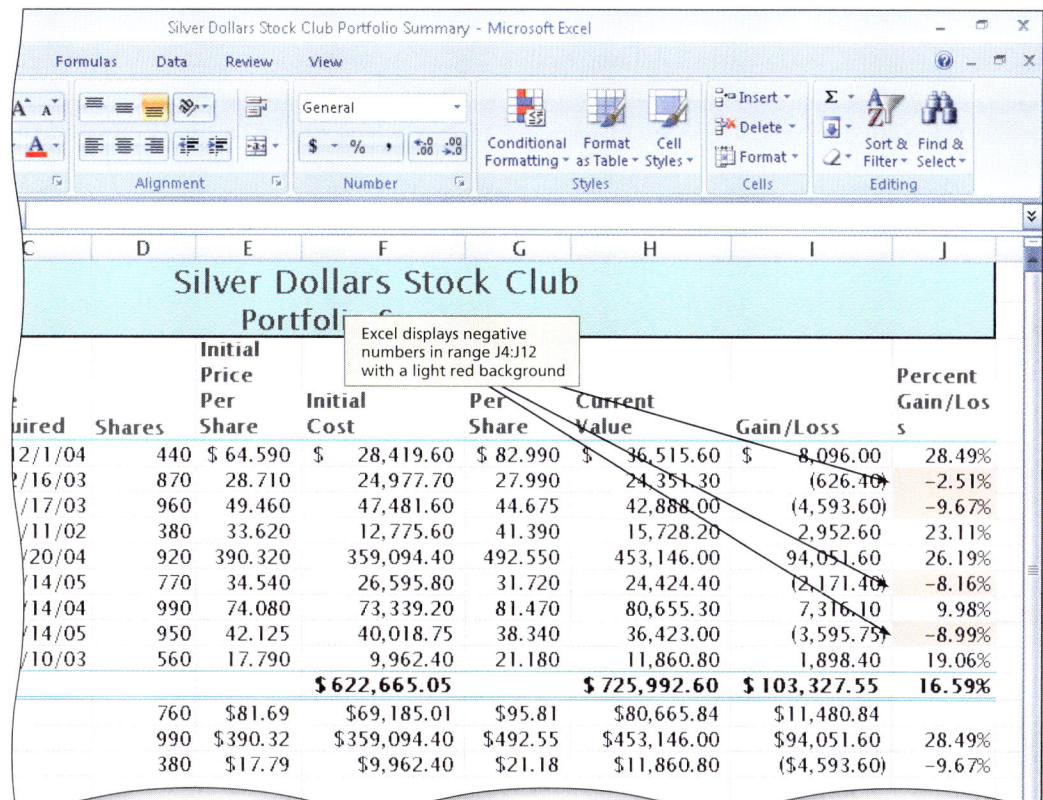

Figure 2–52

Conditional Formatting Operators

As shown in Figure 2–49 on page EX 119, the second text box in the New Formatting Rule dialog box allows you to select a relational operator, such as less than, to use in the condition. The eight different relational operators from which you can choose for conditional formatting in the New Formatting Rule dialog box are summarized in Table 2–5.

BTW

Conditional Formatting
You can assign any format to a cell, a range of cells, a worksheet, or an entire workbook conditionally. If the value of the cell changes and no longer meets the specified condition, Excel suppresses the conditional formatting.

Table 2–5 Summary of Conditional Formatting Relational Operators

Relational Operator	Description
Between	Cell value is between two numbers
Not between	Cell value is not between two numbers
Equal to	Cell value is equal to a number
Not equal to	Cell value is not equal to a number
Greater than	Cell value is greater than a number
Less than	Cell value is less than a number
Greater than or equal to	Cell value is greater than or equal to a number
Less than or equal to	Cell value is less than or equal to a number

BTW

Hidden Columns
Trying to unhide a range of columns using the mouse can be frustrating. An alternative is to use the keyboard: select the columns to the right and left of the hidden columns and then press CTRL+SHIFT+) (RIGHT PARENTHESIS). To use the keyboard to hide a range of columns, press CTRL+0 (ZERO).

Changing the Widths of Columns and Heights of Rows

When Excel starts and displays a blank worksheet on the screen, all of the columns have a default width of 8.43 characters, or 64 pixels. A character is defined as a letter, number, symbol, or punctuation mark in 11-point Calibri font, the default font used by Excel. An average of 8.43 characters in 11-point Calibri font will fit in a cell.

Another measure of the height and width of cells is pixels, which is short for picture element. A **pixel** is a dot on the screen that contains a color. The size of the dot is based on your screen's resolution. At a common resolution of 1024 × 768, 1024 pixels appear across the screen and 768 pixels appear down the screen for a total of 786,432 pixels. It is these 786,432 pixels that form the font and other items you see on the screen.

The default row height in a blank worksheet is 15 points (or 20 pixels). Recall from Chapter 1 that a point is equal to 1/72 of an inch. Thus, 15 points is equal to about 1/5 of an inch. You can change the width of the columns or height of the rows at any time to make the worksheet easier to read or to ensure that Excel displays an entry properly in a cell.

To Change the Widths of Columns

When changing the column width, you can set the width manually or you can instruct Excel to size the column to best fit. **Best fit** means that the width of the column will be increased or decreased so the widest entry will fit in the column. Sometimes, you may prefer more or less white space in a column than best fit provides. Excel thus allows you to change column widths manually.

When the format you assign to a cell causes the entry to exceed the width of a column, Excel automatically changes the column width to best fit. If you do not assign a format to a cell or cells in a column, the column width will remain 8.43 characters. To set a column width to best fit, double-click the right boundary of the column heading above row 1.

The following steps change the column widths: column A to 14.11 characters; columns B and C to best fit; column D to 6.00 characters; columns E, G, and J to 9.00 characters; and columns F, H, and I to 12.67 characters.

- Point to the boundary on the right side of the column A heading above row 1.

- When the mouse pointer changes to a split double arrow, drag until the ScreenTip indicates Width: 14.11 (134 pixels). Do not release the mouse button (Figure 2–53).

Q&A

What happens if I change the column width to zero (0)?

If you decrease the column width to 0, the column is hidden. **Hiding cells** is a technique you can use to hide data that might not be relevant to a particular report or sensitive data that you do not want others to see. To instruct Excel to display a hidden column, position the mouse pointer to the right of the column heading boundary where the hidden column is located and then drag to the right.

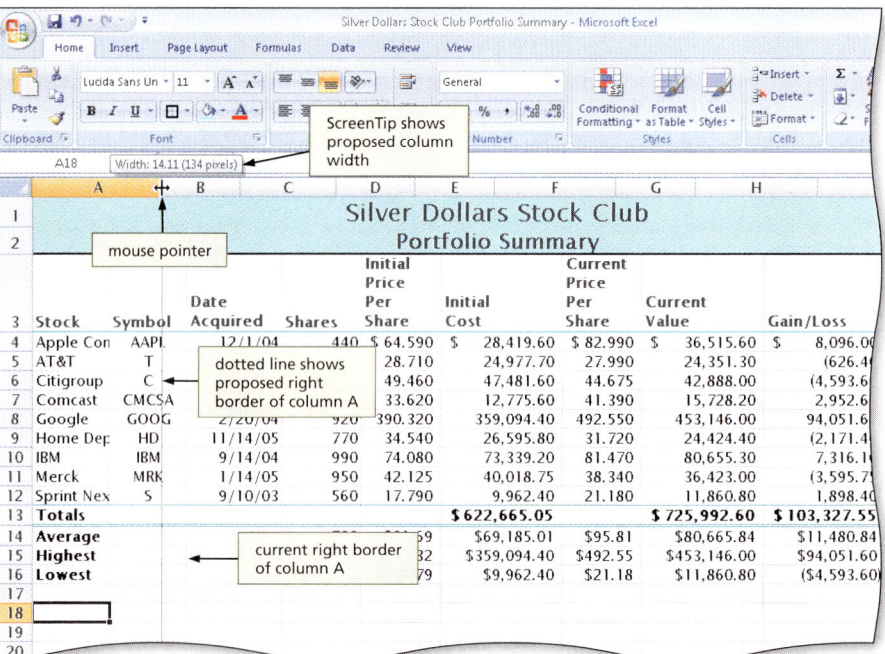

Figure 2–53

2

- Release the mouse button.
- Drag through column headings B and C above row 1.
- Point to the boundary on the right side of column heading C to cause the mouse pointer to become a split double arrow (Figure 2–54).

 What if I want to make a large change to the column width?

If you want to increase or decrease column width significantly, you can right-click a column heading and then use the Column Width command on the shortcut menu to change the column's width. To use this command, however, you must select one or more entire columns.

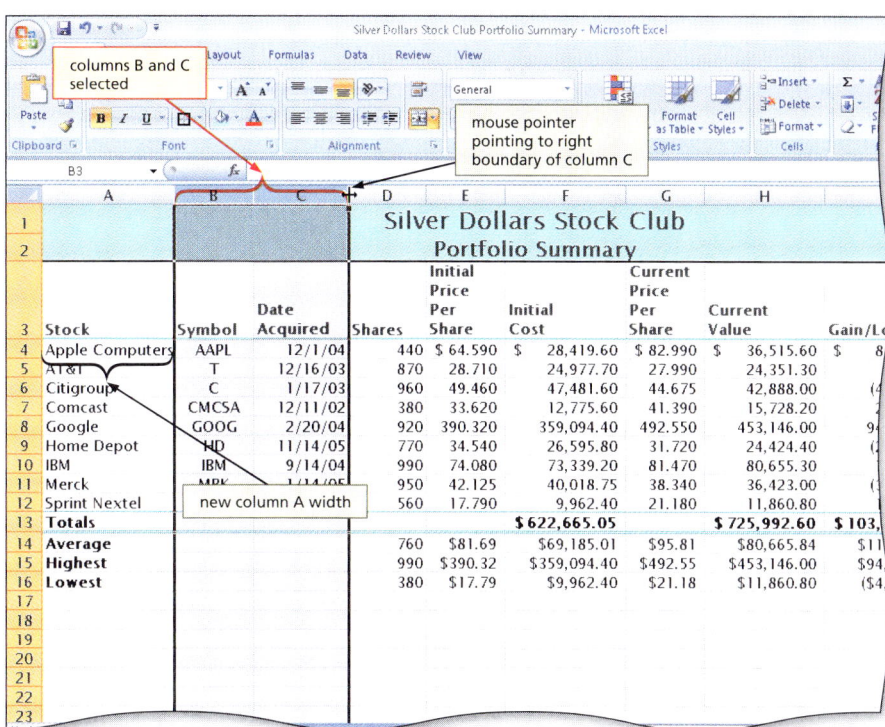

Figure 2–54

3

- Double-click the right boundary of column heading C to change the width of columns B and C to best fit.
- Click the column E heading above row 1.
- While holding down the CTRL key, click the column G heading and then the column J heading above row 1 so that columns E, G, and J are selected.
- If necessary, scroll the worksheet to the right so that the right border of column J is visible. Point to the boundary on the right side of the column J heading above row 1.
- Drag until the ScreenTip indicates Width: 9.00 (88 pixels). Do not release the mouse button (Figure 2–55).

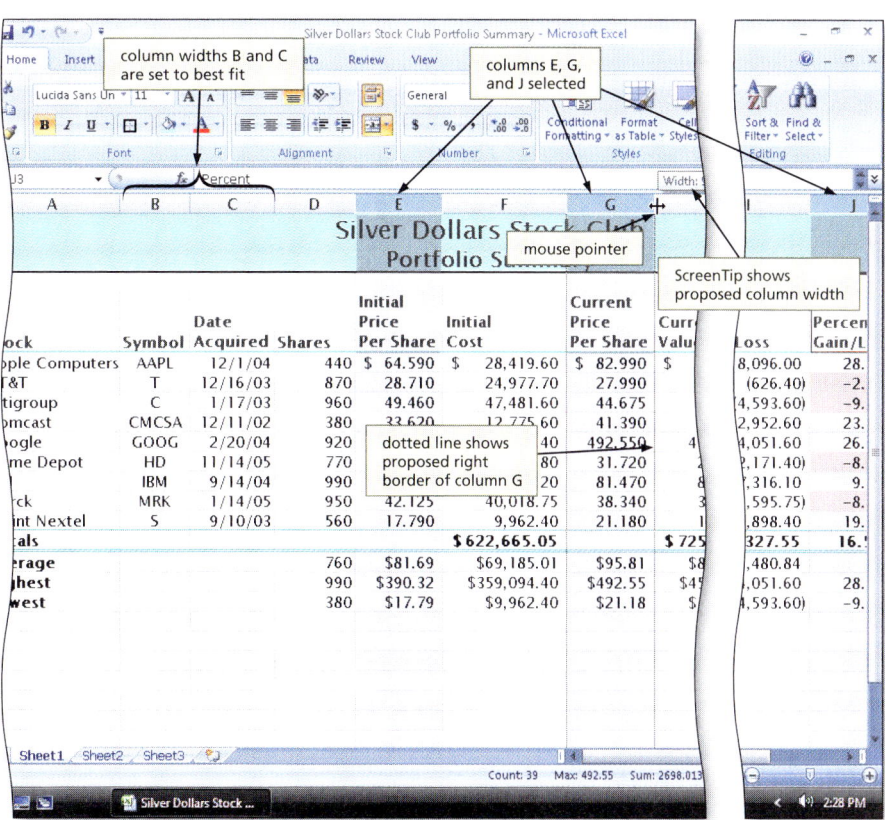

Figure 2–55

EX 124 Excel Chapter 2 Formulas, Functions, Formatting, and Web Queries

4

- Release the mouse button.
- Click the column F heading above row 1 to select column F.
- While holding down the CTRL key, click the column H heading and then the column I heading above row 1, to select columns F, H, and I.
- Point to the boundary on the right side of the column I heading above row 1.
- Drag to the left until the ScreenTip indicates Width: 12.67 (121 pixels). Do not release the mouse button (Figure 2–56).

Figure 2–56

- Release the mouse button.
- Point to the boundary on the right side of the column D heading above row 1.
- Drag to the left until the ScreenTip indicates Width: 6.00 (61 pixels) and then release the mouse button to display the worksheet with the new column widths.
- Click cell A18 to deselect columns F, H, and I (Figure 2–57).

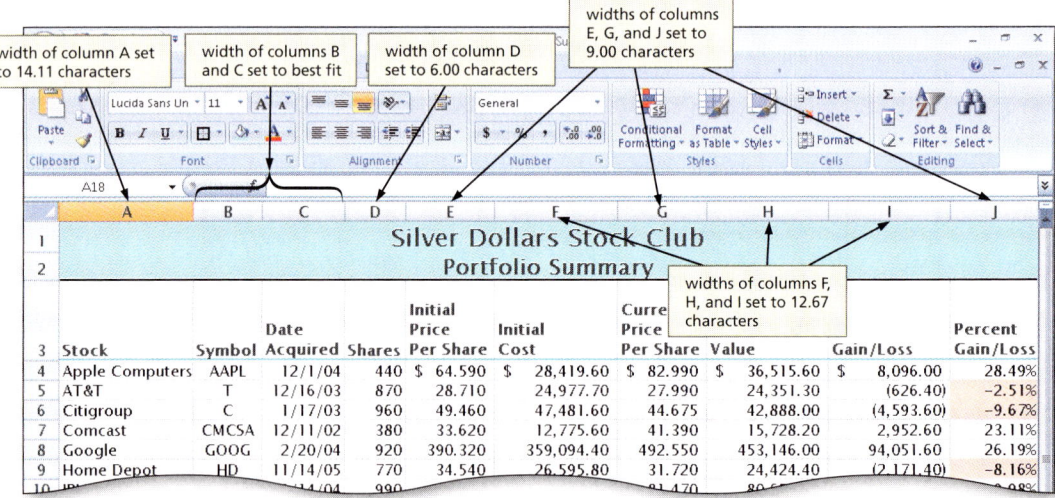

Figure 2–57

Other Ways

1. Right-click column heading or drag through multiple column headings and right-click, click Column Width on shortcut menu, enter desired column width, click OK button
2. Right-click column heading or drag through multiple column headings and right-click, click Format button on Ribbon, click Column Width in Format gallery, enter desired column width, click OK button

To Change the Heights of Rows

When you increase the font size of a cell entry, such as the title in cell A1, Excel automatically increases the row height to best fit so it can display the characters properly. Recall that Excel did this earlier when multiple lines were entered in a cell in row 3, and when the cell style of the worksheet title and subtitle was changed.

You also can increase or decrease the height of a row manually to improve the appearance of the worksheet. The following steps improve the appearance of the worksheet by increasing the height of row 3 to 60.00 points, and increasing the height of row 14 to 26.25 points.

1

- Point to the boundary below row heading 3.

- Drag down until the ScreenTip indicates Height: 60.00 (80 pixels). Do not release the mouse button (Figure 2–58).

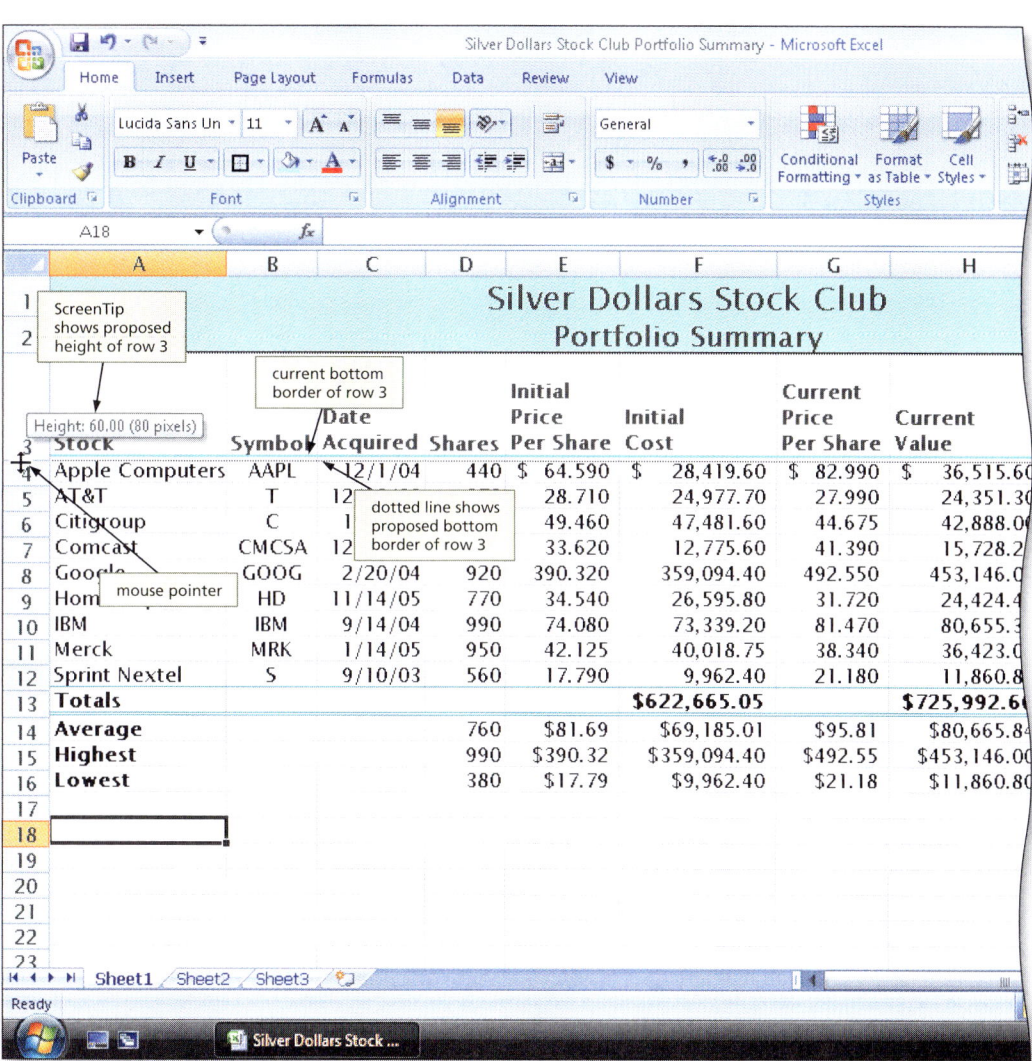

Figure 2–58

2

- Release the mouse button.
- Point to the boundary below row heading 14.
- Drag down until the ScreenTip indicates Height: 26.25 (35 pixels). Do not release the mouse button (Figure 2–59).

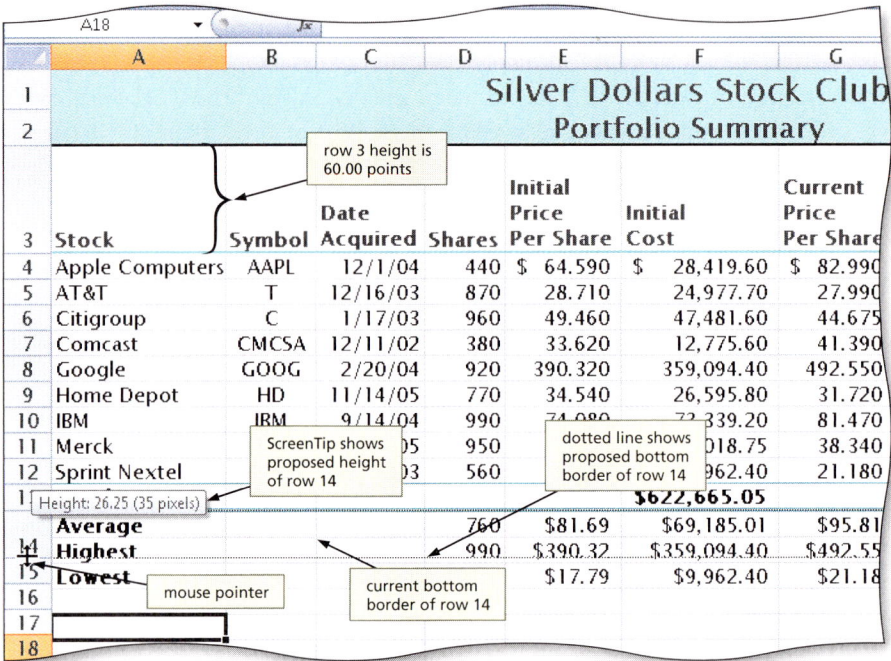

Figure 2–59

3

- Release the mouse button to change the row height of row 14 to 26.25.
- Select cells A3:J3 and then click the Center button on the Ribbon to center the column headings.
- Select cell A18 (Figure 2–60).

 Q&A

Can I hide a row?

Yes. As with column widths, when you decrease the row height to 0, the row is hidden. To instruct Excel to display a hidden row, position the mouse pointer just below the row heading boundary where the row is hidden and then drag down. To set a row height to best fit, double-click the bottom boundary of the row heading.

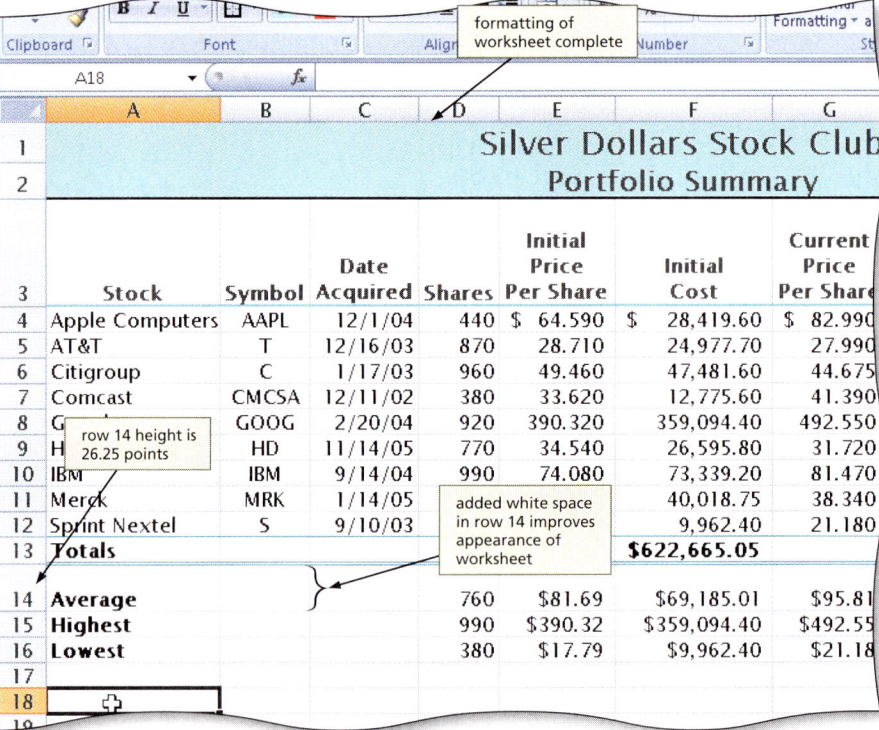

Figure 2–60

Other Ways

1. Right-click row heading or drag through multiple row headings and right-click, click Row Height on shortcut menu, enter desired row height, click OK button

Checking Spelling

Excel has a **spell checker** you can use to check the worksheet for spelling errors. The spell checker looks for spelling errors by comparing words on the worksheet against words contained in its standard dictionary. If you often use specialized terms that are not in the standard dictionary, you may want to add them to a custom dictionary using the Spelling dialog box.

When the spell checker finds a word that is not in either dictionary, it displays the word in the Spelling dialog box. You then can correct it if it is misspelled.

> **BTW**
>
> **Hidden Rows**
> You can use the keyboard to unhide a range of rows by selecting the rows immediately above and below the hidden rows and then pressing CTRL+SHIFT+((LEFT PARENTHESIS). To use the keyboard to hide a range of rows, press CTRL+9.

To Check Spelling on the Worksheet

To illustrate how Excel responds to a misspelled word, the word, Stock, in cell A3 is misspelled purposely as the word, Stcok, as shown in Figure 2–61.

1

- Click cell A3 and then type `Stcok` to misspell the word Stock.
- Click cell A1.
- Click the Review tab on the Ribbon.
- Click the Spelling button on the Ribbon to run the spell checker and display the misspelled word, Stcok, in the Spelling dialog box (Figure 2–61).

Q&A

What happens when the spell checker finds a misspelled word?

When the spell checker identifies that a cell contains a word not in its standard or custom dictionary, it selects that cell as the active cell and displays the Spelling dialog box. The Spelling dialog box (Figure 2–61) lists the word not found in the dictionary and a list of suggested corrections.

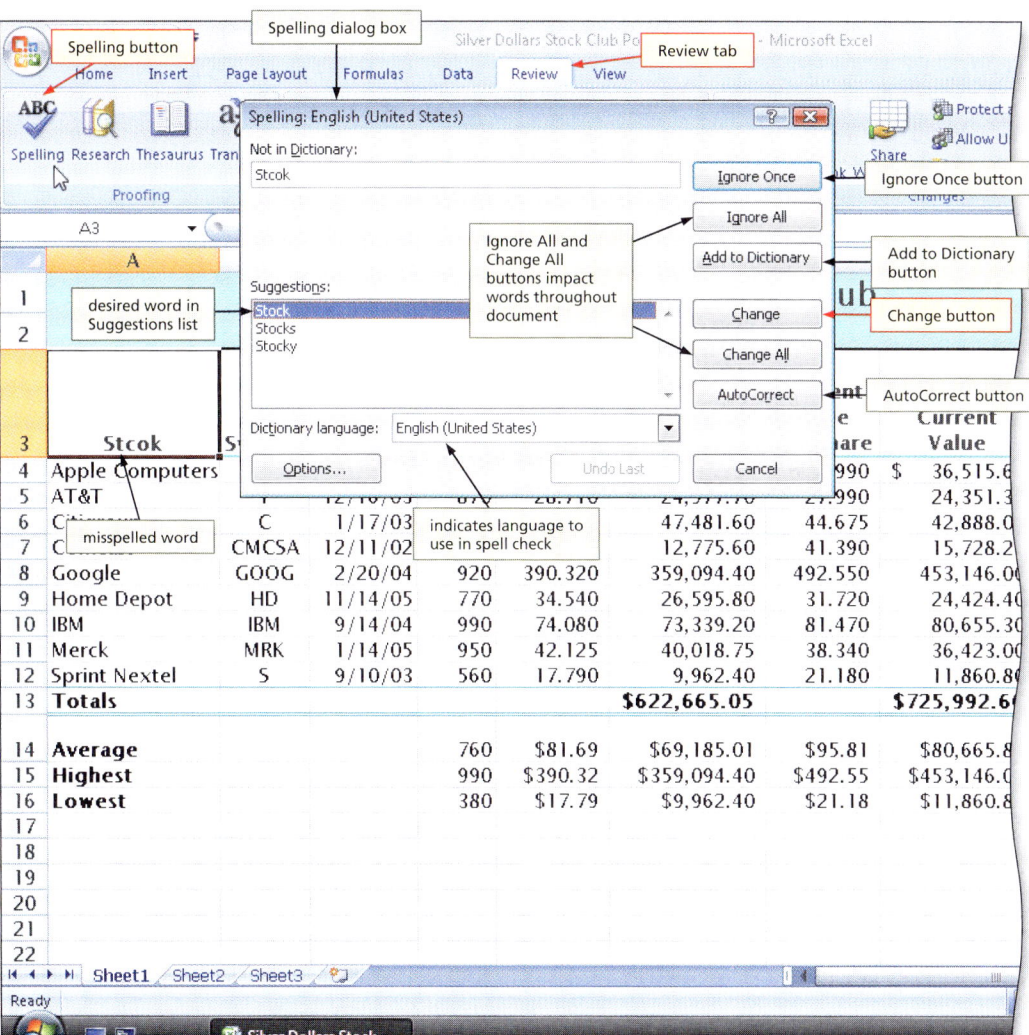

Figure 2–61

2

- With the word Stock highlighted in the Suggestions list, click the Change button to change the misspelled word, Stcok, to the correct word, Stock (Figure 2–62).

- If the Microsoft Office Excel dialog box is displayed, click the OK button.

3

- Select cell A18.

- Click the Home tab on the Ribbon.

- Click the Save button on the Quick Access Toolbar to save the workbook.

Q&A What other actions can I take in the Spelling dialog box?

If one of the words in the Suggestions list is correct, click it and then click the Change button. If none of the suggestions is correct, type the correct word in the Not in Dictionary text box and then click the Change button. To change the word throughout the worksheet, click the Change All button instead of the Change button. To skip correcting the word, click the Ignore Once button. To have Excel ignore the word for the remainder of the worksheet, click the Ignore All button.

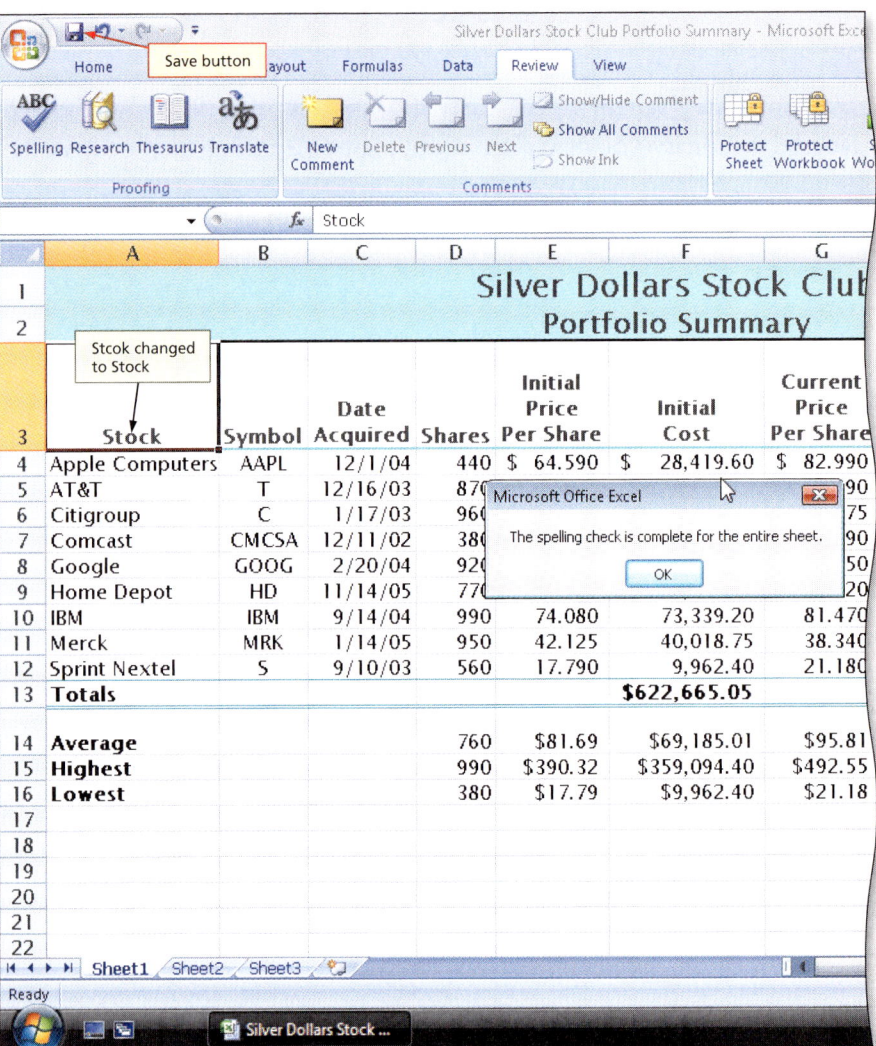

Figure 2–62

Other Ways

1. Press F7

Additional Spell Checker Considerations

Consider these additional guidelines when using the spell checker:
- To check the spelling of the text in a single cell, double-click the cell to make the formula bar active and then click the Spelling button on the Review tab on the Ribbon.
- If you select a single cell so that the formula bar is not active and then start the spell checker, Excel checks the remainder of the worksheet, including notes and embedded charts.
- If you select a cell other than cell A1 before you start the spell checker, Excel will display a dialog box when the spell checker reaches the end of the worksheet, asking if you want to continue checking at the beginning.
- If you select a range of cells before starting the spell checker, Excel checks the spelling of the words only in the selected range.
- To check the spelling of all the sheets in a workbook, click Select All Sheets on the sheet tab shortcut menu and then start the spell checker. To instruct Excel to display the sheet tab shortcut menu, right-click any sheet tab.
- To add words to the dictionary such as your last name, click the Add to Dictionary button in the Spelling dialog box (Figure 2–61 on page EX 127) when Excel identifies the word as not in the dictionary.
- Click the AutoCorrect button (Figure 2–61) to add the misspelled word and the correct version of the word to the AutoCorrect list. For example, suppose you misspell the word, do, as the word, dox. When the spell checker displays the Spelling dialog box with the correct word, do, in the Change to box, click the AutoCorrect button. Then, anytime in the future that you type the word, dox, Excel automatically will change it to the word, do.

> **BTW**
>
> **Spell Checking**
> While Excel's spell checker is a valuable tool, it is not infallible. You should proofread your workbook carefully by pointing to each word and saying it aloud as you point to it. Be mindful of misused words such as its and it's, through and though, and to and too. Nothing undermines a good impression more than a professional looking report with misspelled words.

> **BTW**
>
> **Error Checking**
> Always take the time to check the formulas of a worksheet before submitting it to your supervisor. You can check formulas by clicking the Error Checking button on the Formulas tab on the Ribbon. You also should test the formulas by employing data that tests the limits of formulas. Experienced spreadsheet specialists spend as much time testing a workbook as they do creating it, before placing it into production.

Preparing to Print the Worksheet

Excel allows for a great deal of customization in how a worksheet appears when printed. For example, the margins on the page can be adjusted. A header or footer can be added to each printed page as well. Excel also has the capability to work on the worksheet in Page Layout View. **Page Layout View** allows you to create or modify a worksheet while viewing how it will look in printed format. The default view that you have worked in up until this point in the Excel chapters is called **Normal View**.

> **Plan Ahead**
>
> **Specify how the printed worksheet should appear.**
> Before printing a worksheet, you should consider how the worksheet will appear when printed. In order to fit as much information on the printed page as possible, the margins of the worksheet should be set to a reasonably small width and height. The current Portfolio Summary worksheet will print on one page. If, however, the club added more data to the worksheet, then it may extend to multiple pages. It is, therefore, a good idea to add a page header to the worksheet that prints in the top margin of each page.
>
> In Chapter 1, the worksheet was printed in **portrait orientation**, which means the printout is printed across the width of the page. **Landscape orientation** means the printout is printed across the length of the page. Landscape orientation is a good choice for the Silver Dollars Stock Club Portfolio Summary because the printed worksheet's width is greater than its length.

To Change the Worksheet's Margins, Header, and Orientation in Page Layout View

The following steps change to Page Layout View, narrow the margins of the worksheet, change the header of the worksheet, and set the orientation of the worksheet to landscape.

1
- Click the Page Layout View button on the status bar to view the worksheet in Page Layout View (Figure 2–63).

 What are some key features of Page Layout View?

Page Layout View shows the worksheet divided into pages. A blue background separates each page. The white areas surrounding each page indicate the print margins. The top of each page includes a Header area, and the bottom of each page includes a Footer area. Page Layout View also includes a ruler at the top of the page that assists you in placing objects on the page, such as charts and pictures.

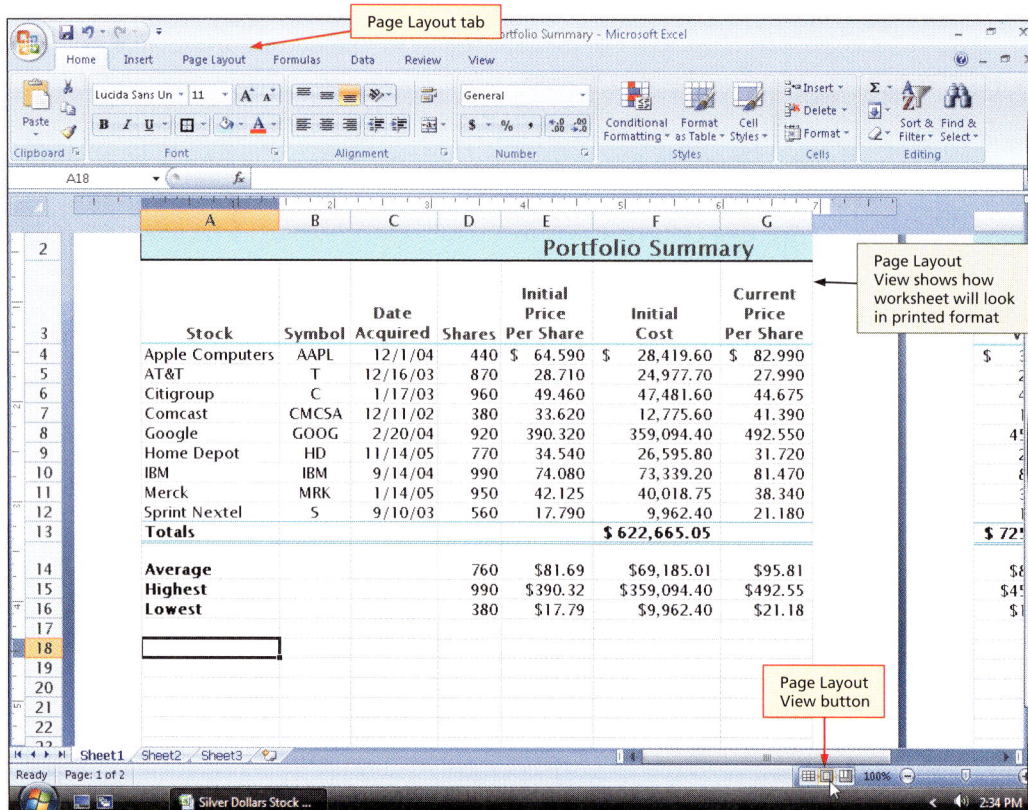

Figure 2–63

2
- Click the Page Layout tab on the Ribbon.
- Click the Margins button on the Ribbon to display the Margins gallery (Figure 2–64).

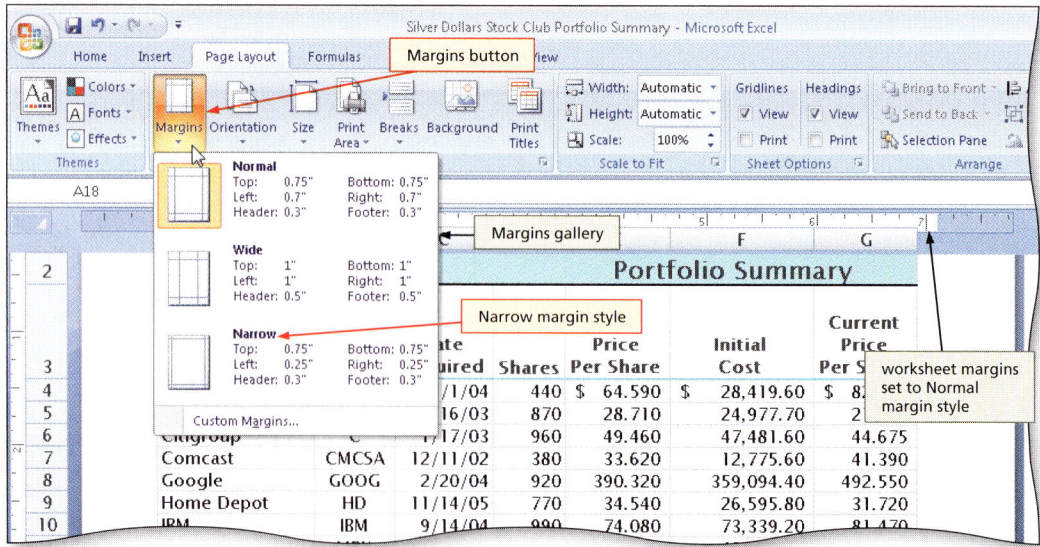

Figure 2–64

3

- Click Narrow in the Margins gallery to change the worksheet margins to the Narrow margin style.

- Drag the scroll bar on the right side of the worksheet to the top so that row 1 of the worksheet is displayed.

- Click above the worksheet title in cell A1 in the Header area.

- Type `Treasurer: Juan Castillo` and then press the ENTER key. Type `castillo_juan37@hotmail.com` to complete the worksheet header (Figure 2–65).

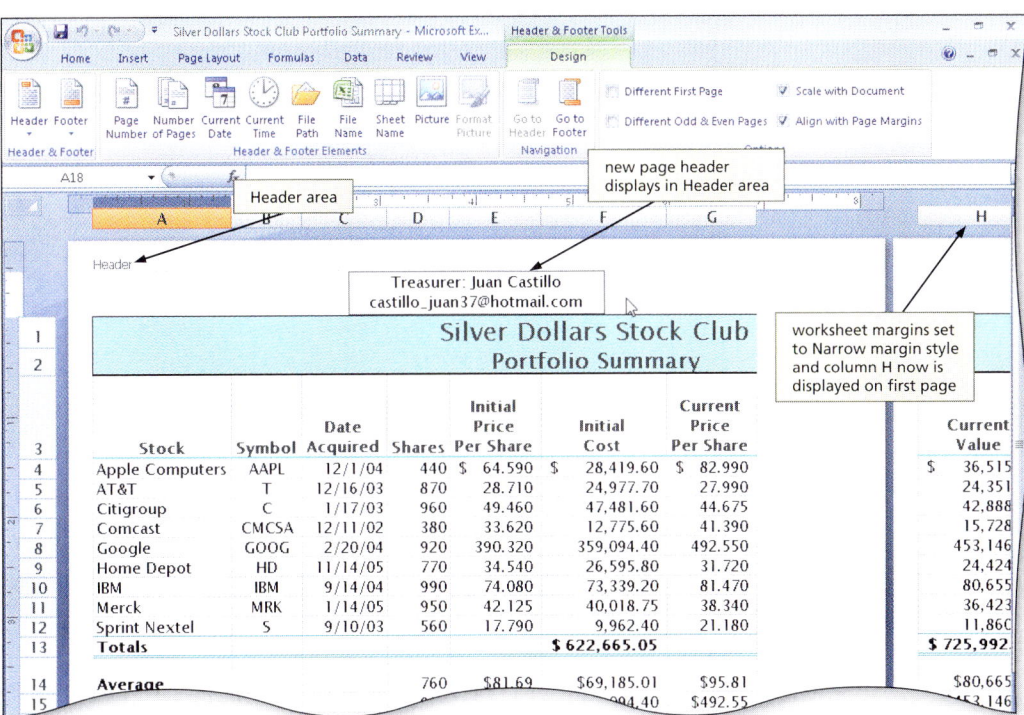

Figure 2–65

4

- Select cell B16 to deselect the header. Click the Orientation button on the Ribbon to display the Orientation gallery.

- Point to Landscape but do not click the mouse button (Figure 2–66).

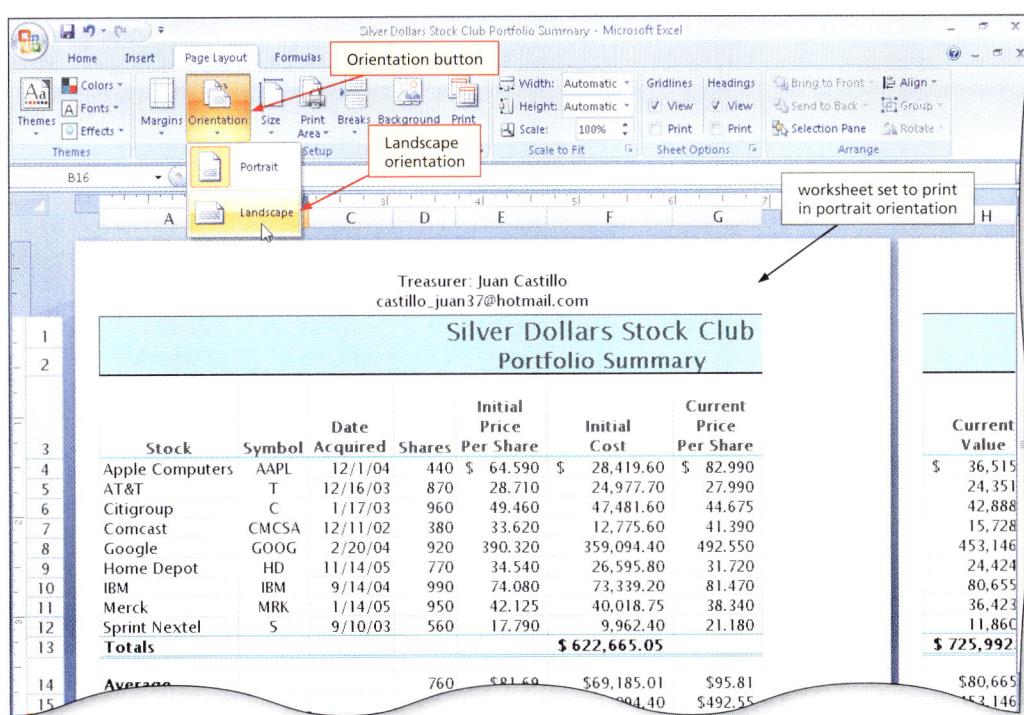

Figure 2–66

- Click Landscape in the Orientation gallery to change the worksheet's orientation to landscape (Figure 2–67).

Q&A Do I need to change the orientation every time I want to print the worksheet?

No. Once you change the orientation and save the workbook, Excel will save the orientation setting for that workbook until you change it. When you open a new workbook, Excel sets the orientation to portrait.

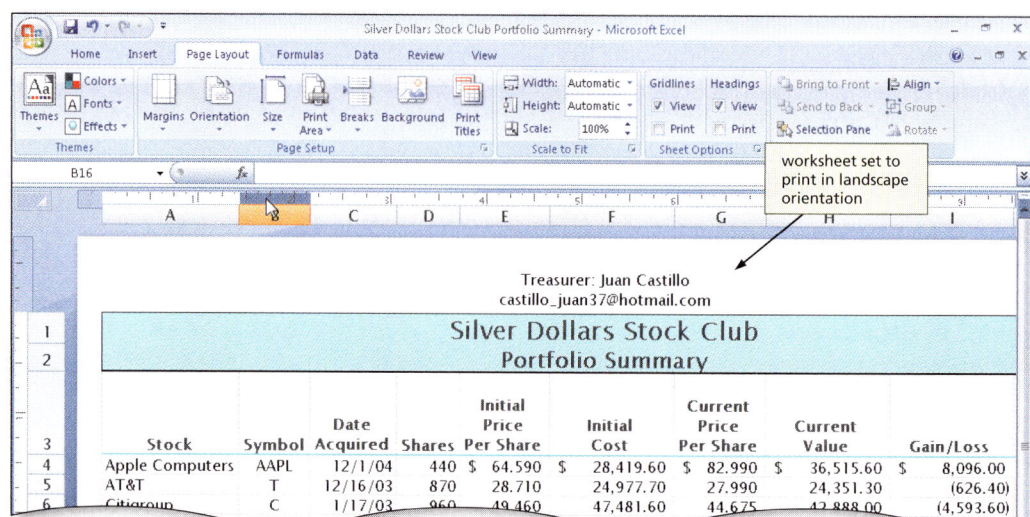

Figure 2–67

Other Ways

1. Click Page Layout tab on Ribbon, click Page Setup Dialog Box Launcher, click Page tab, click Portrait or Landscape, click OK button

Previewing and Printing the Worksheet

In Chapter 1, the worksheet was printed without first previewing it on the screen. By **previewing the worksheet**, however, you see exactly how it will look without generating a printout. Previewing a worksheet using the Print Preview command can save time, paper, and the frustration of waiting for a printout only to discover it is not what you want.

To Preview and Print a Worksheet

The following steps preview and then print the worksheet.

- Click the Office Button and then point to Print on the Office Button menu to display the Print submenu (Figure 2–68).

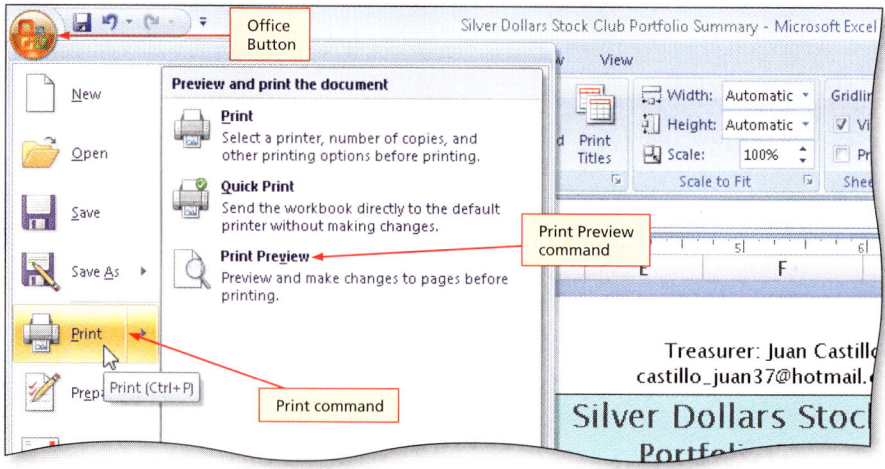

Figure 2–68

Formulas, Functions, Formatting, and Web Queries Excel Chapter 2 EX 133

2

- Click Print Preview on the Print submenu to display a preview of the worksheet in landscape orientation (Figure 2–69).

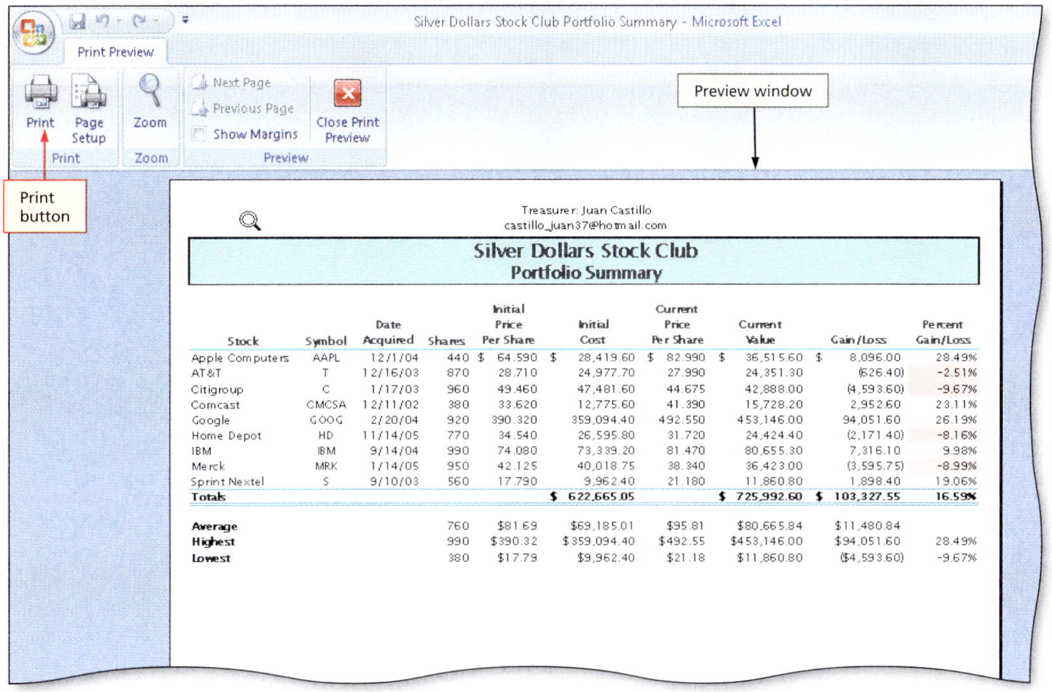

Q&A What is the purpose of the buttons in the Print Preview area?

The Print button displays the Print dialog box and allows you to print the worksheet. The Page Setup button displays the Page Setup dialog box. The Zoom button allows you to zoom in and out of the page displayed in the Preview window. You also can click the previewed page in the Preview window when the mouse pointer shape is a magnifying glass to carry out the function of the Zoom button.

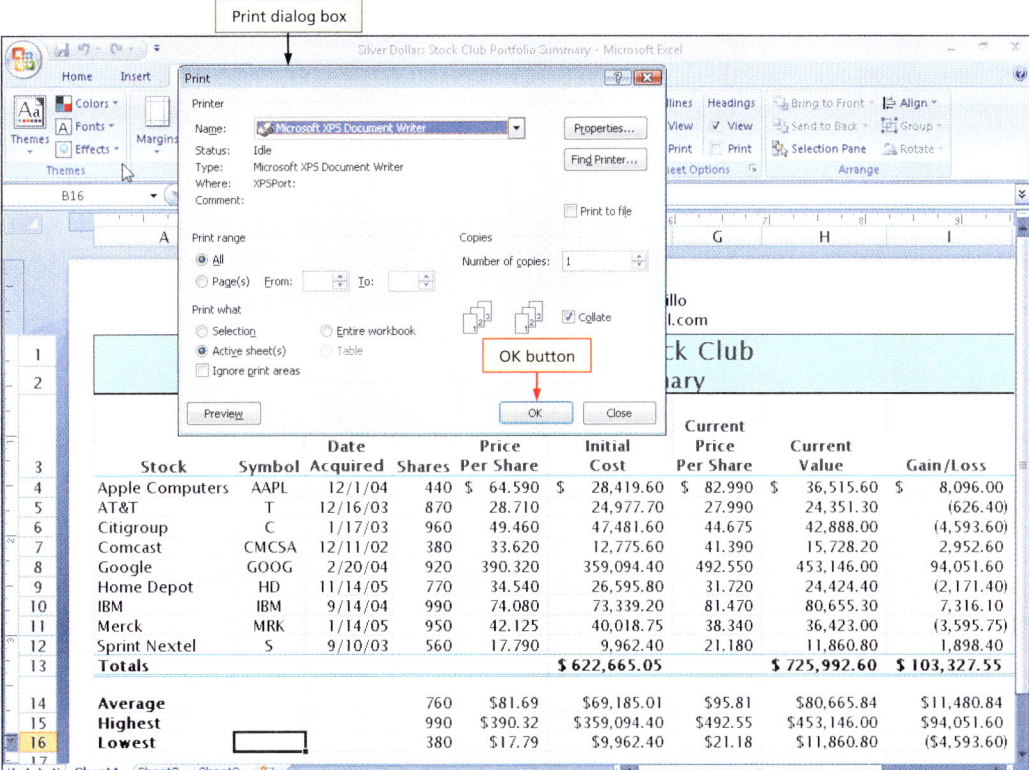

Figure 2–69

3

- Click the Print button to display the Print dialog box (Figure 2–70).

Q&A How can I use the Print dialog box?

When you click the Print command on the Print submenu of the Office Button menu or a Print button in a dialog box or Preview window, Excel displays the Print dialog box shown in Figure 2–70. Excel does not display the Print dialog box when you use the Print button on the Quick Access Toolbar, as was the case in Chapter 1. The Print dialog box allows you to select a printer, instruct Excel what to print, and indicate how many copies of the printout you want.

Figure 2–70

- Click the OK button to print the worksheet (Figure 2–71).

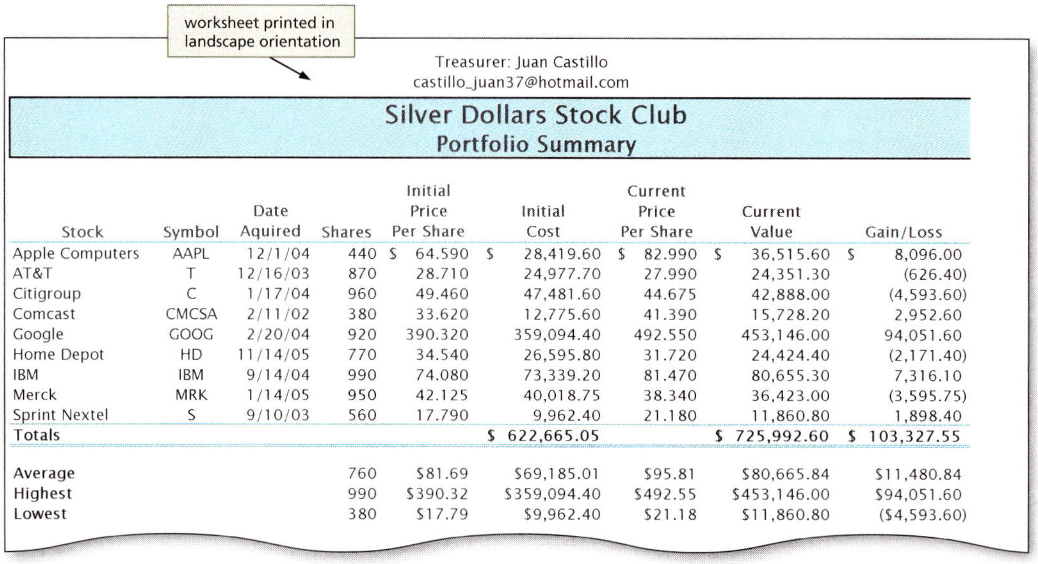

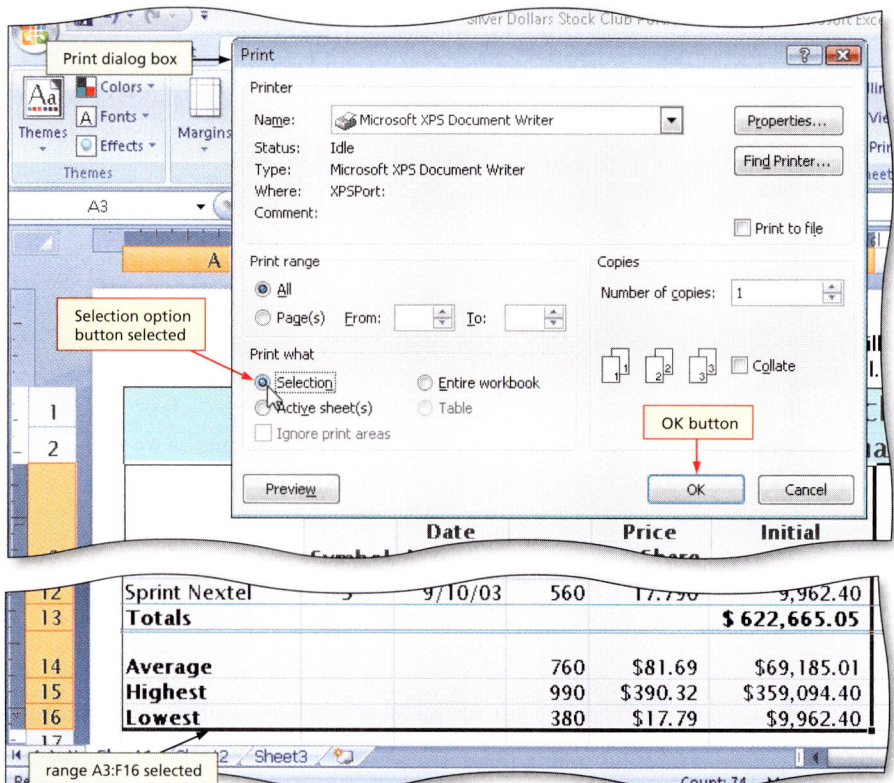

Other Ways

1. Click Page Layout tab on Ribbon, click Page Setup Dialog Box Launcher, click appropriate tab, change desired options, click Print, click OK button

Figure 2–71

To Print a Section of the Worksheet

You might not always want to print the entire worksheet. You can print portions of the worksheet by selecting the range of cells to print and then clicking the Selection option button in the Print what area in the Print dialog box. The following steps print the range A3:F16.

- Select the range A3:F16.

- Click the Office Button and then click Print on the Office Button menu to display the Print dialog box.

- Click Selection in the Print what area to instruct Excel to print only the selected range (Figure 2–72).

Figure 2–72

2

- Click the OK button to print the selected range of the worksheet on the printer (Figure 2–73).

- Click the Normal View button on the status bar.

- Click cell A18 to deselect the range A3:F13.

Q&A What are the options in the Print what area?

The Print what area of the Print dialog box includes four option buttons (Figure 2–72). As shown in the previous steps, the Selection option button instructs Excel to print the selected range. The Active sheet(s) option button instructs Excel to print the active worksheet (the worksheet currently on the screen) or the selected worksheets. Finally, the Entire workbook option button instructs Excel to print all of the worksheets in the workbook.

		header prints	→ Treasurer: Juan Castillo		selected range prints
Stock	Symbol	Date Acquired	Shares	Initial Price Per Share	Initial Cost
Apple Computers	AAPL	12/1/04	440	$ 64.590	$ 28,419.60
AT&T	T	12/16/03	870	28.710	24,977.70
Citigroup	C	1/17/04	960	49.460	47,481.60
Comcast	CMCSA	2/11/02	380	33.620	12,775.60
Google	GOOG	2/20/04	920	390.320	359,094.40
Home Depot	HD	11/14/05	770	34.540	26,595.80
IBM	IBM	9/14/04	990	74.080	73,339.20
Merck	MRK	1/14/05	950	42.125	40,018.75
Sprint Nextel	S	9/10/03	560	17.790	9,962.40
Totals					$ 622,665.05
Average			760	$81.69	$69,185.01
Highest			990	$390.32	$359,094.40
Lowest			380	$17.79	$9,962.40

Figure 2–73

Other Ways

1. Select range, click Page Layout tab on Ribbon, click Print Area button, click Set Print Area, click Quick Print button on Quick Access Toolbar, click Print Area button, click Clear Print Area button

Displaying and Printing the Formulas Version of the Worksheet

Thus far, you have been working with the **values version** of the worksheet, which shows the results of the formulas you have entered, rather than the actual formulas. Excel also can display and print the **formulas version** of the worksheet, which shows the actual formulas you have entered, rather than the resulting values. You can toggle between the values version and formulas version by holding down the CTRL key while pressing the ACCENT MARK (`) key, which is located to the left of the number 1 key on the keyboard.

The formulas version is useful for debugging a worksheet. **Debugging** is the process of finding and correcting errors in the worksheet. Viewing and printing the formulas version instead of the values version makes it easier to see any mistakes in the formulas.

When you change from the values version to the formulas version, Excel increases the width of the columns so the formulas and text do not overflow into adjacent cells on the right. The formulas version of the worksheet thus usually is significantly wider than the values version. To fit the wide printout on one page, you can use landscape orientation, which has already been selected for the workbook, and the Fit to option in the Page sheet in the Page Setup dialog box.

BTW

Values versus Formulas
When completing class assignments, do not enter numbers in cells that require formulas. Most instructors require their students to hand in both the values version and formulas version of the worksheet. The formulas version verifies that you entered formulas, rather than numbers, in formula-based cells.

To Display the Formulas in the Worksheet and Fit the Printout on One Page

The following steps change the view of the worksheet from the values version to the formulas version of the worksheet and then print the formulas version on one page.

- Press CTRL+ACCENT MARK (`).

- When Excel displays the formulas version of the worksheet, click the right horizontal scroll arrow until column J appears to display the worksheet with formulas (Figure 2–74).

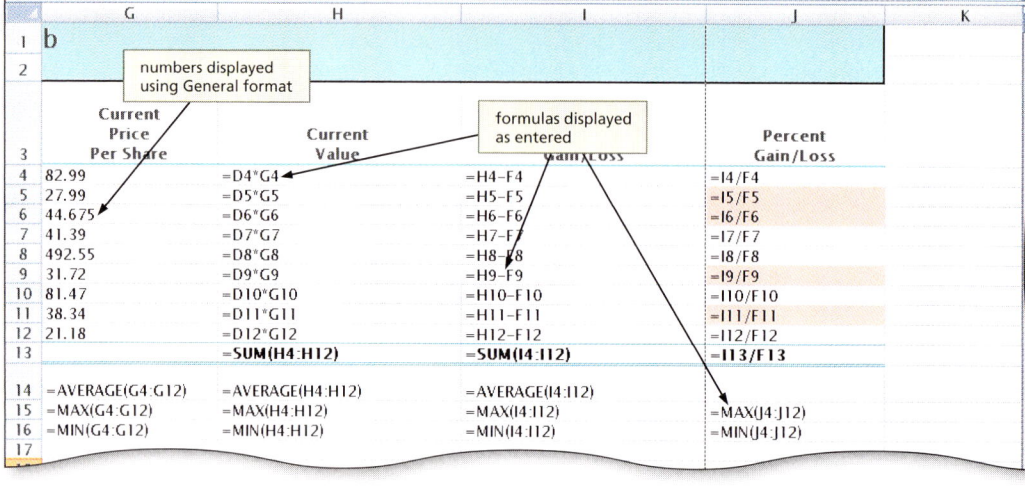

Figure 2–74

- If necessary, click the Page Layout tab on the Ribbon and then click the Page Setup Dialog Box Launcher to display the Page Setup dialog box.

- If necessary, click Landscape to select it and then click Fit to in the Scaling area.

3

- Click the Print button in the Page Setup dialog box to print the formulas in the worksheet on one page in landscape orientation (Figure 2–75).

- When Excel displays the Print dialog box, click the OK button.

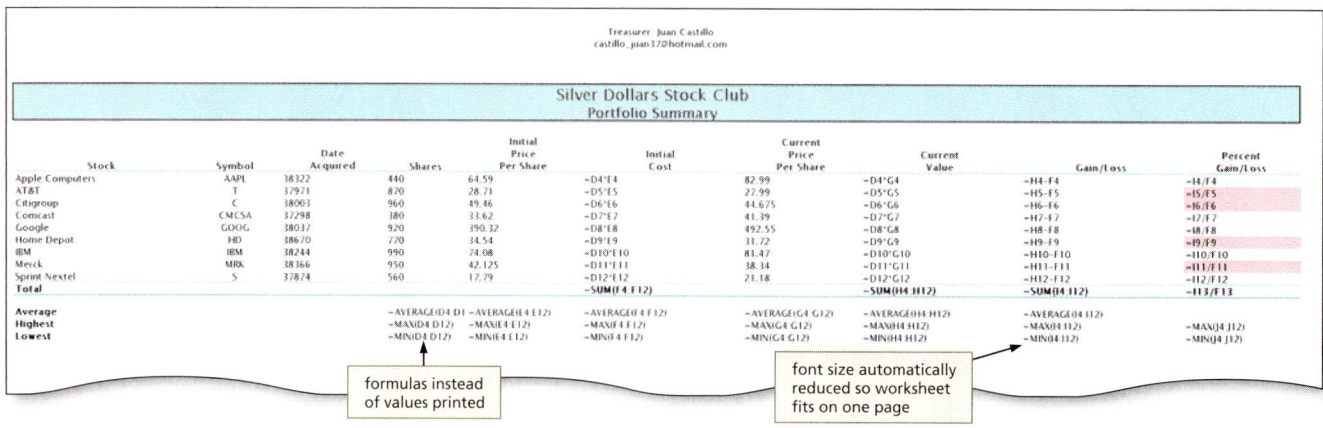

Figure 2–75

- After viewing and printing the formulas version, press CTRL+ACCENT MARK (`) to instruct Excel to display the values version.

- Click the left horizontal scroll arrow until column A appears.

Other Ways

1. Click Show Formulas button on Formulas tab on Ribbon

To Change the Print Scaling Option Back to 100%

Depending on your printer, you may have to change the Print Scaling option back to 100% after using the Fit to option. The following steps reset the Print Scaling option so future worksheets print at 100%, instead of being resized to print on one page.

1 If necessary, click the Page Layout tab on the Ribbon and then click the Page Setup Dialog Box Launcher to display the Page Setup dialog box.

2 Click Adjust to in the Scaling area.

3 If necessary, type `100` in the Adjust to box.

4 Click the OK button to set the print scaling to normal.

5 Click the Home tab on the Ribbon.

Q&A What is the purpose of the Adjust to box in the Page Setup dialog box?

The Adjust to box allows you to specify the percentage of reduction or enlargement in the printout of a worksheet. The default percentage is 100%. When you click the Fit to option, this percentage automatically changes to the percentage required to fit the printout on one page.

Importing External Data from a Web Source Using a Web Query

One of the major features of Excel is its capability of importing external data from Web sites. To import external data from a Web site, you must have access to the Internet. You then can import data stored on a Web site using a **Web query**. When you run a Web query, Excel imports the external data in the form of a worksheet. As described in Table 2–6, three Web queries are available when you first install Excel. All three Web queries relate to investment and stock market activities.

BTW

Web Queries
Most Excel specialists that build Web queries use the worksheet returned from the Web query as an engine to supply data to another worksheet in the workbook. With 3-D cell references, you can create a worksheet similar to the Silver Dollars Stock Club worksheet to feed the Web query stock symbols and get refreshed stock prices in return.

Table 2–6 Excel Web Queries

Query	External Data Returned
MSN MoneyCentral Investor Currency Rates	Currency rates
MSN MoneyCentral Investor Major Indices	Major indices
MSN MoneyCentral Investor Stock Quotes	Up to 20 stocks of your choice

Plan Ahead

Gather information regarding the needed Web query.
As shown in Table 2–6, the MSN Money Central Investor Stock Quotes feature that is included with Excel allows you to retrieve information on up to 20 stocks of your choice. The Web query requires that you supply the stock symbols. The stock symbols are located in column B of the Portfolio Summary worksheet.

To Import Data from a Web Source Using a Web Query

Although you can have a Web query return data to a blank workbook, the following steps have the data for the nine stock symbols in column B of the Portfolio Summary worksheet returned to a blank worksheet in the Silver Dollars Stock Club Portfolio Summary workbook. The data returned by the stock-related Web queries is real time in the sense that it is no more than 20 minutes old during the business day.

- With the Silver Dollars Stock Club Portfolio Summary workbook open, click the Sheet2 tab at the bottom of the window.

- With cell A1 active, click the Data tab on the Ribbon, and then click the Existing Connections button to display the Existing Connections dialog box (Figure 2–76).

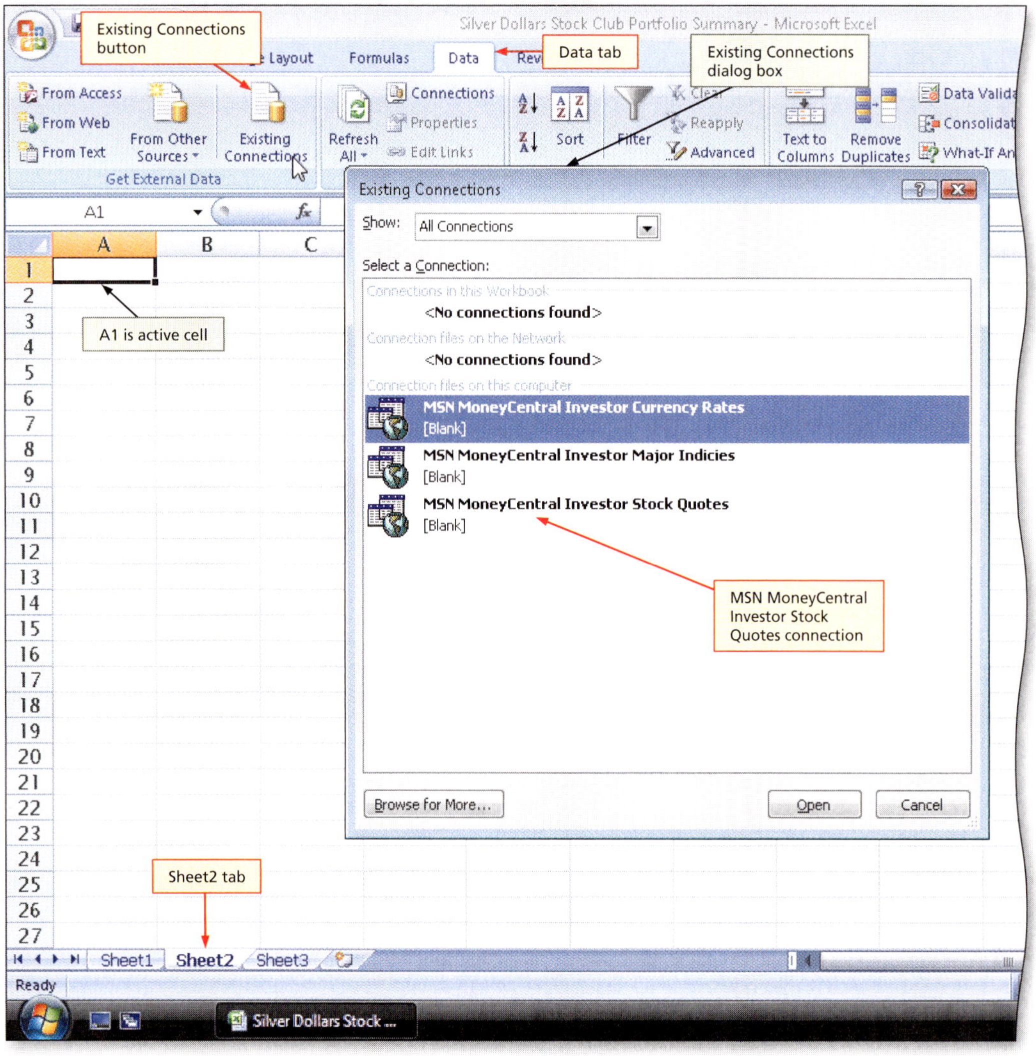

Figure 2–76

Formulas, Functions, Formatting, and Web Queries   Excel Chapter 2   EX 139

2

- Double-click MSN MoneyCentral Investor Stock Quotes to display the Import Data dialog box (Figure 2–77).

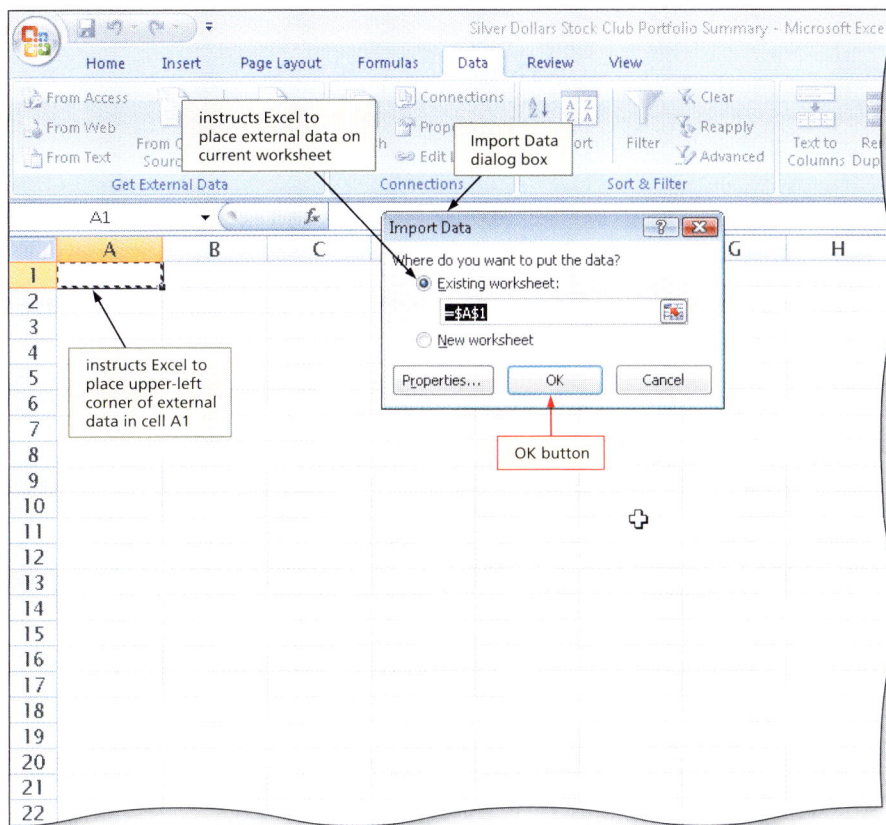

Figure 2–77

3

- Click the OK button.

- When Excel displays the Enter Parameter Value dialog box, type the nine stock symbols aapl t c cmcsa goog hd ibm mrk s in the text box.

- Click the 'Use this value/reference for future refreshes' check box to select it (Figure 2–78).

Q&A What is the purpose of clicking the check box?

Once Excel displays the worksheet, you can refresh the data as often as you want. To refresh the data for all the stocks, click the Refresh All button on the Data tab on the Ribbon. Because the 'Use this value/reference for future refreshes' check box was selected, Excel will continue to use the same stock symbols each time it refreshes.

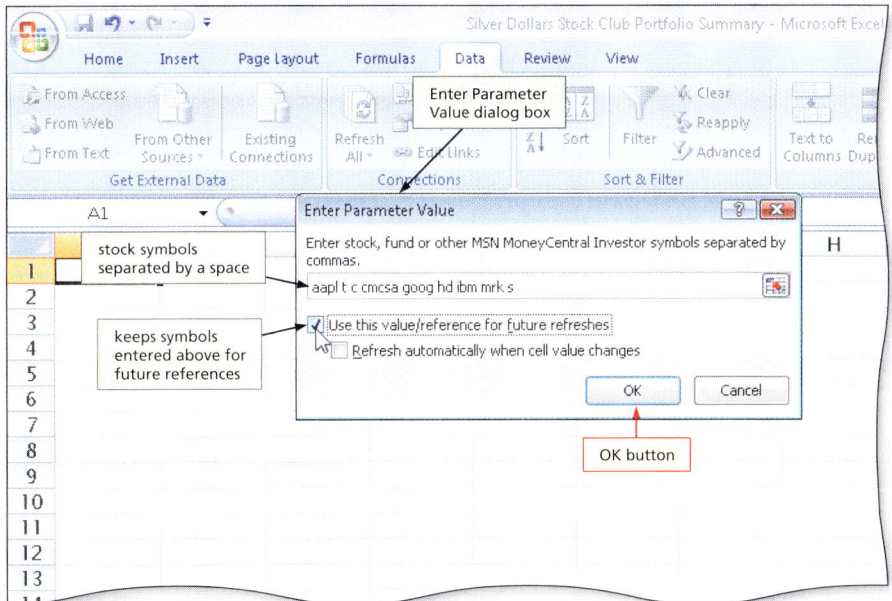

Figure 2–78

4

- Click the OK button to retrieve the stock quotes and display a new worksheet with the desired data (Figure 2–79).

Q&A What composes the new worksheet?

As shown in Figure 2–79, Excel displays the data returned from the Web query in an organized, formatted worksheet, which has a worksheet title, column titles, and a row of data for each stock symbol entered. Other than the first column, which contains the stock name and stock symbol, you have no control over the remaining columns of data returned. The latest price of each stock appears in column D.

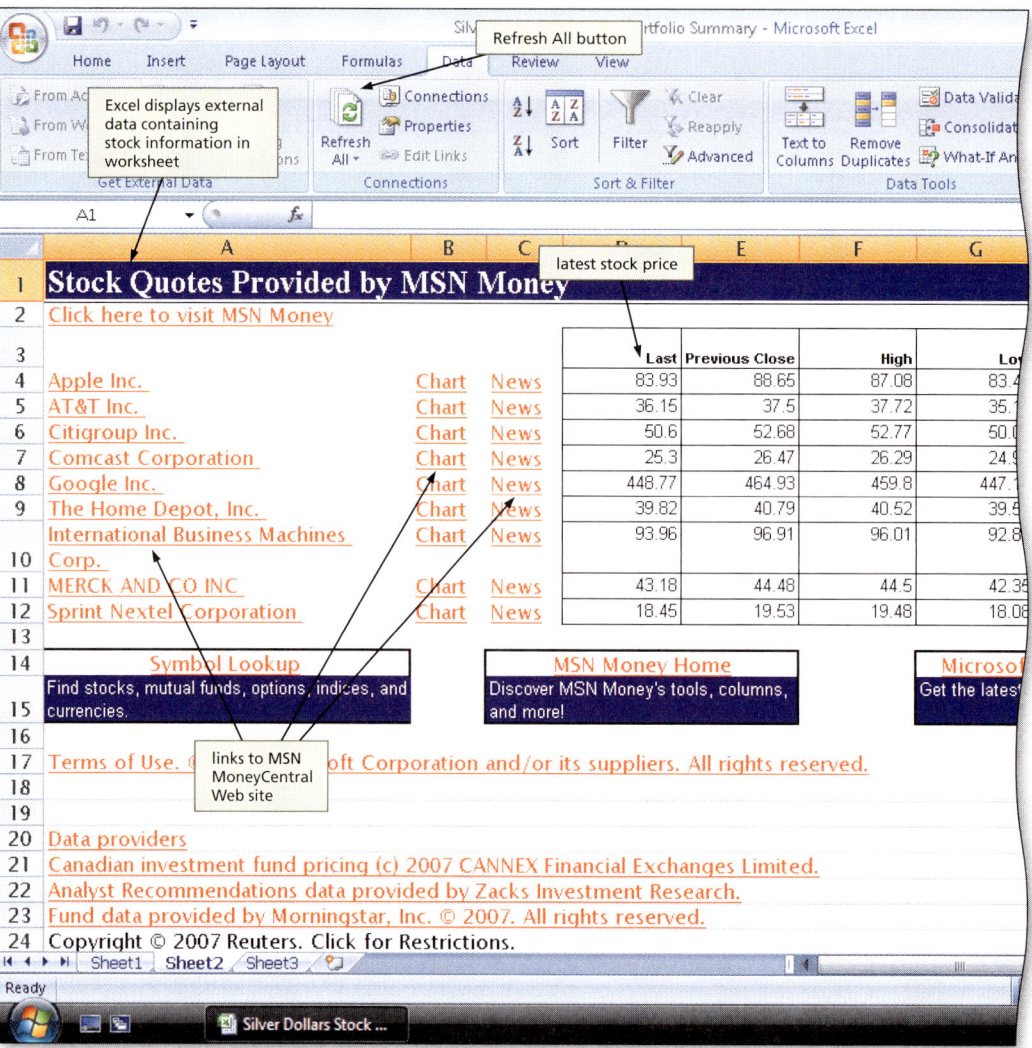

Figure 2–79

Other Ways

1. Press ALT+A, X, select data source

Changing the Worksheet Names

The sheet tabs at the bottom of the window allow you to view any worksheet in the workbook. You click the sheet tab of the worksheet you want to view in the Excel window. By default, Excel presets the names of the worksheets to Sheet1, Sheet2, and so on. The worksheet names become increasingly important as you move towards more sophisticated workbooks, especially workbooks in which you reference cells between worksheets.

Plan Ahead

Choose names for the worksheets.
Use simple, meaningful names for each worksheet. Name the first worksheet that includes the portfolio summary Portfolio Summary. The second worksheet that includes the stock quotes should be named Real-Time Stock Quotes to reflect its contents.

To Change the Worksheet Names

The following steps rename worksheets by double-clicking the sheet tabs.

1

- Double-click the sheet tab labeled Sheet2 in the lower-left corner of the window.

- Type `Real-Time Stock Quotes` as the worksheet name and then press the ENTER key to display the new worksheet name on the sheet tab (Figure 2–80).

Q&A What is the maximum length for a worksheet tab?

Worksheet names can be up to 31 characters (including spaces) in length. Longer worksheet names, however, mean that fewer sheet tabs will show. To view more sheet tabs, you can drag the tab split box (Figure 2–81) to the right. This will reduce the size of the scroll bar at the bottom of the screen. Double-click the tab split box to reset it to its normal position.

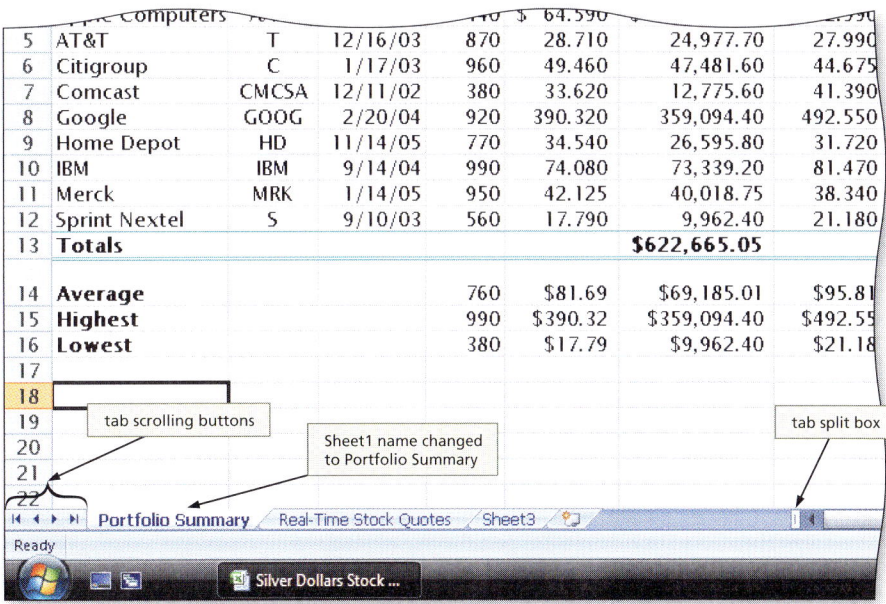

Figure 2–80

Figure 2–81

2

- Double-click the sheet tab labeled Sheet1 in the lower-left corner of the window.

- Type `Portfolio Summary` as the worksheet name and then press the ENTER key to change the name of the worksheet from Sheet 1 to Portfolio Summary (Figure 2–81).

Q&A How can I quickly move between worksheet tabs?

You can use the tab scrolling buttons to the left of the sheet tabs (Figure 2–81) to move between worksheets. The leftmost and rightmost scroll buttons move to the first or last worksheet in the workbook. The two middle scroll buttons move one worksheet to the left or right.

3

- Click the Home tab on the Ribbon.

BTW

Obtaining an E-Mail Account
Several Web sites that allow you to sign up for free e-mail are available. Some choices are MSN Hotmail, Yahoo! Mail, and Google Gmail.

E-Mailing a Workbook from within Excel

The most popular service on the Internet is electronic mail, or **e-mail**, which is the electronic transmission of messages and files to and from other computers using the Internet. Using e-mail, you can converse with friends across the room or on another continent. One of the features of e-mail is the capability to attach Office files, such as Word documents or Excel workbooks, to an e-mail message and send it to a coworker. In the past, if you wanted to e-mail a workbook, you saved the workbook, closed the file, started your e-mail program, and then attached the workbook to the e-mail message before sending it. With Excel, you have the capability of e-mailing a worksheet or workbook directly from within Excel. For these steps to work properly, you must have an e-mail address and one of the following as your e-mail program: Microsoft Outlook, Microsoft Outlook Express, Microsoft Exchange Client, or another 32-bit e-mail program compatible with Messaging Application Programming Interface.

To E-Mail a Workbook from within Excel

The following steps e-mail the Silver Dollars Stock Club Portfolio Summary workbook from within Excel to Juan Castillo at the e-mail address castillo_juan37@hotmail.com.

- With the Silver Dollars Stock Club Portfolio Summary workbook open, click the Office Button and then click Send to display the Send submenu (Figure 2–82).

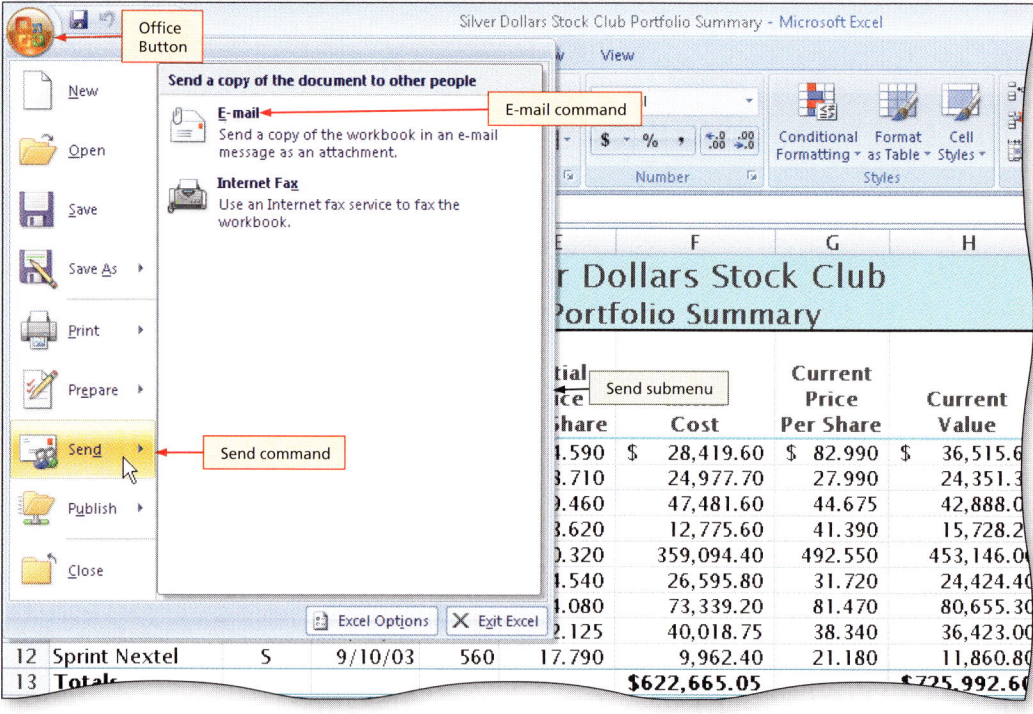

Figure 2–82

②
- Click E-mail on the Send submenu.
- When the e-mail Message window appears, type `castillo_juan37@hotmail.com` in the To text box.
- Type the message shown in the message area in Figure 2–83.

③
- Click the Send button to send the e-mail with the attached workbook to castillo_juan37@hotmail.com.

Q&A How can the recipient use the attached workbook?

Because the workbook was sent as an attachment, Juan Castillo can double-click the attachment in the e-mail to open it in Excel, or he can save it on disk and then open it later.

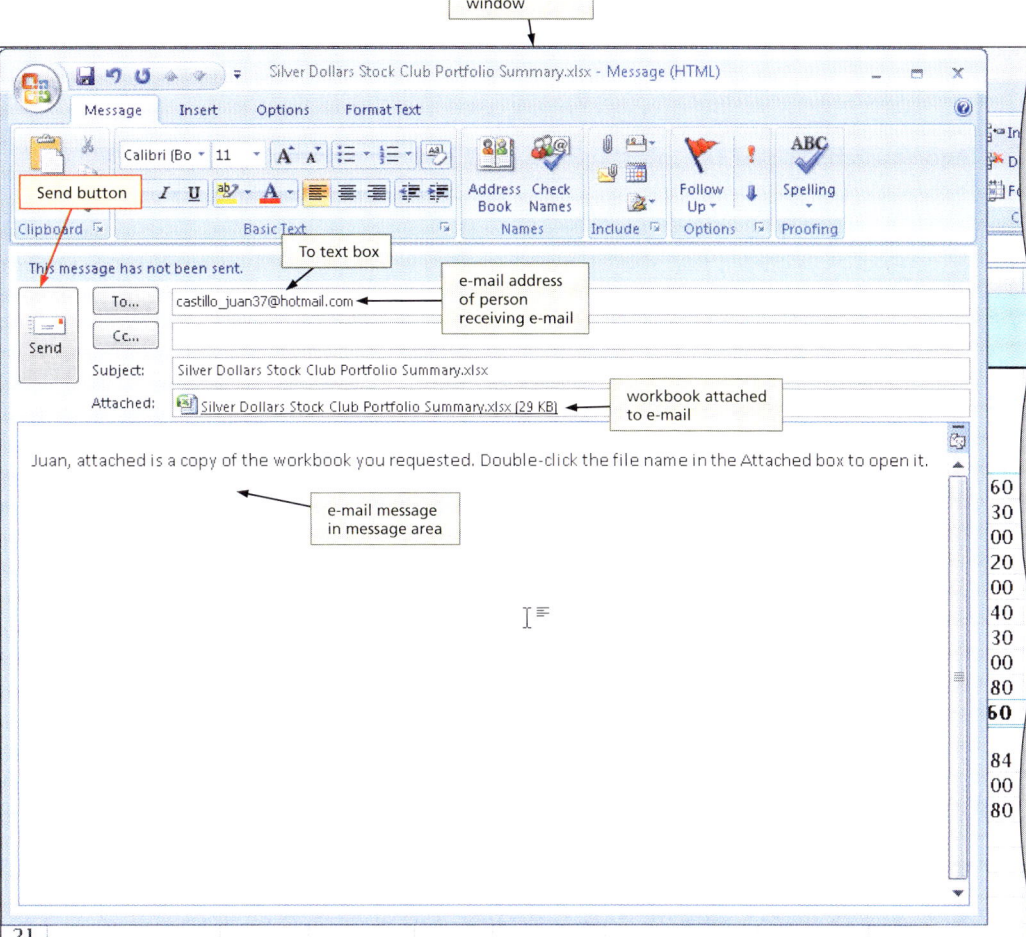

Figure 2–83

To Save the Workbook and Quit Excel

With the workbook complete and e-mailed, the following steps save the workbook and quit Excel.

1. Click the Save button on the Quick Access Toolbar.
2. Click the Close button on the upper-right corner of the title bar.

BTW

Quick Reference
For a table that lists how to complete the tasks covered in this book using the mouse, Ribbon, shortcut menu, and keyboard, see the Quick Reference Summary at the back of this book, or visit the Excel 2007 Quick Reference Web page (scsite.com/dc-off07/qr).

Chapter Summary

In creating the Silver Dollars Stock Club Portfolio Summary workbook, you learned how to enter formulas, calculate an average, find the highest and lowest numbers in a range, verify formulas using Range Finder, draw borders, align text, format numbers, change column widths and row heights, and add conditional formatting to a range of numbers. In addition, you learned to spell check a worksheet, preview a worksheet, print a section of a worksheet, display and print the formulas version of the worksheet using the Fit to option, complete a Web query, rename sheet tabs, and send an e-mail directly from within Excel with the opened workbook as an attachment. The items listed below include all the new Excel skills you have learned in this chapter.

1. Enter a Formula Using the Keyboard (EX 91)
2. Enter Formulas Using Point Mode (EX 93)
3. Copy Formulas Using the Fill Handle (EX 95)
4. Determine the Average of a Range of Numbers Using the Keyboard and Mouse (EX 99)
5. Determine the Highest Number in a Range of Numbers Using the Insert Function Box (EX 101)
6. Determine the Lowest Number in a Range of Numbers Using the Sum Menu (EX 102)
7. Copy a Range of Cells across Columns to an Adjacent Range Using the Fill Handle (EX 104)
8. Verify a Formula Using Range Finder (EX 106)
9. Change the Workbook Theme (EX 109)
10. Change the Background Color and Apply a Box Border to the Worksheet Title and Subtitle (EX 110)
11. Center Data in Cells and Format Dates (EX 113)
12. Apply an Accounting Number Format and Comma Style Format Using the Ribbon (EX 115)
13. Apply a Currency Style Format with a Floating Dollar Sign Using the Format Cells Dialog Box (EX 116)
14. Apply a Percent Style Format and Use the Increase Decimal Button (EX 118)
15. Apply Conditional Formatting (EX 119)
16. Change the Widths of Columns (EX 122)
17. Change the Heights of Rows (EX 125)
18. Check Spelling on the Worksheet (EX 127)
19. Change the Worksheet's Margins, Header, and Orientation in Page Layout View (EX 130)
20. Preview and Print a Worksheet (EX 132)
21. Print a Section of the Worksheet (EX 134)
22. Display the Formulas in the Worksheet and Fit the Printout on One Page (EX 136)
23. Import Data from a Web Source Using a Web Query (EX 138)
24. Change the Worksheet Names (EX 141)
25. E-Mail a Workbook from within Excel (EX 142)

If you have a SAM user profile, you may have access to hands-on instruction, practice, and assessment. Log in to your SAM account (http://sam2007.course.com) to launch any assigned training activities or exams that relate to the skills covered in this chapter.

Learn It Online

Learn It Online is a series of online student exercises that test your knowledge of chapter content and key terms.

Instructions: To complete the Learn It Online exercises, start your browser, click the Address bar, and then enter the Web address `scsite.com/dc-off07/ex2007/learn`. When the Excel 2007 Learn It Online page is displayed, click the link for the exercise you want to complete and then read the instructions.

Chapter Reinforcement TF, MC, and SA
A series of true/false, multiple choice, and short answer questions that test your knowledge of the chapter content.

Flash Cards
An interactive learning environment where you identify chapter key terms associated with displayed definitions.

Practice Test
A series of multiple choice questions that test your knowledge of chapter content and key terms.

Who Wants To Be a Computer Genius?
An interactive game that challenges your knowledge of chapter content in the style of a television quiz show.

Wheel of Terms
An interactive game that challenges your knowledge of chapter key terms in the style of the television show *Wheel of Fortune*.

Crossword Puzzle Challenge
A crossword puzzle that challenges your knowledge of key terms presented in the chapter.

Apply Your Knowledge

Reinforce the skills and apply the concepts you learned in this chapter.

Profit Analysis Worksheet

Instructions Part 1: Start Excel. Open the workbook Apply 2-1 Car-B-Clean Profit Analysis. See the inside back cover of this book for instructions for downloading the Data Files for Students, or contact your instructor for information on accessing the files required in this book. The purpose of this exercise is to open a partially completed workbook, enter formulas and functions, copy the formulas and functions, and then format the worksheet titles and numbers. As shown in Figure 2–84, the completed worksheet analyzes profits by product.

Car-B-Clean Accessories
Profit Analysis

Item	Unit Cost	Unit Profit	Units Sold	Total Sales	Total Profit	% Total Profit
Brush	$ 5.84	$ 3.15	36,751	$ 330,391.49	$ 115,765.65	35.039%
Bucket	7.14	2.75	57,758	571,226.62	158,834.50	27.806%
Drying Cloth	3.52	1.17	42,555	199,582.95	49,789.35	24.947%
Duster	2.55	1.04	78,816	282,949.44	81,968.64	28.969%
Polish	7.19	7.80	57,758	865,792.42	450,512.40	52.035%
Soap	8.52	4.09	50,646	638,646.06	207,142.14	32.435%
Sponge	2.05	1.84	23,154	90,069.06	42,603.36	47.301%
Wax	10.15	7.44	53,099	934,011.41	395,056.56	42.297%
Vacuum	43.91	33.09	17,780	1,369,060.00	588,340.20	42.974%
Totals			418,317	$5,281,729.45	$2,090,012.80	39.571%
Lowest	$2.05	$1.04	17,780	$90,069.06	$42,603.36	24.947%
Highest	$43.91	$33.09	78,816	$1,369,060.00	$588,340.20	52.035%
Average	$10.10	$6.93	46,480	$586,858.83	$232,223.64	

Figure 2–84

Perform the following tasks.

1. Use the following formulas in cells E4, F4, and G4:

   Total Sales (cell E4) = Units Sold * (Unit Cost + Unit Profit) or =D4 * (B4 + C4)

   Total Profit (cell F4) = Units Sold * Unit Profit or = D4 * C4

   % Total Profit (cell G4) = Total Profit / Total Sales or = F4 / E4

   Use the fill handle to copy the three formulas in the range E4:G4 to the range E5:G12.

2. Determine totals for the units sold, total sales, and total profit in row 13. Copy cell G12 to G13 to assign the formula in cell G12 to G13 in the total line.

Continued >

Apply Your Knowledge continued

3. In the range B14:B16, determine the lowest value, highest value, and average value, respectively, for the values in the range B4:B12. Use the fill handle to copy the three functions to the range C14:G16. Delete the average from cell G16, because an average of percentages of this type is mathematically invalid.

4. Format the worksheet as follows:

    a. change the workbook theme to Concourse by using the Themes button on the Page Layout tab on the Ribbon

    b. cell A1 — change to font size 24 with a green (column 6 of standard colors) background and white font color by using the buttons in the Font group on the Home tab on the Ribbon

    c. cell A2 — change to a green (column 6 of standard colors) background and white font color

    d. cells B4:C4, E4:F4, and E13:F13 — Accounting style format with two decimal places and fixed dollar signs (use the Accounting Style button on the Home tab on the Ribbon)

    e. cells B5:C12 and E5:F12 — Comma style format with two decimal places (use the Comma Style button on the Home tab on the Ribbon)

    f. cells D4:D16 — Comma style format with no decimal places

    g. cells G4:G15 — Percent style format with three decimal places

    h. cells B14:C16 and E14:F16 — Currency style format with floating dollar signs (use the Format Cells: Number Dialog Box Launcher on the Home tab on the Ribbon)

5. Switch to Page Layout View and enter your name, course, laboratory assignment number (Apply 2-1), date, and any other information requested by your instructor in the Header area. Preview and print the worksheet in landscape orientation. Change the document properties, as specified by your instructor. Save the workbook using the file name, Apply 2-1 Car-B-Clean Profit Analysis Complete in the format specified by your instructor.

6. Use Range Finder to verify the formula in cell F4.

7. Print the range A3:E16. Press CTRL+ACCENT MARK (`) to change the display from the values version of the worksheet to the formulas version. Print the formulas version in landscape orientation on one page (Figure 2–85) by using the Fit to option in the Page sheet in the Page Setup dialog box. Press CTRL+ACCENT MARK (`) to change the display of the worksheet back to the values version. Do not save the workbook. If requested, submit the three printouts to your instructor.

Instructions Part 2:

1. Do not save the workbook in this part. In column C, use the keyboard to add manually $1.00 to the profit of each product with a unit profit less than $7.00 and $3.00 to the profits of all other products. You should end up with $2,765,603.80 in cell F13.

2. Print the worksheet. Do not save the workbook. If requested, submit the revised workbook in the format specified by your instructor.

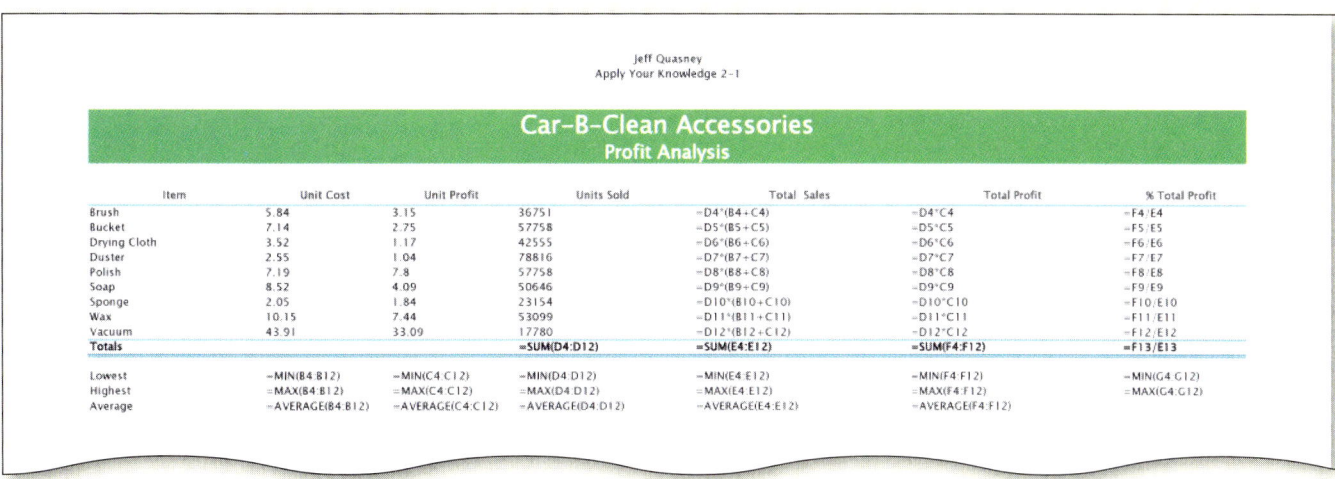

Figure 2–85

Extend Your Knowledge

Extend the skills you learned in this chapter and experiment with new skills. You may need to use Help to complete the assignment.

Applying Conditional Formatting to Cells

Instructions: Start Excel. Open the workbook Extend 2-1 Biology 201 Midterm Scores. See the inside back cover of this book for instructions for downloading the Data Files for Students, or contact your instructor for information on accessing the files required in this book. Perform the following tasks to apply new conditional formatting to the worksheet.

1. Select the range C4:C18. Click the Conditional Formatting button on the Home tab on the Ribbon and then select New Rule in the Conditional Formatting gallery. Select 'Format only top or bottom ranked values' in the Select a Rule Type area (Figure 2–86). Enter a value between 20 and 35 of your choosing in the text box in the Edit the Rule Description area and click the '% of the selected range' check box to select it. Click the Format button and choose a format to assign to this conditional format. Click the OK button in each dialog box to close the dialog boxes and view the worksheet.

2. With range C4:C18 selected, apply a conditional format to the range that highlights scores that are below average.

3. With range D4:D18 selected, apply a conditional format to the range that highlights any grade that is a D or an F.

4. With range B4:B18 selected, apply a conditional format to the range that uses a red color to highlight any duplicate student names.

5. Change the document properties, as specified by your instructor. Change the worksheet header with your name, course number, and other information requested by your instructor. Save the workbook using the file name, Extend 2-1 Biology 201 Midterm Scores Complete, and submit the revised workbook as specified by your instructor.

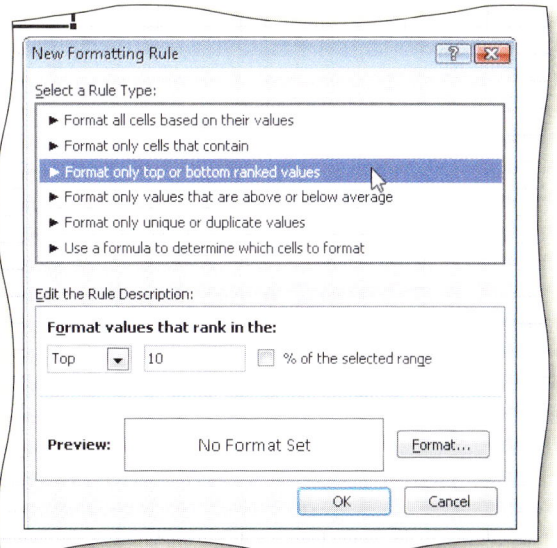

Figure 2–86

Make It Right

Analyze a workbook and correct all errors and/or improve the design.

Correcting Functions and Formulas in a Worksheet

Instructions: Start Excel. Open the workbook Make It Right 2-1 El Centro Diner Payroll Report. See the inside back cover of this book for instructions for downloading the Data Files for Students, or contact your instructor for information on accessing the files required for this book. Correct the following formatting, function, and formula problems (Figure 2–87) in the worksheet.

	A	B	C	D	E	F	G	H	I
1				El Centro Diner					
2				Payroll Report					
3	Employee	Dependents	Rate per Hou	Hours Worked	Gross Pay	Federal Tax	State Tax	Net Pay	% Taxes
4	Vincent Flores	1	$9.90	20.00	$198.00	$34.97	$7.92	$162.03	21.660%
5	Wonda Jefferson	2	11.20	40.00	448.00	80.33	17.92	365.67	21.931%
6	Anthony Sanchez	2	15.90	21.25	337.88	58.31	13.52	277.57	21.257%
7	Alexa Martin	3	11.30	23.50	265.55	39.21	10.62	223.34	18.765%
8	Maria Reyes	1	10.30	21.25	218.88	39.14	8.76	178.73	21.883%
9	Lori Romanoff	2	10.75	40.00	430.00	76.73	17.20	351.27	21.845%
10	Carmen Alvarez	1	12.60	21.50	270.90	49.55	10.84	220.35	22.289%
11	Peter Lane	4	14.50	37.50	543.75	90.21	21.75	449.54	20.591%
12	Claudi Moreno	1	16.00	33.00	528.00	100.97	21.12	426.03	23.122%
13	Wayne Vargas	3	8.00	29.25	234.00	32.90	9.36	198.10	18.059%
14	Totals			287.25	$3,474.95	$602.31	$139.00	$2,852.64	21.333%
15	Average	1.8888889	$12.49	28.67	$360.11	$60.23	$13.90	$294.95	21.140%
16	Highest	4	$16.00	40.00	$543.75	$100.97	$21.75	$449.54	23.122%
17	Lowest	1	$8.00	20.00	$198.00	$32.90	$7.92	$162.03	18.059%

Figure 2–87

1. Adjust the width of column B to 11.25 pixels so that the word in the column header does not wrap.
2. Spell check the worksheet and correct any spelling mistakes that are found, but ignore any spelling mistakes found with the worksheet title and the employee names.
3. The averages in several columns do not include the employee in row 13. Adjust the functions in these cells so that all employees are included in the calculation.
4. The net pay calculation should be:

    Net Pay = Gross Pay – (Federal Taxes + State Taxes)

    Adjust the formulas in the range H4:H13 so that the correct formula is used.
5. The value for the highest value in column C was entered as a number rather than as a function. Replace the value with the appropriate function.
6. The currency values in row 4 should be formatted with the Accounting Number Format button on the Home tab on the Ribbon. They are currently formatted with the Currency format.
7. Delete the function in the cell containing the average of % Taxes because it is mathematically invalid.

8. Change the document properties, as specified by your instructor. Change the worksheet header with your name, course number, and other information requested by your instructor. Save the workbook using the file name, Make It Right 2-1 El Centro Diner Payroll Report Corrected. Submit the revised workbook as specified by your instructor.

In the Lab

Create a workbook using the guidelines, concepts, and skills presented in this chapter. Labs are listed in order of increasing difficulty.

Lab 1: Sales Analysis Worksheet

Problem: You have been asked to build a sales analysis worksheet for Facade Importers that determines the sales quota and percentage of quota met for the sales representatives in Table 2–8. The desired worksheet is shown in Figure 2–88.

Table 2–8 Facade Importers Sales Data			
Sales Representative	Sales Amount	Sales Return	Sales Quota
Polizzi, Bernard	591518	12638	765130
Li, Grace	895050	12015	776381
Volpe, Pamela	716502	18141	733309
Khan, Anwer	709672	22326	566940
Hudson, Emma	802525	11138	712222
Huerta, Teresa	885156	18721	778060

Facade Importers
Sales Analysis

Sales Representative	Sales Amount	Sales Return	Net Sales	Sales Quota	Above Quota
Polizzi, Bernard	$591,518.00	$12,638.00	$578,880.00	$765,130.00	($186,250.00)
Li, Grace	895,050.00	12,015.00	883,035.00	776,381.00	106,654.00
Volpe, Pamela	716,502.00	18,141.00	698,361.00	733,309.00	(34,948.00)
Khan, Anwer	709,672.00	22,326.00	687,346.00	566,940.00	120,406.00
Hudson, Emma	802,525.00	11,138.00	791,387.00	712,222.00	79,165.00
Huerta, Terese	885,156.00	18,721.00	866,435.00	778,060.00	88,375.00
Total	$4,600,423.00	$94,979.00	$4,505,444.00	$4,332,042.00	$173,402.00
Average	$766,737.17	$15,829.83	$750,907.33	$722,007.00	$28,900.33
Highest	$895,050.00	$22,326.00	$883,035.00	$778,060.00	$120,406.00
Lowest	$591,518.00	$11,138.00	$578,880.00	$566,940.00	($186,250.00)
% of Quota Sold ====>	104.00%				

Figure 2–88

Continued >

In the Lab *continued*

Instructions Part 1: Perform the following tasks to build the worksheet shown in Figure 2–88.
1. Apply the Aspect theme to the worksheet by using the Themes button on the Page Layout tab on the Ribbon.
2. Increase the width of column A to 19.00 points and the width of columns B through F to 13.50 points.
3. Enter the worksheet title `Facade Importers` in cell A1 and the worksheet subtitle `Sales Analysis` in cell A2. Enter the column titles in row 3 as shown in Figure 2–88. In row 3, use ALT+ENTER to start a new line in a cell.
4. Enter the sales data described in Table 2–8 in columns A, B, C, and E in rows 4 through 9. Enter the row titles in the range A10:A14 as shown in Figure 2–88 on the previous page.
5. Obtain the net sales in column D by subtracting the sales returns in column C from the sales amount in column B. Enter the formula in cell D4 and copy it to the range D5:D9.
6. Obtain the above quota amounts in column F by subtracting the sales quota in column E from the net sales in column D. Enter the formula in cell F4 and copy it to the range F5:F9.
7. Obtain the totals in row 10 by adding the column values for each salesperson. In the range B11:B13, use the AVERAGE, MAX, and MIN functions to determine the average, highest value, and lowest value in the range B4:B9. Copy the range B11:B13 to the range C11:F13.
8. Determine the percent of quota sold in cell B14 by dividing the total net sales amount in cell D10 by the total sales quota amount in cell E10. Center this value in the cell.
9. If necessary, click the Home tab on the Ribbon. One at a time, merge and center the worksheet title and subtitle across columns A through F. Select cells A1 and A2 and change the background color to red (column 2 in the Standard Colors area on the Fill Color palette). Apply the Title cell style to cells A1 and B1 by clicking the Cell Styles button on the Home tab on the Ribbon and clicking the Title cell style in the Titles and Headings area in the Cell Styles gallery. Change the worksheet title in cell A1 to 28-point white (column 1, row 1 on the Font Color gallery). Change the worksheet subtitle to the same color. Assign a thick box border from the Borders gallery to the range A1:A2.
10. Center the titles in row 3, columns A through F. Apply the Heading 3 cell style to the range A3:F3. Use the Italic button on the Home tab on the Ribbon to italicize the column titles in row 3 and the row titles in the range A10:A14.
11. Apply the Total cell style to the range A10:F10. Assign a thick box to cell B14. Change the background and font colors for cell B14 to the same colors applied to the worksheet title in Step 9.
12. Change the row heights of row 3 to 33.00 points and rows 11 and 14 to 30.00 points.
13. Select cell B14 and then click the Percent Style button on the Home tab on the Ribbon. Click the Increase Decimal button on the Ribbon twice to display the percent in cell B14 to hundredths.
14. Use the CTRL key to select the ranges B4:F4 and B10:F13. That is, select the range B4:F4 and then while holding down the CTRL key, select the range B10:F13. Use the Format Cells: Number Dialog Box Launcher button on the Home tab on the Ribbon to display the Format Cells dialog box to assign the selected ranges a Floating Dollar Sign style format with two decimal places and parentheses to represent negative numbers. Select the range B5:F9 and click the Comma Style button on the Home tab on the Ribbon.
15. Rename the sheet tab as Sales Analysis. Change the document properties, as specified by your instructor. Change the worksheet header with your name, course number, and other information requested by your instructor.

16. Save the workbook using the file name Lab 2-1 Part 1 Facade Importers Sales Analysis. Print the entire worksheet in landscape orientation. Print only the range A3:B10.
17. Display the formulas version by pressing CTRL+ACCENT MARK (`). Print the formulas version using the Fit to option button in the Scaling area on the Page tab in the Page Setup dialog box. After printing the worksheet, reset the Scaling option by selecting the Adjust to option button on the Page tab in the Page Setup dialog box and changing the percent value to 100%. Change the display from the formulas version to the values version by pressing CTRL+ACCENT MARK (`). Do not save the workbook.
18. Submit the assignment as specified by your instructor.

Instructions Part 2: Open the workbook created in Part 1 and save the workbook as Lab 2-1 Part 2 Facade Importers Sales Analysis. Manually decrement each of the six values in the net sales column by $10,000.00 until the percent of quota sold in cell B14 is below, yet as close as possible to, 100%. All six values in column E must be incremented the same number of times. The percent of quota sold in B14 should equal 99.85%. Update the worksheet header and save the workbook. Print the worksheet. Submit the assignment as specified by your instructor.

Instructions Part 3: Open the workbook created in Part 2 and then save the workbook as Lab 2-1 Part 3 Facade Importers Sales Analysis. With the percent of quota sold in cell B14 equal to 99.85% from Part 2, manually decrement each of the six values in the sales return column by $1,000.00 until the percent of quota sold in cell B14 is above, yet as close as possible to, 100%. Decrement all six values in column C the same number of times. Your worksheet is correct when the percent of quota sold in cell B14 is equal to 100.12%. Update the worksheet header and save the workbook. Print the worksheet. Submit the assignment as specified by your instructor.

In the Lab

Lab 2: Balance Due Worksheet

Problem: You are a spreadsheet intern for Jackson's Bright Ideas, a popular Denver-based light fixture store with outlets in major cities across the western United States. You have been asked to use Excel to generate a report (Figure 2–89) that summarizes the monthly balance due. A graphic breakdown of the data also is desired. The customer data in Table 2–9 is available for test purposes.

Table 2–9 Jackson's Bright Ideas Monthly Balance Due Data

Customer	Beginning Balance	Credits	Payments	Purchases
Costa, Dan	160.68	18.70	99.33	68.28
Hernandez, Abraham	138.11	48.47	75.81	46.72
Mc Cartan, John	820.15	32.11	31.23	29.19
Paoli, Pam	167.35	59.32	52.91	33.90
Ramirez, Alberto	568.34	55.17	18.53	36.34
Vaughn, Noah	449.92	25.90	82.05	99.77
Xiong, James	390.73	48.12	19.35	92.13

Continued >

In the Lab *continued*

Instructions Part 1: Create a worksheet similar to the one shown in Figure 2–89. Include the five columns of customer data in Table 2–9 in the report, plus two additional columns to compute a service charge and a new balance for each customer. Assume no negative unpaid monthly balances.

	A	B	C	D	E	F	G
1	Jackson's Bright Ideas						
2	Monthly Balance Due Report						
3	Customer	Beginning Balance	Credits	Payments	Purchases	Service Charge	New Balance
4	Costa, Dan	$160.68	$18.70	$99.33	$68.28	$1.17	$112.10
5	Hernandez, Abraham	138.11	48.47	75.81	46.72	0.38	60.93
6	Mc Cartan, John	820.15	32.11	31.23	29.19	20.81	806.81
7	Paoli, Pam	167.35	59.32	52.91	33.90	1.52	90.54
8	Ramirez, Alberto	568.34	55.17	18.53	36.34	13.60	544.58
9	Vaughn, Noah	449.92	25.90	82.05	99.77	9.40	451.14
10	Xiong, James	390.73	48.12	19.35	92.13	8.89	424.28
11	Totals	$2,695.28	$287.79	$379.21	$406.33	$55.78	$2,490.39
12	Highest	$820.15	$59.32	$99.33	$99.77	$20.81	$806.81
13	Lowest	$138.11	$18.70	$18.53	$29.19	$0.38	$60.93
14	Average	$385.04	$41.11	$54.17	$58.05	$7.97	$355.77

Figure 2–89

Perform the following tasks:

1. Enter and format the worksheet title `Jackson's Bright Ideas` and worksheet subtitle `Monthly Balance Due Report` in cells A1 and A2. Change the theme of the worksheet to the Technic theme. Apply the Title cell style to cells A1 and A2. Change the font size in cell A1 to 28 points. One at a time, merge and center the worksheet title and subtitle across columns A through G. Change the background color of cells A1 and A2 to yellow (column 4 in the Standard Colors area in the Font Color palette). Draw a thick box border around the range A1:A2.

2. Change the width of column A to 20.00 characters. Change the widths of columns B through G to 12.00. Change the heights of row 3 to 36.00 and row 12 to 30.00 points.

3. Enter the column titles in row 3 and row titles in the range A11:A14 as shown in Figure 2–89. Center the column titles in the range A3:G3. Apply the Heading 3 cell style to the range A3:G3. Bold the titles in the range A11:A14. Apply the Total cell style to the range A11:G11. Change the font size of the cells in the range A3:G14 to 12 points.

4. Enter the data in Table 2–9 in the range A4:E10.

5. Use the following formulas to determine the service charge in column F and the new balance in column G for the first customer. Copy the two formulas down through the remaining customers.

    a. Service Charge (cell F4) = 2.75% * (Beginning Balance – Payments – Credits)
       or = 0.0275 * (B4 – D4 – C4)

    b. New Balance (G4) = Beginning Balance + Purchases – Credits – Payments + Service Charge
       or =B4 + E4 – C4 – D4 + F4

6. Determine the totals in row 11.

7. Determine the maximum, minimum, and average values in cells B12:B14 for the range B4:B10 and then copy the range B12:B14 to C12:G14.
8. Use the Format Cells command on the shortcut menu to format the numbers as follows: (a) assign the Currency style with a floating dollar sign to the cells containing numeric data in the ranges B4:G4 and B11:G14; and (b) assign the Comma style (currency with no dollar sign) to the range B5:G10.
9. Use conditional formatting to change the formatting to white font on a red background in any cell in the range C4:C10 that contains a value greater than 50.
10. Change the worksheet name from Sheet1 to Balance Due. Change the document properties, as specified by your instructor. Change the worksheet header with your name, course number, and other information requested by your instructor.
11. Spell check the worksheet. Preview and then print the worksheet in landscape orientation. Save the workbook using the file name, Lab 2-2 Part 1 Jackson's Bright Ideas Monthly Balance Due Report.
12. Print the range A3:D14. Print the formulas version on one page. Close the workbook without saving the changes. Submit the assignment as specified by your instructor.

Instructions Part 2: This part requires that a 3-D Bar chart with a cylindrical shape be inserted on a new worksheet in the workbook. If necessary, use Excel Help to obtain information on inserting a chart on a separate sheet in the workbook.

1. With the Lab 2-2 Part 1 Jackson's Bright Ideas Monthly Balance Due Report workbook open, save the workbook using the file name, Lab 2-2 Part 2 Jackson's Bright Ideas Monthly Balance Due Report. Draw the 3-D Bar chart with cylindrical shape showing each customer's total new balance as shown in Figure 2–90.

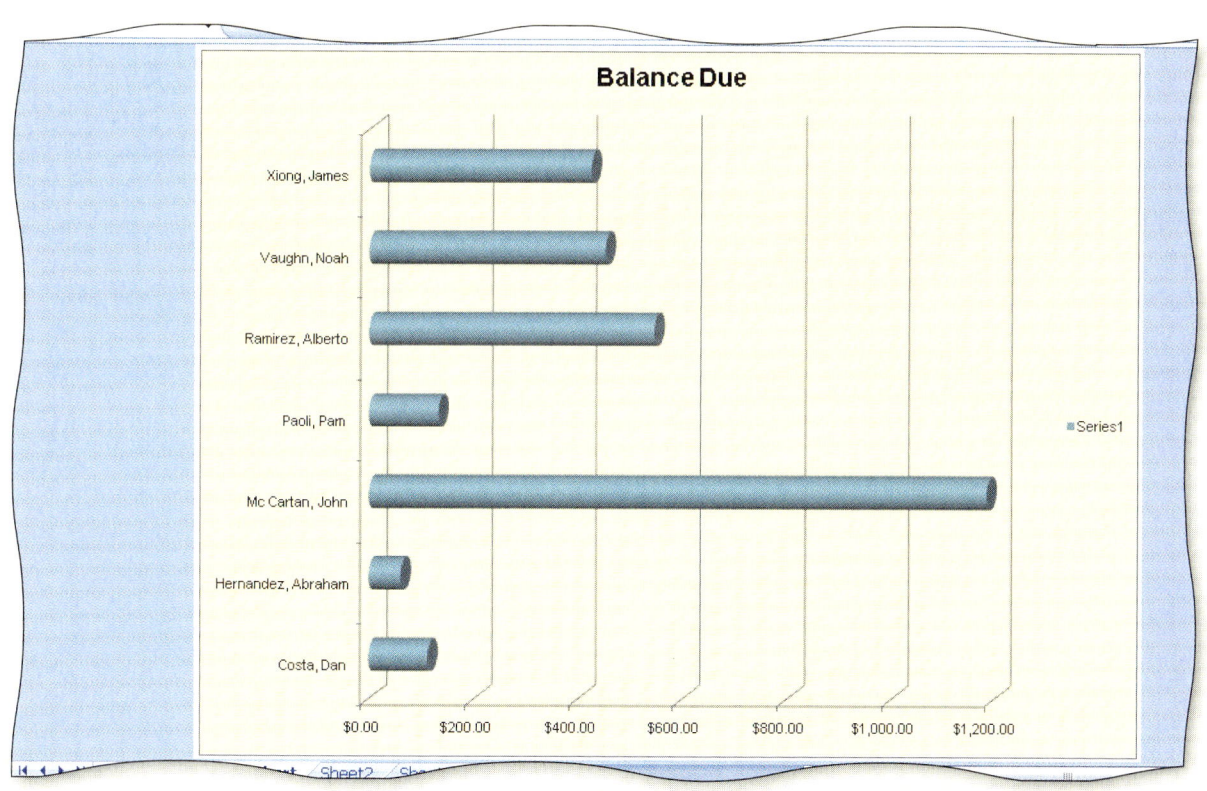

Figure 2–90

2. Use the CTRL key and mouse to select the nonadjacent chart ranges A4:A10 and G4:G10. That is, select the range A4:A10 and then while holding down the CTRL key, select the range G4:G10. The customer names in the range A4:A10 will identify the cylindrical bars, while the data series in the range G4:G10 will determine the length of the bars.

Continued >

In the Lab *continued*

3. Click the Insert tab on the Ribbon. Click the Bar button in the Charts group on the Ribbon and then select Clustered Horizontal Cylinder in the Cylinder area. When the chart is displayed on the worksheet, click the Move Chart button on the Ribbon. When the Move Chart dialog box appears, click New sheet and then type Bar Chart for the sheet name. Click the OK button.

4. When the chart is displayed on the new worksheet, click the chart area, which is a blank area near the edge of the chart, and then click the Format contextual tab. Click the Shape Fill button on the Ribbon and then select Gold, Accent 2, Lighter 80% in the gallery (column 6, row 2). Click the Layout contextual tab. Click the Chart Title button on the Ribbon and then select Above Chart in the Chart Title gallery. If necessary, use the scroll bar on the right side of the worksheet to scroll to the top of the chart. Click the edge of the chart title to select it and then type Balance Due as the chart title.

5. Drag the Balance Due tab at the bottom of the worksheet to the left of the Bar Chart tab to reorder the sheets in the workbook. Preview and print the chart.

6. Click the Balance Due sheet tab. Change the following purchases: customer John Mc Cartan to $406.58, and customer Pam Paoli to $74.99. The company also decided to change the service charge from 2.75% to 3.25% for all customers. After copying the adjusted formula in cell F4 to the range F5:F10, click the Auto Fill Options button and then click Fill without Formatting to maintain the original formatting in the range F5:F10. The total new balance in cell G11 should equal $2,919.01.

7. Select both sheets by holding down the SHIFT key and then clicking the Bar Chart tab. Preview and print the selected sheets. Submit the assignment as requested by your instructor. Save the workbook.

8. Submit the assignment as specified by your instructor.

Instructions Part 3: With your instructor's permission, e-mail the workbook created in this exercise with the changes indicated in Part 2 as an attachment to your instructor. Close the workbook without saving the changes.

In the Lab

Lab 3: Equity Web Queries

Problem: A friend of your family, Benson Yackley, has learned that Excel can connect to the Web, download real-time stock data into a worksheet, and then refresh the data as often as needed. Because you have had courses in Excel and the Internet, he has hired you as a consultant to develop a stock analysis workbook. His portfolio is shown in Table 2–10.

Table 2–10 Benson Yackley's Stock Portfolio	
Company	**Stock Symbol**
Exxon Mobil	XOM
Dell	DELL
Hewlett-Packard	HPQ
Intel	INTC
MetLife	MET
PepsiCo	PEP

Instructions Part 1: Start Excel. If necessary, connect to the Internet. Perform a Web query to obtain multiple stock quotes (Figure 2–91), using the stock symbols in the second column of Table 2–10. Place the results of the Web query in a new worksheet. Rename the worksheet Real-Time Stock Quotes. Change the document properties, as specified by your instructor. Add a header with your name, course number, and other information requested by your instructor. Save the workbook using the file name, Lab 2-3 Part 1 Benson Yackley Equities Online. Preview and then print the worksheet in landscape orientation using the Fit to option.

Click the following links and print the Web page that appears in the browser window: Click here to visit MSN Money; Dell Inc.; Chart (to the right of MetLife, Inc.); and News (to the right of PepsiCo, Inc.). Submit the assignment as specified by your instructor.

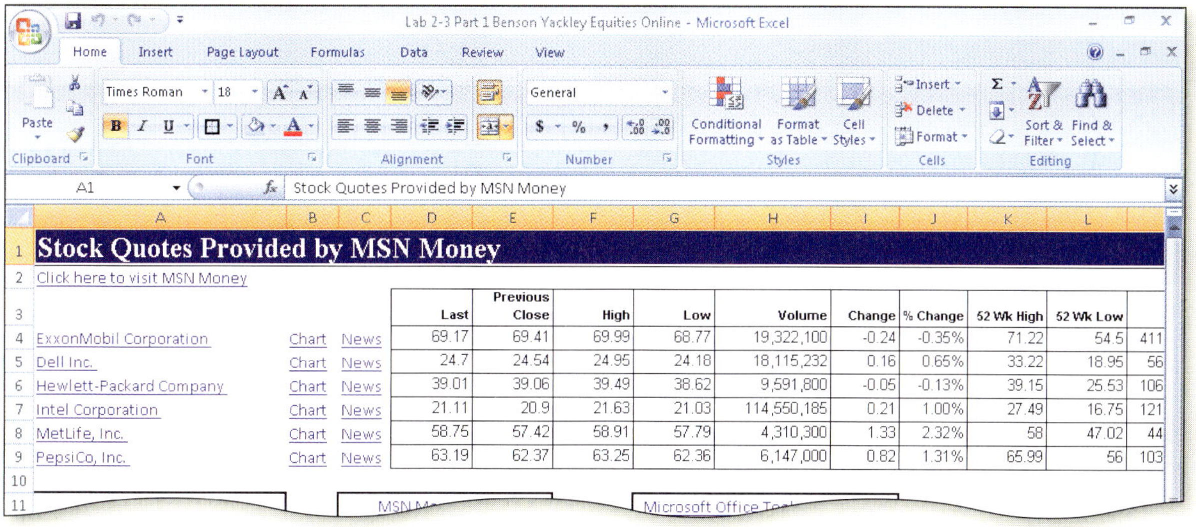

Figure 2-91

Instructions Part 2: While connected to the Internet and with the Lab 2-3 Benson Yackley Equities Online workbook open, create a worksheet listing the major indices and their current values on Sheet2 of the workbook (Figure 2–92). After clicking the Sheet2 tab, create the worksheet by double-clicking MSN MoneyCentral Investor Major Indices in the Existing Connections dialog box. The dialog box is displayed when you click the Existing Connections button on the Data tab on the Ribbon. Rename the worksheet Major Indices. Preview and then print the Major Indices worksheet in landscape orientation using the Fit to option. Save the workbook using the same file name as in Part 1. Submit the assignment as specified by your instructor.

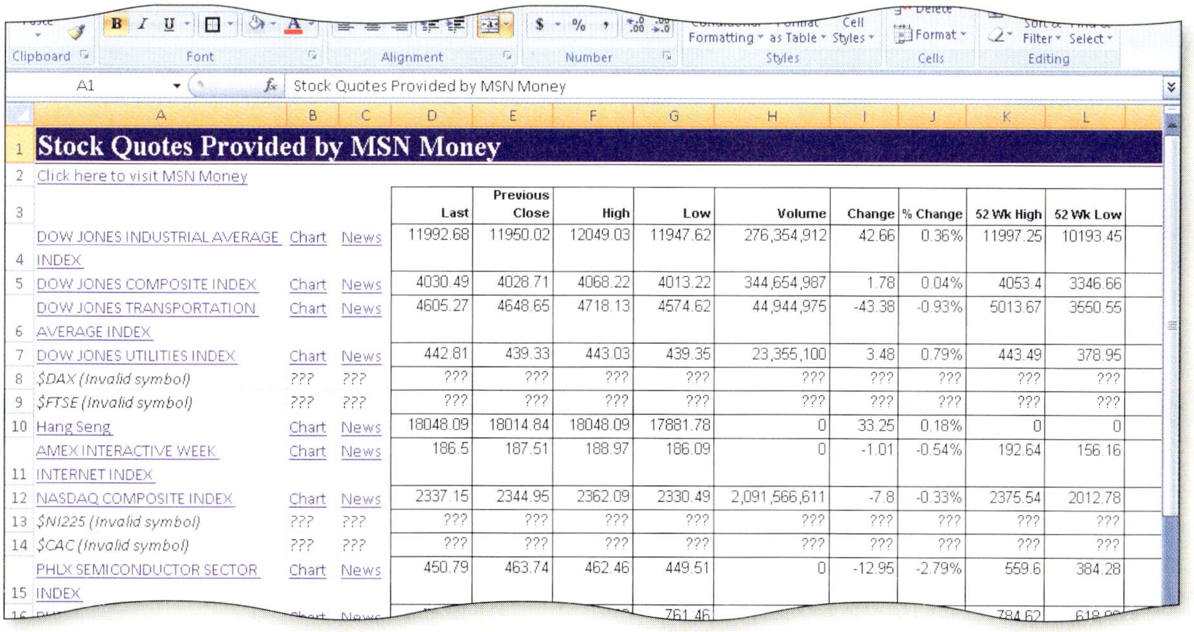

Figure 2-92

Cases and Places

Apply your creative thinking and problem solving skills to design and implement a solution.

• Easier   •• More Difficult

• 1: Design and Create a Weight-Loss Plan Worksheet

As a summer intern working for Choose to Lose, a local weight-loss clinic, you have been asked to create a worksheet that estimates the monthly weight lost for an individual based on recommended average daily activities. You have been given the numbers of calories burned per hour and the average number of hours for each activity (Table 2–11). Use the following formulas:

Formula A: Total Calories Burned per Day = Calories burned per Hour × Average Hours Daily

Formula B: Total Pounds Lost per Month (30 days) = 30 × Total Calories Burned per Day / 3500

Formula C: Average function

Formula D: Max function

Formula E: Min function

Use the concepts and techniques presented in this project to create and format the worksheet. Include an embedded 3-D Pie chart that shows the contribution of each activity to the total calories burned per day. Use Microsoft Excel Help to create a professional looking 3-D Pie chart with title and data labels.

Table 2–11 Activities with Corresponding Calories Burned per Hour and Worksheet Layout				
Activity	Calories Burned per Hour	Average Hours Daily	Total Calories Burned per Day	Total Pounds Lost per Month (30 Days)
Aerobics class	450	0.50	Formula A	Formula B
Brisk walking	350	0.50		
House work	150	1.00		
Office work/sitting	120	6.00		
Sleeping	70	9.00		
Standing	105	2.00		
Swimming	290	0.50		
Tennis	315	0.25		
Walking	240	4.25		
Totals	—		—	—
Average	Formula C			
Highest	Formula D			
Lowest	Formula E			

• 2: Create a Profit Potential Worksheet

You work part-time for Doze-Now, a retailer of sleep-related products. Your manager wants to know the profit potential of their inventory based on the categories of inventory in Table 2–12. Table 2–12 contains the format of the desired report. The required formulas are shown in Table 2–13. Use the concepts and techniques developed in this project to create and format the worksheet. Submit a printout of the values version and formulas version of the worksheet. The company just received a shipment of 175 additional comforters and 273 items of sleepwear. Update the appropriate cells in the Units on Hand column.

Table 2–12 Doze-Now Profit Potential Data and Worksheet Layout

Item	Units on Hand	Average Unit Cost	Total Cost	Average Unit Price	Total Value	Potential Profit
Comforters	216	46.52	Formula A	Formula B	Formula C	Formula D
Night lights	4,283	6.89				
Pillows	691	47.64				
Sleep sound machines	103	45.06				
Sleepwear	489	16.77				
Total		—				
Average	Formula E					
Lowest	Formula F					
Highest	Formula G					

Table 2–13 Doze-Now Profit Potential Formulas

Formula A = Units on Hand * Average Unit Cost

Formula B = Average Unit Cost * (1 / (1 – .58))

Formula C = Units on Hand * Average Unit Price

Formula D = Total Value – Total Cost

Formula E = AVERAGE function

Formula F = MIN function

Formula G = MAX function

Continued >

Cases and Places *continued*

•• 3: Create a Fund-Raising Analysis Worksheet

You are the chairperson of the fund-raising committee for a local charity. You want to compare various fund-raising ideas to determine which will give you the best profit. The data obtained from six businesses about their products and the format of the desired report are shown in Table 2–14. The required formulas are shown in Table 2–15. Use the concepts and techniques presented in this project to create and format the worksheet.

Table 2–14 Fund-Raising Data and Worksheet Layout

Product	Company	Cost per Unit	Margin	Selling Price	Profit per 2000 Sales	Profit per 5000 Sales
Candles	Woodland Farms	$4.75	40%	Formula A	Formula B	Formula C
Candy	Polkandy	3.00	70%			
Coffee	Garcia Coffee	6.50	45%			
Cookie dough	Oh, Dough!	2.90	65%			
Flower bulbs	Early Bloom	2.40	50%			
T-shirts	Zed's Sports	5.75	42%			
Minimum		Formula D				
Maximum		Formula E				

Table 2–15 Band Fund-Raising Formulas

Formula A = Cost per Unit / (1 – Margin)

Formula B = 2000 * (Selling Price – Cost per Unit)

Formula C = 5000 *110% * (Selling Price – Cost per Unit)

Formula D = MIN function

Formula E = MAX function

•• 4: Design and Create a Projected Budget

Make It Personal

For the next six-month period, forecast your income for each month, your base expenditures for each month, and your special expenditures for each month. Base expenditures include expenses that occur each month, such as food and loan payments. Special expenditures include expenses that are out of the ordinary, such as the purchase of gifts, automobile insurance, and medical expenses. With this data, develop a worksheet calculating the amount of remaining money at the end of each month. You can determine this amount by subtracting both expenses from the anticipated income.

Include a total, average value, highest value, and lowest value for income, base expenditures, special expenditures, and remaining money. Use the concepts and techniques presented in this project to create and format the worksheet.

Create a 3-D Pie chart on a separate sheet illustrating the portion each month's special expenditures deducts from the total remaining money after all six months have passed. Use Microsoft Excel Help to create a professional looking 3-D Pie chart with title and data labels.

•• 5: Design and Create a Stock Analysis Worksheet

Working Together

Have each member of your team select six stocks — two bank stocks, two communications stocks, and two Internet stocks. Each member should submit the stock names, stock symbols, and an approximate six-month-old price. Create a worksheet that lists the stock names, symbols, price, and number of shares for each stock (use 350 shares as the number of shares for all stocks). Format the worksheet so that it has a professional appearance and is as informative as possible.

Have the group do research on the use of 3-D references, which is a reference to a range that spans two or more worksheets in a workbook (use Microsoft Excel Help). Use what the group learns to create a Web query on the Sheet2 worksheet by referencing the stock symbols on the Sheet1 worksheet. On the Sheet1 worksheet, change the cells that list current price per share numbers on the Sheet1 worksheet so that they use 3-D cell references that refer to the worksheet created by the Web query on the Sheet2 worksheet. Present your workbook and findings to the class.

Microsoft Office **Access 2007**

1 Creating and Using a Database

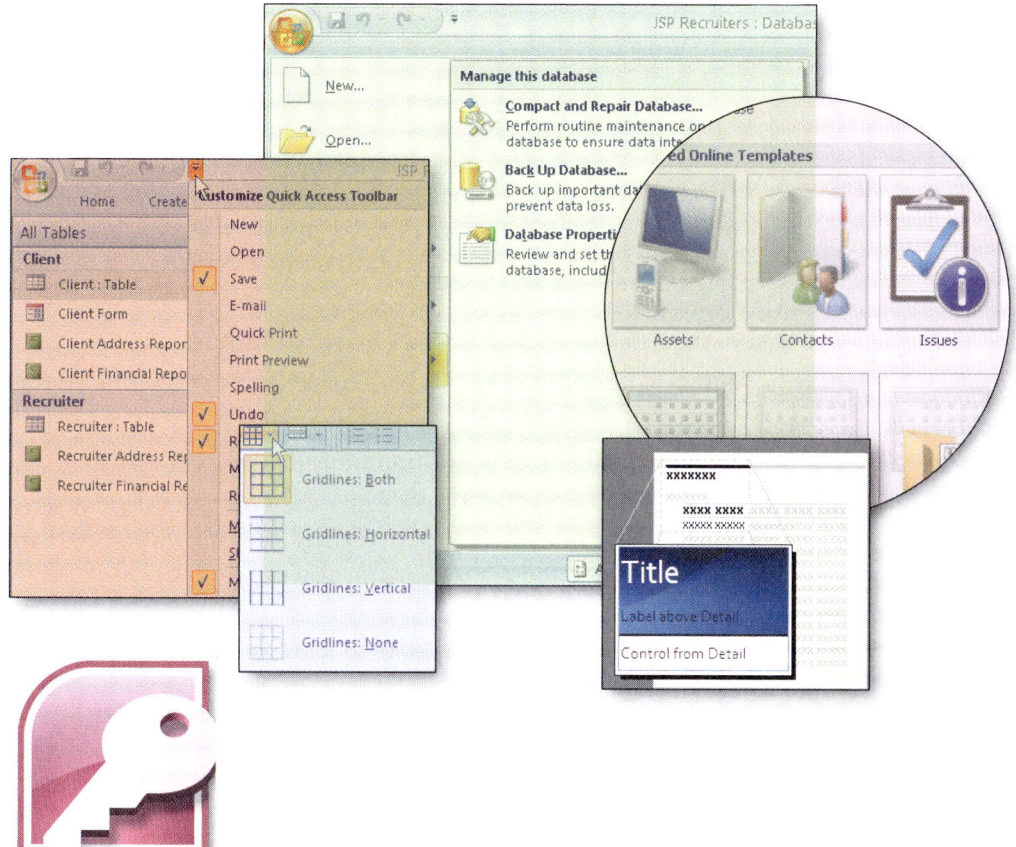

Objectives

You will have mastered the material in this chapter when you can:

- Describe databases and database management systems
- Design a database to satisfy a collection of requirements
- Start Access
- Describe the features of the Access window
- Create a database
- Create a table and add records
- Close a table
- Close a database and quit Access
- Open a database
- Print the contents of a table
- Create and print custom reports
- Create and use a split form
- Use the Access Help system

1 | Creating and Using a Database

What Is Microsoft Office Access 2007?

Microsoft Office Access 2007, usually referred to as simply Access, is a database management system. A database management system, such as Access, is a software tool that allows you to use a computer to create a database; add, change, and delete data in the database; sort the data in the database; retrieve data in the database; and create forms and reports using the data in the database. The term **database** describes a collection of data organized in a manner that allows access, retrieval, and use of that data. Some of the key features in Access are:

- **Data entry and update** Access provides easy mechanisms for adding, changing, and deleting data, including the capability of making mass changes in a single operation.
- **Queries (questions)** Access makes it possible to ask complex questions concerning the data in the database and then receive instant answers.
- **Forms** Access allows the user to produce attractive and useful forms for viewing and updating data.
- **Reports** Access includes report creation tools that make it easy to produce sophisticated reports for presenting data.
- **Web support** Access allows you to save objects, reports, and tables in HTML format so they can be viewed using a browser. You also can import and export documents in XML format as well as share data with others using SharePoint Services.

This version of Access has many new features to help you be more productive. Like the other Office programs, it features a new, improved interface utilizing the Ribbon. The new Navigation Pane makes navigating among the various objects in a database easier and more intuitive than in the past. The new version includes several professionally designed templates that you can use to quickly create a database. Sorting and filtering has been enhanced in this version. The new Layout view allows you to make changes to the design of forms and reports at the same time you are browsing the data. Datasheet view also has been enhanced to make creating tables more intuitive. Split form, a new form object, combines both a datasheet and a form as a single unit. Memo fields now support rich text, and there is a new Attachment data type. Using the Attachment data type, a field can contain an attached file, such as a document, image, or spreadsheet.

Project Planning Guidelines

The process of developing a database that communicates specific information requires careful analysis and planning. As a starting point, establish why the database is needed. Once the purpose is determined, analyze the intended users of the database and their unique needs. Then, gather information about the topic and decide what to include in the database. Finally, determine the database design and style that will be most successful at delivering the message. Details of these guidelines are provided in Appendix A. In addition, each project in this book provides practical applications of these planning considerations.

Project — Database Creation

JSP Recruiters is a recruiting firm that specializes in job placement for health care professionals. Because the recruiters at JSP have previous experience in the health care industry, the firm is able to provide quality candidates for employment in hospitals, clinics, medical laboratories, doctors' offices, and other health care facilities.

JSP Recruiters works with clients in need of health care professionals. It assigns each client to a specific recruiter. The recruiter works with the client to determine the necessary qualifications for each job candidate. The recruiter then contacts and does a preliminary review of the qualifications for each candidate before setting up a job interview between the client and the candidate. If the candidate is hired, the client pays a percentage of the new employee's annual salary to the recruiting firm, which then distributes a percentage of that client fee to the recruiter.

To ensure that operations run smoothly, JSP Recruiters organizes data on its clients and recruiters in a database, managed by Access. In this way, JSP keeps its data current and accurate while the firm's management can analyze the data for trends and produce a variety of useful reports.

In Access, a database consists of a collection of tables, each of which contains information on a specific subject. Figure 1–1 shows the database for JSP Recruiters. It consists of two tables. The Client table (Figure 1–1a) contains information about the clients to whom JSP provides services. The Recruiter table (Figure 1–1b) contains information about the recruiters to whom these clients are assigned.

(a) Client Table

(b) Recruiter Table

Figure 1–1

The rows in the tables are called **records**. A record contains information about a given person, product, or event. A row in the Client table, for example, contains information about a specific client.

The columns in the tables are called fields. A **field** contains a specific piece of information within a record. In the Client table, for example, the fourth field, City, contains the city where the client is located.

The first field in the Client table is the Client Number. JSP Recruiters assigns a number to each client. As is common to the way in which many organizations format client numbers, JSP Recruiters calls it a *number*, although it actually contains letters. The JSP client numbers consist of two uppercase letters followed by a two-digit number.

These numbers are unique; that is, no two clients are assigned the same number. Such a field can be used as a **unique identifier**. This simply means that a given client number will appear only in a single record in the table. Only one record exists, for example, in which the client number is BH72. A unique identifier also is called a **primary key**. Thus, the Client Number field is the primary key for the Client table.

The next seven fields in the Client table are Client Name, Street, City, State, Postal Code, Amount Paid, and Current Due. Note that the default width of the columns cuts off the names of some of the columns. The Amount Paid column contains the amount that the client has paid JSP Recruiters year to date (YTD) prior to the current period. The Current Due column contains the amount due to JSP for the current period. For example, client BL12 is Benton Labs. The address is 12 Mountain in Denton, Colorado. The postal code is 80412. The client has paid $16,500 for recruiting services so far this year. The amount due for the current period is $38,225.

JSP assigns each client a single recruiter. The last column in the Client table, Recruiter Number, gives the number of the client's recruiter.

The first field in the Recruiter table, Recruiter Number, is the number JSP Recruiters assigns to the recruiter. These numbers are unique, so Recruiter Number is the primary key of the Recruiter table.

The other fields in the Recruiter table are Last Name, First Name, Street, City, State, Postal Code, Rate, and Commission. The Rate field contains the percentage of the client fee that the recruiter earns, and the Commission field contains the total amount that JSP has paid the recruiter so far this year. For example, Recruiter 27 is Jaime Fernandez. His address is 265 Maxwell in Charleston, Colorado. The Postal Code is 80380. His commission rate is .09 (9%), and his commission is $9,450.

The recruiter number appears in both the Client table and the Recruiter table. It relates clients and recruiters. For example, in the Client table, you see that the recruiter number for client BL12 is 24. To find the name of this recruiter, look for the row in the Recruiter table that contains 24 in the Recruiter Number column. After you have found it, you know the client is assigned to Camden Reeves. To find all the clients assigned to Camden Reeves, you must look through the Client table for all the clients that contain 24 in the Recruiter Number column. His clients are BH72 (Berls Hospital), BL12 (Benton Labs), FH22 (Family Health), MH56 (Maun Hospital), and WL56 (West Labs).

The last recruiter in the Recruiter table, Jan Lee, has not been assigned any clients yet; therefore, her recruiter number, 34, does not appear on any row in the Client table.

Overview

As you read this chapter, you will learn how to create the database shown in Figure 1–1 on the previous page by performing these general tasks:
- Design the database.
- Create a new blank database.

- Create a table and add the records.
- Preview and print the contents of a table.
- Create a second table and add the records.
- Create four reports.
- Create a form.

Plan Ahead

Database design guidelines.

Database design refers to the arrangement of data into tables and fields. In the example in this chapter the design is specified, but in many cases, you will have to determine the design based on what you want the system to accomplish.

When designing a database, the actions you take and the decisions you make will determine the tables and fields that will be included in the database. As you create a database, such as the project shown in Figure 1–1 on page AC 3, you should follow these general guidelines:

1. **Identify the tables.** Examine the requirements for the database in order to identify the main objects that are involved. There will be a table for each object you identified.

   In one database, for example, the main objects might be departments and employees. Thus, there would be two tables: one for departments and the other for employees. In another database, the main objects might be clients and recruiters. In this case, there would also be two tables: one for clients and the other for recruiters. In still another database, the main objects might be books, publishers, and authors. Here there would be three tables: one for books, a second for publishers, and a third for authors.

2. **Determine the primary keys.** Recall that the primary key is the unique identifier for records in the table. For each table, determine the unique identifier, if there is one. For a Department table, for example, the unique identifier might be the Department Code. For a Book table, the unique identifier might be the ISBN number.

3. **Determine the additional fields.** The primary key will be a field or combination of fields in a table. There typically will be many additional fields, each of which contains a type of data. Examine the project requirements to determine these additional fields. For example, in an Employee table, the additional fields might include such fields as Employee Name, Street Address, City, State, Postal Code, Date Hired, Salary, and so on.

4. **Determine relationships among the tables.** Examine the list of tables you have created to see which tables are related. When you determine two tables are related, include matching fields in the two tables. For example, in a database containing employees and departments, there is a relationship between the two tables because one department can have many employees assigned to it. Department Code could be the matching field in the two tables.

5. **Determine data types for the fields.** For each field, determine the type of data the field can contain. One field, for example, might contain only numbers. Another field might contain currency amounts, while a third field might contain only dates. Some fields contain text data, meaning any combination of letters, numbers and special characters (!, ;, ', &, and so on). For example, in an Employee table, the Date Hired field would contain dates, the Salary field would contain currency amounts, and the Hours Worked field would contain numbers. The other fields in the Employee table would contain text data, such as Employee Name and Department Code.

6. **Identify and remove any unwanted redundancy. Redundancy** is the storing of a piece of data in more than one place. Redundancy usually, but not always, causes problems, such as wasted space, difficulties with update, and possible data inconsistency. Examine each table you have created to see if it contains redundancy and, if so, determine whether the redundancy causes these problems. If it does, remove the redundancy by splitting the table into two tables. For example, you may have a single table of employees. In addition to typical employee data (name, address, earnings, and so on), the table might contain Department Number and Department Name. If so, the Department Name could repeat multiple times.

(continued)

> **Plan Ahead**
>
> *(continued)*
>
> Every employee whose department number is 12, for example, would have the same department name. It would be better to split the table into two tables, one for Employees and one for Department. In the Department table, the Department Name is stored only once.
>
> 7. **Determine a location for the database.** The database you have designed will be stored in a single file. You need to determine a location in which to store the file.
>
> When necessary, more specific details concerning the above guidelines are presented at appropriate points in the chapter. The chapter also will identify the actions performed and decisions made regarding these guidelines during the creation of the database shown in Figure 1–1 on page AC 3.

BTW

Database Design
For more information on database design methods and for techniques for identifying and eliminating redundancy, visit the Access 2007 Database Design Web page (scsite.com/dc-off07/ac2007/dbdesign).

Designing a Database

This section illustrates the database design process by showing how you would design the database for JSP Recruiters from a set of requirements. In this section, you will use a commonly accepted shorthand to represent the tables and fields that make up the database as well as the primary keys for the tables. For each table, you give the name of the table followed by a set of parentheses. Within the parentheses is a list of the fields in the table separated by columns. You underline the primary key. For example,

Product (<u>Product Code</u>, Description, On Hand, Price)

represents a table called Product. The Product table contains four fields: Product Code, Description, On Hand, and Price. The Product Code field is the primary key.

Database Requirements

JSP Recruiters needs to maintain information on both clients and recruiters. It currently keeps this data in the two Word tables and two Excel workbooks shown in Figure 1–2. They use Word tables for address information and Excel workbooks for financial information.

Client Number	Client Name	Street	City	State	Postal Code
AC34	Alys Clinic	134 Central	Berridge	CO	80330
BH72	Berls Hospital	415 Main	Berls	CO	80349
BL12	Benton Labs	12 Mountain	Denton	CO	80412
EA45	ENT Assoc.	867 Ridge	Fort Stewart	CO	80336
FD89	Ferb Dentistry	34 Crestview	Berridge	CO	80330
FH22	Family Health	123 Second	Tarleton	CO	80409
MH56	Maun Hospital	76 Dixon	Mason	CO	80356
PR11	Peel Radiology	151 Valleyview	Fort Stewart	CO	80336
TC37	Tarleton Clinic	451 Hull	Tarleton	CO	80409
WL56	West Labs	785 Main	Berls	CO	80349

(a) Client Address Information (Word Table)

Figure 1–2

(b) Client Financial Information (Excel Workbook)

	A	B	C	D
1	Client Number	Client Name	Amount Paid	Current Due
2	AC34	Alys Clinic	$0.00	$17,500.00
3	BH72	Berls Hospital	$29,200.00	$0.00
4	BL12	Benton Labs	$16,500.00	$38,225.00
5	EA45	ENT Assoc.	$12,750.00	$15,000.00
6	FD89	Ferb Dentistry	$21,000.00	$12,500.00
7	FH22	Family Health	$0.00	$0.00
8	MH56	Maun Hospital	$0.00	$43,025.00
9	PR11	Peel Radiology	$31,750.00	$0.00
10	TC37	Tarleton Clinic	$18,750.00	$31,500.00
11	WL56	West Labs	$14,000.00	$0.00

(c) Recruiter Address Information (Word Table)

Recruiter Number	Last Name	First Name	Street	City	State	Postal Code
21	Kerry	Alyssa	261 Pointer	Tourin	CO	80416
24	Reeves	Camden	3135 Brill	Denton	CO	80412
27	Fernandez	Jaime	265 Maxwell	Charleston	CO	80380
34	Lee	Jan	1827 Oak	Denton	CO	80413

(d) Recruiter Financial Information (Excel Workbook)

	A	B	C	D	E
1	Recruiter Number	Last Name	First Name	Rate	Commission
2	21	Kerry	Alyssa	0.10	$17,600.00
3	24	Reeves	Camden	0.10	$19,900.00
4	27	Fernandez	Jaime	0.09	$9,450.00
5	34	Lee	Jan	0.08	$0.00

Figure 1–2 (continued)

For clients, JSP needs to maintain address data. It currently keeps this address data in a Word table (Figure 1–2a). It also maintains financial data for each client. This includes the amount paid and the current due from the client. It keeps these amounts along with the client name and number in the Excel workbook shown in Figure 1–2b.

JSP keeps recruiter address data in a Word table as shown in Figure 1–2c. Just as with clients, it keeps financial data for recruiters, including their rate and commission, in a separate Excel workbook, as shown in Figure 1–2d.

Finally, it keeps track of which clients are assigned to which recruiters. Currently, for example, clients AC34 (Alys Clinic), FD89 (Ferb Dentistry), and PR11 (Peel Radiology) are assigned to recruiter 21 (Alyssa Kerry). Clients BH72 (Berls Hospital), BL12 (Benton Labs), FH22 (Family Health), MH56 (Maun Hospital), and WL56 (West Labs) are assigned to recruiter 24 (Camden Reeves). Clients EA45 (ENT Assoc.) and TC37 (Tarleton Clinic) are assigned to recruiter 27 (Jaime Fernandez). JSP has an additional recruiter, Jan Lee, whose number has been assigned as 34, but who has not yet been assigned any clients.

Naming Tables and Fields

In designing your database, you must name the tables and fields. Thus, before beginning the design process, you must understand the rules for table and field names, which are:

1. Names can be up to 64 characters in length.
2. Names can contain letters, digits, and spaces, as well as most of the punctuation symbols.
3. Names cannot contain periods (.), exclamation points (!), accent graves (`), or square brackets ([ ]).
4. The same name cannot be used for two different fields in the same table.

The approach to naming tables and fields used in this text is to begin the names with an uppercase letter and to use lowercase for the other letters. In multiple-word names, each word begins with an uppercase letter, and there is a space between words (for example, Client Number). You should know that there are other approaches. Some people omit the space (ClientNumber). Still others use an underscore in place of the space (Client_Number). Finally, some use an underscore in place of a space, but use the same case for all letters (CLIENT_NUMBER or client_number).

> **BTW**
> **Naming Fields**
> Access 2007 has a number of reserved words, words that have a special meaning to Access. You cannot use these reserved words as field names. For example, Name is a reserved word and could not be used in the Client table to describe a client's name. For a complete list of reserved words in Access 2007, consult Access Help.

Identifying the Tables

Now that you know the rules for naming tables and fields, you are ready to begin the design process. The first step is to identify the main objects involved in the requirements. For the JSP Recruiters database, the main objects are clients and recruiters. This leads to two tables, which you must name. Reasonable names for these two tables are:

Client

Recruiter

Determining the Primary Keys

The next step is to identify the fields that will be the primary keys. Client numbers uniquely identify clients, and recruiter numbers uniquely identify recruiters. Thus, the primary key for the Client table is the client number, and the primary key for the Recruiter table is the recruiter number. Reasonable names for these fields would be Client Number and Recruiter Number, respectively. Adding these primary keys to the tables gives:

Client (<u>Client Number</u>)

Recruiter (<u>Recruiter Number</u>)

Determining Additional Fields

> **BTW**
> **Database Design Language (DBDL)**
> DBDL is a commonly accepted shorthand representation for showing the structure of a relational database. You write the name of the table and then within parentheses you list all the columns in the table. If the columns continue beyond one line, indent the subsequent lines.

After identifying the primary keys, you need to determine and name the additional fields. In addition to the client number, the Client Address Information shown in Figure 1–2a on page AC 6 contains the client name, street, city, state, and postal code. These would be fields in the Client table. The Client Financial Information shown in Figure 1–2b also contains the client number and client name, which are already included in the Client table. The financial information also contains the amount paid and the current due. Adding the amount paid and current due fields to those already identified in the Client table and assigning reasonable names gives:

Client (<u>Client Number</u>, Client Name, Street, City, State, Postal Code,
   Amount Paid, Current Due)

Similarly, examining the Recruiter Address Information in Figure 1–2c on page AC 7 adds the last name, first name, street, city, state, and postal code fields to the Recruiter table. In addition to the recruiter number, last name, and first name, the Recruiter Financial Information in Figure 1–2d would add the rate and commission. Adding these fields to the Recruiter table and assigning reasonable names gives:

Recruiter (<u>Recruiter Number</u>, Last Name, First Name, Street, City,
   State, Postal Code, Rate, Commission)

Determining and Implementing Relationships Between the Tables

> **Plan Ahead**
>
> **Determine relationships among the tables.**
> The most common type of relationship you will encounter between tables is the **one-to-many relationship**. This means that each row in the first table may be associated with *many* rows in the second table, but each row in the second table is associated with only *one* row in the first. The first table is called the "one" table and the second is called the "many" table. For example, there may be a relationship between departments and employees, in which each department can have many employees, but each employee is assigned to only one department. In this relationship, there would be two tables, Department and Employee. The Department table would be the "one" table in the relationship. The Employee table would be the "many" table.
>
> To determine relationships among tables, you can follow these general guidelines:
>
> 1. Identify the "one" table.
> 2. Identify the "many" table.
> 3. Include the primary key from the "one" table as a field in the "many" table.

According to the requirements, each client has one recruiter, but each recruiter can have many clients. Thus, the Recruiter table is the "one" table, and the Client table is the "many" table. To implement this one-to-many relationship between recruiters and clients, add the Recruiter Number field (the primary key of the Recruiter table) to the Client table. This produces:

Client (<u>Client Number</u>, Client Name, Street, City, State, Postal Code, Amount Paid,
   Current Due, Recruiter Number)

Recruiter (<u>Recruiter Number</u>, Last Name, First Name, Street, City, State, Postal
   Code, Rate, Commission)

Determining Data Types for the Fields

Each field has a **data type**. This indicates the type of data that can be stored in the field. Three of the most commonly used data types are:

1. **Text** — The field can contain any characters. A maximum number of 255 characters is allowed in a field whose data type is Text.
2. **Number** — The field can contain only numbers. The numbers either can be positive or negative. Fields are assigned this type so they can be used in arithmetic operations. Fields that contain numbers but will not be used for arithmetic operations usually are assigned a data type of Text.
3. **Currency** — The field can contain only monetary data. The values will appear with currency symbols, such as dollar signs, commas, and decimal points, and with

BTW

Currency Symbols
To show the symbol for the Euro (€) instead of the dollar sign, change the Format property for the field whose data type is currency. To change the default symbols for currency, change the settings in the operating system using the Control Panel.

two digits following the decimal point. Like numeric fields, you can use currency fields in arithmetic operations. Access assigns a size to currency fields automatically.

Table 1–1 shows the other data types that are available.

Table 1–1 Additional Data Types	
Data Type	**Description**
Memo	Field can store a variable amount of text or combinations of text and numbers where the total number of characters may exceed 255.
Date/Time	Field can store dates and times.
AutoNumber	Field can store a unique sequential number that Access assigns to a record. Access will increment the number by 1 as each new record is added.
Yes/No	Field can store only one of two values. The choices are Yes/No, True/False, or On/Off.
OLE Object	Field can store an OLE object, which is an object linked to or embedded in the table.
Hyperlink	Field can store text that can be used as a hyperlink address.
Attachment	Field can contain an attached file. Images, spreadsheets, documents, charts, and so on can be attached to this field in a record in the database. You can view and edit the attached file.

In the Client table, because the Client Number, Client Name, Street, City, and State can all contain letters, their data types should be Text. The data type for Postal Code is Text instead of Number, because postal codes are not used in arithmetic operations. You do not add postal codes or find an average postal code, for example. The Amount Paid and Current Due fields both contain monetary data, so their data types should be Currency.

Similarly, in the Recruiter table, the data type for the Recruiter Number, Last Name, First Name, Street, City, State, and Postal Code fields all should be Text. The Commission field contains monetary amounts, so its data type should be Currency. The Rate field contains a number that is not a currency amount, so its data type should be Number.

Identifying and Removing Redundancy

Redundancy means storing the same fact in more than one place. It usually results from placing too many fields in a table — fields that really belong in separate tables — and often causes serious problems. If you had not realized there were two objects, clients and recruiters, for example, you might have placed all the data in a single Client table. Figure 1–3 shows a portion of this table with some sample data. Notice that the data for a given Recruiter (number, name, address, and so on) occurs on more than one record. The data for Camden Reeves is repeated in the figure.

Client Table

Client Number	Client Name	Street	...	Recruiter Number	Last Name	First Name	...
AC34	Alys Clinic	134 Central	...	21	Kerry	Alyssa	...
BH72	Berls Hospital	415 Main	...	24	Reeves	Camden	...
BL12	Benton Labs	12 Mountain	...	24	Reeves	Camden	...
...	...	...	...	...	...	...	...

Figure 1–3

Storing this data on multiple records is an example of redundancy, which causes several problems, including:

1. Wasted storage space. The name of Recruiter 24 (Camden Reeves), for example, should be stored only once. Storing this fact several times is wasteful.

2. More difficult database updates. If, for example, Camden Reeves's name is spelled wrong and needs to be changed in the database, his name would need to be changed in several different places.

3. A possibility of inconsistent data. There is nothing to prohibit the recruiter's last name from being Reeves on client BH72's record and Reed on client BL12's record. The data would be inconsistent. In both cases, the recruiter number is 24, but the last names are different.

The solution to the problem is to place the redundant data in a separate table, one in which the data no longer will be redundant. If, for example, you place the data for recruiters in a separate table (Figure 1–4), the data for each recruiter will appear only once.

Client Table

Client Number	Client Name	Street	...	Recruiter Number
AC34	Alys Clinic	134 Central	...	21
BH72	Berls Hospital	415 Main	...	24
BL12	Benton Labs	12 Mountain	...	24
...	...	...	...	...

Recruiter Table

Recruiter Number	Last Name	First Name	...
21	Kerry	Alyssa	...
24	Reeves	Camden	...
...	...	...	...

Figure 1–4

Notice that you need to have the recruiter number in both tables. Without it, there would be no way to tell which recruiter is associated with which client. The remaining recruiter data, however, was removed from the Client table and placed in the Recruiter table. This new arrangement corrects the problems of redundancy in the following ways:

1. Because the data for each recruiter is stored only once, space is not wasted.

2. Changing the name of a recruiter is easy. You have only to change one row in the Recruiter table.

3. Because the data for a recruiter is stored only once, inconsistent data cannot occur. Designing to omit redundancy will help you to produce good and valid database designs.

You should always examine your design to see if it contains redundancy. If it does, you should decide whether you need to remove the redundancy by creating a separate table.

BTW

Postal Codes
Some organizations with many customers spread throughout the country will, in fact, have a separate table of postal codes, cities, and states. If you call such an organization to place an order, they typically will ask you for your postal code (or ZIP code), rather than asking for your city, state, and postal code. They then will indicate the city and state that correspond to that postal code and ask you if that is correct.

If you examine your design, you'll see that there is one area of redundancy (see the data in Figure 1–1 on page AC 3). Cities and states are both repeated. Every client whose postal code is 80330, for example, has Berridge as the city and CO as the state. To remove this redundancy, you would create a table whose primary key is Postal Code and that contains City and State as additional fields. City and State would be removed from the Client table. Having City, State, and Postal Code in a table is very common, however, and usually you would not take such action. There is no other redundancy in your tables.

Starting Access

If you are using a computer to step through the project in this chapter, and you want your screen to match the figures in this book, you should change your screen's resolution to 1024 × 768. For information about how to change a computer's resolution, read Appendix C.

To Start Access

The following steps, which assume Windows Vista is running, start Access based on a typical installation. You may need to ask your instructor how to start Access for your computer.

- Click the Start button on the Windows Vista taskbar to display the Start menu.

- Click All Programs at the bottom of the left pane on the Start menu to display the All Programs list.

- Click Microsoft Office in the All Programs list to display the Microsoft Office list (Figure 1–5).

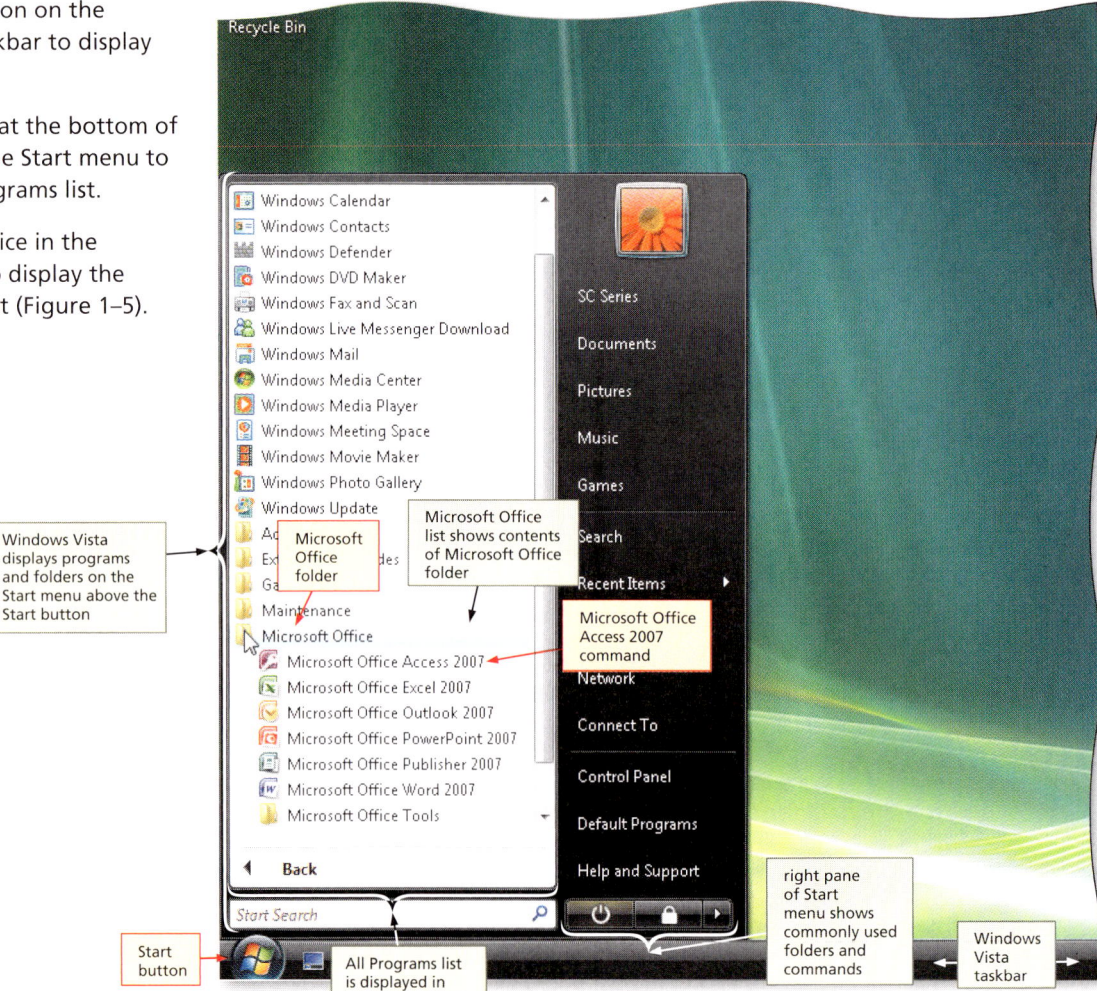

Figure 1–5

❷
- Click Microsoft Office Access 2007 to start Access and display the Getting Started with Microsoft Office Access screen (Figure 1–6).
- If the Access window is not maximized, click the Maximize button next to the Close button on its title bar to maximize the window.

Q&A What is a maximized window?

A maximized window fills the entire screen. When you maximize a window, the Maximize button changes to a Restore Down button.

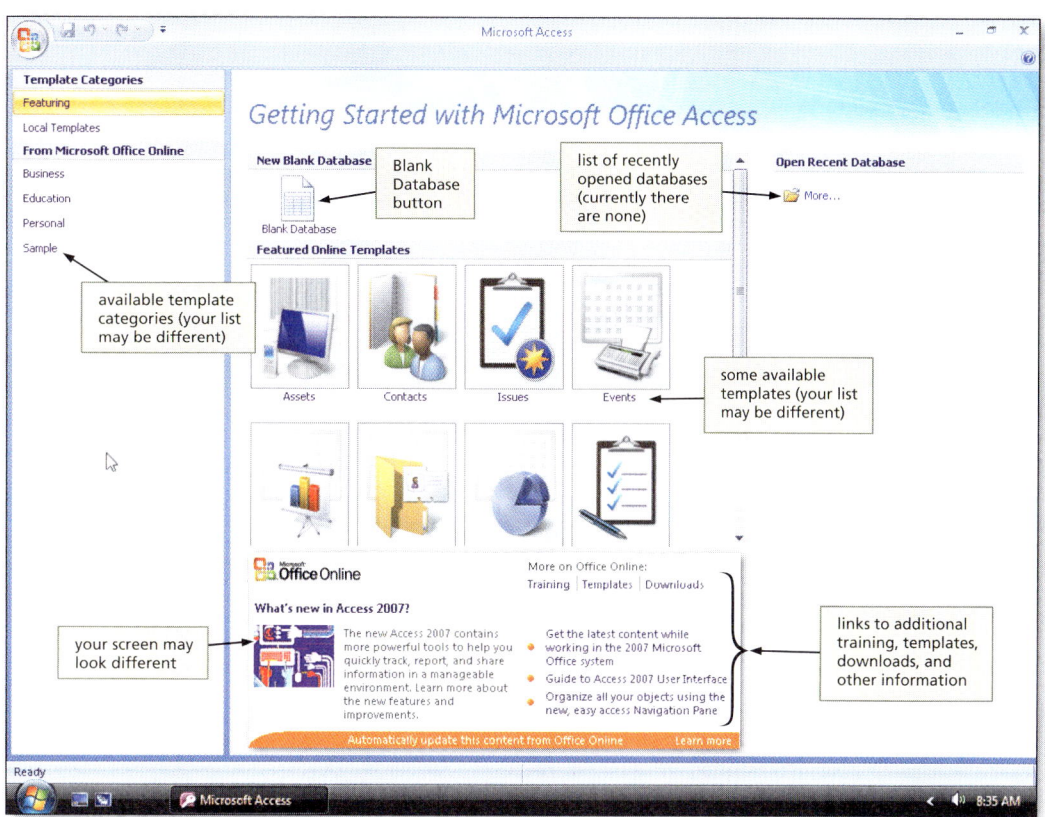

Figure 1–6

Other Ways
1. Double-click Access icon on desktop, if one is present
2. Click Microsoft Office Access 2007 on Start menu

Creating a Database

In Access, all the tables, reports, forms, and queries that you create are stored in a single file called a database. Thus, before creating any of these objects, you first must create the database that will hold them. You can use either the Blank Database option or a template to create a new database. If you already know the tables and fields you want in your database, you would use the Blank Database option. If not, you can use a template. Templates can guide you by suggesting some commonly used databases. If you choose to create a database using a template, you would use the following steps.

To Create a Database Using a Template

1. If the template you wish to use is not already visible on the Getting Started with Microsoft Office Access page, double-click the links in the Template Categories pane to display the desired template.
2. Click the template you wish to use.
3. Enter a file name (or accept the suggested file name) and select a location for the database.
4. Click the Create button to create the database or the Download button to download the database and create the database, if necessary.

When you create a database, the computer places it on a storage medium, such as a USB flash drive, optical disc, or hard disk. A saved database is referred to as a **file**. A **file name** is the name assigned to a file when it is saved.

BTW

Naming Files
File names can be a maximum of 260 characters including the file extension. The file extension for Access 2007 is .accdb. You can use either uppercase or lowercase letters in file names.

> **Plan Ahead**
>
> **Determine where to create the database.**
> When creating a database, you must decide which storage medium to use.
>
> If you always work on the same computer and have no need to transport your database to a different location, then your computer's hard drive will suffice as a storage location. It is a good idea, however, to save a backup copy of your database on a separate medium in case the file becomes corrupted, or the computer's hard drive fails.
>
> If you plan to work on your database in various locations or on multiple computers, then you can consider saving your projects on a portable medium, such as a USB flash drive or optical disc. The projects in this book are stored on a USB flash drive, which saves files quickly and reliably and can be reused. Optical discs are easily portable and serve as good backups for the final versions of projects because they generally can save files only one time.

To Create a Database

Because you already know the tables and fields you want in the JSP Recruiters database, you would use the Blank Database option rather than using a template. The following steps create a database, using the file name JSP Recruiters, on a USB flash drive.

- With a USB flash drive connected to one of the computer's USB ports, click Blank Database to create a new blank database (Figure 1–7).

Figure 1–7

②
- Repeatedly press the DELETE key to delete the default name of Database1.
- Type JSP Recruiters in the File Name text box to replace the default file name of Database1 (your screen may show Database1.accdb). Do not press the ENTER key after typing the file name (Figure 1–8).

Q&A What characters can I use in a file name?

A file name can have a maximum of 260 characters, including spaces. The only invalid characters are the back-slash (\), slash (/), colon (:), asterisk (*), question mark (?), quotation mark ("), less than symbol (<), greater than symbol (>), and vertical bar (|).

③
- Click the 'Browse for a location to put your database' button to display the File New Database dialog box.
- If the Navigation Pane is not displayed in the Save As dialog box, click the Browse Folders button to expand the dialog box.
- If a Folders list is displayed below the Folders button, click the Folders button to remove the Folders list (Figure 1-9).

Q&A Do I have to save to a USB flash drive?

No. You can save to any device or folder. A **folder** is a specific location on a storage medium. You can save to the default folder or a different folder. You also can create your own folders.

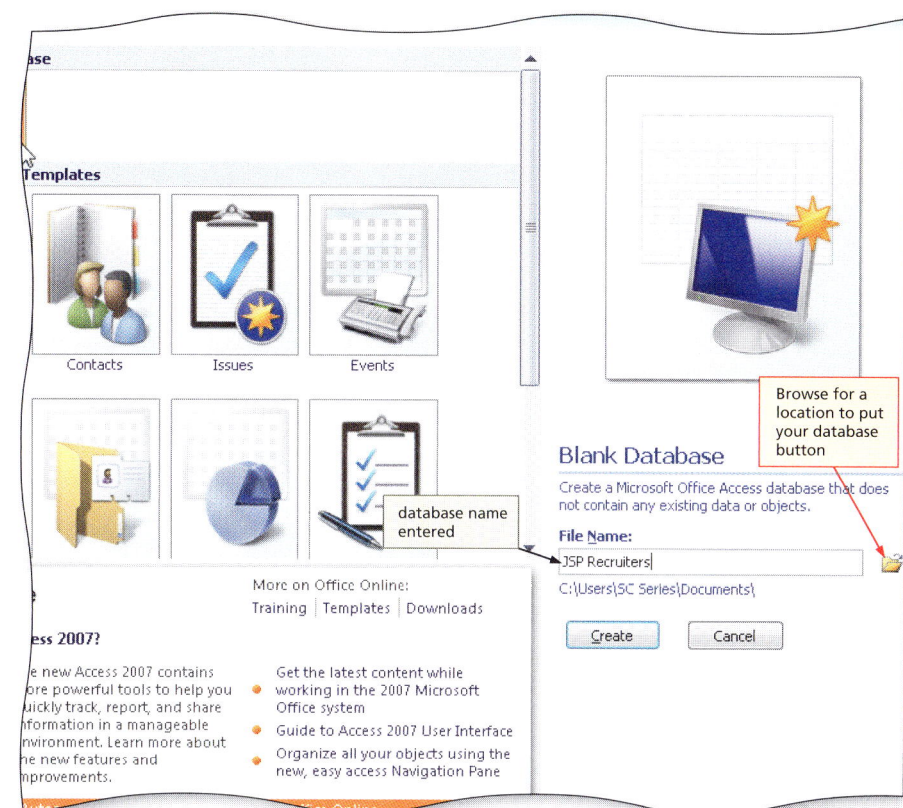

Figure 1–8

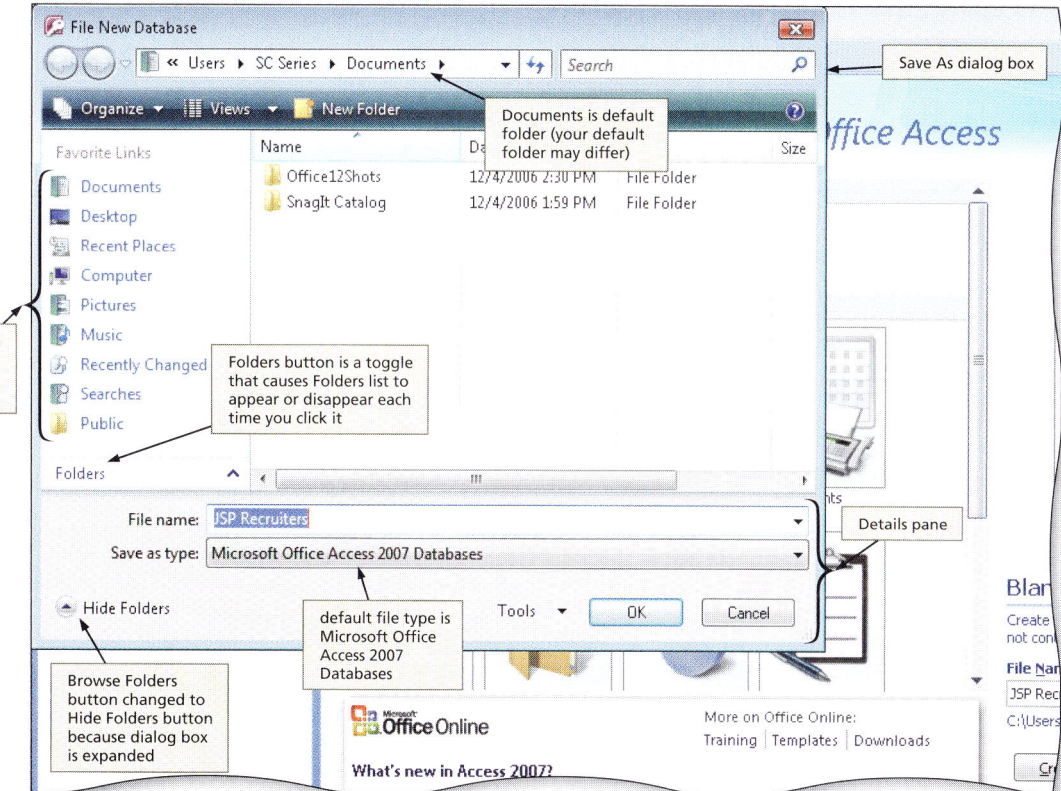

Figure 1–9

4

- If Computer is not displayed in the Favorite Links section, drag the top or bottom edge of the Save As dialog box until Computer is displayed.

- Click Computer in the Favorite Links section to display a list of available drives (Figure 1–10).

- If necessary, scroll until UDISK 2.0 (E:) appears in the list of available drives.

Q&A Why is my list of drives arranged and named differently?

The size of the Save As dialog box and your computer's configuration determine how the list is displayed and how the drives are named.

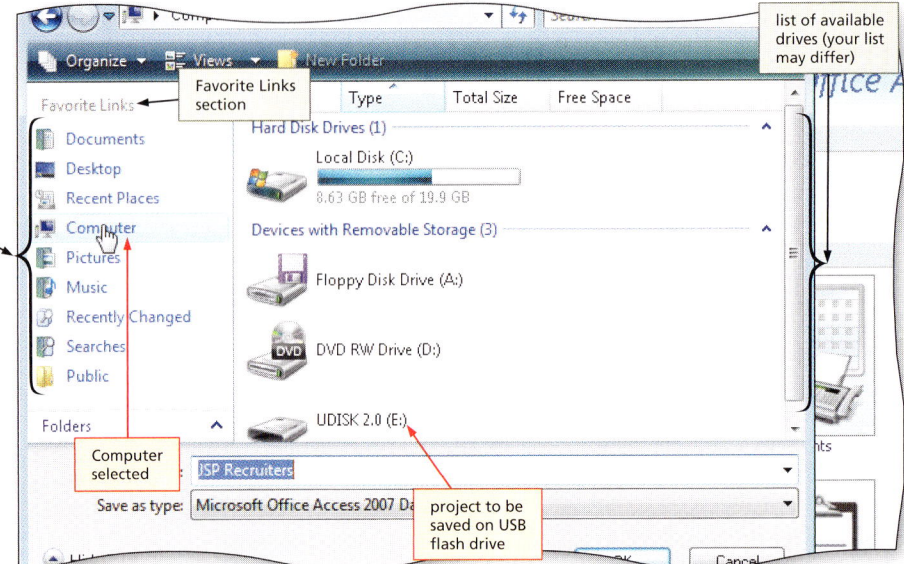

Figure 1–10

Q&A How do I save the file if I am not using a USB flash drive?

Use the same process, but select your desired save location in the Favorite Links section.

5

- Double-click UDISK 2.0 (E:) in the Computer list to select the USB flash drive, Drive E in this case, as the new save location (Figure 1–11).

Q&A What if my USB flash drive has a different name or letter?

It is very likely that your USB flash drive will have a different name and drive letter and be connected to a different port. Verify that the device in your Computer list is correct.

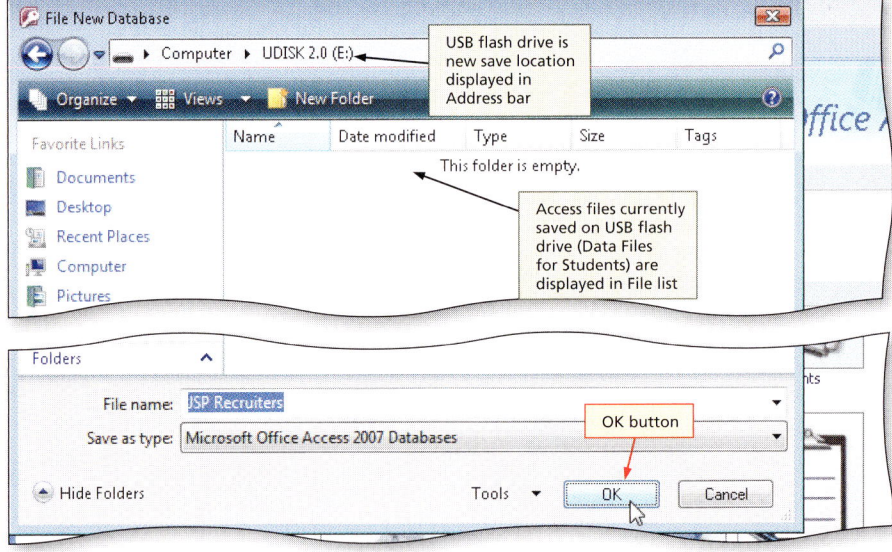

Figure 1–11

6

- Click the OK button to select the USB flash drive as the location for the database and to return to the Getting Started with Microsoft Office Access screen (Figure 1–12).

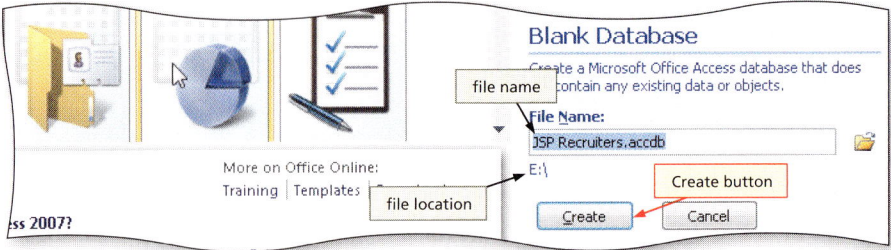

Figure 1–12

7
- Click the Create button to create the database on the USB flash drive with the file name, JSP Recruiters (Figure 1–13).

Q&A How do I know that the JSP Recruiters database is created?

The name of the database appears on the title bar.

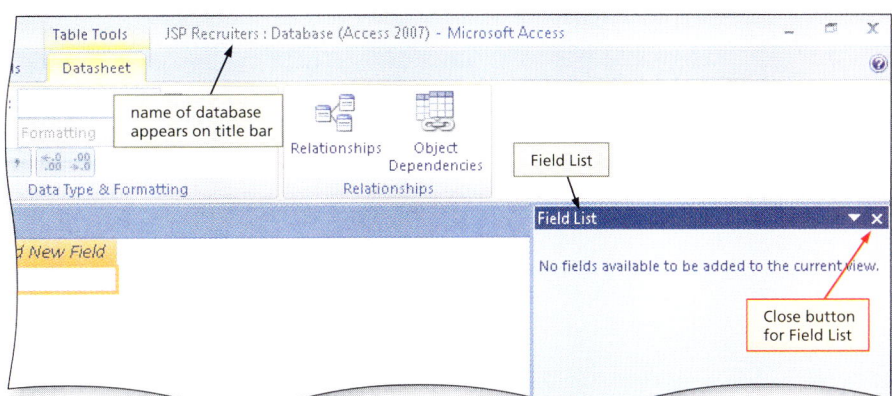

Figure 1–13

8
- If a Field List appears, click its Close button to remove the Field List from the screen (Figure 1–14).

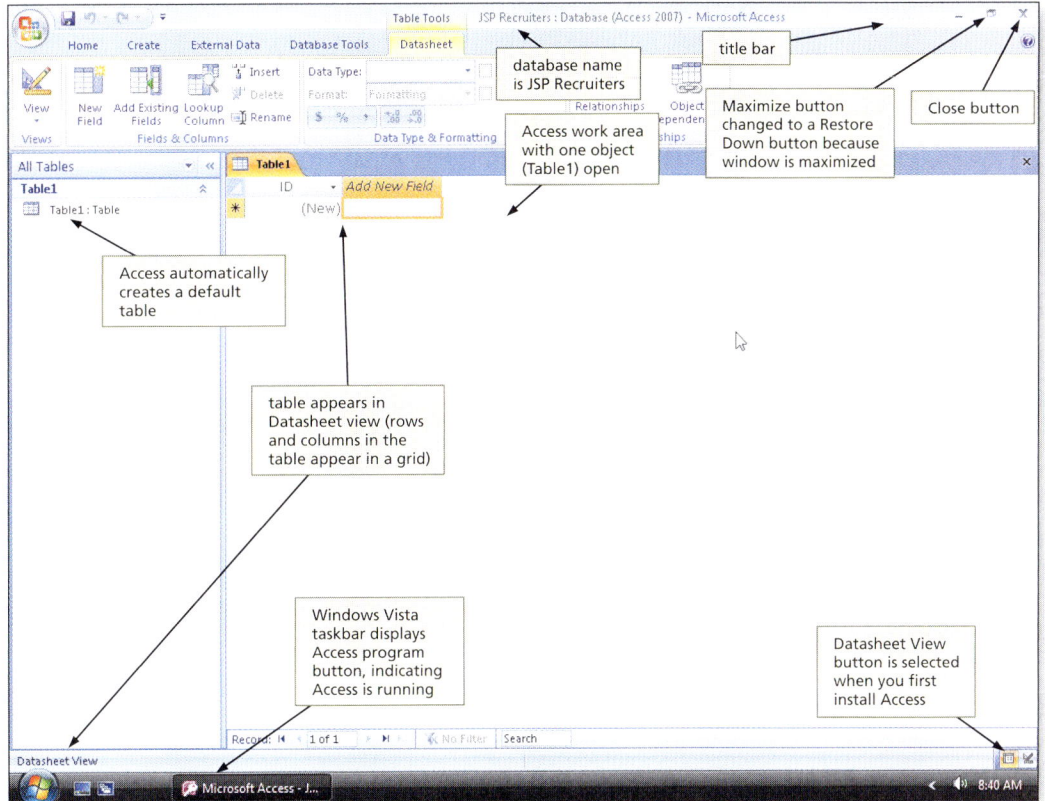

Figure 1–14

The Access Window

The Access window consists of a variety of components to make your work more efficient and documents more professional. These include the Navigation Pane, Access work area, Ribbon, Mini toolbar and shortcut menus, Quick Access Toolbar, and Office Button. Some of these components are common to other Microsoft Office 2007 programs; others are unique to Access.

Other Ways

1. Click Office Button, click Save, type file name, click Computer, select drive or folder, click Save button
2. Press CTRL+S or press SHIFT+F12, type file name, click Computer, select drive or folder, click Save button

Navigation Pane and Access Work Area

You work on objects such as tables, forms, and reports in the **Access work area**. In the work area in Figure 1–14 on the previous page, a single table, Table1, is open in the work area. Figure 1–15 shows a work area with multiple objects open. **Object tabs** for the open objects appear at the top of the work area. You can select one of the open objects by clicking its tab. In the figure, the Client Form is the selected object. To the left of the work area is the Navigation Pane. The Navigation Pane contains a list of all the objects in the database. You use this pane to open an object. You also can customize the way objects are displayed in the Navigation Pane.

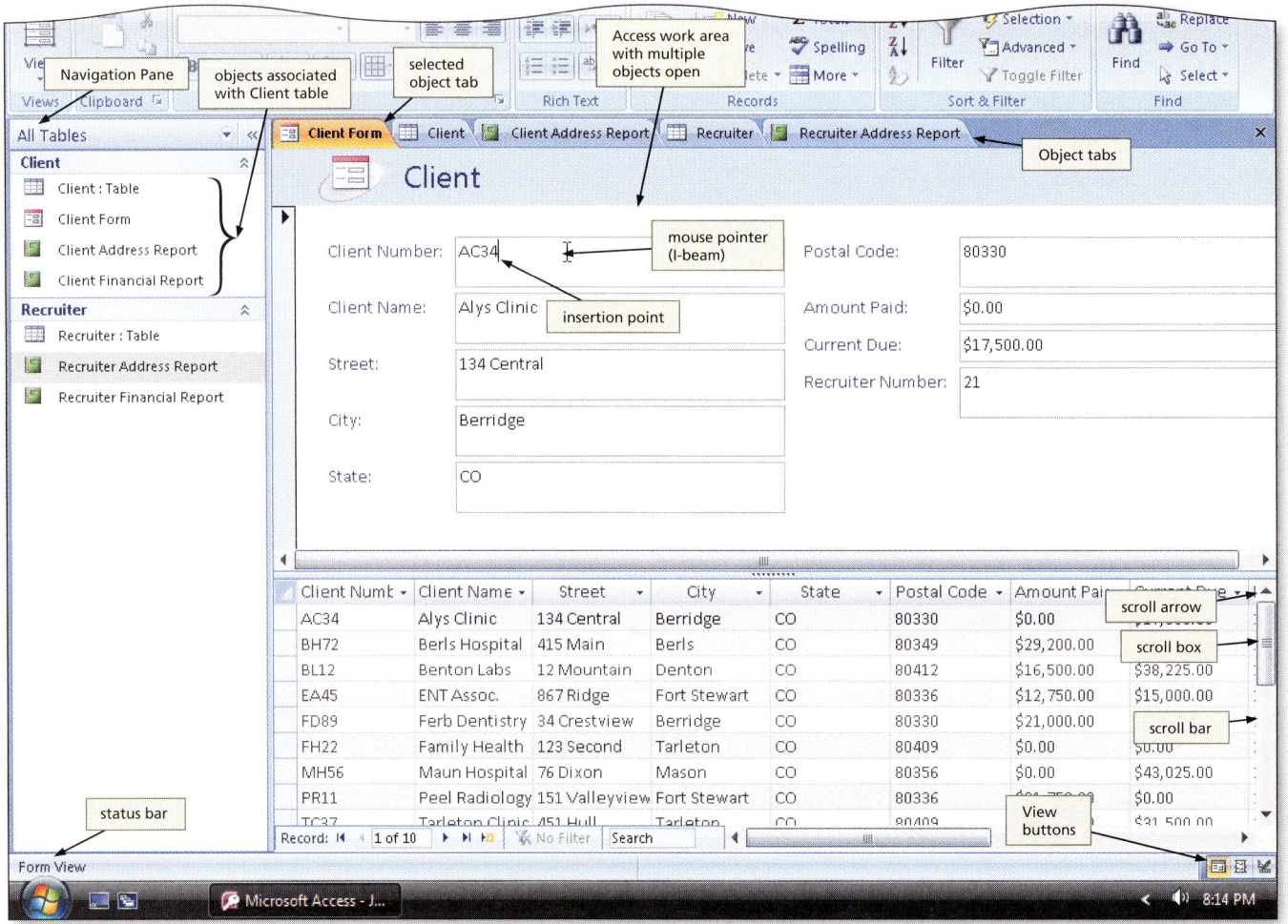

Figure 1–15

The Access work area in Figure 1–15 contains an insertion point, mouse pointer, scroll bar, and status bar. Other work area elements are discussed as they appear.

Insertion Point The **insertion point** is a blinking vertical bar that indicates where text, graphics, and other items will be inserted. As you type, the insertion point moves to the right.

Mouse Pointer The **mouse pointer** becomes different shapes depending on the task you are performing in Access and the pointer's location on the screen. The mouse pointer in Figure 1–15 is the shape of an I-beam.

Scroll Bar You use a **scroll bar** to display different portions of a database object in the Access window. At the right edge of the window is a **vertical scroll bar**. If an object is too wide to fit in the Access window, a **horizontal scroll bar** also appears at the bottom of the window. On a scroll bar, the position of the **scroll box** reflects the location of the portion of the database object that is displayed in the Access window. A **scroll arrow** is located at each end of a scroll bar. To scroll through, or display different portions of the object in the Access window, you can click a scroll arrow or drag the scroll box.

Status Bar The **status bar**, located at the bottom of the Access window above the Windows Vista taskbar, presents information about the database object, the progress of current tasks, and the status of certain commands and keys; it also provides controls for viewing the object. As you type text or perform certain commands, various indicators may appear on the status bar.

The left edge of the status bar in Figure 1–15 shows that the form object is open in Form view. Toward the right edge are View buttons, which you can use to change the view that is currently displayed.

Ribbon

The **Ribbon**, located near the top of the Access window, is the control center in Access (Figure 1–16a). The Ribbon provides easy, central access to the tasks you perform while creating a database object. The Ribbon consists of tabs, groups, and commands. Each **tab** surrounds a collection of groups, and each group contains related commands.

When you start Access, the Ribbon displays four top-level tabs: Home, Create, External Data, and Database Tools. The **Home tab**, called the primary tab, contains the more frequently used commands. To display a different tab on the Ribbon, click the top-level tab. That is, to display the Create tab, click Create on the Ribbon. To return to the Home tab, click Home on the Ribbon. The tab currently displayed is called the **active tab**.

To allow more space in the Access work area, some users prefer to minimize the Ribbon, which hides the groups on the Ribbon and displays only the top-level tabs (Figure 1–16b). To use commands on a minimized Ribbon, click the top-level tab.

Each time you start Access, the Ribbon appears the same way it did the last time you used Access. The chapters in this book, however, begin with the Ribbon appearing as it did at the initial installation of the software. If you are stepping through this chapter on a computer and you want your Ribbon to match the figures in this book, read Appendix C.

> **BTW**
>
> **Minimizing the Ribbon**
> If you want to minimize the Ribbon, right-click the Ribbon and then click Minimize the Ribbon on the shortcut menu, double-click the active tab, or press CTRL+F1. To restore a minimized Ribbon, right-click the Ribbon and then click Minimize the Ribbon on the shortcut menu, double-click any top-level tab, or press CTRL+F1. To use commands on a minimized Ribbon, click the top-level tab.

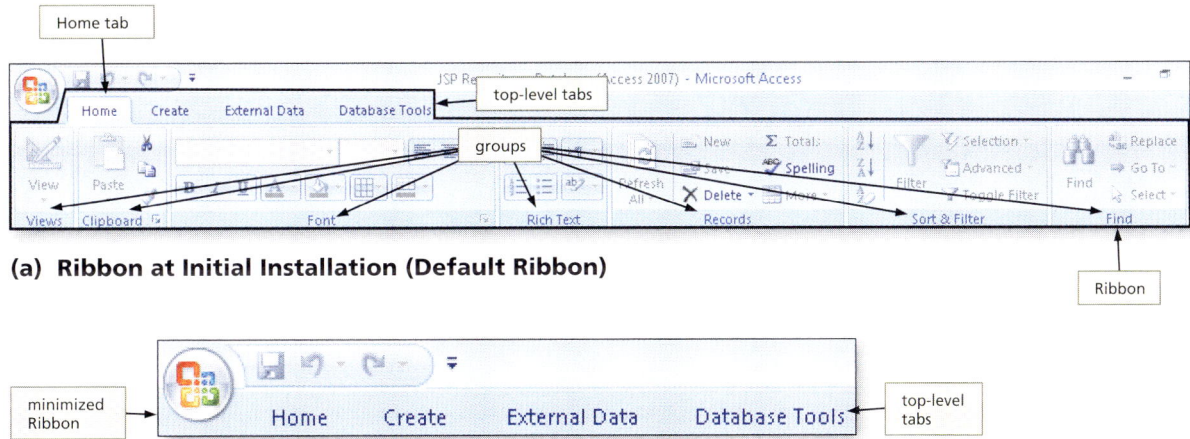

Figure 1–16

In addition to the top-level tabs, Access displays other tabs, called **contextual tabs**, when you perform certain tasks or work with objects such as datasheets. If you are working with a table in Datasheet view, for example, the Table Tools tab and its related subordinate Datasheet tab appear (Figure 1–17). When you are finished working with the table, the Table Tools and Datasheet tabs disappear from the Ribbon. Access determines when contextual tabs should appear and disappear based on tasks you perform. Some contextual tabs have more than one related subordinate tab.

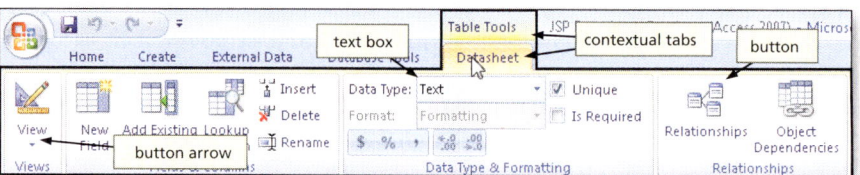

Figure 1–17

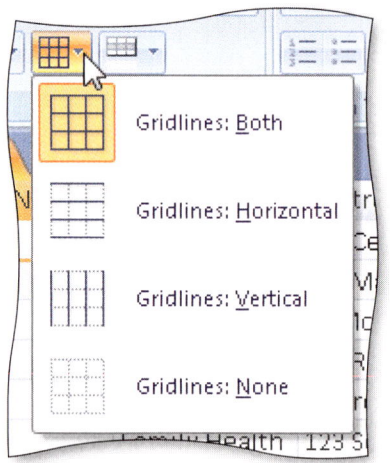

Figure 1–18

Commands on the Ribbon include buttons, boxes (text boxes, check boxes, etc.), and galleries (Figure 1–18). A **gallery** is a set of choices, often graphical, arranged in a grid or in a list. You can scroll through choices on an in-Ribbon gallery by clicking the gallery's scroll arrows. Or, you can click a gallery's More button to view more gallery options on the screen at a time. Some buttons and boxes have arrows that, when clicked, also display a gallery; others always cause a gallery to be displayed when clicked. Many galleries support **live preview**, which is a feature that allows you to point to a gallery choice and see its effect in the database object — without actually selecting the choice.

Some commands on the Ribbon display an image to help you remember their function. When you point to a command on the Ribbon, all or part of the command glows in shades of yellow and orange, and an Enhanced ScreenTip appears on the screen. An **Enhanced ScreenTip** is an on-screen note that provides the name of the command, available keyboard shortcut(s), a description of the command, and sometimes instructions for how to obtain help about the command (Figure 1–19). Enhanced ScreenTips are more detailed than a typical ScreenTip, which usually only displays the name of the command.

The lower-right corner of some groups on the Ribbon has a small arrow, called a **Dialog Box Launcher**, which, when clicked, displays a dialog box or a task pane with additional options for the group (Figure 1–20). When presented with a dialog box, you make selections and must close the dialog box before returning to the database object. A **task pane**, by contrast, is a window that can remain open and visible while you work in the database object.

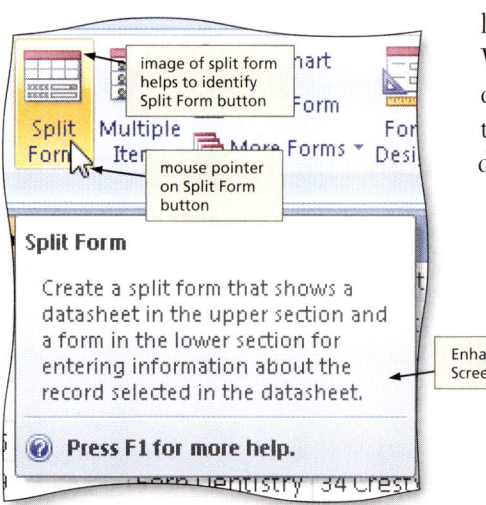

Figure 1–19

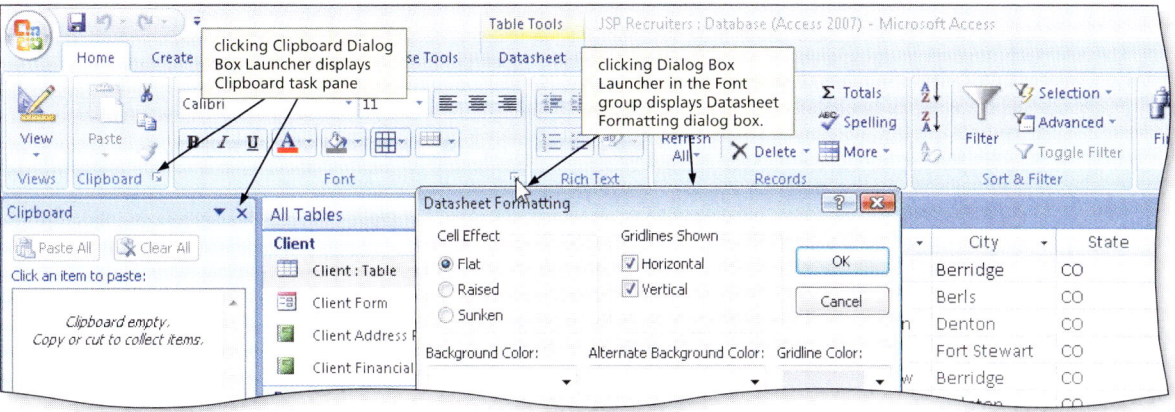

Figure 1–20

Mini Toolbar and Shortcut Menus

The **Mini toolbar**, which appears automatically based on tasks you perform, contains commands related to changing the appearance of text in a database object. All commands on the Mini toolbar also exist on the Ribbon. The purpose of the Mini toolbar is to minimize mouse movement. For example, if you want to use a command that currently is not displayed on the active tab, you can use the command on the Mini toolbar — instead of switching to a different tab to use the command.

When the Mini toolbar appears, it initially is transparent (Figure 1–21a). If you do not use the transparent Mini toolbar, it disappears from the screen. To use the Mini toolbar, move the mouse pointer into the toolbar, which causes the Mini toolbar to change from a transparent to bright appearance (Figure 1–21b).

A **shortcut menu**, which appears when you right-click an object, is a list of frequently used commands that relate to the right-clicked object. When you right-click a table, for example, a shortcut menu appears with commands related to the table (Figure 1–21c).

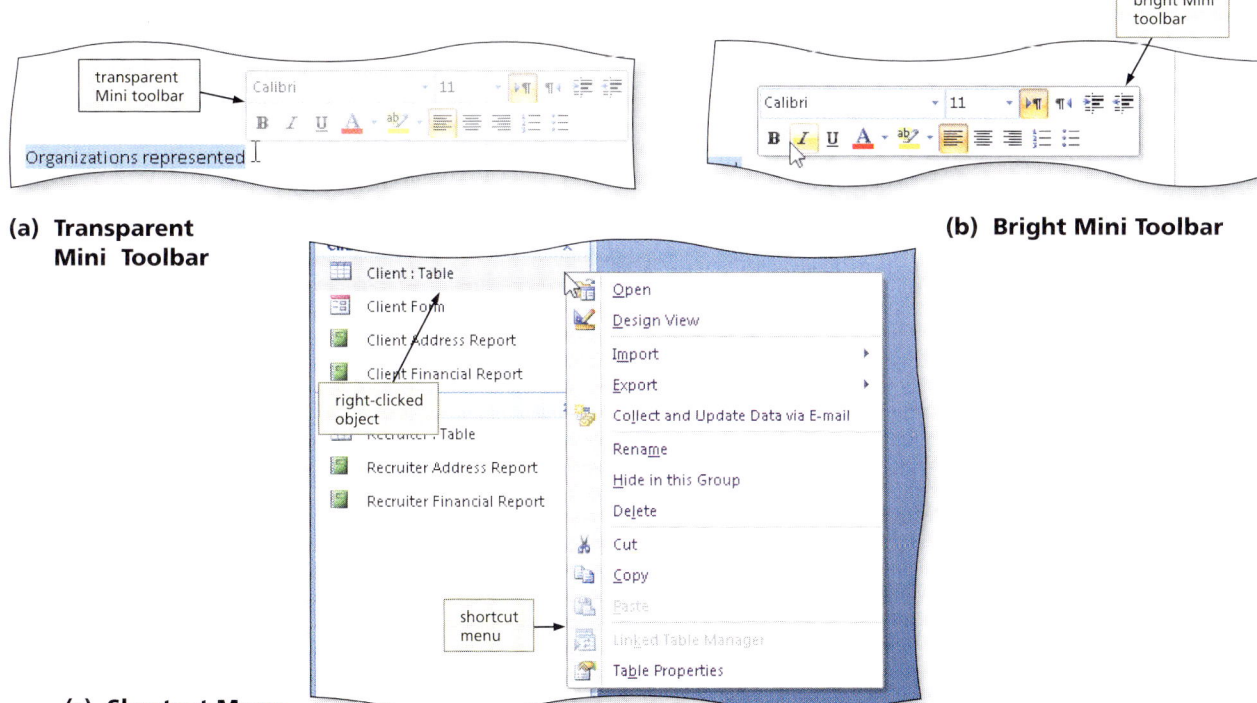

(a) Transparent Mini Toolbar

(b) Bright Mini Toolbar

(c) Shortcut Menu

Figure 1–21

Quick Access Toolbar

The **Quick Access Toolbar**, located by default above the Ribbon, provides easy access to frequently used commands (Figure 1–22a). The commands on the Quick Access Toolbar always are available, regardless of the task you are performing. Initially, the Quick Access Toolbar contains the Save, Undo, and Redo commands. If you click the Customize Quick Access Toolbar button, Access provides a list of commands you quickly can add to and remove from the Quick Access Toolbar (Figure 1–22b).

You also can add other commands to or delete commands from the Quick Access Toolbar so that it contains the commands you use most often. As you add commands to the Quick Access Toolbar, its commands may interfere with the title of the database object on the title bar. For this reason, Access provides an option of displaying the Quick Access Toolbar below the Ribbon (Figure 1–22c).

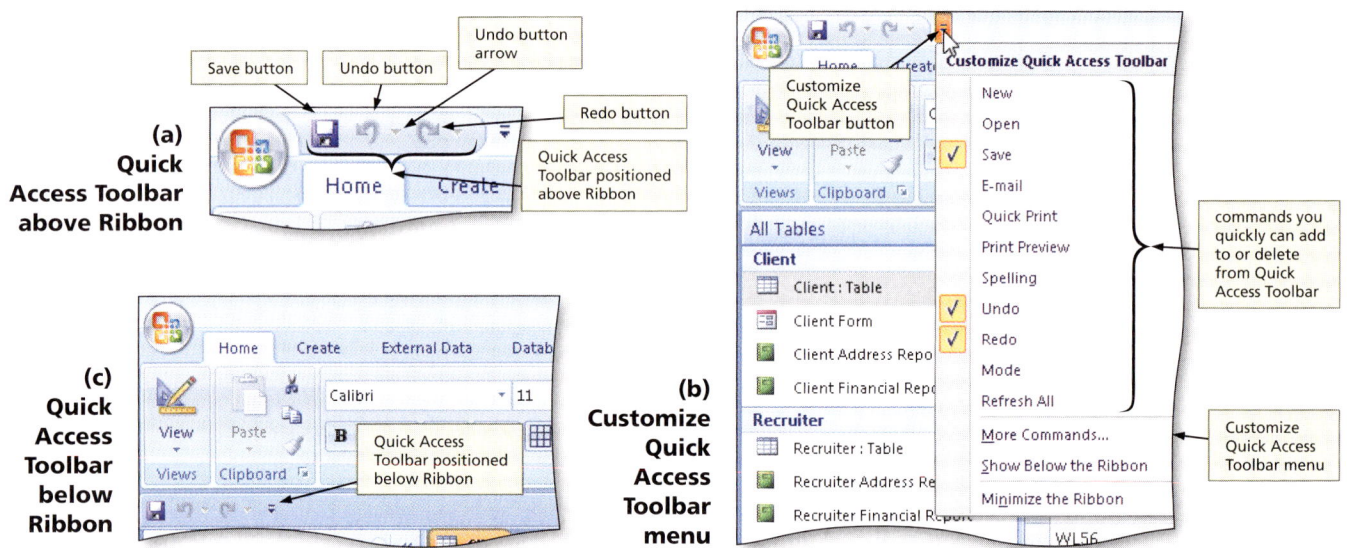

Figure 1–22

Each time you start Access, the Quick Access Toolbar appears the same way it did the last time you used Access. The chapters in this book, however, begin with the Quick Access Toolbar appearing as it did at the initial installation of the software. If you are stepping through this chapter on a computer, and you want your Quick Access Toolbar to match the figures in this book, you should reset your Quick Access Toolbar. For more information about how to reset the Quick Access Toolbar, read Appendix C.

Office Button

While the Ribbon is a control center for creating database objects, the **Office Button** is a central location for managing and sharing database objects. When you click the Office Button, located in the upper-left corner of the window, Access displays the Office Button menu (Figure 1–23). A **menu** contains a list of commands.

When you click the New, Open, and Print commands on the Office Button menu, Access displays a dialog box with additional options. The Save As, Print, Manage, and Publish commands have an arrow to their right. If you point to this arrow, Access displays a **submenu**, which is a list of additional commands associated with the selected command (Figure 1–24). For the Save As, Print, Manage, and Publish commands that do not display a dialog box when clicked, you can point either to the command or the arrow to display the submenu.

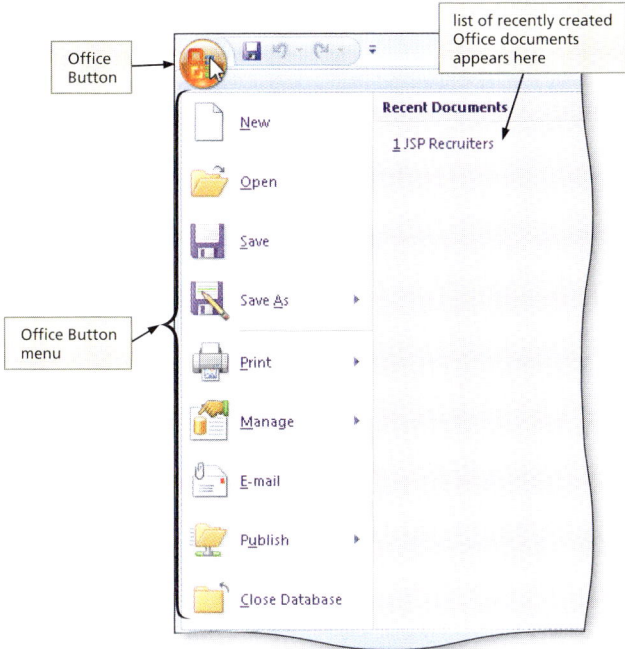

Figure 1–23

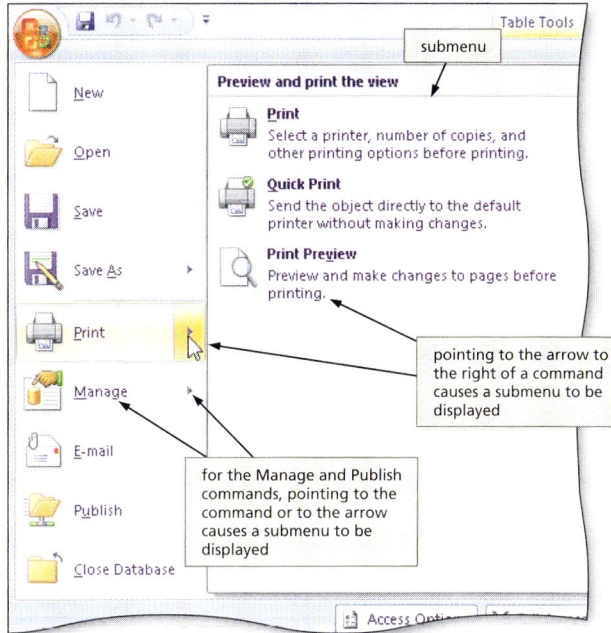

Figure 1–24

Key Tips

If you prefer using the keyboard instead of the mouse, you can press the ALT key on the keyboard to display a **Key Tip badge**, or keyboard code icon, for certain commands (Figure 1–25). To select a command using the keyboard, press its displayed code letter, or **Key Tip**. When you press a Key Tip, additional Key Tips related to the selected command may appear. For example, to select the New command on the Office Button menu, press the ALT key, then press the F key, then press the N key.

To remove the Key Tip badges from the screen, press the ALT key or the ESC key until all Key Tip badges disappear, or click the mouse anywhere in the Access window.

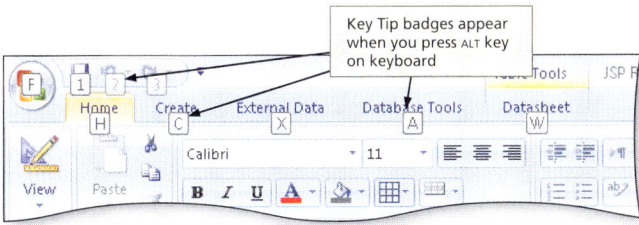

Figure 1–25

Creating a Table

When you first create your database, Access automatically creates a table for you. You can immediately begin defining the fields. If, for whatever reason, you do not have this table or inadvertently delete it, you can create the table by clicking Create on the Ribbon and then clicking the Table button on the Create tab. In either case, you are ready to define the fields.

To Define the Fields in a Table

With the table already created, the next step is to define the fields in the table and to assign them data types. The fields in the Client table are Client Number, Client Name, Street, City, State, Postal Code, Amount Paid, Current Due, and Recruiter Number. The data type for the Amount Paid and Current Due fields is Currency. The data type for all other fields is Text. The following steps define the fields in the table.

1
- Right-click Add New Field to display a shortcut menu (Figure 1–26).

Q&A Why don't I delete the ID field first, before adding other fields?

You cannot delete the primary key in Datasheet view; you only can delete it in Design view. After adding the other fields, you will move to Design view, delete the ID field, and then make the Client Number the primary key.

Q&A Why does my shortcut menu look different?

You right-clicked within the column instead of right-clicking the column heading.

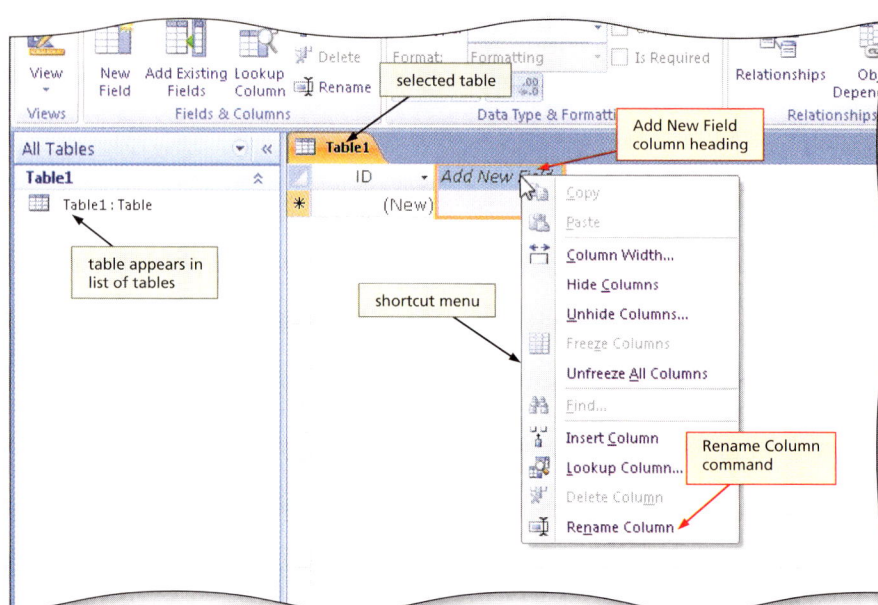

Figure 1–26

2
- Click Rename Column on the shortcut menu to display an insertion point.
- Type `Client Number` to assign a name to the new field.
- Press the DOWN ARROW key to complete the addition of the field (Figure 1–27).

Q&A Why doesn't the whole name appear?

The default column size is not large enough for Client Number to appear in its entirety.

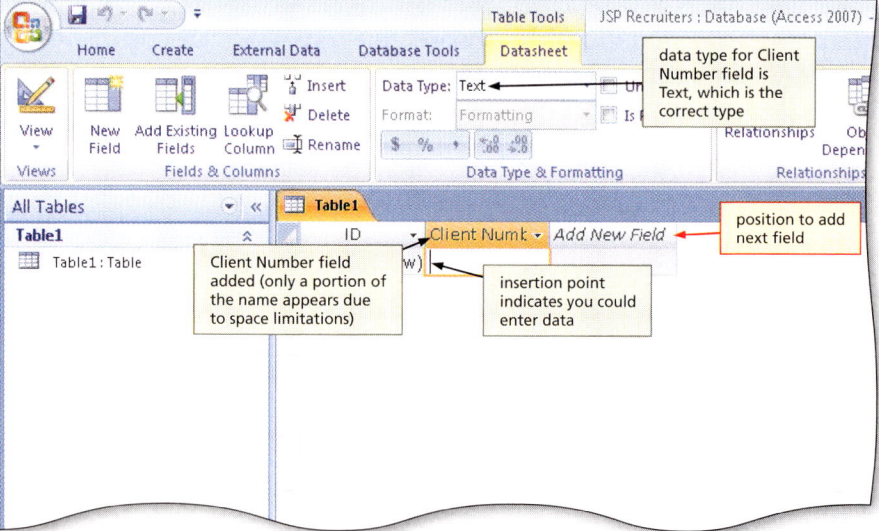

Figure 1–27

3

- Right-click Add New Field to display a shortcut menu, click Rename Column on the shortcut menu to display an insertion point, type Client Name to assign a name to the new field, and then press the DOWN ARROW key to complete the addition of the field.

 Did I have to press the DOWN ARROW key? Couldn't I have just moved to the next field or pressed the ENTER key?

You could have pressed the TAB key or the ENTER key to move to the column heading for the next field. Pressing the DOWN ARROW key, however, completes the entry of the Client Number field and allows you to ensure that the column is assigned the correct data type.

- Using the same technique add the fields in the Client table up through and including the Amount Paid field.

- Click the Data Type box arrow to display the Data Type box menu (Figure 1–28).

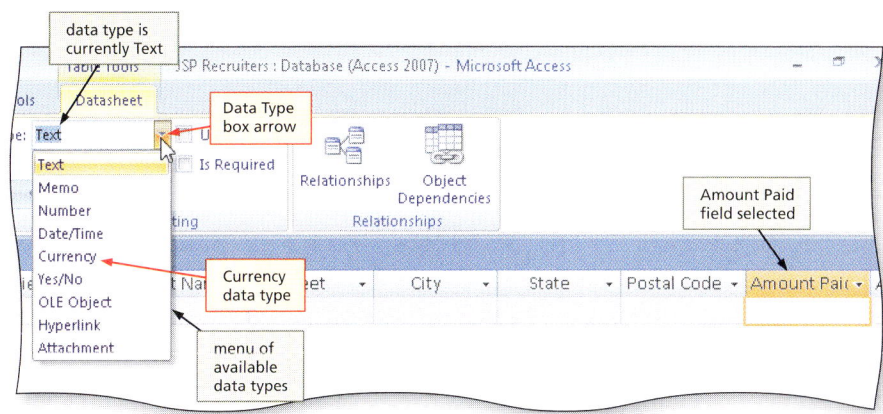

Figure 1–28

4

- Click Currency to select Currency as the data type for the Amount Paid field (Figure 1–29).

 Why does Currency appear twice?

The second Currency is the format, which indicates how the data will be displayed. For the Currency data type, Access automatically sets the format to Currency, which is usually what you would want. You could change it to something else, if desired, by clicking the arrow and selecting the desired format.

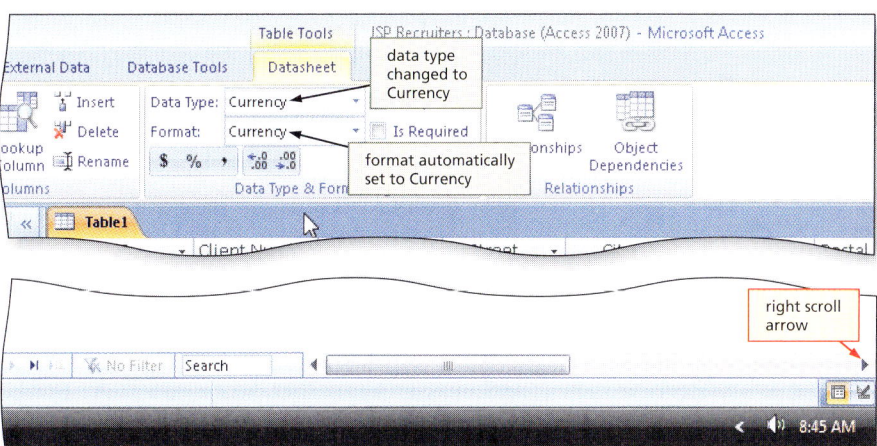

Figure 1–29

5

- Click the right scroll arrow to shift the fields to the left and display the Add New Field column (Figure 1–30).

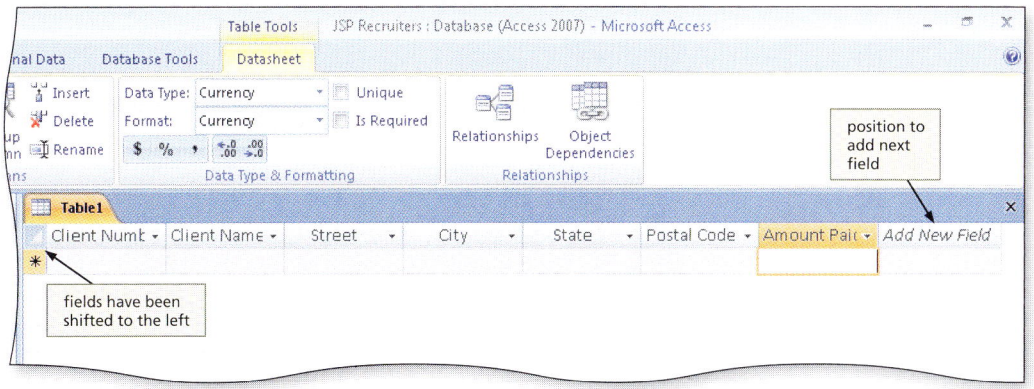

Figure 1–30

6
- Make the remaining entries from the Client table structure shown in Figure 1–31 to complete the structure. Be sure to select Currency as the data type for the Current Due field.

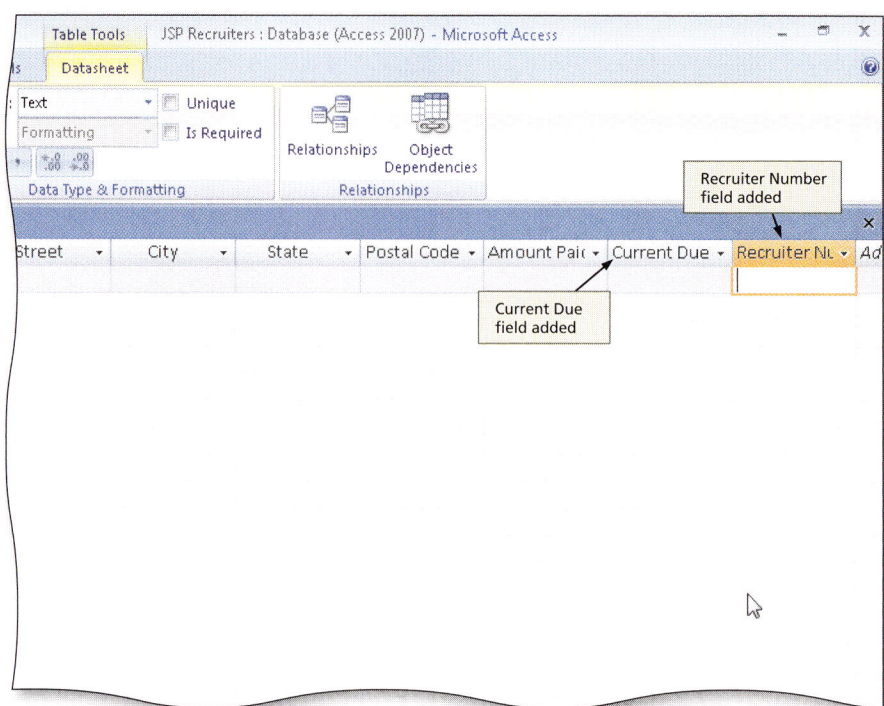

Figure 1–31

BTW

Creating a Table: Table Templates
Access includes table templates that assist you in creating some commonly used tables and fields. To use a template, click Create on the Ribbon and then click the Table Templates button on the Create tab. Click the desired template, make any adjustments you wish to the table that Access creates, and then save the table.

Making Changes to the Structure

When creating a table, check the entries carefully to ensure they are correct. If you discover a mistake while still typing the entry, you can correct the error by repeatedly pressing the BACKSPACE key until the incorrect characters are removed. Then, type the correct characters. If you do not discover a mistake until later, you can use the following techniques to make the necessary changes to the structure:

- To undo your most recent change, click the Undo button on the Quick Access Toolbar. If there is nothing that Access can undo, this button will be dim, and clicking it will have no effect.
- To delete a field, right-click the column heading for the field (the position containing the field name), and then click Delete Column on the shortcut menu.
- To change the name of a field, right-click the column heading for the field, click Rename Column on the shortcut menu, and then type the desired field name.
- To insert a field as the last field, right-click the Add New Field column heading, click Rename Column on the shortcut menu, type the desired field name, click the down arrow, and then ensure the correct data type is already selected.
- To insert a field between existing fields, right-click the column heading for the field that will follow the new field, and then click Insert Column on the shortcut menu. You then proceed just as you do when you insert a field as the last field.

As an alternative to these steps, you may want to start over. To do so, click the Close button for the window containing the table, and then click the No button in the Microsoft Office Access dialog box. Click Create on the Ribbon and then click the Table button to create a table. You then can repeat the process you used earlier to define the fields in the table.

To Save a Table

The Client table structure now is complete. The final step is to save and close the table within the database. At this time, you should give the table a name.

The following steps save the table, giving it the name, Client.

- Click the Save button on the Quick Access Toolbar to save the structure of the table (Figure 1–32).

Q&A I have an extra row between the row containing the field names and the row that begins with the asterisk. What happened? Is this a problem? If so, how do I fix it?

You inadvertently added a record to the table by pressing some key after you pressed the DOWN ARROW key. Even pressing the Spacebar would add a record. You now have a record you do not want and it will cause problems when you attempt to assign a different primary key. To fix it, you need to delete the record, which you will do in Step 3.

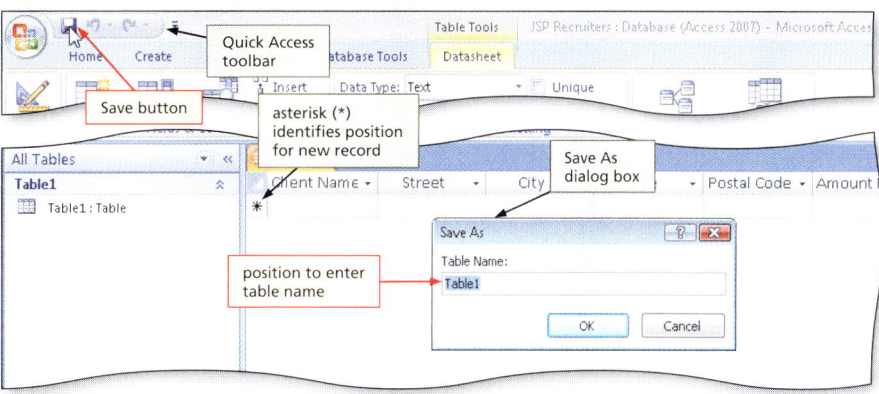

Figure 1–32

- Type Client to change the name to be assigned to the table (Figure 1–33).

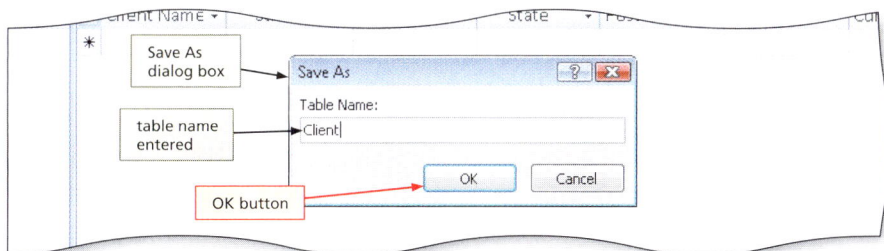

Figure 1–33

- Click the OK button to save the structure with the name, Client (Figure 1–34).

- If you have an additional record between the field names and the asterisk, click the record selector (the box at the beginning of the record), press the DELETE key, and then click the Yes button when Access asks you if you want to delete the record.

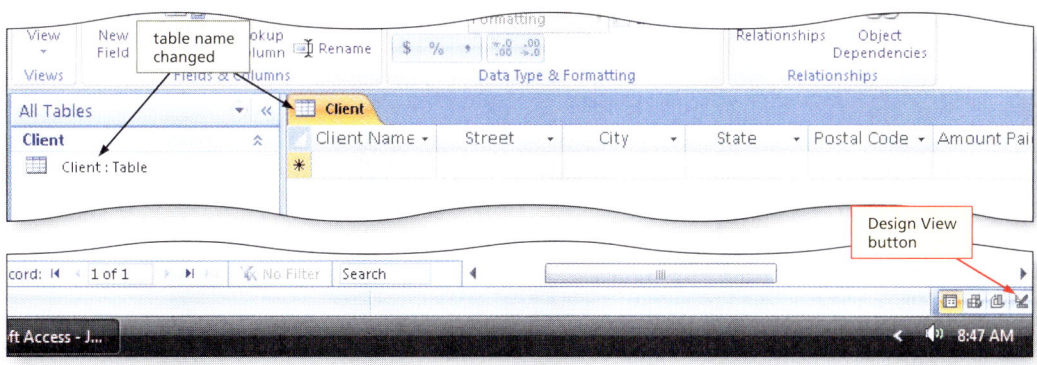

Figure 1–34

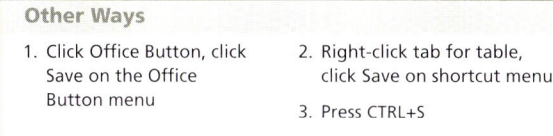

Other Ways
1. Click Office Button, click Save on the Office Button menu
2. Right-click tab for table, click Save on shortcut menu
3. Press CTRL+S

To Change the Primary Key

To change the primary key, you must first delete the ID field that Access created automatically. You then can designate the Client Number field as the primary key. To delete the ID field, the table must appear in Design view rather than Datasheet view. You also can designate the Client Number field as the primary key within Design view. As you define or modify the fields, the **row selector**, the small box or bar that, when you click it, selects the entire row, indicates the field you currently are describing. The following steps move to Design view and then change the primary key.

- Click the Design View button on the status bar to move to Design view.

- Confirm that your data types match those shown in the figure. Make any necessary corrections to the data types (Figure 1-35).

Q&A Did I have to save the table before moving to Design view?

Yes. If you had not saved it yourself, Access would have asked you to save it.

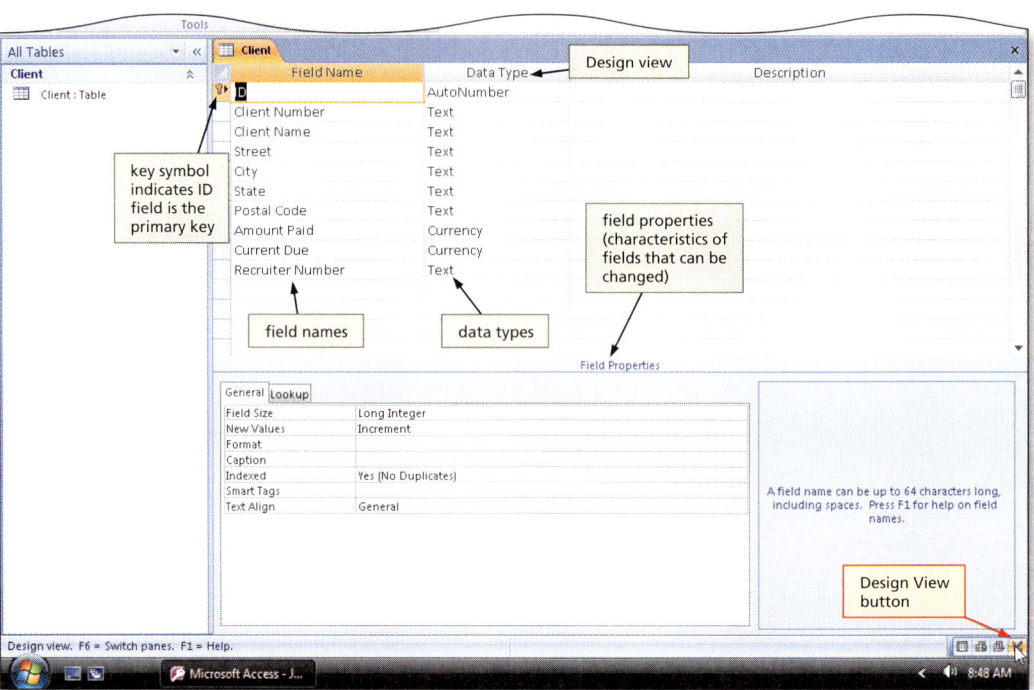

Figure 1–35

- Click the row selector for the ID field to select the field.

- Press the DELETE key to delete the field (Figure 1–36).

Q&A What if I click the row selector for the wrong field before pressing the DELETE key?

Click the No button in the Microsoft Office Access dialog box. If you inadvertently clicked the Yes button, you have deleted the wrong field. You can fix this by clicking the Close button for the Client table, and then clicking the No button when asked if you want to save your changes.

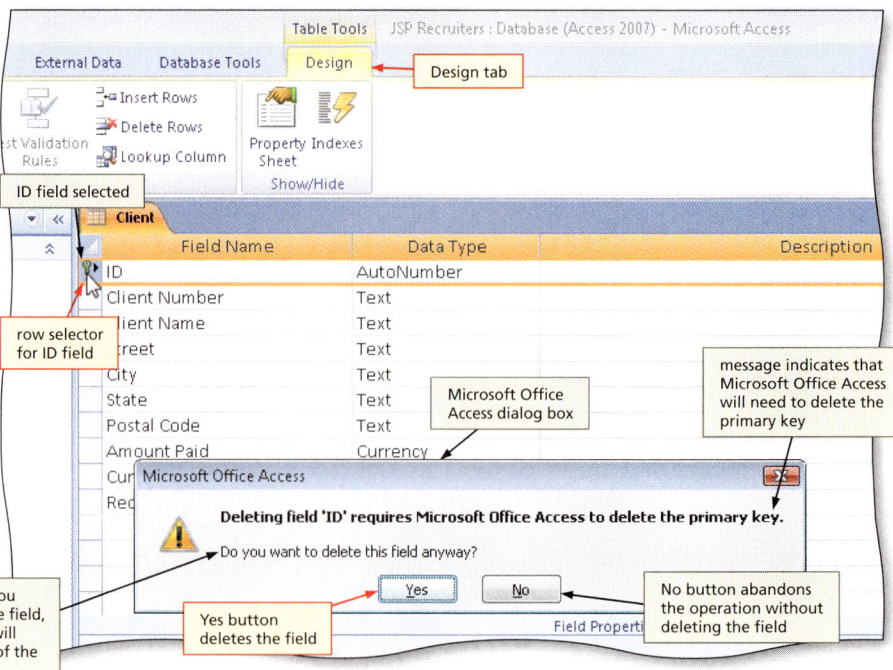

Figure 1–36

3

- Click the Yes button to complete the deletion of the field.

- With the Client Number field selected, click the Primary Key button to designate the Client Number field as the primary key.

- Click the Save button to save the changes (Figure 1–37).

Q&A When I attempted to save the table I got an error message that indicates index or primary key cannot contain a null value. What did I do wrong and how do I fix it?

You inadvertently added a record to the table by pressing some key after you pressed the DOWN ARROW key. To fix it, click the OK button (you will need to do it twice) and then click the Primary Key button to remove the primary key. Click the Save button to save the table and then click the View button near the upper-left corner of the screen to return to datasheet view. Click the little box immediately to the left of the record you added and press the DELETE key. Click the Yes button when Access asks if it is OK to delete the record. Click the View button again and continue with these steps.

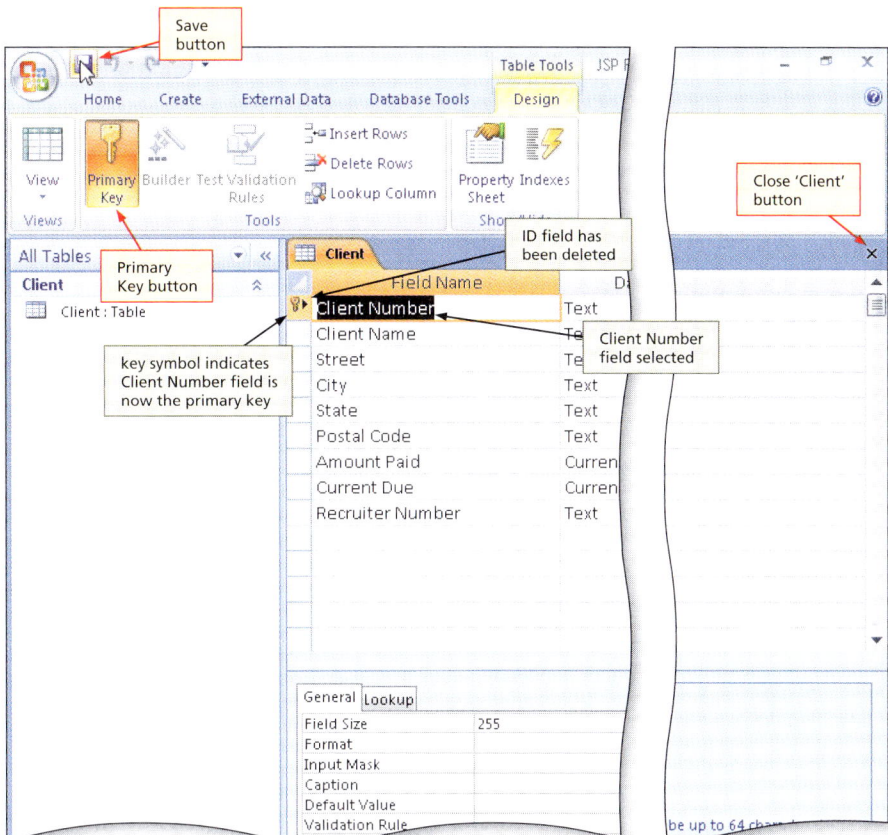

Figure 1–37

4

- Close the Client table by clicking the Close 'Client' button (Figure 1–38).

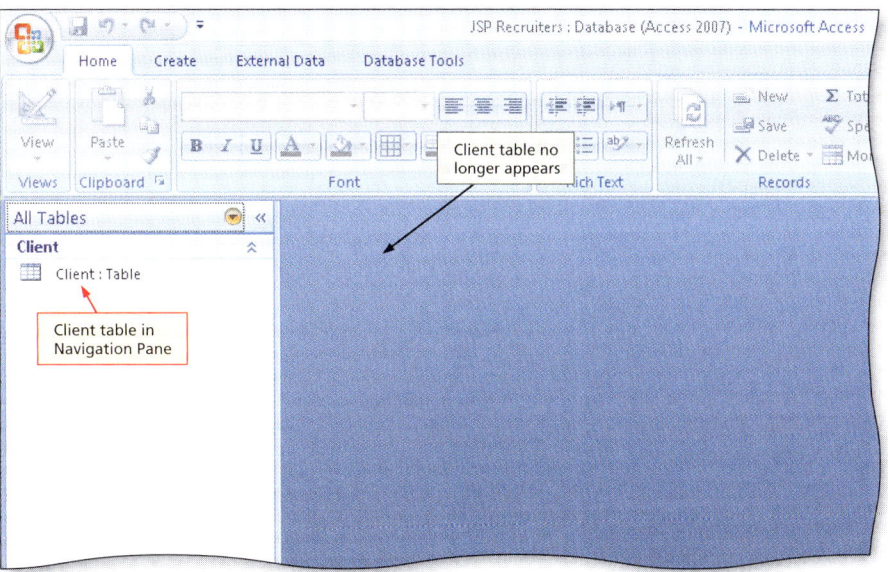

Figure 1–38

To Add Records to a Table

Creating a table by building the structure and saving the table is the first step in a two-step process. The second step is to add records to the table. To add records to a table, the table must be open. When making changes to tables, you work in Datasheet view. In **Datasheet view**, the table is represented as a collection of rows and columns called a **datasheet**.

You often add records in phases. You may, for example, not have enough time to add all the records in one session. The following steps open the Client table in Datasheet view and then add the first two records in the Client table (Figure 1–39).

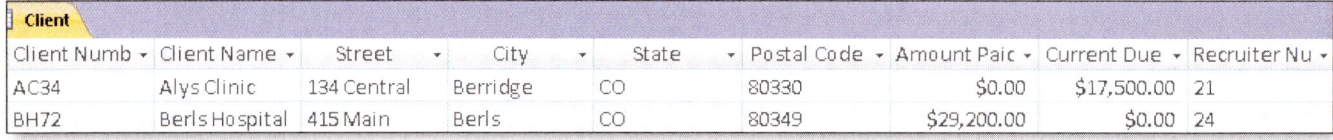

Figure 1–39

- Right-click the Client table in the Navigation Pane to display the shortcut menu (Figure 1–40).

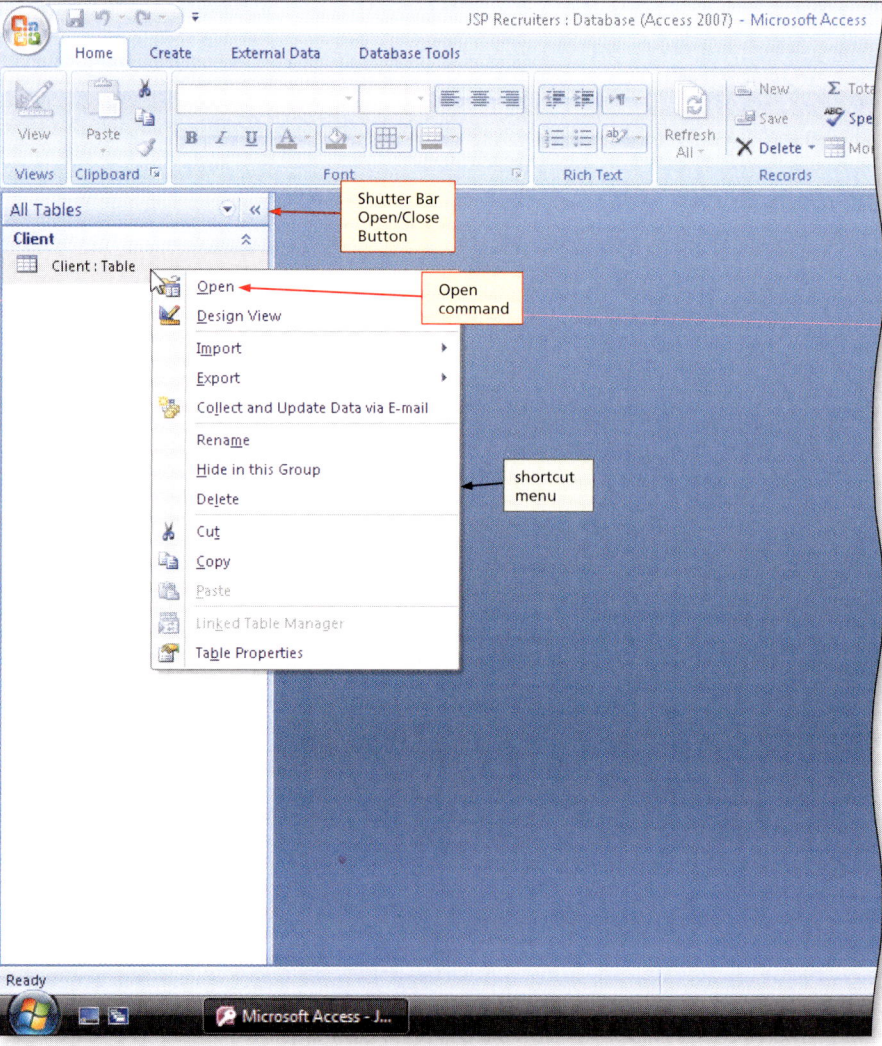

Figure 1–40

- Click Open on the shortcut menu to open the Client table in Datasheet view.

Q&A What if I want to return to Design view?

There are two ways to get to Design view. You could click Design View on the shortcut menu. Alternatively, you could click Open on the shortcut menu to open the table in Datasheet view and then click the Design View button on the Access status bar.

- Click the Shutter Bar Open/Close Button to hide the Navigation Pane (Figure 1–41).

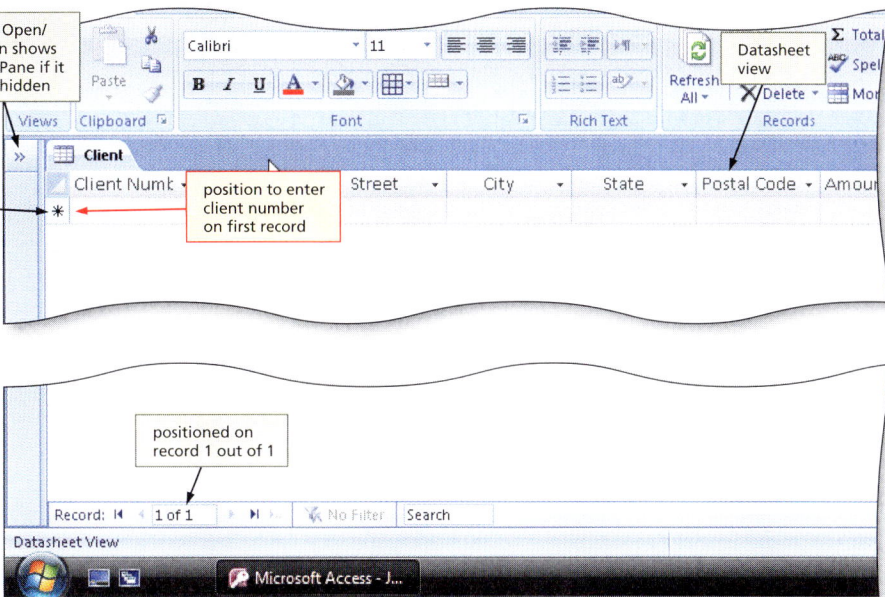

Figure 1–41

- Click in the Client Number field and type AC34 to enter the first client number. Be sure you type the letters in uppercase so they are entered in the database correctly (Figure 1–42).

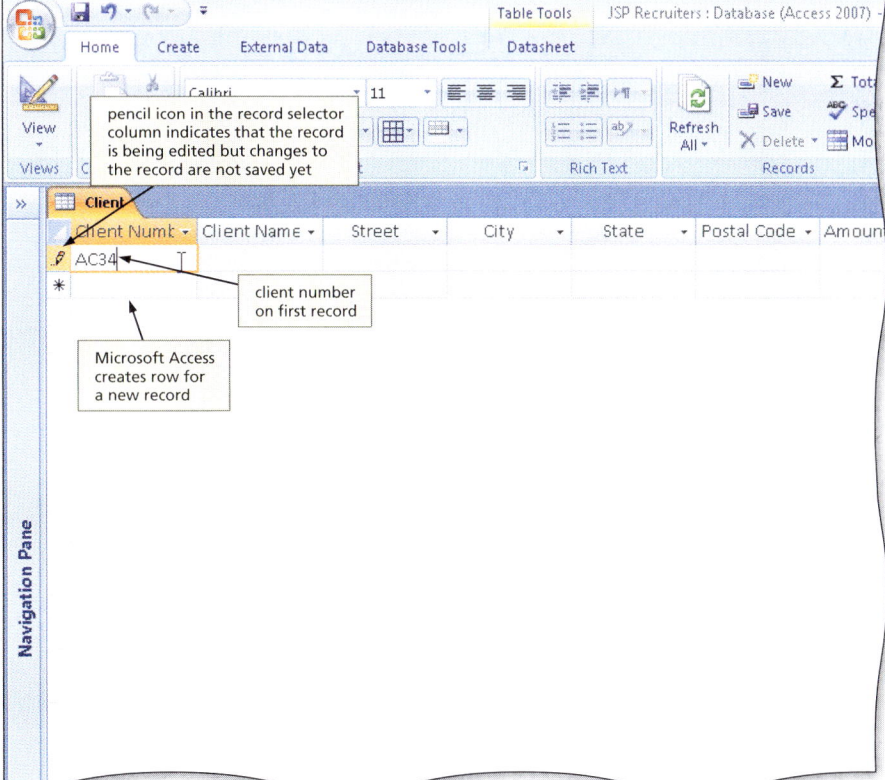

Figure 1–42

4

- Press the TAB key to complete the entry for the Client Number field.
- Enter the client name, street, city, state, and postal code by typing the following entries, pressing the TAB key after each one: `Alys Clinic` as the client name, `134 Central` as the street, `Berridge` as the city, `CO` as the state, and `80330` as the postal code.
- Type `0` to enter the amount paid (Figure 1–43).

Q&A Do I need to type a dollar sign?

You do not need to type dollar signs or commas. In addition, because the digits to the right of the decimal point are both zeros, you do not need to type either the decimal point or the zeros.

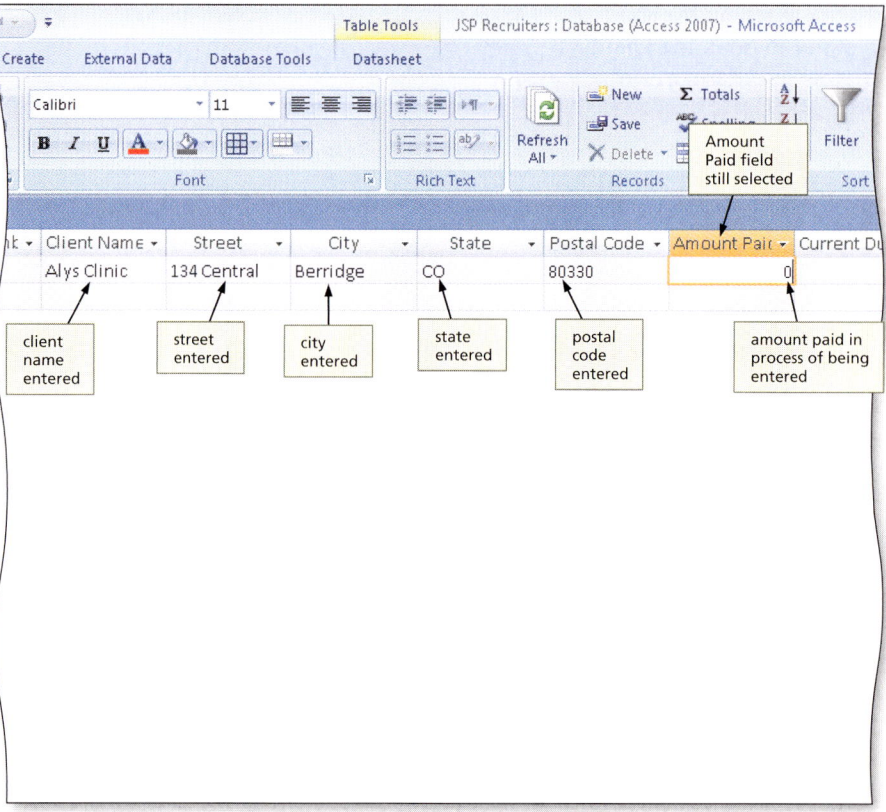

Figure 1–43

5

- Press the TAB key to complete the entry for the Amount Paid field.
- Type `17500` to enter the current due amount and then press the TAB key to move to the next field.
- Type `21` as the Recruiter number to complete data entry for the record (Figure 1–44).

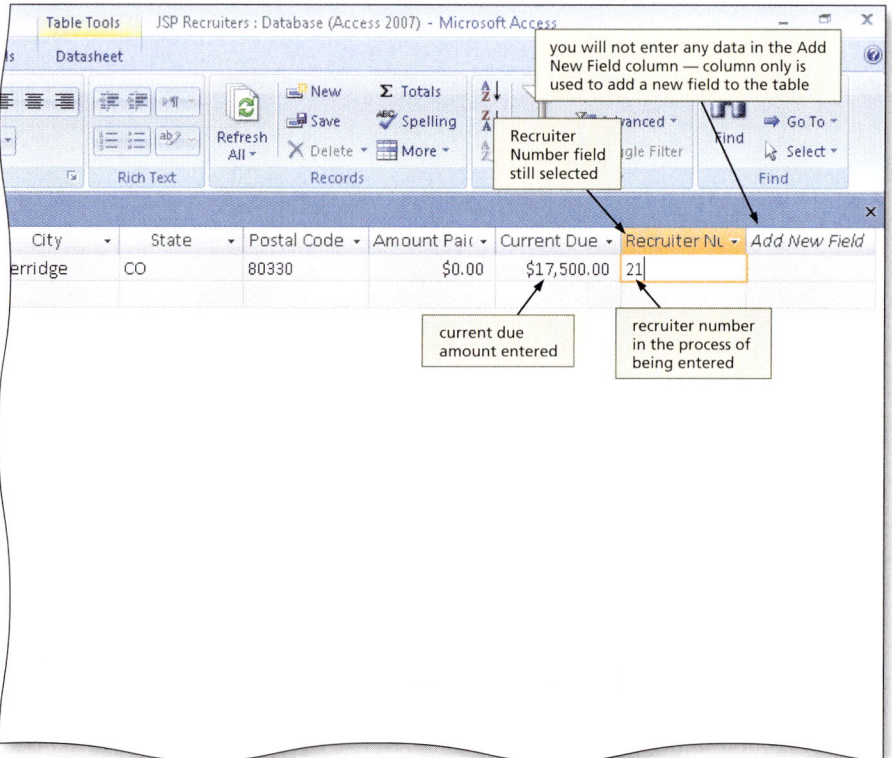

Figure 1–44

6
- Press the TAB key to complete the entry of the first record (Figure 1–45).

Q&A How and when do I save the record?

As soon as you have entered or modified a record and moved to another record, the original record is saved. This is different from other programs. The rows entered in an Excel worksheet, for example, are not saved until the entire worksheet is saved.

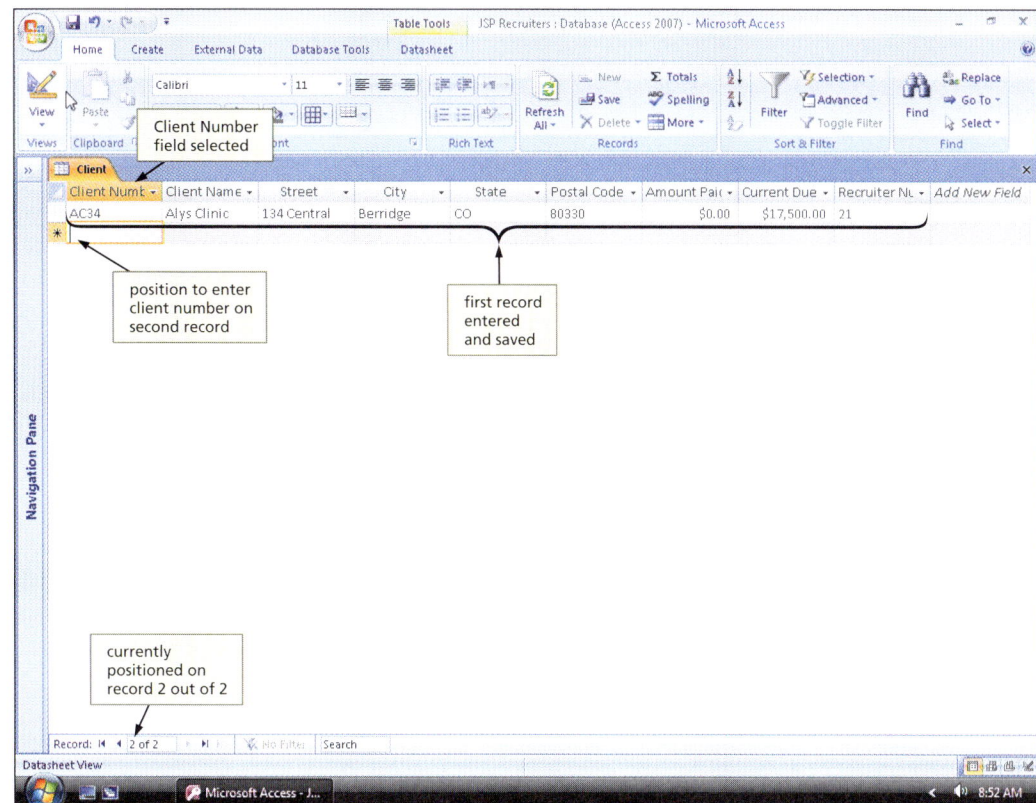

Figure 1–45

7
- Use the techniques shown in Steps 3 through 6 to enter the data for the second record in the Client table (Figure 1–46).

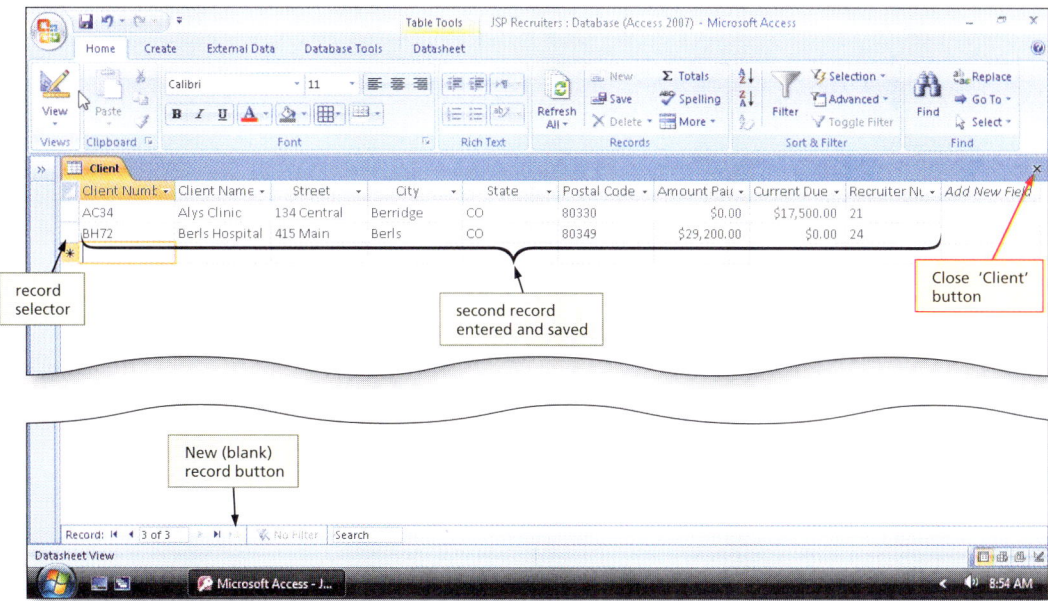

Figure 1–46

Making Changes to the Data

Check your entries carefully to ensure they are correct. If you make a mistake and discover it before you press the TAB key, correct it by pressing the BACKSPACE key until the incorrect characters are removed and then typing the correct characters. If you do not discover a mistake until later, you can use the following techniques to make the necessary corrections to the data:

- To undo your most recent change, click the Undo button on the Quick Access Toolbar. If there is nothing that Access can undo, this button will be dim, and clicking it will have no effect.
- To add a record, click the New (blank) record button, shown in Figure 1–46 on the previous page, and then add the record. Do not worry about it being in the correct position in the table. Access will reposition the record based on the primary key, in this case, the Client Number.
- To delete a record, click the Record selector, shown in Figure 1–46, for the record to be deleted. Then press the DELETE key to delete the record, and click the Yes button when Access asks you to verify that you do indeed wish to delete the record.
- To change the contents of one or more fields in a record, the record must be on the screen. If it is not, use any appropriate technique, such as the UP ARROW and DOWN ARROW keys or the vertical scroll bar, to move to it. If the field you want to correct is not visible on the screen, use the horizontal scroll bar along the bottom of the screen to shift all the fields until the one you want appears. If the value in the field is currently highlighted, you can simply type the new value. If you would rather edit the existing value, you must have an insertion point in the field. You can place the insertion point by clicking in the field or by pressing F2. Once you have produced an insertion point, you can use the arrow keys, the DELETE key, and the BACKSPACE key in making the correction. You also can use the INSERT key to switch between Insert and Overtype mode. When you have made the change, press the TAB key to move to the next field.

If you cannot determine how to correct the data, you may find that you are "stuck" on the record. Access neither allows you to move to any other record until you have made the correction, nor allows you to close the table. If you encounter this situation, simply press the ESC key. Pressing the ESC key will remove from the screen the record you are trying to add. You then can move to any other record, close the table, or take any other action you desire.

AutoCorrect

Not visible in the Access window, the **AutoCorrect** feature of Access works behind the scenes, correcting common mistakes when you complete a text entry in a cell. AutoCorrect makes three types of corrections for you:

1. Corrects two initial capital letters by changing the second letter to lowercase.
2. Capitalizes the first letter in the names of days.
3. Replaces commonly misspelled words with their correct spelling. For example, it changes the misspelled word *recieve* to *receive* when you complete the entry. AutoCorrect will correct the spelling automatically of more than 400 commonly misspelled words.

BTW

Undo and Redo
You also can undo multiple actions. To see a list of recent actions that you can undo, click the down arrow next to the Undo button on the Quick Access Toolbar. To redo the most recent action, click the Redo button on the Quick Access Toolbar. You also can redo multiple actions by clicking the down arrow next to the button.

BTW

Cut, Copy, and Paste
Just as in other Office programs, you can use buttons in the Clipboard group on the Home tab to cut, copy, and paste data. To cut data, select the data to be cut and click the Cut button. To copy data, select the data and click the Copy button. To paste data, select the desired location and click the Paste button.

BTW

AutoCorrect Options
Using the Office AutoCorrect feature, you can create entries that will replace abbreviations with spelled-out names and phrases automatically. For example, you can create the abbreviated entry *dbms* for *database management system*. Whenever you type dbms followed by a space or punctuation mark, Access automatically replaces dbms with database management system. To specify AutoCorrect rules and exceptions to the rules, click Access Options on the Office Button menu and then click Proofing in the Access Options dialog box.

To Close a Table

It is a good idea to close a table as soon as you have finished working with it. It keeps the screen from getting cluttered and prevents you from making accidental changes to the data in the table. The following step closes the Client table.

- Click the Close 'Client' button, shown in Figure 1–46 on page AC 33, to close the table (Figure 1–47).

Figure 1–47

> **Other Ways**
> 1. Right-click tab for table, click Close on shortcut menu

Quitting Access

If you save the object on which you are currently working and then quit Access, all Access windows close. If you have made changes to an object since the last time the object was saved, Access displays a dialog box asking if you want to save the changes you made before it closes that window. The dialog box contains three buttons with these resulting actions:

- Yes button — Saves the changes and then quits Access
- No button — Quits Access without saving changes
- Cancel button — Closes the dialog box and redisplays the database without saving the changes

If no changes have been made to any object since the last time the object was saved, Access will close all windows without displaying any dialog boxes.

To Quit Access

You saved your changes to the table and did not make any additional changes. You are ready to quit Access. The following step quits Access.

1 Click the Close button on the right side of the Access title bar, shown in Figure 1–47 on the previous page, to quit Access.

Starting Access and Opening a Database

Once you have created and later closed a database, you will need to open it in the future in order to use it. Opening a database requires that Access is running on your computer.

To Start Access

The following steps, which assume Windows Vista is running, start Access.

1 Click the Start button on the Windows Vista taskbar to display the Start menu.

2 Click All Programs at the bottom of the left pane on the Start menu to display the All Programs list and then click Microsoft Office in the All Programs list to display the Microsoft Office list.

3 Click Microsoft Office Access 2007 on the Microsoft Office submenu to start Access and display the Getting Started with Microsoft Office Access window (Figure 1–48).

4 If the Access window is not maximized, click the Maximize button on its title bar to maximize the window.

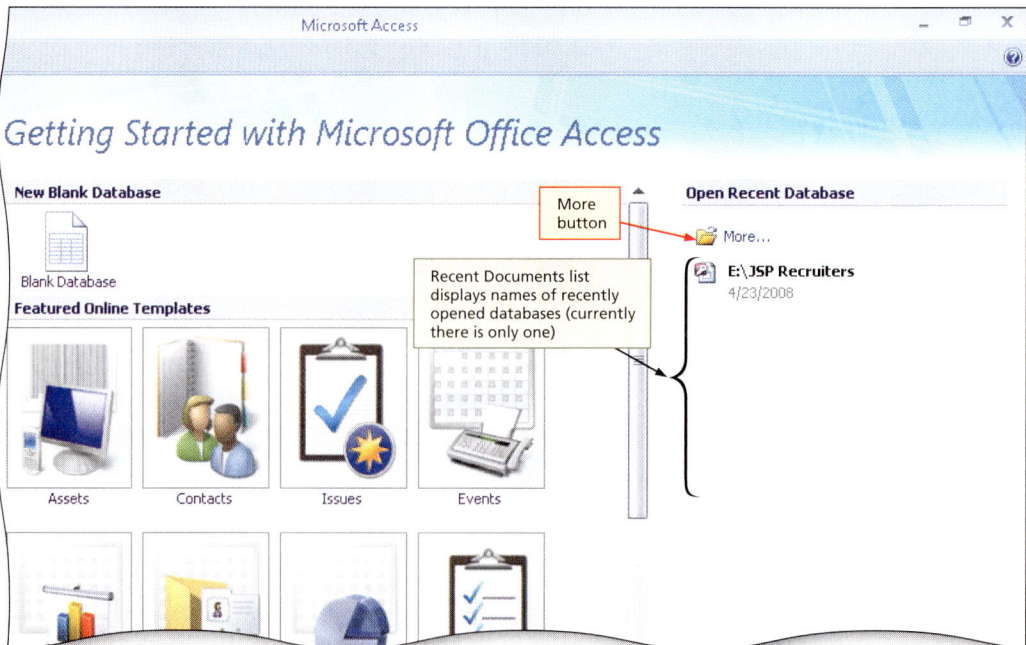

Figure 1–48

To Open a Database from Access

Earlier in this chapter you created your database on a USB flash drive using the file name, JSP Recruiters. There are two ways to open the file containing your database. If the file you created appears in the Recent Documents list, you could click it to open the file. If not, you can use the More button to open the file. The following steps use the More button to open the JSP Recruiters database from the USB flash drive.

1

- With your USB flash drive connected to one of the computer's USB ports, click the More button, shown in Figure 1–48, to display the Open dialog box.

- If the Folders list is displayed below the Folders button, click the Folders button to remove the Folders list.

- If necessary, click Computer in the Favorite Links section.

- Double-click UDISK 2.0 (E:) to select the USB flash drive, Drive E in this case, as the new open location.

- Click JSP Recruiters to select the file name (Figure 1–49).

How do I open the file if I am not using a USB flash drive?

Use the same process, but be certain to select your device in the Look in list. You might need to open multiple folders.

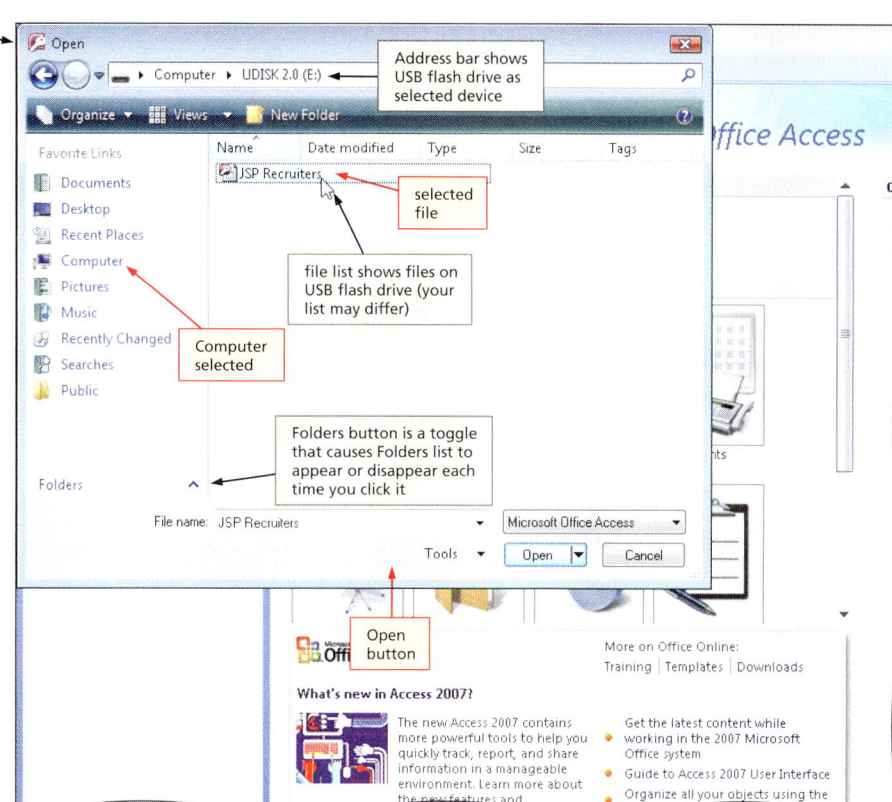

Figure 1–49

2

- Click the Open button to open the database (Figure 1–50).

Why do I see the Access icon and name on the Windows Vista taskbar?

When you open an Access database, an Access program button is displayed on the taskbar. If the contents of a button cannot fit in the allotted button space, an ellipsis appears. If you point to a program button, its entire contents appear in a ScreenTip, which in this case would be the program name followed by the file name.

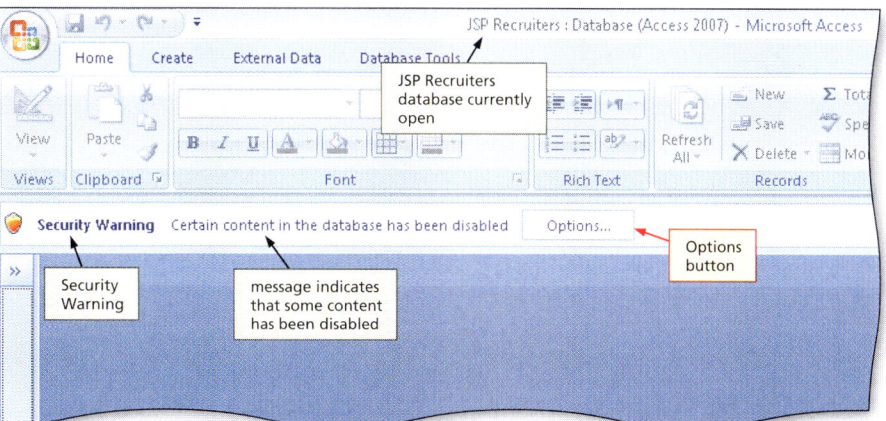

Figure 1–50

- If a Security Warning appears, as shown in Figure 1–50 on the previous page, click the Options button to display the Microsoft Office Security Options dialog box (Figure 1–51).

- Click the 'Enable this content' option button.

- Click the OK button to enable the content.

Q&A When would I want to disable the content?

You would want to disable the content if you suspected that your database might contain harmful content or damaging macros. Because you are the one who created the database and no one else has used it, you should have no such suspicions.

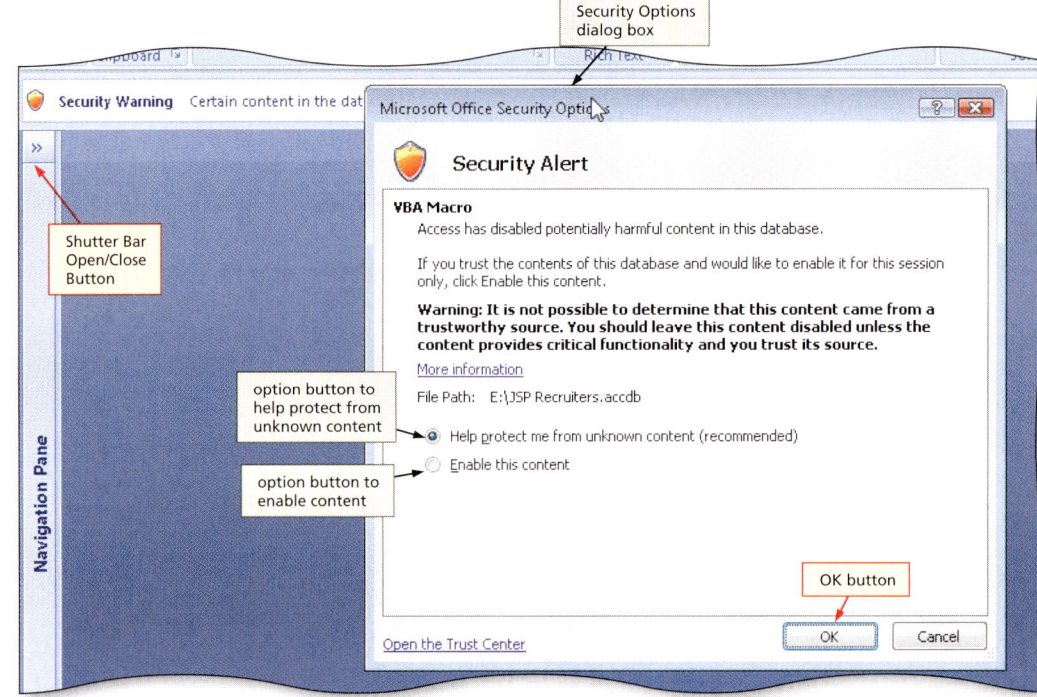

Figure 1–51

Other Ways

1. Click Office Button, double-click file name in Recent Documents list
2. Press CTRL+O, select file name, press ENTER

To Add Additional Records to a Table

You can add records to a table that already contains data using a process almost identical to that used to add records to an empty table. The only difference is that you place the insertion point after the last data record before you enter the additional data. To do so, use the **Navigation buttons**, which are buttons used to move within a table, found near the lower-left corner of the screen when a table is open. The purpose of each of the Navigation buttons is described in Table 1–2.

Table 1–2 Navigation Buttons in Datasheet View	
Button	**Purpose**
First record	Moves to the first record in the table
Previous record	Moves to the previous record
Next record	Moves to the next record
Last record	Moves to the last record in the table
New (blank) record	Moves to the end of the table to a position for entering a new record

The following steps add the remaining records (Figure 1–52) to the Client table.

Client Numb	Client Name	Street	City	State	Postal Code	Amount Paid	Current Due	Recruiter Nu
BL12	Benton Labs	12 Mountain	Denton	CO	80412	$16,500.00	$38,225.00	24
EA45	ENT Assoc.	867 Ridge	Fort Stewart	CO	80336	$12,750.00	$15,000.00	27
FD89	Ferb Dentistry	34 Crestview	Berridge	CO	80330	$21,000.00	$12,500.00	21
FH22	Family Health	123 Second	Tarleton	CO	80409	$0.00	$0.00	24
MH56	Maun Hospital	76 Dixon	Mason	CO	80356	$0.00	$43,025.00	24
PR11	Peel Radiology	151 Valleyview	Fort Stewart	CO	80336	$31,750.00	$0.00	21
TC37	Tarleton Clinic	451 Hull	Tarleton	CO	80409	$18,750.00	$31,500.00	27
WL56	West Labs	785 Main	Berls	CO	80349	$14,000.00	$0.00	24

Figure 1–52

- If the Navigation Pane is hidden, click the Shutter Bar Open/Close Button, shown in Figure 1–51, to show the Navigation Pane (Figure 1–53).

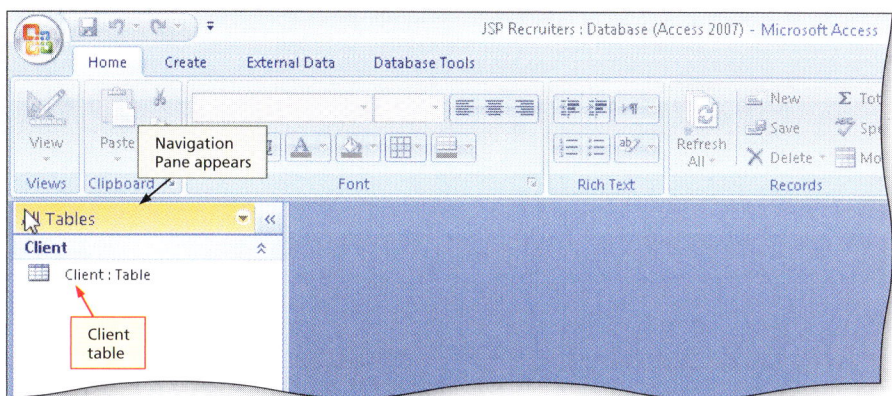

Figure 1–53

- Right-click the Client table in the Navigation Pane to display a shortcut menu.

- Click Open on the shortcut menu to open the Client table in Datasheet view.

- Hide the Navigation Pane by clicking the Shutter Bar Open/Close button (Figure 1–54).

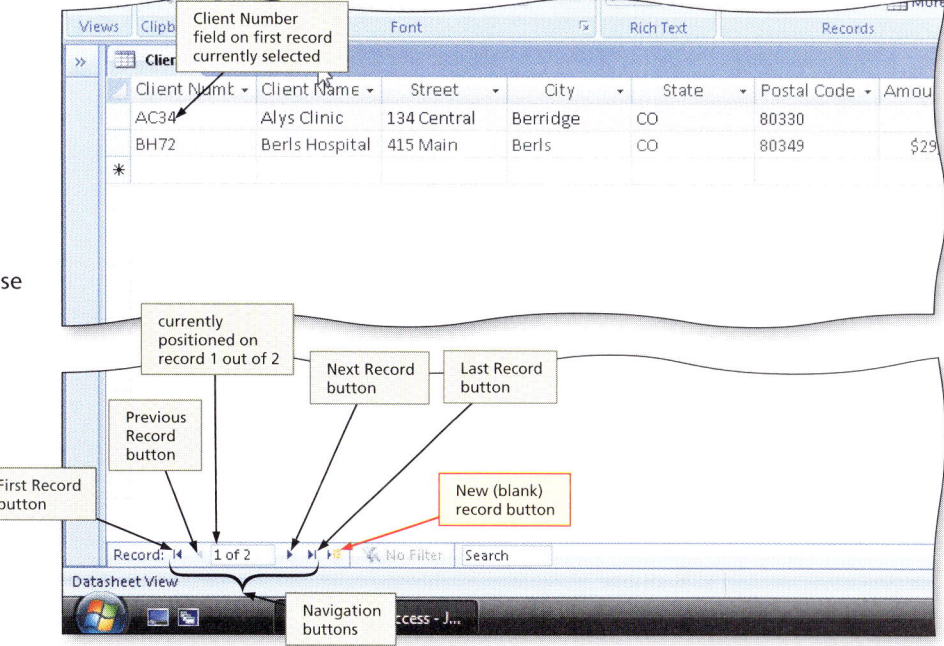

Figure 1–54

- Click the New (blank) record button to move to a position to enter a new record (Figure 1–55).

Q&A Why click the New (blank) record button? Could you just click the Client Number on the first open record and then add the record?

You could click the Client Number on the first open record, provided that record appears on the screen. With only two records in the table, this is not a problem. Once a table contains more records than will fit on the screen, it is easier to click the New (blank) record button.

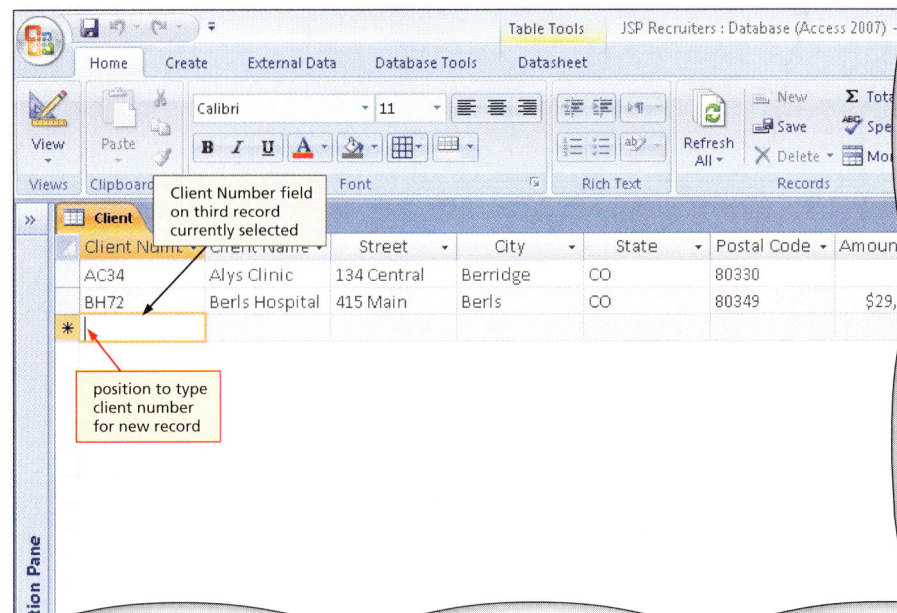

Figure 1–55

- Add the records shown in Figure 1–52 on the previous page, using the same techniques you used to add the first two records (Figure 1–56).

- Click the Close 'Client' button to close the table.

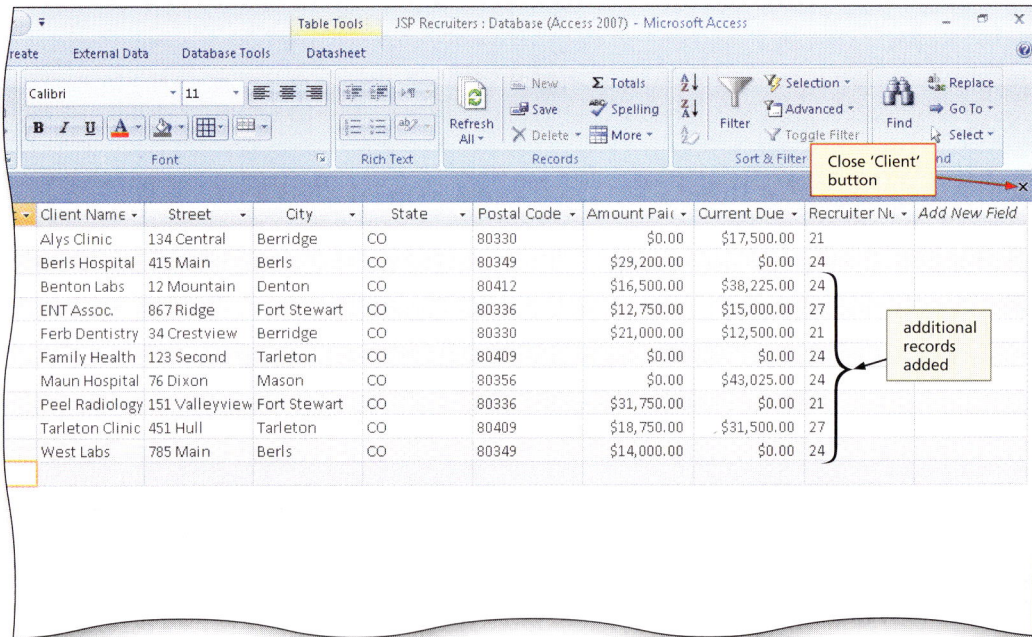

Figure 1–56

Other Ways
1. Click New button in Records group on Ribbon
2. Press CTRL+PLUS SIGN (+)

Previewing and Printing the Contents of a Table

When working with a database, you often will need to print a copy of the table contents. Figure 1–57 shows a printed copy of the contents of the Client table. (Yours may look slightly different, depending on your printer.) Because the Client table is wider substantially than the screen, it also will be wider than the normal printed page in portrait orientation. **Portrait orientation** means the printout is across the width of the page.

Client Number	Client Name	Street	City	State	Postal Code	Amount Paid	Current Due	Recruiter Numb
AC34	Alys Clinic	134 Central	Berridge	CO	80330	$0.00	$17,500.00	21
BH72	Berls Hospital	415 Main	Berls	CO	80349	$29,200.00	$0.00	24
BL12	Benton Labs	12 Mountain	Denton	CO	80412	$16,500.00	$38,225.00	24
EA45	ENT Assoc.	867 Ridge	Fort Stewart	CO	80336	$12,750.00	$15,000.00	27
FD89	Ferb Dentistry	34 Crestview	Berridge	CO	80330	$21,000.00	$12,500.00	21
FH22	Family Health	123 Second	Tarleton	CO	80409	$0.00	$0.00	24
MH56	Maun Hospital	76 Dixon	Mason	CO	80356	$0.00	$43,025.00	24
PR11	Peel Radiology	151 Valleyview	Fort Stewart	CO	80336	$31,750.00	$0.00	21
TC37	Tarleton Clinic	451 Hull	Tarleton	CO	80409	$18,750.00	$31,500.00	27
WL56	West Labs	785 Main	Berls	CO	80349	$14,000.00	$0.00	24

Figure 1–57

Landscape orientation means the printout is across the length (height) of the page. Thus, to print the wide database table, use landscape orientation. If you are printing the contents of a table that fit on the screen, you will not need landscape orientation. A convenient way to change to landscape orientation is to preview what the printed copy will look like by using Print Preview. This allows you to determine whether landscape orientation is necessary and, if it is, to change the orientation easily to landscape. In addition, you also can use Print Preview to determine whether any adjustments are necessary to the page margins.

To Preview and Print the Contents of a Table

The following steps use Print Preview to preview and then print the Client table.

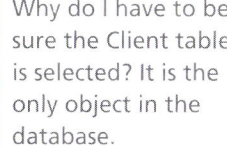

- If the Navigation Pane is hidden, show the Navigation Pane by clicking the Shutter Bar Open/Close Button.

- Be sure the Client table is selected (Figure 1–58).

Q&A Why do I have to be sure the Client table is selected? It is the only object in the database.

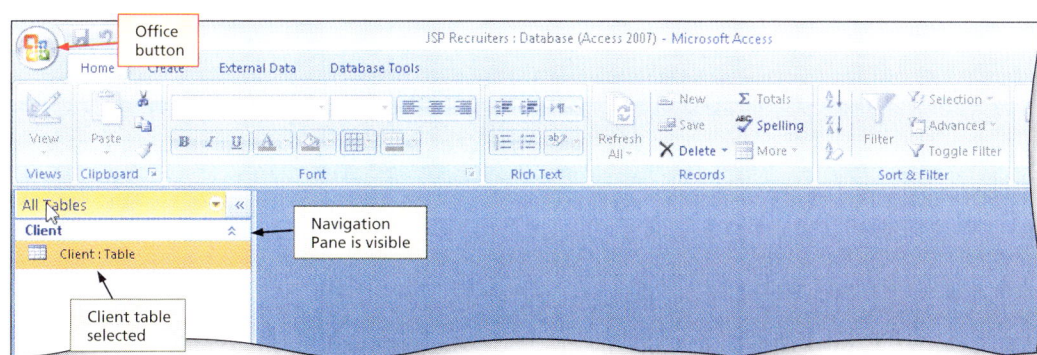

Figure 1–58

There is no issue when the database contains only one object. Ensuring that the correct object is selected is a good habit to form, however, to make sure that the object you print is the one you want.

2

- Click the Office Button to display the Office Button menu.
- Point to the Print command arrow to display the Print submenu (Figure 1–59).

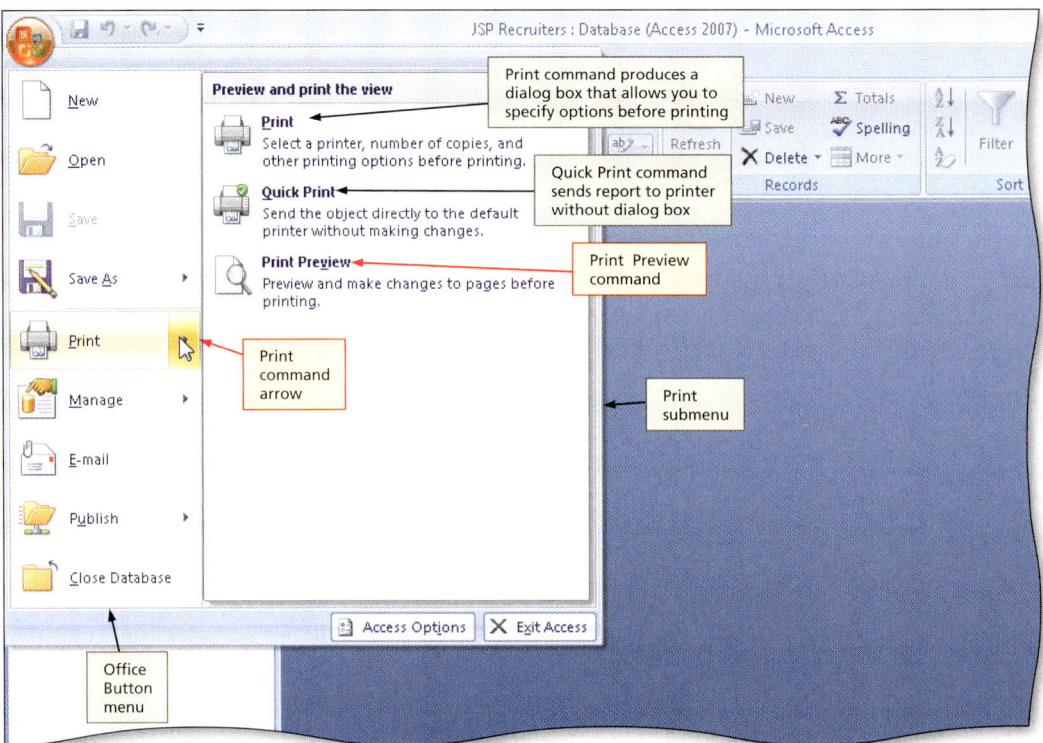

Figure 1–59

3

- Click Print Preview on the Print submenu to display a preview of the report (Figure 1–60).

 I can't read the report. Can I magnify a portion of the report?

Yes. Point the mouse pointer, whose shape will change to a magnifying glass, at the portion of the report that you wish to magnify, and then click. You can return the view of the report to the one shown in the figure by clicking a second time.

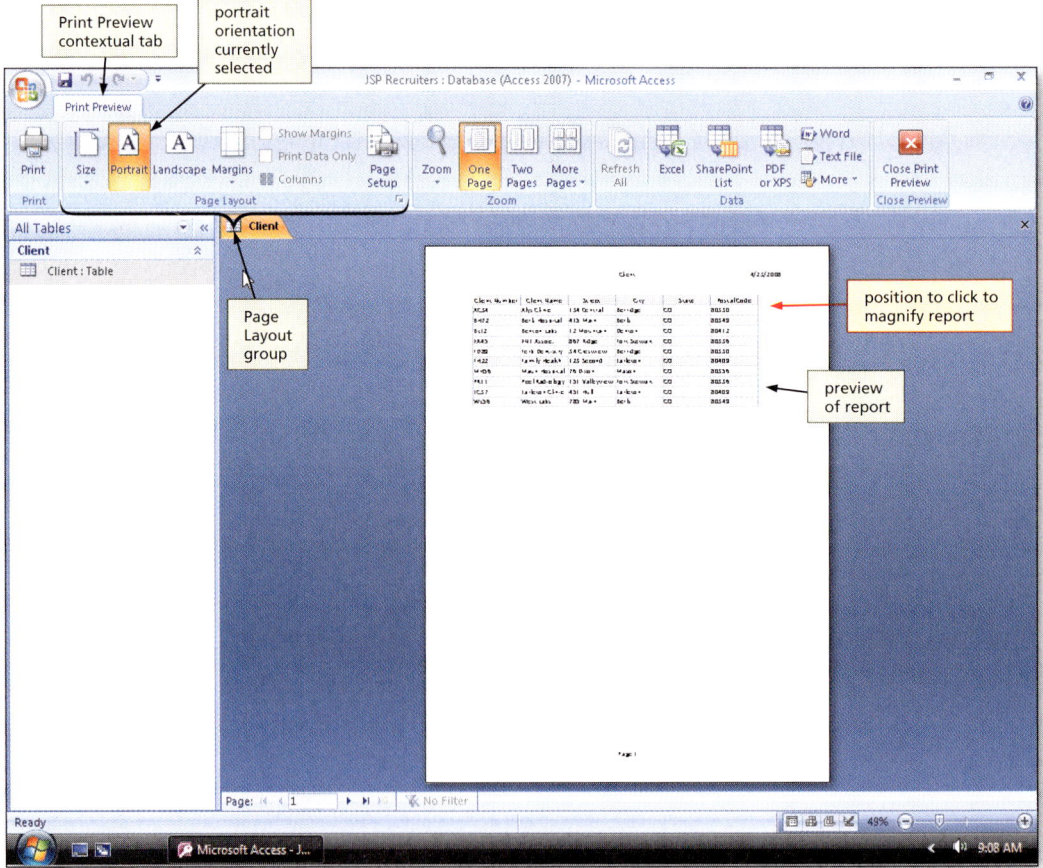

Figure 1–60

4

- Click the mouse pointer in the position shown in Figure 1–60 to magnify the upper-right section of the report (Figure 1–61).

 My report was already magnified in a different area. How can I see the area shown in the figure?

There are two ways. You can use the scroll bars to move to the desired portion of the report. You also can click the mouse pointer anywhere in the report to produce a screen like the one in Figure 1–60, and then click in the location shown in the figure.

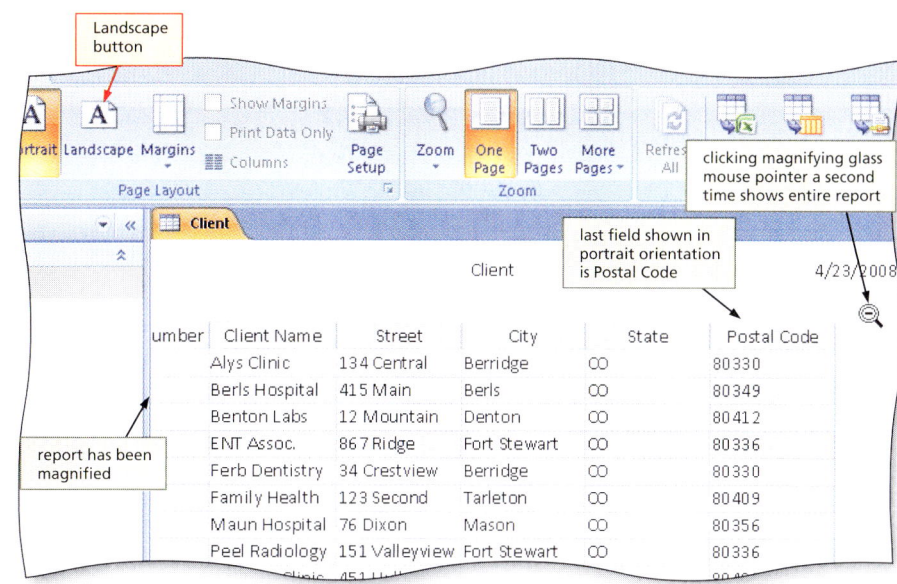

Figure 1–61

5

- Click the Landscape button to change to landscape orientation (Figure 1–62).

6

- Click the Print button on the Print Preview tab to print the report.

- When the printer stops, retrieve the hard copy of the Client table.

- Click the Close Print Preview button to close the Print Preview window.

 How can I print multiple copies of my document other than clicking the Print button multiple times?

Click the Office Button, point to the arrow next to Print on the Office Button menu, click Print on the Print submenu, increase the number in the Number of Copies: box, and then click the OK button.

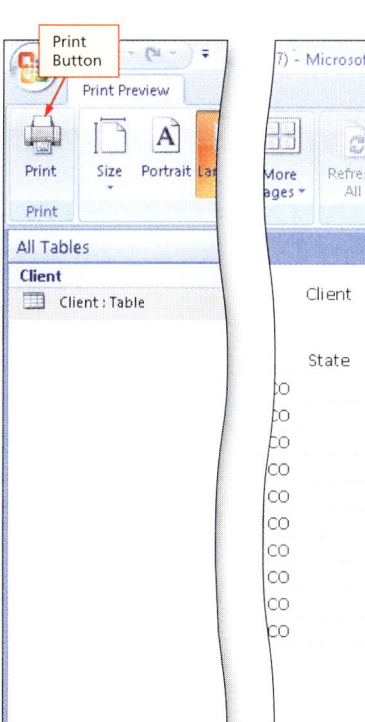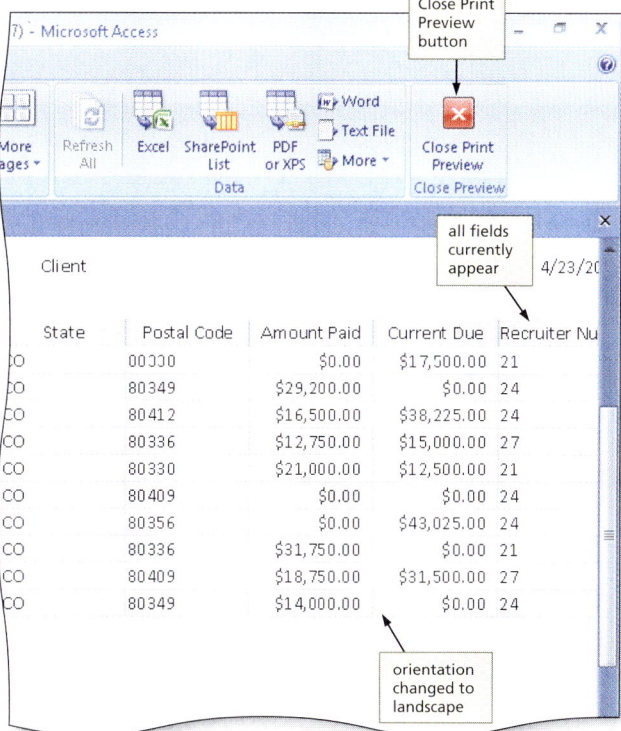

Figure 1–62

How can I print a range of pages rather than printing the whole report?

Click the Office Button, point to the arrow next to Print on the Office Button menu, click Print on the Print submenu, click the Pages option button in the Print Range box, enter the desired page range, and then click the OK button.

Other Ways
1. Press CTRL+P, press ENTER

Creating Additional Tables

The JSP Recruiters database contains two tables, the Client table and the Recruiter table. You need to create the Recruiter table and add records to it. Because you already used the default table that Access created when you created the database, you will need to first create the table. You can then add fields as you did with the Client table.

To Create an Additional Table

The fields to be added are Recruiter Number, Last Name, First Name, Street, City, State, Postal Code, Rate, and Commission. The data type for the Rate field is Number, and the data type for the Commission field is Currency. The data type for all other fields is Text. The following steps create the Recruiter table.

- Click Create on the Ribbon to display the Create tab (Figure 1–63).

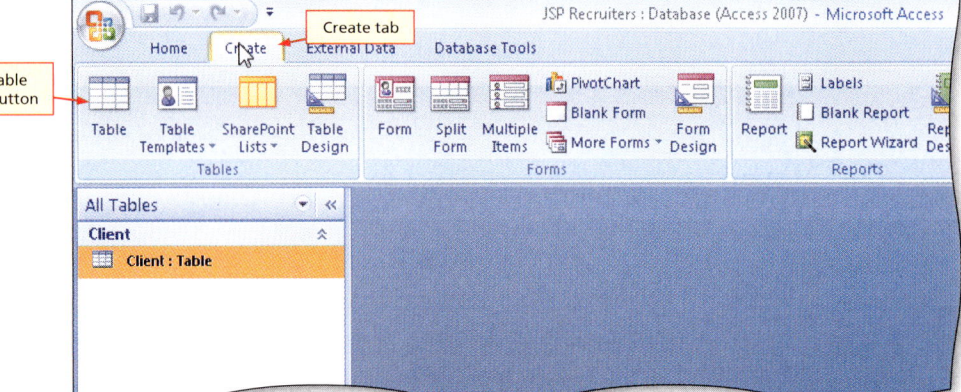

Figure 1–63

- Click the Table button on the Create tab to create a new table (Figure 1–64).

Q&A Could I save the table now so I can assign it the name I want, rather than Table1?

You certainly can. Be aware, however, that you will still need to save it again once you have added all your fields.

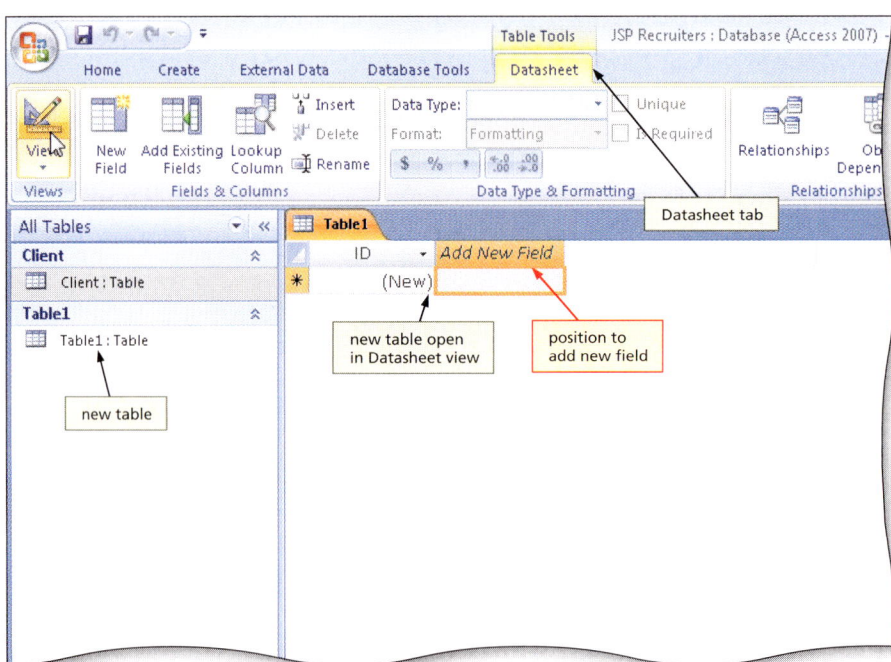

Figure 1–64

- Right-click Add New Field to display a shortcut menu.
- Click Rename Column on the shortcut menu to display an insertion point.
- Type `Recruiter Number` to assign a name to the new field.
- Press the DOWN ARROW key to complete the addition of the field.
- Using the same technique, add the Last Name, First Name, Street, City, State, Postal Code, and Rate fields.
- Click the Data Type box arrow to display the Data Type box menu (Figure 1–65).

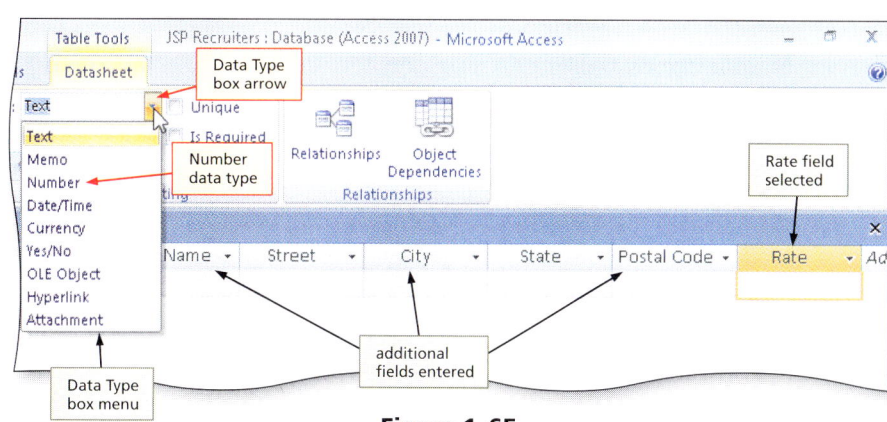

Figure 1–65

- Click Number on the Data Type box menu to select the Number data type and assign the Number data type to the Rate field.
- Add the Commission field and assign it the Currency data type.
- Click the Save button to display the Save As dialog box (Figure 1–66).

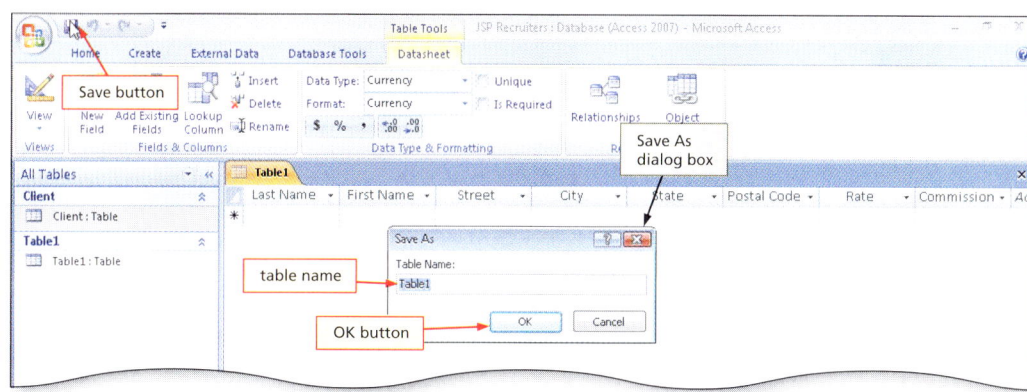

Figure 1–66

- Type `Recruiter` to assign a name to the table.
- Click the OK button (Figure 1–67).

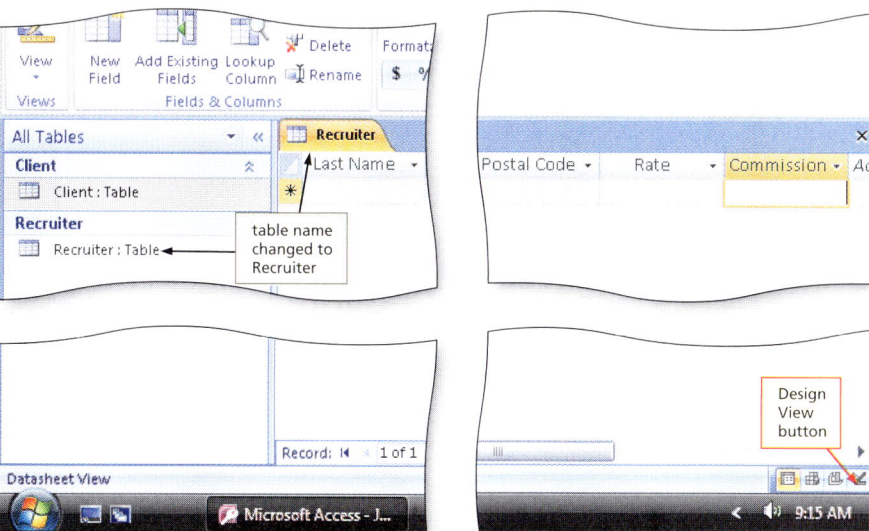

Figure 1–67

To Modify the Primary Key and Field Properties

Fields whose data type is Number often require you to change the field size. Table 1–3 shows the possible field sizes for Number fields.

Table 1–3 Field Sizes for Number Fields	
Field Size	**Description**
Byte	Integer value in the range of 0 to 255.
Integer	Integer value in the range of -32,768 to 32,767.
Long Integer	Integer value in the range of -2,147,483,648 to 2,147,483,647.
Single	Numeric values with decimal places to seven significant digits — requires four bytes of storage.
Double	Numeric values with decimal places to more accuracy than Single — requires eight bytes of storage.
Replication ID	Special identifier required for replication.
Decimal	Numeric values with decimal places to more accuracy than Single — requires 12 bytes of storage.

Because the values in the Rate field have decimal places, only Single, Double, or Decimal would be possible choices. The difference between these choices concerns the amount of accuracy. Double is more accurate than Single, for example, but requires more storage space. Because the rates are only two decimal places, Single is a perfectly acceptable choice.

In addition to changing the field size, you should also change the format to Fixed (a fixed number of decimal places) and the number of decimal places to 2.

The following steps move to Design view, delete the ID field, and make the Recruiter Number field the primary key. They then change the field size of the Rate field to Single, the format to Fixed, and the number of decimal places to 2.

- Click the Design View button on the status bar to move to Design view (Figure 1–68).

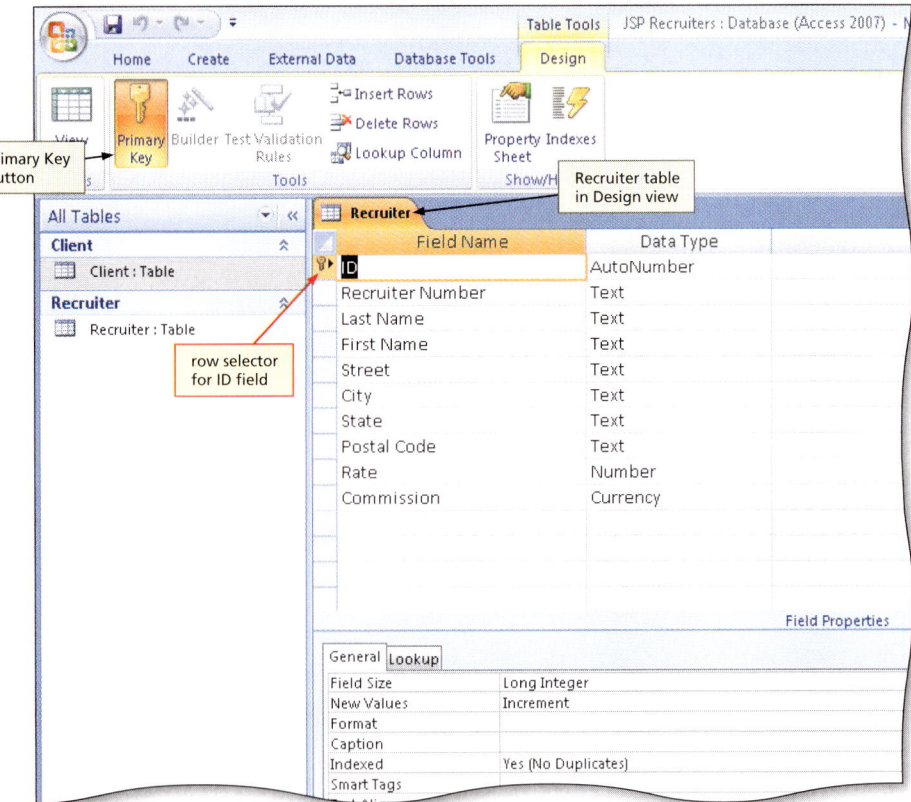

Figure 1–68

Creating and Using a Database   Access Chapter 1   AC 47

2

- Click the row selector for the ID field to select the field.
- Press the DELETE key to delete the field.
- Click the Yes button to complete the deletion of the field.
- With the Recruiter Number field selected, click the Primary Key button to designate the Recruiter Number field as the primary key.
- Click the row selector for the Rate field to select the field (Figure 1–69).

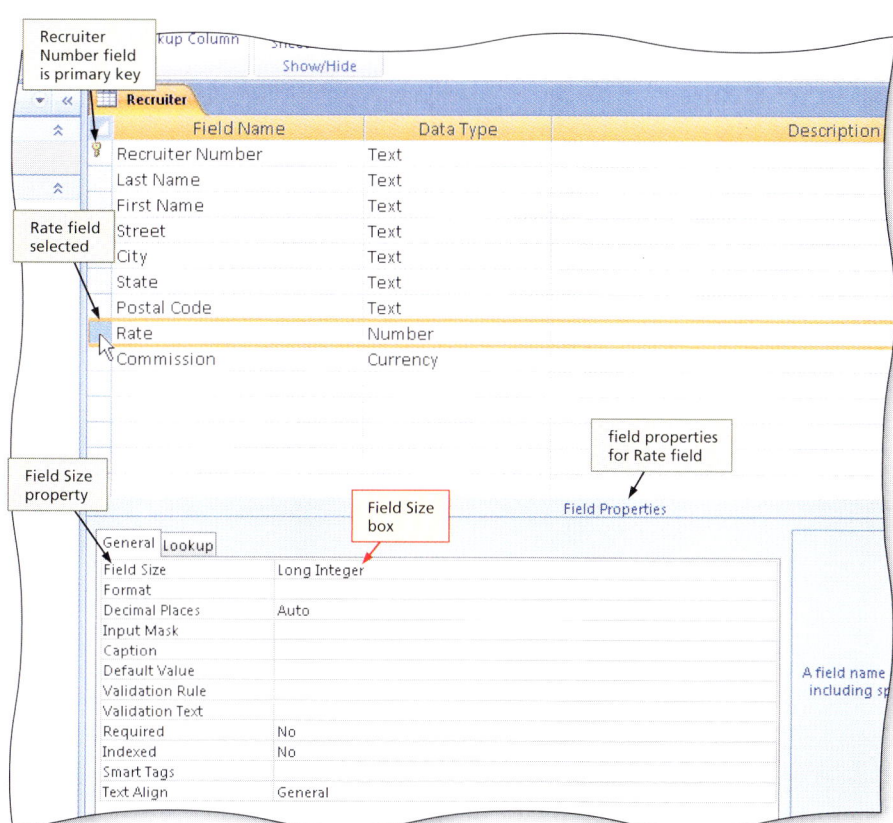

Figure 1–69

3

- Click the Field Size box to display the Field Size box arrow.
- Click the Field Size box arrow to display the Field Size box menu (Figure 1–70).

Q&A What would happen if I left the field size set to Integer?

If the field size is Integer, no decimal places can be stored. Thus a value of .10 would be stored as 0. If you enter your rates and the values all appear as 0, chances are you did not change the field size.

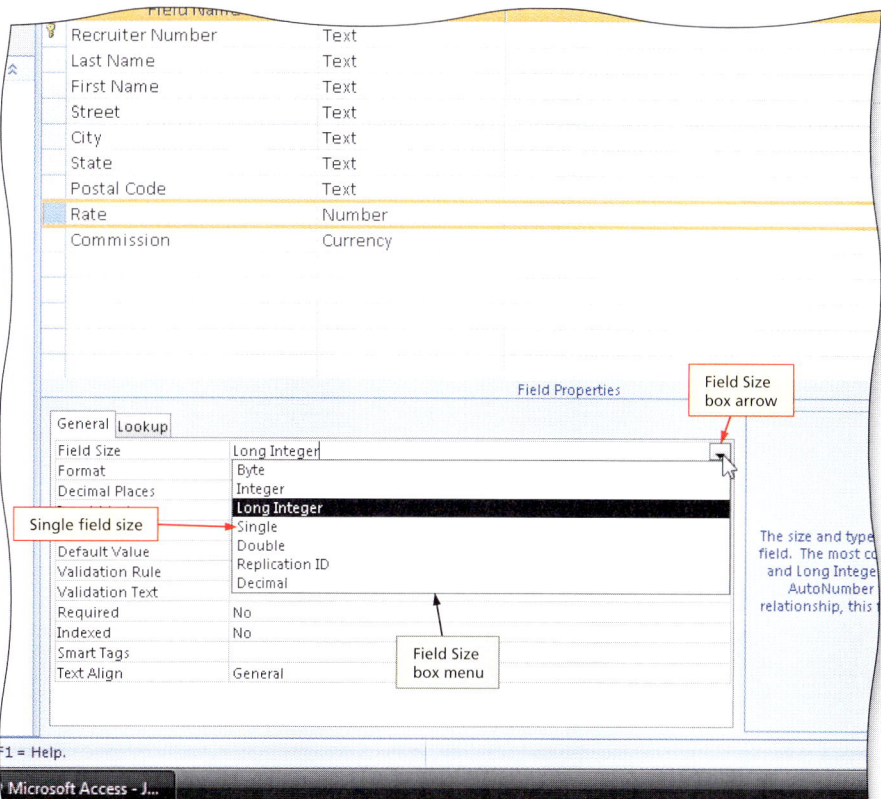

Figure 1–70

- Click Single to select single precision as the field size.
- Click the Format box to display the Format box arrow (Figure 1–71).
- Click the Format box arrow to open the Format box menu.

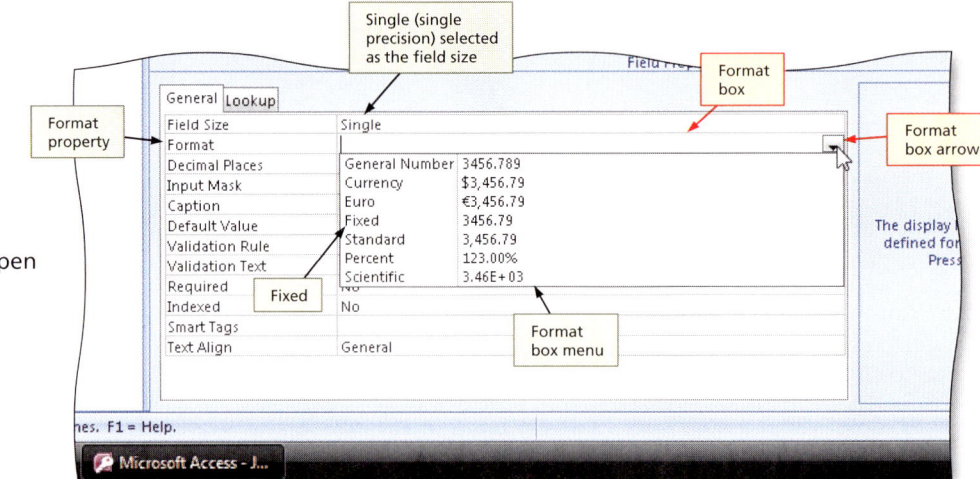

Figure 1–71

- Click Fixed to select fixed as the format.
- Click the Decimal Places box to display the Decimal Places box arrow.
- Click the Decimal Places box arrow to enter the number of decimal places.
- Click 2 to select 2 as the number of decimal places.
- Click the Save button to save your changes (Figure 1–72).

Q&A

What is the purpose of the error checking button?

You changed the number of decimal places. The error checking button gives you a quick way of making the same change everywhere Rate appears. So far, you have not added any data, nor have you created any forms or reports that use the Rate field, so no such changes are necessary.

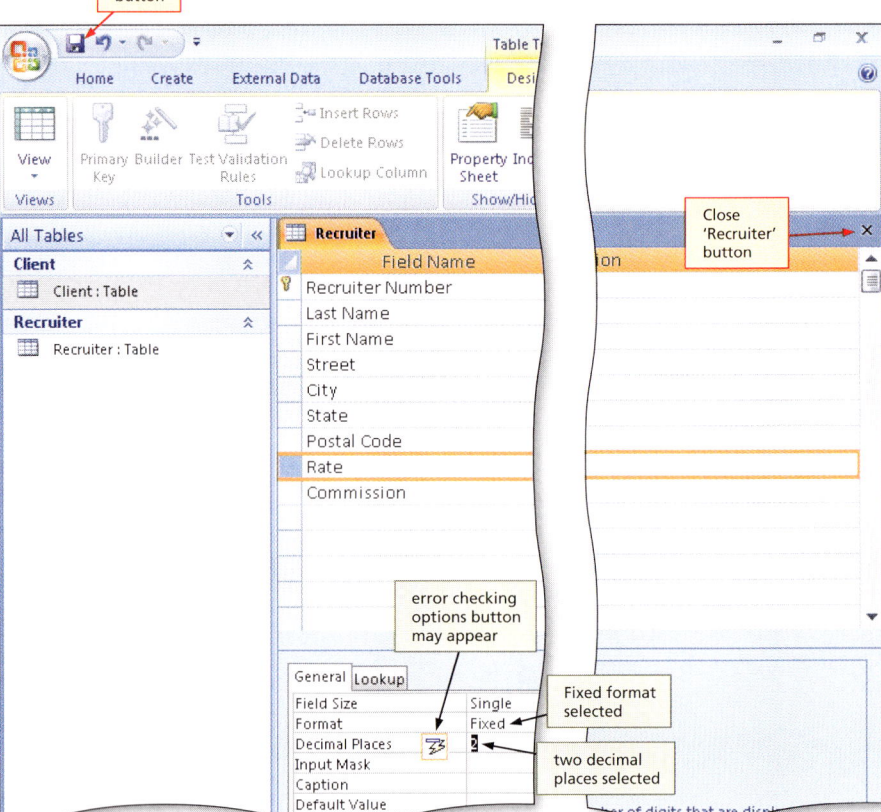

Figure 1–72

- Close the Recruiter table by clicking the Close 'Recruiter' button (Figure 1–73).

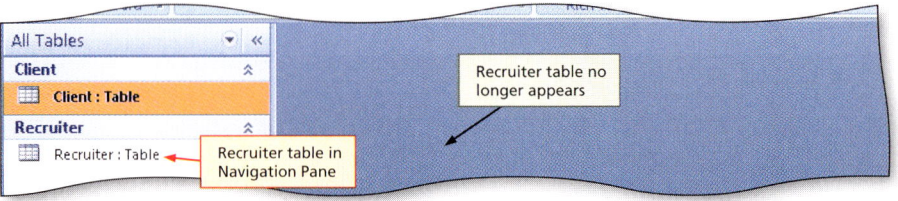

Figure 1–73

Creating and Using a Database   Access Chapter 1   AC 49

To Add Records to an Additional Table

The following steps add the records shown in Figure 1–74 to the Recruiter table.

Recruiter Nu	Last Name	First Name	Street	City	State	Postal Code	Rate	Commission
21	Kerry	Alyssa	261 Pointer	Tourin	CO	80416	0.10	$17,600.00
24	Reeves	Camden	3135 Brill	Denton	CO	80412	0.10	$19,900.00
27	Fernandez	Jaime	265 Maxwell	Charleston	CO	80380	0.09	$9,450.00
34	Lee	Jan	1827 Oak	Denton	CO	80413	0.08	$0.00

Figure 1–74

- Open the Recruiter table in Datasheet view and then hide the Navigation Pane.
- Enter the Recruiter data from Figure 1–74 (Figure 1–75).

Experiment

- Click in the Rate field on any of the records. Be sure the Datasheet tab is selected. Click the Format box arrow and then click each of the formats in the Format box menu to see the effect on the values in the Rate field. When finished, click Fixed in the Format box menu.

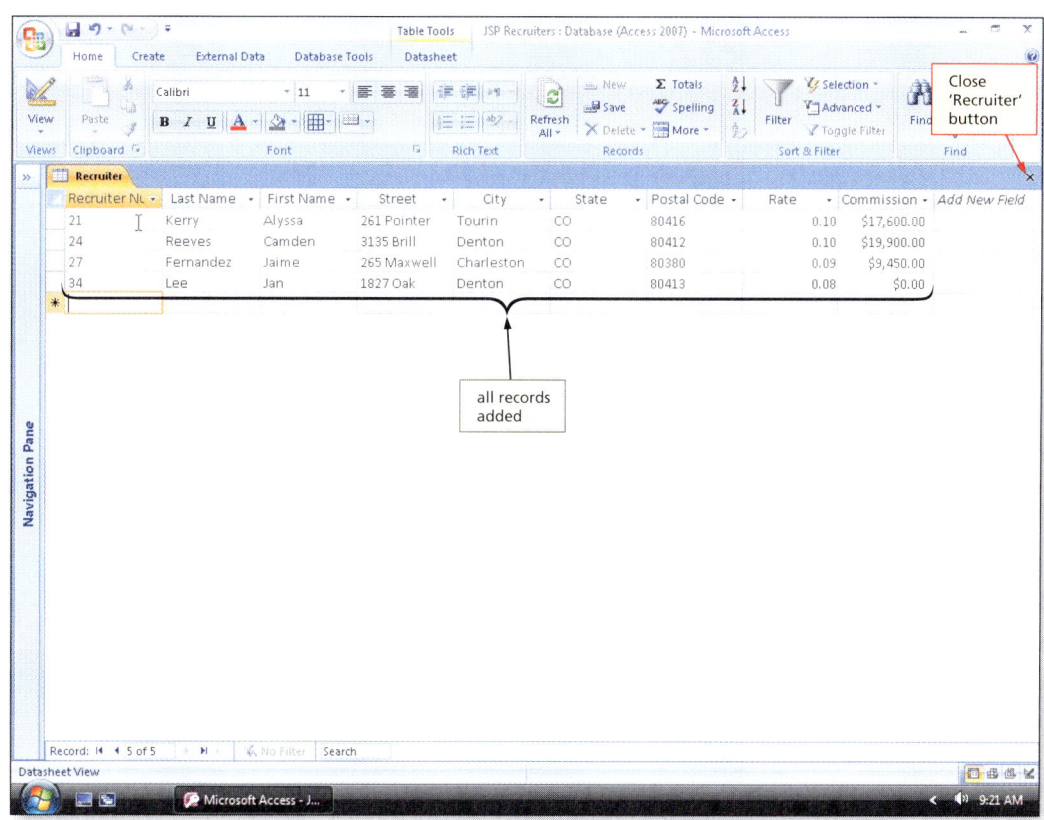

Figure 1–75

- Click the Close 'Recruiter' button to close the table and remove the datasheet from the screen.

Creating a Report

JSP Recruiters needs the following reports. You will create the four reports shown in Figure 1–76 in this section.

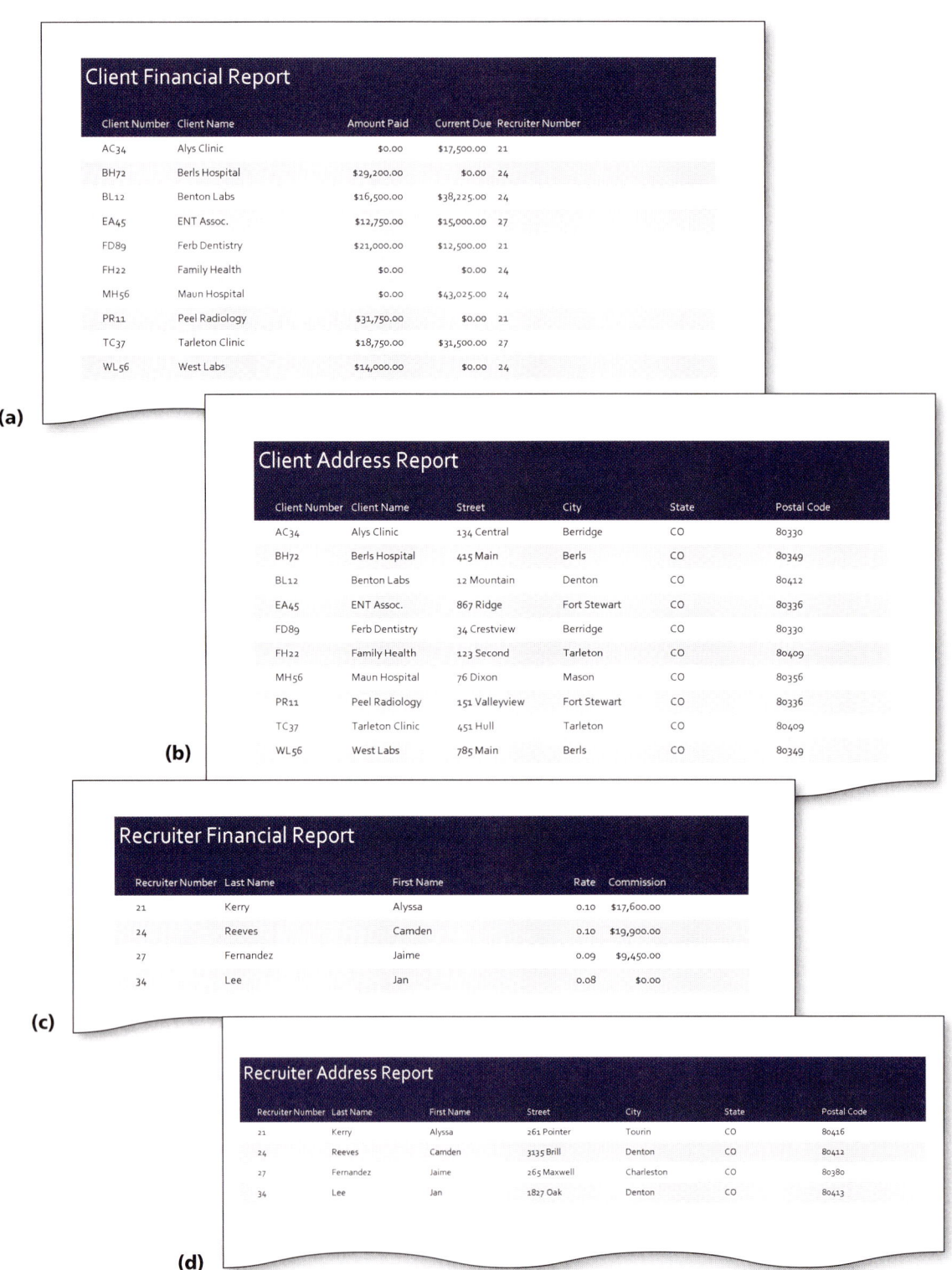

Figure 1–76

To Create a Report

You will first create the report shown in Figure 1–76a. The records in the report are sorted (ordered) by Client Number. To ensure that the records appear in this order, you will specify that the records are to be sorted on the Client Number field. The following steps create the report in Figure 1–76a.

- Be sure the Client table is selected in the Navigation Pane.
- Click Create on the Ribbon to display the Create tab.
- Click the Report Wizard button to display the Report Wizard dialog box (Figure 1–77).

Q&A What would have happened if the Recruiter table were selected instead of the Client table?

The list of available fields would have contained fields from the Recruiter table rather than the Client table.

Q&A If the list contained Recruiter table fields, how could I make it contain Client table fields?

Click the arrow in the Tables/Queries box and then click the Client table in the list that appears.

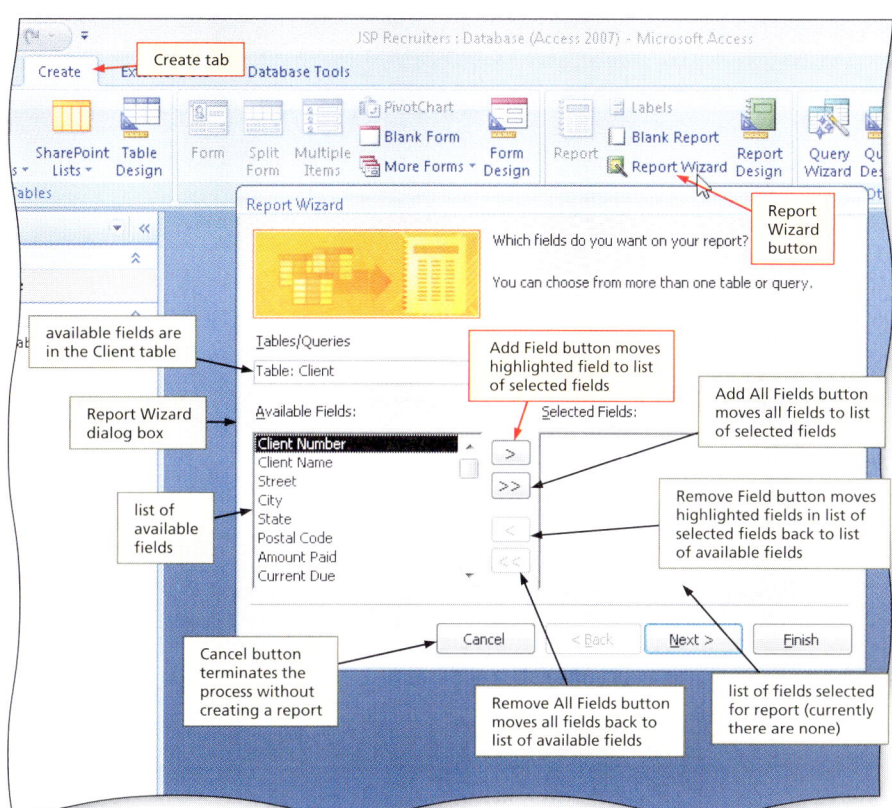

Figure 1–77

- Click the Add Field button to add the Client Number field.
- Click the Add Field button to add the Client Name field.
- Click the Amount Paid field, and then click the Add Field button to add the Amount Paid field.
- Click the Add Field button to add the Current Due field.
- Click the Add Field button to add the Recruiter Number field (Figure 1–78).

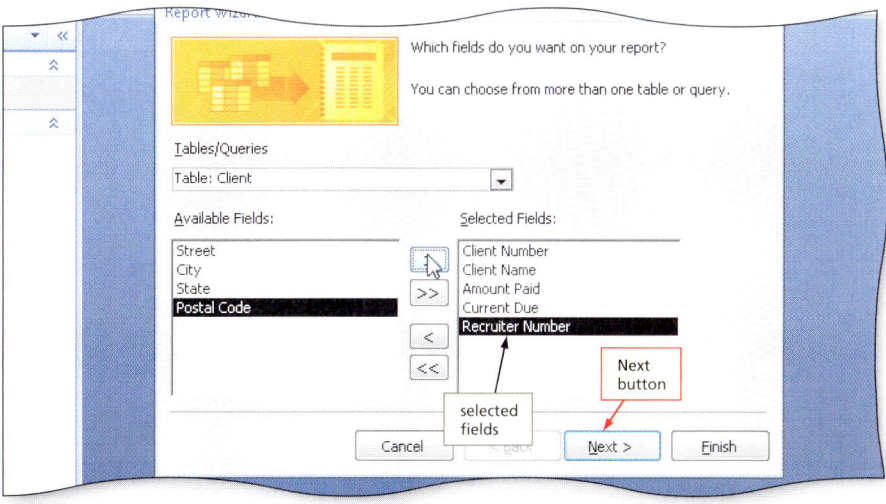

Figure 1–78

3

- Click the Next button to display the next Report Wizard screen (Figure 1–79).

Q&A What is grouping?

Grouping means creating separate collections of records sharing some common characteristic. For example, you might want to group clients in the same Postal code or that have the same recruiter.

Q&A What if I realize that I have selected the wrong fields?

You can click the Back button to return to the previous screen and then correct the list of fields. You also could click the Cancel button and start over.

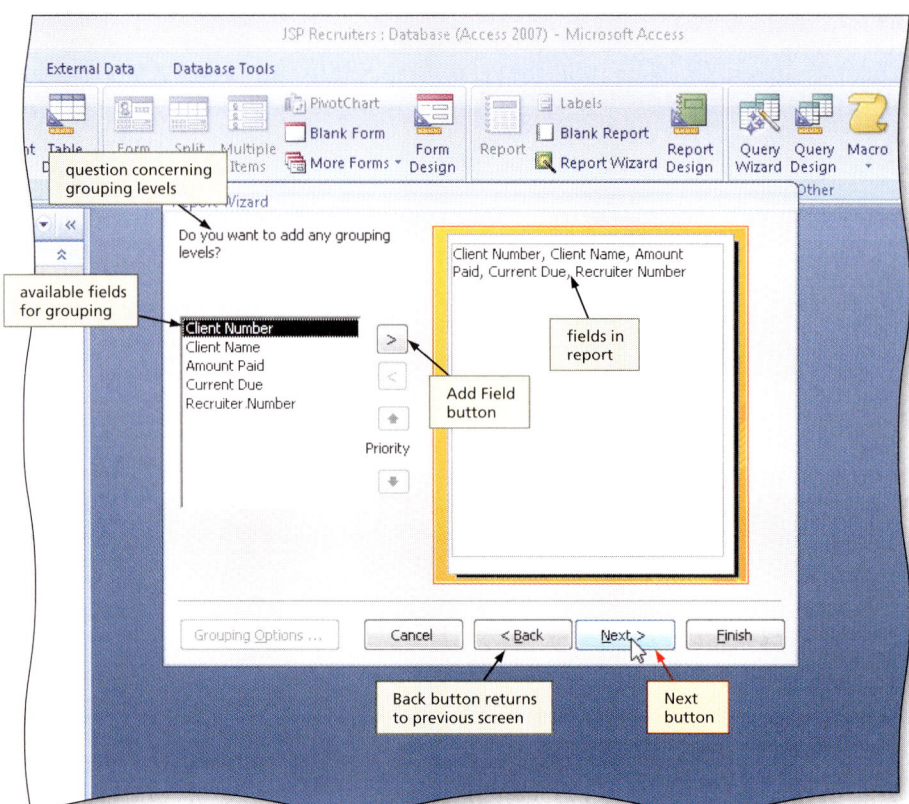

Figure 1–79

4

- Because you will not specify any grouping, click the Next button in the Report Wizard dialog box to display the next Report Wizard screen.
- Click the box arrow in the text box labeled 1 to display a list of available fields for sorting (Figure 1–80).

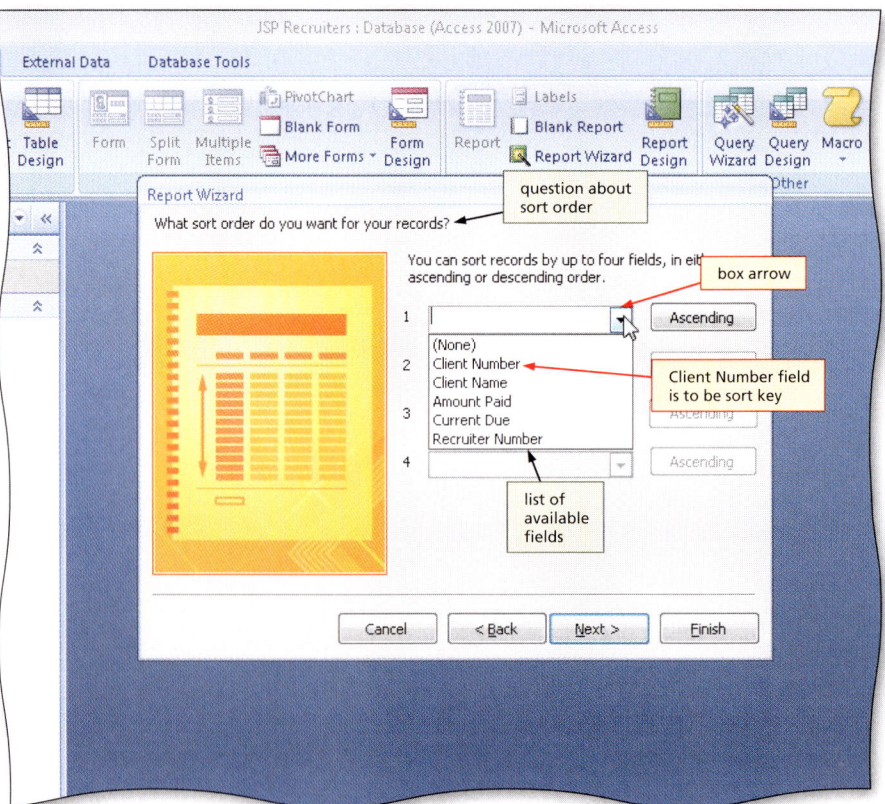

Figure 1–80

5
- Click the Client Number field to select the field as the sort key (Figure 1–81).

  What if I want Descending order?

Click the Ascending button next to the sort key to change Ascending order to Descending. If you decide you want Ascending after all, click the button a second time.

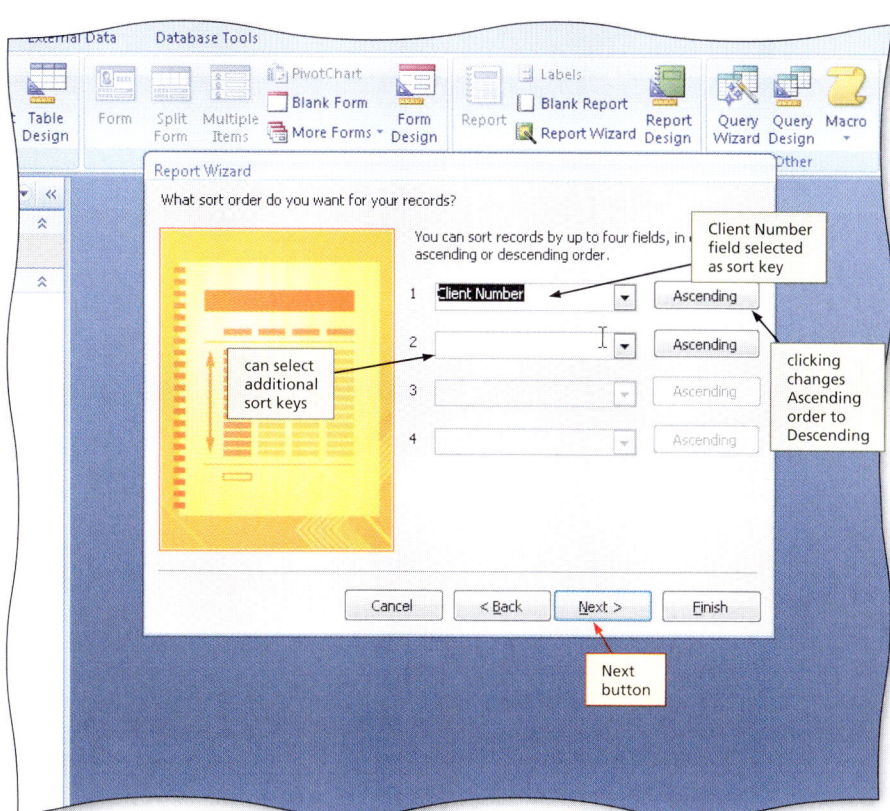

Figure 1–81

6
- Click the Next button to display the next Report Wizard screen (Figure 1–82).

  Experiment

- Click different layouts and orientations and observe the effect on the sample report. When you have finished experimenting, click the Tabular option button for the layout and the Portrait option button for the orientation.

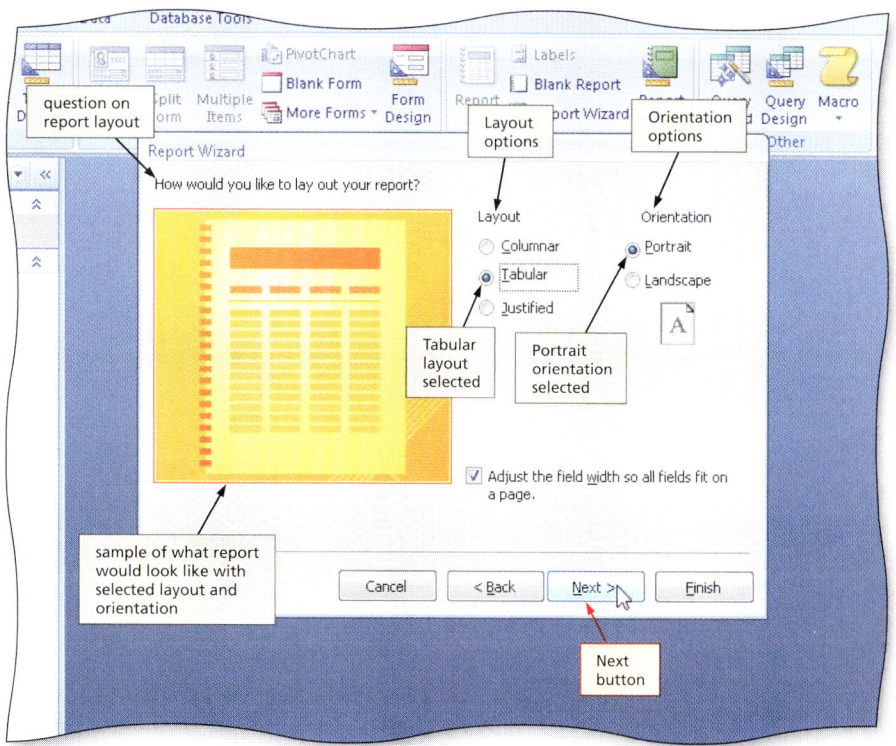

Figure 1–82

- Make sure that Tabular is selected as the Layout. (If it is not, click the Tabular option button to select Tabular layout.)
- Make sure Portrait is selected as the Orientation. (If it is not, click the Portrait option button to select Portrait orientation.)
- Click the Next button to display the next Report Wizard screen (Figure 1–83).

Experiment

- Click different styles and observe the effect on the sample report. When you have finished experimenting, click the Module style.

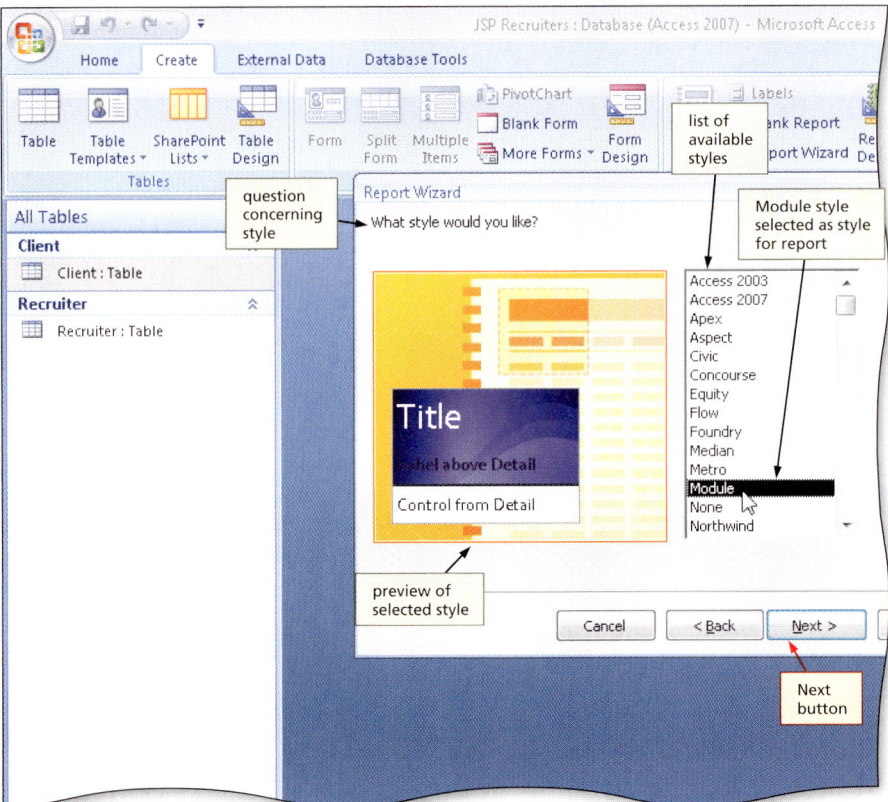

Figure 1–83

- Be sure the Module style is selected. (If it is not, click Module to select the Module style.)
- Click the Next button to display the next Report Wizard screen (Figure 1–84).

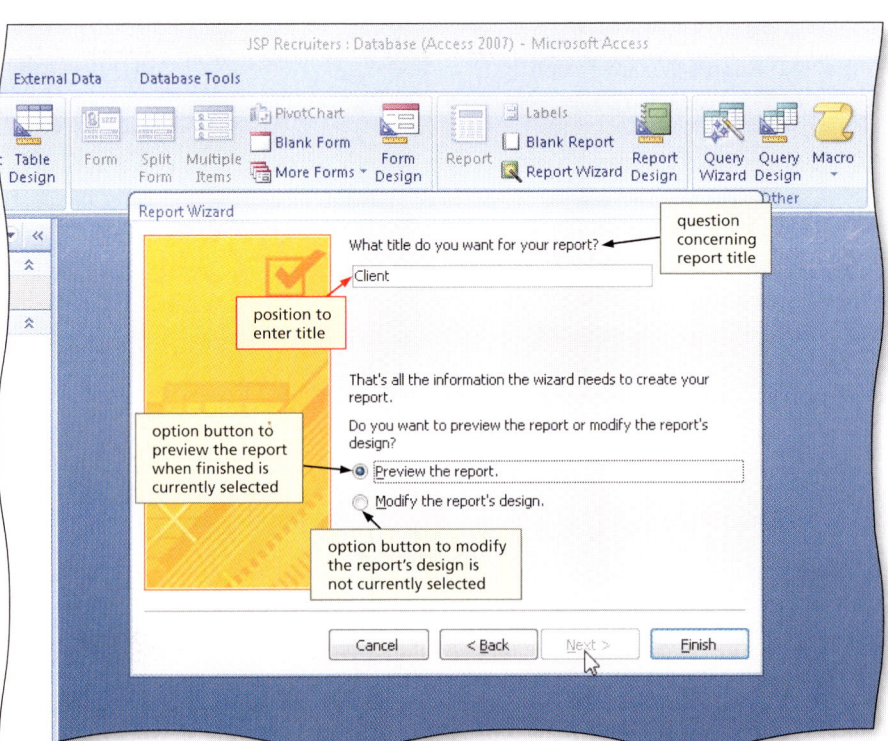

Figure 1–84

9

- Erase the current title, and then type `Client Financial Report` as the new title (Figure 1–85).

Q&A How do I erase the title?

You can highlight the existing title and then press the DELETE key. You can click at the end of the title and repeatedly press the BACKSPACE key. You can click at the beginning of the title and repeatedly press the DELETE key.

Q&A Could I just click after the word, Client, press the Spacebar, and then type Financial Report?

Yes. In general, you can edit the current title to produce the new title using the method with which you are most comfortable.

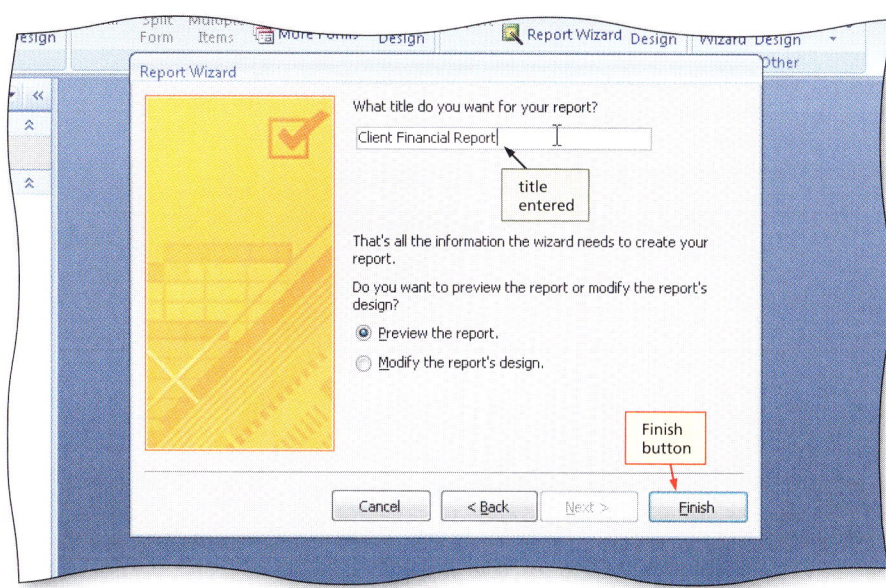

Figure 1–85

- Click the Finish button to produce the report (Figure 1–86).

10

- Click the Close 'Client Financial Report' button to remove the report from the screen.

Q&A Why was it unnecessary for me to save the report?

The Report Wizard saves the report automatically.

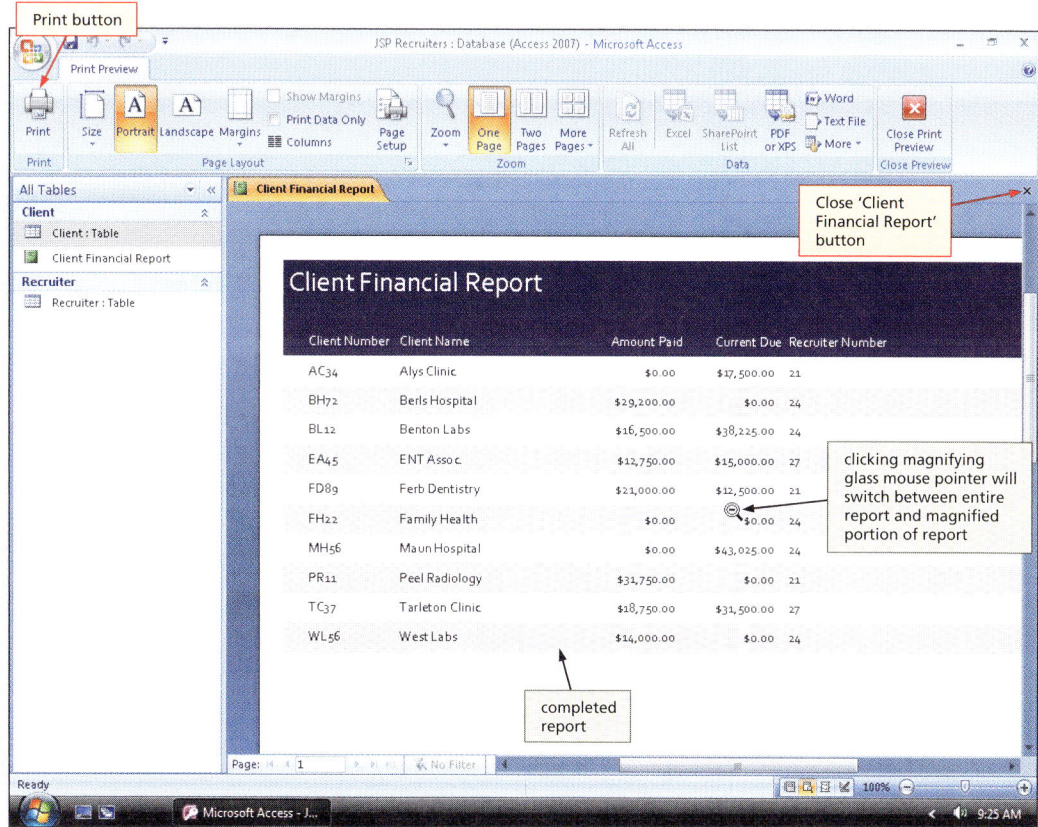

Figure 1–86

BTW

Quick Reference
For a table that lists how to complete the tasks covered in this book using the mouse, Ribbon, shortcut menu, and keyboard, see the Quick Reference Summary at the back of this book, or visit the Access 2007 Quick Reference Web page (scsite.com/dc-off07/qr).

To Print a Report

Once you have created a report, you can print it at any time. The printed layout will reflect the layout you created. The data in the report will always reflect current data. The following step prints the Client Financial Report.

1
- With the Client Financial Report selected in the Navigation Pane, click the Office Button.
- Point to the arrow next to Print on the Office Button menu and then click Quick Print on the Print submenu to print the report.

To Create Additional Reports

The following steps produce the reports shown in Figure 1–76b, Figure 1–76c, and Figure 1–76d on page AC 50.

1 If necessary, click Create on the Ribbon to display the Create tab, and then click the Report Wizard button to display the Report Wizard dialog box.

2 Add the Client Number, Client Name, Street, City, State, and Postal Code fields by clicking each field and then clicking the Add Field button.

3 Click the Next button to move to the screen asking about grouping, and then click the Next button a second time to move to the screen asking about sort order.

4 Click the box arrow in the text box labeled 1, click the Client Number field to select the field as the sort key, and then click the Next button.

5 Make sure that Tabular is selected as the Layout and that Portrait is selected as the Orientation, and then click the Next button.

6 Make sure the Module style is selected, and then click the Next button.

7 Enter `Client Address Report` as the title and click the Finish button to produce the report.

8 Click the Close 'Client Address Report' button to close the Print Preview window.

9 Click the Recruiter table in the Navigation Pane, and then use the techniques shown in Steps 1 through 8 to produce the Recruiter Financial Report. The report is to contain the Recruiter Number, Last Name, First Name, Rate, and Commission fields. It is to be sorted by Recruiter Number. It is to have tabular layout, portrait orientation, and the Module Style. The title is to be Recruiter Financial Report.

10 With the Recruiter table selected in the Navigation Pane, use the techniques shown in Steps 1 through 8 to produce the Recruiter Address Report. The report is to contain the Recruiter Number, Last Name, First Name, Street, City, State, and Postal Code fields. It is to be sorted by Recruiter Number. It is to have tabular layout, landscape orientation, and the Module Style. The title is to be Recruiter Address Report.

11 Click the Close 'Recruiter Address Report' button to close the Print Preview window.

Using a Form to View Data

In Datasheet view, you can view many records at once. If there are many fields, however, only some of the fields in each record might be visible at a time. In **Form view**, where data is displayed in a form on the screen, you usually can see all the fields, but only for one record. To get the advantages from both, many database management systems allow you to easily switch between Datasheet view and Form view while maintaining position within the database. In Access 2007, you can view both a datasheet and a form simultaneously using a split form.

To Create a Split Form

A **split form** combines both a datasheet and a form, thus giving the advantages of both views. The following steps create a split form.

1

- Select the Client table in the Navigation Pane.
- If necessary, click Create on the Ribbon to display the Create tab (Figure 1–87).

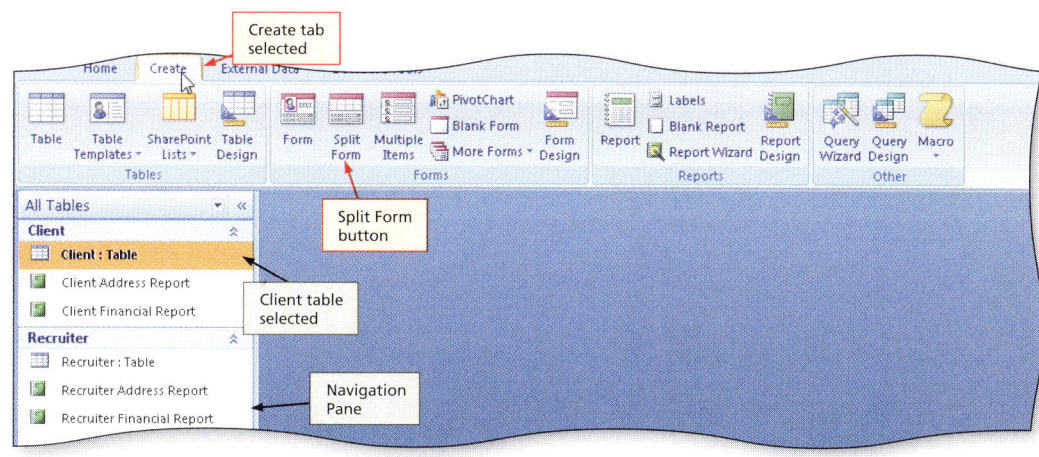

Figure 1–87

2

- Click the Split Form button to create a split form. If a Field List appears, click its Close button to remove the Field List from the screen (Figure 1–88).

Q&A Is the form automatically saved the way the report was created when I used the Report Wizard?

No. You must take specific action if you wish to save the form.

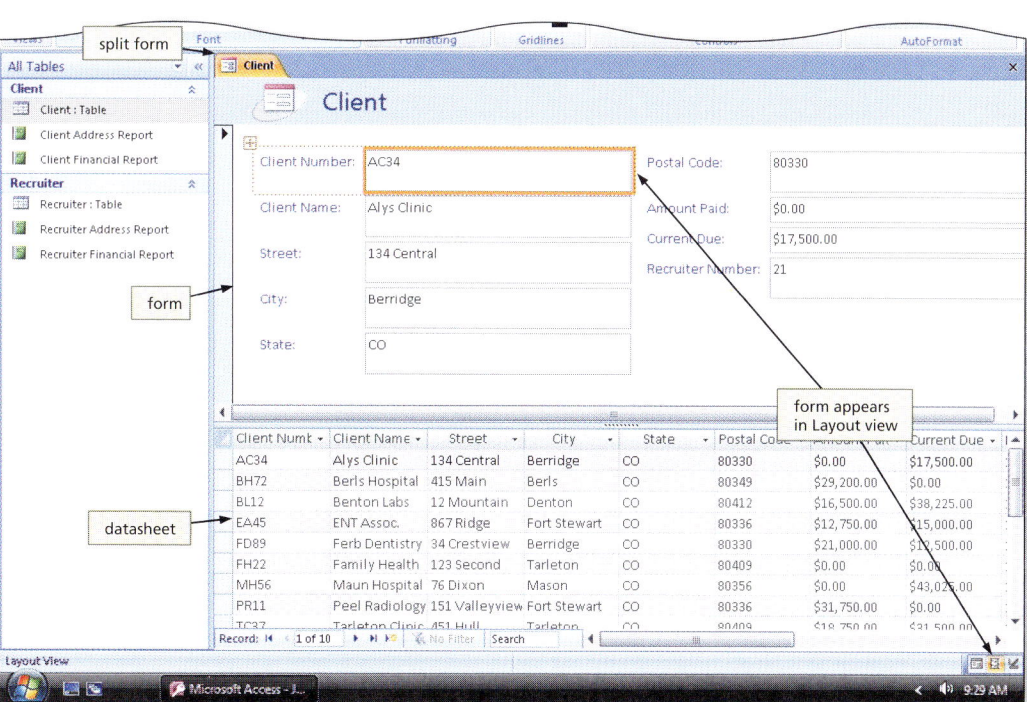

Figure 1–88

- Click the Save button to display the Save As dialog box (Figure 1–89).

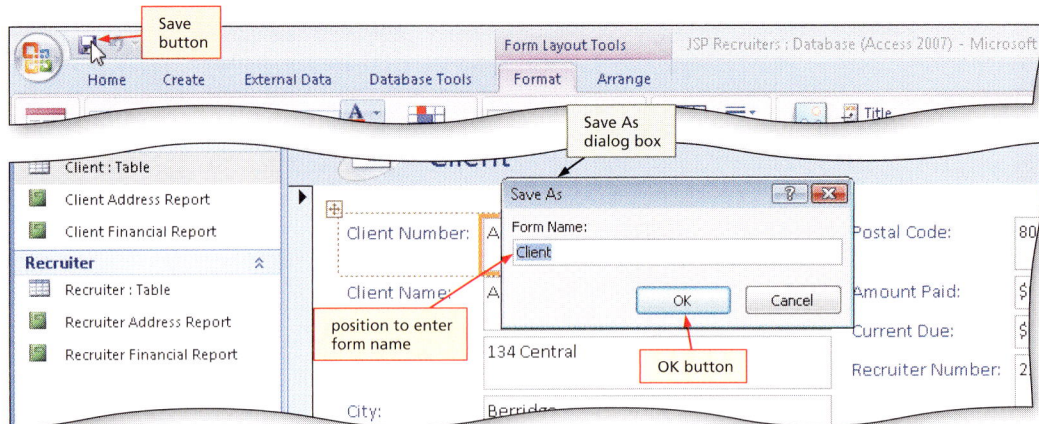

Figure 1–89

- Type Client Form as the form name, and then click the OK button to save the form.

- If the form appears in Layout view, click the Form View button on the Access status bar to display the form in Form view (Figure 1–90).

Q&A How can I recognize Layout view?

There are three ways. The left end of the Status bar will contain the words Layout View. There will be shading around the outside of the selected field in the form. The Layout View button will be selected in the right end of the Status bar.

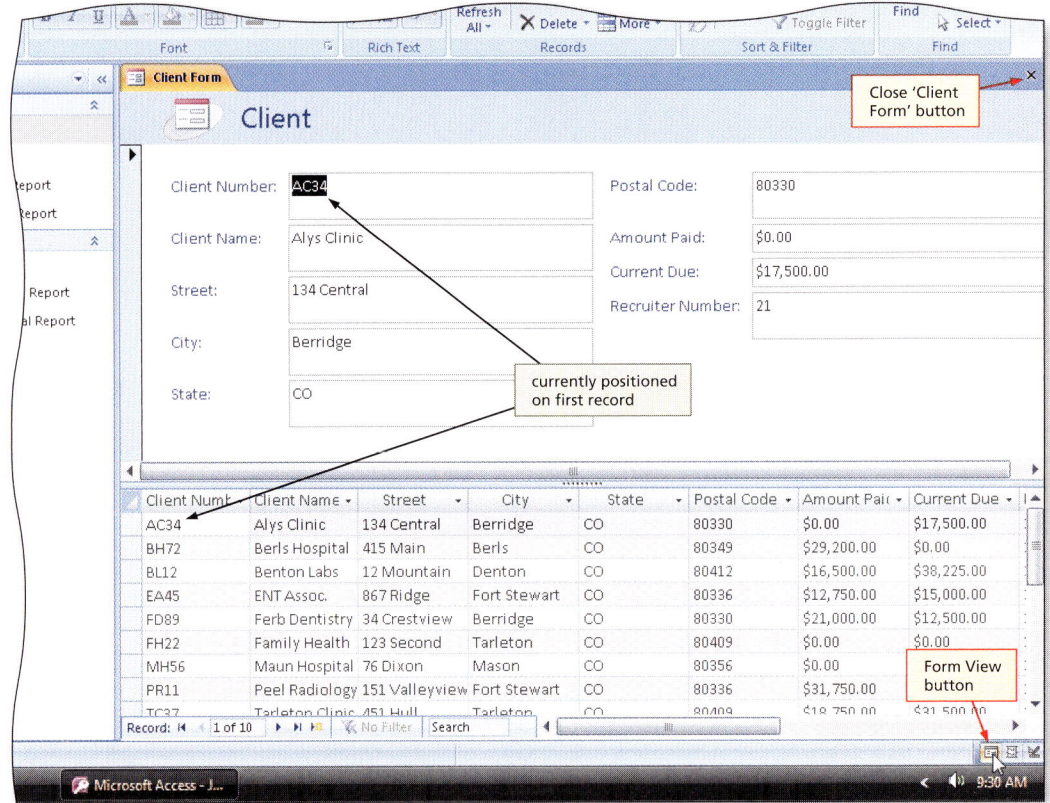

Figure 1–90

To Use a Split Form

After you have saved a form, you can use it at any time by right-clicking the form in the Navigation Pane and then clicking Open in the shortcut menu. If you plan to use the form to enter data, you must ensure you are viewing the form in Form view.

- Click the Next Record button four times to move to record 5 (Figure 1–91).

Q&A I inadvertently closed the form at the end of the previous steps. What should I do?

Right-click the form in the Navigation Pane and then click Open on the shortcut menu.

Q&A Do I have to take any special action for the form to be positioned on the same record as the datasheet?

No. The advantage to the split form is that changing the position on either the datasheet or the form automatically changes the position on the other.

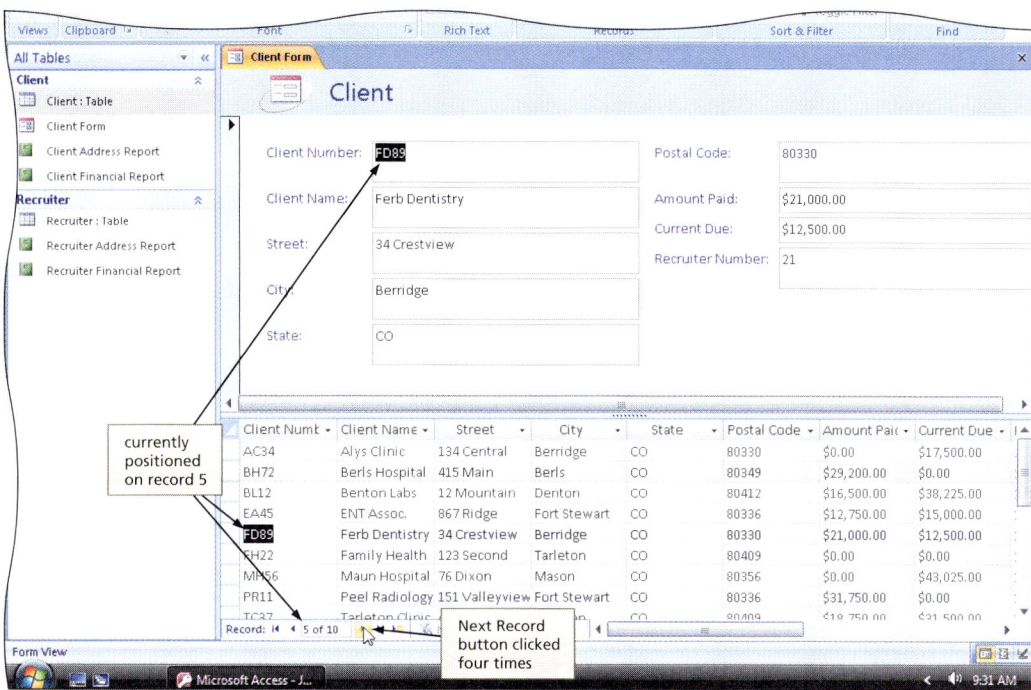

Figure 1–91

- Click the Postal Code field on the second record in the datasheet to select the second record in both the datasheet and the form (Figure 1–92).

Experiment

- Click several fields in various records in the datasheet and observe the effect on the form.

- Click the Close 'Client Form' button to remove the form from the screen.

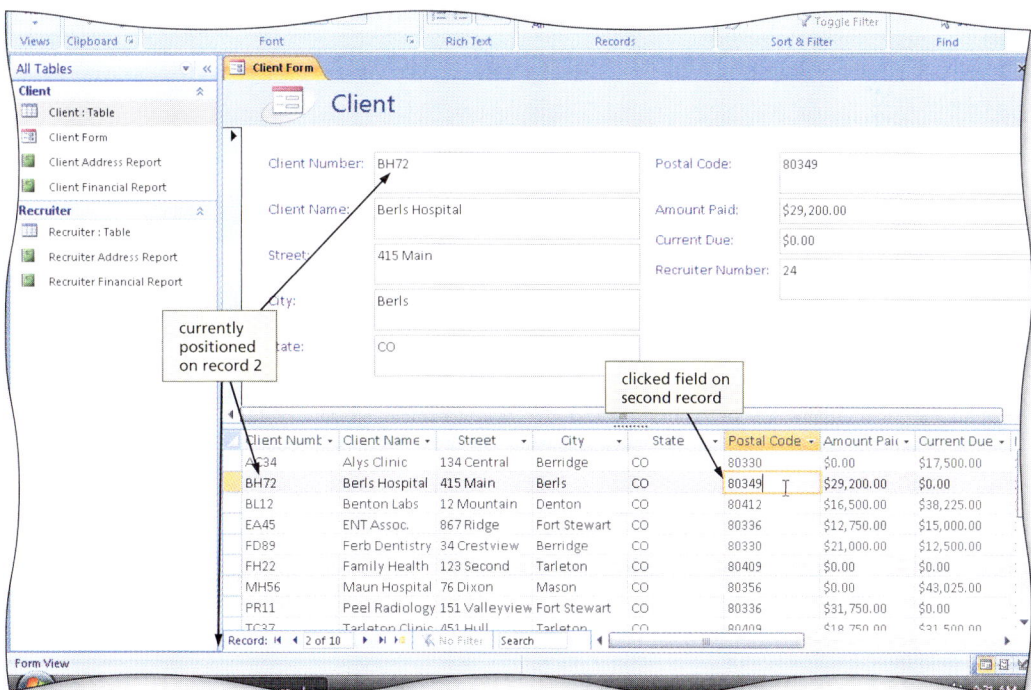

Figure 1–92

Changing Database Properties

Access helps you organize and identify your databases by using **database properties,** which are the details about a file. Database properties, also known as **metadata,** can include such information as the project author, title, or subject. **Keywords** are words or phrases that further describe the database. For example, a class name or database topic can describe the file's purpose or content.

Five different types of document properties exist, but the more common ones used in this book are standard and automatically updated properties. **Standard properties** are associated with all Microsoft Office documents and include author, title, and subject. **Automatically updated properties** include file system properties, such as the date you create or change a file, and statistics, such as the file size.

To Change Database Properties

The Database Properties dialog box contains areas where you can view and enter document properties. You can view and change information in this dialog box at any time while you are working on your database. It is a good idea to add your name and class name as database properties. The following steps use the Properties dialog box to change database properties.

- Click the Office Button to display the Office Button menu.
- Point to Manage on the Office Button menu to display the Manage submenu (Figure 1–93).

Q&A What other types of actions besides changing properties can you take to prepare a database for distribution?

The Manage submenu provides commands to compact and repair a database as well as to back up a database.

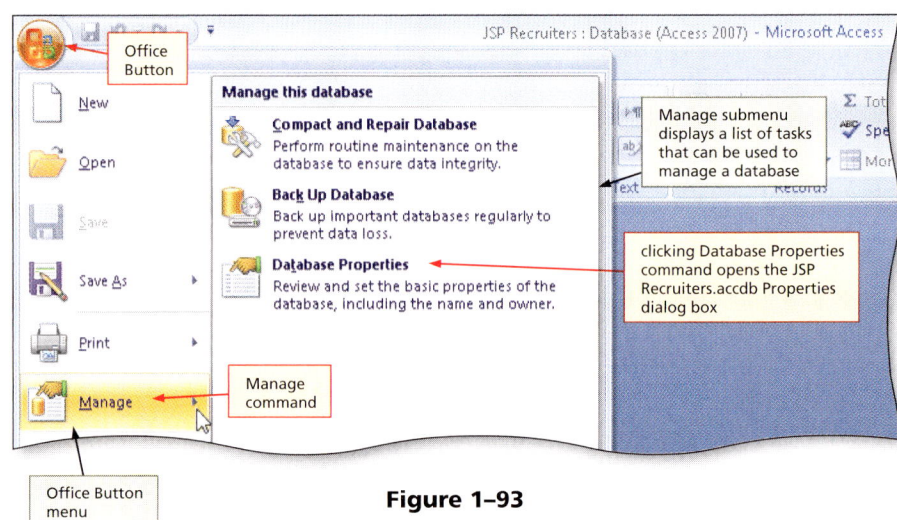

Figure 1–93

- Click Database Properties on the Manage submenu to display the JSP Recruiters.accdb Properties dialog box (Figure 1–94).

Q&A Why are some of the document properties in my Properties dialog box already filled in?

The person who installed Microsoft Office 2007 on your computer or network may have set or customized the properties.

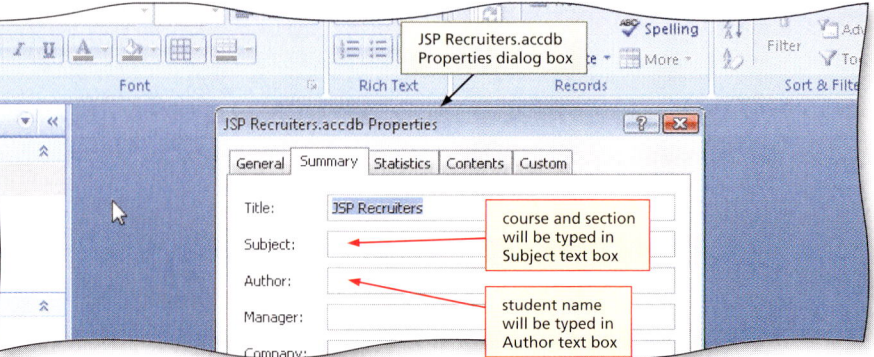

Figure 1–94

3

- If necessary, click the Summary tab.
- Click the Author text box and then type your name as the Author property. If a name already is displayed in the Author text box, delete it before typing your name.
- Click the Subject text box, if necessary delete any existing text, and then type your course and section as the Subject property.
- Click the Keywords text box, if necessary delete any existing text, and then type Healthcare, Recruiter as the Keywords property (Figure 1–95).

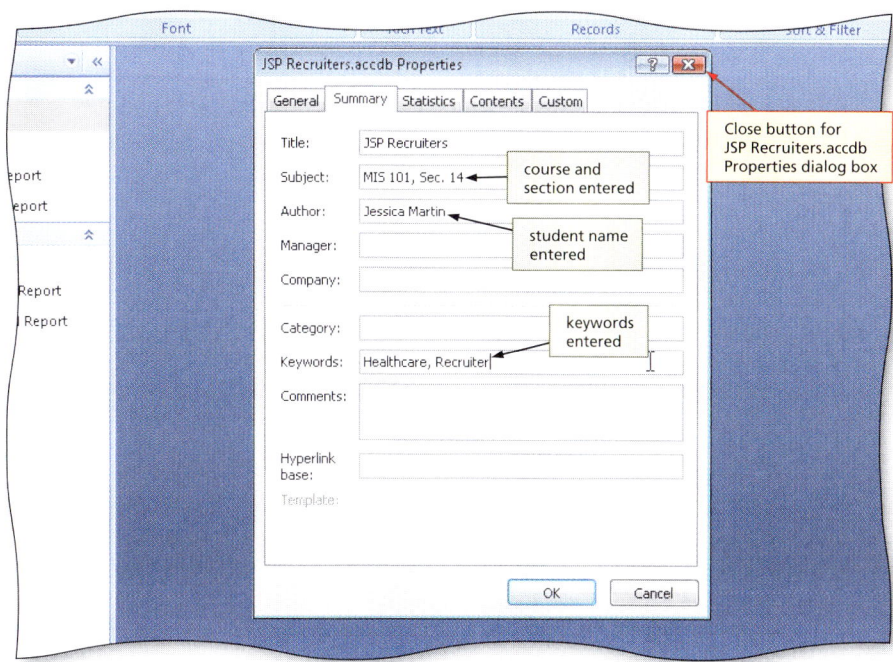

Figure 1–95

Q&A What types of properties does Access collect automatically?

Access records such details as when the database was created, when it was last modified, total editing time, and the various objects contained in the database.

4

- Click the OK button to save your changes and remove the JSP Recruiters.accdb Properties dialog box from the screen.

Access Help

At any time while using Access, you can find answers to questions and display information about various topics through **Access Help**. Used properly, this form of assistance can increase your productivity and reduce your frustrations by minimizing the time you spend learning how to use Access.

This section introduces you to Access Help. Additional information about using Access Help is available in Appendix B.

To Search for Access Help

Using Access Help, you can search for information based on phrases, such as create a form or change a data type, or key terms, such as copy, save, or format. Access Help responds with a list of search results displayed as links to a variety of resources. The following steps, which use Access Help to search for information about creating a form, assume you are connected to the Internet.

- Click the Microsoft Office Access Help button near the upper-right corner of the Access window to open the Access Help window.
- Type create a form in the 'Type words to search for' text box at the top of the Access Help window (Figure 1–96).

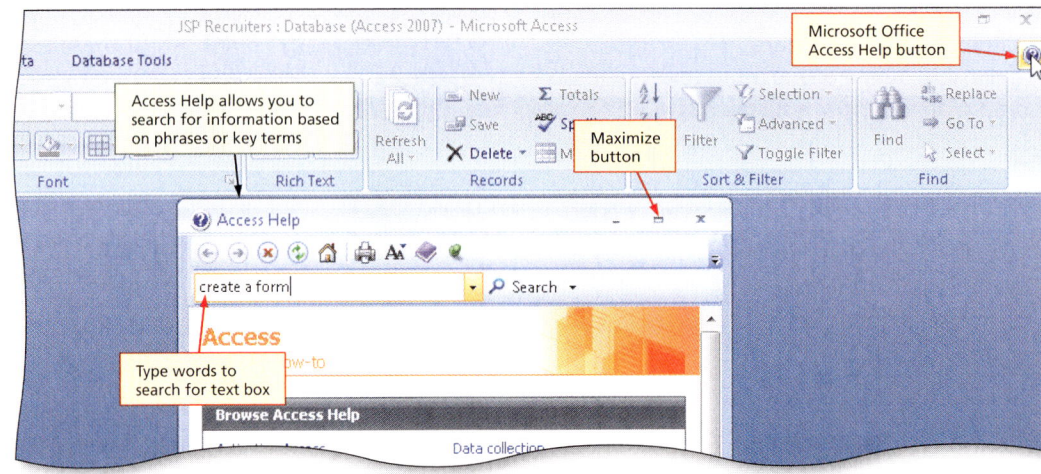

Figure 1–96

- Press the ENTER key to display the search results.
- Click the Maximize button on the Access Help window title bar to maximize the Help window unless it is already maximized (Figure 1–97).

Q&A Where is the Access window with the JSP Recruiters database?

Access is open in the background, but the Access Help window sits on top of the Microsoft Access window. When the Access Help window is closed, the database will reappear.

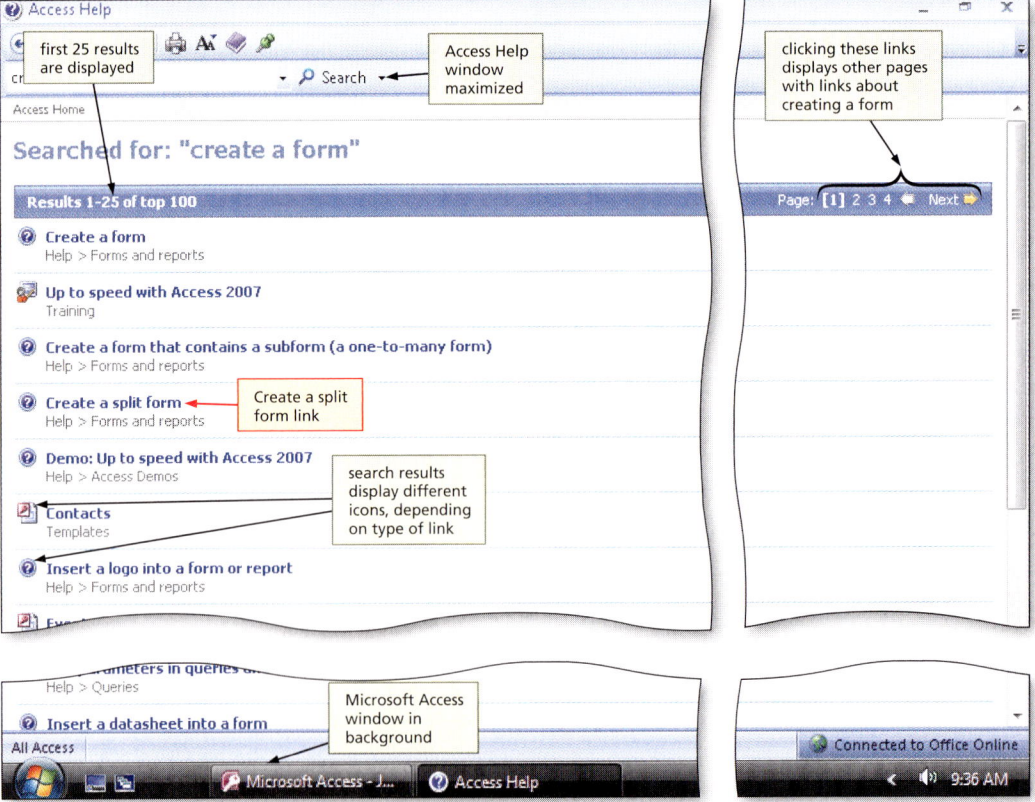

Figure 1–97

3

- Click the 'Create a split form' link to display information regarding creating a split form (Figure 1–98).

 What is the purpose of the buttons at the top of the Access Help window?

Use the buttons in the upper-left corner of the Access Help window to navigate through the Help system, change the display, show the Access Help table of contents, and print the contents of the window.

4

- Click the Close button on the Access Help window title bar to close the Access Help window and make the database active.

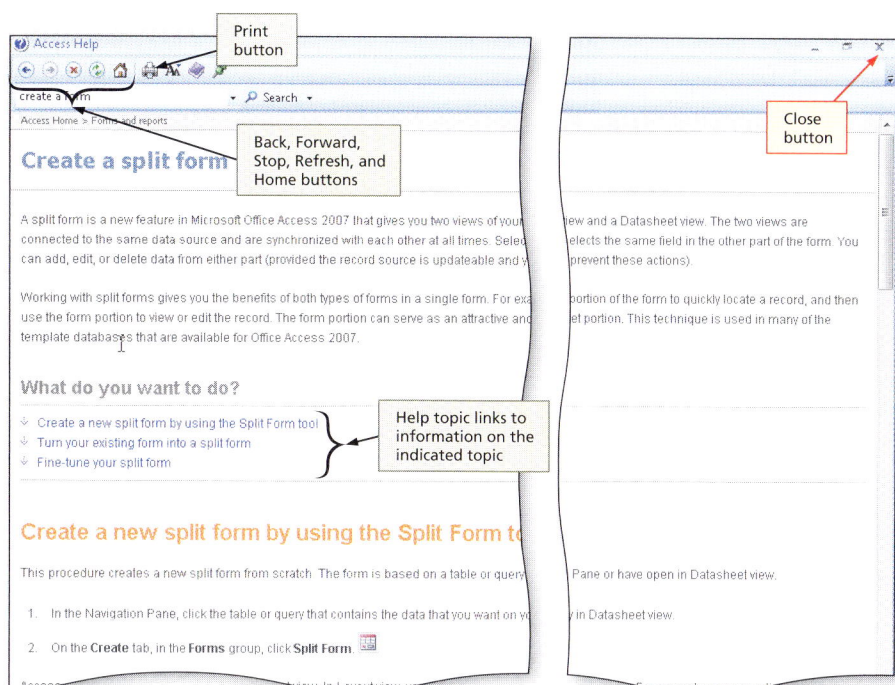

Figure 1–98

Other Ways
1. Press F1

To Quit Access

You saved all your changes and are ready to quit Access. The following step quits Access.

1 Click the Close button on the right side of the Access title bar to quit Access.

Chapter Summary

In this chapter you have learned to design a database, create an Access database, create tables and add records to them, print the contents of tables, create reports, and create forms. The items listed below include all the new Access skills you have learned in this chapter.

1. Start Access (AC 12)
2. Create a Database Using a Template (AC 13)
3. Create a Database (AC 14)
4. Define the Fields in a Table (AC 24)
5. Create a Table Using a Template (AC 26)
6. Save a Table (AC 27)
7. Change the Primary Key (AC 28)
8. Add Records to a Table (AC 30)
9. Close a Table (AC 35)
10. Quit Access (AC 36)
11. Start Access (AC 36)
12. Open a Database from Access (AC 37)
13. Add Additional Records to a Table (AC 38)
14. Preview and Print the Contents of a Table (AC 41)
15. Create an Additional Table (AC 44)
16. Modify the Primary Key and Field Properties (AC 46)
17. Add Records to an Additional Table (AC 49)
18. Create a Report (AC 51)
19. Print a Report (AC 56)

20. Create Additional Reports (AC 56)
21. Create a Split Form (AC 57)
22. Use a Split Form (AC 58)
23. Change Database Properties (AC 60)
24. Search for Access Help (AC 62)
25. Quit Access (AC 63)

 If you have a SAM user profile, you may have access to hands-on instruction, practice, and assessment. Log in to your SAM account (http://sam2007.course.com) to launch any assigned training activities or exams that relate to the skills covered in this chapter.

Learn It Online

Test your knowledge of chapter content and key terms.

Instructions: To complete the Learn It Online exercises, start your browser, click the Address bar, and then enter the Web address scsite.com/dc-off07/ac2007/learn. When the Access 2007 Learn It Online page is displayed, click the link for the exercise you want to complete and then read the instructions.

Chapter Reinforcement TF, MC, and SA
A series of true/false, multiple choice, and short answer questions that test your knowledge of the chapter content.

Flash Cards
An interactive learning environment where you identify chapter key terms associated with displayed definitions.

Practice Test
A series of multiple choice questions that test your knowledge of chapter content and key terms.

Who Wants To Be a Computer Genius?
An interactive game that challenges your knowledge of chapter content in the style of a television quiz show.

Wheel of Terms
An interactive game that challenges your knowledge of chapter key terms in the style of the television show *Wheel of Fortune*.

Crossword Puzzle Challenge
A crossword puzzle that challenges your knowledge of key terms presented in the chapter.

Apply Your Knowledge

Reinforce the skills and apply the concepts you learned in this chapter.

Changing Data, Creating a Form, and Creating a Report
Instructions: Start Access. Open the The Bike Delivers database. See the inside back cover of this book for instructions for downloading the Data Files for Students, or contact your instructor for information on accessing the files required in this book.

The Bike Delivers uses motorbikes to provide courier services for local businesses. The Bike Delivers has a database that keeps track of its couriers and customers. The database has two tables. The Customer table (Figure 1–99a) contains data on the customers who use the services of The Bike Delivers. The Courier table (Figure 1–99b) contains data on the individuals employed by The Bike Delivers.

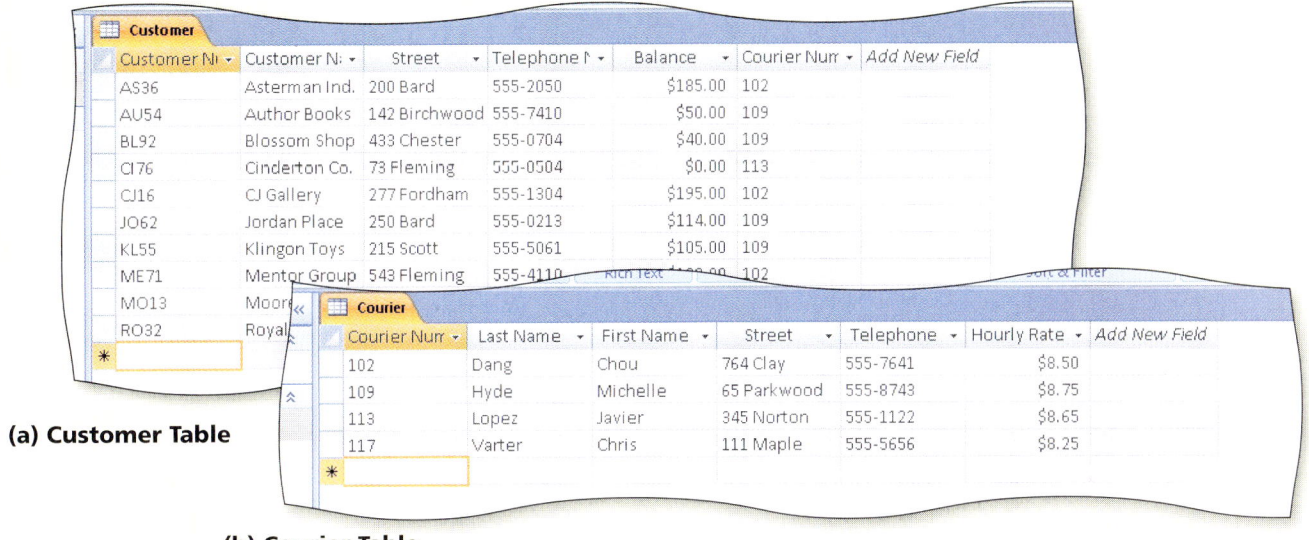

(a) Customer Table

(b) Courier Table

Figure 1–99

Perform the following tasks:
1. Open the Customer table and change the Courier Number for customer KL55 to 113.
2. Close the Customer table.
3. Create a split form for the Courier table. Use the name Courier for the form.
4. Open the form you created and change the street address for Michelle Hyde to 65 Park.
5. Close the Courier form.
6. Create the report shown in Figure 1–100 for the Customer table. The report uses the Module style.
7. Change the database properties, as specified by your instructor. Submit the revised database in the format specified by your instructor.

Figure 1–100

Extend Your Knowledge

Extend the skills you learned in this chapter and experiment with new skills. You may need to use Help to complete the assignment.

Changing Formats and Creating Grouped and Sorted Reports
Instructions: Start Access. Open the Camden Scott College database. See the inside back cover of this book for instructions for downloading the Data Files for Students, or contact your instructor for information on accessing the files required in this book.

Continued >

Extend Your Knowledge *continued*

Camden Scott College is a small liberal arts college. The Human Resources Director has created an Access database in which to store information about candidates applying for faculty positions. You will make some changes to the Candidate table so that it looks like that shown in Figure 1–101 and create a report that both groups records and sorts them in ascending order.

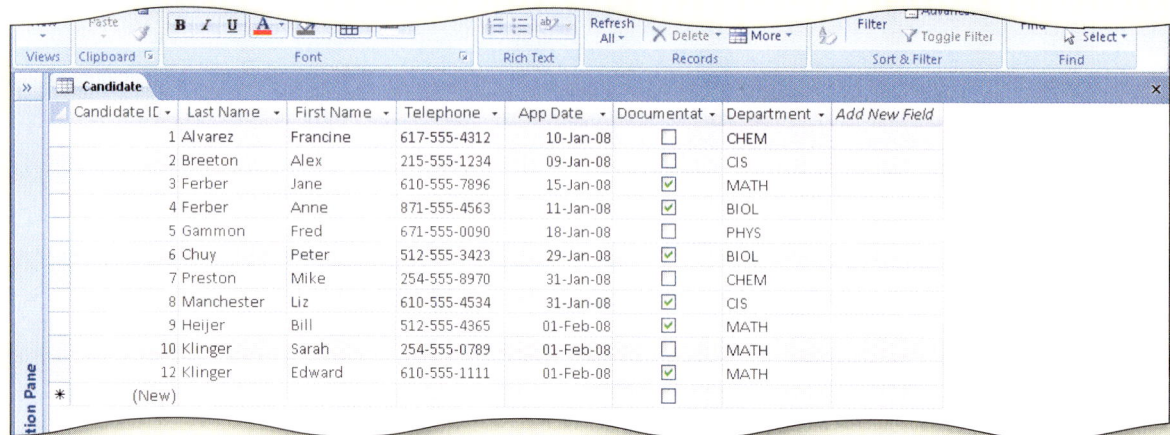

Figure 1–101

Perform the following tasks:

1. Open the Candidate table in Datasheet view and change the column heading for the ID field to Candidate ID.
2. Save the change and open the table in Design view.
3. Select a format for the App Date field that will produce the look shown in Figure 1–101.
4. Change the data type for the Documentation field so that it will match that shown in Figure 1–101.
5. Save the changes.
6. Open the table in Datasheet view. The Human Resources department has received an application from Edward Klinger. Edward applied for the same position as Sarah Klinger on the same date as Sarah. Edward's phone number is 610-555-1111. He did submit all his documentation with his application. Add this record.
7. Add the Quick Print button to the Quick Access Toolbar.
8. Create a report for the Candidate table that lists the Department Code, App Date, Last Name, and First Name. Group the report by Department Code. Sort the report by App Date, Last Name, and then First Name. Choose your own report style and use Candidate by Department as the title of the report.
9. Remove the Quick Print button from the Quick Access Toolbar.
10. Change the database properties, as specified by your instructor. Submit the revised database in the format specified by your instructor.

Make It Right

Analyze a database and correct all errors and/or improve the design.

Correcting Errors in the Table Structure

Instructions: Start Access. Open the SciFi Scene database. See the inside back cover of this book for instructions for downloading the Data Files for Students, or contact your instructor for information on accessing the files required in this book.

SciFi Scene is a database containing information on science fiction books. The Book table shown in Figure 1–102 contains a number of errors in the table structure. You are to correct these errors before any additional records can be added to the table. Book Code, not ID, is the primary key for the Book table. The column heading Titel is misspelled. The On Hand field represents the number of books on hand. The field will be used in arithmetic operations. Only whole numbers should be stored in the field. The Price field represents the price of the book. The current data type does not reflect this information.

Change the database properties, as specified by your instructor. Submit the revised database in the format specified by your instructor.

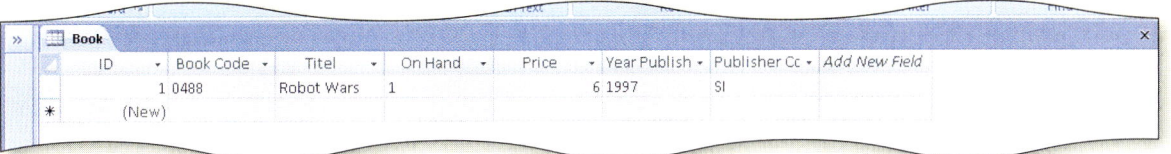

Figure 1–102

In the Lab

Design, create, modify, and/or use a database using the guidelines, concepts, and skills presented in this chapter. Labs are listed in order of increasing difficulty.

Lab 1: Creating the JMS TechWizards Database

Problem: JMS TechWizards is a local company that provides technical services to several small businesses in the area. The company currently keeps its records in two Excel workbooks. One Excel workbook (Figure 1–103a) contains information on the clients that JMS TechWizards serves. The other Excel workbook (Figure 1–103b) contains information on the technicians that JMS employs. JMS would like to store this data in a database and has asked for your help.

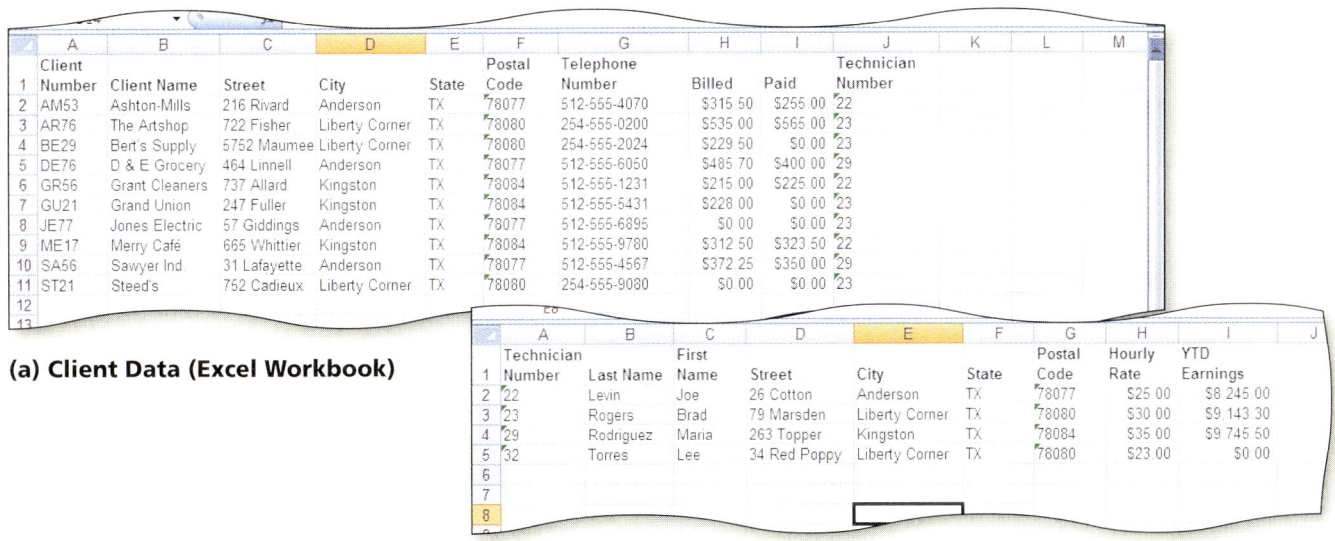

(a) Client Data (Excel Workbook)

(b) Technician Data (Excel Workbook)

Figure 1–103

Continued >

In the Lab *continued*

Instructions: Perform the following tasks:
1. Create a new database in which to store all the objects related to the technical services data. Call the database JMS TechWizards.
2. Create a table in which to store the data related to clients. Use the name Client for the table. The fields for the Client table are: Client Number, Client Name, Street, City, State, Postal Code, Telephone Number, Billed, Paid, and Technician Number. Client Number is the primary key. The Billed and Paid fields are currency data type.
3. Create a table in which to store the data related to technicians. Use the name Technician for the table. The fields for the Technician table are: Technician Number, Last Name, First Name, Street, City, State, Postal Code, Hourly Rate, and YTD Earnings. The primary key for the Technician table is Technician Number. Hourly rate and YTD Earnings are currency data type.
4. Add the data from the Client workbook in Figure 1–103a to the Client table.
5. Add the data from the Technician workbook in Figure 1–103b to the Technician table.
6. Create and save the reports shown in Figure 1–104a for the Client table and Figure 1–104b for the Technician table.
7. Change the database properties, as specified by your instructor. Submit the revised database in the format specified by your instructor.

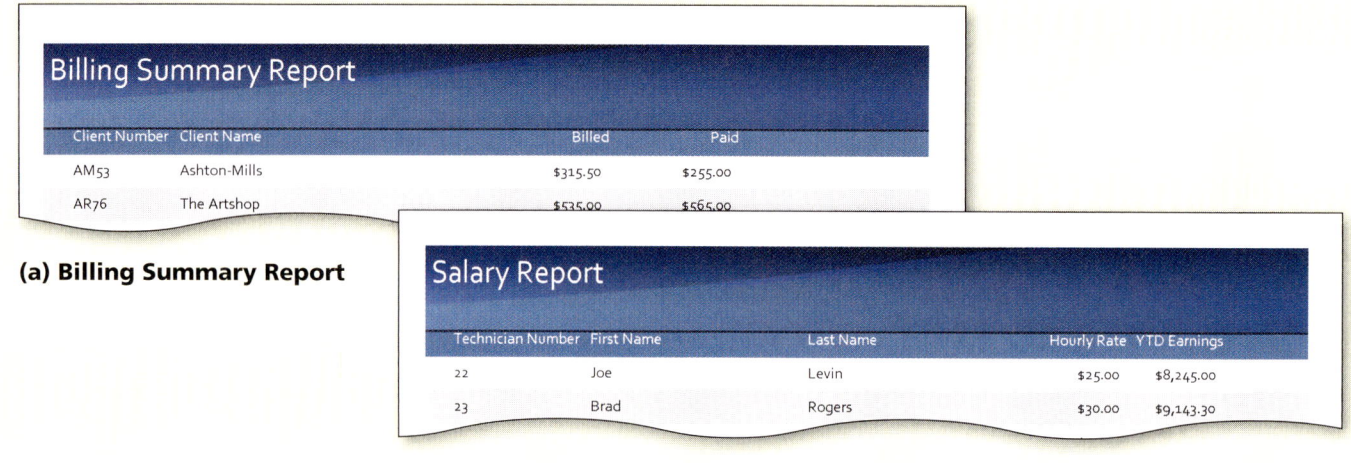

(a) Billing Summary Report

(b) Salary Report

Figure 1–104

In the Lab

Lab 2: Creating the Hockey Fan Zone Database

Problem: Your town has a minor league hockey team. The team store sells a variety of items with the team logo. The store purchases the items from suppliers that deal in specialty items for sports teams. Currently, the information about the items and suppliers is stored in the Excel workbook shown in Figure 1–105. You work part-time at the store, and your boss has asked you to create a database that will store the item and supplier information. You have already determined that you need two tables: an Item table and a Supplier table in which to store the information.

Instructions: Perform the following tasks:
1. Design a new database in which to store all the objects related to the items for sale. Call the database Hockey Fan Zone.

2. Use the information shown in Figure 1–105 to determine the primary keys and determine additional fields. Then, determine the relationships among tables and the data types.
3. Create the Item table using the information shown in Figure 1–105.
4. Create the Supplier table using the information shown in Figure 1–105.
5. Add the appropriate data to the Item table.
6. Add the appropriate data to the Supplier table.
7. Create a split form for the Item table. Use the name Item for the form.
8. Create the report shown in Figure 1–106 for the Item table.
9. Change the database properties, as specified by your instructor. Submit the database in the format specified by your instructor.

Item Number	Description	On Hand	Cost	Selling Price	Supplier Code	Supplier Name	Telephone Number
3663	Ball Cap	30	$11.15	$18.95	LG	Logo Goods	517-555-3853
3683	Bumper Sticker	50	$0.95	$1.50	MN	Mary's Novelties	317-555-4747
4563	Earrings	10	$4.50	$7.00	LG	Logo Goods	517-555-3853
4593	Foam Finger	25	$2.95	$5.00	LG	Logo Goods	517-555-3853
5923	Jersey	12	$21.45	$24.75	AC	Ace Clothes	616-555-9228
6189	Koozies	35	$2.00	$4.00	MN	Mary's Novelties	317-555-4747
6343	Note Cube	7	$5.75	$8.00	MN	Mary's Novelties	317-555-4747
7810	Tee Shirt	32	$9.50	$14.95	AC	Ace Clothes	616-555-9228
7930	Visor	9	$11.95	$17.00	LG	Logo Goods	517-555-3853

Figure 1–105

Inventory Status Report

Item Number	Description	On Hand	Cost
3663	Ball Cap	30	$11.15
3683	Bumper Sticker	50	$0.95
4563	Earrings	10	$4.50
4593	Foam Finger	25	$2.95
5923	Jersey	12	$21.45
6189	Koozies	35	$2.00
6343	Note Cube	7	$5.75
7810	Tee Shirt	32	$9.50
7930	Visor	9	$11.95

Figure 1–106

In the Lab

Lab 3: Creating the Ada Beauty Supply Database

Problem: A distribution company supplies local beauty salons with items needed in the beauty industry. The distributor employs sales representatives who receive a base salary as well as a commission on sales. Currently, the distributor keeps data on customers and sales reps in two Word documents and two Excel workbooks.

Instructions: Using the data shown in Figure 1–107 on the next page, design the Ada Beauty Supply database. Use the database design guidelines in this chapter to help you in the design process.

Continued >

In the Lab *continued*

Customer Number	Customer Name	Street	Telephone
AM23	Amy's Salon	223 Johnson	555-2150
BB34	Bob the Barber	1939 Jackson	555-1939
BL15	Blondie's	3294 Devon	555-7510
CM09	Cut Mane	3140 Halsted	555-0604
CS12	Curl n Style	1632 Clark	555-0804
EG07	Elegante	1805 Boardway	555-1404
JS34	Just Cuts	2200 Lawrence	555-0313
LB20	Le Beauty	13 Devon	555-5161
NC25	Nancy's Place	1027 Wells	555-4210
RD03	Rose's Day Spa	787 Monroe	555-7657
TT21	Tan and Tone	1939 Congress	555-6554

(a) Customer Address Information (Word table)

	A	B	C	D	E
1	Customer Number	Customer Name	Balance	Amount Paid	Sales Rep Num
2	AM23	Amy's Salon	$195.00	$1,695.00	44
3	BB34	Bob the Barber	$150.00	$0.00	51
4	BL15	Blondie's	$555.00	$1,350.00	49
5	CM09	Cut Mane	$295.00	$1,080.00	51
6	CS12	Curl n Style	$145.00	$710.00	49
7	EG07	Elegante	$0.00	$1,700.00	44
8	JS34	Just Cuts	$360.00	$700.00	49
9	LB20	Le Beauty	$200.00	$1,250.00	51
10	NC25	Nancy's Place	$240.00	$550.00	44
11	RD03	Rose's Day Spa	$0.00	$975.00	51
12	TT21	Tan and Tone	$160.00	$725.00	44

(c) Customer Financial Information (Excel Workbook)

Sales Rep Number	Last Name	First Name	Street	City	State	Postal Code
44	Jones	Pat	43 Third	Lawncrest	WA	98084
49	Gupta	Pinn	678 Hillcrest	Manton	WA	98085
51	Ortiz	Gabe	982 Victoria	Lawncrest	WA	98084
55	Sinson	Terry	45 Elm	Manton	WA	98084

(b) Sales Rep Address Information (Word table)

	A	B	C	D	E	F
1	Sales Rep Number	Last Name	First Name	Salary	Comm Rate	Commission
2	44	Jones	Pat	$ 23,000.00	0.05	$613.50
3	49	Gupta	Pinn	$ 24,000.00	0.06	$616.60
4	51	Ortiz	Gabe	$ 22,500.00	0.05	$492.75
5	55	Sinson	Terry	$ 20,000.00	0.05	$0.00

(d) Sales Rep Financial Information (Excel Workbook)

Figure 1–107

When you have completed the database design, create the database, create the tables, and add the data to the appropriate tables. Be sure to determine the correct data types.

Finally, prepare the Customer Status Report shown in Figure 1–108a and the Sales Rep Salary Report shown in Figure 1–108b. Change the database properties, as specified by your instructor. Submit the database in the format specified by your instructor.

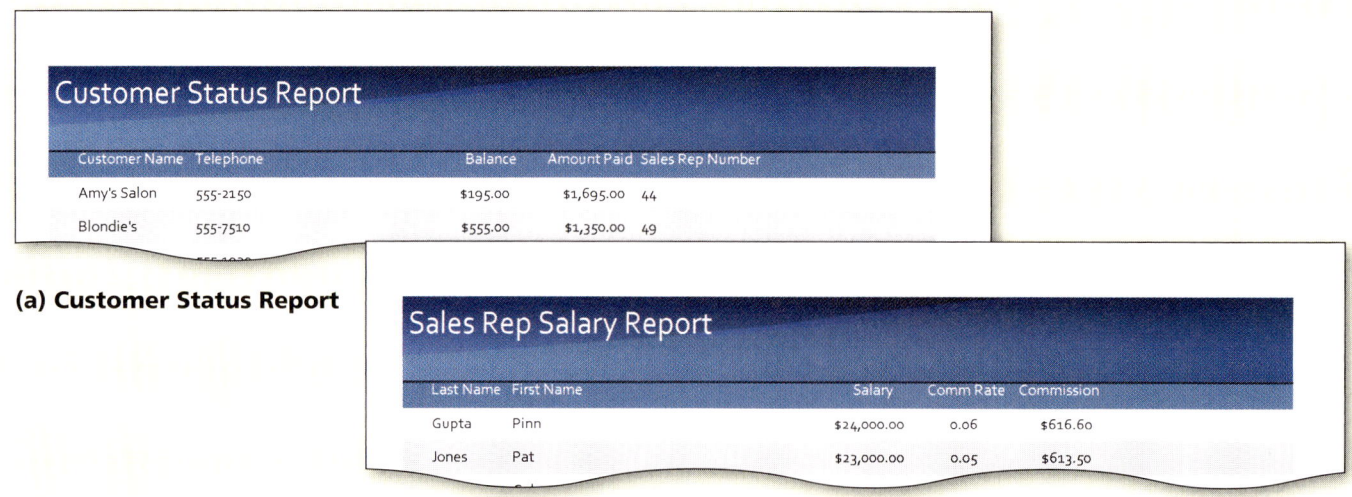

(a) Customer Status Report

(b) Sales Rep Salary Report

Figure 1–108

Cases and Places

Apply your creative thinking and problem solving skills to design and implement a solution.

• Easier   •• More Difficult

• 1: Design and Create an E-Commerce Database

Students often have very little money to furnish dorm rooms and apartments. You and two of your friends have decided to use the skills you learned in your e-commerce class to create a Web site specifically for college students to buy and sell used household furnishings.

Design and create a database to store the data that you need to manage this new business. Then create the necessary tables and enter the data from the Case 1-1 Second-Hand Goods document. See the inside back cover of this book for instructions for downloading the Data Files for Students, or contact your instructor for information on accessing the files required in this book. Submit your assignment in the format specified by your instructor.

• 2: Design and Create a Rental Database

You are a part-time employee of BeachCondo Rentals. BeachCondo Rentals provides a rental service for condo owners who want to rent their units. The company rents units by the week. Currently, the company keeps information about its rentals in an Excel workbook.

Design and create a database to store the rental data. Then create the necessary tables and enter the data from the Case 1-2 BeachCondo Rentals workbook. See the inside back cover of this book for instructions for downloading the Data Files for Students, or contact your instructor for information on accessing the files required in this book. Create an Available Rentals Report that lists the unit number, weekly rate, and owner number. Submit your assignment in the format specified by your instructor.

•• 3: Design and Create a Restaurant Database

Your school is sponsoring a conference that will draw participants from a wide geographical area. The conference director has asked for your help in preparing a database of restaurants that might be of interest to the participants. At a minimum, she needs to know the following: the type of restaurant (vegetarian, fast-food, fine dining, and so on), street address, telephone number, and opening and closing times and days. Because most of the participants will stay on campus, she also would like to know the approximate distance from campus. Additionally, she would like to know about any unique or special features the restaurants may have.

Design and create a database to meet the conference director's needs. Create the necessary tables, determine the necessary fields, enter some sample data, and prepare a sample report to show the director. Submit your assignment in the format specified by your instructor.

•• 4: Design and Create a Database to Help You Find a Job

Make It Personal

Conducting a job search requires careful preparation. In addition to preparing a resume and cover letter, you will need to research the companies for which you are interested in working and contact these companies to let them know of your interest and qualifications.

Microsoft Access includes a Contacts table template that can create a table that will help you keep track of your job contacts. Create a database to keep track of the companies that are of interest to you. Submit your assignment in the format specified by your instructor.

Continued >

Cases and Places *continued*

•• 5: Design a Database that Tracks Student Data

Working Together

Keeping track of students is an enormous task for school administrators. Microsoft Access can help school administrators manage student data. The Database Wizard includes a Students template that can create a database that will maintain many different types of data on students, such as allergies, medications, and emergency contact information.

Have each member of your team explore the features of the Database Wizard and determine individually which tables and fields should be included in a Students database. As a group, review your choices and decide on one common design. Prepare a short paper for your instructor that explains why your team chose the particular database design.

After agreeing on the database design, assign one member to create the database using the Database Wizard. Every other team member should contribute data and add the data to the database. Submit your assignment in the format specified by your instructor.

2 Querying a Database

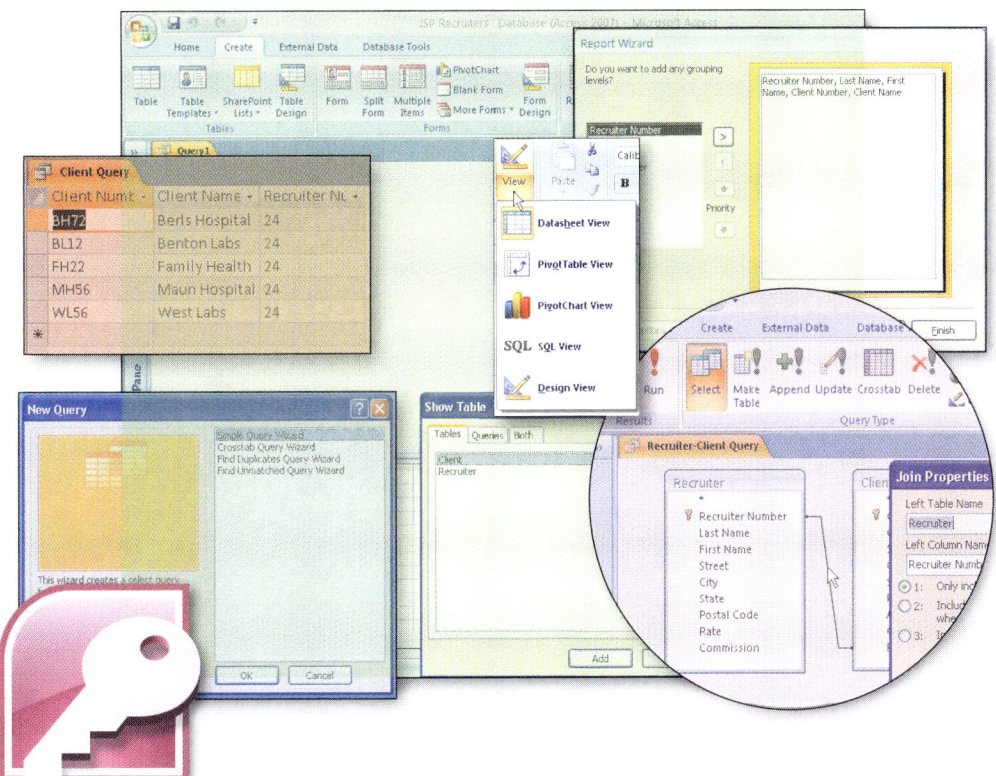

Objectives

You will have mastered the material in this chapter when you can:

- Create queries using the Simple Query Wizard
- Print query results
- Create queries using Design view
- Include fields in the design grid
- Use text and numeric data in criteria
- Create and use parameter queries
- Save a query and use the saved query
- Use compound criteria in queries
- Sort data in queries
- Join tables in queries
- Create a report from a query
- Perform calculations in queries
- Calculate statistics in queries
- Create crosstab queries
- Customize the Navigation Pane

2 Querying a Database

Introduction

A database management system such as Access offers many useful features, among them the capability of answering questions, the answers to which are found in the database. When you pose a question to Access, or any other database management system, the question is called a query. A **query** is simply a question presented in a way that Access can process.

Thus, to find the answer to a question, you first create a corresponding query using the techniques illustrated in this chapter. After you have created the query, you instruct Access to display the query results; that is, to perform the steps necessary to obtain the answer. Access then displays the answer in Datasheet view.

Project — Querying a Database

Organizations and individuals achieve several benefits from storing data in a database and using Access to manage the database. One of the most important benefits is the capability of easily finding the answers to questions such as those shown in Figure 2-1 and the following, which concern the data in the JSP Recruiters database:

1. What are the number, name, the amount paid, and the current due of client FD89?
2. Which clients' names begin with Be?
3. Which clients are located in Berridge?
4. Which clients have a current due of $0.00?
5. Which clients have an amount paid that is more than $20,000.00?
6. Which clients of recruiter 21 have an amount paid that is more than $20,000.00?
7. In what cities are all the clients located?
8. What is the total amount (amount paid + current due) for each client?
9. What is the client number and name of each client, and what is the number and name of the recruiter to whom each client is assigned?

In addition to these questions, JSP Recruiters needs to find information about clients located in a specific city, but they want to enter a different city each time they ask the question. A parameter query would enable this. The agency also has a special way it wants to summarize data. A crosstab query will present the data in the desired form.

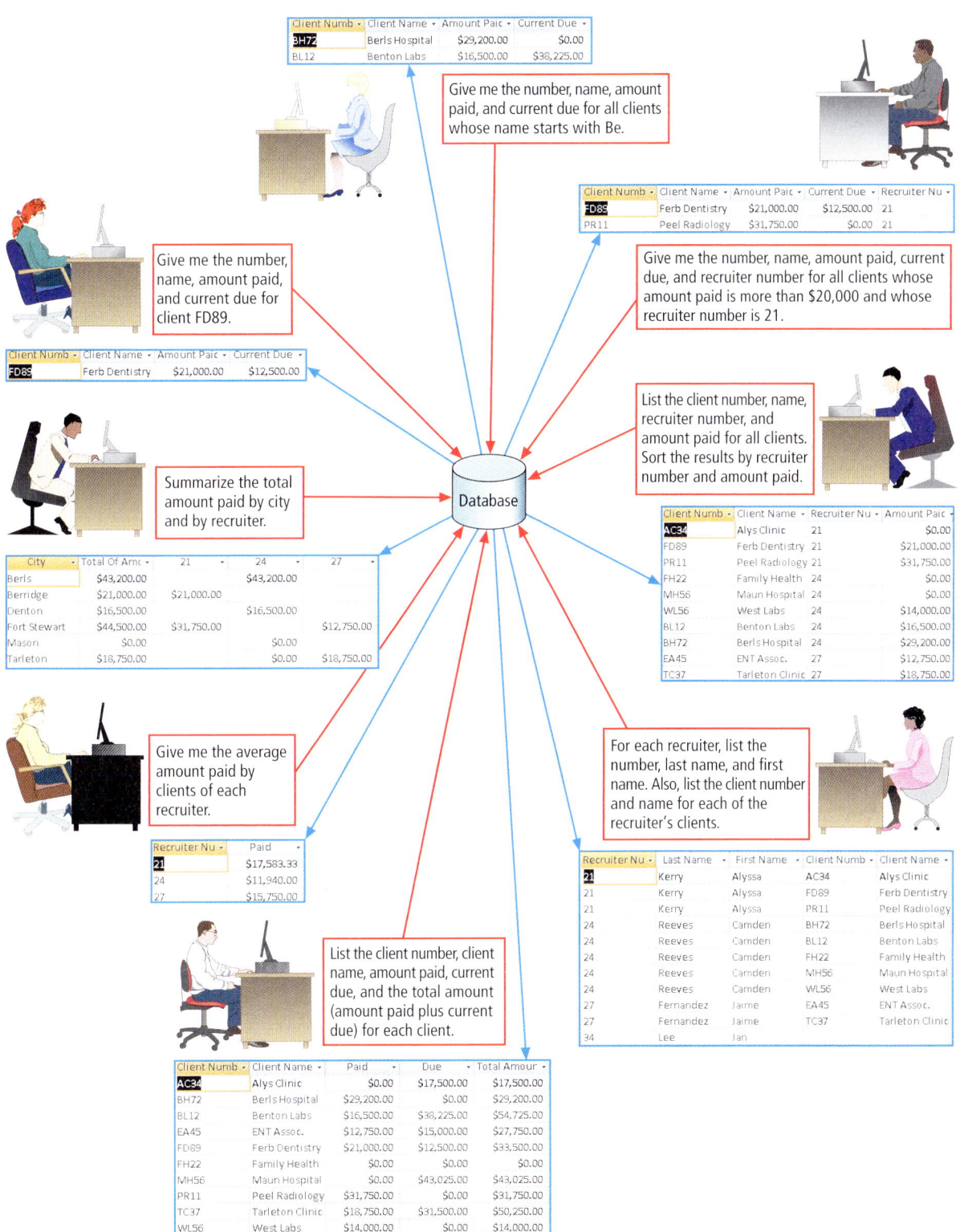

Figure 2–1

Overview

As you read this chapter, you will learn how to query a database by performing these general tasks:

- Create queries using the Simple Query Wizard and Design view
- Use criteria in queries
- Create and use parameter queries
- Sort data in queries
- Join tables in queries
- Perform calculations in queries
- Create crosstab queries

Plan Ahead

Query Design Guidelines

When posing a question to Access, you must design an appropriate query. In the process of designing a query, the decisions you make will determine the fields, tables, criteria, order, and special calculations included in the query. To design a query, you should follow these general guidelines:

1. **Identify the fields.** Examine the question or request to determine which fields from the tables in the database are involved. Examine the contents of these fields to make sure you understand how the data is stored.

2. **Identify restrictions.** Unless the question or request calls for all records, determine the restrictions, that is, the conditions records must satisfy in order to be included in the results.

3. **Determine whether special order is required.** Examine the question or request to determine whether the results must appear in some specific order.

4. **Determine whether more than one table is required.** If all the fields identified in Step 1 are in the same table, no special action is required. If this is not the case, identify all tables represented by those fields.

5. **Determine whether calculations are required.** Examine the question or request to determine whether, in addition to the fields determined in Step 1, calculations must be included. Results of mathematical operations typically are not stored in the database because they can be calculated easily when necessary. Such calculations include individual record calculations (for example, adding the values in two fields) or group calculations (for example, finding the total of the values in a particular field on all the records).

6. **If data is to be summarized, determine whether a crosstab query would be appropriate.** If data is to be grouped by two different types of information, you can use a crosstab query. You will need to identify the two types of information. One of the types will form the row headings and the other will form the column headings in the query results.

When necessary, more specific details concerning the above decisions and/or actions are presented at appropriate points in the chapter.

Starting Access

If you are using a computer to step through the project in this chapter and you want your screen to match the figures in this book, you should change your screen's resolution to 1024 × 768. For information about how to change a computer's resolution, read Appendix C.

To Start Access

The following steps, which assume Windows Vista is running, start Access.

1 Click the Start button on the Windows Vista taskbar to display the Start menu.

2 Click All Programs at the bottom of the left pane on the Start menu to display the All Programs list and then click Microsoft Office in the All Programs list to display the Microsoft Office list.

3 Click Microsoft Office Access 2007 on the Microsoft Office list to start Access and display the Getting Started with Microsoft Office Access window.

4 If the Access window is not maximized, click the Maximize button on its title bar to maximize the window.

To Open a Database

In Chapter 1, you created your database on a USB flash drive using the file name, JSP Recruiters. There are two ways to open the file containing your database. If the file you created appears in the Recent Documents list, you can click it to open the file. If not, you can use the More button to open the file. The following steps use the More button to open the JSP Recruiters database from the USB flash drive.

1 With your USB flash drive connected to one of the computer's USB ports, click the More button to display the Open dialog box.

2 If the Folders list is displayed below the Folders button, click the Folders button to remove the Folders list.

3 If necessary, click Computer in the Favorite Links section and then double-click UDISK 2.0 (E:) to select the USB flash drive, Drive E in this case, as the new open location. (Your drive letter might be different.)

4 Click JSP Recruiters to select the file name.

5 Click the Open button to open the database.

6 If a Security Warning appears, click the Options button to display the Microsoft Office Security Options dialog box.

7 With the option button to enable this content selected, click the OK button to enable the content.

Creating Queries

Queries are simply questions, the answers to which are in the database. Access contains a powerful query feature. Through the use of this feature, you can find the answers to a wide variety of complex questions.

To Use the Simple Query Wizard to Create a Query

Once you have examined the question you wish to ask to determine the fields involved in the question, you can begin creating the query. If there are no restrictions involved in the query, nor any special order or calculations, you can use the Simple Query wizard. The following steps use the Simple Query wizard to create a query to display the number, name, and recruiter number of all clients.

1

- If the Navigation Pane is hidden, click the Shutter Bar Open/Close Button to show the Navigation Pane.

- Be sure the Client table is selected.

- Click Create on the Ribbon to display the Create tab.

- Click the Query Wizard button on the Create tab to display the New Query dialog box (Figure 2–2).

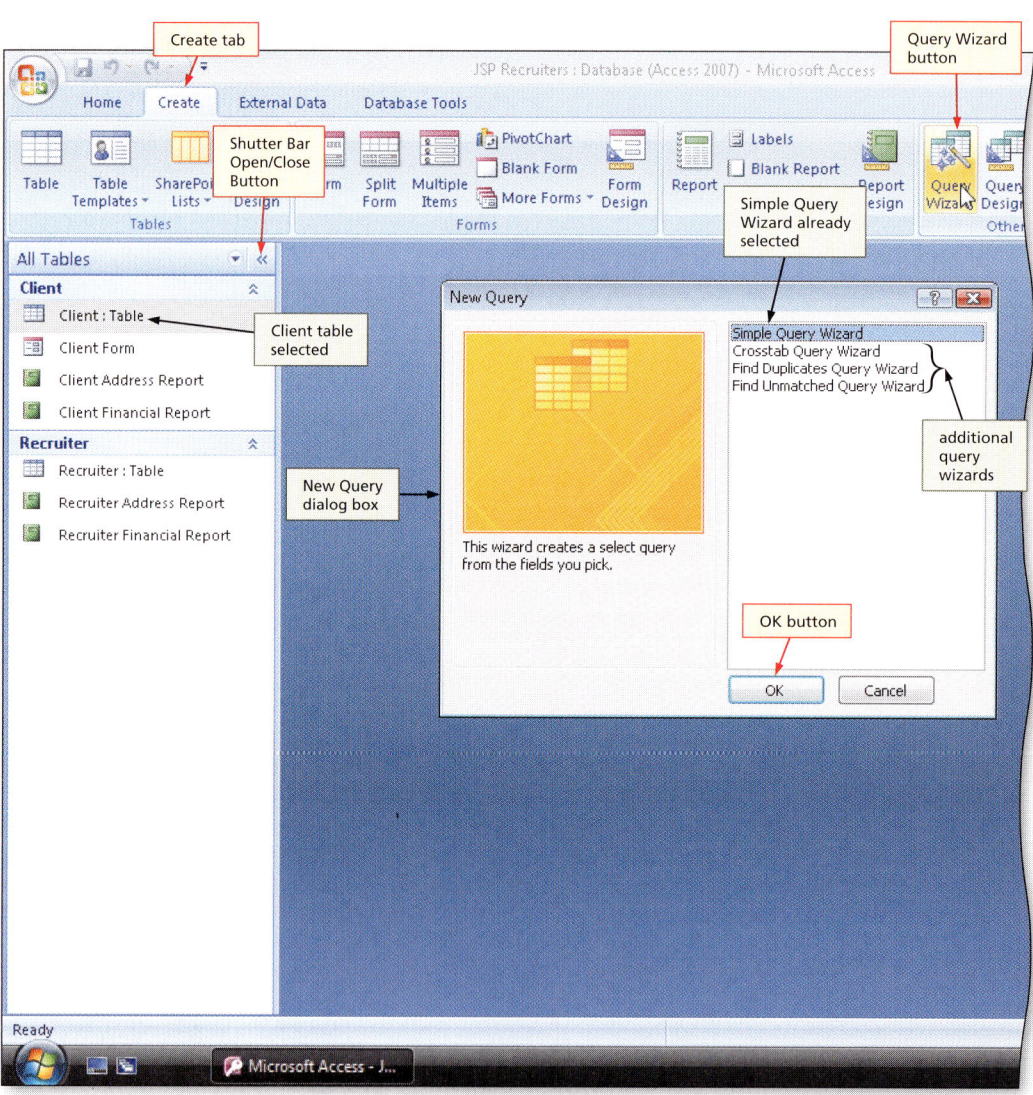

Figure 2–2

2

- Be sure Simple Query Wizard is selected, and then click the OK button to display the Simple Query Wizard dialog box (Figure 2–3).

Q&A This looks like the screen I saw in the Report Wizard. Do I select fields in the same way?

Yes. In fact, you will see a similar screen in other wizards and you always select the fields just as you did in the Report Wizard.

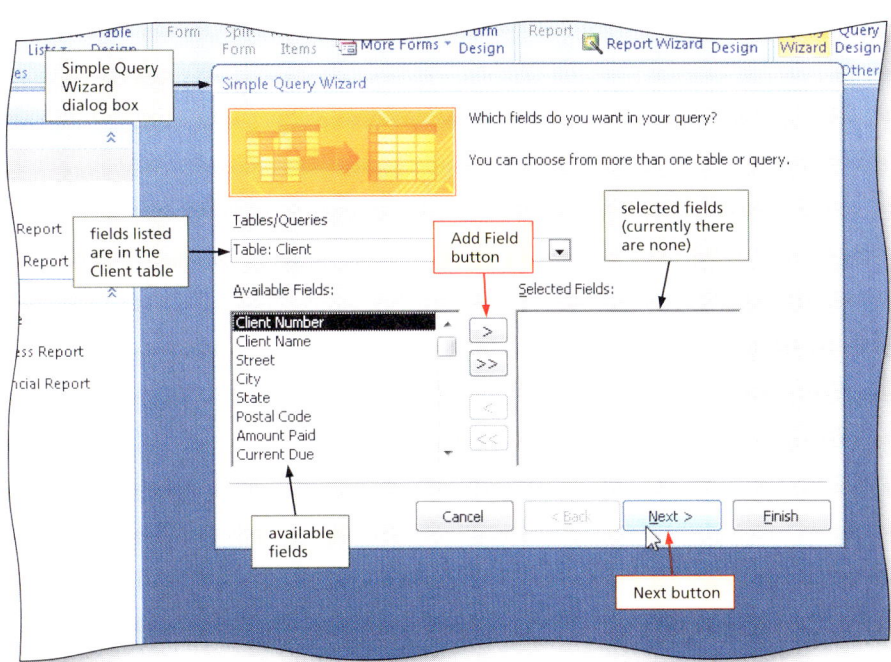

Figure 2–3

3

- Click the Add Field button to add the Client Number field.
- Click the Add Field button a second time to add the Client Name field.
- Click the Recruiter Number field, and then click the Add Field button to add the Recruiter Number field.
- Click the Next button.
- Be sure the title of the query is Client Query.
- Click the Finish button to create the query (Figure 2–4).

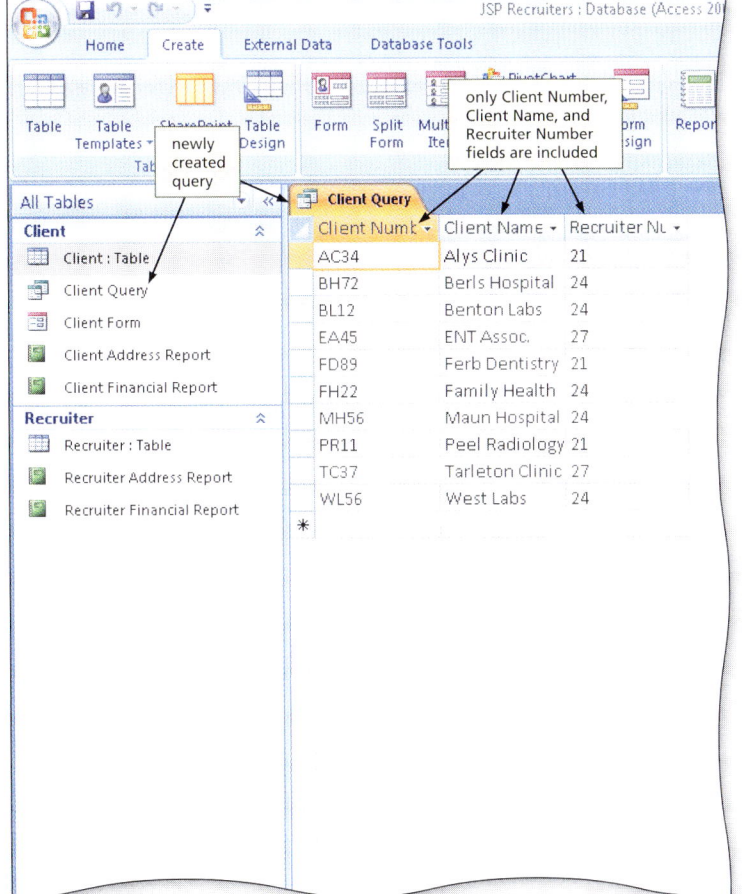

Figure 2–4

4

- Click the Close button for the Client Query to remove the query results from the screen.

Q&A If I want to use this query in the future, do I need to save the query?

Normally you would. The one exception is a query created by the wizard. The wizard automatically saves the query it creates.

Using Queries

After you have created and saved a query, you can use it in a variety of ways:

- To view the results of the query, open it by right-clicking the query in the Navigation Pane and clicking Open on the shortcut menu.
- To print the results with the query open, click the Office Button, point to Print on the Office Button menu, and then click Quick Print on the Print submenu.
- If you want to change the design of the query, right-click the query and then click Design View on the shortcut menu to open the query in Design view.
- To print the query without first opening it, be sure the query is selected in the Navigation Pane and then click the Office Button, point to Print on the Office Button menu, and then click Quick Print on the Print submenu.

You can switch between views of a query by using the View button (Figure 2–5). Clicking the arrow at the bottom of the button produces the View button menu as shown in the figure. You then click the desired view in the menu. The two views you will use in this chapter are Datasheet view (see the results) and Design view (change the design). You also can click the top part of the button, in which case, you will switch to the view identified by the icon on the button. In the figure, the button contains the icon for Design view, so clicking the button would change to Design view. For the most part, the icon on the button represents the view you want, so you can usually simply click the button.

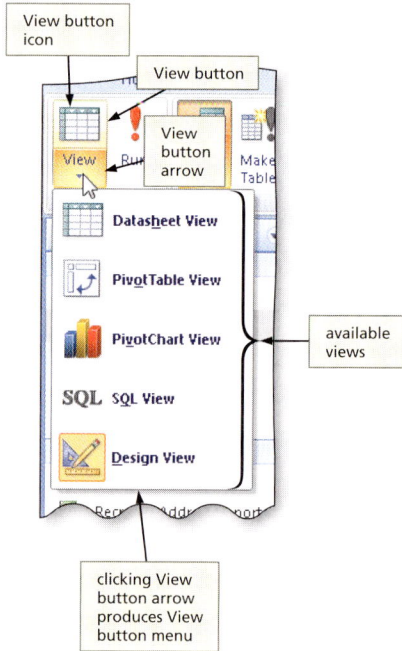

Figure 2–5

To Use a Criterion in a Query

After you have determined the fields to be included in a query, you will determine whether there are any restrictions on the records that are to be included. For example, you might only want to include those clients whose recruiter number is 24. In such a case, you need to enter the 24 as a **criterion**, which is a condition that the records to be included must satisfy. To do so, you will open the query in Design view, enter the criterion below the appropriate field, and then view the results of the query. The following steps enter a criterion to include only the clients of recruiter 24 and then view the query results.

- Right-click Client Query to produce a shortcut menu (Figure 2–6).

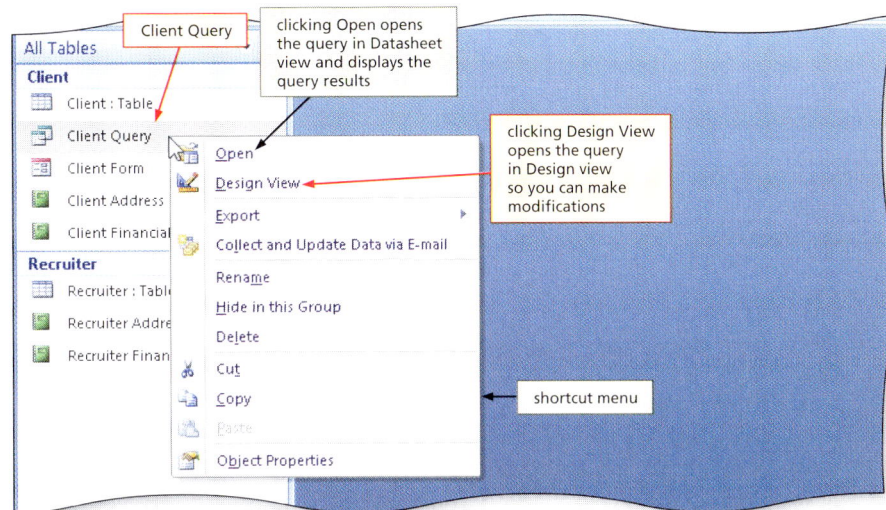

Figure 2–6

- Click Design View on the shortcut menu to open the query in Design view (Figure 2–7). (Your field names may be enclosed in brackets.)

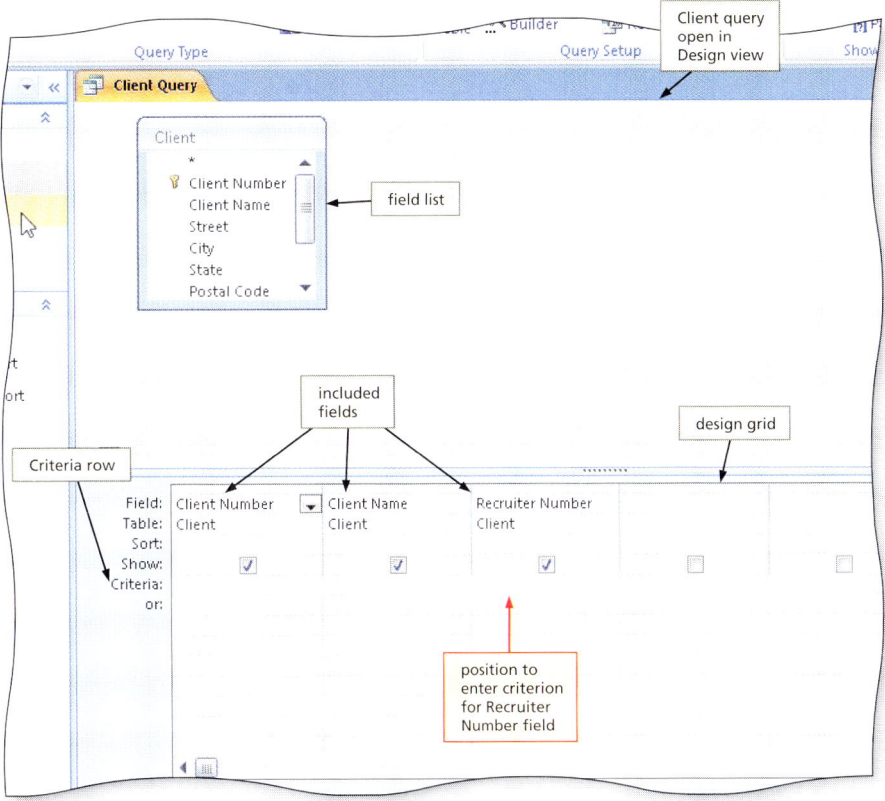

Figure 2–7

- Click the Criteria row in the Recruiter Number column of the grid, and then type 24 as the criterion (Figure 2–8).

Q&A The Recruiter Number field is a text field. Do I need to enclose the value for a text field in quotation marks?

You could, but it is not necessary, because Access inserts the quotation marks for you automatically.

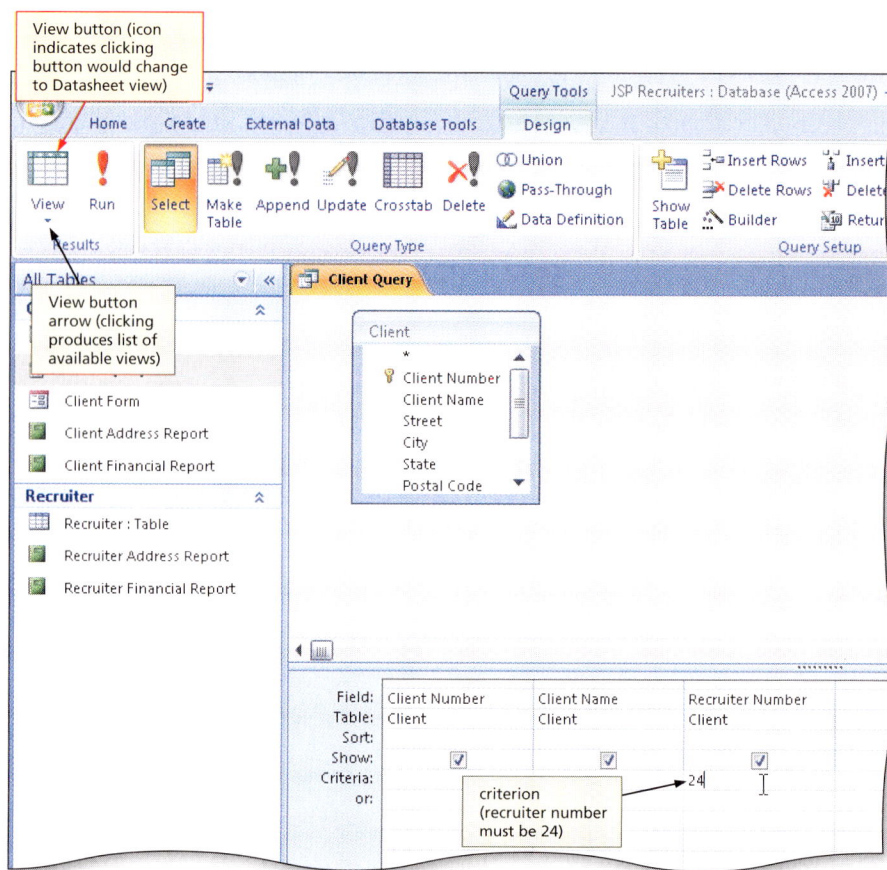

Figure 2–8

- Click the View button to display the results in Datasheet view (Figure 2–9).

Q&A Could I click the View button arrow and then click Datasheet view?

Yes. If the icon representing the view you want appears on the View button, however, it is easier just to click the button.

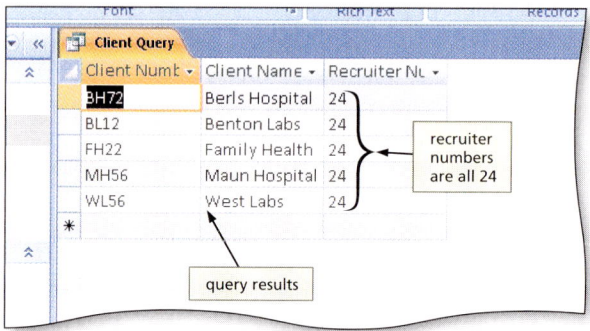

Figure 2–9

- Close the Client Query window by clicking the Close 'Client Query' button.

- When asked if you want to save your changes, click the No button.

Q&A If I saved the query, what would happen the next time I ran the query?

You would see only clients of recruiter 24.

Other Ways

1. Click Run button on Ribbon
2. Click Datasheet View button on status bar

To Print the Results of a Query

To print the results of a query, use the same techniques you learned in Chapter 1 on pages AC 41 and AC 42 to print the data in the table. The following steps print the current query results.

1. With the Client Query selected in the Navigation Pane, click the Office Button.
2. Point to Print on the Office Button menu.
3. Click Quick Print on the Print submenu.

To Create a Query in Design View

Most of the time you will use Design view to create queries. Once you have created a new query in Design view, you can specify fields, criteria, sorting, calculations, and so on. The following steps create a new query in Design view.

1
- Hide the Navigation Pane.
- Click Create on the Ribbon to display the Create tab.
- Click the Query Design button to create a new query (Figure 2–10).

Q&A
Is it necessary to hide the Navigation Pane?

No. It gives you more room for the query, however, so it is usually a good practice to hide it.

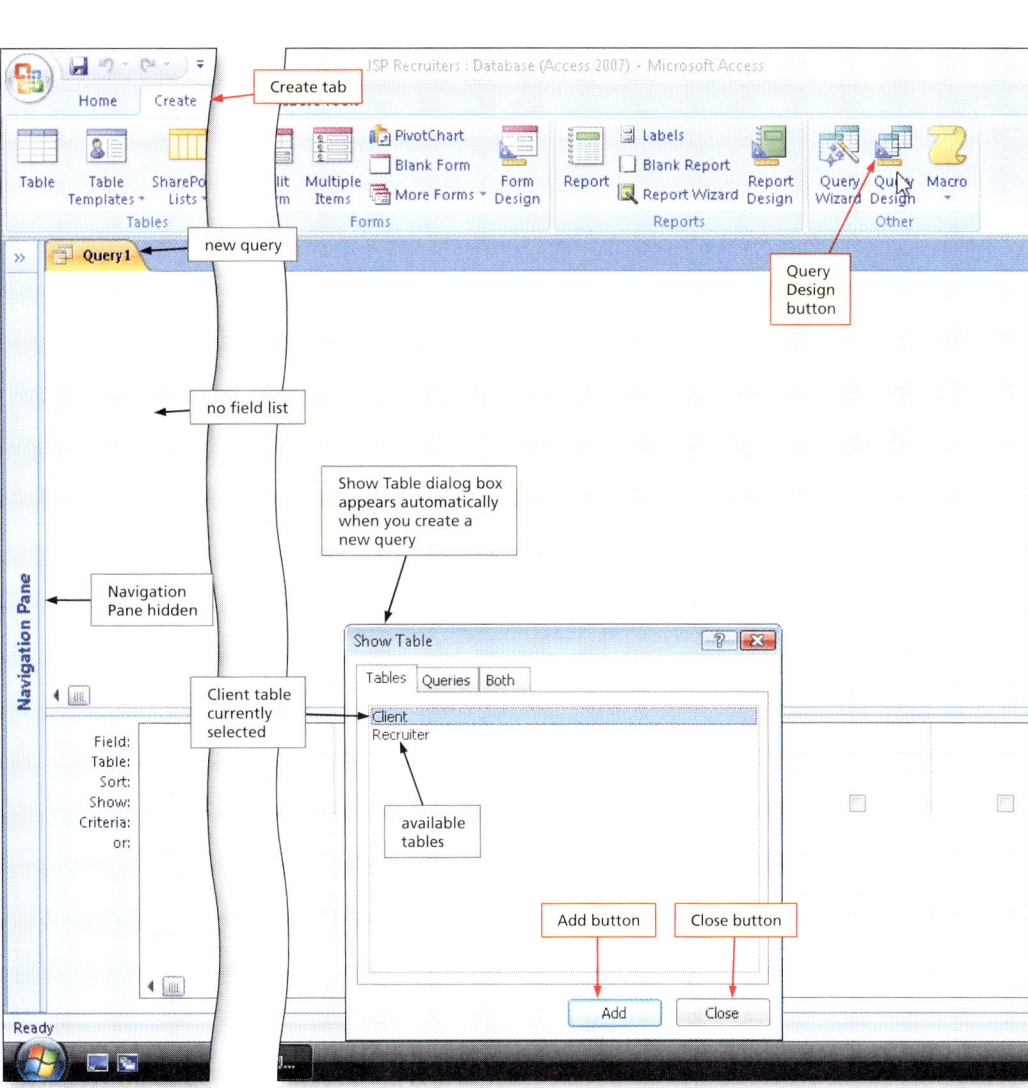

Figure 2–10

2

- With the Client table selected, click the Add button in the Show Table dialog box to add the Client table to the query.

- Click the Close button in the Show Table dialog box to remove the dialog box from the screen.

Q&A What if I inadvertently add the wrong table?

Right-click the table that you added in error and click Remove Table on the shortcut menu. You also can just close the query, indicate that you do not want to save it, and then start over.

- Drag the lower edge of the field box down far enough so all fields in the Client table appear (Figure 2–11).

Q&A How do I drag the lower edge?

Point to the lower edge, press and hold the left mouse button, move the mouse pointer to the new position for the lower edge, and then release the left mouse button. While the mouse pointer points to the lower edge of the field list, its shape changes to a double-headed arrow.

Q&A Is it essential that I resize the field box?

No. You can always scroll through the list of fields using the scroll bar. If you can resize the field box so all fields appear, it is usually more convenient.

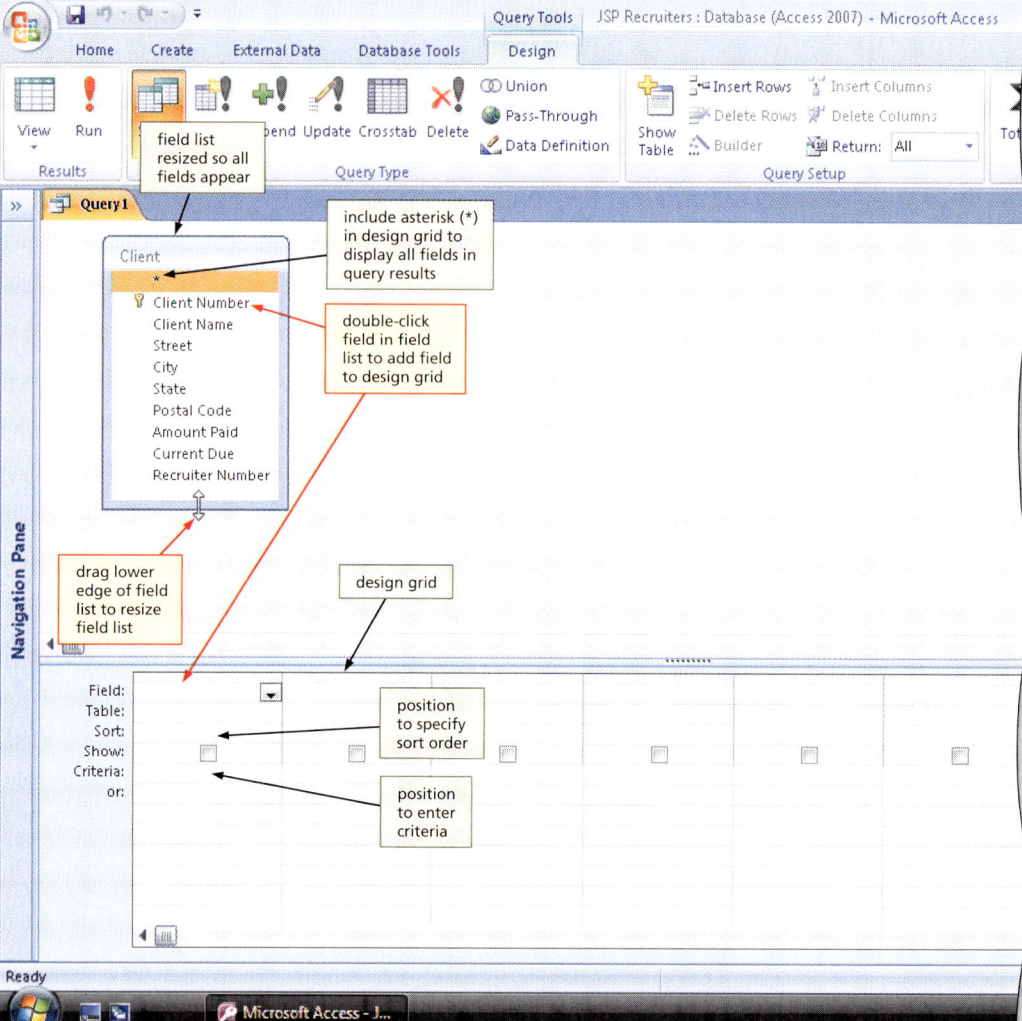

Figure 2–11

To Add Fields to the Design Grid

Once you have a new query displayed in Design view, you are ready to create the query by making entries in the design grid in the lower pane of the window. You add the fields you want included in the Field row in the grid. Only the fields that appear in the design grid will be included in the results of the query. The following step includes the client number, client name, amount paid, and current due for all clients by adding only those fields in the design grid.

1

- Double-click the Client Number field in the field list to add the Client Number field to the query.

Q&A What if I add the wrong field?

Click just above the field name in the design grid to select the column and then press the DELETE key to remove the field.

- Double-click the Client Name field in the field list to add the Client Name field to the query.

- Add the Amount Paid field to the query by double-clicking the Amount Paid field in the field list.

- Add the Current Due field to the query (Figure 2–12).

Q&A What if I want to include all fields? Do I have to add each field individually?

No. Instead of adding individual fields, you can double-click the asterisk (*) to add the asterisk to the design grid.

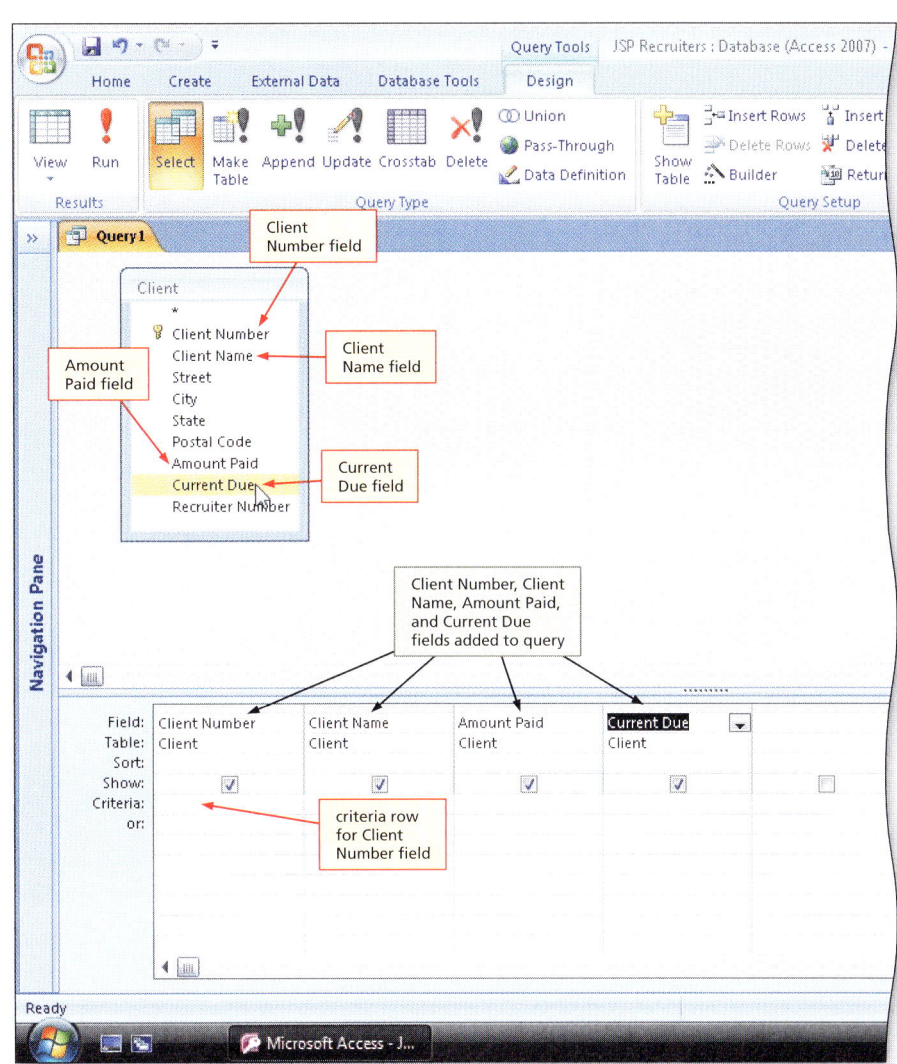

Figure 2–12

Entering Criteria

When you use queries, usually you are looking for those records that satisfy some criterion. In the simple query you created earlier, for example, you entered a criterion to restrict the records that were included to those on which the recruiter number was 24. In another query, you might want the name, amount paid, and current due amounts of the client whose number is FD89, for example, or of those clients whose names start with the letters, Be. You enter criteria in the Criteria row in the design grid below the field name to which the criterion applies. For example, to indicate that the client number must be FD89, you first must add the Client Number field to the design grid. You then would type FD89 in the Criteria row below the Client Number field.

To Use Text Data in a Criterion

To use **text data** (data in a field whose data type is Text) in criteria, simply type the text in the Criteria row below the corresponding field name. The following steps query the Client table and display the client number, client name, amount paid, and current due amount of client FD89.

1
- Click the Criteria row for the Client Number field to produce an insertion point.
- Type FD89 as the criterion (Figure 2–13).

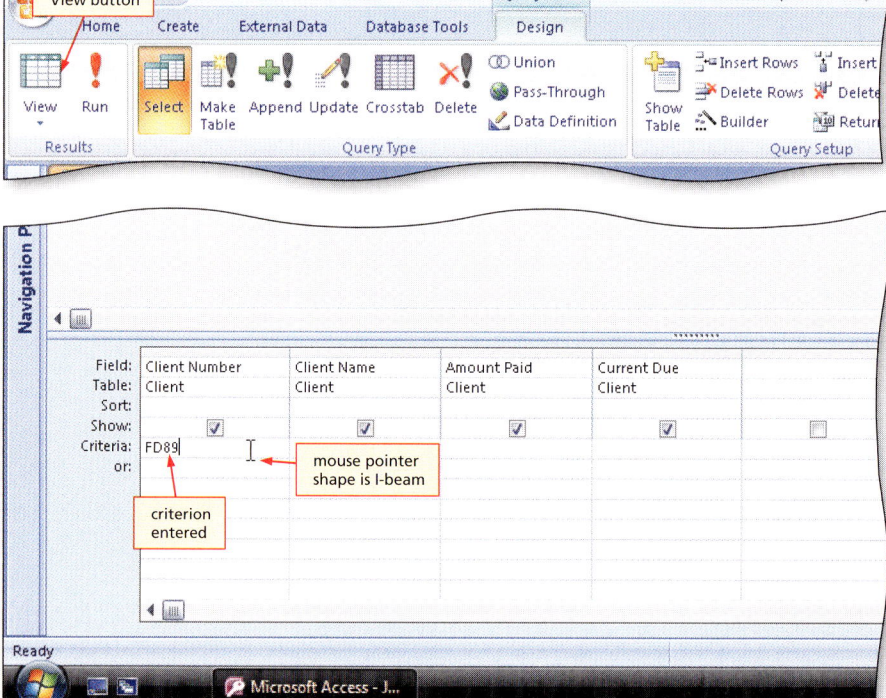

Figure 2–13

2
- Click the View button to display the query results (Figure 2–14).

Q&A I noticed that a View button appears on both the Home tab and the Design tab. Do they both have the same effect?

Yes. Use whichever one you find most convenient.

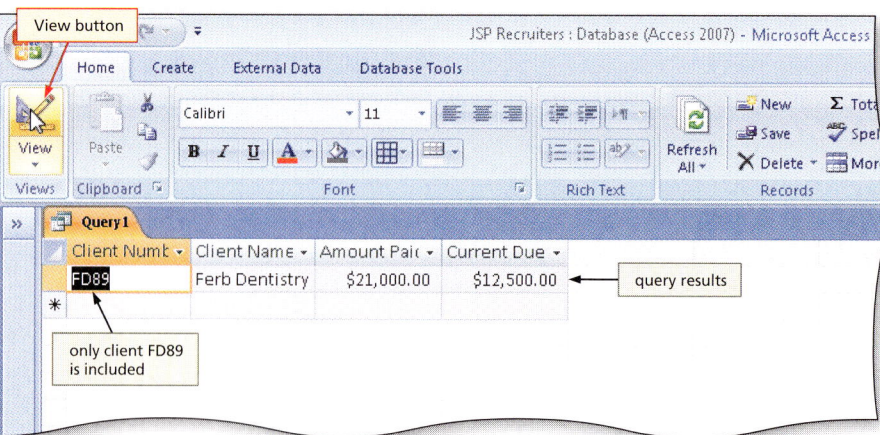

Figure 2–14

To Use a Wildcard

Microsoft Access supports wildcards. **Wildcards** are symbols that represent any character or combination of characters. One common wildcard, the **asterisk** (*), represents any collection of characters. Thus Be* represents the letters, Be, followed by any collection of characters. Another wildcard symbol is the **question mark** (?), which represents any individual character. Thus T?m represents the letter, T, followed by any single character followed by the letter, m, such as Tim or Tom.

The following steps use a wildcard to find the number, name, amount paid, and current due of those clients whose names begin with Be. Because you do not know how many characters will follow the Be, the asterisk is appropriate.

- Click the View button to return to Design view.
- If necessary, click the Criteria row below the Client Number field to produce an insertion point.
- Use the DELETE or BACKSPACE key as necessary to delete the current entry.
- Click the Criteria row below the Client Name field to produce an insertion point.
- Type Be* as the criterion (Figure 2–15).

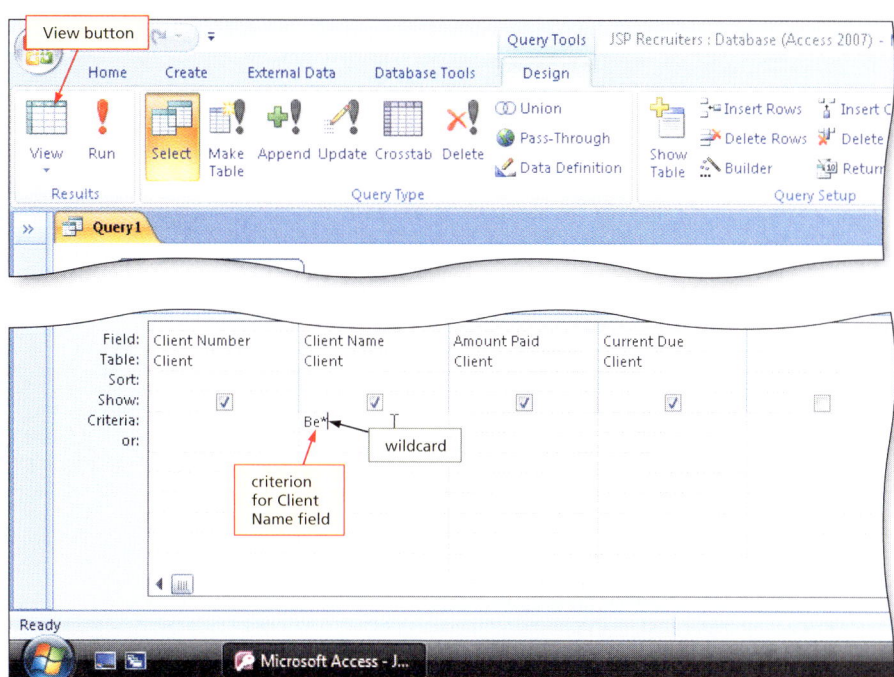

Figure 2–15

- View the query results by clicking the View button (Figure 2–16).

- Vary the case of the letters in the criteria and view the results to determine whether case makes a difference when entering a wildcard.

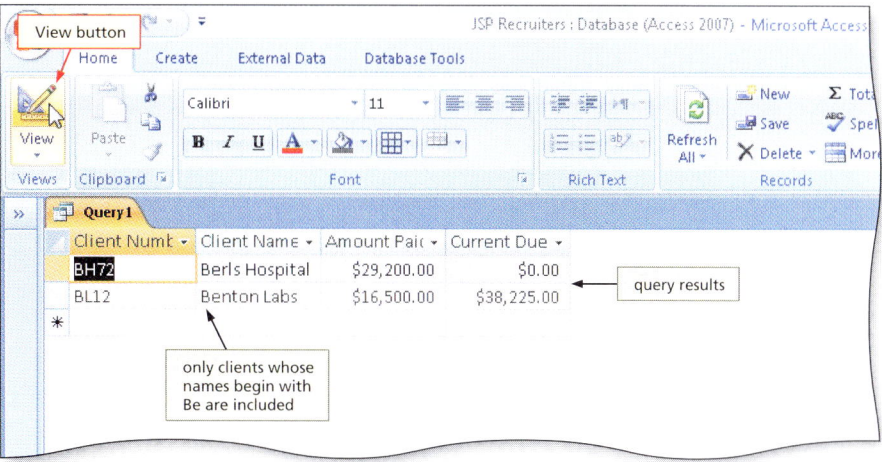

Figure 2–16

To Use Criteria for a Field Not Included in the Results

In some cases, you may have criteria for a particular field that should not appear in the results of the query. For example, you may want to see the client number, client name, amount paid, and current due for all clients located in Berridge. The criteria involve the City field, which is not one of the fields to be included in the results.

To enter a criterion for the City field, it must be included in the design grid. Normally, this also would mean it would appear in the results. To prevent this from happening, remove the check mark from its Show check box in the Show row of the grid. The following steps display the client number, client name, amount paid, and current due for clients located in Berridge.

- Click the View button to return to Design view.
- Erase the criterion in the Client Name field.
- Include the City field in the query.
- Type Berridge as the criterion for the City field (Figure 2–17).

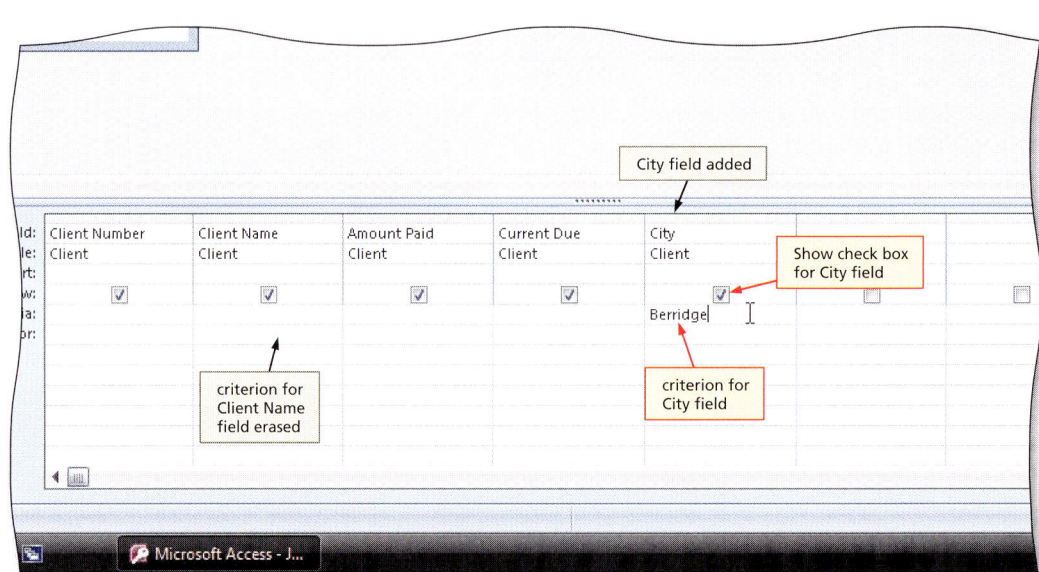

Figure 2–17

- Click the Show check box for the City field to remove the check mark (Figure 2–18).

Q&A Could I have removed the check mark before entering the criterion?

Yes. The order in which you performed the two operations does not matter.

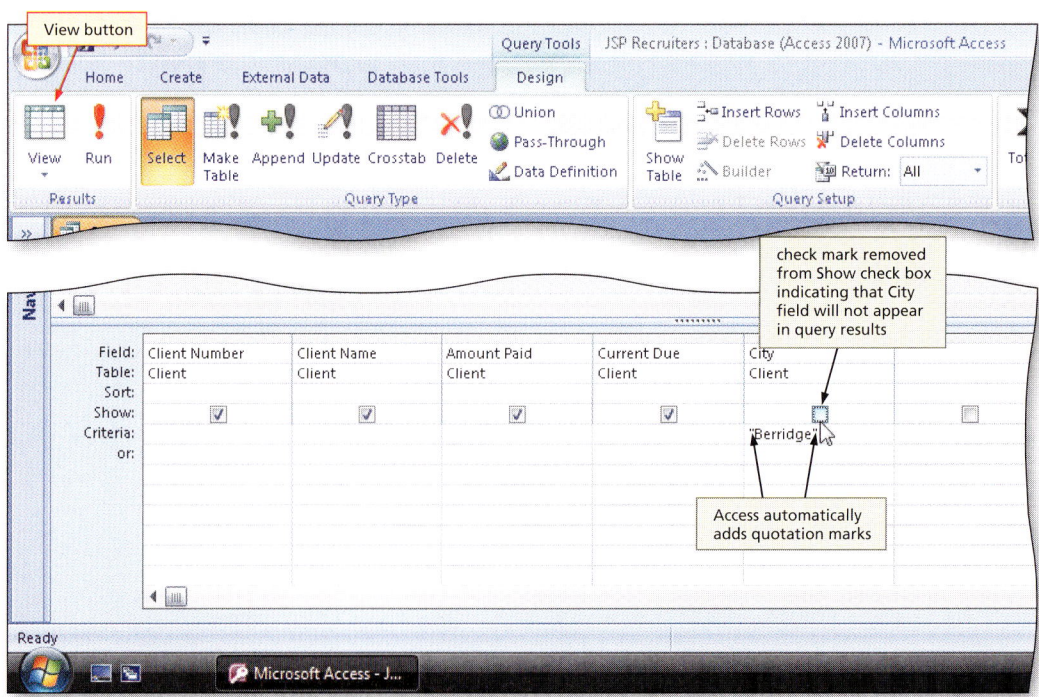

Figure 2–18

- View the query results (Figure 2–19).

🔍 **Experiment**

- Click the View button to return to Design view, enter a different city name, and view the results. Repeat this process with a variety of city names, including at least one city name that is not in the database.

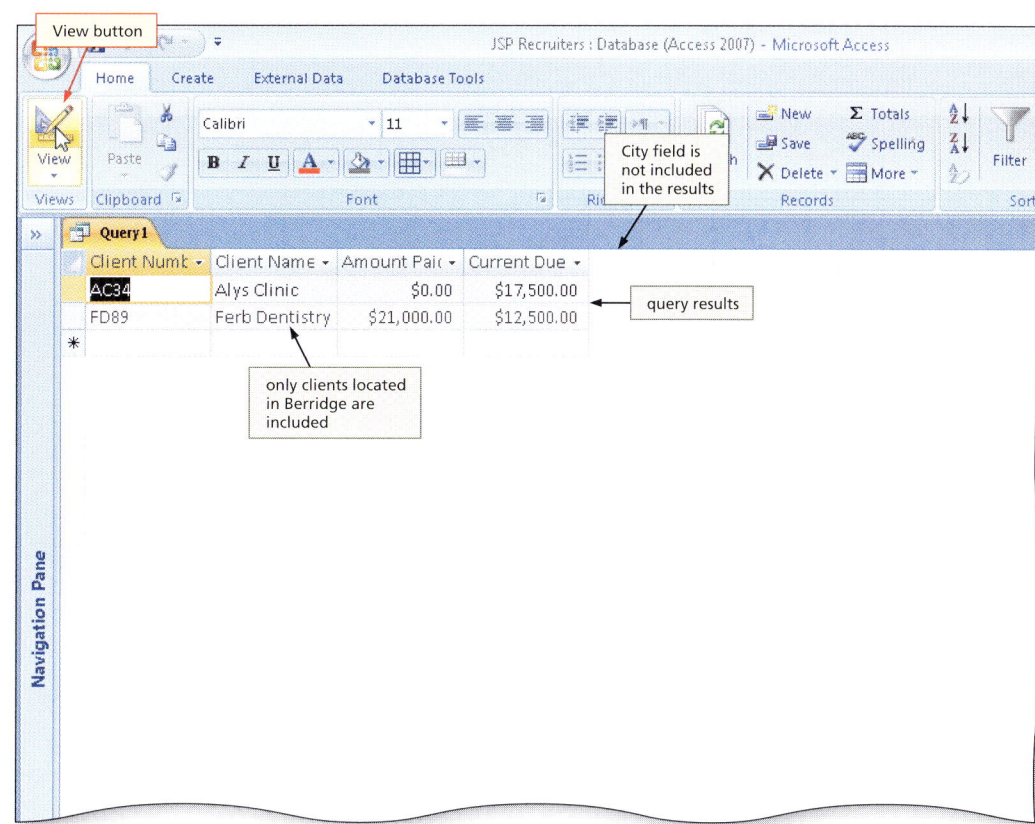

Figure 2–19

Creating a Parameter Query

If you wanted to find clients located in Fort Stewart rather than Berridge, you would either have to create a new query or modify the existing query by replacing Berridge with Fort Stewart as the criterion. Rather than giving a specific criterion when you first create the query, on occasion, you may want to be able to enter part of the criterion when you view the query results and then have the appropriate results appear. For example, to include all the clients located in Berridge, you could enter Berridge as a criterion in the City field. From that point on, every time you ran the query, only the clients in Berridge would appear.

A better way is to allow the user to enter the city at the time the user wants to view the results. Thus a user could view the query results, enter Berridge as the city and then see all the clients in Berridge. Later, the user could use the same query, but enter Fort Stewart as the city, and then see all the clients in Fort Stewart.

To enable this flexibility, you create a **parameter query**, which is a query that prompts for input whenever it is used. You enter a parameter, rather than a specific value, as the criterion. You create a parameter by enclosing a value in a criterion in square brackets. It is important that the value in the brackets does not match the name of any field. If you enter a field name in square brackets, Access assumes you want that particular field and does not prompt the user for input. For example, you could place [Enter City] as the criterion in the City field.

BTW

Removing a Table from a Query
If you add the wrong table to a query or have an extra table in the query, you can remove it by right-clicking the field list for the table and then clicking Remove Table on the shortcut menu.

To Create a Parameter Query

The following steps create a parameter query that prompts the user to enter a city, and then displays the client number, client name, amount paid, and current due for all clients located in that city.

1
- Return to Design view.
- Erase the current criterion in the City column, and then type [Enter City] as the new criterion (Figure 2–20).

Q&A What is the purpose of the square brackets?

The square brackets indicate that the text entered is not text that the value in the column must match. Without the brackets, for example, Access would search for records on which the city is Enter City.

Q&A What if I typed a field name in the square brackets?

Access would simply use the value in that field. In order to create a parameter query, it is essential that the text typed in the square brackets not be a field name.

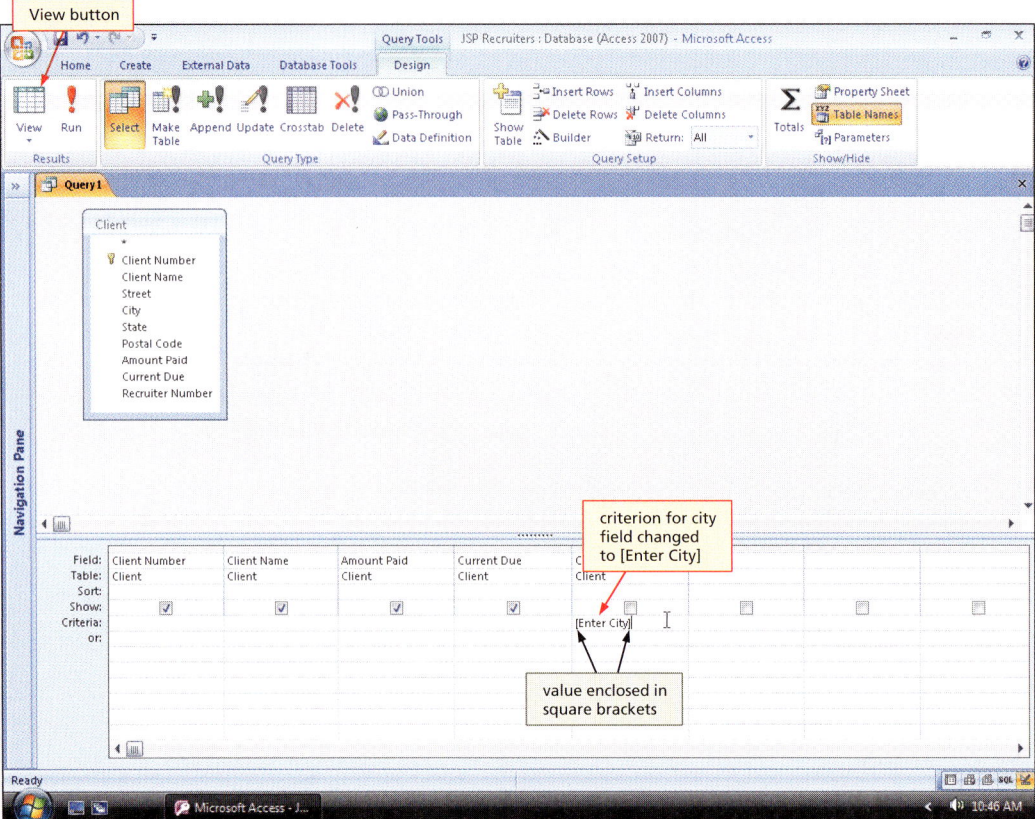

Figure 2–20

2
- Click the View button to display the Enter Parameter Value dialog box (Figure 2–21).

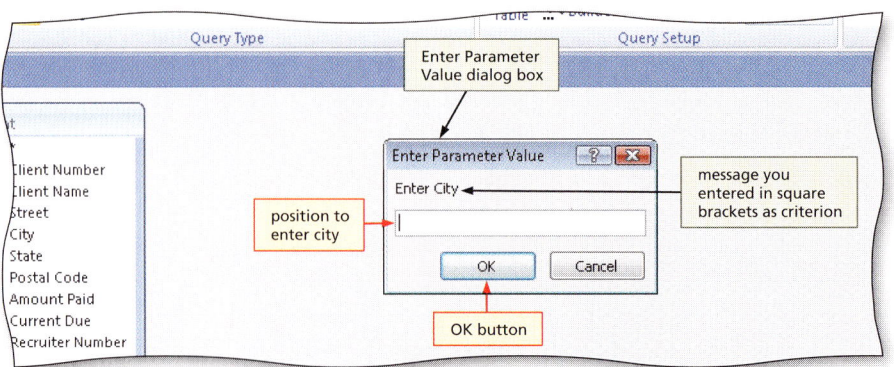

Figure 2–21

3

- Type Fort Stewart as the parameter value in the Enter City text box and then click the OK button (Figure 2–22).

🔍 **Experiment**

- Try other characters between the square brackets. In each case, view the results. When finished, change the characters between the square brackets back to Enter City.

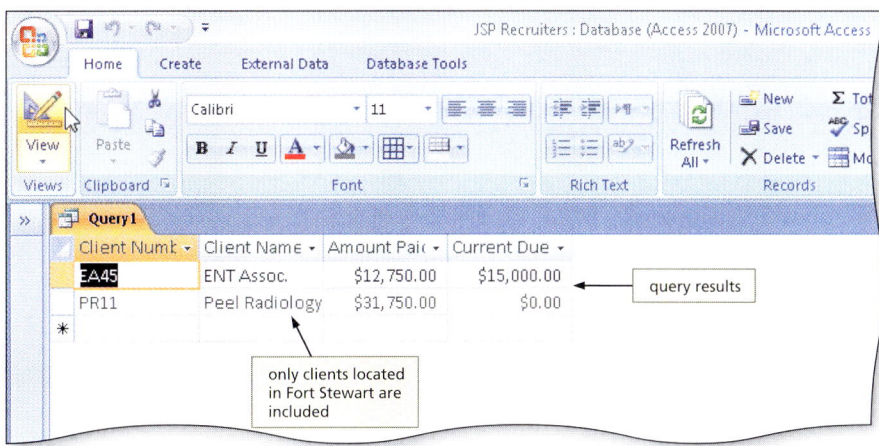

Figure 2–22

Each time you use this query, you will be asked to enter a city. Only clients in the city you enter will be included in the results.

To Save a Query

In many cases, you will want to repeatedly use the queries you construct. By saving the query, you eliminate the need to repeat all your entries. The following steps save the query you just have created and assign it the name Client-City Query.

1

- Click the Save button on the Quick Access Toolbar to open the Save As dialog box.

Q&A Can I also save from Design view?

Yes. You can save the query when you view it in Design view just as you can save the query when you view the query results in Datasheet view.

- Type Client-City Query in the Query Name text box (Figure 2–23).

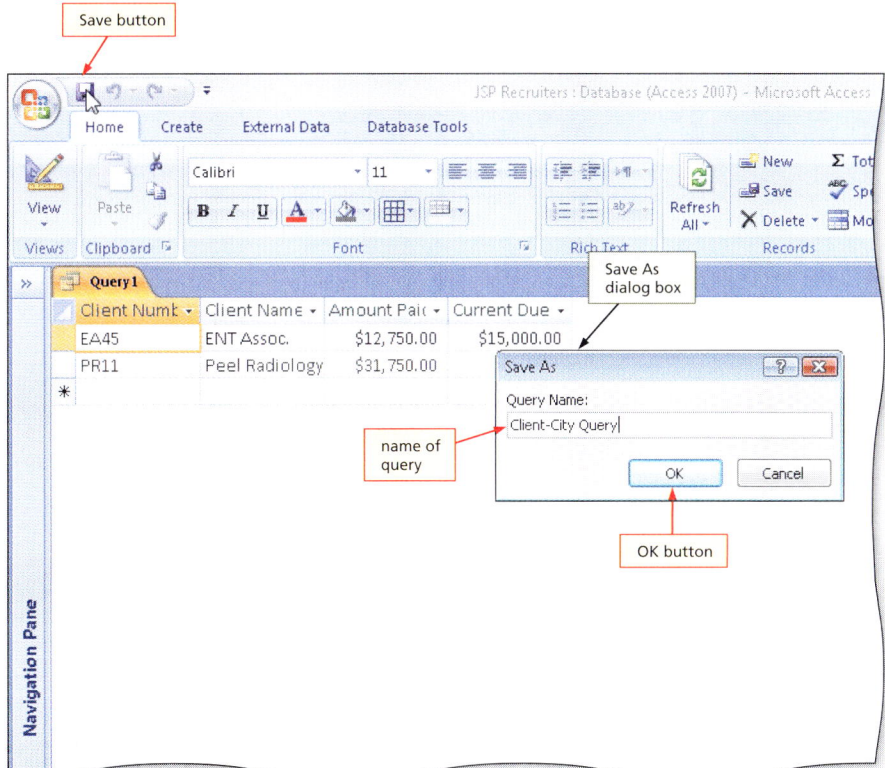

Figure 2–23

- Click the OK button to save the query (Figure 2–24).

- Click the Close 'Client-City Query' button to close the query and remove it from the screen.

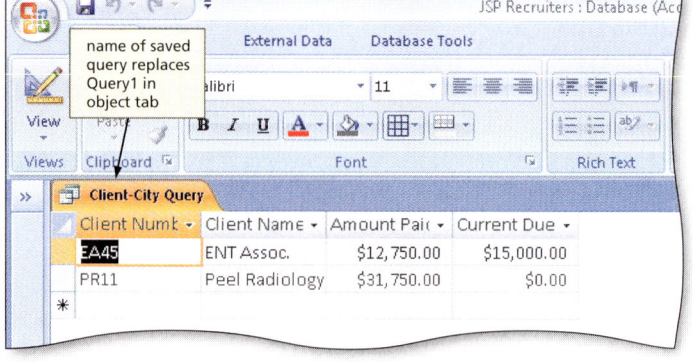
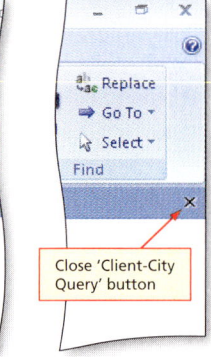

Figure 2–24

Other Ways
1. Right-click tab for query, click Save on shortcut menu
2. Press CTRL+S

To Use a Saved Query

Once you have saved a query, you can use and manipulate it at any time in the future by opening it. When you right-click the query in the Navigation Pane, Access displays a shortcut menu containing commands that allow you to open and change the design of the query. You also can print the results by clicking the Office Button, pointing to Print on the Office Button menu, and then clicking Quick Print on the Print submenu.

The query always uses the data that is currently in the table. Thus, if changes have been made to the data since the last time you ran the query, the results of the query may be different. The following steps use the query named Client-City Query.

- Show the Navigation Pane.
- Right-click the Client-City Query to produce a shortcut menu.
- Click Open on the shortcut menu to open the query and display the Enter Parameter Value dialog box (Figure 2–25).

Q&A What would have happened if there were no parameters?

You would immediately see the results without needing to furnish any additional information.

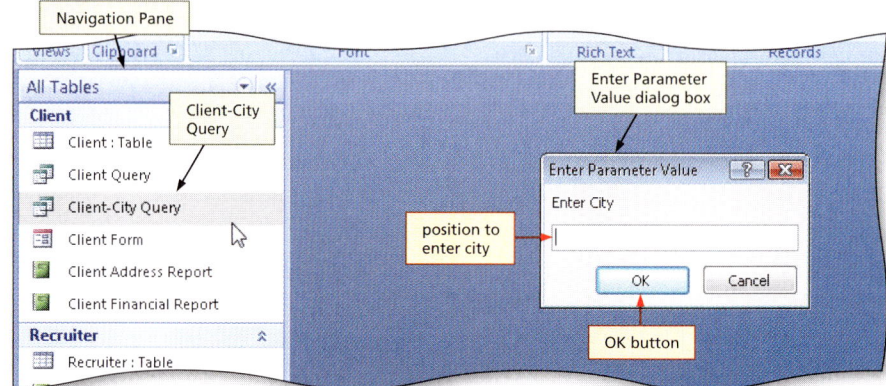

Figure 2–25

- Type `Fort Stewart` in the Enter City text box, and then click the OK button to display the results using Fort Stewart as the city as shown in Figure 2–24.
- Click the Close 'Client-City Query' button, shown in Figure 2–24, to close the query.

To Use a Number in a Criterion

To enter a number in a criterion, type the number without any dollar signs or commas. The following steps display all clients whose current due amount is $0.00.

1

- Hide the Navigation Pane.
- Click Create on the Ribbon to display the Create tab.
- Click the Query Design button to create a new query.
- With the Client table selected, click the Add button in the Show Table dialog box to add the Client table to the query.
- Click the Close button in the Show Table dialog box to remove the dialog box from the screen.
- Drag the lower edge of the field box down far enough so all fields in the Client table are displayed.
- Include the Client Number, Client Name, Amount Paid, and Current Due fields in the query.
- Type 0 as the criterion for the Current Due field (Figure 2–26).

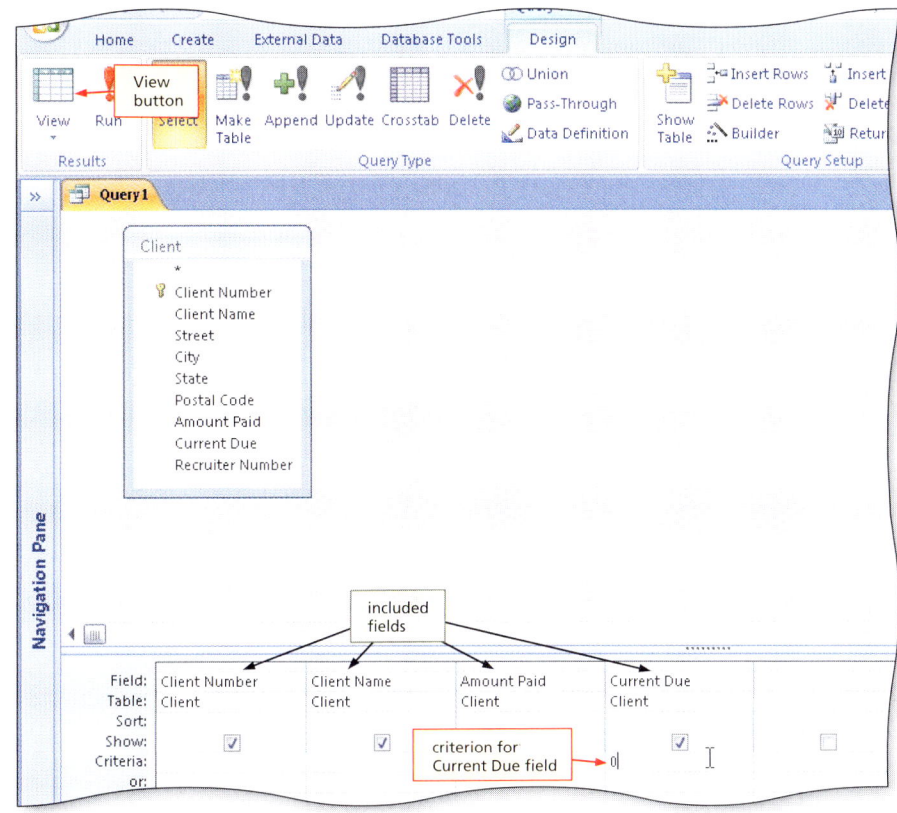

Figure 2–26

Q&A Do I need to enter a dollar sign and decimal point?

No. Access will interpret 0 as $0.00, because the data type for the Current Due field is currency.

2

- View the query results (Figure 2–27).

Q&A Why did Access display the results as $0.00 when I only entered 0?

Access uses the format for the field to determine how to display the result. In this case, the format indicated that Access should include the dollar sign and decimal point.

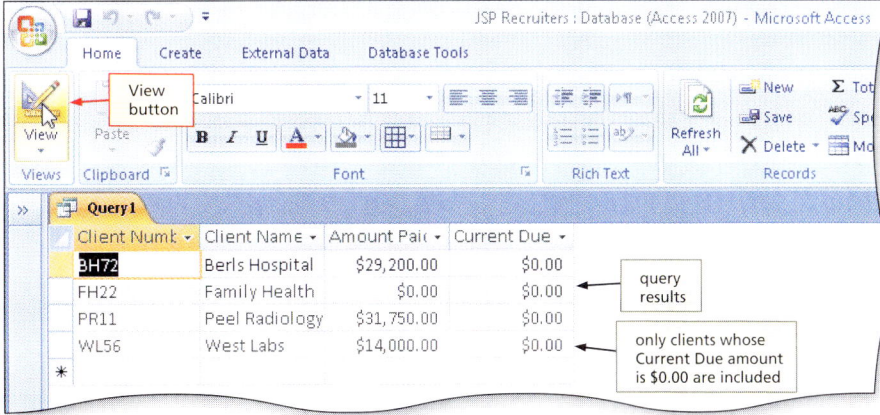

Figure 2–27

To Use a Comparison Operator in a Criterion

Unless you specify otherwise, Access assumes that the criteria you enter involve equality (exact matches). In the last query, for example, you were requesting those clients whose current due amount is equal to 0 (zero). If you want something other than an exact match, you must enter the appropriate **comparison operator**. The comparison operators are > (greater than), < (less than), >= (greater than or equal to), <= (less than or equal to), and NOT (not equal to).

The following steps use the > operator to find all clients whose amount paid is more than $20,000.00.

- Return to Design view.
- Erase the 0 in the Current Due column.
- Type >20000 as the criterion for the Amount Paid field (Figure 2–28).

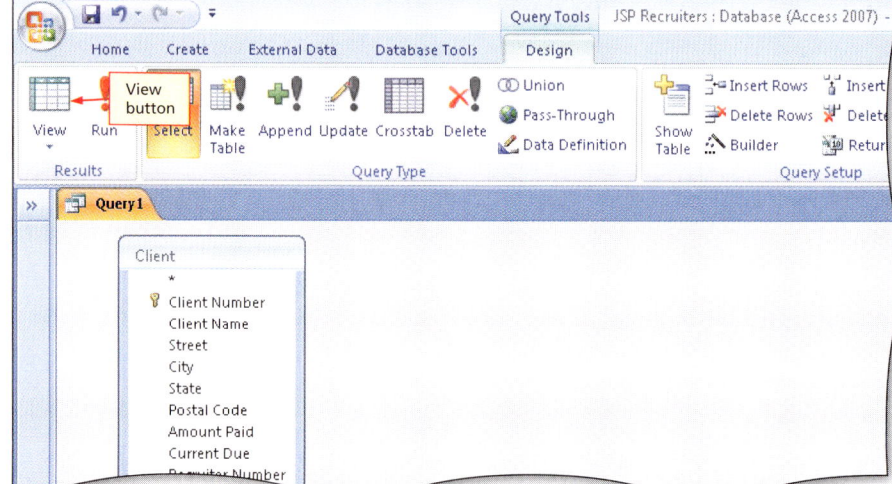
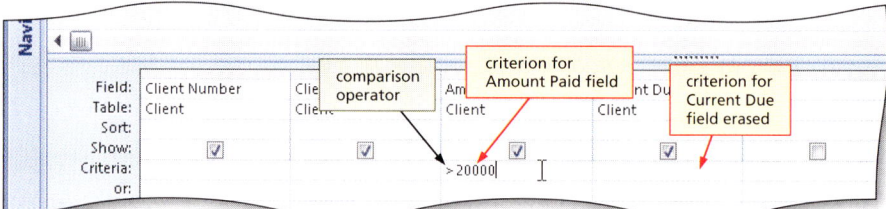

Figure 2–28

- View the query results (Figure 2–29).

- Return to Design view. Try a different criterion involving a comparison operator in the Amount Paid field and view the results. When finished, return to Design view, enter the original criterion (>20000) in the Amount Paid field, and view the results.

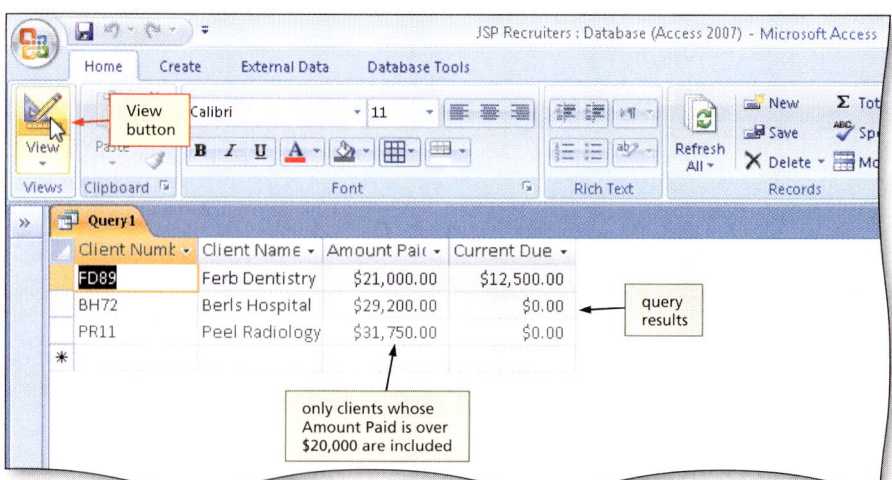

Figure 2–29

Using Compound Criteria

Often you will have more than one criterion that the data for which you are searching must satisfy. This type of criterion is called a **compound criterion**. Two types of compound criteria exist.

In an **AND criterion**, each individual criterion must be true in order for the compound criterion to be true. For example, an AND criterion would allow you to find those clients that have an amount paid greater than $20,000.00 and whose recruiter is recruiter 21.

Conversely, an **OR criterion** is true provided either individual criterion is true. An OR criterion would allow you to find those clients that have an amount paid greater than $20,000.00 or whose recruiter is recruiter 21. In this case, any client whose amount paid is greater than $20,000.00 would be included in the answer, regardless of whether the client's recruiter is recruiter 21. Likewise, any client whose recruiter is recruiter 21 would be included, regardless of whether the client had an amount paid greater than $20,000.00.

> **BTW**
> **The BETWEEN Operator**
> The BETWEEN operator allows you to search for a range of values in one field. For example, to find all clients whose amount paid is between $10,000 and $20,000, you would enter Between 10000 and 20000 in the Criteria row for the Amount Paid field.

To Use a Compound Criterion Involving AND

To combine criteria with AND, place the criteria on the same line. The following steps use an AND criterion to find those clients whose amount paid is greater than $20,000.00 and whose recruiter is recruiter 21.

- Return to Design view.
- Include the Recruiter Number field in the query.
- Type 21 as the criterion for the Recruiter Number field (Figure 2–30).

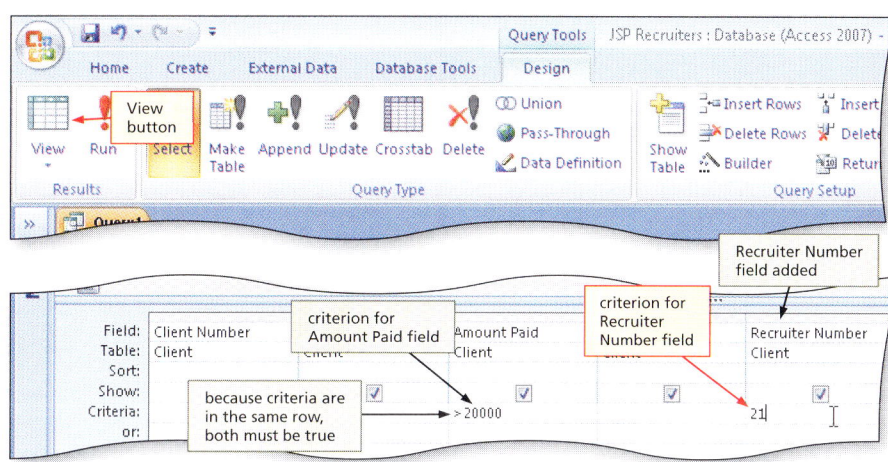

Figure 2–30

- View the query results (Figure 2–31).

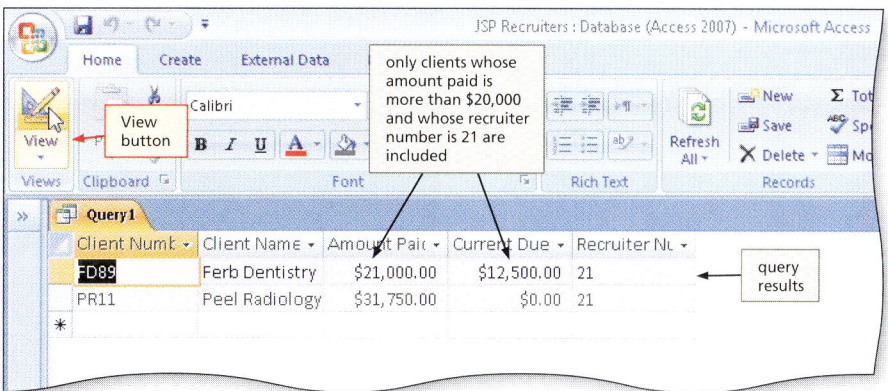

Figure 2–31

To Use a Compound Criterion Involving OR

To combine criteria with OR, the criteria must go on separate lines in the Criteria area of the grid. The following steps use an OR criterion to find those clients whose amount paid is greater than $20,000.00 or whose recruiter is recruiter 21 (or both).

- Return to Design view.
- If necessary, click the Criteria entry for the Recruiter Number field and then use the BACKSPACE key or the DELETE key to erase the entry ("21").
- Click the or: row (the row below the Criteria row) for the Recruiter Number field and then type 21 as the entry (Figure 2–32).

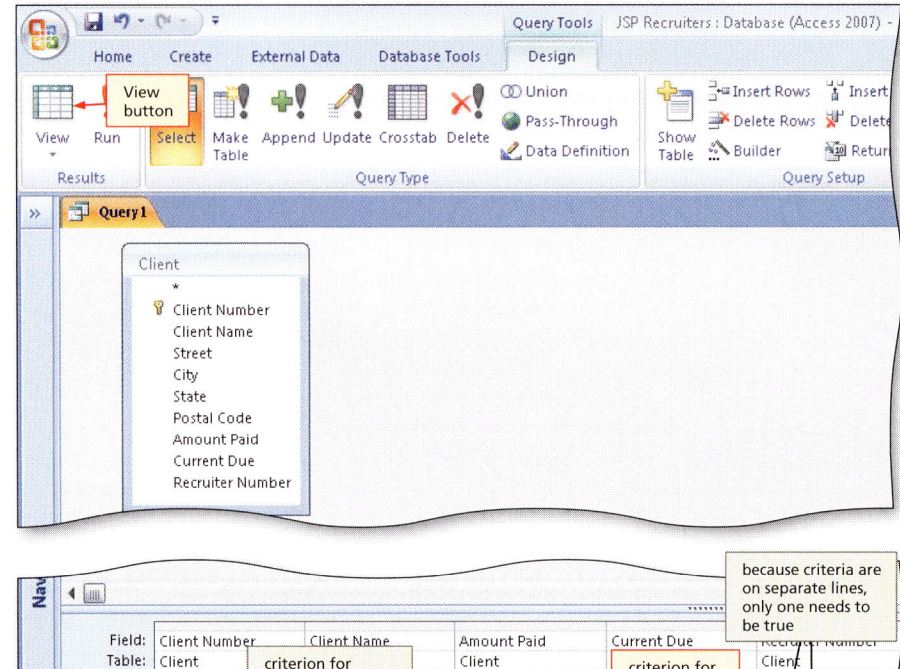

Figure 2–32

- View the query results (Figure 2–33).

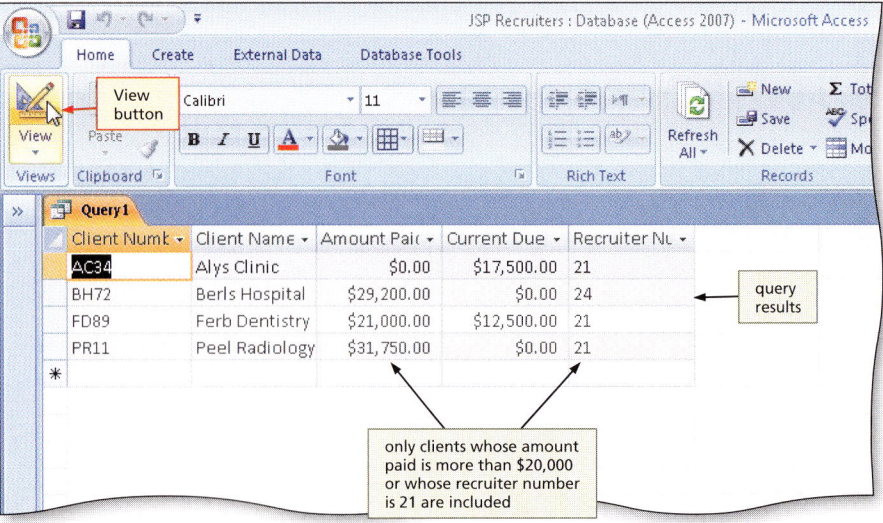

Figure 2–33

Sorting

In some queries, the order in which the records appear really does not matter. All you need to be concerned about are the records that appear in the results. It does not matter which one is first or which one is last.

In other queries, however, the order can be very important. You may want to see the cities in which clients are located and would like them arranged alphabetically. Perhaps you want to see the clients listed by recruiter number. Further, within all the clients of any given recruiter, you might want them to be listed by amount paid from largest amount to smallest.

To order the records in the answer to a query in a particular way, you **sort** the records. The field or fields on which the records are sorted is called the **sort key**. If you are sorting on more than one field (such as sorting by amount paid within recruiter number), the more important field (Recruiter Number) is called the **major key** (also called the **primary sort key**) and the less important field (Amount Paid) is called the **minor key** (also called the **secondary sort key**).

To sort in Microsoft Access, specify the sort order in the Sort row of the design grid below the field that is the sort key. If you specify more than one sort key, the sort key on the left will be the major sort key and the one on the right will be the minor key.

The following are guidelines related to sorting in queries.

> **BTW**
>
> **OR Criteria in a Single Field**
> If you want to combine two criteria with OR in a single field, you can place the criteria on separate lines, or you can place the criteria on the same line with the word OR in between them. For example, to include those records in which the city is Berls or Mason, you could type Berls OR Mason in the Criteria row. You also can use the IN operator, which consists of the word IN followed by the criteria in parentheses. For example, you would type IN (Berls, Mason).

Plan Ahead

> **Determine whether special order is required.**
>
> 1. **Determine whether sorting is required**. Examine the query or request to see if it contains words such as "order" or "sort" that would imply that the order of the query results is important. If so, you need to sort the query.
>
> 2. **Determine the sort key(s)**. If sorting is required, identify the field or fields on which the results are to be sorted. Look for words such as "ordered by" or "sort the results by," both of which would indicate that the specified field is a sort key.
>
> 3. **If using two sort keys, determine major and minor key**. If you are using two sort keys, determine which one is more important. That will be the major key. Look for words such as "sort by amount paid within recruiter number," which imply that the overall order is by recruiter number. Thus, the Recruiter Number field would be the major sort key and the Amount Paid field would be the minor sort key.
>
> 4. **Determine sort order**. Words such as "increasing," "ascending," or "low-to-high" imply Ascending order. Words such as "decreasing," "descending," or "high-to-low" imply Descending order. Sorting in alphabetical order implies Ascending order. If there are no words to imply a particular order, you would typically use Ascending.
>
> 5. **Determine restrictions**. Examine the query or request to see if there are any special restrictions. One common restriction is to exclude duplicates. Another common restriction is to list only a certain number of records, for example to list only the first five records.

To Clear the Design Grid

If the fields you want to include in the next query are different from those in the previous query, it is usually simpler to start with a clear grid, that is, one with no fields already in the design grid. You always can clear the entries in the design grid by closing the query and then starting over. A simpler approach to clearing the entries is to select all the entries and then press the DELETE key. The following steps return to Design view and clear the design grid.

- Return to Design view.
- Click just above the Client Number column heading in the grid to select the column.

Q&A I clicked above the column heading, but the column is not selected. What should I do?

You did not point to the correct location. Be sure the mouse pointer turns to a down-pointing arrow and then click again.

- Hold the SHIFT key down and click just above the Recruiter Number column heading to select all the columns (Figure 2–34).

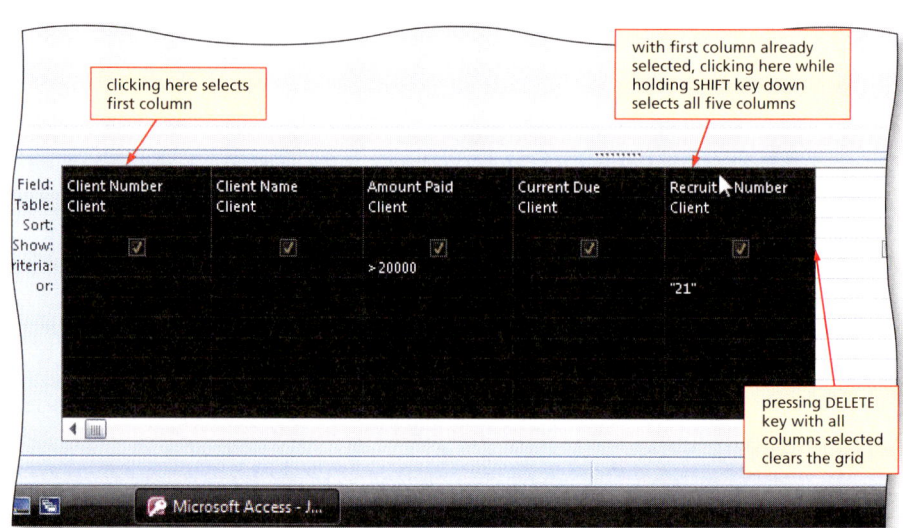

Figure 2–34

- Press the DELETE key to clear the design grid.

To Sort Data in a Query

If you have determined in the design process that a query is to be sorted, you must identify the sort key, that is, the field on which the results are to be sorted. In creating the query, you will need to specify the sort key to Access. The following steps sort the cities in the Client table by indicating that the City field is to be sorted. The steps specify Ascending sort order.

- Include the City field in the design grid.
- Click the Sort row below the City field, and then click the Sort row arrow to display a menu of possible sort orders (Figure 2–35).

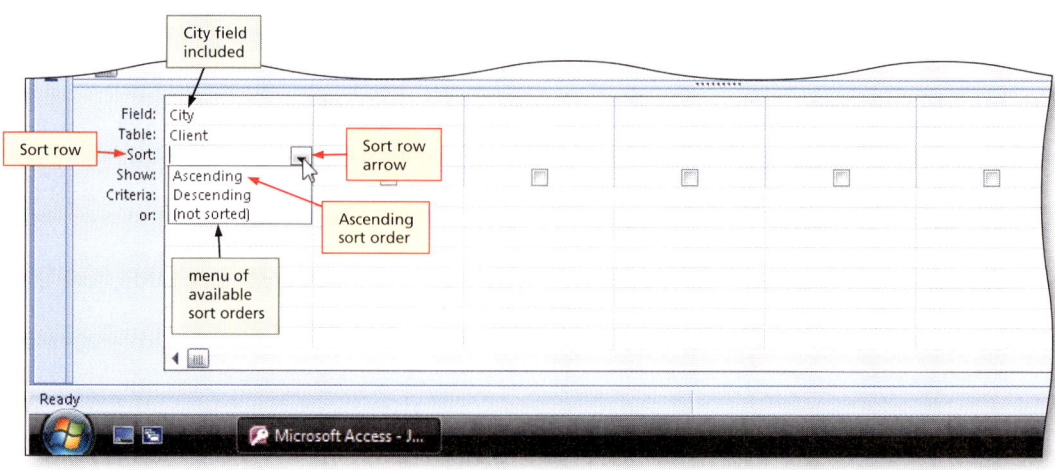

Figure 2–35

2
- Click Ascending to select Ascending sort order (Figure 2–36).

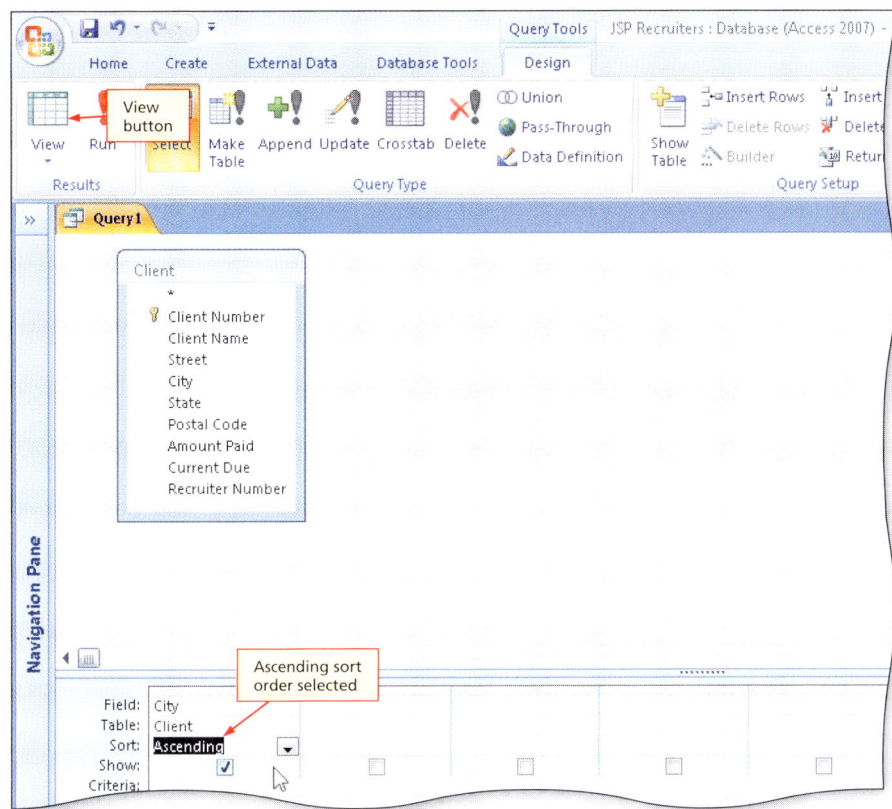

Figure 2–36

3
- View the query results (Figure 2–37).

  Experiment
- Return to Design view and change the sort order to Descending. View the results. Return to Design view and change the sort order back to Ascending. View the results.

Q&A Why do some cities appear more than once?

More than one client is located in those cities.

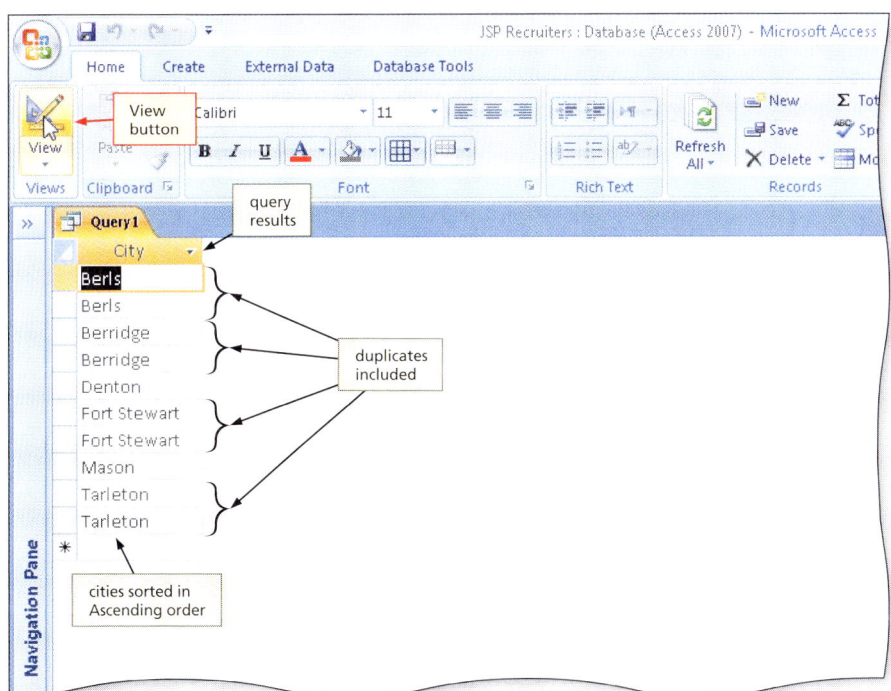

Figure 2–37

To Omit Duplicates

When you sort data, duplicates normally are included. In Figure 2–37 on the previous page, for example, Berridge appeared twice, as did Fort Stewart and Tarleton. These duplicates do not add any value, so you can eliminate them from the results. To eliminate duplicates, display the query's property sheet. A **property sheet** is a window containing the various properties of the object. To omit duplicates, you will use the property sheet to change the Unique Values property from No to Yes.

The following steps produce a sorted list of the cities in the Client table in which each city is listed only once.

- Return to Design view.
- Click the second field in the design grid (the empty field following City).
- If necessary, click Design on the Ribbon to display the Design tab.
- Click the Property Sheet button on the Design tab to display the property sheet (Figure 2–38).

Q&A My property sheet looks different. What should I do?

If your sheet looks different, you clicked the wrong place and will have to close the property sheet and repeat this step.

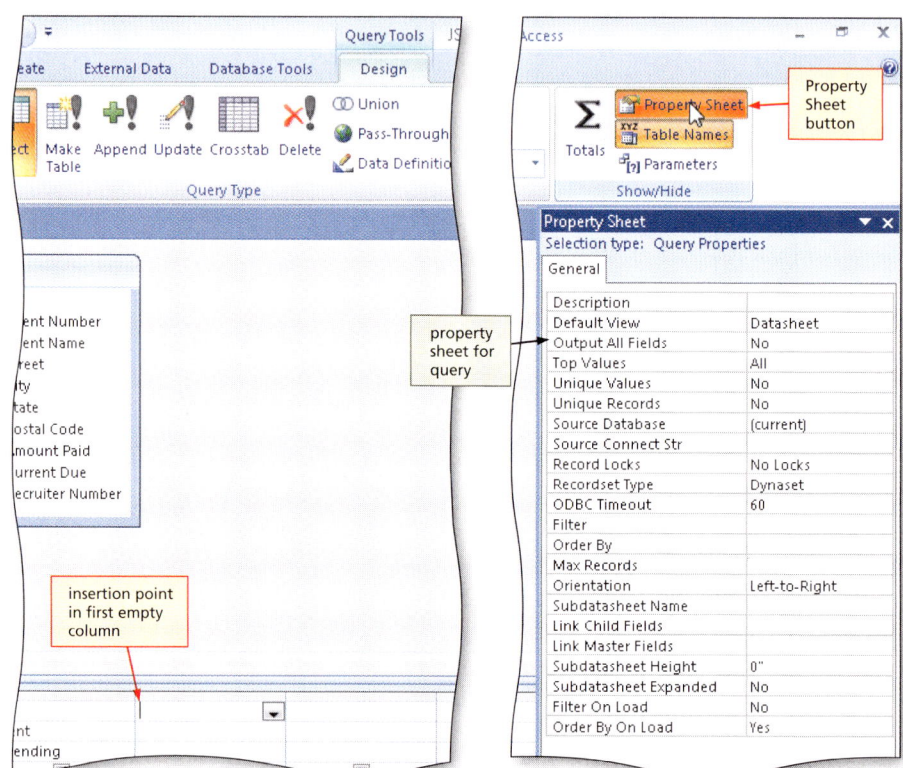

Figure 2–38

- Click the Unique Values property box, and then click the arrow that appears to produce a menu of available choices for Unique Values (Figure 2–39).

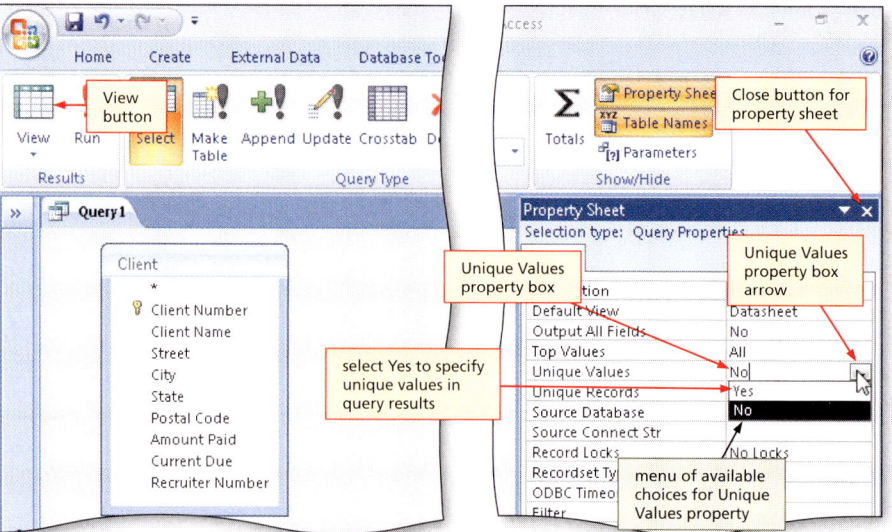

Figure 2–39

- Click Yes and then close the Query Properties sheet by clicking its Close button.
- View the query results (Figure 2–40).

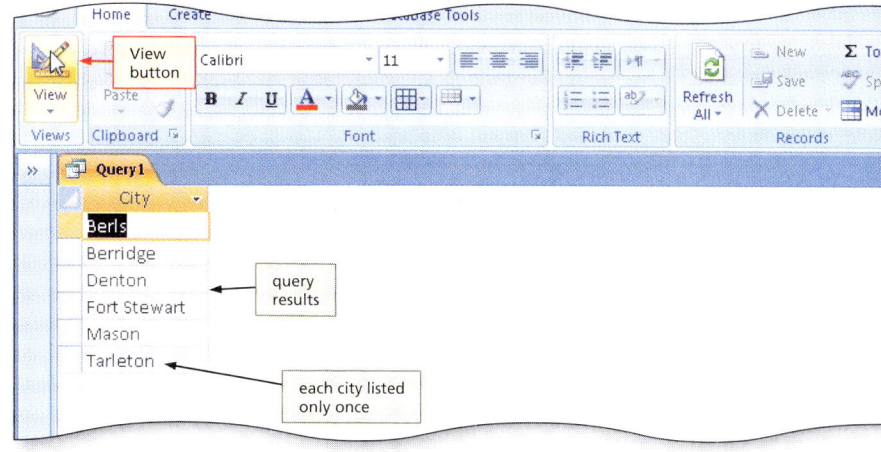

Figure 2–40

Other Ways
1. Right-click second field in design grid, click Properties on shortcut menu

To Sort on Multiple Keys

The following steps sort on multiple keys. Specifically, the data is to be sorted by amount paid (low to high) within recruiter number, which means that the Recruiter Number field is the major key and the Amount Paid field is the minor key.

- Return to Design view.
- Clear the design grid.
- Include the Client Number, Client Name, Recruiter Number, and Amount Paid fields in the query in this order.
- Select Ascending as the sort order for both the Recruiter Number field and the Amount Paid field (Figure 2–41).

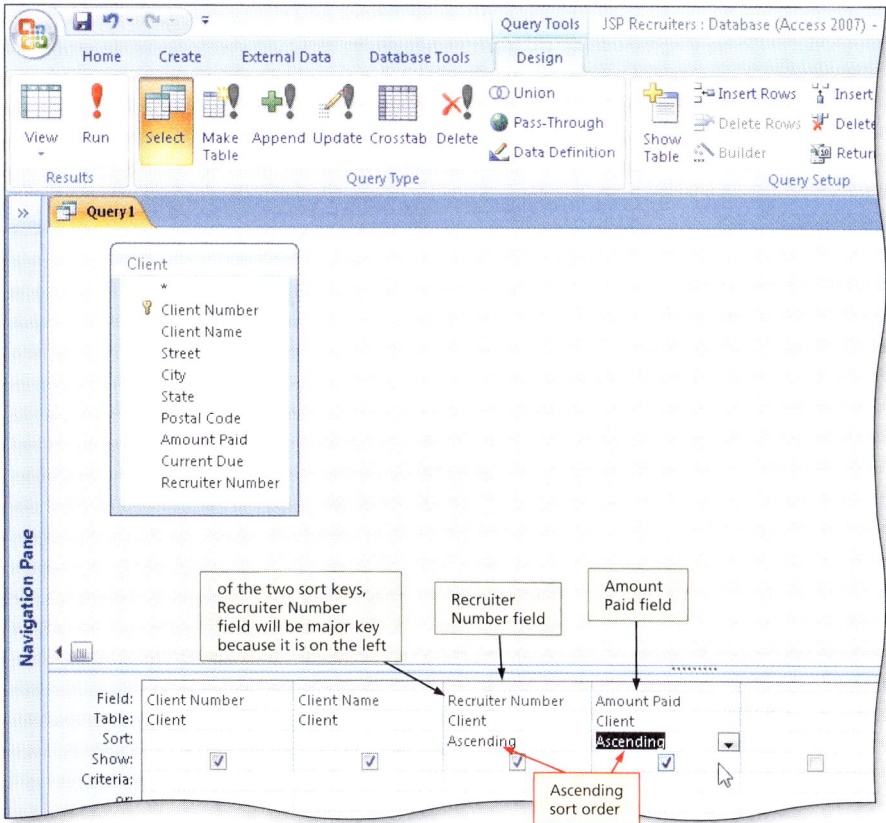

Figure 2–41

2

- View the query results (Figure 2–42).

🔍 **Experiment**

- Return to Design view and try other sort combinations for the Recruiter Number and Amount Paid fields, such as Ascending for Recruiter Number and Descending for Amount Paid. In each case, view the results to see the effect of the changes. When finished, select Ascending as the sort order for both fields.

 Q&A What if the Amount Paid field is to the left of the Recruiter Number?

It is important to remember that the major sort key must appear to the left of the minor sort key in the design grid. If you attempted to sort by amount paid within recruiter number, but placed the Amount Paid field to the left of the Recruiter Number field, your results would be incorrect.

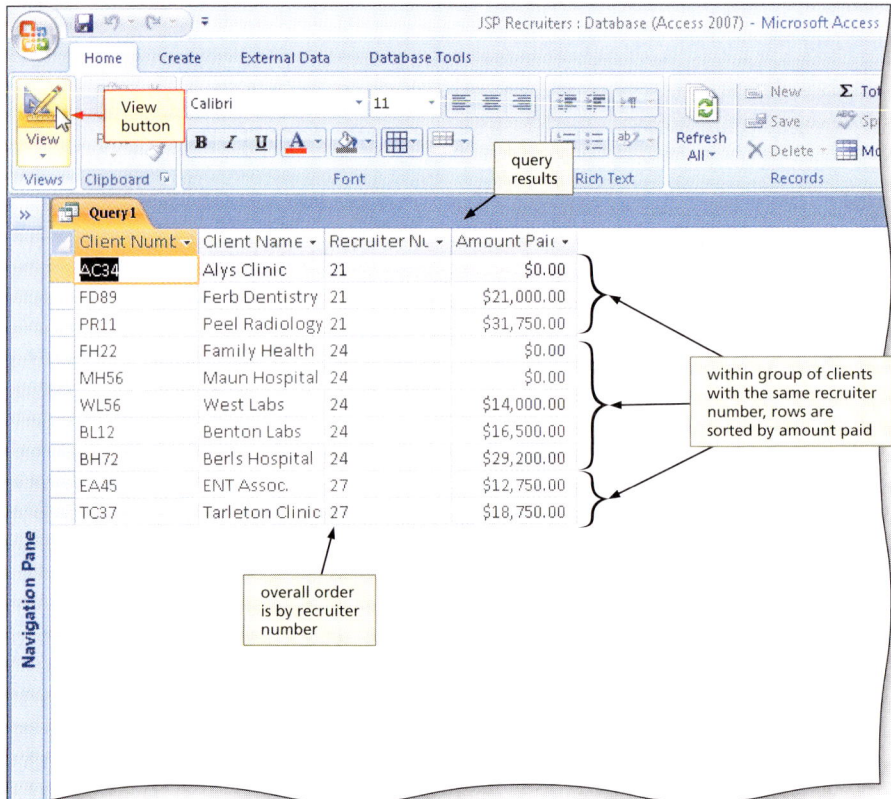

Figure 2–42

To Create a Top-Values Query

Rather than show all the results of a query, you may want to show only a specified number of records or a percentage of records. Creating a **top-values query** allows you to quantify the results. When you sort records, you can limit results to those records having the highest (descending sort) or lowest (ascending sort) values. To do so, first create a query that sorts the data in the desired order. Next, use the Return box on the Design tab to change the number of records to be included from All to the desired number or percentage. The following steps show the first five records that were included in the results of the previous query.

1

- Return to Design view.
- If necessary, click Design on the Ribbon to display the Design tab.
- Click the Return box arrow on the Design tab to display the Return box menu (Figure 2–43).

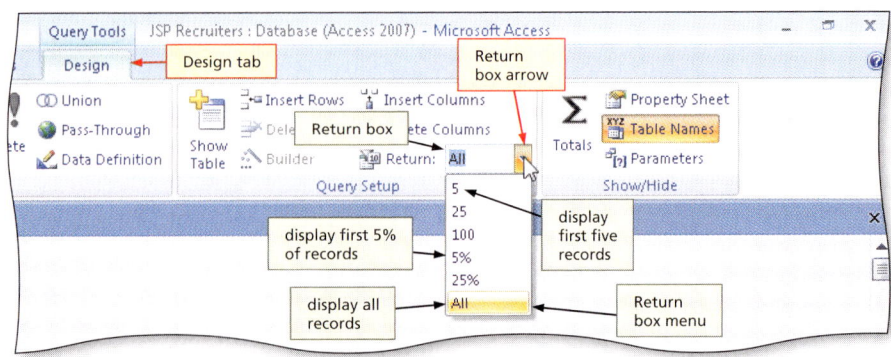

Figure 2–43

2

- Click 5 in the Return box menu to specify that the query results should contain the first five rows.

Q&A Could I have typed the 5? What about other numbers that do not appear in the list?

Yes, you could have typed the 5. For numbers not appearing in the list, you must type the number.

- View the query results (Figure 2–44).

3

- Close the query by clicking the Close 'Query1' button.
- When asked if you want to save your changes, click the No button.

Q&A Do I need to close the query before creating my next query?

Not necessarily. When you use a top-values query, however, it is important to change the value in the Return box back to All. If you do not change the Return value back to All, the previous value will remain in effect. Consequently, you may very well not get all the records you should in the next query. A good practice whenever you use a top-values query is to close the query as soon as you are done. That way, you will begin your next query from scratch, which guarantees that the value is set back to All.

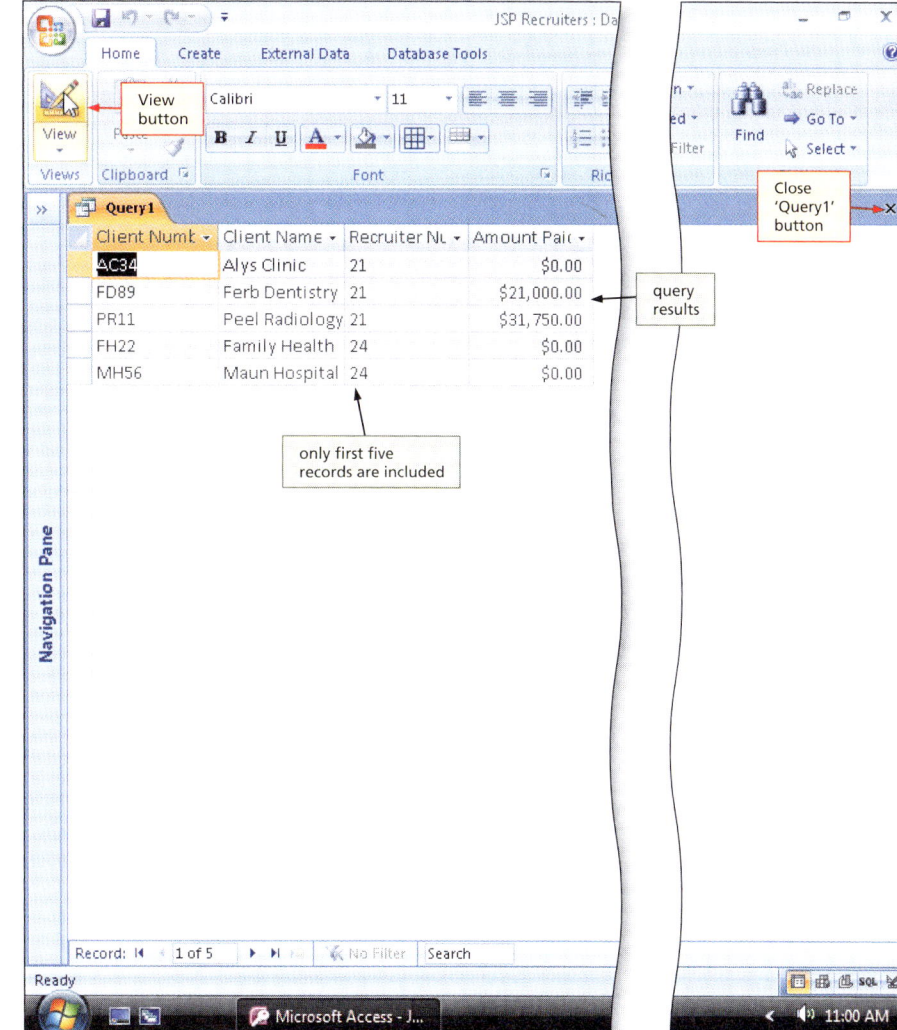

Figure 2–44

Joining Tables

In designing a query, you need to determine whether more than one table is required. If the question being asked involves data from both the Client and Recruiter tables, for example, both tables are required for the query. Such a query may require listing the number and name of each client along with the number and name of the client's recruiter. The client's name is in the Client table, whereas the recruiter's name is in the Recruiter table. Thus, this query cannot be completed using a single table; both the Client and Recruiter tables are required. You need to **join** the tables; that is, to find records in the two tables that have identical values in matching fields (Figure 2–45). In this example, you need to find records in the Client table and the Recruiter table that have the same value in the Recruiter Number fields.

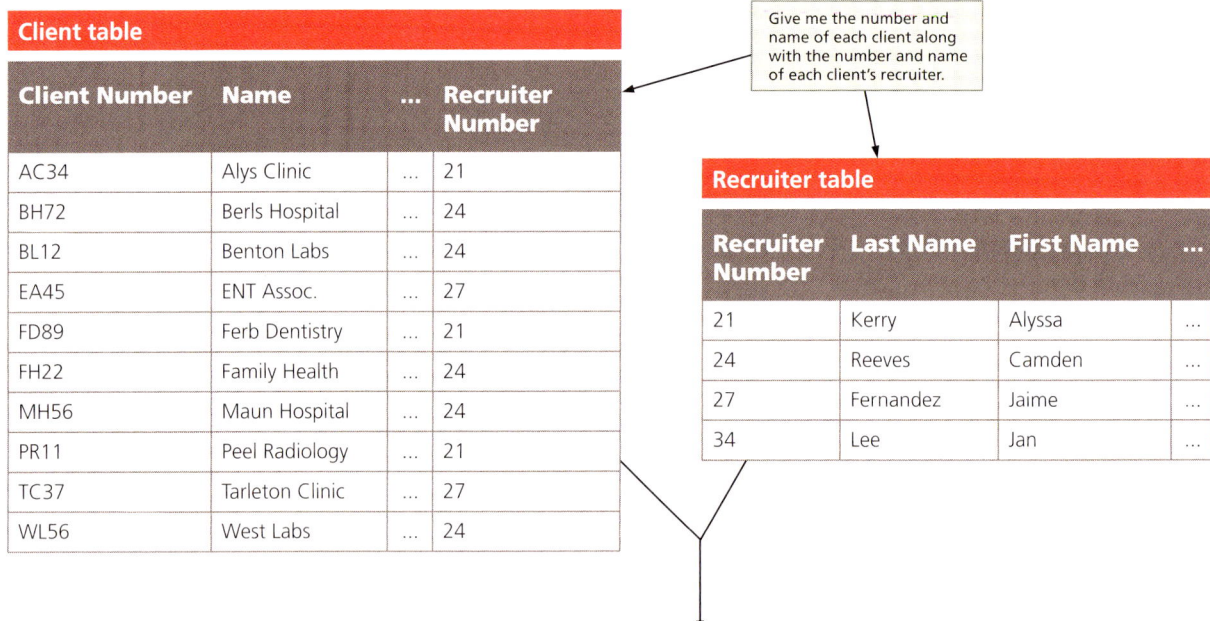

Figure 2–45

> **BTW**
>
> **Join Types**
> The type of join that finds records from both tables that have identical values in matching fields is called an inner join. An inner join is the default join in Access. Outer joins are used to show all the records in one table as well as the common records; that is, the records that share the same value in the join field. In a left outer join, all rows from the table on the left are included. In a right outer join, all rows from the table on the right are included.

The following are guidelines related to joining tables.

Plan Ahead

Determine whether more than one table is required.

1. **Determine whether more than one table is required.** Examine the query or request to see if all the fields involved in the request are in one table. If the fields are in two (or more) tables, you need to join the tables.

2. **Determine the matching fields.** If joining is required, identify the matching fields in the two tables that have identical values. Look for the same column name in the two tables or for column names that are similar.

(continued)

(continued)

Plan Ahead

3. **Determine whether sorting is required.** Queries that join tables often are used as the basis for a report. If this is the case, it may be necessary to sort the results. For example, the Recruiter-Client Report is based on a query that joins the Recruiter and Client tables. The query is sorted by recruiter number and client number.

4. **Determine restrictions.** Examine the query or request to see if there are any special restrictions. For example, the query may only want clients whose current due amount is $0.00.

5. **Determine join properties.** Examine the query or request to see if you only want records from both tables that have identical values in matching fields. If you want to see records in one of the tables that do not have identical values, then you need to change the join properties. When two tables have fields with the same name, you also need to determine which table contains the field to be used in the query. For example, if you want to see all recruiters, even if they have no clients, then you should include the recruiter number from the Recruiter table in the design grid. If you want only records with identical values in matching fields, then it does not matter which matching field you select.

To Join Tables

If you have determined in the design process that you need to join tables, you will first bring field lists for both tables to the upper pane of the Query window. Access will draw a line, called a **join line**, between matching fields in the two tables indicating that the tables are related. You then can select fields from either table. Access joins the tables automatically.

The first step is to create a new query and add the Recruiter table to the query. Then, add the Client table to the query. A join line will appear connecting the Recruiter Number fields in the two field lists. This join line indicates how the tables are related; that is, linked through these matching fields. (If you fail to give the matching fields the same name, Access will not insert the line. You can insert it manually, however, by clicking one of the two matching fields and dragging the mouse pointer to the other matching field.)

The following steps create a new query, add the Client table, and then select the appropriate fields.

1
- Click Create on the Ribbon to display the Create tab.
- Click the Query Design button to create a new query.
- Click the Recruiter table in the Show Table dialog box to select the table.
- Click the Add button to add a field list for the Recruiter table to the query (Figure 2–46).

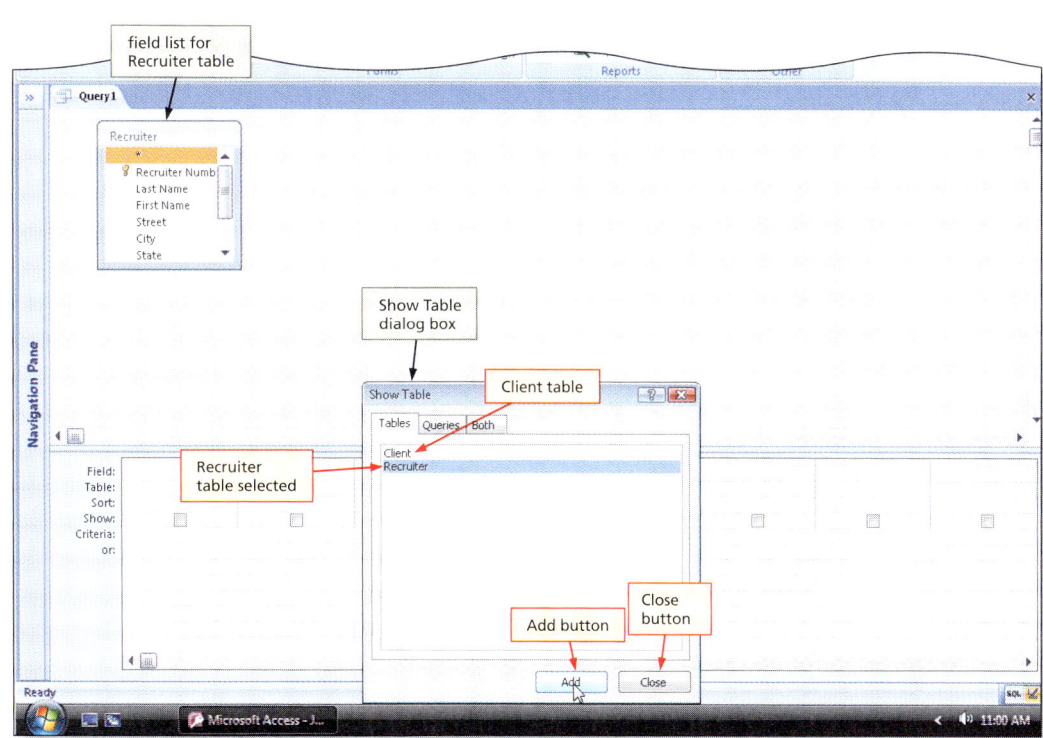

Figure 2–46

2

- Click the Client table in the Show Table dialog box.
- Click the Add button to add a field list for the Client table.
- Close the Show Table dialog box by clicking the Close button.
- Expand the size of the field lists so all the fields in the Recruiter and Client tables appear (Figure 2–47).

Q&A I did not get a join line. What should I do?

Ensure that the names of the matching fields are exactly the same, the data types are the same, and the matching field is the primary key in one of the two tables. If all of these are true and you still do not have a join line, you can produce one by pointing to one of the matching fields and dragging to the other matching field.

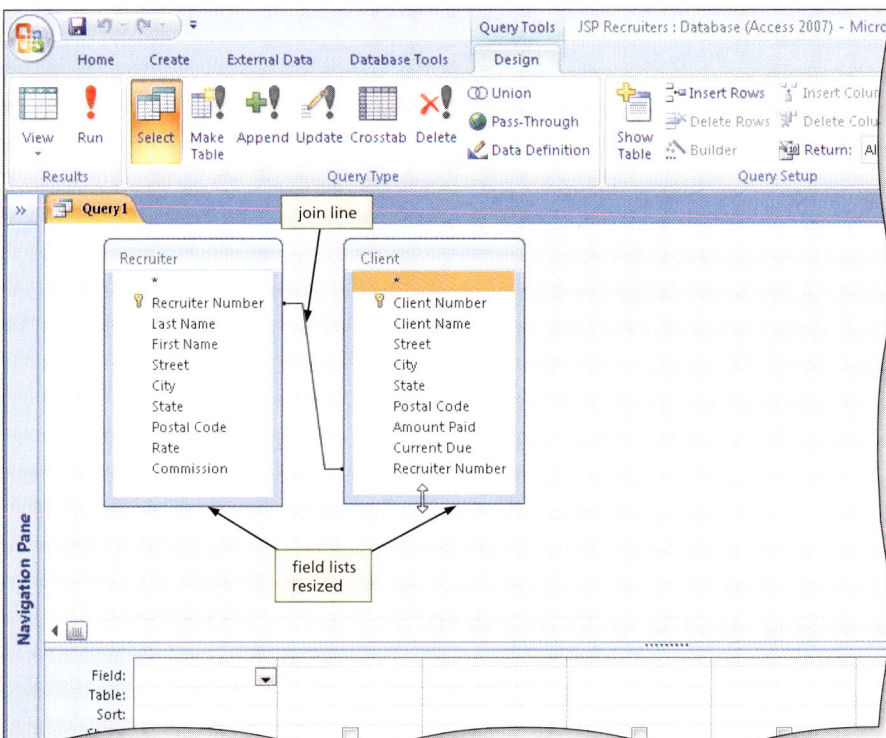

Figure 2–47

3

- In the design grid, include the Recruiter Number, Last Name, and First Name fields from the Recruiter table as well as the Client Number and Client Name fields from the Client table.
- Select Ascending as the sort order for both the Recruiter Number field and the Client Number field (Figure 2–48).

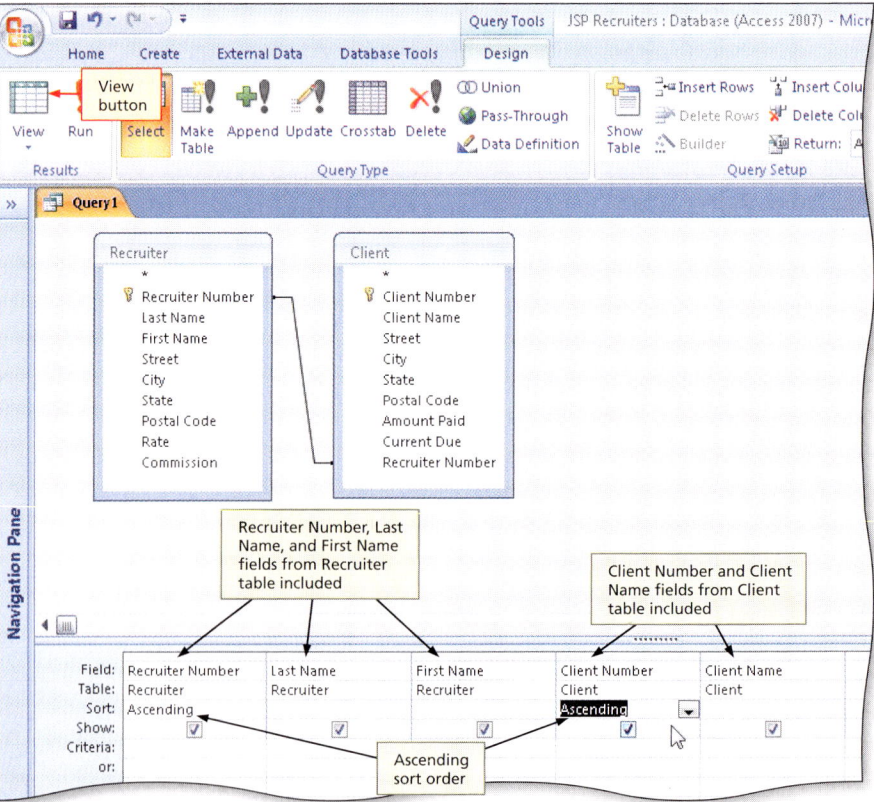

Figure 2–48

4

- View the query results (Figure 2–49).

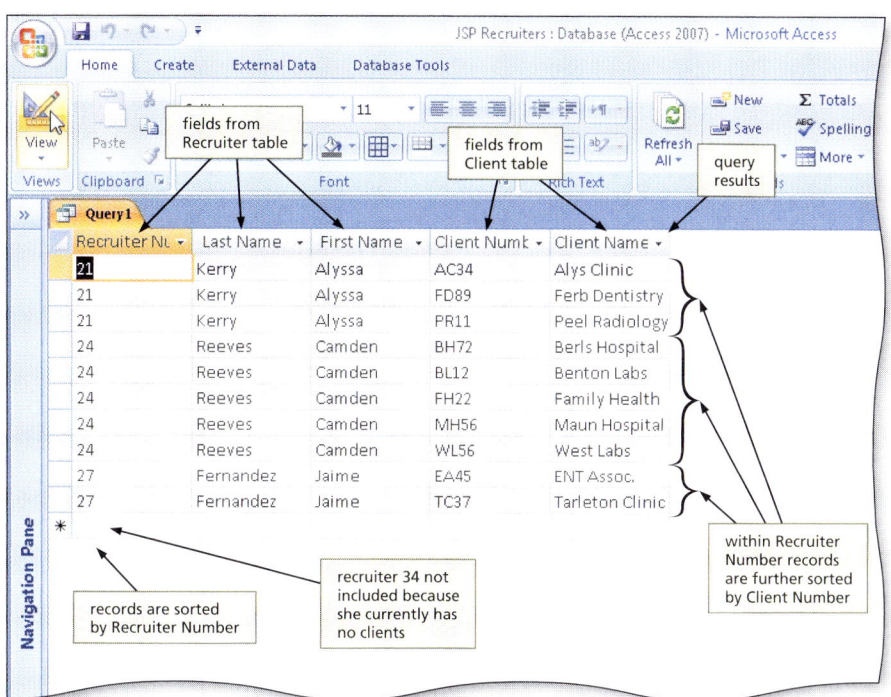

Figure 2–49

To Save the Query

The following steps save the query.

1

- Click the Save button on the Quick Access Toolbar to display the Save As dialog box.
- Type `Recruiter-Client Query` as the query name (Figure 2–50).

2

- Click the OK button to save the query.

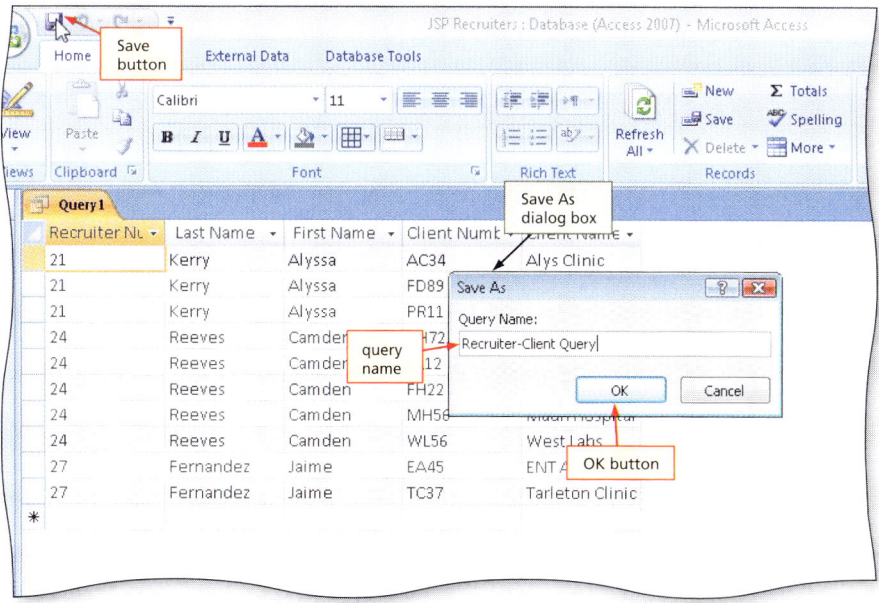

Figure 2–50

To Change Join Properties

Normally records that do not match do not appear in the results of a join query. A recruiter such as Jan Lee, for whom no clients currently exist, for example, would not appear. To cause such a record to be displayed, you need to change the **join properties**, which are the properties that indicate which records appear in a join, of the query, as in the following steps.

1

- Return to Design view.
- Right-click the join line to produce a shortcut menu (Figure 2–51).

Q&A I do not see Join Properties on my shortcut menu. What should I do?

If Join Properties does not appear on your shortcut menu, you did not point to the appropriate portion of the join line. You will need to point to the correct portion and right-click again.

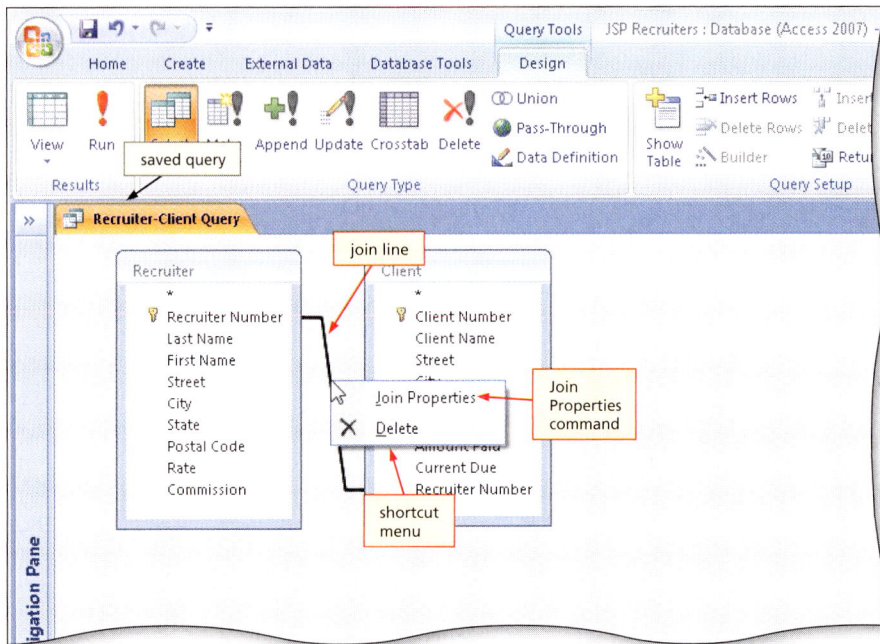

Figure 2–51

2

- Click Join Properties on the shortcut menu to display the Join Properties dialog box (Figure 2–52).

Q&A How do the options in the Join Properties dialog box match the various types of joins described earlier?

Option button 1 gives an inner join, option button 2 gives a left join, and option button 3 gives a right join.

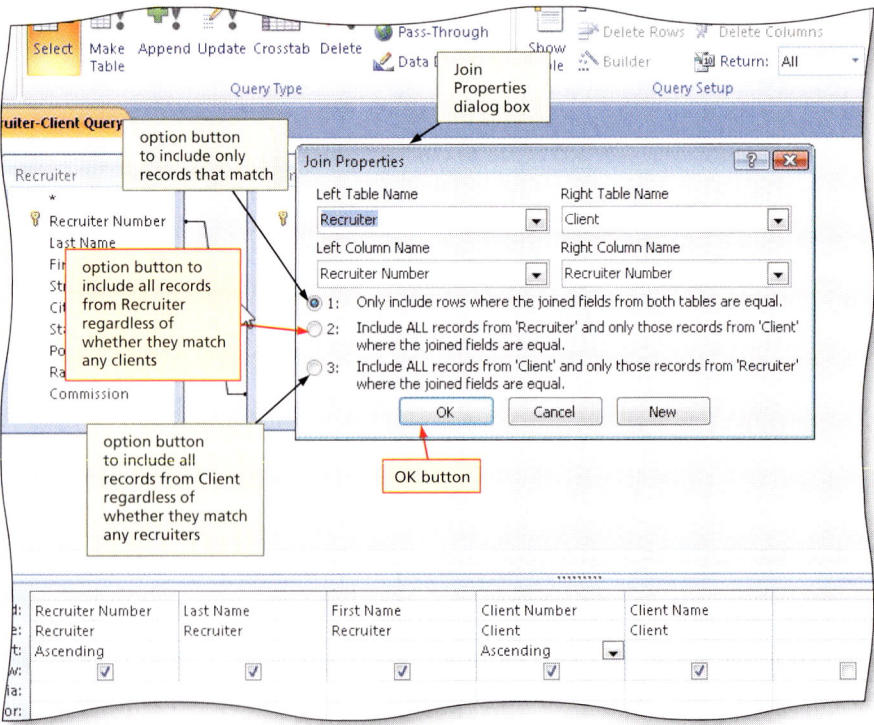

Figure 2–52

- Click option button 2 to include all records from the Recruiter table regardless of whether they match any clients.
- Click the OK button.
- View the query results by clicking the View button (Figure 2–53).
- Click the Save button on the Quick Access Toolbar.

Experiment

- Return to Design view, change the Join properties, and select option button 3. View the results to see the effect of this option. When done, return to Design view, change the Join properties, and once again select option button 2.

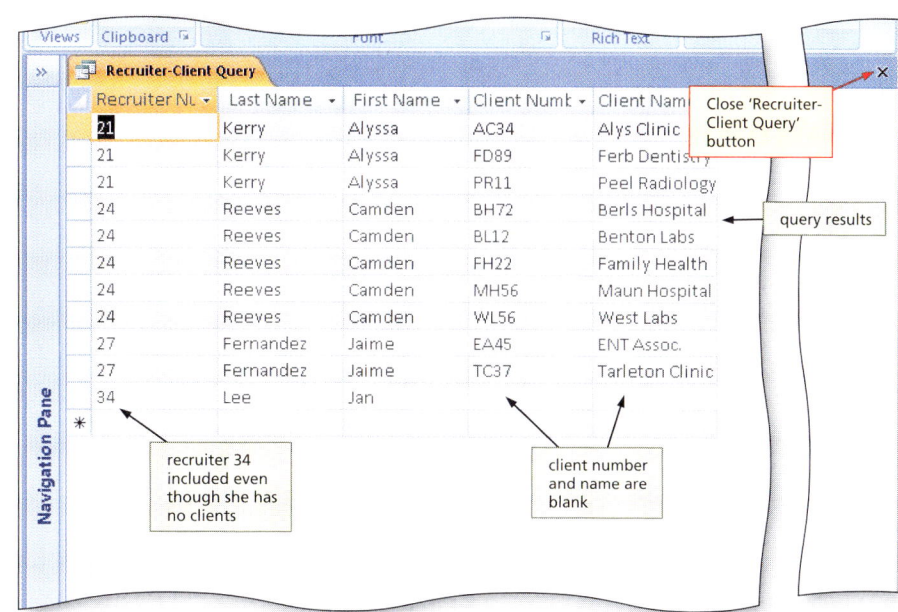

Figure 2–53

- Close the Recruiter-Client Query by clicking the Close 'Recruiter-Client Query' button. Click the No button if asked to save the changes to the query.

To Create a Report Involving a Join

The following steps create the report shown in Figure 2–54. The records in the report are sorted (ordered) by Client Number within Recruiter Number. To ensure that the records appear in this order, the steps specify that the Recruiter Number and Client Number fields are sort keys.

Recruiter-Client Report

Recruiter Number	Last Name	First Name	Client Number	Client Name
21	Kerry	Alyssa	AC34	Alys Clinic
21	Kerry	Alyssa	FD89	Ferb Dentistry
21	Kerry	Alyssa	PR11	Peel Radiology
24	Reeves	Camden	BH72	Berls Hospital
24	Reeves	Camden	BL12	Benton Labs
24	Reeves	Camden	FH22	Family Health
24	Reeves	Camden	MH56	Maun Hospital
24	Reeves	Camden	WL56	West Labs
27	Fernandez	Jaime	EA45	ENT Assoc.
27	Fernandez	Jaime	TC37	Tarleton Clinic
34	Lee	Jan		

Figure 2–54

1
- Show the Navigation Pane and be sure the Recruiter-Client Query is selected in the Navigation Pane.

Q&A I have two copies of Recruiter-Client Query. Does it matter which one I use?

No. There are two copies because the recruiter-Client Query involves two tables. It does not matter which one you select.

- Click Create on the Ribbon to display the Create tab.
- Click the Report Wizard button to display the Report Wizard dialog box (Figure 2–55).

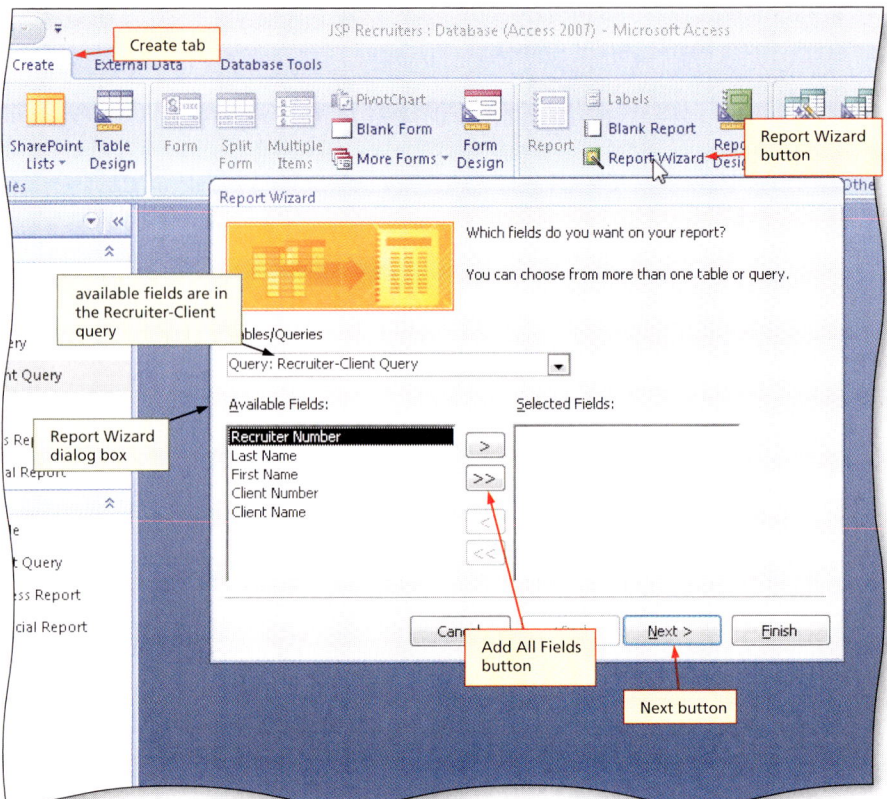

Figure 2–55

2
- Click the Add All Fields button to add all the fields in the Recruiter-Client Query.
- Click the Next button to display the next Report Wizard screen (Figure 2–56).

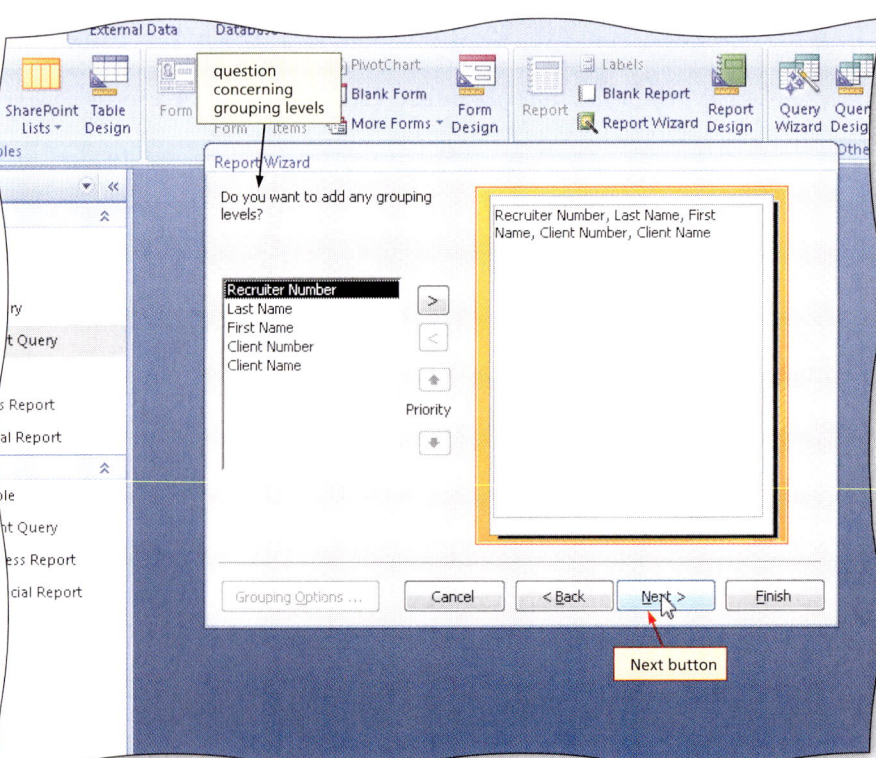

Figure 2–56

- Because you will not specify any grouping, click the Next button in the Report Wizard dialog box to display the next Report Wizard screen.

- Because you already specified the sort order in the query, click the Next button again to display the next Report Wizard screen.

- Make sure that Tabular is selected as the Layout and Portrait is selected as the Orientation.

- Click the Next button to display the next Report Wizard screen.

- Be sure the Module style is selected.

- Click the Next button to display the next Report Wizard screen.

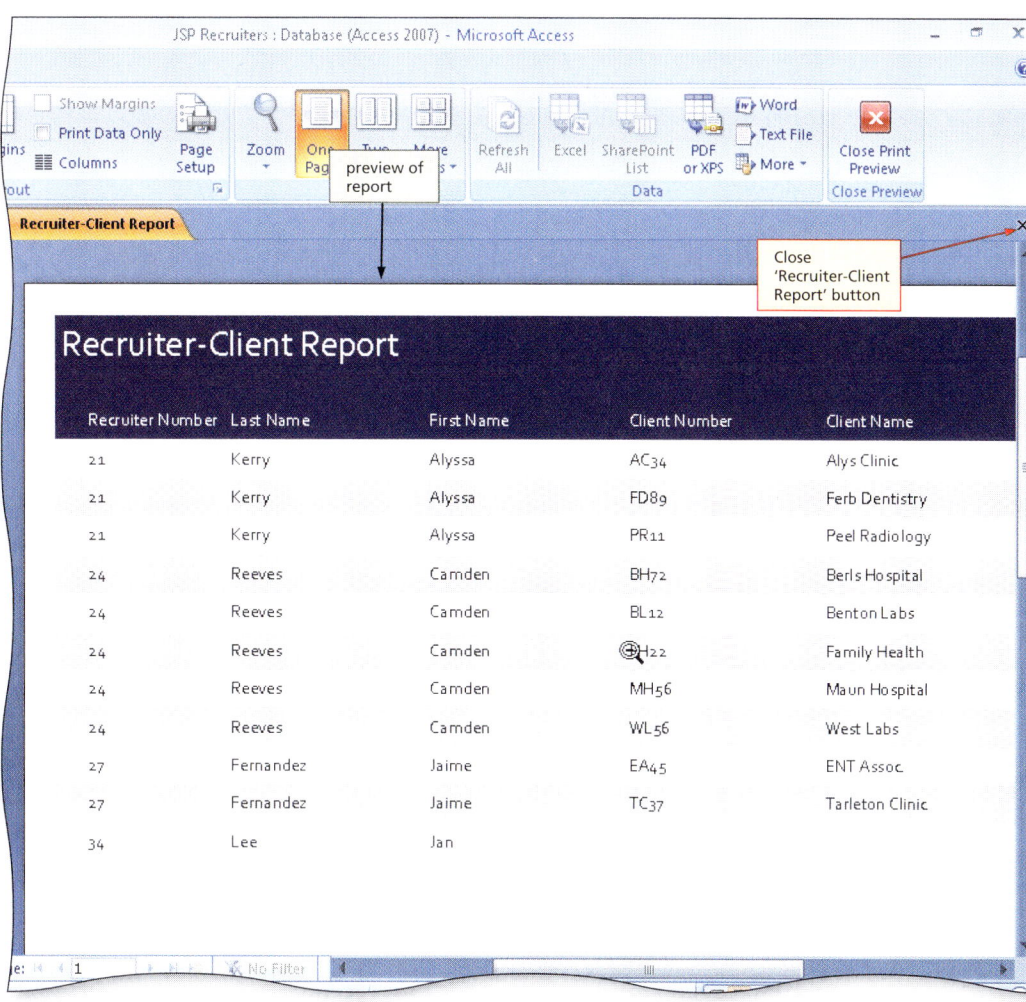

Figure 2-57

- Erase the current title, and then type Recruiter-Client Report as the new title.

- Click the Finish button to produce the report (Figure 2–57).

- Click the Close button for the Recruiter-Client Report to remove the report from the screen.

To Print a Report

Once you have created a report, you can print it at any time. The layout will reflect the layout you created. The data in the report will always reflect current data. The following step prints the Recruiter-Client Report.

1. With the Recruiter-Client Report selected in the Navigation Pane, click the Office Button, point to Print on the Office Button menu, and then click Quick Print on the Print submenu to print the report.

To Restrict the Records in a Join

Sometimes you will want to join tables, but you will not want to include all possible records. For example, you would like to create a report showing only those clients whose Amount Paid is greater than $20,000, but you do not want the Amount Paid field to appear in the results. In such cases, you will relate the tables and include fields just as you did before. You also will include criteria. To include only those clients whose amount paid is more than $20,000.00, you will include >20000 as a criterion for the Amount Paid field.

The following steps modify the Recruiter-Client query to restrict the records that will be included in the join.

- Open the Recruiter-Client Query in Design view and hide the Navigation Pane.
- Add the Amount Paid field to the query.
- Type **>20000** as the criterion for the Amount Paid field and then click the Show check box for the Amount Paid field to remove the check mark (Figure 2–58).

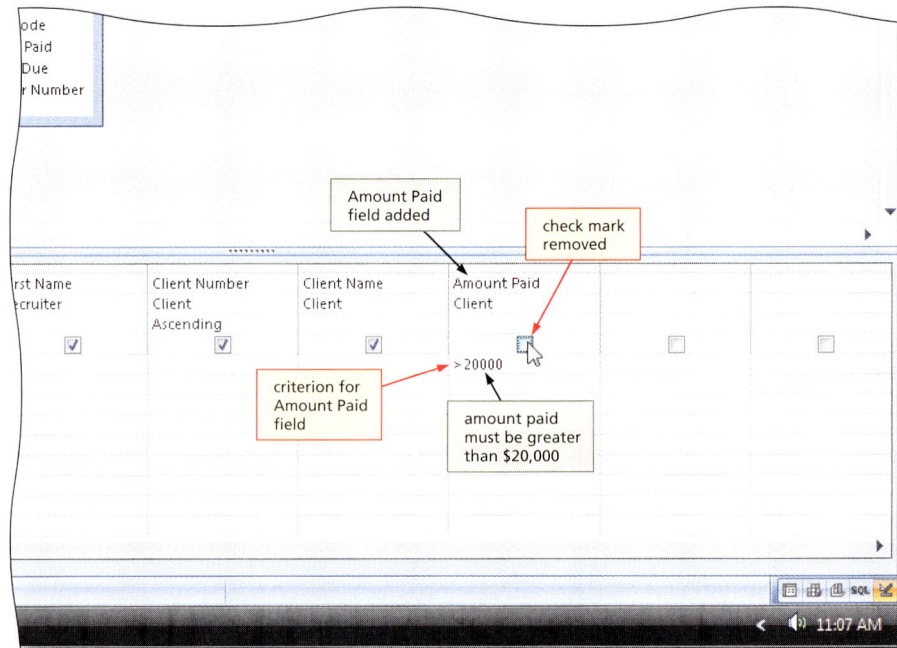

Figure 2–58

- View the query results (Figure 2–59).

- Close the query by clicking the Close 'Recruiter-Client Query' button.
- When asked if you want to save your changes, click the No button.

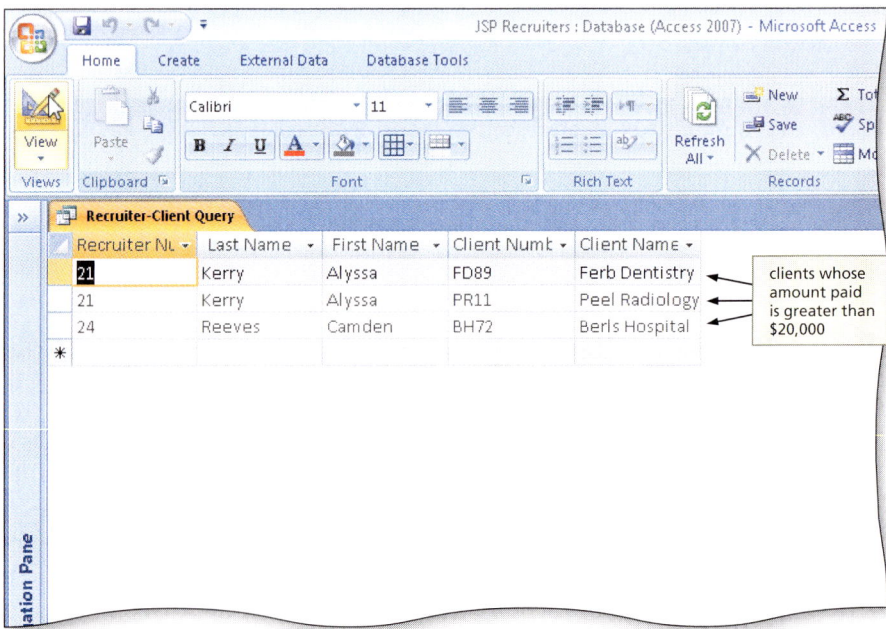

Figure 2–59

Calculations

If you have determined that a special calculation is required for a query, you then need to determine whether the calculation is an individual record calculation (for example, adding the values in two fields) or a group calculation (for example, finding the total of the values in a particular field on all the records).

JSP Recruiters may want to know the total amount (amount paid plus current due) from each client. This would seem to pose a problem because the Client table does not include a field for total amount. You can calculate it, however, because the total amount is equal to the amount paid plus the current due. A field that can be computed from other fields is called a **calculated field**. A calculated field is an individual record calculation.

JSP also may want to calculate the average amount paid for the clients of each recruiter. That is, they want the average for the clients of recruiter 21, the average for the clients of recruiter 24, and so on. This type of calculation is called a group calculation, because it involves groups of records. In this example, the clients of recruiter 21 would form one group, the clients of recruiter 24 would be a second, and the clients of recruiter 27 form a third group.

The following are guidelines related to calculations in queries.

> **BTW**
>
> **Expression Builder**
> Access includes a tool to help you create complex expressions. If you click Build on the shortcut menu (see Figure 2-60 on the next page), Access displays the Expression Builder dialog box. The dialog box includes an expression box, operator buttons, and expression elements. You use the expression box to build the expression. You can type parts of the expression directly and paste operator buttons and expression elements into the box. You also can use functions in expressions.

Plan Ahead

Determine whether calculations are required.

1. **Determine whether calculations are required.** Examine the query or request to see if there are special calculations to be included. Look for words such as "total," "sum," "compute," or "calculate."

2. **Determine a name for the calculated field.** If calculations are required, decide on the name for the field. Assign a name that helps identify the contents of the field. For example, if you are adding the cost of a number of items, the name "Total Cost" would be appropriate. The name, also called an **alias**, becomes the column name when the query is run.

3. **Determine the format for the calculated field.** Determine how the calculated field should appear. If the calculation involves monetary amounts, you would use the currency format. If the calculated value contains decimals, determine how many decimal places to display.

To Use a Calculated Field in a Query

If you have determined that you need a calculated field in a query, you enter a name (alias) for the calculated field, a colon, and then the expression in one of the columns in the Field row. Any fields included in the expression must be enclosed in square brackets [ ]. For the total amount, for example, you will type Total Amount:[Amount Paid]+[Current Due] as the expression.

You can type the expression directly into the Field row. You will not be able to see the entire entry, however, because the Field row is not large enough. The preferred way is to select the column in the Field row and then use the Zoom command on its shortcut menu. When Access displays the Zoom dialog box, you can enter the expression.

You are not restricted to addition in calculations. You can use subtraction (-), multiplication (*), or division (/). You also can include parentheses in your calculations to indicate which calculations should be done first.

The steps on the next page use a calculated field to display the number, name, amount paid, current due, and the total amount for all clients.

1

- Create a query with a field list for the Client table.
- Add the Client Number, Client Name, Amount Paid, and Current Due fields to the query.
- Right-click the Field row in the first open column in the design grid to display a shortcut menu (Figure 2–60).

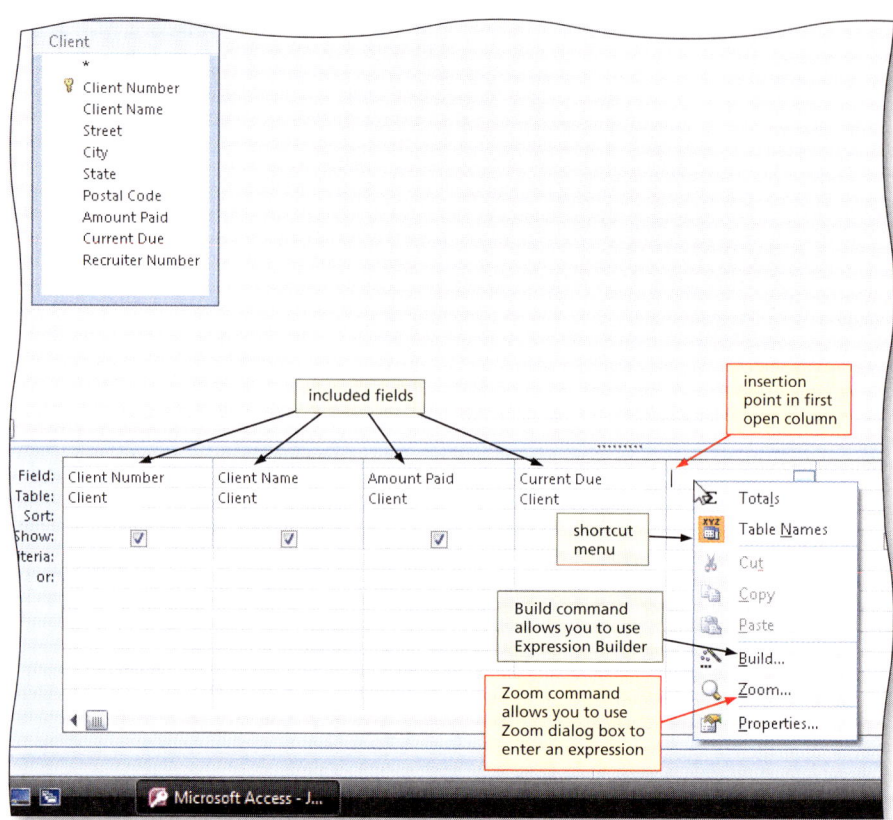

Figure 2–60

2

- Click Zoom on the shortcut menu to display the Zoom dialog box.
- Type `Total Amount:[Amount Paid]+[Current Due]` in the Zoom dialog box (Figure 2–61).

Q&A Do I always need to put square brackets around field names?

If the field name does not contain spaces, square brackets are technically not necessary, although it is still acceptable to use the brackets. It is a good practice, however, to get in the habit of using the brackets.

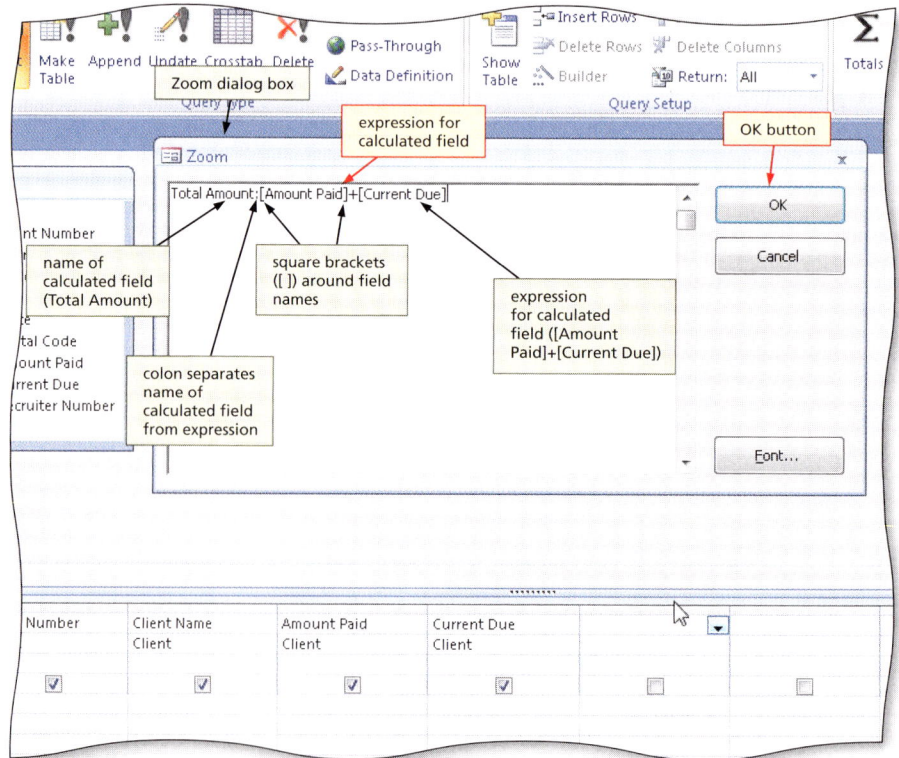

Figure 2–61

3

- Click the OK button to enter the expression (Figure 2–62).

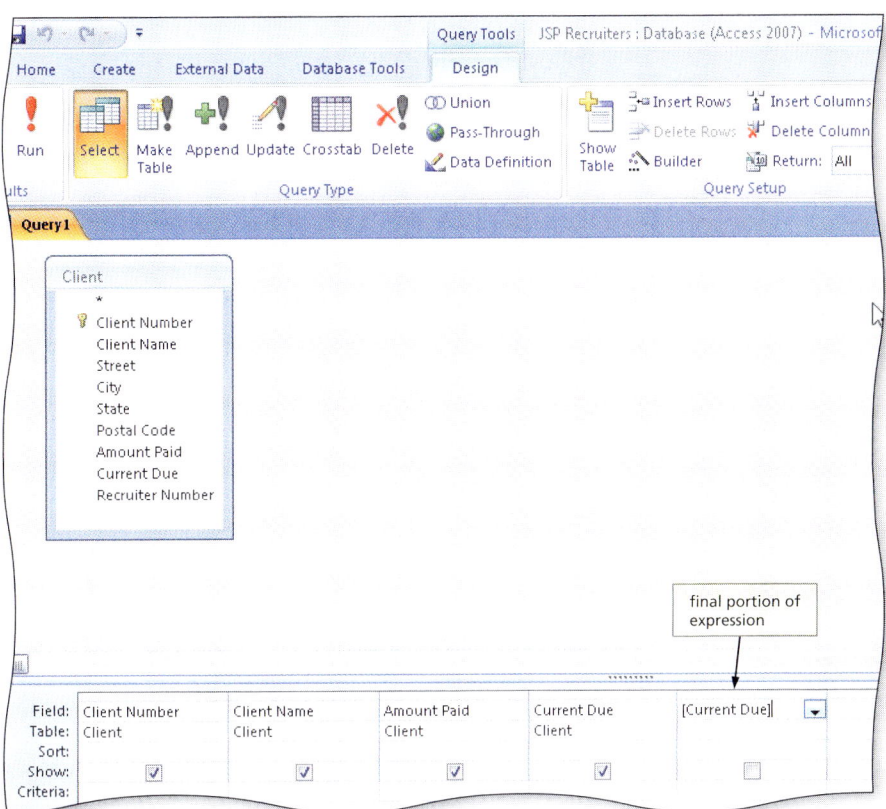

Figure 2–62

4

- View the query results (Figure 2–63).

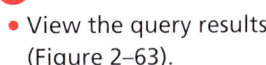 **Experiment**

- Return to Design view and try other expressions. In at least one case, omit the Total Amount and the colon. In at least one case, intentionally misspell a field name. In each case, view the results to see the effect of your changes. When finished, reenter the original expression.

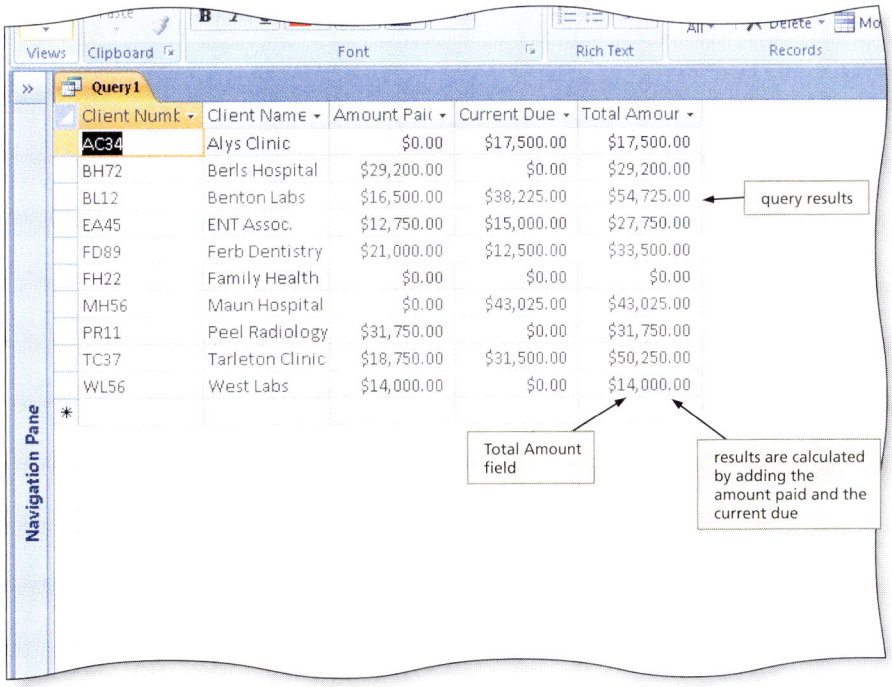

Figure 2–63

Instead of clicking Zoom on the shortcut menu, you can click Build. Access displays the Expression Builder dialog box that provides assistance in creating the expression. If you know the expression you will need, however, it is often easier to enter it using the Zoom command.

To Change a Caption

You can change the way items appear in the results of a query by changing their format. You also can change a query result's heading at the top of a column by changing the caption. Just as when you omitted duplicates, you will make this change by using a property sheet. In the property sheet, you can change the desired property, such as the format, the number of decimal places, or the caption. The following steps change the caption of the Amount Paid field to Paid and the caption of the Current Due field to Due.

- Return to Design view.

- Click Design on the Ribbon to display the Design tab.

- Click the Amount Paid field in the design grid, and then click the Property Sheet button on the Design tab.

- Click the Caption box, and then type Paid as the caption (Figure 2–64).

Q&A My property sheet looks different. What should I do?

If your sheet looks different, you clicked the wrong place and will have to close the property sheet and repeat this step.

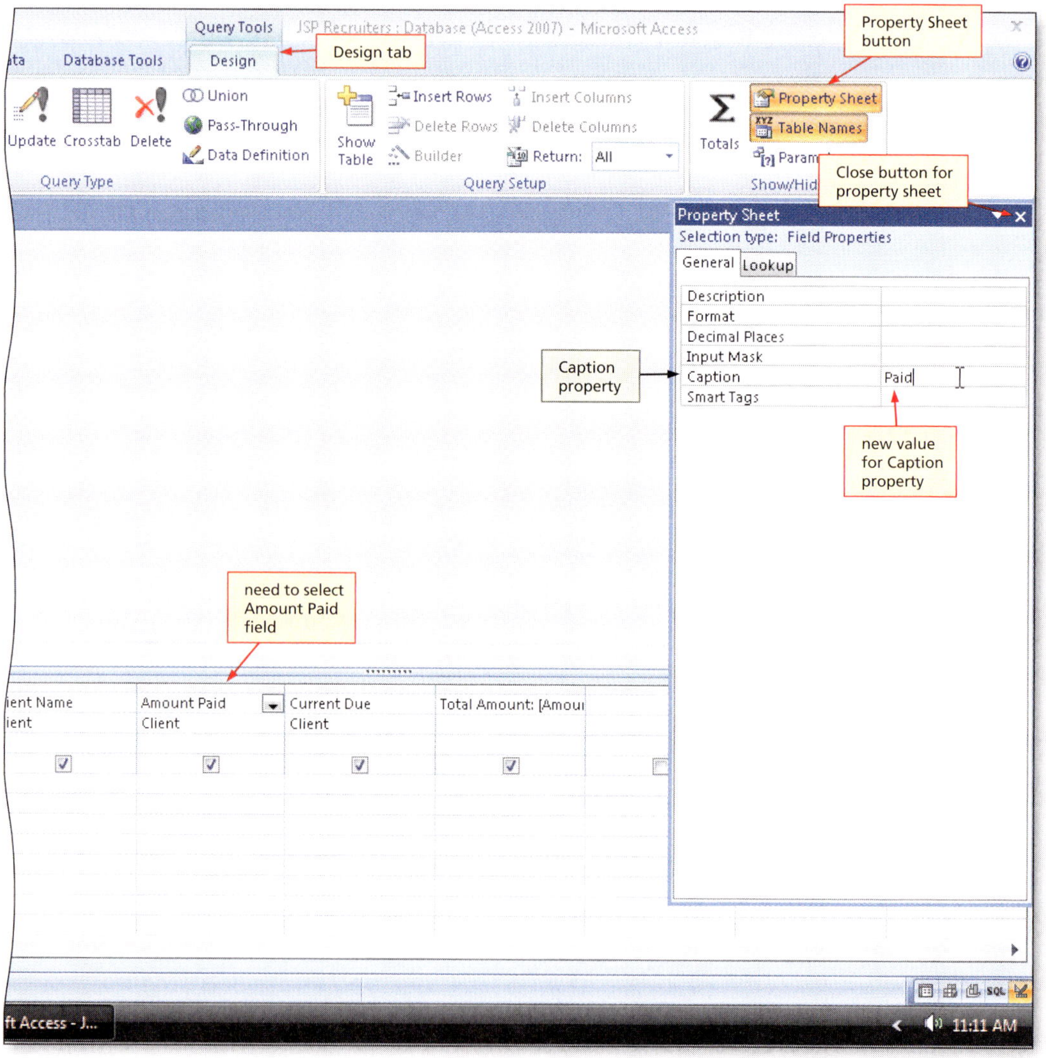

Figure 2–64

- Close the property sheet by clicking its Close button.

- Click the Current Due field in the design grid, and then click the Property Sheet button on the Design tab.

- Click the Caption box, and then type Due as the caption.

- Close the Property Sheet by clicking its Close button.

- View the query results (Figure 2–65).

- Click the Close 'Query1' button to close the query.

- When asked if you want to save your changes, click the No button.

Q&A What would happen if I clicked the Yes button instead of the No button?

If you had saved the query, the changes you made to the properties would be saved in the database along with the query.

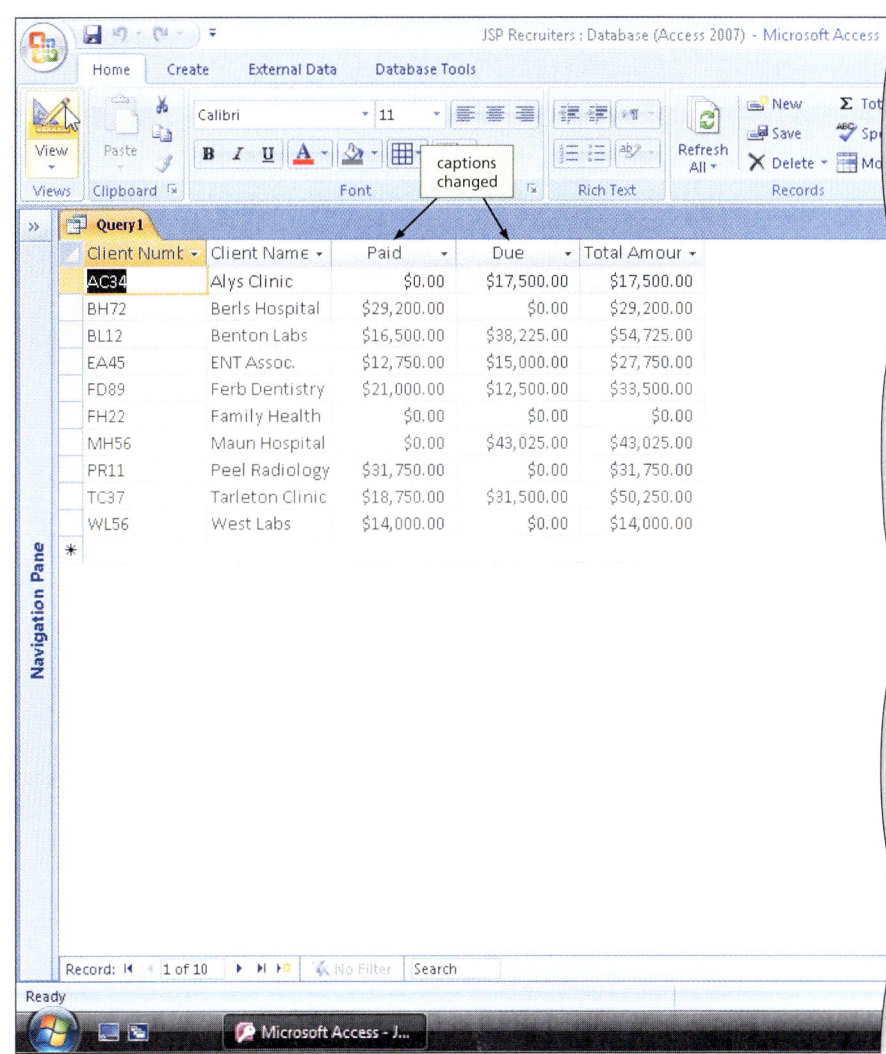

Figure 2–65

Other Ways

1. Right-click field in design grid, click Properties on shortcut menu

Calculating Statistics

For group calculations, Microsoft Access supports several built-in statistics: COUNT (count of the number of records), SUM (total), AVG (average), MAX (largest value), MIN (smallest value), STDEV (standard deviation), VAR (variance), FIRST (first value), and LAST (last value). These statistics are called aggregate functions. An **aggregate function** is a function that performs some mathematical function against a group of records. To use any of these aggregate functions in a query, you include it in the Total row in the design grid. The Total row routinely does not appear in the grid. To include it, click the Totals button on the Design tab.

To Calculate Statistics

The following steps create a new query for the Client table, include the Total row in the design grid, and then calculate the average amount paid for all clients.

- Create a new query with a field list for the Client table.
- If necessary, click Design on the Ribbon to display the Design tab.
- Add the Amount Paid field to the query.
- Click the Totals button on the Design tab to include the Total row in the design grid (Figure 2-66).

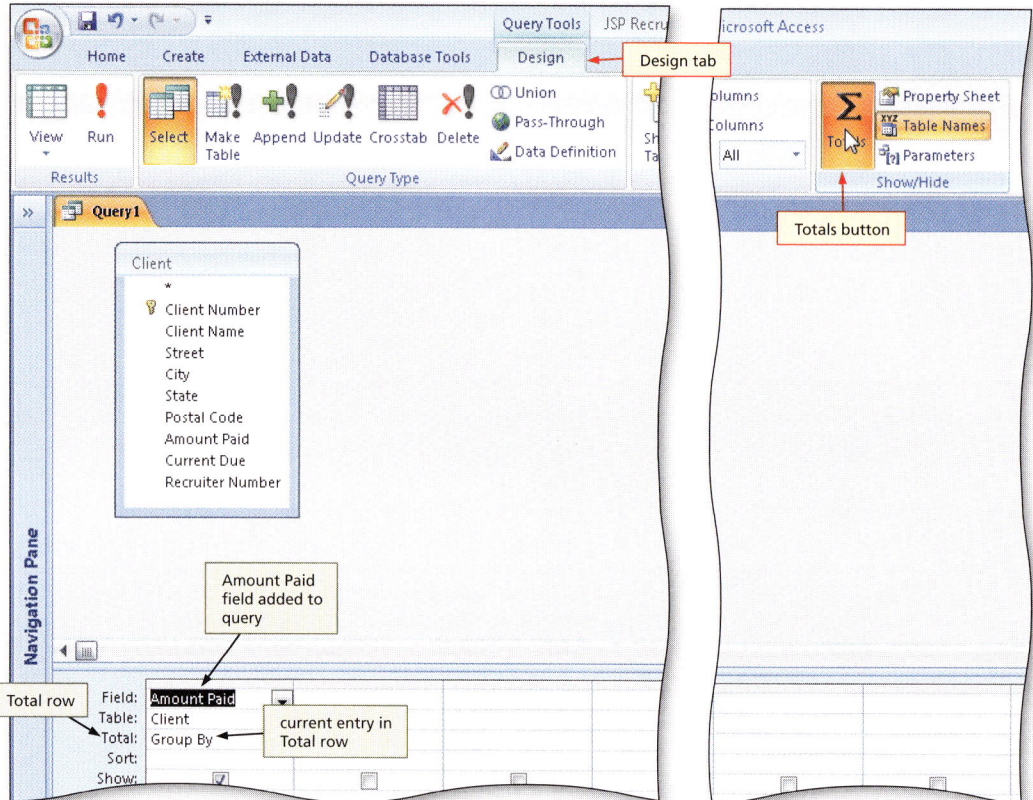

Figure 2–66

- Click the Total row in the Amount Paid column to display the Total box arrow.
- Click the Total box arrow to display the Total list (Figure 2–67).

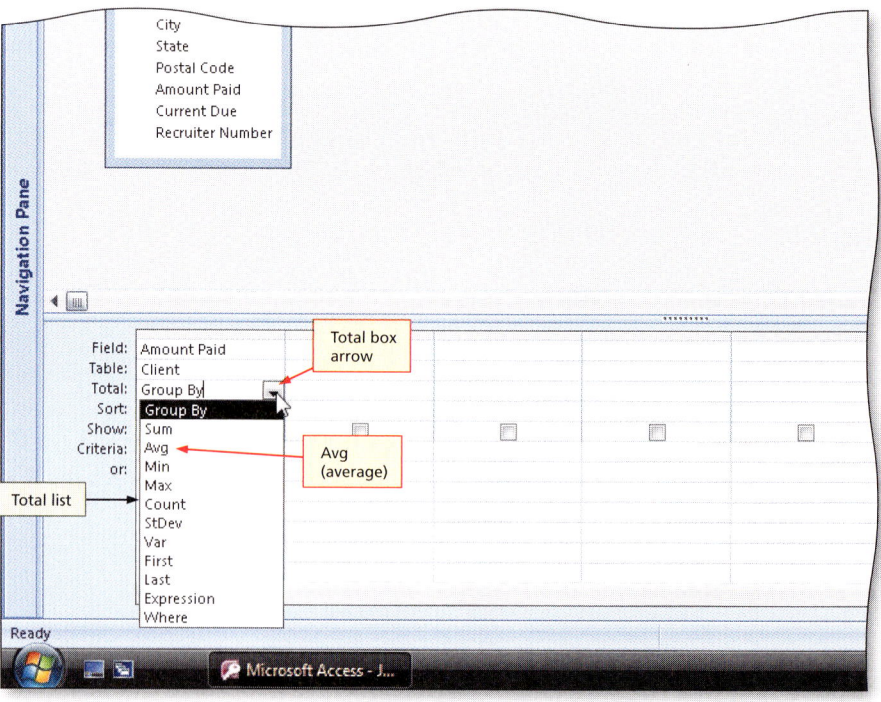

Figure 2–67

3
- Click Avg to indicate that Access is to calculate an average (Figure 2–68).

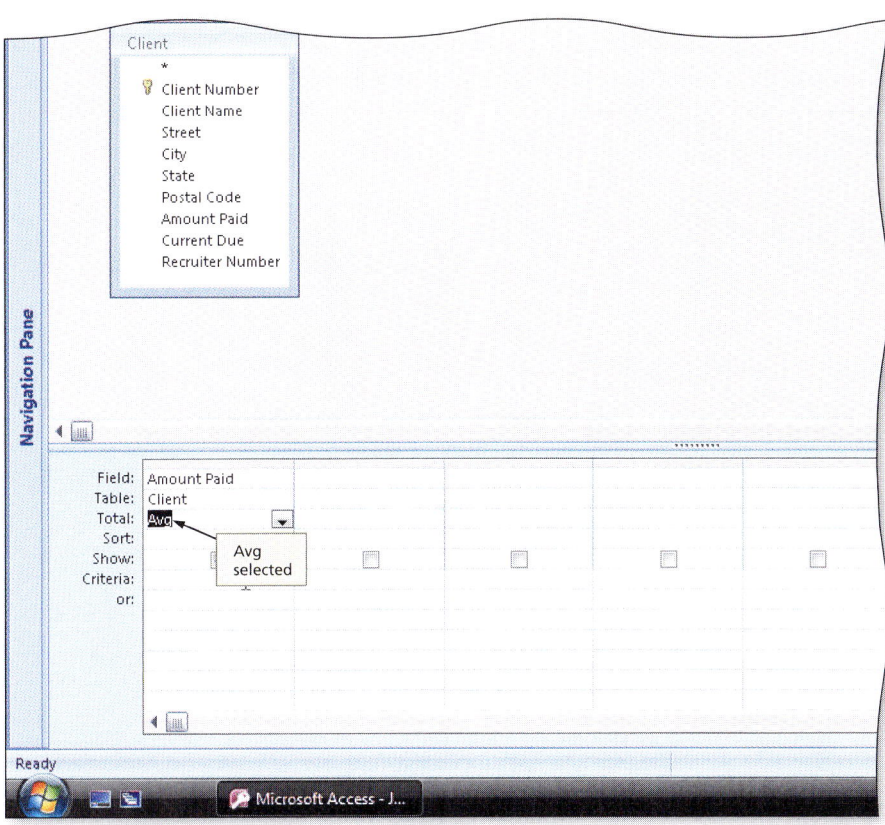

Figure 2–68

4
- View the query results (Figure 2–69).

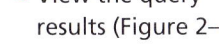 **Experiment**

- Return to Design view and try other aggregate functions. In each case, view the results to see the effect of your selection. When finished, select average once again.

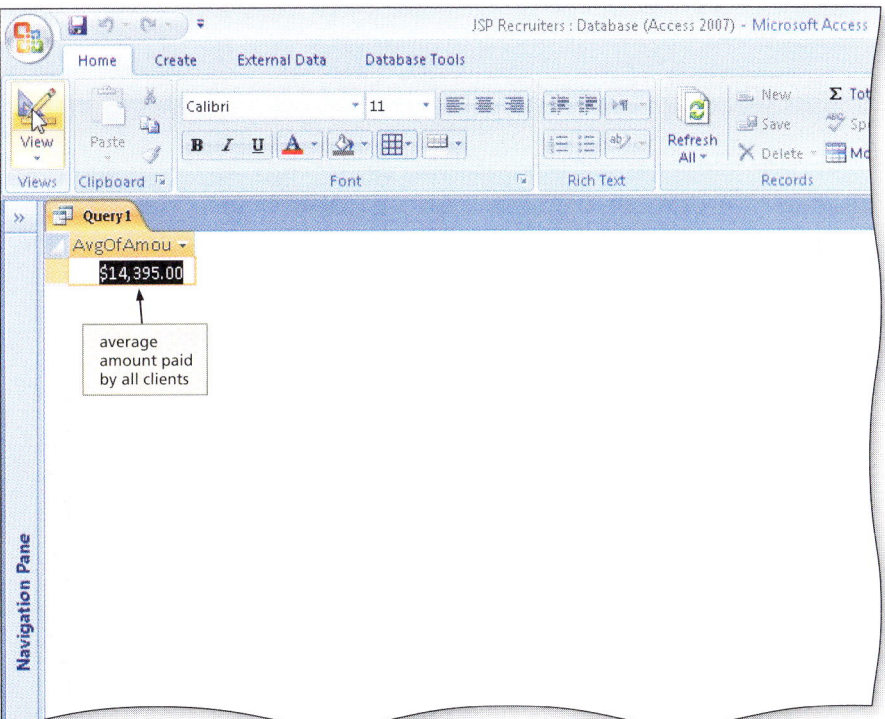

Figure 2–69

To Use Criteria in Calculating Statistics

Sometimes calculating statistics for all the records in the table is appropriate. In other cases, however, you will need to calculate the statistics for only those records that satisfy certain criteria. To enter a criterion in a field, first you select Where as the entry in the Total row for the field, and then enter the criterion in the Criteria row. The following steps use this technique to calculate the average amount paid for clients of recruiter 21.

- Return to Design view.
- Include the Recruiter Number field in the design grid.
- Click the Total box arrow in the Recruiter Number column to produce a Total list (Figure 2–70).

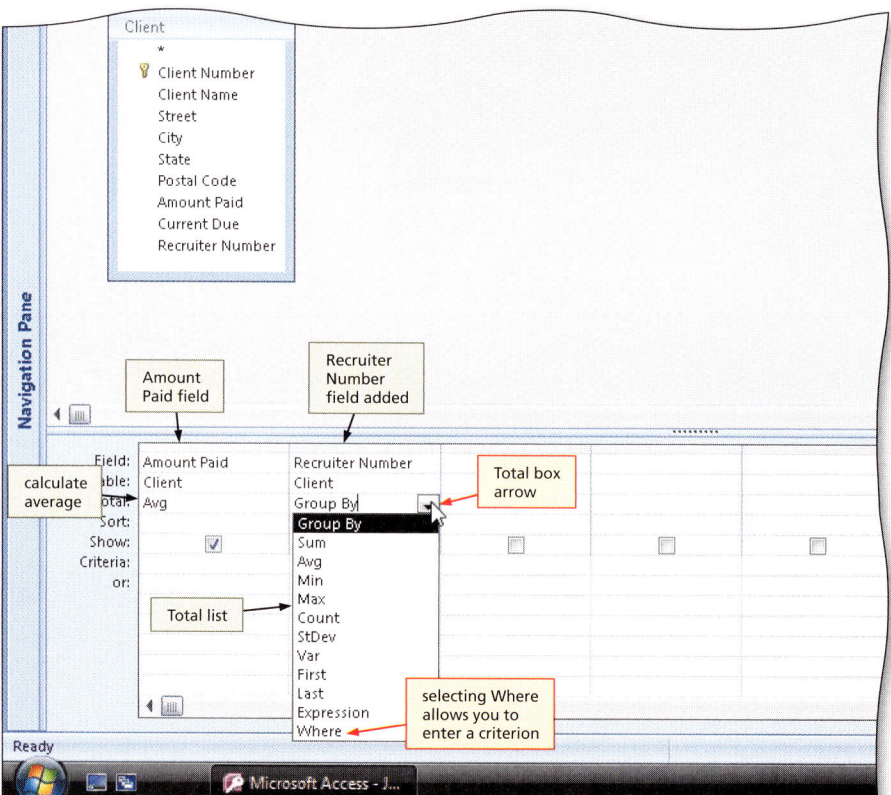

Figure 2–70

- Click Where.
- Type 21 as the criterion for the Recruiter Number field (Figure 2–71).

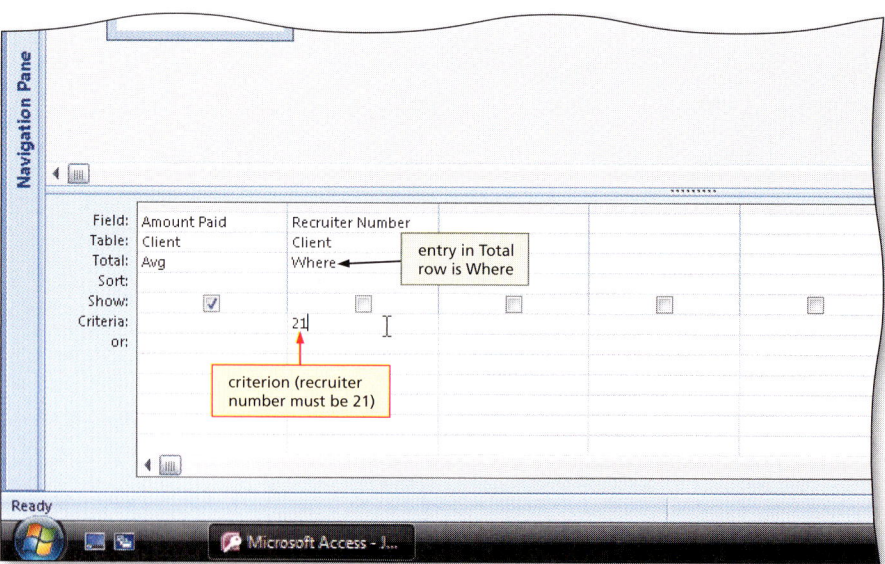

Figure 2–71

- View the query results (Figure 2–72).

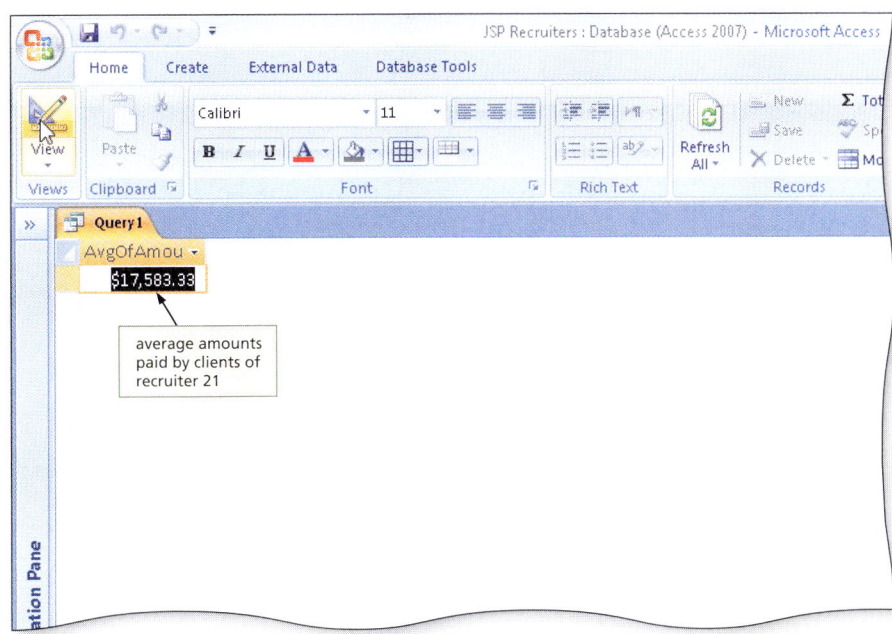

Figure 2–72

To Use Grouping

Another way statistics often are used is in combination with grouping; that is, statistics are calculated for groups of records. You may, for example, need to calculate the average amount paid for the clients of each recruiter. You will want the average for the clients of recruiter 21, the average for clients of recruiter 24, and so on.

Grouping means creating groups of records that share some common characteristic. In grouping by Recruiter Number, for example, the clients of recruiter 21 would form one group, the clients of recruiter 24 would form a second, and the clients of recruiter 27 form a third group. The calculations then are made for each group. To indicate grouping in Access, select Group By as the entry in the Total row for the field to be used for grouping.

The following steps calculate the average amount paid for clients of each recruiter.

- Return to Design view and clear the design grid.
- Include the Recruiter Number field in the query.
- Include the Amount Paid field in the query.
- Select Avg as the calculation in the Total row for the Amount Paid field (Figure 2–73).

Q&A Why was it unnecessary for me to change the entry in the Total Row for the Recruiter Number field?

Group By currently is the entry in the Total row for the Recruiter Number field, which is correct; thus, it was not changed.

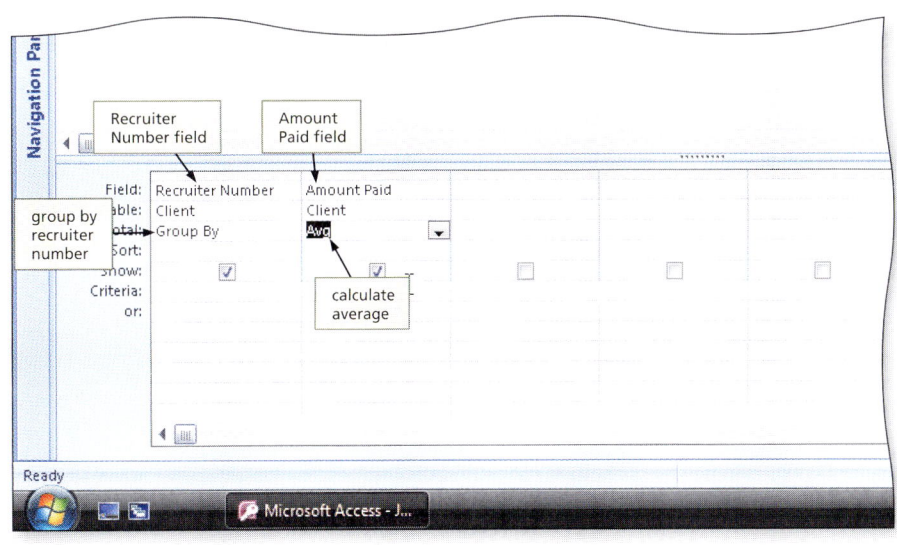

Figure 2–73

2

- View the query results (Figure 2–74).

3

- Close the query.
- Do not save your changes.

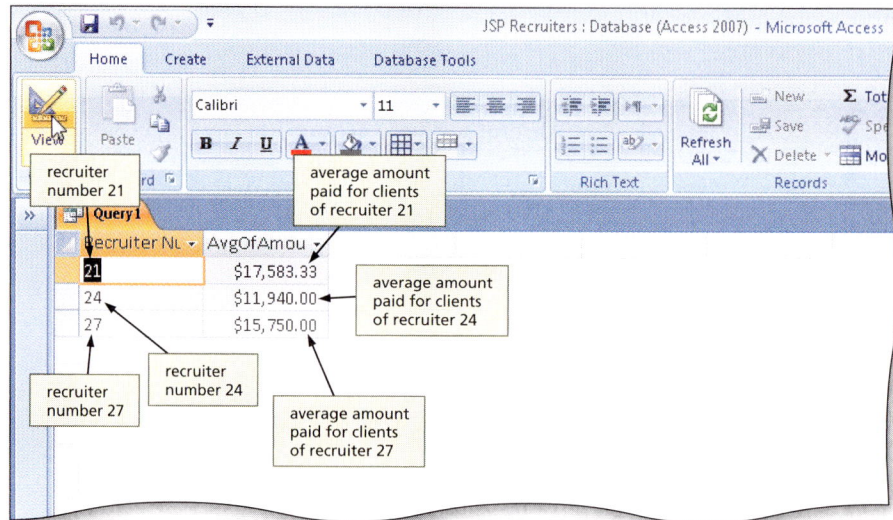

Figure 2–74

Crosstab Queries

Crosstab queries are useful for summarizing data. A crosstab query calculates a statistic (for example, sum, average, or count) for data that is grouped by two different types of information. One of the types will appear down the side of the resulting datasheet, and the other will appear across the top.

For example, if you have determined that a query must summarize the sum of the amounts paid grouped by both city and recruiter number, you could have cities as the row headings, that is, down the side. You could have recruiter numbers as the column headings, that is, across the top. The entries within the data sheet represent the total of the amounts paid. Figure 2–75 shows a crosstab in which the total of amount paid is grouped by both city and recruiter number with cities down the left-hand side and recruiter numbers across the top. For example, the entry in the row labeled Fort Stewart and in the column labeled 21 represents the total of the amount paid by all clients of recruiter 21 who are located in Fort Stewart.

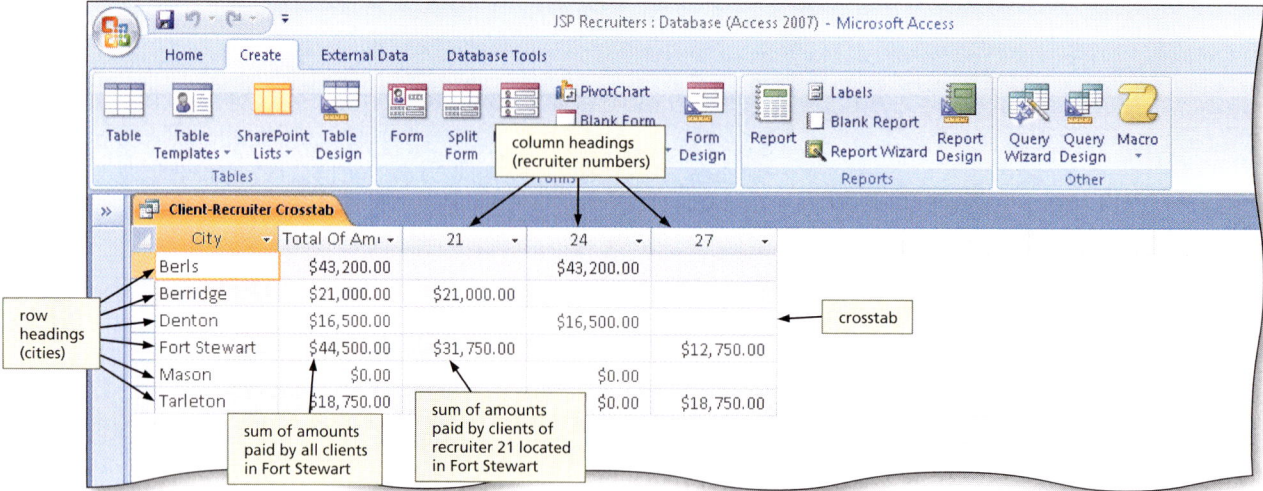

Figure 2–75

To Create a Crosstab Query

The following steps use the Crosstab Query wizard to create a crosstab query.

1
- Click Create on the Ribbon to display the Create tab.
- Click the Query Wizard button to display the New Query dialog box (Figure 2–76).

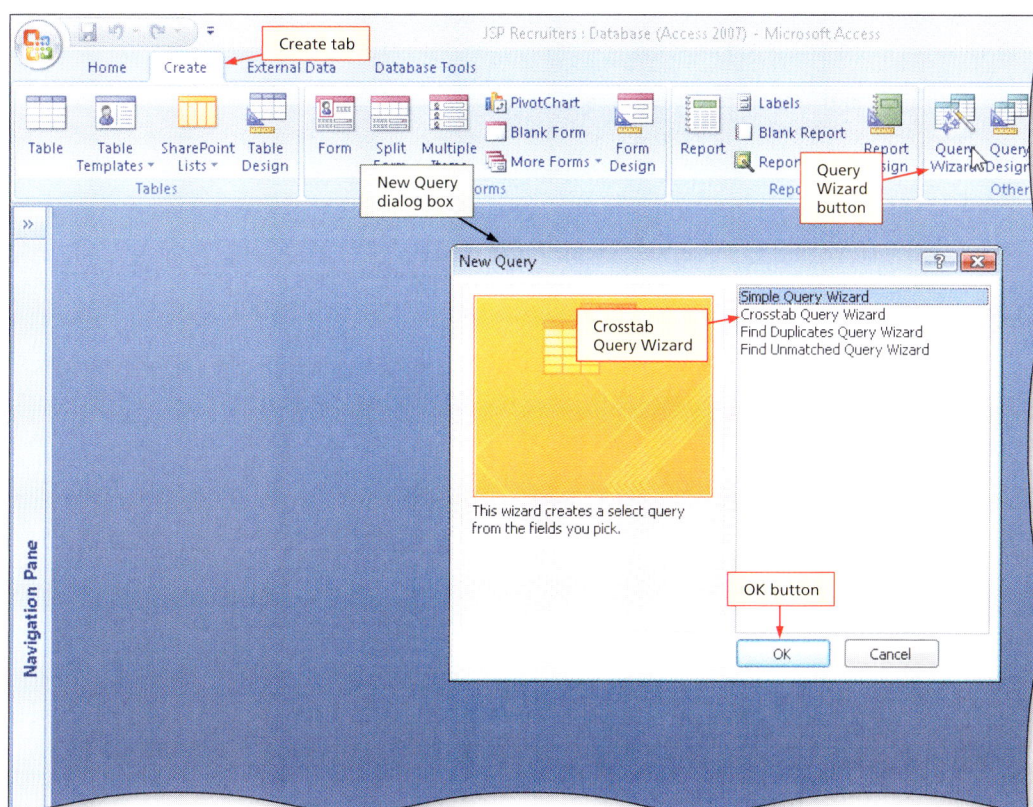

Figure 2–76

2
- Click Crosstab Query Wizard in the New Query dialog box.
- Click the OK button to display the Crosstab Query Wizard (Figure 2–77).

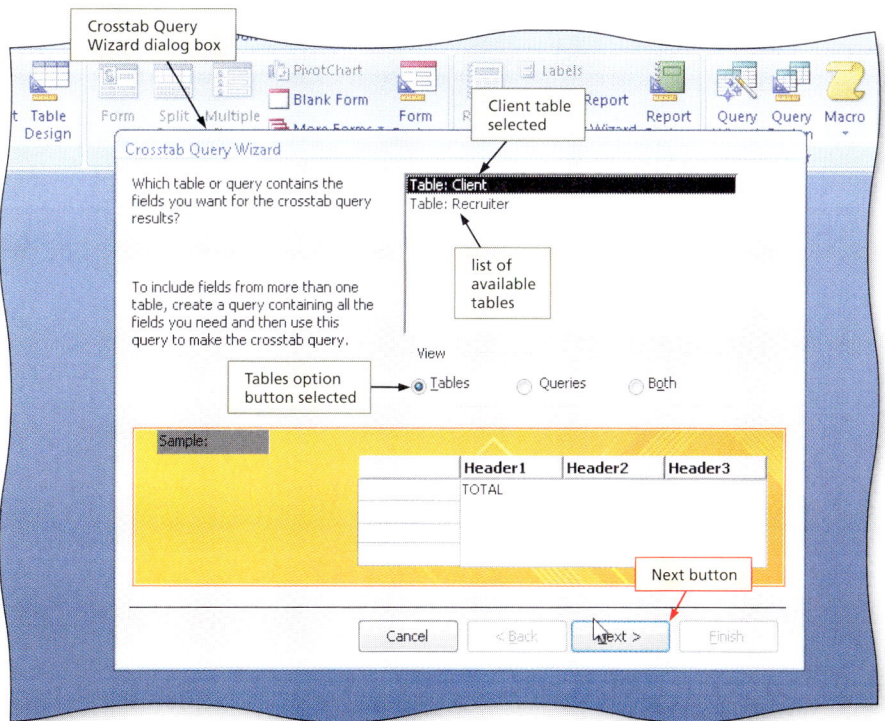

Figure 2–77

3

- With the Tables option button selected and the Client table selected, click the Next button to display the next Crosstab Query Wizard screen.

- Click the City field, and then click the Add Field button to select the City field for row headings (Figure 2–78).

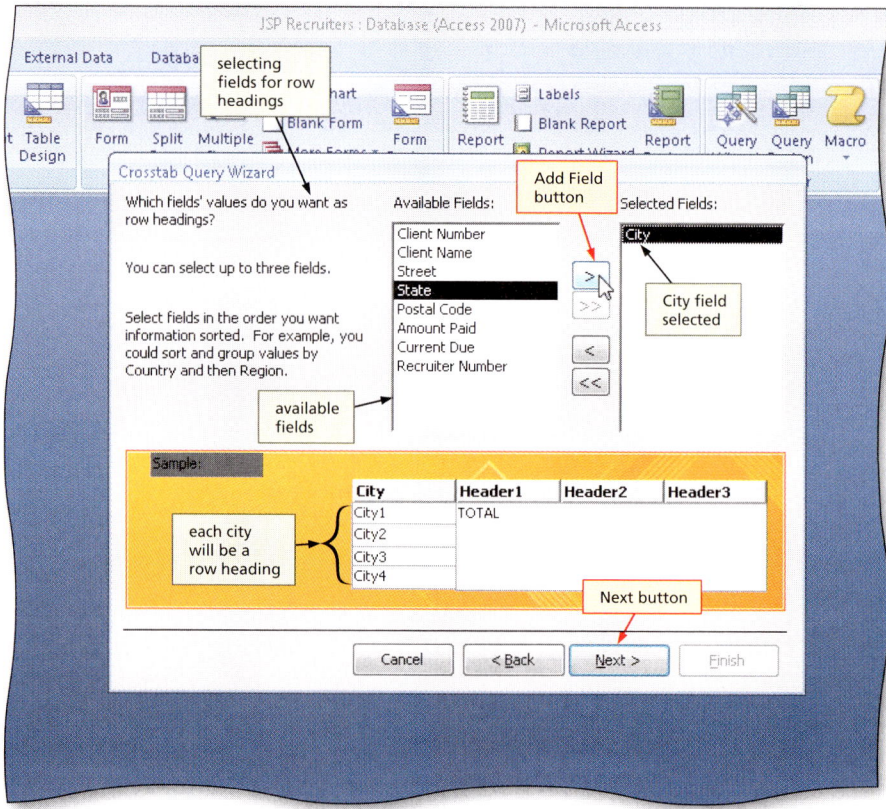

Figure 2–78

4

- Click the Next button to display the next Crosstab Query Wizard screen.

- Click the Recruiter Number field to select the Recruiter Number field for column headings (Figure 2–79).

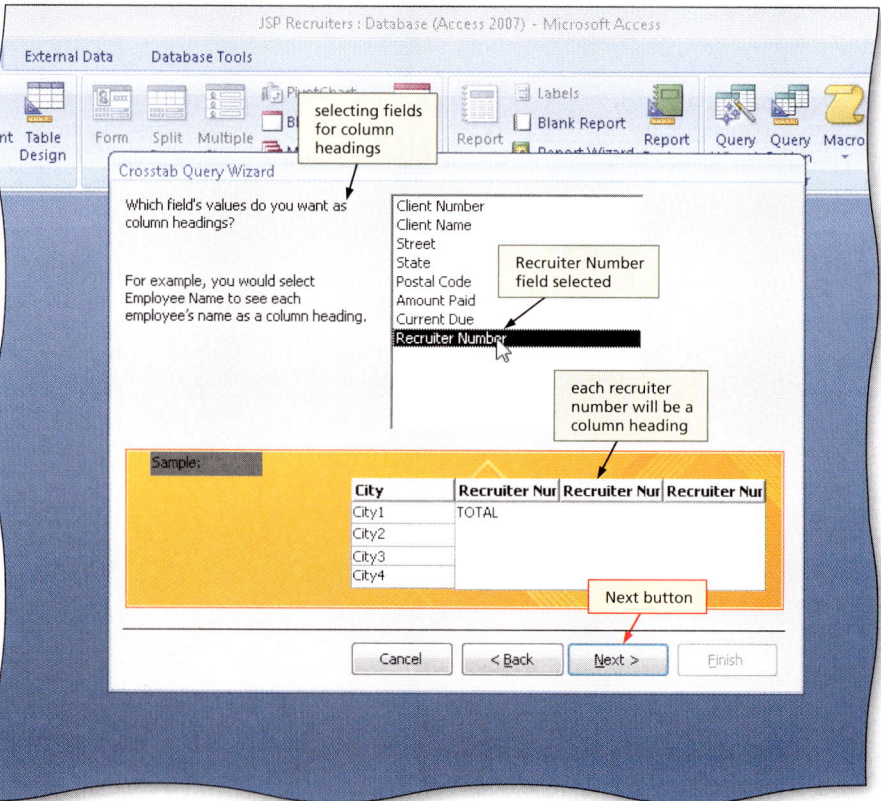

Figure 2–79

5

- Click the Next button to display the next Crosstab Query Wizard screen.
- Click the Amount Paid field to select the Amount Paid field for calculations.

🔎 **Experiment**

- Click other fields. For each field, examine the list of calculations that are available. When finished, click the Amount Paid field again.
- Click Sum to select Sum as the calculation to be performed (Figure 2–80).

 My list of functions is different. What did I do wrong?

Either you clicked the wrong field, or the Amount Paid field has the wrong data type. If you mistakenly assigned it the Text data type for example, you would not see Sum in the list of available calculations.

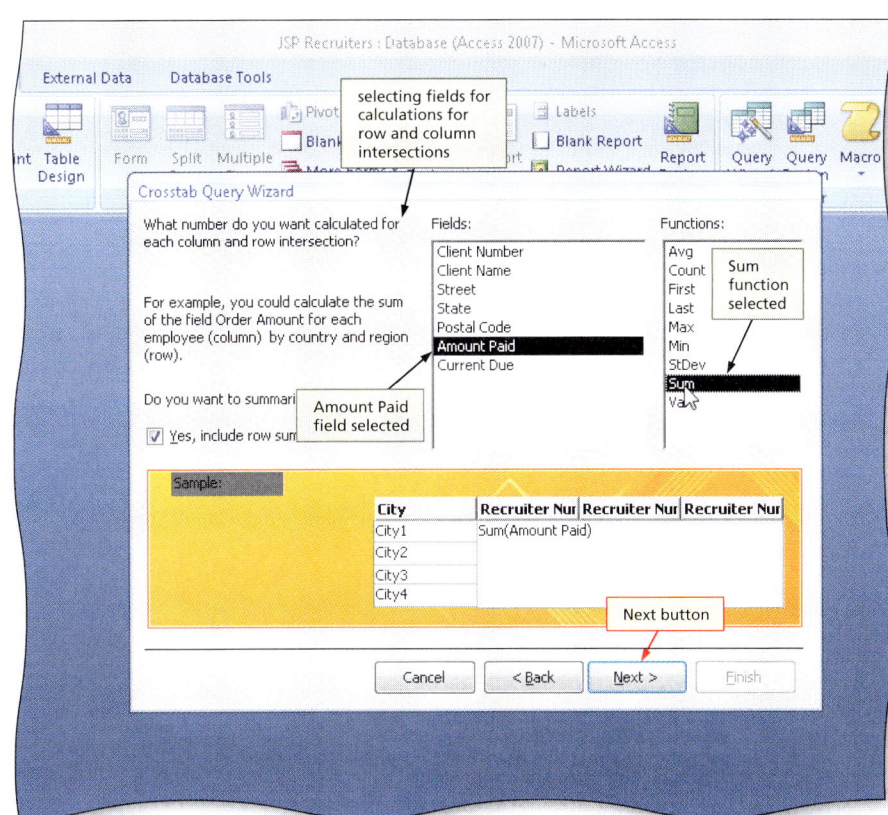

Figure 2–80

6

- Click the Next button to display the next Crosstab Query Wizard screen.
- Type `Client-Recruiter Crosstab` as the name of the query (Figure 2–81).

7

- Click the Finish button to produce the crosstab shown in Figure 2–75 on page AC 122.
- Close the query.

 If I want to view the crosstab at some future date, can I just open the query?

Yes.

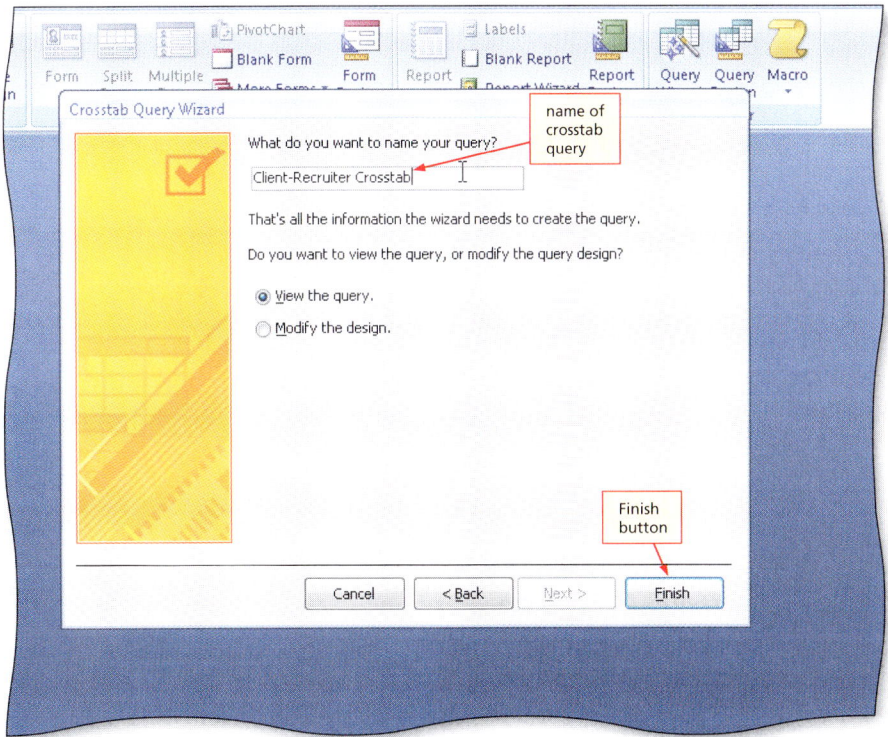

Figure 2–81

To Customize the Navigation Pane

Currently the entries in the Navigation Pane are organized by table. That is, the queries, forms, and reports associated with a particular table appear after the name of the table. In addition, all tables are included. You might want to change the way the information is organized. For example, you might wish to have all the queries appear together, all the forms appear together, and all the reports appear together, regardless of the table on which they are based. The following steps change the organization of the Navigation Pane.

- If necessary, click the Shutter Bar Open/Close Button to show the Navigation Pane.
- Click the Navigation Pane arrow to produce the Navigation Pane menu (Figure 2–82).

Q&A If the Navigation Pane gets too cluttered, can I hide the objects in a group? For example, if the organization is by table, can I hide the objects (forms, queries, reports) for the table group and show only the table name?

Yes. Click the up arrow on the group bar. The objects under the table group will no longer appear and the up arrow will become a down arrow. To redisplay the objects, click the down arrow.

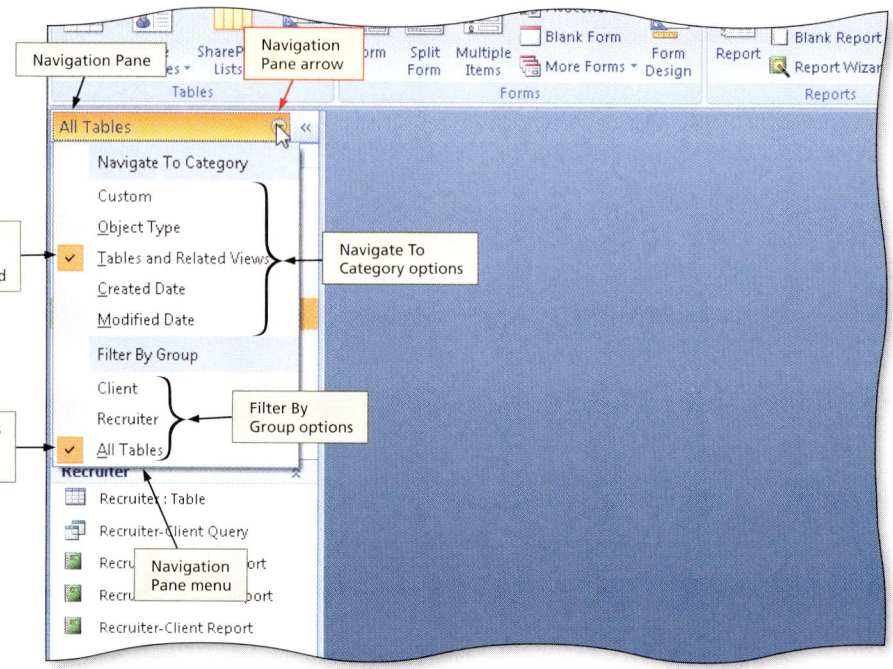

Figure 2–82

- Click Object Type to organize the Navigation Pane by the type of object rather than by table (Figure 2–83).

- Click the Navigation Pane arrow to produce the Navigation Pane menu.
- Click Tables and Related Views to once again organize the Navigation Pane by table.

- Select different Navigate To Category options to see the effect of the option. With each option you select, select different Filter By Group options to see the effect of the filtering. When you have finished experimenting, select the Tables and Related Views Navigate To Category option and the All Tables Filter By Group option.

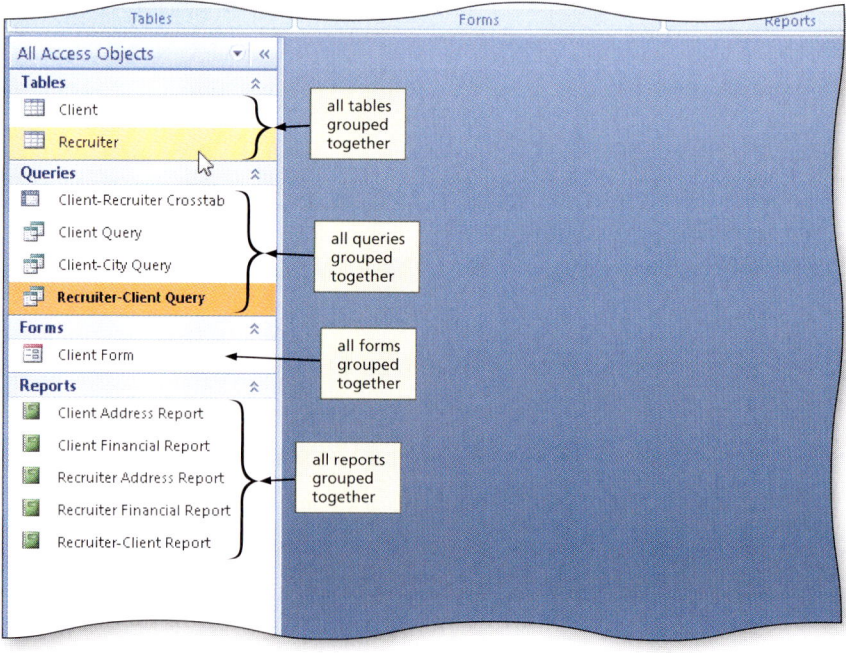

Figure 2–83

To Quit Access

You saved all your changes and are ready to quit Access. The following step quits Access.

 Click the Close button on the right side of the Access title bar to quit Access.

Quick Reference

For a table that lists how to complete the tasks covered in this book using the mouse, Ribbon, shortcut menu, and keyboard, see the Quick Reference Summary at the back of this book, or visit the Access 2007 Quick Reference Web page (scsite.com/dc-off07/qr).

Chapter Summary

In this chapter you have learned to create queries, enter fields, enter criteria, use text and numeric data in queries, use wildcards, use compound criteria, create parameter queries, sort data in queries, join tables in queries, perform calculations in queries, create crosstab queries, and customize the Navigation Pane. The following list includes all the new Access skills you have learned in this chapter.

1. Use the Simple Query Wizard to Create a Query (AC 78)
2. Use a Criterion in a Query (AC 81)
3. Print the Results of a Query (AC 83)
4. Create a Query in Design View (AC 83)
5. Add Fields to the Design Grid (AC 85)
6. Use Text Data in a Criterion (AC 86)
7. Use a Wildcard (AC 87)
8. Use Criteria for a Field Not Included in the Results (AC 88)
9. Create a Parameter Query (AC 90)
10. Save a Query (AC 91)
11. Use a Saved Query (AC 92)
12. Use a Number in a Criterion (AC 93)
13. Use a Comparison Operator in a Criterion (AC 94)
14. Use a Compound Criterion Involving AND (AC 95)
15. Use a Compound Criterion Involving OR (AC 96)
16. Clear the Design Grid (AC 98)
17. Sort Data in a Query (AC 98)
18. Omit Duplicates (AC 100)
19. Sort on Multiple Keys (AC 101)
20. Create a Top-Values Query (AC 102)
21. Join Tables (AC 105)
22. Save the Query (AC 107)
23. Change Join Properties (AC 108)
24. Create a Report Involving a Join (AC 109)
25. Print a Report (AC 111)
26. Restrict the Records in a Join (AC 112)
27. Use a Calculated Field in a Query (AC 113)
28. Change a Caption (AC 116)
29. Calculate Statistics (AC 118)
30. Use Criteria in Calculating Statistics (AC 120)
31. Use Grouping (AC 121)
32. Create a Crosstab Query (AC 123)
33. Customize the Navigation Pane (AC 126)

 If you have a SAM user profile, you may have access to hands-on instruction, practice, and assessment. Log in to your SAM account (http://sam2007.course.com) to launch any assigned training activities or exams that relate to the skills covered in this chapter.

Learn It Online

Test your knowledge of chapter content and key terms.

Instructions: To complete the Learn It Online exercises, start your browser, click the Address bar, and then enter the Web address `scsite.com/dc-off07/ac2007/learn`. When the Access 2007 Learn It Online page is displayed, click the link for the exercise you want to complete and then read the instructions.

Chapter Reinforcement TF, MC, and SA
A series of true/false, multiple choice, and short answer questions that test your knowledge of the chapter content.

Flash Cards
An interactive learning environment where you identify chapter key terms associated with displayed definitions.

Practice Test
A series of multiple choice questions that test your knowledge of chapter content and key terms.

Who Wants To Be a Computer Genius?
An interactive game that challenges your knowledge of chapter content in the style of a television quiz show.

Wheel of Terms
An interactive game that challenges your knowledge of chapter key terms in the style of the television show *Wheel of Fortune*.

Crossword Puzzle Challenge
A crossword puzzle that challenges your knowledge of key terms presented in the chapter.

Apply Your Knowledge

Reinforce the skills and apply the concepts you learned in this chapter.

Using the Query Wizard, Creating a Parameter Query, Joining Tables, and Creating a Report

Instructions: Start Access. Open the The Bike Delivers database that you modified in Apply Your Knowledge in Chapter 1 on page AC 64. (If you did not complete this exercise, contact your instructor for a copy of the modified database.)

Perform the following tasks:

1. Use the Simple Query Wizard to create a query for the Customer table. Include the Customer Name, Balance, and Courier Number in the query. Assign the name, Customer Query, to the query.

2. Create a query for the Customer table and add the Customer Number, Customer Name, Courier Number, and Balance fields to the design grid. Sort the records in descending order by Balance. Add a criterion for the Courier Number field that allows the user to enter a different courier each time the query is run. Save the query as Courier Parameter Query.

3. Create a query that joins the Courier and the Customer tables. Add the Courier Number, First Name, and Last Name fields from the Courier table and the Customer Number and Customer Name fields from the Customer table. Sort the records in ascending order by Courier Number and Customer Number. All couriers should appear in the result even if they currently have no customers. Save the query as Courier-Customer Query.

4. Create the report shown in Figure 2–84. The report uses the Courier-Customer Query.

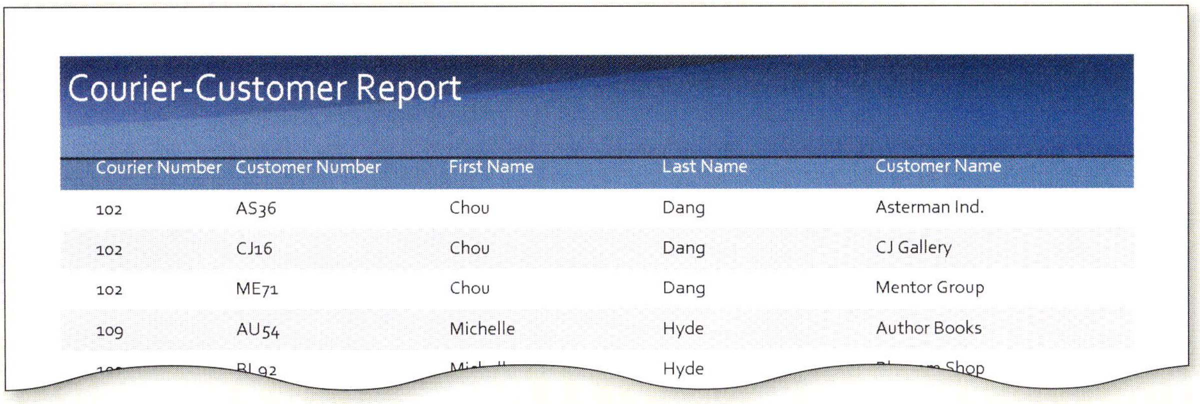

Courier-Customer Report

Courier Number	Customer Number	First Name	Last Name	Customer Name
102	AS36	Chou	Dang	Asterman Ind.
102	CJ16	Chou	Dang	CJ Gallery
102	ME71	Chou	Dang	Mentor Group
109	AU54	Michelle	Hyde	Author Books
109	BL92	Michelle	Hyde	Blossom Shop

Figure 2–84

5. Submit the revised database in the format specified by your instructor.

Extend Your Knowledge

Extend the skills you learned in this chapter and experiment with new skills. You may need to use Help to complete the assignment.

Creating Crosstab Queries, Creating Queries Using Criteria

Instructions: Start Access. Open the Groom n Fluff database. See the inside back cover of this book for instructions for downloading the Data Files for Students, or contact your instructor for information on accessing the files required in this book.

Groom n Fluff is a small pet grooming business. The owner has created an Access database in which to store information about the customers she serves and the pet groomers she employs. You will create the crosstab query shown in Figure 2–85. You also will query the database using specified criteria.

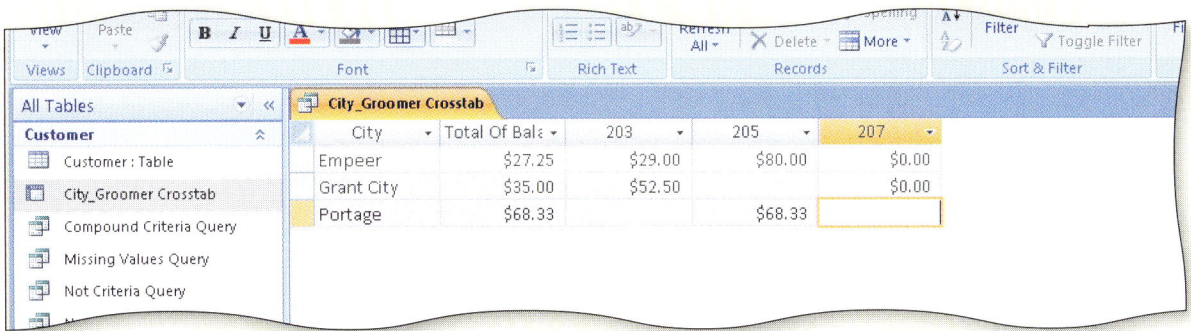

Figure 2–85

Continued >

Extend Your Knowledge continued

Perform the following tasks:
1. Create the crosstab query shown in Figure 2–85 on the previous page. The crosstab groups the average of customers' balances by city and groomer number.
2. Create a query to find all customers who do not live in Grant City. Include the Customer Number, Last Name, and Balance fields in the design grid. Save the query as Not Criteria Query.
3. Create a query to find all customers who do not have a telephone number. Include the Customer Number, Last Name, First Name, Street, and City fields in the query results. Save the query as Missing Values Query.
4. Create a query to find all customers whose balance is between $20.00 and $60.00. Include the Customer Number, Last Name, and Balance fields in the design grid. Save the query as Number Range Query.
5. Create a query to find all customers where the groomer number is 203 or 205 and the balance is greater than $40.00. Include the Customer Number, Last Name, First Name, Balance, and Groomer Number fields in the design grid. Save the query as Compound Criteria Query.
6. Change the database properties, as specified by your instructor. Submit the revised database in the format specified by your instructor.

Make It Right

Analyze a database and correct all errors and/or improve the design.

Correcting Errors in the Query Design

Instructions: Start Access. Open the Keep It Green database. See the inside back cover of this book for instructions for downloading the Data Files for Students, or contact your instructor for information on accessing the files required in this book.

Keep It Green is a database maintained by a small landscaping business. The queries shown in Figure 2–86 contain a number of errors that need to be corrected before the queries run properly. The sort query shown in Figure 2–86a displays the query results in the proper order (First Name, Last Name, Street, City) but it is sorted incorrectly. The query results should be sorted by last name within city in ascending order. Also the caption for the Street field should be Address. Save the query with your changes.

When you try to run the join query for the Keep It Green database, the message shown in Figure 2–86b appears. The query joins the Worker table and the Customer table. It also calculates the total amount for each customer. The query should be sorted in alphabetical order by worker last name and customer last name. Correct the error that is causing the message shown in Figure 2–86b and sort the records properly. Save the query with your changes.

Change the database properties, as specified by your instructor. Submit the revised database in the format specified by your instructor.

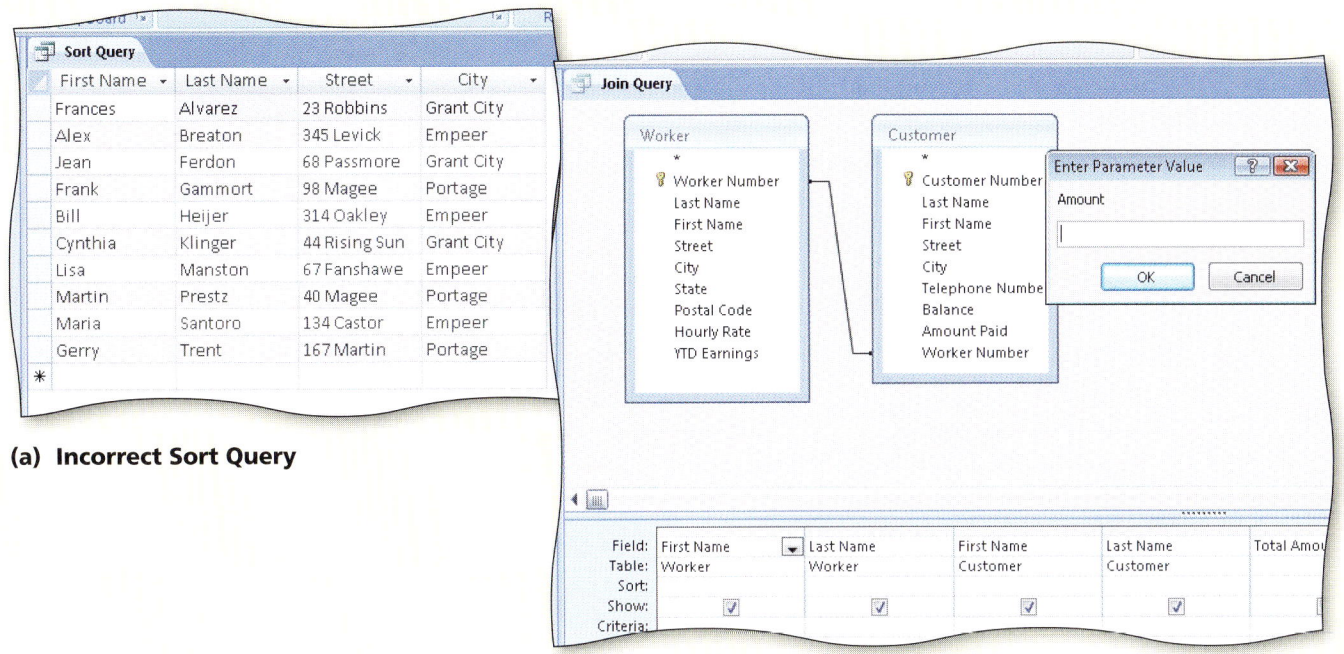

(a) Incorrect Sort Query

(b) Incorrect Join Query

Figure 2–86

In the Lab

Design, create, modify, and/or use a database following the guidelines, concepts, and skills presented in this chapter. Labs are listed in order of increasing difficulty.

Lab 1: Querying the JMS TechWizards Database

Problem: The management of JMS TechWizards has determined a number of questions it wants the database management system to answer. You must obtain answers to the questions posed by management.

Instructions: Use the database created in the In the Lab 1 of Chapter 1 on page AC 67 for this assignment, or contact your instructor for information on accessing the files required for this book. Perform the following tasks:

1. Open the JMS TechWizards database and create a new query for the Client table that includes the Client Number, Client Name, and Technician Number fields in the design grid for all clients where the technician number is 23. Save the query as Lab 2-1 Step 1 Query.

2. Create a query that includes the Client Number, Client Name, and Paid fields for all clients located in Liberty Corner with a paid amount greater than $500.00. Save the query as Lab2-1 Step 2 Query.

3. Create a query that includes the Client Number, Client Name, Street, and City fields for all clients whose names begin with Gr. Save the query as Lab 2-1 Step 3 Query.

4. Create a query that lists all cities in descending order. Each city should appear only once. Save the query as Lab 2-1 Step 4 Query.

5. Create a query that allows the user to enter the city to search when the query is run. The query results should display the Client Number, Client Name, and Billed. Test the query by searching for those records where the client is located in Anderson. Save the query as Client-City Query.

Continued >

In the Lab *continued*

6. Include the Client Number, Client Name, and Billed fields in the design grid. Sort the records in descending order by the Billed field. Display only the top 25 percent of the records in the query result. Save the query as Lab 2-1 Step 6 Query.

7. Join the Technician and the Client table. Include the Technician Number, First Name, and Last Name fields from the Technician table. Include the Client Number, Client Name, and Billed from the Client table. Sort the records in ascending order by technician's last name and client name. All technicians should appear in the result even if they currently have no clients. Save the query as Technician-Client query.

8. Open the Technician-Client query in Design view and remove the Client table. Add the Hourly Rate field to the design grid following the Last Name field. Calculate the number of hours each technician has worked (YTD Earnings/Hourly Rate). Assign the alias Hours Worked to the calculated field. Change the caption for the Hourly Rate field to Rate. Display hours worked as an integer (0 decimal places). Use the Save As command to save the query as Lab 2-1 Step 8 Query.

9. Create a query to display the average billed amount for all clients. Save the query as Lab 2-1 Step 9 Query.

10. Create a query to count the number of clients for technician 23. Save the query as Lab 2-1 Step 10 Query.

11. Create a query to display the average billed amount for each technician. Save the query as Lab 2-1 Step 11 Query.

12. Create the crosstab shown in Figure 2–87. The crosstab groups total of clients' paid amounts by city and technician number. Save the crosstab as City-Technician Crosstab.

13. Submit the revised database in the format specified by your instructor.

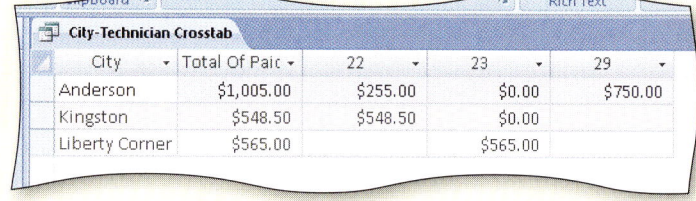

Figure 2–87

In the Lab

Lab 2: Querying the Hockey Fan Zone Database

Problem: The management of the Hockey Fan Zone store has determined a number of questions it wants the database management system to answer. You must obtain answers to the questions posed by management.

Instructions: Use the database created in the In the Lab 2 of Chapter 1 on page AC 68 for this assignment, or contact your instructor for information on accessing the files required for this book. Perform the following tasks:

1. Open the Hockey Fan Zone database and use the query wizard to create a query that includes the Item Number, Description, On Hand, and Cost fields for all records in the Item table. Name the query Lab 2-2 Step 1 Query.

2. Create a query that includes the Item Number, Description, Cost, and Supplier Code fields for all products where the Supplier Code is LG. Save the query as Lab 2-2 Step 2 Query.

3. Create a query that includes the Item Number and Description fields for all products where the description starts with the letter B. Save the query as Lab 2-2 Step 3 Query.
4. Create a query that includes the Item Number and Description field for all products with a cost less than $5.00. Save the query as Lab 2-2 Step 4 Query.
5. Create a query that includes the Item Number and Description field for all products with a selling price greater than $15.00. Save the query as Lab 2-2 Step 5 Query.
6. Create a query that includes all fields for all products with a selling price greater than $10.00 and where the number on hand is fewer than 10. Save the query as Lab 2-2 Step 6 Query.
7. Create a query that includes all fields for all products that have a selling price greater than $15.00 or a supplier code of AC. Save the query as Lab 2-2 Step 7 Query.
8. Join the Supplier table and the Item table. Include the Supplier Code and Supplier Name fields from the Supplier table and the Item Number, Description, On Hand, and Cost fields from the Item table. Sort the records in ascending order by Supplier Code and Item Number. Save the query as Supplier-Item Query. Note that the Report Wizard limits the size of the On Hand column header because it is a number field.
9. Create the report shown in Figure 2–88. The report uses the Supplier-Item query and the Module style.

Supplier-Item Report

Supplier Code	Item Number	Supplier Name	Description	Hand	Cost
AC	5923	Ace Clothes	Jersey	12	$21.45
AC	7810	Ace Clothes	Tee Shirt	32	$9.50
LG	3663	Logo Goods	Ball Cap	30	$11.15
LG	4563	Logo Goods	Earrings	10	$4.50
LG	4593	Logo Goods	Foam Finger	25	$2.95
LG	7930	Logo Goods	Visor	9	$11.95
MN	3683	Mary's Novelties	Bumper Sticker	50	$0.95
MN	6189	Mary's Novelties	Koozies	35	$2.00
MN	6343	Mary's Novelties	Note Cube	7	$5.75

Figure 2–88

10. Create a query that includes the Item Number, Description, On Hand, and Cost fields. Calculate the inventory value (on hand * cost) for all records in the table. Change the caption for the On Hand column to In Stock. Format inventory value as currency with two decimal places. Sort the records in descending order by inventory value. Save the query as Lab 2-2 Step 10 Query.
11. Create a query that calculates and displays the average cost of all items. Save the query as Lab 2-2 Step 11 Query.
12. Create a query that calculates and displays the average cost of items grouped by supplier code. Save the query as Lab 2-2 Step 12 Query.
13. Submit the revised database in the format specified by your instructor.

In the Lab

Lab 3: Querying the Ada Beauty Supply Database

Problem: The management of Ada Beauty Supply has determined a number of questions it wants the database management system to answer. You must obtain answers to the questions posed by management.

Instructions: Use the database created in the In the Lab 3 of Chapter 1 on page AC 69 for this assignment, or contact your instructor for information on accessing the files required for this book. For Part 1 and Part 3, save each query using a format similar to the following: Lab 2-3 Part 1a Query, Lab 2-3 Part 3a Query, and so on. Submit the revised database in the format specified by your instructor.

Instructions Part 1: Create a new query for the Customer table and include the Customer Number, Customer Name, Balance, and Amount Paid fields in the design grid. Answer the following questions: (a) Which customers' names begin with C? (b) Which customers are located on Devon? (c) Which customers have a balance of $0.00? (d) Which customers have a balance greater than $200.00 and have an amount paid less than $800.00? (e) Which two customers have the highest balances? (f) For each customer, what is the total of the balance and amount paid amounts?

Instructions Part 2: Join the Sales Rep and the Customer table. Include the Sales Rep Number, First Name, and Last Name from the Sales Rep table and the Customer Number, Customer Name, and Amount Paid from the Customer table in the design grid. Sort the records in ascending order by Sales Rep Number and Customer Number. All sales reps should appear in the result even if they currently have no customers. Save the query as Sales Rep-Customer Query.

Instructions Part 3: Calculate the following statistics: (a) What is the average balance for customers assigned to sales rep 44? (b) What is the total balance for all customers? (c) What is the total amount paid for each sales rep?

Cases and Places

Apply your creative thinking and problem solving skills to design and implement a solution.

• Easier   •• More Difficult

• 1: Querying the Second Hand Goods Database

Use the Second Hand Goods database you created in Cases and Places 1 in Chapter 1 on page AC 71 for this assignment, or contact your instructor for information on accessing the files required for this book. Create queries for the following:

a. Find the number and description of all items that contain the word Table.
b. Find the item number, description, and condition of the item that has the earliest posting date.
c. Find the total price of each item available for sale. Show the item description and total price.
d. Find the seller of each item. Show the seller's first name and last name as well as the item description, price, quantity, and date posted. Sort the results by item description within seller last name.
e. Create a parameter query that will allow the user to enter an item description when the query is run. The user should see all fields in the query result.
f. Find all items posted between June 1, 2007 and June 4, 2007. The user should see all fields in the query result.

Submit the revised database in the format specified by your instructor.

• 2: Querying the BeachCondo Rentals Database

Use the BeachCondo Rentals database you created in Cases and Places 2 in Chapter 1 on page AC 71 for this assignment, or contact your instructor for information on accessing the files required for this book. Create queries for the following:

a. Find all units that rent for less than $1,000 per week and have at least two bedrooms. The user should see all fields in the query result.
b. Find all units that are on the fourth floor. (Hint: The first digit of the Unit Number field indicates the floor.) Include the Unit Number and the Weekly Rate fields in the query result.
c. Find all units that have more than one bedroom and more than one bathroom and provide linens. Include the Unit Number, Bedrooms, and Weekly Rate fields in the query result.
d. Owner BE20 offers a 15 percent discount on the weekly rate if renters rent for more than one week. What is the discounted weekly rental rate for his units? Your result should include the unit number, bedrooms, bathrooms, sleeps, and discounted weekly rate in your result. Be sure the discounted rate appears as currency.
e. List the owner's first and last name as well as telephone number. Also include the unit number and the weekly rate. All owners should appear in the result even if they currently have no rental units.
f. Find the highest and lowest weekly rate.

Submit the revised database in the format specified by your instructor.

•• 3: Querying the Restaurant Database

Use the restaurant database you created in Cases and Places 3 in Chapter 1 on page AC 71 for this assignment, or contact your instructor for information on accessing the files required for this book. Using the Plan Ahead guidelines presented in this chapter, determine at least five questions the conference director might want to ask the database. Using a word processing program, such as Microsoft Word, write the questions in your own words. Then, design the queries for Access. Run and save each query. Submit the Word document and the revised database in the format specified by your instructor.

Continued >

Cases and Places *continued*

•• 4: Designing Queries to Help in Your Job Search

Make It Personal

Use the contacts database you created in Cases and Places 4 in Chapter 1 on page AC 71 for this assignment, or contact your instructor for information on accessing the files required for this book. Consider your own personal job situation. What questions would you want to ask this database? Using a word processing program, such as Microsoft Word, write the questions in your own words. Can your database answer the questions that you listed? If it can, design the queries for Access. Run and save each query. In your Word document, identify which questions were posed to Access and which questions could not be answered. For questions that could not be answered, explain why your database cannot answer the question. Submit the Word document and the revised database in the format specified by your instructor.

•• 5: Creating Queries to Analyze Data

Working Together

Obtain a copy of the weather page of your local newspaper. As a team, choose 30 cities of interest. Create a database that contains one table and has five fields (City, State or Province, High Temp, Low Temp, Sky). Use the newspaper's abbreviations for Sky; for example, c for cloudy, r for rain and so on. Create queries that do the following:

a. Display the five cities with the highest high temperatures.

b. Calculate the difference between the high and low temperatures for each city.

c. Display the average high and low temperature for all cities.

d. List the states or provinces in your table. Each state or province should appear only once.

Write a one-page paper that explains what the team learned from querying the database and any conclusions you can draw about the data — for example, describe the Sky conditions for the cities with the least difference in high and low temperature. Submit the assignment in the format specified by your instructor.

Microsoft Office **Integration 2007**

Integrating Office 2007 Programs and the World Wide Web

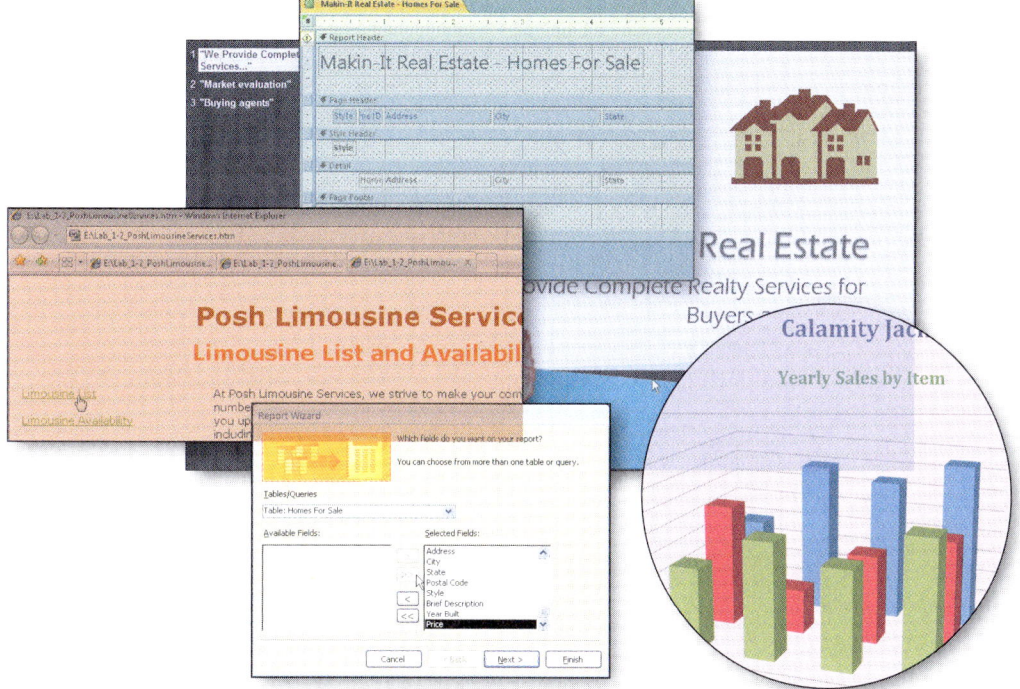

Objectives

You will have mastered the material in this chapter when you can:

- Integrate the Office 2007 programs to create a Web site
- Add hyperlinks to a Word document
- Embed an Excel chart into a Word document
- Add a hyperlink to a PowerPoint slide
- Create Web pages from a PowerPoint presentation
- Add a hyperlink to an Access report
- Create a Web page from an Access report
- Test a Web site in a browser

Integrating Office 2007 Programs and the World Wide Web

Introduction

Integration means joining parts so that they work together or form a whole. In information technology, common usages can include the following:

1. Integration during product development combines activities, programs, or hardware components into a functional unit.
2. Integration in manufacturing can bring different companies' products together into an efficiently working system.
3. Integration in marketing combines products or components to meet objectives such as sharing a common purpose or creating demand. It includes matters such as consistent product pricing and packaging, advertising, and sales campaigns.
4. Integration in product design allows a unifying purpose and/or architecture, such as the Microsoft Office System. (The products also are sold individually, but they are designed with the same larger objectives and/or architecture.)

This Integration chapter will show you how you can use the functionality and productivity tools of the Microsoft Office System.

Project — Integrating Office 2007 Programs and the World Wide Web

Many businesses advertise their products and services on the Internet. Companies find it easy to create Web pages using information already saved in word processing, spreadsheet, database, or presentation software formats. The Web pages shown in Figure 1 include information about the Makin-It Real Estate Company. This small business specializes in selling homes near the local college campus to first-time homebuyers. The owners of the business want to advertise their services and homes for sale on an attractive Web page.

The project in the chapter follows proper design guidelines and uses Office 2007 programs to create the Web pages and other documents shown in Figure 1. The Web page creation capabilities of Microsoft Office 2007 make it simple for you to create an entire Web site using the information available. Word allows you to create and save a document as a Web page. Word also allows you to embed an Excel chart in a document, which can be included in a Web page. PowerPoint provides the same capability and adds a navigation structure for browsing. In addition, an Access report can be saved as a Web page so that users can view database contents online. Several sources of information already exist that can be beneficial to creating a Web page. The following four files of information are supplied to help you get started:

1. A Word document that contains the company letterhead, including logo images, company name, and company address (Figure 1a on page INT 4).
2. An Excel workbook with a bar chart graphically illustrating the company's breakdown of home sales per year (Figure 1b on page INT 4).
3. A PowerPoint presentation that contains general information about the company's services (Figure 1g on page INT 5).
4. An Access database containing information about homes that currently are for sale through the company (Figure 1c on page INT 4).

The Makin-It Real Estate Web site should include the following:

1. A home page with a bar chart that contains the homes sold by the company per year (Figure 1e on page INT 5). Three links also are included on the home page: Company Services, Homes for Sale, and E-Mail for Information.
2. The Homes for Sale Web page (Figure 1d on page INT 4) is created from the Access file. Clicking the Homes for Sale link on the home page accesses this Web page. On this Web page, visitors can view the homes for sale from the company, categorized by the type of home.
3. The PowerPoint Web page (Figure 1g on page INT 5) displays information about services provided by the company. Clicking the Company Services link on the home page accesses this Web page.
4. Using the E-Mail for Information hyperlink, you can create an e-mail message (Figure 1f on page INT 5). E-mail is sent to the e-mail address manager@isp.com.

Overview

As you read this chapter, you will learn how to create the Web pages shown in Figure 1 by performing these general tasks:

- Insert hyperlinks in the Word document
- Embed the Excel chart in the Word document
- Save the Word document as a Web page
- Add a hyperlink to the PowerPoint presentation
- Save the PowerPoint presentation as a Web page
- Create the Access report
- Add a hyperlink to the Access report
- Save the Access report as a Web page
- Test the Web site

INT 4 **Integration Chapter** Integrating Office 2007 Programs and the World Wide Web

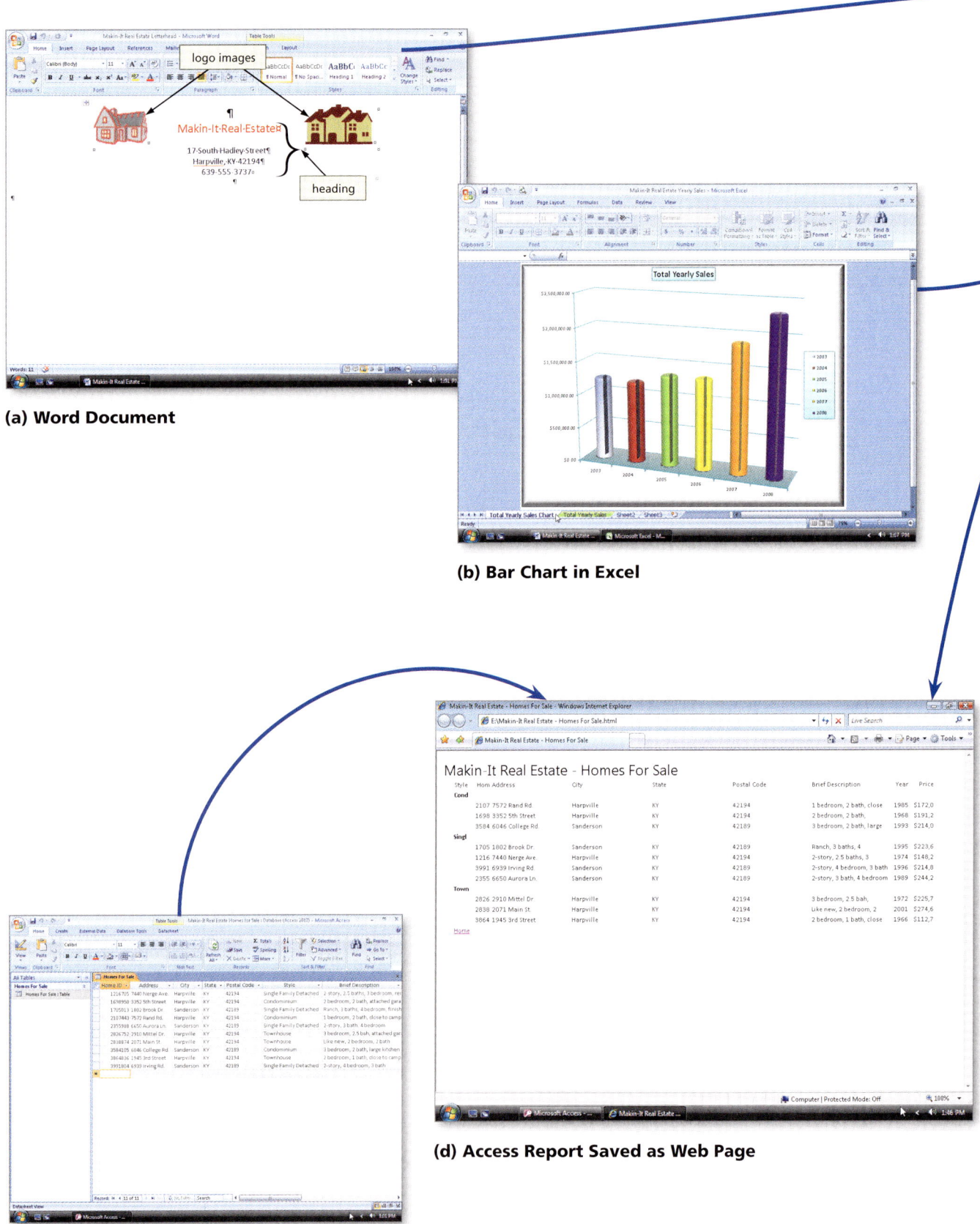

(a) Word Document

(b) Bar Chart in Excel

(c) Access Table

(d) Access Report Saved as Web Page

Figure 1

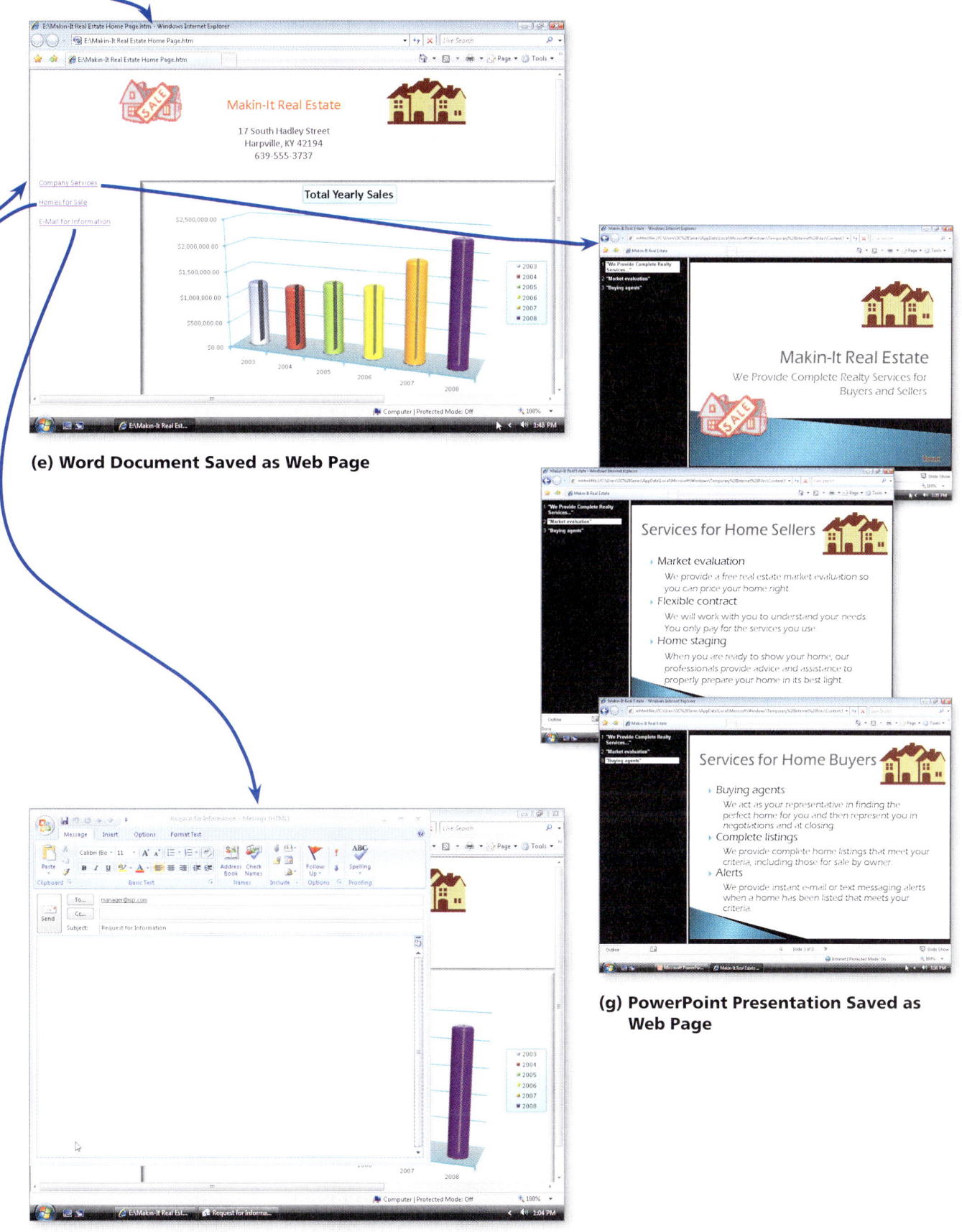

(e) Word Document Saved as Web Page

(f) New E-Mail Message Created from Hyperlink

(g) PowerPoint Presentation Saved as Web Page

Plan Ahead

General Project Decisions
When creating Web pages from many Office 2007 documents, you need to make several decisions that will determine the appearance and characteristics of the finished Web pages. As you create the Web pages shown in Figure 1, you should follow these general guidelines:

1. **Choose hyperlink names and locations.** Decide upon the names of the various Web pages and their location on media before creating the Web pages. For example, the first two hyperlinks in Figure 1e open Web pages named Company Services and Homes for Sale. The third hyperlink, E-Mail for Information, is understood easily by a Web page visitor.

2. **Ascertain the navigational structure of the Web pages.** The arrows shown between the Web pages in Figure 1 are an example of a navigational structure. Determine which pages link to other pages before the Web pages are created. The navigational structure shown in Figure 1 is appropriate for a small Web site.

3. **Determine appropriate file names for Web pages.** File names used for each of the Web pages shown in Figure 1 need to be determined when planning the pages because the file names are used to create the hyperlinks that are needed to navigate the Web pages. When naming these files, appropriate file names should be used. Save all Web pages to the same location so that they are easier to manage.

4. **Organize the layout of the home page.** Follow good design and visual layout principles to create an inviting home page. The page should not be cluttered, and the user should know what to do without the need for instructions.

5. **Plan the layout of the Access report.** Follow good Access report design guidelines to create the Access report. The fact that the report is to be used as a Web page requires additional thought and planning.

BTW

Web Pages
Making information available on the Internet is a key aspect of business today. To facilitate this trend, the Office 2007 programs easily allow you to generate Web pages from existing files. An entire Web site can be created with files from Word, Excel, PowerPoint, or Access by selecting the Web Page file type in the Save As dialog box.

Adding Hyperlinks to a Word Document

The Web site created for Makin-It Real Estate consists of an initial Web page, called the **home page**, (Figure 1e on the previous page) with two hyperlinks to other Web pages, an e-mail link, and a bar chart. Clicking a **hyperlink**, which can be text or an image, allows you to jump to another location. Text is used (Company Services, Homes for Sale, E-Mail for Information) for the three hyperlinks on the Makin-It Real Estate home page. The first hyperlink (Company Services) jumps to a PowerPoint Web page that contains three Web pages that explain the services offered by the company. A second hyperlink (Homes for Sale) jumps to an Access report that provides a list of homes for sale extracted from Makin-It Real Estate's Homes for Sale Access database. This Web page allows inquiries only; updating the database is prohibited. The third hyperlink (E-Mail for Information) creates an e-mail message. In order to place the three hyperlinks to the left of the bar chart, a table will be created in the Word document.

To Start Word, Open an Existing Document, and Save the Document with Another File Name

The first step in this chapter is to open the Word document, Makin-It Real Estate Letterhead, and save it with the new file name, Makin-It Real Estate Home Page.

1 Connect the USB flash drive containing the Data Files for Students to an available USB port on your computer. See the inside back cover of this book for instructions for downloading the Data Files for Students, or contact your instructor for information on accessing the files required in this book.

② Start Word. Click the Office Button and then click Open on the Office Button menu.

③ If necessary, click Computer in the Favorite Links section of the Navigation pane and then double-click UDISK 2.0 (E:) to select the USB flash drive as the new open location. (Your USB drive may have a different name and letter.)

④ Double-click Makin-It Real Estate Letterhead to open the Makin-It Real Estate Letterhead document.

⑤ Click the Office Button and then click Save As on the Office Button menu. Type `Makin-It Real Estate Home Page` in the File name text box and then click the Save button in the Save As dialog box to save the document as Makin-It Real Estate Home Page.

⑥ Click the Web Layout button on the status bar to view the document in Web Layout view (Figure 2).

⑦ If necessary, click the Show/Hide ¶ button on the Home tab to show hidden formatting marks.

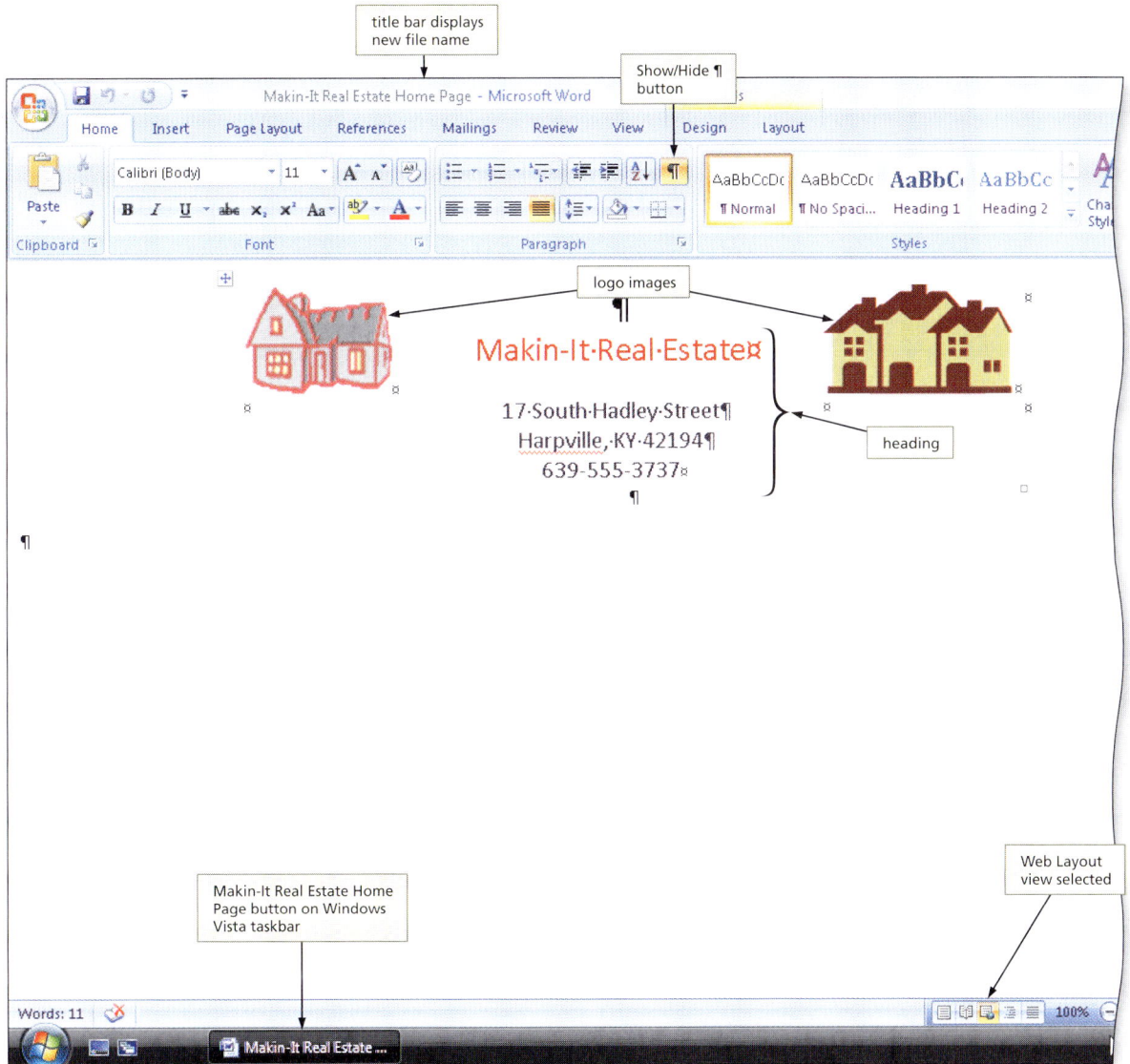

Figure 2

To Insert a Table into a Word Document

The next task is to insert a table with two columns and one row. The left column will contain three hyperlinks. The right column will contain the bar chart.

The following steps add a table to the Makin-It Real Estate Home Page document.

1
- Position the insertion point on the second paragraph mark below the company telephone number.
- Click the Insert tab on the Ribbon and then click the Table button on the Insert tab.
- Drag the mouse pointer through the first two cells in the Table gallery and do not release the mouse button (Figure 3).

2
- Release the mouse button to insert the table and close the Table gallery.

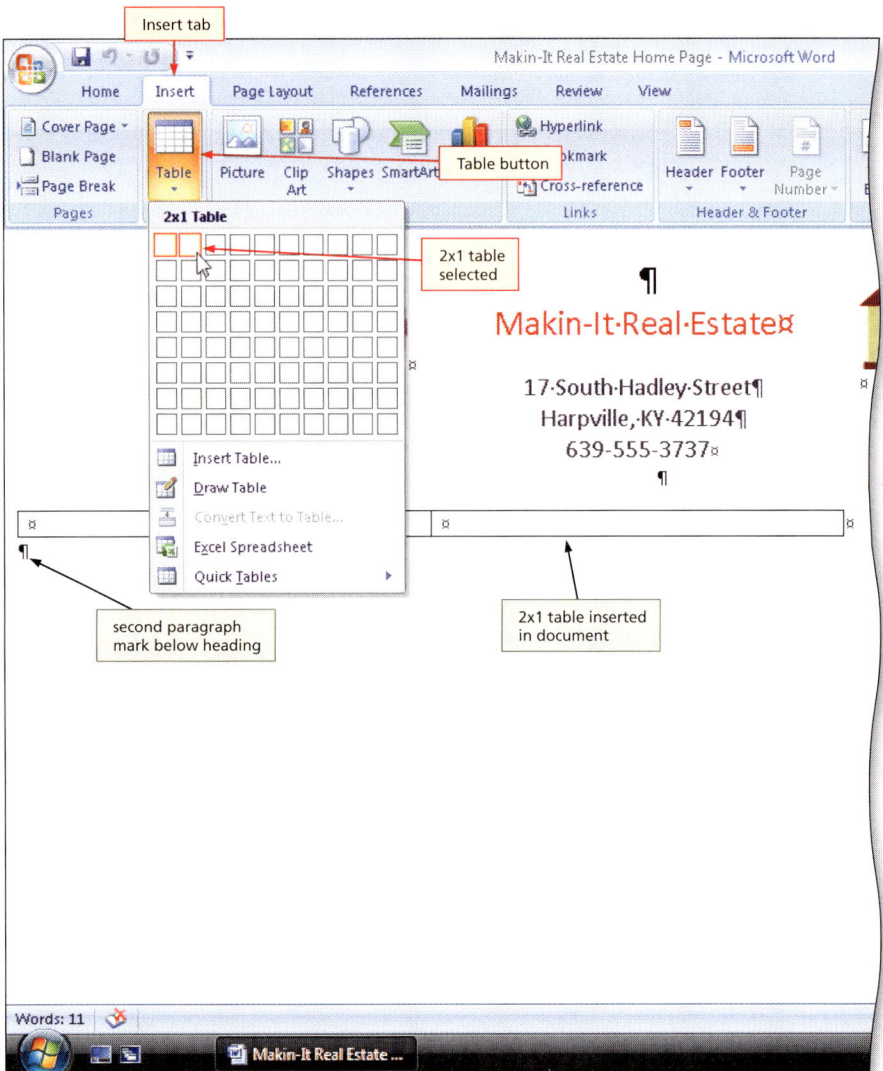

Figure 3

To Remove the Table Border, View Gridlines, and AutoFit the Table Contents

The table border for the new table is not necessary for the Web page. In order to place the contents in the document properly, however, gridlines should be displayed to serve as a guide for inserting the hyperlinks and chart. The cells in the table also should be formatted to adjust their size automatically to accommodate the data inserted in the table. The AutoFit to Contents option allows you to make the columns in a table automatically adjust to the contents. The following steps remove the border of the table, display gridlines in the tables in the document, and set the AutoFit to Contents option for the table. The heading in the document, including the clip art images, is already included in a table.

1
- Select both cells in the new table.
- If necessary, display the Table Tools Design tab.
- Click the Borders button arrow on the Table Tools Design tab to display the Borders gallery (Figure 4).

2
- Click No Border in the Borders gallery to remove the borders from the table.

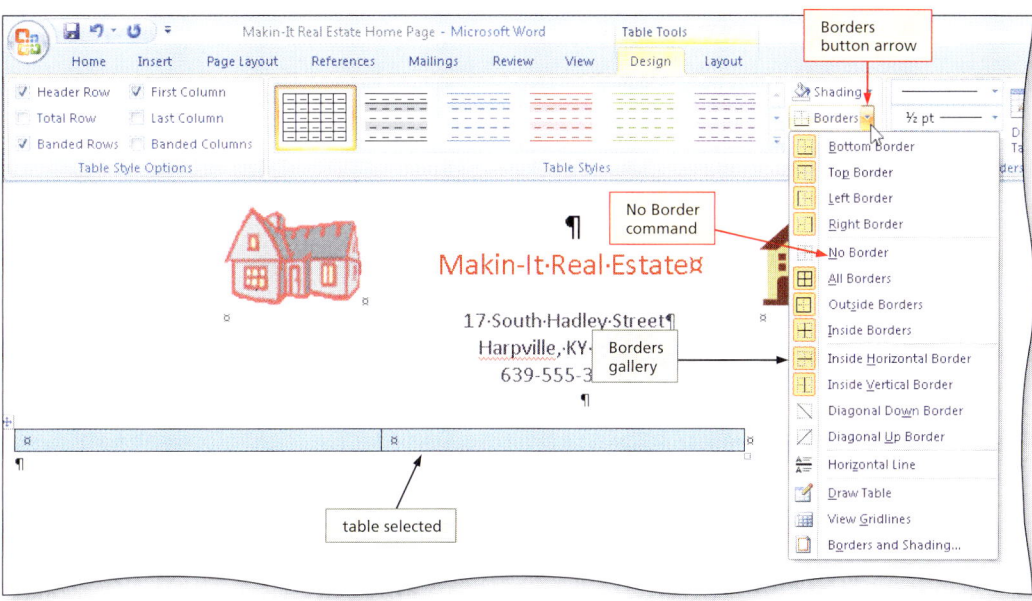

Figure 4

3
- Display the Table Tools Layout tab.
- Click the View Gridlines button on the Table Tools Layout tab to display gridlines in both tables in the document (Figure 5).

Q&A
When should I use gridlines?

Gridlines can be used as a guide when entering text or images. When the document is viewed in your browser or printed, the gridlines do not display or print.

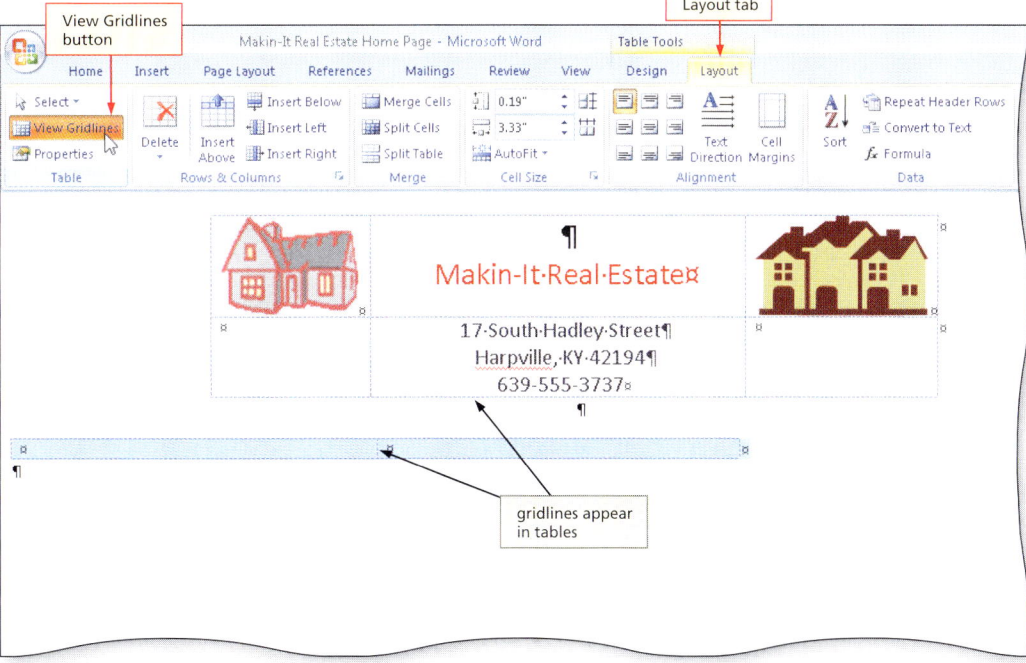

Figure 5

- Click the AutoFit button arrow on the Table Tools Layout tab to display the AutoFit gallery (Figure 6).

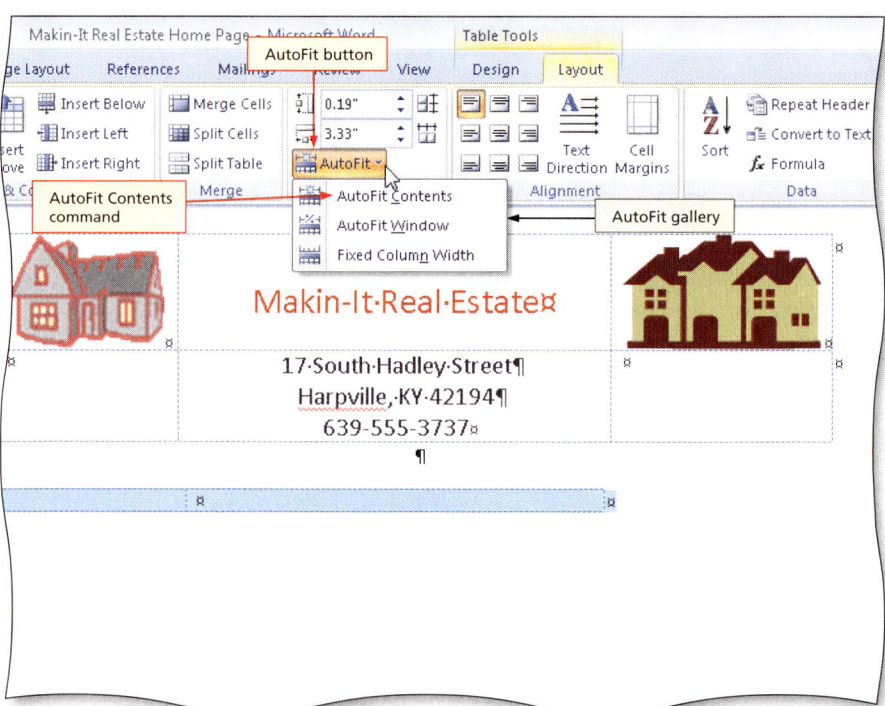

Figure 6

- Click AutoFit Contents in the AutoFit gallery to shrink the selected cells to fit their contents (Figure 7).

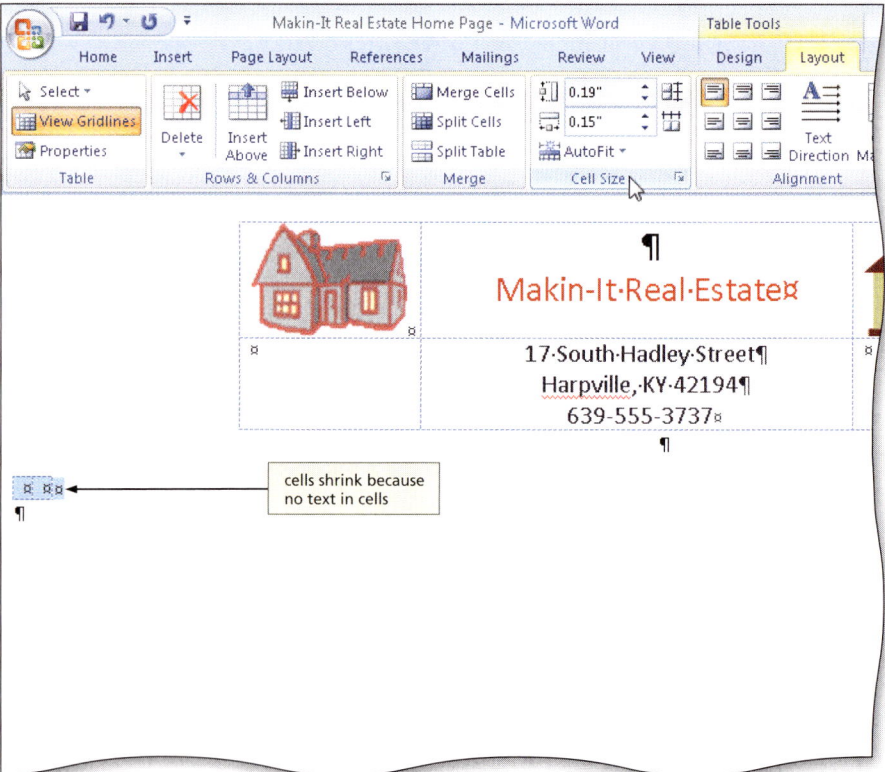

Figure 7

To Insert Text for Hyperlinks

After creating the borderless table, you must insert the three text phrases that will be used as hyperlinks on the home page. These phrases (Company Services, Homes for Sale, and E-Mail for Information) allow the Web page visitor to jump to two other Web pages and create an e-mail message. The following steps add the text phrases that are used as hyperlinks.

- If necessary, click the leftmost cell in the table to place the insertion point in the cell.

- Type `Company Services` and then press the ENTER key twice.
- Type `Homes for Sale` and then press the ENTER key twice.
- Type `E-Mail for Information` but do not press the ENTER key to complete the entry of the three text phrases that will be used as hyperlinks (Figure 8).

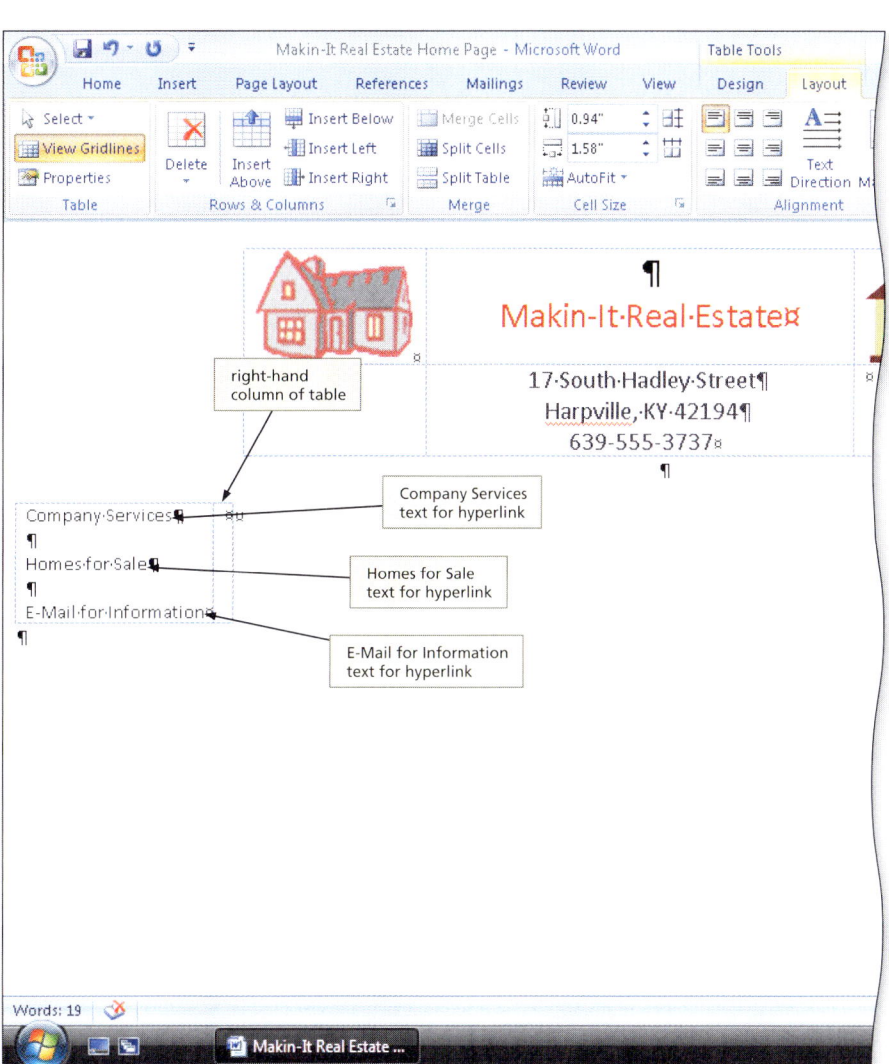

Figure 8

To Create a Hyperlink to PowerPoint Web Pages

The **Insert Hyperlink feature** provides the capability of linking to an existing file or Web page, to a place within the current document, to a newly created document, or to an e-mail address. In this chapter, two hyperlinks (Company Services and Homes for Sale) will be created that link to Web pages. The Company Services hyperlink will jump to a PowerPoint presentation that is saved as a Web page using the Web page name, CompanyServices.htm. The Homes for Sale hyperlink jumps to an Access report page using the Web page name, Homes for Sale.htm.

You will create the report later from an existing Access database. The third text phrase (E-Mail for Information) links to an e-mail address, allowing the Web page visitor to send an e-mail message to the company's manager.

The following steps create a hyperlink for the first text phrase.

1
- Drag through the text, Company Services, in the table to select the text.
- Display the Insert tab.
- Click the Insert Hyperlink button on the Insert tab to display the Insert Hyperlink dialog box.

2
- If necessary, click the Existing File or Web Page button on the Link to bar.
- Type `CompanyServices.htm` in the Address text box (Figure 9).

3
- Click the OK button to assign the hyperlink to the Company Services phrase.

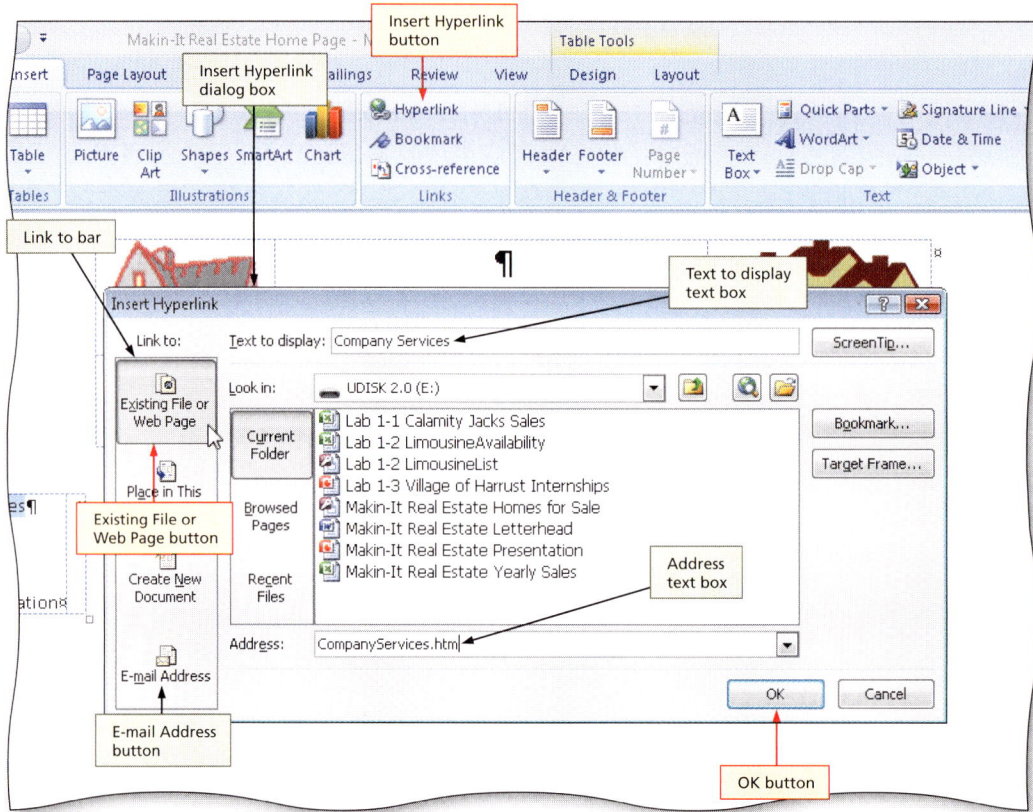

Figure 9

Q&A How does the hyperlink function?

After saving the Word document as a Web page, the visitor clicks the text, Company Services, and the CompanyServices.htm file on the USB flash drive is displayed.

Other Ways
1. Right-click selected words, click Hyperlink on shortcut menu
2. Press CTRL+K

To Insert the Remaining Hyperlinks

The following steps add the remaining two hyperlinks.

1 Drag through the text, Homes for Sale, in the table. Click the Insert Hyperlink button on the Insert tab.

2 Type `Makin-It Real Estate - Homes for Sale.htm` in the Address text box and then click the OK button.

3 Drag through the text, E-Mail for Information. Click the Insert Hyperlink button on the Insert tab and then click the E-mail Address button on the Link to bar.

4 Type `manager@isp.com` in the E-mail address text box.

5 Type `Request for Information` in the Subject box and then click the OK button (Figure 10).

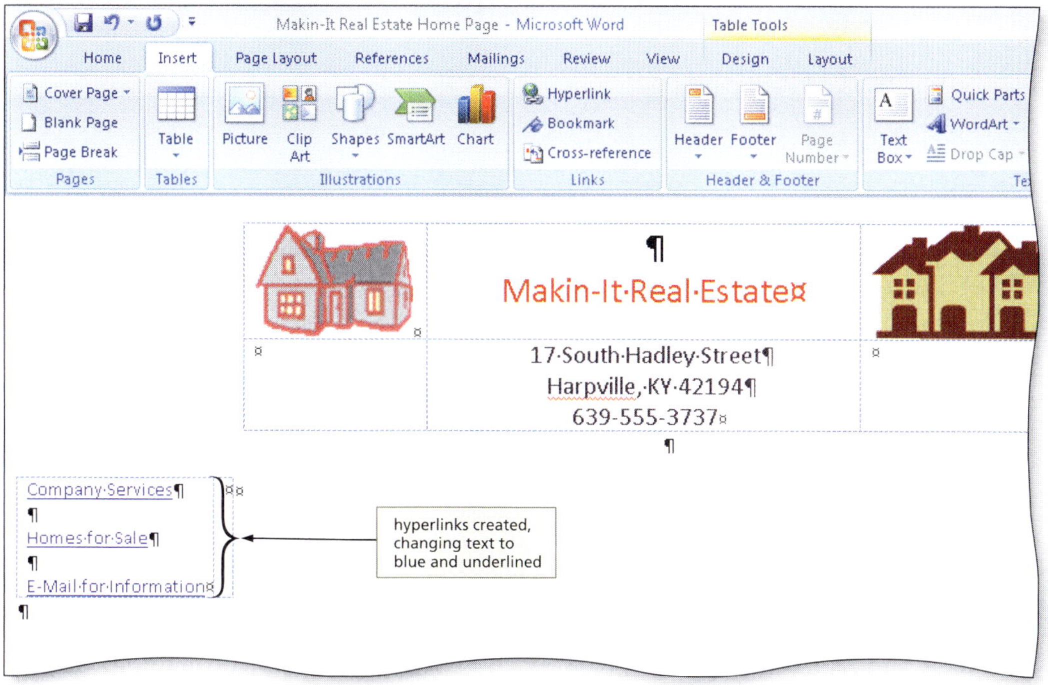

Figure 10

Embedding an Excel Chart into a Word Document

This chapter uses the **Object Linking and Embedding (OLE)** feature of Microsoft Office 2007 to insert the Excel chart into a Word document. OLE allows you to incorporate parts of a document or entire documents from one program into another. The bar chart in Excel is called a **source object** (Figure 1b on page INT 4) and the Makin-It Real Estate Home Page document is the **destination document**. An embedded object becomes part of the destination document. This chapter illustrates using the Paste Special command to embed the Excel object. **Paste Special** inserts an object into Word, but still recognizes the **source program**, the program used to create the object. When you double-click an embedded object, such as the Total Yearly Sales chart, the source program opens within the destination document and allows you to make changes. In this example, Excel is the source program.

To Start Excel and Open an Existing Workbook

The following steps open the Excel workbook in preparation for copying the chart from the workbook.

1. Start Excel. Click the Office Button and then click Open on the Office Button menu.

2. If necessary, click Computer in the Favorite Links section of the Navigation pane and then double-click UDISK 2.0 (E:) to select the USB flash drive as the new open location. (Your USB drive may have a different name and letter.)

3. Double-click Makin-It Real Estate Yearly Sales to open the Makin-It Real Estate Yearly Sales workbook.

BTW

Hyperlinks
Hyperlinks can link to both external locations and internal locations within the current document. To link to a location inside the current document, select the Place in This Document option in the Link to bar in the Insert Hyperlink dialog box. The Microsoft Office 2007 program then will provide a list of locations within the current document to which you can link.

BTW

Embedded Objects
The advantage of using an integrated set of programs, such as Microsoft Office 2007, is the capability of sharing information among programs. The Object Linking and Embedding (OLE) features of Office 2007 make the integration process more efficient. A chart created in Excel can be included in a Word document using OLE. To edit the embedded object, double-click it. The source program then starts and opens the source object for editing.

To Embed an Excel Chart into a Word Document

The following steps embed the Excel bar chart into the Word document.

1
- If necessary, click the Total Yearly Sales Chart tab to make the sheet tab active (Figure 11).

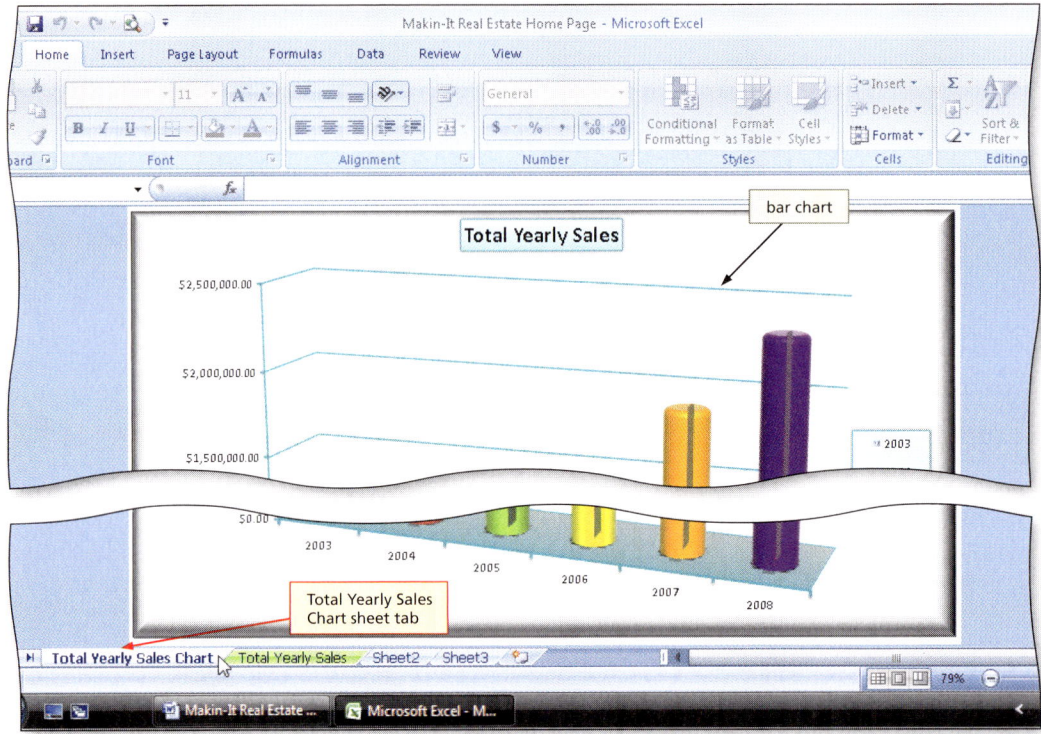

Figure 11

2
- Click the white area around the chart area to select the chart and then click the Copy button on the Home tab to place a copy of the bar chart on the Office Clipboard (Figure 12).

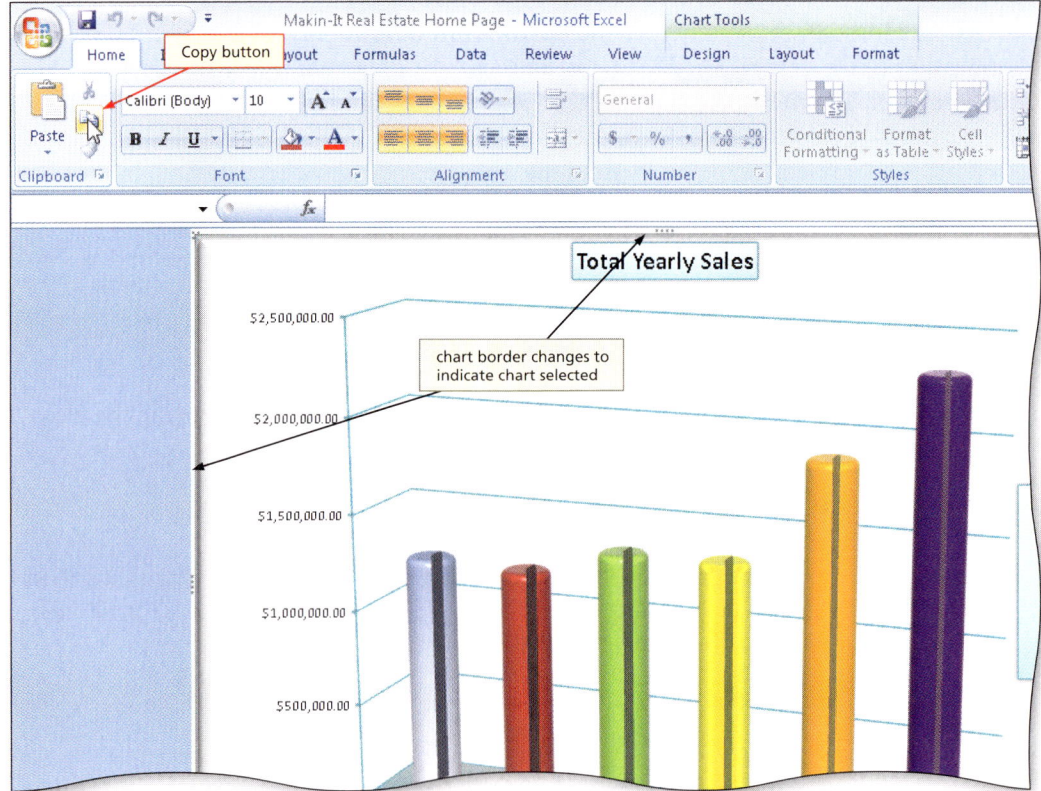

Figure 12

Integrating Office 2007 Programs and the World Wide Web   **Integration Chapter**   INT 15

3

- Click the Makin-It Real Estate Home Page button on the Windows Vista taskbar to switch to the Word document.

- If necessary, click the right cell of the lower table to place the insertion point in the right cell of the table.

- Display the Home tab.

- Click the Paste button arrow on the Home tab to display the Paste gallery (Figure 13).

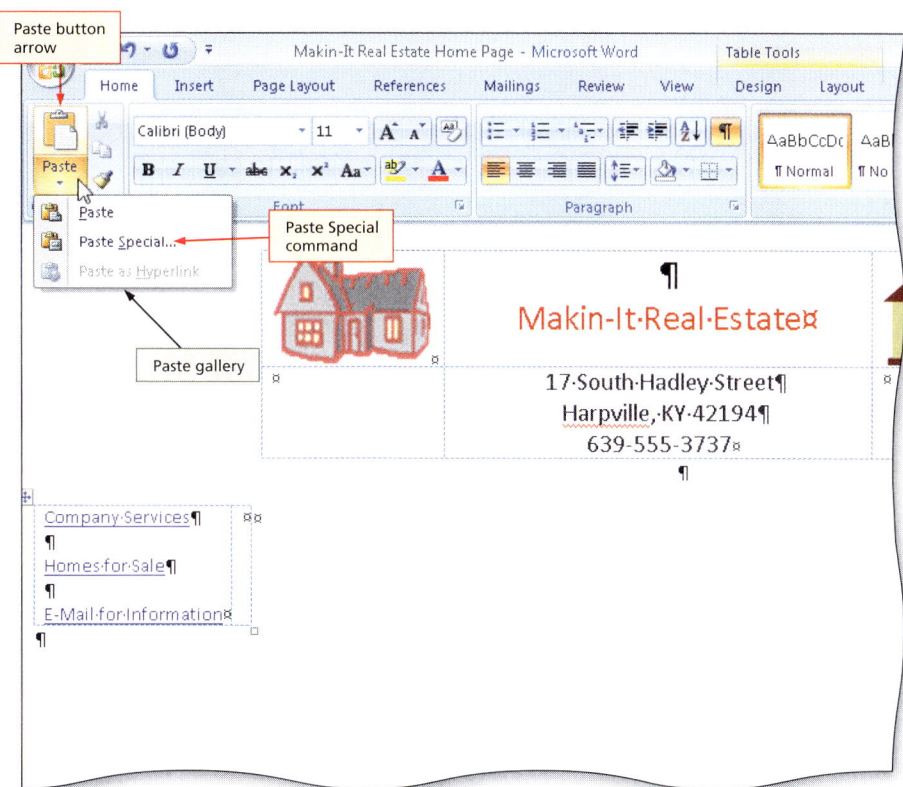

Figure 13

4

- Click Paste Special to display the Paste Special dialog box.

- If necessary, click Microsoft Office Excel Chart Object in the As list (Figure 14).

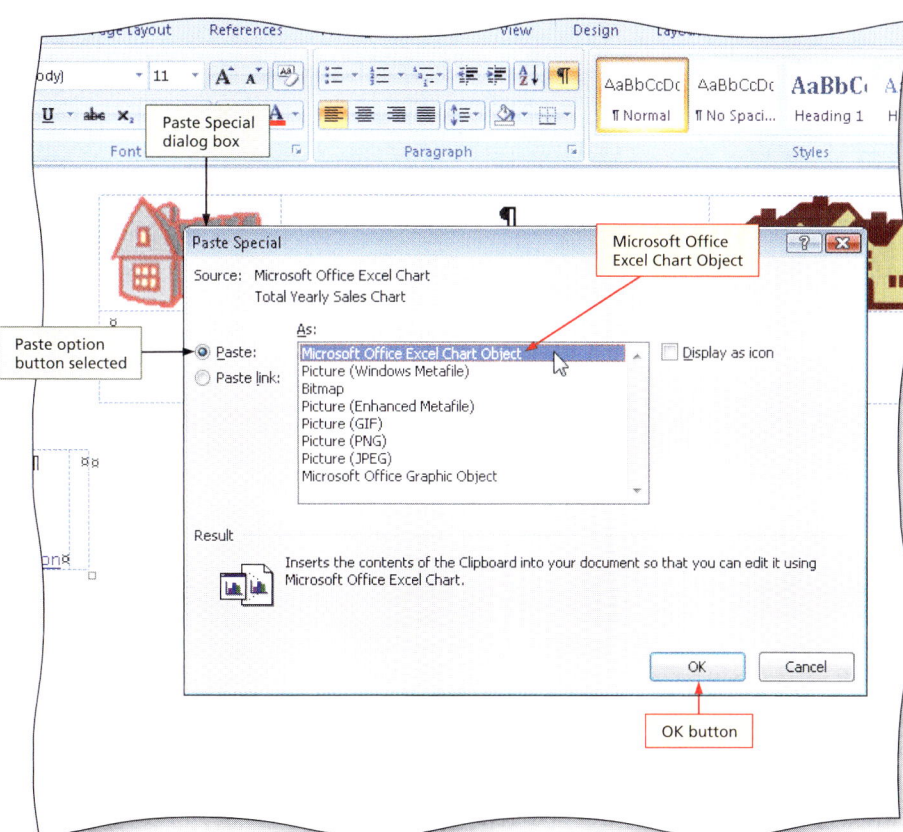

Figure 14

5
- Click the OK button to embed the bar chart into the document (Figure 15).

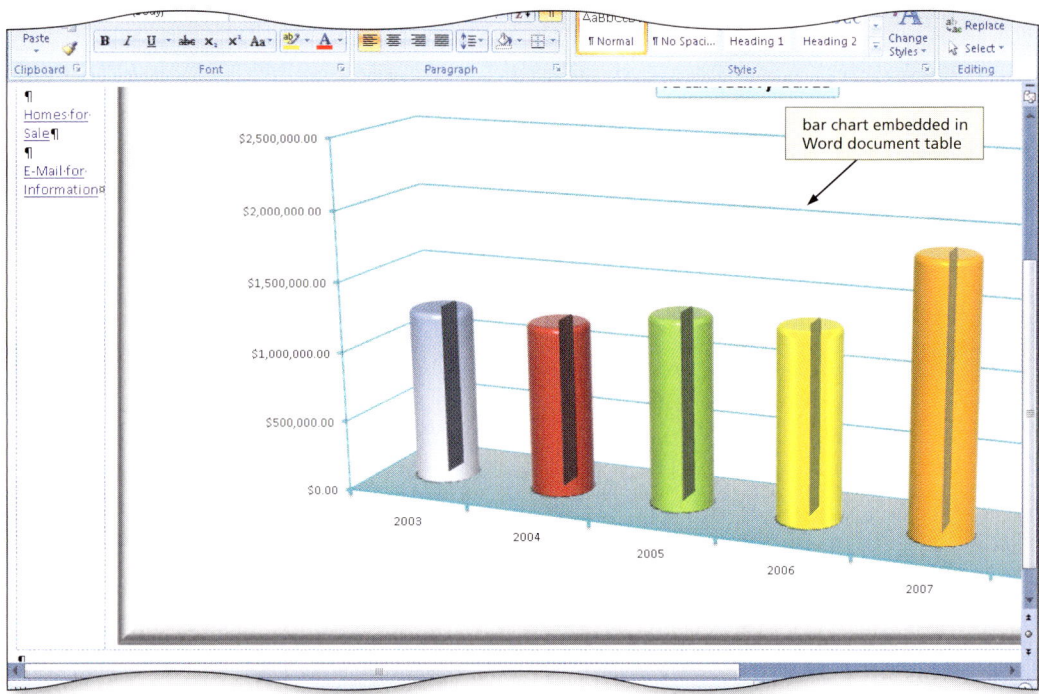

Figure 15

Other Ways
1. Right-click object, on shortcut menu click Copy
2. Press CTRL+C

Copy Methods

All Office 2007 programs allow you to use three methods to copy objects among programs: (1) copy and paste; (2) copy and embed; and (3) copy and link. The first method uses the Copy and Paste buttons. The latter two use the Copy button and the Paste Special command. Table 1 summarizes the differences among the three methods.

BTW

Objects
Objects can be nearly any part of an Office 2007 program or other Windows Vista program. Some examples are an Excel worksheet, a paragraph in a Word document, and a slide in a PowerPoint presentation. As long as you use the Paste Special command to paste data in the Clipboard, you can keep data in its native format.

Table 1 Copy Methods

Method	Characteristics
Copy and paste	The source object becomes part of the destination document. An object may be edited, but the editing features are limited to those of the destination program. An Excel worksheet becomes a Word table. If changes are made to values in the Word table, any original Excel formulas are not recalculated.
Copy and embed	The source object becomes part of the destination document. An object may be edited in the destination document using source editing features. The Excel worksheet remains a worksheet in Word. If you make changes to values in the worksheet with Word active, Excel formulas will be recalculated. If you change the worksheet in Excel without the document open in Word, however, these changes will not display in the Word document the next time you open it.
Copy and link	The source object does not become part of the destination document, even though it appears to be. Instead, a link is established between the two documents, so that when you open the Word document, the worksheet displays within the document, as though it were a part of it. When you attempt to edit a linked worksheet in Word, the computer starts Excel. If you change the worksheet in Excel, the changes also will display in the Word document the next time you open it.

To Change the Size of an Embedded Object

The embedded bar chart slightly exceeds the margins of the Makin-It Real Estate Home Page document. Reducing the size of the bar chart will improve the layout of the document. When an Office 2007 document includes an embedded object from another Office 2007 document, you can edit the object in place. When you edit an object in place, the destination document's program displays commands on the Ribbon from the source document's program. For example, when you edit the Total Yearly Sales chart in the Makin-It Real Estate Home Page, the Ribbon changes so that you can use commands from Excel even though you are working in Word.

The following steps reduce the size of the chart by editing the object in place.

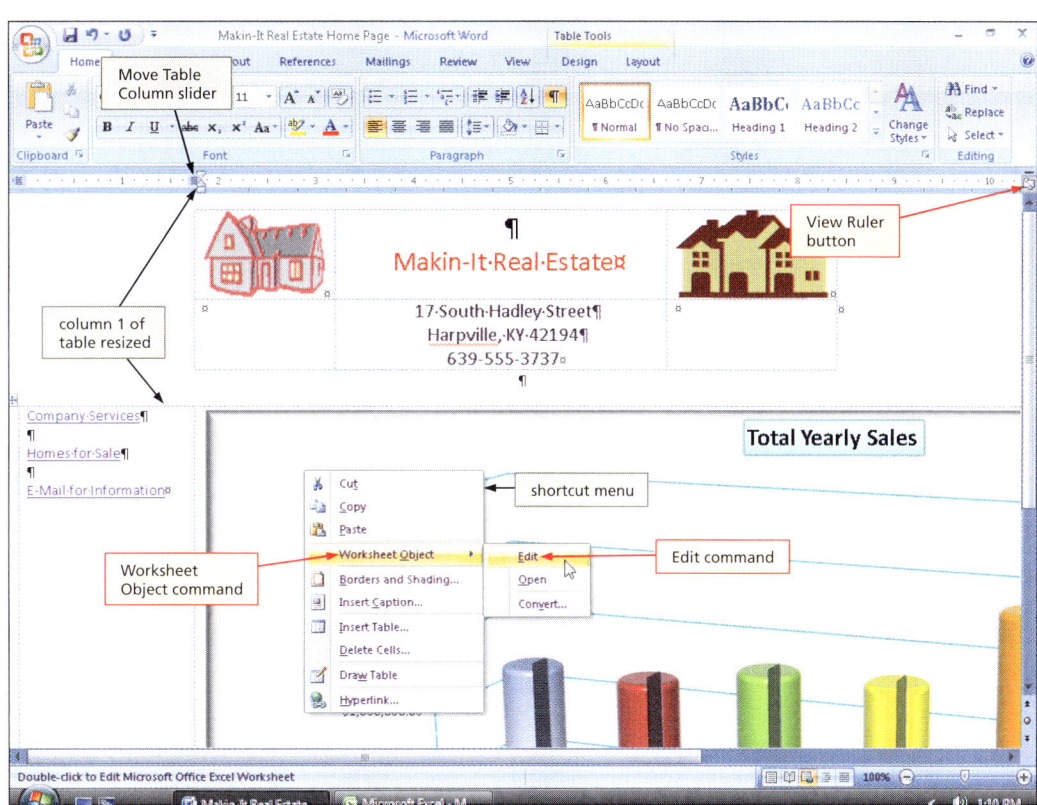

Figure 16

1
- Click the View Ruler button above the vertical scroll box.
- If necessary, use the vertical scroll bar on the right side of the Word window to scroll to the top of the document.
- Drag the Move Table Column slider to the right so that the border aligns with the left border of the upper table.

2
- Right-click the bar chart to display a shortcut menu.
- Click Worksheet Object on the shortcut menu to display the Worksheet Object shortcut menu and then point to Edit (Figure 16).

INT 18 Integration Chapter Integrating Office 2007 Programs and the World Wide Web

3
- Click Edit to begin editing the chart in place.
- Click anywhere in the chart to select it.
- Use the scroll bars on the bottom and right sides of the Word window to scroll to the bottom-right of the chart.
- Drag the lower-right sizing handle of the chart (Figure 17) up and to the left until the chart is sized as shown in Figure 18.

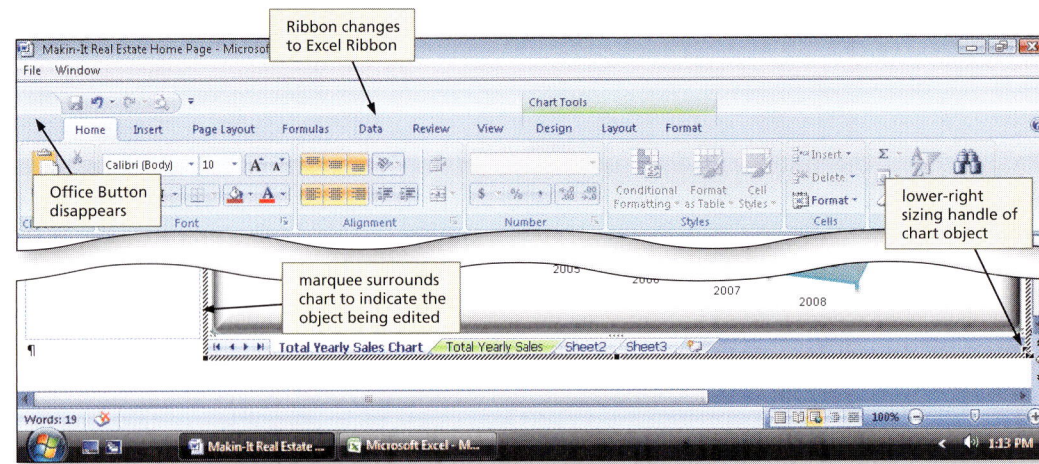

Figure 17

 What happened to the Ribbon?

When you edit an embedded object in place, the destination program, which is Word in this case, displays contextual commands in the Ribbon for the program in which the embedded object was created. You now can edit the Excel chart as though you are working in Excel. This method of editing is much simpler than the entire Excel program opening in order for you to edit the chart.

4
- If necessary, use the scroll bars on the bottom and right sides of the Word window to scroll to the top of the document.
- Click next to the E-Mail for Information hyperlink in the first column of the table to display the Word Ribbon (Figure 18).

Q&A Why did the Word Ribbon appear?

When you are finished editing an embedded object in place, you can click anywhere outside the embedded object in the destination document to reactivate the destination document's Ribbon commands.

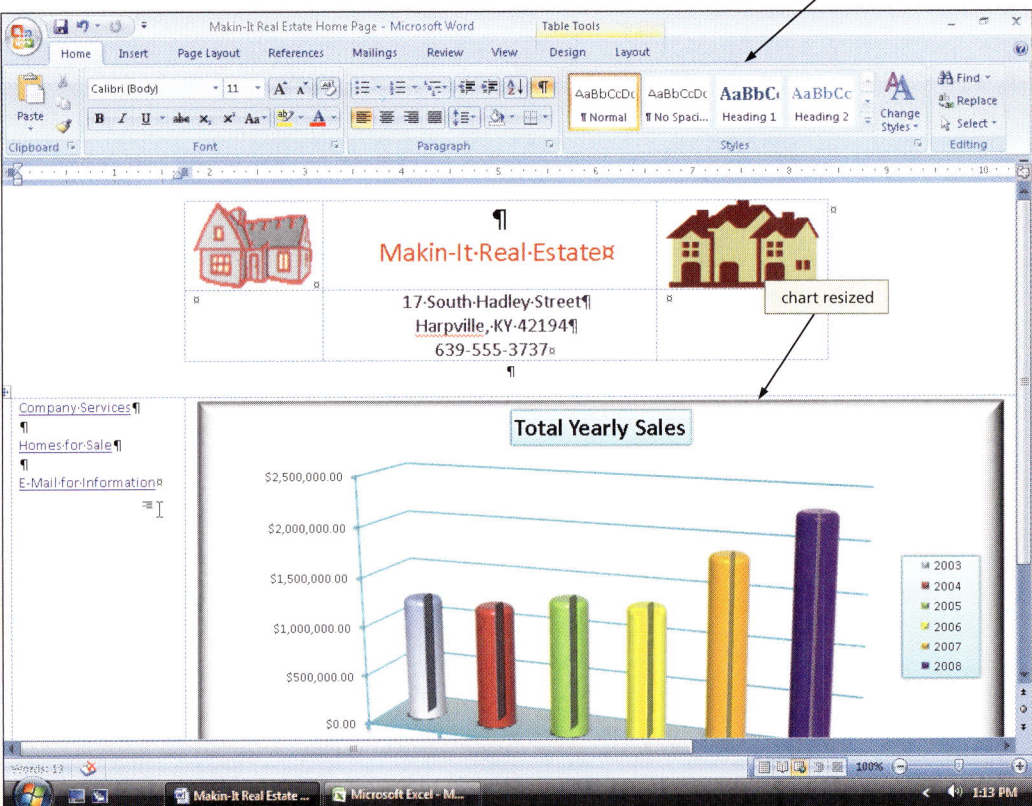

Figure 18

To Quit Excel

With the bar chart embedded in the Word document, you no longer need the Makin-It Real Estate Yearly Sales workbook open. The following steps quit Excel.

1 Right-click the Microsoft Excel - Makin-It Real Estate Yearly Sales button on the Windows Vista taskbar. Click Close on the shortcut menu. If prompted to save changes, click the No button.

2 If the Microsoft Excel dialog box displays regarding saving the large amount of information on the Clipboard, click the No button.

> **BTW**
>
> **Resizing**
> To resize an image proportionally from a corner, you can press and hold down the SHIFT key while dragging a corner sizing handle. To resize vertically, horizontally, or diagonally from the center outward, press and hold down the CTRL key while dragging a sizing handle. To resize proportionally from the center outward, press and hold down the CTRL+SHIFT keys and drag a corner sizing handle.

Viewing the Word Document in Your Browser and Saving It as a Web Page

The next task is to view the Word document in your browser to verify that all information and links in the document are accurate. After verifying its accuracy, you then can save the Word document as an HTML file. Saving the Word document as an HTML file makes it possible for it to be viewed using a browser, such as Internet Explorer.

To Add a Button to the Quick Access Toolbar

Many commands available in Word are not included on any of the tabs on the Ribbon. You can, however, add such commands to the Quick Access Toolbar. One such command allows you to preview a document in a Web browser. This command, Web Page Preview, could be added to the Quick Access Toolbar so that the Web page easily can be previewed. The following steps add the Web Page Preview command to the Quick Access Toolbar.

1
- Click the Customize Quick Access Toolbar button arrow to display the Customize Quick Access Toolbar menu (Figure 19).

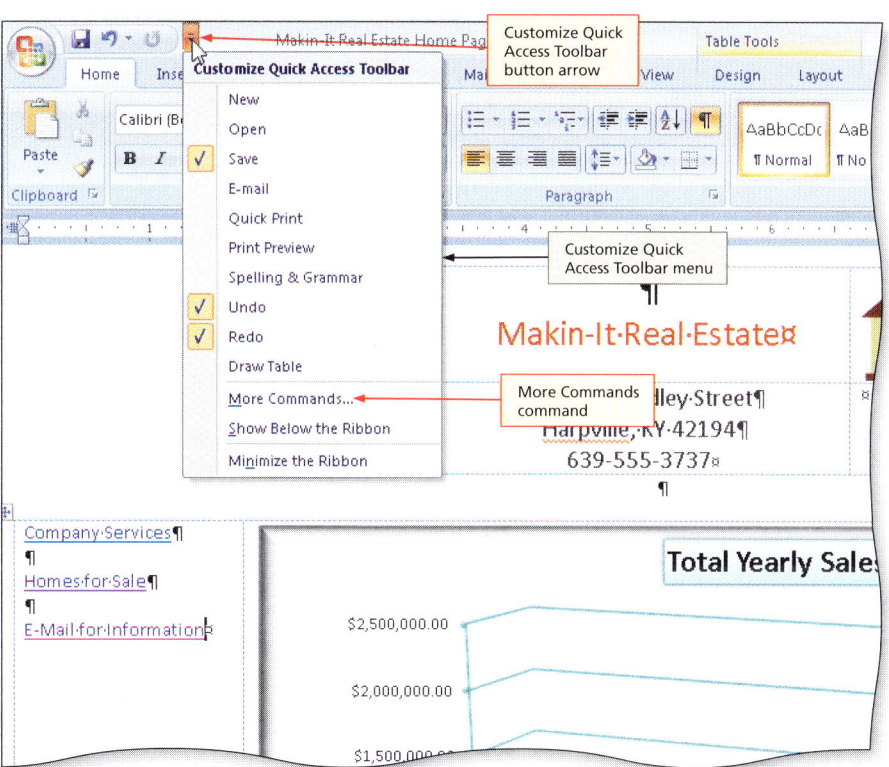

Figure 19

2
- Click More Commands on the Customize Quick Access Toolbar menu.
- When the Word Options dialog box is displayed, click the 'Choose commands from' box arrow to display the Choose commands from list (Figure 20).

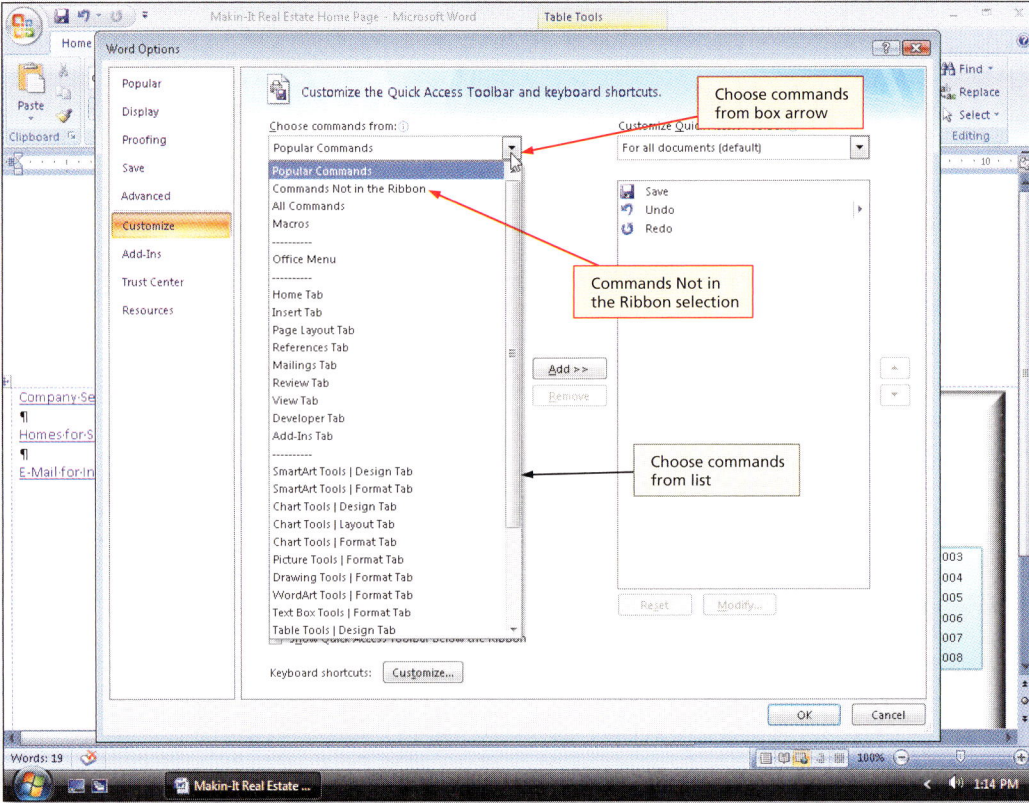

Figure 20

3
- Click Commands Not in the Ribbon in the 'Choose commands from' list to display a list of commands not in the Ribbon (Figure 21).

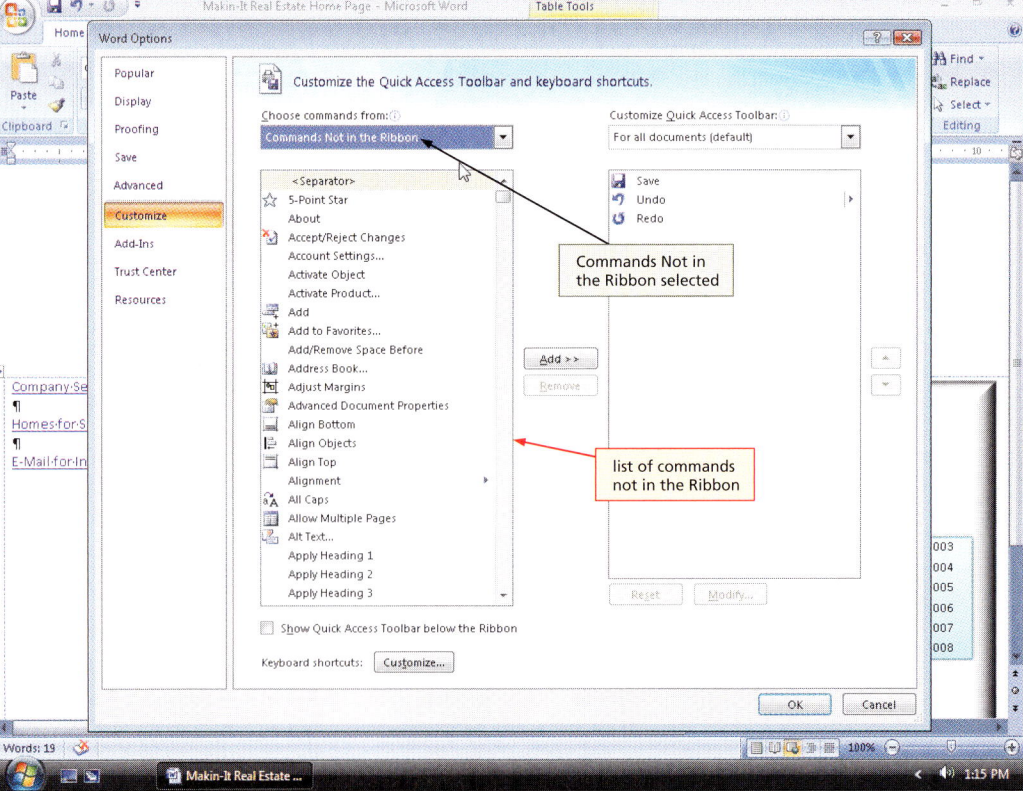

Figure 21

4
- Scroll to the bottom of the list, click Web Page Preview, and then click the Add button to add the button to the Quick Access Toolbar (Figure 22).

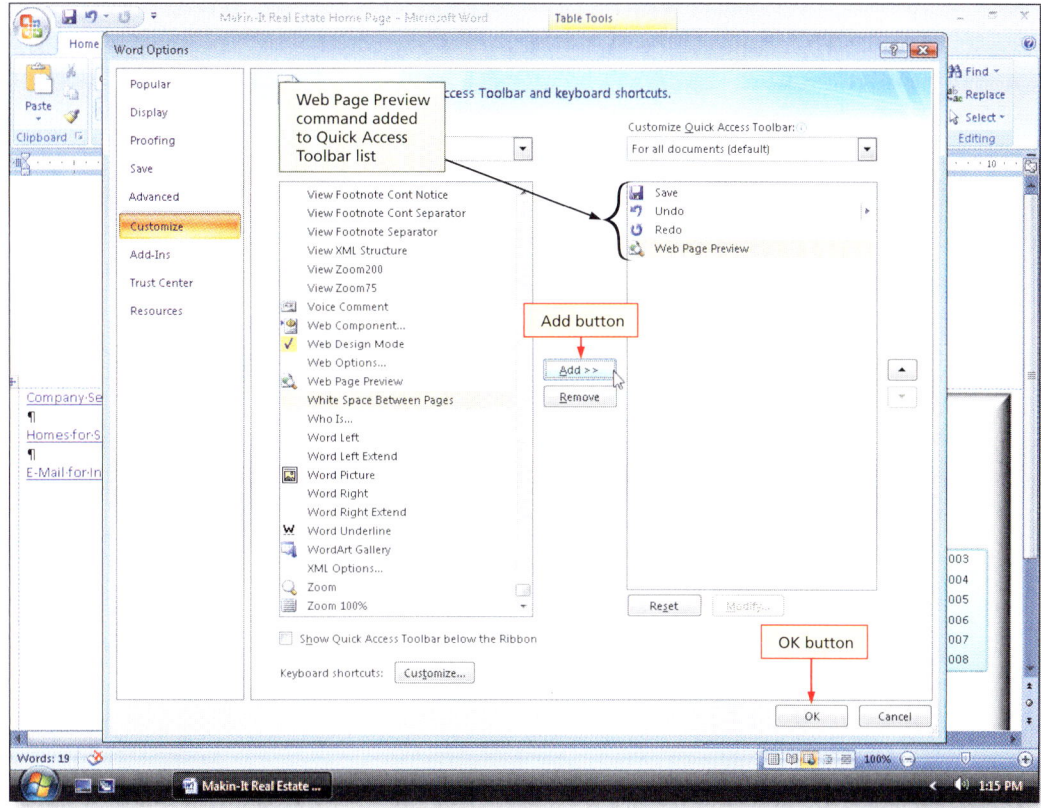

Figure 22

5
- Click the OK button to close the Word Options dialog box (Figure 23).

 Will the Web Page Preview command be on the Quick Access Toolbar the next time that I start Word?

Yes. When you change the Quick Access Toolbar, the changes remain even after you restart Word. If you share a computer with somebody else or if the Quick Access Toolbar becomes cluttered, Word allows you to remove commands from the Quick Access Toolbar. The Web Page Preview button is removed from the Quick Access Toolbar later in this chapter.

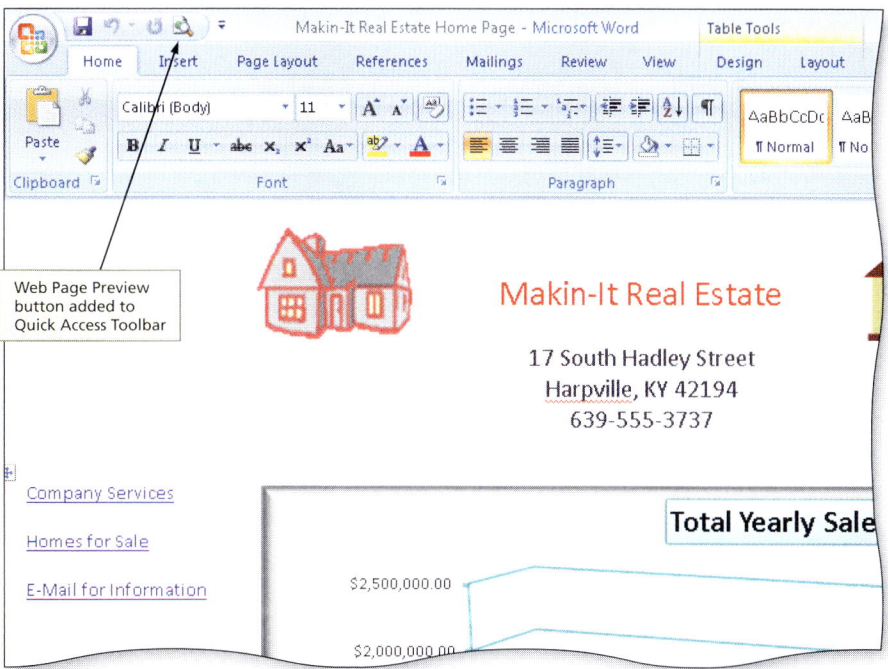

Figure 23

To Preview the Web Page

The following steps preview the document in the browser and then save the Word document as an HTML file.

- Click the Web Page Preview button on the Quick Access Toolbar to display the Web page in your browser. If the security warning appears in the Information bar at the top of the Web page, then click its Close button.

- If necessary, click the Maximize button on your browser's title bar (Figure 24).

- Click the browser's Close button.

Q&A How should I verify the Web page?

Verify that the Web page contains all information necessary and is displayed as shown in Figure 24. The Web page consists of a heading with logo images and the company name, address, and telephone number. A borderless table displays three hyperlinks in the left column and a bar chart in the right column. The E-Mail for Information hyperlink should display a new message when you click it. The other two links, Company Services and Homes for Sale, do not work because the corresponding Web pages are not available until later in this chapter.

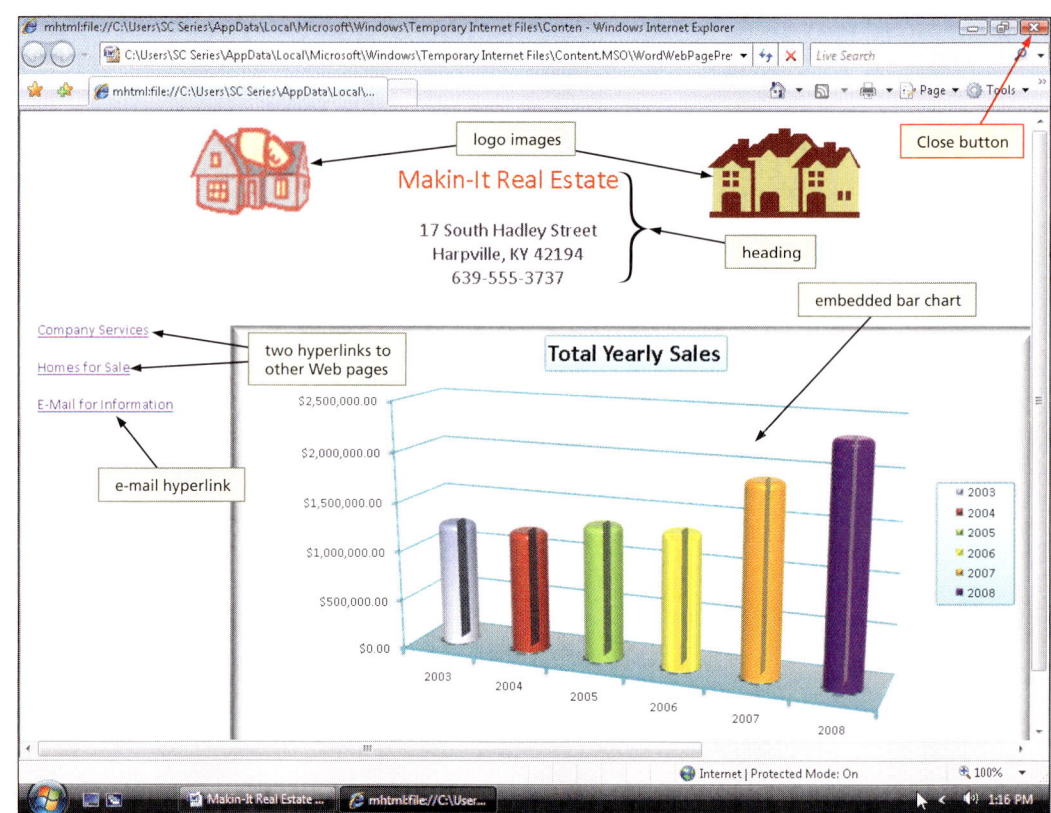

Figure 24

BTW

Web Page Formatting
Because Word provides formatting options that most Web browsers do not support, some text and graphics may look different when you view them on a Web page. When creating documents for the Web, using Web Layout view will ensure that your graphics look the way you want them to when they are viewed as Web pages in a Web browser.

To Save a Document with a New File Name

If the Web page is correct, save it on the USB flash drive as an HTML file. If changes need to be made to the Web page, return to the Word document and correct it. The following steps save the document as a Web page.

1. Click the Office Button and then click the Save As command.
2. Type `Makin-It Real Estate Home Page` in the File name text box if necessary.
3. Select Web Page in the Save as type box.
4. If necessary, click Computer in the Favorite Links section of the Navigation pane and then double-click UDISK 2.0 (E:) to select the USB flash drive as the new open location. (Your USB flash drive may have a different name and letter.)

5 Click the Save button in the Save As dialog box. If the Microsoft Office Word dialog box displays, click the Continue button.

Q&A Why should I save the document as a Web page?

Saving an existing Word document as a Web page allows you quickly to get a Word document ready for copying to the Web or to an intranet. One alternative to this is to write the Hypertext Markup Language (HTML) to develop the Web pages. **HTML** is a programming language used for Web page creation. The home page created earlier in this chapter could be created by writing HTML tags (code). For documents that already are in Word format, the easier method is to use the Word Save as Web Page command. This essentially creates the HTML code for you and saves it in a file. While the HTML code is in the file, you do not need to understand HTML code.

To Reset the Quick Access Toolbar and Quit Word

The necessary work with the Word document is complete. The following steps remove the Web Page Preview button from the Quick Access Toolbar and quit Word.

1 Click the Customize the Quick Access Toolbar button arrow on the Quick Access Toolbar.

2 Click More Commands on the Customize Quick Access Toolbar menu.

3 When the Word Options dialog box is displayed, click the Reset button. If the Reset Customizations dialog box is displayed, click the OK button.

4 Click the OK button on the Word Options dialog box to close it.

5 Click the View Ruler button to close the ruler.

6 Click the Close button on the Microsoft Word title bar.

Q&A Do I need to remove the button from the Quick Access Toolbar?

No. For consistency with this book, reset the Quick Access Toolbar after the added buttons are no longer needed. If you share a computer with others, you should reset the Quick Access Toolbar when you are finished using the computer.

BTW

Web Programming Languages
A number of programming languages can be used to create Web pages. Web pages created using the Save as Web Page command on the File menu can be enhanced with other Web programming languages, such as ASP, DHTML, and JavaScript.

Creating a PowerPoint Presentation Web Page

PowerPoint 2007 allows you to create Web pages from an existing PowerPoint presentation, using the same method used earlier in this chapter to save a Word document as a Web page. The presentation then can be viewed using your browser.

To Start PowerPoint and Open an Existing Presentation

The PowerPoint presentation used in this chapter consists of three slides (Figure 1g on page INT 5). The first slide is a title slide, containing the company name and graphics. Slide 2 consists of information about services for home sellers. Slide 3 includes information about services for home buyers. This information can be used in its present format to enhance a presentation about the company's services. As Web pages, you can use this presentation to address a much wider, global audience on the World Wide Web.

The following steps open an existing PowerPoint presentation.

1. Start PowerPoint. Click the Office Button and then click Open on the Office Button menu.

2. If necessary, click Computer in the Favorite Links section of the Navigation pane and then double-click UDISK 2.0 (E:) to select the USB flash drive as the new open location. (Your USB drive may have a different name and letter.)

3. Double-click Makin-It Real Estate Presentation to open the Makin-It Real Estate Presentation presentation (Figure 25).

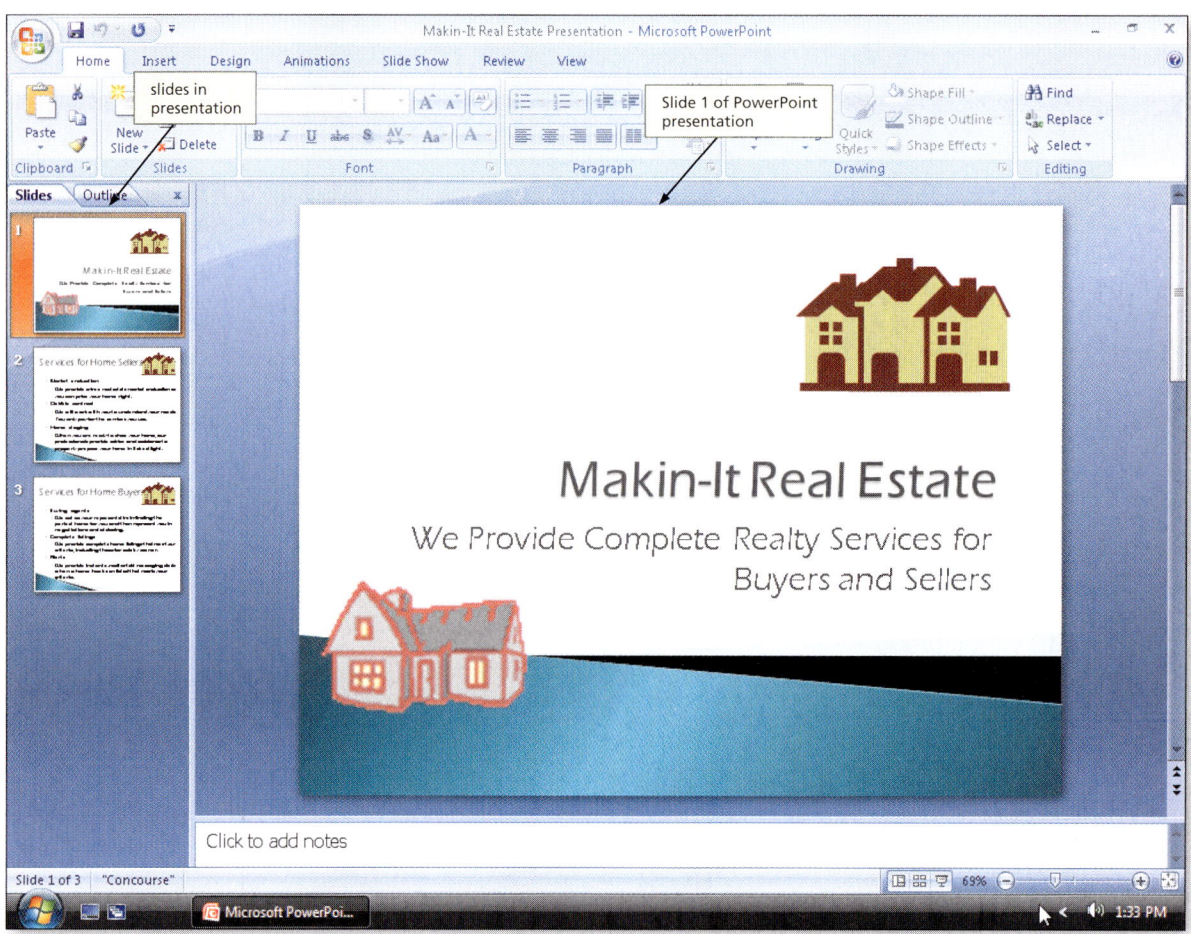

Figure 25

BTW

Keeping Links Fresh
When you create a Web page, it is important to make sure that all of your hyperlinks are functional as time goes on. Links to other pages can become stale, or nonfunctional, if another Web page creator or an external site takes a page offline. Automated tools can help you identify when pages to which you are hyperlinking no longer are available.

To Add Text for a Hyperlink into a PowerPoint Presentation

One of the more important features of Web sites is their capability of linking from one Web page to another using hyperlinks. In earlier steps in this chapter, you added three hyperlinks to the Makin-It Real Estate home page. Once Web page visitors link to the PowerPoint Web pages, however, they cannot return to the home page without using the Back button on the browser's toolbar. This is not a convenient way for Web page visitors to navigate through the Web site. The following steps add a Home link to the first slide of the PowerPoint presentation (Figure 1e on page INT 5).

1. Display the Insert tab.

2. Click Text Box on the Insert tab.

③ Draw the outline of the text box in the location shown on the slide in Figure 26.

④ If necessary, click inside the text box.

⑤ Type Home as the hyperlink text (Figure 26).

Figure 26

To Insert a Hyperlink into a PowerPoint Presentation

After you enter the text for the hyperlink, you can create the hyperlink itself. When clicked, the hyperlink jumps to the Makin-It Real Estate home page created previously in this chapter and saved on the USB flash drive. To create the hyperlink, you will use the Insert Hyperlink button on the Insert tab.

The following steps create the PowerPoint hyperlink.

- Double-click the word, Home, inside the text box you just inserted.

- If necessary, display the Insert tab.
- Click the Insert Hyperlink button on the Insert tab to display the Insert Hyperlink dialog box.

- If necessary, click the Existing File or Web Page button on the Link to bar.
- Type e:\Makin-It Real Estate Home Page.htm in the Address text box. (Your USB drive may have a different name and letter.) Click the OK button to add the hyperlink to the text in the text box (Figure 27).

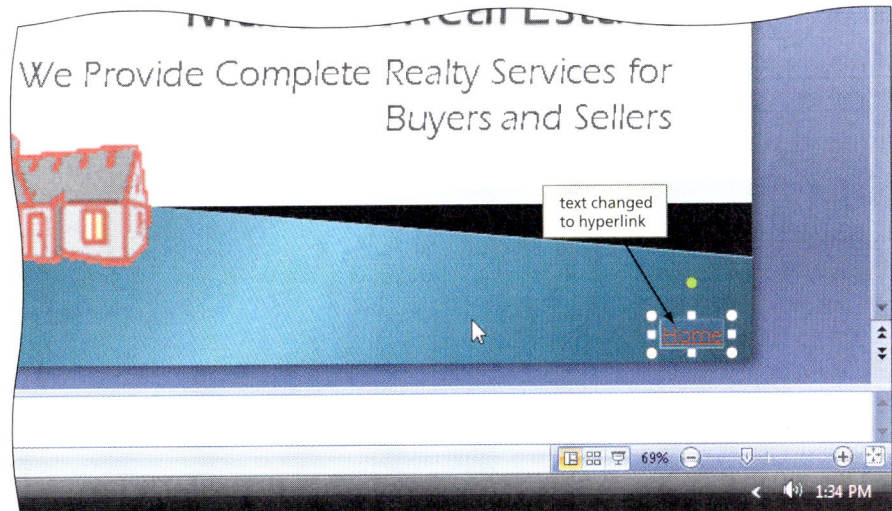

Figure 27

Other Ways
1. Right-click highlighted word, click Hyperlink on shortcut menu
2. Press CTRL+K

To Add a Button to the Quick Access Toolbar and View the Web Page in Your Browser

Just as in the previous section of this chapter, the following steps display the Web page before saving it. It is important to verify all of the Web page navigation features before saving the file. Because the Web Page Preview button is not available on the Quick Access Toolbar, the button must first be added to the Quick Access Toolbar.

1. Click the Customize Quick Access Toolbar button arrow to display the Customize Quick Access Toolbar menu.

2. Click More Commands on the Customize Quick Access Toolbar menu.

3. When the PowerPoint Options dialog box is displayed, click the 'Choose commands from' box arrow to display the Choose commands from list.

4. Click Commands Not in the Ribbon in the Choose commands from list to display a list of commands not in the Ribbon. Scroll to the bottom of the list, click Web Page Preview, and then click the Add button to add the button to the Quick Access Toolbar.

5. Click the OK button to close the PowerPoint Options dialog box.

6. Click the Web Page Preview button on the Quick Access Toolbar to display the Web page in your browser. If the security warning appears in the Information bar at the top of the Web page, then click its Close button.

7. If necessary, click the Maximize button on your browser's title bar (Figure 28).

Figure 28

Using Hyperlinks in PowerPoint

Slide 1 of the PowerPoint presentation Web page contains a hyperlink to the home page of the Makin-It Real Estate Web site. Although you created this hyperlink by adding a text box to the first slide, you also can create hyperlinks from existing text or images in a PowerPoint presentation. For example, one of the logo images on slide 1 could be used as a hyperlink to the home page of the Web site. Using one of those images, however, does not give the Web page visitor a clear idea of where the hyperlink will lead. It is more appropriate to create a hyperlink to the home page from text — for example, Home — that makes sense to the visitor.

In addition to any hyperlinks that are added to the presentation, PowerPoint automatically creates hyperlinks in the left column of the Web page, called the **outline**. Using the Expand/Collapse Outline button below the outline pane, you can expand or collapse the outline and navigate through the Web page presentation (Figure 28). The text in the heading of each slide is used as the phrases for these hyperlinks. When you click a link, you jump to that particular slide within the presentation. The ease of navigation within a PowerPoint Web page is valuable to the Web page visitor.

> **BTW**
> **Web Page Publishing**
> The Web pages created in this project all are stored locally on your computer. Typically, a Web page must be published to a server inside the organization or at your ISP. Microsoft offers a Web Page Publishing Wizard to assist in moving all of the related files and directories that comprise a Web site.

To Save the PowerPoint Presentation as a Web Page

The next step is to save the PowerPoint presentation as a Web page. When you save a PowerPoint presentation as a Web page, the Web page is saved in a default folder. All supporting files, such as backgrounds and images, are organized in this folder automatically. The name of the PowerPoint slide show opened in this section is Makin-It Real Estate Presentation. To simplify the naming of the Web page, the Web page will be saved with the name CompanyServices.htm. PowerPoint uses the name of the saved Web page and adds the string, _files, for the name of the new folder. When saving the current presentation as a Web page, the folder name that PowerPoint Web creates is CompanyServices_files. The default name for the first slide in the presentation is frame.htm. The structure used in the folder organization makes Web page publishing easier because you can keep track of all of the files associated with the Web page. You also can edit the files manually, rather than using PowerPoint.

The steps below save the PowerPoint presentation as a Web page.

> **BTW**
> **Outline**
> The outline pane is displayed by default when you view a presentation in a browser. To hide this pane, click the Outline button while in the browser. Click the Outline button again to redisplay the outline pane.

1. Click the Microsoft PowerPoint button on the Windows Vista taskbar.
2. Click the Office Button and then click the Save As command.
3. If necessary, type `CompanyServices` in the File name text box.
4. Select Web Page in the 'Save as type' box.
5. If necessary, click Computer in the Favorite Links section of the Navigation pane and then double-click UDISK 2.0 (E:) to select the USB flash drive as the new open location. (Your USB flash drive may have a different name and letter.)
6. Click the Save button in the Save As dialog box to save the PowerPoint presentation as a Web page.

To Remove a Button from the Quick Access Toolbar, Quit PowerPoint, and Close Your Browser

After saving the PowerPoint presentation as a Web page, you can remove the Web Page Preview button from the Quick Access Toolbar, quit PowerPoint, and close your browser, as shown in the following steps.

1. Click the Customize the Quick Access Toolbar button arrow on the Quick Access Toolbar.
2. Click More Commands on the Customize Quick Access Toolbar menu.
3. When the PowerPoint Options dialog box is displayed, click the Reset button. If the Reset Customizations dialog box is displayed, click the OK button.
4. Click the OK button on the PowerPoint Options dialog box to close it.
5. Click the Close button on the PowerPoint title bar.
6. Click the Close button on the browser title bar.

BTW

Viewing Web Pages
In addition to Microsoft Windows Vista environments, many environments exist for viewing Web pages. When creating a Web page with special features, such as data access pages, it is important to make sure that the special features are supported within the environment in which the Web page viewers operate. For example, users who view Web pages on Apple Macintosh computers may have a different Web page viewing experience.

Creating a Web Page from an Access Report

The next task in the Makin-It Real Estate Web site creation is to use an Access database to create a report and save it as a Web page. One of the more common purposes of reports is for viewing records in a database via a company's intranet or the World Wide Web. Reports provide a method to make inquiries of large amounts of data in a selective way.

To Start Access and Open an Existing Database

The following steps open an Access database.

1. Start Access. Click the Office Button and then click Open on the Office Button menu.
2. If necessary, click Computer in the Favorite Links section of the Navigation pane and then double-click UDISK 2.0 (E:) to select the USB flash drive as the new open location. (Your USB drive may have a different name and letter.)
3. Double-click Makin-It Real Estate Homes for Sale to open the Makin-It Real Homes for Sale database (Figure 29).

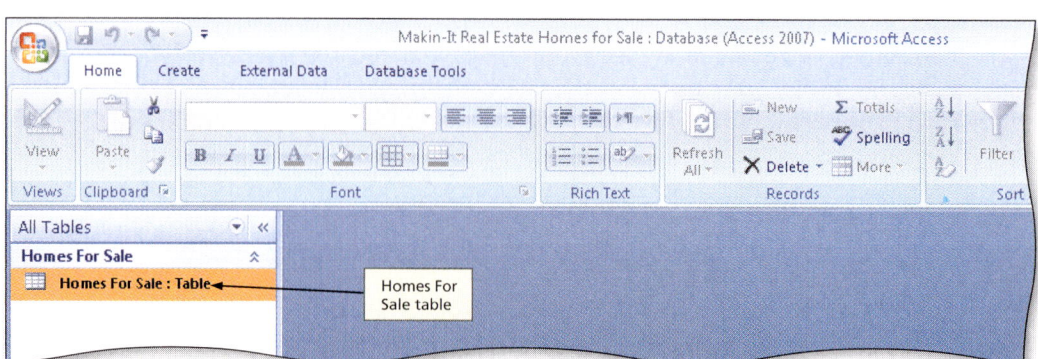

Figure 29

To Create a Report Using the Report Wizard

For the Makin-It Real Estate Web site, you do not want the database to be altered by the Web page visitor in any way. The visitors should be allowed to view only the data. Creating an Access report and then publishing the report as a Web page will achieve this goal. The Web page visitors can view all data, but they cannot change the data itself.

The following steps create a new Access report.

- Display the Create tab.
- Click the Report Wizard button on the Create tab.
- When the Report Wizard dialog box is displayed, click the Add All Fields button to move all the fields in the table to the Selected Fields list (Figure 30).

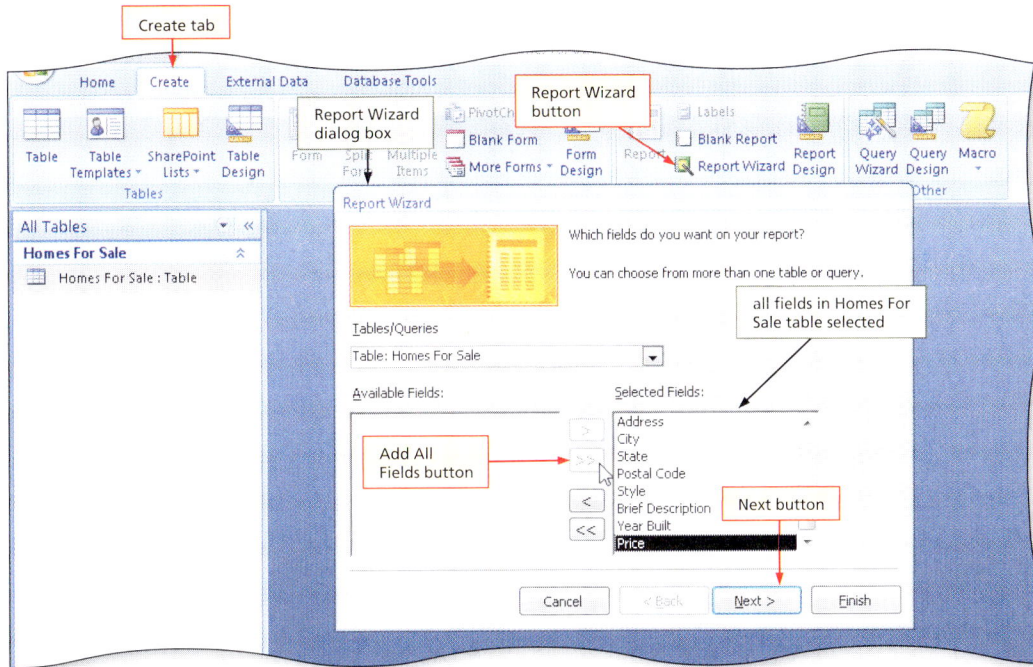

Figure 30

- Click the Next button.
- Click Style in the box on the left and then click the Add button to group the report by Style (Figure 31).

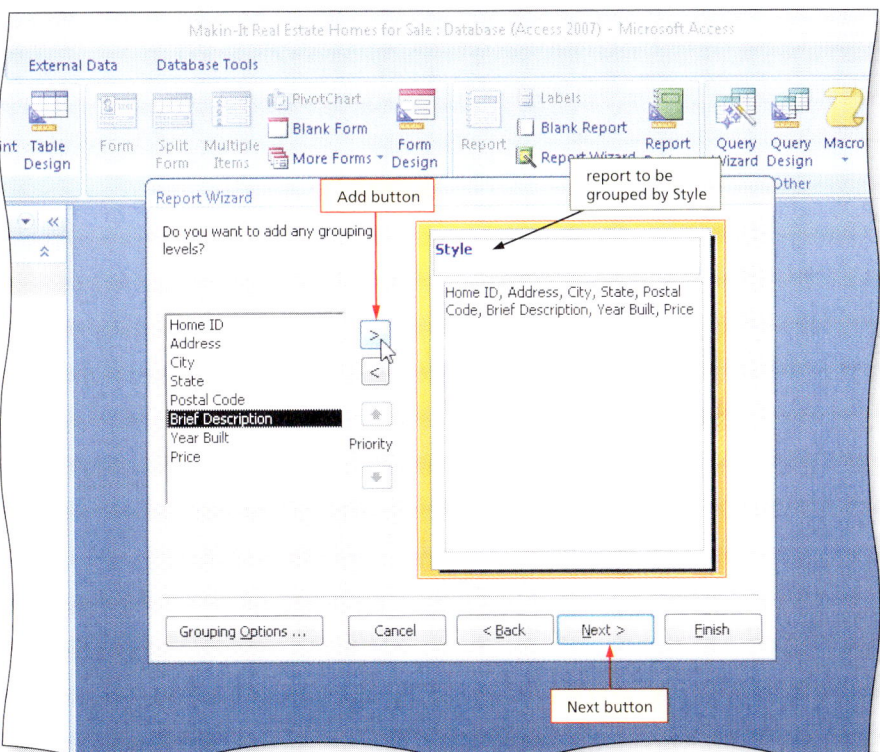

Figure 31

- Click the Next button to display options for sorting records (Figure 32).

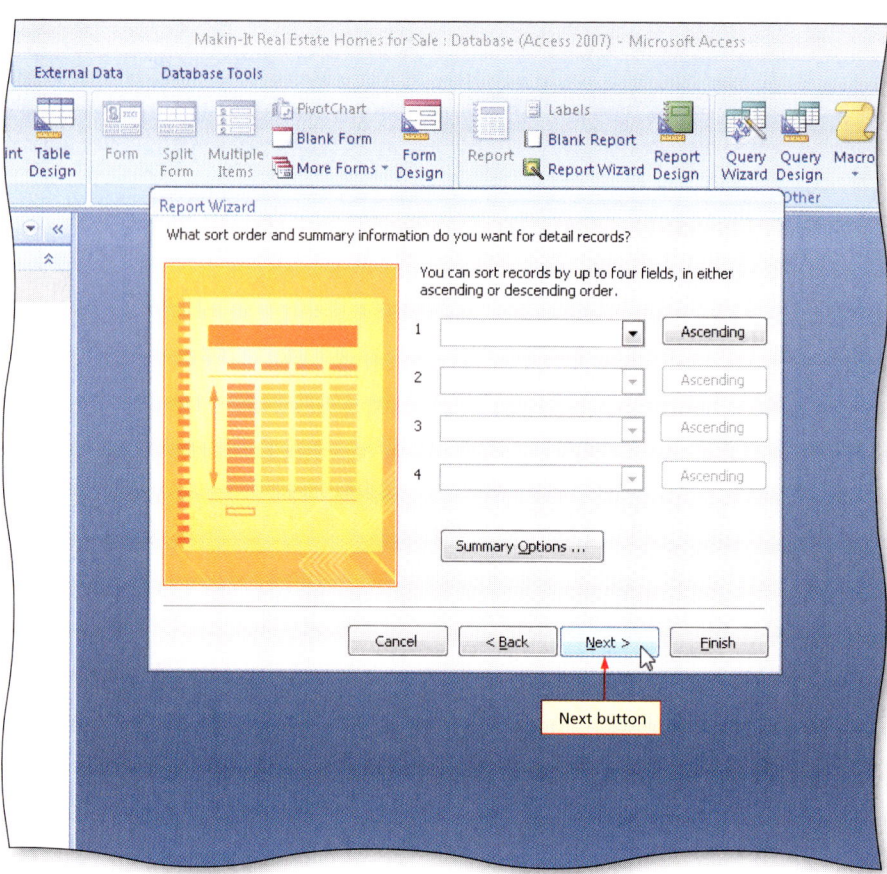

Figure 32

- Click the Next button.
- Click the Landscape option button in the Orientation area to select it (Figure 33).

Q&A Why change the orientation to landscape?

When you plan to use a report as a Web page, set the orientation to landscape so that the report takes up as much horizontal space as possible. If portrait is selected, then the Web page visitor might see a large empty margin on the right side of the page.

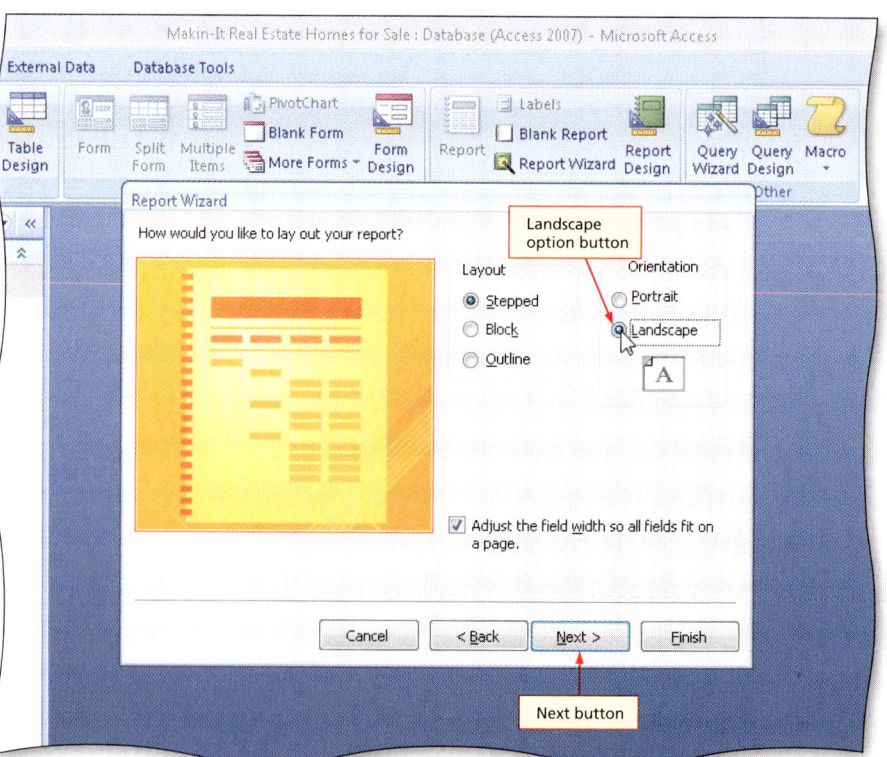

Figure 33

Integrating Office 2007 Programs and the World Wide Web **Integration Chapter** INT 31

- Click the Next button.
- If necessary, click the Access 2007 style in the list on the right (Figure 34).

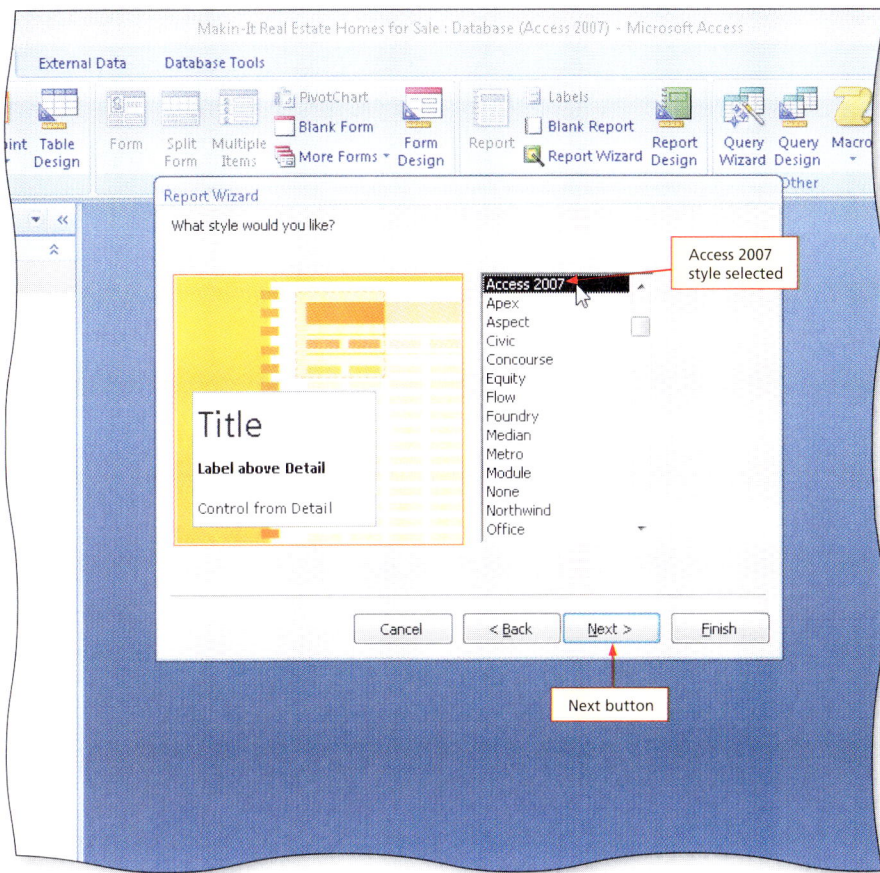

Figure 34

- Click the Next button and then type Makin-It Real Estate - Homes For Sale in the 'What title do you want for your report?' text box.
- If necessary, click the 'Modify the report's design' option button to select it (Figure 35).

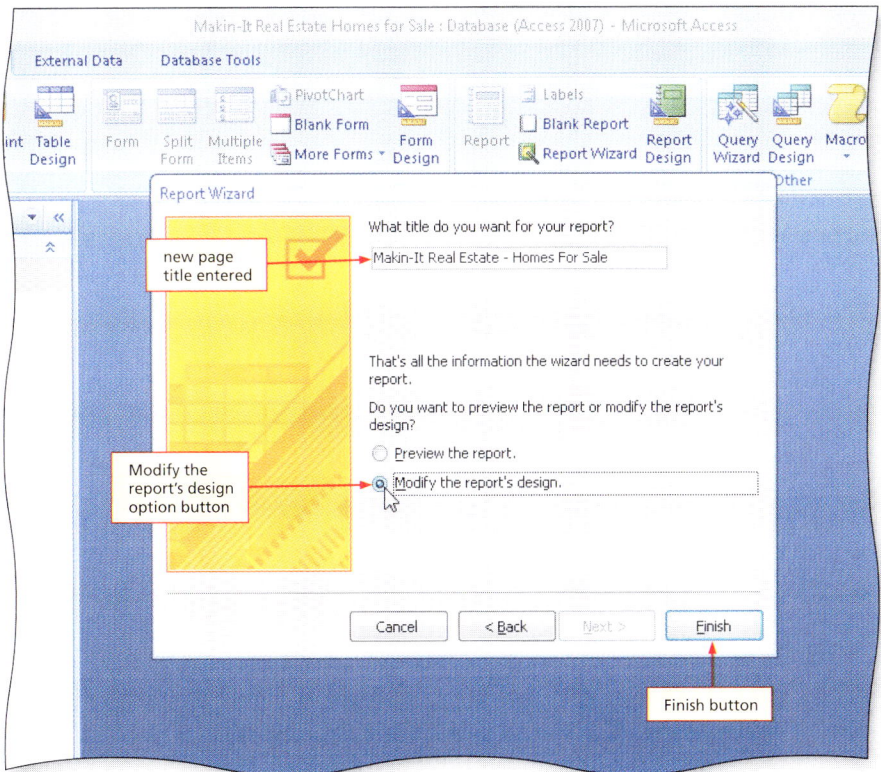

Figure 35

- Click the Finish button to display the report in Design view (Figure 36).

- If necessary, close the Field List task pane.

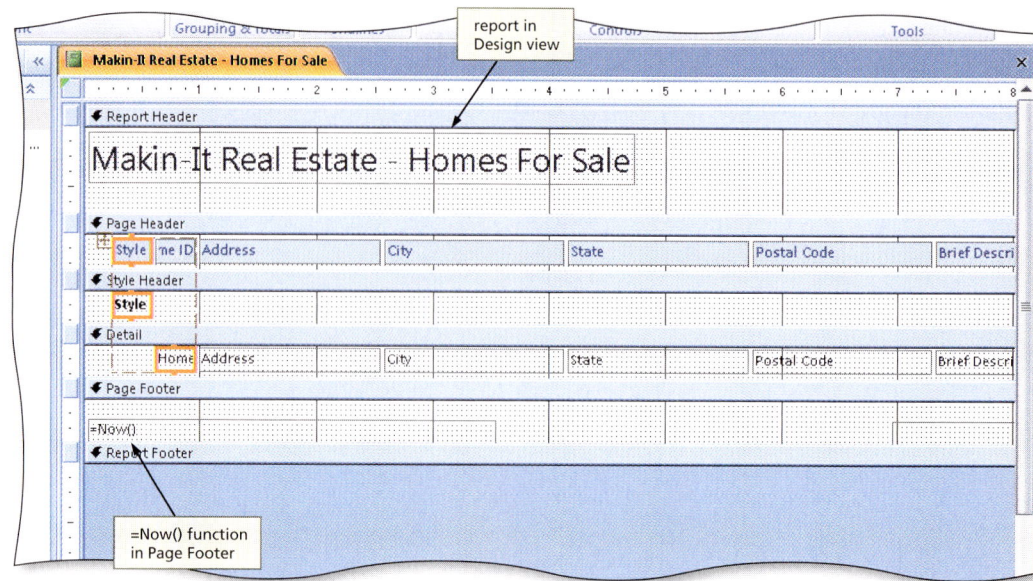

Figure 36

To Add a Hyperlink to a Report and Change the Text Background Color

Just as you did on the PowerPoint Web page, you should add a hyperlink on the report that links to the home page. This allows the Web page visitor to return to the Makin-It Real Estate home page without having to click the Back button on the browser's toolbar repeatedly. When you plan to save a report as a Web page, the background color of the elements of the Web page – such as the report title, column titles, and rows – should be changed to a light color, such as white. Browsers do not properly interpret some default colors used by Access for the background colors. The following steps add a hyperlink to the report and change the background colors of the elements in the report to white.

- Click the rightmost text box in the Page Footer area of the report to select it.

- Press the DELETE key to delete the text box.

- Click the leftmost text box in the Page Footer area of the report to select it.

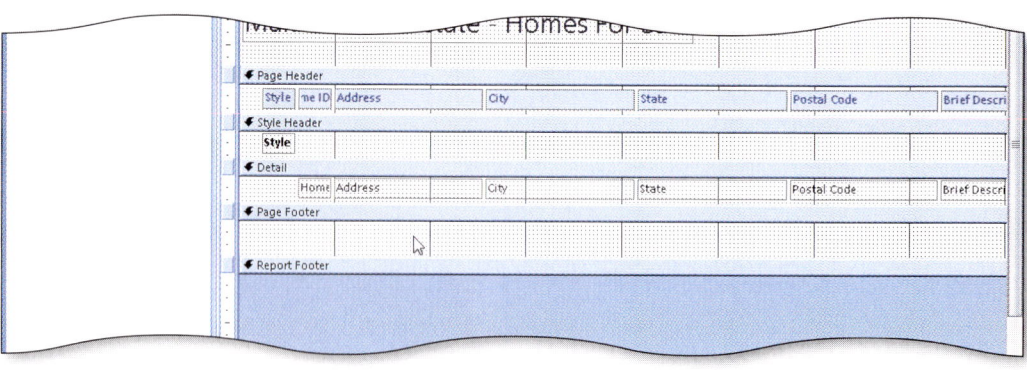

Figure 37

- Press the DELETE key to delete the text box that contains the NOW() function (Figure 37).

Q&A Why should I delete these items?

The report will be saved as a Web page. Web pages should not include page footer items such as page numbers because when the report is displayed in a Web browser, it will display as one long continuous page in the browser. There will never be a second page in the Web browser. A report footer, therefore, would be a good design choice, but not a page footer.

Integrating Office 2007 Programs and the World Wide Web **Integration Chapter** INT 33

2

- Click the Insert Hyperlink button on the Report Design Tools Design tab to display the Insert Hyperlink dialog box.

- If necessary, click the Existing File or Web Page button in the Link to bar.

- Click the 'Text to display' text box and then type Home as the text to display for the hyperlink.

- Click the Address box and then type e:\Makin-It Real Estate Home Page.htm (Figure 38).

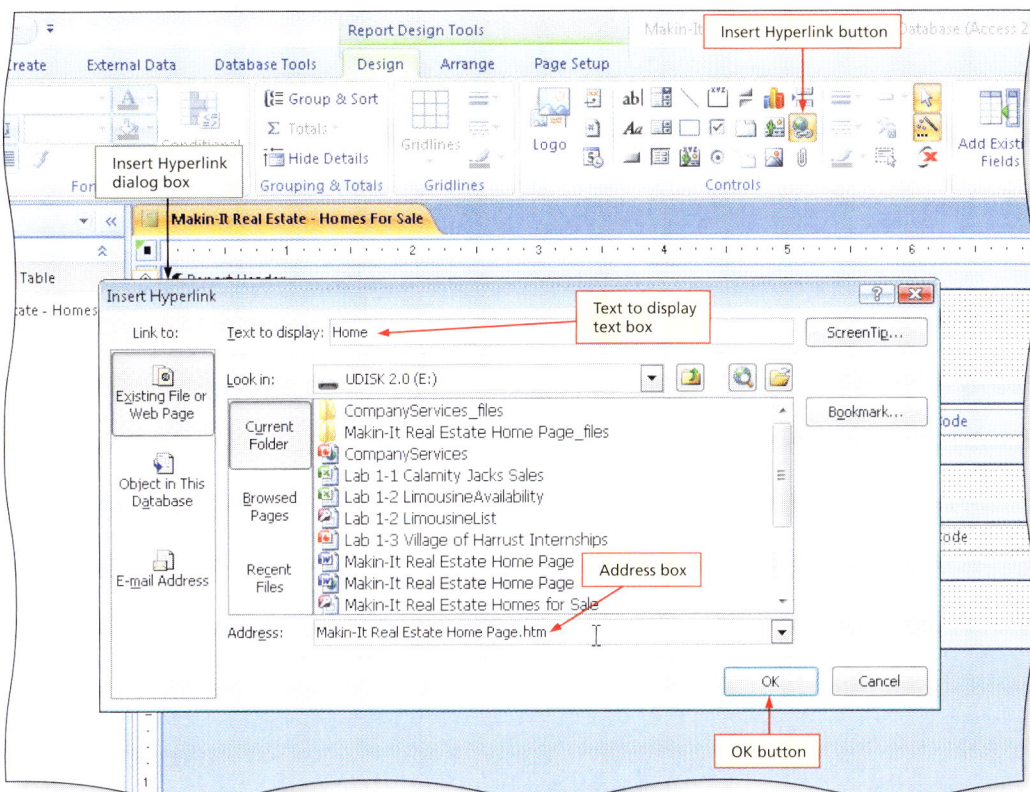

Figure 38

3

- Click the OK button to insert the hyperlink (Figure 39).

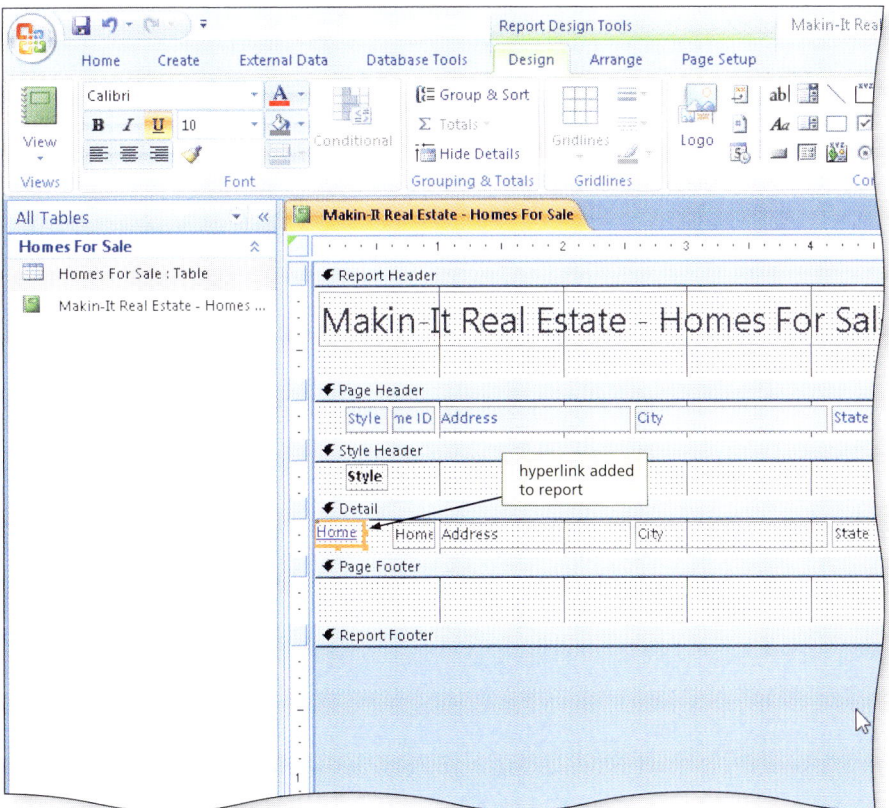

Figure 39

- Drag the hyperlink to the lower-left corner of the Page Footer area of the report (Figure 40).

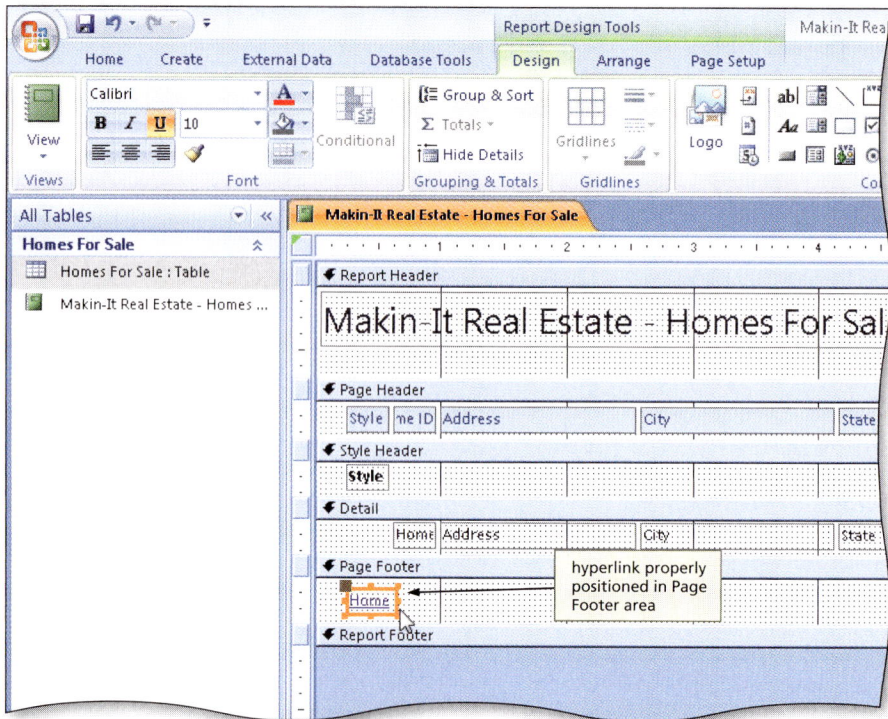

Figure 40

- Click anywhere in the Style header in the Page header area to select it.
- Click the Plus icon in the upper-left corner of the Style header to select all items in the body of the report (Figure 41).

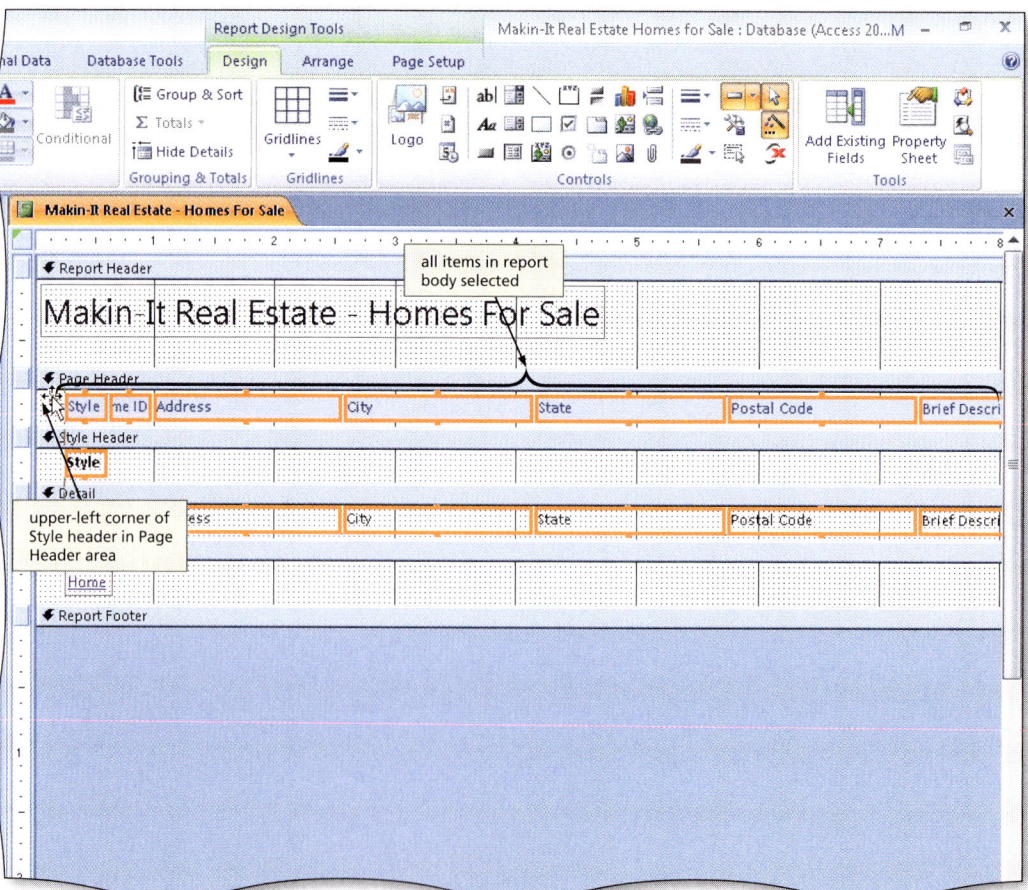

Figure 41

Integrating Office 2007 Programs and the World Wide Web   Integration Chapter   INT 35

6

- Click the Fill/Back Color button arrow on the Report Design Tools Design tab and then click the White color (column 1, row 1) in the Standard Colors area in the Fill/Back Color gallery to change the background color of the selected items to white.

- Click the report title in the Report Header area.

- While holding down the SHIFT key, click the Home hyperlink in the Page Footer area to select it.

- Click the Fill/Back Color button on the Report Design Tools Design tab to change the background color of the selected items to white (Figure 42).

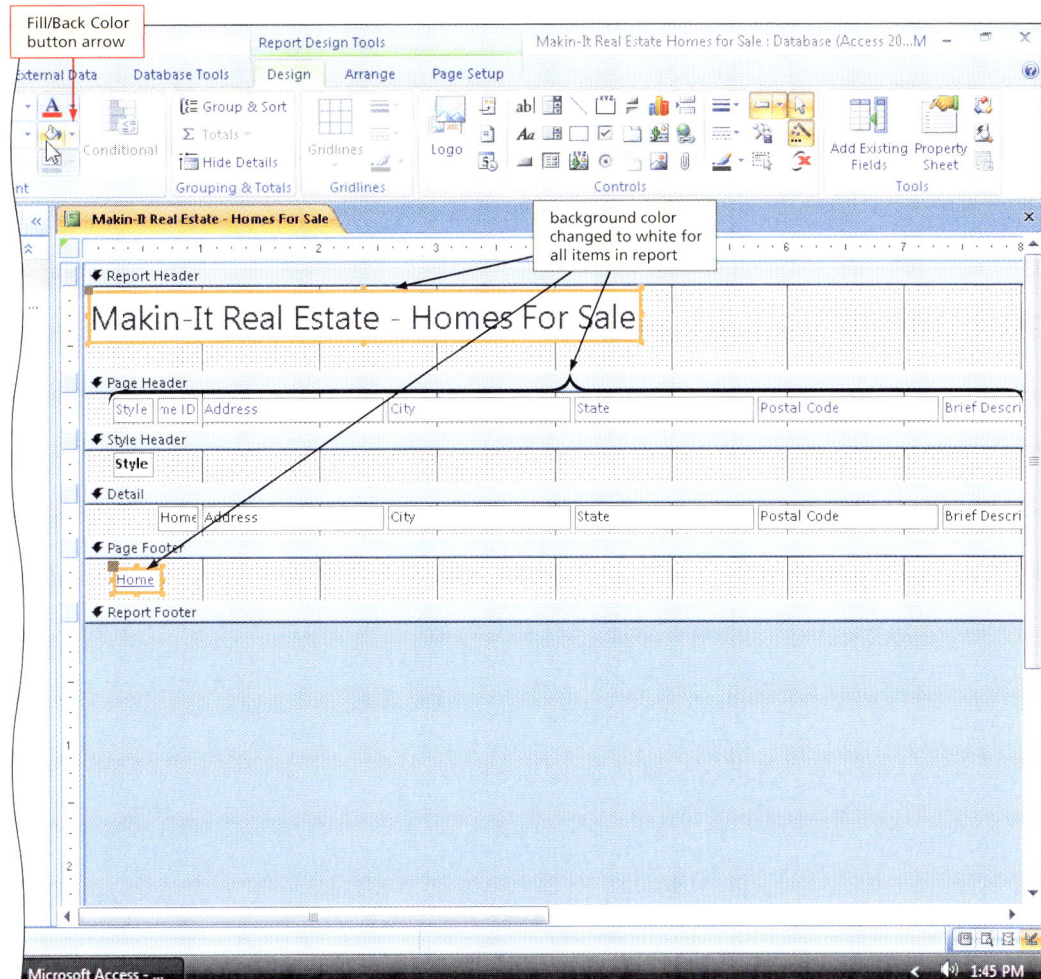

Figure 42

Q&A Why should I change the background color of these items?

Some items do not properly display when a Microsoft Access report is saved as a Web page. These items were transparent by default. The Web browser cannot understand transparency. By assigning a background color, you avoid this problem.

To Save the Report and View It in Your Browser

In other sections of this chapter, you have viewed the Web page, verified that it is correct, and then saved it on a USB flash drive. Unlike Word and PowerPoint, you must save a report as a Web page before you can preview it in your browser.

- Right-click the Makin-It Real Estate - Homes For Sale report in the All Tables list.
- Point to Export on the shortcut menu (Figure 43).

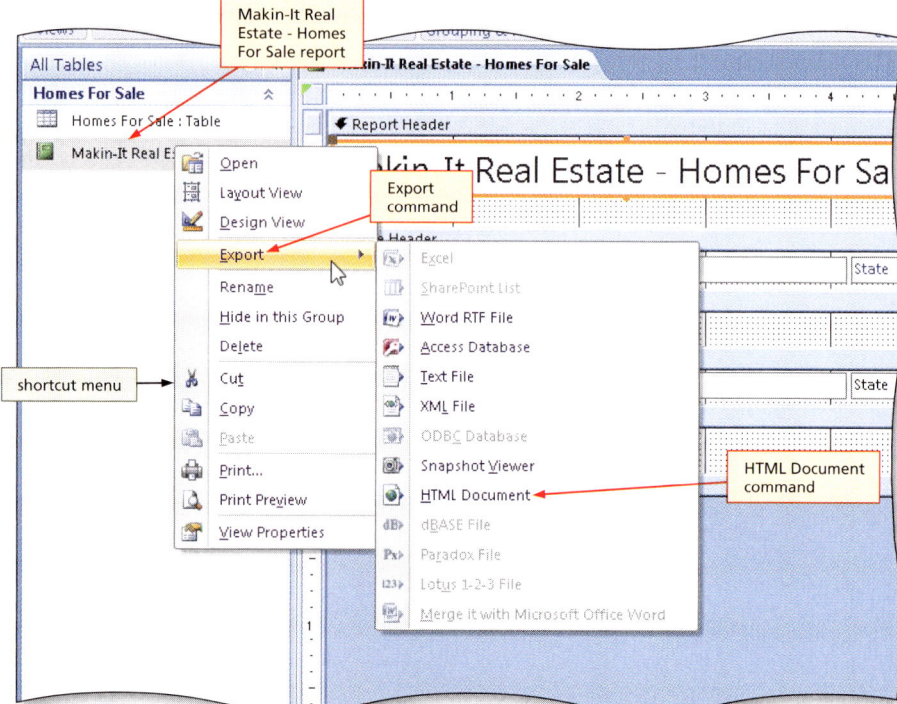

Figure 43

- If necessary, click Export, then click HTML Document.
- When the Export - HTML Document dialog box is displayed, double-click the File name text box and then type `E:\Makin-It Real Estate - Homes For Sale.html` as the file name.
- Click the 'Open the destination file after the export operation is complete' check box to select it (Figure 44).

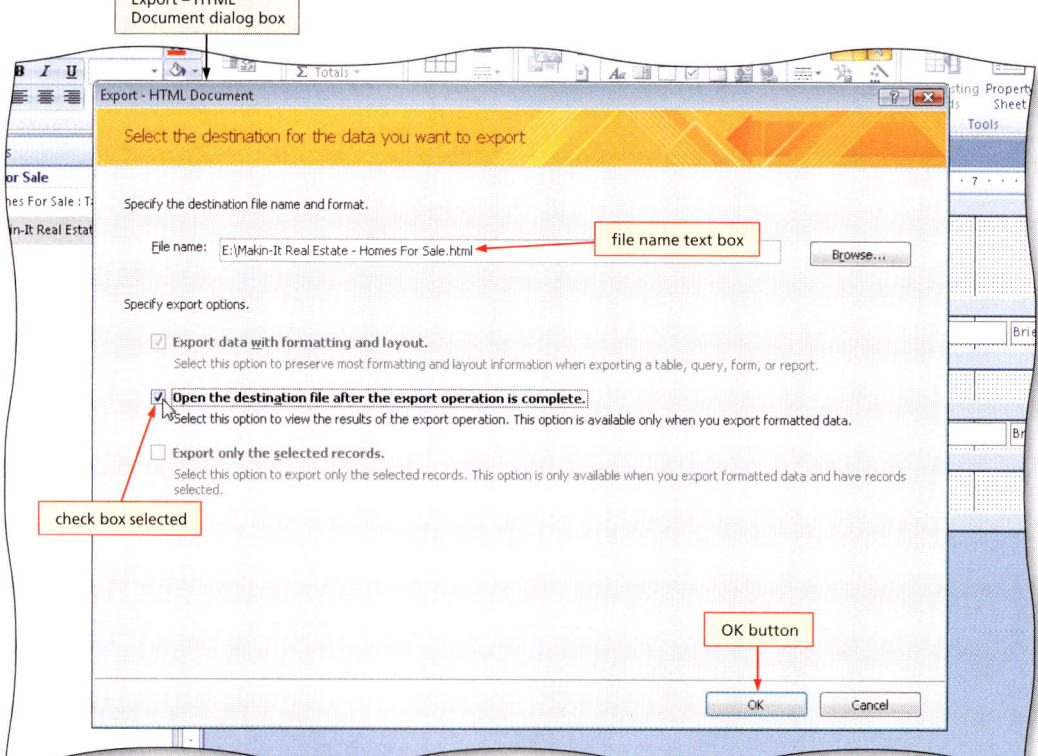

Figure 44

3
- Click the OK button.

- When the HTML Output Options dialog box is displayed, click the OK button to open the report in your browser (Figure 45). If the security warning appears in the Information bar at the top of the Web page, click its Close button.

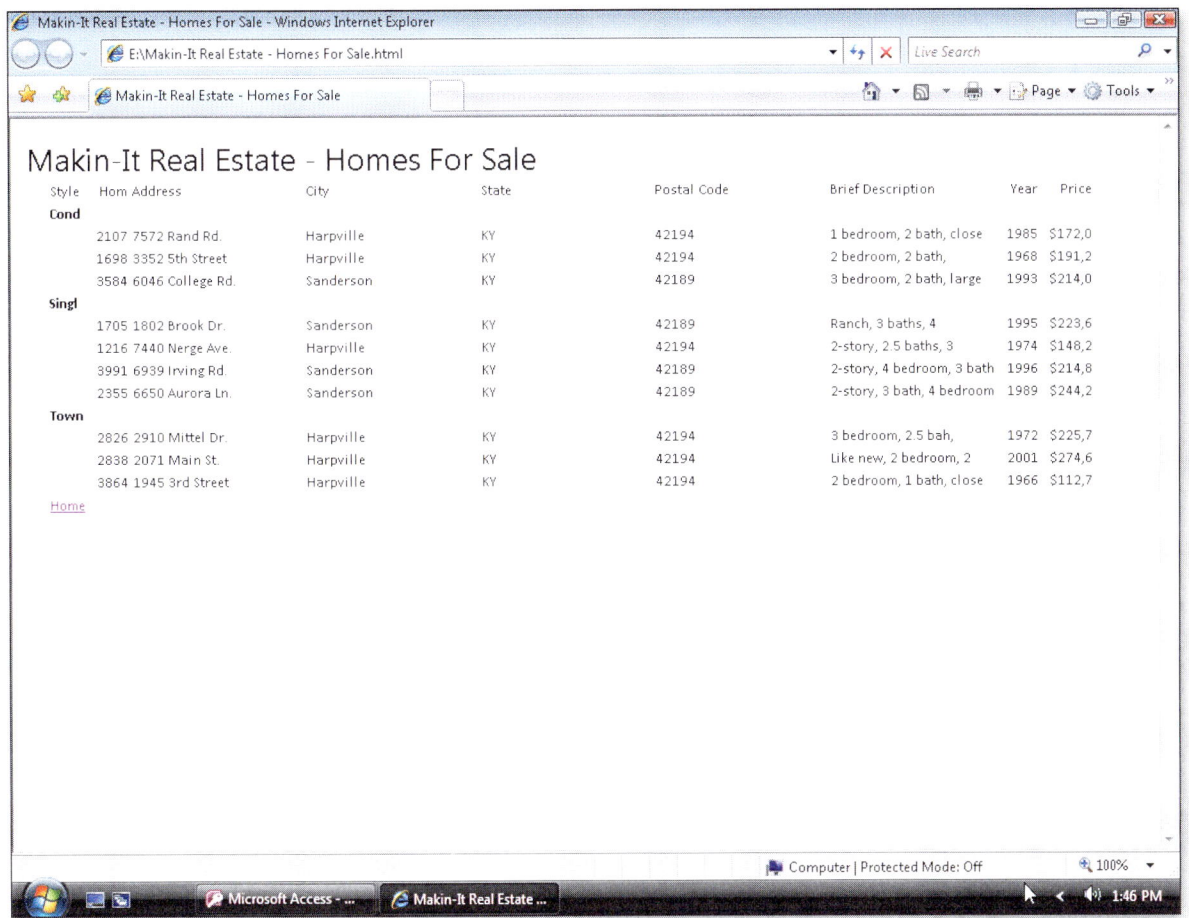

Figure 45

To Close Your Browser and Quit Access

After you preview the report in your browser, you can close your browser and quit Access, as shown in the following steps.

1 Click your browser's Close button.

2 If the Export – HTML Document dialog box is displayed, click the Close button.

3 Click the Close button on the Access title bar to quit Access. Save changes to the report if you are prompted to save the changes.

Testing the Web Site

The Makin-It Real Estate Web site is complete. To ensure that all the links in the Web site are viable, the following steps open the home page and then thoroughly test the entire Web site.

To Test the Web Site

1 Start your browser.

2 Click the Address bar of your browser.

3 Type `e:\Makin-It Real Estate Home Page.htm` in the Address bar, and then press the ENTER key to display the home page of the Makin-It Real Estate Web site in your browser (Figure 46). (Your USB flash drive may have a different drive name and letter.) If the Internet Explorer dialog box appears, click the OK button, right-click the first Internet Explorer button on the Windows Vista taskbar, and then click Close on the shortcut menu. If a security warning appears in the Information bar at the top of the Web page, click its Close button.

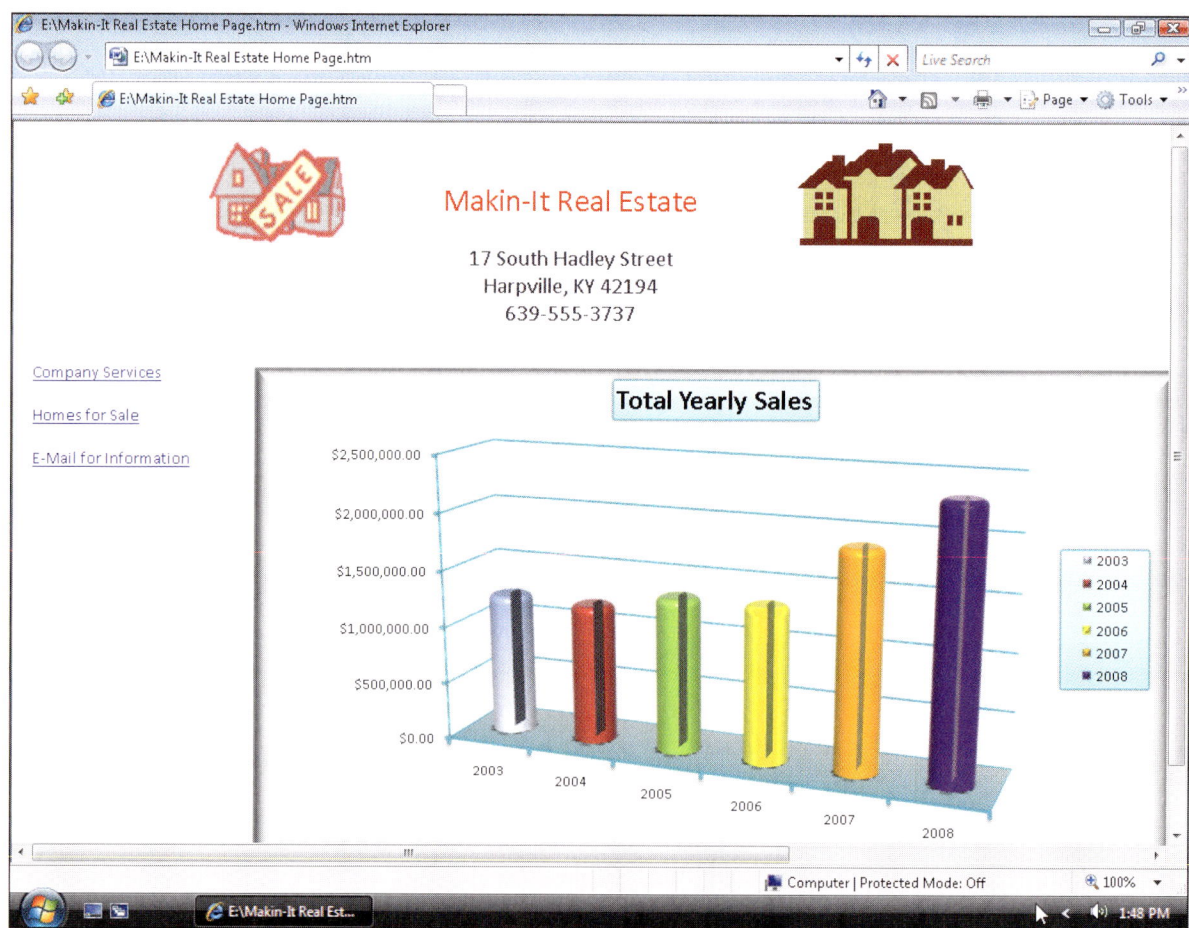

Figure 46

To Verify the Hyperlinks

All hyperlinks should be tested by clicking them and verifying that they jump to the correct Web page. Three hyperlinks are on the home page: Company Services, Homes for Sale, and E-Mail for Information. The following steps test the links.

1. Click the Company Services hyperlink.
2. Click the navigation buttons to view all slides on the Web page.
3. On the first slide on the PowerPoint Web page, click the Home hyperlink.
4. Click the Homes for Sale hyperlink.
5. On the Access report page, click the Home hyperlink.
6. Click the E-Mail for Information hyperlink to display a new e-mail message with `manager@isp.com` in the To text box.

To Quit the E-Mail Program and Close Your Browser

With the hyperlinks verified, the steps on the next page quit the e-mail program and the browser.

1. Click the Close button on your e-mail program's title bar. Click No if asked to save changes.
2. Click the Close button on your browser's title bar.

Chapter Summary

This chapter introduced you to integrating Microsoft Office 2007 programs. You opened an existing Word document and created a two-column, one-row, borderless table. You then inserted three hyperlinks, embedded a Bar chart from an existing Excel worksheet, and saved that document as an HTML file. You then opened an existing PowerPoint presentation, added a hyperlink to the first slide, and saved this presentation as a Web page. Finally, you opened an existing Access database and created a report, which you saved as a Web page. You saved that report and viewed and tested all Web pages and hyperlinks. The items listed below include all the new Office 2007 skills you have learned in this chapter.

1. Insert a Table into a Word Document (INT 8)
2. Remove the Table Border, View Gridlines, and AutoFit the Table Contents (INT 9)
3. Insert Text for Hyperlinks (INT 11)
4. Create a Hyperlink to PowerPoint Web Pages (INT 11)
5. Embed an Excel Chart into a Word Document (INT 14)
6. Change the Size of an Embedded Object (INT 17)
7. Add a Button to the Quick Access Toolbar (INT 19)
8. Preview the Web Page (INT 22)
9. Insert a Hyperlink into a PowerPoint Presentation (INT 25)
10. Create a Report Using the Report Wizard (INT 29)
11. Add a Hyperlink to a Report and Change the Text Background Color (INT 32)
12. Save the Report and View It in Your Browser (INT 36)

Learn It Online

Learn It Online is a series of online student exercises that test your knowledge of chapter content and key terms.

Instructions: To complete the Learn It Online exercises, start your browser, click the Address bar, and then enter the Web address scsite.com/dc-off07/int2007/learn. When the Integration 2007 Learn It Online page is displayed, click the link for the exercise you want to complete and then read the instructions.

Chapter Reinforcement TF, MC, and SA
A series of true/false, multiple choice, and short answer questions that test your knowledge of the chapter content.

Flash Cards
An interactive learning environment where you identify chapter key terms associated with displayed definitions.

Practice Test
A series of multiple choice questions that test your knowledge of chapter content and key terms.

Who Wants To Be a Computer Genius?
An interactive game that challenges your knowledge of chapter content in the style of a television quiz show.

Wheel of Terms
An interactive game that challenges your knowledge of chapter key terms in the style of the television show *Wheel of Fortune*.

Crossword Puzzle Challenge
A crossword puzzle that challenges your knowledge of key terms presented in the chapter.

Integrating Office 2007 Programs and the World Wide Web **Integration Chapter** INT 41

In the Lab

Create a workbook using the guidelines, concepts, and skills presented in this chapter. Labs are listed in order of increasing difficulty.

Lab 1: Creating a Web Page in Word with an Embedded Excel Chart

Problem: As vice president of Calamity Jack's Home Disaster Recovery Service, you have created a worksheet and chart in Excel to analyze the sales for the past year. Create a Web page in Word and embed the chart from the Calamity Jack's Sales workbook on the home page. Add a link to a second Web page and an e-mail link to calamityjacks@isp.com below the chart. Create a second Web page in Word by embedding the Calamity Jack's Sales worksheet.

Instructions: Perform the following tasks.
1. Start Excel by opening the Lab 1-1 Calamity Jack's Sales workbook.
2. Start Word and create a new document in Web Layout view. Add a title and subtitle as shown in the Web page preview of the document in Figure 47. Select the chart in Excel from the Yearly Sales Chart worksheet, copy it, and use the Paste Special dialog box in Word to embed the Microsoft Office Excel Chart Object. Resize the chart so that it fits in the Word window without the need to scroll to see the right edge of the chart.

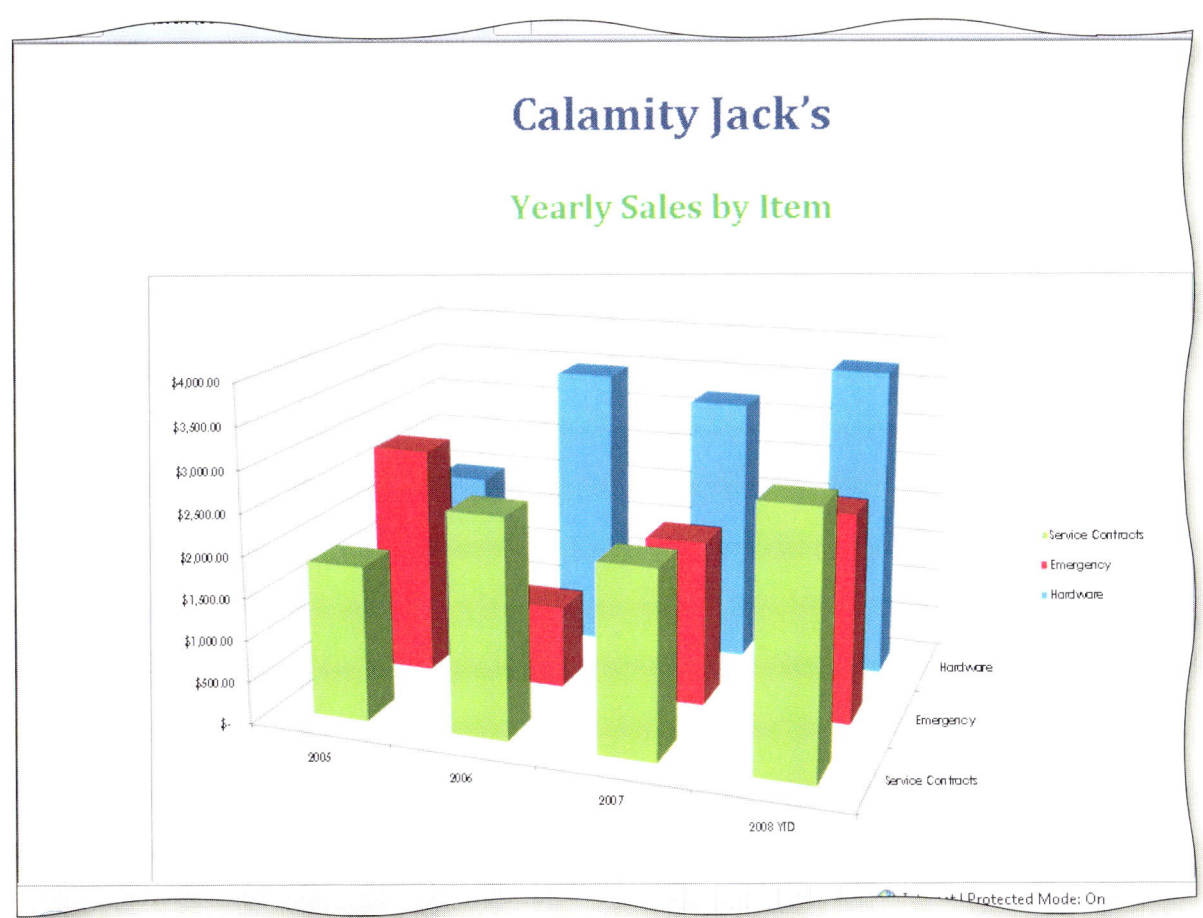

Figure 47

Continued >

In the Lab *continued*

3. Add two hyperlinks to the bottom of the page in a centered table as shown in Figure 47. The first hyperlink should jump to the Web page Lab_1-1_CalamityJacksSales.htm, which is created next. The second hyperlink creates an e-mail message to calamityjacks@isp.com with the subject About Our Company.

4. Save this file as a Web page named Lab_1-1_CalamityJacks.htm.

5. Create a new document in Word in Web Layout view.

6. Embed the Excel worksheet into the Word page. That is, switch to Excel, select the worksheet named Yearly Sales Analysis, select and copy the worksheet to the Clipboard, switch to Word, and use the Paste Special command in the Paste gallery in Word to embed the Excel Worksheet Object.

7. Save this file as a Web page with the name Lab_1-1_CalamityJacksSales.htm.

8. View the Lab_1-1_CalamityJacks.htm file in your browser (Figure 47). Print the Web page. Click the Yearly Sales link to navigate to the Lab_1-1_CalamityJacksSales.htm page (Figure 48).

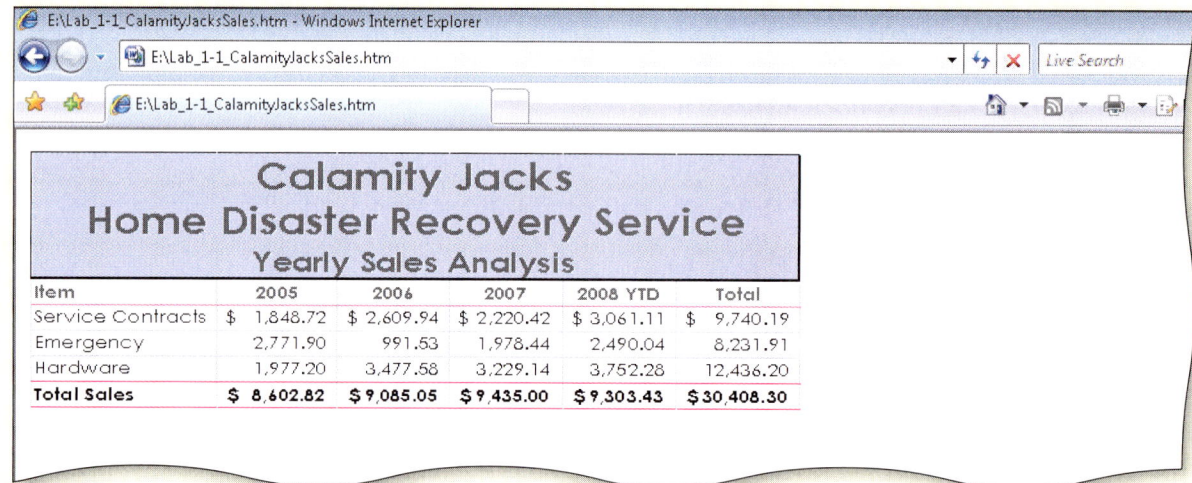

Figure 48

In the Lab

Lab 2: Posh Limousine Rental Web Site with an Access Report and an Excel Worksheet

Problem: As the assistant manager of Posh Limousine Services, Matt Ruginis is responsible for keeping track of limousines that are rented on a per-day basis. He would like you to design a site that allows customers to view the availability of limousines for rent. He also wants an e-mail link for customer questions.

Instructions: Perform the following tasks.
1. Start Word. Create a home page for the Post Limousine Availability Web site (Figure 49). Add a title and a borderless table below the title. In the left column, insert three hyperlinks. The first hyperlink should go to Lab_1-2_LimousineList.htm (Figure 50). The second hyperlink should go to Lab_1-2_LimousineAvailability.htm (Figure 51 on page INT 44). The third hyperlink should start an e-mail message to assistantmanager@isp.com. Type the text in the right column. Save the Web page as Lab_1-2_PoshLimousineServices.htm.

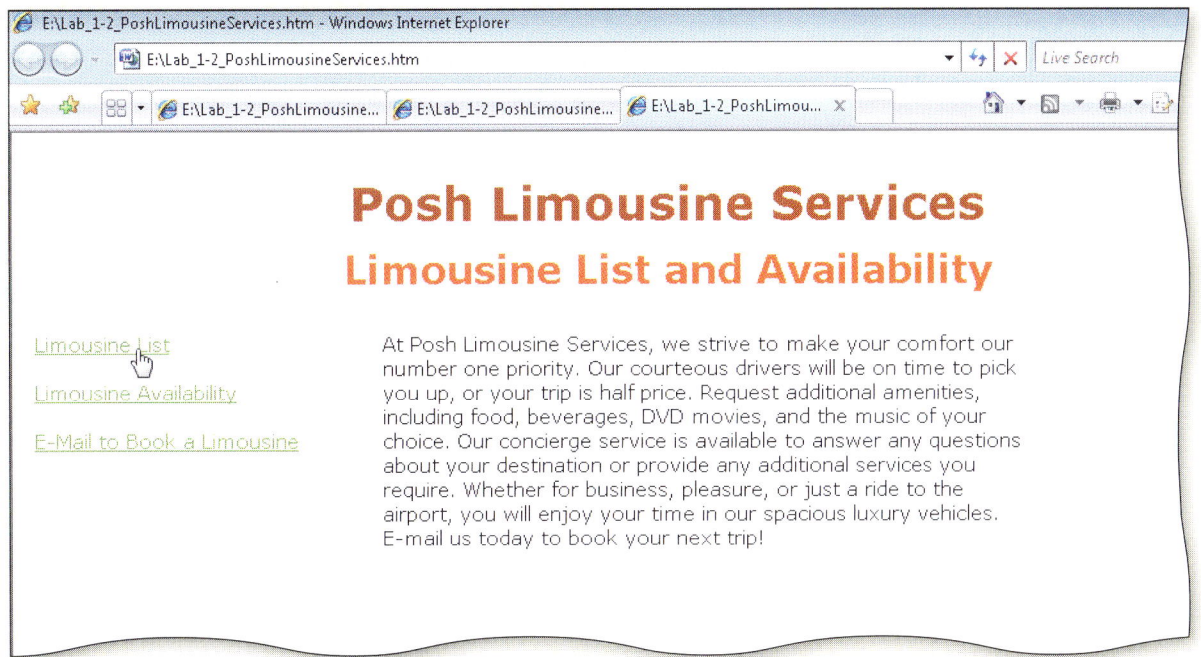

Figure 49

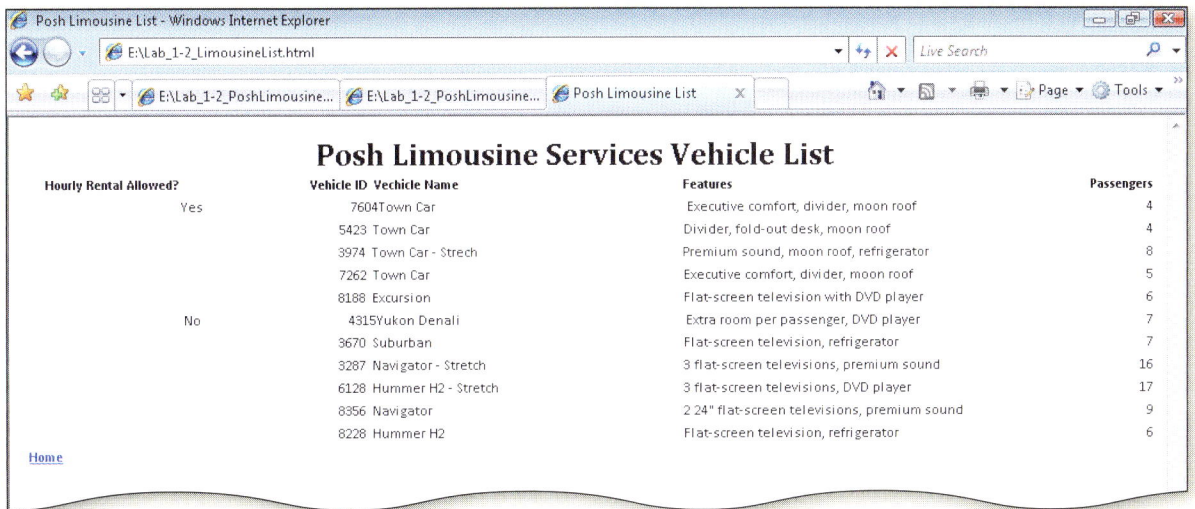

Figure 50

2. Start Access by opening the Lab 1-2 LimousineList.mdb database on the Integration Data Disk. Create an Access Report saved as a Web page from the LimousineList table. Create a grouping level using the Hourly Rental Allowed field. Add a title as shown in Figure 50. Add a link named Home that links to the Lab_1-2_PoshLimousineServices.htm home page at the bottom of the Access Report Web page. Save the Access Report Web page as Lab_1-2_LimousineList.

3. Start Excel by opening the Lab 1-2 LimousineAvailability workbook on the Integration Data Disk. Create a Web page from the workbook by using the Save As command on the Office Button menu and choosing Web Page as the file type. Use the file name, Lab_1-2_LimousineAvailability.htm.

4. View the Lab_1-2_PoshLimousineServices.htm Web page in your browser. Verify that all links operate properly by clicking each one.

Continued >

In the Lab *continued*

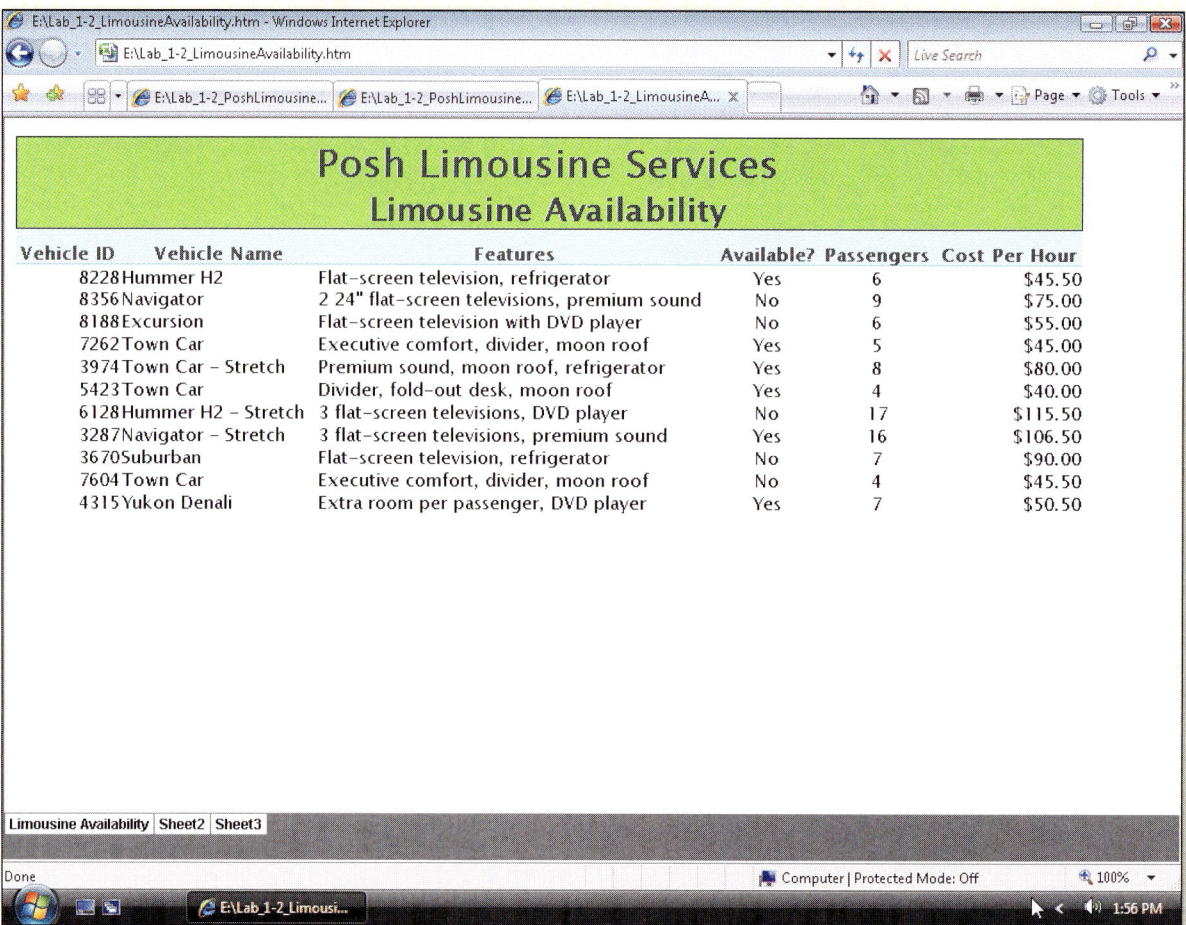

Figure 51

In the Lab

Lab 3: Web Site Incorporating PowerPoint Web Pages

Problem: As a part-time employee with the Village of Harrust, you have been asked to create a Web page that publicizes the village's summer intern program (Figures 52 and 53). The specific information for the internships is located in a PowerPoint presentation, which has four pages.

Instructions: Perform the following tasks.

Start Word. Create the Web page as shown in Figure 52. Insert two hyperlinks. The first hyperlink should link to Lab 1-3 Village of Harrust Internships.htm, and the second should link to an e-mail address at manager@vilharrust.gov. Use clip art to insert the picture of a municipal building. Save this Web page as Lab_1-3_VillageofHarrustHomePage.htm.

Figure 52

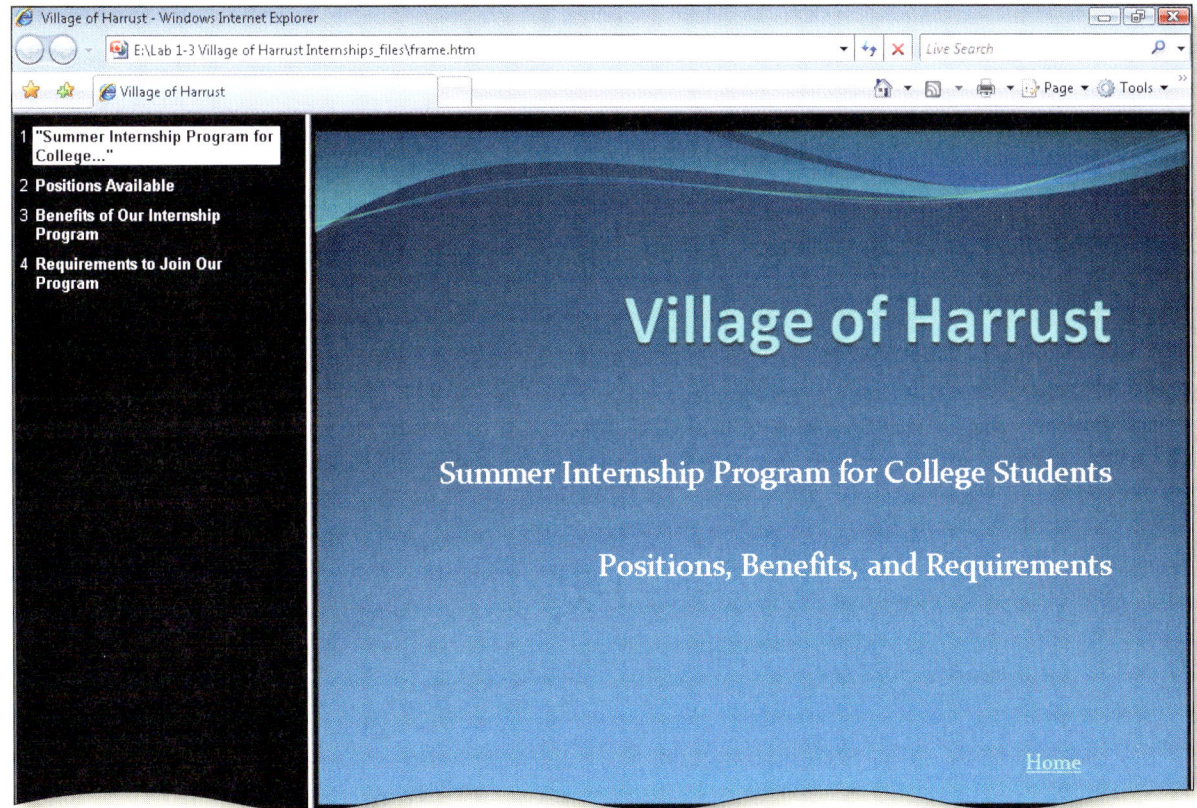

Figure 53

Open the Lab 1-3 PowerPoint presentation Lab 1-3 Village of Harrust Internships. Add a link named Home at the bottom of the first page of the presentation that jumps to the Lab_1-3_VillageofHarrustHomePage.htm Web page. Save the PowerPoint presentation as Web pages on the Integration Data Disk. Name the Web pages Lab 1-3 Village of Harrust Internships.htm. View the Web pages in your browser.

Cases and Places

Apply your creative thinking and problem solving skills to design and implement a solution.

• Easier   •• More Difficult

• 1: Design and Create a Lawn Care Service Web Site

During your summer break, you and your friends decide to get your exercise by providing lawn care services for local residents and businesses. You plan to offer four services, each at a different rate. To mow a small yard with push mowers, you will charge $15 per week for each quarter acre. To mow a large yard with riding mowers, you will charge $22 per week for each quarter acre. To provide weeding and tree pruning, you will charge $20 per week. Additional lawn care service, including dethatching and fertilizing, will cost $50 for the summer per quarter acre. Create a worksheet in Excel that summarizes each of these plans. Create a Web page using Word that embeds the Excel worksheet; the goal of the Web site is to inform new customers of the services provided. Make sure to include an e-mail address on the Web page.

• 2: Analyze the Cost of Internet Access in a Web Page

You have been asked to research the cost of various types of Internet access for local small businesses. Research the different types of Internet access available to small businesses in your area, and determine the following for each: service provider name, service level, speed, contact name, contact telephone number, contract restrictions, and costs. Create an Excel worksheet and charts summarizing your data and graphing the speed and costs for each service provider. Using Word, create a Web page and embed the worksheet on the home page of the Web site. Create another Web page, and embed the chart(s) from Excel. Create a link to the Excel chart(s) Web page and a link to each service provider's Web page.

•• 3: Design and Create a Customer Complaint Web Page

Your housing association has asked you to help to organize and evaluate complaints from residents. Create an Access database and add eight items to it with the following information for each complaint: complaint number, resident ID number, type of complaint, description, date of complaint, resolution date of the complaint, name of staff member who resolved the complaint, and how the complaint was resolved. From this table, create an Access report saved as a Web page using the type of complaint as the grouping level. Include all of the items in the Access database in the Web page. Use a search engine to find relevant links about each type of complaint – such as drainage, landscaping, and noise – that are relevant to housing associations, and create links to one Web page each for each category at the bottom of the Access report Web page.

•• 4: Design and Create a Summer Internship Web Site

Make It Personal

As an intern for your school's placement program, you have been asked to create a Web page on which students can view information about summer internships available in the local area. Using your own field of interest as a guide, create an Access database and add information to the database about prospective summer internships regarding your area of interest. Include the following fields: organization name, preferred major, type of job, job description, number of positions available, and whether the organization has participated in an internship program in the past. From this table, create an Access report and save it as a Web page using the preferred major as the grouping level. Create a Web page using Word that will act as the Web page for the organization list and create a link to the Access report Web page. Be sure to include a link to your e-mail address on the Web page.

•• 5: Design and Create an Informational Web Site about a Foreign Country

Working Together
Gather basic statistical data about a foreign country, including population, important business and industry, and other demographic data. Have one member of your team create an Excel 3-D Pie chart to summarize the demographic information that you find. Have another member create a PowerPoint presentation that contains at least four major points regarding the country that may make the country interesting to potential visitors, including information about business and industry. A third member should create an Access report saved as a Web page that includes information about popular tourist destinations in the country. Embed the Excel chart into one of the PowerPoint slides. Create a link from one of the PowerPoint pages to the Access report Web page. Save the PowerPoint presentation as Web pages. Include relevant links to Web pages regarding the country.

Appendix A
Project Planning Guidelines

Using Project Planning Guidelines

The process of communicating specific information to others is a learned, rational skill. Computers and software, especially Microsoft Office 2007, can help you develop ideas and present detailed information to a particular audience.

Using Microsoft Office 2007, you can create projects such as Word documents, Excel spreadsheets, Access databases, and PowerPoint presentations. Computer hardware and productivity software such as Microsoft Office 2007 minimizes much of the laborious work of drafting and revising projects. Some communicators handwrite ideas in notebooks, others compose directly on the computer, and others have developed unique strategies that work for their own particular thinking and writing styles.

No matter what method you use to plan a project, follow specific guidelines to arrive at a final product that presents information correctly and effectively (Figure A–1). Use some aspects of these guidelines every time you undertake a project, and others as needed in specific instances. For example, in determining content for a project, you may decide that a bar chart communicates trends more effectively than a paragraph of text. If so, you would create this graphical element and insert it in an Excel spreadsheet, a Word document, or a PowerPoint slide.

Determine the Project's Purpose

Begin by clearly defining why you are undertaking this assignment. For example, you may want to track monetary donations collected for your club's fundraising drive. Alternatively, you may be urging students to vote for a particular candidate in the next election. Once you clearly understand the purpose of your task, begin to draft ideas of how best to communicate this information.

Analyze Your Audience

Learn about the people who will read, analyze, or view your work. Where are they employed? What are their educational backgrounds? What are their expectations? What questions do they have?

PROJECT PLANNING GUIDELINES

1. DETERMINE THE PROJECT'S PURPOSE
Why are you undertaking the project?

2. ANALYZE YOUR AUDIENCE
Who are the people who will use your work?

3. GATHER POSSIBLE CONTENT
What information exists, and in what forms?

4. DETERMINE WHAT CONTENT TO PRESENT TO YOUR AUDIENCE
What information will best communicate the project's purpose to your audience?

Figure A–1

Design experts suggest drawing a mental picture of these people or finding photographs of people who fit this profile so that you can develop a project with the audience in mind.

By knowing your audience members, you can tailor a project to meet their interests and needs. You will not present them with information they already possess, and you will not omit the information they need to know.

Example: Your assignment is to raise the profile of your college's nursing program in the community. How much do they know about your college and the nursing curriculum? What are the admission requirements? How many of the applicants admitted complete the program? What percent pass the state Boards?

Gather Possible Content

Rarely are you in a position to develop all the material for a project. Typically, you would begin by gathering existing information that may reside in spreadsheets or databases. Web sites, pamphlets, magazine and newspaper articles, and books could provide insights of how others have approached your topic. Personal interviews often provide perspectives not available by any other means. Consider video and audio clips as potential sources for material that might complement or support the factual data you uncover.

Determine What Content to Present to Your Audience

Experienced designers recommend writing three or four major ideas you want an audience member to remember after reading or viewing your project. It also is helpful to envision your project's endpoint, the key fact you wish to emphasize. All project elements should lead to this ending point.

As you make content decisions, you also need to think about other factors. Presentation of the project content is an important consideration. For example, will your brochure be printed on thick, colored paper or transparencies? Will your PowerPoint presentation be viewed in a classroom with excellent lighting and a bright projector, or will it be viewed on a notebook computer monitor? Determine relevant time factors, such as the length of time to develop the project, how long readers will spend reviewing your project, or the amount of time allocated for your speaking engagement. Your project will need to accommodate all of these constraints.

Decide whether a graph, photograph, or artistic element can express or emphasize a particular concept. The right hemisphere of the brain processes images by attaching an emotion to them, so audience members are more apt to recall these graphics long term rather than just reading text.

As you select content, be mindful of the order in which you plan to present information. Readers and audience members generally remember the first and last pieces of information they see and hear, so you should put the most important information at the top or bottom of the page.

Summary

When creating a project, it is beneficial to follow some basic guidelines from the outset. By taking some time at the beginning of the process to determine the project's purpose, analyze the audience, gather possible content, and determine what content to present to the audience, you can produce a project that is informative, relevant, and effective.

Appendix B
Microsoft Office 2007 Help

Using Microsoft Office Help

This appendix shows how to use Microsoft Office Help. At any time while you are using one of the Microsoft Office 2007 programs, you can use Office Help to display information about all topics associated with the program. To illustrate the use of Office Help, this appendix uses Microsoft Office Word 2007. Help in other Office 2007 programs responds in a similar fashion.

In Office 2007, Help is presented in a window that has Web browser-style navigation buttons. Each Office 2007 program has its own Help home page, which is the starting Help page that is displayed in the Help window. If your computer is connected to the Internet, the contents of the Help page reflect both the local help files installed on the computer and material from Microsoft's Web site. As shown in Figure B–1, two methods for accessing Word's Help are available:

1. Microsoft Office Word Help button near the upper-right corner of the Word window
2. Function key F1 on the keyboard

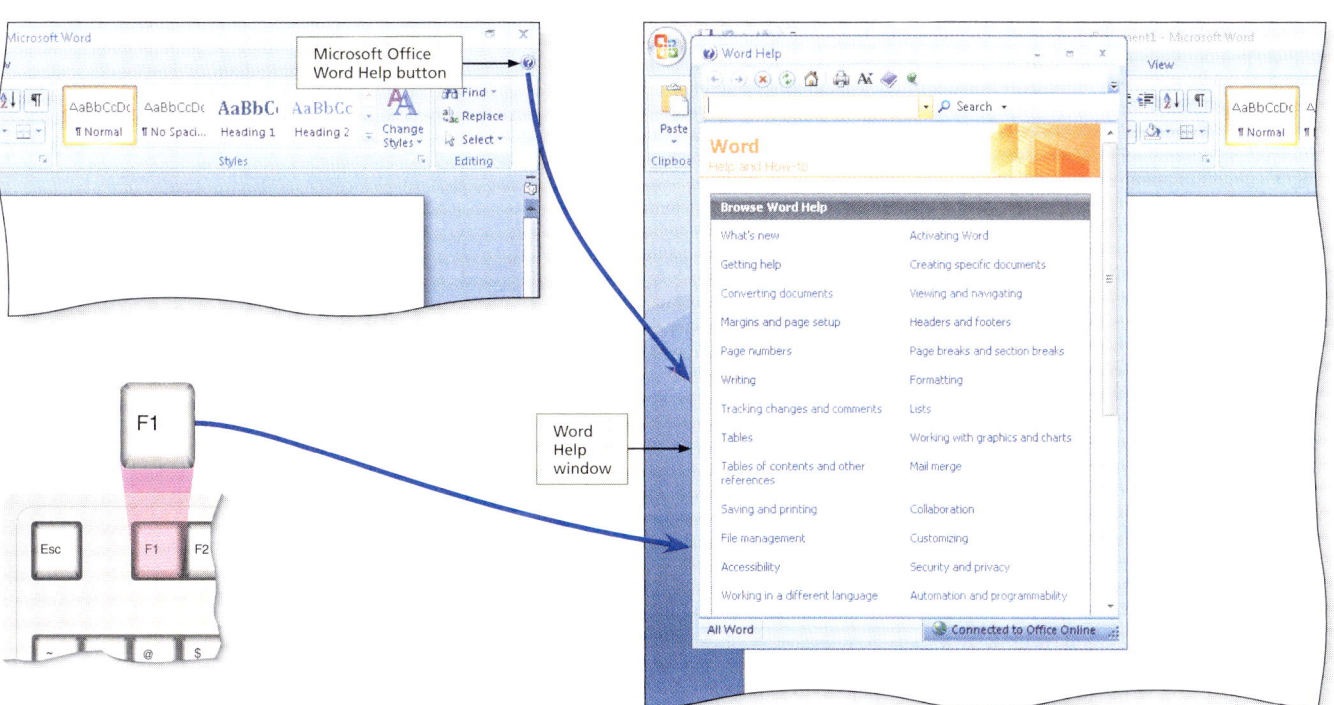

Figure B–1

To Open the Word Help Window

The following steps open the Word Help window and maximize the window.

- Start Microsoft Word, if necessary. Click the Microsoft Office Word Help button near the upper-right corner of the Word window to open the Word Help window (Figure B–2).

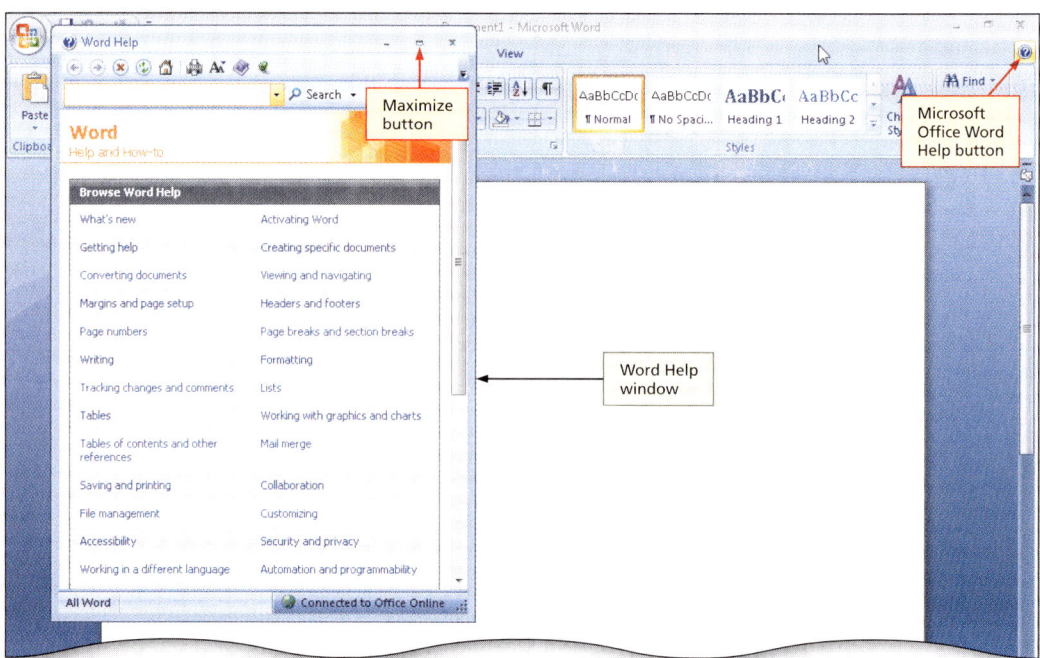

Figure B–2

- Click the Maximize button on the Help title bar to maximize the Help window (Figure B–3).

Figure B–3

The Word Help Window

The Word Help window provides several methods for accessing help about a particular topic and also has tools for navigating around Help. Methods for accessing Help include searching the help content installed with Word or searching the online Office content maintained by Microsoft.

Figure B–3 shows the main Word Help window. To navigate Help, the Word Help window includes search features that allow you to search on a word or phrase about which you want help; the Connection Status button, which allows you to control where Word Help searches for content; toolbar buttons; and links to major Help categories.

Search Features

You can perform Help searches on words or phrases to find information about any Word feature using the 'Type words to search for' text box and the Search button (Figure B–4a). Click the 'Type words to search for' text box and then click the Search button or press the ENTER key to initiate a search of Word Help.

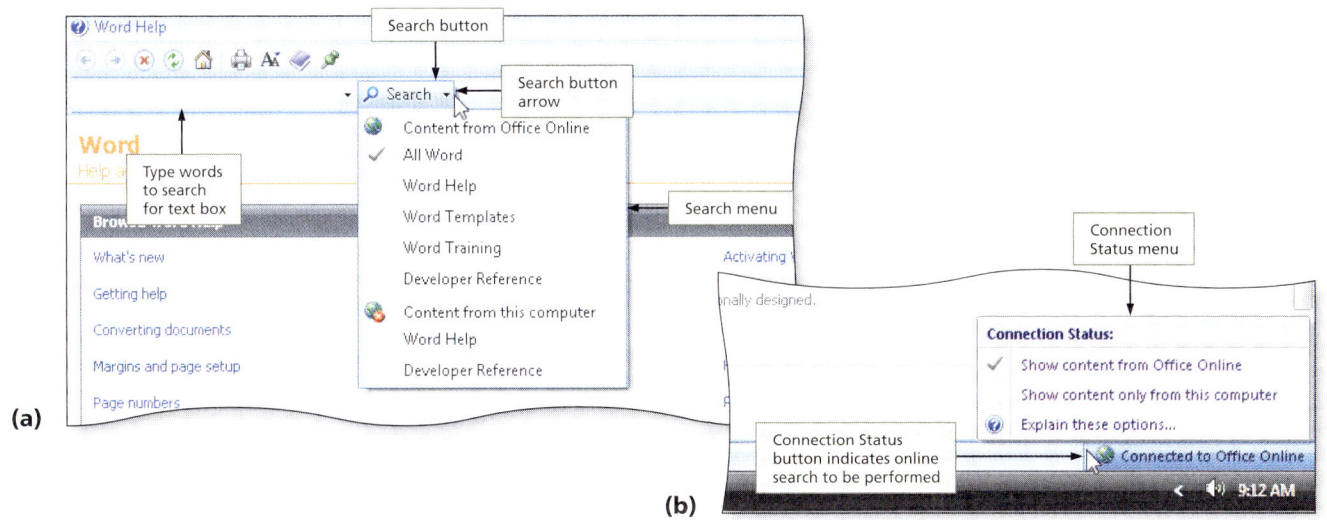

Figure B–4

Word Help offers the user the option of searching the online Help Web pages maintained by Microsoft or the offline Help files placed on your computer when you install Word. You can specify whether Word Help should search online or offline from two places: the Connection Status button on the status bar of the Word Help window, or the Search button arrow on the toolbar. The Connection Status button indicates whether Help currently is set up to work with online or offline information sources. Clicking the Connection Status button provides a menu with commands for selecting online or offline searches (Figure B–4b). The Connection Status menu allows the user to select whether Help searches will return content only from the computer (offline), or content from the computer and from Office Online (online).

Clicking the Search button arrow also provides a menu with commands for an online or offline search (Figure B–4a). These commands determine the source of information that Help searches for during the current Help session only. For example, assume that your preferred search is an offline search because you often do not have Internet access. You would set Connection Status to 'Show content only from this computer'. When you have Internet access, you can select an online search from the Search menu to search Office Online for information for your current search session only. Your search will use the Office Online resources until you quit Help. The next time you start Help, the Connection Status once again will be offline. In addition to setting the source of information that Help searches for during the current Help session, you can use the Search menu to further target the current search to one of four subcategories of online Help: Word Help, Word Templates, Word Training, and Developer Reference. The local search further can target one subcategory, Developer Reference.

In addition to searching for a word or string of text, you can use the links provided on the Browse Word Help area (Figure B–3 on page APP 4) to search for help on a topic. These links direct you to major help categories. From each major category, subcategories are available to further refine your search.

Finally, you can use the Table of Contents for Word Help to search for a topic the same way you would in a hard copy book. The Table of Contents is accessed via a toolbar button.

Toolbar Buttons

You can use toolbar buttons to navigate through the results of your search. The toolbar buttons are located on the toolbar near the top of the Help Window (Figure B–5). The toolbar buttons contain navigation buttons as well as buttons that perform other useful and common tasks in Word Help, such as printing.

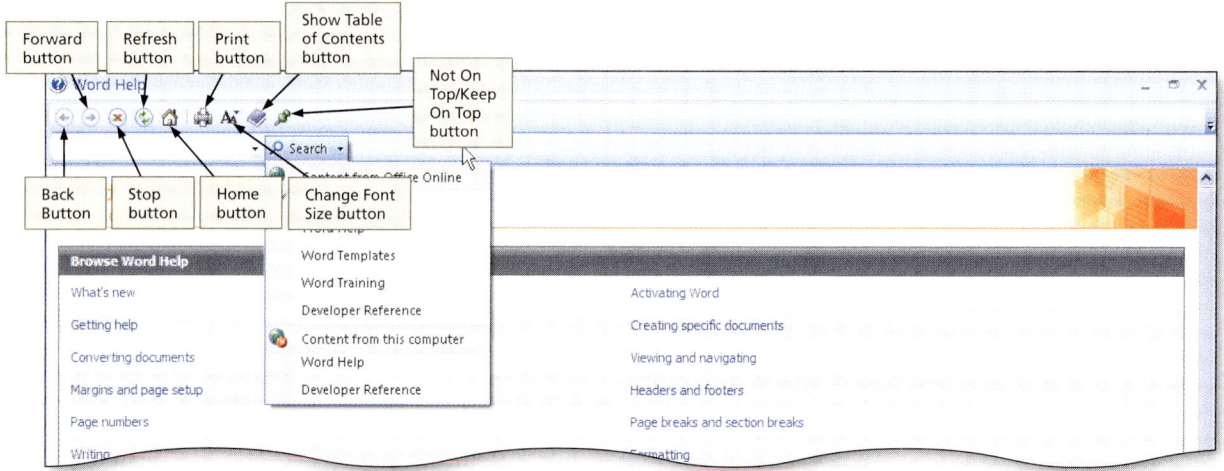

Figure B–5

The Word Help navigation buttons are the Back, Forward, Stop, Refresh, and Home buttons. These five buttons behave like the navigation buttons in a Web browser window. You can use the Back button to go back one window, the Forward button to go forward one window, the Stop button to stop loading the current page, and the Home button to redisplay the Help home page in the Help window. Use the Refresh button to reload the information requested into the Help window from its original source. When getting Help information online, this button provides the most current information from the Microsoft Help Web site.

The buttons located to the right of the navigation buttons — Print, Change Font Size, Show Table of Contents, and Not on Top — provide you with access to useful and common commands. The Print button prints the contents of the open Help window. The Change Font Size button customizes the Help window by increasing or decreasing the size of its text. The Show Table of Contents button opens a pane on the left side of the Help window that shows the Table of Contents for Word Help. You can use the Table of Contents for Word Help to navigate through the contents of Word Help much as you would use the Table of Contents in a book to search for a topic. The Not On Top button is an example of a toggle button, which is a button that can be switched back and forth between two states. It determines how the Word Help window behaves relative to other windows. When clicked, the Not On Top button changes to Keep On Top. In this state, it does not allow other windows from Word or other programs to cover the Word Help window when those windows are the active windows. When in the Not On Top state, the button allows other windows to be opened or moved on top of the Word Help window.

You can customize the size and placement of the Help window. Resize the window using the Maximize and Restore buttons, or by dragging the window to a desired size. Relocate the Help window by dragging the title bar to a new location on the screen.

Searching Word Help

Once the Word Help window is open, several methods exist for navigating Word Help. You can search for help by using any of the three following methods from the Help window:

1. Enter search text in the 'Type words to search for' text box
2. Click the links in the Help window
3. Use the Table of Contents

To Obtain Help Using the 'Type words to search for' Text Box

Assume for the following example that you want to know more about watermarks. The following steps use the 'Type words to search for' text box to obtain useful information about watermarks by entering the word, watermark, as search text. The steps also navigate in the Word Help window.

1

- Type watermark in the 'Type words to search for' text box at the top of the Word Help window.

- Click the Search button arrow to display the Search menu (Figure B-6).

- If it is not selected already, click All Word on the Search menu to select the command. If All Word is already selected, click the Search button arrow again to close the Search menu.

Q&A

Why select All Word on the Search menu?

Selecting All Word on the Search menu ensures that Word Help will search all possible sources for information on your search term. It will produce the most complete search results.

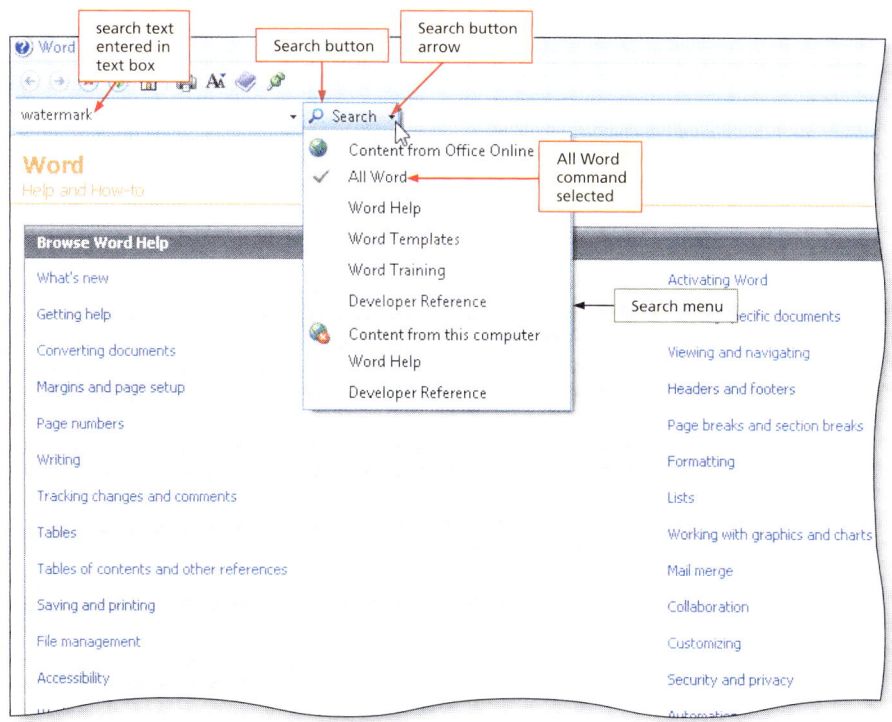

Figure B–6

- Click the Search button to display the search results (Figure B–7).

Q&A Why do my results differ?

If you do not have an Internet connection, your results will reflect only the content of the Help files on your computer. When searching for help online, results also can change as material is added, deleted, and updated on the online Help Web pages maintained by Microsoft.

Q&A Why were my search results not very helpful?

When initiating a search, keep in mind to check the spelling of the search text; and to keep your search very specific, with fewer than seven words, to return the most accurate results.

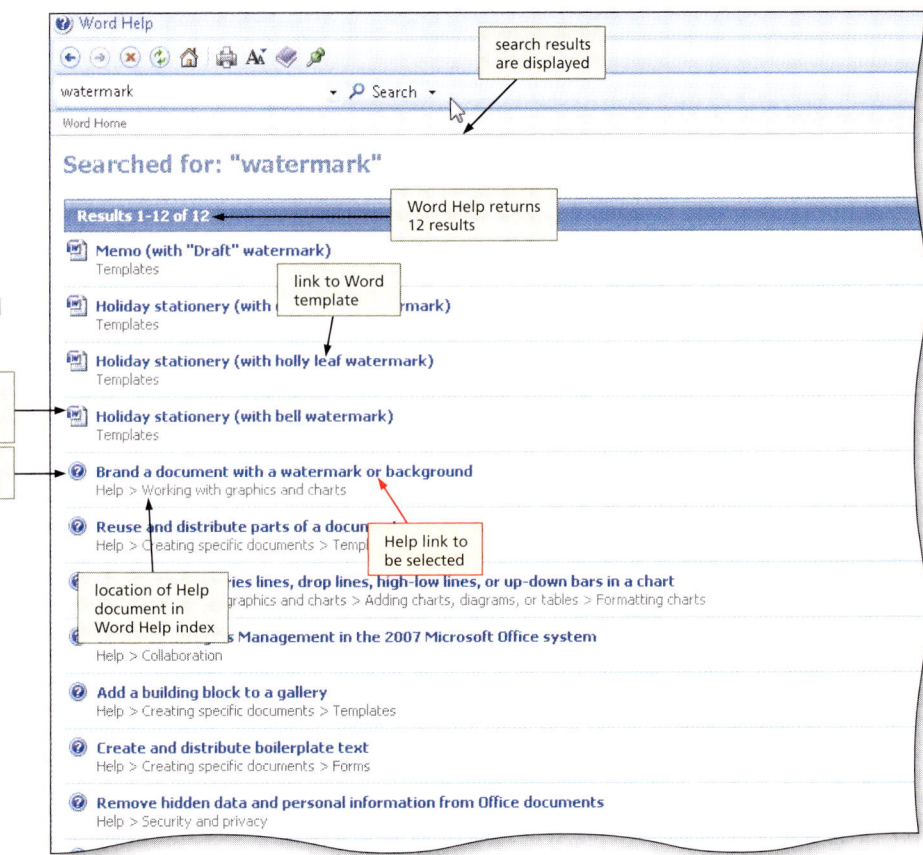

Figure B–7

- Click the 'Brand a document with a watermark or background' link to open the Help document associated with the link in the Help window (Figure B–8).

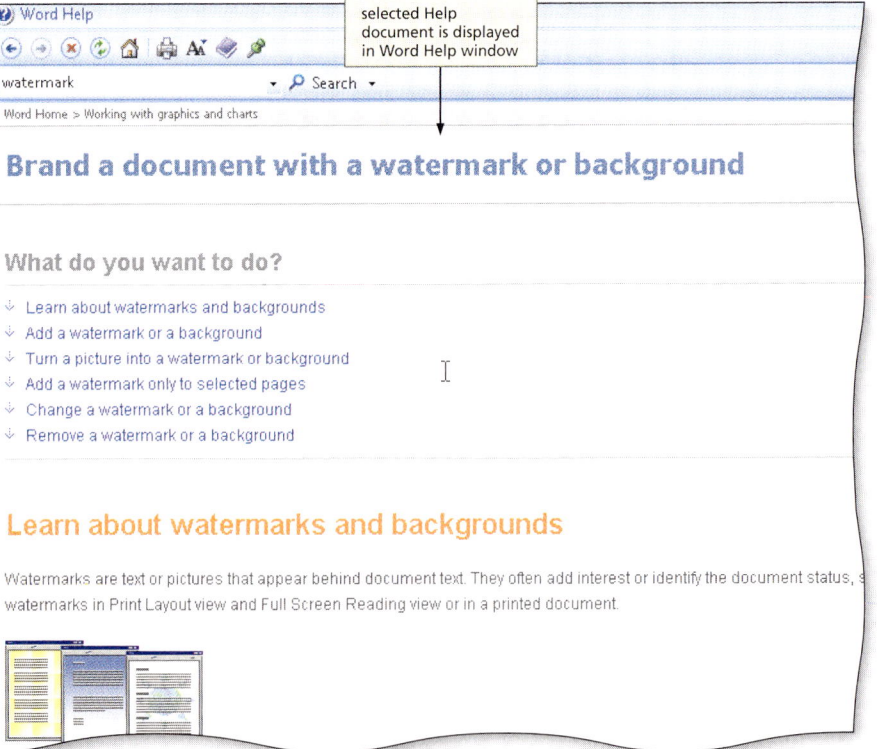

Figure B–8

4

- Click the Home button on the taskbar to clear the search results and redisplay the Word Help home page (Figure B–9).

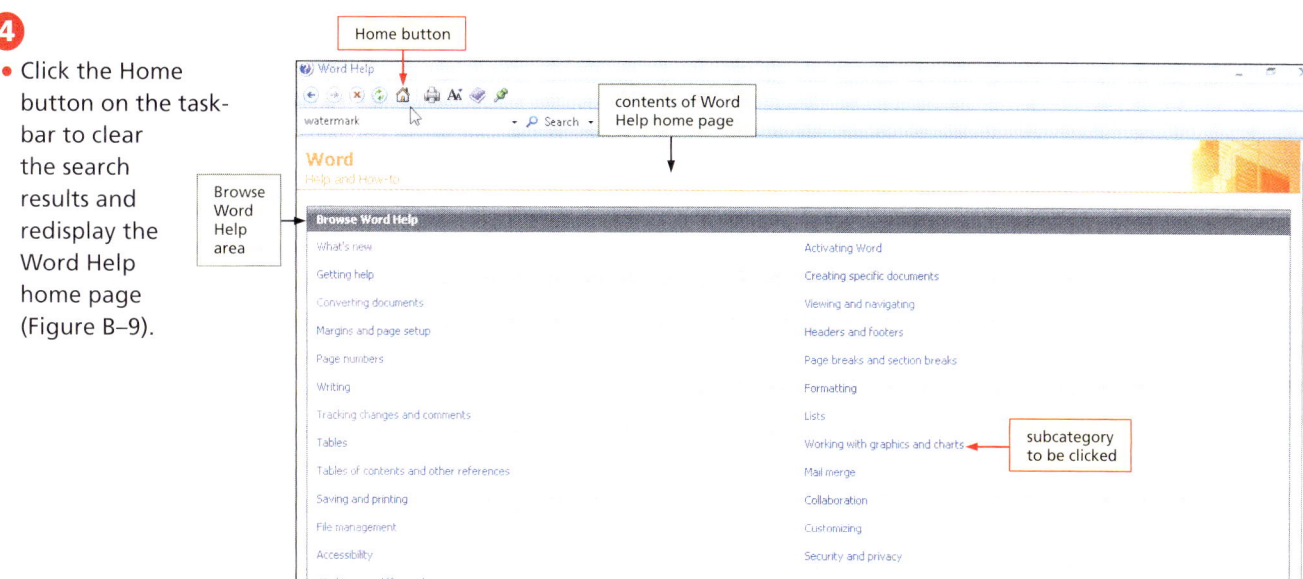

Figure B–9

To Obtain Help Using the Help Links

If your topic of interest is listed in the Browse Word Help area, you can click the link to begin browsing Word Help categories instead of entering search text. You browse Word Help just like you would browse a Web site. If you know in which category to find your Help information, you may wish to use these links. The following step finds the watermark Help information using the category links from the Word Help home page.

1

- Click the 'Working with graphics and charts' link to open the 'Working with graphics and charts' page.

- Click the 'Brand a document with a watermark or background' link to open the Help document associated with the link (Figure B–10).

Q&A What does the Show All link do?

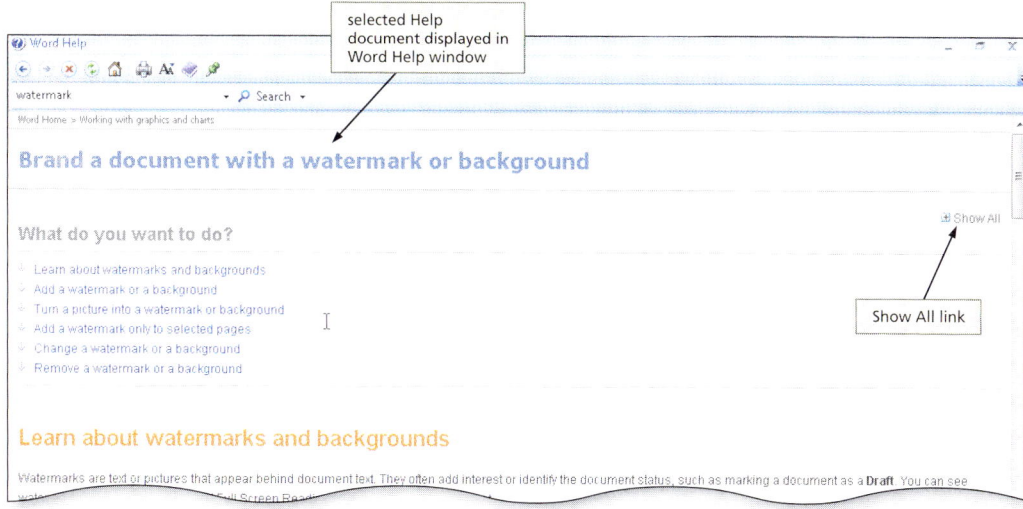

Figure B–10

In many Help documents, additional information about terms and features is available by clicking a link in the document to display additional information in the Help document. Clicking the Show All link opens all the links in the Help document that expand to additional text.

To Obtain Help Using the Help Table of Contents

A third way to find Help in Word is through the Help Table of Contents. You can browse through the Table of Contents to display information about a particular topic or to familiarize yourself with Word. The following steps access the watermark Help information by browsing through the Table of Contents.

1
- Click the Home button on the toolbar.
- Click the Show Table of Contents button on the toolbar to open the Table of Contents pane on the left side of the Help window. If necessary, click the Maximize button on the Help title bar to maximize the window (Figure B–11).

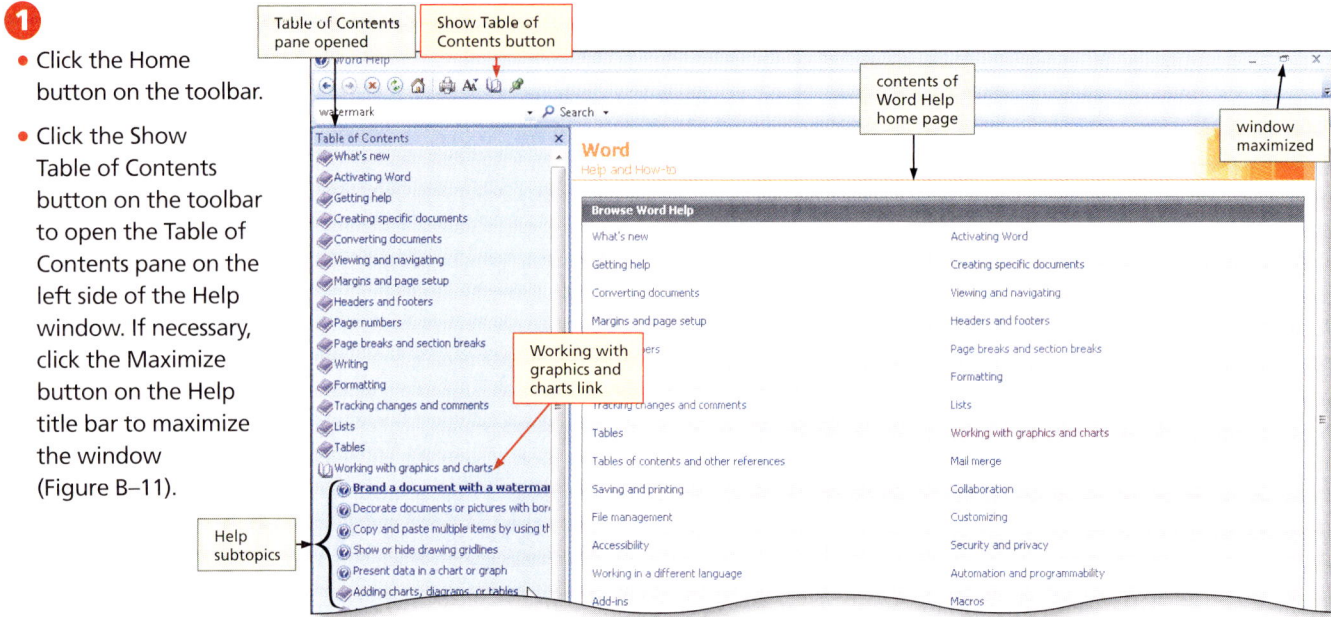

Figure B–11

2
- Click the 'Working with graphics and charts' link in the Table of Contents pane to view a list of Help subtopics.
- Click the 'Brand a document with a watermark or background' link in the Table of Contents pane to view the selected Help document in the right pane (Figure B–12).

 How do I remove the Table of Contents pane when I am finished with it?

The Show Table of Contents button acts as a toggle switch. When the Table of Contents pane is visible, the button changes to Hide Table of Contents. Clicking it hides the Table of Contents pane and changes the button to Show Table of Contents.

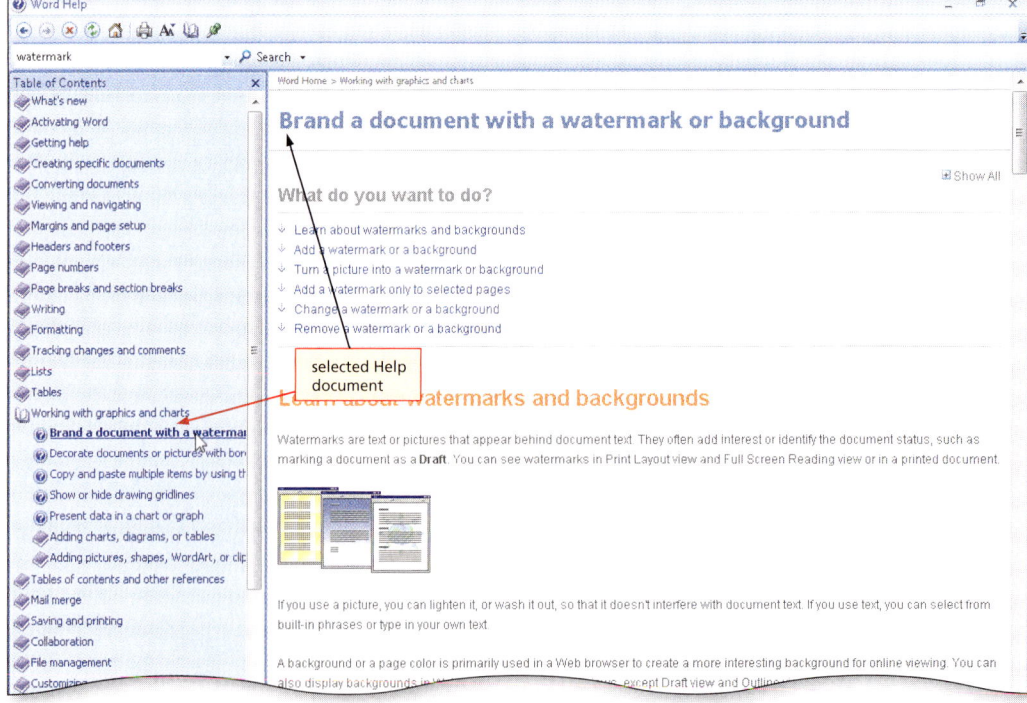

Figure B–12

Obtaining Help while Working in Word

Often you may need help while working on a document without already having the Help window open. For example, you may be unsure about how a particular command works, or you may be presented with a dialog box that you are not sure how to use. Rather than opening the Help window and initiating a search, Word Help provides you with the ability to search directly for help.

Figure B–13 shows one option for obtaining help while working in Word. If you want to learn more about a command, point to the command button and wait for the Enhanced ScreenTip to appear. If the Help icon appears in the Enhanced ScreenTip, press the F1 key while pointing to the command to open the Help window associated with that command.

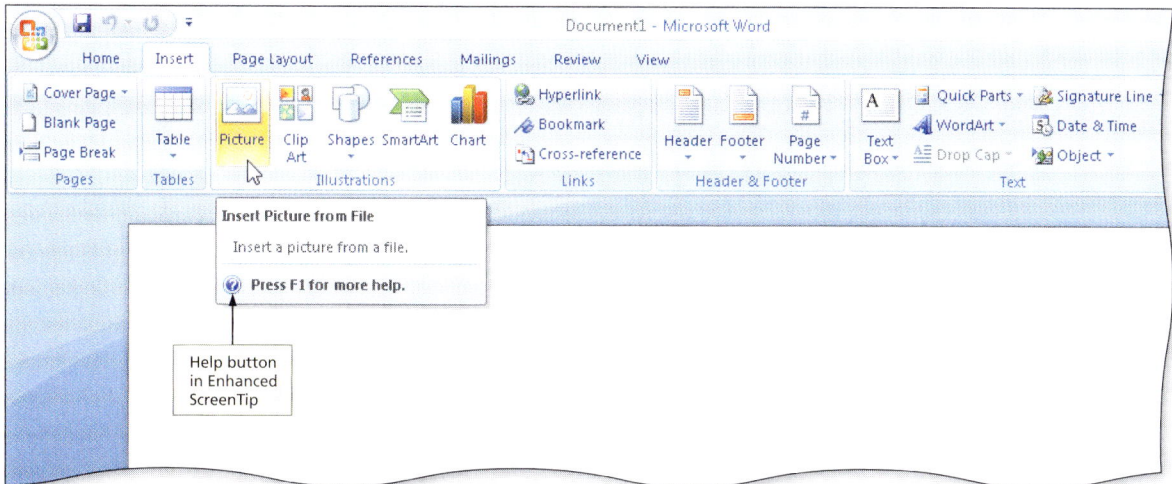

Figure B–13

Figure B–14 shows a dialog box with a Get help button in it. Pressing the F1 key while the dialog box is displayed opens a Help window. The Help window contains help about that dialog box, if available. If no help file is available for that particular dialog box, then the main Help window opens.

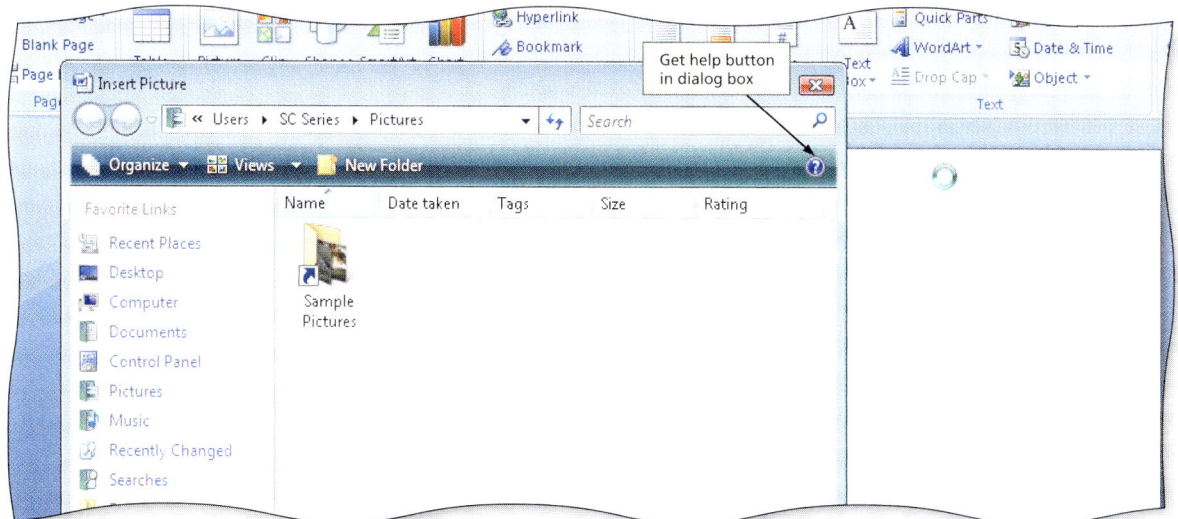

Figure B–14

Use Help

1 Obtaining Help Using Search Text

Instructions: Perform the following tasks using Word Help.

1. Use the 'Type words to search for' text box to obtain help about landscape printing. Use the Connection Status menu to search online help if you have an Internet connection.

2. Click Select page orientation in the list of links in the search results. Double-click the Microsoft Office Word Help window title bar to maximize it. Read and print the information. At the top of the printout, write down the number of links Word Help found.

3. Use the Search menu to search for help offline. Repeat the search from Step 1. At the top of the printout, write down the number of links that Word Help found searching offline. Submit the printouts as specified by your instructor.

4. Use the 'Type words to search for' text box to search for information online about adjusting line spacing. Click the 'Adjust the spacing between a list bullet or number and the text' link in the search results. If necessary, maximize the Microsoft Office 2007 Word Help window. Read and print the contents of the window. Close the Microsoft Office Word Help window. Submit the printouts as specified by your instructor.

5. For each of the following words and phrases, click one link in the search results, click the Show All link, and then print the page: page zoom; date; print preview; Ribbon; word count; and citation. Submit the printouts as specified by your instructor.

2 Expanding on Word Help Basics

Instructions: Use Word Help to better understand its features and answer the questions listed below. Answer the questions on your own paper, or submit the printed Help information as specified by your instructor.

1. Use Help to find out how to customize the Help window. Change the font size to the smallest option and then print the contents of the Microsoft Office Word Help window. Change the font size back to its original setting. Close the window.

2. Press the F1 key. Search for information about tables, restricting the search results to Word Templates. Print the first page of the Search results.

3. Search for information about tables, restricting the search results to Word Help files. Print the first page of the Search results.

4. Use Word Help to find out what happened to the Office Assistant, a feature in the previous version of Word. Print out the Help document that contains the answer.

Microsoft **Office 2007**

Appendix C
Customizing Microsoft Office 2007

This appendix explains how to change the screen resolution in Windows Vista to the resolution used in this book. It also describes how to customize the Word window by changing the Ribbon, Quick Access Toolbar, and the color scheme.

Changing Screen Resolution

Screen resolution indicates the number of pixels (dots) that the computer uses to display the letters, numbers, graphics, and background you see on the screen. When you increase the screen resolution, Windows displays more information on the screen, but the information decreases in size. The reverse also is true: as you decrease the screen resolution, Windows displays less information on the screen, but the information increases in size.

The screen resolution usually is stated as the product of two numbers, such as 1024 × 768 (pronounced "ten twenty-four by seven sixty-eight"). A 1024 × 768 screen resolution results in a display of 1,024 distinct pixels on each of 768 lines, or about 786,432 pixels. The figures in this book were created using a screen resolution of 1024 × 768.

The screen resolutions most commonly used today are 800 × 600 and 1024 × 768, although some Office specialists set their computers at a much higher screen resolution, such as 2048 × 1536.

To Change the Screen Resolution

The following steps change the screen resolution from 1280 × 1024 to 1024 × 768. Your computer already may be set to 1024 × 768 or some other resolution.

- If necessary, minimize all programs so that the Windows Vista desktop appears.

- Right-click the Windows Vista desktop to display the Windows Vista desktop shortcut menu (Figure C–1).

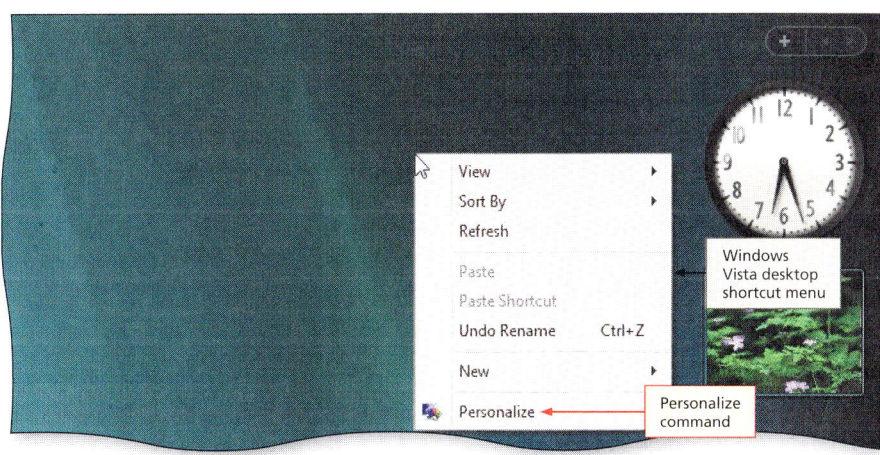

Figure C–1

APP 14 Appendix C Customizing Microsoft Office 2007

2
- Click Personalize on the shortcut menu to open the Personalization window.
- Click Display Settings in the Personalization window to display the Display Settings dialog box (Figure C–2).

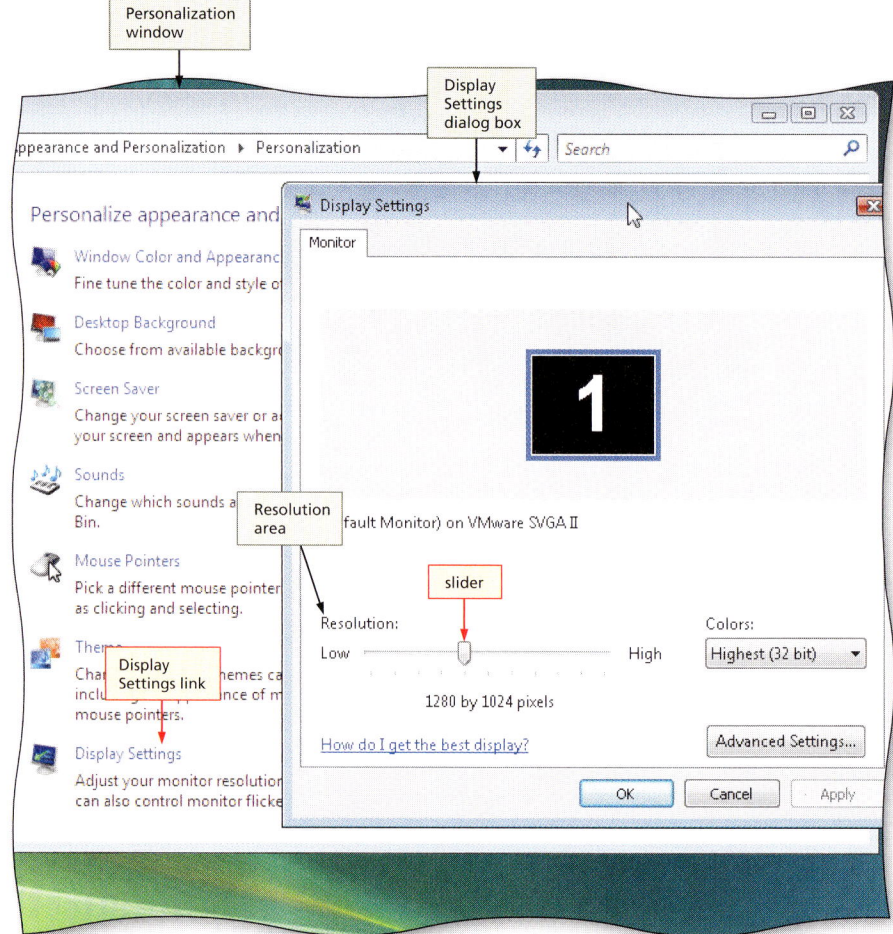

Figure C–2

3
- Drag the slider in the Resolution area so that the screen resolution changes to 1024 × 768 (Figure C–3).

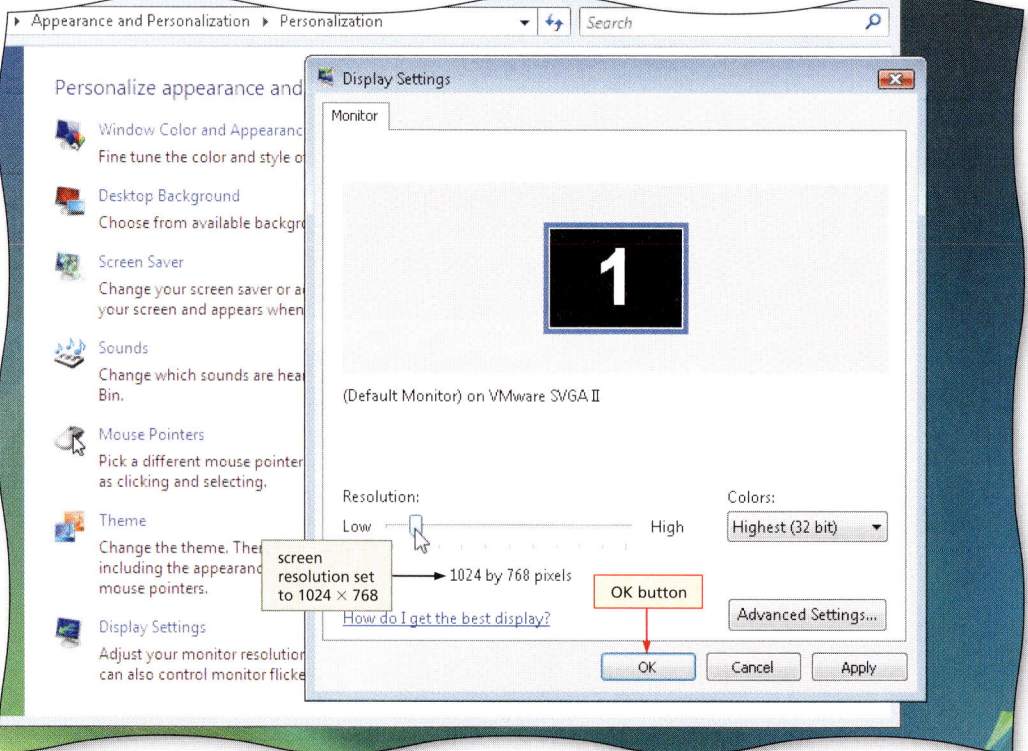

Figure C–3

④
- Click the OK button to change the screen resolution from 1280 × 1024 to 1024 × 768 (Figure C–4).

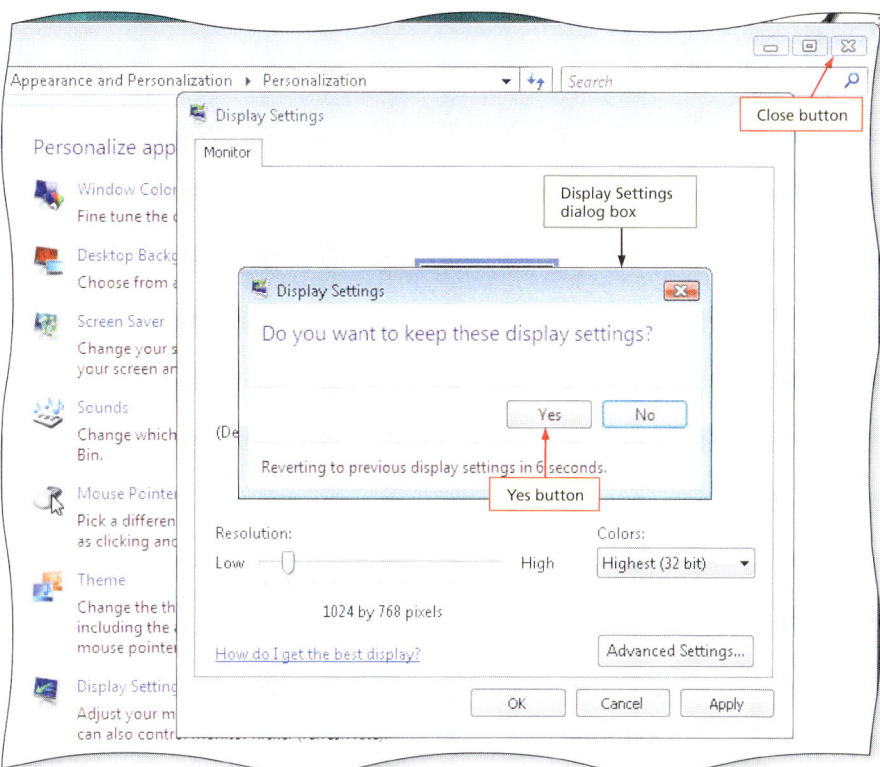

Figure C–4

⑤
- Click the Yes button in the Display Settings dialog box to accept the new screen resolution (Figure C–5).

 What if I do not want to change the screen resolution after seeing it applied after I click the OK button?

You either can click the No button in the inner Display Settings dialog box, or wait for the timer to run out, at which point Windows Vista will revert to the original screen resolution.

- Click the Close button to close the Personalization Window.

Figure C–5

Screen Resolution and the Appearance of the Ribbon in Office 2007 Programs

Changing the screen resolution affects how the Ribbon appears in Office 2007 programs. Figure C–6 shows the Word Ribbon at the screen resolutions of 800 × 600, 1024 × 768, and 1280 × 1024. All of the same commands are available regardless of screen resolution. Word, however, makes changes to the groups and the buttons within the groups to accommodate the various screen resolutions. The result is that certain commands may need to be accessed differently depending on the resolution chosen. A command that is visible on the Ribbon and available by clicking a button at one resolution may not be visible and may need to be accessed using its group button at a different resolution.

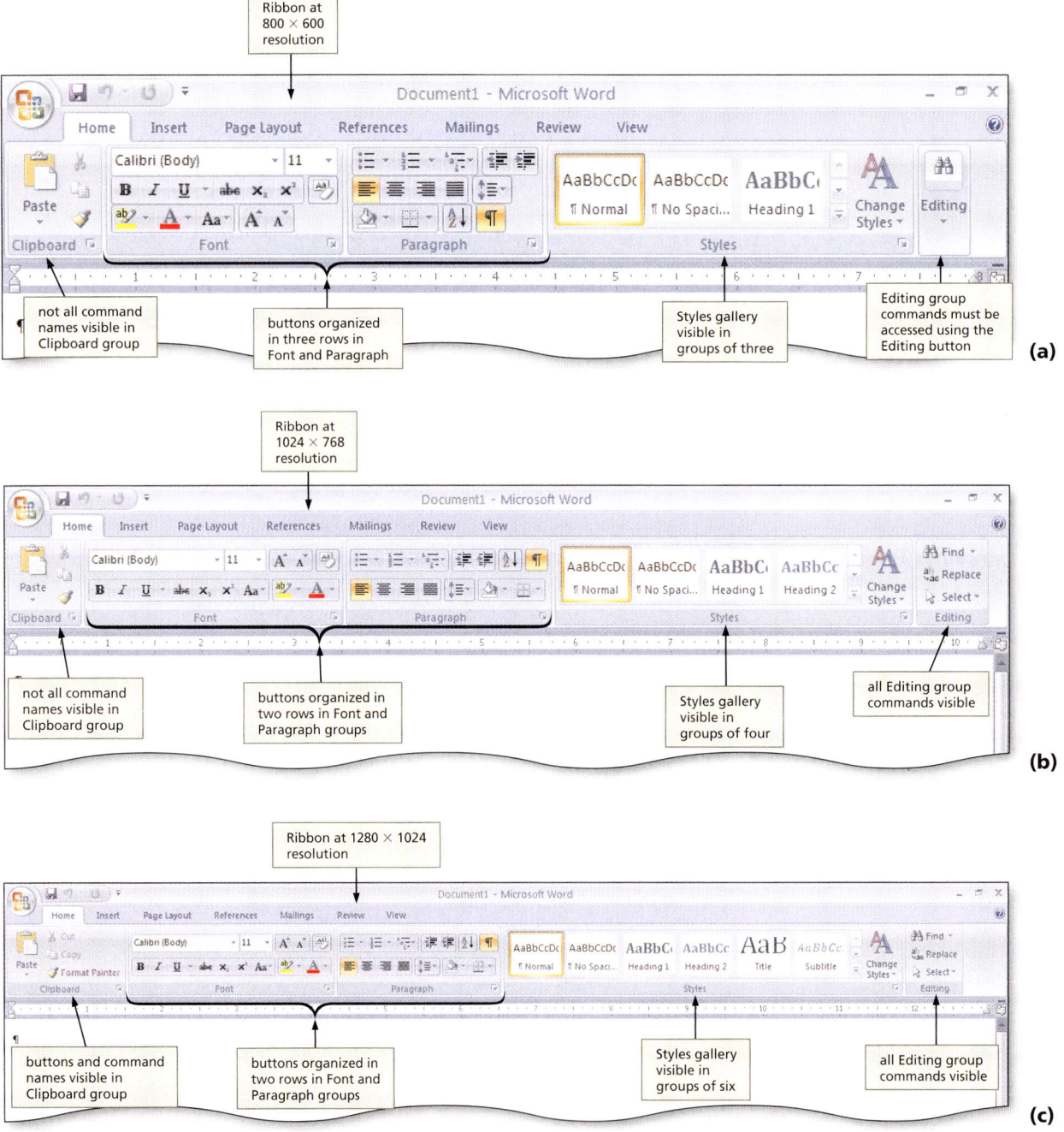

Figure C–6

Comparing the three Ribbons, notice changes in content and layout of the groups and galleries. In some cases, the content of a group is the same in each resolution, but the layout of the group differs. For example, the same buttons appear in the Font and Paragraph groups in the three resolutions, but the layouts differ. The buttons are displayed in three rows at the 800 × 600 resolution, and in two rows in the 1024 × 768 and 1280 × 1024 resolutions. In other cases, the content and layout are the same across the resolution, but the level of detail differs with the resolution. In the Clipboard group, when the resolution increases to 1280 × 1024, the names of all the buttons in the group appear in addition to the buttons themselves. At the lower resolution, only the buttons appear.

Changing resolutions also can result in fewer commands being visible in a group. Comparing the Editing groups, notice that the group at the 800 × 600 resolution consists of an Editing button, while at the higher resolutions, the group has three buttons visible. The commands that are available on the Ribbon at the higher resolutions must be accessed using the Editing button at the 800 × 600 resolution.

Changing resolutions results in different amounts of detail being available at one time in the galleries on the Ribbon. The Styles gallery in the three resolutions presented show different numbers of styles. At 800 × 600, you can scroll through the gallery three styles at a time, at 1024 × 768, you can scroll through the gallery four styles at a time, and at 1280 × 1024, you can scroll through the gallery six styles at a time.

Customizing the Word Window

When working in Word, you may want to make your working area as large as possible. One option is to minimize the Ribbon. You also can modify the characteristics of the Quick Access Toolbar, customizing the toolbar's commands and location to better suit your needs.

To Minimize the Ribbon in Word

The following steps minimize the Ribbon.

- Start Word.
- Maximize the Word window, if necessary.
- Click the Customize Quick Access Toolbar button on the Quick Access Toolbar to display the Customize Quick Access Toolbar menu (Figure C–7).

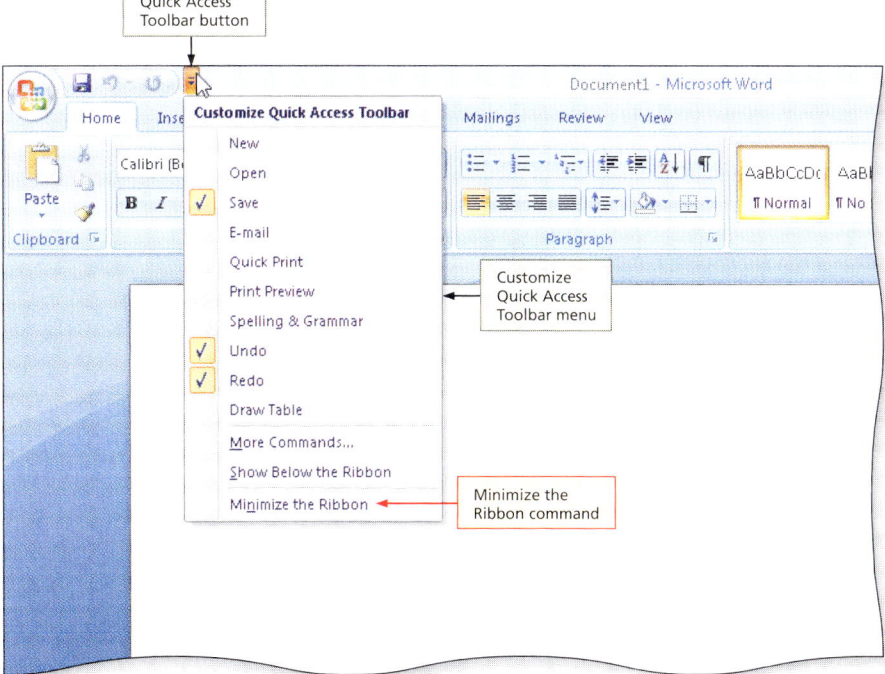

Figure C–7

- Click Minimize the Ribbon on the Quick Access Toolbar to reduce the Ribbon display to just the tabs (Figure C–8).

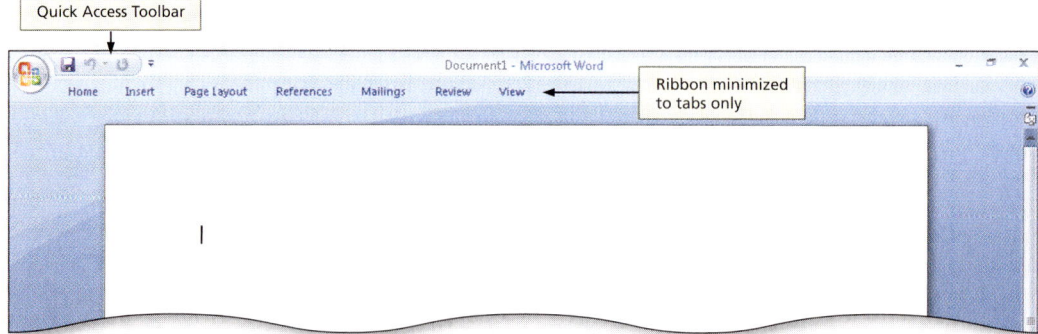

Figure C–8

Other Ways
1. Double-click the active Ribbon tab
2. Press CTRL+F1

Customizing and Resetting the Quick Access Toolbar

The Quick Access Toolbar, located to the right of the Microsoft Office Button by default, provides easy access to some of the more frequently used commands in Word (Figure C–8). By default, the Quick Access Toolbar contains buttons for the Save, Undo, and Redo commands. Customize the Quick Access Toolbar by changing its location in the window and by adding additional buttons to reflect which commands you would like to be able to access easily.

To Change the Location of the Quick Access Toolbar

The following steps move the Quick Access Toolbar to below the Ribbon.

- Double-click the Home tab to redisplay the Ribbon.
- Click the Customize Quick Access Toolbar button on the Quick Access Toolbar menu to display the Customize Quick Access Toolbar menu (Figure C–9).

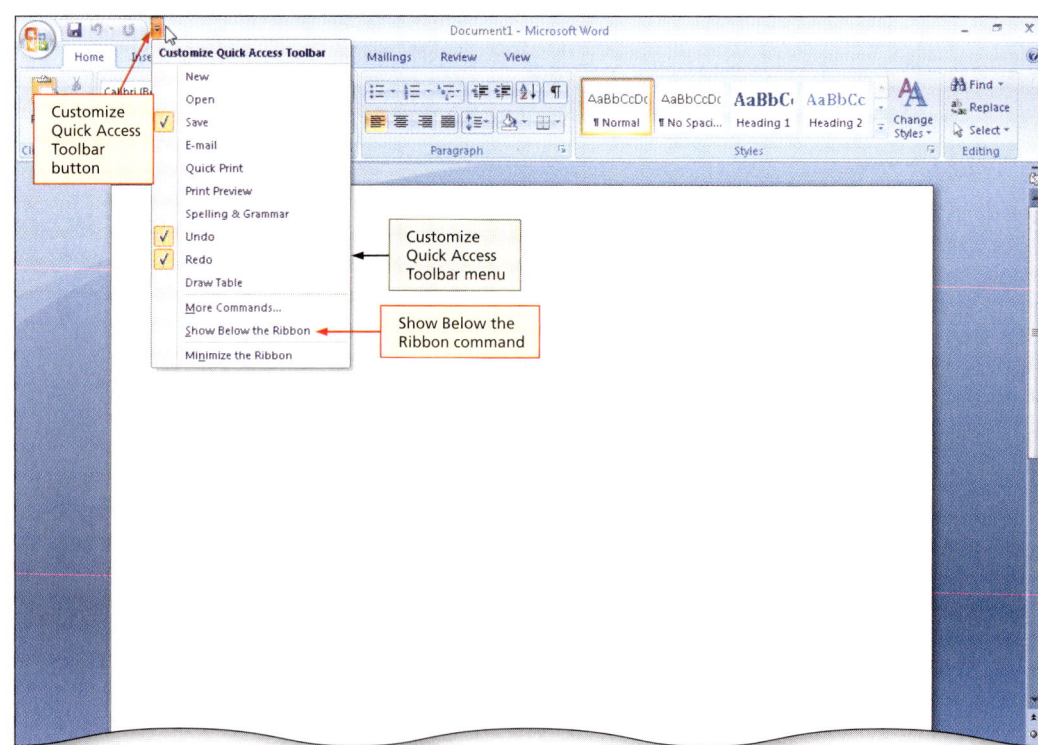

Figure C–9

- Click Show Below the Ribbon on the Quick Access Toolbar menu to move the Quick Access Toolbar below the Ribbon (Figure C–10).

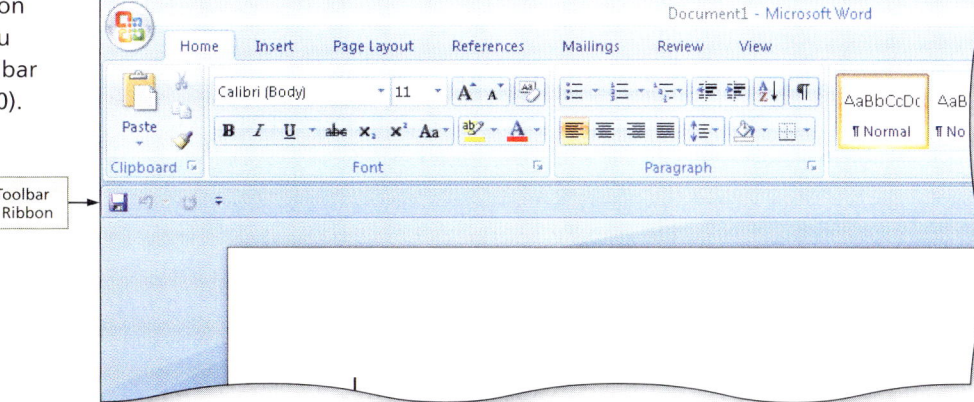

Figure C–10

To Add Commands to the Quick Access Toolbar Using the Customize Quick Access Toolbar Menu

Some of the more commonly added commands are available for selection from the Customize Quick Access Toolbar menu. The following steps add the Quick Print button to the Quick Access Toolbar.

- Click the Customize Quick Access Toolbar button to display the Customize Quick Access Toolbar menu (Figure C–11).

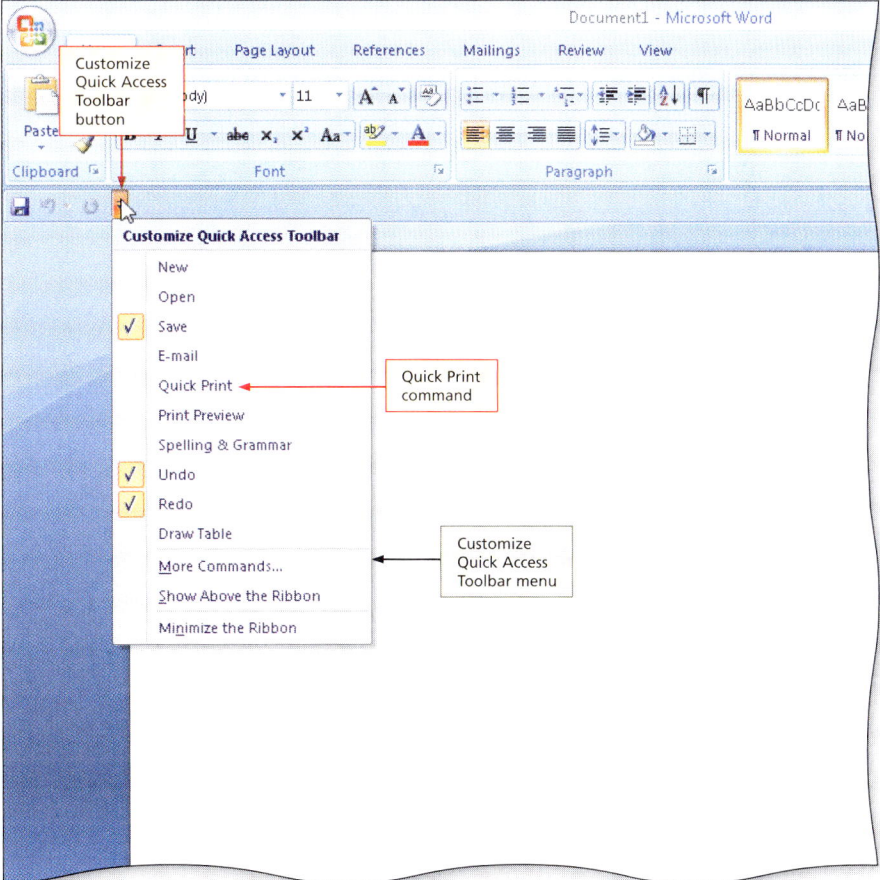

Figure C–11

- Click Quick Print on the Quick Access Toolbar menu to add the Quick Print button to the Quick Access Toolbar (Figure C–12).

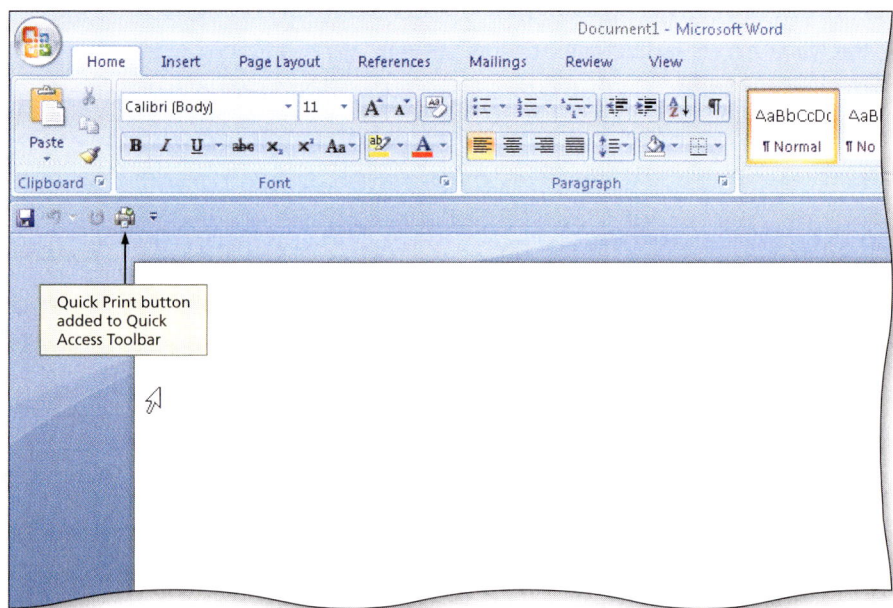

Figure C–12

To Add Commands to the Quick Access Toolbar Using the Shortcut Menu

Commands also can be added to the Quick Access Toolbar from the Ribbon. Adding an existing Ribbon command that you use often to the Quick Access Toolbar makes the command immediately available, regardless of which tab is active.

- Click the Review tab on the Ribbon to make it the active tab.
- Right-click the Spelling & Grammar button on the Review tab to display a shortcut menu (Figure C–13).

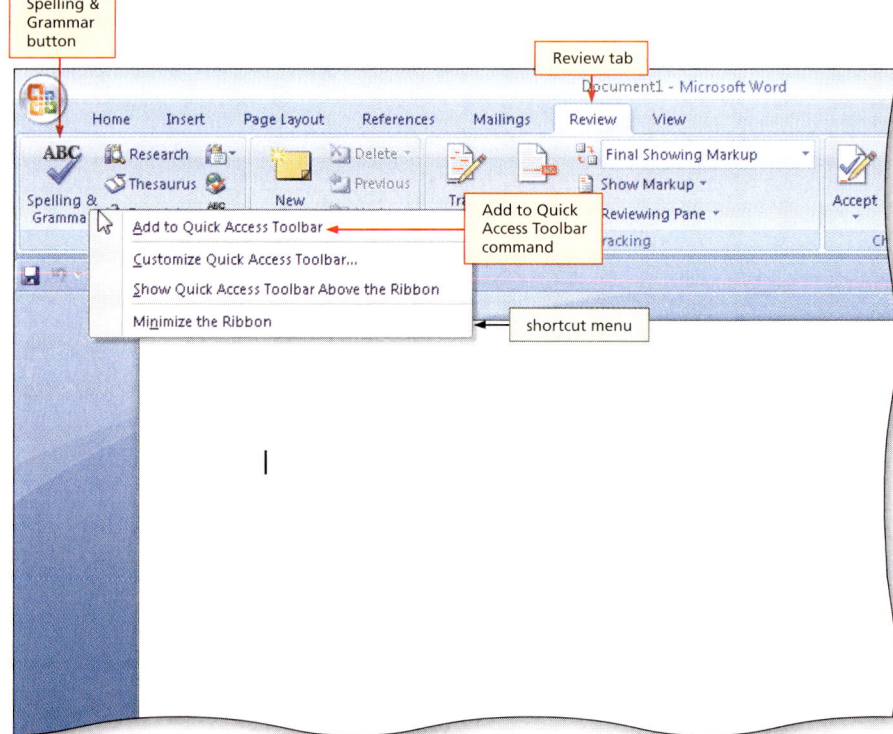

Figure C–13

2
- Click Add to Quick Access Toolbar on the shortcut menu to add the Spelling & Grammar button to the Quick Access Toolbar (Figure C–14).

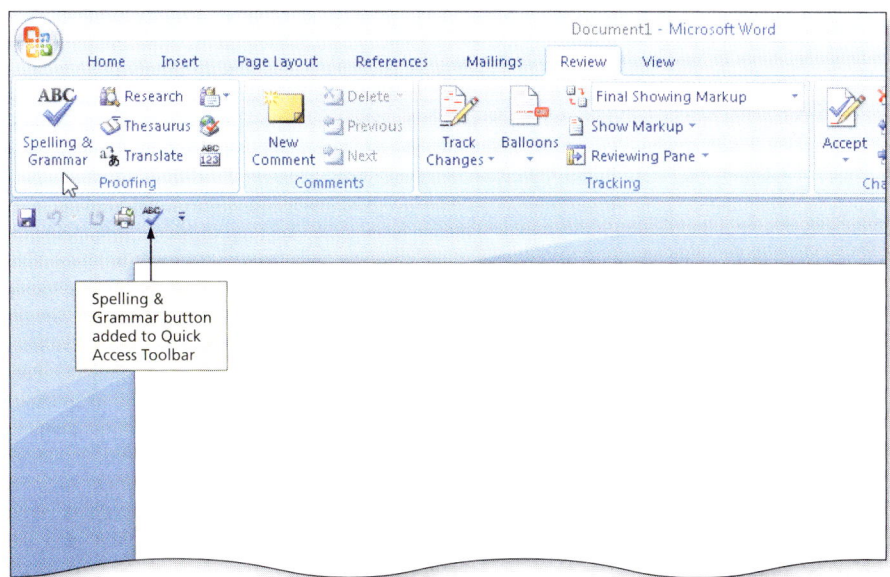

Figure C–14

To Add Commands to the Quick Access Toolbar Using Word Options

Some commands do not appear on the Ribbon. They can be added to the Quick Access Toolbar using the Word Options dialog box.

1
- Click the Office Button to display the Office Button menu (Figure C–15).

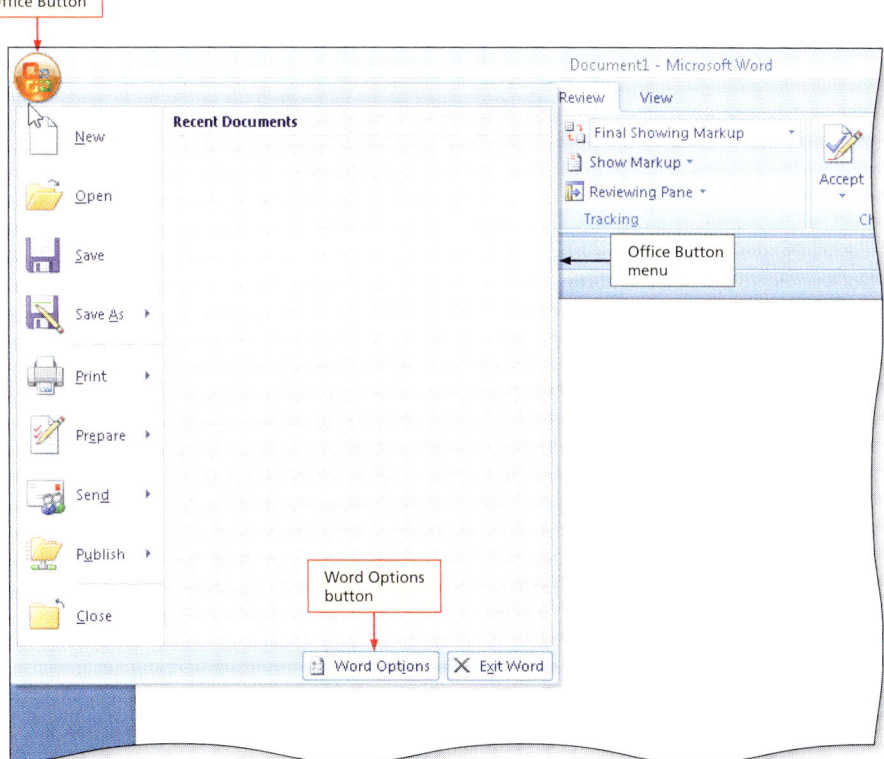

Figure C–15

- Click the Word Options button on the Office Button menu to display the Word Options dialog box (Figure C–16).

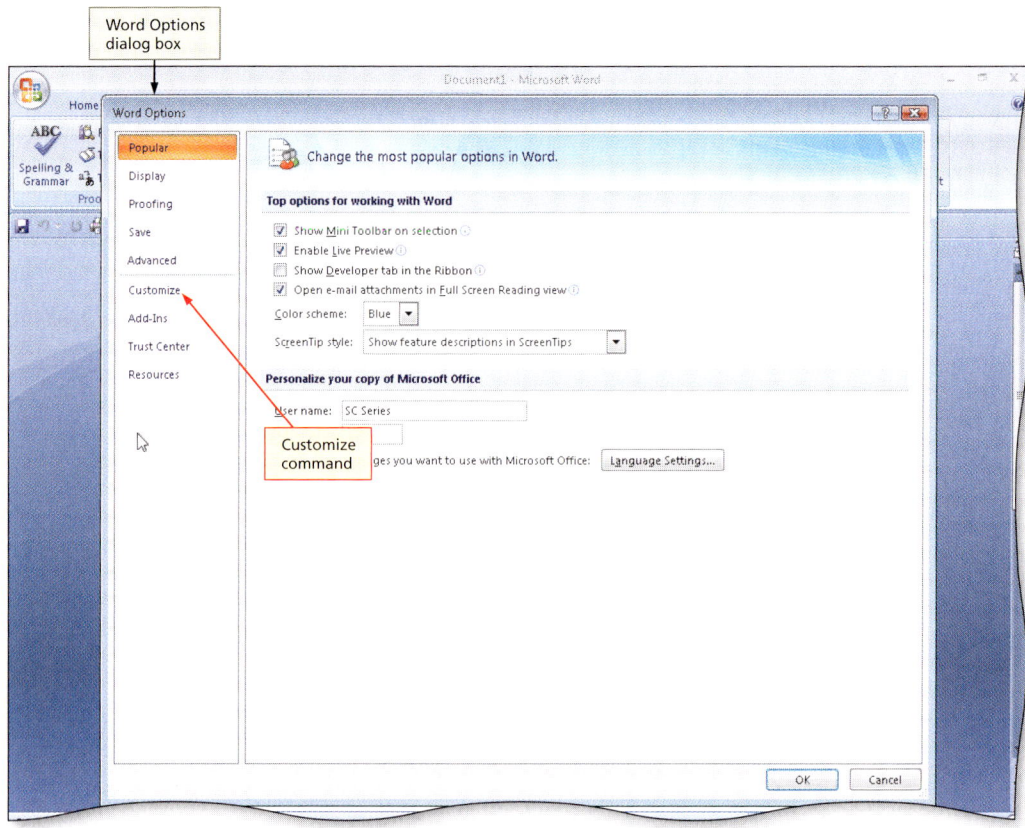

Figure C–16

- Click Customize in the left pane.
- Click 'Choose commands from' box arrow to display the 'Choose commands from' list.
- Click Commands Not in the Ribbon in the 'Choose commands from' list.
- Scroll to display the Web Page Preview command.
- Click Web Page Preview to select it (Figure C–17).

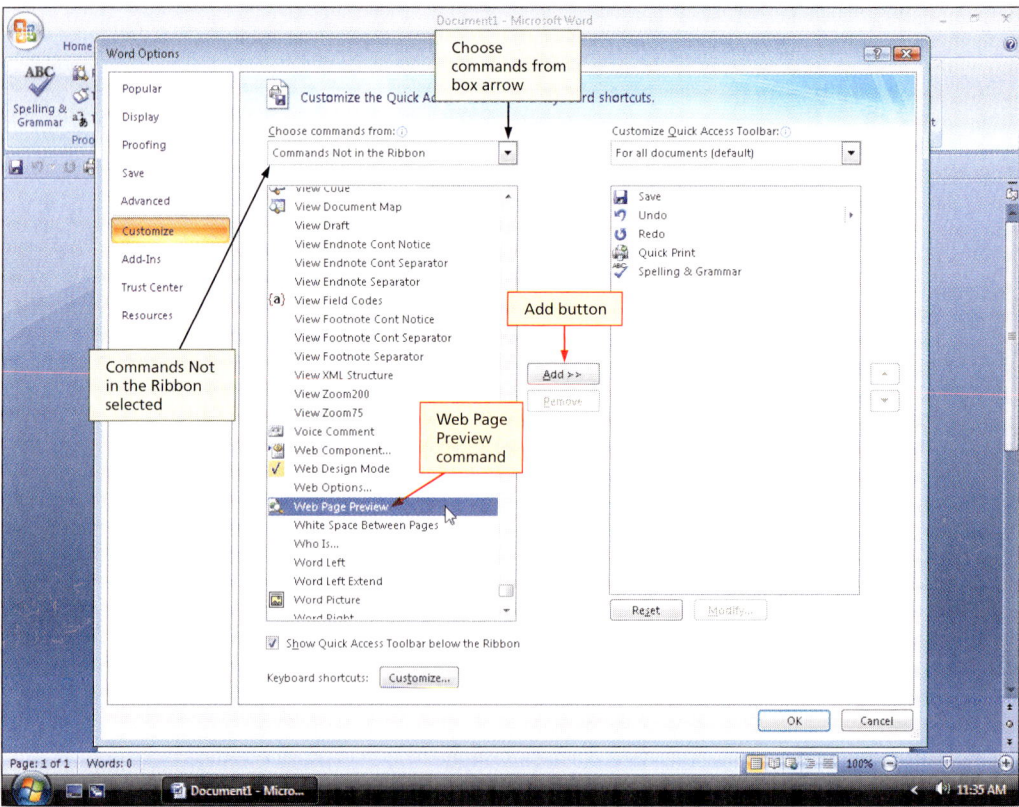

Figure C–17

④
- Click the Add button to add the Web Page Preview button to the list of buttons on the Quick Access Toolbar (Figure C–18).

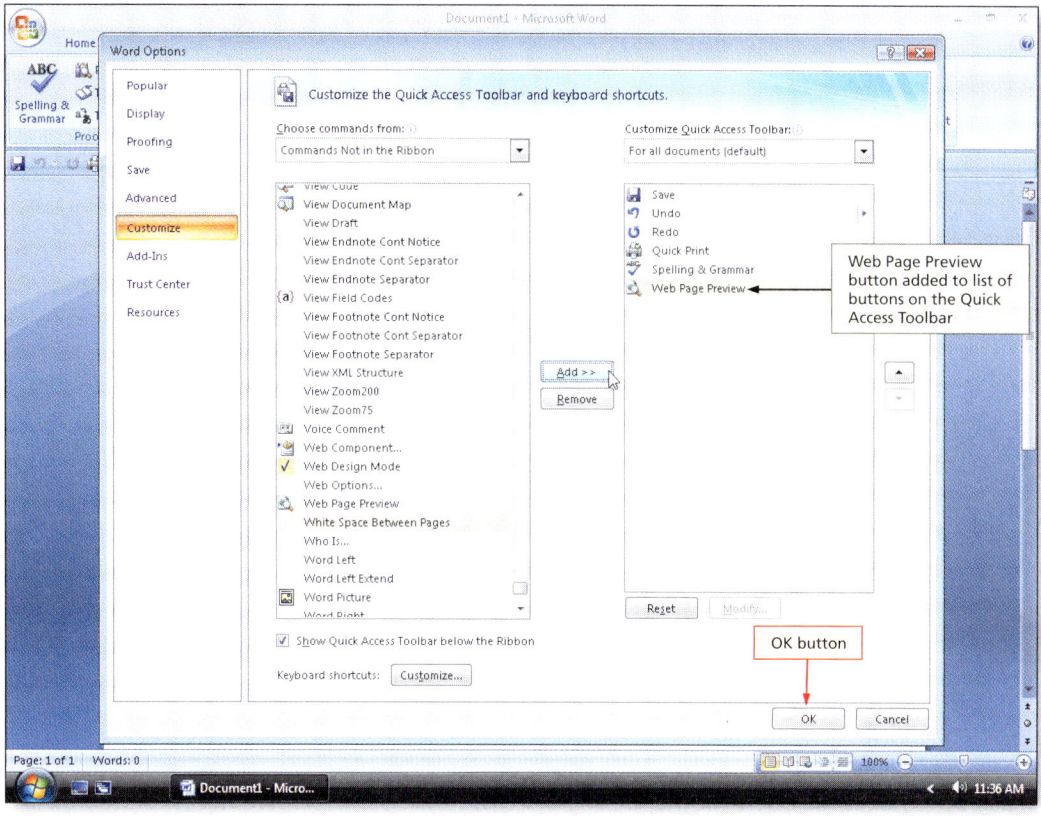

Figure C–18

⑤
- Click the OK button to add the Web Page Preview button to the Quick Access Toolbar (Figure C–19).

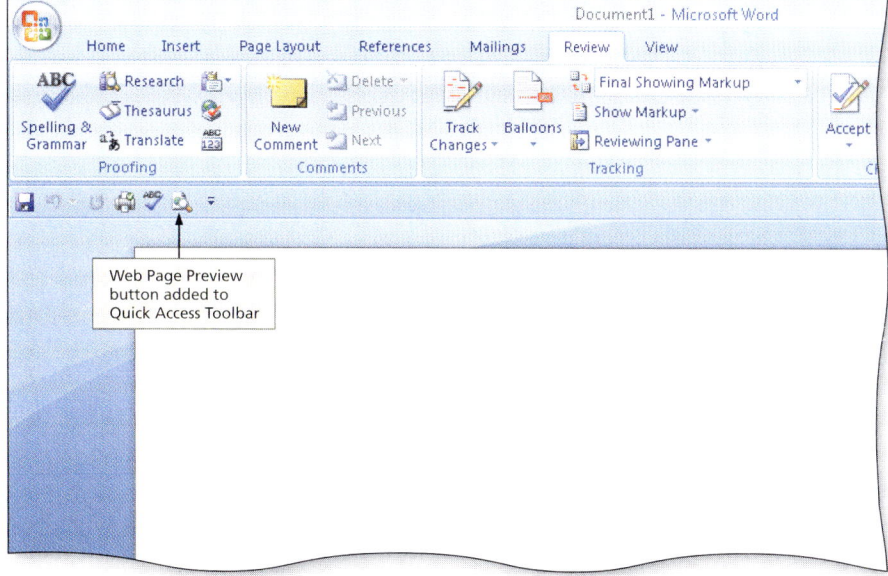

Figure C–19

> **Other Ways**
> 1. Click Customize Quick Access Toolbar button, click More Commands, select commands to add, click Add button, click OK button

To Remove a Command from the Quick Access Toolbar

- Right-click the Web Page Preview button on the Quick Access Toolbar to display a shortcut menu (Figure C–20).

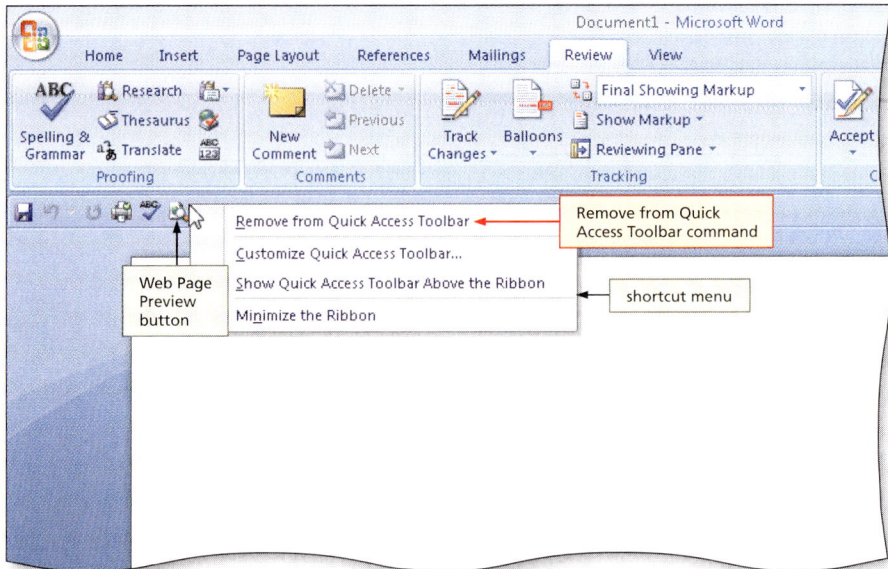

Figure C–20

- Click Remove from Quick Access Toolbar on the shortcut menu to remove the button from the Quick Access Toolbar (Figure C–21).

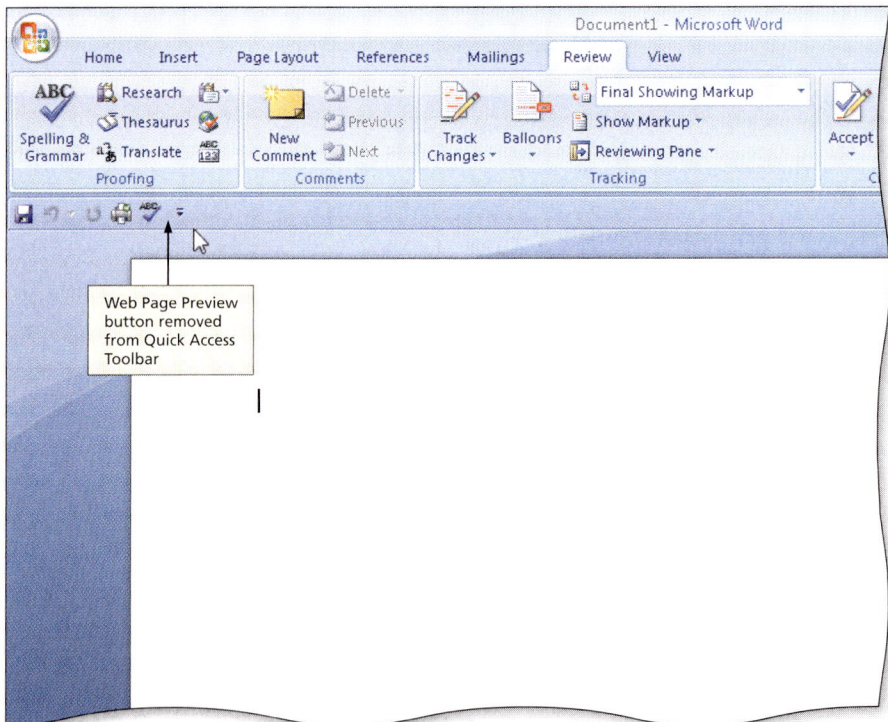

Figure C–21

Other Ways

1. Click Customize Quick Access Toolbar button, click More Commands, click the command you wish to remove in the Customize Quick Access Toolbar list, click Remove button, click OK button
2. If the command appears on the Customize Quick Access Toolbar menu, click the Customize Quick Access Toolbar button, click the command you wish to remove

To Reset the Quick Access Toolbar

1
- Click the Customize Quick Access Toolbar button on the Quick Access Toolbar.

- Click More Commands on the Quick Access Toolbar menu to display the Word Options Dialog box.

- Click the Show Quick Access Toolbar below the Ribbon check box to deselect it (Figure C–22).

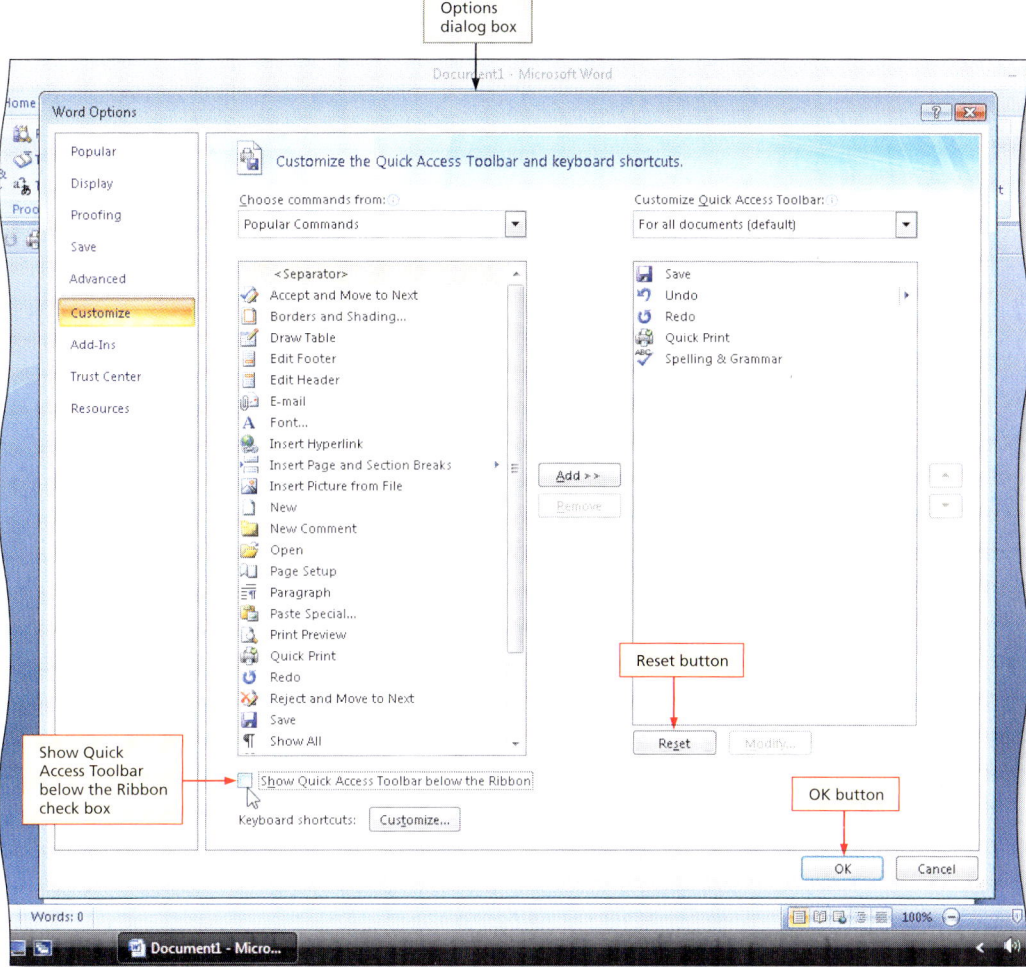

Figure C–22

- Click the Reset button, click the Yes button in the dialog box that appears, and then click the OK button in the Word Options dialog box, to reset the Quick Access Toolbar to its original position to the right of the Office Button, with the original three buttons (Figure C–23).

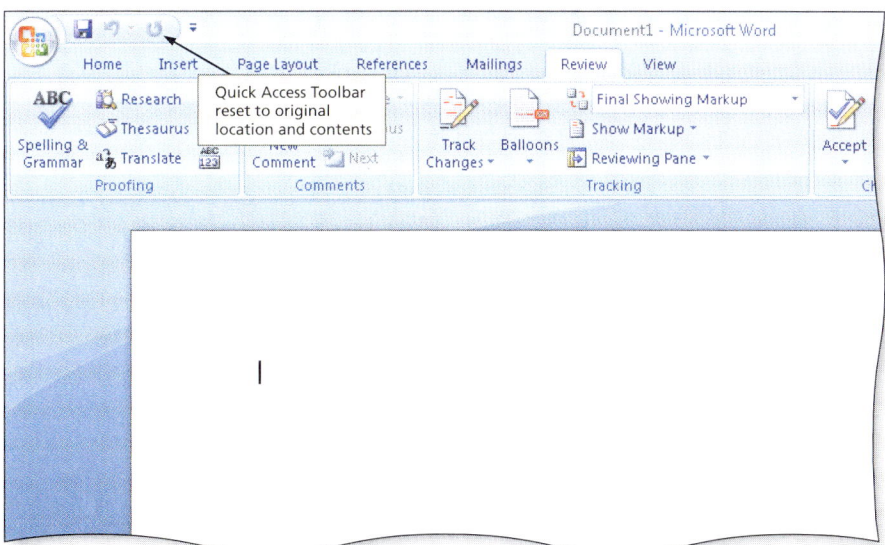

Figure C–23

Changing the Word Color Scheme

The Microsoft Word window can be customized by selecting a color scheme other than the default blue one. Three color schemes are available in Word.

To Change the Word Color Scheme

The following steps change the color scheme.

1
- Click the Office Button to display the Office Button menu.
- Click the Word Options button on the Office Button menu to display the Word Options dialog box.
- If necessary, click Popular in the left pane. Click the Color scheme box arrow to display a list of color schemes (Figure C–24).

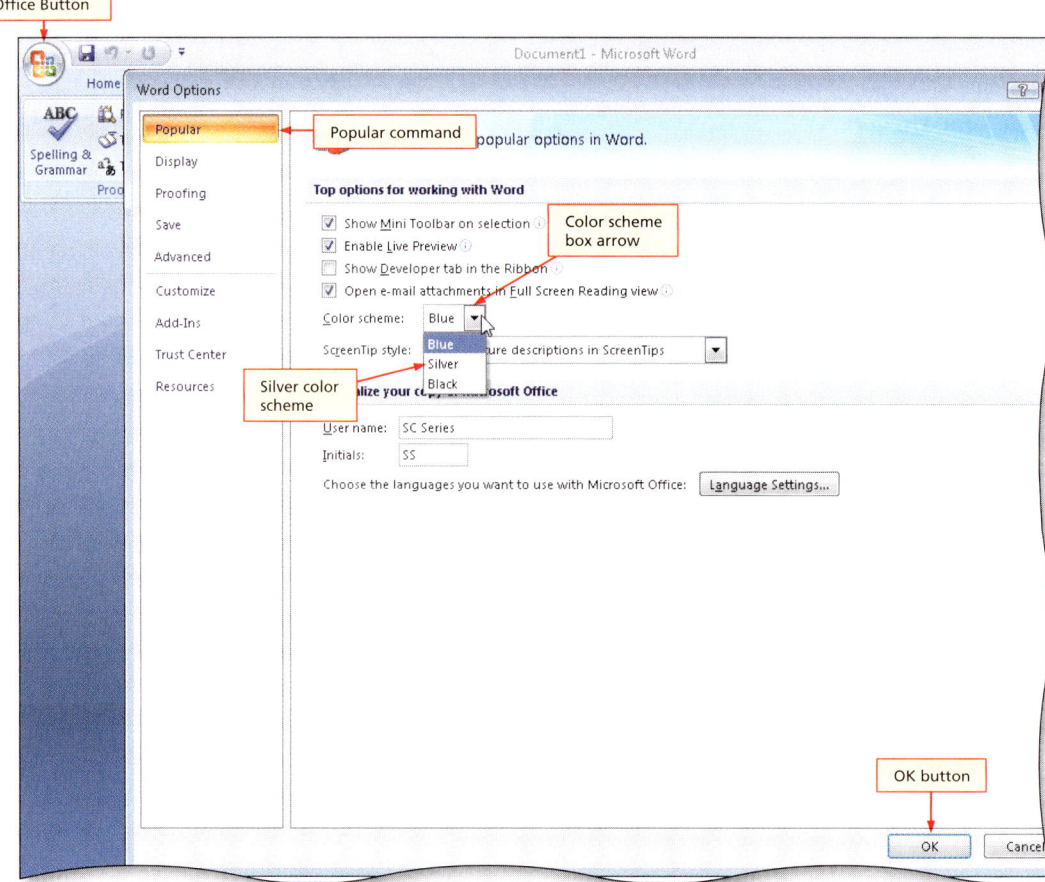

Figure C–24

2
- Click Silver in the list.
- Click the OK button to change the color scheme to silver (Figure C–25).

Q&A How do I switch back to the default color scheme?

Follow the steps for changing the Word color scheme, and select Blue from the list of color schemes.

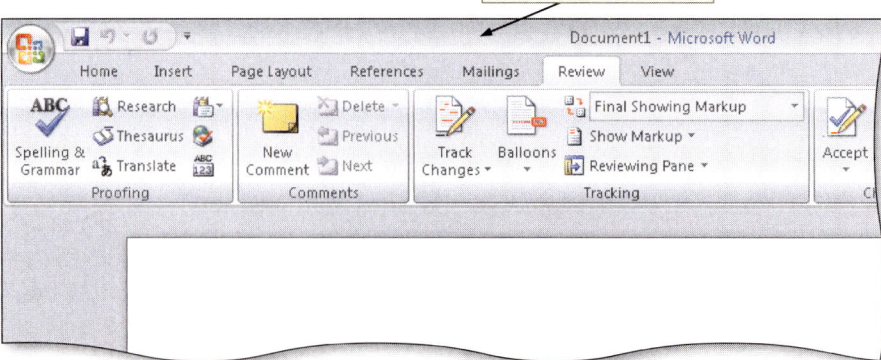

Figure C–25

Index

802.11i: Network standard that conforms to government's security standards and uses more sophisticated encryption techniques than WPA. Sometimes called WPA2. **197**

A

acceptable use policy (AUP), 189
Access 2007
  Access window components, AC 17–23
  creating Web pages from reports, INT 28–37
  opening database from, AC 37–38
  overview of, AC 2–6
  quitting, AC 35–36
  starting, AC 12–13, AC 36
  See also **database**
access control: Security measure that defines who can access a computer, when they can access it, and what actions they can take while accessing the computer. **189**
Access Help
  described, **AC 61**
  searching for, AC 62–63
access provider: Business that provides individuals and companies access to the Internet free or for a fee. 10, **46**
Access window components, AC 17–23
Access work area, **AC 18**
accessibility, alternate text, IE 19
Accessories, WIN 13
Accounting Number format, EX 44, **EX 114**–117
accounting software: Software that helps companies record and report their financial transactions. **107**
  popular (fig.), 100
Acrobat Reader, 61
active cell, **EX 8**
active tab, Ribbon, **WD 7, PPT 9, EX 10, AC 19**
active window (WordPad), **IE 40**
adaptive cruise control, 20
adding
  3-D Clustered Column Chart to worksheet, EX 49–54
  commands to Quick Access Toolbar, APP 19–23

fields to tables, AC 24–26
gadgets to Windows Sidebar, WIN 10–12
hyperlinks to reports, INT 32–35
hyperlinks to Word documents, INT 6
icons to desktop, WIN 16–17
page borders, WD 48–49
records to tables, AC 30–34, AC 38–39, AC 49
shapes, PPT 115–120
slide transitions, PPT 122–124
text for hyperlinks, INT 24–25
See also inserting
add-on Program that extends the capability of a browser; often used to enhance multimedia. *See also* **plug-in**. **61**
Address bar, **IE 13**
Address bar list, **IE 21**
Address bar (Vista), **WIN 18**, WIN 30
address book: List of names and e-mail addresses, created and stored by a user. **65**
addresses
  IP, 48
  searching for street, 71–72
  Web, IE 7–9, 51
Adknowledge, 166
administrator account: Computer account held by computer and network administrators that enables them to access all files and programs on the computer or network, install programs, and specify settings that affect all users on a computer or network. **144**
Adobe Systems, 121
advocacy Web sites, 57
adware: Program that displays an online advertisement in a banner or pop-up window on Web pages, e-mail, or other Internet services. **155, 204, IE 6**
adware remover: Program that detects and deletes adware from a user's computer. **155**
aggregate function, **AC 117**
alias, **AC 113**
All Programs list, WIN 27
Allen, Paul, 29
ALT key, and Key Tips, PPT 15
AltaVista search engine, 81

alternate text, **IE 19**
Amazon company profile, 29
American Psychological Association (APA)
  style, **WD 74**, WD 76
  See also APA documentation style
analog formats, video, 130
AND criterion, **AC 95**
Anderson, Tom, 29
animated slide shows, PPT 122–125
animation: Appearance of motion created by displaying a series of still images in sequence. **59, PPT 122**
anti-spam program: Program that attempts to remove spam before it reaches a user's inbox. **155, 205**
antivirus program: Program that protects a computer against viruses by identifying and removing any computer viruses found in memory, on storage media, or on incoming files. **154, 186**
antivirus software, **IE 7**
APA documentation style, WD 143
  citations, WD 94
  research papers, WD 74, WD 76
  style, **WD 74**, WD 76
Apple, 15, 29, 38, 40, 131
Apple TV, 39
application software: Program designed to make users more productive and/or assist them with personal tasks. **12, 96, WIN 4**
  business software, 100–107
  for communications, 118
  graphics and multimedia software, 108–111
  for home, personal, educational use, 111–116
  learning tools for, 119–120
  overview of, 96–99
  saving files in, 126
  Web applications, 116–117
arguments, **EX 99**
ARPANET, 44
Art gallery, WD 49
arts Web sites, 94
Ask.com, 166
asterisks (*)
  in file names, WD 20
  search wildcard, 55
attaching files to e-mail, 76, EX 143

IND 1

attacks, Internet, 184–189
auction Web sites, 88
audience, for projects, APP 1–2
audio: Music, speech, or any other sound. **60**
 digital products in our lives, 38
audio editing software: Application software that allows a user to modify audio clips, produce studio-quality soundtracks, and add audio to video clips. **110**
 popular (fig.), 108
audit trail: Computer file that records both successful and unsuccessful access attempts. **189**
authentication, 190
Auto Fill options, EX 28
AutoCalculate area
 described, **EX 62**
 determining maximums using, EX 62–63
AutoCorrect dialog box, WD 94
AutoCorrect feature, **WD 91**–94, **EX 19–22**, **AC 34**
AutoCorrect Options button, **WD 92**
AutoFit button
 described, **PPT 19**
 using with tables, INT 9–10
automatic page breaks, **WD 107**
automatic recalculation, EX 96
automatic update: Operating system feature that automatically provides updates to a program. **143**, 164–165
Automatic Update (Windows), **IE 7**
automatically updated properties, **WD 51**, **PPT 44**, **EX 54**, **AC 60**
automobiles
 blogs, 128
 embedded computers in, 20
 LucidTouch sensors, 115
AVERAGE function, EX 98–100, **EX 99**, EX 104–105

B

Back button, **IE 13**, IE 22–25
back door: Program or set of instructions in a program that allow users to bypass security controls when accessing a program, computer, or network. **188**
back up: To make a copy of a file. **196**
 files on offsite Internet server, 214–215
 background, foreground programs, 140

background colors, EX 110–112, INT 35
background repagination, **WD 107**
background styles, **PPT 89**
backslash (\) in file names, WD 20
backup: Duplicate or copy of a file, program, or disk that can be used if the original is lost, damaged, or destroyed. **196**
backup utility: Utility program that allows users to copy, or back up, selected files or an entire hard disk to another storage medium, such as another hard disk, optical disc, USB flash drive, or tape. **152**
banking. See **online banking**
Basic interface (Vista), WIN 6
behavior detection systems, 192
BehaviorIQ, 202
Berners-Lee, Tim, 49, 71
best fit, **EX 122**
BETWEEN operator, AC 95
Bezos, Jeff, 29
bibliographical lists, **WD 113**, WD 117
bibliography, **WD 111**
bibliography style, WD 95–99
Bing Maps, 84, 117
Bing search engine, 81
Biography.com, IE 65
biometric device: Device that authenticates a person's identity by translating a personal characteristic, such as a finger print, into a digital code that then is compared with a digital code stored in a computer verifying a physical or behavioral characteristic. **191**
biometric payment: Payment method where the customer's fingerprint is read by a fingerprint reader that is linked to a payment method such as a checking account or credit card. **191**
black slide, **PPT 39**
BlackBerry, 159, 225
BlackBerry operating system, 149
blog: Informal Web site consisting of time-stamped articles, or posts, in a diary or journal format, usually listed in reverse chronological order. Blog is short for Web log. **10, 56**
 creating your, 34

 personal and business perspectives, 174–175
 Web sites, 82
Blogger, 34, 82
Blogger's Choice Awards Web site, 78
blogging software, 118
blogosphere: Worldwide collection of blogs. **56**, 82
Blogroll, 166
Blu-ray Disc, 6, 157
bold, PPT 25, **WD 34**, **EX 38**
Bold button, EX 38
bookmark: Saved Web address that you access by clicking its name in a list. See also **favorite**. **51**
books Web sites, 88
booting: Process of starting or restarting a computer. **138**
borders
 adding page, WD 48–49
 changing color of picture, WD 45
 printing, WD 54
 worksheet, EX 110–112
botnet: Group of compromised computers connected to a network such as the Internet that is used as part of a network that attacks other networks, usually for nefarious purposes. **187**
breadcrumb trails, **WIN 36**
Bricklin, Dan, 121
Brin, Sergey, 71
broadband: High-speed Internet connection provided through cable, DSL, fiber, radio signals, or satellite. **45**, 221
browser: Application software that allows users to access and view Web pages. See also **Web browser**. **49**
 and chat clients, 67
browsing
 Help topics, WIN 60–61
 the Web, WIN 29–33, IE 15–30
browsing the Web, 49–50
buffer: Segment of memory or storage in which items are placed while waiting to be transferred from an input device or to an output device. **141**
bulleted list, **WD 32**
 adding to slides, PPT 29–31
 developing presentations with, PPT 2–5
 multi-level bulleted list slide, **PPT 33**

bullets, deleting, PPT 32
burning files to optical discs, 164
business, e-mail use in, 169
business software: Application software that assists people in becoming more effective and efficient while performing their daily business activities. **100**
  examples of, 96
  overview of, 101–107
  popular (fig.), 100
business Web sites, 56
business-to-business (B2B) e-commerce, 62, 63
business-to-consumer (B2C) e-commerce, 62
button: Graphical element that is activated to cause a specific action to take place. **98**
  adding to Quick Access Toolbar, INT 19–21, INT 26
  toolbar, APP 6–7
buyer's guide to computers, mobile devices, 217–228

C

cable Internet service: High-speed Internet access provided through the cable television network via a cable modem. **45**
cable modem, 47
calculated field, **AC 113**
calculating
  statistics, AC 117–122
  sums, EX 24–29
calculations
  automatic recalculation, EX 49
  for queries, AC 76
  in spreadsheet software, 103
  See also **formula**
camera. *See* **digital camera**
camera phone: Phone that can send picture messages. **17**
camera pills, 26
Cancel box, **EX 17**
capitalization of sentence's first letter, WD 94
CAPTCHA: Completely Automated Public Turing test to tell Computers and Humans Apart; program used by some Web sites to provide further protection for a user's password by verifying that user input is not computer generated. **190**
captions, changing, AC 116–117

card reader/writer, 5, 6, 219
career Web sites, 93
carpel tunnel syndrome (CTS), 198
cartography Web sites, 84
category axis, **EX 52**
cell, **EX 8**
  bolding, EX 38
  calculating sums, EX 24–29
  centering data in, EX 113–114
  changing style, EX 34–35
  choosing formats, EX 117
  clearing, EX 66
  copying to adjacent, EX 26–28
  editing contents of, EX 64
  entering numbers, EX 22–24
  entering numbers in, EX 22–24
  hiding, EX 122
  merging, EX 40–41
  Normal cell style selection, EX 66
  rotating, shrinking entries in, EX 114
  selecting, entering text, EX 15–22
  selecting using Name box, EX 47
  splitting merged, EX 41
  undoing last entry, EX 65
cell phones, 172–173
cell reference, **EX 8**, EX 96, EX 105
Cell Styles gallery, EX 43
cells, spreadsheet, 103
cellular radio network: High-speed Internet connection for devices with built-in compatible technology or computers with wireless modems. **46**
centered, **WD 26**
centering
  cell entries, EX 40–41
  data in cells, EX 113–114
  page contents vertically, WD 50
  paragraphs, WD 26
  text, WD 112
certificate authority: Authorized person or company that issues and verifies digital certificates. **195–196**
character formatting, **WD 22**
characters
  bold, WD 34
  and filenames, EX 31
  formatting in presentations, PPT 21–26
  nonprinting, WD 14
  shortcut keys for formatting (table), WD 86
  width, WD 18

Chart Tools contextual tab, EX 52
charting, with spreadsheet software, 104
charts
  embedded, EX 49–54
  embedding into Word documents, INT 13–16
  legend, EX 54
  resizing, EX 53
chat: Real-time typed conversation that takes place on a computer. **67**
chat room: Location on an Internet server that permits users to chat with each other. 10, **67**, 118
  emoticons, 69
  personal and business perspectives, 176–177
  checking spelling, WD 125–129
Chess Titans, 140
Chicago Manual of Style (CMS) documentation style, WD 143
children, supervising on Internet, IE 7
chumby, 42
citations
  creating, editing, WD 94–99
  editing, WD 105
  inserting placeholder, WD 101, WD 108
citing Web sites, IE 36
city guides Web sites, 84
clearing
  cells, ranges, entire worksheets, EX 66–67
  design grid, AC 98
  History List, IE 26
click: To move the mouse pointer to a button or link on the computer screen, and then to press and release the left mouse button. **52**, **98**, **WIN 4**
Click and Type feature, **WD 85**
clickjacking: Scam in which an object that can be clicked on a Web site, such as a button, image, or link, contains a malicious program. **205**
client, **WIN 4**
clip art: Collection of drawings, photos, and other images that a user can insert in documents. **101**
  inserting into slides, PPT 95–97
  resizing, PPT 101–102
Clip Art task pane, **PPT 95**

clip art/image gallery: A collection of clip art and photos included with application software. 111, **114**
clip collections, **PPT 95**
clip galleries, 105
Clipboard, **WD 119**
 copying and pasting using, IE 39–41
 displaying, **IE 39**
 using in Office programs, AC 34
clips
 described, **PPT 95**
 importing, PPT 95
 moving, PPT 105
Close button, **WIN 21**, EX 58
closed source operating system (OS), 148
closing
 documents, WD 59–60
 expanded folders, WIN 57
 tables, AC 35
 tabs, WIN 33
 windows, WIN 21, WIN 24
 Windows Help and Support window, WIN 63
cloud storage, 152, 196
codec, 131–132
cold boot: Process of turning on a computer that has been powered off completely. **138**
collapsing folder, WIN 43
colon (:)
 argument and cell references, EX 100
 in file names, WD 20
 in ranges, EX 25
color scheme
 changing, APP 26
 described, **WD 37**
colors
 changing cell entry, EX 39–40
 changing font, PPT 110–111
 changing picture border, WD 45, WD 49
 changing text, PPT 23
 changing theme, WD 39
 (character), **PPT 21**
 red, using, PPT 23
 using in worksheets, EX 108
column charts, 104
column headers, **WIN 19**
column heading, **EX 7**
column width, adjusting, EX 45
columns, changing width, EX 122–126

Comma style format, EX 45, **EX 114**
command: Instruction on a menu that causes a program to perform a specific action. **98, WIN 13**
 adding Ribbon, EX 13
 adding to Quick Access Toolbar, APP 19–23
 getting help on, APP 11
 on Mini toolbar, WD 9–10
 on Office Button, AC 22–23
 Quick Access Toolbar, WD 10–11, PPT 13–14
 on Ribbon, WD 7–9, EX 10, AC 20
Command bar, **WIN 19**, **IE 14**, IE 15
command-line interface: Type of user interface in which a user types commands or presses special keys on the keyboard (such as function keys or key combinations) to enter data and instructions. **139**
communications
 application software for, 118
 digital (feature), 167–180
communications device: Hardware component that enables a computer to send (transmit) and receive data, instructions, and information to and from one or more computers. **6**
comparison operator, **AC 94**
compound criterion, **AC 95**–96
compressing files, 126–127
computer: Electronic device, operating under the control of instructions stored in its own memory, that can accept data, process the data according to specified rules, produce results, and store the results for future use. **3**
 advantages, disadvantages of using, 7–8
 applications in society, 24–27
 buyer's guide to, 217–228
 categories of, 14–20
 components of, 4–7
 construction industry usage of, 120
 described, 3–4
 educational usage, 158
 examples of usage, users, 20–24
 health concerns about using, 198–199
 logging off, WIN 64–65
 logging on, WIN 8–9
 preventing virus infections, 154–155
 recycling old, 14, 202
 starting, shutting down, 138
 transferring videos to, 130–131
 usage of, 2–3
 Web sites, 88
computer addiction: Growing health problem that occurs when the computer consumes someone's entire social life. 7, **199**
computer crime: Any illegal act involving a computer. **182**
computer ethics: Moral guidelines that govern the use of computers and information systems. **199**
See also ethics
computer literacy: Having a current knowledge and understanding of computers and their uses. *See also* **digital literacy**. **3**
computer role-playing game (CRPG), 41
computer security risk: Any event or action that could cause a loss of or damage to computer hardware, software, data, information, or processing capability. **182**
 types of, 182–183
computer virus, **IE 7**
computer vision syndrome: Eyestrain due to prolonged computer usage. **198**
computer-aided design (CAD) software: Sophisticated type of application software that assists a professional user in creating engineering, architectural, and scientific designs. **109**, 120
 popular (fig.), 108
computer-aided manufacturing (CAM): Use of computers to assist with manufacturing processes such as fabrication and assembly. **27**
computer-based training (CBT): Type of education in which students learn by using and completing exercises with instructional software. Also called computer-aided instruction. **115**
ComputerJobs.com, IE 66–67
condition, **EX 118**
conditional formatting, **EX 118**
 applying, EX 119–122
connections, establishing Internet, 142–143
conserving ink, toner, WD 53

consumer-to-consumer (C2C) e-commerce, 62, 63
content aggregator: Business that gathers and organizes Web content and then distributes, or feeds, the content to subscribers for free or a fee. **58**
content filtering: Process of restricting access to certain material on the Web. **207**
content placeholders, PPT 96–97
content sharing, personal and business perspectives, 178–179
contextual spelling errors, WD 126
contextual tabs, Ribbon, WD 8, **PPT 9**, EX 52, **AC 20**
convergence: Term used to refer to the trend of manufacturers offering computers and devices with technologies that overlap. **14**
converting earlier PowerPoint documents, PPT 43
cookie: Small text file that a Web server stores on a computer. **203**
  workings of, 204
copy and embed method, INT 16
copy and link method, INT 16
copy and paste method, **IE 39**, INT 16
copy area, **EX 27**
copying
  cells to adjacent cells, EX 26–28
  and copyright, 201
  files by right-clicking, WIN 52–54
  formulas using fill handle, EX 95–96
  between Office 2007 programs, INT 16
  and pasting using Clipboard, IE 39–47
copyright: Exclusive rights given to authors and artists to duplicate, publish, and sell their materials. **201**, PPT 84
  clips, PPT 97
corporate blogs, 82
correcting
  errors in documents, WD 57–59
  errors with AutoCorrect feature, WD 91–94
  mistakes when typing, PPT 19–20, EX 19–22
  See also undoing actions
counting words, WD 107
CPU (central processing unit): Electronic component on a computer's motherboard that interprets and carries out the basic instructions that operate the computer. *See also* **processor**. **6**
cracker: Someone who accesses a computer or network illegal with the intent of destroying data, stealing information, or other malicious action. **182**
create: To enter text or numbers, insert images, and perform other tasks with a document using an input device such as a keyboard, mouse, or digital pen. **102**
creating
  alphabetical works cited page, WD 111–117
  AutoCorrect entry, WD 93–94
  bibliographical lists, WD 113
  charts, EX 49–54
  citations, WD 94–99
  crosstab queries, AC 122–125
  database tables, AC 44–45
  databases, AC 13–17
  flyers in Word, WD 2–4
  folders, WIN 38–40
  footers, WD 81
  headers, WD 79–83
  multiple home pages, IE 32
  parameter queries, AC 89–91
  PowerPoint Web pages, INT 23–26
  presentations. *See* presentation
  queries, AC 78–80, AC 83–85
  Quick Style, WD 90–91
  reports, AC 50–55
  reports involving joins, AC 109–111
  tables, AC 23–34, AC 26
  top-values query, **AC 102**–103
  transparencies, PPT 62
  Vista user account, WIN 7–8
  worksheets, EX 4
  your blog, 34
crime
  computer issues with, 7
  cybercrimes, 182–183
  identity theft, 10
criterion
  described, **AC 81**
  entering in queries, AC 85–86
  using comparison operators in, AC 94
  using compound, AC 95–96
  using for field not included in results, AC 88–89
  using in calculating statistics, AC 120–121
  using in queries, AC 81–82
  using numbers in, AC 93
crosstab query
  creating, AC 122–125
  planning, AC 76
Currency data type, AC 9–10
currency symbols, AC 9
custom dictionary, WD 127, **PPT 55**, PPT 57
custom layout, **PPT 92**
custom software: Software that performs functions specific to a business or industry, developed by a user or at a user's request. **96**
customizing
  Microsoft Office 2007, APP 13–26
  Navigation Pane, AC 126
  Quick Access Toolbar, APP 18–25
  Windows Sidebar, WIN 11
  Word window, APP 17–18
cutting, **WD 119**
cyberbullying, 69
cybercrime: Online or Internet-based illegal acts. **182**
cyberextortionist: Someone who uses e-mail as a vehicle for extortion. **182**
cyberterrorist: Someone who uses the Internet or network to destroy or damage computers for political reasons. **183**

D

data: Collection of unprocessed items, which can include text, numbers, images, audio, and video. **4**
  centering in cells, EX 113–114
data entry, Access capabilities for, AC 2
data type, **AC 9**
  assigning, AC 24–26
  determining, AC 5
database: Collection of data organized in a manner that allows access, retrieval, and use of that data. **104, AC 2**
  changing data, AC 34
  changing properties, AC 60–61
  creating, AC 13–17
  creating tables, AC 23–34, AC 44–45
  designing, AC 5–12

database (*continued*)
 opening, AC 77
 opening from Access, AC 37–38
 query, AC 74
Database Design Language (DBDL), AC 8
database properties, **AC 60**
database software: Application software used to create, access, and manage a database; add, change, and delete data in the database; sort and retrieve data from the database; and create forms and reports using the data in the database. **104**
 popular (fig.), 100
datasheet, **AC 30**
Datasheet view, **AC 30**, AC 57, AC 82
dates
 date formats, WD 84, EX 88
 sorting in queries, AC 98–99
DBDL (Database Design Language), AC 8
debugging, **EX 135**
decreasing font size, PPT 25–26
decrypt: Process of deciphering encrypted data into a readable form. **195**
defining fields in tables, AC 24–26
definition updates, **IE 7**
defragmenting: Reorganizing a disk so that the files are stored in contiguous sectors, thus speeding up disk access and the performance of the entire computer. **152**
deleting
 bullets from slides, PPT 32
 desktop icons, WIN 25
 fields, AC 26
 files, folders by right-clicking, WIN 56–57
 files accidentally, recovering, 150
 placeholders, PPT 104, PPT 121
 records, AC 27–29, AC 34
 text from documents, WD 58–59
 text from placeholders, PPT 42–43
 text from presentations, PPT 58
 WordArt, PPT 111
demoting (text), **PPT 34**
 denial of service attack: Assault on a computer or network whose purpose is to disrupt computer access to an Internet service such as the Web or e-mail. *See also* **DoS attack**. **187**

Department of Homeland Security, 208
design grid
 adding fields to, AC 85
 clearing, AC 98
Design view, AC 31, AC 80, AC 83–85
designing
 databases, AC 5–12
 queries, AC 76
desktop: On-screen work area that has a graphical user interface. **98**
 adding icons to, WIN 16–17
 deleting icons from, WIN 25
 foreground, background programs on, 140
 opening window using icons, WIN 18
desktop computer: Computer designed so the system unit, input devices, output devices, and any other devices fit entirely on or under a desk or table. **16**, 20, **98**
 buyer's guide to, 218–222
desktop publishing (DTP) software: Application software used by professional designers to create sophisticated documents that can contain text, graphics, and many colors. **109**
 popular (fig.), 108, 111
destination area, **EX 27**
destination drive, **WIN 52**
destination folder, **WIN 52**
destination object, **INT 13**
developer: Person who writes and modifies computer programs. Also called a programmer. **13**
devices, configuring, 142
DeWolfe, Chris, 29
dialog box, **WIN 25**, **EX 11**
Dialog Box Launcher, **WD 9**, **PPT 11**, **EX 11**, **AC 20**
dial-up access: Internet access that takes place when the modem in your computer connects to the Internet via a standard telephone line that transmits data and information using an analog (continuous wave pattern) signal. **46**, 221
dictionary
 custom, PPT 55, PPT 57
 viewing or modifying entries in, WD 127
digital camera: Mobile device that allows users to take pictures and

stores the photographed images digitally, instead of on traditional film. **18**, 20
 buyer's guide to, 227–228
digital certificate: A notice that guarantees a user or a Web site is legitimate. **195**
digital communications (feature), 167–180
digital forensics: The discovery, collection, and analysis of evidence found on computers and networks. **192**
digital formats, video, 130
digital home products in our lives, 42
digital literacy: Having a current knowledge and understanding of computers and their uses. *See also* **computer literacy**. **3**
digital pen operations, 223
digital rights management: Strategy designed to prevent illegal distribution of movies, music, and other digital content. **201**
digital signature: Encrypted code that a person, Web site, or organization attaches to an electronic message to verify the identity of the message sender. **195**
digital video capture device, 219
digital voice communications, personal and business perspectives, 172–173
disabling content, AC 38
disc burning software: Utility program that writes text, graphics, audio, and video files to a recordable or rewritable CD, DVD, or Blu-ray Disc. **157**
Discovering Computers and Microsoft Office 2007 Online Companion, 34–35
disk cleanup: Utility that searches for and removes unnecessary files. **152**
disk defragmenter: Utility that reorganizes the files and unused space on a computer's hard disk so that the operating system accesses data more quickly and programs run faster. **152**
display area (IE), **IE 12**
displaying
 corrections of flagged text, WD 16

folders, WIN 34–36
folders' contents, WIN 54
formatting marks in text, WD 13, WD 77
formulas in worksheets, EX 136
History List, IE 27–30
home page, IE 32
Mini toolbar, PPT 23
Paste Options menu, WD 122
slides out of order, PPT 46–47
Start menu (Vista), WIN 13
Web pages from Favorites Center, IE 41
distance learning: Delivery of education at one location while the learning takes place at other locations. **119**
distributing videos, 134
DivX video file formats, 131
.doc files, WD 18
Document Information Panel, **WD 51, PPT 44, EX 55**
document management software: Application software that provides a means for sharing, distributing, and searching through documents by converting them into a format that can be viewed by any user. **107**
  popular (fig.), 100
document properties, **WD 50**, WD 51, **PPT 43, EX 54**
  changing, WD 130, PPT 124
  changing, saving, WD 50–57
  printing, WD 130–131
document theme, **PPT 8**, PPT 16–17
document window, **WD 6**
documents
  adding hyperlinks to Word, INT 6
  changing settings, WD 77–83
  closing, WD 59–60
  converting from earlier versions of PowerPoint, PPT 43
  creating WordPad, WIN 44–51
  developing word processing, 102
  embedding chart into Word, INT 13–16
  enhancing pages, WD 48–50
  formatting paragraphs, characters, WD 22–40
  inserting, deleting text from, WD 58–59
  inserting pictures in, WD 41–42
  inserting tables into Word, INT 8
  MLA documentation style, WD 76–77

  opening, WD 55–57
  printing, WD 53–54
  saving, WD 18–21, WD 53
  saving as Web pages, INT 19
  sharing, WD 51
  zooming, WD 45–46
.docx files, WD 18
Dolby, Ray, 38
Dolby Laboratories, 38
dollar values
  entering, EX 23, AC 32
  fixed and floating dollar sign, EX 114–115
  floating dollar sign, EX 117
domain highlighting, **IE 14**
domain name: Text version of an IP address. **48, WIN 28, IE 8**
do-not-track list, 53
DoS attack: Assault on a computer or network whose purpose is to disrupt computer access to an Internet service such as the Web or e-mail. *See also* **denial of service attack. 187**
double-click, **WIN 10**
double-space, **WD 78**
down scroll arrow, **WIN 15**
downloading: Process of a computer receiving information, such as a Web page, from a server on the Internet. **50, WIN 40**
  hierarchy of folders, WIN 40–41
  music from iTunes, 60
  sidebar gadgets, WIN 11
drag, **WIN 15**, WD 30
  vs. right-drag, WIN 25
  sizing and moving windows, WIN 22–23
  sizing windows, WIN 23
drag and drop, **PPT 41**
drag-and-drop editing, **WD 119**, WD 121, WD 122
driver: Small program that tells an operating system how to communicate with a specific device. **142**
drives, network, **WIN 37**
driving directions, searching for, 71–72
DRM (digital rights management), 201
DSL: Type of digital technology that provides high-speed Internet connections using regular copper telephone lines. **45**
duplicates, omitting from query results, AC 100–101

duplicating
  slides, PPT 40–41
  See also copying

E

Ease of access button (Vista), **WIN 8**
eBay, 71, 194
e-commerce: Short for electronic commerce; a business transaction that occurs over an electronic network such as the Internet. 23, **62**
EcoSearch, 78
Edison power usage management tool, 216
edit: To make changes to the existing content of a document. **102**
  bibliographical sources, WD 104
  citations, WD 94–99, WD 105
  drag-and-drop editing, **WD 119**
  embedded objects, INT 18
  in-cell editing, EX 64
  sources, citations, WD 109–110
  video, 132
Edit mode, **EX 63**
editions of Windows 7, 146
education
  computer applications in, 24–25
  computer usage in, 158
  learning Web sites, 90
  plagiarism, 36
  trustworthiness of wikis, 56
  Web sites, 57
  word processing, and student laziness, 101
educational software: Application software that teaches a particular skill. **115**
e-learning: Short for electronic learning; delivery of education via some electronic method such as the Internet, networks, or CDs/DVDs. **119**, 158
electronic profiles, 203
electronic storefront: Online business a customer visits that contains product descriptions, graphics, and a shopping cart. **62–63**
e-mail, 10, 118
  accounts, setting up, EX 142
  attaching files to messages, 76
  personal and business perspectives, 168–169
  sending messages, 64
  and spam, 204
  and viruses, 65, 185

e-mail address: Combination of a user name and a domain name that identifies a user so he or she can receive Internet e-mail. **64**

e-mail filtering: Service that blocks e-mail messages from designated sources. **205**

e-mail program: Software used to create, send, receive, forward, store, print, and delete e-mail messages. **63**–**64**

e-mailing workbooks from within Excel, EX 142–143

embedded chart, **EX 49**

embedded computer: Special-purpose computer that functions as a component in a larger product. 15, **19**–20
 improving quality of life, 24

Embedded Linux, 149

embedded operating system: The operating system that resides on a ROM chip inside most PDAs and small devices. 145, **149**

emoticons: Symbols used on the Internet to express emotion. **69**

employee monitoring: The use of computers to observe, record, and review an employee's use of a computer, including communications such as e-mail messages, keyboard activity (used to measure productivity), and Web sites visited. **207**

employment, job-finding Web sites, 93

encryption: Process of converting readable data into unreadable characters to prevent unauthorized access. 144, **195**

encryption algorithm: Set of steps that can convert readable plaintext into unreadable ciphertext. **195**

encryption key: Set of characters that the originator of the encrypted data uses to encrypt the plaintext and the recipient of the data uses to decrypt the ciphertext. **195**

endnote, **WD 99**, WD 100, WD 106

end-user license agreement (EULA), 194

ENERGY STAR program: Program developed by the United States Department of Energy (DOE) and the United States Environmental Protection Agency (EPA) to help reduce the amount of electricity used by computers and related devices. **201**

Enhanced Screen Tip, **WD 9**, **PPT 10**, **EX 11**, **AC 20**

Enter, **EX 9**

Enter box, **EX 17**

ENTER key, moving selection, EX 19

enterprise computing: Term large companies use to refer to the use of a huge network of computers that meets their diverse computing needs. **23**
 software, 100, 107

enterprise user: Computer user working for a business that has hundreds or thousands of employees or customers that work in or do business with offices across a region, the country, or the world. **23**

entertainment, computer usage in, 70

entertainment software: Application software, such as interactive games, videos, and other programs designed to support a hobby or provide amusement and enjoyment. **116**

entertainment Web sites, 57, 80

environment Web sites, 85

Environmental Defense Fund Web site, 85

environmental impact of computers, 7

EPA AirData Web sites, 85

equal sign (=)
 in formulas, EX 91
 in functions, EX 99

ergonomics, 199

error checking button, AC 48

errors
 contextual spelling, WD 126
 correcting in documents, WD 57–59
 correcting in presentations, PPT 58
 correcting on worksheets, EX 63–67
 spell-checking presentations, PPT 55–58

Ethical Hacker Network, 128

ethics
 banning anonymous comments, 69
 computer, 199–202

 government allowing do-not-track list, 53
 government taxing media downloads, 157
 of online mapping services, 117
 privacy of text messages, 207
 recycling of electronics, 14
 trustworthiness of wikis, 56
 word processing, and student laziness, 101

Euro symbol (€), AC 9

e-waste, 14

Excel 2007
 e-mailing workbooks from within, EX 142–143
 embedding chart into Word documents, INT 13–16
 font type, style, size, color, EX 34–46
 formatting worksheets, EX 33–46
 numeric limitations, EX 22
 opening workbook from, EX 60–61
 overview of, EX 2–6
 quitting, EX 58, EX 69
 selecting cell (table), EX 48
 starting, EX 5–6
 workbook. *See* **workbook**
 worksheet. *See* **worksheet**

Excel Help, EX 7, **EX 67**–68

Excel Options button, Office Button menu, EX 58

execute: Process of a computer carrying out the instructions in a program. **12**

exiting
 PowerPoint, PPT 53
 See also quitting

expanding drives, WIN 42

expanding folder windows, WIN 23

exporting favorite Web sites, IE 31

Expression Builder, using, AC 113

external hard disk, 5, 6, 219

eyestrain, easing, 198

F

face recognition systems, 191

FaceBook, 36, 71

FALSE (calculating sums), EX 24

FAQ: List that helps a user find answers to commonly asked questions. **11**

favorite: Saved Web address that you access by clicking its name in a list. *See also* **bookmark**. **51**, **IE 30**
 importing, exporting, IE 31

Favorite Links list, **WIN 19, EX 31**
Favorites bar, **IE 13**, IE 31
Favorites Center
 adding Web pages to, IE 30–31
 displaying, removing Web pages using, IE 33–34
FBI's National Crime Information Center (NCIC), 25
federal privacy laws, 206
Fiber to the Premises (FTTP): Technology that uses fiber-optic cable to provide high-speed Internet access to home and business users. **45**
field, **AC 4**
 adding to design grid, AC 85
 calculated, **AC 113**–116
 defining, AC 24–26
 naming, AC 8
field properties, modifying, AC 46–48
file: Named collection of stored data, instructions, or information. **98**–99, **EX 29, AC 13**
 attaching to e-mail messages, 76
 back up, 196–197
 backing up on offsite Internet server, 214–215
 burning to optical disc, 164
 compressing, zipping, 126–127
 copying, WIN 52–54
 deleting, WIN 56–57
 displaying, organizing, WIN 35–36
 importing, PPT 97–98
 naming, WD 20, PPT 27, AC 13, AC 15
 opening database, AC 37–38
 recovering erased, 150
 renaming, WIN 55
 saving in application software, 126
file compression utility: Utility program that shrinks the size of a file(s), so the file takes up less storage space than the original file. **156**
file formats
 .docx, .doc, WD 18
 that Excel can save in, EX 29
 graphic, 59
 importable to PowerPoint, PPT 97–98
 PDF, 107
 .ppt, PPT 26
 .pptx, PPT 29
 video, 130, 131–132

file management, 143, 151, **WIN 52**–58
file manager: Utility that performs functions related to file and disk management. **151**
file name, **AC 13**, AC 15, **EX 29**, EX 31
file property, PPT 27
file specification, **WIN 29, IE 9**
FileMakerRecovery, 150
fill effects, **PPT 89**
fill handle
 copying formulas using, EX 95–96
 described, **EX 27**
filters, Internet, 155–156
finance
 computer applications in, 25
 Web sites, 86
Find & Select button, EX 48
Find command, PPT 92
finding
 and replacing text, WD 123–126
 specific slides, PPT 92
fingerprint readers, 191, 219, 225
firewall: Hardware and/or software that protects a network's resources from intrusion by users on another network such as the Internet. 186, **188–189**
FireWire port, 130
fireworks software, 108
First Line Indent marker, **WD 88**–89
first-line indent, **WD 88**
Fit to (printing) option, EX 135–137
fixed dollar sign, **EX 114**, EX 115
fixed wireless: High-speed Internet connection that uses a dish-shaped antenna on a house or business to communicate with a tower location via radio signals. **45**
Flash Player, 61
floating dollar sign, **EX 114**, EX 117
flyers, creating, WD 2–4
folder: Specific named location on a storage medium that contains related documents. **151, WD 19, EX 30, AC 15**
 closing expanded, deleting, WIN 57
 displaying contents of, WIN 54
 naming, WIN 38–40
 saving WordPad documents in new, WIN 47–51
 verifying contents of, WIN 52

 working with, organizing, WIN 34–36
folder windows, **WIN 18**
font: Name assigned to a specific design of characters. **102, WD 23, PPT 21**
 changing, WD 29, PPT 109
 changing color, PPT 110–111
 changing theme, WD 39–40
 modifying in cells, EX 34–46
 sans serif, PPT 86
 serif, PPT 108
font color, **EX 34**
Font Color palette, EX 39–40
Font gallery, PPT 109
font set, **WD 37**
font size: Size of the characters in a particular font. **102, WD 23**, WD 28, **EX 34**,
 decreasing, PPT 25–26
 increasing, PPT 24
font style: Font design, such as bold, italic, and underline, that can add emphasis to a font. **102, EX 34**
font type, **EX 34**, EX 36–37
Food Network Web site, 90
footer, **WD 79**, WD 81
footnote, **WD 99**–100, WD 106
Footnote Text style, WD 102–104
foreground, background programs, 140
form, Access capabilities for, AC 2
Form view, **AC 57**
format: To change a document's appearance. **102, PPT 21, EX 33**
 date, WD 84
 file. *See* file formats
 hierarchical, WIN 36
 style, WD 38
Format Cells dialog box, EX 116–117
Format Painter, **PPT 106**, PPT 111–113
formatting
 Auto Fill options, EX 28
 characters in presentations, PPT 21–26
 column titles and rows, EX 42–43
 conditional formatting, EX 118–122
 finding, WD 124
 numbers in worksheet, EX 44–45
 numbers using Ribbon, EX 114–118
 shapes, PPT 115–120

formatting (*continued*)
 using Format Painter, PPT 106
 using Quick Styles, PPT 106–108
 Web page, INT 22–23
 worksheets, EX 33–46, EX 88, EX 107–114
formatting mark
 described, **WD 14**
 hiding, showing in text, WD 13
formatting marks in text, showing or hiding, WD 77
forms
 creating split, AC 57–59
 saving, AC 57–58
formula, **EX 90**
 copying using fill handle, EX 95–96
 displaying in worksheets, EX 136
 entering in worksheets, EX 90–96
 using AVERAGE, MAX, MIN functions, EX 98–106
 verifying using Range Finder, EX 106
formula bar, **EX 12**
formulas version, **EX 135**
Forward button, **IE 13**, IE 22–25
forward slashes (//) in Web addresses, IE 8
frame rate correction tools, 132
FreeUndelete, 150
freeware: Copyrighted software provided at no cost to a user by an individual or a company that retains all rights to the software. **97**
Fry's Web site, 88
FTP: Internet standard that permits file uploading and downloading with other computers on the Internet. **68**, 118
full backup, 197
Full Screen command, IE 12
fun Web sites, 80
function, **EX 82**, **EX 99**
functions
 operating system (OS), 137–145
 spreadsheet software, 103
 using AVERAGE, MAX, MIN, EX 98–106
 utility program, 150
Functions Arguments dialog box, EX 101

G

gadget
 adding to Windows Sidebar, WIN 10–12
 described, **WIN 9**

Gadget Gallery, **WIN 10**
gallery, **WD 8**, **PPT 9**, **EX 10**, **AC 20**
game console: Mobile computing device designed for single-player or multiplayer video games. 15, **18**
gaming, and digital products in our lives, 41
GarageBand software, 40
Gates, Bill, 29
geocaching, 80
Geschke, Charles, 121
ghosting, 153
GIF format, 59
glaucoma, contact lens monitors, 143
Gmail, 64
Go to button, WIN 30
Go To list, **IE 21**
Goggle company profile, 71
good practices, digital communications, 167–180
Google Android, 149
Google Checkout, 63
Google Docs, 57, 117, 158
Google Earth, 117
Google Health, 92
Google Maps, 84
Google search engine, 54, 81
government
 computer applications in, 25
 ethics of allowing do-not-track list, 53
 ethics of taxing media downloads, 157
 Web sites, 87
grammar-checking, WD 13, WD 16–17, WD 125–126
graphic: Digital representation of nontext information such as a drawing, chart, or photo. *See also* **graphical image**. **58**
graphical user interface (GUI): Type of user interface that allows a user to interact with software using text, graphics, and visual images, such as icons. **11**, **139**, **WIN 3**
graphics
 resizing, WD 46
 See also images
graphics software
 examples of, 96
 popular (fig.), 108
grayscale, displaying presentations in, PPT 59–61
greater than symbol (>) in file names, WD 20

green computing: Computer usage that reduces the electricity and environmental waste involved in using a computer. **7**, 128, 166, **201**, 216
green wavy underlined text, WD 16
gridlines, **EX 8**, **INT 9**
group (on Ribbon), **EX 9**
grouping, AC 52, **AC 121–122**
GUI. *See* **graphical user interface (GUI)**

H

hacker: Someone who accesses a computer or network illegally. **182**
hand geometry systems, 191
handheld computer: Computer small enough to fit in one hand. *See also* **Ultra-Mobile PC (UMPC)**. **17**
handheld game consoles, 41
handouts, printing presentations as, PPT 126–130
Hanging Indent marker, **WD 116**
hanging indents, **WD 116**
hard copy, **IE 47**, **WD 53**, **PPT 61**, **EX 57**
hard disk, 6, 219
hard page break, **WD 112**
hardware: Electric, electronic, and mechanical components contained in a computer. **4**
 computer components, considerations, 219–220
 Windows Vista configurations, WIN 6
hardware theft: The act of stealing computer equipment. **193**
hardware vandalism: The act of defacing or destroying computer equipment. **193**
header
 described, **WD 79**
 switching to, WD 80, WD 83
headings, EX 43
head-mounted display (HMD), 39
health
 computer issues with, 7
 concerns of computer use, 198–199
 Web sites, 92
health care, computer applications in, 25–26
healthfinder.gov Web site, 92
help
 Excel Help, EX 7, EX 67–68

PowerPoint Help, PPT 62
Word Help, using, WD 60–61, APP 5–11
hibernate: Operating system function that saves any open documents and programs to a hard disk before removing power from the computer. **138**
hiding
 columns, EX 122
 formatting marks in text, WD 14
 Mini toolbar, PPT 11
 rows, EX 126, EX 127
hiding cells, **EX 122**
hierarchical format, **WIN 36**
high-definition (HD) digital video recorders (DVRs), 39
History List, IE 26–30
hits, search engine, 55
home design/landscaping software: Application software that assists users with the design, remodeling, or improvement of a home, deck, or landscape. 111, **115**
home page: First page that a Web site displays. **50, WIN 28, IE 10**
 displaying, IE 32
Home tab, Ribbon, **WD 7, PPT 9, EX 10, AC 19**
home user: User who spends time on a computer at home. **20**
 computer usage by, 20–21
 Internet workings with cable modem (fig.), 47
home/personal/educational software, 96
homophones, misuse of, WD 126
horizontal ruler, **WD 87**
horizontal scroll bar, **PPT 8, AC 19**
hot spots: Public locations, such as airports, hotels, schools, and coffee shops, that provide Wi-Fi Internet connections to users with mobile computers or devices. **46**
HowStuffWorks Web site, 90
HTML, IE 9–10, **INT 23**
http (Hypertext Transfer Protocol), 51
HTTPS, IE 8
https vs. http, 195
hyperlink: Built-in connection to another related Web page or part of a Web page. *See also* **link**. **52, IE 5, INT 6**
 adding text for, INT 24–25
 adding to reports, INT 32–35
 adding to Word documents, INT 6
 creating to PowerPoint Web pages, INT 11–13
 inserting text for, INT 11
 using in PowerPoint presentations, INT 24–27
 verifying, INT 39
 See also **link**
hypermedia, **IE 5**
Hypertext Markup Language (HTML), **IE 9**–10
Hypertext Transfer Protocol (HTTP), **WIN 28, IE 8**

I

IBackup.com, 214–215
icon: Small image displayed on a computer screen that represents a program, a document, or some other object. **98, WIN 16**
 deleting desktop, WIN 25
 Internet Explorer, IE 10
 opening window using desktop, WIN 18
identifying and removing redundancy, AC 5–6, AC 10–12
identity theft, 10, 192
IE, **IE 10**
iLife software suite, 40
image editing software: Application software that provides the capabilities of paint software and also includes the capability to enhance and modify existing images and pictures. **109**
 popular (fig.), 108, 111
image viewer: Utility program that allows users to display, copy, and print the contents of a graphics file. **151**
images
 resizing, INT 19
 See also pictures
importing
 clips, PPT 95
 external data from Web sources using Web queries, EX 137–140
 favorite Web sites, IE 31
 files to PowerPoint, PPT 97–98
inactive window (WordPad), **IE 40**
in-cell editing, EX 64–65
Increase Decimal button, EX 116
increasing
 Excel window viewing area, EX 9
 font size, PPT 24, EX 38–39
indenting
 hanging indents, WD 116
 paragraphs, WD 87–89
information: Processed data that conveys meaning and is useful to people. **4**
 accuracy, 200–201
 literacy, 79
information privacy: Right of individuals and companies to deny or restrict the collection and use of information about them. **202**
 types and issues, 202–207
information processing cycle: Series of input, process, output, and storage activities performed by a computer. **4**
information theft: Computer security risk that occurs when someone steals personal or confidential information. **195**
informational Web sites, 56
ink, conserving toner and, WD 53, WD 130
inner joins, AC 104
InPrivate Browsing, **IE 27**
input device: Any hardware component that allows users to enter data and instructions into a computer. **4**
 types of, 5
in-Ribbon, **EX 10**
Insert Hyperlink feature, **INT 11**
insert mode, **WD 58**
Insert mode, **EX 64**
Insert tab, EX 51
inserting
 blank lines, WD 15
 citations, WD 96
 clip art, photos into slides, PPT 95–97
 fields to tables, AC 26
 footnote reference mark, WD 100
 hyperlinks into PowerPoint presentations, INT 25
 pictures in documents, WD 41–42
 synonyms, WD 124–125
 text for hyperlinks, INT 11
 text into existing documents, WD 58
 See also adding

insertion point, **WD 6**, **EX 17**, **AC 18**
installing: Process of setting up software to work with the computer, printer, and other hardware components. **12**–13
instant message: Real-time Internet communication where you exchange messages with other connected users. **17**
instant messaging (IM): Real-time Internet communications service that notifies a user when one or more people are online and then allows the user to exchange messages or files or join a private chat room with those people. 10, **66**, 118
  personal and business perspectives, 170–171
  using, 66–67
Instant Search box, WIN 31–32, **IE 15**
integration, **INT 2**
  adding hyperlinks to Word documents, INT 6–10
  copying objects among programs, INT 16
  creating hyperlink to PowerPoint Web pages, INT 11–13
  creating PowerPoint presentation Web page, INT 23–27
  creating Web pages from Access Report, INT 28–37
  embedding Excel chart into Word documents, INT 13–16
  overview of, INT 2–6
  testing Web sites, INT 38–39
  using hyperlinks in PowerPoint, INT 27–28
  viewing Word document, saving as Web page, INT 19–23
intellectual property rights: Rights to which creators are entitled for their work. **201**
Inter@active Pager, 159
Internet: Worldwide collection of networks that connects millions of businesses, government agencies, educational institutions, and individuals. **8**, **44**, **IE 3**
  attacks, 184–189
  connecting to, access providers, 45–46
  establishing connections, 142–143

  filters, 155–156
  making phone calls, 68
  netiquette, 69
  overview of, 8–10, 44–45
  percentage of U.S. households with, 21
  services, 63–69
  transferring videos to, 130–131
  viruses on, 98
  workings of, 47–49
Internet backbone: Major carriers of network traffic on the Internet. **47**, **IE 4**
Internet Explorer (IE), 49, **IE 10**, **WIN 27–28**
  Help, IE 49–51
  overview of, IE 2–3
  printing Web pages, IE 47–49
  quitting, IE 52
  saving information obtained with, IE 35–47
  starting, IE 11–12
Internet Explorer 8, overview of, IE 10–15
Internet Explorer Help, **IE 49**
Internet Explorer menu icon, **IE 13**
Internet Explorer Window, **IE 12**
  components of, IE 12–14
Internet Protocol address, **IE 8**
Internet-enabled: Technology that allows mobile devices to connect to the Internet wirelessly. **16**
intrusion detection software: Program that automatically analyzes all network traffic, assesses system vulnerabilities, identifies any unauthorized intrusions, and notifies network administrators of suspicious behavior patterns or system breaches. **189**
IP address: A number that uniquely identifies each computer or device connected to the Internet. *See also* **Internet Protocol address**. **48**, **IE 8**
iPhone OS, 149
iPods, 38
iris recognition systems, 191
ISP (Internet service provider): Regional or national Internet access provider. **46**
italicized, **WD 36**
italicizing text, PPT 22
iTunes, 60

J

Java, 61
job-finding Web sites, 93
Jobs, Steve, 29
join, **AC 103**
  changing properties, AC 108–109
  creating reports involving a, AC 109–111
  restricting records in, AC 112
  types of, AC 104
join line, **AC 105**, AC 106
join properties, changing, **AC 108**–109
joining tables, AC 103–112
Joint Photographic Experts Group (JPEG), **IE 37**
joystick, 219
JPEG format, 59

K

Key Tip, **WD 12**, **PPT 15**, **EX 15**, **AC 23**
Key Tip badge, **WD 12**, **PPT 15**, **EX 15**, **AC 23**
keyboard, 219, **WIN 3**, 4–5, **WIN 26**
  entering formulas using, EX 91
  scrolling with, WD 43
  selecting ranges, EX 97
keyboard indicators, **EX 9**
keyboard shortcut, **WIN 26**, **IE 13**
keywords, **WD 50**, **PPT 43**, **AC 60**, **EX 54**

L

landscape orientation, INT 30, **PPT 6**, **EX 129**, **AC 41**
landscaping software, 111, **115**
laptop computer: Portable, personal computer often designed to fit on your lap. *See also* **notebook computer**. **16**
last mile, the, **IE 4**
law enforcement
  brain wave, behavior tracking, 192
  computer applications in, 25
  digital forensics, 192
  identity theft, 192
  privacy laws, 206
Layout gallery, **PPT 92**
layouts, **PPT 6**, **PPT 92**
  changing, PPT 92–95
Lazaridis, Mike, 159
learning Web sites, 90
Left Indent marker, **WD 88**–89

left-aligned, WD 85, **EX 18**, EX 22
left-aligned (text), WD 81
legal software: Application software that assists in the preparation of legal documents and provides legal information to individuals, families, and small businesses. **113**
 popular (fig.), 111
legend, **EX 54**
less than symbol (<) in file names, WD 20
level (paragraph), **PPT 19**
Library of Congress Web site, 87
license agreement: An agreement issued by a software manufacturer that gives the user the right to use the software. **194**
line charts, 104
line spacing, **WD 78**, **PPT 32**
line wraps, **PPT 18**
lines
 formatting, WD 31
 selecting, WD 27
link: Built-in connection to another related Web page or part of a Web page. Short for hyperlink. **52**, **IE 5**
 keeping fresh, INT 24
 opening in new tab, WIN 31–32
 printing Web page, IE 49
 using Help, APP 9
 See also **hyperlink**
LinkedIn, 128
Linux: Popular, multitasking UNIX-type operating system. **148**, 159
lists
 bibliographical, WD 113, WD 117
 bulleted, WD 32
 literature Web sites, 94
live preview, **WD 8**, **PPT 9**, **EX 10**, EX 35, **AC 20**
living digitally (feature), 37–42
log on: To access a computer or network as a user. **144**
logging off computers, WIN 64–65
logging on
 described, **WIN 8–9**
 to Vista, WIN 7–8
Louvre Museum Web site, 94
LucidTouch sensors, 115

M

Mac OS X: Multitasking operating system that is the latest version of the Macintosh operating system. **147**

Macintosh operating system: Operating system for Apple's Macintosh computer. **147**
macro viruses, 186
magnifying
 reports, AC 42–43
 See also zooming
mailing list: Group of e-mail names and addresses given a single name. Also called an e-mail list or a distribution list. **66**
mainframe: Large, expensive, powerful computer that can handle hundreds or thousands of connected users simultaneously, storing tremendous amounts of data, instructions, and information. 15, **19**
major key, **AC 97**, AC 101–102
malware: Short for malicious software; programs that act without a user's knowledge and deliberately alter a computer's operations. **98**, **184**
 preventing, 187
manual page break, **WD 112**
manufacturing, computer applications in, 27
mapping software, 111, 115
maps Web sites, 84
margins of documents, WD 50
marketing Web sites, 56
markup language, **IE 10**
MAX function, **EX 101**–102, EX 104–105
Maximize button, **IE 13**, **WIN 20**
maximizing windows, WIN 20, WD 5, PPT 6, EX 7
MBDF virus, 209
McAfee company profile, 209
media
 removable, WIN 37–38
 storage, **6**
media player: Program that allows you to view images and animation, listen to audio, and watch video files on your computer. **156**
media player. *See* **portable media player**
media sharing Web site: Specific type of online social network that enables members to share media such as photos, music, and videos. **57**, 83, 134, 178–179

medicine
 camera pills, 26
 contact lenses monitoring glaucoma, 143
 Wii's use in, 18
memory: Electronic components in a computer that store instructions waiting to be executed and data needed by those instructions. **6**
 management, 137
memory card, 5, 6
memory management: Operating system activity that optimizes the use of random access memory (RAM). **141**
menu: Item on the computer screen that contains a list of commands from which a user can make selections. **98**, **WD 11**, **PPT 14**, **EX 14**, **AC 22**
 described, **WIN 13**
 shortcut. *See* shortcut menu
menu name, **IE 13**
Merge & Center button, EX 40–41
merging cells, **EX 40–41**
message board: Popular Web-based type of discussion group that does not require a newsreader. **69**, 118
metadata, **WD 50**, **PPT 43**, **EX 54**, **AC 60**
microblog: Blog that allows users to publish short messages, usually between 100 and 200 characters, for others to read. **10**, **56**
microphone, 4–5, 219
Microsoft, 29
 company profile, 121
 LucidTouch sensors, 115
 video file formats, 131
 See also specific products
Microsoft Clip Organizer, **PPT 95**
Microsoft Office 2007
 customizing, APP 13–26
 project planning guidelines, APP 1–2
 See also Office 2007
Microsoft Office Access 2007, **AC 2**
 overview of, AC 2–6
 See also Access 2007
Microsoft Office Excel 2007, **EX 2**
 See also Excel 2007
Microsoft Office Help
 overview of, APP 3–4
 Word Help, using, APP 5–11

Microsoft Office PowerPoint 2007
  described, **PPT 2**
  See also PowerPoint 2007
Microsoft Office Word 2007, **WD 2**
  See also Word 2007
Microsoft Windows, **WIN 2**
Microsoft Windows Internet
  Explorer 8, **IE 10**
Microsoft Windows Vista
  described, **WIN 2**
  See also Windows Vista
Microsoft Xbox 360, 18, 41
MIN function, **EX 102**–105
Mini toolbar, **WD 9**–10, WD 28,
  PPT 11, PPT 23, **EX 12**, **AC 21**
Minimize button, **IE 13**
minimizing
  Ribbon, WD 7, PPT 9, EX 10,
    AC 19
  windows, WIN 19
minor key, **AC 97**, AC 101–102
minus sign (−), subtraction operator,
    EX 94
MLA documentation style
  bibliographical lists, WD 113
  citations, WD 94, WD 105
  footnotes, WD 102
  research papers, WD 76–77
  works cited page, WD 111
mobile computer: Personal computer that a user can carry from place to place. 15, **16**, WIN 4
mobile device: Computing device small enough for a user to hold in his or her hand. 15, **16**
  buyer's guide to, 217–228
  types of, 17
mobile users: Users who work on a computer while away from a main office, home office, or school. **22**
  Web sites used by, 47
Mode indicators, **EX 9**
modem, 5, 6, 46, 219
Modern Language Association of
    America (MLA)
  See also MLA documentation style
  style, **WD 74**, WD 76–77
monitor, 5, 219, **WIN 3**
  changing screen resolution, APP
    13–17
monitoring
  computer performance, 143
  customer behavior, conversations,
    202
  glaucoma with contact lenses, 143

Morris Worm, 209
motherboard, 6
mouse, **WIN 3**, 4–5, 219
  dragging, WD 30
  item-selection techniques (table),
    WD 120
  operations, WIN 26, 223
  scrolling with, WD 43
mouse pointer, **WD 7**, WD 33–34,
  PPT 7, **EX 8**, **AC 18**
movie-making software, 114
moving
  clips, PPT 105
  text, WD 119–121
  windows, WIN 22
Mozilla Firefox, **WIN 27**
MP3: Format that reduces an audio file to about one-tenth of its original size, while preserving much of the original quality of the sound. **60**
MP4: Current version of a popular video compression standard. **61**
MSN Money Web site, 86
multi-level bulleted list slide,
  PPT 33
multimedia: Any application that combines text with graphics, animation, audio, video, and/or virtual reality. **58**
  and viruses, 185
multimedia authoring software:
  Software that allows users to combine text, graphics, audio, video, and animation in an interactive application and that often is used for computer-based training and Web-based presentations. **110**
  popular (fig.), 108
multimedia software
  examples of, 96
  popular (fig.), 108
multiprocessing: In reference to operating systems, supports two or more processors running programs at the same time. **141**
multiuser: In reference to operating systems, enables two or more users to run programs simultaneously. **141**
music
  downloading from iTunes, 60
  downloading services, 38
  industry, and digital products, 38
  Web sites, 88

My Collections, **PPT 95**
MySpace, 29, 78, 159

N

Name box, **EX 12**, EX 47
naming
  files, **WD 20**, PPT 27, AC 13,
    AC 15
  folders, WIN 38–40
  tables and fields, AC 8
  worksheets, EX 140–141
NASA's Web site, 91
navigation, scroll arrows, scroll box,
    WIN 15–16
navigation buttons, **IE 13**, IE 22–25
Navigation buttons, **AC 38–39**
Navigation Pane, AC 18, AC 126
Navigation pane (Vista), **WIN 19**
Net: Worldwide collection of networks that links millions of businesses, government agencies, educational institutions, and individuals. *See also* **Internet**. **44**
Net Nanny, 207
netbook: Type of notebook computer that is smaller, lighter, and often not as powerful as a traditional notebook computer. **16**, 224
netiquette: Short for Internet etiquette, the code of acceptable behaviors users should follow while on the Internet. **69**
network: Collection of computers and devices connected together, often wirelessly, via communications devices and transmission media, allowing computers to share resources. **8**, **IE 3**, **WIN 37**
  controlling, 143–144
  overview of, 8–10
network drive, **WIN 37–38**
New Scientist Web site, 91
news Web sites, 55, 89
newsgroup: Online area in which users have written discussions about a particular subject. **68**, 118
Nintendo Wii, 18, 41
No Fly List, 208
nonprinting character, **WD 14**,
  WD 25
Normal style, **WD 23**
Normal view, **PPT 8**, PPT 90–91
normal view, **EX 9**, **EX 129**
Norton AntiVirus, 209
Norton Internet Security, 209

Norton SystemWorks, 157
note reference mark, **WD 99**–100
note taking software: Application software that enables users to enter typed text, handwritten comments, drawings, or sketches anywhere on a page. **106**
  popular (fig.), 100
note text, **WD 99**
notebook computer: Portable, personal computer often designed to fit on your lap. *See also* **laptop computer**. **16**
  buyer's guide to, 222–225
  preventing theft, vandalism, 193
notes in MLA style, WD 76–77
Notes Page view, **PPT 8**
Notes pane, **PPT 8**
number, **EX 22**
  calculating sums, EX 24–29
  entering as text, EX 24
  entering in cells, EX 22–24
  entering in ranges, EX 90
  formatting, using Ribbon, EX 114–118
  formatting in worksheets, EX 44–45
  using in criterion, AC 93
Number data type, AC 9–10

O

Object Linking and Embedding (OLE), **INT 13**
object tabs, **AC 18**
objects
  copy methods, INT 16
  embedding, INT 13–16
  resizing embedded, INT 17–18
Office 2007
  copying objects among programs, INT 16
  integrating programs. *See* integration
  See also specific program
Office Button, **WD 11**, **EX 14**, **PPT 14**–15, **AC 22**
Office Collections, **PPT 95**
Office theme, **PPT 16**
offsite backup, 196
one-to-many relationship, **AC 9**
online: Describes the state of a computer when it is connected to a network. **8**
online auction: E-commerce method that allows consumers to bid on an item being sold by someone else. **63**
  and pirated software, 194
online banking: Online connection to a bank's computer to access account balances, pay bills, and copy monthly transactions to a user's computer. **25, 112**
Online Companion to Discovering Computers and Microsoft Office 2007, 34–35
online Help: Electronic equivalent of a user manual that usually is integrated in a program. **119**
online investing: Use of a computer to buy and sell stocks and bonds online, without using a broker. **25**
online mapping services, 117
online service provider (OSP): Company that provides internet access as well as many members-only features. **46**
online social network: Web site that encourages members in its online community to share their interests, ideas, stories, photos, music, and videos with other registered users. *See also* **Social networking Web site**. **10, 57**
  personal and business perspectives, 176–177
  Web sites, 83
open source operating system, 148
open source software: Software provided for use, modification, and redistribution. **97**
opening
  database from Access, AC 37–38
  databases, AC 77
  documents, WD 55–57
  link in new tab, WIN 31–32
  windows using desktop icons, WIN 18
  workbooks, EX 60–61
operating system: Set of programs that coordinates all the activities among computer hardware devices. **11**
operating system (OS): Set of programs that work together to coordinate all the activities among computer hardware resources. **137, WIN 2**
  closed source vs. open source, 148
  functions, 137–145
  most popular (fig.), 145
  types of, 145–149
operators
  comparison, AC 94
  conditional formatting (table), EX 121
optical discs, 6, 164
optical disc burning software, 40
optical disc creation software, 134
optical disc drives, 5, 219, 223
Options buttons, EX 96–97
OR criterion, **AC 95**–96
order of operations, **EX 92**
organizations, and domain name extensions (table), WIN 29
organizing files and folders, WIN 36
outer joins, AC 104
outlines, viewing Web pages on, **INT 27**
outline pane, INT 27
Outline tab, **PPT 8**
outlines, printing presentations as, PPT 126–130
Outlook e-mail program, 64
output device: Any hardware component that conveys information to one or more people. **5**
  types of, 5
Overtype mode, **EX 64**

P

packed software: Mass-produced, copyrighted retail software that meets the needs of a wide variety of users, not just a single user or company. **96**
Page, Larry, 71
page breaks, WD 107–108, WD 112
Page Layout View, **EX 129**–130
page numbers, formatting, WD 79–82
Page Setup dialog box, EX 133
pages
  adding borders, WD 48–49
  adjusting spacing, WD 78–79
  works cited, WD 111–117
paint software: Application software that allows users to draw pictures, shapes, and other graphical images with various onscreen tools. **109**
  popular (fig.), 108, 111
Palm OS, 149
paragraph formatting, **WD 22**

paragraph mark (¶), WD 14, WD 22
paragraph spacing, **WD 78**
paragraphs, **PPT 19**
  centering, WD 26
  changing spacing above and below, WD 50
  indenting, WD 87–89
  removing space after, WD 79
  right-aligning, WD 81
  selecting, PPT 21–22
  selecting multiple, WD 30
  shortcut keys for formatting (table), WD 86
parameter query, **AC 89**–91
parentheses (())
  and arguments, EX 100
  and order of operations, EX 92
parenthetical citations, **WD 76**
passphrase, 144
password: Private combination of characters associated with a user name that allows access to certain computer resources. **144, 190, WIN 7**
  cookies and, 204
  protection, 191
paste area, **EX 27**
Paste Options menu, **WD 122**
Paste Special, **INT 13**
pasting
  described, **WD 119**
  using Clipboard, IE 39–47
patches, **IE 7**
path, **IE 9, WIN 36**, WIN 37
payload: Destructive event or prank a malicious-logic program is intended to deliver. **184**
PayPal, 63, 71
PCs vs. Apple computers, 15
PDA: Lightweight mobile device that provides personal information management functions such as a calendar, appointment book, address book, calculator, and notepad. *See also* **personal digital assistant**. **17**
PDF: Portable Document Format; a popular file format used by document management software to save converted documents. **107**
performance monitor: Operating system program that assesses and reports information about various computer resources and devices. **143**

personal computer: Computer that can perform all of its input, processing, output, and storage activities by itself and contains a processor, memory, one or more input and output devices, and storage devices. **15**
personal computer maintenance utility: Utility program that identifies and fixes operating system problems, detects and repairs disk problems, and includes the capability of improving a computer's performance. **157**
personal DTP software: Application software that helps home and small office/home office users create newsletters, brochures, advertisements, postcards, greeting cards, letterhead, business cards, banners, calendars, logos, and Web pages **113**
personal finance software: Simplified accounting program that helps home users or small office/home office users manage finances. **112**
  popular (fig.), 111
personal firewall: Utility program that detects and protects a personal computer and its data from unauthorized intrusions. **153, 189**
personal identification number (PIN): Numeric password, either assigned by a company or selected by a user. **191**
personal information manager (PIM): Application software that includes features to help users organize personal information. **106**
  popular software (fig.), 100
personal paint/image editing software: Application software that provides an easy-to-use interface, usually with more simplified capabilities that allows users to draw pictures, shapes, and other images. **114**
personal photo editing software: Application software that allows users to edit digital photos by removing red-eye, erasing blemishes, restoring aged photos, adding special effects, enhancing image quality, or creating electronic photo albums. 111, **114**

personal Web sites, 58
Phanfare Web site, 83
pharming: Scam, similar to phishing, where a perpetrator attempts to obtain your personal and financial information, except they do so via spoofing. **205**
phishing: Scam in which a perpetrator sends an official looking e-mail that attempts to obtain your personal and financial information. 10, **156, 205**
phishing filter: Program that warns or blocks you from potentially fraudulent or suspicious Web sites. **156, 205**
phishing scams, **IE 7**
phone numbers, searching for, 71–72
phones
  business software for, 100, 106–107
  making Internet calls, 68
photo editing software
  popular (fig.), 111
  professional, 109
photo management software: Application software that allows users to view, organize, sort, catalog, print, and share digital photos. **114**
photos
  inserting into slides, PPT 95–100
  resizing, PPT 103
picture message: Photo or other image, sometimes along with sound and text, sent to or from a smart phone or other mobile device. **17**, 118
  personal and business perspectives, 170–171
picture styles, WD 44
Picture Tools and Styles gallery, WD 44–47
Picture with Caption layout, PPT 94
pictures
  changing border colors, WD 45
  copying and pasting from Web pages, IE 42–45
  inserting in documents, WD 41–42
  saving from Web pages, IE 37–38
Pictures folder, **WIN 21**
pie charts, 104
piracy: Unauthorized and illegal duplication of copyrighted material. **193**, 201
  software, 194

pixel, **EX 122**
placeholders, **PPT 7**, PPT 104, PPT 121
placeholders, citation, WD 108
PlagiarismDetect.com, 36
plagiarize, **WD 76**
planning projects, guidelines for, APP 1–2
platforms, 138, 145
player: Software used by a person to listen to an audio file on a computer. **60**
PlayStation 3, 18, 41
Plug and Play: Technology that gives a computer the capability to configure adapter cards and other peripherals automatically as a user installs them. **142**
plug-in: Program that extends the capability of a browser; often used to enhance multimedia. *See also* **add-on**. **61**
 popular (fig.), 61
podcast: Recorded audio stored on a Web site that can be downloaded to a computer or a portable media player such as an iPod. **10**, **60**
point, **WIN 4**, **PPT 21**, WD 23
Point mode, **EX 93**, EX 100
 entering formulas using, EX 93–94
point size, **EX 34**
pointer: Small symbol displayed on a computer screen whose location and shape changes as a user moves a pointing device. **98**
pop-up blocker: Filtering program that stops pop-up ads from displaying on Web pages. **156**
pop-up menu, **PPT 51**
port, 220
portable media player: Mobile device on which you can store, organize, and play digital media. **17**, 20
 buyer's guide to, 226–227
portal: Web site that offers a variety of Internet serves from a single, convenient location. **55**
portrait orientation, **EX 129**, **AC 40**, INT 30
portrait page orientation, PPT 6
positioning graphic images, WD 41–42
possessed object: Any item that a user must carry to gain access to a computer or computer facility. **191**

postage Web sites, 87
postal codes, AC 12
posting student materials, 119
power user: User who requires the capabilities of a workstation or other powerful computer, typically working with multimedia applications and using industry-specific software. **23**
PowerPoint 2007
 overview of, PPT 2–6
 pages, creating hyperlinks to, INT 11–13
 quitting, PPT 130–131
 starting, PPT 5–6
 using hyperlinks in, INT 24–27
 views, PPT 8
 See also **presentation**
PowerPoint Help, **PPT 62**
PowerPoint window, components, PPT 6–16
.ppt files, PPT 26
.pptx files, PPT 29
presentation, **PPT 2**
 adding slides to, PPT 29–31
 background styles for, PPT 89–90
 changing document properties, PPT 43–45
 changing layouts, PPT 92–95
 choosing document theme, PPT 16–17
 corrections to, PPT 58
 creating slides from blank, PPT 84–89
 creating title slide, PPT 18–19
 creating transparencies, PPT 62
 delivery skills, PPT 82
 developing, with bulleted lists, PPT 2–5
 displaying in grayscale, PPT 59–61
 formatting characters in, PPT 21–26
 printing, PPT 61–62
 printing as outlines, handouts, PPT 126–130
 reviewing with different views, PPT 90–91
 saving, PPT 130
 spell-checking, PPT 55–58
 viewing in Slide Show view, PPT 48–52
presentation program, **WIN 27**
presentation software: Application software that allows a user to create visual aids for presentations

to communicate ideas, messages, and other information to a group. **105**
popular (fig.), 100
preventing
 botnets, DoS attacks, back doors, spoofing, 188
 identity theft, 10
 information theft, 195
 malware, 187
 personal information theft, 203
 repetitive strain injury (RSI), WD 43
 software theft, 193–194
 spyware, IE 6–7
 virus infections, 154–155, 185–187
previewing
 documents as Web pages, INT 21–22
 documents before printing, WD 57
 presentations as outlines, handouts, PPT 126–130
 and printing contents of tables, AC 40–43
 worksheets before printing, EX 132–135
Previous Locations button (Vista), **WIN 18**
Previous Page button, WD 119
primary key, **AC 4**, AC 5
 changing, AC 28–29
 determining, AC 8
 modifying, AC 46–48
primary sort key, **AC 97**
print: Placing the copy of a document on paper or some other medium. **102**
Print dialog box, EX 133
Print Layout view, WD 5, **WD 6**
Print Preview, WD 57, EX 60
Print Scaling option, EX 135–137
Print What list, **PPT 126**
printers, 5, 220
 embedded computers in, 20
 spooling, 141–142
 Wordwrap and, WD 14
printing
 document properties, WD 51
 document properties, documents, WD 130–131
 page ranges, AC 43
 presentations, PPT 61–62
 presentations as outlines, handouts, PPT 126–130
 query results, AC 83

printing (*continued*)
  reports, AC 56, AC 111
  table contents, AC 40–43
  Web pages in Internet Explorer, IE 47–49
  worksheets, EX 57–59, EX 132–135
printouts, **IE 47**, **WD 53**, **PPT 61**, **EX 57**
privacy
  computer issues with, 7
  information, 202–207
  laws, 206
  and online mapping services, 117
processor: Electronic component on a computer's motherboard that interprets and carries out the basic instructions that operate the computer. See also **microprocessor**. **6**, 220
product activation: Process that attempts to prevent software piracy by requiring users to provide a software product's 25-character identification number in order to receive an installation identification number. **194**
professional photo editing software: Type of image editing software that allows photographers, videographers, engineers, scientists, and other high-volume digital photo users to edit and customize digital photos. **109**
  popular (fig.), 108
program: Series of related instructions that tells a computer what task(s) to perform and how to perform them. See also **software**. **11**, **WIN 27**
  Accessories, WIN 13
  installing, running, 12–13
  management, 139–141
  starting, running from Windows, 99
programmer: Person who writes and modifies computer programs. See also **developer**. **13**
programming languages, 13
Progressive Casualty Insurance Company, 166
project management software: Application software that allows a user to plan, schedule, track, and analyze the events, resources, and costs of a project. **106**
  popular (fig.), 100

projects
  creating research paper, WD 74–76
  database creation, AC 3–6
  database queries, AC 74–76
  flyer creation, WD 2–4
  integrating Office 2007 programs and the Web, INT 2–6
  planning guidelines, APP 1–2
  presentation with illustrations and a shape, PPT 82–84
  saving, WD 18–21, PPT 26–29, EX 29–32
  worksheet with embedded chart, EX 2–6
  worksheet with formulas, functions, Web queries, EX 82–86
promoting (text), **PPT 34**
proofreading, WD 76, **WD 118**
property sheet, **AC 100**
protocol, **IE 8**, **WIN 28**
public-domain software: Free software that has been donated for public use and has no copyright restrictions. **97**
publishing
  computer applications in, 27
  Web page, INT 27
punctuation, spacing after, WD 106

Q

quarantine: Separate area of a hard disk that holds the infected file until a virus can be removed. **186**
queries, **AC 78**
  changing captions, AC 116–117
  creating, AC 78–80, AC 83–85
  crosstab, AC 122–125
  entering criterion, AC 85–86
  omitting duplicates from, AC 100–101
  parameter, AC 89–91
  printing results of, AC 83
  saving, AC 91–92, AC 107
  sorting, AC 97–103
  sorting dates in, AC 98–99
  top-values, AC 102–103
  using, AC 80–85
  using calculated fields in, AC 113–116
  using criterion for field not included in results, AC 88–89
  using criterion in, AC 81–82
  using saved, AC 92
  using wildcards, AC 87
  Web, EX 137
query, **AC 74**

question mark (?) in file names, WD 20
queue: Lineup of multiple print jobs within a buffer. **142**
Quick Access Toolbar, **WD 10**–11, WD 94, **PPT 13**–14, **EX 13**, **AC 22**
  adding buttons to, INT 19–21
  customizing, APP 18–25
  resetting, APP 25
Quick Print, WD 54, PPT 62
Quick Reference, PPT 126
Quick Style, **WD 36**, WD 90–91, **PPT 106**–108
QuickTime, 61
quitting
  Access, AC 35–36, AC 63
  Excel, EX 58, EX 69
  Internet Explorer (IE), IE 52
  PowerPoint, PPT 52–53, PPT 130–131
  Word, WD 55
  WordPad, IE 47
quotation marks (")
  in file names, WD 20
  using in presentations, PPT 84, PPT 88

R

RAID, 197
RAM
  and booting computers, 138
  described, 220
  and memory management, 141
Range Finder, **EX 106**
ranges
  numeric, EX 90
  selecting with keyboard, EX 97
Ready, **EX 9**
real time: Describes users and the people with whom they are conversing being online at the same time. **66**
real time location system (RTLS): Safeguard used by some businesses to track and identify the location of high-risk or high-value items. **193**
RealMedia file formats, 131
RealPlayer, 60
recalculation
  automatic, EX 96
  with spreadsheet software, 103
Recent Documents list, WD 56, PPT 54, EX 60

Recent Pages list, **IE 21**, IE 25–26
recording
  digital products in our lives, 40
  videos, 130
records, **AC 4**
  adding to tables, AC 30–34, AC 38–39, AC 49
  deleting, AC 27–29, AC 34
  grouping, AC 52, AC 121–122
  restricting in joins, AC 112
  saving, AC 33
Recover My Files, 150
recovering erased files, 150
Recovery Toolbox, 150
Recuva, 150
Recycle Bin, **WIN 9**, WIN 25
recycling of electronics, 14, 202
red wavy underlined text, WD 16
redoing actions, WD 32–33, AC 34
redundancy
  described, **AC 5**
  identifying, removing, AC 5–6, AC 10–12
reference marks, footnote, WD 100
reference software: Application software that provides valuable and thorough information for all individuals. 111, **115**
Refresh button, **IE 20–21**
Refresh button (Vista), **WIN 18**
refreshing
  Web pages, IE 20–21
  worksheet data, EX 139
relational operators, conditional formatting, EX 121
relationships, determining for database, AC 9
relative cell references, **EX 96**
removable media, WIN 37–40
removing
  AutoCorrect Options button from screen, WD 92
  bullets from list or paragraph, WD 32
  commands from Quick Access Toolbar, APP 24
  duplicates from queries, AC 100–101
  gadgets from Windows Sidebar, WIN 12
  italic format, WD 36
  page borders, WD 49
  space after paragraphs, WD 79
  tables from queries, AC 89
  underlining, WD 35

Web pages from Favorites Center, IE 34–35
  See also deleting
renaming
  fields, AC 26
  files by right-clicking, WIN 55
repetitive strain injury (RSI): Injury or disorder of the muscles, nerves, tendons, ligaments, and joints. **198**, WD 43
Replace text as you type feature, WD 94
replacing text, WD 123
reports
  Access capabilities for, AC 2
  adding hyperlinks to, INT 32–35
  creating, AC 50–55
  creating, involving a join, AC 109–111
  creating Web pages from Access, INT 28–37
  magnifying, AC 42–43
  printing, AC 56, AC 111
  saving, AC 55
requirements document, **EX 3**
research
  Web sites, 81
  wikis and academic, 56
Research in Motion (RIM), 159
research papers, **WD 74**
  creating (project), WD 74–76
  proofreading, revising, WD 118–132
Research task pane, using, WD 128–130
reserved words, AC 8
resetting Quick Access Toolbar, APP 25
resizing, **PPT 101**
  charts, EX 53
  clip art, photos, PPT 101–105
  embedded objects, INT 17–18
  graphics, **WD 45**–47
  photos, PPT 103
  shapes, PPT 117–118
resolution, changing screen, WD 4, PPT 5
resources: Hardware, software, data, and information shared using a network. **8**
Restart command (Vista), **WIN 8**
restore: To copy backed up files by copying them to their original location on the computer. **196**
Restore button, **WIN 20**, **IE 13**

restore utility: Program that reverses the backup process and returns backed up files to their original form. **152**
retinal scanners, 191
RFID tags, 193, 216
Ribbon, WD 7–9, **PPT 8**, **EX 9**, **AC 19–20**
  adding commands to Quick Access Toolbar, EX 13
  and changed screen resolution, APP 16–17
  commands, groups, tabs, EX 9–11
  formatting numbers using, EX 114–118
  minimizing, PPT 9
  vs. shortcut keys, WD 86
Ribbon commands, **EX 10**
right-aligned (text), **WD 81**
right-clicking, picture options, IE 37
right-drag, **WIN 25**
Rock and Roll Hall of Fame and Museum Web site, 80
rootkit: Program that hides in a computer and allows someone from a remote location to take full control of the computer. **184**
row heading, **EX 7**
row selector, **AC 28**
rows
  changing height, EX 122–126
  hiding, EX 126, EX 127
RSS 2.0: Really Simple Syndication. Specification that content aggregators use to distribute content to subscribers. **58**
RSS aggregator software, 118
R-Studio, 150
ruler, WD 87, **WD 88**
run: Process of using software. **12**

S

safety, computer issues with, 7
Samsung Alias, 225
sans serif, PPT 86
satellite Internet service: Provides high-speed Internet connections via satellite to a satellite dish that communicates with a satellite modem. **46**
save: To transfer a document from a computer's memory to a storage medium. **102**
  documents, WD 18–21, WD 53
  documents as Web pages, INT 6

save (*continued*)
  documents with new file name, INT 22–23
  files in application software, 126
  forms, AC 57–58
  information obtained with Internet Explorer, IE 35–47
  PowerPoint presentations as Web pages, INT 27
  presentations, PPT 45–46, PPT 130
  projects, WD 18–21, PPT 26–29, EX 29–32
  queries, AC 91–92, AC 107
  records, AC 33
  reports, AC 55, INT 36
  tables, AC 27, AC 44
  Web pages, IE 36–37
  WordPad documents, IE 46–51
  workbooks, EX 5, EX 56–57
Save As dialog box, WIN 48, WIN 51, WD 20–21, WD 53, PPT 28, PPT 46, EX 57
saved queries, using, AC 92
scanners, 4–5, 220
scanners, retinal, 191
science
  computer applications in, 26
  Web sites, 91
screen resolution
  changing, WD 4, PPT 5, APP 13–17
  described, **APP 13**
screen saver: Utility program that causes a display device's screen to show a moving image or blank screen if no mouse activity occurs for a specified time. **153**
ScreenTip, **EX 11**
script kiddie: Someone who accesses a computer or network illegal with the intent of destroying data, stealing information, or other malicious action but does not have the technical skills and knowledge. **182**
scroll, **WD 43**
scroll arrow, **WD 7, PPT 7, PPT 8, EX 9, AC 19**
scroll bar, **WIN 15, WD 7, PPT 8, EX 9, AC 19**
scroll box, **PPT 7, AC 19**
scrolling, WIN 15
Search box (Vista), **WIN 18**
search engine: Program that finds Web sites, Web pages, images, videos, news, and other information related to a specific topic. **53**
  using, 54–55
search text: Word or phrase entered in a search engine's text box that describes the item you want to find. **54**
search tools, widely used (table), 53
search utility: Program that attempts to locate a file on your computer based on criteria you specify. **151**
searching
  Access Help, AC 62–63
  for driving directions, addresses, phone numbers, 71–72
  for Help topics, WIN 62–63, PPT 62
  for information with Research task pane, WD 128–129
  the Web, 53–55
  Word Help, WD 60–61, APP 5–9
secondary sort key, **AC 97**
secure site: Web site that uses encryption techniques to secure its data. **195**
security
  administering, 144
  computer security risks, 182–183
  domain highlighting, IE 14
  Internet concerns, IE 6–7
  national and local, 208
  wireless, 197
Security Warnings, AC 38
Select Browse Object menu, WD 118–119
selecting
  cells, EX 15, EX 47–48
  graphics, WD 46
  groups of words, WD 33–34, PPT 24
  lines, WD 27
  multiple paragraphs, WD 30
  paragraphs, PPT 21–22
  ranges with keyboard, EX 97
  rows, AC 28
  sentences, WD 120
  words, WD 59
selection rectangles around graphics, WD 42, **PPT 101**
selective backup, 197
Semantic Web, 49
sentences, selecting, WD 120
serif fonts, PPT 108

server: Computer that controls access to the hardware, software, and other resources on a network and provides a centralized storage area for programs, data, and information. *See also* **host computer**. 15, **19, WIN 4, WIN 37–38**
  backing up on offsite Internet, 214–215
server operating system: Operating system that organizes and coordinates how multiple users access and share resources on a network. **143**, 145, 148–149
servers, Web, 49
service pack: Free downloadable software updates provided by the software manufacturer to users who have registered and/or activated their software. **143, IE 7**
shadow, **PPT 110**
Shape Quick Style, PPT 119–120
shapes
  adding, formatting, PPT 115–120
  adding text to, PPT 119–120
Shared Collections, **PPT 95**
shareware: Copyrighted software that is distributed at no cost for a trial period. **97**
sharing
  content, personal and business perspectives, 178–179
  documents, WD 51, EX 55
  network resources, 8
sheet tab, **EX 7**
Shockwave Player, 61
shopping cart: Element of an electronic storefront that allows a customer to collect purchases. **63**
shopping Web sites, 88
shortcut keys, **WD 86**
shortcut menu, WIN 17, **WD 10, PPT 12, EX 12, AC 21**
shortcuts, keyboard, WIN 26
showing
  formatting marks in text, WD 14
  and hiding columns, EX 122
  and hiding rows, EX 127
  See also displaying
ShowOffDemo, 216
Shut down button (Vista), **WIN 8**
Shut Down command (Vista), **WIN 8**
Shut down options arrow (Vista), **WIN 8**

signature verification systems, 191
Silverlight, 61
Simple Query Wizard, AC 78–80
Singbox, 39
size, **PPT 21**
sizing
 fonts in cells, EX 39
 text fonts, WD 28
 text with AutoFit, PPT 19
 windows, WIN 22–23
 See also resizing
sizing handles on graphics, WD 42, **PPT 101**
slash (/) in file names, WD 20
Sleep command (Vista), **WIN 8**
sleep mode: Operating system function that saves any open documents and programs to RAM, turns off all unneeded functions, and then places the computer in a low-power state. **138**
slide, **PPT 6**
 adding titles, PPT 31
 adding to presentations, PPT 29–31
 adding transitions, PPT 122–124
 arranging, PPT 41–43
 black, PPT 39
 creating from blank presentation, PPT 84–89
 creating title, PPT 18–19
 displaying out of order, PPT 46–47
 inserting clip art, photos into, PPT 95–97
 moving through in, and out of order, PPT 46–50
 multi-level bulleted list, PPT 33
 replacing text in, PPT 59
slide indicator, **PPT 47**
Slide pane, **PPT 8**
slide show, **PPT 2**
Slide Show view, PPT 48–52, **PPT 49**
slide shows
 ending with closing slide, PPT 40–43
 ending with pop-up menu, PPT 51–52
 running animated, PPT 125
 See also **presentation**
Slide Sorter view, PPT 91
slide transition, **PPT 122**
Slides tab, **PPT 8**
small office/home office (SOHO): Describes any company with fewer than 50 employees, as well as the self-employed who work from home. **22**

smart phone: Internet-enabled telephone that usually also provides personal information management functions. **17**, 172–173
 buyer's guide to, 225–226
smart tag indicator, **EX 96**
smart tags, **EX 96**
Smartlane, 202
SmartScreen Filter, **IE 7**
snaps (chart), **EX 53**
social engineering: Gaining unauthorized access or obtaining confidential information by taking advantage of the trusting human nature of some victims and the naivety of others. **205**
social networking Web site: Web site that encourages members in its online community to share their interests, ideas, stories, photos, music, and videos with other registered users. *See also* **Online social network**. **10**, **57**, 61
soft page breaks, **WD 107**
Softbank, 121
software: Series of related instructions that tells a computer what task(s) to perform and how to perform them. *See also* **program**. **11**
 automatic update, 143
 for desktop computers, 218
 general types of, 11–13
 for home, personal, educational use, 111–116
 used by home users, 20–21
software firewall, **IE 7**
software suite: Collection of individual programs available together as a unit. Business software suites typically include word processing, spreadsheet, e-mail, and presentation graphics software. **106**
software theft: Computer security risk that occurs when someone (1) steals software media, (2) intentionally erases programs, (3) illegally copies a program, or (4) illegally registers and/or activates a program. **193**
Son, Masayosh, 121
Sony PlayStation 3, 18, 41
sort, **AC 97**
sort key, **AC 97**

sorting
 dates in queries, AC 98–99
 on multiple keys, AC 101–102
sorting order, AC 53, AC 97
sound card, 220
source area, **EX 27**
source drive, **WIN 52**
source folder, **WIN 52**
source object, **INT 13**
source program, **INT 13**
sources, bibliographical, WD 96–97, WD 99, WD 101, WD 109
spacing
 above and below paragraphs, WD 50
 adjusting line and page, WD 78–79, PPT 32
 in MLA, APA styles, WD 76–77
 after punctuation, WD 106
 See also line spacing
Spafford, Gene, 209
spam: Unsolicited e-mail message or newsgroups posting sent to many recipients or newsgroups at once. **155**, **204**
speakers, 5, 220
special characters, inserting, PPT 106
spell checker, **EX 127**
spell-checking, WD 13, WD 16–17, WD 125–126, PPT 55–58, EX 127–129
Spelling and Grammar Check icon, WD 13
split forms
 creating, **AC 57–58**
 using, AC 58–59
splitter bar, **PPT 8**
splitting merged cells, EX 41
spoofing: Technique intruders use to make their network or Internet transmission appear legitimate to a victim computer or network. **188**
spooling: Operating system process that sends documents to be printed to a buffer instead of sending them immediately to the printer. The buffer then holds the information waiting to print while the printer prints from the buffer at its own rate of speed. **141**
sports Web sites, 89
spreadsheet. *See* **worksheet**

spreadsheet software: Application software that allows a user to organize data in rows and columns and to perform calculations on the data. **103**
  popular (fig.), 100
  using, 103–104
spyware: Program placed on a computer without the user's knowledge that secretly collects information about the user. **155, 204, IE 6**
spyware remover: Program that detects and deletes spyware and similar programs on a user's computer. **155**
square brackets ([])
  around field names, AC 114
  and parameter queries, AC 89–91
square character, WD 25
Stallman, Richard, 209
stand-alone computers, WIN 4
stand-alone operating system: Complete operating system that works on a desktop computer, notebook computer, or mobile computing device and that also works in conjunction with a network operating system. 145, **146**
standard properties, **WD 51, EX 54, AC 60**
standards, World Wide Web Consortium (W3C), 45
Start button, Windows, 98
Start menu (Vista), **WIN 13**
  opening window using, WIN 21–22
  starting program using, WIN 27–28
start page, **WIN 28**
Start Search box, **WIN 44**
starting
  Access, AC 12–13, AC 36
  Excel, EX 5–6, EX 86–87
  Internet Explorer (IE), IE 11–12
  PowerPoint, PPT 5–6, PPT 53–54
  programs from Windows, WIN 27, 99
  Windows Vista, WIN 7–8
  Word, WD 4–6
  WordPad, WIN 45–46, IE 39–40
statistical functions, EX 98
statistics, calculating, AC 117–122
status bar, **WD 7, PPT 8, EX 9, AC 19**
stock market Web sites, 86

storage device: Hardware used to record (write and/or read) items to and from storage media. **6**
storage media: The physical material on which a computer keeps data, instructions, and information. **6**
streaming: Process of transferring data in a continuous and even flow. **60**
style, **WD 23, PPT 21**
  applying, WD 24–25
  applying picture, WD 44
  background, PPT 89–90
  changing bibliography, WD 95
  changing cell, EX 34–35
  creating Quick Style, WD 90–91
  Footnote Text, WD 102–104
  formats, WD 38
  modifying using Styles task pane, WD 114–115
style sets, changing, WD 37–38
Styles task pane, WD 114–115
subject directory: Search tool that classifies Web pages in an organized set of categories and subcategories. **53**, 55
submenu, **WD 11, EX 14, PPT 15, AC 22**
subscribe: Process of a user adding his or her e-mail name and address to a mailing list. **66**
Suggested Sites feature, IE 30
SUM function, EX 25–29, EX 97
Sum menu, EX 102
sums, calculating, EX 24–29
supercomputer: Fastest, most powerful, and most expensive computer, capable of processing more than 135 trillion instructions in a single second. 15, **19**
surfing the Web: Activity of using links to explore the Web. **52**
surge protector: Device that uses special electrical components to smooth out minor noise, provide a stable current flow, and keep an overvoltage from reaching the computer and other electronic equipment. **196**
S-video, 131
switching
  between Datasheet and Design view, AC 31
  to header, WD 80, WD 83
  between tabs, WIN 33
  between views, PPT 90–91, AC 80

Symantec company profile, 209
Symbian OS, 149
symbols, inserting special characters, PPT 106
synonyms, finding and inserting, **WD 124**–125
system failure: Prolonged malfunction of a computer. **196**
system software: Programs that control or maintain the operations of a computer and its devices. **11, 97, 136**
system unit: Case that contains the electronic components of a computer that are used to process data. 5, **6**

T

tab, **EX 9**
  contextual, WD 8, PPT 9, AC 20
  object, AC 18
  on Ribbon, **PPT 8**
tab row, **IE 15**
tab split box, **EX 9**
tab stops, WD 87
tabbed browsing: Web browser feature where the top of the browser displays a tab (similar to a file folder tab) for each Web page you open. **52**, WIN 31–32
tabbed page, **WIN 31**, WIN 33
Table of Contents (Help), **WIN 62**
tables
  adding records to, AC 30–34, AC 38–39, AC 49
  borders, INT 9
  changing structure, AC 26
  closing, AC 35
  creating, AC 23–34, AC 44–45
  determining relationships, AC 5, AC 9
  inserting into Word documents, INT 8
  joining, AC 103–112
  naming, AC 8
  previewing, printing contents, AC 40–43
  removing from queries, AC 89
  rows, **AC 4**
  saving, AC 27, AC 44
Tablet PC: Special type of notebook computer that resembles a letter-sized slate, which allows a user to write on the screen using a digital pen. **16, 224, 225**

tag names, WD 101
tags
  file properties, WD 20, PPT 27
  smart, **EX 96**
task pane, **PPT 11, EX 11, AC 20**
tax preparation software: Application software that is used to guide individuals, families, or small businesses through the process of filing federal taxes. **113**
  popular (fig.), 111
taxes Web sites, 86
taxing media downloads, 157
TCP/IP, IE 4
technology overload, 7
telecommuting: Work arrangement in which employees work away from a company's standard workplace and often communicate with the office through the computer. **24**
telemedicine: Form of long-distance health care where health-care professionals in separate locations conduct live conferences on the computer. **26**
telesurgery: Surgery in which a surgeon performs an operation on a patient who is not located in the same physical room as the surgeon. **26**
templates
  database, AC 13–17
  table, AC 26
tendonitis, 198
testing Web sites, INT 38–39
text, **EX 15**
  adding for hyperlinks, INT 24–25
  adding to shapes, PPT 119
  alternate, IE 19
  AutoCorrect feature, WD 91–94
  bolding, WD 34
  copying and pasting, IE 42–43
  deleting from placeholders, PPT 42–43
  demoting, promoting, PPT 34
  displaying formatting marks, WD 13, WD 77
  entering, WD 12–14
  entering in cells, EX 18–22
  entering numbers as, EX 24
  finding and replacing, WD 123–126
  formatting specific elements of, PPT 20
  formatting using shortcut keys, WD 86
  grammar-checking, WD 13, WD 16–17, WD 125–126
  inserting for hyperlinks, INT 11
  italicizing, WD 36, PPT 22
  line and paragraph spacing, WD 78
  magnifying (zooming), WD 12
  moving, WD 119–121
  note, WD 99–100
  red or green wavy underlined text, WD 16
  scrolling, WD 43
  search, 54
  selecting with mouse (table), WD 120
  shadowing, PPT 110
  spell-checking, WD 13, WD 16–17, WD 125–126
  underlining, WD 35
  Wordwrap, WD 13–14
  wrapping, EX 88
text boxes, WIN 8
Text data type, AC 9–10
text data, using in criterion, **AC 86**
text message: Short note, typically fewer than 300 characters, sent to or from a smart phone or other mobile device. **17**, 118
  personal vs. business perspective, 170–171
  privacy of employee, 207
  skills, and typing, 118
text placeholders, PPT 31–32
the last mile, **IE 4**
theme, **WD 23, EX 37, EX 107**
  changing colors, fonts, WD 39–40
  document, **PPT 8**, PPT 16–17
  fonts and, EX 34
thesaurus, **WD 124**, WD 125
thumb drive, **WIN 37–38**
thumbnail: Small version of a larger graphic. **59**
title bar: Horizontal space, located at the top of a window, that contains the window's name. **98, IE 13**
Title Slide, **PPT 6**
titles, **EX 19–22**
  adding to slides, PPT 31
  entering worksheet, EX 17–22
  in reports, AC 55
toner, conserving ink and, WD 53, WD 130
toolbar buttons, APP 6–7
tools, widely used search (fig.), 53

top-level domain (TLD): Identifies the type of organization associated with the domain. **48**
  examples of generic (fig.), 48
top-values query, **AC 102**–103
Torvalds, Linus, 159
transferring videos to computers or Internet, 130–131
transitions, slide, PPT 122–124
transparencies, making, PPT 62
transportation industry, computer usage in, 28
travel
  computer applications in, 27
  Web sites, 84
travel and mapping software: Application software that enables users to view maps, determine route directions, and locate points of interest. 111, **115**
Tri-Valley Stables flyer (project), WD 2–4
Trojan horse: Malicious-logic program named after the Greek myth that hides within or looks like a legitimate program. **154**, **184**
TRUE (calculating sums), EX 24
trusted source: Company or person a user believes will not send a virus-infected file knowingly. **185**
TurboTax Online, 57
turning off computers, WIN 66
Turnitin Web site, 36
typing skills, and text messaging, 118
typing text in WordPad document, WIN 47

U

Ultra-Mobile PC (UMPC): Computer small enough to fit in one hand. *See also* **handheld computer**. **17**
unauthorized access: Use of a computer or network without permission. **189**
unauthorized use: Use of a computer or its data for unapproved or possibly illegal activities. **189**
uncompress: To restore a compressed, or zipped, file to its original form. **156**
underlining
  links, IE 18
  words, WD 35
underscore (_) character, WD 35

Undo button, WD 32–33
undoing action, AC 26, AC 34
 with Cancel on shortcut menu, WIN 53
 last cell entry, EX 66–67
 undoing, redoing multiple actions, AC 34
 using BACKSPACE key, IE 17
uninstaller: Utility program that removes a program, as well as any associated entries in the system files. **151**
uninterruptible power supply (UPS): Device that contains surge protection circuits and one or more batteries that can provide power during a temporary or permanent loss of power. **196**
unique identifier, **AC 4**
United States National Park Service Web site, 51
UNIX: Multitasking operating system that now is available for most computers of all sizes. **147**
unsubscribe: Process of a user removing his or her e-mail name and address from a mailing list. **66**
up scroll arrow, **WIN 15**
updating
 Access capabilities for, AC 2
 Windows, 164–165
uploading: Process of transferring documents, graphics, and other objects from a computer to a server on the Internet. **68**
URL: Uniform Resource Locator. Unique address for a Web page. *See also* **Web address**. **51**
U.S. Government Web sites, 87
USAJOBS Web site, 93
USB flash drive, 5, 6, 220, **WIN 37–38**
 plugging into USB port, WIN 38
 saving files to, WD 20–21, EX 30–32
USB hub, 220, 223
USB port, 130, **WIN 37–38**
 plugging USB flash drive into, WIN 38
user: Anyone who communicates with a computer or utilizes the information it generates. **7**
user account, **WIN 7**
user ID: Unique combination of characters, such as letters of the alphabet and/or numbers, that identifies a specific user. *See also* **user name**. **144**
user interface: The portion of software that defines how a user interacts with a computer, including how the user enters data and instructions and how information is displayed on the screen. **138**
 described, WIN 3–4
user name: Unique combination of characters, such as letters of the alphabet and/or numbers, that identifies a specific user. *See also* **user ID**. **65**, **144**, **190**, **WIN 7**
user-friendly, **WIN 3**
utility: Type of system software that allows a user to perform maintenance-type tasks, usually related to managing a computer, its devices, or its programs. **150**
utility program: Type of system software that allows a user to perform maintenance-type tasks usually related to managing a computer, its devices, or its programs. **12**, 98, **150**
 types of, 150–157

V

value axis, **EX 50**
values version, **EX 135**
verifying
 formulas using Range Finder, EX 106
 hyperlinks, INT 39
VeriSign, 159
vertical bar (|), and file names, PPT 27
vertical ruler, **WD 87**
vertical scroll bar, **AC 19**
video: Images displayed in motion. **61**
 digital products in our lives, 39
 digital technology (feature), 129–134
video blog: A blog that contains video clips. **56**
video card, 220
video conferencing, 118, 180
video editing software: Application software that allows a user to modify a segment of video, called a clip. **110**, 132–133
 popular (fig.), 108

video message: Short video clip, usually about 30 seconds, sent to or from a smart phone or other mobile device. **17**, 118
 personal and business perspectives, 170–171
video phone: Phone that can send video messages. **17**
video projectors, 225
view, **PPT 8**
 changing to review presentations, PPT 90–91
 See also specific view
viewing
 datasheets and forms at once, AC 57
 folders, WIN 34–36
 styles assigned to Quick Style, WD 91
 Web pages, INT 28
 Word documents, saving as Web pages, INT 19
virtual memory: A portion of a storage medium, usually the hard disk, that the operating system allocates to function as additional RAM. **141**
virtual reality (VR): Computers used to simulate a real or imagined environment that appears as a three dimensional (3-D) space., **61**
virus: Potentially damaging computer program that affects, or infects, a computer negatively by altering the way the computer works without the user's knowledge or permission. **154**, **184**
 e-mail and, 65, 185
 on Internet, 98
virus definition: Known specific pattern of virus code. *See also* **virus signature**. **186**
virus hoax: E-mail message that warns users of a nonexistent virus or other malware. **187**
virus signature: Known specific pattern of virus code. *See also* **virus definition**. **186**
VisiCalc, 121
Vista. *See* Microsoft Windows Vista
vlog: Short for video blog. **56**
vlogosphere: All vlogs worldwide. **56**
voice verification systems, 191
VoIP: Voice over IP, or Internet Protocol; technology that allows

users to speak to other users over the Internet (instead of the public switched telephone network). **68**, 118, 172–173

W

war driving: Intrusion technique in which an individual attempts to detect wireless networks via their notebook computer or mobile device while driving a vehicle through areas they suspect have a wireless network. **197**
warm boot: Process of using the operating system to restart a computer. **138**
Warnock, John, 121
warranties, computer, 222
watermarks, APP 7–9
Weather Channel Web site, 89
weather Web sites, 89
weather.com, IE 64
Web: Worldwide collection of electronic documents called Web pages, the Web is one of the more popular services on the Internet. *See also* **World Wide Web**. **IE 5**, **10**, **49**
 browsing and navigating the, IE 15–30
 making use of the (feature), 79–94
 searching the, 53–55
Web 2.0: Term used to refer to Web sites that provide a means for users to share personal information, allow users to modify Web site content, and have application software built into the site for visitors to use. **10**, 59
Web 3.0, 49
Web address: Unique address for a Web page. *See also* **URL (Uniform Resource Locator)**. **51**, **IE 7–9**, **WIN 28–30**
 browsing the Web using, IE 16–20
 copying and pasting, IE 39
Web app: Web site that allows users to access and interact with software from any computer or device that is connected to the Internet. *See also* **Web application**. **57**, **116**
Web application: Web site that allows users to access and interact with software from any computer or device that is connected to the

Internet. *See also* **Web app**. **10**, **57**, **96**
 popular, 116–117
Web browser: Application software that allows users to access and view Web pages. *See also* **browser**. **49**, 118, **IE 10**, **WIN 27**
 displaying a home page (fig.), 50
 Internet Explorer. *See* Internet Explorer (IE)
Web cam, 4–5, 80, 220, 224
Web Collections, **PPT 95**
Web conferencing, personal and business perspectives, 176–177
Web filtering software: Program that restricts access to certain material on the Web. **156**, **207**
Web page: Electronic document on the Web, which can contain text, graphics, audio, and video and often has built-in connections to other documents, graphics, Web pages, or Web sites. **10**, **49**, **IE 5**, **WIN 27**
 copying and pasting text, pictures from, IE 42–45
 creating from Access reports, INT 28–37
 creating hyperlink to PowerPoint, INT 11–13
 creating PowerPoint, INT 23–26
 displaying, IE 41
 displaying, removing using Favorites Center, IE 33–35
 examples of, 9
 finding previously displayed, IE 21–30
 generating from existing files, INT 6
 keeping track of favorite, IE 30–35
 navigating, 52
 printing in Internet Explorer, IE 47–49
 saving, IE 36–37
 saving pictures from, IE 37–38
 saving PowerPoint presentations as, INT 27
 saving Word documents in, INT 19
 stopping transfer of, refreshing, IE 20–21
 writing in HTML, INT 23
Web page authoring software: Software used to create Web pages that include graphical images, video, audio, animation,

and other special effects with interactive content. **110**, IE 10
 popular (fig.), 108
Web programming languages, INT 23
Web publishing: Development and maintenance of Web pages. **62**
Web query, **EX 137**
 importing external data from Web source using, EX 137–140
Web server: Computer that delivers requested Web pages to a computer. **49**, **IE 5**
Web site: Document on the Web that contains text, graphics, animation, audio, and video. **10**, **49**, **WIN 28**, **IE 5**
 evaluating content of, 58–59
 types of, 55–58
 used by mobile Internet users, 47
Web site: Collection of related Web pages and associated items, such as documents and pictures, stored on a Web server. **49**, **IE 5**, **10**, **WIN 28**
 accuracy of, 200–201
 adding to Favorites bar, IE 31
 displaying home page, IE 32
 importing external data from, EX 137–140
 personalization, and cookies, 203
 testing, INT 38–39
Web-based training (WBT): Computer-based training that uses Internet technology and consists of application software on the Web. **119**
Welcome Center (Vista), **WIN 9–10**
Welcome screen (Vista), **WIN 8**
wheel, 219
Wi-Fi: Network that uses radio signals to provide Internet connections to wireless computers and devices. **45**
Wi-Fi Protected Access (WPA): Security standard that improves on older security standards by authenticating network users and providing more advanced encryption techniques. **197**
Wii, 18, 41
wiki: Collaborative Web site that allows users to create, add to, modify, or delete the Web site content via their Web browser. **56**

wiki (continued)
  personal and business perspectives, 174–175
wikiCalc, 121
Wikipedia, 56
wildcards, AC 87
window: Rectangular area of a computer screen that displays data or information. 98
  closing Welcome Center, WIN 10
  folder, **WIN 18–19**
  Internet Explorer, IE 12–14
  maximizing, WD 5, EX 7
  opening, closing, sizing, WIN 18–23
  opening using desktop icons, WIN 18
  operations, WIN 26
  PowerPoint, PPT 6–16
Windows
  keeping up-to-date, 164–165
  starting, running program from, 99
Windows 7: Microsoft's fastest, most efficient operating system to date, offering quicker program start up, built-in diagnostics, automatic recovery, improved security, enhanced searching and organizing capabilities, and an easy-to-use interface. **146**
Windows Aero: Windows interface used by computers with more than 1 GB of RAM. **139**, WIN 6
Windows Defender, IE 6
Windows Disk Defragmenter, 152
Windows Embedded CE, 149
Windows Firewall, 153
Windows Help and Support
  described, WIN 2, **WIN 58**
  using, WIN 58–63
Windows Internet Explorer (IE), 49
Windows Live Hotmail, 57, 64
Windows Live Movie Maker, 140
Windows Media Player, 61, 140
Windows Mobile, 149
Windows Photo Viewer, 151
Windows ReadyBoost: Windows feature that can allocate available storage space on removable flash memory devices as additional cache. **141**
Windows Sidebar, **WIN 9**
Windows Vista, **WIN 5**
  basic interface and Aero, WIN 6

desktop described, WIN 9–25
methods for ending sessions (table), WIN 64
operating system editions, WIN 5–6
overview of, WIN 4
starting, logging on, WIN 7–9
wireless Internet service provider: Type of Internet service provider that provides wireless Internet access to computers and mobile devices, such as smart phones and PDAs, with built-in wireless capability or to computers with wireless modems or wireless access devices. **46**
wireless LAN access point, 220
wireless modems, 46
wireless security, 197
Word 2007
  adding hyperlinks to documents, INT 6
  changing color scheme, APP 26
  embedding Excel chart into documents, INT 13–16
  opening documents from, WD 55–57
  overview of, WD 2
  quitting, WD 55
  starting, WD 4–6
  Word Help, using, WD 60–62, APP 5–11
Word Count dialog box, WD 107
Word Help, using, **WD 60**–62, APP 5–11
word processing program, **WIN 27**
word processing software: One of the more widely used types of application software; allows a user to create and manipulate documents containing mostly text and sometimes graphics. Sometimes called a word processor. **101**
  developing documents, 102
  popular (fig.), 100
Word window
  components of, WD 4–12
  customizing, APP 17–18
WordArt, deleting, PPT 111
WordPad, 126, **WIN 44**, **IE 39**
  copying and pasting, IE 39–47
  creating, saving documents, WIN 44–51

saving documents, quitting, IE 46–47
words
  counting, WD 107
  formatting, PPT 21
  selecting groups of, WD 33–34, PPT 24
workbook, **EX 7**
  changing theme, EX 109
  e-mailing from within Excel, EX 142–143
  opening, EX 60–61
  saving, EX 30–32, EX 56–57, EX 90
  viewing worksheets in, EX 140
workplace design, and ergonomics, 199
works cited (MLA style), **WD 77**
works cited page, **WD 111**–117
worksheet: Rows and columns used to organize data in a spreadsheet. **103**, **EX 7**
  adding 3-D Clustered Column Chart, EX 49–54
  adjusting column width, EX 45
  background colors, EX 110–112
  borders, EX 110–112
  changing column widths, row heights, EX 122–126
  clearing, EX 66
  colors, use of, EX 108
  column titles, EX 86–87
  components of, EX 7–8
  correcting errors, EX 63–67
  design considerations, EX 84
  development cycle, EX 4
  displaying formulas in, EX 136
  entering titles, EX 17–18
  formatting, EX 33–46, EX 107–114
  formatting numbers in, EX 44–45
  formulas, and values versions of, EX 135–136
  headings, EX 43
  inserting objects into, EX 51
  planning and development, EX 8, EX 85–86
  print preparation, EX 129–132
  printing, EX 57–59, EX 132–135
  printing sections of, EX 134–135
  refreshing data, EX 139
  renaming, EX 140–141
  spell-checking, EX 127–129
worksheet window, EX 8, **EX 9**
workstations, 23

World Wide Web Consortium (W3C), 45, 71
World Wide Web (WWW): Worldwide collection of electronic documents. *See also* **Web**. **49, IE 5**
  browsing and navigating the, IE 15–30
  browsing the, WIN 29–33
  overview of, IE 5–10
WorldWide Telescope, 59
worm Program that copies itself repeatedly, using up system resources and possibly shutting down the system. **154, 184**

Wozniak, Steve, 29, 159
WPA (Wi-Fi Protected Access), 197
WPA2, 197
wrapping text, EX 88
WWW, **IE 5**

X

x-axis, **EX 52**
Xbox 360, 18, 41

Y

Yahoo! Buzz, 166
Yahoo! Search blog, 166
y-axis, **EX 50**

Yellow Pages Local Directory, 71–72
YouTube, 40, 61, 178

Z

zipped files: Type of compressed files that usually have a .zip extension. **156**
zipping files, 126–127
zombie: Compromised computer whose owner is unaware the computer is being controlled remotely by an outsider. **187**
zooming text, documents, WD 12, WD 45–46
Zuckerberg, Mark, 71

Credits

Chapter 1: Opener © Mark Scott/Getty Images; Collage: PRNewsFoto/Apple; Courtesy of Logitech; Courtesy of D-Link Corporation; Courtesy of Apple; © Hugh Threlfall/Alamy; PRNewsFoto/Polaroid Corporation; PRNewsFoto/Nintendo; Courtesy of SanDisk Corporation; Courtesy of Hewlett-Packard Company; Courtesy of Nokia; Courtesy of Apple; 1-1a © Noel Hendrickson/Getty Images; 1-1b PRNewsFoto/Apple; 1-1d © David L. Moore-Lifestyle/Alamy; 1-1h © Jupiterimages/Comstock Images/Alamy; 1-1i © curved-light/Alamy; 1-1l © Brad Wilson/Getty Images; 1-1n © Jupiterimages/Thinkstock/Alamy; 1-1o Courtesy of Adobe Systems, Inc.; 1-3a Courtesy of Hewlett-Packard Company; 1-3b Courtesy of Logitech; 1-3d Courtesy of Logitech; 1-3e Courtesy of Kingston Technology Corporation; 1-3g Courtesy of SanDisk Corporation; 1-3h Courtesy of SanDisk Corporation; 1-3i Courtesy of LaCie; 1-3j Courtesy of Hewlett-Packard Company; 1-3k Courtesy of Hewlett-Packard Company; 1-4 Courtesy of Seagate Technology; 1-5a © Wm. Baker/GhostWorx Images/Alamy; 1-5b © Jupiterimages/Thinkstock/Alamy; 1-6b PRNewsFoto/Verizon Wireless, Achille Bigliardi; 1-6e Courtesy of Hewlett-Packard Company; 1-6g Courtesy of Apple; 1-6i Courtesy of Hewlett-Packard Company; 1-6k Courtesy of Nokia; 1-6l Courtesy of Palm; 1-6n Courtesy of Hewlett-Packard Company; 1-6p Courtesy of Microsoft Corporation; 1-6r Courtesy of Dell, Inc.; 1-9 © Tony Freeman/PhotoEdit; 1-10b Courtesy of Hewlett-Packard Company; 1-10c Courtesy of Hewlett-Packard Company; 1-10e Courtesy of Kingston Technology Corporation; 1-10f Courtesy of Corel Corporation; 1-10g Courtesy of Hewlett-Packard Company; 1-13b Courtesy of Dell, Inc.; 1-15b iStockphoto; 1-16 Courtesy of MotionPC; 1-17a Courtesy of Apple; 1-17b Courtesy of Nokia; 1-17c Courtesy of Nokia; 1-18a Courtesy of Hewlett-Packard Company; 1-18b Courtesy of Hewlett-Packard Company; 1-19 Courtesy of Apple; 1-20a Courtesy of Sony Electronics Inc.; 1-20b Courtesy of Sony Electronics Inc.; 1-20c iStockphoto; 1-21a © Ian Leonard/Alamy; 1-21b Courtesy of Nintendo Corporation; 1-21c Courtesy of Nintendo Corporation; 1-22 Courtesy of Hewlett-Packard Company; 1-24 Courtesy of IBM Corporation; 1-25a Courtesy of Toyota; 1-25b Courtesy of Toyota; 1-25c Courtesy of Daimler Mercedes-Benz; 1-25d Courtesy of Toyota; 1-25e © Jupiterimages; 1-25f Courtesy of Toyota; 1-26a Courtesy of Intuit; 1-26b © Kin Images/Getty Images; 1-26c Courtesy of Apple; 1-26d © Editorial Image, LLC/Alamy; 1-27a © Dwayne Newton/PhotoEdit; 1-28b © Lester Lefkowitz/Getty Images; 1-28c iStockphoto; 1-28d © Myrleen Ferguson Cate/PhotoEdit; 1-28f © blue jean images/Getty Images; 1-29 © Darryl Bush/San Francisco Chronicle/Corbis; 1-30 © Justin Pumfrey/Getty Images; 1-31 © Thomas Barwick/Getty Images; 1-33 AP Photo/The Post-Tribune, Leslie Adkins; 1-34 © Pigeon Productions SA/Getty images; 1-35a © AP Photo; 1-35d © Reza Estakhrian/Getty Images; 1-37 Courtesy of Garmin Ltd.; Looking Ahead 1-1 iStockphoto; Innovative Computing 1-1 Courtesy of Banner Health; CUW © Digital Vision; Trailblazer 1 © Justin Sullivan/Getty Images; Trailblazer 2 © Rob Kim/Landov. **Special Feature 1:** Page 37: © Synthetic Alan King/Alamy; © Kevork Djansezian/Getty Images; Courtesy of Microsoft Corporation; AP Photo/Mark Lennihan; Tomohiro Ohsumi/Bloomberg via Getty Images; Courtesy of Nintendo of America Inc.; PRNewsFoto/JVC Company of America; PRNewsFoto/Verizon Wireless; Courtesy of Apple; Courtesy of Nero AG; Courtesy of Iomega; Courtesy of Barco; Image copyright 2009, Roca. Used under license from Shutterstock.com; iStockphoto; Courtesy of Sling Media, Inc.; AP Photo/Shizuo Kambayashi; AP Photo/Akira Suemori; Courtesy of Apple; PRNewsFoto/TiVo Inc.; © Markos Dolopikos/Alamy; PRNewsFoto/Logitech; PRNewsFoto/Sony Electronics, Inc.; AP Photo/Paul Sakuma Courtesy of Chumby Industries; Exceptional Innovation, maker of Life|ware™; PRNewsFoto/Memorex; AP Photo/Joerg Sarbach; Figures: 1 PRNewsFoto/Cambridge SoundWorks; 3a © Chris Polk/FilmMagic/Getty Images; 3b AP Photo/Activision; 4-1 © Judith Collins/Alamy; 5 Courtesy of Apple; 6 Courtesy of Myvu Corporation; 7 Courtesy of Sling Media, Inc.; 8a Yoshikazu Tsuno/AFP/Getty Images; 8b; Courtesy of Physical Optics Corporation; 9 PRNewsFoto/TiVo Inc.; 10a Courtesy of LaCie; 10b Courtesy of Nero AG; 11a Courtesy of Facebook; 11b © Colin Young-Wolff/PhotoEdit; 11c PRNewsFoto/JVC Company of America; 12 Courtesy of Apple; 13 PRNewsFoto/SANYO Fisher Company 14a Courtesy of Nintendo of America; 14b Courtesy of Microsoft Corporation; 14c; John MacDougall/AFP/Getty Images 15a Courtesy of Nintendo of America; 15b Daniel Acker/Bloomberg via Getty Images; 16 AP Photo/Eckehard Schulz; 17a Courtesy of Nintendo of America; 17b © Kevork Djansezian/Getty Images; 17c Courtesy of Nintendo of America; 18 AP Photo/The Lawrence Journal-World, Scott McClurg; 19 PRNewsFoto/TiVo Inc.; 20a Exceptional Innovation, maker of Life|ware™; 20b Exceptional Innovation, maker of Life|ware™; 20c Courtesy of NuVo Technologies Inc.; 21 Copyright © Lucid Design Group www.luciddesigngroup.com; 22 Courtesy of ViewSonic Corporation 23 Courtesy of Chumby Industries. **Chapter 2:** Opener © John-Francis Bourke/Getty Images; 2-1e Courtesy of Microsoft Corporation; 2-2b Courtesy of D-Link Corporation; 2-2c Courtesy of Terayon Communication Systems, Inc.; 2-2d © Stephen Chernin/Getty Images; 2-2f Courtesy of Fujitsu Siemens Computers; 2-14b Courtesy of Hewlett-Packard Company; 2-14c Courtesy of Western Digital Corporation; 2-14d Glowimages/Getty Images; 2-14f Courtesy of Hewlett-Packard Company; 2-16 Step 1 © Colin Young-Wolff/PhotoEdit; Step 2 © Mark Evans/iStockphoto; Step 3 © Andrew Lewis/iStockphoto; Step 4 © Alexander Hafemann/iStockphoto; Step 5 Courtesy of Hewlett-Packard Company and Fujitsu-Siemens Computers; Step 6 © Ed Hidden/iStockphoto; Step 7 © Oksana Perkins/iStockphoto; Step 8 © Bill Aron/PhotoEdit; 2-18 Steps 1 & 4 Courtesy of Hewlett-Packard Company; Step 2, Copyright 2005 Sun Microsystems, Inc. All Rights Reserved. Used by permission; Step 3 Courtesy of Juniper Networks Inc.; 2-19 Step 1 Courtesy of Microsoft Corporation; Step 2 Courtesy of Fujitsu-Siemens Computers; Step 3 Courtesy of Microsoft Corporation; Step 4 Courtesy of Acer America, Inc.; Step 5 Courtesy of Hewlett-Packard Company; 2-20a, Courtesy of Sony Electronics Inc.; 2-20b Courtesy of Hewlett-Packard Company; 2-20 center, © Blend Images/Alamy; 2-21a Courtesy of Hewlett-Packard Company; 2-21b Courtesy of Cisco; 2-21c Courtesy of D-Link Corporation; 2-21d Courtesy of Siemens; 2-21e Courtesy of Logitech; CUW © Picture Contact/Alamy; Trailblazer 1 Tech Trailblazer 1, © EPA/Landov; Trailblazer 2 AP Photo/Craig Ruttle. **Special Feature 2:** © Photodisc/Alamy; iStockphoto; © Digital Vision/Alamy; © Digital Vision/Alamy; © Alex Segre/Alamy. **Chapter 3:** Opener: moodboard/Alamy; Collage: Hugh Threlfall/Alamy; Courtesy of Corel

Corporation; Courtesy of Microsoft Corporation; Courtesy of Microsoft Corporation; Courtesy of Microsoft Corporation; Courtesy of Nokia Pinnacle Systems, Inc., a part of Avid Technology, Inc.; Courtesy of Cakewalk Inc.; Courtesy of Intuit Inc. 3-1a Courtesy of Microsoft Corporation; 3-1b Courtesy of Adobe Systems Incorporated; 3-1c Courtesy of Corel Corporation; 3-2a © Brooke Slezak/Getty Images; 3-2c Courtesy of Hewlett-Packard Company; 3-2e Courtesy of Hewlett-Packard Company; 3-11 Courtesy of Microsoft Corporation; 3-12 Courtesy of Computer Systems Odessa Corporation; 3-13 Courtesy of Microsoft Corporation; 3-16 © Artiga Photo/Corbis; 3-17 Courtesy of Quark Inc.; 3-18 Picture Contact/Alamy; 3-19 Courtesy of Cakewalk Inc.; 3-20 Courtesy of SumTotal Systems Inc.; 3-22 Courtesy of Intuit Inc.; 3-22b © Digital Vision/Getty Images; 3-23 Courtesy of Nolo; 3-24 Courtesy of 2nd Story Software, Inc.; 3-26 Courtesy of Corel Corporation; Courtesy of Microsoft Corporation; 3-27Courtesy of Encore, Inc, a Navarre Corporation Company; 3-28 Pinnacle Systems, Inc., a part of Avid Technology, Inc.; 3-29 Courtesy of IMSI/Design; 3-30 Courtesy of Microsoft Corporation; 3-3127Courtesy of Encore, Inc, a Navarre Corporation Company; 3-32a © Bernhard Classen/Alamy; 3-32b © Lon C. Dhiel/PhotoEdit; 3-32c © Fred Prouser/Reuters/Corbis; 3-37 Courtesy of Moodle; CUW iStockphoto; Trailblazer 1AP Photo/Steven Senne; Trailblazer 2 © Tom Wagner/Corbis; Looking Ahead 3-1 Courtesy of Microsoft Corporation; Innovative Computing 3-1 Tetra Images/Getty Images; Web Reserach © Brian Stablyk/Getty Images. **Special Feature 3:** 1a Courtesy of Samsung; 1b Courtesy of Sony Electronics Inc.; 1c PRNewsFoto/VIZIO; 1d Courtesy of Sony Electronics Inc.; 1e © Alex Slobodkin/iStockphoto; 1f iStockphoto; 2a Courtesy of Sony Electronics Inc.; 2b Courtesy of JVC Company of America; 2c © Royalty-Free/CORBIS; 3a Courtesy of Hewlett-Packard Company; 3b © Ben Blankenburg/iStockphoto; 3c Courtesy of Panasonic; 3d Courtesy of JVC Company of America; 4a Courtesy of Pinnacle Systems Inc.; 4b Courtesy of Pinnacle Systems Inc.; 4c © Matej Pribelsky/iStockphoto; 4d Courtesy of Hewlett-Packard Company; 4e Courtesy of Sony Electronics Inc.; 4f © Pete Saloutos/GettyImages; 5 Courtesy of Microsoft Corporation; 7 Courtesy of Pinnacle Systems Inc.; 8 Courtesy of Pinnacle Systems Inc.; 9 Courtesy of Pinnacle Systems Inc. **Chapter 4** Opener: © Stuart O'Sullivan/Getty Images; Collage: Courtesy of Microsoft Corporation; Courtesy of Apple; Courtesy of Apple; PRNewsFoto/AT&T Inc., Courtesy of Symantec Corp; PRNewsFoto/RealNetworks, Inc.; 4-1a © Valeriy Kryvsha/iStockphoto; 4-1i Courtesy of Dell Inc.; 4-1j Courtesy of Hewlett-Packard Company; 4-5a Courtesy of Hewlett-Packard Company; 4-5b Courtesy of Western Digital Corporation; 4-5c Courtesy of TallyGenicom; 4-7 Courtesy of Microsoft Corporation; 4-10 AP Photo/Peter Zschunke; 4-11 Courtesy of KDE e.V.; 4-13 Courtesy of Research in Motion; 4-19 Courtesy of Check Point Software Technologies Ltd.; 4-21 Courtesy of Symantec Corp; 4-22 Courtesy of RealNetworks, Inc.; 4-23 Courtesy of Nero AG; 4-24 Courtesy of Symantec Corp; CUW Keith Morris/Alamy; Trailblazer 1 Photo by Peter DaSilva; Trailblazer 2 © Kim Kulish/CORBIS; Innovative Computing 4-1 Ingram Publishing (Superstock Limited)/Alamy; Looking Ahead 4-1 Tingrui Pan/UC Davis photo; Web Research © Jurgen Reisch/Getty Images. **Special Feature 4:** 1a Courtesy of Microsoft Corporation; 1b © Image Source Black/Alamy; 1c © david hancock/Alamy; 1d Courtesy of Skype; 3a Courtesy of Microsoft Corporation; 3b © Stephen Wilkes/Getty Images; 5c © CAP/Getty Images; 7a © Picturenet/Getty Images; 7b Gary Corbett/Alamy; 7c Courtesy of Research In Motion; 7d Courtesy of Microsoft Corporation; 9a Courtesy of Jive Software; 9c © Jeff Greenberg/Alamy; 11a © David R. Fraizer/PhotoEdit; 11b © Jochen Tack/Alamy; 11c Courtesy of Parliant Corporation; 13a Siemens Press Photo; 13b © Alex Slobodkin/iStockphoto.com; 13c Courtesy of Zoom Technologies; 15c © Reggie Casagrande/Getty Images; 17a Courtesy of NASA; 17b © PhotoAlto/Alamy; 19c AP Photo/Screenshot, Peter Zschunke; 21c Courtesy of Microsoft Corporation; p 154 © John Lund/Drew Kelly/Sam Diephuis/Getty Images; © Photodisc/Alamy; © MIXA Co., Ltd./Alamy. **Chapter 5:** Opener: © Mark Scott/Getty Images; Collage: © Peter Macdiarmid/Getty Images; © TM_Design/Alamy; Courtesy of Microsoft Corporation; Courtesy of Content Watch Inc.; Courtesy of Symantec Corp; Courtesy of McAfee, Inc.; Newscom; © tompiodesign.com/Alamy; Courtesy of Tripp Lite; 5-1a © imagebroker/Alamy; 5-1b © mustafa deliormanli/iStockphoto; 5-1f © Ingvald kaldhussæter/iStockphoto; 5-2b © Christoph Weihs/iStockphoto; 5-2c Image copyright 2009, Ruslan Dashinsky. Used under license from Shutterstock.com; 3-3a Courtesy of McAfee, Inc.; 5-3b Courtesy of McAfee, Inc.; 5-5a Courtesy of SonicWALL, Inc.; 5-5c Courtesy of Check Point Software Technologies Ltd.; 5-5d Courtesy of Fujitsu-Siemens Computers; 5-8 © Paulo Whitaker/Reuters/Landov; 5-9 Courtesy of Kensington Computer Products Group; 5-13 © David Young-Wolff/PhotoEdit; 5-14 Courtesy of MGE UPS SYSTEMS; 5-17 © C Squared Studios/Getty Images; 5-22a Courtesy of Hewlett-Packard Company; 5-26 Courtesy of ContentWatch Inc.; Looking Ahead 5-1 © Ann Cutting/Getty Images; CUW © Ben Edwards/Getty Images; Web Research © Trevor Fisher/iStockphoto. **Special Feature 5:** 1a Courtesy of MotionPC; 1b Courtesy of Dell, Inc.; 1c Courtesy of Sony Electronics, Inc.; 1d Courtesy of Apple; 1e Courtesy of FUJIFILM USA; 1f AP Photo/Paul Sakuma; 1g Courtesy of Apple; 1h Courtesy of Dell, Inc.; Page 218: Courtesy of Hewlett-Packard Company; 2a Courtesy of SanDisk Corporation; 2b Courtesy of Avid Technology; 2c Courtesy of Seagate Technology LLC; 2d Courtesy of Microsoft Corporation; 2e Courtesy of Hewlett-Packard Company; 2f Courtesy of Logitech; 2g Courtesy of Microsoft Corporation; 2h Courtesy of Logitech; 2i Courtesy of US Robotics; 2j © iStockphoto; 2k Courtesy of Microsoft Corporation; 2l Courtesy of Sony Electronics Inc.; 2m Courtesy of Hewlett-Packard Company; 2n Courtesy of Hewlett-Packard Company; 2o Courtesy of Intel Corporation; 2p Courtesy of Kingston Technology Corporation; 2q Courtesy of UMAX; 2r Courtesy of M-Audio/Avid Technology, Inc.; 2s Courtesy of Logitech; 2t Courtesy of Logitech; 2u Courtesy of SanDisk Corporation; 2v Courtesy of Belkin International Inc.; 2x © iStockphoto; Page 222a: Courtesy of Dell, Inc.; Page 222b: Courtesy of Hewlett-Packard Company; Page 222c: Courtesy of Hewlett-Packard Company; 5 PRNewsFoto/Mindjet LLC; 6 Courtesy of Fujitsu-Siemens Computers; 7 Image copyright MadTatyana, 2009. Used under license from Shutterstock.com; Page 225: Courtesy of Nokia; 8 Courtesy of Motion Computing; 9a Courtesy of Verizon Wireless; PRNewsFoto/Verizon Wireless; 9b Courtesy of Verizon Wireless 9c PRNewsFoto/Verizon Wireless; Page 226: Courtesy of Microsoft Corporation; 10 Courtesy of Apple; Page 227: Courtesy of FUJIFILM USA; 11a Courtesy of SanDisk Corporation; 11b Courtesy of Sony Electronics Inc.; 11c Image copyright SasPartout, 2009. Used under license from Shutterstock.com.

Quick Reference Summary

In the Microsoft Office 2007 programs, you can accomplish a task in a number of ways. The following five tables (one each for Microsoft Office Word 2007, Microsoft Office Excel 2007, Microsoft Office Access 2007, Microsoft Office PowerPoint 2007, and Microsoft Office Outlook 2007) provide a quick reference to each task presented in this textbook. The first column identifies the task. The second column indicates the page number on which the task is discussed in the book. The subsequent four columns list the different ways the task in column one can be carried out.

Table 1 Microsoft Office Word 2007 Quick Reference Summary

Task	Page Number	Mouse	Ribbon	Shortcut Menu	Keyboard Shortcut
1.5 Line Spacing	WD 86		Line spacing button on Home tab	Paragraph | Indents and Spacing tab	CTRL+5
AutoCorrect Entry, Create	WD 93	Office Button | Word Options button | Proofing | AutoCorrect Options button			
AutoCorrect Options Menu, Display	WD 92	Point to text automatically corrected, point to small blue box, click AutoCorrect Options button			
Bibliographical List, Create	WD 113		Bibliography button on References tab | Insert Bibliography		
Bibliographical List, Modify Source and Update List	WD 117		Manage Sources button on References tab | select source | Edit button		
Bibliography Style, Change	WD 95		Bibliography Style box arrow on References tab		
Bold	WD 34	Bold button on Mini toolbar	Bold button on Home tab	Font | Font tab | Bold in Font style list	CTRL+B
Bullets, Apply	WD 32	Bullets button on Mini toolbar	Bullets button on Home tab	Bullets	ASTERISK KEY | SPACEBAR
Capital Letters	WD 86		Change Case button on Home tab | UPPERCASE	Font	CTRL+SHIFT+A
Case of Letters, Change	WD 86		Change Case button on Home tab	Font | Font tab	SHIFT+F3

Table 1 Microsoft Office Word 2007 Quick Reference Summary (continued)

Task	Page Number	Mouse	Ribbon	Shortcut Menu	Keyboard Shortcut
Center	WD 26	Center button on Mini toolbar	Center button on Home tab	Paragraph | Indents and Spacing tab	CTRL+E
Citation Placeholder, Insert	WD 101		Insert Citation button on References tab | Add New Placeholder		
Citation, Insert and Create Source	WD 96		Insert Citation button on References tab | Add New Source		
Citation, Edit	WD 98	Click citation, Citation Options box arrow | Edit Citation			
Close Document	WD 60	Office Button | Close			
Count Words	WD 107	Word Count indicator on status bar	Word Count button on Review tab		CTRL+SHIFT+G
Cut	WD 121		Cut button on Home tab	Cut	CTRL+X
Delete Text	WD 59				DELETE
Dictionary, Custom, View or Modify Entries	WD 127	Office Button | Word Options button | Proofing | Custom Dictionaries button			
Dictionary, Set Custom	WD 127	Office Button | Word Options button | Proofing | Custom Dictionaries button | select desired dictionary name | Change Default button			
Document Properties, Set or View	WD 51	Office Button | Prepare | Properties			
Double-Space Text	WD 87		Line spacing button on Home tab	Paragraph | Indents and Spacing	CTRL+2
Double-Underline	WD 35		Font Dialog Box Launcher on Home tab	Font | Font tab	CTRL+SHIFT+D
Find Text	WD 124	Select Browse Object button on vertical scroll bar | Find icon	Find button on Home tab		CTRL+F
Find and Replace Text	WD 123	Select Browse Object button on vertical scroll bar | Find icon | Replace tab	Replace button on Home tab		CTRL+H
First-Line Indent Paragraphs	WD 88	Drag First Line Indent marker on ruler	Paragraph Dialog Box Launcher on Home tab | Indents and Spacing tab	Paragraph | Indents and Spacing tab	TAB
Font Size, Change	WD 28	Font Size box arrow on Mini toolbar	Font Size box arrow on Home tab	Font | Font tab	CTRL+SHIFT+P
Font Size, Decrease 1 Point	WD 86			Font | Font tab	CTRL+[
Font Size, Increase 1 Point	WD 86			Font | Font tab	CTRL+]
Font, Change	WD 29	Font box arrow on Mini toolbar	Font box arrow on Home tab	Font | Font tab	CTRL+SHIFT+F

Table 1 Microsoft Office Word 2007 Quick Reference Summary (continued)

Task	Page Number	Mouse	Ribbon	Shortcut Menu	Keyboard Shortcut
Footnote Reference Mark, Insert	WD 100		Insert Footnote button on References tab		CTRL+ALT+F
Footnote, Delete	WD 106	Delete note reference mark in document window	Cut button Home tab		BACKSPACE | BACKSPACE
Footnote, Edit	WD 106	Double-click note reference mark in document window	Show Notes button on References tab		
Footnote, Move	WD 106	Drag note reference mark in document window	Cut button on Home tab | Paste button on Home tab		
Footnote Style, Modify	WD 102		Click footnote text | Styles Dialog Box Launcher | Manage Styles button | Modify button	Style | Footnote Text | Modify button	
Formatting Marks	WD 14		Show/Hide ¶ button on Home tab		CTRL+SHIFT+*
Graphic, Resize	WD 46	Drag sizing handle	Format tab in Picture Tools tab or Size Dialog Box Launcher on Format tab	Size | Size tab	
Hanging Indent, Create	WD 116	Drag Hanging Indent marker on ruler	Paragraph Dialog Box Launcher on Home tab | Indents and Spacing tab	Paragraph | Indents and Spacing tab	CTRL+T
Hanging Indent, Remove	WD 86		Paragraph Dialog Box Launcher on Home tab | Indents and Spacing tab	Paragraph | Indents and Spacing tab	CTRL+SHIFT+T
Header & Footer, Close	WD 83	Double-click dimmed document text	Close Header and Footer button on Design tab		
Header, Display	WD 80	Double-click dimmed header	Header button on Insert tab | Edit Header		
Help	WD 60 and Appendix B		Office Word Help button		F1
Insertion Point, Move to Beginning of Document	WD 24	Scroll to top of document, click			CTRL+HOME
Insertion Point, Move to End of Document	WD 25	Scroll to bottom of document, click			CTRL+END
Italicize	WD 36	Italic button on Mini toolbar	Italic button on Home tab	Font | Font tab	CTRL+I
Justify Paragraph	WD 86		Justify button on Home tab	Paragraph | Indents and Spacing tab	CTRL+J
Left-Align	WD 86		Align Text Left button on Home tab	Paragraph | Indents and Spacing tab	CTRL+L
Move Selected Text	WD 121	Drag and drop selected text	Cut button on Home tab | Paste button on Home tab	Cut | Paste	CTRL+X; CTRL+V

Table 1 Microsoft Office Word 2007 Quick Reference Summary (continued)

Task	Page Number	Mouse	Ribbon	Shortcut Menu	Keyboard Shortcut
Open Document	WD 56	Office Button | Open			CTRL+O
Page Border, Add	WD 48		Page Borders button on Page Layout tab		
Page Break, Manual	WD 112		Page Break button on Insert tab		CTRL+ENTER
Page Number, Insert	WD 82		Insert Page Number button on Design tab		
Paragraph, Add Space Above	WD 79		Line spacing button on Home tab | Add Space Before (After) Paragraph	Paragraph | Indents and Spacing tab	CTRL+0 (zero)
Paragraphs, Change Spacing Above and Below	WD 50		Spacing Before box arrow on Page Layout tab	Paragraph | Indents and Spacing tab	
Picture Border, Change	WD 45		Picture Border button on Format tab		
Picture Style, Apply	WD 44		Picture Tools and Format tabs | More button in Picture Styles gallery		
Picture, Insert	WD 41		Picture button on Insert tab		
Print Document	WD 54	Office Button | Print | Print			CTRL+P
Print Document Properties	WD 130	Office Button | Print | Print | Print what box arrow			
Quick Style, Create	WD 90		More button in Styles gallery | Save Selection as a New Quick Style	Styles | Save Selection as a New Quick Style	
Quit Word	WD 55	Close button on right side of Word title bar			ALT+F4
Remove character formatting (plain text)	WD 87		Font Dialog Box Launcher on Home tab | Font tab	Font | Font tab	CTRL+SPACEBAR
Remove paragraph formatting	WD 87		Font Dialog Box Launcher on Home tab	Font | Font tab	CTRL+Q
Research Task Pane, Use	WD 128	Hold down ALT key, click word to look up			
Right-Align Paragraph	WD 81		Align Text Right button on Home tab	Paragraph | Indents and Spacing tab	CTRL+R
Rulers, Display	WD 87	View Ruler button on vertical scroll bar	View Ruler on View tab		
Save Document, Same Name	WD 53	Save button on Quick Access Toolbar			CTRL+S
Save New Document	WD 19	Save button on Quick Access Toolbar			CTRL+S
Select Block of Text	WD 33	Click at beginning of text, hold down SHIFT key and click at end of text to select; or drag through text			CTRL+SHIFT+RIGHT ARROW and/or DOWN ARROW

Table 1 Microsoft Office Word 2007 Quick Reference Summary (continued)

Task	Page Number	Mouse	Ribbon	Shortcut Menu	Keyboard Shortcut
Select Browse Object Menu, Use	WD 118	Select Browse Object button on vertical scroll bar			ALT+CTRL+HOME
Select Character(s)	WD 120	Drag through character(s)			CTRL+SHIFT+RIGHT ARROW
Select Entire Document	WD 120	Point to left of text and triple-click			CTRL+A
Select Graphic	WD 46	Click graphic			
Select Line	WD 27	Point to left of line and click			SHIFT+DOWN ARROW
Select Lines	WD 30	Point to left of first line and drag up or down			CTRL+SHIFT+DOWN ARROW
Select Paragraph	WD 90	Triple-click paragraph			SHIFT+DOWN ARROW
Select Paragraphs	WD 30	Point to left of first paragraph, double-click, and drag up or down			
Select Sentence	WD 120	Press and hold down CTRL key and click sentence			CTRL+SHIFT+RIGHT ARROW
Select Word	WD 59	Double-click word			CTRL+SHIFT+RIGHT ARROW
Select Words	WD 33	Drag through words			CTRL+SHIFT+RIGHT ARROW
Single-Space Lines	WD 86		Line spacing button on the Home tab	Paragraph	Indents and Spacing tab	CTRL+1
Small uppercase letters	WD 86		Font Dialog Box Launcher on Home tab	Font tab	Font	Font tab	CTRL+SHIFT+K
Source, Edit	WD 104	Click citation, Citation Options box arrow	Edit Source			
Spelling and Grammar	WD 125	Spelling and Grammar Check icon on status bar	Spelling	Spelling & Grammar button on Review tab	Right-click flagged text	Spelling	F7
Spelling and Grammar Check as You Type	WD 16	Spelling and Grammar Check icon on status bar		Correct word on shortcut menu	
Style Set, Change	WD 37		Change Styles button on Home tab	Style Set on Change Styles menu		
Styles Task Pane, Open	WD 25		Styles Dialog Box Launcher		ALT+CTRL+SHIFT+S
Styles, Apply	WD 24		Styles gallery		
Styles, Modify	WD 90		Styles Dialog Box Launcher		
Subscript	WD 86		Font Dialog Box Launcher on Home tab	Font	Font tab	CTRL+EQUAL SIGN
Superscript	WD 86		Font Dialog Box Launcher on Home tab	Font	Font tab	CTRL+SHIFT+PLUS SIGN
Synonym, Find	WD 124		Thesaurus on Review tab	Synonyms	desired word	SHIFT+F7

Table 1 Microsoft Office Word 2007 Quick Reference Summary (continued)

Task	Page Number	Mouse	Ribbon	Shortcut Menu	Keyboard Shortcut
Theme Colors, Change	WD 39		Change Styles button on Home tab	Colors on Change Styles menu		
Theme Fonts, Change	WD 40		Change Styles button on Home tab	Fonts on Change Styles menu		
Underline	WD 35		Underline button on Home tab	Font	Font tab	CTRL+U
Underline words, not spaces	WD 86				CTRL+SHIFT+W
Zoom	WD 46	Zoom Out and Zoom In buttons on status bar	Zoom button on View tab		

Table 2 Microsoft Office PowerPoint 2007 Quick Reference Summary

Task	Page Number	Mouse	Ribbon	Shortcut Menu	Keyboard Shortcut
Add Shapes	PPT 119		Shapes button on Home tab	select shape		
Add Transition	PPT 122		Transition effect on Animations tab or More button in Transition to This Slide group on Animations tab	select transition		ALT+A	T
Change Size, Clip Art, Photo, or Shape	PPT 101, 103, 117	Drag sizing handles	Dialog Box Launcher in Size group of Format tab	Size tab	enter height and width values or Size group of Format tab	enter height and width values		
Clip Art, Insert	PPT 96	Clip Art icon in slide	Clip Art button on Insert tab		
Demote a Paragraph	PPT 34	Increase List Level button on Mini toolbar	Increase List Level button on Home tab		TAB or ALT+SHIFT+RIGHT ARROW
Display a Presentation in Grayscale	PPT 59		Grayscale button on View tab		ALT+V	C	U
Document Properties	PPT 44	Office Button	Prepare	Properties			
Document Theme, Choose	PPT 16		More button on Design tab	theme		
End Slide Show	PPT 54			End Show	ESC or HYPHEN
Font, Change	PPT 109	Font button or Font box arrow on Mini toolbar	Font button on Home tab or Font arrow on Home tab	select font or Font Dialog Box Launcher on Home tab	Latin text font arrow on Font tab	Font	Latin text font arrow on Font tab	CTRL+SHIFT+F	Font tab	Latin text font arrow

Table 2 Microsoft Office PowerPoint 2007 Quick Reference Summary *(continued)*

Task	Page Number	Mouse	Ribbon	Shortcut Menu	Keyboard Shortcut
Font Color	PPT 23, 110	Font Color button or Font Color arrow on Mini toolbar	Font Color button on Home tab or Font Color arrow on Home tab | select color or Font Dialog Box Launcher on Home tab | Font color button on Font tab | select color	Font | Font color button on Font tab | select color	CTRL+SHIFT+F | Font tab | Font color button | select color
Font Size, Decrease	PPT 25	Decrease Font Size button or Font Size arrow on Mini toolbar	Decrease Font Size button on Home tab or Font Size arrow on Home tab | size	Font Size arrow | Size	CTRL+SHIFT+LEFT CARET (<)
Font Size, Increase	PPT 24	Increase Font Size button or Font Size arrow on Mini toolbar	Increase Font Size button on Home tab or Font Size arrow on Home tab | size	Font size arrow | Size	CTRL+SHIFT+RIGHT CARET (>)
Help	PPT 63 and Appendix B		Office PowerPoint Help button		F1
Insert Photograph	PPT 98, 99	Insert Picture from File icon on slide	Picture button on Insert tab		
Move Clip Art or Photo	PPT 105	Drag			
Next Slide	PPT 47	Next Slide button on vertical scroll bar			PAGE DOWN
Normal View	PPT 91	Normal View button at lower-right PowerPoint window	Normal button on View tab		ALT+V | N
Open Presentation	PPT 54	Office Button | Open | select file			CTRL+O
Previous Slide	PPT 50, 51	Previous Slide button on vertical scroll bar			PAGE UP
Print a Presentation	PPT 61	Office Button | Print			CTRL+P
Print an Outline	PPT 122	Office Button | point to Print | Print Preview | Print What arrow | Outline View			
Promote a Paragraph	PPT 34	Decrease List Level button on Mini toolbar	Decrease List Level button on Home tab		SHIFT+TAB or ALT+SHIFT+ LEFT ARROW
Quit PowerPoint	PPT 53	Double-click Office Button or Close button on title bar or Office Button | Exit PowerPoint		Right-click Microsoft PowerPoint button on taskbar | Close	ALT+F4 or CTRL+Q
Save a Presentation	PPT 27	Save button on Quick Access toolbar or Office Button | Save			CTRL+S or SHIFT+F12
Slide, Add	PPT 29		New Slide button on Home tab or New Slide arrow on Home tab | choose slide type		CTRL+M

Table 2 Microsoft Office PowerPoint 2007 Quick Reference Summary (continued)

Task	Page Number	Mouse	Ribbon	Shortcut Menu	Keyboard Shortcut
Slide, Arrange	PPT 41	Drag slide in Slides tab to new position or in Slide Sorter View drag slide to new position			
Slide, Background	PPT 89		Background Styles button on Design tab | select style	Format Background	
Slide, Duplicate	PPT 40		New Slide arrow on Home tab | Duplicate Selected Slides		
Slide Layout	PPT 92, 94		Layout button on Home tab		
Slide Show View	PPT 49	Slide Show button at lower-right PowerPoint window	Slide Show button on View tab or From Beginning button on Slide Show tab		F5 or ALT+V | W
Slide Sorter View	PPT 91	Slide Sorter View button at lower-right in PowerPoint window	Slide Sorter button on View tab		ALT+V | D
Spelling Check	PPT 55		Spelling button on Review tab		F7
Text, Add Shadow	PPT 110		Text Shadow button on Home tab		
Text, Bold	PPT 25	Bold button on Mini toolbar	Bold button on Home tab		CTRL+B
Text, Change Color	PPT 23	Font Color button or Font Color arrow on Mini toolbar	Font color arrow on Home tab | choose color	Font | Font color button | choose color	
Text, Delete	PPT 42		Cut button on Home tab	Cut	DELETE or CTRL+X or BACKSPACE
Text, Formatting with Quick Styles	PPT 119		Quick Styles button on Home tab | select style		
Text, Italicize	PPT 22	Italic button on Mini toolbar	Italic button on Home tab	Font | Font style arrow | Italics	CTRL+I
Text, Select	PPT 21	Drag to select | double-click to select word | triple-click to select paragraph			SHIFT+DOWN ARROW or SHIFT+RIGHT ARROW
Use Format Painter	PPT 112	Format Painter button on Mini toolbar	Double-click Format Painter button on Home tab | select text with a format you want to copy | select other text to apply previously selected format | press ESC to turn off Format Painter		

Table 2 Microsoft Office PowerPoint 2007 Quick Reference Summary (continued)

Task	Page Number	Mouse	Ribbon	Shortcut Menu	Keyboard Shortcut
Zoom for Printing	PPT 128	Drag Zoom slider on status bar or Office Button | point to Print | Print Preview |	Zoom button on View tab | select zoom		
Zoom for Viewing Slides	PPT 127	Drag Zoom slider on status bar	Zoom button on View tab | select zoom		

Table 3 Microsoft Office Excel 2007 Quick Reference Summary

Task	Page Number	Mouse	Ribbon	Shortcut Menu	Keyboard Shortcut
AutoCalculate	EX 62	Select range | right-click AutoCalculate area | click calculation			
Bold	EX 38	Bold button on Mini toolbar	Bold button on Home tab or Font Dialog Box Launcher on Home tab | Font tab	Format Cells | Font tab | Bold in Font style list	CTRL+B
Borders	EX 111	Borders button on Mini toolbar	Borders button on Home tab or Alignment Dialog Box Launcher on Home tab | Border tab	Format Cells | Border tab	CTRL+1 | B
Cell Style, change	EX 35		Cell Styles button on Home tab		
Center	EX 113	Right-click cell | Center button on Mini toolbar	Center button on Home tab or Alignment Dialog Box Launcher on Home tab	Format Cells | Alignment tab	CTRL+1 | A
Center Across Columns	EX 40	Right-click selection | Merge & Center button on Mini toolbar	Merge & Center button on Home tab or Alignment Dialog Box Launcher on Home tab	Format Cells | Alignment tab	CTRL+1 | A
Chart, Add	EX 50		Dialog Box Launcher in Charts group on Insert tab		F11
Clear Cell	EX 66	Drag fill handle back	Clear button on Home tab	Clear Contents	DELETE
Clear Worksheet	EX 66		Select All button on worksheet | Clear button on Home tab		
Close Workbook	EX 59		Close button on Ribbon or Office Button | Close		CTRL+W
Color Background	EX 110		Fill Color button on Home tab or Font Dialog Box Launcher on Home tab | Fill tab	Format Cells | Fill tab	CTRL+1 | F

Table 3 Microsoft Office Excel 2007 Quick Reference Summary (continued)

Task	Page Number	Mouse	Ribbon	Shortcut Menu	Keyboard Shortcut
Column Width	EX 46, 122	Drag column heading boundary	Home tab | Format button | Column Width	Column Width	ALT+O | C | W
Comma Style Format	EX 44		Comma Style button on Home tab or Number Dialog Box Launcher on Home tab | Accounting	Format Cells | Number tab | Accounting	CTRL+1 | N
Conditional Formatting	EX 119		Conditional Formatting button on Home tab		ALT+O | D
Copy to adjacent cells	EX 27	Select source area | drag fill handle through destination cells	Select source area | click Copy button on Home tab | select destination area | click Paste button on Home tab	Right-click source area | click Copy | right-click destination area | click Paste	
Currency Style Format	EX 116		Currency Style button on Home tab or Format Cells | Number | Currency	Format Cells | Number | Currency	CTRL+1 | N
Cut	EX 64		Cut button on Home tab	Cut	CTRL+X
Date, Format	EX 113		Font Dialog Box Launcher on Home tab | Number tab | Date	Format Cells | Number tab | Date	
Decimal Place, Decrease	EX 115		Decrease Decimal button on Home tab or Number Dialog Box Launcher on Home tab | Number tab | Currency	Format Cells | Number tab | Currency	CTRL+1 | N
Decimal Place, Increase	EX 118		Increase Decimal button on Home tab or Number Dialog Box Launcher on Home tab | Number tab | Currency	Format Cells | Number tab | Currency	CTRL+1 | N
Document Properties, Set or View	EX 55	Office Button | Prepare | Properties			ALT+F | E | P
E-Mail from Excel	EX 142	Office Button | Send | E-Mail			ALT+F | D | E
Embedded Chart, Delete	EX 67				Select chart, press DELETE
Fit to Print	EX 156		Page Setup Dialog Box Launcher on Page Layout tab		ALT+P | SP
Font Color	EX 39	Font Color box arrow on Mini toolbar	Font Color button arrow on Home tab or Font Dialog Box Launcher on Home tab	Format Cells | Font tab	CTRL+1 | F
Font Size, Change	EX 38	Font Size box arrow on Mini toolbar	Font Size box arrow on Home tab or Font Dialog Box Launcher on Home tab	Format Cells | Font tab	CTRL+1 | F
Font Size, Increase	EX 39	Increase Font Size button on Mini toolbar	Increase Font Size button on Home tab		

Table 3 Microsoft Office Excel 2007 Quick Reference Summary (continued)

Task	Page Number	Mouse	Ribbon	Shortcut Menu	Keyboard Shortcut
Font Type	EX 36	Font box arrow on Mini toolbar	Font box arrow on Home tab or Font Dialog Box Launcher in Font group on Home tab	Format Cells	Font tab	CTRL+1	F
Formula Assistance	EX 101	Insert Function button in formula bar	Insert Function button on Formulas tab		CTRL+A after you type function name
Formulas Version	EX 136				CTRL+ACCENT MARK
Full Screen	EX 9		Full Screen button on View tab		ALT+V	U
Function	EX 101	Insert Function button in formula bar	Insert Function button on Formulas tab		SHIFT+F3
Go To	EX 48	Click cell	Find & Select button on Home tab		F5
Help	EX 67 and Appendix B		Microsoft Office Excel Help button on Ribbon		F1
Hide Column	EX 122	Drag column heading boundary	Format button on Home tab	Hide & Unhide or Hide & Unhide button on View tab	Hide	CTRL+0 (zero) to hide CTRL+SHIFT+) to display
Hide Row	EX 126	Drag row heading boundary		Hide	CTRL+9 to hide CTRL+SHIFT+(to display
In-Cell Editing	EX 63	Double-click cell			F2
Margins, Change	EX 130		Margins button on Page Layout tab		
Merge Cells	EX 41		Merge & Center button on Home tab or Alignment Dialog Box Launcher on Home tab	Format Cells	Alignment tab	ALT+O	E	A
New Workbook	EX 67	Office Button	New			CTRL+N
Open Workbook	EX 61	Office Button	Open			CTRL+O
Percent Style Format	EX 118		Percent Style button on Home tab or Number Dialog Box Launcher on Home tab	Percentage	Format Cells	Number tab	Percentage	CTRL+1	N or CTRL+SHIFT+%
Preview Worksheet	EX 132	Office Button	Print	Print Preview			ALT+F	W	V
Print Worksheet	EX 132	Office Button	Print			CTRL+P
Quit Excel	EX 59	Close button on title bar Office Button	Exit Excel			ALT+F4
Range Finder	EX 106	Double-click cell			
Redo	EX 65	Redo button on Quick Access Toolbar			ALT+3 or CTRL+Y
Row Height	EX 125	Drag row heading boundary	Format button on Home tab	Row Height	Row Height	ALT+O	R	E
Save Workbook, New Name	EX 57		Office Button	Save As		ALT+F	A
Save Workbook, Same Name	EX 57	Save button on Quick Access Toolbar	Office Button	Save		CTRL+S

Table 3 Microsoft Office Excel 2007 Quick Reference Summary (continued)

Task	Page Number	Mouse	Ribbon	Shortcut Menu	Keyboard Shortcut
Select All of Worksheet	EX 67	Select All button on worksheet			CTRL+A
Select Cell	EX 15	Click cell or click Name box, type cell reference, press ENTER			Use arrow keys
Shortcut Menu	EX 12	Right-click object			SHIFT+F10
Spell Check	EX 127		Spelling button on Review tab		F7
Split Cell	EX 41		Merge & Center button on Home tab or Alignment Dialog Box Launcher on Home tab	click Merge cells to deselect	Format Cells	Alignment tab	click Merge cells to deselect	ALT+O	E	A
Stock Quotes	EX 138		Existing Connections button on Data tab		ALT+D	D	D
Sum	EX 25	Function Wizard button in formula bar	SUM	Sum button on Home tab	Insert Function button on Formulas tab	ALT+=
Undo	EX 65	Undo button on Quick Access Toolbar			ALT+2, CTRL+Z
Unhide Column	EX 122	Drag hidden column heading boundary to right	Unhide button on View tab	Unhide	ALT+O	C	U
Unhide Row	EX 127	Drag hidden row heading boundary down	Unhide button on View tab	Unhide	ALT+O	R	U
Worksheet Name, Change	EX 141	Double-click sheet tab, type new name		Rename	
Workbook Theme, Change	EX 109		Themes button on Page Layout tab		

Table 4 Microsoft Office Access 2007 Quick Reference Summary

Task	Page Number	Mouse	Ribbon	Shortcut Menu	Keyboard Shortcut
Add New Field	AC 24	Right-click Add New Field in Datasheet	Insert Rows button on Design Tab	Design View	INSERT	
Add Record	AC 30, 38	New (blank) record button	New button on Home tab	Open	Click in field	CTRL+PLUS SIGN (+)
Calculate Statistics	AC 118		Totals button on Design tab		
Change Database Properties	AC 60	Office Button	Manage	Database Properties			
Change Primary Key	AC 28	Delete field	Primary Key button	Design View button on Design tab	select field	Primary Key button		
Clear Query	AC 98				Select all entries	DELETE
Close Object	AC 35	Close button for object		Right-click item	Close	

Table 4 Microsoft Office Access 2007 Quick Reference Summary (continued)

Task	Page Number	Mouse	Ribbon	Shortcut Menu	Keyboard Shortcut
Create Calculated Field	AC 113			Zoom	SHIFT+F2
Create Crosstab Query	AC 123		Query Wizard button on Create tab | Crosstab Query Wizard		
Create Database	AC 14	Blank Database button or Office Button | Save			CTRL+S or SHIFT+F12 or ALT+I
Create Query	AC 78		Query Design button on Create tab		
Create Report	AC 51		Report Wizard button on Create tab		
Create Table	AC 23	Office Button | Save button	Table button on Create tab		CTRL+S or SHIFT+F12
Customize Navigation Pane	AC 126	Navigation Pane arrow | Object Type			
Define Fields in a Table	AC 24		Right-click Add New Field on Datasheet tab | Rename Column	Right-click Add New Field | Rename Column	
Exclude Field from Query Results	AC 112	Show check box			
Field Size	AC 46		Design View button on Design tab | select field | Field Size box		
Format a Calculated Field	AC 116		Property Sheet button on Design tab		
Group in Query	AC 121	Total row or include multiple fields in query			
Include All Fields in Query	AC 85	Double-click asterisk in field list	Query Design button on Create tab | Add All Fields button		
Include Field in Query	AC 85		Query Design button on Create tab | select field | Add Field button		
Join Tables	AC 105		Query Design button on Create tab | bring field lists for tables into upper pane		
Move to First Record	AC 39	First Record button			
Move to Last Record	AC 39	Last Record button			
Move to Next Record	AC 39	Next Record button			
Move to Previous Record	AC 39	Previous Record button			
Omit Duplicates	AC 100	Open Property Sheet, set Unique Values to Yes	Property Sheet button on Design tab | Unique Values	Properties | Unique Values	
Open Database	AC 37	More button | Open button or Office Button | double-click file name			CTRL+O
Open Table	AC 26	Open button		Open	

Table 4 Microsoft Office Access 2007 Quick Reference Summary *(continued)*

Task	Page Number	Mouse	Ribbon	Shortcut Menu	Keyboard Shortcut
Preview Table	AC 41	Office Button | Print | Print Preview			ALT+F, W, V
Print Object	AC 41, 56	Office Button | Print | Quick Print or Print			CTRL+P
Quit Access	AC 36	Close button			
Save Form	AC 58	Office Button | Save			CTRL+S
Save Query	AC 91	Save button or Office Button | Save			CTRL+S
Save Table	AC 27	Save button	Office Button | Save	Save	CTRL+S
Search for Access Help	AC 62 and Appendix B	Microsoft Office Access Help button			F1
Select Fields for Report	AC 51		Report Wizard button on Create tab | Add Field button		
Simple Query Wizard	AC 78		Query Wizard button on Create tab		
Sort Data in Query	AC 98		Select field in Design grid | Ascending		
Sort on Multiple Keys	AC 101	Assign two sort keys			
Split Form	AC 57		Split Form button on Create tab		
Start Access	AC 12	Start button | All Programs | Microsoft Office | Microsoft Office Access 2007			
Switch Between Form and Datasheet Views	AC 57	Form View or Datasheet View button			
Use AND Criterion	AC 95				Place criteria on same line
Use Criterion	AC 81	Right-click query | Design View | Criteria row			
Use OR Criterion	AC 96				Place criteria on separate lines